P9-EDT-113

standard catalog of ®
FORD
1903-2003 3rd Edition

John Gunnell

Published by

krause
publications

700 E. State Street • Iola, WI 54990-0001
Telephone: 715/445-2214

Please call or write for our free catalog of publications.
Our toll-free number to place an order or obtain a free catalog is 800-258-0929
or please use our regular business telephone, 715-445-2214.

Library of Congress Catalog Number: 90-60574
ISBN: 0-87349-452-0

Printed in the United States of America

CONTENTS

Foreword 4
Abbreviations/Photo Credits 5
Body Style Identification Guide 6
Dimensions 10
How To Use This Catalog 11
Catalog Section
    Ford 20
    Edsel 281
    Lincoln 290
    Mercury. 388
    Mustang 544
Price Guide Section
    Ford 605
    Edsel 618
    Lincoln 618
    Mercury 624
    Mustang 634
    Thunderbird. 636
2003 Ford 638

2001 Ford Mustang Bullitt. (FMC)

FOREWORD

The concept behind Krause Publications' Standard Catalog of® series is to compile massive amounts of information about motor vehicles and present it in a standard format which the hobbyist, collector, or professional dealer can use to answer some commonly asked questions. These questions include: What year, make, and model is the vehicle? What did it sell for when new? Is it original or modified? How rare is it? What is special about it? How much is it worth today? Illustrations in the catalogs provide some answers, while the data charts and text present others.

The standardized format presents the following data: (1) a description of the vehicle; (2) where available, a list of standard factory equipment; (3) vehicle and/or engine identification codes and advice on how to interpret these; (4) a chart containing model codes, type descriptions, original retail price, original shipping weight, and available production totals; (5) engine specifications; (6) a concise description of chassis features; (7) technical information regarding the drivetrain and running gear; (8) option lists or a description of accessories seen on vehicles in original period photos; (9) a "thumbnail" history of the vehicle and/or manufacturer; and (10) a price guide for vehicles up to 1994 located at the end of the book featuring data from the *Old Cars Price Guide*.

Standard Catalogs are not history books, encyclopedias, or repair manuals for motor vehicle enthusiasts. They are intended to be collector's guides, much like the popular spotter's guides, buyer's digests, and pricing guides, but utilize a large size, broad scope, and deluxe format. They represent the accumulated efforts of many talented individuals including automotive historians, enthusiasts who lend their expertise, editors, and a production team that transforms piles of facts, figures, and photos into a finished book.

All of the catalogs published to date reflect this unique balance between professional researchers and the materials compiled by hobbyists that possess specialized knowledge regarding their favorite marques. A continuing goal for all future Standard Catalogs is to coordinate efforts so that each section in the book will represent both the skilled prose of a professional writer and the in-depth knowledge, expertise, and enthusiasm of the hobbyist. All automotive enthusiasts are potential contributors to the series, and are encouraged to maintain an ongoing file of new research, corrections to the current Standard Catalog edition, and additional photos that can be used to refine, update, and expand future editions. (All materials received will be returned!)

The long-range goal of Krause Publications is to publish a series of catalogs that are as near to perfect as possible. The feedback and participation of hobby experts is critical to the achievement of this goal. We intend to provide enthusiasts with hours of enjoyable reading, dependable guides in the search for vehicle acquisitions, and essential references when journeying to car shows, wrecking yards, and swap meets. Our diligent efforts combined with the accumulated knowledge of experts will make this goal a reality.

Standard Catalogs currently available include:

The Standard Catalog of® American Cars, 1805-1942
The Standard Catalog of® American Cars, 1946-1975
The Standard Catalog of® American Cars, 1976-1999
The Standard Catalog of® American Light-Duty Trucks
The Standard Catalog of® Buick, 1903-2000
The Standard Catalog of® Cadillac, 1903-2000
The Standard Catalog of® Chevrolet, 1912-1998
The Standard Catalog of® Chevrolet Trucks, 1918-1955
The Standard Catalog of® Chrysler, 1914-2000
The Standard Catalog of® Corvette, 1953-2001
The Standard Catalog of® Ford, 1903-2003
The Standard Catalog of® Imported Cars, 1946-2001
The Standard Catalog of® Light-Duty Ford Trucks, 1905-2002
The Standard Catalog of® Mustang, 1964-2001
The Standard Catalog of® Oldsmobile, 1897-1997
The Standard Catalog of® Pontiac, 1926-2002

To submit information for future editions, contact:

Krause Publications, Automotive Books
700 E. State St., IOLA, WI 54990-0001
(800) 258-0929 • www.krause.com

To receive a free products catalog, contact:

Krause Publications, Products Catalog
700 E. State St., IOLA, WI 54990-0001
(800) 258-0929 • www.krause.com

ABBREVIATIONS

A/C . . . . Air conditioning
A.L.A.M. . . . Assoc. of Licensed Automobile Mfgs.
Adj . . . . Adjustable
Aero . . . . Fastback
AM, FM, AM/FM . . . Radio types
Amp. . . . . Ampere
Approx . . . . Approximate
Auto. . . . . Automatic
Auxil. . . . . Auxiliary
Avail. . . . . Available
Avg. . . . . Average
BxS . . . . Bore x Stroke
Base . . . . Base (usually lowest-priced) model
Bbl. . . . . Barrel (carburetor)
B.H.P. . . . . . Brake horsepower
BSW . . . . . Black sidewall (tire)
Bdrcl. . . . . Broadcloth
Bus. . . . . Business (i.e. Business Coupe)
C.C. . . . . Close-coupled
Cabr. . . . . Cabriolet
Carb. . . . . Carburetor
Cass. . . . Cassette (tape player)
CB . . . . . Citizens Band (radio)
CEO . . . Chief Executive Officer
C.I.D. . . Cubic inch displacement
Clb. . . . . Club (Club Coupe)
Clth. . . . . . . Cloth-covered roof
Col. . . . . Colonnade (coupe body style)
Col. . . . . Column (shift)
Conv/Conv. . . . . . . Convertible
Conv. Sed . . . Convertible Sedan
Corp Limo . Corporate Limousine
Cpe . . . . Coupe
C.R. . . . . . . Compression ratio
Cu. In. . . . . Cubic Inch (displacement)
Cust. . . . . Custom
Cyl. . . . . Cylinder
DeL. . . . . DeLuxe
DFRS . . Dual facing rear seats
Dia . . . . Diameter
Disp . . . . Displacement
Dr. . . . . Door

Ea . . . . Each
E.D. . . . . Enclosed Drive
E.F.I. . Electronic Fuel Injection
E.W.B. . . . Extended Wheelbase
Eight . . . Eight-cylinder engine
8-tr . . . . Eight-track
Encl. . . . . Enclosed
EPA . Environmental Protection Agency
Equip. . . . . Equipment
Exc. . . . . Except
Exec. . . . . Executive
F . . . . Forward (3f - 3 forward speeds)
F.W.D. . . . Four-wheel drive
Fam. . . . . Family
Fml . . . . Formal
"Four" . . . Four-cylinder engine
4WD . . . . Four-wheel drive
4-dr. . . . . Four-door
4-spd. . . . . Four-speed (transmission)
4V . . . . Four-barrel carburetor
FP . . . . Factory Price
Frsm . . . . Foursome
Frt . . . . Front
FsBk . . . . Fastback
Ft. . . . . Foot/feet
FWD . . . . . Front-wheel drive
GBR . . . Glass-belt radial (tire)
Gal. . . . . Gallon
GT . . . . Gran Turismo
G.R. . . . . Gear Ratio
H . . . . Height
H.B. . . . . Hatchback
H.D. . . . . Heavy Duty
HEI . . . . High Energy Ignition
H.O. . . . . High-output
H.P. . . . . Horsepower
HT/HT Hdtp. . . . . . . Hardtop
Hr . . . . Hour
Hwg . . . . Highway
I . . . . Inline
I.D. . . . . Identification
In . . . . Inches
Incl. . . . . Included or Including
Int. . . . . Interior

Lan . Landau (coupe body style)
Lb. or Lbs. . Pound-feet (torque)
LH . . . . Left hand
Lift. . . . . Liftback
Limo . . . . Limousine
LPO . Limited production option
Ltd. . . . . Limited
Lthr. Trm. . . . . . Leather Trim
L.W.B. . . . . . Long Wheelbase
Mag. . . . . Wheel style
Mast. or Mstr. . . . . . . Master
Max. . . . . Maximum
MFI . . . . Multi-port Injection
M.M. . . . . Millimeters
MPG . . . . . Miles per gallon
MPH . . . . . . Miles per hour
N/A . . . . Not Available (or not applicable)
NC . . . . No charge
N.H.P. . . . Net horsepower
No. . . . . Number
Notch or N.B. . . . Notchback
OHC . . Overhead cam (engine)
OHV . . Overhead valve (engine)
O.L. . . . . Overall length
OPEC . . . . Organization of Petroleum Exporting Countries
Opt . . . . Optional
OSRV . . . . Outside rear view
O.W. or O/W . . . Opera Window
OWL . Outline White Letter (tire)
Oz. . . . . Ounce
P . . . . Passenger
PFI . . . . . Port fuel injection
Phae . . . . Phaeton
Pkg. . . . . Package
Prod. . . . . Production
Pwr. . . . . Power
R . . . . Reverse
RBL . . . Raised black letter (tire)
Rbt. . . . . Runabout
Rds . . . . Roadster
Reg . . . . Regular
Remote . . . . . Remote control
Req. . . . . Requires
RH . . . . Right hand drive
Roch. . . Rochester (carburetor)

rpm. . . . Revolutions per minute
RPO . Regular production option
R.S. or R/S . . . . . . Rumbleseat
RV . . . . . Recreational vehicle
RWL . . Raised white letter (tire)
S.A.E. . . . Society of Automobile Engineers
SBR . . . . . . Steel-belted radials
Sed . . . . Sedan
SFI . . Sequential fuel injection
"Six" . . . . . Six-cylinder engine
S.M. . . . . Side Mount
Spd . . . . Speed
Spec . . . . Special
Spt. . . . . Sport
Sq. In. . . . . Square inch
SR . . . . Sunroof
Sta. Wag. . . . . . Station Wagon
Std. . . . . Standard
Sub. . . . . Suburban
S.W.B. . . . . Short Wheelbase
Tach . . . . Tachometer
Tax. . . . Taxable (horsepower)
TBI . Throttle body (fuel) injection
Temp. . . . . Temperature
3S . . . . Three-seat
Trans. . . . . Transmission
Trk. . . . . Trunk
2-Dr. . . . . Two-door
2 V . . . Two-barrel (carburetor)
2WD . . . . . . Two-wheel drive
Univ . . . . Universal
Utl. . . . . Utility
V. . . . . . Venturi (carburetor)
V-6, V-8 . . . . Vee-type engine
VIN . . . . Vehicle Identification Number
W . . . . With
W/O . . . . Without
Wag. . . . . Wagon
w (2w) . Window (two window)
W.B. . . . . Wheelbase
Woodie . . . Wood-bodied car
WLT . . . . . White-letter tire
WSW . . . White sidewall (tire)
W.W. . . . . Whitewalls
W. Whl. . . . . Wire wheel

PHOTO CREDITS

Whenever possible, throughout this Catalog, we have strived to illustrate all cars with photographs that show them in their most original form. All photos gathered from reliable outside sources have an alphabetical code following the caption which indicates the photo source. An explanation of these codes is given below. Additional photos from Krause Publications file are marked accordingly. With special thanks to the editors of the previous *Standard Catalog of American Cars* for their original research and obtaining many of these photos of Chevrolet over the years.

(AA)	Applegate & Applegate
(CH)	Chevrolet
(CP)	Crestline Publishing
(GM)	General Motors
(HAC)	Henry Austin Clark, Jr.
(HFM)	Henry Ford Museum
(IMS)	Indianapolis Motor Speedway

(JAC)	John A. Conde
(JG)	John Gunnell
(NAHC)	National Automotive History Collection
(OCW)	Old Cars Weekly
(PH)	Phil Hall
(RLC)	Robert Lade Collection
(WLB)	William L. Bailey

BODY STYLES

Body style designations describe the shape and character of an automobile. In earlier years automakers exhibited great imagination in coining words to name their products. This led to names that were not totally accurate. Many of those "**car words**" were taken from other fields: mythology, carriage building, architecture, railroading and so on. Therefore, there was no "correct" automotive meaning other than that brought about through actual use. Inconsistencies have persisted into the recent period, though some of the imaginative terms of past eras have faded away. One manufacturer's "sedan" might resemble another's "coupe." Some automakers have persisted in describing a model by a word different from common usage, such as Ford's label for Mustang as a "sedan." Following the demise of the true pillarless hardtop (two- and four-door) in the mid-1970s, various manufacturers continued to use the term "hardtop" to describe their offerings, even though a "B" pillar was part of the newer car's structure and the front door glass may not always have been frameless. Some took on the description "pillared hardtop" or "thin pillar hardtop" to define what observers might otherwise consider, essentially, a sedan. Descriptions in this catalog generally follow the manufacturers' choice of words, except when they conflict strongly with accepted usage.

One specific example of inconsistency is worth noting: the description of many hatchback models as "three-door" and "five-door," even though that extra "door" is not an entryway for people. While the 1976-1999 domestic era offered no real phaetons or roadsters in the earlier senses of the words, those designations continue to turn up now and then, too.

TWO-DOOR (CLUB) COUPE: The Club Coupe designation seems to come from club car, describing the lounge (or parlor car) in a railroad train. The early postwar club coupe combined a shorter-than-sedan body structure with the convenience of a full back seat, unlike the single- seat business coupe. That name has been used less frequently in the 1976-99 period, as most notchback two-door models (with trunk rather than hatch) have been referred to as just "coupes." Moreover, the distinction between two-door coupes and two-door sedans has grown fuzzy.

TWO-DOOR SEDAN: The term sedan originally described a conveyance seen only in movies today: a wheeless vehicle for one person, borne on poles by two men, one ahead and one behind. Automakers pirated the word and applied it to cars with a permanent top, seating four to seven (including driver) in a single compartment. The two-door sedan of recent times has sometimes been called a pillared coupe, or plain coupe, depending on the manufacturer's whim. On the other hand, some cars commonly referred to as coupes carry the sedan designation on factory documents.

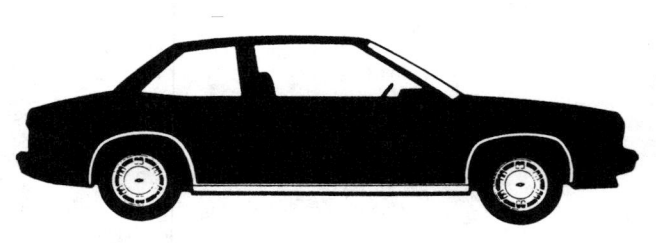

TWO- DOOR (THREE-DOOR) HATCHBACK COUPE: Originally a small opening in the deck of a sailing ship, the term "hatch" was later applied to airplane doors and to passenger cars with rear liftgates. Various models appeared in the early 1950s. but weather-tightness was a problem. The concept emerged again in the early 1970s, when fuel economy factors began to signal the trend toward compact cars. Technology had remedied the sealing difficulties. By the 1980s, most manufacturers produced one or more hatchback models, though the question of whether to call them "two-door" or "three-door" never was resolved. Their main common feature was the lack of a separate trunk "Liftback" coupes may have had a different rear-end shape, but the two terms often described essentially the same vehicle.

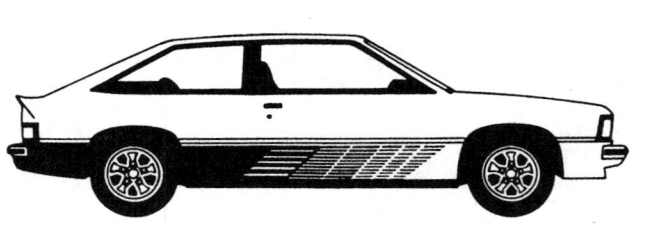

Standard Catalog of® Ford

TWO-DOOR FASTBACK: By definition, a fastback is any automobile with a long, moderately curving, downward slope to the rear of the roof. This body style relates to an interest in streamlining and aerodynamics and has gone in and out of fashion at various times. Some (Mustangs for one) have grown quite popular. Others have tended to turn customers off. Certain fastbacks are, technically, two-door sedans or pillared coupes. Four-door fastbacks have also been produced. Many of these (such as Buick's late 1970s four-door Century sedan) lacked sales appeal. Fastbacks may or may not have a rear-opening hatch.

TWO-DOOR HARDTOP: The term hardtop, as used for postwar cars up to the mid-1970s, describes an automobile styled to resemble a convertible, but with a rigid metal (or fiberglass) top. In a production sense, this body style evolved after World War II, first called "hardtop convertible." Other generic names have included sports coupe, hardtop coupe or pillarless coupe. In the face of proposed rollover standards, nearly all automakers turned away from the pillarless design to a pillared version by 1976-77.

COLONNADE HARDTOP: In architecture, the term colonnade describes a series of columns, set at regular intervals, usually supporting an entablature, roof or series of arches. To meet federal rollover standards in 1974 (standards that never emerged), General Motors introduced two- and four-door pillared body types with arch-like quarter windows and sandwich type roof construction. They looked like a cross between true hardtops and miniature limousines. Both styles proved popular (especially the coupe with louvered coach windows and canopy top) and the term colonnade was applied. As their "true" hardtops disappeared, other manufacturers produced similar bodies with a variety of quarter-window shapes and sizes. These were known by such terms as hardtop coupe, pillared hardtop or opera-window coupe.

FORMAL HARDTOP: The hardtop roofline was a long-lasting fashion hit of the postwar car era. The word "formal" can be applied to things that are stiffly conservative and follow the established rule. The limousine, being the popular choice of conservative buyers who belonged to the Establishment, was looked upon as a formal motorcar. So when designers combined the lines of these two body styles, the result was the Formal Hardtop. This style has been marketed with two or four doors, canopy and vinyl roofs (full or partial) and conventional or opera-type windows, under various trade names. The distinction between a formal hardtop and plain pillared-hardtop coupe (see above) hasn't always followed a strict rule.

CONVERTIBLE: To Depression-era buyers, a convertible was a car with a fixed-position windshield and folding top that, when raised, displayed the lines of a coupe. Buyers in the postwar period expected a convertible to have roll-up windows, too. Yet the definition of the word includes no such qualifications. It states only that such a car should have a lowerable or removable top. American convertibles became extinct by 1976, except for Cadillac's Eldorado, then in its final season. In 1982, though, Chrysler brought out a LeBaron ragtop; Dodge a 400, and several other companies followed it a year or two later.

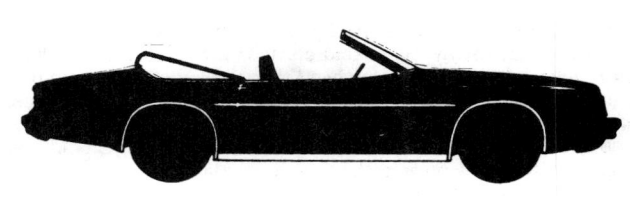

ROADSTER: This term derives from equestrian vocabulary where it was applied to a horse used for riding on the roads. Old dictionaries define the roadster as an open-type car designed for use on *ordinary* roads, with a single seat for two persons and, often, a rumbleseat as well. Hobbyists associate folding windshields and side curtains (rather than roll-up windows) with roadsters, although such qualifications stem from usage, not definition of term. Most recent roadsters are either sports cars, small alternative-type vehicles or replicas of early models.

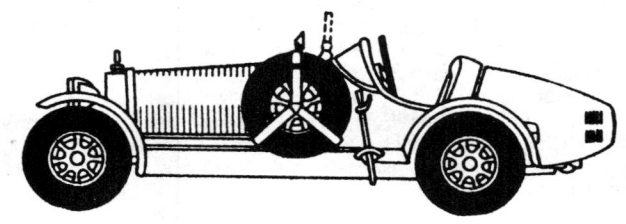

RUNABOUT: By definition, a runabout is the equivalent of a roadster. The term was used by carriage makers and has been applied in the past to light, open cars on which a top is unavailable or totally an add-on option. None of this explains its use by Ford on certain Pinto models. Other than this inaccurate usage, recent runabouts are found mainly in the alternative vehicle field, including certain electric-powered models.

FOUR-DOOR SEDAN: If you took the wheels off a car, mounted it on poles and hired two weightlifters (one in front and one in back) to carry you around in it, you'd have a true sedan. Since this idea isn't very practical, it's better to use the term for an automobile with a permanent top (affixed by solid pillars) that seats four or more persons, including the driver, on two full-width seats.

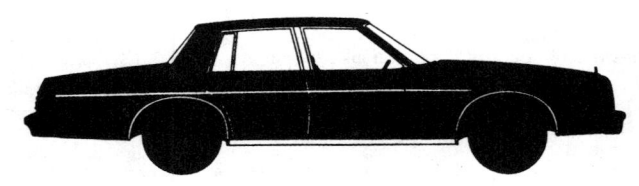

FOUR-DOOR HARDTOP: This is a four-door car styled to resemble a convertible, but having a rigid top of metal or fiberglass. Buick introduced a totally pillarless design in 1955. A year later most automakers offered equivalent bodies. Four-door hardtops have also been labeled sports sedans and hardtop sedans. By 1976, potential rollover standards and waning popularity had taken their toll. Only a few makes still produced a four-door hardtop and those disappeared soon thereafter.

FOUR-DOOR PILLARED HARDTOP: Once the "true" four-door hardtop began to fade away, manufacturers needed another name for their luxury four-doors. Many were styled to look almost like the former pillarless models, with thin or unobtrusive pillars between the doors. Some, in fact, were called "thin-pillar hardtops." The distinction between certain pillared hartops and ordinary (presumably humdrum) sedans occasionally grew hazy.

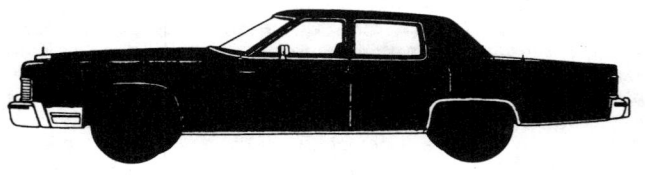

FOUR-DOOR (FIVE-DOOR) HATCHBACK: Essentially unknown among domestic models in the mid-1970s, the four-door hatchback became a popular model as cars grew smaller and front-wheel-drive versions appeared. Styling was similar to the original two-door hatchback, except for — obviously — two more doors. Luggage was carried in the back of the car itself, loaded through the hatch opening, not in a separate trunk.

LIMOUSINE: This word's literal meaning is "a cloak." In France, limousine means any passenger vehicle. An early dictionary defined limousine as an auto with a permanently enclosed compartment for 3-5, with a roof projecting over a front driver's seat. However, modern dictionaries drop the separate compartment idea and refer to limousines as large luxury autos, often chauffeur-driven. Some have a movable division window between the driver and passenger compartments, but that isn't a requirement.

TWO-DOOR STATION WAGON: Originally defined as a car with an enclosed wooden body of paneled design (with several rows of folding or removable seats behind the driver), the station wagon became a different and much more popular type of vehicle in the postwar years. A recent dictionary states that such models have a larger interior than sedans of the line and seats that can be readily lifted out, or folded down, to facilitate light trucking. In addition, there's usually a tailgate, but no separate luggage compartment. The two-door wagon often has sliding or flip-out rear side windows.

FOUR-DOOR STATION WAGON: Since functionality and adaptability are advantages of station wagons, four-door versions have traditionally been sales leaders. At least they were until cars began to grow smaller. This style usually has lowerable windows in all four doors and fixed rear side glass. The term "suburban" was almost synonymous with station wagon at one time, but is now more commonly applied to light trucks with similar styling. Station wagons have had many trade names, such as Country Squire (Ford) and Sport Suburban (Plymouth). Quite a few have retained simulated wood paneling, keeping alive the wagon's origin as a wood-bodied vehicle.

LIFTBACK STATION WAGON: Small cars came in station wagon form too. The idea was the same as bigger versions, but the conventional tailgate was replaced by a single lift-up hatch. For obvious reasons, compact and subcompact wagons had only two seats instead of the three that had been available in many full-size models.

DIMENSIONS

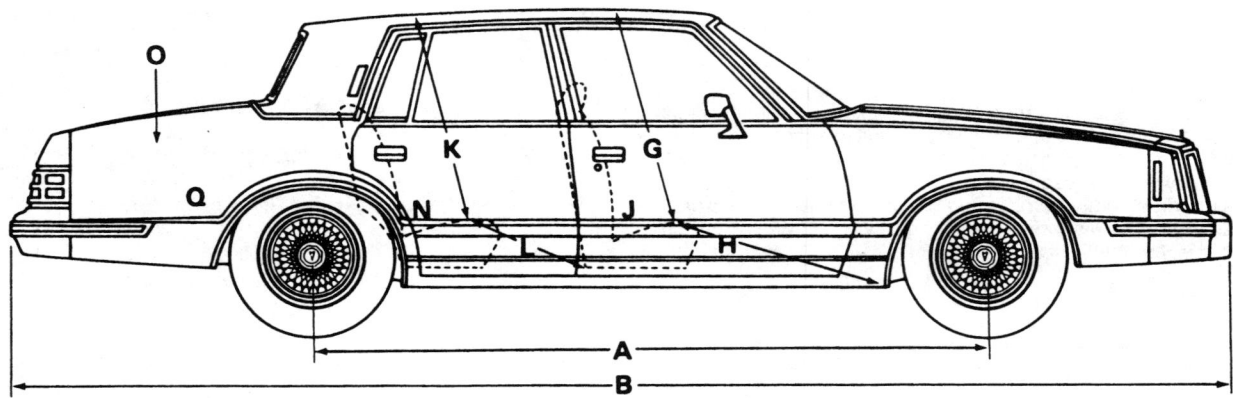

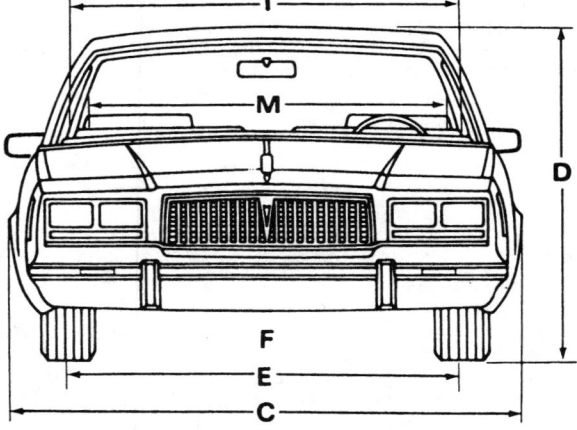

DIMENSIONS
Exterior:
A Wheelbase
B Overall length
C Width
D Overall height
E Tread, front
F Tread, rear

Interior—front:
G Headroom
H Legroom
I Shoulder room
J Hip room

Interior—rear
K Headroom
L Legroom
M Shoulder room
N Hip room
O Trunk capacity (liters/cu. ft.)
P Cargo index volume (liters/cu. ft.)
Q Fuel tank capacity (liters/gallons)

HOW TO USE THIS CATALOG

APPEARANCE AND EQUIPMENT: Word descriptions identify cars by styling features, trim and (to a lesser extent) interior appointments. Most standard equipment lists begin with the lowest-priced model, then enumerate items added by upgrade models and option packages. Most lists reflect equipment available at model introduction.

I.D. DATA: Information is given about the Vehicle Identification Number (VIN) found on the dashboard. VIN codes show model or series, body style, engine size, model year and place built. Beginning in 1981, a standardized 17 symbol VIN is used. Earlier VINs are shorter. Locations of other coded information on the body and / or engine block may be supplied. Deciphering those codes is beyond the scope of this catalog.

SPECIFICATIONS CHART: The first column gives series or model numbers. The second gives body style numbers revealing body type and trim. Not all cars use two separate numbers. Some sources combine the two. Column three tells number of doors, body style and passenger capacity ('4-dr Sed-6P' means four-door sedan, six-passenger). Passenger capacity is normally the maximum. Cars with bucket seats hold fewer. Column four gives suggested retail price of the car when new, or near its introduction date, not including freight or other charges. Column five gives the original shipping weight. The sixth column provides model year production totals or refers to notes below the chart. In cases where the same car came with different engines, a slash is used to separate factory prices and shipping weights for each version. Unless noted, the amount on the left of the slash is for the smallest, least expensive engine. The amount on the right is for the least costly engine with additional cylinders. 'N / A' means data not available.

ENGINE DATA: Engines are normally listed in size order with smallest displacement first. A 'base' engine is the basic one offered in each model at the lowest price. 'Optional' describes all alternate engines, including those that have a price listed in the specifications chart. (Cars that came with either a six or V-8, for instance, list the six as 'base' and V-8 'optional'). Introductory specifications are used, where possible.

CHASSIS DATA: Major dimensions (wheelbase, overall length, height, width and front / rear tread) are given for each model, along with standard tire size. Dimensions sometimes varied and could change during a model year.

TECHNICAL DATA: This section indicates transmissions standard on each model, usually including gear ratios; the standard final drive axle ratio (which may differ by engine or transmission); steering and brake system type; front and rear suspension description; body construction; and fuel tank capacity.

OPTIONAL EQUIPMENT LISTS: Most listings begin with drive-train options (engines, transmissions, steering / suspension and mechanical components) applying to all models. Convenience / appearance items are listed separately for each model, except where several related models are combined into a single listing. Option packages are listed first, followed by individual items in categories: comfort / convenience, lighting / mirrors, entertainment, exterior, interior, then wheels / tires. Contents of some option packages are listed prior to the price; others are described in the Appearance / Equipment text. Prices are suggested retail, usually effective early in the model year. ('N / A' indicates prices are unavailable.) Most items are Regular Production Options (RPO), rather than limited-production (LPO), special-order or dealer-installed equipment. Many options were available only on certain series or body types or in conjunction with other items. Space does not permit including every detail.

HISTORY: This block lists introduction dates, total sales and production amounts for the model year and calendar year. Production totals supplied by auto-makers do not always coincide with those from other sources. Some reflect shipments from the factories rather than actual production or define the model year a different way.

HISTORICAL FOOTNOTES: In addition to notes on the rise and fall of sales and production, this block includes significant statistics, performance milestones, major personnel changes, important dates and places and facts that add flavor to this segment of America's automotive heritage.

1988 MERCURY

GRAND MARQUIS — V-8 — Revised front/rear styling gave the full-size, rear-drive Mercury a new look, as the lineup dropped to four-door sedans and station wagons only. The two-door model was gone. This year's bumpers had an integrated appearance, while wraparound tail lamps highlighted the rear. Wide lower bodyside moldings were standard on both the GS and LS models. Sedans added a half-vinyl roof (rear only). Whitewall P215/75R15 tires became standard on all models. An automatic headlamp on-off warning system also was standard. Joining the option list: an InstaClear heated windshield.

I.D. DATA: Mercury's 17-symbol Vehicle Identification Number (VIN) was stamped on a metal tab fastened to the instrument panel, visible through the windshield. Symbols one to three indicate manufacturer, make and vehicle type. The fourth symbol denotes restraint system. Next comes a letter 'M' (for series), followed by two digits that indicate body type: Model Number, as shown in left column of tables below. (Example: '31' Topaz GS two-door sedan.) Symbol eight indicates engine type. Next is a check digit. Symbol ten indicates model year ('J' 1988). Symbol eleven denotes assembly plant. The final six digits make up the production sequence number, starting with 600001.

TOPAZ (FOUR)

Model No.	Body/ Style No.	Body Type & Seating	Factory Price	Shipping Weight	Prod. Total
31	66D	2-dr. GS Sedan-5P	9166	2565	Note 1
33	66D	2-dr. XR5 Sed-5P	10058	2560	Note 1
36	54D	4-dr. GS Sedan-5P	9323	2608	Note 1
37	54D	4-dr. LS Sedan-5P	10591	2651	Note 1
38	54D	4-dr. LTS Sed-5P	11541	2660	Note 1

NOTE 1: A total of 111,886 Topaz models were produced (16,001 two-door and 95,885 four-door).

ENGINE [Base V-8 (Grand Marquis); Optional (Cougar)]: 90-degree, overhead valve V-8. Cast iron block and head. Displacement: 302 cu. in. (5.0 liters). Bore & stroke: 4.00 x 3.00 in. Compression ratio: 8.9:1. Brake horsepower: (Cougar) 155 at 3400 RPM; (Grand Marquis) 150 at 3200. Torque: (Cougar) 265 lbs.-ft. at 2200 RPM; (Grand Marquis) 270 at 2000. Five main bearings. Hydraulic valve lifters. Sequential fuel injection.

CHASSIS DATA: Wheelbase: (Topaz) 99.9 in.; (Sable) 106.0 in.; (Cougar) 104.2 in.; (Grand Marquis) 114.3 in. Overall Length: (Topaz 2-dr) 176.7 in.; (Topaz 4-dr) 177.0 in.; (Sable) 190.9 in.; (Sable wag) 191.9 in.; (Cougar) 200.8 in.; (Grand Marquis) 213.5 in. (Grand Marquis wag) 218.3 in. Height: (Topaz) 52.8 in.; (Sable) 54.3 in.; (Sable wag) 55.1 in.; (Cougar) 53.8 in.; (Grand Marquis) 55.4 in.; (Grand Marquis wag) 57.0 in. Width: (Topaz 2-dr) 68.3 in.; (Topaz 4-dr) 66.8 in.; (Sable) 70.8 in.; (Cougar) 71.1 in.; (Grand Marquis) 77.5 in.; (Grand Marquis wag) 79.3 in. Front Tread: (Topaz) 54.9 in.; (Sable) 61.6 in.; (Cougar) 58 1 in.; (Grand Marquis) 62.2 in. Rear Tread: (Topaz) 57.6 in.; (Sable) 60.5 in.; (Sable wag) 59.9 in.; (Cougar) 58.5 in.; (Grand Marquis) 62.0 in. Standard Tires: (Topaz) P185/70R14: (Sable) P205/70R14; (Cougar) P215/70R14; (XR-7) P225/60VR15; (Grand Marquis) P215/70R15 SBR WSW.

TECHNICAL: Transmission: Five-speed manual standard on Topaz; three-speed automatic optional. Four-speed overdrive automatic standard on Sable, Cougar and Grand Marquis. Steering: (Grand Marquis) recirculating ball; (others) rack-and-pinion. Front Suspension: (Topaz) MacPherson strut-mounted coil springs w/lower control arms and stabilizer bar; (Cougar) modified MacPherson struts w/lower control arms, coil springs and anti-sway bar; (Sable) MacPherson struts w/control arm, coil springs and anti-sway bar; (Grand Marquis) coil springs with long/short A-arms and anti-sway bar. Rear Suspension: (Topaz) independent quadralink w/MacPherson struts; (Sable) MacPherson struts w/coil springs, parallel suspension arms and anti-sway bar; (Cougar/Grand Marquis) four-link w/coil springs. Brakes: Front disc, rear drums. Body construction: (Grand Marquis) separate body and frame; (others) unibody. Fuel tank: (Topaz) 15.4 gal.; (Topaz 4WD) 13.7 gal.; (Sable) 16 gal.; (Cougar) 22.1 gal.; (Grand Marquis) 18 gal.

GRAND MARQUIS CONVENIENCE/APPEARANCE OPTIONS: Conventional Spare Tire ($73). Automatic Climate Control ($211). Elect Rear Window Defroster ($145). InstaClear Heated Windshield ($250). Pwr Lock Grp ($245). Pwr Decklid Release ($50). 6-Way Pwr Driver's Seat ($251). Dual 6-Way Pwr Seats ($502). w/Pkgs Containing 6-Way Pwr Driver's Seat ($251). Elect AM/FM Stereo Radio w/Cass ($137). High Level Audio System ($472). Premium Sound System ($168). Pwr Antenna ($76). Frt License Plate Bracket (NC). License Plate Frames ($9). Dlx Luggage Rack ($115). Cornering Lamp ($182). Bodyside Protection Moldings ($66). Two-Tone Paint w/Tape Stripes ($159). Formal Coach Vinyl Roof ($665). Hood Accent Paint Stripes ($18). Leather-Wrapped Strg Wheel ($59). F&R Floor Mats ($59). Fingertip Spd Control ($182). Tilt Strg Wheel ($124). Illum Entry System ($82). Light Grp ($46). Dual Illum Visor Mirrors ($109). Tripminder Computer ($215). Pivoting Frt Vent Windows ($79). Dual Facing Rear Seats, sta wag ($173). Cloth Seat Trim, sta wag ($54). Vinyl Seat Trim, sed ($37). Leather Seat Trim ($415). Lckg Wire-Styled Wheel Covers ($183). Turbine Spoke Alum Wheels ($361). Calif. Emission System ($99). Frt Carpet Floor Mats ($26). Eng Block Heater ($18).

HISTORY: Introduced: October 1, 1987, except (Topaz) November 1987. Model year production: 473,400 (total). Calendar year production (U.S.): 293,689. Calendar year sales by U.S. dealers: 486,208 (incl. Tracer). Model year sales by U.S. dealers: 485,613.

FORD
1903-2003

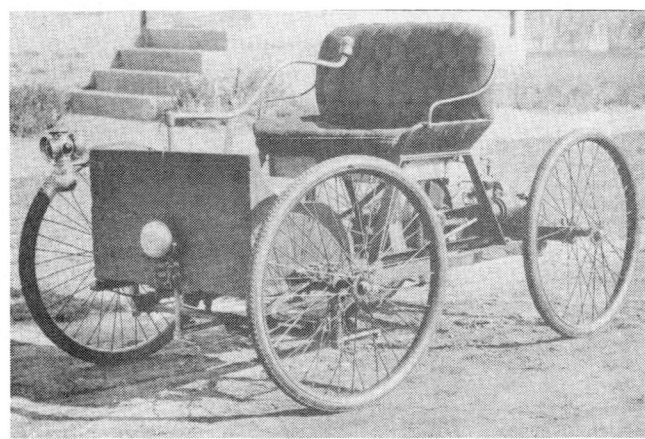

1896 Ford Quadricycle runabout. (HFM)

Henry Ford was born on a farm in rural Michigan on July 30, 1863 and, as his father later said, grew up with "wheels in his head." At age 16 he took himself to Detroit and a variety of machine shop and other jobs that brought him close to engines. In 1888 he married a lovely young farmer's daughter named Clara Jane Bryant and, in 1891, he became an engineer for the Edison Illuminating Co. On Nov. 6, 1893, the Fords' only child, Edsel, was born.

On Christmas Eve in 1893, Henry—with Clara helping to dribble gasoline into the intake valve—tested his first gasoline engine in the kitchen sink of the Ford home. Although for awhile the practical matters of his employment and providing for his family took precedence, Henry Ford already envisioned building an automobile. An acquaintance of his beat him to it, however. Henry was seen cycling behind Charles Brady King when King tested his first gasoline automobile on the streets of Detroit in March 1896.

Henry Ford completed his first car that summer in the shed behind the Ford home, half of the side of which had to be removed to get it out, since its inventor had neglected to consider that the door was too small. Once out, the car—he called it a Quadricycle—performed well. It was driven by a leather belt and a chain, with its two-cylinder, four-stroke horizontal engine producing about four horsepower. It was good for about 20 mph on excursions into the country to the Ford or Bryant farms. Henry drove with Clara sitting beside him and Edsel on her lap.

Henry Ford was on his way to becoming a legend. Although selling the vehicle was not his original intention, when Charles Ainsley offered $200 for it, Ford accepted. He used the money to finance his second car, which was completed in late 1897 or early 1898. In mid-1899, his efforts by now having come to the attention of local businessmen with money to invest—including Detroit's mayor William C. Maybury and William H. Murphy, one of the wealthiest men in town—the Detroit Automobile Co. was organized. Henry Ford was appointed superintendent of a proposed automobile production effort that never came forth.

Initially, Henry Ford couldn't make up his mind about what he wished to build and when he did make his decision, much to the dismay of his backers, it was for a racing car that beat a Winton at Grosse Pointe race track in October 1901. Though only about a dozen cars of any sort had thus far resulted, some of the Ford backers still retained a modicum of faith in their superintendent and a new organization called the Henry Ford Co. resulted on Nov. 30, 1901. By March of 1902, however, disgruntled by a production that was ever forthcoming, but never arriving, even the faithful Ford backers had lost faith.

Ford's backers had brought in one Henry Martyn Leland as a consultant and this infuriated Ford. He left the company abruptly, taking as settlement $900 and William Murphy's promise not to use the Ford name henceforth. Murphy was good to his word; the car that Henry Leland would now build for the former Ford backers was called the Cadillac.

Henry Ford set himself up in a shop elsewhere in town and, with the help of Tom Cooper, built two racing cars called the Arrow and the 999. The latter was a four-cylinder brute displacing an overwhelming 1155.3-cid. Driving it at Grosse Pointe, in June 1903, Barney Oldfield became the first driver to circle a one-mile track in less than a minute (59.6 seconds was his speed). The famous 999 was the first car Oldfield had ever driven and his performance made him a star.

In January 1904, Henry Ford himself drove a revised version of 999 on the ice at Lake St. Clair to a world land speed record of 91.37 mph. Meanwhile, Ford had finally decided to become

1901 Ford runabout. (HFM)

an automobile manufacturer too, with the help of money supplied by coal baron Alexander Young Malcolmson. On June 16, 1903, the Ford Motor Co. evolved from the previous short-lived incorporations of the Ford & Malcomson Co., Ltd., and the Fordmobile Co., Ltd., neither of which had produced any cars. But one month later, in July 1903, the first Ford Model A runabouts were loaded onto freight cars and, in the 15 months to follow, an impressive total of 1,700 cars would be built and sold at $750 ($850 with tonneau) apiece.

These and all subsequent cars from Ford were renegades, unrecognized by the Association of Licensed Automobile Manufacturers. Rebuffed in his initial attempt to obtain an A.L.A.M. license, Ford elected to fight instead. Though others joined him, it was Ford who protested the loudest and whose maverick stance in contesting the monopolistic Selden Patent group made him a folk hero by January 1911 when, finally, the patent was declared ineffective by court decision.

By late 1904, the Model A had evolved into the C, which was different from the A mainly in the moving of its two-cylinder engine up front under a hood. The Model C also had a hood, but its engine was still under the seat, as in the Model A. There was also a new Ford called the Model B, which was a different car altogether, save for the two-speed planetary transmission and gravity lubrication system it shared with predecessor Fords. The B was a vertical inline 24-hp four with shaft drive and a $2,000 price tag. Henry Ford didn't like it at all. It was built mainly because Malcolmson wanted a piece of the upper-price market action.

As early as 1903, Henry Ford had said, "The way to make automobiles is to make one automobile like another, to make them all alike, to make them come through the factory just alike." He was already thinking about a "universal car." The Model B was not that and neither was the two-cylinder 16-hp $1,200 Model F of 1905, nor especially the 40-hp six-cylinder $2,500 Model K introduced later in 1905, a car Henry Ford positively detested—though, with Frank Kulick driving, one did establish a world record for 24 hours of 47.2 mph and 1,135 miles, which bettered the previous mark by 309 miles.

By this time, Ford had taken two steps toward the autonomy he desperately wanted; he made plans to extend his manufacturing to engines and running gear (previously this work had been farmed out, to Dodge Brothers especially) and he bought out Alexander Malcolmson (which meant he'd never be forced into building another expensive Ford). Henry Ford was in control now and knew precisely where he was going. Introduced with the Model K had been the four-cylinder 15/18 hp Model N at $500, underselling the curved dash Oldsmobile (America's best-selling car of that period) and outselling the K by 10 cars to one. By 1906 Ford production topped the 8,000 mark, which was good for first place in the industry; in February the N was joined by the R and was followed by the S in the fall of 1907—good sellers, too.

In October of 1908, the Model T arrived and Henry Ford was through experimenting for almost two decades. This was exactly the car he had wanted to build since 1903. Helping him realize it were Charles Sorensen, Joseph Galamb, Jimmy Smith and especially Childe Harold Wills, whose metallurgical experiments with vanadium steel would result in the lightness with durability that was one of the hallmarks of the Model T. Helping him to set the car up for production was Walter Flanders, who would leave the company, however, before the Ts introduction to become the "F" of the E-M-F.

The Model T Ford was a remarkable automobile, with a 20-hp side-valve four-cylinder engine, two-speed planetary transmission and a 100-in. wheelbase chassis of blessed simplicity and dogged reliability. (The countless jokes that grew up around the Model T were largely that and affectionately told.) Considering its price class, the T was a powerful car with 45 mph possible and it was an economical one too, needing only a gallon of gasoline every 25 miles or so. But more important than what

the Model T was, was what the Model T did. America became a vastly different place in the wake of the Tin Lizzie and, indeed, the Ford concept realized with the Model T revolutionized the world.

The mass production of automobiles had its birth in August 1913 when the Ford final (or chassis) assembly line began to move. Although earlier, Ford and others (notably Ransom Eli Olds) had put together some elements (including sequential positioning of machines, men and material) necessary for mass production, it was only with the moving assembly line that a definitive mass production arrived. At Ford, chassis time was cut from 12-1/2 hours to 1 hour-33 minutes by January 1914, the month Henry Ford introduced the $5 day—and that year Ford produced more than 300,000 Model Ts at the same time the entire rest of the American industry was producing approximately 100,000 less. It was in that year, too, that the Model T—previously available in black, red, green, pearl or French grey—became available in "any color so long as it's black."

Mass production, of course, allowed the Model T to be profitably sold at ever-decreasing prices; introduced at $850, Ford's "Flivver" thereafter enjoyed yearly decreases to a low of $290 in December of 1924. The T's price tag was one of the few things to change during the car's lifetime. The radiator shell was revised from brass to black in 1916, electric lights had been introduced in 1917 and January 1919 brought the option of an electric starter—but that was about all into the mid-1920s. In 1922 the Model T passed the one-million-unit mark in annual sales and it would continue to enjoy million-plus years thereafter, but no longer would the car enjoy its utter dominance of the marketplace.

Everyone at Ford recognized what the emergence of popular competitors such as the Chevrolet meant, except Henry Ford who through clever maneuvering shortly after the First World War—which included his resignation from the company and the placing of his son Edsel in the Ford presidency—had rid himself of all other Ford stockholders and, thus, had no one to answer to but himself. Initially, Ford answered his associates' complaints regarding the Model Ts "old-fashionedness" by introducing balloon tires in 1925 and providing the option of wire wheels and the availability of colors other than black in 1926. Ultimately, by the year following and after the building of 15 million Model Ts, even Henry Ford had to admit that the day of his beloved Tin Lizzie was over. The Ford assembly line was shut down at the end of May 1927; when it was started up again six months later, the Model A was on it.

Like the T, the Model A was a side-valve four, but it was *twice* as powerful at 40 hp and set in a 103.5-in. wheelbase chassis with three-speed sliding gear transmission and four-wheel brakes. The "Tin Lizzie's" planetary gear set and two-wheel brakes had by the mid-1920s become two big marks against it, together with its ungainly appearance. This was nicely rectified in the Model A with sprightly body styling attributable mainly to Henry's son Edsel, who had been guiding Lincoln fortunes since the Ford takeover of that company in 1922.

No car in America had been so feverishly anticipated as the Model A Ford and rumor ran rife during the half-year following the Ford shutdown until Dec. 2, 1927, when the car made its official debut. Interestingly, among the rumors had been that the new car would be a hybrid of the Lincoln and Ford called the Linford. Though there was a pretty Lincoln look to the car, the Model A—with introductory prices as low as $385—was indisputably a Ford. In the four years to follow, Ford and Chevrolet (which had become number one with the Ford shutdown in 1927) divided the production race, with the Model A winning in 1929 and 1930 and Chevy the victor in 1928 and 1931.

Nearly five million Model As had been built by March 31, 1932, when its successor arrived, the Ford V-8, offering 65 hp for as little as $460. Never before had so many cylinders and so much power been offered for so little. Because Ford enjoyed coming up with the revolutionary idea and because experimentation with eight-cylinder engines had been ongoing at the company since the mid-1920s, the V-8 was no doubt the car that Henry Ford would have wished to follow the Model T, although its development status had precluded that in 1927. A refined version of the Model A called the Model B was introduced along with the V-8, but once the latter car got rolling, the four was forgotten altogether.

In 1933 the V-8's wheelbase was increased to 112 in. from the rather short 106.5 in. with which it had been introduced. In 1934, when the Chevrolet went to independent front suspension, Ford was in the seemingly uncomfortable position of having to justify its continued use of all-round transverse leaf suspension (which had been introduced on the T), but a by-now increasingly stubborn Henry Ford explained it away by saying, "We use transverse springs for the same reason that we use round wheels—because we have found nothing better for the purpose."

In 1935, Ford outsold Chevrolet, but for all other years in the 1930s, Chevy was on top. This is not to suggest that the V-8 Ford was an unpopular automobile. It most certainly was popular, its performance potential particularly providing an appeal to the go-faster crowd, whether its member be interested in an illegal fast getaway (as was the bank-robbing Clyde Barrow who wrote Henry Ford a testimonial letter) or a legal one (Ford V-8s virtually ruled stock car racing for several years and Ford racing specials were a mainstay of the Automobile Racing Club of America in the mid-to-late 1930s). But, many average drivers preferred technical advances and more creature comforts than the V-8 had.

In 1936, Chevrolet introduced hydraulic brakes. In 1937, Ford countered with a smaller 60-hp V-8 for a cheaper line of cars, but both it and the traditional V-8 (now at 85 hp) had mechanical brakes. The smaller V-8 was not a success and Ford dealers began clamoring for a six to sell, but they were not to get it for a while. Among numerous other problems the company had now, the labor situation at Ford during the later 1930s was ominous and life threatening. As the Ford Motor Co. moved toward the brink of disaster, an aging Henry Ford—always a mercurial man—grew increasingly recalcitrant. His son Edsel, together with long-time Ford associate Charles Sorensen, became convinced that the Ford Motor Co. could only survive *despite* Henry Ford and not *because* of him.

The Ford V-8 was finally given four-wheel hydraulic brakes for 1939 and the company had a new car that year—another V-8—called the Mercury. About the time it was introduced, Edsel Ford finally convinced his father to produce the car that he and Ford dealers had wanted for several years already. "A Ford Six, At Last" headlined *Business Week* when the new Special was introduced for 1941. It was the first six from Ford since the Model K that Henry had hated so much in 1905, and he had nothing to do with the engine. It was, however, introduced in any color so long as it was black, and the elder Ford may have had something to do with *that*. (Other colors were quickly added, however.)

A pacifist since his peace ship days of the First World War, Henry Ford remained one as World War II approached and, with Charles Lindbergh, was a member of the America First Committee. His son Edsel was not. Prior to Pearl Harbor, the elder Ford had refused to aid the international war effort, believing in military production geared only for American defense purposes. However, following the attack in Hawaii, he ordered a complete changeover to military production even before the War Production Board mandated it.

Personal tragedy would strike Henry Ford soon. On May 26, 1943, his son Edsel, weary and ill from the difficult years when he had become the conscience of the company and an adversary of his father, died of cancer, undulant fever and—as has been written—a broken heart. He was 49 years old. At the funeral Henry Ford stood tight-lipped in grief and, afterwards, he appointed himself president of the Ford Motor Co. He was 80 years old. The Ford Motor Co. lay in chaos now. On Sept. 21,

1946 Ford Super Deluxe Sportsman two-door convertible. (FMC)

1945—with the endorsement of his grandmother and his mother, including a threat by the latter to sell her stock—the eldest son of Edsel Ford became the president of the Ford Motor Co., over Henry Ford's objection. On April 7, 1947, Henry Ford was gone; "The Father of the Automobile Dies," headlined *Life* magazine. It would be Henry Ford II who would guide Ford Motor Co. fortunes in the postwar era.

As was the case with the other major automakers, Ford entered the postwar market with a slightly restyled version of its 1942 models. The car-hungry market responded as if it were a completely new design and public demand dictated that the car remain nearly the same from 1946 through 1948.

When Henry Ford died in 1947, the wheels at Ford Motor Co. began to turn more smoothly and development of the all-new 1949 models began. Gone were the obsolete transverse rear springs and torque tube drive shaft. The new body was much lower, although shorter, than the previous year's models. Once again, the buying public flocked to the Ford showrooms eager to buy the slab-sided offering from Dearborn. Ford wisely decided to continue the same cars, with minor trim changes into the 1950 model year. The basic body style was used again in 1951, only this time the trim changes were more apparent. Model year 1951 also hailed the introduction of one of the most well-proportioned cars ever to come off of the Dearborn assembly lines—the 1951 Ford Victoria. Going hand-in-hand with the introduction of the hardtop Victoria was the introduction of the first fully automatic Ford-O-Matic transmission.

Ford continued to be "the car" to have if you were a performance enthusiast. Even though the old flathead V-8 was outperformed by the new overhead valve offerings from General Motors, many more speed parts were available for the flathead and that was as much a reason for their popularity as anything.

Continuing with a strong second place position in the low-priced field in the early '50s, Ford sales hovered near the one million mark for the first three years of the decade. A significant change, in 1954, was the introduction of the first overhead valve V-8 in Ford's history. Another innovation was the company's

1950 Ford Custom Deluxe two-door convertible. (FMC)

1954 Ford Crestline Sunliner two-door convertible. (FMC)

1957 Ford Fairlane 500 Skyliner two-door retractable hardtop. (FMC)

first ball joint front end. Perhaps the most significant event of the year, however, was the late summer introduction of the Thunderbird. The little two-seater challenged both the European sports cars that American servicemen had fallen in love with during the war and, also, the new Chevrolet Corvette.

Model year 1955 brought the introduction of a beautiful line of new Fairlanes, named after Henry Ford's mansion in Dearborn, Mich. For 1956, Ford once again decided to leave well enough alone in the styling department and offered a beautiful lineup to the public. Even though they looked similar to 1955s, the new models were flashier—an important factor for the 1950s. Ford introduced a sporty two-door station wagon called the Parklane. The great horsepower race of the 1950s was in full swing by 1956 and all manufacturers were offering "power pack" options normally consisting of a four-barrel carburetor, slightly stronger cam and, of course, dual exhaust. Ford offered its version for a new 312-cid V-8.

A high-water mark in the horsepower race, for all manufacturers including Ford, was 1957. Ford offered a supercharged version of the 312-cid V-8. Conservatively rated at 300 hp, these supercharged engines were strong enough to handle any competition. Special "NASCAR" versions—which put out in excess of 340 hp—absolutely dominated the stock car tracks during that year. If the supercharged version of the 312 was a little too wild for your tastes, you could order the engine in several different configurations, including two with twin four-barrel carburetion. Ford also offered the Del Rio Ranch Wagon, in essence a base two-door Ranch Wagon sporting Custom 300 side trim and a fancy interior. They were pleasant cars to look at. The fancier Parklane was discontinued after one year.

Mechanical innovations highlighted Ford model year 1958, while styling changes were made in the trim department. Even though 1957 and 1958 models look considerably different, they are still basically the same car. New for 1958 was the famous "FE" series of 332- and 352-cid V-8s, which grew into the "390" and the awesome "427." Also new for 1958—and offered for the first time in a Ford Division product—was the three-speed Cruise-O-Matic transmission. A novel suspension called Level-Aire-Ride was offered this year only. Quality problems plagued the 1958 models and, as a consequence, only one million were made, the lowest production figure for Ford since 1952.

The following season witnessed the introduction of a car that many consider to be the most beautiful Ford ever built, the 1959 Galaxie. Ford stylists took a Fairlane 500 two-door hardtop and added a Thunderbird inspired roof. The combination was so attractive that it was awarded the Gold Medal for Exceptional Styling at the Brussels World's Fair. With engines of up to 300 hp, they were also spirited performers.

Even though they are not particularly well liked by many, the 1960 Fords were among the smoothest and most aerodynamic cars to come out of Dearborn. With other manufacturers producing engines well into the mid-300-hp range, Ford was being left behind. In response, the company offered a 352-cid 360-hp V-8. While other automakers were offering four-speed manual transmissions, Ford continued to offer only a three-speed manual with overdrive, which undoubtedly helped mileage, but hurt performance. The biggest news for 1960, however, was the introduction of the compact Falcon. The most successful of the compact offerings from the Big Three automakers, the Falcon was extremely simple and straightforward, both in styling and mechanical features.

Throughout the early 1960s, Ford continued on a steady-as-she-goes course, offering the intermediate size Fairlane in 1962. Model year 1963 will be remembered as a high-water mark in the performance books at Ford. Not only was a new V-8 offered in the compact Falcon, but NASCAR and drag racing competition dictated the development and introduction of the most powerful engine ever to come from Dearborn, the incredible 427-cid V-8. This engine was used in racing-only applications, although some did find their way into "street cars." They produced 410 hp with one four-barrel carburetor and 425 hp with two. Ford absolutely dominated NASCAR racing with the 427 for the next four years. Another highlight was the introduction of a car that many consider to be the most beautiful car of the '60s, the 1963-1/2 Galaxie 500 fastback. The body style was designed in answer to the demands of the NASCAR people who had nothing more aerodynamic to drive than the standard notchback Galaxie hardtops.

Nineteen sixty-four saw a continued emphasis by Ford toward total performance. The big Galaxies, Fairlanes, and Falcons continued to offer almost identical product lines and performance options carried over from the 1963-1/2 models. Falcons received the biggest styling changes in spite of the

1959 Ford Fairlane 500 two-door convertible. (FMC)

1963 Ford Thunderbird two-door Sports Roadster. (FMC)

1966 Ford Fairlane GT two-door convertible. (FMC)

midyear introduction of the revolutionary Mustang. (Mustangs are covered in a separate section of this book.)

The 1965 season witnessed introduction of another significant contribution to the low-priced field, the luxurious LTD. Luxury-hungry consumers on a tight budget embraced this plush entry. More than 100,000 were sold during the first year of production. The Fairlane was redesigned in 1965 and the Falcon continued to use the same basic body style introduced in 1964.

The next year saw a slight redesigning in the full-size Ford lineup and, also, the introduction of the limited-production 7-liter Galaxie model as a two-door hardtop or convertible featuring a new 428-cid V-8, Cruise-O-Matic (or four-speed manual) transmission and power front disc brakes as *standard* equipment. With only 8,705 of the hardtops and 2,368 of the convertibles produced, they are highly sought after collector's items today.

The big news in 1966 was the complete redesigning of the intermediate Fairlane series, which was large enough to accommodate big-block Ford V-8s. The full-size Galaxies were restyled for 1967 and presented an attractive package to the buying public. Fairlanes continued to use the same body as in 1966, with only minor restyling. For 1967, NASCAR allowed the use of the intermediate size bodies in Grand National racing. The Fairlanes took the place of the Galaxies on the high banks, with Ford continuing to dominate the big races.

For 1968, the entire lineup received only minor restyling, with the exception of the intermediate Fairlane. Midyear witnessed the introduction of one of the strongest engines ever to come from the Dearborn drawing boards—the incredible Cobra Jet 428. Conservatively rated at 335 hp, its actual output was more in the area of 400 hp. As in the late 1950s, another great horsepower race went into full swing during the late '60s, with each manufacturer trying to out-power the other. Ford was right in the swing of things with the 428 Cobra Jet Fairlane.

Engine and drive train options continued unchanged for 1970 but, in 1971, manufacturers produced the most awesome cars ever introduced to the general public. Ford produced the 429 Super Cobra Jet Torino Cobras and insurance companies started tightening the noose on "Supercar" owners. Experts recognize 1971 as the last year for most true high-performance products from Ford until the 1980s.

Ford made a significant contribution in the economy car field for 1971. In answer to the growing import threat and new subcompacts from AMC and Chevrolet, Ford introduced its successful—but now infamous—Pinto. While competitors, such as the Vega, were plagued with quality control and engineering

1969 Ford Thunderbird four-door Landau sedan. (FMC)

1972 Ford LTD two-door hardtop. (FMC)

1973 Ford Gran Torino Sport two-door hardtop. (FMC)

problems, the simple Pinto continued to be a strong seller until it was finally withdrawn from the market in 1980 to make room for the Escort.

No automaker offered a more complete line than Ford in the 10 years between 1976 and 1986. Offerings ranged from the sub-compact Pinto through the full-size LTD and Thunderbird. Engines reached all the way up to a 460-cid V-8, which would remain available through 1978.

In 1975, the Pinto ran into trouble in the form of serious accusations about fire hazards. Some hideous blazes had resulted from rear-end collisions. Less-vulnerable gas tanks were installed in Pintos built after 1976, but the adverse publicity hurt sales in subsequent years as well.

By 1976, the Maverick was in its next-to-last season, dangling a Stallion package in an attempt to lure youthful drivers. Pinto had one too, but both were for looks rather than action. Ford had high hopes for the Granada, which was introduced in 1975 with Mercedes-like styling and a four-wheel disc brake option. The Torino and Elite made up Ford's mid-size lineup. The Thunderbird not only carried a 202-hp engine, but also came in a selection of luxury paint options to dress up its huge body. Ford sales had shrunk in 1975, but rebounded somewhat this year, partly as a result of the new "California strategy" that delivered special option packages only to West Coast customers.

1976 Granada two-door Sports Coupe. (FMC)

1977 Pinto three-door Runabout. (FMC)

1977 Granada Ghia two-door coupe. (FMC)

The big Thunderbird didn't last much longer. It was replaced in 1977 by a downsized edition that was actually a modification of the new LTD II. The Thunderbird cost far less in this form, but also carried less standard equipment and a modest 302-cid V-8. Production soared far above the level of the last big Thunderbird. The Torino and Elite both faded away and the Maverick was about to do so. The Granada became the first American car to offer a standard four-speed (overdrive) gearbox. GM had downsized its full-size models, but the Ford LTD kept its immense dimensions until 1979.

Few realized it at the time, but the new Fairmont for 1978 soon would serve as the basis for a whole line of FoMoCo rear-drive models. MacPherson struts held up the Fairmont's front end—a suspension style that would grow more common as front-wheel-drive cars arrived. Fairmont power plants ran the gamut: four-cylinder, six-cylinder or V-8. A Euro-styled ES edition became available, but most of the attention went to the Futura Sport Coupe, which was marked by wide B-pillars and a wrap over roofline reminiscent of the Thunderbird's. The Granada tried the Euro route too, with a blackout-trimmed ESS variant. The Pinto Cruising Wagon and Sports Rallye packages seemed less memorable, if practical. The Thunderbird added a Town Landau model, but collectors are more likely to turn to the Diamond Jubilee Edition, offered only in 1978, Ford's 75th anniversary year.

In 1980, Ford shrunk its LTD. The engines shrunk too, with a 302-cid V-8 as standard equipment. The biggest Ford engine was the 351-cid V-8. A luxurious Heritage model took the place of the single-year Diamond Jubilee Thunderbird. The Pinto added equipment and an ESS package and found more customers,

1980 LTD Crown Victoria Country Squire four-door station wagon. (FMC)

while the smaller LTD had trouble in the sales department. The LTD II never caught on and dropped away after 1979. It was the Thunderbird's turn for downsizing in 1980, as a modest 255-cid standard V-8 went under the hood. The best bet for collectors is the year's Silver Anniversary Thunderbird, marking the model's 25th birthday. The Crown Victoria name reappeared in the LTD roster this year, bringing back memories of the sharpest mid-1950s Ford. The LTD also had a new automatic overdrive transmission. Every Ford model endured a loss of sales, but so did most other domestic cars.

Heralding a new Ford era, the front-wheel-drive Escort arrived for 1981 carrying a CHV (hemi) engine. The Escort became Ford's bestseller and, a year later, was America's best-selling car. The Granada slimmed down to the Fairmont's size and used the Fairmont's base four-cylinder engine. After two years powered by a 302-cid V-8 the LTD dropped to a 255-cid V-8. That wasn't the most startling engine change, however, since the Thunderbird now carried a standard six-cylinder power plant.

Sporty performance seemed paramount for the 1982 model year, with the arrival not only of a Mustang GT but a two-seater EXP, based on the Escort platform. Ford now offered its own V-6 engine, while LTDs could get a 351-cid V-8 when destined for police hands. The Thunderbird not only continued the base in-line six, but made a 255-cid V-8 the biggest option. A 20 percent sales decline didn't harm Ford's market share, since other makers weren't finding too many customers either.

The massive Thunderbirds of the 1970s seemed fully forgotten as the 10th generation arrived for 1983. This one was loaded with curves and—before long—a possible turbocharged, fuel-injected four-cylinder engine. With close-ratio five-speed and "quadra-shock" rear suspension. The Thunderbird Turbo Coupe became quite an attraction, helping sales to more than double. A little shuffling of names produced a "new" LTD (closely tied to the dropped Granada), while the big rear-drive became the LTD Crown Victoria.

Turbocharging even hit the EXP and Escort GT for 1984. The EXP altered its form, adding the "bubble back" liftgate from the faded Mercury LN7. Another front-drive model joined up—the compact Tempo with a high-swirl-combustion engine—to replace the Fairmont. Both Tempos and Escorts could be ordered with a Mazda-built diesel—a curious decision, since diesels were on their way out in other makes. Led by the popular Thunderbird, Ford sales hit their highest point since 1979, but the Escort lost its "best-seller" label to Chevrolet's Cavalier.

The LTD continued its high-performance, V-8 engine LX touring sedan into 1985, which was generally a carryover year.

1978 Fairmont four-door sedan. (FMC)

1981 LTD two-door coupe. (FMC)

Tempos now came with standard five-speed gearboxes. Incentive programs helped sales—and Ford's market share—to rise noticeably. A revised Escort emerged before the 1986 model year and included an attractive GT model with a high-output engine.

Not many new models received as much publicity as the front-wheel-drive Taurus, the leader of the 1986 pack. Few cars looked as different from the model they replaced than Taurus did versus the LTD. Plenty of customers liked Taurus's grille-free aero look, as did *Motor Trend*, which awarded the Ford its "Car of the Year" award. Overall sales fell, however, after three years of increases. This left Ford with less than 12 percent of the total market, imports included.

Ford Motor Co. broke records in 1987 with $4.6 billion in net income (better than General Motors) and $71.6 billion in worldwide sales. Earnings from U.S. operations alone hit $3.4 billion. Donald E. Peterson was chairman and CEO for the company, with William Clay Ford, Harold A. Poling and Stanley A. Seneker on his top management team. Thomas J. Wagner took over as Ford Div. general manager. Domestic new car sales climbed six percent, despite a general flatness in the industry.

Leading the sales race was the Escort/EXP series, although the one-year-old Taurus proved the real key to success with its sales more than doubling from 1986. The only change in products was the disappearance of the LTD which, though dropped after 1985, had some 51,000 sales in model year 1986. The popularity of the Taurus made up the difference completely. In fact, all six other Ford car-lines declined somewhat in deliveries.

New for 1987 was a four-wheel-drive Tempo and a five-liter Thunderbird Sport model. The Festiva—a Korean-built captive import—bowed in the spring as a 1988 model, but it was American-made Fords that ruled the market. Model year sales of domestic-built models saw Ford—with 1,422,489 units sold—come in ahead of Chevrolet's 1,390,281. Chevy, however, inched ahead with the Japanese-made Sprint and Spectrum counted. In September, a costly labor agreement helped Ford avert a strike.

Unchanged management guided Ford through 1988, with corporate sales and earnings breaking records for the third year in a row. World sales were $92.4 billion, with $53 billion in net income again topping General Motors. Model year dealer sales of new cars, including the Festiva, rose to 1,535,145 units. This put Ford in first place, ahead of Chevrolet's grand total by 66,000 cars.

The new, Mazda-built Probe and the Festiva accounted for most of Ford's sales increase. Restyled Tempos and Thunderbirds also gained more buyers, while the Escort/EXP, Taurus and Crown Victoria lost some ground. The Escort, however, was still America's number one seller, with the Taurus in second place. Product news focused on the Probe, an Americanized version of Mazda's front-drive 626 with GT trim and a 145-hp turbocharged four available. Other Fords received refinements to drive trains and option packages.

There seemed to be no stopping Ford and 1989 proved it with a 40,000-car sales increase and 4/10ths percent market share increase. Two possible future collector models bowed: the SHO (Super High-Output) Taurus sedan with a standard 24-valve three-liter 220-hp V-6 and the Thunderbird Super Coupe with a 3.8-liter, 215-hp supercharged V-6. They had

1986 Taurus GL four-door station wagon. (FMC)

production runs of 1,558 and 1,243 units, respectively. The Escort approached its three millionth sale since 1981. The Tempo and Taurus dropped slightly in sales, while the Festiva climbed upwards to 60,000 units.

Management changes saw Donald Peterson step down from the chairman's position effective March 1, 1990. Harold Poling replaced him. Philip E. Benton, Jr., became president and chief operating officer. Big corporate news included Ford's 1989 purchase of Jaguar, the English luxury automaker, for $2.5 billion. The Thunderbird marked its 35th anniversary with the start of the 1990 model year and was changed little. Most other models were also largely unaltered, except for a complete updating of the Escort. The new version—designed by Mazda—bowed in the spring of 1990 as a 1991 model. The "old" Escort continued to be built in Edison, N.J., for several months. Other 1990 product changes included a front and rear restyling of the Probe, a Taurus police car package, and a new grille and taillights for the Festiva import. Ford, at the start of the 1990 model year, predicted sales of 1.5 million cars.

In the face of a tough year financially—with a reported loss of $17 million in 1990—Ford maintained a high level of product development. Similar to the early launch of the 1991 Escort in the spring of 1990, Ford introduced its all-new 1992 Crown Victoria lineup—minus a station wagon—in the spring of 1991. The era of the full-size wagon was over at FoMoCo, with this traditional choice of family transportation supplanted by the minivan. The financial slide continued in 1991 with Ford posting a loss of $2.26 billion. The ownership of Jaguar was transferred from FoMoCo's European subsidiary to the parent company in Dearborn, Mich. Ford also became the first Big Three automaker to supply a vehicle to a Japanese maker with its Louisville, Ken.-built Mazda Navajo—a two-door version of the Ford Explorer sport utility vehicle.

The four-wheel-drive model of the Tempo was discontinued in 1992, as was the venerable 5.0-liter V-8 that was now standard in Crown Victoria models. The new, modular 4.6-liter V-8 took its place. The midsize Taurus helped Ford reclaim the title of producer of the United States' best-selling car in 1992. Sales increased by more than 110,000 units over the previous year to elevate Taurus to the top spot and demote the Honda Accord to second with total sales of 409,751 to 329,751, respectively. Overall, Ford recorded an increase of 8.7 percent (141,585 units) in passenger car sales in 1992, while its market share increased 1.6 points to 21.6 percent.

In 1993, Alexander Trotman was named the chairman and CEO of Ford Motor Co., replacing Harold "Red" Poling. The Crown Victoria touring sedan was discontinued, as was the Tempo GLS, Taurus L and base and Sport versions of the Thunderbird. An all-new-design, cab-forward Probe debuted with two new engines: a DOHC 2.0-liter four or DOHC 2.5-liter V-6. Following General Motors' lead, Ford debuted its own credit card—the Ford-Citicorp VISA—in March 1993. Later in the year, Ford consolidated its seven worldwide design operations in Michigan, California, Turin, England, Germany, Australia, and Japan into one group called Ford Corporate Design.

The launch of the 1995 Contour occurred in the spring of 1994, this "world car" being the replacement for the Tempo. The debut of the new 1995 Aspire also occurred early in 1994, with this compact being considered a replacement for the Festiva. In April 1994, FoMoCo Chairman Trotman announced the merger of Ford's North American and European operations and its Automotive Components Group into a single unit called Ford Automotive Operations. The streamlining move was expected to save as much as $3 billion annually. Ford began production of its new AX4N electronically controlled four-speed automatic transmission. The new Ford Windstar minivan also began production in Oakville, Ontario, Canada. In midyear 1994, ground was broken in Dearborn, Mich., for the new Automotive Components Div.'s engineering/testing facility, to be up and running by the fall of 1995.

Ford launched its Ford 2000 global strategy in 1995 to begin a five-year phase of alignment of its worldwide product and processes. Year 2000 goals of the program included trimming the number of power train combinations by 30 percent, reducing the number of vehicle platforms from 24 to 16 and shaving product development time down to 24 months. The all-new-design 1996 Taurus was launched in late 1995, powered by the new Duratec 3.0-liter V-6. The Taurus remained the top-selling automobile in the U.S. in 1995 with 397,000 sales. Ford's announced profits for the year totaled $4.1 billion.

The Taurus SHO sedan was offered with V-8 power for the first time in 1996, using the 3.4-liter engine. The all-new-design 1997 Escort bowed at midyear, but was no longer offered in its long-standing hatchback form. The base Crown Victoria was offered with a natural gas-fueled V-8. The Thunderbird Super Coupe was discontinued at the same time Ford unveiled its "other" sports car—the 1997 Jaguar XK8—which featured an all-alloy DOHC V-8 of Ford design. Ford also debuted its Triton 6.8-liter V-10 engine in the 1996 Econoline van.

In January 1997, Ford launched the 1998 Escort ZX2. It was made available in "Cool" or "Hot" versions, that featured unique body panels and frameless door glass. The compact Aspire was in its final year of being sold in North America. Even bigger news, though, was that there was no 1998 Thunderbird on the drawing board, since the "T-Bird" was being discontinued after 42 years of production. Another long-standing model, the Probe, would also end production at the end of model year 1997.

All 1998 Fords featured both driver's-side and passenger's-side airbags as standard equipment. Safety and security measures were hot marketing tools and Ford offered the SecuriLock anti-theft immobilizer as standard equipment on most new Fords. The rumor mill was going full-speed as to the when the Thunderbird would re-emerge and what form it might take upon that return.

Jack Nasser, a 30-year FoMoCo veteran and former president of Ford Automotive Operations took over as corporate president and chief executive officer on Jan. 1, 1999. Ford's outlook in 1999 was rosy, with $14.9 billion of cash in the bank and plans to acquire a number of automakers to expand the company's line of vehicles. Ford bought Sweden's Volvo car operations for $6.45 billion to become part of its new Premier Automotive Group. Nasser also hooked up with Microsoft's MSN Carpoint service to test market a name-your-price car-buying plan in Florida and opened a plant in Norway to build a two-passenger thermoplastic vehicle named the "Th!nk." In racing history, Ford made news with a four-door Taurus replacing the discontinued Thunderbird on the NASCAR circuit. As far as product, 1999 was a year of mainly refinements for Ford passenger cars, with the Contour getting a "Euro" suspension, the Crown Victoria adding standard antilock brakes, the Escort getting a standard AM/FM stereo cassette and the Taurus switching to five-passenger standard seating.

The 2000 Focus was introduced as an all-new small car to replace the Escort and, eventually Contour. It was available as a three-door hatchback, a sedan, and a wagon. The Escort had no major changes, except that the wagon was dropped. The Contour LX was dropped and the only four-cylinder Contour left was the SE sedan. The high-performance Taurus SHO model was dropped and the remaining models were redesigned in two trim levels: LX and SE with higher horsepower. The Crown Victoria got a new emergency interior trunk release and rear child seat anchors. Ford Motor Co. achieved record volume, revenue, and operating earnings per share and generated strong operating profits and the Focus became the world's best-selling car. Ford acquired Land Rover and integrated it into the company's overall business. But, a major challenge for Ford in 2000 was the headline-making Firestone tire recall that severed Ford's longstanding relationship with Firestone that dated back to the Model T era.

The 2001 Focus was a sophisticated compact aimed at the worldwide market with hatchback, sedan, and wagon. The only Escort left was the ZX2 coupe. It came in a few new colors. The Taurus had minor changes like a child seat tethers, Spruce Green Metallic paint, and an 18-gal. fuel tank. The Crown Victoria featured a more powerful V-8, minor interior improvements, and an optional adjustable pedal assembly. Ford's Firestone tire recall troubles continued with the automaker losing millions on its profitable Explorer SUV and company president and CEO Jack Nasser went on the offensive against Firestone. The quality of Ford's cars and trucks also deteriorated, along with its worker productivity. On Tues., Oct. 30, 2001, Ford Chairman William Clay Ford, Jr., forced the resignation of Nasser, saying that Ford had lost its focus under him. On a more positive note, Ford celebrated a centennial of Ford racing with a special event at the Henry Ford Museum & Greenfield Village during September.

New features for the 2002 Focus included a Personal Safety System and an all-new ZX5 five-door hatchback with the ZX3's Euro styling with the versatility of four doors. A new ZTW wagon included a sporty package and available for the first time were a power moonroof and six-disc in-dash CD changer. You could still get an Escort in 2002, but it was essentially a carryover model with few changes. The Taurus remained available in two body styles: sedan and wagon. A flexible fuel version of the Vulcan engine that ran on E-85 ethanol, regular unleaded gasoline or any combination of the two in the same tank was optional. The year's big news was an all-new two-passenger Thunderbird based on the Lincoln LS platform. In September 2000, Neiman Marcus made the first 200 special edition 2002 Thunderbirds available for early orders in its annual Christmas Book and sold out in two hours and 15 minutes. Ford started taking T-Bird orders on Jan. 8, 2001, the day the car made its regular production debut at the Detroit Auto Show. On November 12, in Las Vegas, the 2002 Ford Thunderbird had captured *Motor Trend* magazine's "Car of the Year" award. Said Jim O'Connor, Ford Div. president. "The all-new Thunderbird celebrates Ford's heritage of innovation and reaffirms our goal to build the best cars on the planet—cars that invoke passion and touch people's hearts and souls."

*(Contributors to the Ford section of this catalog include Robert C. Ackerson who originally compiled the technical data and tables for the prewar section of the **Standard Catalog of American Cars 1805-1942**, James M. Flammang who originally compiled all of the data for the **Standard Catalog of American Cars 1976-1986**, John A. Gunnell who edited the original **Standard Catalog of American Cars 1946-1975**, Beverly Rae Kimes who wrote the prewar histories and compiled the prewar model information for the original **Standard Catalog of American Cars 1805-1942**, Ron Kowalke who edited the second edition of the **Standard Catalog of Fords 1903-1998**, Robert L. Lichty who edited the first edition of the **Standard Catalog of Fords 1903-1990** and John Smith who originally compiled the 1946-1975 data for the **Standard Catalog of American Cars 1946-1975**).*

2002 Ford Thunderbird two-door convertible. (FMC)

1903 FORD

1903 Ford Model A runabout. (OCW)

FORD — MODEL A — TWO: The first production automobile produced by the Ford Motor Company, which was incorporated on June 16, 1903, the Model A was a two-seater runabout capable of a maximum speed of 30 mph.

With a weight of just 1,250 pounds it was an early manifestation of Henry Ford's grasp of the automotive concept that would be fully exhibited in the Model T. As was common to most early automobiles the Model A had a horse buggy (without the horse of course!) appearance. The motor was positioned under the seat and a detachable tonneau provided seating for two additional passengers who gained access to their seats through a rear door.

I.D. DATA: Serial numbers were dash mounted, adjacent to steering column.

Model No.	Body Type & Seating	Factory Price	Shipping Weight	Prod. Total
A	Rbt.-2P	850	1250	Note 1
A	Rbt. w/ton.-2P	950	—	Note 1

NOTE 1: Total production for Model A Series was 670 or 1,708, depending upon the source referred to. Ford officially used the 670 figure.

ENGINE: Opposed. Two. Cast-iron block. B & S: 4 x 4 in. Disp.: 100.4 cid. Brake H.P.: 8. Valve lifters: mechanical. Carb.: Schebler (early), Holley.

CHASSIS: W.B. 72 in.

TECHNICAL: Planetary transmission. Speeds: 2F/1R. Floor controls. Chain drive. Differential, band brakes. Wooden spoke wheels.

HISTORY: Introduced July 1903. On June 19, 1903, Barney Oldfield drove the Ford 999 to a new one-mile record time of 59.6 seconds. Calendar year production: 1,708. Model year production: (1903-1904) 1,700. The president of Ford was John S. Gray.

1904 FORD

FORD — MODELS AC, C — TWO: These two Ford models replaced the Model A in late 1904. Both were powered by a larger engine developing 10-hp. Ford claimed the top speed of both cars was 38 mph. The Model AC was essentially a Model A with the new Model C engine. The Model C had its fuel tank positioned under the hood while that of the AC was located beneath the seat. Both cars had a longer, 78-inch wheelbase than that of the Model A

FORD — MODEL B — FOUR: The Model B was a drastic shift in direction for Henry Ford. With its four-passenger body, polished wood and brass trim, it was an elegant and expensive automobile. Powered by a 24-hp, 318-cubic inch four it was capable of a top speed of 40 mph. In place of the dry cells carried by earlier Fords, the Model B was equipped with storage batteries. A 15-gallon fuel tank was also

fitted. Other features separating the $2,000 Model B from other Fords was its shaft drive and rear hub drum brakes.

I.D. DATA: Location of serial number: dash mounted, adjacent to steering column.

Model No.	Body Type & Seating	Factory Price	Shipping Weight	Prod. Total
Model A	Rbt.-2P	850	1250	Note 1
Model A	Rbt. w/ton.-2P	950	1250	Note 1
Model AC	Rbt.-2P	850	1250	Note 1
Model AC	Rbt. w/ton.-2P	950	1250	Note 1
Model C	Rbt.-2P	850	1250	Note 1
Model C	Rbt. w/ton.-2P	950	1250	Note 1
Model B	2-dr Tr -4P	2000	1700	Note 1

NOTE 1: Total production in 1904 was 1,695 cars. Ford reported building a total of 670 model As and 1900 models A and AC altogether. Other sources show figures that vary.

ENGINE [Model A]: Cylinder layout: opposed. Two. Cast-iron block. B & S: 4 x 4 in. Disp.: 100.4 cid. Brake H.P.: 8. Valve lifters: mechanical. Carb.: Holley.

ENGINE [Model AC, C]: Cylinder layout: opposed. Two. Cast-iron block. B & S: 4-1/4 x 4-1/4 in. Disp; 120.5 cid. Brake H.P.: 10. Valve lifters: mechanical. Carb.: Holley.

ENGINE [Model B]: Inline. Four. Cast-iron block. B & S: 4-1/4 x 5 in. Disp.: 283.5 cid. Brake H.P.; 24. Valve lifters: mechanical. Carb.: Holley.

CHASSIS: [Model A] W.B : 72 in. [Model B] W.B.: 92 in. [Model C, Model AC] W.B.: 78 in. Tires: 28.

1904 Ford Model C runabout with tonneau. (OCW)

1904 Ford Model B. (OCW)

1904 Ford Model B touring. (JAC)

TECHNICAL: [Models A, AC, C] Planetary transmission. Speeds: 2F/1R. Floor shift controls. Cone clutch. Chain drive. Differential band brakes. Wooden spoke wheels. [Model B] Planetary transmission. Speeds: 2F/1R. Floor shift controls. Cone clutch. Shaft drive. Drum brakes. Two rear wheels. Wooden spoke wheels.

HISTORY: Date of Introduction: September 1904 (Model C, AC). Calendar year production: 1695. Model year production: (1904-1905) 1,745. The president of Ford was John S. Gray.

1905 FORD

1905 Ford Model B touring. (OCW)

FORD — MODEL F — TWO: The Ford Models C and B were carried into 1905. The Model C was given light yellow painted running gear in place of the former red finish along with wider 3 x 28 wheels.

In February 1905, these Fords were joined by the Model F powered by a two-cylinder engine developing approximately 16-hp. The Model F had a wheelbase of 84 inches and was fitted with a green body, cream colored wheels and running gear.

I.D. DATA: Serial numbers were dash mounted, adjacent to steering column.

Model No.	Body Type & Seating	Factory Price	Shipping Weight	Prod. Total
C	Rbt.-2P	800	1250	Note 1
C	Rbt w/ton.-4P	950	1250	Note 1
B	2-dr. Tr.-4P	2000	1700	Note 1
F	2-dr. Tr. Car-4P	1000	1400	Note 1
F	2-dr. Dr. Cpe.-2P	1250	—	Note 1

NOTE 1: Total production for 1905 was 1,599 cars.

ENGINE [Model C]: Opposed. Two. Cast-iron block. B & S: 4-1/4 x 4-1/2 in. Disp; 120.5 cid. Brake H.P.: 10. Valve lifters: mechanical. Carb.: Holley.

ENGINE [Model B]: Inline. Four. Cast-iron block. B & S: 4-1/4 x 4 in. Disp.: 283.5 cid. Brake H.P.: 24. Valve lifters: mechanical. Carb.: Holley.

1905 Ford Model B tonneau touring. (RLC)

1905 Ford Model C runabout with tonneau. (OCW)

ENGINE [Model F]: Opposed. Two. Cast-iron block. B & S: 4-1/2 x 4 in. Disp.: 127 cid. Brake H.P.: 16. Valve lifters: mechanical. Carb.: Holley.

CHASSIS: [Model C] W.B.: 78 in. Tires: 28. [Model F] W.B.: 84 in. Tires: 30. [Model B] W.B.: 92 in. Tires: 32.

TECHNICAL: [Model C] Planetary transmission. Speeds: 2F/1R. Floor controls. Cone clutch. Chain drive. Differential band brakes. Wooden spoke wheels. Wheel size: 28. [Model B] Planetary transmission. Speeds: 2F/1R. Floor controls. Cone clutch. Shaft drive. Drum brakes on two rear wheels. Wooden spoke wheels. Wheel size: 32. [Model F] Planetary transmission. Speeds: 2F/1R. Floor controls. Cone clutch. Chain drive. Differential band brakes. Wooden spoke wheels. Wheel size: 30.

OPTIONS: Top. Windshield. Lights.

HISTORY: Introduced February 1905 (Model F). Calendar year production: 1,599. Model year production: (1905-1906) 1,599. The president of Ford was John S. Gray.

1906 FORD

FORD — MODEL K — SIX: Late in 1905 the Model K Ford, priced at $2,500 in touring form, debuted. Since Henry Ford was moving close to the final design of his "car for the multitudes," it's not surprising that he cared little for this expensive automobile. Along with the touring model a roadster version was offered that was guaranteed to attain a 60 mph top speed.

1906 Ford Model K tonneau touring. (RLC)

1906 Ford Model N runabout. (RLC)

FORD — MODEL N — FOUR: The $500 Model N with its front mounted four-cylinder engine developing over 15-hp was capable of 45 mph. Its styling, highlighted by such features as twin nickel-plated front lamps and a boattail rear deck, plus an 84-inch wheelbase, and a reputation for reliability represented a solid step forward by Henry Ford in his quest for a low-priced car for the mass market.

FORD — MODEL F — TWO: The Model F was continued into 1906 unchanged. No longer available were Models B and C.

I.D. DATA: Dash mounted, adjacent to steering column.

Model No.	Body Type & Seating	Factory Price	Shipping Weight	Prod. Total
Model F	2-dr. Tr. Cr.-4P	1100	1400	Note 1
Model K	2-dr. Tr. Cr.-4P	2500	2400	Note 1
Model K	Rbt.-4P	2500	2400	Note 1
Model N	Rbt.-2P	600	800	Note 1

NOTE 1: Total production was 2,798 or 8,729 depending upon the source referred to. Ford Motor Co. records show both figures.

1906 Ford Model N roadster. (OCW)

1906 Ford Model K touring. (JAC)

ENGINE [Model F]: Opposed. Two. Cast-iron block. B & S: 4-1/4 x 4-1/2 in. Disp: 128 cid. Brake H.P.: 10. Valve lifters: mechanical. Carb.: Holley.

ENGINE [Model K]: Inline. Six. Cast-iron block. B & S: 4-1/2 x 4-1/4 in. Disp.: 405 cid. Brake H.P.: 40. Valve lifters: mechanical. Carb.: Holley.

ENGINE [Model N]: Inline Four. Cast-iron block. B & S: 3-3/4 x 3-3/8 in. Disp.: 149 cid. Brake H.P.: 15-18. Valve lifters: mechanical. Carb.: Holley.

CHASSIS: [Series Model F] W.B.: 84 in. Tires: 30. [Series Model N] W.B.: 84 in. Tires: 2-1/2 in. width. [Series Model K] W.B.: 114/120 in.

TECHNICAL: [Model F] Transmission: Planetary. Speeds: 2F/1R. Floor shift controls. Cone clutch. Chain drive. Differential band. Wooden spokes. Wheel size: 30. [Model K] Transmission: Planetary. Speeds 2F/1R. Floor shift controls. Disc clutch. Shaft drive. [Model N] Transmission: Planetary. Speeds 2F/1R. Floor controls. Disc clutch. Chain drive.

OPTIONS: Cowl lamps. Bulb horn. Three-inch wheels (Model N) ($50.00).

HISTORY: Henry Ford became president of the Ford Motor Company, following the death of John S. Gray on July 6, 1906. A racing version of the Model K set a new world's 24 hour record of 1,135 miles averaging 47.2 mph at Ormond Beach.

1907 FORD

1907 Ford six-cylinder roadster. (OCW)

FORD — MODEL K — SIX: The Model K was unchanged for 1907.

FORD — MODEL N — FOUR: The Model N was continued unchanged for 1907. As before it was a handsome automobile with nickel hardware and quarter circle fenders. Volume production didn't begin until late 1907 when the price rose to $600.

FORD — MODEL R — FOUR: The Model R was introduced in February 1907 as a more elaborate version of the Model N with foot boards in place of the Model N's carriage step. A mechanical lubrication system also replaced the forced-feed oiler of the Model N.

FORD — MODEL S — FOUR: The Model S had the same mechanical and appearance features as that of the Model R, in addition to a single seat tonneau.

I.D. DATA: Serial numbers were dash mounted, adjacent to steering column.

Model No.	Body Type & Seating	Factory Price	Shipping Weight	Prod. Total
K	2-dr. Tr. Car-4P	2800	2000	—
K	Rbt.-4P	2800	2000	—
N	Rbt.-2P	600	1050	—
R	Rbt.-2P	750	1400	Note 1
S	Rbt. w/ton.-4P	700	1400	—
S	Rds.-2P	750	—	—

NOTE 1: Total production of the Model R was approximately 2,500 cars.

ENGINE [Model K]: Inline. Six. Cast-iron block. B & S: 4-1/2 x 4-1/4 in. Disp.: 405 cid. Brake H.P.: 40. Valve lifters: mechanical. Carb.: Holley.

ENGINE [Model N, R, S]: Inline. Four. Cast-iron block. B & S: 3-3/4 x 3-3/8 in. Disp.: 149 cid. Brake H.P.: 15-18. Valve lifters: mechanical. Carb.: Holley.

CHASSIS: [Model K] W.B.: 120 in. [Model N, R, S] W.B.: 84 in. Tires: three-in. width.

TECHNICAL: [Model K] Planetary transmission. Speeds: 2F/1R. Floor controls. Disc clutch. Shaft drive. [Model N, R, S] Planetary transmission. Speeds: 2F/1R. Floor controls. Disc clutch. Chain drive.

HISTORY: Calendar year production was 6,775 according to some sources and 14,887 according to others. The president of Ford was Henry Ford.

1907 Ford Model K touring. (OCW)

1907 Ford Model S roadster. (OCW)

1908 Ford Model S roadster. (RLC)

FORD — MODELS K, N, R, S — FOUR: For the 1908 model year Ford continued to produce the K, N, R, and S models until production of the Model T began in October 1908.

I.D. DATA: Serial numbers were dash mounted, adjacent to steering column.

Model No.	Body Type & Seating	Factory Price	Shipping Weight	Prod. Total
K	2-dr. Tr. Cr.-4P	2800	2000	—
K	Rbt.-4P	2800	2000	—
N	Rbt.-2P	600	1050	—
N	Land.-4P	—	—	—
R	Rbt.-2P	750	1400	—
S	Rbt. w/ton.-4P	750	1400	—
S	Rds.-2P	700	—	—

ENGINE [Model K]: Inline. Six. Cast-iron block. B & S: 4-1/2 x 4-1/4 in. Disp.: 405 cid. Brake H.P.: 40. Valve lifters: mechanical. Carb.: Holley.

ENGINE [Model N, R, S]: Inline. Four. Cast-iron block. B & S: 3-3/4 x 3-3/8 in. Disp.: 149 cid. Brake H.P.: 15-18. Valve lifters: mechanical. Carb.: Holley.

CHASSIS: [Model K] W.B.: 120 in. [Model N, R, S] W.B.: 84 in. Tires: three-in. width.

TECHNICAL: [Model K] Planetary transmission. Speeds: 2F/1R. Floor shift controls. Disc clutch. Shaft drive. [Model N, R, S] Planetary transmission. Speeds: 2F/1R. Floor shift controls. Disc clutch. Chain drive.

HISTORY: Calendar year production was 6,015 according to some sources and 10,202 according to others (including early Model T Fords). The president of Ford was Henry Ford.

1908 Ford Model S roadster. (OCW)

1909 FORD

1909 Ford Model T Tourster. (OCW)

1909 Ford Model T touring. (HFM)

FORD — EARLY 1909 — MODEL T: The Model T Ford was introduced in October 1908, and was an entirely new car when compared to Ford's previous models. The engine had four cylinders, cast enbloc with a removable cylinder head, quite unusual for the time. The engine pan was a one-piece steel stamping and had no inspection plate.

The chassis featured transverse springs, front and rear; a rear axle housing that was drawn steel rather than a casting. Rear axles were nontapered, the hubs being held with a key and a pin, with the pin being retained by the hub cap. The front axle was a forged "I" beam with spindles that had integral arms.

The use of vanadium steel almost throughout made for a stronger yet lighter machine that gave the Ford impressive performance for its time.

Wheels were 30 in. with 30 x 3 in. tires on the front, and 30 x 3-1/2 in. on the rear. The wheel hub flanges were 5-1/2 in. diameter (compared with 6 in. from 1911 until the end of production in 1927).

Windshields and tops were optional equipment on the open cars, as were gas headlights, speedometers, robe rails, Prest-o-lite tanks, foot rests, auto chimes, car covers and other accessories that Ford would install at the factory.

The radiator was brass, as were any lamps furnished (oil cowl and tail lamps were standard equipment). The hood had no louvers and was made of aluminum.

Body styles offered were the touring, runabout (roadster), coupe, town car and landaulet.

Bodies were generally made of wood panels over a wood frame, and were offered in red, gray and green, gray being primarily on the runabouts, red on the tourings, and green on the town cars and landaulets.

These early cars (first 2,500) were so unique that they are generally considered a separate subject when discussing the Model T. Essentially, the engines had built-in water pumps, and the first 800 cars came with two foot pedals and two control levers (the second lever being for reverse) instead of the usual three pedals and one lever.

Front fenders were square tipped, with no bills.

FORD — LATE 1909 — MODEL T: Beginning about car number 2500, the Model T became more or less standardized. Through most of 1909 the windshields and tops on the open cars remained optional, but more and more were delivered with this equipment, as well as gas headlights, factory installed. By the end of the year, they were standard.

Body types and styling continued unchanged. Colors continued as in the early production except that both green and red touring cars were produced, along with a mixture of colors in the other models as well. Red was not offered after June 1909. Black was not listed as an available color and only one of the shipping invoices showed black, but early cars extant seem to indicate that black was used. This could be due to oxidation of the top color coat, but black early Fords are an enigma to the Model T student. The one aluminum-paneled touring body, built by Pontiac Body, was discontinued about September 1909.

Fenders were similar in design to the earlier 1909s but now had rounded fronts with small "bills."

The engine no longer had the water pump. It was now cooled by thermosyphon action and set the pattern for all later Model T engines.

I.D. DATA: [Early 1909 (October 1908 to April 1909)] Serial number was between center exhaust ports on side of engine. Starting: 1 (October 1908). Ending: 2500 (approx.) (The first of the non-water pump engines was 2448, built on April 22, 1909, but there was some mixture of the old and the new in production for a short time.) Calendar year engine numbers: 1 to 309. (October to December 1908). Car numbers were stamped on a plate on the front seat kick panel and these were the same as the engine numbers. Other numbers stamped on the body sills, etc. were manufacturer's numbers and not an identifying number. [1909] Serial number was behind the timing gear on the lower right side of the engine. Starting: 2501 (approx.) Ending: 11145 (approx.) (There is no "break" between the 1909 and 1910 cars; 11146 was the first number assembled in October 1909, the beginning of Ford's fiscal year 1910). 1909 calendar year engine numbers: 310 to 14161 (approx.). Car numbers were stamped on a plate on the front seat kick panel and these were the same as the engine numbers. Other numbers stamped on the body sills, etc. were manufacturer's numbers and not an identifying number.

Model No.	Body Type & Seating	Factory Price	Shipping Weight	Prod. Total
T	Tr.-5P	850 (A)	1200	7728 (B)
T	Rbt.-2P	825 (A)	NA	2351 (B)
T	Town Car-7P	1000 (A)	NA	236 (B)
T	Landaulet-7P	950 (A)	NA	298 (B)
T	Cpe.-2P	950 (A)	NA	47 (B)

NOTE: 1,200 pounds was the figure given for the touring car and "others in proportion." The bare chassis weighed about 900 pounds.

All body styles except the roadster had two doors, the front compartment being open and without doors on all but the coupe.

(A) Prices effective October 1, 1908 (at introduction of the Model T).

(B) Fiscal year: October 1, 1908, to September 30, 1909.

ENGINE [Early 1909 (first 2,500)]: L-head. Four. Cast-iron block. B & S: 3-3/4 x 4 in. Disp.: 176.7 cid. C.R.: 4.5:1 (approx.) Brake H.P.: 22 @ 1600 rpm. N.A.C.C. H.P. 22.5. Main bearings: three. Valve lifters: solid. Carb.: Kingston five-ball, Buffalo. Torque: 83 lbs.-ft. @ 900 rpm.

NOTE: The first 2,500 engines had an integral gear-driven water pump and a gear-driven fan. There was no babbitt in the upper half of the main bearings, no inspection plate in the crankcase. Valve stems and lifters are exposed (no cover door).

ENGINE [1909]: L-head. Four. Cast-iron block. B & S: 3-3/4 x 4 in. Disp.: 176.7 cid. C.R.: 4.5:1 (approx.). Brake H.P.: 22 @ 1600 rpm. N.A.C.C. H.P.: 22.5. Main bearings: three. Valve lifters: solid. Carb.: Kingston five-ball, Holley, Buffalo. Torque: 83 lbs.-ft. @ 900 rpm.

NOTE: No water pump, now cooled by thermosyphon action. There was no babbitt in the upper half of the main bearings. No inspection plate in the crankcase. Valve stems and lifters are exposed (no cover door).

CHASSIS: W.B.: 100 in. O.L.: 10 ft. 8 in. (chassis) 11 ft. 2-1/2 in. (car). Front/Rear Tread: 56 in. (60 in. optional until 1916). Tires: 30 x 3 front, 30 x 3-1/2 rear, standard equipment 1909-1925.

NOTE: Chassis essentially identical except those after mid-1913 have a longer rear crossmember.

1909 Ford Model T coupe. (HAC)

TECHNICAL: [Early 1909 (First 800)] Planetary transmission. Speeds: 2F/1R, two pedal controls and two levers on floor. (See "General Comments") Multiple disc clutch (24 discs). Torque tube drive. Straight bevel rear axle. Overall ratio: 3.63:1. Brakes: contracting band in transmission. Hand-operated internal expanding in rear wheels. Foot brake stops driveshaft. Parking brake on two rear wheels. Wheel size: 30 in.

OPTIONS: The basic equipment included three oil lamps only (two side and one tail).

OPTIONS: Windshield. Headlamps. Tops. Horns. Prest-o-lite tanks (instead of the carbide tank). Robe rails. Tire chains. Top boots. Foot rests. Spare tire carriers. Speedometers. Bumpers. No prices were given.

GENERAL COMMENTS

Clutch & Brakes [through car 800]: Clutch pedal gives low when pressed to floor, high when released, neutral in between. Reverse lever puts clutch in neutral and applies reverse brake band. Second lever is the parking brake. [1909-1927] Planetary transmission. Speeds: 2F/1R. Three pedal controls and one lever on floor. Multiple disc clutch (26 discs 1909-1915), (25 discs 1915-1927). Torque tube drive. Straight bevel rear axle. Overall ratio: 3.63:1. Brakes: Contracting band in transmission. Hand-operated internal expanding in rear wheels. Foot brake stops driveshaft. Parking brake on two rear wheels. Wheel size: 30 in. (21 in. optional in 1925, standard in 1926-1927). Drivetrain options: 4.0:1 optional rear axle ratio beginning in 1919.

Clutch & Brakes [after car 800]: Clutch pedal gives low when pressed to floor, high when released, neutral in between. Control lever puts clutch in neutral and applies parking brake. Center foot pedal applies reverse. Third (right-hand) pedal is the service brake, applying transmission brake band.

Model T Wheels: Standard wheels are wooden spoke with demountable rims, an option beginning in 1919. In 1925, 21 in. wood spoke demountable rim wheels were an option; these became standard in 1926. Beginning January 1926 optional 21 in. wire wheels became available. These became standard on some closed cars in calendar year 1927.

In mid-1925 (1926 models) the transmission brake was made about a half-inch wider, and the rear wheel brakes were enlarged to 11 in. with lined shoes. 1909-1925 were seven in. with cast-iron shoes (no lining).

Springs were transverse semi-elliptic, front and rear.

Model T Steering: 3:1 steering gear ratio by planetary gear at top of steering column until mid-1925 when ratio was changed to 5:1.

1910 FORD

FORD — MODEL T: The 1910 Fords were unchanged from 1909, except for a number of mechanical modifications in the rear axle, and the use of one standard color on all models, dark green. The landaulet and coupe were discontinued in 1910 and a new tourabout (basically a touring car using two separate seat sections) was added. All 1910 Model Ts had windshields.

I.D. DATA: Serial number was behind the timing gear on the lower right side of the engine. Starting: 11146 (approx.). Ending: 31532 (approx.). (There is no "break" between the 1910 and 1911 cars. 31533 was the first number assembled in October 1910, the beginning of Ford's fiscal year 1911. The first "1911" car built was a torpedo runabout in which the chassis was assembled October 5, and the final assembly occurred October 26. The first "blue" cars were built during October and are presumed to be "1911" models.) 1910 calendar year engine numbers: 14162 (approx.) to 34901. Car numbers were stamped on a plate on the front seat kick panel and these were the same as the engine numbers. Other numbers stamped on the body sills, etc. were manufacturer's numbers and not an identifying number.

Model No.	Body Type & Seating	Factory Price	Shipping Weight	Prod. Total
T	Tr.-5P	950 (A)	1200	16,890 (B)
T	Tourabout-4P	950 (A)	NA	** (C)
T	Rbt.-2P	900 (A)	NA	1486 (B)
T	Town Car-7P	1200 (A)	NA	377 (B)
T	Landaulet-7P	1100 (A)	NA	2 (B)
T	Cpe-2P	1050 (A)	NA	187 (B)
T	Chassis	NA	900	108 (D)

NOTE: 1,200 pounds was the figure given for the touring car, and "others in proportion." The bare chassis weighed about 900 pounds.

All body styles except the roadster and the tourabout had two doors, the front compartment being open and without doors on all but the coupe. The tourabout was similar to the touring but had two roadster-like seat sections and no doors.

(A) Prices effective October 1, 1909.

(B) Fiscal year, October 1, 1909, to September 30, 1910.

(C)** Tourings and tourabouts grouped. 16,890 is the total of the two.

(D) Chassis not shown in the catalog.

1910 Ford Model T touring. (OCW)

1910 Ford Model T runabout. (OCW)

ENGINE: L-head. Four. Cast-iron block. B & S: 3-3/4 x 4 in. Disp.: 176.7 in. C.R.: 4.5:1 (approx.). Brake H.P.: 22 @ 1600 rpm. N.A.C.C. H.P.: 22.5. Main bearings: three. Valve lifters: solid. Carb.: Kingston five-ball, Holley, Buffalo (early 1910 only). Torque: 83 lbs.-ft. @ 900 rpm.

NOTE: No water pump, now cooled by thermosyphon action. There was no babbitt in the upper half of the main bearings. No inspection plate in the crankcase. Valve stems and lifters are exposed (no cover door).

CHASSIS: [1909-1925] W.B.: 100 in. O.L.: 10 ft. 8 in. (chassis) 11 ft. 2-1/2 in. (car). Front/Rear Tread: 56 in. (60 in. optional until 1916). Tires: 30 x 3 front, 30 x 3-1/2 rear. Standard equipment 1909-1925.

TECHNICAL: Planetary transmission. Speeds: 2F/1R. Three pedal controls and one lever on floor. Multiple disc clutch. Torque tube drive. Straight bevel rear axle. Overall ratio: 3.63:1. Brakes: Contracting band in transmission. Hand-operated internal expanding in rear wheels. Foot brake stops driveshaft. Parking brake on two rear wheels.

NOTE: Additional technical details will be found in the 1909 "General Comments" box.

OPTIONS: The many options listed for 1909 were not available in 1910. Standard equipment for the open cars now included the windshield, gas headlamps and carbide generator, speedometer and top with side curtains.

Interestingly, the more expensive closed cars (landaulet, town car and coupe) were equipped with horn and oil lamps only. Headlamps and speedometer were $80 extra.

1911 FORD

1911 Ford Model T. (OCW)

1911 Ford Model T touring. (OCW)

FORD — MODEL T: Approximately January 1911 the Model T was completely restyled. New fenders, a new but similar radiator, new wheels, new bodies, and during the year, a new engine, front axle and rear axle made the 1911 Ford almost a new beginning.

Bodies were now made with steel panels over a wood framework. A new standard color of dark blue was used on all models.*

Body types continued those offered in 1910. The tourabout and landaulet, while listed in the catalogs, were not produced in 1911. The coupe was phased out, only 45 being built.

Two new bodies were offered, the open runabout and the torpedo runabout, both of which differed considerably from the other models in that they had curved fenders, a longer hood, a lower seating arrangement and a lower and longer steering column. In addition, the gas tank was located on the rear deck, behind the seat. The two cars were similar, the open runabout not having doors while the torpedo had one on each side.

Near the end of the year, and then called a "1912" model, a delivery car was offered.

Fender construction was also new, setting a general pattern for the bulk of Model T production (until 1926). The front fenders had larger "bills" than did the 1910 style.

Lamps were all brass, gas headlights and oil (kerosene) side and tail lamps.

The rear axle housing was redesigned. The earlier pressed steel type had gone through a number of modifications in 1909, 1910 and early 1911 but in mid-year a new type with a cast-iron center section appeared. Axles were now taper end (perhaps changed before the new housing) and the hub flanges were six inches in diameter.

1911 Ford Model T town car. (HAC)

The front axle now used spindles with separate steering arms, and the axle ends were modified to accept the new spindles. The front axle remained relatively unchanged in later years.

* See comments on black cars in 1909.

I.D. DATA: Serial number was behind the timing gear on the lower right side of the engine. Starting: 31533 (approx.). Ending: 70749 (approx.). (There is no "break" between the 1911 and 1912 cars. 70750 was the first number assembled in October 1911, the beginning of Ford's fiscal year 1912.) 1911 calendar year engine numbers: 34901 to 88900 (approx.).

Car numbers were stamped on a plate on the firewall and these might be the same as the engine numbers, Ford now used the engine number to identify all cars. Other numbers stamped on the body sills, etc. were manufacturer's numbers and not an identifying number.

Model No.	Body Type & Seating	Factory Price	Shipping Weight	Prod. Total
T	Tr.-5P	780 (B)	1200	26,405 (C)
T	Trbt.-4P	725 (B)	NA	0 (C)
T	Rbt.-2P	680 (B)	NA	7845 (E)
T	Torp. Rbt.-2P	725 (B)	NA	(E)
T	Open Rbt. 2P	680 (B)	NA	(E)
T	Twn. Car-7P	960 (A)	NA	315 (C)
T	Lan.-7P	1100 (A)	NA	0 (C)
T	Cpe.-2P	840 (A)	NA	45 (C)
T	Chassis	NA	940	248 (D)

NOTE: 1,200 pounds was the figure given for the touring car, with "others in proportion." The bare chassis weighed about 940 pounds.

All body styles except the roadster and the tourabout had two doors, the front compartment being open and without doors on all but the coupe. The tourabout was similar to the touring but had two roadster-like seat sections and no doors.

The coupe, landaulet and tourabout were discontinued before calendar 1911.

(A) Prices for cars without headlamps.

(B) Prices effective October 1, 1910.

(C) Fiscal year, October 1, 1910, to September 30, 1911.

(D) Chassis not shown in catalogs.

(E) Runabouts not broken down by types in production figures.

ENGINE: L-head. Four. Cast-iron block. B & S: 3-3/4 x 4 in. Disp.: 176.7 cid. C.R.: 4.5:1 (approx.). Brake H.P.: 22 @ 1600 rpm. N.A.C.C. H.P.: 22.5. Main bearings: three. Valve lifters: solid. Carb.: Kingston five-ball, Holley 4500, Holley H-1 4550. Torque: 83 lbs.-ft. @ 900 rpm.

NOTE: Thermosyphon. Upper main bearings now babbitted. Valve chambers (two) now enclosed using steel doors held with one stud/nut each. Inspection plate in the crankcase.

CHASSIS: W.B.: 100 in. O.L.: 10 ft. 8 in. (chassis) 11 ft. 2-1/2 in. (car). Front/Rear Tread: 56 in. (60 in. optional until 1916). Tires: 30 x 3 front, 30 x 3-1/2 rear, standard equipment 1909-1925.

1911 Ford Model T touring. (OCW)

TECHNICAL: Planetary transmission. Speeds: 2F/1R. Three pedal controls and one lever on floor. Multiple disc clutch. Torque tube drive. Straight bevel rear axle. Overall ratio: 3.63:1. Brakes: Contracting band in transmission. Hand-operated internal expanding in rear wheels. Foot brake stops driveshaft. Parking brake on two rear wheels.

NOTE: Additional technical details will be found in the 1909 "General Comments" box.

OPTIONS: All cars equipped with headlamps, horn, etc. with no options. Ford even said the warranty, would be voided if any accessories were added, although it's doubtful this ever happened.

1912 FORD

1912 Ford Model T Fordor touring. (RLC)

1912 Ford Model T runabout. (OCW)

FORD — MODEL T: Approximately January 1912 the Model T was again restyled, although the appearance was similar to the 1911 cars. The touring car was now supplied with "fore doors" that enclosed the front compartment. These were removable and many have been lost over the years. The metal side panels of the touring were now relatively smooth from top to bottom, eliminating the "step" under the seats, which marked the 1911s.

The top support straps now fastened to the windshield hinge, rather than to the front of the chassis as they had in prior years.

The torpedo runabout was now based on the standard runabout, and the open runabout was discontinued. While retaining the curved rear fenders, the front fenders were now standard. The hood and steering column were also the same as those used on the other 1912 cars. The front compartment was enclosed in a manner similar to the 1911 torpedo.

The "1912" style year lasted only about nine months, an all new "1913" car appeared about September.

The only color on record for 1912 was dark blue but the existence of black cars of the era seems to indicate that black was available as well.

I.D. DATA: Serial number was behind the timing gear on the lower right side of the engine until about 100000, then just behind the water inlet on the left side of the engine. Also about this time the location was again changed to the standard position above the water inlet, with some mixture of locations for a time. Starting: 70750 (approx.). (Some records show 69877 built on September 30, 1911.) Ending: 157424 (approx.). (There is no "break" between the 1912 and 1913 cars. 157425 was the first number assembled on October 1912, the beginning of Ford's fiscal year 1913.) 1912 calendar year engine numbers: 88901 to 183563. According to Ford records engines with numbers B1 and B12247 were built at the Detroit plant beginning October 1912 and October 1913 but no records exist as to the exact dates. Car numbers were stamped on a plate on the firewall. Other numbers stamped on the body sills, etc. were manufacturer's numbers and not an identifying number. Car numbers no longer agreed with the motor numbers and Ford kept no records of them.

Model No.	Body Type & Seating	Factory Price	Shipping Weight	Prod. Total
T	Tr.-5P	690	1200	50,598 (A)
T	Torp. Runabout-2P	590	NA	13,376 (B)
T	Comm. Rds.-2P	590	NA	(B)
T	Town Car-7P	900	NA	802 (A)
T	Delv. Car-2P	700	NA	1845 (A)
T	Cpe.-2P	NA	NA	19 (C)
T	Chassis	NA	940	2133 (C)

NOTE: 1,200 pounds was the figure given for the touring car, with "others in proportion." The bare chassis weighed about 940 pounds.

The touring cars had three doors (none for the driver).

(A) Fiscal year, October 1, 1911, to September 30, 1912.

(B) Roadster production figures were combined. The total was 13,376.

(C) Coupes and the chassis were not shown in the catalogs.

ENGINE: L-head. Four. Cast-iron block. B & S: 3-3/4 x 4 in. Disp.: 176.7 cid. C.R.: 4.5:1 (approx.). Brake H.P.: 22 @ 1600 rpm. N.A.C.C. H.P.: 22.5. Main bearings: three. Valve lifters: solid. Carb.: Kingston six-ball*, Holley H-1 4550. Torque: 83 lbs.-ft. @ 900 rpm.

NOTE: Thermosyphon. Valve chambers (two) now enclosed using steel doors held with one stud/nut each. Inspection plate in the crankcase. * Kingston carburetor used in limited quantities and does not appear in any of the Ford parts lists.

CHASSIS: W.B. 100 in. O.L.: 10 ft. 8 in. (chassis) 11 ft. 2-1/2 in. (car). Front/Rear Tread: 56 in. (60 in. optional until 1916). Tires: 30 x 3 front, 30 x 3-1/2 rear, standard equipment 1909-1925.

TECHNICAL: Planetary transmission. Speeds: 2F/1R. Three pedal controls and one lever on floor. Multiple disc clutch. Torque tube drive. Straight bevel rear axle. Overall ratio: 3.63:1. Brakes: Contracting band in transmission. Hand-operated internal expanding in rear wheels. Foot brake stops driveshaft. Parking brake on two rear wheels.

NOTE: Additional technical details will be found in the 1909 "General Comments" box.

OPTIONS: The basic equipment included three oil lamps (two side and one tail). Windshield. Headlamps. Tops. Horns. Top boots. Speedometers.

1912 Ford Model T touring. (OCW)

FORD — MODEL T: About September 1912 Ford introduced the second new body in the year, the "1913" models. These were the first to set the "pattern" for the next 12 years. The metal side panels now extended from the firewall to the rear, with one door on the left side (touring car) at the rear, and two doors on the right.

The doors were unique with this new body; they extended clear to the splash apron. There was no metal support between the front and rear sections of the body and this proved to be a severe problem. The body could flex so much that the doors opened while underway. The initial solution to the problem was to add a steel reinforcement across the rear door sills; then heavier body sills, and then both the heavy sills and the steel reinforcement.

The bottom section of the windshield on the open cars now sloped rearwards, the top section being vertical and folding forward.

The fenders followed the pattern of the 1911-12 cars except that they no longer had the "bills" at the front.

Side, tail and headlamps were still oil and gas but were now made of steel (painted black) except for the tops and rims, which were still brass.

The rear axle housings were again redesigned. The center section was now larger (fatter) and the axle tubes were flared and riveted to it.

"Made in USA" now appeared on the radiator under the "Ford." The same notation appeared on many other parts as well and perhaps this was due to the Canadian production. Nineteen-thirteen was the first year in which Ford of Canada manufactured its own engines, etc.

According to Ford data, the 1913 cars were painted dark blue with striping on the early models. As in earlier models, black is a possibility but it is not documented in any Ford literature.

Body styles offered were the touring, runabout and town car. The torpedo with the rear deck mounted gas tank was discontinued. (Ford called the regular runabout a "torpedo" for several years after this.) The delivery car, which had proved to be a sales disaster, was also dropped.

I.D. DATA: Serial number was above the water inlet on the left side of he engine. Starting: 157425 (approx.) October 1912. "1913" cars may have been built earlier. Ending: 248735. (There is no "break" between the 1913 and 1914 cars. The "1914" style touring was introduced about August 1913, which could make the ending number around 320000 for "1913" cars.) 1913 calendar year engine numbers: 183564 to 408347. According to Ford records engines with numbers B1 and B12247 were built at the Detroit plant between October 1912 and October 1913 but no records exist as to the exact dates. Numbers stamped on the body sills, etc. were manufacturer's numbers and not an identifying number.

Model No.	Body Type & Seating	Factory Price	Shipping Weight	Prod. Total
T	3-dr. Tr.-5P	600 (A)	1200	126,715 (B)
T	2-dr. Rbt.-2P	525 (A)	NA	33,129 (B)
T	4-dr. Twn. Car-7P	800 (A)	NA	1,415 (B)
T	Delivery Car-2P	625 (A)	NA	513 (B)
T	2-dr. Cpe.-2P	NA	NA	1 (C)
T	Chassis	NA	960	8,438 (C)

NOTE: 1,200 pounds was the figure given for the touring car, with "others in proportion." The bare chassis weighed about 960 pounds.

(A) October 1, 1912.

(B) Fiscal year, October 1, 1912, to September 30, 1913.

(C) Coupes and the chassis were not shown in the catalogs.

ENGINE: L-head. Four. Cast-iron block. B & S: 3-3/4 x 4 in. Disp.: 176.6 cid. C.R.: 4.0:1 (approx.). Brake H.P.: 20 @ 1600 rpm. N.A.C.C. H.P.: 22.5. Main bearings: three. Valve lifters: solid. Carb.: Kingston Y (4400), Holley S (4450). Torque: 83 lbs.-ft. @ 900 rpm.

NOTE: Thermosyphon. Valve chambers (two) now enclosed using steel doors held with one stud/nut each. Inspection plate in the crankcase.

Camshaft modified for less power (less overlap in timing). Modified cylinder head for slightly lower compression.

CHASSIS: W.B.: 100 in. O.L.: 10 ft. 8 in. (chassis) 11 ft. 2-1/2 in. (car). Front/Rear Tread: 56 in. (60 in. optional until 1916). Tires: 30 x 3 front, 30 x 3-1/2 rear, standard equipment 1909-1925. Chassis essentially identical except those after mid-1913 have a longer rear crossmember.

1913 Ford Model T touring. (HFM)

TECHNICAL: Planetary transmission. Speeds: 2F/1R. Three pedal controls and one lever on floor. Multiple disc clutch. Torque tube drive. Straight bevel rear axle. Overall ratio: 3.63:1. Brakes: Contracting band in transmission. Hand-operated internal expanding in rear wheels. Foot brake stops driveshaft. Parking brake on two rear wheels.

NOTE: Additional technical details will be found in the 1909 "General Comments" box.

OPTIONS: All cars equipped with headlamps, horn, etc. with no options. About 1915 the speedometer was discontinued (and the price reduced). Ford even said the warranty would be voided if any accessories were added, although it's doubtful this ever happened.

1914 FORD

1914 Ford Model T touring. (OCW)

1914 Ford Model T runabout. (OCW)

FORD — MODEL T: The 1914 models looked almost identical to the 1913s but the doors were now inset into the side panels, and the body metal extended across the rear door sills, solving the weakness at that point in the 1913s, and setting the pattern for doors until 1926 models.

The windshield, while similar in appearance to the 1913, now folded to the rear. The windshield support rods were given a bend to clear the folded section.

Fenders were modified and now had embossed reinforcing ribs across the widest part and later in the apron area of both front and rear fenders. Front fenders had no "bill" in most 1914 models but a "bill" was added late in the year. The front fender iron bracket is secured to the fender with four rivets.

Black was now the Ford color, although Ford Archives records seem to indicate blue was still offered. Interestingly, black was never listed as an available color prior to 1914, this in spite of the many seemingly original pre-1914 black Fords. It is possible black was a common color even in 1909 but there is nothing in the records to prove it.

Lamps continued in the pattern of the 1913's, black and brass.

The chassis frame was modified, now had a longer rear crossmember, eliminating the forged body brackets used since 1909.

A bare chassis was added to the Ford line in 1914. In the fall of the year a sedan (commonly called a "centerdoor sedan") and a coupelet (the first "convertible") were introduced but these were "1915 models."

I.D. DATA: Serial number was above the water inlet on the left side of the engine. Starting: 348736 (approx.) October 1913. "1914" cars were built as early as August, which could make the first "1914" cars about 320000. Ending: 670000 (mid-January 1915). The new "1915" Ford was introduced in January at the Highland Park plant, but the "1914" style continued for a time at the branches. There is no clear break point in the style years. 1914 calendar year engine numbers: 408348 to 656063. Numbers stamped on the body sills, etc., were manufacturer's numbers and not an identifying number.

Model No.	Body Type & Seating	Factory Price	Shipping Weight	Prod. Total
T	3-dr. Tr.-5P	550 (A)	1200	165,832 (B)
T	2-dr. Rbt.-2P	500 (A)	NA	35,017 (B)
T	4-dr. Twn. Car-7P	750 (A)	NA	1,699 (B)
T	Chassis	NA	960	119 (B)

NOTE: 1,200 pounds was the figure given for the touring car, with "others in proportion." The bare chassis weighed about 960 pounds.

(A) August 1, 1913.

(B) Fiscal year, October 1, 1913, to July 31, 1914.

ENGINE: L-head. Four. Cast-iron block. B & S: 3-3/4 x 4 in. Disp.: 176.7 cid.. C.R.: 4.0:1 (approx.). Brake H.P.: 20 @ 1600 rpm. N.A.C.C. H.P.: 22.5. Main bearings: three. Valve lifters: solid. Carb.: Kingston Y (4400), Holley G (6040 brass body). Torque: 83 lbs.-ft. @ 900 rpm.

NOTE: Thermosyphon. Valve chambers (two) now enclosed using steel doors held with one stud/nut each. Inspection plate in the crankcase.

CHASSIS: W.B.: 100 in. O.L.: 10 ft. 8 in. (chassis) 11 ft. 2-1/2 in. (car). Front/Rear Tread: 56 in. (60 in. optional until 1916). Tires: 30 x 3 front, 30 x 3-1/2 rear, standard equipment 1909-1925.

TECHNICAL: Planetary transmission. Speeds: 2F/1R. Three pedal controls and one lever on floor. Multiple disc clutch. Torque tube drive. Straight bevel rear axle. Overall ratio: 3.63:1. Brakes: Contracting band in transmission. Hand-operated internal expanding in rear wheels. Foot brake stops driveshaft. Parking brake on two rear wheels.

NOTE: Additional technical details will be found in the 1909 "General Comments" box.

OPTIONS: The basic equipment included three oil lamps. (Two side and one tail.) Windshield. Headlamps. Tops. Horns. Top boots. Speedometers.

1915 & 1916 FORD

1915 Ford Model T. (OCW)

FORD — 1915-1916 — MODEL T: The 1915-style open cars were introduced at the Highland Park plant in January 1915 but the 1914 style continued in some of the branches until as late as April.

The bodies were essentially the same as the 1914 except for the front cowl section. Instead of the exposed wood firewall, the metal cowl curved "gracefully" inward to the hood former. The hood and radiator were the same as earlier (except for the louvers in the hood side panels).

The windshield was now upright, with the top section folding to the rear. Electric headlights were standard, these being of the "typical" size and shape of common Model T Fords until 1927.

Headlight rims were brass. Side lights were now of the rounded style, and interchangeable from side to side. The taillamp was similar but with a red lens in the door, and a clear lens on the side towards the license plate. Side and tail lamps were still kerosene. Side and tail lamps had brass tops and rims but were otherwise painted black. The headlights were powered by the engine magneto.

Fenders in the front again had "bills" and were the same as the later 1914s. While retaining the same style, later the fender iron bracket was revised and now held with three rivets. Rear fenders were now curved to follow the wheel outline. Neither front nor rear fenders were crowned.

The standard horn in 1915 was a bulb type, mounted under the hood. The hood now had louvers, perhaps so that the horn could be heard. Early in the year, though, Ford began using a magneto-powered horn on some production, and by October 1915 all had the new horn.

The sedan was unique. Made of aluminum panels, it required special rear fenders and splash aprons. The gasoline tank was located under the rear seat and proved to be quite unsatisfactory because of the poor fuel flow. The body was redesigned during the year and made of steel panels, and the gasoline tank was relocated under the driver's seat.

1915 Ford Model T touring. (AA)

The coupelet had a folding top but differed from the runabout in that the doors had windows and the windshield was like that in the sedan. It also had a larger turtle deck.

The rear axle was redesigned again, for the last time except for minor modifications. The center section was cast-iron and the axle tubes were straight and inserted into it.

The 1916 Fords were but an extension of the 1915s except for the deletion of the brass trim on the lamps. The hood was now made of steel, and all were equipped with the magneto horn.

"Portholes" were added to the side of the coupelet in an effort to allow the driver a better side view.

The sedan body was redesigned to now use standard fenders and splash aprons, and for a new gas tank under the driver's seat. The new body was all steel.

Body styles offered in 1915 and 1916 were the touring, runabout, sedan, coupelet and town car, in addition to the bare chassis.

I.D. DATA: [1915] Serial number was above the water inlet on the left side of the engine. Starting: 670000 approx. (January 1915) the new "1915" Ford was introduced in January at the Highland Park plant, but the "1914" style continued for a time at the branches. There is no clear break point in the style years. Ending: 856513 (July 24, 1915, end of fiscal 1915). 1915 calendar year engine numbers: 656064 to 1028313. Numbers stamped on the body sills, etc. were manufacturer's numbers and not an identifying number. [1916] Serial number was above the water inlet on the left side of the engine. Starting: 856514 (August 1, 1915). Ending: 1362989 (July 25, 1916, end of fiscal 1916). 1916 calendar year engine numbers: 1028314 to 1614516. Numbers stamped on the body sills, etc. were manufacturer's numbers and not an identifying number.

Model No.	Body Type & Seating	Factory Price	Shipping Weight	Prod. Total
1915				
T	3-dr. Tr.-5P	490 (A)	1500	244,181(B)
T	2-dr. Rbt.-2P	440 (A)	1380	47,116(B)
T	4-dr. Twn. Car-7P	690 (A)	NA	— (B)
T	2-dr. Sed.-5P	975 (A)	1730	989(B)
T	2-dr. Cpe.-2P	750 (A)	1540	2417(B)
T	Chassis	410 (A)	980	13,459(B)

(A) August 1, 1914.

(B) Fiscal year, August 1, 1914, to July 31, 1915.

Model No.	Body Type & Seating	Factory Price	Shipping Weight	Prod. Total
1916				
T	3-dr. Tr.-5P	440 (A)	1510	363,024(B)
T	2-dr. Rbt.-2P	390 (A)	1395	98,633(B)
T	4-dr. Twn. Car-7P	640 (A)	NA	1972(B)
T	2-dr. Sed.-5P	740 (A)	1730	1859(B)
T	2-dr. Cpe.-2P	590 (A)	1540	3532(B)
T	Chassis	360 (A)	1060	1174(B)
T	Ambulance	NA	NA	20,700(C)

(A) Price effective August 1, 1915.

(B) Fiscal year 1916, August 1, 1915, to July 30, 1916.

(C) Built for military.

ENGINE: L-head. Four. Cast-iron block. B & S: 3-3/4 x 4 in. Disp.: 176.7 cid. C.R.: 4.0:1 approx. Brake H.P.: 20 @ 1600 rpm. N.A.C.C. H.P.: 22.5. Main bearings: three. Valve lifters: solid. Carb.: Kingston L (6100), Holley G (6040 brass body). Torque: 83 lbs.-ft. @ 900 rpm.

NOTE: Thermosyphon. Valve chambers (two) now enclosed using steel doors held with one stud/nut each. Inspection plate in the crankcase.

1915 Ford Model T runabout. (OCW)

1916 Ford Model T coupelet. (OCW)

CHASSIS: (1915-1916) W.B.: 100 in. O.L.: 10 ft. 8 in. (chassis) 11 ft. 2-1/2 in. (car). Front/Rear Tread: 56 in. Tires: 30 x 3 front, 30 x 3-1/2 rear, standard equipment 1909-1925.

TECHNICAL: Planetary transmission. Speeds: 2F/1R. Three pedal controls and one lever on floor. Multiple disc clutch (26 discs 1909-1915). (25 discs 1915-1927). Torque tube drive. Straight bevel rear axle. Overall ratio: 3.63:1. Brakes: Contracting band in transmission. Hand-operated internal expanding in rear wheels. Foot brake stops driveshaft. Parking brake on two rear wheels.

NOTE: Additional technical details will be found in the 1909 "General Comments" box.

OPTIONS: The basic equipment included three oil lamps (two side and one tail.) Windshield. Headlamps. Tops. Horns. Top boots.

1917 & 1918 FORD

FORD — 1917-1918 — MODEL T: The Model T for 1917 looked like an all new car but was a rather simple evolution from the 1916. The brass radiator and the small hood were gone, as were all bits of brass trim.

New curved and crowned fenders, a new black radiator shell, and a new hood and hood former were the essential changes. The body itself was unchanged. Lamps were also the same as 1916.

The car continued with minor modifications, such as a different mounting base for the windshield, and new rectangular cross-section top sockets replacing the oval ones used since 1915.

Nickel-plating on the steering gear box, hubcaps and radiator filler neck replaced the earlier brass trim.

A new engine pan came out in 1917 that had a larger front section for a larger fan pulley. The pulley, however, was not enlarged until about 1920.

The "convertible" coupelet was replaced with a "hardtop" coupelet. While the top could no longer fold, the side window posts could be removed (and stored under the seat) giving the car the hardtop look.

During 1917 the Ford Model TT truck chassis was introduced. The town car was discontinued during the year.

I.D. DATA: [1917] Serial number was above the water inlet on the left side of the engine. Starting: 1362990 (August 1, 1916). Ending: 2113501 (July 28, 1917, end of fiscal year 1917). 1917 calendar year engine numbers: 1614517 to 2449179. Numbers stamped on the body sills, etc. were manufacturer's numbers and not an identifying number. [1918] Serial number was above the water inlet on the left side of the engine. Starting: 2113502 (August 1, 1917). Ending: 2756251 (July 27, 1918, end of fiscal year 1918). 1918 calendar year engine numbers: 2449180 to 2831426. Numbers stamped on the body sills, etc. were manufacturer's numbers and not an identifying number.

Model No.	Body Type & Seating	Factory Price	Shipping Weight	Prod. Total
1917				
T	3-dr. Tr.-5P	360 (A)	1480	568,128(B)
T	2-dr. Rbt.-2P	345 (A)	1385	107,240(B)
T	4-dr. Twn. Car-7P	595 (A)	NA	2328(B)
T	2-dr. Sed.-5P	645 (A)	1745	7361(B)
T	2-dr. Cpe.-2P	505 (A)	1580	7343(B)
T	Chassis	325 (A)	1060	41,165(B)
T	Amb.	NA	NA	1452(C)
TT	Truck Chassis	NA	1450	3(D)

(A) Price effective August 1, 1916.

(B) Fiscal year 1917, August 1, 1916, to July 30, 1917.

(C) Built for military.

(D) Apparently a pilot run.

Model No.	Body Type & Seating	Factory Price	Shipping Weight	Prod. Total
1918				
T	3-dr. Tr.-5P	360 (A)	450 (C)	432,519(D)
T	2-dr. Rbt.-2P	345 (A)	435 (C)	73,559(D)
T	4-dr. Twn. Car-7P	595 (A)	NA	2142(D)
T	2-dr. Sed.-5P	645 (A)	1715	35,697(D)
T	2-dr. Cpe.-2P	505 (A)	1580	14,771(D)
T	Chassis	325 (A)	1060	37,648(D)
T	Amb.	NA	NA	2136(E)
TT	Truck Chassis	600 (B)	1450	41,105(D)
T	Del.	NA	NA	399(F)
T	Foreign	NA	NA	24,000(G)

(A) Price effective August 1, 1917.

(B) Price effective October 6, 1917.

(C) Price effective February 21, 1918.

(D) Fiscal year 1918, August 1, 1917, to July 30, 1918.

(E) Built for military.

(F) Not indicated in catalog, perhaps for military.

(G) Cars built in foreign plants and Canada (no breakdown by types).

ENGINE: L-head. Four. Cast-iron block. B & S: 3-3/4 x 4 in. Disp.: 176.7 cid. C.R.: 3.98:1. Brake H.P.: 20 @1600 rpm. N.A.C.C. H.P.: 22.5. Main bearings: three. Valve lifters: solid. Carb.: Kingston L2 (6100), Holley G (6040 iron body). Torque: 83 lbs.-ft. @ 900 rpm.

1917 Ford Model T runabout. (HAC)

1917 Ford Model T touring. (OCW)

1917 Ford Model T. (OCW)

NOTE: Thermosyphon. Valve chambers (two) enclosed using steel doors held with one stud/nut each. Inspection plate in the crankcase.

New cylinder head with slightly lower compression and much larger water jacket.

CHASSIS: [1917-1918] W.B.: 100 in. O.L.: 10 ft. 8 in. (chassis) 11 ft. 2-1/2 in. (car). Front/Rear Tread: 56 in. Tires: 30 x 3 front, 30 x 3-1/2 rear, standard equipment 1909-1925.

TECHNICAL: Planetary transmission. Speeds: 2F/1R. Three pedal controls and one lever on floor. Multiple disc clutch (25 discs 1915-1927). Torque tube drive. Straight bevel rear axle. Overall ratio: 3.63:1. Brakes: Contracting band in transmission. Hand-operated internal expanding in rear wheels. Foot brake stops driveshaft. Parking brake on two rear wheels.

NOTE: Additional technical details will be found in the 1909 "General Comments" box.

OPTIONS: The basic equipment included three oil lamps (two side and one tail.) Windshield. Headlamps. Tops. Horns. Top boots.

1918 Ford Model T center door sedan. (HAC)

1919 & 1920 FORD

1919 Ford Model T touring. (OCW)

FORD — 1919-1920 — MODEL T: The body styling continued unchanged from 1918 but the Ford was finally given a battery and an electric starter. Beginning as standard equipment on the closed cars only, by mid-1919 it became an option on the open cars. This modification required a new engine block, transmission cover, flywheel, etc. but the general design of these items was unchanged except for the modifications needed to adapt the starter and generator.

Also available for the first time from Ford were wheels with demountable rims as standard equipment on the closed cars, and optional on the open models. When demountable wheels were used, all tires were the same size: 30 x 3-1/2.

With the electrical equipment came an instrument panel for the first time on a Model T (as factory equipment) on cars so equipped. Instrumentation consisted of an ammeter. Controls on the panel were the choke knob and the ignition/light switch. Speedometers were dealer installed options.

The coupelet was restyled. While looking the same, the door posts were now integral with the doors, no longer removable.

The rear axle was modified slightly. The oil filler hole was lowered to reduce the amount of oil that could be put in, and thus help the oil leak problem at the rear axles. The center section was milled to accept a gasket between the two halves.

The front radius rod was redesigned and now fastened below the axle, adding strength to the assembly.

1919 Ford Model T coupe. (OCW)

1919 Ford Model T runabout. (HAC)

I.D. DATA: [1919] Serial number was above the water inlet on the left side of the engine. Starting: 2756252 (August 1, 1918). Ending: 3277851 (July 30, 1919, end of fiscal year 1919). 1919 calendar year engine numbers: 2831427 to 3659971. Numbers stamped on the body sills, etc. were manufacturer's numbers and not an identifying number. [1920] Serial number was above the water inlet on the left side of the engine. Starting: 3277852 (August 1, 1919). Ending: 4233351 (July 31, 1920, end of fiscal year 1920). 1920 calendar year engine numbers: 3659972 to 4698419. Numbers stamped on the body sills, etc. were manufacturer's numbers and not an identifying number.

Model No.	Body Type & Seating	Factory Price	Shipping Weight	Prod. Total
T	3-dr. Tr.-5P	525 (B)	1500	286,935(E)
T	2-dr. Rbt.-2P	500 (B)	1390	48,867(E)
T	2-dr. Sed. 5P	875 (A)	1875	24,980(E)
T	2-dr. Cpe.-2P	750 (A)	1685	11,528(E)
T	4-dr. Twn. Car-7P	NA	—	17(G)
T	Chassis	475 (B)	1060	47,125(E)
T	Amb.	NA	2227(F)	
TT	Truck Chassis	550 (C)	1477	70,816(E)
		590 (D)	—	
T	Del.	—	—	5847(G)

(A) Includes starter and demountable wheels.

(B) Price effective August 16, 1918.

(C) Price with solid rubber tires.

(D) Price with pneumatic tires.

(E) Fiscal year 1919, August 1, 1918, to July 30, 1919.

(F) Built for military.

(G) Not indicated in catalog, perhaps for military.

NOTE: Starter was an option on the open cars at $75. Weight 95 lbs. Demountable rims were an additional $25. Weight 55 lbs.

1919 Ford Model T center door sedan. (OCW)

1919 Ford Model T touring. (OCW)

Model No.	Body Type & Seating	Factory Price	Shipping Weight	Prod. Total
1920				
T	3-dr. Tr.-5P	575 (B)	1500	165,929(E)
		675 (A)	1650	367,785(E)
T	2-dr. Rbt.-2P	550 (B)	1390	31,889(E)
		650 (A)	1540	63,514(E)
T	2-dr. Sed.-5P	975 (A)	1875	81,616(E)
T	2-dr. Cpe.-2P	850 (A)	1760	60,215(E)
T	Chassis	525 (B)	1060	18,173(E)
		620 (B)	1210	16,919(E)
TT	Truck Chassis	660 (C)	1477	135,002(E)
		640 (D)		

(A) Includes starter and demountable wheels.

(B) Price effective March 3, 1920.

(C) Price with solid rubber tires.

(D) Price with pneumatic tires.

(E) Fiscal year 1920, August 1, 1919, to July 30, 1920.

NOTE: Starter was an option on the open cars at $75. Weight 95 lbs. Demountable rims were an additional $25. Weight 55 lbs.

ENGINE: L-head. Four. Cast-iron block. B & S: 3-3/4 x 4 in. Disp.: 176.7 cid. C.R.: 3.98:1. Brake H.P.: 20 @ 1600 rpm. N.A.C.C. H.P.: 22.5. Main bearings: three. Valve lifters: solid. Carb.: Kingston L4 (6150). Holley NH (6200). Torque: 83 lbs.-ft. @ 900 rpm.

NOTE: Thermosyphon. Valve chambers (two) enclosed using steel doors held with one stud/nut each. Inspection plate in the crankcase. New lightweight connecting rods.

CHASSIS: [1919-1920] W.B.: 100 in. O.L.: 10 ft. 8 in. (chassis) 11 ft. 2-1/2 in. (car). Front/Rear Tread: 56 in. Tires: 30 x 3 front, 30 x 3-1/2 rear, standard equipment 1909-1925. 30 x 3-1/2 all around with demountable rims 1919-1925.

TECHNICAL: [1919-1920] Planetary transmission. Speeds: 2F/1R. Three pedal controls and one lever on floor. Multiple disc clutch (25 discs 1915-1927). Torque tube drive. Straight bevel rear axle. Overall ratio: 3.63:1. Brakes: Contracting band in transmission. Hand-operated internal expanding in rear wheels. Foot brake stops driveshaft. Parking brake on two rear wheels.

NOTE: Additional technical details will be found in the 1909 "General Comments" box.

OPTIONS: All cars equipped with headlamps, horn, etc. Starter ($75.00). Demountable rims (25.00).

1920-1922 FORD

FORD — MODEL T: Another new body appeared in the open cars in late 1920. It takes an expert to see the difference but different it was. Most noticeable was a new rear quarter panel, now an integral part of the side panel instead of the two-piece assembly used since 1913.

An oval-shaped gas tank (located under the driver's seat) had replaced the previous round type earlier in 1920, and this allowed the seat to be lowered. Seat backs were given a more comfortable angle and the result was a far more comfortable car.

The chassis frame was modified slightly; the runningboard support brackets were now pressed steel channels instead of the forged brackets with a tie rod used since 1909. Otherwise the basic car was like the previous models.

1920 Ford Model T turtledeck roadster. (RLC)

A new pinion bearing spool was used on the rear axle. The earlier type was an iron casting with enclosed mounting studs. The new spool was a forging and used exposed mounting bolts.

Body styles offered during this period were the touring, runabout, coupe-let and sedan, in addition to the chassis and the truck chassis.

I.D. DATA: (1921) Serial number was above the water inlet on the left side of the engine. Starting: 4233352 (August 2, 1920). Ending: 5223135 (July 30, 1921, end of fiscal 1921). 1921 calendar year engine numbers: 4698420 to 5568071. Numbers stamped on the body sills, etc, were manufacturer's numbers and not an identifying number. (1922) Serial number was above the water inlet on the left side of the engine. Starting: 5223136 (August 1, 1921). Ending: 6543606 (September 14, 1922; introduction of first "1923" model). 1922 calendar year engine numbers: 5638072 to 6953071. Numbers stamped on the body sills, etc. were manufacturer's numbers and not an identifying number.

Model No.	Body Type & Seating	Factory Price	Shipping Weight	Prod. Total
1921				
T	3-dr. Tr.-5P	440 (A) 415 (B)	1500	84,970(D)
T	3-dr. Tr.-5P	535 (A) 510 (B)	1650	647,300(E)
T	2-dr. Rbt.-2P	395 (A) 370 (B)	1390	25,918(D)
T	2-dr. Rbt.-2P	490 (A) 465 (B)	1540	171,745(E)
T	2-dr. Sed.-5P	795 (A) 760 (B)	1875	179,734(E)
T	2-dr. Cpe.-2P	745 (A) 695 (B)	1760	129,159(E)
T	Chassis	360 (A) 345 (B)	1060	13,356(D)
T	Chassis	455 (A) 440 (B)	1210	23,436(E)
T	Truck Chassis	545 (C) 495 (B)	1477	118,583(D)
T	Foreign & Canada	NA	NA	42,860(D)

(A) Price effective September 22, 1920.

(B) Price effective June 7, 1921.

(C) Price with pneumatic tires.

(D) August 1, 1920, to December 31, 1921 (Ford began calendar year figures in 1921).

(E) Includes starter and demountable wheels. Demountable rims were an additional $25. Weight 25 lbs.

1920 Ford Model T roadster. (JAC)

NOTE: Starter was an option on the open cars at $70. Weight 95 lbs. Demountable rims were an additional $25. Weight 55 lbs. roadster. (JAC)

Model No.	Body Type & Seating	Factory Price	Shipping Weight	Prod. Total
1922				
T	3-dr. Tr.-5P	355 (A) 348 (B) 298 (C)	1500	80,070 D)
T	3-dr. Tr.-5P	450 (A) 443 (B) 393 (C)	1650	514,333(E)
T	2-dr. Rbt.-2P	325 (A) 319 (B) 269 (C)	1390	31,923(D)
T	2-dr. Rbt.-2P	420 (A) 414 (B) 364 (C)	1540	133,433(E)
T	2-dr. Sed.-5P	660 (A) 645 (B) 595 (C)	1875	146,060(E)
T	4-dr. Sed.-5P	725 (C)	1950	4286(E)
T	2-dr. Cpe.-2P	595 (A) 580 (B) 530 (C)	1760	198,382(E)
T	Chassis	295 (A) 285 (B) 235 (C)	1060	15,228(D)
T	Chassis	390 (A) 380 (B) 330 (C)	1210	23,313(E)
T	Truck chassis	445 (A) 430 (B) 380 (C)	1477	135,629(D)
T	Truck chassis	475 (C)	1577	18,410(E)

(A) Price effective September 2, 1921.

(B) Price effective January 16, 1922.

(C) Price effective October 17, 1922.

(D) January 1, 1922, to December 31, 1922 (includes foreign production).

(E) Includes starter and demountable wheels.

NOTE: Starter was an option on the open cars at $70. Weight 95 lbs.

ENGINE [1920]: L-head. Four. Cast-iron block. B & S: 3-3/4 x 4 in. Disp.: 176.7 cid. C.R.: 3.98:1. Brake H.P.: 20 @ 1600 rpm. N.A.C.C. H.P.: 22.5. Main bearings: three. Valve lifters: solid. Carb.: Kingston L4 (6150), Holley NH (6200). Torque: 83 lbs.-ft. @ 900 rpm.

NOTE: Thermosyphon. Valve chambers (two) enclosed using steel doors held with one stud/nut each. Inspection plate in the crankcase. New lightweight connecting rods.

ENGINE [1921-1922]: L-head. Four. Cast-iron block. B & S: 3-3/4 x 4 in. Disp.: 176.7 cid. C.R.: 3.98:1. Brake H.P.: 20 @ 1600 rpm. N.A.C.C. H.P.: 22.5. Main bearings: three. Valve lifters: solid. Carb.: Kingston L4 (6150), Holley NH (6200). Torque: 83 lbs.-ft. @ 900 rpm.

NOTE: Thermosyphon. Single valve chamber covered with one steel door held with two stud/nuts or bolts. Beginning in 1922 (#5530000—April 1922).

1921 Ford Model T center door sedan. (JAC)

1921 Ford Model T touring. (OCW)

1921 Ford Model T touring. (HFM)

CHASSIS: [1909-1925] W.B.: 100 in. O.L.: 10 ft. 8 in. (chassis) 11 ft. 2-1/2 in. (car). Front/Rear Tread: 56 in. (60 in. optional until 1916). Tires: 30 x 3 front, 30 x 3-1/2 rear, standard equipment 1909-1925. 30 x 3-1/2 all around with demountable rims 1919-1925. 4:40 x 21 optional in late 1925.

NOTE: Chassis essentially identical except those after mid-1913 have a longer rear crossmember.

TECHNICAL: Planetary transmission. Speeds: 2F/1R. Three pedal controls and one lever on floor. Multiple disc clutch (25 discs 1915-1927). Torque tube drive. Straight bevel rear axle. Overall ratio: 3.63:1. Brakes: Contracting band in transmission. Hand-operated internal expanding in rear wheels. Foot brake stops driveshaft. Parking brake on two rear wheels.

NOTE: Additional technical details will be found in the 1909 "General Comments" box.

OPTIONS: No factory options were available.

1922 Ford Model T Fordor sedan. (OCW)

1922 Ford Model T coupe. (OCW)

1923-1925 FORD

1923 Ford Model T touring. (OCW)

1923 Ford Model T coupe. (OCW)

1924 Ford Model T coupe. (JAC)

FORD — 1923 — MODEL T: The 1923 Model T open cars were again restyled. Using the same bodies as the 1921-1922 cars, a new windshield with a sloping angle, and a new "one man" top, the touring and runabout looked all new.

The 1923 model was introduced in the fall of 1922, and was to continue until about June 1923, when another "new" line of Model Ts appeared.

About November 1922, a new "Fordor" sedan was added to the line. The Fordor body was made of aluminum panels over a wood frame.

Instrument panels were now standard on all cars. Non-starter open cars had a blank plate where the ammeter would be.

The early 1923 cars continued the wooden firewall of all previous Fords until early calendar 1923, when the firewall was changed to sheet metal. (This before the styling change in June, mentioned above.)

The starter and generator were standard equipment on all closed cars, as were the demountable wheels. This equipment was optional on the runabout and touring cars.

1923 was the last year for the centerdoor sedan and the coupe with the forward-opening doors. The "1924" Tudor sedan and a new coupe replaced them.

FORD — 1923-1925 — MODEL T: In June of 1923 the Ford line was restyled again. While those cars built after June but before calendar 1924 are commonly called "1923s", Ford referred to them as 1924s.

The open cars continued the same body, windshield and top as the earlier 1923s, but a new higher radiator and larger hood altered the appearance noticeably. The front fenders were given a lip on the front of the apron to blend in with a new valance under the radiator, these giving the car a more "finished" look.

Two new models replaced the centerdoor sedan and the coupe. These were a new coupe, now with an integral rear turtle back, and doors that now opened at the rear. A new Tudor sedan was also introduced, with the doors at the front of the body instead of at the center.

The Fordor sedan was the same as the earlier one except for the new hood and front fenders. Lower body panels were now steel instead of aluminum.

During 1924 the closed car doors were changed to all metal construction, eliminating the wood framing of previous sedan and coupe doors.

In 1924, for the first time Ford offered a "C" cab and a rear platform body on the truck chassis.

The 1924 line continued until about July of 1925 with no major changes except in upholstery material, and construction details.

About May 1925 the roadster/pickup and the closed cab truck appeared.

"Balloon" tires (4:40 x 21 in.) mounted on demountable-rim wooden wheels in either black or natural were added as optional equipment in late 1925.

I.D. DATA: [1923] Serial number was above the water inlet on the left side of the engine. Starting: 6543607 (September 22, 1922, introduction of 1923 model). Ending: 7927374 (June 30, 1923; introduction of "1924" models). 1923 calendar year engine numbers: 6953072 to 9008371. Numbers stamped on the body sills, etc. were manufacturer's numbers

and not an identifying number. [1924] Serial number was above the water inlet on the left side of the engine. Starting: 7927375 (July 2, 1923, introduction of 1924 models). Ending: 10266471 (July 31, 1924, end of fiscal 1924). 1924 calendar year engine numbers: 9008372 to 10994033. Numbers stamped on the body sills, etc. were manufacturer's numbers and not an identifying number. [1925] Serial number was above the water inlet on the left side of the engine. Starting: 10266472 (August 1, 1924, start of fiscal 1925). Ending: 12218728 (July 27, 1925, start of "1926" models). 1925 calendar year engine numbers: 10994034 to 12990076. Numbers stamped on the body sills, etc. were manufacturer's numbers and not an identifying number.

Model No.	Body Type & Seating	Factory Price	Shipping Weight	Prod. Total
1923				
T	3-dr. Tr.-5P	298 (A) 295 (B) 295 (C)	1500	136,441(D)
	3-dr. Tr.-5P	393 (A) 380 (B) 380 (C)	1650	792,651(E)
T	2-dr. Rbt.-2P	269 (A) 265 (B) 265 (C)	1390	56,954(D)
	2-dr. Rbt.-2P	364 (A) 350 (B) 350 (C)	1540	238,638(E)
T	2-dr. Sed.-5P	595 (A) 590 (B) 590 (C)	1875	96,410(E)
T	4-dr. Sed.-5P	725 (A) 685 (B) 685 (C)	1950	144,444(E)
T	2-dr. Cpe.-2P	530 (A) 525 (B) 525 (C)	1760	313,273(E)
T	Chassis	235 (A) 230 (B) 230 (C)	1060	9443(D)
	Chassis	330 (A) 295 (B) 295 (C)	1210	42,874(E)
TT	Truck chassis	380 (A) 370 (B) 370 (C)	1477	197,057(D)
TT	Truck chassis	475 (A) 435 (B) 455 (C)	1577	64,604(E)
TT	Truck w/body	490 (C)	NA	(F)

(A) Price effective October 17, 1922.

(B) Price effective October 2, 1923.

(C) Price effective October 30, 1923.

(D) January 1, 1923, to December 31, 1923 (includes foreign production).

(E) Includes starter and demountable wheels.

(F) Not listed separately from chassis figures.

NOTE: Starter was an option on the open cars at $65. Weight 95 lbs. Demountable rims were an additional $20. Weight 55 lbs. "C" type truck cab, $65. Truck rear bed, $55 if ordered separately.

1924 Ford Model T Fordor sedan. (OCW)

Model No.	Body Type & Seating	Factory Price	Shipping Weight	Prod. Total
1924				
T	3-dr. Tr.-5P	295 (A) 290 (B) 290 (C)	1500	99,523(D)
	3-dr. Tr.-5P	380 (A) 375 (B) 375 (C)	1650	673,579(E)
T	2-dr. Rbt.-2P	265 (A) 260 (B) 260 (C)	1390	43,317(D)
	2-dr. Rbt.-2P	350 (A) 345 (B) 345 (C)	1540	220,955(E)
T	2-dr. Sed.-5P	590 (A) 580 (B) 580 (C)	1875	223,203(E)
T	4-dr. Sed.-5P	685 (A) 660 (B) 660 (C)	1950	84,733(E)
T	2-dr. Cpe.-2P	525 (A) 520 (B) 520 (C)	1760	327,584(E)
T	Chassis	230 (A) 225 (B) 225 (C)	1060	3921(D)
	Chassis	295 (A) 290 (B) 290 (C)	1210	43,980(E)
TT	Truck chassis	370 (A) 365 (B) 365 (C)	1477	127,891(D)
TT	Truck chassis	435 (A) 430 (B) 430 (C)	1577	32,471(E)
TT	Truck w/body	490 (A) 485 (B) 485 (C)	NA	38,840(D)
	Truck w/body	555 (A) 550 (B) 550 (C)	NA	5649(E)
TT	Truck w/stake body	495 (C)	NA	(F)

(A) Price effective October 30, 1923.

(B) Price effective December 2, 1924.

(C) Price effective October 24, 1924.

(D) January 1, 1924, to December 31, 1924 (includes foreign production).

(E) Includes starter and demountable wheels.

(F) Not listed separately from body figures.

NOTE: Starter was an option on the open cars at $65. Weight 95 lbs. Demountable rims were an additional $20. Weight 55 lbs. "C" type truck cab, $65. Truck rear bed, $55 if ordered separately.

Model No.	Body Type & Seating	Factory Price	Shipping Weight	Prod. Total
1925				
T	3-dr. Tr.-5P	290 (A) 290 (B) 290 (C)	1500	64,399(D)
	3 dr. Tr.-5P	375 (A) 375 (B) 375 (C)	1650	626,813(E)
T	2-dr. Rbt.-2P	260 (A) 260 (B) 260 (C)	1390	34,206(D)
	2 dr. Rbt.-2P	345 (A) 345 (B) 345 (C)	1536	264,436(E)
T	2-dr. Pickup-2P	281 (B) 281 (C)	1471	33,795(G)
	2-dr. Pickup-2P	366 (B) 366 (C)	1621	(G)
T	2-dr. Sed.-5P	580 (A) 580 (B) 580 (C)	1875	195,001(E)
T	4-dr. Sed.-5P	660 (A) 660 (B) 660 (C)	1950	81,050(E)
T	2-dr. Cpe.-2P	520 (A) 520 (B) 520 (C)	1760	343,969(E)
T	Chassis	225 (A) 225 (B) 225 (C)	1060	6523(D)
	Chassis	290 (A) 290 (B) 290 (C)	1210	53,450(E)
TT	Truck chassis	365 (A) 365 (B) 365 (C)	1477	186,810(D)

Model No.	Body Type & Seating	Factory Price	Shipping Weight	Prod. Total
TT	Truck chassis	430 (A) 430 (B) 430 (C)	1577	62,496(E)
TT	Truck w/body	485 (A) 485 (B) 485 (C)	NA	192,839(US)
	Truck w/body	550 (A) 550 (B) 550 (C)	NA	(E, F)
TT	Truck w/stake body	495 (A) 495 (B) 495 (C)	NA	(F)

(A) Price effective October 24, 1924.

(B) Price effective March 4, 1925.

(C) Price effective December 31, 1925 (unchanged from March).

(D) January 1, 1925, to December 31, 1925 (includes foreign production).

(E) Includes starter and demountable wheels.

(F) Not listed separately from body figures. (U.S. production only).

(G) Pickups not separate into starter/non-starter. Figure is for total of the two.

NOTE: Starter was an option on the open cars at $65. Weight 95 lbs. Demountable rims were an additional $20. Weight 55 lbs. 21-inch tires and rims $25 extra. Weight 65 lbs. "C" type truck cab, $65. Truck rear bed, $55 if ordered separately. Pickup body for runabout, $25.

ENGINE [1923-1924-1925]: L-head. Four. Cast-iron block. B & S: 3-3/4 x 4 in. Disp.: 176.7 cid. C.R.: 3.98:1. Brake H.P.: 20 @ 1600 rpm. N.A.C.C. H.P.: 22.5. Main bearings: three. Valve lifters: solid. Carb.: Kingston L4 (6150), Holley NH (6200). Torque: 83 lbs.-ft. @ 900 rpm.

NOTE: Thermosyphon. Inspection plate in the crankcase. New light-weight connecting rods.

CHASSIS: [1923-1924-1925] W.B.: 100 in. O.L.: 10 ft. 8 in. (chassis) 11 ft. 2-1/2 in. (car). Front/Rear Tread: 56 in. Tires: 30 x 3 front, 30 x 3-1/2 rear, standard equipment 1909-1925. 30 x 3-1/2 all around with demountable rims 1919-1925. 4:40 x 21 optional in late 1925.

TECHNICAL: Planetary transmission. Speeds: 2F/1R. Three pedal controls and one lever on floor. Multiple disc clutch (26 discs 1909-1915), (25 discs 1915-1927). Torque tube drive. Straight bevel rear axle. Overall ratio: 3.63:1. Brakes: Contracting band in transmission. Hand-operated internal expanding in rear wheels. Foot brake stops driveshaft. Parking brake on two rear wheels.

NOTE: Additional technical details will be found in the 1909 "General Comments" box.

OPTIONS: The basic equipment included three oil lamps only (two side and one tail). Options listed included: Windshield. Headlamps. Tops. Horns. Prest-o-lite tanks (instead of the carbide tank). Robe rails. Tire chains. Top boots. Foot rests. Spare tire carriers. Speedometers. Bumpers. No prices were given.

1925 Ford Model T Tudor sedan. (OCW)

1926 Ford Model T Fordor sedan. (OCW)

1926 Ford Model T Fordor touring. (RLC)

FORD — 1926-1927 — MODEL T: About July 1925 the "Improved Ford" marked the first major restyling of the Model T since 1917. New fenders, runningboards, bodies (except for the Fordor), hoods and even a modified chassis made these Fords unique during the era of the Model T.

The touring was given a door on the driver's side for the first time since 1911 (in U.S. cars, Canadian-built Fords had a driver's side door). The Tudor sedan and the coupe were all new, though similar in style to the 1925s. The Fordor sedan continued the same basic body introduced in late 1922 except for the new cowl, hood, fenders, etc.

The chassis had a new longer rear crossmember, and with a modification of the springs and front spindles, the car was lowered about an inch.

While basically the same running gear as earlier models, the 1926-27 cars had 11-inch rear wheel brake drums, although they were only operated by the "emergency brake" lever. The foot pedals for the low speed and the brake were larger, and the internal transmission brake was made wider for better life and operation.

Initially offered in black, the coupe and the Tudor were later painted a dark green, while the Fordor sedan came in a dark maroon, as standard colors. The open cars continued in black until mid-1926.

In 1926, perhaps as "1927" models (Ford didn't name yearly models consistently), colors were added for the open cars: Gunmetal blue or Phoenix brown. Closed cars were offered in Highland green, Royal maroon, Fawn gray, Moleskin and Drake green. By calendar 1927, any body could be ordered in any standard Ford color. Black could be had on special order on the pickup body, although Commercial green was the standard color. Fenders and runningboards were black on all models.

When introduced in 1925, standard wheels on the closed cars were the 30 x 3-1/2-inch demountables, and 30 x 3-1/2-inch non-demountables on the open cars. By calendar 1926, the 21-inch balloons were standard on all models.

Wire wheels were offered as an option beginning January 1926. By early 1927, many Ford branches were supplying wire wheels as standard equipment on closed cars.

The gasoline tank was now located in the cowl on all models except the Fordor sedan, which continued to have it under the driver's seat.

Model T production ended in May 1927 although Ford continued building engines through the year, then a few at a time until August 4, 1941.

I.D. DATA: [1926] Serial number was above the water inlet on the left side of the engine. Starting: 12218729 (July 27, 1925, start of "1926" models). Ending: 14049029 (July 30, 1926, end of fiscal year 1926). 1926 calendar year engine numbers: 12990077 to 14619254. Numbers stamped on the body sills, etc. were manufacturer's numbers and not an identifying number. [1927] Serial number was above the water inlet on the left side of the engine. Starting: 14049030 (August 2, 1926, start of fiscal 1927). Ending: 15006625 (May 25, 1927, end of Model T Ford car production.)* 1927 calendar year engine numbers: 14619255 to 15076231.* Numbers stamped on the body sills, etc. were manufacturer's numbers and not an identifying number.

*Most records show 15007032 or 15007033 as the last car but the factory records indicate these numbers were built on May 31, 1927, five days after the car assembly line was stopped. Ford continued building engines through 1927 and at a considerable rate until January 1931 (as many as 12,000 per month after the end of the Model T!). Production averaged about 100 per month in 1931, then dropped to less than 10 and ended, finally, on August 4, 1941, with number 15176888.

Model No.	Body Type & Seating	Factory Price	Shipping Weight	Prod. Total
1926				
T	4-dr. Tr.-5P	290 (A)	1633 (D)	
T	4-dr. Tr.-5P	375 (A)	1738	364,409(F)
		380 (B)		
		380 (C)		
T	2-dr. Rbt.-2P	260 (A)	1550 (D)	—
T	2-dr. Rbt.-2P	345 (A)	1655	342,575(F)
		360 (B)		
		360 (C)		
T	2-dr. Pickup-2P	281 (A)	NA (D)	N/L(E)
T	2-dr. Pickup-2P	366 (A)	1736	75,406(F)
		381 (B)		
		381 (C)		
T	2-dr. Sed. 5P	580 (A)	1972	270,331(F)
		495 (B)		
		495 (C)		
T	4-dr. Sed.-5P	660 (A)	2004	102,732(F)
		545 (B)		
		545 (C)		
T	2-dr. Cpe.-2P	520 (A)	1860	288,342(F)
		485 (B)		
		485 (C)		
T	Chassis	225 (A)	1167 (D)	—
T	Chassis	290 (A)	1272	58,223(F)
		300 (B)		
		300 (C)		
TT	Truck chassis	365 (A)	1477	228,496(G)
		325 (B)		
		325 (C)		
TT	Truck chassis	430 (A)	1577	(F)
		375 (B)		
		375 (C)		

Truck Bodies Only

TT 142,852(U.S.)	Open Cab	65	NA	
TT	Closed Cab	85	NA	—(G)
TT	Express Body	55	NA	—(G)
TT	Platform Body	50	—	—(G)
TT	Expr. w/ roof & screen	110	—	—(G)

(A) Price effective January 1, 1926.

(B) Price effective June 6, 1926.

(C) Price effective December 31, 1926 (unchanged from June).

(D) Early models with 30 x 3-1/2-inch non-demountable wheels and no starter.

(E) Available only on special order by calendar 1926.

(F) Includes starter and 21-inch demountable wheels.

(G) Chassis production figures are for U.S. and foreign. Body figures are for U.S. only and are included in the chassis count. Starter production is not listed separately.

NOTE: Starter and demountable wheels are standard on all cars. Starter is optional on the truck. Early 1926 cars with 30 by 3-1/2-inch demountables are 10 pounds lighter. Pickup body for runabout, $25.

1926 Ford Model T touring. (JAC)

Model No.	Body Type & Seating	Factory Price	Shipping Weight	Prod. Total
T	4-dr. Tr.-5P	380	1738	81,181(A)
T	2-dr. Rbt.-2P	360	1655	95,778(A)
T	2-dr. Pickup-2P	381	1736	28,143(A)
T	2-dr. Sed.-5P	495	1972	78,105(A)
T	4 dr. Sed.-5P	545	2004	22,930(A)
T	2-dr. Cpe.-2P	485	1860	69,939(A)
T	Chassis	300	1272	19,280(A)
TT	Truck Chassis	325	1477	83,202(C)
TT	Truck Chassis	375	1577	—(B)

Truck Bodies Only

TT	Open Cab	65	NA	41,318(U.S.)
TT	Closed Cab	85	NA	(C)
TT	Express body	55	NA	(C)
TT	Platform Body	50	NA	(C)
TT	Expr. w/roof & screen	110	NA	(C)

(A) January 1, 1927, to December 31, 1927 (includes foreign production).

(B) Includes starter and demountable wheels.

(C) Chassis production figures are for U.S. and foreign. Body figures are for U.S. only and are included in the chassis count. Starter production is not listed separately.

NOTE: Starter and demountable wheels are standard on all cars. Starter is optional on the truck. Pickup body for runabout, $25.

Automobile production ended May 26, 1927, but trucks continued for some time.

ENGINE: L-head. Four. Cast-iron block. B & S: 3-3/4 x 4 in. Disp.: 176.7 cid. C.R.: 3.98:1. Brake H.P.: 20 @ 1600 rpm. N.A.C.C. H.P.: 22.5. Main bearings: three. Valve lifters: solid. Carb.: Kingston L4 (6150B), Holley NH (6200C), Holley Vaporizer (6250), Kingston Regenerator. Torque: 83 lbs.-ft. @ 900 rpm.

NOTE: Thermosyphon. Single valve chamber covered with one steel door held with two stud/nuts or bolts.

Transmission housing now bolts to the rear of the cylinder. Fan mounted on the water outlet. Later production used nickel-plated head and water connection bolts.

1926 Ford Model T Fordor sedan. (OCW)

1926 Ford Model T Tudor sedan. (HAC)

CHASSIS: W.B. 100 in. O.L.: 10 ft. 8 in. (chassis) 11 ft. 2-1/2 in. (car). Front/Rear Tread: 56 in. Tires: 30 x 3-1/2 all around in early 1926 models. 4:40 x 21 optional in early 1926 and standard in later production.
NOTE: Chassis essentially identical to 1913-1925 except for a much longer rear crossmember. Chassis lowered about an inch by the use of a different front spindle and spring, and a deeper crown in the rear crossmember. In mid-1926 the rear crossmember was made with a flanged edge and the chassis was of heavier steel.

TECHNICAL: Planetary transmission. Speeds: 2F/1R. Three pedal controls and one lever on floor. Multiple disc clutch (25 discs 1915-1927). Torque tube drive. Straight bevel rear axle. Overall ratio: 3.63:1. Brakes: Contracting band in transmission. Hand-operated internal expanding in rear wheels. Foot brake stops driveshaft. Parking brake on two rear wheels.

In January 1926 optional 21-inch wire wheels became available, and these became standard on some closed cars in calendar year 1927.

In mid-1925 (1926 models) the transmission brake was made about a half-inch wider, and the rear wheel brakes were enlarged to 11 inches with lined shoes.

NOTE: Additional technical details will be found in the 1909 "General Comments" box.

1927 Ford Model T touring. (OCW)

1927 Ford Model T roadster. (OCW)

OPTIONS: All cars equipped with headlamps, horn, starter and 21-inch demountable rims after January 1926. Windshield wiper (hand operated) (50 cents).* Windshield wiper (vacuum operated) ($3.50, $2.00 in 1927). Windshield wings (open cars) ($6.50 pair, $2.50 in 1927). Gipsy curtains (open cars) ($3.00 pair, $1.10 in 1927). Top boot (open cars) ($5.00, $4.00 in 1927). Bumpers (front and rear) ($15.00). Wire wheels, set of five ($50.00, $35.00 later 1926). Rear view mirror (open cars) ($.75).* Dash lamp (open cars) ($.60).* Stop light and switch ($2.50). Shock absorbers ($9.00 set).

* Standard on closed cars.

1928 FORD

1928 Ford Model A Tudor sedan. (RLC)

FORD — MODEL A — FOUR: The reverting to a Model A designation for the new Ford symbolized the impact this automobile had upon the Ford Motor Company. A far more complex automobile than the Model T, the Model A contained approximately 6,800 different parts as compared to the less than 5,000 components that comprised the Model T. There were, however, similarities. Both cars had four-cylinder L-head engines and semi-elliptic front and rear transverse springs. But beyond this point the Model A moved far away from the heritage of the Model T. Its engine with a water pump displaced just over 200 cubic inches and with 40-hp was virtually twice as powerful as the Model T's and provided a 65 mph top speed. Superseding the old magneto ignition was a contemporary battery and ignition system. The Model T's planetary transmission gave way to a three-speed sliding gear unit. Other technical advancements found in the Model A included the use of four-wheel mechanical brakes and Houdaille double-action hydraulic shock absorbers.

The styling of the Model A maintained a link with that of the Model T but with a 103-1/2 inch wheelbase, 4.50 x 21 tires and a high belt line, the influence of the Lincoln automobile upon the appearance of the new Ford was unmistakable. Full crown fenders were used and the bodywork of each of the five models initially offered had their body surrounds outlined in contrasting body colors and pin striping. The Model A's two-piece front and rear bumpers were similar to those used on the 1927

Model T but its new radiator shell with its gentle center vee-dip and moderately curved crossbar for the headlights made it impossible to confuse the two Fords.

The first Model A engine was completed on October 20, 1927, and the following day it was installed in the first Model A assembled. From that day (May 25, 1927) Ford announced it would produce a successor to the Model T, public interest had steadily increased to a level that was finally satisfied on December 2, 1927, when the nationwide introduction of the Model A took place. While many industry observers recognized the passing of the Model T as the end of an era, there was equal appreciation for the extraordinary value the Model A represented and an awareness that it was in all ways more than a worthy successor to the Tin Lizzie.

I.D. DATA: Serial numbers were located on top side of frame near clutch pedal. Starting: Oct. 20-Dec. 31, 1927—A1; Jan. 1-Dec. 31, 1928—A5276. Ending: Oct. 20-Dec. 31, 1927—A5275; Jan. 1-Dec. 31, 1928—A810122. Engine numbers were located on boss placed on center of left side of block directly below the cylinder head. A prefix letter A was used and a star is found on either end. Starting: Oct. 20-Dec. 31, 1927—A1; Jan. 1-Dec. 31, 1928—A5276. Ending: Oct. 20-Dec. 31, 1927—A5275; Jan. 1-Dec. 31, 1928—A810122. Model numbers: 1928 models have a date when the body was manufactured stamped on the upper left side of the firewall.

Model No.	Body Type & Seating	Factory Price	Shipping Weight	Prod. Total
A	2-dr. Rds. R/S-2/4P	480	2106	Note 1
A	4-dr. Phae.-4P	460	2140	Note 1
A	2-dr. Bus. Cpe.-2P	550	2225	Note 1
A	2-dr. R/S Cpe.-2/4P	550	2265	Note 1
A	2-dr. Std. Bus. Rds.	480	2050	Note 1
A	2-dr. Spt. Bus. Cpe.-2P	525	NA	Note 1
A	2-dr. Tudor-4P	550	2340	Note 1
A	4-dr. Fordor-4P	585	2386	Note 1
A	4-dr. Taxi Cb.	600	NA	Note 1

NOTE 1: Body style production was recorded only by calendar year. See list at end of Model A section.

ENGINE: Inline. L-head. Four. Cast-iron block. B & S: 3-7/8 x 4-1/4 in. Disp.: 200.5 cid. C.R.: 4.22:1. Brake H.P.: 40 @ 2200 rpm. SAE H.P.: 24.03. Main bearings: three. Valve lifters: mechanical. Carb.: Zenith or Holley double venturi. Torque: 128 lbs.-ft. @ 100 rpm.

CHASSIS: W.B.: 103.5 in. Front/Rear Tread: 56 in. Tires: 4.50 x 21.

TECHNICAL: Sliding gear transmission. Speeds: 3F/1R. Floor shift controls. Dry multiple disc clutch. Shaft drive. 3/4 floating rear axle. Overall ratio: 3.7:1. Mechanical internal expanding brakes on four wheels. Welded wire wheels. Wheel size: 21.

1928 Ford Model A roadster. (AA)

1928 Ford Model A roadster. (BMHV)

1928 Ford Model A Fordor sedan. (JAC)

1928 Ford Model A phaeton. (JAC)

OPTIONS: Single sidemount. External sun shade. Radiator ornament. Wind vanes. Rear view mirror. Rear luggage rack. Radiator stone guard. Spare tire lock.

HISTORY: Introduced December 2, 1927. Innovations: Safety glass installed in all windows. Calendar year production: 633,594. The president of Ford was Edsel Ford.

1929 FORD

FORD — MODEL A — FOUR: The most apparent change made in the Model A's appearance, aside from brighter trim and body paint were the exterior door handles on open models. With production rapidly increasing, more body styles became available. A town car model was introduced on December 13, 1928, followed during 1929 by a wood-bodied station wagon on April 25. Other new styles included a convertible cabriolet, several new four-door sedans and a town sedan. As in 1928 the Model A's base price included many standard equipment features such as a combination tail and stop light, windshield wiper, front and rear bumpers, and a Sparton horn.

I.D. DATA: Serial numbers were located on top side of frame, near clutch pedal. Starting: A 810123. Ending: A 2742695. Engine number location: Boss placed on center of left side of block directly below the cylinder head. Starting: A 810123. Ending: A 2724695.

1929 Ford Model A sport coupe. (AA)

1929 Ford Model A Fordor sedan. (OCW)

Model No.	Body Type & Seating	Factory Price	Shipping Weight	Prod. Total
A	4-dr. Sta. Wag.-4P	650	2500	Note 1
A	2-dr. RS Conv.2-4P	670	2339	Note 1
A	2-dr. RS Spt. Cpe.-2/4P	550	2250	Note 1
A	Mur. Std. Fordor Sed.-4P	625	2497	Note 1
A	Brgg. Std. Fordor Sed.- 4P	625	2497	Note 1
A	Brgg. 2W Std. Sed.-4P	625	2419	Note 1
A	Brgg. Std. Fordor Sed.-4P	625	2497	Note 1
A	Brgg. L.B. Fordor Sed.-4P	625	2500	Note 1
A	2-dr. Tudor Sed.-4P	525	2348	Note 1
A	4-dr. Mur. Twn. Sed.-4P	695	2517	Note 1
A	4-dr. Brgg. Twn. Sed.-4P	695	2517	Note 1
A	2-dr. Std. RS Rds.-2/4P	450	2106	Note 1
A	2-dr. Std. Rds. R/S-2/4P	450	2161	Note 1
A	2-dr. Std. Bus. Cpe.	525	2216	Note 1
A	4-dr. Std. Phae.-4P	460	2203	Note 1
A	4-dr. Std. Cpe.-2P	550	2248	Note 1
A	4-dr. Twn. Cr.-4P	1400	2525	Note 1
A	4-dr. Taxi-4P	800	NA	Note 1

Note 1: Body style production was recorded only by calendar year. See list at end of Model A section.

ENGINE: Inline. L-head. Four. Cast-iron block. B & S: 3-7/8 x 4-1/4 in. Disp.: 200.5 cid. C.R.: 4.22:1. Brake H.P.: 40 @ 2206 rpm. N.A.C.C. H.P.: 24.03. Main bearings: three. Valve lifters: mechanical. Carb.: Zenith or Holley double-venturi. Torque: 128 lbs.-ft. @ 1000 rpm.

CHASSIS: W.B.: 103.5 in. Front/Rear Tread: 56 in. Tires: 4.50 x 21.

TECHNICAL: Sliding gear transmission. Speeds: 3F/1R. Floor shift controls. Dry multiple disc. Shaft drive. 3/4 floating rear axle. Overall ratio: 3.7:1. Mechanical internal expanding brakes on four wheels. Welded wire wheels. Wheel rim size: 21 in.

OPTIONS: Single sidemount. External sun shade. Radiator ornament ($3.00). Wind vanes. Rear view mirror. Rear luggage rack. Radiator stone guard. Spare tire lock.

HISTORY: Introduced January 1929. Calendar year sales: 1,310,147 (registrations). Calendar year production: 1,507,132. The president of Ford was Edsel Ford. Production of the first million Model A Fords was completed on February 4, 1929. The two-millionth Model A Ford was constructed on July 24, 1929.

1929 Ford Model A phaeton. (OCW)

1929 Ford Model A Fordor sedan. (JAC)

1929 Ford Model A town car. (JAC)

1930 FORD

1930 Ford Model A Fordor sedan. (OCW)

FORD — MODEL A — FOUR: The Model A was given a substantial face lift for 1930 and it was effective. Larger 4.75 tires on smaller 19-inch wheels resulted in an overall height reduction, which along with wider fenders, a deeper radiator shell and the elimination of the cowl stanchion all were contributors to the Model A's fresh new look. Replacing the older nickel finish for the Ford's exterior brightwork was both nickel and stainless steel trim. During the year a new victoria model was introduced along with a deluxe version of the phaeton.

I.D. DATA: Serial numbers located on top side of frame near clutch panel. Starting: A 2742696. Ending: A 4237500. Engine numbers located on boss placed on center of left side of block, directly below the cylinder head. Starting Engine No: A 2742696. Ending: A 4237500.

1930 Ford Model A roadster. (AA)

Model No.	Body Type & Seating	Factory Price	Shipping Weight	Prod. Total
35-B	4-dr. Std. Phae-2P	440	2212	Note 1
40-B	2-dr. Std. Rds.	435	2155	Note 1
40-B	2-dr. Del. Rds. R/S-2-4P	495	2230	Note 1
45-B	2-dr. Std. Cpe.	500	2257	Note 1
45-B	2-dr. Del. Cpe.	550	2265	Note 1
50-B	2-dr. Spt. Cpe. R/S-2-4P	530	2283	Note 1
55-B	2-dr. Tudor Sed.	490	2372	Note 1
68-B	2-dr. Cab.	645	2273	Note 1
150-B	4-dr. Sta. Wag.-4P	650	2482	Note 1
155-C	4-dr. Mu'ry Twn. Sed.-4P	640	2495	Note 1
155-D	4-dr. Briggs Twn. Sed.-4P	650	2495	Note 1
165-C	Std. Mu'ry Fordor Sed.-4P	580	2462	Note 1
165-D	Std. Briggs Fordor Sed.-4P	590	2462	Note 1
170-B	Std. Briggs Fordor 2W Sed.-4P	590	2488	Note 1
170-B	Briggs Fordor 2W Sed.-4P	650	2488	Note 1
180-A	4-dr. Del. Phae-4P	645	2285	Note 1
190-A	2-dr. Vict.-4P	580	2375	Note 1

NOTE 1: Body style production was recorded only by calendar year. See list at end of Model A section.

ENGINE: Inline. L-head. Four. Cast-iron block. B & S: 3-7/8 x 4-1/4 in. Disp.: 200.5 cid. C.R.: 4.22:1. Brake H.P.: 40 @ 2200 rpm. Taxable H.P.: 24.03. Main bearings: three. Valve lifters: mechanical. Carb.: Zenith or Holley double-venturi. Torque: 128 lbs.-ft. at 1000 rpm.

CHASSIS: W.B.: 103.5 in. Front/Rear Tread: 56 in. Tires: 4.75 x 19.

1930 Ford Model A phaeton. (JAC)

1930 Ford Model A Budd body touring car. (OCW)

1930 Ford Model A coupe. (JAC)

1930 Ford Model A station wagon. (OCW)

1930 Ford Model A town sedan. (JAC)

TECHNICAL: Sliding gear transmission. Speeds: 3F/1R. Floor shift controls. Dry multiple disc clutch. Shaft drive. 3/4 floating rear axle. Overall ratio: 3.77:1. Mechanical internal expanding brakes on four wheels. Welded wire wheels. Wheel size: 19 in.

OPTIONS: Single sidemount ($20.00). External sun shade. Radiator ornament. Wind vanes. Rear view mirror. Rear luggage rack. Radiator stone guard. Spare tire lock.

HISTORY: January 1930. Calendar year sales: 1,055,097 (registrations). Calendar year production: 1,155,162. The president of Ford was Edsel Ford.

1931 FORD

FORD — MODEL A — FOUR: The final year of Model A production brought revised styling, several new body types and on April 14th production of the 20-millionth Ford, a Fordor sedan. Heading the list of styling changes was a radiator shell with a relief effect, plus

runningboards fitted with single piece slash aprons. In addition to the two- and four-door sedans introduced with a smoother roofline, a revamped cabriolet model was also introduced during 1931. However the star attraction was the convertible sedan that had fixed side window frames over which the top rode up or down on a set of tracks. Standard equipment on the convertible sedan included a side mount.

I.D. DATA: Serial numbers were located on top side of frame, near clutch pedal. Starting: A 4237501. Ending: A 4849340. Engine numbers were located on boss placed on center of left side of block, directly below the cylinder head. Starting: A 4327501. Ending: A 4849340.

1931 Ford Model A Victoria. (OCW)

1931 Ford Model A convertible coupe. (OCW)

1931 Ford Model A Deluxe roadster. (OCW)

1931 Ford Model A victoria coupe. (AA)

1931 Ford Model A roadster. (JAC)

Model No.	Body Type & Seating	Factory Price	Shipping Weight	Prod. Total
A	4-dr. Std. Phae.-4P	435	2212	Note 1
A	2-dr. Std. Rds.	430	2155	Note 1
A	2-dr. Del. Rds.	475	2230	Note 1
A	2-dr. Std. Cpe.	490	2257	Note 1
A	2-dr. Del. Cpe.	525	2265	Note 1
A	2-dr. Spt. Cpe.	500	2283	Note 1
A	2-dr. Std. Tudor Sed.-4P	490	2462	Note 1
A	2-dr. Del. Tudor Sed.-4P	525	2488	Note 1
A	2-dr. Cab	595	2273	Note 1
A	4-dr. Sta. Wag.-4P	625	2505	Note 1
A	4-dr. Mu'ry Twn. Sed.-4P	630	2495	Note 1
A	4-dr. Briggs Twn, Sed.-4P	630	2495	Note 1
A	4-dr. Std. Fordor Sed.-4P	590	2462	Note 1
A	4-dr. Twn. Sed.-4P	630	2495	Note 1
A	4-dr. Del. Fordor Sed.-4P	630	2488	Note 1
A	Mu'ry Std. Fordor Sed.-4P	590	2462	Note 1
A	Briggs Std. Fordor Sed.-4P	590	2462	Note 1
A	Briggs Del. Fordor 2W Sed.-4P	630	2488	Note 1
A	2-dr. Del. Phae.-4P	580	2265	Note 1
A	2-dr. Vic. Cpe.-4P	580	2375	Note 1
A	2-dr. Conv. Sed.-4P	640	2335	Note 1

Note 1: Body style production was recorded only by calendar year. See list at end of Model A section.

ENGINE: Inline. L-head. Four. Cast-iron block. B & S: 3-7/8 x 4-1/4 in. Disp.: 200.5 cid. C.R.: 4.22:1. Brake H.P.: 40 @ 2200 rpm. Taxable H.P.: 24.03. Main bearings: three. Valve lifters: mechanical. Carb.: Zenith or Holley double venturi. Torque: 128 lbs.-ft. @ 1000 rpm.

1931 Ford Model A Fordor sedan. (JAC)

CHASSIS: W.B.: 103.5 in. Front/Rear Tread: 56 in. Tires: 4.75 x 19.

TECHNICAL: Sliding gear transmission. Speeds: 3F/1R. Floor shift controls. Dry multiple disc clutch. Shaft drive. 3/4 floating rear axle. Overall ratio: 3.77:1. Mechanical internal expanding brakes on four wheels. Welded wire wheels. Wheel size: 19 in.

HISTORY: Introduced January 1931. Calendar year sales 528,581 (registrations). Calendar year production: 541,615. The president of Ford was Edsel Ford.

FORD

Model A Domestic Production Figures

(Calendar Year)

	1927	1928	1929	1930	1931	Totals
Phaeton						
standard	221	47,255	49,818	16,479	4076	117,849
deluxe	—	—	—	3946	2229	6175
Roadster						
standard	269	81,937*	191,529	112,901	5499	392,135
deluxe	—	—	—	11,318	52,997	64,315

***Of these, 51,807 were produced without rumbleseat.**

	1927	1928	1929	1930	1931	Totals
Sport Coupe	734	79,099	134,292	69,167	19,700	302,992
Coupe						
standard	629	70,784	178,982	226,027	79,816	556,238
deluxe	—	—	—	28,937	23,067	52,004
Bus.Coupe	—	37,343	37,644	—	—	74,987
Conv. Cabr.	—	—	16,421	25,868	11,801	54,090
Tudor						
standard	1948	208,562	523,922	376,271	148,425	1,259,128
deluxe	—	—	—	—	21,984	21,984
Fordor (two-window)						
standard	—	82,349	146,097	5279	—	233,725
deluxe	—	—	—	12,854	3251	16,105
Fordor (three-window)						
standard	—	—	53,941	41,133	18,127	113,201
town sedan	—	—	84,970	104,935	55,469	245,374
Conv. Sedan	—	—	—	—	4864	4864
Victoria	—	—	—	6306	33,906	40,212
Town Car	—	89	913	63	—	1065
Station Wagon	5	4,954	3510	2848	11,317	
Taxicab	—	264	4,576	10	—	4850

OPTIONS: Single sidemount. External sun shade. Radiator ornament. Wind vanes. Rear view mirror. Rear luggage rack. Radiator stone guard. Spare tire lock.

1932 FORD

FORD — MODEL 18 — EIGHT: Once again Henry Ford made automotive history when, on March 31, 1932, he announced the Ford V-8. This type of engine was not a novelty by that time but when offered at traditional Ford low prices this new engine was a true milestone. Henry Ford had this 221 cid displacement unit developed in traditional Ford-style extreme secrecy—a small workforce operating under relatively primitive conditions—under Henry Ford's close personal supervision.

Its early production life was far from tranquil. Hastily rushed into assembly, many of the 1932 engines experienced piston and bearing failures plus overheating as well as block cracking. However, these problems were soon overcome and for the next 21 years this V-8 would be powering Ford automobiles.

1932 Ford Model 18 V-8 four-door sedan. (OCW)

1932 Ford V-8 DeLuxe three-window coupe. (AA)

1932 Ford V-8 victoria. (BMHV)

The new Ford was extremely handsome. Both front and rear fenders were fully crowned. The soon-to-be classic radiator shell was slightly veed and carried vertical bars. Positioned in the center of the curved headlight tie-bar was Ford's timeless V-8 logo. Apparently sensitive that most of its competitors had longer wheelbases, Ford measured the distance from the center position of the front spring to the center of the rear and claimed it as the V-8's 112-inch wheelbase. Actually its wheelbase was 106 inches.

The new Ford's dash carried all instruments and controls within an engine-turned oval placed in the center of a mahogany colored (early) or walnut (late) grained panel. An anti-theft device was incorporated into the key and ignition switch that was mounted on a bracket attached to the steering column. During the model year Ford incorporated many changes into the design of its new model. One of the most obvious, intended to improve engine cooling, was a switch from a hood with 20 louvers to one with 25.

FORD — MODEL B — FOUR: Somewhat overwhelmed by the public's response to Model 18, the four-cylinder Model B shared the same body as the V-8, minus V-8 emblems on the headlamp tie-bars and with Ford rather than V-8 lettering on its hubcaps.

Both types had single transverse leaf springs front and rear. The locating of the rear spring behind the differential and the use of 18-inch wheels gave the Fords a lower overall height than previous models.

I.D. DATA: Serial numbers located on top side of frame, near clutch pedal. Starting: [Model B] AB 5000001 & up. [Model 18] 18-1. Ending: [Model 18] 18-2031126. Prefix "C" indicates Canadian built. Engine numbers located on boss placed on center of left side of block, directly below the cylinder head [Model B]. Starting: [Model B] AB 5000005 & up. [Model 18] 18-1. Ending: [Model 18] 18-2031126.

Model No.	Body Type & Seating	Factory Price	Shipping Weight	Prod. Total
Ford V-8				
18	2-dr. Rds.	460	2203	520
18	2-dr. Del. Rds.	500	2308	6893
18	4-dr. Phae.	495	2369	483
18	4-dr. Del. Phae.	545	2375	923
18	2-dr. Cpe.	490	2398	28,904
18	2-dr. Spt. Cpe.	535	2405	1982
18	2-dr. Del. Cpe.	575	2493	20,506
18	2-dr. Tudor Sed.-4P	500	2508	57,930
18	2-dr. Del. Tudor Sed.-4P	550	2518	18,836
18	4-dr. Fordor Sed.-4P	590	2538	9310
18	4-dr. Del. Fordor Sed.-4P	645	2568	18,880
18	2-dr. Cab. R/S-2-4P	610	2398	5499
18	2-dr. Vic.-4P	600	2483	7241
18	2-dr. Conv. Sed.-4P	650	2480	842
Ford 4-cyl.				
B	2-dr. Rds.	410	2095	948
B	2-dr. Del. Rds.	450	2102	3719
B	4-dr. Phae.	445	2238	593
B	4-dr. Del. Phae.	495	2268	281
B	2-dr. Cpe.	440	2261	20,342
B	2-dr. Spt. Cpe.	485	2286	739
B	2-dr. Del. Cpe.	425	2364	968
B	2-dr. Tudor Sed.-4P	450	2378	36,553
B	2-dr. Del. Tudor Sed.-4P	500	2398	4077
B	4-dr. Fordor Sed.-4P	540	2413	4116
B	4-dr. Del. Fordor Sed.-4P	595	2432	2620
B	2-dr. Cab.-4P	560	2295	427
B	2-dr. Vic.-4P	550	2344	521
B	2-dr. Conv. Sed.-4P	600	2349	41

ENGINE [Model B]: Inline. L-head. Four. Cast-iron block. B & S: 3-7/8 x 4-1/4 in. Disp.: 200.5 cid. C.R.: 4.6:1. Brake H.P.: 50. Taxable H.P.: 30. Main bearings: three. Valve lifters: mechanical. Carb.: Zenith or Holley double-venturi.

ENGINE [Model 18]: 90 degree V. L-head. Eight. Cast-iron block. B & S: 3-1/16 x 3-3/4 in. Disp.: 221 cid. C.R.: 5.5:1. Brake H.P.: 65 @ 3400 rpm. SAE H.P.: 30. Main bearings: three. Valve lifters: mechanical. Carb.: Special Ford Detroit Lubricator downdraft, single barrel, 1-1/2-in. throat. Torque: 130 lbs.-ft. @ 1250 rpm.

1932 Ford V-8 Tudor sedan. (OCW)

1932 Ford V-8 Deluxe roadster. (JAC)

1932 Ford V-8 Deluxe Fordor sedan. (OCW)

1932 Ford V-8 cabriolet. (PH)

CHASSIS: Model 18 and B. W.B.: 106 in. O.L.: 165-1/2-in. Height: 68-5/8-in. Front/Rear Tread: 55.2/56.7 in. Tires: 5.25 x 18.

TECHNICAL: Sliding gear transmission. Speeds: 3F/1R. Floor shift controls. Single dry plate, molded asbestos lining clutch. Shaft drive. 3/4 floating rear axle. Overall ratio: 4.11:1 (early cars—4.33:1). Mechanical, rod activated brakes on four wheels. Welded wire, drop center rim wheels. Wheel size: 18 in.

OPTIONS: Single sidemount. Dual sidemount. Clock. Trunk rack. Leather upholstery. Mirror. Twin tail lamps. Bedford cord upholstery. Cowl lamps (Standard models).

HISTORY: Introduced April 2, 1932. Mass production of a low-priced one-piece 90 degree V-8 engine block. Calendar year sales: 258,927 (registrations). Calendar year production: 287,285. The president of Ford was Edsel Ford.

1933 FORD

FORD — MODEL 40 — EIGHT: In addition to a longer 112-inch wheelbase, X-member double-drop frame, the Model 40 Ford had valanced front and rear fenders, a new radiator design with vertical bars slanted back to match the rear sweep of the windshield and acorn-shaped headlight shells. Curvaceous one-piece bumpers with a center-dip were used at front and rear. Enhancing the Ford's streamlined appearance were the angled side hood louvers. All models regardless of body color were delivered with black fenders and 17-inch wire spoke wheels.

Accompanying these exterior revisions was a new dash arrangement with a reshaped engine-tuned panel enclosing the gauges placed directly in front of the driver. A similarly shaped glovebox was placed on the passenger's side.

With its teething problems part of the past, the Ford V-8 by virtue of an improved ignition system, better cooling, higher compression ratio and aluminum cylinder heads, developed 75 horsepower.

1933 Ford 5-window coupe. (OCW)

1933 Ford V-8 Deluxe Fordor sedan. (OCW)

FORD — MODEL 40 — FOUR: As before, the four-cylinder Fords were identical to the eight-cylinder models except for their lack of V-8 trim identification.

I.D. DATA: Serial numbers were located on top side of frame near clutch pedal also, left front pillar, forward portion of left frame member, transmission housing. Starting: (V-8) 18-2031127 & up; (four-cylinder, with prefix "B") 5185849 & up. Engine numbers were located on boss placed on center of left side of block, directly below the cylinder head (four-cylinder); on top of clutch housing (V-8). Starting: (V-8) 18-2031127 & up; (four-cylinder) 5185849 & up.

Model No.	Body Type & Seating	Factory Price	Shipping Weight	Prod. Total
Ford V-8				
40	2-dr. Del. Rds. R/S-2/4P	510	2461	4223
40	2-dr. Std. RS Rds.-2/4P	475	2422	126
40	2-dr. Cab R/S-2/4P	585	2545	7852
40	4-dr. Std. Phae.-4P	495	2520	232
40	4-dr. Del. Phae.-4P	545	2529	1483
40	2-dr. 3W Del. Cpe.-2P	540	2538	15,894
40	2-dr. 3W Std. Cpe.-2P	490	2534	6585
40	2-dr. 5W Del. Cpe.-2P	540	2538	11,244
40	2-dr. 5W Std. Cpe.-2P	490	2534	31,797
40	2-dr. Vic.-4P	595	2595	4193
40	2-dr. Del. Tudor Sed.-4P	550	2625	48,233
40	2-dr. Std. Tudor Sed.-4P	500	2621	106,387
40	4-dr. Del. Fordor Sed.-4P	610	2684	45,443
40	4-dr. Std. Fordor Sed.-4P	560	2675	19,602
40	4-dr. Sta. Wag.-4P	640	2635	1654
Ford 4-cyl.				
40	2-dr. Del. Rds. R/S-2/4P	460	2278	101
40	2-dr. Std. RS Rds.-2/4P	425	2268	107
40	2-dr. Cab R/S-2/4P	535	2306	24
40	4-dr. Std. Phae.-4P	445	2281	457
40	4-dr. Del. Phae.-4P	495	2290	241
40	2-dr. 3W Del. Cpe.-2P	490	2220	24
40	2-dr. 3W Std. Cpe.-2P	440	2380	189
40	2-dr. 5W Del. Cpe.-2P	490	2299	28
40	2-dr. 5W Std. Cpe.-2P	440	2220	2148
40	2-dr. Vic.-4P	545	2356	25
40	2-dr. Del. Tudor Sed.-4P	500	2520	85
40	2-dr. Std. Tudor Sed.-4P	450	2503	2911
40	4-dr. Del. Fordor Sed.-4P	560	2590	179
40	4-dr. Std. Fordor Sed.-4P	510	2550	682
40	4-dr. Sta. Wag.-4P	590	2505	359

1933 Ford V-8 DeLuxe coupe. (JAC)

1933 Ford V-8 cabriolet. (OCW)

1933 Ford V-8 victoria. (OCW)

ENGINE [Model B]: Inline. L-head. Four. Cast-iron block. B & S: 3-7/8 x 4-1/4 in. Disp.: 200.5 cid. C.R.: 4.6:1. Brake H.P.: 50. Taxable H.P.: 30. Main bearings: three. Valve lifters: mechanical. Carb.: Zenith or Holley double venturi.

ENGINE [Model 40]: 90 degree V. L-head. Eight. Cast-iron block. B & S: 3-1/16 x 3-3/4 in. Disp.: 221 cid. C.R.: 6.3:1. Brake H.P.: 75 @ 3800 rpm. Main bearings: three. Valve lifters: mechanical. Carb.: Detroit Lubricator downdraft, single barrel 1.25-in. throat.

CHASSIS: [Model 40] W.B.: 112 in. O.L.: 182-9/10 in. Height: 68 in. Front/Rear Tread: 55-1/5/56-7/10 in. Tires: 5.50 x 17.

TECHNICAL: Sliding gear transmission. Speeds: 3F/1R. Floor shift controls. Single dry plate, woven asbestos lining clutch. Shaft drive. 3/4 floating rear axle. Overall ratio: 4.11:1. Mechanical internal expanding brakes on four wheels. Welded spoke wheels, drop center rims. Wheel Size: 17 in.

OPTIONS: Radio. Heater. Clock. Radio antenna. Greyhound radiator ornament. Trunk. Trunk rack. Twin tail lamps. Cowl lamps (standard models). Windshield wings. Dual horns (standard models). Whitewalls. Leather seats. Dual wipers. Steel spare tire cover. Rumbleseat (coupes).

HISTORY: Introduced February 9, 1933. Calendar year sales: 311,113 (registrations). Calendar year production: 334,969. The president of Ford was Edsel Ford. During 1933 Ford conducted a number of economy runs with the Model 40. Under conditions ranging from the Mojave Desert to the Catskill Mountains the Fords averaged between 18.29 and 22.5 mpg.

1934 FORD

FORD — MODEL 40 — EIGHT: Visual changes for 1934 were minor. Different V-8 hubcap emblems (now painted rather than chrome-finished and without a painted surround) were used and the side hood louvers were straight instead of curved. Although the same grille form was continued for 1934 there were changes. The 1934 version had fewer vertical bars and its chrome frame was deeper and flatter. The V-8 grille ornament was placed within an inverted 60 degree triangle and carried a vertical divider. Other exterior alterations included smaller head and cowl light shells, two rather than one hood handles and three instead of two body pin stripes. In addition fenders were painted in body

color on all models. However, black fenders were available as an option. Closed body models featured front door glass that prior to lowering vertically into the door, moved slightly to the rear. This was usually referred to as "clear vision" ventilation.

The dash panel no longer had the engine-turned panel insert. For 1934 this surface was painted.

DeLuxe models were easily distinguished from their Standard counterparts by their pin striping, cowl light, twin horns and two taillights.

The principal change in the design of the Ford V-8 consisted of a Stromberg carburetor in place of the Detroit Lubricator unit and a reshaped air cleaner.

Ford also offered its four-cylinder engine in all models at a price $50 below that of a corresponding V-8 design. This was the final year for this engine's use in a Ford automobile. The engine was designated Model B; the car was designated Model 40.

I.D. DATA: Serial numbers were on top side of frame, near clutch panel. Also left front pillar forward portion of left frame member transmission housing. Starting: 18-451478 and up. Engine numbers on top of clutch housing. Starting: 18-457478 and up.

1934 Ford Deluxe coupe. (OCW)

1934 Ford Model 40 Cabriolet. (OCW)

1934 Ford V-8 victoria. (OCW)

1934 Ford V-8 Deluxe coupe. (OCW)

1934 Ford V-8 station wagon. (AA)

1934 Ford V-8 cabriolet. (JAC)

1934 Ford V-8 Deluxe roadster. (OCW)

Model No.	Body Type & Seating	Factory Price	Shipping Weight	Prod. Total
Ford V-8				
40 V-8	2-dr. Del. Rds.-2P	525	2461	—
40 V-8	4-dr. Phae.-4P	510	2520	373
40 V-8	4-dr. Del. Phae.-4P	550	2529	3128
40 V-8	2-dr. Cab.-2/4P	590	2545	14,496
40 V-8	2-dr. Std. 5W Cpe.-2P	515	2534	47,623
40 V-8	2-dr. Del. 3W Cpe.-2/4P	555	2538	26,348
40 V-8	2-dr. Del. 5W Cpe.-2/4P	555	2538	26,879
40 V-8	2-dr. Tudor-4P	535	2621	124,870
40 V-8	2-dr. Del. Tudor-4P	575	2625	121,696
40 V-8	4-dr. Fordor-4P	585	2675	22,394
40 V-8	4-dr. Del. Fordor-4P	625	2684	102,268
40 V-8	2-dr. Vic.-4P	610	2595	20,083
40 V-8	4-dr. Sta. Wag.-4P	660	2635	2905
Ford 4-cyl.				
40	2-dr. Del. Rds.-2P	475	2278	—
40	4-dr. Phae.-4P	460	2281	377
40	4-dr. Del. Phae.-4P	510	2290	412
40	2-dr. Cab.-2P	540	2306	12
40	2-dr. Std, 5W Cpe.-2P	465	2220	20
40	2-dr. Del. 3W Cpe.-2/4P	505	2220	7
40	2-dr. Del. 5W Cpe.-2/4P	505	2299	3
40	2-dr. Tudor-4P	485	2503	185
40	2-dr. Del. Tudor-4P	525	2520	12
40	4-dr. Fordor-4P	535	2590	405
40	4-dr. Del. Fordor-4P	575	2590	384
40	2-dr. Vic.-4P	560	2356	—
40	4-dr. Sta. Wag.-4P	610	2505	95

ENGINE [Model B]: Inline. L-head. Four. Cast-iron block. B & S: 3-7/8 x 4-1/4 in. Disp.: 200.5 cid. C.R.: 4.6:1. Brake H.P.: 50. Taxable H.P.: 30. Main bearings: three. Valve lifters: mechanical. Carb.: Zenith or Holley double venturi.

ENGINE [Model 40]: 90 degree V. L-head. Eight. Cast-iron block. B & S: 3-1/16 x 3-3/4 in. Disp.: 221 cid. C.R.: 6.3:1. Brake H.P.: 85 @ 3800 rpm. Main bearings: three. Valve lifters: mechanical. Carb.: Stromberg EE-1 two-barrel downdraft. Torque: 150 lbs.-ft. @ 2200 rpm.

CHASSIS: W.B.: 112 in. O.L.: 182.9 in. Height: 68 in. Front/Rear Tread: 55.2/56.7 in. Tires: 5.50 x 17.

TECHNICAL: Sliding gear transmission. Speeds: 3F/1R. Floor shift controls. Single dry plate, woven asbestos lining. Shaft drive. 3/4 floating rear axle. Overall ratio: 4.11:1. Mechanical internal expanding brakes on four wheels. Welded spoke drop center rims. Wheel size: 17 in.

OPTIONS: Radio (ashtray or glovebox door mounted). Heater. Clock. Cigar Lighter. Radio antenna. Seat covers. Spotlight. Cowl lamps (std. models). Trunk. Whitewalls. Greyhound radiator ornament. Special steel spoke wheels. Oversize balloon tires. Bumper guards. Extra horn, black finish (std. models). Dual windshield wiper. Steel tire cover (std. models). Black painted fenders. Two taillights (std. models).

HISTORY: Introduced January 1934. Calendar year production: 563,921. The president of Ford was Edsel Ford. In April 1934 Clyde Barrow wrote his famous (infamous?) letter to Henry Ford in which he told Ford "what a dandy car you make." At the Ford press preview, held on December 6, 1933, Ford served alcoholic beverages for the first time. For the first time since 1930 the Ford Motor Company reported a profit ($3,759,311) for 1934.

1935 FORD

1935 Ford Model 48 3-window coupe. (OCW)

1935 Ford Deluxe Fordor touring sedan. (OCW)

1935 Ford V-8 convertible cabriolet. (AA)

FORD — MODEL 48 — EIGHT: Few Ford enthusiasts would dispute Ford's claim of "Greater Beauty, Greater Comfort, and Greater Safety" for its 1935 models.

The narrower radiator grille lost its sharply veed base and four horizontal bars helped accentuate the 1935 model's new, lower and more streamlined appearance. Fender outlines were now much more rounded and the side hood louvers received three horizontal bright stripes. In profile the Ford windshield was seen to be more sharply sloped then previously. No longer fitted were the old cowl lamps since the parking lamps were integral with the headlamps. The headlight shells were body color painted.

For the first time Ford offered a built-in trunk for its two- and four-door models and all Fords had front-hinged doors front and rear.

Both Standard and DeLuxe versions shared a painted dash finish with the latter Fords having a set of horizontal bars running down the center section. External distinctions were obvious. DeLuxe models had bright windshield and grille trimwork as well as dual exposed horns and twin taillights.

Added to the Ford model lineup was a convertible sedan. No longer available was the victoria.

1935 Ford V-8 Deluxe Fordor touring sedan. (OCW)

1935 Ford V-8 DeLuxe roadster. (JAC)

I.D. DATA: Serial numbers were located on left side of frame near firewall. Starting: 18-1234357. Ending: 18-2207110. Prefix "C" indicates Canadian built. Engine numbers located on top of clutch housing. Starting 18-1234357. Ending: 18-2207110.

Model No.	Body Type & Seating	Factory Price	Shipping Weight	Prod. Total
48	4-dr. Del. Phae.-4P	580	2667	6073
48	2-dr. Del. Rds. R/S-2/4P	550	2597	4896
48	2-dr. Del. RS Cab.-2/4P	625	2687	17,000
48	4-dr. Del. Conv. Sed.-4P	750	2827	4234
48	2-dr. Std. Cpe. 3W-2P	—	2647	—
48	2-dr. Del. Cpe. 3W-2P	570	2647	31,513
48	2-dr. Std. Cpe. 5W-2P	520	2620	78,477
48	2-dr. Del. Cpe. 5W-2P	560	2643	33,065
48	2-dr. Std. Tudor-4P	510	2717	237,833
48	2-dr. Del. Tudor-4P	595	2737	84,692
48	4-dr. Std. Fordor-4P	575	2760	49,176
48	4-dr. Del. Fordor-4P	635	2767	75,807
48	4-dr. Sta. Wag.	670	2896	4536
48	Del. Tudor Sed.-4P	595	2772	87,336
48	Del. Fordor Sed.-4P	655	2787	105,157

ENGINE: 90 degree V. L-head. Eight. Cast-iron block. B & S: 3-1/16 x 3-3/4 in. Disp.: 221 cid. C.R.: 6.3:1. Brake H.P.: 85 @ 3800 rpm. Main bearings: three. Valve lifters: mechanical. Carb.: Stromberg EE-1, two-barrel downdraft. Torque: 144 lbs.-ft. @ 2200 rpm.

CHASSIS: W.B.: 112 in. O.L.: 182-3/4 in. Height: 64-5/8 in. Front/Rear Tread: 55-1/2/58-1/4 in. Tires: 6.00 x 16.

1935 Ford V-8 standard five-window coupe. (OCW)

1935 Ford V-8 Deluxe Tudor sedan. (OCW)

TECHNICAL: Sliding gear transmission. Speeds: 3F/1R. Floor shift controls. Single dry plate, woven asbestos lining clutch. Shaft drive. 3/4 floating rear axle. Overall ratio: 4.33:1. Mechanical, internal expanding brakes on four wheels. Welded spoke, drop center rims on wheels. Wheel size: 16 in.

OPTIONS: Radio. Heater. Clock. Cigar lighter. Radio antenna. Seat covers. Spotlight. Cowl lamps (std. models). Trunk. Luggage rack. Whitewalls. Greyhound radiator ornament. Special steel spoke wheels. Oversize balloon tires. Bumper guards. Extra horns black finish (std. models). Dual windshield wipers. Steel tire cover (std. models). Black painted fenders. Two taillights (standard. models). Banjo type steering wheel. Rumbleseat (coupes and roadsters).

HISTORY: Introduced December 1934. Calendar year registrations: 826,519. Calendar year production: 942,439. The president of Ford was Edsel Ford. Ford was America's best selling car for 1935. A Ford convertible sedan paced the 1935 Indianapolis 500. Ford produced its two-millionth V-8 engine in June 1935.

1936 FORD

1936 Ford Model 68 Club Cabriolet. (OCW)

1936 Ford Model 68 Deluxe Tudor sedan. (OCW)

1936 Ford Model 68 Deluxe 5-window coupe. (OCW)

FORD — MODEL 68 — EIGHT: The 1936 Fords retained the same basic body of the 1935 models but carried a restyled front end and new rear fenders. The grille, consisting only of vertical bars, extended further around the hood sides and the dual horns of the DeLuxe models were placed behind screens set into the fender catwalks.

The convertible sedan with its "flat-back" body was superseded by a version with a built-in luggage compartment or "trunk-back" style during the model year.

In place of wire wheels were new pressed steel, artillery wheels with large 12-inch painted hubcaps and chrome centers carrying a narrow, stylized V-8 logo. The same design was used on the Ford's hood ornament.

Design changes for 1936 included a larger capacity radiator, better engine cooling via new hood side louvers and front vents, and helical-type gears for first and reverse gears. Previously only the second and third gears were of this design. The Ford V-8 now had domed aluminum pistons (replaced by steel versions during the year) and new insert main bearings.

DeLuxe models featured brightwork around the grille, headlamps and windshield as well as dual horns and taillights. Those DeLuxe Fords produced later in the model year also had as standard equipment dual windshield wipers, wheel trim rings, clock and rear view mirror.

1936 Ford Model 68 convertible sedan. (OCW)

1936 Ford V-8 DeLuxe club cabriolet. (AA)

1936 Ford V-8 Deluxe Tudor touring sedan. (OCW)

1936 Ford V-8 Deluxe Fordor touring sedan. (OCW)

1936 Ford V-8 Deluxe five-window coupe. (OCW)

I.D. DATA: Serial numbers were located on left side of frame near firewall. Starting: 18-2207111. Ending: 18-3331856. Prefix "C" indicates Canadian built. Engine numbers were located on top of clutch housing. Starting: 18-2207111. Ending: 18-3331856.

Model No.	Body Type & Seating	Factory Price	Shipping Weight	Prod. Total
68	2-dr. Del. Rds.-2P	560	2561	3862
68	4-dr. Del. Phae.-4P	590	2641	5555
68	2-dr. Cab-4P	625	2649	—
68	2-dr. Clb. Cab.-4P	675	2661	4616
68	4-dr. Conv. Trk. Sed.-4P	780	2916	—
68	4-dr. Conv. Sed.-4P	760	2791	5601
68	2-dr. Del. 3W Cpe.-2P	570	2621	21,446
68	2-dr. Std. 5W Cpe.-2P	510	2599	78,534
68	2-dr. Del. 5W Cpe.-2P	555	2641	29,938
68	2-dr. Std. Tudor Sed.-4P	520	2659	174,770
68	Std. Tudor Tr. Sed.-4P	545	2718	—
68	2-dr. Del. Tudor Sed.-4P	565	2691	20,519
68	Del. Tudor Tr. Sed.-4P	590	2786	125,303
68	4-dr. Std. Fordor Sed.-4P	580	2699	31,505
68	Std. Fordor Tr. Sed.-4P	605	2771	—
68	4-dr. Del. Fordor Sed.-4P	625	2746	42,867
68	Del. Fordor Tr. Sed.-4P	650	2816	159,825
68	4-dr. Sta. Wag.	670	3020	7044

1936 Ford V-8 convertible sedan. (OCW)

1936 Ford V-8 station wagon. (OCW)

ENGINE: 90 degree V. Inline. Eight. Cast-iron block. B & S: 3-1/16 x 3-3/4 in. Disp.: 221 cid. C.R.: 6.3:1. Brake H.P.: 85 @ 3800 rpm. Taxable H.P.: 30. Main bearings: three. Valve lifters: mechanical. Carb.: Ford 679510A two-barrel downdraft. Torque: 148 lbs.-ft. @ 2200 rpm.

CHASSIS: W.B.: 112 in. O.L.: 182-3/4 in. Height: 68-5/8 in. Front/Rear Tread: 55-1/2/58-1/4 in. Tires: 6.00 x 16.

TECHNICAL: Sliding gear transmission. Speeds: 3F/1R. Floor shift controls. Single dry plate, molded asbestos lining clutch. Shaft drive. 3/4 floating rear axle. Overall ratio: 4.33:1. Mechanical, internal expanding brakes on four wheels. Pressed steel wheels, drop center rim. Wheel size: 16 in.

OPTIONS: Radio (five versions from $44.50). Heater (14.00). Clock (9.75). Cigar lighter. Radio antenna. Seat covers. Spotlight. Rumbleseat (coupes, roadster) (20.00). Luggage rack (7.50). Banjo steering wheel. "Spider" wheel covers (3.75 early). Wind wings (10.00). Combination oil-pressure, gas gauge (3.75). Dual windshield wipers (3.00). Leather upholstery. Electric air horns.

HISTORY: Introduced October 1935. Ford was the overall winner of the 1936 Monte Carlo Rally. Calendar year registrations: 748,554. Calendar year production: 791,812. The president of Ford was Edsel Ford.

1936 Ford V-8 Deluxe three-window coupe. (OCW)

1936 Ford V-8 Deluxe phaeton. (OCW)

1937 FORD

1937 Ford Model 60 two-door sedan. (OCW)

FORD — MODEL 78 — EIGHT: The 1937 models were the first Fords to have their headlights mounted in the front fenders and possess an all steel top. The 1937 Ford's styling reflected the strong influence of the Lincoln-Zephyr. The grille with horizontal bars and a center vertical bar cut a sharp vee into the side hood area. As had been the case for many years the side hood cooling vents reflected the grille's general form.

Ford offered sedans with either a "slant-back" or "trunk-back" rear deck. All Ford sedans had access to the trunk area through an external lid.

In addition, a new coupe with a rear seat was introduced. All models had a rear-hinged alligator-type hood.

The operation of the 221 cid V-8 was further improved by the use of a higher capacity water pump, larger insert bearings and cast alloy steel pistons. Replacing the rod-operated mechanical brake system was a version using a cable linkage.

As in previous years Ford offered both Standard and DeLuxe models with the latter possessing interiors with walnut woodgrain window molding and exterior trim brightwork. Standard models had painted radiator grilles and windshield frames. A burl mahogany woodgrain finish was applied to their interior window trim.

1937 Ford V-8 five-window coupe. (AA)

1937 Ford V-8 Tudor sedan. (AA)

Ford introduced a smaller version of its V-8 with a 2-3/5-inch bore and 3-1/5-inch stroke. Its displacement was 136 cubic inches. This 60-hp engine was available only in the Standard Ford models.

I.D. DATA: Serial numbers located on left side of frame near firewall. Starting: [Model 74] 54-6602. [Model 78] 18-3331857. Ending: [Model 74] 54-358334. [Model 78] 18-4186446. Prefix "C" indicates Canadian built. Engine numbers located on top of clutch housing. Starting: [Model 74] 54-6602; [Model 78] 18-3331857. Ending: [Model 74] 54-358334; [Model 78] 18-4186446.

Model No.	Body Type & Seating	Factory Price	Shipping Weight	Prod. Total
78	2-dr. Del. Rds.-2P	696	2576	1250
78	4-dr. Del. Phae.-5P	750	2691	3723
78	2-dr. Del. Cab.	720	2616	10,184
78	2-dr. Del. Clb. Cab.	760	2636	8001
78	4-dr. Del. Conv. Sed.	860	2861	4378
78	2-dr. Del. Cpe. 5W-3P	660	2506	26,738
78	Del. Clb. Cpe. 5W-4P	720	2616	16,992
78	2-dr. Del. Tudor Sed.-5P	675	2656	33,683
78	Del. Tudor Tr. Sed.-5P	700	2679	—
78	4-dr. Del. Fordor Sed.-5P	735	2671	22,885
78	Del. Fordor Tr. Sed.-5P	760	2696	98,687
78	4-dr. Sta. Wag.-5P	755	2991	9304
78	2-dr. Std. Tudor Sed.-5P	610	2616	308,446
78	Std. Tudor Tr. Sed.-5P	635	2648	—
78	4-dr. Std. Fordor Sed.-5P	670	2649	49,062
78	Std. Fordor Tr. Sed.-5P	695	2666	45,531
78	2-dr. Std. Cpe. 5W-3P	585	2496	90,347

NOTE 1: The five standard bodies when ordered with the 60-hp V-8 were designated as Model 74 Fords and weighed over 200 lbs. less.

1937 Ford V-8 station wagon. (JAC)

1937 Ford V-8 Deluxe Fordor touring sedan. (OCW)

1937 Ford V-8 Deluxe roadster. (OCW)

ENGINE [Model 78]: 90 degree V. Inline. Eight. Cast-iron block. B & S: 3-1/16 x 3-3/4 in. Disp.: 221 cid. C.R.: 6.3:1. Brake H.P.: 85 @ 3800 rpm. Taxable H.P.: 30.01. Main bearings: three. Valve lifters: mechanical. Carb.: Stromberg 67-9510A two-barrel downdraft. Torque: 153 lbs.-ft. @ 2200 rpm.

ENGINE [Model 74]: 90 degree V. Inline. Eight. Cast-iron block. B & S: 2-3/5 x 3-1/5 in. Disp.: 136 cid. C.R.: 6.6:1. Brake H.P. 60 @ 3600 rpm. Taxable H.P.: 21.6. Main bearings: three. Valve lifters: mechanical. Carb.: Stromberg 922A-9510A two-barrel downdraft. Torque: 94 lbs.-ft. @ 2500 rpm.

CHASSIS: [Model 74 and 78]. W.B.: 112 in. O.L.: 179-1/2 in. Height: 68-5/8 in. Front/Rear Tread: 55-1/2/58-1/4. Tires: 6.00 x 16 [Model 74] 5.50 x 16.

TECHNICAL: Sliding gear transmission. Speeds: 3F/1R. Floor shift controls. Single dry plate, molded asbestos lining clutch. Shaft drive. 3/4 floating rear axle. Overall ratio: 4.33:1. Mechanical, internal expanding brakes on four wheels. Pressed steel, drop center rim wheels. Wheel size: 16 in.

OPTIONS: Fender skirts. Radio. Heater. Clock (mirror clock and glovebox clock). Cigar lighter. Radio antenna. Seat covers. Side view mirror. Dual wipers. Sport light. Dual taillights (std. on DeLuxe models). Fog lamps. Locking gas cap. Glovebox lock. Defroster. Draft deflectors. Vanity mirror. Wheel trim bands. DeLuxe hubcaps. White sidewall tires. Center bumper guard. DeLuxe steering wheel. Sliding glass panels (station wagon) ($20.00).

HISTORY: Introduced November 1937. First year for 60-hp V-8, first year for rear fender skirts. Calendar year sales: 765,933 (registrations). Calendar year production: 848,608. The president of Ford was Edsel Ford.

1938 FORD

1938 Ford V-8 DeLuxe station wagon. (AA)

1938 Ford Standard four-door sedan. (OCW)

FORD — DELUXE — MODEL 81A — EIGHT: Ford adopted a new marketing strategy for 1938 in which its Standard models carried the same basic front sheet metal used in 1937 while the DeLuxe models were given a substantially revised appearance. A curved grille outline with horizontal bars and a separate set of side hood louvers distinguished the more costly DeLuxe models. Interior alterations consisted of a new instrument panel with a centrally located radio speaker grille and recessed control knobs. As before, the windshield opening knob was centered high on the dash.

FORD — STANDARD — MODEL 82A — EIGHT: The 60-hp Ford V-8 engine was standard only in the three models offered in the Standard line. These Fords were also available with the 221 cid V-8. The Standard Ford grille featured horizontal bars that extended into the side hood region for engine cooling.

I.D. DATA: Serial numbers were located on left frame side member near firewall. Starting: 81A—18-4186447; 82A—54-358335 & up. Ending: 81A—18-4661100. Engine numbers were located on top of clutch housing. Starting: 81A—18-4186447; 82A—54-358335 and up. Ending: 81A—18-4661100.

Model No.	Body Type & Seating	Factory Price	Shipping Weight	Prod. Total
81A	2-dr. Std. Cpe.-2P	625	2575	34,059
81A	2-dr. Std. Tudor Sed.-5P	665	2674	106,117
81A	4-dr. Std. Fordor Sed.-5P	710	2697	30,287
81A	4-dr. Sta. Wag.-5P	825	2981	6944
81A	4-dr. DeL. Phae.-5P	820	2748	1169
81A	2-dr. DeL. Clb. Conv.-5P	800	2719	6080
81A	2-dr. DeL. Conv. Cpe.-3P	770	2679	4702
81A	4-dr. DeL. Conv. Sed.-5P	900	2883	2703
81A	2-dr. DeL. Cpe.-3P	685	2606	22,225
81A	2-dr. DeL. Clb. Cpe.-5P	745	2688	7171
81A	2-dr. DeL. Tudor Sed.-5P	725	2742	101,647
81A	DeL. Fordor Sed.-5P	770	2773	92,020

Note 1: The three Standard bodies when ordered with the 60-hp V-8 were designated as Model 81A Fords.

ENGINE [Model 81A]: 90 degree V. Inline. Eight. Cast-iron block. B & S: 3-1/16 x 3-3/4 in. Disp.: 221 cid. C.R.: 6.12:1. Brake H.P.: 85 @ 3800 rpm. Taxable H.P.: 30. Main bearings: three. Valve lifters: mechanical. Carb.: Chandler-Groves and Stromberg 21A-9510A, two-barrel downdraft. Torque: 146 lbs.-ft. @ 2000 rpm.

ENGINE [Model 82A]: 90 degree V. Inline. Eight. Cast-iron block. B & S: 2-3/5 x 3-1/5 in. Disp.: 136 cid. C.R.: 6.6:1. Brake H.P.: 60 @ 3500 rpm. Taxable H.P.: 21.6. Main bearings: three. Valve lifters: mechanical. Carb.: Chandler-Groves and Stromberg 9221-95101, two-barrel downdraft. Torque: 94 lbs.-ft. @ 2500 rpm.

CHASSIS: Models 81A and 82A. W.B.: 112 in. O.L.: 179-1/2 in. Height: 68-5/8 in. Front/Rear Tread: 55-1/2/58-1/4 in. Tires: 6.00 x 16 (Model 82A—5.50 x 16).

TECHNICAL: Sliding gear transmission. Speeds: 3F/1R. Floor shift controls. Single dry plate, molded asbestos lining clutch. Shaft drive. 3/4 floating rear axle. Overall ratio: 4.33:1. Mechanical, internal expanding brakes on four wheels. Pressed steel wheels, drop-center rims. Wheel size: 16 in.

OPTIONS: Fender skirts. Bumper guards. Radio. Heater. Clock (mirror and glovebox). Cigar lighter. Seat covers. Side view mirror. Dual wipers. Sport light. Dual taillights (Std. models). Fog lights. Locking gas cap. Glovebox lock. Defroster. Draft deflectors. Vanity mirror. Wheel trim bands. DeLuxe hubcaps. White sidewall tires. DeLuxe steering wheel. License plate frame.

HISTORY: Introduced November 1937. Ford secured its second victory in the Monte Carlo Rally. Calendar year registrations: 363,688. Calendar year production: 410,048. The president of Ford was Edsel Ford.

1938 Ford V-8 Standard coupe. (HAC)

1939 Ford Deluxe convertible coupe. (OCW)

1939 Ford V-8 DeLuxe, station wagon. (OCW)

1939 Ford V-8 Deluxe five-window coupe. (OCW)

1939 Ford V-8 Deluxe Tudor sedan. (OCW)

Model No.	Body Type & Seating	Factory Price	Shipping Weight	Prod. Total
922A	2-dr. Std. Cpe.-3P	640	2710	38,197
922A	2-dr. Std. Tudor Sed.-5P	680	2830	124,866
922A	4-dr. Std.. Fordor Sed.-5P	730	2850	—
922A	4-dr. Std. Sta. Wag.-5P	840	3080	3277
91A	2-dr. DeL. Conv. Cpe.-3P	790	2840	10,422
91A	4-dr. DeL. Conv. Sed.-5P	920	2935	3561
91A	2-dr. DeL. Cpe.-3P	700	2752	33,326
91A	2-dr. DeL. Tudor Sed.-5P	745	2867	144,333
91A	DeL. Fordor Sed.-5P	790	2898	—
91A	4-dr. DeL. Sta. Wag.-5P	920	3095	6155

FORD — DELUXE — MODEL 91A — EIGHT: The 1939 Fords were again divided into Standard and DeLuxe models. The former carried the general styling of the 1938 DeLuxe Ford. Thus they had a sharply veed grille with horizontal bars, headlights mounted inboard of the fenders and small side hood louvers. The DeLuxe models had a much more modern appearance. Their teardrop-shaped headlights blended smoothly into the leading edges of the front fenders and a grille set lower in the hood than as previous models carried vertical bars. Simple chrome trim replaced the hood louvers and a smoother body profile was featured. The most significant technical development was the adoption by Ford of Lockheed hydraulic brakes.

FORD — STANDARD — MODEL 922A — EIGHT: Only four body styles were offered in the Standard series. Customers could choose either the 60-hp or 85-hp engines.

Standard models were not equipped with the banjo steering wheel, glovebox lock and clock found on DeLuxe Fords.

I.D. DATA: Serial numbers were located on the left side member near firewall. Starting No.: Model 91A—18-4661001. Model 922A—54506501 & up. Ending: 91A—18-210700. Engine No. location was top of clutch housing. Starting: Model 91A—18-4661001. Model 922A—54-506501 and up. Ending: Model 91A—18-5210700.

NOTE 1: The Standard models were available with the 60-hp or 85-hp engines.

ENGINE [85 hp]: 90 degree V. Inline. Eight. Cast-iron block. B & S: 3-1/16 x 3-3/4 in. Disp.: 221 cid. C.R.: 6.15:1. Brake H.P.: 90 @ 3800 rpm. Taxable H.P.: 30. Main bearings: three. Valve lifters: mechanical. Carb.: Stromberg 21A-951A, two-barrel downdraft. Torque: 155 lbs.-ft. @ 2200 rpm.

ENGINE [60 hp]: 90 degree V. Inline. Eight. Cast-iron block. B & S: 2-3/5 x 3-1/5 in. Disp.: 136 cid. C.R.: 6.6:1. Brake H.P.: 60 @ 3500 rpm. Taxable H.P.: 21.6. Main bearings: three. Valve lifters: mechanical. Carb.: Stromberg 922A-9510A, two-barrel downdraft. Torque: 94 lbs.-ft. @ 2500 rpm.

1939 Ford V-8 DeLuxe Fordor sedan. (OCW)

1939 Ford V-8 Deluxe convertible coupe. (OCW)

1939 Ford V-8 Deluxe convertible sedan. (OCW)

CHASSIS: Series 91A-922A. W.B.: 112 in. O.L.: 179-1/2 in. Height: 68-5/8 in. Front/Rear Tread: 55-1/2/58-1/4 in. Tires: 6.00 x 16 (60-hp 5.50 x 16).

TECHNICAL: Sliding gear transmission. Speeds: 3F/1R. Floor shift controls. Single dry plate, molded asbestos lining clutch. Shaft drive. 3/4 floating rear axle. Overall ratio: 4.33:1. Lockheed hydraulic brakes on four wheels. Pressed steel, drop-center rim on wheels. Wheel size: 16 in.

OPTIONS: Bumper guards. Radio. Heater. Clock. Seat covers. Side view mirror. Sport light. Fog lamps. Locking gas cap. Draft deflectors. Vanity mirror. Wheel dress up rings. DeLuxe hubcaps. White sidewall tires. License plate frames. Fender skirts.

HISTORY: Introduced November 4, 1938. Lockheed hydraulic brakes. Calendar year registrations: 481,496. Calendar year production: 532,152. The president of Ford was Edsel Ford.

1940 FORD

FORD — MODEL 01A — EIGHT: The 1940 Fords featured extremely handsome styling by Eugene Gregorie. All models were fitted with sealed beam headlights and a steering column-mounted shift lever. DeLuxe models had chrome headlight trim rings with the parking light cast into its upper surface. The DeLuxe grille combined a center section with horizontal bars and secondary side grids whose horizontal bars were subdivided into three sections by thicker molding. Hubcaps for these top level Fords featured bright red "Ford DeLuxe" lettering and trim rings finished in the body color. The DeLuxe instrument panel was given a maroon and sand two-tone finish that matched that of the steering wheel. Model 01A carried the 85-hp engine and was available in both Standard and DeLuxe versions.

FORD — MODEL 022A — EIGHT: Distinguishing the 60-hp Standard Fords, the grille and hood were similar to those of the 1939 DeLuxe models. Their headlight shells were finished in the body color and the integral parking lamp lacked the ribbed surround used on the DeLuxe model. The vertical grille bars were painted to match the body color. DeLuxe hubcaps had a series of concentric rings surrounding a blue V-8.

1940 Ford V-8 Deluxe Fordor sedan. (PH)

1940 Ford V-8 DeLuxe station wagon. (OCW)

The Standard dash and steering wheel had a Briarwood brown finish and the instrument panel had a larger speedometer face. Both Standard and DeLuxe Fords had front vent windows.

For the final year the Ford V-8 60 was available for Standard models.

I.D. DATA: Serial numbers located on left frame side member near firewall. Starting: [Model 01A] 18-5210701; [Model 022A] 54-506501 and up. Ending: [Model 01A] 18-5896294. Engine numbers located on top of clutch housing. Starting: [Model 01A] 18-5210701; [Model 022A] 54-506401 and up. Ending: [Model 01A] 18-5896294.

Model No.	Body Type & Seating	Factory Price	Shipping Weight	Prod. Total
022A	2-dr. Std. Cpe.-3P	660	2763	33,693
022A	2-dr. Std. Tudor Sed.-5P	700	2909	150,933
022A	4-dr. Std. Fordor Sed.-5P	750	2936	25,545
022A	4-dr. Std. Sta. Wag.-5P	875	3249	4469
022A	2-dr. Std. Bus. Cpe.-5P	680	2801	16,785
01A	2-dr. Del. Conv. Cpe.-5P	850	2956	23,704
01A	2-dr. Del. Cpe.-3P	721	2791	27,919
01A	2-dr. Del. Tudor Sed.-5P	765	2927	171,368
01A	4-dr. Del. Fordor Sed.-5P	810	2966	91,756
01A	4-dr. Del. Sta. Wag.	950	3262	8730
01A	2-dr. Del. Bus. Cpe.-5P	745	2831	20,183

1940 Ford V-8 Deluxe convertible coupe. (PH)

1940 Ford V-8 Deluxe Tudor sedan. (PH)

1940 Ford Model 01A Deluxe Fordor sedan. (OCW)

ENGINE [85 hp]: 90 degree V. Inline. Eight. Cast-iron block. B & S: 3-1/16 x 3-3/4 in. Disp.: 221 cid. C.R.: 6.15:1. Brake H.P. 85 @ 3800 rpm. Taxable H.P.: 30. Main bearings: three. Valve lifters: mechanical. Carb.: Chandler-Groves 21A-9510A, two-barrel downdraft. Torque: 155 lbs.-ft. @ 2200 rpm.

ENGINE [60 hp]: 90 degree V. Inline. Eight. Cast-iron block. B & S: 2-3/5 x 3-1/5 in. Disp.: 135 cid. C.R.: 6.6:1. Brake H.P.: 60 @ 3500 rpm. Taxable H.P. 21.6. Main bearings: three. Valve lifters: mechanical. Carb.: Chandler-Groves 922A-9510A two-barrel downdraft. Torque: 94 lbs.-ft. @ 2500 rpm.

CHASSIS: 01A and 022A. W.B.: 112 in. O.L.: 188-1/4 in. Height: 68 in. Front/Rear Tread: 55-3/4/58-1/4. Tires: 6.00 x 16. (60-hp 5.50 x 16).

TECHNICAL: Sliding gear transmission. Speeds: 3F/1R. Steering column-mounted shift lever. Single dry plate, molded asbestos lining clutch. Shaft drive. 3/4 floating rear axle. Overall ratio: 4.33:1. Lockheed hydraulic brakes on four wheels. Pressed steel, drop-center rim wheels. Wheel size: 16 in.

OPTIONS: Fender skirts. Bumper guards. Radio. Heater. Cigar lighter. Radio antenna. Seat covers. Side view mirror. Right-hand side mirror. Sport light. Fog lamps. Locking gas cap. Defroster. Vanity mirror. DeLuxe wheel rings. DeLuxe hubcaps. White sidewall tires. Gravel deflectors. License plate frame. Two-tone paint.

HISTORY: Introduced October 1940. Calendar year sales: 542,755 (registrations). Calendar year production: 599,175. The president of Ford was Edsel Ford.

1941 FORD

1941 Ford station wagon. (OCW)

1941 Ford Deluxe two-door sedan. (OCW)

1941 Ford Super DeLuxe club coupe. (AA)

FORD — SUPER DELUXE — SIX or EIGHT: The 1941 Fords were with fresh styling and a revamped chassis easily recognized as new models. All versions were mounted on a longer by two inches wheelbase of 114 inches and by virtue of a wider body featured substantially increased interior dimensions. Emphasizing Ford's rounder, more curved body form was a new three-piece grille that consisted of a neo-traditional vertical center section with two auxillary units set low on either side. Runningboards were continued but due to the body's greater width were far less noticeable than on earlier Fords. Further accentuating the lower and wider nature of the 1941 Ford was the position of the headlights, which were further apart in the fenders.

Super DeLuxe Fords were easily identified by the bright trim on their runningboard edges and chrome grille sections. The Super DeLuxe bumpers had ridges along their bottom edge. A mid-year (March) revision to Super DeLuxe models added bright trimwork to the front and rear fenders, windshield, rear and side windows. Super DeLuxe script was placed in the inboard position of the left front fender. Bright rear taillight surrounds were installed. In addition the standard features of the Super DeLuxe included a trunk light, glovebox mounted clock, bright wheel trimmings, twin visors, wipers and plastic Kelobra grain dash trim. The wheels had either Vermillion or Silver Gray stripes. Seven body styles were offered in Super DeLuxe form.

FORD — DELUXE — SIX or EIGHT: DeLuxe series Fords lacked the trunk light, glovebox clock, wheel trim rings and unique license plate guard found on the Super DeLuxe models. Their instrument panels were finished in Ebony grain and among standard features were a glovebox lock, dual wipers and sun visors. There was no striping in the DeLuxe Ford wheels, which were painted black regardless of body color. Those on the Super DeLuxe models were painted to match the color of the body and fenders. Only the center grille portion was chromed on DeLuxe models.

1941 Ford Super DeLuxe four-door sedan. (OCW)

1941 Ford Super DeLuxe two-door sedan. (OCW)

Both Super DeLuxe and DeLuxe Fords were available with either Ford's V-8 engine, now rated at 90-hp or for $15 less a new 226 cid flathead six also credited with 90-hp. Among its design features were four main bearings, a vibration damper, forged connecting rods, molybdenum-chrome alloy steel valve seat inserts and solid valve lifters. The six-cylinder engine was a mid-year offering and its availability required new hood trim. Prior to the six's introduction the molding was a plain trim piece with horizontal liner. With the availability of two engines it now carried either a V-8 or 6 identification with a blue background.

FORD — STANDARD — SERIES 11A — SIX: The three Standard models were offered only in a Harbor gray finish and without the V-8 engine option. In addition the windshield divider was a black, rather than stainless steel molding and like the DeLuxe Fords, only the center grille section was chromed. In addition the Standard Fords were equipped with a single taillight, horn, windshield wiper and sun visor. Lacking from their interior were such appointments as armrests, dome light, cigarette lighter and glovebox lock.

I.D. DATA: Serial numbers were on left frame member directly behind front engine mount. Starting: six-cyl.: IGA-1; V-8 18-5986295. Ending: six-cyl.: IGA-34800; V-8 18-6769035. Prefix "C" indicates Canadian built. Engine numbers located on top of clutch housing. Starting: six-cyl.: IGA-1; V-8 18-5986295. Ending: six-cyl.: IGA-34800; V-8 18-6769035.

Model No.	Body Type & Seating	Factory Price	Shipping Weight	Prod. Total
Sup. DeL.	2-dr. Conv.-6P	950	3187	30,240
Sup. DeL.	2-dr. Cpe.-3P	775	2969	22,878
Sup. DeL.	2-dr. Cpe.-4P	800	3001	10,796
Sup. DeL.	2-dr. Cpe. Sed.-6P	850	3052	45,977
Sup. DeL.	2-dr. Tudor-6P	820	3110	185,788
Sup. DeL.	4-dr. Fordor-6P	860	3146	88,053
Sup. DeL.	4-dr. Sta. Wag.-6P	1015	3419	9485
DeLuxe	2-dr. Cpe.-3P	730	2953	33,598
DeLuxe	2-dr. Cpe.-4P	750	2981	12,844
DeLuxe	2-dr. Tudor-6P	775	3095	177,018
DeLuxe	4-dr. Fordor-6P	815	3121	25,928
DeLuxe	4-dr. Sta. Wag.-6P	965	3412	6116
Special	2 dr. Cpe.-3P	706	2878	9823
Special	2-dr. Tudor-6P	735	2983	27,189
Special	4-dr. Fordor-6P	775	3033	3838

NOTE: Weights are for V-8 equipped models.

ENGINE [V-8]: 90 degree V. Inline. Eight. Cast-iron block. B & S: 3-1/16 x 3-3/4 in. Disp.: 221 cid. C.R.: 6.15:1. Brake H.P.: 90 @ 3800 rpm. Taxable H.P.: 30. Main bearings: three. Valve lifters: mechanical. Carb.: Ford 21A-9510A two-barrel downdraft. Torque: 156 lbs.-ft. @ 2200 rpm.

1941 Ford DeLuxe two-door sedan. (AA)

ENGINE [Six cylinder]: Inline. L-head. Six. Cast-iron block. B & S: 3-3/10 x 4-2/5 in. Disp.: 225.8 cid. C.R.: 6.7:1. Brake H.P.: 90 @ 3300 rpm. Taxable H.P.: 30. Main bearings: four. Valve lifters: mechanical. Carb.: Ford 1GA-9510A one-barrel. Torque: 180 lbs.-ft. @ 2000 rpm.

CHASSIS: Special, DeLuxe, Super DeLuxe. W.B.: 114 in. O.L.: 194.3 in. Height 68.15 in. Front/Rear Tread: 55.75/58.25 in. Tires: 6.00 x 16.

TECHNICAL: Sliding gear transmission. Speeds: 3F/1R. Column controls. Semi centrifugal, molded asbestos linings. Shaft drive. 3/4 floating rear axle. Overall ratio: 3.78:1. Hydraulic brakes on four wheels. Pressed steel, drop center rim wheels. Wheel size: 16 in.

OPTIONS: Fender skirts ($12.50). Radio. Heater (hot air 23.00, hot water 20.00). Clock. Seat covers. Side view mirror. Passenger side mirror. Sport light. Locking gas cap. Glove compartment lock. Defroster. Vanity mirror. Radio foot control. Wheel trim rings. DeLuxe hubcaps. White sidewall tires. Center bumper guards—front (3.50) rear (2.50). Gravel deflector (1.50).

HISTORY: Introduced September 1941. Calendar year sales: 602,013 (registrations). Calendar year production: 600,814. The president of Ford was Edsel Ford. On April 29, 1941, the 29-millionth Ford was constructed.

1942 FORD

1942 Ford station wagon. (OCW)

1942 Ford Super Deluxe Tudor sedan. (OCW)

1942 Ford Super Deluxe station wagon. (OCW)

FORD — SUPER DELUXE — SIX or V-8: The 1942 Fords were re-designed with fully concealed runningboards plus new front fenders and hood sheet metal. A new grille design featured a narrow center section in conjunction with side grilles considerably larger and more squared off than previous. The Super Deluxe grille had its brightwork accentuated by blue painted grooves. Used only on those top of the line Fords were front and rear bumpers with ridges along their upper surface. The Super DeLuxe script was now positioned just below the left headlight. The taillights on all models were now horizontally positioned but only those on the Super DeLuxe had bright trim plates. Also unique to Super DeLuxe Fords were bright trim surrounds for the windshield, rear window and side windows. Wheel covers were painted to match body color and carried three stripes. Trim rings were standard.

Interior features included an electric clock, left front door armrests, a steering wheel with a full circle horn ring and crank operated front vent windows. The instrument panel was finished in Sequoia grain. Assist cords were installed on sedan and sedan coupe models.

FORD — DELUXE — SERIES 21A: Common to all 1942 Fords was a revised frame design that was lower by one inch than the 1941 version, lower and wider leaf springs, a two inch wider tread and dual lateral stabilizer bars. DeLuxe models were equipped with the bumpers used for the 1941 Super DeLuxe Ford models. Their grille frames were painted body color. Unique to the DeLuxe Ford was its center grille panel with "DeLuxe" spelled out vertically in bright letters before a blue background. Wheel covers were painted to match body color. The DeLuxe instrument panel was finished in Crackle Mahogany grain.

FORD — SPECIAL — SERIES 2GA — SIX: The three Special models shared their grille design and bumpers with the DeLuxe models but lacked the latter's bumper guards. Black wheel covers were standard and like those on all 1942 models, carried blue Ford script.

The transition to a wartime economy brought many material substitutes in the 1942 models. Among the more obvious was the use of plastic interior components and the replacement of nickel by molybdenum in valves, gears and shafts. The final 1942 model Fords were produced on February 10, 1942.

I.D. DATA: Serial numbers located on left frame member directly behind front engine mount. Starting: six-cyl. IGA-34801; V-8 18-6769036. Ending: six-cyl. IGA-227,523; V-8 18-6925878. Prefix "C" indicates Canadian built. Engine numbers were located on top of clutch housing. Starting: six-cyl. IGA-34801; V-8 18-6769036. Ending: six-cyl.—IGA-227523; V-8—18-6925898.

1942 Ford Super Deluxe coupe. (PH)

Model No.	Body Type & Seating	Factory Price	Shipping Weight	Prod. Total
2GA	2-dr. Cpe.-3P	780	2910	1606
2GA	2-dr. Tudor-6P	815	3053	3187
2GA	4-dr. Fordor-6P	850	3093	27,189
21A	2-dr. Cpe.-3P	810	2978	5936
21A	2-dr. Cpe. Sed.-5P	875	3065	5419
21A	2-dr. Tudor-6P	840	3141	27,302
21A	4-dr. Fordor-6P	875	3161	5127
21A	4-dr. Sta. Wag.-6P	1100	3460	567
Sup. DeL.	2-dr. Conv.-5P	1080	3238	2920
Sup. DeL.	2-dr. Cpe.-3P	850	3050	5411
Sup. DeL.	2-dr. Cpe. Sed.-5P	910	3120	13,543
Sup. DeL.	2-dr. Tudor-6P	885	3159	37,199
Sup. DeL.	4-dr. Fordor-6P	920	3200	24,846
Sup. DeL.	4-dr. Sta. Wag.-6P	1100	3468	5483

ENGINE [V-8]: 90 degree V. Inline. Eight. Cast-iron block. B & S: 3-1/16 x 3-3/4 in. Disp.: 221 cid. C.R.: 6.2:1. Brake H.P.: 96 @ 3800 rpm. Taxable H.P.: 30. Main bearings: three. Valve lifters: mechanical. Carb.: Ford 21A-9510A. Torque: 156 lbs.-ft. @ 2200 rpm.

ENGINE [Base Six]: Inline. L-head. Six. Cast-iron block. B & S: 3-3/10 x 4-2/5 in. Disp.: 225.8 cid. C.R.: 6.7:1. Brake H.P.: 90 @ 3300 rpm. Taxable H.P.: 30. Main bearings: four. Valve lifters: mechanical. Carb.: Ford IGA-9510A one-barrel. Torque: 180 lbs.-ft. @ 2000 rpm.

CHASSIS: Special, DeLuxe, Super DeLuxe. W.B.: 114 in. O.L.: 194.4 in. Height: 68.15 in. Front/Rear Tread: 58/60 in. Tires: 6.00 x 16.

TECHNICAL: Sliding gear transmission. Speeds: 3F/1R. Column controls. Semi-centrifugal, molded asbestos lining clutch. Shaft drive. 3/4 floating rear axle. Overall ratio: 3.78:1. Hydraulic brakes on four wheels. Pressed steel wheels, drop center rims. Wheel size: 16 in.

OPTIONS: Fender skirts. Bumper guards (center). Radio ($39.00). Heater (air-23,00, water 20.00). Clock. Side view mirror. Passenger side mirror. Sport light. Locking gas cap. Fog lights. Seat covers. Defroster. Visor-vanity mirror. Radio foot control. Wheel trim rings. White sidewall tires (15.00). Bumper end guards (2.75 a pair). Oil filter (6.14). License plate frames.

HISTORY: Introduced September 12, 1941. Calendar year production 43,407. Model year production: 160,211. The president of Ford was Edsel Ford.

1946 FORD

1946 Ford Super Deluxe convertible. (OCW)

1946 FORDS — OVERVIEW — All 1946 Fords were, in essence, restyled 1942 models utilizing the same drivetrain as the prewar models. The grille was restyled with horizontal bars on the outside of the rectangular opening, instead of the flush-mounted grille of the 1942 model. The remainder of the body was virtually the same as the prewar model.

DELUXE SERIES — (6-CYL/V-8) — The Deluxe series was the base trim level for 1946 and included rubber moldings around all window openings, a horn button instead of a ring, one sun visor and armrests only on the driver's door.

DELUXE SIX-CYLINDER I.D. NUMBERS: Deluxe six-cylinder models began with the designation, "6GA", with production numbers beginning at 1GA-227524 and going to 1GA-326417.

1946 Ford Super Deluxe four-door sedan V-8. (AA)

DELUXE SIX-CYLINDER

Model No.	Body/ Style No.	Body Type & Seating	Factory Price	Shipping Weight	Prod. Total
6GA	73A	4-dr Sed-6P	1198	3167	Note 1
6GA	70A	2-dr Sed-6P	1136	3157	Note 1
6GA	77A	2-dr Cpe-3P	1074	3007	Note 1

NOTE 1: See Deluxe V-8 series listing. Production was counted by series and body style only, with no breakouts by engine type.

DELUXE V-8 I.D. NUMBERS: Deluxe V-8-powered models began with the designation, "69A", with production numbers beginning at 99A-650280 and going to 99A-1412707.

DELUXE V-8

Model No.	Body/ Style No.	Body Type & Seating	Factory Price	Shipping Weight	Prod. Total
69A	73A	4-dr Sed-6P	1248	3220	9,246
69A	70A	2-dr Sed-6P	1165	3190	74,954
69A	77A	2-dr Cpe-3P	1123	3040	10,670

PRODUCTION NOTE: Total series output was 94,870 units. In addition, there were 84 chassis produced with closed drive front end, two chassis produced with open drive front end. Ford does not indicate the number of each model produced with sixes and V-8s. Therefore, all figures given above show total production of each body style with both types of engines.

SUPER DELUXE SERIES — (6-CYL/V-8) — The Super Deluxe series was the top trim level for 1946 and included chrome moldings around all windows, a horn ring, two sun visors, armrests on all doors, passenger assist straps on the interior "B" pillars for easier rear seat egress, horizontal chrome trim on the body and leather interior on the convertible models.

SUPER DELUXE SIX-CYLINDER I.D. NUMBERS: Super Deluxe six-cylinder models began with the same "6GA" designation and used the same production numbers as the Deluxe models.

SUPER DELUXE SIX-CYLINDER

Model No.	Body/ Style No.	Body Type & Seating	Factory Price	Shipping Weight	Prod. Total
6GA	73B	4-dr Sed-6P	1273	3207	Note 1
6GA	70B	2-dr Sed-6P	1211	3157	Note 1
6GA	72B	2-dr Cpe Sed-6P	1257	3107	Note 1
6GA	77B	2-dr Cpe-3P	1148	3007	Note 1
6GA	79B	4-dr Sta Wag-8P	1504	3457	Note 1

NOTE 1: See Super Deluxe V-8 series listing. Production was counted by series and body style only, with no breakouts by engine type.

SUPER DELUXE V-8 I.D. NUMBERS: Super Deluxe V-8 models began with the same "69A" designation and used the same production numbers as the Deluxe models.

1946 Ford Super Deluxe Sportsman two-door convertible V-8. (OCW)

1946 Ford Super Deluxe two-door sedan V-8. (OCW)

1946 Ford Super Deluxe station wagon 6-cyl. (OCW)

SUPER DELUXE V-8

Model No.	Body/ Style No.	Body Type & Seating	Factory Price	Shipping Weight	Prod. Total
69A	73B	4-dr Sed-6P	1322	3240	92,056
69A	70B	2-dr Sed-6P	1260	3190	163,370
69A	72B	2-dr Cpe Sed-6P	1307	3140	70,826
69A	77B	2-dr Cpe-3P	1197	3040	12,249
69A	76	2-dr Conv-6P	1488	3240	16,359
69A	71	2-dr SM Conv 6P	1982	3340	723
69A	79B	4-dr Sta Wag-8P	1553	3490	16,960

NOTE 1: Total series output was 372,543 units. In addition, there were 26 chassis produced with closed drive front end, three chassis produced with open drive front end and eight chassis-only produced. Ford does not indicate the number of each model produced with sixes or V-8s. Therefore, all figures given above show total production of each body style, with both types of engines, except in the case of convertibles, which come only with V-8 power.

ENGINE [Base Six]: L-head. Cast-iron block. Displacement: 226 cid. Bore and stroke: 3.30 x 4.40 inches. Compression ratio: 6.8:1. Brake hp: 90 at 3300 rpm. Carburetor: Holley single-barrel Model 847F. Four main bearings.

ENGINE [V-8]: L-head. Cast-iron block. Displacement: 239 cid. Bore and stroke: 3.19 x 3.75 inches. Compression ratio: 6.6:1. Brake hp: 100 at 3800 rpm. Carburetor: Holley two-barrel Model 94. Three main bearings.

CHASSIS FEATURES: Wheelbase: 114 inches. Overall length: 196.2 inches. Tires: 6.00 x 16.

HISTORY: The "new" postwar Fords were introduced in dealer showrooms on Oct. 22, 1945.

1947 FORD

1947 FORDS — OVERVIEW — 1947 Fords were slightly changed from the previous year. For example, the red tracer paint on the grille was dropped, a hood-mounted emblem was seen up front and relocated circular parking lights looked attractive.

DELUXE SERIES — (6-CYL/V-8) — The Deluxe series was the base trim level for the 1947 Ford and included rubber moldings around all window openings, a horn button instead of a ring, one sun visor and armrests only on the driver's door.

1947 Ford Deluxe two-door coupe 6-cyl. (PH)

1947 Ford Super Deluxe convertible. (OCW)

DELUXE SIX-CYLINDER I.D. NUMBERS: Began with the designation "7GA." Production numbers were 71GA-326418 to 71GA-414366; also (beginning 10/3/47) 77HA-0512 to 77HA-9038.

DELUXE SIX

Model No.	Body/ Style No.	Body Type & Seating	Factory Price	Shipping Weight	Prod. Total
7GA	73A	4-dr Sed-6P	1270	3213	Note 1
7GA	70A	2-dr Sed-6P	1212	3183	Note 1
7GA	77A	2-dr Cpe-3P	1154	3033	Note 1

NOTE 1: See Deluxe V-8 series listing. Production was counted by series and body style only, with no breakouts by engine type.

DELUXE V-8 I.D. NUMBERS: Deluxe V-8 models began with the designation, "79A," with the production numbers beginning at 799A-1412708 and going to 799A-2071231.

DELUXE V-8

Model No.	Body/ Style No.	Body Type & Seating	Factory Price	Shipping Weight	Prod. Total
79A	73A	4-dr Sed-6P	1346	3246	44,563
79A	70A	2-dr Sed-6P	1268	3216	44,523
79A	77A	2-dr Cpe-3P	1230	3066	10,872

NOTE 1: Total series output was 99,958 units. In addition, there were 23 chassis produced with closed drive front ends. Ford does not indicate the number of each model produced with sixes or V-8 engines. Therefore, all production figures given above show total production of each body style with both types of engines.

1947 Ford Super Deluxe Sportsman two-door convertible V-8. (OCW)

1947 Ford Super Deluxe two-door sedan V-8. (PH)

SUPER DELUXE SERIES — (6-CYL/V-8) — The Super Deluxe series was the top trim level for 1947 and included chrome moldings around all windows, a horn ring, two sun visors, armrests on all doors, passenger assist straps on the interior "B" pillars for easier rear seat egress, horizontal chrome trim on body and leather interior on the convertible models.

SUPER DELUXE SIX-CYLINDER I.D. NUMBERS: Super Deluxe six-cylinder models began with the designation, "7GA" and used the same production numbers as the Deluxe models.

SUPER DELUXE SIX

Model No.	Body/ Style No.	Body Type & Seating	Factory Price	Shipping Weight	Prod. Total
7GA	73B	4-dr Sed-6P	1372	3233	Note 1
7GA	70B	2-dr Sed-6P	1309	3183	Note 1
7GA	72B	2-dr Cpe Sed-6P	1330	3133	Note 1
7GA	77B	2-dr Cpe-3P	1251	3033	Note 1
7GA	79B	4-dr Sta Wag-8P	1893	3487	Note 1

NOTE 1: See Super Deluxe V-8 series listing. Production was counted by series and body style only, with no breakouts by engine type.

SUPER DELUXE V-8 I.D. NUMBERS: Super Deluxe V-8 models began with the same "79A" designation and used the same production numbers as the Deluxe models.

SUPER DELUXE V-8

Model No.	Body/ Style No.	Body Type & Seating	Factory Price	Shipping Weight	Prod. Total
79A	73B	4-dr Sed-6P	1440	3266	116,744
79A	70B	2-dr Sed-6P	1382	3216	132,126
79A	72B	2-dr Cpe Sed-6P	1409	3166	80,830
79A	77B	2-dr Cpe-3P	1330	3066	10,872
79A	76B	2-dr Conv-6P	1740	3266	22,159
79A	71B	2-dr SM Conv-6P	2282	3366	2,274
79A	79B	4-dr Sta Wag-8P	1972	3520	16,104

NOTE 1: Total series output was 385,109 units. In addition, there were 23 chassis produced with closed drive front ends. Ford does not indicate the number of each model produced with sixes or V-8s. Therefore, all figures given above show total production of each body style with both types of engines, except in the case of convertibles, which came only with V-8 power.

ENGINE [Base Six]: L-head. Cast-iron block. Displacement: 226 cid. Bore and stroke: 3.30 x 4.40 inches. Compression ratio: 6.8:1. Brake hp: 90 at 3300 rpm. Carburetor: Holley single-barrel Model 847F. Four main bearings.

1947 Ford Super Deluxe station wagon V-8. (OCW)

ENGINE [V-8]: L-head. Cast-iron block. Displacement: 239 cid. Bore and stroke: 3.19 x 3.75 inches. Compression ratio: 6.8:1. Brake hp: 100 at 3600 rpm. Carburetor: Holley two-barrel Model 94. Three main bearings.

CHASSIS FEATURES: Wheelbase: 114 inches. Overall length: 198.2 inches. Tires: 6.00 x 16.

HISTORY: The man who put America on wheels, Henry Ford founder of Ford Motor Co., died at the age of 83 on April 7, 1947.

1948 FORD

1948 FORDS — OVERVIEW — 1948 Fords continued to share the 1946-1947 bodies with only slight trim changes.

DELUXE SERIES — (6-CYL/V-8) — The Deluxe series was the base trim level for 1948 and included rubber moldings around window openings, a horn button instead of horn ring, one sun visor and one armrest only on the driver's door.

DELUXE SIX-CYLINDER I.D. NUMBERS: Deluxe six-cylinder models began with the designation, "87HA," with production numbers beginning at 87HA-0536 and going to 87HA-73901.

DELUXE SIX

Model No.	Body/ Style No.	Body Type & Seating	Factory Price	Shipping Weight	Prod. Total
87HA	73A	4-dr Sed-6P	1270	3213	Note 1
87HA	70A	2-dr Sed-6P	1212	3183	Note 1
87HA	77A	2-dr Cpe-3P	1154	3033	Note 1

NOTE 1: See Deluxe V-8 series listing. Production was counted by series and body style only, with no breakout by engine type.

DELUXE V-8 I.D. NUMBERS: Deluxe V-8-powered models began with the designations "89A," with production numbers beginning with 899A-1984859 and going to 899A-2381447.

DELUXE V-8

Model No.	Body/ Style No.	Body Type & Seating	Factory Price	Shipping Weight	Prod. Total
89A	73A	4-dr Sed-6P	1346	3246	N/A
89A	70A	2-dr Sed-6P	1288	3216	23,356
89A	77A	2-dr Cpe-3P	1230	3066	5,048

NOTE 1: Total series output was 28,404 units (not including the four-door sedan, for which production figures are not available). Ford does not indicate the number of each model produced with sixes or V-8s. Therefore, all production figures given above show total production of each body style with both types of engines.

SUPER DELUXE SERIES — (6-CYL/V-8) — The Super Deluxe series was the top trim level for 1948 and included chrome moldings around the windows, horn ring, two sun visors, armrests on all doors, passenger assist straps on the interior "B" pillar for easier rear seat egress, horizontal chrome trim on the body and leather interior on the convertible models.

SUPER DELUXE SIX-CYLINDER I.D. NUMBERS: Super Deluxe six-cylinder models began with the same "87HA" designation and used the same production numbers as the Deluxe models.

1948 Ford Super Deluxe Sportsman two-door convertible V-8. (OCW)

1948 Ford Super Deluxe four-door sedan V-8. (AA)

1948 Ford Super Deluxe two-door convertible V-8. (OCW)

SUPER DELUXE SIX

Model No.	Body/ Style No.	Body Type & Seating	Factory Price	Shipping Weight	Prod. Total
87HA	73B	4-dr Sed-6P	1372	3233	Note 1
87HA	70B	2-dr Sed-6P	1309	3183	Note 1
87HA	72B	2-dr Cpe Sed-6P	1330	3133	Note 1
87HA	77B	2-dr Cpe-3P	1251	3033	Note 1
87HA	79B	4-dr Sta Wag-8P	1893	3487	Note 1

NOTE 1: See Super Deluxe V-8 series listing. Production was counted by series and body style only, with no breakouts by engine type.

SUPER DELUXE I.D. NUMBERS: Super Deluxe V-8-powered models began with the same "89A" designation and used the same production numbers as the Deluxe models.

SUPER DELUXE V-8

Model No.	Body/ Style No.	Body Type & Seating	Factory Price	Shipping Weight	Prod. Total
89A	73B	4-dr Sed-6P	1440	3266	71,358
89A	70B	2-dr Sed-6P	1382	3216	82,161
89A	72B	2-dr Cpe Sed-6P	1409	3166	44,828
89A	77B	2-dr Cpe-3P	1330	3066	N/A
89A	76B	2-dr Conv-6P	1740	3266	12,033
89A	71B	2-dr SM Conv-6P	2282	3366	28
89A	79B	4-dr Sta Wag-8P	1972	3520	8,912

NOTE 1: Total series output was 219,320 units (not including the two-door coupe, for which production figures are not available). Ford does not indicate the number of each model produced with sixes or V-8 engines. Therefore, all figures given show total production of each body style with both types of engines, except in the case of convertibles, which came only with V-8 power.

ENGINE [Base Six]: L-head. Cast-iron block. Displacement: 226 cid. Bore and stroke: 3.30 x 4.40 inches. Compression ratio: 6.6:1. Brake hp: 95 at 3300 rpm. Carburetor: Holley single-barrel Model 847F. Four main bearings.

ENGINE [V-8]: L-head. Cast-iron block. Displacement: 239 cid. Bore and stroke: 3.19 x 3.75 inches. Compression ratio: 6.8:1. Brake hp: 100 at 3800 rpm. Carburetor: Holley two-barrel Model 94. Three main bearings.

CHASSIS FEATURES: Wheelbase: 114 inches. Overall length: 198.2 inches. Tires: 6.00 x 16.

HISTORY: The actual production run of 1948 Fords, basically retitled 1947 models, ended early, in mid-spring, so retooling could take place for the all-new 1949 Fords. The 1949 Fords were also introduced early, in June 1948.

1949 FORD

1949 Ford two-door sedan. (OCW)

1949 Ford Custom two-door sedan V-8. (AA)

1949 FORDS — OVERVIEW — 1949 represented the first totally new automobile produced by Ford since the end of World War II. The chassis was the wishbone type, with longitudinal rear springs replacing the transverse springs used on earlier models. Styling featured a heavy chrome molding curving from the top of the grille down to the gravel deflector, with 'FORD' in large block letters mounted above the grille molding. There was a horizontal chrome bar in the center of the grille, extending the full width of the opening, with parking lamps mounted on the ends of the bar. In the center of the bar was a large spinner with either a '6' or '8' designation indicating engine choice. The body was slab-sided, eliminating the rear fender bulge altogether. A chrome strip near the bottom of the body extended from the front fender openings back to the gas cap. Models for 1949 included the base Ford series, and the top line Custom series.

FORD SERIES — (6-CYL/V-8) — The Ford series was the base trim level for 1949 and included rubber window moldings, a horn button instead of horn ring, one sun visor and an armrest only on the driver's door.

FORD SIX I.D. NUMBERS: Ford six-cylinder models began with the designation, "98HA," with production numbers beginning at 98HA-101 and going to 98HA-173310.

FORD SIX SERIES

Model No.	Body/ Style No.	Body Type & Seating	Factory Price	Shipping Weight	Prod. Total
98HA	73A	4-dr Sed-6P	1472	2990	Note 1
98HA	70A	2-dr Sed-6P	1425	2945	Note 1
98HA	72A	2-dr Clb Cpe-6P	1415	2925	Note 1
98HA	72C	2-dr Bus Cpe-3P	1333	2871	Note 1

NOTE 1: See Ford V-8 series listing. Production was counted by series and body style only, with no breakout per engine type.

FORD V-8 I.D. NUMBERS: Ford V-8 models began with the designation, "98BA," with production numbers beginning at 98BA-101 and going to 98BA-948236.

FORD V-8 SERIES

Model No.	Body/ Style No.	Body Type & Seating	Factory Price	Shipping Weight	Prod. Total
98BA	73A	4-dr Sed-6P	1546	3030	44,563
98BA	70A	2-dr Sed-6P	1499	2965	126,770
98BA	72A	2-dr Clb Cpe-6P	1523	2965	4,170
98BA	72C	2-dr Bus Cpe-3P	1420	2911	28,946

NOTE 1: Total series output was 204,449 units. Ford does not indicate the number of each model produced with sixes or V-8s. Therefore, all production figures given above show total production of each body style.

CUSTOM SERIES — (6-CYL/V-8) — The Custom series was the top trim level for 1949 and included chrome window moldings, a horn ring, two sun visors, passenger assist straps on the interior B pillars for easier rear seat egress and horizontal chrome trim along the lower half of the body.

CUSTOM SIX I.D. NUMBERS: Custom six-cylinder models began with the same "98HA" designation and used the same production numbers as the Ford series.

1949 Ford Custom two-door station wagon 6-cyl. (OCW)

CUSTOM SIX SERIES

Model No.	Body/ Style No.	Body Type & Seating	Factory Price	Shipping Weight	Prod. Total
98HA	73B	4-dr Sed-6P	1559	2993	Note 1
98HA	70B	2-dr Sed-6P	1511	2948	Note 1
98HA	72B	2-dr Clb Cpe-6P	1511	2928	Note 1
98HA	76	2-dr Conv-6P	1886	3234	Note 1
98HA	79	2-dr Sta Wag-8P	2119	3523	Note 1

NOTE 1: See Custom V-8 series listing. Production was counted by series and body style only with no breakout per engine type.

CUSTOM V-8 I.D. NUMBERS: Custom V-8 models began with the same "98HA" designation and used the same production numbers as the Ford series.

CUSTOM V-8 SERIES

Model No.	Body/ Style No.	Body Type & Seating	Factory Price	Shipping Weight	Prod. Total
98BA	73B	4-dr Sed-6P	1636	3033	248,176
98BA	70B	2-dr Sed-6P	1590	2988	433,316
98BA	72B	2-dr Clb Cpe-6P	1596	2968	150,254
98BA	76	2-dr Conv-6P	1949	3274	51,133
98BA	79	2-dr Sta Wag-8P	2264	3563	31,412

NOTE 1: Total series output was 914,291 units. Ford does not indicate the number of each model produced with sixes or V-8s. Therefore, all production figures given above show total production of each body style.

ENGINE [Base Six]: L-head. Cast-iron block. Displacement: 226 cid. Bore and stroke: 3.30 x 4.40 inches. Compression ratio: 6.6:1. Brake hp: 95 at 3300 rpm. Carburetor: Holley one-barrel Model 847FS. Four main bearings. Serial number code "H."

ENGINE [V-8]: L-head. Cast-iron block. Displacement: 239 cid. Bore and stroke: 3.19 x 3.75 inches. Compression ratio: 6.8:1. Brake hp: 100 at 3600 rpm. Carburetor: Holley two-barrel Model AA-1. Three main bearings. Serial number code "B."

1949 Ford Custom four-door sedan V-8. (OCW)

CHASSIS FEATURES: Three-speed manual transmission with a semi-centrifugal-type clutch; three-speed helical gears and synchronizers for second and third gears was standard equipment. Three-speed with automatic overdrive was optional. The automatic overdrive function cut in at 27 mph and cut out at 21 mph. Approximate drive ratio was 0.70:1. Wheelbase: 114 inches. Overall length: (passenger cars) 196.8 inches; (station wagons) 208 inches. Overall width: 72.8 inches. Rear axle gear ratios with standard transmission: (passenger car) 3.73:1; (station wagon) 3.92:1. Rear axle gear ratio with automatic overdrive: (passenger car) 4.10:1; (station wagon) 4.27:1. Tires: (passenger car) 6.00 x 16; (station wagon) 7.10 x 15.

HISTORY: The 1949 Fords were introduced at the Waldorf-Astoria Hotel in New York City on June 10, 1948, beating General Motors and Chrysler to the punch in the garnering of new-model publicity. Ford also surpassed the million mark in production in 1949 with 1,118,740 units built.

1950 FORD

1950 Ford Custom Deluxe two-door Club Coupe V-8. (AA)

1950 FORDS — OVERVIEW — The 1950 Fords seemed identical to 1949 models, but were said to include "50 improvements for '50." Some of these improvements were: recessed gas filler neck, redesigned hood ornaments, flat-top horn ring, three-bladed cooling fan and push-button handles on exterior doors. An assembly plant designation was used in the serial numbers for the first time. (See NOTE 1).

DELUXE SERIES — (6-CYL/V-8) — The Deluxe series was the base trim level for 1950 and included rubber window moldings, a horn button instead of horn ring, one sun visor, and an armrest only on the driver's door.

DELUXE SIX I.D. NUMBERS: (Ford factory codes) Assembly plant designations were as follows: AT = Atlanta; BF = Buffalo; CS = Chester; CH = Chicago; DL = Dallas; DA = Dearborn; EG = Edgewater; HM = Highland Park; KC = Kansas City; LB = Long Beach; LU = Louisville; MP = Memphis; NR = Norfolk; RH = Richmond; SP = Somerville; SR = Twin City (St. Paul). Deluxe six-cylinder models began with the designation "OHA" followed by an assembly plant code and, finally, the unit's production number according to the final assembly plant. (See NOTE 1). Each plant began at 100001 and went up.

1950 Ford Custom Deluxe four-door sedan V-8. (OCW)

1950 Ford Custom Deluxe two-door convertible V-8. (OCW)

DELUXE SIX SERIES

Model No.	Body/ Style No.	Body Type & Seating	Factory Price	Shipping Weight	Prod. Total
OHA	D73	4-dr Sed-6P	1472	3050	Note 1
OHA	D70	2-dr Sed-6P	1424	2988	Note 1
OHA	D72C	2-dr Bus Cpe-3P	1333	2933	Note 1

NOTE 1: See Deluxe V-8 series listing. Production was counted by series and body style only, with no breakout per engine type.

DELUXE V-8 I.D. NUMBERS: Deluxe V-8 models began with the designation "OBA" followed by an assembly plant code and finally the unit's production number according to the final assembly location (see NOTE 1). Each plant began at 100001 and went up.

DELUXE V-8 SERIES

Model No.	Body/ Style No.	Body Type & Seating	Factory Price	Shipping Weight	Prod. Total
OBA	D73	4-dr Sed-6P	1545	3078	77,888
OBA	D70	2-dr Sed-6P	1498	3026	275,360
OBA	D72C	2-dr Bus Cpe-3P	1419	2965	35,120

NOTE 1: Total series output was 388,368 units. Ford does not indicate the number of each model produced with sixes or V-8s. Therefore, all production figures given above show total production of each body style.

CUSTOM DELUXE SERIES — (6-CYL/V-8) — The Custom Deluxe series was the top trim level and included chrome window moldings, chrome horn ring, two sun visors, armrests on all doors, passenger assist strap on the interior "B" pillars for easier rear seat egress and chrome strips along the lower half of the body, with the model identification at the front edge of the chrome strip.

CUSTOM DELUXE SIX I.D. NUMBERS: Custom Deluxe six-cylinder models began with the same "OHA" designation and used the same production numbers as Deluxe models.

CUSTOM DELUXE SIX SERIES

Model No.	Body/ Style No.	Body Type & Seating	Factory Price	Shipping Weight	Prod. Total
OHA	C73	4-dr Sed-6P	1558	3062	Note 1
OHA	C70	2-dr Sed-6P	1511	2999	Note 1
OHA	C72	2-dr Clb Cpe-6P	1511	2959	Note 1
OHA	C79	4-dr Sta Wag-8P	2028	3491	Note 1

NOTE 1: See Deluxe V-8 series listing. Production was counted by series and body style only, with no breakout per engine type.

CUSTOM DELUXE V-8 I.D. NUMBERS: Custom Deluxe V-8 models began with the same "OBA" designation and used the same production numbers as the Deluxe models.

1950 Ford Custom Deluxe Crestliner two-door sedan V-8. (PH)

1950 Ford Custom Deluxe two-door station wagon V-8. (OCW)

CUSTOM DELUXE V-8 SERIES

Model No.	Body/ Style No.	Body Type & Seating	Factory Price	Shipping Weight	Prod. Total
OBA	C73	4-dr Sed-6P	1637	3093	247,181
OBA	C70	2-dr Sed-6P	1590	3031	396,060
OBA	C70C	2-dr Crestliner-6P	1711	3050	8,703
OBA	C72	2-dr Clb Cpe-6P	1595	3003	85,111
OBA	C76	2-dr Conv-6P	1948	3263	50,299
OBA	C79	2-dr Sta Wag-6P	2107	3531	29,017

NOTE 1: Total series output was 818,371 units. Ford does not indicate the number of each model produced with sixes or V-8s. Therefore, all production figures given above show total production of each body style with both types of engines, except in the case of Crestliners and convertibles, which came only with V-8 power.

ENGINE [Base Six]: L-head. Cast-iron block. Displacement: 226 cid. Bore and stroke: 3.30 x 4.40 inches. Compression ratio: 6.8:1. Brake hp: 95 at 3300 rpm. Carburetor: Holley one-barrel Model 847F5. Four main bearings. Serial number code "H."

ENGINE [V-8]: L-head. Cast-iron block. Displacement: 239 cid. Bore and stroke: 3.19 x 3.75 inches. Compression ratio: 6.8:1. Brake hp: 100 at 3600 rpm. Carburetor: Holley two-barrel Model AA-1. Three main bearings. Serial number code "B."

CHASSIS FEATURES: The standard Ford transmission was a three-speed manual type with semi-centrifugal-type clutch; three-speed helical gearset and synchronizers for second and third gears. A three-speed manual gearbox with automatic overdrive was optional. Specifications were similar to 1949. Wheelbase: (all models) 114 inches. Overall length: (passenger cars) 196.6 inches; (station wagons) 206 inches. Overall width: (all models) 72.8 inches. Tires: (standard) 6.00 x 16; (optional) 6.70 x 15; (station wagon) 7.10 x 15. Rear axle gear ratios with standard transmission: (passenger car) 3.73:1; (station wagon) 3.92:1. Rear axle gear ratio with automatic overdrive: (passenger car) 4.10:1; (station wagon) 4.17:1.

HISTORY: The two-door sedan with short top was the Club Coupe. The Crestliner was a special two-door sedan with vinyl top covering; extra chrome; special steering wheel; special paint and full wheel covers.

1951 FORD

1951 Ford Deluxe two-door sedan V-8. (AA)

1951 Ford Custom convertible. (OCW)

1951 FORDS — OVERVIEW — While the 1951 Fords shared body components with the 1949-1950 models, a few trim changes made a substantial difference in looks. The horizontal bar in the grille had the single large spinner replaced by two smaller spinners that were mounted at the ends of the bar. The taillight lenses were redesigned slightly and the license plate cover was reshaped. Inside, a completely different instrument panel was used and all instruments were grouped in front of the driver.

DELUXE SERIES — (6-CYL/V-8) — The Deluxe series was the base trim level for 1951 and included rubber window moldings, a horn button instead of horn ring, one sun visor and an armrest only on the driver's door.

DELUXE SIX I.D. NUMBERS: (Ford factory codes) Assembly plant designations were as follows: AT = Atlanta; BF = Buffalo; CS = Chester; CH = Chicago; DL = Dallas; DA = Dearborn; EG = Edgewater; HM = Highland Park; KC = Kansas City; LB = Long Beach; LU = Louisville; MP = Memphis; NR = Norfolk; RH = Richmond; SP = Somerville; SR = Twin City (St. Paul). Deluxe six-cylinder model numbers began with the designation "1HA" followed by an assembly plant code and, finally, the unit's production numbers according to the final assembly location (see NOTE 1). All plants began with 100001 and went up.

DELUXE SIX SERIES

Model No.	Body/ Style No.	Body Type & Seating	Factory Price	Shipping Weight	Prod. Total
1HA	73	4-dr Sed-6P	1465	3089	Note 1
1HA	70	2-dr Sed-6P	1417	3023	Note 1
1HA	72C	2-dr Bus Cpe-3P	1324	2960	Note 1

NOTE 1: See Deluxe V-8 series listing. Production was counted by series and body style only with no breakout per engine type.

DELUXE V-8 I.D. NUMBERS: Deluxe V-8 models began with the designation "1BA," assembly code and, finally, the unit's production number, according to the final assembly location (see NOTE 1). All plants began with 100001 and went up.

DELUXE V-8 SERIES

Model No.	Body/ Style No.	Body Type & Seating	Factory Price	Shipping Weight	Prod. Total
1BA	73	4-dr Sed-6P	1540	3114	54,265
1BA	70	2-dr Sed-6P	1492	3062	146,010
1BA	72C	2-dr Bus Cpe-3P	1411	2997	20,343

NOTE 1: Total series output was 220,618 units. Ford does not indicate the number of each model produced with sixes or V-8s. Therefore, all production figures given above show total production of each body style.

1951 Ford Deluxe four-door sedan V-8. (OCW)

1951 Ford Custom Deluxe two-door sedan V-8. (PH)

1951 Ford Custom Deluxe Victoria two-door hardtop V-8. (AA)

CUSTOM DELUXE SERIES — (6-CYL/V-8) — The Custom Deluxe series was the top trim level for 1951 and included chrome window moldings, chrome horn ring, two sun visors, armrests on all doors, passenger assist straps on interior "B" pillars for easier rear seat egress and horizontal chrome strips on the body exterior. The Victoria pillarless two-door hardtop was a new model. The Crestliner two-door sedan with vinyl covered top and special two-tone paint and wheel covers was also continued.

CUSTOM DELUXE SIX I.D. NUMBERS: Custom Deluxe six-cylinder models began with the same "1HA" designation and used the same production numbers as the Deluxe models.

CUSTOM DELUXE SIX SERIES

Model No.	Body/ Style No.	Body Type & Seating	Factory Price	Shipping Weight	Prod. Total
1HA	73	4-dr Sed-6P	1553	3089	Note 1
1HA	70	2-dr Sed-6P	1505	3023	Note 1
1HA	72C	2-dr Clb Cpe-6P	1505	2995	Note 1
1HA	79	2-dr Cty Sq Sta Wag-8P	2029	3510	Note 1

NOTE 1: See Custom Deluxe V-8 series. Production was counted by series and body style only, with no breakouts per engine type.

CUSTOM DELUXE V-8 I.D. NUMBERS: Custom Deluxe V-8 models began with the same "1BA" designation and used the same production numbers as the Deluxe models (see NOTE 1).

1951 Ford Custom Deluxe Country Squire two-door station wagon V-8. (OCW)

1951 Ford Custom Deluxe two-door convertible V-8. (PH)

CUSTOM DELUXE V-8 SERIES

Model No.	Body/ Style No.	Body Type & Seating	Factory Price	Shipping Weight	Prod. Total
1BA	73B	4-dr Sed-6P	1633	3114	232,691
1BA	70B	2-dr Sed-6P	1585	3062	317,869
1BA	70C	2-dr Crestliner-6P	1595	3065	8,703
1BA	72C	2-dr Clb Cpe-6P	1590	3034	53,263
1BA	60	2-dr Vic HT-6P	1925	3188	110,286
1BA	76	2-dr Conv-6P	1949	3268	40,934
1BA	79	2-dr Cty Sq Sta Wag-8P	2110	3550	29,617

NOTE 1: Total series output was 792,763 units. Ford does not indicate the number of each model produced with sixes or V-8s. Therefore, all production figures given above are total production of each body style with both engines, except in the case of Crestliners, Victorias and convertibles, which came only with V-8 power.

ENGINE [Base Six]: L-head. Cast-iron block. Displacement: 226 cid. Bore and stroke: 3.30 x 4.40 inches. Compression ratio: 6.8:1. Brake hp: 95 at 3600 rpm. Carburetor: Holley one-barrel Model 847F5. Four main bearings. Serial number code "H."

ENGINE [V-8]: L-head. Cast-iron block. Displacement: 239 cid. Bore and stroke: 3.19 x 3.75 inches. Compression ratio: 6.8:1. Brake hp: 100 at 3600 rpm. Carburetor: Ford two-barrel Model 8BA. Three main bearings. Serial number code "B."

1951 Ford Custom Deluxe two-door club coupe V-8. (PH)

1951 Ford Custom Deluxe four-door sedan V-8. (PH)

CHASSIS FEATURES: The standard Ford transmission was a three-speed manual-type with semi-centrifugal clutch, three-speed helical gearset and synchronizers for second and third gears. Three-speed transmission with automatic overdrive (see 1949 specifications) was optional at $92 extra. Two-speed Ford-O-Matic transmission was optional at $159 extra. This was a torque converter-type transmission with three-speed (automatic intermediate gear for starting) automatic planetary geartrain and single stage, three element, hydraulic torque converter. Wheelbase: (all models) 114 inches. Overall length: (passenger cars) 196.4 inches; (station wagons) 208 inches. Overall width: (all models) 72.9 inches. Rear axle gear ratios with manual transmission: (standard) 3.73:1; (optional) 4.10:1. Rear axle gear ratio with automatic overdrive: 4.10:1. Rear axle ratio with Ford-O-Matic: 3.31:1. Tires: (standard) 6.00 x 16; (optional) 6.70 x 15 and (station wagon) 7.10 x 15.

HISTORY: The two-door sedan with short top was the Club Coupe. The two-door station wagon was the Country Squire. The Crestliner was a special two-door sedan with vinyl roof covering; extra chrome; special steering wheel; special paint and full wheel covers. The Victoria was a new pillarless two-door hardtop.

1952 FORD

1952 Ford Customline four-door. (OCW)

1952 FORDS — OVERVIEW — 1952 represented the first totally new body for Ford since 1949. The new models featured a one-piece curved windshield, full-width rear window, protruding round parking lights, round three-bladed spinner in the center of the grille bar, simulated scoop on the rear quarter panels, gas filler pipe and neck concealed behind the license plate, redesigned instrument panel and suspended clutch and brake pedals.

MAINLINE SERIES — (6-CYL/V-8) — The Mainline series was the base trim level for 1952 and included rubber window moldings, a horn button instead of horn ring, one sun visor and an armrest only on the driver's door.

MAINLINE SIX I.D. NUMBERS: (Ford factory codes) Assembly plant designations were as follows: AT = Atlanta; BF = Buffalo; CS = Chester; CH = Chicago; DL = Dallas; DA = Dearborn; EG = Edgewater; HM = Highland Park; KC = Kansas City; LB = Long Beach; LU = Louisville; MP = Memphis; NR = Norfolk; RH = Richmond; SP = Somerville; SR = Twin City (St. Paul). Mainline six-cylinder models began with the designation "A2," assembly plant code and, finally, the unit's production number, according to the final assembly location (see NOTE 1). Each plant began at 100001 and went up.

1952 Ford Customline four-door sedan V-8. (OCW)

MAINLINE SIX SERIES

Model No.	Body/ Style No.	Body Type & Seating	Factory Price	Shipping Weight	Prod. Total
A2	73A	4-dr Sed-6P	1530	3173	Note 1
A2	70A	2-dr Sed-6P	1485	3070	Note 1
A2	72C	2-dr Bus Cpe-3P	1389	2984	Note 1
A2	59A	2-dr Sta Wag-6P	1832	3377	Note 1

NOTE 1: See Mainline V-8 series listing. Production was counted by series and body style only, with no breakout per engine type.

MAINLINE V-8 I.D. NUMBERS: Mainline V-8 models began with the designation "B2," assembly plant code and, finally, the unit's production number, according to the final assembly location (see NOTE 1). Each plant began at 100001 and went up.

MAINLINE V-8 SERIES

Model No.	Body/ Style No.	Body Type & Seating	Factory Price	Shipping Weight	Prod. Total
B2	73A	4-dr Sed-6P	1600	3207	41,277
B2	70A	2-dr Sed-6P	1555	3151	79,931
B2	72C	2-dr Bus Cpe-3P	1459	3085	10,137
B2	59A	2-dr Sta Wag-6P	1902	3406	32,566

NOTE 1: Total series output was 163,911 units. Ford does not indicate the number of each model produced with sixes or V-8s. Therefore, all production figures given above show total production of each body style.

CUSTOMLINE SERIES — (6-CYL/V-8) — The Customline series was the intermediate trim level for 1952 and included chrome window moldings, chrome horn ring, two sun visors, armrests on all doors, passenger assist straps on interior "B" pillars for easier rear seat egress, a horizontal chrome strip on the front fenders and a chrome opening on the rear quarter panel scoop.

CUSTOMLINE SIX I.D. NUMBERS: Customline six-cylinder models began with the same "A2" designation and used the same production numbers as the Mainline models (see NOTE 1).

CUSTOMLINE SIX SERIES

Model No.	Body/ Style No.	Body Type & Seating	Factory Price	Shipping Weight	Prod. Total
A2	73B	4-dr Sed-6P	1615	3173	Note 1
A2	70B	2-dr Sed-6P	1570	3070	Note 1
A2	72B	2-dr Clb Cpe-6P	1579	3079	Note 1

NOTE 1: Customline V-8 series listing. Production was counted by series and body style only, with no breakout per engine type.

CUSTOMLINE V-8 I.D. NUMBERS: Customline V-8 models began with the same "B2" designation and used the same production numbers as the Mainline models (see NOTE 1).

CUSTOMLINE V-8 SERIES

Model No.	Body/ Style No.	Body Type & Seating	Factory Price	Shipping Weight	Prod. Total
B2	73B	4-dr Sed-6P	1685	3207	188,303
B2	70B	2-dr Sed-6P	1640	3151	175,762
B2	72B	2-dr Clb Cpe-6P	1649	3153	26,550
B2	79C	4-dr Sta Wag-6P	2060	3617	11,927

NOTE 1: Total series output was 402,542 units. Ford does not indicate the number of each model produced with sixes and V-8s. Therefore, all production figures are total production of each body style.

CRESTLINE SERIES — (V-8) — The Crestline series was the top trim level for 1952 and was offered only with V-8 engines. This series included all trim in the Customline series plus wheel covers and additional chrome trim along the bottom of the side windows.

1952 Ford Crestline Victoria two-door hardtop V-8. (AA)

1952 Ford Mainline two-door Ranch Wagon 6-cyl. (AA)

CRESTLINE I.D. NUMBERS: (V-8 only) Crestline models began with the same "B2" designation and used the same production numbers as the Mainline and Customline V-8 models.

CRESTLINE SERIES

Model No.	Body/ Style No.	Body Type & Seating	Factory Price	Shipping Weight	Prod. Total
B2	60B	2-dr Vic HT-6P	1925	3274	77,320
B2	76B	2-dr Sun Conv-6P	2027	3339	22,534
B2	79B	4-dr Cty Sq Sta Wag-8P	2186	3640	5,426

ENGINE [Base Six]: Overhead valve. Cast-iron block. Displacement: 215 cid. Bore and stroke: 3.56 x 3.60 inches. Compression ratio: 7.0:1. Brake hp: 101 at 3500 rpm. Carburetor: Holley one-barrel Model 847F5. Four main bearings. Serial number code "A."

ENGINE [V-8]: L-head. Cast-iron block. Displacement: 239 cid. Bore and stroke: 3.19 x 3.75 inches. Compression ratio: 7.2:1. Brake hp: 110 at 3800 rpm. Carburetor: Ford two-barrel Model 8BA. Three main bearings. Serial number code "B."

CHASSIS FEATURES: The standard transmission was a three-speed manual-type of the usual design. Three-speed manual with automatic overdrive (see 1949 specifications) was a $102 option. Ford-O-Matic transmission was a $170 option. Ford-O-Matic featured a torque converter transmission with automatic planetary geartrain; single stage three-element hydraulic torque converter; hydraulic mechanical automatic controls with no electrical or vacuum connections; forced air cooling; and power flow through the fluid member at all times. Wheelbase: (all models) 115 inches. Overall length: (all models) 197.8 inches. Overall width: (all models) 73.2 inches. Rear axle gear ratios: (manual transmission) 3.90:1; (overdrive) 4.10:1; (optional overdrive) 3.15:1; (Ford-O-Matic) 3.31:1; (optional with Ford-O-Matic) 3.54:1. Tires: (standard) 6.00 x 16; (optional) 6.70 x 15.

1952 Ford Crestline Country Squire station wagon V-8. (OCW)

CONVENIENCE OPTIONS: A completely new line of custom accessories was brought out by the Ford Motor Co. to match 1952 styling. Several interesting additions on the list were a speed governor; turn indicators; illuminated vanity mirror; engine compartment light; five-tube Deluxe radio; seven-tube Custom radio; spring wound clock; electric clock; color-keyed rubber floor mats; wheel discs; wheel trim rings; rear fender skirts; rocker panel trim strips; hand brake signal lamp and Magic Air heater and defroster.

HISTORY: The Crestline Victoria was a two-door pillarless hardtop. The Sunliner in the same series was a two-door convertible. The four-door all-metal station wagon in the Crestline series was called the Country Squire. It came with woodgrain side trim appliques. The Mainline two-door station wagon was called the Ranch Wagon. The Customline four-door station wagon was called the Country Sedan. This was the first year for the overhead valve six-cylinder engine. The 1952 Fords were introduced to the public on Feb. 1, 1952. Over 32 percent of cars built this year had Ford-O-Matic gear shifting. Over 20 percent of cars built with manual transmissions had the overdrive option. The Ford station wagon led the industry with 30.9 percent of the output for this body style. Of total production for the 1952 calendar year (671,725 units) it was estimated that a full 621,783 Fords were built with V-8 engines!

1953 FORD

1953 Ford Crestline convertible. (OCW)

1953 FORDS — OVERVIEW — 1953 Fords utilized 1952 bodies with moderate trim updating. The grille incorporated a larger horizontal bar with three vertical stripes on either side of a large spinner. The length of this bar was increased and wrapped around the front edges of the fenders. Parking lights were rectangular instead of round. The Ford crest appeared in the center of the steering wheel hub and contained the words, "50th Anniversary 1903-1953."

MAINLINE SERIES — (6-CYL/V-8) — The Mainline series was the base trim level for 1953 and included rubber window moldings, horn button instead of horn ring, one sun visor and an armrest only on the driver's door.

FORD I.D. NUMBERS: Beginning in 1953, Ford adopted a new coding system for serial numbers that can be broken down, as follows: The first symbol designates the engine type: (A) 215 cid six-cylinder; (B) 239 cid V-8. The second symbol designates the model year: '3' for 1953. The third symbol designates the final assembly plant, as follows: A = Atlanta, B = Buffalo; C = Chester; G = Chicago; F= Dearborn; E = Edgewater; H = Highland Park; K = Kansas City; L = Long Beach; M = Memphis; N = Norfolk; R = Richmond; S = Somerville; P = Twin City (St. Paul). The fourth symbol designates body type: C = Sunliner; R = Customline Ranch Wagon; W = Mainline Ranch Wagon; X = Country Sedan; V = Victoria; T = Crestline four-door sedan; G = Mainline and Customline two-door sedan, two-door coupe and four-door sedan. The fifth through tenth digits indicate the number of the unit built at each assembly plant, beginning with 100001. Mainline six-cylinder models began with the designation "A3," followed by assembly plant code, body type and, finally, the unit's production number. Each plant began at 100001 and went up.

MAINLINE SIX SERIES

Model No.	Body/ Style No.	Body Type & Seating	Factory Price	Shipping Weight	Prod. Total
A3	73B	4-dr Sed-6P	1783	3115	Note 1
A3	70A	2-dr Sed-6P	1734	3067	Note 1
A3	72B	2-dr Clb Cpe-6P	1743	3046	Note 1

NOTE 1: See Mainline V-8 series listing. Production was counted by series and body style only, with no breakout per engine type.

1953 Ford Crestline Country Squire station wagon V-8. (OCW)

1953 Ford Crestline Sunliner two-door convertible V-8. (OCW)

1953 Ford Mainline two-door sedan 6-cyl. (OCW)

MAINLINE V-8 I.D. NUMBERS: Mainline V-8 models began with the designation "B3," assembly plant code, body type code, and, finally, the unit's production number, according to the final assembly location (see Ford serial numbers above). Each plant began at 100001 and went up.

MAINLINE V-8 SERIES

Model No.	Body/ Style No.	Body Type & Seating	Factory Price	Shipping Weight	Prod. Total
B3	73A	4-dr Sed-6P	1766	3181	66,463
B3	70A	2-dr Sed-6P	1717	3136	152,995
B3	72C	2-dr Bus Cpe-3P	1614	3068	16,280
B3	59A	2-dr Sta Wag-6P	2095	3408	66,976

NOTE 1: Total series output was 302,714 units. Ford does not indicate the number of each model produced with sixes or V-8s. Therefore, all production figures given above are total production of each body style with both engines.

CUSTOMLINE SERIES — (6-CYL/V-8) — The Customline series was the intermediate trim level for 1953 and included chrome window moldings, chrome horn half-ring, two sun visors, armrests on all doors and passenger assist straps on interior "B" pillars for easier rear seat egress. A horizontal chrome strip on the front fenders and a chrome opening on the rear quarter panel scoop. There was another horizontal chrome strip from the scoop opening to the back of the body.

CUSTOMLINE SIX I.D. NUMBERS: Customline six-cylinder models began with the same "A3" designation and used the same production numbers as the Mainline models.

CUSTOMLINE SIX SERIES

Model No.	Body/ Style No.	Body Type & Seating	Factory Price	Shipping Weight	Prod. Total
A3	73B	4-dr Sed-6P	1783	3115	Note 1
A3	70B	2-dr Sed-6P	1734	3067	Note 1
A3	72B	2-dr Clb Cpe-6P	1743	3046	Note 1

NOTE 1: See Customline V-8 series listing. Production was counted by series and body style only, with no breakout per engine type.

CUSTOMLINE V-8 I.D. NUMBERS: Customline V-8 models began with the same "B3" designation and used the same production numbers as the Mainline models.

CUSTOMLINE V-8 SERIES

Model No.	Body/ Style No.	Body Type & Seating	Factory Price	Shipping Weight	Prod. Total
B3	73B	4-dr Sed-6P	1858	3193	374,487
B3	70B	2-dr Sed-6P	1809	3133	305,433
B3	72B	2-dr Clb Cpe-6P	1820	3121	43,999
B3	79B	4-dr Sta Wag-6P	2267	3539	37,743

NOTE 1: Total series output was 761,662 units. Ford does not indicate the number of each model produced with sixes or V-8s. Therefore, all production figures given above are total production of each body style with both engines, except for station wagons (Country Sedan), which came only with V-8 power.

CRESTLINE SERIES — (V-8) — The Crestline series was the top trim level for 1953 and was offered only with V-8 engines. This series included all trim in the Customline series plus wheel covers and additional chrome trim along the bottom of the side widows.

CRESTLINE I.D. NUMBERS: Crestline models began with the same "B3" designation and used the same production numbers as the Mainline and Customline V-8 models.

CRESTLINE SERIES

Model No.	Body/ Style No.	Body Type & Seating	Factory Price	Shipping Weight	Prod. Total
B3	60B	2-dr Vic HT-6P	2120	3250	128,302
B3	76B	2-dr Sun Conv-6P	2230	3334	40,861
B3	79C	4-dr Cty Sq Sta Wag-6P	2403	3609	11,001

ENGINE [Base Six]: Overhead valve. Cast-iron block. Displacement: 215 cid. Bore and stroke: 3.56 x 3.60 inches. Compression ratio: 7.0:1. Brake hp: 101 at 3500 rpm. Carburetor: Holley one-barrel Model 1904F. Four main bearings. Serial number code "A."

1953 Ford Customline four-door sedan V-8. (AA)

ENGINE [V-8]: L-head. Cast-iron block. Displacement: 239 cid. Bore and stroke: 3.19 x 3.75 inches. Compression ratio: 7.2:1. Brake hp: 110 at 3800 rpm. Carburetor: Holley two-barrel Model 2100. Three main bearings. Serial number code "B."

CHASSIS FEATURES: Three-speed manual transmission was standard. This unit featured a semi-centrifugal-type clutch; three-speed helical gears with synchronizers for second and third gears. Three-speed manual transmission with automatic overdrive was a $108 option. Specifications were the same above with automatic overdrive function cutting in at 27 mph, cutting out at 21 mph. Approximate drive ratio was: 0.70:1. Manual control was provided below the instrument panel. Ford-O-Matic automatic transmission was a $184 option. This was a torque converter-type transmission with automatic planetary geartrain; single stage, three-element hydraulic torque converter; hydraulic-mechanical automatic controls and no electrical or vacuum connections. Power was transmitted through the fluid member at all times. Wheelbase: 115 inches. Overall length: 197.8 inches. Overall width: 74.3 inches. Tires: 6.70 x 15 (standard); 7.10 x 15 (station wagon). Rear axle gear ratios: (standard transmission) 3.90:1; (optional) 4.10:1; (automatic overdrive) 4.10:1; (Ford-O-Matic) 3.31:1.

CONVENIENCE OPTIONS: Power steering ($125). Power brakes ($35). Ford-O-Matic transmission ($184). Overdrive ($108). Six-tube Deluxe radio ($88). Eight-tube Custom radio ($100). Recirculation-type heater ($44). Deluxe heater ($71). Electric clock ($15). Directional signals ($15). Windshield washer ($10). Tinted glass ($23). White sidewall tires ($27).

HISTORY: The Mainline all-metal two-door station wagon was called the Ranch Wagon. The Customline all-metal four-door station wagon was called the Country Sedan. The Crestline all-metal four-door station wagon with woodgrain applique side trim was called the Country Squire. The Victoria was a pillarless two-door hardtop. The Sunliner was a two-door convertible. Introduction of 1953 models took place Dec. 12, 1953. On a model year basis 1,240,000 cars were built, of which 876,300 were estimated to be V-8-powered units. Ford opened a new Technical Service Laboratory at Livonia, Mich., this year. A specially trimmed Sunliner convertible paced the 1953 Indianapolis 500-Mile Race. Master Guide power steering was introduced June 16, 1953.

1954 FORD

1954 Ford Mainline two-door business coupe 6-cyl. (AA)

1954 FORDS — OVERVIEW — 1954 Fords utilized the 1952-1953 bodies with moderate trim updating. The grille incorporated a large horizontal bar with large slots on either side of a centrally located spinner. Round parking lights were located at either end of the horizontal bar. Many new convenience options were added for 1954. Among them were power windows, four-way power seats and power brakes. Ball joints replaced king pins in the front suspension. The big news from Ford Division in 1954, however, was a new V-8 engine, with overhead valves. This new engine was rated at 130 hp, or nearly 25 percent more than the 1953 flathead. Even the introduction of the new V-8 was overshadowed by the biggest news of all; the Feb. 20, 1954, announcement of an all-new personal luxury car called the Thunderbird, which was to be introduced in the 1955 model year.

MAINLINE SERIES — (6-CYL/V-8) — The Mainline series was the base trim level for 1954 and included rubber window moldings, horn button instead of horn ring, one sun visor and an armrest only on the driver's door.

MAINLINE SIX I.D. NUMBERS: Ford's coding system for serial numbers can be broken down, as follows: The first symbol designates the engine type: (A) 223 cid six-cylinder; (U) 239 cid V-8. The second symbol designates the model year: '4' for 1954. The third symbol designates the final assembly plant, as follows: A = Atlanta, B = Buffalo; C = Chester; D = Dallas; G = Chicago; F= Dearborn; E = Edgewater;

H = Highland Park; K = Kansas City; L = Long Beach; M = Memphis; N = Norfolk; R = Richmond; S = Somerville; P = Twin City (St. Paul). The fourth symbol designates body type, as follows: C = Sunliner; F = Skyliner; R = Customline Ranch Wagon; W = Mainline Ranch Wagon; X = Country Sedan; V = Victoria; T = Crestline four-door sedan; Y = Country Squire; G = Mainline and Customline two-door sedan, two-door coupe and four-door sedan. The fifth through tenth digits indicate the number of the unit built at each assembly plant, beginning with 100001. Mainline six-cylinder models began with the designation "A4," followed by assembly plant code, body type code and, finally, the unit's production number according to the final assembly location. Each plant began at 100001 and went up.

MAINLINE SIX SERIES

Model No.	Body/ Style No.	Body Type & Seating	Factory Price	Shipping Weight	Prod. Total
A4	73A	4-dr Sed-6P	1701	3142	Note 1
A4	70A	2-dr Sed-6P	1651	3086	Note 1
A4	72C	2-dr Bus Cpe-3P	1548	3021	Note 1
A4	59A	2-dr Sta Wag-6P	2029	3338	Note 1

NOTE 1: See Mainline V-8 series listing. Production was counted by series and body style only, with no breakout per engine type.

MAINLINE V-8 I.D. NUMBERS: Mainline V-8 models began with the designation "U4," assembly plant code, body type and, finally, the unit's production number, according to the final assembly location. Each plant began at 100001 and went up.

MAINLINE V-8 SERIES

Model No.	Body/ Style No.	Body Type & Seating	Factory Price	Shipping Weight	Prod. Total
U4	73A	4-dr Sed-6P	1777	3263	55,371
U4	70A	2-dr Sed-6P	1728	3207	123,329
U4	72C	2-dr Bus Cpe-3P	1625	3142	10,665
U4	59A	2-dr Sta Wag-6P	2106	3459	44,315

NOTE 1: Total series output was 233,680 units. Ford does not indicate the number of each model produced with sixes and V-8s. Therefore, all production figures given above are total production of each body style with both engines.

CUSTOMLINE SERIES — (6-CYL/V-8) — The Customline series was the intermediate trim level for 1954 and included chrome window moldings, chrome half-horn ring, two sun visors, armrests on all doors, passenger assist straps on interior "B" pillars for easier rear seat egress, a horizontal chrome strip along the entire length of the body and a chrome stone shield near the bottom of the rear quarter panels.

CUSTOMLINE SIX I.D. NUMBERS: Customline six-cylinder models began with the same "A4" designation and used the same production numbers as the Mainline series.

1954 Ford Crestline Skyliner two-door hardtop. (OCW)

1954 Ford four-door Country Sedan V-8. (AA)

1954 Ford Crestline four-door sedan V-8. (PH)

CUSTOMLINE SIX SERIES

Model No.	Body/ Style No.	Body Type & Seating	Factory Price	Shipping Weight	Prod. Total
A4	73B	4-dr Sed-6P	1793	3155	Note 1
A4	70B	2-dr Sed-6P	1744	3099	Note 1
A4	72B	2-dr Clb Cpe-6P	1753	3080	Note 1
A4	59B	2-dr Sta Wag-6P	2122	3344	Note 1
A4	79B	4-dr Sta Wag-6P	2202	3513	Note 1

NOTE 1: Customline V-8 series listing. Production was counted by series and body style only, with no breakout per engine type.

CUSTOMLINE V-8 I.D. NUMBERS: Customline V-8 models began with the same "U4" designation, and used the same production numbers as the Mainline series.

CUSTOMLINE V-8 SERIES

Model No.	Body/ Style No.	Body Type & Seating	Factory Price	Shipping Weight	Prod. Total
U4	73B	4-dr Sed-6P	1870	3276	262,499
U4	70B	2-dr Sed-6P	1820	3220	293,375
U4	72B	2-dr Clb Cpe-6P	1830	3201	33,951
U4	59B	2-dr Sta Wag-6P	2198	3465	36,086
U4	79B	4-dr Sta Wag-6P	2279	3634	48,384

NOTE 1: Total series output was 674,295 units. Ford does not indicate the number of each model produced with sixes or V-8s. Therefore, all production figures given above are total production of each body style with both engines.

CRESTLINE SERIES — (6-CYL/V-8) — The Crestline series was the top trim level for 1954, and included a six-cylinder engine for the first time since the series began in 1950. This series included all the Customline trim plus three chrome hash marks behind the quarter panel stone shields, chrome "A" pillar moldings, additional chrome trim along the bottom of the side windows and wheel covers.

CRESTLINE SIX I.D. NUMBERS: Crestline six-cylinder models began with the same "A4" designation and used the same production numbers as the Mainline and Customline models.

CRESTLINE SIX SERIES

Model No.	Body/ Style No.	Body Type & Seating	Factory Price	Shipping Weight	Prod. Total
A4	73C	4-dr Sed-6P	1898	3159	Note 1
A4	60B	2-dr Vic HT-6P	2055	3184	Note 1
A4	60F	2-dr Sky HT-6P	2164	3204	Note 1
A4	76B	2-dr Sun Conv-6P	2164	3231	Note 1
A4	79C	4-dr Cty Sq Sta Wag-8P	2339	3563	Note 1

NOTE 1: See Mainline V-8 series listing. Production was counted by series and body style only, with no breakout per engine type.

CRESTLINE V-8 I.D. NUMBERS: Crestline V-8 models began with the same "U4" designation and used the same production numbers as the Mainline and Crestline V-8 models.

CRESTLINE V-8 SERIES

Model No.	Body/ Style No.	Body Type & Seating	Factory Price	Shipping Weight	Prod. Total
U4	73C	4-dr Sed-6P	1975	3280	99,677
U4	60B	2-dr Vic HT-6P	2131	3305	95,464
U4	60F	2-dr Sky HT-6P	2241	3325	13,144
U4	76B	2-dr Sun Conv-6P	2241	3352	33,685
U4	76C	4-dr Cty Sq Sta Wag-8P	2415	3684	12,797

NOTE 1: Total series output was 254,767 units. Ford does not indicate the number of each model produced with sixes or V-8s. Therefore, all production figures are total production of each body style with both engines.

CHASSIS FEATURES: Wheelbase: 115 inches. Overall length: (passenger cars) 198.3 inches; (station wagons) 198.1 inches. Overall width: 73.5 inches. Tires: (standard) 6.70 x 15; (station wagon) 7.10 x 15.

ENGINE [Base Six]: Overhead valve. Cast-iron block. Displacement: 223 cid. Bore and stroke: 3.62 x 3.60 inches. Compression ratio: 7.2:1. Brake hp: 115 at 3900 rpm. Carburetor: Holley one-barrel Model 1904F. Four main bearings. Serial number code "A."

ENGINE [V-8]: Overhead valve. Cast-iron block. Displacement: 239 cid. Bore and stroke: 3.50 x 3.10 inches. Compression ratio: 7.2:1. Brake hp: 130 at 4200 rpm. Carburetor: Holley two-barrel Model AA-1. Five main bearings. Serial number code "U."

POWERTRAIN OPTIONS: Three-speed manual transmission was standard equipment. It featured a semi-centrifugal-type clutch; three-speed helical gears and synchronizers for second and third gears. Three-speed with automatic overdrive was optional. Specifications were the same as above with automatic overdrive function cutting in at 27 mph, cutting out at 21 mph. Approximate drive ratio: 0.70:1. Manual control was mounted below the instrument panel. Ford-O-Matic automatic transmission was optional. This was a torque converter-type transmission with automatic planetary geartrain; single stage, three-element hydraulic torque converter; hydraulic-mechanical automatic controls with no electrical or vacuum connections and power flow through the fluid member at all times. Rear axle gear ratios: (Ford) 3.90:1; (Ford with overdrive) 4.10:1; (Ford with Ford-O-Matic) 3.31:1.

CONVENIENCE OPTIONS: Automatic overdrive ($110). Ford-O-Matic transmission ($184). Power steering ($134). Power brakes ($41). Radio ($88-$99). Heater and defroster ($44-$71). Power windows ($102). Power seat ($64). White sidewall tires ($27 exchange). Note: Power windows available on Customline and Crestline only.

HISTORY: Public presentation of the original 1954 Ford line was made Jan. 6, 1954. Three new models, Crestline Skyliner, Crestline Sunliner, and Ranch Wagon were introduced. The Ranch Wagon was a two-door station wagon in the Mainline series but now had Customline appearance features. The Customline two-door sedan with short top was the Club Coupe. The Customline four-door station wagon was the Country Sedan. The Crestline four-door station wagon with woodgrain trim was the Country Squire. The Victoria was a Crestline two-door pillarless hardtop. The Skyliner was a Crestline two-door pillarless hardtop with green tinted plexiglass insert in roof over the front seat. The Sunliner was the Crestline convertible. Of the total 1,165,942 Fords built in the 1954 calendar year, industry sources estimate that 863,096 had V-8 engines installed. The 1,000,000th car of the 1954 production run was turned out Aug. 24, 1954. Production of cars built to 1955 specifications began Oct. 25, 1954.

1954 Ford Crestline Skyliner (glass roof) two-door hardtop V-8. (OCW)

1955 FORD

1955 Ford Club sedan. (OCW)

1955 Ford Thunderbird convertible. (OCW)

1955 FORDS — OVERVIEW — 1955 Fords were totally redesigned, inside and out, from the 1954 version. The bodies were longer, lower and wider. Even though the 1955 models used the same backlighted speedometer, first introduced in 1954, the rest of the instrument panel was new. A new Fairlane series replaced the Crestline as the top trim level. At the front, large round parking lights were mounted in a concave grille underneath the headlights. The Ford crest was mounted above the word Fairlane, in script, on the front of the hood, and again on the doors above the chrome Fairlane stripe. This stripe began at the top of the front fenders, moved back along the top of the fenders, over the side of the doors, into a dip and then to the rear of the car. The Fairlane series also featured chrome eyebrows on the headlight doors. The contemporary interest in horsepower and speed was reflected in two new, larger overhead valve V-8 engines. Perhaps some of the most exciting news was the introduction on Oct. 22, 1954, of the all-new 1955 two-passenger Thunderbird. The announced base price was $2,695.

MAINLINE SERIES — (6-CYL/V-8) — The Mainline series was the base trim level for 1955 and included rubber window moldings, a horn button instead of chrome horn ring, one sun visor and an armrest only on the driver's door.

MAINLINE SIX I.D. NUMBERS: Ford's coding system for serial numbers can be broken down, as follows: The first symbol designates the engine type: (A) 223 cid six-cylinder; (M) 272 cid V-8 with four-barrel carb; (U) 272 cid V-8 with two-barrel carb; (P) 292 cid V-8. The second symbol designates the model year: '5' for 1955. The third symbol designates the final assembly plant, as follows: A = Atlanta, B = Buffalo; C = Chester; D = Dallas; G = Chicago; F= Dearborn; E = Mawah; K = Kansas City; L = Long Beach; M = Memphis; N = Norfolk; R = San Jose; S = Somerville; U = Louisville; P = Twin City (St. Paul). The fourth symbol designates body type, as follows: C = Sunliner; F = Skyliner; R = Ranch Wagon; T = Fairlane (two-door and four-door); X = Country Sedan; V = Victoria; G = Mainline and Customline two-door sedan, two-door coupe and four-door sedan. The fifth through tenth digits indicate the number of the unit built at each assembly plant, beginning with 100001. Mainline six-cylinder models began with the designation "A5" followed by assembly plant code, body type code and, finally, the unit's production number, according to the final assembly location. Each plant began at 100001 and went up.

1955 Ford Thunderbird prototype hardtop. (OCW)

MAINLINE SIX SERIES

Model No.	Body/ Style No.	Body Type & Seating	Factory Price	Shipping Weight	Prod. Total
A5	73A	4-dr Sed-6P	1753	3106	Note 1
A5	70A	2-dr Sed-6P	1707	3064	Note 1
A5	70D	2-dr Bus Cpe-3P	1606	3026	Note 1

NOTE 1: See Mainline V-8 series listing. Production was counted by series and body style only, with no breakout per engine type.

MAINLINE V-8 I.D. NUMBERS: Mainline V-8 models began with the designation "U5" followed by assembly plant code, body type code and, finally, the unit's production number, according to final assembly location. Each plant began at 100001 and went up.

MAINLINE SERIES V-8

Model No.	Body/ Style No.	Body Type & Seating	Factory Price	Shipping Weight	Prod. Total
U5	73A	4-dr Sed-6P	1853	3216	41,794
U5	70A	2-dr Sed-6P	1807	3174	76,698
U5	70D	2-dr Bus Cpe-3P	1706	3136	8,809

NOTE 1: Total series output was 127,301 units. Ford does not indicate the number of each model produced with sixes or V-8s. Therefore, all production figures given above are total production of each body style with both engines.

CUSTOMLINE SERIES — (6-CYL/V-8) — The Customline series was the intermediate trim level for 1955 and included chrome window moldings, chrome horn half-ring, two sun visors, armrests on all doors, passenger assist straps on two-door interior "B" pillars for easier rear seat egress, a horizontal chrome strip along the entire length of the body and Customline, in script, on the rear fenders.

CUSTOMLINE SIX I.D. NUMBERS: Customline six-cylinder models began with the same "A5" designation and used the same production numbers as the Mainline series.

CUSTOMLINE SIX SERIES

Model No.	Body/ Style No.	Body Type & Seating	Factory Price	Shipping Weight	Prod. Total
A5	73B	4-dr Sed-6P	1845	3126	Note 1
A5	70B	2-dr Sed-6P	1801	3084	Note 1

NOTE 1: See Customline V-8 series listing. Production was counted by series and body style only, with no breakout per engine type.

CUSTOMLINE V-8 I.D. NUMBERS: Customline V-8 models began with the same "U5" designation and used the same production numbers as the Mainline series.

1955 Ford Customline two-door sedan V-8. (AA)

1955 Ford Fairlane Crown Victoria two-door hardtop V-8. (PH)

CUSTOMLINE SIX SERIES

Model No.	Body/ Style No.	Body Type & Seating	Factory Price	Shipping Weight	Prod. Total
U5	73B	4-dr Sed-6P	1945	3236	235,417
U5	70B	2-dr Sed-6P	1901	3194	236,575

NOTE 1: Total series output was 471,992 units. Ford does not indicate the number of each model produced with sixes and V-8s. Therefore, all production figures are total production of each body style with both engines.

FAIRLANE SERIES — (6-CYL/V-8) — The Fairlane series was the top trim level for 1955 and included chrome window and "A" pillar moldings (hardtops and Sunliner), chrome eyebrows on the headlight doors and a chrome side sweep molding plus all Customline trim (except the side chrome).

FAIRLANE SIX I.D. NUMBERS: Fairlane six-cylinder models began with the same "A5" designation and used the same production numbers as the Mainline and Customline series.

FAIRLANE SIX SERIES

Model No.	Body/ Style No.	Body Type & Seating	Factory Price	Shipping Weight	Prod. Total
A4	73C	4-dr Twn Sed-6P	1960	3134	Note 1
A4	70C	2-dr Clb Sed-6P	1914	3088	Note 1
A4	60B	2-dr Vic HT-6P	2095	3184	Note 1
A4	64A	2-dr Crn Vic-6P	2202	3246	Note 1
A4	64B	2-dr Crn Vic Sky-6P	2272	3264	Note 1
A4	76B	2-dr Sun Conv-6P	2224	3248	Note 1

NOTE 1: See Fairlane V-8 series listing. Production was counted by series and body style only, with no breakout per engine type.

FAIRLANE V-8 I.D. NUMBERS: Fairlane V-8 models began with the same "U5" designation and used the same production numbers as the Mainline and Customline series.

FAIRLANE V-8 SERIES

Model No.	Body/ Style No.	Body Type & Seating	Factory Price	Shipping Weight	Prod. Total
U5	73C	4-dr Twn Sed-6P	2060	3268	254,437
U5	70C	2-dr Clb Sed-6P	2014	3222	173,311
U5	60B	2-dr Vic HT-6P	2195	3318	113,372
U5	64A	2-dr Crn Vic-6P	2302	3380	33,165
U5	64B	2-dr Crn Vic Sky-6P	2372	3388	1,999
U5	76B	2-dr Sun Conv-6P	2324	3382	49,966

NOTE 1: Total series output was 626,250 units. Ford does not indicate the number of each model produced with sixes or V-8s. Therefore, all production figures given above are total production of each body style with both engines.

1955 Ford Fairlane Skyliner Crown Victoria two-door hardtop V-8. (OCW)

1955 Ford Country Sedan station wagon V-8. (OCW)

STATION WAGON SERIES — (6-CYL/V-8) — Station wagons were, for the first time, included in their own series. The Ranch Wagon was the base trim level two-door wagon. Six- and eight-passenger Country Sedans were the intermediate level and the Country Squire was the top trim level station wagon. The level of trim equipment paralleled the Mainline, Customline and Fairlane series of passenger cars.

STATION WAGON SIX I.D. NUMBERS: Station wagon six-cylinder models began with the same "A5" designation and used the same production numbers as the conventional cars.

STATION WAGON SIX SERIES

Model No.	Body/ Style No.	Body Type & Seating	Factory Price	Shipping Weight	Prod. Total
A5	59A	2-dr RanchWag-6P	2043	3309	Note 1
A5	59B	2-dr Cus Ranch Wag-6P	2109	3327	Note 1
A5	79D	4-dr Cty Sed-6P	2156	3393	Note 1
A5	79B	4-dr Cty Sed-8P	2287	3469	Note 1
A5	79C	4-dr Cty Sq Sta Wag-8P	2392	3471	Note 1

NOTE 1: See station wagon V-8 series listing. Production was counted by series and body style only, with no breakout per engine type.

STATION WAGON V-8 I.D. NUMBERS: Station wagon V-8 models began with the same "U5" designation and used the same production numbers as the conventional cars.

STATION WAGON V-8 SERIES

Model No.	Body/ Style No.	Body Type & Seating	Factory Price	Shipping Weight	Prod. Total
U5	59A	2-dr Ranch Wag-6P	2143	3443	40,493
U5	59B	2-dr Cus Ranch Wag-6P	2209	3461	43,671
U5	79D	4-dr Cty Sed-6P	2256	3527	53,075
U5	79B	4-dr Cty Sed-8P	2387	3603	53,209
U5	79C	4-dr Cty Sq Sta Wag-8P	2492	3605	19,011

NOTE 1: Total series output was 209,459 units. Ford does not indicate the number of each model produced with sixes or V-8s. Therefore, all production figures given above are total production of each body style.

THUNDERBIRD — (V-8) — SERIES 40A — A bright, high-spirited car, the Thunderbird was equipped with the new overhead valve V-8 engine, boosted to higher horsepower with the addition of a four-barrel carburetor and dual exhaust. A host of power-assist options including steering, windows, seat and brakes were available. The three-speed manual transmission was standard equipment, but overdrive and Ford-O-Matic automatic transmissions were optional accessories. Road clearance was only 5-1/2 inches, far less than the conventional Ford cars of the same year. The Thunderbird, with its two-seater personal car appeal, came from the factory with a fiberglass hardtop. A rayon convertible top was an extra-cost option priced at $290. Full-scale production began during the week of Sept. 5, 1954. The 292 cid engine came with two compression ratios: 8.1:1 (193 hp) and 8.5:1 (198 hp). The lower ratio was used with the manual transmission only. The Thunderbird production line operated until Sept. 16, 1955. In addition to being started before the 1954 model run was completed, it continued after the 1956 model year began on Sept. 6, 1955. Only Thunderbirds were being assembled at the start and finish of the 1955 model year run. This means that the first 1500 and the last 500 serial numbers from the series 100001 through 260557 were assigned only to Thunderbirds. The intervening numbers were assigned to the mixed production of Thunderbirds and the regular passenger car lines.

THUNDERBIRD I.D. NUMBERS: (V-8 only) Thunderbirds began with the prefix "P5FH" followed by the serial number starting at 100001.

THUNDERBIRD SERIES

Model No.	Body/ Style No.	Body Type & Seating	Factory Price	Shipping Weight	Prod. Total
P5	40	2-dr Conv-2P	2944	2980	16,155

1955 Ford Fairlane two-door sedan. (OCW)

1955 Ford two-door ranch wagon. (OCW)

ENGINE [Base Six]: Overhead valve. Cast-iron block. Displacement: 223 cid. Bore and stroke: 3.62 x 3.60 inches. Compression ratio: 7.5:1. Brake hp: 120 at 4000 rpm. Carburetor: Holley single-barrel. Four main bearings. Serial number code "A."

ENGINE [V-8]: Overhead valve. Cast-iron block. Displacement: 272 cid. Bore and stroke: 3.62 x 3.30 inches. Compression ratio: 7.6:1. Brake hp: 162 at 4400 rpm. (182 at 4400 rpm. with the four-barrel "Power Pack"). Carburetor: Holley two-barrel. Five main bearings. Serial number code "U" (two-barrel) or "M" (four-barrel).

ENGINE [Thunderbird V-8]: Overhead valve. Cast-iron block. Displacement: 292 cid. Bore and stroke: 3.75 x 3.30 inches. Compression ratio: 8.1:1 (8.5:1 with Ford-O-Matic). Brake hp: 193 at 4400 rpm. (198 at 4400 rpm. with Ford-O-Matic). Carburetor: Holley four-barrel. Five main bearings. Serial number code "P."

FORD CHASSIS FEATURES: Wheelbase: (passenger car) 115.5 inches; (station wagon) 115.5 inches; (Thunderbird) 102 inches. Overall length: (passenger car) 198.5 inches; (station wagon) 197.6 inches; (Thunderbird) 175.3 inches. Overall width: (Ford) 75.9 inches; (Thunderbird) 70.3 inches. Tires: (station wagon) 7.10 x 15 tubeless; (all other cars) 6.70 x 15 tubeless. Front tread: (Ford) 58 inches; (Thunderbird) 56 inches. Rear tread: (Ford) 56 inches; (Thunderbird) 56 inches.

THUNDERBIRD CHASSIS FEATURES: Wheelbase: 102 inches. Overall length: 175.3 inches. Overall width: 70.3 inches. Tires: 6.70 x 15 tubeless.

FORD/THUNDERBIRD OPTIONS: Overdrive transmission ($110). Ford-O-Matic automatic transmission ($178). Radio ($99). Heater ($71). Power brakes ($32). Power seat ($64). Power windows ($102). White sidewall tires ($27 exchange). Soft-top for Thunderbird, in addition to hardtop ($290). Soft-top for Thunderbird, as substitute for hardtop ($75). Power steering ($91). Other standard factory and dealer-installed-type options and accessories. Three-speed manual was standard equipment. It featured a semi-centrifugal-type clutch; three-speed helical gears and synchronizers for second and third gears. Three-speed with automatic overdrive was optional at $110. Specifications were the same as above with automatic overdrive function cutting in at 27 mph and cutting out at 21 mph. Approximate drive ratio: 0.70:1. Manual control below instrument panel.

HISTORY: The Town Sedan is a Deluxe Fairlane four-door sedan. The Club Sedan is a Deluxe Fairlane two-door sedan. The Victoria is a Fairlane two-door pillarless hardtop. The Crown Victoria is a Fairlane two-door pillared hardtop with "tiara" roof trim. The Crown Victoria Skyliner is a similar model with forward half of top constructed from transparent green plexiglass. The Sunliner is the two-door Fairlane convertible. The Ranch Wagon has Mainline level trim; the Custom Ranch Wagon has Customline trim; the Country Sedan is a four-door station wagon with Customline trim and the Country Squire is a Fairlane trim level station wagon with woodgrain side appliques. Production of 1955 Fords began Oct. 25, 1954, and ended August 30, 1955. The 1955 Ford was introduced to the public Nov. 12, 1954. Production of 1955 Thunderbirds began Sept. 7, 1954, and ended Sept. 16, 1955. The 1955 Thunderbird was introduced to the public Oct. 22, 1954. Of the total 1,435,002 cars built from October 1954 to September 1955, the majority were V-8s. During the 1955 calendar year, 1,546,762 Ford V-8s and 217,762 sixes were manufactured. Also on a calendar year basis, 230,000 Fords had power steering; 31,800 had power brakes; 22,575 (of all FoMoCo products) had air conditioning; 197,215 cars had overdrive and 1,014,500 cars had automatic transmissions. The 1955 run was the second best in Ford Motor Co. history, behind 1923 when Model Ts dominated the industry. A new factory in Mahwah, N.J., opened this year, to replace one in Edgewater, N.J. A new factory in San Jose, Calif., replaced a one-third-as-big West Coast plant in Richmond, Calif. A new factory was also opened in Louisville, Ky., replacing a smaller facility in the same city. Robert S. McNamara was vice-president and general manager of Ford Division. Ford Motor Co. engineering had an experimental turbine-powered vehicle this year. It featured a modified 1955 body shell with an altered grille and exhaust system. This car was actually built in 1954 and had a "4" designation in the prefix code to the assigned serial number, which was from the 1954 production serial number series. The car was scrapped after testing was completed.

1956 FORD

1956 FORDS — OVERVIEW — Ford reused the 1955 body, with the exception of differences in the top configuration on two-door hardtops of each year. New models were the Fairlane-level Parklane two-door sport wagon and a Customline Victoria two-door hardtop. Oval parking lights replaced the round units used on the 1955 models and the chrome trim was revised moderately from the previous year. The 1956 models used larger taillights with chrome rings around the lenses. Inside, the 1956 models were completely new. Safety was a popular theme in 1956 and new Fords featured a completely redesigned instrument panel with optional padding and padded sun visors. Also, the steering wheel featured a 2-1/2-inch recessed hub, supposedly designed to lessen injury to the driver in the event of an accident. Seat belts were also offered for the first time in 1956.

1956 Ford Crown Victoria. (OCW)

1956 Ford Country Squire station wagon. (OCW)

MAINLINE SERIES — (6-CYL/V-8) — The Mainline series was the base trim level for 1956 and included rubber window moldings, a horn button instead of horn ring, one sun visor and an armrest on the driver's door only.

MAINLINE SIX I.D. NUMBERS: Ford's coding system for serial numbers can be broken down, as follows: The first symbol designates the engine type: (A) 223 cid six-cylinder; (M) 292 cid V-8; (P) 312 cid V-8; (U) 272 cid V-8. The second symbol designates the model year: '6' for 1956. The third symbol designates the final assembly plant, as follows: A = Atlanta, B = Buffalo; C = Chester; D = Dallas; G = Chicago; F= Dearborn; E = Mawmah; H = Highland Park; K = Kansas City; L = Long Beach; M = Memphis; N = Norfolk; R = San Jose; S = Somerville; U = Louisville; P = Twin City (St. Paul). The fourth symbol designates body type, as follows: C = Sunliner; F = Victoria (Fairlane four-door); R = Customline Ranch Wagon; W = Crown Victoria; X = Country Sedan; V = Victoria (two-door); T = Fairlane (two-and four-door); Y = Country Squire; G = Mainline and Customline two-door sedan, two-door coupe and four-door sedan. The fifth through tenth digits indicate the number of the unit built at each assembly plant, beginning with 100001. Mainline six-cylinder models began with the designation "A6" followed by assembly plant code, body type code and, finally, the unit's production number, according to the final assembly location. Each plant began at 100001 and went up.

MAINLINE SIX SERIES

Model No.	Body/ Style No.	Body Type & Seating	Factory Price	Shipping Weight	Prod. Total
A6	73A	4-dr Sed-6P	1895	3127	Note 1
A6	70A	2-dr Sed-6P	1850	3087	Note 1
A6	70D	2-dr Bus Sed-3P	1748	3032	Note 1

NOTE 1: Total series output was 164,442 units. Ford does not indicate the number of each model produced with sixes or V-8s. See Mainline V-8 chart below.

MAINLINE V-8 I.D. NUMBERS: Mainline V-8 models began with the designation, "U6" (272 cid V-8), "M6" (292 cid V-8), or "P6" (312 cid V-8) followed by assembly plant code, body type code and, finally, the unit's production number, according to the final assembly location. Each plant began with 100001 and went up.

MAINLINE V-8 SERIES

Model No.	Body/ Style No.	Body Type & Seating	Factory Price	Shipping Weight	Prod. Total
U/M/P-6	73A	4-dr Sed-6P	1995	3238	49,448
U/M/P-6	70A	2-dr Sed-6P	1950	3198	106,974
U/M/P-6	70D	2-dr Bus Sed-3P	1848	3143	8,020

NOTE 1: Total series output was 164,442 units. Ford does not indicate the number of each model produced with sixes or V-8s. Therefore, all production figures given above are total production of each body style with both engines.

1956 Ford Customline four-door sedan 6-cyl. (AA)

1956 Ford Customline Victoria two-door hardtop V-8. (PH)

CUSTOMLINE SERIES — (6-CYL/V-8) — The Customline series was the intermediate trim level for 1956 and included chrome window moldings, horn ring, two sun visors, armrests on all doors, passenger assist straps on two-door interior "B" pillars for easier rear seat egress, a chrome strip along the entire length of the body with the series identification just above, and forward of the rear wheel opening. Trunk lid identification consisted of a Ford crest with horizontal chrome bars on either side of the crest.

CUSTOMLINE SIX I.D. NUMBERS: Customline six-cylinder models began with the same "A6" designation and used the same production numbers as the Mainline series.

CUSTOMLINE SIX SERIES

Model No.	Body/ Style No.	Body Type & Seating	Factory Price	Shipping Weight	Prod. Total
A6	73B	4-dr Sed-6P	1985	3147	Note 1
A6	70B	2-dr Sed-6P	1939	3107	Note 1
A6	64D	2-dr Vic-6P	2093	3202	Note 1

NOTE 1: See Customline V-8 series listing. Production was counted by series and body style only, with no breakout per engine type.

CUSTOMLINE V-8 I.D. NUMBERS: Customline V-8 models began with the same "U6," "M6" or "P6" designation and used the same production numbers as the Mainline series.

CUSTOMLINE V-8 SERIES

Model No.	Body/ Style No.	Body Type & Seating	Factory Price	Shipping Weight	Prod. Total
U/M/P-6	73B	4-dr Sed-6P	2086	3258	170,695
U/M/P-6	70B	2-dr Sed-6P	2040	3218	164,828
U/M/P-6	64D	2-dr Vic-6P	2193	3345	33,130

PRODUCTION NOTE: Total series output was 368,653 units. Ford does not indicate the number of each model produced with sixes or V-8s. Therefore, all production figures given above are total production of each body style with both engines.

FAIRLANE SERIES — (6-CYL/V-8) — The Fairlane series was the top trim level for 1956 and included chrome window moldings, chrome "A" pillar moldings on Sunliners, chrome side sweep moldings with simulated exhaust outlets at the back of the trim, Fairlane script below the Ford crest on the hood and a large, V-shaped insignia on the trunk lid. Also, V-8-equipped Fairlanes had rear bumpers with slots in each end for passage of the dual exhaust, which were standard with either V-8 engine.

FAIRLANE SIX-CYLINDER I.D. NUMBERS: Fairlane six-cylinder models began with the same "A6" designation and used the same production numbers as the Mainline and Customline series.

FAIRLANE SIX-CYLINDER SERIES

Model No.	Body/ Style No.	Body Type & Seating	Factory Price	Shipping Weight	Prod. Total
A6	73C	4-dr Twn Sed-6P	2093	3147	Note 1
A6	70C	2-dr Clb Sed-6P	2047	3107	Note 1
A6	57A	4-dr Twn Vic-6P	2249	3297	Note 1
A6	64C	2-dr Clb Vic-6P	2194	3202	Note 1
A6	64A	2-dr Crn Vic-6P	2337	3217	Note 1
A6	64B	2-dr Crn Vic Sky-6P	2407	3227	Note 1
A6	76B	2-dr Sun Conv-6P	2359	3312	Note 1

NOTE 1: See Fairlane V-8 series listing. Production was counted by series and body style only, with no breakout per engine type.

FAIRLANE V-8 I.D. NUMBERS: Fairlane V-8 models began with the same "U6," "M6" or "P6" designations and used the same production numbers as the Mainline and Customline series.

FAIRLANE V-8 SERIES

Model No.	Body/ Style No.	Body Type & Seating	Factory Price	Shipping Weight	Prod. Total
U/M/P-6	73C	4-dr Twn Sed-6P	2194	3290	244,672
U/M/P-6	70C	2-dr Clb Sed-6P	2147	3250	142,629
U/M/P-6	57A	4-dr Twn Vic-6P	2349	3440	32,111
U/M/P-6	64C	2-dr Clb Vic-6P	2294	3345	177,735
U/M/P-6	64A	2-dr Crn Vic-6P	2438	3360	9,209
U/M/P-6	64B	2-dr Crn Vic Sky-6P	2507	3370	603
U/M/P-6	76B	2-dr Sun Conv-6P	2459	3455	58,147

PRODUCTION NOTE: Total series output was 645,306 units. Ford does not indicate the number of each model produced with sixes and V-8s. Therefore, all production figures given above are total production of each body style with both engines.

STATION WAGON SERIES — (6-CYL/V-8) — Station wagons continued as their own series for 1956. The Ranch Wagon was the base trim level two-door station wagon; Country Sedans were the intermediate trim level and Country Squires were the top trim level with simulated woodgrain exterior paneling. The level of equipment paralleled the Mainline, Customline, and Fairlane series of passenger cars.

STATION WAGON SIX-CYLINDER I.D. NUMBERS: Station wagon six-cylinder models began with the same "A6" designation, and used the same production numbers as the conventional cars.

STATION WAGON SIX-CYLINDER SERIES

Model No.	Body/ Style No.	Body Type & Seating	Factory Price	Shipping Weight	Prod. Total
A6	59A	2-dr Ranch Wag-6P	2185	3330	Note 1
A6	59B	2-dr Cus Ranch Wag-6P	2249	3345	Note 1
A6	59C	2-dr Parklane Wag-6P	2428	3360	Note 1
A6	79D	4-dr Cty Sed-6P	2297	3420	Note 1
A6	79B	4-dr Cty Sed-8P	2428	3485	Note 1
A6	79C	4-dr Cty Sq-8P	2533	3495	Note 1

NOTE 1: See station wagon V-8 series listing. Production was counted by series and body style only, with no breakout per engine type.

STATION WAGON V-8 I.D. NUMBERS: Station wagon V-8 models began with the same "U6," "M6" or "P6" designation and used the same production numbers as the passenger cars.

STATION WAGON V-8 SERIES

Model No.	Body/ Style No.	Body Type & Seating	Factory Price	Shipping Weight	Prod. Total
U/M/P-6	59A	2-dr Ranch Wag-6P	2285	3473	48,348
U/M/P-6	59B	2-dr Cus Ranch Wag-6P	2350	3488	42,317
U/M/P-6	59C	2-dr Parklane Wag-6P	2528	3503	15,186
U/M/P-6	79D	4-dr Cty Sed-6P	2397	3536	Note 1
U/M/P-6	79B	4-dr Cty Sed-8P	2528	3628	85,374
U/M/P-6	79C	4-dr Cty Sq-8P	2633	3638	23,221

NOTE 1: The production total for both six-passenger and eight-passenger Country Sedans is combined (85,374) and listed with the latter. No breakout by model is available.

PRODUCTION NOTE: Total series output was 214,446 units. Ford does not indicate the number of each model produced with sixes or V-8 engines. Therefore, all production figures given above are total production of each body style with both engines.

THUNDERBIRD SERIES — (V-8) — Although the 1956 Thunderbird shared the same body as the 1955, there were a few significant changes that make the 1956 model unique. Probably the most visible change is the outside location of the spare tire, which gave much more room in the trunk and, unfortunately, put so much weight behind the rear wheels that handling and steering were adversely affected. Also, the 1956 Thunderbird included wind wings on the windshield, cowl vents on each fender and a different rear bumper configuration with the simplified dual exhaust routed out the ends of the bumper.

THUNDERBIRD V-8 I.D. NUMBERS: Thunderbird models began with the designation "P6" followed by assembly plant code "F" (Dearborn), body type code "H" (Thunderbird) and, finally, the production number beginning at 100001 and going up. Since 1956 Thunderbird production began over a month after the production of other 1956 Fords, the first Thunderbird serial number was later in the sequence.

THUNDERBIRD SERIES

Model No.	Body/ Style No.	Body Type & Seating	Factory Price	Shipping Weight	Prod. Total
M6/P6	40A	2-dr Conv-2P	3151	3088	15,631

ENGINE [Base Six]: Overhead valve. Cast-iron block. Displacement: 223 cid. Bore and stroke: 3.62 x 3.60 inches. Compression ratio: 8.0:1. Brake hp: 137 at 4200 rpm. Carburetor: Holley one-barrel. Four main bearings. Serial number code "A."

1956 Ford Fairlane Town Victoria four-door hardtop V-8. (OCW)

1956 Ford Thunderbird two-door convertible (with hardtop) V-8. (PH)

1956 Ford Thunderbird prototype hardtop. (OCW)

ENGINE [V-8]: Overhead valve. Cast-iron block. Displacement: 272 cid. Bore and stroke: 3.62 x 3.30 inches. Compression ratio: 8.0:1. Brake hp: 173 at 4400 rpm. (176 at 4400 rpm. with Ford-O-Matic). Carburetor: Holley two-barrel. Five main bearings. Serial number code "U."

ENGINE [Thunderbird V-8]: Overhead valve. Cast-iron block. Displacement: 292 cid. Bore and stroke: 3.75 x 3.30 inches. Compression ratio: 6.4:1. Brake hp: 200 at 4600 rpm. (202 at 4600 rpm. with Ford-O-Matic). Carburetor: Holley four-barrel. Five main bearings. Serial number code "M."

ENGINE [Thunderbird Special V-8]: Overhead valve. Cast-iron block. Displacement: 312 cid. Bore and stroke: 3.60 x 3.44 inches. Compression ratio: 6.4:1. Brake hp: 215 at 4600 rpm. (225 at 4600 rpm. with Ford-O-Matic). Carburetor: Holley four-barrel. Five main bearings. Serial number code "P."

FORD CHASSIS FEATURES: Wheelbase: 115.5 inches. Overall length: 198.5 inches (197.6 inches on station wagons). Overall width: 75.9 inches. Tires: 6.70 x 15 four-ply tubeless; 7.10 x 15 four-ply tubeless on Victorias with Ford-O-Matic and on Ranch Wagons, 7.10 x 15 six-ply tubeless on Country Sedans and Country Squire station wagons.

THUNDERBIRD CHASSIS FEATURES: Wheelbase: 102 inches. Overall length: 175.3 inches (185 inches including continental kit). Overall width: 70.3 inches. Tires: 6.70 x 15 four-ply tubeless.

FORD/THUNDERBIRD OPTIONS: Automatic overdrive transmission ($110-$148). Ford-O-Matic transmission ($178-$215). Power steering for Mainline models ($91). Power steering for other models ($51-$64). Power seat ($60). Radio ($100). Heater ($85). Power brakes ($32). Thunderbird V-8 for Fairlane models ($123). Thunderbird Special V-8 for Thunderbirds ($123). Power brakes ($40). Windshield washers ($10). Wire wheel covers ($35). Power windows ($70). Chrome engine dress-up kit ($25). Rear fender shields. Full wheel discs. White sidewall tires. Continental tire kit. Tinted windshield. Tinted glass. Life-Guard safety equipment. Two-tone paint finish. Front and rear bumper guards. Grille guard package. Rear guard package. Rear mount radio antenna. Three-speed manual transmission with a semi-centrifugal-type clutch, three-speed helical gears, and synchronizers for second and third gears standard equipment. Three-speed with automatic overdrive was optional (specifications same as above with automatic overdrive function cutting in at 27 mph, cutting out at 21 mph. Approximate drive ratio: 0.70:1. Manual control below instrument panel.) Ford-O-Matic automatic transmission was optional. This was a torque converter transmission with automatic planetary geartrain; single stage, three-element hydraulic torque converter; hydro-mechanical automatic controls with no electric or vacuum connections and power flow through fluid member at all times. Six-cylinder rear axle ratios: (Ford-O-Matic) 3.22:1; (manual transmission) 3.89:1 and (overdrive) 3.89:1. V-8 rear axle ratios: (Ford-O-Matic) 3.22:1; (manual transmission) 3.78:1 and (overdrive) 3.89:1.

HISTORY: Production of 1956 Fords started Sept. 6, 1955, and the 1956 Thunderbird began production on Oct. 17, 1955. The Parklane station wagon was a Deluxe Fairlane trim level two-door Ranch Wagon. The Crown Victoria Skyliner featured a plexiglass, tinted transparent forward roof, the last year for this type construction. The Sunliner was a two-door convertible. The new Y-block Thunderbird V-8 came with double twin-jet carburetion; integrated automatic choke; dual exhaust; turbo-wedge-shaped combustion chambers and automatic Power Pilot. A 12-volt electrical system and 18-mm anti-fouling spark plugs were adopted this season. Model year sales peaked at 1,392,847 units. Calendar year production hit 1,373,542 vehicles. (Both figures include Thunderbird sales and production).

1957 FORD

1957 Ford Fairlane 500 retractable hardtop. (OCW)

1957 FORDS — OVERVIEW — 1957 Fords were completely restyled and bore only a slight resemblance to earlier models. The new Fairlane series (including Fairlane and Fairlane 500 models) was five inches lower; had a two-and-one-half-inch longer wheelbase and measured more than nine inches longer overall compared to 1956 models. The Custom series (including Custom and Custom 300 models) was three inches longer overall and had a one-half-inch longer wheelbase than the 1956 models. As an aid in lowering the cars, all models had 14-inch wheels for the first time. Other design changes included a rear-opening hood, streamlined wheel openings and the use of windshield posts that sloped rearward at the bottom. Also, all 1957 Fords sported the latest styling craze, tailfins. Ford referred to these as "high-canted fenders." The big news for the year was the introduction of the Skyliner; the only true hardtop convertible in the world. At the touch of a button, an automatic folding mechanism retracted the top into the trunk, creating a true convertible.

CUSTOM SERIES — (6-CYL/V-8) — The Custom series was the base trim level for 1957 and included chrome window moldings, a horn button instead of a horn ring, one sun visor and an armrest on the driver's door only. An abbreviated version of the 1955 Fairlane sweep-type chrome trim began behind the front door and went back along the bodysides.

CUSTOM SIX I.D. NUMBERS: Ford's coding system for serial numbers can be broken down, as follows: The first symbol designates the engine type: (A) 223 cid six-cylinder; (B) 272 cid V-8; (C) 292 cid V-8; (D) 312 cid V-8 (with four-barrel carb); (E) 312 cid V-8 (with dual four-barrel carbs); (F) 312 cid supercharged V-8. The second symbol designates the model year: '7' for 1957. The third symbol designates the final assembly plant, as follows: A = Atlanta, B = Buffalo; C = Chester; D = Dallas; G = Chicago; F= Dearborn; E = Mahwah; K = Kansas City; L = Long Beach; M = Memphis; N = Norfolk; R = San Jose; S = Somerville; U = Louisville; P = Twin City (St. Paul). The fourth symbol designates body type, as follows: C = Fairlane 500 convertible; G = Custom/Custom 300 (two-door and four-door); R = Custom 300 Ranch Wagon; T = Fairlane/Fairlane 500 (two-door and four-door); V = Fairlane/Fairlane 500/Victoria (two-door and four-door); W = Fairlane 500 retractable hardtop; X = Country Sedan; Y = Country Squire. The fifth through tenth digits indicate the number of the unit built at each assembly plant, beginning with 100001. Custom six-cylinder models began with the designation "A7" followed by assembly plant code, body type code and, finally, the unit's production number, according to the final assembly location. Each plant began at 100001 and went up.

1957 Ford Custom 300 four-door sedan 6-cyl. (OCW)

CUSTOM SIX SERIES

Model No.	Body/ Style No.	Body Type & Seating	Factory Price	Shipping Weight	Prod. Total
A7	73A	4-dr Sed-6P	2042	3197	Note 1
A7	70A	2-dr Sed-6P	1991	3154	Note 1
A7	70D	2-dr Bus Cpe-3P	1889	3145	Note 1

NOTE 1: See Custom V-8 series listing. Production was counted by series and body style only, with no breakout per engine type.

CUSTOM V-8 I.D. NUMBERS: Custom V-8 models began with the engine designation code, followed by assembly plant code, body type code and, finally, the unit's production number, according to the final assembly location. Each plant began at 100001 and went up.

CUSTOM V-8 SERIES

Model No.	Body/ Style No.	Body Type & Seating	Factory Price	Shipping Weight	Prod. Total
N/A	73A	4-dr Sed-6P	2142	3319	68,924
N/A	70A	2-dr Sed-6P	2091	3276	116,963
N/A	70D	2-dr Bus Cpe-3P	1979	3267	6,888

PRODUCTION NOTE: Total series output was 192,775 units. Ford does not indicate the number of each model produced with sixes and V-8s. Therefore, all production figures given above are total production of each body style with both engines. "Model numbers" were now equivalent to V-8 engine code designations, which varied with specific powerplant attachments.

CUSTOM 300 MODELS — (6-CYL/V-8) — The Custom 300 was the top trim level in the short wheelbase Custom series and included chrome window moldings; chrome horn ring; two sun visors; armrests on all doors and a slightly modified version of the new Fairlane sweep, featuring a gold anodized insert between two chrome strips. The word 'FORD' was spelled out in block letters above the grille and a small Ford crest appeared on the trunk lid.

CUSTOM 300 SIX I.D. NUMBERS: Custom 300 six-cylinder models began with the same "A7" designation and used the same production numbers as the Custom models.

CUSTOM 300 SIX SERIES

Model No.	Body/ Style No.	Body Type & Seating	Factory Price	Shipping Weight	Prod. Total
A7	73B	4-dr Sed-6P	2157	3212	Note 1
A7	70B	2-dr Sed-6P	2105	3167	Note 1

NOTE 1: See Custom 300 V-8 series listing. Production was counted by series and body style only, with no breakouts per engine type.

CUSTOM 300 V-8 I.D. NUMBERS: Custom 300 V-8 models began with the same engine designations and used the same production numbers as the Custom models.

CUSTOM 300 V-8 SERIES

Model No.	Body/ Style No.	Body Type & Seating	Factory Price	Shipping Weight	Prod. Total
N/A	73B	4-dr Sed-6P	2257	3334	194,677
N/A	70B	2-dr Sed-6P	2205	3289	160,360

PRODUCTION NOTE: Total series output was 355,237 units. Ford does not indicate the number of each model produced with sixes or V-8s. Therefore, all production figures given above are total production of each body style with both engines. "Model Numbers" were equivalent to V-8 engine code designations, which varied with specific powerplant attachments.

FAIRLANE SERIES — (6-CYL/V-8) — The Fairlane model was the base trim level for the longer wheelbase Fairlane series. It included chrome window moldings with slightly less chrome around the "C" pillar than the Fairlane 500 model and a considerably different side stripe than the higher-priced model. The Fairlane side chrome began just behind the front door. It then followed the fin forward to its source, dropped over the side and swept back, at a 45-degree angle, to a point just above the wheel opening. From there it ran straight back to the rear bumper. The word Fairlane appeared in script, on the side of the front fenders, and above the grille. A large, V-shaped Fairlane crest appeared on the trunk lid.

FAIRLANE SIX I.D. NUMBERS: Fairlane six-cylinder models began with the same "A7" designation and used the same production numbers as the Custom series.

FAIRLANE SIX SERIES

Model No.	Body/ Style No.	Body Type & Seating	Factory Price	Shipping Weight	Prod. Total
A7	58A	4-dr Twn Sed-6P	2286	3315	Note 1
A7	64A	2-dr Clb Sed-6P	2235	3270	Note 1
A7	57B	4-dr Twn Vic-6P	2357	3350	Note 1
A7	63B	2-dr Clb Vic-6P	2293	3305	Note 1

NOTE 1: See Fairlane V-8 series listing. Production was counted by series and body style only, with no breakouts per engine type.

FAIRLANE V-8 I.D. NUMBERS: Fairlane V-8 models began with the same engine designations and used the same production numbers as the Custom series.

FAIRLANE V-8 SERIES

Model No.	Body/ Style No.	Body Type & Seating	Factory Price	Shipping Weight	Prod. Total
N/A	56A	4-dr Twn Sed-6P	2386	3437	52,060
N/A	64A	2-dr Clb Sed-6P	2335	3392	39,843
N/A	57B	4-dr Twn Vic-6P	2457	3471	12,695
N/A	63B	2-dr Clb Vic-6P	2393	3427	44,127

PRODUCTION NOTE: Total series output was 148,725 units. Ford does not indicate the number of each model produced with sixes and V-8s. Therefore, all production figures given above are total production of each body style with both engines. "Model Numbers" were now equivalent to V-8 engine code designations, which varied with specific powerplant attachments.

1957 Ford Fairlane 500 Sunliner two-door convertible V-8. (OCW)

1957 Ford Fairlane 500 four-door Town Sedan 6-cyl. (PH)

1957 Ford Fairlane four-door Town Sedan V-8. (AA)

FAIRLANE 500 MODELS — (6-CYL/V-8) — The Fairlane 500 was the top trim level in the Fairlane series and included all the trim used on the Fairlane models plus slightly more chrome on the "C" pillars and different side trim. The side trim was a modified version of the Fairlane sweep, which included a gold anodized insert between two chrome strips. It began on the sides of the front fenders, dipping near the back of the front doors, merging into a strip and following the crest of the fins to the rear of the body.

FAIRLANE 500 SIX I.D. NUMBERS: Fairlane 500 six-cylinder models began with the same "A7" designation and used the same production numbers as the Fairlane models and Custom series.

FAIRLANE 500 SIX SERIES

Model No.	Body/ Style No.	Body Type & Seating	Factory Price	Shipping Weight	Prod. Total
A7	58B	4-dr Twn Sed-6P	2333	3300	Note 1
A7	64B	2-dr Clb Sed-6P	2281	3285	Note 1
A7	57A	4-dr Twn Vic-6P	2404	3365	Note 1
A7	63A	2-dr Clb Vic-6P	2339	3320	Note 1
A7	76B	2-dr Sun Conv-6P	2505	3475	Note 1

NOTE 1: See Fairlane 500 V-8 series listing. Production was counted by series and body style, with no breakouts per engine type.

FAIRLANE 500 V-8 I.D. NUMBERS: Fairlane 500 V-8 models began with the same engine designations and used the same production numbers as the Fairlane models and the Custom series.

FAIRLANE 500 V-8 SERIES

Model No.	Body/ Style No.	Body Type & Seating	Factory Price	Shipping Weight	Prod. Total
N/A	58B	4-dr Twn Sed-6P	2433	3452	193,162
N/A	64B	2-dr Clb Sed-6P	2381	3407	93,753
N/A	57A	4-dr Twn Vic-6P	2504	3487	68,550
N/A	63A	2-dr Clb Vic-6P	2439	3442	183,202
N/A	76B	2-dr Sun Conv-6P	2605	3497	77,728
N/A	51A	2-dr Sky Conv-6P	2942	3916	20,766

PRODUCTION NOTE: Total series output was 637,161 units. Ford does not indicate the number of each model produced with sixes and V-8s. Therefore, all production figures given above are total production of each body style. "Model Numbers" were now equivalent to V-8 engine code designations, which varied with specific powerplant attachments. All convertibles are two-door styles; all Skyliner retractable convertibles are V-8 powered.

STATION WAGON SERIES — (6-CYL/V-8) — The Ranch Wagon was the base trim level two-door station wagon for 1957. Country Sedans were the intermediate level with four-door styling. Country Squires were the top trim level, also with four-door styling. The level of equipment paralleled Custom, Custom 300 and Fairlane 500 models of passenger cars.

1957 Ford Country Sedan nine-passenger station wagon 6-cyl. (PH)

1957 Ford Country Squire nine-passenger station wagon V-8. (OCW)

STATION WAGON SIX I.D. NUMBERS: Station wagon six-cylinder models began with the same "A7" designation and used the same production numbers as the passenger cars.

STATION WAGON SIX SERIES

Model No.	Body/ Style No.	Body Type & Seating	Factory Price	Shipping Weight	Prod. Total
A7	59A	2-dr Ranch Wag-6P	2301	3396	Note 1
A7	59B	2-dr Del Rio-6P	2397	3405	Note 1
A7	79D	4-dr Cty Sed-6P	2451	3468	Note 1
A7	79C	4-dr Cty Sed-9P	2556	3557	Note 1
A7	79E	4-dr Cty Sq-8P	2684	3571	Note 1

NOTE 1: See station wagon V-8 series listing. Production was counted by series and body style, with no breakouts per engine type.

STATION WAGON V-8 I.D. NUMBERS: Station wagon V-8 models began with the same engine designations and used the same production numbers as the passenger cars.

STATION WAGON V-8 SERIES

Model No.	Body/ Style No.	Body Type & Seating	Factory Price	Shipping Weight	Prod. Total
N/A	59A	2-dr Ranch Wag-6P	2401	3520	60,486
N/A	59B	2-dr Del Rio-6P	2497	3527	46,105
N/A	79D	4-dr Cty Sed-6P	2551	3590	135,251
N/A	79C	4-dr Cty Sed-9P	2656	3679	49,638
N/A	79E	4-dr Cty Sq-8P	2784	3693	27,690

PRODUCTION NOTE: Total series output was 319,170 units. Ford does not indicate the number of each model produced with sixes and V-8s. Therefore, all production figures given above are total production of each body style with both engines. "Model Numbers" were now equivalent to V-8 engine code designations, which varied with specific powerplant attachments. The Country Squire had simulated woodgrain exterior paneling.

THUNDERBIRD SERIES — (V-8) — The 1957 model represented the first significant restyling since the Thunderbird was first introduced. A longer rear section provided improved storage space. Riding and handling qualities were greatly enhanced by relocating the spare tire in the trunk. As with the large Fords, 1957 Thunderbirds featured fins on the rear fenders. Inside, the 1957 model used the instrument panel from full-size 1956 Fords, with an engine-turned insert dressing-up the panel.

THUNDERBIRD V-8 I.D. NUMBERS: Thunderbird models began with the engine designation "C7," "D7," "E7," or "F7" (depending on engine choice). The "F7" indicated the supercharged V-8. The assembly plant code was "F" for Dearborn. The body type code was "H" for Thunderbird. The production number was in series, beginning at 100001 and going up.

1957 Ford Thunderbird two-door convertible (with and without hardtop) V-8. (PH)

THUNDERBIRD SERIES

Model No.	Body/ Style No.	Body Type & Seating	Factory Price	Shipping Weight	Prod. Total
C7/D7/E740		2-dr Conv-2P	3408	3134	21,380

ENGINE [Base Six]: Overhead valve. Cast-iron block. Displacement: 223 cid. Bore and stroke: 3.62 x 3.60 inches. Compression ratio: 8.6:1. Brake hp: 144 at 4200 rpm. Carburetor: Holley one-barrel. Four main bearings. Serial number code "A."

ENGINE [V-8]: Overhead valve. Cast-iron block. Displacement: 272 cid. Bore and stroke: 3.62 x 3.30 inches. Compression ratio: 8.6:1. Brake hp: 190 at 4500 rpm. Carburetor: Holley two-barrel. Five main bearings. Serial number code "B."

ENGINE [Thunderbird V-8]: Overhead valve. Cast-iron block. Displacement: 292 cid. Bore and stroke: 3.75 x 3.30 inches. Compression ratio: 9.1:1. Brake hp: 212 at 4500 rpm. Carburetor: Holley four-barrel. Five main bearings. Serial number code "C."

ENGINE [Thunderbird Special V-8]: Overhead valve. Cast-iron block. Displacement: 312 cid. Bore and stroke: 3.80 x 3.44 inches. Compression ratio: 9.7:1. Brake hp: 245 at 4500 rpm. Carburetor: Holley four-barrel. Five main bearings. Serial number code "D."

ENGINE [Thunderbird Special (8V) V-8]: Overhead valve. Cast-iron block. Displacement: 312 cid. Bore and stroke: 3.80 x 3.44 inches. Compression ratio: 9.7:1 (10.0:1 with Racing Kit). Brake hp: 270 at 4800 rpm. (285 at 5000 rpm. with Racing Kit). Carburetor: two Holley four-barrel. Five main bearings. Serial number code "E."

ENGINE [Thunderbird Special Supercharged V-8]: Overhead valve. Cast-iron block. Displacement: 312 cid. Bore and stroke: 3.80 x 3.44 inches. Compression ratio: 8.5:1. Brake hp: 300 at 4800 rpm. (340 at 5300 rpm.—NASCAR version). Carburetor: Holley four-barrel with McCulloch/Paxton centrifugal supercharger. Five main bearings. Serial number code "F."

CHASSIS FEATURES: Wheelbase: (Custom, Custom 300 and station wagon series) 116 inches; (Fairlane, Fairlane 500) 118 inches; (Thunderbird) 102 inches. Overall length: (Custom, Custom 300) 201.6 inches; (Fairlane 500 Skyliner) 210.8 inches; (all other Fairlane and Fairlane 500) 207.7 inches; (station wagons) 203.5 inches; (Thunderbird) 181.4 inches. Tires: (Custom, Custom 300) 7.50 x 14 four-ply tubeless; (Fairlane, Fairlane 500) 7.50 x 14 four-ply tubeless; (Country Sedans and Country Squires) 8.00 x 14; (Thunderbird) 7.50 x 14 four-ply tubeless.

FORD/THUNDERBIRD OPTIONS: Custom engine option, 292 cid V-8 ($439). Ford-O-Matic for Ford ($188); same for Thunderbird ($215). Automatic overdrive transmission for Ford ($108); same for Thunderbird ($146). Power steering ($68). Radio ($100). Heater and defroster ($85). Thunderbird windshield washers ($10). Power windows, Thunderbird ($70). Engine chrome dress-up kit, Thunderbird ($25). Power brakes ($38). Fairlane/station wagon 312 cid V-8 engine option ($43). Rear fender shields (skirts). Two-tone paint. Back-up lamps. Large wheel covers (standard on Fairlane 500). White sidewall tires. Continental tire extension kit. Outside rearview mirror. Lifeguard safety equipment package. Oversized tires. Radio antenna. Non-glare mirror. Three-speed manual transmission (with semi-centrifugal-type clutch, three-speed helical gears and synchronizers for second and third gears) standard. Three-speed with automatic overdrive was optional. Specifications were the same as above with automatic overdrive function cutting in at 27 mph, cutting out at 21 mph. Approximate drive ratio: 0.70:1. Manual control below instrument panel. Ford-O-Matic automatic transmission was optional. This was a torque converter transmission with automatic planetary geartrain; single-stage, three-element hydraulic torque converter; hydro-mechanical automatic controls with no electric or vacuum connections and power flow through fluid member at all times. Six-cylinder rear axle ratios: (Ford-O-Matic) 3.22:1; (manual transmission) 3.89:1 and (automatic overdrive) 4.11:1. V-8 rear axle ratios: (Ford-O-Matic) 3.10:1; (manual transmission) 3.56:1 and (automatic overdrive) 3.70:1.

HISTORY: Introduction of 1957 Fords and Thunderbirds took place in October 1956. The Fairlane 500 Skyliner with retractable hardtop was introduced as a midyear addition to the line. Overdrive or Ford-O-Matic could now be ordered for any car with any engine. Model year production was 1,655,068 vehicles. Calendar year sales amounted to 1,522,406 Fords and Thunderbirds. Ford out-produced Chevrolet this season, to become America's number one automaker of 1957 (model year basis). The Town Victoria was a four-door pillarless hardtop. The Del Rio was a Deluxe two-door Ranch Wagon in Fairlane level trim. The Club Victoria was a two-door pillarless hardtop coupe. The Sunliner was a conventional two-door convertible.

1958 FORD

1958 Ford Custom 300 four-door hardtop. (OCW)

1958 FORDS — OVERVIEW — Even though 1958 Fords shared the same basic body with 1957 models, there were many new styling ideas. A simulated air scoop hood and honeycomb grille were borrowed from Thunderbird stylists. A sculptured rear deck lid, plus dual headlamps, created a much more futuristic looking car than the previous model. Cruise-O-Matic three-speed automatic transmission was offered for the first time in 1958, as were 332 cid and 352 cid V-8s. Also new for 1958 (and offered only in 1958) was the Ford-Aire suspension system for use in Fairlane series cars and station wagons.

CUSTOM 300 SERIES — (6-CYL/V-8) — The Custom 300 series was the base trim level for 1958 and included chrome window moldings, a horn button instead of a horn ring, one sun visor, an armrest on the driver's door only, and a single chrome strip on the bodyside. This molding began on the side of the front fender, continued horizontally to the back of the front door, then turned down and joined a horizontal chrome strip that continued to the back of the body. A top-of-the-line "Styletone" trim option duplicated this side trim, except the lower horizontal strip was a double strip with a gold anodized insert. A mid-level "Special" trim option was also available with a small horizontal chrome strip that turned upward just behind the door.

CUSTOM 300 SIX I.D. NUMBERS: Ford's coding system for serial numbers can be broken down, as follows: The first symbol designates the engine type: (A) 223 cid six-cylinder; (B) 332 cid V-8; (C) 292 cid V-8; (G) 332 cid V-8; (H) 352 cid V-8. The second symbol designates the model year: '8' for 1958. The third symbol designates the final assembly plant, as follows: A = Atlanta, B = Buffalo; C = Chester; D = Dallas; G = Chicago; F= Dearborn; E = Mahwah; K = Kansas City; L = Long Beach, M = Memphis; N = Norfolk; R = San Jose; U = Louisville; P = Twin City (St. Paul). The fourth symbol designates body type, as follows: C = Fairlane 500 convertible; G = Custom 300 (two-door and four-door); R = Custom 300 Ranch Wagon, Del Rio; T = Fairlane/Fairlane 500 (two-door and four-door); V = Fairlane/Fairlane 500/Victoria (two-door and four-door); W = Retractable hardtop; X = Country Sedan; Y = Country Squire. The fifth through tenth digits indicate the number of the unit built at each assembly plant, beginning with 100001. Custom 300 six-cylinder models began with the designation "A8" followed by assembly plant code, body type code, and, finally, the unit's production number, according to the final assembly location. Each plant began at 100001 and went up.

1958 Ford Custom 300 Styletone four-door sedan 6-cyl. (PH)

CUSTOM 300 SIX SERIES

Model No.	Body/ Style No.	Body Type & Seating	Factory Price	Shipping Weight	Prod. Total
A8	73A	4-dr Sed-6P	2119	3227	Note 1
A8	70A	2-dr Sed-6P	2065	3197	Note 1
A8	70D	2-dr Bus Cpe-3P	1977	3174	Note 1

NOTE 1: See Custom V-8 series listing. Production was counted by series and body style only, with no breakout per engine type.

CUSTOM 300 V-8 I.D. NUMBERS: Custom 300 V-8 models began with the engine designation code, assembly plant code, body type code, and, finally, the unit's production number, according to the final assembly location. Each plant began at 100001 and went up.

CUSTOM V-8 SERIES

Model No.	Body/ Style No.	Body Type & Seating	Factory Price	Shipping Weight	Prod. Total
N/A	73A	4-dr Sed-6P	2256	3319	163,366
N/A	70A	2-dr Sed-6P	2202	3289	173,441
N/A	70D	2-dr Bus Cpe-3P	2114	3266	4,062

PRODUCTION NOTE: Total series output was 340,871 units. Ford does not indicate the number of each model produced with sixes or V-8s. Therefore, all production figures given above are total production of each body style with both engines. Individual "model numbers" are not available.

FAIRLANE MODELS — (6-CYL/V-8) — The Fairlane model was the base trim level for the longer wheelbase Fairlane series. It included chrome window moldings, with slightly less chrome around the "C" pillar than Fairlane 500 models. Also a considerably different side stripe was used compared to the higher-priced model. The base Fairlane side chrome had two strips. The lower molding began at the rear of the front wheel opening, then went straight to the back of the front door. From there it began to gradually curve upward. The upper strip began at the front of the fender and went straight back, to the back of the front door. It then began to curve gradually downward, merging with the lower strip directly over the rear wheel opening. A Fairlane script appeared on the rear fenders and directly above the grille opening. Midyear Fairlanes came with an additional sweep spear of anodized aluminum trim centered in the panel created by the aforementioned trim. In addition, midyear Fairlanes featured three porthole trim pieces on the rear where the Fairlane script would appear.

FAIRLANE SIX I.D. NUMBERS: Fairlane six-cylinder models began with the same "A8" designation and used the same production numbers as the Custom 300 series.

FAIRLANE SIX SERIES

Model No.	Body/ Style No.	Body Type & Seating	Factory Price	Shipping Weight	Prod. Total
A8	58A	4-dr Twn Sed-6P	2250	3376	Note 1
A8	64A	2-dr Clb Sed-6P	2198	3307	Note 1
A8	57B	4-dr Twn Vic-6P	2394	3407	Note 1
A8	63B	2-dr Clb Vic-6P	2329	3328	Note 1

NOTE 1: See Fairlane V-8 series listing. Production was counted by series and body style only, with no breakout per engine type.

FAIRLANE V-8 I.D. NUMBERS: Fairlane V-8 models began with the same engine designations and used the same production numbers as the Custom 300 series.

FAIRLANE V-8 SERIES

Model No.	Body/ Style No.	Body Type & Seating	Factory Price	Shipping Weight	Prod. Total
N/A	58A	4-dr Twn Sed-6P	2374	3468	57,490
N/A	64A	2-dr Clb Sed-6P	2320	3399	38,366
N/A	57B	4-dr Twn Vic-6P	2517	3499	5,868
N/A	63B	2-dr Clb Vic-6P	2453	3420	16,416

PRODUCTION NOTE: Total series output was 118,140 units. Ford does not indicate the number of each model produced with sixes or V-8s. Therefore, all production figures given above are total production of each body style with both engines.

FAIRLANE 500 MODELS — (6-CYL/V-8) — The Fairlane 500 models had the top trim level in the Fairlane series. It included all the trim used in the Fairlane models plus slightly more chrome on the "C" pillars and different side trim. The side trim was a double runner chrome strip with a gold anodized insert. The top chrome strip began on the side of the front fender, sloped slightly, and terminated at the top of the rear bumper. The lower molding split from the upper strip where the front door began, dropped in a modified Fairlane sweep and merged with the upper strip at the rear bumper. Fairlane script appeared above the grille and on the trunk lid while the Fairlane 500 script appeared on the rear fenders, above the chrome side trim.

1958 Ford Fairlane 500 Skyliner two-door retractable hardtop V-8. (OCW)

FAIRLANE 500 SIX I.D. NUMBERS: Fairlane 500 six-cylinder models began with the same "A8" designation and used the same production numbers as the Fairlane models and Custom 300 series.

FAIRLANE 500 SIX SERIES

Model No.	Body/ Style No.	Body Type & Seating	Factory Price	Shipping Weight	Prod. Total
A8	58B	4-dr Twn Sed-6P	2403	3380	Note 1
A8	64B	4-dr Clb Sed-6P	2349	3313	Note 1
A8	57A	4-dr Twn Vic-6P	2474	3419	Note 1
A8	63A	2-dr Clb Vic-6P	2410	3316	Note 1
A8	76B	2-dr Sun Conv-6P	2625	3478	Note 1

NOTE 1: See Fairlane 500 V-8 series listing. Production was counted by series and body style, with no breakouts per engine type.

FAIRLANE 500 V-8 I.D. NUMBERS: Fairlane 500 V-8 models began with the same engine designation and used the same production numbers as the Fairlane models and Custom 300 series.

FAIRLANE 500 V-8 SERIES

Model No.	Body/ Style No.	Body Type & Seating	Factory Price	Shipping Weight	Prod. Total
N/A	58B	4-dr Twn Sed-6P	2527	3510	105,698
N/A	64B	2-dr Clb Sed-6P	2473	3443	34,041
N/A	57A	4-dr Twn Vic-6P	2598	3549	36,059
N/A	63A	2-dr Clb Vic-6P	2534	3446	80,439
N/A	76B	2-dr Sun Conv-6P	2749	3637	35,029
N/A	51A	2-dr Sky Conv-6P	3138	4094	14,713

PRODUCTION NOTE: Total series output was 306,429 units. Ford does not indicate the number of each model produced with sixes and V-8s. Therefore, all production figures given above are total production of each body style with both engines. All convertibles are two-door styles; all Skyliner retractable hardtops are V-8 powered.

1958 Ford Ranchero. (OCW)

1958 Ford Country Sedan station wagon 6-cyl. (PH)

STATION WAGON SERIES — (6-CYL/V-8) — The Ranch Wagon was the base trim level two-door and four-door station wagons for 1958. Country Sedans were intermediate level station wagons and Country Squires were the top trim level.

STATION WAGON SIX I.D. NUMBERS: Station wagon six-cylinder models began with the same "A8" designation and used the same production numbers as the passenger cars.

STATION WAGON SIX SERIES

Model No.	Body/ Style No.	Body Type & Seating	Factory Price	Shipping Weight	Prod. Total
A8	59A	2-dr Ranch Wag-6P	2372	3460	Note 1
A8	79A	4-dr Ranch Wag-6P	2426	3543	Note 1
A8	59B	2-dr Del Rio-6P	2478	3504	Note 1
A8	79D	4-dr Cty Sed-8P	2532	3555	Note 1
A8	79C	4-dr Cty Sed-9P	2639	3625	Note 1
A8	79E	4-dr Cty Sq-9P	2769	3672	Note 1

NOTE 1: See station wagon V-8 series listing. Production was counted by series and body style, with no breakouts per engine type.

STATION WAGON V-8 I.D. NUMBERS: Station wagon V-8 models began with the same engine designations and used the same production numbers as the passenger cars.

STATION WAGON V-8 SERIES

Model No.	Body/ Style No.	Body Type & Seating	Factory Price	Shipping Weight	Prod. Total
N/A	59A	2-dr Ranch Wag-6P	2479	3607	34,578
N/A	79A	4-dr Ranch Wag-6P	2533	3670	32,854
N/A	59B	2-dr Del Rio-6P	2585	3631	12,687
N/A	79D	4-dr Cty Sed-6P	2639	3682	68,772
N/A	79C	4-dr Cty Sed-9P	2746	3752	20,702
N/A	79E	4-dr Cty Sq-9P	2876	3799	15,020

PRODUCTION NOTE: Total series output was 164,613 units. Ford does not indicate the number of each model produced with sixes and V-8s. Therefore, all production figures given above are total production of each body style with both engines. The Country Squire station wagon has simulated woodgrain exterior paneling.

THUNDERBIRD SERIES — (V-8) — 1958 was the first year for the four-passenger "Square Birds." The hardtop was introduced on Jan. 13, 1958, with the convertible not showing up until June of 1958. The new personal Thunderbirds were over 16 inches longer and 1,000 pounds heavier than their 1957 counterparts. The new T-bird featured an extended top with squared-off "C" pillar. It had chrome trim along the base of the top and a small Thunderbird crest directly above the trim. A massive, one-piece bumper surrounded a honeycomb grille. The honeycomb look was duplicated in stamped and painted steel around the four circular taillights. A Thunderbird script appeared on the front fenders and five heavy, cast stripes appeared on the door, at the feature line. Inside, bucket seats and a vinyl-covered console were used for the first time in a Thunderbird. Also for the first time, Thunderbirds were offered as either a hardtop or convertible, each being a separate model.

THUNDERBIRD V-8 I.D. NUMBERS: Thunderbird models began with the engine designation "H8," assembly plant code "Y" (Wixom, Mich.), body type code "H" (Thunderbird), and, finally, the unit's production number, beginning at 100001 and going up.

THUNDERBIRD V-8 SERIES

Model No.	Body/ Style No.	Body Type & Seating	Factory Price	Shipping Weight	Prod. Total
H8	63A	2-dr HT-4P	3630	3708	35,758
H8	76A	2-dr Conv-4P	3914	3903	2,134

ENGINE [Base Six]: Overhead valve. Cast-iron block. Displacement: 223 cid. Bore and stroke: 3.62 x 3.60 inches. Compression ratio: 6.6:1. Brake hp: 145 at 4200 rpm. Carburetor: Holley one-barrel. Four main bearings. Serial number code "A."

1958 Ford Thunderbird sport coupe. (FMC)

1958 Ford Thunderbird two-door convertible V-8. (PH)

ENGINE [V-8]: Overhead valve. Cast-iron block. Displacement: 292 cid. Bore and stroke: 3.75 x 3.30 inches. Compression ratio: 9.1:1. Brake hp: 205 at 4500 rpm. Carburetor: Holley two-barrel. Five main bearings. Serial number code "C."

ENGINE [Interceptor V-8]: Overhead valve. Cast-iron block. Displacement: 332 cid. Bore and stroke: 4.00 x 3.30 inches. Compression ratio: 9.5:1. Brake hp: 240 at 4600 rpm. Carburetor: Holley two-barrel. Five main bearings. Serial number code "B."

ENGINE [Interceptor V-8]: Overhead valve. Cast-iron block. Displacement: 332 cid. Bore and stroke: 4.00 x 3.30 inches. Compression ratio: 9.5:1. Brake hp: 265 at 4600 rpm. Carburetor: Holley four-barrel. Five main bearings. Serial number code "G."

ENGINE [Interceptor Special V-8]: Overhead valve. Cast-iron block. Displacement: 352 cid. Bore and stroke: 4.00 x 3.50 inches. Compression ratio: 10.2:1. Brake hp: 300 at 4600 rpm. Carburetor: Holley four-barrel. Serial number code "H."

CHASSIS FEATURES: Wheelbase: (Custom 300 and station wagons) 116 inches; (Fairlane, Fairlane 500)118 inches; (Thunderbird) 113 inches. Overall length: (Custom 300) 202 inches; (station wagons) 202.7 inches; (Skyliner retractable) 211 inches; (other Fairlanes, Fairlane 500s) 207 inches; (Thunderbird) 205 inches. Overall width: (Fords) 78 inches; (Thunderbirds) 77 inches. Tires: (nine-passenger station wagons) 8.00 x 14; (Skyliner retractable) 8.00 x 14; (all other Fords) 7.50 x 14; (Thunderbirds) 8.00 x 14.

CONVENIENCE OPTIONS: Ford-O-Matic drive ($180). Cruise-O-Matic ($197). Ford-Aire suspension ($156). Overdrive ($108). Power brakes ($37). Power steering ($69). Front power windows ($50); on Custom 300 'business' two-door ($64). Front and rear power windows ($101). Manual four-way adjustable seat ($17). Four-way power adjustable seat ($64). Six-tube radio and antenna ($77). Nine-tube Signal-Seeking radio and antenna ($99). White sidewall tires, four-ply size 7.50 x 14 ($33). White sidewall tires, four-ply, size 6.00 x 14 ($50). Wheel covers ($19 and standard on Fairlane 500). Styletone two-tone paint ($22). Tinted glass ($20). Back-up lights ($10). Custom 300 Deluxe interior trim ($24). Electric clock ($15 and standard on Fairlane 500). Windshield washer ($12). Positive action windshield wiper ($11). Lifeguard safety package with padded instrument panel and sun visors ($19). Lifeguard safety package, as above, plus two front seat belts ($33). Polar Air Conditioner, includes tinted glass ($271). Select Air Conditioner, includes tinted glass ($395). Interceptor 265-hp V-8 in Custom 300 ($196); in Fairlane ($163). Interceptor Special 300-hp V-8 in Fairlane 500 ($159); in station wagon ($150). Note: Interceptor engine prices are in place of base six-cylinder prices. Automatic overdrive ($108). Heater and defroster ($80). Heater and defroster in Fairlanes and station wagons ($85). Power steering, Thunderbird ($69). Heater and defroster, Thunderbird ($95). Whitewall tires, Thunderbird ($36 exchange). Leather interior, Thunderbird ($106). Three-speed manual transmission was standard equipment. It featured semi-centrifugal-type clutch; three-speed helical gears, with synchronizers for second and third gears. Three-speed with automatic overdrive was optional. Specifications were the same as above with automatic overdrive function cutting in at 27 mph, cutting out at 21 mph. Approximate drive ratio: 0.70:1. Manual control below instrument panel. Ford-O-Matic automatic transmission was optional. This was a torque converter transmission with automatic planetary geartrain; single-stage, three-element hydraulic torque converter; hydro-mechanical automatic controls with no electrical or vacuum connections and powerflow through fluid member at all times. Cruise-O-Matic automatic transmission was also optional. This unit was the same as Ford-O-Matic, except for having three-speeds forward. It was a high-performance automatic transmission with two selective drive ranges for smooth 1-2-3 full-power stabs, or 2-3 gradual acceleration and axle ratio of 2.69:1 for fuel economy. Six-cylinder rear axle ratios: (Ford-O-Matic) 3.22:1; (manual transmission) 3.89:1 and (automatic overdrive) 4.11:1. V-8 rear axle ratios: (Cruise-O-Matic) 2.69:1; (Ford-O-Matic) 3.10:1; (manual transmission) 3.56:1 and (automatic overdrive) 3.70:1.

HISTORY: Dealer introductions for 1958 Fords were held Nov. 7, 1957. Dealer introductions for 1958 Thunderbirds were held Feb. 13, 1958. Production at three factories—Memphis, Buffalo and Somerville—was phased out this season. In June 1958, a new plant, having capacity equal to all three aforementioned factories, was opened at Loraine, Ohio. On a model year basis, 74.4 percent of all Fords built in the 1958 run had V-8 power. Sixty-eight percent of these cars had automatic transmission. Model year production of Fords and Thunderbirds totaled 967,945 cars. Calendar year sales of Fords and Thunderbirds peaked at 1,038,560 units. The Thunderbird was, along with the Rambler, one of only two U.S. marques to see sales increases for 1958, a recession year in the United States. The Town Victoria was a four-door pillarless hardtop style. The Club Victoria was a two-door pillarless hardtop style. The Custom 300 two-door sedan was also called the business sedan. The Sunliner was a conventional two-door convertible. The Skyliner was a retractable hardtop.

1959 FORD

1959 FORDS — OVERVIEW — 1959 Fords are considered by many to be the most beautifully styled Fords ever built. They were, in fact, awarded the Gold Medal for Exceptional Styling at the Brussels World Fair. With elegance and understated class, the car showed remarkable good taste. At a time when other car manufacturers were attempting to make their cars look like they were capable of interstellar travel or supersonic speeds, Ford exercised restraint. Ford designers merely swept the rear fender feature lines to the back of the car, formed a housing for the back-up lights and curved the lower portion around an oversized taillight for a startling effect. At the front end, the fenders were flattened across the top and housed the dual headlights. They had a sculptured effect at the sides, where they rolled over the side trim. The 1959 Fords were long, low and had an exceptionally flat hood. There was relatively little chrome trim. Bright colors were used. A new 430 cid/350 hp V-8 engine was optional in Thunderbirds and a wider grille extended from side to side. The parking lights were recessed into the bumper and, late in 1958, a new series called the Galaxie was introduced as the top-line model. Galaxie stylists had adapted the roofline of the Thunderbird to the standard Fairlane 500 body and produced truly beautiful results.

CUSTOM 300 SERIES — (6-CYL/V-8) — The Custom 300 series was the base trim level for 1959 and included chrome window moldings, a horn button instead of horn ring, one sun visor, an armrest only on the driver's door and a single chrome strip on the bodyside. The chrome strip followed the lines of the Fairlane sweep, but used only a single strip.

CUSTOM 300 SIX I.D. NUMBERS: Ford's coding system for serial numbers can be broken down, as follows: The first symbol designates the engine type: (A) 223 cid six-cylinder; (B) 332 cid V-8; (C) 292 cid V-8; (H) 352 cid V-8; (J) 430 cid V-8. The second symbol designates the model year: '9' for 1959. The third symbol designates the final assembly plant, as follows: A = Atlanta, C = Chester; D = Dallas; G = Chicago; F= Dearborn; E = Mahwah; H = Loraine; K = Kansas City; L = Long Beach; N = Norfolk; R = San Jose; U = Louisville; P = Twin City (St. Paul). The fourth symbol designates body type, as follows: C = Convertible; G = Custom 300 (two-door and four-door); R = Ranch Wagon, Country Sedan; S = Fairlane 500, Galaxie (two-door and four-door); T = Fairlane (two-door and four-door); V = Fairlane 500 (two-door and four-door); W = Retractable hardtop; Y = Country Squire. The fifth through tenth digits indicate the number of the unit built at each assembly plant, beginning with 100001. Custom 300 six-cylinder models began with the designation "A9" followed by assembly plant code, body type code, and, finally, the unit's production number, according to the final assembly location. Each plant began at 100001 and went up.

1959 Ford Galaxie four-door Town Victoria V-8. (OCW)

CUSTOM 300 SIX SERIES

Model No.	Body/ Style No.	Body Type & Seating	Factory Price	Shipping Weight	Prod. Total
A9	58E	4-dr Sed-6P	2273	3385	Note 1
A9	64F	2-dr Sed-6P	2219	3310	Note 1
A9	64G	2-dr Bus Cpe-3P	2132	3283	Note 1

NOTE 1: See Custom 300 V-8 series listing. Production was counted by series and body style only, with no breakout per engine type.

CUSTOM 300 V-8 I.D. NUMBERS: Custom 300 V-8 models began with the engine designation code, assembly plant code, body type code, and, finally, the unit's production number, according to the final assembly location. Each plant began at 100001 and went up.

CUSTOM 300 V-8 SERIES

Model No.	Body/ Style No.	Body Type & Seating	Factory Price	Shipping Weight	Prod. Total
N/A	56E	4-dr Sed-6P	2391	3466	249,553
N/A	64F	2-dr Sed-6P	2337	3411	228,573

PRODUCTION NOTE: Total series output was 462,210 units. Ford does not indicate the number of each model produced with sixes or V-8s. Therefore, all production figures given above are total production of each body style with both engines.

FAIRLANE MODELS — (6-CYL/V-8) — The Fairlane model was the intermediate trim level for 1959 and included chrome window moldings, a horn ring, two sun visors, armrests on all doors and a more complicated side trim than that found on the Custom series. The trim was a two-piece design, which could feature an optional silver anodized insert between the two pieces forming the 1959 version of the Fairlane sweep.

FAIRLANE SIX I.D. NUMBERS: Fairlane six-cylinder models began with the same "A9" designation and used the same production numbers as the Custom 300 series.

FAIRLANE SIX SERIES

Model No.	Body/ Style No.	Body Type & Seating	Factory Price	Shipping Weight	Prod. Total
A9	58A	4-dr Twn Sed-6P	2411	3415	Note 1
A9	64A	2-dr Clb Sed-6P	2357	3332	Note 1

NOTE 1: See Fairlane V-8 series listing. Production was counted by series and body style, with no breakouts per engine type.

FAIRLANE V-8 I.D. NUMBERS: Fairlane V-8 models began with the same engine designations and used the same production numbers as the Custom 300 series.

FAIRLANE V-8 SERIES

Model No.	Body/ Style No.	Body Type & Seating	Factory Price	Shipping Weight	Prod. Total
N/A	58A	4-dr Twn Sed-6P	2529	3516	64,663
N/A	64A	2-dr Clb Sed-6P	2475	3433	35,126

PRODUCTION NOTE: Total series output was 97,789 units. Ford does not indicate the number of each model produced with sixes or V-8s. Therefore, all production figures given above are total production of each body style with both engines.

FAIRLANE 500 SERIES — (6-CYL/V-8) — Prior to the introduction of the Galaxie, the Fairlane 500 was the top trim level for 1959, and included all the trim used in the Fairlane series, including the optional insert. In addition, a large aluminum panel surrounded the rear wheel opening and ran to the rear bumper. Optional stainless steel fender skirts could be ordered to expand the large expanse of bright metal trim.

1959 Ford Fairlane 500 Skyliner retractable hardtop. (OCW)

1959 Ford Fairlane 500 two-door Club Victoria V-8. (AA)

FAIRLANE 500 SIX I.D. NUMBERS: Fairlane 500 six-cylinder models began with the same "A9" designation and used the same production numbers as the Fairlane models and Custom 300 models.

FAIRLANE 500 SIX SERIES

Model No.	Body/ Style No.	Body Type & Seating	Factory Price	Shipping Weight	Prod. Total
A9	58B	4-dr Twn Sed-6P	2530	3417	Note 1
A9	64B	2-dr Clb Sed-6P	2476	3338	Note 1
A9	57A	4-dr Twn Vic-6P	2602	3451	Note 1
A9	63A	2-dr Clb Vic-6P	2537	3365	Note 1

NOTE 1: See Fairlane 500 V-8 listing. Production was counted by series and body style, with no breakout per engine type.

FAIRLANE 500 V-8 I.D. NUMBERS: Fairlane 500 V-8 models began with the same engine designation and used the same production numbers as the Fairlane models and Custom 300 models.

FAIRLANE 500 V-8 SERIES

Model No.	Body/ Style No.	Body Type & Seating	Factory Price	Shipping Weight	Prod. Total
N/A	58B	4-dr Twn Sed-6P	2648	3518	35,670
N/A	64B	2-dr Clb Sed-6P	2594	3439	10,141
N/A	57A	4-dr Twn Vic-6P	2720	3552	9,308
N/A	63A	2-dr Clb Vic-6P	2655	3466	23,892

PRODUCTION NOTE: Total series output was 79,011 units. Ford does not indicate the number of each model produced with sixes or V-8s. Therefore, all production figures given above are total production of each body style with both engines.

GALAXIE SERIES — (6-CYL/V-8) — Initially, the Fairlane 500 series was the top-of-the-line 1959 Ford. But shortly after new model introductions in late 1958, the Galaxie lineup was introduced offering the same two- and four-door sedans and hardtops as appeared in the Fairlane 500 series, plus it absorbed the Sunliner and Skyliner models. So, while confusing, the Galaxie became the new top-line series for 1959. The only difference between the Galaxie and the Fairlane 500 was the styling of the top. Galaxies used the standard top with a Thunderbird style "C" pillar. The combination created one of the best looking cars ever to come out of Dearborn.

GALAXIE SIX I.D. NUMBERS: Galaxie six-cylinder models used the same "A9" designation and used the same production numbers as the Custom 300, Fairlane and Fairlane 500 models.

GALAXIE SIX SERIES

Model No.	Body/ Style No.	Body Type & Seating	Factory Price	Shipping Weight	Prod. Total
A9	54A	4-dr Twn Sed-6P	2582	3405	Note 1
A9	64H	2-dr Clb Sed-6P	2528	3377	Note 1
A9	75A	4-dr Twn Vic-6P	2654	3494	Note 1
A9	65A	2-dr Clb Vic-6P	2589	3338	Note 1
A9	76B	2-dr Sun Conv-6P	2839	3527	Note 1

NOTE 1: See Galaxie V-8 series listing. Production was counted by series and body style, with no breakouts per engine type.

GALAXIE V-8 I.D. NUMBERS: Galaxie V-8 models began with the same engine designation and used the same production numbers as the Custom 300, Fairlane and Fairlane 500 models.

GALAXIE V-8 SERIES

Model No.	Body/ Style No.	Body Type & Seating	Factory Price	Shipping Weight	Prod. Total
N/A	54A	4-dr Twn Sed-6P	2700	3506	183,108
N/A	64H	2-dr Clb Sed-6P	2646	3478	52,848
N/A	75A	4-dr Twn Vic-6P	2772	3595	47,726
N/A	65A	2-dr Clb Vic-6P	2707	3439	121,869
N/A	51A	2-dr Sky Conv-6P	3346	4064	12,915*
N/A	76B	2-dr Sun Conv-6P	2957	3626	45,868*

PRODUCTION NOTE: Total series output was 464,336 units. Ford does not indicate the number of each model produced with sixes or V-8s. Therefore, all production figures given above are total production of each body style for both engines. The Sunliner is a conventional two-door convertible. The Skyliner is a retractable hardtop convertible and came only with V-8 power. *The Production Totals for both the Skyliner and Sunliner include those models badged as Fairlane 500s released in late 1958 prior to these two convertible models being absorbed into the new, midyear Galaxie series.

STATION WAGON SERIES — (6-CYL/V-8) — The Ranch Wagons were the base trim level two-door and four-door station wagons for 1959. Country Sedans were the intermediate trim level. Country Squires were the top trim level. The level of equipment paralleled Custom 300, Fairlane and Galaxie models of passenger cars.

STATION WAGON SIX I.D. NUMBERS: Station wagon six-cylinder models began with the same "A9" designation and used the same production numbers as the conventional cars.

STATION WAGON SIX SERIES

Model No.	Body/ Style No.	Body Type & Seating	Factory Price	Shipping Weight	Prod. Total
A9	59C	2-dr Ranch Wag-6P	2567	3590	Note 1
A9	71H	4-dr Ranch Wag-6P	2634	3685	Note 1
A9	59D	2-dr Cty Sed-6P	2678	3613	Note 1
A9	71F	4-dr Cty Sed-6P	2745	3718	Note 1
A9	71E	4-dr Cty Sed-9P	2829	3767	Note 1
A9	71G	4-dr Cty Sq-9P	2958	3758	Note 1

NOTE 1: See station wagon V-8 series listing. Production was counted by series and body style, with no breakout per engine.

STATION WAGON V-8 I.D. NUMBERS: Station wagon V-8 models began with the same engine designations and used the same production numbers as the conventional cars.

STATION WAGON V-8 SERIES

Model No.	Body/ Style No.	Body Type & Seating	Factory Price	Shipping Weight	Prod. Total
N/A	59C	2-dr Ranch Wag-6P	2685	3691	45,558
N/A	71H	4-dr Ranch Wag-6P	2752	3786	67,339
N/A	59D	2-dr Cty Sed-6P	2796	3714	8,663
N/A	71F	4-dr Cty Sed-6P	2863	3819	94,601
N/A	71E	4-dr Cty Sed-9P	2947	3868	28,881
N/A	71G	4-dr Cty Sq-9P	3076	3859	24,336

PRODUCTION NOTE: Total series output was 269,378 units. Ford does not indicate the number of each model produced with sixes or V-8s. Therefore, all production figures given above are total production of each body style for both engines.

THUNDERBIRD SERIES — (V-8) — Thunderbird for 1959 saw only a few cosmetic changes to the basic 1958 body style. The honeycomb grille was replaced by a horizontal bar grille and the new look was duplicated in the small grilles behind the taillights. The four side stripes used on the 1958 model were removed and a chrome arrow took their place on the side. The instrument panel dial faces were white for 1959, instead of the black used in previous years.

THUNDERBIRD V-8 I.D. NUMBERS: Thunderbird models began with the engine designation "H9," assembly plant code "Y" (Wixom, Mich.), body type code and, finally, the unit's production number, beginning at 100001 and going up.

THUNDERBIRD V-8 SERIES

Model No.	Body/ Style No.	Body Type & Seating	Factory Price	Shipping Weight	Prod. Total
H9	63A	2-dr HT-4P	3696	3813	57,195
H9	76A	2-dr Conv-4P	3979	3903	10,261

1959 Ford Country Sedan station wagon V-8. (OCW)

1959 Ford Thunderbird two-door hardtop V-8. (AA)

ENGINE [Base Six]: Overhead valve. Cast-iron block. Displacement: 223 cid. Bore and stroke: 3.62 x 3.60 inches. Compression ratio: 8.6:1. Brake hp: 145 at 4000 rpm. Carburetor: Holley one-barrel. Four main bearings. Serial number code "A."

ENGINE [V-8]: Overhead valve. Cast-iron block. Displacement: 292 cid. Bore and stroke: 3.75 x 3.30 inches. Compression ratio: 8.8:1. Brake hp: 200 at 4400 rpm. Carburetor: Holley two-barrel. Five main bearings. Serial number code "C."

ENGINE [Thunderbird 332 Special V-8]: Overhead valve. Cast-iron block. Displacement: 332 cid. Bore and stroke: 4.00 x 3.30 inches. Compression ratio: 8.9:1. Brake hp: 225 at 4400 rpm. Carburetor: Holley two-barrel. Five main bearings. Serial number code "B."

ENGINE [Thunderbird 352 Special V-8]: Overhead valve. Cast-iron block. Displacement: 352 cid. Bore and stroke: 4.00 x 3.50 inches. Compression ratio: 9.6:1. Brake hp: 300 at 4600 rpm. Carburetor: Holley four-barrel. Five main bearings. Serial number code "H."

ENGINE [Thunderbird 430 Special V-8]: (Available only in Thunderbird and with Cruise-O-Matic transmission only). Overhead valve. Cast-iron block. Displacement: 430 cid. Bore and stroke: 4.30 x 4.70 inches. Compression ratio: 10.0:1. Brake hp: 350 at 4400 rpm. Carburetor: Holly four-barrel. Serial number code "J."

CHASSIS FEATURES: Wheelbase: (Fords) 118 inches; (Thunderbird) 113 inches. Overall length: (Skyliner) 208.1 inches; (all other models) 208 inches. Overall width: (Ford) 76.6 inches; (Thunderbird) 77 inches. Tires: (Thunderbird, Skyliner, nine-passenger station wagons and Sunliner with automatic transmission) 6.00 x 14 four-ply tubeless; (all other models) 7.50 x 14 four-ply tubeless.

FORD OPTIONS: Ford-O-Matic Drive ($190). Cruise-O-Matic ($231). Automatic overdrive ($108). Power brakes ($43). Power steering ($75). Front and rear power window lifts ($102). Four-Way power seat ($64). Radio and push-button antenna ($59). Signal-seeking radio and antenna ($83). Fresh Air heater and defroster ($75). Recirculating heater and defroster ($48). White sidewall tires, four-ply, 7.50 x 14 ($33); 8.00 x 14 ($50). Wheel covers as option ($17). Styletone two-tone paint ($26). Tinted glass ($26). Back-up lights ($10). Custom 300 and Ranch Wagon Deluxe ornamentation package ($32). Electric clock ($15). Windshield washer ($14). Two-speed windshield wipers ($7). Lifeguard safety package including padded instrument panel and sun visor ($19); plus pair of front seat safety belts ($21). Polar Air Conditioner, with tinted glass ($271). Select Aire Conditioner, with tinted glass ($404). Heavy-duty 70-amp battery ($6). Equa-Lock differential ($39). Four-way manual seat ($17). Fairlane side molding ($11). Fairlane 500 rocker panel molding. Thunderbird Special 332 cid/225 hp V-8 ($141 over base six). Thunderbird Special 352 cid/300 hp V-8 ($167 over base six). Standard 292 cid two-barrel V-8, all except Skyliner ($118). Three-speed manual transmission was standard. It featured a semi-centrifugal-type clutch; three-speed helical gears and synchronizers for second and third gears. Three-speed with automatic overdrive was optional. Specifications were the same as above with automatic overdrive function cutting in at 27 mph, cutting out at 21 mph. Approximate drive ratio: 0.70:1. Manual control below instrument panel. Ford-O-Matic transmission was also optional. This was a torque converter transmission with automatic planetary geartrain; single-stage, three-element hydraulic torque converter; hydro-mechanical controls with no electric or vacuum connections and power flow through fluid member at all times. Six-cylinder rear axle gear ratios: (Ford-O-Matic) 3.56:1; (manual transmission) 3.56:1; (optional with automatic overdrive) 3.56:1. V-8 rear axle gear ratios: (Ford-O-Matic with 292 cid V-8) 3.10:1; (Ford-O-Matic with 332/352 cid V-8) 2.91:1; (Cruise-O-Matic with 292 cid V-8) 3.10:1; (Cruise-O-Matic with 332 cid V-8) 2.91:1; Cruise-O-Matic with 352 cid V-8) 2.69:1; (manual transmission) 3.56:1. Equa-Lock rear axle gear ratios: 3.70:1 or 3.10:1.

THUNDERBIRD OPTIONS: Dual-Range Cruise-O-Matic transmission ($242). Overdrive ($145). Power brakes ($43). Power steering ($75). Four-way power driver's seat ($86). Front and rear power windows ($102). Heavy-duty 70-amp battery ($8). Fresh Air heater/defroster ($83). Push-button radio and antenna ($105). Select Air Conditioner ($446). Front seat belts ($23). Back-up lights ($110). Tinted glass ($38). Windshield washer ($14). Outside rearview mirror ($5). Conventional two-tone paint ($26). Full wheel covers ($17). Rear fender shields ($27). Five 6.00 x 14 four-ply rayon white sidewall tubeless tires ($36 exchange). Undercoating ($13). Thunderbird Special 350-hp V-8 ($177); leather interior ($106) and other standard dealer-installed accessories.

HISTORY: Dealer introduction for the 1959 Ford line was held Oct. 17, 1958. Thunderbirds were introduced to the public 10 days later. Model year production of Fords and Thunderbird was 1,462,140 units, while calendar year sales peaked at 1,528,592 cars. Special model nomenclature was similar to previous years. In March 1958, Ford reported it had reduced the cost of making an automobile by $94 per unit between 1954 and 1958. On a model year basis, 78.1 percent of all 1959 Fords had V-8 power and 71.7 percent featured automatic transmission.

1960 FORD

1960 FORDS — OVERVIEW — Fords were totally redesigned from the ground up for 1960. They shared nothing with the previous models except engines and drivelines. While 1960 styling was considered controversial by many, it remains one of the smoothest designs ever to come from the Dearborn drawingboards. The new models were longer, lower and wider than their predecessors and were restrained, especially when compared to some of their contemporaries. All 1960 Fords featured a single chrome strip from the top of the front bumper, sweeping up to the top of the front fender, then back, horizontally along the beltline, to the back of the car. There it turned inward and capped the small horizontal fin. Large semi-circular taillights were housed in an aluminum escutcheon panel below the fins and directly above a large chrome bumper. At the front end, a large, recessed mesh grille housed the dual headlights. The Fairlane series contained the word Ford spaced along the recessed section of the full-width hood and used four cast stripes along the rear quarter panel for trim. The Fairlane script was on the sides of the front fenders. The Galaxie series used a Ford crest in script, on the deck lid and on the front fenders. A single chrome strip began near the center of the front door and continued back to the taillights on the side with a ribbed aluminum stone shield behind the rear wheel opening. This season also saw the introduction of the Falcon. Ford's entrant into the compact car race was a pleasingly styled, uncomplicated little car available in two-door and four-door sedans and station wagons. The styling left little doubt that they were Ford products, but was remarkably simple and attractive.

FAIRLANE SERIES — (6-CYL/V-8) — The Fairlane series was the base trim level for 1960 and included chrome moldings around the windshield and rear windows, two sun visors, armrests on all doors and no extra chrome side trim.

FAIRLANE SIX I.D. NUMBERS: The serial number code can be broken down as follows: First symbol indicates year: 0 = 1960. Second symbol identifies assembly plant, as follows: A = Atlanta, C = Chester; D = Dallas; G = Chicago; F= Dearborn; E = Mahwah; H = Loraine; K = Kansas City; L = Long Beach; N = Norfolk; R = San Jose; S = Pilot Plant; T = Metuchen; U = Louisville; P = Twin Cities; Y = Wixom. Third and fourth symbols identify body series (see Body/ Numbers below). Fifth symbol identifies engine code, as follows: V = 223 cid six-cylinder; W = 292 cid V-8 with two-barrel carb; Y = 352 cid V-8 with four-barrel carb; S = 144 cid six-cylinder (Falcon); J = 430 cid V-8 (Thunderbird). The last six digits are the unit's production number, beginning at 100001 and going up, at each of the assembly plants. Fairlane six-cylinder models began with the number 0 followed by the assembly plant code, body type code, engine designation and, finally, the unit's production number, according to the final assembly location.

FAIRLANE SIX SERIES

Model No.	Body/ Style No.	Body Type & Seating	Factory Price	Shipping Weight	Prod. Total
V	32	4-dr Sed-6P	2311	3605	Note 1
V	31	2-dr Sed-6P	2257	3531	Note 1
V	32	2-dr Bus Cpe-3P	2170	3504	Note 1

NOTE 1: See Fairlane V-8 series listing. Production was counted by series and body style only, with no breakout per engine type.

FAIRLANE V-8 I.D. NUMBERS: Fairlane V-8 models began with the number '0', followed by assembly plant code, body type code, engine designation code and, finally, the unit's production number.

1960 Ford Fairlane 500 four-door sedan 6-cyl. (OCW)

FAIRLANE V-8 SERIES

Model No.	Body/ Style No.	Body Type & Seating	Factory Price	Shipping Weight	Prod. Total
N/A	32	4-dr Sed-6P	2424	3706	110,373
N/A	31	2-dr Sed-6P	2370	3632	93,561
N/A	33	2-dr Bus Cpe-3P	2283	3605	1,733

PRODUCTION NOTE: Total series output was 205,667 units. This figure included 572 Custom 300 four-door sedans and 302 Custom 300 two-door sedans that were used in fleets (taxis, police cruisers, etc.). Ford does not indicate the number of each model produced with sixes and V-8s. Therefore, all production figures given above are total production of each body style with both engines.

FAIRLANE 500 SERIES — (6-CYL/V-8) — The Fairlane 500 was the intermediate trim level and included all the Fairlane trim plus five "delta wing" chrome stripes on the rear fenders (only on two-door Club Sedans) and the Fairlane crest on the hood.

FAIRLANE 500 SIX I.D. NUMBERS: Fairlane 500 six-cylinder models used the same serial number sequence as the Fairlane models.

FAIRLANE 500 SIX SERIES

Model No.	Body/ Style No.	Body Type & Seating	Factory Price	Shipping Weight	Prod. Total
V	42	4-dr Twn Sed-6P	2388	3609	Note 1
V	41	2-dr Clb Sed-6P	2334	3535	Note 1

NOTE 1: See Fairlane 500 V-8 series listing. Production was counted by series and body style only, with no breakout per engine type.

FAIRLANE 500 V-8 I.D. NUMBERS: Fairlane 500 V-8 models used the same serial number sequence as the Fairlane models.

FAIRLANE 500 V-8 SERIES

Model No.	Body/ Style No.	Body Type & Seating	Factory Price	Shipping Weight	Prod. Total
N/A	42	4-dr Twn Sed-6P	2501	3710	153,234
N/A	41	2-dr Clb Sed-6P	2447	3636	91,041

PRODUCTION NOTE: Total series output was 244,275 units. Ford does not indicate the number of each produced with sixes or V-8s. Therefore, all production figures given above are total production of each body style with both engines.

GALAXIE AND GALAXIE SPECIAL SERIES — (6-CYL/V-8) — The Galaxie and Galaxie Special series were the top trim level for 1960 and included chrome "A" pillar moldings, chrome window moldings, horizontal chrome strip on the side of the body, ebbed aluminum stone shields behind the rear wheels, Galaxie script on the front fenders and trunk lid and the Ford crest on the hood. The Galaxie Special series included the Starliner and Sunliner with all the high-level trim, except that the Galaxie script on the trunk lid was replaced with either the Sunliner or Starliner script.

GALAXIE AND GALAXIE SPECIAL SIX I.D. NUMBERS: Galaxie and Galaxie Special six-cylinder models used the same serial number sequence as the Fairlane series.

GALAXIE AND GALAXIE SPECIAL SIX SERIES

Model No.	Body/ Style No.	Body Type & Seating	Factory Price	Shipping Weight	Prod. Total
V	52	4-dr Twn Sed-6P	2603	3633	Note 1
V	51	2-dr Clb Sed-6P	2549	3552	Note 1
V	54	4-dr Twn Vic-6P	2788	3752	Note 1
V	53	2-dr Star HT-6P	2610	3566	Note 1
V	55	2-dr Sun Conv-6P	2860	3750	Note 1

NOTE 1: See Galaxie and Galaxie Special V-8 series listing. Production was counted by series and body style only, with no breakout per engine type.

1960 Ford Galaxie Special Sunliner two-door convertible V-8. (PH)

GALAXIE AND GALAXIE SPECIAL V-8 I.D. NUMBERS Galaxie and Galaxie Special V-8 models used the same serial number sequence as the Fairlane series.

GALAXIE AND GALAXIE SPECIAL V-8 SERIES

Model No.	Body/ Style No.	Body Type & Seating	Factory Price	Shipping Weight	Prod. Total
N/A	52	4-dr Twn Sed-6P	2716	3734	103,784
N/A	51	2-dr Clb Sed-6P	2662	3653	31,866
N/A	54	4-dr Twn Vic-6P	2901	3853	40,215
N/A	53	2-dr Star HT-6P	2723	3667	68,641
N/A	55	2-dr Sun Conv-6P	2973	3841	44,762

PRODUCTION NOTE: Total series output was 289,268 units. Ford does not indicate the number of each model produced with sixes or V-8s. Therefore, all production figures given above are total production of each body style with both engines.

STATION WAGON SERIES — (6-CYL/V-8) — The Ranch Wagon was the base trim level station wagon, Country Sedans were the intermediate level of equipment and Country Squires were the top trim level. The level of equipment paralleled Fairlane, Fairlane 500 and Galaxie models of passenger cars.

STATION WAGON SIX I.D. NUMBERS: Station wagon six-cylinder models used the same serial number sequence as Fairlane and Galaxie models of passenger cars.

1960 Ford Country Squire nine-passenger station wagon V-8. (PH)

1960 Ford Ranchero. (OCW)

STATION WAGON SIX SERIES

Model No.	Body/ Style No.	Body Type & Seating	Factory Price	Shipping Weight	Prod. Total
V	61	2-dr Ranch Wag-6P	2586	3830	Note 1
V	62	4-dr Ranch Wag-6P	2656	3947	Note 1
V	64	4-dr Cty Sed-6P	2752	3961	Note 1
V	66	4-dr Cty Sed-9P	2837	4007	Note 1
V	68	4-dr Cty Sq-9P	2967	4021	Note 1

STATION WAGON V-8 I.D. NUMBERS: Station wagon V-8 models used the same serial number sequence as Fairlane and Galaxie models of passenger cars.

STATION WAGON V-8 SERIES

Model No.	Body/ Style No.	Body Type & Seating	Factory Price	Shipping Weight	Prod. Total
N/A	61	2-dr Ranch Wag-6P	2699	3931	27,136
N/A	62	4-dr Ranch Wag-6P	2769	4048	43,872
N/A	64	4-dr Cty Sed-6P	2865	4062	59,302
N/A	66	4-dr Cty Sed-9P	2950	4108	19,277
N/A	68	4-dr Cty Sq-9P	3080	4122	22,237

PRODUCTION NOTE: Total series output was 171,824 units. Ford does not indicate the number of each model produced with sixes or V-8s. Therefore, all production figures given above are total production of each body style with both engines.

FALCON SERIES — (6-CYL) — The Falcon was Ford's contribution to the compact car field. While being nearly three feet shorter overall than the full-size Fords, the Falcon offered an interior spacious enough for occupants more than six-feet tall. The compact station wagon offered more than enough cargo space for the majority of buyers. Falcon styling was simple and ultra-conservative. The body was slab-sided, with just a slightly recessed feature line. Two single headlights were mounted inside the grille opening and the grille itself was an aluminum stamping consisting of horizontal and vertical bars. The name Ford appeared on the hood, in front of the power bulge-type simulated scoop. At the rear, the word Falcon, in block letters, appeared between the two round taillights. Power was supplied by a 144 cid six-cylinder engine. Transmission choices included the standard three-speed synchromesh manual transmission or optional two-speed Ford-O-Matic automatic transmission.

FALCON SIX I.D. NUMBERS: Falcon models used the same serial number sequence as the full-size Fords, except the engine code was "S."

FALCON SIX SERIES

Model No.	Body/ Style No.	Body Type & Seating	Factory Price	Shipping Weight	Prod. Total
S	58A	4-dr Sed-6P	1974	2317	167,896
S	64A	2-dr Sed-6P	1912	2282	193,470
S	71A	4-dr Sta Wag-6P	2287	2575	46,758
S	59A	2-dr Sta Wag-6P	2225	2540	27,552

PRODUCTION NOTE: Total series output was 435,676 units.

1960 Ford Falcon four-door sedan 6-cyl. (PH)

1960 Ford Falcon two-door station wagon 6-cyl. (PH)

1960 Ford Falcon two-door sedan 6-cyl. (PH)

THUNDERBIRD SERIES — (V-8) — The 1960 Thunderbird used the same body as the previous two years, with only trim updating. This was the last of the 'Square Birds,' with the highly sculptured fender and body lines. The grille was the same pattern of small squares used in 1957 and was located behind a large horizontal chrome bar with three vertical dividers. The grille pattern was duplicated behind the taillights. Three taillights were used per side, instead of two, as in previous years. The Thunderbird script, unique to 1960, appeared on the door. Script in other years was sometimes shared (1963-'64). The 430 cid V-8 was again an option available only with automatic transmission. The most significant change for 1960 was the addition of a manually-operated sun roof and 2,536 cars were produced with this option.

THUNDERBIRD V-8 I.D. NUMBERS: Thunderbird models began with the number '0', assembly plant code 'Y' (Wixom), body type code, engine type code 'Y' or 'J' and, finally, the unit's production number beginning at 100001 and going up.

THUNDERBIRD V-8 SERIES

Model No.	Body/ Style No.	Body Type & Seating	Factory Price	Shipping Weight	Prod. Total
Y/J	71	2-dr HT Cpe-4P	3755	3799	80,938
Y/J	73	2-dr Conv-4P	4222	3897	11,860

ENGINE [Falcon Base Six]: Overhead valve. Cast-iron block. Displacement: 144 cid. Bore and stroke: 3.50 x 2.50 inches. Compression ratio: 8.7:1. Brake hp: 85 at 4200 rpm. Carburetor: Holley one-barrel. Four main bearings. Serial number code "S" ("D" on export models).

ENGINE [Ford Base Six]: Overhead valve. Cast-iron block. Displacement: 223 cid. Bore and stroke: 3.62 x 3.60 inches. Compression ratio: 8.4:1. Brake hp: 145 at 4000 rpm. Carburetor: Holley single barrel. Four main bearings. Serial number code "V."

ENGINE [V-8]: Overhead valve. Cast-iron block. Displacement: 292 cid. Bore and stroke: 3.75 x 3.30 inches. Compression ratio: 8.8:1. Brake hp: 185 at 4200 rpm. Carburetor: Holley two-barrel. Five main bearings. Serial number code "W."

ENGINE [Interceptor V-8]: Overhead valve. Cast-iron block. Displacement: 352 cid. Bore and stroke: 4.00 x 3.50 inches. Compression ratio: 8.9:1. Brake hp: 235 at 4400 rpm. Carburetor: Holley two-barrel. Five main bearings. Serial number code "X" ("G" on export models).

ENGINE [Interceptor Special V-8]: Overhead valve. Cast-iron block. Displacement: 352 cid. Bore and stroke: 4.00 x 3.50 inches. Compression ratio: 9.6:1. Brake hp: 300 at 4600 rpm. Carburetor: Holley four-barrel. Five main bearings. Serial number code "Y."

ENGINE [Interceptor Special V-8]: Overhead valve. Cast-iron block. Displacement: 352 cid. Bore and stroke: 4.00 x 3.50 inches. Compression ratio: 10.6:1. Brake hp: 360 at 6000 rpm. Carburetor: Holley four-barrel. Five main bearings. Serial number code "R."

1960 Ford Thunderbird two-door hardtop (with sun roof option) V-8. (OCW)

1960 Ford Thunderbird two-door convertible V-8. (PH)

ENGINE [Thunderbird Special V-8]: Overhead valve. Cast-iron block. Displacement: 430 cid. Bore and stroke: 4.30 x 3.50 inches. Compression ratio: 10.2:1. Brake hp: 350 at 4400 rpm. Carburetor: Holley four-barrel. Five main bearings. Serial number code "J."

CHASSIS FEATURES: Wheelbase: (Fords and Thunderbird) 119 inches; (Falcon) 109.5 inches. Overall length: (Fords) 213.7 inches; (Thunderbird) 205.32 inches; (Falcon passenger cars) 181.2 inches; (Falcon station wagons) 189 inches. Overall width: (Fords) 81.5 inches; (Thunderbird) 77 inches; (Falcon) 70 inches. Overall height: (Fords) 55 inches; (Thunderbird) 52.5 inches; (Falcon) 54.5 inches. Tires: (Ford passenger cars, closed body) 7.50 x 14; (Ford convertibles and station wagons and Thunderbird) 8.00 x 14; (Falcon passenger cars) 6.00 x 13; (Falcon station wagon) 6.50 x 13.

FORD OPTIONS: Standard 185-hp V-8 engine ($113). Two-barrel 235-hp V-8 ($147.80). Four-barrel 300-hp V-8 ($177.40). Polar Air conditioning, including tinted glass and V-8 ($271). Select Air air conditioning, including tinted glass and V-8 ($404). Back-up lights ($11). Heavy-duty 70-amp battery ($8). Equa-Lock differential ($39). Electric clock ($15). Fresh Air heater/defroster ($75). Recirculating heater/defroster ($47). Four-way manual seat ($11). Rocker panel molding ($14). Padded dash and visors ($25). Two-tone paint ($19). Power brakes ($43). Power seat ($64). Power steering ($77). Front and rear power windows ($102). Push-button radio and antenna ($59). Front seat belts ($21). Tinted glass ($43). Cruise-O-Matic ($211). Ford-O-Matic with six-cylinder ($180). Ford-O-Matic with V-8 ($190). Overdrive ($108). Wheel covers ($17). Windshield washer ($14). Two-speed windshield wipers ($10). Tires—Ford offered numerous tire options such as white sidewall and oversized models.

FALCON OPTIONS: Heavy-duty battery ($8). Deluxe trim package ($66). Fresh Air heater/defroster ($68). Two-tone paint ($17). Manual radio and antenna ($54). Safety equipment: padded dash and visors ($19). Front seat safety belts ($21). Whitewall tires ($29). Automatic transmission ($159). Wheel covers ($18). Windshield washer ($13). Electric windshield wiper ($10).

THUNDERBIRD OPTIONS: Cruise-O-Matic ($242). Overdrive ($145). Radio and antenna ($113). Fresh Air heater ($83). Air conditioner ($466). Tinted glass ($38). White sidewall tires, rayon, size 8.00 x 14 ($36). White sidewall tires, nylon, size 8.00 x 14 ($64). Engine, V-8, 350 hp ($177). Power steering ($75). Power windows ($102). Power brakes ($43). Four-Way power driver's seat ($92). Outside, left or right mirror ($5). Back-up lights ($10). Windshield washers ($14). Rear fender shield ($27). Front seat belts ($23). Leather interior

($106). Heavy-duty 70-amp battery, standard on convertible, on other models ($8). Two-tone paint ($26). Underseal ($14). Sliding roof for hardtop ($212).

HISTORY: All three lines of 1960 Fords were introduced to the public on Oct. 8, 1959. Falcon station wagons were added to the new compact series in March 1960. Although Ford did not provide production breakouts by engine type, trade publications recorded that 67.5 percent of all Fords (excluding Thunderbirds and Falcons) had V-8 engines installed. All Falcons were sixes and all Thunderbirds were V-8 powered. Automatic transmissions were installed in 67.1 percent of all Fords, 44.5 percent of all Falcons and 97.9 percent of all Thunderbirds built during the model run. Ford's share of the overall automobile market dropped to 22.55 percent this year, compared to 27.33 percent in 1959. Model year production peaked at 911,034 Fords, 435,676 Falcons and 92,843 Thunderbirds. Model year series production was as follows: (Custom 300) 900; (Fairlane) 204,700; (Fairlane 500) 244,300; (Galaxie) 289,200; (station wagon) 171,800; (Thunderbird) 92,800. Just 297,400 six-cylinder Fords were produced for the model year.

1961 FORD

1961 FORDS — OVERVIEW — 1961 saw the third major restyling of the full-size Ford line in as many years. From the beltline down, the 1961 Fords were completely new. The upper body structure was retained from the 1960 lineup. A full-width concave grille with a horizontal dividing bar highlighted front end styling. The Ford name, in block letters, replaced the crest used in previous years on Fairlane models and the series designation appeared on the front fenders, behind the headlights. The horizontal full-length fin, used in 1960, was replaced with a smaller canted fin, nearly identical in size and shape to the fin used on 1957-1958 Custom series cars. Large, round taillights were used once again. A horizontal chrome strip, similar to one used on 1960 models, was used once again. It was complemented by a ribbed, aluminum stone guard on the Galaxie series. The year 1961 saw the beginning of the great horsepower race of the 1960s, and Ford cracked the magic 400 barrier with a new engine, the 390 cid/401 hp V-8. The Falcon continued virtually unchanged from 1960, with only an updated convex grille in place of the concave unit used the previous year. A 170 cid six-cylinder engine became optional throughout the line. The biggest styling changes for 1961 took place in the Thunderbird series. Replacing the 1958-1960 'Square Bird' was a much longer, more rounded Thunderbird. A massive front bumper surrounded the grille, which was stamped aluminum and carried a horizontal grid pattern. A single chrome strip began at the top of the front bumpers, swept up and back, and outlined the small, canted fins back to the taillights. Four cast stripes were stacked on the side, immediately in front of the taillights. A smooth deck lid replaced the heavily sculptured lid used during the previous three years. Two large, round taillights replaced the six lights used in 1960. Beginning in 1961, Cruise-O-Matic transmission, power steering and power brakes became standard equipment on all Thunderbirds.

FAIRLANE SERIES — (6-CYL/V-8) — The Fairlane series was the base trim level for 1961 and included chrome moldings around the windshield and rear window, two sun visors, a horn button instead of horn ring, armrest on all doors and no extra side chrome.

FAIRLANE SIX I.D. NUMBERS: The serial number code can be broken down as follows: First symbol indicates year: 1 = 1961. Second symbol identifies assembly plant, as follows: A = Atlanta; C = Chester; D = Dallas; G = Chicago; F = Dearborn; E = Mawah; H = Loraine; J = Los Angeles; K = Kansas City; L = Long Beach; N = Norfolk; R = San Jose; S = Pilot Plant; T = Metuchen; U = Louisville; P = Twin Cities; W = Wixom. Third and fourth symbols identify body series (see Body/Numbers below). Fifth symbol identifies engine code, as follows: U = 170 cid six-cylinder; V = 223 cid six-cylinder; W = 292 cid V-8; X = 352 cid V-8 with two-barrel carb; Z = 390 cid V-8 with four-barrel carb; S = 144 cid six-cylinder. The last six digits are the unit's production number, beginning at 100001 and going up, at each of the assembly plants. Fairlane six-cylinder models began with the number '1' followed by the assembly plant code, body type code, engine designation 'V' and, finally, the unit's production number according to the final assembly location. Each plant began at 100001 and went up.

FAIRLANE SIX SERIES

Model No.	Body/ Style No.	Body Type & Seating	Factory Price	Shipping Weight	Prod. Total
V	32	4-dr Twn Sed-6P	2315	3585	Note 1
V	31	4-dr Clb Sed-6P	2261	3487	Note 1

NOTE 1: See Fairlane V-8 series listing. Production was counted by series and body style only, with no breakouts per engine type.

1961 Ford Fairlane four-door Town Sedan 6-cyl. (OCW)

FAIRLANE V-8 I.D. NUMBERS: Fairlane V-8 models began with the number '1,' followed by assembly plant code, body type code, engine designation code and, finally, the unit's production number according to final assembly location. Each plant began at 100001 and went up.

FAIRLANE V-8 SERIES

Model No.	Body/ Style No.	Body Type & Seating	Factory Price	Shipping Weight	Prod. Total
N/A	32	4-dr Twn Sed-6P	2431	3683	66,924
N/A	31	2-dr Clb Sed-6P	2377	2685	97,208

PRODUCTION NOTE: Total series output was 164,132 units. This figure includes 303 Custom 300 four-door sedans and 49 Custom 300 two-door sedans that were used in fleet service (taxis, police cruisers, etc.). Ford does not indicate the number of each model produced with sixes or V-8s. Therefore, all production figures given above are total production of each body style with both engines.

FAIRLANE 500 SERIES — (6-CYL/V-8) — The Fairlane 500 was the intermediate trim level and included all the Fairlane trim plus a chrome horn ring and a single horizontal chrome strip running from the back of the front wheelwell to the rear bumper.

FAIRLANE 500 SIX I.D. NUMBERS: Fairlane 500 six-cylinder models used the same serial number sequence as the Fairlane models.

FAIRLANE 500 SIX SERIES

Model No.	Body/ Style No.	Body Type & Seating	Factory Price	Shipping Weight	Prod. Total
V	42	4-dr Twn Sed-6P	2430	3593	Note 1
V	41	2-dr Clb Sed-6P	2376	3502	Note 1

NOTE 1: See Fairlane 500 V-8 series listing. Production was counted by series and body style, with no breakouts per engine type.

FAIRLANE 500 V-8 I.D. NUMBERS: Fairlane 500 V-8 models used the same serial number sequence as the Fairlane models.

FAIRLANE 500 V-8 SERIES

Model No.	Body/ Style No.	Body Type & Seating	Factory Price	Shipping Weight	Prod. Total
N/A	42	4-dr Twn Sed-6P	2546	3691	98,917
N/A	41	4-dr Clb Sed-6P	2492	3600	42,468

PRODUCTION NOTE: Total series output was 141,385 units. Ford does not indicate the number of each model produced with sixes or V-8s. Therefore, all production figures given above are total production of each body style with both engines.

GALAXIE SERIES — (ALL ENGINES) — The Galaxie series was the top trim level for 1961 and included chrome 'A' pillar moldings; chrome window moldings; horizontal chrome strip on the side of the body; ribbed aluminum stone shield behind the rear wheel opening; a stamped aluminum escutcheon panel between the taillights (duplicating the pattern of the grille) and either Galaxie, Starliner or Sunliner script on the trunk lid.

GALAXIE SIX I.D. NUMBERS: Galaxie six-cylinder models used the same serial number sequence as the Fairlane series.

GALAXIE SIX SERIES

Model No.	Body/ Style No.	Body Type & Seating	Factory Price	Shipping Weight	Prod. Total
V	52	4-dr Twn Sed-6P	2590	3570	Note 1
V	51	2-dr Clb Sed-6P	2536	3488	Note 1
V	54	4-dr Twn Vic-6P	2662	3588	Note 1
V	57	2-dr Clb Vic-6P	2597	3545	Note 1
V	53	2-dr Star HT-6P	2597	3517	Note 1
V	55	2-dr Sun Conv-6P	2847	3694	Note 1

NOTE 1: See Galaxie V-8 series listing. Production was counted by series and body style, with no breakouts per engine type.

1961 Ford Galaxie Starliner two-door hardtop. (OCW)

GALAXIE V-8 I.D. NUMBERS: Galaxie V-8 models used the same serial number sequence as the Fairlane series.

GALAXIE V-8 SERIES

Model No.	Body/ Style No.	Body Type & Seating	Factory Price	Shipping Weight	Prod. Total
N/A	52	4-dr Twn Sed-6P	2706	3668	141,823
N/A	51	2-dr Clb Sed-6P	2652	3586	27,760
N/A	54	4-dr Twn Vic-6P	2778	3686	30,342
N/A	57	2-dr Clb Vic-6P	2713	3643	75,437
N/A	53	2-dr Star HT-6P	2713	3615	29,669
N/A	55	2-dr Sun Conv-6P	2963	3792	44,614

PRODUCTION NOTE: Total series output was 349,665 units. Ford does not indicate the number of each model produced with sixes or V-8s. Therefore, all production figures are total production of each body style with each engine.

1961 Ford Galaxie Starliner two-door hardtop V-8. (PH)

1961 Ford Country Squire station wagon V-8. (OCW)

STATION WAGON SERIES — (6-CYL/V-8) — The Ranch Wagon was the base trim level station wagon, Country Sedans were the intermediate level and Country Squires were the top trim level. The level of equipment paralleled Fairlane, Fairlane 500 and Galaxie models of passenger cars.

STATION WAGON SIX I.D. NUMBERS: Station wagon six-cylinder models used the same serial number sequence as Fairlane, Fairlane 500 and Galaxie series passenger cars.

STATION WAGON SIX SERIES

Model No.	Body/ Style No.	Body Type & Seating	Factory Price	Shipping Weight	Prod. Total
V	61	2-dr Ranch Wag-6P	2586	3816	Note 1
V	62	4-dr Ranch Wag-6P	2656	3911	Note 1
V	64	4-dr Cty Sed-6P	2752	3934	Note 1
V	66	4-dr Cty Sed-9P	2656	3962	Note 1
V	67	4-dr Cty Sq-6P	2941	3930	Note 1
V	68	4-dr Cty Sq-9P	3011	3966	Note 1

NOTE 1: See station wagon V-8 series listing. Production was counted by series and body style, with no breakouts per engine type.

STATION WAGON V-8 I.D. NUMBERS: Station wagon V-8 models used the same serial number sequence as Fairlane, Fairlane 500 and Galaxie models of passenger cars.

STATION WAGON V-8 SERIES

Model No.	Body/ Style No.	Body Type & Seating	Factory Price	Shipping Weight	Prod. Total
N/A	61	2-dr Ranch Wag-6P	2702	3914	12,042
N/A	62	4-dr Ranch Wag-6P	2772	4009	30,292
N/A	64	4-dr Cty Sed-6P	2868	4032	46,311
N/A	66	4-dr Cty Sed-9P	2972	4060	16,356
N/A	67	4-dr Cty Sq-6P	3057	4036	16,961
N/A	68	4-dr Cty Sq-9P	3127	4064	14,657

PRODUCTION NOTE: Total series output was 136,619 units. Ford does not indicate the number of each model produced with sixes or V-8s. Therefore, all production figures given above are total production of each body style with both engines.

FALCON SERIES — (6-CYL) — The Falcon continued unchanged from 1961, with the exception of a new convex grille. A new 170 cid six-cylinder engine was added to the lineup and the Futura two-door sedan was added to give a sporty flair to the compact car line. The Futura was the same body shell, but equipped with a bucket seat interior and a center console.

FALCON SIX I.D. NUMBERS: Falcon models used the same serial number sequence as the full-size Fords, except the engine code was either 'S' or 'U.'

FALCON SIX SERIES

Model No.	Body/ Style No.	Body Type & Seating	Factory Price	Shipping Weight	Prod. Total
S/U	12	4-dr Sed-6P	1974	2289	159,761
S/U	11	2-dr Sed-6P	1912	2254	149,982
S/U	17	2-dr Futura Sed-5P	2160	2322	44,470
S/U	22	4-dr Sta Wag-6P	2268	2558	87,933
S/U	21	2-dr Sta Wag-6P	2225	2525	32,045

PRODUCTION NOTE: Total series output was 474,191 units.

THUNDERBIRD SERIES — (V-8) — The 1961 Thunderbirds were totally new cars. They were longer, lower, wider and heavier than the previous year's model. Cruise-O-Matic automatic transmission, power steering, power brakes and the new 390 cid V-8 engine were standard equipment on all Thunderbirds for 1961.

1961 Ford Falcon four-door sedan 6-cyl. (PH)

1961 Ford Thunderbird two-door hardtop V-8. (OCW)

THUNDERBIRD V-8 I.D. NUMBERS: Thunderbird models began with the number '1,' assembly plant code 'Y' (Wixom), body type code, engine type code 'Z' and, finally, the unit's production number beginning at 100001 and going up.

THUNDERBIRD V-8 SERIES

Model No.	Body/ Style No.	Body Type & Seating	Factory Price	Shipping Weight	Prod. Total
Z	71	2-dr HT Cpe-4P	4170	3958	62,535
Z	73	2-dr Conv-4P	4637	4130	10,516

ENGINE [Falcon Base Six]: Overhead valve. Cast-iron block. Displacement: 144 cid. Bore and stroke: 3.50 x 2.50 inches. Compression ratio: 6.7:1. Brake hp: 65 at 4200 rpm. Carburetor: Holley one-barrel. Four main bearings. Serial number code "S" ("D" on export models).

ENGINE [Falcon Six]: Overhead valve. Cast-iron block. Displacement: 170 cid. Bore and stroke: 3.50 x 2.94 inches. Compression ratio: 8.7:1. Brake hp: 101 at 4400 rpm. Carburetor: Holley one-barrel. Four main bearings. Serial number code "U."

ENGINE [Ford Base Six]: Overhead valve. Cast-iron block. Displacement: 223 cid. Bore and stroke: 3.62 x 3.60 inches. Compression ratio: 6.4:1. Brake hp: 135 at 4000 rpm. Carburetor: Holley one-barrel. Four main bearings. Serial number code "V."

ENGINE [V-8]: Overhead valve. Cast-iron block. Displacement: 292 cid. Bore and stroke: 3.75 x 3.30 inches. Compression ratio: 8.8:1. Brake hp: 175 at 4200 rpm. Carburetor: Holley two-barrel. Five main bearings. Serial number code "W" ("T" on export models).

ENGINE [Interceptor V-8]: Overhead valve. Cast-iron block. Displacement: 352 cid. Bore and stroke: 4.00 x 3.50 inches. Compression ratio: 8.9:1. Brake hp: 220 at 4400 rpm. Carburetor: Holley two-barrel. Five main bearings. Serial number code "X."

ENGINE [Thunderbird V-8]: Overhead valve. Cast-iron block. Displacement: 390 cid. Bore and stroke: 4.05 x 3.78 inches. Compression ratio: 9.6:1. Brake hp: 300 at 4600 rpm. Carburetor: Holley four-barrel. Five main bearings. Serial number code "Z."

1961 Ford Thunderbird two-door convertible V-8. (OCW)

ENGINE [Thunderbird Special V-8]: Overhead valve. Cast-iron block. Displacement: 390 cid. Bore and stroke: 4.05 x 3.78 inches. Compression ratio: 10.6:1. Brake hp: 375 at 6000 rpm. Carburetor: Holley four-barrel. Five main bearings. Serial number code "Z" and "Q" ("R" on export models).

ENGINE [Thunderbird Special (6V) V-8]: Overhead valve. Cast-iron block. Displacement: 390 cid. Bore and stroke: 4.05 x 3.78 inches. Compression ratio: 10.6:1. Brake hp: 401 at 6000 rpm. Carburetor: three Holley two-barrel. Five main bearings. Serial number code "Z."

CHASSIS FEATURES: Wheelbase: (Thunderbird) 113 inches; (Falcon) 109.5 inches; (all other models) 119 inches. Overall length: (Thunderbird) 205 inches; (Falcon station wagon) 189 inches; (other Falcons) 181.2 inches; (all other models) 209.9 inches. Front tread: (Fords and Thunderbird) 61 inches; (Falcon) 55 inches. Rear tread: (Fords and Thunderbird) 60 inches; (Falcon) 54.5 inches. Tires: (Ford station wagons and Thunderbird) 8.00 x 14; (Fords) 7.50 x 14; (Falcon station wagon) 6.50 x 13; (other Falcons) 6.00 x 13.

FALCON CONVENIENCE OPTIONS: Back-up lights ($11). Heavy-duty battery ($8). Crankcase vent system ($6). Deluxe trim package ($78). Engine, 170 cid/101 hp ($37). Fresh Air heater/defroster ($73). Station wagon luggage rack ($35). Two-tone paint ($19). Manual radio and antenna ($54). Safety equipment, including padded dash and visors ($22); plus front seat belts ($21). Electric tailgate windows for station wagons ($30). Automatic transmission ($163). Wheel covers ($16). Windshield washer ($14). Electric windshield wiper ($10). Numerous oversize and white sidewall tire options.

FORD CONVENIENCE OPTIONS: Standard 175-hp V-8 engine ($116). Two-barrel, 220-hp V-8 ($148). Four-barrel, 300-hp V-8 ($197). Polar Air air conditioner, including tinted glass ($271). Select Aire air conditioner, including tinted glass ($436). Back-up lights ($11). Heavy-duty, 70-amp battery ($8). Crankcase vent system ($6). Equa-Lock differential ($39). Electric clock ($15). Magic-Aire heater/defroster ($75). Recirculating heater/defroster ($47). Four-way manual seat ($17). Rocker panel molding ($16). Padded dash and visors ($24). Two-tone paint ($22). Power brakes ($43). Power seat ($64). Power steering ($82). Power tailgate window ($32). Front and rear power windows ($102). Push-button radio and antenna ($59). Front seat belts ($21). Tinted glass ($43). Cruise-O-Matic transmission ($212). Ford-O-Matic transmission with six-cylinder engine ($180). Ford-O-Matic transmission with V-8 engine ($190). Overdrive transmission ($108). Wheel covers ($19). Windshield washer ($14). Two-speed windshield wipers ($12). Plus numerous oversize and white sidewall tire options with price variations by style, engine and use of air conditioning.

THUNDERBIRD CONVENIENCE OPTIONS: Radio and antenna ($113). Fresh Air heater ($83). Select Aire air conditioner ($463). Tinted glass ($43). White sidewall tires, rayon 8.00 x 14 ($42); nylon ($70). Power windows ($106). Four-way driver's power seat ($92). Outside left- or right-hand mirror ($5). Windshield washers ($14). Rear fender shields ($27). Front seat belts ($23). Leather interior ($106). Heavy-duty, 70-amp battery ($8). Two-tone paint ($26). Equa-Lock differential ($39). Movable steering control ($25). Note: Crankcase ventilation system standard on California cars only.

HISTORY: Lee A. Iacocca was in his second season at the Ford helm this year. Calendar year output totaled 1,362,186 cars. Market penetration was up to 24 percent as model year production peaked at 163,600 Fairlanes; 141,500 Fairlane 500s; 349,700 Galaxies; 136,600 station wagons; 73,000 Thunderbirds; 129,700 standard Falcons; 224,500 Deluxe Falcons and 135,100 Falcon station wagons. Dealer introduction dates were Sept. 29, 1960, for Fords and Falcons, Nov. 12, 1960, for Thunderbirds. The full-size line production totals included 201,700 six-cylinder cars, while all Falcons were sixes and all Thunderbirds V-8s.

1961 Ford Thunderbird. (OCW)

1962 FORD

1962 Ford Galaxie 500 XL. (OCW)

1962 FORDS — OVERVIEW — In 1962, Ford continued its policy of making major styling changes in least one line. The 1962 Galaxies and full-size line were restyled and the end result is recognized as one of the cleaner designs to come from Dearborn. Except for one horizontal feature line at the beltline, the body was slab-sided. The model designation was carried in script along the rear fender. Ford continued the tradition of large round taillights throughout the entire line, with the taillights on Galaxies being separated by a stamped aluminum escutcheon panel. The model designation was spelled out, in block letters, across the trunk lid. At the front end, a full-width grille carried a horizontal grid pattern and was capped on each end by the dual headlights. The Ford crest was centered at the front of the hood throughout the full-size line. The Falcon line continued unchanged from the previous year except for the addition of an updated grille. The convex grille bars carried a vertical pattern. Also, a woodgrained version of the Falcon four-door station wagon was added to the Deluxe series and was known as the Falcon Squire. A Futura two-door sedan bucket seat sport model was also added to the Deluxe line. Like the Falcon line, the 1962 Thunderbirds received only minor cosmetic changes for the new year. The new T-birds had a smooth hood without the two ridges characteristic only of 1961 models. The 1962 taillights were also slightly different than the previous year's, with a chrome ring around the center of the lens. The big news for 1962 was the introduction of the intermediate-size Fairlane. The new model was nearly 12 inches shorter than the full-size Galaxie, yet was nearly eight inches longer than the compact Falcon. At the time of their introduction, the Fairlanes were compared to the 1949-1950 Fords in length and width. They were nearly identical, but were considerably lower. No one would ever guess the Fairlane was anything but a Ford. They utilized the characteristic round taillights, 'high canted' fenders and a grille that was nearly identical to the Galaxie line. This year saw a continuation of the great 1960's horsepower race and to do combat with the General Motors and Chrysler offerings, Ford introduced the famous 406 cid/405 hp V-8. The re-sizing of the Fairlane also brought the introduction of a completely new line of small V-8 engines. At 221 cid, the new base V-8 was the same displacement as the first Ford flathead V-8. It was of thin wall casting design and was the first in a series of lightweight V-8s.

GALAXIE SERIES — (6-CYL/V-8) — The Galaxie series was the base trim level for 1962 and included chrome moldings around the windshield and rear window, two sun visors, a chrome horn ring, armrests on all doors and a single horizontal chrome strip at the beltline.

GALAXIE SIX I.D. NUMBERS: The serial number code can be broken down as follows: First symbol indicates year: 2 = 1962. Second symbol identifies assembly plant, as follows: A = Atlanta; D = Dallas; G = Chicago; F = Dearborn; E = Mahwah; H = Loraine; J = Los Angeles; K = Kansas City; L = Long Beach; N = Norfolk; R = San Jose; S = Pilot Plant; T = Metuchen; U = Louisville; P = Twin Cities; W = Wayne; Y = Wixom; Z = St. Louis. Third and fourth symbols identify body series (see Body/ Numbers below). Fifth symbol identifies engine code, as follows: U = 170 cid six-cylinder; V = 223 cid six-cylinder; W = 292 cid V-8; X = 352 cid V-8 with two-barrel carb; Z = 390 cid V-8 with four-barrel carb; S = 144 cid six-cylinder; M or Q = 390 cid V-8 (high performance); B or G = 406 cid V-8 (high performance). The last six digits are the unit's production number, beginning at 100001 and going up, at each of the assembly plants. Galaxie six-cylinder models began with the number '2' followed by the assembly plant code, body type code, engine designation 'V' and, finally, the unit's production number according to the final assembly location. Each plant began at 100001 and went up.

GALAXIE SIX SERIES

Model No.	Body/ Style No.	Body Type & Seating	Factory Price	Shipping Weight	Prod. Total
V	52	4-dr Sed-6P	2507	3583	Note 1
V	51	2-dr Sed-6P	2453	3478	Note 1

NOTE 1: See Galaxie V-8 series listing. Production was counted by series and body style only, with no breakouts per engine type.

GALAXIE V-8 I.D. NUMBERS: Galaxie V-8 models began with the number '2' followed by the assembly plant code, body type code, engine designation code and, finally, the unit's production number according to the final assembly location. Each plant began at 100001 and went up.

GALAXIE V-8 SERIES

Model No.	Body/ Style No.	Body Type & Seating	Factory Price	Shipping Weight	Prod. Total
N/A	52	4-dr Sed-6P	2616	3684	115,594
N/A	51	2-dr Sed-6P	2562	3589	54,930

PRODUCTION NOTE: Total series output was 170,524 units. Ford does not indicate the number of each model produced with sixes or V-8s. Therefore, all production figures given above are total production of each body style with both engines.

GALAXIE 500 SERIES — (6-CYL/V-8) — The Galaxie 500 series was the top trim level for 1962 and included chrome 'A' pillar moldings, chrome window moldings, a color-keyed horizontal chrome strip at the beltline, chrome rocker panel moldings, quarter panel moldings and a chrome trim strip with a Ford crest at the base of the 'S' pillar, on the top.

GALAXIE 500 SIX I.D. NUMBERS: Galaxie 500 six-cylinder models used the same serial number sequence as the Galaxie series.

GALAXIE 500 SIX SERIES

Model No.	Body/ Style No.	Body Type & Seating	Factory Price	Shipping Weight	Prod. Total
V	62	4-dr Twn Sed-6P	2667	3566	Note 1
V	61	2-dr Clb Sed-6P	2613	3476	Note 1
V	64	4-dr Twn Vic-6P	2739	3577	Note 1
V	63	2-dr Clb Vic-6P	2674	3505	Note 1

NOTE 1: See Galaxie 500 V-8 series listing. Production was counted by series and body style with no breakouts per engine type.

GALAXIE 500 V-8 I.D. NUMBERS: Galaxie 500 V-8 models used the same serial number sequence as the Galaxie series.

GALAXIE 500 V-8 SERIES

Model No.	Body/ Style No.	Body Type & Seating	Factory Price	Shipping Weight	Prod. Total
N/A	62	4-dr Twn Sed-6P	2776	3679	174,195
N/A	61	2-dr Clb Sed-6P	2722	3567	27,824
N/A	64	4-dr Twn Vic-6P	2848	3688	30,778
N/A	63	2-dr Clb Vic-6P	2783	3616	87,562
N/A	65	2-dr Sun Conv-6P	3033	3782	42,646

PRODUCTION NOTE: Total series output was 404,600 units. Ford does not indicate the number of each model produced with sixes or V-8s. Therefore, all production figures are total production of each body style with each engine.

GALAXIE 500XL SERIES — (V-8) — The Galaxie 500XL series was new for 1962, and was the sporty series of the Galaxie line. The "XLs" included all the top level trim of the Galaxie 500 models, but offered bucket seats and a floor-mounted shift lever, as well as an engine-turned insert in the instrument panel and on the side stripe.

1962 Ford Galaxie 500 four-door Town Sedan V-8. (OCW)

1962 Ford Galaxie 500 Sunliner convertible. (OCW)

GALAXIE 500XL V-8 I.D. NUMBERS:
Galaxie 500XL models used the same serial number sequence as the Galaxie and Galaxie 500 series.

GALAXIE 500XL V-8 SERIES

Model No.	Body/ Style No.	Body Type & Seating	Factory Price	Shipping Weight	Prod. Total
N/A	63A	2-dr Clb Vic-6P	3106	3625	28,412
N/A	76B	2-dr Sun Conv-5P	3358	3804	13,183

PRODUCTION NOTE: Total series output was 41,595 units.

STATION WAGON SERIES — (6-CYL/V-8) — The Ranch Wagon was the base trim level station wagon, Country Sedans were the intermediate level and Country Squires were the top trim level. The level of equipment paralleled Galaxie, Galaxie 500 and Galaxie 500XL models of passenger cars.

STATION WAGON SIX I.D. NUMBERS: Station wagon six-cylinder models used the same serial number sequence as the Galaxie series of passenger cars.

STATION WAGON SIX SERIES

Model No.	Body/ Style No.	Body Type & Seating	Factory Price	Shipping Weight	Prod. Total
V	71	4-dr Ranch Wag-6P	2733	3905	Note 1
V	72	4-dr Cty Sed-6P	2829	3928	Note 1
V	74	4-dr Cty Sed-9P	2933	3946	Note 1
V	78	4-dr Cty Sq-9P	3088	3959	Note 1

NOTE 1: See station wagon V-8 series listing. Production was counted by series and body style, with no breakouts per engine type.

STATION WAGON V-8 I.D. NUMBERS: Station wagon V-8 models used the same serial number sequence as the Galaxie series of passenger cars.

STATION WAGON V-8 SERIES

Model No.	Body/ Style No.	Body Type & Seating	Factory Price	Shipping Weight	Prod. Total
N/A	71	4-dr Ranch Wag-6P	2842	4016	33,674
N/A	72	4-dr Cty Sed-6P	2938	4039	47,635
N/A	74	4-dr Cty Sed-9P	3042	4057	16,562
N/A	78	4-dr Cty Sq-9P	3197	4057	15,666

PRODUCTION NOTE: Total series output was 129,651 units. Ford does not indicate the number of each model produced with sixes or V-8s. Therefore, all production figures given above are total production of each body style with both engines.

FAIRLANE SERIES — (6-CYL/V-8) — The Fairlane was the new intermediate size line of Ford for 1962. With styling similar to the 1961 full-size Fords there was no doubt of the Fairlane's heritage. The Fairlane line included the base Fairlane models and the top Fairlane 500 models. The new models also introduced the famous 221 series small-block Ford V-8, with the new thin-wall casting technique, producing the lightest complete V-8 engine of the time.

FAIRLANE SERIES — (6-CYL/V-8) — The Fairlane was the base trim level of the line and included chrome windshield and rear window moldings, a horn button instead of horn ring, armrests on all doors, a single horizontal Fairlane sweep-type strip (which followed the belt level feature line), the Ford crest on the hood and the word Ford in block letters, on the trunk lid.

FAIRLANE SIX I.D. NUMBERS: Fairlane six-cylinder models began with the number "2" followed by the assembly plant code, body type code, engine designation 'U' and, finally, the unit's production number according to the final assembly location. Each plant began at 100001 and went up.

1962 Ford Fairlane 500 four-door sedan V-8. (AA)

1962 Ford Fairlane 500 two-door Sports Coupe V-8. (OCW)

FAIRLANE SIX SERIES

Model No.	Body/ Style No.	Body Type & Seating	Factory Price	Shipping Weight	Prod. Total
U	32	4-dr Sed-6P	2216	2791	Note 1
U	31	2-dr Sed-6P	2154	2757	Note 1

NOTE 1: See Fairlane V-8 series listing. Production was counted by series and body style only, with no breakouts per engine type.

FAIRLANE V-8 I.D. NUMBERS: Fairlane V-8 models began with the number '2' followed by the assembly plant code, body type code, engine designation code 'L' and, finally, the unit's production number according to final assembly location. Each plant began at 100001 and went up.

FAIRLANE V-8 SERIES

Model No.	Body/ Style No.	Body Type & Seating	Factory Price	Shipping Weight	Prod. Total
L	32	4-dr Sed-6P	2319	2949	45,342
L	31	2-dr Sed-6P	2257	2915	34,264

PRODUCTION NOTE: Total series output was 79,606 units. Ford does not indicate the number of each model produced with sixes or V-8s. Therefore, all production figures given above are total production of each body style with each engine.

FAIRLANE 500 SERIES — (6-CYL/V-8) — The Fairlane 500 models were the top trim level of the line and included chrome window moldings, a chrome horn ring, armrests on all doors, simulated chrome inserts on the door upholstery, a two-piece chrome Fairlane sweep with a ribbed aluminum insert and two sun visors. The Sport Coupe two-door sedan, introduced midyear, included bucket seats and special identification.

FAIRLANE 500 SIX I.D. NUMBERS: Fairlane 500 six-cylinder models used the same serial numbers sequence as the Fairlane models.

FAIRLANE 500 SIX SERIES

Model No.	Body/ Style No.	Body Type & Seating	Factory Price	Shipping Weight	Prod. Total
U	42	4-dr Sed-6P	2507	2808	Note 1
U	41	2-dr Sed-6P	2304	2774	Note 1
U	47	2-dr Spt Cpe-5P	2504	2870	Note 1

NOTE 1: See Fairlane 500 V-8 series listing. Production was counted by series and body style, with no breakouts per engine type.

FAIRLANE 500 V-8 I.D. NUMBERS: Fairlane 500 V-8 models used the same serial number sequence as the Fairlane models.

FAIRLANE 500 V-8 SERIES

Model No.	Body/ Style No.	Body Type & Seating	Factory Price	Shipping Weight	Prod. Total
L	42	4-dr Sed-6P	2407	2966	129,258
L	41	2-dr Sed-6P	2345	2932	68,624
L	47	2-dr Spt Cpe-5P	2607	3002	19,628

PRODUCTION NOTE: Total series output was 217,510 units. Ford does not indicate the number of each model produced with sixes or V-8s. Therefore, all production figures given above are total production of each body style with each engine.

FALCON SERIES — (6-CYL) — The Falcon continued unchanged from 1961, with the exception of a new convex grille with vertical bars and a new Galaxie-style top configuration. There were two separate Falcon lines for 1962: the standard and Deluxe series, rather than the Deluxe trim package, which was optional on all 1960 and 1961 Falcons. Also new was the Falcon Squire station wagon.

STANDARD FALCON I.D. NUMBERS: The standard series Falcon used the same serial number sequence as the full-size Fords, except the engine code was either 'S' or 'U.'

1962 Ford Falcon Deluxe Squire station wagon 6-cyl. (OCW)

STANDARD SERIES FALCON

Model No.	Body/ Style No.	Body Type & Seating	Factory Price	Shipping Weight	Prod. Total
S/U	12	4-dr Sed-6P	2047	2299	Note 1
S/U	11	2-dr Sed-6P	1985	2262	Note 1
S/U	22	4-dr Sta Wag-6P	2341	2595	Note 1
S/U	21	2-dr Sta Wag-6P	2298	2559	Note 1

NOTE 1: See Deluxe Falcon listing. Production was counted by body style, with no breakouts per level of trim.

DELUXE FALCON I.D. NUMBERS: Deluxe Falcon models used the same serial number sequence as the full-size Fords, except the engine code was either 'S' or 'U.'

DELUXE SERIES FALCON

Model No.	Body/ Style No.	Body Type & Seating	Factory Price	Shipping Weight	Prod. Total
S/U	12	4-dr Sed-6P	2133	2319	126,041
S/U	11	2-dr Sed-6P	2071	2282	143,650
S/U	17	2-dr Futura Sed-5P	2232	2347	17,011
S/U	22	4-dr Sta Wag-6P	2427	2621	66,819
S/U	21	2-dr Sta Wag-6P	2384	2584	Note 1
S/U	26	4-dr Sq Wag-6P	2603	2633	22,583

PRODUCTION NOTE: Total series output was 396,129 units. Ford does not indicate the total number of standard models and Deluxe models produced. Therefore, all production figures are total production of each body style with both levels of trim.

THUNDERBIRD SERIES — (V-8) — Except for minor exterior trim changes, the 1962 Thunderbirds were identical to their 1961 counterparts. The new Landau hardtop featured a vinyl top as standard equipment. It was the first time such a top was offered on the Thunderbird line. Also new for 1962 was the Sports Roadster. In an attempt to bring back the sporty appearance of the old two-seat T-birds, Ford offered the Thunderbird convertible with a fiberglass tonneau cover for the back seats. The cover included two streamlined headrest, which contributed to a sleek looking car when the top was down. The 390 cid "M" series engine was a new option for 1962.

1962 Ford Falcon Deluxe four-door sedan 6-cyl. (OCW)

1962-1/2 Ford Falcon Futura two-door sedan 6-cyl. (PH)

THUNDERBIRD I.D. NUMBERS: Thunderbird models began with the number '2,' assembly plant code 'Y' (Wixom), body type code, engine type code 'Z' and, finally, the unit's production number beginning at 100001 and going up.

THUNDERBIRD SERIES

Model No.	Body/ Style No.	Body Type & Seating	Factory Price	Shipping Weight	Prod. Total
Z	83	2-dr HT Cpe-6P	4321	4132	68,127
Z	83	2-dr Lan HT Cpe-4P	4398	4144	Note 1
Z	85	2-dr Conv-4P	4788	4370	9,844
Z	85/89	2-dr Spt Rds Conv-4P	5439	4471	Notes 1 & 2

NOTE 1: Total series output was 78,011 units. Ford does not indicate the number of Landau hardtops and Sports Roadsters produced, separate from the standard hardtops and convertibles. Therefore, all production figures are total production of each.

NOTE 2: The Body/ Number for the Sports Roadster was "85" for the first 558 units at which time it was changed to "89" for the balance of that model year's production. The change to "89" took place with serial number 2Y 89 Z 127027. The last "85" Sports Roadster serial number was 2Y 85 Z 114640.

ENGINE [Falcon Base Six]: Overhead valve. Cast-iron block. Displacement: 144 cid. Bore and stroke: 3.50 x 2.50 inches. Compression ratio: 6.7:1. Brake hp: 65 at 4200 rpm. Carburetor: Holley one-barrel. Seven main bearings. Serial number code "S."

ENGINE [Falcon Six]: Overhead valve. Cast-iron block. Displacement: 170 cid. Bore and stroke: 3.50 x 2.94 inches. Compression ratio: 8.7:1. Brake hp: 101 at 4400 rpm. Carburetor: Holley one-barrel. Seven main bearings. Serial number code "U."

ENGINE [Ford Base Six]: Overhead valve. Cast-iron block. Displacement: 223 cid. Bore and stroke: 3.62 x 3.60 inches. Compression ratio: 8.4:1. Brake hp: 138 at 4200 rpm. Carburetor: Holley one-barrel. Four main bearings. Serial number code "V."

ENGINE [Fairlane V-8]: Overhead valve. Cast-iron block. Displacement: 221 cid. Bore and stroke: 3.50 x 2.87 inches. Compression ratio: 8.7:1. Brake hp: 145 at 4400 rpm. Carburetor: Holley two-barrel. Five main bearings. Serial number code "L."

ENGINE [Ford V-8]: Overhead valve. Cast-iron block. Displacement: 292 cid. Bore and stroke: 3.75 x 3.30 inches. Compression ratio: 8.8:1. Brake hp: 170 at 4200 rpm. Carburetor: Holley two-barrel. Five main bearings. Serial number code "W."

ENGINE [Interceptor V-8]: Overhead valve. Cast-iron block. Displacement: 352 cid. Bore and stroke: 4.00 x 3.50 inches. Compression ratio: 8.9:1. Brake hp: 220 at 4300 rpm. Carburetor: Holley two-barrel. Five main bearings. Serial number code "X."

ENGINE [Interceptor 390 V-8]: Overhead valve. Cast-iron block. Displacement: 390 cid. Bore and stroke: 4.05 x 3.78 inches. Compression ratio: 9.6:1. Brake hp: 300 at 4600 rpm. Carburetor: Holley four-barrel. Five main bearings. Serial number code "Z."

ENGINE [Thunderbird 390 V-8]: Overhead valve. Cast-iron block. Displacement: 390 cid. Bore and stroke: 4.05 x 3.78 inches. Compression ratio: 10.5:1. Brake hp: 340 at 5000 rpm. Carburetor: Three Holley two-barrel. Five main bearings. Serial number code "M."

ENGINE [Thunderbird 406 V-8]: Overhead valve. Cast-iron block. Displacement: 406 cid. Bore and stroke: 4.13 x 3.78 inches. Compression ratio: 11.4:1. Brake hp: 385 at 5800 rpm. Carburetor: Holley four-barrel. Five main bearings. Serial number code "B."

ENGINE [Thunderbird Special 406 V-8]: Overhead valve. Cast-iron block. Displacement: 406 cid. Bore and stroke: 4.13 x 3.78 inches. Compression ratio: 11.3:1. Brake hp: 405 at 4800 rpm. Carburetor: Three Holley two-barrel. Five main bearings. Serial number code "G."

1962 Ford Thunderbird two-door Sports Roadster V-8. (AA)

1962 Ford Thunderbird two-door hardtop V-8. (OCW)

CHASSIS FEATURES: Wheelbase: (Falcon) 109.5 inches; (Fairlane) 115.5 inches (Thunderbird) 113 inches; (all others) 119 inches. Overall length: (Falcon station wagons) 189 inches; (other Falcons) 181.1 inches; (Fairlanes) 197.6 inches; (all Fords) 209.3 inches; (Thunderbird) 205 inches. Tires: (Fairlane six and Falcon station wagons) 6.50 x 13; (Falcon) 6.00 x 13; (Fairlane V-8) 7.00 x 14; (Fairlane '260' V-8) 7.00 x 13; (Ford station wagons) 8.00 x 14; (other Fords) 7.50 x 14.

FALCON CONVENIENCE OPTIONS: Back-up lights ($11). Heavy-duty battery ($8). Squire bucket seats and console ($120). Crankcase ventilation system ($6). Deluxe trim package ($87). Engine, 170 cid/101 hp ($38). Tinted glass ($27). Windshield tinted glass ($13). Station wagon luggage rack ($39). Two-tone paint ($19). Push-button radio and antenna ($59). Safety equipment, including padded dash and front visors ($22). Seat safety belts ($21). Electric tailgate windows ($30). Automatic transmission ($163). Vinyl trim for sedan (Deluxe trim package required) ($25). Wheel covers ($16). Windshield washer ($14). Electric windshield wiper ($10).

FORD CONVENIENCE OPTIONS: Polar Air air conditioning with V-8 ($271). Select Aire air conditioning with V-8 ($361). Back-up lights, standard Galaxie 500 ($11). Heavy-duty battery, 70-amp ($8). Crankcase ventilation system ($6). Equa-Lock differential ($39). Electric clock, standard Galaxy 500 ($15). Re-circulating heater and defroster ($28 deduct option). Chrome luggage rack ($39). Four-way manual seat ($17). Rocker panel molding ($16). Padded dash and visors ($24). Two-tone paint ($22). Power brakes ($43). Power seat ($64). Power steering ($82). Power tailgate window ($32). Front and rear power windows ($102). Push-button radio and antenna ($59). Front seat belts ($21). Tinted glass ($40). Tinted windshield ($22). Cruise-O-Matic transmission ($212). Ford-O-Matic with six-cylinder ($180). Ford-O-Matic with V-8 ($190). Overdrive transmission ($108). Four-speed manual transmission, 375-hp or 401-hp V-8 required ($188). Vinyl trim, Galaxie 500 except convertible ($26). Deluxe wheel covers ($26). Wheel covers ($19). Windshield washer and wipers, two-speed ($20).

THUNDERBIRD CONVENIENCE OPTIONS: Radio and antenna ($113). Engine, 340-hp Tri-carb V-8 ($242). Select Aire air conditioning ($415). Tinted glass ($43). Rayon white sidewall tires, 6.00 x 14 ($42). Nylon white sidewall tires, 6.00 x 14 ($70). Power windows ($106). Four-way power seat, driver or passenger ($92). Outside rearview mirror ($5). Windshield washers ($14). Rear fender shields ($27). Front seat belts ($23). Seat bolsters and inserts, leather ($106). Heavy-duty battery, 70-amp ($6). Two-tone paint ($26). Chrome wire wheels ($373).

1962 Ford Thunderbird Landau two-door hardtop V-8. (OCW)

HISTORY: The 1962 Falcon was introduced Sept. 29, 1961. The 1962 Galaxie and station wagon lines appeared the same day. The new Thunderbirds were introduced Oct. 12, 1961. The Fairlane series did not debut until Nov. 16, 1961. Ford announced the introduction of the first transistorized ignition system, for production cars, in March 1962. A total of 30,216 Fairlanes had the 260 cid V-8 installed. A total of 722,647 Galaxies, 386,192 Fairlanes, 381,559 Falcons and 75,536 Thunderbirds were built this year, second only to the record production season 1955. Midyear models included the Galaxie 500/XL hardtop and convertible, the Fairlane 500 Sport Sedan and the Falcon Sport Futura. Lee A. Iacocca was vice-president and general manager of the Ford Division again this year. In a historic move, Ford built 10 Galaxie "factory lightweight" drag racing cars late in model year 1962.

1963 FORD

1963 FORDS — OVERVIEW — In 1963, for the fifth year in-a-row, the full-size Ford line was completely restyled. As in 1962, the sides were devoid of any sculpture lines, except for the beltline feature line. The model designation was carried in script on the fender immediately behind the front wheel opening. Once again, the taillights were large round units mounted at the top of the rear fenders, with a stamped aluminum escutcheon panel being used on the Galaxie 500 series. The model designation was spelled out in block letters across the trunk lid. The grille was a full-width aluminum stamping, again carrying a horizontal grid, and featuring a large Ford crest in the center, which was actually the hood release. The word 'FORD' was spelled out in block letters across the front of the hood. For 1963, the famous small-block 260 cid and 289 cid engines replaced the old 292 cid Y-block, which had been in continuous production since 1956 as the standard V-8. Also, with the other carmakers continuing to escalate the horse-power race, Ford introduced the most powerful engines in its history: the 410 hp and 425 hp 427 cid big-blocks.

FORD 300 SERIES — (6-CYL/V-8) — The Ford 300 was the base trim level for 1963 and included chrome moldings around the windshield and rear window, two sun visors, a chrome horn ring, armrests on all doors, and no chrome side trim.

FORD 300 SIX I.D. NUMBERS: The serial number code can be broken down as follows: First symbol indicates year: 3 = 1963. Second symbol identifies assembly plant, as follows: A = Atlanta; D = Dallas; G = Chicago; F = Dearborn; E = Mahwah; H = Loraine; J = Los Angeles; K = Kansas City; L = Long Beach; N = Norfolk; R = San Jose; S = Pilot Plant; T = Metuchen; U = Louisville; P = Twin Cities; W = Wayne; Y = Wixom; Z = St. Louis. Third and fourth symbols identify body series (see Body/ Numbers below). Fifth symbol identifies engine code, as follows: U = 170 cid six-cylinder; T = 200 cid six-cylinder; V = 223 cid six-cylinder; L = 221 cid V-8; F = 260 cid V-8; C = 289 cid V-8; X = 352 cid V-8 with two-barrel carb; Z = 390 cid V-8 with four-barrel carb; S = 144 cid six-cylinder; M = 390 cid V-8 (high performance); B or G = 406 cid V-8 (high performance); Q or R = 427 cid V-8 (high performance). The last six digits are the unit's production number, beginning at 100001 and going up, at each of the assembly plants. Ford 300 six-cylinder models began with the number '3,' followed by the assembly plant code, engine designation 'V' and, finally, the unit's production number, according to the final assembly location. Each plant began at 100001 and went up.

FORD 300 SIX SERIES

Model No.	Body/ Style No.	Body Type & Seating	Factory Price	Shipping Weight	Prod. Total
V	54	4-dr Sed-6P	2378	3645	Note 1
V	53	2-dr Sed-6P	2324	3565	Note 1

NOTE 1: See Ford 300 V-8 series listing. Production was counted by series and body only, with no engine breakouts.

1963 Ford Galaxie two-door sedan V-8. (PH)

FORD 300 V-8 I.D. NUMBERS: Ford 300 V-8 models began with the number '3' followed by the assembly plant code, body type code, engine designation code and, finally, the unit's production number according to the final assembly location. Each plant began at 100001 and went up.

FORD 300 V-8 SERIES

Model No.	Body/ Style No.	Body Type & Seating	Factory Price	Shipping Weight	Prod. Total
N/A	54	4-dr Sed-6P	2387	3640	44,142
N/A	53	2-dr Sed-6P	2433	3560	26,010

PRODUCTION NOTE: Total series output was 70,152 units. Ford does not indicate the number of each model produced with sixes or V-8s. Therefore, all production figures given above are total production of each body style with both engines.

GALAXIE SERIES — (6-CYL/V-8) — The Galaxie was the intermediate trim level for 1963 and included all the 300 series trim plus a single chrome strip running horizontally along the lower bodysides and two chrome fender ornaments on the front fenders.

GALAXIE SIX I.D. NUMBERS: Galaxie six-cylinder models used the same serial number sequence as the '300' series.

GALAXIE SIX SERIES

Model No.	Body/ Style No.	Body Type & Seating	Factory Price	Shipping Weight	Prod. Total
V	52	4-dr Sed-6P	2507	3665	Note 1
V	51	2-dr Sed-6P	2453	3575	Note 1

NOTE 1: See Galaxie V-8 series listing. Production was counted by series and body only, with no engine breakouts.

GALAXIE V-8 I.D. NUMBERS: Galaxie V-8 models used the same serial number sequence as the '300' series.

GALAXIE V-8 SERIES

Model No.	Body/ Style No.	Body Type & Seating	Factory Price	Shipping Weight	Prod. Total
N/A	52	4-dr Sed-6P	2616	3660	82,419
N/A	51	2-dr Sed-6P	2562	3850	30,335

PRODUCTION NOTE: Total series output was 112,754 units. Ford does not indicate the number of each model produced with sixes or V-8s. Therefore, all production figures given above are total production of each body style with both engines.

GALAXIE 500 SERIES — (6-CYL/V-8) — The Galaxie 500 series was the top trim level for 1963 and included chrome 'A' pillar moldings, chrome window moldings, two horizontal chrome strips on the side: one at the feature line and another, shorter one, beginning at the front of the front door and going to the back of the car, where it swept up and merged with the upper strip. Between the two chrome pieces, just in front of the taillights, were six cast 'hash marks.'

GALAXIE 500 SIX I.D. NUMBERS: Galaxie 500 six-cylinder models used the same serial number sequence as the '300' and Galaxie series.

GALAXIE 500 SIX SERIES

Model No.	Body/ Style No.	Body Type & Seating	Factory Price	Shipping Weight	Prod. Total
V	62	4-dr Twn Sed-6P	2667	3685	Note 1
V	61	2-dr Clb Sed-6P	2613	3605	Note 1
V	64	4-dr Twn Vic-6P	2739	3700	Note 1
V	63	2-dr Clb Vic-6P	2674	3620	Note 1
V	66	2-dr FsBk Cpe-6P	2674	3620	Note 1
V	65	2-dr Sun Conv-6P	2924	3775	Note 1

NOTE 1: See Galaxie 500 V-8 series listing. Production was counted by series and body only, with no engine breakouts.

1963-1/2 Ford Galaxie 500XL two-door fastback hardtop V-8. (PH)

1963 Ford Galaxie 500XL Sunliner two-door convertible V-8. (AA)

GALAXIE 500 V-8 I.D. NUMBERS: Galaxie 500 V-8 models used the same serial number sequence as the '300' and Galaxie series.

GALAXIE 500 V-8 SERIES

Model No.	Body/ Style No.	Body Type & Seating	Factory Price	Shipping Weight	Prod. Total
N/A	62	4-dr Twn Sed-6P	2776	3680	205,722
N/A	61	2-dr Clb Sed-6P	2722	3600	21,137
N/A	64	4-dr Twn Vic-6P	2848	3695	26,558
N/A	63	2-dr Clb Vic-6P	2783	3615	49,733
N/A	66	2-dr FsBk Cpe-6P	2783	3615	100,500
N/A	65	2-dr Sun Conv-6P	3033	3770	36,876

PRODUCTION NOTE: Total series output was 440,526 units. Ford does not indicate the number of each model produced with sixes or V-8s. Therefore, all production figures given above are total production of each body style with both engines.

GALAXIE 500XL SERIES — (V-8) — Galaxie 500XL models used the same serial number sequence as the Galaxie and Galaxie 500 series.

GALAXIE 500XL V-8 SERIES

Model No.	Body/ Style No.	Body Type & Seating	Factory Price	Shipping Weight	Prod. Total
N/A	62	4-dr Twn Vic-5P	3333	3750	12,596
N/A	67	2-dr Clb Vic-5P	3626	3670	29,713
N/A	68	2-dr FsBk Cpe-5P	3268	3670	33,870
N/A	69	2-dr Sun Conv-5P	3518	3820	18,551

PRODUCTION NOTE: Total series output was 94,730 units.

STATION WAGON SERIES — (6-CYL/V-8) — The Country Sedans were the base trim level station wagons for 1963, with the Country Squires being the top trim level. The trim paralleled the Galaxie and Galaxie 500 models of passenger cars.

STATION WAGON SIX I.D. NUMBERS: Station wagon six-cylinder models used the same serial number sequence as Galaxie and Galaxie 500 series of passenger cars.

STATION WAGON SIX SERIES

Model No.	Body/ Style No.	Body Type & Seating	Factory Price	Shipping Weight	Prod. Total
V	72	4-dr Cty Sed-6P	2829	3990	Note 1
V	74	4-dr Cty Sed-9P	2933	4005	Note 1
V	76	4-dr Cty Sq-6P	3018	4005	Note 1
V	78	4-dr Cty Sq-9P	2933	4015	Note 1

NOTE 1: See station wagon V-8 series listing. Production was counted by series and body only, with no engine breakouts.

STATION WAGON V-8 I.D. NUMBERS: Station wagon V-8 models used the same serial number sequence as Galaxie and Galaxie 500 models of passenger cars.

1963 Ford Country Squire nine-passenger station wagon V-8. (OCW)

STATION WAGON V-8 SERIES

Model No.	Body/ Style No.	Body Type & Seating	Factory Price	Shipping Weight	Prod. Total
N/A	72	4-dr Cty Sed-6P	2938	3985	64,954
N/A	74	4-dr Cty Sed-9P	3042	4000	22,250
N/A	76	4-dr Cty Sq-6P	3127	4000	19,922
N/A	78	4-dr Cty Sq-9P	3197	4010	19,246

PRODUCTION NOTE: Total series output was 126,372 units. Ford does not indicate the number of each model produced with sixes or V-8s. Therefore, all production figures given above are total production of each body style with both engines.

FAIRLANE SERIES — (6-CYL/V-8) — The 1963 Fairlane was a carryover from the 1962 model year, with minor changes in chrome trim. The addition of two-door hardtop models added a sporty touch to the conservative Fairlane lineup. They were the Fairlane 500 two-door hardtop and the Fairlane 500 Sport Coupe.

FAIRLANE SIX I.D. NUMBERS: Fairlane six-cylinder models began with the number '3' followed by the assembly plant code, body type code, engine designation "U" and, finally, the unit's production number according to the final assembly location. Each plant began at 100001 and went up.

FAIRLANE SIX SERIES

Model No.	Body/ Style No.	Body Type & Seating	Factory Price	Shipping Weight	Prod. Total
U	32	4-dr Sed-6P	2216	2855	Note 1
U	31	2-dr Sed-6P	2154	2815	Note 1
U	38	4-dr Ranch Wag-6P	2525	3195	Note 1

NOTE 1: See Fairlane V-8 series listing. Production was counted by series and body only, with no engine breakouts.

FAIRLANE V-8 I.D. NUMBERS: Fairlane V-8 models began with the number '3' followed by the assembly plant code, body type code, engine designation code and, finally, the unit's production number according to the final assembly location. Each plant began at 100001 and went up.

FAIRLANE V-8 SERIES

Model No.	Body/ Style No.	Body Type & Seating	Factory Price	Shipping Weight	Prod. Total
N/A	32	4-dr Sed-6P	2319	2987	44,454
N/A	31	2-dr Sed-6P	2257	2924	28,984
N/A	38	4-dr Ranch Wag-6P	2628	3327	24,006

PRODUCTION NOTE: Total series output was 97,444 units. Ford does not indicate the number of each model produced with sixes or V-8s. Therefore, all production figures given above are total production of each body style with both engines.

FAIRLANE 500 SERIES — (6-CYL/V-8) — The Fairlane 500 models were the top trim level of the line and included chrome window moldings, a chrome horn ring, armrests on all doors, a version of the 'Fairlane sweep', three chrome exhaust pods located on the rear fenders, just ahead of the taillights, and a stamped aluminum escutcheon panel between the taillights, with the Ford crest situated in the center, on the gasoline filler cap.

FAIRLANE 500 SIX I.D. NUMBERS: Fairlane 500 six-cylinder models used the same serial number sequence as the Fairlane models.

1963 Ford Fairlane 500 two-door hardtop. (OCW)

1963 Ford Fairlane 500 four-door Ranch Wagon V-8. (OCW)

FAIRLANE 500 SIX SERIES

Model No.	Body/ Style No.	Body Type & Seating	Factory Price	Shipping Weight	Prod. Total
U	42	4-dr Sed-6P	2304	2670	Note 1
U	41	2-dr Sed-6P	2242	2830	Note 1
U	43	2-dr HT Cpe-6P	2324	2850	Note 1
U	47	2-dr Spt Cpe-5P	2504	2870	Note 1
U	48	4-dr Ranch Wag-8P	2613	3210	Note 1
U	49	4-dr Squire-6P	2781	3220	Note 1

NOTE 1: See Fairlane V-8 series listing. Production was counted by series and body only, with no engine breakouts.

FAIRLANE 500 V-8 I.D. NUMBERS: Fairlane 500 V-8 models used the same serial number sequence as the Fairlane models.

FAIRLANE 500 V-8 SERIES

Model No.	Body/ Style No.	Body Type & Seating	Factory Price	Shipping Weight	Prod. Total
N/A	42	4-dr Sed-6P	2407	3002	103,175
N/A	41	2-dr Sed-6P	2345	2962	34,764
N/A	43	2-dr HT Cpe-6P	2427	2982	41,641
N/A	47	2-dr Spt Cpe-5P	2607	3002	28,268
N/A	48	4-dr Ranch Wag-6P	2716	3342	29,612
N/A	49	4-dr Squire-6P	2884	3352	7,983

PRODUCTION NOTE: Total series output was 246,443 units, including 277 Fairlane Squires with optional bucket seat interiors. Ford does not indicate the number of each model produced with sixes or V-8s. Therefore, all production figures given above are total production of each body style with both engines.

FALCON SERIES — (6-CYL/V-8) — The Falcon line continued to use the body shell introduced in 1960, but was updated with a new convex grille featuring a horizontal grid pattern, chrome side trim, and slightly revised taillight lenses, with additional chrome around the inside of the lens. The Deluxe models of 1962 were replaced by the Futura models for 1963 and included the addition of a two-door hardtop and a convertible. They offered V-8 power for the first time in the series' history.

STANDARD FALCON SERIES — (6-CYL) — Falcon standard series cars were the base trim level for 1963 and included chrome windshield and rear window moldings, two horns, two sun visors, armrests on the front doors only and a horn button instead of a chrome horn ring.

STANDARD FALCON I.D. NUMBERS: Falcon standard series cars used the same serial number sequence as the full-size Fords and the Fairlane.

STANDARD FALCON SERIES

Model No.	Body/ Style No.	Body Type & Seating	Factory Price	Shipping Weight	Prod. Total
N/A	02	4-dr Sed-6P	2047	2345	62,365
N/A	01	2-dr Sed-6P	1985	2305	70,630

1963-1/2 Ford Falcon Futura Sprint two-door hardtop V-8. (PH)

1963 Ford Falcon Futura two-door convertible 6-cyl. (AA)

FUTURA SERIES — (6-CYL/V-8)

FUTURA SERIES — (6-CYL/V-8) — The Futura series was the top trim level for 1963 and included a chrome horn ring; rear armrests and ashtrays; two horns; Futura wheel covers instead of hubcaps; the round 'Futura' symbol on the top 'C' pillar; chrome side window moldings; chrome windshield and rear window moldings; a horizontal chrome strip between the taillights; and a horizontal arrow-style chrome strip on the bodyside. The Sport Coupe and Sprint versions also included wire wheel covers, full console and bucket seats. In addition, the Sprint offered a 260 cid V-8, monitored by a dash-mounted tachometer. Initially, a few Sprints were powered by sixes although the aforementioned '260' V-8 was considered standard equipment.

FUTURA I.D. NUMBERS: Futura models used the same serial number sequence as the full-size Fords, Fairlane models and standard series Falcons.

FUTURA SERIES

Model No.	Body/ Style No.	Body Type & Seating	Factory Price	Shipping Weight	Prod. Total
N/A	16	4-dr Sed-6P	2165	2355	31,736
N/A	19	2-dr Sed-6P	2116	2315	16,674
N/A	17	2-dr Sed-5P	2237	2350	10,344
N/A	18	2-dr HT Cpe-6P	2198	2455	17,524
N/A	18	2-dr Spt HT-5P	2319	2490	10,972
N/A	15	2-dr Conv-6P	2470	2655	18,942
N/A	15	2-dr Spt Conv-5P	2591	2690	12,250

SPRINT V-8 SUBSERIES

N/A	18	2-dr Sprint HT-5P	2603	2875	10,479
N/A	15	2-dr Sprint Conv-5P	2837	2998	4,602

PRODUCTION NOTE: Total series output was 265,518 units. Ford does not indicate the number of each model produced with sixes or V-8s. Therefore, all production figures given above are total production of each body style with both engines, with the exception of the V-8-only Sprint subseries.

THUNDERBIRD SERIES — (V-8) — While using the same body as the 1961-1962 T-birds, the 1963 model is the most easily recognizable of the entire series. The major difference in the 1963 model was a mid-body feature line that moves back, horizontally, from the front of the car and then dips down near the back of the front door. Three sets of five cast 'hash marks' are used on the side of the door, just ahead of the feature line dip. A single exhaust system was included as standard equipment for the first and only time and a 390 cid/340 hp V-8 was again an option. It featured three two-barrel carburetors. In January 1963, a Limited Edition Thunderbird Landau was introduced and was available only with white exterior color, maroon top, white steering wheel and white leather interior. This model is often referred to as the Monaco Edition, as it was introduced in the principality of Monaco.

1963 Ford Falcon Futura Sprint two-door convertible V-8. (OCW)

1963 Ford Thunderbird convertible. (OCW)

THUNDERBIRD I.D. NUMBERS: Thunderbird models began with number '3,' assembly plant code 'Y' (Wixom), body type code, engine type code 'P' or 'M' and, finally, the unit's production number, beginning at 100001 and going up.

THUNDERBIRD SERIES

Model No.	Body/ Style No.	Body Type & Seating	Factory Price	Shipping Weight	Prod. Total
P/M	83	2-dr HT Cpe-4P	4445	4195	42,806
P/M	87	2-dr Lan HT-4P	4548	4320	14,139
P/M	85	2-dr Conv-4P	4912	4205	5,913
P/M	89	2-dr Spt Rds-4P	5563	4395	455

PRODUCTION NOTE: Total series output was 63,313 units.

ENGINE [Falcon Base Six]: Overhead valve. Cast-iron block. Displacement: 144 cid. Bore and stroke: 3.50 x 2.50 inches. Compression ratio: 8.7:1. Brake hp: 85 at 4200 rpm. Carburetor: Holley single barrel. Seven main bearings. Serial number code "S" (export code 2).

ENGINE [Falcon/Fairlane Six]: Overhead valve. Cast-iron block. Displacement: 170 cid. Bore and stroke: 3.50 x 2.94 inches. Compression ratio: 8.7:1. Brake hp: 101 at 4400 rpm. Carburetor: Holley one-barrel. Seven main bearings. Serial number code "U" (export code 4).

ENGINE [Ford Base Six]: Overhead valve. Cast-iron block. Displacement: 200 cid. Bore and stroke: 3.68 x 3.13 inches. Compression ratio: 8.7:1. Brake hp: 116 at 4400 rpm. Carburetor: one-barrel. Four main bearings. Serial number code "T."

ENGINE [Ford Six]: Overhead valve. Cast-iron block. Displacement: 223 cid. Bore and stroke: 3.62 x 3.60 inches. Compression ratio: 8.4:1. Brake hp: 138 at 4200 rpm. Carburetor: Holley one-barrel. Four main bearings. Serial number code "V" (export code 5; taxi code E).

ENGINE [Fairlane V-8]: Overhead valve. Cast-iron block. Displacement: 221 cid. Bore and stroke: 3.75 x 3.30 inches. Compression ratio: 8.8:1. Brake hp: 145 at 4400 rpm. Carburetor: Holley two-barrel. Five main bearings. Serial number code "L" (export code 3).

ENGINE [Challenger 260 V-8]: Overhead valve. Cast-iron block. Displacement: 260 cid. Bore and stroke: 3.80 x 2.87 inches. Compression ratio: 8.7:1. Brake hp: 164 at 4400 rpm. Carburetor: Holley two-barrel. Five main bearings. Serial number code "F" (export code 6).

ENGINE [Challenger 289 V-8]: Overhead valve. Cast-iron block. Displacement: 289 cid. Bore and stroke: 3.00 x 2.87 inches. Compression ratio: 6.6:1. Brake hp: 195 at 4400 rpm. Carburetor: Holley two-barrel. Five main bearings. Serial number code "C."

ENGINE [High Performance Challenger 289 V-8]: Overhead valve. Cast-iron block. Displacement: 289 cid. Bore and stroke: 3.00 x 2.67 inches. Compression ratio: 10.5:1. Brake hp: 271 at 6000 rpm. Carburetor: Holley four-barrel. Five main bearings. Serial number code "K."

ENGINE [Interceptor V-8]: Overhead valve. Cast-iron block. Displacement: 352 cid. Bore and stroke: 4.00 x 3.50 inches. Compression ratio: 8.9:1. Brake hp: 220 at 4300 rpm. Carburetor: Holley two-barrel. Five main bearings. Serial number code "X."

ENGINE [Thunderbird V-8]: Overhead valve. Cast-iron block. Displacement: 390 cid. Bore and stroke: 4.05 x 3.78 inches. Compression ratio: 9.6:1. Brake hp: 300 at 4600 rpm. Carburetor: Holley four-barrel. Five main bearings. Serial number code "P" (export code 9).

ENGINE [Thunderbird V-8]: Overhead valve. Cast-iron block. Displacement: 390 cid. Bore and stroke: 4.05 x 3.76 inches. Compression ratio: 9.6:1. Brake hp: 330 at 5000 rpm. Carburetor: Holley four-barrel. Five main bearings. Serial number code "Z."

ENGINE [Thunderbird Special "Six-Barrel" V-8]: Overhead valve. Cast-iron block. Displacement: 390 cid. Bore and stroke: 4.05 x 3.76 inches. Compression ratio: 10.5:1. Brake hp: 340 at 5000 rpm. Carburetor: three Holley two-barrel. Five main bearings. Serial number code "M."

1963 Ford Thunderbird Landau two-door hardtop V-8. (OCW)

ENGINE [Thunderbird 406 V-8]: Overhead valve. Cast-iron block. Displacement: 406 cid. Bore and stroke: 4.13 x 3.76 inches. Compression ratio: 11.4:1. Brake hp: 385 at 5600 rpm. Carburetor: Holley four-barrel. Five main bearings. Serial number code "B."

ENGINE [Thunderbird Special "Six-Barrel" V-8]: Overhead valve. Cast-iron block. Displacement: 406 cid. Bore and stroke: 4.13 x 3.78 inches. Compression ratio: 11.4:1. Brake hp: 405 at 5800 rpm. Carburetor: three Holley two-barrel. Five main bearings. Serial number code "G."

ENGINE [Thunderbird High-Performance V-8]: Overhead valve. Cast-iron block. Displacement: 427 cid. Bore and stroke: 4.23 x 3.78 inches. Compression ratio: 11.5:1. Brake hp: 410 at 5600 rpm. Carburetor: Holley four-barrel. Five main bearings. Serial number code "Q."

ENGINE [Thunderbird High-Performance 8V V-8]: Overhead valve. Cast-iron block. Displacement: 427 cid. Bore and stroke: 4.23 x 3.78 inches. Compression ratio: 11.5:1. Brake hp: 425 at 6000 rpm. Carburetor: two Holley four-barrel. Five main bearings. Serial number code "R."

NOTE: Export engines have lower compression and less horsepower.

FORD CHASSIS FEATURES: Wheelbase: 119 inches. Overall length: 209.0 inches. Tires: 7.50 x 14 four-ply tubeless blackwalls (8.00 x 14 four-ply tubeless blackwalls on station wagons).

FAIRLANE CHASSIS FEATURES: Wheelbase: 115.5 inches. Overall length: 197.6 inches (201.8 inches on station wagons). Tires: 6.50 x 13 four-ply blackwall tubeless (7.00 x 14 four-ply blackwall tubeless on station wagons).

FALCON CHASSIS FEATURES: Wheelbase: 109.5 inches. Overall length: 181.1 inches. Tires: 6.00 x 13 four-ply tubeless blackwall (6.50 x 13 four-ply tubeless on station wagons and convertibles).

THUNDERBIRD CHASSIS FEATURES: Wheelbase: 113 inches. Overall length: 205 inches. Tires: 8.00 x 14 four-ply tubeless whitewalls.

FORD OPTIONS: Popular '300' and Galaxie series options included the 289 cid V-8 engine ($109). Cruise-O-Matic automatic transmission ($212). Power steering ($81). Power brakes ($43). White sidewall tires ($33). Popular Galaxie 500 and Galaxie 500XL options included the 390 cid V-8 engine ($246). Cruise-O-Matic automatic transmission ($212). Four-speed manual transmission ($188). Power steering ($81). Power brakes ($43). Two-tone paint ($22). White sidewall tires ($33). Windshield washers ($20). Back-up lights ($10). Electric clock ($14). Radio ($58). AM/FM radio ($129). Popular station wagon options included power tailgate window ($32). Luggage rack ($45). Electric clock ($14). There were 758 Country Squires produced with the optional bucket seat interior at $141 extra. Popular Fairlane and Fairlane 500 options included the 260 cid engines ($103 or $154). Ford-O-Matic automatic transmission ($189). Four-speed manual transmission with V-8s ($188). AM radio ($58). Power steering ($81). Power tailgate window on station wagons ($32). Luggage rack on station wagons ($45). Two-tone paint ($22). White sidewall tires ($34). Padded dashboard and sun visors ($24). Popular Falcon options included the 170 cid six-cylinder engine ($437). The 260 cid V-8 ($158 or $196). Ford-O-Matic automatic transmission ($163). Four-speed manual transmission ($90 with six-cylinder or $188 with V-8). Power tailgate window on station wagons ($29). Two-tone paint ($19). AM radio ($58). White sidewall tires ($29). Back-up lights ($10). Deluxe trim package for sedans ($37). Popular Thunderbird options included power windows ($106). Power seats ($92). Passenger power seats ($92). AM/FM radio ($83). Tinted glass ($43). Windshield washers ($13). Wire wheels ($343).

HISTORY: The "Fairlane 500 Sport Coupe" was a two-door pillarless hardtop. The "Falcon Sprint" was a compact, high-performance V-8-powered Falcon. The "Galaxie Fastback" was a full-size two-door hardtop with more gently sloping roofline than conventional hardtop, to produce less wind resistance. Ford built 50 Galaxie "factory lightweight" race cars this year. A team of specially prepared 1963 Falcon Sprint hardtops terrorized the European rally circuit, with some very un-Falconlike performance.

1964 FORD

1964 FORDS — OVERVIEW — As is the case in the previous six years, the 1964 Fords were totally restyled. This year it wasn't just the regular Ford that came under the stylist's brush, but the entire line from the compact Falcon to the prestigious Thunderbird. Engine choices remained virtually unchanged for 1964.

FORD CUSTOM SERIES — (6-CYL/V-8) — Full-size Fords were completely revamped for 1964. They were recognizable as Ford products only because of their traditional large, round taillights. The grille carried a horizontal grid highlighted with three vertical ribs. The Ford name, in block letters, was seen on all models, but side trim differed considerably. A sheet metal feature line began on the front fender at beltline level. It continued horizontally, to the rear of the car, and dipped down. A lower sheet metal feature line began behind the front wheels and continued, horizontally, toward the rear of the car. There it swept upward and merged with the upper feature line. All models using optional large displacement V-8s earned the engine designation symbol on the lower front fender. The Custom series was the base trim level. It included chrome windshield and rear window moldings, two sun visors, a chrome horn ring, armrests on all doors and three cast 'stripes' on the front fenders, just behind the headlights.

CUSTOM SIX I.D. NUMBERS: The serial number code can be broken down as follows: First symbol indicates year: 4 = 1964. Second symbol identifies assembly plant, as follows: A = Atlanta; D = Dallas; G = Chicago; F = Dearborn; E = Mahwah; H = Loraine; J = Los Angeles; K = Kansas City; L = Long Beach; N = Norfolk; R = San Jose; S = Pilot Plant; T = Metuchen; U = Louisville; P = Twin Cities; W = Wayne; Y = Wixom; Z = St. Louis. Third and fourth symbols identify body series (see Body/ Numbers below). Fifth symbol identifies engine code, as follows: U = 170 cid six-cylinder; T = 200 cid six-cylinder; V = 223 cid six-cylinder; L = 221 cid V-8; F = 260 cid V-8; C = 289 cid V-8; D = 289 cid V-8 with four-barrel carb; K = 289 cid V-8 (high performance); X = 352 cid V-8 with four-barrel carb; Z = 390 cid V-8 with four-barrel carb; S = 144 cid six-cylinder; M = 390 cid V-8 (high performance); Q or R = 427 cid V-8 (high performance). The last six digits are the unit's production number, beginning at 100001 and going up, at each of the assembly plants. Custom six-cylinder models began with the number '4' followed by the assembly plant code, engine designation 'V' and, finally, the unit's production number according to the final assembly location. Each plant began at 100001 and went up.

CUSTOM SIX SERIES

Model No.	Body/ Style No.	Body Type & Seating	Factory Price	Shipping Weight	Prod. Total
V	54	4-dr Sed-6P	2404	3621	Note 1
V	53	2-dr Sed-6P	2350	3521	Note 1

NOTE 1: See Custom V-8 series listing. Production was counted by series and body only, with no engine breakout.

CUSTOM V-8 I.D. NUMBERS: Custom V-8 models began with the number '4,' followed by the assembly plant code, body type code, engine designation code and, finally, the unit's production number according to the final assembly location. Each plant began at 100001 and went up.

1964 Ford Galaxie 500 four-door Town Sedan V-8. (OCW)

CUSTOM V-8 SERIES

Model No.	Body/ Style No.	Body Type & Seating	Factory Price	Shipping Weight	Prod. Total
N/A	54	4-dr Sed-6P	2513	3617	57,964
N/A	53	2-dr Sed-6P	2459	3527	41,359

PRODUCTION NOTE: Total series output was 99,323 units. Ford does not indicate the number of each model produced with sixes or V-8s. Therefore, all production figures given above are total production of each body style with both engines.

CUSTOM 500 SERIES — (6-CYL/V-8) — The Custom 500 was the upper trim level of the base-line Custom series and included chrome windshield and rear window moldings; nylon carpeting (instead of the rubber mats used in the Custom models); armrests with ashtrays on all doors; two sun visors and all trim used in the Custom models plus a single horizontal chrome strip on the exterior bodyside.

CUSTOM 500 SIX I.D. NUMBERS: Custom 500 six-cylinder models used the same serial number sequence as the Custom models.

CUSTOM 500 SIX SERIES

Model No.	Body/ Style No.	Body Type & Seating	Factory Price	Shipping Weight	Prod. Total
V	52	4-dr Sed-6P	2507	3661	Note 1
V	51	2-dr Sed-6P	2453	3561	Note 1

NOTE 1: See Custom 500 V-8 series listing. Production was counted by series and body only, with no engine breakout.

CUSTOM 500 V-8 I.D. NUMBERS: Custom 500 V-8 models used the same serial number sequence as the Custom models.

CUSTOM 500 V-8 SERIES

Model No.	Body/ Style No.	Body Type & Seating	Factory Price	Shipping Weight	Prod. Total
N/A	52	4-dr Sed-6P	2616	3657	68,828
N/A	51	2-dr Sed-6P	2562	3557	20,619

PRODUCTION NOTE: Total series output was 89,447 units. Ford does not indicate the number of each model produced with sixes or V-8s. Therefore, all production figures given above are total production of each body style with both engines.

GALAXIE 500 SERIES — (6-CYL/V-8) — The Galaxie 500 was the top trim level for 1964 and included all Custom trim, plus chrome fendertop ornamentation, chrome window frames, the Ford crest on the roof 'C' pillar and a full-length chrome strip (which split at the rear of the front doors and included an aluminum insert forward of that point). 'Galaxie 500', in script, was included in the aluminum insert, at the front of the stripe. A stamped aluminum insert also highlighted the rear treatment and included 'Galaxie 500' in script on the right side of the insert. Two-tone vinyl trim was used on the side of the doors and on the seats.

GALAXIE 500 SIX I.D. NUMBERS: Galaxie 500 six-cylinder models used the same serial number sequence as the Custom series.

GALAXIE 500 SIX SERIES

Model No.	Body/ Style No.	Body Type & Seating	Factory Price	Shipping Weight	Prod. Total
V	62	4-dr Twn Sed-6P	2667	3676	Note 1
V	61	2-dr Clb Sed-6P	2613	3576	Note 1
V	64	4-dr Twn Vic-6P	2739	3691	Note 1
V	66	2-dr Clb Vic-5P	2674	3586	Note 1
V	65	2-dr Sun Conv-5P	2936	3761	Note 1

NOTE 1: See Galaxie 500 V-8 series listing. Production was counted by series and body only, with no engine breakout.

1964 Ford Galaxie 500XL two-door Club Victoria V-8. (PH)

1964 Ford Galaxie 500XL four-door Town Victoria V-8. (OCW)

GALAXIE 500 V-8 I.D. NUMBERS: Galaxie 500 V-8 models used the same serial number sequence as the Custom series.

GALAXIE 500 V-8 SERIES

Model No.	Body/ Style No.	Body Type & Seating	Factory Price	Shipping Weight	Prod. Total
N/A	62	4-dr Twn Sed-6P	2776	3672	196,805
N/A	61	2-dr Clb Sed-6P	2722	3572	13,041
N/A	64	4-dr Twn Vic-6P	2848	3667	49,242
N/A	66	2-dr Clb Vic-5P	2763	3582	206,996
N/A	65	2-dr Sun Conv-5P	3045	3757	37,311

PRODUCTION NOTE: Total series output was 505,397 units. Ford does not indicate the number of each model produced with sixes or V-8s. Therefore, all production figures given above are total production of each body style with both engines.

GALAXIE 500XL SERIES — (V-8) — Galaxie 500XL included all the trim features of the Galaxie models plus bucket seats and floor-mounted transmission shifter; polished door trim panels; dual-lens courtesy/warning lights in the doors; rear reading lights in hardtops and Galaxie 500XL badges on the body exterior. The 289 cid/195 hp V-8 engine was standard on all XLs.

GALAXIE 500 XL I.D. NUMBERS: Galaxie 500XLs used the same serial number sequence as the Custom and Galaxie 500 series.

GALAXIE 500XL SERIES

Model No.	Body/ Style No.	Body Type & Seating	Factory Price	Shipping Weight	Prod. Total
N/A	60	4-dr Twn Vic-5P	3287	3722	14,661
N/A	68	2-dr Clb Vic-5P	3222	3622	58,306
N/A	69	2-dr Conv-5P	3484	3787	15,169

PRODUCTION NOTE: Total series output was 88,136 units.

STATION WAGON SERIES — (6-CYL/V-8) — The Country Sedans were the base trim level station wagons for 1964, with the Country Squires being the top trim level. The trim paralleled the Galaxie 500 and Galaxie 500XL models of passenger cars.

STATION WAGON SIX I.D. NUMBERS: Station wagon six-cylinder models used the same serial number sequence as Custom and Galaxie 500 series of passenger cars.

1964 Ford Galaxie 500XL two-door convertible V-8. (OCW)

1964 Ford Country Squire station wagon V-8. (OCW)

STATION WAGON SIX SERIES

Model No.	Body/Style No.	Body Type & Seating	Factory Price	Shipping Weight	Prod. Total
V	72	4-dr Cty Sed-6P	2829	3975	Note 1
V	74	4-dr Cty Sed-9P	2933	3985	Note 1
V	76	4-dr Cty Sq-6P	3018	3990	Note 1
V	78	4-dr Cty Sq-9P	3088	4000	Note 1

NOTE 1: See station wagon V-8 series listing. Production was counted by series and body only, with no engine breakout.

STATION WAGON V-8 I.D. NUMBERS: Station wagon V-8 models used the same serial number sequence as Custom and Galaxie 500 models of passenger cars.

STATION WAGON V-8 SERIES

Model No.	Body/Style No.	Body Type & Seating	Factory Price	Shipping Weight	Prod. Total
N/A	72	4-dr Cty Sed-6P	2938	3971	68,578
N/A	74	4-dr Cty Sed-9P	3042	3981	25,661
N/A	76	4-dr Cty Sq-6P	3127	3986	23,570
N/A	78	4-dr Cty Sq-9P	3197	3996	23,120

PRODUCTION NOTE: Total series output was 140,929 units. Ford does not indicate the number of each model produced with sixes or V-8s. Therefore, all production figures given above are total production of each body style with both engines.

FAIRLANE SERIES — (6-CYL/V-8) — The 1964 Fairlane styling featured new sheet metal for the bodysides and rear, which seemed to add to the Fairlane's 'Total Performance' image. The rear fenders featured a smoother top than in 1963, with a complete absence of fins. The sides were sculptured into a convex shape, which flowed forward from the sides of the taillights and terminated in a chrome scoop. The grille carried the familiar horizontal grid with thin vertical dividers.

FAIRLANE SIX I.D. NUMBERS: Fairlane six-cylinder models began with number '4' followed by the assembly plant code, body type code, engine designation code and, finally, the unit's production number according to the final assembly location. Each plant began at 100001 and went up.

FAIRLANE SIX SERIES

Model No.	Body/Style No.	Body Type & Seating	Factory Price	Shipping Weight	Prod. Total
U/T	32	4-dr Sed-6P	2224	2828	Note 1
U/T	31	2-dr Sed-6P	2183	2788	Note 1
U/T	38	2-dr Ranch Wag-6P	2520	3223	Note 1

NOTE 1: See Fairlane V-8 series listing. Production was counted by series and body only, with no engine breakout.

1964 Ford Fairlane 500 Custom station wagon V-8. (OCW)

1964 Ford Fairlane 500 two-door Sports Coupe V-8. (OCW)

FAIRLANE V-8 I.D. NUMBERS: Fairlane V-8 models began with the number '4' followed by the assembly plant code, body type code, engine designation 'U' or 'T' and, finally, the unit's production number according to the final assembly location. Each plant began at 100001 and went up.

FAIRLANE V-8 SERIES

Model No.	Body/Style No.	Body Type & Seating	Factory Price	Shipping Weight	Prod. Total
N/A	32	4-dr Sed-6P	2324	2962	36,693
N/A	31	2-dr Sed-6P	2283	2922	20,421
N/A	38	2-dr Ranch Wag-6P	2620	3357	20,980

PRODUCTION NOTE: Total series output was 78,094 units. Ford does not indicate the number of each model produced with sixes or V-8s. Therefore, all production figures given above are total production of each body style with both engines.

FAIRLANE 500 SERIES — (6-CYL/V-8) — The Fairlane 500 models were the top trim level of the line and included chrome window moldings; a chrome horn ring; armrests on all doors and a twin-spear side molding running the full length of the body (with an accent color of red, black or white, between the spears). In addition, chrome fendertop ornaments and the Ford crest appeared on the 'C' pillar of the more Deluxe model of the series. Fairlane 500 models also had carpeting.

FAIRLANE 500 SIX I.D. NUMBERS: Fairlane 500 six-cylinder models used the same serial number sequence as the Fairlane models.

FAIRLANE 500 SIX SERIES

Model No.	Body/Style No.	Body Type & Seating	Factory Price	Shipping Weight	Prod. Total
U/T	42	4-dr Twn Sed-6P	2306	2843	Note 1
U/T	41	2-dr Clb Sed-6P	2265	2813	Note 1
U/T	43	2-dr HT Cpe-6P	2330	2858	Note 1
U/T	47	2-dr HT Spt Cpe-5P	2491	2878	Note 1
U/T	48	4-dr Cus Sta Wag-6P	2601	3243	Note 1

NOTE 1: See Fairlane 500 V-8 series listing. Production was counted by series and body only, with no engine breakouts.

FAIRLANE 500 V-8 I.D. NUMBERS: Fairlane 500 V-8 models used the same serial number sequence as the Fairlane models.

FAIRLANE 500 V-8 SERIES

Model No.	Body/Style No.	Body Type & Seating	Factory Price	Shipping Weight	Prod. Total
N/A	42	4-dr Twn Sed-6P	2406	3051	86,919
N/A	41	2-dr Clb Sed-6P	2365	2913	23,477
N/A	43	2-dr HT Cpe-6P	2430	2992	42,733
N/A	47	2-dr HT Spt Cpe-5P	2591	3012	12,431
N/A	46	4-dr Cus ta Wag-6P	2701	3377	24,962

PRODUCTION NOTE: Total series output was 199,522 units. Ford does not indicate the number of each model produced with sixes or V-8s. Therefore, all production figures given above are total production of each body style with both engines.

FALCON SERIES — (6-CYL/V-8) — The 1964 Falcons reflected the 'Total Performance' image in their new styling. A more aggressive, angled grille led a completely restyled body. As in 1963, the base trim level was the standard series, and the top trim level was the Futura. The highly sculptured bodysides gave the 1964 Falcons a racy appearance and added rigidity to the sheet metal. A convex feature line began on the front fenders, but sloped slightly and increased in width gradually, until it met the taillights. The word 'Ford' was spelled out across the hood in block letters and 'Falcon' was spelled out in block letters between the taillights. The new grille featured a rectangular design that was angularly recessed and complemented the side profile. As in past years, the Falcons continued to use single headlamps.

Standard Falcon cars were the base trim level for 1964. They included chrome windshield and rear window moldings, twin horns, two sun visors, armrests on the front doors only and a horn button instead of a chrome horn ring.

STANDARD FALCON I.D. NUMBERS — (6-CYL/V-8) — Standard series Falcons used the same serial number sequence as the full-size Fords and the Fairlane line.

STANDARD FALCON SERIES

Model No.	Body/ Style No.	Body Type & Seating	Factory Price	Shipping Weight	Prod. Total
N/A	02	4-dr Sed-6P	2040	2400	54,254
N/A	01	2-dr Sed-6P	1985	2365	64,852

NOTE: The Production Totals listed include those Falcons equipped with Deluxe trim, with a breakdown as follows: Standard four-door sedan (27,722); Deluxe four-door sedan (26,532); Standard two-door sedan (36,441); Deluxe two-door sedan (28,411).

FALCON FUTURA SERIES — (6-CYL/V-8) — The Futura series was the top trim level for 1964 and included a chrome horn ring; rear armrests with ashtrays: twin horns; Futura wheel covers (instead of hubcaps); chrome hood ornament; Futura symbol on the front fender; chrome side window moldings; chrome windshield and rear window moldings; two horizontal sloping chrome strips on the bodyside and four cast 'hash marks' on the rear fender in front of the taillights. The Sprint versions of the Futura hardtop and convertible also featured a V-8 engine, bucket seats and wire wheel covers.

FALCON FUTURA I.D. NUMBERS: Futura models used the same serial number sequence as the full-size Fords, Fairlanes and standard series Falcons.

FALCON FUTURA SERIES

Model No.	Body/ Style No.	Body Type & Seating	Factory Price	Shipping Weight	Prod. Total
N/A	16	4-dr Sed-6P	2165	2410	38,032
N/A	19	2-dr Sed-6P	2116	2375	16,261
N/A	17	2-dr Sed-6P	2237	2350	212
N/A	17	2-dr HT Cpe-6P	2198	2515	32,608
N/A	11	2-dr Spt HT-5P	2314	2545	8,322
N/A	15	2-dr Conv-6P	2470	2710	13,220
N/A	12	2-dr Spt Conv-5P	2586	2735	2,980

SPRINT V-8 SUBSERIES

Model No.	Body/ Style No.	Body Type & Seating	Factory Price	Shipping Weight	Prod. Total
N/A	13	2-dr Sprint HT-5P	2425	2813	13,830
N/A	14	2-dr Sprint Conv-5P	2660	3008	4,278

PRODUCTION NOTE: Total series output was 130,103 units. This figure includes 285 Sprint hardtops built without consoles, 626 Sprint convertibles built with bench seats. Ford does not indicate the number of each model produced with sixes or V-8s. Therefore all production figures given above, except for Sprint models, are total production of each body style with both engines. The Sprint models came only with V-8 engines.

1964 Ford Falcon Sprint convertible. (OCW)

1964 Ford Falcon Squire station wagon V-8. (PH)

FALCON STATION WAGON SERIES — (6-CYL/V-8) — Falcon station wagons became a separate series for the first time in 1964 and included the base standard series, the intermediate Deluxe series and the top-line Squire wagon.

FALCON STATION WAGON I.D. NUMBERS: Falcon station wagons used the same serial number sequence as the full-size Fords, Fairlanes and Falcon sedans.

FALCON STATION WAGON SERIES

Model No.	Body/ Style No.	Body Type & Seating	Factory Price	Shipping Weight	Prod. Total
N/A	22	4-dr Sta Wag-6P	2349	2695	17,779
N/A	21	2-dr Sta Wag-6P	2315	2660	6,034
N/A	24	4-dr DeL Sta Wag-6P	2435	2715	20,697
N/A	26	4-dr Squire Sta Wag-6P	2611	2720	6,766

PRODUCTION NOTE: Total series output was 51,276 units. Ford does not indicate the number of each model produced with sixes or V-8s. Therefore, all production figures given above are total production of each body style with both engines.

THUNDERBIRD SERIES — (V-8) — The 1964 Thunderbirds were also completely restyled and featured longer hoods and shorter roof lines than previous offerings. The side panels were highly sculptured. They had mirror-image feature lines at the beltline and lower bodyside. The front end was more aggressive and featured a larger power dome (scoop) on the hood. The headlights were spaced farther apart than in previous years. The rear of the 1964 T-bird featured rectangular taillights set within a massive bumper. The Thunderbird name, in script, was located just behind the front wheels on the front fenders and Thunderbird, in block letters, was spaced along the front of the hood. The factory-built Sports Roadster was dropped, but dealers continued to add this kit, as an option, on a few 1964 Thunderbirds.

THUNDERBIRD I.D. NUMBERS: Thunderbird models began with the number '4,' assembly plant code 'Y' (Wixom), body type code, engine type code 'Z' and, finally, the unit's production number, beginning at 100001 and going up.

THUNDERBIRD SERIES

Model No.	Body/ Style No.	Body Type & Seating	Factory Price	Shipping Weight	Prod. Total
Z	83	2-dr HT Cpe-4P	4486	4431	60,552
Z	87	2-dr Landau-4P	4589	4586	22,715
Z	85	2-dr Conv-4P	4853	4441	9,198

PRODUCTION NOTE: Total series output was 92,465 units.

ENGINE [Falcon Base Six]: Overhead valve. Cast-iron block. Displacement: 144 cid. Bore and stroke: 3.50 x 2.50 inches. Compression ratio: 8.7:1. Brake hp: 85 at 4200 rpm. Carburetor: Holley one-barrel. Seven main bearings. Serial number code "S."

ENGINE [Falcon/Fairlane Six]: Overhead valve. Cast-iron block. Displacement: 170 cid. Bore and stroke: 3.50 x 2.94 inches. Compression ratio: 8.7:1. Brake hp: 101 at 4400 rpm. Carburetor: Holley one-barrel. Seven main bearings. Serial number code "U."

ENGINE [Ford Base Six]: Overhead valve. Cast-iron block. Displacement: 223 cid. Bore and stroke: 3.62 x 3.60 inches. Compression ratio: 8.4:1. Brake hp: 138 at 4200 rpm. Carburetor: Holley one-barrel. Four main bearings. Serial number code "V."

ENGINE [V-8]: Overhead valve. Cast-iron block. Displacement: 260 cid. Bore and stroke: 3.80 x 2.87 inches. Compression ratio: 8.8:1. Brake hp: 164 at 4400 rpm. Carburetor: Holley two-barrel. Five main bearings. Serial number code "F."

1964 Ford Thunderbird Landau two-door hardtop V-8. (OCW)

1964 Ford Thunderbird two-door convertible (with optional tonneau cover) V-8. (OCW)

ENGINE [Challenger 289 V-8]: Overhead valve. Cast-iron block. Displacement: 289 cid. Bore and stroke: 4.00 x 2.87 inches. Compression ratio: 9.0:1. Brake hp: 195 at 4400 rpm. Carburetor: Holley two-barrel. Five main bearings. Serial number code "C."

ENGINE [Challenger 289 Four-Barrel V-8]: Overhead valve. Cast-iron block. Displacement: 289 cid. Bore and stroke: 4.00 x 2.87 inches. Compression ratio: 9.8:1. Brake hp: 225 at 4800 rpm. Carburetor: Holley four-barrel. Five main bearings. Serial number code "A."

ENGINE [High-Performance Challenger 289 V-8]: Overhead valve. Cast-iron block. Displacement: 289 cid. Bore and stroke: 4.00 x 2.87 inches. Compression ratio: 10.5:1. Brake hp: 271 at 6000 rpm. Carburetor: Holley four-barrel. Five main bearings. Serial number code "K."

ENGINE [Interceptor V-8]: Overhead valve. Cast-iron block. Displacement: 352 cid. Bore and stroke: 4.00 x 3.50 inches. Compression ratio: 9.3:1. Brake hp: 250 at 4400 rpm. Carburetor: Holley four-barrel. Five main bearings. Serial number code "X."

ENGINE [Thunderbird V-8]: Overhead valve. Cast-iron block. Displacement: 390 cid. Bore and stroke: 4.05 x 3.78 inches. Compression ratio: 10.1:1. Brake hp: 300 at 4600 rpm. Carburetor: Holley four-barrel. Five main bearings. Serial number code "Z."

ENGINE [Thunderbird Police Special V-8]: Overhead valve. Cast-iron block. Displacement: 390 cid. Bore and stroke: 4.05 x 3.78 inches. Compression ratio: 10.1:1. Brake hp: 330 at 5000 rpm. Carburetor: Holley four-barrel. Five main bearings. Serial number code "P."

ENGINE [Thunderbird High-Performance V-8]: Overhead valve. Cast-iron block. Displacement: 427 cid. Bore and stroke: 4.23 x 3.78 inches. Compression ratio: 11.5:1. Brake hp: 410 at 5600 rpm. Carburetor: Holley four-barrel. Five main bearings. Serial number code "Q."

ENGINE [Thunderbird Super High-Performance V-8]: Overhead valve. Cast-iron block. Displacement: 427 cid. Bore and stroke: 4.23 x 3.78 inches. Compression ratio: 11.5:1. Brake hp: 425 at 6000 rpm. Carburetor: Two Holley four-barrel. Five main bearings. Serial number code "R."

CHASSIS FEATURES: Wheelbase: (full-size Fords) 119 inches; (Fairlane) 115.5 inches; (Falcon) 109.5 inches; (Thunderbird) 113.2 inches. Overall length: (full-size Fords) 209.9 inches; (Fairlane passenger models) 197.6 inches; (Fairlane station wagons) 201.8 inches; (Falcon Sprint) 181.1 inches; (Falcon passenger cars) 181.6 inches; (Falcon station wagons) 189 inches; (Thunderbird) 205.4 inches. Tires: (Ford Custom) 7.00 x 14; (Ford station wagons) 8.00 x 14; (all other Fords) 7.50 x 14; (Fairlane passenger cars) 6.50 x 14; (Fairlane station wagons) 7.00 x 14; (Falcon Sprint) 6.50 x 13; (Falcon convertible) 6.50 x 13; (Falcon station wagons) 6.50 x 13; (regular Falcons) 6.00 x 13; (Thunderbird) 8.15 x 15.

FORD OPTIONS: Popular Custom and Galaxie series options included 289 cid V-8 engine ($109). 390 cid V-8 engine ($246). Cruise-O-Matic automatic transmission ($189 or $212). Four-speed manual transmission ($188). Power steering ($86). Power brakes ($43). Power windows ($102). Tinted windshield ($21). AM radio ($58). Vinyl roof on two-door Victorias ($75). Wheel covers ($45). White sidewall tires ($33). Popular station wagon options included the 390 cid V-8 engine ($246). Cruise-O-Matic automatic transmission ($212). Power steering ($86). Power brakes ($43). Power tailgate window ($32). Luggage rack ($45). White sidewall tires ($33). Electric clock ($14). Radio ($58 for AM, $129 for AM/FM).

FAIRLANE OPTIONS: 260 cid V-8 engine ($100). The 289 cid V-8 engine ($145). 390 cid V-8. 427 cid V-8. Ford-O-Matic automatic transmission ($189). Cruise-O-Matic automatic transmission ($189). Four-speed manual transmissions with V-8 engines ($188). AM radio ($58). Power steering ($86). Power tailgate window on station wagons ($32). Luggage rack on station wagons ($45). Two-tone paint ($22). White sidewall tires ($33). Wheel covers ($18). Vinyl roof on two-door hardtops ($75).

FALCON OPTIONS: 170 cid six-cylinder engine ($17). The 260 cid V-8 engine ($170). Ford-O-Matic automatic transmission ($177). Four-speed manual transmission ($92 with six-cylinder; $188 with V-8). AM radio ($58). Two-tone paint ($19). White sidewall tires ($30). Back-up lights ($10). Deluxe trim package for standard sedans ($43). Popular Falcon station wagon options included all those for sedans, plus power tailgate window ($30).

THUNDERBIRD OPTIONS: Air conditioning ($415). Tinted windows ($43). Leather seats ($106). Power seats ($184). Power windows ($108). AM/FM radio ($83). White sidewall tires ($42). Fiberglass tonneau cover for convertibles ($269). Deluxe wheel covers ($16).

HISTORY: The full-size Fords, Fairlanes and Falcons were introduced Sept. 27, 1963, and the Mustang appeared in dealer showrooms on April 17, 1964. Model year production peaked at 1,015,697 units. Calendar year production of 1,787,535 cars was recorded. The entire lineup of 1964 Fords received *Motor Trend* magazine's "Car of the Year" award. Lee A. Iacocca was the chief executive officer of the company this year. Note also that Ford introduced the famous Fairlane Thunderbolt drag cars and also the single-overhead cam hemi-engine that Ford tried to use for NASCAR racing. It was disallowed due to insufficient number produced for homologation.

1965 FORD

1965 FORDS — OVERVIEW — As well as several of the lines being completely restyled once again for 1965, the new "Total Performance" Ford lineup represented five full car-lines, with 44 models—the widest choice of models in Ford Division's history.

The 1965 full-size Fords were billed as the "Newest since 1949." Luxury and comfort were featured with the big Fords, which used rear coil springs for the first time and featured new interior styling. "Silent Flow" ventilation systems were standard on four-door hardtops. In keeping with the new luxury image, the Galaxie 500 LTD interior trim option was offered for the first time for two- and four-door hardtops. Completely restyled once again, the full-size Fords possessed incredibly clean styling with sharp, square lines and almost no curves. The new grille featured thin horizontal bars that followed the leading edge contour of the hood and were framed by the new vertical dual headlights. From the side, a single, horizontal feature line divided the less prominent beltline and lower body lines. As in 1964, all full-size Fords carried the engine designation symbol on the front fender behind the front wheel, for the larger, optional V-8 engines.

FORD CUSTOM SERIES — (6-CYL/V-8) — The Custom series was the base trim level full-size Ford for 1965, and included chrome windshield and rear window moldings, two sun visors, a chrome horn ring, armrests on all doors, and the "Custom" name on the front fender. The taillights were round lenses in a rectangular housing. The Ford name appeared in block letters across the front of the hood and on the vertical section of the trunk lid.

1965 Ford Galaxie 500XL two-door convertible V-8. (OCW)

CUSTOM SIX I.D. NUMBERS: The serial number code can be broken down, as follows: First symbol indicates year: 5 = 1965. Second symbol identifies assembly plant, as follows: A = Atlanta; B = Oakville, Ontario, Canada; D = Dallas; F = Dearborn; E = Mahwah; H = Loraine; J = Los Angeles; K = Kansas City; L = Long Beach; N = Norfolk; R = San Jose; S = Pilot Plant; T = Metuchen; U = Louisville; P = Twin Cities; W = Wayne; Y = Wixom; Z = St. Louis. Third and fourth symbols identify body series (see Body/ Numbers below). Fifth symbol identifies engine code, as follows: U = 170 cid six-cylinder; T = 200 cid six-cylinder; V = 240 cid six-cylinder; F = 260 cid V-8; C = 289 cid V-8; D = 289 cid V-8 with four-barrel carb; K = 289 cid V-8 (high performance); X = 352 cid V-8 with four-barrel carb; Z = 390 cid V-8 with four-barrel carb; L or M = 427 cid V-8 (overhead cam); R = 427 cid V-8 (high performance). The last six digits are the unit's production number, beginning at 100001 and going up, at each of the assembly plants. Custom six-cylinder models began with the number "5" followed by the assembly plant code, engine designation code "V," and, finally, the unit's production number according to the final assembly location. Each plant began at 100001 and went up.

CUSTOM SIX SERIES

Model No.	Body/ Style No.	Body Type & Seating	Factory Price	Shipping Weight	Prod. Total
V	54	4-dr Sed-6P	2366	3350	Note 1
V	62	2-dr Sed-6P	2313	3278	Note 1

NOTE 1: See Custom V-8 series listing. Production was counted by series and body only, with no engine breakouts.

CUSTOM V-8 I.D. NUMBERS: Custom V-8 models began with the number "5" followed by the assembly plant code, body type code, engine designation code and, finally, the unit's production number according to the final assembly location. Each plant began at 100001 and went up.

CUSTOM V-8 SERIES

Model No.	Body/ Style No.	Body Type & Seating	Factory Price	Shipping Weight	Prod. Total
N/A	54	4-dr Sed-6P	2472	3400	96,393
N/A	62	2-dr Sed-6P	2420	3328	49,034

PRODUCTION NOTE: Total series output was 145,427 units. Ford does not indicate the number of each model produced with sixes and V-8s. Therefore, all production figures are total production of each body style with both engines.

CUSTOM 500 SERIES — (6-CYL/V-8) — The Custom 500 was the upper trim level of the base-line Custom series and included chrome windshield and rear window moldings; nylon carpeting instead of the rubber mats used in the Custom models; armrests, with ashtrays, on all doors; two sun visors and all the trim used in the Custom models plus a short horizontal chrome strip along the front fender and front door.

CUSTOM 500 SIX I.D. NUMBERS: Custom 500 six-cylinder models used the same serial number sequence as the Custom models.

CUSTOM 500 SIX SERIES

Model No.	Body/ Style No.	Body Type & Seating	Factory Price	Shipping Weight	Prod. Total
V	54B	4-dr Sed-6P	2467	3380	Note 1
V	62B	2-dr Sed-6P	2414	3308	Note 1

NOTE 1: See Custom 500 V-8 series listing. Production was counted by series and body only, with no engine breakouts.

CUSTOM 500 V-8 I.D. NUMBERS: Custom 500 V-8 models used the same serial number sequence as the Custom models.

CUSTOM 500 V-8 SERIES

Model No.	Body/ Style No.	Body Type & Seating	Factory Price	Shipping Weight	Prod. Total
N/A	54B	4-dr Sed-6P	2573	3430	71,727
N/A	62B	2-dr Sed-6P	2520	3358	19,603

PRODUCTION NOTE: Total series output was 91,330 units. Ford does not indicate the number of each model produced with sixes and V-8s. Therefore, all production figures are total production of each body style with both engines.

GALAXIE 500 SERIES — (6-CYL/V-8) — The Galaxie 500 was the intermediate trim level for 1965, and included all the Custom trim plus a chrome hood ornament, Ford crest in the center of the trunk lid, chrome window frames, the Ford crest on the roof "C" pillar, 'Galaxie 500', in block letters, at the front of the front fenders, chrome rocker panel trim, hexagonal taillights with chrome 'cross-hairs' trim and back-up lights. Two-tone vinyl trim was used on the insides of the doors and on the seats.

1965 Ford Galaxie 500 four-door sedan V-8. (OCW)

GALAXIE 500 SIX I.D. NUMBERS: Galaxie 500 six-cylinder models used the same serial number sequence as the Custom series.

GALAXIE 500 SIX SERIES

Model No.	Body/ Style No.	Body Type & Seating	Factory Price	Shipping Weight	Prod. Total
V	54A	4-dr Sed-6P	2623	3412	Note 1
V	57B	4-dr HT-6P	2708	3452	Note 1
V	63B	2-dr HT-6P	2630	3352	Note 1
V	76A	2-dr Conv-6P	2889	3556	Note 1

NOTE 1: See Custom 500 V-8 series listing. Production was counted by series and body only, with no engine breakouts.

GALAXIE 500 V-8 I.D. NUMBERS: Galaxie 500 V-8 models used the same serial number sequence as the Custom series.

GALAXIE 500 V-8 SERIES

Model No.	Body/ Style No.	Body Type & Seating	Factory Price	Shipping Weight	Prod. Total
N/A	54A	4-dr Sed-6P	2730	3462	181,183
N/A	57B	4-dr HT-6P	2815	3502	49,982
N/A	63B	2-dr HT-6P	2737	3402	157,284
N/A	76A	2-dr Conv-6P	2996	3616	31,930

PRODUCTION NOTE: Total series output was 420,379 units. Ford does not indicate the number of each model produced with sixes and V-8s. Therefore, all production figures are total production of each body style with both engines.

GALAXIE 500XL SERIES — (V-8) — Galaxie 500XL was the sport trim version of the Galaxie 500 two-door hardtop and two-door convertible, and included all Galaxie 500 trim plus bucket seats and floor-mounted shift lever, polished door trim panels with carpeting on the lower portion of the doors, dual-lens courtesy/warning lights in the door panels, rear reading lights in hardtops and Galaxie 500XL badges on the body exterior. The 289 cid/200 hp V-8 engine and Cruise-O-Matic automatic transmission were standard in both XL body styles.

GALAXIE 500XL I.D. NUMBERS: Galaxie 500XLs used the same serial number sequence as the Custom and Galaxie series.

GALAXIE 500XL SERIES

Model No.	Body/ Style No.	Body Type & Seating	Factory Price	Shipping Weight	Prod. Total
N/A	63C	2-dr HT-5P	3167	3507	28,141
N/A	76B	2-dr Conv-5P	3426	3675	9,849

PRODUCTION NOTE: Total series output was 37,990 units.

GALAXIE 500 LTD SERIES — (V-8) — The Galaxie 500 LTD was the new top trim level for 1965, and included all the Galaxie 500 trim plus 289 cid/200 hp V-8 engine and Cruise-O-Matic automatic transmission as standard equipment. Also included were thickly padded seats, with 'pinseal' upholstery, simulated walnut appliques on the lower edge of the instrument panel, Gabardine finish headlining and sun visors, front and rear door courtesy/warning lights, courtesy lights in the rear roof pillars on the interior and under the instrument panel, glovebox and ashtray lights and a self regulating clock.

1965 Ford Galaxie 500XL two-door hardtop V-8. (PH)

1965 Ford Galaxie 500 LTD four-door hardtop V-8. (PH)

GALAXIE 500 LTD I.D. NUMBERS:
Galaxie 500 LTD used the same serial number sequence as the Custom and Galaxie 500 series.

GALAXIE 500 LTD SERIES

Model No.	Body/ Style No.	Body Type & Seating	Factory Price	Shipping Weight	Prod. Total
N/A	57F	4-dr HT-6P	3245	3588	68,038
N/A	63F	2-dr HT-6P	3167	3496	37,691

PRODUCTION NOTE: Total series output was 105,729 units.

STATION WAGONS SERIES — (6-CYL/V-8) — The Ranch Wagon was once again the base trim level station wagon for 1965, with the Country Sedans being the intermediate level and the Country Squires being the top trim level. The trim paralleled the Custom 500, Galaxie 500 and Galaxie 500 LTD models of passenger cars.

STATION WAGON SIX I.D. NUMBERS: Station wagon six-cylinder models used the same serial number sequence as Custom and Galaxie 500 series of passenger cars.

STATION WAGON SIX SERIES

Model No.	Body/ Style No.	Body Type & Seating	Factory Price	Shipping Weight	Prod. Total
V	71D	4-dr Ranch Wag-6P	2707	3841	Note 1
V	71B	4-dr Cty Sed-6P	2797	3851	Note 1
V	71C	4-dr Cty Sed-10P	2899	3865	Note 1
V	71E	4-dr Cty Sq-6P	3041	3895	Note 1
V	71A	4-dr Cty Sq-10P	3109	3909	Note 1

NOTE 1: See station wagon V-8 series listing. Production was counted by series and body only, with no engine breakouts.

STATION WAGON V-8 I.D. NUMBERS: Station wagon V-8 models used the same serial number sequence as Custom and Galaxie 500 models of passenger cars.

STATION WAGON V-8 SERIES

Model No.	Body/ Style No.	Body Type & Seating	Factory Price	Shipping Weight	Prod. Total
N/A	71D	4-dr Ranch Wag-6P	2813	3891	30,817
N/A	71B	4-dr Cty Sed-6P	2904	3901	59,693
N/A	71C	4-dr Cty Sed-10P	3005	3915	32,344
N/A	71E	4-dr Cty Sq-6P	3147	3945	24,308
N/A	71A	4-dr Cty Sq-10P	3216	3959	30,502

PRODUCTION NOTE: Total series output was 177,664 units. Ford does not indicate the number of each model produced with sixes and V-8s. Therefore, all production figures are total production of each body style with both engines.

FAIRLANE SERIES — (6-CYL/V-8) — The Fairlane was the base trim level for the line and included chrome windshield and rear window moldings, chrome horn ring, front and rear armrests, cigarette lighter, vinyl coated rubber floor mats, and the Fairlane name in block letters at the front of the front fenders. The 1965 Fairlane featured new sheet metal below the beltline for new front, rear and side appearance. Overall length and width were increased resulting in the first total restyling of the line since its introduction in 1962. The front end featured a wide horizontal grille and horizontal dual headlights. The hood incorporated a small peak in the center that swept forward over the leading edge and met a similar accent line in the grille. Overall profile was changed with a higher fender line that carried farther back, for a more massive look. For the first time since its introduction, Fairlane taillights were not round, but, rather, rectangular and were accented with chrome 'cross-hairs' accents across the lens face. The optional back-up lights were mounted in the center of the lens.

FAIRLANE SIX I.D. NUMBERS: Fairlane six-cylinder models began with the number "5" followed by the assembly plant code, body type code, engine designation "T" and, finally, the unit's production number according to the final assembly location. Each plant began at 100001 and went up.

FAIRLANE SIX SERIES

Model No.	Body/ Style No.	Body Type & Seating	Factory Price	Shipping Weight	Prod. Total
T	54A	4-dr Sed-6P	2223	2858	Note 1
T	62A	2-dr Sed-6P	2183	2806	Note 1
T	71D	4-dr Sta Wag-6P	2512	3183	Note 1

NOTE 1: See Fairlane V-8 series listing. Production was counted by series and body only, with no engine breakouts.

FAIRLANE V-8 I.D. NUMBERS: Fairlane V-8 models began with the number "5" followed by the assembly plant code, body type code, engine designation code and, finally, the unit's production number according to the final assembly location. Each plant began at 100001 and went up.

FAIRLANE V-8 SERIES

Model No.	Body/ Style No.	Body Type & Seating	Factory Price	Shipping Weight	Prod. Total
N/A	54A	4-dr Sed-6P	2329	3055	25,376
N/A	62A	2-dr Sed-6P	2288	2998	13,685
N/A	71D	4-dr Sta Wag-6P	2618	3375	13,911

PRODUCTION NOTE: Total series output was 52,974 units. Ford does not indicate the number of each model produced with sixes and V-8s. Therefore, all production figures are total production of each body style with both engines.

FAIRLANE 500 SERIES — (6-CYL/V-8) — The Fairlane 500 models were the top trim level of the line and included chrome window moldings, a chrome horn ring and front and rear armrest, a Ford crest on the roof "C" pillar, a chrome hood ornament and a single horizontal chrome strip with an aluminum insert. Ford appeared, in block letters, across the rear escutcheon panel, with two chrome strips between the taillights and a Ford crest in the center of the panel. The Fairlane 500 models also used carpet instead of the vinyl floor mats found in Fairlane models.

FAIRLANE 500 SIX I.D. NUMBERS: Fairlane 500 six-cylinder models used the same serial number sequence as the Fairlane models.

FAIRLANE 500 SIX SERIES

Model No.	Body/ Style No.	Body Type & Seating	Factory Price	Shipping Weight	Prod. Total
T	54B	4-dr Sed-6P	2303	2863	Note 1
T	62B	2-dr Sed-6P	2263	2806	Note 1
T	65A	2-dr HT-6P	2327	2877	Note 1
T	65B	2-dr Spt Cpe-5P	2484	2888	Note 1
T	71B	4-dr Sta Wag-6P	2592	3220	Note 1

NOTE 1: See Fairlane 500 V-8 series listing. Production was counted by series and body only, with no engine breakouts.

1965 Ford Fairlane 500 two-door Sports Coupe V-8. (OCW)

1965 Ford Fairlane 500 station wagon V-8. (PH)

FAIRLANE 500 V-8 I.D. NUMBERS: Fairlane 500 V-8 models used the same serial number sequence as the Fairlane models.

FAIRLANE 500 V-8 SERIES

Model No.	Body/ Style No.	Body Type & Seating	Factory Price	Shipping Weight	Prod. Total
N/A	54B	4-dr Sed-6P	2409	3055	77,836
N/A	62B	2-dr Sed-6P	2369	2997	16,092
N/A	65A	2-dr HT-6P	2432	3069	41,405
N/A	65B	2-dr Spt Cpe-5P	2590	3080	15,141
N/A	71B	4-dr Sta Wag-6P	2697	3412	20,506

PRODUCTION NOTE: Total series output was 170,980 units. Ford does not indicate the number of each model produced with sixes and V-8s. Therefore, all production figures are total production of each body style with both engines.

FALCON SERIES — (6-CYL/V-8) — Falcons were the base trim level for 1965, and included chrome windshield and rear window moldings, two horns, two sun visors, armrests on the front doors only, and a horn button instead of a chrome horn ring. While continuing to use the 1964 body shell, trim changes made the 1965 Falcon look considerably different than the previous year. The grille was a thin horizontal bar design, which was divided into two sections by a wider vertical bar at the center. A vertical, three-colored crest was used on the center divider. The round taillights utilized chrome 'cross-hairs' for accent, and the optional back-up lights were mounted in the center of the lens. A new Falcon emblem with black, paint-filled Falcon letters was attached to the front fender behind the wheel opening.

FALCON I.D. NUMBERS: Falcons used the same serial number sequence as the full-size Fords and the Fairlane line.

FALCON SERIES

Model No.	Body/ Style No.	Body Type & Seating	Factory Price	Shipping Weight	Prod. Total
N/A	54A	4-dr Sed-6P	2038	2410	30,186
N/A	62A	2-dr Sed-6P	1977	2370	35,858

FUTURA SERIES — (6-CYL/V-8) — The Futura series was the top Falcon trim level for 1965 and included a chrome horn ring; armrests front and rear, with ashtrays; two horns; Futura wheel covers (instead of hubcaps); a chrome hood ornament; Futura symbol on the front fender behind the wheelwell; chrome windshield and rear window moldings and side window moldings; a full-length, spear-type chrome-molding, with either red, white or black painted insert.

FUTURA I.D. NUMBERS: Futura models used the same serial number sequence as the full-size Fords, Fairlanes and Falcons.

FUTURA SERIES

Model No.	Body/ Style No.	Body Type & Seating	Factory Price	Shipping Weight	Prod. Total
N/A	54B	4-dr Sed-6P	2146	2410	33,985
N/A	62B	2-dr Sed-6P	2099	2375	11,670
N/A	63B	2-dr HT-6P	2179	2395	24,451
N/A	63B	2-dr Spt Cpe-5P	2226	2380	1,303
N/A	76A	2-dr Conv-6P	2428	2675	6,191
N/A	76B	2-dr Conv-5P	2481	2660	124

SPRINT V-8 SUBSERIES

Model No.	Body/ Style No.	Body Type & Seating	Factory Price	Shipping Weight	Prod. Total
N/A	63D	2-dr Sprint HT-5P	2425	2813	2,806
N/A	76D	2-dr Sprint Conv-5P	2660	3008	300

PRODUCTION NOTE: Total series output was 174,548 units, including 13,824 four-door sedans and 13,850 two-door sedans with the Deluxe trim option in the Falcon model line. Ford does not indicate the number of each model with sixes and V-8s. Therefore, all production figures are total production of each body style with both engines.

NOTE 2: Models 63D and 76D have bucket seats.

1965 Ford Falcon Futura two-door convertible V-8. (OCW)

1965 Ford Falcon Futura two-door Sports Coupe V-8. (PH)

FALCON STATION WAGON SERIES — (6-CYL/V-8) — Falcon station wagons included the Falcon as the base trim level, Futura as the intermediate level and Squire as the top trim level.

FALCON STATION WAGON I.D. NUMBERS: Falcon station wagons used the same serial number sequence as the full-size Fords, Fairlanes and Falcon sedans.

FALCON STATION WAGON SERIES

Model No.	Body/ Style No.	Body Type & Seating	Factory Price	Shipping Weight	Prod. Total
N/A	71A	4-dr Sta Wag-6P	2317	2680	14,911
N/A	59A	2-dr Sta Wag-6P	2284	2640	4,891
N/A	71B*	4-dr Futura Wag-6P	2453	2670	12,548
N/A	71C	4-dr Sq Wag-6P	2608	2695	6,703

PRODUCTION NOTE: Total series output was 39,053 units. Ford does not indicate the number of each model produced with sixes and V-8s. Therefore, all production figures are total production of each body style with both engines. *Confusing is Ford's use of the 71B identification for both the Falcon Futura four-door station wagon and the Fairlane 500 four-door station wagon.

THUNDERBIRD SERIES — (V-8) — Except for minor trim changes, the 1965 Thunderbird was the same as the 1964 model. Disc brakes and sequential turn signals were added to the 1965 list of features, as well as reversible keys and keyless locking system. Also available were vacuum-operated, power door locks (introduced as part of an optional safety group in 1964) and a remote trunk release. A simulated chrome scoop was incorporated into the front fenders, immediately to the rear of the front wheel openings. A new Thunderbird crest replaced the Thunderbird name across the front of the hood. A restyled Thunderbird emblem was used on the roof "C" pillar and new wheel covers were used. The new horizontal grille featured six vertical bars and eight horizontal bars. Late in the year, a "Special Landau" version of the Thunderbird was offered. It had a parchment-colored vinyl interior and vinyl top and either a special white or "Emberglo" (copper) exterior finish.

1965 Ford Falcon Squire station wagon 6-cyl. (PH)

1965 Ford Thunderbird two-door convertible V-8. (OCW)

THUNDERBIRD I.D. NUMBERS: Thunderbird models began with the number "5," assembly plant code "Y" (Wixom), body type code, engine type code "Z" and, finally, the unit's production number according to final assembly location. Each plant began at 100001 and went up.

THUNDERBIRD SERIES

Model No.	Body/ Style No.	Body Type & Seating	Factory Price	Shipping Weight	Prod. Total
Z	63A	2-dr HT-4P	4394	4470	42,652
Z	63B	2-dr Landau-4P	4495	4478	25,474
Z	76A	2-dr Conv-4P	4851	4588	6,846

PRODUCTION NOTE: Total series output was 74,972 units.

ENGINE [Falcon/Fairlane Base Six]: Overhead valve. Cast-iron block. Displacement: 170 cid. Bore and stroke: 3.50 x 2.94 inches. Compression ratio: 9.1:1. Brake hp: 105 at 4400 rpm. Carburetor: Holley single-barrel. Seven main bearings. Serial number code "U."

ENGINE [Falcon/Fairlane Six]: Overhead valve. Cast-iron block. Displacement: 200 cid. Bore and stroke: 3.68 x 3.13 inches. Compression ratio: 9.2:1. Brake hp: 120 at 4400 rpm. Carburetor: Holley single-barrel. Seven main bearings. Serial number code "T."

ENGINE [Ford Base Six]: Overhead valve. Cast-iron block. Displacement: 240 cid. Bore and stroke: 4.00 x 3.18 inches. Compression ratio: 9.2:1. Brake hp: 150 at 4000 rpm. Carburetor: Holley one-barrel. Seven main bearings. Serial number code "V."

ENGINE [Challenger 289 V-8]: Overhead valve. Cast-iron block. Displacement: 289 cid. Bore and stroke: 4.00 x 2.87 inches. Compression ratio: 9.3:1. Brake hp: 200 at 4400 rpm. Carburetor: Holley two-barrel. Five main bearings. Serial number code "C."

ENGINE [Challenger 289 4V V-8]: Overhead valve. Cast-iron block. Displacement: 289 cid. Bore and stroke: 4.00 x 2.87 inches. Compression ratio: 10.0:1. Brake hp: 225 at 4800 rpm. Carburetor: Holley four-barrel. Five main bearings. Serial number code "A."

ENGINE [High-Performance 289 V-8]: Overhead valve. Cast-iron block. Displacement: 289 cid. Bore and stroke: 4.00 x 2.87 inches. Compression ratio: 10.5:1. Brake hp: 271 at 6000 rpm. Carburetor: Holley four-barrel. Five main bearings. Serial number code "K."

ENGINE [Interceptor V-8]: Overhead valve. Cast-iron block. Displacement: 352 cid. Bore and stroke: 4.00 x 3.50 inches. Compression ratio: 9.3:1. Brake hp: 250 at 4400 rpm. Carburetor: Holley four-barrel. Five main bearings. Serial number code "X."

ENGINE [Thunderbird V-8]: Overhead valve. Cast-iron block. Displacement: 390 cid. Bore and stroke: 4.05 x 3.78 inches. Compression ratio: 10.0:1. Brake hp: 300 at 4600 rpm. Carburetor: Holley four-barrel. Five main bearings. Serial number code "Z."

ENGINE [Thunderbird Interceptor Special V-8]: Overhead valve. Cast-iron block. Displacement: 390 cid. Bore and stroke: 4.05 x 3.78 inches. Compression ratio: 10.0:1. Brake hp: 330 at 5000 rpm. Carburetor: Holley four-barrel. Five main bearings. Serial number code "P."

ENGINE [Thunderbird Super High-Performance V-8]: Overhead valve. Cast-iron block. Displacement: 427 cid. Bore and stroke: 4.23 x 3.78 inches. Compression ratio: 11.5:1. Brake hp: 425 at 6000 rpm. Carburetor: Two Holley four-barrel. Serial number code "R."

ENGINE ["SOHC 427" 4V V-8]: Hemispherical combustion chambers with overhead valves and overhead camshafts for each engine bank. Cast-iron block and cylinder heads. Displacement: 427 cid. Bore and stroke: 4.23 x 3.78 inches. Compression ratio: 12.1:1. Brake hp: 616 at 7000 rpm. Carburetor: Holley four-barrel. Five main bearings. (Code L: $2,500.)

ENGINE ["SOHC 427" 8V V-8]: Hemispherical combustion chambers with overhead valves and overhead camshafts for each engine bank. Cast-iron block and cylinder heads. Displacement: 427 cid. Bore and stroke: 4.23 x 3.78 inches. Compression ratio: 12.1:1. Brake hp: 657 at 7500 rpm. Carburetor: Two Holley four-barrel. Five main bearings. Code "M."

FORD CHASSIS FEATURES: Wheelbase: 119 inches. Overall length: 210 inches. Tires: 7.35 x 15 four-ply tubeless blackwall (8.15 x 15 four-ply tubeless blackwall on station wagons).

FAIRLANE CHASSIS FEATURES: Wheelbase: 116 inches. Overall length: 198.4 inches (203.2 inches on station wagons). Tires: 6.94 x 14 four-ply tubeless blackwall (7.35 x 14 four-ply tubeless on station wagons).

FALCON CHASSIS FEATURES: Wheelbase: 109.5 inches. Overall length: 181.6 inches (190 on station wagons). Tires: 6.50 x 13 (7.00 x 13 on station wagons). All tires were four-ply tubeless blackwall.

THUNDERBIRD CHASSIS FEATURES: Wheelbase: 113.2 inches. Overall length: 205.4 inches. Tires: 8.15 x 15 four-ply tubeless blackwall.

FORD OPTIONS: Popular Custom and Custom 500 model options included the 289 cid V-8 engine ($109). Cruise-O-Matic automatic transmission ($189). Power steering ($97). AM radio ($58). Wheel covers ($25). White sidewall tires ($34). Popular Galaxie 500 and Galaxie 500XL options included the 390 cid V-8 engine ($246). Cruise-O-Matic automatic transmission ($190); four-speed manual transmission ($188 - no charge on XLs). Power steering ($97). Power brakes ($43). Power windows ($102). Tinted windshield ($40). Air conditioning ($36). AM radio ($58). Vinyl roof ($76). Wheel covers ($26). White sidewall tires ($34). Popular LTD options included the 390 cid V-8 engine ($137). Power steering ($97). Power brakes ($43). Power windows ($102). Tinted windshield ($40). Air conditioning ($364). AM radio ($72). AM/FM radio ($142). Vinyl roof ($76). White sidewall tires ($34). Popular station wagon options included the 390 cid V-8 engine ($246). Cruise-O-Matic automatic transmission ($190). Power steering ($97). Power brakes ($43). Tinted windows ($40). Power tailgate window ($32). Luggage rack ($45). AM radio ($58). White sidewall tires ($34). Wheel covers ($25). A Borg-Warner T-10 four-speed transmission was replaced, for 1965, with the Ford produced T&C 'top-loader' four-speed.

FAIRLANE OPTIONS: 289 cid V-8 engine ($108), or high-performance 289 cid V-8 ($430). Cruise-O-Matic automatic transmission ($190); four-speed manual transmission ($188). AM radio ($58). Power steering ($86). Power tailgate window on station wagons ($32). Luggage rack on station wagons ($45). Two-tone paint ($22). White sidewall tires ($34). Wheel covers ($22). Vinyl roof on two-door hardtops ($76).

FALCON OPTIONS: 200 cid six-cylinder engine ($45), or 289 cid V-8 engine ($153). Cruise-O-Matic automatic transmission ($182 or $172 with six-cylinder). Front bucket seats ($69). AM radio ($58). Two-tone paint ($19). White sidewall tires ($30). Sprint package ($222, $273 on convertibles). Popular Falcon station wagon options included all those of the sedans plus the following: Power tailgate window ($30). Luggage rack ($45).

THUNDERBIRD OPTIONS: Air conditioning ($425). Tinted windows ($43). Leather seats ($106). Power seats ($184). Power windows ($106). AM/FM radio ($84). White sidewall tires ($44). Vacuum trunk release ($13). Deluxe wheel covers ($16).

HISTORY: Model names were dropped for 1965, in favor of designating the car by its actual body style, i.e., "Club Victoria" became "two-door hardtop," and "Sunliner" became "two-door convertible", etc. The 427 cid single-overhead cam engine was installed in the Fairlane Thunderbolt drag cars.

1965 Ford Thunderbird two-door hardtop V-8. (PH)

1966 FORD

1966 Ford Galaxie 500 '7-Litre' two-door convertible V-8. (PH)

1966 FORDS — OVERVIEW — For 1966, Ford continued its policy of major restyling in several of the model lines. While 1965 and 1966 full-size Fords bear a resemblance to each other, they are quite different cars. The hood is the only interchangeable exterior body component. The 1966 models featured more rounded lines than the previous year, even though the feature lines were in the same location.

FORD CUSTOM SERIES — (6-CYL/V-8) — The Custom series was the base trim level full-size Ford for 1966 and included chrome windshield and rear window moldings; two sun visors; a chrome horn ring; armrests on all doors; and the Custom name, in script, on the rear fender. The taillights had square lenses, with centrally-mounted back-up lights surrounded by a chrome bezel. The Ford name appeared, in block letters, across the front of the hood and across the vertical section of the trunk lid.

CUSTOM SIX I.D. NUMBERS: The serial number code can be broken down, as follows: First symbol indicates year: 6 = 1966. Second symbol identifies assembly plant, as follows: A = Atlanta; B = Oakville, Ontario, Canada; C = Ontario, Canada; D = Dallas; G = Chicago; F = Dearborn; E = Mahwah; H = Loraine; J = Los Angeles; K = Kansas City; N = Norfolk; R = San Jose; S = Pilot Plant; T = Metuchen; U = Louisville; P = Twin Cities; W = Wayne; Y = Wixom; Z = St. Louis. Third and fourth symbols identify body series (see Body/ Numbers below). Fifth symbol identifies engine code, as follows: U = 200 cid six-cylinder; T = 200 cid six-cylinder; V = 240 cid six-cylinder; K = 289 cid V-8 (high performance); X = 352 cid V-8 with four-barrel carb; Y = 390 cid V-8; Z = 390 cid V-8 with four-barrel carb; S = 390 cid V-8 with four-barrel carb (GT version); M = 410 cid V-8 with four-barrel carb; R = 427 cid V-8 (high performance); Q = 428 cid V-8 with four-barrel carb. The last six digits are the unit's production number, beginning at 100001 and going up, at each of the assembly plants. Custom six-cylinder models began with the number '6,' followed by the assembly plant code, engine designation code 'V' and, finally, the unit's production number according to the final assembly location. Each plant began at 100001 and went up.

CUSTOM SIX SERIES

Model No.	Body/ Style No.	Body Type & Seating	Factory Price	Shipping Weight	Prod. Total
V	54B	4-dr Sed-6P	2415	3433	Note 1
V	62B	2-dr Sed-6P	2363	3333	Note 1

NOTE 1: See Custom V-8 series listing. Production was counted by series and body style, with no engine breakouts.

CUSTOM V-8 I.D. NUMBERS: Custom V-8 models began with the number '6' followed by the assembly plant code, body type code, engine designation code and, finally, the unit's production number according to the final assembly location. Each plant began at 100001 and went up.

CUSTOM V-8 SERIES

Model No.	Body/ Style No.	Body Type & Seating	Factory Price	Shipping Weight	Prod. Total
N/A	54B	4-dr Sed-6P	2539	3477	72,245
N/A	62B	2-dr Sed-6P	2487	3377	32,292

PRODUCTION NOTE: Total series output was 104,537 units. Ford does not indicate the number of each model produced with sixes or V-8s. Therefore, all production figures given above are total production of each body style with both engines.

CUSTOM 500 SERIES — (6-CYL/V-8) — The Custom 500 was the upper trim level of the base line Custom series and included chrome windshield and rear window moldings; nylon carpeting instead of the rubber mats used in the Custom models; armrests (with ashtrays) on

all doors; two sun visors and all trim used in the Custom models. There was also a horizontal chrome strip along the side feature line and the designation '500' in a die-cast block with black-painted background, in front of the Custom script. A small Ford crest was located in the chrome side strip, on the front of the front fenders.

CUSTOM 500 SIX I.D. NUMBERS: Custom 500 six-cylinder models used the same serial number sequence as the Custom models.

CUSTOM 500 SIX SERIES

Model No.	Body/ Style No.	Body Type & Seating	Factory Price	Shipping Weight	Prod. Total
V	54B	4-dr Sed-6P	2514	3444	Note 1
V	62B	2-dr Sed-6P	2464	3375	Note 1

NOTE 1: See Custom 500 V-8 series listing. Production was counted by series and body style, with no engine breakouts.

CUSTOM 500 V-8 I.D. NUMBERS: Custom 500 V-8 models used the same serial number sequence as the Custom models.

CUSTOM 500 V-8 SERIES

Model No.	Body/ Style No.	Body Type & Seating	Factory Price	Shipping Weight	Prod. Total
N/A	54B	4-dr Sed-6P	2639	3488	109,449
N/A	62B	2-dr Sed-6P	2588	3419	28,789

PRODUCTION NOTE: Total series output was 138,238 units. Ford does not indicate the number of each model produced with sixes or V-8s. Therefore, all production figures given above are total production of each body style with both engines.

GALAXIE 500 SERIES — (6-CYL/V-8) — The Galaxie 500 was the intermediate trim level for 1966 and included all the Custom trim plus a chrome hood ornament; Ford crest in the feature line on the front fender; stamped aluminum rocker panel moldings; and a stamped aluminum insert, between two chrome strips on the vertical section of the trunk lid, with Ford in block letters, spaced evenly across. Two-tone vinyl trim was used on the inside of the doors and on the seats. Simulated wood appliques were used on the instrument panel trim pieces.

GALAXIE 500 SIX I.D. NUMBERS: Galaxie 500 six-cylinder models used the same serial number sequence as the Custom and Custom 500 models.

GALAXIE 500 SIX SERIES

Model No.	Body/ Style No.	Body Type & Seating	Factory Price	Shipping Weight	Prod. Total
V	54A	4-dr Sed-6P	2658	3456	Note 1
V	57B	4-dr FsBk Sed-6P	2743	3526	Note 1
V	63B	2-dr FsBk Cpe-6P	2685	3437	Note 1
V	76A	2-dr Conv-6P	2914	3633	Note 1

NOTE 1: See Galaxie 500 V-8 series listing. Production was counted by series and body style, with no engine breakouts.

GALAXIE 500 V-8 I.D. NUMBERS: Galaxie 500 V-8 models used the same serial number sequence as the Custom and Custom 500 series.

GALAXIE 500 V-8 SERIES

Model No.	Body/ Style No.	Body Type & Seating	Factory Price	Shipping Weight	Prod. Total
N/A	54A	4-dr Sed-6P	2784	3500	171,886
N/A	57B	4-dr FsBk Sed-6P	2869	3570	54,886
N/A	63B	2-dr FsBk Cpe-6P	2791	3481	198,532
N/A	76A	2-dr Conv-6P	3041	3677	27,454

PRODUCTION NOTE: Total series output was 452,758 units. Ford does not indicate the number of each model produced with sixes or V-8s. Therefore, all production figures given above are total production of each body style with both engines.

1966 Ford Galaxie 500 two-door fastback hardtop V-8. (OCW)

1966 Ford Galaxie 500 four-door sedan V-8. (OCW)

GALAXIE 500XL SERIES — (V-8) — Galaxie 500XL was the sport trim version of the Galaxie 500 two-door hardtop and two-door convertible and included all Galaxie 500 trim plus bucket seats and floor-mounted shift lever; polished door trim with carpeting on the lower position of the doors; dual-lens, courtesy/warning lights in the door panels; rear reading lights (in hardtops) and Galaxie 500XL badges on the body exterior. The 289 cid/200-hp V-8 engine and Cruise-O-Matic automatic transmission were standard in both 'XL' body styles.

GALAXIE 500XL I.D. NUMBERS: Galaxie 500XLs used the same serial number sequence as the Custom and Galaxie series.

GALAXIE 500XL SERIES

Model No.	Body/ Style No.	Body Type & Seating	Factory Price	Shipping Weight	Prod. Total
N/A	63C	2-dr FsBk-5P	3208	3616	25,715
N/A	76B	2-dr Conv-5P	3456	3761	6,360

PRODUCTION NOTE: Total series output was 32,075 units.

GALAXIE 500 7-LITRE SERIES — (V-8) — The '7-Litre' was the high-performance version of the Galaxie 500XL and was equipped with the 428 cid/345-hp V-8 engine as standard equipment along with the Cruise-O-Matic automatic transmission. The four-speed manual transmission was available as a no-cost option for those who chose to be even more sporting. Along with the 428 cid engine, standard equipment also included a Sport steering wheel (of simulated English walnut); bucket seats; floor shift; low restriction dual exhaust; and a non-silenced air cleaner system. Also standard were power disc brakes.

GALAXIE 500 7-LITRE I.D. NUMBERS: Galaxie 500 7-Litres used the same serial number sequence as the Custom and Galaxie series.

GALAXIE 500 7-LITRE SERIES

Model No.	Body/ Style No.	Body Type & Seating	Factory Price	Shipping Weight	Prod. Total
Q	63D	2-dr FsBk Cpe-5P	3596	3914	8,705
Q	76D	2-dr Conv-5P	3844	4059	2,368

PRODUCTION NOTE: Total series output was 11,073 units.

GALAXIE 500 LTD SERIES — (V-8) — The Galaxie 500 LTD was the top trim level for 1966 and included all the Galaxie 500 trim, plus the 289 cid/200-hp V-8 engine; Cruise-O-Matic automatic transmission; thickly padded seats (with 'pinseal' upholstery); simulated walnut appliques on the lower edge of the instrument panel (and in the door inserts); Gabardine finish headliner and sun visors; front and rear door courtesy/warning lights; courtesy lights on the rear interior roof pillars and under the instrument panel; glovebox and ashtray lights and a self-regulating clock.

GALAXIE 500 LTD I.D. NUMBERS: Galaxie 500 LTDs used the same serial number sequence as the Custom and Galaxie 500 series

GALAXIE 500 LTD SERIES.

Model No.	Body/ Style No.	Body Type & Seating	Factory Price	Shipping Weight	Prod. Total
N/A	57F	4-dr HT Sed-6P	3278	3649	69,400
N/A	63F	2-dr FsBk Cpe-6P	3201	3601	31,696

PRODUCTION NOTE: Total series output was 101,096 units.

1966 Ford Galaxie 500 '7-Litre' two-door hardtop V-8. (OCW)

1966 Ford Galaxie 500 LTD four-door hardtop V-8. (OCW)

STATION WAGON SERIES — (6-CYL/V-8) — The Ranch Wagon was the base trim level station wagon for 1966. The Country Sedans were the intermediate level and the Country Squires were the top trim level. The trim paralleled the Custom 500, Galaxie 500 and Galaxie 500 LTD models of passenger cars.

STATION WAGON SIX I.D. NUMBERS: Station wagon six-cylinder models used the same serial number sequence as Custom and Galaxie 500 series of passenger cars.

STATION WAGON SIX SERIES

Model No.	Body/ Style No.	Body Type & Seating	Factory Price	Shipping Weight	Prod. Total
V	71D	4-dr Ranch Wag-6P	2793	3919	Note 1
V	71B	4-dr Cty Sed-6P	2882	3934	Note 1
V	71C	4-dr Cty Sed-9P	2999	3975	Note 1
V	71E	4-dr Cty Sq-6P	3182	4004	Note 1
V	71A	4-dr Cty Sq-9P	3265	4018	Note 1

NOTE 1: See station wagon V-8 series listing. Production was counted by series and body style, with no engine breakouts.

STATION WAGON V-8 I.D. NUMBERS: Station wagon V-8 models used the same serial number sequence as Custom and Galaxie 500 models of passenger cars.

STATION WAGON V-8 SERIES

Model No.	Body/ Style No.	Body Type & Seating	Factory Price	Shipping Weight	Prod. Total
N/A	71D	4-dr Ranch Wag-6P	2900	3963	33,306
N/A	71B	4-dr Cty Sed-6P	2989	3978	55,616
N/A	71C	4-dr Cty Sed-9P	3105	4019	36,633
N/A	71E	4-dr Cty Sq-6P	3289	4048	27,645
N/A	71A	4-dr Cty Sq-9P	3372	4062	47,953

PRODUCTION NOTE: Total series output was 201,153 units. Ford does not indicate the number of each model produced with sixes and V-8s. Therefore, all production figures given above are total production of each body style with both engines.

FAIRLANE SERIES — (6-CYL/V-8) — The Fairlane was the base trim level for 1966 and included chrome windshield and rear window moldings; chrome rain gutter molding; chrome horn ring; front and rear armrests; cigarette lighter and vinyl-coated rubber floor mats. Major restyling was given to the Fairlane lineup, which included 13 different models. They were longer, lower and wider, and featured new suspensions both front and rear. The full-width grille featured a horizontal grid with a large divider bar and the Fairlane crest in the center of the grille. The headlights were vertically stacked and angled back, at the bottom, for a more aggressive look. A full-length horizontal feature line was used for emphasis and the model designation, in block letters, was located on the rear fender. The taillights were rectangular and featured a chrome ring around the outside and around the centrally located back-up lights. Engine choices ranged from the 200 cid/120-hp six-cylinder engine up to the mighty 390 cid/335-hp 'GT' V-8 engine. For the first time, three convertibles were added to the lineup of hardtops and sedans.

FAIRLANE SIX I.D. NUMBERS: Fairlane six-cylinder models began with the number '6' followed by the assembly plant code, body type code, engine designation 'T' and, finally, the unit's production number according to the final assembly location. Each plant began at 100001 and went up.

FAIRLANE SIX SERIES

Model No.	Body/ Style No.	Body Type & Seating	Factory Price	Shipping Weight	Prod. Total
T	54	4-dr Sed-6P	2280	2792	Note 1
T	62	2-dr Sed-6P	2240	2747	Note 1
T	71	4-dr Sta Wag-6P	2589	3182	Note 1

NOTE 1: See Fairlane V-8 series listing. Production was counted by series and body style, with no engine breakouts.

FAIRLANE V-8 I.D. NUMBERS: Fairlane V-8 models began with the number '6' followed by the assembly plant code, body type code, engine designation code and, finally, the unit's production number according to the final assembly location. Each plant began at 100001 and went up.

FAIRLANE V-8 SERIES

Model No.	Body/ Style No.	Body Type & Seating	Factory Price	Shipping Weight	Prod. Total
N/A	54A	4-dr Sed-6P	2386	2961	26,170
N/A	62A	2-dr Sed-6P	2345	2916	13,498
N/A	71D	4-dr Sta Wag-6P	2694	3351	12,379

PRODUCTION NOTE: Total series output was 52,047 units. Ford does not indicate the number of each model produced with sixes or V-8s. Therefore, all production figures given above are total production of each body style with both engines.

FAIRLANE 500 SERIES — (6-CYL/V-8) — The Fairlane 500 was the intermediate trim level for 1966 and included all the Fairlane trim plus polished aluminum rocker panel moldings, a Fairlane crest in the center of the grille, color-keyed carpets (front and rear), and Fairlane 500 identification, in block letters, on the rear fenders. A Fairlane crest and Fairlane script also appeared on the right-hand vertical section of the trunk lid.

FAIRLANE 500 SIX I.D. NUMBERS: Fairlane 500 six-cylinder models used the same serial number sequence as the Fairlane models.

FAIRLANE 500 SIX SERIES

Model No.	Body/ Style No.	Body Type & Seating	Factory Price	Shipping Weight	Prod. Total
T	54B	4-dr Sed-6P	2357	2798	Note 1
T	62B	2-dr Sed-6P	2317	2754	Note 1
T	63B	2-dr HT Cpe-6P	2378	2856	Note 1
T	76B	2-dr Conv-6P	2603	3084	Note 1
T	71B	4-dr Sta Wag-6P	2665	3192	Note 1
T	71E	4-dr Sq Sta Wag-6P	2796	3200	Note 1

NOTE 1: See Fairlane 500 V-8 series listing. Production was counted by series and body style, with no engine breakouts.

FAIRLANE 500 V-8 I.D. NUMBERS: Fairlane 500 V-8 models used the same serial number sequence as the Fairlane models.

1966 Ford Fairlane 500 convertible. (OCW)

1966 Ford Fairlane 500 four-door sedan 6-cyl. (OCW)

1966 Ford Fairlane 500 station wagon 6-cyl. (OCW)

FAIRLANE 500 V-8 SERIES

Model No.	Body/ Style No.	Body Type & Seating	Factory Price	Shipping Weight	Prod. Total
N/A	54B	4-dr Sed-6P	2463	2967	68,635
N/A	62B	2-dr Sed-6P	2423	2923	14,118
N/A	63A	2-dr HT Cpe-6P	2484	3025	75,947
N/A	76B	2-dr Conv-6P	2709	3253	9,299
N/A	71B	4-dr Sta Wag-6P	2770	3361	19,826
N/A	71E	4-dr Sq Sta Wag-6P	2901	3369	11,558

PRODUCTION NOTE: Total series output was 199,383 units. Ford does not indicate the number of each model produced with sixes or V-8s. Therefore, all production figures given above are total production of each body style with both engines.

FAIRLANE 500XL SERIES — (6-CYL/V-8) — The Fairlane 500XL was the sporty version of the Fairlane 500 series and included all the Fairlane 500 features plus bucket seats and console; special name plaques and exterior trim; Deluxe wheel covers; red safety lights and white courtesy lights in the door armrests.

FAIRLANE 500XL SIX I.D. NUMBER: Fairlane 500XL six-cylinder models used the same serial number sequence as the Fairlane and Fairlane 500 models.

FAIRLANE 500XL SIX SERIES

Model No.	Body/ Style No.	Body Type & Seating	Factory Price	Shipping Weight	Prod. Total
T	63C	2-dr HT Cpe-5P	2543	2884	Note 1
T	76C	2-dr Conv-5P	2768	3099	Note 1

NOTE 1: See Fairlane 500XL V-8 series listing. Production was counted by series and body style, with no engine breakouts.

FAIRLANE 500XL V-8 I.D. NUMBERS: Fairlane 500XL V-8 models used the same serial number sequence as the Fairlane and Fairlane 500 models.

1966 Ford Fairlane 500 Squire station wagon 6-cyl. (OCW)

1966 Ford Fairlane 500XL GT two-door convertible V-8. (OCW)

FAIRLANE 500XL V-8 SERIES

Model No.	Body/ Style No.	Body Type & Seating	Factory Price	Shipping Weight	Prod. Total
N/A	63C	2-dr HT Cpe-5P	2649	3053	23,942
N/A	76C	2-dr Conv-5P	2874	3268	4,560
N/A	63D	2-dr GT HT-5P	2843	3493	33,015
N/A	76D	2-dr GT Conv-5P	3068	3070	4,327

PRODUCTION NOTE: Total series output was 65,844 units. Ford does not indicate the number of each model produced with sixes or V-8s. Therefore, all production figures given above are total production of each body style with both engines.

NOTE 2: The Fairlane GT models came only with the 390 cid V-8 engine.

FALCON SERIES — (6-CYL/V-8) — The Falcons were the base trim level of the compact Falcon line for 1966 and included chrome windshield, rear window and rain gutter moldings; twin horns and sun visors; armrests on the front doors only and a horn button, instead of a chrome horn ring. The Falcon series also received a total restyling for 1966, with a longer hood, shorter trunk and rounder lines than in 1965. The two-door hardtops were discontinued for 1966, with the Futura Sports Coupe carrying the sporty image for the year. The Falcon script was located behind the front wheelwell on the front fender, and Ford was spelled out, in block letters, across the front of the hood. Falcon was spelled out, in block letters, across the vertical section of the trunk lid.

1966 Ford Fairlane 500XL two-door hardtop V-8. (OCW)

1966 Ford Fairlane 500XL two-door convertible V-8. (OCW)

FALCON I.D. NUMBERS: Falcons used the same serial number sequence as the full-size Ford and the Fairlane line.

FALCON SERIES

Model No.	Body/ Style No.	Body Type & Seating	Factory Price	Shipping Weight	Prod. Total
N/A	54A	4-dr Sed-6P	2114	2559	34,685
N/A	62A	2-dr Sed-6P	2060	2519	41,432
N/A	71A	4-dr Sta Wag-6P	2442	3037	16,653

PRODUCTION NOTE: Total series output was 92,770 units. Ford does not indicate the number of each model produced with sixes or V-8s. Therefore, all production figures given above are total production of each body style with both engines.

FUTURA SERIES — (6-CYL/V-8) — The Futura series was the top trim level for 1966 and included all the standard Falcon features plus a cigarette lighter; rear armrests and ashtrays; chrome horn ring; nylon carpeting; special Futura moldings, trim, emblems and nameplates; and chrome side window frames. In addition, the Sports Coupe also featured the 200 cid/120-hp six-cylinder engine; bucket seats in front; special nameplates and special wheel covers.

FUTURA I.D. NUMBERS: Futura models used the same serial number sequence as the full-size Fords, Fairlanes and Falcons.

1966 Ford Falcon Futura two-door Sports Coupe V-8. (OCW)

1966 Ford Falcon Futura station wagon 6-cyl. (OCW)

1966 Ford Falcon Futura four-door sedan 6-cyl. (OCW)

FALCON FUTURA SERIES

Model No.	Body/ Style No.	Body Type & Seating	Factory Price	Shipping Weight	Prod. Total
N/A	54B	4-dr Sed-6P	2237	2567	34,039
N/A	62B	2-dr Clb Cpe-6P	2183	2527	21,997
N/A	62C	2-dr Spt Cpe-5P	2328	2597	20,289
N/A	71B	4-dr Sta Wag-6P	2553	3045	13,574

PRODUCTION NOTE: Total series output was 89,899 units. Ford does not indicate the number of each model produced with sixes or V-8s. Therefore, all production figures are total production of each body style with both engines.

THUNDERBIRD SERIES — (V-8) — Even though it used the body shell of the previous two years, the 1966 Thunderbird looked completely new. The grille was more sharply angled back and featured an eggcrate backing for a massive Thunderbird emblem that appeared to float in the grille. At the rear, a single, massive taillight stretched from side to side with a single back-up light being part of the Thunderbird emblem in the center of the lens. The name Thunderbird appeared, in script, just ahead of the taillights on the rear fender. Another Thunderbird emblem appeared on the roof 'C' pillar. More horsepower was available in the form of the optional 428 cid/345-hp V-8 engine.

THUNDERBIRD I.D. NUMBERS: Thunderbird models began with the number '6,' assembly plant code 'Y' (Wixom), body type code, engine type codes 'Z' or 'Q' and, finally, the unit's production number, beginning at 100001 and going up.

THUNDERBIRD SERIES

Model No.	Body/ Style No.	Body Type & Seating	Factory Price	Shipping Weight	Prod. Total
Z/Q	63A	2-dr HT Cpe-4P	4395	4386	13,389
Z/Q	63B	2-dr HT Twn Sed-4P	4451	4359	15,633
Z/Q	63D	2-dr Landau-4P	4552	4367	35,105
Z/Q	76A	2-dr Conv-4P	4845	4496	5,049

PRODUCTION NOTE: Total series output was 69,176 units.

ENGINE [Falcon/Fairlane Base Six]: Overhead valve. Cast-iron block. Displacement: 170 cid. Bore and stroke: 3.50 x 2.94 inches. Compression ratio: 9.1:1. Brake hp: 105 at 4400 rpm. Carburetor: Holley one-barrel. Seven main bearings. Serial number code "4."

ENGINE [Falcon/Fairlane Six]: Overhead valve. Cast-iron block. Displacement: 200 cid. Bore and stroke: 3.68 x 3.13 inches. Compression ratio: 9.2:1. Brake hp: 120 at 4400 rpm. Carburetor: Holley one-barrel. Seven main bearings. Serial number "U."

ENGINE [Ford Base Six]: Overhead valve. Cast-iron block. Displacement: 240 cid. Bore and stroke: 4.00 x 3.18 inches. Compression ratio: 9.2:1. Brake hp: 150 at 4000 rpm. Carburetor: Holley one-barrel. Seven main bearings. Serial number code "V" (police code "B"; taxi code "E)."

ENGINE [Challenger 289 V-8]: Overhead valve. Cast-iron block. Displacement: 289 cid. Bore and stroke: 4.00 x 2.87 inches. Compression ratio: 9.3:1. Brake hp: 200 at 4400 rpm. Carburetor: Holley two-barrel. Five main bearings. Serial number code "C."

1966 Ford Thunderbird two-door Landau hardtop V-8. (OCW)

1966 Ford Thunderbird two-door hardtop V-8. (OCW)

1966 Ford Thunderbird two-door convertible V-8. (OCW)

ENGINE [Challenger 289 V-8]: Overhead valve. Cast-iron block. Displacement: 289 cid. Bore and stroke: 4.00 x 2.87 inches. Compression ratio: 10.0:1. Brake hp: 225 at 4800 rpm. Carburetor: Holley four-barrel. Five main bearings. Serial number code "A."

ENGINE [High-Performance 289 V-8]: Overhead valve. Cast-iron block. Displacement: 289 cid. Bore and stroke: 4.00 x 2.87 inches. Compression ratio: 10.5:1. Brake hp: 271 at 6000 rpm. Carburetor: Holley four-barrel. Five main bearings. Serial number code "K."

ENGINE [Interceptor V-8]: Overhead valve. Cast-iron block. Displacement: 352 cid. Bore and stroke: 4.00 x 3.50 inches. Compression ratio: 9.3:1. Brake hp: 250 at 4400 rpm. Carburetor: Holley four-barrel. Five main bearings. Serial number code "X."

ENGINE [Thunderbird V-8]: Overhead valve. Cast-iron block. Displacement: 390 cid. Bore and stroke: 4.05 x 3.78 inches. Compression ratio: 9.5:1. Brake hp: 275 at 4400 rpm. Carburetor: Holley two-barrel. Five main bearings. Serial number codes "Y" or (Special) "H."

ENGINE [Thunderbird Four-Barrel V-8]: Overhead valve. Cast-iron block. Displacement: 390 cid. Bore and stroke: 4.05 x 3.78 inches. Compression ratio: 10.5:1. Brake hp: 315 at 4600 rpm. Carburetor: Holley four-barrel. Five main bearings. Serial number code "Z."

ENGINE [GT 390 V-8]: Overhead valve. Cast-iron block. Displacement: 390 cid. Bore and stroke: 4.05 x 3.78 inches. Compression ratio: 11.0:1. Brake hp: 335 at 4800 rpm. Carburetor: Holley four-barrel. Five main bearings. Serial number code "S."

ENGINE [Thunderbird High-Performance V-8]: Overhead valve. Cast-iron block. Displacement: 427 cid. Bore and stroke: 4.23 x 3.78 inches. Compression ratio: 11.0:1. Brake hp: 410 at 5600 rpm. Carburetor: Holley four-barrel. Five main bearings. Serial number code "W."

ENGINE [Thunderbird Super High-Performance V-8]: Overhead valve. Cast-iron block. Displacement: 427 cid. Bore and stroke: 4.23 x 3.78 inches. Compression ratio: 11.5:1. Brake hp: 425 at 6000 rpm. Carburetor: Two Holley four-barrel. Five main bearings. Serial number code "R."

ENGINE [Thunderbird Special V-8]: Overhead valve. Cast-iron block. Displacement: 428 cid. Bore and stroke: 4.13 x 3.98 inches. Compression ratio: 10.5:1. Brake hp: 345 at 4600 rpm. Carburetor: Holley four-barrel. Five main bearings. Serial number code "Q."

ENGINE ["SOHC 427" 4V V-8]: Hemispherical combustion chambers with overhead valves and overhead camshafts for each engine bank. Cast-iron block and cylinder heads. Displacement: 427 cid. Bore and stroke: 4.23 x 3.78 inches. Compression ratio: 12.1:1. Brake hp: 616 at 7000 rpm. Carburetor: Holley four-barrel. Five main bearings. Engine was only available "over the counter" for $2,500.

ENGINE ["SOHC 427" 8V V-8]: Hemispherical combustion chambers with overhead valves and overhead camshafts for each engine bank. Cast-iron block and cylinder heads. Displacement: 427 cid. Bore and stroke: 4.23 x 3.78 inches. Compression ratio: 12.1:1. Brake hp: 657 at 7500 rpm. Carburetor: Two Holley four-barrel. Five main bearings.

ENGINE [Police Interceptor V-8]: Overhead valve. Cast-iron block. Displacement: 428 cid. Bore and stroke: 4.13 x 3.98 inches. Compression ratio: 10.5:1. Brake hp: 360 at 5400 rpm. Carburetor: Holley four-barrel. Five main bearings. Serial number code "P."

FORD CHASSIS FEATURES: Wheelbase: 119 inches. Overall length: 210 inches (210.9 inches on station wagons). Tires: 7.35 x 15 four-ply tubeless blackwall (8.45 x 15 four-ply tubeless blackwall on station wagons).

FAIRLANE CHASSIS FEATURES: Wheelbase: 116 inches (113 inches on station wagons). Overall length: 197 inches (199.8 inches on station wagons). Tires: 6.95 x 14 four-ply tubeless blackwall (7.75 x 14 four-ply tubeless blackwall on station wagons).

FALCON CHASSIS FEATURES: Wheelbase: 110.9 inches (113 inches on station wagons). Overall length: 184.3 inches (198.7 inches on station wagons). Tires: 6.50 x 13 four-ply tubeless blackwall (7.75 x

1966 Ford Country Squire station wagon V-8. (OCW)

THUNDERBIRD CHASSIS FEATURES: Wheelbase: 113.2 inches. Overall length: 205.4 inches. Tires: 8.15 x 15 four-ply tubeless blackwall.

FORD OPTIONS: Popular Custom and Custom 500 options included the 289 cid V-8 engine ($106). Cruise-O-Matic automatic transmission ($184). Power steering ($94). AM radio ($57). Wheel covers ($22). White sidewall tires ($33). Popular Galaxie 500/Galaxie 500XL/Galaxie 500 7-Litre/Galaxie 500 LTD options included the 390 cid V-8 engine ($101 for two-barrel engine, $153 for four-barrel engine and not available in 7-Litre models). Power steering ($94). Power brakes ($42). Power windows ($99). Tinted windshield ($21). Air conditioning ($353). AM radio ($57). AM/FM radio ($133). Vinyl roof on two-door hardtops ($74); on four-door hardtops ($83). White sidewall tires ($33). Popular station wagon options included all those in the Galaxie 500 models plus power tailgate window ($31). Luggage rack ($44). Third passenger seat ($29).

FAIRLANE/FAIRLANE 500 OPTIONS: 289 cid V-8 engine ($105 and not available on GT). 390 cid V-8 engine ($206 and standard on GT). Cruise-O-Matic automatic transmission ($184 with 289 cid V-8; $214 with 390 cid V-8). Four-speed manual transmission ($183). AM radio ($57). Power steering ($84). Power tailgate window on station wagons ($31). Luggage rack on station wagons ($44). Two-tone paint ($21). White sidewall tires ($33). Wheel covers ($21). Vinyl roof on two-door hardtops ($76).

FALCON OPTIONS: 200 cid six-cylinder engine ($26). The 289 cid V-8 engine ($131). Cruise-O-Matic automatic transmission ($167 with six-cylinder engine; $156 with 289 cid V-8). Power Steering ($84). Power tailgate on station wagons ($44). AM radio ($57). Vinyl roof on two-door models ($74). Wheel covers ($21). White sidewall tires ($32).

THUNDERBIRD OPTIONS: Air conditioning ($413). The 428 cid V-8 engine ($64). Six-Way power seats ($193). Power windows ($103). Cruise control ($129). AM/FM radio ($82). Two-tone paint ($25). White sidewall tires with red stripe ($43).

HISTORY: The full-size Fords were introduced Oct. 1, 1966, and all the Ford lines appeared in dealer showrooms the same day. Model year production peaked at 2,093,832 units. Calendar year sales of 2,038,415 cars were recorded. Donald N. Frey was the chief executive officer of the company this year. On a calendar year sales basis, Ford was the number two maker in America this year and held a 23.71 percent share of total market. Only 237 Ford Motor Co. products, of all types, had 427 cid V-8s installed during the 1966 calendar year. A positive note was the performance of the Ford GT-40 in the European Grand Prix racing circuit. A trio of these cars, running at LeMans, finished first, second and third. It was the first time American entries had ever captured the championship honors in the prestigious race.

1967 FORD

1967 FORDS — OVERVIEW — As in the previous 10 years, Ford continued to restyle at least one of the model lines. The 1967 full-size Fords were completely restyled from the previous year, sharing only drivetrains with the 1966 models. The new models were more rounded, with rounder tops and fenders. At the front end, stacked quad

headlights were used once again, but the grille was all new. It was a double-stamped aluminum piece, featuring horizontal bars, divided by five vertical bars. The center portion of the grille projected forward and this point was duplicated in the forward edge of the hood and in the bumper configuration. The bodyside feature lines were in the same location as the 1966 models, but were somewhat less pronounced. The taillights were vertically situated rectangular units with chrome moldings and chrome cross-hairs surrounding the standard equipment back-up lights. All 1967 Fords are easily recognizable by the Energy-Absorbing steering wheels used in every model. A large, deeply padded hub predominates the wheel. Also, all 1967 Fords were equipped with a dual brake master cylinder for the first time.

FORD CUSTOM SERIES — (6-CYL/V-8) — The Custom series was the base trim level Ford for 1967 and included chrome windshield and rear window moldings; a chrome horn ring; nylon carpeting; the Custom name in script on the front fenders and the Ford name, in block letters, spaced across the front of the hood and across the vertical section of the trunk lid.

CUSTOM SIX I.D. NUMBERS: The serial number code can be broken down, as follows: First symbol indicates year: 7 = 1967. Second symbol identifies assembly plant, as follows: A = Atlanta; B = Oakville, Ontario, Canada; C = Ontario, Canada; D = Dallas; G = Chicago; F = Dearborn; E = Mahwah; H = Loraine; J = Los Angeles; K = Kansas City; N = Norfolk; R = San Jose; S = Pilot Plant; T = Metuchen; U = Louisville; P = Twin Cities; W = Wayne; Y = Wixom; Z = St. Louis. Third and fourth symbols identify body series (see Body/ Numbers below). Fifth symbol identifies engine code, as follows: U = 170 cid six-cylinder; T = 200 cid six-cylinder; V = 240 cid six-cylinder; C = 289 cid V-8; K = 289 cid V-8 (high performance); H or Y = 390 cid V-8; Z = 390 cid V-8 with four-barrel carb; S = 390 cid V-8 with four-barrel carb (GT version); R or W = 427 cid V-8 (high performance); Q = 428 cid V-8 with four-barrel carb. The last six digits are the unit's production number, beginning at 100001 and going up, at each of the assembly plants. Custom six-cylinder models began with the number '7' followed by the assembly plant code, engine designation code 'V' and, finally, the unit's production number according to the final assembly location. Each plant began at 100001 and went up.

CUSTOM SIX SERIES

Model No.	Body/ Style No.	Body Type & Seating	Factory Price	Shipping Weight	Prod. Total
V	54E	4-dr Sed-6P	2496	3469	Note 1
V	62E	2-dr Sed-6P	2441	3411	Note 1

NOTE 1: See Custom V-8 series listing. Production was counted by series and body style, with no engine breakouts.

CUSTOM V-8 I.D. NUMBERS: Custom V-8 models began with the number '7' followed by the assembly plant code, body type code, engine designation code, and, finally, the unit's production number according to the final assembly location. Each plant began at 100001 and went up.

CUSTOM V-8 SERIES

Model No.	Body/ Style No.	Body Type & Seating	Factory Price	Shipping Weight	Prod. Total
N/A	54E	4-dr Sed-6P	2602	3507	41,417
N/A	62E	2-dr Sed-6P	2548	3449	18,107

PRODUCTION NOTE: Total series output was 59,524 units. Ford does not indicate the number of each model produced with sixes or V-8s. Therefore, all production figures given above are total production of each body style with both engines.

CUSTOM 500 SERIES — (6-CYL/V-8) — The Custom 500 was the upper trim level of the base line Custom series and included all the Custom trim plus special Custom 500 exterior trim and choice of four different interior upholsteries.

CUSTOM 500 SIX I.D. NUMBERS: Custom 500 six-cylinder models used the same serial number sequence as the Custom models.

1967 Ford Galaxie 500 four-door sedan V-8. (OCW)

CUSTOM 500 SIX SERIES

Model No.	Body/ Style No.	Body Type & Seating	Factory Price	Shipping Weight	Prod. Total
V	54B	4-dr Sed-6P	2551	3471	Note 1
V	62B	2-dr Sed-6P	2595	3513	Note 1

NOTE 1: See Custom 500 V-8 series listing. Production was counted by series and body style only, with no breakout per engine type.

CUSTOM 500 V-8 I.D. NUMBERS: Custom 500 V-8 models used the same serial number sequence as the Custom models.

CUSTOM 500 V-8 SERIES

Model No.	Body/ Style No.	Body Type & Seating	Factory Price	Shipping Weight	Prod. Total
N/A	54B	4-dr Sed-6P	2701	3509	83,260
N/A	62B	2-dr Sed-6P	2659	3451	18,146

PRODUCTION NOTE: Total series output was 101,406 units. Ford does not indicate the number of each model produced with sixes or V-8s. Therefore, all production figures given above are total production of each body style with both engines.

GALAXIE 500 SERIES — (6-CYL/V-8) — The Galaxie 500 was the intermediate trim level for 1967 and included all the Custom series trim plus stamped aluminum lower bodyside moldings; chrome side window moldings; simulated woodgrain appliques on the instrument panel and inner door panels and a stamped aluminum trim panel on the vertical section of the trunk lid. The name, Galaxie 500, in block letters, was located on the rear fenders and the Ford crest was located on the trunk lid above the aluminum trim panel.

GALAXIE 500 SIX I.D. NUMBERS: Galaxie 500 six-cylinder models used the same serial number sequence as the Custom series.

GALAXIE 500 SIX SERIES

Model No.	Body/ Style No.	Body Type & Seating	Factory Price	Shipping Weight	Prod. Total
V	54A	4-dr Sed-6P	2732	3481	Note 1
V	57B	4-dr FsBk Sed-6P	2808	3552	Note 1
V	63B	2-dr FsBk Cpe-6P	2755	3484	Note 1
V	76A	2-dr Conv-6P	3003	3660	Note 1

NOTE 1: See Galaxie 500 V-8 series listing. Production was counted by series and body style only, with no breakout per engine type.

GALAXIE 500 V-8 I.D. NUMBERS: Galaxie 500 V-8 models used the same serial number sequence as the Custom and Custom 500 models.

GALAXIE 500 V-8 SERIES

Model No.	Body/ Style No.	Body Type & Seating	Factory Price	Shipping Weight	Prod. Total
N/A	54A	4-dr Sed-6P	2838	3519	130,063
N/A	57B	4-dr FsBk Sed-6P	2743	3526	57,087
N/A	63B	2-dr FsBk Cpe-6P	2861	3522	197,388
N/A	76A	2-dr Conv-6P	3110	3704	19,068

PRODUCTION NOTE: Total series output was 403,606 units. Ford does not indicate the number of each model produced with sixes or V-8s. Therefore, all production figures given above are total production of each body style with both engines.

GALAXIE 500XL SERIES — (V-8) — The Galaxie 500XL was the sport trim version of the two-door fastback and two-door convertible and included the 289 cid/200-hp V-8 engine and SelectShift Cruise-O-Matic automatic transmission as standard equipment. Also, the model line included bucket seats and front console; all Galaxie 500 trim; special ornamentation; automatic courtesy and warning lights in the door panels and chrome trim on the foot pedals.

GALAXIE 500XL I.D. NUMBERS: Galaxie 500XLs used the same serial number sequence as the Custom and Galaxie series.

1967 Ford Galaxie 500XL two-door convertible V-8. (PH)

1967 Ford Galaxie 500XL two-door fastback hardtop V-8. (PH)

GALAXIE 500XL SERIES

Model No.	Body/ Style No.	Body Type & Seating	Factory Price	Shipping Weight	Prod. Total
N/A	63C	2-dr FsBk Cpe-5P	3243	3594	18,174
N/A	76B	2-dr Conv-5P	3493	3704	5,161

PRODUCTION NOTE: Total series output was 23,335 units.

LTD SERIES — (V-8) — The LTD was the top trim level full-size Ford for 1967 and was considered its own series for the first time since introduced in 1965. LTDs included all the Galaxie 500 trim plus the 289 cid/200-hp V-8 engine and SelectShift Cruise-O-Matic automatic transmission as standard equipment. Other regular features were flow-through ventilation system, distinctive LTD trim and ornamentation, special wheel covers, simulated woodgrain on the instrument panel and door panels, automatic courtesy and warning lights in the doors, deep-foam cushioning in the seating surfaces, pull-down armrests front and rear, color-keyed steering wheel and vinyl top on two-door hardtops.

LTD I.D. NUMBERS: LTDs used the same serial number sequence as the Custom and Galaxie series.

LTD SERIES

Model No.	Body/ Style No.	Body Type & Seating	Factory Price	Shipping Weight	Prod. Total
N/A	54F	4-dr Sed-6P	3298	3795	12,491
N/A	57F	4-dr HT Sed-6P	3363	3676	51,978
N/A	63F	2-dr HT Cpe-6P	3362	3626	46,036

PRODUCTION NOTE: Total series output was 110,505 units.

STATION WAGON SERIES — (6-CYL/V-8) — The Ranch Wagon was the base trim level station wagon for 1967, with the Country Sedans being the intermediate level and the Country Squires being the top trim level. The trim paralleled the Custom 500, Galaxie 500 and LTD models of passenger cars.

STATION WAGON SIX I.D. NUMBERS: Station wagon six-cylinder models used the same serial number sequence as Custom and Galaxie 500 series of passenger cars.

1967 Ford LTD two-door hardtop V-8. (OCW)

1967 Ford LTD four-door hardtop V-8. (PH)

1967 Ford Country Squire station wagon V-8. (OCW)

STATION WAGON SIX SERIES

Model No.	Body/ Style No.	Body Type & Seating	Factory Price	Shipping Weight	Prod. Total
V	71D	4-dr Ranch Wag-6P	2836	3911	Note 1
V	71B	4-dr Cty Sed-6P	2935	3924	Note 1
V	71C	4-dr Cty Sed-9P	3061	4004	Note 1
V	71E	4-dr Cty Sq-6P	3234	3971	Note 1
V	71A	4-dr Cty Sq-9P	3359	4011	Note 1

NOTE 1: See station wagon V-8 series listing. Production was counted by series and body style only, with no breakout per engine type.

STATION WAGON V-8 I.D. NUMBERS: Station wagon V-8 models used the same serial number sequence as the Custom and Galaxie 500 series of passenger cars.

STATION WAGON V-8 SERIES

Model No.	Body/ Style No.	Body Type & Seating	Factory Price	Shipping Weight	Prod. Total
N/A	71D	4-dr Ranch Wag-6P	2943	3949	23,932
N/A	71B	4-dr Cty Sed-6P	2042	3962	50,818
N/A	71C	4-dr Cty Sed-9P	3168	4042	34,377
N/A	71E	4-dr Cty Sq-6P	3340	4009	25,600
N/A	71A	4-dr Cty Sq-9P	3466	4049	44,024

PRODUCTION NOTE: Total series output was 178,751 units. Ford does not indicate the number of each model produced with sixes or V-8s. Therefore, all production figures given above are total production of each body style with both engines.

FAIRLANE MODELS — (6-CYL/V-8) — The Fairlane was the base trim level for 1967 and included chrome windshield and rear window moldings; chrome rain gutter moldings; a chrome horn ring; front and rear armrests; cigarette lighter; vinyl-coated rubber floor mats and a single horizontal chrome trim strip along the bodyside, with the Fairlane name, in block letters, at the forward end. The Fairlane continued to use the body introduced in 1966 with minor trim changes. The new grille was a single aluminum stamping instead of the two grilles used in the previous model and the taillights were divided horizontally by the back-up light, instead of vertically as in 1966.

FAIRLANE SIX I.D. NUMBERS: Fairlane six-cylinder models began with the number '7' followed by the assembly plant code, body type code, engine designation 'T' and, finally, the unit's production number according to the final assembly location. Each plant began at 100001 and went up.

FAIRLANE SIX SERIES

Model No.	Body/ Style No.	Body Type & Seating	Factory Price	Shipping Weight	Prod. Total
T	54	4-dr Sed-6P	2339	2782	Note 1
T	62	2-dr Sed-6P	2297	2747	Note 1
T	71	4-dr Sta Wag-6P	2643	3198	Note 1

NOTE 1: See Fairlane V-8 series listing. Production was counted by series and body style only, with no breakout per engine type.

FAIRLANE V-8 I.D. NUMBERS: Fairlane V-8 models began with the number '7' followed by the assembly plant code, body type code, engine designation code and, finally, the unit's production number according to the final assembly location. Each plant began at 100001 and went up.

FAIRLANE V-8 SERIES

Model No.	Body/ Style No.	Body Type & Seating	Factory Price	Shipping Weight	Prod. Total
N/A	54A	4-dr Sed-6P	2445	2951	19,740
N/A	62A	2-dr Sed-6P	2402	2916	10,628
N/A	71D	4-dr Sta Wag-6P	2748	3387	10,881

PRODUCTION NOTE: Total series output was 41,249 units. Ford does not indicate the number of each model produced with sixes or V-8s. Therefore, all production figures given above are total production of each body style with both engines.

1967 Ford Fairlane 500 four-door sedan V-8. (OCW)

FAIRLANE 500 SERIES — (6-CYL/V-8) — The Fairlane 500 was the intermediate trim level for 1967 and included all the Fairlane trim plus special Fairlane 500 trim and moldings; color-keyed carpet front and rear and a choice of four nylon and vinyl upholsteries. Also included was a stamped aluminum lower bodyside molding that contained the Fairlane name, in block letters, at the forward edge and another aluminum stamping containing the Ford name, in block letters, located on the vertical section of the trunk lid.

FAIRLANE 500 SIX I.D. NUMBERS: Fairlane 500 six-cylinder models used the same serial number sequence as the Fairlane models.

FAIRLANE 500 SIX SERIES

Model No.	Body/ Style No.	Body Type & Seating	Factory Price	Shipping Weight	Prod. Total
T	54B	4-dr Sed-6P	2417	2802	Note 1
T	62B	2-dr Sed-6P	2377	2755	Note 1
T	63B	2-dr HT Cpe-6P	2439	2842	Note 1
T	76B	2-dr Conv-6P	2664	3159	Note 1
T	71B	4-dr Sta Wag-6P	2718	3206	Note 1
T	71E	4-dr Sq Sta Wag-6P	2902	3217	Note 1

NOTE 1: See Fairlane 500 V-8 series listing. Production was counted by series and body style only, with no breakout per engine type.

FAIRLANE 500 V-8 I.D. NUMBERS: Fairlane 500 V-8 models used the same serial number sequence as the Fairlane models.

1967 Ford Fairlane 500 Squire station wagon V-8. (OCW)

1967 Ford Fairlane 500XL two-door hardtop V-8. (OCW)

1967 Ford Fairlane 500XL GTA two-door hardtop V-8. (OCW)

FAIRLANE 500 V-8 SERIES

Model No.	Body/ Style No.	Body Type & Seating	Factory Price	Shipping Weight	Prod. Total
N/A	54B	4-dr Sed-6P	2522	2971	52,552
N/A	62B	2-dr Sed-6P	2482	2924	8,473
N/A	63B	2-dr HT Cpe-6P	2545	3011	70,135
N/A	76B	2-dr Conv-6P	2770	3328	5,428
N/A	71B	4-dr Sta Wag-6P	2824	3375	15,902
N/A	71E	4-dr Sq Sta Wag-6P	3007	3386	8,348

PRODUCTION NOTE: Total series output was 159,838 units. Ford does not indicate the number of each model produced with sixes or V-8s. Therefore, all production figures given above are total production of each body style with both engines.

FAIRLANE 500XL SERIES — (6-CYL/V-8) — The Fairlane 500XL was the sporty version of the Fairlane 500 series and included all the Fairlane 500 features plus bucket seats and console; special name plaques and exterior trim; Deluxe wheel covers; and red safety lights and white courtesy lights in the lower interior door panels.

FAIRLANE 500XL SIX I.D. NUMBERS: Fairlane 500XL six-cylinder models used the same serial number sequence as the Fairlane and Fairlane 500 models.

FAIRLANE 500XL SIX SERIES

Model No.	Body/ Style No.	Body Type & Seating	Factory Price	Shipping Weight	Prod. Total
T	63C	2-dr HT Cpe-5P	2619	2870	Note 1
T	76C	2-dr Conv-5P	2843	3187	Note 1

NOTE 1: See Fairlane 500XL V-8 series listing. Production was counted by series and body style only, with no breakout per engine type.

FAIRLANE 500XL V-8 I.D. NUMBERS: Fairlane 500XL V-8 models used the same serial number sequence as the Fairlane and Fairlane 500 models.

FAIRLANE 500XL V-8 SERIES

Model No.	Body/ Style No.	Body Type & Seating	Factory Price	Shipping Weight	Prod. Total
N/A	63C	2-dr HT Cpe-5P	2724	3039	14,871
N/A	76C	2-dr Conv-5P	2950	3356	1,943
N/A	63D	2-dr GT HT Cpe-5P	2839	3301	18,670
N/A	76D	2-dr GT Conv-5P	3064	3607	2,117

PRODUCTION NOTE: Total series output was 37,601 units. Ford does not indicate the number of each model produced with sixes or V-8s. Therefore, all production figures given above are total production of each body style with both engines.

1967 Ford Fairlane 500XL GTA two-door convertible V-8. (OCW)

1967 Ford Falcon sports coupe. (OCW)

FALCON SERIES — (6-CYL/V-8) — The Falcons were the base trim level of the compact Falcon line for 1967 and included chrome windshield, rear window and rain gutter moldings, armrests on the front doors only and a horn button, instead of the chrome horn ring found on Futura models. The Falcon name, in script, was located on the rear fender, just ahead of the taillights and, in block letters, across the vertical section of the trunk lid. Like the Fairlane lineup, the 1967 Falcons continued to use the body introduced in 1966, with only minor trim changes. The most noticeable change in the two years, was the scoop-like indentations behind the front wheel openings, on the front fenders. The grille was nearly identical, with a horizontal and vertical dividing bar being the only difference.

FALCON I.D. NUMBERS: Falcons used the same serial number sequence as the full-size Ford and Fairlane lines.

FALCON SERIES

Model No.	Body/ Style No.	Body Type & Seating	Factory Price	Shipping Weight	Prod. Total
N/A	54A	4-dr Sed-6P	2167	2551	13,554
N/A	62A	2-dr Sed-6P	2118	2520	16,082
N/A	71A	4-dr Sta Wag-6P	2497	3030	5,553

PRODUCTION NOTE: Total series output was 35,198 units. Ford does not indicate the number of each model produced with sixes or V-8s. Therefore, all production figures given above are total production of each body style with both engines.

FUTURA SERIES — (6-CYL/V-8) — The Futura series was the top trim level for 1967 and included all the standard Falcon features plus a cigarette lighter; armrests and ashtrays on all doors; a chrome horn ring; nylon carpeting; special Futura moldings; trim, emblems and nameplates and chrome side window trim. In addition, the Sports Coupe offered front bucket seats, special nameplates, a map light, ashtray, glovebox and trunk lights, 7.35 x 14 tires, a 'side accent stripe,' remote-control outside driver's mirror and Deluxe seat belts.

FUTURA I.D. NUMBERS: Futura models used the same serial number sequence as the full-size Fords, Fairlanes and Falcons.

FUTURA SERIES

Model No.	Body/ Style No.	Body Type & Seating	Factory Price	Shipping Weight	Prod. Total
N/A	54B	4-dr Sed-6P	2322	2559	11,254
N/A	62B	2-dr Sed-6P	2280	2528	6,287
N/A	62C	2-dr HT Spt Cpe-5P	2437	3062	7,053
N/A	71B	4-dr Sq Wag-6P	2609	2556	4,552

PRODUCTION NOTE: Total series output was 29,146 units. Ford does not indicate the number of each model produced with sixes or V-8s. Therefore, all production figures given above are total production of each body style with both engines.

1967 Ford Falcon Futura station wagon 6-cyl. (OCW)

1967 Ford Thunderbird two-door hardtop V-8. (OCW)

THUNDERBIRD SERIES — (V-8) — The 1967 Thunderbirds were totally restyled once again. The front end featured a full-width grille with hidden headlights and a large Thunderbird emblem floating in the center of the grille. As in 1966, the rear end featured a large, single taillight lens with a horizontal trim strip in the center. In addition, there were backup lights, in the center of the strip, giving the impression of a large round taillight. For the first time in the Thunderbird's history, a four-door sedan, called the 'Landau Sedan,' was offered. This Landau was different than the sedans in that the rear doors opened to the front, given the nickname 'suicide doors.'

THUNDERBIRD I.D. NUMBERS: Thunderbird models began with the number '7,' assembly plant code 'Y' (Wixom), body type code, engine type code 'Z' or 'Q' and, finally, the unit's production number, beginning at 100001 and going up.

THUNDERBIRD SERIES

Model No.	Body/ Style No.	Body Type & Seating	Factory Price	Shipping Weight	Prod. Total
Z/Q	65A	2-dr HT-4P	4603	4348	15,567
Z/Q	65B	2-dr Landau-4P	4704	4256	37,422
Z/Q	57B	4-dr Landau-4P	4825	4348	24,967

PRODUCTION NOTE: Total series output was 77,956 units.

ENGINE [Falcon/Fairlane Base Six]: Overhead valve. Cast-iron block. Displacement: 200 cid. Bore and stroke: 3.68 x 3.13 inches. Compression ratio: 9.2:1. Brake hp: 120 at 4400 rpm. Carburetor: Holley one-barrel. Seven main bearings. Serial number codes 'T' or 'U.'

ENGINE [Ford Base Six]: Overhead valve. Cast-iron block. Displacement: 240 cid. Bore and stroke: 4.00 x 3.18 inches. Compression ratio: 9.2:1. Brake hp: 150 at 4000 rpm. Carburetor: Holley one-barrel. Seven main bearings. Serial number code 'V' (police code 'B'; taxi code 'E).'

ENGINE [Challenger 289 V-8]: Overhead valve. Cast-iron block. Displacement: 289 cid. Bore and stroke: 4.00 x 2.87 inches. Compression ratio: 9.3:1. Brake hp: 200 at 4400 rpm. Carburetor: Holley two-barrel. Five main bearings. Serial number code 'C.'

ENGINE [Challenger 289 V-8]: Overhead valve. Cast-iron block. Displacement: 289 cid. Bore and stroke: 4.00 x 2.87 inches. Compression ratio: 10.0:1. Brake hp: 225 at 4800 rpm. Carburetor: Holley four-barrel. Five main bearings. Serial number code 'A.'

ENGINE [High-Performance 289 V-8]: Overhead valve. Cast-iron block. Displacement: 289 cid. Bore and stroke: 4.00 x 2.87 inches. Compression ratio: 10.5:1. Brake hp: 271 at 6000 rpm. Carburetor: Holley four-barrel. Five main bearings. Serial number code 'K.'

ENGINE [Thunderbird V-8]: Overhead valve. Cast-iron block. Displacement: 390 cid. Bore and stroke: 4.05 x 3.76 inches. Compression ratio 9.5:1. Brake hp: 275 at 4400 rpm. Carburetor: Holley two-barrel. Five main bearings. Serial number codes 'Y' or (Special) 'H.'

ENGINE [Thunderbird Four-Barrel V-8]: Overhead valve. Cast-iron block. Displacement: 390 cid. Bore and stroke: 4.05 x 3.78 inches. Compression ratio: 10.5:1. Brake hp: 315 at 4600 rpm. Carburetor: Holley four-barrel. Five main bearings. Serial number code 'Z.'

ENGINE [GT 390 V-8]: Overhead valve. Cast-iron block. Displacement: 390 cid. Bore and stroke: 4.05 x 3.78 inches. Compression ratio: 11.0:1. Brake hp: 335 at 4800 rpm. Carburetor: Holley four-barrel. Five main bearings. Serial number code 'S.'

ENGINE [Thunderbird High-Performance V-8]: Overhead valve. Cast-iron block. Displacement: 427 cid. Bore and stroke: 4.23 x 3.78 inches. Compression ratio: 11.0:1. Brake hp: 410 at 5600 rpm. Carburetor: Holley four-barrel. Five main bearings. Serial number code 'W.'

ENGINE [Thunderbird Super High-Performance V-8]: Overhead valve. Cast-iron block. Displacement: 427 cid. Bore and stroke: 4.23 x 3.78 inches. Compression ratio: 11.5:1. Brake hp: 425 at 6000 rpm. Carburetor: Two Holley four-barrel. Five main bearings. Serial number code 'R.'

ENGINE [Thunderbird Special V-8]: Overhead valve. Cast-iron block. Displacement: 428 cid. Bore and stroke: 4.13 x 3.98 inches. Compression ratio: 10.5:1. Brake hp: 345 at 4600 rpm. Carburetor: Holley four-barrel. Five main bearings. Serial number code 'Q.'

ENGINE ["SOHC 427" 4V V-8]: Hemispherical combustion chambers with overhead valves and overhead camshafts for each engine bank. Cast-iron block and cylinder heads. Displacement: 427 cid. Bore and stroke: 4.23 x 3.78. Compression ratio: 12.1:1. Brake hp: 616 at 7000 rpm. Carburetion: Holley four-barrel. Five main bearings. Engine was only available "over the counter" for $2,500.

ENGINE ["SOHC 427" 8V V-8]: Hemispherical combustion chambers with overhead valves and overhead camshafts for each engine bank. Cast-iron block and cylinder heads. Displacement: 427 cid. Bore and stroke: 4.23 x 3.78 inches. Compression ratio: 12.1:1. Brake hp: 657 at 7500 rpm. Carburetor: Two Holley four-barrel. Five main bearings. Availability as 4V version.

ENGINE [Police Interceptor V-8]: Overhead valve. Cast-iron block. Displacement: 428 cid. Bore and stroke: 4.13 x 3.98 inches. Compression ratio: 10.5:1. Brake hp: 360 at 5400 rpm. Carburetor: Holley four-barrel. Five main bearings. Serial number code 'P.'

NOTE: A tunnel-port 427 was available as an over-the-counter kit, with tunnel-port intake on special cylinder heads and special intake manifold.

FORD CHASSIS FEATURES: Wheelbase: 119 inches. Overall length: (station wagons) 213.9 inches; (other models) 213 inches. Tires: (sedans) 7.75 x 15 four-ply tubeless blackwall; (hardtops) 8.15 x 15 four-ply tubeless blackwall; (station wagons) 8.45 x 15 four-ply tubeless blackwall.

FAIRLANE CHASSIS FEATURES: Wheelbase: (station wagons) 113 inches; (other models) 116 inches. Overall length: (station wagons) 199.8 inches; (other models) 197 inches. Tires: (hardtops and station wagons) 7.15 x 14 four-ply tubeless blackwall; (other models) 6.95 x 14 four-ply tubeless blackwall.

FALCON CHASSIS FEATURES: Wheelbase: (station wagons) 113 inches; (other models) 110.9 inches. Overall length: (station wagons) 197 inches; (other models) 184.3 inches. Tires: (Sports Coupe) 7.35 x 14 four-ply tubeless blackwall; (station wagons) 7.75 x 14 four-ply tubeless blackwall; (other models) 6.50 x 13 four-ply tubeless blackwall.

THUNDERBIRD SERIES CHASSIS FEATURES: Wheelbase: (four-door Landau) 117 inches; (other models) 115 inches. Overall length: (four-door Landau) 209.9 inches; (other models) 206.9 inches. Tires: 8.15 x 15 four-ply tubeless blackwall.

FORD OPTIONS: 289 cid/200-hp V-8 engine ($107). 390 cid/275-hp V-8 engine ($78 in XLs and LTDS; $184 in all others). 390 cid/315-hp V-8 engine ($158 in XLs and LTDS; $265 in all others). Cruise-O-Matic automatic transmission ($188 to $220 depending on engine choice). Four-speed manual transmission ($184). Power steering ($95). Power brakes ($42). Tinted windshield ($21). Air conditioning ($356). AM radio ($57). AM/FM radio ($134). Vinyl roof on two-door hardtops ($74); on four-door hardtops ($83). White sidewall tires ($35).

STATION WAGON OPTIONS: Included all those in the Custom and Galaxie 500 models, plus power tailgate window ($32). Luggage rack ($44). Deluxe adjustable luggage rack ($63).

FAIRLANE OPTIONS: Included the 289 cid/200-hp V-8 engine ($106, standard on GT models). 390 cid V-8 engines ($184 for two-barrel version, $264 for four-barrel version). Cruise-O-Matic automatic transmission ($188 to $220 depending on engine choice). Four-speed manual transmission ($184). AM radio ($57). Power steering ($84). Power tailgate window in station wagons ($32). Luggage rack on station wagons ($44). Two-tone paint ($22). White sidewall tires ($34). Wheel covers ($41). Vinyl roofs on two-door hardtops ($74).

1967 Ford Thunderbird Landau two-door hardtop V-8. (OCW)

1967 Ford Thunderbird four-door Landau Sedan V-8. (AA)

FALCON OPTIONS: Included the 200 cid six-cylinder engine ($26). 289 cid V-8 engine ($132). 289 cid four-barrel carb V-8 engine ($183). Cruise-O-Matic automatic transmission ($187). Four-speed manual transmission ($184). Power steering ($84). Power tailgate window on station wagons ($32). Tinted windshield ($21). Luggage rack on station wagons ($44). AM radio ($57). Eight-track stereo tape ($128). Two-tone paint ($19). Vinyl roof on two-door sedans ($74). Wheel covers ($21). White sidewall tires ($32).

THUNDERBIRD OPTIONS: Included the 428 cid/345-hp V-8 engine ($91). Six-Way power seats ($98—driver's seat only). Power windows ($104). Cruise Control ($130). Air conditioning ($421). AM/8-track stereo radio ($128). AM/FM radio ($90). AM/FM multiplex stereo radio ($164). Two-tone paint ($25). White sidewall tires with red band ($52).

HISTORY: The 1967 Fords were introduced Sept. 30, 1966. The grand total of assemblies for the 1967 model year was 1,742,311 units. This included 877,128 Fords, 233,688 Fairlanes, 76,500 Falcons, 472,121 Mustangs and 77,956 Thunderbirds. Calendar year production for all the above lines peaked at 240,712 units. As far as sales and production it was a good year for America's number two automaker. However, vice-president and general manager M.S. McLaughlin did have other things to deal with, such as a 57-day United Auto Worker's strike. It was the longest lasting labor dispute in Ford history and culminated in a three-year contract agreement that included unprecedented wage and benefits packages.

1968 FORD

1968 Ford Galaxie 500 convertible. (OCW)

1968 FORDS — OVERVIEW — For the first time in 10 years, only one of the Ford lines received major restyling. The remainder of the model lineup stayed basically the same as in 1967. The 1968 full-size Fords were basically 1967 body shells with updated front ends. The two years look completely different, to be sure, but there is little that changed behind the windshield. The new grillework was less protruding than the 1967 version and offered hidden headlights on the upper lines. It was a honeycomb grille with a single, centrally located vertical dividing bar. The Ford name, in block letters, and the Ford crest, in a small emblem on the driver's side headlight door, appeared. The rooflines were a little more formal than the previous year and the taillights, although retaining the same shape, were divided horizontally by the back-up lights, rather than vertically. The large, padded hub used on the steering wheels of all 1967 Fords, was replaced by a more conventional pad covering the entire center spoke. More federally mandated safety regulations appeared in the form of front and rear fender marker lights. Power-wise, the mighty 427 cid V-8 engine was detuned to 390-hp by limiting carburetion to a single four-barrel and replacing the wild solid-lifter camshaft with a more timid hydraulic rider cam. At midyear, the 427 was discontinued and replaced by the equally famous and powerful Cobra Jet 428 and Super Cobra Jet 428 V-8s. These engines dominated the Super Stock classes at the drag races in 1968, when installed in the light Mustang bodies. Also, the new lightweight '385' series engines, displacing 429 cid, became the top power option in the big Thunderbirds.

FORD CUSTOM SERIES — (6-CYL/V-8) — The Custom series was the base trim level Ford for 1968 and included chrome windshield and rear window moldings; a chrome horn ring; nylon carpeting; the Custom name, in script, on the rear fenders; and Ford in block letters, across the front of the hood.

CUSTOM SIX I.D. NUMBERS: The serial number code can be broken down, as follows: First symbol indicates year: 8 = 1968. Second symbol identifies assembly plant, as follows: A = Atlanta; B = Oakville, Ontario, Canada; C = Ontario, Canada; D = Dallas; G = Chicago; F = Dearborn; E = Mahwah; H = Loraine; J = Los Angeles; K = Kansas City; N = Norfolk; R = San Jose; S = Pilot Plant; T = Metuchen; U = Louisville; P = Twin Cities; W = Wayne; X = St. Thomas, Ontario, Canada; Y = Wixom; Z = St. Louis. Third and fourth symbols identify body series (see Body/ Numbers below). Fifth symbol identifies engine code, as follows: U = 170 cid six-cylinder; T = 200 cid six-cylinder; V = 240 cid six-cylinder; C = 289 cid V-8; F = 302 cid V-8; J = 302 cid V-8 with four-barrel; Y = 390 cid V-8; Z = 390 cid V-8 with four-barrel carb; S = 390 cid V-8 with four-barrel carb (GT version); W = 427 cid V-8 (high performance); Q = 428 cid V-8 with four-barrel carb; R = 428 cid Super Cobra Jet V-8 with four-barrel carb; N = 429 cid V-8 with four-barrel carb. The last six digits are the unit's production number, beginning at 100001 and going up, at each of the assembly plants. Custom six-cylinder models began with the number '8,' followed by the assembly plant code, engine designation 'V' and, finally, the unit's production number, according to the final assembly location. Each plant began at 100001 and went up.

CUSTOM SIX SERIES

Model No.	Body/ Style No.	Body Type & Seating	Factory Price	Shipping Weight	Prod. Total
V	54E	4-dr Sed-6P	2642	3478	Note 1
V	62E	2-dr Sed-6P	2584	3451	Note 1

NOTE 1: See Custom V-8 series listing. Production was counted by series and body style only, with no breakout per engine type.

CUSTOM V-8 I.D. NUMBERS: Custom V-8 models began with the number '8' followed by the assembly plant code, body type code, engine designation code and, finally, the unit's production number, according to the final assembly location. Each plant began at 100001 and went up.

CUSTOM V-8 SERIES

Model No.	Body/ Style No.	Body Type & Seating	Factory Price	Shipping Weight	Prod. Total
N/A	54E	4-dr Sed-6P	2749	3518	45,980
N/A	62E	2-dr Sed-6P	2691	3491	18,485

PRODUCTION NOTE: Total series output was 64,465 units. Ford does not indicate the number of each model produced with sixes or V-8s. Therefore, all production figures given above are total production of each body style with both engines.

CUSTOM 500 SERIES — (6-CYL/V-8) — The Custom 500 was the upper trim level of the base line Custom series and included all the Custom trim plus special Custom 500 exterior trim, a single horizontal chrome strip along the bodyside feature line and choices of four different upholsteries on the interior.

CUSTOM 500 SIX I.D. NUMBERS: Custom 500 six-cylinder models used the same serial number sequence as the Custom models.

CUSTOM 500 SIX SERIES

Model No.	Body/ Style No.	Body Type & Seating	Factory Price	Shipping Weight	Prod. Total
V	54B	4-dr Sed-6P	2741	3491	Note 1
V	62B	2-dr Sed-6P	2699	3440	Note 1

NOTE 1: See Custom 500 V-8 series listing. Production was counted by series and body style only, with no breakout per engine type.

1968 Ford Galaxie 500 two-door hardtop V-8. (OCW)

CUSTOM 500 V-8 I.D. NUMBERS: Custom 500 V-8 models used the same serial number sequence as the Custom models.

CUSTOM 500 V-8 SERIES

Model No.	Body/ Style No.	Body Type & Seating	Factory Price	Shipping Weight	Prod. Total
N/A	54B	4-dr Sed-6P	2848	3531	49,398
N/A	62B	2-dr Sed-6P	2806	3480	8,938

PRODUCTION NOTE: Total series output was 58,336 units. Ford does not indicate the number of each model produced with sixes or V-8s. Therefore, all production figures given above are total production of each body style with both engines.

GALAXIE 500 SERIES — (6-CYL/V-8) — The Galaxie 500 was the intermediate trim level for 1968 and included all the Custom series trim plus stamped aluminum rocker panel moldings; simulated woodgrain appliques on the instrument panel and inner door panels and a stamped aluminum trim panel on the vertical section of the trunk lid. The name Ford in block letters, was located on the vertical section of the trunk, on the passenger side of the car. The name Galaxie 500, in script, was located on the rear fenders, just in front of the taillights.

GALAXIE 500 SIX I.D. NUMBERS: Galaxie 500 six-cylinder models used the same serial number sequence as the Custom series.

GALAXIE 500 SIX SERIES

Model No.	Body/ Style No.	Body Type & Seating	Factory Price	Shipping Weight	Prod. Total
V	54A	4-dr Sed-6P	2864	3496	Note 1
V	57B	4-dr HT Sed-6P	2936	3542	Note 1
V	63B	2-dr FsBk Cpe-6P	2881	3514	Note 1
V	65C	2-dr HT Cpe-6P	2916	3520	Note 1
V	76A	2-dr Conv-6P	3108	3659	Note 1

NOTE 1: See Galaxie 500 V-8 series listing. Production was counted by series and body style only, with no breakout per engine type.

GALAXIE 500 V-8 I.D. NUMBERS: Galaxie 500 V-8 models used the same serial number sequence as the Custom series.

GALAXIE 500 V-8 SERIES

Model No.	Body/ Style No.	Body Type & Seating	Factory Price	Shipping Weight	Prod. Total
N/A	54A	4-dr Sed-6P	2971	3536	117,877
N/A	57B	4-dr HT Sed-6P	3043	3582	55,461
N/A	63B	2-dr FsBk Cpe-6P	2988	3554	69,760
N/A	65C	2-dr HT Cpe-6P	3023	3560	84,332
N/A	76A	2-dr Conv-6P	3215	3699	11,832

PRODUCTION NOTE: Total series output was 339,262 units. Ford does not indicate the number of each model produced with sixes or V-8s. Therefore, all production figures given above are total production of each body style with both engines.

GALAXIE 500XL SERIES — (V-8) — The Galaxie 500XL was the sport trim version of the Galaxie 500 two-door fastback and two-door convertible and included the 302 cid/210-hp V-8 engine and Select-Shift Cruise-O-Matic automatic transmission as standard equipment. Also, the model line included bucket seats and front console; hidden headlights; special 'XL' crest in the center of the hood; automatic courtesy and warning lights in the door panels and chrome trim on the foot pedals.

GALAXIE 500XL I.D. NUMBERS: Galaxie 500XLs used the same serial number sequence as the Custom series and standard Galaxie 500 models.

GALAXIE 500XL SERIES

Model No.	Body/ Style No.	Body Type & Seating	Factory Price	Shipping Weight	Prod. Total
N/A	63C	2-dr FsBk Cpe-5P	3092	3608	50,048
N/A	76B	2-dr Conv-5P	3321	3765	6,066

PRODUCTION NOTE: Total series output was 56,114 units.

1968 Ford Galaxie 500XL GT two-door fastback hardtop V-8. (PH)

1968 Ford LTD two-door hardtop V-8. (PH)

1968 Ford LTD four-door hardtop V-8. (PH)

LTD SERIES — (V-8) — The LTD was the top trim level full-size Ford for 1968 and included all the Galaxie 500 trim plus the 302 cid/210-hp V-8 engine and Select-Shift Cruise-O-Matic automatic transmission as standard equipment. Also included in the LTD package was flow-through ventilation; distinctive LTD trim and ornamentation; special wheel covers; simulated woodgrain appliques on the instrument panel and inner door panels; automatic courtesy and warning lights in the doors; deep-foam cushioning in the seating surfaces; pull-down armrests, front and rear; color-keyed steering wheel; and vinyl top on two-door hardtops.

LTD I.D. NUMBERS: LTDs used the same serial number sequence as the Custom and Galaxie series.

LTD SERIES

Model No.	Body/ Style No.	Body Type & Seating	Factory Price	Shipping Weight	Prod. Total
N/A	54C	4-dr Sed-6P	3135	3596	22,834
N/A	57F	4-dr HT Sed-6P	3206	3642	61,755
N/A	65A	2-dr HT Cpe-6P	3153	3679	54,163

PRODUCTION NOTE: Total series output was 138,752 units.

STATION WAGON SERIES — (6-CYL/V-8) — The Ranch Wagon was the base trim level station wagon for 1968, with the Custom Ranch Wagons and the Country Sedans being the intermediate trim level and the Country Squires being the top trim level. The trim paralleled the Custom, Custom 500, Galaxie 500 and LTD models of passenger cars.

STATION WAGON SIX I.D. NUMBERS: Station wagon six-cylinder models used the same serial number sequence as Custom and Galaxie 500 series of passenger cars.

STATION WAGON SIX SERIES

Model No.	Body/ Style No.	Body Type & Seating	Factory Price	Shipping Weight	Prod. Total
V	71D	4-dr Ranch Wag-6P	3000	3905	Note 1
V	71H	4-dr Cus Wag-6P	3063	3915	Note 1
V	71J	4-dr Cus Wag-9P	3176	3961	Note 1
V	71B	4-dr Cty Sed-6P	3181	3924	Note 1
V	71C	4-dr Cty Sed-9P	3295	3981	Note 1

NOTE 1: See station wagon V-8 series listing. Production was counted by series and body style only, with no breakout per engine type.

1968 Ford LTD Country Squire station wagon V-8. (PH)

STATION WAGON V-8 I.D. NUMBERS: Station wagon V-8 models used the same serial number sequence as the Custom and Galaxie 500 series of passenger cars.

STATION WAGON V-8 SERIES

Model No.	Body/ Style No.	Body Type & Seating	Factory Price	Shipping Weight	Prod. Total
N/A	71D	4-dr Ranch Wag-6P	3107	3945	18,237
N/A	71H	4-dr Cus Wag-6P	3170	3955	18,181
N/A	71J	4-dr Cus Wag-9P	3283	4001	13,421
N/A	71B	4-dr Cty Sed-6P	3288	3964	39,335
N/A	71C	4-dr Cty Sed-9P	3402	4021	29,374
N/A	71E	4-dr Cty Sq-6P	3539	4013	33,994
N/A	71A	4-dr Cty Sq-9P	3619	4059	57,776

PRODUCTION NOTE: Total series output was 210,318 units. Ford does not indicate the number of each model produced with sixes and V-8s. Therefore, all production figures given above are total production of each body with both engines. It was during 1968 that Ford gained the title 'Wagon Master,' because of the outstanding sales record of that particular body style in all the lines.

FAIRLANE MODELS — (6-CYL/V-8) — The Fairlane was the base trim level for 1968 and included chrome windshield and rear window moldings; chrome rain gutters and side window frames; a chrome horn ring; front and rear armrests; cigarette lighter; vinyl-coated rubber floor mats and the Fairlane name, in script, on the side of the rear fender. The Ford name was spelled out, in block letters, across the front of the hood and across the vertical section of the trunk lid. The Fairlane line was the one chosen for major restyling for the new year. It was undoubtedly one of the nicest looking Fairlanes ever to come out of Detroit. It had a full-width grille, containing horizontally mounted quad headlights, and smooth sides with a single horizontal feature line running front to rear. The taillights were vertically situated rectangular units with a centrally located back-up light. The word Ford was spaced evenly across the trunk lid in block letters. The top-line Fairlane models for 1968 were called Torino, with the Fairlane 500 being demoted to intermediate trim level.

FAIRLANE SIX I.D. NUMBERS: Fairlane six-cylinder models began with the number '8' followed by the assembly plant code, body type code, engine designation 'T' and, finally, the unit's production number according to the final assembly location. Each plant began at 100001 and went up.

FAIRLANE SIX SERIES

Model No.	Body/ Style No.	Body Type & Seating	Factory Price	Shipping Weight	Prod. Total
T	54A	4-dr Sed-6P	2464	2889	Note 1
T	65A	2-dr HT Cpe-6P	2456	2931	Note 1
T	71B	4-dr Sta Wag-6P	2770	3244	Note 1

NOTE 1: See Fairlane V-8 series listing. Production was counted by series and body style only, with no breakout per engine type.

FAIRLANE V-8 I.D. NUMBERS: Fairlane V-8 models began with the number '8' followed by the assembly plant code, body type code, engine designation code and, finally, the unit's production number according to the final assembly location. Each plant began at 100001 and went up.

FAIRLANE V-8 SERIES

Model No.	Body/ Style No.	Body Type & Seating	Factory Price	Shipping Weight	Prod. Total
N/A	54A	4-dr Sed-6P	2551	3083	18,146
N/A	65A	2-dr HT Cpe-6P	2544	3125	44,683
N/A	71B	4-dr Sta Wag-6P	2858	3422	14,800

PRODUCTION NOTE: Total series output was 77,629 units. Ford does not indicate the number of each model produced with sixes or V-8s. Therefore, all production figures given above are total production of each body style with both engines.

1968 Ford Fairlane 500 two-door convertible V-8. (OCW)

1968 Ford Fairlane Torino GT two-door convertible V-8. (OCW)

FAIRLANE 500 SERIES — (6-CYL/V-8) — The Fairlane 500 was the intermediate trim level for 1968 and included all the Fairlane trim plus special Fairlane 500 trim and moldings, color-keyed carpeting front and rear, and a choice of four nylon and vinyl upholsteries. Also included was an aluminum dividing bar, in the center of the vertical portion of the trunk lid, and a horizontal dividing bar, in the center of the grille. The Fairlane 500 name, in script, appeared on the rear fender, just ahead of the taillights.

FAIRLANE 500 SIX I.D. NUMBERS: Fairlane 500 six-cylinder models used the same serial number sequence as the Fairlane models.

FAIRLANE 500 SIX SERIES

Model No.	Body/ Style No.	Body Type & Seating	Factory Price	Shipping Weight	Prod. Total
T	54B	4-dr Sed-6P	2520	2932	Note 1
T	63B	2-dr FsBk Cpe-6P	2543	2994	Note 1
T	65B	2-dr HT Cpe-6P	2568	2982	Note 1
T	76B	2-dr Conv-6P	2822	3136	Note 1
T	71D	4-dr Sta Wag-6P	2857	3274	Note 1

NOTE 1: See Fairlane 500 V-8 series listing. Production was counted by series and body style only, with no breakout per engine type.

FAIRLANE 500 V-8 I.D. NUMBERS: Fairlane 500 V-8 models used the same serial number sequence as the Fairlane models.

FAIRLANE 500 V-8 SERIES

Model No.	Body/ Style No.	Body Type & Seating	Factory Price	Shipping Weight	Prod. Total
N/A	54B	4-dr Sed-6P	2631	3121	42,390
N/A	63B	2-dr FsBk Cpe-6P	2653	3177	32,452
N/A	65B	2-dr HT Cpe-6P	2679	3136	33,282
N/A	76B	2-dr Conv-6P	2910	3323	3,761
N/A	71D	4-dr Sta Wag-6P	2968	3466	10,190

PRODUCTION NOTE: Total series output was 122,075 units. Ford does not indicate the number of each model produced with sixes or V-8s. Therefore, all production figures given above are total production of each body style with both engines.

FAIRLANE TORINO SERIES — (6-CYL/V-8) — The Fairlane Torino was the top trim level for 1968 and included all the Fairlane 500 trim plus a lower bodyside molding, special emblems and trim inside and out and a Torino crest on the 'C' pillars of the two-door hardtop and four-door sedan.

1968 Ford Fairlane Torino GT two-door fastback hardtop V-8. (OCW)

1968 Ford Fairlane Torino two-door hardtop V-8. (PH)

1968 Ford Fairlane Torino four-door sedan V-8. (OCW)

FAIRLANE TORINO SIX I.D. NUMBERS: Fairlane Torino six-cylinder models used the same serial number sequence as the Fairlane and Fairlane 500 models.

FAIRLANE TORINO SIX SERIES

Model No.	Body/ Style No.	Body Type & Seating	Factory Price	Shipping Weight	Prod. Total
T	54C	4-dr Sed-6P	2688	2965	Note 1
T	65C	2-dr HT Cpe-6P	2710	3001	Note 1
T	71E	4-dr Sq Sta Wag-6P	3032	3336	Note 1

NOTE 1: See Torino V-8 series listing. Production was counted by series and body style only, with no breakout per engine type.

FAIRLANE TORINO V-8 I.D. NUMBERS: Fairlane Torino V-8 models used the same serial number sequence as the Fairlane and Fairlane 500 models.

FAIRLANE TORINO V-8 SERIES

Model No.	Body/ Style No.	Body Type & Seating	Factory Price	Shipping Weight	Prod. Total
N/A	54C	4-dr Sed-6P	2776	3159	17,962
N/A	65C	2-dr HT Cpe-6P	2798	3195	35,964
N/A	71E	4-dr Sq Sta Wag-6P	3119	3514	14,773

PRODUCTION NOTE: Total series output was 68,699 units. Ford does not indicate the number of each model produced with sixes or V-8s. Therefore, all production figures given above are total production of each body style with both engines.

FAIRLANE TORINO GT SERIES — (V-8) — The Fairlane Torino GT was the sporty version of the Fairlane 500 series and included all the Fairlane 500 features plus the 302 cid/210-hp V-8 engine, bucket seats and console, special name plaques and exterior trim, Deluxe wheel covers and red safety and white courtesy lights on the interior door panels, as standard equipment.

FAIRLANE TORINO GT I.D. NUMBERS: Fairlane GT V-8 models used the same serial number sequence as the Fairlane, Fairlane 500 and Fairlane Torino models.

1968 Ford Fairlane Torino Squire station wagon V-8. (PH)

1968 Ford Falcon Futura station wagon V-8. (OCW)

FAIRLANE TORINO GT SERIES

Model No.	Body/ Style No.	Body Type & Seating	Factory Price	Shipping Weight	Prod. Total
N/A	63D	2-dr FsBk Cpe-5P	2747	3208	74,135
N/A	65D	2-dr HT Cpe-5P	2772	3194	23,939
N/A	76D	2-dr Conv-5P	3001	3352	5,310

PRODUCTION NOTE: Total series output was 103,384 units.

FALCON SERIES — (6-CYL/V-8) — The Falcons were the base trim level of the compact Falcon line for 1968 and included chrome windshield, rear window and rain gutter moldings; armrests on the front doors only; and a horn button, instead of the chrome horn ring found on the Futura models. The Falcon name, in script, appeared on the rear fenders, just ahead of the taillights and in block letters, across the vertical section of the trunk lid. The 1968 Falcons again used the same body shell as the previous two years, with only minor trim changes. The most noticeable change in the entire car is that the taillights were square, instead of the round type used on the car since its introduction in 1960. The grille was a stamped aluminum piece, with a rectangular mesh pattern, divided by the Falcon crest in the center. The simulated exhaust port, used on the front fender of the 1967 Falcons, was not continued into the year 1968.

FALCON SERIES I.D. NUMBERS: Falcons used the same serial number sequence as the full-size Fords and the Fairlane lines.

FALCON SERIES

Model No.	Body/ Style No.	Body Type & Seating	Factory Price	Shipping Weight	Prod. Total
N/A	54A	4-dr Sed-6P	2301	2714	29,166
N/A	62A	2-dr Sed-6P	2252	2659	36,443
N/A	71A	4-dr Sta Wag-6P	2617	3132	15,576

PRODUCTION NOTE: Total series output was 81,185 units. Ford does not indicate the number of each model produced with sixes or V-8s. Therefore, all production figures given above are total production of each body style with both engines.

1968 Ford Falcon Futura two-door Sports Coupe V-8. (OCW)

1968 Ford Falcon Futura four-door sedan 6-cyl. (OCW)

FUTURA SERIES — (6-CYL/V-8) — The Futura series was the top trim level for 1968 and included all the standard Falcon features plus a cigarette lighter; armrests and ashtrays on all doors; a chrome horn ring; nylon carpeting; special Futura moldings; trim, emblems and nameplates; and chrome side window frames. In addition, the Sports Coupe offered front bucket seats; special nameplates; a map light; ashtray; glovebox and trunk lights; 7.35 x 14 tires; a side chrome accent stripe; remote control outside driver's mirror; and Deluxe seat belts.

FUTURA I.D. NUMBERS: Futura models used the same serial number sequence as the full-size Fords, Fairlanes and Falcons.

FUTURA SERIES

Model No.	Body/ Style No.	Body Type & Seating	Factory Price	Shipping Weight	Prod. Total
N/A	54B	4-dr Sed-6P	2456	2719	18,733
N/A	62B	2-dr Sed-6P	2415	2685	10,633
N/A	62C	2-dr Spt Cpe-5P	2541	2713	10,077
N/A	71B	4-dr Sq Sta Wag-6P	2728	3123	10,761

PRODUCTION NOTES: Total series output was 50,204 units. Ford does not indicate the number of each model produced with sixes and V-8s. Therefore, all production figures given above are total production of each body style with both engines.

THUNDERBIRD SERIES — (V-8) — The 1968 Thunderbird was a restyled version of the 1967 model, with minor trim updating. The grille and taillights were slightly revised from the 1967 offering and new wheel covers completed the face-lifting of the Thunderbird for 1968.

THUNDERBIRD I.D. NUMBERS: Thunderbird models began with the number '8,' assembly plant code 'Y' (Wixom), body type code, engine type code 'Z' or 'N' and, finally, the unit's production number, beginning at 100001 and going up.

THUNDERBIRD SERIES

Model No.	Body/ Style No.	Body Type & Seating	Factory Price	Shipping Weight	Prod. Total
N/Z	65A	2-dr HT Cpe-6P	4716	4366	9,977
N/Z	65B	2-dr Landau-4P	4845	4372	33,029
N/Z	57B	4-dr Landau-4P	4924	4458	21,925

PRODUCTION NOTE: Total series output was 64,931 units. This figure includes 4,557 two-door hardtops, 13,924 two-door Landau hardtops and 17,251 four-door Landau hardtops equipped with bench seats.

ENGINE [Falcon/Fairlane Base Six]: Overhead valve. Cast-iron block. Displacement: 170 cid. Bore and stroke: 3.50 x 2.94 inches. Compression ratio: 8.7:1. Brake hp: 100 at 4000 rpm. Carburetor: Holley one-barrel. Seven main bearings. Serial number code 'U.'

ENGINE [Falcon/Fairlane Six]: Overhead valve. Cast-iron block. Displacement: 200 cid. Bore and stroke: 3.68 x 3.13 inches. Compression ratio: 8.8:1. Brake hp: 115 at 3800 rpm. Carburetor: Holley one-barrel. Seven main bearings. Serial number code 'T' (export code '2).'

ENGINE [Ford Base Six]: Overhead valve. Cast-iron block. Displacement: 240 cid. Bore and stroke: 4.00 x 3.18 inches. Compression ratio: 9.2:1. Brake hp: 150 at 4000 rpm. Carburetor: Holley one-barrel. Seven main bearings. Serial number code 'V' (police code 'B'; taxi code 'E'; export code '5).'

ENGINE [Challenger 289 V-8]: Overhead valve. Cast-iron block. Displacement: 289 cid. Bore and stroke: 4.00 x 2.87 inches. Compression ratio: 8.7:1. Brake hp: 195 at 4600 rpm. Carburetor: Holley two-barrel. Five main bearings. Serial number code 'C.'

ENGINE [302 V-8]: Overhead valve. Cast-iron block. Displacement: 302 cid. Bore and stroke: 4.00 x 3.00 inches. Compression ratio: 9.0:1. Brake hp: 210 at 4000 rpm. Carburetor: Motorcraft two-barrel. Five main bearings. Serial number code 'F' (export code '6).'

1968 Ford Thunderbird two-door hardtop V-8. (OCW)

1968 Ford Thunderbird Landau two-door hardtop V-8. (PH)

ENGINE [302 Four-Barrel V-8]: Overhead valve. Cast-iron block. Displacement: 302 cid. Bore and stroke: 4.00 x 3.00 inches. Compression ratio: 10.0:1. Brake hp: 230 at 4800 rpm. Carburetor: Motorcraft four-barrel. Five main bearings. Serial number code 'J.'

ENGINE [Thunderbird V-8]: Overhead valve. Cast-iron block. Displacement: 390 cid. Bore and stroke: 4.05 x 3.78 inches. Compression ratio: 9.5:1. Brake hp: 265 at 4400 rpm. Carburetor: two-barrel. Five main bearings. Serial number code 'Y.'

ENGINE [Thunderbird V-8]: Overhead valve. Cast-iron block. Displacement: 390 cid. Bore and stroke: 4.05 x 3.78 inches. Compression ratio: 10.5:1. Brake hp: 280 at 4400 rpm. Carburetor: two-barrel. Five main bearings. Serial number code 'X.'

ENGINE [Thunderbird Four-Barrel V-8]: Overhead valve. Cast-iron block. Displacement: 390 cid. Bore and stroke: 4.05 x 3.78 inches. Compression ratio: 10.5:1. Brake hp: 315 at 4600 rpm. Carburetor: Motorcraft four-barrel. Five main bearings. Serial number code 'Z.'

ENGINE [GT 390 V-8]: Overhead valve. Cast-iron block. Displacement: 390 cid. Bore and stroke: 4.05 x 3.78 inches. Compression ratio: 10.5:1. Brake hp: 325 at 4800 rpm. Carburetor: Holley four-barrel. Five main bearings Serial number code 'S.'

ENGINE [Thunderbird High-Performance V-8]: Overhead valve. Cast-iron block. Displacement: 427 cid. Bore and stroke: 4.23 x 3.78 inches. Compression ratio: 10.9:1. Brake hp: 390 at 4600 rpm. Carburetor: Motorcraft four-barrel. Five main bearings. Serial number code 'W.'

ENGINE [Cobra Jet 428 V-8]: Overhead valve. Cast-iron block. Displacement: 428 cid. Bore and stroke: 4.13 x 3.98 inches. Compression ratio: 10.7:1. Brake hp: 335 at 5600 rpm. Carburetor: Holley four-barrel. Five main bearings. Police version code 'P.'

ENGINE [Super Cobra Jet 428 V-8]: Overhead valve. Cast-iron block. Displacement: 428 cid. Bore and stroke: 4.13 x 3.98 inches. Compression ratio: 10.5:1. Brake hp: 360 at 5400 rpm. Carburetor: Holley four-barrel. Serial number code 'R.'

ENGINE [Thunderbird 428 V-8]: Overhead valve. Cast-iron block. Displacement: 428 cid. Bore and stroke: 4.13 x 3.98 inches. Compression ratio: 10.5:1. Brake hp: 340 at 5400 rpm. Carburetor: Motorcraft four-barrel. Serial number code 'Q.'

ENGINE [Thunder-Jet 429 V-8]: Overhead valve. Cast-iron block. Displacement: 429 cid. Bore and stroke: 4.36 x 3.59 inches. Compression ratio: 10.5:1. Brake hp: 360 at 4600 rpm. Carburetor: Motorcraft four-barrel. Serial number code 'N.'

FORD CHASSIS FEATURES: Wheelbase: 119 inches. Overall length: (station wagons) 213.9 inches; (other models) 213.3 inches. Tires: (hardtops) 8.15 x 15 four-ply tubeless blackwall; (station wagons) 8.45 x 15 four-ply tubeless blackwall; (other models) 7.75 x 15 four-ply tubeless blackwall.

FAIRLANE CHASSIS FEATURES: Wheelbase: (station wagons) 113 inches; (other models) 116 inches; Overall length: (station wagons) 203.9 inches; (other models) 201 inches. Tires: (station wagons) 7.75 x 14 tubeless blackwall; (GT) F870-14; (other models) 7.35 x 14 tubeless blackwall.

FALCON CHASSIS FEATURES: Wheelbase: (station wagons) 113 inches; (other models) 110.9 inches. Overall length: (station wagons) 198.7 inches; (other models) 184.3 inches. Tires: (station wagons) 7.75 x 14 four-ply tubeless blackwall; (other models) 6.95 x 14 four-ply tubeless blackwall.

THUNDERBIRD CHASSIS FEATURES: Wheelbase: (four-door Landau) 117 inches; (other models) 115 inches. Overall length: (four-door Landau) 209.9 inches; (other models) 206.9 inches. Tires: (four-door Landau) 8.45 x 15 tubeless blackwall; (other models) 8.15 x 15 four-ply tubeless blackwall.

1968 Ford Thunderbird four-door Landau Sedan V-8. (PH)

FORD OPTIONS: 302 cid/210-hp V-8 engine ($110). 390 cid/265-hp V-8 engine ($78 in XLs and LTDs; $184 in others). 390 cid/315-hp V-8 engine ($158 in XLs and LTDs; $265 in others). Cruise-O-Matic automatic transmission ($188 to $220, depending on engine choice). Power steering ($95). Power brakes ($42). Tinted windshield ($95). Air conditioning ($356). AM radio ($57). AM/FM stereo radio ($134). Vinyl roof ($74 on two-door hardtops, $83 on four-door models). White sidewall tires ($35).

STATION WAGON OPTIONS: All the above plus power tailgate window ($32). Luggage rack ($44). Deluxe adjustable luggage rack ($63).

FAIRLANE/TORINO OPTIONS: 302 cid/210-hp V-8 engine ($107, standard on GT models). 390 cid V-8 engine ($184 for two-barrel version; $264 for the four-barrel version). Cruise-O-Matic automatic transmission ($188 to $220, depending on engine choice). Four-speed manual transmission ($184). AM radio ($57). Power steering ($84). Power tailgate window in station wagons ($32). Luggage rack on station wagons ($44). Two-tone paint ($22). White sidewall tires ($34). Wheel covers ($41). Vinyl roofs on two-door hardtops ($74).

FALCON OPTIONS: 200 cid six-cylinder engine ($26). 289 cid V-8 engine ($132). 302 cid V-8 engine ($183). Cruise-O-Matic automatic transmission ($187). Four-speed manual transmission ($184). Power steering ($84). Power tailgate window on station wagons ($32). Tinted windshield ($21). Luggage rack on station wagons ($44). AM radio ($57). Eight-track stereo tape player ($128) Two-tone paint ($19). Vinyl roof on two-door sedans ($74). Wheel covers ($21). White sidewall tires ($32).

THUNDERBIRD OPTIONS: 429 cid Thunder-Jet V-8 engine. Six-Way power driver's seat ($98). Power windows ($104). Cruise Control ($130). Air conditioning ($421). AM/8-track stereo radio ($128). AM/FM Multiplex stereo radio ($164). Two-tone paint ($25). White sidewall tires with red band ($52).

HISTORY: Ford products captured over 20 checkered flags in NASCAR stock car racing during 1968, with Ford driver David Pearson taking the overall championship. In USAC competition, Ford pilot A.J. Foyt was the top driver of the year. Benny Parsons and Cale Yarborough also made Ford racing history this year, driving Fairlanes and Torinos in ARCA contests. A specially-trimmed Torino convertible paced the 52nd Indianapolis 500-Mile race. The new Fords were introduced to the public on Sept. 22, 1967. In Europe, Ford GT-40s competed in the international class races, attempting to repeat the success of 1966, when similar machines finished first, second and third at LeMans. Early in 1968, Semon E. 'Bunkie' Knudsen became the chief executive officer of Ford Motor Co. Knudsen had held a similar position with Pontiac and Chevrolet during some of the most exciting years in automotive history.

1969 FORD

1969 Ford Custom 500 four-door sedan 6-cyl. (PH)

1969 Ford Galaxie 500 two-door fastback hardtop V-8. (OCW)

1969 FORDS — OVERVIEW — The year 1969 started out as a scramble for new Ford Motor Co. products. It was almost to the point where a scorecard was needed to keep track of all the models. A new series on the scene was the Cobra, Ford's performance line in the Fairlane series. The big news for 1969 came at midyear introduction time, when the Maverick was introduced. The Maverick was designed to be direct competition for the Volkswagen and was intended to influence those who liked a small and economical car. With a base price of $1,995 it was the only Ford under $2,000. For the first time, economy was heavily promoted, with Ford announcing that the Maverick would average 22 mpg. By design, the Maverick was introduced April 17, 1969, exactly five years to the day, after the phenomenally successful Mustang.

FORD CUSTOM SERIES — (6-CYL/V-8) — The 1969 full-size Fords were totally restyled and shared nothing with the previous year's offering. The lines of the new models were even rounder than in 1968. They looked more like big luxury cars, than Fords. Luxury, in fact, was highly promoted. Velour interiors and vinyl tops were the order of the day in the LTD lineup. All full-size Fords shared the same body lines, with the LTD receiving its own front end treatment, thus further segregating it from the 'ordinary' Galaxies. The Custom series was the base trim level Ford for 1969 and included chrome windshield and rear window moldings; a chrome horn ring; nylon carpeting; the Custom name, in script, on the rear fender (just in front of the rear marker light); the Ford name, in block letters, across the rear escutcheon panel; and a single horizontal chrome strip along the center of the body.

CUSTOM SIX I.D. NUMBERS: The serial number code can be broken down, as follows: First symbol indicates year: 9 = 1969. Second symbol identifies assembly plant, as follows: A = Atlanta; B = Oakville, Ontario, Canada; C = Ontario, Canada; D = Dallas; G = Chicago; F = Dearborn; E = Mahwah; H = Loraine; J = Los Angeles; K = Kansas City; N = Norfolk; R = San Jose; S = Pilot Plant; T = Metuchen; U = Louisville; P = Twin Cities; W = Wayne; X = St. Thomas, Ontario, Canada; Y = Wixom; Z = St. Louis. Third and fourth symbols identify body series (see Body/ Numbers below). Fifth symbol identifies engine code, as follows: U = 170 cid six-cylinder; T = 200 cid six-cylinder; V = 240 cid six-cylinder; L = 250 cid six-cylinder; F = 302 cid V-8; G = 302 cid Boss V-8 with four-barrel carb; H = 351 cid V-8; M = 351 cid V-8 with four-barrel carb; Y = 390 cid V-8; S = 390 cid V-8 with four-barrel carb; Q = 428 cid V-8 with four-barrel carb; R = 428 cid Super Cobra Jet V-8 with four-barrel carb; K = 429 cid V-8; N = 429 cid V-8 with four-barrel carb; Z = 429 cid Boss V-8 with four-barrel carb. The last six digits are the unit's production number, beginning at 100001 and going up, at each of the assembly plants. Custom six-cylinder models began with the number '9' followed by the assembly plant code, engine designation 'V' and, finally, the unit's produchon number according to the final assembly location. Each plant began at 100001 and went up.

CUSTOM SIX SERIES

Model No.	Body/ Style No.	Body Type & Seating	Factory Price	Shipping Weight	Prod. Total
V	54E	4-dr Sed-6P	2674	3608	Note 1
V	62E	2-dr Sed-6P	2632	3585	Note 1
V	71D	4-dr Ranch Wag-6P	3074	4069	Note 1

NOTE 1: See Custom V-8 series listing. Production was counted by series and body style only, with no breakout per engine type.

CUSTOM V-8 I.D. NUMBERS: Custom V-8 models began with the number '9' followed by the assembly plant code, body type code, engine designation code and, finally, the unit's production number according to the final assembly location. Each plant began at 100001 and went up.

CUSTOM V-8 SERIES

Model No.	Body/ Style No.	Body Type & Seating	Factory Price	Shipping Weight	Prod. Total
N/A	54E	4-dr Sed-6P	2779	3648	45,653
N/A	62E	2-dr Sed-6P	2737	3625	15,439
N/A	71D	4-dr Ranch Wag-6P	3179	4109	17,489

PRODUCTION NOTE: Total series output was 78,581 units. Ford does not indicate the number of each model produced with sixes or V-8s.

Therefore, all production figures given above are total production of each body style with both engines.

CUSTOM 500 SERIES — (6-CYL/V-8) — The Custom 500 was the upper trim level of the base line Custom series and included all the Custom trim plus special Custom 500 exterior trim and choices of four different upholsteries on the interior.

CUSTOM 500 SIX I.D. NUMBERS: Custom 500 six-cylinder models used the same serial number sequence as the Custom models.

CUSTOM 500 SIX SERIES

Model No.	Body/ Style No.	Body Type & Seating	Factory Price	Shipping Weight	Prod. Total
V	54B	4-dr Sed-6P	2773	3620	Note 1
V	62B	2-dr Sed-6P	2731	3570	Note 1
V	71H	4-dr Ranch Wag-6P	3138	4082	Note 1
V	71J	4-dr Ranch Wag-10P	3251	4132	Note 1

NOTE 1: See Custom 500 V-8 series listings. Production was counted by series and body style only, with no breakout per engine type.

CUSTOM 500 V-8 I.D. NUMBERS: Custom 500 V-8 models used the same serial number sequence as the Custom models.

CUSTOM 500 V-8 SERIES

Model No.	Body/ Style No.	Body Type & Seating	Factory Price	Shipping Weight	Prod. Total
N/A	54B	4-dr Sed-6P	2878	3660	45,761
N/A	62B	2-dr Sed-6P	2836	3610	7,585
N/A	71H	4-dr Ranch Wag-6P	3243	4122	16,432
N/A	71J	4-dr Ranch Wag-10P	3556	4172	11,563

PRODUCTION NOTE: Total series output was 81,341 units. Ford does not indicate the number of each model produced with sixes or V-8s. Therefore, all production figures given above are total production of each body style with both engines.

GALAXIE 500 SERIES — (6-CYL/V-8) — The Galaxie 500 was the intermediate trim level for 1969 and included all the Custom series trim plus stamped aluminum lower bodyside moldings and pleated interior trim.

GALAXIE 500 SIX I.D. NUMBERS: Galaxie 500 six-cylinder models used the same serial number sequence as the Custom series.

GALAXIE 500 SIX SERIES

Model No.	Body/ Style No.	Body Type & Seating	Factory Price	Shipping Weight	Prod. Total
V	54A	4-dr Sed-6P	2897	3670	Note 1
V	64B	2-dr FsBk Cpe-6P	2913	3680	Note 1
V	65C	2-dr FT Cpe-6P	2965	3635	Note 1
V	57B	4-dr HT Sed-6P	2966	3705	Note 1
V	76A	2-dr Conv-6P	3142	3840	Note 1
V	71B	4-dr Cty Sed-6P	3257	4067	Note 1
V	71C	4-dr Cty Sed-10P	3373	3092	Note 1

NOTE 1: See Galaxie 500 V-8 series listing. Production was counted by series and body style only, with no breakout per engine type.

GALAXIE 500 V-8 I.D. NUMBERS: Galaxie 500 V-8 models used the same serial number sequence as the Custom series.

GALAXIE 500 V-8 SERIES

Model No.	Body/ Style No.	Body Type & Seating	Factory Price	Shipping Weight	Prod. Total
N/A	54A	4-dr Sed-6P	3002	3710	104,606
N/A	63B	2-dr FsBk Cpe-6P	3018	3720	63,921
N/A	65C	2-dr FT Cpe-6P	3070	3675	71,920
N/A	57B	4-dr HT Sed-6P	3071	3745	64,031
N/A	76A	2-dr Conv-6P	3247	3880	6,910
N/A	71B	4-dr Cty Sed-6P	3362	4107	36,287
N/A	71C	4-dr Cty Sed-10P	3487	4132	11,563

PRODUCTION NOTE: Total series output was 359,238 units. Ford does not indicate the number of each model produced with sixes or V-8s. Therefore, all production figures given above are total production of each body style with both engines.

GALAXIE 500XL SERIES — (6-CYL/V-8) — The Galaxie 500XL was the sport trim version of the Galaxie 500. It came in 'Sportsroof' (two-door fastback coupe) and convertible styles. Standard equipment included bucket seats; wheel covers; die-cast grille; retractable headlights; pleated, all-vinyl interior trim; and five vertical 'hash marks' at the forward part of the front fenders, in addition to all the standard Galaxie 500 trim.

1969 Ford Galaxie 500 two-door convertible V-8. (OCW)

1969 Ford Galaxie 500XL GT two-door convertible V-8. (PH)

GALAXIE 500XL SIX I.D. NUMBERS: The Galaxie 500XL six-cylinder models used the same serial number sequence as the Custom, Custom 500 and Galaxie 500 series.

GALAXIE 500XL SIX SERIES

Model No.	Body/ Style No.	Body Type & Seating	Factory Price	Shipping Weight	Prod. Total
V	63C	2-dr FsBk Cpe-5P	3052	3785	Note 1
V	76B	2-dr Conv-5P	3280	3935	Note 1

NOTE 1: See Galaxie 500XL V-8 series listing. Production was counted by series and body style only, with no breakout per engine data.

GALAXIE 500XL V-8 I.D. NUMBERS: The Galaxie 500XL V-8 models used the same serial number sequence as the Custom, Custom 500 and Galaxie 500 series.

GALAXIE 500XL V-8 SERIES

Model No.	Body/ Style No.	Body Type & Seating	Factory Price	Shipping Weight	Prod. Total
N/A	63C	2-dr FsBk Cpe-5P	3157	3825	54,557
N/A	76B	2-dr Conv-5P	3385	3975	7,402

PRODUCTION NOTE: Total series output was 61,959 units. Ford does not indicate the number of each model produced with sixes or V-8s. Therefore, all production figures given above are total production of each body style with both engines.

1969 Ford Galaxie 500XL two-door fastback hardtop V-8. (OCW)

1969 Ford LTD two-door "Formal" hardtop V-8. (OCW)

1969 Ford LTD Country Squire station wagon V-8. (OCW)

LTD SERIES — (V-8) — The LTD was the top trim level full-size Ford for 1969 and included all the Galaxie 500 trim plus the 302 cid/220-hp V-8 engine; SelectShift Cruise-O-Matic automatic transmission; electric clock; bright exterior moldings; and dual accent paint stripes. The LTD station wagon models (Country Squires) also had simulated woodgrain appliques on the bodysides. All LTDs also came with retractable headlights and die-cast grilles.

LTD I.D. NUMBERS: LTDs used the same serial number sequence as the Custom, Custom 500 and Galaxie 500 series.

LTD SERIES

Model No.	Body/ Style No.	Body Type & Seating	Factory Price	Shipping Weight	Prod. Total
N/A	54C	4-dr Sed-6P	3192	3745	63,709
N/A	57F	4-dr Sed-6P	3261	3840	113,168
N/A	65A	2-dr FT Cpe-6P	3234	3745	111,565
N/A	71E	4-dr Cty Sq-6P	3644	4202	46,445
N/A	71A	4-dr Cty Sq-10P	3721	4227	82,790

PRODUCTION NOTE: Total series output was 417,677 units.

FAIRLANE MODELS — (6-CYL/V-8) — The Fairlane was the base trim level for 1969 and included chrome windshield and rear window moldings; chrome rain gutters and side window frames; a chrome horn ring; front and rear armrests; cigarette lighter; vinyl-coated rubber floor mats; and the Fairlane name, in script, on the passenger side of the escutcheon panel. The Ford name was spelled out, in block letters, across the front of the hood and on the vertical section of the trunk lid. Performance was the key word in the Fairlane lineup for 1969. Visually all models, except four-door sedans, looked fast. And most of them were. When equipped with the Cobra Jet 428, the Fairlanes were awesome as well as beautiful. They shared the same body as the 1968 models, with only minor trim updating. The taillights were revised slightly and were squarer in shape than the 1968 type. The grille was revised slightly, with a more prominent center dividing bar than in 1968. At midyear introduction time, the Torino Talladega Special was released in extremely limited quantities, to qualify the body style for use in NASCAR racing. The front end was extended several inches and used a flat grille, mounted at the front of the opening, rather than several inches back, as on standard models. Also, the rear bumper from a standard Fairlane was used up front, because it was more aerodynamic than the original front bumper. All Torino Talladega Specials were equipped with the Cobra Jet 428 engine and offered a choice of either SelectShift Cruise-O-Matic automatic transmission, or the bulletproof 'top-loader' four-speed manual gearbox.

1969 Ford Fairlane 500 two-door convertible V-8. (OCW)

FAIRLANE SIX I.D. NUMBERS: Fairlane six-cylinder models began with the number '9' followed by the assembly plant code, body type code, engine designation 'T' and, finally, the unit's production number according to the final assembly location. Each plant began at 100001 and went up.

FAIRLANE SIX SERIES

Model No.	Body/ Style No.	Body Type & Seating	Factory Price	Shipping Weight	Prod. Total
T	54A	4-dr Sed-6P	2471	3010	Note 1
T	65A	2-dr HT Cpe-6P	2482	3025	Note 1
T	71B	4-dr Sta Wag-6P	2824	3387	Note 1

NOTE 1: See Fairlane V-8 series listing. Production was counted by series and body style only, with no breakout per engine data.

FAIRLANE V-8 I.D. NUMBERS: Fairlane V-8 models began with the number '9' followed by the assembly plant code, body type code, engine designation code and, finally, the unit's production number according to the final assembly location. Each plant began at 100001 and went up.

FAIRLANE V-8 SERIES

Model No.	Body/ Style No.	Body Type & Seating	Factory Price	Shipping Weight	Prod. Total
N/A	54A	4-dr Sed-6P	2561	3120	27,296
N/A	65A	2-dr HT Cpe-6P	2572	3133	85,630
N/A	71D	4-dr Sta Wag-6P	2914	3387	10,882

PRODUCTION NOTE: Total series output was 123,808 units. Ford does not indicate the number of each model produced with sixes and V-8s. Therefore, all production figures given above are total production of each body style with both engines.

FAIRLANE 500 SERIES — (6-CYL/V-8) — The Fairane 500 was the intermediate trim level for 1969 and included all Fairlane trim plus special 500 trim and moldings; color-keyed carpeting (front and rear); and a choice of four nylon and vinyl upholsteries. Also included was an aluminum trim panel in the center of the rear escutcheon panel, between the taillights. The Fairlane 500 name, in script, appeared on the side of the rear fender, just in front of the taillights.

FAIRLANE 500 SIX I.D. NUMBERS: The Fairlane 500 six-cylinder model used the same serial number sequence as the Fairlane models.

FAIRLANE 500 SIX SERIES

Model No.	Body/ Style No.	Body Type & Seating	Factory Price	Shipping Weight	Prod. Total
T	54B	4-dr Sed-6P	2551	3029	Note 1
T	65B	2-dr FT Cpe-6P	2609	3036	Note 1
T	63B	2-dr FsBk Cpe-6P	2584	3083	Note 1
T	76B	2-dr Conv-6P	2834	3220	Note 1
T	71B	4-dr Sta Wag-6P	2934	3415	Note 1

NOTE 1: See Fairlane 500 V-8 series listing. Production was counted by series and body style only, with no breakout per engine type.

FAIRLANE 500 V-8 I.D. NUMBERS: The Fairlane 500 V-8 models used the same serial number sequence as the Fairlane models.

FAIRLANE 500 V-8 SERIES

Model No.	Body/ Style No.	Body Type & Seating	Factory Price	Shipping Weight	Prod. Total
N/A	54B	4-dr Sed-6P	2641	3135	40,888
N/A	65B	2-dr FT Cpe-6P	2699	3143	28,179
N/A	63B	2-dr FsBk Cpe-6P	2674	3190	29,849
N/A	76B	2-dr Conv-6P	2924	3336	2,264
N/A	71B	4-dr Sta Wag-6P	3024	3523	12,869

PRODUCTION NOTE: Total series output was 114,049 units. This figure includes 3,379 Formal Hardtop coupes (FT Cpe) produced with bucket seats; 7,345 Sportsroofs (FsBk Cpe) produced with bucket seats and 219 convertibles produced with bucket seats. Ford does not indicate the number of each model produced with sixes or V-8s. Therefore, all production figures are total production of each body style.

1969 Ford Fairlane Torino four-door sedan V-8. (OCW)

1969 Ford Fairlane Torino two-door "Formal" hardtop V-8. (OCW)

FAIRLANE TORINO SERIES — (6-CYL/V-8) — The Fairlane Torino was the top trim level for 1969 and included all the Fairlane 500 trim plus a polished aluminum rocker panel molding; special emblems and trim (inside and out) and a Torino crest on the 'C' pillars on the two-door hardtop and four-door sedan versions.

FAIRLANE TORINO SIX I.D. NUMBERS: Fairlane Torino six-cylinder models used the same serial number sequence as the Fairlane and Fairlane 500 models.

FAIRLANE TORINO SIX SERIES

Model No.	Body/ Style No.	Body Type & Seating	Factory Price	Shipping Weight	Prod. Total
T	54C	4-dr Sed-6P	2716	3075	Note 1
T	65C	2-dr FT Cpe-6P	2737	3090	Note 1
T	71E	4-dr Sq Sta Wag-6P	3090	3450	Note 1

NOTE 1: See Fairlane Torino V-8 series listing. Production was counted by series and body style only, with no breakout per engine type.

FAIRLANE TORINO V-8 I.D. NUMBERS: Fairlane Torino V-8 models used the same serial number sequence as the Fairlane and Fairlane 500 models.

FAIRLANE TORINO V-8 SERIES

Model No.	Body/ Style No.	Body Type & Seating	Factory Price	Shipping Weight	Prod. Total
N/A	54C	4-dr Sed-6P	2806	3180	11,971
N/A	65C	2-dr FT Cpe-6P	2827	3195	20,789
N/A	71E	4-dr Sq Sta Wag-6P	3180	3556	14,472

PRODUCTION NOTE: Total series output was 47,232 units. Ford does not indicate the number of each model produced with sixes or V-8s. Therefore, all production figures given above are total production of each body style with both engines.

1969 Ford Fairlane Torino GT Cobra two-door SportsRoof hardtop V-8. (PH)

1969 Ford Torino GT convertible. (OCW)

FAIRLANE TORINO GT SERIES — (V-8) — The Fairlane Torino GT was the sporty version of the Fairlane 500 series and included all the Fairlane 500 features plus the 302 cid/220-hp V-8 engine; bucket seats and console; special name plaques and exterior trim; styled steel wheels; lower bodyside striping on two-door hardtop and two-door convertible versions; and a bodyside 'C' stripe on the two-door Sportsroof (FsBk Cpe) version. A high-performance version of this model, known as the Torino Cobra, was also offered. It included the 428 cid/335-hp V-8 engine and four-speed manual transmission as standard equipment as well as F70-14 wide oval tires.

FAIRLANE TORINO GT I.D. NUMBERS: The Fairlane Torino GTs used the same serial number sequence as the Fairlane and Fairlane 500 models.

FAIRLANE TORINO GT SERIES

Model No.	Body/ Style No.	Body Type & Seating	Factory Price	Shipping Weight	Prod. Total
N/A	65D	2-dr FT Cpe-5P	2848	3173	17,951
N/A	63D	2-dr FsBk Cpe-5P	2823	3220	61,319
N/A	76D	2-dr Conv-5P	3073	3356	2,552

FAIRLANE TORINO GT COBRA SUB-SERIES

Model No.	Body/ Style No.	Body Type & Seating	Factory Price	Shipping Weight	Prod. Total
N/A	65A	2-dr HT Cpe-5P	3208	3490	N/A
N/A	63B	2-dr FsBk Cpe-5P	3183	3537	N/A

1969 Ford Fairlane Torino GT two-door SportsRoof hardtop V-8. (OCW)

1969-1/2 Ford Fairlane Torino GT Talladega Special two-door SportsRoof hardtop V-8. (PH)

PRODUCTION NOTE: Total series output was 81,822 units, including the Cobra models (for which separate production figures are not available). Ford does not indicate the number of each model produced with sixes or V-8s. Therefore, all production figures are total production of each body style with both engines.

FALCON SERIES — (6-CYL/V-8) — The Falcons were the base trim level for 1969 and included chrome windshield, rear window and rain gutter moldings; armrests on the front doors only and a horn button, instead of the chrome ring found on the Futura models. The Falcon name, in script, appeared on the rear fendersides and on the vertical section of the trunk lid (on the passenger side). Falcons continued to use the same body style as in the previous three years, with no major changes in either sheet metal or trim. An optional V-8, new safety steering wheel and redesigned side marker lamps were the most noticeable revisions from the past. A full-width anodized aluminum grille helped impart a 'big car' appearance.

FALCON SERIES I.D. NUMBERS: Falcons used the same serial number sequence as the full-size Fords and the Fairlane lines.

FALCON SERIES

Model No.	Body/ Style No.	Body Type & Seating	Factory Price	Shipping Weight	Prod. Total
N/A	54A	4-dr Sed-6P	2316/2431	2735	22,719
N/A	62A	2-dr Sed-6P	2226/2381	2700	29,263
N/A	71A	4-dr Sta Wag-6P	2643/2733	3110	11,568

PRODUCTION NOTE: Total series output was 63,550 units. Ford does not indicate the number of each model produced with sixes or V-8s. Therefore, all production figures are total production of each body style with both engines.

NOTE 2: The prices above the slash are for sixes/below the slash for V-8s.

FUTURA SERIES — (6-CYL/V-8) — The Futura series was the top trim level for 1969 and included all the standard Falcon features plus a cigarette lighter; armrests and ashtrays on all doors; a chrome horn ring; nylon carpeting; special Futura moldings, trim, emblems and nameplates; and chrome side window frames. In addition, the Sports Coupe offered front bucket seats; special nameplates; a map light; ashtray, glovebox and trunk lights; 7.35 x 14 tires; a side chrome accent stripe; polished aluminum rocker panel moldings and wheelwell trim; a remote-control outside driver's mirror; and Deluxe seat belts.

FUTURA SERIES I.D. NUMBERS: Futura models used the same serial number sequence as the full-size Fords, Fairlanes and Falcon models.

1969 Ford Falcon Futura sports coupe. (OCW)

1969 Ford Falcon Futura four-door sedan 6-cyl. (OCW)

1969 Ford Falcon Futura station wagon 6-cyl. (OCW)

FUTURA SERIES

Model No.	Body/ Style No.	Body Type & Seating	Factory Price	Shipping Weight	Prod. Total
N/A	54B	4-dr Sed-6P	2481/2571	2748	11,850
N/A	62B	2-dr Sed-6P	2444/2534	2715	6,482
N/A	62C	2-dr Spt Cpe-5P	2581/2671	2738	5,931
N/A	71B	4-dr Sta Wag-6P	2754/2844	3120	7,203

PRODUCTION NOTE: Total series output was 31,466 units. Ford does not indicate the number of each model produced with sixes or V-8s. Therefore, all production figures are total production of each body style with both engines.

NOTE 2: The prices above slash are for sixes/below the slash for V-8s.

MAVERICK SERIES — (6-CYL) — The Maverick was the midyear introduction model for 1969. It used a Falcon chassis and 170 cid six-cylinder engine to power the only body style available—a two-door sedan.

MAVERICK SERIES I.D. NUMBERS: The Mavericks used the same serial number sequence as the full-size Fords, Fairlanes and Falcons.

MAVERICK SERIES

Model No.	Body/ Style No.	Body Type & Seating	Factory Price	Shipping Weight	Prod. Total
T	91	2-dr Sed-6P	1995	2411	127,833

PRODUCTION NOTE: Total series output was 127,833 units.

THUNDERBIRD SERIES — (V-8) — The Thunderbird continued to use the same body as the previous two years with minor trim changes and new frontal and taillight arrangements. The grille featured a horizontal division bar with the Thunderbird emblem in the center and three vertical moldings. The taillights of the 1969 Thunderbirds were large rectangular units, with a single back-up light mounted in the center of the escutcheon panel. A power-operated sun roof was once again offered in the Thunderbird Sun Roof Landau.

THUNDERBIRD I.D. NUMBERS: Thunderbird models began with the number '9,' assembly plant code 'Y' (Wixom), body type code, engine type code 'N' or 'Z' and, finally, the unit's production number, beginning at 100001 and going up.

THUNDERBIRD SERIES

Model No.	Body/ Style No.	Body Type & Seating	Factory Price	Shipping Weight	Prod. Total
N/Z	65C	2-dr HT-4P	4807	4348	5,913
N/Z	65D	2-dr Landau-4P	4947	4360	27,664
N/Z	57C	4-dr Landau-4P	5026	4460	15,650

PRODUCTION NOTE: Total series output was 49,227 units. This figure includes 2,361 hardtops equipped with bucket seats; 12,425 Landau hardtops equipped with bucket seats and 1,961 Landau four-doors equipped with bucket seats.

1969 Ford Thunderbird two-door hardtop V-8. (OCW)

1969 Ford Thunderbird two-door Sun Roof Landau hardtop V-8. (OCW)

ENGINE [Falcon Base Six]: Overhead valve. Cast-iron block. Displacement: 170 cid. Bore and stroke: 3.50 x 2.94 inches. Compression ratio: 8.7:1. Brake hp: 100 at 4000 rpm. Carburetor: Holley one-barrel. Seven main bearings. Serial number code 'U.'

ENGINE [Falcon/Fairlane Six]: Overhead valve. Cast-iron block. Displacement: 200 cid. Bore and stroke: 3.68 x 3.13 inches. Compression ratio: 8.8:1. Brake hp: 115 at 3800 rpm. Carburetor: Motorcraft one-barrel. Seven main bearings. Serial number code 'T' (export code '2').'

ENGINE [Ford Base Six]: Overhead valve. Cast-iron block. Displacement: 240 cid. Bore and stroke: 4.00 x 3.18 inches. Compression ratio: 9.2:1. Brake hp: 150 at 4000 rpm. Carburetor: Motorcraft one-barrel. Seven main bearings. Serial number code 'V' (police code 'B'; taxi code 'E'; export code '5').'

ENGINE [Ford Six]: Overhead valve. Cast-iron block. Displacement: 250 cid. Bore and stroke: 3.68 x 3.91 inches. Compression ratio: 9.0:1. Brake hp: 155 at 4000 rpm. Carburetor: Motorcraft one-barrel. Seven main bearings. Serial number code 'L' (export code '3').'

ENGINE [302 V-8]: Overhead valve. Cast-iron block. Displacement: 302 cid. Bore and stroke: 4.00 x 3.00 inches. Compression ratio: 9.5:1. Brake hp: 220 at 4600 rpm. Carburetor: Motorcraft two-barrel. Five main bearings. Serial number code 'F' (police/taxi code 'D').'

ENGINE [BOSS 302 V-8]: Overhead valve. Cast-iron block. Displacement: 302 cid. Bore and stroke: 4.00 x 3.00 inches. Compression ratio: 10.5:1. Brake hp: 290 at 5600 rpm. Carburetor: Holley four-barrel. Five main bearings. Serial number code 'G.'

ENGINE [351 V-8]: Overhead valve. Cast-iron block. Displacement: 351 cid. Bore and stroke: 4.00 x 3.50 inches. Compression ratio: 9.5:1. Brake hp: 250 at 4600 rpm. Carburetor: Motorcraft two-barrel. Five main bearings. Serial number code 'H.'

ENGINE [351 Four-Barrel V-8]: Overhead valve. Cast-iron block. Displacement: 351 cid. Bore and stroke: 4.00 x 3.50 inches. Compression ratio: 10.7:1. Brake hp: 290 at 4800 rpm. Carburetor: Motorcraft four-barrel. Five main bearings. Serial number code 'M.'

ENGINE [Interceptor V-8]: Overhead valve. Cast-iron block. Displacement: 390 cid. Bore and stroke: 4.05 x 3.78 inches. Compression ratio: 9.5:1. Brake hp: 265 at 4400 rpm. Carburetor: Motorcraft two-barrel. Five main bearings. Serial number code 'Y.'

ENGINE [390 V-8]: Overhead valve. Cast-iron block. Displacement: 390 cid. Bore and stroke: 4.05 x 3.78 inches. Compression ratio: 10.5:1. Brake hp: 320 at 4600 rpm. Carburetor: Holley four-barrel. Five main bearings. Serial number code 'S.'

ENGINE [Cobra Jet 428 V-8]: Overhead valve. Cast-iron block. Displacement: 428 cid. Bore and stroke: 4.13 x 3.98 inches. Compression ratio: 10.6:1. Brake hp: 335 at 5200 rpm. Carburetor: Holley four-barrel. Five main bearings. Serial number code 'Q.'

ENGINE [Super Cobra Jet 428 V-8]: Overhead valve. Cast-iron block. Displacement: 428 cid. Bore and stroke: 4.13 x 3.98 inches. Compression ratio: 10.5:1. Brake hp: 360 at 5400 rpm. Carburetor: Holley four-barrel. Five main bearings. Serial number code 'P.'

ENGINE [Thunder-Jet 429 V-8]: Overhead valve. Cast-iron block. Displacement: 429 cid. Bore and stroke: 4.36 x 3.59 inches. Compression ratio: 10.5:1. Brake hp: 320 at 4500 rpm. Carburetor: Motorcraft two-barrel. Five main bearings. Serial number code 'K.'

ENGINE [Thunder-Jet 429 Four-Barrel V-8]: Overhead valve. Cast-iron block. Displacement: 429 cid. Bore and stroke: 4.36 x 3.59 inches. Compression ratio: 10.5:1. Brake hp: 360 at 4600 rpm. Carburetor: Motorcraft four-barrel. Five main bearings. Serial number code 'N.'

ENGINE [Boss 429 V-8]: Overhead valve. Cast-iron block. Displacement: 429 cid. Bore and stroke: 4.36 x 3.59 inches. Compression ratio: 11.3:1. Brake hp: 375 at 5600 rpm. Carburetor: Holley four-barrel. Five main bearings. Serial number code 'Z.'

FORD CHASSIS FEATURES: Wheelbase: 121 inches. Overall length: (station wagons) 216.9 inches; (other models) 213.9 inches. Tires: (station wagons) 9.00 x 15 four-ply tubeless blackwall; (other models) 8.25 x 15 four-ply tubeless blackwall.

FAIRLANE CHASSIS FEATURES: Wheelbase: (station wagons) 113 inches; (other models) 116 inches. Overall length: (station wagons) 203.9 inches; (other models) 201 inches. Tires: (convertibles) 7.50 x 14 four-ply blackwall; (Cobra) F70-14; (other models) 7.35 x 14 four-ply tubeless blackwall.

FALCON CHASSIS FEATURES: Wheelbase: (station wagons) 113 inches; (other models) 110.9 inches. Overall length: (station wagon) 198.7 inches; (other models) 184.3 inches. Tires: (station wagons) 7.75 x 14 four-ply tubeless blackwall; (Sports Coupe) 7.35 x 14 four-ply tubeless blackwall; (other models) 6.95 x 14 four-ply tubeless blackwall.

MAVERICK CHASSIS FEATURES: Wheelbase: 103 inches. Overall length: 179.4 inches. Tires: 6.00 x 13 four-ply tubeless blackwall.

THUNDERBIRD CHASSIS FEATURES: Wheelbase: (four-door Landau) 117 inches; (other models) 115 inches. Overall length: (four-door Landau) 209.9 inches; (other models) 206.9 inches. Tires: (four-door Landau) 6.45 x 15 four-ply tubeless; (other models) 8.15 x 15 four-ply tubeless whitewall.

FORD OPTIONS: 390 cid/265-hp V-8 engine ($58). 429 cid/320-hp V-8 engine ($163). 429 cid/360-hp V-8 engine ($237). Cruise-O-Matic automatic transmission ($222). Power steering ($100). Power brakes ($65—front discs). Tinted windshield ($45). Air conditioning ($369). AM radio ($61). AM/FM stereo radio ($181). Vinyl roof ($100). White sidewall tires ($33).

FAIRLANE/FAIRLANE TORINO OPTIONS: 302 cid/220-hp V-8 engine (no charge). 351 cid V-8 engine ($84). Cruise-O-Matic automatic transmission ($222). Four-speed manual transmission ($194, standard on Cobra). AM radio ($61). Power steering ($100). Power tailgate window on station wagons ($35). Luggage rack on station wagons ($47). Two-tone paint ($27). White sidewall tires ($34). Vinyl roof on two-door hardtops and four-door sedans ($90).

FALCON OPTIONS: 200 cid six-cylinder engine ($26). 302 cid V-8 engine ($79). Cruise-O-Matic automatic transmission ($175). Power steering ($89). Power tailgate window on station wagons ($35). Tinted windshield ($32). AM radio ($61). Wheel covers ($21).

MAVERICK OPTIONS: Cruise-O-Matic automatic transmission ($175). AM radio ($61). White sidewall tires ($34).

THUNDERBIRD OPTIONS: 429 cid Thunder-Jet V-8 engine ($237). Six-Way power seats ($99). Power windows ($109). Cruise-Control ($97). Air conditioning ($427). Climate Control air conditioning ($499). AM/FM stereo radio ($150). AM/8-track stereo ($128). Exterior Protection Group on two-doors ($25); on four-doors ($29).

1969 Ford Torino Squire station wagon. (OCW)

HISTORY: The 1969 Ford lines were publicly introduced on Sept. 27, 1968. Calendar year production for America's number two automaker hit the 1,743,442 unit level this year. A total of 1,880,384 Fords were registered as new cars during calendar year 1969. Semon E. Knudsen remained as president of the company and continued to actively pursue a strong high-performance image. Stock car driver Richard Petty was enticed to drive for Ford in 1969, after a long and successful association with Plymouth. He captured the checkered flag in the Riverside 500 Grand National Race. David Pearson, also driving Fords, won the NASCAR championship with 26 Grand National victories. Their stock cars were streamlined Torino Talladega Specials that sold for $3,680. A total of 754 were built during January and February of 1969. It was the next to last season for the compact Falcon, which could not be modified to meet federal safety regulations at reasonable cost. The Falcon nameplate was used on a budget priced Torino added as a late-year model in 1970, then dropped entirely. Ford called its fastback cars 'Sportsroof' models and used the name "Squire" on its fanciest station wagons.

1970 FORD

1970 FORDS — OVERVIEW — For model year 1970, Ford continued to expand its lineup with more and more models within each series. The full-size Fords were only slightly restyled for 1970, with a revamped rear end treatment. The taillights of the new model were positioned lower in the body and the grille was updated.

FORD CUSTOM SERIES — (6-CYL/V-8) — The Custom series was the base trim level for 1970 and included chrome windshield and rear window moldings; nylon carpeting; the Custom name, in script, on the rear fenders and the Ford name, in block letters, across the front of the hood and in the rear escutcheon panel. The Custom 500 models offered the same trim, with the addition of a horizontal chrome strip along the mid-section of the body and a brushed aluminum trim strip at the front of the hood.

CUSTOM SIX I.D. NUMBERS: The serial number code can be broken down, as follows: First symbol indicates year: 0 = 1970. Second symbol identifies assembly plant, as follows: A = Atlanta; B = Oakville, Ontario, Canada; D = Dallas; G = Chicago; F = Dearborn; E = Mahwah; H = Loraine; J = Los Angeles; K = Kansas City; L = Michigan Truck; N = Norfolk; R = San Jose; S = Pilot Plant; T = Metuchen; U = Louisville; P = Twin Cities; W = Wayne; X = St. Thomas, Ontario, Canada; Y = Wixom. Third and fourth symbols identify body series (see Body/Numbers below). Fifth symbol identifies engine code, as follows: U = 170 cid six-cylinder; T = 200 cid six-cylinder; V = 240 cid six-cylinder; L = 250 cid six-cylinder; F = 302 cid V-8; G = 302 cid Boss V-8 with four-barrel carb; H = 351 cid V-8; M = 351 cid V-8 with four-barrel carb; X = 390 cid V-8; Y = 390 cid V-8; S = 390 cid V-8 with four-barrel carb; R = 428 cid Super Cobra Jet V-8 with four-barrel carb; C = 429 cid V-8; J = 429 cid V-8; K = 429 cid V-8; N = 429 cid V-8 with four-barrel carb; Z = 429 cid Boss V-8 with four-barrel carb. The last six digits are the unit's production number, beginning at 100001 and going up, at each of the assembly plants. Custom six-cylinder models began with the number '0' followed by the assembly plant code, engine designation 'V' and, finally, the unit's production number, according to the final assembly location. Each plant began at 100001 and went up.

CUSTOM SIX SERIES

Model No.	Body/ Style No.	Body Type & Seating	Factory Price	Shipping Weight	Prod. Total
V	54E	4-dr Sed-6P	2771	3527	Note 1
V	54B	4-dr Sed-6P	2872	3567	Note 1

NOTE 1: See Custom V-8 series listing. Production was counted by series and body style only, with no breakout per engine type.

CUSTOM V-8 I.D. NUMBERS: Custom V-8 models began with the number '0' followed by the assembly plant code, body type code, engine designation code and, finally, the unit's production number according to the final assembly location. Each plant began at 100001 and went up.

CUSTOM V-8 SERIES

Model No.	Body/ Style No.	Body Type & Seating	Factory Price	Shipping Weight	Prod. Total
N/A	54E	4-dr Sed-6P	2850	3563	42,849
N/A	71D	4-dr Ranch Wag-6P	3305	4079	15,086
N/A	54B	4-dr Sed-6P	2951	3603	41,261
N/A	71H	4-dr Ranch Wag-6P	3368	4049	15,304
N/A	71J	4-dr Ranch Wag-10P	3481	4137	9,943

PRODUCTION NOTE: Total series output was 124,443 units. Ford does not indicate the number of each model produced with sixes or V-8s. Therefore, all production figures given above are total production of each body style with both engines.

GALAXIE 500 SERIES — (6-CYL/V-8) — The Galaxie 500 was the intermediate trim level for 1970 and included all the Custom trim plus a pleated vinyl interior; chrome side window and rain gutter moldings; and polished aluminum wheel opening moldings.

GALAXIE 500 SIX I.D. NUMBERS: Galaxie 500 six-cylinder models used the same serial number sequence as the Custom series.

GALAXIE 500 SIX SERIES

Model No.	Body/ Style No.	Body Type & Seating	Factory Price	Shipping Weight	Prod. Total
V	54A	4-dr Sed-6P	3026	3540	Note 1
V	57B	4-dr HT Sed-6P	3096	3611	Note 1
V	65C	2-dr FT Cpe-6P	3094	3550	Note 1
V	63B	2-dr FsBk Cpe-6P	3043	3549	Note 1

NOTE 1: See Galaxie 500 V-8 series listing. Production was counted by series and body style only, with no breakout per engine type.

GALAXIE 500 V-8 I.D. NUMBERS: Galaxie 500 V-8 models used the same serial number sequence as the Custom series.

GALAXIE 500 V-8 SERIES

Model No.	Body/ Style No.	Body Type & Seating	Factory Price	Shipping Weight	Prod. Total
N/A	54A	4-dr Sed-6P	3137	3661	101,784
N/A	57B	4-dr HT Sed-6P	3208	3732	53,817
N/A	65C	2-dr FT Cpe-6P	3205	3671	57,059
N/A	63B	2-dr FsBk Cpe-6P	3154	3670	50,825
N/A	71B	4-dr Cty Sed-6P	3488	4089	32,209
N/A	71C	4-dr Cty Sed-10P	3600	4112	22,645

PRODUCTION NOTE: Total series output was 318,339 units. Ford does not indicate the number of each model produced with sixes or V-8s. Therefore, all production figures given above are total production of each body style with both engines.

FORD XL SERIES — (V-8) — The Ford XL was the sport trim version of the full-size two-door convertible and two-door fastback models and included the features of the Galaxie 500s, plus the 302 cid V-8 engine; bucket seats; special wheel covers; LTD style die-cast grille; retractable headlights; pleated, all-vinyl interior trim; and the XL designation, in block letters, in the center of the front of the hood.

FORD XL I.D. NUMBERS: Ford XLs used the same serial number sequence as the Custom and Galaxie 500 series.

1970 Ford Galaxie 500 four-door sedan V-8. (OCW)

1970 Ford XL convertible. (OCW)

1970 Ford XL two-door SportsRoof hardtop V-8. (OCW)

FORD XL SERIES

Model No.	Body/ Style No.	Body Type & Seating	Factory Price	Shipping Weight	Prod. Total
N/A	63C	2-dr FsBk Cpe-6P	3293	3750	27,251
N/A	76B	2-dr Conv-5P	3501	3983	6,348

PRODUCTION NOTE: Total series output was 33,599 units.

1970 Ford LTD Brougham two-door hardtop V-8. (OCW)

1970 Ford LTD four-door hardtop V-8. (OCW)

1970 Ford LTD two-door hardtop V-8. (OCW)

FORD LTD SERIES — (V-8) — The LTD was the top trim level full-size Ford for 1970 and included all the Galaxie 500 trim plus the 351 cid/250-hp V-8 engine; Cruise-O-Matic automatic transmission; electric clock; bright exterior moldings; and dual accent paint stripes. The LTD station wagon models (Country Squires) also included simulated woodgrain appliques on the bodysides. All LTDs also included retractable headlights and a die-cast grille. The absolute top trim level for 1970 was the LTD Brougham two- and four-door hardtops and four-door sedan. These were LTDs with more lavish interiors than the regular LTD offered. Exterior trim remained the same as the standard LTD.

FORD LTD I.D. NUMBERS: LTDs used the same serial number sequence as the Custom and Galaxie 500 series.

FORD LTD SERIES

Model No.	Body/ Style No.	Body Type & Seating	Factory Price	Shipping Weight	Prod. Total
N/A	54C	4-dr Sed-6P	3307	3701	78,306
N/A	57F	4-dr HT Sed-6P	3385	3771	90,390
N/A	65A	2-dr HT Cpe-6P	3356	3727	96,324
N/A	71E	4-dr Cty Sq Sta Wag-6P	3832	4139	39,837
N/A	71A	4-dr Cty Sq Sta Wag-10P	3909	4185	69,077

LTD BROUGHAM SUB-SERIES

Model No.	Body/ Style No.	Body Type & Seating	Factory Price	Shipping Weight	Prod. Total
N/A	54	4-dr Sed-6P	3502	3829	N/A
N/A	57	4-dr HT Sed-6P	3579	4029	N/A
N/A	65	2-dr HT Cpe-6P	3537	3855	N/A

PRODUCTION NOTE: Total series output was 373,934 units. Production is not broken down between LTD models and LTD Brougham models. Therefore, production figures represent total LTD model production.

FAIRLANE SERIES — (6-CYL/V-8) — The Fairlane was the base trim level of the intermediate Fairlane series and included chrome windshield, rear window and rain gutter moldings; front and rear door armrests; cigarette lighter; nylon carpeting; the Fairlane 500 name, in script, on the rear fenders above the side marker lights; two chrome 'hash marks' on the front fenders, behind the front wheel opening; and the Ford name, in block letters, on the driver's side of the hood and across the escutcheon panel. The Fairlane series was completely restyled, with a sleek body shell and rounded fender contours. The mid-year 1969 introduction of the Maverick caused Falcon sales to plummet. For the first half of 1970, the Falcon Futura was offered (unchanged from their 1969 counterparts) as two-door and four-door sedan versions as well as a station wagon. The midyear introduction of the revised Falcon (the Futura name was dropped completely) was nothing more than the lowest-price Fairlane model. It was available only as a two-door sedan, although all the high-performance engine options were offered in it.

1970 Ford Country Squire. (OCW)

1970-1/2 Ford Falcon two-door sedan V-8. (OCW)

1970 Ford Falcon Futura two-door sedan (built only for the first half of model year) 6-cyl. (OCW)

FAIRLANE 500 SIX I.D. NUMBERS: Fairlane 500 six-cylinder models began with the number '0' followed by the assembly plant code, body type code, engine designation 'L' and, finally, the unit's production number according to the final assembly location. Each plant began at 100001 and went up.

FAIRLANE 500 SIX SERIES

Model No.	Body/ Style No.	Body Type & Seating	Factory Price	Shipping Weight	Prod. Total
FALCON SUB-SERIES					
L	54A	4-dr Sed-6P	2500	3116	Note 1
L	62A	2-dr Sed-6P	2460	3100	Note 1
L	71D	4-dr Sta Wag-6P	2767	3155	Note 1
FAIRLANE 500 SUB-SERIES					
L	54B	4-dr Sed-6P	2627	3116	Note 1
L	65B	2-dr HT Cpe-6P	2660	3128	Note 1
L	71B	4-dr Sta Wag-6P	2957	3508	Note 1

NOTE 1: See Fairlane 500 V-8 series listing. Production was counted by series and body style only, with no breakout per engine type.

FAIRLANE 500 V-8 I.D. NUMBERS: Fairlane 500 V-8 models began with the number '0' followed by the assembly plant code, body type code, engine designation code and, finally, the unit's production number according to the final assembly location. Each plant began at 100001 and went up.

1970 Ford Falcon Futura four-door sedan (built only for the first half of model year) 6-cyl. (OCW)

1970 Ford Falcon Futura station wagon (built only for the first half of model year) V-8. (OCW)

1970 Ford Fairlane 500 two-door hardtop V-8. (PH)

FAIRLANE 500 V-8 SERIES

Model No.	Body/ Style No.	Body Type & Seating	Factory Price	Shipping Weight	Prod. Total
N/A	54A	4-dr Sed-6P	2528	3216	30,443
N/A	62A	2-dr Sed-6P	2479	3200	26,071
N/A	71D	4-dr Sta Wag-6P	2856	3255	10,539
N/A	54B	4-dr Sed-6P	2716	3216	25,780
N/A	65B	2-dr HT Cpe-6P	2750	3228	70,636
N/A	71B	4-dr Sta Wag-6P	3047	3608	13,613

PRODUCTION NOTE: Total series output was 177,091 units. Ford does not indicate the number of each model produced with sixes or V-8s. Therefore, all production figures given above are total production of each body style with both engines.

TORINO SERIES — (6-CYL/V-8) — The Torino was the intermediate trim level for the intermediate size Torino series, which now stood apart from the Fairlane lineup. Torinos included all the Fairlane 500 trim plus a single horizontal chrome strip along the bodyside. The Torino name appeared, in script, on the driver's side of the hood and in block letters on the side of the front fenders, behind the front wheel opening.

TORINO SIX I.D. NUMBERS: Torino six-cylinder models used the same serial number sequence as the Fairlane 500 models.

TORINO SIX SERIES

Model No.	Body/ Style No.	Body Type & Seating	Factory Price	Shipping Weight	Prod. Total
L	54C	4-dr Sed-6P	2689	3158	Note 1
L	57C	4-dr HT Sed-6P	2795	3189	Note 1
L	65C	2-dr HT Cpe-6P	2722	3173	Note 1
L	63C	2-dr FsBk Cpe-6P	2810	3211	Note 1
L	71C	4-dr Sta Wag-6P	3074	3553	Note 1

NOTE 1: See Torino V-8 series listing. Production was counted by series and body style only, with no breakout per engine type.

1970 Ford Torino two-door hardtop 6-cyl. (OCW)

1970-1/2 Ford Torino two-door SportsRoof hardtop 6-cyl. (PH)

1970 Ford Torino Brougham two-door hardtop V-8. (OCW)

TORINO V-8 I.D. NUMBERS: Torino V-8 models used the same serial number sequence as the Fairlane 500 models.

TORINO V-8 SERIES

Model No.	Body Style No.	Body Type & Seating	Factory Price	Shipping Weight	Prod. Total
N/A	54C	4-dr Sed-6P	2778	3258	30,117
N/A	57C	4-dr HT Sed-6P	2885	3289	14,312
N/A	65C	2-dr HT Cpe-6P	2812	3273	49,826
N/A	63C	2-dr FsBk Cpe-6P	2899	3311	12,490
N/A	71C	4-dr Sta Wag-6P	3164	3653	10,613

PRODUCTION NOTE: Total series output was 117,358 units. Ford does not indicate the number of each model produced with sixes or V-8s. Therefore, all production figures given above are total production of each body style with both engines.

TORINO BROUGHAM SERIES — (V-8) — The Torino Brougham was the top trim level of the Torino series for 1970 and included all the Torino trim plus polished aluminum wheelwell and rocker panel moldings; retractable headlights; wheel covers; and the 302 cid/220-hp V-8 engine. The station wagon version included all of the above features plus simulated woodgrain appliques and power front disc brakes.

TORINO BROUGHAM I.D. NUMBERS: Torino Brougham models used the same serial number sequence as the Fairlane 500 and Torino models.

TORINO BROUGHAM SERIES

Model No.	Body/ Style No.	Body Type & Seating	Factory Price	Shipping Weight	Prod. Total
N/A	57E	4-dr HT Sed-6P	3078	3309	14,543
N/A	65E	2-dr HT Cpe-6P	3006	3293	16,911
N/A	71E	4-dr Sq Sta Wag-6P	3379	3673	13,166

PRODUCTION NOTE: Total series output was 44,620 units.

1970 Ford Torino Brougham four-door hardtop V-8. (OCW)

1970 Ford Torino GT SportsRoof. (OCW)

TORINO GT AND COBRA SERIES — (V-8) — The Torino GT was the sport version of the Torino series and included all the Torino trim plus hood scoop; trim rings with hubcaps; courtesy lights; carpeting; padded seats; GT emblems; 302 cid/220-hp V-8 engine and E70-14 fiberglass-belted white sidewall tires (F70-14 tires on convertible versions). The Torino Cobra was the high-performance version of the Torino series and included all the Torino trim plus the 429 cid/360-hp V-8 engine; four-speed manual transmission; competition suspension; seven-inch wide wheels with hubcaps; black center hood; hood locking pins; bright exterior moldings; courtesy lights; Cobra emblems; and F70-14 fiberglass-belted black sidewall tires with raised white letters. The powerful Cobra models offered a functional hood scoop and rear window louvers as part of the Cobra package.

TORINO GT AND TORINO COBRA I.D. NUMBERS: Torino GT and Cobra models used the same serial number sequence as Fairlane 500 and Torino models.

TORINO GT AND COBRA SERIES

TORINO GT

Model No.	Body/ Style No.	Body Type & Seating	Factory Price	Shipping Weight	Prod. Total
N/A	63F	2-dr FsBk Cpe-6P	3105	3366	56,819
N/A	76F	2-dr Conv-6P	3212	3490	3,939

TORINO GT COBRA

Model No.	Body/ Style No.	Body Type & Seating	Factory Price	Shipping Weight	Prod. Total
N/A	63H	2-dr FsBk Cpe-6P	3270	3774	7,675

PRODUCTION NOTE: Total series output was 68,433 units.

1970 Ford Torino GT two-door convertible V-8. (OCW)

1970 Ford Torino GT Cobra two-door SportsRoof hardtop V-8. (OCW)

MAVERICK SERIES — (6-CYL) — The Maverick, a midyear introduction model for 1969, was back for 1970. It again used a Falcon chassis and 170 cid six-cylinder engine and came only as a two-door sedan. Customer demand was so great for the 1969 version that Ford officials decided to leave a good thing alone and continued to offer the same car for 1970.

MAVERICK I.D. NUMBERS: The Maverick used the same serial number sequence as the full-size Fords, Fairlanes and Falcons.

MAVERICK SERIES

Model No.	Body/ Style No.	Body Type & Seating	Factory Price	Shipping Weight	Prod. Total
T	91	2-dr Sed-6P	1995	2411	451,081

PRODUCTION NOTE: Total series output was 451,081 units.

THUNDERBIRD SERIES — (V-8) — The 1970 Thunderbird featured a new grille, with a protruding center section, which was found to be delicate and caused insurance companies to charge high premiums to Thunderbird owners. The entire car was lower than in previous years and featured an inverted 'U' taillight arrangement. The length and lowness of the new Thunderbird was accented by a single horizontal feature line along the mid-section of the body. Color-keyed wheel covers added to the rich look of the new Thunderbirds.

THUNDERBIRD I.D. NUMBERS: Thunderbird models began with the number '0,' assembly plant code 'Y' (Wixom), body type code, engine type code 'N' and, finally, the unit's production number, beginning at 100001 and going up.

THUNDERBIRD SERIES

Model No.	Body/ Style No.	Body Type & Seating	Factory Price	Shipping Weight	Prod. Total
N	65C	2-dr HT-4P	4961	4354	5,116
N	65D	2-dr Landau-4P	5104	4630	36,847
N	57C	4-dr Landau-4P	5182	4464	8,401

PRODUCTION NOTE: Total series output was 50,364 units. This figure includes 1,925 two-door hardtops equipped with bucket seats; 16,953 two-door Landau hardtops equipped with bucket seats and 5,005 four-door Landau hardtops equipped with bucket seats.

ENGINE [Maverick Base Six]: Overhead valve. Cast-iron block. Displacement: 170 cid. Bore and stroke: 3.50 x 2.94 inches. Compression ratio: 9.0:1. Brake hp: 105 at 4400 rpm. Carburetor: Holley one-barrel. Seven main bearings. Serial number code 'U.'

ENGINE [Maverick Six]: Overhead valve. Cast-iron block. Displacement: 200 cid. Bore and stroke: 3.68 x 3.13 inches. Compression ratio: 8.0:1. Brake hp: 120 at 4400 rpm. Carburetor: Motorcraft one-barrel. Seven main bearings. Serial number code 'T.'

ENGINE [Ford Base Six]: Overhead valve. Cast-iron block. Displacement: 240 cid. Bore and stroke: 4.00 x 3.18 inches. Compression ratio: 9.2:1. Brake hp: 150 at 4000 rpm. Carburetor: Motorcraft one-barrel. Seven main bearings. Serial number code 'V.'

ENGINE [Ford Six]: Overhead valve. Cast-iron block. Displacement: 250 cid. Bore and stroke: 3.68 x 3.91 inches. Compression ratio: 9.0:1. Brake hp: 155 at 4400 rpm. Carburetor: Motorcraft one-barrel. Seven main bearings. Serial number code 'L.'

ENGINE [302 V-8]: Overhead valve. Cast-iron block. Displacement: 302 cid. Bore and stroke: 4.00 x 3.00 inches. Compression ratio: 9.5:1. Brake hp: 220 at 4600 rpm. Carburetor: Motorcraft two-barrel. Five main bearings. Serial number code 'F.'

ENGINE [Boss 302 V-8]: Overhead valve. Cast-iron block. Displacement: 302 cid. Compression ratio: 10.6:1. Brake hp: 290 at 5800 rpm. Carburetor: Holley four-barrel. Five main bearings. Serial code number 'G.'

1970 Ford Maverick. (OCW)

ENGINE [351 V-8]: Overhead valve. Cast-iron block. Displacement: 351 cid. Bore and stroke: 4.00 x 3.50 inches. Compression ratio: 9.5:1. Brake hp: 250 at 4600 rpm. Carburetor: Motorcraft two-barrel. Five main bearings. Serial number code 'H.'

ENGINE [351 Four-Barrel V-8]: Overhead valve. Cast-iron block. Displacement: 351 cid. Bore and stroke: 4.00 x 3.50 inches. Compression ratio: 11.0:1. Brake hp: 300 at 5400 rpm. Carburetor: Motorcraft four-barrel. Five main bearings. Serial number code 'M.'

ENGINE [390 V-8]: Overhead valve. Cast-iron block. Displacement: 390 cid. Bore and stroke: 4.05 x 3.78 inches. Compression ratio: 9.5:1. Brake hp: 270 at 4400 rpm. Carburetor: Motorcraft two-barrel. Five main bearings. Serial number code 'X.'

ENGINE [Cobra Jet 428 V-8]: Overhead valve. Cast-iron block. Displacement: 428 cid. Bore and stroke: 4.13 x 3.98 inches. Compression ratio: 10.6:1. Brake hp: 335 at 5200 rpm. Carburetor: Holley four-barrel. Five main bearings.

ENGINE [Super Cobra Jet 428 V-8]: Overhead valve. Cast-iron block. Displacement: 428 cid. Bore and stroke: 4.13 x 3.98 inches. Compression ratio: 10.5:1. Brake hp: 360 at 5400 rpm. Carburetor: Holley four-barrel. Five main bearings. Serial number code 'R.'

ENGINE [Thunder-Jet 429 V-8]: Overhead valve. Cast-iron block. Displacement: 429 cid. Bore and stroke: 4.36 x 3.59 inches. Compression ratio: 10.5:1. Brake hp: 320 at 4400 rpm. Carburetor: Motorcraft two-barrel. Five main bearings. Serial number code 'K.'

ENGINE [Thunder-Jet 429 Four-Barrel V-8]: Overhead valve. Cast-iron block. Displacement: 429 cid. Bore and stroke: 4.36 x 3.59 inches. Compression ratio: 10.5:1. Brake hp: 360 at 4600 rpm. Carburetor: Motorcraft four-barrel. Five main bearings. Serial number code 'N.'

ENGINE [Police Interceptor 429 V-8]: Overhead valve. Cast-iron block. Displacement: 429 cid. Bore and stroke: 4.36 x 3.59 inches. Compression ratio: 11.3:1. Brake hp: 370 at 5400 rpm. Carburetor: Holley four-barrel. Five main bearings.

ENGINE [Boss 429 V-8]: Overhead valve. Cast-iron block. Displacement: 429 cid. Bore and stroke: 4.36 x 3.59 inches. Compression ratio: 11.3:1. Brake hp: 375 at 5600 rpm. Carburetor: Holley four-barrel. Five main bearings. Serial number code 'Z.'

NOTE: Ram Air Boss 429 cid V-8: Same specifications as Boss 429.

FORD CHASSIS FEATURES: Wheelbase: 121 inches. Overall length: (station wagons) 216.9 inches; (other models) 213.9 inches. Tires: (Custom six-cylinder) F78-15 four-ply blackwall tubeless; (Custom and Custom 500 V-8) G78-15 four-ply tubeless blackwall; (Galaxie 500 and LTD) H78-15 four-ply tubeless blackwall.

1970-1/2 Ford Maverick "Grabber" two-door sedan 6-cyl. (PH)

1970 Ford Torino Brougham Squire station wagon V-8. (OCW)

FAIRLANE 500/TORINO CHASSIS FEATURES: Wheelbase: (station wagon) 114 inches; (other models) 117 inches. Overall length: (station wagon) 209 inches; (other models) 206.2 inches. Tires: (convertibles) F70-14 four-ply tubeless blackwall; (station wagon) G78-14; (GT) E70-14; (other models) E78-14.

THUNDERBIRD CHASSIS FEATURES: Wheelbase: (two-doors) 114.7 inches; (other models) 117.1 inches. Overall length: 215 inches. Tires 215-15 radial blackwalls.

FORD OPTIONS: Power disc brakes ($65). Power steering ($105). Air conditioning ($389). Cruise-O-Matic automatic transmission ($201-$222). Tinted windshield ($45). AM radio ($61). AM/FM radio ($240). Vinyl roof ($105). White sidewall tires ($34). Custom series 390 cid/265-hp V-8 engine ($131). Galaxie 500/XL/LTD 390 cid/265-hp V-8 engine ($86). Custom series 429 cid/320-hp V-8 engine ($213). Galaxie 500/XL/LTD 429 cid/320-hp V-8 engine ($168). LTD Luxury trim package ($104).

FAIRLANE/TORINO OPTIONS: Power steering ($100). Air conditioning ($389). Cruise-O-Matic automatic transmission ($201-$222). Four-speed manual transmission ($194). AM radio ($61). Station wagon power tailgate window ($35). Station wagon rooftop luggage rack ($46). White sidewall tires ($34). Vinyl roof on two- and four-door hardtops and sedan ($95). Fairlane/Torino 351 cid V-8 engine ($45).

PINTO OPTIONS: 122 cid/100-hp four-cylinder overhead cam engine ($50). Cruise-O-Matic automatic transmission ($175). AM radio ($61). Chrome window moldings ($60). White sidewall tires ($33).

THUNDERBIRD OPTIONS: Air conditioning ($427). Six-Way power seats ($198). Power side windows ($110). Cruise-Control ($97). Air conditioning with Climate Control ($499). AM/FM stereo radio ($150). AM radio with 8-track tape player ($150). Brougham interior package ($162). Limited-edition Fiera Brougham option package ($304).

1970 Ford Thunderbird two-door hardtop V-8. (OCW)

1970 Ford Thunderbird four-door Landau Sedan V-8. (OCW)

HISTORY: The full-size Fords were introduced in September 1969 and the Falcon and Torino appeared in dealer showrooms at midyear. Model year production peaked at 1,326,533 units. Calendar year production of 1,647,918 cars was recorded. Due to the new reverse-curve Torino rear window design (and increased competition from the aerodynamic Dodge Daytona and Plymouth Superbird), Ford elected to race 1969 models this year. Only six checkered flags were taken by FoMoCo stock car drivers. The DeTomaso Pantera, an Italian-built specialty sports car powered by a 351 cid/310-hp Ford 'Cleveland' V-8 made its debut in 1970. During the early months of 1970, the Falcon compact was still marketed in three styles, two- and four-door sedans and station wagons, but was replaced by the larger Fairlane-based '70-1/2 Falcon during the summer.

1971 FORD

1971 Ford Galaxie 500 four-door hardtop 6-cyl. (OCW)

1971 FORDS — OVERVIEW — The complete restyling of two model lines and the introduction of the sub-compact Pinto line characterized 1971, a year that also saw the end of two Ford trademarks. The Fairlane was dropped, along with the 'FE' series big-block V-8 engine. The Fairlane name ceased to exist with the end of the 1970 model year and the big-block engine, in 390 cid and 428 cid sizes, was gradually phased-out during the production run. It was replaced by a new 400 cid 'Cleveland' V-8 and the 429 cid V-8.

FORD CUSTOM SERIES — (6-CYL/V-8) — The full-size Fords received a total restyling. The grille was a full-width horizontal unit, with a larger, vertical center section that protruded forward. The hood peaked at the center section of the grille and became wider toward the windshield. The Custom series was the base trim level full-size Ford for 1971 and included chrome windshield and rear window moldings; nylon carpeting and the Custom name, in block letters, on the rear fenders and rear escutcheon panel. The Custom 500 models included all the Custom trim plus polished aluminum wheelwell moldings; argent and chrome appliques on the instrument panel; rear deck moldings; and Custom 500 ornamentation. The Custom and Custom 500 models were available with either the 240 cid/140-hp six-cylinder engine or the 302 cid/210-hp V-8 engine as standard equipment.

CUSTOM I.D. NUMBERS: The serial number code can be broken down, as follows: First symbol indicates year: 1 = 1971. Second symbol identifies assembly plant, as follows: A = Atlanta; B = Oakville, Ontario, Canada; D = Dallas; G = Chicago; F = Dearborn; E = Mahwah; H = Loraine; J = Los Angeles; K = Kansas City; N = Norfolk; R = San Jose; S = Allen Park; T = Metuchen; U = Louisville; P = Twin Cities; W = Wayne; X = St. Thomas, Ontario, Canada; Y = Wixom; Z = St. Louis. Third and fourth symbols identify body series (see Body/ Numbers below). Fifth symbol identifies engine code, as follows: W = 98 cid four-cylinder; X = 122 cid four-cylinder; U = 170 cid six-cylinder; T = 200 cid six-cylinder; V = 240 cid six-cylinder; L = 250 cid six-cylinder; D = 302 cid HO V-8; F = 302 cid V-8; G = 302 cid Boss V-8 with four-barrel carb; H = 351 cid V-8; M = 351 cid V-8 with four-barrel carb; Q = 351 cid V-8; R = 351 cid Boss V-8; Y = 390 cid V-8; S = 400 cid V-8; C = 429 cid V-8; J = 429 cid V-8; K = 429 cid V-8; N = 429 cid V-8 with four-barrel carb; P = 429 cid V-8. The last six digits are the unit's production number, beginning at 100001 and going up, at each of the assembly plants. Custom models began with the number '1' followed by the assembly plant code, engine designation code and, finally, the unit's production number according to the final assembly location. Each plant began at 100001 and went up.

CUSTOM SERIES

Model No.	Body/ Style No.	Body Type & Seating	Factory Price	Shipping Weight	Prod. Total
BASE CUSTOM					
N/A	54B	4-dr Sed-6P	3288/3363	3683/3724	41,062
N/A	71B	4-dr Ranch Wag-6P	3890	4190	16,696
CUSTOM 500					
N/A	54D	4-dr Sed-6P	3426/3501	3688/3729	33,765
N/A	71D	4-dr Ranch Wag-6P	3982	4215	25,957

PRODUCTION NOTE: Total series output was 117,480 units. The price and weight to the left of the slash indicate six-cylinder-equipped models and the price and weight to the right of the slash indicate V-8-powered models.

GALAXIE 500 SERIES — (6-CYL/V-8) — The Galaxie 500 was the intermediate trim level full-size Ford for 1971 and included all the Custom trim plus woodgrain appliques on the interior doors and instrument panel; bodyside moldings, with black-painted inserts; radical polished aluminum wheelwell moldings; chrome window frames; deck and rear quarter extension moldings; Galaxie 500 ornamentation; 351 cid/240-hp V-8 engine; and F78-15 belted black sidewall tires (H78-15 tires on Country Sedan).

GALAXIE 500 SERIES I.D. NUMBERS: Galaxie 500 models used the same serial number sequence as the Custom series.

GALAXIE 500 SERIES

Model No.	Body/ Style No.	Body Type & Seating	Factory Price	Shipping Weight	Prod. Total
N/A	54F	4-dr Sed-6P	3246/3367	3668/3826	98,130
N/A	57F	4-dr HT Sed-6P	3665/3786	3723/3881	46,595
N/A	65F	2-dr HT Cpe-6P	3628/3749	3668/3826	117,139
N/A	71F	4-dr Cty Sed-6P	4074	4241	60,487
N/A	71D	4-dr Cty Sed-10P	4188	4291	N/A

PRODUCTION NOTE: Total series output was 322,351 units. This figure does not include the 10-passenger four-door Country Sedan, for which separate production figure breakouts are not available. The price and weight to the left of the slash indicate six-cylinder-equipped models and the price and weight to the right of the slash indicate V-8-powered models.

FORD LTD SERIES — (V-8) — A more formal roof line was used in the LTD series and the interiors were completely restyled, with the emphasis on luxury or a luxury appearance in the lower-priced lines. The taillights were rectangular and were located at either end of the rear escutcheon panel, with the LTDs featuring an additional red plastic reflector in the center. This gave the illusion of a single full-width taillight. The LTD was the top trim level full-size Ford for 1971 and included all the Galaxie 500 trim plus power front disc brakes; electric clock; luxury seat trim (except convertibles); left-hand outside rearview mirror; nylon carpeting; power top on convertibles; and G78-15 belted tires, in place of F78-15 on convertibles. The LTD Country Squire station wagons also included wheel covers; power tailgate window; simulated woodgrain appliques on the bodyside panels; pleated vinyl trim; and H78-15 belted black sidewall tires. The LTD Brougham series included all the LTD trim plus wheel covers; unique Brougham seat trim; Deluxe steering wheel; front door courtesy light; cut-pile carpeting; front seat center armrest and polished seat side shields; rear door courtesy light switches; special LTD 'C' pillar ornamentation; and high-back bucket seats on the two-door hardtop.

LTD I.D. NUMBERS: LTDs used the same serial number sequence as the Custom and Galaxie 500 series.

1971 Ford LTD Country Squire station wagon V-8. (OCW)

1971 Ford LTD Brougham two-door hardtop V-8. (OCW)

1971 Ford LTD Brougham four-door hardtop V-8. (OCW)

LTD SERIES

Model No.	Body/ Style No.	Body Type & Seating	Factory Price	Shipping Weight	Prod. Total
BASE LTD					
N/A	53H	4-dr Sed-6P	3931	3913	92,260
N/A	57H	4-dr HT Sed-6P	3969	3908	48,166
N/A	65H	2-dr FT Cpe-6P	3923	3853	103,896
N/A	76H	2-dr Conv-6P	4094	4091	5,750
N/A	71H	4-dr Cty Sq-6P	4308	4308	130,644
N/A	71H	4-dr Cty Sq-10P	4496	4358	N/A
LTD BROUGHAM					
N/A	53K	4-dr Sed-6P	4094	3949	26,186
N/A	57K	4-dr HT Sed-6P	4140	3944	27,820
N/A	65K	2-dr HT Cpe-6P	4097	3883	43,303

PRODUCTION NOTE: Total series output was 478,025 units. This figure includes the four-door, 10-passenger Country Squire, for which separate production figure breakouts are not available.

1971 Ford LTD two-door hardtop. (OCW)

1971 Ford Torino 500 four-door hardtop V-8. (OCW)

1971 Ford Torino Brougham four-door hardtop V-8. (OCW)

TORINO AND TORINO 500 SERIES — (6-CYL/V-8) — Torinos for 1971 were merely 1970 bodies with updated trim and a slightly revised grille. Standard equipment on the base Torino series included chrome windshield, rear window and rain gutter moldings; front and rear armrests on the doors; and the Torino name, in block letters, on the rear fenders. The Torino 500 series had all the base Torino trim plus color-keyed carpeting; cloth and vinyl interior trim; Argent-painted eggcrate grille and polished aluminum wheelwell and rocker panel moldings.

TORINO AND TORINO 500 I.D. NUMBERS: Torino and Torino 500s began with the number '1' followed by the assembly plant code, body type code, engine designation code and, finally, the unit's production number according to the final assembly location. Each plant began at 100001 and went up.

TORINO AND TORINO 500 SERIES

Model No.	Body/ Style No.	Body Type & Seating	Factory Price	Shipping Weight	Prod. Total
BASE TORINO					
N/A	54A	4-dr Sed-6P	2672/2767	3141/3220	29,501
N/A	62A	2-dr HT Cpe-6P	2706/2801	3151/3230	37,518
N/A	71D	4-dr Sta Wag-6P	3023/2950	3498/3577	21,570
TORINO 500					
N/A	54C	4-dr Sed-6P	2855/2950	3146/3225	35,650
N/A	57C	4-dr HT Sed-6P	2959/3054	3210/3289	12,724
N/A	65C	2-dr HT Cpe-6P	2887/2982	3156/3235	89,966
N/A	63C	2-dr FsBk Cpe-6P	2943/3038	3212/3291	11,150
N/A	71C	4-dr Sta Wag-6P	3170/3265	3560/3639	23,270

PRODUCTION NOTE: Total series output was 261,349 units. The price and weight to the left of the slash indicate six-cylinder-equipped models and the price and weight to the right of the slash indicate V-8-powered models.

1971 Ford Torino GT two-door SportsRoof hardtop V-8. (OCW)

1971 Ford Torino Brougham Squire station wagon V-8. (OCW)

1971 Ford Torino Cobra two-door hardtop V-8. (OCW)

TORINO BROUGHAM/TORINO GT/TORINO COBRA SERIES — (V-8) — The Torino Brougham was the top trim level Torino for 1971 and included all the Torino 500 equipment plus wheel covers; chrome exterior moldings; soundproofing package; Brougham ornamentation; cloth interior trims (in a choice of four colors); and 302 cid/210-hp V-8 engine. The Squire wagon also included power front disc brakes; simulated woodgrain paneling on the bodysides; and G78-14 belted black sidewall tires. The Torino GT was the sporty version of the Brougham series and included all the basic Brougham trim plus color-keyed outside racing mirrors (remote control on left-hand mirror); GT identification on the grille and rocker panels; simulated hood scoop; hubcaps with trim rings; chrome trim on the foot pedals; full-width taillight; and E70-14 white sidewall Wide-Oval tires. The convertible also had a power top. The Torino Cobra was the high-performance version of the Brougham series and included all the Brougham trim plus 351 cid/285-hp 'Cleveland' V-8 engine; four-speed manual transmission with Hurst shifter; special Cobra identification; heavy-duty suspension; seven-inch wide, Argent-painted wheels with chrome hubcaps; black grille and lower escutcheon panel; black-finished hood with non-reflective paint; polished aluminum wheelwell moldings; F70-14 white sidewall Wide-Oval tires; 55-amp heavy-duty battery; dual exhaust and pleated vinyl seat trim.

TORINO BROUGHAM/TORINO GT/TORINO COBRA I.D. NUMBERS: Torino Brougham/GT/Cobra models used the same serial number sequence as the Torino and Torino 500 series.

TORINO BROUGHAM/TORINO GT/TORINO COBRA SERIES

Model No.	Body/ Style No.	Body Type & Seating	Factory Price	Shipping Weight	Prod. Total
N/A	57E	4-dr Brgm HT Sed-6P	3248	3345	4,408
N/A	65E	2-dr Brgm HT Cpe-6P	3175	3390	8,593
N/A	71E	4-dr Sq Sta Wag-6P	3560	3663	15,805
N/A	63F	2-dr GT Spt Cpe-6P	3150	3346	31,641
N/A	76F	2-dr GT Conv-6P	3408	3486	1,613
N/A	63H	2-dr Cobra HT Cpe-6P	3295	3594	3,054

PRODUCTION NOTE: Total series output was 65,114 units.

1971 Ford Maverick. (OCW)

1971 Ford Maverick four-door sedan 6-cyl. (OCW)

1971 Ford Maverick 'Grabber' two-door sedan V-8. (OCW)

MAVERICK SERIES — (6-CYL/V-8) — The 1971 Maverick was unchanged from the previous two years, except for the addition of a four-door sedan and a 'Grabber' version of the two-door sedan. Also the 302 cid V-8 engine was available for the first time. The '302' proved to be a brisk performer in the small body and the special edition of the two-door sedan, called the 'Grabber,' was introduced to further enhance the performance image.

MAVERICK I.D. NUMBERS: Maverick used the same serial number sequence as the full-size Fords and Torinos.

MAVERICK SERIES

Model No.	Body/ Style No.	Body Type & Seating	Factory Price	Shipping Weight	Prod. Total
N/A	54A	4-dr Sed-6P	2235/2404	2610/2803	73,208
N/A	62A	2-dr Sed-6P	2175/2344	2478/2671	159,726
N/A	62D	2-dr Grabber-6P	2354/2523	2570/2763	38,963

PRODUCTION NOTE: Total series output was 271,697 units. The price and weight to the left of the slash indicate six-cylinder-equipped models and the price and weight to the right of the slash indicate V-8-powered models.

PINTO SERIES — (4-CYL) — The Pinto was Ford's new sub-compact offering, built to serve the ever-growing small car market and compete with imports and domestic sub-compacts such as Chevrolet's Vega and American Motor's Gremlin. It came only as a two-door sedan at first. Standard equipment included: ventless door windows; highback, slim line bucket seats; all-vinyl upholstery; two-pod instrument cluster; glovebox; interior dome light; floor-mounted transmission controls; rack and pinion steering; hot water heater; Direct-Aire Ventilation system and 6.00 x 13 rayon blackwall tires. In mid-season, a three-door Runabout was added to the Pinto line. Its standard equipment was the same as above plus fold-down rear seat with load floor color-keyed carpeting and passenger compartment color-keyed carpeting. Pintos were available with either a British-built 1600cc overhead valve four-cylinder engine, or a second, more powerful (and much more popular) German-built 2000cc engine, which was also a four. Both engines used a four-speed manual transmission, but only the larger engine was available with the three-speed Cruise-O-Matic transmission. While good fuel economy was the main objective of the new Pinto, those equipped with the larger engine and four-speed manual transmission provided quite brisk performance by any standards.

PINTO I.D. NUMBERS: Pintos used the same serial number sequence as the full-size Fords, Torinos and Mavericks.

PINTO SERIES

Model No.	Body/ Style No.	Body Type & Seating	Factory Price	Shipping Weight	Prod. Total
N/A	62B	2-dr Sed-4P	1919	1949	288,606
N/A	64B	2-dr Rbt-4P	2062	1994	63,796

PRODUCTION NOTE: Total series output was 352,402 units.

1971 Ford Pinto. (OCW)

THUNDERBIRD SERIES — (V-8) — The Thunderbird was essentially a 1970 model with only slight trim revisions. The grille had slightly wider bright metal blades at every third rung, giving a horizontally segmented look. There were also nine vertical division bars. New front side marker lamps with a one-piece lens were used. In addition, the front bumper wraparound edge was more massive.

THUNDERBIRD I.D. NUMBERS: Thunderbirds began with the number '1,' assembly plant code 'Y' (Wixom), body type code, engine code 'N' and, finally, the unit's production number, beginning at 100001 and going up.

THUNDERBIRD SERIES

Model No.	Body/ Style No.	Body Type & Seating	Factory Price	Shipping Weight	Prod. Total
N	65A	2-dr HT Cpe-4P	5295	4399	9,146
N	65B	2-dr Landau-4P	5438	4370	20,356
N	57C	4-dr Landau-4P	5516	4509	6,553

PRODUCTION NOTE: Total series output was 36,055 units. This figure includes 2,992 two-door hardtops equipped with bucket seats; 8,133 two-door Landau hardtops equipped with bucket seat and 4,238 four-door Landau hardtops equipped with the split bench seat.

ENGINE [Pinto Base Four]: Overhead cam. Cast-iron block. Displacement: 98 cid. Bore and stroke: 3.19 x 3.06 inches. Compression ratio: 8.4:1. Brake hp: 75 at 5000 rpm. Carburetor: one-barrel. Five main bearings. Serial number code 'W.'

ENGINE [Pinto Four]: Overhead cam. Cast-iron block. Displacement: 122 cid. Bore and stroke: 3.58 x 3.03 inches. Compression ratio: 9.0:1. Brake hp: 100 at 5600 rpm. Carburetor: Ford/Weber two-barrel. Five main bearings. Serial number code 'X.'

ENGINE [Maverick Base Six]: Overhead valve. Cast-iron block. Displacement: 170 cid. Bore and stroke: 3.50 x 2.94 inches. Compression ratio: 8.7:1. Brake hp: 100 at 4200 rpm. Carburetor: Motorcraft one-barrel. Seven main bearings. Serial number code 'U.'

ENGINE [Maverick Six]: Overhead valve. Cast-iron block. Displacement: 200 cid. Bore and stroke: 3.68 x 3.13 inches. Compression ratio: 8.7:1. Brake hp: 115 at 4000 rpm. Carburetor: Motorcraft one-barrel. Seven main bearings. Serial number code 'T.'

ENGINE [Ford/Maverick Base Six]: Overhead valve. Cast-iron block. Displacement: 250 cid. Bore and stroke: 3.68 x 3.91 inches. Compression ratio: 9.0:1. Brake hp: 145 at 4000 rpm. Carburetor: Motorcraft one-barrel. Seven main bearings. Serial number code 'L.'

ENGINE [Ford Six]: Overhead valve. Cast-iron block. Displacement: 240 cid. Bore and stroke: 4.00 x 3.18 inches. Compression ratio: 8.9:1. Brake hp: 140 at 4000 rpm. Carburetor: Motorcraft one-barrel. Seven main bearings. Serial number code 'V.'

1971 Ford Thunderbird two-door Landau hardtop V-8. (OCW)

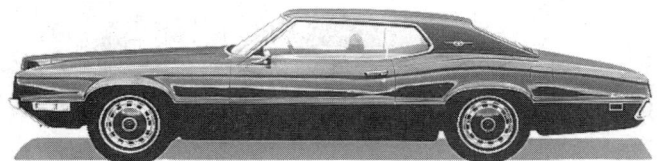

1971 Ford Thunderbird. (OCW)

ENGINE [302 V-8]: Overhead valve. Cast-iron block. Displacement: 302 cid. Bore and stroke: 4.00 x 3.00 inches. Compression ratio: 9.0:1. Brake hp: 210 at 4600 rpm. Carburetor: Motorcraft two-barrel. Five main bearings. Serial number code 'F.'

ENGINE [351 'Cleveland' Two-Barrel V-8]: Overhead valve. Cast-iron block. Displacement: 351 cid. Bore and stroke: 4.00 x 3.50 inches. Compression ratio: 9.0:1. Brake hp: 240 at 4600 rpm. Carburetor: Motorcraft two-barrel. Five main bearings. Serial number code 'H.'

ENGINE [351 'Cleveland' Four-Barrel V-8]: Overhead valve. Cast-iron block. Displacement: 351 cid. Bore and stroke: 4.00 x 3.50 inches. Compression ratio: 10.7:1. Brake hp: 285 at 5400 rpm. Carburetor: Holley four-barrel. Five main bearings. Serial number code 'M.'

ENGINE [Boss 351 V-8]: Overhead valve. Cast-iron block. Displacement: 351 cid. Bore and stroke: 4.00 x 3.50 inches. Compression ratio: 11.1:1. Brake hp: 330 at 5400 rpm. Carburetor: Holley four-barrel. Five main bearings. Serial number code 'R.'

ENGINE [390 V-8]: Overhead valve. Cast-iron block. Displacement: 390 cid. Bore and stroke: 4.05 x 3.78 inches. Compression ratio: 8.6:1. Brake hp: 225 at 4400 rpm. Carburetor: Motorcraft two-barrel. Five main bearings. Serial number code 'Y.'

ENGINE [400 'Cleveland' V-8]: Overhead valve. Cast-iron block. Displacement: 400 cid. Bore and stroke: 4.00 x 4.00 inches. Compression ratio: 9.0:1. Brake hp: 260 at 4400 rpm. Carburetor: Motorcraft two-barrel. Five main bearings. Serial number code 'S.'

ENGINE [Thunder-Jet 429 Four-Barrel V-8]: Overhead valve. Cast-iron block. Displacement: 429 cid. Bore and stroke: 4.36 x 3.59 inches. Compression ratio: 10.5:1. Brake hp: 360 at 4600 rpm. Carburetor: Motorcraft four-barrel. Five main bearings. Serial number code 'N.'

ENGINE [Cobra Jet 429 V-8]: Overhead valve. Cast-iron block. Displacement: 429 cid. Bore and stroke: 4.36 x 3.59 inches. Compression ratio: 11.3:1. Brake hp: 370 at 5400 rpm. Carburetor: Holley four-barrel. Five main bearings. Serial number code 'C.'

ENGINE [Super Cobra Jet 429 V-8]: Overhead valve. Cast-iron block. Displacement: 429 cid. Bore and stroke: 4.36 x 3.59 inches. Compression ratio: 11.3:1. Brake hp: 375 at 5600 rpm. Carburetor: Holley four-barrel (with Ram-Air induction). Five main bearings. Serial number code 'J.'

FORD CHASSIS FEATURES: Wheelbase: 121 inches. Overall length: 216.2 inches (219.2 inches on station wagons). Tires: F78-15 belted black sidewall (G78-15 on Galaxie 500s and LTDs and H78-15 on station wagons).

TORINO CHASSIS FEATURES: Wheelbase: 117 inches (114 on station wagons). Overall length: 206.2 inches (209 on station wagons). Tires: E78-14 belted blackwall (unless noted).

MAVERICK CHASSIS FEATURES: Wheelbase: 103 inches. Overall length: 179.4 inches. Tires: 6.45 x 14 (6.50 x 14 on V-8 models).

PINTO CHASSIS FEATURES: Wheelbase: 94 inches. Overall length: 163 inches. Tires: 6.00 x 13 belted black sidewall.

THUNDERBIRD CHASSIS FEATURES: Wheelbase: 115 inches (117 inches on four-door Landau hardtops). Overall length: 215 inches. Tires: H78-15 belted black sidewall.

FORD OPTIONS: 400 cid/260-hp V-8 engine. 390 cid/255-hp V-8 engine ($98). 429 cid/320-hp V-8 engine ($168). 429 cid/360-hp V-8 engine ($268). Cruise-O-Matic automatic transmission ($217 to $238, depending on engine choice). Power steering ($115). Power front disc brakes ($52). Tinted windshield ($54). Air conditioning ($420). Cruise control ($84). AM radio ($66). AM/FM radio ($240). Vinyl roof on passenger cars ($113); on station wagons ($142). White sidewall tires ($34).

TORINO OPTIONS: 351 cid/240-hp V-8 engine ($45). 351 cid/285-hp V-8 engine ($93). 429 cid/370-hp Cobra Jet V-8 engine, in Cobra ($279); in all other Torinos ($372). Cruise-O-Matic automatic transmission, base Torino ($217); Cobra ($238). Four-speed manual transmission ($250). AM radio ($66). Power steering ($115). Power tailgate window on station wagons ($35). Luggage rack on station wagon ($52). Vinyl roof ($95). White sidewall tires ($34).

MAVERICK OPTIONS: 200 cid/115-hp six-cylinder engine ($39). 250 cid/145-hp six-cylinder engine ($79). 302 cid/210-hp V-8 engine. Cruise-O-Matic automatic transmission ($183). AM radio ($61). Power steering ($95). White sidewall tires ($34).

PINTO OPTIONS: 122 cid/100-hp four-cylinder overhead cam engine ($50). Cruise-O-Matic automatic transmission ($175). AM radio ($61). Chrome window moldings ($60). White sidewall tires ($33).

THUNDERBIRD OPTIONS: Six-Way power seats ($207). Power windows ($133). Cruise Control ($97). Air conditioning ($448); with Climate Control ($519). AM/FM stereo radio ($150); or AM/8-track stereo ($150). Electric rear window defogger ($48).

HISTORY: The full-size Fords were introduced Sept. 18, 1970, and the other lines appeared in dealer showrooms the same day. Model year production peaked at 1,910,924 units. Calendar year production of 2,176,425 cars was recorded. (Note: The model year figure includes only Fords, Torinos, Mavericks, Pintos and Thunderbirds while the calendar year figure covers all passenger and station wagon models.) The Pinto Runabout was a two-door hatchback coupe. The more expensive full-size Ford four-door sedans were advertised as 'pillared hardtops' this year. Fords captured only three NASCAR races in 1971, as the performance era wound to its close. Lee Iacocca became the president of Ford Motor Co. this season.

1972 FORD

1972 FORDS — OVERVIEW — For 1972, only two of the model lines received major restyling: the Torino and Thunderbird. All others either remained the same or received only minor trim changes. It was a significant year in the respect that all engines were required to run on regular gasoline requiring a maximum compression ratio of around 9.0:1. Also, engines were no longer rated at brake horsepower. Beginning in 1972, all engines were rated in SAE net horsepower or the theoretical power after deducting for the drain caused by the accessories and transmission. This fact not withstanding, the 351 'Cleveland' V-8 still generated nearly 300 nhp, making it one of the most powerful engines being produced that year. Pollution requirements and rising insurance rates, plus the lower compression ratios, meant considerably restricted performance. As a result, 1971 is almost universally considered to be the end of the Ford muscle car era.

FORD CUSTOM AND CUSTOM 500 SERIES — (6-CYL/V-8) — For 1972, the full-size Fords received only minor trim updating in the form of a slightly restyled grille set within the same grille opening. There was also a slightly more protective front bumper. The rest of the body styling remained unchanged. The Custom was the base trim level for 1971 and included chrome windshield and rear window moldings; nylon carpeting; ignition key warning buzzer; 351 cid V-8 engine and Cruise-O-Matic automatic transmission (six-cylinder versions were available for fleet and taxi use, but will not be covered here). Power steering and F78-15 belted black sidewall tires were also standard. The Custom 500 versions included all the Custom trim plus lower back panel and wheel lip moldings, and cloth and vinyl seating surfaces. Station wagons also included H78-15 belted black sidewall tires and power tailgate window.

1972 Ford Galaxie 500 four-door hardtop V-8. (OCW)

1972 Ford LTD Country Squire station wagon V-8. (OCW)

CUSTOM I.D. NUMBERS: The serial number code can be broken down, as follows: First symbol indicates year: 2 = 1972. Second symbol identifies assembly plant, as follows: A = Atlanta; B = Oakville, Ontario, Canada; E = Mahwah; F = Dearborn; G = Chicago; H = Loraine; J = Los Angeles; K = Kansas City; N = Norfolk; P = Twin Cities; R = San Jose; S = Allen Park; T = Metuchen; U = Louisville; W = Wayne; X = St. Thomas, Ontario, Canada; Y = Wixom; Z = St. Louis. Third and fourth symbols identify body series (see Body/Numbers below). Fifth symbol identifies engine code, as follows: W = 98 cid four-cylinder; X = 122 cid four-cylinder; U = 170 cid six-cylinder; T = 200 cid six-cylinder; V = 240 cid six-cylinder; L = 250 cid six-cylinder; F = 302 cid V-8; H = 351 cid V-8; Q = 351 cid V-8; R = 351 cid Boss V-8; S = 400 cid V-8; N = 429 cid V-8 with four-barrel carb; A = 460 cid V-8. The last six digits are the unit's production number, beginning at 100001 and going up, at each of the assembly plants. Custom models began with the number '2,' followed by the assembly plant code, engine designation code and, finally, the unit's production number according to the final assembly location. Each plant began at 100001 and went up.

CUSTOM SERIES

Model No.	Body/ Style No.	Body Type & Seating	Factory Price	Shipping Weight	Prod. Total
BASE CUSTOM					
N/A	54B	4-dr Sed-6P	3288	3759	33,014
N/A	71B	4-dr Ranch Wag-6P	3806	4317	13,064
CUSTOM 500					
N/A	54D	4-dr Sed-6P	3418	3764	24,870
N/A	71D	4-dr Ranch Wag-6P	3895	4327	16,834

PRODUCTION NOTE: Total series output was 87,782 units. Station wagon production was not broken out between six- and 10-passenger models.

GALAXIE 500 SERIES — (6-CYL/V-8) — The Galaxie 500 was the intermediate trim level full-size Ford for 1972 and included all the Custom 500 trim plus wheel lip and deck lid moldings, rocker panel moldings and woodgrain appliques on the instrument panel.

GALAXIE 500 I.D. NUMBERS: Galaxie 500 models used the same serial number sequence as the Custom series.

GALAXIE 500 SERIES

Model No.	Body/ Style No.	Body Type & Seating	Factory Price	Shipping Weight	Prod. Total
N/A	54F	4-dr Sed-6P	3685	3826	104,167
N/A	57F	4-dr HT Sed-6P	3720	3881	28,939
N/A	65F	2-dr HT Cpe-6P	3752	3826	80,855
N/A	71F	4-dr Cty Sed-6P	4028	4308	55,238

PRODUCTION NOTE: Total series output was 269,199 units. Station wagon production was not broken out between six- and 10-passenger models.

FORD LTD SERIES — (V-8) — The LTD was the top trim level full-size Ford for 1972 and included all the Galaxie 500 trim plus power front disc brakes; electric clock; luxury seat trim (except convertibles); rear bumper guards; woodgrain accents on interior door panels; front door courtesy lights; chrome trim on foot pedals; chrome armrest bases; F78-15 belted black sidewall tires on two-door hardtops; and G78-15 tires on all others, except station wagons. Country Squire station wagons also included full wheel covers and reflective rear woodgrain paneling, in addition to the woodgrain paneling on the bodysides. LTD Brougham included all the standard LTD features plus full wheel covers; rocker panel moldings; unique Brougham seat and door trim; highback, flight-bench seats with center armrest; cut-pile carpeting; rear door courtesy light switches; front end rear dual armrests; and G78-15 belted black sidewall tires.

1972 Ford LTD two-door convertible V-8. (OCW)

1972 Ford LTD two-door hardtop. (OCW)

LTD I.D. NUMBERS: LTDs used the same serial number sequence as the Custom and Galaxie 500 series.

LTD SERIES

Model No.	Body/ Style No.	Body Type & Seating	Factory Price	Shipping Weight	Prod. Total
BASE LTD					
N/A	53H	4-dr Sed-6P	3906	3913	104,167
N/A	57H	4-dr HT Sed-6P	3941	3908	33,742
N/A	65H	2-dr HT Cpe-6P	3898	3853	101,048
N/A	76H	2-dr Conv-6P	4073	4091	4,234
N/A	71H	4-dr Cty Sq-6P	4318	4308	121,419
LTD BROUGHAM					
N/A	53K	4-dr Sed-6P	4047	3949	36,909
N/A	57K	4-dr HT Sed-6P	4090	3944	23,364
N/A	65K	2-dr HT Cpe-6P	4050	3883	50,409

PRODUCTION NOTE: Total series output was 475,292 units. Station wagon production was not broken out between six- and 10-passenger models.

TORINO SERIES — (6-CYL/V-8) — Two basic lines of intermediate-size Ford Torinos remained. Both the base Torino models and the top-line Gran Torinos were restyled from end-to-end. The Torino models featured chrome windshield, rear window and rain gutter moldings; highback bench seats; all-vinyl seat and door trim; floor mats; hubcaps with trim rings; 250 cid six-cylinder engine and three-speed manual transmission. The Torino station wagon also included power front disc brakes and three-way tailgate. The Gran Torino was the top trim level for 1972 and included all the Torino trim plus manual front disc brakes; cloth and vinyl trim on seats and interior door panels; carpeting; lower bodyside, wheelwell and deck lid moldings; dual-note horn; trunk mat; Deluxe steering wheel and chrome trim on the foot pedals. The Gran Torino Squire station wagon also included the 302 cid/140-hp V-8 engine; Deluxe pleated vinyl interior trim; wheel covers; and woodgrain appliques on the bodysides, tailgate and instrument panel. The Gran Torino Sport was the sporty version of the Gran Torino line and included all the Gran Torino features plus the 302 cid/140-hp V-8 engine; pleated, all-vinyl trim; hood scoops; color-keyed dual racing mirrors and a unique grille. The Torino's 'Coke bottle' shape was even more pronounced for 1972, than in previous years. There were rounded front fender profiles, and a rear fenderline that swept up toward the roof 'C' pillar, then tapered toward the rear of the car. Behind the car was a massive rear bumper, which housed rectangular taillights at each end. The grille was slightly reminiscent of the Cobra, being a large oval between the quad headlights. Automotive writer Tom McCahill observed that he thought the 1972 Torinos looked like "land-locked tunas sucking air." The top profile of the four-door sedans was rounder than in previous years, and the two-door fastback 'Sportsroof' featured an extremely low roofline.

TORINO AND GRAN TORINO I.D. NUMBERS: Torino and Gran Torino models began with the number '2' followed by the assembly plant code, body type code, engine designation code and, finally, the unit's production number according to the final assembly location. Each plant began at 100001 and went up.

Model No.	Body/ Style No.	Body Type & Seating	Factory Price	Shipping Weight	Prod. Total
BASE TORINO					
N/A	53B	4-dr HT Sed-6P	2641/2731	3469/3548	33,486
N/A	65B	2-dr HT Cpe-6P	2673/2762	3369/3448	33,530
N/A	71B	4-dr Sta Wag-6P	2955/3045	3879/3958	22,204

1972 Ford Torino two-door hardtop V-8. (OCW)

1972 Ford Gran Torino Sport. (FMC)

TORINO AND GRAN TORINO SERIES

GRAN TORINO

Model No.	Body/Style No.	Body Type & Seating	Factory Price	Shipping Weight	Prod. Total
N/A	65D	2-dr HT-6P	2878/2967	3395/3474	132,284
N/A	71D	4-dr Sta Wag-6P	3096/3186	3881/3960	45,212
N/A	53D	4-dr Plrd HT-6P	2856/2947	3476/3555	102,300
N/A	63R	2-dr FsBk Cpe-6P	3094	3496	60,794
N/A	65R	2-dr Spt HT Cpe-6P	3094	3474	31,239
N/A	71K	4-dr Sq Sta Wag-6P	3486	4042	35,595

PRODUCTION NOTE: Total series output was 496,645 units. The prices and weights to the left of the slash are for six-cylinder-equipped models and the prices and weights to the right of the slash are for V-8-powered models.

MAVERICK SERIES — (6-CYL/V-8) — The Maverick series was unchanged from the 1971 models.

MAVERICK I.D. NUMBERS: Mavericks used the same serial number sequence as the full-size Fords and Torino models.

MAVERICK SERIES

Model No.	Body/Style No.	Body Type & Seating	Factory Price	Shipping Weight	Prod. Total
N/A	54A	4-dr Sed-6P	2245/2406	2833/2826	73,686
N/A	62A	2-dr Sed-6P	2190/2350	2538/2731	145,931
N/A	62D	2-dr Grabber-6P	2359/2519	2493/2786	35,347

1972 Ford Gran Torino Squire station wagon V-8. (OCW)

1972 Ford Gran Torino two-door hardtop. (OCW)

PRODUCTION NOTE: Total series output was 254,964 units. The prices and weights to the left of the slash are for six-cylinder-equipped models and the prices and weights to the right of the slash are for V-8-powered models.

PINTO SERIES — (4-CYL) — The Pintos were unchanged from the 1971 models, with the exception of a larger rear window on Runabout models and the addition of a two-door station wagon.

PINTO I.D. NUMBERS: Pintos used the same serial number sequence as the full-size Fords, Torinos and Mavericks.

1972 Ford Maverick four-door sedan V-8. (OCW)

1972 Ford Maverick two-door sedan 6-cyl. (OCW)

1972 Ford Maverick "Grabber" two-door sedan V-8. (OCW)

1972-1/2 Ford Maverick two-door sedan (with Sprint Decor option) V-8. (PH)

PINTO SERIES

Model No.	Body/ Style No.	Body Type & Seating	Factory Price	Shipping Weight	Prod. Total
N/A	62B	2-dr Sed-4P	1960	1968	181,002
N/A	64B	2-dr Runabout-4P	2078	2012	197,920
N/A	73B	2-dr Sta Wag-4P	2265	2293	101,483

PRODUCTION NOTE: Total series output was 480,405 units.

THUNDERBIRD SERIES — (V-8) — Thunderbirds were completely restyled for 1972, a year that witnessed the introduction of the largest Thunderbirds ever. They were based on the Lincoln Continental Mark IV chassis and used the Mark IV body, with only minor changes, inside and outside. While the Thunderbird had lost most of its sportiness, it had gained all the luxury features of the Continental. The grille was a centrally located opening featuring horizontal grille bars between the quad headlights. The top had a low profile, with a large 'C' pillar. At the rear, a single taillight lens was used once again, giving a massive appearance.

THUNDERBIRD I.D. NUMBERS: Thunderbirds began with the number '2,' assembly plant code 'J' (Los Angeles) or 'Y' (Wixom), body type code, engine code 'A' or 'N' and, finally, the unit's production number, beginning at 100001 and going up.

1972 Ford Pinto runabout. (OCW)

THUNDERBIRD SERIES

Model No.	Body/ Style No.	Body Type & Seating	Factory Price	Shipping Weight	Prod. Total
A/N	65K	2-dr HT-6P	5293	4420	57,814

PRODUCTION NOTE: Total series output was 57,814 units.

ENGINE [Pinto Base Four]: Overhead cam. Cast-iron block. Displacement: 98 cid. Bore and stroke: 3.19 x 3.06 inches. Compression ratio: 8.0:1. Net hp: 54 at 4600 rpm. Carburetor: Motorcraft one-barrel. Five main bearings. Serial number code 'W.'

ENGINE [Pinto Four]: Overhead cam. Cast-iron block. Displacement: 122 cid. Bore and stroke: 3.58 x 3.03 inches. Compression ratio: 8.2:1. Net hp: 86 at 5400 rpm. Carburetor: Ford/Weber two-barrel. Five main bearings. Serial number code 'X.'

ENGINE [Maverick Base Six]: Overhead valve. Cast-iron block. Displacement: 170 cid. Bore and stroke: 3.50 x 2.94 inches. Compression ratio: 8.3:1. Net hp: 82 at 4400 rpm. Carburetor: Motorcraft one-barrel. Seven main bearings. Serial number code 'U.'

ENGINE [Ford Base Six]: Overhead valve. Cast-iron block. Displacement: 240 cid. Bore and stroke: 4.00 x 3.18 inches. Compression ratio: 8.5:1. Net hp: 103 at 3800 rpm. Carburetor: Motorcraft one-barrel. Seven main bearings. Serial number code 'V.'

ENGINE [Maverick/Torino Six]: Overhead valve. Displacement: 250 cid. Bore and stroke: 3.68 x 3.91 inches. Compression ratio: 8.0:1. Net hp: 98 at 3400 rpm. Carburetor: Motorcraft one-barrel. Seven main bearings. Serial number code 'L.'

ENGINE [302 V-8]: Overhead valve. Cast-iron block. Displacement: 302 cid. Bore and stroke: 4.00 x 3.00 inches. Compression ratio: 8.5:1. Net hp: 140 at 4000 rpm. Carburetor: Motorcraft two-barrel. Five main bearings. Serial number code 'F.'

ENGINE [351 'Windsor' V-8]: Overhead valve. Cast-iron block. Displacement: 351 cid. Bore and stroke: 4.00 x 3.50 inches. Compression ratio: 8.3:1. Net hp: 153 at 3800 rpm. Carburetor: Motorcraft two-barrel. Five main bearings.

ENGINE [351 'Cleveland' V-8]: Overhead valve. Cast-iron block. Displacement: 351 cid. Bore and stroke: 4.00 x 3.50 inches. Compression ratio: 8.6:1. Net hp: 163 at 3800 rpm. Carburetor: Motorcraft two-barrel. Five main bearings. Serial number code 'H.'

ENGINE [351 'Cleveland' Four-Barrel V-8]: Overhead valve. Cast-iron block. Displacement: 351 cid. Bore and stroke: 4.00 x 3.50 inches. Compression ratio: 8.6:1. Net hp: 248 at 5400 rpm. Carburetor: Holley four-barrel. Five main bearings.

1972 Ford Pinto two-door sedan (with Luxury Decor Group option) 4-cyl. (OCW)

1972 Ford Pinto Runabout two-door hatchback 4-cyl. (OCW)

1972 Ford Pinto Squire two-door station wagon 4-cyl. (OCW)

ENGINE [351 HO 'Cleveland' V-8]: Overhead valve. Cast-iron block. Displacement: 351 cid. Bore and stroke: 4.00 x 3.50 inches. Compression ratio: 8.6:1. Net hp: 266 at 5400 rpm. Carburetor: Holley four-barrel. Five main bearings. Serial number code 'Q.'

ENGINE [400 'Cleveland' V-8]: Overhead valve. Cast-iron block. Displacement: 400 cid. Bore and stroke: 4.00 x 4.00 inches. Compression ratio: 8.5:1. Net hp: 172 at 4000 rpm. Carburetor: Motorcraft two-barrel. Five main bearings. Serial number code 'S.'

ENGINE [Thunderbird 429 V-8]: Overhead valve. Cast-iron block. Displacement: 429 cid. Bore and stroke: 4.36 x 3.59 inches. Compression ratio: 8.5:1. Net hp: 212 at 4400 rpm. Carburetor: Motorcraft four-barrel. Five main bearings. Serial number code 'N.'

ENGINE [Thunderbird 460 V-8]: Overhead valve. Cast-iron block. Displacement: 460 cid. Bore and stroke: 4.36 x 3.85 inches. Compression ratio: 8.5:1. Net hp: 224 at 4400 rpm. Carburetor: Motorcraft four-barrel. Five main bearings. Serial number code 'A.'

FORD CHASSIS FEATURES: Wheelbase: 121 inches. Overall length: 216.2 inches (219.2 inches on station wagons). Tires: F78-15 belted black sidewall (G78-15 on Galaxie 500 and LTDs and H78-15 on station wagons).

TORINO/GRAN TORINO CHASSIS FEATURES: Wheelbase: (four-door models) 118 inches; (other models) 114 inches. Overall length: (two-door models) 203.7 inches; (four-door models) 207.3 inches; (station wagons) 211.6 inches. Tires: (Torino two-door models) E78-14; (Gran Torino and Torino four-door models) F78-14; (station wagons) H78-14; (Gran Torino Sport hardtop) E70-14; (Gran Torino Sport Sportsroof) F70-14. All tires were belted black sidewall.

MAVERICK CHASSIS FEATURES: Wheelbase: 103 inches. Overall length: 179.4 inches. Tires: (V-8) C78-14 tubeless blackwall; (other models) 6.45 x 14 tubeless blackwall.

1972 Ford LTD Brougham two-door hardtop. (FMC)

PINTO CHASSIS FEATURES: Wheelbase: 94 inches. Overall length: 163 inches. Tires: 6.00 x 13 rayon black sidewall (A78-13; A70-13 and 175R13 tires were optional).

THUNDERBIRD CHASSIS FEATURES: Wheelbase: 120.4 inches. Overall length: 214 inches. Tires: 215R15 belted Michelin radial blackwalls.

FORD OPTIONS: 400 cid/172-hp V-8 engine ($95). 429 cid/205-hp V-8 engine ($222). Power front disc brakes, standard on LTDs ($50). Tinted windshield ($53). Air conditioning ($409); with Climate Control ($486). Cruise Control ($99). AM radio ($64). AM/FM stereo radio ($234). Vinyl roof ($110); on station wagons ($148). White sidewall tires ($34).

TORINO/GRAN TORINO OPTIONS: 351 cid/163-hp 'Cleveland' V-8 engine ($44). 351 cid/248-hp 'Cleveland' V-8 engine, two-door models only ($127). 429 cid/205-hp V-8 engine ($99). Cruise-O-Matic automatic transmission ($21 to $211, depending on engine choice). Four-speed manual transmission ($200). AM radio ($64). AM/FM stereo radio ($208). Power steering ($112). Power tailgate window on station wagons ($34). Luggage rack on station wagons ($77). Vinyl roof ($93). White sidewall tires ($34).

MAVERICK OPTIONS: 200 cid six-cylinder ($38). 250 cid six-cylinder engine ($77). 302 cid V-8 engine. Cruise-O-Matic automatic transmission ($177). AM radio ($59). Power steering ($92). White sidewall tires ($34).

PINTO OPTIONS: 122 cid/86-hp four-cylinder overhead cam engine ($49). Cruise-O-Matic automatic transmission ($170). AM radio ($59). Chrome window moldings. Luxury Decor Group ($137). Wheel covers ($23). White sidewall tires ($42).

THUNDERBIRD OPTIONS: Six-Way power seats ($201). Power windows ($130). Cruise Control ($103). Tilt steering wheel ($51). Climate Control air conditioning ($505). AM/FM stereo radio ($146). Electric rear window defogger ($36). Power sun roof ($505). Vinyl roof ($137). Turnpike convenience group ($132).

HISTORY: The 1972 Ford line was introduced Sept. 24, 1971. New options appearing this season included electric sliding sun roofs; electric deck lid release, tailgate power lock and bodyside moldings with vinyl inserts. Sun roofs were installed on 0.6 percent of all 1972 FoMoCo products, including Lincolns and Mercurys. As far as the Ford lines—Ford Torino/Maverick Pinto/Club Wagon/Thunderbird—were concerned model year output peaked at 1,855,201 vehicles this year. The calendar year production total was counted as 1,868,016 units. Henny Ford II was Ford Motor Co. board chairman and Lee Iacocca was the firm's president. Ford Division (also called Ford Marketing Corp.) was headed by J.B. Naughton, who held the title of vice-president and divisional general manager. The year 1972 was a sales record-breaker and marked the first time in history that Ford dealers sold more than three million cars and trucks.

1972 Ford Thunderbird with Landau roof option, V-8.. (OCW)

1973 Ford LTD four-door hardtop. (OCW)

1973 Ford Galaxie 500 four-door hardtop sedan V-8. (OCW)

1973 FORDS — OVERVIEW — For 1973, the full-size Fords were the only models to receive significant restyling. The rest of the Ford lines received only minor trim updating. More federally mandated safety requirements were initiated. They were reflected in the form of massive 'park bench' safety bumpers. These bumpers were supposed to be able to tolerate a direct impact at five mph without damage. Pollution standards were tightened. The existing engines were further de-tuned or more emissions control equipment was added, making for some of the poorest performing and least fuel efficient engines ever built. The Arab embargo of oil products imported from the Middle East also brought fuel economy into the spotlight and manufacturers began striving for improved mileage at the expense of performance and efficiency.

FULL-SIZE FORD SERIES — (V-8) — Full-size Fords were restyled for 1973. The emphasis was placed on a more rounded profile, similar to the Torino series of the previous year. The 'Mercedes style' grille was the current craze and big Fords had their own version, complete with a spring-loaded hood ornament on the high trim-level models. At the rear, two rectangular taillights were used on all models and were similar to those used on the lower-priced lines of the 1972 full-size Fords. The Custom 500 was the base trim level Ford for 1973 and included chrome windshield and rear window moldings; nylon carpeting; ignition key warning buzzer; 351 cid V-8 engine; Cruise-O-Matic automatic transmission; power steering; and G78-15 belted black sidewall tires. The Galaxie 500 was the intermediate trim level and included all the Custom 500 features plus lower back panel wheel lip moldings; cloth and vinyl seating surfaces; rocker panel moldings; and woodgrain appliques on the instrument panel. The LTD was the top trim level and included all the Galaxie 500 features plus deep-cushioned low-back bench seats; electric clock; Deluxe two-spoke steering wheel; chrome trim on the foot pedals; polished aluminum trim around the rear edge of the hood; bodyside moldings with vinyl inserts; and HR78-15 steel-belted radial tires. The LTD Brougham had all the LTD features plus highback Flight-Bench seats with center armrests; ashtray and front door courtesy lights; full wheel covers; cut-pile carpeting; carpeted lower door panels; polished rocker panel moldings and extensions; automatic seatback release (on two-door models); vinyl roof; and color-keyed seat belts. The Ranch Wagon contained all the features of the Galaxie 500 models plus J78-15 tires. The Country Sedan contained all the features found in the Ranch Wagon plus dual note horn; woodgrain appliques on the instrument panel and front and rear door panels; special sound package; bodyside moldings and a chrome-plated grille. The Country Squires contained all the features found in the LTDs plus J78-15 tires and 400 cid V-8 engine.

FORD I.D. NUMBERS: The serial number code can be broken down, as follows: First symbol indicates year: 3 = 1973. Second symbol identifies assembly plant, as follows: A = Atlanta; B = Oakville, Ontario, Canada; E = Mahwah; F = Dearborn; G = Chicago; H = Loraine; J = Los Angeles; K = Kansas City; N = Norfolk; P = Twin Cities; R = San Jose; S = Allen Park; T = Metuchen; U = Louisville; W = Wayne; X = St. Thomas, Ontario, Canada; Y = Wixom; Z = St. Louis. Third and fourth symbols identify body series (see Body/ Numbers below). Fifth symbol identifies engine code, as follows: X = 122 cid four-cylinder; T = 200 cid six-cylinder; L = 250 cid six-cylinder; F = 302 cid V-8; H = 351 cid V-8; Q = 351 cid Cobra Jet V-8 with four-barrel carb; R = 351 cid HO V-8; S = 400 cid V-8; N = 429 cid V-8 with four-barrel carb; A = 460 cid V-8. The last six digits are the unit's production number, beginning at 100001 and going up, at each of the assembly plants. Fords began with the number '3' followed by the assembly plant code, engine designation code and, finally, the unit's production number according to the final assembly location. Each plant began at 100001 and went up.

FORD SERIES

Model No.	Body/ Style No.	Body Type & Seating	Factory Price	Shipping Weight	Prod. Total
CUSTOM 500					
N/A	53D	4-dr Sed-6P	3606	4078	42,549
N/A	71D	4-dr Ranch Wag-6P	4050	4550	22,432
GALAXIE 500					
N/A	53F	4-dr Sed-6P	3771	4110	85,654
N/A	57F	4-dr HT Sed-6P	3833	4120	25,802
N/A	65F	2-dr HT Cpe-6P	3778	4059	70,808
N/A	71F	4-dr Cty Sed Sta Wag-6P	4164	4581	51,290
LTD					
N/A	53H	4-dr Sed-6P	3958	4150	122,851
N/A	57H	4-dr HT Sed-6P	4001	4160	28,608
N/A	65H	2-dr HT Cpe-6P	3950	4100	120,864
N/A	71H	4-dr Cty Sq Sta Wag-6P	4401	4642	142,933
LTD BROUGHAM					
N/A	53K	4-dr Sed-6P	4113	4179	49,553
N/A	57K	4-dr HT Sed-6P	4103	4189	22,268
N/A	65K	2-dr HT Cpe-6P	4107	4128	68,901

PRODUCTION NOTE: Total series output was 941,054 units.

NOTE 2: The LTD four-door sedan was called a "pillared hardtop."

1973 Ford LTD Brougham two-door hardtop V-8. (OCW)

1973 Ford LTD Country Squire station wagon V-8. (OCW)

1973 Ford Gran Torino Brougham four-door sedan V-8. (OCW)

TORINO SERIES

Model No.	Body/ Style No.	Body Type & Seating	Factory Price	Shipping Weight	Prod. Total
N/A	53B	4-dr Sed-6P	2701/2796	3597/3683	37,524
N/A	65B	2-dr HT Cpe-6P	2732/2826	3528/3615	28,005
N/A	71B	4-dr Sta Wag-6P	3198	4073	23,982

GRAN TORINO SERIES

Model No.	Body/ Style No.	Body Type & Seating	Factory Price	Shipping Weight	Prod. Total
N/A	53D	4-dr Sed-6P	2890/2984	3632/3719	98,404
N/A	65D	2-dr HT Cpe-6P	2921/3015	3570/3656	138,962
N/A	71D	4-dr Sta Wag-6P	3344	4096	60,738
N/A	71K	4-dr Sq Sta Wag-6P	3559	4124	40,023
N/A	63R	2-dr Spt FsBk Cpe-5P	3154	3670	51,853
N/A	65R	2-dr Spt HT Cpe-5P	3154	3652	17,090

GRAN TORINO BROUGHAM

Model No.	Body/ Style No.	Body Type & Seating	Factory Price	Shipping Weight	Prod. Total
N/A	53K	4-dr Sed-6P	3051/3140	3632/3719	N/A
N/A	65K	2-dr HT Cpe-6P	3071/3160	3590/3656	N/A

PRODUCTION NOTE: Total series output was 496,581 units. Separate breakouts were not available for Gran Torino Broughams. Styles 53B, 53D and 53K were called four-door pillared hardtops.

NOTE 2: Prices and weights above slash are for sixes/below slash for V-8s.

MAVERICK SERIES — (6-CYL/V-8) — The Maverick series was basically unchanged from the 1972 models. There was, however, a slightly new appearance up front because of the flatter, reinforced bumper.

MAVERICK I.D. NUMBERS: Mavericks used the same serial number sequence as full-size Fords and Torino models.

MAVERICK SERIES

Model No.	Body/ Style No.	Body Type & Seating	Factory Price	Shipping Weight	Prod. Total
N/A	54A	4-dr Sed-6P	2297/2419	2737/2900	110,382
N/A	62A	2-dr Sed-6P	2240/2362	2642/2800	148,943
N/A	62D	2-dr Grabber-6P	2419/2541	2697/2855	32,350

PRODUCTION NOTE: Total series output was 291,675 units. The prices and weights to the left of the slash indicate six-cylinder-equipped models and the prices and weights to the right of the slash indicate V-8-powered models.

1973 Ford Gran Torino two-door hardtop V-8. (OCW)

TORINO AND GRAN TORINO SERIES — (6-CYL/V-8) — The 1973 Torino and Gran Torino models were slightly modified from 1972 specifications. New was a revised grille with the opening more rectangular than the 1972 version, which blended well with the large front bumper. Improvements included larger standard rear brakes, an interior hood release and optional spare tire lock. The Torino models were the base trim level and featured chrome windshield, rear window and rain gutter moldings; highback bench seats; all-vinyl seat and door trim; floor mats; hubcaps; 250 cid six-cylinder engine and three-speed manual transmission. The Torino station wagon also included power front disc brakes and three-way tailgate. The Gran Torino was the top trim level for 1973 and included all the Torino trim plus manual front disc brakes; cloth and vinyl trim on seats and interior door panels; carpeting; lower bodyside, wheelwell and deck lid moldings; dual note horns; trunk mat; Deluxe two-spoke steering wheel; and chrome trim on the foot pedals. The Gran Torino Squire station wagon also included the 302 cid/138-hp V-8 engine; Deluxe pleated vinyl interior trim; wheel covers and woodgrain appliques on the bodysides, tailgate and instrument panel. The Gran Torino Sport was the sporty version of the Gran Torino line and included all the Gran Torino features plus the 302 cid/138-hp V-8 engine; pleated, all-vinyl trim; hood scoops; color-keyed dual racing mirrors and a unique grille.

TORINO AND GRAN TORINO I.D. NUMBERS: The Torino and Gran Torino models began with the number '3' followed by the assembly plant code, body type code, engine designation code and, finally, the unit's production number according to the final assembly location. Each plant began at 100001 and went up.

1973 Ford Gran Torino Squire station wagon V-8. (OCW)

1973 Ford Gran Torino sport. (OCW)

1973 Ford Maverick 'Grabber' two-door sedan V-8. (OCW)

1973 Ford Maverick two-door sedan 6-cyl. (OCW)

1973 Ford Pinto Squire two-door station wagon 4-cyl. (OCW)

PINTO SERIES — (4-CYL) — The Pinto exterior remained basically the same as in the 1972 model year with the exception of front and rear bumpers. Front bumper guards were made standard equipment this year (but deleted in later years). Pinto styles included the two-door (sometimes called three-door) Runabout, which had a large rear hatch with gas-operated springs, plus the two-door sedan and station wagon. Because of the bumper design changes, the Pinto was actually about one-and-one-half inches longer this year, although the bumper-to-bumper body length was not changed.

PINTO I.D. NUMBERS: Pintos used the same serial number sequence as the full-size Fords, Torinos and Mavericks.

PINTO SERIES

Model No.	Body/Style No.	Body Type & Seating	Factory Price	Shipping Weight	Prod. Total
N/A	62B	2-dr Sed-4P	1997	2124	116,146
N/A	64B	2-dr Runabout-4P	2120	2162	150,603
N/A	73B	2-dr Sta Wag-4P	2319	2397	217,763

PRODUCTION NOTE: Total series output was 484,512 units.

1973 Ford Pinto Runabout two-door hatchback 4-cyl. (OCW)

THUNDERBIRD SERIES — (V-8) — The 1973 Thunderbird continued to use the same body as introduced in 1972 with a few minor changes. An opera window was added to help eliminate the blind spot created by the massive 'C' pillar. Other product improvements included suspension system refinements; increased front and rear headroom; and steel belted radial tires with white sidewalls as standard equipment. An inside hood release and spare tire lock were also new. The 1973 Thunderbird had an eggcrate grille in place of the bar-type used the previous year. The two headlamps on either side of the grille were mounted in individual, square-shaped bezels. An unslotted bumper with vertical grille guards and new fender-notched parking lamp treatment were seen. The remainder of the car was unchanged.

THUNDERBIRD I.D. NUMBERS: Thunderbirds began with the number '3,' assembly plant code 'J' (Los Angeles) or 'Y' (Wixom), body type code, engine designation code 'A' or 'N' and, finally, the unit's production number, beginning at 100001 and going up.

THUNDERBIRD SERIES

Model No.	Body/Style No.	Body Type & Seating	Factory Price	Shipping Weight	Prod. Total
A/N	65K	2-dr HT Cpe-6P	5577	4572	87,269

ENGINE [Pinto Base Four]: Overhead cam. Cast-iron block. Displacement: 122 cid. Bore and stroke: 3.58 x 3.03 inches. Compression ratio: 8.2:1. Net hp: 86 at 5400 rpm. Carburetor: Ford/Weber two-barrel. Five main bearings. Serial number code 'X.'

1973 Ford Pinto Runabout two-door hatchback (with Sports Accent option) 4-cyl. (OCW)

ENGINE [Maverick Base Six]: Overhead valve. Cast-iron block. Displacement: 200 cid. Bore and stroke: 3.68 x 3.13 inches. Compression ratio: 8.3:1. Net hp: 84 at 3800 rpm. Carburetor: Motorcraft single-barrel. Seven main bearings. Serial number code 'T.'

ENGINE [Maverick/Torino Six]: Overhead valve. Cast-iron block. Displacement: 250 cid. Bore and stroke: 3.68 x 3.91 inches. Compression ratio: 8.0:1. Net hp: 88 at 3200 rpm. Carburetor: Motorcraft single-barrel. Seven main bearings. Serial number code 'L.'

ENGINE [302 V-8]: Overhead valve. Cast-iron block. Displacement: 302 cid. Bore and stroke: 4.00 x 3.00 inches. Compression ratio: 8.0:1. Net hp: 135 at 4200 rpm. Carburetor: Motorcraft two-barrel. Five main bearings. Serial number code 'F.'

ENGINE [351 'Windsor' V-8]: Overhead valve. Cast-iron block. Displacement: 351 cid. Bore and stroke: 4.00 x 3.50 inches. Compression ratio: 8.0:1. Net hp: 156 at 3800 rpm. Carburetor: Motorcraft two-barrel. Five main bearings.

ENGINE [351 'Cleveland' V-8]: Overhead valve. Cast-iron block. Displacement: 351 cid. Bore and stroke: 4.00 x 3.50 inches. Compression ratio: 8.0:1. Net hp: 154 at 4000 rpm. Carburetor: Motorcraft two-barrel. Five main bearings. Serial number code 'H.'

ENGINE [351 'Cobra Jet Cleveland' V-8]: Overhead valve. Cast-iron block. Displacement: 351 cid. Bore and stroke: 4.00 x 3.50 inches. Compression ratio: 8.0:1. Net hp: 266 at 5400 rpm. Carburetor: Holley four-barrel. Five main bearings. Serial number code 'Q.'

ENGINE [400 'Cleveland' V-8]: Overhead valve. Cast-iron block. Displacement: 400 cid. Bore and stroke: 4.00 x 4.00 inches. Compression ratio: 8.0:1. Net hp: 163 at 3800 rpm. Carburetor: Motorcraft two-barrel. Five main bearings. Serial number code 'S.'

ENGINE [Thunderbird 429 V-8]: Overhead valve. Cast-iron block. Displacement: 429 cid. Bore and stroke: 4.36 x 3.59 inches. Compression ratio: 8.0:1. Net hp: 201 at 4400 rpm. Carburetor: Motorcraft four-barrel. Five main bearings. Serial number code 'N.'

ENGINE [Thunderbird 460 V-8]: Overhead valve. Cast-iron block. Displacement: 460 cid. Bore and stroke: 4.36 x 3.85 inches. Compression ratio: 8.0:1. Net hp: 219 at 4400 rpm. Carburetor: Motorcraft four-barrel. Five main bearings. Serial number code 'A.'

ENGINE NOTE: Beginning with the 250 cid six-cylinder engine, Ford rated each engine with two or three different horsepower ratings, depending on the model each engine was installed in. Ratings shown in the engine section represent the lowest rating for each engine (except the '460,' which shows the highest rating). As body size and weight increased between models, horsepower ratings increased correspondingly (i.e.: 302 cid V-8 rated at 135-hp in Maverick and 138-hp in Gran Torino). Most engine ratings varied between one and five horsepower, with the 460 cid V-8 varying 17-hp.

FORD CHASSIS FEATURES: Wheelbase: 121 inches. Overall length: 216.2 inches (219.2 inches on station wagons). Tires: F78-15 belted black sidewall (G78-15 on Galaxie 500 and LTDs and H78-15 on station wagons).

1973 Ford Thunderbird two-door hardtop V-8. (OCW)

1973 Ford Maverick four-door sedan 6-cyl. (OCW)

TORINO/GRAN TORINO CHASSIS FEATURES: Wheelbase: (four-door models) 118 inches; (other models) 114 inches. Overall length: (two-door models) 203.7 inches; (four-door models) 207.3 inches; (station wagons) 211.6 inches. Tires: (Torino two-door models) E78-14; (Gran Torino and Torino four-door models) F78-14; (station wagons) H78-14; (Gran Torino Sport hardtop) E70-14; (Gran Torino Sport fastback) F70-14. All tires were belted black sidewall.

MAVERICK CHASSIS FEATURES: Wheelbase: 103 inches. Overall length: 179.4 inches. Tires: (V-8) C78-14 tubeless blackwall; (other models) 6.45 x 14 tubeless blackwall.

PINTO CHASSIS FEATURES: Wheelbase: 94 inches. Overall length: 163 inches. Tires: 6.00 x 13 rayon black sidewall (A78-13; A70-13 and 175R13 tires were optional).

THUNDERBIRD CHASSIS FEATURES: Wheelbase: 120.4 inches. Overall length: 214 inches. Tires: 215R15 belted Michelin radial blackwalls.

FORD OPTIONS: 400 cid/172-hp V-8 engine ($95). 429 cid/205-hp V-8 engine ($222). 460 cid/202-hp V-8 engine ($222). Power front disc brakes, standard on LTDs ($50). Tinted windshield ($53). Air conditioning ($409); with Climate Control ($486). Cruise Control ($99). AM radio ($64). AM/FM stereo radio ($234). Vinyl roof ($110); on station wagons ($148). White sidewall tires ($34).

TORINO/GRAN TORINO OPTIONS: 351 cid/159-hp 'Cleveland' V-8 engine ($44). 400 cid/168-hp 'Cleveland' V-8 engine ($127). 429 cid/197-hp V-8 engine ($99). Cruise-O-Matic automatic transmission ($211). Four-speed manual transmission ($200). AM radio ($64). AM/FM stereo radio ($206). Power steering ($112). Power tailgate window on station wagons ($34). Luggage racks on station wagons ($77). Vinyl roof ($93). White sidewall tires ($34).

MAVERICK OPTIONS: 200 cid six-cylinder engine ($77). 302 cid/135-hp V-8 engine (N/A). Cruise-O-Matic automatic transmission ($177). AM radio ($59). Power steering ($92). White sidewall tires ($33).

PINTO OPTIONS: Cruise-O-Matic automatic transmission ($170). AM radio ($59). Luxury decor group ($137). Wheel covers ($23). White sidewall tires ($42).

THUNDERBIRD OPTIONS: Six-Way power seats ($201). Power windows ($130). Cruise Control ($103). Tilt steering wheel ($51). Climate Control air conditioning ($505). AM/FM stereo radio ($146). Electric rear window defogger ($36). Power sun roof ($505). Vinyl roof ($137). Turnpike convenience group ($132).

HISTORY: The 1973 Ford line was publicly introduced on Sept. 22, 1972. Highlights of the year included the new impact-absorbing bumpers and an increased emphasis on making cars theft and vandal-proof. For example, a new fixed length type radio antenna was adopted; inside hood release mechanisms became a regular feature in some models; and a spare tire lock was a new, extra-cost option. The Ford LTD was honored, by *Motor Trend* magazine, as the "Full-size Sedan of the Year" while *Road Test* magazine went further, calling it the "Car of the Year." Important FoMoCo executives included Board Chairman Henry Ford II; Corporate President Lee Iacocca and Ford Marketing Corp. Vice-President and Divisional General Manager B.E. Bidwell.

1974 FORD

1974 FORDS — (OVERVIEW) — The 1974 Fords were basically 1973 models with refinements and slight trim updating. Emphasis continued to be placed on a luxury look and the addition of safety equipment. More federally mandated safety requirements were initiated, primarily in the form of massive rear 'safety' bumpers designed to withstand direct impact, at five mph, without damage. When combined with the front safety bumpers adopted in 1973, the weight of a typical car was up nearly 350 pounds! Pollution standards were also further tightened, which, when combined with the weight increases, made 1974 models generally more sluggish than any available in the recent past. Pintos and Mavericks saw little technical innovation and all other lines were now limited to just V-8s under the hood. Torinos could be had with '302,' '351,' '400' and '460' engines. The bigger cars came with a base 351 cid V-8 or one of three options. They were a higher output '351,' the '400' or the '460.' The latter engine was the only one offered in Thunderbirds, as the powerful '429' was gone for all time.

FULL-SIZE FORDS — (V-8) — The full-size Fords were slightly re-trimmed versions of 1973 models. The main difference between cars of the two years appeared at the front. Extension caps were no longer used on the front fender corners, so that the vertical parking lamp lens was taller than the previous type and had a ribbed appearance. The overall shape of the grille was the same, but inserts with a finer mesh pattern were used. Also, the central section—below the protruding area of the hood—was surrounded by a rectangular housing that segmented it from the rest of the grille. This gave more of a 'Mercedes-Benz' look to the front of the car, or what some refer to as neo-classical styling. To heighten this image, a stand-up hood ornament was added to models with high-level trims. The profile of the 1974 Ford was much the same as previously seen, except that an upper, full-length horizontal feature line paralleled the upper body edge. It swept from the top of the parking lamps to the rear of the car. In addition, the lower feature line now continued ahead of the forward wheel opening. Newly designed wheel covers were seen and the rear end treatment was also enriched. The Custom 500 was the base trim level offering and included chrome windshield and rear window moldings; nylon carpeting; ignition key warning buzzer; power steering; automatic transmission; G78-15 belted black sidewall tires and the 351 cid engine. The Galaxie 500 was the intermediate trim level and included all Custom 500 features plus lower back panel and wheel lip moldings; cloth and vinyl seats; rocker panel moldings; and woodgrain appliques on the instrument panel. The LTD was the top trim level and included all the Galaxie 500 features plus deep cushioned, low-back bench seats; electric clock; Deluxe two-spoke steering wheel; chrome trim on the foot pedals; polished aluminum trim for the rear hood edge; and HR78-15 steel-belted radial tires. The LTD Brougham had all LTD features plus highback Flight-Bench seats with center armrest, ashtray and front door courtesy lights; full wheel covers; cut-pile carpeting and carpeted lower door panels; polished rocker panel moldings (with extensions); automatic seatback release (in two-door styles); vinyl roof and color-keyed seat belts. The Ranch Wagon contained all the features of the Custom 500 plus J78-15 tires. The Country Sedan added a dual note horn; woodgrain instrument panel applique; woodgrain front and rear door panel trim; special sound insulation package; bodyside moldings and a special chrome-plated grille. The Country Squire contained all features found in LTDs plus J78-15 tires and a base 400 cid V-8.

FORD I.D. NUMBERS: The serial number code can be broken down, as follows: First symbol indicates year: 4 = 1974. Second symbol identifies assembly plant, as follows: A = Atlanta; B = Oakville, Ontario, Canada; E = Mahwah; F = Dearborn; G = Chicago; H = Loraine; J = Los Angeles; K = Kansas City; N = Norfolk; P = Twin Cities; R = San Jose; S = Allen Park; T = Metuchen; U = Louisville; W = Wayne; X = St. Thomas, Ontario, Canada; Y = Wixom; Z = St. Louis. Third and fourth symbols identify body series (see Body/ Numbers below). Fifth symbol identifies engine code, as follows: X = 122 cid four-cylinder; Y = 139 cid V-8; T = 200 cid six-cylinder; L = 250 cid six-cylinder; F = 302 cid V-8; H = 351 cid V-8; Q = 351 cid Cobra Jet V-8 with four-barrel carb; S = 400 cid V-8; A = 460 cid V-8. The last six digits are the unit's production number, beginning at 100001 and going up, at each of the assembly plants. Fords began with the number '4' followed by the assembly plant code, engine designation code and, finally, the unit's production number, according to final assembly location. Each plant began at 100001 and went up.

FULL-SIZE FORD SERIES

Model No.	Body/ Style No.	Body Type & Seating	Factory Price	Shipping Weight	Prod. Total
CUSTOM 500/RANCH WAGON					
N/A	53D	4-dr Sed-6P	3911	4180	128,941
N/A	71D	4-dr Sta Wag-6P	4417	4654	12,104
GALAXIE 500/COUNTRY SEDAN					
N/A	53F	4-dr Sed-6P	4093	4196	49,661
N/A	57F	4-dr HT Sed-6P	4166	4212	11,526
N/A	65F	2-dr HT Cpe-6P	4140	4157	34,214
N/A	71F	4-dr Cty Sed Sta Wag-6P	4513	4690	22,400
LTD/COUNTRY SQUIRE					
N/A	53H	4-dr Sed-6P	4299	4262	72,251
N/A	57H	4-dr HT Sed-6P	4367	4277	12,375
N/A	65H	2-dr HT Cpe-6P	4318	4215	73,296
N/A	71H	4-dr Cty Sq Sta Wag-6P	4827	4742	64,047

1974 Ford LTD four-door hardtop sedan V-8. (OCW)

LTD BROUGHAM

N/A	53K	4-dr Sed-6P	4576	4292	30,203
N/A	57K	4-dr HT Sed-6P	4646	4310	11,371
N/A	65K	2-dr HT Cpe-6P	4598	4247	39,084

PRODUCTION NOTES: Total series output was 519,916 units. Styles 53F, 53H and 53K were called four-door pillared hardtops. An LTD station wagon, which was essentially the Country Squire without the wood trim, was also offered, but no breakout in production is available.

TORINO AND GRAN TORINO SERIES — (V-8) — New grilles, front bumpers and some optional revisions in roof pillar treatments characterized the Torino models of 1974. The grille used a finer mesh and was now segmented by seven vertical division bars, with the parking lamps hidden behind the insert instead of being mounted on it. The bumper had a slightly more prominent center protrusion with the rubber-faced guards moved a bit closer together. Opera window treatments could be ordered, at extra cost, to 'fancy-up' the rear pillar of coupes. Side trim was revised to eliminate the wide, horizontally ribbed decorative panels used on high-trim models the previous season. Introduced at midyear was the Gran Torino Elite series featuring full-length side trim with vinyl inserts; a chrome center molding across the grille; single headlamps (in square bezels); and parking lamps notched into the corners of front fenders. Stand-up hood ornaments were seen on many 1974 Torino models. The Torino series was the base trim level and featured windshield, rear window and rain gutter moldings; highback bench seats; all-vinyl upholstery and trim; floor mats; hubcaps; three-speed manual transmission; HR78-14 tires (G78-14 on hardtops); and a base 302 cid V-8. The Torino station wagon also included power front disc brakes; H78-14 tires and a three-way tailgate. The Gran Torino was the top trim level and included all the above items plus manual front disc brakes; cloth and vinyl seat trims; carpeting; lower bodyside, wheelwell and deck lid moldings; dual note horn; trunk mat; Deluxe two-spoke steering wheel and chrome foot pedal trim. The Gran Torino Squire station wagon also had Deluxe pleated vinyl interior trim; wheel covers; woodgrain bodyside appliques; woodgrain tailgate trim; and woodgrain dashboard inserts. The Gran Torino Sport was the sporty version of the Gran Torino line. Its standard extras included pleated, all-vinyl trim; hood scoops; color-keyed dual outside racing mirrors and a unique grille.

TORINO AND GRAN TORINO I.D. NUMBERS: The Torino and Gran Torino models began with the number '4' followed by the assembly plant code, body type code, engine designation code and, finally, the unit's production number according to the final assembly location. Each plant began at 100001 and went up.

TORINO AND GRAN TORINO SERIES

Model No.	Body/ Style No.	Body Type & Seating	Factory Price	Shipping Weight	Prod. Total
TORINO					
N/A	53B	4-dr Sed-6P	3176	3793	31,161
N/A	65B	2-dr HT Cpe-6P	3310	3509	22,738
N/A	71B	4-dr Sta Wag-6P	3755	4175	15,393
GRAN TORINO					
N/A	53D	4-dr Sed-6P	3391	3847	72,728
N/A	65D	2-dr HT Cpe-6P	3485	3647	76,290
N/A	71D	4-dr Sta Wag-6P	3954	4209	29,866

1974 Ford Gran Torino Brougham two-door hardtop V-8. (PH)

1974-1/2 Ford Gran Torino Elite two-door hardtop V-8. (PH)

GRAN TORINO SPORT/SQUIRE

Model No.	Body/ Style No.	Body Type & Seating	Factory Price	Shipping Weight	Prod. Total
N/A	71K	4-dr Sq Sta Wag-6P	4237	4250	22,837
N/A	65R	2-dr HT Spt Cpe-5P	3761	3771	23,142

GRAN TORINO BROUGHAM

N/A	53K	4-dr Sed-6P	3903	3887	11,464
N/A	65K	2-dr HT Cpe-6P	3912	3794	26,402

GRAN TORINO ELITE

N/A	65M	2-dr HT Cpe-6P	4374	4092	96,604

PRODUCTION NOTES: Total series output was 426,086 units. Styles 53D and 53K were called four-door pillared hardtops.

MAVERICK SERIES — (6-CYL/V-8) — The Maverick had a slight frontal restyling for 1974 as energy-absorbing bumpers were adopted this year. A horizontal slot appeared in the center of the face bar, where the license plate indentation had formerly been positioned. Deluxe models featured side moldings with vinyl inserts; wheel cutout trim moldings and, on cars with vinyl roofs, a Maverick nameplate on the rear roof pillar. On all models, a similar nameplate was carried at the left-hand side of the grille.

MAVERICK I.D. NUMBERS: Mavericks used the same serial number system as other Ford products.

MAVERICK SERIES

Model No.	Body/ Style No.	Body Type & Seating	Factory Price	Shipping Weight	Prod. Total
N/A	54A	4-dr Sed-6P	2824/2982	2851/3014	137,728
N/A	62A	2-dr Sed-6P	2742/2949	2739/2902	139,818
N/A	62D	2-dr Grabber-6P	2923/3081	2787/2950	23,502

PRODUCTION NOTE: Total series output was 301,048 units. The prices and weights to the left of the slash are for sixes/to the right of the slash for V-8s.

PINTO SERIES — (4-CYL) — This was the year that energy-absorbing bumpers were added to the Pinto, too. This brought an obvious change to the front of the car, as the air slot opening in the gravel pan could no longer be seen. Also eliminated was the center-mounted license plate holder. It didn't look right with the massive new bumper, but then, hardly anything else did either. The bumper was plain on the base trim models, but came with rubber faced vertical guards and a black vinyl impact strip on models with the Deluxe Decor package. Pinto station wagons could be had with optional trim packages that included simulated woodgrain exterior paneling and rooftop luggage racks.

PINTO I.D. NUMBERS: Pintos used the same serial number system as full-size Fords, Torinos and Mavericks.

1974 Ford Maverick four-door sedan (with Luxury Decor package) 6-cyl. (OCW)

1974 Ford Pinto Runabout two-door hatchback (with Luxury Decor package) 4-cyl. (OCW)

PINTO SERIES

Model No.	Body/ Style No.	Body Type & Seating	Factory Price	Shipping Weight	Prod. Total
N/A	62B	2-dr Sed-4P	2527	2372	132,061
N/A	64B	2-dr Hatch-4P	2631	2402	174,754
N/A	73B	2-dr Sta Wag-4P	2771	2576	237,394

PRODUCTION NOTES: Total series output was 544,209 units. The two-door hatchback coupe was called the Pinto Runabout.

THUNDERBIRD SERIES — (V-8) — The Thunderbird was left pretty much alone for 1974, except that the 460 cid V-8 was now standard under the hood. The side script plate was in its same location—above the side molding at the trailing edge of the front fender—but was slightly larger in size.

THUNDERBIRD I.D. NUMBERS: Thunderbirds began with the number '4' followed by the assembly plant code 'J' (Los Angeles) or 'Y' (Wixom), body type code, engine designation code 'A' and, finally, the unit's production number, beginning at 100001 and going up.

THUNDERBIRD SERIES

Model No.	Body/ Style No.	Body Type & Seating	Factory Price	Shipping Weight	Prod. Total
A	65K	2-dr HT Cpe-6P	7221	4825	58,443

ENGINE [Pinto Base Four]: Overhead cam. Cast-iron block. Displacement: 122 cid. Bore and stroke: 3.58 x 3.03 inches. Compression ratio: 8.2:1. Net hp: 86 at 5400 rpm. Carburetor: Ford/Weber two-barrel. Five main bearings. Serial number code 'X.'

ENGINE [Pinto Four]: Overhead cam. Cast-iron block. Displacement: 139 cid. Bore and stroke: 3.78 x 3.13 inches. Compression ratio: 8.6:1. Net hp: 80. Carburetor: Motorcraft two-barrel. Five main bearings. Serial number code 'Y.'

ENGINE [Maverick Base Six]: Overhead valve. Cast-iron block. Displacement: 200 cid. Bore and stroke: 3.68 x 3.13 inches. Compression ratio: 8.3:1. Net hp: 84 at 3800 rpm. Carburetor: Motorcraft one-barrel. Seven main bearings. Serial number code 'T.'

ENGINE [Maverick Six]: Overhead valve. Cast-iron block. Displacement: 250 cid. Bore and stroke: 3.68 x 3.91 inches. Compression ratio: 8.0:1. Net hp: 91 at 3200 rpm. Carburetor: Motorcraft one-barrel. Seven main bearings. Serial number code 'L.'

ENGINE [302 V-8]: Overhead valve. Cast-iron block. Displacement: 302 cid. Bore and stroke: 4.00 x 3.00 inches. Compression ratio: 8.0:1. Net hp: 140 at 3800 rpm. Carburetor: Motorcraft two-barrel. Five main bearings. Serial number code 'F.'

ENGINE [351 'Windsor' V-8]: Overhead valve. Cast-iron block. Displacement: 351 cid. Bore and stroke: 4.00 x 3.50 inches. Compression ratio: 8.2:1. Net hp: 163 at 4200 rpm. Carburetor: Motorcraft two-barrel. Five main bearings.

ENGINE [351 'Cleveland' V-8]: Overhead valve. Cast-iron block. Displacement: 351 cid. Bore and stroke: 4.00 x 3.50 inches. Compression ratio: 8.0:1. Net hp: 162 at 4000 rpm. Carburetor: Motorcraft two-barrel. Five main bearings. Serial number code 'H.'

ENGINE [351 'Cleveland' Four-Barrel V-8]: Overhead valve. Cast-iron block. Displacement: 351 cid. Bore and stroke: 4.00 x 3.50 inches. Compression ratio: 7.9:1. Net hp: 255 at 5600 rpm. Carburetor: Motorcraft four-barrel. Five main bearings. Serial number code 'Q.'

ENGINE [400 V-8]: Overhead valve. Cast-iron block. Displacement: 400 cid. Bore and stroke: 4.00 x 4.00 inches. Compression ratio: 6.0:1. Net hp: 170 at 3400 rpm. Carburetor: Motorcraft two-barrel. Five main bearings. Serial number code 'S.'

1974 Ford Thunderbird two-door hardtop V-8. (PH)

ENGINE [Thunderbird 460 V-8]: Overhead valve. Cast-iron block. Displacement: 460 cid. Bore and stroke: 4.36 x 3.85 inches. Compression ratio: 8.0:1. Net hp: 220 at 4000 rpm. (215-hp when '460' is optioned in other Fords). Carburetor: Carter four-barrel. Five main bearings. Serial number code 'A.'

FORD CHASSIS FEATURES: Wheelbase: 121 inches. Overall length: (passenger cars) 223 inches; (station wagons) 226 inches. Width: 80 inches. Tires: Refer to text.

TORINO CHASSIS FEATURES: Wheelbase: (two-door model) 114 inches; (four-door model) 118 inches. Overall length: (two-door model) 212 inches; (four-door model) 216 inches; (station wagon) 222 inches. Width: (passenger cars) 80 inches; (station wagon) 79 inches. Tires: Refer to text.

MAVERICK CHASSIS FEATURES: Wheelbase: (two-door model) 103 inches; (four-door model) 109.9 inches. Overall length: (two-door model) 187 inches; (four-door model) 194 inches. Width: 71 inches. Tires: (two-door model) 6.45 x 14; (four-door model) C78-14; (Grabber) D70-14.

PINTO CHASSIS FEATURES: Wheelbase: 94.2 inches. Overall length: (passenger car) 169 inches; (station wagon) 179 inches. Width: 70 inches. Tires: (passenger car) 6.00 x 13; (station wagon) A78-13.

THUNDERBIRD CHASSIS FEATURES: Wheelbase: 120.4 inches. Overall length: 225 inches. Width: 80 inches. Tires: LR78-15.

FORD OPTIONS: 400 cid/170-hp V-8, in Country Squires (standard); in other models ($94). 460 cid/215-hp V-8 ($304). Tinted glass ($55). Air conditioning, standard type ($426); with Climate Control ($506). Cruise Control ($103). AM radio ($67). AM/FM radio ($243). Vinyl roof on passenger cars ($115); on station wagons ($148); on LTD Brougham (standard). White sidewall tires ($33). AM/FM stereo with tape player ($378). Power seats ($106). Power windows ($134). Sun roof ($516). Country Squire Brougham option ($202). Country Squire Luxury package option ($545). Brougham Luxury Package option ($380).

TORINO OPTIONS: 351 cid/162-hp 'Cleveland' V-8 ($46). 400 cid/170-hp V-8 ($140). 460 cid/215-hp V-8 ($245). 351 cid/225-hp 'Cleveland' four-barrel V-8 ($132). Cruise-O-Matic transmission; with small V-8 ($219); with '460' V-8 ($241). AM radio ($67). AM/FM stereo radio ($217). Power steering ($117). Power disc brakes, on station wagons (standard); on passenger cars ($71). Power tailgate window ($35). Station wagon luggage rack ($80). Vinyl roof ($96). White sidewall tires ($33). Station wagon third passenger seat ($67). Sun roof ($490). AM/FM stereo radio with tape player ($378).

MAVERICK OPTIONS: 250 cid six ($42). 302 cid/140-hp V-8 ($122). Cruise-O-Matic transmission ($212). AM radio ($61). Power steering ($106). White sidewall tires ($33). Vinyl top ($83). Air conditioning ($383). Luxury Decor Group, except Grabber ($332).

PINTO OPTIONS: 140 cid/90-hp four ($52). Cruise-O-Matic transmission ($212). AM radio ($61). AM/FM stereo radio ($222). Luxury Decor Group ($137). Full wheel covers ($23). Forged aluminum wheels ($154). White sidewall tires ($44). Vinyl top ($83). Air conditioning ($383). Squire station wagon package ($241).

THUNDERBIRD OPTIONS: Six-Way power seats ($105). Cruise Control ($107). Climate Control air conditioning ($74). Electric rear window defogger ($85). Power moon roof ($798). Sun roof ($525). AM/FM radio with stereo tape ($311). Turnpike Convenience Group, includes Cruise Control, trip odometer and manual reclining passenger seat ($138). Burgundy Luxury Group package ($411).

OPTIONAL EQUIPMENT NOTES: Cruise-O-Matic automatic transmission and power front disc brakes were standard equipment on Torino station wagons. Automatic transmission, power steering and power front disc brakes were standard equipment on LTD, Custom 500, Galaxie and Thunderbird. Air conditioning, power windows and AM radio were also standard equipment in Thunderbirds.

Ford's 1974 model year resulted in 1,843,340 assemblies, including Falcon Club Wagons (the Falcon Club Wagon was a light truck that Ford included, statistically, with passenger car production). Calendar year output was 1,716,975 units again including the Falcon Club Wagon. The chief executives of the company were unchanged from 1973. Model year declines of some 130,000 units were caused by lagging buyer interest in 'big' Fords and Thunderbirds.

1975 FORD

1975 Ford LTD Landau two-door hardtop coupe (with opera windows) V-8. (OCW)

1975 FORDS — OVERVIEW — With the exception of the slightly restyled full-size Fords, the 1975 models were, once again, basically the same as the year before. The big Fords were attractively face lifted with the addition of a larger Mercedes-style grille and new taillights. The most significant change occurred with the two-door hardtop model. The true pillarless hardtop was replaced by a coupe with fixed quarter windows and large 'opera' windows. The 1975 Torinos were unchanged from the previous year. The Gran Torino name was dropped and this car was now called the Elite. Once again, the Maverick and Pinto were unchanged, except for some minor grille updating in each line. The big news for 1975 was the addition of the new Granada series. The Granada was a new intermediate size car offered in four-door sedan and two-door sedan versions. As Ford was proud to point out, the four-door had more than a passing resemblance to the Mercedes-Benz. Granadas could be fitted with options that created anything from a taxi to a mini-limousine. They came powered by engines ranging from the sedate 250 cid six-cylinder to the 351 cid 'Windsor' V-8. The latter engine produced not-so-sedate performance and these Granadas were, in fact, among the fastest of the 1975 Fords. The Thunderbird was exactly the same car as produced in 1974, with one small exception. The Thunderbird steering wheel had slightly different spokes (as did the steering wheels on all new Fords, except the Pinto). Pollution standards were stiffened once again and, in 1975, all cars were required to burn unleaded gasoline. The majority of the new models came with catalytic converters on the exhaust systems, to help reduce emissions and contaminates.

FULL-SIZE FORD SERIES — (V-8) — The Custom 500 was the base trim level Ford for 1975. It included chrome windshield and rear window moldings; nylon carpeting; ignition key warning buzzer; 351 cid V-8 engine; Cruise-O-Matic automatic transmission; power steering and G78-15 belted black sidewall tires. The LTD was the intermediate trim level. It included all the Custom 500 features plus hood lip moldings; cloth and vinyl seating surfaces; rocker panel moldings; and woodgrain appliques on the instrument panel. The LTD Brougham was the top trim level and included all the LTD features plus deep cushioned lowback bench seats; electric clock; Deluxe two-spoke steering wheel; chrome trim on the foot pedals; polished aluminum trim around the rear edge of the hood; bodyside moldings with vinyl inserts; and HR78-15 steel-belted radial tires. The LTD Landau had all the Brougham features plus highback Flight Bench seats (with center armrests); ashtray and front door courtesy lights; full wheel covers; cut-pile carpeting; carpeted lower door panels; polished rocker panel moldings with extensions; automatic seatback release (on two-door models); vinyl roof and color-keyed seat belts. The Ranch Wagon contained all the features of the LTD models plus JR78-15 steel-belted radial tires. The Country Sedan contained all the features found on the Ranch Wagon plus dual note horn; woodgrain appliques on the instrument panel and front and rear door panels; special sound package; bodyside moldings and a chrome-plated grille. The Country Squires contained all the features found in the LTD Country Sedans plus JR78-15 steel-belted radial tires and the 400 cid V-8 engine.

FORD I.D. NUMBERS: The serial number code can be broken down, as follows: First symbol indicates year: 5 = 1975. Second symbol identifies assembly plant, as follows: A = Atlanta; B = Oakville, Ontario, Canada; E = Mahwah; F = Dearborn; G = Chicago; H = Loraine; J = Los Angeles;

K = Kansas City; P = Twin Cities; R = San Jose; S = Allen Park; T = Metuchen; U = Louisville; W = Wayne; X = St. Thomas, Ontario, Canada; Y = Wixom; Z = St. Louis. Third and fourth symbols identify body series (see Body/ Numbers below). Fifth symbol identifies engine code, as follows: Y = 139 cid V-8; T = 200 cid six-cylinder; L = 250 cid six-cylinder; F = 302 cid V-8; H = 351 cid V-8; S = 400 cid V-8; A = 460 cid V-8. The last six digits are the unit's production number, beginning at 100001 and going up, at each of the assembly plants. Fords began with the number '5' followed by the assembly plant code, engine designation code and, finally, the unit's production number according to the final assembly location. Each plant began at 100001 and went up.

FORD SERIES

Model No.	Body/ Style No.	Body Type & Seating	Factory Price	Shipping Weight	Prod. Total
CUSTOM 500					
N/A	53D	4-dr Sed-6P	4380	4377	31,043
N/A	71D	4-dr Ranch Wag-6P	4970	4787	6,930
LTD					
N/A	53H	4-dr Sed-6P	4615	4408	82,382
N/A	60H	2-dr O/W Cpe-6P	4656	4359	47,432
N/A	71H	4-dr Cty Sed Sta Wag-6P	5061	4803	22,935
LTD BROUGHAM					
N/A	53K	4-dr Sed-6P	5016	4419	32,327
N/A	60K	2-dr O/W Cpe-6P	5050	4391	24,005
N/A	71K	4-dr Cty Sq Sta Wag-6P	5340	4845	41,550
LTD LANDAU					
N/A	53L	4-dr Sed-6P	5370	4446	32,506
N/A	60L	2-dr O/W Cpe-6P	5401	4419	26,919

PRODUCTION NOTE: Total series output was 348,029 units. The new body type designation O/W Cpe indicates the two-door coupe with opera windows.

TORINO/GRAN TORINO/ELITE SERIES — (V-8) — The Torino line was the same as the previous year. The Torino models were the base trim level and featured chrome windshield, rear widow and rain gutter moldings; highback bench seats; all-vinyl seat and door trim; floor mats; hubcaps; 302 cid V-8 engine and three-speed manual transmission. The Torino station wagon also included power front disc brakes and three-way tailgate. The Gran Torino was the intermediate trim level for 1975 and included all the Torino features plus manual front disc brakes; cloth and vinyl trim on seats and interior door panels; carpeting; lower bodyside, wheelwell and deck lid moldings; dual note horn; trunk mat; Deluxe two-spoke steering wheel and chrome trim on the foot pedals. The Gran Torino Squire station wagon also included the 351 cid/148-hp V-8 engine, Cruise-O-Matic automatic transmission, Deluxe pleated vinyl interior trim, wheel covers and woodgrain appliques on the bodysides, tailgate and instrument panel. The Gran Torino Brougham was the highest trim level and included all the Gran Torino features plus power front disc brakes; power steering; cloth seating surfaces; bodyside moldings and padded vinyl top. The Elite continued to offer the same features as in 1974.

1975 Ford Gran Torino Brougham four-door sedan V-8. (OCW)

1975 Ford Elite two-door hardtop V-8. (PH)

TORINO/GRAN TORINO/ELITE I.D. NUMBERS: The Torino, Gran Torino and Elite models began with the number '5' followed by assembly plant code, body type code, engine designation code and, finally, the unit's production number according to the final assembly location. Each plant began at 100001 and went up.

TORINO/GRAN TORINO/ELITE SERIES

Model No.	Body/ Style No.	Body Type & Seating	Factory Price	Shipping Weight	Prod. Total
TORINO					
N/A	53B	4-dr Sed-6P	3957	4059	22,928
N/A	65B	2-dr O/W Cpe-6P	3954	3987	13,394
N/A	71B	4-dr Sta Wag-6P	4336	4412	13,291
GRAN TORINO					
N/A	53D	4-dr Sed-6P	4258	4090	53,161
N/A	65D	2-dr O/W Cpe-6P	4234	3998	35,324
N/A	71D	4-dr Sta Wag-6P	4593	4456	23,951
TORINO BROUGHAM					
N/A	53K	4-dr Sed-6P	4791	4163	5,929
N/A	65K	2-dr O/W Cpe-6P	4759	4087	4,849
TORINO SPORT					
N/A	65R	2-dr Spt HT-5P	4744	4044	5,126
ELITE					
N/A	65M	2-dr HT Cpe-6P	4721	4160	123,372

PRODUCTION NOTE: Total series output was 318,482 units.

MAVERICK SERIES — (6-CYL/V-8) — Originally scheduled to be replaced by the new Granada, the Maverick's existence was extended after the energy scare of 1974. The sedans and the sporty Grabber featured refinements to interior and exterior trim; thicker, cut-pile carpeting; a Deluxe steering wheel as standard equipment and a 200 cid base six. Ford block lettering was added along the hood lip and the slot in the center of the front bumper was slightly decreased in width. New options included power disc brakes and a deck lid-mounted luggage rack. A catalytic converter was required with the base engine, while the optional 250 cid six or 302 cid V-8 came without this unpopular piece of equipment. Radial tires were also added to the regular equipment list. Buyers were given a choice of blue, black or tan interior combinations (as in the past) or new, light green trim.

MAVERICK I.D. NUMBERS: Mavericks used the same serial number sequence as the full-size Fords and Torino models.

MAVERICK SERIES

Model No.	Body/ Style No.	Body Type & Seating	Factory Price	Shipping Weight	Prod. Total
N/A	54A	4-dr Sed-6P	3025/3147	2820/2971	90,695
N/A	62A	2-dr Sed-6P	3061/3183	2943/3094	63,404
N/A	62D	2-dr Grabber-6P	3224/3346	2827/2979	8,473

PRODUCTION NOTE: Total series output was 162,572 units. The prices and weights to the left of the slash apply to six-cylinder-equipped models and the prices and weights to the right of the slash apply to V-8-powered models.

PINTO SERIES — (4-CYL/V-6) — Changes to the Pinto were also of the minor type this year. There was little reason to go any further, since good fuel economy was helping sell the car. The optional 2.8-liter V-6 was available only with Cruise-O-Matic attachments and only in the hatchback and station wagon, but wasn't popular. Only 16 percent of all buyers added optional six-cylinder engines. Some other new accessories included power steering; power front disc brakes and a fuel-economy warning light. Standard motivation came from a U.S. built 2.3-liter inline four-cylinder engine equipped with either a four-speed manual or three-speed automatic transmission.

1975 Ford Maverick two-door sedan 6-cyl. (OCW)

1975 Ford Pinto Runabout two-door hatchback 4-cyl. (OCW)

PINTO SERIES

Model No.	Body/ Style No.	Body Type & Seating	Factory Price	Shipping Weight	Prod. Total
N/A	62B	2-dr Sed-4P	2769	2495	64,081
N/A	64B	2-dr Hatch-4P	2967/3220	2528/2710	68,919
N/A	73B	2-dr Sta Wag-4P	3094/3347	2692/2874	90,763

PRODUCTION NOTE: Total series output was 223,763 units. The prices and weights to the left of the slash apply to four-cylinder-equipped models and the prices and weights to the right of the slash apply to V-6-powered models.

GRANADA SERIES — (6-CYL/V-8) — Ford referred to the Granada as a 'precision-sized' compact car. It was built off the Maverick four-door platform and came as a two-door coupe and four-door sedan. Its styling had a luxury flavor and was heavily influenced by European design themes. Even as a base model, it was quite elegant amongst cars in its class. The super-rich Ghia-optioned Granada went a step further where luxury was concerned. The 200 cid inline six was the base Granada powerplant when attached to the three-speed manual gearbox. Ghias came standard with a 250 cid inline six; digital clock; Deluxe sound package and wide range of fancy seating surfaces. The base model could be ordered with the bigger six. Two-barrel V-8s, of 302- or 351 cid, were provided in both levels. Dealer sales of Granadas in the United States peaked at 241,297 cars, cutting substantially into the popularity of Mustang II.

GRANADA I.D. NUMBERS: Granadas used the same serial number sequence as full-size Fords, Torinos, Mavericks and Pintos.

GRANADA SERIES

Model No.	Body/ Style No.	Body Type & Seating	Factory Price	Shipping Weight	Prod. Total
BASE					
N/A	54H	4-dr Sed-6P	3756/3784	3293/3355	118,168
N/A	66H	2-dr Sed-6P	3698/3826	3230/3306	100,810
GHIA					
N/A	54K	4-dr Sed-6P	4240/4326	3361/3423	43,652
N/A	66K	2-dr Sed-6P	4182/4268	3311/3373	40,028

PRODUCTION NOTE: Total series output was 302,649 units. The prices and weights to the left of the slash apply to six-cylinder-equipped models and the prices and weights to the right of the slash apply to V-6-powered models.

1975 Ford Granada Ghia four-door sedan 6-cyl. (OCW)

1975 Ford Granada Ghia two-door sedan 6-cyl. (OCW)

THUNDERBIRD SERIES — (V-8) — The Thunderbird had certainly come a long way since its 'two-seater' days. It was now FoMoCo's top-of-the-line personal/luxury car. A highly promoted new feature was the Sure-Trac rear brake anti-skid device. There were other chassis refinements, such as four-wheel power disc brakes and the Hydro-Boost hydraulic brake boosting system. Standard features included automatic transmission; power steering; power brakes; power windows; air conditioning and AM/FM radio. Optional, for collector types, were Silver or Copper Luxury Groups with a special heavy-grained half-vinyl roof, velour or leather seats, Deluxe trunk lining and specific wheel covers.

THUNDERBIRD I.D. NUMBERS: Thunderbirds began with the number '5' followed by assembly plant code 'J' (Los Angeles) or 'Y' (Wixom), body type code, engine designation code 'A' and, finally, the unit's production number, beginning at 100001 and going up.

THUNDERBIRD SERIES

Model No.	Body/ Style No.	Body Type & Seating	Factory Price	Shipping Weight	Prod. Total
A	65K	2-dr HT Cpe-6P	7701	4893	42,685

ENGINE [Pinto Base Four]: Overhead cam. Cast-iron block. Displacement: 139 cid. Bore and stroke: 3.78 x 3.13 inches. Compression ratio: 8.6:1. Net hp: 83. Carburetor: Motorcraft two-barrel. Five main bearings. Serial number code 'Y.'

ENGINE [Pinto Base Six]: Overhead valve. Cast-iron block. Displacement: 169 cid. Bore and stroke: 3.50 x 2.70 inches. Compression ratio: 8.0:1. Net hp: 97. Carburetor: Holley two-barrel. Four main bearings. Serial number code 'Z.'

ENGINE [Maverick Base Six]: Overhead valve. Cast-iron block. Displacement: 200 cid. Bore and stroke: 3.68 x 3.13 inches. Compression ratio: 8.3:1. Net hp: 75 at 3200 rpm. Carburetor: Motorcraft one-barrel. Seven main bearings. Serial number code 'T.'

ENGINE [Maverick/Granada Six]: Overhead valve. Cast-iron block. Displacement: 250 cid. Bore and stroke: 3.68 x 3.91 inches. Compression ratio: 8.0:1. Net hp: 72 at 2900 rpm. Carburetor: Motorcraft one-barrel. Seven main bearings. Serial number code 'L.'

ENGINE [302 V-8]: Overhead valve. Cast-iron block. Displacement: 302 cid. Bore and stroke: 4.00 x 3.00 inches. Compression ratio: 8.0:1. Net hp: 129 at 3800 rpm. Carburetor: Motorcraft two-barrel. Five main bearings. Serial number code 'F.'

ENGINE [351 'Windsor' V-8]: Overhead valve. Cast-iron block. Displacement: 351 cid. Bore and stroke: 4.00 x 3.50 inches. Compression ratio: 8.2:1. Net hp: 143 at 3600 rpm. Carburetor: Motorcraft two-barrel. Five main bearings.

ENGINE [351 'Modified' V-8]: Overhead valve. Cast-iron block. Displacement: 351 cid. Bore and stroke: 4.00 x 3.50 inches. Compression ratio: 8.0:1. Net hp: 148 at 3800 rpm. Carburetor: Motorcraft two-barrel. Five main bearings. Serial number code 'H.'

ENGINE [400 V-8]: Overhead valve. Cast-iron block. Displacement: 400 cid. Bore and stroke: 4.00 x 4.00 inches. Compression ratio: 8.0:1. Net hp: 158 at 3800 rpm. Carburetor: Motorcraft two-barrel. Five main bearings. Serial number code 'S.'

ENGINE [Thunderbird 460 V-8]: Overhead valve. Cast-iron block. Displacement: 460 cid. Bore and stroke: 4.36 x 3.65 inches. Compression ratio: 8.0:1. Net hp: 218 at 4000 rpm. Carburetor: Motorcraft four-barrel. Five main bearings. Serial number code 'A.'

FORD CHASSIS FEATURES: Wheelbase: 121 inches. Overall length: (passenger cars) 224 inches; (station wagon) 226 inches. Width: 80 inches. Tires: HR78-15.

TORINO CHASSIS FEATURES: Wheelbase: (two-door model) 114 inches; (four-door model) 118 inches. Overall length: (two-door model) 214 inches; (four-door model) 218 inches; (station wagon) 223 inches. Width: 80 inches. Tire: HR78-14.

1975 Ford Granada four-door sedan V-8. (OCW)

MAVERICK CHASSIS FEATURES: Wheelbase: (two-door model) 103 inches; (four-door model) 109.9 inches. Overall length: (two-door model) 187 inches; (four-door model) 194 inches. Width: 71 inches. Tires: (Grabber) DR70-14; (other two-door model) BR78-14; (four-door model) CR78-14.

PINTO CHASSIS FEATURES: Wheelbase: (passenger cars) 94.4 inches; (station wagon) 94.7 inches. Overall length: (passenger cars) 169 inches; (station wagon) 179 inches. Width: 70 inches. Tires: (all models) BR78-13B.

GRANADA CHASSIS FEATURES: Wheelbase: 109.9 inches. Overall length: (base models) 198 inches; (Ghia) 200 inches. Width: 74 inches. Tires: (Ghia four-door) ER78-14; (other models) DR78-14.

THUNDERBIRD CHASSIS FEATURES: Wheelbase: 120.4 inches. Overall length: 226 inches. Width: 80 inches. Tires: LR78-15.

FORD OPTIONS: 400 cid/158-hp V-8 engine ($94, standard on Country Squires). 460 cid/218-hp V-8 engine ($304). Tinted glass ($55). Air conditioning ($426). Climate Control ($506). Cruise Control ($103). AM radio ($67). AM/FM stereo radio ($243). Vinyl roof ($115), on station wagons ($148); on LTD Landau (standard). White sidewall tires ($33).

TORINO/GRAN TORINO/ELITE OPTIONS: 400 cid/158-hp V-8 engine ($54). 460 cid/218-hp V-8 engine ($245). AM radio ($67). AM/FM stereo radio ($217). Power steering ($117). Power front disc brakes ($71); on station wagons (standard). Power tailgate window on station wagons ($35). Luggage rack on station wagons ($80). Vinyl top ($96). Air conditioning ($426). White sidewall tires ($33).

MAVERICK OPTIONS: 302 cid/129-hp V-8 engine. Cruise-O-Matic automatic transmission ($212). AM radio ($61). Power steering ($106). Luxury Decor Package ($392). White sidewall tires ($33).

PINTO OPTIONS: 169 cid V-6 engine ($229). Cruise-O-Matic automatic transmission ($212). AM radio ($61). AM/FM stereo radio ($222). Luxury Decor Group ($137). Forged aluminum wheels ($154). White sidewall tires ($33).

1975 Ford Thunderbird two-door hardtop (with Copper Luxury package) V-8. (OCW)

GRANADA OPTIONS: 302 cid/129-hp V-8 engine ($85). 351 cid/143-hp 'Windsor' V-8 engine (N/A). Cruise-O-Matic automatic transmission ($222). Power steering ($106). Power brakes ($45). AM radio ($61). AM/FM stereo radio ($222). Vinyl roof ($83). Air conditioning ($426). White sidewall tires ($33).

THUNDERBIRD OPTIONS: Six-Way power seats ($105). Cruise Control ($107); with Turnpike Convenience Group (standard). Climate-Control air conditioning ($74). Electric rear window defroster ($85). Power moon roof ($798). Turnpike Convenience Group includes: Cruise-Control, trip odometer and manual passenger seat recliner ($138).

HISTORY: The 1975 Ford line was introduced Sept. 27, 1974. Model year sales, by United States dealers, included 282,130 Pintos; 142,964 Mavericks; 241,297 Granadas; 158,798 Torinos; 102,402 Elites; 297,655 LTDs and 37,216 Thunderbirds. The production of 1975 models, in U.S. factories, hit 1,302,205 cars. Calendar year production of Fords, in this country, peaked at 1,302,644 units. Top executives influencing Ford Division policy were Henry Ford II, Lee Iacocca and B.E. Bidwell. It was the final season for the long-lasting Custom 500 nameplate.

1976 FORD

1976 Ford Pinto Stallion hatchback coupe. (F)

Not much was dramatically different at Ford for 1976, after some significant changes a year earlier. Full-size models had been restyled in 1975, gaining a Mercedes-like grille. The Granada mid-size was new that year, with obvious Mercedes styling touches, while the Elite name went on the former Gran Torino. Pillarless two-door hardtop models had faded away by 1975, replaced by a new six-window coupe style with fixed quarter windows and large opera windows. Installation of catalytic converters expanded for 1976, accompanied by ample gas mileage boosts. Fuel economy improvements this year resulted from revised carburetor calibrations and lower rear axle ratios. All models used no-lead gas. The model lineup was the same as 1975, except that Custom 500 (equivalent to LTD) was now available only to fleet buyers. Special Pinto (and Mustang) models were produced for West Coast consumption. Corporate body colors for 1976 were: black, silver metallic, medium slate blue metallic, candyapple red, dark red, bright red, medium blue metallic, bright blue metallic, bright dark blue metallic, light blue, bright medium blue, dark yellow green metallic, dark jade metallic, light or dark green, copper metallic, medium chestnut metallic, dark brown metallic, saddle bronze metallic, tan, yellow orange, bright yellow, cream, dark yellow, chrome yellow, light gold, light jade, medium green gold, medium ginger metallic, dark brown, medium orange metallic, tangerine, and white. Additional colors were available on certain models, including diamond bright and diamond flare finishes, as well as three crystal metallic colors.

PINTO — FOUR/V-6 — Ford's subcompact, introduced in 1971, had a new front-end look this year. Appearance changes included a new argent-painted egg crate grille of one-piece corrosion-resistant plastic, bright bezels for the single round headlamps, bright front lip hood molding, and 'Ford' block letters centered above the grille. That new grille was peaked and angled forward slightly, with a tighter crosshatch pattern than before, and held square inset parking lamps. Backup lights were integral with the horizontal tail lamps. Bodies held front and rear side marker lights. For the first time, standard interiors had a choice of all vinyl or sporty cloth-and-vinyl. Four new interior trim fabrics were offered, along with a new bright red interior color. Three four-passenger bodies were offered: two-door sedan, "three-door" Runabout hatchback, and two-door wagon. Wagons had flipper rear compartment windows and a liftgate-open warning light, as well as tinted glass. Major fuel economy improvements resulted from catalysts, new carburetor calibrations, and a lower (3.18:1) rear axle ratio with the standard 140 cid (2.3-liter) OHC four and fully synchronized four-speed manual gearbox with floor shift lever. Optional was a 170.8 cid (2.8-liter) two-barrel V-6, which came only with Cruise-O-Matic transmission. Pinto's front suspension used independent short/long arms with ball joints. At the rear were longitudinal semi-elliptic leaf springs with rubber Iso-clamps at the axle. Rear springs had four leaves except wagons, five leaves. Pinto had front disc/rear drum brakes, rack-and-pinion steering, and unibody construction. New this year was a low-budget Pony MPG two-door, wearing minimal chrome trim and plain hubcaps. The fuel economy leader Pinto, dubbed an "import fighter," had a 3.00:1 axle ratio, a slip-clutch cooling fan, and new calibrations for the 2.3 liter engine. Pinto standard equipment included a heater/defroster with DirectAire ventilation, bucket seats, mini-console, inside hood release, dome light, glovebox, dual padded sunvisors, and B78x13 tires. Runabouts and wagons had a fold-down back seat and deluxe seatbelts. Six-cylinder models required automatic transmission. Runabouts had a carpeted load area. A new Squire option for Runabouts added simulated woodgrain vinyl paneling on bodyside and lower back panel, similar to the Squire wagon option. Squire also displayed bright surround and B-pillar moldings as well as belt, drip and window frame moldings. Targeting younger drivers was a sporty new Stallion option featuring special silver body paint and taping, black window and door moldings, and blacked-out wiper arms, hood, grille and lower back panel. Black tape treatment went on rocker panel and wheel lip areas; Stallion (horse) decals on front fenders. Stallion also included dual racing mirrors, styled steel wheels with trim rings, A70 x 13 tires with raised white letters, and a "competition" handling suspension. A Luxury Decor Group included woodtone instrument panel appliqué, custom steering wheel, passenger door courtesy light switch, and rear seat ashtray. Joining the individual option list this year were an AM radio with tape player, the half-vinyl roof, rocker panel moldings, and leather-wrapped steering wheel.

MAVERICK — SIX/V-8 — Initially scheduled for disappearance when the new Granada arrived in 1975, Maverick hung on a while longer as concern about the fuel crisis continued. This year's grilled was a forward-slanting horizontal-bar design, split into two sections by a center vertical divider bar. Rectangular park/signal lamps were mounted in the bright argent plastic grille; backup lights integral with the tail lamps. Single round headlamps continued. The front bumper held twin slots, and the hood showed a sculptured bulge. Inside was a new foot-operated parking brake. Front disc brakes were now standard. Base engine was the 200 cid (3-3 liter) inline six with one-barrel carburetor. Options: 250 cid six with one-barrel, or the 302 V-8 with two-barrel. All three came with either three-speed manual or automatic transmission. Maverick's fuel tank had grown from 16 to 19.2 gallons during the 1975 model year. Gas mileage was improved by lowering rear axle ratio to 2.79:1, recalibrating engines and adding back-pressure modulation of the EGR system. The compact, unibodied Maverick used a ball-joint front suspension with short and long arms. Hotchkiss rear suspensions had longitudinal semi-elliptic (three-leaf) springs. Standard equipment included fully-synchronized three-speed column shift, C78 x 14 bias-ply tires, hubcaps, ventless windows with curved glass, front/rear side marker lights. European-type armrest with door pull assist handle, and lockable glovebox. A padded instrument panel held two round cluster pods for gauges. Standard bench seats were trimmed in Random stripe cloth and vinyl. Two-doors had a flipper rear quarter window. A Stallion dress-up package, similar to Pinto's, included black grille and moldings; unique paint/tape treatment on hood, grille, decklid, lower body, and lower back panel; plus large Stallion decal on front quarter panel. The package also included dual outside mirrors, raised white-letter steel-belted radials on styled steel wheels, and "competition" suspension. Two-doors had a new optional three-quarter vinyl roof; four-doors, as "halo" vinyl roof. Other options included individually reclining bucket seats; paint stripes that extended along bodyside and over the roof (on vinyl-topped two-doors); and AM and AM/FM radios with stereo tape players.

1976 Ford Pinto Squire hatchback coupe. (OCW)

1976 Ford Maverick four-door with luxury décor option. (OCW)

GRANADA — SIX/V-8 — Ford called Granada "the most successful new-car nameplate in the industry in 1975," after its debut. For 1976, fuel economy improved and the "precision-size" compact held a new standard vinyl bench seat and door trim, but not much changed otherwise. Granada's chromed grille showed a 6x5 pattern of wide holes, with a 2 x 2 pattern within each hole. On each side of the single round headlamps were small, bright vertical sections patterned like the grille. Wide-spaced 'Ford' letters stood above the grille. On the fender extensions were wraparound front parking lights and signal/marker lenses. Hoods held a stand-up ornament. Each wraparound tri-color horizontal-style taillamp was divided into an upper and lower section, with integral side marker lights. Backup lamps sat inboard of the tail lamps. Sporting a tall, squared-off roofline and European-influenced design, the five-passenger Granada strongly resembled a Mercedes up front. Ford hardly hit that fact, bragging that "Its looks and lines remind you of the Mercedes 280 and the Cadillac Seville." Bodies featured bright wraparound bumpers, plus bright moldings on windshield, backlight, drip rail, door belt, door frame, and wheel lip. Two-door Granadas had distinctive opera windows. Four-doors had a bright center pillar molding with color-keyed insert. Two-and four-door sedans were offered, in base or Ghia trim. Standard equipment included a three-speed manual transmission, front disc/rear drum brakes, heater/defroster, inside hood release. DR78 x 14 blackwall steel-belted radials, anti-theft decklid lock, buried walnut woodtone instrument panel appliqués, locking glovebox, two rear seat ashtrays, lighter, and full wheel covers. Base engine was the 200 cid (3.3-liter) inline six with one-barrel carb. Optional: a 250 cid six, 302 cid V-8, and 351 cid V-8. Granada Ghia added a Ghia ornament on the opera window glass; color-keyed bodyside molding with integral wheel lip molding; left-hand remote-control mirror; dual accent paint stripes on bodyside, hood and decklid; trunk carpeting; and lower back panel appliqué color-keyed to the vinyl roof. Inside Ghia was a "floating pillow" sew design on independent reclining or flight bench seats, map pockets and assist handle on back of front seats, day/night mirror, and luxury steering wheel with woodtone appliqué on the rim. Under Ghia's hood was the larger 250 cid six-cylinder engine. For economy, axle ratios were reduced to 2.75:1 and 2.79:1. Granada's front suspension used short/long control arms with ball joints and coil springs. At the rear were semi-elliptic four-leaf springs. Steering was the recirculating ball type. Four-wheel power disc brakes had become optional during the 1975 model year, along with Sure-Trak anti-skid brakes, power seats, Traction-Lok axle, power moonroof, and space-saver spare tire. Those continued for 1976. New options this year included speed control, tilt steering wheel, AM radio with stereo tape player, power door locks, and heavy-duty suspension. A Luxury Decor option (for four-door Ghia only) included black/tan two-tone paint, four-wheel disc brakes, lacy-spoke cast aluminum wheels, large Ghia badge on C-pillar, and front/rear bumper rub strips. Inside, that option had velour cloth and super-soft vinyl upholstery with larger door armrest, soft glovebox and ashtray doors, rear center armrest, console with warning lights, leather-wrapped steering wheel, and lighted visor vanity mirror. A Sports Sedan package for two-doors included a floor shift lever, special paint, color-keyed wheels, pin stripes, and leather-wrapped steering wheel. Mercury's Monarch was Granada's corporate twin, differing only in grille/taillamp design and trim details. Both evolved from the Maverick platform.

TORINO — V-8 — Nine models made up the mid-size Torino lineup this year; base, Gran Torino and Brougham two- and four-doors, and a trio of wagons. Gran Torino Sport was dropped. Two-doors rode a 114 in. wheelbase; four-doors measured 118 in. between hubs. The similar-size Elite was a separate model (below). Fuel economy was improved by recalibrating engine spark and back-pressure EGR, and lowering the rear axle ratio to 2.75:1. Five body colors were new. Torino and Gran Torino got a new saddle interior. Appearance was similar to 1975. Side-by-side quad round headlamps flanked a one-piece plastic grille with tiny crosshatch pattern, divided into six sections by vertical bars. Clear vertical parking/signal lamps hid behind twin matching outer sections, making eight in all. "Ford block letters stood above the grille. Two-door Torinos retained the conventional pillarless design, while four-doors were referred to as "pillared hardtops." Bodies held frameless, ventless curved side glass. Standard engine was the 351 cid (5.8-liter) V-8 with two-barrel carburetor and solid-state ignition, SelectShift Cruise-O-Matic, power front disc/rear drum brakes, power steering, and HR78 x 14 steel-belted radial tires were standard. Two V-8s were optional: a 400 cid two-barrel and the big 460 four-barrel. Torino's front suspension used single lower control arms, strut bar and ball joints. Coil springs brought up the rear. Bodies sat on a separate torque box perimeter-type frame. Standard equipment included a cloth/vinyl front bench seat with adjustable head restraints, vinyl door trim panels, recessed door handles, day/night mirror, heater/defroster, and inside hood release. Broughams had a split bench set. Torino and Gran Torino wore hubcaps; Broughams added wheel covers, as well as opera windows and a vinyl roof. Wagons had a three-way tailgate and locking storage compartment. Squire wagons added a power tailgate window, full wheel covers, and woodgrain paneling with side rails. New options included a bucket seat console (on Gran Torino two-door); opera windows for the base Torino two-door (as well as other models); space-saver spare tire; and engine immersion heater. Also optional: an automatic parking brake release and electric decklid release.

ELITE — V-8 — Although the Elite nameplate arrived just a year earlier, its body had been around a while longer, then called Gran Torino. Appearance changes were slight this year on the pillarless two-door hardtop body, which rode a 114 in. wheelbase. Elite sported a "luxury" sectioned grille with vertical bars and horizontal center bar. Its floating egg crate design formed a two-row, eight-column arrangement. Each of the 16 "holes" held a crosshatch pattern. The grille protruded forward in segments, and the bumper extended forward at its center and ends. A stand-up hood ornament held the Elite crest. Single round headlamps in square housings with bright bezels, while vertical parking/signal lamps sat in front fendertip extensions. Wide vinyl-insert bodyside moldings were color-keyed to the vinyl roof. Large wraparound tail lamps had bright bezels and integral side marker lights (with red reflector on lower back panel appliqué). On the rear roof pillar were two tiny side-by-side opera windows, the rear of regular quarter windows. Bodies also displayed bright tapered wide wheel lip moldings. Six body colors were new, while a standard gold vinyl roof replaced the former brown. Either a full vinyl roof or a new half-vinyl version was available, at no extra charge. To boost gas mileage, the standard axle changed from 3.00:1 to 2.75:1. Standard equipment included the 351 cid (5.8-liter) two-barrel V-8 with SelectShift Cruise-O-Matic, power steering and brakes, four-wheel coil springs, and HR78 x 15 SBR tires. The standard bench seat had Westminster pleated knit cloth and vinyl trim. Woodtone accented the instrument cluster/panel, steering wheel and door panels. Also standard: front bumper guards, heater/defroster, DirectAire ventilation, clock, full wheel covers, and bright window moldings. An Interior Decor group included individually adjustable split bench seats with choice of cashmere-like cloth or all-vinyl trim, shag carpeting, visor vanity mirror, dual-note horn, and eight-pod instrument panel with tachometer. Bucket seats with console and floor shift became optional this year. Other new options: space-saver spare tire, turbine-spoke cast aluminum wheels, AM/FM stereo search radio, electric decklid release, automatic parking brake release, and engine immersion heater.

1976 Ford Granada Ghia sedan. (F)

1976 Ford Gran Torino two-door hardtop. (F)

1976 Ford Elite. (OCW)

FULL-SIZE LTD/CUSTOM 500 — V-8 — LTD was the only full-size Ford available to private buyers this year, as the Custom 500 badge went on fleet models only. The ten-model lineup included two- and four-door base. Brougham and Landau LTD models; Custom 500 four-door and wagon; and base and Country Squire LTD wagons. Four-doors were called "pillared hardtops." Landau and Country squire models had hidden headlamps. Brougham and Landau two-doors carried half-vinyl roofs; four-doors got a "halo" vinyl roof. Front-end appearance changed slightly with a switch to dark argent paint on the secondary surface of the chromed grille. Otherwise, little change was evident other than a new wheel cover design. LTD's crosshatch grille peaked slightly forward. Headlamp doors held a horizontal emblem. Tri-section wraparound front parking/signal lenses stood at fender tips. On the hood was a stand-up ornament. Two-doors had a six-window design, with narrow vertical windows between the front and rear side windows. Vinyl-insert bodyside moldings were standard. All models had a reflective rear appliqué. Six body colors were new. At mid-year, Country Squire lost the long horizontal chrome strip along its woodgrain bodyside panel. Base engine was the two-barrel 351 cid (5.8-liter) V-8, but wagons carried the 400 cid engine. A 460 V-8 with dual exhausts was optional on all models. Standard equipment included power steering and brakes, SelectShift Cruise-O-Matic, steel-belted radials, power ventilation system, and front bumper guards. Brougham, Landau and wagon also had rear guards. Police models with the 460 V-8 and three-speed automatic had first-gear lockout. Front suspensions used single lower arms with strut bar and ball joints. At the rear were coil springs with three-link rubber cushion and track bar. Rear axle ratios changed to 2.75:1 and engines were recalibrated, in an attempt to boost gas mileage. Wagons had a fuel tank of only 21 gallons, versus 24.3 gallons on hardtops. An 8-gallon auxiliary tank was available. Wagons now had standard hydro-boost rear brakes. A parking brake warning light became standard on all models. Decklid and ignition switch locks offered improved anti-theft protection. Other new options: four-wheel power disc brakes, adjustable-level air shocks, dual-tone paint treatment (Brougham and Landau) in four combinations, and AM/FM search radio. Inside were standard full-width bench seats with cloth/vinyl trim; cut-pile carpeting; full-length padded armrests; and woodtone instrument panel and door appliqués. LTD bodies held bright belt, drip and wheel lip moldings. Landau added concealed headlamps, a convenience group, half vinyl roof (on two-door), front cornering lamps, wide color-keyed bodyside moldings, and unique narrow center pillar windows. Also on Landaus: padded door panels with woodtone accents, fold-down center armrests, and a digital clock.

THUNDERBIRD — V-8 — Apart from a trio of trim/paint Luxury Group packages, not much was new on the personal-luxury Thunderbird for 1976. T-Bird's bulged-out grille consisted of rectangular holes in a crosshatch pattern, with 'Thunderbird' block letters above. Quad round headlamps in squarish housings didn't fit snugly together but were mounted separately, with a little body-colored space between each pair. Large sectioned wraparound parking and cornering lamps stood at fender tips. T-Bird's opera windows were less tall than most, and narrow roll-down rear windows also were installed. Full-width segmented-design tail lamps had four-bulbs in each pod. Standard equipment included the big 460 cid (7.5-liter) V-8 with four-barrel carburetor, SelectShift Cruise-O-Matic, 2.75:1 rear axle, SelectAire condition, vinyl roof, vinyl-insert bodyside moldings, JR78 x 15 steel-belted radials, power steering and brakes, power windows, and cornering lamps. Rear suspension, as before, was the "stabul" four-link system. Inside was a baby burled walnut woodtone instrument panel appliqué and new AM radio. Also standard: automatic parking brake release, front and rear bumper guards with white insert rub strips, split bench seats with fold-down armrests, remote-control left mirror, full wheel covers, twin padded pull-down arm-rests, lined luggage area, and courtesy lights. New options included a power lumbar seat, AM/FM search radio, AM/FM quadrasonic 8 track tape player, engine block heater, and Kasman cloth interior trim. An automatic headlamp dimmer was added to the Light Group. Also available: a power-operated moonroof made with one-way glass. The new Creme/Gold Luxury Group featured two-tone paint (gold glamour paint on bodyside and creme accent on hood, deck, greenhouse and bodyside molding). Also included was a gold padded half-vinyl roof, deep-dish aluminum wheels, and gold Thunderbird emblem in opera window. Inside was a choice of two-tone Creme/Gold leather or gold media velour seating surface. The right-hand instrument panel was finished with gold appliqué. A Bordeaux Luxury Group included Bordeaux glamour paint, fully padded half-vinyl roof in silver or dark red, wide bodyside moldings to match the vinyl roof, dual hood and bodyside paint stripes, and simulated wire wheel covers. Inside was a choice of red leather or red media velour. There was also a Lipstick (red) package with white striping. Thunderbirds came in 21 colors, including the Luxury Group choices.

I.D. DATA: Ford's 11-symbol Vehicle Identification Number (VIN) is stamped on a metal tab fastened to the instrument panel, visible through the windshield. The first digit is a model year code ('6' 1976). The second letter indicates assembly plant: 'A' Atlanta, GA; 'B' Oakville, Ontario (Canada); 'E' Mahwah, NJ; 'G' Chicago; 'H' Lorain; Ohio; 'J' Los Angeles; 'K' Kansas City, MO; 'P' Twin Cities, Minn.; 'R' San Jose, CA; 'T' Metuchen, NJ; 'U' Louisville, KY; 'W' Wayne, MI; 'Y' Wixom, MI. Digits three and four are the body serial code, which corresponds to the Model Numbers shown in the tables below (e.g. '10' Pinto 2-dr. sedan). The fifth symbol is an engine code: 'Y' L4-140 2Bbl.; 'Z' V6-170 2Bbl.; 'T' L6-200 1Bbl.; 'L' L6-250 1Bbl.; 'F' V8-302 2Bbl.; 'H' V8-351 2Bbl.; 'S' V8-400 2Bbl.; 'A' V8-460 4Bbl.; 'C' Police V8-460 4Bbl. Finally, digits 6-11 make up the consecutive unit number of cars built at each assembly plant. The number begins with 100001. A Vehicle Certification Label on the left front door lock face panel or door pillar shows the manufacturer, month and year of manufacture, GVW, GAWR, certification statement, VIN, body code, color code, trim code, axle code, transmission code, and domestic (or foreign) special order code.

PINTO (FOUR/V-6)

Model No.	Body/ Style No.	Body Type & Seating	Factory Price	Shipping Weight	Prod. Total
10	62B	2-dr. Sedan-4P	3025/3472	2452/2590	92,264
10	62B	2-dr. Pony Sed-4P	2895/----	2450/----	Note 1
11	64B	2-dr. Hatch-4P	3200/3647	2482/2620	92,540
11	64B	2-dr. Sqr Hatch-4P	3505/3952	2518/2656	Note 2
12	73B	2-dr. Sta Wag-4P	3365/3865	2635/2773	105,328
12	73B	2-dr. Sqr Wag-4P	3671/4171	2672/2810	Note 2

Note 1: Pony production included in base sedan figure.

Note 2: Squire Runabout hatchback and Squire Wagon production are included in standard Runabout and station wagon totals.

MAVERICK (SIX/V-8)

Model No.	Body/ Style No.	Body Type & Seating	Factory Price	Shipping Weight	Prod. Total
91	62A	2-dr. Sedan-4P	3117/3265	2763/2930	60,611
92	54A	4-dr. Sedan-5P	3189/3337	2873/3040	79,076

GRANADA (SIX/V-8)

| 82 | 66H | 2-dr. Sedan-5P | 3707/3861 | 3119/3226 | 161,618 |
| 81 | 54H | 4-dr. Sedan-5P | 3798/3952 | 3168/3275 | 287,923 |

GRANADA GHIA (SIX/V-8)

| 84 | 66K | 2-dr. Sedan-5P | 4265/4353 | 3280/3387 | 46,786 |
| 83 | 54K | 4-dr. Sedan-5P | 4355/4443 | 3339/3446 | 52,457 |

TORINO (V-8)

25	65B	2-dr. HT Cpe-6P	4172	3976	34,518
27	53B	4-dr. HT Sed-6P	4206	4061	17,394
40	71B	4-dr. Sta Wag-6P	4521	4409	17,281

GRAN TORINO (V-8)

30	65D	2-dr. HT Cpe-6P	4461	3999	23,939
31	53D	4-dr. HT Sed-6P	4495	4081	40,568
42	71D	4-dr. Sta Wag-6P	4769	4428	30,596
43	71K	4-dr. Sqr Wag-6P	5083	4454	21,144

1976 Ford LTD Landau four-door pillared hardtop. (F)

GRAN TORINO BROUGHAM (V-8)

| 32 | 65K | 2-dr. HT Cpe-6P | 4883 | 4063 | 3,183 |
| 33 | 53K | 4-dr. HT Sed-6P | 4915 | 4144 | 4,473 |

ELITE (V-8)

| 21 | 65H | 2-dr. HT Cpe-6P | 4879 | 4169 | 146,475 |

CUSTOM 500 (V-8)

52	60D	2-dr. Pill. HT-6P	N/A	N/A	7,037
53	53D	4-dr. Pill. HT-6P	4493	4298	23,447
72	71D	4-dr. Ranch Wag-6P	4918	4737	4,633

LTD (V-8)

62	60H	2-dr. Pill. HT-6P	4780	4257	62,844
63	53H	4-dr. Pill. HT-6P	4752	4303	108,168
74	71H	4-dr. Sta Wag-6P	5207	4752	30,237
74	71H	4-dr. DFRS Wag-10P	5333	4780	Note 3
76	71K	4-dr. Ctry Sqr-6P	5523	4809	47,379
76	71K	4-dr. DFRS Sqr-10P	5649	4837	Note 3

NOTE 3: Wagons with dual-facing rear seats (a $126 option) are included in standard station wagon and Country Squire wagon totals.

LTD BROUGHAM (V-8)

| 68 | 60K | 2-dr. Pill. HT-6P | 5299 | 4299 | 20,863 |
| 66 | 53K | 4-dr. Pill. HT-6P | 5245 | 4332 | 32,917 |

LTD LANDAU (V-8)

| 65 | 60L | 2-dr. Pill. HT-6P | 5613 | 4346 | 29,673 |
| 64 | 53L | 4-dr. Pill. HT-6P | 5560 | 4394 | 35,663 |

THUNDERBIRD (V-8)

| 87 | 65K | 2-dr. HT Cpe-6P | 7790 | 4808 | 52,935 |

FACTORY PRICE AND WEIGHT NOTE: For Maverick and Granada, prices and weights to left of slash are for six-cylinder, to right for V-8 engine. For Pinto, prices and weights to left of slash are for four-cylinder, to right for V-6 engine.

ENGINE [Base Four (Pinto)]: Inline. Overhead cam. Four-cylinder. Cast-iron block and head. Displacement: 140 cid (2.3 liters). Bore & stroke: 3.78 x 3.13 in. Compression ratio: 9.0:1 Brake horsepower: 92 at 5000 rpm. Torque: 121 lbs.-ft. at 3000 rpm. Five main bearings. Hydraulic valve lifters. Carburetor: 2Bbl. Holley-Weber 9510. VIN Code: Y.

ENGINE [Optional V-6 (Pinto)]: 60-degree, overhead-valve V-6. Cast-iron block and head. Displacement: 170.8 cid (2.8 liters). Bore & stroke: 3.66 x 2.70 in. Brake horsepower: 103 at 4400 rpm. Torque: 149 lbs.-ft. at 2800 rpm. Four main bearings. Solid valve lifters. Carburetor: 2Bbl. Motorcraft 9510 (D6ZE-BA). VIN Code: Z.

ENGINE [Base Six (Maverick, Granada)]: Inline. Overhead valve. Six-cylinder. Cast-iron block and head. Displacement: 200 cid (3.3 liters). Bore & stroke: 3.68 x 3.13 in. Compression ratio: 8.3:1. Brake horsepower: 81 at 3400 rpm. Torque: 151 lbs.-ft. at 1700 rpm. Seven main bearings. Hydraulic valve lifters. Carburetor: 1Bbl. Carter YFA 9510. VIN Code: T.

ENGINE [Base Six (Granada Ghia); Optional (Maverick, Granada)]: Inline. Overhead valve. Six-cylinder. Cast-iron block and head. Displacement: 250 cid (4.1 liters). Bore & stroke: 3.68 x 3.91 in. Compression ratio: 8.0:1 Brake horsepower: 87 at 3600 rpm. (Maverick/Ghia, 90 at 3000). Torque: 190 lbs.-ft. at 2000 rpm. (Ghia, 187 at 1900). Seven main bearings. Hydraulic valve lifters. Carburetor: 1Bbl. Carter YFA 9510. VIN Code: L.

ENGINE [Optional V-8 (Maverick, Granada)]: 90-degree, overhead valve V-8. Cast-iron block and head. Displacement: 302 cid (5.0 liters). Bore & stroke: 4.00 x 3.00 in. Compression ratio: 8.0:1. Brake horsepower: 138 at 3600 rpm. (Granada, 134 at 3600). Torque: 245 lbs.-ft. at 2000 rpm. (Granada, 242 at 2000). Five main bearings. Hydraulic valve lifters. Carburetor: 2Bbl. Ford 2150A 9510. VIN Code: F.

ENGINE [Base V-8 (Torino, Elite, LTD); Optional (Granada)]: 90-degree, overhead valve V-8. Cast-iron block and head. Displacement: 351 cid (5.8 liters). Bore & stroke: 4.00 x 3.50 in. Compression ratio: 8.0:1. (Torino, 8.1:1). Brake horsepower: 152 at 3800 rpm. (Torino, 154 at 3400). Torque: 274 lbs.-ft. at 1600 rpm. (Torino, 286 at 1800). Five main bearings. Hydraulic valve lifters. Carburetor: 2Bbl. Ford 2150A. VIN Code: H.

ENGINE [Base V-8 (500/LTD wagon); Optional (Torino, Elite, LTD)]: 90-degree, overhead valve V-8. Cast-iron block and head. Displacement: 400 cid (6.6 liters). Bore & stroke: 4.00 x 4.00 in. Compression ratio: 8.0:1. Brake horsepower: 180 at 3800 rpm. Torque: 336 lbs.-ft. at 1800 rpm. Five main bearings. Hydraulic valve lifters. Carburetor: 2Bbl. Ford 2150A. VIN Code: S.

ENGINE [Base V-8 (Thunderbird); Optional (Torino, Elite, LTD)]: 90-degree, overhead valve V-8. Cast-iron block and head. Displacement: 460 cid (7.5 liters). Bore & stroke: 4.36 x 3.85 in. Compression ratio: 8.0:1. Brake horsepower: 202 at 3800 rpm. Torque: 352

lbs.-ft. at 1600 rpm. Five main bearings. Hydraulic valve lifters. Carburetor: 4Bbl. Motorcraft 9510 or Ford 4350A9510. VIN Code: A.

NOTE: A Police 460 cid V-8 was also available for LTD.

CHASSIS DATA: Wheelbase: (Pinto) 94.5 in.; (Pinto wag) 94.8 in.; (Maverick 2dr.) 103.0 in.; (Maverick 4dr.) 109.9 in.; (Granada) 109.9 in.; (Torino) 114.0 in.; (Torino 4 dr./wag) 118.0 in.; (Elite) 114.0 in.; (Custom 500/LTD) 121.0 in.; (TBird) 120.4 in.; Overall length: (Pinto) 169.0 in.; (Pinto wag) 178.8 in.; (Maverick 2dr.) 187.0 in.; (Maverick 4dr.) 193.9 in.; (Granada) 197.7 in.; (Torino 2dr.) 213.6 in.; (Torino 4dr) 217.6 in.; (Torino wag) 222.6 in.; (Elite) 216.1 in.; (LTD 2dr.) 223.9 in.; (LTD wag) 225.6 in.; (TBird) 225.7 in. Height: (Pinto) 50.6 in.; (Pinto wag) 52.0 in.; (Maverick) 52.9 in.; (Granada) 53.3-53.4 in.; (Torino 2dr.) 52.6 in.; (Torino 4dr.) 53.3 in.; (Torino wag) 54.9 in.; (Elite) 53.1 in.; (LTD 2dr.) 53.7 in.; (LTD 4dr.) 54.8 in.; (LTD wag) 56.7 in.; (TBird) 52.8 in. Width: (Pinto) 69.4 in.; (Pinto wag) 69.7 in.; (Maverick) 70.5 in.; (Granada) 74.0 in.; (Granada Ghia) 74.5 in.; (Torino) 79.3 in.; (Torino wag) 79.9 in.; (Elite) 78.5 in.; (LTD) 79.5 in.; (LTD wag) 79.9 in.; (TBird) 79.7 in. front Tread: (Pinto) 55.0 in.; (Maverick) 56.5 in.; (Granada) 58.5 in.; (Torino) 63.4 in. (Elite) 63.0 in.; (LTD) 64.1 in. (TBird) 62.9 in. Rear Tread: (Pinto) 55.8 in.; (Maverick) 56.5 in.; (Granada) 57.7 in.; (Torino) 63.5 in.; (Torino wag) 63.1 in.; (Elite) 3.1 in.; (LTD) 64.3 in. (TBird) 62.8 in. Standard Tires: (Pinto) A78 x 13 or B78 x 13; (Maverick) C78 x 14, except DR78 x 14 w/V-8 engine; (Granada) DR78 x 14; (Torino) HR78 x 14; (Elite) HR78 x 15; (LTD) HR78 x 15 exc. wagon. JR78 x 15; (TBird) JR78 x 15.

TECHNICAL: Transmission: Three-speed manual transmission (column shift) standard on Maverick/Granada. Gear ratios: (1st) 2.99:1; (2nd) 1.75:1; (3rd) 1.00:1; (Rev) 3.17:1. Four-speed floor shift standard on Pinto: (1st) 3.65:1; (2nd) 1.97:1; (3rd) 1.37:1; (4th) 1.00:1; (Rev) 3.66:1 or 3.95:1. Pinto station wagon: (1st) 4.07:1; (2nd) 2.57:1; (3rd) 1.66:1; (4th) 1.00:1; (Rev) 3.95:1. Select-Shift three-speed automatic standard on other models, optional on all; column lever but floor shift optional on Maverick, Granada, Torino and Elite (standard on Pinto). Pinto (L4140) automatic gear ratios: (1st 2.47:1; (2nd) 1.47:1; (3rd) 1.00:1; (Rev) 2.11:1. Pinto (V-6)/Maverick/Granada/Torino (V8351)/Elite (V8351) auto. gear ratios: (1st) 2.46:1; (2nd) 1.46:1; (3rd) 1.00:1; (Rev) 2.20:1. Torino/Elite/LTD/TBird (V8400/460): auto. (1st) 2.46:1; (2nd) 1.46:1; (3rd) 1.00:1; (Rev) 2.18:1. LTD (V8351): (1st) 2.40:1; (2nd) 1.47:1; (3rd) 1.00:1; (Rev) 2.00:1 Standard final drive ratio: (Pinto four) 3.18:1 w/4 spd. 3.18:1 or 3.40:1 w/auto.; (Pinto Pony) 3.00:1; (Pinto V-6) 3.40:1; (Maverick) 2.79:1; (Granada) 2.79:1 or 2.75:1 w/3spd and 2.75:1, 3.00:1 or 3.07:1 w/auto.; (Torino/Elite) 2.75:1; (LTD/T-Bird) 2.75:1 exc. Police 460 V-8, 3.00:1. Steering: (Pinto) rack and pinion; (others) recirculating ball. Front Suspension: (Pinto/Maverick/Granada) rigid axle w/semi-elliptic leaf springs; (Torino/Elite) rigid axle w/lower trailing arms, upper oblique torque arms and coil trailing links and anti-sway bar; (Torino/Elite/LTD/Thunderbird) coil springs with single lower control arm, lower trailing links, strut bar and anti-sway bar. Rear Suspension: (Pinto/Maverick/Granada) rigid axle w/semi elliptic leaf springs; (Torino/Elite) rigid axle w/lower trailing arms, upper oblique torque arms and coil springs; (LTD) rigid axle w/lower trailing radius arms, upper torque arms and coil springs, three-link w/track bar; (Thunderbird) "stabul" four-link system with coil springs and anti-sway bar. Brakes: front disc, rear drum; four-wheel discs available on Granada, LTD and Thunderbird. Ignition: Electronic. Body construction: (Pinto/Maverick/Granada) unibody; (Torino/Elite/LTD) separate body and perimeter box frame; (Thunderbird) separate body and perimeter frame with torque box. Fuel tank: (Pinto) 13 gal.; (Pinto wag) 14 gal.; (Maverick/Granada) 19.2 gal.; (Torino/Elite) 26.5 gal.; (Torino wag) 21.3 gal.; (LTD) 24.3 gal. exc. wagon. 21 gal.; (TBird) 26.5 gal.

DRIVETRAIN OPTIONS: Engines: 250 cid, 1Bbl. six: Maverick/Granada ($96). 302 cid, 2Bbl. V-8: Granada ($154); Granada Ghia ($88). 351 cid, 2Bbl. V-8: Granada ($200); Granada Ghia ($134). 400 cid, 2Bbl. V-8; Torino/Elite/LTD ($100). 460 cid, 4Bbl. V-8: Torino/Elite ($292); LTD ($353); LTD wagon ($251). Dual exhaust: TBird ($72). Transmission/Different: SelectShift Cruise-O-Matic: Pinto ($186); Maverick/Granada ($245). Floor shift lever: Maverick/Granada ($27). Traction-Lok differential: Granada ($48); Torino/Elite ($53); LTD ($54); TBird ($55). Optional axle ratio: Pinto/Maverick/Granada ($13); Torino/Elite/LTD/TBird ($14). Power Accessories: Power brakes: Pinto ($54); Maverick ($53); Granada ($57). Four-wheel power disc brakes: Granada ($210); LTD ($170); TBird ($184). Sure-Track brakes: Granada ($227); TBird ($378). Power steering: Pinto ($117); Maverick/Granada ($124). Suspension: H.D. susp.: Maverick ($16); Granada ($29); LTD ($18); TBird ($29). H.D. handling susp.: Torino ($18-$32); Elite ($92). Adjustable air shock absorbers: LTD ($43). Other: Engine block heater: Pinto/Maverick/Granada ($17); Torino/Elite/LTD/TBird ($18). H.D. battery: Maverick/Granada ($14); LTD ($17). H.D. electrical system: Torino ($29); Elite ($80). Extended-range fuel tank: LTD ($99). Trailer towing pkg. (light duty): Granada ($42); LTD ($53). Trailer towing pkg. (medium duty): Torino/Elite ($59); LTD ($46-$145). Trailer towing pkg. (heavy duty): Torino ($87-$121); Elite ($121); LTD ($132-230); TBird ($92). California emission system: Maverick/Granada ($46); Torino/Elite/LTD/TBird ($50). High-altitude option: Torino/Elite/LTD/TBird ($13).

1976 Ford Maverick Stallion coupe. (F)

PINTO CONVENIENCE/APPEARANCE OPTIONS: Option Packages: Stallion option ($283). Luxury decor group ($241). Convenience light group ($70-$102). Protection group ($73-$134). Comfort/Convenience: Air conditioner ($420). Rear defroster, electric ($70). Tinted glass ($46). Leather-wrapped steering wheel ($33). Dual color-keyed mirrors ($42). Entertainment: AM radio ($71); w/stereo tape player ($192). AM/FM radio ($129). AM/FM stereo radio ($173). Exterior: Sunroof, manual ($230). Half vinyl roof ($125). Metallic glow paint ($54). Roof luggage rack ($52-$75). Rocker panel moldings ($19). Wheels: Forged aluminum wheels ($82-$172). Styled steel wheels ($92-$119). Wheel covers ($28). Trim rings ($29). Tires: A78 x 13 WSW. A70 x 13 RWL. B78 x 13 BSW/WSW. BR78 x 13 SBR BSW/WSW. BR70 x 13 RWL.

MAVERICK CONVENIENCE/APPEARANCE OPTIONS: Option Packages: Stallion option ($329). Exterior decor group ($99). Interior decor group ($106). Luxury decor group ($508). Luxury interior decor ($217). Deluxe bumper group ($28-$61). Convenience group ($34-$64). Protection group ($24-$39). Light group ($22-$34). Security lock group ($16). Comfort/Convenience: Air cond. ($420). Rear defogger ($40). Tinted glass ($45-$59). Fuel monitor warning light ($18). Dual color-keyed mirrors ($13-$25). Entertainment: AM radio ($71); w/tape player ($192). AM/FM radio ($128). AM/FM stereo radio ($210); w/tape player ($299). Exterior: Vinyl roof ($94). Metallic glow paint ($54). Lower bodyside paint ($55). Bodyside or bodyside-roof accent paint stripe ($27). Decklid luggage rack ($51). Rocker panel moldings ($19). Bumper guards, front or rear ($17). Interior: Reclining bucket seats ($147). Cloth bucket seat trim ($24). Vinyl seat trim ($25). Color-keyed deluxe seatbelts ($17). Wheels: Forged aluminum wheels ($98-$187). Styled steel wheels ($59-$89). Hubcap trim rings ($35) except (NC) wit decor group. Tires: C78 x 14 WSW. BR78 x 14 BSW. CR78 x 14 BSW/WSW. DR78 x 14 BSW/WSW. DR70 x 14 RWL. Space-saver spare ($13) except (NC) with radial tires.

GRANADA CONVENIENCE/APPEARANCE OPTIONS: Option Packages: Sports sedan option ($482). Exterior decor group ($128). Interior decor group ($181). Luxury decor group ($642). Convenience group ($31-$75). Deluxe bumper group ($61). Light group ($25-$37). Protection group ($24-$39). Visibility group ($30-$47). Security lock group ($17). Comfort/Convenience: Air cond. ($437). Rear defogger ($43). Rear defroster, electric ($76). Fingertip speed control ($96). Power windows ($95-$133). Power door locks ($63-$88). Power four-way seat ($119). Tinted glass ($47). Leather-wrapped steering wheel ($14-$33). Luxury steering wheel ($18). Tilt steering wheel ($54). Fuel monitor warning light ($18). Digital clock ($40). Horns and Mirrors: Dual-note horn ($6). Color-keyed outside mirrors ($29-$42). Lighted visor vanity mirror ($40). Entertainment: AM radio ($71); w/tape player ($192). AM/FM radio ($142). AM/FM stereo radio ($210); w/tape player ($299). Exterior: Power moonroof ($786). Power sunroof ($517). Vinyl or half vinyl roof ($102). Metallic glow paint ($54). Bodyside/decklid paint stripes ($27). Bodyside/decklid accent moldings ($28). Black vinyl insert bodyside moldings. ($35). Rocker panel moldings ($19). Decklid luggage rack ($51). Interior: Console ($65). Reclining seats ($60). Leather seat trim ($181). Deluxe cloth seat trim ($88). Trunk carpeting ($20). Trunk dress-up ($33). Color-keyed seatbelts ($17). Wheels: Styled steel wheels ($41-$60); w/trim rings ($76-$95). Lacy spoke aluminum wheels ($112-$207). Tires: E78 x 14 BSW/WSW. DR78 x 14 WSW. ER78 x 14 BSW/WSW. FR78 x 14 BSW/WSW. Space-saver spare (NC).

1976 Ford Gran Torino Brougham four-door pillared hardtop. (F)

1976 Ford Granada sedan (with Exterior Decor Group option). (OCW)

1976 Ford Thunderbird two-door hardtop. (F)

TORINO/ELITE CONVENIENCE/APPEARANCE OPTIONS: Option Packages: Squire Brougham option: Torino ($184). Interior decor group: Elite ($384). Accent group: Torino ($45). Deluxe bumper group ($50-$67). Light group ($41-$43). Convenience group: Torino ($33-$84); Elite ($49). Protection group ($26-$42). Security lock group ($18). Comfort/Convenience: Auto-temp control air cond. ($88). Anti-theft alarm system ($84). Rear defroster, electric ($99). Windshield/rear window defroster, Power windows ($104-$145). Power tailgate window: Torino wag ($43). Power door locks ($68-$109). Electric decklid release ($17). Six-way power seat ($130). Automatic seatback release ($30). Reclining passenger seat ($70). Leather-wrapped steering wheel ($36). Luxury steering wheel ($20). Tilt steering wheel ($59). Fuel sentry vacuum gauge ($13-$32). Fuel monitor warning light ($20). Electric clock: Torino ($18). Horns and Mirrors: Dual-note horn ($7). Remote driver's mirror, chrome ($14). Remote-control color-keyed mirrors ($32-$46). Lighted visor vanity mirror ($43). Entertainment: Am radio ($78). AM/FM stereo radio ($229); w/tape player ($326). AM/FM stereo search radio: Elite ($386). Dual rear speakers ($39). Exterior: Power moonroof: Elite ($859). Power sunroof ($545). Vinyl roof: Torino ($112); Elite (NC). Opera windows: Torino ($50). Fender skirts: Torino ($41). Rocker panel moldings ($26). Vinyl-insert bodyside moldings: Torino ($38). Metallic glow paint ($59). Dual accent paint stripes ($29). Bumper guards, front or rear: Torino ($18). Luggage rack: Torino ($82-$91). Interior; Bucket seats ($146) exc. Elite w/decor group (NC). Rear-facing third seat: Torino wag ($104). Vinyl bench seat trim: Torino ($22). Pleated vinyl bench seat trim ($22-$28). Duraweave vinyl seat trim: Torino ($55). Vinyl split bench seat: Torino (NC). Color-keyed seatbelts ($18). Trunk trim ($36). Wheels; Deluxe wheel covers: Torino ($37). Luxury wheel covers ($58-$95). Wire wheel covers: Elite ($99). Magnum 500 wheels w/trim rings: Torino ($141-$178). Turbine spoke cast aluminum wheels: Elite ($226). Torino Tires: H78 x 14 BSW/WSW. HR78 x 14 WSW. HR78 x 14 six-ply BSW/WSW. JR78 x 14 WSW. HR78 x 15 BSW/WSW. Space-saver spare (NC). Elite Tires: HR78 x 15 SBR WSW ($39). HR70 x 15 SBR WSW ($59). Space-saver spare (NC).

LTD CONVENIENCE/APPEARANCE OPTIONS: Option Packages: Landau luxury group ($472-$708). Brougham option: wagon ($396); Squire ($266). Harmony color group ($99). Convenience group ($97-$104). Light group ($76-$79). Deluxe bumper group ($41-$59). Protection group ($47-$78). Security lock group ($18). Comfort/Convenience: Air cond. ($353); w/auto-temp control ($486). Anti-theft alarm system ($566). Rear defogger ($43). Rear defroster, electric ($83). Fingertip speed control ($87-$107). Power windows ($108-$161). Power mini-vent and side windows ($232). Power door locks ($68-$109). Six-way power driver's seat ($132); driver and passenger ($259). Automatic seatback release ($30). Tinted glass ($64). Luxury steering wheel ($20). Tilt steering wheel ($59). Fuel monitor warning light ($20). Electric clock ($18). Digital clock ($25-$43). Lighting, Horns and Mirrors: Cornering lamps ($43). Dual-note horn ($6). Driver's remote mirror ($14). Entertainment: AM radio ($78). AM/FM stereo radio ($229); w/tape player ($326). AM/FM stereo search radio ($386). Dual rear speakers ($39). Exterior: Sunroof, manual ($632). Full vinyl roof ($126) exc. wagon ($151) and Brougham/Landau two-door (NC). Half vinyl roof ($126). Fender skirts ($42). Metallic glow paint ($59). Dual accent paint stripes ($29). Rocker panel moldings ($26). Vinyl-insert bodyside moldings ($41). Rear bumper guards ($18). Luggage rack ($82-$96). Interior: Dual-facing rear seats: wagon ($126). Split bench seat w/passenger recliner ($222). Leather interior trim ($141). All-vinyl seat ($22). Duraweave vinyl trim ($55). Recreation table ($58). Color-keyed seatbelts ($18). Deluxe cargo area ($83-$126). Lockable side stowage compartment ($43). Luggage area trim ($36). Wheels; Full wheel covers ($30). Deluxe wheel covers ($63-$93). Tires: H78 x 15 BSW/WSW. J78 x 15 BSW/WSW. HR78 x 15 WSW. JR78 x 15 BSW/WSW. LR78 x 15 BSW/WSW.

THUNDERBIRD CONVENIENCE/APPEARANCE OPTIONS: Option Packages: Bordeaux luxury group ($624-$700). Creme/gold luxury group ($717-$793). Lipstick luxury group ($337-$546). Turnpike group ($180). Convenience group ($84). Protection group ($79-$87). Light group ($164). Power lock group ($86). Security lock group ($18). Comfort/Convenience: Auto-temp control air cond. ($88). Anti-theft alarm system ($84). Rear defroster, electric ($99). Windshield/rear window defroster, electric ($355). Fingertip speed control ($120). Tinted glass ($29-$66). Power mini-vent windows ($79). Six-way power driver's seat ($132); driver and passenger ($250). Power lumber support seats ($86). Reclining passenger seat ($70). Automatic seatback release ($30). Tilt steering wheel ($68). Fuel monitor warning light ($20). Lighting and Mirrors: Cornering lamps ($43). Lighted driver's visor vanity mirror ($43). Entertainment: AM/FM stereo radio ($145); w/tape player ($249). AM/FM stereo search radio ($298). AM/FM quadrasonic radio w/tape player ($382). Power antenna ($39). Exterior: Power moonroof ($879); sunroof ($716). Starfire paint ($204). Wide color-keyed vinyl-insert bodyside molding ($121). Dual bodyside/hood paint stripes ($33). Interior: Leather trim ($239). Kasman cloth trim ($96). Super-soft vinyl seat trim ($55). Trunk dress-up ($59). Wheels: Deluxe wheel covers ($67). Simulated wire wheel covers ($88) exc. with creme/gold group ($163 credit). Deep-dish aluminum wheels ($251) exc. with Bordeaux/lipstick luxury group ($163). Tires: JR78 x 15 SBR WSW ($41). LR78 x 15 SBR wide WSW ($59). Space-saver spare ($86).

HISTORY: Introduced: October 3, 1975. Model year production: 1,861,537 (incl. Mustangs). Total production for the U.S. market of 1,714,258 units. (incl. Mustangs) consisted of 342,434 four-cylinder, 390,750 sixes and 981,074 V-8s. Calendar year production (U.S.): 1,459,109 (incl. Mustangs). Calendar year sales by U.S. dealers: 1,682,583 (incl. Mustangs); total sales gave Ford a 19.9 percent share of the market. Model year sales by U.S. dealers: N/A.

NOTE: Totals do not include Club Wagons.

HISTORY: Ford sales had declined sharply in the 1975 model year, down over 21 percent. That left Ford with only a 22 percent market share. Full-size models had sold best. Even the success of the Granada (new for 1975) wasn't as great as anticipated. Continuing their interest in small, economical cars, Ford had introduced Pinto Pony and Mustang II MPG models late in the 1975 model year. Sales swung upward again for the 1976 model year, even though few major changes were evident in the lineup. Part of the reason was Ford's new "California strategy," which offered special option packages for West Coast buyers only, in an attempt to take sales away from the imports. It proved quite successful this year. Prices took a sizable jump as the model year began, then were cut back in January. Production fell for Pinto, Mustang II and Maverick in the 1976 model year, but overall production zoomed up almost 19 percent - especially due to Granada demand. Model year sales followed a similar pattern, up 18.5 percent for the year. Major changes in Ford personnel had taken place late in the 1975 model year. Henry Ford II, Lee Iacocca and B.E. Bidwell were the top Ford executives. Pinto was once described as "a car nobody loved, but everybody bought." This was the last year of the allegedly unsafe Pinto gas tank and filler neck, which had resulted in a number of highly publicized and grotesque accident-caused fires that led to massive product-liability lawsuits. The new Maverick Stallion was meant to look like a '60s muscle car, but offered no more performance than other Mavericks. Granada, on the other hand, had proven to be one of the fastest Fords, at least with a "Windsor" 351 cid V-8 under its hood.

1977 FORD

Biggest news for 1977 was the downsizing of Thunderbird (which had actually grown a bit in the past few years). Torino and Elite were dropped, and Pinto restyled with a sportier look. Maverick hung on for one more season without change, and nothing dramatic happened to

Granada or LTD. Later in the model year, though, a new A bodied LTD II replaced the abandoned Torino. On the mechanical side, Dura-Spark ignition was supposed to help meet the more stringent emissions standards.

PINTO — FOUR/V-6 — Revised front and rear styling hit Ford's subcompact, offered again in two-door sedan, "three-door" Runabout and station wagon form. Up front was a new "soft" nose with sloping hood and flexible fender extension and store deflector assembly. The new horizontal-bar crosshatch grille, made of rigid plastic, tilted backward. Twin vertical rectangular park/signal lamps stood on each side of the bright grille, with recessed round headlamps at the outside. Soft urethane headlamp housings were taller than before, but the grille itself was narrower. As in the previous design. 'Ford' letters stood above the grille. At the rear of the two-door sedan and three-door Runabout were new, larger horizontal dual-lens tail lamps. New extruded anodized aluminum bumpers went on the front and rear. New body colors were added, and a new vinyl roof grain was available. Runabouts had a new optional all-glass third door. Inside was new cloth trim, optional on the base high-back bucket seats. A new lower (2.73:1) rear axle ratio went with the standard OHC 140 cid (2.3-liter) four-cylinder engine, which hooked up to a wide-ratio four-speed manual gearbox. The low-budget Pony came with rack-and-pinion steering, front disc brakes, all-vinyl or cloth/vinyl high-back front bucket seats, mini-console, color-keyed carpeting, and argent hubcaps. The base two-door sedan included a color-keyed instrument panel and steering wheel, bright backlight trim, plus bright drip and belt moldings. Runabouts had a fold-down rear seat, rear liftgate, and rubber mat on the loaded floor. All models except the Pony could have a 170.8 cid (2.8-liter) V-6 instead of the four. Pinto got a shorter manual-transmission shift lever to speed up gear-changes. A new Sports option included a tachometer, ammeter and temperature gauge, new soft-rim spots steering wheel, front stabilizer bar, higher-rate springs, and higher axle ratio. A new Cruising Wagon, styled along the lines of the Econoline Cruising Van, aimed at youthful buyers. It included a front spoiler, blanked rear quarters with glass portholes, styled wheels, Sports Rallye equipment, and carpeted rear section. Other major new options included a flip-up removable sunroof, manual four-way bucket seat, Runabout cargo area cover, two-tone paint, simulated wire wheel covers, and high-altitude option. An Interior Decor Group included Alpine cloth plaid trim on low-back bucket seats.

MAVERICK — SIX/V-8 — For its final season, Maverick changed little except for some new body and interior colors, two new vinyl roof colors, and a new vinyl-insert bodyside molding. New options included wire wheel covers, four-way manual bucket seats, and high-altitude option. The optional 302 V-8 got a new variable-Venturi carburetor. All engines gained Dura-Spark ignition. There was also a new wide-ratio three-speed manual shift. Revised speedometers showed miles and kilometers. The Decor Group added a halo vinyl roof. Standard powerplant was the 200 cid (3.3-liter) six; optional, either a 250 cid six or 302 cid V-8. Standard equipment included front disc brakes (manual), three-speed column-shift manual transmission, foot parking brake with warning light, and 19.2-gallon gas tank. The full-width bench seat had Random stripe cloth and vinyl trim. Also standard: color-keyed carpeting; armrests with door pull assist handle; flip-open rear quarter windows; bright hubcaps; and bright drip rail and wheel lip moldings.

1977 Ford Pinto three-door Runabout (with optional wire wheels). (F)

1977 Ford Pinto two-door runabout. (OCW)

1977 Ford Maverick coupe. (F)

1977 Ford Maverick sedan. (OCW)

GRANADA — SIX/V-8 — Styling of the Mercedes-emulating Granada remained similar to 1976, with nine new body colors available. According to Ford's catalog, that carryover design "Looks like cars costing three times as much." A new full-synchronized four-speed manual transmission with overdrive fourth gear became standard, replacing the former three-speed. That made Granada the first domestic model to offer an overdrive four-speed as standard equipment (except in California, where it was unavailable). Actually, it was the old three-speed gearbox with an extra gear hooked on. Base engine was the 200 cid (3.3-liter) inline six with Dura-Spark ignition. Also standard were front disc brakes, inside hood release, wiper/washer control on the turn signal lever. DR78 x 14 steel-belted radial tires, hood ornament, vinyl-trim bench seats, cigar lighter, and full wheel covers. Two-doors displayed opera lamps. Granada Ghia added a left-hand emote-control mirror, wide color-keyed vinyl-insert bodyside moldings (integral with wheel lip moldings), flight bench seats, and unique wire-style wheel covers. Alternate engine choices were the 250 cid inline six, 302 V-8 and 351 V-8. A new variable-Venturi carburetor for the 302 V-8 was used only in California. Four basic models were offered: Granada and Ghia two- and four-door sedans. A Sport Coupe package with Odense-grain half-vinyl roof became available later. It included white-painted styled steel wheels with bright trim rings, louvered opera window appliqué, color-keyed lower back panel appliqué, and rubber bumper guards (front/rear) with wide rub strips. Sport Coupes also had new taillamp lenses with black surround moldings; black wiper arms and window moldings; color-keyed sport mirrors; leather-wrapped sports steering wheel; and reclining bucket seats in simulated perforated vinyl. New Granada options included four-way manual bucket seats, automatic-temperature-control air conditioning, illuminated entry, front cornering lamps, simulated wire wheel covers, white lacy-spoke cast aluminum wheels, wideband whitewall radials, electric trunk lid release, and high-altitude option.

1977 Ford Granada Sports Coupe. (F)

1977 Ford Granada sedan. (JG)

1977-1/2 Ford Granada Sports Coupe (with opera-window louvers). (PH)

LTD II — V-8 — Serving as a replacement for the abandoned Torino, the new A-bodied LTD II had similar dimensions, and long-hood styling that wasn't radically different. Wheelbase was 114 inches for the two-door, 118 inches for four-door models. Overall length ranged from 215.5 to 223.1 inches. The goal, according to Ford, was to combine "LTD's traditional high level of workmanship with Mustang's sporty spirit." A wide choice of models was offered: 'S', base and Brougham in two-door hardtop, four-door pillared hardtop or four-door wagon body styles (same selection as Torino). Wagons were offered only this year, and LTD II would last only into the 1979 model year. Among the more noticeable styling features were vertically-stacked quad rectangular headlamps, and doors with a straight beltline. Sharply-tapered opera windows on wide roof pillars stood to the rear of (and higher than) the regular quarter windows of two-doors (except for the 'S' model). Four-doors were also a six-window design. Wraparound parking/signal lamps were fendertip-mounted, and the hood ornament was new. The chrome-plated grille had a crosshatch pattern similar to the full-size LTD, but with a sharper peak. Angled, sharp-edged wraparound vertical tail lamps stood at rear quarter panel tips. Inside, LTD II had new seat trim and new styles, plus new-look door trim and instrument cluster. Standard engine dropped from the 351 of the last Torino to a 302 V-8, now with Dura-Spark ignition and a lower axle ratio. Standard equipment on the budget-priced 'S' included Select-Shift automatic transmission; power brakes and steering; coolant recovery system; and Kirsten cloth/vinyl bench seat. The basic LTD II had Ardmore cloth/vinyl flight bench seat, deluxe door trim, rear panel appliqué, hood ornament, and rocker panel and wheel lip moldings. The top-line Brougham added Doral cloth/vinyl split bench seats, dual horns, electric clock, dual accent paint stripes, and wide color-keyed vinyl-insert bodyside moldings. Standard engine was the 302 cid V-8 with two-barrel carb (351 in California) hooked to SelectShift Cruise-O-Matic. Important new options included the opera windows, illuminated entry, day/date quartz clock, sports steering wheel, cornering lamps, monaural AM/FM radio, stereo radio with quadrasonic tape player, wide whitewall radials, wire wheel covers, and (for two-doors) a half-vinyl roof. Announced for mid-year introduction was a Brougham Creme/Blue package, offered in Creme or dark blue metallic body color with creme or blue vinyl roof. Creme vinyl split-bench seats had blue accent straps and welts.

LTD/CUSTOM 500 — V-8 — Rivals may have shrunk their big cars, but Ford's remained fully full-size once again. According to the factory, that gave LTD a "wider stance, and more road-hugging weight." New colors and fabrics entered LTD interiors this year, but not much else was different. Powertrain changes included improved 351 and 400 cid V-8s with new Dura-Spark ignition, as well as lower rear axle ratios and standard coolant recovery system. New options included illuminated entry, quadrasonic tape player, simulated wire wheel covers, forged aluminum wheels, and wide whitewall radial tires. LTD Brougham was dropped, but the top-rung Landau model took over its position in the pricing lineup. Six basic models were available: LTD and Landau two-and four-door, LTD wagon, and Country Squire wagon. As in 1976, the Custom 500 was for fleet buyers only. LTD's front end looked similar to 1976. A crosshatch grille had four horizontal divider bars and 15 vertical bars, with 'Ford' block letters across the upper header. Three-section wraparound parking/signal lamps stood at fender tips. Standard LTD equipment included a 351 cid (5.8-liter) V-8 with Dura-Spark ignition, SelectShift automatic transmission, power brakes and steering, front bumper guards, Redondo cloth/vinyl bench seat, glovebox and ashtray lamps, hood ornament, and bright hubcaps. Vinyl-insert moldings highlighted door belt, drip, hood, rear, rocker panels, and wheel lips. Landau models added concealed headlamps, as well as an Ardmore cloth/vinyl flight bench seat, electric clock, half or full vinyl roof, rear bumper guards, full wheel covers, wide color-keyed bodyside moldings, and dual-note horn. A Landau Creme and Blue package was announced for mid-year, with choice of color combinations. Creme body color came with a creme or blue vinyl roof; dark blue body with creme or blue vinyl roof. Inside was a creme super-soft vinyl luxury group, and split bench seats with blue welts.

THUNDERBIRD — V-8 — All-new sheetmetal and sharp downsizing to a 114 inch wheelbase helped conceal the fact that the shrunken Thunderbird was essentially an adaptation of the newly-introduced LTD II. Even if buyers noticed, they might not have cared, since T-Bird's price was also sharply cut by about $2700 from its 1976 level. However, this Thunderbird had less standard equipment and more options than before. Overall length was cut by 10 inches in this new "contemporary" package, ranking as mid-rather than full-size, but with the same six-passenger capacity. This year's side view was much different. A chrome wrapover roof molding with little beveled-glass opera windows stood on the wide, solid B-pillars between the door window and large far-rear coach window, with thin C-pillar. Both of those rear side windows sat higher than the door window. Distinctive features also included concealed headlamps behind large flip-up doors, and functional fender louvers. The chrome-plated crosshatch grille with bright surround design was similar to the prior design, but with dominant horizontal bars. Park/signal lenses stood at front fender tips. At the rear were new tall, full-width tail lamps and a sculptured decklid. A 'Thunderbird' nameplate stood on the deck section that extended down between the tail lamps. The hinged grille's lower edge was designed to swing rearward under impact, to avoid damage from slow-speed collision. A smaller engine was installed this year: the 302 cid (5.0-liter) V-8 with new Dura-Spark ignition; but California buyers got a 351 V-8. Both the 351 and 400 cid V-8s were optional. To improve handling, Thunderbird had higher-rate rear springs, larger front stabilizer bar, and standard rear stabilizer bar. Standard fittings included HR78x15 steel-belted radial tires, SelectShift automatic transmission, power steering and brakes, coolant recovery system, Wilshire cloth/vinyl bench seats, AM radio, electric clock, wheel covers, and hood ornament. Moldings for roof wrapover, wheel lips, rocker panels, hood rear, and belt also were standard. Inside was a new five-pod instrument cluster with European-type graphics and simulated burled woodgrain. Sew style of the standard bench seat was new, with optional split-bench and bucket seats. Town Landau added an aluminum roof wrapover appliqué; unique stripes on upper bodysides, hood/grille opening panel, headlamp doors and decklid; accent paint on wheels and fender louvers; die-cast hood ornament with color-coordinated acrylic insert; and 'Town Landau' script silk-screened on opera windows. Also included: turbine-spoke cast aluminum wheels, dual sport mirrors, cornering lamps. Town Landau plaque at the right of the instrument panel, and an owner's nameplate in 22K gold finish. Major new options included an illuminated entry system, day/date quartz clock, leather-wrapped sports steering wheel, console, turbine-style cast aluminum wheels, automatic-temperature air conditioning, and front and rear vinyl roof. An optional Exterior Decor Group could accent T-Bird's wrapover roof treatment. An Interior Decor Group contained Aardmore and Kasman Knit cloth upholstery, fold-down center armrests, reclining passenger seat, passenger visor vanity mirror, and color-keyed seatbelts. A Silver/Lipstick feature package, announced for mid-year, featured Silver metallic or Lipstick Red body color with Silver or Lipstick Red vinyl roof. Inside was a Dove Gray all-vinyl decor group with either split-bench or bucket seats, with Lipstick Red accent straps and welts. Dove Gray door and quarter trim, and Lipstick carpet molding.

1977 Ford LTD Landau four-door pillared hardtop. (F)

1977 Ford LTD II hardtop coupe. (F)

I.D. DATA: As before, Ford's 11-symbol Vehicle Identification Number (VIN) is stamped on a metal tab fastened to the instrument panel, visible through the windshield. Coding is similar to 1976. Model year code changed to '7' for 1977. Code 'Y' for Wixom assembly plant was dropped. One engine code was added: 'Q' modified V8-351 2Bbl.

PINTO (FOUR/V-6)

Model No.	Body/ Style No.	Body Type & Seating	Factory Price	Shipping Weight	Prod. Total
10	62B	2-dr. Sedan-4P	3237/3519	2315/2438	48,863
10	62B	2-dr. Pony Sed-4P	3099/----	2313/----	Note 1
11	64B	2-dr. Hatch-4P	3353/3635	2351/2414	74,237
12	73B	2-dr. Sta. Wag-4P	3548/3830	2515/2638	79,449
12	73B	2-dr. Sqr Wag-4P	3891/4172	2552/2675	Note 2

NOTE 1: Pony production included in base sedan figure.

NOTE 2: Squire Wagon production is included in standard station wagon total.

PINTO PRODUCTION NOTE: Totals include 22,548 Pintos produced as 1978 models but sold as 1977 models (6,599 two-door sedans, 8,271 hatchback Runabouts and 7,678 station wagons).

MAVERICK (SIX/V-8)

91	62A	2-dr. Sedan-4P	3322/3483	2782/2947	40,086
92	54A	4-dr. Sedan-5P	3395/3556	2887/3052	58,420

GRANADA (SIX/V-8)

82	66H	2-dr. Sedan-5P	4022/4209	3124/3219	157,612
81	54H	4-dr. Sedan-5P	4118/4305	3174/3269	163,071

GRANADA GHIA (SIX/V-8)

84	66K	2-dr. Sedan-5P	4452/4639	3175/3270	34,166
83	54K	4-dr. Sedan-5P	4548/4735	3229/3324	35,730

1977 Ford LTD II Brougham pillared hardtop. (OCW)

LTD II (V-8)

30	65D	2-dr. HT Cpe-6P	4785	3789	57,449
31	53D	4-dr. Pill. HT-6P	4870	3904	56,704
42	71D	4-dr. Sta Wag-6P	5064	4404	23,237
43	71K	4-dr. Squire Wag-6P	5335	4430	17,162

LTD II 'S' (V-8)

Model No.	Body/ Style No.	Body Type & Seating	Factory Price	Shipping Weight	Prod. Total
25	65B	2-dr. HT Cpe-6P	4528	3789	9,531
27	53B	4-dr. Pill. HT-6P	4579	3894	18,775
40	71B	4-dr. Sta Wag-6P	4,806	4393	9,636

LTD II BROUGHAM (V-8)

32	65K	2-dr. HT Cpe-6P	5121	3898	20,979
33	53K	4-dr. Pill. HT-6P	5206	3930	18,851

CUSTOM 500 (V-8)

52	60D	2-dr. Pill. HT-6P	N/A	N/A	4,139
53	53D	4-dr. Pill. HT-6P	N/A	N/A	5,582
72	71D	4-dr. Ranch Wag-6P	N/A	N/A	1,406

LTD (V-8)

62	60H	2-dr. Pill. HT-6P	5128	4190	73,637
63	53H	4-dr. Pill. HT-6P	5152	4240	160,255
74	71H	4-dr. Sta Wag-6P	5415	4635	90,711
76	71K	4-dr. Ctry Sqr-6P	5866	4674	Note 3

NOTE 3: Country Squire production, and that of wagons with dual-facing rear seats (a $134 option for both standard and Country Squire wagon), is included in basic wagon totals.

LTD LANDAU (V-8)

65	60L	2-dr. Pill. HT-6P	5717	4270	44,396
64	53L	4-dr. Pill. HT-6P	5742	4319	65,030

THUNDERBIRD (V-8)

87	60H	2-dr. HT Cpe-6P	5063	3907	318,140

THUNDERBIRD TOWN LANDAU (V-8)

87	60H	2-dr. HT Cpe-6P	7990	4104	Note 4

NOTE 4: Town Landau production is included in basic Thunderbird total.

FACTORY PRICE AND WEIGHT NOTE: For Maverick and Granada, prices and weights to left of slash are for six-cylinder, to right for V-8 engine. For Pinto, prices and weights to left of slash are for four-cylinder, to right for V-6 engine.

ENGINE [Base Four (Pinto)]: Inline. Overhead cam. Four-cylinder. Cast-iron block and head. Displacement: 140 cid (2.3 liters). Bore & stroke: 3.78 x 3.13 in. Compression ratio: 9.0:1. Brake horsepower: 89 at 4800 rpm. Torque: 120 lbs.-ft. at 3000 rpm. Five main bearings. Hydraulic valve lifters. Carburetor: 2Bbl. Motorcraft 5200. VIN Code: Y.

ENGINE [Optional V-6 (Pinto)]: 60-degree, overhead-valve V-6. Cast-iron block and head. Displacement: 170.8 cid (2.8 liters). Bore & stroke: 3.66 x 2.70 in. Compression ratio: 8.7:1. Brake horsepower: 93 at 4200 rpm. Torque: 140 lbs.-ft. at 2600 rpm. Four main bearings. Solid valve lifters. Carburetor: 2Bbl. Motorcraft 2150. VIN Code: Z.

ENGINE [Base Six (Maverick, Granada)]: Inline. Overhead valve. Six-cylinder. Cast-iron block and head. Displacement: 200 cid (3.3 liters). Bore & stroke: 3.68 x 3.13 in. Compression ratio: 8.5:1. Brake horsepower: 96 at 4400 rpm. Torque: 151 lbs.-ft. at 2000 rpm. Seven main bearings. Hydraulic valve lifters. Carburetor: 1Bbl. Carter YFA. VIN Code: T.

ENGINE [Base Six (Granada Ghia); Optional (Maverick, Granada)]: Inline. Overhead valve. Six-cylinder. Cast-iron block and head. Displacement: 250 cid (4.1 liters). Bore & stroke: 3.68 x 3.91 in. Compression ratio: 8.1:1. Brake horsepower: 98 at 3400 rpm. Torque: 182 lbs.-ft. at 1800 rpm. Seven main bearings. Hydraulic valve lifters. Carburetor: 1Bbl. Carter YFA. VIN Code: L.

ENGINE [Base V-8 (LTD II, Thunderbird); Optional (Maverick, Granada)]: 90-degree, overhead valve V-8. Cast-iron block and head. Displacement: 302 cid (5.0 liters). Bore & stroke: 4.00 x 3.00 in. Compression ratio: 8.4:1. Brake horsepower: 130-137 at 3400-3600 rpm. (some Granadas, 122 at 3200). Torque: 243-245 lbs.-ft. at 1600-1800 rpm. (some Granadas, 237 at 1600). Five main bearings. Hydraulic valve lifters. Carburetor: 2Bbl. Motorcraft 2150. VIN code: F.

NOTE: Horsepower and torque ratings of the 302 V-8 varied slightly, according to model.

ENGINE [Optional V-8 (LTD II. Thunderbird)]: 90-degree, overhead valve V-8, Cast-iron block and head. Displacement: 351 cid (5.8 liters). Bore & stroke: 4.00 x 3.50 in. Compression ratio: 8.3:1. Brake horsepower: 149 at 3200 rpm. Torque: 291 lbs.-ft. at 1600 rpm. Five main bearings. Hydraulic valve lifters. Carburetor: 2Bbl. Motorcraft 2150. Windsor engine. VIN Code: H.

1977 Ford Thunderbird Town Landau hardtop coupe. (F)

ENGINE [Optional V-8 (Granada)]: Same as 351 cid V-8 above, but Brake H.P.: 135 at 3200 rpm. Torque: 275 lbs.-ft. 1600 rpm.

ENGINE [V-8 (LTD II wagon, LTD); Optional (Granada Ghia, LTD II. Thunderbird)]: Same as 351 cid V-8 above, but Compression: 8.0:1. Brake H.P.: 161 at 3600 rpm. Torque: 285 lbs.-ft. at 1800 rpm. VIN Code: Q.

ENGINE [Base V-8 (LTD wagon): Optional (LTD II. Thunderbird, LTD)]: 90-dgree, overhead valve V-8. Cast-iron block and head. Displacement: 400 cu. in (6.6 liters). Bore & stroke: 4.00 x 4.00 in. Compression ratio: 8:0.1. Brake horsepower: 173 at 3800 rpm. Torque: 326 lb. at 1600 rpm. Five main bearings. Hydraulic valve lifters. Carburetor: 2Bbl. Motorcraft 2150. VIN Code: S.

ENGINE [Optional V-8 (LTD)]: 90-degree, overhead valve V-8. Cast-iron block and head. Displacement: 460 cu. in (7.5 liters). Bore & stroke: 4.36 x 3.85 in. Compression ratio: 8.0:1. Brake horsepower: 197 at 4000 rpm. Torque: 353 lbs.-ft. at 2000 rpm. Five main bearings. Hydraulic valve lifters. Carburetor: 4Bbl. Motorcraft 4350. VIN Code: A.

NOTE: A Police 460 cid V-8 was also available for LTD.

CHASSIS DATA: Wheelbase: (Pinto) 94.5 in.: (Pinto wag) 94.8 in.: (Maverick 2 dr.) 103.0 in.: (Maverick 4 dr.) 109.9 in.: (Granada) 109.9 in.: (LTD II 2 dr.) 1140.0 in: (LTD II 4 dr./wag) 118.0 in.: (Custom 500/LTD) 121.0 in.: (TBird) in. Overall Length: (Pinto) 169.0 in.: (Pinto wag) 178.8 in.: (Maverick 2 dr.) 187.0 in.: (Maverick 4 dr.) 193.9 in. (Granada) 197.7 in. (LTD II 2 dr.) 215.5 in.: (LTD II 4 dr.) 219.5 in.: (LTD II wag) 223.1 in. (LTD) 224.1 in.: (LTD wag) 225.6 in.: (TBird) 215.5 in. Height: (Pinto) 50.6 in.: (Pinto wag) 52.0 in.: (Maverick) 53.4-53.5 in.: (Granada 53.2-53.5 in.: (LTD II 2dr.) 52.6 in.: (LTD II 4dr.) 53.3 in.: (LTD II wag) 54.9 in.: (LTD 2dr.) 53.8 in.: (LTD 4dr.) 54.8 in.: (LTD wag) 56.7 in.: (TBird) 53.0 in. Width: (Pinto) 69.4 in.: (Pinto wag) 69.7 in.: (Maverick) 70.5 in.: (Granada) 74.0 in.: (Granada 4dr.) 74.5 in.: (LTD II) 78.0 in.: (LTD II wag) 79.6 in.: (LTD) 79.5 in.: (LTD wag) 79.9 in.: (TBird) 78.5 in. Front Tread: (Pinto 55.0 in.: (Maverick) 56.5 in.: (Granada) 59.0 in.: (LTD II) 63.6 in. (LTD) 64.1 in. (TBird) 63.2 in. Rear Tread (Pinto) 55.8 in.: (Maverick) 56.5 in.: (Granada) 57.7 in. (LTD 63.5 in.: (LTD) 64.3 in. (TBird) 63.1 in. Standard Tires: (Pinto) A78 x 13; Maverick C78 x 14, except DR78 x 14 w/V-8 engine: (Granada) DR78 x 14 SBR BSW; (LTD II) HR78 x 14 SBR; (LTD) HR 78 x 15 exc. wagon, JR78 x 15; (TBird) HR 78 x 15 SBR BSW.

TECHNICAL: Transmission: Three-speed manual transmission (column shift) standard on Maverick. Gear ratios: (1st) 3.56:1; (2nd) 1.90:1 (3rd) 1.00:1; (Rev) 3.78:1 Four-Speed overdrive manual standard on Granada: (1st) 3.29:1; (2nd) 1.84:1; (3rd) 1.00:1; (4th) 0.81:1; (Rev) 3.29.1. Four-speed floor shift standard on Pinto: (1st) 3.98:1; (2nd) 2.14:1 (3rd) 2.14:1; (4th) 1.00:1; (Rev) 3.99:1 Pinto station wagon: (1st) 3.65:1; (2nd) 1.97:1; (3rd) 1.37:1; (4th) 1.00:1; (Rev) 3.66:1. Select-Shift three-speed automatic standard on other models, optional on all. Pinto automatic gear ratios: (1st) 2.46-2.47:1; (2nd) 1.46-1.47.1; (3rd) 1.00:1; (Rev) 2.11:1 or 2.19:1. Maverick/Granada/LTD II/LTD/TBird gear ratios: (1st) 2.46:1; (2nd) 1.46:1; (3rd) 1.00:1; (Rev) 2.14:1 to 2.19:1. LTD II/LTD/TBird w/V8351 or V8400: (1st) 2.40:1; (2nd) 1.47:1; (3rd) 1.00:1; (Rev) 2.00:1. Standard final drive ratio: (Pinto four) 2.73:1 w/4spd, 3.18:1 w/auto.: (Pinto V-6) 3.00:1; (Maverick) 2.79:1 or 3.00:1; (Granada) 3.00:1 or 3.4.1: (LTD 11) 2.50:1; (LTD) 2.47:1; (TBird) 2.50:1 exc. w/V8400, 3.00:1. Steering: (Pinto) rack and pinion; (others) recirculating ball. Front Suspension: (Pinto) coil springs with short/long control arms, lower leading arms, and anti-sway bar on wagon; (others) coil springs with control arms lower trailing links and anti-sway bar. Rear Suspension: (Pinto/Maverick/Granada) rigid axle w/semi-elliptic leaf springs; (LTD II/Thunderbird) rigid axle w/lower trailing radius arms, upper oblique torque arms, coil springs and anti-sway bar; (LTD) rigid axle w/lower trailer radius arms, upper torque arms and coil springs, three-link w/track bar. Brakes: Front disc, rear drum; four-wheel discs available on Granada and LTD. Ignition: Electronic. Body construction: (Pinto/Maverick/Granada) unibody; (LTD II/LTD/TBird) separate body and perimeter box frame. Fuel tank: (Pinto) 13 gal.; (Pinto wag) 14 gal.: (Maverick/Granada) 19.2 gal.: (LTD 11) 26 gal. exc. wag, 21.3 gal.: (LTD) 24.2 gal. exc. wagon, 21 gal.; (TBird) 26.5 gal.

1977 Ford LTD Country Squire wagon. (JG)

DRIVETRAIN OPTIONS: Engines: 170 cid V-6: Pinto ($289) .250 cid, 1Bbl. six: Maverick/Granada ($102). 302 cid, 2Bbl. V-8: Maverick ($161): Granada ($164) 351 cid, 2Bbl. V-8: Granada ($212); LTD II/TBird ($66). 400 cid, 2Bbl. V-8: LTD II/TBird ($155): LTD II wagon ($100): LTD ($107). 460 cid, 4Bbl. V-8: LTD ($297); LTD wagon ($189). Transmission/Differential: SelectShift Cruise-O-Matic: Pinto ($196): Maverick/Granada ($259). Floor shift lever: Granada ($28). Traction-Lok differential: LTD ($57); TBird ($54). Optional axle ratio: Pinto ($14); TBird ($14); LTD ($16). Power Accessories: Power brakes: Pinto ($58): Maverick ($57); Granada ($60). Four-wheel power disc brakes: Granada ($222); LTD ($180). Power steering: Pinto ($124); Maverick/Granada ($131). Suspension: H.D. susp.: Maverick ($17); Granada ($38); LTD ($20). Handling susp.: TBird ($79). H.D. handling susp.: LTD 11 ($9-$33), Adjustable air shock absorbers: LTD ($46). Other: H.D. battery: Pinto/Maverick ($16); LTD II/TBird ($17); LTD ($18). H.D. alternator: LTD II/TBird ($45). Trailer towing pkg. (heavy duty): LTD 11 ($93-$151); LTD ($125); TBird ($138). California emission system: Maverick/Granada ($48); LTD ($53); TBird ($70). High-altitude option Pinto/Maverick/Granada ($39): LTD ($42); TBird ($22).

PINTO CONVENIENCE/APPEARANCE OPTIONS: Option Packages: Cruising wagon option, incl. bodyside tape stripe ($416). Sports Rallye pkg. ($89). Exterior decor group ($122 $128). Interior decor group ($160). Convenience light group ($73-$108). Deluxe bumper group ($65). Protection group ($122-$142). Comfort/Convenience: Air conditioner ($446). Rear defroster, electric ($73). Tinted glass ($48). Dual sport mirrors ($45). Entertainment: AM radio ($76). w/stereo tape player ($204). AM/FM radio ($135). AM/FM stereo radio ($184). Exterior: Sunroof, manual ($243). Flip-up open air roof ($147). Half vinyl roof ($133). Glass third door ($13). Metallic glow paint ($58). Two-tone paint/tape treatment ($5-$51). Special paint/tape w/luggage rack: cruising wag ($58). Black narrow vinyl-insert bodyside moldings ($37). Roof luggage rack ($80). Rocker panel moldings ($20). Interior: Four-way driver's seat ($33). Load floor carpet ($23). Cargo area cover ($30). Wheels: Wire wheel covers ($79-$119). Forged aluminum wheels ($57-$183). Styled steel wheels ($98-$127). Wheel covers ($29). Tires: A78 x 13 WSW. A70 x 13 RWL. B78 x 13 BSW/WSW. BR78 x 13 BSW/WSW. BR70 x 13 RWL.

MAVERICK CONVENIENCE/APPEARANCE OPTIONS: Option Packages: Exterior decor group ($105). Interior decor group ($112). Deluxe bumper group ($65).Convenience group ($49-$67). Protection group ($34-$41). Light group ($36). Comfort/Convenience: Air cond ($446). Rear defogger ($42). Tinted glass ($47-$63). Dual sport mirrors ($14-$27). Entertainment: AM radio ($76). w/tape player ($204). AM/FM radio ($135). AM/FM stereo radio ($222). w/tape player ($317). Exterior: Vinyl roof ($100). Metallic glow paint ($58). Wide vinyl-insert bodyside moldings ($64). Bumper guards, front and rear ($36). Interior: Four-way reclining driver's bucket seat ($33). Reclining vinyl bucket seats ($129). Cloth reclining bucket seats ($25). Vinyl seat trim ($27). Wheels: Wire wheel covers ($86-$119). Lacy spoke aluminum wheels ($218-$251). Styled steel wheels ($100-$131). Tires: C78 x 14 WSW ($33). CR78 x 14 SBR BSW ($89). CR78 x 14 SBR WSW ($121). DR78 x 14 SBR BSW ($89-$112). DR78 x 14 SBR WSW ($121-$144). Space-saver spare ($14) except (NC) with radial tires.

LTD II CONVENIENCE/APPEARANCE OPTIONS: Option Packages: Squire Brougham option ($203). Sports instrumentation group ($103-$130). Exterior decor group ($225-$276). Accent group ($58). Deluxe bumper group ($72). Light group ($46-$49). Convenience group ($49-$67). Power lock group ($92-$125). Comfort/Convenience: Air cond. ($505); w/auto-temp control ($546). Rear defroster, electric ($87). Fingertip speed control ($93-$114). Illuminated entry system ($51). Tinted glass ($57). Power windows ($114-$158). Power tailgate window: wag ($43). Six-way power seat ($143). Leather-wrapped steering wheels ($39-$61). Tilt steering wheel ($63). Day/date clock ($20-$39). Lighting and Mirrors: Cornering lamps ($43). Remote driver's mirror, chrome ($14). Dual sports mirrors ($51). Entertainment: AM radio ($72). AM/FM radio ($132). AM/FM stereo radio ($192); w/tape player ($266); w/quadrasonic tape player ($399). AM/FM stereo search radio ($349).

Dual rear speakers ($43). Exterior: Full vinyl roof ($111-$162). Half vinyl roof ($111). Opera windows ($51). Vinyl-insert bodyside moldings ($39). Metallic glow paint ($62). Two-tone paint ($49-$88) exc. Brougham (NC). Rear-facing third seat: wag ($100). Vinyl seat trim ($22). Color-keyed seatbelts ($18). Wheels: Deluxe wheel covers ($36). Luxury wheel covers ($59-$95). Wire wheel covers ($99). Turbine spoke cast aluminum wheels ($234-$270). Tires: H78 x 14 SBR WSW ($45). HR78 x 14 wide-band WSW ($16-$61). JR78 x 14 SBR WSW ($26-$71). HR78 x 15 SBR WSW ($45).

LTD CONVENIENCE/APPEARANCE OPTIONS: Option Packages: Landau luxury group ($403-$563). Convenience group ($88-$136). Light group ($36-$38). Deluxe bumper group ($43-$63). Protection group ($50-$59). Comfort/Convenience: Air cond. ($514): w/auto-temp control ($600). Rear defogger ($46). Rear defroster, electric ($88). Fingertip speed control ($92-$113). Illuminated entry system ($54). Power windows ($114-$170). Power mini-vent and side windows ($246). Power door locks ($72-$116) Six-way power driver's seat ($139); driver and passenger ($275). Tinted glass ($68). Tilt steering wheel ($63). Electric clock ($20). Digital clock ($26-$46). Lighting and Mirrors: Cornering lamps ($46). Driver's remote mirror ($16). Lighted visor vanity mirror ($42-$46). Entertainment: AM radio ($83). AM/FM radio ($147). AM/FM stereo radio ($242); w/tape player ($346); w/quadrasonic tape player ($450). AM/FM stereo search radio ($409). Dual rear speakers ($42). Exterior: Full vinyl roof ($134) exc. Landau two-door (NC). Half vinyl roof ($134). Fender skirts ($45). Metallic glow paint ($63). Dual accent paint stripes ($30). Rocker panel moldings ($28). Vinyl-insert bodyside moldings ($43). Rear bumper guards ($20). Luggage rack ($101). Interior: Dual-facing rear seats: wagon ($134). Split bench seat w/passenger recliner ($149). Leather seat trim ($236). All-vinyl seat trim ($23). Duraweave vinyl trim ($59). Color-keyed seatbelts ($20). Lockable side storage compartment ($46). Wheels: Full wheel covers ($32). Deluxe wheel covers ($67-$99) Wire wheel covers ($105-$131). Deep-dish aluminum wheels ($251-$283). Tires: HR78 x 15 SBR WSW. JR78 x 15 SBR BSW/WSW/wide WSW. LR78 x 15 SBR WSW.

THUNDERBIRD CONVENIENCE/APPEARANCE OPTIONS: Option Packages: Interior luxury group ($724). Exterior decor group ($317-$368) Interior decor group ($299). Deluxe bumper group ($72). Instrumentation group ($103-$111). Convenience group ($88-$96). Protection group ($43-$47). Light group ($46). Power lock group ($92). Comfort/Convenience: Air cond. ($505): auto-temp ($546). Rear defroster, electric ($87). Fingertip speed control ($93-$114). Illuminated entry system ($51). Tinted glass ($61). Power windows ($124). Six-way power seat ($143). Automatic setback release ($32). Leather-wrapped steering wheel ($39-$61). Tilt steering wheel ($63). Day/date clock ($20). Lighting and Mirrors: Cornering lamps ($43). Driver's remote mirror, chrome ($14). Dual sport mirrors ($51). Lighted passenger visor vanity mirror ($42-$46). Entertainment: AM/FM radio ($59). AM/FM stereo radio ($120); w/tape player ($193); w/quadrasonic tape player ($326). AM/FM stereo search radio ($276). AM radio delete ($72) credit). Dual rear speakers ($43). Exterior: Power moonroof ($888). Vinyl roof, two-piece ($132). Metallic glow paint ($62). Two-paint ($49). Bright wide bodyside moldings ($39). Black vinyl-insert bodyside moldings ($39). Wide color-keyed vinyl-insert bodyside moldings ($51). Dual accent paint stripes ($39).Interior: Bucket seats w/console ($158) exc. (NC) w/decor group. Leather seat trim ($241). Vinyl seat trim ($22). Color-keyed seatbelts ($18). Wheels: Wire wheel covers ($99) exc. w/decor group ($47 credit). Turbine spoke aluminum wheels ($88-$234). Tires: HR78 x 15 SBR WSW ($45). HR78 x 15 SBR wide WSW ($61). HR70 x 15 SBR WSW ($67). Spacesaver spare (NC).

HISTORY: Introduced: October 1, 1976. Model year production: 1,840,427 (incl. Mustangs). Total passenger-car production for the U.S. market of 1,703,945 units (incl. Mustangs) included 236,840 four-cylinder, 262,840 sixes and 1,184,225 V-8s. Calendar year production (U.S.): 1,714,783 (incl. Mustangs). Calendar year sales by U.S. dealers: 1,824,035 (incl. Mustangs). Model year sales by U.S. dealers: 1,749,529 (incl. Mustangs).

NOTE: Totals above do not include Club Wagons. of which 32,657 were sold in the model year.

HISTORY: Both the new LTD II and the shrunken Thunderbird were meant to rival Chevrolet's Monte Carlo and Pontiac Grand Prix. Far more T-Birds came off the line for 1977 than had their predecessors the year before: 301,787 of the new downsized versions versus just 48,196 of the '76 biggies. While Thunderbird's price was cut dramatically this year, LTD cost nearly 7 percent more than in 1976. Since gasoline prices weren't rising, Ford's lineup of relatively small cars wasn't doing as well as hoped. Slight price cuts of smaller models, after their 1977 introduction, didn't help. As a result, plants producing smaller Fords shut down nearly two months earlier for the '78 changeover than did those turning out full-size models. During the model year, Maverick production halted, to be replaced by the new Fairmont compact. A UAW strike against Ford during the model year didn't affect production much, as it was nearly identical to 1976 output. Since the California strategy of special models available on the West coast had been successful the year before, Ford continued that approach.

1978 FORD

1978 Ford Pinto three-door hatchback. (F)

Ford's diamond jubilee (75th anniversary) was celebrated for an entire year, topped off by the Diamond Jubilee Edition Thunderbird. New this year was the compact Fairmont, replacing the Maverick which had not been selling well. Granada gained a restyle for the first time since its 1975 debut. Thunderbird now offered a sports decor package. A Pulse Air or Thermactor II emissions control device replaced the complicated standard Thermactor air pump system.

PINTO — FOUR/V-6 — New body and interior colors made up most of the changes in Ford's rear-drive subcompact model. Pintos now carried split-cushion 'bucket' style rear seats. New options included white-painted forged aluminum wheels and an accent stripe treatment in four color combinations. New interior colors were jade. tangerine and blue. Seven body colors were available, as well as vinyl roofs in jade or chamois. Pinto's model lineup was the same as before: two-door sedan, three-door hatchback Runabout, and station wagon. Base engine remained the 140 cid (2.3-liter) overhead-cam four, with four-speed manual gearbox. The optional 2.8-liter V-6 engine got a new lightweight plastic fan. Optional power rack-and-pinion steering added a new variable-ratio system similar to that used on Fairmont/Zephyr. A Sports Rallye Package included a tachometer, sport steering wheel, front stabilizer bar, heavy-duty suspension. and 3.18:1 axle, The Rallye Appearance package contained dual racing mirrors, black front spoiler, gold accent stripes, and blacked-out exterior moldings. The Cruising Wagon option returned, with front spoiler, graphic multi-colored paint striping, cargo area carpeting, styled steel wheels, dual sport mirrors, and steel side panels with round tinted porthole windows near the rear. At mid-year a panel delivery Pinto was added, with full-length flat cargo floor and metal side panels. Most regular production options were available on the panel Pinto (plus a rear-window security screen).

1978 Ford Pinto three-door Runabout (with Rallye Appearance Package). (OCW)

1978 Ford Pinto station wagon (with Exterior Decor Package). (OCW)

1978 Ford Fairmont. (OCW)

1978 Ford Fairmont Futura Sport Coupe. (F)

FAIRMONT — FOUR/SIX/V-8 — With the demise of Maverick came a new, more modern compact model. Fairmont and Zephyr (its corporate twin from Mercury) shared the new unitized "Fox" body/chassis platform which began development in the early 1970s and would later carry a number of other FoMoCo models. Fairmont was designed with an emphasis on efficiency and fuel economy, achieved by means of reduced weight and improved aerodynamics. At the same time, Ford wanted to make the best use of interior space, combining the economy of a compact with the spaciousness of a mid-size. Fairmont also offered easy serviceability and maintenance, with a roomy engine compartment and good accessibility. Styling was influenced by Ford's Ghia design studios in Turin, Italy, with clean, straightforward lines. Zephyr differed only in grille design and trim details. The standard Fairmont grille had two horizontal bars and one vertical divider over a subdued crosshatch pattern. Single rectangular headlamps flanked vertical rectangular signal lamps. A single bright molding surrounded the headlamps, park/signal lamps, and grille. Tail lamps contained integral backup lamps. Doors and front seatbacks were thinner than Maverick's.

Fairmont also had a higher roofline and lower beltline. Under the chassis was a new suspension system using MacPherson struts and coil springs up front, and four-link coil spring design at the rear. Front coil springs were mounted on lower control arms instead of around the struts, as in other applications. Rack-and-pinion steering could have unique variable-ratio power assist at extra cost. Base engine was the 140 cid (2.3-liter) "Lima" four, as used in Pintos and Mustangs the first four-cylinder powerplant in a domestic Ford compact. Options included a 250 cid (3.3-liter) inline six and 302 cid (5.0-liter) V-8. A four-speed manual gearbox was standard, but V-8 models required automatic. Four-cylinder models had standard low-back bucket seats, while sixes and eights held a bench seat. Bodies sported bright grille, headlamp and parking lamp bezels; plus bright windshield, backlight and drip moldings. Standard equipment included B78 x 14 blackwall tires, hubcaps, and bright left-hand mirror. Wagons had CR78 x 14 tires. Wheelbase was 105.5 inches. The opening model lineup included two- and four-door sedans and a station wagon. An ES option (Euro styled), added later, displayed a blacked-out grille and cowl grille, rear quarter window louvers, black window frames and lower back panel, and turbine-spoked wheel covers. Also included: a sports steering wheel, color-keyed interior trim, and unique black instrument panel with gray engine turnings. Its specially-tuned suspension included a rear stabilizer bar. Vent louvers were also available as an individual option. A different looking Futura Sport Coupe, with roofline reminiscent of Thunderbird, joined the original sedans and wagon in December, touted as a sporty luxury model. Futura's unique styling features included quad rectangular headlamps above rectangular parking lamps, a large-pattern crosshatch grille, hood ornament, bright window frames, slanted rear end with wraparound tail lamps, wide wrapover roof design, and horizontal louvers in center roof pillars. The coupe, which borrowed a subtitle formerly used on the 1960s Falcon, also added accent paint striping, black luggage area, full-length vinyl bodyside moldings with bright inserts, bright belt moldings, wheel lip moldings, and deluxe wheel covers. Inside, the five-passenger Futura had pleated vinyl bucket seats, woodtone appliqués on the dash, and color-keyed seatbelts. William P.

Benton, Ford's vice-president (and Ford Division General Manager) said Fairmont Futura "has the best fuel economy in its class, leg, shoulder and hip room of a mid-size car, and responsive handling, plus a rich new look and an array of luxury touches." Four-cylinder powered, with four-speed manual shift, it could deliver 26 MPG on the EPA scale. Options included a divided vinyl roof and seven two- tone combinations, plus color-keyed turbine wheel covers.

GRANADA — SIX/V-8 — Granada and its twin, the Mercury Monarch, took on a fresh look this year with new bright grilles, rectangular headlamps, parking lamps, front bumper air spoiler, wide wheel lip moldings, new wraparound tail lamps, and lower back panel appliqués. Also new on two-doors were "twindow" opera windows split by a bright center bar. This was the first major restyle since the pair's 1974 debut, and the first quad rectangular headlamps in the Ford camp. The spoiler and hood-to-grille-opening panel seal, and revised decklid surface, helped reduce aerodynamic drag. The new crosshatch grille showed a tight pattern, split into sections by two horizontal dividers. A 'Ford' badge went on the lower driver's side of the grille. Rectangular headlamps stood above nearly-as-large rectangular parking lamps, both in a recessed housing. Two-door and four-door sedans were offered again, in base or Ghia trim. Granada Ghia had wide bodyside moldings. A new ESS (European Sports Sedan) option package included a blackout vertical grille texture as well as black rocker panels, door frames and bodyside moldings; black rubber bumper guards and wide rub strips; and a unique interior. ESS had color-keyed wheel covers, a heavy-duty suspension, dual sport mirrors, decklid and hood pin striping. leather-wrapped steering wheel. FR78 x 14 SBR tires, and individual reclining bucket seats. ESS also had unique half- covered, louvered quarter windows. Low on the cowl was an 'ESS' badge, above 'Granada' script. Other options included an AM/FM stereo with cassette tape player, and a 40-channel CB transceiver. Five new Granada colors were offered this year, and a valino vinyl roof came in three new color choices. The base 200 cid six from 1977 was replaced by a 250 cid (4.1-liter) version. with 302 cid (5.0 liter) V-8 optional. The V-8 could now have a variable-venturi carburetor. The bigger 351 cid V-8 was abandoned.

1978 Ford Granada Ghia two-door sedan. (OCW)

1978 Ford Granada ESS sedan. (PH)

1978 Ford LTD II "S" hardtop coupe. (OCW)

1978 Ford LTD II Brougham hardtop coupe. (F)

LTD II — V-8 — Station wagons left the LTD II lineup this year, since the new Fairmont line included a wagon. Otherwise, models continued as before in 'S', base and Brougham series. Broughams had a full-length bodyside trim strip. Standard engine was again the 302 cid (5.0-liter) V-8 with Cruise-O-Matic transmission, power front disc brakes, and power steering. Options included the 351 and 400 cid V-8 engines, a heavy-duty trailer towing package (for the 400 V-8), and a Sports Appearance package. Two-doors could either have a solid panel at the rear, or the extra (higher) far rear coach-style window. A new bumper front spoiler, hood-to-grille-opening panel seal, revised decklid surface, and new fuel tank air deflector were supposed to cut aerodynamic drag and boost economy. Bumper-to-fender shields were new, too. A revised low-restriction fresh-air intake went on V-8 engines. A new mechanical spark control system was limited to the 351M and 400 cid V-8s. Newly optional this year: a 40-channel CB radio. Mercury Cougar was corporate twin to the LTD II.

LTD/CUSTOM 500 — V-8 — Full-size Fords were carried over for 1978, with new body colors available but little change beyond a new front bumper spoiler, rear floorpan air deflector, and other aerodynamic additions. The decklid also was new. As before, LTD came in two-door or four-door pillared hardtop form, as well as plain-bodyside and Country Squire (simulated wood paneled) station wagons. Custom 500 was the fleet model, sold in Canada. Station wagons could now have optional removable auxiliary cushions for the dual facing rear seats. Among the more than 70 options were new two-tone body colors for the LTD Landau. Air conditioners now allowed the driver to control heating and cooling. A downsized LTD would arrive for 1979, so this was a waiting season.

THUNDERBIRD — V-8 — Styling of Ford's personal luxury coupe was similar to that of the downsized 1977 model. Six new body colors, four vinyl roof colors, bold striped cloth bucket seat trim, and new russet interior trim were offered. But the biggest news was the limited-production Diamond Jubilee Edition, commemorating Ford's 75th anniversary. Billed as "the most exclusive Thunderbird you can buy," it included several items never before offered on a Thunderbird. Diamond Jubilee had a unique monochromatic exterior in Diamond Blue metallic or Ember metallic; distinctive matching thickly-padded vinyl roof and color-keyed grille texture; unique quarter-window treatment; accent striping; jewel-like hood ornament; cast aluminum wheels; and bodyside moldings. 'Diamond Jubilee Edition' script went in the opera windows, a hand-painted 'D.J.' monogram on the door (with owner's initials). Also included were color-keyed bumper guard/rub strips and turbine aluminum wheels. Inside was unique "biscuit" style cloth split bench seat trim, leather-covered steering wheel, twin illuminated visor vanity mirrors, seatbelt warning chimes, "Super sound" package, and other luxury options. Even the keys were special. Diamond Blue models had a blue luxury cloth interior; Ember bodies had a chamois-color interior. Standard features also included whitewall tires, AM/FM stereo search radio with power antenna, dual sport mirrors, manual passenger recliner, and a hand-stitched leather-covered instrument panel pad above the tachometer and gauge set. Finishing off the interior were ebony woodtone appliqués, and 22K gold-finish owner's nameplate. Thunderbird's Town Landau, introduced as a mid-year 1977 model, continued in 1978. Its roofline displayed a brushed aluminum wrapover appliqué. Also included were pin striping, script on the opera windows, a color-coordinated jewel-like hood ornament, cast aluminum wheels with accent paint, wide vinyl-insert bodyside moldings, six-way power driver's seat, power windows and door locks, cornering lamps, and interior luxury group. Town Landau came in 14 body colors. Standard fittings also included whitewall tires, accent stripes, lighted visor vanity mirror, and dual sport mirrors. Inside were crushed velour split bench seats with fold-down center armrests. Six velour trim colors were available, along with optional leather seating surfaces. Dashes held buried walnut woodtone appliqués. Also on Town Landau: SelectAire conditioner, AM/FM stereo search radio, day/date clock, and trip odometer. Thunderbird's Sports Decor Group included a bold blackout grille, unique imitation decklid straps, paint stripes, twin remote mirrors, spoke-style wheels, and tan vinyl root with color-keyed rear window moldings. New options included a power radio antenna and 40-channel CB. Standard engine remained the 302 cid (5.0-liter) V-8 with SelectShift automatic, power steering and brakes. Both 351 and 400 cid V-8s were optional. Cougar XR7 was Thunderbird's Mercury counterpart.

1978-1/2 Ford Thunderbird (with T-roof Convertible option). (OCW)

I.D. DATA: As before, Ford's 11-symbol Vehicle Identification Number (VIN) is stamped on a metal tab fastened to the instrument panel, visible through the windshield. Coding is similar to 1976-77. Model year code changed to '8' for 1978.

PINTO (FOUR/V-6)

Model No.	Body/Style No.	Body Type & Seating	Factory Price	Shipping Weight	Prod. Total
10	62B	2-dr. Sedan-4P	3336/3609	2337/2463	62,317
10	62B	2-dr. Pony Sed-4P	2995/----	2321/----	Note 1
11	64B	3-dr. Hatch-4P	3451/3724	2381/2507	74,313
12	73B	2-dr. Sta Wag-4P	3794/4067	2521/2637	52,269
12	73B	2-dr. Sqr Wag-4P	4109/4382	2555/2672	Note 2

NOTE 1: Pony production included in base sedan figure.

NOTE 2: Squire Wagon production is included in standard station wagon total.

PINTO PRODUCTION NOTE: Totals do not include 22,548 Pintos produced as 1978 models but sold as 1977s (see note following 1977 listing).

FAIRMONT (FOUR/SIX)

Model No.	Body/Style No.	Body Type & Seating	Factory Price	Shipping Weight	Prod. Total
93	36R	2-dr. Spt Cpe-5P	4044/4164	2605/2648	116,966
91	66B	2-dr. Sedan-5P	3589/3709	2568/2611	78,776
92	54B	4-dr. Sedan-5P	3663/3783	2610/2653	136,849
94	74B	4-dr. Sta Wag-5P	4031/4151	2718/2770	128,390

FAIRMONT ENGINE NOTE: Prices shown are for four-cylinder and six-cylinder engines. A V-8 cost $199 more than the six.

GRANADA (SIX/V-8)

Model No.	Body/Style No.	Body Type & Seating	Factory Price	Shipping Weight	Prod. Total
81	66H	2-dr. Sedan-5P	4264/4445	3087/3177	110,481
82	54H	4-dr. Sedan-5P	4342/4523	3122/3212	139,305

GRANADA GHIA (SIX/V-8)

Model No.	Body/Style No.	Body Type & Seating	Factory Price	Shipping Weight	Prod. Total
81	66K	2-dr. Sedan-5P	4649/4830	3147/3237	Note 3
82	54K	4-dr. Sedan-5P	4728/4909	3230/3320	Note 3

GRANADA ESS (SIX/V-8)

Model No.	Body/Style No.	Body Type & Seating	Factory Price	Shipping Weight	Prod. Total
81	N/A	2-dr. Sedan-5P	4836/5017	3145/3235	Note 3
82	N/A	4-dr. Sedan-5P	4914/5095	3180/3270	Note 3

NOTE 3: Granada Ghia and ESS production is included in base Granada totals above.

LTD II (V-8)

Model No.	Body/Style No.	Body Type & Seating	Factory Price	Shipping Weight	Prod. Total
30	65D	2-dr. HT Cpe-6P	5069	3773	76,285
31	53D	4-dr. Pill. HT-6P	5169	3872	64,133

LTD II 'S' (V-8)

Model No.	Body/Style No.	Body Type & Seating	Factory Price	Shipping Weight	Prod. Total
25	65B	2-dr. HT Cpe-6P	4814	3746	9,004
27	53B	4-dr. Pill. HT-6P	4889	3836	21,122

1978 Ford Fairmont station wagon. (JG)

LTD II BROUGHAM (V-8)

30	65K	2-dr. HT Cpe-6P	5405	3791	Note 4
31	53K	4-dr. Pill. HT-6P	5505	3901	Note 4

NOTE 4: Brougham production is included in LTD II totals above.

LTD LANDAU (V-8)

64	60L	2 dr. Pill. HT-6P	5898	4029	27,305
65	53L	4 dr. Pill. HT 6P	5973	4081	39,836

CUSTOM 500 (V-8)

52	60D	2-dr. Pill. HT-6P	N/A	N/A	1,359
53	53D	4-dr. Pill. HT-6P	N/A	N/A	3,044
72	71D	4-dr. Ranch Wag-6P	N/A	N/A	1,196

PRODUCTION NOTE: Custom 500 was produced for sale in Canada. Totals include an LTD 'S' two-door and Ranch wagon for sale in U.S.

LTD (V-8)

62	60H	2-dr. Pill. HT-6P	5335	3972	57,466
63	53H	4-dr. Pill. HT-6P	5410	4032	112,392
74	71H	4-dr. Sta Wag-6P	5797	4532	71,285
74	71K	4-dr. Ctry Sqr-6P	6207	4576	Note 5

NOTE 5: Country Squire production, and that of wagons with dual-facing rear seats (a $143 option for both standard and Country Squire wagon), is included in basic wagon totals.

THUNDERBIRD (V-8)

87	60H	2-dr. HT Cpe-6P	5411	3907	333,757

THUNDERBIRD TOWN LANDAU (V-8)

87/607	60H	2-dr. HT Cpe-6P	8420	4104	Note 6

NOTE 6: Town Landau production is included in basic Thunderbird total.

THUNDERBIRD DIAMOND JUBILEE EDITION (V-8)

87/603	60H	2-dr. HT Cpe-6P	10106	4200	18,994

FACTORY PRICE AND WEIGHT NOTE: Pinto/Fairmont prices and weights to left of slash are for four-cylinder, to right for six-cylinder engine. For Granada, prices and weights to left of slash are for six-cylinder, to right for V-8 engine.

ENGINE [Base Four (Pinto, Fairmont)]: Inline. Overhead cam. Four-cylinder. Cast-iron block and head. Displacement: 140 cid (2.3 liters). Bore & stroke: 3.78 x 3.13 in. Compression ratio: 9.0:1. Brake horsepower: 88 at 4800 rpm. Torque: 118 lbs.-ft. at 2800 rpm. Five main bearings. Hydraulic valve lifters. Carburetor: 2Bbl. Motorcraft 5200. VIN Code: Y.

ENGINE [Optional V-6 (Pinto)]: 60-degree, overhead-valve V-6. Cast-iron block and head. Displacement: 170.8 cid (2.8 liters). Bore & stroke: 3.66 x 2.70 in. Compression ratio: 8.7:1. Brake horsepower: 90 at 4200 rpm. Torque: 143 lbs.-ft. at 2200 rpm. Four main bearings. Solid valve lifters. Carburetor: 2Bbl. Motorcraft 2150. VIN Code: Z.

ENGINE [Optional Six (Fairmont)]: Inline. Overhead valve. Six-cylinder. Cast-iron block and head. Displacement: 200 cid (3.3 liters). Bore & stroke: 3.68 x 3.13 in. Compression ratio: 8.5:1. Brake horsepower: 85 at 3600 rpm. Torque: 154 lbs.-ft. at 1600 rpm. Seven main bearings. Hydraulic valve lifters. Carburetor: 1Bbl. Carter YFA. VIN Code: T.

ENGINE [Base Six (Granada)]: Inline. Overhead valve. Six-cylinder. Cast-iron block and head. Displacement: 250 cid (4.1 liters). Bore & stroke: 3.68 x 3.91 in. Compression ratio: 8.5:1. Brake horsepower: 97 at 3200 rpm. Torque: 210 lbs.-ft. at 1400 rpm. Seven main bearings. Hydraulic valve lifters. Carburetor: 1Bbl. Carter YFA. VIN Code: L.

ENGINE [Base V-8 (LTD II, Thunderbird, LTD); Optional (Fairmont, Granada)]: 90-degree, overhead valve V-8. Cast-iron block and head. Displacement: 302 cid (5.0 liters). Bore & stroke: 4.00 x 3.00 in. Compression ratio: 8.4:1. Brake horsepower: 134 at 3400 rpm. (Fairmont, 139 at 3600). Torque: 248 lbs.-ft. at 1600 rpm. (Fairmont, 250 at 1600). Five main bearings. Hydraulic valve lifters. Carburetor: 2Bbl. Motorcraft 2150. VIN Code: F.

ENGINE [Base V-8 (LTD wagon); Optional (LTD II, LTD)]: 90-degree, overhead valve V-8. Cast-iron block and head. Displacement: 351 cid (5.8 liters). Bore & stroke: 4.00 x 3.50 in. Compression ratio: 8.3:1. (LTD, 8.0:1). Brake horsepower: 144 at 3200 rpm. (LTD, 145 at 3400). Torque: 277 lbs.-ft. at 1600 rpm. (LTD, 273 at 1800). Five main bearings. Hydraulic valve lifters. Carburetor: 2Bbl. Motorcraft 2150. Windsor engine. VIN Code: H.

ENGINE [Optional V-8 (LTD II, Thunderbird)]: Modified version of 351 cid V-8 above Compression: 8.0:1. Brake H.P.: 152 at 3600 rpm. Torque: 278 lbs.-ft. at 1800 rpm. VIN Code: Q.

ENGINE [Optional V-8 (LTD II, Thunderbird, LTD)]: 90-degree, overhead valve V-8. Cast-iron block and head. Displacement: 400 cid (6.6 liters). Bore & stroke: 4.00 x 4.00 in. Compression ratio: 8.0:1. Brake horsepower: 166 at 3800 rpm. (LTD, 160 at 3800). Torque: 319 lbs.-ft. at 1800 rpm. (LTD, 314 at 1800). Five main bearings. Hydraulic valve lifters. Carburetor: 2Bbl. Motorcraft 2150. VIN Code: S.

ENGINE [Optional V-8 (LTD)]: 90-degree, overhead valve V-8. Cast-iron block and head. Displacement: 460 cid (7.5 liters). Bore & stroke: 4.36 x 3.85 in. Compression ratio: 8.0:1. Brake horsepower: 202 at 4000 rpm. Torque: 348 lbs.-ft. at 2000 rpm. Five main bearings. Hydraulic valve lifters. Carburetor: 4Bbl. Motorcraft 4350. VIN Code: A.

NOTE: A Police 460 cid V-8 was also available for LTD.

CHASSIS DATA: Wheelbase: (Pinto) 94.5 in.; (Pinto wag) 94.8 in.; (Fairmont) 105.5 in.; (Granada) 109.9 in.; (LTD II 2dr.) 114.0 in.; (LTD II 4dr.) 118.0 in.; (Custom 500/LTD) 121.0 in.; (TBird) 114.0 in. Overall Length: (Pinto) 169.3 in.; (Pinto wag) 179.1 in.; (Fairmont) 193.8 in. exc. Futura coupe, 195.8 in.; (Granada) 197.7 in.; (LTD II 2dr.) 215.5in.; (LTD II 4dr.) 219.5 in.; (LTD) 224.1 in.; (LTD wag) 225.7 in.; (LTD Landau) 226.8in.; (TBird) 215.5 in. Height: (Pinto) 50.6 in.; (Pinto wag) 52.1 in.; (Fairmont) 53.5in.; (Fairmont Futura cpe) 52.2 in.; (Fairmont wag) 54.7 in.; (Granada) 53.2-53.3 in.; (LTD II 2dr.) 52.6 in.; (LTD II 4dr.) 53.3 in.; (LTD 2dr.) 53.8 in.; (LTD 4dr.) 54.8 in.; (LTD wag) 56.7 in.; (TBird) 53.0 in. Width: (Pinto) 69.4 in.; (Pinto wag) 69.7 in.; (Fairmont) 71.0 in.; (Granada) 74.0 in.; (LTD II) 78.6 in.; (LTD) 79.5 in.; (LTD wag) 79.7 in.; (TBird) 78.5 in. Front Tread: (Pinto) 55.0 in.; (Fairmont) 56.6 in.; (Granada) 59.0 in.; (LTD II) 63.6 in. (LTD) 64.1 in. (TBird) 63.2 in. Rear Tread: (Pinto) 55.8 in.; (Fairmont) 57.0 in.; (Granada) 57.7 in.; (LTD II) 63.5 in.; (LTD) 64.3 in. (TBird) 63.1 in. Standard Tires: (Pinto) A78 x 13; (Fairmont) B78 x 14, except CR78 x 14 on wagon; (Granada) DR78 x 14 SBR BSW; (Granada Ghia) ER78 x 14; (LTD II) HR78 x 14 SBR BSW; (LTD) HR78 x 15 exc. wagon, JR78 x 15 and 2dr. w/V8-302 engine, GR78 x 15; (TBird) HR78 x 15 SBR BSW.

TECHNICAL: Transmission: Three-speed manual transmission standard on Fairmont six. Gear ratios: (1st) 3.56:1; (2nd) 1.90:1; (3rd) 1.00:1; (Rev) 3.78:1. Four-speed overdrive manual standard on Granada (1st) 3.29:1; (2nd) 1.84:1; (3rd) 1.00:1; (4th) 0.81:1; (Rev) 3.29:1. Four-speed floor shift standard on Pinto/Fairmont four: (1st) 3.98:1; (2nd) 2.14:1; (3rd) 1.42:1; (4th) 1.00:1; (Rev) 3.99:1. SelectShift three-speed automatic standard on other models, optional on all. Pinto/Fairmont four-cylinder automatic gear ratios: (1st) 2.47:1; (2nd) 1.47:1; (3rd) 1.00:1; (Rev) 2.11:1. LTD II/TBird w/VB351 or V8400: (1st) 2.40:1; (2nd) 1.47:1; (3rd) 1.00:1; (Rev) 2.00:1; Other models, (1st) 2.46:1; (2nd) 1.46:1; (3rd) 1.00:1; (Rev) 2.18:1 to 2.20:1. Standard final drive ratio: (Pinto) 2.73:1 w/4spd; (Fairmont) 3.08:1 or 2.73:1 w/manual, 2.47:1 w/auto.; (Granada) 3.00:1 w/4spd, 2.47:1 w/auto. (LTD II) 2.75:1 or 2.50:1; (LTD) 2.75:1 or 2.47:1; (TBird) 2.75:1 w/V8302, 2.50:1 w/other V-8 engines. Steering: (Pinto/Fairmont) rack and pinion; (others) recirculating ball. Front Suspension: (Pinto) coil springs with short/long control arms, lower leading arms, and anti-sway bar on wagon; (Fairmont) MacPherson struts with coil springs mounted on lower control arms; (others) coil springs w/lower trailing links and anti-sway bar. Rear Suspension: (Pinto/Granada) rigid axle w/semi-elliptic leaf springs; (Fairmont) four-link coil springs; (LTD II/TBird) rigid axle w/lower trailing radius arms, upper oblique torque arms, coil springs and anti-sway bar; (LTD) rigid axle w/lower trailing radius arms, upper torque arms and coil springs, three-link w/track bar. Brakes: Front disc, rear drum; four-wheel discs available on Granada and LTD. Ignition: Electronic. Body construction: (Pinto/Fairmont/Granada) unibody; (LTD II/LTD/TBird) separate body and perimeter box frame. Fuel tank: (Pinto) 13 gal.; (Pinto wag) 14 gal.; (Fairmont) 16 gal.; (Granada) 18 gal.; (LTD II) 21 gal.; (LTD) 24.2 gal. exc. wagon, 21 gal.; (TBird) 21 gal.

1978-1/2 Ford Thunderbird Diamond Jubilee hardtop coupe. (F)

DRIVETRAIN OPTIONS: Engines: 170 cid V-6: Pinto ($273). 200 cid, 1Bbl. six: Fairmont ($120). 302 cid, 2Bbl. V-8: Fairmont ($319); Granada ($181). 351 cid, 2Bbl. V-8: LTD II/LTD/TBird ($157). 400 cid, 2Bbl. V-8: LTD II/LTD/TBird ($283); LTD wagon ($126). 460 cid, 4Bbl. V-8: LTD ($428); LTD wagon ($271). Transmission/Differential: SelectShift Cruise-O-Matic: Pinto ($281); Fairmont ($368); Fairmont wagon ($281); Granada ($193). Floor shift lever: Fairmont/Granada ($30). First-gear lockout delete: LTD/LTD II ($7). Traction-Lok differential: LTD II/TBird ($59): LTD ($62). Optional axle ratio: Pinto ($13); LTD ($14). Brakes & Steering: Power brakes: Pinto ($64); Fairmont/Granada ($63). Four-wheel power disc brakes: Granada ($300); LTD ($187-$197). Power steering: Pinto ($131); Fairmont ($140); Granada ($148). Semi-metallic front disc pads: LTD/LTD II ($8). Suspension: H.D. susp.: Granada ($27); LTD ($65); TBird ($20). Handling susp.: Fairmont ($30). H. D. handling susp.: LTD II ($36). Adjustable air shock absorbers: LTD ($50). Other: H.D. battery: Fairmont ($17); LTD II/LTD/TBird ($18). H.D. alternator LTD II/LTD/TBird ($50). Trailer towing pkg. (heavy duty): LTD II/TBird ($184); LTD ($139). California emission system: Pinto/Fairmont/Granada ($69); LTD II/TBird ($75); LTD ($138-$295). High-attitude option (NC).

PINTO CONVENIENCE/APPEARANCE OPTIONS: Option Packages: Cruising wagon option ($365-$401). Cruising wagon paint/tape treatment ($59). Sports Rallye pkg. ($76- $96). Rallye appearance pkg. ($176-$201). Exterior decor group ($30-$40). Interior decor group ($149-$181). Interior accent group ($28-$40). Convenience/light group ($81-$143). Deluxe bumper group ($70). Protection group ($83-$135). Comfort/Convenience: Air conditioner ($459). Rear defroster, electric ($77). Tinted glass ($53); windshield only ($25). Cigar lighter ($5). Trunk light ($5). Driver's sport mirror ($16). Dual sport mirrors ($49). Day/night mirror ($7). Entertainment: AM radio ($65); w/digital clock ($47-$119); w/stereo tape player ($119-$192). AM/FM radio ($48-$120). AM/FM stereo radio ($89-$161). Exterior: Flip-up open air roof ($167). Half vinyl roof ($125). Glass third door ($25). Metallic glow paint ($40). Two-tone paint/tape treatment ($40-$49). Accent tape stripe ($49-$59). Black narrow vinyl-insert bodyside moldings ($39). Bumper guards ($37). Roof luggage rack ($59). Rocker panel moldings ($22). Lower bodyside protection ($30). Interior: Four-way driver's seat ($33). Load floor carpet ($23). Cargo area cover ($25). Wheels: Wire wheel covers ($90). Forged aluminum wheels ($173-$252); white ($187-$265). Styled steel wheels ($78). Tires: A78 x 13 WSW. A70 x 13 RWL. B78 x 13 BSW/WSW. BR78 x 13 BSW/WSW. BR70 x 13 RWL.

FAIRMONT CONVENIENCE/APPEARANCE OPTIONS: Option Packages: ES option: sedan ($300). Squire option ($365). Exterior decor group ($214). Exterior accent group ($96). Interior decor group ($176-$301). Interior accent group ($89-$94). Deluxe bumper group ($70). Convenience group ($29-$60). Appearance protection group ($36-$47). Light group ($35-$40). Comfort/Convenience: Air cond. ($465). Rear defroster ($47). Rear defroster, electric ($84). Tinted glass ($52); windshield only ($25). Sport steering wheel ($36). Electric clock ($18). Cigar lighter ($6). Interval wipers ($29). Liftgate wiper/washer: wag ($78). Trunk light ($4). Left remote mirror ($19). Dual bright mirrors ($13-$36). Day/night mirror ($8). Entertainment: AM radio ($72); w/8track tape player ($192). AM/FM radio ($120). AM/FM stereo radio ($176); w/8track or cassette player ($243). Exterior: Vinyl roof ($89-$124). Metallic glow paint ($46). Two-tone paint ($42). Accent paint stripe ($30) exc. Futura (NC). Pivoting front vent windows ($37-$60). Rear quarter vent louvers ($33). Bodyside moldings ($39). Rocker panel moldings ($22). Bumper guards, front and rear ($37). Luggage rack ($72). Lower bodyside protection ($30-$42). Interior: Bucket seat, non-reclining ($72). Bench seat ($72 credit). Cloth seat trim ($19-$37). Vinyl seat trim ($22). Lockable side storage box ($19). Wheels: Hubcaps w/trim rings ($34) exc. Futura (NC). Deluxe wheel covers ($33). Turbine wheel covers ($33-$66). Wire wheel covers ($48-$114). Cast aluminum wheels ($210-$276). Tires: BR78 x 14 WSW. BR78 x 14 BSW/WSW. C78 x 14 BSW/WSW. CR78 x 14 BSW/WSW. DR78 x 14 SBR BSW/WSW/RWL.

1978 Ford Fairmont two-door sedan. (OCW)

GRANADA CONVENIENCE/APPEARANCE OPTIONS: Option Packages: Luxury interior group ($476). Interior decor group ($211). Convenience group ($30-$89). Deluxe bumper group ($70). Light group ($30-$43). Cold weather group ($37-$54). Heavy-duty group ($37-$54). Protection group ($25-$43). Visibility group ($4-$58). Comfort/Convenience: Air cond. ($494); auto-temp ($535). Rear defogger ($47). Rear defroster, electric ($84). Fingertip speed control ($55-$102). Illuminated entry system ($49). Power windows ($116-$160). Power door locks ($76-$104). Power decklid release ($19). Auto. parking brake release ($8). Power four-way seat ($90). Tinted glass ($54); windshield only ($25). Tilt steering wheel ($58). Digital clock ($42). Lighting and Mirrors: Cornering lamps ($42). Trunk light ($4). Left remote mirror ($14). Dual remote mirrors ($31-$46). Dual sport mirrors ($42-$53). Day/night mirror ($8). Lighted right visor vanity mirror ($34). Entertainment: AM radio ($72); w/tape player ($192). AM/FM radio ($135). AM/FM stereo radio ($176); w/8 track or cassette player ($243); w/quadrasonic tape ($365). AM/FM stereo search radio ($319). CB radio ($270). Exterior: Power moonroof ($820). Full or half vinyl roof ($102). Metallic glow paint ($46). Bodyside/decklid paint stripes ($29). Bodyside accent moldings ($33). Vinyl insert bodyside moldings ($39). Rocker panel moldings ($23). Interior: Console ($75). Four-way driver's seat ($33). Reclining seats (NC). Leather seat trim ($271). Flight bench seat (NC). Cloth flight bench seat ($54). Deluxe cloth seat/door trim: Ghia/ESS ($99). Color-keyed seatbelts ($19). Wheels: Deluxe wheel covers ($37) exc. Ghia/ESS (NC). Wire wheel covers ($59-$96). Styled steel wheels w/trim rings ($59-$96). Lacy spoke aluminum wheels ($205-$242); white ($218-$255). Tires: DR78 x 14 SBR WSW. ER78 x 14 SBR BSW/WSW. FR78 x 14 SBR BSW/WSW/wide WSW. Inflatable spare (NC).

LTD II CONVENIENCE/APPEARANCE OPTIONS: Option Packages: Sports appearance pkg. ($216-$363). Sports instrumentation group ($111-$138). Sports touring pkg. ($287-$434). Deluxe bumper group ($76). Light group ($49-$54). Convenience group ($107-$139). Power lock group ($100-$132). Front protection group ($46-$58). Comfort/Convenience: Air cond. ($543); w/auto-temp control ($588). Rear defroster, electric ($93). Fingertip speed control ($104-$117). Illuminated entry system ($54). Tinted glass ($62); windshield only ($28). Power windows ($126-$175). Power door locks ($71-$101). Six-way power seat ($149). Auto. parking brake release ($9). Leather-wrapped steering wheel ($51-$64). Tilt steering wheel ($70). Electric clock ($20). Day/date clock ($22-$42). Lighting, Horns and Mirrors: Cornering lamps ($46). Trunk light ($4). Dual-note horn ($7). Remote driver's mirror ($16). Dual chrome mirrors ($7). Dual sport mirrors ($29-$58). Lighted visor vanity mirror ($33-$37). Entertainment: AM radio ($79). AM/FM radio ($132). AM/FM stereo radio ($192); w/tape player ($266); w/quadrasonic tape player ($399). AM/FM stereo search radio ($349). CB radio ($295). Dual rear speakers ($46). Exterior: Full or half vinyl roof ($112). Opera windows ($51). Vinyl-insert bodyside moldings ($42). Wide bright bodyside moldings ($42). Rocker panel moldings ($29). Metallic glow paint ($62) exc. (NC) w/sports pkg. Two-tone paint ($53). Dual accent paint stripes ($33). Lower bodyside protection ($33). Interior: Bucket seats w/console ($211) exc. Brougham ($37). Vinyl seat trim ($24). Cloth/vinyl seat trim ($24). Front floor mats ($20). H.D. floor mats ($9). Color-keyed seatbelts ($21). Wheels: Deluxe wheel covers ($38). Luxury wheel covers ($62-$100). Wire wheel covers ($105-$143) exc. (NC) w/sports pkg. Cast aluminum wheels ($196-$301). Tires: HR78 x 14 SBR WSW ($46). HR78 x 14 wide-band WSW ($66). HR78 x 14 SBR RWL ($62). HR78 x 15 SBR WSW ($68). Inflatable spare (NC).

1978 Ford Fairmont ES Sport Coupe. (JG)

1978 Ford LTD Landau pillared sedan. (F)

LTD CONVENIENCE/APPEARANCE OPTIONS: Option Packages: Landau luxury group ($457-$580). Convenience group ($96-$146). Light group ($26-$38). Deluxe bumper group ($50-$72). Protection group ($45-$53). Comfort/Convenience: Air cond. ($562): w/auto-temp control ($607). Rear defogger ($50). Rear defroster, electric ($93). Fingertip speed control ($104-$117). Illuminated entry system ($54). Power windows ($129-$188). Power door locks ($82-$153). Six-way power driver's seat ($149); driver and passenger ($297). Tinted glass ($75); windshield only ($28). Tilt steering wheel ($70). Auto. parking brake release ($8). Electric clock ($21). Digital clock ($28-$49). Lighting, Horns and Mirrors: Cornering lamps ($46). Trunk light ($4). Dual-note horn ($7). Driver's remote mirror ($16). Dual remote mirrors ($32-$47). Lighted visor vanity mirror ($33-$37). Entertainment: AM radio ($79). AM/FM radio ($132). AM/FM stereo radio ($192); w/tape player ($266). w/quadrasonic tape player ($399). AM/FM stereo search radio ($349). Dual rear speakers ($46). Exterior: Power moonroof ($896). Full vinyl roof ($141) exc. Landau two-color (NC). Half vinyl roof ($141). Metallic glow paint ($62). Dual accent paint stripes ($33). Rocker panel moldings ($29). Vinyl-insert bodyside moldings ($42). Rear bumper guards ($22). Luggage rack ($80). Interior: Dual-facing rear seats: wagon ($143). Split bench seat w/passenger recliner ($141-$233). Leather seat trim ($296). All-vinyl seat trim ($24). Duraweave vinyl trim ($50). H.D. floor mats ($9). Color-keyed seatbelts ($21). Lockable side stowage compartment ($33). Wheels: Full wheel covers ($38). Deluxe or color-keyed wheel covers ($61-$99). Wire wheel covers ($99-$137). Deep-dish aluminum wheels ($263-$301). Tires: GR78 x 15 SBR WSW. HR78 x 15 SBR BSW/WSW. JR78 x 15 SBR BSW/WSW/wide WSW. LR78 x 15 SBR WSW.

THUNDERBIRD CONVENIENCE/APPEARANCE OPTIONS: Option Packages: Sports decor group ($396-$446). Interior luxury group ($783). Exterior decor group ($332-$382). Interior decor group ($316). Deluxe bumper group ($76). Sports instrumentation group ($111-$118). Convenience group ($93-$103). Protection group ($46-$50). Light group ($49). Power lock group ($100). Sound insulation pkg. ($29). Comfort/Convenience: Air cond. ($543); auto-temp ($588) exc. special editions ($45). Rear defroster, electric ($93). Fingertip speed control ($104-$117). Illuminated entry system ($54). Tinted glass ($66); windshield only ($28). Power windows ($126). Six-way power seat ($149). Automatic seatback release ($33). Auto. parking brake release ($9). Leather-wrapped steering wheel ($51-$64). Tilt steering wheel ($70). Day/date clock ($22). Lighting and Mirrors: Cornering lamps ($46). Trunk light ($4). Driver's remote mirror, chrome ($16). Dual sport mirrors ($8-$58). Lighted visor vanity mirror ($33-$37). Entertainment: AM/FM radio ($53). AM/FM stereo radio ($113); w/tape player ($187); w/quadrasonic tape player ($320) exc. special editions ($50). AM/FM stereo search radio ($270). CB radio ($295). AM radio delete ($79 credit). Power antenna ($45). Dual rear speakers ($46). Exterior: Power moonroof ($691). Vinyl roof, two-piece ($138). Metallic glow paint ($62). Two-tone paint ($53). Dual accent paint stripes ($46). Bright wide bodyside moldings ($42). Vinyl bodyside moldings ($42). Wide color-keyed bodyside moldings ($54). Rocker panel moldings ($29). Bumper guards ($42). Interior Bucket seats w/console ($211) exc. ($187) w/decor group. Leather/vinyl seat trim ($296). Vinyl seat trim ($24). Front floor mats ($20). Trunk trim ($39). Color-keyed seatbelts ($21). Wheels: Wire wheel covers ($105). Styled wheels ($146). Tires: GR78 x 15 WSW ($46). HR78 x 15 BSW ($22). HR78 x 15 SBR WSW ($20-$68). HR78 x 15 SBR wide WSW ($88). HR70 x 15 SBR WSW ($22-$90). Inflatable spare (NC).

HISTORY: Introduced: October 7, 1977 except Fairmont Futura Coupe, December 2, 1977. Model year production: 1,929,254 (incl. Mustangs). Total passenger-car production for the U.S. market of 1,777,291 units (incl. Mustangs) included 285,878 four-cylinder, 511,500 sixes and 979,913 V-8s. Calendar year production (U.S.): 1,698,136 (incl. Mustangs). Calendar year sales by U.S. dealers: 1,768,753 (incl. Mustangs). Model year sales by U.S. dealers: 1,830,417 (incl. Mustangs).

NOTE: Totals above do not include Club Wagons, of which 43,917 were sold in the model year; or imported Fiestas, which recorded sales of 81,273).

HISTORY: Model year sales increased modestly for 1978, though production slipped a bit. Major recalls of more than 4 million vehicles, however (and investigations of many more), did Ford's reputation no good. Most serious were the Pintos recalled for gas tanks that might burst into flame, followed by automatic transmissions that were alleged to jerk suddenly from "park" to "reverse" (a situation that never was fully resolved). At this time, too, Ford president Lee Iacocca was replaced by Philip Caldwell; and Iacocca reemerged within a few months as the new head of Chrysler. The new compact Fairmont sold far better than its predecessor Maverick: 417,932 Fairmonts versus just 105,156 Mavericks sold in 1977. Fairmont sold even better as a first-year car than had Mustang when it was introduced. 1977 had been Thunderbird's best sales year, and it sold well in 1978 too. Granada and LTD II sales plummeted for the model year. Fairmont was "the most successful new-car nameplate ever introduced by a domestic manufacturer and Ford's top selling car line in 1978," said Walter S.

Walla, Ford Division General Manager. It was also highly rated by the auto magazines. Readers of *Car and Driver* called it 'most significant new American car for 1978. Computer-assisted design techniques had been used to develop the Fairmont/Zephyr duo, along with over 320 hours of wind-tunnel testing. Corporate Average Fuel Economy (CAFE) standards began this year. Automakers' fleets would be required to meet a specified average miles-per-gallon rating each year for the next decade, with 27.5 MPG the ultimate goal. Fairmont, in fact, was designed with the CAFE ratings in mind, which required that Fords average 18 MPG. This year's model introduction meetings had been held in the Detroit and Dearborn area for the first time since 1959. More than 15,000 dealers, general managers and spouses attended. The international emphasis was highlighted by a 'flags of the world of Ford' display at the world headquarters, in a special ceremony. On the import front, Ford began to import the tiny front-wheel drive Fiesta from its German plant.

1979 FORD

1979 Ford Pinto three-door Runabout. (F)

Full-size Fords finally received their expected downsizing, two years later than equivalent General Motors models. Mustang (listed separately) also offered some big news for 1979 with a total restyle. Pinto got a more modest alteration, while Thunderbird switched grilles. CAFE standards rose from 18 to 19 MPG this year, prompting powertrain refinements. The 2.3-liter four on Pinto/Fairmont got an aluminum or plastic fan, oil filler cap and rear cover plate. The 2.8-liter V-6 got a new camshaft design. An aluminum intake manifold went on the 302 cid V-8 in LTD and some Granadas. The 351 cid V-8 ('W' version), optional in LTD, LTD II and Thunderbird, lost up to 40 pounds by switching to an aluminum intake manifold, water pump and rear cover.

1979 Ford Pinto ESS three-door hatchback. (PH)

1979 Ford Pinto Cruising Wagon. (PH)

1979 Ford Pinto Squire station wagon. (OCW)

PINTO — FOUR/V-6 — Restyling brought the subcompact Pinto a new front-end look with single rectangular headlamps in bright housings, as well as a new sloping hood and fenders, and horizontal-style argent grille. Single vertical parking lamps stood inboard of the headlamps, which were recessed farther back than the parking lamps. The slat-style grille contained three horizontal divider bars. 'Ford' block letters stood at the hood front. New sculptured-look front/rear aluminum bumpers had black rub strips and end sections. Small backup lenses were at inner ends of the new sedan/ Runabout horizontal-design tail lamps, extending through the upper, center and lower sections. Full wheel covers took on a new design. Inside, a new instrument panel and pad held rectangular instrument pods. The redesigned cluster now included a speedometer graduated in miles and kilometers, fuel gauge, and warning lights with symbols. New body and interior colors were available. As before, two-door sedan, 'three-door' hatchback Runabout and station wagon models were offered. A Cruising Package became optional on both Runabouts and wagons, featuring multi-color bodyside paint/tape treatment and black louvers on the wagon's liftgate window. There was also a new ESS option for sedans and Runabouts, with black grille and exterior accents, black-hinged glass third door, wide black bodyside moldings, and sports-type equipment. Other new options included lacy-spoke cast aluminum wheels, AM/FM stereo radio with cassette, separate light and convenience groups (formerly combined), heavy-duty battery, and a revised Exterior Decor group. Pinto's standard equipment list grew longer this year, adding an AM radio, power brakes, electric rear defroster, and tinted glass. The low-budget Pony lacked some of these extras. Standard engine remained the 140 cid (2.3-liter) overhead-cam four, with four-speed gearbox; automatic and V-6 optional. Oil-change intervals were raised to 30,000 miles. The V-6 added a higher-performance camshaft, while V-6 automatic transmissions were meant to offer higher rpm. shift points to improve acceleration.

1979 Ford Fairmont Squire wagon. (F)

1979 Ford Fairmont two-door sedan. (OCW)

1979 Ford Granada sedan (with optional two-tone paint and cast aluminum wheels). (OCW)

FAIRMONT — FOUR/SIX/V-8 — Appearance of the year-old compact didn't change this year. Model lineup included two-door and four-door sedans, a station wagon, and the uniquely-styled Futura coupe. Seven new body colors and four new vinyl roof colors were available. Availability of the distinctive tu-tone paint treatment was expanded to sedans, as well as the Futura. A four-speed overdrive manual transmission with new single-rail shifter design replaced the former three-speed, with either the 200 cid (3.3-liter) inline six or 302 cid (5.0-liter) V-8. (V-8s formerly came only with automatic.) Base engine remained the 140 cid (2.3-liter) four, with non-overdrive four-speed manual gearbox. The six was now offered on California wagons. Ignition and door locks were modified to improve theft-resistance. A lower axle ratio (2.26:1) came with the V-8 and automatic. Inside was a new dark walnut woodtone instrument cluster appliqué. New options included tilt steering, new-design speed control, performance instruments (including tachometer and trip odometer), ultra-fidelity premium sound system, remote decklid release, styled steel wheels with trim rings, and flip-up open-air roof. Wide vinyl-insert bodyside moldings were available on Futura. The Futura Sports Group included unique tape striping, charcoal argent grille and color-keyed turbine wheel covers, but dispensed with the usual hood ornament. Futura again sported a unique front end with quad rectangular headlamps, wrapover roof pillar, wide tapered B-pillars, and wraparound tail lamps. Fairmont's ES package was offered again. It included a blackout grille, black cowl grille, bright belt moldings, black window frames and quarter window vent louvers, black/bright bodyside moldings. dual black sail-mount sport mirrors (left remote), turbine wheel covers, handling suspension with rear stabilizer bar, and 5.5 inch wheels.

GRANADA — SIX/V-8 — Billed as 'An American Classic' (playing on its Mercedes lookalike origins), Granada changed little for 1979. Few customers had chosen four-wheel disc brakes, so that option was dropped. Both the standard 250 cid (3.3-liter) inline six and 302 cid (5.0-liter) V-8 came with a four-speed overdrive manual gearbox that used a new enclosed single-rail shift mechanism. As before, two- and four-door sedans were produced, in base, Ghia or ESS trim. Four new body colors and two new vinyl roof colors were offered, along with a paint and tape treatment option. Base models got all-bright versions of the '78 Ghia wheel cover. A thin, contemporary wheel lip molding replaced Ghia's former wider moldings. Ghia seats had a new sew style, as well as all-vinyl door trim with carpeted lower panels. Leather/vinyl trim was now available with bucket seats in the Interior Decor group. New soft Rossano cloth became optional on the base flight bench seat. New Wilshire cloth luxury trim was available. Bright moldings replaced the color-keyed moldings on the vinyl roof. A new light-weight aluminum intake manifold went on V-8s in four-doors. Electronic voltage regulators were new. Ignition locks offered improved theft-resistance. New options included tone-on-tone paint in five color combinations. Dropped were white lacy-spoke aluminum wheels, Traction-Lok axle, and the Luxury Interior Group. This year's ESS option was identified by 'Granada' script above the 'ESS' badge, rather than below, on the lower cowl. Granada ESS had blacked-out grille and exterior trim, color-keyed wheel covers and dual mirrors, decklid and hood pinstriping, individually reclining bucket seats with Euro headrests, and leather-wrapped steering wheel. Optional speed control for the ESS included a black leather-wrapped steering wheel.

1979 Ford Granada Ghia coupe. (F)

1979 Ford Granada ESS sedan. (OCW)

1979 Ford LTD II hardtop coupe (with Sports Appearance Package). (OCW)

LTD II — V-8 — Not enough buyers had found LTD II appealing, so this would be its third and final season. Not much was new this year, except for a redesigned front bumper spoiler, corrosion-resistant plastic battery tray, and electronic voltage regulator. Seven body colors were new, as were front and full vinyl roofs. Broughams had new interior fabric selections. All models had standard flight bench seating with fold-down center armrest. The 400 cid V-8 option was abandoned. Base engine remained the 302 cid (5.0-liter) V-8, with 351 V-8 optional. Automatic transmission was standard. A newly optional 27.5 gallon gas tank suggested that LTD II's economy problems hadn't quite been corrected by the use of a lighter weight front bumper this year, or by carburetor refinements, Rear bumper guards became standard, and the ignition lock was modified. The Sports Touring Package included two-tone paint with tape breaks on the bodyside/hood/lower back panel, as well as a grille badge and Magnum 500 wheels with HR78 x 14 RWL tires. A Sports Appearance Group for two-doors had bold tri-color tape stripes. As before, two-door hardtop and four-door pillared hardtop bodies were offered, in base, Brougham or 'S' trim. The low-cost 'S' model had an upgraded bench seat and woodtone instrument panel appliqué this year.

LTD — V-8 — Substantial downsizing made this year's LTD the ninth all-new full-size model in the company's history. Still built with body-on-frame construction, it was intended to be space-efficient as well as fuel-efficient, a result of over 270 hours of wind-tunnel testing. Riding a 114.4 inch wheelbase (7 inches shorter than before), the reduced LTD managed to increase its former interior space while shrinking on the outside. A conventional sedan design replaced the former pillared hardtop style. Door openings grew larger, and doors thinner. Both the cowl and hood were lower. So was the car's beltline. Glass area expanded. Overall, the new design was slightly taller and more boxy. Inside, LTD's seating position was higher. LTD's tighter crosshatch grille was split into two side-by-side sections by a narrow vertical divider, and topped by a wide upper bar. The grille looked flatter than before. 'Ford' letters went on the driver's side of the upper grille header. Base models displayed single rectangular headlamps with outboard fendertip signal lamps, while quad rectangular head-lamps above rectangular park/signal lamps went on Landau and Squire models. Front marker lenses wrapped around fender sides, matching the headlamps and parking lamps. A tall. narrow ornament

adorned the hood. Two-doors were four-window design with a slim coach-style quarter window. Landaus had new rear-pillar coach lamps. Country Squire wagons showed a new woodtone appliqué treatment. Large vertical rectangular tail lamps were rather wide, each with a small backup lens below. The recessed license plate housing was in the decklid's center, with 'Ford' letters on left of decklid. Inside were thin-back seats with foam padding over flex-o-lator cushion support, and a four-spoke soft-rim steering wheel. A steering-column stalk held the dimmer, horn and wiper/washer controls. Door-lock plungers moved to the armrests to improve theft-resistance. Lockable side stowage compartments were standard on wagons. Base engine, except on wagons with California emissions, was the 302 cid (5.0-liter) V-8. That engine had a new single accessory-drive belt operating the fan/water pump, alternator, and power steering pump. A variable-venturi carburetor became standard on both the 302 and the optional 351 V-8 engines. Up front was a new short/long arm coil spring front suspension with link-type stabilizer bar; at the rear, a new four-bar link coil spring setup. Front disc brakes used a new pin-slider design. LTD's option list still included speed control, tilt steering, automatic temperature-control air conditioning, heavy-duty trailer towing package, and the 351 V-8. along with other popular extras. New options this year were: special handling suspension system, premium stereo sound, digital clock with time/date/elapsed time, flight bench seating with dual reclining seatbacks, power antenna, and 40-channel CB radio. Also available: window-frame-mounted mirrors, bumper rub strips, electronic AM/FM stereo search radio with Quadrasonic 8 tape player, AM/FM stereo radio with cassette. tu-tone paint/tape treatment, and Exterior Accent Group. The Convenience Group added a trip odometer and low fuel/low washer fluid warning lights. A "resume" feature was added to the fingertip speed control; a left-hand recliner added to split bench seats. Options dropped included the 400 and 460 V-8 engines, Traction-Lok, four-wheel disc brakes, leather seat trim, color-keyed wheel covers, deep-dish aluminum wheels, and fender skirts.

1979 Ford LTD Country Squire station wagon. (F)

1979 Ford LTD Landau sedan. (OCW)

1979 Ford Thunderbird Heritage Edition hardtop coupe. (F)

1979 Ford Thunderbird hardtop coupe. (OCW)

THUNDERBIRD — V-8 — A much bolder, heavier-looking box-texture grille greeted Thunderbird customers this year. A large 4x4 grid pattern (just three horizontal and three vertical bars) stood in front of thin vertical bars. A new spoiler went below the front bumper. Clear fender-tip parking lamps with adjoining amber marker lenses each held three horizontal divider strips. Separate large rectangular tail lamps, replacing the former full-width units, were essentially a rectangle within a rectangle, with T-bird emblem in the center. A single backup lamp stood between them, centered over new standard rear bumper guards. Thunderbird also had a new electronic voltage regulator, and carburetor refinements on the standard 302 cid (5.0-liter) V-8. Door and ignition locks were modified for theft protection. Eight body colors, five vinyl roof colors, and four interior trim colors were new. Standard seating was now the flight bench design with Rossano cloth seating surfaces and large fold-down front armrest. Front fenders held a vertical set of 'louvers.' Bodysides showed narrow opera windows, with large rear swept-back side windows. Headlamp covers held a wide insignia, plus 'Thunderbird' script on the left one, A posh new Heritage model replaced the Diamond Jubilee edition. 'Heritage' script went on the huge blank C-pillar, as that model had no large rear side window. Heritage had two monochromatic body color themes in maroon or light medium blue, with formal padded vinyl roof. Equipment included 36-ounce cut-pile carpeting, split bench seats in soft velour cloth (or optional leather seating surfaces), leather-wrapped steering wheel, sports instrument panel with tachometer and gauges, driver's lighted visor vanity mirror, and AM/FM stereo radio. Town Landau had a brushed aluminum wrapover appliqué, color-keyed hood ornament, cast aluminum wheels with accent paint, and wide vinyl-insert bodyside moldings. New options included an extended-range 27.5-gallon gas tank (standard on Town Landau and Heritage), AM/FM stereo radio with cassette, mud/stone deflectors, and ultra-soft leather/vinyl upholstery (for Heritage). Bucket seats and a console could be ordered separately, or as a no-cost extra with the Interior Decor Group.

I.D. DATA: Ford's 11-symbol Vehicle Identification Number (VIN) is stamped on a metal tab fastened to the instrument panel, visible through the windshield. The first digit is a model year code ('9' 1979). The second letter indicates assembly plant: 'A' Atlanta, GA; 'B' Oakville, Ontario (Canada); 'E' Mahwah, NJ; 'G' Chicago; 'H' Lorain, Ohio; 'J' Los Angeles; 'K' Kansas City, MO; 'S' St. Thomas, Ontario; 'T' Metuchen, NJ; 'U' Louisville, KY; 'W' Wayne, MI. Digits three and four are the body serial code, which corresponds to the Model Numbers shown in the tables below (e.g., '10' Pinto 2-dr. sedan). The fifth symbol is an engine code: 'Y' L4-140 2Bbl.; 'Z' V6-170 2Bbl.; 'T' L6-200 1Bbl.; 'L' L6-250 1Bbl.; 'F' V8-302 2Bbl.; 'H' V8-351 2Bbl. Finally, digits 6-11 make up the consecutive unit number of cars built at each assembly plant. The number begins with 100001. A Vehicle Certification Label on the left front door lock face panel or door pillar shows the manufacturer, month and year of manufacture, GVW. GAWR, certification statement, VIN, body code, color code, trim code, axle code, transmission code, and special order code.

1979 Ford Fairmont Futura sedan. (F)

PINTO (FOUR/V-6)

Model No.	Body/ Style No.	Body Type & Seating	Factory Price	Shipping Weight	Prod. Total
10	62B	2-dr. Sedan-4P	3629/3902	2346/2446	75,789
10	41E	2-dr. Pony Sed-4P	3199/----	2329/----	Note 1
11	64B	3-dr. Hatch-4P	3744/4017	2392/2492	69,383
12	738	2-dr. Sta Wag-4P	4028/4301	2532/2610	53,846
12	41E	2-dr. Pony Wag-4P	3633/----	N/A	Note 1
12	73B	2-dr. Sqr Wag-4P	4343/4616	2568/2646	Note 2

NOTE 1: Pony production included in base sedan and wagon figures.

NOTE 2: Squire Wagon production is included in standard station wagon total.

FAIRMONT (FOUR/SIX)

93	36R	2-dr. Spt Cpe-5P	4071/4312	2546/2613	106,065
91	66B	2-dr. Sedan-5P	3710/3951	2491/2558	54,798
92	54B	4-dr. Sedan-5P	3810/4051	2544/2611	133,813
94	74B	4-dr. Sta Wag-5P	4157/4398	2674/2741	100,691

FAIRMONT ENGINE NOTE: Prices shown are for four-cylinder and six-cylinder engines. A V-8 cost $283 more than the six.

GRANADA (SIX/V-8)

Model No.	Body/ Style No.	Body Type & Seating	Factory Price	Shipping Weight	Prod. Total
81	66H	2-dr. Sedan-5P	4342/4625	3051/3124	76,850
82	54H	4-dr. Sedan-5P	4445/4728	3098/3169	105,526

GRANADA GHIA (SIX/V-8)

81/602	66K	2-dr. Sedan-5P	4728/5011	3089/3160	Note 3
82/602	54K	4-dr. Sedan-5P	4830/5113	3132/3203	Note 3

GRANADA ESS (SIX/V-8)

81/433	N/A	2-dr. Sedan-5P	4888/5161	3105/3176	Note 3
82/433	N/A	4-dr. Sedan-5P	4990/5273	3155/3226	Note 3

NOTE 3: Granada Ghia and ESS production is included in base Granada totals above.

LTD II (V-8)

30	65D	2-dr. HT Cpe-6P	5445	3797	18,300
31	53D	4-dr. Pill. HT-6P	5569	3860	19,781

LTD II 'S' (V-8)

25	65B	2-dr. HT Cpe-6P	5198	3781	834
27	53B	4-dr. Pill. HT-6P	5298	3844	9,649

PRODUCTION NOTE: LTD 'S' was for fleet sale only.

LTD II BROUGHAM (V-8)

30	65K	2-dr. HT Cpe-6P	5780	3815	Note 4
31	53K	4-dr. Pill. HT-6P	5905	3889	Note 4

NOTE 4: Brougham production is included in LTD II totals above.

LTD (V-8)

62	66H	2-dr. Sedan-6P	5813	3421	54,005
63	54H	4-dr. Sedan-6P	5913	3463	117,730
74	74H	4-dr. Sta Wag-6P	6122	3678	37,955
74	74K	4-dr. Ctry Sqr-6P	6615	3719	29,932

LTD PRODUCTION NOTES: Production of wagons with dual-facing rear seats (a $145-$149 option for both standard and Country Squire wagon) is included in base wagon totals. Totals also include production of Custom 500 models for Canadian market (2,036 two-doors, 4,567 four-doors and 1,568 wagons).

LTD LANDAU (V-8)

64	66K	2-dr. Sedan-6P	6349	3472	42,314
65	54K	4-dr. Sedan-6P	6474	3527	74,599

THUNDERBIRD (V-8)

87	60H	2-dr. HT Cpe-6P	5877	3893	284,141

THUNDERBIRD TOWN LANDAU (V-8)

Model No.	Body/ Style No.	Body Type & Seating	Factory Price	Shipping Weight	Prod. Total
87/607	60H	2-dr. HT Cpe-6P	8866	4284	Note 5

THUNDERBIRD HERITAGE EDITION (V-8)

87/603	60H	2-dr. HT Cpe-6P	10687	4178	Note 5

NOTE 5: Town Landau and Heritage production is included in basic Thunderbird total.

FACTORY PRICE AND WEIGHT NOTE: Pinto/Fairmont prices and weights to left of slash are for four-cylinder, to right for six-cylinder engine. For Granada, prices and weights to left of slash are for six-cylinder, to right for V-8 engine.

ENGINE [Base Four (Pinto, Fairmont)]: Inline. Overhead cam. Four-cylinder. Cast-iron block and head. Displacement: 140 cid (2.3 liters). Bore & stroke: 3.78 x 3.13 in. Compression ratio: 9.0:1. Brake horsepower: 88 at 4800 rpm. Torque: 118 lbs.-ft. at 2800 rpm. Five main bearings. Hydraulic valve lifters. Carburetor: 2Bbl. Motorcraft 5200, VIN Code: Y.

ENGINE [Optional V-6 (Pinto)]: 60-degree, overhead-valve V-6. Cast-iron block and head. Displacement: 170.8 cid (2.8 liters). Bore & stroke: 3.66 x 2.70 in. Compression ratio: 8.7:1. Brake horsepower: 102 at 4400 rpm. Torque: 138 lbs.-ft. at 3200 rpm. Four main bearings. Solid valve lifters. Carburetor: 2Bbl. Motorcraft 2150 or 27OOVV. VIN Code: Z.

ENGINE [Optional Six (Fairmont)]: Inline. Overhead valve. Six-cylinder. Cast-iron block and head. Displacement: 200 cid (3.3 liters). Bore & stroke: 3.68 x 3.13 in. Compression ratio: 8.5: 1. Brake horsepower: 85 at 3600 rpm. Torque: 154 lb.-ft, at 1600 rpm. Seven main bearings. Hydraulic valve lifters. Carburetor: 1Bbl. Carter YFA or Holley 1946. VIN Code: T.

ENGINE [Base Six (Granada)]: Inline. Overhead valve. Six-cylinder. Cast-iron block and head. Displacement: 250 cid (4.1 liters). Bore & stroke: 3.68 x 3.91 in. Compression ratio: 8.6:1. Brake horsepower: 97 at 3200 rpm. Torque: 210 lbs.-ft. at 1400 rpm. Seven main bearings. Hydraulic valve lifters, Carburetor: 1Bbl. Carter YFA. VIN Code: L.

ENGINE [Base V-8 (LTD II, Thunderbird, LTD); Optional (Fairmont, Granada)]: 90-degree, overhead valve V-8. Cast-iron block and head. Displacement: 302 cid (5.0 liters). Bore & stroke: 4.00 x 3.00 in. Compression ratio: 8.4:1. Brake horsepower: (LTD) 129 at 3600 rpm.; (LTD II/TBird) 133 at 3400; (Fairmont) 140 at 3600; (Granada) 137 at 3600. Torque: (LTD) 223 lbs.-ft. at 2600 rpm.; (LTD II/TBird) 245 at 1600; (Fairmont) 250 at 1800; (Granada) 243 at 2000. Five main bearings. Hydraulic valve lifters. Carburetor: 2Bbl. Motorcraft 2150 or 27OOVV. VIN Code: F.

ENGINE [Optional V-8 (LTD, Thunderbird)]: 90-degree, overhead valve V-8. Cast-iron block and head. Displacement: 351 cid (5.8 liters). Bore & stroke: 4.00 x 3.50 in. Compression ratio: 8.3:1. Brake horsepower: 135 or 142 at 3200 rpm. Torque: 286 lbs.-ft. at 1400 rpm. Five main bearings. Hydraulic valve lifters. Carburetor: 2Bbl. Motorcraft 72OOVV. Windsor engine. VIN Code: H.

ENGINE [Optional V-8 (LTD II, LTD, Thunderbird)]: Modified version of 351 cid V-8 above Compression: 8.0:1. Brake H.P.: 151 at 3600 rpm. Torque: 270 lbs.-ft. at 2200 rpm. Carb: Motorcraft 2150.

1979 Ford LTD Landau sedan. (F)

CHASSIS DATA: Wheelbase: (Pinto) 94.5 in.; (Pinto wag) 94.8 in.; (Fairmont) 105.5 in.; (Granada) 109.9 in.; (LTD II 2dr.) 114.0 in.; (LTD II 4dr.) 118.0 in.; (LTD) 114.4 in.; (TBird) 114.0 in. Overall Length: (Pinto) 168.8 in.; (Pinto wag) 178.6 in.; (Fairmont) 193.8 in, exc. Futura coupe, 195.8 in.; (Granada) 197.8 in.; (LTD II 2dr.) 217.2 in.; (LTD II 4dr.) 221.2 in.; (LTD) 209.0 in.; (LTD wag) 212.9 in.; (TBird) 217.2 in. Height: (Pinto) 50.6 in.; (Pinto wag) 52.1 in.; (Fairmont) 53.5 in.; (Fairmont Futura cpe) 52.3 in.; (Fairmont wag) 54.4 in.; (Granada) 53.2 in.; (LTD II 2dr.) 52.6 in.; (LTD II 4dr.) 53.3 in.; (LTD) 54.5 in.; (LTD wag) 56.7 in.; (TBird) 52.8 in. Width: (Pinto) 69.4 in.; (Pinto wag) 69.7 in.; (Fairmont) 71.0 in.; (Granada) 74.0 in.; (LTD II) 78.6 in.; (LTD) 77.5 in.; (LTD wag) 79.3 in.; (TBird) 78.5 in. Front Tread: (Pinto) 55.0 in.; (Fairmont) 56.6 in.; (Granada) 59.0 in.; (LTD II) 63.6 in. (LTD) 62.2 in. (TBird) 63.2 in. Rear Tread: (Pinto) 55.8in.; (Fairmont) 57.0 in.; (Granada) 57.7 in.; (LTD II) 63.5 in.; (LTD) 62.0 in. (TBird) 63.1in. Standard Tires: (Pinto) A78 x 13; (Fairmont) B78 x 14, except CR78 x 14 on wagon; (Granada) DR78 x 14 SBR BSW; (Granada Ghia) ER78 x 14; (LTD II) HR78 x 14 SBR BSW; (LTD) FR78 x 14 SBR SSW exc. wagon, GR78 x 14; (TBird) GR78 x 15 SBR BSW.

TECHNICAL: Transmission: Four-speed manual standard on Pinto/Fairmont four: (1st) 3.98:1; (2nd) 2.14:1; (3rd) 1.42:1; (4th) 1.00:1; (Rev) 3.99:1. Four-speed overdrive manual standard on Fairmont/Granada six/V-8. Six-cylinder: (lst) 3.29:1; (2nd) 1.84:1; (3rd) 1.00:1; (4th) 0.81:1; (Rev) 3.29:1. V-8 ratios: (1st) 3.07:1; (2nd) 1.72:1; (3rd) 1.00:1; (4th) 0.70:1; (Rev) 3.07:1. Three-speed automatic standard on other models, optional on all, Pinto/Fairmont four-cylinder (and Fairmont six) gear ratios: (1st) 2.47:1; (2nd) 1.47:1; (3rd) 1.00:1; (Rev) 2.11:1. LTD II/TBird w/V8-351: (1st) 2.40:1; (2nd) 1.47:1; (3rd) 1.00:1; (Rev) 2.00:1. Other models: (1st) 2.46:1; (2nd) 1.46:1; (3rd) 1.00:1; (Rev) 2.18:1 to 2.20:1. Standard final drive ratio: (Pinto) 2.73:1 or 3.08:1; (Fairmont) 3.08:1 exc. 2.73:1 w/six and auto., 2.26:1 w/V-8 and auto.; (Granada) 3.00:1 w/4spd; (LTD II) 2.75:1 or 2.47:1; (LTD) 2.26:1 exc. wag, 2.73:1 or 2.26:1; (TBird) 2.75:1 exc. w/V8-351, 2.47:1. Steering: Pinto/Fairmont) rack and pinion; (others) recirculating ball. Front Suspension: (Pinto) coil springs with short/long control arms, and anti-sway bar with V-6; (Fairmont) MacPherson struts with coil springs on lower control arms and link-type anti-sway bar; (Granada/LTD II/TBird) coil springs with short/long control arms and anti-sway bar; (LTD) long/short control arms w/coil springs and link-type stabilizer. Rear Suspension: (Pinto/Granada) rigid axle w/semi-elliptic leaf springs; (Fairmont) four-bar link coil springs; (LTD II/TBird) rigid axle w/lower trailing radius arms, upper oblique torque arms, coil springs and anti-sway bar; (LTD) rigid axle w/four-bar link and helical coil springs. Brakes: Front disc, rear drum. Ignition: Electronic. Body construction: (Pinto/Fairmont/Granada) unibody; (LTD II/LTD/TBird) separate body and perimeter box frame. Fuel tank: (Pinto) 11.7 gal.; (Pinto wag) 14 gal.; (Fairmont) 16 gal.; (Granada) 18 gal.; (LTD II) 21 gal.; (LTD) 19 gal. exc. wagon, 20 gal.; (TBird) 21 gal. exc. 27.5 gal. on Town Landau and Heritage.

DRIVETRAIN OPTIONS: Engines: 170 cid V-6: Pinto ($273). 200 cid, 1Bbl six: Fairmont ($241). 302 cid, 2Bbl. V-8: Fairmont ($524); Granada ($283). 351 cid, 2Bbl. V-8: LTD II/LTD/TBird ($263). Transmission/Differential: Cruise-O-matic trans.: Pinto ($307); Fairmont ($401); Fairmont wagon ($307); Granada ($307). Floor shift lever: Fairmont/Granada ($31). Traction-Lok differential: LTD II/TBird ($64). Optional axle ratio: Pinto ($13); LTD ($18). Brakes & Steering: Power brakes: Pinto/Fairmont/Granada ($70). Power steering: Pinto ($141); Fairmont ($149); Granada ($155). Suspension: H.D. susp.: Fairmont ($19-$25); Granada ($20); LTD II ($41); LTD/TBird ($22). Handling susp.: Fairmont ($41); LTD ($42). Adjustable air shock absorbers: LTD ($54). Other: H.D. battery ($18-$21). H.D. alternator: LTD II/LTD ($50). Engine block heater ($13-$14). Trailer towing pkg. (heavy duty): LTD ($161-$192). California emission system: Pinto ($69); Fairmont/Granada ($76); others ($83). High-altitude option ($33-$36).

PINTO CONVENIENCE/APPEARANCE OPTIONS: Option Packages: ESS pkg. ($236-$261). Cruising pkg. ($330-$566); tape delete ($55 credit). Sport pkg. ($96-$110). Exterior decor group ($20-$40). Interior decor group ($137-$207). Interior accent group ($5-$40). Convenience group ($24-$61). Deluxe bumper group ($52). Protection group ($33-$36). Light group ($25-$37). Comfort/Convenience: Air conditioner ($484). Rear defroster ($84). Tinted glass ($59). Cigar lighter ($5). Trunk light ($5). Driver's sport mirror ($18). Dual sport mirrors ($52). Day/night mirror ($10). Entertainment: AM radio: Pony ($65). AM radio w/digital clock ($47-$119); w/stereo tape player ($119-$192). AM/FM radio ($48-$120). AM/FM stereo radio ($89-$161); w/cassette player ($157-$222). Radio flexibility option ($90). Exterior: Flip-up open air roof ($199). Glass third door ($25). Metallic glow paint ($41). Two-tone paint/tape treatment ($76). Accent tape stripe ($76). Black narrow vinyl-insert bodyside moldings ($39). Premium bodyside moldings ($10-$48). Rear bumper guards ($19). Roof luggage rack ($63). Mud/stone deflectors ($23). Lower bodyside protection ($30). Interior: Four-way driver's seat ($35). Load floor carpet ($24). Cargo area cover ($28). Front floor mats ($18). Wheels: Wire wheel covers ($99). Forged aluminum wheels ($217-$289); white ($235-$307). Lacy spoke alum. wheels ($217-$289). Styled steel wheels ($54). Tires: A78 x 13 WSW ($43). BR78 x 13 BSW ($148); WSW ($191). BR70 x 13 RWL ($228).

1979 Ford Fairmont Futura Sport Coupe. (F)

FAIRMONT CONVENIENCE/APPEARANCE OPTIONS: Option Packages: ES option ($329). Futura sports group ($102). Ghia pkg. ($207-$498). Squire option ($399). Exterior decor group ($223). Exterior accent group ($82). Interior decor group ($170-$311). Interior accent group ($80-$84). Instrumentation group ($77). Deluxe bumper group ($57). Convenience group ($33-$65). Appearance protection group ($36-$47). Light group ($27-$43). Comfort/Convenience: Air cond. ($484). Rear defogger ($51). Rear defroster, electric ($90). Fingertip speed control ($104-$116). Power windows ($116-$163). Power door locks ($73-$101). Power decklid release ($22). Power seat ($94). Tinted glass ($59); windshield only ($25). Sport steering wheel ($39). Tilt steering ($69-$81). Electric clock ($20). Cigar lighter ($7). Interval wipers ($35). Rear wiper/washer ($63). Map light ($7). Trunk light ($7). Left remote mirror ($17). Dual bright mirrors ($37-$43). Day/night mirror ($10). Entertainment: AM radio ($72); w/8track tape player ($192). AM/FM radio ($120). AM/FM stereo radio ($176); w/8 track or cassette player ($243). Premium sound system ($67). Radio flexibility ($93). Exterior: Flip-up open air roof ($199). Full vinyl roof ($90). Metallic glow paint ($48). Two-tone paint ($51); special ($51-$207). Accent stripe ($28). Pivoting front vent windows ($48). Rear quarter vent louvers ($35). Vinyl bodyside moldings ($39); wide black vinyl ($41). Rocker panel moldings ($25). Bright window frames ($18). Bumper guards, rear ($20). Luggage rack ($76). Lower bodyside protection ($30-$42). Interior: Vinyl bucket seats, non-reclining ($72). Bench seat ($72 credit). Cloth/vinyl seat trim ($20-$42). Vinyl seat trim ($24). Front floor mats ($18). Lockable side storage box ($20). Wheels: Hubcaps w/trim rings ($37). Deluxe wheel covers ($37). Turbine wheel covers ($39-$76). Wire wheel covers ($50-$127). Styled steel wheels ($40-$116). Cast aluminum wheels ($251-$327). Tires: B78 x 14 WSW. BR78 x 14 BSW/WSW. C78 x 14 BSW/WSW. CR78 x 14 BSW/WSW. DR78 x 14 SBR BSW/WSW/RWL.

GRANADA CONVENIENCE/APPEARANCE OPTIONS: Option Packages: Interior decor group ($211). Convenience group ($35-$94). Deluxe bumper group ($78). Light group ($41-$46). Cold weather group ($30-$60). Heavy-duty group ($18-$60). Protection group ($24-$47). Visibility group ($5-$70). Comfort/Convenience: Air cond. ($514); auto-temp ($555). Rear defogger ($51). Rear defroster, electric ($90). Fingertip speed control ($104-$116). Illuminated entry system ($52). Power windows ($120-$171). Power door locks ($78-$110). Power decklid release ($22). Auto. parking brake release ($8). Power four-way seat ($94). Tinted glass ($64); windshield only ($25). Tilt steering wheel ($69). Digital clock ($47). Lighting and Mirrors: Cornering lamps ($43). Trunk light ($7). Left remote mirror ($17). Dual remote mirrors ($37-$54). Dual sport mirrors ($46-$63). Day/night mirror ($11). Lighted right visor vanity mirror ($36). Entertainment: AM radio ($72); w/tape player ($192). AM/FM radio ($135). AM/FM stereo radio ($176); w/8 track or cassette player ($243); w/quadrasonic tape ($365). AM/FM stereo search radio ($319). CB radio ($270). Radio flexibility ($93). Exterior: Power moonroof ($899). Full or half vinyl roof ($106). Metallic glow paint ($48). Bodyside/decklid paint stripes ($36). Two-tone paint/tape ($163). Bodyside accent moldings ($43). Black vinyl insert bodyside moldings ($39). Rocker panel moldings ($25). Lower bodyside protection ($31). Interior: Console ($99). Four-way driver's seat ($34). Reclining seats (NC). Leather seat trim ($271). Flight bench seat (NC). Cloth/vinyl flight bench seat ($54). Deluxe cloth/vinyl trim (NC). Front floor mats ($18). Color-keyed seatbelts ($19). Wheels: Deluxe wheel covers ($41) exc. Ghia/ESS (NC). Wire wheel covers ($108) exc. Ghia/ESS ($67). Styled steel wheels w/trim rings ($83-$124). Cast aluminum wheels ($248-$289). Tires: DR78 x 14 SBR WSW. ER78 x 14 SBR BSW/WSW. FR78 x 14 SBR BSW/WSW/wide WSW. Inflatable spare (NC).

LTD II CONVENIENCE/APPEARANCE OPTIONS: Option Packages: Sports appearance pkg.: 2dr. ($301-$449). Sports instrumentation group ($121-$151). Sports touring pkg.: 2dr. ($379-$526). Deluxe bumper group ($63). Light group ($51-$57). Convenience group ($120-$155). Power lock group ($111-$143). Protection group ($49-$61). Comfort/Convenience: Air cond. ($562); w/auto-temp control ($607). Rear defroster, electric ($99). Fingertip speed control ($113-$126). Illuminated entry system ($57). Tinted glass ($70); windshield only ($28). Power windows ($132-$187). Six-way power seat ($163). Tilt steering wheel ($75). Electric clock ($22). Day/date clock ($22-$45). Lighting, Horns and Mirrors: Cornering lamps ($49). Dual-note

horn ($9). Remote driver's mirror ($18). Dual sport mirrors ($9-$68). Lighted visor vanity mirror ($34-$39). Entertainment: AM radio ($79). AM/FM radio ($132). AM/FM stereo radio ($192); w/tape player ($266); w/quadrasonic tape player ($399). AM/FM stereo search radio ($349). CB radio ($295). Dual rear speakers ($46). Radio flexibility ($105). Exterior: Full or half vinyl roof ($116). Opera windows ($54). Vinyl-insert bodyside moldings ($42). Wide bright bodyside moldings ($42-$71). Rocker panel moldings ($29). Metallic glow paint ($64) exc. (NC) w/sports pkg. Two-tone paint ($82). Dual accent paint stripes ($33). Front bumper guards ($26). Mud/stone deflectors ($25). Lower bodyside protection ($33-$46). Interior: Bucket seats w/console ($211) exc. Brougham ($37). Vinyl seat trim ($26). Cloth/vinyl seat trim ($26). Front floor mats ($20). H.D. floor mats ($9). Color-keyed seatbelts ($22). Wheels/Tires: Deluxe wheel covers ($45). Luxury wheel covers ($66-$111). Wire wheel covers ($116-$161) exc. (NC) w/sports pkg. Cast aluminum wheels ($200-$361). HR78 x 14 SBR WSW ($47). GR78 x 15 SBR WSW ($48).

LTD CONVENIENCE/APPEARANCE OPTIONS: Option Packages: Interior luxury group: Landau ($705); Country Squire ($758). Exterior accent group ($29-$66). Convenience group ($68-$99). Light group ($32-$41). Protection group ($46-$55). Comfort/Convenience: Air cond. ($597); w/auto-temp control ($642). Rear defogger ($57). Rear defroster, electric ($100). Fingertip speed control ($113-$126). Illuminated entry system ($57). Power windows ($137-$203). Power door locks ($87-$161). Power driver's seat ($164); driver and passenger ($329). Tinted glass ($83); windshield only ($28). Tilt steering wheel ($76). Auto. parking brake release ($8). Electric clock ($24). Digital clock ($32-$55). Lighting. Horns and Mirrors: Cornering lamps ($49). Trunk light ($4). Dual-note horn ($9). Driver's remote mirror, door or sail mount ($18). Dual remote mirrors ($37-$55). Lighted visor vanity mirror ($36-$41). Entertainment: AM radio ($79). AM/FM radio ($132). AM/FM stereo radio ($192); w/tape player ($266). AM/FM stereo search radio w/quadrasonic tape player ($432). CB radio ($295). Power antenna ($47). Dual rear speakers ($46). Deluxe sound pkg. ($55); luxury pkg. ($42). Premium sound system ($74-$158). Radio flexibility ($105). Exterior: Full or half vinyl roof ($143). Metallic glow paint ($64). Two-tone paint/tape ($86-$118). Hood striping ($14). Rocker panel moldings ($29). Vinyl-insert bodyside moldings ($43). Bumper guards, front or rear ($26). Bumper rub strips ($54). Luggage rack ($113). Lower bodyside protection ($33-$46). Interior: Dual-facing rear seats: wagon ($145-$149). Flight bench seat ($99). Dual flight bench seat recliner ($58). Split bench seat w/passenger recliner ($187-$233). All-vinyl seat trim ($26). Duraweave vinyl trim ($52). Front floor mats ($20). H.D. floor mats ($9). Trunk trim ($41-$46). Color-keyed seatbelts ($24). Wheels: Full wheel covers ($39). Luxury wheel covers ($64). Wire wheel covers ($145). Tires: FR78 x 14 WSW ($47). GR78 x 14 BSW ($30). GR78 x 14 WSW ($47-$77). HR78 x 14 (wagon): BSW ($30); WSW ($77). Conventional spare ($13).

THUNDERBIRD CONVENIENCE/APPEARANCE OPTIONS: Option Packages: Sports decor group ($459-$518). Interior luxury group ($816). Exterior decor group ($346-$405). Interior decor group ($322). Sports instrumentation group ($87-$129). Convenience group ($108-$117). Protection group ($49-$53). Light group ($51). Power lock group ($111). Luxury sound insulation ($30). Comfort/Convenience: Air cond. ($562); auto-temp ($607) exc. Twn Lan/Heritage ($45). Rear defroster ($99). Fingertip speed control ($113-$126). Illuminated entry system ($57). Tinted glass ($70); windshield only ($28). Power windows ($132). Six-way power seat ($163). Automatic seatback release ($36). Seatbelt warning chime ($22). Tilt steering wheel ($75). Day/date clock ($24). Lighting and Mirrors: Cornering lamps ($49). Driver's remote mirror, chrome ($18). Dual sport mirrors ($9-$68). Lighted visor vanity mirror ($34-$39). Entertainment: AM/FM radio ($53). AM/FM stereo radio ($113); w/tape player ($187); w/quadrasonic tape player ($320) exc. Twn Lan/Heritage ($50). AM/FM stereo search radio ($270). CB radio ($295). AM radio delete ($79 credit). Power antenna ($47). Dual rear speakers ($46). Radio flexibility ($105). Exterior: T-Roof ($747). Power moonroof ($691). Vinyl roof, two-piece ($132). Metallic glow paint ($64). Two-tone paint ($82). Dual accent paint stripes ($46). Bright wide bodyside moldings ($42). Vinyl bodyside moldings ($42). Wide color-keyed vinyl bodyside moldings ($53). Rocker panel moldings ($29). Bumper rub strips ($37). Mud/stone deflectors ($25). Lower bodyside protection ($33-$46). Interior: Bucket seats w/console ($211) exc. ($37) w/decor group. Leather seat trim ($243-$309). Vinyl seat trim ($26). Front floor mats ($20). Trunk trim ($43). Color-keyed seatbelts ($22). Wheels/Tires: Wire wheel covers ($118). Styled wheels ($166). Cast aluminum wheels ($150-$316). GR78 x 15 WSW ($47). HR78 x 15 BSW ($25). HR78 x 15 WSW ($72). HR70 x 15 WSW ($29-$100). Inflatable spare (NC).

HISTORY: Introduced: October 6, 1978. Model year production: 1,835,937 (incl. Mustangs). Total passenger-car production for the U.S. market of 1,670,106 units (incl. Mustangs) included 448,627 four-cylinder, 485,842 sixes and 735,637 V-8s. Calendar year production (U.S.): 1,345,427 (incl. Mustangs). Calendar year sales by U.S. dealers: 1,499,098 (incl. Mustangs). Model year sales by U.S. dealers: 1,541,600 (incl. Mustangs).

NOTE: Totals above do not include Club Wagons, of which 42,449 were sold in the model year; or imported Fiestas, which recorded sales of 77,733.

HISTORY: To attempt to meet the CAFE requirement of 19 MPG gas mileage this year, Ford pushed sales of the new downsized LTD. Buyers seemed to want the big V-8 rather than economical fours and sixes, prompting Ford to increase the price of the V-8 model. LTD sales fell rather sharply, putting the reduced-size model far behind Caprice/Impala. LTD II production ceased in January 1979, amid flagging sales. Sales declined considerably for model year 1979, down 15 percent. A gasoline crisis in mid-year didn't help; but mainly, Ford had lagged behind other companies in downsizing its big-car lineup. Pinto sales were good, even though the outmoded design couldn't truly rival the new subcompacts. And sales of the new Mustang were most impressive-nearly 70 percent above the final figure for its second-generation predecessor. A replacement for the Pinto was scheduled for 1981, dubbed 'Erika.' That would, of course, be changed to Escort by the time the new front-drive subcompact was introduced. Not until then would Ford have a true rival to Chevrolet's Chevette. Lee Iacocca had been fired by Henry Ford II soon after the model year began. Philip Caldwell then became president.

1980 FORD

1980 Ford Pinto three-door hatchback. (JG)

Ford's emphasis this year lay in economy, highlighted by its new lockup overdrive automatic transmission. The 1980 CAFE goal for automakers' fleets was 20 MPG (up from 19 MPG in 1979). Thunderbird was the star of the lineup in its new downsized form. LTD II was gone, and Pinto was in its final season. On the powerplant front, a turbocharged four was announced as a Fairmont option, but didn't quite materialize, presumably due to mechanical difficulties. A smaller (255 cid) V-8 replaced the former 302 as a Fairmont option, and became standard on the new mid-size Thunderbird. LTD's new automatic overdrive transmission boasted an economy improvement of 19 percent over a comparable 1979 model.

PINTO-FOUR — All Pintos had four-cylinder engines for 1980, as the optional V-6 disappeared. The standard 140 cid (2.3-liter) four received improvements to boost its highway gas mileage. Styling was virtually identical to 1979, with seven new body colors and three new interior trim colors available. The low-budget Pony now wore steel-belted radial tires. Batteries were maintenance-free, and cars carried a restyled scissors jack. Radios played a Travelers' Advisory band, and the station wagon's Cruising Package option was revised. This was Pinto's final season, as the new front-drive Escort was ready for production. The Rallye Pack option, introduced late in 1979 on hatchback and wagon, was expanded this year. Model lineup continued as before: two-door sedan, 'three-door' hatchback Runabout, two-door station wagon, and Pony sedan or wagon. Pony lacked the base model's tinted glass, rear defroster, AM radio, bumper rub strips, and vinyl-insert bodyside moldings, as well as bright window frame, belt and B-pillar moldings. Pinto's ESS package included a charcoal grille and headlamp doors, black windshield and backlight moldings, dual black racing mirrors, glass third door with black hinges, blackout paint treatment, black wheel lip moldings, 'ESS' fender insignia, and black window frames. The price was $281 to $313.

FAIRMONT — **FOUR/SIX/V-8** — Powerplants were the major news in the Fairmont arena this year. Most notable was the announcement of a turbocharged four, but evidently that one never quite made production. A new 255 cid (4.2-liter) V-8 did, though, replacing the former 302 option. It was available only with automatic. Both the 255 and the 200 cid (3.3-liter) inline six had a new lightweight starter. Base engine remained the 140 cid (2.3-liter) four, with four-speed manual gearbox. Manual-shift transmissions had a new self-adjusting clutch. New high-pressure P-metric steel-

belted radial tires became standard on all models. A mini spare tire and maintenance-free battery were standard, while all radios added a Travelers' Advisory band. Fairmont came in nine new body colors and two new two-tone color schemes (with accent color in the bodyside center). A four-door sedan joined the Futura coupe at mid-year, wearing the unique Futura crosshatch grille. Futuras had standard halogen headlamps (except where prohibited by state laws). Otherwise, styling was similar to 1978-79. The Futura coupe had a woodgrain dash appliqué, quad halogen headlamps, trunk light, bright window frame moldings, vinyl bodyside moldings, and wheel lip and door belt moldings. The Futura sports group, priced at $114, included color-keyed turbine wheel covers, charcoal/argent grille, and youth-oriented tape stripes; the customary hood ornament, louvers and accent stripe were deleted. The optional sport steering wheel switched from brushed aluminum to black finish. Fairmont's $378 ES sedan option package included a blackout grille, front/rear rub strips, black cowl grille, black window frames and quarter window vent louvers, and vinyl-insert bodyside moldings. Also included: dual black remote sport mirrors, turbine wheel covers, black sport steering wheel, rear bumper guards, handling suspension, and black lower back panel.

1980 Ford Pinto three-door hatchback (with Rallye Pack option). (PH)

1980-1/2 Ford Fairmont Futura sedan. (OCW)

1980 Ford Fairmont two-door sedan (turbocharged). (PH)

1980 Ford Fairmont Futura Sport Coupe (turbocharged). (PH)

1980 Ford Granada Ghia sedan. (F)

GRANADA — SIX/V-8 — Apart from seven new body colors and three new vinyl roof colors, little changed on the compact Granada sedans. A new lightweight starter went under the hood, a better scissors jack in the trunk, and Ardmore cloth upholstery on the seats. Maintenance-free batteries were standard. Joining the option list were a heavy-duty 54-amp battery, mud/stone guards, and revised electronic search stereo radios and tape players. 'Tu-tone' paint cost $180. Standard engine was the 250 cid (4.1-liter) inline six. with 302 cid (5.0-liter) V-8 optional. California Granadas required the new 255 cid V-8. Granada came in two-or four-door sedan form again: base, Ghia or ESS trim. Granada Ghia carried dual body/hood/decklid accent stripes, black/argent lower back panel appliqué, left remote mirror, wide vinyl-insert bodyside moldings, and burled walnut woodtone door trim. The sporty Granada ESS held a blacked-out grille, dual remote mirrors, black bodyside moldings with bright inserts, black rocker panel paint, hood/decklid paint stripes, bucket seats with chain mail vinyl inserts, leather-wrapped steering wheel, louvered opera window appliqué, and wide wheel lip moldings.

LTD — V-8 — Reshuffling of the model lineup hit the full-size line for 1980. This year's selection included budget-priced LTD 'S', base LTD, and LTD Crown Victoria sedans. An 'S' edition also joined the LTD (plain-body) and Country Squire (woodgrain) station wagon choices, Crown Victoria (same name as the mid-1950s high-line Ford) replaced the former Landau as top-of-the-line sedan. A new four-speed automatic transmission with overdrive top gear became optional on all models with the 351 cid (5.8-liter) V-8, and on sedans with the base 302 (5.0-liter) V-8. Also new this year: standard P-metric radial tires with higher pressure, standard maintenance-free battery, and halogen headlamps (except LTD 'S'). Crown Victoria and Country Squire carried a new wide hood ornament design, while standard LTDs had no ornament at all. Country Squire wagons had simulated woodgrain panels with planking lines. New black rocker panel moldings and lower bright moldings with rear extensions went on the Crown Victoria. So did a new rear half vinyl roof with 'frenched' seams and brushed aluminum roof wrapover moldings. Both LTD and Crown Vic sedans displayed new decklid tape stripes. Front bumper guards were standard. New options included the Traction-Lok axle: cast aluminum wheels; auto-headlamp on/off/delay system; leather-wrapped luxury steering wheel; and electronic stereo search radio with cassette player and Dolby sound. Appearance was similar to 1979. Each checkerboard grille section had a 15 x 7 hole pattern (30 across), topped by a heavy upper header bar. 'S' had a different front end and grille, with round headlamps and parking lamps inset into the grille. Other models showed quad headlamps. Bodyside beltline striping was higher this year. Two-door opera windows had a more vertical look. LTD had three police packages available: 302 cid V-8, regular 351 V-8, and high-output 351 (with dual exhausts and modified camshaft). Police packages included heavy-duty alternators, a 2.26:1 axle for the 5.0 liter (3.08:1 for the 5.8 liter), 71 ampere-hour battery, heavy-duty power brakes, 140 MPH speedometer, heavy-duty suspension, GR70 x 15 blackwall police radials, and conventional spare tire. Police automatic transmissions had a first-gear lockout and oil cooler.

1980 Ford LTD Crown Victoria sedan. (F)

1980 Ford Thunderbird Silver Anniversary hardtop coupe. (PH)

THUNDERBIRD — V-8 — For its 25th year in the lineup, Thunderbird got a new size and a new standard engine. This year's version rode a 108.4 inch wheelbase (formerly 114) and carried a standard 255 cid (4.2-liter) V-8. That engine had the same stroke as the 302 V-8 (now optional), but a smaller bore. For the first time in a decade and a half, this Thunderbird also wore a unitized body, essentially a stretch of the Fairmont platform. Instead of the former six-passenger capacity, the ninth-generation edition was intended for just four. It weighed over 700 pounds less than before. Modified MacPherson struts made up the front suspension, with four-bar-link coil springs at the rear. Thunderbird had power-assisted, variable-ratio rack-and-pinion steering. Axle ratios were lowered, to boost mileage. A new four-speed overdrive automatic transmission was optional with the 302 V-8. Styling features included traditional concealed headlamps, full-width wraparound tail lamps, a lower beltline, unique (but traditional) wraparound parking lamps, and a strong mid-bodyside sculpture theme. Single opera windows to the rear of a wrapover roof band on the solid wide C-pillars held a Thunderbird emblem. At front and rear were soft color-keyed urethane bumper systems. The eggcrate grille showed an 8 x 6 "hole" pattern, with the pattern repeated in a bumper slot below. Trim panels on the headlamp covers extended outward and around the fender sides to contain side marker lenses. Taillamp panels had a notch at the center, and wide Thunderbird emblem on each lens. Base and Town Landau models were offered at first. Town Landau added air conditioning, autolamp delay system, tinted glass, jewel-like hood ornament, electronic instrument cluster, cornering lamps, dual remote mirrors, and owner's nameplate with 22K gold finish. Also included: upper bodyside/hood/grille paint/tape striping, AM/FM stereo search radio, padded half-vinyl roof with wrapover band and coach lamps, power driver's seat, power windows, and turbine-spoke cast aluminum wheels. A Silver Anniversary model, added at mid-year, came in a selection of color combinations: Silver Anniversary Glow (with black wrapover band and silver vinyl roof, or silver band and black roof); Black (with silver wrapover and black vinyl roof, or black wrapover and silver roof); Light Gray (silver wrapover band and black vinyl roof); Red Glow (silver wrapover and red vinyl roof); Midnight Blue metallic (silver wrapover band and midnight blue vinyl roof); or Black Silver Glow two-tone (silver wrapover and black vinyl roof). All Silver Anniversary models had Dove Gray interiors, plus standard automatic overdrive transmission. Three distinct roof treatments were available: base, Exterior Luxury Group (on Town Landau), and Silver Anniversary. T-Birds also had new high-pressure P-metric radial tires, maintenance-free battery, mini spare tire, new wheels and covers, new two-tier instrument panel, and a four-spoke soft-rim steering wheel. Dual seatback recliners went on all split bench seats. Sculptured window-frame-mounted mirrors were optional. Other new options included: electronic instrument cluster including digital speedometer; TR type low-profile wide aspect ratio tires on cast aluminum wheels with special suspension tuning; keyless entry system; electronic garage door opener; diagnostic warning light system; six-speaker premium sound system; and flip-up removable moon roof. Many of these extras were standard on Town Landau and/or Silver Anniversary. Thunderbird's mate over at Mercury was the Cougar XR7.

I.D. DATA: As before, Ford's 11-symbol Vehicle Identification Number (VIN) is stamped on a metal tab fastened to the instrument panel, visible through the windshield. Coding is the same as 1979, except engine codes (symbol five) changed as follows: 'A' L4-140 2Bbl.; 'A' turbo L4-140 2Bbl.; 'B' L6-200 1Bbl.; 'C' L6-250 1Bbl.; 'D' V8-255 2Bbl.; 'F' V8-302 2Bbl.; 'G' V8-351 2Bbl. Model year code changed to 'O' for 1980.

PINTO (FOUR)

Model No.	Body/ Style No.	Body Type & Seating	Factory Price	Shipping Weight	Prod. Total
10	62B	2-dr. Sedan-4P	4223	2385	84,053
10	41E	2-dr. Pony Sed-4P	3781	2377	Note 1
11	64B	3-dr. Hatch-4P	4335	2426	61,842
12	73B	2-dr. Sta Wag-4P	4622	2553	39,159
12	41E	2-dr. Pony Wag-4P	4284	2545	Note 1
12/604	73B	2-dr. Sqr Wag-4P	4937	2590	Note 2

NOTE 1: Pony production included in base sedan and wagon figures. Panel deliver Pintos also were produced.

NOTE 2: Squire Wagon production is included in standard station wagon total.

1980 Ford Fairmont Squire station wagon. (F)

Model No.	Body/ Style No.	Body Type & Seating	Factory Price	Shipping Weight	Prod. Total
FAIRMONT (FOUR/SIX)					
91	66B	2-dr. Sedan-5P	4435/4604	2571/----	45,074
92	54B	4-dr. Sedan-5P	4552/4721	2599/----	143,118
94	74B	4-dr. Sta Wag-5P	4721/4890	2722/----	77,035
FAIRMONT FUTURA (FOUR/SIX)					
93	36R	2-dr. Spt Cpe-5P	4837/5006	2612/----	51,878
92	N/A	4-dr. Sedan-5P	5070/5239	N/A	5,306

FAIRMONT ENGINE NOTE: Prices shown are for four-cylinder and six-cylinder engines. A 255 cid V-8 cost $119 more than the six.

GRANADA (SIX/V-8)					
81	66H	2-dr. Sedan-5P	4987/5025	3063/3187	60,872
82	54H	4-dr. Sedan-5P	5108/5146	3106/3230	29,557
GRANADA GHIA (SIX/V-8)					
81/602	66K	2-dr. Sedan-5P	5388/5426	3106/3230	Note 3
82/602	54K	4-dr. Sedan-5P	5509/5547	3147/3271	Note 3
GRANADA ESS (SIX/V-8)					
81/933	N/A	2-dr. Sedan-5P	5477/5515	3137/3261	Note 3
82/933	N/A	4-dr. Sedan-5P	5598/5636	3178/3302	Note 3

NOTE 3: Granada Ghia and ESS production is included in base Granada totals above.

GRANADA ENGINE NOTE: Prices shown are for six-cylinder and V-8 255 engines. A 302 cid V-8 cost $150 more than the 255 V-8.

LTD (V-8)					
62	66H	2-dr. Sedan-6P	6549	3447	15,333
63	54H	4-dr. Sedan-6P	6658	3475	51,630
74	74H	4-dr. Sta Wag-6P	7007	3717	11,718
LTD 'S' (V-8)					
N/A	66D	2-dr. Sedan-6P	N/A	N/A	553
61	54D	4-dr. Sedan-6P	6320	2464	19,283
72	74D	4-dr. Sta Wag-6P	6741	3707	3,490
LTD CROWN VICTORIA (V-8)					
64	66K	2-dr. Sedan-6P	7070	3482	7,725
65	54K	4-dr. Sedan-6P	7201	3524	21,962
76	74K	4-dr. Ctry Sqr-6P	7426	3743	9,868

1980 Ford Granada sedan. (JG)

1980 Ford LTD sedan. (JG)

LTD PRODUCTION NOTE: Production of wagons with dual-facing rear seats (a $146-$151 option for both standard and Country Squire wagon) is included in basic wagon totals.

THUNDERBIRD (V-8)					
87	66D	2-dr. HT Cpe-4P	6432	3118	156,803
THUNDERBIRD TOWN LANDAU (V-8)					
87/607	66D	2-dr. HT Cpe-4P	10036	3357	Note 4
THUNDERBIRD SILVER ANNIVERSARY (V-8)					
87/603	66D	2-dr. HT Cpe-4P	11679	3225	Note 4

NOTE 4: Town Landau and Silver Anniversary production is included in basic Thunderbird total.

FACTORY PRICE AND WEIGHT NOTE: Fairmont prices and weights to left of slash are for four-cylinder, to right for six-cylinder engine. Granada prices and weights to left of slash are for six-cylinder, to right for 255 cid V-8 engine.

ENGINE [Base Four (Pinto, Fairmont)]: Inline. Overhead cam. Four-cylinder. Cast-iron block and head. Displacement: 140 cid (2.3 liters). Bore & stroke: 3.78 x 3.13 in. Compression ratio: 9.0:1. Brake horsepower: 88 at 4600 rpm. Torque: 119 lbs.-ft. at 2600 rpm. Five main bearings. Hydraulic valve lifters. Carburetor: 2Bbl. Motorcraft 5200. VIN Code: A.

ENGINE [Optional Six (Fairmont)]: Inline. Overhead valve. Six-cylinder. Cast-iron block and head. Displacement: 200 cid (3.3 liters). Bore & stroke: 3.68 x 3.13 in. Compression ratio: 8.6:1. Brake horsepower: 91 at 3800 rpm. Torque: 160 lbs.-ft. at 1600 rpm. Seven main bearings. Hydraulic valve lifters. Carburetor: 1Bbl. Holley 1946. VIN Code: B.

ENGINE [Base Six (Granada)]: Inline. Overhead valve. Six-cylinder. Cast-iron block and head. Displacement: 250 cid (4.1 liters). Bore & stroke: 3.68 x 3.91 in. Compression ratio: 8.6:1. Brake horsepower: 90 at 3200 rpm. Torque: 194 lbs.-ft. at 1660 rpm. Seven main bearings. Hydraulic valve lifters. Carburetor: 1Bbl. Carter YFA. VIN Code: C.

ENGINE [Base V-8 (Thunderbird); Optional (Fairmont, Granada)]: 90-degree, overhead valve V-8. Cast-iron block and head. Displacement: 255 cid (4.2 liters). Bore & stroke: 3.68 x 3.00 in. Compression ratio: 8.8:1. Brake horsepower: (Fairmont) 119 at 3800 rpm.; (Thunderbird) 115 at 3800. Torque: (Fairmont) 194 lbs.-ft. at 2200 rpm.; (third) 194 at 2200. Five main bearings. Hydraulic valve lifters. Carburetor: 2Bbl. Motorcraft 2150. VIN Code: D.

ENGINE [Base V-8 (LTD, Thunderbird Silver Anniversary); Optional (Granada, Thunderbird)]: 90-degree, overhead valve V-8. Cast-iron block and head. Displacement: 302 cid (5.0 liters). Bore & stroke: 4.00 x 3.00 in. Compression ratio: 8.4:1. Brake horsepower: (LTD) 130 at 3600 rpm.; (third) 131 at 3600; (Granada) 134 at 3600. Torque: (LTD) 230 lbs.-ft. at 1600 rpm.; (third) 231 at 1600; (Granada) 232 at 1600. Five main bearings. Hydraulic valve lifters. Carburetor: 2Bbl. Motorcraft 2150 or 2700VV. VIN Code: F.

ENGINE [Optional V-8 (LTD)]: 90-degree, overhead valve V-8. Cast-iron block and head. Displacement: 351 cid (5.8 liters). Bore & stroke: 4.00 x 3.50 in. Compression ratio: 8.3:1. Brake horsepower: 140 at 3400 rpm. Torque: 265 lbs.-ft. at 2000 rpm. Five main bearings. Hydraulic valve lifters. Carburetor: 2Bbl. Motorcraft 7200VV. Windsor engine. VIN Code: G.

NOTE: A high-output version of the 351 cid V-8 was available for police use.

CHASSIS DATA: Wheelbase: (Pinto) 94.5 in.; (Pinto wag) 94.8 in.; (Fairmont) 105.5 in.; Granada) 109.9 in.; (LTD) 114.3 in.; (third) 108.4 in. Overall Length: (Pinto) 170.8 in.; (Pinto wag) 180.6 in.; (Fairmont) 195.5 in. exc. Futura coupe, 197.4 in.; (Granada) 199.7 in.; (LTD) 209.3 in.; (LTD wag) 215.0 in.; (third) 200.4 in. Height: (Pinto) 50.5 in.; (Pinto wag) 52.0 in.; (Fairmont) 52.9 in.; (Fairmont Futura cpe) 51.7 in.; (Fairmont wag) 54.2 in.; (Granada) 53.2-53.3 in.; (LTD) 54.7 in.; (LTD wag) 57.4 in.; (third) 53.0 in. Width: (Pinto) 69.4 in.; (Pinto wag) 69.7 in.; (Fairmont) 71.0 in.; (Granada) 74.5 in.; (LTD) 77.5 in.; (LTD wag) 79.3 in.; (third) 74.1 in. Front Tread: (Pinto) 55.0 in.; (Fairmont) 56.6 in.; (Granada) 59.0 in.; (LTD) 62.2 in. (third) 58.1 in. Rear Tread: (Pinto) 55.8 in.; (Fairmont) 57.0 in.; (Granada) 57.7 in.; (LTD) 62.0 in. (third) 57.0 in. Standard Tires: (Pinto) BR78 x 13 SBR exc. Pony, A78 x 13; (Fairmont) P175/75R14; (Granada) DR78 x 14 SBR BSW exc. Ghia, ER78 x 14 and ESS, FR78 x 14; (LTD) P205/75R14 BSW exc. wagon, P215/75R14; (third) P185/75R14 SBR BSW.

TECHNICAL: Transmission: Four-speed manual standard on Pinto/Fairmont four (1st) 3.98:1; (2nd) 2.14:1; (3rd) 1.42:1; (4th) 1.00:1; (Rev) 3.99:1. Four-speed overdrive manual standard on Fairmont/Granada six: (1st) 3.29:1; (2nd) 1.84:1; (3rd) 1.00:1; (4th) 0.81:1; (Rev) 3.29:1. Three-speed automatic standard on other models, optional on all. Pinto/Fairmont four-cylinder gear ratios: (1st)

2.47:1: (2nd) 1.47:1; (3rd) 1.00:1; (Rev) 2.11:1. Other models: (1st) 2.46:1; (2nd) 1.46:1; (3rd) 1.00:1; (Rev) 2.18:1 to 2.20:1. Four-speed overdrive automatic available on Thunderbird w/V8-302 and LTD: (lst) 2.47:1; (2nd) 1.47:1; (3rd) 1.00:1; (4th) 0.67:1; (Rev) 2.00:1. Standard final drive ratio: (Pinto) 3.08:1 w/4spd; (Fairmont) 3.08:1 exc. 2.73:1 w/six and auto.; (Granada) 3.00:1 w/4spd, 2.79:1 w/V-8 and auto.; (LTD) 2.26:1 exc. wag 2.73: 1, and 3.08:1 w/4spd overdrive auto.; (third) 2.26:1 ex, w/4spd auto., 3.08:1. Steering: (Pinto/Fairmont/third) rack and pinion; (others) recirculating ball. Front Suspension: (Pinto) coil springs with short/long control arms, and anti-sway bar with V-6; (Fairmont) MacPherson struts with coil springs on lower control arms and link-type anti-sway bar; (Granada) coil springs with short/long control arms and anti-sway bar; (LTD) long/short control arms w/coil springs and link-type stabilizer; (Thunderbird) modified MacPherson struts. Rear Suspension: (Pinto/Granada) rigid axle w/semi-elliptic leaf springs; (Fairmont/third) four-bar link coil springs; (LTD) rigid axle w/four-bar link and helical coil springs. Brakes: Front disc, rear drum. Ignition: Electronic. Body construction: (Pinto/Fairmont/Granada/third) unibody: (LTD) separate body and perimeter box frame. Fuel tank: (Pinto) 13 gal. exc. wag, 14 gal.; (Fairmont) 16 gal.; (Granada) 18 gal.; (LTD) 19 gal.; (third) 17.5 gal.

DRIVETRAIN OPTIONS: Engines: Turbo 140 cid four: Fairmont ($481). 200 cid six: Fairmont ($169). 255 cid V-8: Fairmont ($288); Granada ($38). 302 cid V-8: Granada ($188); third ($150). 351 cid V-8: LTD ($150). Transmission/Differential: Select-shift auto. trans.: Pinto/Fairmont/Granada ($340). Four-speed overdrive automatic trans.: LTD/third ($138). Floor shift lever: Fairmont/Granada ($38). Traction-Lok differential: LTD ($69). Optional axle ratio: Pinto/Fairmont ($15); LTD ($19). Brakes/Steering/Suspension: Power brakes: Pinto/Fairmont/Granada ($78). Power steering: Pinto ($160); Fairmont/Granada ($165). H.D. susp.: Granada/LTD/third ($23). Handling susp.: Fairmont ($44); LTD ($43). Adjustable air shock absorbers: LTD ($55). Other: H.D. battery ($20-$21). Engine block heater ($15). Trailer towing pkg., heavy duty: LTD ($164-$169). California emission system: Pinto/Fairmont ($253); Granada ($275); LTD ($235); third ($238). High-altitude option ($36).

PINTO CONVENIENCE/APPEARANCE OPTIONS: Option Packages: ESS pkg. ($281-$313). Cruising pkg. ($355-$606); tape delete ($70 credit). Rally pack: hatch ($369); wagon ($625). Sport pkg. ($103-$118). Exterior decor group ($24-$44). Interior decor group ($165-$238). Interior accent group ($5-$50). Convenience group ($26-$118). Protection group ($36-$40). Light group ($41). Comfort/Convenience: Air conditioner ($538). Rear defroster, electric ($96). Tinted glass ($65). Cigar lighter ($8). Trunk light ($5). Driver's remote mirror ($18). Dual sport mirrors ($58). Day/night mirror ($11). Entertainment: AM radio: Pony ($80). AM/FM radio ($65-$145). AM/FM stereo radio ($103-$183); w/cassette player ($191-$271). Radio flexibility option ($60). Exterior: Flip-up open air roof ($206-$219). Glass third door ($31). Metallic glow paint ($45). Two-tone paint/tape ($80). Accent tape stripe ($80). Black narrow vinyl-insert bodyside moldings ($43). Premium bodyside moldings ($11-$54). Bumper rub strips ($34). Roof luggage rack ($71). Mud/stone deflectors ($25). Lower bodyside protection ($34). Interior: Four-way driver's seat ($38). Load floor carpet ($28). Cargo area cover ($30). Front floor mats ($19). Wheels/Tires: Wire wheel covers ($104). Forged aluminum wheels ($225-$300); white ($256-$331). Lacy spoke alum. wheels ($225-$300). Styled steel wheels ($56). BR78 x 13 WSW ($50). BR70 x 13 RWL ($87).

FAIRMONT CONVENIENCE/APPEARANCE OPTIONS: Option Packages: ES option ($378). Futura sports group ($114). Ghia pkg.: Futura cpe ($193); std. sedan ($566). Squire option ($458). Exterior decor group ($260). Exterior accent group ($95). Interior decor group ($184-$346). Interior accent group ($110-$115). Instrument cluster ($85). Convenience group ($29-$51). Appearance protection group ($46-$53). Light group ($30-$48). Comfort/Convenience: Air cond. ($571). Rear defroster, electric ($101). Fingertip speed control ($116-$129). Power windows ($135-$191). Power door locks ($88-$125). Power decklid release ($25). Power seat ($111). Tinted glass ($71). Sport steering wheel ($43). Leather-wrapped steering wheel ($44). Tilt steering ($78-$90). Electric clock ($25). Cigar lighter ($8). Interval wipers ($39). Rear wiper/washer ($79). Left remote mirror ($19). Dual bright remote mirrors ($54-$60). Entertainment: AM radio ($93). AM/FM radio ($145). AM/FM stereo radio ($183); w/8 track player ($259); w/cassette player ($271). Premium sound system ($94). Radio flexibility ($63). Exterior: Flip-up open air roof ($219). Full or half vinyl roof ($118). Metallic glow paint ($54). Two-tone paint ($56); metallic ($154-$169). Accent stripe ($33). Pivoting front vent windows ($50). Rear quarter vent louvers ($41). Vinyl insert bodyside moldings ($44); wide black vinyl ($45). Rocker panel moldings ($30). Bright window frames ($24). Bumper guards, rear ($23). Bumper rub strips ($40). Luggage rack ($88). Mud/stone deflectors ($25). Lower bodyside protection ($34-$48). Interior: Non-reclining bucket seats ($31-$50). Bench seat ($50 credit). Cloth/vinyl seat trim ($28-$44). Vinyl seat trim ($25). Front floor mats ($19), Lockable side storage box ($23). Wheels/Tires: Hubcaps w/trim rings ($41). Deluxe wheel covers ($41).

Turbine wheel covers ($43); argent ($43-$84). Wire wheel covers ($74-$158). Styled steel wheels ($49-$133). Cast aluminum wheels ($268-$351). P175/75R14 WSW ($50). P185/75R14 BSW ($31); WSW ($81); RWL ($96). Conventional spare ($37).

GRANADA CONVENIENCE/APPEARANCE OPTIONS: Option Packages: Interior decor group ($243). Convenience group ($39-$108). Light group ($46-$51). Cold weather group ($31-$65). Heavy-duty group ($20-$65). Protection group ($29-$53). Visibility group ($6-$66). Comfort/Convenience: Air cond. ($571); auto-temp ($634). Rear defroster, electric ($101). Fingertip speed control ($116-$129). Illuminated entry system ($58). Power windows ($136-$193). Power door locks ($89-$125). Power decklid release ($25). Power four-way seat ($111). Tinted glass ($71). Tilt steering wheel ($78). Digital clock ($54). Lighting and Mirrors: Cornering lamps ($50). Dual remote mirrors ($41-$60). Dual sport mirrors ($50-$69). Lighted right visor vanity mirror ($41). Entertainment: AM radio ($93). AM/FM radio ($145). AM/FM stereo radio ($183); w/8track player ($259); w/cassette ($271). AM/FM stereo search radio ($333); w/8 track ($409); w/cassette and Dolby ($421). Radio flexibility ($63). Exterior: Power moonroof ($998). Full or half vinyl roof ($118). Metallic glow paint ($54). Bodyside/decklid paint stripes ($49). Two-tone paint/tape ($180). Bodyside accent moldings ($50). Black vinyl insert bodyside moldings ($44). Rocker panel moldings ($30). Bumper rub strips ($41). Mud/stone deflectors ($25). Lower bodyside protection ($34). Interior: Console ($110). Four-way driver's seat ($38). Reclining bucket seats (NC). Deluxe cloth/vinyl seat (NC). Flight bench seat (NC). Cloth/vinyl flight bench seat ($60). Leather seat trim ($277). Front floor mats ($19). Color-keyed seatbelts ($23). Wheels: Luxury wheel covers ($46) exc. Ghia (NC). Wire wheel covers ($119) exc. Ghia/ESS ($73). Styled steel wheels w/trim rings ($91-$138). Cast aluminum wheels ($275-$321). Tires: DR78 x 14 SBR WSW. ER78 x 14 SBR BSW/WSW. FR78 x 14 SBR BSW/WSW/wide WSW. Inflatable spare ($37).

LTD CONVENIENCE/APPEARANCE OPTIONS: Option Packages: Interior luxury group ($693-$741). Convenience group ($68-$98). Power lock group ($114-$166). Light group ($33-$43). Protection group ($48-$58). Comfort/Convenience: Air cond. ($606); w/auto-temp control ($669). Rear defroster, electric ($103). Fingertip speed control ($116). Illuminated entry system ($58). Power windows ($140-$208). Power door locks ($89-$120). Power driver's seat ($168); driver and passenger ($335). Tinted glass ($85). Autolamp on/off delay ($63). Leather-wrapped steering wheel ($44). Tilt steering wheel ($78). Auto. parking brake release ($10). Electric clock ($24). Digital clock ($38-$61). Seatbelt chime ($23). Interval wipers ($40). Lighting, Horns and Mirrors: Cornering lamps ($48). Trunk light ($5). Dual-note horn ($10). Driver's remote mirror ($19). Dual remote mirrors ($38-$56). Lighted right visor vanity mirror ($35-$41); pair ($42-$83). Entertainment: AM radio ($93). AM/ FM radio ($145). AM/FM stereo radio ($183); w/8track tape player ($259); w/cassette ($271). AM/FM stereo search radio ($333); w/8track ($409); w/cassette ($421). CB radio ($316). Power antenna ($49). Dual rear speakers ($40). Premium sound system ($94). Radio flexibility ($66). Exterior: Full or half vinyl roof ($145). Metallic glow paint ($65). Two-tone paint/tape ($75). Dual accent paint stripes ($33). Hood striping ($14). Pivoting front vent windows ($50). Rocker panel moldings ($29). Vinyl-insert bodyside moldings ($45). Bumper guards, rear ($26). Bumper rub strips ($56). Luggage rack ($115). Lower bodyside protection ($34-$46). Interior: Dual-facing rear seats: wagon ($146-$151). Flight bench seat ($56). Leather split bench seat ($349). Dual flight bench seat recliners ($55). Split bench seat w/ recliners ($173-$229). All-vinyl seat trim ($28). Duraweave vinyl trim ($50). Front floor mats ($19); front/rear ($30). Trunk trim ($46-$51). Trunk mat ($14). Color-keyed seatbelts ($24). Wheels/Tires: Luxury wheel covers ($70). Wire wheel covers ($138). Cast aluminum wheels ($310). P205/75Rl4 WSW ($50). P215/75R14 BSW ($29); WSW ($50-$79). P225/75R14 WSW ($79-$107). P205/75R15 WSW ($55-$87). Conventional spare ($37).

1980 Ford LTD Country Squire station wagon. (OCW)

1980 Ford Thunderbird Town Landau hardtop coupe. (PH)

THUNDERBIRD CONVENIENCE/APPEARANCE OPTIONS: Option Packages: Exterior luxury group ($489). Interior luxury group ($975). Exterior decor group ($359). Interior decor group ($348). Protection group ($39-$43). Light group ($35). Power lock group ($113). Comfort/Convenience: Air cond. ($571); auto-temp ($634) exc. Twn Lan/Anniv. ($63). Rear defroster ($101). Fingertip speed control ($116-$129). Illuminated entry system ($58). Keyless entry ($106-$119). Garage door opener w/lighted vanity mirrors ($130-$171). Autolamp on/off delay ($63). Tinted glass ($71); windshield only ($29). Power windows ($136). Four-way power seat ($111). Six-way power driver's seat ($166). Auto. parking brake release ($10). Leather-wrapped steering wheel ($44). Tilt steering wheel ($78). Electronic instrument cluster ($275-$313). Diagnostic warning lights ($50). Digital clock ($38). Interval wipers ($39). Lighting, Horns and Mirrors: Cornering lamps ($50). Trunk light ($5). Dual-note horn ($9). Driver's remote mirror, chrome ($18). Dual remote mirrors ($69). Lighted right visor vanity mirror ($35-$41). Entertainment: AM/ FM radio ($53). AM/FM stereo radio ($90); w/8track player ($166); w/cassette ($179). AM/FM stereo search radio ($240); w/8 track ($316) exc. Twn Lan/Anniv. ($76); w/cassette ($329) exc. Twn Lan/Anniv. ($89). CB radio ($316). AM radio delete ($81 credit). Power antenna ($49). Dual rear speakers ($38). Premium sound system ($119-$150). Radio flexibility ($66). Exterior: Flip-up open-air roof ($219). Vinyl half roof ($133). Metallic glow paint ($60). Two-tone paint/tape ($106-$163). Dual accent bodyside paint stripes ($40). Hood/bodyside paint stripes ($16-$56). Wide vinyl bodyside moldings ($54). Wide door belt moldings ($31-$44). Rocker panel moldings ($30). Mud/stone deflectors ($25). Lower bodyside protection ($34-$46). Interior: Bucket seats w/console ($176) exc. (NC) w/decor group. Recaro buckets w/console ($166-$254) exc. Twn Lan (NC). Leather seat trim ($318-$349). Vinyl seat trim ($26). Front floor mats ($19). Trunk trim ($44). Color-keyed seatbelts ($23). Wheels/Tires: Wire wheel covers ($50-$138). Luxury wheel covers ($88). P195/75R14 BSW ($26); WSW ($50). TR WSW tires on alum. wheels: base ($441-$528). Conventional spare ($37).

HISTORY: Introduced: October 12, 1979. Model year production: 1,167,581 (incl. Mustangs). Total passenger-car production for the U.S. market of 1,048,044 units (incl. Mustangs) included 426,107 four-cylinder, 334,298 sixes and 287,639 V-8s. Of the fours. 1,158 were Fairmont turbos (and 12,052 Mustang turbos). Calendar year production (U.S.): 929,639 (incl. Mustangs). Calendar year sales by U.S. dealers: 1,074,675 (incl. Mustangs). Model year sales by U.S. dealers: 1,124,192 (incl. Mustangs, but not incl. 68,841 imported Fiestas).

NOTE: Starting this year, Club Wagons (vans) were no longer classed as passenger cars.

HISTORY: Early in 1980, the "Erika" subcompact to come for 1981 was renamed Escort (and Mercury Lynx). Sales for the model year fell over 28 percent, touching every car in the lineup but headed by LTD's 43 percent drop. LTD was advertised during this period as rivaling Rolls-Royce for smooth, quiet ride qualities. The restyled and downsized Thunderbird didn't find many buyers either. Two assembly plants closed during 1980, at Mahwah, New Jersey, and Los Angeles. Still, Ford expected to spend $2 billion for expansion and retooling at other domestic facilities. Foremost hope for the future was the new Escort being readied for 1981 introduction. Philip E. Benton became head of the Ford Division, following the retirement of Walter S. Walla.

1981 FORD

The new front-wheel drive Escort 'world car' arrived for 1981, to assist Ford in reaching a healthy share of subcompact buyers. Granada had all-new sheetmetal with shorter wheelbase and length, but claimed six-passenger capacity. Fairmont Futura added a wagon,

while there was a new top-of-the-line Thunderbird. Several Ford models could be ordered with either a four, six or eight-cylinder engine. New base powertrain for the full-size LTD was the small (255 cid) V-8. Corporate body colors for 1981 were: Black, Bright Bittersweet, Candyapple Red, Medium or Bright Red, Light Medium Blue, Medium Dark Brown, Bright Yellow, Cream, Chrome Yellow, Tan, Antique Cream, Pastel Chamois, Fawn, and White. Also available was a selection of metallics including: Silver, Medium Gray, Light Pewter, Medium Pewter, Maroon, Dark Blue, Bright Blue, Medium Dark Spruce, Dark Brown, Dark Pine, and Dark Cordovan. Some Ford products also could choose from up to nine "Glamour" colors and 16 clearcoat polish paint selections.

ESCORT — FOUR — Because it evolved from Ford's international experience, the new front-wheel-drive Escort was called a 'world car.' It was also dubbed 'international' size, as Ford's attempt to rival the imports. A $3 billion development program had been initiated in the early 1970s to produce Escorts for sale both in the U.S. and Europe. The engine alone cost $1 billion to develop. The U.S. version of the all-new overhead-cam, Compound Valve Hemispherical (CVH) engine had to meet federal emissions standards, too. The transverse-mounted engine was called hemi-head because of its hemispherical-shaped combustion chambers, calling to mind some far more muscular hemis of past decades. Displacing just 97.6 cid, it was the smallest engine in American Ford history. Cylinder head and intake manifold were aluminum. The CVH design put the spark plug close to the center of the combustion chamber. Escort had many maintenance-free features, including self-adjusting brakes, lubed-for-life wheel bearings and front suspension, preset carb mixtures, hydraulic valve lifters, fixed caster and camber settings at the front end, and self-adjusting clutches. Ford General Manager Phillip E. Benton Jr. said 'all of the Escort's major components and systems such as the engine, transaxle suspension and body were especially designed for the car, with no carryover parts or components.' 'Three-door' hatchback and four-door liftgate bodies were offered. Both were 65.9 inches wide, on a 94.2 inch wheelbase. Five trim levels included base, L, GL, GLX and a sporty SS. Escort's four-speed manual transaxle was fully synchronized, with wide-ratio gearing. Optional three-speed automatic used a new split-torque design in intermediate and high, which divided torque between the converter and a direct mechanical hookup to the dual driveshafts. Escort had four-wheel independent suspension, rack-and-pinion steering, standard halogen headlamps, maintenance-free battery, fluidic windshield washer, and inertia seatback release. Front suspension used MacPherson struts with strut-mounted coil springs and a stabilizer bar. At the rear were independent trailing arms with modified MacPherson struts and coil springs, mounted on stamped lower control arms. P-metric (P155/80R) radial tires rode 13 in. steel wheels, with cast aluminum wheels optional. The hatchback Escort was 7 inches shorter than the old Pinto Runabout, while the wagon was 15 inches shorter than the Pinto version. Seats were higher than Pinto's, and glass area greatly enlarged. Escort's eggcrate grille had a 7 x 4 hole pattern. Recessed single rectangular headlamps sat in bright housings. Outboard were wraparound park/signal lamps. Wraparound tail lamps were angled at the front edge. Backup lamps stood inboard, toward the license plate housing. 'Ford' and 'Escort' lettering went on the hatch lid, below large sloping, curved hatch glass. Wagons had vertical wraparound tail lamps and a less-sloped rear window. Standard equipment for the base Escort included an AM radio, two-speed wipers, lighter, three-speed heater/defroster, inside hood release, high-back vinyl front bucket seats, bench-type folding rear seat, argent grille, bright bumpers, door-mounted driver's mirror, day/night mirror, courtesy lights, and semi-styled steel wheels with black hub covers and lug covers. Bright moldings went on the windshield surround, drip rail, and rear window surround. Escort L added bright headlamp housings, a bright grille, bright driver's mirror, matte black rocker panel paint, bodyside paint stripe, and bright belt molding. Escort GL included deluxe bumper rub strips and end caps, bright window frame moldings, vinyl-insert bodyside moldings with argent stripe, bright wheel hub covers and trim rings, bright lower back surround molding, high-back reclining bucket seats, four-spoke "soft feel" steering wheel, console, visor vanity mirror, and rear ashtrays. Escort GLX added dual color-keyed remote control sport mirrors, bumper guards, low-back reclining bucket seats, woodtone instrument cluster appliqué, console with graphic warning display, digital clock, roof grab handles, locking glovebox, styled steel wheels with bright trim rings, interval wipers, and P165/80R13 blackwall SBR tires. Escort SS included black bumpers, argent stripe bumper end caps, black grille and headlamp housings, blackout moldings and rocker panel paint, dual black remote sport mirrors, bodyside/rear tape striping with decal, styled steel wheels with bright trim rings and argent hub covers, high-back reclining vinyl bucket seats, handling suspension, and instrumentation group. Options included a console with graphic display module, intermittent wipers, and pivoting front vent windows. Gas mileage estimates reached 30 MPG city and 44 MPG highway. Early criticisms from the press and elsewhere prompted Ford to deliver a number of running changes right from the start, in an attempt to increase the car's refinement. First-year versions suffered several recalls. Mercury Lynx was Escort's corporate twin.

1981 Ford Escort GLX three-door hatchback. (F)

1981 Ford Escort GLX four-door Liftgate. (JG)

1981 Ford Fairmont sedan. (F)

FAIRMONT — FOUR/SIX/V-8 — In addition to the usual sedans and Futura coupe, Fairmont delivered a station wagon this year under the Futura badge. The four-door, steel-sided wagon had Futura's quad rectangular headlamps and distinctive grille, as well as body brightwork and an upgraded interior. Squire (woodgrain) trim was available at extra cost. Fairmonts also added new standard equipment, including power front disc brakes, bucket seats, deluxe sound package to reduce road noise, dual-note horn, bright window frames, visor vanity mirror, glovebox lock, and rear seat ashtray. The option list expanded to include a console with diagnostic warning lights and digital clock (as on Mustang), illuminated entry system, Traction-Lok rear axle (V-8 only), lighted visor vanity mirror, and Michelin TR type tires. Both the 200 cid (3.3-liter) six and 255 cid (4.2-liter) V-8 now had a viscous-clutch fan drive. Base engine remained the 140 cid (2.3-liter) four, with four-speed manual gearbox. The elusive turbo four was no longer listed as a possibility. Neither was the six with four-speed manual gearbox. That four-speed now had a self-adjusting clutch. Fairmont's base four-cylinder produced EPA estimates of 34 MPG highway and 23 MPG city. Fairmont's new grille had a tight crosshatch pattern, with two horizontal dividers to split it into three rows, each two 'holes' high. As before, large vertical parking lamps stood inboard of the rectangular headlamps. Wide (non-wraparound) tail lamps had vertical ribbing, with backup lenses at inner ends. Four-doors had a six-window design with narrow quarter windows that tapered to a point at the top. Wagons carried vertical wraparound tail lamps, with backup lenses alongside the license plate.

1981 Ford Granada GLX sedan. (F)

1981 Ford Granada GL coupe. (JG)

GRANADA — FOUR/SIX/V-8 — For its final two years in the lineup, Granada received an aerodynamic restyle that was supposed to deliver a 21 percent improvement in fuel economy. Ford called it 'the industry's most changed American-built sedan for 1981.' This Granada was 3 inches shorter than its predecessor, but with more leg, hip and shoulder room inside, and more luggage space. Wheelbase was Fairmont-sized. In fact, Granada's chassis was based on the familiar 'Fox' platform, with coil springs all around. The fully unitized body weighed 400 pounds less than the 1980 version. Drag coefficient rated a low 0.44. Under this year's hood was a standard 140 cid (2.3-liter) OHC four, as in Fairmont and Mustang, with four-speed manual shift. Also available: the 200 cid (3.3-liter) inline six and 255 cid (4.2-liter) V-8. Automatic was standard with the bigger engines. New for 1981 was a MacPherson strut front suspension, a pin-slider front disc brake system, front bucket seats on all models, revised instrument panel with two-pod instrument cluster, and stalk-mounted controls for turn signals, horn, dimmer, and wiper. P-metric steel-belted radial tires rode 14 in. stamped steel wheels. Granada also sported halogen headlamps. Three Granada series were offered: L, GL and GLX (replacing base, Ghia and ESS). As before, body styles included only the two- and four-door sedans. The new upright bright grille had a tight crosshatch pattern with wide slots in 10 x 10 hole arrangement, with 'Ford' lettering on the upper header bar (driver's side). Quad rectangular headlamps were used, with wraparound marker lenses and small horizontal amber parking lamps set in the front bumper. Wide tail lamps (full-width except for the recessed license plate area) had backup lamps halfway toward the center. Each taillamp was divided into an upper and lower segment. Pinstripes flowed along the hood creases, and there was a stand-up see-through hood ornament. A small square badge was mounted ahead of the front door. Mercury Cougar was Granada's corporate companion.

LTD — V-8 — Full-size Fords no longer carried a standard full-size engine. LTD's new standard powertrain consisted of the 255 cid (4.2-liter) V-8 and automatic overdrive transmission, which had been introduced in 1980 as an option on LTD and Thunderbird. That transmission also featured a lockup clutch torque converter. Three-speed automatic was abandoned. Two other V-8s were optional: 302 cid (5.0-liter) or 351 cid (5.8-liter), both with two-barrel carburetors. The latter produced 145 horsepower. A high-output 351 delivering 20 more horsepower was available only for police cars. LTD's lineup included four-door sedans in base, 'S' and Crown Victoria trim; two-door sedans in base and Crown Vic; and four-door wagons in all three series. Switching to a smaller base powerplant didn't seem to help mileage enormously, as the EPA estimate was a modest 16 MPG. New standard equipment included halogen headlamps on 'S' models, and separate ignition and door keys. Remote mirrors were now door-mounted rather than sail-mounted. Joining the option list were puncture-resistant tires and a convex remote-control passenger mirror. Country Squire switched from a seatbelt buzzer to chime. Appearance was the same as 1980. Tail lamps had vertical ribbing, with small backup lenses below. The license plate was recessed in the decklid. Rear marker lenses followed the angle of quarter panel tips.

THUNDERBIRD — SIX/V-8 — Some Thunderbird enthusiasts were doubtless shocked by the news: this year's edition carried a standard six-cylinder engine. The old familiar inline six at that, displacing just 200 cid (3.3-liter). It came with standard SelectShift automatic. (Actually, the inline six had become a credit option during the 1980 model year.) The formerly standard 255 cid (4.2-liter) V-8 became optional, as was a 302 cid (5.0-liter) engine and automatic overdrive transmission for either V-8. Base models were better trimmed this year. In fact, all models offered items that had formerly been part of the Exterior Luxury Group. New standard equipment included halogen headlamps, viscous fan clutch, vinyl-insert bodyside moldings, wide door belt moldings, remote control left mirror, and deluxe color-keyed seatbelts. Automatic temperature-control air conditioners added a defog mode. Three Thunderbird series were offered: base, Town Landau and Heritage (replacing the former Silver Anniversary model). Town Landau also added equipment, including luxury wheel covers and a color-keyed wrapover band with small opera windows for the rear half-vinyl roof (similar to the treatment used on the 1980 Silver Anniversary Thunderbird). Heritage carried a standard 255 cid V-8. Appearance was similar to 1980, except that the front bumper no longer held a lower grille pattern. Huge full-width tail lamps held

Thunderbird emblems on each side. The decklid protruded halfway between each taillamp half. The license plate sat in a recessed opening low on the bumper. With wrapover roof band, opera windows were tiny. New options included a convertible-like Carriage Roof, Traction-Lok axle, pivoting front vent windows, convex remote mirror (passenger side), and self-sealing puncture-resistant tires.

I.D. DATA: Ford had a new 17-symbol Vehicle Identification Number (VIN), again stamped on a metal tab fastened to the instrument panel, visible through the windshield. Symbols one to three indicates manufacturer, make and vehicle type: '1FA' Ford passenger car. The fourth symbol ('B') denotes restraint system. Next comes a letter 'P', followed by two digits that indicate body type: Model Number, as shown in left column of tables below. (Example: '91' Fairmont two-door sedan.) Symbol eight indicates engine type: '2' L4-98 2Bbl.; 'A' L4-140 2Bbl.; 'B' L6-200 1Bbl.; 'D' V8-255 2Bbl.; 'F' V8-302 2Bbl.; 'G' V8-351 2Bbl. Next is a check digit. Symbol ten indicates model year ('B' 1981). Symbol eleven is assembly plant: 'A' Atlanta. GA; 'B' Oakville, Ontario (Canada); 'G' Chicago; 'H' Lorain, Ohio; 'K' Kansas City, MO; 'X' St. Thomas, Ontario; 'T' Metuchen, NJ; 'U' Louisville, KY; 'W' Wayne, MI. The final six digits make up the sequence number, starting with 100001. A Vehicle Certification Label on the left front door lock face panel or door pillar shows the manufacturer, month and year of manufacture, GVW, GAWR, certification statement, VIN, and codes for such items as body type, color, trim, axle, transmission, and special order information.

ESCORT (FOUR)

Model No.	Body/Style No.	Body Type & Seating	Factory Price	Shipping Weight	Prod. Total
05	61D	3-dr. Hatch Sed-4P	5158	1962	Note 1
08	74D	4-dr. Liftgate-4P	5731	2074	Note 1
05/60Q	61D	3-dr. L Hatch-4P	5494	1964	Note 1
08/60Q	74D	4-dr. L Liftgate-4P	5814	2075	Note 1
05/60Z	61D	3-dr. GL Hatch-4P	5838	1987	Note 1
08/60Z	74D	4-dr. GL Lift-4P	6178	2094	Note 1
05/602	61D	3-dr. GLX Hatch-4P	6476	2029	Note 1
08/602	74D	4-dr. GLX Lift-4P	6799	2137	Note 1
05/936	61D	3-dr. SS Hatch-4P	6139	2004	Note 1
08/936	74D	4-dr. SS Lift-4P	6464	2114	Note 1

NOTE 1: Total Escort production came to 192,554 three-door hatchbacks and 128,173 four-door liftbacks. Breakdown by trim level not available.

Escort Body Type Note: Hatchback Escorts are variously described as two- or three-door; Liftgate models are sometimes referred to as station wagons.

FAIRMONT (FOUR/SIX)

20	66	2-dr. 'S' Sed-5P	5701/5914	N/A	N/A
20	66B	2-dr. Sedan-5P	6032/6245	2564/2617	23,066
21	54B	4-dr. Sedan-5P	6151/6364	2614/2667	104,883
23	74B	4-dr. Sta Wag-5P	6384/6597	2721/2788	59,154

FAIRMONT FUTURA (FOUR/SIX)

22	36R	2-dr. Coupe-5P	6347/6560	2619/2672	24,197
21/605	54B	4-dr. Sedan-5P	6361/6574	2648/2701	Note 2
23/605	74B	4-dr. Sta Wag-5P	6616/6829	2755/2822	Note 2

NOTE 2: Production totals listed under base Fairmont sedan and wagon also include Futura models.

GRANADA (FOUR/SIX)

26	66D	2-dr. L Sedan-5P	6474/6687	2707/2797	35,057
27	54D	4-dr. L Sedan-5P	6633/6848	2750/2840	86,284
26/602	66D	2-dr. GL Sed-5P	6875/7088	2728/2818	Note 3
27/602	54D	4-dr. GL Sed-5P	7035/7248	2777/2867	Note 3
26/933	66D	2-dr. GLX Sed-5P	6988/7201	2732/2822	Note 3
27/933	54D	4-dr. GLX Sed-5P	7148/7361	2784/2874	Note 3

NOTE 3: Granada GL and GLX production is included in base Granada totals above.

1981 Ford Escort three-door hatchback. (JG)

1981 Ford Fairmont Futura Squire station wagon. (JG)

FAIRMONT/GRANADA ENGINE NOTE: Prices shown are for four- and six-cylinder engines. A 255 cid V-8 cost $50 more than the six.

LTD (V-8)

32	66H	2-dr. Sedan-6P	7607	3496	6,279
33	54H	4-dr. Sedan-6P	7718	3538	35,932
38	74H	4-dr. Sta Wag-6P	8180	3719	10,554
39	74K	4-dr. Ctry Sqr-6P	8640	3737	9,443

LTD 'S' (V-8)

Model No.	Body/Style No.	Body Type & Seating	Factory Price	Shipping Weight	Prod. Total
31	54D	4-dr. Sedan-6P	7522	3490	17,490
37	74D	4-dr. Sta Wag-6P	7942	3717	2,465

LTD CROWN VICTORIA (V-8)

34	66K	2-dr. Sedan-6P	8251	3496	11,061
35	54K	4-dr. Sedan-6P	8384	3538	39,139

LTD PRODUCTION NOTE: Production of wagons with dual-facing rear seats (a $143 option) is included in basic wagon totals.

THUNDERBIRD (SIX/V-8)

42	66D	2-dr. HT Cpe-4P	7551/7601	3004/3124	86,693

THUNDERBIRD TOWN LANDAU (SIX/V-8)

42/60T	66D	2-dr. HT Cpe-4P	8689/8739	3067/3187	Note 4

THUNDERBIRD HERITAGE (V-8)

42/607	66D	2-dr. HT Cpe-4P	11355	3303	Note 4

NOTE 4: Town Landau and Heritage production is included in basic Thunderbird total.

MODEL NUMBER NOTE: Some sources include a prefix 'P' ahead of the two-digit model number.

FACTORY PRICE AND WEIGHT NOTE: Fairmont/Granada prices and weights to left of slash are for four-cylinder, to right for six-cylinder engine. Thunderbird prices and weights to left of slash are for six-cylinder, to right for V-8 engine.

ENGINE [Base Four (Escort)]: Inline. Overhead cam. Four-cylinder. Cast-iron block; aluminum head. Displacement: 97.6 cid (1.6 liters). Bore & stroke: 3.15 x 3.13 in. Compression ratio: 8.8:1. Brake horsepower: 65 at 5200 rpm. Torque: 85 lbs.-ft. at 3000 rpm. Five main bearings. Hydraulic valve lifters. Carburetor: 2Bbl. Holley-Weber 5740. VIN Code: 2.

ENGINE [Base Four (Fairmont, Granada)]: Inline. Overhead cam. Four-cylinder. Cast-iron block and head. Displacement: 140 cid (2.3 liters). Bore & stroke: 3.78 x 3.13 in. Compression ratio: 9.0:1. Brake horsepower: 88 at 4600 rpm. Torque: 118 lbs.-ft. at 2600 rpm. Five main bearings. Hydraulic valve lifters. Carburetor: 2Bbl. Holley 6500. VIN Code: A.

ENGINE [Base Six (Thunderbird); Optional (Fairmont, Granada)]: Inline. Overhead valve. Six-cylinder. Cast-iron block and head. Displacement: 200 cid (3.3 liters). Bore & stroke: 3.68 x 3.13 in. Compression ratio: 8.6:1. Brake horsepower: 88 at 3800 rpm. Torque: 154 lbs.-ft. at 1400 rpm. Seven main bearings. Hydraulic valve filters. Carburetor: 1Bbl. Holley 1946. VIN Code: B.

1981 Ford Thunderbird Town Landau hardtop coupe. (JG)

1981 Ford Escort GLX Squire wagon. (JG)

ENGINE [Base V-8 (LTD); Optional (Fairmont, Granada, Thunderbird)]: 90-degree, overhead valve V-8. Cast-iron block and head. Displacement: 255 cid (4.2 liters). Bore & stroke: 3.68 x 3.00 in. Compression ratio: 8.2:1. Brake horsepower: 115 at 3400 rpm.; (LTD, 120 at 3400). Torque: 195 lbs.-ft. at 2200 rpm.; (LTD, 205 at 2600). Five main bearings. Hydraulic valve lifters. Carburetor: 2Bbl. Motorcraft 2150 or 72OOVV. VIN Code: D.

ENGINE [Optional V-8 (LTD, Thunderbird)]: 90-degree, overhead valve V-8. Cast-iron block and head. Displacement: 302 cid (5.0 liters). Bore & stroke: 4.00 x 3.00 in. Compression ratio: 8.4:1. Brake horsepower: 130 at 3400 rpm. Torque: 235 lbs.-ft. at 1600 rpm.; (LTD, 235 at 1800). Five main bearings. Hydraulic valve lifters. Carburetor: 2Bbl. Motorcraft 2150 or 72OOVV. VIN Code: F.

ENGINE [Optional V-8 (LTD)]: 90-degree, overhead valve V-8. Cast-iron block and head. Displacement: 351 cid (5.8 liters). Bore & stroke: 4.00 x 3.50 in. Compression ratio: 8.3:1. Brake horsepower: 145 at 3200 rpm. Torque: 270 lbs.-ft. at 1800 rpm. Five main bearings. Hydraulic valve lifters. Carburetor: 2Bbl. Motorcraft 72OOVV. Windsor engine. VIN Code: G.

NOTE: A high-output version of the 351 cid V-8 was available. Brake H.P.: 165 at 3600 rpm. Torque: 285 lbs.-ft. at 2200 rpm.

CHASSIS DATA: Wheelbase: (Escort) 94.2 in.; (Fairmont/Granada) 105.5 in.; (LTD) 114.3 in.; (third) 108.4 in. Overall Length: (Escort hatch) 163.9 in.; (Escort Lift) 165.0 in.; (Fairmont) 195.5 in. exc. Futura coupe, 197.4 in.; (Granada) 196.5 in.; (LTD) 209.3 in.; (LTD wag) 215.0 in.: (third) 200.4 in. Height: (Escort) 53.3 in.; (Fairmont) 52.9 in.; (Fairmont Futura 2dr.) 51.7 in.; (Fairmont wag) 54.2 in.; (Granada) 53.0 in.; (LTD) 54.7 in.; (LTD wag) 57.4 in.; (third) 53.0 in. Width: (Escort) 65.9 in.; (Fairmont/Granada) 71.0 in.; (LTD) 77.5 in.; (LTD wag) 79.3 in.; (third) 74.1 in. Front Tread: (Escort) 54.7 in.; (Fairmont/Granada) 56.6 in.; (LTD) 62.2 in.; (third) 58.1 in. Rear Tread: (Escort) 56.0 in.; (Fairmont/Granada) 57.0 in.; (LTD) 62.0 in.; (third) 57.0 in. Standard Tires: (Escort) P155/80R13 SBR BSW; (Fairmont/Granada) P175/75R14 SBR BSW; (LTD) P205/75R14 SBR WSW exc. wagon, P215/75R14; (third) P195/75R14 SBR WSW.

TECHNICAL: Transmission: Four-speed manual standard on Fairmont/Granada four: (1st) 3.98:1; (2nd) 2.14:1; (3rd) 1.42:1; (4th) 1.00:1; (Rev) 3.99:1. Four-speed manual transaxle standard on Escort: (1st) 3.58:1; (2nd) 2.05:1; (3rd) 1.21:1; (4th) 0.81:1; (Rev) 3.46:1. Three-speed automatic standard on other models, optional on Escort. Gear ratios on Fairmont/Granada four, Fairmont six and some TBirds: (1st) 2.47:1; (2nd) 1.47:1; (3rd) 1.00:1; (Rev) 2.11:1. Other models: (1st) 2.46:1; (2nd) 1.46:1; (3rd) 1.00:1; (Rev) 2.19:1. Four-speed overdrive automatic standard on LTD, available on Thunderbird V-8: (1st) 2.40:1; (2nd) 1.47:1; (3rd) 1.00:1; (4th) 0.67:1; (Rev) 2.00:1. Standard final drive ratio: (Escort) 3.59:1 w/4spd, 3.31:1 w/auto.; (Fairmont/Granada) 3.08:1 exc. 2.73:1 w/six, 2.26:1 w/V-8; (LTD) 3.08:1. (third) 2.73:1 w/six and auto., 2.26:1 w/255 V-8 and 3spd auto., 3.08:1 w/4spd manual. Drive Axle: (Escort) front; (others) rear. Steering: (LTD) recirculating ball; (others) rack and pinion. Front Suspension: (Escort/Granada) MacPherson strut-mounted coil springs with lower control arms and stabilizer bar: (Fairmont/Thunderbird) modified MacPherson struts with lower control arms, coil springs and link-type anti-sway bar; (LTD) long/short control arms w/coil springs and link-type stabilizer bar. Rear Suspension: (Escort) independent trailing arms w/modified MacPherson struts and coil springs on lower control arms; (Fairmont/Granada/LTD) four-link live axle with coil springs: (Thunderbird) four-link live axle system with coil springs and anti-sway bar. Brakes: Front disc, rear drum. Ignition: Electronic. Body construction: (LTD) separate body and frame; (others) unibody. Fuel tank: (Escort) 10 gal.; (Fairmont/Granada) 14 or 16 gal.; (LTD) 20 gal.; (third) 18 gal.

DRIVETRAIN OPTIONS: Engines: 200 cid six: Fairmont/Granada ($213). 255 cid V-8: Fairmont/Granada ($263); third ($50). 302 cid V-8: third ($91) exc. Heritage ($41); LTD sedan ($41). 351 cid V-8: LTD sedan ($83); LTD wagon ($41). H.O. 351 cid V-8: LTD ($139-$180). Transmission/Differential: Automatic transaxle: Escort ($344). Select-shift auto. trans.: Fairmont/Granada ($349). Four-speed overdrive

automatic trans.: third ($162). Floor shift lever: Fairmont/Granada ($43). Traction-Lok differential: Fairmont/Granada/third ($67); LTD ($71). Optional axle ratio: Escort ($15); Granada ($16). Brakes/Steering/Suspension: Power brakes: Escort ($79). Power steering: Escort ($163); Fairmont/Granada ($168). H.D. susp.: Fairmont/Granada ($22); LTD/third ($23). Handling susp.: Escort ($37); Fairmont/LTD ($45). Adjustable air shock absorbers: LTD ($57). Other: H.D. battery ($20). H.D. alternator: LTD ($46). Extended-range gas tank: Escort ($32). Engine block heater ($16). Trailer towing pkg., heavy duty: LTD ($176). California emission system ($46). High-altitude option ($38).

ESCORT CONVENIENCE/APPEARANCE OPTIONS: Option Packages: Squire wagon pkg. ($256). instrument group ($77). Protection group ($49). Light group ($39). Comfort/Convenience: Air conditioner ($530). Rear defrostor, electric ($102). Fingertip speed control ($132). Tinted glass ($70); windshield only ($28). Digital clock ($52). Intermittent wipers ($41). Rear wiper/washer ($100). Dual remote sport mirrors ($56). Entertainment: AM/FM radio ($63). AM/FM stereo radio ($100); w/cassette player ($187). Dual rear speakers ($37). Premium sound ($91). AM radio delete ($61 credit). Exterior: Flip-up open air roof ($154-$228). Metallic glow paint ($45). Two-tone paint/tape ($104). Front vent windows, pivoting ($55). Remote quarter windows ($95). Vinyl insert bodyside moldings ($41). Bumper guards, front or rear ($23). Bumper rub strips ($34). Roof luggage rack ($74). Roof air deflector ($26). Lower bodyside protection ($60). Interior: Console ($98). Low-back reclining bucket seats ($30). Reclining front seatbacks ($55). Cloth/vinyl seat trim ($28); vinyl (NC). Deluxe seatbelts ($23). Wheels/Tires: Wheel trim rings ($44). Aluminum wheels ($193-$330). Pl55/80R13 WSW ($55). P165/80R13 BSW ($19); WSW ($55-$74).

FAIRMONT CONVENIENCE/APPEARANCE OPTIONS: Option Packages: Squire option ($200). Interior luxury group ($232-$256). Instrument cluster ($88). Appearance protection group ($50). Light group ($43). Comfort/Convenience: Air cond. ($585). Rear defroster, electric ($107). Fingertip speed control ($132). Illuminated entry ($60). Power windows ($140-$195). Power door locks ($93-$132). Remote decklid release ($27). Power seat ($122). Tinted glass ($76); windshield only ($29). Leather-wrapped steering wheel ($49). Tilt steering ($80-$93). Electric clock ($23). Interval wipers ($41). Rear wiper/washer ($85). Lighting and Mirrors: Map light ($9); dual-beam ($13). Trunk light ($6). Left remote mirror ($15). Dual bright remote mirrors ($55). Lighted visor vanity mirror ($43). Entertainment: AM/FM radio ($51). AM/FM stereo radio ($88); w/8 track player ($162); w/cassette player ($174). Twin rear speakers ($37). Premium sound system ($91). Radio flexibility ($61). AM radio delete ($61 credit). Exterior: Flip-up open air roof ($228). Full or half vinyl roof ($115). Metallic glow paint ($55). Two-tone paint ($128-$162). Accent paint stripe ($34). Pivoting front vent windows ($55). Liftgate assist handle: wag ($16). Rocker panel moldings ($30). Bumper guards, rear ($23). Bumper rub strips ($43). Luggage rack: wagon ($90). Lower bodyside protection ($37-$49) Interior Console ($168). Bench seat ($24 credit). Cloth seat trim ($28-$54). Flight bench seat (NC); w/vinyl trim ($26). Front floor mats ($18-$20). Locking storage box ($24). Deluxe seatbelts ($23). Wheels/Tires: Wire wheel covers ($76-$117). Styled steel wheels ($52-$94). P175/75R14 WSW ($55). P185/75R14 WSW ($86). P190/65R390 BSW on TRX alum. wheels ($470-$512). Conventional spare ($39).

GRANADA CONVENIENCE/APPEARANCE OPTIONS: Option Packages: Interior sport group ($282-$295). Light group ($45). Cold weather group ($67). Protection group ($51). Comfort/Convenience: Air cond. ($585). Rear defroster ($107). Fingertip speed control ($89-$132). Illuminated entry system ($60). Power windows ($140-$195). Power door locks ($93-$132). Power decklid release ($27). Power flight bench seat ($122); split bench ($173). Tinted glass ($76); windshield only ($29). Steering wheel: sport ($26-$39); leather-wrapped ($49); tilt ($80-$94). Electric clock ($23). Interval wipers ($41). Lighting and Mirrors: Cornering lamps ($51). Map light ($13). Trunk light ($6). Remote right mirror ($52). Lighted right visor vanity mirror ($43). Entertainment: AM/FM radio ($51). AM/FM stereo radio ($88); w/8track player ($162); w/cassette ($174). Premium sound ($91). Radio flexibility ($61). AM radio delete ($61 credit). Exterior: Flip-up open-air roof ($228). Full or half vinyl roof ($115). Metallic glow paint ($55). Bodyside/decklid paint stripes ($50). Two-tone paint ($146-$162). Pivoting front vent windows ($55). Vinyl insert bodyside moldings ($45). Bumper guards, rear ($23). Bumper rub strips ($43). Mud/stone deflectors ($26). Lower bodyside protection ($37). Interior: Console ($168). Split bench seat: GL/GLX ($178). Cloth seat trim ($45-$62). Flight bench seat (NC). Front floor mats ($18-$20). Color-keyed seatbelts ($23). Wheels/Tires: Luxury wheel covers: L ($43); GL/GLX (NC). Wire wheel covers ($124); GL/GLX ($80). Cast aluminum wheels ($308-$350). P175/75R14 WSW ($55). P185/75R14 SSW ($32); WSW ($86); RWL ($102). 190/65R390 BSW on TRX aluminum wheels ($468-$512). Conventional spare ($39).

LTD CONVENIENCE/APPEARANCE OPTIONS: Option Packages: Interior luxury group ($693-$765). Convenience group ($70-$101). Power lock group ($93-$176). Light group ($37). Protection group

($57). Comfort/Convenience: Air cond. ($624); w/auto-temp control ($687). Rear defroster, electric ($107). Fingertip speed control ($135). Illuminated entry system ($59). Power windows ($143-$211). Power driver's seat ($173); driver and passenger ($346). Tinted glass ($87); windshield only ($29). Autolamp on/off delay ($65). Leather-wrapped steering wheel ($45). Tilt steering wheel ($80). Auto. parking brake release ($10). Electric clock ($23). Digital clock ($40-$63). Seatbelt chime ($23). Interval wipers: fleet only ($41). Lighting and Mirrors: Cornering lamps ($48). Remote right mirror ($39). Lighted right visor vanity mirror ($38); pair ($43-$80). Entertainment: AM/FM radio ($51). AM/FM stereo radio ($88); w/8track tape player ($162) exc. Crown Vic ($74); w/cassette ($174) exc. Crown Vic ($87). AM/FM stereo search radio ($234) exc. Crown Vic ($146); w/8 track ($221-$309); w/cassette ($233-$321). Power antenna ($48). Dual rear speakers ($39). Premium sound system ($116-$146). Radio flexibility ($65). AM radio delete ($61 credit). Exterior: Full or half vinyl roof ($141). Metallic glow paint ($67). Two-tone paint/tape ($44-$78). Dual accent paint stripes ($34). Hood striping ($15). Pivoting front vent windows ($55). Rocker panel moldings: Ctry Squire ($29). Vinyl-insert bodyside moldings ($44). Bumper guards, rear ($27). Bumper rub strips ($46). Luggage rack ($84). Lower bodyside protection ($34-$46). Interior: Dual-facing rear seats: wagon ($146). Cloth/vinyl flight bench seat ($59). Leather seating ($361). Dual flight bench seat recliners ($56). Cloth/vinyl split bench seating ($178-$237). All-vinyl seat trim: Crown Vic/Ctry Squire ($28); Duraweave vinyl ($54). Front floor mats ($20). Trunk trim ($45). Wheels/Tires: Luxury wheel covers ($72). Wire wheel covers ($135). Cast aluminum wheels ($338). P215/75R14 WSW ($30). P225/75R14 WSW ($30-$61). P205/75R15 WSW ($10-$40); puncture-resistant ($95-$125). Conventional spare ($39).

1981 Ford LTD Crown Victoria sedan. (JG)

1981 Ford Thunderbird Heritage hardtop coupe. (F)

THUNDERBIRD CONVENIENCE/APPEARANCE OPTIONS: Option Packages: Interior luxury group ($1039) exc. Town Landau ($584). Exterior decor group ($341). Interior decor group ($349). Protection group ($45). Light group ($30). Power lock group ($120). Comfort/Convenience: Air cond. ($585); auto-temp ($652) exc. Twn Lan/Heritage ($67). Rear defroster ($107). Fingertip speed control ($132). Illuminated entry system ($60). Keyless entry ($122). Garage door opener w/lighted vanity mirrors ($134-$177). Autolamp on/off delay ($65) Tinted glass ($76); windshield only ($29). Power windows ($140). Four-way power seat ($122). Six-way power driver's seat ($173). Auto. parking brake release ($10). Leather-wrapped steering wheel ($45). Tilt steering wheel ($80). Electronic instrument cluster ($282-$322). Diagnostic warning lights: base ($51). Digital clock ($40). Interval wipers ($41). Lighting and Mirrors: Cornering lamps ($51). Remote right mirror ($52). Lighted right visor vanity mirror ($41). Entertainment: AM/FM radio ($51). AM/FM stereo radio ($88); w/8 track player ($74-$162); w/cassette ($87-$174). AM/FM stereo search radio ($146-$234); w/8track ($221-$309) exc. Heritage ($74); w/cassette ($233-$321) exc. Heritage ($87). Power antenna ($48). Dual rear speakers ($37). Premium sound system ($116-$146). Radio flexibility ($65). AM radio delete ($61 credit). Exterior: Carriage roof ($902). Flip-up open-air roof ($228). Vinyl half roof ($130). Metallic glow paint ($70). Two-tone paint ($111-$180). Dual accent bodyside paint stripes: base ($41). Hood/bodyside paint stripes ($16-$57). Pivoting front vent windows ($55). Wide door belt moldings ($45). Rocker panel moldings ($30). Mud/stone deflectors ($26). Lower bodyside protection ($34-$48). Interior: Bucket seats w/console ($182) exc. (NC) w/decor group. Recaro bucket seats w/console ($376-$461) exc. Heritage ($213). Leather seat trim ($359). Vinyl seat trim ($28-$29). Front floor mats ($13); carpeted ($20). Trunk trim ($44). Wheels/Tires: Wire wheel covers ($38-$135). Luxury wheel covers ($98). Self-sealing tires ($85). TR WSW tires on alum. wheels ($428-$563). Conventional spare ($39).

HISTORY: Introduced: October 3, 1980. Model year production: 1,054,976 (incl. Mustangs). Total passenger-car production for the U.S. market of 1,030,915 units (incl. Mustangs) included 531,507 four-cylinder, 287,673 sixes and 211,735 V-8s. (Total includes 71,644 early '82 EXPS, all four-cylinder.) Calendar year production (U.S.): 892,043 (incl. Mustangs). Calendar year sales by U.S. dealers: 977,220 (incl. Mustangs). Model year sales by U.S. dealers: 1,058,044 (incl. Mustangs, 27,795 leftover Pintos and 41,601 early '82 EXPS, but not incl. 47,707 imported Fiestas).

HISTORY: Escort quickly managed to become the best-selling Ford model, selling 284,633 examples. Obviously, Escort was primed to compete with Chevrolet's five-year-old Chevette. Otherwise, sales slumped somewhat. The restyled and downsized Granada sold better than in 1980, however, finding 105,743 buyers. Total model year sales were down over 7 percent, but that wasn't so bad considering the 28 percent decline from 1979 to 1980 (which also saw Ford/Lincoln/Mercury's market share shrink to a record low 16.5 percent). Mustang didn't sell nearly as well as hoped. even with a series of rebates offered during the year, dropping 29.5 percent for the model year. Model year production was closer to the 1980 figure, down just over 3 percent as opposed to a whopping 39 percent decline in the previous season. Calendar year production and sales both fell too, but not to a shocking level. This was a bad year all around for the industry. Car prices and interest rates had been rising steadily during this inflationary period, while the country also remained in a recession economy. Escort evolved from the 'Erika' project, which first began in 1972. The goal: to produce a car that could be revised to suit both European and American tastes, using parts that could either be provided locally or imported. Both a 1.3-liter and 1.6-liter engine were planned, but only the bigger one found its way under domestic Escort hoods. Ford spent some $640 million to renovate its Dearborn, Michigan, plant to manufacture Escort's 1.6-liter CVH engine. The engines were also built at a Ford facility in Wales. Additional future production was planned for Lima, Ohio, and for a new plant to be built in Mexico. The 1981 CAFE goal was 22 MPG.

1982 FORD

In addition to the new high-performance Mustang GT, 1982 brought a new two-seater EXP to the Ford fold, the first two-passenger model since the '55 Thunderbird. Escort added a four-door hatchback sedan, while Granada added a station wagon. Otherwise, 1982 was largely a carryover year. Ford's first domestic V-6 engine became available this year in Granada and Thunderbird. Weighing only a few pounds more than a four, it had an aluminum head, intake manifold and front cover. Ford's famous script returned this year after a long absence, in the form of a blue oval emblem at the front and rear of each model. Fairmont/Granada/Thunderbird sixes now had lockup torque converters in their SelectShift automatics, which worked in all three forward speeds. The government's fuel economy (CAFE) standard this year was 24 MPG.

ESCORT — FOUR — A new four-door hatchback sedan joined Escort's initial 'three-door' (actually two-door) hatchback and four-door liftback wagon. Base and SS wagons were dropped. L, GL and GLX Escorts now had bright headlamp housings. Power front disc brakes had become standard on wagons late in the 1981 model year, and continued this year. New stainless steel wheel trim rings (formerly stamped aluminum) arrived on GL, GLX and GT models. Escort had a new low-restriction exhaust and larger (P165/80R13) tires in all series. Ford's oval script emblem replaced 'Ford' block letters on the liftgate, which also held 'Escort' lettering. An electric hatch release was now standard on GLX hatchbacks (optional elsewhere). There was a running change in the four-speed manual transaxle, with different third and fourth gear ratios. Third gear changed from 1.23:1 to 1.36:1, and fourth from 0.81:1 to 0.95:1. Air-conditioned models included a switch that disconnected the unit for an instant when the gas pedal was floored. Like other Ford models, this year's Escort also displayed the blue script oval up front. Otherwise, appearance was similar to 1981. Base Escorts had an argent painted grille, wraparound amber parking lamps, single rectangular halogen headlamps, short black bumper end caps, semi-styled steel wheels with black and argent hub covers, and black wheel nut covers. Sedans had wraparound tricolor tail lamps; red tail lamps went on wagons. Inside were vinyl high-back front bucket seats, a black two-spoke steering wheel, black instrument panel with ashtray, bronzetone cluster, and color-keyed soft-feel pad. Escort L added bright headlamp doors, bright grille with integral Ford oval, brushed center-pillar appliqué, matte black rocker panels, bodyside paint stripes, black taillamp extensions, an 'L' badge on the liftgate, and blackout front end. Escort GL added deluxe bumper end caps and rub strips, 'GL' badge in back, front air dam, vinyl-insert bodyside moldings with argent insert, and bright window frame and lower back surround moldings. Inside, the GL had high-back reclining bucket seats and a four-spoke soft-feel color-keyed steering wheel. GLX stepped upward with interval wipers, dual color-keyed remote sport mirrors, 'GLX' badge, front and rear bumper guards, low-back reclining bucket seats in GLX vinyl or cloth/vinyl, woodtone instrument cluster appliqué, P165/80R13 tires. and console with graphic warning display. Escort GT (formerly SS) added a handling suspension, black bumpers with deluxe rub strips and deluxe end caps, front air dam, roof grab handles, black grille and headlamp doors, and Ford oval on the black grille's header bar. Blackout treatment went on windshield molding, drip moldings, quarter window and door frames, quarter window moldings, dual remote sport mirrors, door handles and lock covers, center pillar appliqué, rocker panels, belt and back window moldings, lower back surround molding, and taillamp extensions. Bodyside and rear end tape stripes showed an identifying decal. New options included shearling and leather (or leather alone) seat inserts, and an AM/FM stereo with 8 track player. The optional Squire exterior now had lighter-color walnut woodtone trim. Escorts had a larger (11.3 gallon) gas tank this year. EPA ratings reached 31 MPG city (47 MPG highway) on the base Escort with four-speed.

1982 Ford Escort GLX five-door hatchback. (PH)

1982 Ford EXP three-door hatchback. (F)

1982 Ford Fairmont Futura sedan. (JG)

EXP — FOUR — First shown at the Chicago Auto Show, then introduced in April as an early '82 model, EXP was the first two-seater Ford offered in 25 years. Comparing EXP to the original Thunderbird, Ford Division General Manager Louis E. Latalf said: 'We're introducing another two-seater with the same flair, but the EXP will be a very affordable, very fuel efficient car matched to the lifestyles of the eighties.' For comparison, the sporty new coupe weighed a thousand pounds less than the original Thunderbird. EXP was also 2 inches lower and 5 inches shorter. EXP's rakish non-boxy body rode an Escort/Lynx 94.2 inch wheelbase, with that car's front-drive running gear, four-wheel independent suspension, and dashboard. EXP was longer, lower and narrower than Escort. Performance wasn't (yet) its strong suit, however, since EXP weighed about 200 pounds more than Escort but carried the same small engine. Standard features included steel-belted radial tires, power front disc/rear drum brakes, halogen headlamps, rack-and-pinion steering, reclining high-back bucket seats, four-spoke sport steering wheel, and easy-to-read instrument panel and console with full instrumentation. Underhood was the 97.6 cid (1.6-liter) CVH engine with standard four-speed overdrive manual transaxle. Several standard equipment additions were incorporated as a running change. They included tinted glass, an electronic day/date digital clock, power liftgate release, maintenance-free 48 ampere-hour battery, engine compartment light, ashtray light, and headlamps-on warning buzzer. Both EXP and Mercury's LN7, its corporate cousin, had a sharply-sloped windshield, wheel arches with prominent lips, and wide bodyside moldings not far below the top of the wheel opening line. Biggest difference was in the back end. Ford's coupe was a notchback with lift-up hatch, while Mercury's LN7 fielded a big 'bubbleback' back window. EXP's minimalist grille consisted merely of twin side-by-side slots in the sloped front panel (LN7 had ten). Single quad headlamps sat in 'eyebrow' housings. Large wraparound tail lamps came to a point on the quarter panel. Parking lamps stood in the bumper, well below the headlamps. Priced considerably higher than Escort, EXP carried an ample list of standard equipment. It included power brakes, tachometer, engine gauges, full carpeting, electric back window defroster, power hatchback release, digital clock, and cargo area security shade. Manual-transaxle models had a sport-tuned exhaust. Automatic models had a wide-open-throttle cutout switch for the optional air conditioning compressor clutch. A rather modest option list included a flip-up open-air roof, premium stereo system, and leather (or shearling and leather) seating surfaces. An optional TR handling package included special wheels and Michelin TRX tires in P165/70R365 size, and a larger-diameter front stabilizer bar. Shock valving, spring rates and caster/camber settings were modified for firmer ride and tighter handling. As the full model year began, Ford offered an optional (no-extra-cost) 4.05:1 final drive ratio for better performance. Later came a close-ratio gearbox with 3.59:1 final drive ratio, intended for the same purpose. Finally, in March 1982, an 80-horsepower edition of the CVH four became available. It had higher (9.0:1) compression, a bigger air cleaner intake, lower-restriction exhaust and dual-outlet exhaust manifold, larger carburetor venturis, and higher-lift camshaft.

FAIRMONT FUTURA — FOUR/SIX/V-8 — All Fairmont models acquired the Futura name this year as the lineup shrunk to a single series: just a two-and four-door sedan, and sport coupe, the station wagon was dropped, and the 255 cid (4.2-liter) V-8 was available only in police and taxi packages. Base engine was the 140 cid (2.3-liter) four, with 3.3-liter inline six optional. Optional SelectShift automatic with the six included a new lockup torque converter. Fairmont's new front end look featured a bold grille with strong divider forming a 6x2 grid, with each 'hole' containing a tight internal crosshatch pattern. Quad rectangular headlamps now stood above quad park/signal lamps, like LTD but without its wraparound side marker lenses. Instead, Fairmont had small marker lenses set low on front fenders. The rear held the same vertically-ribbed tail lamps as before. Front fenders held a Futura badge. Deluxe wide lower bodyside moldings met partial wheel lip moldings. Interiors held new high-gloss woodtone door trim and instrument panel appliqués (formerly walnut). In back was a new deep-well trunk. AM radios added dual front speakers, and a new flash-to-pass feature was added to the headlamp lever. There was also a new gas cap tether. The former optional sweep-hand electric clock switched to quartz-type, and the available extended-range fuel tank held 20 gallons (formerly 16). Discontinued options were the leather-wrapped steering wheel, vinyl front floor mats, and right lighted visor vanity mirror.

GRANADA — FOUR/SIX/V-6 — Following its major restyle and downsizing for 1981, Granada looked the same this year but added a pair of station wagons (L and GL series). New station wagon options included a luggage rack, two-way liftgate (with flip-up window), rear wiper/washer, and Squire package. Fuel filler caps were now tethered. Flash-to-pass control on the steering column was new this year. Sedans could get an optional extended-range fuel tank. No more V-8s went under Granada hoods. An optional 'Essex' 232 cid (3.8-liter) V-6 producing 112 horsepower was said to offer V-8 power; and it weighed just four pounds more than the base 140 cid (2.3-liter) four. An inline six also remained available (standard on wagons). The V-6 got an EPA rating of 19 MPG city and 26 MPG highway. A new torque converter clutch providing a direct connection became standard on SelectShift automatic for the six and V-6 engines. This would be Granada's final season, but its basic design carried on in the form of a restyled LTD.

LTD — V-8 — After a long history, the 351 cid (5.8-liter) V-8 no longer was available for private full-size Fords, but continued as an option for police models. Little changed on this year's LTD lineup, apart from seven new body colors. Ford ovals were added to front grilles and rear decklids (or tailgates). All monaural radios had dual front speakers and wiring for rear speakers. The sweep-hand clock added quartz operation. A new medium-duty trailer towing option replaced the former heavy-duty one. New optional wire wheel covers incorporated a locking feature. Base engine was a 255 cid (4.2-liter) V-8; optional, the 302 cid (5.0-liter) V-8. Also optional for 1982 was a Tripminder computer that combined a trip odometer with quartz clock to show vehicle speed, real or elapsed time, and fuel flow. Touching buttons could display instant or average MPG, amount of fuel used, trip mileage, average trip speed, and total trip time. Thunderbird could also get one. With 114.3 inch wheelbase, LTD was the biggest Ford. Wide amber parking lamps stood below quad headlamps. Amber marker lenses had a large section above a smaller one, to follow the line of the headlamp/parking lamp. The fine checkerboard grille pattern was divided by a vertical center bar, with Ford oval at driver's side. An 'Automatic Overdrive' badge went ahead of the door. Vertically ribbed tail lamps held 'LTD' lettering, with small backup lamps below the tail lamps. 'LTD' letters also decorated the 'C' pillar.

THUNDERBIRD — SIX/V-6/V-8 — Engine choices grew smaller yet on the '82 Thunderbird, as the familiar 302 cid (5.0-liter) V-8 was abandoned. The 200 cid (3.3-liter) inline six became standard on base 'birds, new 232 cid (3.8-liter) V-6 optional, with 255 cid (4.2-liter) V-8 the biggest that could be bought. SelectShift transmission with the inline six had a new lockup torque converter. Three models were offered again: base, Town Landau, and Heritage. Thunderbird's gas tank grew from 18 to 21 gallons. Exterior trim had more black-accented areas. A new optional Tripminder computer not only showed time and speed, but figured and displayed elapsed time, distance traveled, average or present MPG, fuel used, and average speed. There was a new wire wheel cover option with locking feature, and a new luxury vinyl roof option (standard on Town Landau). Appearance was similar to 1981, with the same huge tail lamps. Concealed headlamps again had a clear lens-like trim panel on each cover, which extended outward far around the fender to form large wraparound signal/marker lenses. Those lenses were all clear except for an amber section toward the wheel. The crosshatch grille had an 8 x 6 pattern of wide holes. 'Thunderbird' lettering was set in the grille header. A wide see-through hood ornament held a Thunderbird insignia. That emblem also highlighted lenses and back pillars.

I.D. DATA: Ford's 17-symbol Vehicle Identification Number (VIN) again was stamped on a metal tab fastened to the instrument panel, visible through the windshield. The first three symbols ('1FA') indicate manufacturer, make and vehicle type. The fourth symbol ('B') denotes restraint system. Next comes a letter 'P', followed by two digits that indicate body type: Model Number, as shown in left column of tables below. (Example: '05' Escort two-door hatchback.) Symbol eight indicates engine type: '2' L4-98 2Bbl.; 'A' L4-140 2Bbl.; 'B' or 'T' L6-200 1Bbl.; '3' V6-232 2Bbl.; 'D' V8-255 2Bbl.; 'F' V8-302 2Bbl.; 'G' V8-351 2Bbl. Next is a check digit. Symbol ten indicates model year ('C' 1982). Symbol eleven is assembly plant: 'A' Atlanta, GA; 'B' Oakville, Ontario (Canada); 'G' Chicago; 'H' Lorain, Ohio; 'K' Kansas City, MO; 'X' St. Thomas, Ontario; 'Z' St. Louis, MO; 'R' San Jose, CA; 'T' Edison. NJ; 'W' Wayne, Mi. The final six digits make up the sequence number, starting with 100001. A Vehicle Certification Label on the left front door lock face panel or door pillar shows the manufacturer, month and year of manufacture. GVW, GAWR, certification statement, VIN, and codes for such items as body type, color, trim, axle, transmission, and special order information.

ESCORT(FOUR)

Model No.	Body/ Style No.	Body Type & Seating	Factory Price	Shipping Weight	Prod. Total
05	61D	2-dr. Hatch-4P	5462	1920	Note 1
06	58D	4-dr. Hatch-4P	5668	N/A	Note 1
05	61D	2-dr. L Hatch-4P	6046	1926	Note 1
06	58D	4-dr. L Hatch-4P	6263	2003	Note 1
08	74D	4-dr. L Sta Wag-4P	6461	2023	Note 1
05	61D	2-dr. GL Hatch-4P	6406	1948	Note 1
06	58D	4-dr. GL Hatch-4P	6622	2025	Note 1
08	74D	4-dr. GL Sta Wag-4P	6841	2043	Note 1
05	61D	2-dr. GLX Hatch-4P	7086	1978	Note 1
06	58D	4-dr. GLX Hatch-4P	7302	2064	Note 1
08	74D	4-dr. GLX Sta Wag-4P	7475	2079	Note 1
05	61D	2-dr. GT Hatch-4P	6706	1963	Note 1

NOTE 1: Total Escort production came to 165,660 two-door hatchbacks, 130,473 four-door hatchbacks, and 88,999 station wagons. Breakdown by trim level not available. Bodies are sometimes referred to as three-door and five-door.

EXP (FOUR)

Model No.	Body/ Style No.	Body Type & Seating	Factory Price	Shipping Weight	Prod. Total
01	67D	3-dr. Hatch Cpe-2P	7387	2047	98,256

FAIRMONT FUTURA (FOUR/SIX)

Model No.	Body/ Style No.	Body Type & Seating	Factory Price	Shipping Weight	Prod. Total
22	36R	2-dr. Spt Cpe-5P	6517/7141	2597/2682	17,851
20	66B	2-dr. Sedan-5P	5985/6619	2574/2659	8,222
21	54B	4-dr. Sedan-5P	6419/7043	2622/2707	101,666

GRANADA (FOUR/SIX/V-6)

Model No.	Body/ Style No.	Body Type & Seating	Factory Price	Shipping Weight	Prod. Total
26	66D	2-dr. L Sedan-5P	7126/7750	2673/2791	12,802
27	54D	4-dr. L Sedan-5P	7301/7925	2705/2823	62,339
28	74D	4-dr. L Sta Wag-5P	----/7983	----/2965	45,182
26	66D	2-dr. GL Sed-5P	7543/8167	2699/2817	Note 2
27	54D	4-dr. GL Sed-5P	7718/8342	2735/2853	Note 2
28	74D	4-dr. GL Wag-5P	----/8399	----/2995	Note 2
26	66D	2-dr. GLX Sed-5P	7666/8290	2717/2835	Note 2
27	54D	4-dr. GLX Sed-5P	7840/8464	2753/2871	Note 2

NOTE 2: Granada GL and GLX production is included in basic Granada L totals above.

FAIRMONT/GRANADA ENGINE NOTE: Prices shown are for four- and six-cylinder engines. Six-cylinder price includes $411 for the required automatic transmission. A 232 cid V-6 cost $70 more than the inline six in a Granada.

LTD (V-8)

Model No.	Body/ Style No.	Body Type & Seating	Factory Price	Shipping Weight	Prod. Total
32	66H	2-dr. Sedan-6P	8455	3496	3,510
33	54H	4-dr. Sedan-6P	8574	3526	29,776
38	74H	4-dr. Sta Wag-6P	9073	3741	9,294

LTD 'S' (V-8)

| 31 | 54D | 4-dr. Sedan-6P | 8312 | 3522 | 22,182 |
| 37 | 74D | 4-dr. Sta Wag-6P | 8783 | 3725 | 2,973 |

LTD CROWN VICTORIA (V-8)

34	66K	2-dr. Sedan-6P	9149	3523	9,287
35	54K	4-dr. Sedan-6P	9294	3567	41,405
39	74K	4-dr. Ctry Sqr-6P	9580	3741	9,626

THUNDERBIRD (SIX/V-8)

| 42 | 66D | 2-dr. HT Cpe-4P | 8492/8733 | 3000/3137 | 45,142 |

THUNDERBIRD TOWN LANDAU (SIX/V-8)

| 42/60T | 66D | 2-dr. HT Cpe-4P | 9703/9944 | 3063/3200 | Note 3 |

THUNDERBIRD HERITAGE (V-6/V-8)

| 42/607 | 66D | 2-dr. HT Cpe-4P | 12742/12742 | 3235/3361 | Note 3 |

NOTE 3: Town Landau and Heritage production is included in basic Thunderbird total.

1982 Ford Granada GL Squire station wagon. (JG)

1982 Ford Fairmont Futura sedan. (JG)

MODEL NUMBER NOTE: Some sources include a prefix 'P' ahead of the two-digit model number.

FACTORY PRICE AND WEIGHT NOTE: Fairmont/Granada prices and weights to left of slash are for four-cylinder, to right for six-cylinder engine. Thunderbird prices and weights to left of slash are for inline six-cylinder, to right for V-8 engine. Thunderbird could also have a V-6 engine (standard on the Heritage) for the same price as the V-8.

ENGINE [Base Four (Escort, EXP)]: Inline. Overhead cam. Four-cylinder. Cast-iron block and aluminum head. Displacement: 97.6 cid (1.6 liters). Bore & stroke: 3.15 x 3.13 in. Compression ratio: 8.8:1. Brake horsepower: 70 at 4600 rpm. Torque: 89 lbs.-ft. at 3000 rpm. Five main bearings. Hydraulic valve lifters. Carburetor: 2Bbl. Motorcraft 740. VIN Code: 2.

NOTE: An 80-horsepower high-output version of the 1.6-liter four arrived later in the model year.

ENGINE [Base Four (Fairmont, Granada)]: Inline. Overhead cam. Four-cylinder. Cast-iron block and head. Displacement: 140 cid (2.3 liters). Bore & stroke: 3.78 x 3.13 in. Compression ratio: 9.0:1. Brake horsepower: 86 at 4600 rpm. Torque: 117 lbs.-ft. at 2600 rpm. Five main bearings. Hydraulic valve lifters. Carburetor: 2Bbl. Holley 6500 or Motorcraft 5200. VIN Code: A.

ENGINE [Base Six (Granada wagon, Thunderbird); Optional (Fairmont, Granada)]: Inline. Overhead valve. Six-cylinder. Cast-iron block and head. Displacement: 200 cid (3.3 liters). Bore & stroke: 3.68 x 3.13 in. Compression ratio: 8.6:1. Brake horsepower: 87 at 3800 rpm. Torque: 151-154 lbs.-ft. at 1400 rpm. Seven main bearings. Hydraulic valve lifters. Carburetor: 1Bbl. Holley 1946. VIN Code: B or T.

ENGINE [Optional V-6 (Granada, Thunderbird)]: 90-degree, overhead valve V-6. Cast-iron block and aluminum head. Displacement: 232 cid (3.8 liters). Bore & stroke: 3.80 x 3.40 in. Compression ratio: 8.65:1. Brake horsepower: 112 at 4000 rpm. Torque: 175 lbs.-ft. at 2000 rpm. Four main bearings. Hydraulic valve lifters. Carburetor: 2Bbl. Motorcraft 2150. VIN Code: 3.

ENGINE [Base V-8 (LTD); Optional (Thunderbird)]: 90-degree, overhead valve V-8. Cast-iron block and head. Displacement: 255 cid (4.2 liters). Bore & stroke: 3.68 x 3.00 in. Compression ratio: 8.2:1. Brake horsepower: 122 at 3400 rpm.; (third, 120 at 3400). Torque: 209 lbs.-ft. at 2400 rpm.; (third, 205 at 1600). Five main bearings. Hydraulic valve lifters. Carburetor: 2Bbl. Motorcraft 2150 or 7200VV. VIN Code: D.

NOTE: The 255 cid V-8 was also offered in Fairmont police cars.

ENGINE [Base V-8 (LTD wagon); Optional (LTD sedan)]: 90-degree, overhead valve V-8. Cast-iron block and head. Displacement: 302 cid (5.0 liters). Bore & stroke: 4.00 x 3.00 in. Compression ratio: 8.4:1. Brake horsepower: 132 at 3400 rpm. Torque: 236 lbs.-ft. at 1800 rpm. Five main bearings. Hydraulic valve lifters. Carburetor: 2Bbl. Motorcraft 2150A or 7200VV. VIN Code: F.

ENGINE [High-Output Police V-8 (LTD)]: 90-degree, overhead valve V-8. Cast-iron block and head. Displacement: 351 cid (5.8 liters). Bore & stroke: 4.00 x 3.50 in. Compression ratio: 8.3:1. Brake horsepower: 165 at 3600 rpm. Torque: 285 lbs.-ft. at 2200 rpm. Five main bearings. Hydraulic valve lifters. Carburetor: 2Bbl. VV. VIN Code: G.

CHASSIS DATA: Wheelbase: (Escort/EXP) 94.2 in.; (Fairmont/Granada) 105.5 in.; (LTD) 114.3 in.; (third) 108.4 in. Overall Length: (Escort hatch) 163.9 in.; (Escort wagon) 165.0 in.; (EXP) 170.3 in.; (Fairmont) 195.5 in. exc. Futura coupe, 197.4 in.; (Granada) 196.5 in.; (LTD) 209.3 in.; (LTD wag) 215.0 in.; (LTD Crown Vic) 211.0 in.; (third) 200.4 in. Height: (Escort hatch) 53.1 in.; (Escort wag) 53.3 in.; (EXP) 50.5 in.; (Fairmont) 52.9 in.; (Futura cpe) 51.7 in.; (Granada) 53.0 in.; (Granada wag) 54.2 in.; (LTD) 54.7 in.; (LTD wag) 57.4 in.; (third) 53.3 in. Width: (Escort) 65.9 in.; (EXP) 63.0 in.; (Fairmont/Granada) 71.0 in.; (LTD) 77.5 in.; (LTD wag) 79.3 in.; (third) 74.1 in. Front Tread: (Escort/EXP) 54.7 in.; (Fairmont/Granada) 56.6 in.; (LTD) 62.2 in. (third) 58.1 in. Rear Tread: (Escort/EXP) 56.0 in.; (Fairmont/Granada) 57.0

in.; (LTD) 62.0 in. (third) 57.0 in. Standard Tires: (Escort/EXP) P165/80R13 SBR BSW; (Fairmont/Granada) P175/75R14 SBR BSW; (LTD) P205/75R14 SBR WSW exc. wagon, P215/75R14; (third) P195/75R14 SBR WSW.

TECHNICAL: Transmission: Four-speed manual standard on Fairmont/Granada four: (1st) 3.98:1; (2nd) 2.14:1; (3rd) 1.42:1; (4th) 1.00:1; (Rev) 3.99:1. Four-speed manual transaxle standard on Escort/EXP: (1st) 3.58:1; (2nd) 2.05:1; (3rd) 1.21:1 or 1.36:1; (4th) 0.81:1 or 0.95:1; (Rev) 3.46:1. Three-speed automatic standard on Fairmont/Granada and third six: (lst) 2.46:1 or 2.47:1; (2nd) 1.46:1 or 1.47:1; (3rd) 1.00:1; (Rev) 2.11:1 or 2.19:1. Escort/EXP three-speed automatic: (1st) 2.79:1; (2nd) 1.61:1; (3rd) 1.00:1; (Rev) 1.97:1. Four-speed overdrive automatic standard on LTD and Thunderbird V-6/V-8: (lst) 2.40:1; (2nd) 1.47:1; (3rd) 1.00:1; (4th) 0.67:1; (Rev) 2.00:1. Standard final drive ratio: (Escort/EXP) 3.59:1 w/4spd, 3.31:1 w/auto.; (Fairmont/Granada four) 3.08:1; (Fairmont/Granada six) 2.73:1; (Granada V-6) 2.47:1; (LTD) 3.08:1 exc. w/V8-351, 2.73:1; (third six) 2.73:1; (third V-6/V-8) 3.08:1. Drive Axle: (Escort/EXP) front; (others) rear. Steering: (LTD) recirculating ball; (others) rack and pinion. Front Suspension: (Escort/EXP) MacPherson strut-mounted coil springs and stabilizer bar; (Fairmont/Granada/third) modified MacPherson struts with lower control arms, coil springs and anti-sway bar; (LTD) long/short control arms w/coil springs and stabilizer bar. Rear Suspension: (Escort/EXP) independent trailing arms w/modified MacPherson struts and coil springs on lower control arms; (others) four-link rigid axle with coil springs. Brakes: Front disc, rear drum; power assisted (except Escort). Ignition: Electronic. Body construction: (Escort/EXP/Fairmont/Granada/third) unibody; (LTD) separate body and frame. Fuel tank: (Escort/EXP) 11.3 gal.; (Fairmont/Granada) 16 gal.; (LTD) 20 gal.; (third) 21 gal.

DRIVETRAIN OPTIONS: Engines: H.O. 1.6-liter four: Escort ($57). Fuel-saver 1.6-liter four: Escort (NC). Fuel-saver 140 cid four: Fairmont (NC). 200 cid six: Fairmont/Granada ($213). 232 cid V-6: Granada ($283) exc. wagon ($70); Thunderbird ($241). 255 cid V-8: third ($241) exc. Heritage (NC). 302 cid V-8: LTD sedan ($59). Transmission/Differential: Automatic transaxle: Escort/EXP ($411). Auto. transmission.: Fairmont/Granada ($411). Floor shift lever: Fairmont/Granada ($49). Traction-Lok differential: Fairmont/Granada/third ($76); LTD ($80). Optional axle ratio: Escort/EXP/Fairmont/Granada (NC). Brakes & Steering: Power brakes: Escort ($93). Power steering: Escort/EXP ($190); Fairmont/Granada ($195). Suspension: H.D. susp.: Granada ($24); LTD/third ($26). Handling susp.: Escort ($139-$187) exc. GLX ($41); Fairmont ($52); LTD ($49). TR performance susp. pkg.: EXP ($405) w/TR sport aluminum wheels; ($204) w/steel wheels. Other: H.D. battery ($22-$26): H.D. alternator: EXP ($27); LTD ($52). Extended-range gas tank: Fairmont/Granada ($46). Engine block heater ($17-$18). Trailer towing pkg., medium duty: LTD ($200-$251). California emission system ($64-$65). High-altitude emissions (NC).

ESCORT CONVENIENCE/APPEARANCE OPTIONS: Option Packages: Squire wagon pkg. ($293). Instrument group ($87). Appearance protection group ($55). Light group ($30). Comfort/Convenience: Air conditioner ($611). Rear defroster, electric ($120). Remote liftgate release ($30). Tinted glass ($82); windshield only ($32). Digital clock ($57). Interval wipers ($48). Rear wiper/washer ($117). Dual remote sport mirrors ($66). Entertainment: AM radio ($61). AM/FM radio ($76) exc. base ($137). AM/FM stereo radio ($106) exc. base ($167); w/cassette or 8- track player ($184) exc. base ($245). Dual rear speakers ($39). Exterior: Metallic glow paint ($61). Two-tone paint/tape ($122-$161). Front vent windows, pivoting ($60). Remote quarter windows ($109). Vinyl-insert bodyside moldings ($45). Bumper guards. front or rear ($26). Bumper rub strips ($41). Luggage rack ($93). Roof air deflector ($29). Lower bodyside protection ($68). Interior: Console ($111). Low-back reclining bucket seats ($33-$98). High-back reclining bucket seats ($65). Cloth/vinyl seat trim ($29); vinyl (NC). Shearling/leather seat trim ($109-$138). Deluxe seatbelts ($24). Wheels/Tires: Wheel trim rings ($48). Aluminum wheels ($232-$377). P165/80R13 WSW ($58).

1982 Ford LTD two-door sedan. (OCW)

EXP CONVENIENCE/APPEARANCE OPTIONS: Comfort/Convenience: Appearance protection group ($48). Air conditioner ($611). Fingertip speed control ($151). Tinted glass ($82). Right remote mirror ($41). Entertainment: AM/FM radio ($76). AM/FM stereo radio ($106); w/cassette or 8track player ($184). Premium sound ($105). AM radio delete ($37 credit). Exterior: Flip-up open air roof ($276). Metallic glow paint ($51). Two-tone paint/tape ($122). Luggage rack ($93). Lower bodyside protection ($68). Interior: Low-back bucket seats ($33). Cloth/vinyl seat trim ($29); vinyl (NC). Leather seat trim ($138). Shearling/leather seat trim ($138). Wheels/Tires: Cast aluminum wheels ($232). P165/80R13 RWL ($72).

FAIRMONT/GRANADA CONVENIENCE/APPEARANCE OPTIONS: Option Packages: Granada Squire option ($282). Interior luxury group: Fairmont ($282). Instrument cluster: Fairmont ($100). Cold weather group: Granada ($77). Appearance protection group ($57-$59). Light group ($49-$51). Comfort/Convenience: Air cond. ($676). Rear defroster, electric ($124). Fingertip speed control ($155). Illuminated entry ($68). Power windows ($165-$235). Power door locks ($106-$184). Remote decklid release: Fairmont ($32). Power seat: Fairmont ($139). Power split bench seat: Granada ($196). Tinted glass: Granada ($88). Tinted windshield ($32). Leather-wrapped steering wheel: Granada ($55). Tilt steering ($95). Quartz clock ($32). Interval wipers ($48). Liftgate wiper/washer: wagon ($99). Lighting and Mirrors: Cornering lamps: Granada ($59). Map light: Fairmont ($10); Granada dual-beam ($15). Trunk light ($7). Left remote mirror: Fairmont ($22). Dual bright remote mirrors: Fairmont ($65); right only, Granada ($60). Lighted right visor vanity mirror ($46); pair ($91). Entertainment: AM/FM radio ($39-$54). AM/FM stereo radio ($85); w/8track or cassette player ($172). Twin rear speakers: Fairmont ($39). Premium sound system ($105). AM radio delete ($61 credit). Exterior: Flip-up open air roof ($276). Full or half vinyl roof ($137-$140). Metallic glow paint ($63). Two-tone paint ($105-$144). Accent paint stripes ($39-$57). Pivoting front vent windows ($63). Two-way liftgate: wag ($105). Rocker panel moldings: Fairmont ($33). Protective bodyside moldings: Granada ($49). Bumper guards, rear ($28). Bumper rub strips ($50). Luggage rack: Granada ($115). Lower bodyside protection ($41). Interior: Console ($191). Vinyl flight bench seat: Fairmont ($29) w/interior luxury. Cloth/vinyl seat trim: Fairmont ($29). Vinyl seat trim: Granada ($29). Flight bench seat (NC). Split bench seat: Granada ($230). Front floor mats ($13-$22). Wheels/Tires: Luxury wheel covers: Granada ($49) exc. GL/GLX (NC). Wire wheel covers ($80-$152). Turbine wheel covers: Fairmont ($54). Styled steel wheels: Fairmont ($54-$107). Cast aluminum wheels: Granada ($348-$396). P175/75R14 WSW ($66). P185/75R14 BSW: Granada ($38). P185/75R14 WSW ($104) exc. wagon ($66). P185/75R14 RWL: Granada ($121) exc. wagon ($83). P190/65R390 BSW on TRX alum. wheels ($529-$583). Conventional spare ($51).

LTD CONVENIENCE/APPEARANCE OPTIONS: Option Packages: Interior luxury group ($727-$807). Convenience group ($90-$116). Power lock group ($106-$201). Light group ($43). Protection group ($67). Comfort/Convenience: Air cond. ($695); w/auto-temp control ($761). Rear defroster, electric ($124). Fingertip speed control ($155). Illuminated entry system ($68). Power windows ($165-$240). Power driver's seat ($198); driver and passenger ($395). Tinted glass ($102); windshield only ($32). Autolamp on/off delay ($73). Leather-wrapped steering wheel ($51). Tilt steering wheel ($95). Auto. parking brake release ($12). Tripminder computer ($215-$293). Quartz clock ($32). Digital clock ($46-$78). Seatbelt chime ($27). Interval wipers ($48). Lighting and Mirrors: Cornering lamps ($55). Remote right mirror ($43). Lighted right visor vanity mirrors ($46-$91). Entertainment: AM/FM radio ($41-$54). AM/FM stereo radio ($85); w/8track or cassette tape player ($172) exc. Crown Vic ($87). AM/FM stereo search radio ($232) exc. Crown Vic ($146); w/8track or cassette ($233-$318). Power antenna ($55). Dual rear speakers ($41). Premium sound system ($133-$167). AM radio delete ($61 credit). AM/FM delete: Crown Vic ($152 credit). Exterior: Full or half vinyl roof ($165). Metallic glow paint ($66). Two-tone paint/tape ($66-$105). Dual accent bodyside paint stripes ($39). Hood striping ($17). Pivoting front vent windows ($63). Rocker panel moldings ($32). Vinyl-insert bodyside moldings ($51). Bumper guards, rear ($30). Bumper rub strips ($52). Luggage rack ($104). Lower bodyside protection ($39-$52). Interior: Dual-facing rear seats: wagon ($167). Leather seating ($412). Dual flight bench seat recliners ($65). Split bench seating ($139-$204). All-vinyl seat trim ($28); Duraweave vinyl ($62). Front floor mats ($15-$21). Trunk trim ($49). Wheels/Tires: Luxury wheel covers ($82). 15 in. wheel covers ($49). Wire wheel covers ($152). Cast aluminum wheels ($384). P215/75R14 WSW ($36). P225/75R14 WSW ($36-$73). P205/75R15 WSW ($11-$47); puncture-resistant ($112-$148). Conventional spare ($51).

THUNDERBIRD CONVENIENCE/APPEARANCE OPTIONS: Option Packages: Interior luxury group ($1204) exc. Town Landau ($683). Exterior decor group ($385). Interior decor group ($372). Protection group ($51). Light group ($35). Power lock group ($138). Comfort/Convenience: Air cond. ($676); auto-temp ($754) exc. Heritage ($78). Rear defroster ($126). Fingertip speed control ($155). Illuminated entry system ($68). Keyless entry ($139). Tripminder computer ($215-$261). Autolamp on/off delay ($73). Tinted glass ($88); windshield

only ($32). Power windows ($165). Six-way power driver's seat ($198). Auto. parking brake release ($12). Leather-wrapped steering wheel ($51). Tilt steering wheel ($95). Electronic instrument cluster ($321-$367). Diagnostic warning lights ($59). Digital clock ($46). Interval wipers ($48). Lighting and Mirrors: Cornering lamps ($59). Remote right mirror ($60). Lighted right visor vanity mirrors ($46-$91). Entertainment: AM/FM radio ($39-$54). AM/FM stereo radio ($85); w/8track or cassette player ($87-$172). AM/FM stereo search radio ($146-$232); w/8track or cassette ($318). Twn Lan ($233) and Heritage ($87). Power antenna ($55). Dual rear speakers ($39). Premium sound system ($133-$167). AM radio delete ($61 credit). Exterior: Carriage roof ($766-$973). Flip-up open-air roof ($276). Vinyl rear half roof ($156-$320). Metallic glow paint ($80). Two-tone paint ($128-$206). Dual accent bodyside paint stripes ($49). Hood/bodyside paint stripes ($16-$65). Pivoting front vent windows ($63). Wide door belt moldings ($51). Rocker panel moldings ($33). Lower bodyside protection ($39-$54). Interior: Bucket seats w/console ($211) exc. (NC) w/decor group. Split bench seat ($208). Luxury split bench ($124). Recaro bucket seats w/console ($405-$523) exc, Heritage ($222). Leather seat trim ($409). Vinyl seat trim ($28-$30). Front floor mats, carpeted ($22). Trunk trim ($48). Wheels/Tires: Wire wheel covers ($45-$152). Luxury wheel covers ($107). Self-sealing tires ($106). TR WSW tires on alum. wheels ($490-$643). Conventional spare ($51).

HISTORY: Introduced: September 24, 1981 except EXP, April 9, 1981. Model year production: 1,035,063 (incl. Mustangs). Total production for the U.S. market of 888,669 units (incl. Mustangs) included 461,524 four-cylinder, 251,145 sixes and 176,000 V-8s. Calendar year production (U.S.): 690,655 (incl. Mustangs). Calendar year sales by U.S. dealers: 925,490 (incl. Mustangs). Model year sales by U.S. dealers: 888,633 (incl. Mustangs).

HISTORY: Escort became the best selling domestic car this model year, finding 321,952 buyers (up over 13 percent from 1981). Still, total Ford Division sales for the model year declined by close to 20 percent: only 888,633 versus 1,105,751 in 1981. And 1981 had posted a loss as well. FoMoCo's market share held at the depressing 16.5 percent level of the prior year. *Car and Driver* readers had voted Escort 'Most Significant New Domestic Car' for 1981, and it beat Chevrolet's Chevette this year. Granada gained sales in its recently downsized form, but other models did not. Mustang dropped by almost one-third, Fairmont and Thunderbird by more than 40 percent. EXP did not sell as well as hoped for after its spring 1981 debut, so within a couple of months incentives were being offered. Sales rose a bit later, partly due to a more peppy high-output EXP 1.6-liter engine that debuted in mid-year. Two new plants (San Jose, California, and St. Thomas, Ontario) were assigned to assemble the Escort/EXP subcompacts. Escort was also assembled at Wayne, Michigan, and Edison, New Jersey. Production of Thunderbird for the model year fell dramatically, by more than half. As the 1983 model year began, Ford offered what was then low-interest financing (10.75 percent rate) to customers who would buy one of the leftover '82 models. In January 1982, the UAW agreed to an alternating-shift arrangement at certain plants. Workers would work 10 days, then take 10 days off. That way, a skilled work force remained available for the day when increased production again became necessary. Ford's advertising theme at this time was: "Have you driven a Ford lately?"

1983 FORD

A dramatically modern 10th-generation Thunderbird showed the aero styling that was becoming the standard for sporty-and even luxury-models. Escort added a revised GT model, based on the European XR3. The high-output 1.6-liter four, added at mid-year 1982, could power both Escort and EXP. The new short-wheelbase LTD sedan was basically a rebodied Granada. The LTD nameplate also continued on the bigger LTD Crown Victoria.

1983 Ford EXP HO Sport Coupe. (JG)

1983 Ford Escort GT three-door hatchback. (F)

ESCORT — FOUR — America's best selling car in 1982 lost its base model this year, dropping to four series. That made Escort L the new base model, with stepups to GL, GLX, and a sporty GT. The new GT was said to be more akin to the high-performance XR3, which had been the image car of the European Escort line. Its 1.6-liter four had multi-port fuel injection. GT also carried five-speed manual shift with 3.73:1 final drive, a TR performance suspension with Michelin TRX tires, functional front and rear spoilers, molded wheel lip extensions (flares), and flared tailpipe extension. GT standards also included foglamps (below the bumper), flat black exterior trim, unique taillamp treatment, a new reclining sport seat, specially-tuned exhaust, special steering wheel, and console and full instrumentation featuring arc yellow graphics. GT was claimed to run 0-60 MPH in about 11 seconds. The high-output carbureted 97.6 cid (1.6-liter) four, introduced as a 1982.5 option, continued available on any Escort except the GT. The base 1.6-liter had new fast-burn technology to improve fuel economy. Escort might have any of three suspension levels: base, handling, and TRX performance. All manual-shift models had a standard upshift indicator that showed when to shift into the next higher gear for best mileage. All Escorts now had all-season SBR tires and a larger (13-gallon) gas tank. Five-speed was available with either the high output or EFI engine. Escort's Fuel-Saver package came with economy 3.04:1 final drive and wide-ratio four-speed gearbox. Apart from minor details, appearance was the same as 1982. GL and GLX had a new wide bodyside molding with argent stripe (introduced at mid-year 1982). GLX no longer had front and rear bumper guards. GL now had standard low-back reclining bucket seats. All except L had a new locking gas filler door with inside release. Optional knit vinyl seat trim replaced regular vinyl on GL and GLX. New Escort options were: remote-controlled convex right-hand mirror, remote-release fuel filler door (standard on upper Escorts), and P175/80R13 tires. Other options included a luggage rack for hatchbacks, roof air deflector, shearling and leather seat trim, and dual rear speakers.

EXP — FOUR — This year's EXP looked the same, but had a wider choice of engines and transaxles. Standard powertrain was a refined 97.6 cid (1.6-liter) four with two-barrel carburetor and fast-burn capability, hooked to four-speed manual transaxle with overdrive fourth gear. The high-output 1.6-liter introduced as a 1982.5 option was available with either automatic or a new optional five-speed gearbox. That engine produced 80 horsepower, versus 70 for the base four. Newly optional this year was a multi-port fuel-injected version of the four. Acceleration to 60 MPH was supposed to be cut by three seconds with the new powerplant. Five-speed gearboxes came with 3.73:1 final drive ratio. Shift control for the optional automatic transaxle was revised to a straight-line pattern. EXP had a larger (13-gallon) gas tank. Interiors were more color-keyed this year, including the console and instrument panel (which had arc yellow gauge graphics); the former panel was black. Seats had a new sew style and more porous knit vinyl that would be cooler in summer. A remote-control locking fuel filler door was now standard. New options included a right-hand remote-control convex mirror, remote fuel door release, sport performance bucket seats, and P175/80R13 tires. Michelin TRX tires and TR wheels were now available with base suspension. The luggage

rack, 4.05:1 drive ratio and conventional remote right mirror were deleted from the option list. As before, a Ford script oval stood above the twin grille slots. 'EXP' letters and Ford oval decorated the decklid. Small backup lenses were near inner ends of full-width wraparound tail lamps.

LTD — FOUR/SIX/V-6 — The familiar LTD nameplate took on two forms for 1983: a new, smaller five-passenger model, and the old (larger) LTD Crown Victoria (listed below). This new LTD was built on the 'L' body shell. Among its features were gas-pressurized shocks and struts, as introduced in 1982 on the new Continental. LTD came in a single well-equipped series: just a four-door sedan and wagon. Sedans carried the 140 cid (2.3-liter) four with four-speed as base powertrain; wagons, the 250 cid (3.3-liter) inline six with three-speed automatic. A 3.8-liter 'Essex' V-6 became optional, with four-speed overdrive automatic. So was a propane-powered four, intended to attract fleet buyers. The base 2.3-liter engine had a new single-barrel carburetor and fast-burn technology. LTD had flash-to-pass on the headlamp lever, as well as rack-and-pinion steering. Wheelbase was 105.5 inches, just like the Granada it replaced. In fact this was the familiar Fairmont platform, in yet another variant. Aerodynamic design features included a 60-degree rear-window angle, addition of a front valance and spoiler, and aero-styled decklid. Drag coefficient was claimed to be 0.38 (low for a sedan). LTD's sloping front end displayed a slanted grille that consisted of thin vertical strips dominated by three heavier horizontal divider bars. A Ford oval adorned the center of the heavy upper header bar. Quad rectangular headlamps were deeply recessed. Park lamps sat below the bumper strip; wraparound side markers at front fender tips. The sloping rear end held horizontal tricolor wraparound tail lamps with upper and lower segments, and back-up lenses halfway toward the center (similar to 1982 Granada). Standard wide vinyl-insert bodyside moldings met with bright partial wheel lip moldings. The instrument panel stemmed from the 1982 Thunderbird. Tire tread design was the wraparound European style, with all-season capability. Mercury Marquis was LTD's corporate twin. Both measured somewhere between compact and mid-size.

FAIRMONT FUTURA — FOUR/SIX — For its final season, Fairmont continued with little change. The lineup had been simplified into a single series for the 1982 model year. This time, the 4.2-liter V-8 was dropped completely, leaving only a base four and optional inline six. The 140 cu. (2.3-liter) switched from 1Bbl. to 2Bbl. carburetion and added fast-burn technology and long-reach spark plugs, plus a redesigned exhaust manifold. Two-and four-door sedans were offered again, along with a two-door coupe. A low-budget 'S' series also was introduced. The Traction-Lok axle was now available with TR-type tires. New options included a 100-amp alternator (LPO option). Flight bench seating and a headlamp-on warning buzzer were added to the interior luxury group. Dual rear speakers were discontinued as an option. Radios got a new look and graphics. In short, not much change. For 1984, the rear-drive Fairmont, which had sold quite well during its six-year life and remained popular with fleet and taxi buyers, would be replaced by the new front-drive Tempo.

LTD CROWN VICTORIA — V-8 — Full-size Fords carried on with little change and a longer name. The model lineup first consisted of two-and four-door sedans and Country Squire (woodgrain) station wagon, in just one luxury level. Later came a low budget 'S' pair of sedans and plain-bodied wagon. Base engine was the fuel-injected 302 cid (5.0-liter) V-8 with four-speed overdrive automatic. Base tires grew one size, to P215/75R14. Country Squire now had a standard AM/FM radio. All models had a new fuel cap tether. The right-hand remote mirror option was now a convex type. A new, bolder double-crosshatch design grille had a 12x4 hole pattern with internal crosshatching in each hole, and a heavy upper header. The Ford script oval sat at the left portion of the grille. Quad rectangular headlamps stood above rectangular parking lamps, and the assembly continued around the fender tips to enclose signal/marker lenses. Sedans also had a new taillamp design. Country Squire had revised woodtone appearance without the former planking lines. New options included a remote-control locking fuel door, locking wire wheel covers, and new-generation electronic radios. Two trailer-towing packages were offered. Options deleted were dual rear speakers, monaural AM/FM radio, full and half vinyl roofs, seatbelt reminder chime, rear bumper guards, and dual flight bench recliner seats.

THUNDERBIRD — V-6/V-8 — In its tenth and smaller form, Thunderbird took on a striking aero look. 'Conceived for today with an eye on tomorrow' was the way the factory catalog described it. The new version was built on the 'S' shell, with 104 inch wheelbase (down from 108). Extensive aerodynamic testing resulted in an air drag coefficient of 0.35 (lower than any tested domestic competitor in its class). Aero design features included concealed drip moldings, a sloping hood, tapered fenders and quarter panels, sharply raked windshield and backlight, contoured parking lamps, and integrated decklid spoiler. Inside, Thunderbird had a standard deep-well luggage compartment, assist straps, storage bins integral with door trim panels, and a console with padded armrest/lid. Engineering features of the new design included gas-pressurized, modified MacPherson struts at the front suspension and gas shocks at the four-bar-link rear. Base engine was the 232 cid (3.8-liter) V-6 with SelectShift three-speed automatic and locking torque converter. Optional: a fuel-injected 302 cid (5.0-liter) V-8 with four-speed overdrive automatic. The Town Landau series was deleted. So was the 4.2-liter V-8 and the inline six. Flash-to-pass became standard. So was variable-ratio, power rack-and-pinion steering. Much more curvaceous and smooth than former 'Birds, the new one had exposed quad rectangular halogen headlamps in deeply recessed housings, with cornering/marker lenses at the edge of each headlamp housing. Parking lamps were well below the front bumper strip. The sloping grille showed an eggcrate (8x6) pattern and heavy upper header. Full-width wraparound tail lamps met the recessed license plate housing in a sloping back panel. Backup lenses stood near the center of each taillamp. Trim was minimal, with little of the former Thunderbird's sculptured look. Wide bodyside moldings continued all around the car to meet the bumper rub strips. Options included electric remote outside mirrors, an automatic-dimming rearview mirror, pivoting front vent windows, keyless entry, clearcoat metallic paint, remote locking fuel door, voice alert, and a canvas-wrapped emergency kit containing tools and first aid items (which stored in a quarter-panel well). Mercury Cougar was similar in design, but with a different side-window look. The new Thunderbird was expected to appeal to younger buyers than previous editions. All the more so a little later when the Turbo Coupe appeared. Louis E. Lataif spoke for Ford in calling it 'the ultimate road machine-a complete high-performance package.' The turbocharged 2.3-liter four was Ford's first use of a 'blow-through' design. That put the turbocharger ahead of the throttle, giving faster response by maintaining slight pressure in the intake system. This helped overcome the low-speed lag of conventional turbos. The engine also had Bosch multi-port fuel injection, forged-aluminum pistons, an oil cooler, aluminum rocker covers, and the fourth generation (EECIV) of electronic engine control systems. Compression was cut to 8.0:1 from the usual 9.5:1. Standard was a five-speed manual transmission with performance-type close-ratio gearing. Fifth gear was a 0.86:1 overdrive. The shift linkage had a short throw between gears. Turbos had a 3.45:1 final drive ratio, A new Ford rear suspension called 'quadra-shock' was offered for the first time on the Turbo Coupe. It was a special four-bar-link coil spring system with two hydraulic axle dampers mounted horizontally toward the rear, between brackets on axle and body rail. Like other models, Turbo Coupe had gas-pressurized struts and shocks. The unique front fascia included two recessed Marchal foglamps. A wide charcoal-color bodyside molding and bumper rub strip system encircled the whole car. Headlamp housings were black. There was also a special fluted B-pillar molding, and other charcoal or black accents. Goodyear Eagle P205/70HR14 blackwall performance tires rode unique aluminum wheels. Turbo Coupe's instrument panel was special black and brushed finish, including a tachometer with boost and overboost lights; plus a row of diagnostic warning lights and a digital clock. Controls for the dual electric mirrors were on the console. Standard fittings included a leather-wrapped steering wheel and shift knob, Traction-Lok axle, bodyside and decklid paint stripes, black door handles and lock bezels, and charcoal headlamp doors. Lear-Siegler articulated bucket seats had inflatable lumbar support along with open-mesh head restraints. Turbo Coupe's special handling suspension with performance tires was available on other models. Illuminated entry was now standard on the Heritage model, as were dual bright electric remote-control mirrors, electronic instruments, tinted glass, lighted vanity mirrors, and a premium sound system. Also included: tilt steering, digital clock, power locks, autolamp on/off/delay system, bodyside moldings, bumper rub strip extensions, wire wheel covers, a special grille ornament, and striping on hood, bodyside and decklid. Heritage seats wore velour cloth trim and a Thunderbird seatback emblem. Front seats held a Velcro-closed driver's map pocket. The instrument panel displayed Prima Vera woodtone appliqués. Heritage had unique quarter windows and electro-luminiscent coach lamps. Customers later received an anodized aluminum plaque with their signature.

I.D. DATA: Ford's 17-symbol Vehicle Identification Number (VIN) again was stamped on a metal tab fastened to the instrument panel, visible through the windshield. The first three symbols ('1FA') indicate manufacturer, make and vehicle type. The fourth symbol ('B') denotes restraint system. Next comes a letter 'P', followed by two digits that indicate body type: Model Number, as shown in left column of tables below. (Example: '04' Escort L two-door hatchback; the numbering system changed this year.) Symbol eight indicates engine type: '2' L4-98 2Bbl.; '4' H.O. L4-98 2Bbl.; '5' L4-98 EFI; 'A' L4-140 1Bbl.; 'D' Turbo L4-140 EFI; 'X' L6-200 1Bbl.; '3' V6-232 2Bbl.; 'F' V8-302 2Bbl.; 'G' V8-351 2Bbl. Next is a check digit. Symbol ten indicates model year ('D' 1983). Symbol eleven is assembly plant: 'A' Atlanta, GA; 'B' Oakville, Ontario (Canada); 'G' Chicago, IL; 'H' Lorain, Ohio; 'K' Kansas City, MO; 'X' St. Thomas, Ontario; 'Z' St. Louis, MO; 'R' San Jose, CA; 'T' Edison, NJ; 'W' Wayne, MI. The final six digits make up the sequence number, starting with 100001. A Vehicle Certification Label on the left front door lock face panel or door pillar shows the manufacturer, month and year of manufacture, GVW, GAWR, certification statement, VIN, and codes for such items as body type, color, trim, axle, transmission, and special order information.

1983 Ford LTD four-door sedan. (JG)

ESCORT (FOUR)

Model No.	Body/ Style No.	Body Type & Seating	Factory Price	Shipping Weight	Prod. Total
04	61D	2-dr. L Hatch-4P	5639	1932	Note 1
13	58D	4-dr. L Hatch-4P	5846	1998	Note 1
09	74D	4-dr. L Sta Wag-4P	6052	2026	Note 1
05	61D	2-dr. GL Hatch-4P	6384	1959	Note 1
14	58D	4-dr. GL Hatch-4P	6601	2025	Note 1
10	74D	4-dr. GL Sta Wag-4P	6779	2052	Note 1
06	61D	2-dr. GLX Hatch-4P	6771	1993	Note 1
15	58D	4-dr. GLX Hatch-4P	6988	2059	Note 1
11	74D	4-dr. GLX Sta Wag-4P	7150	2083	Note 1
07	61D	2-dr. GT Hatch-4P	7339	2020	Note 1

NOTE 1: Total Escort production came to 151,386 two-door hatchbacks, 84,649 four-door hatchback sedans, and 79,335 station wagons. Breakdown by trim level not available. Bodies are sometimes referred to as three-door and five-door.

EXP (FOUR)

01	67D	3-dr. Hatch Cpe-2P	6426	2068	19,697
01/301B	67D	3-dr. HO Cpe-2P	7004	N/A	Note 2
01/302B	67D	3-dr. HO Spt Cpe-2P	7794	N/A	Note 2
01/303B	67D	3-dr. Luxury Cpe-2P	8225	N/A	Note 2
01/304B	67D	3-dr. GT Cpe-2P	8739	N/A	Note 2

NOTE 2: Production of step-up models is included in basic EXP total above.

FAIRMONT FUTURA (FOUR/SIX)

37	36R	2-dr. Coupe-4P	6666/7344	2601/2720	7,882
35	66B	2-dr. Sedan-5P	6444/7122	2582/2701	3,664
36	54B	4-dr. Sedan-5P	6590/7268	2626/2745	69,287

FAIRMONT 'S' (FOUR)

35/41K	66B	2-dr. Sedan-5P	5985/6663	2569/2688	Note 3
36/41K	54B	4-dr. Sedan-5P	6125/6803	2613/2732	Note 3

NOTE 3: Fairmont 'S' production is included in Futura sedan totals above.

LTD (FOUR/SIX)

Model No.	Body/ Style No.	Body Type & Seating	Factory Price	Shipping Weight	Prod. Total
39	54D	4-dr. Sedan-5P	7777/8455	2788/2874	111,813
39/60H	54D	4-dr. Brghm-5P	8165/8843	2802/2888	Note 4
40	74D	4-dr. Sta Wag-5P	----/8577	----/2975	43,945

NOTE 4: Brougham production is included in basic sedan total.

FAIRMONT/LTD ENGINE NOTE: Prices shown are for four-and six-cylinder engines. Six-cylinder price includes $439 for the required automatic transmission. A 232 cid V-6 cost $70 more than the inline six in an LTD.

1983 Ford LTD Country Squire station wagon. (JG)

1983 Ford Thunderbird hardtop coupe. (F)

LTD CROWN VICTORIA (V-8)

42	66K	2-dr. Sedan-6P	10094	3590	11,414
43	54K	4-dr. Sedan-6P	10094	3620	81,859
44	74K	4-dr. Ctry Sqr-6P	10253	3773	20,343
43/41K	54K	4-dr. 'S' Sed-6P	9130	N/A	Note 5
44/41K	74K	4-dr. 'S' Wag-6P	9444	N/A	Note 5
44/41E	74K	4-dr. Sta Wag-6P	10003	N/A	Note 5

NOTE 5: Production of 'S' models and basic station wagon is included in basic sedan and Country Squire totals above.

THUNDERBIRD (V-6/V-8)

46	66D	2-dr. HT Cpe-4P	9197/9485	2905/2936	121,999

THUNDERBIRD HERITAGE (V-6/V-8)

46/607	66D	2-dr. HT Cpe-4P	12228/12516	3027/----	Note 6

THUNDERBIRD TURBO COUPE (FOUR)

46/934	66D	2-dr. HT Cpe-4P	11790	N/A	Note 6

NOTE 6: Turbo Coupe and Heritage production is included in basic Thunderbird total.

MODEL NUMBER NOTE: Some sources include a prefix 'P' ahead of the two-digit model number.

FACTORY PRICE AND WEIGHT NOTE: Fairmont/LTD prices and weights to left of slash are for four-cylinder, to right for six-cylinder engine. Thunderbird prices and weights to left of slash are for V-6, to right for V-8 engine.

ENGINE [Base Four (Escort, EXP)]: Inline, Overhead cam, Four-cylinder. Cast-iron block and aluminum head. Displacement: 98 cid (1.6 liters). Bore & stroke: 3.15 x 3.13 in. Compression ratio: 8.8:1. Brake horsepower: 70 at 4600 rpm. Torque: 88 lbs.-ft. at 2600 rpm. Five main bearings, Hydraulic valve lifters. Carburetor: 2Bbl. Motorcraft 740. VIN Code: 2.

ENGINE [Optional Four (Escort, EXP)]: High-output version of 1.6-liter four above Horsepower: 80 at 5400 rpm. Torque: 88 lbs.-ft. at 3000 rpm. VIN Code: 4.

ENGINE [Base Four (Escort GT); Optional (Escort, EXP)]: Fuel-injected version of 1.6-liter four above Compression ratio: 9.5:1. Horsepower: 88 at 5400 rpm. Torque: 94 lbs.-ft. at 4200 rpm. VIN Code: 5.

ENGINE [Base Four (Fairmont, LTD)]: Inline. Overhead cam. Four-cylinder. Cast-iron block and head. Displacement: 140 cid (2.3 liters). Bore & stroke: 3.78 x 3.13 in. Compression ratio: 9.0: 1. Brake horse-power: 90 at 4600 rpm. Torque: 122 lbs.-ft. at 2600 rpm. Five main bearings. Hydraulic valve lifters. Carburetor: 1Bbl. Carter YFA. VIN Code: A.

NOTE: A 140 cid (2.3-liter) propane four was also available for LTD.

ENGINE [Turbocharged Four (Thunderbird Turbo Coupe)]: Same as 140 cid four above, with fuel injection and turbocharger Compression ratio: 8.0:1. Horsepower: 142 at 5000 rpm. Torque: 172 lbs.-ft. at 3800 rpm. VIN Code: D.

ENGINE [Optional Six (Fairmont, LTD)]: Inline. Overhead valve. Six-cylinder. Cast-iron block and head. Displacement: 200 cid (3.3 liters). Bore & stroke: 3.68 x 3.13 in. Compression ratio: 8.6:1. Brake horse-power: 92 at 3800 rpm. Torque: 156 lbs.-ft. at 1400 rpm. Seven main bearings. Hydraulic valve lifters. Carburetor: 1Bbl. Holley 1946. VIN Code: X.

ENGINE [Base V-6 (Thunderbird); Optional (LTD)]: 90-degree, over-head valve. Cast-iron block and aluminum head. Displacement: 232 cid (3.8 liters). Bore & stroke: 3.80 x 3.40 in. Compression ratio: 8.65:1. Brake horsepower: 110 at 3800 rpm. Torque: 175 lbs.-ft. at 2200 rpm. Four main bearings. Hydraulic valve lifters. Carburetor: 2Bbl. Motorcraft 2150 or 7200VV. VIN Code: 3.

1983 Ford Thunderbird Turbo coupe. (JG)

ENGINE [Base V-8 (Crown Victoria); Optional (LTD, Thunderbird)]: 90-degree, overhead valve V-8. Cast-iron block and head. Displace-ment: 302 cid (5.0 liters). Bore & stroke: 4.00 x 3.00 in. Compression ratio: 8.4:1. Brake horsepower: 130 at 3200 rpm. Torque: 240 lbs.-ft. at 2000 rpm. Five main bearings. Hydraulic valve lifters. Electronic fuel injection. VIN Code: F.

NOTE: Crown Victoria also announced a high-output version rated 145 horsepower at 3600 rpm., 245 lbs.-ft. at 2200 rpm.

ENGINE [High-Output Police V-8 (Crown Victoria)]: 90-degree, overhead valve V-8. Cast-iron block and head. Displacement: 351 cid (5.8 liters). Bore & stroke: 4.00 x 3.50 in. Compression ratio: 8.3:1. Brake horsepower: 165 at 3600 rpm. Torque: 290 lbs.-ft. at 2200 rpm. Five main bearings. Hydraulic valve lifters. Carburetor: 2Bbl. VV. VIN Code: G.

CHASSIS DATA: Wheelbase: (Escort/EXP) 94.2 in.; (Fairmont/LTD) 105.5 in.; (Crown Vic) 114.3 in.; (TBird) 104.0 in. Overall Length: (Es-cort) 163.9 in.; (Escort wagon) 165.0 in.; (EXP) 170.3 in.; (Fairmont) 195.5 in. exc. Futura coupe, 197.4 in.; (LTD) 196.5 in.; (Crown Vic) 211.1 in.; (TBird) 197.6 in. Height: (Escort) 53.3 in.; (EXP) 50.5 in.; (Fairmont) 52.9 in.; (Futura cpe) 51.7 in.; (LTD) 53.6 in.; (LTD wag) 54.3 in.; (Crown Vic) 55.3 in.; (Crown Vic wag) 56.8 in.; (TBird) 53.2 in. Width: (Escort/EXP) 65.9 in.; (Fair-mont/LTD) 71.0 in.; (Crown Vic) 77.5 in.; (Crown Vic wag) 79.3 in.; (TBird) 71.1 in. Front Tread: (Escort/EXP) 54.7 in.; (Fairmont/LTD) 56.6 in.; (Crown Vic) 62.2 in. (TBird) 58.1 in. Rear Tread: (Escort/EXP) 56.0 in.; (Fairmont/LTD) 57.0 in.; (Crown Vic) 62.0 in. (TBird) 58.5 in. Standard Tires: (Escort/EXP) P165/80R13 SBR BSW; (Escort GT/EXP luxury cpe) P165/70R365 Michelin TRX; (Fairmont) P175/75R14 SBR BSW; (LTD) P185/75R14 SBR BSW; (Crown Vic) P215/75R14 SBR WSW; (TBird) P195/75R14 SBR WSW; (TBird Turbo Cpe) P205/70HR14.

TECHNICAL: Transmission: Four-speed manual standard on LTD: (1st) 3.98:1; (2nd) 2.14:1; (3rd) 1.49:1; (4th) 1.00:1 Rev 3.99:1. Escort four-speed manual transaxle (1st) 3.23:1; (2nd) 1.90:1; (3rd) 1.23:1; (4th) 0.81:1; (Rev) 3.46:1. Four-speed manual on Escort/EXP: (1st) 3.58:1; (2nd) 2.05:1; (3rd) 1.23:1 or 1.36:1; (4th) 0.81:1 or 0.95:1; (Rev) 3.46:1. Five-speed manual on Escort/EXP: (1st) 3.60:1; (2nd) 2.12:1; (3rd) 1.39:1; (4th) 1.02:1; (5th) 1.02:1; (Rev) 3.62:1. (Note: separate final drive for 5th gear.) TBird Turbo Coupe five-speed: (1st) 4.03:1; (2nd) 2.37:1; (3rd) 1.50:1; (4th) 1.00:1; (5th) 0.86:1; (Rev) 3.76:1. TBird Turbo Coupe five-speed with 3.73:1 axle ratio: (lst) 3.76:1; (2nd) 2.18:1; (3rd) 1.36:1; (4th) 1.00:1; (5th) 0.86:1; (Rev) 3.76:1. Three-speed automatic standard on LTD and TBird six: (1st) 2.46:1 or 2.47:1; (2nd) 1.46:1 or 1.47:1; (3rd) 1.00:1; (Rev) 2.11:1 or 2.19:1. Escort/EXP three-speed automatic: (1st) 2.79:1; (2nd) 161:1; (3rd) 1.00:1; (Rev) 1.97:1. Four-speed overdrive automatic standard on LTD V-6, Crown Victoria and Thunderbird V-8: (1st) 2.40:1 (2nd) 1.47:1; (3rd) 1.00:1; (4th) 0.67:1; (Rev) 2.00:1. Standard final drive ratio: (Escort/EXP) 3.59:1 w/4spd, 3.04:1 w/fuel saver, 3.73:1 w/5spd, 3.31:1 w/auto.; (Fairmont) 3.08:1 exc. w/six, 2.73:1; (LTD four) 3.45:1 (LTD six) 2.73:1; (LTD V-6) 3.08:1; (Crown Vic) 3.08:1; (TBird) 3.45:1 w/5spd, 2.47:1 w/3spd automatic, 3.08:1 w/4spd auto. Drive Axle: (Escort/EXP) front; (others) rear. Steering: (Crown Vic) recirculating ball; (others) rack and pinion. Front Suspension: (Escort/EXP) MacPherson struts with lower control arms, coil springs and stabilizer bar; (Fairmont/LTD/TBird) modified MacPherson struts with lower con-trol arms, coil springs and anti-sway bar; (Crown Vic) long/short control arms w/coil springs and stabilizer bar. LTD and TBird had gas-filled shock absorbers. Rear Suspension: (Escort/EXP) independent trailing arms w/modified MacPherson struts and coil springs on lower control arms: (Fairmont/LTD/Crown Vic) rigid axle w/four-link coil springs; (Thunderbird) four-link rigid axle with coil springs and electronic level control; (TBird Turbo Coupe) 'quadra-shock' four-bar-link assembly with two hydraulic, horizontal axle dampers. Gas-filled shocks on LTD and TBird. Brakes: Front disc, rear drum: power assisted (except Es-cort). Ignition: Electronic. Body construction: (Crown Vic) separate body and frame; (others) unibody. Fuel tank: (Escort/EXP) 13.0 gal.; (Fairmont/LTD) 16.0 gal.; (Crown Vic) 18.0 gal.; (Crown Vic wagon) 18.5 gal.; (TBird) 21 gal.

1983 Ford LTD Brougham sedan. (JG)

DRIVETRAIN OPTIONS: Engines: H.O. 1.6-liter four: Escort ($70-$73); EXP GT ($70). Fuel-saver 1.6-liter four: Escort (NC). Turbo 140 cid four: LTD ($896). 200 cid six: Fairmont/LTD ($239). 232 cid V-6: LTD ($309) exc. wagon ($70). 302 cid V-8: Thunderbird ($288). Transmission/Differential: Close-ratio four-speed trans.: Escort (NC). Five-speed manual trans.: Escort ($76). Automatic transaxle: Escort/base EXP ($439) exc. GT and other EXP ($363). Select-shift auto. transmission.: Fairmont/LTD ($439). Overdrive auto. trans.: LTD ($615) exc. wagon ($176); Thunderbird ($176). Floor shift lever: Fairmont/LTD ($49). Traction-Lok differential: Fairmont/LTD/Crown Vic/TBird ($95). Optional axle ratio: Fairmont (NC). Brakes & Steering: Power brakes: Escort ($95). Power steering: Escort/EXP ($210): Fairmont/LTD ($218). Suspension: H.D. susp.: Fairmont ($24); Crown Vic/TBird ($26). Handling susp.: Escort ($199) exc. GLX ($41); Fairmont ($52); Crown Vic ($49). TR performance susp. pkg.: Escort ($41) w/Michelin TRX tires: EXP luxury or GT ($41). Other: H.D. battery ($26). H.D. alternator: EXP ($27). Extended-range gas tank: Fairmont/LTD ($46). Engine block heater ($17-$18). Trailer towing pkg., medium duty: Crown Vic ($200-$251); heavy duty ($251-$302). Trailer towing pkg.: TBird ($251). California emission system ($46-$76). High-altitude emissions (NC).

ESCORT CONVENIENCE/APPEARANCE OPTIONS: Option Packages: Squire wagon pkg. ($350). Instrument group ($87). Appearance protection group ($39). Light group ($43). Comfort/Convenience: Air conditioner ($624). Rear defroster, electric ($124). Fingertip speed control ($170). Tinted glass ($90); windshield only, LPO ($38). Digital clock ($57). Interval wipers ($49). Rear wiper/washer ($117). Dual remote sport mirrors ($67). Entertainment: AM radio: L ($61). AM/FM radio ($82) exc. L ($143). AM/FM stereo radio ($109) exc. base ($170): w/cassette or 8 track player ($199) exc. L ($260). Premium sound ($117). Exterior: Flip-up open-air roof ($217-$310). Clearcoat metallic paint ($305). Metallic glow paint ($51). Two-tone paint/tape ($134-$173). Dual bodyside paint stripes ($39). Front vent windows, pivoting ($60). Remote quarter windows ($109). Vinyl-insert bodyside moldings ($45). Bumper guards, front or rear ($28). Bumper rub strips ($41). Luggage rack ($93). Lower bodyside protection ($68). Interior: Console ($111). Fold-down center armrest ($55). Low-back reclining bucket seats: L ($98). High-back reclining bucket seats: L ($65). Vinyl low-back reclining bucket seats: GL/GLX ($24). Vinyl high-back bucket seats: L ($24). Color-keyed front mats ($22). Wheels/Tires: Wheel trim rings ($54). Cast aluminum wheels ($226-$383). TR sport aluminum wheels ($568) exc. GLX ($411) and GT ($201). TR styled steel wheels ($210-$367). P165/80R13 SBR WSW ($59). P175/80R13 SBR BSW ($20); WSW ($78).

EXP CONVENIENCE/APPEARANCE OPTIONS: Comfort/Convenience: Air conditioner ($624). Rear defroster: base ($124). Tinted glass: HO ($90). Entertainment: AM/FM radio ($82). AM/FM stereo radio ($109); w/cassette or 8track player ($199) exc. luxury cpe ($90). Premium sound ($117). AM radio delete ($37 credit). AM/FM stereo delete: luxury cpe ($145 credit). AM/FM stereo/cassette delete: GT ($235 credit). Exterior: Flip-up open air roof ($310). Metallic glow paint ($51). Two-tone paint/tape ($146). Sport tape stripe ($41). Lower bodyside protection ($68). Interior: Low-back sport cloth or knit vinyl bucket seats (NC). Low-back sport performance seats ($173). Leather/vinyl seat trim ($144). Shearling low-back bucket seats ($227). Wheels: TR sport aluminum wheels: GT (NC).

FAIRMONT CONVENIENCE/APPEARANCE OPTIONS: Option Packages: Interior luxury group ($294). Instrument cluster ($100). Appearance protection group ($32-$60). Light group ($55). Comfort/Convenience: Air cond. ($724). Rear defroster, electric ($135). Fingertip speed control ($170). Illuminated entry ($82). Power windows ($180-$255). Power door locks ($120-$170). Remote decklid release ($40). Four-way power seat ($139). Tinted glass ($105). Tinted windshield ($38). Tilt steering ($105). Quartz clock ($35). Interval wipers ($49). Lighting and Mirrors: Trunk light ($7). Left remote mirror: S ($22). Dual bright remote mirrors: S ($68). Lighted visor vanity mirrors, pair ($100). Entertainment: AM radio: S ($61). AM/FM radio ($59-$120). AM/FM

stereo radio ($109-$170); w/8 track or cassette player ($199-$260). Premium sound system ($117). AM radio delete ($61 credit). Exterior: Flip-up open air roof ($310). Full or half vinyl roof ($152). Metallic glow paint ($63). Two-tone paint ($117-$156). Accent paint stripes: S ($39). Pivoting front vent windows ($63). Rocker panel moldings ($33). Bumper guards, rear ($28). Bumper rub strips ($50). Lower bodyside protection ($41). Interior: Console ($191). Cloth/vinyl seat trim ($35). Bench seat (NC). Front floor mats ($15-$24). Wheels/Tires: Wire wheel covers ($87-$152). Turbine wheel covers: S ($66). Styled steel wheels ($60-$126). Steel wheels, 5.5 in.: fleet LPO ($18-$74). P175/75R14 SBR WSW ($72). P185/75R14 BSW: fleet ($44). P185/75R14 WSW ($116). P190/65R390 Michelin BSW TRX ($535-$601).

LTD CONVENIENCE/APPEARANCE OPTIONS: Option Packages: Squire option ($282). Brougham decor option: wagon ($363). Power lock group ($170-$210). Cold weather group ($77). Appearance protection group ($60). Light group ($38). Comfort/Convenience: Air cond. ($724); auto-temp ($802). Rear defroster, electric ($135). Fingertip speed control ($170). Illuminated entry ($76). Autolamp on-off delay ($73). Power windows ($255). Six-way power driver's seat ($207): dual ($415). Tinted glass ($105). Tinted windshield: fleet ($38). Leather-wrapped steering wheel ($59). Tilt steering ($105). Electronic instrument cluster ($289-$367). Tripminder computer ($215-$293). Digital clock ($78). Diagnostic warning lights ($59). Auto. parking brake release ($12). Interval wipers ($49). Liftgate wiper/washer: wagon ($99). Lighting and Mirrors: Cornering lamps ($60). Map light: fleet ($15). Right remote convex mirror ($60). Lighted visor vanity mirrors ($51-$100). Entertainment: AM/FM radio ($59). AM/FM stereo radio ($109); w/8 track or cassette player ($199). Electronic-tuning AM/FM stereo radio ($252); w/cassette ($396). Premium sound system ($117-$151). AM radio delete ($61 credit). Exterior: Flip-up open air roof ($310). Full vinyl roof ($152). Metallic glow paint ($63). Two-tone paint ($117). Pivoting front vent windows ($63). Two-way liftgate: wag ($105). Protective bodyside moldings, LPO ($49). Bumper guards, rear ($28). Bumper rub strips ($56). Luggage rack: wagon ($126). License frames ($9). Lower bodyside protection ($41). Interior: Console ($100). Vinyl seat trim ($35). Split bench seat (NC). Individual seats w/console ($61). Leather seat trim ($415). Front floor mats ($23). Wheels/Tires: Luxury wheel covers ($55). Wire wheel covers ($159-$198). Styled wheels ($178). Cast aluminum wheels ($402). P185/75R14 BSW ($38); WSW ($72). P195/75R14 WSW ($72-$116). Puncture-sealant P195/75R14 WSW ($228). Conventional spare ($63).

CROWN VICTORIA CONVENIENCE/APPEARANCE OPTIONS: Option Packages: Interior luxury group ($830-$911). Convenience group ($95-$116). Power lock group ($123-$220). Light group ($48). Protection group ($68). Comfort/Convenience: Air cond. ($724); w/auto-temp control ($802). Rear defroster, electric ($135). Fingertip speed control ($170). Illuminated entry system ($76). Power windows ($180-$255). Power driver's seat ($210); driver and passenger ($420). Remote fuel door lock ($24). Tinted glass ($105); windshield only, fleet ($38). Autolamp on/off delay ($73). Leather-wrapped steering wheel ($59). Tilt steering wheel ($105). Auto. parking brake release ($12). Tripminder computer ($215-$261). Quartz clock: S ($35). Digital clock ($61-$96). Interval wipers ($49). Lighting and Mirrors: Cornering lamps ($60). Remote right mirror ($43). Lighted visor vanity mirrors ($100). Entertainment: AM/FM stereo radio: S ($106); w/8 track or cassette tape player ($112-$218). AM/FM stereo search radio ($166-$272); w/8 track or cassette ($310-$416). Power antenna ($60). Premium sound system ($145-$179). AM radio delete: S ($61 credit). AM/FM delete ($152 credit). Exterior: Metallic glow paint ($77). Two-tone paint/tape ($78). Dual accent bodyside paint stripes: S ($39). Pivoting front vent windows ($63). Rocker panel moldings: Ctry Squire ($32). Vinyl-insert bodyside moldings ($55). Bumper rub strips ($52). Luggage rack: Ctry Sq ($110). License frames ($9). Lower bodyside protection ($39-$52). Interior: Dual-facing rear seats: Ctry Sq ($167). Leather seat trim ($418). Split bench seating ($139). All-vinyl seat trim ($34); Duraweave vinyl, wagon ($96). Carpeted floor mats ($33). Trunk trim ($49). Wheels/Tires: Luxury wheel covers ($88). 15 in. wheel covers: S ($49). Wire wheel covers ($159-$198). Cast aluminum wheels ($390). P225/75R14 WSW ($42-$43). P205/75R15 WSW ($17); puncture-resistant ($130). Conventional spare ($63).

THUNDERBIRD CONVENIENCE/APPEARANCE OPTIONS: Option Packages: Interior luxury group: base ($1170). Exterior accent group ($343). Luxury carpet group ($48-$72). Traveler's assistance kit ($65). Light group ($35). Power lock group ($172). Comfort/Convenience Air cond. ($732); auto-temp ($802). Rear defroster ($135). Fingertip speed control ($170). Illuminated entry system ($82). Keyless entry ($163) exc Heritage ($88). Anti-theft system ($159). Remote fuel door lock ($26). Tinted glass ($105); windshield only, LPO ($38). Power windows ($193). Six-way power driver's seat ($222); dual ($444). Auto. parking brake release ($12). Leather-wrapped steering wheel ($59). Tilt steering wheel ($105). Electronic instrument cluster ($321-$382). Electronic voice alert ($67) Diagnostic warning lights ($59). Digital clock ($61). Interval wipers ($49). Lighting and Mirrors: Cornering lamps ($68). Dual electric remote mirrors ($94). Electronic dimming day/night mirror ($77). Lighted visor vanity mirrors, pair ($106). Entertainment: AM/FM stereo radio: base ($109); w/8-track or cassette player ($199) exc. Turbo Cpe ($90). Electronic-tuning AM/FM stereo search radio ($144-$252); w/cassette ($396) exc. Turbo Cpe ($288) and Heritage ($144). Power antenna ($66). Premium sound system ($179). AM radio delete ($61 credit). Exterior: Flip-up open-air roof ($310). Clearcoat paint ($152). Two tone paint/tape ($148-$218). Charcoal lower accent treatment: Turbo Cpe ($78). Hood paint stripe ($16). Dual accent bodyside/decklid paint stripes ($55). Hood/deck-lid/bodyside paint stripes ($71). Pivoting front vent windows ($76). Wide bodyside moldings: base ($57). Bright rocker panel moldings ($39). Bumper rub strip extensions ($52). License frames ($9). Lower bodyside protection ($39-$54). Interior: Articulated seats ($183-$427). Leather seat trim ($415-$659). Vinyl seat trim ($37). Front floor mats, carpeted ($22). Wheels/Tires: Wire wheel covers ($45-$159); locking ($84-$198) exc. Heritage ($20). Luxury wheel covers ($113). Styled wheels ($65-$178). Puncture sealing tires ($124). P205/70R14 performance WSW ($62). P205/70HR14 performance BSW ($152). TRX performance BSW ($471-$649) exc. Turbo Cpe ($154). Conventional spare ($63).

HISTORY: Introduced: October 14, 1982, except Thunderbird, February 17, 1983, and Thunderbird Turbo Coupe, April 1, 1983. Model year production: 928,146 (incl. Mustangs). Total production for the U.S. market of 914,666 units (incl. Mustangs and 55,314 early '84 Tempos) included 423,532 four-cylinder, 313,353 sixes and 177,781 V-8s. That total included 12,276 turbo fours. Calendar year production (U.S.): 1,008,799 (incl. Mustangs). Calendar year sales by U.S. dealers: 1,060,314 (incl. Mustangs). Model year sales by U.S. dealers: 996,694 (incl. Mustangs and 70,986 early '84 Tempos).

HISTORY: Once again, Escort was the best-selling car in the country. That helped Ford's model year sales to rise 12 percent over 1982, but the total stood well below the 1981 total of 1.1 million. Next in line for sales honors were the new smaller LTD and full-size LTD Crown Victoria. The new aero-styled T-Bird sold far more copies than its predecessor—more than twice the 1982 total. Ford still ranked No. 2 in the domestic auto industry, but Oldsmobile had become a potent contender for that spot. Ford was judged second in the industry in quality, behind the Lincoln-Mercury division but ahead of rival GM and Chrysler. Low-rate (10.75 percent) financing was extended in December 1982 to include '83 models as well as the leftover 1982s. Continuing demand kept the big rear-drive Ford alive, as did improved fuel supplies. The new Tempo was introduced in May 1983, but as an early '84 model.

1984 FORD

Ford was trying hard to conquer the youth market-especially the affluent young motorist with offerings such as the SVO Mustang, Thunderbird Turbo Coupe, and new turbo EXP. Fairmont was gone after a six-year run, but the brand-new Tempo took its place in the compact market. Horn buttons returned to the steering wheel hub once again on most models. The inline six finally disappeared. The turbocharged 1.6-liter four, available for Escort and EXP, featured a high-lift camshaft and EEC-IV electronic controls. It delivered boost up to 8 PSI, raising horsepower by some 35 percent.

1984 Ford EXP Turbo coupe. (JG)

1984 Ford Escort LX station wagon. (PH)

ESCORT — FOUR — Diesel power was the first big news under Ford subcompact hoods, as the company's first passenger-car diesel engine became available on both Escort and Tempo. Produced by Mazda, the 2.0-liter diesel four came with five-speed manual (overdrive) transaxle. A little later came a different kind of four: a turbocharged, fuel-injected version of Escort's 97.6 cid (1.6-liter) engine, ready for the GT model. Turbos hooked up to a five-speed manual gearbox, in a package that included firmer suspension and special wheels/tires. Three other 1.6-liter engines were available: base carbureted, high-output, and fuel-injected. Model availability was revised. In addition to the carryover L and GL, and the sporty GT, there was a new LX (replacing GLX). LX had the fuel-injected four, TR suspension, blackout body trim, overhead console with digital clock. full instruments (including tach), and five-speed transaxle. Appearance changes were limited to details. Escort GT now sported black polycarbonate bumpers. Inside was a new soft-feel instrument panel with integral side-window demisters, and new steering wheel. Escort's horn button moved to the center of the steering wheel. A new-design rear seat, standard on GL, GT and LX, folded down to form a flatter load floor. Each side could fold independently. LX bodies showed dark moldings with "discreet" bright accents. Power ventilation replaced the 'ram air' system. New Escort options were: overhead console with digital clock; floor console with graphic warning display module and covered storage area; new electronic radios; graphic equalizer; tilt steering; and power door locks. A lighted visor vanity mirror was added to the light group.

EXP — FOUR — Turbocharged power brought EXP a strong performance boost this year. The new turbo model had a unique front air dam and rear decklid spoiler, with easy-to-spot taped 'Turbo' nomenclature on doors and rear bumper. It also had two-tone paint with black lower section, unique C-pillar appliqué, black wheel flares, and black rocker panel moldings. The turbo package also included a tighter suspension with Koni shock absorbers, Michelin P185/65R365 TRX tires on new cast aluminum wheels, and five-speed manual transaxle. Base powertrain was upgraded to the high-output 1.6-liter engine, also mated to five-speed manual. EXP had a completely revised exterior. The silhouette was altered dramatically by adding a 'bubbleback' liftgate. EXP also had new blackout tail lamps, color-keyed bumper rub strips and mirrors, and a revised front air dam. Both the liftgate and tail lamps came from Mercury's LN7, companion to EXP that was discontinued this year. Inside was a standard overhead console with digital clock, new instrument panel with performance cluster and tachometer, and new steering wheel with center horn control. Cloth low-back bucket seats became standard. Styled steel wheels were a new design. New options included a tilt steering wheel, electronic radios with graphic equalizer, clearcoat paint, and illuminated visor vanity mirror. Options deleted were: shearling and leather seat trims, AM/FM stereo with 8 track, and AM/FM monaural radio. Both EXP and Escort had a new clutch/starter interlock system. New competitors for EXP included Honda's CRX and Pontiac Fiero.

1984 Ford Tempo L sedan (with diesel engine). (PH)

1984 Ford LTD Brougham sedan. (PH)

TEMPO — FOUR — Ford's second front-drive model, replacement for the departed rear-drive Fairmont, arrived as an early '84 model, wearing what Ford called 'rakish contemporary styling.' General Manager Louis E. Lataif said 'it continues the modern aerodynamic design theme established with the '83 Thunderbird, but with its own particular flair.' Less enthusiastic observers sometimes referred to Tempo's aero shape as a 'jellybean' design. Aircraft-type door configurations were indeed shared with the '83 Thunderbird. Door tops extended up into the roof to create a wraparound effect. That also eliminated the need for an exterior drip molding, and allowed easier entry/exit. Tempo's body-color plastic grille consisted of three horizontal slots, one above the other, with a Ford oval at the center of the middle one. Alongside the grille were single quad recessed halogen headlamps. Tapered amber wraparound signal/marker lenses started at the outer end of each headlamp housing. Horizontal tail lamps at ends of rear panels tapered down in a curve on the quarter panels. A bodyside 'character line' ran just below the beltline, sweeping upward a pit at the back. The nose was sloped; the rear end stubby. Two-and four-door sedans were offered, on a 99.9 inch wheelbase, the latter with six-window design and rounded window corners. Tempo came in L, GL and GLX trim. This was essentially a stretched version of Escort's chassis, but with a different suspension. A new 140 cid (2.3-liter) HSC (high swirl combustion) four-cylinder engine was developed specially for Tempo. Displacement was identical to the familiar 2.3-liter four used in Fairmont/LTD, but bore/stroke dimensions differed in this OHV design, which actually evolved from the old inline six. This was the first production fast-burn engine, controlled by an EEC-IV onboard computer as used in the Thunderbird Turbo Coupe. The engine had 9.0:1 compression and was announced as producing 90 horsepower (though later sources give a lower rating), For this year only, a carburetor was used. Tempo could have either a close-ratio five-speed manual or automatic transaxle, or a Fuel Saver four-speed (which was standard). In addition to rack-and-pinion steering, Tempo had fully independent quadra-link rear suspension using MacPherson struts; also a MacPherson strut front suspension and stabilizer bar. Power front disc brakes were standard. Inside, Tempo had low-back bucket seats with cloth trim; color-keyed molded door trim panels with integral storage bins; a storage bin above the radio (on the instrument panel); color-keyed vinyl sunvisors with elastic band on driver's side; a carpeted package tray; and a consolette. An optional TR handling package included Michelin P185/65R365 TRX tires on new-design cast aluminum wheels, and a special handling suspension. Other notable options included a factory-installed anti-theft system, remote-release fuel filler door, illuminated entry, light-duty trailer towing package, and electronic AM/FM stereo search sound systems. Several changes were made for the full 1984 model year. Most noteworthy was the addition of a 2.0-liter diesel option with five-speed manual overdrive. The horn button was relocated to the steering wheel; fuel tank enlarged; and two options were added (tachometer and sport performance seat). Mercury's Topaz was nearly identical except for trim and the list of options available.

1984 Ford LTD sedan. (JG)

1984 Ford LTD Crown Victoria sedan. (JG)

LTD — FOUR/V-6/V-8 — Though basically unchanged after its 1983 debut, LTD received a few fresh touches that included argent accents on bodyside moldings and (optional) bumper rub strips, and a revised instrument panel woodtone appliqué, A new A-frame steering wheel with center horn button replaced the former four-spoke design. Headlamp doors now had dark argent paint, instead of light argent. Parking and turn lamp lenses switched from clear white to amber, and bulbs from amber to clear. The most noteworthy new body feature was the unique formal roof treatment added to the Brougham four-door sedan. It had a distinctive solid rear pillar and 'frenched' back window treatment, and included a full Cambria cloth roof. The inline six-cylinder engine finally disappeared. Manual transmission with the base 140 cid (2.3-liter) four was dropped. A 302 cid (5.0-liter) EFL high-output V-8 was available only on police sedans. That made a 232 cid (3.8-liter) V-6, now fuel-injected, the only regular option (standard on wagons). All engines added EECIV controls. Propane power was available again, but found few takers. Base and Brougham sedans were offered again, along with a station wagon. Base models could get some of Brougham's expanded standard trim as part of the Interior Luxury Group. Power steering and three-speed automatic were made standard, with four-speed automatic available in V-6 models. New LTD options included a flight bench seat (said to be the single most requested feature).

LTD CROWN VICTORIA — V-8 — Crown Vic's new grille featured a light argent second surface, and a new optional Brougham roof for the four-door had a formal look. It included a padded full vinyl top, a more upright rear window with 'frenched' treatment, and electro-luminiscent coach lamps on the center pillar. Interiors had a new vinyl grain pattern, Otherwise, the full-size Ford was a carryover, available again as a two- or four-door sedan, and pair of wagons. The Crown Victoria station wagon was just a Country Squire without simulated wood trim. The wide grille had a 12 x 4 hole crosshatch pattern (plus a 2 x 2 pattern within each segment). Wide amber parking lamps went below the quad headlamps. Amber signal/marker lenses consisted of a large lens above a small one. 'LTD Crown Victoria' lettering went ahead of the front door, just above the crease line. Sole standard engine was the 302 cid (5.0-liter) fuel-injected V-8. The high-performance 351 cid (5.8-liter) V-8 with variable-venturi carburetor was available only with police package.

THUNDERBIRD — FOUR/V-6/V-8 — Visible changes were few on Ford's personal luxury coupe, but the model lineup was revised. The Heritage series was renamed elan (Ford didn't capitalize the name). And a new Fila model was developed in conjunction with Fila Sports, Inc., an Italian manufacturer of apparel for active leisure sports (mainly tennis and skiing). Fila had exclusive light oxford gray over charcoal paint, with unique red and blue tape stripes emulating the graphics of the company's logo. Bright trim was minimal, with body-color grille and wheels, and charcoal windshield and backlight moldings. Inside, Fila had charcoal components. Articulated seats were trimmed in oxford white leather, with perforated leather inserts; or oxford gray luxury cloth with perforated cloth inserts. Turbo Coupe added charcoal greenhouse moldings and a new viscous clutch fan, as well as a starter/clutch interlock system and oil-temperature warning switch. All Thunderbirds now had standard bumper rub strip extensions, and a modified appearance of the birds on tail lamps. Electronic fuel injection went on the base 232 cid (3.8-liter) V-6. Counterbalanced springs replaced the hood's prior prop rod. Steering wheels (except Turbo Coupe's) were now A frame design, with horn button in the center. Sole engine option was the 302 cid (5.0-liter) fuel-injected V-8. Turbo Coupe retained the 140 cid (2.3-liter) turbocharged four, but now came with automatic transmission as well as the five-speed manual gearbox. Each model had a slightly curved 8 x 6 hole crosshatch grille pattern with wide Thunderbird insignia in the tall header bar, Staggered, recessed quad headlamps flanked the grille, Amber (formerly clear) parking lamps were set into the bumper. Small amber wraparound marker lenses were used. 'Thunderbird' insignias went on back pillars. Mercury Cougar was mechanically identical, but a bit different in styling.

I.D. DATA: Ford's 17-symbol Vehicle Identification Number (VIN) again was stamped on a metal tab fastened to the instrument panel, visible through the windshield. The first three symbols ('1FA') indicate manufacturer, make and vehicle type. The fourth symbol ('B') denotes restraint system. Next comes a letter 'P', followed by two digits that indicate body type: Model Number, as shown in left column of tables below. (Example: '04' Escort L two-door hatchback). Symbol eight indicates engine type: '2' L4-98 2Bbl.; '4' H.O. L4-98 2Bbl.; '5' L4-98 EFI; '8' Turbo L4-98 FI; 'H' Diesel L4-121; 'A' L4-140 1Bbl.; 'R' or 'J' HSC L4-140 1Bbl.; '6' Propane L4-140; 'W' Turbo L4-140 EFI; '3' V6-232 2Bbl.; 'F' V8-302 2Bbl.; 'G' V8-351 2Bbl. Next is a check digit. Symbol ten indicates model year ('E' 1984). Symbol eleven is assembly plant: 'A' Atlanta, GA; 'B' Oakville, Ontario (Canada); 'G' Chicago; 'H' Lorain, Ohio; 'K' Kansas City, MO; 'X' St. Thomas, Ontario; 'Z' St. Louis, MO; 'T' Edison, NJ; 'W' Wayne, Mi. The final six digits make up the sequence number, starting with 100001. A Vehicle Certification Label on the left front door lock face panel or door pillar shows the manufacturer, month and year of manufacture, GVW, GAWR, certification statement, VIN, and code for such items as body type and color, trim, axle ratio, transmission, and special order data.

ESCORT (FOUR)

Model No.	Body/ Style No.	Body Type & Seating	Factory Price	Shipping Weight	Prod. Total
04	61D	2-dr. Hatch-4P	5629	1981	Note 1
13	58D	4-dr. Hatch-4P	5835	2024	Note 1
04	61D	2-dr. L Hatch-4P	5885	1981	Note 1
13	58D	4-dr. L Hatch-4P	6099	2034	Note 1
09	74D	4-dr. L Sta Wag-4P	6313	2066	Note 1
05	61D	2-dr. GL Hatch-4P	6382	2033	Note 1
14	58D	4-dr. GL Hatch-4P	6596	2086	Note 1
10	74D	4-dr. GL Sta Wag-4P	6773	2115	Note 1
15	58D	4-dr. LX Hatch-4P	7848	2137	Note 1
11	74D	4-dr. LX Sta Wag-4P	7939	2073	Note 1

ESCORT GT (FOUR)

07	61D	2-dr. Hatch-4P	7593	2103	Note 1
07	61D	2 dr. Turbo Hatch-4P	N/A	2239	Note 1

1984 Ford Tempo GLX sedan. (JG)

NOTE 1: Total Escort production came to 184,323 two-door hatchbacks, 99,444 four-door hatchback sedans, and 88,756 station wagons. Breakdown by trim level not available. Bodies are sometimes referred to as three-door and five-door.

DIESEL ENGINE NOTE: Diesel-powered Escorts came in L and GL trim, priced $558 higher than equivalent gasoline models.

EXP (FOUR)

01/A80	67D	3-dr. Hatch Cpe-2P	6653	2117	23,016
01/A81	67D	3-dr. Luxury Cpe-2P	7539	2117	Note 2
01/A82	67D	3-dr. Turbo Cpe-2P	9942	2158	Note 2

NOTE 2: Production of luxury and turbo coupe models is included in basic EXP total above.

TEMPO (FOUR)

18	66D	2-dr. L Sedan-5P	6936	2249	Note 3
21	54D	4-dr. L Sedan-5P	6936	2308	Note 3
19	66D	2-dr. GL Sed-5P	7159	2276	Note 3
22	54D	4-dr. GL Sed-5P	7159	2339	Note 3
20	66D	2-dr. GLX Sed-5P	7621	2302	Note 3
23	54D	4-dr. GLX Sed-5P	7621	2362	Note 3

NOTE 3: Total Tempo production came to 107,065 two-doors and 295,149 four-doors.

DIESEL ENGINE NOTE: Diesel-powered Tempos cost $558 more than equivalent gasoline models.

LTD (FOUR/V-6)

39	54D	4-dr. Sedan-5P	8605/9014	2804/2881	154,173
39/60H	54D	4-dr. Brghm-5P	9980/10389	2812/2889	Note 4
40	74D	4-dr. Sta Wag-5P	----/9102	----/2990	59,569

NOTE 4: Brougham production is included in basic sedan total.

LTD CROWN VICTORIA (V-8)

42	66K	2-dr. Sedan-6P	10954	3546	12,522
43	54K	4-dr. Sedan-6P	10954	3587	130,164

Model No.	Body/ Style No.	Body Type & Seating	Factory Price	Shipping Weight	Prod. Total
44	74K	4-dr. Ctry Sqr-6P	11111	3793	30,803
43/41	54K	4-dr. 'S' Sed-6P	9826	N/A	Note 5
44/41K	74K	4-dr. 'S' Wag-6P	10136	N/A	Note 5
44/41E	74K	4-dr. Sta Wag-6P	10861	N/A	Note 5

NOTE 5: Production of 'S' models and basic station wagon is included in basic sedan and Country Squire totals above.

THUNDERBIRD (V-6/V-8)

46	66D	2-dr. HT Cpe-4P	9633/10253	2890/3097	170,533
46/607	66D	2-dr. Elan Cpe-4P	12661/13281	2956/3163	Note 6
46/606	66D	2-dr. Fila Cpe-4P	14471/14854	3061/3268	Note 6

1984 Ford LTD Country Squire station wagon. (JG)

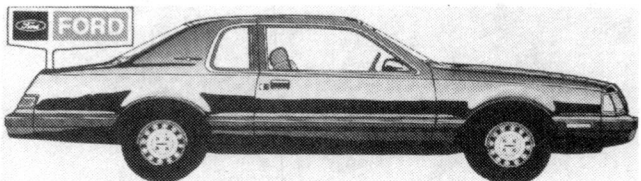

1984 Ford Thunderbird hardtop coupe. (JG)

1984 Ford Thunderbird Turbo Coupe. (PH)

THUNDERBIRD TURBO COUPE (FOUR)

46/934 66D 2-dr. HT Cpe-4P 12330 2938 Note 6

NOTE 6: Turbo Coupe and Elan/Fila production is included in basic Thunderbird total.

MODEL NUMBER NOTE: Some sources include a prefix 'P' ahead of the two-digit model number

FACTORY PRICE AND WEIGHT NOTE: LTD prices and weights to left of slash are for four-cylinder, to right for V-6 engine. Thunderbird prices and weights to left of slash are for V-6, to right for V-8 engine.

ENGINE [Base Four (Escort)]: Inline. Overhead cam. Four-cylinder. Cast-iron block and aluminum head. Displacement: 97.6 cid (1.6 liters). Bore & stroke: 3.15 x 3.13 in. Compression ratio: 9.0:1. Brake horsepower: 70 at 4600 rpm. Torque: 88 lbs.-ft. at 2600 rpm. Five main bearings. Hydraulic valve lifters. Carburetor: 2Bbl. Motorcraft 740. VIN Code: 2.

ENGINE [Base Four (EXP); Optional (Escort)]: High-output version of 1.6-liter four above Horsepower: 80 at 5400 rpm. Torque: 88 lbs.-ft. at 3000 rpm. VIN Code: 4.

ENGINE [Base Four (Escort LX, GT); Optional (Escort, EXP)]: Fuel-injected version of 1.6-liter four above Horsepower: 84 at 5200 rpm. Torque: 90 lbs.-ft. at 2800 rpm. VIN Code: 5.

ENGINE [Turbo Four (Escort, EXP)]: Same as 1.6-liter four above, with fuel injection and turbocharger Compression ratio: 8.0:1. Horsepower: 120 at 200 rpm. Torque: 120 lbs.-ft. at 3400 rpm. VIN Code: 8.

ENGINE [Diesel Four (Escort, Tempo)]: Inline. Overhead cam. Four-cylinder. Cast-iron block and aluminum head. Displacement: 121 cid (2.0 liters). Bore & stroke: 3.39 x 3.39 in. Compression ratio: 22.5:1. Brake horsepower: 52 at 4000 rpm. Torque: 82 lbs.-ft. at 2400 rpm. Five main bearings. Solid valve lifters. Fuel injection. VIN Code: H.

ENGINE [Base Four (Tempo)]: Inline. Overhead valve. Four-cylinder. Cast-iron block and head. Displacement: 140 cid (2.3 liters). Bore & stroke: 3.70 x 3.30 in. Compression ratio: 9.0:1. Brake horsepower: 84 at 4400 rpm. Torque: 118 lbs.-ft. at 2600 rpm. Five main bearings. Hydraulic valve lifters. Carburetor: 1Bbl. Holley 6149. High Swirl Combustion (HSC) design. VIN Code: R (U.S.) or J (Mexico).

ENGINE [Base Four (LTD)]: Inline. Overhead cam. Four-cylinder. Cast-iron block and head. Displacement: 140 cid (2.3 liters). Bore & stroke: 3.78 x 3.13 in. Compression ratio: 9.0:1. Brake horsepower: 88 at 4000 rpm. Torque: 122 lbs.-ft. at 2400 rpm. Five main bearings. Hydraulic valve lifters. Carburetor: 1Bbl. Carter YFA. VIN Code: A.

ENGINE [Propane Four (LTD)]: Same as 140 cid four above, but for propane fuel Compression ratio: 10.0:1. Brake horsepower: 88 at 4000 rpm. Torque: 122 lbs.-ft. at 2400 rpm. VIN Code: 6.

ENGINE [Turbocharged Four (Thunderbird Turbo Coupe)]: Same as 140 cid four above, with fuel injection and turbocharger Compression ratio: 8.0:1. Horsepower: 145 at 4600 rpm. Torque: 180 lbs.-ft. at 3600 rpm. VIN Code: W.

ENGINE [Base V-6 (Thunderbird); Optional (LTD)]: 90-degree, overhead valve V-6. Cast-iron block and aluminum head. Displacement: 232 cid (3.8 liters). Bore & stroke: 3.80 x 3.40 in. Compression ratio: 8.7:1. Brake horsepower: 120 at 3600 rpm. Torque: 205 lbs.-ft. at 1600 rpm. Four main bearings. Hydraulic valve lifters. Throttle-body fuel injection. VIN Code: 3.

ENGINE [Base V-8 (Crown Victoria); Optional (Thunderbird)]: 90-degree, overhead valve V-8. Cast-iron block and head. Displacement: 302 cid (5.0 liters). Bore & stroke: 4.00 x 3.00 in. Compression ratio: 8.4:1. Brake horsepower: 140 at 3200 rpm. Torque: 250 lbs.-ft. at 1600 rpm. Five main bearings. Hydraulic valve lifters. Electronic fuel injection (TBI). VIN Code: F.

NOTE: Crown Victoria wagons had a high-output 302 cid V-8 rated 155 horsepower at 3600 rpm. 265 lbs.-ft. at 2000 rpm.

1984 Ford Escort GL five-door hatchback. (JG)

1984 Ford Tempo GLX coupe. (JG)

ENGINE [High-Output Police V-8 (Crown Victoria)]: 90-degree, overhead valve V-8. Cast-iron block and head. Displacement: 351 cid (5.8 liters). Bore & stroke: 4.00 x 3.50 in. Compression ratio: 8.3:1. Brake horsepower: 180 at 3600 rpm. Torque: 285 lbs.-ft. at 2400 rpm. Five main bearings. Hydraulic valve lifters. Carburetor: 2Bbl. VV. VIN Code: G.

CHASSIS DATA: Wheelbase: (Escort/EXP) 94.2 in.; (Tempo) 99.9 in.; (LTD) 105.6 in.; (Crown Vic) 114.3 in.; (TBird) 104.0 in. Overall Length: (Escort) 163.9 in.; (Escort wagon) 165.0 in.; (EXP) 170.3 in.; (Tempo) 176.2 in.; (LTD) 196.5 in.; (Crown Vic) 21 1.1 in.; (Crown Vic wag) 215.0 in.: (TBird) 197.6 in. Height: (Escort) 53.3-53.4 in.; (EXP) 50.5 in.; (Tempo 2dr.) 52.7 in.; (Tempo 4dr.) 52.7 in.; (LTD) 53.6 in.; (LTD wag) 54.3 in.; (Crown Vic) 55.3 in.; (Crown Vic wag) 56.8 in.; (TBird) 53.2 in. Width: (Escort/EXP) 65.9 in.; (Tempo) 66.2 in.; (LTD) 71.0 in.; (Crown Vic) 77.5 in.; (Crown Vic wag) 79.3 in.; (TBird) 71.1 in. Front Tread: (Escort/EXP) 54.7 in.; (Tempo) 54.7 in.; (LTD) 56.6 in.; (Crown Vic) 62.2 in. (TBird) 58.1 in. Rear Tread: (Escort/EXP) 56.0 in.; (Tempo) 57.6 in.; (LTD) 57.0 in.; (Crown Vic) 62.0 in. (TBird) 58.5 in. Standard Tires: (Escort/EXP) P165/80R13 SBR BSW; (Escort GT) P165/70R15 Michelin TRX; (Escort Turbo GT) P185/65R15 Michelin TRX; (Tempo) P175/80R13 SBR BSW; (LTD) P185/75R14; (Crown Vic) P215/75R14 SBR WSW; (TBird) P195/75R14 SBR WSW; (TBird Turbo Cpe) P205/70HR14 BSW.

TECHNICAL: Transmission: Four-speed manual standard on Tempo: (1st) 3.23:1; (2nd) 1.92:1; (3rd) 1.23:1; (4th) 0.81:1; (Rev) 3.46:1. Escort four-speed manual transaxle: (1st) 3.23:1; (2nd) 1.90:1; (3rd) 1.23:1; (4th) 0.81:1; (Rev) 3.46:1. Alternate Escort four-speed manual: (1st) 3.58:1; (2nd) 2.05:1; (3rd) 1.23:1 or 1.36:1; (4th) 0.81:1 or 0.95:1; (Rev) 3.46:1. Five-speed manual on Escort/EXP/Tempo: (1st) 3.60:1; (2nd) 2.12:1; (3rd) 1.39:1; (4th) 1.02:1; (5th) 1.02:1; (Rev) 3.62:1. (Note: separate final drive for 5th gear.) Tempo diesel five-speed manual: (1st) 3.93:1; (2nd) 2.12:1; (3rd) 1.39:1; (4th) 1.02:1; (5th) 0.98:1; (Rev) 3.62:1. TBird Turbo Coupe five-speed: (1st) 4.03:1; (2nd) 2.37:1; (3rd) 1.50:1; (4th) 1.00:1; (5th) 0.86:1; (Rev) 3.76:1. Three-speed automatic standard on LTD: (1st) 2.46:1 or 2.47:1; (2nd) 1.46:1 or 1.47:1; (3rd) 1.00:1; (Rev) 2.11:1 or 2.19:1. Escort/EXP/Tempo three-speed automatic: (1st) 2.79:1; (2nd) 1.61:1; (3rd) 1.00:1; (Rev) 1.97:1. Four-speed overdrive automatic standard on LTD propane four, Crown Victoria and Thunderbird: (1st) 2.40:1; (2nd) 1.47:1; (3rd) 1.00:1; (4th) 0.67:1; (Rev) 2.00:1. Standard final drive ratio: (Escort/EXP) 3.59:1 w/4spd, 3.73:1 w/5spd, 3.31:1 w/auto., 3.52:1 w/diesel; (Tempo) 3.04:1 w/4spd, 3.33:1 w/5spd, 3.23:1 w/auto., 3.73:1 w/diesel; (LTD four) 3.27:1; (LTD V-6) 2.73:1 or 3.27:1; (LTD propane four) 3.08:1; (Crown Vic) 3.08:1; (TBird) 3.45:1 w/5spd, 2.73:1 w/3spd automatic and V-6, 3.27:1 w/4spd auto. and V-6, 3.08:1 w/4spd auto. and V-8, 3.73:1 w/turbo and auto. Drive Axle: (Escort/EXP/Tempo) front; (others) rear. Steering: (Crown Vic) recirculating ball; (others) rack and pinion. Front Suspension: (Escort/EXP) MacPherson struts with lower control arms, coil springs and stabilizer bar; (Tempo) MacPherson struts with stabilizer bar; (LTD/TBird) modified MacPherson struts with lower control arms, coil springs and anti-sway bar; (Crown Vic) long/short control arms w/coil springs and stabilizer bar. LTD and TBird had gas-filled struts. Rear Suspension: (Escort/EXP) independent trailing arms w/modified MacPherson struts and coil springs on lower control arms; (Tempo) fully independent quadra-link with MacPherson struts; (LTD/Crown Vic) rigid axle w/four-link coil springs; (Thunderbird) four-link rigid axle with coil springs and electronic level control; (TBird Turbo Coupe) 'quadra-shock' four-bar-link assembly with two hydraulic, horizontal axle dampers. Gas-filled shocks on LTD and TBird. Brakes: Front disc, rear drum: power assisted (except Escort). Ignition: Electronic. Body construction: (Crown Vic) separate body and frame; (others) unibody. Fuel tank: (Escort/EXP) 13.0 gal.; (Tempo) 14.0 gal.; (LTD) 16.0 gal.; (Crown Vic) 20.0 gal.; (TBird) 21 gal.

DRIVETRAIN OPTIONS: Engines: Fuel-saver 1.6-liter four: Escort (NC). Propane 140 cid four: LTD ($896). 232 cid V-6: LTD ($409). 302 cid V-8: Thunderbird ($383). Transmission/Differential: Five-speed manual trans.: Escort/Tempo ($76). Automatic transaxle: Escort ($439) exc, LX/GT and EXP ($363); Tempo ($439). Auto. transmission.: TBird Turbo Cpe ($315). Overdrive auto. trans.: LTD/TBird ($237). Traction-Lok differential: LTD/Crown Vic/TBird ($95). Brakes & Steering: Power brakes: Escort ($95). Power steering: Escort/EXP ($215); Tempo ($223). Suspension: H.D. susp.: Tempo (NC); Crown

Vic/TBird ($26). Handling susp.: Escort L ($199); Escort GL ($95). Soft ride susp. pkg.: Tempo (NC). Other: H.D. battery ($27). H.D. alternator: EXP ($27); LTD ($52). Extended-range gas tank: LTD ($46). Engine block heater ($18). Trailer towing pkg.: LTD ($398); Crown Vic ($200-$251); TBird ($251). California emission system: Escort/EXP ($46); others ($99). High-attitude emissions (NC).

ESCORT CONVENIENCE/APPEARANCE OPTIONS: Option Packages: Squire wagon pkg. ($373). Instrument group ($87). Power door lock group ($124-$176). Light group ($67). Comfort/Convenience: Air conditioner ($643). Rear defroster, electric ($130). Fingertip speed control ($176). Tinted glass ($95); windshield only ($48). Tilt steering ($104). Overhead console w/digital clock ($82). Interval wipers ($50). Rear wiper/washer ($120) exc. LX ($46). Dual remote sport mirrors ($68). Entertainment: AM radio: L ($39). AM/FM radio ($82) exc. L ($121). AM/FM stereo radio ($109) exc. L ($148); w/cassette player ($204) exc. L ($243). Electronic-tuning AM/FM stereo ($252-$291); w/cassette ($396-$435). Graphic equalizer ($176). Premium sound ($117). Exterior: Flip-up open-air roof ($315). Clearcoat metallic paint (NC). Glamour paint ($51). Dual bodyside paint stripes ($39). Front vent windows, pivoting ($63). Vinyl-insert bodyside moldings ($45). Bumper guards, front or rear ($28). Bumper rub strips ($48). Luggage rack ($100). Lower bodyside protection ($68). Interior: Console ($111). Vinyl seat trim ($24). Color-keyed front mats ($22). Wheels/Tires: Wheel trim rings ($54). Cast aluminum wheels ($279). TR aluminum wheels ($201). Styled steel wheels ($104 credit). P165/80R13 SBR WSW ($59). P175/80R13 SBR BSW (NC).

EXP CONVENIENCE/APPEARANCE OPTIONS: Comfort/Convenience: Air conditioner ($643). Fingertip speed control ($176). Tinted glass ($95). Tilt steering ($104). Lighted visor vanity mirror ($50). Entertainment: AM/FM stereo radio ($109); w/cassette player ($204) exc. luxury cpe ($95). Electronic-tuning AM/FM stereo ($252) exc. luxury cpe ($144) and Turbo ($49); w/cassette ($396) exc. luxury ($288) and Turbo ($193). Graphic equalizer ($176). Premium sound ($117). AM radio delete ($39 credit). AM/FM stereo delete: luxury cpe ($148 credit). AM/FM stereo/cassette delete: Turbo ($243 credit). Exterior: Flip-up open air roof ($315). Clearcoat paint ($161). Lower two-tone paint/tape ($146). Sport tape stripe ($41). Stripe delete (NC). Medium bodyside moldings ($45). Lower bodyside protection ($68). Interior: Low-back knit vinyl bucket seats (NC). Sport performance seats ($173). Front floor mats ($22). Wheels: TR aluminum wheels ($369). TR styled steel wheels ($168). Cast aluminum wheels ($238). P165/80R13 RWL ($90). P165/70R365 TRX (NC).

TEMPO CONVENIENCE/APPEARANCE OPTIONS: Option Packages: TR performance pkg. w/aluminum wheels ($366-$424). Sport appearance group: GL 2dr. ($299). Power lock group ($202-$254). Appearance protection group ($71). Light/convenience group ($50-$85). Comfort/Convenience: Air cond. ($743). Rear defroster, electric ($140). Fingertip speed control ($176). Illuminated entry ($82). Anti-theft system ($159). Power windows ($272). Power decklid release ($41). Six-way power seat ($224). Tinted glass ($110); windshield ($48). Tilt steering ($110). Sport instrument cluster ($71-$87). Digital clock ($61). Interval wipers ($50). Lighting and Mirrors: Left remote mirror ($23); right ($70). Dual sport remote mirrors ($93). Lighted visor vanity mirrors, pair ($100-$112). Entertainment: AM/FM radio ($59). AM/FM stereo radio ($109); w/cassette player ($204). Electronic-tuning AM/FM stereo ($252); w/cassette ($396). Premium sound system ($117). AM radio delete ($39 credit). Exterior: Flip-up open air roof ($315). Metallic glamour glow paint ($63). Black lower body accent paint ($78-$194). Narrow bodyside moldings ($61). Bumper guards, front/rear ($56). Bumper rub strips ($56). Interior: Console ($111). Fold-down front armrest ($55). Vinyl seat trim ($35). Carpeted front floor mats ($13). Trunk trim ($30). Wheels/Tires: Luxury wheel covers ($59). Styled steel wheels ($59) exc. GL/GLX (NC). P175/80R13 WSW ($72).

1984 Ford Thunderbird Elan hardtop coupe. (JG)

1984 Ford Thunderbird FILA hardtop coupe. (JG)

LTD CONVENIENCE/APPEARANCE OPTIONS: Option Packages: Squire option ($282). Brougham decor option: wagon ($363). Interior luxury group ($388). Power lock group ($213-$254). Cold weather group ($77). Light group ($38). Police pkg. ($859-$1387). Taxi pkg. ($860). H.D. fleet pkg. ($210). Comfort/Convenience: Air cond. ($743); auto-temp ($809). Rear defroster, electric ($140). Fingertip speed control ($176). Illuminated entry ($82). Autolamp on-off delay ($73). Power windows ($272). Six-way power driver's seat ($224); dual ($449). Tinted glass ($110). Tinted windshield ($48). Leather-wrapped steering wheel ($59). Tilt steering ($110). Electronic instrument cluster ($289-$367). Tripminder computer ($215-$293). Digital clock ($78). Diagnostic warning lights ($83). Interval wipers ($50). Liftgate wiper/washer: wagon ($99). Lighting and Mirrors: Cornering lamps ($68). Right remote convex mirror ($61). Lighted visor vanity mirrors ($57-$106). Entertainment: AM/FM stereo radio ($109); w/cassette player ($204). Electronic-tuning AM/FM stereo radio w/cassette ($396). Premium sound system ($151). AM radio delete ($39 credit). Exterior: Full vinyl roof ($152). Metallic glow paint ($63). Two-tone paint ($117). Pivoting front vent windows ($79). Two-way liftgate: wag ($105). Protective bodyside moldings ($55). Bumper guards. rear ($28). Bumper rub strips ($56). Luggage rack: wagon ($126). Lower bodyside protection ($41). Interior: Vinyl seat trim ($35). Split or flight bench seat (NC). Individual seats w/console ($61). Leather seat trim ($415). Front floor mats, carpeted ($23). Wheels/Tires: Luxury wheel covers ($55). Wire wheel covers ($165); locking ($204). Styled wheels ($178). Styled steel wheels w/trim rings ($54). P185/75R14 WSW ($72). P195/75R14 BSW ($38); WSW ($116). Puncture-sealant P195/75R14 WSW ($240). Conventional spare ($63).

LTD CROWN VICTORIA CONVENIENCE/APPEARANCE OPTIONS: Option Packages: Interior luxury group ($954-$1034). Convenience group ($109-$134). Power lock group ($140-$238). Light group ($48). Protection group ($68). Police pkg. ($279-$398). Comfort/Convenience: Air cond. ($743); w/auto-temp control ($809). Rear defroster, electric ($140). Fingertip speed control ($176). Illuminated entry system ($82). Power windows ($198-$272). Power driver's seat ($227); driver and passenger ($454). Remote fuel door lock ($35). Tinted glass ($110); windshield only ($48). Autolamp on/off delay ($73). Leather-wrapped steering wheel ($59). Tilt steering wheel ($110). Auto. parking brake release ($12). Tripminder computer ($215-$261). Digital clock ($61). Interval wipers ($50). Lighting and Mirrors: Cornering lamps ($68). Remote right mirror ($46). Lighted visor vanity mirrors ($106). Entertainment: AM/FM stereo radio: S ($106); w/cassette tape player ($112-$204). Electronic-tuning AM/FM stereo radio w/cassette ($166) exc. S ($416). Power antenna ($66). Premium sound system ($151-$179). Radio delete ($148 credit). Exterior: Metallic glow paint ($77). Two-tone paint ($117). Dual accent bodyside paint stripes ($39). Pivoting front vent windows ($79). Rocker panel moldings ($18-$38). Vinyl-insert bodyside moldings ($61). Bumper rub strips ($59). Luggage rack ($110). Lower bodyside protection ($39-$52). Interior: Dual-facing rear seats: Ctry Sq ($167). Leather seat trim ($418). Split bench seating ($139). All-vinyl seat trim ($34); Duraweave vinyl ($96). Carpeted front floor mats ($21). Trunk trim ($49). Wheels/Tires: Wire wheel covers ($165); locking ($204). Cast aluminum wheels ($390). P225/75R14 WSW ($42-$43). P205/75R15 WSW ($17); puncture-sealant ($178). P215/75R14 BSW ($66 credit). Conventional spare ($63).

THUNDERBIRD CONVENIENCE/APPEARANCE OPTIONS: Option Packages: Interior luxury group ($1223). Exterior accent group ($299). Luxury carpet group ($72). Traveler's assistance kit ($65). Light group ($35). Power lock group ($177). Comfort/Convenience: Air cond. ($743); auto-temp ($809). Rear defroster ($140). Fingertip speed control ($176). Illuminated entry system ($82). Keyless entry ($116-$198). Anti-theft system ($159). Remote fuel door lock ($37). Tripminder computer ($215-$276). Autolamp on/off delay ($73). Tinted glass ($110); windshield only ($48). Power windows ($198). Six-way power driver's seat ($227); dual ($454) exc. Fila ($227). Auto. parking brake release ($12). Leather-wrapped steering wheel ($59). Tilt steering wheel ($110). Electronic instrument cluster ($321-$382). Electronic voice alert ($67). Diagnostic warning lights ($89). Low oil warning light ($24). Digital clock: base ($61). Interval wipers ($50). Lighting and Mirrors: Cornering lamps ($68). Electro-luminiscent coach lamps ($84). Dual electric remote mirrors ($86). Electronic-dimming day/night mirror ($77). Lighted visor vanity mirrors, pair ($106). Entertainment: AM/FM stereo radio: base ($109); w/cassette player ($204) exc. Turbo Cpe ($95). Electronic-tuning AM/FM stereo search radio ($144-$252); w/cassette ($396) exc. Turbo Cpe ($288) and Elan ($144). Power antenna ($66). Premium sound system ($179). AM radio delete ($39 credit). Exterior: Flip-up open-air roof ($315). Metallic clearcoat paint ($183). Two-tone paint/tape ($148-$218). Charcoal lower accent treatment ($78). Hood paint stripe ($16). Dual accent bodyside/decklid paint stripes ($55). Hood/decklid/bodyside paint stripes ($71). Pivoting front vent windows ($79). Wide bodyside moldings ($57). Rocker panel moldings ($39). License frames ($9). Lower bodyside protection ($39-$54). Interior: Articulated seats ($183-$427). Leather seat trim ($415). Vinyl seat trim ($37). Front floor mats, carpeted ($22). Wheels/Tires: Wire wheel covers, locking ($26-$204). Luxury wheel covers ($113). Styled wheels ($65-$178). Puncture-sealing tires ($124). P205/70R14 BSW (NC). P205/70R14 WSW ($62). P205/70HR14 performance BSW ($152). Cast aluminum TRX wheels w/BSW performance tires ($471-$649) exc. Turbo Cpe ($154). Conventional spare ($63).

HISTORY: Introduced: September 22, 1983, except Tempo, May 1983. Model year production: 1,496,997 (incl. Mustangs). Total production for the U.S. market of 1,294,491 units (incl. Mustangs) included 711,698 four-cylinder, 323,985 sixes and 258,808 V-8s. That total included 25,581 turbo fours and 24,879 diesel engines. Calendar year production (U.S.): 1,145,028 (incl. Mustangs). Calendar year sales by U.S. dealers: 1,300,644 (incl. Mustangs). Model year sales by U.S. dealers: 1,262,498 (incl. Mustangs).

HISTORY: Sales hit their highest mark since 1979 for the model year. That was a 27 percent jump over 1983. Thunderbird showed the strongest rise. Escort lost its title as top-selling car in the nation to Chevrolet's Cavalier. EXP sales had never been promising, and declined again this year, even after the turbo edition had been offered. Escort/Tempo's 2.0-liter diesel, from Mazda Motor Corp., showed sluggish sales as well. As an indication of the importance placed upon advertising to the youth market, Edsel B. Ford II was named advertising manager in late 1983. Tempo design had begun in 1979 under a 'Topaz' project (the name ultimately given to the Mercury version).

1985 FORD

1985 Ford Escort (1st series) GL five-door hatchback (with diesel engine). (PH)

Thunderbird enjoyed a modest restyle, but nothing too dramatic occurred for the 1985 model year. LTD had added a high-performance, V-8 powered LX touring sedan late in the '84 season, which continued this year. Base models were upgraded, now including as standard various popular items that were formerly optional. Such simplification of the model lineup cut production costs and (presumably) made selection easier for buyers. Manual gearboxes for Escort and Thunderbird were improved. Tempo now had a standard fuel-injected 2.3-liter four and five-speed transaxle, as well as a high-performance engine option.

ESCORT — FOUR — Reverse gear on both the four-and five-speed manual transaxle moved to a new position this year, intended to make shifting easier. On five-speeds, it moved from the upper left to the lower right. (The change began on Thunderbird Turbo Coupe and Mustang SVO for '84.) Mechanical radios had a new flat-face design. Starting in mid-year 1984, clearcoat paints were made available on the Escort L and GL. Otherwise, little was new on Ford's subcompact two-and four-door hatchbacks as the model year began. Later on, though, a restyled 1985.5 Escort appeared, powered by a new 1.9-liter four-cylinder engine. Standard engine for the first series was again

the CVH 97.6 cid (1.6-liter) carbureted four, with four-speed gearbox. A high-output version was available, as well as one with electronic fuel injection and another with a turbocharger. The 2.0-liter diesel was offered again, too. Five-speed manual and three-speed automatic transmissions were available. Escort's three-row grille design had thin vertical bars across each row to form a crosshatch pattern, with Ford oval in the center. Base and L Escorts had a bright grille and blackout front-end treatment, halogen headlamps, heater/defroster, four-speed gearbox, rack-and-pinion steering, short black bumper end caps, bright bumpers, side window demisters, day/night mirror, and cloth/vinyl high-back reclining front bucket seats. Bright moldings went on the windshield surround, backlight, belt, headlamps and drip rail; color-keyed moldings on the A pillar. Escort L had a brushed aluminum B-pillar appliqué. Wagons and diesels had standard power brakes. Escort GL added a front air dam, long black bumper end caps,with argent stripe, remote locking fuel door, dual bodyside paint stripes, AM radio, low-back seats, and additional bright moldings. Escort LX included front/rear bumper guards, power brakes, blackout body treatment, digital clock, foglamps, locking glovebox, TR performance suspension and styled steel wheels, black tri-oval steering wheel, and five-speed manual transaxle. GT models carried wide black bodyside moldings with argent striping, dual black remote racing mirrors, power brakes, TR performance suspension, tape stripes and decals, five-speed transaxle, black wheel spats, remote liftgate release, foglamps, and sport-tuned exhaust. Turbo GT had aluminum TR wheels; non-turbos, steel wheels with bright trim rings. Turbos also had standard power steering.

EXP — FOUR — Like the Escort sedans, the two-seater EXP got a revised location for reverse gear (below fifth gear). Radios and cassette players showed a new flat-face design. Base engine was the fuel-injected 97.6 cid (1.6-liter) four. The Turbo Coupe was available again, wearing aluminum wheels with low-profile performance tires and Koni shock absorbers. This was EXP's final season in its original form. Standard equipment included an AM radio, tinted rear-window glass, halogen headlamps, digital clock, power brakes, tachometer, handling suspension, remote locking fuel door, black bumper rub strips, black left-hand remote sport mirror, and black moldings. Inside were low-back cloth/vinyl reclining bucket seats. EXP's Luxury Coupe added an AM/FM stereo radio, interval wipers, luxury cloth seats with four-way (manual) driver's side adjuster, remote liftgate release, dual remote mirrors, rear defroster, and tinted glass. Turbo Coupe included a front air dam, black rocker panel moldings, AM/FM stereo with cassette, lower tu-tone paint/tape treatment, power steering, TR suspension and aluminum wheels, wheel spats, and rear spoiler.

TEMPO — FOUR — Throttle-body fuel injection was added to Tempo's 2300 HSC (High Swirl Combustion) engine after a year of carburetion. A new high-output version had a new cylinder head and intake manifold, and drove a special 3.73:1 final drive ratio. Five-speed manual overdrive transaxles were now standard in all Tempo series, with revised reverse gear position (now below fifth gear). GLX Tempos now had a sport instrument cluster, front center armrest, power lock group, illuminated entry, light convenience group, tinted glass, AM/FM stereo radio, power steering, and tilt steering wheel. Just before the '85 model year, the fuel tank grew from 14 to 15.2 gallons. There were new see-through reservoirs for brake, power steering and washer fluid levels. This year's instrument panel included side window demisters, plus contemporary flat-face radio design and a storage shelf. New options included graphic equalizer, clearcoat metallic paints, and styled road wheels (standard on GL and GLX). Tempo again came in three series: L, GL and GLX. Base Tempos came with AM radio, cloth/vinyl reclining low-back bucket seats, bodyside accent stripes, dual decklid stripes (two-doors), power brakes, bright bumpers with black end caps, and black left-hand mirror. GL added a blackout back panel treatment, bumper end cap extensions, bumper rub strips, digital clock, map pocket, black bodyside moldings, styled wheels, interval wipers, and dual striping on four-door decklids. A high-performance Sport GL performance option included the high-output (HSO) engine, seven-spoke aluminum wheels with locking lug nuts, P185/70R14 blackwall tires, improved suspension components, graduated bodyside taping, dual remote mirrors. sport performance cloth seats, and gray bumpers with blue inserts.

1985 Ford Tempo GL coupe (with Sports option package). (PH)

1985 Ford LTD LX Brougham sedan. (PH)

LTD — FOUR/V-6/V-8 — Modest restyling gave LTD a new horizontal grille for its third season, plus new sedan tail lamps. Otherwise, only minor trim changes were evident. The new grille had three horizontal bars, with the Ford script oval incorporated into the body. As before, the whole front end was angled, and displayed a large upper grille header bar. The new tail lamps had a larger lighted area, LTD also had new black vinyl-clad bodyside moldings with argent accent stripe, and a new. smoother-looking brushed stainless B-pillar molding. Base models wore new deluxe wheel covers. The base 140 cu in. (2.3-liter) engine added low-friction piston rings, with a boost in compression. Wagons had a standard 232 cid (3.8-liter) V-6. Standard tires grew one size, to 195/75R14 all-season tread. New options included dual electric remote mirrors and black vinyl rocker panel moldings. Optional styled road wheels changed color to light argent. Joining the base and Brougham sedan and LTD wagon later in the model year was a new high-performance LX touring sedan. It carried a high-output version of the fuel-injected 302 cid (5.0-liter) V-8, coupled to four-speed over-drive automatic transmission and a 3.27:1 Traction-Lok rear axle. The performance sedan also had a special handling suspension with rear stabilizer bar, fast 15:1 steering gear, and Goodyear Eagle GT performance tires. LX had its own distinctive look, highlighted by body-color grille, charcoal and red-orange accents, twin chromed exhaust extensions and styled road wheels. Inside LX was a center console with floor shifter, tachometer, and unique front bucket seats with inflatable lumbar support. Both base and Brougham sedans had an AM radio, SelectShift automatic transmission, locking glovebox, power brakes and steering, reclining split-bench seating with cloth upholstery, left-hand remote mirror, dual bodyside and hood accent stripes, and bright moldings. Brougham added a digital clock, light group, seat-back map pockets. lighted visor vanity mirror (passenger), luxury cloth upholstery, automatic parking brake release, and luxury door trim panels with cloth inserts.

LTD CROWN VICTORIA — V-8 — Except for an aluminum front bumper on station wagons and some new body and vinyl roof colors, full-size Fords showed no significant body change. To improve the ride, Crown Vic got new gas-filled shock absorbers, pressurized with nitrogen. An ignition diagnostics monitor was added to the EEC-IV electronic engine controls. The horn control moved from the stalk to the center of the steering wheel. Flash-to-pass was added this year. A single key was now used for door and ignition locks. Lower bodyside panels now had urethane coating for extra corrosion protection. Model lineup for the biggest rear-drives remained the same: two- and four-door sedan (standard or 'S'), along with plain-bodied and Country Squire (woodgrain) wagons. The sole 302 cid (5.0-liter) V-8 engine, with fuel injection, came with four speed automatic overdrive transmission. A new optional automatic load leveling suspension (available later in the model year) used an electronic sensor and air-adjustable rear shocks. With a heavy-duty trailer towing package, Crown Vic and Country Squire could again tow trailers up to 5,000 pounds. Standard equipment included chrome bumpers with guards, left-hand remote-control mirror, dual-note horn, cloth/vinyl reclining flight bench seating, power steering and brakes, and deluxe wheel covers. The budget-priced 'S' models lacked such items as the padded half (rear) vinyl roof, dual accent tape striping, quartz clock, brushed lower decklid appliqué, and various moldings. 'S' models had an AM radio; others an AM/FM stereo.

1985 Ford LTD Crown Victoria two-door sedan. (PH)

THUNDERBIRD — FOUR/V-6/V-8 — A new color-keyed grille and full-width wraparound tail lamps with inboard backup lamps made up the evident changes on Ford's personal luxury coupe. There was also a new Thunderbird emblem, which appeared on taillamp lenses, C-pillars and upper grille header. Inside was a new instrument panel with digital speedometer and analog gauges, door trim panels, and a third rear seatbelt. Standard interiors had a shorter center console, so three people could sit in back. Turbo Coupe's 140 cid (2.3-liter) four-cylinder engine got electronic boost control and higher flow-rate fuel injectors for more power, water-cooled bearings, and a new five-speed gearbox with revised gear ratios. Standard tire size was now 205/70R14 except for Turbo Coupe, which wore performance 225/60VR15 tires on seven inch wheels. Joining the option list were power front seat recliners for comfort and a graphic equalizer to improve audio entertainment. Fully electronic instruments were optional on all Thunderbirds except the Turbo Coupe. Base 'birds had the standard 232 cid (3.8-liter) V-6 with three-speed automatic transmission, power steering and brakes, mini spare tire, knit cloth 60/40 split bench reclining seats, AM/FM stereo radio, quartz clock, and bumper rub strips. Bright moldings went on the drip rail, windshield surround, backlight, and windows. Charcoal bodyside moldings had vinyl inserts. Thunderbird Elan added wide bodyside moldings, power windows, interval wipers, dual electric remote mirrors, diagnostic warning lights. digital clock. tinted glass, AM/FM stereo with cassette, decklid and bodyside accent stripes, and a light group. Fila included the autolamp delay system, speed control, leather-wrapped tilt steering wheel, four-speed overdrive automatic transmission, cast aluminum wheels, electronic-tuning radio with cassette, cornering lamps, power locks, illuminated entry, and articulated sport seats. The driver's seat had six-way power adjustment and power lumbar support. Fila also had a color-keyed grille instead of the usual brightwork, as well as charcoal paint with dark charcoal lower accents and charcoal windshield/back-light moldings.

1985 Ford Thunderbird Turbo Coupe. (PH)

I.D. DATA: Ford's 17-symbol Vehicle Identification Number (VIN) again was stamped on a metal tab fastened to the instrument panel, visible through the windshield. Coding was similar to 1984. Model year code changed to 'F' for 1985. Engine code 'W' for HSC L4-140 FI was added; code '6' for propane four dropped. A Vehicle Certification Label on the left front door lock face panel or door pillar shows the manufacturer. month and year of manufacture, GVW, GAWR, certification statement, VIN, and codes for such items as body type, color, trim, axle, transmission, and special order information.

ESCORT (FOUR)

Model No.	Body/ Style No.	Body Type & Seating	Factory Price	Shipping Weight	Prod. Total
04/41P	61D	2-dr. Hatch-4P	5620	1981	Note 1
13/41P	58D	4-dr. Hatch-4P	5827	2034	Note 1
04	61D	2-dr. L Hatch-4P	5876	1981	Note 1
13	58D	4-dr. L Hatch-4P	6091	2034	Note 1
09	74D	4-dr. L Sta Wag-4P	6305	2066	Note 1
05	61D	2-dr. GL Hatch-4P	6374	2033	Note 1
14	58D	4-dr. GL Hatch-4P	6588	2086	Note 1
10	74D	4-dr. GL Sta Wag-4P	6765	2115	Note 1
15	58D	4-dr. LX Hatch-4P	7840	2137	Note 1
11	74D	4-dr. LX Sta Wag-4P	7931	2073	Note 1

ESCORT GT (FOUR)

07	61D	2-dr. Hatch-4P	7585	2103	Note 1
07/935	61D	2-dr. Turbo Hatch-4P	8680	2239	Note 1

1985.5 ESCORT - Second Series (FOUR)

31	N/A	2-dr. Hatch-4P	5856	2089	Note 1
31	N/A	2-dr. L Hatch-4P	6127	2096	Note 1
36	N/A	4-dr. L Hatch-4P	6341	2154	Note 1
34	N/A	4-dr. L Sta Wag-4P	6622	2173	Note 1
32	N/A	2-dr. GL Hatch-4P	6642	2160	Note 1
37	N/A	4-dr. GL Hatch-4P	6855	2214	Note 1
35	N/A	4-dr. GL Sta Wag-4P	7137	2228	Note 1

NOTE 1: Ford reported production of the second (1985.5) Escort series at 100,554 two-door hatchbacks, 48,676 four-door hatchback

sedans, and 36,998 station wagons, but did not include the initial series. Other sources give total Escort production for the model year of 212,960 two-doors, 111,385 four-doors, and 82,738 wagons. Breakdown by trim level not available. Bodies are sometimes referred to as three-door and five-door.

DIESEL ENGINE NOTE: Diesel-powered Escorts came in L and GL trim. priced $558 higher than equivalent gasoline models.

EXP (FOUR)

01/A80	67D	3-dr. Hatch Cpe-2P	6697	2117	26,462
01/A81	67D	3-dr. Luxury Cpe-2P	7585	2117	Note 2
01/A82	67D	3-dr. Turbo Cpe-2P	9997	N/A	Note 2

NOTE 2: Production of luxury and turbo coupe models is included in basic EXP total above.

TEMPO (FOUR)

18	66D	2-dr. L Sedan-5P	7052	2249	Note 3
21	54D	4-dr. L Sedan-5P	7052	2308	Note 3
19	66D	2-dr. GL Sed-5P	7160	2276	Note 3
22	54D	4-dr. GL Sed-5P	7160	2339	Note 3
20	66D	2-dr. GLX Sed-5P	8253	2302	Note 3
23	54D	4-dr. GLX Sed-5P	8302	2362	Note 3

NOTE 3: Total Tempo production came to 72,311 two-doors and 266,776 four-doors. A turbocharged Tempo GTX, priced at $9870, was announced but apparently not produced.

DIESEL ENGINE NOTE: Diesel-powered Tempos cost $479 more than equivalent gasoline models.

LTD (FOUR/V-6)

39	54D	4-dr. Sedan-5P	8874/9292	2804/2881	162,884
39/60H	54D	4-dr. Brghm-5P	9262/9680	2812/2889	Note 4
40	74D	4-dr. Sta Wag-5P	----/9384	----/2990	42,642

LTD LX BROUGHAM (V-8)

39/938	54D	4-dr. Sedan-5P	11421	N/A	Note 4

NOTE 4: Brougham production is included in basic sedan total.

LTD CROWN VICTORIA (V-8)

42	66K	2-dr. Sedan-6P	11627	3546	13,673
43	54K	4-dr. Sedan-6P	11627	3587	154,612
44	74K	4-dr. Ctry Sqr-6P	11809	3793	30,825
43/41K	54K	4-dr. 'S' Sed-6P	10609	N/A	Note 5
44/41K	74K	4-dr. 'S' Wag-6P	10956	N/A	Note 5
44/41E	74K	4-dr. Sta Wag-6P	11559	N/A	Note 5

NOTE 5: Production of 'S' models and basic station wagon is included in basic sedan and Country Squire totals above.

Police Model Note: Crown Victoria 'S' police models sold for $10,929 with the 302 cid V-8 and $11,049 with 351 cid V-8 engine.

THUNDERBIRD (V-6/V-8)

Model No.	Body/ Style No.	Body Type & Seating	Factory Price	Shipping Weight	Prod. Total
46	66D	2-dr. HT Cpe-5P	10249/10884	2890/3097	151,851
46/607	66D	2-dr. Elan Cpe-5P	1916/12551	2956/3163	Note 6
46/606	66D	2-dr. Fila Cpe-5P	14974/15609	3061/3268	Note 6

THUNDERBIRD TURBO COUPE (FOUR)

46/934	66D	2-dr, HT Cpe-5P	13365	2938	Note 6

NOTE 6: Turbo Coupe and Elan/Fila production is included in basic Thunderbird total.

MODEL NUMBER NOTE: Some sources include a prefix 'P' ahead of the two-digit model number.

FACTORY PRICE AND WEIGHT NOTE: LTD prices and weights to left of slash are for four-cylinder, to right for V-6 engine. Thunderbird prices and weights to left of slash are for V-6, to right for V-8 engine.

ENGINE [Base Four (Escort)]: Inline. Overhead cam. Four-cylinder. Cast-iron block and aluminum head. Displacement: 97.6 cid (1.6 liters). Bore & stroke: 3.15 x 3.13 in. Compression ratio: 9.0:1. Brake horsepower: 70 at 4600 rpm. Torque: 88 lb.-ft, at 2600 rpm. Five main bearings. Hydraulic valve lifters. Carburetor: 2Bbl. Holley 740. VIN Code: 2.

NOTE: Second Series Escorts, introduced at mid-year, carried a new 1.9-liter engine; see 1986 listing for specifications.

ENGINE [Base Four (EXP): Optional (Escort)]: High-output version of 1.6-liter four above Horsepower: 80 at 5400 rpm. Torque: 88 lbs.-ft. at 3000 rpm. VIN Code: 4.

ENGINE [Base Four (Escort LX/GT): Optional (Escort)]: Fuel-injected version of 1.6-liter four above Horsepower 84 at 5200 rpm. Torque: 90 lbs.-ft. at 2800 rpm. VIN Code: 5.

1985 Ford EXP Luxury Coupe. (PH)

ENGINE [Turbo Four (Escort, EXP)]: Same as 1.6-liter four above, with fuel injection and turbocharger Compression ratio: 8.0:1. Horsepower: 120 at 5200 rpm. Torque: 120 lbs.-ft. at 3400 rpm. VIN Code: B.

ENGINE [Diesel Four (Escort, Tempo)]: Inline. Overhead cam. Four-cylinder, Cast-iron block and aluminum head. Displacement: 121 cid (2.0 liters). Bore & stroke: 3.39 x 3.39 in. Compression ratio: 22.5: 1. Brake horsepower: 52 at 4000 rpm. Torque: 82 lbs.-ft. at 2400 rpm. Five main bearings. Solid valve lifters. Fuel injection. VIN Code: H.

ENGINE [Base Four (Tempo)]: Inline. Overhead valve. Four-cylinder. Cast-iron block and head. Displacement: 140 cid (2.3 liters). Bore & stroke: 3.70 x 3.30 in. Compression ratio: 9.0:1. Brake horsepower: 86 at 4000 R. P.M. Torque: 124 lbs.-ft. at 2800 rpm. Five main bearings. Hydraulic valve lifters. Throttle-body fuel injection. High Swirl Combustion (HSC) design. VIN Code: X.

ENGINE [Optional Four (Tempo)]: High-output version of HSC four above Horsepower: 100 at 4600 rpm. Torque: 125 lbs.-ft. at 3200 rpm. VIN Code: S. BASE FOUR (LTD): Inline. Overhead cam. Four-cylinder. Cast-iron block and head. Displacement: 140 cid (2.3 liters). Bore & stroke: 3.78 x 3.13 in. Compression ratio: 9.5:1. Brake horsepower: 88 at 4000 rpm. Torque: 122 lbs.-ft. at 2400 rpm. Five main bearings. Hydraulic valve lifters. Carburetor: 1Bbl. Carter YFA. VIN Code: A.

ENGINE [Propane Four (LTD)]: Same as 140 cid four above, but for propane fuel Compression ratio: 10.0:1. Brake horsepower: 88 at 4000 rpm. Torque: 122 lbs.-ft. at 2400 rpm. VIN Code: 6.

ENGINE [Turbocharged Four (Thunderbird Turbo Coupe)]: Same as 140 cid four above, with fuel injection and turbocharger Compression ratio: 8.0:1. Horsepower: 155 at 4600 rpm. Torque: 190 lbs.-ft. at 2800 rpm. VIN Code: W.

ENGINE [Base V-6 (LTD wagon, Thunderbird); Optional (LTD)]: 90-degree: overhead valve V-6. Cast-iron block and aluminum head. Displacement: 232 cid (3.8 liters). Bore & stroke: 3.80 x 3.40 in. Compression ratio: 8.7:1. Brake horsepower: 120 at 3600 rpm. Torque: 205 lbs.-ft. at 1600 rpm. Four main bearings. Hydraulic valve lifters. Throttle-body fuel injection. VIN Code: 3.

ENGINE [Base V-8 (Crown Victoria); Optional (Thunderbird)]: 90-degree, overhead valve V-8. Cast-iron block and head. Displacement: 302 cid (5.0 liters). Bore & stroke: 4.00 x 3.00 in. Compression ratio: 8.4:1. Brake horsepower: 140 at 3200 rpm. Torque: 250 lbs.-ft. at 1600 rpm. Five main bearings. Hydraulic valve lifters. Electronic fuel injection (TBI). VIN Code: F.

ENGINE [Optional High-Output V-8 (Crown Victoria)]: Same as 302 cid V-8 above, except Horsepower: 155 at 3600 rpm. Torque: 265 lbs.-ft. at 2000 rpm. BASE V-8 (LTD LX): Same as 302 cid V-8, above, except Compression ratio: 8.3:1. Horsepower: 165 at 3800 rpm. Torque: 245 lbs.-ft. at 2000 rpm.

ENGINE [High-Output Police V-8 (Crown Victoria)]: 90-degree, overhead valve V-8. Cast-iron block and head. Displacement: 351 cid (5.8 liters). Bore & stroke: 4.00 x 3.50 in. Compression ratio: 8.3:1. Brake horsepower: 180 at 3600 rpm. Torque: 285 lbs.-ft. at 2400 rpm. Five main bearings. Hydraulic valve lifters. Carburetor: 2Bbl. 7200VV. VIN Code: G.

CHASSIS DATA: Wheelbase: (Escort/EXP) 94.2 in.; (Tempo) 99.9 in.; (LTD) 105.6 in.; (Crown Vic) 114.3 in.; (TBird) 104.0 in. Overall Length: (Escort) 163.9 in.; (Escort wagon) 165.0 in.: (EXP) 170.3 in.: (Tempo) 176.2 in.; (LTD) 196.5 in.; (Crown Vic) 211.0 in.; (Crown Vic wag) 215.0 in.; (TBird) 197.6 in. Height: (Escort) 53.3-53.4 in.; (EXP) 50.5 in.; (Tempo) 52.7 in.; (LTD) 53.8 in.; (LTD wag) 54.4 in.; (Crown Vic) 55.3 in,; (Crown Vic wag) 56.8 in.; (TBird) 53.2 in. Width:

(Escort/EXP) 65.9 in.; (Tempo) 68.3 in.: (LTD) 71.0 in.; (Crown Vic) 77.5 in.; (Crown Vic wag) 79.3 in.; (TBird) 71.1 in. Front Tread: (Escort/EXP/Tempo) 54.7 in.; (LTD) 56.6 in.; (Crown Vic) 62.2 in. (TBird) 58.1 in. Rear Tread: (Escort/EXP) 56.0 in.; (Tempo) 57.6 in.; (LTD) 57.0 in.: (Crown Vic) 62.0 in. (TBird) 58.5 in. Standard Tires: (Escort/EXP) P165/80R13 SBR BSW; (Escort L) P175/80R13; (Escort LX/GT) P165/70R365 Michelin TRX; (Escort/EXP Turbo) P185/65R365 Michelin TRX; (Tempo) P175/80R13 SBR BSW; (LTD) P195/75R14 SBR BSW exc. LX and police, P205/70HR14 Goodyear Eagle BSW; (Crown Vic) P215/75R14 SBR WSW; (TBird) P205/70R14 SBR BSW; (TBird Turbo Cpe) P225/60VR15 performance BSW.

TECHNICAL: Transmission: Escort four-speed manual transaxle: (Ist) 3.23:1; (2nd) 1.92:1; (3rd) 1.23:1; (4th) 0.81:1; (Rev) 3.46:1. Alternate Escort four-speed manual: (1st) 3.58:1 (2nd) 2.05:1; (3rd) 1.23:1; (4th) 0.81:1; (Rev) 3.46:1. Five-speed manual on Escort/EXP/Tempo: (Ist) 3.60:1; (2nd) 2.12:1; (3rd) 1.39:1; (4th) 1.02:1; (5th) 1.02:1; (Rev) 3.62:1. (Note: separate final drive for 5th gear.) Escort/Tempo diesel five-speed manual (1st) 3.93:1; (2nd) 2.12:1; (3rd) 1.39:1; (4th) 0.98:1; (5th) 0.98:1; (Rev) 3.62:1; TBird Turbo Coupe five-speed: (1st) 4.03:1; (2nd) 2.37:1; (3rd) 1.49:1; (4th) 1.00:1; (5th) 0.81:1; (Rev) 3.76:1. Three-speed automatic standard on LTD, Thunderbird turbo/V-6: (1st) 2.46:1 or 2.47:1 (2nd) 1.46:1 or 1.47:1 (3rd) 1.00:1 (Rev) 2.11:1 or 2.19:1. Escort/EXP/Tempo three-speed automatic: (Ist) 2.79:1; (2nd) 1.61:1; (3rd) 1.00:1; (Rev) 1.97:1. Four-speed overdrive automatic standard on LTD V-6, Crown Victoria and Thunderbird: (Ist) 2.40:1; (2nd) 1.47:1; (3rd) 1.00:1; (4th) 0.67:1; (Rev) 2.00:1. Standard final drive ratio: (Escort/EXP) 3.59:1 w/4spd, 3.73:1 w/5spd, 3.31:1 w/auto., 3.52:1 w/diesel; (Tempo) 3.33:1 w/5spd, 3.23:1 w/auto., 3.73:1 w/diesel or H.O. engine; (LTD four) 3.27:1 (LTD V-6) 2.73:1 w/3spd auto.; (Crown Vic) 3.08:1; (TBird) 3.45:1 w/turbo, 2.73:1 w/3spd automatic and V-6, 3.27:1 w/4spd auto. and V-6, 3.08:1 w/V-8. Drive Axle: (Escort/EXP/Tempo) front; (others) rear. Steering: (Crown Vic) recirculating ball; (others) rack and pinion. Front Suspension: (Escort/EXP/Tempo) MacPherson struts with lower control arms, coil springs and stabilizer bar; (LTD/TBird) modified MacPherson struts with lower control arms, coil springs and anti-sway bar; (Crown Vic) long/short control arms w/coil springs and stabilizer bar. LTD, Crown Vic and TBird had gas-filled struts/shocks. Rear Suspension: (Escort/EXP) independent trailing arms w/modified MacPherson struts and coil springs on lower control arms; (Tempo) fully independent quadra-link with MacPherson struts; (LTD/Crown Vic/TBird) rigid axle w/four-link coil springs; (TBird Turbo Coupe) 'quadra-shock' four-bar-link assembly with two hydraulic, horizontal axle dampers. Gas-filled shocks on LTD, Crown Vic and TBird. Brakes: Front disc, rear drum; power assisted (except Escort). Ignition: Electronic. Body construction: (Crown Vic) separate body and frame; (others) unibody. Fuel tank: (Escort/EXP) 13.0 gal.; (Tempo) 15.2 gal.; (LTD) 16.0 gal.; (Crown Vic) 18.0 gal.; (Crown Vic wag) 18.5 gal.; (TBird) 20.6 gal.

DRIVETRAIN OPTIONS: Engines: H.O. 1.6-liter four: Escort ($73). 232 cid V-6: LTD ($418). 302 cid V-8: Thunderbird ($398). Transmission/Differential: Five-speed manual trans.: Escort ($76). Automatic transaxle: Escort ($439) exc. LX/GT and EXP ($363); Tempo ($266-$363). Auto. transmission.: TBird Turbo Cpe ($315). First gear lockout delete: LTD, Crown Vic 'S' ($7). Overdrive auto. trans.: TBird ($237). Traction-Lok differential: LTD/Crown Vic/TBird ($95). Brakes/Steering/Suspension: Power brakes: Escort ($95). Power steering: Escort/EXP ($215); Tempo ($223). H.D. susp.: Crown Vic/TBird ($26); LTD LPO ($43). Handling susp.: Escort L ($199); Escort GL ($95); Crown Vic ($49). Auto. load leveling: Crown Vic ($200). Other: H.D. battery ($27). H.D. alternator: Escort/EXP ($27). Extended-range gas tank: LTD ($46). Engine block heater ($18). Trailer towing pkg.: Crown Vic ($251-$302); TBird ($251). California emission system: Escort/EXP ($46); others ($99). High-altitude emissions (NC).

ESCORT CONVENIENCE/APPEARANCE OPTIONS: Option Packages: Squire wagon pkg. ($373). Instrument group ($87). Convenience group ($206-$341). Light group ($67). Comfort/Convenience: Air conditioner ($643). Rear defroster, electric ($139). High-capacity heater ($76). Fingertip speed control ($176). Power door locks ($124-$176). Tinted glass ($95); windshield only LPO ($48). Tilt steering ($104). Overhead console w/digital clock ($82). Interval wipers ($50). Rear wiper/washer ($120) exc. LX ($46). Dual remote sport mirrors ($68). Entertainment: AM radio: base/L ($39). AM/FM radio ($82) exc. base/L ($121). AM/FM stereo radio ($109) exc. base/L ($148); w/cassette player ($148) exc. base/L ($295). Electronic-tuning AM/FM stereo w/cassette ($409-$448). Premium sound ($138). Exterior: Flip-up open-air roof ($315). Clearcoat metallic paint ($91) exc. LX/GT (NC). Two-tone paint/tape ($134-$173). Dual bodyside paint stripes ($39). Front vent windows, pivoting ($63). Vinyl-insert bodyside moldings ($45). Bumper guards, front or rear ($28). Bumper rub strips ($48). Luggage rack: wag ($100). Interior: Console ($111). Vinyl seat trim ($24). Cloth/vinyl low-back bucket seats: L ($33). Color-keyed front mats ($22). Wheels/Tires: Wheel trim rings ($54). Cast aluminum wheels ($279). TR aluminum wheels: LX/GT ($201). Styled steel wheels fleet only ($104 credit). P165/80R13 SBR WSW ($59).

1985 Ford Tempo GLX sedan. (JG)

EXP CONVENIENCE/APPEARANCE OPTIONS: Comfort/Convenience: Air conditioner ($643). Fingertip speed control ($176). Tinted glass ($95). Tilt steering ($104). Lighted visor vanity mirror ($50). Entertainment: AM/FM stereo radio: base ($109); w/cassette player ($256) exc. luxury cpe ($148). Electronic-tuning AM/FM stereo w/cassette ($409) exc. luxury cpe ($300) and Turbo ($152). Premium sound ($138). AM radio delete ($39 credit). AM/FM stereo delete: luxury cpe ($148 credit). AM/FM stereo/cassette delete: Turbo ($295 credit). Exterior: Flip-up open air roof ($315). Clearcoat paint ($91). Lower two-tone paint/tape ($146). Paint/tape delete LPO (NC), Medium bodyside moldings: Turbo ($45). Lower bodyside protection ($68). Interior: Four-way driver's seat: base ($55). Low-back vinyl bucket seats: base (NC). Cloth sport performance seats: luxury cpe ($173). Front floor mats ($22). Wheels/Tires: TR aluminum wheels: luxury cpe ($370). TR styled steel wheels: luxury cpe ($168). Cast aluminum wheels: luxury cpe ($238). P165/80R13 RWL ($90). P165/70R365 Michelin TRX (NC).

TEMPO CONVENIENCE/APPEARANCE OPTIONS: Option Packages: Sport performance pkg.: GL ($900-$911). Power lock group ($202-$254). Luxury option group: GL/LX ($755-$855). Select option group: GL ($401). Comfort/Convenience: Air bag, driver's side: GL 4dr. fleet only ($815). Air cond. ($743). Rear defroster, electric ($140). Fingertip speed control: GL/GLX ($176). Power windows ($272). Power decklid release ($40). Remote fuel door release LPO ($26). Six-way power driver's seat ($224). Tinted glass ($110); windshield fleet ($48). Tilt steering: GL ($110). Sport instrument cluster ($87). Dual sport remote mirrors ($93). Entertainment: AM/FM stereo radio: L/GL ($109); w/cassette player ($148-$256). Electronic-tuning AM/FM stereo w/cassette ($152-$409). Graphic equalizer ($107-$218). AM radio delete ($39 credit). Exterior: Clearcoat paint ($91). Lower body accent paint ($78-$118). Interior: Vinyl seat trim LPO ($35). Leather seat trim: GLX ($300). Carpeted front floor mats fleet ($13). Wheels/Tires: Styled wheels: L ($73). P175/80R13 WSW ($72).

LTD CONVENIENCE/APPEARANCE OPTIONS: Option Packages: Squire option ($282). Interior luxury group: wagon ($388). Power lock group ($213-$254). Light group ($38). Police pkg. ($901-$1429). Taxi pkg. ($860). Comfort/Convenience: Air cond. ($743); auto-temp ($809). Fingertip speed control ($176). Illuminated entry ($82). Auto-lamp on-off delay ($73). Power windows ($272). Six-way power driver's seat ($224); dual ($449). Tinted glass ($110). Tinted windshield fleet ($48). Leather-wrapped steering wheel ($59). Tilt steering ($110). Tripminder computer ($215-$293). Digital clock ($78). Diagnostic warning lights ($89). Auto. parking brake release LPO ($12). Interval wipers ($50). Liftgate wiper/washer: wagon ($99). Lighting and Mirrors: Cornering lamps ($68). Right remote convex mirror ($61). Dual electric remote mirrors ($96). Lighted visor vanity mirrors ($57-$106). Entertainment: AM/FM stereo radio ($109); w/cassette player ($256). Electronic-tuning AM/FM stereo radio w/cassette ($409). Premium sound system ($138). AM radio delete ($39 credit), Exterior: Formal roof, cloth or vinyl ($848). Full vinyl roof ($152). Two-tone paint ($117). Pivoting front vent windows ($79). Two-way liftgate: wag ($105). Bright protective bodyside moldings w/vinyl insert ($55). Rocker panel moldings ($40). Bumper guards, rear ($28). Bumper rub strips ($56). Luggage rack: wagon ($126). Lower bodyside protection ($41). Interior: Vinyl seat trim ($35). Flight bench seat (NC). Front floor mats, carpeted ($23). Wheels/Tires: Luxury wheel covers ($55). Wire wheel covers, locking ($204). Cast aluminum wheels: LX ($224). Styled wheels ($178). Styled steel wheels w/trim rings fleet ($54). P195/75R14 WSW ($72). P205/70R14 WSW ($134). Puncture-sealant P195/75R14 WSW ($202). Conventional spare LPO ($63).

NOTE: Many LTD options listed above were not available for the LX Brougham.

1985 Ford Thunderbird Elan hardtop coupe. (JG)

LTD CROWN VICTORIA CONVENIENCE/APPEARANCE OPTIONS: Option Packages, Interior luxury group ($949-$1022). Convenience group ($109-$134). Power lock group ($140-$238). Light group ($48). Comfort/Convenience: Air cond. ($743); w/auto temp control ($809). Rear defroster, electric ($140). Fingertip speed control ($176). Illuminated entry system ($82). Power windows ($198-$272). Power driver seat ($227); driver and passenger ($454). Remote fuel door lock ($35). Tinted glass ($110): windshield only LPO ($48). Autolamp on/off delay ($73). Leather-wrapped steering wheel ($59). Tilt steering wheel ($110). Auto. parking brake release ($12). Tripminder computer ($215-$261). Quartz clock: S ($35). Digital clock ($61-$96). Interval wipers ($50). Lighting and Mirrors: Cornering lamps ($68). Remote right mirror ($46). Lighted visor vanity mirrors ($106). Entertainment: AM/FM stereo radio: S ($109); w/cassette tape Player ($148-$256). Electronic-tuning AM/FM stereo radio w/cassette ($300) exc. S LPO ($409). Power antenna ($66). Premium sound system ($168). Radio delete: AM ($39 credit); AM/FM ($148 credit). Exterior: Fully padded Brougham vinyl roof ($793). Two-tone paint/tape ($117). Dual accent bodyside paint stripes: S LPO ($39). Pivoting front vent windows ($79). Rocker panel moldings ($18-$38). Vinyl-insert bodyside moldings ($61). Bumper rub strips ($59). Luggage rack: wagon ($110). License frames ($9). Interior: Dual-facing rear seats: wagon ($167). Leather split bench seat ($418). Cloth/vinyl split bench seating ($139). All-vinyl seat trim ($34); Duraweave vinyl, wagon ($96). Carpeted front/rear floor mats ($33). Trunk trim ($37). Wheels/Tires: Wire wheel covers, locking ($204). Cast aluminum wheels ($390). P205/75R15 WSW ($17); puncture-sealant ($178). P215/70R15 WSW ($79). Conventional spare ($63).

THUNDERBIRD CONVENIENCE/APPEARANCE OPTIONS: Option Packages: Light group ($35). Power lock group ($213). Comfort/Convenience: Air cond. ($743); auto-temp ($905). Rear defroster ($140). Fingertip speed control ($176). Illuminated entry system ($82). Keyless entry ($116-$198). Anti-theft system ($159). Tripminder computer ($215-$276). Autolamp on/off delay ($73). Tinted glass ($110); windshield only LPO ($48). Power windows ($198). Six-way power driver's seat ($227); dual ($454) exc. Fila ($227). Dual power seat recliners ($189). Auto. parking brake release: base ($12). Leather-wrapped steering wheel ($59). Tilt steering wheel ($110). Electronic instrument cluster ($270-$330). Diagnostic warning lights ($89). Low oil warning light: base ($24). Digital clock: base ($61). Interval wipers ($50). Lighting and Mirrors: Cornering lamps ($68). Dual electric remote mirrors ($96). Electronic dimming day/night mirror ($77). Lighted visor vanity mirrors, pair ($106). Entertainment: AM/FM stereo radio w/cassette player ($148). Electronic-tuning AM/FM stereo search radio w/cassette ($300) exc. Elan ($152). Power antenna ($66). Graphic equalizer ($252). Premium sound system ($168). AM/FM radio delete ($148 credit). Exterior: Flip-up open-air roof ($315). Metallic clearcoat paint ($183). Two-tone paint/tape ($163-$218). Hood paint stripe ($16). Dual accent bodyside/decklid paint stripes: base ($55). Hood/decklid/bodyside paint stripes: base ($71). Pivoting front vent windows ($79). Wide bodyside moldings: base ($57). Bright rocker panel moldings ($39). License frames ($9). Interior: Articulated sport seats ($183-$427). Heated seats ($157). Leather seat trim ($415). Vinyl seat trim: base ($37). Front floor mats, carpeted ($22). Wheels/Tires: Wire wheel covers, locking ($204). Cast aluminum wheels ($343). Styled wheels ($178). P205/70R14 WSW ($62). P215/70R14 WSW ($99). P215/70HR14 performance BSW ($215). Conventional spare ($63).

HISTORY: Introduced: October 4, 1984. Model year production: 1,265,221 (incl. Mustangs, but with incomplete Escort total from Ford). Total production in the U.S. market of 1,389,103 units (incl. Mustangs) included, 828,320 four-cylinder, 270,461 sixes and 290,322 V-8s. That total included 24,708 turbo fours and 10,246 diesel engines. Calendar year production (U.S.): 1,098,532 (incl. Mustangs). Calendar year sales by U.S. dealers: 1,386,195 (incl. Mustangs). Model year sales by U.S. dealers: 1,443,993 (incl. Mustangs).

HISTORY: Sales rose 14 percent for the 1985 model year, partly as a result of incentive programs late in the season. Ford's market share rose to a healthy 17.2 percent, up from 16 percent the year before. All seven series showed an increase, led by Escort which revealed a 21 percent rise. Tempo did well, too. Ford raised prices only 1.3 percent (average) this year, though Crown Victoria went up over 6 percent and Mustangs were actually cheaper.

1986 FORD

The new front-drive, mid-size Taurus was the big news for 1986. Its aerodynamic styling went considerably beyond the Tempo design, taking its cue from European Fords. Taurus hardly resembled the rear-drive LTD that it was meant to replace. Mercury's Sable was similar, but with its own set of body panels and features. A reworked Escort had appeared as a mid-year 1985 model, but the restyled EXP two-seater wouldn't arrive until later in this model year.

1986 Ford Escort LX wagon. (JG)

ESCORT — FOUR — This year's Escort actually arrived as a 1985.5 model, carrying a bigger (1.9-liter) four-cylinder engine under its hood. The model lineup was revised. An LX series replaced the former GL, and the temporarily-abandoned GT was reintroduced. Pony was the name for the base hatchback (same name as the low-budget Pinto of the late 1970s). 'Official' diesel models were dropped, but the 2.0-liter diesel engine remained available as an option. A new two-slot body-color grille held the Ford script oval in the center of the single horizontal bar. Aero-style headlamps met the amber wraparound parking lenses. Wraparound tail lamps had two horizontal ribs. Inside was a new black four-spoke steering wheel. Options included tilt steering, speed control, and an instrumentation group. Escort's base engine was carbureted, hooked to a four-speed manual transaxle. Automatic shift was optional. As before, Escort had four-wheel independent suspension. Pony had standard power brakes, day/night mirror, dome light, cloth/vinyl low-back reclining bucket seats, and P175/80R13 tires. Escort L added an AM radio and load floor carpet. LX included remote fuel door lock, remote liftgate release, wide vinyl bodyside moldings, bumper rub strips, and styled steel wheels. In addition to a high-output 1.9-liter engine with port fuel injection and five-speed manual transaxle, Escort GT had a performance suspension with new front and rear stabilizer bars, as well as P195/60HR15 tires on eight-spoke aluminum wheels. Also included: front and rear body-color partial fascias; foglamps; console with graphic display; leather-wrapped steering wheel; body-color wheel spats with integral rocker panel moldings; rear spoiler; and body-color narrow bodyside moldings. One easy-to-spot styling feature was GT's offset grille, with slots occupying just two-thirds of the panel instead of full-width. A 'GT' decal sat on the solid passenger side of the 'grille' panel.

EXP — FOUR — After a brief absence from the lineup, the two-seater EXP returned in restyled form with a sleek new front-end design, including air dam and aero headlamps. Also new was a bubble-back styled rear hatch with integral spoiler. Otherwise, the new four-window coupe design looked similar to 1985 at the rear, but markedly different up front. Ford's blue script oval stood above a single-slot grille. Aero headlamps met wraparound marker lenses. Parking lamps were mounted below, in the bumper region, alongside a wide center slot. Large 'EXP' recessed lettering was easy to spot on the wide C pillar. Wraparound full-width tail lamps (split by the license plate's recessed housing) were divided into upper/lower segments, and tapered downward to a point on each quarter panel. Luxury Coupe and Sport Coupe versions were offered, with 1.9-liter fast-burn four, five-speed manual transaxle, and four-wheel independent suspension. Luxury Coupe had the carbureted engine, along with a tachometer and trip odometer, reclining low-back bucket seats trimmed in cloth/vinyl (or all vinyl), AM/FM stereo radio, overhead console, and left remote mirror. A fuel-injected high-output version of the four went into the Sport Coupe, which also had special handling components, performance bucket seats, center console with graphic systems monitor, foglamps, dual electric mirrors, and low-profile 15 in. handling tires on cast aluminum wheels. Special Option Groups contained such items as speed control, flip-up open air roof, and premium sound system.

1986 Ford Tempo LX coupe. (JG)

1986 Ford Taurus LX sedan. (JG)

TEMPO — FOUR — After only two seasons in the lineup, Tempo got new front and rear styling. The new grille consisted simply of twin wide slots below a blue Ford oval in the sloping, body-colored center panel. Aerodynamic halogen headlamps continued outward to meet clear parking lamps, wrapping around to amber side marker lenses that tapered downward to a rounded 'point.' (The former Tempo had conventional recessed headlamps.) Tempo also had a color-keyed lower front valence panel. Wide, dark gray bodyside moldings held bright inserts. This year's tail lamps were wraparound full-width style. Dark gray partial front and rear bumper covers had side extensions with bright insert. Completing the look were aero-style mirrors. Inside was a new-design four-spoke deep-dish steering wheel. A push-pull headlamp switch replaced the toggle unit. New door sill scuff plates were added. A new LX series replaced the GLX. Both GL and LX tires were upgraded to 14 inch size. Sport GL went to 15 inches, and had red interior accent colors to replace the former blue. New options included P185/70R14 whitewalls, decklid luggage rack, 2.0-liter diesel (except in California), and premium sound system. Diesel power was an option rather than a distinct model. Also available: a supplemental air bag restraint system, sport instrument cluster, and lower accent paint treatment. In addition to the basic GL and LX models, Select GL and Sport GL packages were offered. GL included full cloth reclining front bucket seats, power front disc/rear drum brakes, and such conveniences as interval wipers and a digital clock. Tempo LX included styled wheels, tilt steering, power door locks, a full array of courtesy lights, bright argent lower back panel appliqué, and AM/FM stereo radio (which could be deleted). A Select GL package added power steering, tinted glass, dual sail-mounted remote electric mirrors, and AM/FM stereo radio (also open to deletion for credit). Sport GL had a special handling suspension, as well as a high specific output (HSO) version of the standard 2300 HSC (high swirl combustion) four. All had a standard five-speed manual transaxle. Automatic was optional on GL and Select GL, as was the 2.0-liter diesel four with five-speed.

TAURUS — FOUR/V-6 — Most striking of the aerodynamic new midsize, front-drive Taurus's styling features was the lack of a grille. The solid body-colored panel between aero halogen headlamps held nothing other than a Ford oval, set in a larger oval opening. The only other opening up front was a wide center air-intake slot, far down between horizontally-ribbed bumper segments. Those wide single-section headlamps (with integrated turn signal lamps) continued around the fender side to meet small amber lenses. Clear side marker lenses were farther down, below the bodyside/bumper molding. The 'Taurus' nameplate (and model identification) went low on the door, in or just below the bodyside molding. At the rear were wraparound tail lamps. Taurus wagons had narrow vertical tail lamps, and center high-mount stoplamp above the liftgate. That distinctive liftgate design had a back window that tapered inward at the top. Taurus had flush-mounted glass all around, and shingled one-piece doors. Aero styling gave an impressive drag coefficient: as low as 0.33 for the sedan. Four series were offered: L, GL, LX, and (later) a sporty MT5, in six-window sedan or wagon form. Base engine was a new 153 cid (2.5-liter) fuel-injected HSC four, though early models came only with the 183 cid (3.0-liter) V-6. Later optional (standard on GL/LX and wagons), that V-6 had multi-port fuel injection. The 2.5-liter four could have a three-speed automatic transaxle with centrifugally locking clutch; the V-6 turned to a four-speed overdrive automatic transaxle. A five-speed manual transaxle was available only with the four. The four-cylinder engine was derived from Tempo's High Swirl Combustion design. Sedans had fully independent MacPherson strut suspension, front and rear. Wagons had independent short and long arm type rear suspension, which was more compact to add cargo space. Polycarbonate bumpers were corrosion-proof and resilient. The driver-oriented instrument panel featured a swept-away design with three analog backlit instrument clusters. An electronic cluster was optional. Tactile-type switches had raised or depressed sections so drivers could determine the function by touch. Windshield wipers had 20 in. blades and an articulated driver's side arm for a full wipe all the way to the pillar. Standard equipment included power brakes and steering, gas-filled shocks and struts, all-season steel-belted

radials, driver's side footrest, locking glovebox, dual-note horn, black left-hand remote mirror, AM radio, and reclining cloth flight bench seats. Wagons had a 60/40 split fold-down rear seat, cargo tie-downs, rear bumper step pad, and dual cargo area lights. MT5 came with five-speed manual transaxle and floor shift lever, and included interval wipers, electronic-tuning AM/FM stereo with digital clock, tinted glass, tachometer, dual electric remote mirrors, color-keyed rocker panel moldings, and bucket seats. MT5 sedans had blackout treatment on 'B' and 'C' pillars. Taurus GL was similar to MT5 but with four-speed automatic and without a tachometer. The top-ranked LX had air conditioning, remote fuel door release, cornering lamps, power locks, black/bright bodyside moldings, power cloth split bench seats with adjustable front lumbar support, tilt steering, power windows, and lighted visor vanity mirrors. Options included an Insta-Clear heated windshield, power moonroof, keyless entry, and electronic climate control. Wagons could get a rear-facing third seat, liftgate wiper/washer, and folding load floor extension that could also serve as a picnic table. Preferred Equipment Packages included such options as speed control, rear window defroster, air conditioning, and electronic entertainment systems. At first glance, Taurus looked very much like the related Mercury Sable, developed under the same program; but the sedans shared no sheetmetal at all. Wagons differed up front, but were the same from the windshield on back. The pair did share drivetrains and running gear, plus most equipment.

LTD — FOUR/V-6 — Ford's rear-drive mid-size was scheduled for abandonment at mid-year. now that the front-drive Taurus had arrived. For its final partial season, the 232 cid (3.8-liter) V-6 became standard (though the four was listed as a credit option). The high-performance LX sedan didn't make the lineup this year, and not much was new apart from the newly required center high-mount stop lamp. Quite a few low-rate options were dropped, and the four-speed automatic overdrive transmission became optional. LTD was virtually identical to Mercury Marquis, both riding the old Granada platform. Models included base and Brougham sedans, and the base wagon.

LTD CROWN VICTORIA — V-8 — Big rear-drives had more than a spark of life remaining in Ford's plans. Crown Victoria added a new sedan and wagon series this year: the top-level LX and Country Squire LX. Each model incorporated a standard (previously optional) interior luxury group. LX had reclining split bench seats upholstered in velour cloth or vinyl (leather seating surfaces optional). Equipment included power windows and a digital clock, as well as a variety of luxury trim extras. Sequential multi-port fuel injection replaced the former central injection on the standard 302 cid (5.0-liter) V-8 engine, which came with four-speed overdrive automatic. No options were available, except the 351 cid V-8 for police models. The 302 got a number of internal changes, including fast-burning combustion chambers, higher compression, roller tappets, low-tension piston rings, and viscous clutch cooling fan. Wagons now had a mini spare tire rather than the conventional one. All series had automatic parking brake release, a tethered gas cap, and right-hand visor mirror. A rear bumper step pad became standard on wagons. The new high-mount brake lamp was mounted on the package tray on sedans, on tailgate of wagons. Standard equipment included an AM/FM stereo radio with four speakers, quartz clock, front/rear courtesy lights, cloth flight bench seat with dual recliners, and remote driver's mirror. Split bench seats were optional. P205/75R15 tires became standard this year. Seven exterior colors were new, along with five vinyl roof colors. Country Squire's simulated woodgrain panels switched from cherry to dark cherry. Optional this year were dual electric remote mirrors for LX and a conventional spare tire for wagons. Traction-Lok axle was now included with the heavy-duty trailer towing packages. Preferred Equipment Packages grouped such options as six-way power driver's seat, power lock group, and speed control. Styling was similar to 1985. Full-size Fords had an upright crosshatch grille with relatively large holes in a 12x4 pattern. Quad rectangular headlamps stood above amber park/signal lenses, and the whole assembly continued outward to meet twin amber lenses around the fender tips. The entire front end showed a straight-up, symmetrical design. Small marker lenses sat quite low on the front fenders, just ahead of wheel openings. Red rear side marker lenses were vertical, near quarter panel tips. In back, each squarish vertical taillamp consisted of four raised segments.

1986 Ford Thunderbird hardtop coupe. (JG)

1986 Ford Thunderbird Turbo Coupe. (PH)

1986 Ford LTD Crown Victoria Country Squire station wagon. (JG)

THUNDERBIRD — FOUR/V-6/V-8 — Thunderbird dropped down to three models this year as the Fila series left the lineup. Both the base 232 cid (3.8-liter) V-6 and optional 302 cid (5.0-liter) V-8 engines now had viscous engine mounts (which had been standard on the 2.3-liter turbo in 1985). The V-8 switched to multi-port fuel injection and added roller tappets, low-tension piston rings, and fast-burn combustion chambers. P215/70R14 blackwalls were now standard (except on Turbo Coupe). V-6 models came with three-speed SelectShift automatic; V-8s with four-speed overdrive automatic. All models now had an electronic-tuning AM/FM stereo radio. Six body colors and three interior trim colors were new. Elan's interior cloth trim was revised for a plusher appearance. A woodtone instrument panel appliqué was added. Standard equipment included variable-ratio power rack-and-pinion steering, power front disc/rear drum brakes, and gas-pressurized shocks and struts. Inside were reclining cloth split bench seats. Thunderbird elan (accent over the e) had upgraded trim and such conveniences as power windows, dual electric remote mirrors, interval wipers, system sentry, a digital clock, and lighted visor mirrors. Turbo Coupe again carried the 2.3-liter turbocharged four, with five-speed close-ratio manual shift and special Goodyear performance tires. Articulated front sport seats adjusted several ways. New options were: power moonroof (delayed availability) and a collapsible spare tire (including a 12-volt air compressor that plugged into the lighter). Preferred Equipment Packages included such extras as illuminated entry, electronic instrument cluster, and a power lock group. Styling was similar to 1985. Recessed, staggered quad rectangular headlamps were flanked by amber wraparound signal/marker lenses at matching height. Thunderbird's grille had four thin, bright horizontal bars over a blackout pattern. Small amber parking lamps were down in the bumper rub strip. Wraparound tail lamps again held a Thunderbird emblem in each lens. Emblems also went on the C pillar and grille header. Thunderbird was similar to Mercury's Cougar.

I.D. DATA: Ford's 17-symbol Vehicle Identification Number (VIN) again was stamped on a metal tab fastened to the instrument panel, visible through the windshield. The first three symbols ('1FA') indicate manufacturer, make and vehicle type. The fourth symbol ('B') denotes restraint system. Next comes a letter 'P', followed by two digits that indicate body type: Model Number, as shown in first column of tables below. (Example: '31' Escort L two-door hatchback.) Symbol eight indicates engine type: '9' L4-113 2Bbl.; 'J' H.O. L4-113 FI; 'H' Diesel L4-121; 'X' HSC L4-140 FI; 'S' H.O. HSC L4-140 FI; 'W' Turbo L4-140 EFI; 'D' L4-153 FI; 'U' V6-183 FI; '3' V6-232 2Bbl.; 'F' V8-302 2Bbl.; 'G' V8-351 2Bbl. Next is a check digit. Symbol ten indicates model year ('G' 1986). Symbol eleven is assembly plant: 'A' Atlanta, GA; 'B' Oakville, Ontario (Canada); 'G' Chicago; 'H' Lorain, Ohio; 'K' Kansas City, MO; 'X' St. Thomas, Ontario; 'T' Edison, NJ; 'W' Wayne, MI. The final six digits make up the sequence number, starting with 100001. A Vehicle Certification Label on the left front door lock face panel or door pillar shows the manufacturer, month and year of manufacture, GVW, GAWR, certification statement, VIN, and codes for such items as body type, color, trim, axle, transmission, and special order information.

ESCORT (FOUR)

Model No.	Body/ Style No.	Body Type & Seating	Factory Price	Shipping Weight	Prod. Total
31/41P	N/A	2-dr. Pony Hatch-4P	6052	2089	Note 1
31	N/A	2-dr. L Hatch-4P	6327	2096	Note 1
36	N/A	4-dr. L Hatch-4P	6541	2154	Note 1
34	N/A	4-dr. L Sta Wag-4P	6822	2173	Note 1
32	N/A	2-dr. LX Hatch-4P	7284	2160	Note 1
37	N/A	4-dr. LX Hatch-4P	7448	2214	Note 1
35	N/A	4-dr. LX Sta Wag-4P	7729	2228	Note 1
33	N/A	2-dr. GT Hatch-4P	8112	2282	Note 1

NOTE 1: For the model year, a total of 228,013 two-door hatchbacks, 117,300 four-door hatchback sedans, and 84,740 station wagons were produced. Breakdown by trim level not available. Bodies are sometimes referred to as three-door and five-door.

EXP (FOUR)

01	N/A	2-dr. Spt Cpe-2P	7186	N/A	Note 2
01/931	N/A	2-dr. Luxury Cpe-2P	8235	N/A	Note 2

NOTE 2: Total EXP production was 30,978.

TEMPO (FOUR)

19	66D	2-dr. GL Sed-5P	7358	2363	Note 3
22	54D	4-dr. GL Sed-5P	7508	2422	Note 3
20	66D	2-dr. GLX Sed-5P	8578	2465	Note 3
23	54D	4-dr. GLX Sed-5P	8777	2526	Note 3

NOTE 3: Total Tempo production came to 69,101 two-doors and 208,570 four-doors.

TAURUS (FOUR/V-6)

29	54D	4-dr. L Sedan-6P	9645/10256	2749/2749	Note 4
30	74D	4-dr. L Sta Wag-6P	----/10763	----/3067	Note 4
29/934	54D	4-dr. MT5 Sed-6P	10276/----	2759/----	Note 4
30/934	74D	4-dr. MT5 Wag-6P	10741/----	2957/----	Note 4
29/60D	54D	4-dr. GL Sedan-6P	----/11322	----/2909	Note 4
30/60D	74D	4-dr. GL Wag-6P	----/11790	----/3108	Note 4
29/60H	54D	4-dr. LX Sedan-6P	----/13351	----/3001	Note 4
30/60H	74D	4-dr. LX Wag-6P	----/13860	----/3198	Note 4

NOTE 4: Total Taurus production came to 178,737 sedans and 57,625 station wagons.

LTD (FOUR/V-6)

39	54D	4-dr. Sedan-5P	9538/10032	2801/2878	58,270
39	54D	4-dr. Brghm-5P	9926/10420	2806/2883	Note 5
40	74D	4-dr. Sta Wag-5P	----/10132	----/2977	14,213

NOTE 5: Brougham production is included in basic sedan total.

LTD CROWN VICTORIA (V-8)

42	66K	2-dr. Sedan-6P	13022	3571	6,559
43	54K	4-dr. Sedan-6P	12562	3611	97,314
44	74K	4-dr. Ctry Sqr-6P	12655	3834	20,164
44/41E	74K	4-dr. Sta Wag-6P	12405	3795	Note 6
43/41K	54K	4-dr. 'S' Sed-6P	12188	3591	Note 6
44/41K	74K	4-dr. 'S' Wag-6P	12468	3769	Note 6

LTD CROWN VICTORIA LX (V-8)

42/60H	66K	2-dr. Sedan-6P	13752	3608	Note 6
43/60H	54K	4-dr. Sedan-6P	13784	3660	Note 6
44/41E/ 6	60H	74K	4-dr. Sta Wag-6P	13567	3834 Note 6
44/60H	74K	4-dr. Ctry Sqr-6P	13817	3873	Note 6

NOTE 6: Production of 'S' and LX models and basic station wagon is included in basic sedan and Country Squire totals above.

Police Crown Victoria Note: A Police model (P43/41K/55A) 'S' sedan cost $11,813 with 302 cid V-8, or $11,933 with 351 cid V-8 engine.

THUNDERBIRD (V-6/V-8)

Model No.	Body/ Style No.	Body Type & Seating	Factory Price	Shipping Weight	Prod. Total
46	66D	2-dr. HT Cpe-5P	11020/11805	2923/3101	163,965
46	66D	2-dr. Elan Cpe-5P	12554/13339	2977/3155	Note 7

THUNDERBIRD TURBO COUPE (FOUR)

46	66D	2-dr. HT Cpe-5P	14143	3016	Note 7

NOTE 7: Turbo Coupe and Elan production is included in basic Thunderbird total.

MODEL NUMBER NOTE: Some sources include a prefix 'P' ahead of the two-digit model number.

FACTORY PRICE AND WEIGHT NOTE: LTD and Taurus prices and weights to left of slash are for four-cylinder, to right for V-6 engine. Thunderbird prices and weights to left of slash are for V-6, to right for V-8 engine.

ENGINE [Base Four (Escort)]: Inline. Overhead cam. Four-cylinder. Cast-iron block and aluminum head. Displacement: 113 cid (1.9 liters). Bore & stroke: 3.23 x 3.46 in. Compression ratio: 9.0:1. Brake horsepower: 86 at 4800 rpm. Torque: 100 lbs.-ft. at 3000 rpm. Five main bearings. Hydraulic valve lifters. Carburetor: 2Bbl. Holley 740. VIN Code: 9.

ENGINE [Base Four (Escort GT); Optional (Escort)]: High-output, multi-port fuel-injected version of 1.9-liter four above Horsepower: 108 at 5200 rpm. Torque: 114 lbs.-ft. at 4000 rpm. VIN Code: J.

ENGINE [Diesel Four (Escort, Tempo)]: Inline. Overhead cam. Four-cylinder. Cast-iron block and aluminum head. Displacement: 121 cid (2.0 liters). Bore & stroke: 3.39 x 3.39 in. Compression ratio: 22.7:1. Brake horsepower: 52 at 4000 rpm. Torque: 82 lbs.-ft. at 2400 rpm. Five main bearings. Solid valve lifters. Fuel injection. VIN Code: H.

ENGINE [Base Four (Tempo)]: Inline. Overhead valve. Four-cylinder. Cast-iron block and head. Displacement: 140 cid (2.3 liters). Bore & stroke: 3.70 x 3.30 in. Compression ratio: 9.0:1. Brake horsepower: 86 at 4000 rpm. Torque: 124 lbs.-ft. at 2800 rpm. Five main bearings. Hydraulic valve lifters. Throttle-body fuel injection. High Swirl Combustion (HSC) design. VIN Code: X.

ENGINE [Optional Four (Tempo)]: High-output version of HSC four above Horsepower: 100 at 4600 rpm. Torque: 125 lbs.-ft. at 3200 rpm. VIN Code: S.

ENGINE [Base Four (Thunderbird Turbo Coupe)]: Inline. Overhead cam. Four-cylinder. Cast-iron block and head. Displacement: 140 cid (2.3 liters). Bore & stroke: 3.78 x 3.13 in. Compression ratio: 8.0:1. Brake horsepower: 155 at 4600 rpm. (145 at 4400 with automatic). Torque: 190 lbs.-ft. at 2800 rpm. (180 at 3000 with automatic). Five main bearings. Hydraulic valve lifters. Port fuel injection. VIN Code: W.

ENGINE [Base Four (late Taurus)]: Inline. Overhead valve. Four-cylinder. Cast-iron block and head. Displacement: 153 cid (2.5 liters). Bore & stroke: 3.70 x 3.60 in. Compression ratio: 9.0:1. Brake horsepower: 88 at 4600 rpm. Torque: 130 lbs.-ft. at 2800 rpm. Five main bearings. Hydraulic valve lifters. Electronic fuel injection. VIN Code: D.

ENGINE [Base V-6 (Taurus LX/wagon); Optional (Taurus)]: 60-degree, overhead valve V-6. Cast-iron block and head. Displacement: 183 cid (3.0 liters). Bore & stroke: 3.50 x 3.10 in. Compression ratio: 9.25:1. Brake horsepower: 140 at 4800 rpm. Torque: 160 lbs.-ft. at 3000 rpm. Four main bearings. Hydraulic valve lifters. Multi-port fuel injection. VIN Code: U.

ENGINE [Base V-6 (LTD, Thunderbird)]: 90-degree, overhead valve V-6. Cast-iron block and aluminum head. Displacement: 232 cid (3.8 liters). Bore & stroke: 3.80 x 3.40 in. Compression ratio: 8.7:1. Brake horsepower: 120 at 3600 rpm. Torque: 205 lbs.-ft. at 1600 rpm. Four main bearings. Throttle-body fuel injection. VIN Code: 3.

ENGINE [Base V-8 (Crown Victoria); Optional (Thunderbird)]: 90-degree, overhead valve V-8. Cast-iron block and head. Displacement: 302 cid (5.0 liters). Bore & stroke: 4.00 x 3.00 in. Compression ratio: 8.9:1. Brake horsepower: 150 at 3200 rpm. Torque: 270 lbs.-ft. at 2000 rpm. Five main bearings. Hydraulic valve lifters. Sequential (port) fuel injection. VIN Code: F.

ENGINE [High-Output Police V-8 (Crown Victoria)]: 90-degree, overhead valve V-8. Cast-iron block and head. Displacement: 351 cid (5.8 liters). Bore & stroke: 4.00 x 3.50 in. Compression ratio: 8.3:1. Brake horsepower: 180 at 3600 rpm. Torque: 285 lbs.-ft. at 2400 rpm. Five main bearings. Hydraulic valve lifters. Carburetor: 2Bbl. VIN Code: G.

CHASSIS DATA: Wheelbase: (Escort/EXP) 94.2 in.; (Tempo) 99.9 in.; (Taurus) 106.0 in.; (LTD) 105.6 in.; (Crown Vic) 114.3 in.; (TBird) 104.0 in. Overall Length: (Escort) 166.9 in.; (Escort wagon) 168.0 in.; (EXP) 168.4 in.; (Tempo) 176.2 in.; (Taurus) 188.4 in.; (Taurus wag) 191.9 in.; (LTD) 196.5 in.; (Crown Vic) 211.0 in.; (Crown Vic wag) 215.0 in.; (TBird) 197.6 in. Height: (Escort) 53.3-53.5 in.; (EXP) 50.9 in.; (Tempo) 52.7 in.; (Taurus) 54.4 in.; (Taurus wag) 55.2 in.; (LTD) 53.8 in.; (LTD wag) 54.4 in.; (Crown Vic) 55.3 in.; (Crown Vic wag) 56.8 in.; (TBird) 53.2 in. Width: (Escort/EXP) 65.9 in.; (Tempo) 68.3 in.; (Taurus) 70.7 in.; (LTD) 71.0 in.; (Crown Vic) 77.5 in.; (Crown Vic wag) 79.3 in.; (TBird) 71.1 in. Front Tread: (Escort/EXP/Tempo) 54.7 in.; (Taurus) 61.5 in.; (LTD) 56.6 in.; (Crown Vic) 62.2 in. (TBird) 58.1 in. Rear Tread: (Escort/ EXP) 56.0 in.; (Tempo) 57.6 in.; (Taurus) 60.5 in.; (Taurus wag) 59.9 in.; (LTD) 57.0 in.; (Crown Vic) 62.0 in.; (TBird) 58.5 in. Standard Tires: (Escort Pony/L) P165/80R13 BSW; (Escort L wag/LX) P175/80R13; (Escort GT) P195/60HR15 BSW; (EXP) P185/70R14 SBR; (Tempo) P185/80R14 SBR BSW; (Taurus) P195/70R14 BSW; (Taurus GL/LX) P205/70R14; (LTD) P195/75R14 BSW; (Crown Vic) P205/75R15 SBR WSW; (TBird) P215/70R14 SBR BSW; (TBird Turbo Cpe) P225/60VR15 Goodyear unidirectional 'Gatorback' BSW.

TECHNICAL: Transmission: Four-speed manual transaxle standard on Escort Pony/L; five-speed standard on Escort LX/GT, EXP, Tempo, and Thunderbird Turbo Coupe. Gear ratios N/A. Three-speed automatic standard on LTD, Thunderbird turbo/V-6: (1st) 2.46:1 or 2.47:1; (2nd) 1.46:1 or 1.47:1; (3rd) 1.00:1; (Rev) 2.11:1 or 2.19:1. Taurus

four/Escort/Tempo three-speed automatic: (1st) 2.79:1; (2nd) 1.61:1-1.62:1; (3rd) 1.00:1; (Rev) 1.97:1. Four-speed overdrive automatic standard on LTD V-6, Crown Victoria and Thunderbird: (1st) 2.40:1; (2nd) 1.47:1; (3rd) 1.00:1; (4th) 0.67:1; (Rev) 2.00:1. Taurus V-6 four-speed overdrive automatic: (lst) 2.77:1; (2nd) 1.54:1; (3rd) 1.00:1; (4th) 0.69:1; (Rev) 2.26:1. Standard final drive ratio: (Escort) 3.52:1 w/4spd, 2.85:1 w/fuel saver, 3.73:1 w/5spd, 3.23:1 w/auto., 3.52:1 w/diesel; (EXP) N/A; (Tempo) 3.23:1 exc. 3.73:1 w/diesel or H.O. engine; (Taurus four) 3.23:1; (Taurus V-6) 3.37:1; (LTD) 2.73:1 w/3spd auto., 3.27:1 w/4spd auto.; (Crown Vic) 2.73:1; (TBird) 3.45:1 w/turbo, 2.73:1 w/3spd automatic and V-6, 3.27:1 w/4spd auto. and V-6, 3.08:1 w/V-8. Drive Axle: (Escort/EXP/Tempo/Taurus) front; (others) rear. Steering: (Crown Vic) recirculating ball; (others) rack and pinion. Front Suspension: (Escort/EXP/Tempo) MacPherson struts with lower control arms, coil springs and stabilizer bar; (EXP) N/A; (Taurus) MacPherson struts with control arms, coil springs and stabilizer bar; (LTD/TBird) modified MacPherson struts with lower control arms, coil springs and anti-sway bar; (Crown Vic) long/short control arms w/coil springs and stabilizer bar. LTD, Crown Vic and TBird had gas-filled struts/shocks. Rear Suspension: (Escort/EXP) independent trailing arms w/modified MacPherson struts and coil springs on lower control arms; (EXP) N/A; (Tempo) fully independent trailing quadra-link with MacPherson struts; (Taurus) MacPherson struts w/parallel suspension arms and coil springs; (Taurus wag) upper/lower control arms, coil springs and stabilizer bar; (LTD/Crown Vic/TBird) rigid axle w/four links and coil springs; (TBird Turbo Coupe) 'quadra-shock' four-bar-link assembly with two hydraulic, horizontal axle dampers. Gas-filled shocks on LTD, Crown Vic and TBird. Brakes: Front disc, rear drum (power assisted). Ignition: Electronic. Body construction: (Crown Vic) separate body and frame; (others) unibody. Fuel tank: (Escort) 10.0 gal.; (Escort wag) 13.0 gal.; (EXP) N/A; (Tempo) 15.2 gal.; (Taurus/LTD) 16.0 gal.; (Crown Vic) 18.0 gal.; (Crown Vic wag) 18.5 gal.; (TBird) 20.6 gal.

DRIVETRAIN OPTIONS: Engines: Diesel 2.0-liter four: Escort ($591); Tempo ($509). 140 cid four: LTD ($494 credit). 182 cid V-6: Taurus L sed ($611). 302 cid V-8: Thunderbird ($548). Transmission/Differential: Five-speed manual trans.: Escort ($76). Automatic transaxle: Escort ($466) exc. LX/GT and EXP ($390); Tempo ($448). Auto. transmission.: TBird Turbo Cpe ($315). Floor shift lever: Taurus GL/LX (NC). First gear lockout delete: Crown Vic ($7). Overdrive auto. trans.: TBird ($237); LTD ($245). Traction-Lok differential: LTD/Crown Vic/TBird ($100). Steering/Suspension: Power steering: Escort/EXP ($226); Tempo ($223). H.D. susp.: Escort/Taurus/Crown Vic ($26); LTD ($43). Handling susp.: Crown Vic ($49). Auto. load leveling: Crown Vic ($200). Other: H.D. battery ($27). H.D. alternator: Escort/EXP ($27); Crown Vic ($54). Extended-range gas tank: Taurus/LTD ($46). Engine block heater ($18). Trailer towing pkg.: Crown Vic ($377-$389). California emission system: Escort/EXP ($46); others ($99). High-altitude emissions (NC).

ESCORT CONVENIENCE/APPEARANCE OPTIONS: Option Packages: Instrument group ($87). Climate control/convenience group ($742-$868). Premium convenience group ($306-$390). Protection convenience group ($131-$467). Select L pkg. ($397). Light group ($67). Comfort/Convenience: Air conditioner ($657). Rear defroster, electric ($135). Fingertip speed control ($176). Tinted glass ($99). Tilt steering ($115). Overhead console w/digital clock ($82). Interval wipers ($50). Rear wiper/washer ($126). Dual remote sport mirrors ($68). Entertainment: AM radio ($39). AM/FM stereo radio ($109) exc. base ($148). w/cassette player ($256) exc. base/L ($295) and GT ($148). Radio delete: L/LX ($39 credit); GT ($148 credit). Premium sound ($138). Exterior: Clearcoat paint ($91). Two-tone paint ($61-$156). Front vent windows, pivoting ($63). Wide vinyl bodyside moldings ($45). Bumper guards, front/rear ($56). Bumper rub strips ($48). Luggage rack: wag ($100). Interior: Console ($111). Vinyl seat trim ($24). Wheels/Tires: Bright wheel trim rings ($54). Styled wheels ($128-$195). P165/80R13 SBR WSW ($59). Full-size spare ($63).

1986 Ford Escort GT hatchback coupe. (PH)

1986 Ford EXP Sport coupe. (F)

EXP CONVENIENCE/APPEARANCE OPTIONS: Option Packages: Climate control/convenience group ($841-$868). Sun/Sound group ($612). Convenience group ($300-$455). Comfort/Convenience: Air conditioner ($657). Rear defroster ($135). Fingertip speed control ($176). Console w/graphic systems monitor ($111). Tinted glass ($99). Tilt steering ($115). Interval wipers ($50). Dual electric remote mirrors ($88). Lighted visor vanity mirror ($50). Entertainment: AM/FM stereo radio w/cassette player ($148). Premium sound ($138). Radio delete ($148 credit). Exterior: Flip-up open air roof ($315). Clearcoat paint ($91). Interior: Cargo area cover ($59). Vinyl seat trim ($24).

TEMPO CONVENIENCE/APPEARANCE OPTIONS: Option Packages: Sport GL pkg. ($934). Select GL pkg. ($340-$423). Power lock group ($207-$259). Power equipment group ($291-$575). Convenience group ($224-$640). Comfort/Convenience: Air bag restraint system ($815). Air cond. ($743). Rear defroster, electric ($145). Fingertip speed control ($176). Power windows ($207-$282). Six-way power driver's seat ($234). Tinted glass ($113); windshield ($48). Tilt steering ($115). Sport instrument cluster ($87). Dual electric remote mirrors ($111). Entertainment: AM/FM stereo radio ($109) w/cassette player ($148-$256). Electronic-tuning AM/FM stereo w/cassette ($171-$279) exc. w/Sport GL pkg. ($23). Premium sound ($138). Radio delete ($39-$295 credit). Exterior: Clearcoat metallic paint ($91). Lower body accent paint ($78). Decklid luggage rack ($100). Interior: Console ($116). Front center armrest ($55). Vinyl seat trim ($35). Leather seat trim ($300). Wheels/Tires: Styled wheels ($178). P185/70R14 WSW ($72).

TAURUS CONVENIENCE/APPEARANCE OPTIONS: Option Packages: Exterior accent group ($49-$99). Power lock group ($180-$221). Light group ($48-$51). Comfort/Convenience: Air cond. ($762). Electronic climate control air cond.: GL ($945); LX ($183). Rear defroster ($145). Insta-clear windshield ($250); N/A on MT5. Fingertip speed control ($176). Illuminated entry ($82). Keyless entry ($202). Power windows ($282). Six-way power driver's seat ($237); dual ($473). Remote fuel door release: MT5/GL ($37). Tinted glass: L ($115); windshield only LPO ($48). Leather-wrapped steering wheel ($59). Tilt steering ($115). Electronic instrument cluster ($305); N/A on MT5. Autolamp on/off delay ($73). Diagnostic warning lights ($89). Auto. parking brake release: L/GL ($12). Digital clock: L ($78). Interval wipers: L ($50). Rear wiper/washer: wag ($124). Lighting and Mirrors: Cornering lamps ($68). Dual electric remote mirrors: L ($59-$96). Dual lighted visor vanity mirrors ($104-$116). Entertainment: Electronic-tuning AM/FM stereo radio: L/MT5 ($157). Electronic-tuning AM/FM stereo w/cassette/Dolby ($127-$284). Power antenna ($71). Premium sound system ($168). Radio delete: L ($39 credit); others ($196 credit). Exterior: Power moonroof ($701). Clearcoat paint ($183). Bodyside/decklid paint stripe ($57). Rocker panel moldings: L ($55). Luggage rack delete: L wag LPO ($105 credit). Interior: Bucket seats (NC). Split bench seating: L ($276). Vinyl seat trim ($39). Leather seat trim: LX sed ($415). Rear-facing third seat: wag ($155). Reclining passenger seat ($45). Load floor extension: wag ($66). Cargo area cover: wag ($66). Carpeted floor mats ($43). Wheels/Tires: Luxury wheel covers ($65). Styled wheels, 14 in. ($113-$178). Cast aluminum wheels, 15 in. ($326-$390). P195/70R14 WSW ($72). P205/70R14 BSW ($38); WSW ($72-$110). P205/65R15 BSW ($46-$84); WSW ($124-$162). Conventional spare ($63).

LTD CONVENIENCE/APPEARANCE OPTIONS: Option Packages: Squire option ($282). Interior luxury group ($388). Power lock group ($218-$259). Light group ($38). Comfort/Convenience: Air cond. ($762). Rear defroster ($145). Fingertip speed control ($176). Autolamp on-off delay ($73). Power windows ($282). Six-way power driver's seat ($234). Tinted glass ($115). Tinted windshield ($48). Leather-wrapped steering wheel ($59). Tilt steering ($115). Digital clock ($78). Auto. parking brake release ($12). Interval wipers ($50). Lighting and Mirrors: Cornering lamps ($68). Right remote convex mirror ($61). Dual electric remote mirrors ($96). Lighted visor vanity mirrors ($57-$106). Entertainment: AM/FM stereo radio ($109); w/cassette player ($256). Premium sound system ($138). AM radio delete ($39 credit). Exterior: Full vinyl roof ($152). Clearcoat metallic paint ($183). Two-tone paint w/tape stripe ($117). Pivoting front vent windows ($79). Two-way liftgate: wag ($105). Rocker panel moldings ($40). Bumper guards, rear ($28). Bumper rub strips ($56). Luggage rack: wagon

($126). Lower bodyside protection ($41). Interior: Vinyl seat trim ($35). Flight or split bench seat (NC). Front floor mats, carpeted ($23). Wheels/Tires: Luxury wheel covers ($55). Wire wheel covers, locking ($212). Styled wheels ($178). Styled steel wheels w/trim rings ($54). P195/75R14 WSW ($72). P205/70R14 WSW ($134). Conventional spare ($63).

LTD CROWN VICTORIA CONVENIENCE/APPEARANCE OPTIONS: Option Packages: Convenience group ($109-$134). Power lock group ($143-$243). Light group ($48). Police pkg. ($291-$411). Comfort/Convenience: Air cond. ($762); w/auto-temp control ($828). Rear defroster, electric ($145). Fingertip speed control ($176). Illuminated entry system ($82). Power windows ($282). Power six-way driver's seat ($237); driver and passenger ($473). Tinted glass ($115); windshield only ($48). Autolamp on/off delay ($73). Leather-wrapped steering wheel ($59). Tilt steering wheel ($115). Tripminder computer ($215-$261). Quartz clock: S ($35). Digital clock ($61-$96). Interval wipers ($50). Lighting and Mirrors: Cornering lamps ($68). Remote right convex mirror ($46). Dual electric remote mirrors ($100). Entertainment: AM/FM stereo radio: S ($109); w/cassette tape player ($148-$256). Electronic-tuning AM/FM stereo radio w/cassette ($300) exc. S ($409). Premium sound system ($168). Radio delete: AM ($39 credit); AM/FM ($148 credit). Exterior: Brougham vinyl roof ($793). Two-tone paint/tape ($117). Dual accent bodyside stripes ($39). Pivoting front vent windows ($79). Rocker panel moldings ($18-$38). Vinyl-insert bodyside moldings ($61). Bumper rub strips ($59). Luggage rack: wagon ($110). Interior: Dual-facing rear seats: wagon ($167). Leather seat trim ($433). Reclining split bench seats ($144). All-vinyl seat trim ($35); Duraweave vinyl ($100). Carpeted front floor mats ($21); front/rear ($33). H.D. floor covering ($27). Wheels/Tires: Wire wheel covers, locking ($205). Cast aluminum wheels ($390). P205/75R15 puncture-sealant ($161). P215/70R15 WSW ($62). Conventional spare ($63).

THUNDERBIRD CONVENIENCE/APPEARANCE OPTIONS: Option Packages: Light group ($35). Power lock group ($220). Comfort/Convenience: Air cond. ($762); auto-temp ($924). Rear defroster ($145). Fingertip speed control ($176). Illuminated entry system ($82). Keyless entry ($198). Anti-theft system ($159). Tripminder computer ($215-$276). Autolamp on/off delay ($73). Tinted glass ($115); windshield only ($49). Power windows ($207). Six-way power driver's seat ($238); dual ($476). Dual power seat recliners ($189). Leather-wrapped steering wheel ($59). Tilt steering wheel ($115). Electronic instrument cluster ($270-$330). Diagnostic warning lights ($89). Digital clock ($61). Interval wipers ($50). Lighting and Mirrors: Cornering lamps ($68). Dual electric remote mirrors ($96). Lighted visor vanity mirrors, pair ($106). Entertainment: Power antenna ($71). Graphic equalizer ($218). Premium sound system ($168). AM/FM radio delete ($196 credit). Exterior: Power moonroof ($701). Metallic clearcoat paint ($183). Two-tone paint/tape ($163-$218). Dual accent paint stripes ($55). Pivoting front vent windows ($79). Wide bodyside moldings ($57). Interior: Articulated sport seats ($183). Leather seat trim ($415). Soft vinyl seat trim ($37). Front floor mats, carpeted ($22). Wheels/Tires: Wire wheel covers, locking ($212). Cast aluminum wheels ($343). Styled wheels ($178). P215/70R14 WSW ($62). Conventional spare ($63). Inflatable spare ($122).

HISTORY: Introduced: October 3, 1985, except Taurus, December 26, 1985, and EXP, mid-year. Model year production: 1,559,959 (incl. Mustangs). Total production for the U.S. market of 1,424,374 units (incl. Mustangs) included 845,607 four-cylinder, 380,402 sixes and 198,365 V-8s. That total included 23,658 turbo fours and 7,144 diesel engines. Calendar year production (U.S.): 1,221,956 (incl. Mustangs). Calendar year sales by U.S. dealers: 1,397,141 (incl. Mustangs). Model year sales by U.S. dealers: 1,332,097 (incl. Mustangs).

1986 Ford Taurus GL station wagon. (JG)

1986 Ford LTD Crown Victoria sedan. (JG)

HISTORY: Sales fell this model year, after three straight years of rises. Moreover, Ford's market share shrunk markedly (from 13.1 percent overall in 1985 to just 11.9 percent in '86). Ford's share when considering only domestic-built autos declined less sharply, from 17.2 percent down to 16.5 percent. Only Mustang showed a sales increase. Escort continued as America's best seller. The Escort/ EXP duo found 416,147 buyers this year. Tempo was the second best-selling Ford, for the third year in a row. Crown Vic hung on because of continuing popularity of full-size rear-drives, partly due to moderated gas prices. Throughout the year, low-interest financing was offered, at record-breaking rates. Ford offered a new three-year unlimited mileage powertrain warranty (with deductibles). Because of production delays, the new Taurus (and related Mercury Sable) weren't introduced until December 1985. The new aero mid-size sold well, however. V-6 engines for Taurus were in short supply, keeping production from reaching an even higher level. Taurus was the result of a $3 billion development program, and was named *Motor Trend* magazine's 'Car of the Year.' Even before production, it got a lot of publicity. Auto show attendees were even asked their opinions on whether Taurus should or should not have a conventional grille. (Those who preferred a solid panel eventually 'won'.)' Ford claimed that a 1985 owner survey showed that "Ford makes the best-built American cars," based on reports of problems people had with 1981-84 models. Ford's main slogan at this time: 'Quality is Job 1.'

1987 FORD

Once again, Ford's subcompact Escort ranked number one in sales for the model year. Also for the 1987 model year, Taurus became the second best-selling passenger car in the country. As soon as the mid-size Taurus began its rise to become a hot seller, Ford's LTD left the lineup for good. Sales of the full-size, rear-drive LTD Crown Victoria slid this year, but its place in the lineup was assured regardless. Tempo added a four-wheel-drive option this year, while Thunderbird took on some new sheet metal and glass (but kept its same overall profile).

ESCORT — FOUR — Fuel injection replaced the carburetor on Escort's base 1.9-liter four-cylinder engine. As before, Escort GT was powered by a high-output version of the four, with multi-point injection. Some shuffling of model designations and the deletion of the LX series meant this year's offering consisted of Pony, GL and GT models. Automatic motorized front seat belts were introduced during the model year. Joining the option list: a fold-down center armrest and split fold-down rear seat.

EXP — FOUR — Ford's tiny two-seater came in two forms: Luxury Coupe with the base 1.9-liter four-cylinder engine, or Sport Coupe with the high-output powerplant. EXP enjoyed a restyling for reintroduction as a 1986.5 model, after a brief departure from the lineup. Rather than a distinct model, EXP was now considered part of the Escort series.

1987 Ford Escort GL hatchback sedan. (FMC)

1987 Ford Tempo All-Wheel-Drive sedan. (FMC)

TEMPO — FOUR — Front-drive only through its first three seasons, the compact Tempo added a part-time four-wheel-drive option this year. "Shift-on-the-fly" capability allowed engagement of 4WD while in motion, simply by touching a dashboard switch. Models with that option, which was intended for use only on slippery roads, got an "All Wheel Drive" nameplate. 4WD models also included the high-output version of the 2.3-liter four-cylinder engine. Power steering was now standard on all Tempos, while the driver's airbag became a regular production option (RPO) instead of a limited-production item. A revised three-speed automatic transmission contained a new fluid-linked converter, eliminating the need for a lockup torque converter.

TAURUS — FOUR/V-6 — Sales of the aero-styled front-drive Taurus began to take off soon after its mid-1986 debut, so little change was needed for the 1987 model year. Base powerplant for the L and MT5 series, and the GL sedan, was a 2.5-liter four, with a 3.0-liter V-6 optional in all except the MT5. Other models had the V-6 as standard, with four-speed overdrive automatic transmission. The MT5 came with a standard five-speed gearbox: L/GL with a three-speed automatic. Mercury's Sables, with similar styling, were all V-6 powered this year.

LTD CROWN VICTORIA — V-8 — Only a few equipment changes arrived with the '87 full-size Fords. Air conditioning, tinted glass and a digital clock were now standard equipment. Two- and four-door sedans and a four-door station wagon, in base and LX trim levels, were all powered by a 5.0-liter V-8 with four-speed overdrive automatic transmission.

THUNDERBIRD — FOUR/V-6/V-8 — Even though the personal-luxury coupe's profile didn't undergo a dramatic alteration, the sheetmetal was all new this year. So were aero-style headlamps and flush-fitting side glass, as well as full-width tail lamps. A new sport model with 5.0-liter V-8 joined the lineup, and the former Elan was now called LX. A 232 cid (3.8-liter) V-6 hooked to four-speed overdrive automatic was the standard powertrain for base and LX models, with V-8 optional. The former three-speed automatic was gone. T-Bird's Turbo Coupe got a boost under the hood from the intercooled 2.3-liter four, which was formerly seen in the Mustang SVO. The Turbo also had Automatic Ride Control, functional hood scoops, 16-inch unidirectional tires, a standard five-speed manual gearbox, and four-wheel disc brakes with anti-lock system.

1987 Ford Taurus LX sedan. (FMC)

1987 Ford LTD Crown Victoria LX sedan. (FMC)

1987 Ford Thunderbird Turbo Coupe. (FMC)

I.D. DATA: Ford's 17-symbol Vehicle Identification Number (VIN) was stamped on a metal tab fastened to the instrument panel, visible through the windshield. The first three symbols ('1FA') indicate manufacturer, make and vehicle type. The fourth symbol ('B') denotes restraint system. Next comes a letter 'P', followed by two digits that indicate Model Number, as shown in left column of tables below. (Example: '20'-Escort Pony two-door hatchback). Symbol eight indicates engine type. Next is a check digit. Symbol ten indicates model year ('H' 1987). Symbol eleven is assembly plant. The final six digits make up the sequence number, starting with 100001.

ESCORT (FOUR)

Model No.	Body/ Style No.	Body Type & Seating	Factory Price	Shipping Weight	Prod. Total
20	61D	2-dr. Pony Hatch-4P	6436	2180	Note 1
21	61D	2-dr. GL Hatch-4P	6801	2187	Note 1
25	58D	4-dr. GL Hatch-4P	7022	2222	Note 1
28	74D	4-dr. GL Sta Wag-4P	7312	2274	Note 1
23	61D	2-dr. GT Hatch-4P	8724	2516	Note 1

NOTE 1: For the model year, a total of 206,729 two-door hatchbacks. 102,187 four-door hatchback sedans, and 65,849 station wagons were built.

EXP (FOUR)

18	N/A	2-dr. Spt Cpe-2P	8831	2388	Note 2
17	N/A	2-dr. Luxury Cpe-2P	7622	2291	Note 2

NOTE 2: Total EXP production was 25,888.

TEMPO (FOUR)

31	66D	2-dr. GL Sed-5P	8043	2462	Note 3
36	54D	4-dr. GL Sed-5P	8198	2515	Note 3
32	66D	2-dr. LX Sed-5P	9238	2562	Note 3
37	54D	4-dr. LX Sed-5P	9444	2617	Note 3
33	66D	2-dr. Spt GL Sed-5P	8888	2667	Note 3
38	54D	4-dr. Spt GL Sed-5P	9043	2720	Note 3
34	66D	2-dr. AWD Sed-5P	9984	2667	Note 3
39	54D	4-dr. AWD Sed-5P	10138	2720	Note 3

NOTE 3: Total Tempo production came to 70,164 two-doors and 212,468 four-doors.

TAURUS (FOUR/V-6)

50	54D	4-dr. L Sedan-6P	10491/11163	----/2982	Note 4
55	74D	4-dr. L Sta Wag-6P	-----/11722	----/3186	Note 4
51	54D	4-dr. MT5 Sed-6P	11966/-----	2886/----	Note 4
56	74D	4-dr. MT5 Wag-6P	12534/-----	3083/----	Note 4
52	54D	4-dr. GL Sedan-6P	11498/12170	----/3045	Note 4
57	74D	4-dr. GL Wag-6P	-----/12688	----/3242	Note 4
53	54D	4-dr. LX Sedan-6P	-----/14613	----/3113	Note 4
58	74D	4-dr. LX Wag-6P	-----/15213	----/3309	Note 4

NOTE 4: Total Taurus production came to 278,562 sedans and 96,201 station wagons.

LTD CROWN VICTORIA (V-8)

70	66K	2-dr. Sed-6P	14727	3724	5,527
73	54K	4-dr. Sed-6P	14355	3741	105,789
78	74K	4-dr. Ctry Sqr-6P	14507	3920	17,562
76	74K	4-dr. Sta Wag-6P	14235	3920	Note 5
72	54K	4-dr. 'S' Sed-6P	13860	3708	Note 5
75	74K	4-dr. 'S' Sta Wag-6P	14228	3894	Note 5

LTD CROWN VICTORIA LX (V-8)

71	66K	2-dr. Sed-6P	15421	3735	Note 5
74	54K	4-dr. Sed-6P	15454	3788	Note 5
77	74K	4-dr. Sta Wag-6P	15450	4000	Note 5
79	74K	4-dr. Ctry Sqr-6P	15723	4000	Note 5

NOTE 5: Production of 'S' and LX models and basic station wagon is included in basic sedan and Country Squire totals above.

1987 Ford LTD Country Squire station wagon. (FMC)

THUNDERBIRD (V-6/V-8)

60	66D	2-dr. HT Cpe-5P	12972/13611	3133/3176	Note 6
61	66D	2-dr. Spt Cpe-5P	-----/15079	----/3346	Note 6
62	66D	2-dr. LX Cpe-5P	15383/16022	3176/3315	Note 6

THUNDERBIRD TURBO COUPE (FOUR)

64	66D	2-dr. HT Cpe-5P	16805	3380	Note 6

NOTE 6: Total production, 128,135 Thunderbirds.

FACTORY PRICE AND WEIGHT NOTE: Taurus prices and weights to left of slash are for four-cylinder, to right for V-6 engine. Thunderbird prices and weights to left of slash are for V-6, to right for V-8 engine.

ENGINE [Base Four (Escort)]: Inline. Overhead cam. Four-cylinder. Cast-iron block and aluminum head. Displacement: 113 cid (1.9 liters). Bore & stroke: 3.23 x 3.46 in. Compression ratio: 9.0:1. Brake horsepower: 90 at 4600 rpm. Torque: 106 lbs.-ft. at 3400 rpm. Five main bearings. Hydraulic valve lifters. Throttle-body fuel injection.

ENGINE [Base Four (Escort GT, EXP Spt coupe)]: High-output, MFI version of 1.9-liter four above - Horsepower: 115 at 5200 rpm. Torque: 120 lbs.-ft. at 4400 rpm.

ENGINE [Diesel Four (Escort)]: Inline. Overhead cam. Four-cylinder. Cast-iron block and aluminum head. Displacement: 121 cid (2.0 liters). Bore & stroke: 3.39 x 3.39 in. Compression ratio: 22.7:1. Brake horsepower: 58 at 3600 rpm. Torque: 84 lbs.-ft. at 3000 rpm. Five main bearings. Solid valve lifters. Fuel injection.

ENGINE [Base Four (Tempo)]: Inline. Overhead valve. Four-cylinder. Cast-iron block and head. Displacement: 140 cid (2.3 liters). Bore & stroke: 3.70 x 3.30 in. Compression ratio: 9.0:1. Brake horsepower: 86 at 3800 rpm. Torque: 120 lbs.-ft. at 3200 rpm. Five main bearings. Hydraulic valve lifters. Throttle-body fuel injection. High Swirl Combustion (HSC) design.

ENGINE [Base Four (Tempo 4WD or Sport)]: High-output version of HSC four above - Horsepower: 94 at 4000 rpm. Torque: 126 lbs.-ft. at 3200 rpm.

ENGINE [Base Four (Thunderbird Turbo Coupe)]: Inline. Overhead cam. Four-cylinder. Cast-iron block and head. Displacement: 140 cid (2.3 liters). Bore & stroke: 3.78 x 3.13 in. Compression ratio: 8.0:1. Brake horsepower: 190 at 4600 rpm. (150 at 4400 with automatic). Torque: 240 lbs.-ft. at 3400 rpm. (200 at 3000 with automatic). Five main bearings. Hydraulic valve lifters. Port fuel injection.

ENGINE [Base Four (Taurus)]: Inline. Overhead valve. Four-cylinder. Cast-iron block and head. Displacement: 153 cid (2.5 liters). Bore & stroke: 3.70 x 3.60 in. Compression ratio: 9.0:1. Brake horsepower: 90 at 4400 rpm. Torque: 140 lbs.-ft. at 2800 rpm. Five main bearings. Hydraulic valve lifters. Throttle-body fuel injection.

ENGINE [Base V-6 (Taurus LX): Optional (Taurus)]: 60-degree, overhead valve V-6. Cast-iron block and head. Displacement: 182 cid (3.0 liters). Bore & stroke: 3.50 x 3.10 in. Compression ratio: 9.3:1. Brake horsepower: 140 at 4800 rpm. Torque: 160 lbs.-ft. at 3000 rpm. Four main bearings. Hydraulic valve lifters. Multi-port fuel injection.

1987 Ford Escort GL station wagon. (FMC)

1987 Ford Taurus LX station wagon. (FMC)

ENGINE [Base V-6 (Thunderbird)]: 90-degree, overhead valve V-6. Cast-iron block and aluminum head. Displacement: 232 cid (3.8 liters). Bore & stroke: 3.80 x 3.40 in. Compression ratio: 8.7:1. Brake horsepower: 120 at 3600 rpm. Torque: 205 lbs.-ft. at 1600 rpm. Four main bearings. Hydraulic valve lifters. Throttle-body fuel injection.

ENGINE [Base V-8 (LTD Crown Victoria); Optional (Thunderbird)]: 90-degree, overhead valve V-8. Cast-iron block and head. Displacement: 302 cid (5.0 liters). Bore & stroke: 4.00 x 3.00 in. Compression ratio: 8.9:1. Brake horsepower: 150 at 3200 rpm. Torque: 270 lbs.-ft. at 2000 rpm. Five main bearings. Hydraulic valve lifters. Sequential (port) fuel injection.

CHASSIS DATA: Wheelbase: (Escort/EXP) 94.2 in.; (Tempo) 99.9 in.; (Taurus) 106.0 in.: (Crown Vic) 114.3 in.; (T-Bird) 104.2 in. Overall Length: (Escort) 166.9 in.; (Escort wagon) 168.0 in.; (EXP) 168.4 in.; (Tempo) 176.5 in.; (Taurus) 188.4 in.; (Taurus wag) 191.9 in.; (Crown Vic) 211.0 in.; (Crown Vic wag) 215.0 in.; (T-Bird) 202.1 in. Height: (Escort) 53.3-53.5 in.; (EXP) 50.9 in.; (Tempo) 52.7 in.; (Taurus) 54.3 in.; (Taurus wag) 55.1 in.; (Crown Vic) 55.3 in.; (Crown Vic wag) 57.1 in.; (T-Bird) 53.4 in. Width: (Escort/ EXP) 65.9 in.; (Tempo) 68.3 in.; (Taurus) 70.6 in.; (Crown Vic) 77.5 in.; (Crown Vic wag) 79.3 in.; (T-Bird) 71.1 in. Front Tread: (Escort/EXP) 54.7 in.; (Tempo) 54.9 in.; (Taurus) 61.5 in.; (Crown Vic) 62.2 in.; (T-Bird) 58.1 in. Rear Tread: (Escort/EXP) 56.0 in.; (Tempo) 57.6 in.; (Taurus) 60.5 in.; (Taurus wag) 59.9 in.; (Crown Vic) 62.0 in.; (T-Bird) 58.5 in. Standard Tires: (Escort Pony) P165/80R13; (Escort GL 4dr/wag) P165/80R13; (Escort GT) P195/60HR15; (EXP) P185/70R14; (Tempo) P185/70R14; (Taurus) P195/70R14; (Taurus GL/LX) P205/70R14; (Crown Vic) P205/75R15; (T-Bird) P215/70R14; (T-Bird Spt) P215/70HR14; (T-Bird Turbo Cpe) P225/60VR16 Goodyear Eagle GT "Gatorback."

TECHNICAL: Transmission: Four-speed manual transaxle standard on Escort. Five-speed standard on Escort GT, EXP, Tempo, Taurus MT5 and Thunderbird Turbo. Three-speed automatic standard on Taurus L/GL. Four-speed overdrive automatic standard on Taurus LX/Crown Vic/T-Bird. Drive Axle: (Escort/EXP/Tempo/Taurus) front; (others) rear. Steering: (Crown Vic) recirculating ball; (others) rack/pinion. Front Suspension: (Escort/EXP/Tempo) MacPherson struts with lower control arms, coil springs and stabilizer bar; (Taurus) MacPherson struts with control arms, coil springs and stabilizer bar; (T-Bird) modified MacPherson struts with lower control arms, coil springs and anti-sway bar; (Crown Vic) upper/lower control arms w/coil springs and stabilizer bar. Rear Suspension: (Escort/EXP) trailing arms w/modified MacPherson struts and coil springs on lower control arms; (Tempo) independent trailing four-link with MacPherson struts; (Taurus sedan) MacPherson struts w/parallel suspension arms and coil springs; (Taurus wag) upper/lower control arms, coil springs and stabilizer bar; (Crown Vic/T-Bird) rigid axle w/four links and coil springs. Brakes: Front disc, rear drum (power assisted) except (Thunderbird Turbo Coupe) four-wheel discs with anti-lock. Body construction: (Crown Vic) separate body and frame; (others) unibody. Fuel tank: (Escort/EXP) 13.0 gal.; (Tempo) 15.4 gal.; (Tempo 4WD) 13.7 gal.; (Taurus) 16.0 gal.; (Crown Vic) 18.0 gal.; (T-Bird) 22.1 gal.

DRIVETRAIN OPTIONS: Engines: Diesel 2.0-liter four: Escort (NC). 3.0-liter V-6: Taurus L/GL ($672). 5.0-liter V-8: Thunderbird ($639). Transmission/Differential: Five-speed manual trans.: Escort ($76). Automatic transaxle: Escort GL ($490); EXP ($415); Tempo ($482). Auto. transmission: T-Bird Turbo Cpe ($515). Traction-Lok differential: Crown Vic ($100). Steering/Suspension: Power steering: Escort/EXP ($235). H.D./handling susp.: Taurus/Crown Vic ($26). Auto. load leveling: Crown Vic ($200). Trailer towing pkg.: Crown Vic ($387-$399).

ESCORT/EXP CONVENIENCE/APPEARANCE OPTIONS: Premium Equipment Group. Bumper guards and rub strips, overhead console with digital clock, tachometer, trip odometer and coolant temperature gauge, dual power mirrors, power steering, GL w/gas engine ($496). GL w/diesel engine ($409). Front & rear bumper guards ($56). Bumper rub strips ($48). Overhead console w/clock ($82). Tachometer, trip odometer & coolant temp gauge ($87). Dual power

mirrors ($88). Power steering ($235). Climate Control Group; Air conditioning, heavy-duty battery, rear defogger, tinted glass, intermittent wipers; GL w/gas engine, EXP Luxury Coupe ($920). GL w/diesel, GT or EXP Sport Coupe ($893). Air conditioning ($688). Heavy-duty battery ($27). Rear defogger ($145). Tinted glass ($105). Intermittent wipers ($55). Luxury Group; Light/Security Group, front center armrest, cruise control, split folding rear seatback, tilt steering column; GL ($395). Light/Security Group, GL ($91). GT ($67). Front center armrest, Escort ($55). Cruise control ($176). Split folding rear seatback, Escort ($49). Tilt steering column ($124). Convenience Group: Cargo area cover, dual power mirrors, dual visor mirrors, (lighted right), cruise control, power steering, tilt steering column, EXP Luxury Coupe ($473). EXP Sport Coupe ($309). Cargo area cover, EXP ($59). Dual power mirrors, EXP ($88). Visor mirrors (lighted right), EXP ($50). Sun and Sound Group. Overhead console w/graphic systems monitor, removable sunroof, AM/FM ST w/cassette, premium Sound System, EXP Luxury Coupe ($597). EXP Sport Coupe ($566). Console w/graphic systems monitor, EXP ($56). Removable sunroof, EXP ($355). AM/FM ST w/cassette, EXP ($148). Premium Sound System ($138). Luggage rack ($110). Clearcoat paint, GL & EXP ($91). AM radio ($39). AM/FM Stereo, Pony ($159). GL ($120). AM/FM Stereo w/cassette, AM/FM stereo, Pony ($306). GL ($267). GT, EXP ($148). Cast aluminum wheels ($293). Styled road wheels ($195). Rear wiper/washer ($126).

TEMPO CONVENIENCE/APPEARANCE OPTIONS: Select GL Pkg. Tinted glass, dual power mirrors w/AM/FM Stereo ED ($191). W/o radio ($124). Tinted glass ($120). Dual power mirrors ($111). AM/FM Stereo ET radio ($93). Power Equipment Group. Power Lock Group (includes remote fuel filler and trunk releases), power driver's seat, power windows: 2-door GL, Sport or All Wheel Drive ($560). 4-door GL, Sport or All Wheel Drive ($635). LX 2-door ($323). LX 4-door ($347). Power Lock Group, 2-doors ($237). 4-doors ($288). Power driver's seat ($251). Power windows, 2-doors ($223). 4-doors ($296). Convenience Group: Front center armrest, Premium Sound System, AM/FM ST ET cassette, speed control, tilt steering column: GL ($643). Select GL ($565). Sport GL ($418). LX ($371). All Wheel Drive ($510). Front center armrest ($55). Premium Sound System ($138). AM/FM Stereo ET cassette, GL ($250). LX or Select GL ($157). Speed control ($176). Tilt steering column ($124). Lower accent paint treatment ($78). Air bag, GL ($815). LX ($751). Air conditioning ($773). Console ($116). Rear defogger ($145). Sport instrument cluster ($87). Decklid luggage rack ($115). AM/FM Stereo ($93). AM/FM Stereo ET cassette, GL ($250). LX, Select GL or All Wheel Drive ($157). AM delete, GL ($65 credit). AM/FM ST delete LX or All-Wheel Drive ($157 credit). Sport GL or w/Convenience Group ($315 credit). Styled road wheels ($178). Calif. emission pkg ($99). Clearcoat metallic paint ($91). All vinyl seat trim ($35).

TAURUS CONVENIENCE/APPEARANCE OPTIONS: Exterior accent group, MT5 sedan ($91). MT5 wagon ($49). Automatic air conditioning, LX ($183). GL ($945). Manual air conditioning ($788). Autolamp system ($73). Heavy-duty battery ($27). Cargo area cover, wagons ($66). Digital clock ($78). Cornering lamps ($68). Rear defogger ($145). Engine block heater ($18). Remote fuel door & decklid release ($91), w/remote liftgate release, wagons ($41). Extended range fuel tank ($46). Tinted glass ($120). Illuminated entry system ($82). Electronic instrument cluster ($351). Keyless entry system ($202). Light group, L, GL & MT5 sedans ($48). L, GL & MT5 wagons ($52). Diagnostic alert lights ($89). Load floor extension, wagons ($66). Power door locks ($195). Dual power mirrors, L sedan ($96). L wagon ($59). Dual illuminated visor mirrors, L ($116). GL & MT5 ($104). Rocker panel moldings ($55). Power moonroof ($741). Clearcoat paint ($183). Automatic parking brake release ($12). AM/FM Stereo ET radio ($141). AM/FM Stereo w/cassette, L ($268). GL, MT5 & LX ($137). Premium sound system ($168). Power antenna ($76). AM radio delete, L ($65 credit). AM/FM stereo delete GL, MT5 & LX ($206 credit). Rear-facing third seat, wagons ($155). Reclining passenger seat ($45). Power driver's seat ($251). Dual power seats, LX ($502). Others ($251). Speed control ($176). Tilt steering column ($124). Leather-wrapped steering wheel ($59). Paint stripe ($57). Sliding vent windows ($79). Rear wiper/washer, wagons ($126). Finned wheel covers, L, GL & MT5 ($65). Locking spoked wheel covers, L, GL & MT5 ($205). LX ($140). Aluminum wheels, L, GL & MT5 ($390). LX ($326). Styled road wheels, L, GL & MT5 ($178). LX ($113). Power windows ($296). Insta-Clear windshield ($250). Intermittent wipers ($55). Calif. emissions pkg ($99). Split bench seats ($276). Leather seat trim ($415). Vinyl seat trim ($39).

LTD CROWN VICTORIA CONVENIENCE/APPEARANCE OPTIONS: Conventional spare tire ($73). Automatic A/C & rear defogger ($211). Autolamp system ($73). Heavy-duty battery ($27). Bumper rub strips ($59). Convenience group: Remote decklid or tailgate release, intermittent wipers, trip odometer, low fuel & oil warning lights; exc. LX ($135), w/Power Lock Group ($85). Cornering lamps ($68). Rear defogger ($145). Engine block heater ($18). Illuminated entry system ($82). Light group ($48). Power lock group: Power door locks, remote fuel door release, 2-doors ($207). 4-doors & wagons ($257). Deluxe luggage rack ($115). Right remote mirror ($46). Vinyl insert bodyside moldings ($66). Two-tone paint/tape treatment ($117). AM/FM Stereo w/cassette ($137). Power antenna ($76). AM/FM radio delete ($206 credit). Premium Sound System ($168). Power driver's seat ($251). Dual power seats ($502). Dual facing rear seats, wagon ($173). Cruise control ($176). Leather-wrapped steering wheel ($59). Tilt steering column ($124). Tripminder computer ($215). Pivoting front vent windows ($79). Locking wire wheel covers ($212). Cast aluminum wheels ($390). Power windows & mirrors ($393). Intermittent wipers ($55). Brougham half vinyl roof ($665). Split bench seat ($139). All-vinyl seat trim ($34). Duraweave vinyl seat trim ($96). Leather seat trim ($418). P215/70R15 tires ($72).

THUNDERBIRD CONVENIENCE/APPEARANCE OPTIONS: Heavy-duty battery ($27). Electronic Equipment Group: Keyless entry system, automatic climate control, base ($634). Sport, Turbo Coupe ($365). LX ($577). Luxury Light/Convenience Grp: Autolamp system, cornering lamps, lighted visor mirrors, illuminated entry system, Light group, base ($461). Base w/Electronic Equipment ($379). Sport & Turbo ($426). Sport & Turbo w/Electronic Equipment ($344). LX ($244). Dual power seats, base, LX & Sport ($302). LX w/articulated seats, Turbo ($251). Power antenna ($76). Digital clock, base ($61). Rear defogger ($145). Engine block heater ($18). Power Lock Grp: Power door locks, remote fuel filler & trunk releases ($249). Dual power mirrors ($96). Power moonroof, base, Sport or Turbo ($841). LX or w/Luxury/Light Group ($741). AM/FM Stereo delete ($206 credit). AM/FM Stereo ET cassette ($137). Graphic Equalizer ($218). Premium Sound System ($168). Power driver's seat ($251). Speed control ($176). Leather-wrapped steering wheel ($59). Tilt steering column ($124). Locking wire wheel covers. LX ($90). Cast aluminum wheels, LX ($221). Base ($343). Styled road wheels ($122). Power windows ($222). Intermittent wipers ($55). Calif. emissions pkg ($99). Two-tone paint, base ($218). LX ($163). Clearcoat paint ($183). Articulated sport seats (std. Turbo) ($183). Vinyl trim ($37). Leather trim ($415).

HISTORY: Introduced: October 2, 1986. Model year production: 1,474,116 (total), incl. Mustangs. Calendar year production (U.S.): 1,317,787 (incl. Mustangs). Calendar year sales by U.S. dealers: 1,389,886 (incl. Mustangs). Model year sales by U.S. dealers: 1,422,489 (incl. Mustangs).

1988 FORD

Escort and EXP started off the year in their former form, but were replaced by a modestly modified Second Series in the spring. For the first time in nearly a decade, the full-size LTD Crown Victoria got a notable restyling. Tempo earned a more modest restyle, while Taurus added some performance with a new engine choice. During 1987, Taurus had become Ford's top seller, displacing the Escort. In addition to the domestic models, Ford now offered a Korean-built Festiva subcompact, designed by Mazda.

ESCORT — FOUR — For the first half of the model year, Escort continued with little change except that an automatic transmission became optional for the base Pony. The diesel engine option was dropped during the 1987 model year. Also during the model year, motorized automatic front shoulder belts were made standard. A facelifted Second Series Escort arrived at mid-year. Changes at that time included new fenders, tail lamps, bodyside moldings, quarter panels and plastic bumpers, plus a switch to 14-inch tires. The upgraded GT got a new grille and rear spoiler.

EXP — FOUR — Only one model remained for the first half of the model year, the Luxury Coupe, as the Sport Coupe dropped out. A Second Series EXP arrived at mid-year, but this would be the final season for the subcompact two-seater.

1988-1/2 Ford Escort GT hatchback coupe. (FMC)

1988 Ford Escort GL three-door hatchback. (PH)

1988 Ford Tempo sedan (with all-wheel-drive). (PH)

1988 Ford Tempo GLS sedan. (PH)

TEMPO — FOUR — Restyling of Ford's compact sedans included a new two-slot grille aero-styled headlamps (integrated with parking lamps and side marker lenses), wraparound tail lamps, and new bumpers. The four-door also got mostly new body panels and new window designs, while the two-door changed a bit less. A new analog instrument panel contained a standard temperature gauge. Motorized front shoulder belts automatically pivoted around the seats. Under the hood, multi-point fuel injection was now used on both the standard and high-output 2.3-liter four-cylinder engines. The standard four got a boost of 12 horsepower. All Wheel Drive was now available only in the four-door model. The high-output engine was standard in the GLS series and the AWD this year.

1988 Ford Taurus LX station wagon. (PH)

1988 Ford Taurus LX sedan. (PH)

TAURUS — FOUR/V-6 — Performance fans had a new engine to choose from under Taurus hoods this year: a 3.8-liter V-6. Horsepower was the same as that of the 3.0-liter V-6, but the bigger engine developed 55 more pound-feet of torque. All models except the base L and MT5 sedans could get the 3.8-liter powerplant, which came only with four-speed overdrive automatic transmission. The MT5 wagon was dropped this year, so only the MT5 sedan came with the four-cylinder engine and five-speed manual transmission. L/GL sedans also had the four as standard, but with three-speed automatic. All station wagons (and the LX sedans) had a standard 3.0-liter V-6 with four-speed automatic. Taurus L models had some equipment additions, including a dual reclining split front bench seat, dual power mirrors, trip odometer, electronically-tuned stereo radio, and tinted glass.

LTD CROWN VICTORIA — V-8 — No two-doors remained in the full-size Ford lineup for 1988. The four-door sedans and wagons got a front and rear restyle (including new grille and hood, bumpers with rub strips, and trunk lid). Sedans also gained wraparound tail lamps. Whitewall P215/70R15 tires became standard, along with intermittent wipers, a trip odometer, low fuel and oil-level warning lights, an automatic headlamp on/off system, and front-door map pockets. Base models added a remote-control mirror on the passenger side. Joining the options was the Insta-Clear heated windshield. Both base and LX models were powered by a 150-horsepower, 5.0-liter V-8 engine with four-speed overdrive automatic.

THUNDERBIRD — FOUR/V-6/V-8 — Multi-point fuel injection replaced the former single-point system in Thunderbird's base V-6 engine this year, boosting horsepower by 20. Inside that engine was a new balance shaft to produce smoother running. Dual exhausts were now standard with the 5.0-liter V-8, which was standard on the Sport model and optional on the base/LX editions. As before, the Turbo Coupe carried a turbocharged 2.3-liter four. Also standard on the Turbo: a five-speed gearbox, anti-lock braking, electronic ride control and 16-inch tires. Sport models switched from a standard electronic instrument cluster to analog gauges, and came with articulated sport seats.

1988 Ford LTD Crown Victoria sedan. (PH)

1988 Ford Thunderbird coupe. (FMC)

1988-1/2 Ford Escort LX station wagon. (PH)

I.D. DATA: Ford's 17-symbol Vehicle Identification Number (VIN) was stamped on a metal tab fastened to the instrument panel, visible through the windshield. The first three symbols ('1FA') indicate manufacturer, make and vehicle type. The fourth symbol denotes restraint system. Next comes a letter 'P', followed by two digits that indicate Model Number, as shown in left column of tables below. (Example: '20' - Escort Pony two-door hatchback). Symbol eight indicates engine type. Next is a check digit. Symbol ten indicates model year ('J' 1988). Symbol eleven is assembly plant. The final six digits make up the sequence number, starting with 100001.

ESCORT (FOUR)

Model No.	Body/ Style No.	Body Type & Seating	Factory Price	Shipping Weight	Prod. Total
20	61D	2-dr. Pony Hatch-4P	6632	2180	Note 1
21	61D	2-dr. GL Hatch-4P	6949	2187	Note 1
25	58D	4-dr. GL Hatch-4P	7355	2222	Note 1
28	74D	4-dr. GL Sta Wag-4P	7938	2274	Note 1
23	61D	2-dr. GT Hatch-4P	9055	2516	Note 1
90	61D	2-dr. Pony Hatch-4P	6747	N/A	Note 1
91	61D	2-dr. LX Hatch-4P	7127	2258	Note 1
95	58D	4-dr. LX Hatch-4P	7457	2295	Note 1
98	74D	4-dr. LX Sta Wag-4P	8058	2307	Note 1
93	61D	2-dr. GT Hatch-4P	9093	N/A	Note 1

EXP (FOUR)

17	N/A	2-dr. Luxury Cpe-2P	8073	2291	Note 1

EXP SECOND SERIES (FOUR)

88	N/A	2-dr. Luxury Cpe-2P	8201	2359	Note 1

NOTE 1: Total production of both series, including EXP, was 422,035 (251,911 two-door, 113,470 four-door and 56,654 station wagons).

TEMPO (FOUR)

31	66D	2-dr. GL Sed-5P	8658	2536	Note 2
36	54D	4-dr. GL Sed-5P	8808	2585	Note 2
37	54D	4-dr. LX Sed-5P	9737	2626	Note 2
39	54D	4-dr. AWD Sed-5P	10413	2799	Note 2
33	66D	2-dr. GLS Sed-5P	9249	2552	Note 2
38	54D	4-dr. GLS Sed-5P	9400	2601	Note 2

NOTE 2: Total Tempo production came to 313,262 (49,930 two-door and 263,332 four-door.)

TAURUS (FOUR/V-6)

50	54D	4-dr. L Sedan-6P	11699/12731	N/A/3005	Note 3
55	74D	4-dr. L Sta Wag-6P	-----/12884	----/3182	Note 3
51	54D	4-dr. MT5 Sed-6P	12835/-----	2882/----	Note 3
52	54D	4-dr. GL Sedan-6P	12200/12872	----/3049	Note 3
57	74D	4-dr. GL Wag-6P	-----/13380	----/3215	Note 3
53	54D	4-dr. LX Sedan-6P	-----/15295	----/3119	Note 3
58	74D	4-dr. LX Wag-6P	-----/15905	----/3288	Note 3

NOTE 3: Total Production was 387,577 (294,576 sedans and 93,001 wagons.)

LTD CROWN VICTORIA (V-8)

73	54K	4-dr. Sedan-6P	15218	3779	Note 4
72	54K	4-dr. 'S' Sed-6P	14653	3742	Note 4
76	74K	4-dr. Sta Wag-6P	15180	3991	Note 4
78	74K	4-dr. Ctry Sqr-6P	15613	3998	Note 4

LTD CROWN VICTORIA LX (V-8)

74	54K	4-dr. Sedan-6P	16134	3820	Note 4
77	74K	4-dr. Sta Wag-8P	16210	3972	Note 4
79	74K	4-dr. Ctry Sqr-8P	16643	4070	Note 4

NOTE 4: Total production came to 110,249 sedans and 14,940 station wagons.

THUNDERBIRD (V-6/V-8)

60	66D	2-dr. HT Cpe-5P	13599/14320	3215/3345	Note 5
61	66D	2-dr. Spt Cpe-5P	-----/16030	----/3450	Note 5
62	66D	2-dr. LX Cpe-5P	15885/16606	3259/3389	Note 5

THUNDERBIRD TURBO COUPE (FOUR)

| 64 | 66D | 2-dr. HT Cpe-5P | 17250 | 3415 | Note 5 |

NOTE 5: Total production came to 147,243 Thunderbirds.

FACTORY PRICE AND WEIGHT NOTE: Taurus prices and weights to left of slash are for four-cylinder, to right for V-6 engine. Thunderbird prices and weights to left of slash are for V-6, to right for V-8 engine.

ENGINE [Base Four (Escort)]: Inline. Overhead cam. Four-cylinder. Cast-iron block and aluminum head. Displacement: 113 cid (1.9 liters). Bore & stroke: 3.23 x 3.46 in. Compression ratio: 9.0:1. Brake horsepower: 90 at 4600 rpm. Torque: 106 lbs.-ft. at 3400 rpm. Five main bearings. Hydraulic valve lifters. Throttle-body duel injection.

ENGINE [Base Four (Escort GT)]: High-output. MFI version of 1.9-liter four above except: Horsepower: 115 at 5200 rpm. Torque: 120 lbs.-ft. at 4400 rpm.

ENGINE [Base Four (Tempo)]: Inline. Overhead valve. Four-cylinder. Cast-iron block and head. Displacement: 140 cid (2.3 liter). Bore & stroke: 3.70 x 3.30 in. Compression ratio: 9.0:1. Brake horsepower: 98 at 4400 rpm. Torque: 124 lbs.-ft. at 2200 rpm. Five main bearings. Hydraulic valve lifters. Multi-point fuel injection. High Swirl Combustion (HSC) design.

ENGINE [Base Four (Tempo 4WD or Sport)]: High-output version of HSC four above except: Brake horsepower: 100 at 4400 rpm. Torque: 130 lbs.-ft. at 2600 rpm.

ENGINE [Base Four (Thunderbird Turbo Coupe)]: Inline. Overhead cam. Four-cylinder. Cast-iron block and head. Displacement: 140 cid (2.3 liters). Bore & stroke: 3.78 x 3.13 in. Compression ratio: 8.0:1. Brake horsepower: 190 at 4600 rpm. (150 at 4400 with automatic). Torque: 240 lbs.-ft. at 3400 rpm. (200 at 3000 with automatic). Five main bearings. Hydraulic valve lifters. Port fuel injection.

ENGINE [Base Four (Taurus)]: Inline. Overhead valve. Four-cylinder. Cast-iron block and head. Displacement: 153 cid (2.5 liters). Bore & stroke: 3.70 x 3.60 in. Compression ratio: 9.0:1. Brake horsepower: 90 at 4000 rpm. Torque: 130 lbs.-ft. at 2600 rpm. Five main bearings. Hydraulic valve lifters. Throttle-body fuel injection.

ENGINE [Base V-6 (Taurus LX/Wagons); Optional (Taurus L sedan)]: 60-degree, overhead valve V-6. Cast-iron block and head. Displacement: 182 cid (3.0 liters). Bore & stroke: 3.50 x 3.10 in. Compression ratio: 9.3:1. Brake horsepower: 140 at 4800 rpm. Torque: 160 lbs.-ft. at 3000 rpm. Four main bearings. Hydraulic valve lifters. Multi-port fuel injection.

ENGINE [Base V-6 (Thunderbird); Optional (Taurus)]: 90-degree, overhead valve V-6. Cast-iron block and aluminum head. Displacement: 232 cid (3.8 liters). Bore & stroke: 3.80 x 3.40 in. Compression ratio: 9.0:1. Brake horsepower: 140 at 3800 rpm. Torque: (Taurus) 215 lbs.-ft. at 2200 RPM; (T-bird) 215 lbs.-ft. at 2400 rpm. Four main bearings. Hydraulic valve lifters. Multi-point fuel injection.

ENGINE [Base V-8 (LTD Crown Victoria); Optional (Thunderbird)]: 90-degree, overhead valve V-8. Cast-iron block and head. Displacement: 302 cid (5.0 liters). Bore & stroke: 4.00 x 3.00 in. Compression ratio: 8.9:1. Brake horsepower: (Crown Vic) 150 at 3200 RPM; (T-bird) 155 at 3400 rpm. Torque: (Crown Vic) 270 lbs.-ft. at 2000 RPM; (T-bird) 265 lbs.-ft. at 2200 rpm. Five main bearings. Hydraulic valve lifters. Sequential (port) fuel injection.

CHASSIS DATA: Wheelbase: (Escort/EXP) 94.2 in.; (Tempo) 99.9 in.; (Taurus) 106.0 in.; (Crown Vic) 114.3 in.; (T-bird) 104.2 in. Overall Length: (Escort) 166.9 in.; (Escort wagon) 168.0 in.; (EXP) 168.4 in.; (Tempo) 176.5 in.; (Taurus) 188.4 in.; (Taurus wag) 191.9 in.; (Crown Vic) 211.0 in.; (Crown Vic wag) 216.0 in.; (T-bird) 202.1 in. Height: (Escort) 53.3-53.5 in.; (EXP) 50.9 in.; (Tempo) 52.7 in.; (Taurus) 54.3 in.; (Taurus wag) 55.1 in.; (Crown Vic) 55.5 in.; (Crown Vic wag) 57.0 in.; (T-bird) 53.4 in. Width: (Escort/EXP) 65.9 in.; (Tempo) 68.3 in.; (Taurus) 70.6 in.; (Crown Vic) 77.5 in.; (Crown Vic wag) 79.3 in.; (T-bird) 71.1 in. Front Tread: (Escort/EXP) 54.7 in.; (Tempo) 54.9 in.; (Taurus) 61.5 in.; (Crown Vic) 62.2 in.; (T-bird) 58.1 in. Rear Tread: (Escort/EXP) 56.0 in.; (Tempo) 57.6 in.; (Taurus) 60.5 in.; (Taurus wag) 59.9 in.; (Crown Vic) 62.0 in.; (T-bird) 58.5 in. Standard Tires: (Escort Pony) P175/80R13; (Escort GL 4-dr/wag) P165/80R13; (Second Series Escort) P175/70R14; (Escort GT) P195/60HR15; (EXP) P185/70R14; (Tempo) P185/70R14; (Taurus) P195/70R14; (Taurus LX) P205/70R14; (Crown Vic) P205/70R15; (T-Bird) P215/70R14; (T-bird Spt) P215/70HR14; (T-bird Turbo Cpe) P225/60VR16 Goodyear Eagle GT.

TECHNICAL: Transmission: Four-speed manual transaxle standard on Escort. Five-speed standard on Escort GT, EXP Tempo, Taurus MT5 and Thunderbird Turbo. Three-speed automatic standard on Taurus L/GL. Four-speed overdrive automatic standard on Taurus LX/wagons, Crown Vic and T-bird. Drive Axle: (Escort/EXP/Tempo/Taurus) front; (others) rear. Steering: (Crown Vic) recirculating ball; (others) rack/pinion. Front Suspension: (Escort/EXP/Tempo)

MacPherson struts with lower control arms, coil springs and stabilizer bar; (Taurus) MacPherson struts with control arms, coil springs and stabilizer bar; (T-bird) modified MacPherson struts with lower control arms, coil springs and anti-sway bar; (Crown Vic) upper/lower control arms w/coil springs and stabilizer bar. Rear Suspension: (Escort/EXP) trailing arms w/modified MacPherson struts and coil springs on lower control arms; (Tempo) independent trailing four-link with MacPherson struts; (Taurus sedan) MacPherson struts w/parallel suspension arms and coil springs; (Taurus wag) upper/lower control arms, coil springs, and stabilizer bar; (Crown Vic/T-Bird) rigid axle w/four links and coil springs. Brakes: Front disc, rear drum (power assisted). Body construction: (Crown Vic) separate body and frame; (others) unibody. Fuel tank: (Escort/EXP) 13.0 gal.; (Tempo) 15.4 gal.; (Tempo 4WD) 13.7 gal.; (Taurus) 16.0 gal.; (Crown Vic) 18.0 gal.; (T-Bird) 22.1 gal.

DRIVETRAIN OPTIONS: Engines: 3.0-liter V-6: Taurus L ($672). 3.8-liter V-6: Taurus LX, L/GL wagons ($396); other Taurus ($1068). 5.0-liter V-8: Thunderbird ($721). Transmission/Differential: Five-speed manual trans.: Escort ($76). Automatic transaxle: Escort GL ($490); EXP ($415); Tempo ($482). Auto. transmission: T-Bird Turbo Cpe ($515). Traction-Lok differential: Crown Vic ($100). Steering/Suspension: Power steering: Escort/EXP ($235). H.D./handling susp.: Escort/Taurus/Crown Vic ($26). Auto load leveling: Crown Vic ($195). Trailer towing pkg.: Crown Vic ($387-$399).

ESCORT/EXP CONVENIENCE/APPEARANCE OPTIONS: EXP Special Value Pkg. ($961). Escort GT Special Value Pkg. ($815). 4 Spd. Man. Transaxle Pkg., Transaxle, 4 Spd Man., Wide Vinyl Bodyside moldings, Elect. AM/FM Stereo, Elect. Digital Clock/Overhead Console, Power Steering, Tinted Glass, Interval Wipers. Bumper Guards, Bumper Rub Strips, Rear Defroster, Instrumentation Grp., Light/Security Grp, Dual Elect. Remote Cntrl Mirrors, Trim Rings/Center Hubs ($582). Auto. Transaxle Pkg., Wide Vinyl Bodyside Mldgs., Elect. AM/FM Stereo Radio, Digital Clock/Overhead Console, Tinted Glass, Interval Wipers, Bumper Guards, Bumper Rub Strips, Instrumentation Grip, Dual Elect. Remote-Control Mirrors, Trim Rings/Center Hubs ($823). Sun & Sound Group (EXP) Console w/Graphic Systems Monitor ($56). Flip-Up Open Air Roof ($355). Elect. AM/FM Stereo Radio ($137). Premium Sound System ($138). EXP Lux Coupe ($586). Manual Air Cond. ($688). Frt. Center Armrest ($55). H.D. Battery ($27). F&R Bumper Guards ($56). Bumper Rub Strips ($48). Cargo Area Cover ($70). Tu-Tone Paint ($159). Elect. Digital Clock/Overhead Console ($82). Rr. Window Defrost ($145). Tinted Glass ($105). Instrumentation Grp. ($87). Light/Security Grp., GL ($91); GT ($67). Dlx Luggage Rack ($115). Color-Keyed Remote-Cntrl. Mirrors ($88). Wide Vinyl Bodyside Moldings ($50). Clearcoat Paint, GL/EXP ($91); GT (Tu-Tone) ($152). AM Radio ($39). Electronic AM/FM Stereo, Pony ($206); GL ($167). Elect. AM/FM Cass. Tape, Pony ($343); GL ($304); GT & EXP ($137). Premium Sound System ($138). Speed Control ($182). Split Fold Down Rr. Seat ($49). Tilt Wheel ($124). Trim Rings/Center Hubs ($67). Vinyl Trim ($37). Styled Road Wheels ($195). Interval Windshield Wipers ($55). Rr. Window Wiper/Washer ($126). H.D. Alternator ($27). Frt. Lic. Plate Bracket (NC). Calif. Emissions System (NC). Engine Block Heater ($18). Full Size Spare Tire ($73). TIRES: P165/80R13 WSW ($73).

TEMPO CONVENIENCE/APPEARANCE OPTIONS: Preferred Equip. Pkgs.: 2-Door GL ($245); 4-Door GL ($295); 4-Door GL ($1013); 4-Door LX ($748); 4-Door LX ($984). Manual Air Conditioner ($773). Frt. Center Armrest ($55). Rr. Window Defroster ($145). Sport Instrument Cluster ($87). Decklid Luggage Rack ($115). Pwr. Lock Group, 2-Door Models ($237); 4-Door Models ($287). Dual Electric Remote Control Mirrors ($111). AM/FM Stereo Radio w/Cass ($141). Power Driver's Seat ($251). Premium Sound System ($138). Speed Control ($182). Tilt Steering Wheel ($124). Supplemental Air Bag Restraint System, GL ($815); LX ($751). Polycast Wheels ($176). Power Side Windows, 4 Dr ($296). Calif. Emissions ($99). Clearcoat Metallic Paint ($91). Lower Accent Paint Treatment ($159). All Vinyl Seat & Trim ($37). H.D. Battery ($27). Frt. Lic. Plate Bracket (NC). Eng. Block Heater ($94). Styled Steel Wheels/Trim Rings (NC). TIRES: P185/70R14 WSW ($82).

1988 Ford Escort hatchback sedan. (FMC)

1988 Ford LTD Country Squire station wagon. (PH)

1988 Ford Thunderbird Turbo Coupe. (PH)

TAURUS CONVENIENCE/APPEARANCE OPTIONS: Preferred Equip. Pkgs., L (201A) ($1203); 4-Dr. GL Sedan (203A) ($1366), (204A) ($1808); 4-Dr. GL Wagon (203A) ($1316). (204A) ($1758); LX (207A) ($559). (208A) ($1495); 4-Dr. MT5 Sedan (212A) ($972). Elect. Climate Control Air Conditioning, L or GL ($971); LX or Pkgs. 201A, 203A or 204A ($183). Manual Air Cond. ($788). Autolamp System ($73). H.D. Battery ($27). Cargo Area Cover ($66). Electronic Digital Clock ($78). Cornering Lamps ($68). Rr. Window Defroster ($145). Eng. Block Heater ($18). F&R Floor mats ($43). Remote Fuel Door/Decklid Release, Sdns ($91). Remote Fuel Door Release, Wgns ($41). Extended Range Fuel Tank ($46). Illum. Entry System ($82). Diagnostic ($89). Electronic, LX ($239); All Other, exc. MT5 ($351). Keyless Entry System, w/Pkg. 207A ($121); All Other ($202). Light Group ($59). Load Flr Extension, "Picnic Table" ($66). Power Door Locks ($195). Dual Illum Visor Mirrors: L ($116). GL or MT5 ($104). Rocker Panel Moldings ($55). Power Moonroof ($741). Clearcoat Paint ($183). Auto Parking Brake Release ($12). High Level audio System, w/Pkg 207A ($167), w/Pkg 212A ($335). All Other ($472). Elect. AM/FM Stereo Search Radio w/Cass ($137). Premium Sound System ($168). Power Radio Antenna ($76). Rr. Facing Third Seat ($155). 6-Way Pwr. Driver Seat ($251). 6-Way Dual Pwr. Seats, LX or Pkg 204A or 212A ($251); All Other ($502). Speed Control ($182). Tilt Steering Column ($124). Leather-Wrapped Strg. Wheel ($59). Paint Stripe ($57). Rr. Window Washer/Wiper ($126). Calif. Emissions ($99). Bucket Seats (NC). Leather Seat Trim, LX ($415); GL & MT5 ($518); Vinyl Seat Trim, L ($51); All Other ($37). Frt. Lic. Plate Bracket (NC). Frt. Floor Mats ($26). Bolt-on Lux. wheel covers, w/Pkg. 203A or 204A ($21); All Other ($85). Finned Wheelcovers ($65). Custom 15-inch (Locking) wheelcovers, L or GL ($212); LX, or Pkg. 203A or 204A ($148); Pkgs. 207A or 208A ($34); MT5 ($127). Cast Alum. Wheels, L or GL ($227); MT5 ($141); LX, or Pkg. 203A or 204A ($162); Pkgs. 207A or 208A ($49). Styled Road Wheels, L or GL ($178); MT5 ($93); LX or Pkg. 203A or 204A ($113). Pwr. Side Windows ($296). Insta-Clear Windshield ($250). Interval Windshield Wipers ($55). TIRES: P205/70R14 WSW Tires ($82). P205/65R15 BSW Tires ($65). P205/65R15 WSW Tires ($146). Conventional Spare Tire ($73).

LTD CROWN VICTORIA CONVENIENCE/APPEARANCE OPTIONS: Preferred Equip. Pkgs., 4-Dr. LTD Crown Victoria (110A) ($472). 4-Dr. LTD Crown Victoria LX (111A) ($699). 4-Dr. LTD Crown Victoria LX (112A) ($988); 4-Dr. LTD Crown Victoria LX (113A) ($1564); 4-Dr. LTD Crown Victoria & Country Squire Wgn (130A) ($587). (131A) ($1385); 4-Dr. LTD Country Squire Wagon (130A) ($472), (131A) ($1270); 4-Dr. LTD Crown Victoria LX & Country Squire LX Wgn (132A) ($756); (133A) ($1191); 4-Dr. LTD Crown Victoria S (120A) ($352), (121A) ($1085). Auto. Temp. Control Air Cond. w/Pkgs. 110A, 111A, 112A, 130A, 131A or 132A ($66); All Other ($211). High Level Audio System, w/Pkg. 112A or 132A ($335); w/Pkg. 113A or 133A ($167); Other Models ($472). H.D. Battery ($27). Frt. License Plate Bracket (NC). Cornering Lamps ($68). Rr. Window Defroster ($145). F&R Color-Keyed Carpet Floor Mats ($43). Eng. Block Heater ($18). Illum. Entry System ($82). Light Group ($59). Power Lock Group ($245). Dlx Luggage Rack ($115). Vinyl Insert Bodyside Moldings ($66). Tu-Tone Paint/Tape Treatment ($159). Elect. AM/FM Stereo Search Radio w/Cass. Tape Player & Dolby Noise Reduction System ($137). Pwr. Radio Antenna ($76). Premium Sound System ($168). Pwr. 6-Way Driver Seat ($251). Dual Control Power Seats w/Pkgs. 111A, 112AS, 113A, 131A, 132A or 133A ($251); Other Models ($502). Dual Facing Rr. Seats ($173). Speed Control ($182). Leather-Wrapped Steering Wheel ($59). Tilt Steering Wheel ($124). Tripminder Computer ($215). Pivoting Frt. Vent Windows ($79). Lckg. Wire Style Wheelcovers ($212). Cast Alum. Wheels ($390). Pwr. Side Windows, incl. Dual Elect. Remote Mirrors ($379). Insta-Clear Windshield ($250). Brghm Hall Vinyl Roof ($665). Calif. Emissions ($99). All Vinyl Seat Trim ($37). Duraweave Vinyl Seat Trim ($96). Leather Seat Trim ($415). 100 Ampere Alternator ($52). F&R Bumper Guards ($62). Remote Decklid Release ($50). First Gear Lock-Out Delete ($7). Frt. Floor Mats (Color-Keyed) ($26). H.D. Blk. Floor Covering F&R ($27). Dual Accent Bodyside Paint Stripes ($61). Dlx. 15-inch Wheelcovers ($49).

THUNDERBIRD CONVENIENCE/APPEARANCE OPTIONS: Preferred Equip. Pkgs., Standard Model (151A) ($1273). Premium Sound System Added & Rear Defroster Deleted ($1296). Graphic Equalizer Added & Rr. Defroster Deleted ($1346); Sport (154A) ($852). Premium Sound System Added & Rr. Defroster Deleted ($885). Graphic Equalizer Added & Rr. Defroster Deleted ($925); LX (162A) ($804). Premium Sound System Added & Rr. Defroster Deleted ($827). Graphic Equalizer Added & Rr. Defroster Deleted ($877); Turbo Coupe (157A) (NC). Premium Sound System Added & Rr. Defroster Deleted ($23). Graphic Equalizer Added & Rr. Defroster Deleted ($72). H.D. Battery, 58 Amp ($27). Electronic Equip. Group, Base ($634); Sport & Turbo Coupe ($365); LX ($577). Frt. Floor Mats ($33). Luxury Light/Convenience Group, Base ($472); Base w/Electronic Equip. Grp. ($390); Sport & Turbo Coupe ($426); Sport & Turbo Cpe w/Electronic Equip. Grp. ($344); LX ($244). Dual Pwr. Seats, LX or 151A ($302); 154A or 157A ($251). Pwr. Antenna ($76). Premium Luxury Pkg. w/151A ($832); Turbo Coupe w/157A & Sport w/154A ($669). Frt. License Plate Bracket (NC). Rr. Window Defroster ($145). Eng. Block Heater ($18). Illum. Entry System ($82). Power Lock Grp ($237). Dual Electronic Remote Cntrl. Mirrors ($96). Power Moonroof, Base Turbo Cpe & Spt ($841); LX, or w/Lux./Light Group ($741). Elect. AM/FM Stereo w/Cass. Tape Player ($137). Graphic Equalizer ($218). Premium Sound System ($168). Power, 6-Way Driver Seat ($251). Dual Power Seats, Base ($554); Turbo Cpe or Sport ($502). Speed Control ($182). Leather-Wrapped Strg. Wheel ($59). Tilt Strg Wheel ($124). Bodyside & Decklid Stripes ($55). Lckg. Wire Style Wheelcovers, LX or w/151A (Over Styled Road Wheels) ($90); Base (Over Luxury Wheelcovers) ($212). Cast Alum Wheels, LX, Spt or w/151A ($89); Base ($211). Styled Road Wheels ($122). Pwr. Side Windows ($222). Interval Windshield Wipers ($55). Calif. Emissions System ($99). Tu-Tone Paint Treatment, Base ($213); LX, or w/151A (Over Bodyside & Decklid Stripes, or LX) ($159). Clearcoat Paint ($183). Leather Trim ($415). TIRES: P215/70R14 WSW Tires ($73). Conventional Spare Tire ($73).

HISTORY: Introduced: October 1, 1987, except (Tempo) November 1987 and (Escort/EXP Second Series) May 12, 1988. Model year production: 1,606,531 total (incl. Mustangs). Calendar year production (U.S.) 1,305,883 (incl. Mustangs). Calendar year sales by U.S. dealers: 1,527,504 (incl. Mustangs). Model year sales by U.S. dealers: 1,471,343 (incl. Mustangs).

1989 FORD

While the subcompact EXP dropped out of Ford's lineup, a new sporty coupe arrived: the Probe, a product of a joint venture between Ford and Mazda, but built in Michigan. Also new this year was a totally restyled Thunderbird, including a Super Coupe with supercharged V-6 engine. That SC was named *Motor Trend* magazine's 'Car Of The Year.' Taurus also jumped on the performance bandwagon with a "Super High Output" engine in its SHO edition, cutting 0-60 mph time down to the 8-second neighborhood.

1989 Ford Escort GT hatchback coupe. (FMC)

ESCORT — FOUR — Following its mild face lift during the 1988 model year, the front-drive Ford subcompact entered 1989 with little change. With the EXP two-seater gone, the remaining Escort lineup included only the Pony and GT (both in two-door hatchback form only), and the LX (in three body styles). This year's models has gas-charged struts. The base 1.9-liter four produced 90 horsepower, while the GT's high-output version delivered 115 horsepower, with multi-point fuel injection.

TEMPO — FOUR — Little change was evident on this year's compact Tempo sedan, which received a notable aero face lift a year earlier. GL models added nitrogen-pressurized shock absorbers. GLS had a new standard front center armrest. All models got an emissions-system warning light. A stretchable cargo tie-down net went into GLX, LX and All-Wheel Drive models.

PROBE — FOUR — Instead of serving as a replacement for the long-lived rear-drive Mustang, the new Probe became a separate model with its own following. Body and interior of the front-drive, two-door hatchback coupe were designed by Ford. Chassis and powertrain were shared with the Mazda MX-6 coupe, which is no surprise since both were produced at the same plant in Flat Rock, Michigan. Three models were available: base and GL, powered by a 110-horsepower Mazda 2.2-liter (12-valve) four: and the GT, with a turbocharged/intercooled variant of the four, rated 145 horsepower. A five-speed manual gearbox was standard; four-speed automatic optional on GL/LX. Standard equipment also included cloth reclining front bucket seats (driver's seat height-adjustable), power brakes and steering, tachometer, gauges, AM/FM stereo radio, tinted backlight and quarter windows, cargo cover, full console, and a digital clock. The LX added full tinted glass, intermittent wipers, tilt steering column (and instrument cluster), power mirrors, overhead console (with map light), lumbar/bolster adjustments on the driver's seat, rear defogger, and remote fuel door/liftgate releases. The sporty GT, available only with five-speed, also added front/rear disc brakes, alloy wheels, automatically-adjustable performance suspension, fog lamps, its own front/rear fascia, and P195/60VR15 tires on alloy wheels. Both front seats had lumbar adjustment. Only the GT could get optional anti-lock braking.

TAURUS — FOUR/V-6 — Most of the attention this year went to the new Taurus SHO, a high-performance model with special dual-overhead-cam 3.0-liter V-6 (four valves per cylinder) that churned out 220 horsepower. The engine was built by Yamaha, and the sole transmission was a Mazda-built five-speed manual (designed by Ford). SHO also included disc brakes on all four wheels, a special handling suspension, dual exhaust, and P215/65R15 performance tires on aluminum alloy wheels. For a distinctive look, the SHO added a set of rather subtle ground-effects body panels, including wheel spats, headed by a front air dam with fog lamps. Interior touches included a leather-wrapped steering wheel, analog gauges, special power front sport seats with lumbar adjustment, 140-mph speedometer, 8000-rpm tachometer, a rear defogger, cruise control, console with cup holders and armrest, and power windows. With the demise of the MT5 model, SHO was the only Taurus available with manual shift. Other models had slight revisions to grille, headlamps and tail lamps.

LTD CROWN VICTORIA — V-8 — Since it enjoyed a significant face lift a year earlier, the full-size rear-drive Ford returned with little change for 1989. Base and LX trim levels were offered, a four-door sedan and station wagon body styles, all powered by a 150-horsepower 5.0-liter V-8 with four-speed overdrive automatic. Standard equipment included air conditioning, tinted glass and automatic headlamp on/off. On the dashboard, an engine-systems warning light replaced the former low-oil indicator.

1989 Ford Taurus SHO sedan. (FMC)

1989 Ford LTD Crown Victoria sedan. (FMC)

THUNDERBIRD — V-6 — Still rear-drive and arriving a little later than the other Ford models, the sharply restyled Thunderbird rode a much longer (113-inch) wheelbase but was nearly an inch lower and 3.4 inches shorter than its predecessor. Width grew by 1.6 inches, and the interior gained considerable room. All four wheels now had independent suspension. The Turbo Coupe was gone, so both base and LX 'Birds had the 232 cid (3.8-liter) V-6 engine with four-speed over-drive automatic. Both rode 15-inch tires this year, instead of the former 14-inchers. The LX featured digital instruments (including a tachometer) and speed-sensitive power steering. The base 'Bird had analog gauges. All models came with air conditioning and power windows. Cloth reclining front bucket seats, tinted glass, intermittent wipers, dual remote mirrors, a full-length console, visor mirrors, power brakes/steering and AM/FM stereo radio were standard. The LX added a power driver's seat, illuminated entry system, power locks, cruise control, power mirrors, folding rear armrest, lighted visor mirrors, radio with cassette player, leather-wrapped steering wheel (with tilt column) and remote gas door and decklid releases. The V-8 engine option was gone, but performance fans had a much different choice: the new Super Coupe, with a supercharged (intercooled) version of the V-6 under its hood and a standard five-speed manual gearbox. Aero body flaring and dual exhausts made the SC distinctive, while standard four-wheel disc brakes came with anti-locking (optional on the base and LX models). An Automatic Adjustable Suspension allowed selection of shock-absorber damping for a soft or firm ride. Performance tires were 16-inch size. Inside were analog instruments, including a tachometer and boost gauge, plus power articulated front seats with inflatable lumbar bolsters and adjustable backrest wings. Also on the SC: fog lamps, soft-feel steering wheel, power mirrors and a folding rear armrest.

I.D. DATA: Ford's 17-symbol Vehicle Identification Number (VIN) was stamped on a metal tab fastened to the instrument panel, visible through the windshield. The first three symbols ('1FA')indicate manufacturer, make and vehicle type. The fourth symbol denotes restraint system. Next comes a letter (usually 'P'), followed by two digits that indicate Model Number, as shown in left column of tables below. (Example: '90' Escort Pony two-door hatchback). Symbol eight indicates engine type. Next is a check digit. Symbol ten indicates model year ('K' 1989). Symbol eleven denotes assembly plant. The final six digits make up the sequence number, starting with 000001 (except Probe, 500001).

ESCORT (FOUR)

Model No.	Body/ Style No.	Body Type & Seating	Factory Price	Shipping Weight	Prod. Total
90	N/A	2-dr. Pony Hatch-4P	6964	2235	Note 1
91	N/A	2-dr. LX Hatch-4P	7349	2242	Note 1
95	N/A	4-dr. LX Hatch-4P	7679	2313	110,631
98	N/A	4-dr. LX Sta Wag-4P	8280	2312	30,888
93	N/A	2-dr. GT Hatch-4P	9315	2442	Note 1

NOTE 1: Production of two-door hatchbacks totaled 201,288 with no further breakout available.

TEMPO (FOUR)

Model No.	Body/Style No.	Body Type & Seating	Factory Price	Shipping Weight	Prod. Total
31	66D	2-dr. GL Sed-5P	9057	2529	Note 1
36	54D	4-dr. GL Sed-5P	9207	2587	Note 2
37	54D	4-dr. LX Sed-5P	10156	2628	Note 2
39	54D	4-dr. AWD Sed-5P	10860	2787	Note 2
33	66D	2-dr. GLS Sed-5P	9697	2545	Note 1
38	54D	4-dr. GLS Sed-5P	9848	2603	Note 2

NOTE 1: Production of two-door sedans totaled 23,719 with no further breakout available.

NOTE 2: Production of four-door sedans totaled 217,185 with no further breakout available.

PROBE (FOUR)

20	N/A	2-dr. GL Cpe-4P	10459	2715	Note 1
21	N/A	2-dr. LX Cpe-4P	11443	2715	Note 1
21	N/A	2-dr. GT Cpe-4P	13593	2870	Note 1

NOTE 1: Production of two-door coupes totaled 162,889 with no further breakout available.

TAURUS (FOUR/V-6)

50	54D	4-dr. L Sedan-6P	11778/12450	2901/3020	Note 1
55	74D	4-dr. L Sta Wag-6P	-----/13143	----/3172	Note 2
52	54D	4-dr. GL Sedan-6P	12202/12874	2927/3046	Note 1
57	74D	4-dr. GL Sta Wag-6P	-----/13544	----/3189	Note 2
53	54D	4-dr. LX Sedan-6P	-----/15282	----/3076	Note 1
58	74D	4-dr. LX Sta Wag-6P	-----/16524	----/3220	Note 2
54	54D	4-dr. SHO Sed-6P	-----/19739	----/3078	Note 1

NOTE: Taurus prices and weights to left of slash are for four-cylinder, to right for V-6 engine.

NOTE 1: Production of four-door sedans totaled 284,175 with no further breakout available.

NOTE 2: Production of station wagons totaled 87,013 with no further breakout available.

LTD CROWN VICTORIA (V-8)

73	54K	4-dr. Sedan-6P	15851	3730	Note 1
72	54K	4-dr. 'S' Sed-6P	15434	3696	Note 1
76	74K	4-dr. Sta Wag-6P	16209	3941	Note 2
78	74K	4-dr. Ctry Sqr-6P	16527	3935	Note 2

NOTE 1: Production of four-door sedans totaled 110,437 with no further breakout available.

NOTE 2: Production of station wagons totaled 12,549 with no further breakout available.

LTD CROWN VICTORIA LX (V-8)

74	54K	4-dr. Sedan-6P	16767	3770	Note
77	74K	4-dr. Sta Wag-8P	17238	3915	Note
79	74K	4-dr. Ctry Sqr-8P	17556	4013	Note

NOTE: See production figures for Crown Victoria models above.

THUNDERBIRD (V-6)

60	N/A	2-dr. HT Cpe-5P	14612	3542	Note 1
62	N/A	2-dr. LX Cpe-5P	16817	3554	Note 1
64	N/A	2-dr. Super Cpe-5P	19823	3701	Note 1

NOTE 1: Production of two-door coupes totaled 107,996 with no further breakout available.

ENGINE [Base Four (Escort)]: Inline. Overhead cam. Four-cylinder. Cast-iron block and aluminum head. Displacement: 113 cid (1.9 liters). Bore & stroke: 3.23 x 3.46 in. Compression ratio: 9.0:1. Brake horsepower: 90 at 4600 rpm. Torque: 106 lbs.-ft. at 3400 rpm. Five main bearings. Hydraulic valve lifters. Throttle-body fuel injection.

ENGINE [Base Four (Escort GT)]: High-output. MFI version of 1.9-liter four above except: Brake horsepower: 110 at 5400 rpm. Torque: 115 lbs.-ft. at 4200 rpm.

1989 Ford Taurus LX station wagon. (OCW)

ENGINE [Base Four (Probe)]: Inline. Overhead cam. Four-cylinder. Cast-iron block. Displacement: 133 cid (2.2 liters). Bore & stroke: 3.39 x 3.70 in. Compression ratio: 8.6:1. Brake horsepower: 110 at 4700 rpm. Torque: 130 lbs.-ft. at 3000 rpm. Hydraulic valve lifters. Port fuel injection.

ENGINE [Turbocharged Four (Probe GT)]: Same as 2.2-liter four above, with turbocharger and intercooler: Compression ratio: 7.8:1. Brake horsepower: 145 at 4300 rpm. Torque: 190 lbs.-ft. at 3500 rpm.

ENGINE [Base Four (Tempo)]: Inline. Overhead valve. Four cylinder. Cast-iron block and head. Displacement: 140 cid (2.3 liters). Bore & stroke: 3.70 x 3.30 in. Compression ratio: 9.0:1. Brake horsepower: 98 at 4400 rpm. Torque: 124 lbs.-ft. at 2200 rpm. Five main bearings. Multi-point fuel injection. High Swirl Combustion (HSC) design.

ENGINE [Base Four (Tempo 4WD or Sport)]: High-output version of HSC four above except: Brake horsepower: 100 at 4400 rpm. Torque: 130 lbs.-ft. at 2600 rpm.

ENGINE [Base Four (Taurus)]: Inline. Overhead valve. Four cylinder. Cast-iron block and head. Displacement: 153 cid (2.5 liters). Bore & stroke: 3.70 x 3.60 in. Compression ratio: 9.0:1. Brake horsepower: 90 at 4400 rpm. Torque: 130 lbs.-ft. at 2600 rpm. Five main bearings. Hydraulic valve lifters. Throttle body fuel injection.

ENGINE [Base V-6 (Taurus LX/wagons); Optional (Taurus)]: 60-degree, overhead valve V-6. Cast-iron block and head. Displacement: 182 cid (3.0 liters). Bore & stroke: 3.50 x 3.10 in. Compression ratio: 9.3:1. Brake horsepower: 140 at 4800 rpm. Torque: 160 lbs.-ft. at 3000 rpm. Four main bearings. Hydraulic valve lifters. Multi-port fuel injection.

ENGINE [Base V-6 (Taurus SHO)]: Dual-overhead-cam V-6 (24 valve). Cast-iron block and head. Displacement: 182 cid (3.0 liters). Bore & stroke: 3.50 x 3.10 in. Compression ratio: 9.8:1. Brake horsepower: 220 at 6000 rpm. Torque: 200 lbs.-ft. at 4800 rpm. Four main bearings. Hydraulic valve lifters. Sequential fuel injection.

ENGINE [Base V-6 (Thunderbird); Optional: (Taurus)]: 90-degree, overhead valve V-6. Cast-iron block and aluminum head. Displacement: 232 cid (3.8 liters). Bore & stroke: 3.80 x 3.40 in. Compression ratio: 9.0:1. Brake horsepower: 140 at 3800 rpm. Torque: (Taurus) 215 lbs.-ft. at 2200 RPM; (T-Bird) 215 lbs.-ft. at 2400 rpm. Four main bearings. Hydraulic valve lifters. Port fuel injection.

ENGINE [Supercharged V-6 (Thunderbird Super Coupe)]: Same as 232 cid (3.8-liter) V-6 above, except: Compression ratio: 8.2:1. Brake horsepower: 210 at 4000 rpm. Torque: 315 lbs.-ft. at 2600 rpm.

ENGINE [Base V-8 (LTD Crown Victoria)]: 90-degree, overhead valve V-8. Cast-iron block and head. Displacement: 302 cid (5.0 liters). Bore & stroke: 4.00 x 3.00 in. Compression ratio: 8.9:1. Brake horsepower: 150 at 3200 rpm. Torque: 270 lbs.-ft. at 2000 rpm. Five main bearings. Hydraulic valve lifters. Sequential (port) fuel injection.

CHASSIS DATA: Wheelbase: (Escort) 94.2 in.; (Tempo) 99.9 in.; (Probe) 99.0 in.; (Taurus) 106.0 in.; (Crown Vic) 114.3 in.; (T-Bird) 113.0 in. Overall length: (Escort) 166.9 in.; (Escort wagon) 168.0 in.; (Tempo) 176.5 in.; (Probe) 177.0 in.; (Taurus) 188.4 in.; (Taurus wag) 191.9 in.; (Crown Vic) 211.0 in.; (Crown Vic Wag) 216.0 in.; (T-Bird) 198.7 in. Height: (Escort) 53.3-53.5 in.; (Tempo) 52.7 in.; (Probe) 51.8 in.; (Taurus) 54.3 in.; (Taurus wag) 55.1 in.; (Crown Vic) 55.5 in.; (Crown Vic wag) 57.0 in.; (T-Bird) 52.7 in. Width: (Escort) 65.9 in.; (Tempo) 68.3 in.; (Probe) 67.9 in.; (Taurus) 70.6 in.; (Crown Vic) 77.5 in.; (Crown Vic wag) 79.3 in.; (T-Bird) 72.7 in. Front Tread: (Escort) 54.7 in.; (Tempo) 54.9 in.; (Probe) 57.3 in.; (Taurus) 61.5 in.; (Crown Vic) 62.2 in.; (T-Bird) 61.4 in. Rear Tread: (Escort) 56.0 in.; (Tempo) 57.6 in.; (Probe) 57.7 in.; (Taurus) 60.5 in.; (Taurus wag) 59.9 in.; (Crown Vic) 62.0 in.; (T-Bird) 60.2 in. Standard Tires: (Escort Pony) P175/70R14; (Escort GT) P195/60HR15; (Tempo) P185/70R14; (Probe) P185/70SR14; (Probe GT) P195/60VR15; (Taurus) P195/70R14; (Taurus LX) P205/70R14; (Taurus SHO) P215/65R15; (Crown Vic) P215/70R15; (T-Bird) P205/70R15; (T-Bird Super Cpe) P225/60VR16.

TECHNICAL: Transmission: Four-speed manual transaxle standard on Escort Pony. Five-speed standard on Escort LX wagon and GT, Tempo, Probe, Taurus SHO and Thunderbird Super Coupe. Three-speed automatic standard on Taurus four. Four speed overdrive automatic standard on Taurus V-6, Crown Vic and T-Bird. Drive Axle: (Crown Vic/T-Bird) rear; (others) front. Steering: (Crown Vic) recirculating ball; (others) rack/pinion. Front Suspension: (Escort/Tempo) MacPherson struts with lower control arms, coil springs and stabilizer bar; (Probe) MacPherson struts with asymmetrical control arms, strut-mounted coil springs and stabilizer bar; (Taurus) MacPherson struts with control arms, coil springs and stabilizer bar; (Crown Vic) upper/lower control arms w/coil springs and stabilizer bar; (T-Bird) independent long spindle with short/long arms, coil springs and stabilizer bar. Rear Suspension: (Escort) trailing arms w/modified MacPherson struts and coil springs on lower control arms; (Tempo) independent trailing four-link with MacPherson struts; (Probe) independent struts, four-bar with single trailing arms, coil springs and stabilizer bar; (Taurus sedan) MacPherson struts w/parallel suspension arms and coil springs; (Taurus wag) upper/lower control arms, coil springs and stabilizer bar; (Crown Vic) rigid axle w/four links and coil springs; (Thunderbird) independent with upper/lower arms, coil springs and stabilizer bar. Brakes: Front disc, rear drum (power assisted) except (Probe GT, Taurus SHO and T-Bird Super Coupe) front/rear disc. Body construction: (Crown Vic) separate body and frame; (others) unibody. Fuel tank: (Escort) 13.0 gal.; (Tempo) 15.4 gal.; (Tempo 4WD) 13.7 gal.; (Probe) 15.1 gal.; (Taurus) 16.0 gal.; (Crown Vic) 18.0 gal.; (T-Bird) 19.0 gal.

DRIVETRAIN OPTIONS: Engines: 3.0-liter V-6: Taurus L/GL sed ($672). 3.8-liter V-6: Taurus GL wagon ($400); other Taurus ($1072). Transmission/Differential: Five-speed manual trans.: Escort LX sed ($76). Automatic transaxle: Escort ($490) except LX wagon ($415); Tempo ($515); Probe ($617). Automatic transmission: T-Bird Super Coupe ($539). Traction-Lok differential: Crown Vic/T-Bird ($100); T-Bird SC ($21). Steering/Suspension: Power steering: Escort ($235). H.D./handling susp.: Taurus/Crown Vic ($26). Auto load leveling: Crown Vic ($195). Trailer towing pkg: Crown Vic ($387-$399).

ESCORT CONVENIENCE/APPEARANCE OPTIONS: (330A) Escort GT Special Value Pkg. ($815). LX Series (320A) 5 Spd Manual Transaxle Pkg incl: Power Steering, Electronic Digital Clock, Overhead Console, Rr Window Defroster, Tinted Glass, Instrumentation Grp, Light Security Grp, Dual Electric Remote Cntrl, Mirrors, Wide Vinyl Bodyside Moldings, Electronic AM/FM Stereo Radio, Luxury Wheel Covers, Interval Windshield Wipers, 2- & 4-Dr LX hatchback ($560). 4-Dr LX Wagon ($484). (321A) Automatic Transaxle Pkg incl: all 320A except Auto. Transaxle instead of 5 Spd Manual, 2- & 4-Dr LX hatchback ($938). 4-Dr LX Wgn ($863). Manual Air Conditioner ($720). H.D. Battery ($27). Digital Clock, Overhead Console ($82). Rr Window Defroster ($150). Tinted Glass ($105). Instrumentation Grp. ($87). Light/Security Grp, LX ($91). GT ($67). Dlx Luggage Rack ($115). Color-Keyed Elect. Remote Control Mirrors ($98). Wide Vinyl Bodyside Moldings ($50). Clearcoat Paint, LX ($91). GT (incl Tu-Tone) ($183). Tu-Tone Paint ($91). AM Radio ($54). Elect. AM/FM Stereo, Pony ($206). LX ($152). Elect. AM/FM Cass Tape, Pony ($343). LX ($289). GT & EXP ($137). Premium Sound System ($138). Speed Control ($191). Split Fold Down Rr Seat ($50). Pwr Steering ($235). Tilt Steering ($124). Luxury Wheel Covers ($71). Vinyl Trim ($37). Polycast Wheels ($193). Interval Windshield Wipers ($55). Rr Window Wiper/Washer ($126). H.D. Alternator ($27). Frt License Plate Bracket (NC). Calif. Emissions System (NC). Eng Block Heater ($20). Full Size Spare Tire ($73). P175/70R14 WSW Tires, LX ($73).

1989 Ford Escort LX station wagon. (OCW)

1989 Ford Tempo AWD sedan. (OCW)

1989 Ford Probe GT. (OCW)

TEMPO CONVENIENCE/APPEARANCE OPTIONS: Preferred Equip Pkgs: (226A) 2-Dr GL ($449). 4-Dr GL ($499). (227A) 4-Dr GL ($1250). (229A) 2-Dr GLS ($1220). (229A) 4-Dr GLS ($1270). (233A) 4-Dr LX ($863). (234A) 4-Dr LX ($1099). (232A) 4-Dr AWD ($352). Manual Air Conditioner ($807). Rr Window Defroster ($150). Sport Instrument Cluster ($87). Decklid Luggage Rack ($115). Pwr Lock Grp, 2-Dr ($246). 4-Dr ($298). Dual Elect. Remote Control Mirrors ($121). AM/FM Stereo Radio w/Cass ($137). Power Driver's Seat ($261). Premium Sound System ($138). Speed Control ($191). Sports Appearance Grp ($1178). Tilt Steering Wheel ($124). Supplemental Air Bag Restraint System, GL ($815). LX ($751). Polycast Wheels ($193). 4-Dr Power Side Windows ($306). Calif. Emissions ($100). Clearcoat Metallic Paint ($91). Lower Accent Paint Treatment ($159). All Vinyl Seat & Trim ($37). Frt Lic Plate Bracket (NC). Eng Block Heater ($20). Styled Steel Wheels/Trim Rings (NC). Tires: P185/70R14 WSW ($82).

PROBE CONVENIENCE/APPEARANCE OPTIONS: Preferred Equip Pkgs: (251A) Tinted Glass, Interval Wipers, Light Grp, Dual Electric Remote Grp, Tilt Strg Column & Cluster, Rr Window Defroster ($334). (253A) Electronic Instrument Cluster, Elect. Control Air Cond, Illum Entry, Leather-Wrapped Strg Wheel & Transaxle Shift Knob, Pwr Driver's seat, Trip Computer, Rr Washer/Wiper, Walk-in Passenger Seat, Pwr Windows, Spd Control, Pwr Dr Locks, AM/FM Electronic Cass w/Prem Sound/Pwr Antenna ($2214). (261A) Anti-Lock Braking System, Electronic Air Cond, Illum Entry, Leather-Wrapped Strg Wheel & Transaxle Shift Knob, Pwr Driver's Seat, Trip Computer, Vehicle Maintenance Monitor (Overhead Console), Rr Washer/Wiper, Walk-in Passenger Seat, Pwr Windows, Spd Control, Pwr Dr Locks, AM/FM Electronic Cass w/Prem Sound/Pwr Antenna ($2621). Air Conditioner Manual, w/Pkg 250A, incl tinted glass ($927). Other models ($807). Rr Window Defroster ($150). Pwr Dr Locks ($155). Speed Control ($191). Flip-up Open Air Roof ($355). Alum Wheels, w/GL ($290). w/LX ($237). AM/FM Elect. Stereo Radio w/Premium Sound ($168). AM/FM Elect. Cass. w/Premium Sound/Pwr Antenna ($344). AM/FM Prem Electronic Cass w/Premium Sound/CD player, Pwr Antenna w/Pkgs 251A, 252A, or 260A ($1052). W/Pkgs 253A or 261A ($708). Frt Lic Plate Bracket (NC). Calif. Emission System (NC). Eng Block Heater ($20).

TAURUS CONVENIENCE/APPEARANCE OPTIONS: GL (204A) ($1749). LX (207A) ($777). (208A) Sedan ($1913). (208A) Wagon ($1513). SHO (211A) ($533). Elect. Climate Control Air Conditioning Pkg 202A ($971). SHO, LX or Pkg 204A ($183). Air Cond, Manual ($807). Autolamp System ($73). H.D. Battery ($27). Cargo Area Cover ($66). Cornering Lamps ($68). Rr Window Defroster ($150). Eng Block Heater ($20). F&R Floor Mats ($43). Remote Fuel Door/Decklid or Liftgate Release ($91). Extended Range Fuel Tank ($46). Illum Entry System ($82). Diagnostic Instrument Cluster ($89). Electronic Instruments, LX ($239). GL ($351). Keyless Entry System w/Pkg 207A or 211A ($137). Other Models ($218). Light Group ($59). Load Flr Extension, "Picnic Table" ($66). Power Door Locks ($205). Dual Illum Visor Mirrors ($100). Rocker Panel Moldings ($55). Power Moonroof ($741). Auto Parking Brake Release ($12). High Level Audio System w/Pkg 204A ($335). W/Pkg 207A ($167). Other Models ($472). Elect. AM/FM Stereo Search Radio w/Cass ($137). Premium Sound System ($168). Power Radio Antenna ($76). JBL Audio System ($488). Rr Facing Third Seat ($155). 6-Way Pwr Driver Seat ($261). Dual 6-Way Pwr Seats, LX or Pkg 204A or 211A ($261). Other Models ($502). Speed Control ($191). Tilt Steering Column ($124). Leather-Wrapped Strg Wheel ($63). Paint Stripe ($61). Rr Window Washer/Wiper ($126). Finned Wheel Covers ($65). Custom 15-inch (Locking) Wheel Covers, w/Pkg 202A ($212). W/Pkg 204A ($148). Cast Alum Wheels, L or GL ($279). LX or Pkg 204A ($215). Pkgs 207A or 208A ($49). Styled Road Wheels, GL ($193). LX or 204A ($128). Pwr Side Windows ($306). Insta-Clear Windshield ($250). Interval Windshield Wipers ($55). Calif. Emission System ($100). Bucket Seats (NC). Leather Seat Trim, LX & SHO ($489). GL

($593). Vinyl Seat trim, L ($51). GL ($37). Ft Lic Plate Bracket (NC). Frt Floor Mats ($26). Bolt-on Luxury Wheel Covers w/Pkg 204A ($21). Other Models ($85). Tires: P205/70R14 WSW ($82). P205/65R15 BSW ($65). P205/65R15 WSW ($146). Conventional Spare Tire ($73).

CROWN VICTORIA CONVENIENCE/APPEARANCE OPTIONS: 4-Dr LTD Crown Victoria LX (111A) ($383). 4-Dr LTD Crown Victoria LX (112A) ($938). 4-Dr LTD Crown Victoria LX (113A) ($1514). 4-Dr LTD Crown Victoria Wgn & Country Squire Wgn (131A) ($1280). 4-Dr LTD Crown Victoria LX Wgn & Country Squire LX Wgn (132A) ($688). 4-Dr LTD Crown Victoria LX Wgn & Country Squire LX Wgn (133A) ($1191). 4-Dr LTD Crown Victoria S (120B) ($66). 4-Dr LTD Crown Victoria S (121A) ($802). Auto Temp Control Air Cond w/Pkgs 111A, 112A, 131A or 132A ($66). Other Models ($216). High Level Audio System w/Pkg 112A or 132A ($335). W/Pkg 113A or 133A ($167). Other Models ($472). H.D. Battery ($27). Frt License Plate Bracket (NC). F&R Bumper Guards ($62). Cornering Lamps ($68). Rr Window Defroster ($150). Color-Keyed Floor Mats, F&R ($43). Eng Block Heater ($20). Illum Entry System ($82). Light Group ($59). Power Lock Group ($255). Vinyl Insert Bodyside Moldings ($66). Clearcoat Paint ($226). Tu-Tone Paint/Tape Treatment ($159). Elect AM/FM Stereo Search Radio w/Cass Tape Player & Dolby Noise Reduction System ($137). Pwr Radio Antenna ($76). Premium Sound System ($168). Pwr, 6-Way Driver Seat ($261). Dual Control, Power Seats w/Pkgs 112A, 131A, or 132A ($251). Other Models ($522). Dual Facing Rr Seat, Wags ($173). Speed Control ($191). Leather-Wrapped Steering Wheel ($63). Tilt Steering Wheel ($124). Tripminder Computer ($215). Pivoting Frt Vent Windows ($79). Vinyl Roof Delete ($200 credit). Style Lckg Wire Wheel Covers ($228). Cast Alum Wheels ($40). Pwr Side Windows incl: Dual Elect. Remote Mirrors ($389). Insta-Clear Windshield ($250). Brghm Half Vinyl Roof ($665). Calif. Emission System ($100). All Vinyl Seat Trim ($37). Duraweave Vinyl Seat Trim ($96). Leather Seat Trim ($489). 100 Ampere Alternator ($52). Electronic Digital Clock ($96). Remote Decklid Release ($50). First Gear Lock-Out Delete ($7). Frt Floor Mats (Color-Keyed) ($26). H.D. Blk, F&R Floor Covering ($27). Dual Accent Bodyside Paint Stripes ($61). Dlx, 15-inch Wheel Covers ($49).

THUNDERBIRD CONVENIENCE/APPEARANCE OPTIONS: (151B) Standard, Dual Electric Remote Mirrors, Bright Window Mldgs, Elect AM/FM Stereo Radio w/Cass Player/Clock, Spd Cntrl & Tilt Strg Wheel, Pwr Lock Group, 6-Way Pwr Driver's seat, 6-Way Pwr Pass Seat, Styled Wheel Covers, Rr Window Defroster, Lux Light/Convenience Grp ($1235). (162A) LX, Rr Window Defrost, 6-Way Pwr Pass Seat, Cast Alum Wheels w/BSW P215/70R15 Tires, Premium Luxury Grp, (Lux Light/Convenience Grp, Floor Mats, Keyless Entry System, Electronic Prem Cass Radio w/Premium Sound, Pwr Antenna) ($735). (157B) Super Coupe: Elect. AM/FM Stereo Radio w/Cass Player/Clock, Spd Control & Tilt Strg Wheel, Pwr Lock Grp, 6-Way Pwr Driver's Seat, 6-Way Pwr Pass Seat, Rr Window Defroster (NC). (161B) Premium Luxury Group, Floor Mats, Keyless Entry System, Lux Light/Convenience Grp, Elect. Prem Cass Radio w/Premium Sound, Pwr Antenna ($420). Super Coupe w/Pkg 157B ($761). Anti-Lock Brake System ($1085). Anti-Theft System ($183). Pwr Moonroof Base w/41X & Super Cpe w/o Lux Light/Conv Grp ($841). LX, or Super Cpe w/Lux Light/Convenience Grp or w/Pkg 151B ($741). Clearcoat Paint ($183). JBL Audio System ($488). Compact Disc Player ($491). Locking Wire Style Wheel Covers LX w/41X, or w/Pkg 151B ($127). Base Model w/41X ($212). LX (NC). Calif. Emissions System ($100). Leather Trim, LX ($489). Super Coupe ($622). Frt License Plate Bracket (NC). Cold Weather Grp (eng block heater, 72 ampere H.D. battery, 75 ampere H.D. alternator, Rear Window Defroster, Base & LX) ($45). Super Coupe ($18). Cast Alum Wheels w/Upsized P215/70R15 BSW Tires w/Pkg 151B ($213). Base Model w/41X ($299). Tires: P205/70R14 WSW ($73). Eagle GT+4 P225/60VR16 BSW all-season performance, Super Coupe ($73). Conventional Spare Tire, Base or LX ($73).

HISTORY: Introduced: October 6, 1988, except (Thunderbird) December 26, 1988, and (Probe) May 12, 1989. Model year production: 1,234,954 (U.S.) and 1,505,908 (total) (incl. Mustangs). Calendar year sales by U.S. dealers: 1,433,550 (incl. Mustangs). Model year sales by U.S. dealers: 1,512,007 (incl. Mustangs).

1990 FORD

Escort and Taurus had been edged out by an import (Honda Accord) as America's best selling car for calendar year 1989, but a new Escort was being readied for the 1991 model year. The sporty Probe hatchback coupe, introduced for 1989, gained a V-6 engine this year for one of its models. Anti-lock braking was available on both Probe and Taurus models. Performance continued to play a strong role in the Ford lineup, with the availability of the Taurus SHO, Probe GT and Thunderbird Super Coupe.

1990 Ford Escort LX station wagon. (OCW)

1990 Ford Escort GT three-door hatchback. (OCW)

ESCORT — FOUR — Not much was new in the Ford subcompact for 1990, since an all-new version was expected for '91. Rear shoulder belts became standard this year, to complement the motorized front belts. The model lineup was unchanged: Pony two-door hatchback, LX in three body styles, and sporty GT two-door hatchback. The GT version of the 1.9-liter four-cylinder engine produced 110 horsepower, versus 90 horsepower for the base powerplant.

TEMPO — FOUR — Little was new this year for the popular compact Ford sedans, except for the addition of standard floor mats and footwell and trunk lights. Polycast wheels got a fresh look. As before, two versions of the 2.3-liter four-cylinder engine were available, and Tempo came in three trim levels (plus the All Wheel Drive four-door). A five-speed manual gearbox was standard, except in the 4WD, which had standard three-speed automatic.

1990 Ford Probe LX coupe. (OCW)

1990 Ford Probe GT coupe. (OCW)

1990 Ford Taurus SHO sedan. (OCW)

PROBE — FOUR/V-6 — Most significant of the changes for the sporty Ford front-drive coupe, based on a Mazda MX-6 chassis, was the appearance of a V-6 engine choice. Only the GL came with a standard Mazda-built four-cylinder this year. Probe's GT again carried a turbocharged/intercooled four, and LX got the 140-horsepower, 3.8-liter V-6. This year, too, the GT could have the four-speed overdrive automatic transmission instead of the standard five-speed manual gearbox. Four-wheel disc brakes went on the LX, with anti-lock braking optional. Front seatbelts were now motorized, and back seats also held shoulder belts. As for appearance, all Probes got new tail lamps and front/rear fascias. New bodyside moldings and cladding adorned the GT, which also earned a restyle for its alloy wheels. Inside the GT was a new soft-feel steering wheel, while other models got leather on the wheel and gearshift knob. Leather upholstery became optional this year, and both LX and GT tires were bigger than before.

TAURUS — FOUR/V-6 — Anti-lock braking joined the Taurus sedan option list this year, and all models got a standard airbag (with tilt steering) on the driver's side. Inside, the instrument panel was revised and now held coin and cup holders. Otherwise, the popular mid-size front-drive sedans and wagons continued as before, in three trim levels plus the performance-oriented SHO. All but the L sedan could have an optional 3.8-liter V-6 engine instead of the 2.5-liter four or 3.0-liter V-6. Both V-6 engines came with four-speed overdrive automatic. SHO continued its special double-overhead-cam, 24-valve version of the 3.0 V-6, available only with five-speed manual gearbox. New to the option list: a compact-disc player.

LTD CROWN VICTORIA — V-8 — No major changes were evident in the full-size Ford, but quite a few minor revisions appeared. An airbag was now standard on the driver's side, and a coolant temperature gauge went on the revised instrument panel. Map pockets departed from the doors, but the glove compartment grew in size. A split bench seat replaced the formerly standard full bench arrangement, and all back seats held shoulder belts. New standard equipment also included power windows and mirrors, plus tilt steering. Departing from the option list: the Tripminder computer and pivoting front vent windows. Crown Vics came in a dozen colors this year, including five new ones. Sole powertrain continued to be the 5.0-liter V-8 with four-speed overdrive automatic.

1990 Ford LTD Country Squire station wagon. (OCW)

1990 Ford LTD Crown Victoria sedan. (OCW)

1990 Ford Thunderbird Super Coupe. (OCW)

1990-1/2 Ford Thunderbird 35th Anniversary Edition Super Coupe. (OCW)

THUNDERBIRD — V-6 — Following its striking 1989 redesign, the rear-drive personal coupe changed little for '90 except for the availability of two new option packages (Power Equipment and Luxury Groups). Base and LX models again carried a standard 3.8-liter V-6 with four-speed overdrive automatic. The Super Coupe held a supercharged (intercooled) version of the V-6, rated at 210 horsepower, with standard five-speed manual gearbox.

I.D. DATA: Ford's 17-symbol Vehicle Identification Number (VIN) was stamped on a metal tab fastened to the instrument panel, visible through the windshield. The first three symbols ('1FA') indicate manufacturer, make, and vehicle type. The fourth symbol denotes restraint system. Next comes a letter (usually 'P'), followed by two digits that indicate Model Number, as shown in the left column of tables below. (Example: '90' Escort Pony two-door hatchback). Symbol eight indicates engine type. Next is a check digit. Symbol ten indicates model year ('L' 1990). Symbol eleven denotes assembly plant. The final six digits make up the sequence number, starting with 000001 (except Probe, 500001).

ESCORT (FOUR)

Model No.	Body/ Style No.	Body Type & Seating	Factory Price	Shipping Weight	Prod. Total
90	N/A	2-dr. Pony Hatch-4P	7423	2083	N/A
91	N/A	2-dr. LX Hatch-4P	7827	2090	N/A
95	N/A	4-dr. LX Hatch-4P	8157	2144	N/A
98	N/A	4-dr. LX Sta Wag-4P	8758	2177	N/A
93	N/A	2-dr. GT Hatch-4P	9842	2519	N/A

TEMPO (FOUR)

31	66D	2-dr. GL Sed-5P	9505	2418	Note 1
36	54D	4-dr. GL Sed-5P	9655	2467	Note 2
37	54D	4-dr. LX Sed-5P	10607	2508	Note 2
39	54D	4-dr. AWD Sed-5P	11330	2689	Note 2
33	66D	2-dr. GLS Sed-5P	10180	2434	Note 1
38	54D	4-dr. GLS Sed-5P	10328	2483	Note 2

NOTE 1: Production of two-door sedans totaled 8,551 with no further breakout available.

NOTE 2: Production of four-door sedans totaled 209,875 with no further breakout available.

PROBE (FOUR/V-6)

20	N/A	2-dr. GL Cpe-4P	11574	2715	Note 1
21	N/A	2-dr. LX Cpe-4P	13113	2715	Note 1
21	N/A	2-dr. GT Cpe-4P	14838	2715	Note 1

NOTE: Probe LX had a V-6 engine.

NOTE 1: Production of two-door coupes totaled 109,898 with no further breakout available.

TAURUS (FOUR/V-6)

50	54D	4-dr. L Sedan-6P	12594/13290	2765/2885	Note 1
55	74D	4-dr. L Sta Wagon-6P	-----/13983	----/3062	Note 2
52	54D	4-dr. GL Sedan-6P	13067/13763	3049/3169	Note 1
57	74D	4-dr. GL Sta Wag-6P	-----/14433	----/3095	Note 2
53	54D	4-dr. LX Sedan-6P	-----/16095	----/2999	Note 1
58	74D	4-dr. LX Sta Wag-6P	-----/17338	----/3233	Note 2
54	54D	4-dr. SHO Sed-6P	-----/21505	----/2985	Note 1

NOTE: Taurus prices and weights to left of slash are for four-cylinder, to right for V-6 engine.

NOTE 1: Production of four-door sedans totaled 233,153 with no further breakout available.

NOTE 2: Production of station wagons totaled 75,531 with no further breakout available.

LTD CROWN VICTORIA (V-8)

73	54K	4-dr. Sedan-6P	17106	3611	N/A
72	54K	4-dr. 'S' Sed-6P	16479	3591	N/A
76	74K	4-dr. Sta Wag-6P	17512	3795	N/A
78	74K	4-dr. Ctry Sqr-6P	17830	3834	N/A

LTD CROWN VICTORY LX (V-8)

74	54K	4-dr. Sedan-6P	17743	3660	N/A
77	74K	4-dr. Sta Wag-8P	18262	3834	N/A
79	74K	4-dr. Ctry Sqr-8P	18580	3873	N/A

THUNDERBIRD (V-6)

60	N/A	2-dr. HT Cpe-5P	15076	3267	Note 1
62	N/A	2-dr. LX Cpe-5P	17310	3311	Note 1
64	N/A	2-dr. HT Super Cpe-5P	20394	3467	Note 1

NOTE 1: Production of two-door coupes totaled 104,602 with no further breakout available.

ENGINE [Base Four (Escort)]: Inline. Overhead cam. Four-cylinder. Cast-iron block and aluminum head. Displacement: 113 cid (1.9 liters). Bore & stroke: 3.23 x 3.46 in. Compression ratio: 9.0:1. Brake horsepower: 90 at 4600 rpm. Torque: 106 lbs.-ft. at 3400 rpm. Five main bearings. Hydraulic valve lifters. Throttle-body fuel injection.

ENGINE [Base Four (Escort GT)]: High-output, MFI version of 1.9-liter four above except: Brake horsepower: 110 at 5400 rpm. Torque: 115 lbs.-ft. at 4200 rpm.

ENGINE [Base Four (Probe)]: Inline. Overhead cam. Four-cylinder. Cast-iron block. Displacement: 133 cid (2.2 liters). Bore & stroke: 3.39 x 3.70 in. Compression ratio: 8.6:1. Brake horsepower: 110 at 4700 rpm. Torque: 130 lbs.-ft. at 3000 rpm. Hydraulic valve lifters. Port fuel injection.

ENGINE [Turbocharged Four (Probe GT)]: Same as 2.2-liter four above, with turbocharger and intercooler: Compression ratio: 7.8:1. Brake horsepower: 145 at 4300 rpm. Torque: 190 lbs.-ft. at 3500 rpm.

ENGINE [Base Four (Tempo)]: Inline. Overhead valve. Four cylinder. Cast-iron block and head. Displacement: 140 cid (2.3 liters). Bore & stroke: 3.70 x 3.30 in. Compression ratio: 9.0:1. Brake horsepower: 98 at 4400 rpm. Torque: 124 lbs.-ft. at 2200 rpm. Five main bearings. Hydraulic valve lifters. Port fuel injection.

ENGINE [Base Four (Tempo 4WD or Sport)]: High-output version of HSC four above except: Brake horsepower: 100 at 4400 rpm. Torque: 130 lbs.-ft. at 2600 rpm.

ENGINE [Base Four (Taurus)]: Inline. Overhead valve. Four-cylinder. Cast-iron block and head. Displacement 153 cid (2.5 liters). Bore & stroke: 3.70 x 3.60 in. Compression ratio: 9.0:1. Brake horsepower: 90 at 4400 rpm. Torque: 130 lbs.-ft. at 2600 rpm. Five main bearings. Hydraulic valve lifters. Throttle-body fuel injection.

1990 Ford Taurus LX sedan. (OCW)

ENGINE [Base V-6 (Probe LX, Taurus LX/wagons); Optional (Taurus)]: 60-degree, overhead valve V-6. Cast-iron block and head. Displacement: 182 cid (3.0 liters). Bore & stroke: 3.50 x 3.10 in. Compression ratio: 9.3:1. Brake horsepower: 140 at 4800 rpm. Torque: 160 lbs.-ft. at 3000 rpm. Four main bearings. Hydraulic valve lifters. Multi-port fuel injection.

ENGINE [Base V-6 (Taurus SHO)]: Dual-overhead-cam V-6 (24 valve). Cast-iron block and head. Displacement: 182 cid (3.0 liters). Bore & stroke: 3.50 x 3.10 in. Compression ratio: 9.8:1. Brake horsepower: 220 at 6200 rpm. Torque: 200 lbs.-ft. at 4800 rpm. Four main bearings. Hydraulic valve lifters. Sequential fuel injection.

ENGINE [Base V-6 (Thunderbird); Optional (Taurus)]: 90-degree, overhead valve V-6. Cast-iron block and aluminum head. Displacement: 232 cid (3.8 liters). Bore & stroke: 3.80 x 3.40 in. Compression ratio: 9.0:1. Brake horsepower: 140 at 3800 rpm. Torque: (Taurus) 215 lbs.-ft. at 2200 rpm; (Thunderbird) 215 lbs.-ft. at 2400 rpm. Four main bearings. Hydraulic valve lifters. Port fuel injection.

ENGINE [Supercharged V-6 (Thunderbird Super Coupe)]: Same as 232 cid (3.8 liter) V-6 above, except: Compression ratio: 8.2:1. Brake horsepower: 210 at 4000 rpm. Torque: 315 lbs.-ft. at 2600 rpm.

ENGINE [Base V-8 (LTD Crown Victoria)]: 90-degree, overhead valve V-8. Cast-iron block and head. Displacement: 302 cid (5.0 liters). Bore & stroke: 4.00 x 3.00 in. Compression ratio: 8.9:1. Brake horsepower: 150 at 3200 rpm. Torque: 270 lbs.-ft. at 2000 rpm. Five main bearings. Hydraulic valve lifters. Sequential (port) fuel injection.

CHASSIS DATA: Wheelbase: (Escort) 94.2 in.; (Tempo) 99.9 in.; (Probe) 99.0 in.; (Taurus) 106.0 in.; (Crown Vic) 114.3 in.; (T-Bird) 113.0 in. Overall Length: (Escort) 169.4 in.; (Tempo 2-dr) 176.7 in.; (Tempo 4-dr) 177.0 in.; (Probe) 177.0 in.; (Taurus) 188.4 in.; (Taurus wag) 191.9 in.; (Crown Vic) 211.0 in.; (Crown Vic wag) 215.7 in.; (T-Bird) 198.7 in. Height: (Escort) 53.7 in.; (Escort wag.) 53.4 in.; (Tempo) 52.8 in.; (Probe) 51.8 in.; (Taurus) 54.6 in.; (Taurus wag) 55.4 in.; (Crown Vic) 55.6 in.; (Crown Vic wag) 56.5 in.; (T-Bird) 52.7 in. Width: (Escort) 65.9 in.; (Tempo) 68.3 in.; (Probe) 67.9 in.; (Probe GT) 68.3 in.; (Taurus) 70.8 in.; (Crown Vic) 77.5 in.; (Crown Vic wag) 79.3 in.; (T-Bird) 72.7 in. Front Tread: (Escort) 54.7 in.; (Tempo) 54.9 in.; (Probe) 57.3 in.; (Taurus) 61.5 in.; (Crown Vic) 62.2 in.; (T-Bird) 61.6 in. Rear Tread: (Escort) 56.0 in.; (Tempo) 57.6 in.; (Probe) 57.7 in.; (Taurus) 60.5 in.; (Taurus wag) 59.9 in.; (Crown Vic) 63.3 in.; (T-Bird) 60.2 in. Standard Tires: (Escort) P175/70R14; (Escort GT) P195/60HR15; (Tempo) P185/70R14; (Probe) P185/70R14; (Probe LX) P195/70R14; (Probe GT) P205/60VR15; (Taurus) P195/70R14; (Taurus LX) P205/70R14; (Taurus SHO) P215/65R15; (Crown Vic) P215/70R15; (T-Bird) P205/70R15; (T-Bird Super Cpe) P225/60VR16.

1990 Ford Escort LX four-door hatchback and two-door hatchback. (OCW)

1990 Ford Ford Tempo four-door. (OCW)

1990 Ford Thunderbird LX Coupe. (OCW)

TECHNICAL: Transmission: Four-speed manual transaxle standard on Escort Pony. Five-speed standard on Escort LX wagon and GT, Tempo, Probe, Taurus SHO, and Thunderbird Super Coupe. Three-speed automatic standard on Taurus four. Four-speed overdrive automatic standard on Taurus V-6, Crown Vic, and T-Bird. Drive Axle: (Crown Vic/T-Bird) rear; (others) front. Steering: (Crown Vic) recirculating ball; (others) rack/pinion. Front Suspension: (Escort/Tempo) MacPherson struts with lower control arms, coil springs, and stabilizer bar; (Probe) MacPherson struts with asymmetrical control arms, strut-mounted coil springs, and stabilizer bar; (Taurus) MacPherson struts with control arms, coil springs, and stabilizer bar; (Crown Vic) upper/lower control arms w/coil springs and stabilizer bar; (T-Bird) independent long spindle with short/long arms, coil springs, and stabilizer bar. Rear Suspension: (Escort) trailing arms w/modified MacPherson struts and coil springs on lower control arms; (Tempo) independent trailing four-link with MacPherson struts; (Probe) independent struts, four-bar with single trailing arms, coil springs, and stabilizer bar; (Taurus sedan) MacPherson struts w/parallel suspension arms and coil springs; (Taurus wag) upper/lower control arms, coil springs, and stabilizer bar; (Crown Vic) rigid axle w/four links and coil springs; (Thunderbird) independent with upper/lower arms, coil springs, and stabilizer bar. Brakes: Front disc, rear drum (power assisted) except (Probe LX/GT, Taurus SHO, and T-Bird Super Coupe) front/rear disc. Body construction: (Crown Vic) separate body and frame; (others) unibody. Fuel tank: (Escort) 13.0 gal.; (Tempo) 15.9 gal.; (Tempo 4WD) 14.2 gal.; (Probe) 15.1 gal.; (Taurus) 16.0 gal.; (Crown Vic) 18.0 gal.; (T-Bird) 19.0 gal.

DRIVETRAIN OPTIONS: Engines: 3.0-liter V-6: Taurus L/GL sed ($696). 3.8-liter V-6: Taurus GL wagon/LX sed ($400); Taurus GL sed ($1096). Transmission/Differential: Five-speed manual trans.: Escort LX sed ($76). Automatic transaxle: Escort ($515) except LX wagon ($439); Tempo ($539); Probe ($617). Automatic transmission: T-Bird Super Coupe ($539). Traction-Lok differential: Crown Vic/T-Bird ($100). Steering/Suspension/Brakes: Power steering: Escort Pony/LX ($235). Variable-assist power steering: Taurus ($104). H.D./handling susp.: Taurus/Crown Vic ($26). Auto load leveling: Crown Vic ($195). Trailer towing pkg.: Crown Vic ($378-$405). Anti-lock brakes: Probe LX/GT ($924): Taurus ($985); Thunderbird ($1085).

TEMPO CONVENIENCE/APPEARANCE OPTIONS: Preferred Equip Pkgs: 2-Dr GL (226A) incl 5 Spd Manual, Air Cond., Rr Window Defroster, Light Group, Power Lock Grp, pwr decklid release, remote fuel filler door, Dual Elect. Remote Control Mirrors, Tilt Wheel ($486); 4-Dr GL ($538). (229A) Special Value GLS 5 Spd Manual, Air Conditioner, Pwr Lock Grp, pwr decklid release, remote fuel filler door, Tilt Strg Wheel, Pwr Driver's Seat, Prem Sound System, Spd Control, 2-Dr GLS ($1267); 4-Dr GLS ($1319). (233A) Special Value LX, Auto Transaxle, Air Conditioner, Rr Defroster, Decklid Luggage Rack, 4-Dr LX ($911). Special Value AWD, Auto Transaxle, Rr Window Defroster, Power Lock Grp, pwr decklid release, remote fuel filler door, Tilt Strg Wheel, Pwr Side Windows, 4-Dr AWD ($378). Air Conditioner ($807). Frt Center Armrest ($55). Rr Window Defroster ($150). Spt Instrument Cluster ($87). Light Grp, ashtray, glovebox, eng compartment, dome, door switches & map light ($38). Decklid Luggage Rack ($115). Pwr Lock Grp, pwr dr locks, pwr decklid release, remote fuel filler door (NC); 2-Dr ($246); 4-Dr ($298). Dual Elect. Remote Control Mirrors ($121). Elect. AM/FM Stereo Radio w/Cass ($137). Pwr Driver's Seat ($261). Premium Sound System (4 spkrs & amplifier) ($138). Speed Control ($191). Sports Appearance Grp ($1178). Tilt Steering Wheel ($124). Supplemental Air Bag Restraint System, GL ($815); LX or GL w/226A ($690). Polycast Wheels ($193). Pwr Side Windows (4-Dr) ($306). Calif. Emission System ($100). Clearcoat Metallic Paint ($91). Lower Accent Paint Treatment ($159). All Vinyl Seat Trim ($37). Frt License Plate Bracket (NC). Engine Block Heater ($20). Styled Steel Wheels/Trim Rings (NC). P185/70R14 WSW Tires ($82).

ESCORT CONVENIENCE/APPEARANCE OPTIONS: LX Series (302A) 5 Spd Manual Transaxle Pkg, Electronic Digital Clock/Overhead Console, Rr Window Defroster, Tinted Glass, Instrumentation Grp incl. odometer, temp gauge, white graphics, Light/Security Grp incl. illum pass side visor mirror, glovebox light, cargo compartment lights (incl liftgate light switch), eng compartment light, ashtray light, rear door courtesy light switch (4-dr only), headlamps-on chimes, remote liftgate release (hatchback only), Dual

Elect. Remote Cntrl Mirrors, Vinyl Bodyside Moldings, Elect. AM/FM Stereo Radio, Pwr Strg, Luxury Wheel Covers, Interval Wipers, 2- & 4-Dr LX hatchback ($562); 4-Dr LX Wgn ($486). (321A) Auto Transaxle Pkg, all equipment in 320A but Auto Transaxle 2- & 4-Dr LX hatchback ($965); 4-Dr LX Wgn ($889). Preferred Equipment Pkg GT (330A) incl HO 4-Cyl Eng, 5 Spd Transaxle, Air Cond, Rr Defroster, Tinted Glass, Light Security Grp, Elect. AM/FM Stereo Radio Cass, Spd Control, Tilt Strg Wheel, Interval Wipers ($829). Air Conditioner ($720). HD Battery ($27). Electronic Digital Clock/Overhead Console ($82). Rr Window Defroster ($150). Tinted Glass ($105). Instrumentation Group (tachometer, trip odometer, temp gauge, white graphics) ($87). Light/Security Grp, illum pass side visor mirror, glovebox light, cargo compartment light (incl. liftgate light switch), eng compart. light, ashtray light, rear door courtesy light switch (4-dr), headlamps-on chimes, remote liftgate release (hatchback only), LX ($78); GT ($67). Dlx Luggage Rack ($115). Color-Keyed Electric Remote Cntrl Mirrors ($98). Vinyl Bodyside Moldings ($50). Clearcoat Paint, LX ($91); GT (incl tu-tone paint) ($183). Tu-Tone Paint ($91). AM Radio ($54). Elect. AM/FM Stereo, Pony ($206); LX ($152). Elect. AM/FM Cass Tape Player, Pony ($343); LX ($289); GT ($137). Premium Sound System ($138). Speed Control ($191). Split Fold Down Rr Seat ($50). Tilt Steering Wheel ($124). Luxury Wheel Covers ($71). Vinyl Trim ($37). Polycast Wheels ($193). Interval Windshield Wipers ($55). Rear Window Wiper/Washer ($126). H.D. Alternator ($27). Frt License Plate Bracket (NC). Calif. Emissions System (NC). Eng Block Heater ($20). Full Size Spare Tire ($73). P175/70R14 WSW Tires, LX ($73).

PROBE CONVENIENCE/APPEARANCE OPTIONS: Preferred Equip Pkgs (251A) Tinted Glass, Tilt Strg Column & Cluster, Rr Defroster, Convenience Grp incl Interval Wipers, Light Grp incl glovebox light, underhood lights, fade-to-off dome lamp, headlamps-on warning light, Dual Electric Remote Mirrors ($158). (253A) Electronic Instrument Cluster, Electronic Air Cond Illum. Entry, Pwr Driver's Seat, Trip Computer, Rr Washer/Wiper, Walk-in Pass Seat, Pwr Windows, Spd Control, Pwr Dr Locks, AM/FM Elect. Cass w/Premium Sound/Pwr Antenna, Cargo Tie Down Net ($2088). (261A) Anti-Lock Braking System, Electronic Air Cond, Illum Entry, Pwr Driver's Seat, Trip Computer, Vehicle Maintenance Monitor (Overhead Console), Rr Washer/Wiper, Walk-in Pass Seat, Pwr Windows, Spd Control, Pwr Dr Locks, AM/FM Elect. Cass w/Premium Sound/Pwr Antenna, Dual Illum Visor Vanity Mirrors, Cargo Tie Down Net ($2795). Air Conditioner w/Pkg 250A incl tinted glass ($927); Other Models ($807). Rr Window Defroster ($150). Leather Seating Surface Trim ($489). Pwr Dr Locks ($155). Speed Control ($191). Flip-Up Open Air Roof ($355). Alum Wheels, w/GL (Pkgs 250A or 251A) ($313); w/LX (Pkg 252A or 253A) ($252). Pwr Windows ($241). AM/FM Elect. Stereo Radio w/Premium Sound ($168). AM/FM Elect. Cass w/Premium Sound/Pwr Antenna ($344). AM/FM Premium Elect. Cass w/Premium Sound/CD Player/Pwr Antenna w/Pkgs 251A, 252A, or 260A ($1052); w/Pkgs 253A or 261A ($709). Calif. Emission System (NC). Frt License Plate Bracket (NC). Eng Block Heater ($20).

TAURUS CONVENIENCE/APPEARANCE OPTIONS: Preferred Equip Pkg GL (202A) 4-cyl. Engine, Auto Transaxle, Air Cond, Spd Control, Remote Decklid/Liftgate & Fuel Dr Releases, dual beam map light, eng compartment light, dual courtesy lights, headlamps-on reminder chime, Rr Defroster, Rocker Panel Mldgs, Paint Stripe, Pwr Dr Locks, 6-Way Pwr Driver's Seat, Finned Wheel Covers, Power Windows ($1688). LX (207A) 3.0-liter V-6, Air Cond, Rr Window Defroster, Pwr Dr Locks, Elect. AM/FM Stereo Radio w/Cass, 6-Way Pwr Driver's Seat, Pwr Windows, Cast Alum Wheels (styled wheels may be substituted), Auto Lamp System, F&R Flr Mats, Illum Entry System, Premium Sound System, Leather-Wrapped Strg Wheel ($748). LX Sedan (208A) 3.8-liter V-6, Spd Control, Remote Decklid/Liftgate & Fuel Dr Releases, dual beam map light, eng compartment light, dual courtesy lights, headlamps-on reminder chime, Rocker Panel Moldings, Paint Stripe, Pwr Dr Locks, Cast Alum Wheels, Autolamp System, Flr Mats, Leather-Wrapped Strg Wheel, Elect. Climate Cntrl air cond, Anti-Lock Braking System, High Level Audio System, Elect. Instrument Cluster, Keyless Entry System, Pwr Radio Antenna, 6-Way Pwr Dual Control Seats ($3099); LX Wagon ($1714). SHO (211A) DOHC 3.0-liter V-6, 5 Spd Manual, Air Cond, Spd Control, Remote Decklid/Liftgate & Fuel Dr. Releases, dual beam map light, eng compartment light, dual courtesy lights, headlamps-on reminder chime, Rr Window Defroster, Pwr Dr. Locks, 6-Way Pwr Driver's Seat, Pwr Side Windows, Cast Alum Wheels, Autolamp System, F&R Flr Mats, Illum Entry Syst, Leather-Wrapped Strg Wheel, Anti-Lock Braking System, High Level Audio System ($533). (212A) DOHC 3.0-liter V-8, 5 Spd Man, Spd Control, Remote Decklid/Liftgate & Fuel Dr Releases, Light Grp, Rear Defroster, Pwr Door Locks, Power Windows, Cast Alum Wheels, Autolamp System. F&R Flr Mats, Leather-Wrapped Strg Wheel. Elect. Climate Control Air Cond, Anti-Lock Braking System, Keyless Entry System, Power Radio Antenna, JBL Audio System, 6-Way Pwr Dual Control Seats, Leather Seat Trim, Power Moonroof ($2724). Conventional Spare Tire ($73). Electronic Air Conditioning, Pkg 202A ($990); SHO, LX, or Pkg 204A ($183). Manual Air Conditioning ($807). Autolamp System ($73). HD Battery ($27). Cargo Area Cover ($66). Cornering Lamps ($68). Rr Window Defroster ($150). Engine Block Heater ($20). F&R Floor Mats ($43). Remote Decklid & Fuel Door, Sedans ($91); Wgns (Fuel dr only) ($41). Extended Range Fuel Tank ($46). Illum Entry System ($82). Diagnostic Instrument Cluster ($89). Elect. Instrument Cluster, LX ($239); GL ($351). Keyless Entry System w/Pkg 207A or 211A ($137); Other Models ($218). Light Grp: dual beam map light, eng compartment light, dual courtesy lights, headlamps-on reminder chime ($59). "Picnic Table" Load Floor Extension ($66). Pwr Door Locks ($205). Dual Illum Visor Mirrors ($100). Rocker Panel Moldings ($55). Pwr Moonroof ($741). Clearcoat Paint ($188). Automatic Parking Brake Release ($12). CD Player ($491). High Level Audio System w/Pkg 204A ($335); w/Pkg 207A ($167); Other Models ($472). Elect. AM/FM Stereo Search Radio w/Cass Player ($137). Premium Sound System ($168). Pwr Radio Antenna ($76). JBL Audio System ($488). Rear Facing Third Seat, Wgns ($155). 6-Way Pwr Driver's Seat ($261). Dual 6-Way Power Seats, LX or Pkg. 204A or 211A ($261); Other Models ($522). Speed Control ($191). Leather-Wrapped Steering Wheel ($63). Paint Stripe ($61). Rr. Window Washer/Wiper ($126). Finned Wheel Covers ($65). Cast Aluminum Wheels, GL ($279); LX, or Pkg 204A ($215). Styled Road Wheels, GL ($193); LX or Pkg 204A ($128). Pwr Side Windows ($306). Insta-Clear Windshield ($250). Calif. Emission System ($100). Bucket Seats (NC). Leather Seat Trim, LX & SHO ($489); GL ($593). Vinyl Seat Trim, L ($51); GL ($37). Frt License Plate Bracket (NC). Frt Floor Mats ($26). Tilt Steering Column-Delete ($76 credit). P205/70R14 WSW ($82). P205/65R15 BSW ($65). P205/65R15 WSW ($146).

LTD CROWN VICTORIA CONVENIENCE/APPEARANCE OPTIONS:
4-Dr LTD Crown Victoria LX (112A) Auto OD Trans, F&R Bumper Guards, Rr Window Defroster, Spd Control, Pwr Lock Grp, Elect. AM/FM Stereo Radio Cass, Light Grp ($420). (113A) all equipment in 112A plus 6-Way Pwr Driver's Seat, Cast Alum Wheels, Light Grp, Cornering Lamps, Illum Entry System, Leather-Wrapped Strg Wheel ($859). (114A) Auto OD Trans, F&R Bumper Guards, Spd Control, Power Lock Grp, Cast Alum Wheels, Light Grp, Cornering Lamps, F&R Flr Mats (Color-keyed), Illum Entry System, Leather-Wrapped Steering Wheel, Auto Climate Control Air Cond, High Level Audio System, Power Antenna, Dual 6-Way Power Seats ($1490). 4-Dr LTD Crown Victoria Wgn & Country Squire Wgn (131A) Auto OD Trans, Bumper Guards (NC). Rear Defroster, Spd Control, Power Lock Grp, Elect. AM/FM Stereo Radio Cass, 6-Way Pwr Driver's Seat, Dual Facing Rr Seats ($938). 4-Dr LTD Crown Victoria Wgn & Country Squire LX Wgn (133A) all equipment in (131A) plus Cast Alum Wheels, HD battery, Cornering Lamps, F&R Color-Keyed Mats, Illum Entry System, Leather-Wrapped Strg Wheel ($779). (134A) all equipment in (133A) except Rr Defroster, Elect. AM/FM Stereo Cass, 6-Way Pwr Driver's Seat plus Auto Climate Control Air Cond, High Level Audio, Pwr Radio Antenna, Dual 6-Way Power Seats ($1117). Auto Temp Air Conditioner w/Pkgs 112A, 113A, 131A or 133A ($66); Other Models ($216). HD Battery ($27). Frt License Plate Bracket (NC). F&R Bumper Guards ($62). Cornering Lamps ($68). Rr Window Defroster ($150). F&R Color-Keyed Floor Mats ($43). Eng Block Heater ($20). Illum Entry System ($82). Light Grp: dual beam map light, dual courtesy lights, eng compartment light ($59). Pwr Lock Grp: pwr dr locks, pwr mirrors on base, remote control electric decklid release on sdn, pwr doorgate lock on wgn ($255). Vinyl Insert Bodyside Moldings ($66). Clearcoat Paint ($230). Tu-Tone Paint/Tape Treatment ($159). High Level Audio System w/Pkg 112A, 113A, 131A or 133A ($335); Other Models ($472). Elect. AM/FM Stereo Radio w/Cass Player ($137). Pwr Radio Antenna ($76). Premium Sound System ($168). 6-Way Pwr Driver's Seat ($261). Dual 6-Way Pwr Seats w/Pkgs 113A, 131A or 133A ($261); Other Models ($522). Dual Facing Rear Seats ($173). Speed Control ($191). Leather-Wrapped Steering Wheel ($63). Vinyl Roof Delete ($200 credit). Locking Wire Style Wheel Covers ($184). Cast Alum Wheels ($440). Insta-Clear Windshield ($250). Brghm Half Vinyl Roof ($665). Calif. Emission System ($100). All-Vinyl Seat Trim ($37). Duraweave Vinyl Seat Trim ($96). Leather Seat Trim ($489).

THUNDERBIRD CONVENIENCE/APPEARANCE OPTIONS:
Preferred Equipment Pkg (151A) Standard Elect. AM/FM Stereo Radio w/Cass Player/Clock, Rr Window Defroster, 6-Way Pwr Pass Seat, Pwr Lock Grp, 6-Way Pwr Driver's Seat, Frt Flr Mats, Keyless Entry, Luxury Group incl Bright Window Mldgs, Spd Control & Tilt Strg Wheel, Dual Elect. Remote Mirrors, Styled Road Wheel Covers, Luxury Light Convenience Grp, Cast Alum Wheels w/P215/70R15 BSW Tires ($1288). LX (155A) Rear Defroster, 6-Way Pwr Pass Seat, Keyless Entry System, Elect. Premium Radio Cass w/Premium Sound, Pwr Antenna, Frt Flr Mats, Luxury Grp incl Bright Window Mldgs, Spd Control & Tilt Strg Wheel, Dual Elect. Remote Mirrors, Styled Road Wheel Covers, Luxury Light/Convenience Grp, Cast Alum Wheels w/P215/70R15 BSW Tires ($819). Anti-Theft System ($183). Keyless Entry Base Model w/o Luxury Grp, or Super Cpe w/o Lux/Light Convenience Grp ($219); LX, Base w/Luxury Grp, or Super Cpe w/Luxury Light/Convenience Grp ($137). Frt. Floor Mats ($33). Luxury Light/Convenience Grp (Cornering Lamps, Dual Illum Visor Vanity Mirrors, Illum Entry System, Autolamp System, Auto Day/Night Mirror, Vehicle Maintenance Monitor) ($426). Pwr Moonroof, Super Coupe w/o Luxury Light/Convenience Grp ($841); Base, LX or Super Coupe w/Luxury Light/Convenience Grp ($741). Clearcoat Paint ($188). Elect. Premium Radio Cass w/Premium Sound, base Model w/o Pkg 151A, Super Cpe w/o Pkg 157A ($442); w/Pkg 151A or 157A ($305).

JBL Audio System ($488). Compact Disc Player ($491). Power Antenna ($76). Calif. Emission System ($100). Leather Seating Surfaces Trim, LX ($489). Super Coupe ($622). Frt License Plate Bracket (NC). Cold Weather Grp, eng block heater, H.D. battery, H.D. alternator, rear window defroster, base model w/o 151A, LX w/o 155A or Super Cpe w/Manual Trans & w/o 157A ($195); Super Cpe w/Auto Trans & w/o 157A ($168); Pkgs 151A, 155A, or Super Cpe w/Pkg 157A & Manual Trans ($45); Super Cpe w/Pkg 157A & Auto Trans ($18). Locking Wire Wheel Covers, base model w/Pkg 151A ($143); Base w/o 151A ($228). LX w/Pkg 155A & P205/70R15 WSW Tires (NC). Cast Alum Wheels w/P215/70R15 BSW Tires, base model w/Pkg 151A ($213); w/o Pkg 151A ($298). P205/70R15 WSW LX & Base ($73). Eagle GT+4 P225/60R16 95V All-Season Perf, Super Coupe ($73). Conventional Spare Tire, base or LX ($73).

HISTORY: U.S. model year production: 1,258,428 (incl. Mustangs). Calendar year sales by U.S. dealers: 1,880,389 (incl. Mustangs).

1991 FORD

1991 Ford Escort GT three-door hatchback. (OCW)

Coming off a year where Ford's U.S. automotive operations lost a reported $17 million, and predictions for an even tougher year for sales in 1991, Ford maintained a high level of product development throughout the year. An all-new (1992) Crown Victoria was introduced in early-1991 as was the all-new Escort for 1991, which was actually launched in the spring of 1990. The new Escort's design was primarily contributed by Mazda Motor Corp. in Japan. The car was built in both Mexico and domestically in Wayne, Mich. Other developments at Ford included powertrain and functional improvements including the addition of a 5.0-liter V-8 in the Thunderbird and an electronically controlled automatic transaxle for the Taurus. Anti-lock brakes were now standard on the Taurus LX line of cars.

ESCORT — FOUR — All new for 1991, the Escort featured a revamped profile with a lower cowl and belt that provided more glass area and improved visibility. Inside, the new Escort featured an ergonomically-designed, wraparound instrument panel and a larger interior package offered five-passenger seating capacity (up from four the year previous). Available in three series, Pony, LX and GT, models offered were a Pony two-door hatchback, LX two- and four-door hatchbacks and station wagon, and GT two-door hatchback. The Pony and LX versions were powered by the upgraded 1.9-liter four-cylinder engine, which was now rated at 88 horsepower. The GT used the Mazda-produced 127-hp DOHC 1.8-liter four. The five-speed manual transmission was standard and the four-speed automatic was optional on all Escorts. Four-wheel disc brakes were standard on the GT.

1991 Ford Escort LX station wagon. (OCW)

TEMPO — FOUR — The Tempo received several functional improvements for 1991 to reduce the amount of noise and vibration transmitted into the interior. Included in these upgrades were front structure enhancements, new engine mount bracket, new fan and new front spring isolators. The five-passenger Tempo was available in four series: GL (two- and four-door sedans), GLS (two- and four-door sedans), LX (four-door sedan) and the four-door Tempo four-wheel-drive sedan. A driver's side airbag was again offered as an option on four-door GL and LX models. The 2.3-liter HSC (high swirl combustion) four-cylinder engine was the standard powerplant on GL and LX models. An HSO (higher specific output) version of the 2.3-liter four was used with the GLS and four-wheel-drive Tempos. A three-speed automatic transaxle was standard on four-wheel-drive models while a five-speed manual was the base unit for all other Tempos.

1991 Ford Tempo GL sedan. (OCW)

1991 Ford Taurus LX sedan. (OCW)

PROBE – FOUR/V-6 — The two-door Probe was again offered in three series in 1991: GL, LX and GT. Prove GL continued using the 2.2-liter, 12-valve electronically fuel-injected four-cylinder engine. The Probe LX again used the 3.0-liter electronically fuel-injected V-6 engine. The Probe GT was powered by the turbocharged 2.2-liter electronically fuel-injected four. The five-speed manual overdrive transmission was standard and the four-speed automatic with overdrive was optional equipment. Anti-lock brakes were optional on the LX model's four-wheel power disc brakes. The GT model's handling suspension featured sport-tuned performance components and a computerized Automatic Adjusting Suspension.

TAURUS — FOUR/V-6 — The Taurus underwent significant functional improvements for 1991. Available in four series, L, GL, LX and the SHO sedan, the LX sedans and station wagons came standard with anti-lock brakes while the Taurus SHO sedan received new 16-inch cast aluminum wheels mounted with Goodyear GT+4 performance tires, a larger clutch with lower pedal effort and modifications to the five-speed transaxle for smoother shifting. A new package was offered for 1991, the Taurus "L-Plus," which came equipped with air conditioning, rear window defroster, power locks and automatic transaxle. The Taurus GL's option list included bucket seats, floor-mounted shifter and a console for added storage. All Taurus models came standard with driver's side airbags. The Taurus L and GL sedans were powered by the 2.5-liter four-cylinder engine which received sequential electronic multi-port fuel injection and a 15-hp boost to 105-hp for 1991. Taurus L and GL station wagons and LX sedan used the 3.0-liter V-6 engines that also received sequential electronic multi-port fuel injection. The Taurus SHO sedan came standard with the 220-hp DOHC 3.0-liter 24-valve V-6. The LX station wagon was powered by the 3.8-liter V-6. All except the aforementioned SHO model used the electronic overdrive four-speed automatic transaxle.

1991 Ford Taurus LX station wagon. (OCW)

1991 Ford Taurus SHO sedan. (OCW)

1991 Ford LTD Country Squire station wagon. (OCW)

LTD CROWN VICTORIA — **V-8** — Awaiting the spring 1991 launch of the all-new 1992 Crown Victoria models, the 1991 models were essentially carry-overs from the year previous. The three series of sedans were again offered: base, 'S' and LX, and, for the final time, the Crown Victoria and Country Squire station wagons were available. All models were powered by the 5.0-liter V-8 mated to a four-speed automatic overdrive transmission.

THUNDERBIRD — **V-6/V-8** — The Thunderbird two-door coupe was again offered in three series: base, LX and Super Coupe (SC). The 3.8-liter V-6 was the standard engine for base and LX models while V-8 power returned to the Thunderbird in 1991 with the 200-hp 5.0-liter V-8 optional in the base and LX models with four-speed automatic transmission. A 210-hp supercharged version of the 3.8-liter V-6 was used in the SC model with the five-speed manual transmission standard and the four-speed automatic overdrive unit optional. Base Thunderbirds received luxurious cloth-seat inserts. LX models got leather accents and new vinyl-and-cloth inserts in place of woodgrain trim panels. The SC model received a new trim style that included the Thunderbird emblem embroidered on upper seat backs. A new electronic automatic temperature control system was optional on the LX and SC models.

I.D. DATA: Ford's 17-symbol Vehicle Identification Number (VIN) was stamped on a metal tab fastened to the instrument panel, visible through the windshield. The first three symbols indicate manufacturer, make and vehicle type. The fourth symbol denotes restraint system. Next comes a letter (usually 'P'), followed by two digits that indicate Model Number, as shown in left column of tables below. (Example: '10' Escort Pony two-door hatchback). Symbol eight indicates engine type. Next is a check digit. Symbol ten indicates model year ('M' 1991). Symbol eleven denotes assembly plant. The final six digits make up the sequence number, starting with 000001 (except Probe, 500001).

1991 Ford Thunderbird LX coupe. (OCW)

1991 Ford Thunderbird Super Coupe. (OCW)

ESCORT (FOUR)

Model No.	Body/ Style No.	Body Type & Seating	Factory Price	Shipping Weight	Prod. Total
P	10	2-dr. Pony Hatch-5P	7976	2287	Note 1
P	11	2-dr. LX Hatch-5P	8667	2312	Note 1
P	14	4-dr. LX Hatch-5P	9095	2355	114,944
P	15	4-dr. LX Sta Wag-5P	9680	2411	57,337
P	12	2-dr. GT Hatch-5P	11484	2458	Note 1

NOTE 1: Production of two-door hatchback models totaled 182,445 with no further breakout available.

TEMPO (FOUR)

P	30	2-dr. L Sed-5P	8306	NA	Note 1
P	35	4-dr. L Sed-5P	8449	NA	Note 2
P	31	2-dr. GL Sed-5P	9541	2529	Note 1
P	36	4-dr. GL Sed-5P	9691	2587	Note 2
P	37	4-dr. LX Sed-5P	10663	2628	Note 2
P	39	4-dr. AWD Sed-5P	11390	2808	Note 2
P	33	2-dr. GLS Sed-5P	10358	2545	Note 1
P	38	4-dr. GLS Sed-5P	10506	2603	Note 2

NOTE 1: Production of two-door sedan models totaled 4,876 with no further breakout available.

NOTE 2: Production of four-door sedan models totaled 180,969 with no further breakout available.

PROBE (FOUR/V-6 in LX only)

T	20	2-dr. GL Cpe-4P	11691	2730	Note 1
T	21	2-dr. LX Cpe-4P	13229	2970	Note 1
T	22	2-dr. GT Cpe-4P	14964	3000	Note 1

NOTE 1: Production of two-door coupe models totaled 73,200 with no further breakout available.

TAURUS (FOUR/V-6)

P	50	4-dr. L Sed-6P	13352/13873	3049/3097	Note 1
P	55	4-dr. L Sta Wag-6P	-----/14874	----/3276	Note 2
P	52	4-dr. GL Sed-6P	13582/14103	3062/3110	Note 1

Model No.	Body/ Style No.	Body Type & Seating	Factory Price	Shipping Weight	Prod. Total
P	57	4-dr. GL Sta Wag-6P	----/14990	----/3283	Note 2
P	53	4-dr. LX Sedan-6P	----/17373	----/3170	Note 1
P	58	4-dr. LX Sta Wag-6P	----/18963	----/3345	Note 2
P	54	4-dr. SHO Sed-6P	----/22071	----/3463	Note 1

NOTE: Taurus prices and weights to left of slash are for four-cylinder, to right for V-6 engine.

NOTE 1: Production of four-door sedan models totaled 218,311 with no further breakout available.

NOTE 2: Production of station wagon models totaled 62,786 with no further breakout available.

LTD CROWN VICTORIA (V-8)

P	73	4-dr. Sed-6P	18227	3822	Note 1
P	72	4-dr. 'S' Sed-6P	17045	3822	Note 1
P	76	4-dr. Sta Wag-6P	18083	4028	Note 2
P	78	4-dr. Ctry Sqr-6P	18335	4047	Note 2

LTD CROWN VICTORIA LX (V-8)

P	74	4-dr. Sed-6P	18863	3841	Note 1
P	77	4-dr. Sta Wag-8P	18833	4021	Note 2
P	79	4-dr. Ctry Sqr-8P	19085	4082	Note 2

NOTE 1: Production of four-door sedan models totaled 91,315 with no further breakout available.

NOTE 2: Production of station wagon models totaled 8,000 with no further breakout available.

THUNDERBIRD (V-6/V-8)

P	60	2-dr. Cpe-5P	15318/16398	3550/3732	Note 1
P	62	2-dr. LX Cpe-5P	17734/18814	3572/3742	Note 1
P	64	2-dr. Super Cpe-5P	20999/-----	3767/----	Note 1

NOTE: Thunderbird prices and weights to left of slash for V-6, to right for V-8.

NOTE 1: Production of two-door coupe models totaled 77,688 with no further breakout available.

ENGINE [Base Four (Escort)]: Inline. Overhead cam. Four-cylinder. Cast-iron block and aluminum head. Displacement: 113 cid (1.9 liters). Bore & stroke: 3.23 x 3.46 in. Compression ratio: 9.0:1. Brake horsepower: 90 at 4600 rpm. Torque: 106 lbs.-ft. at 3400 rpm. Five main bearings. Hydraulic valve lifters. Sequential fuel injection.

ENGINE [Base Four (Escort GT)]: High-output, DOHC MFI version of 1.9-liter four above. Horsepower: 127 at 6500 rpm. Torque: 114 lbs.-ft. at 4500 rpm.

1991 Ford Escort GT. (OCW)

ENGINE [Base Four (Probe)]: Inline. Overhead cam. Four-cylinder. Cast-iron block. Displacement: 133 cid (2.2 liters). Bore & stroke: 3.39 x 3.70 in. Compression ratio: 8.6:1. Brake horsepower: 110 at 4700 rpm. Torque: 130 lbs.-ft. at 3000 rpm. Hydraulic valve lifters. Multi-port fuel injection.

ENGINE [Turbocharged Four (Probe GT)]: Same as 2.2-liter four above, with turbocharger and intercooler - Compression ratio: 7.8:1. Horsepower: 145 at 4300 rpm. Torque: 190 lbs.-ft. at 3500 rpm.

ENGINE [Base Four (Tempo)]: Inline. Overhead valve. Four-cylinder. Cast-iron block and head. Displacement: 140 cid (2.3 liters). Bore & stroke: 3.70 x 3.30 in. Compression ratio: 9.0:1. Brake horsepower: 98 at 4400 rpm. Torque: 124 lbs.-ft. at 2200 rpm. Five main bearings. Hydraulic valve lifters. Multi-port fuel injection. High Swirl Combustion (HSC) design.

ENGINE [Base Four (Tempo 4WD)]: High-output version of HSC four above - Horsepower: 100 at 4400 rpm. Torque: 130 lbs.-ft. at 2600 rpm.

ENGINE [Base Four (Taurus)]: Inline. Overhead valve. Four-cylinder. Cast-iron block and head. Displacement: 153 cid (2.5 liters). Bore & stroke: 3.70 x 3.60 in. Compression ratio: 9.0:1. Brake horsepower: 105 at 4400 rpm. Torque: 140 lbs.-ft. at 2400 rpm. Five main bearings. Hydraulic valve lifters. Sequential fuel injection.

ENGINE [Base V-6 (Probe LX/Taurus L and GL wagons/Taurus LX sedan): Optional (Taurus L and GL sedans)]: 60-degree, overhead valve V-6. Cast-iron block and head. Displacement: 182 cid (3.0 liters). Bore & stroke: 3.50 x 3.10 in. Compression ratio: 9.3:1. Brake horsepower: (Probe LX) 145 at 4800 RPM; (all others) 140 at 4800 rpm. Torque: (Probe LX) 165 lbs.-ft. at 3400 RPM; (all others) 160 lbs.-ft. at 3000 rpm. Four main bearings. Hydraulic valve lifters. (Probe LX) Multi-port fuel injection; (all others) Sequential fuel injection.

ENGINE [Base V-6 (Taurus SHO)]: Dual-overhead-cam V-6 (24 valve). Cast-iron block and head. Displacement: 182 cid (3.0 liters). Bore & stroke: 3.50 x 3.15 in. Compression ratio: 9.8:1. Brake horsepower: 220 at 6200 rpm. Torque: 200 lbs.-ft. at 4800 rpm. Four main bearings. Hydraulic valve lifters. Sequential fuel injection.

ENGINE [Base V-6 (Thunderbird and Thunderbird LX): Optional: (Taurus GL sedan and wagon/Taurus LX sedan)]: 90-degree, overhead valve V-6. Cast-iron block and aluminum head. Displacement: 232 cid (3.8 liters). Bore & stroke: 3.80 x 3.40 in. Compression ratio: 9.0:1. Brake horsepower: 140 at 3800 rpm. Torque: (Taurus) 215 lbs.-ft. at 2200 RPM; (Thunderbird) 215 lbs.-ft. at 2400. Four main bearings. Hydraulic valve lifters. Sequential fuel injection.

ENGINE [Supercharged V-6 (Thunderbird Super Coupe)]: Same as 232 cid (3.8-liter) V-6 above, except - Compression ratio: 8.2:1. Horsepower: 210 at 4000 rpm. Torque: 315 lbs.-ft. at 2600 rpm.

ENGINE [Base V-8 (LTD Crown Victoria): Optional: (Thunderbird and Thunderbird LX)]: 90-degree, overhead valve V-8. Cast-iron block and head. Displacement: 302 cid (5.0 liters). Bore & stroke: 4.00 x 3.00 in. Compression ratio: (LTD Crown Vic) 8.9:1; (Thunderbird) 9.0:1. Brake horsepower: (LTD Crown Vic) 150 at 3200 RPM; (Thunderbird) 200 at 4000 rpm. Torque: (LTD Crown Vic) 270 lbs.-ft. at 2000 RPM; (Thunderbird) 275 lbs.-ft. at 3000 rpm. Five main bearings. Hydraulic valve lifters. Sequential fuel injection.

CHASSIS DATA: Wheelbase: (Escort) 98.4 in.; (Tempo) 99.9 in.; (Probe) 99.0 in.: (Taurus) 106.0 in.; (Crown Vic) 114.3 in.; (T-Bird) 113.0 in. Overall Length: (Escort) 170.0 in.; (Escort wag) 171.3 in.; (Tempo two-door) 176.7 in.; (Tempo four-door) 177.0 in.; (Probe) 177.0 in.; (Taurus) 188.4 in.; (Taurus wag) 191.9 in.; (Crown Vic) 211.0 in.; (Crown Vic wag) 215.7 in.; (T-Bird) 198.7 in. Height: (Escort) 52.5 in.; (Escort wag) 53.6 in.; (Tempo two-door) 52.8 in.; (Tempo four-door) 52.9 in.; (Probe) 51.8 in.; (Taurus) 54.1 in.; (Taurus wag) 55.4 in.; (Crown Vic) 55.6 in.; (Crown Vic wag) 56.5 in.; (T-Bird) 52.7 in. Width: (Escort) 66.7 in.; (Tempo) 68.3 in.; (Probe) 67.9 in.; (Probe GT) 68.3 in.; (Taurus) 70.8 in.; (Crown Vic) 77.5 in.; (Crown Vic wag) 79.3 in.; (T-Bird) 72.7 in. Front Tread: (Escort) 56.5 in.; (Tempo) 54.9 in.; (Probe) 57.3 in.; (Taurus) 61.6 in.; (Crown Vic) 62.2 in.; (T-Bird) 61.6 in. Rear Tread: (Escort) 56.5 in.; (Tempo) 57.6 in.; (Probe) 57.7 in.; (Taurus) 60.5 in.; (Crown Vic) 63.3 in.; (T-Bird) 60.2 in. Standard Tires: (Escort Pony) P175/70R13; (Escort GT) P185/60HR15; (Tempo) P185/70R14; (Probe) P185/70SR14; (Probe LX) P195/70R14; (Probe GT) P205/60VR15; (Taurus) P205/70R14; (Taurus LX) P205/70R14; (Taurus SHO) P215/60R16; (Crown Vic) P215/70R15; (T-Bird) P205/70R15; (T-Bird Super Cpe) P225/60R16.

TECHNICAL: Transmission: Five-speed manual transaxle standard on Escort, Tempo, Probe, Taurus SHO and Thunderbird Super Coupe. Three-speed automatic standard on Tempo four-wheel-drive. Four-speed overdrive automatic standard on Taurus, Crown Vic and T-Bird. Drive Axle: (Crown Vic/T-Bird) rear; (others) front. Steering: (Crown Vic) recirculating ball; (others) rack/pinion. Front Suspension: (Escort/Tempo) MacPherson struts with lower control arms, coil springs and stabilizer bar; (Probe) MacPherson struts with asymmetrical control arms, strut-mounted coil springs and stabilizer bar; (Taurus) MacPherson struts with control arms, coil springs and stabilizer bar; (Crown Vic) upper/lower control arms w/coil springs and stabilizer bar; (T-Bird) independent long spindle with short/long arms, coil springs and stabilizer bar. Rear Suspension: (Escort) trailing arms w/modified MacPherson struts and coil springs on lower control arms; (Tempo) independent trailing four-link with MacPherson struts; (Probe) independent struts, four-bar with single trailing arms, coil springs and stabilizer bar. (Taurus sedan) MacPherson struts w/parallel suspension arms and coil springs; (Taurus wag) upper/lower control arms, coil springs and stabilizer bar; (Crown Vic) rigid axle w/four links and coil springs; (Thunderbird) independent with upper/lower arms, coil springs and stabilizer bar. Brakes: Front disc, rear drum (power assisted) except (Escort GT, Probe LX and GT, Taurus SHO and T-Bird Super Coupe) front/rear disc. Body construction: (Crown Vic) separate body and frame; (others) unibody. Fuel tank: (Escort) 11.9 gal.; (Tempo) 15.9 gal.; (Tempo 4WD) 14.2 gal.; (Probe) 15.1 gal.; (Taurus) 16.0 gal.; (Crown Vic) 18.0 gal.; (T-Bird) 19.0 gal.

DRIVETRAIN OPTIONS: Engines: 3.0-liter V-6: Taurus L and GL sed ($521). 3.8-liter V-6: Taurus GL ($1276). 5.0-liter V-8: Thunderbird and LX cpe ($1080). Transmission/Differential: Three-speed automatic transaxle: Tempo (except stnd in 4WD) ($563). Four-speed automatic transaxle: Escort ($732); Probe ($732); T-Bird Super Coupe ($595). Traction-Lok differential: Crown Vic/T-Bird (base and LX only) ($100). Steering/Suspension/Brakes: Power steering: Escort (LX and GT only) ($235). H.D./handling susp.: Crown Vic ($26). Auto. load leveling susp.: Crown Vic ($250). Trailer towing pkg: Crown Vic ($405). Anti-lock brakes: Probe (LX and GT only) ($924); Taurus ($985); T-Bird (includes Traction-Lok ($1085).

ESCORT CONVENIENCE/APPEARANCE OPTIONS: Preferred Equip Pkg LX Series: Pwr Steering, Light Grp, Elect Rr Window Defroster ($185). Preferred Equip Pkg GT Series: Elect Rr Window Defroster, Man Air Cond, Lux Convenience Grp ($496). Calif. Emission System ($70). Air Cond (LX and GT only) ($744). Rr Window Defroster ($160). Light/Convenience Grp: incl dual map, cargo area, underhood and ignition key, dual illum visor vanity mirrors, dual pwr mirrors ($290). Lux Convenience Grp: incl tilt steering wheel, cruise control, pwr door locks, (stnd on GT): LX ($251-$334); GT ($336). Pwr Moonroof (LX and GT only) ($549). Clearcoat Paint ($91). AM/FM Stereo radio (Pony only) ($245). AM/FM Cass radio: Pony ($400); LX ($155). Premium sound syst ($138). Pwr Steering (LX and GT only) ($235). Wagon Grp: incl dlx luggage rack and rear window wiper/washer ($241).

TEMPO CONVENIENCE/APPEARANCE OPTIONS: Preferred Equip Pkg GL Series: Man Air Cond, Light Grp, Dual Elect Remote Control Mirrors and Tilt Steering Wheel ($294). Preferred Equip Pkg GL two-door models: Incls all GL Series items plus Rr Window Defroster, Frnt Center Armrest, F&R Flr Mats, Pwr Lock Grp, Elect AM/FM Stereo Radio w/Cass & Clock, Auto FLC Transaxle and Polycast Wheels ($1346). Preferred Equip Pkg GL four-door models: same as

1991 Ford Escort LX sedan. (OCW)

GL two-door equipment ($1388). Preferred Equip Grp SRS GL Series: same as GL two-door equipment minus Tilt Steering Wheel, Elect AM/FM Stereo Radio w/Cass & Clock and Polycast Wheels ($1377). Preferred Equip Pkg GLS two-door models: Man Air Cond, Tilt Steering Wheel and Pwr Lock Grp ($1366). Preferred Equip Pkg GLS four-door models: same as GL two-door equipment ($1408). Preferred Equip Pkg LX Series: Man Air Cond, Rr Window Defroster, Elect AM/FM Stereo Radio w/Cass & Clock and Auto FLC Transaxle ($1060). Preferred Equip Pkg 4WD Series: Tilt Steering Wheel, Rr Window Defroster, Elect AM/FM Stereo Radio w/Cass & Clock and Pwr Lock Grp ($533). Calif. Emission Syst ($100). Man Air Cond ($817). Frnt Center Armrest ($55). Rr Window Defroster ($160). Flr Mats F&R ($33). Instrument Cluster ($87). Light Grp ($38). Pwr Lock Grp: two-door ($276); four-door ($318). Luggage Rack ($115). Dual Elect Remote Mirrors ($121). Clearcoat Paint ($91). Elect AM/FM Stereo Radio w/Cass & Clock ($155). Pwr Driver's Seat ($290). Premium Sound System ($138). Spd Control ($210). Tilt Steering Wheel ($135). Airbag (driver's side only): SRS GL ($815); LX ($690). Polycast Wheels ($193). Pwr Side Windows (four-door only) ($315). Eng Block Htr ($20). P185/70R14 WSW Tires ($82).

PROBE CONVENIENCE/APPEARANCE OPTIONS: Preferred Equip Pkg GL Series: Tinted Glass, Tilt Strg Column & Cluster, Rr Window Defroster, Convenience Grp incl Interval Wipers, Light Grp, Dual Electric Remote Mirrors ($179). Preferred Equip Pkg LX Series: Man Air Cond, Illum Entry Syst, Rr Washer/Wiper, Walk-in Pass Seat, Pwr Windows, Spd Control, Pwr Dr Locks, Elect AM/FM w/Cass/Prem Sound/Pwr Antenna, Cargo Tie Down Net ($1545). Preferred Equip Pkg GT Series: same as LX Series ($1645). Man Air Cond ($937, incls Tinted Glass). Electronics Grp: LX ($82); GT ($182). Rr Window Defroster ($160). Leather Bucket Seats (LX and GT only) ($489). Pwr Driver's Seat (LX and GT only) ($290). Pwr Dr Locks ($195). Spd Control ($210). Anti-lock Brakes (LX and GT only) ($924). Flip-Up Open Air Roof (LX and GT only) ($355). Aluminum Wheels: GL ($313); LX ($376). Pwr Windows (LX and GT only) ($260). Tinted Glass ($120, stnd LX and GT). Elect AM/FM Stereo Radio w/Cass & Premium Sound ($368). AM/FM Electronic Cass w/CD Player & Premium Sound/Pwr Antenna ($709). Calif. Emissions System ($100). Eng Block Heater ($20).

TAURUS CONVENIENCE/APPEARANCE OPTIONS: Preferred Equip Pkg L Plus Series: Pwr Door Locks, Man Air Cond, Rr Window Defroster and Paint Stripe ($964). Preferred Equip Pkg GL Sed: Pwr Door Locks, Man Air Cond, Rr Window Defroster, Paint Stripe, Pwr Windows and Pwr 6-way Driver's Seat ($1804). Preferred Equip Pkg GL Wagon: same as GL Sedan ($1754). Preferred Equip Pkg LX Series: Rr Window Defroster, Paint Stripe, Elect AM/FM Stereo Radio w/Cass, Spd Control, Cast Alum Wheels w/P205 15-in. tires, Autolamp Syst, Flr Mats F&R, Leather-wrapped Strg Wheel, Illum Entry Syst and Premium Sound Syst ($795). Preferred Equip Pkg LX Sed: Rr Window Defroster, Paint Stripe, Spd Control, Cast Alum Wheels w/P205 15-in. tires, Autolamp Syst, Flr Mats F&R, Leather-wrapped Strg Wheel, Anti-lock Brakes, Elect Climate Control Air Cond, High-Level Audio Syst, Keyless Entry, Pwr Antenna, Dual Control 6-Way Pwr Seats, Elect Instrument Cluster, Variable Spd Sensitive Pwr Assist Strg and 3.8-liter V-6 w/automatic overdrive trans ($3336). Preferred Equip Pkg LX Wagon: same as LX Sedan ($2781). Preferred Equip Pkg SHO Sed: Elect Climate Control Air Cond, Dual Control 6-Way Pwr Seats, Autolamp Syst, Flr Mats F&R, Keyless Entry Syst, High Level Audio System and Pwr Radio Antenna ($724). Conventional Spare Tire ($73). Elect Air Cond: GL ($1000); SHO or LX ($183). Man Air Cond ($817). Autolamp System ($73). HD Battery ($27). Cargo Area Cover ($56). Cornering Lamps ($68). Rr Window Defroster ($160). Engine Blk Heater ($20). Floor Mats, F&R ($43). Remote Decklid & Fuel Door, Sedans ($91); Wagons (fuel door only) ($41). Ext Range Fuel Tank ($46). Illum Entry Syst ($82, NA on L Series). Elect Instrument Cluster, LX ($239); GL ($351). Keyless Entry System (GL or LX only) ($218). Light Grp (L or GL only) ($59). "Picnic Table" Load Floor Extension ($66, wagons only). Pwr Door Locks ($226, L Plus only). Dual Illum Visor Mirrors ($100). Rocker Panel Moldings ($55). Pwr Moonroof ($776). Clearcoat Paint ($188). Auto Parking Brake Release ($12). Elect AM/FM Stereo Radio w/Cass Player ($155). Pwr Antenna ($82). Rr Facing Third Seat ($155, wagons only). Dual Control 6-Way Pwr Seats ($290). Spd Control ($210). Leather-Wrapped Strg Wheel ($63). Paint Stripe ($61). Rr Window Washer/Wiper ($126, wagons only). HD Susp ($26). Variable Pwr Assist Spd Sensitive Strg ($104). Finned Wheel Covers ($65). Cast Aluminum Wheels: LX ($279); GL or L Plus ($344). Styled Road Wheels: LX ($128); GL or L Plus ($193). Insta-Clear Windshield ($305). Calif. Emissions Syst ($100). Leather Bucket Seats w/console: LX or SHO ($489); GL ($593). Vinyl Split Bench Seat: L or GL ($37). Frnt Floor Mats ($26). P205/70R14 WSW ($82).

LTD CROWN VICTORIA CONVENIENCE/APPEARANCE OPTIONS: Same as those listed in 1990 section (new, 1992 LTD Crown Victoria launched in spring 1991—see 1992 listing for that model's equipment pricing).

THUNDERBIRD CONVENIENCE/APPEARANCE OPTIONS: Preferred Equip Pkg Base Series: Elect AM/FM Stereo Radio w/Cass Player & Clock, Rr Window Defroster, 6-Way Pwr Driver's Seat, Luxury Grp incl Bright Window Mldgs, Spd Control & Tilt Strg Wheel, Dual Elect Remote Mirrors, Styled Road Wheel Covers and Cast Alum Wheels w/P215/70R15 BSW Tires ($796). Preferred Equip Pkg LX Series: Rr Window Defroster, 6-Way Pwr Pass Seat, Luxury Grp incl Bright Window Mldgs, Spd Control & Tilt Strg Wheel, Dual Elect Remote Mirrors, Styled Road Wheel Covers and Cast Alum Wheels w/P215/70R15 BSW Tires, Keyless Entry System, Elect Premium Radio Cass w/Prem Sound, Pwr Antenna, Frt Floor Mats, Autolamp Grp, Cornering Lamps and Elect Auto Temp Control ($977). Preferred Equip Pkg Super Coupe Series: same as Base Series equipment (except wheels) plus Elect Auto Temp Control and Pwr Antenna ($739). Anti-Theft System ($245). Keyless Entry ($219). Frt Floor Mats ($33). Light/Convenience Grp: base ($146); Super Coupe ($100). Elect AM/FM Stereo Radio w/Cass & Clock ($155). Elect Radio Cass w/Premium Sound ($460). Ford JBL Audio System ($526). Pwr Antenna ($82). CD Player ($491). Calif. Emissions System ($100). Anti-lock Brakes ($1085). Autolamp Grp ($176). Cornering Lamps ($68). Rr Window Defroster ($160). Elect Auto Temp Control ($162, LX or Super Coupe only). Elect Instrument Cluster ($270, LX only). Leather Bucket Seats: LX ($489); Super Coupe ($622). 6-Way Pwr Driver's Seat ($290). Pass Seat ($290). Vehicle Maint Monitor ($89). Spd Control & Tilt Strg Wheel ($345). Cold Weather Grp: ($205). Locking Wire Wheel Covers: base ($228); LX ($143). Cast Alum Wheels: base ($299); LX ($214). P205/70R15 WSW Tires ($73). Eagle GT4 P225/60R16 All-Season Perf Tires ($73). Conv Spare Tire, Base or LX ($73).

HISTORY: U.S. model year production totaled 1,162,256 (including Mustang). U.S. calendar year production totaled 772,971 (including Mustang) for a 14.2 percent of industry market share. The Taurus, Escort and Tempo all ranked in the Top 10—second, fifth and tenth, respectively—in U.S. car sales for calendar year 1991.

1992 FORD

In addition to the all-new, 1992 Crown Victoria introduced in the spring of 1991, Ford's 1992 lineup included a redesigned Taurus series, two new four-door Escort sedans as well as a Crown Victoria Touring Sedan. The Taurus received a sleeker body design and revamped, more ergonomic interior. The Escort series added LX and LX-E sedans, both providing five-passenger seating. The LX-E was a performance model with styled aluminum wheels, sport suspension and a 127-hp 1.8-liter DOHC four-cylinder engine. The Pony hatchback previously available in the Escort series was dropped. The new Crown Victoria line no longer offered station wagons, instead adding the Touring Sedan as a top-of-the-line performance model. It was powered by the 210-hp V-8 and rode on a handling suspension. Other changes to the Ford lineup for 1992 included a 3.0-liter V-6 added to the Tempo GLS, a front end treatment similar to the Super Coupe for the Thunderbird LX and Sport models and the Probe LX offered with a Sport option.

ESCORT—FOUR—Totally redesigned the year previous, the Escort was basically unchanged for 1992 with the exception of a revamped lineup. The Escort Pony was dropped and an LX sedan and performance-minded LX-E sedan were added. The lineup now consisted of four series: base (three-door hatchback), LX (three- and five-door hatchbacks, four-door sedan and station wagon), LX-E (four-door sedan) and GT (three-door hatchback). The new LX and LX-E sedans came standard with split fold-down rear seats. The LX model also came standard with 14-inch wheels, two-speed interval wipers, four-wheel independent suspension, rack-and-pinion steering, color-keyed bumpers and AM/FM stereo radio. The LX-E sedan shared the 16-valve DOHC 1.8-liter four-cylinder engine found in the GT model. Standard equipment on the LX-E included 14-inch styled aluminum wheels, modified GT front seats and door trim, four-wheel disc brakes and a sport suspension. Base engine for Escorts was the 1.9-liter four with sequential fuel injection. A five-speed manual transaxle was standard on Escorts, with the electronic four-speed automatic overdrive transaxle optional.

1992 Ford Tempo GL sedan. (OCW)

1992 Ford Tempo GLS sedan. (OCW)

1992 Ford Tempo GLS coupe. (OCW)

1992 Ford Taurus. (OCW)

1992 Ford Taurus SHO sedan. (OCW)

TEMPO — FOUR — The big news for Tempo buyers in 1992 was the 140-hp 3.0-liter V-6 offered as standard equipment on the GLS and optional on the GL and LX series. All V-6-equipped Tempos offered a touring suspension with performance tires, tuned gas shock absorbers and a rear stabilizer bar. The Tempo GLS came equipped with sport suspension. The four-wheel-drive Tempo offered previously was discontinued. Tempo was available as a two- or four-door sedan in the GL series, a two- or four-door sedan in the GLS series, and a four-door sedan in the LX series. The base powerplant was the 2.3-liter four-cylinder engine, which added sequential electronic fuel injection as an upgrade. Both the GL and LX series received minor exterior refinements as well as a single-belt accessory drive system to reduce noise and vibration. The GLS was restyled using new bumper and bodyside cladding, fog lamps, bright exhaust tips, 15-inch aluminum wheels and performance tires and, on the two-door GLS a decklid spoiler. Other 1992 Tempo refinements included a color-keyed grille and color-keyed bodyside moldings that gave Tempo a monochromatic look. Standard equipment included the five-speed manual transaxle.

PROBE — FOUR/V-6 — Probe returned with its three series lineup in 1992, GL, LX and GT, but added an LX Sport option model that featured a rear deck spoiler, 15-inch aluminum wheels and performance tires. Two new "tropical" colors were offered to Probe buyers, Calypso green and Bimini blue. Probe GL continued using the 2.2-liter, 12-valve electronically fuel-injected four-cylinder engine. The LX and LX Sport were powered by a 3.0-liter electronically fuel-injected V-6 engine. The Probe GT used the turbocharged 2.2-liter electronically fuel-injected four. The five-speed manual overdrive transaxle was standard and the four-speed automatic with overdrive was optional equipment. Anti-lock brakes were optional on the LX, LX Sport and GT, all equipped with four-wheel power disc brakes as standard equipment. The same trio of coupes also came equipped with tilt steering column/instrument panel, while the LX driver's seat offered manual adjustments for tilt, lumbar support and side bolsters.

TAURUS — V-6 — The 1992 Taurus had a virtually all-new body as well as receiving improvements in interior appointments. The Taurus SHO sedan was also restyled to emphasize its performance character. Taurus for 1992 consisted of four-door sedans and station wagons in the L, GL and LX series as well as the aforementioned SHO sedan model. In addition to the exterior redesign, Taurus models' exterior trim was also new including ornamentation, bumpers and rocker panel moldings. The Taurus' overall length was increased 3.8 inches from the year previous. Nine new exterior colors were offered and other changes included tinted outside rearview mirrors, new wheel covers and new aluminum wheels. Inside the Taurus, changes included the addition of an optional passenger side airbag, a "flow-through" dashboard, more legible gauges and larger, illuminated power window switches. A four-cylinder engine was no longer available in a Taurus. Standard powertrain for the L, GL and LX sedans and L and GL wagons was the 140-hp 3.0-liter V-6 with sequential electronic fuel injection and the electronically controlled four-speed automatic overdrive transaxle. The LX wagon was powered by the 3.8-liter V-6, which was optional on other Taurus models. It, too, used the four-speed automatic. The SHO sedan used a DOHC 220-hp 24-valve 3.0-liter V-6 and a five-speed manual transaxle. The redesign of the SHO sedan included a more aggressive look via color-keyed bodyside and rocker panel moldings, flared mud spats, a unique grille with integrated fog lamps, a special rear bumper and 16-inch aluminum wheels.

1992 Ford Probe GT coupe. (OCW)

1992 Ford Crown Victoria Touring Sedan. (OCW)

1992 Ford Thunderbird LX coupe. (OCW)

CROWN VICTORIA — V-8 — The all-new, 1992 Crown Victoria design was introduced in the spring the year previous. A Touring Sedan was added to the lineup in 1992, but the station wagon models offered previously were discontinued. Also, with the new design, a revision of the name was in order as the Crown Vic line no longer used the LTD prefix. The three model line consisted of four-door sedans in base, LX and Touring Sedan trim levels. The Crown Victoria models all featured speed-sensitive steering, four-wheel disc brakes, a rear stabilizer bar and standard driver's side airbag. Anti-lock brakes and traction control were standard equipment on the Touring Sedan and optional on the base and LX sedans. Additional options included a rear air-suspension and passenger side airbag. Performance and efficiency were improved in the Crown Vic due to a new 4.6-liter modular V-8, rated at 190-hp. The Touring Sedan was powered by a 210-hp version of the 4.6-liter V-8. The four-speed automatic overdrive transmission was used in all Crown Vics.

THUNDERBIRD — V-6/V-8 — Styling changes for the Thunderbird LX and Sport coupes highlighted the list of new features for Ford's 1992 Thunderbird lineup. The LX and Sport models featured a new aerodynamic front end treatment similar to the Super Coupe. The Thunderbird lineup was comprised of base, LX and Sport coupes and the Super Coupe. Also new-for-'92 were color-keyed bodyside moldings on the base, LX and Sport coupes and full-width taillamp illumination. Four new exterior colors were offered: Cayman green, Dark Plum, Opal gray and Silver Metallic. The 3.8-liter V-6 with sequential electronic fuel injection was again the standard engine for base and LX models. The 200-hp 5.0-liter V-8 again powered the Sport coupe, while the 210-hp supercharged version of the 3.8-liter V-6 with the five-speed manual transmission was used in the Super Coupe. The four-speed automatic overdrive transmission was used in all other Thunderbirds. Standard equipment in base and LX coupes included air conditioning, tinted glass, a full-length console with floor-mounted shift, power front-disc brakes, power rack-and-pinion steering and four-wheel independent suspension. Standard on the Super Coupe were anti-lock brakes, adjustable suspension, articulated sport seats and a performance analog instrument cluster. A vehicle maintenance monitor was optional on all Thunderbirds.

I.D. DATA: Ford's 17-symbol Vehicle Identification Number (VIN) was stamped on a metal tab fastened to the instrument panel, visible through the windshield. The first three symbols indicate manufacturer, make and vehicle type. The fourth symbol denotes restraint system. Next comes a letter (usually 'P'), followed by two digits that indicate Model Number, as shown in left column of tables below. (Example: '10' Escort two-door hatchback). Symbol eight indicates engine type. Next is a check digit. Symbol ten indicates model year ('N' - 1992). Symbol eleven denotes assembly plant. The final six digits make up the sequence number, starting with 000001.

ESCORT (FOUR)

Model No.	Body/ Style No.	Body Type & Seating	Factory Price	Shipping Weight	Prod. Total
P	10	2-dr. Hatch-5P	8355	2287	Note 1
P	11	2-dr. LX Hatch-5P	9055	2312	Note 1
P	14	4-dr. LX Hatch-5P	9483	2355	57,651*
P	13	4-dr. LX Sed-5P	9795	2364	Note 2
P	15	4-dr. LX Sta Wag-5P	10067	2411	58,950*
P	16	4-dr. LX-E Sed-5P	11933	2464	Note 2
P	12	2-dr. GT Hatch-5P	11871	2458	Note 1

NOTE 1: Production of two-door hatchback models totaled 81,023* with no further breakout available.

NOTE 2: Production of four-door sedan models totaled 62,066* with no further breakout available.

* NOTE: All Escort total production figures include 1993 models that were introduced early in 1992.

TEMPO (FOUR/V-6 in GLS only)

P	31	2-dr. GL Sed-5P	9987	2532	Note 1
P	36	4-dr. GL Sed-5P	10137	2600	Note 2
P	37	4-dr. LX Sed-5P	11115	2626	Note 2
P	33	2-dr. GLS Sed-5P	12652	2601	Note 1
P	38	4-dr. GLS Sed-5P	12800	2659	Note 2

NOTE 1: Production of two-door sedan models totaled 35,149 with no further breakout available.

NOTE 2: Production of four-door sedan models totaled 172,191 with no further breakout available.

PROBE (FOUR/V-6 in LX only)

T	20	2-dr. GL Cpe-4P	12257	2730	Note 1
T	21	2-dr. LX Cpe-4P	13257	2970	Note 1
T	22	2-dr. GT Cpe-4P	14857	3000	Note 1

NOTE 1: Production of two-door coupe models totaled 41,035* with no further breakout available.

* NOTE: Probe total production figure includes 1993 models that were introduced early in 1992.

TAURUS (V-6)

P	50	4-dr. L Sed-6P	14980	3111	Note 1
P	55	4-dr. L Sta Wag-6P	16013	3262	Note 2
P	52	4-dr. GL Sed-6P	15280	3117	Note 1
P	57	4-dr. GL Sta Wag-6P	16290	3264	Note 2
P	53	4-dr. LX Sedan-6P	17775	3193	Note 1
P	58	4-dr. LX Sta Wag-6P	19464	3388	Note 2
P	54	4-dr. SHO Sed-6P	23839	3309	Note 1

NOTE 1: Production of four-door sedan models totaled 274,289 with no further breakout available.

NOTE 2: Production of station wagon models totaled 67,828 with no further breakout available.

CROWN VICTORIA (V-8)

Model No.	Body/ Style No.	Body Type & Seating	Factory Price	Shipping Weight	Prod. Total
P	73	4-dr. Sed-6P	19563	3748	Note 1
P	74	4-dr. LX Sed-6P	20887	3769	Note 1
P	75	4-dr. Tour Sed-6P	23832	3850	Note 1

NOTE 1: Production of four-door sedan models totaled 136,949 with no further breakout available.

THUNDERBIRD (V-6/V-8)

P	60	2-dr. Cpe-5P	16345/17425	3514/3772	Note 1
P	60	2-dr. Sport Cpe	-----/18611	-----/3686	Note 1
P	62	2-dr. LX Cpe-5P	18783/19863	3566/3719	Note 1
P	64	2-dr. Super Cpe-5P	22046/-----	3768/-----	Note 1

NOTE 1: Production of two-door coupe models totaled 73,892 with no further breakout available.

ENGINE [Base Four (Escort)]: Inline. Overhead cam. Four-cylinder. Cast-iron block and aluminum head. Displacement: 113 cid (1.9 liters). Bore & stroke: 3.23 x 3.46 in. Compression ratio: 9.0:1. Brake horsepower: 88 at 4400 rpm. Torque: 108 lbs.-ft. at 3800 rpm. Five main bearings. Hydraulic valve lifters. Sequential fuel injection.

ENGINE [Base Four (Escort GT)]: High-output, DOHC MFI version of 1.9-liter four above. Horsepower: 127 at 6500 rpm. Torque: 114 lbs.-ft. at 4500 rpm.

ENGINE [Base Four (Probe)]: Inline. Overhead cam. Four-cylinder. Cast-iron block. Displacement: 133 cid (2.2 liters). Bore & stroke: 3.39 x 3.70 in. Compression ratio: 8.6:1. Brake horsepower: 110 at 4700 rpm. Torque: 130 lbs.-ft. at 3000 rpm. Hydraulic valve lifters. Multiport fuel injection.

ENGINE [Turbocharged Four (Probe GT)]: Same as 2.2-liter four above, with turbocharger and intercooler - Compression ratio: 7.8:1. Horsepower: 145 at 4300 rpm. Torque: 190 lbs.-ft. at 3500 rpm.

ENGINE [Base Four (Tempo)]: Inline. Overhead valve. Four-cylinder. Cast-iron block and head. Displacement: 140 cid (2.3 liters). Bore & stroke: 3.70 x 3.30 in. Compression ratio: 9.0:1. Brake horsepower: 96 at 4400 rpm. Torque: 128 lbs.-ft. at 2600 rpm. Five main bearings. Hydraulic valve lifters. Sequential fuel injection.

ENGINE [Base V-6 (Tempo GLS/Probe LX/Taurus L and GL/Taurus LX sedan): Optional (Tempo GL and Tempo LX)]: 60-degree, overhead valve V-6. Cast-iron block and head. Displacement: 182 cid (3.0 liters). Bore & stroke: 3.50 x 3.10 in. Compression ratio: 9.3:1. Brake horsepower: (Probe LX) 145 at 4800 RPM; (all others) 140 at 4800 rpm. Torque: (Probe LX) 165 lbs.-ft. at 3400 RPM; (all others) 165 lbs.-ft. at 3000 rpm. Four main bearings. Hydraulic valve lifters. (Probe LX) Multi-port fuel injection; (all others) Sequential fuel injection.

1992 Ford Escort LX-E sedan. (OCW)

ENGINE [Base V-6 (Taurus SHO)]: Dual-overhead-cam V-6 (24 valve). Cast-iron block and head. Displacement: 182 cid (3.0 liters). Bore & stroke: 3.50 x 3.15 in. Compression ratio: 9.8:1. Brake horsepower: 220 at 6200 rpm. Torque: 200 lbs.-ft. at 4800 rpm. Four main bearings. Hydraulic valve lifters. Sequential fuel injection.

ENGINE [Base V-6 (Thunderbird and Thunderbird LX): Optional: (Taurus GL/Taurus LX sedan)]: 90-degree, overhead valve V-6. Cast-iron block and aluminum head. Displacement: 232 cid (3.8 liters). Bore & stroke: 3.80 x 3.40 in. Compression ratio: 9.0:1. Brake horsepower: 140 at 3800 rpm. Torque: (Taurus) 215 lbs.-ft. at 2200 RPM; (Thunderbird) 215 lbs.-ft. at 2400. Four main bearings. Hydraulic valve lifters. Sequential fuel injection.

ENGINE [Supercharged V-6 (Thunderbird Super Coupe)]: Same as 232 cid (3.8-liter) V-6 above, except - Compression ratio: 8.2:1. Horsepower: 210 at 4000 rpm. Torque: 315 lbs.-ft. at 2600 rpm.

ENGINE [Base V-8 (Crown Victoria)]: Modular, overhead valve V-8. Displacement: 281 cid (4.6 liters). Bore & stroke: 3.60 x 3.60. Compression ratio: 9.0:1. Brake horsepower: 190 at 4200 rpm. Torque: 260 lbs.-ft. at 3200 rpm.

ENGINE [Base V-8 (Thunderbird Sport); Optional (Thunderbird and Thunderbird LX)]: 90-degree, overhead valve V-8. Cast-iron block and head. Displacement: 302 cid (5.0 liters). Bore & stroke: 4.00 x 3.00 in. Compression ratio: 9.0:1. Brake horsepower: 200 at 4000 rpm. Torque: 275 lbs.-ft. at 3000 rpm. Five main bearings. Hydraulic valve lifters. Sequential fuel injection.

CHASSIS DATA: Wheelbase: (Escort) 98.4 in.; (Tempo) 99.9 in.; (Probe) 99.0 in.: (Taurus) 106.0 in.; (Crown Vic) 114.4 in.; (T-Bird) 113.0 in. Overall Length: (Escort) 170.0 in.; (Escort wag) 171.3 in.; (Tempo two-door) 176.7 in.; (Tempo four-door) 177.0 in.; (Probe) 177.0 in.; (Taurus) 192.0 in.; (Taurus wag) 193.1 in.; (Crown Vic) 212.4 in.; (T-Bird) 198.7 in. Height: (Escort) 52.5 in.; (Escort wag) 53.6 in.; (Tempo two-door) 52.8 in.; (Tempo four-door) 52.9 in.; (Probe) 51.8 in.; (Taurus) 54.1 in.; (Taurus wag) 55.5 in.; (Crown Vic) 56.7 in.; (T-Bird) 52.7 in. Width: (Escort) 66.7 in.; (Tempo) 68.3 in.: (Probe) 67.9 in.; (Probe GT) 68.3 in.; (Taurus) 71.2 in.; (Crown Vic) 77.8 in.; (T-Bird) 72.7 in. Front Tread: (Escort) 56.5 in.; (Tempo) 54.9 in.; (Probe) 57.3 in.; (Taurus) 61.6 in.; (Crown Vic) 62.8 in.; (T-Bird) 61.6 in. Rear Tread: (Escort) 56.5 in.; (Tempo) 57.6 in.; (Probe) 57.7 in.; (Taurus) 60.5 in.; (Tempo wag) 59.9 in.; (Crown Vic) 63.3 in.; (T-Bird) 60.2 in. Standard Tires: (Escort) P175/70R13; (Escort LX) P175/65R14; (Escort LX-E) P185/65R14; (Escort GT) P185/60R15; (Tempo) P185/70R14; (Probe) P195/70R14; (Probe GT) P205/60VR15; (Taurus) P205/70R14; (Taurus SHO) P215/60R16; (Crown Vic) P215/70R15; (T-Bird) P205/70R15; (T-Bird Sport Cpe) P215/65R15; (T-Bird Super Cpe) P225/60ZR16.

TECHNICAL: Transmission: Five-speed manual transaxle standard on Escort, Tempo, Probe, Taurus SHO and Thunderbird Super Coupe. Four-speed overdrive automatic standard on Taurus, Crown Vic and T-Bird. Drive Axle: (Crown Vic/T-Bird) rear; (others) front. Steering: (Crown Vic) recirculating ball; (others) rack/pinion. Front Suspension:

(Escort) Independent MacPherson strut w/strut-mounted coil springs; (Tempo) Independent MacPherson strut w/strut-mounted coil springs, forged lower control arms, cast steering knuckle and stabilizer bar; (Probe) Independent MacPherson struts with lower asymmetrical control arms, upper strut-mounted coil springs and stabilizer bar; (Taurus) Independent MacPherson strut w/strut-mounted coil springs, stabilizer bar, tension strut and lower control arm; (Crown Vic) Independent short/long arm w/ball joints, coil springs and stabilizer bar; (T-Bird) Short/long arm w/double isolated tension strut, coil springs and stabilizer bar. Rear Suspension: (Escort) Independent, strut-type and Twin Trapezoidal Links with trailing arms and upper strut-mounted coil springs; (Tempo) Fully independent MacPherson strut w/coil spring offset on shock strut, parallel suspension arms and tension struts; (Probe) independent struts, four-bar with single trailing arms, upper strut-mounted coil springs and stabilizer bar. (Taurus sedan) Independent MacPherson struts w/coil spring on shock strut, tension strut, parallel suspension arms and two-piece forged/cast spindle; (Taurus wagon) Independent short/long arm w/spring on lower control arm, stamped tension strut w/two-piece forged/cast spindle; (Crown Vic) Rigid axle w/four links and coil springs; (T-Bird) H-arm independent, coil springs and stabilizer bar. Brakes: Front disc, rear drum (power assisted) except (Escort LX-E and GT, Probe LX and GT, Taurus LX and SHO, Crown Victoria and T-Bird Super Coupe) front/rear disc. Body construction: (Crown Vic) separate body and frame; (others) unibody. Fuel tank: (Escort) 11.9 gal.; (Tempo) 15.9 gal.; (Probe) 15.1 gal.; (Taurus) 16.0 gal.; (Taurus SHO) 18.4 gal.; (Crown Vic) 20.0 gal.; (T-Bird) 18.0 gal.

DRIVETRAIN OPTIONS: Engines: 3.0-liter V-6: Tempo GL and LX sed ($685). 3.8-liter V-6: Taurus GL and LX sed ($555). 5.0-liter V-8: Thunderbird and LX cpe ($1080). Transmission/Differential: Four-speed automatic transaxle: Escort ($732); Probe ($732); T-Bird Super Coupe ($595). Traction-Lok differential: T-Bird (base, Sport and LX only) ($100). Steering/Suspension/Brakes: Power steering: Escort (LX only) ($261). Trailer towing pkg: Crown Vic ($205). Anti-lock brakes: Probe (LX and GT only) ($595); Taurus ($595); T-Bird (includes Traction-Lok) ($695).

ESCORT CONVENIENCE/APPEARANCE OPTIONS: Preferred Equip Pkg LX Series: Pwr Steering, Light Grp incl Dual Elect Remote Control Mirrors, Rr Window Defroster ($248). Preferred Equip Pkg LX-E Series: Man Air Cond, Rr Window Defroster, Lux Convenience Grp ($554). Preferred Equip Pkg GT Series: Man Air Cond, Rr Window Defroster, Lux Convenience Grp ($554). Calif. Emission System ($72). Air Cond (LX, LX-E and GT only) ($759). Rr Window Defroster ($170). Light/Convenience Grp: incl Dual Elect Remote Control Mirrors, Remote Fuel Door Release, Remote Decklid Release ($317). Lux Convenience Grp: incl Tilt Steering Wheel, Cruise Control, Pwr Door Locks, Tach (stnd on GT): LX/LX-E sed, GT ($369); LX/LX-E hatch and wagon ($428). Pwr Moonroof (LX, LX-E and GT only) ($549). Clearcoat Paint ($91). Dual Elect Remote Control Mirrors ($98). Remote Fuel Door/Decklid Release ($101). Comfort Grp: incl Air Cond and Pwr Strg (base Escort only) ($841). AM/FM Stereo radio (base Escort only) ($312). AM/FM Cass radio: base Escort ($467); LX ($155). Premium sound syst ($138). Pwr Steering (LX only) ($261). Wagon Grp: incl Dlx Luggage Rack, Light/Convenience Grp and Rear Window Wiper/Washer (LX wagon only) ($250).

TEMPO CONVENIENCE/APPEARANCE OPTIONS: Preferred Equip Pkg GL Series: Man Air Cond, Light Grp, Dual Elect Remote Control Mirrors and Tilt Steering Wheel ($304). Preferred Equip Pkg GL two-door models: Incls all GL Series items plus Rr Window Defroster, Frnt Center Armrest, F&R Flr Mats, Pwr Lock Grp, Elect AM/FM Stereo Radio w/Cass & Clock, Auto FLC Transaxle and Polycast Wheels ($1305). Preferred Equip Pkg GL four-door models: same as GL two-door equipment ($1345). Preferred Equip Pkg SRS GL Series: same as GL two-door equipment plus Driver's Side Airbag, but minus Tilt Steering Wheel, Elect AM/FM Stereo Radio w/Cass & Clock and Polycast Wheels ($1081). Preferred Equip Pkg GLS two-door models: Tilt Steering Wheel, Rr Window Defroster, Dual Elect Remote Control Mirrors, Flr Mats F&R, Premium Sound Syst and Pwr Lock Grp ($642). Preferred Equip Pkg GLS four-door models: same as GLS two-door equipment ($682). Preferred Equip Pkg LX Series: Man Air Cond, Rr Window Defroster, Elect AM/FM Stereo Radio w/Cass & Clock and Auto FLC Transaxle ($1755). Calif. Emission Syst ($100). Man Air Cond ($817). Frnt Center Armrest ($59). Rr Window Defroster ($170). Flr Mats F&R ($33). Instrument Cluster ($87). Light Grp ($38). Pwr Lock Grp: two-door ($311); four-door ($351). Luggage Rack ($115). Dual Elect Remote Mirrors ($115). Clearcoat Paint ($91). Elect AM/FM Stereo Radio w/Cass & Clock ($155). Pwr Driver's Seat ($305). Premium Sound System ($138). Spd Control ($224). Tilt Steering Wheel ($145). Airbag (driver's side only): GL ($369); LX ($224). Polycast Wheels ($193). Pwr Side Windows (four-door only) ($330). Eng Block Htr ($20). P185/70R14 WSW Tires ($82).

PROBE CONVENIENCE/APPEARANCE OPTIONS: Preferred Equip Pkg GL Series: Tinted Glass, Tilt Strg Column & Cluster, Rr Window Defroster, Dual Illum Visor Vanity Mirrors, Convenience Grp incl Interval Wipers, Light Grp, Dual Electric Remote Mirrors ($308). Preferred Equip Pkg LX Series: same as GL Series equipment plus Air Cond and Elect AM/FM w/Cass/Prem Sound/Pwr Antenna ($1842). Preferred Equip Pkg GT Series: same as LX Series equipment ($1397). Man Air Cond ($937, incls Tinted Glass). Rr Window Defroster ($170). Leather Bucket Seats (LX and GT only) ($523). Pwr Driver's Seat (LX and GT only) ($305). Pwr Dr Locks (GL only) ($210). Spd Control ($224). Anti-lock Brakes (LX and GT only) ($595). Flip-Up Open Air Roof (LX and GT only) ($355). Aluminum Wheels (GL only) ($313). Pwr Windows (LX and GT only) ($485). Vehicle Maint Monitor ($146). Trip Computer ($215). Tilt Strg Column w/Gauge Cluster ($205). Sport Option (LX only) ($445). Illum Entry Syst (LX and GT only) ($82). Convenience Grp I ($213). Convenience Grp II: GL ($188); LX or GT ($323). Instrument Cluster ($463). Tinted Glass ($120, stnd LX and GT). Elect AM/FM Stereo Radio w/Cass & Premium Sound ($372). AM/FM Electronic Cass w/CD Player & Premium Sound/Pwr Antenna ($1080). Calif. Emissions System ($72). Eng Block Heater ($20).

TAURUS CONVENIENCE/APPEARANCE OPTIONS: Preferred Equip Pkg L Series: Man Air Cond and Rr Window Defroster ($686). Preferred Equip Pkg GL Series: Pwr Door Locks, Man Air Cond, Rr Window Defroster, Elect AM/FM Stereo Radio w/Cass, Spd Control, Dlx Wheel Covers, Cargo Tie-Down Net, Flr Mats, Light Grp, Pwr Windows and Pwr 6-way Driver's Seat ($2023). Preferred Equip Pkg LX Sed: Rr Window Defroster, Spd Control, Flr Mats F&R, Leather-wrapped Strg Wheel, Elect AM/FM Stereo Radio w/Cass, Cargo Area Cover, "Picnic Table" Load Flr Extension, Keyless Entry Syst and Pwr Antenna ($454). Preferred Equip Pkg LX Wagon: same as LX Sedan equipment except Rr Window Washer/Wiper ($655). Preferred Equip Pkg SHO Sed: Elect Climate Control Air Cond and Keyless Entry Syst ($219). Conventional Spare Tire ($73). Elect Air Cond (LX and SHO only) ($183). Man Air Cond (L and GL only) ($841). Pass Side Airbag ($488). Anti-lock Brakes (stnd SHO sedan) ($595). CD Player ($491). High Level Audio Syst ($502). Cargo Area Cover ($66, wagons only). Cargo Tie-Down Net ($44, GL only). Rr Window Defroster ($170). Engine Blk Heater ($20). Floor Mats, F&R ($45). Remote Decklid & Fuel Door Release (GL only) ($101). Remote Keyless Entry Syst (LX and SHO only) ($146). Light Grp (GL only) ($59). "Picnic Table" Load Floor Extension ($90, wagons only). Pwr Door Locks (L and GL only) ($257). Pwr Moonroof ($776, LX and SHO only). Elect AM/FM Stereo Radio w/Cass ($171). Pwr Antenna ($102, LX only). Rr Facing Third Seat ($155, wagons only). Dual Control 6-Way Pwr Seats ($305, LX and SHO only). 6-Way Pwr Driver's Seat ($305, GL only). Spd Control ($224). Leather-Wrapped Strg Wheel ($96). Rr Window Washer/Wiper ($135, wagons only). Cast Aluminum Wheels (GL only) ($239). HD Battery ($27). Calif. Emissions Syst ($100). Leather Bucket Seats w/console: LX ($515); GL ($618). Leather Split Bench Seat (LX only) ($515). Leather Bucket Seats (SHO sedan only) ($515). Frt Floor Mats ($26). P205/65R15 BSW ($150, GL only).

1992 Ford Probe LX coupe. (OCW)

1992 Ford Escort GT three-door hatchback. (OCW)

CROWN VICTORIA CONVENIENCE/APPEARANCE OPTIONS: Preferred Equip Pkg base series: Rr Window Defroster, Color-Keyed Flr Mats, F&R, Illum Entry Syst, Light/Decor Grp, Pwr Lock Grp, Elect AM/FM Stereo Radio w/Cass, Remote Fuel Door Release, 6-Way Pwr Driver's Seat, Leather-wrapped Strg Wheel, Spd Control, Spare Tire Cover, Trunk Cargo Net and Locking Spoked Wheel Covers ($943). Preferred Equip Pkg LX Series: Rr Window Defroster, Color-Keyed Flr Mats, F&R, Illum Entry Syst, Pwr Lock Grp, Elect AM/FM Stereo Radio w/Cass, Pwr Antenna, 6-Way Pwr Driver's Seat, Leather-wrapped Strg Wheel, Spd Control, Cornering Lamps and Cast Alum Wheels ($827). Preferred Equip Pkg Touring Sedan: Rr Window Defroster, Pwr Lock Grp, Cornering Lamps, Pwr Antenna, High Level Audio Syst and Illum Keyless Entry Syst ($961). Calif. Emissions Syst ($100). Leather Split Bench Seat: LX ($555); Touring Sed ($339). Conv Spare Tire ($85). Pass Airbag ($488). Anti-lock Brakes (stnd Touring Sed) ($695). HD Battery ($27). Cornering Lights ($68). Elect Rr Window Defroster ($170). Electronic Grp: ($516). Color-Keyed Flr Mats F&R ($46). 41G Handling & Perf Pkg incl Elect Traction Control, Cast Alum Wheels, Alum Driveshaft and Dual Exhaust ($1172). Eng Block Htr ($25). Illum Entry Syst ($82). Illum Keyless Entry Syst ($146). Light/Decor Grp (base Crown Vic only) ($222). Pwr Lock Grp ($310). Elect AM/FM Stereo Radio w/Cass ($155). High Level Audio Syst: LX ($335); Touring Sed ($490). Ford JBL Audio Syst ($526). Pwr Antenna ($85). Rr Air Suspension ($285). Remote Fuel Door Release (base Crown Vic only) ($41). 6-Way Pwr Driver's Seat ($305). Dual 6-Way Pwr Seat ($779). Cruise Control, incl Leather-wrapped Strg Wheel ($321). Trailer Towing Pkg: base Crown Vic ($490); LX ($205). Trunk Cargo Net ($44). Cast Alum Wheels: LX ($440); Touring Sed (NC). Locking Spoked Wheel Covers (base Crown Vic only) ($311). Insta-Clear Windshield (NA base Crown Vic) ($305).

THUNDERBIRD CONVENIENCE/APPEARANCE OPTIONS: Preferred Equip Pkg base series: Elect AM/FM Stereo Radio w/Cass Player & Clock, Rr Window Defroster, 6-Way Pwr Driver's Seat, Rr Window Defroster, Luxury Grp incl Spd Control & Tilt Strg Wheel, Dual Elect Remote Mirrors, Styled Road Wheel Covers and Cast Alum Wheels ($762). Preferred Equip Pkg Sport Series: same as base Thunderbird equipment except Cast Alum Wheels are stnd (NC). Preferred Equip Pkg LX Series: Rr Window Defroster, Luxury Grp incl Spd Control & Tilt Strg Wheel, Dual Elect Remote Mirrors, Styled Road Wheel Covers and Cast Alum Wheels, Keyless Entry System, Elect Premium Radio Cass w/Prem Sound, Frt Floor Mats, Autolamp Grp, Cornering Lamps and Elect Auto Temp Control ($1038). Preferred Equip Pkg Super Coupe Series: same as Sport Series equipment plus Elect Auto Temp Control, Pwr Lock Grp and Pwr Antenna ($858). Anti-Theft System ($245). Illum Keyless Entry (base T-Bird and LX only) ($82). Frt Floor Mats ($33). Light/Convenience Grp: base T-Bird or Sport ($146); Super Coupe ($100). Elect AM/FM Stereo Radio w/Cass (base T-Bird or LX) ($155). Elect Radio Cass w/Premium Sound ($460). Ford JBL Audio System ($526). Pwr Antenna ($82). CD Player ($491). Calif. Emissions System ($100). Anti-lock Brakes, incl Traction-Lok Axle ($695). Traction-Lok Axle ($100). Autolamp Grp ($193). Rr Window Defroster ($170). Elect Instrument Cluster ($270, LX only). Leather Bucket Seats: LX ($515); Super Coupe ($648). 6-Way Pwr Driver's Seat ($305); Pass Seat ($305). Vehicle Maint Monitor ($89). Lux Grp incl Spd Control & Tilt Strg Wheel ($561). Cold Weather Grp: ($205). Pwr Lock Grp (base T-Bird or LX only) ($311). Pwr Moonroof ($876). Cast Alum Wheels: base T-Bird ($306); LX ($221). P225/60ZR16 All-Season Perf Tires (Super Coupe only) ($73). Conv Spare Tire (base T-Bird or LX only) ($73).

HISTORY: U.S. model year production totaled 758,865 (including Mustang). U.S. calendar year production totaled 922,488 (including Mustang) for a 16.3 percent of industry market share. The Taurus was the best selling car in the United States in 1992, with 409,751 units sold compared to 329,751 for the Honda Accord which finished second.

1993 FORD

Leading the "what's new" parade at Ford in 1993 was the total redesign of the Probe. It now featured a cab forward design and was available in base and GT versions. The Probe series used two new powerplants, a 2.0-liter 16-valve DOHC four-cylinder engine or a 2.5-liter 24-valve DOHC V-6. Several models that were offered the year previous were discontinued. These were the Tempo GLS, Taurus L, Crown Victoria Touring Sedan and both the base and Sport versions of the Thunderbird coupe. For Taurus buyers, the SHO (Super High Output) sedan could be ordered with a 3.2-liter V-6 and automatic transaxle. An electronically controlled automatic overdrive transmission was now available on the Crown Victoria.

1993 Ford Escort LX five-door hatchback. (OCW)

1993 Ford Escort LX three-door hatchback. (OCW)

ESCORT — FOUR — For 1993, Escort's lineup again consisted of four series: base (three-door hatchback), LX (three- and five-door hatchbacks, four-door sedan and station wagon), LX-E (four-door sedan) and GT (three-door hatchback). Key design refinements consisted of six new exterior colors, new grilles, taillamp treatment, wheel covers and color-keyed bumpers and bodyside moldings on many models. The LX three-door hatchback was offered with a Sport Appearance Group option that included a rear spoiler, 14-inch aluminum wheels, full cloth seats, tachometer and sport steering wheel. The Escort GT featured a new rear spoiler, new aluminum wheels, sport steering wheel and a new rocker panel treatment. Standard equipment on all 1993 Escorts included side-window demisters, electronic engine controls and ignition, an engine-malfunction indicator light, tinted glass, inside hood release and front and rear stabilizer bars. Base engine for base and LX model Escorts was the 1.9-liter four with sequential fuel injection. A five-speed manual transaxle was standard on Escorts, with the electronic four-speed automatic overdrive transaxle optional. The LX-E sedan shared the 16-valve DOHC 1.8-liter four-cylinder engine found in the GT model.

1993 Ford Tempo GL sedan. (OCW)

1993 Ford Probe GT coupe. (OCW)

TEMPO — FOUR — Tempo's ranks were thinned a bit in 1993 with the GLS series offered previously being discontinued. The lineup now consisted of two- and four-door sedans in the GL series and a four-door sedan in LX trim. Tempo's base powerplant was again the 2.3-liter four-cylinder engine with sequential electronic fuel injection. The five-speed manual transaxle was standard equipment with the three-speed automatic transaxle optional. Also optional was a 3.0-liter V-6. Standard equipment included an AM/FM stereo radio with digital electronic clock. Models with the five-speed manual transaxle received a new leather-wrapped shift knob. The Tempo LX featured dual electric remote control mirrors, polycast 14-inch wheels with performance tires, illuminated entry system, power lock group, trip odometer, tachometer and upgraded cloth seat trim with seatback pockets.

PROBE — FOUR/V-6 — Introduced in 1988, the 1993 version of the Probe was all-new including an increase in length, width, wheelbase and tread. The Probe now utilized a cab forward design, which moved the passenger compartment closer to the front of the car resulting in a shorter front overhang, increased windshield slope and greater interior space. The sporty coupe was available in two series: base or GT. The base coupe was powered by a new DOHC 2.0-liter four-cylinder engine with four valves per cylinder and an aluminum cylinder head. It was rated at 115-hp. The GT coupe used a DOHC 2.5-liter V-6 with four valves per cylinder with cast aluminum engine block and cylinder head. It was rated at 164-hp. A five-speed manual transaxle was standard equipment on both coupes and an electronically controlled four-speed automatic transaxle was optional. A driver's side airbag was standard equipment on Probe. The GT version's standard equipment included a leather-wrapped steering wheel, adjustable power lumbar and seat-back side bolster front seats, fog lamps, cargo net and four-wheel disc brakes. Anti-lock brakes were optional on both coupes. A new center console/armrest with storage area was standard on the GT and optional on the base Probe.

1993 Ford Taurus LX station wagon. (OCW)

1993 Ford Taurus SHO sedan. (OCW)

TAURUS — V-6 — Taurus for 1993 underwent several refinements after undergoing a major redesign the year previous. For the first time, an optional automatic transaxle was offered on the SHO sedan. This automatic unit was coupled to a DOHC 3.2-liter V-6 with four valves per cylinder. The DOHC 3.0-liter V-6 mated to a five-speed manual transaxle remained as the base powertrain for the SHO model. Among other changes for the SHO model was the addition of a decklid spoiler with an integrated light-emitting diode (LED) stop lamp. In addition to the SHO sedan, Taurus was offered in both sedan and station wagon versions in the GL and LX series. The L series offered the year previous was discontinued. The GL sedan and wagon and LX sedan were again powered by the 3.0-liter V-6 with sequential electronic fuel injection. The LX wagon was again powered by the 3.8-liter V-6, which was optional on other Taurus models (except the SHO sedan). The four-speed automatic overdrive transaxle was the standard unit on Taurus with the five-speed manual unit optional, just the opposite of the SHO sedan. Body-color bumpers and bodyside moldings as well as new seat trim were added to the GL series. On the LX, exterior color choices expanded from six to ten monochromatic colors, and a new floor-mounted console was added. A driver's side airbag was standard equipment on all Taurus models with the passenger-side airbag and anti-lock brakes (standard on SHO sedan) both optional.

CROWN VICTORIA — V-8 — With the Touring Sedan offered in the previous year discontinued, the 1993 Crown Victoria lineup was now two series: base and LX with each offering a four-door sedan. New features included a chrome grille; color-coordinated, wide bodyside moldings and a decklid appliqué located between the two tail lamps. The modular 4.6-liter V-8 again was the standard engine, now coupled to an electronically controlled four-speed automatic transmission (introduced late in 1992). This unit featured an overdrive lock-out function for improved acceleration on demand. The Crown Victoria again featured as standard equipment speed-sensitive steering, four-wheel disc brakes and driver's side airbag. A passenger-side airbag, anti-lock brakes and traction control were optional. The Crown Vic's trunk provided 20 cubic feet of space—the largest in its class. The optional trailer-towing package included a dual exhaust system that boosted horsepower to 210 (from the standard 190-hp) and allowed for a Class III towing capacity up to 5,000 pounds. The LX sedan featured new cloth seats and optional cast aluminum wheels in both 15- or 16-inch sizes. An important safety feature incorporated into the Crown Vic was the brake shift interlock, which required the brake to be depressed before the car could be put into gear. Other features for 1993 included an express-down feature that allowed the driver-side power window to be run down completely with one touch of a button. Also added was a driver's foot rest.

THUNDERBIRD — V-6/V-8 — Compared to the previous year, the 1993 Thunderbird lineup was cut in half with the discontinuation of the base and Sport coupes. Remaining were the LX coupe and Super Coupe. The 3.8-liter V-6 with sequential electronic fuel injection was again the standard engine for the LX model. The High Output 5.0-liter V-8 was optional. The 210-hp supercharged version of the 3.8-liter V-6 with the five-speed manual transmission was again used in the Super Coupe. The four-speed automatic overdrive transmission was standard on the LX and optional on the Super Coupe. Speed-sensitive rack-and-pinion steering, air conditioning, tinted glass and power windows were standard equipment on every Thunderbird. The Super Coupe's list of standard features also included anti-lock brakes, Trac-tion-Lok axle, adjustable suspension and an electronic AM/FM stereo radio with cassette. All LX models offered color-keyed exterior mirrors, leather-wrapped steering wheel and shift knob and optional 15-inch cast aluminum wheels.

1993 Ford Crown Victoria LX sedan. (OCW)

1993 Ford Thunderbird LX coupe. (OCW)

I.D. DATA: Ford's 17-symbol Vehicle Identification Number (VIN) was stamped on a metal tab fastened to the instrument panel, visible through the windshield. The first three symbols indicate manufacturer, make and vehicle type. The fourth symbol denotes restraint system. Next comes a letter (usually 'P'), followed by two digits that indicate Model Number, as shown in left column of tables below. (Example: '10' Escort two-door hatchback). Symbol eight indicates engine type. Next is a check digit. Symbol ten indicates model year ('P' - 1993). Symbol eleven denotes assembly plant. The final six digits make up the sequence number, starting with 100001.

ESCORT (FOUR)

Model No.	Body/ Style No.	Body Type & Seating	Factory Price	Shipping Weight	Prod. Total
P	10	2-dr. Hatch-5P	8355	2285	Note 1
P	11	2-dr. LX Hatch-5P	9364	2306	Note 1
P	14	4-dr. LX Hatch-5P	9797	2354	58,909
P	13	4-dr. LX Sed-5P	10041	2359	Note 2
P	15	4-dr. LX Sta Wag-5P	10367	2403	157,239
P	16	4-dr. LX-E Sed-5P	11933	2440	Note 2
P	12	2-dr. GT Hatch-5P	11871	2440	Note 1

NOTE 1: Production of two-door hatchback models totaled 89,761 with no further breakout available.

NOTE 2: Production of four-door sedan models totaled 69,796 with no further breakout available.

TEMPO (FOUR)

Model No.	Body/ Style No.	Body Type & Seating	Factory Price	Shipping Weight	Prod. Total
P	31	2-dr. GL Sed-5P	10267	2511	52,129
P	36	4-dr. GL Sed-5P	10267	2569	Note 1
P	37	4-dr. LX Sed-5P	12135	2613	Note 1

NOTE 1: Production of four-door sedan models totaled 154,762 with no further breakout available.

PROBE (FOUR/V-6 in GT only)

Model No.	Body/ Style No.	Body Type & Seating	Factory Price	Shipping Weight	Prod. Total
T	20	2-dr. Cpe-4P	12845	2619	Note 1
T	22	2-dr. GT Cpe-4P	15174	2815	Note 1

NOTE 1: Production of two-door coupe models totaled 119,769 with no further breakout available.

TAURUS (V-6)

Model No.	Body/ Style No.	Body Type & Seating	Factory Price	Shipping Weight	Prod. Total
P	52	4-dr. GL Sed-6P	15491	3083	Note 1
P	57	4-dr. GL Sta Wag-6P	16656	3255	Note 2
P	53	4-dr. LX Sedan-6P	18300	3201	Note 1
P	58	4-dr. LX Sta Wag-6P	19989	3368	Note 2
P	54	4-dr. SHO Sed-6P	24829	3354	Note 1

NOTE 1: Production of four-door sedan models totaled 350,802 with no further breakout available.

NOTE 2: Production of station wagon models totaled 76,502 with no further breakout available.

CROWN VICTORIA (V-8)

Model No.	Body/ Style No.	Body Type & Seating	Factory Price	Shipping Weight	Prod. Total
P	73	4-dr. Sed-6P	19972	3793	Note 1
P	74	4-dr. LX Sed-6P	21559	3799	Note 1

NOTE 1: Production of four-door sedan models totaled 100,179 with no further breakout available.

THUNDERBIRD (V-6/V-8)

Model No.	Body/ Style No.	Body Type & Seating	Factory Price	Shipping Weight	Prod. Total
P	62	2-dr. LX Cpe-5P	15797/16883	3536/3689	Note 1
P	64	2-dr. Super Cpe-5P	22030/-----	3760/----	Note 1

NOTE: Figures to the left of slash are for V-6/to right of slash are for V-8.

NOTE 1: Production of two-door coupe models totaled 129,712 with no further breakout available.

ENGINE [Base Four (Escort)]: Inline. Overhead cam. Four-cylinder. Cast-iron block and aluminum head. Displacement: 113 cid (1.9 liters). Bore & stroke: 3.23 x 3.46 in. Compression ratio: 9.0:1. Brake horsepower: 88 at 4400 rpm. Torque: 108 lbs.-ft. at 3800 rpm. Five main bearings. Hydraulic valve lifters. Sequential fuel injection.

ENGINE [Base Four (Escort LX-E and Escort GT)]: High-output. Inline. Dual overhead cam. Four-cylinder. Cast-iron block and aluminum head. Displacement: 109 cid (1.8 liters). Bore & stroke: 3.27 x 3.35 in. Compression ratio: 9.0:1. Brake horsepower: 127 at 6500 rpm. Torque: 114 lbs.-ft. at 4500 rpm. Five main bearings. Hydraulic valve lifters. Multi-port fuel injection.

ENGINE [Base Four (Probe)]: Inline. Dual overhead cam. Four-cylinder. Cast-iron block and aluminum head. Displacement: 122 cid (2.0 liters). Bore & stroke: 3.27 x 3.62 in. Compression ratio: 9.0:1. Brake horsepower: 115 at 5500 rpm. Torque: 124 lbs.-ft. at 3500 rpm. Hydraulic valve lifters. Sequential fuel injection.

ENGINE [Base Four (Tempo)]: Inline. Overhead valve. Four-cylinder. Cast-iron block and head. Displacement: 140 cid (2.3 liters). Bore & stroke: 3.70 x 3.30 in. Compression ratio: 9.0:1. Brake horsepower: 96 at 4200 rpm. Torque: 126 lbs.-ft. at 2600 rpm. Five main bearings. Hydraulic valve lifters. Sequential fuel injection.

ENGINE [Base V-6 (Probe GT)]: Dual overhead cam V-6 (24 valve). Aluminum block and head. Displacement: 153 cid (2.5 liters). Bore & stroke: 3.33 x 2.92 in. Compression ratio: 9.2:1. Brake horsepower: 164 at 6000 rpm. Torque: 156 lbs.-ft. at 4000 rpm. Four main bearings. Hydraulic valve lifters. Sequential fuel injection.

ENGINE [Base V-6 (Taurus GL/Taurus LX sedan): Optional (Tempo GL/Tempo LX)]: 60-degree, overhead valve V-6. Cast-iron block and head. Displacement: 182 cid (3.0 liters). Bore & stroke: 3.50 x 3.10 in. Compression ratio: 9.3:1. Brake horsepower: 135 at 4800 rpm. Torque: 165 lbs.-ft. at 3250 rpm. Four main bearings. Hydraulic valve lifters. Sequential fuel injection.

ENGINE [Base V-6 (Taurus SHO)]: Dual-overhead-cam V-6 (24 valve). Cast-iron block and head. Displacement: 182 cid (3.0 liters). Bore & stroke: 3.50 x 3.15 in. Compression ratio: 9.8:1. Brake horsepower: 220 at 6200 rpm. Torque: 200 lbs.-ft. at 4800 rpm. Four main bearings. Hydraulic valve lifters. Sequential fuel injection.

ENGINE [Base V-6 (Taurus LX wagon/Thunderbird LX); Optional (Taurus GL/Taurus LX sedan)]: 90-degree, overhead valve V-6. Cast-iron block and aluminum head. Displacement: 232 cid (3.8 liters). Bore & stroke: 3.80 x 3.40 in. Compression ratio: 9.0:1. Brake horsepower: 140 at 3800 rpm. Torque: (Taurus) 215 lbs.-ft. at 2200 RPM; (Thunderbird) 215 lbs.-ft. at 2400. Four main bearings. Hydraulic valve lifters. Sequential fuel injection.

ENGINE [Supercharged V-6 (Thunderbird Super Coupe)]: Same as 232 cid (3.8-liter) V-6 above, except - Compression ratio: 8.2:1. Horsepower: 210 at 4000 rpm. Torque: 315 lbs.-ft. at 2600 rpm.

ENGINE [Base V-8 (Crown Victoria)]: Modular, overhead cam V-8. Displacement: 281 cid (4.6 liters). Bore & stroke: 3.60 x 3.60. Compression ratio: 9.0:1. Brake horsepower: 190 at 4600 rpm. Torque: 260 lbs.-ft. at 3200 rpm. Sequential fuel injection.

ENGINE [Optional V-8 (Crown Victoria)]: Same as 281 cid (4.6-liter) V-8 above, except - Brake horsepower: 210 at 4600 rpm. Torque: 270 lbs.-ft. at 3400 rpm.

ENGINE [Optional V-8: (Thunderbird LX/Thunderbird Super Coupe)]: High Output, 90-degree, overhead valve V-8. Cast-iron block and head. Displacement: 302 cid (5.0 liters). Bore & stroke: 4.00 x 3.00 in. Compression ratio: 9.0:1. Brake horsepower: 200 at 4000 rpm. Torque: 275 lbs.-ft. at 3000 rpm. Five main bearings. Hydraulic valve lifters. Sequential fuel injection.

CHASSIS DATA: Wheelbase: (Escort) 98.4 in.; (Tempo) 99.9 in.; (Probe) 102.9 in.: (Taurus) 106.0 in.; (Crown Vic) 114.4 in.; (T-Bird) 113.0 in. Overall Length: (Escort) 170.0 in.; (Escort wag) 171.3 in.; (Tempo two-door) 176.7 in.; (Tempo four-door) 177.0 in.; (Probe) 178.9 in.; (Taurus) 192.0 in.; (Taurus wag) 193.1 in.; (Crown Vic) 212.4 in.; (T-Bird) 198.7 in. Height: (Escort) 52.5 in.; (Escort wag) 53.6 in.; (Tempo two-door) 52.8 in.; (Tempo four-door) 52.9 in.; (Probe) 51.8 in.; (Taurus) 54.1 in.; (Taurus wag) 55.5 in.; (Crown Vic) 56.8 in.; (T-Bird) 52.5 in. Width: (Escort) 66.7 in.; (Tempo) 68.3 in.; (Probe) 69.8 in.; (Taurus) 71.2 in.; (Crown Vic) 77.8 in.; (T-Bird) 72.7 in. Front Tread: (Escort) 56.5 in.; (Tempo) 54.9 in.; (Probe) 59.4 in.; (Taurus) 61.6 in.; (Crown Vic) 62.8 in.; (T-Bird) 61.6 in. Rear Tread: (Escort) 56.5 in.; (Tempo) 57.6 in.; (Probe) 59.4 in.; (Taurus) 60.5 in.; (Taurus wag) 59.9 in.; (Crown Vic) 63.3 in.; (T-Bird) 60.2 in. Standard Tires: (Escort) P175/70R13; (Escort LX) P175/65R14; (Escort LX-E) P185/60R14; (Escort GT) P185/60R15; (Tempo) P185/70R14; (Probe) P195/65R14; (Probe GT) P225/50VR16; (Taurus) P205/70R14; (Taurus LX) P205/65R15; (Taurus SHO) P215/60R16; (Crown Vic) P215/70R15; (T-Bird LX) P205/70R15; (T-Bird Super Cpe) P225/60ZR16.

1993 Ford Escort LX station wagon. (OCW)

TECHNICAL: Transmission: Five-speed manual transaxle standard on Escort, Tempo, Probe, Taurus SHO and Thunderbird Super Coupe. Four-speed overdrive automatic standard on Taurus, Crown Vic and T-Bird. Drive Axle: (Crown Vic/T-Bird) rear; (others) front. Steering: (Crown Vic) recirculating ball; (others) rack/pinion. Front Suspension: (Escort) Independent MacPherson strut w/strut-mounted coil springs; (Tempo) Independent MacPherson strut w/strut-mounted coil springs, forged lower control arms and cast steering knuckle; (Probe) Independent strut-type with lower A-type control arms, upper strut-mounted coil springs and stabilizer bar; (Taurus) Independent MacPherson strut front drive w/strut-mounted coil springs, stabilizer bar, tension strut and lower control arm; (Crown Vic) Independent short/long arm w/ball joints, coil springs and stabilizer bar; (T-Bird) Short/long arm w/double isolated tension strut, coil springs and stabilizer bar. Rear Suspension: (Escort) Independent, strut-type and Twin Trapezoidal Links with trailing arms and upper strut-mounted coil springs; (Tempo) Fully independent MacPherson strut w/coil spring offset on shock strut, parallel suspension arms and tension struts; (Probe) Independent strut-type, Quadra-link, upper strut-mounted coil springs and stabilizer bar. (Taurus sedan) Independent MacPherson struts w/coil spring on shock strut, stabilizer bar, tension strut, parallel suspension arms and two-piece cast spindle w/forged stem; (Taurus wagon) Independent short/long arm w/spring on lower control arm, stamped tension strut w/two-piece forged/cast spindle; (Crown Vic) Rigid axle w/four links and coil springs; (T-Bird) H-arm independent, coil springs and stabilizer bar. Brakes: Front disc, rear drum (power assisted) except (Escort LX-E and GT, Probe GT, Taurus SHO, Crown Victoria and T-Bird Super Coupe) front/rear disc. Body construction: (Crown Vic) separate body and frame; (others) unibody. Fuel tank: (Escort) 11.9 gal.; (Tempo) 15.9 gal.; (Probe) 15.5 gal.; (Taurus) 16.0 gal.; (Taurus SHO) 18.4 gal.; (Crown Vic) 20.0 gal.; (T-Bird) 18.0 gal.

DRIVETRAIN OPTIONS: Engines: 3.0-liter V-6: Tempo ($685). 3.8-liter V-6: Taurus GL and LX sed ($555). 5.0-liter V-8: Thunderbird LX and Super Coupe ($1080). Transmission/Differential: Three-speed automatic transaxle: Tempo ($563). Four-speed automatic transaxle: Escort ($732); Probe ($732); T-Bird Super Coupe ($595). Traction-Lok differential: T-Bird (LX only) ($100). Steering/Suspension/Brakes: Power steering: Escort (LX only) ($261). Heavy Duty Suspension: Taurus (N/A SHO) ($26). Trailer towing pkg: Crown Vic ($205). Anti-lock brakes: Probe (GT only) ($595); Taurus (stnd SHO) ($595); Crown Vic (w/Elect Traction Assist) ($695); T-Bird (includes Traction-Lok) ($695).

ESCORT CONVENIENCE/APPEARANCE OPTIONS: Preferred Equip Pkg LX Series: Pwr Steering, Light Grp incl Dual Elect Remote Control Mirrors, Rr Window Defroster ($248). Preferred Equip Pkg LX-E Series: Man Air Cond, Rr Window Defroster, Spd Control, Tilt Strg and Tach ($554). Preferred Equip Pkg GT Series: Man Air Cond, Rr Window Defroster, Spd Control, Tilt Strg and Tach ($554). Calif. Emission System ($72). Air Cond (LX, LX-E and GT only) ($759). Rr Window Defroster ($170). Light/Convenience Grp: incl Dual Elect Remote Control Mirrors, Remote Fuel Door Release, Remote Decklid Release ($317). Lux Convenience Grp: incl Tilt Steering Wheel, Cruise Control, Pwr Door Locks, Tach (stnd on GT): LX-E and GT ($369); LX ($428). Pwr Moonroof ($549). Clearcoat Paint ($91). Dual Elect Remote Control Mirrors (LX only) ($98). Remote Fuel Door/Decklid Release ($101). Comfort Grp: incl Air Cond and Pwr Strg (base Escort only) ($841). AM/FM Stereo radio (base Escort only) ($312). AM/FM Cass radio: base Escort ($467); LX ($155). Premium sound syst ($138). Pwr Steering (LX only) ($261). Wagon Grp: incl Dlx Luggage Rack, Light/Convenience Grp and Rear Window Wiper/Washer (LX wagon only) ($250). Sport Appearance Grp: incl 14-inch alum wheels, GT strg wheel & tach, full cloth seats, liftgate spoiler and appliqués ($757). Iris Decor Grp (GT only): incl clearcoat Iris exterior color, color-keyed wheels, leather-wrapped strg wheel, and seat, door and front flr mats w/embroidered GT trim ($365).

TEMPO CONVENIENCE/APPEARANCE OPTIONS: Preferred Equip Pkg GL Series: Man Air Cond, Light Grp, Dual Elect Remote Control Mirrors and Tilt Steering Wheel ($304). Preferred Equip Pkg GL two-door models: Incls all GL Series items plus Rr Window Defroster, Frnt Center Armrest, F&R Flr Mats, Pwr Lock Grp, Elect AM/FM Stereo Radio w/Cass & Clock, Auto FLC Transaxle and Polycast Wheels ($1305). Preferred Equip Pkg GL four-door models: same as GL two-door equipment ($1345). Preferred Equip Grp SRS GL Series: same as GL equipment plus Driver's Side Airbag, but minus Tilt Steering Wheel, Elect AM/FM Stereo Radio w/Cass & Clock and Polycast Wheels: two-door ($1081); four-door ($1121). Preferred Equip Pkg LX Series: Man Air Cond, Rr Window Defroster, Elect AM/FM Stereo Radio w/Cass & Clock and Auto FLC Transaxle ($1005). Calif. Emission Syst ($100). Man Air Cond ($817). Frnt Center Armrest ($59). Rr Window Defroster ($170). Flr Mats F&R ($33). Instrument Cluster ($87). Light Grp ($38). Pwr Lock Grp: two-door ($311); four-door ($351). Luggage Rack ($115). Dual Elect Remote Mirrors ($121). Clearcoat Paint ($91). Elect AM/FM Stereo Radio w/Cass & Clock ($155). Pwr Driver's Seat ($305). Premium Sound System ($138). Spd Control ($224). Tilt Steering Wheel ($145). Airbag (driver's side only): GL ($369); LX ($224). Polycast Wheels ($193). Pwr Side Windows (four-door only) ($330). Eng Block Htr ($20). P185/70R14 WSW Tires ($82).

PROBE CONVENIENCE/APPEARANCE OPTIONS: Preferred Equip Pkg base series (251A): Tilt Strg Column, Rr Window Defroster, Convenience Grp incl Interval Wipers, Light Grp, Dual Electric Remote Mirrors ($395). Preferred Equip Pkg base series (253A): same as 251A plus Man Air Cond, Elect AM/FM Radio w/Cass and Premium Sound, Color-Keyed Bodyside Mldgs, Remote Keyless Entry, Spd Control, Pwr Grp ($2421). Preferred Equip Pkg GT Series (261A): same as 251A plus Man Air Cond and Elect AM/FM Radio w/Cass and Premium Sound ($1451). Preferred Equip Pkg GT Series (263A): same as 253A plus Anti-lock Brakes, Rr Wiper/Washer and Heated Dual Elect Remote Control Mirrors ($2898). Man Air Cond ($817). Rr Window Defroster ($170). Leather Bucket Seats: base ($712); GT ($523). Cloth Bucket Seats (stnd GT) ($189). Pwr Driver's Seat ($305). Spd Control ($224). Anti-lock Brakes: base ($774); GT ($595). Pwr Sliding Roof ($648). Keyless Entry Syst ($137). Anti-theft Syst ($200). Convenience Grp: incl Tinted Glass, Interval Wipers, Courtesy Lights and Headlamp Warning Chime ($374). Pwr Grp: incl Pwr Door Locks and Pwr Windows w/Dual Express Down ($510). Light Grp: incl Dual Illum Visor Vanity Mirrors, Fade-to-Off Dome Lamp and Illum Entry ($249). Frnt Color-Keyed Flr Mats ($33). Dual Elect Remote Control Mirrors ($106). Color-Keyed Bodyside Mldgs ($50). Rr Wiper/Washer Syst ($182). Man Driver's Seat Adj ($37). Pwr Antenna ($85). Elect AM/FM Stereo Radio w/Cass & Premium Sound ($339). AM/FM Electronic Cass w/CD Player & Premium Sound ($840). Calif. Emissions System ($100). Eng Block Heater ($20). P205/55R15 BSW Tires (base only) ($450).

TAURUS CONVENIENCE/APPEARANCE OPTIONS: Preferred Equip Pkg GL Series (203A): Man Air Cond and Rr Window Defroster ($686). Preferred Equip Pkg GL Series (204A): same as 203A plus Pwr Door Locks, Elect AM/FM Stereo Radio w/Cass, Spd Control, Dlx Wheel Covers, Cargo Tie-Down Net, Flr Mats F&R, Light Grp, Pwr Windows and Pwr 6-way Driver's Seat ($2412). Preferred Equip Pkg LX Series: Rr Window Defroster, Spd Control, Flr Mats F&R, Leather-wrapped Strg Wheel, Elect AM/FM Stereo Radio w/Cass, Cargo Area Cover (wagon), "Picnic Table" Load Flr Extension (wagon), Keyless Entry Syst and Pwr Antenna ($501). Elect Air Cond (LX only) ($183). Conventional Spare Tire ($73). Elect Air Cond (LX only) ($183). Man Air Cond (GL only) ($841). Pass Side Airbag ($488). Anti-lock Brakes (stnd SHO sedan) ($595). Cargo Area Cover ($66, wagons only). Cargo Tie-Down Net ($44, GL only). Rr Window Defroster ($170). Engine Blk Heater ($20). Floor Mats, F&R ($45). Remote Deck-lid & Fuel Door Release (GL only) ($101). Remote Keyless Entry Syst (LX and SHO only) ($193). Light Grp (GL only) ($59). "Picnic Table" Load Floor Extension ($90, wagons only). Pwr Door Locks (GL only) ($257). Pwr Moonroof (LX and SHO only) ($776). Elect AM/FM Stereo Radio w/Cass ($171). Audio Digital CD Player ($491). JBL Audio Syst ($526). Pwr Antenna ($102, LX only). Rr Facing Third Seat ($155, wagons only). Dual Control 6-Way Pwr Seats ($305, LX and SHO only). 6-Way Pwr Driver's Seat ($305, GL only). Spd Control ($224). Leather-Wrapped Strg Wheel ($96). Rr Window Washer/Wiper ($135, wagons only). Cellular Phone ($779). Lux Convenience Grp: incl JBL Audio Syst, Pwr Moonroof and Dual Pwr Seats ($1407). GL Decor Equip Grp: incl Upgraded Cloth Trim, Spd Sensitive Pwr Strg, Paint Stripe and Dual Visor Mirrors ($389). Cast Aluminum Wheels (GL only) ($239). HD Battery ($27). Calif. Emissions Syst ($100). Leather Bucket Seats w/console: LX ($515); GL ($618). Leather Split Bench Seat (LX only) ($515). Leather Bucket Seats (SHO sedan only) ($515). Heavy Duty Suspension (N/A SHO) ($26). Frt Floor Mats ($45). P205/65R15 BSW ($150).

CROWN VICTORIA CONVENIENCE/APPEARANCE OPTIONS: Preferred Equip Pkg base series (111A): Color-Keyed Flr Mats F&R, Illum Entry and Convenience Grp ($559). Preferred Equip Pkg LX Series (113A): same as 111A plus Audio Grp, Exterior Decor Grp, Leather-wrapped Strg Wheel and Light/Decor Grp ($1082). Preferred Equip Pkg LX Series (114A): same as 113A plus LX Lux Grp ($3581). Calif. Emissions Syst ($100). Leather Split Bench Seat ($555). Conv Spare Tire ($85). Pass Airbag ($488). Anti-lock Brakes w/Elect Traction Assist ($695). 41G Handling & Perf Pkg (LX only) incl Elect Traction Control, Revised Springs/Shocks/Stabilizer Bar, Pwr Strg Cooler, P225/60R16 BSW Touring Tires, 16-inch Cast Alum Wheels and Dual Exhaust ($1905). Eng Block Htr ($25). Illum Entry Syst ($82). Illum Keyless Entry Syst ($196). Light/Decor Grp (base only) ($240). Cellular Phone ($779). Exterior Decor Grp (LX only) ($508). Convenience Grp incl Rr Window Defroster, Pwr Lock Grp, Spd Control and Trunk Cargo Net: base ($807); LX ($704). Exterior Decor Grp (LX only) incl Cast Alum Wheels and Cornering Lamps ($508). Elect AM/FM Stereo Radio w/Cass ($171). High Level Audio Syst (LX only) ($335). Ford JBL Audio Syst ($526). LX Luxury Grp incl Anti-lock Brakes w/Elect Traction Assist, High Level Audio Syst, Elect Grp, Rr Air Suspension, Remote Keyless Entry and Dual Pwr Seats ($2820). Rr Air Suspension ($285). Leather-wrapped Strg Wheel (LX only) ($96). Trailer Towing Pkg: base ($490); LX ($205). 6-Way Pwr Driver's Seat (base only) ($305). Dual Pwr Seats (LX only) ($504).

THUNDERBIRD CONVENIENCE/APPEARANCE OPTIONS: Preferred Equip Pkg LX Series: Rr Window Defroster, Dual Illum Visor Mirrors, Cast Alum Wheels and Elect Auto Temp Control ($620). Preferred Equip Pkg Super Coupe Series: Rr Window Defroster, Dual Illum Visor Mirrors, Cast Alum Wheels, Elect Auto Temp Control, Pwr Lock Grp, 6-Way Pwr Driver's Seat and Spd Control ($1055). Calif. Emission Syst ($95). Leather Bucket Seats: LX ($490); Super Coupe ($615). Anti-Theft System ($235). Remote Keyless Entry: LX ($215); Super Coupe ($295). Frt Floor Mats ($30). Elect AM/FM Stereo Radio w/Cass w/Premium Sound ($370). Ford JBL Audio System ($500). Trunk Mounted CD Changer ($785). Anti-lock Brakes ($565). Cold Weather Grp: LX ($300); Super Coupe ($180). Pwr Moonroof ($740). Tri-Coat Paint ($225). Traction Assist (LX only) ($210). Cellular Phone ($530). Luxury Grp incl Autolamp Grp, Illum Entry, Light Grp, 6-Way Pwr Pass Seat and Integrated Warning Module: LX ($580); Super Coupe ($555).

HISTORY: U.S. model year production totaled 1,118,265 (including Mustang). U.S. calendar year production totaled 1,026,338 (including Mustang) for a 17.2 percent of industry market share. For the second consecutive year, Taurus was the best selling car in the United States in 1993, with 360,448 units sold compared to 330,030 for the Honda Accord which finished second. Alex J. Trotman was named chairman and CEO of Ford Motor Co. on Nov. 1, 1993. He succeeded Harold A. "Red" Poling who retired.

1994 FORD

1994 Ford Escort LX sedan. (PH)

1993 Ford Taurus LX sedan. (OCW)

The Tempo was in its final year in 1994 as a Ford product, and it was a short year at that with production halted in the spring. At that point, production geared up for the all-new Contour, which debuted as a 1995 model. Another new Ford model debuted in the spring of 1994, that being the import (produced in South Korea) Aspire, which replaced the Ford Festiva. Both of these foreign-produced compact models are not within the scope of this book and are not covered in detail. The Escort LX-E model offered previously was discontinued. Dual airbags became standard equipment on the Probe, Taurus, Crown Victoria and Thunderbird. A driver's side airbag was standard on the Escort and Tempo offered a driver's side airbag as optional equipment on the models powered by the 2.3-liter four-cylinder engine. The 5.0-liter V-8 offered previously as an option engine in the Thunderbird was replaced by the modular 4.6-liter V-8.

ESCORT — FOUR — Escort's 1994 lineup was the same as the year previous except for the discontinuation of the LX-E four-door sedan. Returning were three series as follows: base (three-door hatchback), LX (three- and five-door hatchbacks, four-door sedan and station wagon) and GT (three-door hatchback). A driver's side airbag became standard equipment and a compact disc player was optional on the GT model. Standard engine for base and LX model Escorts was again the 1.9-liter four-cylinder powerplant with sequential fuel injection. A five-speed manual transaxle was standard on Escorts, with the electronic four-speed automatic overdrive transaxle optional. The GT model again used the 16-valve DOHC 1.8-liter four-cylinder engine with multi-port fuel injection.

1994 Ford Tempo LX sedan. (OCW)

TEMPO — FOUR — In its final half year (production halted in spring of 1994) of production, Tempo returned unchanged from the year previous. The lineup again consisted of two- and four-door sedans in the GL series and a four-door sedan in LX trim. Tempo's base powerplant was again the 2.3-liter four-cylinder engine with sequential electronic fuel injection. The five-speed manual transaxle was standard equipment with the three-speed automatic transaxle optional, except on the GL two-door sedan. Again optional across-the-board was a 3.0-liter V-6. A driver's side airbag was optional on all Tempos equipped with the 2.3-liter four.

1994 Ford Taurus SHO sedan. (OCW)

1994 Ford Taurus GL sedan. (OCW)

1994 Ford Probe GT coupe. (PH)

1994 Ford Taurus GL station wagon. (OCW)

PROBE — FOUR/V-6 — After its redesign the year previous, Probe returned in 1994 with its lineup unchanged. Probe was again available in two series: base or GT. The base coupe was again powered by the DOHC 2.0-liter four-cylinder engine. The GT coupe again used the all-aluminum DOHC 2.5-liter V-6. A five-speed manual transaxle was standard equipment on both coupes and an electronically controlled four-speed automatic transaxle was optional. Along with a driver's side airbag, a passenger side supplemental restraint system (SRS) was now standard equipment on Probe.

TAURUS — V-6 — The lineup for Taurus in 1994 also remained unchanged from the year previous. Taurus was again offered in both sedan and station wagon versions in the GL and LX series as well as the SHO sedan. The GL sedan and wagon and LX sedan were again powered by the 3.0-liter V-6 with sequential electronic fuel injection. The LX wagon was again powered by the 3.8-liter V-6, which was again the option engine on other Taurus models (except the SHO sedan). The four-speed automatic overdrive transaxle was the standard unit on Taurus GL and LX models. The SHO sedan used the DOHC 3.0-liter V-6 as its base unit coupled to a five-speed manual transaxle. The DOHC 3.2-liter V-6 was the option engine on SHO models, this unit mated to a four-speed automatic overdrive transaxle. The passenger side supplemental restraint system (SRS) was now standard equipment on all Taurus models.

CROWN VICTORIA — V-8 — The Crown Vic returned in 1994 with its two series—base and LX—each offering a four-door sedan. The modular 4.6-liter V-8 again was the standard engine, coupled to an electronically controlled four-speed automatic overdrive transmission. A passenger's side airbag became standard equipment in Crown Vics.

THUNDERBIRD — V-6/V-8 — The LX coupe and Super Coupe were again the offerings in the 1994 Thunderbird lineup. The 3.8-liter V-6 with sequential electronic fuel injection was again the standard engine for the LX model. The 210-hp supercharged version of the 3.8-liter V-6 with the five-speed manual transmission was again used in the Super Coupe. The four-speed automatic overdrive transmission was standard on the LX and optional on the Super Coupe. The 4.6-liter V-8 replaced the previously offered 5.0-liter V-8 as the option engine for the LX coupe. Dual airbags became standard equipment in Thunderbirds.

1994 Ford Crown Victoria LX sedan. (PH)

1994 Ford Thunderbird LX coupe. (PH)

I.D. DATA: Ford's 17-symbol Vehicle Identification Number (VIN) was stamped on a metal tab fastened to the instrument panel, visible through the windshield. The first three symbols indicate manufacturer, make and vehicle type. The fourth symbol denotes restraint system. Next comes a letter (usually 'P'), followed by two digits that indicate Model Number, as shown in left column of tables below. (Example: '10' Escort two-door hatchback). Symbol eight indicates engine type. Next is a check digit. Symbol ten indicates model year ('R' - 1994). Symbol eleven denotes assembly plant. The final six digits make up the sequence number, starting with 100001.

ESCORT (FOUR)

Model No.	Body/ Style No.	Body Type & Seating	Factory Price	Shipping Weight	Prod. Total
P	10	2-dr. Hatch-5P	9035	2304	Note 1
P	11	2-dr. LX Hatch-5P	9890	2325	Note 1
P	14	4-dr. LX Hatch-5P	10325	2419	39,837
P	13	4-dr. LX Sed-5P	10550	2371	49,052
P	15	4-dr. LX Sta Wag-5P	10880	2419	108,372
P	12	2-dr. GT Hatch-5P	12300	2447	Note 1

NOTE 1: Production of two-door hatchback models totaled 87,888 with no further breakout available.

TEMPO (FOUR)

Model No.	Body/ Style No.	Body Type & Seating	Factory Price	Shipping Weight	Prod. Total
P	31	2-dr. GL Sed-5P	10735	2511	32,050
P	36	4-dr. GL Sed-5P	10735	2569	Note 1
P	37	4-dr. LX Sed-5P	12560	2569	Note 1

NOTE 1: Production of four-door sedan models totaled 110,399 with no further breakout available.

PROBE (FOUR/V-6 in GT only)

Model No.	Body/ Style No.	Body Type & Seating	Factory Price	Shipping Weight	Prod. Total
T	20	2-dr. Cpe-4P	13685	2690	Note 1
T	22	2-dr. GT Cpe-4P	16015	2921	Note 1

NOTE 1: Production of two-door coupe models totaled 85,505 with no further breakout available.

TAURUS (V-6)

Model No.	Body/ Style No.	Body Type & Seating	Factory Price	Shipping Weight	Prod. Total
P	52	4-dr. GL Sed-6P	16140	3104	Note 1
P	57	4-dr. GL Sta Wag-6P	17220	3253	Note 2
P	53	4-dr. LX Sedan-6P	18785	3147	Note 1
P	58	4-dr. LX Sta Wag-6P	20400	3296	Note 2
P	54	4-dr. SHO Sed-6P	24715	3395	Note 1

NOTE 1: Production of four-door sedan models totaled 288,737 with no further breakout available.

NOTE 2: Production of station wagon models totaled 55,135 with no further breakout available.

CROWN VICTORIA (V-8)

Model No.	Body/ Style No.	Body Type & Seating	Factory Price	Shipping Weight	Prod. Total
P	73	4-dr. Sed-6P	19300	3786	Note 1
P	74	4-dr. LX Sed-6P	20715	3794	Note 1

NOTE 1: Production of four-door sedan models totaled 100,983 with no further breakout available.

THUNDERBIRD (V-6/V-8)

Model No.	Body/ Style No.	Body Type & Seating	Factory Price	Shipping Weight	Prod. Total
P	62	2-dr. LX Cpe-5P	16830/17860	3570/3711	Note 1
P	64	2-dr. Super Cpe-5P	22240/-----	3758/----	Note 1

NOTE: Figures to the left of slash are for V-6/to right of slash are for V-8.

NOTE 1: Production of two-door coupe models totaled 120,320 with no further breakout available.

ENGINE [Base Four (Escort)]: Inline. Overhead cam. Four-cylinder. Cast-iron block and aluminum head. Displacement: 113 cid (1.9 liters). Bore & stroke: 3.23 x 3.46 in. Compression ratio: 9.0:1. Brake horsepower: 88 at 4400 rpm. Torque: 108 lbs.-ft. at 3800 rpm. Five main bearings. Hydraulic valve lifters. Sequential fuel injection.

ENGINE [Base Four (Escort GT)]: High-output. Inline. Dual overhead cam. Four-cylinder. Cast-iron block and aluminum head. Displacement: 109 cid (1.8 liters). Bore & stroke: 3.27 x 3.35 in. Compression ratio: 9.0:1. Brake horsepower: 127 at 6500 rpm. Torque: 114 lbs.-ft. at 4500 rpm. Five main bearings. Hydraulic valve lifters. Multi-port fuel injection.

ENGINE [Base Four (Probe)]: Inline. Dual overhead cam. Four-cylinder. Cast-iron block and aluminum head. Displacement: 122 cid (2.0 liters). Bore & stroke: 3.27 x 3.62 in. Compression ratio: 9.0:1. Brake horsepower: 118 at 5500 rpm. Torque: 127 lbs.-ft. at 4500 rpm. Hydraulic valve lifters. Multi-port fuel injection.

ENGINE [Base Four (Tempo)]: Inline. Overhead valve. Four-cylinder. Cast-iron block and head. Displacement: 140 cid (2.3 liters). Bore & stroke: 3.70 x 3.30 in. Compression ratio: 9.0:1. Brake horsepower: 96 at 4200 rpm. Torque: 126 lbs.-ft. at 2600 rpm. Five main bearings. Hydraulic valve lifters. Sequential fuel injection.

ENGINE [Base V-6 (Probe GT)]: Dual overhead cam V-6 (24 valve). Aluminum block and head. Displacement: 153 cid (2.5 liters). Bore & stroke: 3.33 x 2.92 in. Compression ratio: 9.2:1. Brake horsepower: 164 at 5600 rpm. Torque: 160 lbs.-ft. at 4000 rpm. Four main bearings. Hydraulic valve lifters. Multi-port fuel injection.

ENGINE [Base V-6 (Taurus GL/Taurus LX sedan); Optional (Tempo GL/Tempo LX)]: 60-degree, overhead valve V-6. Cast-iron block and head. Displacement: 182 cid (3.0 liters). Bore & stroke: 3.50 x 3.15 in. Compression ratio: 9.3:1. Brake horsepower: 140 at 4800 rpm. Torque: 165 lbs.-ft. at 3250 rpm. Four main bearings. Hydraulic valve lifters. Sequential fuel injection.

ENGINE [Base V-6 (Taurus SHO)]: Dual-overhead-cam V-6 (24 valve). Cast-iron block and head. Displacement: 182 cid (3.0 liters). Bore & stroke: 3.50 x 3.15 in. Compression ratio: 9.8:1. Brake horsepower: 220 at 6200 rpm. Torque: 200 lbs.-ft. at 4800 rpm. Four main bearings. Hydraulic valve lifters. Sequential fuel injection.

ENGINE [Base V-6 (Taurus LX wagon/Thunderbird LX); Optional: (Taurus GL/Taurus LX sedan)]: 90-degree, overhead valve V-6. Cast-iron block and aluminum head. Displacement: 232 cid (3.8 liters). Bore & stroke: 3.80 x 3.40 in. Compression ratio: 9.0:1. Brake horsepower: (Taurus) 140 at 3800 rpm. Torque: (Taurus) 215 lbs.-ft. at 2200 RPM; (Thunderbird) 215 lbs.-ft. at 2400. Four main bearings. Hydraulic valve lifters. Sequential fuel injection.

ENGINE [Supercharged V-6 (Thunderbird Super Coupe)]: Same as 232 cid (3.8-liter) V-6 above, except - Compression ratio: 8.2:1. Horsepower: 210 at 4000 rpm. Torque: 330 lbs.-ft. at 2500 rpm.

ENGINE [Base V-8 (Crown Victoria); Optional (Thunderbird LX)]: Modular, overhead valve V-8. Displacement: 281 cid (4.6 liters). Bore & stroke: 3.60 x 3.60. Compression ratio: 9.0:1. Brake horsepower: (Crown Vic) 190 at 4600 RPM; (Thunderbird) 205 at 4500 rpm. Torque: (Crown Vic) 260 lbs.-ft. at 3200 RPM; (Thunderbird) 265 lbs.-ft. at 3200 rpm. Sequential fuel injection.

CHASSIS DATA: Wheelbase: (Escort) 98.4 in.; (Tempo) 99.9 in.; (Probe) 102.8 in.: (Taurus) 106.0 in.; (Crown Vic) 114.4 in.; (T-Bird) 113.0 in. Overall Length: (Escort) 170.0 in.; (Escort wag) 171.3 in.; (Tempo two-door) 176.7 in.; (Tempo four-door) 177.0 in.; (Probe) 178.7 in.; (Taurus) 192.0 in.; (Taurus wag) 193.1 in.; (Crown Vic) 212.4 in.; (T-Bird) 200.3 in. Height: (Escort) 52.5 in.; (Escort wag) 53.6 in.; (Tempo two-door) 52.8 in.; (Tempo four-door) 52.9 in.; (Probe) 51.6 in.; (Taurus) 54.1 in.; (Taurus wag) 55.5 in.; (Crown Vic) 56.8 in.; (T-Bird) 52.5 in. Width: (Escort) 66.7 in.; (Tempo) 68.3 in.: (Probe) 69.8 in.; (Taurus) 70.7 in.; (Crown Vic) 77.8 in.; (T-Bird) 72.7 in. Front Tread: (Escort) 56.5 in.; (Tempo) 54.9 in.; (Probe) 59.4 in.; (Taurus) 61.6 in.; (Crown Vic) 62.8 in.; (T-Bird) 61.6 in. Rear Tread: (Escort) 56.5 in.; (Tempo) 57.6 in.; (Probe) 59.4 in.; (Taurus) 60.5 in.; (Taurus wag) 59.9 in.; (Crown Vic) 63.3 in.; (T-Bird) 60.2 in. Standard Tires: (Escort) P175/70R13; (Escort LX) P175/65R14; (Escort GT) P185/60R15; (Tempo) P185/70R14; (Probe) P195/65R14; (Probe GT) P225/50VR16; (Taurus) P205/65R15; (Taurus SHO) P215/60ZR16; (Crown Vic) P215/70R15; (T-Bird LX) P205/70R15; (T-Bird Super Cpe) P225/60ZR16.

TECHNICAL: Transmission: Five-speed manual transaxle standard on Escort, Tempo, Probe, Taurus SHO and Thunderbird Super Coupe. Four-speed overdrive automatic standard on Taurus, Crown Vic and T-Bird. Drive Axle: (Crown Vic/T-Bird) rear; (others) front. Steering: (Crown Vic) recirculating ball; (others) rack/pinion. Front Suspension: (Escort) Independent MacPherson strut w/strut-mounted coil springs; (Tempo) Independent MacPherson strut w/strut-mounted coil springs, forged lower control arms and cast steering knuckle; (Probe) Independent strut-type with lower A-type control arms, upper strut-mounted coil springs and stabilizer bar; (Taurus) Independent MacPherson strut front drive w/strut-mounted coil springs, stabilizer bar, tension strut and lower control arm; (Crown Vic) Independent short/long arm w/ball joints, coil springs and stabilizer bar; (T-Bird) Short/long arm w/double isolated tension strut, coil springs and stabilizer bar. Rear Suspension: (Escort)

Independent, strut-type and Twin Trapezoidal Links with trailing arms and upper strut-mounted coil springs; (Tempo) Fully independent MacPherson strut w/coil spring offset on shock strut, parallel suspension arms and tension struts; (Probe) Independent strut-type, Quadra-link, upper strut-mounted coil springs and stabilizer bar. (Taurus sedan) Independent MacPherson struts w/coil spring on shock strut, stabilizer bar, tension strut, parallel suspension arms and two-piece cast spindle w/forged stem; (Taurus wagon) Independent short/long arm w/spring on lower control arm, stamped tension strut w/two-piece forged/cast spindle; (Crown Vic) Rigid axle w/four links and coil springs; (T-Bird) H-arm independent, coil springs and stabilizer bar. Brakes: Front disc, rear drum (power assisted) except (Escort GT, Probe GT, Taurus SHO, Crown Victoria and T-Bird Super Coupe) front/rear disc. Body construction: (Crown Vic) separate body and frame; (others) unibody. Fuel tank: (Escort) 11.9 gal.; (Tempo) 15.9 gal.; (Probe) 15.5 gal.; (Taurus) 16.0 gal.; (Taurus SHO) 18.4 gal.; (Crown Vic) 20.0 gal.; (T-Bird) 18.0 gal.

DRIVETRAIN OPTIONS: Engines: 3.0-liter V-6: Tempo ($655). 3.8-liter V-6: Taurus GL and LX sed ($630). 4.6-liter V-8: Thunderbird LX ($515). Transmission/Differential: Three-speed automatic transaxle: Tempo ($535). Four-speed automatic transaxle: Escort ($790); Probe ($790); T-Bird Super Coupe ($790). Traction Assist: T-Bird (LX only) ($210). Steering/Suspension/Brakes: Power steering: Escort (LX only) ($250). Rear Air Suspension: Crown Vic (LX only) ($270). Heavy Duty Suspension: Taurus (N/A SHO) ($26). Trailer towing pkg: Crown Vic ($690). Anti-lock brakes: Escort ($565); Probe ($735); Probe GT ($565); Taurus (stnd SHO) ($565); Crown Vic (w/Elect Traction Assist) ($665); T-Bird ($565).

ESCORT CONVENIENCE/APPEARANCE OPTIONS: Preferred Equip Pkg LX Series (320A): Pwr Steering, Light/Convenience Grp and Rr Window Defroster ($235). Preferred Equip Pkg LX Series (321A): Man Air Cond, Rr Window Defroster, Light/Convenience Grp, Pwr Steering, Elect AM/FM Stereo Radio w/Cass & Clock, Clearcoat Paint and (wagon only) Luggage Rack and Rr Window Wiper/Washer ($1850). Preferred Equip Pkg GT Series: Man Air Cond, Rr Window Defroster and Luxury/Convenience Grp ($530). Calif. Emission System ($70). Air Cond (LX and GT only) ($725). Rr Window Defroster ($160). Light/Convenience Grp: incl Dual Elect Remote Control Mirrors, Remote Fuel Door Release, Remote Decklid Release ($205). Lux Convenience Grp: incl Tilt Strg Wheel, Spd Control and Tach (stnd on GT) ($410). Pwr Moonroof ($525). Clearcoat Paint ($85). Comfort Grp: incl Air Cond and Pwr Strg (base Escort only) ($800). AM/FM Stereo radio (base Escort only) ($300). AM/FM Cass radio: base Escort ($465); LX ($165). Elect AM/FM Stereo Radio w/CD Player: base ($740); LX ($445); GT ($280). Premium sound syst ($138). Pwr Steering (LX only) ($250). Wagon Grp: incl Dlx Luggage Rack, Light/Convenience Grp and Rr Window Wiper/Washer (LX wagon only) ($240). Sport Appearance Grp: incl 14-inch alum wheels, tach, full cloth seats, liftgate spoiler and appliqués ($720). Sunrise Red Decor Grp (GT only) incl clearcoat Sunrise Red exterior color, color-keyed wheels, cloth bucket seats and front flr mats w/embroidered GT trim ($350). Anti-lock Brakes ($565). Pwr Equip Grp: incl Pwr Door Locks, Pwr Windows and Tach ($520).

TEMPO CONVENIENCE/APPEARANCE OPTIONS: Preferred Equip Pkg GL Series (225A): Man Air Cond, Light Grp, Dual Elect Remote Control Mirrors and Rr Window Defroster ($310). Preferred Equip Pkg GL Series (226A): same as 225A plus Elect AM/FM Stereo Radio w/Cass & Clock, Auto Trans, Frt Center Armrest, Flr Mats F&R, Pwr Lock Grp, Polycast Wheels and Tilt Strg Wheel ($1255). Preferred Equip Pkg GL Series (227A): same as 226A plus Driver's Side Airbag ($1190). Preferred Equip Pkg LX Series: Man Air Cond, Rr Window Defroster, 3.0-liter V-6 & Auto Trans, Elect AM/FM Stereo Radio w/Cass & Clock and Decklid Luggage Rack ($960). Calif. Emission Syst ($95). Man Air Cond ($780). Frt Center Armrest ($55). Rr Window Defroster ($160). Flr Mats F&R ($45). Instrument Cluster ($85). Light Grp ($35). Pwr Lock Grp: two-door ($295); four-door ($335). Luggage Rack ($110). Dual Elect Remote Mirrors ($115). Clearcoat Paint ($85). Elect AM/FM Stereo Radio w/Cass & Clock ($150). Pwr Driver's Seat ($290). Premium Sound System ($135). Spd Control ($215). Tilt Strg Wheel ($140). Airbag (driver's side only): GL ($465); LX ($325). Polycast Wheels ($185). Pwr Side Windows (four-door only) ($315). Eng Block Htr ($20). P185/70R14 WSW Tires (GL and LX only) ($80).

1994 Ford Taurus LX sedan. (PH)

1994 Ford Taurus LX station wagon. (OCW)

PROBE CONVENIENCE/APPEARANCE OPTIONS: Preferred Equip Pkg base series (251A): Tilt Strg Column, Rr Window Defroster, Convenience Grp incl Interval Wipers, Light Grp, Dual Electric Remote Mirrors and Tinted Glass ($370). Preferred Equip Pkg base series (253A): same as 251A plus Man Air Cond, Elect AM/FM Radio w/Cass and Premium Sound, Color-Keyed Bodyside Mldgs, Illum Entry Syst, Spd Control, Pwr Grp and Fade-to-Off Dome Lamp ($2340). Preferred Equip Pkg GT Series (261A): Man Air Cond, Elect AM/FM Stereo Radio w/Cass & Premium Sound, Tilt Strg Column, Rr Window Defroster, Convenience Grp incl Interval Wipers, Light Grp, Dual Electric Remote Mirrors and Tinted Glass ($1385). Preferred Equip Pkg GT Series (263A): same as 261A plus Color-Keyed Bodyside Mldgs, Illum Entry Syst, Spd Control, Pwr Grp and Fade-to-Off Dome Lamp ($2790). Man Air Cond ($780). Leather Bucket Seats (GT only) ($500). Pwr Driver's Seat ($290). Anti-lock Brakes: base ($735); GT ($565). Pwr Sliding Roof ($615). Feature Car Pkg (GT only): incl Wild Orchid Exterior Finish and Unique Flr Mats and Bucket Seat Trim ($215). Sport Edition Option (base only): incl GT fascia w/foglamps, 15-inch Alum Wheels and P205/55R15 Tires ($760). Anti-theft Syst ($190). Pwr Grp: incl Pwr Door Locks and Pwr Windows w/Dual Express Down ($700). Light Grp: incl Dual Illum Visor Vanity Mirrors, Fade-to-Off Dome Lamp and Illum Entry ($395). Frt Color-Keyed Flr Mats ($30). Dual Elect Remote Control Mirrors ($175). Color-Keyed Bodyside Mldgs ($50). Rr Wiper/Washer Syst ($175). Man Driver's Seat Height Adj ($35). Pwr Antenna ($80). Elect AM/FM Stereo Radio w/Cass & Premium Sound ($325). Elect AM/FM Stereo Radio w/CD Player & Premium Sound ($800). Calif. Emissions System ($95). Eng Block Heater ($20). P205/55R15 BSW Tires (base only) ($430).

TAURUS CONVENIENCE/APPEARANCE OPTIONS: Preferred Equip Pkg GL Series (203A): Man Air Cond and Rr Window Defroster ($650). Preferred Equip Pkg GL Series (204A): same as 203A plus Pwr Door Locks, Elect AM/FM Stereo Radio w/Cass, Spd Control, Dlx Wheel Covers, Flr Mats F&R, Pwr Windows and Pwr 6-way Driver's Seat ($2070). Elect Air Cond (LX only) ($175). Anti-lock Brakes (stnd SHO sedan) ($565). Engine Blk Heater ($20). Floor Mats, F&R ($45). Remote Keyless Entry Syst: GL ($390); LX ($215). "Picnic Table" Load Floor Extension ($85, wagons only). Pwr Door Locks (GL only) ($245). Elect AM/FM Stereo Radio w/Cass ($165). High Level Audio Syst (LX and SHO only) ($315). CD Player (LX and SHO only) ($470). JBL Audio Syst (LX and SHO only) ($500). Rr Facing Third Seat ($150, wagons only). Dual Control Pwr Seats (LX only) ($290). 6-Way Pwr Driver's Seat ($290). Spd Control ($215). Cellular Phone ($500). Lux Convenience Grp: incl JBL Audio Syst, Pwr Moonroof, Keyless Entry Syst and Dual Pwr Seats ($1555). LX Convenience Grp: incl Pwr Moonroof and Dual Pwr Seats ($1030). Cast Aluminum Wheels (GL only) ($230). Calif. Emissions Syst ($95). Leather Bucket Seats w/console: LX ($495); GL ($595). Leather Split Bench Seat (LX only) ($495). Leather Bucket Seats (SHO sedan only) ($495). Heavy Duty Suspension (N/A SHO) ($26). Heavy Duty Battery (N/A SHO) ($30). Conventional Spare Tire (LX only) ($70). Pwr Side Windows ($340).

CROWN VICTORIA CONVENIENCE/APPEARANCE OPTIONS: Preferred Equip Pkg base series: Color-Keyed Flr Mats F&R, Rr Window Defroster, Pwr Lock Grp, Trunk Cargo Net, Spd Control, Illum Entry Syst and Spare Tire Cover ($695). Preferred Equip Pkg LX Series (113A): Color-Keyed Flr Mats F&R, Rr Window Defroster, Pwr Lock Grp, Cornering Lamps, Spd Control, Illum Entry Syst, Leather-wrapped Strg Wheel, Elect AM/FM Stereo Radio w/Cass, Cast Alum Wheels, Pwr Antenna and Light/Decor Grp ($295). Preferred Equip Pkg LX Series (114A): same as 113A plus Dual Control Pwr Seats, High Level Audio Syst, Anti-lock Brakes w/Elect Traction Assist, Rr Air Suspension, Auto Temp Control Air Cond, Tripminder Computer, Elect Digital Instrumentation, HD Battery, Remote Keyless Entry and Elect Auto Dim Mirror ($2295). Calif. Emissions Syst ($95). Leather Split Bench Seat (LX only) ($625). Conv Spare Tire ($80). Anti-lock Brakes w/Elect Traction Assist ($665). 41G Handling & Perf Pkg (LX only) incl Elect Traction Control, Revised Springs/Shocks/Stabilizer Bar, Pwr Strg Cooler, P225/60R16 BSW Touring Tires, 16-inch Cast Alum Wheels and Dual Exhaust ($1765). Eng Block Htr ($25). Illum Entry Syst ($80). Remote Keyless Entry Syst (LX only) ($215).

Light/Decor Grp (LX only) ($225). Cellular Phone (LX only) ($745). Exterior Decor Grp (LX only) ($485). Convenience Grp incl Rr Window Defroster, Pwr Lock Grp, Spd Control and Trunk Cargo Net: base ($770); LX ($670). Exterior Decor Grp (LX only) incl Cast Alum Wheels and Cornering Lamps ($485). Elect AM/FM Stereo Radio w/Cass ($165). High Level Audio Syst (LX only) ($315). Ford JBL Audio Syst ($500). LX Luxury Grp incl Anti-lock Brakes w/Elect Traction Assist, High Level Audio Syst, Elect Grp, Rr Air Suspension, Remote Keyless Entry and Dual Pwr Seats ($2720). Rr Air Suspension (LX only) ($270). Leather-wrapped Strg Wheel (LX only) ($90). Trailer Towing Pkg: (LX Only) ($395). 6-Way Pwr Driver's Seat ($290). Dual Pwr Seats (LX only) ($480). Dlx Wheel Covers ($45). Rr Window Defroster ($160). Color-Keyed Flr Mats F&R ($45).

THUNDERBIRD CONVENIENCE/APPEARANCE OPTIONS: Preferred Equip Pkg LX Series: Rr Window Defroster, Dual Illum Visor Mirrors, Cast Alum Wheels and Elect Auto Temp Control (NC). Preferred Equip Pkg Super Coupe Series: Rr Window Defroster, Dual Illum Visor Mirrors, Cast Alum Wheels, Elect Auto Temp Control, Pwr Lock Grp, 6-Way Pwr Driver's Seat and Spd Control (NC). Calif. Emission Syst ($95). Leather Bucket Seats: LX ($490); Super Coupe ($615). Anti-Theft System ($235). Remote Keyless Entry: LX ($215); Super Coupe ($295). Frt Floor Mats ($30). Elect AM/FM Stereo Radio w/Cass & Premium Sound ($370). Ford JBL Audio System ($500). Trunk Mounted CD Changer ($785). Anti-lock Brakes ($565). Cold Weather Grp: LX ($300); Super Coupe ($180). Pwr Moonroof ($740). Tri-Coat Paint ($225). Traction Assist (LX only) ($210). Cellular Phone ($530). Luxury Grp incl Autolamp Grp, Illum Entry, Light Grp, 6-Way Pwr Pass Seat and Integrated Warning Module: LX ($580); Super Coupe ($555). P225/60ZR16 BSW Tires ($70).

HISTORY: U.S. model year production totaled 1,307,534 (including Mustang). U.S. calendar year production totaled 1,220,512 (including Mustang) for a 18.5 percent of industry market share. For the third consecutive year, Taurus was the best selling car in the United States in 1994, with 397,037 units sold compared to 367,615 for the Honda Accord which finished second. Ford recorded an auto industry-record net income of $5.308 billion for 1994, more than double its 1993 net of $2.5 billion.

1995 FORD

With the Tempo discontinued, its 1995 replacement model debuted early in 1994 and was called the Contour. Offered in three series, each with a four-door sedan, the Contour was an example of Ford's new wave of "World Cars" (Contour/Mercury Mystique/Ford Mondeo—the European version of the Contour—all based on the same platform). The Contour used either the Zetec 2.0-liter four-cylinder engine (GL or LX sedans) or the Duratec 2.5-liter V-6 (SE sedan). Other new models in Ford's 1995 lineup included a Taurus SE sedan. The Crown Victoria received several revisions including a modified grille and tail lamps on its exterior and a new instrument panel inside. The Thunderbird now offered speed-sensitive steering as a standard feature with either the 4.6-liter V-8 or supercharged 3.8-liter V-6.

ESCORT — FOUR — The six models of Escort offered the year previous returned for 1995. The lineup again was comprised of the base three-door hatchback; LX three- and five-door hatchback, four-door sedan and station wagon and GT three-door hatchback. The passenger-side airbag was now standard equipment on the Escort. Also inside, all models featured a new instrument panel. The tachometer that was previously standard on the LX sedan was discontinued. Standard engine for base and LX model Escorts was again the 1.9-liter four-cylinder powerplant with sequential fuel injection. A five-speed manual transaxle was again standard on Escorts, with the electronic four-speed automatic overdrive transaxle optional. The GT model again used the 16-valve DOHC 1.8-liter four-cylinder engine with multi-port fuel injection.

1995 Ford Escort GT three-door hatchback. (OCW)

1995 Ford Contour GL sedan. (OCW)

CONTOUR — FOUR/V-6 — The Contour was Ford's replacement for the discontinued Tempo as well as being its initial offering of a "global car"—a concept whereby technology and expertise within Ford's worldwide operations were brought together to produce vehicles for multiple markets. The front-wheel-drive Contour was offered in three series: GL, LX and SE, each a four-door sedan with five-passenger capacity. It featured "safety cell" body construction, with high-tensile boron steel door beams, a cross-car beam running between the windshield pillars and a reinforced subframe. The Contour's cab forward design incorporated a low-mounted cowl and hood for better aerodynamics and a low 0.31 Cd (coefficient of drag). The GL and LX sedans used the Zetec DOHC, 16-valve 2.0-liter four-cylinder engine rated at 125-hp. The SE sedan was powered by the all-aluminum, modular Duratec 2.5-liter V-6—the smallest and lightest V-6 engine to that point in time. Both powerplants were controlled by Ford's engine controller EEC-IV, and featured distributorless ignition, sequential fuel-injection with mass-air flow and knock sensors. Base transaxle on all Contours was the MTX75 five-speed manual while the CD4E electronically controlled four-speed automatic was optional. Dual airbags were standard equipment as was solar reflective glass all-around to reduce interior heat build-up.

PROBE — FOUR/V-6 — Probe's lineup again consisted of a coupe in base or GT series. Changes for 1995 included a minor interior redesign, modified tail lamps and rear bumper and new aluminum wheels for the GT model. The base coupe was again powered by the DOHC 2.0-liter four-cylinder engine. The GT coupe again used the all-aluminum DOHC 2.5-liter V-6. A five-speed manual transaxle was again standard equipment on both coupes and an electronically controlled four-speed automatic transaxle was optional.

1995 Ford Escort LX station wagon. (OCW)

1995 Ford Probe GT coupe. (OCW)

1995 Ford Taurus SE sedan. (OCW)

TAURUS — V-6 — With the addition of an SE series sedan, the 1995 Taurus lineup expanded to six models in four series: GL, SE, LX and SHO. The SE and SHO series each offered a four-door sedan while the GL and LX series each were comprised of both a sedan and station wagon. The base 3.0-liter V-6 offered in the GL and SE series and LX sedan received an upgrade. New standard equipment for Taurus models included a rear window defroster, manual air conditioning, tinted glass and low fuel light. The LX wagon was again powered by the 3.8-liter V-6, which was again the option engine on other Taurus models (except the SHO sedan). The four-speed automatic overdrive transaxle was the standard unit on Taurus GL, SE and LX models. The SHO sedan used the DOHC 3.0-liter V-6 as its base unit coupled to a five-speed manual transaxle. The SHO sedan was also available with the DOHC 3.2-liter V-6 when ordered with the four-speed automatic overdrive transaxle. An all-new design 1996 Taurus was launched in June 1995.

CROWN VICTORIA — V-8 — The Crown Victoria four-door sedan was again available in base or LX series. The Crown Vic was revised inside and out receiving a new instrument panel, door panels and seats as well as modified tail lamps, grille, bumpers and bodyside moldings. New standard features included a battery saver and heated rearview mirror. The modular 4.6-liter V-8 and electronically controlled four-speed automatic overdrive transmission were again the standard powertrain units.

THUNDERBIRD — V-6/V-8 — Thunderbird was again offered as an LX coupe or Super Coupe. Several features previously available were discontinued including anti-theft alarm, engine block heater, Traction-Lok axle and heavy-duty battery. Speed-sensitive steering was added as a standard feature when the LX was ordered with the optional 4.6-liter V-8 or with the Super Coupe's base supercharged 3.8-liter V-6. The five-speed manual transaxle was used with the Super Coupe while the four-speed automatic overdrive transmission was standard on the LX and optional on the SC. The 3.8-liter V-6 with sequential electronic fuel injection was again the standard engine for the LX model.

1995 Ford Crown Victoria LX sedan. (OCW)

1995 Ford Thunderbird LX coupe. (OCW)

I.D. DATA: Ford's 17-symbol Vehicle Identification Number (VIN) was stamped on a metal tab fastened to the instrument panel, visible through the windshield. The first three symbols indicate manufacturer, make and vehicle type. The fourth symbol denotes restraint system. Next comes a letter (usually 'P'), followed by two digits that indicate Model Number, as shown in left column of tables below. (Example: '10' Escort two-door hatchback). Symbol eight indicates engine type. Next is a check digit. Symbol ten indicates model year ('S' - 1995). Symbol eleven denotes assembly plant. The final six digits make up the sequence number, starting with 100001 (Contour 000001).

ESCORT (FOUR)

Model No.	Body/ Style No.	Body Type & Seating	Factory Price	Shipping Weight	Prod. Total
P	10	2-dr. Hatch-5P	9560	2316	Note 1
P	11	2-dr. LX Hatch-5P	10415	2355	Note 1
P	14	4-dr. LX Hatch-5P	11020	2385	50,233
P	13	4-dr. LX Sed-5P	10850	2404	62,713
P	15	4-dr. LX Sta Wag-5P	11405	2451	115,960
P	12	2-dr. GT Hatch-5P	12700	2459	Note 1

NOTE 1: Production of two-door hatchback models totaled 91,875 with no further breakout available.

CONTOUR (FOUR/V-6)

P	65	4-dr. GL Sed-5P	13310/14390	2769/NA	Note 1
P	66	4-dr. LX Sed-5P	13995/15040	2808/NA	Note 1
P	67	4-dr. SE Sed-5P	-----/15695	----/2994	Note 1

NOTE: Figures to the left of slash are for four-cylinder/to right of slash are for V-6.

NOTE 1: Production of four-door sedan models totaled 178,832 with no further breakout available.

PROBE (FOUR/V-6 in GT only)

T	20	2-dr. Cpe-4P	14180	2690	Note 1
T	22	2-dr. GT Cpe-4P	16545	2921	Note 1

NOTE 1: Production of two-door coupe models totaled 58,226 with no further breakout available.

TAURUS (V-6)

P	52	4-dr. GL Sed-6P	17585	3118	Note 1
P	57	4-dr. GL Sta Wag-6P	18680	3285	Note 2
P	52	4-dr. SE Sed-6P	17955	3118	Note 1
P	53	4-dr. LX Sedan-6P	19400	3186	Note 1
P	58	4-dr. LX Sta Wag-6P	21010	3363	Note 2
P	54	4-dr. SHO Sed-6P	25140	3377	Note 1

NOTE 1: Production of four-door sedan models totaled 345,244 with no further breakout available.

NOTE 2: Production of station wagon models totaled 50,494 with no further breakout available.

CROWN VICTORIA (V-8)

P	73	4-dr. Sed-6P	20160	3762	Note 1
P	74	4-dr. LX Sed-6P	21970	3779	Note 1

NOTE 1: Production of four-door sedan models totaled 98,309 with no further breakout available.

THUNDERBIRD (V-6/V-8)

P	62	2-dr. LX Cpe-5P	17225/18355	3536/3673	Note 1
P	64	2-dr. Super Cpe-5P	22735/-----	3758/----	Note 1

NOTE: Figures to the left of slash are for V-6/to right of slash are for V-8.

NOTE 1: Production of two-door coupe models totaled 114,823 with no further breakout available.

ENGINE [Base Four (Escort)]: Inline. Overhead cam. Four-cylinder. Cast-iron block and aluminum head. Displacement: 113 cid (1.9 liters). Bore & stroke: 3.23 x 3.46 in. Compression ratio: 9.0:1. Brake horsepower: 88 at 4400 rpm. Torque: 108 lbs.-ft. at 3800 rpm. Five main bearings. Hydraulic valve lifters. Sequential fuel injection.

ENGINE [Base Four (Escort GT)]: High-output. Inline. Dual overhead cam. Four-cylinder. Cast-iron block and aluminum head. Displacement: 109 cid (1.8 liters). Bore & stroke: 3.27 x 3.35 in. Compression ratio: 9.0:1. Brake horsepower: 127 at 6500 rpm. Torque: 114 lbs.-ft. at 4500 rpm. Five main bearings. Hydraulic valve lifters. Multi-port fuel injection.

ENGINE [Base Four (Probe)]: Inline. Dual overhead cam. Four-cylinder. Cast-iron block and aluminum head. Displacement: 122 cid (2.0 liters). Bore & stroke: 3.27 x 3.62 in. Compression ratio: 9.0:1. Brake horsepower: 118 at 5500 rpm. Torque: 127 lbs.-ft. at 4500 rpm. Hydraulic valve lifters. Multi-port fuel injection.

ENGINE [Base Four (Contour)]: Inline. Dual overhead cam. Four-cylinder (16 valve). Cast-iron block and aluminum head.

Displacement: 121 cid (2.0 liters). Bore & stroke: 3.34 x 3.46 in. Compression ratio: 9.6:1. Brake horsepower: 125 at 5500 rpm. Torque: 125 lbs.-ft. at 4500 rpm. Sequential fuel injection.

ENGINE [Base V-6 (Probe GT)]: Dual overhead cam V-6 (24 valve). Aluminum block and head. Displacement: 153 cid (2.5 liters). Bore & stroke: 3.33 x 2.92 in. Compression ratio: 9.2:1. Brake horsepower: 164 at 5600 rpm. Torque: 160 lbs.-ft. at 4000 rpm. Four main bearings. Hydraulic valve lifters. Multi-port fuel injection.

ENGINE [Base V-6 (Contour SE); Optional (Contour GL/Contour LX)]: Modular, dual overhead cam V-6 (24 valve). Aluminum block and head. Displacement: 155 cid (2.5 liters). Bore & stroke: 3.24 x 3.13 in. Compression ratio: 9.7:1. Brake horsepower: 170 at 6200 rpm. Torque: 165 lbs.-ft. at 5000 rpm. Sequential fuel injection.

ENGINE [Base V-6 (Taurus GL/Taurus SE/Taurus LX sedan)]: Overhead valve V-6. Cast-iron block and head. Displacement: 182 cid (3.0 liters). Bore & stroke: 3.50 x 3.15 in. Compression ratio: 9.3:1. Brake horsepower: 140 at 4800 rpm. Torque: 165 lbs.-ft. at 3250 rpm. Four main bearings. Hydraulic valve lifters. Sequential fuel injection.

ENGINE [Base V-6 (Taurus SHO)]: Dual-overhead-cam V-6 (24 valve). Cast-iron block and head. Displacement: 182 cid (3.0 liters). Bore & stroke: 3.50 x 3.15 in. Compression ratio: 9.8:1. Brake horsepower: 220 at 6200 rpm. Torque: 200 lbs.-ft. at 4800 rpm. Four main bearings. Hydraulic valve lifters. Sequential fuel injection.

ENGINE [Base V-6 (Taurus LX wagon/Thunderbird LX); Optional: (Taurus GL/Taurus SE/Taurus LX sedan)]: 90-degree, overhead valve V-6. Cast-iron block and aluminum head. Displacement: 232 cid (3.8 liters). Bore & stroke: 3.80 x 3.40 in. Compression ratio: 9.0:1. Brake horsepower: (Taurus) 140 at 4800 RPM; (Thunderbird) 140 at 3800 rpm. Torque: (Taurus) 215 lbs.-ft. at 2200 RPM; (Thunderbird) 215 lbs.-ft. at 2400. Four main bearings. Hydraulic valve lifters. Sequential fuel injection.

ENGINE [Supercharged V-6 (Thunderbird Super Coupe)]: Same as 232 cid (3.8-liter) V-6 above, except - Compression ratio: 8.5:1. Horsepower: 230 at 4400 rpm. Torque: 330 lbs.-ft. at 2500 rpm.

ENGINE [Base V-8 (Crown Victoria); Optional (Thunderbird LX)]: Modular, overhead valve V-8. Displacement: 281 cid (4.6 liters). Bore & stroke: 3.60 x 3.60. Compression ratio: 9.0:1. Brake horsepower: (Crown Vic) 190 at 4250 RPM; (Thunderbird) 205 at 4500 rpm. Torque: (Crown Vic) 260 lbs.-ft. at 3200 RPM; (Thunderbird) 265 lbs.-ft. at 3200 rpm. Sequential fuel injection.

CHASSIS DATA: Wheelbase: (Escort) 98.4 in.; (Contour) 106.5 in.; (Probe) 102.8 in.: (Taurus) 106.0 in.; (Crown Vic) 114.4 in.; (T-Bird) 113.0 in. Overall Length: (Escort) 170.0 in.; (Escort wag) 171.3 in.; (Contour) 183.9 in.; (Probe) 178.7 in.; (Taurus) 192.0 in.; (Taurus wag) 193.1 in.; (Crown Vic) 212.4 in.; (T-Bird) 200.3 in. Height: (Escort) 52.5 in.; (Escort wag) 53.6 in.; (Contour) 54.5 in.; (Probe) 51.6 in.; (Taurus) 54.1 in.; (Taurus wag) 55.5 in.; (Crown Vic) 56.8 in.; (T-Bird) 52.5 in. Width: (Escort) 66.7 in.; (Contour) 69.1 in.; (Probe) 69.8 in.; (Taurus) 71.2 in.; (Crown Vic) 77.8 in.; (T-Bird) 72.7 in. Front Tread: (Escort) 56.5 in.; (Contour) 59.2 in.; (Probe) 59.4 in.; (Taurus) 61.6 in.; (Crown Vic) 62.8 in.; (T-Bird) 61.6 in. Rear Tread: (Escort) 56.5 in.; (Contour) 58.5 in.; (Probe) 59.4 in.; (Taurus) 60.5 in.; (Taurus wag) 59.9 in.; (Crown Vic) 63.3 in.; (T-Bird) 60.2 in. Standard Tires: (Escort) P175/70R13; (Escort LX) P175/65R14; (Escort GT) P185/60R15; (Contour) P185/70R14S; (Contour SE) P205/60R15T; (Probe) P195/65R14; (Probe GT) P225/50VR16; (Taurus) P205/65R15; (Taurus SHO) P215/60ZR16; (Crown Vic) P215/70R15; (T-Bird LX) P205/70R15; (T-Bird Super Cpe) P225/60ZR16.

1995 Ford Contour SE sedan. (OCW)

TECHNICAL: Transmission: Five-speed manual transaxle standard on Escort, Contour, Probe, Taurus SHO and Thunderbird Super Coupe. Four-speed overdrive automatic standard on Taurus, Crown Vic and Thunderbird LX. Drive Axle: (Crown Vic/T-Bird) rear; (others) front. Steering: (Crown Vic) recirculating ball; (others) rack/pinion. Front Suspension: (Escort) Independent MacPherson strut w/strut-mounted coil springs; (Contour) Independent, subframe-mounted MacPherson strut; (Probe) Independent strut-type with lower A-type control arms, upper strut-mounted coil springs and stabilizer bar; (Taurus) Independent MacPherson strut front drive w/strut-mounted coil springs, stabilizer bar, tension strut and lower control arm; (Crown Vic) Independent short/long arm w/ball joints, coil springs and stabilizer bar; (T-Bird) Short/long arm w/double isolated tension strut, coil springs and stabilizer bar. Rear Suspension: (Escort) Independent, strut-type and Twin Trapezoidal Links with trailing arms and upper strut-mounted coil springs; (Contour) Quadra-link independent w/passive rear-wheel steering (compliance understeer); (Probe) Independent strut-type, Quadra-link, upper strut-mounted coil springs and stabilizer bar. (Taurus sedan) Independent MacPherson struts w/coil spring on shock strut, stabilizer bar, tension strut, parallel suspension arms and two-piece cast spindle w/forged stem; (Taurus wagon) Independent short/long arm w/spring on lower control arm, stamped tension strut w/two-piece forged/cast spindle; (Crown Vic) Rigid axle w/four links and coil springs; (T-Bird) H-arm independent, coil springs and stabilizer bar. Brakes: Front disc, rear drum (power assisted) except (Escort GT, Contour SE, Probe GT, Taurus SHO, Crown Victoria and T-Bird Super Coupe) front/rear disc. Body construction: (Crown Vic) separate body and frame; (others) unibody. Fuel tank: (Escort) 11.9 gal.; (Contour) 15.0 gal.; (Probe) 15.5 gal.; (Taurus) 16.0 gal.; (Taurus SHO) 18.4 gal.; (Crown Vic) 20.0 gal.; (T-Bird) 18.0 gal.

DRIVETRAIN OPTIONS: Engines: 2.5-liter DOHC V-6: Contour GL ($1080); Contour LX ($1045). 3.8-liter V-6: Taurus GL, Taurus SE and Taurus LX sed ($630). 4.6-liter V-8: Thunderbird LX ($615). Transmission/Differential: Four-speed automatic transaxle: Escort ($815); Contour ($815); Probe ($790); T-Bird Super Coupe ($790). Traction Assist: T-Bird ($210). Steering/Suspension/Brakes: Power steering: Escort (LX only) ($250). Rear Air Suspension: Crown Vic (LX only) ($270). Heavy Duty Suspension: Taurus (N/A SHO) ($26). Trailer towing pkg: Crown Vic ($795). Anti-lock brakes: Escort GT ($565); Contour ($565); Probe ($735); Probe GT ($565); Taurus (w/o SHO) ($565); Crown Vic (w/Elect Traction Assist) ($665); T-Bird LX ($565).

ESCORT CONVENIENCE/APPEARANCE OPTIONS: Preferred Equip Pkg LX Series (320M): Pwr Steering, Light/Convenience Grp, Sport Appearance Grp and Rr Window Defroster ($190). Preferred Equip Pkg LX Series (321M): Man Air Cond, Rr Window Defroster, Light/Convenience Grp, Sport Appearance Grp, Pwr Steering, Elect AM/FM Stereo Radio w/Cass & Clock and (wagon only) Luggage Rack and Rr Window Wiper/Washer ($1185). Preferred Equip Pkg LX Series (322M): Auto Trans, Man Air Cond, Rr Window Defroster, Light/Convenience Grp, Sport Appearance Grp, Pwr Steering, Elect AM/FM Stereo Radio w/Cass & Clock and (wagon only) Luggage Rack and Rr Window Wiper/Washer ($2000). Preferred Equip Pkg GT Series: Man Air Cond and Rr Window Defroster ($435). Calif. Emission System ($95). Integrated Child Seat (LX only) ($135). Air Cond (LX and GT only) ($785). Rr Window Defroster ($160). Light/Convenience Grp: incl Dual Elect Remote Control Mirrors (LX only) ($160). Lux Convenience Grp: incl Tilt Strg Wheel, Spd Control and Tach (stnd on GT): LX ($410); GT ($460). Pwr Moonroof ($525). Clearcoat Paint ($85). Comfort Grp: incl Air Cond and Pwr Strg (base only) ($860). Elect AM/FM Stereo Radio (base only) ($300). Elect AM/FM Stereo Radio w/Cass: base ($465); LX ($165). Elect AM/FM Stereo Radio w/CD Player: base ($625); LX ($325); GT ($160). Premium sound syst ($60). Pwr Steering (LX only) ($250). Wagon Grp: incl Dlx Luggage Rack, Light/Convenience Grp and Rr Window Wiper/Washer (LX wagon only) ($240). Sport Appearance Grp: incl 14-inch alum wheels, tach, full cloth seats, liftgate spoiler and appliqués ($720). Ultra Violet Decor Grp (GT only): incl clearcoat metallic Ultra Violet exterior color, color-keyed wheels, cloth bucket seats and front flr mats w/embroidered GT trim ($400). Anti-lock Brakes (GT only) ($565). Elect Dual Remote Control Mirrors ($95). Pwr Equip Grp: incl Pwr Door Locks, Pwr Windows and Tach ($520).

CONTOUR CONVENIENCE/APPEARANCE OPTIONS: Preferred Equip Pkg GL Series (235A): Man Air Cond, Rr Window Defroster, Heated Ext Mirrors, AM/FM Stereo Radio w/Cass and Full-length Console ($850). Preferred Equip Pkg GL Series (236A): same as 235A plus Pwr Door Locks, Light Grp incl Dual Illum Visor Mirrors and Illum Entry Syst ($1310). Preferred Equip Pkg GL Series (240A): same as 236A plus Pwr Windows and 2.5-liter V-6 Engine Pkg ($2530). Preferred Equip Pkg LX Series (237A): Man Air Cond, Rr Window Defroster, Pwr Locks, Pwr Windows, Light Grp incl Dual Illum Visor Mirrors and Illum Entry Syst ($1350). Preferred Equip Pkg LX Series (238A): same as 237A plus 2.5-liter V-6 Engine Pkg ($2245). Preferred Equip Pkg SE Series (239A): Air Cond, Rr Window Defroster, Pwr Windows, Pwr Door Locks, Light Grp incl Dual Illum Visor Mirrors and Illum Entry Syst ($1350). Calif. Emission Syst ($95). Door Lock/Light Grp incl Pwr Door Locks, Dual Illum Visor Mirrors and Illum Entry Syst

($345). Lock Syst w/Keyless Remote ($160). Pwr Moonroof ($595). Pwr Driver's Seat: LX ($330); SE ($290). Pwr Windows ($340). Elect AM/FM Stereo Radio w/Cass ($130). Elect AM/FM Stereo Radio w/CD Player ($270). All Spd Traction Control w/Anti-lock Brakes ($800). Anti-lock Brakes ($565). Man Air Cond ($780). Rr Window Defroster ($160). Carpeted Flr Mats F&R ($45). Leather Bucket Seats: LX ($645); SE ($595). Spd Control ($215). 14-inch Alum Wheels (GL and LX only) ($265).

PROBE CONVENIENCE/APPEARANCE OPTIONS: Preferred Equip Pkg base series (251A): Man Air Cond, AM/FM Stereo Radio w/Cass and Tinted Glass ($560). Preferred Equip Pkg base series (253A): same as 251A plus Tilt Strg, Interval Wipers, Dual Remote Pwr Mirrors, Rr Window Defroster and Console ($2545). Preferred Equip Pkg GT Series (261A): Man Air Cond, Elect AM/FM Stereo Radio w/Cass & Premium Sound, Tilt Strg, Rr Window Defroster, Interval Wipers, Spd Control, Color-Keyed Bodyside Mldgs, Tinted Glass, Color-Keyed Flr Mats F&R and Dual Electric Remote Mirrors ($1790). Preferred Equip Pkg GT Series (263A): same as 261A plus Anti-lock Brakes, Remote Keyless Entry, Dual Illum Visor Mirrors, Pwr Windows, Pwr Driver's Seat and Fade-to-Off Dome Lamp ($3495). Man Air Cond ($895). Leather Bucket Seats (GT only) ($500). Pwr Driver's Seat (GT only) ($290). Anti-lock Brakes: base ($735); GT ($565). Anti-theft Syst (GT only) ($190). Elect AM/FM Stereo Radio w/Cass & Clock (base only) ($165). Elect AM/FM Stereo Radio w/Cass & Premium Sound ($405). Elect AM/FM Stereo Radio w/CD Player & Premium Sound: base ($430); GT ($270). Color-Keyed Bodyside Mldgs ($50). Color-Keyed Flr Mats F&R ($30). Pwr Sliding Roof ($615). Rr Decklid Spoiler ($235). Rr Window Wiper/Washer Syst (GT only) ($130). SE Appearance Pkg incl GT front fascia, 15-inch alum wheels, P205/55R15 BSW Tires and SE Graphics ($530). Calif. Emissions System ($95). Eng Block Heater ($20). 15-inch Alum Wheels (base only) ($450). 16-inch Chrome Wheels (GT only) ($390).

TAURUS CONVENIENCE/APPEARANCE OPTIONS: Preferred Equip Pkg GL Series (204A): Pwr Door Locks, Elect AM/FM Stereo Radio w/Cass, Spd Control, Dlx Wheel Covers, Flr Mats F&R, Pwr Windows and Pwr 6-way Driver's Seat ($775). Note: 204A Pkg for GL Series with 3.8-liter engine ($1275). Preferred Equip Pkg SE Series (205A): Pwr Door Locks, Pwr Windows, Elect AM/FM Stereo Radio w/Cass, Pwr Driver's Seat, Sport Bucket Seats, Cast Alum Wheels, Flr Mats F&R and Console ($1045). Note: 205A Pkg for SE Series with 3.8-liter engine ($1545). Preferred Equip Pkg LX Series (208A): Spd Control, Remote Keyless Entry, Elect AM/FM Stereo Radio w/Cass & Pwr Antenna, Leather-wrapped Strg Wheel, Flr Mats F&R and (wagon) Rr Window Washer/Wiper, Load Flr Extension and Cargo Area Cover ($545). Elect Air Cond (LX only) ($175). Anti-lock Brakes (stnd SHO sedan) ($565). Engine Blk Heater ($20). Floor Mats, F&R ($45). Remote Keyless Entry Syst: GL ($295); SE ($390); LX or SHO ($215). "Picnic Table" Load Flr Extension ($85, wagons only). Pwr Door Locks (GL and SE only) ($245). Elect AM/FM Stereo Radio w/Cass ($165). High Level Audio Syst (LX and SHO only) ($315). Audio Digital CD Player (LX and SHO only) ($375). JBL Audio Syst (LX and SHO only) ($500). Rr Facing Third Seat ($150, wagons only). Dual Control Pwr Seats (LX and SHO only) ($290). 6-Way Pwr Driver's Seat (LX only) ($290). Spd Control ($215). Cellular Phone ($500). Lux Convenience Grp: incl JBL Audio Syst, Pwr Moonroof, Keyless Entry Syst and Dual Pwr Seats ($1555). LX Convenience Grp: incl Pwr Moonroof and Dual Pwr Seats ($1030). GL Equip Grp: incl Spd Sensitive Pwr Strg, Paint Stripe, Dual Visor Mirrors and Secondary Visor ($245). Decklid Spoiler (SE only) ($270). Pwr Side Windows (GL and SE only) ($340). Cast Aluminum Wheels (GL only) ($230). Calif. Emissions Syst ($95). Leather Bucket Seats w/console: LX ($495); GL ($595). Leather Split Bench Seat (LX only) ($495). Leather Bucket Seats (SE and SHO sedan only) ($495). Heavy Duty Suspension (N/A SHO) ($26). Heavy Duty Battery (N/A SHO) ($30). Dlx Wheel Covers (GL only) ($80). Conventional Spare Tire (GL and LX only) ($70).

CROWN VICTORIA CONVENIENCE/APPEARANCE OPTIONS: Preferred Equip Pkg base series (111A): Color-Keyed Flr Mats F&R, Pwr Lock Grp, Spoked Wheel Covers, Spd Control and Illum Entry Syst ($745). Preferred Equip Pkg LX Series (113A): Color-Keyed Flr Mats F&R, Pwr Lock Grp, Cornering Lamps, Spd Control, Illum Entry Syst, Leather-wrapped Strg Wheel, Elect AM/FM Stereo Radio w/Cass, Cast Alum 12-spoke Wheels, Light Decor Grp and Light/Decor Grp ($320). Preferred Equip Pkg LX Series (114A): same as 113A plus Dual Control Pwr Seats, High Level Audio Syst, Anti-lock Brakes w/Elect Traction Assist, Rr Air Suspension, Auto Temp Control Air Cond, Tripminder Computer, Elect Digital Instrumentation, HD Battery, Remote Keyless Entry and Elect Auto Dim Mirror ($2300). Elect Auto Temp Control Air Cond ($175). Calif. Emissions Syst ($95). Leather Split Bench Seat (LX only) ($645). Conv Spare Tire ($80). Anti-lock Brakes w/Elect Traction Assist ($665). 41G Handling & Perf Pkg (LX only) incl Revised Springs/Shocks/Stabilizer Bar, Pwr Strg Cooler, P225/60R16 BSW Touring Tires, 16-inch Cast Alum Wheels and Dual Exhaust ($1100). Eng Block Htr ($25). Remote Keyless Entry Syst (LX only) ($215). Light/Decor Grp (LX only) ($225). Elect AM/FM Stereo Radio w/Cass ($185). High Level Audio Syst (LX only) ($360). Ford JBL Audio Syst ($500). Rr Air Suspension (LX only) ($270). Trailer Towing Pkg: base ($500); LX ($795). 6-Way Pwr Driver's Seat (base only) ($360). Dual Pwr Seats ($360). Color-Keyed Flr Mats F&R ($45). P215/70R15 WSW Tires ($80).

THUNDERBIRD CONVENIENCE/APPEARANCE OPTIONS: Preferred Equip Pkg LX Series: Rr Window Defroster, P215/70R15 Tires, Cast Alum Wheels and Elect Auto Temp Control (NC). Preferred Equip Pkg Super Coupe Series: Rr Window Defroster, Pwr Lock Grp, 6-Way Pwr Driver's Seat and Spd Control (NC). Calif. Emission Syst ($95). Leather Bucket Seats: LX ($490); Super Coupe ($615). Remote Keyless Entry: LX ($215); Super Coupe ($295). Frt Floor Mats ($30). Elect AM/FM Stereo Radio w/Cass & Premium Sound ($290). Elect AM/FM Stereo Radio w/CD Changer ($430). Anti-lock Brakes (stnd Super Coupe) ($565). Pwr Moonroof ($740). Tri-Coat Paint ($225). Traction Assist (LX only) ($210). Cellular Phone ($530). 6-Way Pwr Pass Seat ($290). Luxury Grp incl Autolamp Grp, Illum Entry Syst, Light Grp and Integrated Warning Module: LX ($350); Super Coupe ($325). HD Battery ($25). P225/60ZR16 BSW Tires ($70).

HISTORY: U.S. model year production totaled 1,179,436 (including Mustang but excluding Crown Victoria). U.S. calendar year production totaled 1,010,997 (including Mustang) for a 15.9 percent of industry market share. For the fourth consecutive year, Taurus was the best selling car in the United States in 1995, with 366,266 units sold compared to 341,384 for the Honda Accord which finished second.

1996 FORD

1996 Ford Contour SE sedan. (OCW)

1996 Ford Escort LX three-door hatchback (with Sport Appearance Package). (OCW)

1995 Ford Contour LX sedan. (OCW)

Ford entered the 1996 model year with an all-new design Taurus offered in three series: GL, LX and SHO. The front-drive Taurus, available in four-door sedan and station wagon versions, was longer, wider and had a more rounded body than its previous edition. Powerplants for each series were new, the GL models using the revised Vulcan 3.0-liter V-6, the LX using the Duratec 3.0-liter V-6 and the SHO sedan powered by the 3.4-liter V-8. The Thunderbird was reduced to one coupe, the LX model, with the discontinuation of the Super Coupe. Design-wise, the Thunderbird now sported a revised hood, headlights, grille and bumper covers. Its standard 3.8-liter V-6 was modified as was its optional 4.6-liter V-8. Crown Victoria buyers could now order a 4.6-liter V-8 fueled by natural gas. The Escort underwent several refinements even though an all-new design, 1997 model would debut in May 1996. The Sport Appearance Package offered previously could now also be ordered on LX models. Escort's drive ratio was increased to improve acceleration.

ESCORT — FOUR — With an all-new design, 1997 model to be launched in the spring of 1996, the 1996 Escort lineup was carried over from the year previous. Again offered were the base three-door hatchback; LX three- and five-door hatchbacks, four-door sedan and station wagon and GT three-door hatchback. Escort's drive ratio was increased from 3.55:1 to 4.06:1 for improved acceleration. Integrated child seats were made optional equipment in all Escort models. The previously offered Sport Appearance Package was now available on LX series models. Standard engine for base and LX model Escorts was again the 1.9-liter four-cylinder powerplant with sequential fuel injection. A five-speed manual transaxle was again standard on Escorts, with the electronic four-speed automatic overdrive transaxle optional. The GT model again used the 16-valve DOHC 1.8-liter four-cylinder engine, now equipped with electronic fuel injection.

CONTOUR — FOUR/V-6 — The Contour was basically unchanged from its debut the year previous. It was again offered as a four-door sedan in three series: GL, LX and SE. The Contour's seats were revised to increase rear passenger leg room. The GL and LX sedans again used the Zetec DOHC, 16-valve 2.0-liter four-cylinder engine. The SE sedan was again powered by the modular, DOHC Duratec 2.5-liter V-6, which was the option engine for the GL and LX models. Contours again used the five-speed manual transaxle as base unit and electronically controlled four-speed automatic transaxle as the option unit.

PROBE — FOUR/V-6 — Half of the option packages offered previously on Probe's base or GT coupes were discontinued, leaving only two—one for each series—for 1996. The base coupe was again powered by the DOHC 2.0-liter four-cylinder engine. The GT coupe again used the DOHC 2.5-liter V-6. A five-speed manual transaxle was again standard equipment on both coupes and an electronically controlled four-speed automatic transaxle was optional.

1996 Ford Taurus GL sedan. (OCW)

1996 Ford Taurus GL station wagon. (OCW)

1996 Ford Taurus SHO sedan. (OCW)

TAURUS — V-6/V-8 — The all-new design, 1996 Taurus was launched in September 1995 and was available in three series: GL, LX and SHO. The GL and LX series each were comprised of both a sedan and station wagon while the SHO model was a four-door sedan. This new Taurus was longer, wider and more rounded than the previous year's version. Standard features included an integrated control panel that governed audio and climate systems, electronic four-speed automatic transaxle and dual airbags. An antitheft system and air filtration system were standard in LX and SHO models. GL models were capable of seating six due to a front flip-fold central console seat. Anti-lock brakes were optional for GL and LX models. The GL series used the revised Vulcan 3.0-liter V-6 rated at 145-hp. LX models were powered by the Duratec DOHC 3.0-liter V-6 rated at 200-hp. The SHO sedan used the DOHC 3.4-liter V-8 rated at 240-hp. The option engine for the GL sedan was a flex-fuel 3.0-liter V-6. The electronically controlled four-speed automatic transaxle was the standard unit for all Taurus models except the SHO sedan which used the five-speed manual transaxle.

CROWN VICTORIA — V-8 — Base or LX four-door sedans again comprised the Crown Victoria lineup, returning for 1996 basically unchanged after undergoing refinement the year previous. Changes included the Crown Vic's variable assist power steering receiving an upgrade and the addition of an option engine, the 178-hp 4.6-liter V-8 fueled by natural gas. Base powertrain was again the modular 4.6-liter V-8 and electronically controlled four-speed automatic overdrive transmission.

1996 Ford Crown Victoria LX sedan. (OCW)

1996 Ford Thunderbird LX coupe. (OCW)

THUNDERBIRD — V-6/V-8 — The Thunderbird was reduced to a one-model series, the LX coupe, in 1996 with the discontinuation of the Super Coupe. The LX model received a restyling in the hood, grille, headlight and bumper cover areas. The standard 3.8-liter V-6 was upgraded and was now rated at 145-hp. Optional was a revised 4.6-liter V-8. An antitheft system and traction control returned as optional equipment after not being offered the year previous. The four-speed automatic overdrive transmission was standard.

I.D. DATA: Ford's 17-symbol Vehicle Identification Number (VIN) was stamped on a metal tab fastened to the instrument panel, visible through the windshield. The first three symbols indicate manufacturer, make and vehicle type. The fourth symbol denotes restraint system. Next comes a letter (usually 'P'), followed by two digits that indicate Model Number, as shown in left column of tables below. (Example: '10' Escort two-door hatchback). Symbol eight indicates engine type. Next is a check digit. Symbol ten indicates model year ('T' - 1996). Symbol eleven denotes assembly plant. The final six digits make up the sequence number, starting with 100001.

ESCORT (FOUR)

Model No.	Body/ Style No.	Body Type & Seating	Factory Price	Shipping Weight	Prod. Total
P	10	2-dr. Hatch-5P	10065	2323	Note 1
P	11	2-dr. LX Hatch-5P	10910	2356	Note 1
P	14	4-dr. LX Hatch-5P	11345	2398	11,807
P	13	4-dr. LX Sed-5P	11515	2378	13,439
P	15	4-dr. LX Sta Wag-5P	11900	2444	35,199
P	12	2-dr. GT Hatch-5P	13205	2455	Note 1

Note 1: Production of two-door hatchback models totaled 64,964 with no further breakout available.

CONTOUR (FOUR/V-6)

Model No.	Body/ Style No.	Body Type & Seating	Factory Price	Shipping Weight	Prod. Total
P	65	4-dr. GL Sed-5P	13785/14865	2773/2875	Note 1
P	66	4-dr. LX Sed-5P	14470/15515	2815/2939	Note 1
P	67	4-dr. SE Sed-5P	-----/16170	----/2934	Note 1

NOTE: Figures to the left of slash are for four-cylinder/to right of slash are for V-6.

NOTE 1: Production of four-door sedan models totaled 167,555 with no further breakout available.

PROBE (FOUR/V-6 in GT only)

Model No.	Body/ Style No.	Body Type & Seating	Factory Price	Shipping Weight	Prod. Total
T	20	2-dr. Cpe-4P	13930	2690	Note 1
T	22	2-dr. GT Cpe-4P	16450	2921	Note 1

NOTE 1: Production of two-door coupe models totaled 30,125 with no further breakout available.

TAURUS (V-6/V-8 in SHO only)

Model No.	Body/ Style No.	Body Type & Seating	Factory Price	Shipping Weight	Prod. Total
P	52	4-dr. GL Sed-6P	18600	3347	Note 1
P	57	4-dr. GL Sta Wag-6P	19680	3511	Note 2
P	53	4-dr. LX Sedan-6P	20980	3355	Note 1
P	58	4-dr. LX Sta Wag-6P	22000	3531	Note 2
P	54	4-dr. SHO Sed-6P	25930	3544	Note 1

NOTE 1: Production of four-door sedan models totaled 348,671 with no further breakout available.

NOTE 2: Production of station wagon models totaled 45,439 with no further breakout available.

CROWN VICTORIA (V-8)

Model No.	Body/ Style No.	Body Type & Seating	Factory Price	Shipping Weight	Prod. Total
P	73	4-dr. Sed-6P	20955	3780	Note 1
P	74	4-dr. LX Sed-6P	22675	3791	Note 1

NOTE 1: Production of four-door sedan models totaled 108,252 with no further breakout available.

THUNDERBIRD (V-6/V-8)

Model No.	Body/ Style No.	Body Type & Seating	Factory Price	Shipping Weight	Prod. Total
P	62	2-dr. LX Cpe-5P	17485/18615	3561/3689	85,029

NOTE: Figures to the left of slash are for V-6/to right of slash are for V-8.

ENGINE [Base Four (Escort)]: Inline. Overhead cam. Four-cylinder. Cast-iron block and aluminum head. Displacement: 113 cid (1.9 liters). Bore & stroke: 3.23 x 3.46 in. Compression ratio: 9.0:1. Brake horsepower: 88 at 4400 rpm. Torque: 108 lbs.-ft. at 3800 rpm. Five main bearings. Hydraulic valve lifters. Sequential fuel injection.

ENGINE [Base Four (Escort GT)]: High-output. Inline. Dual overhead cam. Four-cylinder. Cast-iron block and aluminum head. Displacement: 109 cid (1.8 liters). Bore & stroke: 3.27 x 3.35 in. Compression ratio: 9.0:1. Brake horsepower: 127 at 6500 rpm. Torque: 114 lbs.-ft. at 4500 rpm. Five main bearings. Hydraulic valve lifters. Electronic fuel injection.

ENGINE [Base Four (Probe)]: Inline. Dual overhead cam. Four-cylinder. Cast-iron block and aluminum head. Displacement: 122 cid (2.0 liters). Bore & stroke: 3.27 x 3.62 in. Compression ratio: 9.0:1. Brake horsepower: 118 at 5500 rpm. Torque: 127 lbs.-ft. at 4500 rpm. Hydraulic valve lifters. Sequential fuel injection.

ENGINE [Base Four (Contour)]: Inline. Dual overhead cam. Four-cylinder (16 valve). Cast-iron block and aluminum head. Displacement: 121 cid (2.0 liters). Bore & stroke: 3.34 x 3.46 in. Compression ratio: 9.6:1. Brake horsepower: 125 at 5500 rpm. Torque: 125 lbs.-ft. at 4500 rpm. Sequential fuel injection.

ENGINE [Base V-6 (Probe GT)]: Dual overhead cam V-6 (24 valve). Aluminum block and head. Displacement: 153 cid (2.5 liters). Bore & stroke: 3.33 x 2.92 in. Compression ratio: 9.2:1. Brake horsepower: 164 at 5600 rpm. Torque: 160 lbs.-ft. at 4000 rpm. Four main bearings. Hydraulic valve lifters. Sequential fuel injection.

ENGINE [Base V-6 (Contour SE); Optional (Contour GL/Contour LX)]: Modular, dual overhead cam V-6 (24 valve). Aluminum block and head. Displacement: 155 cid (2.5 liters). Bore & stroke: 3.24 x 3.13 in. Compression ratio: 9.7:1. Brake horsepower: 170 at 6200 rpm. Torque: 165 lbs.-ft. at 5000 rpm. Sequential fuel injection.

ENGINE [Base V-6 (Taurus GL)]: Overhead valve V-6. Cast-iron block and head. Displacement: 182 cid (3.0 liters). Bore & stroke: 3.50 x 3.15 in. Compression ratio: 9.3:1. Brake horsepower: 140 at 4800 rpm. Torque: 165 lbs.-ft. at 3250 rpm. Four main bearings. Hydraulic valve lifters. Sequential fuel injection.

ENGINE [Base V-6 (Taurus LX)]: Dual-overhead-cam V-6 (24 valve). Aluminum block and head. Displacement: 182 cid (3.0 liters). Bore & stroke: 3.50 x 3.15 in. Compression ratio: 9.3:1. Brake horsepower: 200 at 5750 rpm. Torque: N/A. Four main bearings. Hydraulic valve lifters. Sequential fuel injection.

ENGINE [Base V-6 (Thunderbird LX)]: 90-degree, overhead valve V-6. Cast-iron block and aluminum head. Displacement: 232 cid (3.8 liters). Bore & stroke: 3.80 x 3.40 in. Compression ratio: 9.0:1. Brake horsepower: 145 at 4000 rpm. Torque: N/A. Four main bearings. Hydraulic valve lifters. Sequential fuel injection.

ENGINE [Base V-8 (Taurus SHO)]: Dual overhead cam (32 valve) V-8. Aluminum block and head. Displacement: 207 cid (3.4 liters). Bore & stroke: 3.50 x 3.15 in. Compression ratio: 9.8:1. Brake horsepower: 224 at 6500 rpm. Torque: N/A. Sequential fuel injection.

ENGINE [Base V-8 (Crown Victoria)]: Modular, overhead cam V-8. Displacement: 281 cid (4.6 liters). Bore & stroke: 3.60 x 3.60. Compression ratio: 9.0:1. Brake horsepower: 190 at 4250 rpm. Torque: 260 lbs.-ft. at 3200 rpm. Sequential fuel injection.

ENGINE [Optional V-8 (Thunderbird LX)]: same as 4.6-liter V-8 above, except - Dual overhead cam. Brake horsepower: 205 at 4500 rpm. Torque: 265 lbs.-ft. at 3200 rpm.

CHASSIS DATA: Wheelbase: (Escort) 98.4 in.; (Contour) 106.5 in.; (Probe) 102.8 in.: (Taurus) 108.5 in.; (Crown Vic) 114.4 in.; (T-Bird) 113.0 in. Overall Length: (Escort) 170.0 in.; (Escort wag) 171.3 in.; (Contour) 183.9 in.; (Probe) 178.7 in.; (Taurus) 197.5 in.; (Crown Vic) 212.0 in.; (T-Bird) 200.3 in. Height: (Escort) 52.5 in.; (Escort wag) 53.6 in.; (Contour) 54.5 in.; (Probe) 51.6 in.; (Taurus) 55.1 in.; (Crown Vic) 56.8 in.; (Taurus) 73.0 in.; (T-Bird) 52.5 in. Width: (Escort) 66.7 in.; (Contour) 69.1 in.: (Probe) 69.8 in.; (Taurus) 73.0 in.; (Crown Vic) 77.8 in.; (T-Bird) 72.7 in. Front Tread: (Escort) 56.5 in.; (Contour) 59.2 in.; (Probe) 59.4 in.; (Taurus) 61.6 in.; (Crown Vic) 62.8 in.; (T-Bird) 61.6 in. Rear Tread: (Escort) 56.5 in.; (Contour) 58.5 in.; (Probe) 59.4 in.; (Taurus) 61.4 in.; (Taurus wag) 61.8 in.; (Crown Vic) 63.3 in.; (T-Bird) 60.2 in. Standard Tires: (Escort) P175/70R13; (Escort LX) P175/65R14; (Escort GT) P185/60R15; (Contour) P185/70R14S; (Contour SE) P205/60R15T; (Probe) P195/65R14; (Probe GT) P225/50VR16; (Taurus) P205/65R15; (Taurus SHO) P225/55VR16; (Crown Vic) P215/70R15; (T-Bird LX) P205/70R15.

TECHNICAL: Transmission: Five-speed manual transaxle standard on Escort, Contour, Probe and Taurus SHO. Four-speed overdrive automatic standard on Taurus, Crown Vic and Thunderbird. Drive Axle: (Crown Vic/T-Bird) rear; (others) front. Steering: (Crown Vic) recirculating ball; (others) rack/pinion. Front Suspension: (Escort)

Independent MacPherson strut w/strut-mounted coil springs; (Contour) Independent, subframe-mounted MacPherson strut; (Probe) Independent strut-type with lower A-type control arms, upper strut-mounted coil springs and stabilizer bar; (Taurus) Independent MacPherson strut front drive w/strut-mounted coil springs, stabilizer bar, tension strut and lower control arm; (Crown Vic) Independent short/long arm w/ball joints, coil springs and stabilizer bar; (T-Bird) Short/long arm w/double isolated tension strut, coil springs and stabilizer bar. Rear Suspension: (Escort) Independent, strut-type and Twin Trapezoidal Links with trailing arms and upper strut-mounted coil springs; (Contour) Quadra-link independent w/passive rear-wheel steering (compliance understeer); (Probe) Independent strut-type, Quadra-link, upper strut-mounted coil springs and stabilizer bar. (Taurus sedan) Independent MacPherson struts w/coil spring on shock strut, stabilizer bar, tension strut, parallel suspension arms and two-piece cast spindle w/forged stem; (Taurus wagon) Independent short/long arm w/spring on lower control arm, stamped tension strut w/two-piece forged/cast spindle; (Crown Vic) Rigid axle w/four links and coil springs; (T-Bird) H-arm independent, coil springs and stabilizer bar. Brakes: Front disc, rear drum (power assisted) except (Escort GT, Contour SE, Probe GT, Taurus SHO and Crown Victoria) front/rear disc. Body construction: (Crown Vic) separate body and frame; (others) unibody. Fuel tank: (Escort) 11.9 gal.; (Contour) 14.5 gal.; (Probe) 15.5 gal.; (Taurus) 18.0 gal.; (Crown Vic) 20.0 gal.; (T-Bird) 18.0 gal.

DRIVETRAIN OPTIONS: Engines: 2.5-liter DOHC V-6: Contour GL ($1080); Contour LX ($1045). Flex-fuel (methanol or ethanol) 3.0-liter V-6: Taurus GL sedan only ($1165). Natural Gas-powered 4.6-liter V-8: base Crown Vic only ($6165). DOHC 4.6-liter V-8: Thunderbird LX ($1130). Transmission/Differential: Four-speed automatic transaxle: Escort ($815); Contour ($815); Probe ($815). Traction Assist: T-Bird ($210). Steering/Suspension/Brakes: Power steering: Escort (stnd GT) ($250). Rear Air Suspension: Crown Vic (LX only) ($270). Heavy Duty Suspension: Taurus (GL wagon only) ($25). Trailer towing pkg: Crown Vic ($795). Anti-lock brakes: Escort GT ($570); Contour ($570); Probe ($740); Probe GT ($570); Taurus (stnd SHO) ($570); Crown Vic (w/Elect Traction Assist) ($670); T-Bird LX ($570).

ESCORT CONVENIENCE/APPEARANCE OPTIONS: Preferred Equip Pkg LX Series (320M): Pwr Steering, Light/Convenience Grp, Sport Appearance Grp and Rr Window Defroster: two-door ($250); four-door ($200). Preferred Equip Pkg LX Series (321M): Man Air Cond, Elect AM/FM Stereo Radio w/Cass & Clock and (wagon only) Luggage Rack and Rr Window Wiper/Washer: two-door ($1195); four-door hatch ($760); wagon ($205). Preferred Equip Pkg LX Series (322M): Auto Trans, Man Air Cond, Elect AM/FM Stereo Radio w/Cass & Clock and (wagon only) Luggage Rack and Rr Window Wiper/Washer: two-door ($2010); four-door sed ($1405); four-door hatch ($1575); wagon ($1020). Preferred Equip Pkg GT Series: Man Air Cond and Rr Window Defroster ($445). Calif. Emission System ($100). Integrated Child Seat (LX only) ($135). Air Cond ($785). Rr Window Defroster ($170). Light/Convenience Grp: incl Dual Elect Remote Control Mirrors ($160). Luxury Convenience Grp: incl Tilt Strg Wheel, Leather-wrapped Strg Wheel, Spd Control and Tach (stnd on GT): LX ($465); GT ($460). Pwr Moonroof ($525). Clearcoat Paint ($85). Comfort Grp: incl Air Cond and Pwr Strg (base only) ($860). Elect AM/FM Stereo Radio (base only) ($300). Elect AM/FM Stereo Radio w/Cass: base ($465); LX ($165). Elect AM/FM Stereo Radio w/CD Player: base ($625); LX ($325); GT ($160). Premium sound syst ($60). Pwr Steering (stnd GT) ($250). Wagon Grp: incl Luggage Rack, Light/Convenience Grp and Rr Window Wiper/Washer (LX wagon only) ($240). Sport Appearance Grp: incl 14-inch alum wheels, tach, liftgate spoiler and appliqués ($720). Anti-lock Brakes (GT only) ($570). Elect Dual Remote Control Mirrors ($95). Pwr Equip Grp: incl Pwr Door Locks, Pwr Windows and Tach: LX ($520); GT ($460). Integrated Child's Seat (LX only) ($135).

CONTOUR CONVENIENCE/APPEARANCE OPTIONS: Preferred Equip Pkg GL Series (235A): Man Air Cond, Rr Window Defroster, Heated Ext Mirrors, AM/FM Stereo Radio w/Cass and Full-length Console ($870). Preferred Equip Pkg GL Series (236A): same as 235A plus Pwr Door Locks, Light Grp incl Dual Illum Visor Mirrors and Illum Entry Syst and Spd Control ($1330). Preferred Equip Pkg GL Series (240A): same as 236A plus Pwr Windows and 2.5-liter V-6 Engine Pkg ($3365). Preferred Equip Pkg LX Series (238A): 2.5-liter V-6, Air Cond, Rr Window Defroster, Spd Control, Pwr Locks, Pwr Windows, Light Grp incl Dual Illum Visor Mirrors and Illum Entry Syst ($3060). Preferred Equip Pkg SE Series (239A): Air Cond, Rr Window Defroster, Spd Control, Pwr Windows, Pwr Door Locks, Light Grp incl Dual Illum Visor Mirrors and Illum Entry Syst ($1370). Calif. Emission Syst ($100). Door Lock/Light Grp incl Pwr Door Locks, Dual Illum Visor Mirrors and Illum Entry Syst ($345). Lock Syst w/Keyless Remote ($190). Pwr Moonroof ($595). Pwr Windows ($340). Elect AM/FM Stereo Radio w/Cass ($130). Elect AM/FM Stereo Radio w/CD Player ($270). All Spd Traction Control w/Anti-lock Brakes ($805). Anti-lock Brakes ($570). Man Air Cond ($780). Rr Window Defroster ($170). Carpeted Flr Mats F&R ($45). Pwr Driver's Seat (LX and SE only) ($330). Leather Bucket Seats: LX ($645); SE ($595). Rr Split Folddown Seat (GL only) ($205). Sport Pkg: GL ($495); LX (420). Spd Control ($215). 15-inch Alum Wheels (GL and LX only) ($425).

1996 Ford Probe SE coupe. (OCW)

PROBE CONVENIENCE/APPEARANCE OPTIONS: Preferred Equip Pkg base series: SE Appearance Pkg, Man Air Cond, AM/FM Stereo Radio w/Cass, Interval Wipers, Rr Window Defroster and Tinted Glass ($1120). Preferred Equip Pkg GT Series: Man Air Cond, Rr Window Defroster, Interval Wipers, Tinted Glass, Anti-lock Brakes, Pwr Windows, Pwr Door Locks, Decklid Spoiler and Dual Electric Remote Mirrors ($1905). Man Air Cond ($895). Leather Bucket Seats (GT only) ($500). Pwr Driver's Seat (GT only) ($290). Convenience Grp incl Dual Pwr Mirrors: base ($740); GT ($570). Pwr Convenience Grp incl Pwr Door Locks and Pwr Windows ($485). Driver Comfort Grp incl Tilt Strg and Spd Control ($355). Anti-lock Brakes: base ($740); GT ($570). Elect AM/FM Stereo Radio w/Cass & Clock (base only) ($165). Elect AM/FM Stereo Radio w/CD Player & Premium Sound ($430). Color-Keyed Bodyside Mldgs ($50). Color-Keyed Flr Mats F&R ($30). Pwr Sliding Roof (only) ($615). Remote Keyless Entry ($270). Rr Decklid Spoiler ($235). Interval Wipers ($60). SE Appearance Pkg incl GT front fascia, 15-inch alum wheels, P205/55R15 BSW Tires and SE Graphics ($530). Calif. Emissions System ($100). Eng Block Heater ($20). 16-inch Chrome Wheels (GT only) ($390).

TAURUS CONVENIENCE/APPEARANCE OPTIONS: Preferred Equip Pkg GL Series (204A): Pwr Door Locks, AM/FM Stereo Radio w/Cass, Spd Control, Air Filtration Syst and Flr Mats F&R ($240). Preferred Equip Pkg GL Series (205A): same as 204A plus Pwr Driver's Seat, Light Grp, Cargo Net and Alum Wheels: sed ($840); wag ($880). Preferred Equip Pkg LX Series (208A): Spd Control and Flr Mats F&R ($150). Preferred Equip Pkg LX Series (209A): same as 208A plus 4-wheel Disc Brakes w/Anti-lock and Remote Keyless Entry w/Perimeter Antitheft Syst ($860). Preferred Equip Pkg LX Series (210A): same as 209A plus Elect Temp Control Air Cond, Alum Wheels and Sound Syst Upgrade: sed ($1915); wag ($1730). Preferred Equip Pkg SHO Series: Pwr Moonroof, Elect Temp Control Air Cond, Remote Keyless Entry w/Perimeter Antitheft Syst and JBL Audio Syst ($1325). Elect Temp Control Air Cond (LX and SHO only) ($175). Anti-lock Brakes (stnd SHO) ($570). Pwr Moonroof (LX and SHO only) ($740). Air Filtration Syst (GL only) ($30). Daytime Running Lights ($40). Remote Keyless Entry Syst ($190). Elect AM/FM Stereo Radio w/Cass (GL only) ($175). Elect AM/FM Stereo Radio w/Cass & Premium Sound (LX wag only) ($315). Trunk-mounted CD Changer (LX and SHO only) ($595). JBL Audio Syst (LX and SHO seds only) ($500). Rr Facing Third Seat ($200, wagons only). Pwr Driver's Seat (GL only) ($340). Cellular Phone ($650). Light Grp (GL only) ($45). Wagon Grp incl Rr Window Washer/Wiper and Cargo Cover ($255). Chrome Wheels (LX and SHO only) ($580). Cast Aluminum Wheels (GT only) ($315). Calif. Emissions Syst ($100). Leather Seats w/console (LX only) ($990). Leather Sport Bucket Seats (SHO sedan only) ($1190). Heavy Duty Suspension (GL wag only) ($25). Conventional Spare Tire (GL and LX only) ($125).

CROWN VICTORIA CONVENIENCE/APPEARANCE OPTIONS: Preferred Equip Pkg base series (111A): Color-Keyed Flr Mats F&R, Pwr Lock Grp, Spoked Wheel Covers, Spd Control and Illum Entry Syst ($60). Preferred Equip Pkg LX Series (113A): Color-Keyed Flr Mats F&R, Pwr Lock Grp, Cornering Lamps, Spd Control, Illum Entry Syst, Leather-wrapped Strg Wheel, Elect AM/FM Stereo Radio w/Cass, Cast Alum 12-spoke Wheels and Light/Decor Grp ($640). Preferred Equip Pkg LX Series (114A): same as 113A plus Dual Control Pwr Seats, High Level Audio Syst, Anti-lock Brakes w/Elect Traction Assist, Rr Air Suspension, Auto Temp Control Air Cond, Tripminder Computer, Elect Digital Instrumentation, HD Battery, Remote Keyless Entry and Elect Auto Dim Mirror ($3385). Natural Gas-fueled 4.6-liter V-8 (base only) ($6165). Elect Auto Temp Control Air Cond ($175). Calif. Emissions Syst ($100). Leather Split Bench Seat (LX only) ($645). Conv Spare Tire ($80). Anti-lock Brakes w/Elect Traction Assist (LX only) ($670). 41G Handling & Perf Pkg (LX only) incl Revised Springs/Shocks/Stabilizer Bar, Pwr Strg Cooler, P225/60R16 BSW Touring Tires, 16-inch Cast Alum Wheels and Dual Exhaust ($1100). Eng Block Htr ($25). Remote Keyless Entry Syst (LX only) ($240). Light/Decor Grp (LX only) ($225). Elect AM/FM Stereo Radio w/Cass ($185). High Level Audio Syst (LX only) ($360). Rr Air Suspension (LX only) ($270). Spd Control (w/Natural Gas-fueled 4.6-liter V-8 only) ($215). Pwr Lock Grp (w/Natural Gas-fueled 4.6-liter V-8 only) ($305). 6-Way Pwr Driver's Seat (base only) ($360). Dual Pwr Seats ($360). Color-Keyed Flr Mats F&R ($45). P215/70R15 WSW Tires ($80).

THUNDERBIRD CONVENIENCE/APPEARANCE OPTIONS: Preferred Equip Pkg LX Series (155A): Rr Window Defroster, P215/70R15 Tires and Cast Alum Wheels (NC). Preferred Equip Pkg LX Series (157A): 4.6-liter V-8, Spd Sensitive Pwr Strg, Battery Upgrade, 6-Way Pwr Driver's Seat, Illum Entry Syst and Leather-wrapped Strg Wheel ($835). Calif. Emission Syst ($100). Leather Bucket Seats ($490). Remote Keyless Entry ($270). Frt Floor Mats ($30). Elect AM/FM Stereo Radio w/Cass & Premium Sound ($290). Elect AM/FM Stereo Radio w/CD Player & Premium Sound ($430). Anti-lock Brakes ($570). Antitheft Syst ($145). Pwr Moonroof ($740). Sport Option incl 16-inch Alum Wheels, P225/65R16 BSW Tires, Modified Stabilizer Bars and Revised Spring Rates ($210). Tri-Coat Paint ($225). Traction Assist ($210). Pwr Driver's Seat ($290). Luxury Grp incl Elect Semi-Auto Temp Control Air Cond, Dual Illum Visor Mirrors, Light Grp and Integrated Warning Module ($495). 15-inch Chrome Wheels ($580).

HISTORY: U.S. model year production totaled 829,427 (including Mustang but excluding Crown Victoria). U.S. calendar year production totaled 1,069,764 (including Mustang) for a 17.6 percent of industry market share. For the fifth consecutive year, Taurus was the best selling car in the United States in 1996, with 401,049 units sold compared to 382,298 for the Honda Accord which finished second. The Escort was also ranked as the best-selling small car with 284,644 units sold compared to 278,574 for Saturn which finished second.

1997 FORD

The all-new-design, 1997 Escort sedan and station wagon models made their debut in the spring of 1996. The lineup was trimmed considerably from what was offered previously, with the new-design Escort offered as a base four-door sedan or LX four-door sedan or station wagon. The Contour was slated for a re-do in 1998 so changes were minimal on the 1997 models. A Sport Package was optional on the Contour GL or LX models, which included aluminum wheels, foglamps and Sport badging. The Probe GT also received a GTS Sport Appearance Group that included dual racing stripes, a rear deck spoiler and 16-inch chrome wheels. This was the final year for Probe production. Taurus added a base G sedan midyear during the previous year, with no major changes occurring in that series in 1997. The venerable Crown Victoria's steering gear was modified to provide more stability. The Thunderbird, also in its final year of production, received a redesigned instrument panel and console and also could be purchased with a Sport Package that featured upgraded suspension and 16-inch aluminum wheels. The Ford Aspire (not covered in this catalog due to its import status) was also in its last year of sale in the United States.

1997 Ford Escort LX sedan. (OCW)

1997 Ford Probe GT coupe. (OCW)

ESCORT — FOUR — The all-new Escort featured one-piece bodyside construction, which allowed for 25 percent more torsional rigidity and better road "feel" over the previous version. Available in four-door sedan (base and LX versions as well as an LX sedan with optional Sport Package) and station wagon (LX only) models, the 1997 Escort featured side impact protection and dual airbags as standard equipment. Four inches longer than before, the Escort sedan provided 100 cubic feet of interior passenger and cargo space while the Escort station wagon offered 120 cubic feet. The Escort featured an Integrated Control Panel that put audio and climate controls in easy-to-use locations as well as solar-tinted glass to reduce glare. Ford's new small car offered 100,000-mile tune-up intervals on its new 2.0-liter four-cylinder engine with Split Port Induction, rated at 110-hp and 125 pound-feet of torque. The standard five-speed manual transaxle as well as the optional four-speed automatic transaxle were both improved for better shift quality and improved performance. Optional equipment included four-wheel anti-lock brakes, trunk-mounted CD player and remote keyless entry.

CONTOUR — FOUR/V-6 — The addition of a base four-door sedan as well as an optional Sport model in GL or LX versions topped the list of changes for the 1997 Contour. Offered in base, GL, LX and SE trim, all four-door sedans, new features for Contour included an interior trunk light, a tilt-column steering wheel, power antenna, illuminated visor mirrors (LX and SE sedans only) and optional 15-inch alloy wheels (GL and LX sedans only). The Contour Sport featured an exclusive Alpine green clearcoat body color (as well as standard Contour colors), leather-wrapped steering wheel and shift knob, 15-inch alloy wheels, foglamps, Sport badging and Sport graphics on front floor mats. The base, GL and LX sedans were powered by the DOHC 2.0-liter four-cylinder engine. The SE sedan was again powered by the modular, DOHC 2.5-liter V-6, which was the option engine for the GL and LX models. Contours again used the five-speed manual transaxle as standard equipment while the electronically controlled four-speed automatic transaxle was optional.

PROBE — FOUR/V-6 — In its ninth and final year of production, Probe was again offered in base and GT coupe versions. An optional GTS Sport Appearance Package was added to the GT coupe for 1997, and consisted of dual racing stripes running the length of the car, GTS decals, a rear spoiler and 16-inch chrome wheels. The base coupe was again powered by the DOHC 2.0-liter four-cylinder engine. The GT coupe again used the DOHC 2.5-liter V-6. A five-speed manual transaxle was again standard equipment on all Probes and an electronically controlled four-speed automatic transaxle was optional.

TAURUS — V-6/V-8 — The introduction of a base G four-door sedan midyear in 1996 expanded the 1997 Taurus lineup, which now was comprised of the aforementioned G, GL, LX and SHO four-door sedans as well as GL and LX station wagons. Totally redesigned the previous year, the 1997 Taurus was only slightly revised. The GL series' Vulcan 3.0-liter V-6 received an upgraded catalytic configuration, engine recalibrations and a secondary air-injection system that enabled it to qualify as a low-emission vehicle (LEV) in California. This 3.0-liter V-6 also offered two flexible fuel packages (introduced midyear in 1996). One permitted use of up to 85 percent methanol and the other permitted use of up to 85 percent ethanol. Taurus offered 101.5 cubic feet of interior room. The G and GL series used the aforementioned Vulcan 3.0-liter V-6. The LX series was again powered by the Duratec DOHC 3.0-liter V-6. The SHO sedan again used the DOHC 3.4-liter V-8. The AX4N electronically controlled four-speed automatic transaxle was the standard unit for all Taurus models. Features of the SHO sedan included a color-keyed rear spoiler, flared rocker panel design, 16-inch/five-spoke cast aluminum wheels and dual exhaust.

CROWN VICTORIA — V-8 — Four-door sedan models in base or LX trim were again the Crown Victoria offerings for 1997. New features included improved steering gear to enhance on-center road "feel" and stability as well as several new color selections. The Crown Victoria NGV (natural gas vehicle) returned after being introduced in 1996. Using a modified version of the Crown Vic's standard 4.6-liter V-8, the NGV model produced 175-hp at 4500 rpm and 235 lbs.-ft. of torque at 3500 rpm. The electronically controlled four-speed automatic over-drive transmission was again used in all Crown Vics.

THUNDERBIRD — V-6/V-8 — In its final appearance after 42 years of continuous production, Thunderbird was again available only as an LX coupe but offered several new features in 1997. Inside, a new instrument cluster arranged key engine functions in three separate displays. A decklid spoiler (introduced midyear in 1996) included an integrated stoplight. Also, three new exterior colors were offered: Light Prairie tan, Light Denim blue and Arctic green. Light Prairie tan was also a new interior color. A new Sport Package was optional and included 16-inch wheels and upgraded suspension. Other new optional equipment included a power sliding moonroof and 15-inch/seven-spoke chrome wheels. The LX coupe was again powered by the 3.8-liter V-6 with the 4.6-liter V-8 as the option engine. An improved 4R70W four-speed automatic overdrive transmission was standard and offered better corrosion protection.

I.D. DATA: Ford's 17-symbol Vehicle Identification Number (VIN) was stamped on a metal tab fastened to the instrument panel, visible through the windshield. The first three symbols indicate manufacturer, make and vehicle type. The fourth symbol denotes restraint system. Next comes a letter (usually 'P'), followed by two digits that indicate Model Number, as shown in left column of tables below. (Example: '10' Escort four-door sedan). Symbol eight indicates engine type. Next is a check digit. Symbol ten indicates model year ('V' - 1997). Symbol eleven denotes assembly plant. The final six digits make up the sequence number, starting with 000001.

ESCORT (FOUR)

Model No.	Body/ Style No.	Body Type & Seating	Factory Price	Shipping Weight	Prod. Total
P	10	4-dr. Sed-5P	11015	2457	Note 1
P	13	4-dr. LX Sed-5P	11515	2503	Note 1
P	15	4-dr. LX Sta Wag-5P	12065	2571	71,610

NOTE 1: Production of four-door sedan models totaled 251,894 with no further breakout available.

CONTOUR (FOUR/V-6)

P	65	4-dr. Sed-5P	13460/-----	2769/----	Note 1
P	65	4-dr. GL Sed-5P	14285/15520	2769/NA	Note 1
P	66	4-dr. LX Sed-5P	14915/16115	2769/2808	Note 1
P	67	4-dr. SE Sed-5P	-----/16615	----/2994	Note 1

NOTE: Figures to the left of slash are for four-cylinder/to right of slash are for V-6.

NOTE 1: Production of four-door sedan models totaled 79,951 with no further breakout available.

PROBE (FOUR/V-6 in GT only)

T	20	2-dr. Cpe-4P	14280	2690	Note 1
T	22	2-dr. GT Cpe-4P	16780	2921	Note 1

NOTE 1: Production of two-door coupe models totaled 16,821 with no further breakout available.

TAURUS (V-6/V-8 in SHO only)

P	51	4-dr. G Sed-6P	17995	3329	Note 1
P	52	4-dr. GL Sed-6P	18985	3329	Note 1
P	57	4-dr. GL Sta Wag-6P	20195	3480	Note 2
P	53	4-dr. LX Sedan-6P	21610	3326	Note 1
P	58	4-dr. LX Sta Wag-6P	22715	3480	Note 2
P	54	4-dr. SHO Sed-6P	26460	3440	Note 1

NOTE 1: Production of four-door sedan models totaled 384,844 with no further breakout available.

NOTE 2: Production of station wagon models totaled 13,958 with no further breakout available.

CROWN VICTORIA (V-8)

Model No.	Body/ Style No.	Body Type & Seating	Factory Price	Shipping Weight	Prod. Total
P	73	4-dr. Sed-6P	21475	3776	Note 1
P	74	4-dr. LX Sed-6P	23195	3780	Note 1

NOTE 1: Production of four-door sedan models totaled 123,833 with no further breakout available.

THUNDERBIRD (V-6/V-8)

P	62	2-dr. LX Cpe-5P	17885/19015	3561/3644	73,814

NOTE: Figures to the left of slash are for V-6/to right of slash are for V-8.

ENGINE [Base Four (Escort)]: Inline. Overhead cam. Four-cylinder. Cast-iron block and aluminum head. Displacement: 122 cid (2.0 liters). Bore & stroke: 3.33 x 3.46 in. Compression ratio: 9.2:1. Brake horsepower: 110 at 5000 rpm. Torque: 125 lbs.-ft. at 3750 rpm. Sequential fuel injection.

1997 Ford Crown Victoria LX sedan. (OCW)

ENGINE [Base Four (Probe)]: Inline. Dual overhead cam. Four-cylinder. Cast-iron block and aluminum head. Displacement: 122 cid (2.0 liters). Bore & stroke: 3.27 x 3.62 in. Compression ratio: 9.0:1. Brake horsepower: 118 at 5500 rpm. Torque: 127 lbs.-ft. at 4500 rpm. Sequential fuel injection.

ENGINE [Base Four (Contour)]: Inline. Dual overhead cam. Four-cylinder. Cast-iron block and aluminum head. Displacement: 121 cid (2.0 liters). Bore & stroke: 3.34 x 3.46 in. Compression ratio: 9.6:1. Brake horsepower: 125 at 5500 rpm. Torque: 130 lbs.-ft. at 4000 rpm. Sequential fuel injection.

ENGINE [Base V-6 (Probe GT)]: Dual overhead cam V-6 (24 valve). Aluminum block and head. Displacement: 153 cid (2.5 liters). Bore & stroke: 3.33 x 2.92 in. Compression ratio: 9.2:1. Brake horsepower: 164 at 5600 rpm. Torque: 160 lbs.-ft. at 4000 rpm. Sequential fuel injection.

ENGINE [Base V-6 (Contour SE); Optional (Contour GL/Contour LX)]: Modular, dual overhead cam V-6 (24 valve). Aluminum block and head. Displacement: 155 cid (2.5 liters). Bore & stroke: 3.24 x 3.13 in. Compression ratio: 9.7:1. Brake horsepower: 170 at 6250 rpm. Torque: 165 lbs.-ft. at 4250 rpm. Sequential fuel injection.

ENGINE [Base V-6 (Taurus G/Taurus GL)]: Overhead valve V-6. Cast-iron block and head. Displacement: 182 cid (3.0 liters). Bore & stroke: 3.50 x 3.15 in. Compression ratio: 9.3:1. Brake horsepower: 145 at 5250 rpm. Torque: 170 lbs.-ft. at 3250 rpm. Sequential fuel injection.

ENGINE [Base V-6 (Taurus LX)]: Dual-overhead-cam V-6 (24 valve). Aluminum block and head. Displacement: 182 cid (3.0 liters). Bore & stroke: 3.50 x 3.15 in. Compression ratio: 9.3:1. Brake horsepower: 200 at 5750 rpm. Torque: 200 lbs.-ft. at 4500 rpm. Sequential fuel injection.

ENGINE [Base V-6 (Thunderbird LX)]: 90-degree, overhead valve V-6. Cast-iron block and aluminum head. Displacement: 232 cid (3.8 liters). Bore & stroke: 3.80 x 3.40 in. Compression ratio: 9.0:1. Brake horsepower: 145 at 4000 rpm. Torque: 215 lbs.-ft. at 2750 rpm. Sequential fuel injection.

ENGINE [Base V-8 (Taurus SHO)]: 60-degree, dual overhead cam (32 valve) V-8. Aluminum block and head. Displacement: 207 cid (3.4 liters). Bore & stroke: 3.50 x 3.15 in. Compression ratio: 9.8:1. Brake horsepower: 235 at 6100 rpm. Torque: 230 lbs.-ft. at 4800 rpm. Sequential fuel injection.

ENGINE [Base V-8 (Crown Victoria)]: Modular, overhead valve V-8. Displacement: 281 cid (4.6 liters). Bore & stroke: 3.60 x 3.60. Compression ratio: 9.0:1. Brake horsepower: 190 at 4250 rpm. Torque: 265 lbs.-ft. at 3200 rpm. Sequential fuel injection.

ENGINE [Optional V-8 (Thunderbird LX)]: same as 4.6-liter V-8 above, except - Dual overhead cam. Brake horsepower: 205 at 4250 rpm. Torque: 280 lbs.-ft. at 3000 rpm.

CHASSIS DATA: Wheelbase: (Escort) 98.4 in.; (Contour) 106.5 in.; (Probe) 102.8 in.; (Taurus) 108.5 in.; (Crown Vic) 114.4 in.; (T-Bird) 113.0 in. Overall Length: (Escort) 174.7 in.; (Escort wag) 172.7 in.; (Contour) 183.9 in.; (Probe) 178.7 in.; (Taurus) 197.5 in.; (Taurus wag) 199.6 in.; (Crown Vic) 212.0 in.; (T-Bird) 200.3 in. Height: (Escort) 53.3 in.; (Escort wag) 53.9 in.; (Contour) 54.5 in.; (Probe) 51.6 in.; (Taurus) 55.1 in.; (Taurus wag) 57.6 in.; (Crown Vic) 56.8 in.; (T-Bird) 52.5 in. Width: (Escort) 67.0 in.; (Contour) 69.1 in.; (Probe) 69.8 in.; (Taurus) 73.0 in.; (Crown Vic) 77.8 in.; (T-Bird) 72.7 in. Front Tread: (Escort) 56.5 in.; (Contour) 59.2 in.; (Probe) 59.4 in.; (Taurus) 61.6 in.; (Crown Vic) 62.8 in.; (T-Bird) 61.6 in. Rear Tread: (Escort) 56.5 in.; (Contour) 58.5 in.; (Probe) 59.4 in.; (Taurus) 61.4 in.; (Taurus wag) 61.8 in.; (Crown Vic) 63.3 in.; (T-Bird) 60.2 in. Standard Tires: (Escort) P185/65R14; (Contour) P185/70R14; (Contour SE) P205/60R15; (Probe) P195/65R14; (Probe GT) P225/50R16; (Taurus) P205/65R15; (Taurus SHO) P225/55VR16; (Crown Vic) P215/70R15; (T-Bird LX) P205/70R15.

TECHNICAL: Transmission: Five-speed manual transaxle standard on Escort, Contour and Probe. Four-speed overdrive automatic standard on Taurus, Crown Vic and Thunderbird. Drive Axle: (Crown

Vic/T-Bird) rear; (others) front. Steering: (Crown Vic) recirculating ball; (others) rack/pinion. Front Suspension: (Escort) Independent MacPherson strut w/strut-mounted coil springs; (Contour) Independent, subframe-rubber-mounted MacPherson strut w/strut-mounted coil springs, lower control A-arms and cast steering knuckles; (Probe) Independent MacPherson strut-type with lower A-type control arms, upper strut-mounted coil springs w/cross-member and stabilizer bar; (Taurus) Independent MacPherson strut front drive w/strut-mounted coil springs, stabilizer bar, lower control arm and cast knuckle; (Crown Vic) Independent short/long arm w/ball joints, coil springs and stabilizer bar; (T-Bird) Short/long arm w/double isolated tension strut, coil springs and stabilizer bar. Rear Suspension: (Escort) Independent, Quadra-link w/stabilizer bar; (Contour) Independent, Quadra-link strut w/coil spring on shock strut, mounted to rigid subframe; (Probe) Independent strut-type, Quadra-link, upper strut-mounted coil springs and stabilizer bar. (Taurus sedan) Independent Quadra-link w/coil spring on shock strut, stabilizer bar, tension strut, parallel suspension arms and two-piece cast spindle w/forged stem; (Taurus wagon) Independent short/long arm w/spring on lower control arm, stabilizer bar, tension strut and cast spindle w/pressed-in forged stem and integrated ball joints; (Crown Vic) Rigid axle w/four links and coil springs; (T-Bird) H-arm independent, coil springs and stabilizer bar. Brakes: Front disc, rear drum (power assisted) except (Contour SE, Probe GT, Taurus GL wagon/Taurus LX wagon/Taurus SHO, Crown Victoria and Thunderbird LX) front/rear disc. Body construction: (Crown Vic) separate body and frame; (others) unibody. Fuel tank: (Escort) 12.7 gal.; (Contour) 14.5 gal.; (Probe) 15.5 gal.; (Taurus) 16.0 gal.; (Crown Vic) 20.0 gal.; (T-Bird) 18.0 gal.

DRIVETRAIN OPTIONS: Engines: 2.5-liter DOHC V-6: Contour GL ($1235); Contour LX ($1200). Flex-fuel (methanol or ethanol) 3.0-liter V-6: Taurus GL sedan only ($1165). Natural Gas-powered 4.6-liter V-8: Crown Vic ($6165). DOHC 4.6-liter V-8: Thunderbird LX ($1130). Transmission/Differential: Four-speed automatic transaxle: Escort ($815); Contour ($815); Probe ($895). Traction Assist: T-Bird ($210). Traction-Lok Axle: T-Bird ($95). Suspension/Brakes: Heavy Duty Suspension: Taurus (GL wagon only) ($25). Anti-lock brakes: Escort ($570); Contour ($570); Probe ($820); Probe GT ($650); Taurus (stnd SHO) ($600); Crown Vic (w/Elect Traction Assist) ($695); T-Bird LX ($570).

ESCORT CONVENIENCE/APPEARANCE OPTIONS: Preferred Equip Pkg LX Series (317A): Air Cond, Driver's Door Remote Entry and Rr Window Defroster ($765). Preferred Equip Pkg LX Series (318A): Air Cond, Driver's Door Remote Entry, Dual Pwr Mirrors, Pwr Locks w/Anti-theft, Pwr Windows and Rr Window Defroster ($1390). Calif. Emission System ($170). Integrated Child Seat (LX only) ($135). Air Cond ($795). Rr Window Defroster ($190). Elect AM/FM Stereo Radio w/Cass ($165). Elect AM/FM Stereo Radio w/CD Player (LX only) ($515). Wagon Grp: incl Luggage Rack and Rr Window Wiper/Washer (LX wagon only) ($240). Sport Pkg: incl 14-inch alum wheels, oval-tipped exhaust, unique sport seats w/rear integrated headrests, tach, liftgate spoiler and appliqués ($495). Anti-lock Brakes ($570). Dual Pwr Mirrors (LX only) ($95). Flr Mats F&R ($45).

1997 Ford Escort LX station wagon. (OCW)

1997 Ford Contour SE sedan. (OCW)

1997 Ford Taurus LX sedan. (OCW)

CONTOUR CONVENIENCE/APPEARANCE OPTIONS: Preferred Equip Pkg base series (230A): Rr Window Defroster, Full-length Console and Elect AM/FM Stereo Radio w/Cass ($410). Preferred Equip Pkg GL Series (236A): Rr Window Defroster, Full-length Console, Spd Control, Light Grp, Pwr Door Locks and Elect AM/FM Stereo Radio w/Cass ($1310). Preferred Equip Pkg GL Series (240A): same as 236A plus Pwr Windows and 2.5-liter V-6 Engine Pkg ($2685). Preferred Equip Pkg LX Series (238A): Pwr Windows, 2.5-liter V-6 Engine Pkg, Rr Window Defroster, Full-length Console, Spd Control, Light Grp, Pwr Door Locks and Elect AM/FM Stereo Radio w/Cass ($2415). Preferred Equip Pkg SE Series (239A): Pwr Windows, Rr Window Defroster, Full-length Console, Spd Control, Light Grp, Pwr Door Locks and Elect AM/FM Stereo Radio w/Cass ($1385). Calif. Emission Syst ($100). Remote Keyless Entry Syst (NA base) ($190). Pwr Moonroof (NA base) ($595). Pwr Windows (LX and SE only) ($340). Elect AM/FM Stereo Radio w/Cass & Premium Sound: GL ($315); LX and SE ($130). Elect AM/FM Stereo Radio w/CD Player & Premium Sound: GL ($455); LX and SE ($270). Anti-lock Brakes ($570). Air Cond ($795). Rr Window Defroster ($190). Carpeted Flr Mats F&R (NA base) ($45). Pwr Driver's Seat (LX and SE only) ($330). Leather Bucket Seats: LX ($645); SE ($595). Rr Split Fold-down Seat (GL only) ($205). Sport Pkg incl 15-inch/six-spoke alum wheels, leather-wrapped strg wheel & shift knob, foglamps and tach: GL ($495); LX ($420). Spd Control ($215). 15-inch Alum Wheels (GL and LX only) ($425). 2.0-liter Four-Cylinder Gaseous Fuel Prep ($260).

PROBE CONVENIENCE/APPEARANCE OPTIONS: Preferred Equip Pkg base series: Air Cond and AM/FM Stereo Radio w/Cass & Clock ($740). Preferred Equip Pkg GT Series: Air Cond and AM/FM Stereo Radio w/Cass & Clock ($740). Calif. Emissions System ($170). Man Air Cond w/Tinted Glass ($895). Leather Bucket Seats ($500). Pwr Driver's Seat ($290). Convenience Grp incl Interval Wipers, Spd Control, Tilt Strg and Console: base ($430); GT ($375). Luxury Grp incl Pwr Side Windows, Pwr Door Locks, Elect Dual Remote Mirrors and Remote & Illum Keyless Entry ($615). Anti-lock Brakes: base ($820); GT ($650). Elect AM/FM Stereo Radio w/Cass & Clock ($165). Elect AM/FM Stereo Radio w/Cass & Premium Sound ($170). Elect AM/FM Stereo Radio w/CD Player & Premium Sound ($620). Color-Keyed Bodyside Mldgs ($60). Color-Keyed Front Flr Mats ($30). Pwr Sliding Roof ($615). Rr Decklid Spoiler ($235). GTS Sport Appearance Grp incl rear decklid spoiler, tape stripes and 16-inch chrome wheels w/P225/50VR15 BSW Tires ($745). 15-inch Alum Wheels w/P205/55HR15 BSW Tires (base only) ($470). 16-inch Chrome Wheels w/P225/50VR16 BSW Tires ($390).

TAURUS CONVENIENCE/APPEARANCE OPTIONS: Preferred Equip Pkg GL Series (204A): Pwr Door Locks, AM/FM Stereo Radio w/Cass, Spd Control, Air Filtration Syst and Flr Mats F&R ($250). Preferred Equip Pkg GL Series (205A): same as 204A plus Pwr Driver's Seat, Light Grp and Alum Wheels ($850). Preferred Equip Pkg LX Series (209A): 4-wheel Disc Brakes w/Anti-lock, Spd Control, Flr Mats F&R, Air Filtration Syst and Remote Keyless Entry w/Perimeter Antitheft Syst ($720). Preferred Equip Pkg LX Series (210A): same as 209A plus Elect Temp Control Air Cond, Alum Wheels and Sound Syst Upgrade: sed ($1710); wag ($1630). Preferred Equip Pkg SHO Series: Pwr Moonroof, Elect Temp Control Air Cond, Pwr Heated Mirrors, Remote Keyless Entry w/Perimeter Antitheft Syst and MACH Audio Syst ($1210). Calif. Emissions Syst ($170). Elect Temp Control Air Cond ($210). Anti-lock Brakes (stnd SHO) ($600). Pwr Moonroof (LX and SHO only) ($740). Air Filtration Syst ($30). Daytime Running Lights ($40). Remote Entry Syst (GL only) ($190). Remote Entry Syst w/Perimeter Anti-theft Syst (LX and SHO only) ($440). Elect AM/FM Stereo Radio w/Cass (G and GL only) ($185). Trunk-mounted CD Changer (LX and SHO only) ($595). MACH Audio Syst: LX sed ($400); LX wag and SHO ($320). Rr Facing Third Seat ($200, wagons only). Pwr Driver's Seat (GL only) ($340). Cellular Phone (NA G) ($650). Light Grp (GL only) ($45). Wagon Grp incl Rr Window Washer/Wiper and Cargo Cover ($295). Chrome Wheels (LX and SHO only) ($580). Cast Aluminum Wheels (GL only) ($315). Leather Seats w/console (LX only) ($990). Leather Sport Bucket Seats w/console (SHO sedan only) ($1190). Heavy Duty Suspension (GL wag only) ($25).

1997 Ford Thunderbird LX coupe. (OCW)

CROWN VICTORIA CONVENIENCE/APPEARANCE OPTIONS: Preferred Equip Pkg base series (111A): Color-Keyed Flr Mats F&R, Pwr Lock Grp, Spoked Wheel Covers, Spd Control and Illum Entry Syst ($60). Preferred Equip Pkg LX Series (113A): Color-Keyed Flr Mats F&R, Pwr Lock Grp, Cornering Lamps, Spd Control, Illum Entry Syst, Leather-wrapped Strg Wheel, Elect AM/FM Stereo Radio w/Cass, Cast Alum 12-spoke Wheels and Light/Decor Grp ($640). Preferred Equip Pkg LX Series (114A): same as 113A plus Elect Auto Temp Control Air Cond, Anti-lock Brakes w/Elect Traction Assist, Pwr Pass Seat, High Level Audio Syst, Elect Digital Instrumentation, Remote Keyless Entry and Elect Auto Dim Mirror ($2965). Calif. Emissions Syst ($170). Natural Gas-fueled 4.6-liter V-8 ($6165). Elect Auto Temp Control Air Cond ($175). Leather Split Bench Seat (LX only) ($735). Anti-lock Brakes w/Elect Traction Assist ($695). 41G Handling & Perf Pkg (LX only) incl Revised Springs/Shocks/Stabilizer Bar, Pwr Strg Cooler, P225/60R16 BSW Touring Tires, 16-inch Cast Alum Wheels and Dual Exhaust ($1100). Eng Block Htr ($25). Remote Keyless Entry Syst (LX only) ($240). Light/Decor Grp ($225). Elect AM/FM Stereo Radio w/Cass ($185). High Level Audio Syst: base ($545); LX ($360). 6-Way Pwr Driver's Seat ($360). Pwr Pass Seat (LX only) ($360). Color-Keyed Flr Mats F&R ($45). Conventional Spare Tire ($80). P215/70R15 WSW Tires ($80).

THUNDERBIRD CONVENIENCE/APPEARANCE OPTIONS: Preferred Equip Pkg LX Series (155A): Rr Window Defroster, P215/70R15 Tires and Cast Alum Wheels (NC). Preferred quip Pkg LX Series (157A): same as 155A plus 4.6-liter V-8, 6-Way Pwr Driver's Seat, Illum Entry Syst and Leather-wrapped Strg Wheel & Shift Knob ($840). Calif. Emission Syst ($170). Leather Bucket Seats ($490). Remote Illum Keyless Entry ($270). Frnt Floor Mats ($30). Elect AM/FM Stereo Radio w/Cass & Premium Sound ($290). Elect AM/FM Stereo Radio w/CD Player & Premium Sound ($430). Anti-lock Brakes ($570). Antitheft Syst ($145). Pwr Moonroof ($740). Sport Option incl 16-inch Alum Wheels, P225/60R16 BSW Tires, Modified Stabilizer Bars, Larger Frnt Disc Brake Rotors, Revised Spring Rates and Rr Decklid Spoiler ($450). Rr Decklid Spoiler ($250). Leather-wrapped Strg Wheel & Shift Knob ($90). Tri-Coat Paint ($225). Traction Assist ($210). Traction-Lok Axle ($95). Pwr Driver's Seat ($290). Luxury Grp incl Elect Semi-Auto Temp Control Air Cond, Dual Illum Visor Mirrors and Pwr Antenna ($395). 15-inch Chrome Wheels ($580).

HISTORY: U.S. model year production totaled 1,116,975 (including Mustang).

1997 Ford Taurus GL station wagon. (OCW)

1998 FORD

After 42 years of production, Ford's automotive institution known around the world as the Thunderbird was not continued for the 1998 model year. This was one of several sweeping changes at Ford as model lineups were juggled substantially from the year previous. Also discontinued after nine years of production was the Probe. New models from the blue oval were the Escort ZX2 two-door coupe, available in either base/"Cool" or upscale/"Hot" versions and the high-performance Contour SVT four-door sedan, a limited edition product of Ford's Special Vehicle Team. The aforementioned juggling of lineups was due to Ford slimming each model line to two series. (Contour and Taurus were the exceptions with their LX and SE series bolstered by the SVT and SHO sedans, respectively.) On the safety front, second-generation driver and passenger airbags became standard equipment on all models. The SecuriLock anti-theft immobilizer also became standard equipment on most Ford automobiles.

ESCORT — FOUR — The Escort lineup was revised for 1998 with the previously offered base Escort and LX station wagon discontinued and a new SE series introduced. Escort was now available as an LX four-door sedan or SE four-door sedan or station wagon. Ford also introduced an all-new two-door coupe named the ZX2, which was affiliated with the Escort in that the two shared key components. This performance coupe was aimed at younger buyers and was available in two versions: "Cool" or "Hot". The ZX2 used the Zetec 2.0-liter four-cylinder engine, rated at 130-hp, mated to a five-speed manual transaxle. Optional equipment included anti-lock brakes, premium sound system, power windows, power moonroof, remote entry system and automatic transaxle. A Sport Package was also offered with the ZX2, which featured 15-inch aluminum wheels, rear spoiler, foglamps, upgraded bucket seats and special badging. The Escort, after being totally redesigned in 1997, received several improvements. The upgrades included a new electronically controlled four-speed automatic transaxle that provided for more throttle response, chrome-plated wheel covers, a sensor added to the powerplant to reduce engine noise and emissions controls added to contain the non-tailpipe hydrocarbons generated during both refueling and driving. The SE series' list of standard equipment included air conditioning, rear defroster, driver's door remote entry system and dual power mirrors. The Escort again used the 2.0-liter four-cylinder engine with Split Port Induction. Standard transaxle was the five-speed manual with the option unit being the electronically controlled four-speed automatic with overdrive.

CONTOUR — FOUR/V-6 — Ford touted the 1998 Contour as receiving more than 100 customer-driven refinements. The biggest change was that the base and GL sedans offered previously were dropped. Contour's lineup now consisted of an LX or SE four-door sedan. If neither of those models were "zippy" enough, a buyer could opt for the limited edition Contour SVT four-door sports sedan. Ford's Special Vehicle Team (SVT) announced it would build 5,000 Contour SVT sports sedans per year, each fitted with an exclusive 195-hp version of the Duratec DOHC 2.5-liter V-6 with 10.0:1 compression ratio and 2.25-inch stainless steel dual exhaust and coupled to a MTX-75 five-speed manual transaxle. Announced top speed of the SVT sports sedan was 143 mph. Standard features of the Contour SVT included four-wheel disc brakes with a four-channel/four-sensor antilock system, five-spoke cast aluminum wheels, leather interior surfaces including seats/steering wheel/shifter knob and air filtration system. Standard equipment on the Contour LX and SE sedans included air conditioning, dual power mirrors and full wheel covers with the SE model adding color-keyed mirrors, rear defroster, power locks and windows and speed control. LX and SE sedans were again powered by the Zetec DOHC 2.0-liter four-cylinder engine. The modular, DOHC 2.5-liter V-6 was the option engine for both. The five-speed manual transaxle was again standard equipment while the electronically controlled four-speed automatic transaxle was optional.

1998 Ford Escort SE sedan (with Sport Package). (OCW)

1998 Ford Taurus SE station wagon. (OCW)

1998 Ford Taurus LX sedan. (OCW)

TAURUS — V-6/V-8 — The Taurus lineup was overhauled in 1998 with the previously offered G and GL models discontinued and the SE series introduced. Taurus was now available as an LX four-door sedan, SE four-door sedan or station wagon or the high-performance SHO sedan. The LX and SE models received a more assertive fascia, new fluted park/turn lamps and a more consistent monochrome treatment for tail lamps and rear appliqué. A new Sport Group was available on the SE sedan, which included the Duratec V-6 engine, SecuriLock anti-theft system, rear decklid spoiler and chrome bolt-on wheel covers. The LX and SE series used the Vulcan 3.0-liter V-6, rated at 145-hp, and four-speed automatic overdrive transaxle as base powertrain. Optional for both series was the Duratec 3.0-liter V-6, rated at 200-hp, coupled to the electronically controlled AX4N non-synchronous four-speed automatic overdrive transaxle. The SHO sedan again used the DOHC 3.4-liter V-8 mated to the AX4N four-speed automatic. The two flex fuel (methanol or ethanol) 3.0-liter V-6 engines that debuted in 1997 were again offered in LX or SE sedans only. Taurus models also received the second generation driver and passenger airbags as standard equipment.

CROWN VICTORIA — V-8 — The Crown Victoria offered the lone unchanged lineup from Ford for 1998. Again available as a four-door sedan in base or LX trim, several new features were added including all-new Watt's linkage rear and revised front suspensions, larger front brakes and tires (16-inch instead of the previous 15-inch), SecuriLock anti-theft system and optional all-speed traction control. The Crown Vic's exterior was redesigned comprising a new front fascia and larger headlamps as well as new wraparound tail lamps. The 4.6-liter V-8, rated at 200-hp, and the electronically controlled four-speed automatic overdrive transmission were again the standard powertrain. Buyers opting for the Handling & Performance Package (41G) received 15 extra horsepower (215) and 10 additional pound-feet of torque. The Crown Victoria NGV (powered by a 4.6-liter V-8 fueled by natural gas) was also offered again in 1998.

1998 Ford Crown Victoria LX sedan. (OCW)

I.D. DATA: Ford's 17-symbol Vehicle Identification Number (VIN) was stamped on a metal tab fastened to the instrument panel, visible through the windshield. The first three symbols indicate manufacturer, make and vehicle type. The fourth symbol denotes restraint system. Next comes a letter (usually 'P'), followed by two digits that indicate Model Number, as shown in left column of tables below. (Example: '10' Escort LX four-door sedan). Symbol eight indicates engine type. Next is a check digit. Symbol ten indicates model year ('W' - 1998). Symbol eleven denotes assembly plant. The final six digits make up the sequence number, starting with 000001.

ESCORT (FOUR)

Model No.	Body/ Style No.	Type & Seating	Factory Price	Shipping Weight	Prod. Total
P	10	4-dr. LX Sed-5P	11280	2468	*
P	13	4-dr. SE Sed-5P	12580	NA	*
P	15	4-dr. SE Sta Wag-5P	13780	2531	*

ESCORT ZX2 SUB-SERIES (FOUR)

P	11/41V	2-dr. Cool Cpe-5P	11580	2478	*
P	11	2-dr. Hot Cpe-5P	13080	NA	*

CONTOUR (FOUR/V-6)

P	66	4-dr. LX Sed-5P	14460/NA	2811/NA	*
P	67	4-dr. SE Sed-5P	15785/NA	3030/NA	*
P	68	4-dr. SVT Sports Sed-5P	22405	3068	5,000

NOTE: Figures to the left of slash are for four-cylinder/to right of slash are for V-6.

NOTE: SVT sport sedan powered by V-6 only. Ford announced it would build approximately 5,000 SVTs per year, but no actual production figure was available when this book was printed.

TAURUS (V-6/V-8 in SHO only)

P	52	4-dr. LX Sed-6P	18245	3353	*
P	52/60E	4-dr. SE Sedan-6P	19445	3294	*
P	57	4-dr. SE Sta Wag-6P	21105	3457	*
P	54	4-dr. SHO Sed-6P	28920	NA	*

CROWN VICTORIA (V-8)

P	73	4-dr. Sed-6P	20935	NA	*
P	74	4-dr. LX Sed-6P	23135	NA	*

*NOTE: Production figures for 1998 Ford automobiles were not available at the time this book was printed.

ENGINE [Base Four (Escort)]: Inline. Overhead cam. Four-cylinder. Cast-iron block and aluminum head. Displacement: 122 cid (2.0 liters). Bore & stroke: 3.33 x 3.46 in. Compression ratio: 9.2:1. Brake horsepower: 110 at 5000 rpm. Torque: 125 lbs.-ft. at 3750 rpm. Split Port induction.

ENGINE [Base Four (Escort ZX2)]: Inline. Dual overhead cam. Four-cylinder. Cast-iron block and aluminum head. Displacement: NA in cid (2.0 liters). Bore & stroke: NA. Compression ratio: 9.6:1. Brake horsepower: 130 at 5750 rpm. Torque: 127 lbs.-ft. at 4250 rpm. Sequential fuel injection.

ENGINE [Base Four (Contour)]: Inline. Dual overhead cam. Four-cylinder. Cast-iron block and aluminum head. Displacement: 121 cid (2.0 liters). Bore & stroke: 3.34 x 3.46 in. Compression ratio: 9.6:1. Brake horsepower: 125 at 5500 rpm. Torque: 130 lbs.-ft. at 4000 rpm. Sequential fuel injection.

ENGINE [Base V-6 (Contour SVT)]: 60-degree dual overhead cam V-6. Aluminum block and head. Displacement: 155 cid (2.5 liters). Bore & stroke: 3.21 x 3.08 in. Compression ratio: 10.0:1. Brake horsepower: 195 at 6625 rpm. Torque: 165 lbs.-ft. at 5625 rpm. Sequential fuel injection.

ENGINE [Optional V-6 (Contour LX/Contour SE)]: Modular, dual overhead cam V-6. Aluminum block and head. Displacement: 155 cid (2.5 liters). Bore & stroke: 3.24 x 3.13 in. Compression ratio: 9.7:1. Brake horsepower: 170 at 6250 rpm. Torque: 165 lbs.-ft. at 4250 rpm. Sequential fuel injection.

ENGINE [Base V-6 (Taurus)]: Overhead valve V-6. Cast-iron block and head. Displacement: 182 cid (3.0 liters). Bore & stroke: 3.50 x 3.15 in. Compression ratio: 9.3:1. Brake horsepower: 145 at 5250 rpm. Torque: 170 lbs.-ft. at 3250 rpm. Sequential fuel injection.

ENGINE [Optional V-6 (Taurus)]: Dual-overhead-cam V-6. Aluminum block and head. Displacement: 182 cid (3.0 liters). Bore & stroke: 3.50 x 3.15 in. Compression ratio: 9.3:1. Brake horsepower: 200 at 5750 rpm. Torque: 200 lbs.-ft. at 4500 rpm. Sequential fuel injection.

ENGINE [Base V-8 (Taurus SHO)]: 60-degree, dual overhead cam V-8. Aluminum block and head. Displacement: 207 cid (3.4 liters). Bore & stroke: 3.50 x 3.15 in. Compression ratio: 9.8:1. Brake horsepower: 235 at 6100 rpm. Torque: 230 lbs.-ft. at 4800 rpm. Sequential fuel injection.

ENGINE [Base V-8 (Crown Victoria)]: Modular, overhead cam V-8. Displacement: 281 cid (4.6 liters). Bore & stroke: 3.60 x 3.60. Compression ratio: 9.0:1. Brake horsepower: 190 at 4250 rpm. Torque: 265 lbs.-ft. at 3200 rpm. Sequential fuel injection.

CHASSIS DATA: Wheelbase: (Escort/ZX2) 98.4 in.; (Contour) 106.5 in.; (Taurus) 108.5 in.; (Crown Vic) 114.4 in. Overall Length: (Escort) 174.7 in.; (Escort wag) 172.7 in.; (ZX2) 175.2 in.; (Contour) 184.6 in.; (Taurus) 197.5 in.; (Taurus wag) 199.6 in.; (Crown Vic) 212.0 in. Height: (Escort) 53.3 in.; (Escort wag) 53.9 in.; (ZX2) 52.3 in.; (Contour) 54.5 in.; (Taurus) 55.1 in.; (Taurus wag) 57.6 in.; (Crown Vic) 56.8 in. Width: (Escort) 67.0 in.; (ZX2) 67.4 in.; (Contour) 69.1 in.; (Taurus) 73.0 in.; (Crown Vic) 77.8 in. Front Tread: (Escort/ZX2) 56.5 in.; (Contour) 59.2 in.; (Taurus) 61.6 in.; (Crown Vic) 62.8 in. Rear Tread: (Escort/ZX2) 56.5 in.; (Contour) 58.5 in.; (Taurus) 61.4 in.; (Taurus wag) 61.8 in.; (Crown Vic) 63.3 in. Standard Tires: (Escort/ZX2) P185/65R14; (Contour) P185/70R14; (Contour SVT) P205/55ZR16; (Taurus) P205/65R15; (Taurus SHO) P225/55ZR16; (Crown Vic) P225/60SR16.

TECHNICAL: Transmission: Five-speed manual transaxle standard on Escort, ZX2 and Contour. Four-speed overdrive automatic standard on Taurus and Crown Vic. Drive Axle: (Crown Vic) rear; (others) front. Steering: (Crown Vic) recirculating ball; (others) rack/pinion. Front Suspension: (Escort/ZX2) Independent MacPherson strut w/strut-mounted coil springs; (Contour) Independent, subframe-rubber-mounted MacPherson strut w/strut-mounted coil springs, lower control A-arms and cast steering knuckles; (Contour SVT) MacPherson struts, lower A-arms, coil springs, tube shock dampers and stabilizer bar; (Taurus) Independent MacPherson strut front drive w/strut-mounted coil springs, stabilizer bar, lower control arm and cast aluminum knuckle w/integral balljoint; (Crown Vic) Independent short/long arm w/ball joints, coil springs and stabilizer bar. Rear Suspension: (Escort/ZX2) Independent, Quadra-link w/stabilizer bar; (Contour) Independent, Quadra-link strut w/coil spring on shock strut, mounted to rigid subframe; (Contour SVT) Independent Quadra-link design, coil springs, tube shock dampers and stabilizer bar; (Taurus sedan) Independent Quadra-link w/coil spring on shock strut, stabilizer bar, tension strut, parallel suspension arms and two-piece cast spindle w/forged stem; (Taurus wagon) Independent short/long arm w/spring on lower control arm, stabilizer bar, tension strut and cast spindle w/pressed-in forged stem and integrated ball joints; (Crown Vic) Watt's linkage. Brakes: Front disc, rear drum (power assisted) except (Contour SVT, Taurus SE wagon/Taurus SHO and Crown Victoria) front/rear disc. Body construction: (Crown Vic) separate body and frame; (others) unibody. Fuel tank: (Escort/ZX2) 12.7 gal.; (Contour) 14.5 gal.; (Taurus) 16.0 gal.; (Crown Vic) 20.0 gal.

1998 Ford Escort ZX2 coupe. (OCW)

1998 Ford Contour SE sedan. (OCW)

DRIVETRAIN OPTIONS: Engines: 2.5-liter DOHC V-6: Contour LX/Contour SE ($495). Flex-fuel (methanol or ethanol) 3.0-liter V-6: Taurus LX/Taurus SE sedan ($1165). Duratec 3.0-liter V-6: Taurus LX/Taurus SE ($495). Natural Gas-powered 4.6-liter V-8: Crown Vic ($6165). Transmission/Differential: Four-speed automatic transaxle: Escort/Escort ZX2 ($815); Contour LX/Contour SE ($815). Suspension/Brakes: Heavy Duty Suspension: Taurus (SE wagon only) ($25). Anti-lock brakes: Escort/Escort ZX2 ($400); Contour LX/Contour SE ($500); Taurus (stnd SHO) ($600); Crown Vic (w/Elect Traction Control) ($775).

ESCORT CONVENIENCE/APPEARANCE OPTIONS: (51S) Appearance Grp incl Leather-wrapped Strg Wheel, 14-inch Chrome Bolt-on Wheel Covers and Bright Tip Exhaust: SE sed ($155); SE wag ($120). (50A) Comfort Grp incl Spd Control, Tilt Strg Col, Dual Map Lights and Dual Visor Mirrors (SE only) ($345). (60A) Pwr Grp incl Pwr Locks, Pwr Windows and All-door Remote Entry w/Anti-theft (SE only) ($395). (51W) SE Wagon Grp incl Dlx Luggage Rack, Rr Window Wiper/Washer and Cargo Area Cover ($295). (434) Sport Grp incl 14-inch Alum Wheels, Rr Spoiler, Tach, Bright Tip Exhaust, Rr Seats w/Integrated Headrest (SE sed only) ($495). Calif. Emission System ($170). Man Air Cond ($795). Integrated Child's Seat (SE wag only) ($135). Rr Window Defroster ($190). Elect AM/FM Stereo Radio w/Cass ($185). Elect AM/FM Stereo Radio w/Cass & Premium Sound ($255). Elect AM/FM Stereo Radio w/Cass & Premium Sound & CD Changer (SE sed only) ($515). Smoker's Pkg incl ashtray and cigarette lighter ($15). Driver's Door Remote Entry w/Panic Alarm ($135). Anti-lock Brakes ($400). Flr Mats F&R ($55). 14-inch Alum Wheels (SE only) ($265).

ESCORT ZX2 CONVENIENCE/APPEARANCE OPTIONS: Man Air Cond ($795). (50A) Comfort Grp incl Spd Control, Tilt Strg Col, Dual Map Lights and Dual Visor Mirrors (Hot Cpe only) ($345). (51S) Appearance Grp incl Leather-wrapped Strg Wheel, 14-inch Chrome Bolt-on Wheel Covers and Bright Tip Exhaust (Hot Cpe only) ($155). (41G) Sport Pkg incl 15-inch Alum Wheels, Foglamps, Spoiler, Bright Tip Exhaust and Upgraded Seats (Hot Cpe only) ($595). Driver's Door Remote Entry w/Panic Alarm (Cool Cpe only) ($135). (60A) Pwr Grp incl Pwr Locks, Pwr Windows and All-door Remote Entry w/Anti-theft (Hot Cpe only) ($395). Pwr Sliding Moonroof (Hot Cpe only) ($595). Rr Window Defroster ($190). Calif. Emission System ($170). Flr Mats F&R (Hot Cpe only) ($55). Elect AM/FM Stereo Radio w/Cass ($185). Elect AM/FM Stereo Radio w/Cass & Premium Sound ($255). Elect AM/FM Stereo Radio w/Cass & Premium Sound & CD Changer (Hot Cpe only) ($515). Smoker's Pkg incl ashtray and cigarette lighter ($15). 14-inch/five-spoke Alum Wheels ($265).

CONTOUR CONVENIENCE/APPEARANCE OPTIONS: (53C) SE Comfort Grp incl 10-Way Pwr Driver's Seat, Eight-spoke Alum Wheels, Leather-wrapped Strg Wheel, Foglights, Intermittent Wipers, Dual Illum Vanity Mirrors and Pwr Antenna (SE only) ($795). (53S) SE Sport Grp incl Duratec 2.5-liter V-6, P205/60TGR15 BSW Tires, 12-spoke Alum Wheels, Tach, Leather-wrapped Strg Wheel, Sport Flr Mats, Rr Spoiler, Intermittent Wipers, Foglights, Dual Illum Vanity Mirrors and Sport Cloth Bucket Seats (SE only) ($1000). Calif. Emission Syst ($170). Rr Window Defroster (stnd SE) ($190). Anti-lock Brakes (stnd SVT) ($500). 2.0-liter Four-Cylinder Gaseous Fuel Prep (LX and SE only) ($260). Remote Keyless Entry Syst (SE only) ($190). Carpeted Flr Mats F&R ($55). Pwr Moonroof (SE and SVT only) ($595). Leather Seats w/Split-Fold Rr Seat (SE only) ($895). 60/40 Split-Fold Rr Seat (SE only) ($205). 10-Way Pwr Driver's Seat (stnd SVT) ($350). Elect AM/FM Stereo Radio w/Cass & Premium Sound (SE only) ($135). Elect AM/FM Stereo Radio w/Premium Sound & CD Player: SE ($275); SVT ($140). Pwr Antenna (SE only) ($95). Integrated Child's Seat ($135). Smoker's Pkg incl ashtray and cigarette lighter ($15). 15-inch/Eight-spoke Alum Wheels (SE only) ($425). 15-inch Wheels w/Simulated Bolt-on Covers (SE only) ($135).

TAURUS CONVENIENCE/APPEARANCE OPTIONS: (60S) SE Sport Grp incl Duratec 3.0-liter V-6, Rr Spoiler and Chrome Wheel Covers (SE sed only) ($695). (P53) SE Comfort Grp incl Duratec 3.0-liter V-6, Pwr Driver's Seat, Elect Temp Control Air Cond, 12-spoke Alum Wheels, Leather-wrapped Strg Wheel, Pwr Antenna, Remote Entry Keypad w/Perimeter Anti-theft and Illum Pass Side Visor Mirror: SE sed ($1450); SE wag ($1285). (P53/60S) SE Comfort & Sport Grp incl same as P53 and 60S packages plus 12-spoke Chrome Wheels (SE sed only) ($2000). Calif. Emissions Syst ($170). Anti-lock Brakes (stnd SHO) ($600). Pwr Moonroof (stnd SHO) ($740). Daytime Running Lights ($40). Flr Mats F&R (stnd SHO) ($55). Light Grp incl Dual Courtesy Lights (stnd SHO) ($45). Pwr Dual Heated Mirrors (SE only) ($35). Pwr Door Locks (LX only) ($275). Remote Keyless Entry Syst w/Keyfobs (LX only) ($190). Elect AM/FM Stereo Radio w/Cass (LX only) ($185). CD Changer (SE only) ($350). MACH Audio Syst: SE sed ($400); SE wag ($320). Cloth Bucket Seats (SE only) ($105). Leather Bucket Seats (SE only) ($895). Pwr Driver's Seat (SE only) ($350). Dual Pwr Seats (SE only) ($350). Integrated Child's Seat (SE wag only) ($135). Wagon Grp incl Cargo Area Cover and Cargo Net (SE wag only) ($140). Rr Facing Third Seat (SE wag only) ($200). Heavy Duty Suspension (SE wag only) ($25). Conventional Spare Tire ($105). Five-spoke Alum Wheels (LX and SE only) ($315).

1998 Ford Contour SVT sedan. (OCW)

1999 Ford Escort SE four-door sedan. (FMC)

CROWN VICTORIA CONVENIENCE/APPEARANCE OPTIONS: (65C) Comfort Grp incl Elect Auto Temp Control Air Cond, 12-spoke Alum Wheels, Pwr Pass Seat and Leather-wrapped Strg Wheel (LX only) ($900). (65E) Comfort Grp Plus incl 65C plus Elect Instrumentation, Anti-lock Brakes w/Traction Control and Premium Audio Syst (LX only) ($2200). Calif. Emissions Syst ($170). Anti-lock Brakes w/Traction Control ($775). 41G Handling & Perf Pkg (LX only) incl Revised Springs/Shocks/Stabilizer Bar, P225/60TR16 BSW Touring Tires, 16-inch Cast Alum Wheels, Rr Air Suspension and Dual Exhaust (LX only) ($935). Remote Keyless Entry Syst (base only) ($240). Elect AM/FM Stereo Radio w/Cass (base only) ($185). Elect AM/FM Stereo Radio w/CD Player (LX only) ($140). Premium Audio Syst ($360). 6-Way Pwr Driver's Seat (base only) ($360). Leather Split-Bench Seat (LX only) ($735). Color-Keyed Flr Mats F&R ($55). Conventional Spare Tire ($120). P225/60SR16 WSW Tires ($80). P225/60VR16 WSW Tires (NGV only) ($170). Universal Garage Door Opener (LX only) ($115).

HISTORY: The four-door Taurus was selected as the model to replace the discontinued Thunderbird on the NASCAR circuit. This was the first time in NASCAR's history a production four-door automobile was allowed as an accepted body style.

1999 FORD

ESCORT — FOUR — The 1999 Escort had no major changes. Ford's entry-level car again combined style and fun in a small-size car. With the optional ZX2 Sport Group the Escort buyer received special wheels, special seats and a spoiler. For those who considered performance a priority, the ZX2 featured a 130-hp, 16-valve, double overhead cam Zetec engine and a sporty suspension. The wagon model increased the Escort's rear cargo area to 63.4 cu. ft. Standard equipment for the Escort LX included dual second-generation airbags, power-assisted front disc/rear drum brakes, side window demisters, the 2.0-liter split port induction (SPI 2000) four-cylinder engine, single exhaust with tip, flush Solar-Tinted windshield and backlight, semi-flush Solar-Tinted windows, a heater and defroster, a flow-through ventilation system with a four-speed blower, a soft "vinyl feel" dashboard with knee bolsters, an integrated climate control and audio control panel, a separate clock, a storage bin, Power Point with tethered covered cap, child safety rear door locks, left- and right-hand manual black exterior mirrors, driver and passenger visor mirrors, an AM/FM stereo with premium speakers, low-back cloth front seats, split-folding 60/40 rear seat with dual release pull tabs, a four-spoke steering wheel, power rack-and-pinion steering, a temperature gauge, P185/65R14 black sidewall tires, a five-speed manual transmission, a trip odometer, two-speed windshield wipers with intermittent feature and 14 x 5.5-in. semi styled steel wheels with full luxury bolt-through wheel covers. In addition to or in place of LX equipment, the Escort SE featured CFC-free manual temperature control air conditioning, a rear window defroster, dual black outside power mirrors, an AM/FM cassette stereo with premium speakers, keyless remote entry with perimeter anti-theft, and (on wagons only) a rear window wiper/washer. The Cool series coupe also included the 2.0-liter DOHC 16-valve Zetec four-cylinder engine, frameless door glass, low-back cloth front bucket seats with driver side memory recline, a tachometer, a temperature gauge, and a trip odometer. The Hot series coupe added CFC-free manual temperature control air conditioning, a rear window defroster, power mirrors, a stereo cassette system with premium speakers and a remote keyless entry system with panic alarm.

I.D. DATA: Ford's 17-symbol Vehicle Identification Number (VIN) was stamped on a metal tab fastened to the instrument panel, visible through the windshield. The first symbol indicates the nation of origin: 1=United States; 2=Canada; 3=Mexico. The second symbol indicates manufacturer: F=Ford Motor Co.; The third symbol indicates vehicle type: A=passenger car. The fourth symbol indicates type of restraint system: B=driver and passenger airbags and active belts (except Escort ZX2 coupe); F=driver and passenger airbags and active belts; K=driver and passenger airbags and active belts in all outboard positions; L=driver and passenger airbags and front passive belts, rear active belts. The fifth symbol indicates designation: P=Ford; T=Imported from outside North America or non-Ford car marketed by Ford in North America. The sixth and seventh symbols indicate body type: 10=Escort LX four-door sedan; 13=Escort SE four-door sedan; 15=Escort SE four-door station wagon; 52=Taurus LX four-door sedan; 53=Taurus SE two-valve four-door sedan; 54=Taurus SE four-valve four-door sedan; 58=Taurus SE four-door station wagon; 65=Contour LX four-door sedan; 67=Contour SE four-door sedan; 68=Contour SVT four-door sedan; 71=Crown Vicrtoria Police Interceptor four-door sedan; 72=Crown Victoria "S" (Fleet) four-door sedan; 73=Crown Victoria four-door sedan; 74=Crown Victoria LX four-door sedan. The eighth symbol indicates engine: [Escort] P=2.0-liter I-4 with EFI; [Taurus] S=3.0-liter DOHC V-6 with EFI; U=3.0-liter V-6 with EFI; 2=flexible fuel 3.0-liter V-6 with EFI. [Contour] G=2.5-liter DOHC V-6 with EFI; L=2.5-liter DOHC V-6 with EFI; Z=2.0-liter DOHC I-4 with EFI; 3=2.0-liter DOHC I-4 with EFI. [Crown Victoria] W=4.6-liter SOHC V-8 with EFI (Romeo engine plant). The ninth symbol is a check digit. The 10th symbol indicates model year: Y=2000. The 11th symbol indicates assembly plant: A=Hapeville (Atlanta), Ga.; F=Dearborn, Mich.; G=Chicago, Ill.; K=Claycomo (Kansas City), Mo.; M=Cuautitlan, Mexico; R=Hermosillo, Mexico; W=Wayne, Mich.; X=Talbotville (St. Thomas), Ontario, Canada. The last six symbols are the sequential production number starting at 100001 at each factory.

Model No.	Body/ Style No.	Body Type & Seating	Factory Price	Shipping Weight	Prod. Total
ESCORT LX (FOUR)					
P	10	4d Sedan-5P	11,870	2,468	Note1
ESCORT SE (FOUR)					
P	13	4d Sedan-5P	13,350	2,468	Note 1
P	15	4d Wagon-5P	14,550	2,531	Note 2
ESCORT ZX2 COOL SERIES (FOUR)					
P	11/41V	2d Coupe-5P	12,075	2,478	Note 3

1999 Ford Escort ZX2 Hot Series two-door coupe. (FMC)

1999 Ford Contour SE Sport Coupe four-door sedan. (FMC)

ESCORT ZX2 HOT SERIES (FOUR)

P	11	2d Coupe-5P	13,755	2,478	Note 3

Note 1: Model year production in the U.S., Canada and Mexico for the U.S. market of four-door sedans was 170,715.

Note 2: Model year production in the U.S., Canada and Mexico for the U.S. market of four-door wagons was 22,621.

Note 3: Model year production in the U.S., Canada and Mexico for the U.S. market of two-door coupes was 94,175.

Note 4: Total Escort model year production in the U.S., Canada and Mexico for the U.S. market was 287,511.

CONTOUR — FOUR/CONTOUR SVT — V-6 — In its 1999 sales catalog, Ford noted that the Contour had been named an "All Star" by Automobile Magazine for four years in a row. The base and GL models were dropped from the lineup. Contour offerings now consisted of an LX or SE four-door sedan. If neither of those models were "zippy" enough, a buyer could opt for the limited edition Contour SVT four-door sports sedan. Ford's Special Vehicle Team (SVT) announced it would build 5,000 Contour SVT sports sedans per year, each fitted with an exclusive 195-hp version of the Duratec DOHC 2.5-liter V-6 with 10.0:1 compression ratio and 2.25-in. stainless steel dual exhaust and coupled to a MTX-75 five-speed manual transaxle. Announced top speed of the SVT sports sedan was 143 mph. A European front suspension design was adopted for improved ride and handling. The front seats were redesigned to give more rear seat foot and leg room. Second generation airbags, redesigned front brakes and a larger fuel tank, which were made standard late in 1998, continued in use on the 1999 models. Standard equipment on the Contour LX included dual second generation airbags, air conditioning, a fixed antenna mounted on the rear quarter panel, power front disc and rear drum brakes, an electric digital clock, childproof rear door locks, the 2.0-liter DOHC Zetec 16-valve I-4, semi flush exterior glass with Solar-Tint, a heater and defroster with a four-speed blower control, a soft touch dashboard with knee bolsters and four positive shutoff registers, a backlit cluster with 130-mph speedometer, analog gauges (including a trip odometer, a fuel gauge, a high-beam warning light, a coolant temperature gauge and a low-oil-pressure light, turn signal indicator lights, a handbrake-on warning light, a catalyst malfunction light and a seat belt reminder light), left- and right-hand power body-color exterior mirrors, a day/night rearview mirror, an AM/FM stereo, individual manual two-way adjustable front bucket seats with reclining seat backs and cloth trim and a driver's side armrest attached to the seat, a tilt steering column, a soft touch steering wheel with center horn control, power rack-and-pinion steering, a driver's side covered visor mirror and passenger side uncovered visor mirror, P185/70R14S black sidewall tires, a five-speed manual transmission with overdrive, single-speed windshield wipers with intermittent feature and fluidic washers and 14-in. wheel covers with full bolt-on appearance. In addition to or in place of LX equipment, the Contour SE featured a rear window defroster, power door locks, an AM/FM stereo radio with cassette player, speed control, power windows with express-down driver's window, rear window lockout, illuminated switches on all doors and a tachometer. In addition to or in place of LX equipment, the Contour SVT featured a power antenna mounted on the rear quarter panel, power four-wheel disc brakes with Dacromat finished rotors and unique front calipers, an antilock braking system, the 2.5-liter DOHC high-output Duratec 24-valve V-6 with passive anti-theft system (PATS), a unique Quasi-Dual exhaust system with low back pressure mufflers, a unique instrument cluster with a white-faced 160-mph speedometer, an electronic AM/FM stereo radio with cassette player and premium sound system, unique sport front seats with special bolstering and perforated leather seating areas and a 10-way power driver's seat, a split-folding 60/40 rear seat with simulated bucket design and integral headrests, armrest and perforated leather seating surfaces, carpeted rear seat backs, a leather-wrapped steering wheel with center horn control, cloth-covered sun visors, P215/50R16Z directional-rated tires, variable intermittent windshield wipers with fluidic washers and five-spoke 16-in. cast-aluminum wheels.

Model No.	Body/ Style No.	Body Type & Seating	Factory Price	Shipping Weight	Prod. Total
CONTOUR LX (FOUR)					
P	65	4d Sedan-5P	14,995	2,744	Note 5
CONTOUR LX (V-6)					
P	65	4d Sedan-5P	15,590	—	Note 5
CONTOUR SE (FOUR)					
P	66	4d Sedan-5P	16,490	2,744	Note 5
CONTOUR SE (V-6)					
P	66	4d Sedan-5P	16,890	—	Note 5
CONTOUR SVT (V-6)					
P	68	4d Sports Sed-5P	22,940	3,068	Note 5

Note 5: Model year production in the U.S., Canada and Mexico for the U.S. market of four-door sedans was 139,380.

Note 6: Approximately 5,000 Contour SVT Sports Sedans were included in the total given in Note 5.

TAURUS — V-6/V-8 — For 1999, five-passenger seating became standard in the Taurus, but six-passenger seating was a no-charge option. The suspension was revised for a smoother ride and the 16-in. wheels used on the SHO model were made available at extra cost on LX and SE models. Standard equipment on the Taurus LX included dual second generation airbags, CFC-free manual temperature control air conditioning, a fixed whip antenna mounted on the rear quarter panel, power front disc/rear drum brakes, an electric digital clock with dimming feature, a rear window defroster and defogger, the 3.0-liter two-valve six-cylinder engine, complete Solar-Tinted glass, a backlit instrument panel cluster with positive shut-off climate control registers, a full-width windshield defroster and side window demisters, a dual grain instrument panel finish for reduced glare, a temperature gauge, a fuel gauge, a 110-mph speedometer (120-mph with Duratec V-6 or 150-mph in SHO), a warning light for low brake, a "fluids-low" alert light, a million mile odometer, a tachometer, an integrated control panel (with radio and climate controls, rear defroster control and clock controls), rear door child safety locks, black exterior mirrors, an interior day/night mirror, an electronic AM/FM stereo radio, five-passenger seating with dual recliners, front arm rests and front seat map pockets, two-way headrests, a mini console, a fixed rear seat back, a tilt steering column, a color-keyed four-spoke soft feel steering wheel with center horn engagement, power rack-and-pinion steering with variable assist, cloth-covered sun visors with covered vanity mirrors, P205/65R15 all-season tires, an electronic four-speed automatic transmission with overdrive, two-speed intermittent windshield wipers, full wheel covers, illuminated power side windows with lockout switch and driver's side express down and accessory delay. In addition to or in place of standard LX equipment, the Taurus SE featured remote keyless entry, illuminated door controls for power accessories, colored-keyed remote-control outside mirrors (heated on the SHO model), an electronic AM/FM stereo with full logic stereo cassette player and four speakers and a 60/40 split-folding rear seat. In addition, the SE wagon only featured a power antenna, four-wheel disc brakes, a unique liftgate latch and a rear washer/wiper. In addition to or in place of SE equipment, the Taurus SHO Sport Sedan featured electronic temperature control air conditioning, four-wheel disc brakes, the 3.4-liter four-valve V-8, a unique dual exhaust system with oval-styled outlets, a MACH audio system with six speakers, a six-way power leather driver's sport bucket seat with adjustable lumbar support, front seat map pockets, two-way headrests, a front console, a SecuriLock™ passive anti-theft system with coded key, a leather-wrapped four-spoke steering wheel with center horn engagement, precision power rack-and-pinion steering with ZF variable assist, driver and passenger sun visors with illuminated visor mirrors, P225/55ZR16 all-season low-profile sport handling tires, an automatic transmission with overdrive lockout switch on the shifter, aerodynamic Autobahn windshield wipers and chromed cast five-spoke aluminum wheels.

Model No.	Body/ Style No.	Body Type & Seating	Factory Price	Shipping Weight	Prod. Total
TAURUS LX (V-6)					
P	52	4d Sedan-6P	17,995	3,329	Note 7
TAURUS SE (V-6)					
P	53	4d Sedan-6P	18,995	3,329	Note 7
P	58	4d Wagon-6P	19,995	3,480	Note 8
TAURUS SE COMFORT (V-6)					
P	53	4d Sedan-6P	20,495	3,353	Note 7
P	58	4d Wagon-6P	21,495	3,480	Note 8
TAURUS SHO (V-8)					
P	54	4d Sedan-6P	29,550	3,326	Note 7

Note 7: Model year production in the U.S., Canada and Mexico for the U.S. market of four-door sedans was 385,227.

1999 Ford Taurus SE four-door Sport sedan. (FMC)

Note 8: Model year production in the U.S., Canada and Mexico for the U.S. market of four-door wagons was 38,129.

Note 9: Total Taurus model year production in the U.S., Canada and Mexico for the U.S. market was 423,356.

CROWN VICTORIA — V-8 — The 1999 Crown Victorias got antilock brakes as standard equipment and traction control became a free-standing option. The Crown Victoria was also now made available as a dedicated natural gas-fueled vehicle. Standard equipment on the base Crown Victoria included dual airbags, manual air conditioning with positive shut-off registers, a radio antenna hidden in the rear window defroster, the SecuriLock™ passive anti-theft system, a brake/shift interlock, power four-wheel disc antilock brakes, rear seat child safety latches, an electric digital clock with dimming feature, a rear window defroster, the 4.6-liter OHC sequential fuel-injected V-8, a stainless steel exhaust system, a gauge cluster with analog gauges (voltmeter, oil pressure, water temperature and fuel), full Solar-Tinted glass, woodgrain instrument panel appliqués, side window demisters, power door locks, dual remote-control fold-away power exterior mirrors with color-keyed finish, a day/night inside rearview mirror, an electronic AM/FM stereo with cassette and door-mounted speakers, a cloth-trimmed split bench front seat with center fold-down armrest and reclining seatbacks (two-way manual adjusting type with 10-in. track travel), a sound insulation package, speed control, a color-keyed steering wheel with center horn blow, speed sensitive variable-assist power steering (not available in cars with the natural gas engine), cloth-covered sun visors with retention clips, a tilt steering column with stalk-mounted controls, P225/60SR16 all-season black sidewall tires, an ECT automatic transmission with overdrive lockout, a trip odometer, dual-jet interval windshield wipers, deluxe wheel covers, HSLA 16 x 7-in. wheel rims and power windows with driver side ex-press down. In addition to or in place of base Crown Victoria equip-ment, the LX featured remote keyless entry (except with natural gas engine), a split bench seat with fold-down center armrest trimmed in Luxury cloth (with power lumbar adjustment and six-way power ad-justment on the driver's side, plus a power back recliner) and chrome-plated, locking cross-spoke wheel covers.

Model No.	Body/ Style No.	Body Type & Seating	Factory Price	Shipping Weight	Prod. Total
CROWN VICTORIA (Gas V-4)					
P	73	4d Sedan-5P	22,510	3,917	Note 10
CROWN VICTORIA LX (Gas V-8)					
P	74	4d Sedan-5P	24,530	3,917	Note 10
CROWN VICTORIA (Natural V-8)					
P	73	4d Sedan-5P	28,675	—	Note 10
CROWN VICTORIA LX (Natural V-8)					
P	74	4d Sedan-5P	30,695	—	Note 10

Note 10: Model year production in the U.S., Canada and Mexico for the U.S. market of four-door sedans was 118,882.

ESCORT ENGINES

ENGINE [Base LX/SE]: Inline. Overhead cam. Four-cylinder. Cast-iron block and aluminum head. Displacement: 122 cid (2.0 liters). Bore & stroke: 3.33 x 3.46 in. Compression ratio: 9.2:1. Brake horsepower: 110 at 5000 rpm. Torque: 125 lbs.-ft. at 3750 rpm. Split Port induction.

ENGINE [Base ZX2]: Inline. Double overhead cam. Four-cylinder. Cast-iron block and aluminum head. Displacement: 121 cid (2.0 liters). Bore & stroke: 3.34 x 3.46 in. Compression ratio: 9.6:1. Brake horse-power: 130 at 5750 rpm. Torque: 127 lbs.-ft. at 4250 rpm. Sequential fuel injection.

CONTOUR ENGINES

ENGINE [Base LX/SE]: Inline. Double overhead cam. Four-cylinder. Cast-iron block and aluminum head. Displacement: 121 cid (2.0 liters). Bore & stroke: 3.34 x 3.46 in. Compression ratio: 9.6:1. Brake horse-power: 125 at 5500 rpm. Torque: 130 lbs.-ft. at 4000 rpm. Sequential fuel injection.

ENGINE [Base SVT]: 60-degree double overhead cam V-6. Aluminum block and head. Displacement: 155 cid (2.5 liters). Bore & stroke: 3.24 x 3.13 in. Compression ratio: 10.0:1. Brake horsepower: 200 at 6625 rpm. Torque: 165 lbs.-ft. at 5625 rpm. Sequential fuel injection.

ENGINE [Optional LX/SE]: Modular, double overhead cam V-6. Alu-minum block and head. Displacement: 155 cid (2.5 liters). Bore & stroke: 3.24 x 3.13 in. Compression ratio: 9.7:1. Brake horsepower: 170 at 6250 rpm. Torque: 165 lbs.-ft. at 4250 rpm. Sequential fuel injection.

TAURUS ENGINES

ENGINE [Base LX/SE]: Overhead valve V-6. Cast-iron block and head. Displacement: 182 cid (3.0 liters). Bore & stroke: 3.50 x 3.15 in. Compression ratio: 9.3:1. Brake horsepower: 145 at 5250 rpm. Torque: 170 lbs.-ft. at 3250 rpm. Sequential fuel injection.

ENGINE [Optional LX/SE]: Double overhead cam V-6. Aluminum block and head. Displacement: 182 cid (3.0 liters). Bore & stroke: 3.50 x 3.15 in. Compression ratio: 10.0:1. Brake horsepower: 200 at 5750 rpm. Torque: 200 lbs.-ft. at 4500 rpm. Sequential fuel injection.

ENGINE [Optional Ethanol V-6 LX/SE]: Double overhead cam flexi-ble-fuel V-6. Aluminum block and head. Displacement: 182 cid (3.0 liters). Bore & stroke: 3.50 x 3.15 in. Compression ratio: 10.0:1. Brake horsepower: 200 at 5750 rpm. Torque: 200 lbs.-ft. at 4500 rpm. ETH.

ENGINE [Base SHO]: 60-degree, double overhead cam V-8. Aluminum block and head. Displacement: 207 cid (3.4 liters). Bore & stroke: 3.2 x 3.1 in. Compression ratio: 9.8:1. Brake horsepower: 235 at 6100 rpm. Torque: 230 lbs.-ft. at 4800 rpm. Sequential fuel injection.

CROWN VICTORIA ENGINE

ENGINE [Base]: Modular, overhead valve V-8. Displacement: 281 cid (4.6 liters). Bore & stroke: 3.60 x 3.60. Compression ratio: 9.0:1. Brake horsepower: 190 at 4250 rpm. Torque: 265 lbs.-ft. at 3200 rpm. Se-quential fuel injection.

1999 Ford Crown Victoria LX four-door sedan. (FMC)

1999 Ford Escort SE four-door wagon. (FMC)

1999 Ford Contour SE four-door sedan. (FMC)

ESCORT CHASSIS: Wheelbase: (all) 98.4 in. Overall length: (LX/SE sedan) 174.7 in.; (SE wagon) 172.7 in.; (ZX2 coupe) 175.2 in. Overall width: (LX/SE sedan) 67 in.; (SE wagon) 67 in.; (ZX2 coupe) 67.4 in. Overall height: (LX/SE sedan) 53.3 in.; (LX/SE wagon) 53.9 in.; (ZX2 coupe) 52.3 in. Front tread: (all) 56.5 in. Rear tread: (all) 56.5 in.

CONTOUR CHASSIS: Wheelbase: (all) 106.5 in.; Overall length: (all) 184.6 in. Overall width: (all) 69.1 in.; Overall height: (all) 54.4 in. Front tread: (all) 59.2 in. Rear tread: (all) 58.5 in.

TAURUS CHASSIS: Wheelbase: (all) 108.5 in. Overall length: (sedan) 197.5 in.; (wagon) 199.6 in. Overall width: (all) 73 in. Overall height: (sedan) 55.1 in.; (wagon) 57.6 in. Front tread: 61.6 in. Rear tread: 61.4 in.

CROWN VICTORIA CHASSIS: Wheelbase: (all) 114.7 in. Overall length: (all) 212 in. Overall width: (all) 78.2 in. Overall height: (all) 56.8 in. Front tread: (all) 62.8 in. Rear tread: (all) 63.3 in.

ESCORT TECHNICAL: Standard transmission: five-speed manual transaxle. Drive axle: front. Steering: rack-and-pinion. Front suspension: independent MacPherson strut with strut-mounted coil springs. Rear suspension: independent, Quadra-link with stabilizer bar. Brakes: front disc, rear drum (power assisted). Body construction: unibody. Fuel tank: 12.7 gallons.

CONTOUR TECHNICAL: Standard transmission: five-speed manual transaxle. Drive axle: front. Steering: rack-and-pinion. Front suspension: (LX/SE) independent, subframe rubber mounted MacPherson strut with strut-mounted coil springs, lower control A-arms and cast steering knuckles; (SVT) MacPherson struts, lower A-arms, coil springs, tube shock dampers and stabilizer bar. Rear suspension: (LX/SE) independent, Quadra-link strut with coil spring on shock strut, mounted to rigid subframe; (SVT) independent Quadra-link design, coil springs, tube shock dampers and stabilizer bar. Brakes: front disc, rear drum (power assisted), except SVT has four-wheel discs. Body construction: unibody. Fuel tank: 14.5 gallons.

TAURUS TECHNICAL: Standard transmission: Four-speed overdrive automatic. Drive axle: front. Steering: rack-and-pinion. Front suspension: independent MacPherson strut front drive with strut-mounted coil springs, stabilizer bar, lower control arm and cast aluminum knuckle with integral ball joint. Rear suspension: (sedan) independent Quadra-link with coil spring on shock strut, stabilizer bar, tension strut, parallel suspension arms and two-piece cast spindle with forged stem; (wagon) independent short/long arm with spring on lower control arm, stabilizer bar, tension strut and cast spindle with pressed-in forged stem and integrated ball joints. Brakes: front disc, rear drum (power assisted) except Taurus SE wagon and Taurus SHO have four-wheel discs. Body construction: unibody. Fuel tank: 16.0 gallons.

1999 Ford Taurus SE four-door wagon. (FMC)

1999 Ford Crown Victoria four-door sedan. (FMC)

CROWN VICTORIA TECHNICAL: Standard transmission: four-speed overdrive automatic. Drive axle: rear. Steering: re-circulating ball. Front suspension: independent short/long arm with ball joints, coil springs and stabilizer bar. Rear suspension: Watt's linkage. Brakes: four-wheel disc. Body construction: separate body and frame. Fuel tank: 20.0 gallons.

ESCORT OPTIONS: 572 air conditioning, standard in SE ($795). 552 antilock braking system ($400). 57Q rear window defroster, standard in SE ($190). 422 California emissions (no cost). 12Y front and rear floor mats ($55). 41H engine block heater ($20). 58H AM/FM stereo with cassette ($185). 586 ETR AM/FM stereo cassette with premium sound, for ZX2 Hot coupe only ($95). 919 AM/FM stereo cassette with premium sound and six disc CD changer ($295). 144 remote keyless entry ($165). 50A SE comfort group, includes speed control, tilt steering and dual map lights, SE only ($345). 60A SE power group, includes power locks and power windows ($345). J unique sport bucket seats (no cost). 63B smoker's package ($15). 434 Sport package includes 14-in. aluminum wheels, rear deck lid spoiler, bright exhaust pipe tips, unique seats with rear integrated headrests, leather-wrapped steering wheel and Sport badging, SE sedan only ($495). 44T four-speed overdrive automatic transmission ($815). 64P 14-in. aluminum wheels ($265). 50A ZX2 Hot coupe series power group, includes power windows with one-touch down feature on driver's side and power door locks ($345). 60A ZX2 Hot coupe series Sport group includes rear deck lid spoiler, bright exhaust tips, unique seats with rear headrests with ZX2 script, 15-in. aluminum wheels, Sport badging and leather-wrapped steering wheel ($595). 13B power sliding moonroof for Hot coupe only ($595). 13K rear deck lid spoiler for coupes, requires 41G if ordered for Hot coupe ($195). 44T four-speed overdrive transmission with 16-valve Zetec 2.0-liter DOHC engine, ZX2 only ($815). 64Z aluminum wheels for Hot coupe only ($265). 53V Wheels and Tunes package, includes 14-in. aluminum wheels, 58H radio, 12Y floor mats and 13K spoiler for ZX2, not available on Hot coupe ($450).

CONTOUR OPTIONS: 153 front license plate bracket (no cost). 552 antilock braking system, standard on SVT ($500). 57Q rear window defroster ($190). 422 California emissions system (no cost). 428 high-altitude emissions system (no cost). 99Z 2.0-liter four-cylinder gaseous fuel preparation package, includes four-wheel disc brakes and P195/65R14 tires, requires automatic transmission ($260). 99L 2.5-liter Duratec V-6, includes tachometer, P195/65R15 black sidewall performance tires, four-wheel antilock brakes and SecuriLock anti-theft system, requires 5S on SE only ($70 credit). 41H engine block heater ($20). 12Y floor mats, front and rear ($55). 13B moonroof SE ($595; no charge SVT). 58P premium sound system with ETR AM/FM stereo, cassette and amplifier ($135). 585 ETR AM/FM stereo with CD player and premium sound, in SE ($275; no charge in SVT). 58H AM/FM stereo cassette in LX only, standard in SE ($185). 91H power antenna ($95). 143 remote keyless entry, includes illuminated entry system ($190). 53C SE Comfort group, includes power driver's seat, 15-in. 12-spoke aluminum wheels, leather-wrapped steering wheel, leather shift knob, fog lamps, variable interval windshield wipers, illuminated visor mirror and power antenna ($795). 53S Sport group, included 2.5-liter V-6, five-speed manual transmission, 15-in. eight-spoke aluminum wheels, a tachometer, a leather-wrapped steering wheel, a leather-wrapped shift knob, sport floor mats, a rear deck lid spoiler, body cladding, variable fixed interval windshield wipers, an illuminated vanity mirror, fog lamps, Sport cloth bucket seats and Sport badging ($1,000). 28 leather seating surfaces ($895). 219 60/40 split folding rear seat in SE ($205). 21A six-way power driver's seat, in SE ($350). 63B smoker's package ($15). 525 speed control in LX ($215). 553 traction control, requires 2.5-liter engine and antilock brakes ($175). 44T ECT automatic transmission, in LX and SE ($815). 64X 15-in. eight-spoke cast-aluminum wheels, includes P205/60R15 black sidewall tires, on SE ($425).

TAURUS OPTIONS: 153 front license plate bracket (no cost). 552 antilock braking system, standard on SHO ($600). 902 power door locks in LX ($275). 422 California emissions system (no cost). 428 high-altitude emissions system (no cost). 992 3.0-liter flexible fuel (ethanol) V-6 on LX/SE with column shift only ($1,165). 41H engine block heater ($35). 943 light group ($45). 12Y floor mats, front and rear

($55). 54P heated exterior mirrors, standard on SHO ($35). 13B power moonroof, includes unique map lamps in overhead console ($740). 58H ETR AM/FM stereo, cassette with four speakers ($185). 916 Ford Mach audio system with six speakers in SE ($320; no charge in SHO). 919 trunk-mounted six-disc CD changer ($350). 143 remote keyless entry ($190). 60E SE Comfort group, includes 3.0-liter four, overdrive automatic transmission, power driver's seat with adjustable lumbar support, electronic temperature control air conditioning, 12-spoke bright cast aluminum wheels, leather-wrapped steering wheel, automatic headlamps, remote entry with keypad and perimeter anti-theft, light group, illuminated visor mirrors, five-passenger seating, floor console and floor shift ($1,000 with sport group; $1,500 without Sport group). 60S SE Sport group includes 3.0-liter four-valve V-6, automatic overdrive transmission, rear deck lid spoiler, five-spoke aluminum wheels, five-passenger seating, floor console and floor shift ($750). 186 five-passenger seating with center seating console, column shift and secondary power point ($105). 184 six-passenger seating with center seating console, column shift and secondary power point (no cost). M leather bucket seats, requires 21A power seat ($895). 21A power driver's seat with power lumbar adjustment in SE ($395). 21J dual power seats in SE, requires 60E SE Comfort package ($350). 214 rear facing vinyl third seat in wagon ($200). 216 integrated rear child seat, SE wagon only ($135). 525 speed control ($215). 508 conventional spare tire ($125). 96W wagon group, includes cargo net and cargo area cover, SE wagon only ($140). 64C five-spoke aluminum wheels, includes locking lug nut package, LX/SE only ($395). 649 chrome 12-spoke wheels, includes locking lug nut kit (no cost). 641 16-in. bright cast-aluminum five-spoke wheels, includes P225/55ZR16 all-season low-profile tires ($580).

CROWN VICTORIA OPTIONS: 153 front license plate bracket (no cost) 65C LX Comfort group, includes electronic automatic temperature control air conditioning, 12-spoke aluminum wheels, power passenger seat with power lumbar and recliners, auto dim mirror with compass and leather-wrapped steering wheel ($900). 65E LX Comfort Plus group, includes Comfort group plus electronic instrumentation, leather trim seats and premium sound system ($2,150). 422 California emissions (no cost). 999 4.6-liter natural gas engine, includes engine compression light and P225/60VR16 tires, but deletes standard auto headlamp system and SecuriLock anti-theft system, and remote keyless entry on LX ($6,165). 41G Handling and Performance package, includes revised springs, shocks and stabilizer bar, P225/60TR16 black sidewall touring tires, 16-in. cast-aluminum wheels, rear air suspension, dual exhausts with 2154-hp/275-ft.-lbs. rating and 3.27:1 axle ($615-$935 depending upon other options ordered). 12H front color-keyed carpeting ($30). 12Q rear color-keyed carpeting ($25). 585 single CD player replacing cassette ($140). 919 trunk-mounted six-disc CD changer ($350). 586 premium sound system ($360). 144 remote keyless entry ($240). L leather seating surfaces on split bench seat ($735). 21A six-way power driver's seat, includes power lumbar and recliner ($360). 508 conventional spare tire ($120). T2A P225/60R16 white sidewall tires ($80 above regular tires). T23 P225/60VR15 white sidewall tires, requires natural gas engine (no cost). 553 traction control ($175). 175 universal garage door opener ($115).

HISTORY: Jack Nasser, a 30-year FoMoCo veteran and former president of Ford Automotive Operations took over as corporate president and chief executive officer on Jan. 1, 1999. At the time it was announced that he would be working as a team with 41-year-old William Clay Ford, Jr., who was named non-executive chairman. It was predicted that Nasser would run day-to-day operations of the company for the next 14 years, although things turned out differently. Shortly before this edition of the Standard Catalog of Ford 1903-2003 went to press, Nasser was fired by Mr. Ford. In any case, Ford's outlook in 1999 was rosy, with $14.9 billion of cash in the bank and plans to acquire a number of automakers to expand the company's line of vehicles. Rumors began to circulate that Ford was poised to buy Sweden's Volvo car operations in March of 1999. The purchase did take place and cost Ford $6.45 billion. Nasser envisioned Volvo and other brands as part of a new Premier Automotive Group within the Ford family. He also hooked up with Microsoft's MSN Carpoint service, teamed with Priceline.com to test market a name-your-price car-buying plan in Florida and opened a plant in Norway to build a two-passenger thermoplastic vehicle named the "Th!nk." Meanwhile, in racing history, Ford made additional news when the four-door Taurus was selected as the model to replace the discontinued Thunderbird on the NASCAR stock car circuit. This was the first time in NASCAR's history that a production four-door automobile was approved as an accepted body style for modification into a racing car.

2000 FORD

FOCUS — FOUR — The Focus was introduced during 2000 as an all-new small car intended to replace the Escort and, eventually, the Contour. It was available in three body styles: a three-door hatchback

coupe, a four-door sedan and a four-door wagon. Standard equipment on the ZX3 hatchback included a 2.0-liter DOHC inline four-cylinder engine, a five-speed manual transmission, P195/60R15 tires, a spacesaver spare tire, a steel spare wheel, four-wheel disc brakes, front and rear stabilizer bars, front seat belt pre-tensioners, child seat anchors, an emergency release in the trunk, two front headrests, a remote vehicle anti-theft system, front fog lights, intermittent windshield wipers, a rear window wiper and defogger, front bucket seats, premium cloth upholstery, a height-adjustable driver's seat, a split bench rear seat with split-folding back, rear seat heat ducts, an AM/FM stereo and four speakers, power steering, remote control dual outside mirrors, front and rear cupholders, front door pockets, a 12-volt power outlet, a front storage console, dual visor-vanity mirrors, a leather-wrapped steering wheel, alloy shift knob trim, front and rear floor mats, a tachometer, a clock and a low-fuel indicator. In addition to or instead of ZX3 equipment, the LX sedan featured a four-cylinder SOHC engine, P185/65R14 tires, full wheel covers, a front stabilizer bar only, rear door child safety locks and an AM/FM cassette stereo. In addition to or in place of LX sedan equipment, the SE sedan featured P195/60R15 tires, variable intermittent wipers, remote power door locks, power windows with one touch down driver's window, power outside rearview mirrors, an AM/FM CD stereo and a multi-CD player located in the dash. In addition to or in place of ZX3 hatchback equipment, the SE wagon featured a four-speed automatic transmission, rear door child safety locks, variable intermittent wipers, a roof rack, remote power door locks, one-touch power windows, power mirrors and air conditioning. In addition to or instead of ZX3 hatchback equipment, the Focus ZTS four-door sedan featured P205/50R16 tires, antilock brakes, rear door child safety locks, variable intermittent wipers, a driver's seat with adjustable lumbar support, remote power door locks, one-touch power windows, power mirrors, cruise control, a tilt/telescope steering column, air conditioning, front reading lights, simulated wood dash trim and simulated wood door trim.

I.D. DATA: Ford's 17-symbol Vehicle Identification Number (VIN) was stamped on a metal tab fastened to the instrument panel, visible through the windshield. The first symbol indicates the nation of origin: 1=United States; 2=Canada; 3=Mexico. The second symbol indicates manufacturer: F=Ford Motor Co.; The third symbol indicates vehicle type: A=passenger car. The fourth symbol indicates type of restraint system: B=driver and passenger airbags and active belts (except Escort ZX2 coupe); F=driver and passenger airbags and active belts; K= driver and passenger airbags and active belts in all outboard positions. The fifth symbol indicates designation: P=Ford; T=Imported from outside North America or non-Ford car marketed by Ford in North America. The sixth and seventh symbols indicate body type: 13=Escort LX four-door sedan; 30=Focus ECO three-door coupe; 31=Focus ZX3 three-door coupe; 33=Focus LX four-door sedan; 34=Focus SE four-door sedan; 36=Focus SE four-door station wagon; 38=Focus ZTS four-door sedan; 52=Taurus LX four-door sedan; 53=Taurus SE two-valve four-door sedan; 54=Taurus SE four-valve four-door sedan; 55=Taurus SE SVG four-door sedan; 56=Taurus SE four-door Comfort sedan; 58=Taurus SE four-door station wagon; 59=Taurus SE four-door Comfort station wagon; 66=Contour SE four-door sedan; 68=Contour SVT four-door sedan; 71=Crown Victoria Police Interceptor four-door sedan; 72=Crown Victoria "S" (Fleet) four-door sedan; 73=Crown Victoria four-door sedan; 74=Crown Victoria LX four-door sedan. The eighth symbol indicates engine: [Escort] P=2.0-liter I-4 with EF/SPI; [Taurus] S=3.0-liter DOHC V-6 with EFI; U=3.0-liter V-6 with EFI; 2=flexible fuel 3.0-liter V-6 with EFI. [Contour] G=2.5-liter DOHC V-6 with EFI; L=2.5-liter DOHC V-6 with EFI; Z=2.0-liter DOHC I-4 with EFI; 3=2.0-liter DOHC I-4 with EFI. [Crown Victoria] W=4.6-liter SOHC V-8 with EFI (Romeo engine plant). The ninth symbol is a check digit. The 10th symbol indicates model year: Y=2000. The 11th symbol indicates assembly plant: A=Hapeville (Atlanta), Ga.; F=Dearborn, Mich.; G=Chicago, Ill.; K=Claycomo (Kansas City), Mo.; M=Cuautitlan Mexico; R=Hermosillo Mexico; W=Wayne, Mich.; X=Talbotville (St. Thomas), Ontario Canada. The last six symbols are the sequential production number starting at 100001 at each factory.

2000 Ford Focus four-door sedan. (FMC)

2000 Ford Escort ZX2 two-door coupe. (FMC)

Model No.	Body/ Style No.	Body Type & Seating	Factory Price	Shipping Weight	Prod. Total
FOCUS ZX3 (FOUR)					
P	31	3d Hatchback-5P	12,280	2,551	—
FOCUS LX (FOUR)					
P	33	4d Sedan-5P	12,540	2,564	—
FOCUS SE (FOUR)					
P	34	4d Sedan-5P	13,980	2,564	—
P	36	4d Wagon-5P	15,795	2,717	—
FOCUS ZTS (FOUR)					
P	38	4d Sedan-5P	15,580	2,564	—

ESCORT — FOUR — The 2000 Escort series had no major changes, except that the station wagon was dropped. Standard equipment for the Escort SE included dual second-generation airbags, power-assisted front disc/rear drum brakes, side window demisters, a rear window defroster, the 2.0-liter split port induction (SPI 2000) four-cylinder engine, single exhaust with tip, flush Solar-Tinted windshield and backlight, semi-flush Solar-Tinted windows, a heater and defroster, CFC-free manual temperature control air conditioning, a soft "vinyl feel" dashboard with knee bolsters, an integrated climate control and audio control panel, a separate clock, a storage bin, Power Point with tethered covered cap, child safety rear door locks, dual black outside power mirrors, driver and passenger visor mirrors, an AM/FM cassette stereo with premium speakers, keyless remote entry with perimeter anti-theft, low-back cloth front seats, split-folding 60/40 rear seat with dual release pull tabs, a four-spoke steering wheel, power rack-and-pinion steering, a temperature gauge, P185/65R14 black sidewall tires, a five-speed manual transmission, a trip odometer, two-speed windshield wipers with intermittent feature and 14 x 5.5-in. semi styled steel wheels with full luxury bolt-through wheel covers. The ZX2 coupe also included the 2.0-liter DOHC 16-valve Zetec four-cylinder engine, frameless door glass, low-back cloth front bucket seats with driver side memory recline, a tachometer, a temperature gauge, an AM/FM stereo cassette, power mirrors, a rear window defroster, a rear spoiler and a trip odometer. A performance-oriented S/R package was optional on the Escort ZX2 and the Sport optioned version now featured a 60/40 split-folding seatback, a passive anti-theft system and remote keyless entry, but leather seats were no longer available.

Model No.	Body/ Style No.	Body Type & Seating	Factory Price	Shipping Weight	Prod. Total
ESCORT SE (FOUR)					
P	13	4d Sedan-5P	12,440	2,468	—
ESCORT ZX2 (FOUR)					
P	11	2d Coupe-5P	12,200	2,478	—

CONTOUR — FOUR/ CONTOUR SVT — V-6 — For the 2000 model year the Contour LX series was dropped. The only four-cylinder model available was the Contour SE four-door sedan. This model was also available in a three-car V-6 series, along with the Contour Sport four-door sedan and the Contour SVT four-door sedan. Standard equipment on the Contour SE included dual second generation airbags, air conditioning, rear window defroster, power door locks, a fixed antenna mounted on the rear quarter panel, power front disc and rear drum brakes, an electric digital clock, childproof rear door locks, the 2.0-liter DOHC Zetec 16-valve I-4, semi flush exterior glass with Solar-Tint, a heater and defroster with a four-speed blower control, a soft touch dashboard with knee bolsters and four positive shutoff registers, a backlit cluster with 130-mph speedometer, analog gauges (including a trip odometer, a fuel gauge, a high-beam warning light, a coolant temperature gauge and a low oil pressure light, turn signal indicator lights, a handbrake-on warning light, a catalyst malfunction light and a seat belt reminder light), left- and right-hand power body-color exterior mirrors, a day/night rearview mirror, an AM/FM stereo with cassette player, speed control, one-touch power windows, illuminated switches on all doors, individual manual two-way adjustable front

bucket seats with reclining seat backs and cloth trim and a driver's side armrest attached to the seat, a tilt steering column, a tachometer, a soft touch steering wheel with center horn control, power rack-and-pinion steering, a driver's side covered visor mirror and passenger side uncovered visor mirror, P185/70R14S black sidewall tires, a five-speed manual transmission with overdrive, single-speed windshield wipers with intermittent feature and fluidic washers and 14-in. wheel covers with full bolt-on appearance. In addition to or in place of LX equipment, the Contour SVT featured a power antenna mounted on the rear quarter panel, power four-wheel disc brakes with Dacromat finished rotors and unique front calipers, an antilock braking system, the 2.5-liter DOHC high-output Duratec 24-valve V-6 with passive anti-theft system (PATS), a unique quasi-dual exhaust system with low back pressure mufflers, a unique instrument cluster with a white-faced 160-mph speedometer, an electronic AM/FM stereo radio with cassette player and premium sound system, unique sport front seats with special bolstering and perforated leather seating areas and a 10-way power driver's seat, a split-folding 60/40 rear seat with simulated bucket design and integral headrests, armrest and perforated leather seating surfaces, carpeted rear seat backs, a leather-wrapped steering wheel with center horn control, cloth-covered sun visors, P215/50R16Z directional rated tires, variable intermittent windshield wipers with fluidic washers and five-spoke 16-in. cast-aluminum wheels.

Model No.	Body/ Style No.	Body Type & Seating	Factory Price	Shipping Weight	Prod. Total
CONTOUR SE (FOUR)					
P	66	4d Sedan-5P	17,290	2,769	—
CONTOUR SE (GASEOUS FUEL FOUR)					
P	66	4d Sedan-5P	22,365	2,850	—
CONTOUR SE (V-6)					
P	66	4d Sedan-5P	17,785	2,774	—
CONTOUR SE SPORT OPTION (V-6)					
P	66	4d Sedan-5P	17,405	2,774	—
CONTOUR SVT (V-6)					
P	68	4d Sedan-5P	23,275	3,068	—

TAURUS — V-6/V-8 — For enthusiasts, the big news for 2000 was that the high-performing SHO model was dropped. The remaining cars were redesigned and offered in two trim levels: LX and SE. Both engines used in these cars—the 3.0-liter Vulcan V-6 and the 3.8-liter Duratec V-6—had higher horsepower and torque ratings. Trunk space in the Taurus sedan was significantly increased thanks to a new rear deck design. A restyled roofline increased interior headroom in the front and rear. Sedans had new front and rear fascias, while wagons had a new front fascia. Ford introduced a new "Personal Safety System" that included dual-stage airbags, a crash severity sensor, a belt-use sensor and a driver seat position sensor. Child seat tether anchors and the SecuriLock™ passive anti-theft system were made standard on all Taurus models. New options included front side-impact airbags and all-speed traction control combined with antilock braking. Also new was a power adjustable pedal system. Standard equipment in the LX sedan included a V-6 engine, a four-speed automatic transmission, P215/60R16 all-season tires, a spacesaver spare, full wheel covers, a four-wheel independent suspension, a front stabilizer bar, front and rear solid disc brakes, front seat belt pre-tensioners, rear door child safety locks, child seat anchors, an emergency release in the trunk, two front headrests, variable intermittent windshield wipers, a rear defogger, five-passenger seating with cloth upholstered bucket front seats and rear bench seat, rear seat heating ducts, power door locks, one-touch power windows, power mirrors, an AM/FM stereo system with four speakers, a mast antenna, speed-proportional power steering, a tilt-adjustable steering wheel, front cupholders, a remote trunk lid release, front seatback storage, a front 12-volt power outlet, a front console with storage space, retained accessory power, air conditioning, front reading lights, dual visor-vanity mirrors, a trunk light, a tachometer, a clock and a low-fuel warning indicator. In addition to or instead of LX sedan equipment, the SE sedan included alloy rims, remote power door locks, and AM/FM cassette stereo system and cruise control. The SES sedan also added ABS brakes, six-passenger seating with a split front bench seat, a six-way power driver's seat with adjustable lumbar support, an AM/FM cassette CD stereo and dual illuminating vanity mirrors. The SEL sedan added the Duratec V-6, a remote vehicle anti-theft system dusk-sensing headlights, digital keypad power door locks, heated mirrors, an AM/FM cassette and six CD stereo system with multi-CD located in dash, a climate control system and a leather-wrapped steering wheel. In addition to LX sedan equipment, the SE station wagon featured alloy rims, front and rear stabilizer bars, front disc/rear drum brakes, a front center lap belt, a roof rack, rear window wipers, six-passenger seating with a split front bench seat and a split-folding rear seat, remote power door locks, an AM/FM cassette sound system, a power radio antenna, cargo area lighting and cargo tie downs.

2000 Ford Escort four-door sedan. (FMC)

Model No.	Body/ Style No.	Body Type & Seating	Factory Price	Shipping Weight	Prod. Total
TAURUS LX (V-6)					
P	52	4d Sedan-6P	18,245	3,329	—
TAURUS SE (V-6)					
P	53	4d Sedan-6P	19,295	3,329	—
P	58	4d Wagon-6P	20,450	3,480	—
TAURUS SE (FLEXIBLE FUEL V-6)					
P	—	4d Sedan-6P	19,295	—	—
P	—	4d Wagon-6P	20,450	—	—
TAURUS SES (V-6)					
P	55	4d Sedan-6P	20,170	3,353	—
TAURUS SEL (V-8)					
P	56	4d Sedan-6P	21,445	3,340	—

CROWN VICTORIA — V-8 — The 2000 Crown Victoria got a new emergency interior trunk release and rear child seat anchors. Standard equipment on the base Crown Victoria included dual airbags, manual air conditioning with positive shut-off registers, a radio antenna hidden in the rear window defroster, the SecuriLock™ passive anti-theft system, a brake/shift interlock, power four-wheel disc antilock brakes, rear seat child safety latches, an electric digital clock with dimming feature, a rear window defroster, the 4.6-liter OHC sequential fuel-injected V-8, a stainless steel exhaust system, a gauge cluster with analog gauges (voltmeter, oil pressure, water temperature and fuel), full Solar Tinted glass, woodgrain instrument panel appliqués, side window demisters, power door locks, dual remote-control fold-away power exterior mirrors with color-keyed finish, a day/night inside rearview mirror, an electronic AM/FM stereo with cassette and door-mounted speakers, a cloth-trimmed split bench front seat with center fold-down armrest and reclining seatbacks (two-way manual adjusting type with 10-in. track travel), a sound insulation package, speed control, a color-keyed steering wheel with center horn blow, speed sensitive variable-assist power steering (not available in cars with the natural gas engine), cloth-covered sun visors with retention clips, a tilt steering column with stalk-mounted controls, P225/60SR16 all-season black sidewall tires, an ECT automatic transmission with overdrive lockout, a trip odometer, dual-jet interval windshield wipers, deluxe wheel covers, HSLA 16 x 7-in. wheel rims and power windows with driver side express down. In addition to or in place of base Crown Victoria equipment, the LX featured remote keyless entry (except with natural gas engine), a split bench seat with fold-down center armrest trimmed in Luxury cloth (with power lumbar adjustment and six-way power adjustment on the driver's side, plus a power back recliner) and chrome-plated, locking cross-spoke wheel covers.

Model No.	Body/ Style No.	Body Type & Seating	Factory Price	Shipping Weight	Prod. Total
CROWN VICTORIA POLICE INTERCEPTOR (GAS V-8)					
P	71	4d Sedan-5P	—		——
CROWN VICTORIA "S" FLEET OPTION (GAS V-8)					
P	72	4d Sedan-5P	—		——
CROWN VICTORIA (GAS V-8)					
P	73	4d Sedan-5P	22,635	3,908	—
CROWN VICTORIA (NATURAL GAS V-8)					
P	73	4d Sedan-5P	28,800	3,990	—
CROWN VICTORIA LX (GAS V-8)					
P	74	4d Sedan-5P	24,750	3,908	—
CROWN VICTORIA LX (NATURAL GAS V-8)					
P	74	4d Sedan-5P	30,915	3,990	—

FOCUS ENGINES

ENGINE [Base LX/SE/ZX3]: Inline. Overhead cam. Four-cylinder. Cast-iron block and aluminum head. Displacement: 121 cid (2.0 liters). Bore & stroke: 3.39 x 3.52 in. Compression ratio: 9.4:1. Brake horsepower: 110 at 5000 rpm. Torque: 125 lbs.-ft. at 3750 rpm. Split Port induction.

ENGINE [Base ZTS]: Inline. Double overhead cam. Four-cylinder. Cast-iron block and aluminum head. Displacement: 121 cid (2.0 liters). Bore & stroke: 3.39 x 3.52 in. Compression ratio: 9.6:1. Brake horsepower: 130 at 5750 rpm. Torque: 135 lbs.-ft. at 4500 rpm. Sequential fuel injection.

ESCORT ENGINES

ENGINE [Base SE]: Inline. Overhead cam. Four-cylinder. Cast-iron block and aluminum head. Displacement: 121 cid (2.0 liters). Bore & stroke: 3.39 x 3.52 in. Compression ratio: 9.4:1. Brake horsepower: 110 at 5000 rpm. Torque: 125 lbs.-ft. at 3750 rpm. Split Port induction.

ENGINE [Base ZX2]: Inline. Double overhead cam. Four-cylinder. Cast-iron block and aluminum head. Displacement: 121 cid (2.0 liters). Bore & stroke: 3.39 x 3.52 in. Compression ratio: 9.6:1. Brake horsepower: 130 at 5750 rpm. Torque: 135 lbs.-ft. at 4500 rpm. Sequential fuel injection.

CONTOUR ENGINES

ENGINE [Base SE]: Inline. Double overhead cam. Four-cylinder. Cast-iron block and aluminum head. Displacement: 121 cid (2.0 liters). Bore & stroke: 3.39 x 3.52 in. Compression ratio: 9.6:1. Brake horsepower: 125 at 5500 rpm. Torque: 130 lbs.-ft. at 4000 rpm. Sequential fuel injection.

ENGINE [Base SVT]: 60-degree double overhead cam V-6. Aluminum block and head. Displacement: 155 cid (2.5 liters). Bore & stroke: 3.24 x 3.13 in. Compression ratio: 10.0:1. Brake horsepower: 200 at 6625 rpm. Torque: 167 lbs.-ft. at 5625 rpm. Sequential fuel injection.

ENGINE [Optional SE]: Modular. Double overhead cam V-6. Aluminum block and head. Displacement: 155 cid (2.5 liters). Bore & stroke: 3.24 x 3.13 in. Compression ratio: 9.7:1. Brake horsepower: 170 at 6250 rpm. Torque: 165 lbs.-ft. at 4250 rpm. Sequential fuel injection.

TAURUS ENGINES

ENGINE [Base LX/SE]: Overhead valve V-6. Cast-iron block and head. Displacement: 182 cid (3.0 liters). Bore & stroke: 3.50 x 3.15 in. Compression ratio: 9.3:1. Brake horsepower: 155 at 4900 rpm. Torque: 185 lbs.-ft. at 3950 rpm. Sequential fuel injection.

ENGINE [Optional SE/Comfort Wagon]: Double overhead cam V-6. Aluminum block and head. Displacement: 182 cid (3.0 liters). Bore & stroke: 3.50 x 3.15 in. Compression ratio: 10.0:1. Brake horsepower: 200 at 5750 rpm. Torque: 200 lbs.-ft. at 4500 rpm. Sequential fuel injection. VIN code S.

ENGINE [Optional SE SVG]: Double overhead cam flexible-fuel V-6. Aluminum block and head. Displacement: 182 cid (3.0 liters). Bore & stroke: 3.50 x 3.15 in. Compression ratio: 10.0:1. Brake horsepower: 200 at 5750 rpm. Torque: 200 lbs.-ft. at 4500 rpm.

CROWN VICTORIA ENGINE

ENGINE [Base]: Modular, overhead valve V-8. Displacement: 281 cid (4.6 liters). Bore & stroke: 3.60 x 3.60. Compression ratio: 9.0:1. Brake horsepower: 200 at 4250 rpm. Torque: 275 lbs.-ft. at 3000 rpm. Sequential fuel injection.

ENGINE [Natural Gas]: Modular, overhead valve V-8. Displacement: 281 cid (4.6 liters). Bore & stroke: 3.60 x 3.60. Compression ratio: 9.0:1. Brake horsepower: 175 at 4250 rpm. Torque: 235 lbs.-ft. at 3000 rpm. Natural gas engine.

FOCUS CHASSIS: Wheelbase: 103 in. Overall length: (hatchback) 168.1 in.; (sedan) 174.9 in.; (wagon) 174.9 in. Overall width: (all) 66.9 in. Overall height: (wagon) 53.9 in.; (others) 56.3 in.

ESCORT CHASSIS: Wheelbase: (all) 98.4 in. Overall length: (SE sedan) 174.7 in.; (ZX2 coupe) 175.2 in. Overall width: (sedan) 67 in.; (ZX2 coupe) 67.4 in. Overall height: (SE sedan) 53.3 in.; (ZX2 coupe) 52.1 in. Front tread: (all) 56.5 in. Rear tread: (all) 56.5 in.

CONTOUR CHASSIS: Wheelbase: (all) 106.5 in.; Overall length: (all) 184.6 in. Overall width: (all) 69.1 in.; Overall height: (all) 54.4 in. Front tread: (all) 59.2 in. Rear tread: (all) 58.5 in.

TAURUS CHASSIS: Wheelbase: (all) 108.5 in. Overall length: (sedan) 197.5 in.; (wagon) 199.6 in. Overall width: (all) 73 in. Overall height: (sedan) 56.1 in.; (wagon) 58 in. Front tread: 61.6 in. Rear tread: 61.4 in.

CROWN VICTORIA CHASSIS: Wheelbase: (all) 114.7 in. Overall length: (all) 212 in. Overall width: (all) 78.2 in. Overall height: (all) 56.8 in. Front tread: (all) 62.8 in. Rear tread: (all) 63.3 in.

2000 Ford Crown Victoria four-door sedan. (FMC)

FOCUS TECHNICAL: Standard transmission: five-speed manual transaxle. Drive axle: front. Steering: rack-and-pinion. Front suspension: (all) independent MacPherson struts with coil springs and stabilizer bar (all). Rear suspension: (all) independent control blade multilink design with coil springs and shock absorbers (2.0L SOHC)/stabilizer bar (2.0L DOHC Zetec). Brakes: ventilated front disc, rear drum (power assisted). Body construction: unibody. Fuel tank: 13.2 gallons.

ESCORT TECHNICAL: Standard transmission: five-speed manual transaxle. Drive axle: front. Steering: rack-and-pinion. Front suspension: independent MacPherson strut with strut-mounted coil springs. Rear suspension: independent, Quadra-link with stabilizer bar. Brakes: front disc, rear drum (power assisted). Body construction: unibody. Fuel tank: 12.7 gallons.

CONTOUR TECHNICAL: Standard transmission: five-speed manual transaxle. Drive axle: front. Steering: rack-and-pinion. Front suspension: (LX/SE) independent, subframe rubber mounted MacPherson strut with strut-mounted coil springs, lower control A-arms and cast steering knuckles; (SVT) MacPherson struts, lower A-arms, coil springs, tube shock dampers and stabilizer bar. Rear suspension: (LX/SE) independent, Quadra-link strut with coil spring on shock strut, mounted to rigid subframe; (SVT) independent Quadra-link design, coil springs, tube shock dampers and stabilizer bar. Brakes: front disc, rear drum (power assisted), except SVT has four-wheel discs. Body construction: unibody. Fuel tank: 14.5 gallons.

TAURUS TECHNICAL: Standard transmission: Four-speed overdrive automatic. Drive axle: front. Steering: rack-and-pinion. Front suspension: independent MacPherson strut front drive with strut-mounted coil springs, stabilizer bar, lower control arm and cast aluminum knuckle with integral ball joint. Rear suspension: (sedan) independent Quadra-link with coil spring on shock strut, stabilizer bar, tension strut, parallel suspension arms and two-piece cast spindle with forged stem; (wagon) independent short/long arm with spring on lower control arm, stabilizer bar, tension strut and cast spindle with pressed-in forged stem and integrated ball joints. Brakes: front disc, rear drum (power assisted) except Taurus SE wagon and Taurus SHO have four-wheel discs. Body construction: unibody. Fuel tank: 17.0 gallons.

CROWN VICTORIA TECHNICAL: Standard transmission: four-speed overdrive automatic. Drive axle: rear. Steering: re-circulating ball. Front suspension: independent short/long arm with ball joints, coil springs and stabilizer bar. Rear suspension: Watt's linkage. Brakes: four-wheel disc. Body construction: separate body and frame. Fuel tank: 20.0 gallons.

2000 Ford Taurus SE four-door Sport sedan. (FMC)

2000 Ford Contour SVT four-door sedan. (FMC)

FOCUS OPTIONS: (ZX3 hatchback) 44A four-speed overdrive automatic transmission ($815). 47D AdvanceTrac ($1,225). 572 air conditioning ($795). 552 antilock braking system ($400). 422 California emissions requirements (no cost). 13A manual moonroof ($446). 93N non-California emissions (no cost). 60A power group ($740). 50P premium group ($1,095). 59M side airbags ($350). (LX sedan) 44A four-speed overdrive automatic transmission ($815). 572 air conditioning ($795). 552 antilock braking system ($400). 422 California emissions requirements (no cost). 93N non-California emissions (no cost). 59M side airbags ($350). (SE sedan) 44A four-speed overdrive automatic transmission ($815). 552 antilock braking system ($400). 422 California emissions requirements (no cost). 93N non-California emissions (no cost). 50A SE Comfort group ($345). 434 SE sports group ($470). 59M side airbags ($350). (ZTS sedan) 44A four-speed overdrive automatic transmission ($815). 47D AdvanceTrac ($1,225). 422 California emissions requirements (no cost). 93N non-California emissions (no cost). 59M side airbags ($350). 8 low-back bucket seats with unique leather trim and map pockets ($695). (SE wagon) 445 five-speed manual transmission (no cost). 552 antilock braking system ($400). 422 California emissions requirements (no cost). 93N non-California emissions (no cost). 50A SE Comfort group ($345). 59M side airbags ($350).

ESCORT OPTIONS: 572 air conditioning, standard in SE ($795). 552 antilock braking system ($400). 57Q rear window defroster, standard in SE ($190). 422 California emissions (no cost). 12Y front and rear floor mats ($55). 41H engine block heater ($20). 58H AM/FM stereo with cassette ($185). 586 ETR AM/FM stereo cassette with premium sound, for ZX2 Hot coupe only ($95). 919 AM/FM stereo cassette with premium sound and six disc CD changer ($295). 144 remote keyless entry ($165). 50A SE comfort group, includes speed control, tilt steering and dual map lights, SE only ($345). 60A SE power group, includes power locks and power windows ($345). J unique sport bucket seats (no cost). 63B smoker's package ($15). 434 Sport package includes 14-in. aluminum wheels, rear deck lid spoiler, bright exhaust pipe tips, unique seats with rear integrated headrests, leather-wrapped steering wheel and Sport badging, SE sedan only ($495). 44T four-speed overdrive automatic transmission ($815). 64P 14-in. aluminum wheels ($265). 50A ZX2 Hot coupe series power group, includes power windows with one-touch down feature on driver's side and power door locks ($345). 60A ZX2 Hot coupe series Sport group includes rear deck lid spoiler, bright exhaust tips, unique seats with rear headrests with ZX2 script, 15-in. aluminum wheels, Sport badging and leather-wrapped steering wheel ($595). 13B power sliding moon roof for Hot coupe only ($595). 13K rear deck lid spoiler for coupes, requires 41G if ordered for Hot coupe ($195). 44T four-speed automatic overdrive transmission with 16-valve Zetec 2.0-liter DOHC engine, ZX2 only ($815). 64Z aluminum wheels for Hot coupe only ($265). 53V Wheels and Tunes package, includes 14-in. aluminum wheels, 58H radio, 12Y floor mats and 13K spoiler for ZX2, not available on Hot coupe ($450).

CONTOUR OPTIONS: 153 front license plate bracket (no cost). 552 antilock braking system, standard on SVT ($500). 57Q rear window defroster ($190). 422 California emissions system (no cost). 428 high-altitude emissions system (no cost). 99Z 2.0-liter four-cylinder gaseous fuel preparation package, includes four-wheel disc brakes and P195/65R14 tires, requires automatic transmission ($260). 99L 2.5-liter Duratec V-6, includes tachometer, P195/65R15 black sidewall performance tires, four-wheel antilock brakes and SecuriLock™ anti-theft system, requires 5S on SE only ($70 credit). 41H engine block heater ($20). 12Y floor mats, front and rear ($55). 13B moonroof SE ($595; no charge SVT). 58P premium sound system with ETR AM/FM stereo, cassette and amplifier ($135). 585 ETR AM/FM stereo with CD player and premium sound, in SE ($275; no charge in SVT). 58H AM/FM stereo cassette in LX only, standard in SE ($185). 91H power antenna ($95). 143 remote keyless entry, includes illuminated entry system ($190). 53C SE Comfort group, includes power driver's seat, 15-in. 12-spoke aluminum wheels, leather-wrapped steering wheel, leather shift knob, fog lamps, variable interval windshield wipers, illuminated visor mirror and power antenna ($795). 53S Sport group, included 2.5-liter V-6, five-speed manual transmission, 15-in. eight-spoke aluminum wheels, a tachometer, a leather-wrapped steering wheel, a leather-wrapped shift knob, sport floor mats, a rear deck lid spoiler, body cladding, variable fixed interval windshield wipers, an illuminated vanity mirror, fog lamps, Sport cloth bucket seats and Sport badging ($1,000). 28 leather seating surfaces ($895). 219 60/40 split-folding rear seat in SE ($205). 21A six-way power driver's seat, in SE ($350). 63B smoker's package ($15). 525 speed control in LX ($215). 553 traction control, requires 2.5-liter engine and antilock brakes ($175). 44T ECT automatic transmission, in LX and SE ($815). 64X 15-in. eight-spoke cast-aluminum wheels, includes P205/60R15 black sidewall tires, on SE ($425).

TAURUS OPTIONS: 153 front license plate bracket (no cost). 552 antilock braking system, standard on SHO ($600). 902 power door locks in LX ($275). 422 California emissions system (no cost). 428 high-altitude emissions system (no cost). 992 3.0-liter flexible fuel (ethanol) V-6 on LX/SE with column shift only ($1,165). 41H engine block heater ($35). 943 light group ($45). 12Y floor mats, front and rear ($55). 54P heated exterior mirrors, standard on SHO ($35). 13B power moonroof, includes unique map lamps in overhead console ($740). 58H ETR AM/FM stereo, cassette with four speakers ($185). 916 Ford Mach audio system with six speakers in SE ($320; no charge in SHO). 919 trunk-mounted six-disc CD changer ($350). 143 remote keyless entry ($190). 60E SE Comfort group, includes 3.0-liter four, overdrive automatic transmission, power driver's seat with adjustable lumbar support, electronic temperature control air conditioning, 12-spoke bright cast aluminum wheels, leather-wrapped steering wheel, automatic headlamps, remote entry with keypad and perimeter anti-theft, light group, illuminated visor mirrors, five-passenger seating, floor console and floor shift ($1,000 with Sport group; $1,500 without Sport group). 60S SE Sport group includes 3.0-liter four-valve V-6, automatic overdrive transmission, rear deck lid spoiler, five-spoke aluminum wheels, five-passenger seating, floor console and floor shift ($750). 186 five-passenger seating with center seating console, column shift and secondary power point ($105). 184 six-passenger seating with center seating console, column shift and secondary power point (no cost). M leather bucket seats, requires 21A power seat ($895). 21A power driver's seat with power lumbar adjustment in SE ($395). 21J dual power seats in SE, requires 60E SE Comfort package ($350). 214 rear facing vinyl third seat in wagon ($200). 216 integrated rear child seat, SE wagon only ($135). 525 speed control ($215). 508 conventional spare tire ($125). 96W wagon group, includes cargo net and cargo area cover, SE wagon only ($140). 64C five-spoke aluminum wheels, includes locking lug nut package, LX/SE only ($395). 649 chrome 12-spoke wheels, includes locking lug nut kit (no cost). 641 16-in. bright cast-aluminum five-spoke wheels, includes P225/55ZR16 all-season low-profile tires ($580).

CROWN VICTORIA OPTIONS: 153 front license plate bracket (no cost) 65C LX Comfort group, includes electronic automatic temperature control air conditioning, 12-spoke aluminum wheels, power passenger seat with power lumbar and recliners, auto dim mirror with compass and leather-wrapped steering wheel ($900). 65E LX Comfort Plus group, includes Comfort group plus electronic instrumentation, leather trim seats and premium sound system ($2,150). 422 California emissions (no cost). 999 4.6-liter natural gas engine, includes engine compression light and P225/60VR16 tires, but deletes standard auto headlamp system and SecuriLock™ anti-theft system, and remote keyless entry on LX ($6,165). 41G Handling and Performance package, includes revised springs, shocks and stabilizer bar, P225/60TR16 black sidewall touring tires, 16-in. cast-aluminum wheels, rear air suspension, dual exhausts with 2154-hp/275-ft.-lbs. rating and 3.27:1 axle ($615-$935 depending upon other options ordered). 12H front color-keyed carpeting ($30). 12Q rear color-keyed carpeting ($25). 585 single CD player replacing cassette ($140). 919 trunk-mounted six-disc CD changer ($350). 586 premium sound system ($360). 144 remote keyless entry ($240). L leather seating surfaces on split bench seat ($735). 21A six-way power driver's seat, includes power lumbar and recliner ($360). 508 conventional spare tire ($120). T2A P225/60R16 white sidewall tires ($80 above regular tires). T23 P225/60VR15 white sidewall tires, requires natural gas engine (no cost). 553 traction control ($175). 175 universal garage door opener ($115).

HISTORY: In the year 2000, Ford Motor Co. made substantial accomplishments, but also faced unprecedented challenges. The automaker achieved record volume, revenue and operating earnings per share and generated strong operating profits. Individual product successes included the Ford Focus, becoming the world's best-selling car. During 2000, Ford acquired another strong global brand in Land Rover and successfully integrated it into the company's overall business. The Automotive Consumer Services Group—Ford's principal source of vehicle service and customer support worldwide—had record revenues and was a strong contributor to customer satisfaction. Ford Financial—which included Ford Credit and Primus Financial Services—achieved earnings of $1.54 billion, up 22 percent. Ford's Hertz rental car unit posted a record income for the ninth year in a row. A major challenge for Ford in 2000 was the headline-making Firestone tire recall. Ford dealers, suppliers and union partners were called upon to identify bad tires and find replacements months ahead of the original Firestone schedule. Ford said that, "Customer safety guided all of our actions," but the recall severed Ford's longstanding relationship with Firestone that dated back to the Model T era. Ford changed to covering tires

under its vehicle warranty program, which was not a common industry practice before the Firestone recall. The company planned to introduce a tire pressure monitoring system in the 2002 Ford Explorer and eventually in all of its light trucks and sport utility vehicles. Ford also worked with the U.S. government and the auto industry to create an "early warning system" with a linked computer database of tire information. During 2000, Ford Motor Co. continued to be overly dependent on its North American earnings. With business conditions softening and competition getting more intense in the United States, correcting this imbalance became a critical goal for the automaker, which implemented a long-term European Turnaround Strategy that was aggressive, but achievable. The strategy included the introduction of at least 45 new products in the next five years and the taking of action to improve its performance in South America.

2001 FORD

2001 Ford Focus SE four-door station wagon. (FMC)

2001 Ford Excort ZX2 two-door coupe. (FMC)

2001 Ford Taurus LX four-door Sport sedan. (FMC)

2001 Ford Crown Victoria four-door sedan. (FMC)

2001 Ford Focus ZX3 three-door hatchback. (FMC)

FOCUS — FOUR — The 2001 Ford Focus featured "smart design and spirited driving" according to Ford. It was a sophisticated compact aimed at the worldwide market and available in three-door hatchback, four-door sedan and four-door wagon styles. The sedan was merchandised in LX, SE and ZTS trim lines. Standard equipment for the ZX3 hatchback included a 2.0-liter DOHC 16-valve 130-hp four-cylinder engine, a five-speed manual transmission, front-wheel drive, four-wheel independent suspension with front and rear stabilizer bars, a tachometer, a low-fuel indicator, a clock, 15-in. alloy wheel rims, P195/60R15 tires, a spacesaver spare on a steel spare wheel, intermittent windshield wipers, a rear window wiper, a rear defogger, ventilated front disc/rear drum brakes, child seat anchors, a center rear three-point safety belt, front seat belt pre-tensioners, an emergency interior trunk release, two front seat headrests, power steering, front and rear cupholders, a front 12-volt power outlet, remote driver and passenger mirrors, a front console with storage space, five-passenger seating with premium cloth-trimmed front bucket seats, height adjustable driver and passenger seats, a split rear bench seat with split-folding seatbacks, rear seat heating ducts, dual visor-vanity mirrors, alloy trim on the gearshift knob, a leather-wrapped steering wheel, front and rear floor mats, an AM/FM CD stereo and a four-speaker sound system. Standard equipment for the Focus LX sedan included a 2.0-liter SOHC 8-valve 110-hp four-cylinder engine, a five-speed manual transmission, front-wheel drive, four-wheel independent suspension with front stabilizer bar, a clock, a low-fuel indicator, 14-in. wheel rims, P185/65R14 tires, a spacesaver spare on a steel spare wheel, full wheel covers, intermittent windshield wipers, a rear defogger, ventilated front disc/rear drum brakes, rear door child safety locks, child seat anchors, a center rear three-point safety belt, front seat belt pre-tensioners, an emergency interior trunk release, two front seat headrests, an engine immobilizer, a remote anti-theft system, power steering, front and rear cupholders, a front 12-volt power outlet, remote driver and passenger mirrors, front door pockets, a front console with storage space, five-passenger seating with cloth-trimmed front bucket seats, height adjustable driver and passenger seats, a split rear bench seat with split-folding seatbacks, rear seat heating ducts, dual visor-vanity mirrors, front and rear floor mats, an AM/FM cassette stereo and a four-speaker sound system. Standard equipment for the Focus SE sedan included a 2.0-liter SOHC 8-valve 110-hp four-cylinder engine, a five-speed manual transmission, front-wheel drive, four-wheel independent suspension with front stabilizer bar, a clock, a low-fuel indicator, 15-in. alloy wheel rims, P195/60R15 tires, a spacesaver spare on a steel spare wheel, variable intermittent windshield wipers, a rear defogger, ventilated front disc/rear drum brakes, rear door child safety locks, child seat anchors, a center rear three-point safety belt, front seat belt pre-tensioners, an emergency interior trunk release, two front seat headrests, an engine immobilizer, a remote anti-theft system, remote power door locks, one touch power windows, power mirrors, power steering, front and rear cupholders, a front 12-volt power outlet, front door pockets, a front console with storage space, five-passenger seating with cloth-trimmed front bucket seats, height adjustable driver and passenger seats, a split rear bench seat with split-folding seatbacks, rear seat heating ducts, air conditioning, dual visor-vanity mirrors, front and rear floor mats, an AM/FM CD stereo and a four-speaker sound system. Standard equipment for the Focus Street sedan included a 2.0-liter SOHC 8-valve 110-hp four-cylinder engine, a five-speed manual transmission, front-wheel drive, four-wheel independent suspension with front and rear stabilizer bars, a clock, a low-fuel indicator, 16-in. wheel rims, P205/65R16 tires, a spacesaver spare on a steel spare wheel, variable intermittent windshield wipers, a rear defogger, ventilated front disc/rear drum brakes, rear door child safety locks, child seat anchors, a center rear three-point safety belt, front seat belt pre-tensioners, an emergency interior trunk release, two front seat headrests, an engine immobilizer, a remote anti-theft system, remote power door locks, one touch power windows, power steering, front and rear cupholders, a front 12-volt power outlet, power driver and passenger mirrors, front door pockets, a front console with storage space, five-passenger seating with cloth-trimmed front bucket seats, height adjustable driver and passenger seats, a split rear bench seat with split-folding seatbacks, rear seat heating ducts, air conditioning, dual visor-vanity mirrors, front and rear floor mats, an AM/FM six CD stereo (with multi-CD located in dash) and a four-speaker sound system. Standard equipment for the Focus ZTS sedan included a 2.0-liter DOHC 16-valve 130-hp four-cylinder engine, a five-speed manual transmission, front-wheel drive, four-wheel independent suspension with front and rear stabilizer bars, a clock, a tachometer, a low-fuel indicator, 16-in. wheel rims, P205/50R16 tires, a spacesaver spare on a steel spare wheel, variable intermittent windshield wipers, a rear defogger, ventilated front disc/rear drum ABS brakes, rear door child safety locks, child seat anchors, a center rear three-point safety belt, front seat belt pre-tensioners, an emergency interior trunk release, two front seat headrests, an engine immobilizer, a remote anti-theft system, front fog lights, remote power door locks, one touch power windows, power steering, cruise control, a tilt/telescope steering wheel, front and rear cupholders, a front 12-volt power outlet, power driver and passenger mirrors, front door pockets, a front console with storage space, five-passenger seating with premium cloth-trimmed front bucket seats, height adjustable driver and passenger seats (with adjustable lumbar support on driver's seat), a split rear bench seat with split-folding seatbacks, rear seat heating ducts, air conditioning, dual visor-vanity mirrors, front reading lights, a leather-wrapped steering wheel, simulated wood dash trim, simulated wood door trim, front and rear floor mats, an AM/FM CD stereo and a four-speaker sound system. Standard equipment for the Focus SE wagon included a 2.0-liter DOHC 16-valve 130-hp four-cylinder engine, a four-speed automatic transmission, front-wheel drive, four-wheel independent suspension with front and rear stabilizer bars, a clock, a low-fuel indicator, 15-in. wheel rims, P195/60R15 tires, a spacesaver spare on a steel spare wheel, variable intermittent windshield wipers, a rear defogger, a roof rack, a rear window wiper, ventilated front disc/rear drum brakes, rear door child safety locks, child seat anchors, a center rear three-point safety belt, front seat belt pre-tensioners, an emergency interior hatch release, two front seat headrests, a remote anti-theft system, an engine immobilizer, remote power door locks, one touch power windows, power steering, front and rear cupholders, a front 12-volt power outlet, power driver and passenger mirrors, front door pockets, a front console with storage space, five-passenger seating with cloth-trimmed front bucket seats, height adjustable driver and passenger seats, a split rear bench seat with split-folding seatbacks, rear seat heating ducts, air conditioning, dual visor-vanity mirrors, front and rear floor mats, an AM/FM CD stereo and a four-speaker sound system. Standard equipment for the Focus Street wagon included a 2.0-liter DOHC 16-valve 130-hp four-cylinder engine, a four-speed automatic transmission, front-wheel drive, four-wheel independent suspension with front and rear stabilizer bars, a clock, a low-fuel indicator, 16-in. wheel rims, P205/50R16 tires, a spacesaver spare on a steel spare wheel, variable intermittent windshield wipers, a rear defogger, a roof rack, a rear window wiper, ventilated front disc/rear drum brakes, rear door child safety locks, child seat anchors, a center rear three-point safety belt, front seat belt pre-tensioners, an emergency interior hatch release, two front seat headrests, a remote anti-theft system, an engine immobilizer, remote power door locks, one touch power windows, power steering, front and rear cupholders, a front 12-volt power outlet, power driver and passenger mirrors, front door pockets, a front console with storage space, five-passenger seating with cloth-trimmed front bucket seats, height adjustable driver and passenger seats, a split rear bench seat with split-folding seatbacks, rear seat heating ducts, air conditioning, dual visor-vanity mirrors, front and rear floor mats, an AM/FM six CD stereo (with in-dash multi-CD) and a four-speaker sound system.

I.D. DATA: Ford's 17-symbol Vehicle Identification Number (VIN) was stamped on a metal tab fastened to the instrument panel, visible through the windshield. The first symbol indicates the nation of origin: 1=United States; 2=Canada; 3=Mexico. The second symbol indicates manufacturer: F=Ford Motor Co.; The third symbol indicates vehicle type: A=passenger car. The fourth symbol indicates type of restraint system: B=driver and passenger airbags and active belts (except Escort ZX2 coupe); F=driver and passenger airbags and active belts; K=driver and passenger airbags and active belts in all outboard positions. The fifth symbol indicates designation: P=Ford; T=Imported from outside North America or non-Ford car marketed by Ford in North America. The sixth and seventh symbols indicate body type: 11=Escort ZX2 two-door coupe; 31=Focus ZX3 three-door coupe; 33=Focus LX four-door sedan; 34=Focus SE/Focus Street four-door sedan; 36=Focus SE/Focus Street four-door station wagon; 38=Focus ZTS four-door sedan; 52=Taurus LX four-door sedan; 53=Taurus SE two-valve four-door sedan; 55=Taurus SE SVG four-door sedan; 56=Taurus SEL four-door sedan; 58=Taurus SE four-door station wagon; 73=Crown Victoria four-door sedan; 74=Crown Victoria LX four-door sedan. The eighth symbol indicates engine: [Escort] P=2.0-liter I-4 with EF/SPI; [Taurus] S=3.0-liter DOHC V-6 with EFI; U=3.0-liter V-6 with EFI; 2=flexible fuel 3.0-liter V-6 with EFI. [Contour] G=2.5-liter DOHC V-6 with EFI; L=2.5-liter DOHC V-6 with EFI; Z=2.0-liter DOHC I-4 with EFI; 3=2.0-liter DOHC I-4 with EFI. [Crown Victoria] W=4.6-liter SOHC V-8 with EFI (Romeo engine plant). The ninth symbol is a check digit. The 10th symbol indicates model year: Z=2001. The 11th symbol indicates assembly plant: A=Hapeville (Atlanta), Ga.; F=Dearborn, Mich.; G=Chicago, Ill.; K=Claycomo (Kansas City), Mo.; M=Cuautitlan Mexico; R=Hermosillo Mexico; W=Wayne, Mich.; X=Talbotville (St. Thomas), Ontario Canada. The last six symbols are the sequential production number starting at 100001 at each factory.

2001 Ford Taurus SEL four-door sedan. (FMC)

Model No.	Body/ Style No.	Body Type & Seating	Factory Price	Shipping Weight	Prod. Total
FOCUS ZX3 (FOUR)					
P	31	3d Hatchback-5P	12,905	2,551	—
FOCUS LX (FOUR)					
P	33	4d Sedan-5P	13,220	2,564	—
FOCUS SE (FOUR)					
P	34	4d Sedan-5P	14,320	2,564	—
P	36	4d Wagon-5P	17,015	2,717	—
FOCUS STREET (FOUR)					
P	34	4d Sedan-5P	14,810	2,564	—
P	36	4d Wagon-5P	17,015	2,717	—
FOCUS ZTS (FOUR)					
P	38	4d Sedan-5P	16,030	2,564	—

ESCORT — FOUR — The only Escort model remaining in 2001 was the ZX2 two-door coupe. It came in a few new colors and that was about the extent of any changes. The S/R high-performance option was no longer available. Standard equipment included a 2.0-liter DOHC 16-valve 130-hp four-cylinder engine, a five-speed manual transmission, front-wheel drive, four-wheel independent suspension with front and rear stabilizer bars, a tachometer, a low-fuel indicator, a clock, an external temperature indicator, 15-in. wheel rims, P185/60TR15 tires, a spacesaver spare on a steel spare wheel, variable intermittent windshield wipers, a rear defogger, a rear spoiler, front disc/rear drum brakes, child seat anchors, an emergency interior trunk release, daytime running lights, power door locks, power mirrors, power steering, front cupholders, a front 12-volt power outlet, front door pockets, a front console with storage space, four-passenger seating with cloth-trimmed front bucket seats, a split-folding rear seat, rear seat heating ducts, dual visor-vanity mirrors and an AM/FM cassette stereo.

Model No.	Body/ Style No.	Body Type & Seating	Factory Price	Shipping Weight	Prod. Total
ESCORT ZX2 (FOUR)					
P	11	2d Coupe-5P	12,830	2,478	—

TAURUS — V-6/V-8 — After being restyled in 2000, the Taurus had minor changes for 2001. A LATCH (lower anchor and tether for children) arrangement for child safety belts was standard on all models. A new Spruce Green Metallic color was offered and fuel tank capacity was increased to 18 gallons. SES models got a six-disc CD changer. Power door locks and a rear deck lid spoiler were available on the Taurus LX. Standard equipment in the Taurus LX sedan included a 3.0-liter 12-valve 155-hp V-6 engine, a four-speed automatic transmission, front-wheel drive, four-wheel independent suspension, a front stabilizer bar, a tachometer, a low-fuel indicator, a clock, P215/60R16 all-season tires on 16-in. steel rims, a spacesaver spare on a spare steel wheel, full wheel covers, variable intermittent wipers, a rear defogger, ventilated front disc/rear drum brakes, front seat belt pre-tensioners, rear door child safety locks, child seat anchors, an emergency inside trunk release, a center rear lap belt, two front headrests, an engine immobilizer, power door locks, one-touch power windows, power mirrors, speed-proportional power steering, a tilt-adjustable steering wheel, front cupholders, a remote trunk lid release, front seatback storage, a front 12-volt power outlet, a front console with storage space, retained accessory power, five-passenger seating with cloth-trimmed front bucket seats, a rear bench seat, rear seat heating ducts, air conditioning, front reading lights, dual visor-vanity mirrors, a trunk light, an AM/FM stereo, a mast antenna and a four-speaker sound system. Standard equipment in the Taurus SE sedan included a 3.0-liter 12-valve 155-hp V-6 engine, a four-speed automatic transmission, front-wheel drive, four-wheel independent suspension, a front stabilizer bar, a tachometer, a low-fuel indicator, a clock, P215/60R16 all-season tires on 16-in. alloy rims, a spacesaver spare on a spare steel wheel, variable intermittent wipers, a rear defogger, ventilated front disc/rear drum brakes, front seat belt pre-tensioners, rear door child safety locks, child seat anchors, an emergency inside trunk release, a center rear lap belt, two front headrests, an

engine immobilizer, remote power door locks, one-touch power windows, power mirrors, cruise control, speed-proportional power steering, a tilt-adjustable steering wheel, front cupholders, a remote trunk lid release, front seatback storage, a front 12-volt power outlet, a front console with storage space, retained accessory power, five-passenger seating with cloth-trimmed front bucket seats, a rear bench seat, rear seat heating ducts, air conditioning, front reading lights, dual visor-vanity mirrors, a trunk light, an AM/FM cassette stereo, a mast antenna and a four-speaker sound system. Standard equipment in the Taurus SEL sedan included a 3.0-liter 24-valve 200-hp V-6 engine, a four-speed automatic transmission, front-wheel drive, four-wheel independent suspension, a front stabilizer bar, a tachometer, a low-fuel indicator, a clock, P215/60R16 all-season tires on 16-in. alloy rims, a spacesaver spare on a spare steel wheel, variable intermittent wipers, a rear defogger, ventilated front disc/rear drum ABS brakes, front seat belt pre-tensioners, rear door child safety locks, child seat anchors, an emergency inside trunk release, center front and rear lap belts, two front headrests, an engine immobilizer, a remote anti-theft system, dusk-sensing headlights, digital keypad power door locks, one-touch power windows, heated power mirrors, cruise control, speed-proportional power steering, a tilt-adjustable steering wheel, front cupholders, a remote trunk lid release, front seatback storage, a front 12-volt power outlet, retained accessory power, six-passenger seating with cloth-trimmed front split bench seat with six-way power and adjustable lumbar support on driver's side, a split-folding rear bench seat, rear seat heating ducts, a climate control system, a leather-wrapped steering wheel, front reading lights, dual illuminated visor-vanity mirrors, a trunk light, an AM/FM cassette six-CD stereo with multi-CD located in dash, a mast antenna and a four-speaker sound system. Standard equipment in the Taurus SES sedan included a 3.0-liter 12-valve 155-hp V-6 engine, a four-speed automatic transmission, front-wheel drive, four-wheel independent suspension, a front stabilizer bar, a tachometer, a low-fuel indicator, a clock, P215/60R16 all-season tires on 16-in. alloy rims, a spacesaver spare on a spare steel wheel, variable intermittent wipers, a rear defogger, ventilated front disc/rear drum ABS brakes, front seat belt pre-tensioners, rear door child safety locks, child seat anchors, an emergency inside trunk release, center front and rear lap belts, two front headrests, an engine immobilizer, remote power door locks, one-touch power windows, power mirrors, cruise control, speed-proportional power steering, a tilt-adjustable steering wheel, front cupholders, a remote trunk lid release, front seatback storage, a front 12-volt power outlet, retained accessory power, six-passenger seating with cloth-trimmed front split bench seat with six-way power and adjustable lumbar support on driver's side, a split-folding rear bench seat, rear seat heating ducts, air conditioning, front reading lights, dual illuminated visor-vanity mirrors, a trunk light, an AM/FM cassette CD stereo, a mast antenna and a four-speaker sound system. Standard equipment in the Taurus SE wagon included a 3.0-liter 12-valve 155-hp V-6 engine, a four-speed automatic transmission, front-wheel drive, four-wheel independent suspension, front and rear stabilizer bars, a tachometer, a low-fuel indicator, a clock, cargo tie downs, P215/60R16 all-season tires on 16-in. alloy rims, a spacesaver spare on a spare steel wheel, variable intermittent wipers, a rear defogger, a roof rack, a rear window wiper, ventilated front disc/rear solid disc brakes, front seat belt pre-tensioners, rear door child safety locks, child seat anchors, center front and rear lap belts, two front headrests, an engine immobilizer, remote power door locks, one-touch power windows, power mirrors, cruise control, speed-proportional power steering, a tilt-adjustable steering wheel, front cupholders, front seatback storage, a front 12-volt power outlet, retained accessory power, six-passenger seating with cloth-trimmed front split bench seat, a split-folding rear bench seat, rear seat heating ducts, air conditioning, front reading lights, dual illuminated visor-vanity mirrors, a cargo area light, an AM/FM cassette CD stereo, a power antenna and a four-speaker sound system.

2001 Ford Taurus SES four-door Sport sedan. (FMC)

2001 Ford Taurus SE four-door station wagon. (FMC)

Model No.	Body/ Style No.	Body Type & Seating	Factory Price	Shipping Weight	Prod. Total
TAURUS LX (V-6)					
P	52	4d Sedan-6P	19,175	3,354	—
TAURUS SE (V-6)					
P	53	4d Sedan-6P	19,325	3,354	—
P	58	4d Wagon-6P	21,105	3,516	—
TAURUS SES (V-6)					
P	55	4d Sedan-6P	20,965	3,354	—
TAURUS SEL (V-8)					
P	56	4d Sedan-6P	22,450	3,354	—

CROWN VICTORIA — V-8 — The 2001 Crown Victoria offered a more powerful V-8 engine. There were also minor interior improvements and an optional adjustable pedal assembly. A crash sensor, safety belt pre-tensioners, dual-stage airbags and seat-position sensor enhanced the safety of the driver and passengers. Standard equipment for the base Crown Victoria included a 4.6-liter SOHC 16-valve 220-hp V-8, a four-speed automatic transmission, rear-wheel drive, a front independent suspension, front and rear stabilizer bars, a clock, a low-fuel indicator, P225/60SR16 all-season tires on 16 x 7-in. steel rims, a spacesaver spare tire on a steel spare wheel, variable intermittent windshield wipers, a rear window defogger, front disc/rear drum brakes, front seat belt pre-tensioners, rear door child safety locks, an emergency interior trunk release, front and rear center lap belts, two front headrests, an engine immobilizer, one touch power windows, power door locks, power mirrors, cruise control, speed-proportional power steering, a tilt-adjustable steering wheel, steering wheel mounted cruise controls, a remote trunk release, front door map pockets, six-passenger seating with a cloth-trimmed split front bench seat, a rear bench seat, air conditioning, a trunk light, a wood-trimmed dash, an AM/FM cassette stereo with four speakers and an element radio antenna. Standard equipment for the base Crown Victoria LX included a 4.6-liter SOHC 16-valve 220-hp V-8, a four-speed automatic transmission, rear-wheel drive, a front independent suspension, front and rear stabilizer bars, a clock, a low-fuel indicator, P225/60SR16 all-season tires on 16 x 7-in. steel rims, a spacesaver spare tire on a steel spare wheel, variable intermittent windshield wipers, a rear window defogger, front disc/rear drum brakes, front seat belt pre-tensioners, rear door child safety locks, an emergency interior trunk release, front and rear center lap belts, two front headrests, an engine immobilizer, one touch power windows, remote power door locks, power mirrors, cruise control, speed-proportional power steering, a tilt-adjustable steering wheel, steering wheel mounted cruise controls, a remote trunk release, front door map pockets, front seatback storage, six-passenger seating with a cloth-trimmed split front bench seat with six-way power and adjustable lumbar support on driver's side, a rear bench seat with folding center armrest, air conditioning, front reading lights, dual illuminated visor-vanity mirrors, a trunk light, a wood-trimmed dash, an AM/FM cassette stereo with four speakers and an element radio antenna.

Model No.	Body/ Style No.	Body Type & Seating	Factory Price	Shipping Weight	Prod. Total
CROWN VICTORIA (V-8)					
P	73	4d Sedan-5P	22,935	3,946	—
CROWN VICTORIA LX (V-8)					
P	74	4d Sedan-5P	25,050	3,946	—

FOCUS ENGINES

ENGINE [Base LX/SE/Street Sedans]: Inline. Overhead cam. Four-cylinder. Cast-iron block and aluminum head. Displacement: 121 cid (2.0 liters). Bore & stroke: 3.39 x 3.52 in. Compression ratio: 9.4:1. Brake horsepower: 110 at 5000 rpm. Torque: 125 lbs.-ft. at 3750 rpm. Split Port induction.

ENGINE [Base ZX3 Hatchback/ZTS Sedan/SE Wagon]: Inline. Double overhead cam. Four-cylinder. Cast-iron block and aluminum head. Displacement: 121 cid (2.0 liters). Bore & stroke: 3.39 x 3.52 in. Compression ratio: 9.6:1. Brake horsepower: 130 at 5750 rpm. Torque: 135 lbs.-ft. at 4500 rpm. Sequential fuel injection.

ESCORT ENGINES

ENGINE [ZX2]: Inline. Double overhead cam. Four-cylinder. Cast-iron block and aluminum head. Displacement: 121 cid (2.0 liters). Bore & stroke: 3.39 x 3.52 in. Compression ratio: 9.6:1. Brake horsepower: 130 at 5750 rpm. Torque: 135 lbs.-ft. at 4500 rpm. Sequential fuel injection.

TAURUS ENGINES

ENGINE [Base LX/SE]: Overhead valve V-6. Cast-iron block and head. Displacement: 182 cid (3.0 liters). Bore & stroke: 3.50 x 3.15 in. Compression ratio: 9.3:1. Brake horsepower: 155 at 4900 rpm. Torque: 185 lbs.-ft. at 3950 rpm. Sequential fuel injection.

ENGINE [Base SEL]: Double overhead cam flexible-fuel V-6. Aluminum block and head. Displacement: 182 cid (3.0 liters). Bore & stroke: 3.50 x 3.15 in. Compression ratio: 10.0:1. Brake horsepower: 200 at 5750 rpm. Torque: 200 lbs.-ft. at 4500 rpm.

CROWN VICTORIA ENGINE

ENGINE [Base]: Modular, overhead valve V-8. Displacement: 281 cid (4.6 liters). Bore & stroke: 3.60 x 3.60. Compression ratio: 9.0:1. Brake horsepower: 220 at 4750 rpm. Torque: 265 lbs.-ft. at 4000 rpm. Sequential fuel injection.

FOCUS CHASSIS: Wheelbase: 103 in. Overall length: (hatchback) 168.1 in.; (sedan) 174.9 in.; (wagon) 174.9 in. Overall width: (all) 66.9 in. Overall height: (wagon) 53.9 in.; (others) 56.3 in.

ESCORT CHASSIS: Wheelbase: 98.4 in. Overall length: 175.2 in. Overall width: 67.4 in. Overall height: 52.3 in. Front tread: (all) 56.5 in. Rear tread: (all) 56.5 in.

TAURUS CHASSIS: Wheelbase: (all) 108.5 in. Overall length: (sedan) 197.5 in.; (wagon) 199.6 in. Overall width: (all) 73 in. Overall height: (sedan) 56.1 in.; (wagon) 58 in. Front tread: 61.6 in. Rear tread: 61.4 in.

CROWN VICTORIA CHASSIS: Wheelbase: (all) 114.7 in. Overall length: (all) 212 in. Overall width: (all) 78.2 in. Overall height: (all) 56.8 in. Front tread: (all) 62.8 in. Rear tread: (all) 63.3 in.

FOCUS TECHNICAL: Standard transmission: five-speed manual transaxle. Drive axle: front. Steering: rack-and-pinion. Front suspension: (all) independent MacPherson struts with coil springs and stabilizer bar (all). Rear suspension: (all) independent control blade multi-link design with coil springs and shock absorbers (2.0L SOHC)/stabilizer bar (2.0L DOHC Zetec). Brakes: ventilated front disc, rear drum (power assisted). Body construction: unibody. Fuel tank: 13.2 gallons.

ESCORT TECHNICAL: Standard transmission: five-speed manual transaxle. Drive axle: front. Steering: rack-and-pinion. Front suspension: independent MacPherson strut with strut-mounted coil springs. Rear suspension: independent, Quadra-link with stabilizer bar. Brakes: front disc, rear drum (power assisted). Body construction: unibody. Fuel tank: 12.7 gallons.

TAURUS TECHNICAL: Standard transmission: four-speed overdrive automatic. Drive axle: front. Steering: rack-and-pinion. Front suspension: independent MacPherson strut front drive with strut-mounted coil springs, stabilizer bar, lower control arm and cast aluminum knuckle with integral ball joint. Rear suspension: (sedan) independent Quadra-link with coil spring on shock strut, stabilizer bar, tension strut, parallel suspension arms and two-piece cast spindle with forged stem; (wagon) independent short/long arm with spring on lower control arm, stabilizer bar, tension strut and cast spindle with pressed-in forged stem and integrated ball joints. Brakes: front disc, rear drum (power assisted) except Taurus SE wagon and Taurus SHO have four-wheel discs. Body construction: unibody. Fuel tank: 18.0 gallons.

CROWN VICTORIA TECHNICAL: Standard transmission: four-speed overdrive automatic. Drive axle: rear. Steering: re-circulating ball. Front suspension: independent short/long arm with ball joints, coil springs and stabilizer bar. Rear suspension: Watt's linkage. Brakes: four-wheel disc. Body construction: separate body and frame. Fuel tank: 19.0 gallons.

FOCUS OPTIONS: (ZX3 hatchback) 44A four-speed overdrive automatic transmission ($815). 47D AdvanceTrac ($1,225). 572 air conditioning ($795). 552 antilock braking system ($400). 422 California emissions requirements (no cost). 13A manual moonroof ($446). 93N non-California emissions requirements (no cost). 60A power group ($740). 50P premium group ($1,095). 59M side airbags ($350). (LX sedan) 44A four-speed overdrive automatic transmission ($815). 572 air conditioning ($795). 552 antilock braking system ($400). 422 California emissions requirements (no cost). 93N non-California emissions requirements (no cost). 59M side airbags ($350). (SE sedan) 44A four-speed overdrive automatic transmission ($815). 552 antilock braking system ($400). 422 California emissions requirements (no cost). 93N non-California emissions requirements (no cost). 50A SE Comfort group ($345). 434 SE sports group ($470). 59M side airbags ($350). (Street sedan) 44A four-speed overdrive automatic transmission ($815). 47D AdvanceTrac ($1,225). 552 antilock braking system ($400). 422 California emissions requirements (no cost). 93N non-California emissions requirements (no cost). 50A SE comfort group ($345). 434 SE sports group ($470). 59M side airbags ($350). 67A Street Edition Feature Car package ($775). (ZTS sedan) 44A four-speed overdrive automatic transmission ($815). 47D AdvanceTrac ($1,225). 422 California emissions requirements (no cost). 93N non-California emissions requirements (no cost). 59M side airbags ($350). 8 low-back bucket seats with unique leather trim and map pockets ($695). (SE wagon) 445 five-speed manual transmission (no cost). 552 antilock braking system ($400). 422 California emissions requirements (no cost). 93N non-California emissions requirements (no cost). 50A SE Comfort group ($345). 59M side airbags ($350). (Street wagon) 445 five-speed manual transmission (no cost). 47D AdvanceTrac ($1,225). 552 antilock braking system ($400). 422 California emissions requirements (no cost). 93N non-California emissions requirements (no cost). 50A SE Comfort group ($345). 434 SE sports group ($470). 59M side airbags ($350). 67A Street Edition Feature Car package ($775).

ESCORT OPTIONS: (ZX2) 64A 14-in. five-spoke chrome wheels ($595). 44T four-speed overdrive automatic transmission ($815). 919 AM/FM stereo cassette with six-disc compact CD changer ($295). 552 antilock braking system ($400). 422 California emissions requirements (no cost). 50A comfort group ($395). 12Y front and rear floor mats ($55). 572 manual air conditioning ($795). 93N non-California emissions requirements (no cost). 60A power group ($395). 13B power moonroof ($595). "A" unique leather sport bucket seats ($395).

TAURUS OPTIONS: (LX sedan) 992/44L 3.0-liter flexible fuel ethanol V-6 (no cost). 184 six-passenger seating (no cost). 552 antilock braking system ($600). 422 California emissions requirements (no cost). 12H front floor mats ($30). 93N non-California emissions requirements (no cost). 12Q rear floor mats ($25). 61B side impact airbags ($390). (SE sedan) 992/44L 3.0-liter flexible fuel ethanol V-6 (no cost). 184 six-passenger seating (no cost). 585 AM/FM stereo with single CD player ($140). 59C adjustable pedals ($120). 553 All-Speed traction control ($175). 552 antilock braking system ($600). 422 California emissions requirements (no cost). 12H front floor mats ($30). 93N non-California emissions requirements (no cost). 21A power driver's seat with manual lumbar adjustment ($395). 12Q rear floor mats ($25). 61B side impact airbags ($390). 46S 60/40 split-folding rear seat ($140). (SEL sedan) 185 five-passenger seating ($105). 59C adjustable pedals ($120). 553 All-Speed traction control ($175). 422 California emissions requirements (no cost). 12H front floor mats ($30). J leather seating surfaces ($895). 916 MACH premium sound system ($320). 93N non-California emissions requirements (no cost). 21J power passenger's seat ($350). 12Q rear floor mats ($25). 13K rear spoiler ($230). 61B side impact airbags ($390). (SES sedan) 992/44L 3.0-liter flexible fuel ethanol V-6 (no cost). 99S/44L 3.0-liter four-valve V-6 ($695). 185 five-passenger seating ($105). 59C adjustable pedals ($120). 553 All-Speed traction control ($175). 422 California emissions requirements (no cost). 12H front floor mats ($30). 54P heated mirrors ($35). 93N non-California emissions requirements (no cost). 13B power moonroof ($890). 53A premium audio group ($530). 12Q rear floor mats ($25). 13K rear spoiler ($230). 61B side impact airbags ($390). (SE wagon) 992/44L 3.0-liter flexible fuel ethanol V-6 (no cost). 99S/44L 3.0-liter four-valve V-6 ($695). 585 AM/FM stereo single CD player ($140). 59C adjustable pedals ($120). 553 All-Speed traction control ($175). 552 antilock braking system ($600). 422 California emissions requirements (no cost). FE9 federal emissions (no cost). 12H front floor mats ($30). 54P heated mirrors ($35). J leather seating surfaces ($895). 93N non-California emissions requirements (no cost). 21A power driver's seat with manual lumbar adjustment ($395). 53A premium audio group ($530). 12Q rear floor mats ($25). 85A SES group ($1,040). 61B side impact airbags ($390). 96W Wagon group ($300).

2001 Ford Crown Victoria LX four-door sedan. (FMC)

CROWN VICTORIA OPTIONS: (Base sedan) 999 4.6-liter natural gas V-8 with automatic overdrive transmission ($6,165). 21A six-way power driver's seat ($360). 552 antilock braking system ($600). 553 antilock braking system with traction control ($775). 422 California emissions requirements (no cost). 508 conventional spare tire ($120). 508 conventional spare tire ($105). 585 electronic AM/FM stereo with single CD player ($140). 153 front license plate bracket (no cost). 12Y front and rear floor mats ($55). 41G Handling and Performance package ($935). 93N non-California emissions requirements (no cost). T2A P225/60SR15 white sidewall tires ($80). 144 remote keyless entry system ($240). (LX sedan) 999 4.6-liter natural gas V-8 with automatic overdrive transmission ($6,165). 60R five-passenger sport appearance package ($995). 552 antilock braking system ($600). 553 antilock braking system with traction control ($775). 422 California emissions requirements (no cost). 65C Comfort group ($900). 65E Comfort Plus group ($1,900). 508 conventional spare tire ($120). 508 conventional spare tire ($105). 585 electronic AM/FM stereo with single CD player ($140). 153 front license plate bracket (no cost). 12Y front and rear floor mats ($55). 41G Handling and Performance package ($740). 41G Handling and Performance package ($615). 41G Handling and Performance package ($615). L split bench seat with leather seating surfaces ($795). 93N non-California emissions requirements (no cost). T2A P225/60SR15 white sidewall tires ($80). 59C power adjustable pedals ($120). 586 premium electronic AM/FM stereo with cassette ($360). 919 trunk-mounted six-disc CD changer ($350). 175 universal garage door opener ($115).

HISTORY: On Tues., Oct. 30, 2001, Ford Motor Co. Chairman William Clay Ford, Jr., forced the resignation of Jacques Nasser, the company's president and chief executive officer. Ford hinted that the company had lost its focus in several areas. Nasser's resignation ended a stormy three-year relationship between the earthy and outspoken native of the Middle East who grew up in Australia and the 44-year-old Ford family member. It also highlighted a stressful season for Ford, which lost more than $1 billion between April and November and had no clear sign that things would improve by 2002. Ford said that his company needed to focus on its core business of making cars and trucks. Ford's troubles started with the massive Firestone tire recall during 2000. With millions of dollars of lost sales for one of its most profitable vehicles (the Explorer SUV) at stake, Nasser went on the offensive against Firestone. This led to a split between the two companies, ending one of the oldest business and personal relationships in U.S. corporate history. Henry Ford and Harvey Firestone were Bill Ford's great-grandfathers. But, tires weren't the only problem. The quality of Ford's cars and trucks had deteriorated and productivity at its manufacturing facilities slipped. The introductions of the new Ford Escape mini-SUV and the redesigned 2002 Ford Explorer were delayed in an effort to avoid recalls, which still occurred. With Nasser's resignation, William Clay Ford, Jr., became chairman and CEO. Nick Scheele, a group vice president at the company's North American operation, was named chief operating officer and began work immediately on a recovery plan. Carl Reichardt, a retired chairman and CEO of Wells Fargo & Co., was named vice chairman of the board and chairman of the finance committee. Reichardt, 70, an old friend of the Ford family, took charge of Ford's financial operations. On a more positive note, Ford Motor Co. celebrated a centennial of Ford motor sports during 2001, with a big celebration taking place at the Henry Ford Museum & Greenfield Village during September.

2002 FORD

FOCUS — FOUR — Since its introduction in Europe in 1999 and in the U.S. in 2000 model, the Focus had won praise for its performance, handling and package ingenuity. The Focus was made available for 2002 in four distinct body styles: a ZX3 two-door hatchback, a four-door sedan, a four-door wagon and a new ZX5 four-door hatchback. New features for the 2002 Focus included a Personal Safety System. The all-new ZX5 five-door hatchback had the European styling of the ZX3 with the versatility of four doors. The new ZTW wagon included a sporty package that added more style to the versatile wagon. Available for the first time on all body styles was a power moonroof and a six-disc in-dash CD changer. Inside, Focus buyers found improved cup holders designed to accept larger cups, an added rear-seat map pocket on LX, SE and ZX3 models and "kangaroo" seat pouches on the ZTS. Colors added for 2002 included Grabber Green Clearcoat Metallic, French Blue Clearcoat Metallic and Liquid Grey Clearcoat Metallic. All Focus models employed efficient design and package engineering to maximize interior room for passengers and cargo. The high roofline increased front and rear headroom, while the long wheelbase offered greater interior volume and contributed to a smoother ride. A 2.0L SOHC in-line four-cylinder was standard on Focus LX and SE. It produced 110-hp and 125 lbs.-ft. of torque. This engine was matched with an IB5 five-speed manual transaxle that used synthetic lubricant to help ensure durability and smooth shifting in cold weather. The 2.0-liter DOHC Zetec inline four-cylinder engine was standard on Focus ZX3, ZTS and wagon models and optional on the Focus SE sedan. It delivered 130-hp and 135 lbs.-ft. of torque. This engine was matched with a MTX75 five-speed manual transaxle designed with low-friction needle-roller bearings and using low-viscosity mineral oil to help improve fuel economy and performance. A four-speed electronically controlled automatic overdrive transaxle was available on all models.

FOCUS ZX3 HATCHBACK: Standard equipment included a bumper-color 5-mph front bumper, a black deck lid handle, black door handles with integral front key locks, fog lamps, a flush windshield and backlight with Solar-Tint glass, semi-flush side glass, fixed rear quarter glass, aerodynamic halogen headlamps, front side markers in bumper and front turn indicators in grille, black-finished manual outside rearview mirrors, color-keyed door frame moldings, black beltline moldings, black rocker panel moldings, black body side moldings, a PVC coating on the lower body sides, a PVC underbody coating, clearcoat paint, 15-in. five-spoke aluminum wheels, dual front second-generation air-bags, manual front belts with pre-tensioners and adjustable D-rings, manual outboard rear belts, LATCH system in rear, a full-length center console with two front cupholders, pen storage, a storage area with cupholder, an alloy shift knob (manual transmission only), courtesy lights with theater dimming feature, soft feel vinyl door trim, vinyl covered door trim insert panels, a non-locking glove box, front and rear grab handles, a soft feel instrument panel with climate and radio controls in center stack position, a storage tray, a coin holder and trinket tray, alloy appearance on center stack bezel, a carpeted and removable package tray cover, an AM/FM stereo single disc CD player with digital clock and four speakers, sport bucket seats with tip/slide feature and driver side height adjustment, unique ZX3 seat fabric, single seat map pockets, a 60/40 split-folding rear seat with flip-up rear cushion, a four-spoke leather-wrapped sport steering wheel, a tachometer, driver and passenger visor-vanity mirrors with flap closings, a 110-amp. alternator, a maintenance-free battery, a battery saver, a power-assisted front disc/rear drum brake system, a self-energizing rear linkage clutch, a rear window defroster, side window demisters, electronic engine controls, an electronic ignition system, the 2.0-liter Zetec four-cylinder engine, a single exhaust tip tailpipe, front-wheel drive, a 13.2-gallon fuel tank, a headlamps-on warning chime, an inside hood release, a single-note horn, an interior trunk or liftgate release, a low-fuel warning light, a 12V-power point, rear seat heat ducts, the SecuriLock™ passive anti-theft system, front and rear stabilizer bars, power rack-and-pinion steering, a MacPherson strut independent front suspension, a control blade short/long arm independent rear suspension, a temperature gauge, P195/60R15 tires, a mini spare tire, a five-speed transaxle, a trip odometer, two-speed windshield wipers with fixed intermittent feature and a rear window wiper and washer.

FOCUS LX SEDAN: Standard equipment included a bumper-color 5-mph front bumper, a black deck lid handle, black door handles with integral front key locks, a flush windshield and backlight with Solar-Tint glass, semi-flush side glass, aerodynamic halogen headlamps, front side markers in bumper and front turn indicators in grille, black-finished manual outside rearview mirrors, color-keyed door frame moldings, black beltline moldings, black body side moldings, a PVC coating on the lower body sides, a PVC underbody coating, clearcoat paint, 14-in. five-spoke steel wheels, dual front second-generation airbags, manual front belts with pre-tensioners and adjustable D-rings, manual outboard rear belts, LATCH system in rear, a full-length center console with two front cupholders, pen storage, a storage area with cupholder, courtesy lights with theater dimming feature, soft feel vinyl door trim, vinyl covered door trim insert panels, a non-locking glove box, front and rear grab handles, a soft feel instrument panel with climate and radio controls in center stack position, a storage tray, a coin holder and trinket tray, an AM/FM stereo cassette with digital clock and four speakers, low-back cloth bucket seats with driver's seat height adjustment and a single map pocket, a 60/40 split-folding rear seat with flip-up rear cushion, a four-spoke soft feel steering wheel, driver and passenger visor-vanity mirrors with flap closings, a 110-amp. alternator, a maintenance-free battery, a battery saver, a power-assisted front disc/rear drum brake system, a self-energizing rear linkage clutch, a rear window defroster, side window demisters, electronic engine controls, an electronic ignition system, the 2.0-liter SPI four-cylinder engine, front-wheel drive, a 13.2-gallon fuel tank, a headlamps-on warning chime, an inside hood release, a single-note horn, an interior trunk or liftgate release, child safety rear door locks, a low-fuel warning light, a 12V-power point, rear seat heat ducts, the SecuriLock™ passive anti-theft system, a front stabilizer bar, power rack-and-pinion steering, a MacPherson strut independent front suspension, a control blade short/long arm independent rear suspension, a temperature gauge, P185/65R14 tires, a mini spare tire, a five-speed transaxle, a trip odometer and two-speed windshield wipers with fixed intermittent feature.

FOCUS SE SEDAN: Standard equipment included a bumper-color 5-mph front bumper, a black deck lid handle, black door handles with integral front key locks, a flush windshield and backlight with Solar-Tint glass, semi-flush side glass, aerodynamic halogen headlamps, front

side markers in bumper and front turn indicators in grille, black-finished power outside rearview mirrors, color-keyed door frame moldings, black beltline moldings, body-color side moldings, a PVC coating on the lower body sides, a PVC underbody coating, clearcoat paint, 15-in. five-spoke aluminum wheels, dual front second-generation airbags, manual front belts with pre-tensioners and adjustable D-rings, manual outboard rear belts, LATCH system in rear, a full-length center console with two front cupholders, pen storage, a storage area with cupholder, a driver's armrest with storage, courtesy lights with theater dimming feature, soft feel vinyl door trim, vinyl covered door trim insert panels, a non-locking glove box, front and rear grab handles, a soft feel instrument panel with climate and radio controls in center stack position, a storage tray, a coin holder and trinket tray, power door locks, an AM/FM stereo single disc CD player with digital clock and four speakers, low-back cloth bucket seats with driver's seat height adjustment and a single map pocket, a 60/40 split-folding rear seat with flip-up rear cushion, a four-spoke soft feel steering wheel, driver and passenger visor-vanity mirrors with flap closings, one touch power windows, air conditioning, remote keyless entry, a 110-amp. alternator, a maintenance-free battery, a battery saver, a power-assisted front disc/rear drum brake system, a self-energizing rear linkage clutch, a rear window defroster, side window demisters, electronic engine controls, an electronic ignition system, the 2.0-liter SPI four-cylinder engine, a single exhaust tip tailpipe, front-wheel drive, a 13.2-gallon fuel tank, a headlamps-on warning chime, an inside hood release, a single-note horn, an interior trunk or liftgate release, child safety rear door locks, a low-fuel warning light, a 12V-power point, rear seat heat ducts, the SecuriLock™ passive anti-theft system, a front stabilizer bar, power rack-and-pinion steering, a MacPherson strut independent front suspension, a control blade short/long arm independent rear suspension, a temperature gauge, P195/60R15 tires, a mini spare tire, a five-speed transaxle, a trip odometer and variable intermittent windshield wipers.

FOCUS ZTS SEDAN: Standard equipment included a bumper-color 5-mph front bumper, a chrome deck lid handle, black door handles with integral front key locks, fog lamps, a flush windshield and backlight with Solar-Tint glass, semi-flush side glass, aerodynamic halogen headlamps, front side markers in bumper and front turn indicators in grille, black-finished power outside rearview mirrors, color-keyed door frame moldings, black beltline moldings, body-color side moldings, a PVC coating on the lower body sides, a PVC underbody coating, clearcoat paint, 16-in. six-spoke aluminum wheels, dual front second-generation airbags, manual front belts with pre-tensioners and adjustable D-rings, manual outboard rear belts, LATCH system in rear, pen storage, a storage area with cupholder, a driver's armrest with storage, courtesy lights with theater dimming feature and map reading lights, soft feel vinyl door trim, vinyl covered door trim insert panels, a non-locking glove box, front and rear grab handles, a soft feel instrument panel with climate and radio controls in center stack position, a storage tray, a coin holder and trinket tray, dark brushed aluminum appearance on instrument panel center stack bezel, power door locks, an AM/FM stereo single disc CD player with digital clock and four speakers, low-back cloth bucket seats with driver's seat height adjustment and lumbar support, dual map pockets and "kangaroo" pouch, a 60/40 split-folding rear seat with flip-up rear cushion, a four-spoke leather-wrapped soft feel, tilt/telescope steering wheel, a tachometer, driver and passenger visor-vanity mirrors with flap closings, one touch power windows, air conditioning, remote keyless entry, a 110-amp. alternator, a maintenance-free battery, a battery saver, a power-assisted front disc/rear drum brake system, a self-energizing rear linkage clutch, a rear window defroster, side window demisters, electronic engine controls, an electronic ignition system, the 2.0-liter Zetec four-cylinder engine, a single exhaust tip tailpipe, front-wheel drive, a 13.2-gallon fuel tank, a headlamps-on warning chime, an inside hood release, a single-note horn, an interior trunk or liftgate release, child safety rear door locks, a low-fuel warning light, a 12V-power point, rear seat heat ducts, the SecuriLock™ passive anti-theft system, speed control, front and rear stabilizer bars, power rack-and-pinion steering, a MacPherson strut independent front suspension, a control blade short/long arm independent rear suspension, a temperature gauge, P205/50R16 tires, a mini spare tire, a five-speed transaxle, a trip odometer and variable intermittent windshield wipers.

FOCUS ZX5 HATCHBACK: Standard equipment included a bumper-color 5-mph front bumper, a chrome liftgate handle, black door handles with integral front key locks, fog lamps, a flush windshield and backlight with Solar-Tint glass, semi-flush side glass, aerodynamic halogen headlamps, front side markers in bumper and front turn indicators in grille, black-finished power outside rearview mirrors, color-keyed door frame moldings, black beltline moldings, body-color side moldings, a PVC coating on the lower body sides, a PVC underbody coating, clearcoat paint, 16-in. six-spoke aluminum wheels, dual front second-generation airbags, manual front belts with pre-tensioners and adjustable D-rings, manual outboard rear belts, LATCH system in rear, a full-length center console with two cupholders, pen storage, a storage area with cupholder, a driver's armrest with storage, courtesy lights with theater dimming feature and map reading lights, soft feel vinyl door trim, vinyl covered door trim insert panels, a non-locking glove box, front and rear grab handles, a soft feel instrument panel with climate and radio controls in center stack position, a storage tray, a coin holder and trinket tray, dark brushed aluminum appearance on instrument panel center stack bezel, power door locks, an AM/FM stereo with six disc in-dash CD player with digital clock and four speakers, sport bucket seats with driver's seat height adjustment, dual map pockets and "kangaroo" pouch, a 60/40 split-folding rear seat with flip-up rear cushion, a four-spoke leather-wrapped soft feel, tilt/telescope steering wheel, a tachometer, driver and passenger visor-vanity mirrors with flap closings, one touch power windows, air conditioning, remote keyless entry, a 110-amp. alternator, a maintenance-free battery, a battery saver, a power-assisted front disc/rear drum brake system, a self-energizing rear linkage clutch, a rear window defroster, side window demisters, electronic engine controls, an electronic ignition system, the 2.0-liter Zetec four-cylinder engine, a single exhaust tip tailpipe, front-wheel drive, a 13.2-gallon fuel tank, a headlamps-on warning chime, an inside hood release, a single-note horn, an interior trunk or liftgate release, child safety rear door locks, a low-fuel warning light, a 12V-power point, rear seat heat ducts, the SecuriLock™ passive anti-theft system, speed control, front and rear stabilizer bars, power rack-and-pinion steering, a MacPherson strut independent front suspension, a control blade short/long arm independent rear suspension, a temperature gauge, P205/50R16 tires, a mini spare tire, a five-speed transaxle, a trip odometer, variable intermittent windshield wipers and a rear window wiper/washer.

FOCUS SE WAGON: Standard equipment included a bumper-color 5-mph front bumper, a black liftgate handle, black door handles with integral front key locks, a flush windshield and backlight with Solar-Tint glass, semi-flush side glass, aerodynamic halogen headlamps, front side markers in bumper and front turn indicators in grille, a luggage rack, black-finished power outside rearview mirrors, color-keyed door frame moldings, black beltline moldings, body-color side moldings, a PVC coating on the lower body sides, a PVC underbody coating, clearcoat paint, 15-in. multi-spoke aluminum wheels, dual front second-generation airbags, manual front belts with pre-tensioners and adjustable D-rings, manual outboard rear belts, LATCH system in rear, a cargo area cover, a full-length center console with two cupholders, pen storage, a storage area with cupholder, a driver's armrest with storage, courtesy lights with theater dimming feature, soft feel vinyl door trim, vinyl covered door trim insert panels, a non-locking glove box, front and rear grab handles, a soft feel instrument panel with climate and radio controls in center stack position, a storage tray, a coin holder and trinket tray, power door locks, an AM/FM stereo with single disc CD player with digital clock and four speakers, low-back cloth bucket seats with driver's height adjustment, single map pockets, a 60/40 split-folding rear seat with flip-up rear cushion, a four-spoke soft feel steering wheel, driver and passenger visor-vanity mirrors with flap closings, one touch power windows, air conditioning, remote keyless entry, a 110-amp. alternator, a maintenance-free battery, a battery saver, a power-assisted front disc/rear drum brake system, side window demisters, electronic engine controls, an electronic ignition system, the 2.0-liter Zetec four-cylinder engine, a single exhaust tip tailpipe, front-wheel drive, a 13.2-gallon fuel tank, a headlamps-on warning chime, an inside hood release, a single-note horn, an interior trunk or liftgate release, child safety rear door locks, a low-fuel warning light, a 12V-power point, rear seat heat ducts, the SecuriLock™ passive anti-theft system, a rear stabilizer bar, power rack-and-pinion steering, a MacPherson strut independent front suspension, a control blade short/long arm independent rear suspension, a temperature gauge, P195/60R15 tires, a mini spare tire, a four-speed automatic transmission, a trip odometer, variable intermittent windshield wipers and a rear window wiper/washer.

FOCUS ZTW WAGON: Standard equipment included a bumper-color 5-mph front bumper, black door handles with integral front key locks, fog lamps, a flush windshield and backlight with Solar-Tint glass, semi-flush side glass, aerodynamic halogen headlamps, front side markers in bumper and front turn indicators in grille, a luggage rack, black-finished power outside rearview mirrors, color-keyed door frame moldings, black beltline moldings, body-color side moldings, a PVC coating on the lower body sides, a PVC underbody coating, clearcoat paint, 16-in. six-spoke aluminum wheels, dual front second-generation airbags, manual front belts with pre-tensioners and adjustable D-rings, manual outboard rear belts, LATCH system in rear, a cargo area cover, a full-length center console with two cupholders, pen storage, a storage area with cupholder, a driver's armrest with storage, courtesy lights with theater dimming feature and map reading lights, soft feel vinyl door trim, vinyl covered door trim insert panels, a non-locking glove box, front and rear grab handles, a soft feel instrument panel with climate and radio controls in center stack position, a storage tray, a coin holder and trinket tray, a dark brushed aluminum center stack appearance, power door locks, an AM/FM stereo with single disc CD player with digital clock and four speakers, low-back leather bucket seats with driver's seat height adjustment and lumbar support, a 60/40 split-folding rear seat with flip-up rear cushion, a four-spoke leather-wrapped soft feel, tilt/telescope steering wheel, a tachometer, driver and passenger visor-vanity mirrors with flap closings, one touch power windows, air conditioning, remote keyless entry, a 110-amp. alterna-

tor, a maintenance-free battery, a battery saver, a power-assisted front disc/rear drum brake system, a battery saver, a power-assisted front disc/rear drum brake system, a rear defroster, side window demisters, electronic engine controls, an electronic ignition system, the 2.0-liter Zetec four-cylinder engine, a single exhaust tip tailpipe, front-wheel drive, a 13.2-gallon fuel tank, a headlamps-on warning chime, an inside hood release, a single-note horn, an interior trunk or liftgate release, child safety rear door locks, a low-fuel warning light, a 12V-power point, rear seat heat ducts, the SecuriLock™ passive anti-theft system, speed control, front and rear stabilizer bars, power rack-and-pinion steering, a MacPherson strut independent front suspension, a control blade short/long arm independent rear suspension, a temperature gauge, P205/50R16 tires, a mini spare tire, a four-speed automatic transmission, a trip odometer, variable intermittent windshield wipers and a rear window wiper/washer.

I.D. DATA: Ford's 17-symbol Vehicle Identification Number (VIN) was stamped on a metal tab fastened to the instrument panel, visible through the windshield. panel, visible through the windshield. The first symbol indicates the nation of origin: 1=United States; 2=Canada; 3=Mexico. The second symbol indicates manufacturer: F=Ford Motor Co.; The third symbol indicates vehicle type: A=passenger car. The fourth symbol indicates type of restraint system: B=driver and passenger airbags and active belts (except Escort ZX2 coupe); F=driver and passenger airbags and active belts; K= driver and passenger airbags and active belts in all outboard positions. The fifth symbol indicates designation: P=Ford; T=Imported from outside North America or non-Ford car marketed by Ford in North America. The sixth and seventh symbols indicate body type: 11=Escort ZX2 two-door coupe; 31=Focus ZX3 three-door coupe; 33=Focus LX four-door sedan; 34=Focus SE/Focus Street four-door sedan; 36=Focus SE/Focus Street four-door station wagon; 38=Focus ZTS four-door sedan; 52=Taurus LX four-door sedan; 53=Taurus SE two-valve four-door sedan; 55=Taurus SE SVG four-door sedan; 56=Taurus SEL four-door sedan; 58=Taurus SE four-door station wagon; 73=Crown Victoria four-door sedan; 74=Crown Victoria LX four-door sedan. The eighth symbol indicates engine: [Escort] P=2.0-liter I-4 with EF/SPI; [Taurus] S=3.0-liter DOHC V-6 with EFI; U=3.0-liter V-6 with EFI; 2=flexible fuel 3.0-liter V-6 with EFI. [Contour] G=2.5-liter DOHC V-6 with EFI; L=2.5-liter DOHC V-6 with EFI; Z=2.0-liter DOHC I-4 with EFI; 3=2.0-liter DOHC I-4 with EFI. [Crown Victoria] W=4.6-liter SOHC V-8 with EFI (Romeo engine plant). The ninth symbol is a check digit. The 10th symbol indicates model year: Z=2001. The 11th symbol indicates assembly plant: A=Hapeville (Atlanta), Ga.; F=Dearborn, Mich.; G=Chicago, Ill.; K=Claycomo (Kansas City), Mo.; M=Cuautitlan, Mexico; R=Hermosillo, Mexico; W=Wayne, Mich.; X=Talbotville (St. Thomas), Ontario, Canada. The last six symbols are the sequential production number starting at 100001 at each factory.

Model No.	Body/ Style No.	Body Type & Seating	Factory Price	Shipping Weight	Prod. Total
FOCUS ZX3 (FOUR)					
P	31	3d Hatchback-5P	12,935	2,551	—
FOCUS ZX3 POWER PREMIUM (FOUR)					
P	31	3d Hatchback-5P	14,970		2,551—
FOCUS ZX3 PREMIUM (FOUR)					
P	31	3d Hatchback-5P	14,030	2,551	
FOCUS LX (FOUR)					
P	33	4d Sedan-5P	13,250	2,551	
FOCUS LX PREMIUM (FOUR)					
P	33	4d Sedan-5P	14,095	2,551	
FOCUS SE (FOUR)					
P	34	4d Sedan-5P	14,840	2,551	
P	36	4d Wagon-5P	17,045	2,551	—
FOCUS SE COMFORT (FOUR)					
P	34	4d Sedan-5P	15,185	2,551	—
P	36	4d Wagon-5P	17,390	2,551	—
FOCUS SE COMFORT (ZETEC FOUR)					
P	34	4d Sedan-5P	15,435	2,551	
FOCUS ZTS (FOUR)					
P	38	4d Sedan-5P	15,760	2,551	
FOCUS ZK5 (FOUR)					
P	—	5d Hatchback-5P	16,135	2,600	
FOCUS ZTW (FOUR)					
P	38	4d Wagon-5P	18,225	2,551	—

ESCORT — FOUR — The Escort didn't make it into Ford Motor Co.'s 2002 electronic press kits, but you could still get one in 2002. It was essentially a carryover model with few, if any, changes from the previous year's model. It was offered in ZX2 coupe, Deluxe ZX2 coupe and Premium ZX2 coupe trim levels all utilizing the same regular-grade-fuel 2.0-liter 16-valve inline four-cylinder gasoline engine that produced 130-hp at 5300 rpm and 135 ft.-lbs. of torque at 4500 rpm.

ESCORT ZX2: Standard equipment included a 2.0-liter DOHC 16-valve 130-hp four-cylinder engine, a five-speed manual transmission, front-wheel drive, four-wheel independent suspension, front and rear stabilizer bars, a tachometer, a low-fuel indicator, a clock, 15-in. alloy wheel rims, P185/60R15 all-season tires, a spacesaver spare on a steel spare wheel, variable intermittent windshield wipers, a rear defogger, a rear spoiler, front disc/rear drum brakes, power mirrors, power steering, front and rear cupholders, a remote trunk release, front door pockets, a front 12-volt power outlet, a front console with storage space, four-passenger seating with cloth trimmed sport bucket seats, a split-folding rear seat, dual visor-vanity mirrors and an AM/FM cassette stereo with four speakers.

ESCORT ZX2 DELUXE: Standard equipment included a 2.0-liter DOHC 16-valve 130-hp four-cylinder engine, a five-speed manual transmission, front-wheel drive, four-wheel independent suspension, front and rear stabilizer bars, a tachometer, a low-fuel indicator, a clock, 15-in. alloy wheel rims, P185/60R15 all-season tires, a spacesaver spare on a steel spare wheel, variable intermittent windshield wipers, a rear defogger, a rear spoiler, front disc/rear drum brakes, power mirrors, cruise control, power steering, a leather-wrapped tilt-adjustable steering wheel, front and rear cupholders, a remote trunk release, front door pockets, a front 12-volt power outlet, a front console with storage space, four-passenger seating with cloth trimmed sport bucket seats, a split-folding rear seat, air conditioning, front reading lights, dual visor-vanity mirrors and an AM/FM cassette stereo with four speakers.

ESCORT ZX2 PREMIUM: Standard equipment included a 2.0-liter DOHC 16-valve 130-hp four-cylinder engine, a five-speed manual transmission, front-wheel drive, four-wheel independent suspension, front and rear stabilizer bars, a tachometer, a low-fuel indicator, a clock, 15-in. alloy wheel rims, P185/60R15 all-season tires, a spacesaver spare on a steel spare wheel, variable intermittent windshield wipers, a rear defogger, a rear spoiler, front disc/rear drum brakes, remote power door locks, one touch power windows, power mirrors, cruise control, power steering, a leather-wrapped tilt-adjustable steering wheel, front and rear cupholders, a remote trunk release, front door pockets, a front 12-volt power outlet, a front console with storage space, four-passenger seating with cloth trimmed sport bucket seats, a split-folding rear seat, air conditioning, front reading lights, dual visor-vanity mirrors, front and rear floor mats and an AM/FM cassette stereo with four speakers.

Model No.	Body/ Style No.	Body Type & Seating	Factory Price	Shipping Weight	Prod. Total
ESCORT ZX2 (FOUR)					
P	11	2d Coupe-5P	12,990	2,478	—
ESCORT ZX2 DELUXE (FOUR)					
P	11	2d Coupe-5P	14,035	2,478	—
ESCORT ZX2 PREMIUM (FOUR)					
P	11	2d Coupe-5P	14,490	2,478	—

TAURUS — V-6/V-8 — The 2002 Taurus remained an outstanding family vehicle with a focus on safety, quality, convenience and comfort. It was available in two body styles, a four-door sedan and a four-door wagon. The 2002 Taurus featured a contemporary aerodynamic design. The 3.0-liter OHV Vulcan V-6 produced 155-hp and 185 lbs.-ft. of torque, while the 3.0-liter DOHC 24-valve Duratec V-6 produced 200-hp and 200 lbs.-ft. of torque. A flexible fuel version of the Vulcan engine that ran on E-85 ethanol, regular unleaded gasoline or any combination of the two in the same tank was optional. The Taurus offered a spacious interior with a high level of convenience items. The sedan came with a choice of five- or six-passenger seating and offered available 60/40 split fold-down rear seatbacks for flexibility in carrying passengers and cargo. A rear-facing third seat was available on the wagon. Taurus' Personal Safety System is able to adjust the deployment of the dual-stage front airbags to help protect the front occupants. The system determined how many airbags should deploy and at what level, depending on the severity of the accident and safety belt usage. The system used an electronic crash severity sensor, a PSS restraint control module, a driver's seat position sensor, safety belt pre-tensioners, energy management retractors and front outboard safety belt usage sensors to help it protect the driver and right front passenger in certain frontal collisions. The Taurus also offered an optional side airbag supplemental restraint system for enhanced protection. The new LATCH child-safety seat system (Lower Anchors and Tethers for Children) helped to improve the connection of a LATCH-compatible child safety seat. The SecuriLock™ passive anti-theft system used an electronically coded ignition key to start the vehicle. The vehicle would not start if the key did not have the code. An available perimeter anti-theft system monitored the doors, hood and deck lid against unauthorized entry. All doors locked automatically when they were closed, the ignition was on, the transaxle was in gear and the brake pedal was depressed. New 2002 Taurus features included an LED rear high-mount stop lamp on all series. An auto-dimming rearview mirror with a compass was available on SES and SEL models. Security approach lamps were standard on SE, SES and SEL models. An AM/FM stereo single CD player was a new no-cost option on SE sedans and wagons. Power adjustable accelerator and brake pedals were made standard in 2002 SEL sedans and wagons. Six-passenger seating with flip-fold storage console made standard (five-passenger seating was still standard in the SES Deluxe and SEL models). Floor mats became standard in all series. SE, SES and SEL models got a new cargo net. Added colors for 2002 included Matador Red Clearcoat Metallic, True Blue Clearcoat Metallic, Arizona Beige Clearcoat Metallic and Dark Shadow Grey Clearcoat Metallic. All Taurus models had an 18-gallon fuel tank.

TAURUS LX SEDAN: Standard equipment included 5-mph front and rear bumpers, body-color flush mounted door handles, a body-color front fascia, multi reflector halogen headlamps, black-finished electric control mirrors, body-color side moldings, flush black window moldings, black rocker panel moldings, clearcoat paint, monochromatic taillights with red turn signals, locking wheel covers, a front ashtray, color-keyed 13.5-oz. Carpeting with built-in foot rest, electronic digital clock with dimmer feature, a color-keyed integral center console with cupholders and cassette storage, chrome interior door handles, front and rear floor mats, a glove box, rear grab handles, grocery bag hooks in trunk, two-tone instrument panel with backlit cluster, positive shut-off climate control registers, side window demisters, a windshield defroster, an integrated control panel with climate and radio controls, a rear defroster, a light group with dual-beam map and dome lamps, a dome light switch on all doors, warning lights and chimes, a low-fuel indicator, a delayed-off dome lamp, front door courtesy lights, an ashtray light, a luggage compartment light, a fully-trimmed low-liftover luggage compartment, day/night rearview mirrors, dual second-generation airbags, an electronic AM/FM full-logic stereo with four speakers, six-passenger seating with dual recliners, a front armrest, seat map pockets, two-way headrests, a center seat console, a driver position sensor, a front safety belt use detector, seat belts, a tilt steering column, a color-keyed four-spoke steering wheel, cloth covered sun visors, dual visor-vanity mirrors, air conditioning, quarter panel air extractors, a 130-amp/ alternator, a fixed whip antenna mounted on the quarter panel, a 58-amp. low-maintenance battery, a battery saver, power assisted front disc/rear drum brakes, chimes, a crash-severity sensor, a deck lid release, a rear window defogger/defroster, electronic engine controls, an emergency inside trunk release, the 3.0-liter two-valve Vulcan V-6, front-wheel drive, an 18-gallon fuel tank, a fuel shut-off switch, Solar-Tinted glass, rear seat heat ducts, a hood with gas-assist struts and a remote release, a dual-note horn, instrumentation (including temperature and fuel gauges, a 110-mph speedometer, a low brake fluid warning, a trip odometer, an odometer and a tachometer), rear door child safety locks, illuminated power door lock controls, a foot-operated parking brake, two 12-volt power points (outlets), the SecuriLock™ passive anti-theft system, a column-mounted gearshift with soft feel handle, power rack-and-pinion steering, MacPherson strut independent front suspension with nitrogen gas pressurized struts and a front stabilizer bar, an independent rear quadra-link suspension with nitrogen gas pressurized struts, deck lid tie-down provisions, P21560R16 all-season tires, a mini spare tire, an electronic four-speed automatic overdrive transaxle, a transaxle oil cooler, two-speed variable intermittent windshield wipers and one touch power windows with lock-out switch and illuminated controls.

TAURUS SE SEDAN: Standard equipment included 5-mph front and rear bumpers, body-color flush mounted door handles, a body-color front fascia, multi reflector halogen headlamps, a perimeter lighting system with remote keyless entry, body-color electric control mirrors, body-color side moldings, flush black window moldings, black rocker panel moldings, clearcoat paint, monochromatic taillights with red turn signals, 16-in. five-spoke wheels, a front ashtray, a cargo net, color-keyed 13.5-oz. Carpeting with built-in foot rest, electronic digital clock with dimmer feature, a color-keyed integral center console with cupholders and cassette storage, chrome interior door handles, front and rear floor mats, a glove box, rear grab handles, grocery bag hooks in trunk, two-tone instrument panel with backlit cluster, positive shut-off climate control registers, side window demisters, a windshield defroster, an integrated control panel with climate and radio controls, a rear defroster, a light group with dual-beam map and dome lamps, a dome light switch on all doors, warning lights and chimes, a low-fuel indicator, a delayed-off dome lamp, front door courtesy lights, an ashtray light, a luggage compartment light, a fully-trimmed low-liftover luggage compartment, day/night rearview mirrors, dual second-generation airbags, an electronic AM/FM full-logic stereo cassette with four speakers, six-passenger seating with dual recliners, a front armrest, seat map pockets, two-way headrests, a center seat console, a driver position sensor, a front safety belt use detector, seat belts, a tilt steering column, a color-keyed four-spoke steering wheel, cloth covered sun visors, dual visor-vanity mirrors, air conditioning, quarter panel air extractors, a 130-amp/ alternator, a fixed whip antenna mounted on the quarter panel, a 58-amp. low-maintenance battery, a battery saver, power assisted front disc/rear drum brakes, chimes, a crash-severity sensor, a deck lid release, a rear window defogger/defroster, electronic engine controls, an emergency inside trunk release, the 3.0-liter two-valve Vulcan V-6, front-wheel drive, an 18-gallon fuel tank, a fuel shut-off switch, Solar-Tinted glass, rear seat heat ducts, a hood with gas-assist struts and a remote release, a dual-note horn, instrumentation (including temperature and fuel gauges, a 110-mph speedometer, a low brake fluid warning, a trip odometer, an odometer and a tachometer), rear door child safety locks, illuminated power door lock controls, a foot-operated parking brake, two 12-volt power points (outlets), remote keyless entry, the SecuriLock™ passive anti-theft system, a column-mounted gear shifter with soft feel handle, speed control, power rack-and-pinion steering, MacPherson strut independent front suspension with nitrogen gas pressurized struts and a front stabilizer bar, an independent rear quadra-link suspension with nitrogen gas pressurized struts, deck lid tie-down provisions, P21560R16 all-season tires, a mini spare tire, an electronic four-speed automatic overdrive transaxle, a transaxle oil cooler, two-speed variable intermittent windshield wipers and one touch power windows with lock-out switch and illuminated controls.

TAURUS SES SEDAN: Standard equipment included 5-mph front and rear bumpers, body-color flush mounted door handles, a body-color front fascia, multi reflector halogen headlamps, a perimeter lighting system with remote keyless entry, body-color electric control mirrors, body-color side moldings, flush black window moldings, black rocker panel moldings, clearcoat paint, monochromatic taillights with red turn signals, 16-in. five-spoke wheels, a front ashtray, a cargo net, color-keyed 13.5-oz. Carpeting with built-in foot rest, electronic digital clock with dimmer feature, a color-keyed integral center console with cupholders and cassette storage, chrome interior door handles, front and rear floor mats, a glove box, rear grab handles, grocery bag hooks in trunk, two-tone instrument panel with backlit cluster, positive shut-off climate control registers, side window demisters, a windshield defroster, an integrated control panel with climate and radio controls, a rear defroster, a light group with dual-beam map and dome lamps, a dome light switch on all doors, warning lights and chimes, a low-fuel indicator, a delayed-off dome lamp, front door courtesy lights, an ashtray light, a luggage compartment light, a fully-trimmed low-liftover luggage compartment, day/night rearview mirrors, dual second-generation airbags, an electronic AM/FM full-logic stereo and single in-dash CD player with four speakers, six-passenger seating with dual recliners, a front armrest, seat map pockets, two-way headrests, a center seat console, a six-way power driver's seat with lumbar support, a 60/40 rear seat with folding seatbacks, a driver position sensor, a front safety belt use detector, seat belts, a tilt steering column, a color-keyed four-spoke steering wheel, cloth covered sun visors, dual illuminated visor-vanity mirrors, air conditioning, quarter panel air extractors, a 130-amp/ alternator, a fixed whip antenna mounted on the quarter panel, a 58-amp. low-maintenance battery, a battery saver, power assisted front disc/rear drum antilock brakes, chimes, a crash-severity sensor, a deck lid release, a rear window defogger/defroster, electronic engine controls, an emergency inside trunk release, the 3.0-liter two-valve Vulcan V-6, front-wheel drive, an 18-gallon fuel tank, a fuel shut-off switch, Solar-Tinted glass, rear seat heat ducts, a hood with gas-assist struts and a remote release, a dual-note horn, instrumentation (including temperature and fuel gauges, a 110-mph speedometer, a low brake fluid warning, a trip odometer, an odometer and a tachometer), rear door child safety locks, illuminated power door lock controls, a foot-operated parking brake, two 12-volt power points (outlets), remote keyless entry, the SecuriLock™ passive anti-theft system, a column-mounted gear shifter with soft feel handle, speed control, power rack-and-pinion steering, MacPherson strut independent front suspension with nitrogen gas pressurized struts and a front stabilizer bar, an independent rear quadra-link suspension with nitrogen gas pressurized struts, deck lid tie-down provisions, P21560R16 all-season tires, a mini spare tire, an electronic four-speed automatic overdrive transaxle, a transaxle oil cooler, two-speed variable intermittent windshield wipers and one touch power windows with lock-out switch and illuminated controls.

TAURUS SE WAGON: Standard equipment included a rear flip-up backlight with gas cylinders, 5-mph front and rear bumpers, a rear 5-mph impact-absorbing shape in body color, body-color flush mounted door handles, a body-color front fascia, multi reflector halogen headlamps, a perimeter lighting system with remote keyless entry, a luggage rack, body-color electric control mirrors, body-color side moldings, flush black windshield and backlight moldings, bright side door window moldings, black rocker panel moldings, clearcoat paint, monochromatic taillights with red turn signals, 16-in. five-spoke wheels, a front ashtray, a cargo area cover, color-keyed 13.5-oz. Carpeting with built-in foot rest, electronic digital clock with dimmer feature, a color-keyed integral center console with cupholders and cassette storage, chrome interior door handles, front and rear floor mats, a glove box, rear grab handles, two-tone instrument panel with backlit cluster, positive shut-off climate control registers, side window

demisters, a windshield defroster, an integrated control panel with climate and radio controls, a rear defroster, a light group with dual-beam map and dome lamps, a dome light switch on all doors, warning lights and chimes, a low-fuel indicator, a delayed-off dome lamp, front door courtesy lights, an ashtray light, a luggage compartment light, a liftgate-activated cargo area courtesy light, a fully-trimmed low-liftover luggage compartment, day/night rearview mirrors, dual second-generation airbags, an electronic AM/FM full-logic stereo and single in-dash CD player with four speakers, six-passenger seating with dual recliners (with third row fold-down rear seat for eight-passenger capacity), a front armrest, seat map pockets, two-way headrests, a center seat console, a six-way power driver's seat with lumbar support, a 60/40 rear seat with folding seatbacks, a driver position sensor, a front safety belt use detector, seat belts, a tilt steering column, a color-keyed four-spoke steering wheel, an under-floor stowage compartment, a right quarter stowage compartment, cloth covered sun visors, air conditioning, quarter panel air extractors, a 130-amp/ alternator, a power automatic antenna mounted on the quarter panel, a 58-amp. low-maintenance battery, a battery saver, ABS four-wheel disc brakes, chimes, a crash-severity sensor, a rear window defogger/defroster, electronic engine controls, the 3.0-liter two-valve Vulcan V-6, front-wheel drive, an 18-gallon fuel tank, a fuel shut-off switch, Solar-Tinted glass, rear seat heat ducts, a hood with gas-assist struts and a remote release, a dual-note horn, instrumentation (including temperature and fuel gauges, a 110-mph speedometer, a low brake fluid warning, a trip odometer, an odometer and a tachometer), rear door child safety locks, a unique station wagon liftgate latch, a night latch, an exterior release handle, illuminated power door lock controls, a foot-operated parking brake, two 12-volt power points (outlets), remote keyless entry, the SecuriLock™ passive anti-theft system, a column-mounted gear shifter with soft feel handle, speed control, power rack-and-pinion steering, MacPherson strut independent front suspension with nitrogen gas pressurized struts and a front stabilizer bar, independent short/long arm rear suspension with nitrogen gas pressurized shock absorbers, progressive-rate springs, a rear stabilizer bar, P21560R16 all-season tires, a mini spare tire, an electronic four-speed automatic overdrive transaxle, a transaxle oil cooler, two-speed variable intermittent windshield wipers, a rear wiper/washer and one touch power windows with lock-out switch and illuminated controls.

TAURUS SEL WAGON: Standard equipment included a 5-mph front and rear bumpers, body-color flush mounted door handles, a body-color front fascia, multi reflector halogen headlamps, a perimeter lighting system with remote keyless entry, body-color electric control mirrors, body-color side moldings, bright side door window moldings, black rocker panel moldings, clearcoat paint, monochromatic taillights with red turn signals, 16-in. five-spoke machined wheels, a front ashtray, a cargo net, color-keyed 13.5-oz. Carpeting with built-in foot rest, electronic digital clock with dimmer feature, a color-keyed integral center console with cupholders and cassette storage, chrome interior door handles, front and rear floor mats, a glove box, grocery bag hooks, rear grab handles, two-tone instrument panel with backlit cluster, positive shut-off climate control registers, side window demisters, a windshield defroster, an integrated control panel with climate and radio controls, a rear defroster, a light group with dual-beam map and dome lamps, a dome light switch on all doors, warning lights and chimes, a low-fuel indicator, a delayed-off dome lamp, front door courtesy lights, an ashtray light, a luggage compartment light, a fully-trimmed low-liftover luggage compartment, day/night rearview mirrors, dual second-generation airbags, an electronic AM/FM full-logic stereo cassette player with four speakers, a six-disc CD changer, five-passenger seating with dual recliners, a front armrest, seat map pockets, two-way headrests, a center seat console, a six-way power driver's seat with lumbar support, a 60/40 rear seat with folding seatbacks, a driver position sensor, a front safety belt use detector, seat belts, a tilt steering column, a color-keyed four-spoke leather-wrapped steering wheel, cloth covered sun visors, dual illuminated visor-vanity mirrors, electronic temperature control, quarter panel air extractors, a 130-amp. alternator, a fixed whip antenna mounted on the quarter panel, a 58-amp. low-maintenance battery, a battery saver, power front disc/rear drum brakes, chimes, a crash-severity sensor, a deck lid release, a rear window defogger/defroster, electronic engine controls, an emergency inside trunk release, the 3.0-liter four-valve Duratec V-6, front-wheel drive, an 18-gallon fuel tank, a fuel shut-off switch, Solar-Tinted glass, rear seat heat ducts, a hood with gas-assist struts and a remote release, a dual-note horn, instrumentation (including temperature and fuel gauges, a 110-mph speedometer, a low brake fluid warning, a trip odometer, an odometer and a tachometer), rear door child safety locks, a night latch, an exterior release handle, illuminated power door lock controls, a foot-operated parking brake, two 12-volt power points (outlets), remote keyless entry with keypad, the SecuriLock™ passive anti-theft system, a column-mounted gear shifter with soft feel handle, speed control, power rack-and-pinion steering, MacPherson strut independent front suspension with nitrogen gas pressurized struts and a front stabilizer bar, independent rear quadra-link suspension with nitrogen gas pressurized struts, P21560R16 all-season tires, a mini spare tire, an electronic four-speed automatic overdrive transaxle, a transaxle oil cooler, two-speed variable intermittent windshield wipers and one touch power windows with lock-out switch and illuminated controls.

Model No.	Body/Style No.	Body Type & Seating	Factory Price	Shipping Weight	Prod. Total
TAURUS LX (V-6)					
P52		4d Sedan-6P	19,375	3,336	—
TAURUS SE (V-6)					
P	53	4d Sedan-6P	20,185	3,336	—
P	58	4d Wagon-6P	22,120	3,502	—
TAURUS SE DELUXE (V-6)					
P	58	4d Wagon-6P	22,745	3,502	—
TAURUS SE PREMIUM (V-6)					
P	58	4d Wagon-6P	23,435	3,502	—
TAURUS SES (V-6)					
P	55	4d Sedan-6P	21,200	3,336	—
TAURUS SES DELUXE (V-6)					
P	55	4d Sedan-6P	22,300	3,336	—
TAURUS SEL DELUXE (V-8)					
P	55	4d Sedan-6P	23,070	3,336	—
P	58	4d Wagon-6P	23,320	3,502	—
TAURUS SEL PREMIUM (V-8)					
P	56	4d Sedan-6P	23,640	3,336	—

CROWN VICTORIA — V-8 — Standard equipment on the base Crown Victoria included a 4.6-liter SOHC 16-valve 220-hp V-8, a four-speed automatic transmission, rear-wheel drive, a front independent suspension, front and rear stabilizer bars, a clock, a low-fuel indicator, P225/60SR16 all-season tires on 16 x 7-in. steel rims, a spacesaver spare tire on a steel spare wheel, variable intermittent windshield wipers, a rear window defogger, front disc/rear drum brakes, front seat belt pre-tensioners, rear door child safety locks, an emergency interior trunk release, front and rear center lap belts, two front headrests, an engine immobilizer, one touch power windows, power door locks, power mirrors, cruise control, speed-proportional power steering, a tilt-adjustable steering wheel, steering wheel mounted cruise controls, a remote trunk release, front door map pockets, six-passenger seating with a cloth-trimmed split front bench seat, a rear bench seat, air conditioning, a trunk light, a wood-trimmed dash, an AM/FM cassette stereo with four speakers and an element radio antenna. Standard equipment on the base Crown Victoria LX included a 4.6-liter SOHC 16-valve 220-hp V-8, a four-speed automatic transmission, rear-wheel drive, a front independent suspension, front and rear stabilizer bars, a clock, a low-fuel indicator, P225/60SR16 all-season tires on 16 x 7-in. steel rims, a spacesaver spare tire on a steel spare wheel, variable intermittent windshield wipers, a rear window defogger, front disc/rear drum brakes, front seat belt pre-tensioners, rear door child safety locks, an emergency interior trunk release, front and rear center lap belts, two front headrests, an engine immobilizer, one touch power windows, remote power door locks, power mirrors, cruise control, speed-proportional power steering, a tilt-adjustable steering wheel, steering wheel mounted cruise controls, a remote trunk release, front door map pockets, front seatback storage, six-passenger seating with a cloth-trimmed split front bench seat with six-way power and adjustable lumbar support on driver's side, a rear bench seat with folding center armrest, air conditioning, front reading lights, dual illuminated visor-vanity mirrors, a trunk light, a wood-trimmed dash, an AM/FM cassette stereo with four speakers and an element radio antenna.

Model No.	Body/Style No.	Body Type & Seating	Factory Price	Shipping Weight	Prod. Total
CROWN VICTORIA (V-8)					
P	73	4d Sedan-5P	22,935	3,946	—
CROWN VICTORIA LX (V-8)					
P	74	4d Sedan-5P	25,050	3,946	—

THUNDERBIRD — (V-8) — Motoring excitement returned to Ford showrooms with the introduction of the all-new two-passenger Thunderbird, a throwback to the original roadster that wore the T-Bird nameplate. The all-new sporty car was a production version of the Thunderbird concept car that stole the spotlight at auto shows in 1999 and 2000. It was based on the Lincoln LS platform. In September 2000, the upscale retailer Neiman Marcus made 200 special edition 2002 Thunderbirds available for early orders in its annual Christmas Book, a catalog of exclusive gifts. The black and silver cars were priced at $41,995 and sold out in a record time of two hours and 15 minutes, even though buyers had to wait until the fall of 2001 for deliveries to begin. Ford officially opened the order banks for the 2002 Thunderbird on Monday, Jan. 8, 2001, the day the car made its regular production debut at the North American International Auto Show in Detroit. The dramatically designed 2002 version was also a two-seat, rear-wheel-drive, V-8-powered, convertible roadster that reflected a feeling of boldness and confidence in its design. The Thunderbird featured obvious visual cues that tied it to the classic cars of the past, but with a decidedly modern interpretation. It came standard as a convertible and offered an optional removable top with classic porthole windows. The removable top weighed 83 lbs. and was intended for easy removal and installation. A secure pin-and-bolt system at the two front attachment points and two clamps at the rear connected the removable top to the car. The two-place interior reflected the exterior design and the car's romantic heritage, but also offered the comfort and convenience today's customers demanded. Thunderbird specifications included a 107.2-in. wheelbase and 3.9-liter DOHC V-8 engine. The designers of the modern Thunderbird took great care to borrow classic styling cues, but to never lose the modern look. Among other details, the car's two-seat configuration, hood scoop, round headlamps, egg-crate grille and porthole windows all paid homage to the past. The new T-Bird utilized a rigid, computer-engineered chassis and a fine-tuned four-wheel independent suspension system employing lightweight materials to reduce unsprung weight and improve response. Its rack-and-pinion steering gear was a variable-assist design, providing lower turning efforts at parking speeds and higher-level road feel at highway speeds. Standard equipment included an all-aluminum 3.9-liter DOHC V-8 that produced an estimated 252-hp, a new generation power train electronic controller (PTEC), a specially engineered close-ratio five-speed automatic transmission, 17 x 7.5-in. cast aluminum wheels, P235/50VR17 all-season tires, a space saver spare tire, four-wheel independent suspension, front and rear stabilizer bars, four-wheel antilock disc brakes (with electronic brake force distribution, vented rotors, and dual piston calipers), an airbag deactivation switch, child seat anchors, an inside-the-trunk emergency release, two front seat headrests, a remote vehicle anti-theft system, auto delay off headlights, variable intermittent windshield wipers, a power convertible top, a glass rear window, a rear window defogger, bucket front seats, leather upholstery, a six-way power driver's seat with adjustable lumbar support, a two-way power passenger seat, remote power door locks, one touch power windows, power outside rearview mirrors, an AM/FM stereo with six-disc CD changer (multi CD located in dashboard), a 180-watts eight speaker sound system, an element radio antenna, cruise control, power steering, a leather-wrapped tilt and telescopic steering wheel with audio and cruise controls on the center hub, front cupholders, front door pockets, a front console with storage space, retained accessory power, dual zone climate controls, front reading lights, dual visor-vanity mirrors, front floor mats, a luggage compartment light, a trip odometer, a clock and a low-fuel warning indicator. Ford said that it was scheduling the assembly of approximately 25,000 Thunderbirds per year at its Wixom Assembly Plant in Michigan.

THUNDERBIRD PREMIUM — (V-8) — Standard equipment included an all-aluminum 3.9-liter DOHC V-8 that produced an estimated 252-hp, a new generation power train electronic controller (PTEC), a specially engineered close-ratio five-speed automatic transmission, 17 x 7.5-in. chrome alloy wheels, P235/50VR17 all-season tires, a space saver spare tire, four-wheel independent suspension, front and rear stabilizer bars, four-wheel antilock disc brakes (with electronic brake force distribution, vented rotors, and dual piston calipers), all-speed traction control, an airbag deactivation switch, child seat anchors, an inside-the-trunk emergency release, two front seat headrests, a remote vehicle anti-theft system, auto delay off headlights, variable intermittent windshield wipers, a power convertible top, a glass rear window, a rear window defogger, bucket front seats, leather upholstery, a six-way power driver's seat with adjustable lumbar support, a two-way power passenger seat, remote power door locks, one touch power windows, power outside rearview mirrors, an AM/FM stereo with six-disc CD changer (multi CD located in dashboard), a 180-watts eight speaker sound system, an element radio antenna, cruise control, power steering, a leather-wrapped tilt and telescopic steering wheel with audio and cruise controls on the center hub, front cupholders, front door pockets, a front console with storage space, retained accessory power, dual zone climate controls, front reading lights, dual visor-vanity mirrors, front floor mats, a luggage compartment light, a trip odometer, a clock and a low-fuel warning indicator.

THUNDERBIRD NIEMAN MARCUS EDITION — (V-8) — The 2002 Neiman Marcus Edition featured a unique elegant silver and black color theme, a removable top with the Thunderbird insignia etched into the porthole window, an all-aluminum 3.9-liter DOHC 252-hp V-8 with new generation PTEC, a specially engineered close-ratio five-speed automatic transmission with special silver gearshift knob, 17 x 7.5-in. chrome alloy wheels, P235/50VR17 all-season tires, a space saver spare tire, four-wheel independent suspension, front and rear stabilizer bars, four-wheel antilock disc brakes (with electronic brake force distribution, vented rotors, and dual piston calipers), all-speed traction control, an airbag deactivation switch, child seat anchors, an inside-the-trunk emergency release, two front seat headrests, a remote vehicle anti-theft system, auto delay off headlights, variable intermittent windshield wipers, a power convertible top, a glass rear window, a rear window defogger, bucket front seats, leather upholstery, Neiman Marcus emblems on the instrument panel, a six-way power driver's seat with adjustable lumbar support, a two-way power passenger seat, remote power door locks, one touch power windows, power outside rearview mirrors, an AM/FM stereo with six-disc CD changer (multi CD located in dashboard), a 180-watts eight speaker sound system, an element radio antenna, cruise control, power steering, a special silver tilt and telescopic steering wheel with audio and cruise controls on the center hub, front cupholders, front door pockets, a front console with storage space, retained accessory power, dual zone climate controls, front reading lights, dual visor-vanity mirrors, front floor mats with Neiman Marcus emblems, a luggage compartment light, a trip odometer, a clock and a low-fuel warning indicator. Collectors were also issued a special vehicle identification number (VIN) as a guarantee of authenticity.

Model No.	Body/ Style No.	Body Type & Seating	Factory Price	Shipping Weight	Prod. Total
THUNDERBIRD (V-8)					
P	73	2d Roadster-5P	35,495	3,775	—
THUNDERBIRD PREMIUM (V-8)					
P	74	2d Roadster-5P	38,995	3,775	—
THUNDERBIRD NIEMAN MARCUS EDITION (V-8)					
P	74	2d Roadster-5P	41,995	3,863	—

Note 1: Weight is 3,863 lbs. with removable hardtop; standard on Neiman Marcus Edition.

FOCUS ENGINES

ENGINE [Standard LX/SE Sedans]: Inline. Overhead cam. Four-cylinder. Cast-iron block and aluminum head. Displacement: 121 cid (2.0 liters). Bore & stroke: 3.39 x 3.52 in. Compression ratio: 9.4:1. Brake horsepower: 110 at 5000 rpm. Torque: 125 lbs.-ft. at 3750 rpm. Split Port induction.

ENGINE [Standard Hatchbacks/ZTS Sedan/Wagons]: Inline. Double overhead cam. Four-cylinder. Cast-iron block and aluminum head. Displacement: 121 cid (2.0 liters). Bore & stroke: 3.39 x 3.52 in. Compression ratio: 9.6:1. Brake horsepower: 130 at 5300 rpm. Torque: 135 lbs.-ft. at 4500 rpm. Sequential fuel injection.

ESCORT ENGINES

ENGINE [ZX2]: Inline. Double overhead cam. Four-cylinder. Cast-iron block and aluminum head. Displacement: 121 cid (2.0 liters). Bore & stroke: 3.39 x 3.52 in. Compression ratio: 9.6:1. Brake horsepower: 130 at 5750 rpm. Torque: 135 lbs.-ft. at 4500 rpm. Sequential fuel injection.

TAURUS ENGINES

ENGINE [Base LX/SE]: Overhead valve V-6. Cast-iron block and head. Displacement: 182 cid (3.0 liters). Bore & stroke: 3.50 x 3.15 in. Compression ratio: 9.3:1. Brake horsepower: 155 at 4900 rpm. Torque: 185 lbs.-ft. at 3950 rpm. Sequential fuel injection.

ENGINE [Base SEL]: Double overhead cam flexible-fuel V-6. Aluminum block and head. Displacement: 182 cid (3.0 liters). Bore & stroke: 3.50 x 3.15 in. Compression ratio: 10.0:1. Brake horsepower: 200 at 5750 rpm. Torque: 200 lbs.-ft. at 4500 rpm.

CROWN VICTORIA ENGINE

ENGINE [Base]: Modular, overhead valve V-8. Displacement: 281 cid (4.6 liters). Bore & stroke: 3.60 x 3.60. Compression ratio: 9.0:1. Brake horsepower: 220 at 4750 rpm. Torque: 265 lbs.-ft. at 4000 rpm. Sequential fuel injection.

THUNDERBIRD ENGINE

ENGINE [Standard]: DOHC V-8. Aluminum block and head. Displacement: 240 cid (3.9 liters). Bore & stroke: 3.39 x 3.35 in. Compression ratio: 10.55:1. Brake horsepower: 252 at 6100 rpm. Torque: 261 lbs.-ft. at 4300 rpm. Sequential multiport electronic fuel injection.

FOCUS CHASSIS: Wheelbase: (all) 103 in. Overall length: (all) 168.1 in. Overall width: (all) 66.9 in. Overall height: (all) 56.3.9 in. Front and rear tread: (all) 58.5 in.

ESCORT CHASSIS: Wheelbase: 98.4 in. Overall length: 175.2 in. Overall width: 67.4 in. Overall height: 52.3 in. Front tread: (all) 56.5 in. rear tread: (all) 56.5 in.

TAURUS CHASSIS: Wheelbase: (all) 108.5 in. Overall length: (sedan) 197.6 in.; (wagon) 197.7 in. Overall width: (all) 73 in. Overall height: (sedan) 56.1 in.; (wagon) 58 in. Front tread: 61.6 in. Rear tread: 62.1 in.

CROWN VICTORIA CHASSIS: Wheelbase: (all) 114.7 in. Overall Length: (all) 212 in. Overall width: (all) 78.2 in. Overall height: (all) 56.8 in. Front Tread: (all) 62.8 in. Rear Tread: (all) 63.3 in.

THUNDERBIRD CHASSIS: Wheelbase: 107.2 in. Overall Length: 186.3 in. Overall width: 72 in. Overall height: (all) 52.1 in. Front Tread: (all) 60.5 in. Rear Tread: (all) 60.2 in.

FOCUS TECHNICAL: Standard transmission: five-speed manual transaxle. Drive axle: front. Steering: rack-and-pinion. Front suspension: (all) independent MacPherson struts with coil springs and stabilizer bar (all). Rear suspension: (all) independent control blade multilink design with coil springs and shock absorbers (2.0L SOHC)/stabilizer bar (2.0L DOHC Zetec). Brakes: ventilated front disc, rear drum (power assisted). Body construction: unibody. Fuel tank: 13.2 gallons.

ESCORT TECHNICAL: Standard transmission: five-speed manual transaxle. Drive axle: front. Steering: rack-and-pinion. Front suspension: independent MacPherson strut with strut-mounted coil springs. Rear suspension: independent, Quadra-link with stabilizer bar. Brakes: front disc, rear drum (power assisted). Body construction: unibody. Fuel tank: 12.7 gallons.

TARAUS TECHNICAL: Standard transmission: four-speed overdrive automatic. Drive axle: front. Steering: power engine-speed sensitive variable-assist rack-and-pinion. Front suspension: independent MacPherson struts with coil springs and stabilizer bar. Rear suspension: MacPherson strut with strut-mounted coil springs, stabilizer bar, tension struts and parallel control arms (sedan); independent unequal length control arms with variable rate coil springs on lower control arms, upper control arms, stabilizer bar, shock absorbers and tension struts (wagon). Brakes: (front) power disc, available antilock braking system; (rear) power drum (disc on wagon), available antilock braking system (ABS). Body construction: unibody. Fuel tank: 18.0 gallons.

CROWN VICTORIA TECHNICAL: Standard transmission: four-speed overdrive automatic. Drive axle: rear. Steering: re-circulating ball. Front suspension: independent short/long arm with ball joints, coil springs and stabilizer bar. Rear suspension: Watt's linkage. Brakes: four-wheel disc. Body construction: separate body and frame. Fuel tank: 19.0 gallons.

THUNDERBIRD TECHNICAL: Standard transmission: special close-ratio five-speed automatic with overdrive. Drive axle: rear. Steering: Power, speed-sensitive, variable-assist rack-and-pinion with 18.0:1 overall ratio and 35.2-ft. curb-to-curb turn circle; 3.0 turns lock-to-lock. Frame: Cross-car beam and three bolted-on X-braces. Front suspension: Independent unequal-length control arms, coil springs, shock absorbers and stabilizer bar. Rear suspension: Independent unequal-length control arms, with anti-lift design, coil springs, shock absorbers and stabilizer bar. Front brakes: Power disc with ABS, outside rotor diameter 11.8 in., inside rotor diameter 7.17 in., total swept area 277.0 sq. in. Rear brakes: Power disc, with ABS, outside rotor diameter 11.3 in., inside rotor diameter 7.83 in., total swept area 211.1 sq. in. Fuel tank: 18 gal.

FOCUS OPTIONS: (ZX3 hatchback) 572 air conditioning ($795). 552 antilock braking system (no cost). 422 California emissions requirements (no cost). 59M side airbags ($350). (ZX3 premium power hatchback) 44A four-speed overdrive automatic transmission ($815). 47D ABS brakes with AdvanceTrac ($1,625). 552 antilock braking system ($400). 422 California emissions requirements (no cost). 13B power moonroof ($595). (ZX3 premium hatchback) 44A four-speed overdrive automatic transmission ($815). 581 AM/FM stereo with six-disc in-dash CD player ($280). 552 antilock braking system ($400). 422 California emissions requirements (no cost). 59M side airbags ($350). (LX sedan) 552 antilock braking system ($400). 422 California emissions requirements (no cost). 59M side airbags ($350). (LX premium sedan) 44A four-speed overdrive automatic transmission ($815). 552 antilock braking system ($400). 422 California emissions requirements (no cost). 59M side airbags ($350). (SE sedan) 44A four-speed overdrive automatic transmission ($815). 552 antilock braking system ($400). 422 California emissions requirements (no cost). 59M side airbags ($350). (SE comfort sedan) 44A four-speed overdrive automatic transmission ($815). 581 AM/FM stereo with six-disc in-dash CD player ($280). 552 antilock braking system ($400). 422 California emissions requirements (no cost). 13B power moonroof ($595). 59M side airbags ($350). (SE comfort sedan with Zetec engine) 44A four-speed overdrive automatic transmission ($815). 581 AM/FM stereo with six-disc in-dash CD player ($280). B3W in-dash CD changer regional discount ($280 credit). 552 antilock braking system ($400). 422 California emissions requirements (no cost). 13B power moonroof ($595). 59M side airbags ($350). (SE wagon) 445 five-speed manual transmission ($815). 552 antilock braking system ($400). 422 California emissions requirements (no cost). 59M side airbags ($350). (ZTS sedan) 44A four-speed overdrive automatic transmission ($815). 47D ABS brakes with AdvanceTrac ($1,625). 581 AM/FM stereo with six-disc in-dash CD player ($280). B3W in-dash CD changer regional discount ($280 credit). 552 antilock braking system ($400). 422 California emissions requirements (no cost). 8 leather seating ($695). 13B power moonroof ($595). 59M side airbags ($350). (SE comfort wagon) 445 five-speed manual transmission ($815). 552 antilock braking system ($400). 422 California emissions requirements (no cost). 13B power moonroof ($595). 59M side airbags ($350). (ZX5) 44A four-speed overdrive automatic transmission ($815). 47D ABS brakes with AdvanceTrac ($1,625). 552 antilock braking system ($400). 422 California emissions requirements (no cost). U leather seating ($695). 13B power moonroof ($595). 59M side airbags ($350). (ZTW wagon) 445 five-speed manual transmission ($815). 47D ABS brakes with AdvanceTrac ($1,625). 552 antilock braking system ($400). 422 California emissions requirements (no cost). 13B power moonroof ($595). 59M side airbags ($350).

ESCORT OPTIONS: (ZX2) 44T four-speed overdrive automatic transmission ($815). 552 antilock braking system ($400). 422 California emissions requirements (no cost). 12Y front and rear floor mats ($55). 572 manual air conditioning ($795). (ZX2 Deluxe) 44T four-speed overdrive automatic transmission ($815). 552 antilock braking system ($400). 422 California emissions requirements (no cost). 13B power moonroof ($595). (ZX2 Premium) 64A 14-in. five-spoke chrome wheels ($595). 44T four-speed overdrive automatic transmission ($815). 919 AM/FM cassette with six-disc CD changer ($295). 552 antilock braking system ($400). 422 California emissions requirements (no cost). 13B power moonroof ($595). A unique leather sport bucket seats ($367).

TAURUS OPTIONS: (LX sedan) 58H AM/FM stereo cassette ($185). 552 antilock braking system ($600). 422 California emissions (no cost). 93N non-California emissions (no cost). (SE sedan) 59C adjustable pedals ($120). 552 antilock braking system ($600). 422 California emissions (no cost). 53S no charge SE Value package discount ($535 credit). 93N non-California emissions (no cost). 53S SE Value package discount (no cost). 85R safety package ($565). 46S 60/40 split-folding rear seat ($140). (SE wagon) 59C adjustable pedals ($120). 422 California emissions (no cost). 93N non-California emissions (no cost). 85R safety package ($565). (SE Deluxe wagon) 59C adjustable pedals ($120). 422 California emissions (no cost). 93N non-California emissions (no cost). 85R safety package ($565). (SE Premium wagon) 59C adjustable pedals ($120). 422 California emissions (no cost). 93N non-California emissions (no cost). 85R safety package ($565). (SES Sedan) 59C adjustable pedals ($120). 422 California emissions (no cost). J leather seating surfaces ($895). 96L Luxury and Convenience package ($185). 85R safety package ($565). 13B no-cost power moonroof discount ($895 credit). J no-cost power moonroof and leather seating surfaces discount ($895 credit). J no-cost power moonroof and leather seating surfaces discount ($895 credit). 93N non-California emissions (no cost). 13B power moonroof ($895). 53A premium audio group ($530). 90T SES sport package ($290). (SES Deluxe Sedan) 59C adjustable pedals ($120). 422 California emissions (no cost). J leather seating surfaces ($895). 96L Luxury and Convenience package ($185). 13B no-cost power moonroof discount ($895 credit). J no-cost power moonroof and leather seating surfaces discount ($895 credit). J no-cost power moonroof and leather seating surfaces discount ($895 credit). 93N non-California emissions (no cost). 13B power moonroof ($895). 53A premium audio group ($530). 90T SES sport package ($290). (SEL Sedan) 184 six-passenger seating with flip-fold center console ($105 credit). 422 California emissions (no cost). J leather seating surfaces ($895). 96L Luxury and Convenience package ($185). 916 MACH premium sound system ($320). 13B no-cost power moonroof discount ($895 credit). J no-cost power moonroof and leather seating surfaces discount ($895 credit). J no-cost power moonroof and leather seating surfaces discount ($895 credit). 93N non-California emissions (no cost). 13B power moonroof ($895). 13K rear deck lid spoiler ($230). 85R safety package ($565). (SEL Deluxe Sedan) 184 six-passenger seating with flip-fold center console ($105 credit). 422 California emissions (no cost). 53D Duratec engine package ($1,120). J leather seating surfaces ($895). 96L Luxury and Convenience package ($185). 916 MACH premium sound system ($320). 13B no-cost power moonroof discount ($895 credit). J no-cost power moonroof and leather seating surfaces discount ($895 credit). 93N non-California emissions (no cost). 13K rear deck lid spoiler ($230). 85R safety package ($565). (SEL Premium Sedan) 422 California emissions (no cost). J leather seating surfaces ($895). 96L Luxury and Convenience package ($185). 916 MACH premium sound system ($320). 916 MACH premium sound system no charge ($320 credit). 13B no-cost power moonroof discount ($895 credit). J no-cost power moonroof and leather seating surfaces discount ($895 credit). J no-cost power moonroof and leather seating surfaces discount ($895 credit). 93N non-California emissions (no cost). 13B power moonroof ($895). 21J power passenger seat ($350). 3K rear deck lid spoiler ($230). 85R safety package ($565).

CROWN VICTORIA OPTIONS: (Base sedan) 999 4.6-liter natural gas V-8 with automatic overdrive transmission ($6,165). 21A siz-way power driver's seat ($360). 552 antilock braking system ($600). 553 antilock braking system with traction control ($775). 422 California emissions (no cost). 508 conventional spare tire ($120). 508 conventional spare tire ($105). 585 electronic AM/FM stereo with single CD player ($140). 153 front license plate bracket (no cost). 12Y front and rear floor mats ($55). 41G Handling and Performance package ($935). 93N non-California emissions (no cost). T2A P225/60SR15 white sidewall tires ($80). 144 remote keyless entry system ($240). (LX sedan) 999 4.6-liter natural gas V-8 with automatic overdrive transmission ($6,165). 60R five-passenger sport appearance package ($995). 552 antilock braking system ($600). 553 antilock braking system with trac-

tion control ($775). 422 California emissions (no cost). 65C Comfort group ($900). 65E Comfort Plus group ($1,900). 508 conventional spare tire ($120). 508 conventional spare tire ($105). 585 electronic AM/FM stereo with single CD player ($140). 153 front license plate bracket (no cost). 12Y front and rear floor mats ($55). 41G Handling and Performance package ($740). 41G Handling and Performance package ($615). 41G Handling and Performance package ($615). L split bench seat with leather seating surfaces ($795). 93N non-California emissions (no cost). T2A P225/60SR15 white sidewall tires ($80). 59C power adjustable pedals ($120). 586 premium electronic AM/FM stereo with cassette ($360). 919 trunk-mounted six-disc CD changer ($350). 175 universal garage door opener ($115).

THUNDERBIRD OPTIONS: (Deluxe Roadster) 68B black accent group ($295), 422 California emissions (no cost). 68C complete interior color accent package ($800). 68D partial interior color accent package ($595). 51P auxiliary parking lamps (no cost). (Deluxe Roadster with hardtop) 68B black accent group ($295), 422 California emissions (no cost). 68C complete interior color accent package ($800). 68D partial interior color accent package ($595). 51P auxiliary parking lamps (no cost). 553 all-speed traction control ($230). (Neiman Marcus Edition with hardtop) 68B black accent group ($295), 422 California emissions (no cost). 68C complete interior color accent package ($800). 68D partial interior color accent package ($595). 51P auxiliary parking lamps (no cost). 553 all-speed traction control ($230). (Premium Roadster) 68B black accent group ($295), 422 California emissions (no cost). 68C complete interior color accent package ($800). 68D partial interior color accent package ($595). 51P auxiliary parking lamps (no cost). (Premium Roadster with hardtop) 68B black accent group ($295), 422 California emissions (no cost). 68C complete interior color accent package ($800). 68D partial interior color accent package ($595). 51P auxiliary parking lamps (no cost).

HISTORY: Ford Motor Co. entered 2002 with William Clay Ford Jr. at its helm. The Thunderbird Custom—a one-of-a-kind project car that brought a new look to the roadster through subtle design changes—was introduced at the 2001 Pebble Beach Concours d'Elegance in Monterey, Calif. The Custom was designed to be a contemporary interpretation of the customizing and hot-rod movement of the 1950s. It started as a 2002 Ford Thunderbird. Ford designers were asked to develop design renderings of new possibilities for future years. One sketch featured several unique elements, including a blacked-out grille, more pronounced belt line and big chrome wheels with knock-off hubs. The sketch looked so good, Ford decided to build it. Changes included doubling the size of the recesses for the characteristic chevrons on the Thunderbird's front fender and adding a black mesh insert behind them to accentuate their presence. The car was painted with several coats of Dark Shadow Gray Metallic lacquer for a deep glossy finish. The iconic egg-crate grille was recessed slightly—an old customizer's trick—and painted in the same color as the body. It further was accentuated with a chrome bezel surrounding the grille. To achieve a longer, more relaxed exterior appearance for the car, the design team lowered the coil-spring suspension one inch front and rear making it appear higher in front and lower in the rear. The exhaust system was retuned to give the car a low baritone "burble" at idle and a more aggressive performance tone during acceleration. Chrome tailpipe extensions—two and one-half inches in diameter at the tip—were prominent from the side or rear view. Halibrand created a unique interpretation of its classic "Kidney Bean 5" polished chrome wheel featuring five spokes with kidney bean-shaped "windows" that create a strobing effect through the wheel when the car is in motion. The wheel hubs are set off by three-arm knock-offs, a classic custom touch. Aggressively treaded Michelin Pilot Sport Z-rated 18-in. tires finished the look, virtually filling the wheel wells. The Thunderbird Custom had a black convertible top that stored below a removable two-piece, ebony leather-wrapped tonneau cover. The interior featured a two-tone theme with sienna and ebony leather, set off by engine-turned aluminum accent panels. The door sill plate was wrapped in a thin layer of sienna leather with an opening in the middle exposing the Thunderbird logo etched in aluminum. The door panels featured sienna leather armrests and upper sills with engine-turned aluminum accents. The bucket seats were covered in sienna leather and featured plush side bolsters and adjustable head restraints. The seating surfaces were covered with perforated sienna leather in the familiar Thunderbird tuck-and-roll style. The steering wheel and shift knob were tightly wrapped and stitched in sienna leather. The shifter bezel featured an engine-turned aluminum background. The center stack was finished in Dark Shadow Gray matching the exterior. It flowed into a one-of-a-kind white-on-black Thunderbird instrument cluster. The instrument panel was finished in precision-stitched, ebony leather. On November 12, in Las Vegas, Nev., it was announced that the 2002 Ford Thunderbird had captured *Motor Trend* magazine's "Car of the Year" award. The award was announced during the *Motor Trend* International Auto Show. In the 50-year lifespan of *Motor Trend*, no other model has won more "Car of the Year" honors than the Thunderbird, which has twice as many wins as its closest competitor. "We're especially honored that Ford Thunderbird was chosen *Motor Trend's* 'Car of the Year' for the fourth time," said Jim O'Connor, Ford Div. president. "The all-new Thunderbird celebrates Ford's heritage of innovation and reaffirms our goal to build the best cars on the planet—cars that invoke passion and touch people's hearts and souls."

1911 Ford Model T Touring. (OCW)
Owned by Edith Kettelson of Louisburg, Minnesota.

1922 Ford center-door sedan. (OCW)
Owned by Ron Cloat of Peoria, Illinois.

1923 Ford Model T Roadster. (OCW)
Owned by Harold Sorlie of Mt. Prospect, Illinois.

1929 Ford Model A. (OCW)
Owned by Doyce Caudill of Belleville, Michigan.

1930 Ford Model A Roadster. (OCW)

1934 Ford Cabriolet. (OCW)
Owned by James Cular of Lafayette, New Jersey.

1936 Ford Model 740 convertible sedan. (OCW)
Owned by Bill Wiseman.

1940 Ford Deluxe two-door convertible. (OCW)

1946 Ford Super Deluxe Station Wagon. (OCW)

1950 Ford Deluxe coupe. (OCW)
Owned by Bud Louis of Waukesha, Wisconsin.

1951 Ford Custom Deluxe convertible. (OCW)

1955 Ford Fairlane Crown Victoria V-8. (OCW)

1956 Ford Fairlane Sunliner convertible. (OCW)

1957 Ford Fairlane two-door hardtop. (OCW)

1963 Ford Falcon Futura convertible. (OCW)

1964 Ford Galaxie 500 XL two-door hardtop. (OCW)

1965 Ford Galaxie 500 XL two-door hardtop. (OCW)

1970 Ford Maverick. (OCW)

1975 Ford LTD Landau hardtop. (OCW)

1978 Ford Pinto. (OCW)

1992 Ford Crown Victoria. (FMC)

1992 Ford Taurus LX station wagon. (FMC)

1993 Ford Probe. (FMC)

1993 Ford Crown Victoria LX. (FMC)

1993 Ford Escort LX. (FMC)

1996 Ford Taurus. (FMC)

1997 Ford Escort. (FMC)

1997 Ford Contour SE. (FMC)

1997 Ford Taurus. (FMC)

1937 Lincoln Model K Brunn convertible. (Blackhawk)

1960 Lincoln Continental two-door convertible. (OCW)

1964 Lincoln Continental four-door convertible. (OCW)

1978 Lincoln Continental Town Car. (OCW)

1992 Lincoln Town Car Signature Series. (FMC)

1993 Lincoln Mark VIII. (FMC)

1995 Lincoln Continental. (FMC)

1997 Lincoln Town Car. (FMC)

1997 Lincoln Mark VIII. (FMC)

1948 Mercury station wagon. (OCW)

1951 Mercury convertible. (OCW)

1955 Mercury Montclair two-door hardtop. (OCW)

1967 Mercury Monterey S55 two-door hardtop. (OCW)
Owned by Lewis Weinstein of Morristown, New Jersey.

1971 Mercury Marquis Brougham. (OCW)

1971 Mercury Comet. (OCW)

1976 Mercury Bobcat. (OCW)

1978 "Macho" Cougar XR-7. (OCW)

1991 Mercury Tracer. (FMC)

1992 Mercury Grand Marquis LS. (FMC)

1993 Mercury Cougar XR7. (FMC)

1993 Mercury Capri. (FMC)

1996 Mercury Sable. (FMC)

1997 Mercury Mystique. (FMC)

1965 Ford Mustang convertible. (OCW)

1975 Ford Mustang II Ghia. (OCW)

1983 Ford Mustang LX convertible. (OCW)

1993 Ford Mustang GT. (FMC)

1955 Ford Thunderbird. (OCW)

1955 Ford Thunderbird. (OCW)

1958 Ford Thunderbird convertible. (OCW)
Owned by Carl Tomasello of Rockaway, New Jersey.

1960 Ford Thunderbird convertible. (OCW)

1963 Ford Thunderbird convertible. (OCW)

1965 Ford Thunderbird. (OCW)

1973 Ford Thunderbird. (OCW)

1975 Ford Thunderbird. (OCW)

1978 Ford Thunderbird. (OCW)

1983 Ford Thunderbird. (FMC)

1993 Ford Thunderbird. (FMC)

EDSEL

1958-1960

Two models—a Citation two-door hardtop and a Citation convertible—dramatically illustrated the distinctive styling of the 1958 Edsel line. The line consisted of 18 models in four series: Ranger, Pacer, Corsair and Citation. (PH)

As early as 1948, Ford Motor Co., under the direction of Henry Ford II, realized that its coverage of the automotive sales spectrum was lacking. At General Motors, the one-step-up buyer could move from Chevrolet to Pontiac, then on to Oldsmobile and Buick, before topping out at Cadillac. Even Mopar buyers had three steps between Plymouth and Imperial. At Ford, it was Ford, Mercury then Lincoln. Many one-step-up sales were being lost to the competition.

This was the seed for the Edsel. Active planning was shelved in the early 1950s due to the Korean Conflict, but in late 1954, the marketing planners were once again looking toward a new make for FoMoCo. In 1955, a Special Products Div. was formed under which this new car would be developed.

An entire new branch of FoMoCo was formed to produce this vehicle. It was not an arm of Ford or Mercury, but shared some basic components with both. Selected by FoMoCo chief stylist George Walker to head up the project was designer Roy Brown. His goal was to create a car that looked like no other and would be immediately recognizable a block away. Developed under the code name "E-car" ("E" meant experimental), it featured a classic-inspired vertical center grille flanked by two horizontal side grilles and high-mounted headlights.

A graceful gull-wing effect represented the rear view and three distinct color areas—body, roof and scallops—were incorporated into the side views.

Under the leadership of R.E. Krafve, the Special Products Div. developed the E-car, with release dates pushed back several times before the fall of 1957 was decided on. Heading the sales department was J.C. "Larry" Doyle, who was general sales

and marketing manager. He organized 24 sales districts and signed nearly 1,200 dealerships by opening day.

Just to select this new car's name was to prove a challenge. Under the direction of the Foote, Cone & Belding advertising agency, the division's account executive, Dave Jenkins, compiled a list of 18,000 possible names. Edsel was not among them!

On Nov. 19, 1956, after much negotiating with the Ford family, the name Edsel was decided on. From the initial list the top four selections of Citation, Corsair, Pacer, and Ranger were used to name each of the Edsel series.

Shortly after the naming of the Edsel, the model lineup was announced. There were to be 18 models in four basic series, including five station wagons. The Ranger was the price leader, followed by the Pacer. Both of these cars were mounted on the Ford Fairlane 118-in. wheelbase. The Corsair and Citation models were based on the 1957-1958 Mercury chassis with a special 124-in. wheelbase. A two-door Roundup station wagon, along with the four-door Villager wagons, were trimmed on a par with the Ranger, while the wood-trimmed upscale Bermuda station wagon shared many of the Pacer's touches.

Production started on July 15, 1957 in four assembly plants. Producing the Ford-based models were FoMoCo's Mahwah, N.J., Louisville, Ky. and San Jose, Calif., facilities. Producing the senior cars at the beginning was the Somerville, Mass. factory. By Aug. 19, 1957, both the Wayne, Mich. and Los Angeles, Calif. plants were brought on line.

In late August 1957, the media was given a grand showing of the Edsel in Dearborn, Mich., at Ford Motor Co.'s expense. There were rare reviews of the cars and some 75 editors from across the country drove specially-prepared Pacers back to their hometowns.

On Sept. 4, 1957, the Edsel—billed as "The Newest Thing on Wheels"—was released to the general public. Nearly 4,000 sales were reported that first day, which sounded great. However, sales soon plummeted and, within a month, the writing on the wall was already showing.

The junior Edsels were powered by the E-400 V-8, with 361 cid and a 303-hp rating. It was part of the FE series of Ford engines introduced in 1958. For the senior Corsair and Citation models, the E-475 with 410 cid and 345-hp kept them moving. There were no optional power plants for 1958 Edsels.

On senior cars, Edsel's exclusive Teletouch push-button transmission was standard. This same unit was optional on junior cars and was installed in about 90 percent of those models, where the automatic transmission was actually based on the three-speed Ford-O-Matic. Proposed was a counterpart to the new Ford Cruise-O-Matic, but outside of a few prototypes, none were ever produced.

What went wrong with the Edsel? In C. Gayle Warnock's book *The Edsel Affair*, he cites production problems. All Edsels were built at either Ford or Mercury plants and, at a ratio of 10:1 in some cases. Assembly line workers didn't like the odd changes required for Edsels and plant managers looked upon the car as a production problem for their divisions. This led to poor production quality in delivered cars.

By October 1957, the sales picture started to look dismal. An economic recession had a lot of purse strings tied shut and, at that time of year, many dealers were offering great deals on the 1957 clearance models.

In early January 1958, the Edsel Div. was involved in a reorganization. It was then placed in the new Mercury-Edsel-Lincoln Div. of Ford Motor Co.

Disenchanted dealers were dropping like flies. Prior to the Edsel's release, many established Ford and Mercury dealers couldn't get Edsel franchises. Now, they didn't want them! Only 63,110 of the 1958 Edsels were produced, a far cry from the 200,000 predicted by R.E. Krafve in January 1957.

The Edsel lineup was drastically cut back for 1959. It was down to 10 models. Only the Ranger, Villager, and Corsair nameplates remained. This year, both the Ranger and Corsair models were based on the Ford Fairlane. The Villager was based on the Ford station wagon and was available in both six- and nine-passenger forms.

Styling was toned-down a bit from the 1958 look, but was still distinctively Edsel. Cost-cutting in the design was seen by incorporating the 1958 Continental taillights and back-up lights into the 1959 Edsel units, thereby saving tooling costs on two plastic molds.

Edsel production in 1959 was limited to the Louisville plant and quality was considered pretty good. While the marketing goal of the 1958 Edsel had been to fit into the medium-priced car range, for the 1959 model year the aim was to stay just above the "low-priced three." Released on Halloween day, Edsel's slogan this year was "Makes History by Making Sense."

Standard power for the Ranger series was now the 292 cid Y-block V-8 available in Fords since 1955. Standard in the Villager station wagons and Corsair series was the 332 cid V-8, also identical to that used in Fords. As a delete-option, a 223 cid six-cylinder engine could be ordered for both the Ranger and Villager. An extra-cost option was the 361 cid V-8, which was held over from 1958.

Despite the more conventional car, the name Edsel seemed already tainted and just 44,861 of the 1959 models were built.

On Oct. 15, 1959, the 1960 Edsels were put on sale. Now limited officially to just seven models, there were five Rangers and two Villagers. Basically, the 1960 models were little more than face-lifted Fords. Using a more elaborate chrome-plated die-cast grille than Fords, the Edsel resembled the 1959 Pontiac in side trim and grille treatment. Standard power for all 1960 models was the 292 cid V-8, with the six as a delete-option in all models except the convertible. The 300-hp version of the Ford 352 cid V-8 was available as an extra-cost option in all models.

On Nov. 19, 1959, Ford Motor Co. announced the end of the Edsel line. It was stated that poor sales and steel shortages caused the decision, but there may have been deeper reasons within the corporation that caused the cut. As late as September 1959, a new compact car called the Comet was being readied for marketing as an Edsel.

The 1960 Edsel was not a bad car and *Automotive News* selected it as the "Best Buy" for 1960 domestic cars. Unfortunately, this article was published in December, after the Edsel had ceased to exist. So close to the 1960 Ford is the 1960 Edsel, that counterfeits have been produced. In considering the purchase of such a car, great care should be taken to research the sale.

*(Contributors to the Edsel section of this catalog include Dale Rapp, who originally compiled the technical data and tables for the 1958-1960 Edsel section of the **Standard Catalog of American Cars 1946-1975**, Phil Skinner, who wrote the Edsel introduction to the **Standard Catalog of Ford 1903-1998**, John A. Gunnell who edited the original **Standard Catalog of American Cars 1946-1975**, Ron Kowalke who edited the second edition of the **Standard Catalog of Ford 1903-1998** and Robert L. Lichty, who edited the first edition of the **Standard Catalog of Ford 1903-1998**.)*

1959 Edsel Corsair four-door hardtop. (FMC)

1958 EDSEL

1958 Edsel Ranger four-door sedan, V-8. (OCW)

1958 Edsel Ranger two-door sedan, V-8. (AA)

RANGER — (V-8) — SERIES A — The all-new 1958 Edsel, said to be the product of nine years of planning, was publicly launched on Sept. 4, 1957, as a product of the Edsel Division of Ford Motor Co. Although obviously based on contemporary Fords and Mercurys, the Edsel was described as being, "Entirely new to the industry." It was aimed at the medium-priced car field and came in four different lines with prices from $2,484 to a high of $3,796. The two lower-priced series, Ranger and Pacer, were built off the 118-inch wheelbase platform that 1958 Fords utilized. The two higher-priced lines, Corsair and Citation, were on a 124-inch wheelbase and had what was, essentially, a stretched Mercury chassis and sheet metal. Station wagons shared the 116-inch Ford wheelbase used on Ford wagons and Custom models. When compared to Ford and Mercury counterparts, on a model-for-model basis, the Edsels offered more power, more luxury, more standard equipment and more radical styling. They were intended to enter the sales battle against cars such as Buick, Oldsmobile and Chrysler New Yorker, which Ford previously had no distinct product to compete with. In trying to make the Edsel into a car that buyers would view as something really different, Ford went to the trouble of establishing a separate Edsel Division with headquarters in Ecorse Township, Mich. It was the first time in automotive history that any major manufacturer had set up a large dealer organization (1,200 to 1,400 outlets) prior to the introduction and marketing of a completely new line of automobiles. Also, the Edsel's radical styling was part of the effort to give the new model its own personality. The frontal treatment was conceived as a modern interpretation of a classic Packard's tall, vertical center grille. There were smaller grilles at each side. Unfortunately, the public thought that the center grille looked like a horse collar and that's what it was soon being called. The "horse collar" grille split the center of the car and was flanked by twin rectangular openings having horizontal grille bars and parking lamps at the outboard ends. Both the grille and the lamps wrapped around the front body corners. The front bumper was also split and had a concave indention that took on a projectile-like contour. The center of the hood had a broad peak or bulge that protruded to meet the horse collar. The name Edsel, in bright block letters, ran vertically down the center of the grille inside a horse collar-shaped inner molding. The top of the hood was decorated with a stand-up hood ornament. Two headlamps were placed in each fender, being horizontally positioned and set into oval-shaped openings. Bodyside styling had a sort of reverse-angled, fin-shaped feature line running along the front fender and door. At the rear was a sporty-looking indentation, usually referred to as a 'cove'. It was outlined with a thin chrome molding and had large, block letters inside. They spelled out the new car's name. Body panels and rooflines on the smaller models had a Ford look, while those on the big Edsels came straight from the Mercury studio. The rear end reverted to a more radical theme with a split-style bumper, boomerang-shaped horizontal tail lamps and the deck lid depressed below the level of the flat, rounded fendertops. Station wagons of all types had certain styling distinctions, which are described in the outline of the station wagon series below. The Ranger was the base trim-level Edsel. Rangers could be identified by suitable model signature script placed above and ahead of the front wheel openings; lack of front fender and rocker panel trim; lack of upper body edge reveal moldings; and a slightly plainer appearance in general. Ranger sedans were equipped with front and rear armrests; three ashtrays; two coat hooks; black rubber floor mats and white vinyl headliners. Trims available for these cars were Code A (green cloth), Code B (blue cloth) and Code C (gray and black cloth). Ranger hardtops were equipped the same as sedans, except for the style of upholstery. Trims available for both two- and four-door pillarless styles were Code K (white vinyl and green cloth), Code M (white vinyl and blue cloth) and Code N (white vinyl and black cloth). Three-speed manual transmission with column controls, a 361 cid/303-hp V-8 with four-barrel carburetor and 8.00 x 14 four-ply tires were featured as well.

EDSEL I.D. NUMBERS: Encoded information designating engine, model year, assembly plant, body style and consecutive unit production number was found on the upper line of the data plate, affixed to the left-hand front door post of all 1958 Edsels. The first symbol was a letter designating the type of engine, as follows: W = 361 cid V-8 or X = 410 cid V-8. The second symbol indicated model year: 8 = 1958. The third symbol was another letter, designating assembly plant, as follows: U = Louisville, Ky.; R = San Jose, Calif.; S = Somerville, Mass.; E = Madwah, N.J.; W = Wayne, Mich., and J = Los Angeles, Calif. The fourth symbol was another letter, which designated the style of the body, as follows: C = Ranger two-door sedan; F = Ranger/Pacer four-door sedan; G = Ranger/Pacer two-door hardtop; H = Ranger/Pacer four-door hardtop; R = Pacer two-door convertible; S = Roundup station wagon; T = six-passenger Villager/Bermuda station wagon; V = Villager/Bermuda station wagon; W = Corsair/Citation two-door hardtop; X = Corsair/Citation four-door hardtop; Y = Citation two-door convertible. The following symbols (six numbers) were the consecutive unit production number. Consecutive numbers at each plant began at 700001 and up. Additional encoded information designating body type, exterior color, interior trim, date of assembly, transmission type and rear axle was listed on the lower part of the data plate. The body type codes consisted of two numbers followed by a single letter, as shown in the second column of the specifications charts below. The exterior color code consisted of three letters: the first indicating main body color, the second indicating top color and the third indicating the color that the cove (or scallop) was painted. The codes and colors were as follows: A = Jet black; B = silver-gray metallic; C = Ember red; D = turquoise (N/A on Ranger/Villager/Roundup); E = Snow white (Pacer/Ranger station wagons only) or E = Frost white (Corsair/Citation only); F = Powder blue; H = Royal blue metallic; J = Ice green; K = Spring green; L = Spruce green; M = Charcoal brown metallic; N = Driftwood (Pacer/Ranger station wagons only); Q = Jonquil yellow; R = Unset coral (Pacer/Ranger station wagons only); T = Chalk pink (Corsair/Citation only); U = Copper metallic (Corsair/Citation only); X = Gold metallic (Corsair/Citation only). The interior trim code was a single letter, as described in text covering each model. The date code consisted of one or two numbers and a letter. The numbers designated the day of the month that the car was built. The letter indicated the month of production: G = July 1957; H = August 1957; J = September 1957; K = October 1957; L = November 1957; M = December 1957; A = January 1958 (*); B = February 1958; C = March 1958; D = April 1958; E = May 1958; F = June 1958; U = July 1958 and V = August 1958. (* NOTE: A few cars have been found with a month code of N. This represented January 1958 as does the letter A). Transmission codes were numerical, as follows: 1 = standard manual; 2 = overdrive; 3 = column-lever automatic; and 4 = Teletouch push-button automatic. A letter was used to designate different rear axles, as follows: A = 2.91:1; B = 3.32:1; C = 3.70:1 and D = 3.89:1.

RANGER SERIES

Model No.	Body/ Style No.	Body Type & Seating	Factory Price	Shipping Weight	Prod. Total
A	64A	2-dr Sed-6P	2484	3729	4,615
A	58A	4-dr Sed-6P	2557	3805	6,576
A	63A	2-dr HT Cpe-6P	2558	3724	5,546
A	57A	4-dr HT Sed-6P	2643	3796	3,077

1958 Edsel Pacer two-door hardtop, V-8. (OCW)

1958 Edsel Pacer two-door convertible, V-8. (OCW)

1958 Edsel Corsair four-door hardtop sedan, V-8. (PH)

PACER — (V-8) — SERIES B — The Pacer represented the second step up in the Edsel product lineup. It used the same body as Rangers, with slightly more trim, extra equipment and fancier upholstery fittings. Pacers could be externally identified by the Pacer front fender script and the use of a slightly curved, fin-shaped molding on the sides of front fenders and doors. Available body styles were similar to those in the Ranger series, except that the two-door sedan wasn't available. A two-door convertible was. Pacer sedans were equipped with four built-in armrests; two ashtrays; cigarette lighter; two coat hooks; chromed inside rearview mirror; one-third/two-thirds design front seat; color-keyed rubber floor mats and a white vinyl headliner. Trims available in the sedan were: D = brown cloth; E = green cloth and F = blue cloth. Pacer hardtops carried the same equipment as sedans, but different trims were used. They were, as follows: R = white vinyl and brown cloth; S = white vinyl and coral cloth; AX = white vinyl and red cloth; AY = white vinyl and turquoise cloth; T = green cloth and vinyl and V = blue cloth and vinyl. Pacer convertibles came with four built-in armrests; three ashtrays; cigarette lighter; courtesy lights under instrument panel; rear armrest lights and chrome inside rearview mirror. They also had one-third/two-thirds seat designs, color-keyed rubber floor mats and vinyl-coated convertible tops in a choice of black, white, turquoise or coral. Convertible interior trims were, as follows: AJ = white and coral vinyl; AN = white and black vinyl; AV = white and turquoise vinyl; AZ = white and red vinyl.

PACER SERIES B

Model No.	Body/ Style No.	Body Type & Seating	Factory Price	Shipping Weight	Prod. Total
B	58B	4-dr Sed-6P	2700	3826	6,083
B	63B	2-dr HT Cpe-6P	2770	3773	6,139
B	57B	4-dr HT Sed-6P	2828	3857	4,959
B	76B	2-dr Conv-6P	3766	4311	1,876

CORSAIR — (V-8) — SERIES A — The third step up in the 1958 Edsel lineup was the Corsair series, which was comprised of two- and four-door hardtops on the 124-inch wheelbase. Cars in this line had the look of contemporary Mercurys with greater overall length and a roof styled with an overhanging rear edge and wraparound backlight. For identification, there was Corsair front fender script; fin-shaped side moldings across the upper mid-section of front fenders and doors; chrome outline moldings on the rear fender cove; bright Edsel block lettering within the rear fender cove; Edsel block lettering positioned vertically within the horse collar center grille; rocker panel moldings and heavy chrome trim along the edge of the roof and rear body pillars. Vertical guards were optional on each of the front bumpers, being positioned quite close to the horse collar grille. The Corsair and Citation shared many chassis and inner body components with the 1958 Mercury, but little with Fords. Therefore, only a few components from the Ranger/Pacer series would interchange with the Corsair/Citation series. Examples of parts that were common between the two types included the hood ornaments; center and side grilles; front bumpers and starter. Standard equipment on Corsair hardtops included built-in front and rear armrests; ashtrays; cigarette lighter; two coat hooks; courtesy lights on the instrument panel; chromed inside rearview mirror; one-third/two-thirds design front seat; white vinyl headliner and color-keyed floor carpeting. Trim codes available for Corsairs were: B = blue cloth and vinyl; C = white vinyl and turquoise cloth; D = green cloth and vinyl; E = white vinyl and gold cloth; X = gray vinyl and red cloth and Y = white vinyl and copper cloth.

CORSAIR SERIES A

Model No.	Body/ Style No.	Body Type & Seating	Factory Price	Shipping Weight	Prod. Total
A	63A	2-dr HT Cpe-6P	3311	4134	3,312
A	57A	4-dr HT Sed-6P	3390	4235	5,880

CITATION — (V-8) — SERIES B — The Citation was the top-of-the-line Edsel offering. It shared the Corsair body, but came with more DeLuxe interiors and trim. There was Citation front fender script; model medallions on the rear roof pillars and a special decorative arrangement within the coves on the rear fender sides. Inside the cove an additional projectile-shaped beauty panel was formed by chrome outline moldings. Also, a large medallion was placed directly below the upper inner molding towards the rear. On most cars the inner beauty panel was finished in one color and the cove was done in another, which often matched the color of the roof. It was then possible to select a third color for the main body itself. A wide variety of two-tone or three-tone combinations could be achieved with the 161 colors available for the big Edsels. Standard equipment on Citation hardtops included all items found on Corsairs plus padded dashboard; electric clock and glove compartment light. Interior trims available in Citation hardtops were: AA = black vinyl and gray cloth; H = blue cloth and vinyl; J = white vinyl and turquoise cloth; K = green cloth and vinyl; L = white vinyl and gold cloth; Z = pink vinyl and brown cloth; AB = white vinyl and copper cloth. The Citation convertible came with the same equipment as hardtops plus dual exhaust and vinyl-coated convertible tops available in black, white, turquoise and copper. Convertible color schemes were as follows: AC = brown and pink vinyl; AD = red and white vinyl; AE = copper and white vinyl; S = turquoise and white vinyl; T = gold and white vinyl.

CITATION SERIES B

Model No.	Body/ Style No.	Body Type & Seating	Factory Price	Shipping Weight	Prod. Total
B	63B	2-dr HT Cpe-6P	3500	4136	2,535
B	57B	4-dr HT Sed-6P	3580	4230	5,112
B	76B	2-dr Conv-6P	3766	4311	930

1958 Edsel Citation four-door hardtop sedan, V-8. (OCW)

1958 Edsel Citation two-door convertible, V-8. (OCW)

STATION WAGONS — (V-8) — MIXED SERIES CODING

— The 1958 Edsel station wagons were all built off the 116-inch wheelbase Ford station wagon platform and utilized the basic sheet metal of two- or four-door Ford station wagons. Front end sheet metal was shared with the Edsel Ranger/Pacer series. The station wagons had completely different (Ford) rear fenders and vertical taillights housed in chrome, boomerang-shaped bezels. Three models were available. The Roundup was a two-door station wagon with seating for six. A Roundup script was placed at the front fender tip and a projectile-shaped contrast panel was formed by a chrome outline molding. The projectile went from the rear of the car to the middle of the front door. All station wagons were equipped with four armrests; ashtrays; cigarette lighter; two coat hooks; dome and courtesy lights and white vinyl headliner. The Roundup came with black rubber floor mats and a conventional split front seat (as used in Ford two-door sedans). The Villager station wagon was a four-door model that came with six- or nine-passenger seating. It had all items that were standard on the Roundup plus a solid front bench seat. Trim codes available for both station wagons discussed above were: BA = white and green vinyl; BB = white and blue vinyl; BC = black vinyl and gold Saran; BD = red vinyl with gold Saran. The Bermuda was the top-line station wagon. It had four doors and either six- or nine-passenger seating. Bermudas had simulated woodgrain exterior paneling; color-keyed rubber floor mats; one-third/two-thirds design front seats and chromed inside rearview mirror. Trim included: AT = two-tone blue vinyl; AJ = white and coral vinyl; AS = two-tone green vinyl; AU = driftwood vinyl and brown Saran and AV = white and turquoise vinyl.

STATION WAGON SERIES

Model No.	Body/ Style No.	Body Type & Seating	Factory Price	Shipping Weight	Prod. Total
ROUNDUP					
N/A	59A	2-dr Sta Wag-6P	2841	3761	924
VILLAGER					
N/A	79C	4-dr Sta Wag-6P	2898	3827	2,054
N/A	79A	4-dr Sta Wag-9P	2955	3900	1,735
BERMUDA					
N/A	79D	4-dr Sta Wag-6P	3155	3853	892

ENGINE [(Ranger/Pacer/Station Wagon Series) V-8]: Overhead valve. Cast-iron block. Displacement: 361 cid. Bore and stroke: 4.05 x 3.50 inches. Compression ratio: 10.5:1. Brake hp: 303 at 4600 rpm. Five main bearings. Hydraulic valve lifters. Carburetor: four-barrel Model B8E-9510A. Note: This engine was the 352 cid Ford V-8 with a slight overbore. The block and heads were painted yellow. The air cleaner and valve covers were painted white. There were red 'E 400' markings on the valve covers to designate torque (not horsepower).

ENGINE [(Corsair/Citation Series) V-8]: Overhead valve. Cast-iron block. Displacement: 410 cid. Bore and stroke: 4.20 x 3.70 inches. Compression ratio: 10.5:1. Brake hp: 345 at 4600 rpm. Five main bearings. Hydraulic valve lifters. Carburetor: four-barrel Model EDH9510-A.

1958 Edsel Bermuda station wagon, V-8. (PH)

1958 Edsel Villager station wagon, V-8. (OCW)

CHASSIS FEATURES: Wheelbase: (Ranger/Pacer) 118 inches; (all station wagons) 116 inches; (Corsair/Citation) 124 inches. Overall length: (Ranger/Pacer) 213.1 inches; (all station wagons) 205.4 inches; (Corsair/Citation) 218.8 inches. Front tread: (Ranger/Pacer) 59.44 inches; (station wagons) 58.97 inches; (Corsair/Citation) 59.38 inches. Rear tread: (Ranger/ Pacer) 59 inches; (station wagons) 56.40 inches; (Corsair/Citation) 59 inches. Tires: (Corsair/Citation) 8.50 x 14; (all others) 8.00 x 14.

OPTIONS: Power steering ($84.95). Power brakes ($38.25). Power windows ($100.95). Four-Way power seats ($76.45). Dial-A-Temp heater and defroster ($92.45). Dial-A-Temp air conditioning with heater, on Ranger/Pacer ($417.70); on Corsair/Citation ($460.15). Push-button radio with manual antenna ($95.25). Station-seeking radio with electric antenna ($143.90). Rear seat speaker ($16). Tachometer ($14.95). Electric clock, standard in Citation ($15.94). Compass push-button chassis lubricator, on Corsair/Citation only ($42.50). Padded instrument panel ($22.65). Front seat belts. Windshield washer ($11.50). Tinted glass ($34). Back-up lights ($8.50). Full wheel covers ($12.75). Full wheel covers with appliques and spinner. Front bumper guards. Rear bumper guards. Engine compartment light. Glove compartment light. Luggage compartment light. Inside non-glare rearview mirror. Rocker panel moldings. Hooded outside mirror. Foam front seat cushion, standard in Corsair/Citation ($21.25). Foam rear seat cushion. Carpeting, standard in Corsair/Citation ($12.30). License plate frames. Courtesy lights. Oil filter, standard with Corsair/Citation ($9.15). Paper air cleaner. Two-tone paint on top or scallop or top and scallop ($17). Tri-tone paint. Size 8.00 x 14 whitewall tires, Ranger/Pacer ($40.35). Corsair/Citation ($44.25). Size 8.50 x 14 whitewall tires. Undercoating. Vacuum-booster windshield wipers ($11.70). Electric windshield wipers. Rear-mounted antenna, single or dual. Excess speed warning light. Parking brake warning light. Fuel level warning light. Oil level warning light. Open door warning light. Padded sun visors (included in padded dash safety package). Exhaust deflector, single or dual. Seat covers. Contour floor mats, front and rear. Locking fuel tank cap. Curb signals. Traffic light reflector. Standard-style outside mirror, left and right. Spotlight, left and right. Electric luggage compartment opener. Rear door safety locks, four-doors only. Fuel and vacuum booster pump. Extra-cooling radiator and fan. Three-speed manual transmission with column lever control was standard in Rangers, Pacers and all station wagons. Three-speed automatic transmission with push-button Teletouch Drive was standard and mandatory in Corsair/Citation. Overdrive transmission, in Ford-based models only ($127.45). Three-speed automatic transmission with column lever control ($217.70). Three-speed automatic transmission with Teletouch control in Ford-based models ($231.40). Dual exhaust, on Citation convertible (standard equipment); on other models ($23.45).

HISTORY: The Edsel received one of the best and longest lasting new car buildups in automotive history. As early as Aug. 7, 1956, Ford announced that its Special Products Division was in the process of establishing five regional sales offices through which to market an all-new car called the Edsel. The following October 15, the company appointed 24 district sales managers to oversee Edsel sales in major cities. On Jan. 11, 1957, Ford informed the world that the Edsel would be far more radical than any of its other products and that equally radical sales techniques would be adopted in the marketing of the car. Ten days later, corporate officials predicted 200,000 sales in the first year and set their sights accordingly. After having named the car publicly on Nov. 19, 1956, Ford released the names and characteristics of each Edsel series on Feb. 5, 1957. To build even more interest, a March 10, 1957, press release identified five factories where Edsels were to be assembled, adding that a sixth factory, on the West Coast, would be added soon. Edsel production began in July 1957 under the direction of R.E. Krafve, a Ford Motor Co. vice-president who was named general manager of the Edsel Division. The new division built 3,729 units in July; 19,876 units in August; 18,815 units in September; 7,566 units in October; 2,483 units in November and 2,138 units in December for a total of 54,607 cars in calendar 1957. Model year output was recorded as 63,110 cars for only 1.5 percent of the total U.S. market. Of this figure, 4,900 cars were built at Wayne, Mich.;

6,400 at Mahwah, N.J.; 33,300 at Louisville, Ky.; 5,600 at San Jose, Calif.; 11,400 at Somerville, Mass.; and 1,500 at Los Angeles. In mid-January 1958, Ford combined the operations of Edsel, Mercury, Lincoln and English Ford to create a new Mercury-Edsel-Lincoln Division. Of all Edsels built in 1958, 91.9 percent had automatic transmission; 48.7 percent had power steering; 43.3 percent had power brakes; 7.6 percent had power seats; 5.6 percent had power windows; 80.3 percent had radios; 89.4 percent had a heater; 73.2 percent had white sidewall tires; 32.9 percent had tinted glass; 61.4 percent had windshield washers; 43.3 percent had back-up lights; 28.4 percent had dual exhaust; 1.6 percent had air conditioning; two percent had overdrive and all had V-8 engines. Although universally recognized as a failure in the area of sales, it is interesting to note that, in its first year, the Edsel set an all-time record for deliveries of a brand new medium-priced automobile.

1959 EDSEL

RANGER — (V-8) — The Edsel Marketing Division had expected to sell 200,000 cars during 1958 but soon admitted that there was a problem. The company went on record as saying that the Edsel had an "identity crisis." Since the first models covered such a wide market spectrum, buyers were unable to determine exactly where the Edsel fit in. Consequently, the Pacer and Citation series were discontinued for 1959. More emphasis was placed on slotting the remaining models into the top end of the low-priced field. As previously indicated, the Edsel line joined Lincolns, Mercurys and English Fords in the new M-E-L marketing division. Upon instituting this regrouping, Henry Ford II, the president of the corporation, said, "Unified direction of the organizations responsible for the five M-E-L Division product lines (which included English Anglia, Prefect, Consul, Zephyr and Zodiac cars and Thames Van trucks) will strengthen the profit potential of our dealers and assist in increasing the company's efficiency." J.J. Nance was named general manager of M-E-L at its formation, but on Sept. 4, 1959, Ben D. Mills was appointed to the same post. Edsel launched its new 1959 program with the theme of "a new kind of car." Economy was stressed more than before. The Ranger was built off a new 120-inch wheelbase platform, with a 292 cid V-8 engine as base powerplant. It shared some common sheet metal with the 1959 Ford. Overall styling changes were quite obvious, although the original theme was not totally disregarded either. The horse collar grille was retained in a modified form. It was now filled with horizontal blades and an Edsel badge at the top. The stand-up hood ornament disappeared and the parking lamps were moved into the split front bumpers. The side grilles each had three stacks of short, prominent moldings. There were also less noticeable moldings in between. They ran from the grille to the dual, horizontal headlamps. The hood still had a broad peak above the top of the grille. The front of the body was flatter and more shelf-like and the concave cove at the rear was nearly gone. A different type of sweep spear treatment was used. It had a distinct scallop shape for each car line. On Rangers, it consisted of a full-length upper molding, combined with a lower molding that ran to the door, then dipped in a curved 'V' and continued in a taper to the rear where it rejoined the top molding. The area between the moldings was often painted in a color other than that used on the main body. It often matched the roof's color. The two-tone paint combinations consisted of a contrasting color being placed in the side scallop and on the roof. Widely spaced block letters spelled out Edsel in chrome, with a few letters on each side of the front door break line. A Ranger script was placed near the rear body corner, under the sweep spear. The rear end still had a wing-like image, but no longer with the taillights in the wings. They were now placed into the rear deck latch panel, slightly above the horizontal centerline. The taillights consisted of three circular lenses placed horizontally against chrome grille panels housed in wedge-shaped chrome surrounds. A massive one-piece bumper (with a dip below the license plate) ran fully across the rear of the cars. The deck lid still had a wide center depression with a simulated chrome air vent at the rear. Roof treatments looked like those on the big 1958 Edsels, with a rear overhang and a large wraparound backlight with angular looking edges. A grooved aluminum trim plate was used on the rear roof pillar. Standard equipment on all models included an air cleaner; positive action windshield wipers; front foam seat cushions; electric clock; cigarette lighter and carpeting (except station wagons). Rangers were also equipped with four armrests; front and rear ashtrays; two coat hooks; color-keyed vinyl headliner and a conventional split front seatback. Trim codes on this series were: 23 = two-tone green vinyl and signet cloth; 24 = two-tone blue vinyl and signet cloth; 25 = white and buff vinyl and gold puff cloth; 50 = silver and black vinyl with black surf cloth. (Surf cloth was leftover 1958 Edsel material.) Around January 1959, a four-pointed star cloth, originally made for 1957 Mercurys, was introduced. In March 1959, the trim code was changed to 501. In May 1959, the cloth used in this option was changed to black Signet cloth.

1959 Edsel Ranger four-door sedan, V-8. (OCW)

EDSEL I.D. NUMBERS: The numbering system and code locations were basically the same as on 1958 Edsels. The first symbol in the top row of codes on the data plate designated engine type, as follows: A = six-cylinder; C = 292 cid V-8; B = 332 cid V-8; W = 361 cid V-8. The second symbol indicated model year: 9 = 1959. Third symbols were the same for each Ford factory but Edsels were now built only at Louisville, Ky. (Code U). Body style and consecutive numbering systems were unchanged, although fewer codes were used in 1959. On the lower row of codes, body type designations were as listed in the specification charts below. Exterior color codes were as follows: A = Jet black; S = Moonrise gray; C = gold metallic; D = Redwood metallic; E = Snow white; F = President red; G = Talisman red; H = Desert tan; J = Velvet maroon; K = Platinum gray metallic; L = Star blue metallic; M = Jet Stream blue; N = Light aqua; P = blue aqua; Q = Petal yellow; R = Mist green; S = Jadeglint green metallic. Interior trim codes are explained in the text. Date codes were as before except that only the letters of normal progression are used. Transmission codes were the same as before, although few types were available. Axle codes were changed, as follows: 1 = 3.10:1; 2 = 3.56:1; 3 = 3.70:1; 4 = 3.89:1; 5 = 2.91:1 and 6 = 2.69:1.

RANGER SERIES V-8

Model No.	Body/ Style No.	Body Type & Seating	Factory Price	Shipping Weight	Prod. Total
N/A	64C	2-dr Sed-6P	2629	3545	7,778
N/A	58D	4-dr Sed-6P	2684	3775	12,814
N/A	63F	2-dr HT Cpe-6P	2691	3690	5,474
N/A	57F	4-dr HT Sed-6P	2756	3680	2,352

NOTE 1: The prices and weights given above are for Ranger V-8s.
NOTE 2: For sixes: subtract $84/deduct 99 pounds.

CORSAIR — (V-8) — The Corsair was now nothing more than a Ranger with a larger engine and longer list of standard features. Both series were built off the same platform. The biggest external difference between the two lines was the placement of side trim and variations in the body styles offered. The upper sweep spear molding on Corsairs actually started as a front hood lip accent, moved around the edge of the front fender, then began a long, subtle curve to the taillights. Upon hitting the taillight, it moved back across the quarter panel, then curved upward and tapered to a point of the front fender tip. The area between the two moldings, at the rear, was filled with a scallop-shaped contrast panel, also outlined in chrome. A medallion was positioned at the forward tip of the 'scallop'. There was also a series identification script on the lower rear quarter panel, under the trim. Standard equipment on closed body styles included all Ranger items, except a one-third/two-thirds-type seat design was used. Trim combinations included all of the following: 38 = aqua vinyl and Reception cloth; 39 = Redwood vinyl and Reception cloth; 40 = gold vinyl and black Reception cloth; 51 = black vinyl and black mesh cloth; 53 = green vinyl and green Reception cloth and 54 = blue vinyl and Reception cloth. Code 39 Redwood vinyl and Reception cloth was an alternate choice. Standard equipment on the Corsair convertible was the same as for closed cars plus dual exhaust and a vinyl-coated top with vinyl boot. The ragtops featured all-vinyl interior trims in the following combinations: 41 = gold and white; 42 = black, white and silver; 43 = turquoise and white; 44 = black and red.

1959 Edsel Corsair two-door convertible, V-8. (OCW)

CORSAIR SERIES V-8

Model No.	Body/ Style No.	Body Type & Seating	Factory Price	Shipping Weight	Prod. Total
N/A	58B	4-dr Sed-6P	2812	3695	3,301
N/A	63B	2-dr HT Cpe-6P	2819	3780	2,315
N/A	57B	4-dr HT Sed-6P	2885	3710	1,694
N/A	76E	2-dr Conv-6P	3072	3790	1,343

STATION WAGONS — (V-8) — VILLAGER SERIES — Only the Villager station wagon survived into 1959. It shared frontal treatments and side trim with the Ranger line of passenger models. Distinct styling was seen at the rear. The taillights consisted of two circular lenses set against a chrome grillework that was housed in a short, horizontal oval, which was banded in chrome. At the lower portion of the rear body, a full-width, oval-shaped beauty panel stretched across the Villager. It contained Edsel block lettering at its center and backup lights at each outboard end. The panel was usually (or always) painted a contrasting color, matching the sweep spear insert. A chrome outline molding encircled the panel and incorporated a rectangular nameplate at the top center. It earned the Villager name in block letters against a color field. Directly above this ornament, a combination lock button and handle was positioned. Villager rear fender tops formed a small, crisp taillfin and the bumper was a distinctive type, which was reshaped at the center to hold the license plate. Only the four-door station wagon was available and it came with either six- or nine-passenger seating. Standard equipment included four armrests; two ashtrays; cigarette lighter; color-keyed rubber floor mats; printed cardboard headliner with chrome bows and a solid-back bench seat. Available interior trims were: 30 = two-tone green vinyl and Gold puff cloth; 31 = white and red vinyl and gold puff cloth; 32 = buff and white vinyl and straw vinyl and 52 = two-tone blue vinyl with gold puff cloth.

VILLAGER SERIES

Model No.	Body/ Style No.	Body Type & Seating	Factory Price	Shipping Weight	Prod. Total
N/A	71E	4-dr Sta Wag-6P	2971	3840	5,687
N/A	71F	4-dr Sta Wag-9P	3055	3930	2,133

NOTE 1: The prices and weights given above are for Villager V-8s.
NOTE 2: For sixes: subtract $84/deduct 99 pounds.

ENGINE [(Ranger Series) V-8]: Overhead valve. Cast-iron block. Displacement: 292 cid. Bore and stroke: 3.75 x 3.30 inches. Compression ratio: 8.8:1. Brake hp: 200 at 4400 rpm. Five main bearings. Hydraulic valve lifters. Carburetor: two-barrel Model B9A9510-A. Note: This engine was available as standard equipment in Rangers only. It came with the cylinder block and heads painted black, the air cleaner and valve covers painted gold.

ENGINE [(Optional Ranger SIX)]: Inline. Overhead valve. Cast-iron block. Displacement: 223 cid. Bore and stroke: 3.62 x 3.60 inches. Compression ratio: 8.4:1. Brake hp: 145 at 4000 rpm. Four main bearings. Hydraulic valve lifters. Carburetor: one-barrel Model B9A9510-F. Note: This engine was available, as a delete option, only in the Ranger series. It came with the cylinder block and head painted black and air cleaner and valve cover painted red.

ENGINE [(Corsair Series) V-8]: Overhead valve. Cast-iron block. Displacement: 332 cid. Bore and stroke: 4.00 x 3.30 inches. Compression ratio: 8.9:1. Brake hp: 225 at 4400 rpm. Five main bearings. Hydraulic valve lifters. Carburetor: two-barrel Model PB9E9510-8.

1959 Edsel Villager station wagon, V-8. (OCW)

1959 Edsel Corsair four-door hardtop, V-8. (OCW)

CHASSIS FEATURES: Wheelbase: (Villager) 118 inches; (all others) 120 inches. Overall length: (Villager) 210.1 inches; (all others) 210.9 inches. Front tread: (all models) 59 inches. Rear tread: (all models) 56.4 inches. Tires: (Ranger with standard shift) 7.50 x 14 four-ply; (all others) 8.00 x 14 four-ply.

OPTIONS: Power brakes ($42.25). Four-Way power seat ($70.20). Power steering ($81.80). Power windows ($102.05). Lever-Temp heater ($74.45). Polar-Aire air conditioning with Dial-Temp heater/defroster ($431.20). Dial-Temp heater/defroster ($90.10). Back-up lights ($9.42). Eight-tube push-button radio ($64.95). Signal-Seeking radio ($89.20). Rear seat radio speaker ($10.70). Safety Package, including padded windshield header and dashboard ($20.60). Wheel covers ($16.60). Wheel covers with applique ($28). Windshield washer ($13.95). Tinted glass ($37.90). Two-tone top paint ($21.55). Electric windshield wipers ($3.40). Size 8.00 x 14 four-ply white sidewall tire ($35.68). Rocker panel molding ($17). Heavy-duty rear springs ($4.86). Heavy-duty front springs ($6.50) Heavy-duty shock absorbers ($14.60). Seat belts. Single or dual rear-mounted radio antenna. Continental tire carrier. Engine compartment light. Luggage compartment light. Courtesy lights. Contour floor mats. Fuel tank lock. Curb signals. Inside non-glare rearview mirror. License plate frames. Traffic light reflectors. Standard-type outside rearview mirror. Hooded-type outside rearview mirror. Single or dual spotlights. Seat covers. Rear door safety locks. Parking brake warning light. Station wagon rooftop carrier. Compass. Tissue dispenser. Letter container. Remote control outside rearview mirror. Also available was the Visibility Group option package including: back-up lights; windshield washer; hooded outside rearview mirror; courtesy and glovebox lights and non-glare inside rearview mirror ($35.40). A three-speed manual transmission with column control was standard equipment with the 233-, 292- and 332 engines. Two-speed Mile-O-Matic transmission was optional on all models with any engine, but was rarely used in attachment with the 361 cid Super Express V-8 ($189.60). Three-speed Dual Drive automatic transmission was optional only with the 361 cid Super Express V-8 ($230.80). Overdrive transmission was not officially listed as a factory option for 1959 Edsels. However, at least three 1959 models are known to have been specially ordered and factory-built with such attachments. In such cases, the space on the data plate for the transmission code is left blank. Dual exhaust on convertible (standard equipment); on other V-8 models ($31.90). Heavy-duty clutch ($17).

HISTORY: The 1959 Edsel lineup was publicly introduced on Oct. 31, 1958. Model year output peaked at 44,891 units, for 0.8 percent market penetration. Calendar year production hit 29,677 units. Ben D. Mills was the general manager of the Mercury-Edsel-Lincoln Division. All Edsels made to 1959 specifications were assembled at the Louisville assembly plant. On a model year basis, 80.5 percent of all Edsels had automatic transmissions; 30.5 percent had power steering; 18.9 percent had power brakes; 2.3 percent had power seats; 1.5 percent had power windows; 75.5 percent had radios; 95 percent had heater/defrosters; 72.1 percent had white sidewall tires; 8.2 percent had tinted glass; 19.8 percent had windshield washers; 12.2 percent had electric windshield wipers; 31.7 percent had backup lights; 2.9 percent had dual exhaust; 2.2 percent had air conditioning; 77.6 percent had V-8 engines and 22.4 percent had six-cylinder engines. Production during calendar year 1959 included 5,880 cars in January; 3,819 in February; 4,035 in March; 4,031 in April; 2,959 in May; 2,575 in June; 1,971 in July and 1,561 in August.

1960 EDSEL

EDSEL RANGER — (V-8) — In February 1959, Henry Ford II attempted to dispel the rumors circulating in the auto industry about the Edsel's forthcoming demise. Ford Motor Co.'s president assured the world that the Edsel was to be a permanent member of the Ford family of cars. He said that he was certain the Edsel would prove successful and profitable in the long run and also revealed that the introduction date for 1960 models had already been set. These cars made their debut in October and featured a completely new body with numerous engineering improvements. Features included a lower silhouette, longer overall length and greater body width. Offered only in Ranger and Villager configurations, the 1960 Edsel provided engines ranging from the 145-hp six to a 300-hp V-8. The horse collar grille was abandoned and in its place was an attractive design with dual headlamps 'floating' against a chrome grid. The grille was split at the center by a pinch-waist panel. A one-piece front bumper appeared on Edsels for the first time and incorporated a license plate housing at the center. The front parking lamps were integrated into the fenders in projectile-shaped housings. The new Edsel profile was straight from the Ford studios, with the exception of trim and decorations. A thin chrome molding swept from behind the upper front wheel cutout to the extreme lower corner of the rear body. Edsel block letters were placed above the molding at the trailing edge of the rear fender, while Ranger or Villager script appeared on the cowlside. At the rear, there was a wide, horizontal deck latch panel with a concave indentation and Edsel block lettering spaced across the center portion. Twin, vertical tail lamps were positioned at each end of the car. They were somewhat oval-shaped, with the top portion rising higher than the upper edge of the deck. The deck lid and rear fendertop surfaces were formed into two narrow bulges on each side, which mated with the tail lamps. The rear bumper was a one-piece unit, with a center license plate indentation and vertical side ribs directly below the vertical taillamp lenses. Standard equipment on all models included an electric clock; air cleaner; front foam cushion; oil filter; positive-action windshield wipers; cigarette lighter; turn signals and carpets (except on station wagons). In addition, the Ranger convertible featured a DeLuxe trim package and standard dual exhaust. Also found inside all Rangers were four armrests; front and rear ashtrays; two coat hooks and vinyl color-keyed headlinings. Standard trims available in Ranger sedans and hardtops were: 20 = silver vinyl and black pebble cloth; 22 = blue vinyl and black pebble cloth; 23 = green vinyl and brown pebble cloth; 24 = gold vinyl and brown pebble cloth; 25 = red vinyl and black pebble cloth. Also available in these styles were DeLuxe combinations including: 11 = silver vinyl and gray Champagne cloth; 15 = red vinyl and gray Champagne cloth and 17 = turquoise vinyl and Champagne cloth. The DeLuxe combinations used in Ranger convertibles were: 54 = two-tone Gold vinyl; 55 = red and silver vinyl; 56 = black vinyl and 57 = two-tone turquoise vinyl.

EDSEL I.D. NUMBERS: Code locations were basically the same as on previous models. The first symbol indicated model year: 0 = 1960. The second symbol indicated the assembly plant: U = Louisville, Ky. The third and fourth symbols indicated body style: 11 = two-door sedan; 12 = four-door sedan; 13 = two-door hardtop; 14 = four-door hardtop; 15 = convertible; 17 = six-passenger station wagon; 18 = nine-passenger station wagon. The fifth symbol indicated the engine: V = 223 cid six; W = 292 cid V-8; Y = 352 cid V-8. The following numbers were the sequential production number starting at 700001 and ending at 703197. On the lower row of codes, Body Type designations were as listed in the second column of the specifications charts below. Exterior color codes were: A = black velvet; C = turquoise; E = Cadet blue metallic; F = Hawaiian blue; H = Alaskan gold metallic; J = Regal red; K = turquoise metallic; M = Polar white; N = Sahara beige; Q = Lilac metallic; R = Buttercup yellow; T = Sherwood green metallic; U = Bronze rose metallic; W = Sea Foam green; Z = Cloud silver metallic. Interior trim codes are explained in the text. Date codes were as in 1959. (Actually, all production took place during 1959.) Transmission codes were unchanged. Axle codes were as follows: 1 = 3.56:1; 2 = 3.89:1; 3 = 3.10:1; 6 = 2.91:1; A = 3.56:1 with Equa-Lock; B = 3.89:1 with Equa-Lock and C = 3.10:1 with Equa-Lock.

RANGER SERIES V-8

Model No.	Body/ Style No.	Body Type & Seating	Factory Price	Shipping Weight	Prod. Total
N/A	64A	2-dr Sed-6P	2643	3601	777
N/A	58A	4-dr Std Sed-6P	2697	3700	1,126
N/A	58B	4-dr Del Sed-6P	2736	3700	162
N/A	63A	2-dr Std HT-6P	2705	3641	243
N/A	63B	2-dr Del HT-6P	2743	3641	52
N/A	57A	4-dr Std HT-6P	2770	3718	104
N/A	57B	4-dr Del HT-6P	2809	3718	31
N/A	76B	2-dr Conv-6P	3000	3836	76

NOTE 1: Style Number suffix A = standard trim.
NOTE 2: Style Number suffix B = DeLuxe interior trim.
NOTE 3: Prices shown for Deluxes are standard retail + Deluxe option price.
NOTE 4: Prices and weights are for V-8s; six-cylinder engine was delete option.
NOTE 5: For sixes: subtract $97/deduct 99 pounds.

1960 Edsel Villager station wagon, V-8. (OCW)

STATION WAGON — (V-8) — VILLAGER SERIES — The Edsel station wagon for 1960 had the same general styling seen on the passenger cars. As usual, however, there were slight changes at the rear to accommodate the station wagon body structure. This amounted to the upper rear fender feature line running straight across above the tail lamps, and then sweeping back to intersect the top of the concave lower panel. There was Edsel block lettering within the center of the lower panel, a Villager script directly above (on the tailgate) and, at the top of the gate, a chrome ornament that served as a handle containing the lock and latch mechanisms. As in the past, the station wagon continued to offer an access arrangement with the upper tailgate and lower drop-down tailgate. The 1960 Villager came only in four-door styles, with a choice of six- or nine-passenger seating configurations. Villagers had the same standard equipment as other lines, except that color-keyed rubber floor mats and printed cardboard headliners were utilized. Interior trims included: 32 = blue vinyl and ivy-stripe rib cloth; 33 = green vinyl and ivy-stripe rib cloth; 35 = red vinyl and ivy-stripe rib cloth; 50 = silver and black vinyl.

VILLAGER SERIES

Model No.	Body/ Style No.	Body Type & Seating	Factory Price	Shipping Weight	Prod. Total
N/A	71F	4-dr Sta Wag-6P	2989	4029	216
N/A	71E	4-dr Sta Wag-9P	3072	4046	59

NOTE 1: Prices/weights are for V-8s; six-cylinder engine was delete option.
NOTE 2: For sixes: subtract $97/deduct 99 pounds.

ENGINE [(Ranger Series) V-8]: Overhead valve. Cast-iron block. Displacement: 292 cid. Bore and stroke: 3.75 x 3.30 inches. Compression ratio: 8.8:1. Five main bearings. Hydraulic valve lifters. Carburetor: two-barrel Model B9A9510-A. Note: The cylinder block and heads were painted black. The valve covers and air cleaner were painted red.

1960 Edsel Ranger four-door sedan, V-8. (PH)

1960 Edsel Ranger two-door convertible, V-8. (PH)

ENGINE [(Optional Ranger SIX)]: Inline. Overhead valve. Cast-iron block. Displacement: 223 cid. Bore and stroke: 3.62 x 3.60 inches. Compression ratio: 8.4:1. Brake hp: 145 at 4000 rpm. Four main bearings. Hydraulic valve lifters. Carburetor: one-barrel Model B9A9510-F. Note: This engine was available, as a delete option, only in the Ranger series. It came with the cylinder block and head painted black and air cleaner and valve cover painted red.

CHASSIS FEATURES: Wheelbase: (all models) 120 inches. Overall length: (Ranger) 216 inches; (Villager) 214.8 inches. Front tread: 61 inches. Rear tread: 60 inches. Tires: (Villager) 8.00 x 14; (Ranger) 7.50 x 14.

OPTIONS: Power steering ($81.80). Power brakes ($43.25). Power windows ($102.05). Four-Way power seat ($70.20). Lever-Temp heater and defroster ($74.45). Lever-Temp air conditioning with tinted glass and heater ($403.80). Polar-Air air conditioner. Back-up lights ($9.50). Push-button radio ($64.95). Rear seat speaker, except convertibles ($10.70). Single or dual rear-mounted antenna. Rocker panel moldings, except Villager ($17). Tinted glass ($37.90). Two-tone paint ($17). Full wheel covers ($16.60). Wheel covers with applique and spinner ($30.10). Windshield washer ($13.85). Electric windshield wipers ($8.40). Whitewall tires ($35.70). Inside non-glare rearview mirror. Standard outside mirror. Hooded outside mirror. Single spotlight with mirror. Remote-control outside mirror. Padded instrument panel. Padded sun visors. Courtesy lights. Glovebox light. Luggage compartment light. Parking brake warning light. Equa-lock differential. Seat belts. Heavy-duty cooling system. Fender skirts. Tissue dispenser. Litter bag. Locking fuel cap. Remote-control deck lid opener. Luggage rack. Villager license plate frames. Rubber floor mats, front and rear. Rear door safety locks, four-door. A three-speed manual transmission was standard on all base models, but cars with the optional 352 cid 'Super Express' V-8 included automatic transmission as a mandatory option. Two-speed Mile-O-Matic automatic transmission, available in any model ($189.60). Three-speed Dual-Power drive automatic transmission, available with the 'Super Express' 352 cid V-8 only ($230.80). The 352 cid/300 hp 'Super Express' V-8, available as optional equipment over the base V-8 ($58). Note: Dual exhaust were standard equipment with the 'Super Express' V-8. This engine was painted black, with the valve covers and air cleaner finished in turquoise.

OPTION PACKAGES: DeLuxe trim package ($38.60). Visibility Group, includes back-up lights; windshield washer; inside non-glare mirror; outside hooded mirror ($30.90). Convenience Group A, includes heater and defroster; radio; Mile-O-Matic Drive; two-tone paint and full wheel covers ($362.60). Convenience Group B, includes heater and defroster; radio; Dual-Power drive; two-tone paint; wheel covers with applique and white sidewall tires ($453).

HISTORY: The 1960 Edsels were introduced on Oct. 15, 1959. The Edsel was discontinued on Nov. 19, 1959. Model year output amounted to 2,846 cars, all of which were built in calendar year 1959. Of these, 889 were made in September; 1,767 were made in October and 190 were built in November. All assemblies were made at the Louisville factory. Since the first Edsel was built, in 1957, a total of 110,847 were made. After Nov. 19, 1959, Ben D. Mills became general manager of Ford Motor Co.'s new Lincoln/Mercury Division. The much heralded—and now famous—Edsel was no more.

1960 Edsel Ranger two-door convertible, V-8. (OCW)

LINCOLN
1921-2003

The 1941 Lincoln lineup included (back-to-front) the new-that-year eight-passenger Custom sedan, the Lincoln-Continental Coupe and the Lincoln-Zephyr four-door sedan. (LMD)

He named the company for the president for whom he had first voted in 1864; initially, it was not intended for automobile manufacture at all and its organization was the product of circumstance. In early 1917, Henry Martyn Leland had walked out of Cadillac, following unpleasant words both he and his son Wilfred had with William C. Durant of General Motors.

A lot of people left GM that way, the confrontation in this case being, according to the Lelands, the reluctance of Durant to convert Cadillac to Liberty aviation engine production for the war effort. Already Henry Leland was 74 years old, but his stature in the industry and his passionate patriotism resulted in his new Lincoln Motor Co. being given a government contract to build some 6,000 Liberty engines and a $10,000,000 advance to do it. The Armistice came too quickly for the Lelands to have established a solid footing with their new company. Faced with a huge factory, a workforce of about 6,000 men and mounting debts, they made a quite logical decision. The man who had given America the Cadillac motorcar would now provide the country with the Lincoln.

Capital stock for the venture—$6.5 million of it—was subscribed within three hours of being placed on sale. This was a terrific beginning; unfortunately, it would prove to be one of only two high points the Lelands would enjoy during their short tenure with the car. The other was the trade press response to the engineering of the Lincoln itself. Like any Leland product, the Lincoln was precision built. Its 60-degree V-8 with its characteristic fork-and-blade connecting rods, was rugged and compact. The engine developed 81 hp and ensured 70-mph performance. Full-pressure lubrication and a massive torque tube drive highlighted the chassis.

Unfortunately, two factors convened to make the Lincoln less appealing. First, its coachwork had been assigned to Leland's son-in-law, whose previous speciality seems to have been ladies millinery. The Lincoln look was strictly old-hat—even dowdy—with styling reminiscent of the prewar era past, not a breath of the flapper flamboyance that would mark the 1920s. Second, because of late supplier deliveries and Leland's penchant for engineering perfection, the car was delayed, arriving in the marketplace in September 1920—not the planned January. It missed an entire selling season and hit the postwar recession.

The Lelands were convinced they could set matters right and contacted Brunn, in Buffalo, N.Y., about coachwork. Still, the Lincoln board directors could only see the figures—3,407 cars produced by Feb. 4, 1922, vis-a-vis the projected 6,000 for the first year alone. So, on that day, over the vigorous objection of the Lelands, the directors put the company into receivership and up for sale. It was bought for $8 million by Henry Ford.

Though the car hadn't appealed to many customers, Ford took a fancy to the Lincoln for several intertwined reasons. His Model T was America's best-selling cheap car by leagues; offering a luxury automobile at over 10 times the price (the Lincoln was introduced as a $5,000 range car) probably tweaked his interest and certainly that of his son Edsel, whose refined sense of the aesthetic was certainly not satisfied with his father's "Tin Lizzie." Moreover, in 1902, Henry Leland had made his Cadillac out of the frazzled remains of a company Henry Ford himself had started and which he left in disgust after, among other vexations, listening to Leland's uncomplimentary comments about his car. Buying out Leland now must have been a splendid satisfaction. It may have been further vengeance or the genuine admiration Ford had for Henry Leland, but initially the plan was for the Lelands to remain with the company.

It was a marriage made in hell, however, and the Lelands left after four months, seeing Henry Ford thereafter only in court during the lawsuit they instituted regarding reimbursement to original creditors and stockholders. Meanwhile, Edsel Ford became the president of the Lincoln Motor Co. By December 1922, just 10 months after the Ford purchase of the company, 5,512 Lincolns had been sold; over 2,000 more cars than the Lelands had delivered in 17 months. The Lelands' fears to the contrary, the product had not been compromised; indeed it had been improved, with aluminum pistons and better cylinder head cooling immediately and an increase in wheelbase to 136 in. (from 130) for 1923. Sales that year rose to 7,875.

Under Ford aegis, the Lincoln remained a robust car, favored by the Detroit Police Flying Squad among other progressive law enforcement agencies, the cars for the police sometimes being provided four-wheel brakes, which production versions wouldn't have until 1927. Perhaps more importantly, under Edsel Ford's direction, the Lincoln became a beautiful car, with series production of designs from the masters of America's coachbuilding craft. By 1929, the Model L Lincoln was up to 90 hp and 90 mph. Leading it down the road was a graceful greyhound mascot, selected by Edsel and produced by Gorham. In 1931 the Model K (that designation having been used on Henry Ford's first foray into the luxury car field in 1908, incidentally) replaced the Model L. It was a refined V-8 offering 120 hp, a 145-in. wheelbase and duo-servo brakes. Clearly, it was an interim model.

In 1932 the Ford became a V-8 and, though the Lincoln Model K V-8 was continued that year, the Lincoln grabbing the headlines was the new V-12 Model KB with 447.9 cu. in., 150 hp and 95-plus miles-per-hour performance. Interestingly, the more expensive and custom-built KB (with price tags ranging from $4,300-$7,200) fared rather well against the V-8 Model K (at $2,900-$3,350) that year, with 1,641 of the former built, 1,765 of the latter. In 1933, the V-8 was replaced by a smaller 382 cid 125-hp V-12 designated KA and set in a 136-in. wheelbase chassis, as opposed to the KB's145 inches. But that depth-of-Depression year brought sales of only 587 KBs and 1,420 KAs.

Building two different engines for a plummeting luxury car market didn't make a great deal of sense and, in 1934, both were dropped and replaced with a 414 cid 150-hp unit with aluminum cylinder heads. All Lincolns into the early postwar years would be V-12 powered, though precious few of them would be of the K series, as sales of these big Lincolns continued to dwindle while the 1930s wore on. Just 120 of the big Ks would be built in 1939-1940, the most famous of which was President Roosevelt's "Sunshine Special." Roosevelt carried forth a presidential preference for Lincolns that had begun with Calvin Coolidge and that would endure to the Clinton era.

But prestige was not what made Lincoln financially respectable in the later 1930s. The Zephyr did. When it arrived for 1936, Lincoln sales soared from under 4,000 cars in 1935 to over 22,000. Originally intended to use a modified version of the Ford V-8, the Zephyr instead—at Edsel Ford's direction—became a 75-degree 267 cid 110-hp V-12 with aluminum alloy heads, cast steel pistons and a reputation for sluggishness and unreliability it has had ever to live with, not always fairly. (The engine was used in England in the Allard, Atalanta and Brough Superior.)

The Zephyr chassis, with its transverse springs and mechanical four-wheel brakes, represented a specification only to be whispered about, but the synchromesh gear box was fine and the unitized construction was worthy of a shout, as was the fresh (and later imitated) styling of John Tjaarda of Briggs, which was refined for production by E.T. "Bob" Gregorie of Lincoln. With some models listing under $1,500, the Zephyr was the lowest-priced V-12 offered on the American market since Errett Lobban Cord's Auburn of the early 1930s. It didn't change appreciably

in the years to follow, though 1938 saw the gearshift lever spring from the dashboard. The year 1939 brought hydraulic brakes and, in 1940, the by-now-popular column-mounted gearshift arrived on the Zephyr.

With the demise of the big K in 1940—the last cars carrying prophetic black cloisonne emblems replacing the former red or blue—there was room for a new car in the Lincoln lineup, though the one that arrived did so rather by accident. It was in September of 1938 that, returning from a trip to Europe, Edsel Ford asked Bob Gregorie to design a special custom job for him that would be "strictly continental." Whether a Lincoln or Ford would be used—or the chassis of the company's new car called Mercury—was a matter decided in favor of the first named. And thus it was that the Continental was born of the Zephyr.

Ford's personal Continental engendered such comment wherever he took it that production seemed a good and viable idea. On Oct. 2, 1939, the new Continental cabriolet was introduced at the Ford Rotunda in Dearborn, Mich., as a model of the Lincoln-Zephyr. A coupe followed in May 1940 and, in September of that year, the word "Zephyr" was dropped; the car became simply the Lincoln Continental. A total of 1,990 Continentals were built before the war put an end to all automobile production. Postwar the Continental would return, but without Edsel Ford. Henry's son, whose unerring good taste had made a ravishing beauty of the Lincoln, died on May 26, 1943.

Like most American cars, the 1946-1948 Lincolns were warmed-over prewar models. When you had a gorgeous automobile such as the Continental, that wasn't bad. It was one of those rare cars that became an instant classic. Although highly regarded for its styling, sales were not good, but the Continental *did* help Lincoln's image.

When the first postwar Lincolns debuted in early 1948 (as 1949 models), the company had nothing to compare with the Continental. The top-of-the-line Cosmopolitan looked too much like the standard Lincoln series, which in turn resembled Mercury, with which it shared bodies.

In 1952, Lincoln dramatically changed the appearance of all its cars. The new Lincolns bore no resemblance to the previous year's models, but shared the corporate look all 1952 Ford Motor Co. cars. Although Lincolns had participated in previous Pan American Road Races, this was the first year the make dominated the event, winning the first four spots with 1953 models. The "hot car" image nurtured by the racing victories was fully exploited by the company. As an ad for 1955 models read, "The first function of a fine car is outstanding performance." Fortunately for Lincoln, the Pan American Road Race was discontinued in 1954. Its days as a road race winner were about to end when Chrysler came out with its potent 300 Letter Car in 1955.

The Lincoln Continental returned in 1956 as the beautiful Mark II, which captured the spirit of the original Continental, although it was thoroughly modern in design. Despite early waiting lists, it suffered the same fate as its predecessor: low demand. The 1956 Continental was also attractive. If anyone had doubts about Continental's status as a prestige automobile, they were vanquished this year.

The 1957 Continental Mark II two-door hardtop was a classic-looking Lincoln product. (LMD)

Regrettably, Lincoln styling was jazzed up a bit for 1957. The following year, the Continental model was completely changed and its lines were shared by its Capri and Premiere stable mates. The 1958 to 1960 models were the largest American cars of the postwar era. In certain parts of the country, owners were obligated by law to place red reflectors on the rear of their new Lincolns and amber clearance lights on the front. These huge Lincolns came on the automotive scene at a time when Detroit was being widely criticized for building cars that were too big. Continental sales declined in 1958 and continued to drop until the restyled 1961 models were introduced.

As in 1956, the 1961 Continental showed the world just how beautiful a production American automobile could be. Stylistically, it was one of the most influential cars of the decade. Continental kept the same basic styling until 1969. One benefit of this styling consistency was that it established a "Continental look." Cadillac had long been aware of the value of continuity in styling, something early postwar Continentals did not have. With an easily identifiable look all its own, Ford Motor Co. was able to make its less expensive cars classier by giving them Continental styling traits.

In the spring of 1968, the 1969 Continental Mark III was introduced. The Mark III proved to be popular and a sales success. Its design would influence Continental styling throughout the 1970s.

Descriptions of Lincoln in 1976 and beyond sound more like they belong in a fashion magazine than an automobile catalog. Bill Blass? Givenchy? Pucci and Cartier? Each of those internationally known apparel designers put his name and ideas on a designer series "Mark" Lincoln. Each displayed the designer's signature on opera windows, as well as a golden plate on the dash. Affluent customers must have liked the idea, just as ordinary folks wore jeans with designer names on the back pocket. Lincoln sales leaped upward this year.

As the era began, just two basic models made up the Lincoln lineup; Continental and Mark IV, both powered by FoMoCo's 460 cid V-8. Mark was known not only for fashionable signatures, but for its Rolls-Royce style vertical bar grille. Town Car and Town Coupe options added even greater luxury to Continentals.

Downsizing hit bodies and engines alike in 1977 as the 400 V-8 became standard, its big brother an option. Styling carried on traditional Lincoln cues, including hidden headlamps and simulated spare tire hump on the reduced Mark V coupe. Continentals adopted the Town Car name and added a *Williamsburg* special edition. Another breed of Lincoln arrived later in the year: the compact Versailles, ready to battle Cadillac's Seville on a Granada-size platform. Early Versailles models carried a standard 351 cid V-8, but dropped to a 302 cid V-8 for 1978. In honor of Ford's 75th anniversary, Lincoln produced the Mark V in a distinctive Diamond Jubilee Edition.

Collector's Series versions of both Continental and Mark V joined up for 1979, as Versailles got a bit of restyling. The 400 cid V-8 was now the largest Lincoln power plant, since the big 460 cid unit disappeared. Further downsizing came in 1980, when the Continental and the new Mark VI managed to look more alike than ever before. The Mark VI's headlamps remained hidden, while the Continental's were now exposed. Base engine for both was now the 302 cid V-8, with Ford's 351 cid V-8 as an option. A year later, the Mark VI came in both the customary designer series and a similarly luxurious Signature series. Versailles, which was never able to attract enough buyers (perhaps because of its modest origins and high price), dropped out of the Lincoln lineup after 1980.

A new Continental for 1982 weighed less than the old Versailles and could even be ordered with a V-6 instead of the traditional Lincoln V-8. The former Continental design continued under the Town Car badge, as a four-door sedan only. The Mark VI still offered three designer models and a Signature series.

The Continental line added two designer models of its own for 1983 and dropped that V-6 engine. Lincoln sales climbed appreciably for the model year.

The 1976 Lincoln Continental four-door sedan. (LMD)

The 1978 Lincoln-Versailles four-door sedan. (LMD)

The Continental Mark VII took a dramatically different form for 1984: an aero-styled wedge shape, far removed from its Mark forerunners. It was also shorter. A Mark VII LSC model added capable handling to traditional Lincoln luxury. Both the Continental and the Mark VII could get a turbo diesel engine, though not too many customers seemed to want one and it didn't last long.

A performance Lincoln? That was the Mark VII LSC, adding more such extras for 1985, including big Eagle GT blackwall tires. Antilock braking became optional on both Mark and Continental in 1985 and standard the next year. All three models offered designer and Signature series. The Town Car continued as the "big" conventional Lincoln, reaching record sales levels in 1985 and again in 1986. Plenty of Lincoln buyers, it seemed, preferred the old familiar comforts.

Lincoln-Mercury Div. built three cars under the Lincoln nameplate in 1987. Lincoln Town Cars, Mark VII coupes and Continentals were all assembled at a plant in Wixom, Mich., which operated two shifts and built an average 40 cars per hour between Aug. 1, 1986, and Aug. 4, 1987. A total of 159,320 Lincolns were sold during the 1987 model year. The popularity of the Town Car and Mark VII increased slightly, while the Continental lost about 9,000 customers from 1986. Part of this decrease could be attributed to the fact that a totally new Continental was in the works.

The 1979 Collectors Series four-door sedan and Continental Mark V two-door hardtop. (LMD)

The 1990 model year marked the 50th anniversary of the Continental nameplate. Ross Roberts, then Lincoln-Mercury general manager, posed with the special 50th Anniversary Lincoln Continental four-door sedan and a 1940 Lincoln Continental Cabriolet. The original Continental was based on the Zephyr and was created after Edsel Ford asked designers to come up with a car with a "Continental" look—long, low and sleek. (LMD)

Thomas J. Wagner was general manager of the division headquartered in Detroit's Renaissance Center. Edsel B. Ford II was active in the company as general marketing manager. Product news included a revised Givenchy designer package for the rear-drive Continental sedan. The Mark VII rear-wheel-drive coupe came in base and LSC versions, with a high-output version of the 5.0-liter Lincoln V-8 in the latter car. A Bill Blass Designer Series Mark VII was available again. The rear-drive Town Car received a new compact disc player option and continued to come in Signature and Cartier editions.

In 1988, Ross H. Roberts took over as general manager of Lincoln-Mercury Div. The Continental became a front-wheel-drive sedan that was dramatically different from its predecessors. It was all new and more aerodynamic, with a standard 3.8-liter V-6, a four-speed automatic transaxle, a four-wheel independent suspension and all-disc antilock brakes. Priced upwards from $26,602, the new model came in standard or Signature trim levels. Even with production starting three months into the model year, the updated Lincoln still sold 33,507 units, over twice as many cars as in 1987. Lincoln Town Cars received a new grille and hood ornament, revised interior trim and an electronic AM/FM radio. The wheel covers and rear styling were updated, too. Base-priced at $24,897, the car earned 126,642 sales, down nearly 9,500 from 1987. Declining in sales by about half as much was the Mark VII, which came in sporty LSC and fancy Bill Blass models. They were priced from $26,904. The LSC got sporty new road wheels and leather seats as a no-cost option. The grille and hood ornament were reworked and a JBL sound system was a new-for-1988 option.

During 1989, Lincoln Town Car sales tapered off to 117,806, while the Mark VII coupe's sales climbed to 27,030. In its first full season, the Continental realized 59,054 customers, making Lincoln dealers very happy. From sales of 180,712 cars in 1987, the annual total was now up to 203,890. New for 1989 was a driver/passenger airbag system for the Continental, an optional anti-theft system for Mark VIIs and new models of the Town Car. Cartier editions had a half-vinyl top and two-tone finish, while Signature versions boasted a half-vinyl coach roof. Mark VIIs came in LSC (with analog gauges) and Bill Blass (with electronic instrumentation) models.

For 1990, the Town Car was totally updated. This all-new aerodynamic luxo-mobile had flush aircraft-inspired doors, airbags, speed-sensitive steering, load leveling and an automatic radio antenna. Starting at $28,541, all three editions—base, Signature and Cartier—had a 5.0-liter V-8 linked to a four-speed overdrive transaxle. A new grille, hood ornament, tail lamps,

and power antenna were seen on the just-under-$30,000 Continental. The Mark VII, also about $30,000, got an airbag system, safer new seat belts, new seats, and a message center.

A new 4.6-liter V-8 was under the hoods of each of the Town Car models in 1991. The Town Cars all rode on a revised front suspension and had four-wheel disc brakes as standard equipment while anti-lock brakes with traction assist was optional. Continentals received an improved 3.8-liter V-6 teamed with a new electronically controlled four-speed automatic overdrive transmission. The Bill Blass edition of the Mark VII featured several upgrades including an improved suspension.

Lee Miskowski replaced Ross Roberts as general manager of the Lincoln-Mercury Div. in 1992. The Continental was now available in Executive ($32,263) or Signature ($34,253) trim and new standard equipment included a passenger-side airbag. There was an Executive version of the Town Car this year, with prices starting at $31,211. Town Cars also featured a passenger-side airbag as standard equipment.

An all-new Mark VIII debuted in 1993, this single model replaced the Mark VII Bill Blass and LSC coupes. The Mark VIII sported a wheelbase of 113 in. and weighed 3,741 lbs. It also increased in price by about $5,000 ($37,265) over the Mark VII. It was powered by the 32-valve DOHC 4.6-liter V-8 and featured the new-for-1993 4R70W four-speed automatic overdrive transmission. Dual airbags and anti-lock brakes were standard features. Sales of the Mark VIII totaled 31,852, compared to just 8,115 for the previous year's Mark VII. Town Cars and Continentals received remote keyless entry as a new standard item. Unfortunately, sales for each of those series slid 5.2 percent and 26.7 percent, respectively.

A redesigned, 1994 Continental series was launched early in 1993. The new-look Executive and Signature models featured solar glass for all windows and rebound suspension springs all-around. Mark VIIIs got remote memory recall for seats and mirrors and a price increase to $38,675. Keith C. Magee replaced Lee Miskowski as general manager of Lincoln-Mercury Div.

For 1995, the Executive and Signature models of the Continental series were both dropped and an all-new Continental was launched late in 1994. This was the first V-8-powered front-wheel-drive Lincoln and used the company's InTech DOHC 4.6-liter engine rated at 260 hp. The $41,375 Continental offered a memory profile system that governed three levels of power steering and suspension damping. Dual airbags and antilock brakes were standard equipment. Sales of the new Continental reached 40,708 compared to 32,145 for both versions sold the year previous. The Town Car was "gussied up" both front and rear and this model received an anti-theft system as standard equipment.

Both the Mark VIII and Town Car were offered in Diamond Anniversary Editions for 1996. A Luxury Sport Coupe version of the Mark VIII was released midyear in 1995 as a limited production (5,000) 1996 model. The Continental now also featured an anti-theft system as a standard item. Continentals also offered Lincoln's RESCU (remote emergency satellite cellular unit) that could be used for emergency roadside assistance. In April 1996, James G. O'Connor replaces Keith Magee as vice-president and general manager of Lincoln-Mercury Div.

All-speed traction control became standard equipment on Continental and Mark VIII models for 1997. The Luxury Sport Coupe version of the Mark VIII was continued, while all models in the series received a retuned suspension, a more prominent hood, a more distinctive grille and high-intensity discharge headlamps.

Lincoln's flagship automobile, the Town Car, had an all-new design for 1998. Still available in three models—Executive, Signature and Cartier—the all-four-door-sedan series featured a re-engineered full perimeter steel frame, Watt's Linkage rear suspension and an optional touring package for a firmer ride. The Continental featured daytime running lamps and de-powered dual airbags as standard equipment. The Mark VIII was again available in both base and Luxury Sport Coupe versions as well as a Collector's Edition. This limited-production Mark VIII was available in either Cordovan or White Pearlescent exterior colors with gold Collector's Edition badging.

January 1999 was a big month for Lincoln, as the Lincoln-Mercury Div. announced plans to move its headquarters from Detroit, Mich. To Irvine, Calif. Mark Hutchins became president of the division in 1999, with Jim Rogers serving as his general marketing manager and Gary Lessuisse in charge of dealer relations. In the product realm, the Continental gained 15 hp, and front side-impact airbags became standard in the Town Car. The Navigator—Lincoln's first Sport Utility Vehicle—was treated to adjustable pedals, an optional Alpine stereo system and other refinements. The all-new Lincoln LS entered production at the Lincoln plant in Wayne, Mich., and was introduced in the spring of 1999 as a 2000 model. Other than the LS, there were no major changes in the 2000 lineup, but all models got an added emphasis on safety and a satellite navigational system was added to the Navigator's options list.

The 2001 Lincoln LS, Navigator and Town Car earned the U.S. government's highest safety grade for frontal crashes, as rated by the National Highway and Traffic Safety Administration (NHTSA). Lincoln showcased a stunning MK 9 coupe concept vehicle during the US Open Tennis Championships, which took Aug. 27-Sept. 9, 2001 at the company's 8,000-sq. ft. 'Lincoln Innovations' pavilion on the grounds of the USTA National Tennis Center. Also in August, AutoPacific—an automotive marketing and product consulting firm—gave the 2001 Lincoln Navigator its top vehicle satisfaction award in both the SUV and Total Truck categories.

For 2002, Lincoln introduced the all-new Lincoln Blackwood to join the LS, Navigator, Town Car, and Continental in Lincoln dealer showrooms. Based on a 1999 concept vehicle, the assembly line version of the Blackwood was a limited-production vehicle that hoped to broaden appeal of Lincoln's model lineup. Lincoln's recent new-product releases had been extremely successful in broadening the brand's appeal among affluent consumers. Seventy percent of Lincoln Navigator buyers and 60 percent of Lincoln LS customers had never owned a Lincoln before. In addition, the median age for these customers was in the mid-50s, substantially lower than the mid-60s median age of Lincoln's customers in the traditional luxury car market segment.

Lincoln's 2002 sedans offered a new Vehicle Communication System (VCS) as an option. The VCS telematics system was built around a full transportable digital/analog Motorola Timeport phone with voice activiation and hands-free functionality. Features included automatic emergency services notification upon airbag deployment, emergency, route and points of interest assistance, and news and information services.

Lincoln Mercury president Mark Hutchins also announced some key appointments for the 2002 model year. Effective Dec. 1, 2001. Ann Kalass became marketing communications manager, Pat Petroske became Orlando regional manager and Jennifer Moneagle was appointed regional manager for the Memphis, Tenn., region.

*(Contributors to the Lincoln section of this catalog include Robert C. Ackerson who originally compiled the technical data and tables for the prewar section of the **Standard Catalog of American Cars 1805-1942**, James M. Flammang who originally compiled all of the data for the **Standard Catalog of American Cars 1976-1986**, John A. Gunnell who edited the original **Standard Catalog of American Cars 1946-1975**, Beverly Rae Kimes who wrote the prewar histories and compiled the prewar model information for the original **Standard Catalog of American Cars 1805-1942**, Ron Kowalke who edited the second edition of the **Standard Catalog of Fords 1903-1998**, Robert L. Lichty who edited the first edition of the **Standard Catalog of Fords 1903-1990** and Charles Webb who originally compiled the 1946-1975 data for the **Standard Catalog of American Cars 1946-1975**).*

1929 Lincoln Phaeton. (OCW)

1921 LINCOLN

1921 Lincoln Model L coupe. (AA)

LINCOLN — MODEL L — EIGHT: The styling of the first Lincoln was conservative to the point of being uninspired. However in terms of its design, the Lincoln was an automobile of grandeur. Rightly identified in automotive history as the "Master of Precision," its creator, Henry M. Leland, was 75 years old when the company he and his son founded produced its first automobile. Leland had already made his mark in the automotive industry as a supplier of engines to Ransom E. Olds, the creator of the first Cadillac in 1903 and the prime force behind their quality. Under Leland's presidency Cadillac won the 1908 Dewar Trophy in England, introduced its self-starter and all-electric system in 1912 and two years later the first American 90 degree V-8 automobile engine to be produced in quantity.

After breaking with William Durant in 1917 Leland proceeded to form the Lincoln Motor Company to produce Liberty aircraft engines for the U.S. government. However this effort came to a close after 6,500 engines had been delivered. The next step in Leland's career was the development and production of the Lincoln automobile, of which its engine and chassis design attracted considerable attention. Key engine features included a 60 degree instead of 90 degree vee and fork and blade connecting rods. The chassis was noted for its strong torque-tube drive and Alemite lubrication fittings.

I.D. DATA: Serial numbers were on right side of cowl, top of clutch housing and transmission case. Starting: 1 (1920), 835 (1921). Ending: 834 (1920), 3151 (1921). Engine numbers were on left side of crankcase between cylinders 1 and 2. Starting: 1 (1920), 835 (1921). Ending: 834 (1920), 3151 (1921).

Model No.	Body Type & Seating	Factory Price	Shipping Weight	Prod. Total
101	4-dr. Tr. (perm top)-7P	4600	—	1015
102	2-dr. Rds.-3P	—	—	78
103	4-dr. Phae.-5P	—	—	278
104	2-dr. Cpe.-4P	—	—	451
105	4-dr. Sed.-5P	—	—	352
106	4-dr. Limo. gls. part-7P	6600	—	101
107	4-dr. Twn. Brgm.-7P	6600	—	10
108	4-dr. Sed.-7P	—	—	26
109	4-dr. Twn. Car-7P	6600	—	19
110	4-dr. Berl. gls. part-7P	—	—	6
111	2-dr. Brunn Rds.-3P	—	—	68
112	2-dr. Brunn Phae. Del.-7P	—	—	196
113	4-dr. Sed.-4P	—	—	50
114	4-dr. Judkins Sed. gls. part-7P	—	—	29
115	4-dr. Judkins Berl. gls. part-5P	—	—	25
122	Chassis only	4000	—	253

ENGINE: 60 degree V, L-head. Eight. Cast-iron block. B & S: 3-3/8 x 5 in. Disp.: 357.8 cid C.R.: 4.8:1. Brake H.P.: 81 @ 2600 R.P.M. Main bearings: three. Valve lifters: mechanical. Carb.: Stromberg updraft.

CHASSIS: [Types 101-105 and 107] W.B.: 130 in. Frt/Rear Tread: 60 in. Tires: 33 x 5. [Types 106, 108-115, 122] W.B.: 136 in. Frt/Rear Tread: 60 in. Tires: 33 x 5.

TECHNICAL: Sliding gear transmission. Speeds: 3F/1R. Floor shift controls. Multiple disc, dry plate clutch. Shaft drive. Full floating rear axle. Overall ratio: 4.58:1. Mechanical brakes on two rear wheels. Twelve spoke wooden artillery wheels, demountable rims. Wheel size: 23 in.

OPTIONS: Front bumper. Rear bumper. Dual sidemount. Sidemount cover(s).

HISTORY: Introduced September 1920. A Lincoln won a Los Angeles to Phoenix race in April 1921. Innovations: circuit breaker electrical system, Alemite pressure gun lubrication, automatic tire pump, thermostatic radiator shutters, sealed cooling system with condenser tank. Calendar year production: 2,957 (1920 and 1921). Model year sales: 674. Model year production: 2,957. The president of Lincoln was Henry Martyn Leland. Considerable discrepancies exist in early production and sales records for the Lincolns. Thus these and subsequent figures should be considered only approximate levels.

1922 LINCOLN

LINCOLN — MODEL L — EIGHT: The postwar depression that overwhelmed William Durant's best efforts to retain control of General Motors and put Henry Ford to a severe test forced the Lincoln Motor Company into receivership in November 1921. Subsequently the firm was purchased by Henry Ford for $8 million on February 4, 1922.

Changes in the Lincoln's design were minor. The acquisition of Lincoln by Ford was made evident by a new radiator badge that had the Lincoln name sandwiched by "Ford Detroit" and placed within an oval shell. The older more ornate, version had carried the words "Leland Built." Design changes included an improved cylinder head for better engine cooling (on cars after serial number 7820) and the use of aluminum in place of the older cast-iron versions. Also phased in after car number 8500 was a new timing chain and sprockets.

In June 1922 both Henry Leland and his son acrimoniously left Lincoln and Edsel Ford became the company's president. Under total Ford control the above noted engineering changes were made as well as a price reduction of $1,000 on all models with non-custom bodies. Aided by the economy's recovery these moves caused a major reversal in Lincoln sales, which after totalling only 150 cars in January and February reached 5,512 for the remaining 10 months of 1922.

I.D. DATA: Serial numbers were located on right side of cowl, top of clutch housing and transmission case. Starting: 3152. Ending: 8709. Engine numbers were located on left side of crankcase between cylinder 1 and 2. Starting: 3152. Ending: 8709.

1922 Lincoln Model L town car. (OCW)

1922 Lincoln Model L touring. (OCW)

1922 Lincoln Model L Brunn seven-passenger touring. (OCW)

1923 Lincoln Model L Brunn Deluxe seven-passenger touring. (OCW)

Model No.	Body Type & Seating	Factory Price	Shipping Weight	Prod. Total
101	4-dr. Tr. (perm top)-7P	3800	—	483
102	2-dr. Rds.-3P	—	—	6
103	4-dr. Phae.-5P	—	—	37
104	2-dr. Cpe.-4P	3900	—	441
105	4-dr. Sed.-5P	4200	—	344
107	4-dr. Twn. Brgm.-7P	—	—	2
109	4-dr. Twn. Car-7P	—	—	12
111	2-dr. Brunn Rds.-3P	3800	—	178
112	4-dr. Brunn Phae. Delx.-4P	3800	—	771
113	4-dr. Sed.-4P	3800	—	353
114	4-dr. Judkins Sed. gls. part.-7P	—	—	22
115	4-dr. Judkins Berl. gls. part.-5P	—	—	29
116	4-dr. FW Sed.-7P	—	—	6
117	4-dr. Brunn Sed.-7P	4900	—	718
118	4-dr. Brunn Limo. gls. part.-7P	—	—	554
119	4-dr. FW Limo. gls. part.-7P	5800	—	20
120	4-dr. Brunn Twn. Car-7P	7200	—	6
121	4-dr. Brunn Limo. gls. part.-7P	5100	—	2
122	Chassis	3400	—	287
124A	4-dr. Tr.-7P	3300	—	1136
125	4-dr. Sed.-4P	5200	—	59
126	2-dr. Brunn Cpe.-2P	4400	—	1
127	4-dr. Judkins Sed.-4P	—	—	104
128	4-dr. Judkins Berline-4P	200	—	74
129	4-dr. Brunn Sed.-5P	4700	—	1
702	2-dr. Judkins. Cpe.-2P	—	—	1

ENGINE: 60 degree V, L-head. Eight. Cast-iron block. B & S: 3-3/8 x 5 in. Disp.: 357.8 cid C.R.: 4.8:1. Brake H.P.: 90 @ 2800 R.P.M. Main bearings: three. Valve lifters: mechanical. Carb.: Stromberg updraft.

CHASSIS: [Series 101-105] W.B.: 130 in. Frt/Rear Tread 60 in. Tires: 33 x 5. [All others] W.B.: 136 in. Frt/Rear Tread: 60 in. Tires: 33 x 5.

TECHNICAL: Sliding gear transmission. Speeds: 3F/1R. Floor shift controls. Multiple disc, dry plate clutch. Shaft drive. Full floating rear axle. Overall ratio: 4.58:1. Mechanical brakes on two rear wheels. Twelve spoke wooden artillery wheels, demountable rims. Wheel size: 23 in.

OPTIONS: Front bumper. Rear bumper. Dual sidemount. Sidemount cover(s).

HISTORY: Introduced January 1922. Calendar year production: 5,512. The president of Lincoln was Edsel Ford—after June 1922.

1923 LINCOLN

LINCOLN — MODEL L — EIGHT: After the Ford takeover, the Lincoln Motor Company became an independent operation whose stock was 100 percent owned by the Ford Motor Company. However, with the Lelands completely out of the picture, it was absorbed into Ford.

Principal changes for 1923 were headlined by the elimination of the 130-inch wheelbase chassis. During the model year a number of changes occurred, including the use of Houdaille hydraulic shock absorbers.

I.D. DATA: Serial numbers were located on the right side of cowl, top of clutch housing and transmission case. Starting: 8710. Ending: 16434. Engine numbers were located on left side of crankcase between cylinders 1 and 2. Starting: 8710. Ending: 16434.

Model No.	Body Type & Seating	Factory Price	Shipping Weight	Prod. Total
111	2-dr. Brunn Rds.-2P	3800	NA	54
112	4-dr. Brunn Del. Phae.-4P	3800	—	15
117	4-dr. Brunn Sed.-7P	4900	—	971
118	4-dr. Brunn Limo.-7P	—	—	563
120	4-dr. Brunn Fwn. Car-6P	—	—	50
121	4-dr. Brunn Limo. gls. part-7P	—	—	18
122	Chassis	—	—	177
123A	4-dr. Brunn Phae.-4P	—	—	1061
124A	4-dr. Tr.-4P	—	—	1182
125	4-dr. Judkins Sed.-4P	—	—	365
126	2-dr. Brunn Cpe.-4P	—	—	816
127	4-dr. Judkins Sed. 3W-4P	—	—	532
128	4-dr. Judkins Ber. gls. part-4P	—	—	238
129	4-dr. Brunn Sed.-5P	—	—	1195
130	2-dr. Brunn Rds.-3P	—	—	48
131	4-dr. Brunn Cab.-6P	—	—	14
132	4-dr. Judkins Sed. 2W-4P	—	—	93
133	4-dr. Judkins Sed. 3W-4P	—	—	269
	4-dr. FW Cab. Coll. Tp.-7P	6200	—	—

ENGINE: 60 degree V, L-head. Eight. Cast-iron block. B & S: 3-3/8 x 5 in. Disp.: 357.8 cid C.R.: 4.8:1. Brake H.P.: 90 @ 2800 R.P.M. Taxable H.P.: 39.2. Main bearings: three. Valve lifters: mechanical. Carb.: Stromberg 03 updraft.

CHASSIS: W.B.: 136 in. Frt/Rear Tread: 60 in. Tires: 33 x 5.

TECHNICAL: Sliding gear transmission. Speeds: 3F/1R. Floor shift controls. Multiple disc, dry plate clutch. Shaft drive. Full floating rear axle. Overall ratio: 4.58:1; opt. 4.90:1. Mechanical brakes on two rear wheels (Lincolns for police use had four-wheel brakes). Twelve spoke wooden artillery wheels with demountable rims. Wheel size: 23 in.

1923 Lincoln Model L touring. (OCW)

1923 Lincoln Model L five-passenger coupe. (HAC)

OPTIONS: Front bumper. Rear bumper. Dual sidemount. Sidemount cover(s). Drum headlights.

HISTORY: Introduced January 1923. Calendar year registrations: 7,875. Calendar year production: 7,875. The company president was Edsel Ford.

1924 LINCOLN

1924 Lincoln Model L Brunn seven-passenger touring. (OCW)

LINCOLN — MODEL L — EIGHT: Although there was no single styling change in the Lincoln's appearance that could even remotely be regarded as revolutionary, the sum total of the revisions made for 1924 resulted in a more modern and decidedly more attractive appearance. All models had as standard equipment the nickel-plated drum-style headlights that had been optional in 1923. A higher radiator with a nickel-plated shell enabled a smoother hoodline to be used. The radiator shutters were now vertical instead of horizontal. The Lincoln's oval grille emblem no longer carried the "Ford Detroit" lettering. On all models except Type 702 (a Judkins-bodied coupe) new fenders with a smoother and wider design were installed.

Although no changes were made in the Lincoln's engine's basic specifications a new cam reshaped for smoother valve operation was installed.

I.D. DATA: Serial numbers were located on right side of cowl, top of clutch housing and transmission case. Starting: 16435. Ending: 23614. Engine numbers were located on left side of crankcase between cylinders 1 and 2. Starting: 16435. Ending: 23614.

Model No.	Body Type & Seating	Factory Price	Shipping Weight	Prod. Total
117	4-dr. Brunn Sed.-7P	—	—	271
118	4-dr. Brunn Limo.-7P	5100	—	128
120	4-dr. Brunn Twn. Car-6P	—	—	12
121	4-dr. Brunn Limo.-7P	—	—	8
122	Chassis	3600	—	79
123A	4-dr. Brunn Phae.-4P	4000	—	829
124A	4-dr. Tr.-7P	4000	—	601
126	2-dr. Brunn Cpe.-4P	4600	—	424
127	4-dr. Judkins Sed. 3W-4P	4800	—	2
128	4-dr. Judkins Ber.-4P	400	—	111
129	4-dr. Brunn Sed.-5P	4900	—	351
130	2 dr. Brunn Rds.-3P	4000	—	188
131	2-dr. Brunn Cab-6P	—	—	13
132	4 dr. Judkins Sed. 2W-4P	—	—	358
133	4-dr. Judkins Sed. 3W-4P	—	—	889
134	4-dr. Judkins Sed.-7P	—	—	846

1924 Lincoln Model L touring. (OCW)

1924 Lincoln Model 130 Brunn roadster. (OCW)

Model No.	Body Type & Seating	Factory Price	Shipping Weight	Prod. Total
135	4-dr. Brunn Limo.-7P	6400	—	482
136	4-dr. Brunn Sed.-5P	—	—	928
137	4-dr. Brunn Cab-5P	—	—	6
138	4-dr. Brunn Twn. Car-5P	6400	—	8
139	4-dr. FW Limo.-7P	6000	—	29
140	4-dr. Judkins Ber.-4P	5400	—	20
140	4-dr. Brunn Open Drive Limo.-5P	6400	—	—

ENGINE: 60 degree V, L-head. Eight. Cast-iron block. B & S: 3-3/8 x 5 in. Disp.: 357.8 cid C.R.: 4.8:1. Brake H.P.: 90 @ 2800 R.P.M. Taxable H.P.: 39.2. Main bearings: three. Valve lifters: mechanical. Carb.: Stromberg 03 updraft.

CHASSIS: W.B.: 136 in. Frt/Rear Tread: 60 in. Tires: 33 x 5.

OPTIONS: Front bumper. Rear bumper. Dual sidemount. Sidemount cover(s). Natural wood finish wheels. Disc wheels. Rudge-Whitworth wire wheels. Painted radiator shell.

1924 Lincoln Model L Fleetwood Inside Drive Limousine. (OCW)

TECHNICAL: Sliding gear transmission. Speeds: 3F/1R. Floor shift controls. Multiple disc, dry plate clutch. Shaft drive. Full floating rear axle. Overall ratio: 4.58:1, opt. 4.90:1. Mechanical brakes on two rear wheels (Lincolns for police use had four-wheel brakes). Twelve spoke wooden artillery wheels, demountable rims. Wheel size: 23 in.

HISTORY: Introduced January 1924. Calendar year registrations: 5,672. Calendar year production: 7,053. The president of Ford was Edsel Ford. The 1924 models were the first Lincolns to have a spark setting mark on the clutch ring and fly wheel.

1925 LINCOLN

1925 Lincoln 7-passenger sedan. (OCW)

Model No.	Body Type & Seating	Factory Price	Shipping Weight	Prod. Total
145A	4-dr. Brunn Brgm. gls. part.-7P	—	—	15
146	4-dr. Dietrich Sed.-5P	—	—	1095
147A	4-dr. Dietrich Sed.-7P	—	—	398
147B	4-dr. Dietrich Berl.-7P	—	—	214
148A	4-dr. Dietrich Brgm.-6P	6800	—	3
149A	4-dr. Dietrich Coll. Cab.	—	—	12
150A	Burial C'ch.	—	—	1
702	2-dr. Judkins Cpe.-2P	5100	—	345
2557	Special	—	—	2
2686	Special Rds.	—	—	11
1230	4-dr. Spt. Phae.-4P	—	—	106
	4-dr. Brunn Twn. C.-5P	6400	—	
	4-dr. Brunn Open-D Limo.	6400	—	
	4-dr. FW Limo.-7P	6000	—	
	4-dr. Judkins Berl. 3W-4P	5400	—	

ENGINE: 60 degree V, L-head. Eight. Cast-iron block. B & S: 3-3/8 x 5 in. Disp.: 357.8 cid C.R.: 4.8:1. Brake H.P.: 90 @ 2800 R.P.M. Taxable H.P.: 39.2. Main bearings: three. Valve lifters: mechanical. Carb.: Stromberg 03 updraft.

CHASSIS: W.B.: 136 in. Frt/Rear Tread: 60 in. Tires: 33 x 5.

TECHNICAL: Sliding gear transmission. Speeds: 3F/1R. Floor shift controls. Multiple disc, dry plate clutch. Shaft drive. Full floating rear axle. Overall ratio: 4.58:1; opt. 4.90:1. Mechanical brakes on two rear wheels (Lincolns for police use had four-wheel brakes). Twelve spoke wooden artillery wheels with demountable rims. Wheel size: 23 in.

1925 Lincoln Model L touring. (OCW)

LINCOLN — MODEL L — EIGHT: The absence of cowl lights made it easy to identify the 1925 Lincoln. Also giving them a distinctive appearance was the Gorham-produced greyhound radiator ornament. Initially this was an option but during the year it was included in the Lincoln's standard equipment. Other changes included a longer and smoother operating emergency brake lever plus factory installed front and rear bumpers for all models. Early in the model year run a steering ratio of 15:1 replaced the older 12-2/3:1 ratio.

I.D. DATA: Serial numbers were located on right side of cowl, top of clutch housing and transmission case. Starting: 23615. Ending: 32029. Engine numbers were located on left side of crankcase between cylinder 1 and 2. Starting: 23615. Ending: 32029.

Model No.	Body Type & Seating	Factory Price	Shipping Weight	Prod. Total
122	Chassis	3800	—	121
123A	4-dr. Brunn Phae.-4P	4000	—	689
123B	4-dr. Brunn Spt. Phae.-4P	—	—	25
123C	4-dr. Brunn Spt. Phae. TC-4P	—	—	1
124A	4-dr. Tr.-7P	4000	—	418
124B	4-dr. Brunn Spt. Tr. TC-7P	4200	—	324
124C	4-dr. Brunn Spt. Tr.-7P	—	—	3
126	2-dr. Brunn Cpe.-4P	4600	—	204
128	4-dr. Judkins Berl.-4P	5600	—	31
130	2-dr. Brunn Rds.-2P	4000	—	126
132	4-dr. Judkins Sed. 2W-4P	—	—	146
133	4-dr. Judkins Sed. 3W-4P	—	—	548
134	4-dr. Brunn Sed.-7P	—	—	829
135	4-dr. Brunn Limo. gls. part.-7P	—	—	443
136	4-dr. Brunn Sed.-5P	—	—	541
137	4-dr. Brunn Cab.-5P	6600	—	58
138	4-dr. Brunn Twn. C.-7P	—	—	18
139	4-dr. FW Limo.-7P	—	—	297
140	4-dr. Judkins Berl. gls. part. 2W-4P	—	—	248
141	2-dr. LeBaron. Cpe. Rds.-2P	—	—	95
142	4-dr. Holbrook Coll. Cab-7P	7200	—	11
143	2-dr. Brunn Cpe.-4P	—	—	470
144A	4-dr. LeBaron. Trk. Sed. 2W-4P	—	—	159
144B	4-dr. LeBaron. Trk. Sed. 3W-4P	—	—	433

1925 Lincoln Model L Brunn four-passenger coupe. (OCW)

1925 Lincoln Model L LeBaron dual cowl sport phaeton. (OCW)

1925 Lincoln Model L Brunn seven-passenger touring. (OCW)

OPTIONS: Dual sidemount. Sidemount cover(s). Natural wood finish wheels. Disc wheels. Rudge-Whitworth wire wheels. Painted radiator shell. 7.00 x 21 balloon tires.

HISTORY: Introduced January 1925. Calendar year registrations: 6,808. Calendar year production: 8,451. The company president was Edsel Ford.

1926 LINCOLN

1926 Lincoln Model 74 7-passenger phaeton. (OCW)

1926 Lincoln Model L Dietrich Club Roadster. (OCW)

LINCOLN — MODEL L — EIGHT: Exterior changes were virtually non-existent in the Lincoln's appearance but a number of interior revisions and engine modifications contributed to the best sales year yet for Lincoln. During the model year a non-movable 19-inch wheel with a smaller cross section and molded to form finger grips on its lower surface replaced the older tilt-type 18-inch unit. The headlight tilting lever was now located below the horn button on the hub and both the wheel and spokes were of black walnut construction.

Beneath the Lincoln hood, a new centrifugal-type carburetor air cleaner was readily noticeable. A new distributor cam that Lincoln said provided more efficient high-speed operation was standard.

I.D. DATA: Serial numbers were located on right side of cowl, top of clutch housing and transmission case. Starting: 32030. Ending: 39899. Engine numbers were located on left side of crankcase between cylinders 1 and 2. Starting: 32030. Ending: 39899.

Model No.	Body Type & Seating	Factory Price	Shipping Weight	Prod. Total
122	Chassis	—	—	154
123A	4-dr. Phae.-4P	4000	—	147
123B	4-dr. Spt. Phae.-4P	4500	—	283
123C	4-dr. Brunn Spt. Phae. TC-4P	—	—	41
124A	4-dr. Tr.-7P	—	—	93
124B	4-dr. Brunn Spt. Tr. TC-7P	4500	—	324
124C	4-dr. Brunn Spt. Tr.-7P	—	—	12
130	2-dr. Brunn Rds.-3P	—	—	99
136	4-dr. Brunn Sed.-5P	6400	—	3
137	4-dr. Brunn Cab-5P	6600	—	52
139	4-dr. FW Limo.-7P	6000	—	60
140	4-dr- Judkins Berl 2W gls. part.-4P	5400	—	273
141	2-dr. LeBaron. Cpe. Rds. Aux. St.-2P	—	—	150
142	4-dr. Holbrook Coll. Cab-7P	7200	—	13
143	2-dr. Brunn Cpe.-4P	—	—	308
144A	4-dr. LeBaron. Trk. Sed. 2W- 4P	4800	—	513
144B	4-dr. LeBaron. Trk. Sed. 3W- 4P	4800	—	1350
145A	4-dr. Brunn Brgm. gls. part.-7P	6400	—	42
145B	4-dr. Brunn Open Limo.	—	—	3
146	4-dr. Dietrich Sed.-5P	6800	—	558
147A	4-dr. Dietrich Sed.-7P	—	—	1590
147B	4-dr. Dietrich Berl.-7P	6800	—	1180
148A	4-dr. Dietrich Brgm.-6P	6800	—	2
149A	4-dr. Dietrich Coll. Cab-5P	7200	—	2
150A	Burial C'ch.	—	—	8
150B	150" wb Chassis	—	—	37
151	2-dr. Locke. Rds.-2P	—	—	101
152	4-dr. Dietrich Sed.-5P	—	—	653
153A	4-dr. Holbrook Coll. Cab-5P	7200	—	10
154	2-dr. Dietrich Clb. Rds.-2P	—	—	263
155	4-dr. LeBaron. Coll. Spt. Cab-5P	—	—	7
157	4-dr. Willoughby Land.-6P	6700	—	10
702	2-dr. Judkins Cpe.-2P	5300	—	371

ENGINE: 60 degree V, L-head. Eight. Cast-iron block. B & S: 3-3/8 x 5 in. Disp.: 357.8 cid C.R.: 4.8:1. Brake H.P.: 90 @ 2800 R.P.M. Taxable H.P.: 39.2. Main bearings: three. Valve lifters: mechanical. Carb.: Stromberg 03 updraft.

CHASSIS: W.B.: 136 in. Frt/ Rear Tread: 60 in. Tires: 33 x 5.

TECHNICAL: Sliding gear transmission. Speeds: 3F/1R. Floor shift controls. Multiple disc, dry plate clutch. Shaft drive. Full floating rear axle. Overall ratio: 4.58:1, opt. 4.90:1. Mechanical brakes on two rear wheels (Lincolns for police use had four-wheel brakes). Twelve spoke wooden artillery wheels, demountable rims. Wheel size: 23 in.

OPTIONS: Dual sidemount. Sidemount cover(s). Natural wood finish wheels. Disc wheels. Buffalo wire wheels. 7.00 x 21 balloon tires. Monogram ($5.00). Tonneau cowl & rear windshield ($400.00).

HISTORY: Introduced January 1926. Calendar year registrations: 7,711. Calendar year production: 8,787. The president of Lincoln was Edsel Ford.

1926 Lincoln Model L seven-passenger sedan. (JAC)

1926 Lincoln Model L Locke sport roadster. (JAC)

1927 LINCOLN

1927 Lincoln Model L three-window sedan. (OCW)

LINCOLN — MODEL L — EIGHT: Identifying the 1927 Lincolns were bullet-shaped headlight shells enclosing new lamps with dual filaments providing high and low beams in place of the older tilting beam arrangement. Also updated were the Lincoln's rear lights that now consisted of a red lens-taillight, amber lens-brake light and a white lens-backup light. Another revision taking place during 1927 was the use of runningboards with black-ribbed rubber rather than a linoleum covering. Although not easily detected, the 1927 Lincolns were one inch lower than previously, due to new 32 x 6.75 tires and a 112-inch reduction in spring camber. A new instrument panel placed all instruments within an oval surface.

After offering front wheel brakes for police use since 1923, Lincoln installed mechanical four-wheel brakes on all its 1927 models. This was described as a "six brake system" in reference to the hand brake control over the rear brakes and the operation of the front and rear brakes by the foot pedal.

The technical changes for 1927 included a new lighter weight clutch system with fewer parts plus a standard equipment "coincidental lock" for the ignition and steering wheel.

I.D. DATA: Serial numbers were located on right side of cowl, top of clutch housing and transmission case. Starting: 39900. Ending: 47499. Engine numbers were located on left side of crankcase between cylinders 1 and 2. Starting: 39900. Ending: 47499.

Model No.	Body Type & Seating	Factory Price	Shipping Weight	Prod. Total
122	Chassis	3500	—	83
123B	4-dr. Brunn Spt. Phae.-4P	4700	—	8
123C	4-dr. Brunn Spt. Phae. TC-4P	—	—	1
124A	4-dr. Tr.-7P	—	—	2
124B	4-dr. Brunn Spt. Tr. TC-7P	—	—	6
143	2-dr. Brunn Cpe.-4P	—	—	46
144A	4-dr. LeBaron. Trk. Sed. 2W-4P	4600	—	400
144B	4-dr. LeBaron. Trk. Sed. 3W-4P	4800	—	926
145A	4-dr. Brunn Brgm.-7P	6800	—	63
146	4-dr. Dietrich Sed.-5P	5100	—	3
147A	4-dr. Dietrich Sed.-7P	5300	—	1193

1927 Lincoln Model L Locke sport roadster. (OCW)

Model No.	Body Type & Seating	Factory Price	Shipping Weight	Prod. Total
147B	4-dr. Dietrich Ber.-7P	—	—	1005
150B	150" wb Chassis	3700	—	22
151	2-dr. Locke Rds.-2P	4600	—	178
152	4-dr. Dietrich Sed.-5P	—	—	917
153A	4-dr. Holbrook Coll. Cab-5P	7200	—	7
154	2-dr. Dietrich Cpe. R/S-2P	—	—	580
155	4-dr. LeBaron. Coll. Spt. Cab-5P	7300	—	7
156	2-dr. LeBaron. Cpe.-4P	—	—	293
157	4-dr. Willoughby Ber.-6P	—	—	12
158	4-dr. Judkins Ber.-5P	—	—	100
159	4-dr. Brunn Cab-5P	—	—	54
160	4-dr. Willoughby Limo.-7P	6000	—	164
161	4-dr. Judkins Ber.-5P	—	—	352
162A	4-dr. LeBaron. Cab 2W-5P	—	—	—
162B	4-dr. LeBaron. Lan. 3W-5P	—	—	Note 1
162C	4-dr. LeBaron. Brgm. 3W-5P	—	—	Note 1
	4-dr. Brunn Cab-7P	—	—	—
	4-dr. Brunn Brgm.-7P	—	—	—
	4-dr. Judkins Ber. 2W-4P	5500	—	—
	4-dr. Holbrook Cab-7P	7400	—	—
	4-dr. LeBaron Cab-7P	7600	—	—
	4-dr. Willoughby Ber. Land.-6P	6500	—	—
163A	4-dr. Locke. Spt. Phae.-4P	—	—	167
163B	4-dr. Locke. Dbl. Cowl Spt. Phae.-4P	—	—	90
164A	4-dr. Locke. Spt. Tr.-7P	—	—	173
702	2-dr. Judkins Cpe.-2P	5300	—	205
	Custom Cars	—	—	72

NOTE 1: Total combined production for the LeBaron Landaulette and LeBaron Brougham was 20.

ENGINE: 60 degree V, L-head. Eight. Cast-iron block. B & S: 3-3/8 x 5 in. Disp.: 357.8 cid C.R.: 4.8:1. Brake H.P.: 90 @ 2800 R.P.M. Taxable H.P.: 39.2. Main bearings: three. Valve lifters: mechanical. Carb.: Stromberg 03 updraft.

CHASSIS: W.B.: 136 in. Frt/Rear Tread: 60 in. Tires: 32 x 6.75.

1927 Lincoln Model L Locke dual cowl phaeton. (HAC)

1927 Lincoln Model L roadster. (OCW)

TECHNICAL: Sliding gear transmission. Speeds: 3F/1R. Floor shift controls. Multiple disc, dry plate clutch. Shaft drive. Full floating rear axle. Overall ratio: 4.58:1, opt. 4.90:1. Mechanical internal expanding brakes on four wheels. Twelve spoke wooden artillery wheels, demountable rims. Wheel size: 20 in.

OPTIONS: Dual sidemount. Sidemount cover(s). Natural wood finish wheels. Steel disc wheels. Buffalo wire wheels. Monogram. Tonneau cowl and rear windshield.

HISTORY: Introduced January 1927. Innovations: four wheel mechanical brakes, dual filament headlights. Calendar year registrations: 6,460. Calendar year production: 7,149. The president of Lincoln was Edsel Ford.

1928 LINCOLN

1928 Lincoln Model L Locke sport phaeton. (OCW)

LINCOLN — MODEL L — EIGHT: Lincoln did not endorse the concept of model years, explaining, "There are no yearly or periodic Lincoln models; the Lincoln has reached such a state of development that drastic changes are neither necessary or desirable. Whenever it is possible to achieve an improvement in the Lincoln it is made interchangeable with previous design." This philosophy was illustrated by the use of new mufflers during 1928 that dealers were able to retrofit to earlier Lincolns.

Of greater importance was the use of a larger engine that began late in 1927 and was carried over into 1928. By virtue of a 1/8 inch bore increase the Lincoln V-8 now displaced 384.8 cubic inches. Other changes occurring at this time included a slight boost in compression ratio to 4.81:1, larger 1-7/8 inch rather than 1-3/4 inch intake valves, a reshaped combustion chamber and the use of counterweights on the crankshaft. Also debuting in 1928 was an engine oil filter and conical valve springs. Other technical changes included new steering tube bearings and lighterweight rear axle.

Appearance revisions consisted of cowl lights shaped in the form of Lincoln's front and rear lamps, chrome-plated bumpers and five-stud, steel spoke wheels.

I.D. DATA: Serial numbers were located on right side of cowl, top of clutch housing and transmission case. Starting: 47500. Ending: 54500. Numbers were located on left side of crankcase between cylinders 1 and 2. Starting: 47500. Ending: 54500.

1928 Lincoln Model L Locke Sport roadster. (OCW)

Model No.	Body Type & Seating	Factory Price	Shipping Weight	Prod. Total
122	Chassis	—	—	105
144A	4-dr. LeBaron. Trk. Sed. 2W-4P	4800	—	263
144B	4-dr. LeBaron. Trk. Sed. 3W-4P	4800	—	529
145A	4-dr. Brunn Brgm.-7P	6400	—	3
147A	4-dr. Dietrich Sed.-7P	5000	—	1023
147B	4-dr. Dietrich Ber.-7P	5200	—	709
150A	150" wb Chassis	—	—	24
151	2-dr. Locke. Rds.-2P	4600	—	65
152	4-dr. Dietrich Sed.-5P	4800	—	835
153A	4-dr. Holbrook Coll. Cab.-5P	7200	—	8
154	2-dr. Dietrich Cpe. R/S-2P	4600	—	54
155	4-dr. LeBaron. Coll. Spt. Cab.-5P	7300	—	9
156	2-dr. LeBaron. Cpe.-4P	4600	—	230
157	4-dr. Willoughby Ber.-6P	6500	—	6
159	4-dr. Brunn Cab.-5P	6600	—	12
160	4-dr. Willoughby Limo.-7P	6000	—	483
161	4-dr. Judkins Ber.-5P	5500	—	348
162A	4-dr. LeBaron. Cab. 2W-5P	7350	—	Note 1
162B	4-dr. LeBaron. Lan. 3W-5P	7350	—	Note 1
162C	4-dr. LeBaron. Brgm. 3W-5P	—	—	Note 1
163A	4-dr. Locke. Spt. Phae.-4P	4600	—	226
163B	4-dr. Locke. Dbl. Cwl. Spt. Phae.-4P	—	—	150
164A	4-dr. Lke. Sport Tr.-7P	4600	—	323
165	2-dr. Clb. Rds. R/S-2P	—	—	347
166	4-dr. Brunn Brgm.-7P	—	—	86
167	4-dr. Dietrich Conv. Sed.-5P	—	—	38
168A	4-dr. Sed.-7P	—	—	1
168B	4-dr. Limo.-7P	—	—	1
169A	4-dr. Twn. 2W Sed.-5P	—	—	88
169B	4-dr. Twn. 3W Sed.-5P	—	—	140
170	2-dr. Judkins Cpe.-2P	—	—	14
171	4-dr. Dietrich Conv. Cpe.-4P	6500	—	6
172	4-dr. Judkins Ber.-5P	—	—	1
702	2-dr. Judkins Cpe.-2P	5000	—	110
	Custom	—	—	59

NOTE 1: Total combined production of the LeBaron Cabriolet, LeBaron Landaulette, and LeBaron Brougham was 66.

ENGINE: 60 degree V, L-head. Eight. Cast-iron block. B & S: 3-1/2 x 5 in. Disp.: 384.8. C.R.: 4.81:1. Brake H.P.: 90 @ 2800 R.P.M. Taxable H.P.: 39.2. Main bearings: three. Valve lifters: mechanical. Carb.: Stromberg 03 updraft.

CHASSIS: W.B.: 136 in. Frt/Rear Tread: 60 in. Tires: 32 x 6.75. Opt. 20 x 7.00.

TECHNICAL: Sliding gear transmission. Speeds: 3F/1R. Floor shift controls. Multiple disc, dry plate clutch. Shaft drive. Full floating rear axle. Overall ratio: 4.58:1, opt. 4.90:1. Mechanical internal expanding brakes on four wheels. Steel spoke wheels. Wheel size: 20 in.

OPTIONS: Dual sidemount. Sidemount cover(s). Wooden artillery wheels. Steel disc wheels (all-welded "safety wheels"). Buffalo wire wheels. Monogram. Tonneau cowl and windshield.

1928 Lincoln Model L club roadster. (HAC)

HISTORY: Introduced January 1928. Innovations: standard oil filter, counterbalanced crankshaft. Calendar year registrations: 6,039. Calendar year production: 6,362. The president of Lincoln was Edsel Ford.

1929 LINCOLN

1929 Lincoln phaeton. (OCW)

LINCOLN — MODEL L — EIGHT: The 1929 Lincoln's appearance was highlighted by a higher, narrower and somewhat squarer radiator shell topped by a larger filler cap. In addition, the old leather windshield visor was replaced by a dark glass version. Many models had laminated safety glass and all 1928 Lincolns had twin windshield wipers.

Interior changes consisted of a new engine temperature gauge (which corresponded with the repositioning of the cigar lighter to the dashboard from its previous instrument panel location) and an electric rather than spring-wound clock.

Technical changes were not extensive, consisting of the use of rubber engine mounts, increased (from 30 to 50 pounds) oil pressure and a stronger starter-generator.

I.D. DATA: Serial numbers were located on right side of cowl, top of clutch housing and transmission case. Starting: 54501. Ending: 61699. Engine numbers were located on left side of crankcase between cylinders 1 and 2. Starting: 54501. Ending: 61699.

Model No.	Body Type & Seating	Factory Price	Shipping Weight	Prod. Total
122	Chassis	3300	—	75
150B	150" wb Chassis	3500	—	43
151	2-dr. Locke Rds.-2P	4650	—	7
153A	4-dr. Holbrook Coll. Cab.-5P	6800	—	2
155	4-dr. LeBaron Coll, Spt. Cab.-5P	7400	—	3

1929 Lincoln Model L LeBaron Arrow phaeton. (OCW)

Model No.	Body Type & Seating	Factory Price	Shipping Weight	Prod. Total
156	2-dr. LeBaron Cpe.-4P	5300	—	138
157	4-dr. Willoughby Ber.-6P	5		
160	4-dr. Willoughby Limo.-7P	6200	—	155
162A	4-dr. LeBaron Cab. 2W-5P	7400	—	Note 1
162B	4-dr. LeBaron Lan. 3W-5P	—	—	Note 1
162C	4-dr. LeBaron Brgm. 3W-5P	—	—	Note 1
163A	4-dr. Locke Spt. Phae.-4P	4650	—	88
163B	4-dr. Locke Dbl. Cwl. Spt. Phae.-4P	—	—	58
164A	4-dr. Locke Spt. Tr.-7P	—	—	88
164B		—	—	18
165	2-dr. Clb. Rds. R/S-2P	4900	—	225
166	4-dr. Brunn Brgm.-7P	7400	—	78
167	4-dr. Dietrich Conv. Sed.-7P	6900	—	60
168A	4-dr. Sed.-7P	5100	—	1380
168B	4-dr. Limo.-7P	5300	—	837
169A	4-dr. Twn. 2W Sed.-5P	4900	—	658
169B	4-dr. Twn. 3W Sed.-5P	—	—	1513
170	2-dr. Judkins Cpe.-2P	5200	—	270
171	4-dr. Dietrich Conv. Cpe.-4P	6000	—	69
172	4-dr. Judkins Ber.-5P	5800	—	360
173A	4-dr. Sed. 2W-5P	4900	—	22
173B	4-dr. Sed. 3W-5P	4900	—	436
174	4-dr. Willoughby Limo.-7P	6200	—	228
175	4-dr. Brunn Brgm.-5P	7200	—	50
176A	4-dr. Spt. Phae.-4P	4650	—	92
176B	4-dr. Spt. Phae. Dbl. Cwl.-4P	5050	—	42
177	4-dr. Spt. Tr.-7P	4650	—	174
178	4-dr. LeBaron Spt. Sed.-5P	—	—	42
179	2-dr. Cpe.-4P	4800	—	209
180	4-dr. Brunn Brgm. 2W-7P	7200	—	24
181	2-dr. Dietrich Conv. Cpe.-4P	6500	—	8
182	4-dr. Dietrich Conv. Sed.-5P	6900	—	10
183	4-dr. Sed.-5P	5000	—	27
184	4-dr. LeBaron Brgm.-5P	—	—	2

NOTE 1: Total combined production of the LeBaron Cabriolet, LeBaron Landaulette, and LeBaron Brougham was 74.

1929 Lincoln Model L roadster. (AA)

1929 Lincoln Model L town sedan. (JAC)

1929 Lincoln Model L convertible coupe. (OCW)

1930 Lincoln Model L roadster. (DW)

1929 Lincoln Model L phaeton. (JAC)

ENGINE: 60 degree V, L-head. Eight. Cast-iron block. B & S: 3-1/2 x 5 in. Disp.: 384.8 cid C.R.: 4.81:1. Brake H.P.: 90 @ 2800 R.P.M. Taxable H.P.: 39.2. Main bearings: three. Valve lifters: mechanical. Carb.: Stromberg 03 updraft.

CHASSIS: [Model L] W.B.: 136 in. Frt/Rear Tread: 60 in. Tires: 32 x 6.75. Opt. 20 x 7.00.

TECHNICAL: Sliding gear transmission. Speeds: 3F/1R. Floor shift controls. Multiple disc, dry plate clutch. Shaft drive. Full floating rear axle. Overall ratio: 4.58:1, opt. 4.90:1. Mechanical external expanding brakes on four wheels. Steel spoke wheels. Wheel size: 20 in.

OPTIONS: Dual sidemount. Sidemount cover(s). Wooden artillery wheels. Steel disc wheels. Buffalo wire wheels. Monogram. Tonneau cowl and windshield.

HISTORY: Introduced January 1, 1929. Calendar year sales: 6,399 (6,151 registrations). Calendar year production: 7,672. Model year production: 7,641. The president of Lincoln was Edsel Ford.

1930 LINCOLN

1930 Lincoln Model L coupe. (OCW)

1930 Lincoln Model L seven-passenger sedan. (JAC)

LINCOLN — MODEL L — EIGHT: With the L series Lincoln scheduled for replacement in 1931 only minor changes were to be found in the Lincoln's format for 1930. The Brunn seven-passenger brougham, Willoughby six-passenger landaulet and the seven-passenger cabriolets by Brunn and Holbrook were no longer available. An open, convertible model took the place of the club roadster. Lincoln made a concession to modern tastes by offering fenders painted to match body colors for the first time. More precise control was now provided by the adoption of worm and roller type steering.

I.D. DATA: Serial numbers were located on right side of cowl, top of clutch housing and transmission case. Starting: 61700. Ending: 66000. Engine numbers were located on left side of crankcase between cylinders 1 and 2. Starting: 61700. Ending: 66000.

Model No.	Body Type & Seating	Factory Price	Shipping Weight	Prod. Total
122	Chassis	—	—	30
165	2-dr. Clb. Rds. R/S-2P	—	—	12
172	4 dr. Judkins Ber.-5P	5600	—	72
174	4-dr. Willoughby Limo.-7P	—	—	244
175	4-dr. Brunn Brgm.-5P	—	—	44
176A	4-dr. Spt. Phae.-4P	—	—	53
176B	4-dr. Spt. Phae. Dbl. Cwl.-4P	—	—	90
177	4-dr. Spt. Tr.-7P	—	—	79
178	4-dr. LeBaron Spt. Sed.-5P	5300	—	8
179	2-dr. Cpe.-4P	—	—	275
180	4-dr. Brunn Brgm. 2W-7P	—	—	68
181	2-dr. Dietrich Conv. Cpe.-4P	—	—	42
182	4-dr. Dietrich Conv. Sed.-5P	—	—	40
183	4 dr. Sed.-5P	—	—	541
184	4 dr. LeBaron Brgm.-5P	—	—	49
185	2 dr. LeBaron Conv. Rds.-2P	6900	—	100
186	4-dr. Judkins Ber.-5P	5600	—	100
187	4-dr. Willoughby Panel Brgm.-4P	7000	—	5
188	2-dr. Derham Conv. Rds.-2P	—	—	1
189	4-dr. Derham Conv. Phae.-5P	6000	—	21
190	2-dr. Judkins Cpe.-2P	5000	—	25
191	2-dr. Locke Spt. Rds.-2P	4500	—	15

1930 Lincoln Model L LeBaron convertible roadster. (JAC)

1930 Lincoln Model L Brunn five-passenger brougham. (OCW)

ENGINE: 60 degree V, L-head. Eight. Cast-iron block. B & S: 3-1/2 x 5 in. Disp.: 384.8 cid C.R.: 4.81:1. Brake H.P.: 90 @ 2800 R.P.M. Taxable H.P. 39.2. Main bearings: three. Valve lifters: mechanical. Carb.: Stromberg 03 updraft.

CHASSIS: W.B.: 136 in. Frt/Rear Tread: 60 in. Tires: 32 x 6.75; opt. 20 x 7.00.

TECHNICAL: Sliding gear transmission. Speeds: 3F/1R. Floor shift controls. Multiple disc clutch. Shaft drive. Full floating rear axle. Overall ratio: 4.58:1, opt. 4.90:1. Mechanical external expanding brakes on four wheels. Steel spoke wheels. Wheel size: 20 in.

OPTIONS: Dual sidemount. Sidemount cover(s). Wooden artillery wheels. Steel disc wheels. Buffalo wire wheels. Monogram. Tonneau cowl and windshield.

HISTORY: Introduced January 1930. Calendar year registrations: 4,356. Calendar year production: 3,515. Model year production: 3,212. The president of Lincoln was Edsel Ford.

1930 Lincoln Model L Judkins two-window berline. (JAC)

1930 Lincoln phaeton. (OCW)

1931 LINCOLN

1931 Lincoln Model K Judkins two-passenger coupe. (JAC)

LINCOLN — SERIES 201 — MODEL K — EIGHT: The Model K represented a dramatic shift away from the confines of the Model L design, although that car's great engine in updated form was continued.

The use of a new 145-inch wheelbase frame with six crossmembers and cruciform braces plus 7.00 x 19 tires gave the new Lincoln a low, sleek profile. Accentuating this look were numerous other styling changes. A new peaked radiator shape, a longer hood plus higher windows were key contributors. Only slightly less dramatic were the new bowl-shaped headlight shells and imposing dual trumpet horns with town and country settings. The graceful flow of the Lincoln fenders plus the rounded form of the front and rear bumpers were further examples of a well-coordinated design.

Both freewheeling and synchromesh on second and third gears were introduced on the 1931 models. In addition, a new double dry disc clutch was installed. Lincoln retained both a floating rear axle and torque tube drive with slight revisions. The old steel rod and Perrot braking system was replaced by a cable-operated Bendix Duo-Servo system. Also introduced in 1931 were double-acting Houdaille hydraulic shock absorbers at all four wheels.

In addition to a new Stromberg carburetor and more efficient manifolding, the Lincoln V-8 was now fitted with five main bearings plus separate generator and starter units. A mechanical fuel pump replaced the obsolete vacuum system.

I.D. DATA: Serial numbers were located on the right side of cowl, top of clutch housing and transmission case. Starting: 66001. Ending: 70000. Engine numbers were located on left side of crankcase between cylinders 1 and 2. Starting: 66001. Ending: 70000.

Model No.	Body Type & Seating	Factory Price	Shipping Weight	Prod. Total
201	Chassis	—	—	61
202-A	4-dr. Dbl. Cwl. Spt. Phae.-5P	4600	5245	77
202-B	4-dr. Spt. Phae.-5P	4400	5175	60
203	4-dr. Spt. Tr.-7P	4400	5250	45
204-A	4-dr. Twn. Sed. 2W-5P	4600	5205	211
204-B	4-dr. Twn. Sed. 3W-5P	4600	5205	447
205	4-dr. Sed.-5P	4700	5440	552
206	2-dr. Cpe.-5P	4600	5235	225
207-A	4-dr. Sed.-7P	4900	5420	521
207-B	4-dr. Limo.-7P	5100	5370	387
207-C	4-dr. Limo.-7P	5100	5370	14
208-A	4-dr. All. W. Non-Clp. Brunn Cab-5P	7400	5340	30
208-B	4-dr. All W. Semi-Clp. Brunn Cab-5P	7400	5440	—
209	4-dr. All. W. Brgm. Brunn-5P	7200	5370	34
210	4-dr. Dietrich Conv. Cpe.-4P	6400	5220	25
211	4-dr. Dietrich Sed.-5P	6800	5250	65
212	4-dr. Derham Phae.-4P	6200	5040	11
213-A	4-dr. Judkins Ber. 2W-4P	5800	5420	—
213-B	4-dr. Judkins Ber. 3W-4P	5800	5460	171
214	2-dr. LeBaron Conv. Cpe.-2/4P	4700	5070	275
215	4-dr. Willoughby Limo.-6P	6100	5370	151
216	4-dr. Willoughby Panel Brgm.-7P	7400	5400	15
217-A	4-dr. All W. Non-Up LeBaron Cab-7P	7100	5320	Note 1
217-B	4-dr. All W. Semi-Clp. LeBaron Cab-7P	7300	5420	Note 1
218	2-dr. Judkins Cpe.-2P	5200	5180	86
219	2-dr. Dietrich Cpe.-2P	—	—	35
220	150" wb Chassis	—	—	3
221	155" wb Chassis	—	—	3
	Special	—	—	26
	RHD	—	—	21

1931 Lincoln touring. (OCW)

1931 Lincoln Model K town sedan. (JAC)

1931 Lincoln Model K Murphy dual cowl phaeton. (OCW)

NOTE 1: Total combined production of the All Weather Non-Up LeBaron Cabriolet and All Weather Semi-Clp. LeBaron Cabriolet was 21.

ENGINE: 60 degree V, L-head. Eight. Cast-iron block. B & S: 3-1/2 x 5 in. Disp.: 384.8 cid C.R.: 4.95:1. Brake H.P.: 120 @ 2900 R.P.M. N.A.C.C. H.P.: 43. Main bearings: five. Valve lifters: mechanical. Carb.: Stromberg DD3 downdraft two-barrel.

CHASSIS: W.B.: 145 in. Frt/ Rear Tread: 60 in. Tires: 19 x 7.00.

TECHNICAL: Sliding gear transmission. Speeds: 3F/1R. Floor shift controls. Double dry disc clutch. Shaft drive. Full floating rear axle. Overall ratio: 4.58:1; 4.90:1, 4.23:1 (standard). Bendix Duo Servo mechanical brakes on four wheels. Steel spoke wheels. Wheel size: 19 in.

OPTIONS: Dual sidemount.

HISTORY: Introduced January 1931. Innovations: First American use of a two-barrel downdraft carburetor. Freewheeling was introduced on the 1931 Lincolns. Calendar year registrations: 3,466. Calendar year production: 3,592. Model year production: 3,540. The president of Lincoln was Edsel Ford.

1932 LINCOLN

LINCOLN — SERIES 501 — MODEL KA — EIGHT: Lincoln significantly altered its marketing stance in 1932. The KA series models were priced lower than previous K models and were offered in seven standard body styles. On a 136-inch wheelbase chassis the KA Lincoln featured a sharply pointed front grille, one-piece front and rear bumpers and thermostatically-operated hood shutters.

1932 Lincoln Model KB Brunn all-weather cabriolet. (OCW)

1932 Lincoln Model KB Murphy dual cowl sport phaeton. (OCW)

LINCOLN — SERIES 231 — MODEL KB — TWELVE: The KB shared the modern appearance of the medium-priced KA but since it represented a new peak of Lincoln excellence the KB had many distinctive features. Its cloisonne emblem was blue (that of the KA was red), its radiator shell was noticeably thinner and of course its wheelbase was 145 inches. As was the case with the 1931 Model K, the KA was available in 9 standard and 14 factory custom bodies. Of even greater interest was the KA's new V-12 engine. The terms "massive" and "rugged" have often been applied to this engine with good reason. Displacement was 447.9 cubic inches, installed weight exceeded a 1-1/2 ton and the valves measured two inches in diameter. The forged-steel crankshaft was carried in seven main bearings.

I.D. DATA: Serial numbers were located on the right side of cowl, top of clutch housing and transmission case. Starting: KA-70001; [KB] KB-1. Ending: KA-72041; [KB] KB-1666. Engine numbers were located on left side of crankcase between cylinders 1 and 2. Starting: KA-70001, [KB] KB-1. Ending: KA-72041; [KB] KB-1666.

1932 Lincoln Model KB Dietrich sport berline. (OCW)

1932 Lincoln Model KB V-12 Dietrich coupe. (OCW)

1932 Lincoln Model KB Brunn Double Entry (Doublentree) sport sedan. (OCW)

1932 Lincoln Model KB Willoughby seven-passenger limousine. (OCW)

Model No.	Body Type & Seating	Factory Price	Shipping Weight	Prod. Total
Series 501 KA				
501	Chassis	—	—	7
502	2-dr. Cpe.-2P	3200	5220	—
502	2-dr. Cpe.-2/4P	3245	5090	86
503		—	—	40
504	4-dr. Twn. Sed.-4P	3100	5450	147
505	4-dr. Sed.-5P	3200	5430	921
506	2-dr. Vict.-5P	3200	5345	265
507-A	4-dr. Sed.-7P	3300	5435	508
507-B	4-dr. Limo.-7P	3350	5520	122
508	4-dr. Phae.-4P	3000	5145	29
510	2-dr. Rds.-2P	2900	4925	—
	RHD	—	—	5

1932 Lincoln Model KB LeBaron convertible roadster. (OCW)

1932 Lincoln Model KA Murray five-passenger sedan. (OCW)

1932 Lincoln Model KA Murray town sedan. (OCW)

Model No.	Body Type & Seating	Factory Price	Shipping Weight	Prod. Total
Series 231 KB				
231	Chassis	—	—	18
232-A	4-dr. Murphy Double Cwl. Spt. Phae.-4P	4500	5625	30
232-B	4-dr. Murphy. Spt. Phae.-4P	4300	5600	13
233	4-dr. Spt. Tr.-7P	4300	5720	24
234-A	4-dr. Twn. Sed. 2W-5P	4500	5740	123
234-B	4-dr. Twn. Sed. 3W-5P	4500	5740	200
235	4-dr. Sed.-5P	4600	5750	216
236	2-dr. Cpe.-5P	4400	5750	83
237-A	4-dr. Sed.-7P	4700	5855	266
237-B	4-dr. Limo.-7P	4900	5885	41
237-C	4 dr. Limo.-7P	4900	5885	135
238	4-dr. Brunn all w. Cab.-5P	7200	5585	14
239	4-dr. Brunn all w. Brgm.-7P	7000	5920	13
240	4-dr. Dietrich Spt. Ber.-5P	6500	5605	8
241	4-dr. Dietrich Conv. Sed.-5P	6400	5720	20
242-A	2 dr. Dietrich Cpe.-2/4P	5150	5710	—
242-B	2 dr. Dietrich Cpe. 2P	5000	5710	17
243-A	4-dr. Judkins Ber. 2W-5P	5700	5860	—
243-B	4-dr. Judkins Ber. 3W-5P	5700	5860	74
244-A	2-dr. Judkins Cpe.-2/4P	5350	5610	—
245	4-dr. Willoughby Limo.-7P	5900	5950	64
246	4 dr. Willoughby Pan. Brgm.-4P	7100	5855	4
247	4-dr. Waterhouse Conv. Vict.-5P	5900	5470	10
248	2-dr. Conv. Rds.-2/4P	4600	5535	112
249	2-dr. Murphy Spt. Rds.	6800	5605	3
250	150" wb Chassis	—	—	1
	Specials	—	—	3
	RHD	—	—	10

ENGINE [Series KA]: 60 degree V, L-head. Eight. Cast-iron block. B & S: 3-1/2 x 5 in. Disp.: 384.8 cid C.R.: 5.23:1. Brake H.P.: 125 @ 2900 R.P.M. Main bearings: five. Valve lifters: mechanical. Carb.: Stromberg DD3 downdraft two-barrel.

ENGINE [Series KB]: 60 degree V, L-head. Twelve. Cast-iron block. B & S: 3-1/4 x 4-1/2 in. Disp.: 447.9 cid C.R.: 5.25:1. Brake H.P.: 150 @ 3400 R.P.M. Taxable H.P.: 50.7. Main bearings: seven. Valve lifters: mechanical. Carb.: Stromberg DD downdraft two-barrel. Torque: 292 lbs.-ft. @ 1200 R.P.M.

CHASSIS: [Series KA] W.B.: 136 in. Frt/Rear Tread: 60 in. Tires: 18 x 7.00. [Series KB] W.B.: 145 in. O.L.: 214 in. Frt/Rear Tread: 60 in. Tires: 18 x 7.50.

1932 Lincoln Model KA Dietrich four-passenger sport phaeton. (OCW)

1932 Lincoln Model KA Murray five-passenger victoria. (OCW)

1932 Lincoln Model KA V-8 touring. (OCW)

TECHNICAL: Sliding gear transmission. Speeds: 3F/1R. Floor shift controls. Double dry disc clutch. Shaft drive. Full floating rear axle. Overall ratio: 4.58:1; 4.90:1; 4.23:1 (standard). Bendix Duo-Servo mechanical brakes on four wheels. Steel spoke wheels. Wheel size: 18 in.

OPTIONS: Dual sidemount.

HISTORY: Calendar year registrations: 3,179. Calendar year production: 3,388. Model year production: Series 501 (KA)-2132, Series 231 (KB)-1515. The company president of Lincoln was Edsel Ford.

1932 Lincoln Model KA coupe. (AA)

1932 Lincoln Model KA V-8 Opera coupe. (OCW)

1933 Lincoln 7-passenger limousine. (OCW)

LINCOLN — SERIES 511 — MODEL KA — TWELVE: Lincoln concluded the era of the classic V-8 engine with its fork and blade connecting rods by introducing a new 67 degree V-12 for the KA series. Its displacement was 381.7 cubic inches. Aluminum pistons were installed and the crankshaft was carried in four bearings. The detachable cylinder heads were constructed of cast-iron. This engine, while based upon the KB V-12, was simpler and less expensive to produce.

A total of 12 models were available in KA form and their styling was once again substantially revised. Lincoln adopted hood louvers rather than shutters for both KA and KB models and an elegant chrome mesh grille sloped backward for a more streamlined profile. Early models continued to use the older clamshell type fenders but midway through the model year valanced-type versions were adopted and Lincoln agreed to retro-fit them to the early 1933 models at no cost to owners.

LINCOLN — SERIES 251 — MODEL KB — TWELVE: The KB had the same basic styling of the KA but its considerably larger size and available custom bodywork left no chance of being mistaken for a KA. A new double-drop frame was introduced for 1933.

1933 Lincoln Model KB coupe. (HAC)

1933 Lincoln Model KB five-passenger town sedan. (OCW)

1933 Lincoln Model KB Brunn convertible victoria. (AA)

I.D. DATA: Serial numbers were located on right side of cowl, top of clutch housing and transmission case. Starting: [KA] KA1 [KB] KB2001. Ending: [KA] KA1 140; [KB] KB2604. Engine numbers were located on left side of crankcase between cylinders 1 and 2. Starting: [KA] KA1, [KB] KB2001. Ending: [KA] KA1140, [KB] KB2604.

Model No.	Body Type & Seating	Factory Price	Shipping Weight	Prod. Total
Series 511 KA				
511	Chassis	—	—	7
512-A	2-dr. Cpe.-2/4P	3145	5210	Note 1
512-B	2-dr. Cpe.-2P	3100	5190	Note 1
513-A	2-dr. Conv. Rds.-2/4P	3200	5050	85
514	4-dr. Twn. Sed.-5P	3100	5235	201
515	4-dr. Sed.-5P	3200	5270	320
516	2-dr. Vict.-5P	3200	5200	109
517-A	4-dr. Sed.-7P	3300	5440	190
517-B	4-dr. Limo.-7P	3350	5465	111
518-A	4-dr. Dbl. Cwl. Phae.-5P	3200	5040	12
518-B	4-dr. Phae.-5P	3000	5030	12
519	4-dr. Phae.-7P	3200	5040	10
520 A	2-dr. Rds.-2/4P	2745	5030	Note 2
520-B	2-dr. Rds.-2P	2700	5020	Note 2
	Specials	—	—	1
	RHD	—	—	4
Series 251 KB				
251	Chassis	—	—	4
252-A	2-dr. Dbl. Cwl. Spt. Phae.-4P	4400	5500	9
252-B	4-dr. Spt. Phae.-4P	4200	5410	6
253	4-dr. Spt. Tr.-7P	4300	5500	6
254-A	4-dr. Twn. Sed. 2W-5P	4400	5590	39
254 B	4-dr. Twn. Sed. 3W-5P	4400 5590		41
255	4-dr. Sed.-5P	4500	5790	52
256	4-dr. Vict. Cpe.-5P	4300	5710	18
257-A	4-dr. Sed.-7P	4600	5820	110
257-B	4-dr. Limo.-7P	4800	5840	105
258-C	4-dr. Brunn Non. Clp. Cab.-7P	6900	5685	—
258-D	4-dr. Brunn Smi. Clp. Cab.-5P	6900	5685	8
14	4-dr. Brunn Brgm.-7P	6900	5730	13
260	2-dr. Brunn Conv. Cpe.-5P	5700	5470	—
260	2-dr. Dietrich Spt. Ber.-5P	—	—	15
261	4-dr. Dietrich Conv. Sed.-5P	6100	5600	15
263-A	4-dr. Judkins Ber. 2W-4P	5500	5710	Note 3
263-A	4-dr. Judkins Ber. 3W-4P	5500	5710	Note 3
264-D	2-dr. Judkins Cpe.-2P	5000	5720	12
265-B	4-dr. Willoughby Limo.-7P	5700	5840	40
266-B	4-dr. Willoughby Panel Brgm.	7000	5840	2
267-B	2-dr. LeBaron Conv. Rds.-2/4P	4500	5490	37
2197	2-dr. Dietrich Cpe.-2P	4900	—	8
1308	4-dr. Judkins Sed. Limo.-7P	5800	—	—
	155" wb Chassis	—	—	1
	Specials	—	—	16
	RHD	—	—	3

NOTE 1: Total combined production of the Series 511 KA two-door coupes was 44.

NOTE 2: Total combined production of the Series 511 KA two-door roadsters was 12.

NOTE 3: Total combined production of the Series 251 KB four-door Judkins Berline (2W and 3W) was 36.

ENGINE [KA]: 67 degree V, L-head. Twelve. Cast-iron block. B & S: 3 x 4-1/2 in. Disp.: 381.7. Brake H.P.: 125 @ 3400 R.P.M. N.A.C.C. H.P.: 43.2. Main bearings: four. Valve lifters: mechanical. Carb.: Stromberg EE22 downdraft, two-barrel.

1933 Lincoln Model KB Judkins sedan limousine. (OCW)

1933 Lincoln Model KB five-passenger sedan. (OCW)

ENGINE [KB]: 65 degree V, L-head. Twelve. Cast-iron block. B & S: 3-1/4 x 4-1/2 in. Disp.: 447.9. C.R.: 5.25:1. Brake H.P.: 150 @ 3400 R.P.M. N.A.C.C. H.P.: 50.7. Main bearings: seven. Valve lifters: mechanical. Carb.: Stromberg DD downdraft two-barrel. Torque: 292 lbs.-ft. @ 1200 R.P.M.

CHASSIS: [Series KA] W.B.: 136 in. Frt/Rear Tread: 60 in. Tires: 18 x 7.00. [Series KB] W.B.: 145 in. O.L.: 214 in. Frt/Rear Tread: 60 in. Tires: 18 x 7.50.

TECHNICAL: Sliding gear transmission. Speeds: 3F/1R. Floor shift controls. Double dry disc clutch. Shaft drive. Full floating rear axle. Overall ratio: 4.58:1, 4.90:1, 4.23:1 (standard). Bendix Duo-Servo mechanical brakes on four wheels. Steel spoke wheels. Wheel size: 18 in. Drivetrain options: Freewheeling standard on KB, optional on KA.

OPTIONS: Dual sidemounts.

HISTORY: Calendar year production: 2,007. Model year production: 1,647 (1,114-KA, 533-KB). The president of Lincoln was Edsel Ford.

1934 LINCOLN

LINCOLN — SERIES 521 — MODEL KA — TWELVE: In effect there was only a single Lincoln series for 1934. However the use of KA and KB prefixes for serial numbers as well as the use of different series numbers for the 136-inch and 145-inch wheelbase chassis warrants their separation into KA and KB series.

Lincoln styling was little changed for 1934. Radiator shells in both series were now painted body color instead of being chrome plated and all models had hood shutters rather than louvers. Smaller headlights further enhanced the Lincoln's refined front end appearance.

LINCOLN — SERIES 271 — MODEL KB — TWELVE: The Senior Lincoln shared a draftless ventilation system with the KA models. In addition, all 1934 Lincolns were fitted with asymmetric headlights that had an additional passing feature in which only the left headlight would be lowered. Powering these 145-inch wheelbase Lincolns was a larger version of the KA V-12. Among its features were aluminum cylinder heads providing a 6.28:1 compression ratio and an engine oil cooler.

1934 Lincoln Model KB Willoughby sport sedan. (OCW)

I.D. DATA: Serial numbers were located on right side of cowl, top of clutch housing and transmission case. Starting: 136-inch wheelbase KA1501, 145-inch wheelbase KB3001. Ending: 136-inch wheelbase KA3176, 146-inch wheelbase KB3744. Engine numbers were located on left side of crankcase between cylinders 1 and 2. Starting: 136-inch wheelbase KA1501, 145-inch wheelbase KB3001. Ending: 136-inch wheelbase KA3176, 145-inch wheelbase KB3744.

Model No.	Body Type & Seating	Factory Price	Shipping Weight	Prod. Total
Series 521 (136" wb)				
521	Chassis —	—	21	
522-A	2-dr. Cpe.-2/4P	3250	4959	Note 1
522-B	2-dr. Cpe.-2P	3200	4929	Note 1
523	2-dr. Conv. Rds.-2/4P	3400	3934	75
524	4-dr. Twn. Sed.-5P	3450	5044	450
525	4-dr. Sed.-5P	3400	5044	425
526	2-dr. Vict.-5P	3400	5029	115
527-A	4-dr. Sed.-7P	3500	5203	275
527-B	4-dr. Limo.-7P	3550	5228	175
531	4-dr. Conv. Sed. Phae.	3900	5029	75
	RHD	—	—	8
Series 271 (145" wb)				
271	Chassis	—	—	12
272-A		—	—	2
272-B		—	—	—
273	4-dr. Tr.-7P	4200	5125	20
277-A	4-dr. Sed.-7P	4500	5510	210
277-B	4-dr. Limo.-7P	4700	5570	215
278-A	4-dr. Brunn Semi-Clp. Cab.-5P	6800	5335	—
278-B	4-dr. Brunn Non Clp Cab-5P	6800	5315	13
279	4-dr. Brunn Brgm.-7P	6800	5480	15
280	2 dr. Brunn Conv. Cpe-5P	5600	5045	Note 2
280 ?	2 dr. Dietrich Conv. Rd.	—	—	Note 2
281	4-dr. Dietrich Conv. Sed.-5P	5600	5330	25
282	4-dr. Judkins Sed. Limo.-7P	5700	5605	Note 3
282 ?	2-dr. Dietrich Cpe.-2P	—	—	Note 3
283-A	-dr. Judkins Ber. 2W-4P	5400	5495	37
283-B	4-dr. Judkins Ber. 3W-4P	5400	5520	17
285	4-dr. Willoughby Limo.-7P	5600	5605	77
287	2-dr. LeBaron Conv. Rds.-2/4P	4400	5085	45
	Special	—	—	7
	RHD	—	—	5

NOTE 1: The total combined production of the Series 521 two-door coupes was 60.

NOTE 2: The total combined production of the Series 271 Brunn convertible coupe and Dietrich convertible roadster was 25.

NOTE 3: The total combined production of the Series 271 Judkins sedan limousine and Dietrich coupe was 27.

1934 Lincoln Model KB LeBaron roadster. (JAC)

1934 Lincoln Model KB touring. (JAC)

1934 Lincoln Model KB Judkins two-window berline. (JAC)

ENGINE: 67 degree V, L-head. Twelve. Cast-iron block. B & S: 3-1/8 x 4-1/2 in. Disp.: 414 cid C.R.: 6.38:1. Brake H.P.: 150 @ 3800 R.P.M. Taxable H.P.: 46.8. Main bearings: four. Valve lifters: mechanical. Carb.: Stromberg EE22 downdraft two-barrel.

CHASSIS: [Series 521] W.B.: 136 in. Frt/Rear Tread: 60 in. Tires: 18 x 7.00. [Series 271] W.B.: 145 in. O.L.: 214 in. Height: 72 in. Frt/Rear Tread: 60 in. Tires: 18 x 7.50.

TECHNICAL: Sliding gear transmission. Speeds: 3F/1R. Floor shift controls. Double dry disc clutch. Shaft drive. Full floating rear axle. Overall ratio: 4.58:1, 4.90:1, 4.23:1 (standard). Bendix Duo-Servo mechanical brakes on four wheels. Steel spoke wheels. Wheel size: 18 in.

OPTIONS: Dual sidemounts.

HISTORY: Calendar year registrations: 3,024. Model year production: 2,411 (1,671—136-inch wheelbase, 740—145-inch wheelbase). The president of Lincoln was Edsel Ford.

1935 LINCOLN

LINCOLN — SERIES 301 — MODEL K — TWELVE: The long wheelbase Lincolns were available in three factory body styles for 1935. Other configurations were offered as in earlier years by Brunn, LeBaron, Judkins and Willoughby. Whereas the new bodies were moved forward 4-1/2 inches on the 136-inch wheelbase models, those for the 145-inch wheelbase version were moved a full nine inches to the front. In either case Lincoln claimed the result was an improved ride and a lower center of gravity.

Technical changes, while less dramatic than the Lincoln's new appearance, were still noteworthy. A new cam provided a smoother level of operation and along with a new exhaust system contributed to improved performance and a lower overall noise level.

Transmission changes included the use of helical cut gears for second and third plus the use of needle roller bearings in the clutch. A fully automatic spark control was also a first-time feature for the Lincoln.

1935 Lincoln Model K LeBaron convertible coupe. (AA)

1935 Lincoln Model K LeBaron convertible sedan. (JAC)

LINCOLN — SERIES 541 — MODEL K — TWELVE: Lincoln limited the use of the 136-inch wheelbase chassis in 1935 to its two-door factory custom and five-passenger standard bodies. The exceptions to this policy was the availability of the LeBaron coupe, sedan, phaeton and convertible roadster plus a Brunn convertible victoria with this wheelbase.

Regardless of their wheelbase all Lincolns had new styling dominated by a more rounded, softer appearance. A sloping rear deck, similar to that of the 1934 Willoughby Sport Sedan was adopted, as was a honeycomb mesh radiator grille. With the radiator cap now placed under the hood, the Lincoln's greyhound hood ornament was permanently mounted. Other changes enabling the 1935 Lincolns to be quickly perceived as new models were their one-piece bumpers with twin vertical bars, horizontal hood ventilators extending nearly to the windshield and smaller headlights that were further elongated to add another element of fleetness. Their shells were now body-color painted.

Interior changes were highlighted by a new dash with two large dials containing the instruments and a placement was provided for a radio. The glovebox was also enlarged.

I.D. DATA: Serial numbers were located on right side of cowl, top of clutch housing and transmission case. Starting: K 3501. Ending: K 4919. Engine numbers were located on left side of crankcase between cylinders 1 and 2. Starting: K 3501. Ending: K 4919.

1935 Lincoln Judkins limousine. (OCW)

1935 Lincoln convertible coupe. (OCW)

1935 Lincoln LeBaron two-passenger coupe. (OCW)

1935 Lincoln Willoughby sport sedan. (OCW)

1935 Lincoln five-passenger sedan. (OCW)

1935 Lincoln Judkins sedan limousine. (OCW)

1935 Lincoln Brunn seven-passenger Brougham. (OCW)

1935 Lincoln five-passenger sedan. (OCW)

Model No.	Body Type & Seating	Factory Price	Shipping Weight	Prod. Total
Series 541 (136" wb)				
541	Chassis	—	—	1
542	2-dr. LeBaron Conv. Rds.-2/4P	4600	5335	30
543	4-dr. Sed. 2W-5P	4300	5690	170
544	4-dr. Sed. 3W-5P	4300	5680	278
545	2-dr. Cpe.-5P	4200	5535	44
546	2-dr. LeBaron Conv. Sed. Phae.-5P	5000	5665	20
547	2-dr. Brunn Conv. Vict.-5P	5500	5440	15
548	2-dr. LeBaron Cpe.-2P	4600	5335	23
	RHD	—	—	5
Series 301 (145" wb)				
301	Chassis	—	—	8
302	4-dr. Tr.-7P	4200	5155	15
303-A	4-dr. Sed.-7P	4600	5840	351
303-B	4-dr. Limo.-7P	4700	5935	282
304-A	4-dr. Brunn Semi-Clp. Cab-5P	—	—	13
304-B	4-dr. Brunn Non-Clp. Cab-5P	—	—	13
305	4-dr. Brunn Brgm.-7P	—	—	10
307	4-dr. LeBaron Conv. Sed.-5P	5500	5965	20
308	4-dr. Judkins Limo.-7P	—	—	18
309-A	4-dr. Judkins Ber. 2W-5P	—	—	34
309-B	4-dr. Judkins Ber. 3W-5P	—	—	13
310	4-dr. Willoughby Limo.-7P	—	—	40
311	4-dr. Willoughby Spt. Sed.-5P	—	—	5
8	Specials	—	—	8
	RHD	—	—	18

ENGINE: 67 degree V, L-head. Twelve. Cast-iron block. B & S: 3-1/8 x 4-1/2 in. Disp.: 414 cid C.R.: 6.38:1. Brake H.P.: 150 @ 3800 R.P.M. Taxable H.P.: 46.8. Main bearings: four. Valve lifters: mechanical. Carb.: Stromberg EE22 downdraft two-barrel.

1935 Lincoln Brunn semi-collapsible cabriolet. (OCW)

1935 Lincoln Brunn convertible victoria. (OCW)

CHASSIS: [Series 541] W.B.: 136 in. Frt/Rear Tread: 60 in. Tires: 17 x 7.50. [Series 301] W.B.: 145 in. O.L.: 214. Frt/Rear Tread: 60 in. Tires: 17 x 7.50.

TECHNICAL: Sliding gear transmission. Speeds: 3F/1R. Floor shift controls. Double dry disc clutch. Shaft drive. Full floating rear axle. Overall ratio: 4.58:1, 4.90:1, 4.23:1 (standard). Bendix Duo-Servo mechanical brakes on four wheels. Steel spoke wheels. Wheel size: 17 in.

OPTIONS: Dual sidemounts. Radio. Heater. Clock.

HISTORY: Model year production: 1,411 (Series 541-581, Series 301-830). The president of Lincoln was Edsel Ford.

1936 LINCOLN

LINCOLN-ZEPHYR — TWELVE: The Lincoln-Zephyr was both one of the most handsome American cars of the Thirties and one of the most revolutionary. The word teardrop was applicable to its overall form, taillights, fender skirts and grille emblem. The sloping rear deck, curved side window corners, simple grille form with horizontal bars in combination with headlights fully molded into the front fenders were successfully coordinated in an appearance that gave life to the expression "streamlined."

The dramatic exterior appearance of the Zephyr was mirrored by its interior motif. Twin circular dials containing the oil temperature, fuel, battery gauges and the speedometer was reminiscent of earlier Lincolns. In the dash center was a circular ashtray and directly beneath two large dials were the controls for the instrument panel light, throttle, choke and cigarette lighter. The dual windshield wipers were operated by a button just above the ashtray. The starter button was to the driver's left while the steering wheel hub contained the switch controlling the exterior lights. A steering wheel/ignition lock was installed on the steering column.

The Zephyr's pleated upholstery was available in taupe broadcloth or tan bedford cord. Leather was offered as an option.

The engineering design format of the Zephyr was headed by its integral body frame construction and all steel roof, the first offered by Ford Motor Company. Suspension was by transverse springs with solid front and rear axles.

To power the Lincoln-Zephyr a V-12 was developed from the Ford V-8 design. In essence the Zephyr engine was a 75 degree version of the Ford V-8 with four additional cylinders. Twin water pumps were used as was a single downdraft carburetor. Other key features included alloy steel pistons, aluminum cylinder heads and a one-piece block casting.

1936 Lincoln Zephyr four-door sedan. (OCW)

1936 Lincoln five-passenger (three-window) sedan. (OCW)

1936 Lincoln convertible sedan. (OCW)

1936 Lincoln 7-passenger touring. (OCW)

I.D. DATA: Serial numbers were located on right side of cowl, top of clutch housing and transmission case. Starting: H1. Ending: H15528. Engine on left side of crankcase between cylinder 1 and 2. Starting: H1. Ending: H15528.

Model No.	Body Type & Seating	Factory Price	Shipping Weight	Prod. Total
902	4-dr. Sed.-6P	1320	3349	12,272
902	4-dr. Sed. RHD-6P	—	—	908
903	2-dr. Sed.-6P	1275	3289	1814

ENGINE: 75 degree V, L-head. Twelve. Cast-iron block. B & S: 2-3/4 x 3-3/4 in. Disp.: 267.3 cid C.R.: 6.7:1. Brake H.P.: 110 @ 3900 R.P.M. Taxable H.P.: 36.3. Main bearings: four. Valve lifters: mechanical. Carb.: Stromberg downdraft two-barrel. Torque: 186 lbs.-ft. @ 2000 R.P.M.

CHASSIS: W.B.: 122 in. O.L.: 202.5 in. Height: 69 in. Frt/Rear Tread: 55.5/58.25 in. Tires: 16 x 7.00.

TECHNICAL: Sliding gear transmission. Speeds: 3F/1R. Floor shift controls. Single dry plate, centrifugal clutch. Shaft drive. 3/4 floating rear axle. Overall ratio: 4.44:1. Mechanical brakes on four wheels. Pressed steel, drop-center rims wheels. Wheel size: 23 in. Drivetrain options: Columbia two-speed rear axle.

OPTIONS: Clock. Leather upholstery. Fitted luggage.

HISTORY: Introduced November 1935. Innovations: aerodynamic design, low priced V-12 motoring, float indicator for oil level. Model year production; 14,994. The president of Lincoln was Edsel Ford.

1936 Lincoln seven-passenger touring. (OCW)

1936 Lincoln Model K LeBaron coupe. (AA)

1936 Lincoln Judkins five-passenger berline. (OCW)

1936 Lincoln Willoughby seven-passenger limousine. (OCW)

LINCOLN — SERIES 300 — MODEL K — TWELVE: All Lincolns, regardless of wheelbase carried the K label and a 300 series model number. Changes in the year old body shell consisted of a more sharply (27 degrees instead of 20 degrees) rearward sloping windshield, a grille with more prominent horizontal bars and fenders with smoother and more rounded edges. Substantially changing the Lincoln's front end appearance was the lowering of the headlights. Standard pressed steel wheels with larger hubcaps replaced the older wire version. A new interior feature was the under dash placement of the handbrake.

1936 Lincoln Brunn semi-collapsible cabriolet. (OCW)

1936 Lincoln LeBaron convertible sedan-phaeton. (OCW)

1936 Lincoln LeBaron convertible sedan. (OCW)

1936 Lincoln Brunn seven-passenger Brougham. (OCW)

Mechnical changes included the use of dual windshield wiper motors, a five rather than four engine mount system and an all-helical gear transmission.

I.D. DATA: Serial numbers were located on right side of cowl, top of clutch housing and transmission case. Starting: K 5501. Ending: K 7014. Engine numbers were located on left side of crankcase between cylinders 1 and 2. Starting: Same as serial number. Ending: Same as serial number.

Model No.	Body Type & Seating	Factory Price	Shipping Weight	Prod. Total
321	145" wheelbase Chassis	—	—	9
322	136" wheelbase Chassis	—	—	6
323	4-dr. Tr.-7P	4200	5276	8
324-A	4-dr. Sed. 2W-5P	4300	5426	103
324-B	4-dr. Sed. 3W-5P	4300	5476	297
326	2-dr. Cpe.-5P	4200	5266	36
327-A	4-dr. Sed.-7P	4600	5591	368
327-B	4-dr. Limo.-7P	4700	5641	370
328	2-dr. Brunn Conv. Vict.-5P	5500	5176	10
329-A	4-dr. Brunn Non Clp. Cab.-5P	—	—	10
329-B	4-dr. Brunn SC Cab.-5P	—	—	10
330	2-dr. LeBaron Conv. Rds.-2/4P	4700	5136	20
331	4-dr. Brunn Brgm.-7P	—	—	20
332	2-dr. LeBaron Cpe.-2/4P	4700	5126	25
333	4-dr. LeBaron Conv. Sed. Phae.-5P	5000	5296	30
334	4-dr. LeBaron Conv. Sed.-5P	5500	5381	15
335	4-dr. Judkins Sed. Limo.-7P	—	—	26
337-A	4-dr. Judkins Ber. 2W-5P	—	—	51
337-B	4-dr. Judkins Ber. 3W-5P	—	—	13
339	4-dr. Willoughby Limo.-7P	—	—	62
341	4-dr. Willoughby Spt. Sed.-5P	—	—	11
	RHD (136" wb)	—	—	4
	RHD (145" wb)	—	—	15
	Specials	—	—	15

1936 Lincoln Brunn convertible victoria. (OCW)

1936 Lincoln five-passenger (two-window) sedan. (OCW)

ENGINE: 67 degree V, L-head. Twelve. Cast-iron block. B & S: 3-1/8 x 4-1/2 in. Disp. 414 cid C.R.: 6.38:1. Brake H.P.: 150 @ 3800 R.P.M. Taxable H.P.: 46.8: Main bearings: four. Valve lifters: mechanical. Carb.: Stromberg EE22 downdraft two-barrel.

CHASSIS: W.B.: 136/145 in. Frt/Rear Tread: 60 in. Tires: 17 x 7.50.

TECHNICAL: Sliding gear transmission. Speeds: 3F/1R. Floor shift control. Double dry disc clutch. Shaft drive. Full floating rear axle. Overall ratio: 4.58:1, 4.90:1, 4.23:1 (standard). Bendix Duo-Servo mechanical brakes on four wheels. Pressed steel disc wheels. Wheel size: 17 in.

OPTIONS: Dual sidemounts. Radio. Heater. Clock.

HISTORY: Model year production: 1,515. The president of Lincoln was Edsel Ford.

1937 LINCOLN

1937 Lincoln Zephyr sedan. (OCW)

LINCOLN-ZEPHYR — TWELVE: The positive public reaction to the original Lincoln-Zephyr was underscored by a doubling of its popularity in 1937. As expected of a new car beginning its second year the Zephyr wasn't radically changed for 1937. However a new instrument panel with twin glove compartments bracketing a center console carrying the controls and instruments was featured. The speedometer was placed within a large circular dial with a smaller unit positioned directly below containing the clock. On either side were vertical dials with the fuel and oil level gauges placed in the unit to the left. The right side unit enclosed the temperature and battery gauges.

Easier access to the trunk was provided by a revised spare tire bracket that now folded outward when the trunk lid was opened.

Styling changes, while limited in scope, made it easy to identify a 1937 Lincoln-Zephyr. The grille now carried five pairs of vertical bars and a new side molding swept upward from the grille bar prior to extending along the upper belt line in its way to the rear deck. In addition, the front bumper was slightly less veed than previously and a more ornate set of hood vents were used that matched the grille texture.

1937 Lincoln Judkins two-window berline. (OCW)

1937 Lincoln seven-passenger sedan. (OCW)

I.D. DATA: Serial numbers were located on right side of cowl, top of clutch housing and transmission case. Starting: H15529. Ending: H45529. Engine numbers were located on left side of crankcase between cylinders 1 and 2. Starting: H15529. Ending: H45529.

Model No.	Body Type & Seating	Factory Price	Shipping Weight	Prod. Total
700	2-dr. Cpe. Sed.-6P	1245	3329	1500
720	2-dr. Cpe.-6P	1165	3214	5199
730	4-dr. Sed.-6P	1265	3369	23,159
737	4-dr. Twn. Limo.-6P	1425	3398	139

ENGINE: 75 degree V, L-head. Twelve. Cast-iron block. B & S: 2-3/4 x 3-3/4 in. Disp.: 267.3 cid C.R.: 6.7:1. Brake H.P.: 110 @ 3900 R.P.M. N.A.C.C. H.P.: 36.3. Main bearings: four. Valve lifters: mechanical. Carb.: Stromberg downdraft two-barrel. Torque 186 lbs.-ft. @ 2000 R.P.M.

CHASSIS: W.B.: 122 in. O.L.: 202.5 in. Height: 69 in. Frt/Rear Tread: 55.5/58.25 in. Tires: 16 x 7.00.

TECHNICAL: Sliding gear transmission. Speeds: 3F/1R. Floor shift controls. Single dry plate, centrifugal clutch. Shaft drive. 3/4 floating rear axle. Overall ratio: 4.44:1. Mechanical brakes on four wheels. Pressed steel wheels, drop center rims. Wheel size: 16 in. Drivetrain options: Columbia two-speed rear axle.

OPTIONS: Radio. Heater. Leather upholstery. Fitted luggage.

HISTORY: Calendar year production: 29,293. Model year production: 29,997. The company president was Edsel Ford.

LINCOLN — MODEL K — TWELVE: Lincoln continued to place a priority on custom body styles with a total of 17 versions available, along with four standard body types in 1937. For the first time the Lincoln V-12 was fitted with hydraulic valve lifters. Other technical changes for 1937 included a positioning of the V-12 further forward on the chassis as well as the use of altered engine mounts.

New styling that blended the headlights into the front fender form and gave the Lincolns even more of a rounded, smooth appearance represented the last major changes that would be made in the design of the K Lincoln.

1937 Lincoln Model K Brunn convertible sedan. (JAC)

1937 Lincoln LeBaron convertible sedan. (OCW)

1937 Lincoln LeBaron convertible. (OCW)

1937 Lincoln Willoughby seven-passenger limousine, PH

I.D. DATA: Serial numbers were located on right side of cowl, top of clutch housing and transmission case. Starting: K7501. Ending: K8490. Engine numbers were located on left side of crankcase between cylinders 1 and 2. Starting: K7501. Ending: K8490.

Model No.	Body Type & Seating	Factory Price	Shipping Weight	Prod. Total
353	4-dr. Willoughby Tr.-7P	5550	—	7
354-A	4-dr. Sed. 2W-5P	4450	5492	48
354-B	4-dr. Sed. 3W-5P	4450	5522	136
356	2-dr. Willoughby Cpe.-5P	5550	—	6
357-A	4-dr. Sed.-7P	4750	5697	212
357 B	4-dr. Limo.-7P	4850	5647	248
358	2-dr. Brunn Conv. Vict.-5P	5550	5346	13
359-A	4-dr. Brunn Non-Clp. Cab-5P	6650	—	10
359-B	4-dr. Brunn Semi-Clp. Cab	6750	5646	7
360	2-dr. LeBaron Conv. Rds.-2/4P	4950	—	15
361	4-dr. Brunn Brgm.-7P	6750	5681	29
362	2-dr. LeBaron Cpe.-2P	4950	5172	24
363-A	4-dr. LeBaron Conv. Sed part.-5P	5650	—	12
363-B	4-dr. LeBaron Conv. Sed.-5P	5450	5547	37
365	4-dr. Judkins Sed. Limo.-7P	5950	5732	27
367-A	4-dr. Judkins Ber. 2W-5P	5650	5622	47
367-B	4-dr. Judkins Ber. 3W-5P	5750	5682	19
369	4-dr. Willoughby Limo.-7P	5850	5801	60
371	4-dr. Willoughby Spt. Sed.-5P	6850	—	6
373	4-dr. Willoughby Pnl. Brgm.-5P	7050	—	4
375	4-dr. Brunn Tr. Cab-5P	6950	—	10

ENGINE: 67 degree V, L-head. Twelve. Cast-iron block. B & S: 3-1/8 x 4-1/2 in. Disp.: 414 cid C.R.: 6.38:1. Brake H.P.: 150 @ 3800 R.P.M. Taxable H.P.: 46.8. Main bearings: four. Valve lifters: hydraulic. Carb.: Stromberg EE22 downdraft two-barrel.

1937 Lincoln Brunn seven-passenger Brougham. (OCW)

CHASSIS: W.B.: 136 in./145 in. Frt/Rear Tread: 60 in. Tires: 17 x 7.50.

TECHNICAL: Sliding gear transmission. Speeds: 3F/1R. Floor shift controls. Double dry disc clutch. Shaft drive. Full floating rear axle. Overall ratio: 4.58:1, 4.90:1, 4.23:1 (standard). Bendix Duo-Servo mechanical brakes on four wheels. Pressed steel disc wheels. Wheel size: 17 in.

OPTIONS: Dual sidemounts. Radio. Heater. Clock. Cigar lighter.

HISTORY: Model year production: 977. The president of Lincoln was Edsel Ford.

1938 LINCOLN

1938 Lincoln-Zephyr convertible sedan. (AA)

1938 Lincoln-Zephyr convertible coupe. (OCW)

LINCOLN-ZEPHYR — TWELVE: The Lincoln-Zephyr received a major styling revision utilizing new front sheet metal and rear fenders as well as a longer, 125-inch wheelbase. The grille now was divided and consisted of thin, horizontal chrome bars. This design set the theme for the rest of the Lincoln Zephyr's exterior body trim. The narrow belt line molding enhanced the low profile of the Zephyr, which was further accentuated by the four-side hood bars. Furthering the integration of the Zephyr's various body trim components into an extremely coherent styling format was the unobtrusive hood ornament that flowed downward to accentuate the two-piece grille design. At the rear the fenders were like those up front, larger and more elongated than previously. The teardrop-shaped headlights were incorporated into the smooth form of the fenders.

Following up on the construction of three prototype convertible sedans were two production open models, a convertible coupe and convertible sedan.

Interior revisions were numerous. The metal surrounds for the seats used in 1936 and 1937 were removed, a larger banjo-type, 18-inch steering wheel was installed and a new biscuit upholstery pattern was introduced. Closed model seats were available in striped tan broadcloth or tan bedford cloth as well as tan leather. The convertible models were upholstered in tan leather and whipcord. Lincoln once again rearranged the Zephyr's dash gauges for gas, oil, temperature and battery functions. Pointing the way to the column-mounted shift lever, which Lincoln would introduce in 1940, was a convoluted shift handle that protruded from the center console.

1938 Lincoln-Zephyr four-door sedan. (OCW)

I.D. DATA: Serial numbers were located on right side of cowl, top of clutch housing and transmission case. Starting: H45530. Ending: H64640. Engine numbers were located on left side of crankcase between cylinders 1 and 2. Starting: H45530. Ending: H64640.

Model No.	Body Type & Seating	Factory Price	Shipping Weight	Prod. Total
700	2-dr. Cpe. Sed.-6P	1355	3409	800
720	2-dr. Cpe.-6P	1295	3294	2600
730	4-dr. Sed.-6P	1375	3444	14,520
737	4-dr. Twn. Limo.-6P	1550	3474	130
740	4-dr. Conv. Sed.-6P	1790	3724	461
760-B	2-dr. Conv. Cpe.-6P	1650	3489	600

ENGINE: 75 degree V, L-head. Twelve. Cast-iron block. B & S: 2-3/4 x 3-3/4 in. Disp.: 267.3 cid Overall ratio: 6.7:1. Brake H.P.: 110 @ 3900 R.P.M. Taxable H.P.: 36.3. Main bearings: four. Valve lifters: hydraulic. Carb.: Chandler Gloves AA1 downdraft two-barrel. Torque: 186 lbs.-ft. @ 2000 R.P.M.

CHASSIS: W.B.: 125 in. O.L.: 210 in. Height: 63-1/4 in. Frt/Rear Tread 55-1/2/58-1/4. Tires: 16 x 7.00.

TECHNICAL: Sliding gear transmission. Speeds: 3F/1R. Floor located controls. Single dry plate clutch. Shaft drive. 3/4-floating rear axle. Overall ratio: 4.44:1. Mechanical brakes on four wheels. Pressed steel wheels, drop center rim. Wheel size: 16 in. Drivetrain options: Columbia two-speed rear axle.

OPTIONS: Bumper guards. Radio. Heater. Leather upholstery. Wind wings. Whitewall tires. Fitted luggage.

HISTORY: Calendar year production: 19,751. Model year production: 19,111. The president of Lincoln was Edsel Ford. A Zephyr sedan was second among 26 entrants in the 1938 Gilmore Economy run with a 23.47 mpg.

LINCOLN — MODEL K — TWELVE: The 1938 K Lincoln's grille was given a new look via the use of 18 rather than 30 horizontal bars as used previously. Due to the elimination of thermostatically controlled hood shutters, the side engine louvers were also revised. Built-in trunks were found on all standard sedan models and both the side belt line molding and exterior door handles were of stainless steel construction.

Minor changes to the Lincoln's upholstery plus rheostat dash-panel lighting highlighted the Lincoln's interior.

Technical changes consisted of improved synchromesh and brakes with a greater resistance to fading.

I.D. DATA: Serial numbers were located on right side of cowl, top of clutch housing and transmission case. Starting: K9001. Ending: K9450. Engine numbers were located on left side of crankcase between cylinders 1 and 2. Starting K9001. Ending: K9450.

1938 Lincoln Model K. (OCW)

1938 Lincoln Model K Willoughby 7-passenger touring. (RLC)

1938 Lincoln Brunn convertible victoria. (OCW)

Model No.	Body Type & Seating	Factory Price	Shipping Weight	Prod. Total
403	4-dr. Willoughby Tr.-7P	5900	—	5
404-A	4-dr. Sed.-2W-5P	4900	5527	9
404-B	4-dr. Sed.- 3W-5P	4900	5532	49
406	2-dr. Willoughby Cpe.-5P	5900	5407	4
407-A	4-dr. Sed.-7P	5100	5672	78
407-B	4-dr. Limo.-7P	5200	5762	91
408	4-dr. Brunn Conv. Vict.-5P	5900	5322	8
409-A	4-dr. Brunn Sm. Clp. Cab.-5P	7000	5716	6
409-B	4-dr. Brunn Non. Clp. Cab.-5P	6900	5696	5
410	2-dr. LeBaron Conv. Rds.-2/4P	5300	—	8
411	4-dr Brunn Brgm.-5P	7000	5806	13
412	2-dr. LeBaron Cpe.-2P	5300	5227	12
413-A	4-dr. LeBaron Conv. Sed.-5P	5800	5462	15

ENGINE: 67 degree V, L-head. Twelve. Cast-iron block. B & S: 2-1/8 x 4-1/2 in. Disp.: 414 cid C.R. 6.38:1. Brake H.P.: 150 @ 3800 R.P.M. Taxable H.P.: 46.8. Main bearings: four. Valve lifters: hydraulic. Carb.: Stromberg EE1 downdraft two-barrel.

CHASSIS: W.B.: 136/145 in. O.L.: 213 in. Frt/Rear Tread: 60 in. Tires: 17 x 7.50.

TECHNICAL: Sliding gear transmission. Speeds: 3F/1R. Floor shift controls. Double dry disc clutch. Shaft drive. Full floating rear axle. Overall ratio: 4.58:1. Bendix Duo-Servo mechanical brakes on four wheels. Pressed steel disc wheels. Wheel size: 17 in.

OPTIONS: Dual sidemounts. Sidemount cover(s). Radio. Heater. Clock. Cigar lighter.

HISTORY: Model year production: 416. The president of Lincoln was Edsel Ford.

1939 LINCOLN

LINCOLN-ZEPHYR — TWELVE: The use of hydraulic brakes highlighted the Lincoln-Zephyr's technical changes for 1939. The other change of any consequence was the use of a voltage-regulator rather than a generator cut out. This feature was also found on Zephyrs produced towards the end of the 1938 model run.

Among styling changes found on the 1939 Lincoln-Zephyr was a larger grille shape with vertical bars, two rather than four side hood bars and a more vertical front prow. The lower body panels now enclosed the runningboards. Both the front and rear bumpers were reshaped. The front unit had a two-part center section while at the rear the bumper was less pointed than previously.

1939 Lincoln-Zephyr convertible coupe. (AA)

The Zephyr's dash continued to feature symmetrically positioned dual gloveboxes and ashtrays plus the centrally located speedometer. For 1939 this circular panel also contained the gauges for battery oil, fuel and engine temperature. A battery condition gauge replaced the ammeter.

Once again a new upholstery scheme was used with vertical pleats and the optional leather option was offered in tan, red, gray and brown. In addition a new custom interior option (standard on the town limousine) was offered.

I.D. DATA: Serial numbers were located on right side of cowl, top of clutch housing and transmission case. Starting: H64641. Ending: H85640. Engine numbers were located on left side of crankcase between cylinders 1 and 2. Starting: H64641. Ending: H85640.

Model No.	Body Type & Seating	Factory Price	Shipping Weight	Prod. Total
H-70	2-dr. Cpe. Sed.-6P	1330	3600	800
H-72	2-dr. Cpe.-6P	1320	3520	2500
H-73	4-dr. Sed.-6P	1360	3620	16,663
	4-dr. Tun.-Limo.-6P	1700	3670	95
H-74	4-dr. Conv. Sed.-6P	1790	3900	302
H-76	2-dr. Conv. Cpe.-6P	1700	3790	640

ENGINE: 75 degree V, L-head. Twelve. Cast-iron block. B & S: 2 3/4 x 3-3/4 in. Disp.: 267.3 cid C.R.: 6.7:1. Brake H.P.: 110 @ 3900 R.P.M. Taxable H.P.: 36.3. Main bearings: four. Valve lifters: hydraulic. Carb.: Stromberg downdraft two-barrel. Torque: 186 lbs.-ft. @ 2000 R.P.M.

CHASSIS: W.B.: 125 in. O.L.: 210 in. Height: 69-1/2 in. Frt/Rear Tread: 55-1/2/58-1/4 in. Tires: 16 x 7.00.

TECHNICAL: Sliding gear transmission. Speeds: 3F/1R. Floor shift controls. Single dry disc plate clutch. Shaft drive. 3/4 floating rear axle. Overall ratio: 4.44:1. Bendix hydraulic internal expanding brakes on four wheels. Pressed steel, dropped center wheels. Wheel size: 16 in. Drivetrain options: Columbia two-speed rear axle.

OPTIONS: Bumper guards. Radio. Heater. Leather upholstery. Wind wings. Whitewall tires. Fitted luggage. Custom interior.

HISTORY: Calendar year production: 22,578. Model year production: 21,000. The president of Lincoln was Edsel Ford.

LINCOLN — MODEL K — TWELVE: Changes in the Lincoln K were limited to the use of a different model Stromberg carburetor and wider steel wheel rims with steel spokes added to the back side for greater strength.

Specific production figures for the last of the K Lincoln are unavailable. If any were built in 1940 they were unchanged from the 1939 version.

1939 Lincoln Zehpyr convertible coupe. (OCW)

1939 Lincoln Model K Willoughby limousine. (OCW)

I.D. DATA: Serial numbers were located on right side of cowl, top of clutch housing and transmission case. Starting: K9451. Ending: K9674. Engine numbers were located on left side of crankcase between cylinder 1 and 2. Starting: K9451. Ending: K9674.

Model No.	Body Type & Seating	Factory Price	Shipping Weight	Prod. Total
403	4-dr. Tr.-7P—	—		1
404-A	4-dr. Sed. 2W-5P	4800	5735	2
404-B	4-dr. Sed. 3W-5P	4800	5740	12
406	2-dr. Willoughby Cpe.-5P	5800	5615	1
407-A	4-dr. Sed.-7P	5000	5880	25
407-B	4-dr. Limo.-7P	5100	5970	58
408	2-dr. Brunn Conv. Vict.-5P	5800	5530	2
409-A	4-dr. Brunn Non. Clp. Cab.-5P	6800	6010	1
409-B	4-dr. Brunn Smi. Cpl. Cab.-5P	6900	6030	1
410	2-dr. LeBaron Conv. Rds.-2/4P	5200	5505	2
411	4-dr Brunn Brgm.-7P	6900	6120	2
412	2-dr. LeBaron Cpe.-2P	5200	5425	4
413-A	4-dr. LeBaron Conv. Sed.-5P	5700	5670	3
413-B	4-dr. LeBaron Conv. Sed. Part.-5P	5900	5780	6
415	4-dr. Judkins Limo.-7P	6200	5950	2
417-A	4-dr. Judkins Ber. 2W-5P	5900	5770	2
417-B	4-dr. Judkins Ber. 3W-5P	6000	5840	1
419	4-dr. Willoughby Limo.-7P	6100	6140	4
421	4-dr. Willoughby Spt. Sed.-5P	6900	6030	1
423	4-dr. Willoughby Pnl. Brgm.-5P	—	—	1
425	4-dr. Brunn Tr. Cab.-5P	7100	5870	2

ENGINE: 67 degree V, L-head. Twelve. Cast-iron block. B & S: 3-1/8 x 4-1/2 in. Disp.: 414 cid C.R.: 6.38:1. Brake H.P.: 150 @ 3800 R.P.M. Taxable H.P.: 46.8. Main bearings: four. Valve lifters: hydraulic. Carb.: Stromberg downdraft two-barrel.

CHASSIS: W.B.: 136/145 in. Frt/Rear Tread: 60 in. Tires: 17 x 7.50.

TECHNICAL: Sliding gear transmission. Speeds: 3F/1R. Floor shift controls. Double dry disc clutch. Shaft drive. Full floating rear axle. Overall ratio: 4.58:1, 4.90:1, 4.23:1 (standard). Bendix Duo-Servo mechanical brakes on four rear wheels. Wheel size: 17 in.

OPTIONS: Dual sidemounts. Sidemount cover(s). Radio. Heater. Clock. Cigar lighter.

HISTORY: Model year production: 133. The president of Lincoln was Edsel Ford.

1939 Lincoln Model K Willoughby 7-passenger. (OCW)

1939 Lincoln Model K LeBaron convertible sedan. (OCW)

1940 LINCOLN

1940 Lincoln Zephyr four-door sedan. (OCW)

1940 Lincoln Zephyr convertible coupe. (OCW)

LINCOLN-ZEPHYR — TWELVE: The use of a redesigned body shell for the Zephyr, which was to remain in use until 1949, cushioned the demise of the K Lincolns and buoyed the Lincoln-Zephyr into the mainstream of Lincoln's marketing strategy. The major styling features for 1940 consisted of larger (by 22 percent) glass area, front window vent windows and the inboard positioning of the taillight. In addition, the one-piece rear window, lack of runningboards and the use of sealed-beam headlights made it easy to identify the 1940 Lincoln-Zephyr.

Once again a rearranged instrument panel was introduced for the Lincoln-Zephyr. The circular case for the speedometer and instruments was now located directly behind the steering column (which for the first time carried the "Finger-Tip Gearshift") and a single, large glovebox was placed in front of the passenger seat. The optional radio was installed on the upper dash panel just above the centrally located radio grille. To the left of the speaker was the clock.

1940 Lincoln-Zephyr sedan coupe. (OCW)

1940 Lincoln Zephyr coupe. (OCW)

All interior appointments had a mahogany metal finish and a two-spoke steering wheel was installed.

By virtue of a large 2-7/8 inch bore the Zephyr's engine now displaced 292 cubic inches and was rated at 120 hp.

In addition to the production model Lincoln-Zephyrs, a small number of custom-built versions were constructed during 1940. Three of these carried Brunn town car bodies. In addition three Custom series limousines were completed.

CONTINENTAL — TWELVE: The outstanding nature of the Lincoln-Zephyr's styling was further demonstrated by its transformation into one of America's most beautiful classics, the Continental. Compared to the Zephyr, the Continental was three inches lower and had a longer, by seven inches, hood. During the 1940 model run many styling developments took place. These included the installation of a spare tire cover, rear bumper splash shields and rubber rear fender gravel shields. Also changed was the location of the license bracket, which was moved from the body to the bumper. Continentals were fitted with the instrument panel of the Lincoln-Zephyr Town Limousine and featured a gold colored finish for the interior trim and hardware.

With the exception of a side-mounted engine air cleaner the Continental's mechanical composition was essentially that of other Lincoln-Zephyrs. However Continental engines had polished aluminum heads and manifolds and chromed acorn cylinder head nuts.

1940 Lincoln Continental coupe. (AA)

1940 Lincoln Continental cabriolet. (JAC)

1940 Lincoln Continental convertible. (OCW)

I.D. DATA: Serial numbers were located on right side of cowl, top of clutch housing and transmission case. Starting: H85641. Ending: H107687. Engine numbers were located on left side of crankcase between cylinders 1 and 2. Starting: H85641. Ending: H107687.

Model No.	Body Type & Seating	Factory Price	Shipping Weight	Prod. Total
72A	2-dr. Cpe.-2P	1360	3375	1256
72AS	2-dr. Cpe.-4P	1400	3465	316
73	4-dr. Sed.-6P	1400	3535	15,764
	4-dr. Twn. Sed.-7P	1740	3575	98
76	2-dr. Conv. Cpe.-6P	1770	3635	700
77	2-dr. Clb. Cpe.-6P	1400	3465	3500
H-32	4-dr. Limo.-7P	—	—	4
H-36	4-dr. Brunn Twn. Car-5P	—	—	4
56	2-dr. Cont. Cab.-5P	2840	3615	350
57	2-dr. Cont. Cpe.-5P	—	—	54

ENGINE: 75 degree V, L-head. Twelve. Cast-iron block. B & S: 2-7/8 x 3-3/4 in. Disp : 292 cid C.R.: 7.2:1. Brake H.P.: 120 @ 3500 R.P.M. Taxable H.P.: 39.3. Main bearings: four. Valve lifters: hydraulic. Carb.: Holley downdraft two-barrel. Torque: 220 lbs.-ft. @ 2000 R.P.M.

CHASSIS: W.B.: 125 in. O.L.: 209-1/2 in. Height: 69-1/2 in. (Continental 63). Frt/Rear Tread: 55-1/2/58-1/4 in. Tires: 16 x 7.00.

TECHNICAL: Sliding gear transmission. Speeds: 3F/1R. Column shift controls. Single dry plate clutch. Shaft drive. 3/4 floating rear axle. Overall ratio: 4.44:1. Bendix hydraulic internal expanding brakes on four wheels. Pressed steel, dropped center wheels. Wheel size: 4-1/2K-16. Drivetrain options: Columbia two-speed rear axle.

OPTIONS: Bumper guards. Radio. Heater. Leather upholstery. Wind wings. Whitewall tires. Fitted luggage. Custom interior.

HISTORY: Introduced October 2, 1939. Calendar year production: 24,021. Model year production: 22,046. The president of Lincoln was Edsel Ford.

1941 LINCOLN

1941 Lincoln Continental coupe. (OCW)

1941 Lincoln Zephyr coupe. (OCW)

1941 Lincoln-Zephyr four-door sedan. (AA)

LINCOLN — ZEPHYR — TWELVE: Lincolns for 1941 were available as either Zephyr, Custom or Continental models with the Zephyr providing the basic styling engineering platform for all three versions.

The new Zephyrs had a wide grille outline molding, front fender mounted parking lights, more heavily chromed and reshaped taillights and a combined trunk lid and rear deck light. The front and rear bumpers were also slightly altered and a new hubcap design was introduced.

Interior alterations were similarly of a minor nature. The clock and ashtray were now circular in shape as were the door handles. Additional upholstery fabrics were also available.

For the first time Borg-Warner overdrive was optional and a power top was standard on the convertible model.

1941 Lincoln Continental cabriolet. (HFM)

1941 Lincoln Continental eight-passenger Custom Sedan. (OCW)

LINCOLN — CONTINENTAL — TWELVE: Since the Continental had used the Zephyr's new styling for its 1940 debut, only superficial appearance changes distinguished the 1941 version, although separate tooling was now used for the Continental. Both interior and exterior door handles were of the push-button type and the same styling changes found of the 1941 Zephyr models were also carried over to the Continental. Lincoln Continental script was found both on the hood and spare tire hubcap of the 1941 model. Road hubcaps carried Lincoln V-12 inscriptions. During the 1941 model run minor refinements took place in the appearance of the Continental's hood ornament, V-12 emblem and taillight form. Both turn signals and vacuum window lifts were standard. Interior selection consisted of blue cord/leather, green cord/leather and tan cord matched with either tan or red leather. All-leather upholstery was available in colors of green, black, blue, red or tan. The instrument panel had a mahogany finish.

LINCOLN — CUSTOM — TWELVE: With a wheelbase 13 inches longer than the other 1941 Lincolns and a more luxurious interior the Custom series represented a reasonable reincarnation of the K Lincoln spirit. The Custom carried a Continental hood ornament and Zephyr club coupe front doors. The Custom's side hood molding had previously been used on the 1940 Lincoln-Zephyr.

Custom interiors were of a high quality. A pin stripe broadcloth upholstery was available in blue, green and tan-brown. A cord pattern was offered in tan-brown. Optional custom interiors were also available.

I.D. DATA: Serial numbers were located on right side of cowl, top of clutch housing and transmission case. Starting: H 107688. Ending: H129690. Engine numbers were located on left side of crankcase between cylinders 1 and 2. Starting: H107688. Ending: H129690.

Model No.	Body Type & Seating	Factory Price	Shipping Weight	Prod. Total
Lincoln-Zephyr				
72A	2-dr. Cpe.-3P	1432	3560	972
72B	2-dr. Cpe.-5P	1464	3580	178
73	4-dr. Sed.-6P	1493	3710	14,469
76	2-dr. Conv. Cpe.-6P	1801	3840	725
77	2-dr. Clb. Cpe.-6P	1493	3640	3750
36	4-dr. Brunn Twn. Cr.-5P	—	—	5
Lincoln-Continental				
56	2-dr. Cab-5P	2778	3860	400
57	2-dr. Cpe.-5P	2727	3890	850
Lincoln-Custom				
31	4-dr. Sed.-7P	2622	4250	355
32	4-dr. Limo.-7P	2751	4270	295

ENGINE: 75 degree V, L-head. Twelve. Cast-iron block. B & S: 2-7/8 x 3-3/4 in. Disp.: 292 cid C.R.: 7.2:1. Brake H.P.: 120 @ 3500 R.P.M. Taxable H.P.: 39.3. Main bearings: four. Valve lifters: hydraulic. Carb.: Holley downdraft two-barrel. Torque: 220 lbs.-ft. @ 2000 R.P.M.

CHASSIS: [Zephyr] W.B.: 125 in. O.L.: 210 in. Height: 69-1/2 in. Frt/Rear Tread: 55-1/2/60-3/4 in. Tires: 16 x 7.00. [Custom] W.B.: 138 in. O.L. 225.3 in. Height: 70.5. Frt/Rear Tread: 55-1/2/60-3/4 in. Tires: 16 x 7.00 [Continental] W.B.: 125 in. O.L.: 209-8/10 in. Height: 63 in. Frt/Rear Tread: 55-1/2/60-3/4 in. Tires: 16 x 7.00.

TECHNICAL: Sliding gear transmission. Speeds: 3F/1R. Column shift controls. Single dry plate clutch. Shaft drive. 3/4 floating rear axle. Overall ratio: 4.44:1. Bendix Hydraulic, internal expanding brakes on four wheels. Pressed steel, dropped center wheels. Wheel size: 5K-16. Drivetrain options: Columbia two-speed rear axle. Borg-Warner overdrive.

1941 Lincoln Continental convertible cabriolet. (RLC)

OPTIONS: Bumper guards, Radio. Heater. Custom interior ($100.00). Leather upholstery. Wind wings. Whitewall tires. Fitted luggage.

HISTORY: Calendar year production: 17,756. Model year production: 21,994 (Lincoln-Zephyr: 20,094, Lincoln-Continental: 1,250, Lincoln Custom: 650).. The president of Lincoln was Edsel Ford. In the 1941 Gilmore Economy Run the first-place winner was a Lincoln Custom with a 10-miles-per-gallon average of 57.827 or 21.03 mpg. The second-place car was a Lincoln Zephyr at 57.749 t.m.p.g. or 22.96 mpg. Both cars had Columbia two-speed rear axles and Borg-Warner overdrive.

1942 LINCOLN

1942 Lincoln-Zephyr four-door sedan. (OCW)

LINCOLN-ZEPHYR — TWELVE: The 1942 Lincoln-Zephyr was longer, wider and lower. A two-part grille with horizontal bars accentuated the Lincoln's more massive form. Adding to the popular horizontal-line styling theme common to so many 1942 automobiles were the new headlight trim plates containing the parking and directional lights. Common to all 1942 Lincolns were exterior push-button door latches.

Although chassis revisions included longer front springs and a wider front tread, the big technical news was the availability of the Liquimatic two-speed automatic transmission. This complex and ultimately unsuccessful venture combined overdrive, a fluid coupling and a semi-automatic transmission.

CONTINENTAL — TWELVE: Common to all 1942 Lincolns was a larger, 306-cubic inch V-12 rated at 130 hp. A lower 7.0:1 compression ratio was specified and cast-iron heads replaced the aluminum versions. The Continental also shared the Zephyr's new styling format.

1942 Lincoln Continental four-door sedan. (RLC)

1942 Lincoln Continental cabriolet. (AA)

1942 Lincoln Continental coupe. (OCW)

CUSTOM — TWELVE: The Custom shared a rearranged dashboard with the Zephyr. The circular speedometer was placed just to the right of the steering column with a panel containing fuel, temperature, oil and battery gauges to its immediate left. A large radio speaker grille occupied the center section. A clock, whose size and shape matched that of the speedometer plus a Lincoln plaque, provided design symmetry on the right side of the dash.

I.D. DATA: Serial numbers were located on right side of cowl, top of clutch housing and transmission case. Starting: H129691. Ending: H36254. Engine numbers were located on left side of crankcase between cylinders 1 and 2. Starting: H129691. Ending: H136254.

Model No.	Body Type & Seating	Factory Price	Shipping Weight	Prod. Total
Lincoln-Zephyr				
72-A	2-dr. Cpe.-3P	1748	3790	Note 1
72-B	2-dr. Cpe.-5P	—	3790	Note 1
73	4-dr. Sed.-6P	1801	3980	4418
76	2-dr. Conv. Cpe.-6P	2274	4190	191
77-A	2-dr. Clb. Cpe.-6P	1801	3810	253
Lincoln Continental				
56	2-dr. Cab.-5P	3174	4020	136
57	2-dr. Cpe.-5P	3174	4060	200
Lincoln Custom				
31	4-dr. Sed.-7P	3117	4380	47
32	4-dr. Limo.-7P	3248	4400	66

NOTE 1: The total combined production of these models was 1,236.

ENGINE: 75 degree V, L-head. Twelve. Cast-iron block. B & S: 2-15/16 x 3-3/4 in. Disp.: 292 cid C.R.: 7.0:1. Brake H.P.: 130 @ 4000 R.P.M. Taxable H.P.: 39.9. Main bearings: four. Valve lifters: hydraulic. Carb.: Holley downdraft two-barrel. Torque 220 lbs.-ft. @ 2000 R.P.M.

CHASSIS: [Zephyr] W.B.: 125 in. O.L.: 218.7 in. Height: 68-1/2. Frt/Rear Tread: 59/60-3/4 in. Tires: 15 x 7.00. [Custom] W.B.: 138 in. Frt/Rear Tread 59/60-3/4 in. Tires: 15 x 7.00. [Continental] W.B.: 125 in. O.L.: 217 in. Height: 63-1/10 (Cabriolet). Frt/Rear Tread: 59/60-3/4 in. Tires: 15 x 7.00.

TECHNICAL: Sliding gear transmission. Speeds: 3F/1R. Column shift controls. Single dry plate clutch. Shaft drive. 3/4 floating rear axle. Overall ratio: 4.22:1. Bendix hydraulic, internal expanding brakes on four wheels. Pressed steel, dropped center wheels. Drivetrain options: Columbia two-speed rear axle. Borg-Warner overdrive. Liquimatic ($189.00).

OPTIONS: Bumper guards. Radio. Heater. Clock. Custom interior ($95.00). Leather upholstery. Wind wings. Whitewall tires. Fitted luggage.

HISTORY: Introduced September 30, 1942. Innovations: Liquimatic transmission. Calendar year production: 1,276. Model year production: 6,547 (Zephyr: 6,098, Continental: 336, Custom: 113). The president of Lincoln was Edsel Ford. 1942 model year production ended January 31, 1942.

1946 LINCOLN

LINCOLN SERIES — SERIES 66H — The new 1946 Lincolns were warmed over 1942s. They had a more massive bumper, different nameplate on the sides of the hood and a heavier grille with horizontal and vertical bars. The push-button Continental style door openers introduced on the 1942 models were kept.

1946 Lincoln two-door convertible V-12. (OCW)

1946 Lincoln four-door sedan V-12. (AA)

LINCOLN I.D. NUMBERS: Serial numbers were the same as engine numbers. They ranged from H136625 to H138051; H138052 to H152839. The first letter (H) indicates the series (66H).

LINCOLN

Model No.	Body/ Style No.	Body Type & Seating	Factory Price	Shipping Weight	Prod. Total
66H	73	4-dr Sed-6P	2337	3980	Note 1
66H	76	2-dr Conv-6P	2883	4210	Note 1
66H	77	2-dr Clb Cpe-6P	2318	3380	Note 1

NOTE 1: Total production of all body types was 16,645 units with no breakouts.

CONTINENTAL SERIES — SERIES 66H — The Continental was a luxurious, beautiful, handcrafted automobile built for boulevard cruising. The 1946 model received a larger, criss-cross pattern grille and a heavier bumper. Lincoln Continental was written in chrome on the side of the hood.

CONTINENTAL

Model No.	Body/ Style No.	Body Type & Seating	Factory Price	Shipping Weight	Prod. Total
66H	52	2-dr Conv-5P	4474	4090	201
66H	57	2-dr Club Cpe-5P	4392	4100	265

ENGINE [V-12]: L-head. Cast-iron block. Displacement: 305 cid. Bore and stroke: 2.93 x 3.75 inches. Compression ratio: 7.2:1. Brake hp: 130 at 3600 rpm. Four main bearings. Carburetor: Chandler-Grove two-barrel.

1946 Lincoln-Continental two-door cabriolet V-12. (OCW)

CHASSIS FEATURES: Wheelbase: 125 inches. Overall length: 216 inches. Front tread: 59 inches. Rear tread: 60.6 inches. Tires: 7.00 x 15.

OPTIONS: Custom interior ($149 in Lincoln sedan and coupe). Radio. Whitewall tires. Heater. A three-speed manual transmission was standard. Overdrive was optional.

HISTORY: The 1946 Continental was the pace car at the 1946 Indianapolis 500. This beautiful car was introduced to the press on Sept. 13, 1945. Only 569 cars were made by the end of the calendar year, although a total of 13,496 were built in calendar year 1946. Model year production of 16,645 helped Lincoln place 16th in the domestic sales race.

1947 LINCOLN

1947 Lincoln two-door convertible V-12. (OCW)

LINCOLN SERIES — SERIES 76H — Styling changes for 1947 were minor. The push-button door handles were replaced by conventional ones. The word 'Lincoln' was written in chrome on both sides of the hood. The raised hexagon center wheel covers of the previous year were replaced by plainer ones.

LINCOLN I.D. NUMBERS: Serial numbers were the same as engine numbers. They ranged from 7H152840 to 7H174289.

LINCOLN

Model No.	Body/ Style No.	Body Type & Seating	Factory Price	Shipping Weight	Prod. Total
76H	73	4-dr Sed-6P	2554	4015	Note 1
76H	76	2-dr Conv-6P	3142	4245	Note 1
76H	77	2-dr Clb Cpe-6P	2533	3915	Note 1

NOTE 1: Total production of all body types was 19,891 units with no breakouts.

CONTINENTAL SERIES — SERIES 76H — The best way to tell a 1947 Continental from a 1946 (or 1948) is to ask the owner. The only exterior changes were in the wheel covers and, in mid-model year, the hood ornament. Mechanical improvements were made to the generator and starter drive.

CONTINENTAL

Model No.	Body/ Style No.	Body Type & Seating	Factory Price	Shipping Weight	Prod. Total
76H	52	2-dr Conv-5P	4746	4135	738
76H	57	2-dr Clb Cpe-5P	4662	4125	831

ENGINE [V-12]: L-head. Cast-iron block. Displacement: 305 cid. Bore and stroke: 2.93 x 3.75 inches. Compression ratio: 7.2:1. Brake hp: 130 at 3600 rpm. Four main bearings. Carburetor: Chandler-Grove two-barrel.

1947 Lincoln-Continental two-door Club Coupe V-12. (TVB)

1947 Lincoln Continental two-door cabriolet V-12. (OCW)

CHASSIS FEATURES: Wheelbase: 125 inches. Overall length: 216 inches. Front tread. 59 inches. Rear tread: 60.6 inches. Tires: 7.00 x 15.

OPTIONS: Custom interior, in Lincoln sedan and coupe ($168). White-wall tires. Radio. Heater. A three-speed manual transmission was standard and overdrive was optional.

HISTORY: The year 1947 was the best yet for Lincoln-Continental sales. Production hit 1,569 vehicles, but calendar year production of Lincolns and Continentals was 29,275. Lincoln came in 18th in domestic sales.

1948 LINCOLN

1948 Lincoln four-door sedan. (OCW)

1948 Lincoln two-door convertible V-12. (OCW)

1948 Lincoln Continental two-door cabriolet V-12. (OCW)

LINCOLN SERIES — SERIES 876H — Lincoln Division was working frantically to bring out the new postwar model. So the 1948s were basically just leftover 1947 models.

LINCOLN I.D. NUMBERS: Serial numbers were the same as engine numbers. They ranged from 8H174290 to 8H182129.

LINCOLN

Model No.	Body/ Style No.	Body Type & Seating	Factory Price	Shipping Weight	Prod. Total
876H	73	4-dr Sed-6P	2554	4015	Note 1
876H	76	2-dr Conv-6P	3142	4245	Note 1
876H	77	2-dr Clb Cpe-6P	2533	3915	Note 1

NOTE 1: Total production of all body types was 6,470 with no break-outs.

CONTINENTAL SERIES — SERIES 876H — The Continental was virtually unchanged for 1948.

CONTINENTAL

Model No.	Body/ Style No.	Body Type & Seating	Factory Price	Shipping Weight	Prod. Total
876H	56	2-dr Conv-6P	4746	4135	452
876H	57	2-dr Clb Cpe-6P	4662	4125	847

ENGINE [V-12]: L-head. Cast-iron block. Displacement: 305 cid. Bore and stroke: 2.93 x 3.75 inches. Compression ratio: 7.2:1. Brake hp: 130 at 3600 rpm. Four main bearings. Carburetor: Chandler-Grove two-barrel.

CHASSIS FEATURES: Wheelbase: 125 inches. Overall length: 216 inches. Front tread: 59 inches. Rear tread: 60.6 inches. Tires: 7.00 x 15.

OPTIONS: Custom interior ($168 in Lincoln sedan and coupe). White-wall tires. Radio. Heater. A three-speed manual transmission was standard. Overdrive was optional.

1948 Lincoln Continental two-door Club Coupe V-12. (OCW)

HISTORY: In 1951, the Museum of Modern Art selected the Continental as one of eight automotive 'works of art'. Eight years later, *TIME* magazine ranked it in its top 10 choice of the 100 best-designed commercial products. The 1948 model year began on Nov. 1, 1947, and lasted only six months. Calendar year sales were 43,938 units. Model year production was 1,299 Continentals. This made Lincoln the 17th largest U.S. automaker.

1949 LINCOLN

1949 Lincoln Cosmopolitan. (OCW)

LINCOLN SERIES — SERIES 9EL — The first all-new postwar Lincolns were introduced on April 22, 1948. They had a more streamlined appearance than the 1948 models. However, the new, two-piece windshield seemed a bit out of sync with the 'modern' styling. At a distance it was hard to tell a Lincoln from a Mercury. Recessed headlights and a shinier front end set it apart.

LINCOLN I.D. NUMBERS: Serial numbers were the same as engine numbers. They started at 9EL1 and went up to 9EL73559. Cosmopolitan numbers ranged from 9EH1 to 9EH73563.

LINCOLN

Model No.	Body/ Style No.	Body Type & Seating	Factory Price	Shipping Weight	Prod. Total
9EL	72	2-dr Clb Cpe-6P	2527	3959	Note 1
9EL	74	4-dr Spt Sed-6P	2575	4009	Note 1
9EL	76	2-dr Conv-6P	3116	4224	Note 1

NOTE 1: Total 9EL series production was 38,384 units with no breakouts.

1949 Lincoln four-door sedan V-8. (AA)

1949 Lincoln Cosmopolitan two-door Club Coupe V-8. (OCW)

1949 Lincoln Cosmopolitan four-door Sport Sedan V-8. (OCW)

1949 Lincoln Cosmopolitan two-door convertible V-8. (OCW)

COSMOPOLITAN SERIES — SERIES 9EH — The Continental was gone. The new top-of-the-line Lincoln was the Cosmopolitan. While it resembled the standard series, most of the sheet metal was different. A one-piece windshield and what appeared to be a huge horizontal gob of chrome on each front fender, were a couple of its main distinguishing features. Power windows and power seats were standard.

COSMOPOLITAN

Model No.	Body/ Style No.	Body Type & Seating	Factory Price	Shipping Weight	Prod. Total
9EH	72	2-dr Clb Cpe-6P	3186	4194	7,685
9EH	73	4-dr Twn Sed-6P	3238	3274	7,302
9EH	74	4-dr Spt Sed-6P	3238	4259	18,906
9EH	76	2-dr Conv-6P	3948	4419	1,230

NOTE 1: The Town Sedan was the only 1949 Lincoln with fastback styling.

ENGINE [V-8]: L-head. Cast-iron block. Displacement: 336.7 cid. Bore and stroke: 3.50 x 4.37 inches. Compression ratio: 7.0:1. Brake hp: 152 at 3600 rpm. Carburetor: Holley two-barrel.

CHASSIS FEATURES: Wheelbase: (Lincoln) 121 inches; (Cosmopolitan) 125 inches. Overall length: (Lincoln) 213 inches; (Cosmopolitan) 220.5 inches. Front tread: 58.5 inches. Rear tread: 60 inches. Tires: 8.20 x 15.

OPTIONS: Handbrake signal. Radio. Vacuum antenna. Power windows. Heater. A three-speed manual transmission was standard. 'Touch-O-Matic' overdrive was optional. Late in the model year, Hydra-Matic automatic transmission became optional.

HISTORY: Lincolns won two of the nine National Association for Stock Car Auto Racing (NASCAR) Grand National races held in 1949. The 1949 Lincoln's recessed headlights were originally planned to be hidden. The 1949 Lincolns were introduced April 22, 1948. Model year production was 73,507 cars. Calendar year assemblies totaled 33,132 units. Lincoln came in 17th in sales for the second year running.

1950 LINCOLN

LINCOLN SERIES — SERIES 0EL — A new horizontal bar grille with vertical elements enhanced the appearance of the standard Lincoln. Its name was in the same location on the front fender as last year, but it was larger. In mid-model year, the Lido Coupe was added to the line. It featured a vinyl top and custom interior.

1950 Lincoln two-door Club Coupe V-8. (AA)

1950 Lincoln Cosmopolitan convertible. (OCW)

LINCOLN I.D. NUMBERS: 0EL series serial numbers ranged from 50LP5001L to 50LP20082L and 50LA5001L to 50LA72521L. Lincoln Cosmopolitan serial numbers ranged from 50LP5001H to 50LP15701H. Assembly plant codes: LA = Los Angeles; LP = Lincoln Plant; SL = St. Louis.

LINCOLN

Model No.	Body/ Style No.	Body Type & Seating	Factory Price	Shipping Weight	Prod. Total
0EL	L-72	2-dr Clb Cpe-6P	2529	4090	Note 1
0EL	L-72C	2-dr Lido Cpe-6P	2721	4145	Note 1
0EL	L-74	4-dr Spt Sed-6P	2576	4115	11,714

NOTE 1: Total production of body styles L-72 and L-72C was 5,748 with no breakouts.

COSMOPOLITAN SERIES — SERIES 0EH — The Cosmopolitan received a new grille and dash for 1950. Its name was now written in chrome on the lower front fenders. The Cosmopolitan Capri had a padded leather roof and custom interior. It also had an additional horizontal gob of chrome on the rear quarter panels parallel to the ones on the front fenders. The Capri was introduced to make up for Continental's lack of a two-door hardtop.

1950 Lincoln Cosmopolitan two-door Club Coupe V-8. (OCW)

COSMOPOLITAN

Model No.	Body/ Style No.	Body Type & Seating	Factory Price	Shipping Weight	Prod. Total
0EH	H-72	2-dr Clb Cpe-6P	3187	4375	1,315
0EH	H-72C	2-dr Capri Cpe-6P	3406	4385	509
0EH	H-74	4-dr Spt Sed-6P	3240	4410	8,332
0EH	H-76	2-dr Conv-6P	3950	4640	536

ENGINE [V-8]: L-head. Cast-iron block. Displacement: 336.7 cid. Bore and stroke: 3.50 x 4.37 inches. Compression ratio: 7.0:1. Brake hp: 152 at 3600 rpm. Carburetor: Holley 885-FFC two-barrel.

CHASSIS FEATURES: Wheelbase: (Lincoln) 121 inches; (Cosmopolitan) 125 inches. Overall length: (Lincoln) 213.8 inches; (Cosmopolitan) 212.2 inches. Front tread: 58.5 inches. Rear tread: 60 inches. Tires: (Lincoln) 8.00 x 15; (Cosmopolitan) 8.20 x 15.

OPTIONS: Heater. Power windows (standard in Cosmopolitan). Power antenna. Whitewall tires. Radio. A three-speed manual transmission was standard. Overdrive and Hydra-Matic automatic transmission were extra-cost options.

HISTORY: Lincolns won two of the 19 NASCAR Grand National races held in 1950.

1951 LINCOLN

1951 Lincoln four-door Sport Sedan (with late-in-year bodyside trim revision) V-8. (TVB)

LINCOLN SERIES — SERIES 1EL — The front of the 1951 Lincoln looked like a 1950 model that had gotten into a fight...and lost. The grille bar only extended from the center section between the bumper guards. A forward slanting, vertical piece was added to the front fender side chrome. The word Lincoln was written behind it. The glamorous Lido coupe came with a canvas or vinyl roof, fender skirts, rocker panel molding and custom interior.

LINCOLN I.D. NUMBERS: Series 1EL serial numbers began with either 41LP5001L or 51LA5001L. Cosmopolitan serial numbers ranged from 51LP5001H to 51LP20813H.

LINCOLN

Model No.	Body/ Style No.	Body Type & Seating	Factory Price	Shipping Weight	Prod. Total
1EL	L-72B	2-dr Clb Cpe-6P	2505	4065	Note 1
1EL	L-72C	2-dr Lido Cpe-6P	2702	4100	Note 1
1EL	L-74	4-dr Spt Sed-6P	2553	4130	12,279

NOTE 1: Total production for body styles L-72B and L-72C was 4,482 units with no breakouts.

1951 Lincoln Cosmopolitan four-door Sport Sedan V-8. (OCW)

1951 Lincoln Cosmopolitan convertible. (OCW)

COSMOPOLITAN SERIES — SERIES 1EH — Except for the chrome rocker panels, the new Cosmopolitan looked pretty much like the standard Lincoln. The distinctive gob of chrome on the front fenders of the previous two years was mercifully removed. Also, the Cosmopolitan name was placed on the upper front fenders. Next to the convertible, the snazziest model was the Capri coupe. It featured a canvas or vinyl roof, Deluxe upholstery and (like all Cosmopolitans) fender skirts.

COSMOPOLITAN

Model No.	Body/ Style No.	Body Type & Seating	Factory Price	Shipping Weight	Prod. Total
1EH	H-72B	2-dr Clb Cpe-6P	3129	4340	1,476
1EH	H-72C	2-dr Capri Cpe-6P	3350	4360	1,251
1EH	H-74	4-dr Spt Sed-6P	3182	4415	12,229
1EH	H-76	2-dr Conv-6P	3891	4615	857

ENGINE [V-8]: L-head. Cast-iron block. Displacement: 336.7 cid. Bore and stroke: 3.50 x 4.38 inches. Compression ratio: 7.0:1. Brake hp: 154 at 3600 rpm. Carburetor: Holley 885-FFC two-barrel.

CHASSIS FEATURES: Wheelbase: (Lincoln) 121 inches; (Cosmopolitan) 125 inches. Overall length: (Lincoln) 214.8 inches; (Cosmopolitan) 222.5 inches. Front tread: 58.5 inches. Rear tread: 60 inches. Tires (Lincoln) 8.00 x 15; (Cosmopolitan) 8.20 x 15.

OPTIONS: Heater. Power windows. Whitewall tires. Radio. A three-speed manual transmission was standard. Overdrive and Hydra-Matic automatic transmission were optional.

HISTORY: This season's dealer introductions were staged for Nov. 15, 1950. Production of models built to 1951 specifications was quartered at Detroit and Los Angeles assembly plants, although a new factory in Wayne, Mich., was nearly completed this season and went into operation for production of 1952 Lincolns. In November 1951, the 125-inch wheelbase series was discontinued. Benson Ford was the general manager of the Lincoln-Mercury Division this year.

1952 LINCOLN

COSMOPOLITAN SERIES — SERIES 2H — Lincoln was completely restyled for 1952. It had a lean, racy look. The bumper and grille were integrated instead of being recessed, the headlights seemed to stick out slightly from the fenders. Side trim consisted of a nearly full-length spear that divided a wide, slanted rear fender molding. The large vertical taillights were vaguely similar to last year's. A wraparound windshield and rear window added a 'modern' touch to the car's styling. New ball-joint suspension improved its handling and ride.

LINCOLN I.D. NUMBERS: Cosmopolitan serial numbers ranged from 52LP5001H to 52WA29217H. Capri serial numbers ranged from 52LA5001H to 52LA7761H; 52SL5001H to 52SL5072H plus those found in the Cosmopolitan I.D. numbers section. Assembly plant code: LA = Los Angeles; LP = Lincoln plant; SL = St. Louis; WA = Wayne, Mich.

COSMOPOLITAN

Model No.	Body/ Style No.	Body Type & Seating	Factory Price	Shipping Weight	Prod. Total
2H	60C	2-dr HT Spt Cpe-6P	3293	4155	4,545
2H	73A	4-dr Sed-6P	3198	4125	Note 1

NOTE 1: Total production for Cosmopolitan and Capri four-door sedans was 15,854 with no breakouts.

1952 Lincoln Cosmopolitan four-door sedan V-8. (AA)

CAPRI SERIES — SERIES 2H — The Capri was now Lincoln's top-of-the-line model. The sedan featured fabric and leather upholstery. Like the Cosmopolitan that it resembled, its gas tank filler was hidden behind the rear license plate.

CAPRI

Model No.	Body/ Style No.	Body Type & Seating	Factory Price	Shipping Weight	Prod. Total
2H	60A	2-dr HT Cpe-6P	3518	4235	5,681
2H	73B	4-dr Sed-6P	3331	4140	Note 1
2H	76A	2-dr Conv-6P	3665	4350	1,191

NOTE 1: Total production for Cosmopolitan and Capri four-door sedans was 15,854 with no breakouts.

ENGINE [V-8]: Overhead valve. Cast-iron block. Displacement: 317.4 cid. Bore and stroke: 3.8 x 3.5 inches. Compression ratio: 7.5:1. Brake hp: 160 at 3900 rpm. Carburetor: Holley two-barrel.

CHASSIS FEATURES: Wheelbase: 123 inches. Overall length: 214 inches. Front tread: 58.5 inches. Rear tread: 58.5 inches. Tires: 8.00 x 15.

1952 Lincoln Capri convertible. (OCW)

1952 Lincoln Capri two-door hardtop (prototype with no hood ornament) V-8. (AA)

1952 Lincoln Capri four-door sedan V-8. (OCW)

OPTIONS: Heater. Power front seat and power windows (both standard in convertible). Whitewall tires. Radio. Spotlight. Grille guard. Hydra-Matic automatic transmission was standard. A 'maximum duty kit' was available for owners who wanted to race their Lincolns.

HISTORY: Lincolns came in first, second, third and fourth at the 1952 Pan American Road Race in Mexico. However, 1953 models were used.

1953 LINCOLN

COSMOPOLITAN SERIES — SERIES 8H — With the exception of an emblem inside a chrome 'V' on the upper section of the grille and the word Lincoln printed across the face of the hood, styling was basically the same as the previous year.

LINCOLN I.D. NUMBERS: Serial numbers in 1953 ranged from 53WA5001H to 53WA39566H; 53LA5001H to 53LA10995H. Assembly plant code: LA = Los Angeles; LP = Lincoln Plant; SL = St. Louis; WA = Wayne, Mich.

COSMOPOLITAN

Model No.	Body/ Style No.	Body Type & Seating	Factory Price	Shipping Weight	Prod. Total
8H	60C	2-dr HT Spt Cpe-6P	3322	4155	6,562
8H	73A	4-dr Sed-6P	3226	4135	7,560

1953 Lincoln Capri two-door convertible V-8. (OCW)

CAPRI SERIES — SERIES 8H — The most expensive series continued to be the Capri. Except for the chrome rocker panels, it was difficult to tell them from Cosmopolitans.

CAPRI

Model No.	Body/ Style No.	Body Type & Seating	Factory Price	Shipping Weight	Prod. Total
8H	60A	2-dr HT Cpe-6P	3549	4165	12,916
8H	73B	4-dr Sed-6P	3453	4150	11,352
8H	76A	2-dr Conv-6P	3699	4310	2,372

ENGINE [V-8]: Overhead valve. Cast-iron block. Displacement: 317.5 cid. Bore and stroke: 3.8 x 3.5 inches. Compression ratio: 8.0:1. Brake hp: 205 at 4200 rpm. Five main bearings. Carburetor: Holley 2140 four-barrel.

CHASSIS FEATURES: Wheelbase: 123 inches. Overall length: 214.1 inches. Front tread: 58.5 inches. Rear tread: 58.5 inches. Tires: 8.00 x 15; (convertible) 8.20 x 15.

OPTIONS: Power brakes. Four-way power seat. Power steering. Electric windows. Tinted windows. Whitewall tires. Radio. Hydra-Matic automatic transmission was standard.

HISTORY: For the second year in-a-row, Lincolns captured the top four spots at the Pan American Road Race. A fire at General Motors' Livonia, Mich., transmission plant stopped production of the Hydra-Matic-equipped Lincolns for 55 days. This reportedly caused Lincoln to lose 7,000 sales. Eighty-seven percent of 1953 Lincolns had power brakes and 69 percent had power steering.

1954 LINCOLN

COSMOPOLITAN SERIES — Lincolns grew an inch in length and width this year. The Lincoln name was now written on the front fenders. The wide, slanted rear fender chrome piece was replaced by a rear fender stone shield. The straight, side molding was higher and longer than that used on the 1953s. The company emblem and 'V' were on the face of the hood and the top bumper/grille bar was straight.

LINCOLN I.D. NUMBERS: Serial numbers ranged from 54WA5001H to 54WA36840H and 54LA5001H to 54LA9891H. Assembly plant code: LA = Los Angeles; LP = Lincoln Plant; SL = St. Louis; WA = Wayne, Mich.

COSMOPOLITAN

Model No.	Body/ Style No.	Body Type & Seating	Factory Price	Shipping Weight	Prod. Total
N/A	60C	2-dr HT Spt Cpe-6P	3625	4155	2,994
N/A	73A	4-dr Sed-6P	3522	4135	4,447

1954 Lincoln Cosmopolitan four-door sedan V-8. (PH)

1954 Lincoln Capri two-door hardtop V-8. (OCW)

1954 Lincoln Capri convertible. (OCW)

CAPRI SERIES — Except for the chrome rocker panels and roof trim, it was hard to tell a Capri from a Cosmopolitan without looking at the nameplate.

CAPRI

Model No.	Body/ Style No.	Body Type & Seating	Factory Price	Shipping Weight	Prod. Total
N/A	60A	2-dr HT Cpe-6P	3869	4250	14,003
N/A	73B	4-dr Sed-6P	3711	4245	13,598
N/A	76A	2-dr Conv-6P	4031	4310	1,951

ENGINE [V-8]: Overhead valve. Cast-iron block. Displacement: 317.5 cid. Bore and stroke: 3.8 x 3.5 inches. Compression ratio: 8.0:1. Brake hp: 205 at 4200 rpm. Five main bearings. Carburetor: Holley 2140 four-barrel.

CHASSIS FEATURES: Wheelbase: 123 inches. Overall length: 215 inches. Tires: 8.00 x 15; (convertible) 8.20 x 15.

CONVENIENCE OPTIONS: Power brakes. Power steering. Four-Way power seat. Tinted glass. Whitewall tires. Radio. Heater. Hydra-Matic automatic transmission was standard.

HISTORY: Lincolns took first and second place at the 1954 Pan American Road Race.

1955 LINCOLN

CUSTOM SERIES — The 1955 Lincoln was a refined version of the 1954 model. Removal of the lower vertical bars on the grille gave it a cleaner look. The headlight treatment seemed very Ford-like. The Lincoln name was (as in 1953) printed on the front of the hood. Although the full-length side chrome spear remained, the rear fender stone shield was changed. The taillight design and hood ornament were also new. Custom two-door hardtops came with chrome rocker panels.

LINCOLN I.D. NUMBERS: Serial numbers ranged from 55WA5001H to 55WA28595H and 55LA5001H to 55LA8519H. Assembly plant code: LA = Los Angeles; LP = Lincoln Plant; SL = St. Louis; WA = Wayne, Mich.

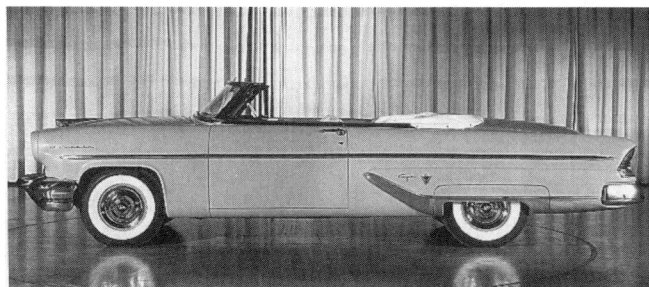

1955 Lincoln Capri two-door convertible V-8. (PH)

1955 Lincoln Capri two-door hardtop V-8. (PH)

CUSTOM

Model No.	Body/ Style No.	Body Type & Seating	Factory Price	Shipping Weight	Prod. Total
N/A	60C	2-dr HT Spt Cpe-6P	3666	4185	1,362
N/A	73A	4-dr Sed-6P	3563	4235	2,187

CAPRI SERIES — Its nameplate, chrome rocker panels and a different rear roof pillar trim distinguished the exterior of the Capri from the lower-priced Custom. The convertible had leather upholstery.

CAPRI

Model No.	Body/ Style No.	Body Type & Seating	Factory Price	Shipping Weight	Prod. Total
N/A	60A	2-dr HT Cpe-6P	3910	4305	11,462
N/A	73B	4-dr Sed-6P	3752	4245	10,724
N/A	76A	2-dr Conv-6P	4072	4415	1,487

ENGINE [V-8]: Overhead valve. Cast-iron block. Displacement: 341 cid. Bore and stroke: 3.93 x 3.50 inches. Compression ratio: 8.5:1. Brake hp: 225 at 4400 rpm. Carburetor: Holley four-barrel.

CHASSIS FEATURES: Wheelbase: 123 inches. Overall length: 215.6 inches. Tires: 8.00 x 15; (convertible and cars with air conditioning) 8.20 x 15.

CONVENIENCE OPTIONS: Air conditioning. Power steering. Power brakes. Power windows. Tinted glass. Heater. Radio. Power seats. Whitewall tires. Turbo-Drive automatic transmission was standard.

HISTORY: Ninety-three percent of 1955 Lincolns had power steering; 94 percent had power brakes; 91 percent had power seats; 82 percent had power windows; 98 percent had radios; 99 percent had heaters and 89 percent had tinted glass. This was the first year Lincoln used its own automatic transmission. It had been equipping cars with GM's Hydra-Matic. Also, on April 18, 1955, Lincoln became a separate division of the Ford Motor Co. Since October 1945 it had been part of the Lincoln-Mercury Division.

1956 LINCOLN

CAPRI SERIES — Lincoln was attractively restyled for 1956. It was based on the XL-500 and XM-800 concept cars. It had hooded headlights and a bumper-integrated, center horizontal bar grille with thinner horizontal bars above and below it. Taillight treatment was similar to last year. Bumper ports beneath the taillights served as exhaust exits. A full-length tire-level side molding was incorporated onto the standard fender skirts. All 1956 Lincolns came equipped with power steering, automatic transmission and dual exhaust.

LINCOLN I.D. NUMBERS: Serial numbers ranged from 56WA5001L to 56WA480056 and 56LA5001L to 56LA12288L. Assembly plant code: LA = Los Angeles; LP = Lincoln Plant; SL = St. Louis; WA = Wayne, Mich.

CAPRI

Model No.	Body/ Style No.	Body Type & Seating	Factory Price	Shipping Weight	Prod. Total
N/A	60E	2-dr HT Spt Cpe-6P	4119	4305	4,355
N/A	73A	4-dr Sed-6P	4212	4315	4,436

PREMIERE SERIES — It's easy to see why the Premiere hardtop was able to win an award from the Industrial Designers Institute for excellence in automotive design. Outside of rear fender medallions and fancier wheel covers, it was difficult to tell the Premiere from the less costly Capri. Like all Ford Motor Co. products in 1956, the Premiere had a lot of safety features. Improved door latches, deep-dish steering wheel, and heavily padded seatbacks and door panels. Power windows and four-way power front seat were standard.

PREMIERE

Model No.	Body/ Style No.	Body Type & Seating	Factory Price	Shipping Weight	Prod. Total
N/A	60B	2-dr HT Cpe-6P	4601	4357	19,619
N/A	73B	4-dr Sed-6P	4601	4347	19,465
N/A	76B	2-dr Conv-6P	4747	4452	2,447

MARK II SERIES — The Lincoln-Continental returned this year with the introduction of the Mark II. It made its debut on Oct. 6, 1955, at the Paris Auto Show. A long hood, short deck, restrained use of chrome and near perfect proportions helped the Mark II show the world just how beautiful a production American automobile could be. Like its predecessors, it was an instant classic. Yet it was not an imitation of the original. The Mark II was unmistakably modern in design. Being priced in the then lofty $10,000 range seemed to only accentuate how special this car was.

MARK II

Model No.	Body/ Style No.	Body Type & Seating	Factory Price	Shipping Weight	Prod. Total
N/A	60A	2-dr Spt Cpe-6P	9966	4825	2,550

ENGINE [Base V-8]: Overhead valve. Cast-iron block. Displacement: 368 cid. Bore and stroke: 4.00 x 3.65 inches. Compression ratio: 9.0:1. Brake hp: 285 at 4600 rpm. Carburetor: Lincoln four-barrel.

1956 Lincoln Premiere two-door convertible V-8. (PH)

1956 Lincoln Continental Mark II two-door hardtop V-8. (OCW)

1956 Lincoln Continental two-door hardtop. (OCW)

ENGINE [Mark II V-8]: Overhead valve. Cast-iron block. Displacement: 368 cid. Bore and stroke: 4.00 x 3.65 inches. Compression ratio: 10.0:1. Brake hp: 300 at 4800 rpm. Carburetor: Carter four-barrel.

CHASSIS FEATURES: [Lincoln] Wheelbase: 126 inches. Overall length: 223 inches. Overall width: 79.9 inches. Tires: 8.00 x 15; (convertible and cars with air conditioning) 8.20 x 15. [Mark II] Wheelbase: 126 inches. Overall length: 218.5 inches. Overall width: 77.5 inches. Tires: 8.00 x 15; (cars with air conditioning) 8.20 x 15.

CONVENIENCE OPTIONS: [Lincoln] Air conditioning. Power brakes. Push-button lubrication. Power windows. Power Four-Way front seat. Automatic headlight dimmer. Heater. Radio. Whitewall tires. Turbo-Drive automatic transmission was standard. [Mark II] The only option was air conditioning. Power steering, power brakes, power seat, radio, whitewall tires and a heater were all standard equipment.

HISTORY: Ninety-eight percent of 1956 Lincolns were equipped with power brakes; 85 percent had power seats; 86 percent had power windows; 94 percent had radios; 99 percent had heaters and 98 percent had whitewall tires. In 1956, Lincoln switched from a six-volt to a 12-volt electrical system.

1957 LINCOLN

1957 Lincoln Capri four-door sedan V-8. (OCW)

CAPRI SERIES — Lincolns received a face lift this year that was stylistically equivalent to putting a beehive hairdo on the Mona Lisa. The main change included the addition of two more headlights (actually they functioned as auxiliary lights), wider parking and signal lights, full-length center bodyside chrome and exaggerated tailfin-enclosed taillights.

LINCOLN I.D. NUMBERS: Serial numbers ranged from 57WA5001L to 57WA46232L. Assembly plant code: LA = Los Angeles; LP = Lincoln Plant; SL = St. Louis; WA = Wayne, Mich.

CAPRI

Model No.	Body/ Style No.	Body Type & Seating	Factory Price	Shipping Weight	Prod. Total
N/A	57A	4-dr Lan HT Sed-6P	5294	4538	1,451
N/A	58A	4-dr Sed-6P	2794	4349	1,476
N/A	60A	2-dr HT Cpe-6P	4649	4373	2,973

PREMIERE SERIES — Except for the nameplate and star medallion on the front fenders, exterior differences between the Premiere and Capri were nil. Advertising promoted the 300-hp V-8 as a 'safety feature'. Power seats, power steering, electric windows and power brakes were standard.

1957 Lincoln Capri two-door hardtop V-8. (OCW)

1957 Lincoln Premiere Landau four-door hardtop V-8. (AA)

PREMIERE

Model No.	Body/Style No.	Body Type & Seating	Factory Price	Shipping Weight	Prod. Total
N/A	57B	4-dr Lan HT Sed-6P	5294	4538	11,223
N/A	58B	4-dr Sed-6P	5294	4527	5,139
N/A	60B	2-dr HT Cpe-6P	5149	4451	15,185
N/A	76B	2-dr Conv-6P	5381	4676	3,676

MARK II SERIES — This was the second and last year for the beautiful Mark II. Outside of a slightly lighter frame, it was identical to the previous year's model. Two convertibles were specially built. Power steering, power brakes, carpeting, radio, heater, power seats, power windows and whitewall tires were standard.

MARK II

Model No.	Body/Style No.	Body Type & Seating	Factory Price	Shipping Weight	Prod. Total
N/A	60A	2-dr HT Spt Cpe-6P	9695	4797	444
N/A	76A	2-dr Conv-4P	10,000	N/A	2

ENGINE [Base V-8]: Overhead valve. Cast-iron block. Displacement: 368 cid. Bore and stroke: 4.00 x 3.65 inches. Compression ratio: 10.0:1. Brake hp: 300 at 4800 rpm. Carburetor: Carter four-barrel.

1957 Lincoln Premiere two-door convertible V-8. (PH)

1957 Lincoln Continental Mark II two-door hardtop V-8. (AA)

ENGINE [Mark II V-8]: Overhead valve. Cast-iron block. Displacement: 368 cid. Bore and stroke: 4.00 x 3.65 inches. Compression ratio: 10.0:1. Brake hp: 300 at 4800 rpm. Carburetor: Carter four-barrel.

CHASSIS FEATURES: [Lincoln] Wheelbase: 126 inches. Overall length: 224.6 inches. Front tread: 58.5 inches. Rear tread: 60 inches. Tires: 8.00 x 15; (convertible and with air conditioning) 8.20 x 15. [Mark II] Wheelbase: 126 inches. Overall length: 218.5 inches. Overall width: 77.5 inches. Tires: 8.00 x 15; (with air conditioning) 8.20 x 15.

CONVENIENCE OPTIONS: [Lincoln] Air conditioning. Tinted glass. Whitewall tires. Front license plate frame. Padded instrument panel. Seat belts. Spotlight. Power vent windows. Three-tone leather trim. Six-Way power seat. Auxiliary driving lights. Electric door locks. Automatic headlight dimmer. Town and Country radio. Power radio antenna. Push-button lubrication. Dual control heater. Padded sun visors. Directed power differential. [Mark II] Air conditioning.

HISTORY: Only 22 percent of 1957 Lincolns came equipped with air conditioning.

1958 LINCOLN

1958 Lincoln Premiere Landau four-door hardtop V-8. (OCW)

CAPRI SERIES — The Capri was totally restyled for 1958. It had a unique roof design, slanting headlight pods, stylized front and rear bumpers and wraparound front and rear windows. The grille was mainly horizontal, with several vertical accent bars that seemed to make the car look wider than it already was. The side chrome spears were lower and not as long as those used on the previous year's model. Automatic transmission; power steering; power brakes; windshield washers; padded instrument panel and a V-8 engine were standard on all 1958 Lincolns.

LINCOLN I.D. NUMBERS: Serial numbers ranged from H8Y()400001 to H8Y()429624. The first letter (H) stood for the 430 cid V-8 with four-barrel carburetor. The first letter (J) stood for the same engine with three two-barrel carburetors. The second digit (8) referred to the year (1958). The 'Y' referred to the Wixom, Mich., assembly plant. The fourth digit indicated the series and body styles as follows: 'A' = 1958-1959 Capri two-door hardtop; 1959 four-door sedan; 1959 four-door hardtop sedan. 'B' = 1958 Capri four-door hardtop; 1959 Premiere four-door sedan; 1959 Premiere four-door hardtop; 1959 Premiere two-door hardtop; 1959 Continental. 'D' = 1959 Premiere four-door hardtop. 'E' or 'F' = 1958 Continental two-door hardtop. 'K' = Capri four-door sedan. 'L' = 1958 Premiere four-door sedan. 'M' = 1958 Continental four-door sedan. The fifth digit ('4') refers to the Lincoln Division. The last five digits are the production numbers.

CAPRI SERIES

Model No.	Body/Style No.	Body Type & Seating	Factory Price	Shipping Weight	Prod. Total
N/A	53A	4-dr Sed-6P	4951	4799	1,184
N/A	57A	4-dr Lan HT Sed-6P	4951	4810	3,084
N/A	63A	2-dr HT Cpe-6P	4803	4735	2,591

PREMIERE SERIES — A chrome rocker panel, a star at the forward tip of the side chrome spear and its distinct nameplate were the easiest ways to tell the Premiere series from the lower-priced Capri. Buyers could get either leather and fabric or all-fabric upholstery.

PREMIERE SERIES

Model No.	Body/Style No.	Body Type & Seating	Factory Price	Shipping Weight	Prod. Total
N/A	53B	4-dr Sed-6P	5505	4802	1,660
N/A	57B	4-dr HT Sed-6P	5505	4798	5,572
N/A	63B	2-dr HT Cpe-6P	5259	4734	3,043

1958 Lincoln Continental Mark III two-door convertible V-8. (OCW)

CONTINENTAL MARK III — The Mark II of 1956-1957 had as much in common with the new Mark III as a thoroughbred Kentucky Derby winner has with TV's "Mr. Ed," the talking horse. A criss-cross pattern aluminum grille, full-length lower-body molding and a grid pattern rear panel were exclusive to the Mark III. The coupe and four-door had an unusual rear window that could be lowered. The coupe's roof style was shared with the convertible. The Mark III had the same standard equipment as Premieres and Capris.

CONTINENTAL SERIES

Model No.	Body/ Style No.	Body Type & Seating	Factory Price	Shipping Weight	Prod. Total
N/A	54A	4-dr Sed-6P	6012	4888	1,283
N/A	65A	2-dr HT Cpe-6P	5765	4802	2,328
N/A	68A	2-dr Conv-6P	6223	4927	3,048
N/A	75A	4-dr HT Sed-6P	6012	4884	5,891

ENGINE [V-8]: Overhead valve. Cast-iron block. Displacement: 430 cid. Bore and stroke: 4.29 x 3.70 inches. Compression ratio: 10.5:1. Brake hp: 375 at 4800 rpm. Carburetor: Holley 4150 four-barrel.

CHASSIS FEATURES: Wheelbase: 131 inches. Overall length: 229 inches. Tires: 9.00 x 14; [Optional on Mark III] 9.50 x 14.

OPTIONS: Special paint ($39.10). Air conditioner and heater ($610.70). Power windows ($120.40). Power vent windows ($66). Power Six-Way seat over manual ($106.50). Six-Way power seat over Four-Way ($45.20). Whitewall tires, five, rayon ($55.50); five nylon whitewall tires ($85.40). Tinted glass ($48.40). Automatic headlight dimmer ($49.50). Translucent sun visors ($26.90). Power lubricator ($43). Leather interior, except standard in convertible ($100). Seat belts ($23.70). Air suspension. Directed power differential. A 430 cid V-8 with three two-barrel carburetors and 400 hp at 4600 rpm was available at extra cost.

HISTORY: One of the least popular options in 1958 was air suspension. Only two percent of Lincolns came with it. Lincoln switched to unitized body construction this year. The chassis was eliminated. The suspension, driveline and engine units were fastened to the body structure.

1959 LINCOLN

CAPRI SERIES — The 1959 Capri was a couple of inches shorter than the previous year's model but at 227 inches, nobody confused it with a Rambler American. The canted headlights were integrated into the restyled grille. Side chrome was a bit gaudier. Brushed-aluminum trim covered the lower quarter panel and was connected to a chrome spear above the rear tires, which continued almost to the front fender. The rear panel pattern was redesigned.

LINCOLN I.D. NUMBERS: Serial numbers ranged from H9Y()400001 and up. The first letter (H) stood for the 430 cid V-8 with four-barrel carburetor. The first letter (J) stood for the same engine with three

two-barrel carburetors. The second digit (9) referred to the year (1959). The 'Y' referred to the Wixom, Mich., assembly plant. The fourth digit indicated the series and body styles as follows: 'A' = 1958-1959 Capri two-door hardtop; 1959 four-door sedan; 1959 four-door hardtop sedan. 'B' = 1958 Capri four-door hardtop; 1959 Premiere four-door sedan; 1959 Premiere four-door hardtop; 1959 Premiere two-door hardtop; 1959 Continental. 'D' = 1959 Premiere four-door hardtop. 'E' or 'F' = 1958 Continental two-door hardtop. 'K' = 1958 Capri four-door sedan. 'L' = 1958 Premiere four-door sedan. 'M' = 1958 Continental four-door sedan. The fifth digit ('4') refers to the Lincoln Division. The last five digits are the production numbers.

CAPRI SERIES

Model No.	Body/ Style No.	Body Type & Seating	Factory Price	Shipping Weight	Prod. Total
N/A	53A	4-dr Sed-6P	5090	5030	1,312
N/A	57A	4-dr HT Sed-6P	5090	5000	4,417
N/A	63A	2-dr HT Cpe-6P	4902	4925	2,200

PREMIERE SERIES — Once again, the best way to identify a Premiere was to look for its nameplate. On the outside, it looked the same as the lowest-priced Lincoln series. All 1959 Lincolns were equipped with automatic transmission; power brakes; power steering; dual exhaust; electric clock; windshield washer and remote-control outside mirror. In addition, Premieres came with power windows, rear license plate frame and Four-Way power front seat.

PREMIERE SERIES

Model No.	Body/ Style No.	Body Type & Seating	Factory Price	Shipping Weight	Prod. Total
N/A	53B	4-dr Sed-6P	5594	5030	1,282
N/A	57B	4-dr HT Sed-6P	5594	5015	4,606
N/A	63B	2-dr HT Cpe-6P	5347	4920	1,963

1959 Lincoln Premiere four-door hardtop sedan V-8 (PH).

1959 Lincoln Premiere two-door hardtop V-8. (OCW)

1959 Lincoln Continental Mark IV two-door convertible V-8. (OCW)

1959 Lincoln Continental Mark IV Landau four-door hardtop V-8. (OCW)

1959 Lincoln Continental Mark IV four-door Executive Limousine V-8. (PH)

CONTINENTAL MARK IV — The Mark IV featured a criss-cross pattern grille, full-length lower body molding (but no side spear), four taillights and reverse slant rear window that could be lowered. Even the back window of the convertible was made of glass and was retractable. Mark IVs were equipped with Six-Way power seats; tinted glass; Travel-Tuner radio with dual speakers; power vent windows and were available in three metallic paints exclusive to the series.

CONTINENTAL SERIES

Model No.	Body/ Style No.	Body Type & Seating	Factory Price	Shipping Weight	Prod. Total
N/A	23A	4-dr Exec Limo-6P	10,230	5450	49
N/A	23B	4-dr Fml Sed-6P	9208	5450	78
N/A	54A	4-dr Sed-6P	6845	5155	955
N/A	65A	2-dr HT Cpe-6P	6598	5050	1,703
N/A	68A	2-dr Conv-6P	7056	5175	2,195
N/A	75A	4-dr HT Sed-6P	6845	5155	6,146

ENGINE [V-8]: Overhead valve. Cast-iron block. Displacement: 430 cid. Bore and stroke: 4.29 x 3.70 inches. Compression ratio: 10.0:1. Brake hp: 350 at 4400 rpm. Carburetor: Carter AFB-2853S four-barrel.

CHASSIS FEATURES: Wheelbase: 131 inches. Overall length: 227.1 inches. Tires: 9.50 x 14.

OPTIONS: Travel Tuner radio ($144.20). FM tuner radio ($114). Leather upholstery ($85). Remote control trunk release ($40). Power lubricator ($40). Electronic headlight dimmer ($51). Power vents ($65). Six-Way power seats ($98). Tinted glass ($48). Power windows ($94.70). Air conditioner with heater ($385). Directed power differential ($52).

HISTORY: Almost all 1959 Lincolns (99.6 percent) had a radio and 40.8 percent came with an air conditioner.

1960 LINCOLN

LINCOLN SERIES — The biggest changes for 1960 were a full-length mid-body chrome spear; larger tailfins wrapped in chrome; new instrument panel; altered horizontal theme grille; more conventional style front bumper and Ford-like square roofline. The back-up and taillights were rectangular. All 1960 Lincolns came with power brakes; power steering; heater and defroster; undercoating; whitewall tires; clock; radio; windshield washer; padded dash; center rear armrest and dual exhaust.

LINCOLN I.D. NUMBERS: Lincoln serial numbers contained 11 digits. The first indicated model year, as follows: '0' = 1960. The second indicated the assembly plant as follows: 'Y' = Wixom, Mich.; 'S' = Allen Park, Mich. The third and fourth digits referred to the series and Body/ model numbers. The fifth indicated engine as follows: 430 cid V-8 with two-barrel carb. The last six digits were the sequential vehicle production numbers.

LINCOLN SERIES

Model No.	Body/ Style No.	Body Type & Seating	Factory Price	Shipping Weight	Prod. Total
N/A	53A	4-dr Sed-6P	5441	5016	1,093
N/A	57A	4-dr HT Sed-6P	5441	5012	4,397
N/A	63A	2-dr HT Cpe-6P	5253	4929	1,670

PREMIERE SERIES — The Premiere looked virtually the same as the standard Lincoln, except for a small front fender medallion. All Premieres came with power windows, rear compartment reading lights and four-way power seats.

PREMIERE SERIES

Model No.	Body/ Style No.	Body Type & Seating	Factory Price	Shipping Weight	Prod. Total
N/A	53B	4-dr Sed-6P	5945	5072	1,010
N/A	57B	4-dr HT Sed-6P	5945	5068	4,200
N/A	63B	2-dr HT Cpe-6P	5696	4987	1,364

CONTINENTAL MARK V — A criss-cross "dot-in-a-square" pattern grille; circular tail and back-up lights; lower front fender chrome bars and a reverse slanted, retractable rear window, set the top-of-the-line Mark V apart from the other series. Standard features included a Six-Way power seat, tinted glass and power vent windows.

CONTINENTAL SERIES

Model No.	Body/ Style No.	Body Type & Seating	Factory Price	Shipping Weight	Prod. Total
N/A	23A	4-dr Exec Limo-6P	10,230	5495	34
N/A	23B	4-dr Town Car-6P	9207	5286	136
N/A	54A	4-dr Sed-6P	6854	5157	807
N/A	65A	2-dr HT Cpe-6P	6598	5070	1,461
N/A	68A	2-dr Conv-6P	7056	5176	2,044
N/A	75A	4-dr HT Sed-6P	6845	5153	6,604

ENGINE [V-8]: Overhead valve. Cast-iron block. Displacement: 430 cid. Bore and stroke: 4.29 x 3.70 inches. Compression ratio: 10.0:1. Brake hp: 315 at 4100 rpm. Carburetor: Carter ABD-2965S two-barrel.

CHASSIS FEATURES: Wheelbase: 131 inches. Overall length: 227.2 inches. Overall width: 80.3 inches. Tires: 9.50 x 14.

1959 Lincoln Continental convertible. (OCW)

1960 Lincoln Continental Mark V four-door Executive Limousine V-8. (OCW)

1960 Lincoln Continental Mark V two-door convertible V-8. (OCW)

OPTIONS: Air conditioner with heater ($475.20). Electronic headlight dimmer ($56). Electric door locks, on two-doors ($39.45); on four-doors ($63.65). Power lubricator ($46.90). FM radio attachment ($129). Four-Way power seat ($87). Six-Way power seat, over a manual seat ($118.95). Six-Way power seat over a Four-Way power seat ($49.50). Power vent windows ($75.60). Remote control trunk lid ($45.60). Chrome curb guard ($26.90). Directed power differential ($57.50).

HISTORY: Almost half of all 1960 Lincolns (49 percent) came equipped with an air conditioner. Lincolns had a new Hotchkiss rear suspension.

1961 LINCOLN

1961 Lincoln Continental convertible. (OCW)

CONTINENTAL SERIES — For 1961, only one Lincoln series was offered, the Lincoln-Continental. And what a series it was! Once again, Lincoln proved it could produce a strikingly beautiful car. The 1961 Continental became one of the most influential automobile designs of the 1960s. The four headlights were embedded in a criss-cross pattern grille (with emphasis on the horizontal bars). The front and rear wraparound bumpers blended well into the overall design. Side trim was limited to full-length upper body molding and a chrome rocker panel. The rear doors opened to the center. All 1961 Continentals had automatic transmission; a radio with rear speaker; heater; power brakes; power steering; power windows; walnut applique or padded instrument panel; carpeting and power door locks.

LINCOLN I.D. NUMBERS: The Vehicle Identification Number is stamped on the right inner fender apron under hood. First symbol: 1=1961. Second symbol indicates assembly plant: Y=Wixom, Mich. Third and fourth symbols indicate model and series: 82 = Continental sedan; 86 = Continental convertible. Fifth symbol indicates engine: H=430 cid/300 hp V-8 and K=low-compression Export version of 430 cid V-8. Last six symbols are sequential production number. Body plate riveted to front body pillar between door hinges gives body, color, trim, date, engine, transmission and axle codes.

1961 Lincoln Continental four-door sedan V-8. (OCW)

CONTINENTAL SERIES

Model No.	Body/ Style No.	Body Type & Seating	Factory Price	Shipping Weight	Prod. Total
82	53A	4-dr Sed-6P	6067	4927	22,303
86	74A	4-dr Conv-6P	6713	5215	2,857

ENGINE [V-8]: Overhead valve. Cast-iron block. Displacement: 430 cid. Bore and stroke: 4.29 x 3.70 inches. Compression ratio: 10.0:1. Brake hp: 300 at 4100 rpm. Carburetor: Carter ABD two-barrel.

CHASSIS FEATURES: Wheelbase: 123 inches. Overall length: 212.4 inches. Tires: (sedan) 9.00 x 14; (convertible) 9.50 x 14.

OPTIONS: Air conditioner with heater ($504.60). Six-Way power seat ($118.95). Speed control ($96.80). Special interior trim ($100). Tinted glass ($53.65). Directed power differential ($57.50).

HISTORY: Sixty-five percent of 1961 Continentals were equipped with an air conditioner. Every new Continental underwent a 12-mile road test before it left the factory. The Industrial Design Institute awarded the designers of the 1961 Lincoln-Continental a bronze medal. Few other automobiles have ever been so honored.

1962 LINCOLN

1962 Lincoln Continental four-door convertible V-8. (OCW)

CONTINENTAL SERIES — Removal of the front bumper guards, the use of a new type of individual headlight trim, a narrower center grille bar and a semi-honeycomb style grille treatment (repeated on the rear panel) were the main changes for 1962. The new Continentals were also slightly lower, longer and narrower than the 1961 models. Broadcloth upholstery was standard in the sedan, all-vinyl in the convertible. Such as the previous year's model, the convertible top retracted into the trunk. All Continentals had power brakes; automatic transmission; power steering; power windows; a radio with a rear speaker; carpeting; electric clock; power door locks; walnut applique or padded instrument panel; dual exhaust and folding center armrests.

LINCOLN I.D. NUMBERS: The Vehicle Identification Number is stamped on the right inner fender apron under hood. First symbol: 2=1962. Second symbol indicates assembly plant: Y=Wixom, Mich.

Third and fourth symbols indicate model and series: 82=Continental sedan; 86=Continental convertible. Fifth symbol indicates engine: H=430 cid/300 hp V-8 and K=low-compression Export version of 430 cid V-8. Last six symbols are sequential production number. Body plate riveted to front body pillar between door hinges gives body, color, trim, date, engine, transmission and axle codes.

CONTINENTAL SERIES

Model No.	Body/ Style No.	Body Type & Seating	Factory Price	Shipping Weight	Prod. Total
82	53A	4-dr Sed-6P	6074	4929	27,849
86	74A	4-dr Conv-6P	6720	5213	3,212

NOTE 1: Four Lincoln-Continental four-door hardtops (model number 84, body code 57C) may have been built.

ENGINE [V-8]: Overhead valve. Cast-iron block. Displacement: 430 cid. Bore and stroke: 4.29 x 3.70 inches. Compression ratio: 10.0:1. Brake hp: 300 at 4100 rpm. Carburetor: Carter ABD two-barrel.

CHASSIS FEATURES: Wheelbase: 123 inches. Overall length: 213 inches. Tires: (sedan) 9.00 x 14; (convertible) 9.50 x 14.

OPTIONS: Air conditioner and heater ($505.60). Automatic headlight dimmer ($45.60). Special interior trim ($100). Power vent windows ($75.60). Electric radio antenna ($32.60). Automatic trunk release ($53.40). Six-Way power seat ($118.95). Speed control ($96.80). Tinted glass ($53.65). Directed power differential ($57.50).

HISTORY: Almost three out of four 1962 Continentals were sold with air conditioning, 96 percent came with power seats.

1963 LINCOLN

1963 Lincoln Continental four-door sedan V-8. (OCW)

CONTINENTAL SERIES — A different rear panel design and new grille treatment were the main changes for 1963. The Continental was also about a third of an inch longer. The dash was changed slightly to give more knee room. All new Continentals came equipped with automatic transmission; power brakes; power windows; heater; Six-Way power seat; power radio antenna; radio with rear speaker; dual exhaust; carpeting; electric clock; power steering; walnut applique or padded instrument panel; power vent windows; chrome curb guards; visor vanity mirror; remote control outside rearview mirror and power door locks.

LINCOLN I.D. NUMBERS: The Vehicle Identification Number is stamped on the right inner fender apron under hood. First symbol: 3=1963. Second symbol indicates assembly plant: Y=Wixom, Mich. Third and fourth symbols indicate model and series: 82=Continental sedan; 86=Continental convertible. Fifth symbol indicates engine: N=430 cid/320 hp V-8 and 7=low-compression Export version of 430 cid V-8. Last six symbols are sequential production number. Body plate riveted to front body pillar between door hinges gives body, color, trim, date, engine, transmission and axle codes.

1963 Lincoln Continental four-door convertible V-8. (OCW)

CONTINENTAL

Model No.	Body/ Style No.	Body Type & Seating	Factory Price	Shipping Weight	Prod. Total
82	53A	4-dr Sed-6P	6270	4950	28,095
86	74A	4-dr Conv-6P	6916	5360	3,138

ENGINE [V-8]: Overhead valve. Cast-iron block. Displacement: 430 cid. Bore and stroke: 4.29 x 3.70 inches. Compression ratio: 10.0:1. Brake hp: 320 at 4600 rpm. Carburetor: Carter AFB four-barrel.

CHASSIS FEATURES: Wheelbase: 123 inches. Overall length: 213.3 inches. Tires: (sedan) 9.00 x 14; (convertible) 9.50 x 14.

OPTIONS: Air conditioner and heater ($504.60). Tinted glass ($53.65). Power trunk lock ($53.40). Speed control ($96.80). Front seat belts ($16.80). Automatic headlight dimmer ($45.60). AM/FM push-button radio ($84.70). Special leather trim, except standard in convertible ($100). Directed power differential ($57.50).

HISTORY: Seventy-three percent of all 1963 Continentals had air conditioners, 94.4 percent had tinted glass and 20.6 percent had a locking differential.

1964 LINCOLN

1964 Lincoln Continental four-door convertible V-8. (PH)

CONTINENTAL SERIES — The Continental grew a bit in 1964. Still, styling changes continued to be mild. Among them were a new dash; full-length lower body molding; flat side glass; horizontal theme rear end trim and the replacement of the thick center grille bar, formerly connecting the headlights, by five vertical bars. All Continentals were equipped with automatic transmission; radio; power seats; power windows; power brakes and power steering.

LINCOLN I.D. NUMBERS: The Vehicle Identification Number is stamped on the right inner fender apron under hood. First symbol: 4=1964. Second symbol indicates assembly plant: Y=Wixom, Mich. Third and fourth symbols indicate model and series: 82=Continental sedan; 86=Continental convertible. Fifth symbol indicates engine: N=430 cid/320 hp V-8 and 7=low-compression Export version of 430 cid V-8. Last six symbols are sequential production number. Body plate riveted to front body pillar between door hinges gives body, color, trim, date, engine, transmission and axle codes.

CONTINENTAL

Model No.	Body/ Style No.	Body Type & Seating	Factory Price	Shipping Weight	Prod. Total
82	53A	4-dr Sed-6P	6292	5055	32,969
86	74A	4-dr Conv-6P	6938	5393	3,328

ENGINE [V-8]: Overhead valve. Cast-iron block. Displacement: 430 cid. Bore and stroke: 4.29 x 3.70 inches. Compression ratio: 10.0:1. Brake hp: 320 at 4600 rpm. Carburetor: Carter C3VE-9510B four-barrel.

1964 Lincoln Continental four-door sedan V-8. (OCW)

CHASSIS FEATURES: Wheelbase: 126 inches. Overall length: 216.3 inches. Width: 76.6 inches. Tires: 9.15 x 15.

OPTIONS: Air conditioner and heater ($504.60). Speed control ($96.80). Tinted glass ($53.65). AM/FM push-button radio ($84.70). Power trunk lock ($53.40). Automatic headlight dimmer ($45.60). Movable steering wheel. Directed power differential.

HISTORY: One of the least popular Lincoln options in 1964 was the movable steering wheel. Only seven percent of the cars came with this feature.

1965 LINCOLN

1965 Lincoln Continental convertible. (OCW)

CONTINENTAL SERIES — The Continental received a relatively major face lift in 1965. Although basic styling remained the same, it had a flat horizontal grille theme and wraparound signal lights. The hood was also new. Among the many standard features were automatic transmission; power steering; dual exhaust; visor vanity mirror; trip odometer; transistorized radio with rear speaker; undercoating; walnut applique or padded instrument panel; heater and defroster; Six-Way power seat; power radio antenna; remote control outside rearview mirror; power brakes; carpeting; windshield washer and power door locks.

LINCOLN I.D. NUMBERS: The Vehicle Identification Number is stamped on the right inner fender apron under hood. First symbol: 5=1965. Second symbol indicates assembly plant: Y=Wixom, Mich. Third and fourth symbols indicate model and series: 82=Continental sedan; 86=Continental convertible. Fifth symbol indicates engine: N=430 cid/320 hp V-8 and 7=low-compression Export version of 430 cid V-8. Last six symbols are sequential production number. Body plate riveted to front body pillar between door hinges gives body, color, trim, date, engine, transmission and axle codes.

CONTINENTAL

Model No.	Body/ Style No.	Body Type & Seating	Factory Price	Shipping Weight	Prod. Total
82	53A	4-dr Sed-6P	6292	5075	36,824
86	74A	4-dr Conv-6P	6798	5475	3,356

ENGINE [V-8]: Overhead valve. Cast-iron block. Displacement: 430 cid. Bore and stroke: 4.29 x 3.70 inches. Compression ratio: 10.0:1. Brake hp: 320 at 4600 rpm. Carburetor: Carter C3VE-9510B four-barrel.

CHASSIS FEATURES: Wheelbase: 126 inches. Overall length: 216.3 inches. Width: 78.6 inches. Tires: 9.15 x 15.

1965 Lincoln Continental four-door sedan V-8. (OCW)

OPTIONS: Air conditioner and heater ($504.50). Vinyl roof ($104.30). Individually adjustable front seats ($281.40). Power trunk lock ($53.40). Automatic headlight dimmer ($45.60). Emergency flasher ($12.80). AM/FM push-button radio ($84.70). Speed control ($96.80). Movable steering wheel ($60.00). Special leather trim, except standard in convertible ($100). Tinted glass ($53.65). Door edge guards ($6.90). Closed crankcase emission reduction system ($5.30). Directed power differential ($57.50).

HISTORY: Only about one in four 1965 Continentals had a movable steering wheel, but 90.6 percent were sold with air conditioning.

1966 LINCOLN

1966 Lincoln Continental two-door hardtop V-8. (PH)

CONTINENTAL SERIES — The Continental grew another four inches in 1966. The turn signals returned to the bumper, which now extended to the front tire openings. An emblem was on the front fender above the bumper. For the first time in five years, the taillights did not wrap around the rear fenders. Other changes included a return to curved side glass and a new instrument panel. Among the many standard features were automatic transmission; power seats; power steering; front disc brakes; power windows; carpeting and windshield washer.

LINCOLN I.D. NUMBERS: The Vehicle Identification Number is stamped on the right inner fender apron under hood. First symbol: 6=1966. Second symbol indicates assembly plant: Y=Wixom, Mich. Third and fourth symbols indicate model and series: 82=Continental sedan; 86=Continental convertible; 89=Continental two-door hardtop. Fifth symbol indicates engine: G=462 cid/340 hp V-8. Last six symbols are sequential production number. Body plate riveted to front body pillar between door hinges gives body, color, trim, date, engine, transmission and axle codes.

1966 Lincoln Continental four-door convertible V-8. (OCW)

1966 Lincoln Continental. (OCW)

1966 Lincoln Continental four-door sedan V-8. (OCW)

CONTINENTAL

Model No.	Body/ Style No.	Body Type & Seating	Factory Price	Shipping Weight	Prod. Total
82	53A	4-dr Sed-6P	5750	5085	35,809
86	74A	4-dr Conv-6P	6383	5480	3,180
89	65A	2-dr HT Cpe-6P	5485	4985	15,766

ENGINE [V-8]: Overhead valve. Cast-iron block. Displacement: 462 cid. Bore and stroke: 4.38 x 3.83 inches. Compression ratio: 10.25:1. Brake hp: 340 at 4600 rpm. Carburetor: Carter C6VF-9510B four-barrel.

CHASSIS FEATURES: Wheelbase: 126 inches. Overall length: 220.9 inches. Width: 79.7 inches. Tires: 9.15 x 15.

OPTIONS: Air conditioner and heater ($504.60). Vinyl roof ($104.30). Individually adjustable front seats ($281.40). Power trunk lock ($53.40). Automatic headlight dimmer ($45.60). AM/FM push-button radio ($84.70). Speed control ($96.80). Movable steering wheel ($60.00). Tinted glass ($53.65). Directed power differential. 3.00:1 rear axle were optional.

HISTORY: Slightly more than one in three Continentals had a movable steering wheel, 93.5 percent came with air conditioning, 14.3 percent with a locking differential and 97.7 percent with tinted glass.

1967 LINCOLN

1967 Lincoln Continental two-door hardtop V-8 (PH).

1967 Lincoln Continental four-door sedan V-8. (OCW)

CONTINENTAL SERIES — Styling changes for 1967 were minor. Once again the center section of the grille was slightly protruding. The grille pattern featured horizontal bars accentuated by vertical ones. All new Continentals were equipped with automatic transmissions; power steering; power brakes; power windows; visor vanity mirror; trip odometer; front and rear seat belts; Two-Way power seat; dual exhaust; carpeting; electric clock; remote control outside mirror; windshield washer and heater and defroster. The convertible also had leather trim, remote control trunk release and rear glass window.

LINCOLN I.D. NUMBERS: The Vehicle Identification Number is stamped on the right inner fender apron under hood. First symbol: 7=1967. Second symbol indicates assembly plant: Y=Wixom, Mich. Third and fourth symbols indicate model and series: 82=Continental sedan; 86=Continental convertible; 89=Continental two-door hardtop. Fifth symbol indicates engine: G=462 cid/340 hp V-8; 7=Export version. Last six symbols are sequential production number. Body plate riveted to front body pillar between door hinges gives body, color, trim, date, engine, transmission and axle codes.

CONTINENTAL

Model No.	Body/ Style No.	Body Type & Seating	Factory Price	Shipping Weight	Prod. Total
82	53A	4-dr Sed-6P	5795	5049	32,331
86	74A	4-dr Conv-6P	6449	5505	2,276
89	65A	2-dr HT Cpe-6P	5553	4940	11,060

ENGINE [V-8]: Overhead valve. Cast-iron block. Displacement: 462 cid. Bore and stroke: 4.38 x 3.83 inches. Compression ratio: 10.25:1. Brake hp: 340 at 4600 rpm. Carburetor: Carter 4362 four-barrel.

CHASSIS FEATURES: Wheelbase: 126 inches. Overall length: 220.9 inches. Width: 79.7 inches. Tires: 9.15 x 15.

POWERTRAIN OPTIONS: SelectShift Turbo Drive automatic transmission was standard. Directed power differential and a high torque axle were optional at extra cost.

1967 Lincoln Continental Lehman-Peterson four-door limousine V-8. (OCW)

1967 Lincoln Continental. (OCW)

OPTIONS: Manual air conditioner ($471.05). Air conditioner with automatic temperature control ($523.55). Leather with vinyl trim, standard in convertible ($124.30). Automatic headlight dimmer ($50.05). Emission control exhaust ($50). Speed actuated power door locks, in convertible and sedan ($68.50); in coupe ($44.85). Six-Way power seat ($83.23). Six-Way power seat with passenger side recliner and power adjustable headrest ($181.68). Two-Way contour power seat, individually adjustable, with passenger side recliner ($290.58). Individually adjustable power contour seat, Six-Way for driver, Two-Way reclining for passenger ($373.86). Power vent windows ($71.64). AM radio with power antenna ($161.27). AM/FM signal seeking radio with power antenna ($244.54). AM radio and stereosonic tape system with power antenna ($244.54). Shoulder belts ($32). Embassy roof for coupe ($131.60); for sedan ($136.85). Tilting steering wheel ($58.74). Remote control trunk release with warning light ($33.19). Tinted glass ($52.53). Speed control ($94.77).

HISTORY: Most 1967 Continentals, 96.5 percent, were sold with air conditioning.

CONTINENTAL SERIES — A new hood accentuated the protruding center section of the 1968 Lincoln-Continental grille. Wraparound signal lights, similar to those on the 1965 models, and wraparound taillights resumed. Otherwise, styling was little changed from the previous year. All 1968 Continentals were equipped with automatic transmission; power steering; seat belts; remote-control outside rearview mirror; windshield washer; power windows; dual exhaust; electric clock; padded instrument panel; four-way emergency flashers; power disc brakes and Two-Way power seat.

LINCOLN I.D. NUMBERS: The Vehicle Identification Number is on a tag on the dashboard, visible through windshield. First symbol: 8=1968. Second symbol indicates assembly plant: Y=Wixom, Mich. Third and fourth symbols indicate model and series: 82=Continental sedan; 80=Continental two-door hardtop; 89=Mark III two-door hardtop. Fifth symbol indicates engine: A=460 cid/365 hp V-8; 1=Export version of 460 cid V-8; G=462 cid/340 hp V-8; 7=462 cid Export V-8. Last six symbols are sequential production number. Body plate riveted to front body pillar between door hinges gives body, color, trim, date, engine, transmission and axle codes.

CONTINENTAL

Model No.	Body/ Style No.	Body Type & Seating	Factory Price	Shipping Weight	Prod. Total
80	65A	2-dr HT Cpe-6P	5736	4883	9,415
82	53A	4-dr Sed-6P	5970	4978	29,719

CONTINENTAL MARK III SERIES — The big news at Lincoln was the introduction of the Mark III. It arrived in April of 1968, as a 1969 model. It was a personal luxury car in the long hood, short deck tradition. The rear deck spare tire hump was also reminiscent of the first 'Mark'. Among the many standard features were all items available on the Continental, plus individually adjustable front seats; front and rear center folding armrests; Flow-Thru ventilation system and rear lamp monitoring system.

CONTINENTAL MARK III

Model No.	Body/ Style No.	Body Type & Seating	Factory Price	Shipping Weight	Prod. Total
89	65A	2-dr HT Cpe-5P	6585	4739	Note 1

NOTE 1: Mark III is considered a 1969 production vehicle; see 1969 for first year production total.

ENGINE [Base V-8]: Overhead valve. Cast-iron block. Displacement: 462 cid. Bore and stroke: 4.38 x 3.83 inches. Compression ratio: 10.25:1. Brake hp: 340 at 4600 rpm. Carburetor: Carter C8VF-9510E four-barrel.

ENGINE [Mark III V-8]: Overhead valve. Cast-iron block. Displacement: 460 cid. Bore and stroke: 4.36 x 3.85 inches. Compression ratio: 10.5:1. Brake hp: 365 at 4600 rpm. Carburetor: four-barrel.

CHASSIS FEATURES: Wheelbase: 126 inches. Overall length: 221 inches. Tires: 9.15 x 15.

OPTIONS: Manual control air conditioner ($503.90). Air conditioner with automatic temperature control ($523.55). Remote control right-hand outside mirror ($13.15). Automatic headlight dimmer ($50.05). Front seat shoulder belts ($32). Rear seat shoulder belts ($32). Tinted glass ($52.53). Rear window defogger ($42.50). Spare tire cover ($10.95). Manually adjustable head rests ($52.50). Power door locks in coupe ($47.45); in sedan ($68.50). Combination AM radio with stereosonic tape system, including two front and rear speakers and power antenna ($244.54). AM/FM signal-seeking radio with power antenna ($244.54). Vinyl covered roof ($136.85). Automatic ride leveler suspension ($97.15). Individually adjustable contour seats with Six-Way power for driver, Two-Way power reclining passenger side ($334.46). Six-Way power bench seat ($83.28). Six-Way power seat with reclining passenger side ($142.28). Tilting steering wheel ($66.95). Speed control ($94.77). Powervent windows ($71.64). Stereosonic tape system ($130.10). Leather with vinyl trim ($137.26). Five four-ply dual chamber whitewall tires ($196.80). Directed power differential. High torque (3.00:1) axle.

HISTORY: Most 1968 Lincolns, 75.6 percent, had a vinyl top, 98.7 percent had air conditioning and 99.3 percent came with tinted glass. The one-millionth Lincoln, a four-door sedan, was built this year. The new Continental Mark III was introduced in April 1968.

1968 Lincoln Continental two-door hardtop V-8. (OCW)

CONTINENTAL SERIES — The most noticeable changes made to the 1969 Lincoln were a revised grille pattern and the appearance of the Continental name printed above the grille. This was the last year the basic 1961 Continental body shell (and unit body construction) was used. Among the standard features were automatic transmission; power steering; power brakes; self-adjusting front disc brakes; dual exhaust; vanity mirror; power windows and Two-Way power seat.

LINCOLN I.D. NUMBERS: The Vehicle Identification Number is on a tag on the dashboard, visible through windshield. First symbol: 9=1969. Second symbol indicates assembly plant: Y=Wixom, Mich. Third and fourth symbols indicate model and series: 82=Continental sedan; 80=Continental two-door hardtop; 89=Mark III two-door hardtop. Fifth symbol indicates engine: A=460 cid/365 hp V-8. Last six symbols are sequential production number. Body plate riveted to front body pillar between door hinges gives body, color, trim, date, engine, transmission and axle codes.

CONTINENTAL

Model No.	Body/ Style No.	Body Type & Seating	Factory Price	Shipping Weight	Prod. Total
80	65A	2-dr HT Cpe-6P	5813	4916	9,032
82	53A	4-dr Sed-6P	6046	5011	29,351

CONTINENTAL MARK III SERIES — Production of the new Continental Mark III coupe continued from April 1968 without interruption, with all cars in the series considered 1969 models. The new car was a far cry from its namesake, the Mark III of 1958. Rather, it was a personal luxury car in the long hood, short deck tradition of the Mark I. The rear deck spare tire hump was also reminiscent of the first 'Mark'. However, basic styling was in tune with that of standard Lincolns. Among the many standard features offered on the Mark III were the same items available on the Continental plus individually adjustable front seats; front and rear center folding armrests; Flow-Thru ventilation system and rear lamp monitoring system.

1969 Lincoln Continental Mk III. (OCW)

CONTINENTAL MARK III

Model No.	Body/ Style No.	Body Type & Seating	Factory Price	Shipping Weight	Prod. Total
89	65A	2-dr HT Cpe-5P	6741	4475	30,858

ENGINE [V-8]: Overhead valve. Cast-iron block. Displacement: 460 cid. Bore and stroke: 4.36 x 3.85 inches. Compression ratio: 10.5:1. Brake hp: 365 at 4600 rpm. Carburetor: Autolite C8VF-9510J four-barrel.

CHASSIS FEATURES: Wheelbase: (Continental) 126 inches; (Mark III) 117.2 inches. Overall length: (Continental) 224 inches; (Mark III) 216 inches. Tires: (Continental) 9.15 x 15; (Mark III) 8.55 x 15.

OPTIONS: Manual air conditioner ($503.70). Automatic temperature control air conditioner ($523.30). Automatic headlight dimmer ($51.20). Rear window defogger with environment control in Continental ($42). Rear window defogger in Mark III ($26.30). Rear window defroster in Mark III ($85.30). Remote-control deck lid release ($40.70). Leather with vinyl interior ($137.80). Power door locks in two-doors ($47.30); in four-doors ($68.20). Six-Way power seat in Continental ($89.20). Six-Way power seat in Mark III ($179.70). Six-Way power seat with reclining passenger side seat, in Continental ($149.60); in Mark III ($238.70). Power vent windows in Continental ($72.20). AM radio with power antenna ($161.40). AM/FM signal seeking radio with power antenna in Continental ($244). AM radio/stereosonic tape system with power antenna, in Continental ($245.30); in Mark III ($258.40). AM/FM radio with power antenna, in Continental ($288.60); in Mark III ($326.60). Vinyl roof ($152.20). Individually adjustable seats, in Continental ($334.50). Speed control ($94.50). Sure-Track brake system in Mark III ($195.80). Tilting steering wheel ($72.20). Tinted glass ($56.40). Town Car interior in Continental ($249.20). Four-ply fiberglass belted 9.15 x 15 whitewall tires ($196.80). Directed power differential. High torque axle.

HISTORY: All but 0.3 percent of Mark IIIs had an air conditioner. Just over one in three came with a movable steering wheel. The vast majority of 1969 Continentals, 83.8 percent were sold with a vinyl roof.

1970 LINCOLN

1970 Lincoln Continental. (OCW)

1970 Lincoln Continental Mark III two-door hardtop V-8. (OCW)

CONTINENTAL SERIES — The Continental was restyled for 1970. A resemblance to past models was clearly evident. Hidden headlights, a protruding grille (with horizontal grille pieces) and wraparound front fenders gave it a sort of refined 'Batmobile' look. The Continental also had a new bumper-integrated taillight rear end treatment. The doors were wider on both the hardtop and sedan. The sedan's rear door now opened in the conventional way. Standard equipment included: automatic transmission; fender skirts; custom pin stripe; padded windshield pillar; map and reading lights; cut-pile carpeting; electric clock; vanity mirror; simulated woodgrain dash panel applique; power windows; power steering; power front disc brakes; front and rear ashtrays and cigarette lighters; Two-Way power bench seat and flashing side marker lights.

LINCOLN I.D. NUMBERS: The Vehicle Identification Number is on a tag on the dashboard, visible through windshield. First symbol: 9=1969. Second symbol indicates assembly plant: Y=Wixom, Mich. Third and fourth symbols indicate model and series: 82=Continental sedan; 80=Continental two-door hardtop; 89=Mark III two-door hardtop. Fifth symbol indicates engine: A=460 cid/365 hp V-8. Last six symbols are sequential production number. Body plate riveted to front body pillar between door hinges gives body, color, trim, date, engine, transmission and axle codes.

CONTINENTAL

Model No.	Body/ Style No.	Body Type & Seating	Factory Price	Shipping Weight	Prod. Total
81	65A	2-dr HT Cpe-6P	5976	4669	3,073
82	53A	4-dr Sed-6P	6211	4719	28,622

CONTINENTAL MARK III SERIES — The biggest changes in the 1970 Mark III were hidden windshield wipers and new wheel covers. The signal and taillights were also altered. The parking lights now remained on when the headlights were being used. Inside, the seats, door panels and steering wheel were redesigned. The previous diamond tufted seats and door panels were replaced with a crosshatched design. Extensive use of genuine walnut veneers were used in place of and in addition to the simulated rosewood or oak previously used. They were used on the instrument panel, front and rear side panels and the steering wheel. In addition to the items standard on the Continental, the Mark III also came equipped with: Sure-Track brake system; Cartier electric chronometer; head console with warning lights; spare tire cover; rear lamp monitor system and vinyl roof.

CONTINENTAL MARK III

Model No.	Body/ Style No.	Body Type & Seating	Factory Price	Shipping Weight	Prod. Total
89	65A	2-dr HT Cpe-6P	7281	4675	21,432

ENGINE [V-8]: Overhead valve. Cast-iron block. Displacement: 460 cid. Bore and stroke: 4.36 x 3.85 inches. Compression ratio: 10.5:1. Brake hp: 365 at 4600 rpm. Carburetor: four-barrel.

CHASSIS FEATURES: Wheelbase: (Continental) 127 inches; (Mark III) 117.2 inches. Overall length: (Continental) 224 inches; (Mark III) 216 inches. Tires: (Continental) 9.15 x 15; (Mark III) 225 x 15.

OPTIONS: Manual air conditioner ($503.70). Automatic temperature control air conditioner ($523.20). Automatic headlight dimmer ($51.20). Cross-Country ride package in Continental ($17.10). Automatic ride control ($97.10). Sun roof in Mark III ($459.10). Leather with vinyl interior, in Mark III ($164.00); in Continental ($157.40). 'Moondust' paint ($131.20). Remote control deck lid release in Mark III ($40.70). Power door locks in Mark III ($47.30). Six-Way power seat in Continental ($89.20); in Mark III ($179.70). Six-Way power seat with reclining passenger side seat, in Continental ($149.60); in Mark III ($242.70). Twin Comfort Six-Way/Two-Way power seats in Continental ($220.40). Twin Comfort Six-Way/Two-Way power seats with reclining passenger seat ($280.70). AM radio with power antenna ($161.40). AM/FM radio with power antenna ($301.70). AM radio with Stereosonic tape system and power antenna ($296.50). Traction Lok differential. High ratio rear axle.

HISTORY: All but four percent of 1970 Continentals came with an air conditioner and tinted glass. Most Marks IIIs, 83.9 percent, had a tilting steering wheel. Many chassis parts on Lincoln's new body, mounted on a frame construction, were interchangeable with full-size Mercurys and Fords. The 1970 Mark III was the first American car to come with steel-belted radial tires as standard equipment.

1971 LINCOLN

1971 Lincoln Continental. (OCW)

CONTINENTAL SERIES — Styling was little changed from 1970. Unlike the previous year, the grille's horizontal bars were not extended to the headlight covers. This toned down the front end a bit. Standard equipment included: automatic temperature control air conditioning; automatic transmission; power front disc brakes; power steering; Two-Way power seat; fender skirts; cut-pile carpeting; carpeted luggage compartment; folding center armrests in front and rear; remote-control outside mirror; vanity mirror; tinted glass; electric clock; trip odometer and power ventilation system.

LINCOLN I.D. NUMBERS: The Vehicle Identification Number is on a tag on the dashboard, visible through windshield. First symbol: 1=1971. Second symbol indicates assembly plant: Y=Wixom, Mich. Third and fourth symbols indicate model and series: 82=Continental sedan; 81=Continental two-door hardtop; 89=Mark III two-door hardtop. Fifth symbol indicates engine: A=460 cid/365 hp V-8. Last six symbols are sequential production number. Body plate riveted to front body pillar between door hinges gives body, color, trim, date, engine, transmission and axle codes.

CONTINENTAL

Model No.	Body/ Style No.	Body Type & Seating	Factory Price	Shipping Weight	Prod. Total
81	65A	2-dr HT Cpe-6P	7172	5032	8,205
82	53A	4-dr Sed-6P	7419	5072	27,346

CONTINENTAL MARK III SERIES — The Mark III was virtually unchanged for 1971. It had the same standard features as the Continental plus high-back front seats with individual armrests; Cartier chronometer; monitor system for brakes; spare tire cover and vinyl roof (five vinyl top covers were available).

CONTINENTAL MARK III

Model No.	Body/ Style No.	Body Type & Seating	Factory Price	Shipping Weight	Prod. Total
89	65A	2-dr HT Cpe-5P	8421	5003	27,091

ENGINE [V-8]: Overhead valve. Cast-iron block. Displacement: 460 cid. Bore and stroke: 4.36 x 3.85 inches. Compression ratio: 10.5:1. Brake hp: 365 at 4600 rpm. Carburetor: four-barrel.

1971 Lincoln Continental Mark III two-door hardtop V-8. (OCW)

CHASSIS FEATURES: Wheelbase: (Continental) 127 inches. (Mark III) 117.2 inches. Overall length: (Continental) 225 inches; (Mark III) 216.1 inches. Tread width: (Continental) 64.3 inches; (Mark III) 62.3 inches. Tires: 225 x 15 steel belted Michelin.

OPTIONS: Sure-Track brake system, standard in Mark III; in Continental ($196.80). Front bumper guards, in Continental ($19.70). Rear window defogger ($31.50). Automatic headlight dimmer ($51.20). Automatic load adjuster, in Continental ($97.10). Power deck lid release, in Mark III ($46.00). Power door locks, in Mark III ($49.90). Lock release group, in Continental ($106.30). 'Moondust' metallic paint ($131.20). Six-Way power seat in Continental ($91.90) in Mark III ($183.70). Six-Way power bench seat with recliner, in Continental ($152.50). Six-Way power seat with reclining passenger seat, in Mark III ($242.70). Six-Way/Two-Way Twin Comfort power seat, in Continental ($223.00). Rear window defroster ($85.30). Six-Way/Two-Way Twin Comfort power seat, in Mark III ($246.60). Six-Way/Two-Way power Twin Comfort seat with passenger recliner, in Continental ($263.30). Cross-Country ride package ($17.10). Speed control ($94.50). AM signal-seeking radio ($161.40). AM/FM stereo radio ($306.90). AM radio with stereo tape system ($301.70). Vinyl roof, in Continental ($156.10). Leather seat trim, in Continental ($173.20); in Mark III ($183.70). Tilting steering wheel ($72.20). Luxury wheel covers, in Continental ($59.10). Intermittent windshield wipers, in Continental ($26.30). Traction-Lok differential. Higher ratio rear axle.

HISTORY: Only 12.3 percent of 1971 Continentals had a locking differential. Most Mark IIIs, 88 percent, came with a tilting steering wheel. Nineteen seventy-one was the 50th anniversary of Lincoln and to observe the occasion a limited production model called the Golden Anniversary Town Car was offered for sale.

1972 LINCOLN

1972 Lincoln Continental four-door sedan V-8. (OCW)

CONTINENTAL SERIES — Full-length upper body moldings and a new criss-cross pattern grille were the most noticeable styling changes for 1972. A hood ornament with the Lincoln emblem was also added. Standard equipment included: fender skirts; automatic temperature control air conditioning; power front disc brakes; cut-pile carpeting; electric clock; carpeted luggage compartment; left-hand remote-control outside rearview mirror; front and rear armrests; tinted glass; visor vanity mirror; AM radio with power antenna; Two-Way power seat; power ventilation; power windows and seat belts.

LINCOLN I.D. NUMBERS: The Vehicle Identification Number is on a tag on the dashboard, visible through windshield. First symbol: 2=1972. Second symbol indicates assembly plant: Y=Wixom, Mich. Third and fourth symbols indicate model and series: 82=Continental sedan; 81=Continental two-door hardtop 89=Mark IV two-door hardtop. Fifth symbol indicates engine: A=460 cid V-8. Last six symbols are sequential production number. Body plate riveted to front body pillar between door hinges gives body, color, trim, date, engine, transmission and axle codes.

1972-1/2 Lincoln Continental Town Car four-door sedan V-8. (PH)

1972 Lincoln Continental Mark IV two-door hardtop V-8. (OCW)

CONTINENTAL

Model No.	Body/ Style No.	Body Type & Seating	Factory Price	Shipping Weight	Prod. Total
81	65A	2-dr HT Cpe-6P	7068	4906	10,408
82	53A	4-dr Sed-6P	7302	4958	35,561

CONTINENTAL MARK IV SERIES — The new Mark IV was four inches longer, about half an inch lower and a fraction of an inch wider than the previous year's Mark III. The radiator-style grille was longer and used fewer vertical bars. It also bore a Mark IV emblem with a hood ornament on top. A new roof design featured an oblong opera window. Four rectangular bumper integrated taillights replaced the vertical wraparound ones. The distinctive spare tire hump on the trunk remained. The Mark IV had more leg and shoulder room for rear seat passengers. In addition to the standard features offered on the Continental, the Mark IV was equipped with Sure-Track power brake system; spare tire cover; luxury wheel covers; Cartier electric clock; Six-Way power Twin Comfort lounge seat; vinyl roof and automatic seatback release.

CONTINENTAL MARK IV

Model No.	Body/ Style No.	Body Type & Seating	Factory Price	Shipping Weight	Prod. Total
89	65A	2-dr HT Cpe-6P	8640	4792	48,591

ENGINE [Base V-8]: Overhead valve. Cast-iron block. Displacement: 460 cid. Bore and stroke: 4 36 x 3.85 inches. Compression ratio: 8.5:1. SAE nhp: 212 at 4400 rpm. Carburetor: four-barrel.

ENGINE [Mark IV V-8]: Overhead valve. Cast-iron block. Displacement: 460 cid. Bore and stroke: 4.36 x 3.85 inches. Compression ratio: 8.5:1. SAE nhp: 224 at 4400 rpm. Carburetor: four-barrel.

CHASSIS FEATURES: Wheelbase: (Continental) 127 inches; (Mark IV) 120.4 inches. Overall length: (Continental) 225 inches; (Mark IV) 220.1 inches. Tires: 225 x 15 Michelin radial.

CONVENIENCE OPTIONS: Sure-Track brake system, on Continental ($191.83). Opera window, in Mark IV ($81.84). Front bumper guards ($19.19). Rear window defroster ($83.13). Automatic headlight dimmer ($49.88). Cornering lamps, in Mark IV ($35.81). 'Moondust' metallic paint ($127.88). Power lock/release group, in Continental ($103.59). Lock convenience group, in Mark IV ($93.36). AM/FM stereo radio ($141.96). AM radio with stereo tape player ($136.84). Seats with leather trim, in Continental ($168.80); in Mark IV ($179.04). Leather trimmed seats with passenger recliner ($61.39 extra in Mark IV). Six-Way power bench seat with passenger recliner ($148.35 Continental). Six-Way power bench seat in Continental ($89.52). Six-Way/Two-Way power Twin Comfort seats, in Continental ($217.50). Six-Way/Two-Way power Twin Comfort seats with passenger recliner in Continental ($276.23). Tilting steering wheel ($70.35). Town Car package for Continental four-door sedan ($446.67). Town Car package with leather trim for Continental four-door sedan ($635.47). Speed control ($92.08). Vinyl roof, on Continental ($152.19). Luxury wheel covers, on Continental ($57.56). Traction-Lok differential. High-ratio rear axle.

HISTORY: Most 1972 Continentals, 77.3 percent, came with a tilting steering wheel.

1973 LINCOLN

CONTINENTAL SERIES — The Continental name was printed above the grille of the 1973 model. It hadn't been seen in this location for three years. An improved bumper with bumper guards was another change. Otherwise, the new Continental looked virtually the same as the previous year's model. Among the standard features were: automatic transmission; power steering; white sidewall tires; Deluxe wheel covers; dual custom stripes; power windows; Two-Way power seat; AM radio with power antenna; cut-pile carpeting; seat belt warning buzzer; electric clock; folding center armrests in front and rear; carpeted luggage compartment; tinted glass; remote control left-hand outside mirror; visor mounted vanity mirror; spare tire lock and cornering lights.

LINCOLN I.D. NUMBERS: The Vehicle Identification Number is on a tag on the dashboard, visible through windshield. First symbol: 3=1973. Second symbol indicates assembly plant: Y=Wixom, Mich. Third and fourth symbols indicate model and series: 82=Continental sedan; 81=Continental two-door hardtop; 89=Mark IV two-door hardtop. Fifth symbol indicates engine: A=460 cid V-8. Last six symbols are sequential production number. Body plate riveted to front body pillar between door hinges gives body, color, trim, date, engine, transmission and axle codes.

CONTINENTAL

Model No.	Body/ Style No.	Body Type & Seating	Factory Price	Shipping Weight	Prod. Total
81	65A	2-dr HT Cpe-6P	7230	5016	13,348
82	53A	4-dr Sed-6P	7474	5049	45,288

CONTINENTAL MARK IV SERIES — The main changes to the new Mark IV were restyled, wraparound signal lights and an improved front bumper that covered the lower part of the grille (this area had been exposed in 1972). The Mark IV featured the same standard items as the Continental plus vinyl roof; opera windows; Twin Lounge seats with Six-Way power; cloth and vinyl upholstery; deep cut-pile carpeting; reading lights; carpeted spare tire cover; Cartier electric clock; inside hood latch release; Sure-Track brake system and customer monograms.

CONTINENTAL MARK IV

Model No.	Body/ Style No.	Body Type & Seating	Factory Price	Shipping Weight	Prod. Total
89	65A	2-dr HT Cpe-6P	8984	4908	69,437

ENGINE [Base V-8]: Overhead valve. Cast-iron block. Displacement: 460 cid. Bore and stroke: 4.36 x 3.85 inches. Compression ratio: 8.0:1. SAE nhp: 208 at 4400 rpm. Carburetor: four-barrel.

ENGINE [Mark IV V-8]: Overhead valve. Cast-iron block. Displacement: 460 cid. Bore and stroke: 4.36 x 3.85 inches. Compression ratio: 8.0:1. SAE nhp: 220 at 4400 rpm. Carburetor: four-barrel.

CHASSIS FEATURES: Wheelbase: (Continental) 127 inches; (Mark IV) 120.4 inches. Overall length: (Continental) 229.5 inches; (Mark IV) 224 inches. Tires: 230R15 steel-belted radial.

1973 Lincoln Continental four-door sedan V-8. (OCW)

1973 Lincoln Continental Mark IV two-door hardtop V-8. (OCW)

OPTIONS: Town Car package including power vent windows; rear door quarter armrest inserts; 'C' pillar lights and vinyl covered 'B' pillar, on four-door models; also, on both two- and four-door models, including vinyl roof; seatback robe cords; seatback carpet inserts; personalized owner's initials; distinctive Town Car insignia; flocked headlining and sun visors and glovebox vanity mirror, for two-door Continentals ($567); for four-door Continentals ($635). Sun roof ($611.28). Rear window defroster ($83.13). Remote control right-hand mirror ($26.67). Tilting steering wheel ($70.35). Automatic headlight dimmer ($49.88). Mark IV Silver Luxury group, including silver grained vinyl roof, red interior and silver 'moondust' metallic paint ($400). AM/FM stereo radio ($141.96). AM radio with stereo tape system ($136.84). Continental seats with leather trim ($168.80). Speed control ($92.08). Seats with leather trim and passenger recliner ($240.43). Six-Way/Two-Way Twin Comfort power seats, in Continental ($217.40). Six-Way/Two-Way Twin Comfort power seats with recliner, in Continental ($276.23). Six-Way power bench seat in Continental ($89.52). Six-Way power bench seat with recliner, in Continental ($148.35). Bodyside vinyl insert molding ($33.25). Interval windshield wipers ($25.57). Traction-Lok differential. High-ratio rear axle.

HISTORY: Ninety-three percent of 1973 Mark IVs came with a tilting steering wheel.

1974 LINCOLN

CONTINENTAL SERIES — The Continental received a minor, but attractive face lift this year. New wraparound signal lights, clean headlight doors and a vertical bar style grille seemed to have been influenced by the Mark IV. Standard features included power windows; power ventilation system; Six-Way power seat; automatic temperature control; AM radio with power antenna; Cartier electric clock; visor-mounted vanity mirror; tinted glass; automatic parking brake release; Deluxe wheel covers; spare tire lock; remote control outside rearview mirror; power steering; fender skirts; power front disc brakes; cornering lights and carpeted luggage compartment.

LINCOLN I.D. NUMBERS: The Vehicle Identification Number is on a tag on the dashboard, visible through windshield. First symbol: 4=1974. Second symbol indicates assembly plant: Y=Wixom, Mich. Third and fourth symbols indicate model and series: 82=Continental sedan; 81=Continental two-door hardtop; 89=Mark IV two-door hardtop. Fifth symbol indicates engine: A=460 cid V-8. Last six symbols are sequential production number. Body plate riveted to front body pillar between door hinges gives body, color, trim, date, engine, transmission and axle codes.

CONTINENTAL

Model No.	Body/ Style No.	Body Type & Seating	Factory Price	Shipping Weight	Prod. Total
81	65A	2-dr HT Cpe-6P	8053	5366	7,318
82	53A	4-dr Sed-6P	8238	5361	29,351

CONTINENTAL MARK IV SERIES — The Mark IV's styling was virtually unchanged for 1974. However, new sound insulation and thicker carpeting helped give it a quieter ride. In addition to most of the standard features offered on Continentals, the Mark IV came equipped with Sure-Track power brake system; carpeted spare tire cover; digital clock; rear bumper guard; luxury steering wheel; front and rear rub strips; vinyl roof; Six-Way Twin Comfort power seat and engine compartment light.

CONTINENTAL MARK IV

Model No.	Body/ Style No.	Body Type & Seating	Factory Price	Shipping Weight	Prod. Total
89	65A	2-dr HT Cpe-6P	10,194	5362	57,316

1974 Lincoln Continental Town Car four-door sedan V-8. (OCW)

1974 Lincoln Continental Mark IV two-door hardtop V-8. (OCW)

ENGINE [Base V-8]: Overhead valve. Cast-iron block. Displacement: 460 cid. Bore and stroke: 4.36 x 3.85 inches. Compression ratio: 8.0:1. SAE net hp: 215 at 4000 rpm. Carburetor: four-barrel.

ENGINE [Mark IV V-8]: Overhead valve. Cast-iron block. Displacement: 460 cid. Bore and stroke: 4.36 x 3.85 inches. Compression ratio: 8.0:1. SAE net hp 220 at 4000 rpm. Carburetor: four-barrel.

CHASSIS FEATURES: Wheelbase: (Continental) 127.2 inches; (Mark IV) 120.4 inches. Overall length: (Continental) 232.6 inches; (Mark IV) 228.4 inches. Tires: (Continental) 234R-15 steel-belted radial; (Mark IV) 230 x 15 steel-belted radial.

OPTIONS: Anti-theft alarm system ($77). Sure-Track brake system, on Continental ($191.82). Quick Defrost defroster, in Mark IV ($306.70). Rear window defroster ($83.13). Dual exhaust, on Mark IV ($52). Right-hand remote control outside rearview mirror ($26.67). Illuminated visor vanity mirror ($86.70). Body side moldings with vinyl insert ($33.25). 'Moondust' metallic paint ($127.88). 'Diamond Fire' metallic paint ($167). AM/FM Multiplex radio ($141.96). AM/FM Multiplex radio with stereo tape system, in Continental ($26.33); in Mark IV ($127.37). Speed control ($92.08). Bench seat with passenger recliner, in Continental ($58.83). Six-Way Twin Comfort power seat, in Continental ($217.15). Six-Way Twin Comfort power seat with passenger recliner, in Continental ($278.48). Tilting steering wheel ($70.35). Sun roof ($611.28). Power sun roof with steel panel, in Mark IV ($611.28). Space Saver spare tire for Mark IV ($77.40). Leather interior trim, in Mark IV ($179.04); in Continental ($168.80). Mark IV velour interior trim ($179.70). Vinyl roof on Continental ($152.19). Luxury wheel covers on Continental ($76). Power vent windows, in Continental four-door ($68). Interval windshield wipers ($25.57). Mark IV Silver Luxury package including silver grained vinyl roof, silver metallic paint, red leather or velour interior, or silver leather interior ($400). As above, with power glass sun roof ($777.40). Mark IV Gold Luxury package including gold grained vinyl roof, gold 'diamond fire' metallic paint, tan leather interior with brown suede accents and tan components ($438 Mark IV). As above with power glass sun roof ($770.40). Town Car package including vinyl roof; Six-Way power bench seat in vinyl with leather seating surfaces; full-width head restraints; front seatback robe cords; carpeted front seatbacks; glovebox; vanity mirror; distinctive insignia; flocked headlining and sun visors; and personalized initials, in two-door Continentals ($567.47); in four-door Continentals ($635.47). Traction-Lok differential and high ratio rear axle were optional.

HISTORY: A Mark IV equipped with the Gold Luxury Package was designated as "America's Consummate Luxury Car."

1975 LINCOLN

1975 Lincoln Continental. (OCW)

1975 Lincoln Continental Mark IV Landau two-door hardtop V-8. (OCW)

CONTINENTAL SERIES — Several changes were made to the Continental for 1975. Among these were a new roof design; new taillights; rotary valve steering gear; new brakes; Continental name written in chrome on the rear fenders; full-length lower body molding; a vertical bar grille containing several heavier accent bars and the extension of the grille below the upper front bumper. Some of the many standard Continental features included: power steering; power front disc brakes; solid-state ignition; automatic temperature control; air conditioning; tinted glass; power windows; AM/FM Multiplex stereo radio with power antenna; Cartier digital clock; vinyl roof; power door locks; power trunk lid release; tilting steering wheel; trip odometer; door edge guards; Deluxe wheel covers; Six-Way cloth and vinyl power seat; cut-pile carpeting; door-closing assist straps; folding center armrests; visor mounted vanity mirror; left-hand remote-control outside rearview mirror; spare tire cover and lock; personalized initials and license plate frames.

LINCOLN I.D. NUMBERS: The Vehicle Identification Number is on a tag on the dashboard, visible through windshield. First symbol: 5=1975. Second symbol indicates assembly plant: Y=Wixom, Mich. Third and fourth symbols indicate model and series: 82=Continental sedan; 81=Continental two-door hardtop; 89=Mark IV two-door hardtop. Fifth symbol indicates engine: A=460 cid V-8. Last six symbols are sequential production number. Body plate riveted to front body pillar between door hinges gives body, color, trim, date, engine, transmission and axle codes.

CONTINENTAL

Model No.	Body/ Style No.	Body Type & Seating	Factory Price	Shipping Weight	Prod. Total
81	60B	2-dr HT Cpe-6P	9214	5219	21,185
82	53B	4-dr Sed-6P	9656	5229	33,513

CONTINENTAL MARK IV SERIES — The 1975 Mark IV was a virtual clone of the previous year's model. However, there was a new Landau vinyl roof option. It featured a 'frenched' rear window and bright chrome band vaguely reminiscent of the 1955-1956 Ford Crown Victorias. Standard features included most of those offered on the Continental plus four-wheel disc brakes; wiper-mounted windshield washers; speed control; Six-Way power Twin Comfort lounge seats with cloth upholstery and engine compartment light.

CONTINENTAL MARK IV

Model No.	Body/ Style No.	Body Type & Seating	Factory Price	Shipping Weight	Prod. Total
89	65A	2-dr HT Cpe-6P	11,082	5145	47,145

ENGINE [Base V-8]: Overhead valve. Cast-iron block. Displacement: 460 cid. Bore and stroke: 4.36 x 3.85 inches. Compression ratio: 8.0:1. SAE net hp: 215 at 4000 rpm. Carburetor: four-barrel.

ENGINE [Mark IV V-8]: Overhead valve. Cast-iron block. Displacement: 460 cid. Bore and stroke: 4.36 x 3.85 inches. Compression ratio: 8.0:1. SAE net hp: 220 at 4000 rpm. Carburetor: four-barrel.

1975 Lincoln Continental Town Car four-door sedan V-8. (OCW)

CHASSIS FEATURES: Wheelbase: (Continental) 127.2 inches; (Mark IV) 120.4 inches. Overall length: (Continental) 232.9 inches; (Mark IV) 228.1 inches. Tires: (Continental/Mark IV) 230 x 15 steel-belted radial.

CONVENIENCE OPTIONS: Town Car/Town Coupe package included power vent windows; coach lamps; exterior nameplate; Six-Way power seat with leather seating surfaces; special seat trim and door panels; deep cut-pile carpeting; glovebox vanity mirror; luggage compartment carpeting and interior nameplate with gold accent, in Continental two-door ($567.47); in Continental four-door ($635.47). Mark IV Silver Luxury group ($400). Lipstick and White Mark IV luxury group ($400). Mark IV forged aluminum wheels ($287). AM/FM stereo radio with tape player ($139). Leather interior trim, in Continental ($168.80); in Mark IV ($179.04). Rear window defroster ($83.13). Speed-control, on Continental ($92.08). Six-Way Twin Comfort seat with passenger recliner, in Mark IV ($61.39). Add $97.40 for above with power lumbar back support. 'Moondust' metallic paint ($141.96). 'Aqua Blue Diamond Fire' metallic paint ($167). Right-hand remote control outside rearview mirror ($26.67). Power sun roof ($611.28). Mark IV power sun roof with glass panel ($777.40). Space Saver spare tire ($77.40). Anti-theft alarm system ($77). Traction-Lok differential and high-ratio rear axle were optional.

HISTORY: New Luxury Group packages offered on the 1975 Mark IV were: Blue Diamond (Aqua Blue Diamond Fire finish); Lipstick and White (white exterior with white leather interior and lipstick red interior accents); and Jade (dark Jade metallic finish). Also, a Mark IV Spring Edition option, called Versailles, offered deep pillow-style upholstery in crushed Majestic cloth; matching door trim panels and headlining; illuminated vanity mirrors on each sun visor and unique two-tone bodyside and deck lid stripes.

1976 LINCOLN

1976 Lincoln Continental. (OCW)

Lincoln entered the mid-1970s with a pair of big luxury cars. Continental had received a significant face lift for 1975 and continued in that form this year. Mark IV also showed little change for 1976, but added a set of Designer models, signed by well-known names in the fashion world, to lure affluent buyers. Quite a few previously standard items were made optional for 1976, to keep base prices down.

CONTINENTAL — V-8 — Not much changed in the Continental luxury lineup, which had been substantially redesigned a year earlier, except for several new options and some revisions in standard equipment. A number of former standard items became optional. As before, two body styles were produced: a traditional four-door sedan and distinctive coupe. Posher Town Car and Town Coupe packages also were offered. Wheelbase was 127.2 inches. Continental had a wide six-section vertical-bar grille, with pattern repeated in twin side-by-side bumper slots below. A nameplate decorated the door of the left concealed headlamp. Horizontally-ribbed wraparound park/signal lights stood at fender tips, with separate cornering lamps. The bright Continental star stand-up hood ornament had a fold-down feature. A gold Continental star was laminated into the glass of the two-door's large fixed quarter windows. Front doors held a plaque for owner's initials. Rear fender skirts had bright moldings. The vertical two-pod taillamp assembly had a bright frame and integral side marker light and reflector, with full-width red lower back panel appliqué. Continental also had bright 'Lincoln Continental' script and 'Lincoln' block letters. Four body colors were added, and the distinctive Jade Green interior was now available in all models. Inside was a standard Cartier-signed digital clock, and the instrument panel had a simulated buried walnut appliqué. Town Car had special identification on the front fender; Town Coupe, on rear pillar. Both had a vinyl roof and coach lamps on the center pillar, with a new roof band. Interiors had leather seating surfaces and vinyl upholstery. Above the glovebox door was a gold-color Lincoln Town Coupe or Town Car nameplate. For 1976, both Town Coupe and Town Car could be ordered with a coach roof in 14 color choices. It was a thickly-padded vinyl half-roof, rolled and tucked at the rear and quarter windows. A wide molding extended over the roof at the center pillar. Town Car and Town Coupe interiors had loose-pillow seating. Leather and vinyl bench seats were standard in both with Twin Comfort Lounge seats optional in velour or leather and vinyl. Continental had a separate body on perimeter frame and helical coil spring rear suspension with three-link, rubber-insulated cushioned pivots. Sole engine was the big 460 cid (7.5-liter) V-8. New options included two radio packages: AM/FM stereo search, and the same thing with quadrasonic tape player (an industry first). Forged aluminum wheels were also optional. So was a four-note horn. Four-doors had a new optional opera window set.

MARK IV — V-8 — Lincoln's personal luxury coupe rode a 120.4 inch wheelbase and its 'classic' styling changed little this year. New trims and options were available, and the standard equipment list was altered. Most noteworthy, though, was the addition of four Designer Series models, each named for a famous fashion designer: Bill Blass, Cartier, Hubert de Givenchy, and Emilio Pucci. Appearance was similar to 1975, including the expected concealed headlamps. Mark's traditional radiator-style, classic-look grille was rather narrow, made up of thin vertical bars, with a heavy upper header bar that extended down along the grille sides. Its resemblance to Rolls-Royce was no accident. Above the grille was a bright Continental star stand-up hood ornament. Combination wraparound parking and turn signal lamps were inset in leading edges of front tenders. The padded halo vinyl roof had color-keyed surround moldings, with vinyl-clad color-keyed rear window molding. Tiny oval opera windows to the rear of the quarter windows. in the wide rear pillar, held Continental star ornaments. Identification consisted of 'Continental' block letters and script, as well as 'Mark IV' block letters and plaque. Doors displayed the buyer's initials. Bright rocker panel moldings and extensions were included. The simulated spare tire had 'Continental' lettering around the upper perimeter. Horizontal wraparound tail lamps stood just above the bumper. Inside were standard Twin Comfort Lounge seats in cloth and vinyl. Mark had the same 460 cid (7.5-liter) V-8 as Continental, with standard 2.75:1 rear axle ratio. A Traction-Lok differential was available, as was a new engine block heater. A number of formerly standard items were made optional, including an AM/FM stereo radio, power door locks, power decklid release, tilt steering column, speed control, paint stripes, and appearance protection group. There were four new optional luxury group interiors: gold/cream, red/rose, light jade/dark jade, and jade/white. Other new colors included dark jade (with a Versailles option), gold, and dove gray. Standard body colors were: black, dove gray, dark red, dark blue metallic, light blue, dark jade metallic, dark brown metallic, cream, tan, and white. Thirteen additional colors were optional. Turning to the Designer Series, the Cartier had dove gray body paint and a Valino grain landau vinyl roof; red and white paint/tape stripes; dove gray bodyside molding; and Twin Comfort Lounge seats in either dove gray Versailles cloth or gray leather seating surfaces. Opera windows carried the golden Cartier signature. Bill Blass had a blue metallic body, cream Normande grain landau vinyl roof, cream and gold paint/tape stripes, and either cream or dark blue bodyside moldings. Twin Comfort seats were either blue majestic cloth or blue leather, with cream accent straps and buttons. The Givenchy Mark displayed aqua blue (turquoise) Diamond Fire body paint, with white Normande grain landau vinyl roof. black and white paint/tape stripes, and white or aqua blue bodyside moldings. Twin Comfort seats wore aqua blue velour cloth or aqua blue leather. Dark red Moondust (burgundy) body paint went on the Pucci, which also had a silver Normande grain landau vinyl roof, silver and lipstick red custom paint/tape stripes. and red or silver bodyside moldings. Twin Comfort seats carried dark red majestic cloth. All four Designer editions had forged aluminum wheels. All had the designer's signature on the opera window, and on a 22K gold plate on the instrument panel (which also carried the owner's name).

1976 Lincoln Continental Town Coupe. (L)

1976 Lincoln Continental Mark IV coupe. (L)

1976 Lincoln Continental sedan. (L)

I.D. DATA: Lincoln's 11-symbol Vehicle Identification Number (VIN) is stamped on a metal tab fastened to the instrument panel, visible through the windshield. The first digit is a model year code ('6' 1976). The second letter indicates assembly plant: 'Y' Wixom, Mi. Digits three and four are the body serial code, which corresponds to the Model Numbers shown in the tables below: '81' Continental 2-dr. HT coupe; '82' Continental 4-dr. HT sedan; '89' Mark IV 2-dr. HT coupe. The fifth symbol is an engine code: 'A' V8-460 4Bbl. Finally, digits 6-11 make up the consecutive unit number, starting with 800001. A Vehicle Certification Label on the left front door lock face panel or door pillar shows the manufacturer, month and year of manufacture, GVW, GAWR, certification statement, VIN, body code, color code, trim code, axle code, transmission code, and domestic (or foreign) special order code.

Model No.	Body/ Style No.	Body Type & Seating	Factory Price	Shipping Weight	Prod. Total
CONTINENTAL (V-8)					
81	60B	2-dr. HT Cpe-6P	9142	5035	24,663
82	53B	4-dr. Sedan-6P	9293	5083	43,983
MARK IV (V-8)					
89	65D	2-dr. HT Cpe-6P	11060	5051	56,110

ENGINE [Base V-8]: 90-degree, overhead valve V-8. Cast-iron block and head. Displacement: 460 cid (7.5 liters). Bore & stroke: 4.36 x 3.85 in. Compression ratio: 8.0:1. Brake horsepower: 202 at 3800 rpm. Torque: 352 lbs.-ft. at 1600 rpm. Five main bearings. Hydraulic valve lifters. Carburetor: 4Bbl. Motorcraft 4350 (9510).

CHASSIS DATA: Wheelbase: (Continental) 127.2 in.; (Mark IV) 120.4 in. Overall Length: (Cont.) 232.9 in.; (Mark IV) 228.1 in. Height: (Cont. 2-dr.) 55.3 in.; (Cont. 4-dr.) 55.5 in.; (Mark IV) 53.5 in. Width: (Cont.) 80.3 in.; (Mark IV) 79.8 in. Front Tread: (Cont.) 64.3 in.; (Mark IV) 63.1 in. Rear Tread: (Cont.) 64.3 in.; (Mark IV) 62.6 in. Standard Tires: KR78 x 15 SBR WSW.

TECHNICAL: Transmission: Select Shift three-speed manual transmission (column shift) standard. Gear ratios: (1st) 2.46:1; (2nd) 1.46:1; (3rd) 1.00:1; (Rev) 2.18:1. Standard final drive ratio: 2.75:1. Steering: Recirculating ball, power-assisted. Suspension: Independent front coil springs w/lower trailing links and anti-sway bar; rigid rear axle w/lower trailing radius arms, upper oblique torque arms, coil springs. and transverse linkage (anti-sway) bar. Brakes: Front disc, rear drum. Ignition: Electronic. Body construction: Separate body on perimeter-type (ladder) frame. Fuel tank: (Continental) 24.2 gal.; (Mark IV) 26.5 gal.

DRIVETRAIN OPTIONS: Differential: Higher axle ratio: Cont. ($33). Higher axle ratio w/dual exhausts: Mark ($87). Traction-Lok differential ($61). Brakes & Steering: Sure track brakes ($263). Four-wheel disc brakes: Cont. ($172). Other: Engine block heater ($19). Extended-range fuel tank: Cont. ($100). Trailer towing pkg. III: Mark ($127).

CONVENIENCE/APPEARANCE OPTIONS: Option Packages: Town Car option: Cont. ($731). Town Coupe option: Cont. ($731). Versailles option: Mark ($1033). Mark IV Designer series (Cartier, Blass or Pucci): leather ($1500). Versailles cloth ($2000). Mark IV Givenchy Designer series: leather or velour ($1500). Mark IV luxury group: gold-cream, red rose, dark/light jade, jade-white, saddle-white, lipstick-white, or blue diamond paint ($477-$552). Power lock convenience group ($87-$113). Appearance protection group ($53-$61). Headlamp convenience group ($101). Comfort/Convenience: Rear defroster, electric ($81). Quick-defroster: Mark ($360). Speed control ($117).

Power vent windows ($80). Tilt steering wheel ($69). Fuel economy light ($27). Intermittent wipers ($28). Anti-theft alarm ($115). Security lock group ($11-$17). Lighting, Horn and Mirrors: Coach lamps: Cont. ($60). Four-note horn ($17). Right remote mirror ($31). Lighted visor vanity mirrors ($100). Entertainment: AM/FM stereo radio ($148); w/quadrasonic 8-track tape player ($387). AM/FM stereo radio w/tape player: Cont. ($288). Search-tune AM/FM stereo radio ($300). Exterior: Sunroof ($701). Moonroof ($885). Vinyl roof: Cont. ($168). Landau vinyl roof ($113-$512). Coach vinyl roof: Cont. Twn Car/Cpe ($333). Opera windows: Cont. ($84). Moondust paint ($147). Diamond fire paint ($193). Custom paint stripes ($29). Narrow vinyl-insert moldings ($41). Premium bodyside moldings ($113-$143). Interior: Leather interior: Cont. ($220); Mark ($235 credit). Velour seats: Cont. Twn Car/Cpe ($187 credit). Bench seat w/passenger recliner: Cont. ($76). Twin comfort seats: Cont. ($259); w/passenger recliner ($335). Power lumbar seat: Mark ($93). Passenger recliner seat: Mark ($76). Trunk trim option: Cont. ($61). Wheels and Tires: Luxury wheel covers: Cont. ($83). Forged aluminum wheels ($300). LR78 x 15 SBR WSW ($44). Space saver spare: Mark ($96).

HISTORY: Introduced: October 3, 1975. Model year production: 124,756. Calendar year production: 124,880. Calendar year sales by U.S. dealers: 122,003. Model year sales by U.S. dealers: 122,317.

HISTORY: Sales rose by 43 percent for both Lincoln models in the 1976 model year. That made Continental the industry's most successful car (according to Lincoln-Mercury). Production of the new Versailles was scheduled to begin in April 1977, targeted to compete with Cadillac's Seville.

1977 LINCOLN

1977 Lincoln Versailles sedan. (JG)

In the first wave of powerplant downsizing, the restyled Mark lost its big 460 cid standard V-8 and switched to a modest 400 cid version. Continental soon did likewise, keeping the big V-8 as an option. A whole new model arrived later in the season: the Versailles, based on the Ford Granada/Mercury Monarch platform but far most costly, ready to compete with Cadillac's Seville. Standard Continental/Mark colors were: black, dove gray, midnight blue, dark jade metallic, cream, cordovan metallic, light cordovan, and white. Optional: dark red, ice blue, ember, or cinnamon gold Moondust; and silver, black, yellow gold, light jade, or (Mark V only) rose Diamond Fire, Versailles introduced clearcoat paint to domestic cars.

1977 Lincoln Continental Williamsburg Town Car. (PH)

VERSAILLES — V-8 — Lincoln hardly wanted to be left behind when Cadillac's new Seville was attracting plenty of customers. Versailles was its response, introduced very late in the model year (not until spring) as a 1977.5 model. The idea was to combine traditional Lincoln styling with a smaller, more efficient chassis. That was accomplished by turning to the compact Granada/Monarch platform, adding a number of luxury Lincoln touches and vastly improved quality control. Versailles had a radiator-style vertical-bar grille not unlike Continental's (with small emblem in the center of the upper header bar); quad rectangular (exposed) headlamps above clear quad parking/signal lamps: a decklid lid similar in shape to Mark V (with simulated spare tire bulge); and fully padded vinyl roof with "frenched" rear window. Clear wraparound and amber side marker lenses on front fenders matched the height of the headlamp/parking lamp housing and were enclosed by the same bright molding. A stand-up hood ornament featured the Continental star. Full-length high-luster bodyside moldings had color-keyed vinyl inserts. On the center pillars were Continental-style coach lamps; up top, a padded vinyl roof with Valino pattern (six color choices). At the rear were simple wraparound horizontal tail lamps. Forged aluminum wheels were uniquely styled. Versailles came in three metallic colors (cordovan, cinnamon gold and light silver), plus five non-metallic (white, midnight blue, wedgewood blue, light chamois, and midnight cordovan). A lower body two-tone option came in four colors: medium silver metallic, midnight blue, midnight cordovan, or cinnamon gold. Inside were standard flight bench seats, leather-covered armrests, a hand-wrapped leather instrument panel crash pad, and woodgrain cluster and trim panel appliqués. Standard equipment included a collapsible spare tire, dual lighted vanity mirrors, digital clock from Cartier, AM/FM stereo search radio, and four-way power seat. A relatively small option list included an illuminated outside thermometer, tilt steering wheel, power decklid release, remote right-hand mirror, whitewalls, power door locks, speed control, forged aluminum wheels, leather/vinyl trim, visor-mounted garage door opener, glass moonroof, CB radio, and illuminated entry. Under the hood (at first) was a 351 cid (5.8-liter) two-barrel V-8 with DuraSpark ignition and SelectShift automatic, hooked to standard 2.50:1 rear axle ratio. California versions carried a 302 cid V-8, which would soon become standard everywhere. Versailles featured unibody construction and a lightweight aluminum hood. Front suspension consisted of helical coil springs (spring over upper arm) with ball joints and drag strut. The Hotchkiss rear had semi-elliptic leaf springs. Four-wheel power disc brakes were standard. Engineering features aimed at refinement and smooth, quiet ride. They included matched, balanced driveline parts, low-friction lower ball joints, double-isolated shocks, reinforced chassis areas, and plenty of insulation. Balanced forged aluminum wheels wore Michelin-X radials. Quality control at the plant was strengthened to the point of dynamometer testing of the engine/transmission, a rigorous water spray test to pinpoint body leaks, and a simulated road test. Bodies received the first clearcoat paint on a regular production car.

CONTINENTAL — V-8 — Model lineup of the big Continental was the same as 1976, including the posh Town Coupe and Town Car options. The restyled front end retained the 'classic' vertical chrome-plated grille, but in a narrower form similar to Mark V, along with concealed headlamps and integral parking/turn signal lamps in front fender extensions. Otherwise, appearance was similar to 1976. The strong vertical theme was enhanced by crisp lines of the hood, front fenders, and parking lamps. Continentals had black bumper guard pads and rub strips, a bright stand-up hood ornament, cornering lamps, bright rocker moldings with rear quarter extension, bright full-length fender peak moldings, and rear fender skirts. Premium bodyside moldings had a new vinyl insert grain. Rear quarter windows on two-doors had a Continental star laminated into the glass, Rear ends displayed a full-width red reflective lower back panel appliqué, vertical two-pod taillamp assembly, and hinged Continental star on the decklid. Five body colors were new. Inside were new head restraints and two new interior colors, as well as a new high-gloss simulated walnut grain on instrument panel, steering wheel, and other components. New options included illuminated entry, fixed-glass moon roof, and CB radio. Base engine announced at first was the big old 460 cid (7.5-liter) V-8, but a 400 cid (6.6-liter) two-barrel V-8 engine with SelectShift automatic later became standard, the 460 four-barrel optional. New DuraSpark ignition gave higher spark plug voltage at startup and low idle speeds, which allowed the wider spark gap needed for burning modern (lean) mixtures. Town Car and Town Coupe added a new Valino grain full vinyl roof and center pillar; coach lamps; and 'Town Coupe' script on rear pillar (or 'Town Car' on front fender). Both had leather seating surfaces, with 'loose pillow' design. They also had power vent windows and a six-way power seat. A new special edition also was announced: the Town Car Williamsburg series, in silver or cordovan. It combined two different shades of the same color to give a longer and lower appearance. The silver model had new medium gray metallic paint on bodysides, combined with silver diamond fire on hood, roof and rear deck. The cordovan model had new midnight cordovan bodyside paint, with cordovan metallic hood, roof and rear deck. The silver Williamsburg model also had a silver Valino grain full vinyl roof, dual silver paint stripes, and dove gray natural-grain leather-and-vinyl or media velour upholstery. Cordovan versions carried a cordovan Valino grain vinyl roof, cordovan paint stripes, and cordovan leather-and-vinyl or media velour upholstery. Both Williamsburgs had six-way power Twin Comfort Lounge seats, reclining passenger seat, power vent windows, personalized instrument panel nameplate, lighted visor vanity mirror, carpeted luggage compartment, and dual-beam dome/map lamp.

MARK V — V-8 — A new Mark version arrived for 1977, similar to its predecessor but weighing more than 300 pounds less. Downsized, that is, but hardly drastically. Styling was described as 'evolutionary,' carrying on such familiar details as concealed headlamps, simulated-tire decklid hump, and little horizontal oval porthole windows on the sail panels (with Continental star laminated in the glass). But this version had all-new sheetmetal, grille, bumpers, functional triple fender louvers at the cowl, and vertical tail lamps. The overall look was more angular than before, described as 'sculptured styling.' As before, Mark V had a 'classic' (radiator-style) chrome-plated vertical-bar grille, with heavier upper header bar. Front bumper guards were farther apart. Vertical tail lamps had thin horizontal trim strips. Mark also had a bright star stand-up hood ornament, blade-like vertical parking lamps, black bumper guard pads and rub strips, premium bodyside moldings with Corinthian grain vinyl insert (choice of color), cornering lamps, bright wheel lip moldings, and personalized owner's initials. The standard roof was painted metal. Interiors held Twin Comfort Lounge seats in pleated design with soft ultravelour fabric. The new instrument panel had a high-gloss walnut woodgrain appliqué, new lenses with cut crystal appearance, jewelry-like instrument faces, and new Cartier day/date clock. Other standard features included an AM/FM monaural radio with four speakers, power antenna, two-spoke steering wheel, automatic-temperature-control air conditioning, power windows and six-way driver's seat, tinted glass, and four lighted ashtrays with lighters. Standard Mark V colors were black, white, dove gray, midnight blue, dark jade metallic, cream, cordovan metallic, and light cordovan. Optional Moondust colors were dark red, ice blue, cinnamon gold, or ember. Optional Diamond Fire colors: black, rose, silver, light jade, or yellow gold. Base powerplant was reduced to a 400 cid (6.6-liter) two-barrel V-8 with Dura-Spark ignition. Standard equipment included SelectShift three-speed automatic, four-wheel power disc brakes, Michelin steel-belted radial whitewalls, space-saver spare tire, and power steering. The big 460 V-8 remained available as an option. Other new options included illuminated entry, heated left-hand remote mirror (packaged with electric rear defroster), turbine-style cast aluminum wheels, CB radio, and high-altitude option. Like its predecessor, Mark V was available in Designer models. Bill Blass had midnight blue paint; chamois-color landau vinyl roof with pigskin grain (full vinyl roof optional); pigskin-grain leather-and-vinyl interior in new chamois color; chamois or midnight blue bodyside molding; dual chamois paint stripes on bodyside and decklid, with Bill Blass insignia on front fender; Bill Blass name in opera window; and optional (no extra charge) 22K gold finished instrument panel nameplate with customer's name engraved. Turbine style cast aluminum wheels and six-way power passenger's seat also were included. Cartier's version was similar but with dove gray paint and landau vinyl roof, and dove gray leather-and-vinyl (or majestic velour) interior. Also dove gray bodyside moldings, and a single thin dark red bodyside paint stripe. Decklids held a Cartier interlocking-C logo; opera windows, a Cartier signature. The Emilio Pucci model came in black Diamond Fire paint with white landau roof in Cayman grain patent-leather look. A white leather and vinyl interior had black components. Pucci also had black bodyside moldings, a three-quarter length bodyside tape stripe, and Pucci signature in the opera window. Mark's Givenchy edition was painted dark jade metallic, with a unique forward half-vinyl roof in chamois-color pigskin. Interiors were dark jade majestic cloth or leather and vinyl. Chamois-color bodyside moldings and dual paint stripes went on bodyside, hood and decklid. Hood and decklid stripes terminated in a double-G Givenchy insignia. There was also a series of luxury groups: cordovan, midnight blue/cream, gold/cream, light jade/dark jade, red/rose, and majestic velour.

I.D. DATA: Lincoln's 11-symbol Vehicle Identification Number (VIN) is stamped on a metal tab fastened to the instrument panel, visible through the windshield. The first digit is a model year code ('7' 1977). The second letter indicates assembly plant: 'Y' Wixom, MI; 'W' Wayne, MI. Digits three and four are the body serial code, which corresponds to the Model Numbers shown in the tables below: '81' Continental 2-dr. HT coupe; '82' Continental 4-dr. sedan; '84' Versailles 4-dr. sedan; '89' Mark V 2-dr. HT coupe. The fifth symbol is an engine code: 'H' V8-351 2Bbl.; 'S' V8-400 2Bbl.; 'A' V8-460 4Bbl. Finally, digits 6-11 make up the consecutive unit number, starting with 800001. A Vehicle Certification Label on the left front door lock face panel or door pillar shows the manufacturer, month and year built, GVW, GAWR, VIN, body code, color code, trim code, axle code, transmission code, and special order coding.

1977 Lincoln Continental Mark V coupe. (L)

Model No.	Body/ Style No.	Body Type & Seating	Factory Price	Shipping Weight	Prod. Total
VERSAILLES (V-8)					
84	54M	4-dr. Sedan-5P	11500	3800	15,434
CONTINENTAL (V-8)					
81	60B	2-dr. HT Cpe-6P	9474	4836	27,440
82	53B	4-dr. Sedan-6P	9636	4880	68,160
MARK V (V-8)					
89	65D	2-dr. HT Cpe-6P	11396	4652	80,321

ENGINE [Base V-8 (Versailles)]: 90-degree, overhead valve V-8. Cast-iron block and head. Displacement: 351 cid (5.8 liters). Bore & stroke: 4.00 x 3.50 in. Compression ratio: 8.1:1. Brake horsepower: 135 at 3200 rpm. Torque: 275 lbs.-ft. at 1600 rpm. Five main bearings. Hydraulic valve lifters. Carburetor: 2Bbl. Motorcraft 2150. VIN Code: H.

ENGINE [Base V-8 (Mark V, later Continental)]: 90-degree, overhead valve V-8. Cast-iron block and head. Displacement: 400 cid (6.6 liters). Bore & stroke: 4.00 x 4.00 in. Compression ratio: 8.0:1. Brake horsepower: 179 at 4000 rpm. Torque: 329 lbs.-ft. at 1600 rpm. Five main bearings. Hydraulic valve lifters. Carburetor: 2Bbl. Motorcraft 2150. VIN Code: S.

ENGINE [Base V-8 (early Continental); Optional (Mark V)]: 90-degree, overhead valve V-8. Cast-iron block and head. Displacement: 460 cid (7.5 liters). Bore & stroke: 4.36 x 3.85 in. Compression ratio: 8.0:1. Brake horsepower: 208 at 4000 rpm. Torque: 356 lbs.-ft. at 2000 rpm. Five main bearings. Hydraulic valve lifters. Carburetor: 4Bbl. Motorcraft 4350. VIN Code: A.

CHASSIS DATA: Wheelbase: (Versailles) 109.9 in.; (Continental) 127.2 in.; (Mark V) 120.4 in. Overall Length: (Versailles) 200.9 in.; (Cont.) 233.0 in.; (Mark V) 230.3 in. Height: (Versailles) 54.1 in.; (Cont. 2-dr.) 55.0 in.; (Cont. 4-dr.) 55.2 in.; (Mark V) 53.0 in. Width: (Versailles) 74.5 in.; (Cont. 2-dr.) 79.7 in.; (Cont. 4-dr.) 80.0 in.; (Mark V) 79.7 in. Front Tread: (Versailles) 59.0 in.; (Cont.) 64.3 in.; (Mark V) 63.1 in. Rear Tread: (Versailles) 57.7 in.; (Cont.) 64.3 in.; (Mark V) 62.6 in. Standard Tires: N/A; (Continental) KR78 x 15 SBR WSW; (Mark V) JR78 x 15 SBR WSW.

TECHNICAL: Transmission: SelectShift three-speed manual transmission (column shift) standard. Gear ratios: (1st) 2.46:1; (2nd) 1.46:1; (3rd) 1.00:1; (Rev) 2.18:1. Standard final drive ratio: (Versailles) 2.50:1; (Continental) 2.75:1 except with V8-460, 2.50:1; (Mark V) 3.00:1. Steering: Recirculating ball, power-assisted. Suspension: (Versailles) front spring over upper arm w/ball joints and drag struts and coil springs, Hotchkiss rear w/semi-elliptic leaf springs; (others) independent front coil springs w/lower trailing links and anti-sway bar; rigid rear axle w/lower trailing radius arms, upper oblique torque arms, coil springs, and transverse linkage (anti-sway) bar. Brakes: Four-wheel disc except Continental, front disc and rear drum. Ignition: Electronic. Body construction: (Versailles) unibody; (others) separate body on perimeter-type ladder frame. Fuel Tank: (Versailles) N/A; (Continental) 24.2 gal.; (Mark V) 26 gal.

1977 Lincoln Continental Town Car. (L)

DRIVETRAIN OPTIONS: 460 cid V-8 engine: Mark ($133). Dual exhausts: Mark ($71). Higher axle ratio: Mark ($21). Traction-Lok differential ($65). Four-wheel disc (Sure Track) brakes: Cont. ($461). Sure Track brakes: Mark ($280). Engine block heater ($20). Trailer towing pkg.: Mark ($68-$89). California emission system ($54).

CONTINENTAL/MARK V CONVENIENCE/APPEARANCE OPTIONS: Option Packages: Town Car option: Cont. ($913). Town Coupe option: Cont. ($913). Williamsburg Limited Edition: Cont. (N/A). Mark V Cartier Designer series: leather ($1600); cloth ($2100). Mark V Bill Blass or Emilio Pucci Designer series ($1600). Mark V Givenchy Designer series: leather vinyl ($1600); velour ($2100). Power lock convenience group ($92-$120). Appearance protection group ($57-$65). Headlamp convenience group ($107). Defroster group ($107). Interior light group ($106-$120). Comfort/Convenience: Rear defroster: Cont. ($86). Speed control ($124). Illuminated entry system ($55). Six-way power seat: Cont. ($139); w/recliner ($219) exc. ($81) with Town Car/Cpe. Reclining passenger seat: Mark ($80). Six-way power passenger seat: Mark ($143). Power lumbar seat: Mark ($187). Twin comfort power seats: Cont. ($354-$493). Power vent windows ($85). Tilt steering wheel ($73). Intermittent wipers: Cont. ($30). Lighting and Mirrors: Coach lamps: Cont. ($64). Right remote mirror ($33). Entertainment: AM/FM stereo radio ($143): w/quadrasonic 8-track tape player ($396). AM/FM stereo search radio ($304). CB radio ($285). Exterior: Fixed glass moonroof: Cont. ($954). Power glass moonroof ($938). Steel roof: Mark ($271 credit). Coach roof: Cont. ($522) exc. ($285) with Town Car/Cpe. Full vinyl roof: Cont. ($178); Mark ($187) exc. ($271 credit) w/Designer series. Opera windows: Cont. ($89). Moondust paint ($155). Diamond fire paint ($205). Custom paint stripes ($31). Rocker panel moldings: Mark ($28). Narrow vinyl-insert moldings: Cont. ($44). Premium bodyside moldings: Cont. ($120). Interior: Leather interior trim: Mark ($252). Velour seats: Cont. Twn Car/Cpe ($198 credit). Wheels: Luxury wheel covers: Cont. ($88). Forged aluminum wheels: Cont. ($230-$318). Turbine spoke wheels: Cont. ($237-$325).

NOTE: Versailles option list not available: similar to 1978.

HISTORY: Introduced: October 1, 1976, except Versailles, March 28, 1977. Model year production: 191,355. Calendar year production: 211,439. Calendar year sales by U.S. dealers: 181,282. Model year sales by U.S. dealers: 164,208.

HISTORY: Continental was the biggest car on the domestic market, as well as the worst guzzler. It weighed a whopping 5,000 pounds at the curb. The restyled Mark V sold strongly, up by one-third over the score of the last Mark IV. Versailles cost nearly three times as much as the related Mercury Monarch, and not everyone agreed that it was worth the extra price, even with the luxury features and tight construction. The new compact was 32 inches shorter and half a ton lighter than a Continental sedan but cost nearly $2,000 more. Only 8,169 Versailles found buyers in its short opening season. Stretch limousines were produced by various manufacturers, including AHA Manufacturing Co. in Mississauga, Ontario. That firm did a 12-inch stretch to 139 inch wheelbase, an 18-inch stretch to 145 inches, and even a massive 157 inch version.

1978 LINCOLN

Versailles turned to a smaller V-8 engine in its first complete season, while both Continental and Mark carried on with 400 and 460 cid V-8s. Mark V offered a new Diamond Jubilee Edition to help commemorate FoMoCo's 75th anniversary.

1978 Lincoln Versailles. (OCW)

1978 Lincoln Continental Town Car. (OCW)

VERSAILLES — V-8 — After beginning life in spring 1977 with a 351 cid V-8, Versailles switched to a 302 cid (5.0-liter) V-8 with variable-venturi carburetor for the 1978 model year. That engine had been formerly been installed in California Versailles. Appearance of the four-door sedan was nearly identical this year, and mechanical changes were modest: just an improved power steering pump and new electronic engine control system. Versailles had a Continental-style grille, horizontal parking lamps, sculptured aluminum hood with bright Continental star ornament, center-pillar coach lamps, special forged aluminum wheels, and simulated spare tire on the decklid. The fully padded vinyl roof had a 'frenched' rear window. Bumper guards had vertical rub strips and a wide horizontal rub strip. Bodies featured a clearcoat paint finish, as well as high-luster wide upper bodyside moldings with vinyl insert. At the rear were horizontal wraparound tail lamps and low-profile bumper guards. Inside touches included leather covering on the instrument panel, steering wheel and armrests. This year's colors were white, midnight blue, wedgewood blue, light chamois, cordovan metallic, light silver metallic, cinnamon gold metallic, dark red metallic, or medium silver metallic in two-tones only. There was a new wire wheel cover option, as well as a remote-mount 40-channel CB radio and lighted outside thermometer. SelectShift automatic transmission was standard, with a 2.50:1 axle ratio.

CONTINENTAL — V-8 — Not too much was new on the big Continental, except for different wheel covers. The sculptured bodyside got a new, more contemporary rear fender skirt and wheel lip molding (to match the rocker molding). Interiors had a new wide center folding armrest and revised door armrests. The instrument panel had a new high gloss woodtone appliqué, as well as restyled knobs and controls and a padded glovebox door. The 'classic' vertical-bar grille and concealed headlamps continued, as did the Town Coupe and Town Car option packages. This year's body colors were black, white, midnight blue, wedgewood blue, midnight jade, cream, cordovan metallic, dark champagne, midnight cordovan, and dove gray. Optional glamour metallic colors were: dark red, silver, ice blue, light jade, light gold, crystal apricot, champagne, and cinnamon gold. The 400 cid (6.6-liter) V-8 offered improved fuel economy with a low-restriction fresh-air intake, and a new mechanical spark control system. The 460 cid (7.5-liter) V-8 was optional again, except in California. Under the hood was a new electronic voltage regulator and maintenance-free battery; on the dash, a low windshield washer fluid warning light. New options included an integral garage door opener, lighted outside thermometer, and wire wheel covers. The optional CB radio introduced in 1977 now had 40 channels.

MARK V — V-8 — Lincoln's personal luxury coupe was limited mainly to mechanical refinements and new standard wheel covers this year, but a special version was offered: the Diamond Jubilee Edition, to commemorate Ford's 75th anniversary. That one came in a choice of special Diamond Blue or Jubilee Gold clearcoat metallic paint. It had a Valino grain landau vinyl roof with matching Valino grain accent molding. Vertical grille bars were color-keyed to the body color, as was the unique hood ornament. There was also a special paint stripe on the hood. Front and rear bumper guard pads had horizontal rub strips color-keyed to the body color. Bright-edged fender louvers and coach lamps were included, and the special opera windows (very small oval, as usual) had 'Diamond Jubilee Edition' script and a simulated diamond chip laminated in the beveled glass. Turbine style cast aluminum wheels were color-keyed to the body. Unique bodyside paint striping was interrupted on the door by personalized customer's initials. On the decklid contour was distinctive Valino grain padded vinyl, with 'Continental' letters spelled out on the simulated spare tire cover. A Valino grain vinyl insert also went in the trunk lock cover. Inside were Diamond Jubilee leather/cloth bucket seats in unique sew style with power lumbar support, along with real and simulated ebony woodgrain inserts. Extras even went so far as unique keys with woodtone appliqué insert, plus a leather-bound owner's manual and a leather-bound tool kit. A leather-covered console held an umbrella. Diamond Jubilee had dual wide-band whitewall steel-belted radials, illuminated entry, interval wipers, tilt steering, and other extras. Two engines were offered again on Mark V: the 400 cid (6.6-liter) V-8 with SelectShift and 2.75:1 rear axle, or the 460 V-8 with 2.50:1 axle. Body colors were: black, white, midnight blue, wedgewood blue, midnight jade, cream, cordovan metallic, dark champagne, light champagne, midnight cordovan, and dove gray. Moondust metallic colors were optional: dark red, light silver, ice blue, light jade, light gold, crystal apricot, and cinnamon gold. Joining the option list were a digital miles-to-empty indicator, integral garage door opener, lighted outside ther-mometer, wire wheel covers, and power retractable CB antenna. The four Designer Series were available again. Bill Blass sported midnight cordovan body color with light champagne landau vinyl roof in Valino grain. The Cartier edition came in light champagne body color with light champagne landau vinyl roof. (A standard metal-finished roof was offered at no extra cost; full vinyl roof at extra cost.) Both had light champagne bodyside moldings. Mark's Pucci edition came in light silver metallic body color, with black landau vinyl roof in Cayman grain for a patent-leather look. It had black bodyside moldings and unique paint/tri-tone tape stripes, plus Pucci logo. Givenchy came in midnight jade body color, with unique forward half-vinyl roof in light chamois color pigskin. Jade leather and vinyl interior trim had a unique broad lace insert in the seatback, embroidered in the double-G Givenchy logo. Bodyside moldings and dual paint stripes were cham-ois-colored on the Givenchy.

I.D. DATA: As before, Lincoln's 11-symbol Vehicle Identification Num-ber (VIN) is stamped on a metal tab fastened to the instrument panel, visible through the windshield. Coding is similar to 1977. Model year code changed to '8' for 1978. Engine code 'H' (V8-351) was replaced by 'F' (V8-302 2Bbl.).

Model No.	Body/ Style No.	Body Type & Seating	Factory Price	Shipping Weight	Prod. Total
VERSAILLES (V-8)					
84	54M	4-dr. Sedan-5P	12529	3759	8,931
CONTINENTAL (V-8)					
81	60B	2-dr. HT Cpe-6P	9974	4659	20,977
82	53B	4-dr. Sedan-6P	10166	4660	67,110
MARK V (V-8)					
89	65D	2-dr. HT Cpe-6P	12099	4567	72,602

Mark V Production Note: Of the total shown, 5,159 were the Diamond Jubilee edition. A total of 16,537 Marks had one of the four Designer packages (8,520 Cartier, 3,125 Pucci, 917 Givenchy, and 3,975 Bill Blass).

ENGINE [Base V-8 (Versailles)]: 90-degree, overhead valve V-8. Cast-iron block and head. Displacement: 302 cid (5.2 liters). Bore & stroke: 4.00 x 3.00 in. Compression ratio: 8.4:1. Brake horsepower: 133 at 3600 rpm. Torque: 243 lbs.-ft. at 1600 rpm. Five main bearings. Hydraulic valve lifters. Carburetor: 2Bbl. variable-venturi Motorcraft 2150. VIN Code: F.

ENGINE [Base V-8 (Continental, Mark V)]: 90-degree, overhead valve V-8. Cast-iron block and head. Displacement: 400 cid (6.6 liters). Bore & stroke: 4.00 x 4.00 in. Compression ratio: 8.0:1. Brake horse-power: 166 at 3800 rpm. Torque: 319 lbs.-ft. at 1800 rpm. Five main bearings. Hydraulic valve lifters. Carburetor: 2Bbl. Motorcraft 2150. VIN Code: S.

ENGINE [Optional V-8 (Continental, Mark V)]: 90-degree, overhead valve V-8. Cast-iron block and head. Displacement: 460 cid (7.5 liters). Bore & stroke: 4.36 x 3.85 in. Compression ratio: 8.0:1. Brake horse-power: 210 at 4200 rpm. Torque: 357 lbs.-ft. at 2200 rpm. Five main bearings. Hydraulic valve lifters. Carburetor: 4Bbl. Motorcraft 4350. VIN Code: A.

1978 Lincoln Continental Mark V coupe. (L)

1978 Lincoln Continental sedan. (L)

CHASSIS DATA: Wheelbase: (Versailles) 109.9 in.; (Continental) 127.2 in.; (Mark V) 120.4 in. Overall Length: (Versailles) 200.9 in.; (Cont.) 233.0 in.; (Mark V) 230.3 in. Height: (Versailles) 54.1 in.; (Cont. 2-dr.) 55.0 in.; (Cont. 4-dr.) 55.2 in.; (Mark V) 52.9 in. Width: (Ver-sailles) 74.5 in.; (Cont. 2-dr.) 79.7 in.; (Cont. 4-dr.) 80.0 in.; (Mark V) 79.7 in. Front Tread: (Versailles) 59.0 in.; (Cont.) 64.3 in.; (Mark V) 63.2 in. Rear Tread: (Versailles) 57.7 in.; (Cont.) 64.3 in.; (Mark V) 62.6 in. Standard Tires: (Versailles) FR78 x 14 SBR WSW; (Conti-nental) 225 x 15 SBR WSW; (Mark V) Michelin 225/230 x 15 SBR WSW.

TECHNICAL: Transmission: SelectShift three-speed manual trans-mission (column shift) standard. Gear ratios: (1st) 2.46:1; (2nd) 1.46:1; (3rd) 1.00:1; (Rev) 2.18:1. Standard final drive ratio: (Versailles) 2.50:1; (Continental/Mark) 2.75:1 except with V8-460, 2.50:1. Steer-ing: Recirculating ball, power-assisted. Suspension/Brakes/Body: same as 1977. Fuel Tank: (Versailles) 19.2 gal.; (Continental) 24.2 gal.; (Mark V) 25 gal.

DRIVETRAIN OPTIONS: 460 cid V-8 engine: Cont./Mark ($187). Dual exhausts: Cont. /Mark ($75). Floor shift selector: Versailles ($33). Higher axle ratio: Cont. ($21). Traction-Lok differential: Cont./Mark ($67). Four-wheel disc (Sure Track) brakes: Cont. ($496). Sure Track brakes: Mark ($296). Engine block heater ($20). Trailer towing pkg.: Cont. ($33-$67). Class III trailer towing pkg.: Mark ($72-$95). Califor-nia emission system ($76). High-altitude option (NC).

VERSAILLES CONVENIENCE/APPEARANCE OPTIONS: Appear-ance protection group ($76). Reclining bucket seat group ($467). Power lock group ($147). Defroster group ($115). Rear defroster, elec-tric ($88). Garage door opener ($87). Illuminated outside thermometer ($27). Tilt steering wheel ($77). AM/FM stereo radio w/8 track tape player ($84 credit); w/quadrasonic 8 track ($87). 40 channel CB radio ($321). Power glass panel moonroof ($1027). Dual-shade paint ($59). Protective bodyside moldings ($48). Lower bodyside protection ($33). Leather interior trim ($295). Wire wheel covers (NC).

CONTINENTAL/MARK V CONVENIENCE/APPEARANCE OPTIONS: Option Packages: Mark V Diamond Jubilee edition ($8000). Williams-burg Limited Edition: Cont. ($1525-$1725). Town Car option: Cont. ($1440). Town Coupe option: Cont. ($1440). Mark V Cartier Designer series: leather/vinyl or velour cloth ($1800). Mark V Emilio Pucci or Givenchy Designer series: leather/vinyl ($1800). Mark V Bill Blass Designer series: leather/vinyl ($1800); ultra-velour cloth ($1533). Mark V luxury groups ($680), but ($775) w/Moondust paint. Power lock con-venience group ($115-$147). Appearance protection group ($69-$76). Headlamp convenience group ($133). Defroster group ($115). Interior light group ($108-$127). Comfort/Convenience: Speed control ($127). Illuminated entry system ($63). Six-way power seat: Cont. ($151); w/recliner ($236). Reclining passenger seat: Mark ($85). Six-way power passenger seat: Mark ($151). Power lumbar seat: Mark ($107). Twin comfort power seats: Cont. ($547). Power vent windows ($89). Illuminated outside thermometer ($27). Miles-to-empty fuel indicator ($125). Garage door opener ($87). Tilt steering wheel ($77). intermit-tent wipers ($35). Lighting and Mirrors: Coach lamps: Cont. ($63). Map/dome light ($19). Right remote mirror ($37). Entertainment: AM/FM stereo radio ($144); w/8 track tape player ($203); w/quadra-sonic 8-track player ($373). AM/FM stereo search radio ($287). 40 channel CB radio ($321). Exterior: Fixed-glass moonroof: Mark ($1027). Power glass panel moonroof ($1027). Landau vinyl roof: Mark ($484). Steel roof: Mark V Cartier ($261 credit). Coach roof: Cont. ($547) exc. ($269) with Town Car/Cpe or ($332) w/Williamsburg. Full vinyl roof: Cont. ($215); Mark ($223) exc. ($261 credit) w/Designer series. Opera windows: Cont. ($93). Moondust paint ($189). Custom paint stripes ($53). Rocker panel moldings: Mark ($29). Narrow vinyl-insert moldings: Cont. ($48). Premium bodyside moldings: Cont. ($128). Lower bodyside protection ($33). Interior: Leather interior trim ($267-$295). Velour seats (leather delete): Cont. Twn Car/Cpe ($200 credit). Wheels and Tires: Wire wheel covers ($233). Forged aluminum wheels ($333) exc. (NC) w/Designer Mark. Turbine spoke wheels ($333). Dual wide-band whitewall tires ($52).

1978 Lincoln Continental Mark V Diamond Jubilee coupe. (L)

HISTORY: Introduced: October 7, 1977. Model year production: 169,620. Calendar year production: 189,523. Calendar year sales by U.S. dealers: 188,487. Model year sales by U.S. dealers: 184,299. Although Versailles production for the model year dropped sharply, sales this year weren't too far short of twice the total in its first (brief) season: 15,061 versus 8,169. Continental sales rose somewhat for the model year (94,242 versus 83,125), while Mark V gained only modestly. To meet Lincoln-Mercury sales-weighted CAFE requirements, sales of the full-size models had to be held in check, but the company counted on Versailles in its second year.

1979 LINCOLN

Both Continental and Mark V added a new Collector's Series, but otherwise changed little for 1979. Versailles enjoyed a modest, though much-needed restyle, and was the first domestic model to get halogen headlamps. The big 460 cid V-8 disappeared, making a 400 V-8 the biggest Lincoln powerplant.

VERSAILLES — V-8 — Subtle restyling added eight inches to the Versailles roofline, giving it a more square, formal 'town car' look. Topped with Valino grain vinyl, the roof was fully padded, with a 'frenched' back window. Cavalry twill vinyl also was available, with convertible-style back window. New roof accents included a brushed stainless steel wrapover molding, and matching brushed-finish center-pillar appliqués with restyled integral coach lamps. Quarter windows were enlarged and door frames revised, allowing wider back doors to open farther. Versailles also added padded vinyl over the simulated spare tire shape on the decklid contour, which carried 'Lincoln' block letters. Wide wraparound tail lamps met that 'spare.' Versailles was the first domestic car with standard halogen headlamps, which cast a 'whiter' light. The standard 302 cid (5.0-liter) V-8 had been the first engine to be equipped with electronic engine control (EEC-I) and variable-venturi carburetor, and continued in that form. Standard equipment included such tempting touches as air conditioning, power windows, four-wheel disc brakes, and speed control. A new electronic AM/FM stereo radio had seek/scan and a Quadrasonic 8 tape player. Wire wheel covers were a no-cost option, with aluminum wheels standard.

1979 Lincoln Versailles "Moon Roof" option sedan. (JG)

1979 Lincoln Versailles "Convertible" option sedan. (JG)

1979 Lincoln Continental "Collectors Series" sedan. (L)

1979 Lincoln Continental Mark V "Bill Blass" coupe. (L)

CONTINENTAL — V-8 — Lincoln's big rear-drive was largely a carryover for 1979, though a Collector's Series was added. Lincoln-Mercury called it the "pinnacle of Lincoln Continental prestige." Some styling features came from the 1978 Mark V Diamond Jubilee Edition, including special paint and a gold-colored grille. Both Town Car and Town Coupe option packages were still available. Wheelbase continued at the lengthy 127 inches. Collector's Series Continentals offered a choice of white or midnight blue clearcoat metallic body paint, with coach roof color-keyed to the body (replacing the full vinyl roof that would otherwise be standard). Up front were gold painted vertical grille bars. Turbine-style cast aluminum wheels were painted midnight blue between the spokes and the bodyside held unique paint stripes, along with premium lower bodyside moldings keyed to the body color. (Bodyside moldings on other Continentals had a Corinthian grain vinyl insert in customer's choice of color.) 'Collector's Series' script went on the lower corner of the rear pillar of that model. The customary 'Town Car' script on front fender was deleted, and the Collector's Series did not include opera windows. Collector's interior choices were luxury cloth or leather-and-vinyl seat trim in midnight blue. There was a woodtone appliqué insert in the steering wheel rim and hub, and a unique hub ornament. Also included: plush midnight blue Tiffany cut-pile carpeting; leather-bound tool kit (containing tools); leather-bound owner's manual; umbrella; power mini-vent windows; illuminated entry; speed control; 63 ampere-hour maintenance-free battery; interval windshield wipers; and a remote-control garage door opener. A Williamsburg option for the Town Car was offered again, in a choice of seven dual-shade color combinations. Williamsburgs included a full vinyl roof, either leather-and-vinyl or velour interior, Twin Comfort Lounge seats, power vent windows, premium bodyside moldings, and so forth. Continental came with the 400 cid (6.6-liter) two-barrel V-8, SelectShift automatic, and 2.47:1 rear axle. Interiors showed expanded use of woodtone appliqués on the instrument panel, which added a fuel warning light to replace the former washer fluid light. A new electronic AM/FM stereo radio had digital frequency display.

MARK V — V-8 — Like Continental, Mark V added a Collector's Series with golden grille this year, to replace the previous Diamond Jubilee Edition. It came with a choice of white or midnight blue clearcoat metallic paint. Standard Collector's equipment included a landau vinyl roof with matching accent moldings. gold-painted vertical grille bars, unique hood ornament and paint stripe, color-keyed front/rear bumper guard pads and horizontal rub strips, bright-edged fender louvers, and coach lamps. 'Collector's Series' script decorated the rear pillar. Turbine aluminum wheels were painted midnight blue between the spokes. A unique bodyside paint stripe was interrupted by the owner's initials on the door. Opera windows were deleted on the Collector's Series, but the decklid lock cover had a vinyl insert. Inside, Mark Collector's had midnight blue power bucket seats in unique sew style (or optional Twin Comfort Lounge seats in white or dark blue leather-and-vinyl). It also had a leather-covered instrument panel, ebony woodtone appliqué insert in steering wheel rim and hub, blue plush carpeting, leather-covered padded console, leather-bound tool kit and owner's manual, unique keys with woodtone appliqué insert, power vent windows, illuminated entry, interval wipers, and a number of other luxury touches. Otherwise, Mark V appearance changed little. Padded vinyl now decorated the simulated spare tire on the decklid, which had 'Continental' lettering spaced around its rim. Mark V had only the 400 cid (6.6-liter) two-barrel V-8, with 2.47:1 rear axle ratio. Not much else was different beyond new door/ignition locks and an improved heater.

Four Designer Series were offered again, with modest revisions. Bill Blass had a distinctive two-tone paint treatment with hood, decklid and upper bodysides in white: lower bodysides and decklid contour in midnight blue metallic. A white carriage roof had a bright die-cast rear pillar ornament. (If ordered with optional full vinyl roof, the Bill Blass name was in the opera windows.) Blass also had dark blue bodyside moldings and dual gold paint stripes on bodysides and decklid, along with color-keyed turbine-style cast aluminum wheels. Cartier again came in the popular light champagne paint with matching landau vinyl roof, though a standard metal-finished roof was available at no extra cost. It had light champagne bodyside moldings, and a single thin, dark red paint stripe on bodysides. A Cartier interlocking-C logo went on the decklid, and Cartier signature in opera windows. Emilio Pucci's edition had turquoise metallic body paint, a full vinyl roof in midnight blue, white leather-and-vinyl interior trim with midnight blue accents, midnight blue bodyside moldings, Pucci signature in opera windows, and Pucci logo as part of the tri-tone tape stripes. Pucci also had wire wheel covers, whereas the other three had turbine-style cast aluminum wheels. The Givenchy model came in a new crystal blue metallic body paint with crystal blue front half-vinyl roof. Also included: dark crystal blue bodyside moldings and dual tape stripes on bodysides, hood and decklid. Those hood and decklid stripes terminated in a double-G logo. There was also the signature in opera windows. Designer models also had a new electronic-search AM/FM stereo radio with Quadrasonic 8 tape player. Mark's Luxury Group series expanded to nine colors this year, from seven in 1978. One of the new ones was white leather-and-vinyl seats with color-keyed components.

I.D. DATA: As before, Lincoln's 11-symbol Vehicle Identification Number (VIN) is stamped on a metal tab fastened to the instrument panel, visible through the windshield. Coding is similar to 1977-78. Model year code changed to '9' for 1979. Engine code 'A' (V8-460) was dropped. Consecutive unit (sequence) numbers began with 600001.

Model No.	Body/ Style No.	Body Type & Seating	Factory Price	Shipping Weight	Prod. Total
VERSAILLES (V-8)					
84	54M	4-dr. Sedan-5P	12939	3684	21,007
CONTINENTAL (V-8)					
81	60B	2-dr. HT Cpe-6P	10985	4639	16,142
82	53B	4-dr. Sedan-6P	11200	4649	76,458
MARK V (V-8)					
89	65D	2-dr. HT Cpe-6P	13067	4589	75,939

PRICE NOTE: Collector's Series Continental and Mark V were listed as option packages, but also given initial prices as separate models: Continental $16,148 with leather interior, $15,936 with cloth; Mark V $21,326 with bucket seats, $20,926 with Twin Comfort seats.

1979 Lincoln Versailles "Valino Brougham" option sedan. (JG)

1979 Lincoln Continental Mark V "Luxury Group" coupe. (L)

1979 Lincoln Continental "Collector's Series" coupe. (OCW)

ENGINE [Base V-8 (Versailles)]: 90-degree, overhead valve V-8. Cast-iron block and head. Displacement: 302 cid (5.2 liters). Bore & stroke: 4.00 x 3.00 in. Compression ratio: 8.4:1. Brake horsepower: 130 at 3600 rpm. Torque: 237 lbs.-ft. at 1600 rpm. Five main bearings. Hydraulic valve lifters. Carburetor: 2Bbl. variable-venturi Motorcraft 2150. VIN Code: F.

ENGINE [Base V-8 (Continental, Mark V)]: 90-degree, overhead valve V-8. Cast-iron block and head. Displacement: 400 cid (6.6 liters). Bore & stroke: 4.00 x 4.00 in. Compression ratio: 8.0:1. Brake horsepower: 159 at 3400 rpm. Torque: 315 lbs.-ft. at 1800 rpm. Five main bearings. Hydraulic valve lifters. Carburetor: 2Bbl. Motorcraft 2150. VIN Code: S.

CHASSIS DATA: Wheelbase: (Versailles) 109.9 in.; (Continental) 127.2 in.; (Mark V) 120.3 in. Overall Length: (Versailles) 201.0 in.; (Cont.) 233.0 in.; (Mark V) 230.3 in. Height: (Versailles) 54.1 in.; (Cont. 2-dr.) 55.2 in.; (Cont. 4-dr.) 55.4 in.; (Mark V) 53.1 in. Width: (Versailles) 74.5 in.; (Cont. 2-dr.) 79.6 in.; (Cont. 4-dr.) 79.9 in.; (Mark V) 79.7 in. Front Tread: (Versailles) 59.0 in.; (Cont.) 64.3 in.; (Mark V) 63.2 in. Rear Tread: (Versailles) 57.7 in.; (Cont.) 64.3 in.; (Mark V) 62.6 in. Standard Tires: (Versailles) FR78 x 14 SBR WSW; (Continental, Mark V) 225 x 15 SBR WSW.

TECHNICAL: Transmission: SelectShift three-speed manual transmission (column shift) standard. Gear ratios: (1st) 2.46:1; (2nd) 1.46:1; (3rd) 1.00:1; (Rev) 2.18:1. Standard final drive ratio: 2.47:1. Steering/Suspension/Brakes/Body: same as 1977-78. Fuel Tank: (Versailles) 19.2 gal.; (Continental) 24.2 gal.; (Mark V) 25 gal.

DRIVETRAIN OPTIONS: Floor shift selector: Versailles ($36). Higher axle ratio: Cont./Mark ($23). Traction-Lok differential: Cont./Mark ($71). Sure Track disc brakes: Cont. ($525). Sure Track brakes: Mark ($313). H.D. battery: Cont. ($21). Engine block heater ($21). Trailer towing pkg.: Cont. ($71). Class III trailer towing pkg.: Mark ($84-$107). California emission system ($84). High-altitude option: Cont./Mark (NC).

VERSAILLES CONVENIENCE/APPEARANCE OPTIONS: Appearance protection group ($87). Reclining bucket seat group ($491). Power lock group ($155). Defroster group ($121). Rear defroster, electric ($101). Garage door opener ($92). Illuminated outside thermometer ($28). Tilt steering wheel ($81). AM/FM stereo radio w/standard 8 track or cassette tape player ($168 credit). 40 channel CB radio ($321). Power glass panel moonroof ($1088). Full vinyl or coach roof: Valino grain or Cavalry twill (NC). Dual-shade paint ($63). Protective bodyside moldings ($51). Premium bodyside moldings ($77). Lower bodyside protection ($35). Leather/vinyl interior trim ($312). Wire wheel covers (NC).

1979 Lincoln Versailles "French Window" option sedan. (L)

CONTINENTAL/MARK V CONVENIENCE/APPEARANCE OPTIONS:
Option Packages: Collector's series: Continental ($4736-$5163); Mark ($7859-$8259). Williamsburg Limited Edition: Cont. ($1617-$1829). Town Car option: Cont. ($1527). Town Coupe opt. on: Cont. ($1527). Mark V Cartier Designer series: leather/vinyl or velour cloth ($1945). Mark V Emilio Pucci Designer series: leather/vinyl interior ($1525). Mark V Bill Blass Designer series: leather/vinyl interior w/carriage roof ($2775); w/full vinyl roof ($1809). Mark V Givenchy Designer series w/broadcloth interior ($2145). Mark V luxury groups ($743), but ($843) w/Moondust paint, Power lock convenience group ($121-$156). Appearance protection group ($80-$91). Headlamp convenience group ($140). Defroster group ($121). Interior light group ($115-$135). Comfort/Convenience: Rear defroster ($101). Speed control ($140). Illuminated entry system ($65). Six-way power seat: Cont. ($160); w/recliner ($251). Reclining passenger seat: Mark ($91). Six-way power passenger seat: Mark ($159). Power lumbar seat: Mark ($113). Twin comfort power seats: Cont. ($580). Power vent windows ($95). Illuminated outside thermometer ($28). Miles-to-empty fuel indicator: Mark ($133). Garage door opener ($92). Tilt steering wheel ($81). Intermittent wipers ($40). Lighting and Mirrors: Coach lamps: Cont. ($67). Map/dome light ($20). Right remote mirror ($39). Entertainment: AM/FM stereo radio ($144); w/8 track tape player ($203); w/cassette player ($203) exc. ($204 credit) w/Collector's. AM/FM stereo search radio w/quadrasonic 8 track player ($407). 40 channel CB radio ($321). Exterior: Fixed-glass moonroof: Cont. ($1088). Power glass panel moonroof ($1088) exc. ($555) w/Cont. Collector's. Carriage roof: Mark ($1201). Landau vinyl roof: Mark ($513). Coach roof: Cont. ($580) exc. ($285) with Town Car/Cpe or ($352) w/Williamsburg. Full vinyl roof: Cont. ($228); Mark ($236). Opera windows: Cont. ($99). Moondust paint ($201). Custom paint stripes ($56). Rocker panel moldings: Mark ($31). Narrow vinyl-insert moldings: Cont. ($51). Premium bodyside moldings: Cont. ($136). Lower bodyside protection ($35). Interior: Leather interior trim ($312-$333). Velour seats (leather delete): Cont. Twn Car/Cpe ($212 credit). Wheels and Tires: Wire wheel covers ($247). Forged aluminum wheels ($373). Turbine spoke wheels ($373). Dual wide-band whitewall tires ($54). Inflatable spare tire (NC).

HISTORY: Introduced: October 6, 1978. Model year production: 189,546. Calendar year production: 151,960. Calendar year sales by U.S. dealers: 131,271. Model year sales by U.S. dealers: 149,717.

HISTORY: The big Continental was about to be replaced by a new smaller, lighter version. Sales fell for the model year, quite sharply for the two big Lincolns. Mark V sales had been more than double Cadillac Eldorado's, but the freshly-downsized Eldo threatened Lincoln's supremacy in that league.

1980 LINCOLN

Weights of both big Lincolns dropped considerably as Continental took on an all-new form and Mark VI was similarly redesigned. Each was nearly 800 pounds lighter than its predecessor. New suspensions kept the luxury ride, and both got a new deep-well trunk. Electronic engine control systems were standard on all Lincolns. So was a new four-speed automatic overdrive transmission, which had a mechanical lockup in (overdrive) fourth gear. Continental and Mark were more similar than before, essentially two versions of one modernized traditional design, with Mark the upscale edition. Both rode a 'Panther' platform based on the 1979 LTD/Marquis. Base engines also shrunk, down to 302 cid (5.0-liter) size, with 351 cid (5.8-liter) V-8 optional. Other new technical features on both models included halogen headlamps, P-metric radial tires, and a fluidic windshield washer system. A new electronic instrument panel with message center was standard on Mark VI, optional on Continental. It included a digital speedometer, graphic fuel gauge, vehicle warning system and trip computer. Optional on both was keyless entry, operated by a panel of calculator-type push buttons in a preprogrammed sequence. All these changes applied to the upper Lincolns, as the smaller Versailles was in its final season.

VERSAILLES — V-8 — Only a handful of changes hit the compact Lincoln sedan in its final year. Under the hood was a new starter; in the trunk, an improved jack. Five body colors were new, as well as three vinyl roof colors. So were standard Twin Comfort Lounge seats with recliners. Two Versailles options were dropped: the floor-mounted shift lever and the full vinyl roof. Standard engine was again the 302 cid (5.0-liter V-8) with variable-venturi carburetor. The enlarged and ample standard equipment list included halogen headlamps, leather-wrapped steering wheel, six-way power driver's seat, auto-temp air conditioning, tinted glass, four-wheel disc brakes, new electronic AM/FM stereo search radio and day/date/elapsed time digital clock, and Michelin tires. Appearance was the same as 1979.

1980 Lincoln Versailles "French Window" sedan. (JG)

1980 Lincoln Versailles "Convertible" option sedan. (L)

CONTINENTAL — V-8 — For the first time in a decade, an all-new Lincoln arrived, featuring a formal roofline, wider swing-away grille, and full-width tail lamps. Again built with separate body and frame construction, Continental lost close to 800 pounds. The aero-styled body was more than a foot shorter, now riding a 117.4-inch wheelbase. A traditional Lincoln "classic" vertical-bar chrome-plated grille was now flanked by exposed quad rectangular halogen headlamps, rather than the former concealed lights. The grille was wider than the former version, though not as tall. As before, its pattern repeated in a single bumper slot. Integral parking/turn signal lamps were in front fender extensions, with cornering lamps standard. Bright bumper guards had black pads, and black bumper rub strips held white accent stripes. On the hood was a bright Continental star ornament, bright rear edge molding, and paint stripes. At the rear was a full-width red reflective lower back panel appliqué (with bright surround molding), vertical tail lamps with bright surround moldings, and bumper-mounted backup lamps. Power vent windows and a full vinyl roof with padded rear roof pillar were standard. Inside was a restyled three-pod instrument cluster with new engine temperature gauge. As before, two- and four-door models were offered. Town Car and Town Coupe had their script in the rear quarter window. Both had coach lamps, seatback robe cords, and map pockets. The Williamsburg Town Car series was replaced by individual dual-shade paint options. New dual-shade paint treatments came in five combinations: black with light pewter metallic, maroon with silver metallic, dark cordovan metallic with bittersweet metallic, dark blue metallic with light pewter metallic, or dark champagne metallic with medium fawn metallic. That dual-treatment included upper body paint stripes and premium bodyside moldings. The new standard 302 cid (5.0-liter) V-8 had electronic fuel injection and third-generation electronic engine controls (EEC-III). Standard four-speed automatic transmission (basically a three-speed with 0.67:1 overdrive gear tacked on) would slip into overdrive at about 35 MPH. A single poly "V" belt on the optional 351 cid (5.8-liter) V-8 drove the water pump, fan, alternator, and power steering pump. Axle ratio was 3.08:1 with the 302 engine, 2.73:1 with the 351 (same as Mark VI). The big 400 cid V-8 was gone. The new coil-spring front suspension used long and short arms, with a stabilizer bar. At the rear was a new four-link coil spring suspension. Michelin P-metric steel-belted radials were standard. Gas cylinders eased opening of both hood and decklid. An electronic AM/FM stereo search radio was standard. New options included an electronic instrument cluster (with "message center" and 11-function monitor), keyless entry (with five door-mounted push buttons), Premium Sound System, and lacy-spoke aluminum wheels. Optional speed control added a "resume" feature.

MARK VI — V-8 — This year, a four-door sedan joined the customary Mark luxury coupe in its freshly downsized form. While the shrunken Mark rode a 114.4-inch wheelbase, though, the sedan's was three inches longer (same as Continental). The coupe lost six inches of wheelbase and 14 inches in overall length, as well as close to 700 pounds. Styling was undeniably Lincoln, evolved from Mark V, including Rolls-Royce style grille, oval opera windows on wide C-pillars (with Continental star), and easy-to-spot decklid bulge. While the similarly downsized Continental switched to exposed quad headlamps, Mark kept its halogen headlamps hidden behind closed (larger) doors. Body features included a fully padded vinyl roof with "frenched" rear window, wide bright stainless steel/aluminum rocker panel moldings, and standard power vent windows. Four-doors had center-pillar coach lamps. Front fender louvers had bright edges and a simulated adjuster. Premium bodyside moldings came with vinyl insert in choice of colors. Mark also had bright bumper guards with black pads, black bumper rub strips with white accent stripe, bright Continental star hood ornament, and a bright hood rear-edge molding. Slightly taller vertical wraparound parking/signal lights stood again at fender tips. This year's vertical-bar grille pattern was repeated in a wide bumper slot below. Inside was a four-spoke color-keyed steering wheel. Base engine was now the 302 cid (5.0-liter) V-8, with 351 cid variable-venturi V-8 optional. Four-speed overdrive automatic was standard. Unequal-length A-arms replaced the former the single arm with drag strut at the front suspension. The four-link rear suspension had shocks angled ahead of the axle. Standard electronic instruments could be deleted. In the trunk was a new mini spare tire. Once again, Mark VI two-doors came in four Designer Series, Bill Blass, painted dark blue metallic on the lower areas, with white upper accents, had a white carriage roof. Leather seating surfaces were midnight blue with white accents (or vice versa). Blass also had dark blue bodyside moldings, dual gold paint stripes on bodyside and decklid contour, Blass logo on rear roof pillar and decklid contour, and color-keyed lacy-spoke cast aluminum wheels. The light/medium pewter metallic Cartier, with medium pewter landau roof, had light pewter bodyside moldings and a single thin, dark red paint stripe on bodyside and decklid. A Cartier logo went on the decklid above the Mark VI script, and Cartier signature in the opera windows. Leather or luxury cloth seating came in light and medium pewter colors. Mark's light/medium fawn metallic Pucci had medium fawn bodyside moldings, tri-band bodyside and decklid contour tape stripes, Pucci signature in opera window, and Pucci logo on rearward fender louver. Givenchy offered bittersweet bodyside moldings, dual bittersweet hood tape stripes, and light fawn bodyside and decklid paint stripes with integral hood/decklid Givenchy logo. Givenchy lettering decorated the opera windows. Body paint was two-tone light fawn and bittersweet metallic, with full vinyl roof in light fawn. Twin Comfort Lounge seats with leather seating surfaces were bittersweet color, accented with Givenchy buttons on seatbacks. Givenchy had wire wheel covers. A new top-of-the-line Signature Series Mark VI (replacing the Collector's Edition) came in dark red or silver metallic paint on both two- and four-door bodies. It had a color-keyed Cavalry twill landau vinyl roof, color-keyed bumper rub strips, body-color accent on parking lamp lenses, vinyl roof wrapover molding with bright accents and coach lamps, and two-tone bodyside and hood accent stripes. 'Signature Series' script went on the rear roof pillar, an owner's monogram on front door. The decklid contour had a padded vinyl treatment. Inside, Signature had dark red leather or cloth seating surfaces, an owner's Signature nameplate on the dash, and plush Allure carpeting on the floor, cowl side, lower doors, center pillar, and in the trunk. Many Mark VI options were standard on the Signature Series, including speed control, six-way power seats, driver and passenger recliners, keyless entry, and Premium Sound System.

I.D. DATA: Lincoln's 11-symbol Vehicle Identification Number (VIN) is stamped on a metal tab fastened to the instrument panel, visible through the windshield. The first digit is a model year code ('O' 1980). The second letter indicates assembly plant: 'Y' Wixom, MI; 'W' Wayne, MI. Digits three and four are the body serial code, which corresponds to the Model Numbers shown in the tables below: '81' Continental 2-dr. coupe; '82' Continental 4-dr. sedan; '84' Versailles 4-dr. sedan; '89' Mark VI 2-dr. coupe; '90' Mark VI 4-dr. sedan; '96' Mark VI Signature Series. The fifth symbol is an engine code: 'F' V8-302 2Bbl. or EFI; 'G' V8-351 2Bbl. Finally, digits 6-11 make up the consecutive unit number, starting with 600001. A Vehicle Certification Label on the left front door lock face panel or door pillar shows the manufacturer, month and year built, GVW, GAWR, VIN, body code, color code, trim code, axle code, transmission code, and special order coding.

Model No.	Body/ Style No.	Body Type & Seating	Factory Price	Shipping Weight	Prod. Total
VERSAILLES (V-8)					
84	54M	4-dr. Sedan-6P	14674	3661	4,784
CONTINENTAL (V-8)					
81	66D	2-dr. Coupe-6P	12555	3843	7,177
82	54D	4-dr. Sedan-6P	12884	3919	24,056

1980 Lincoln Continental Town Coupe. (PH)

1980 Lincoln Continental Town Car. (PH)

Model No.	Body/ Style No.	Body Type & Seating	Factory Price	Shipping Weight	Prod. Total
MARK VI (V-8)					
89	66D	2-dr. Coupe-6P	15424	3892	20,647
90	54D	4-dr. Sedan-6P	15824	3988	18,244
MARK VI SIGNATURE SERIES (V-8)					
96	66D	2-dr. Coupe-6P	20940	3896	N/A
96	54D	4-dr Sedan-6P	21309	3993	N/A

ENGINE [Base V-8 (Versailles)]: 90-degree, overhead valve V-8. Cast-iron block and head. Displacement: 302 cid (5.2 liters). Bore & stroke: 4.00 x 3.00 in. Compression ratio: 8.4:1. Brake horsepower: 132 at 3600 rpm. Torque: 232 lbs.-ft. at 1400 rpm. Five main bearings. Hydraulic valve lifters. Carburetor: 2Bbl. Motorcraft 2150. VIN Code: F.

ENGINE [Base V-8 (Continental, Mark VI)]: Same as 302 cid V-8 above, but with electronic fuel injection. Brake H.P.: 129 at 3600 rpm. Torque: 231 lbs.-ft. at 2000 rpm.

ENGINE [Optional V-8 (Continental, Mark VI)]: 90-degree, overhead valve V-8. Cast-iron block and head. Displacement: 351 cid (5.8 liters). Bore & stroke: 4.00 x 3.50 in. Compression ratio: 8.3:1. Brake horsepower: 140 at 3400 rpm. Torque: 265 lbs.-ft. at 2000 rpm. Five main bearings. Hydraulic valve lifters. Carburetor: 2Bbl. Motorcraft 72OOVV. VIN Code: G.

CHASSIS DATA: Wheelbase: (Versailles) 109.9 in.; (Continental) 117.4 in.; (Mark VI 2dr.) 114.4 in.; (Mark VI 4dr.) 117.4 in. Overall Length: (Versailles) 200.7 in.; (Cont.) 219.2 in.; (Mark 2dr.) 216.0 in.; (Mark 4dr.) 219.2 in. Height: (Versailles) 54.1 in.; (Cont./Mark 2dr.) 55.1 in.; (Cont./Mark 4dr.) 55.8 in. Width: (Versailles) 74.5 in.; (Cont./Mark) 78.1 in. Front Tread: (Versailles) 59.0 in.; (Cont./Mark) 62.2 in. Rear Tread: (Versailles) 57.7 in.; (Cont./Mark) 62.0 in. Standard Tires: (Versailles) FR78 x 14 SBR WSW; (Continental, Mark) Michelin P205/75R15 SBR WSW.

TECHNICAL: Transmission: SelectShift three-speed manual transmission (column shift) standard on Versailles. Gear ratios: (1st) 2.46:1; (2nd) 1.46:1; (3rd) 1.00:1; (Rev) 2.19:1. Four-speed automatic overdrive standard on Continental and Mark VI: (1st) 2.40:1; (2nd) 1.47:1; (3rd) 1.00:1; (4th) 0.67:1; (Rev) 2.00:1. Standard final drive ratio: (Versailles) 2.47:1; (Cont./Mark) 3.08:1 except 2.73:1 w/V8-351. Steering: Recirculating ball, power-assisted. Suspension: (Versailles) front spring over upper arm w/ball joints and drag struts and coil springs, Hotchkiss rear w/semi-elliptic leaf springs; (Continental/Mark VI) long/short A arm front w/coil springs and anti-sway bar, four-link coil spring rear. Brakes: (Versailles) four-wheel disc; (others) front disc and rear drum; all power-assisted. Ignition: Electronic. Body construction: (Versailles) unibody; (others) separate body and frame. Fuel Tank: (Versailles) 19.2 gal.; (others) 20.0 gal.

DRIVETRAIN OPTIONS: 351 cid V-8 engine: Cont./Mark ($160). Optional axle ratio ($24). Traction-Lok differential: Cont./Mark ($110). H.D. battery: Cont./Mark ($23). Engine block heater ($23). Trailer towing pkg.: Cont. ($97-$137); Mark ($140-$180). California emission system ($253). High-altitude option: Versailles (NC).

1980 Lincoln Continental Mark VI coupe. (PH)

1980 Lincoln Continental Mark VI sedan. (PH)

1981 Lincoln Continental Town Car. (L)

VERSAILLES CONVENIENCE/APPEARANCE OPTIONS: Appearance protection group ($84-$88). Reclining bucket seat group ($416). Power lock group ($169). Defroster group ($132). Rear defroster, electric ($109). Garage door opener ($99). Illuminated outside thermometer ($31). Tilt steering wheel ($81). AM/FM stereo search radio w/8 track tape player ($81); w/cassette player ($95). 40 channel CB radio ($356). Power glass panel moonroof ($1128). Coach roof, Valino grain (NC). Dual-shade paint ($80). Protective bodyside moldings ($53). Premium bodyside moldings ($83). Lower bodyside protection ($35). Padded decklid appliqué delete (NC). Leather/vinyl interior trim ($416). Wire wheel covers (NC).

CONTINENTAL/MARK VI CONVENIENCE/APPEARANCE OPTIONS: Option Packages: Mark VI Signature Series ($5485-$5516). Fashion Accent series: Cont. ($600). Town Car option: Cont. ($1089). Town Coupe option: Cont. ($1089). Mark VI Cartier Designer series: leather/vinyl or luxury cloth interior ($2191). Mark VI Emilio Pucci Designer series ($2191). Mark VI Bill Blass Designer series w/carriage roof ($2809); w/full vinyl roof ($1825). Mark VI Givenchy Designer series ($1739). Mark VI luxury groups ($1044). Headlamp convenience group ($141). Defroster group ($132). Comfort/Convenience: Rear defroster ($109). Speed control ($149). Illuminated entry system ($67). Keyless entry ($253-$293). Power door locks ($103-$143). Remote decklid release ($27). Six-way power flight bench seat: Cont. ($171); w/recliners ($312). Reclining passenger seat: Mark ($91); both ($139). Twin comfort six-way power seats: Mark ($171). Twin comfort lounge power seats: Cont. ($1044-$1089) exc. ($45) with Town Car/Cpe. Electronic instrument panel: Cont. ($707): Mark ($707 credit). Garage door opener ($99). Leather-wrapped steering wheel ($47). Tilt steering wheel ($83). Intermittent wipers ($43). Lighting and Mirrors: Coach lamps: Cont. ($71). Touring lamps: Mark ($67). Right remote mirror ($44). Lighted visor vanity mirror ($123). Entertainment: AM/FM stereo search radio w/cassette ($95) or 8 track player ($81). 40 channel CB radio ($356). Premium sound system ($160). Exterior: Power glass panel moonroof ($1128) exc. ($817-$888) w/Mark Signature. Carriage roof: Mark ($984). Landau vinyl roof: Mark ($240-$311). Coach vinyl roof: Cont. ($367) exc. ($296) with Town Car/Cpe. Moondust paint ($232). Dual-shade paint: Cont. ($360). Custom paint stripes: Mark ($53). Door edge guards ($16-$24). Premium bodyside moldings: Cont. ($144). Rocker panel molding delete: Mark ($76 credit). Padded decklid appliqué delete: Mark Signature (NC). License plate frames: rear ($8); front/rear ($16). Lower bodyside protection ($35). Interior: Leather interior trim: Cont. ($368-$435). Floor mats: front ($35); rear ($19). Trunk mat ($15). Wheels and Tires: Wire wheel covers ($255). Lacy spoke or turbine spoke aluminum wheels ($396) exc. Givenchy ($141). Wide-band whitewall tires ($36). Conventional spare tire ($40).

NOTE: Mark VI Signature Series was listed first as an option package (with prices shown above), then as a separate model.

HISTORY: Introduced: October 12, 1979. Model year production: 74,908. Calendar year production: 52,793. Calendar year sales by U.S. dealers: 69,704. Model year sales by U.S. dealers: 87,468.

HISTORY: This was the final year for Versailles, which was expensive and guzzled gas. its price rose once again, and sales fell to a mere 4,784 for the year. In fact, sales of all three models fell sharply. The total for Lincoln dropped 42 percent. Evidently, downsizing of the 'big' Lincolns wasn't enough to attract customers in this difficult period for the industry.

1981 LINCOLN

Without changing appreciably in appearance, the Continental of 1980 became this year's 'Town Car,' adding more power/comfort choices. A new top-rung Signature Series was added. New options included wire-spoke aluminum wheels and self-sealing tires. Versailles was dropped after 1980 due to diminished sales. So was the 351 cid V-8, leaving only the fuel-injected 302 powerplant.

TOWN CAR — V-8 — Now called the Lincoln Town Car, the former Continental (downsized for 1980) aimed harder at connoisseurs of luxury motoring. Town Car had new standard Twin Comfort Lounge seats with six-way power driver's seat. Coach lamps and premium bodyside moldings were added as standard. Town Car came in 18 body colors: 11 standard, seven optional. Standard auto-temp air conditioning added a 'mix' mode, while the optional electronic instrument panel included a message center with fuel economy data. New options were: self-sealing whitewalls, dual-shade paint colors with vinyl roof matching the upper bodyside, Class 11 trailer towing package. dual power remote mirrors, and wire-spoke aluminum wheels. Coach and carriage roofs were available. Base (and only) engine was the fuel-injected 302 cid (5.0-liter) V-8, with four-speed automatic overdrive transmission and 3.08:1 rear axle. The 351 cid V-8 disappeared. Appearance was similar to 1980, except that the grille pattern no longer repeated in a bumper slot. Both the two-door and four-door rode a 117.3-inch wheelbase. The new top-level Signature Series was posher yet. It included a coach roof, 'Signature Series' script on rear roof pillar (and instrument panel), six-way power Twin Comfort Lounge front seats in special 'pillowed' sew style, seatback robe cords and map pockets, and padded center-pillar upper trim panel with lower carpeting.

MARK VI — V-8 — Six important options became standard this year: power door locks, power decklid release, intermittent wipers, tilt steering wheel, speed control, and right remote-control mirror. Mark's electronic instrument panel with message center had a new instantaneous fuel economy function. A mix mode was added to the standard automatic-temperature-control air conditioning. Four-doors had new dual-shade paint options. New options this year were: puncture-resistant self-sealing wide whitewalls; power remote mirrors; Class 11 trailer towing package; and wire-spoke aluminum wheels. The wire wheels and power mirrors became standard on Signature Series, which was otherwise a carryover. Two-doors could have a carriage roof in diamond-grain or Cambria fabric. Of the 21 body colors offered on Mark VI, seven were new: five new standard colors and two optional Moondust colors. Eleven colors in all were standard, eight optional (Moondust), and two offered only on the Signature Series. New interior colors were: nutmeg, light fawn, medium fawn, and gold. Powertrain was the same as Town Car's: 302 cid (5.0-liter) fuel-injected V-8 with four-speed overdrive automatic and 3.08:1 axle ratio. No other choices were available. Appearance was unchanged following the 1980 re-style. The Designer Series quartet was revised this year. Cartier came in medium pewter metallic body color. Its interior was luxury group sew style in choice of leather with vinyl or luxury cloth, pewter colored with Cartier logo buttons. The landau vinyl roof was medium pewter. Cartier had dark red accent stripes on bodyside and decklid, and medium pewter bodyside moldings. Standard wheels were color-keyed lacy-spoke aluminum. Mark's Givenchy model had its upper bodyside in black, lower bodyside in dark pewter. Leather with vinyl or luxury cloth interior was pewter colored, with Givenchy logo buttons. Also included: a black landau vinyl roof; red and gold dual accent stripes on hood, bodyside and decklid; black bodyside moldings; and new wire-spoke aluminum wheels. Pucci's edition came in medium fawn metallic, with light fawn interior and Pucci buttons on the seatbacks. It had a fawn full vinyl roof, tri-tone accent stripes on bodyside and decklid. light fawn bodyside moldings, and wire-spoke aluminum wheels. Finally, Bill Blass had its upper bodyside in dark blue metallic, lower bodyside in light fawn metallic. Interior was dark blue with light fawn bolsters and Blass seat buttons; carriage vinyl roof in midnight blue cloth. The Bill Blass had dual dark blue accent stripes on the bodyside, light fawn accent stripes on decklid contour, and light fawn bodyside moldings; plus color-keyed lacy-spoke aluminum wheels.

1981 Lincoln Continental Mark VI sedan. (L)

1981 Lincoln Continental Mark VI coupe. (PH)

I.D. DATA: Lincoln had a new 17-symbol Vehicle Identification Number (VIN) this year, again fastened to the instrument panel, visible through the windshield. The first three symbols indicate manufacturer, make and vehicle type: '1LN' Lincoln; '1MR' Continental (Mark). The fourth symbol ('B') denotes restraint system. Next comes a letter 'P', followed by two digits that indicate body type: '93' 2dr. Town Car; '94' 4dr. Town Car; '95' 2dr. Mark VI; '96' 4dr. Mark VI. Symbol eight indicates engine type ('F' V8-302). Next is a check digit. Symbol ten indicates model year ('B' 1981). Symbol eleven is assembly plant ('Y' Wixom, MI). The final six digits make up the sequence number, starting with 600001. A Vehicle Certification Label on the left front door lock face panel or door pillar shows the manufacturer, month and year built, GVW, GAWR, VIN, and codes for body type, color, trim, axle, transmission, and special order information.

Model No.	Body/ Style No.	Body Type & Seating	Factory Price	Shipping Weight	Prod. Total
TOWN CAR (V-8)					
93	66D	2-dr. Coupe-5P	13707	3884	4,935
94	54D	4-dr. Sedan-6P	14068	3958	27,904
MARK VI (V-8)					
95	66D	2-dr. Coupe-5P	16858	3899	18,740
96	54D	4-dr. Sedan-6P	17303	3944	17,958
MARK VI SIGNATURE SERIES (V-8)					
95	66D	2-dr. Coupe-5P	22463	3990	N/A
96	54D	4-dr. Sedan-6P	22838	4035	N/A

ENGINE [Base V-8 (Town Car, Mark VI)]: 90-degree, overhead valve V-8. Cast-iron block and head. Displacement: 302 cid (5.2 liters). Bore & stroke: 4.00 x 3.00 in. Compression ratio: 8.4:1. Brake horsepower: 130 at 3400 rpm. Torque: 230 lbs.-ft. at 2200 rpm. Five main bearings. Hydraulic valve lifters. Electronic fuel injection. VIN Code: F.

CHASSIS DATA: Wheelbase: (2dr.) 114.3 in.: (4dr.) 117.3 in. Overall Length: (Town Car) 219.0 in.; (Mark 2dr.) 216.0 in.; (Mark 4dr.) 219.1 in. Height: (2dr.) 55.4 in.; (4dr.) 56.1 in. Width: 78.1 in. Front Tread: 62.2 in. Rear Tread: 62.0 in. Standard Tires: Michelin P205/75R15 SBR WSW.

TECHNICAL: Transmission: Four-speed automatic overdrive standard. Gear ratios: (1st) 2.40:1; (2nd) 1.47:1; (3rd) 1.00:1; (4th) 0.67:1; (Rev) 2.00:1. Standard final drive ratio: 3.08:1. Steering: Recirculating ball, power-assisted. Suspension: Upper/lower front control arms w/coil springs and anti-sway bar, four-link coil spring rear. Brakes: Front disc and rear drum, power-assisted. Ignition: Electronic. Body construction: Separate body and frame. Fuel Tank: 18 gal.

DRIVETRAIN OPTIONS: Traction-Lok differential ($108). H.D. battery ($22). Engine block heater ($22). Trailer towing pkg. ($141-$180). California emission system ($47).

CONVENIENCE/APPEARANCE OPTIONS: Option Packages: Town Car Signature Series ($1144). Mark VI Designer series: Cartier ($2031); Emilio Pucci ($2160); Bill Blass ($3015); Givenchy ($2372). Mark VI luxury groups ($1044). Headlamp convenience group ($149). Defroster group ($135). Comfort/Convenience: Speed control w/resume: Town Car ($153). Illuminated entry system ($67). Keyless entry: Town Car ($257-$294): Mark ($123) Power door locks: Town ($106-$143). Remote decklid release: Town Car ($27). Driver/passenger recliners: Mark ($138); passenger only ($90). Twin comfort six-way power seats: Mark ($170). Twin comfort lounge power seats: Town Car ($260). Twin comfort lounge power seats w/dual recliners: Town ($309) exc. ($48) w/Signature Series. Electronic instrument panel: Town ($706); Mark, delete ($706 credit). Garage door opener ($99). Leather-wrapped steering wheel ($47). Tilt steering wheel: Town ($83). Intermittent wipers: Town ($44). Lighting and Mirrors: Touring lamps: Mark ($67). Right remote mirror: Town ($46). Dual power remote mirrors: Town ($148); Mark ($99). Lighted visor vanity mirrors, pair ($126). Entertainment: AM/FM stereo search radio w/8 track player ($81); w/cassette and Dolby ($95). 40 channel CB radio ($356). Premium sound system ($160). Exterior: Power glass panel moonroof ($1122). Carriage roof, diamond-grain or Cambria fabric ($984). Vinyl coach roof ($240-$315). Moondust paint ($236). Dual-shade paint Town Car or Mark 4dr. ($246). Custom paint stripes: Mark ($53).

Door edge guards ($16-$23). Rocker panel molding delete: Mark ($141 credit). License plate frames: rear ($9); front/rear ($16). Lower bodyside protection ($35). Interior: Leather interior trim: Town ($378-$440); Mark ($470). Floor mats: front ($35); rear ($20). Trunk mat ($16). Wheels and Tires: Wire spoke aluminum wheels ($756) exc. Blass/Cartier ($342). Lacy spoke aluminum wheels ($414) exc. Givenchy/Pucci ($342 credit). Turbine spoke aluminum wheels ($414) exc. Givenchy/Pucci ($342 credit) and Blass/Cartier (NC). Self-sealing whitewall tires ($105). Conventional spare tire ($39).

HISTORY: Introduced: October 3, 1980. Model year production: 69.537. Calendar year production: 64,185. Calendar year sales by U.S. dealers: 63,830. Model year sales by U.S. dealers: 65,248 (plus 334 leftover Versailles models).

HISTORY: Sales were disappointing for the 1981 model year, down by some 25 percent. The Town Car at least came fairly close to its 1980 sales total, but Mark VI found more than 10,000 fewer buyers (down to 34,210).

1982 LINCOLN

1982 Lincoln Continental Signature Series sedan. (PH)

A new, smaller Continental debuted this year, weighing less than the old Versailles. Three models now made up the Lincoln lineup: four-door Continental, four-door (Lincoln) Town Car, and Mark VI coupe.

CONTINENTAL — V-6/V-8 — An all-new 'contemporary size' Continental took on the name used by Lincoln for four decades. This modern version rode a 108.7-inch wheelbase and weighed less than 3,600 pounds at the curb. It was 18 inches shorter and 500 pounds lighter than the former version. Base price of $21,302 was considerably higher than either the Town Car or Mark. Four-door bodied only, Continental came in base model, Signature Series, and Givenchy Designer Series. Under the hood, the 302 cid (5.0-liter) V-8 was standard, but a 232 cid (3.8-liter) V-6 was now available as a no-cost option. Four-speed overdrive automatic was the standard transmission. Continental had variable-ratio power rack-and-pinion steering, four-wheel disc brakes, and a modified MacPherson strut front suspension with stabilizer bar. Nitrogen-pressurized shock absorbers went at all four corners (first time on a domestic car). Standard features included an electronic instrument panel with message center, all-electronic AM/FM stereo search radio, self-sealing steel-belted radials, speed control, illuminated entry, tilt steering, rear defroster, power door locks, power windows, power antenna, interval wipers, and dual power heated outside mirrors (with thermometer in the left one). Six-way power Twin Comfort Lounge front seats had manual recliners. The modest option list included keyless entry and a power glass moonroof. Styling was unmistakably Lincoln, starting with the traditional 'classic' vertical-style grille and 'Continental' decklid treatment. Continental had front bumper guards. front and rear bumper rub strips with accent stripe, a Lincoln star hood ornament, and flush-mounted bright windshield molding. Each pair of exposed quad rectangular headlamps met wraparound signal lenses at the fender tips, with cornering and side marker lamps in a single housing. Bumper-mounted backup lamps stood on each side of the license plate bracket. 'Lincoln' script went on the decklid, 'Continental' script on front fenders. There was also a Lincoln Continental rear roof pillar ornament and rear side marker lamps. Front cornering and side marker lamps fit in a single housing. Forged aluminum wheels were standard. Continental's Signature Series had 'Signature Series' script on rear roof pillar, coach lamps in center roof pillar, and wire-spoke aluminum wheels. A bright/brushed full-length narrow upper bodyside molding replaced the standard accent stripe. The owner's identification kit included a signature plate for the instrument panel, and two sets of initials for the outside of front doors. Those items were sent directly to the buyer. The dual-shade paint treatment on Signature Series came in three special color combinations. A Givenchy Designer Series had dual-shade paint in unique black/medium dark mulberry metallic. Givenchy's rear roof pillar ornament replaced the usual

Lincoln Continental ornament and Signature Series script. There was also 'Givenchy' script in the rear quarter window glass. Interior was mulberry cloth luxury cloth or leather. Signature and Designer Series had a new trouble light mounted in the trunk.

MARK VI — V-8 — Appearance of Lincoln's personal luxury coupe and sedan was similar to 1981, with the exception of two new optional specialty roofs: a coach roof (rear half) for two-doors, and a full roof for four-doors. Specialty roofs included a large C-pillar, accented by small vertical quarter windows and slim coach lamps. Roof rear half and moldings could be covered in either Bayville grain vinyl, diamond grain vinyl, Valino vinyl, or Cambria cloth. As before, Mark had concealed headlamps. A simulated spare tire bulge on the decklid, and (on two-doors) tiny horizontal oval opera windows. Standard equipment was similar to 1981, including air conditioning, four-speed overdrive automatic, power brakes and steering, and the fuel-injected 302 cid (5.0-liter) V-8. Eleven paint colors were added, along with three new dual-shade combinations. Both the Givenchy and Cartier Designer Series were scheduled to disappear, but Givenchy reappeared a bit later. The optional leather-wrapped steering wheel was no longer available. A dual exhaust system had become optional in late 1981 and continued this year. Mark's Signature Series came in 13 monotone paint colors, with color-keyed Valino grain coach roof. It also had color-keyed bumper rub strips with white accent stripes. Body-color accents went on parking lamp lenses, and 'Signature Series' script on the C-pillar. This year's Designer Series consisted only of a Bill Blass two-door and Pucci four-door (and later, a Givenchy two-door). The Bill Blass had a choice of three paint and roof treatments: two-tone white with red bodyside accent color, and white diamond-grain vinyl carriage roof; all-white paint with white diamond-grain vinyl carriage roof; or all-black with black Cambria cloth carriage roof. Blass also had black bodyside moldings and dual accent stripes, and double red accent stripes on the decklid contour. The Bill Blass logo went on C-pillar and decklid. Mark VI Pucci models came in two-tone pastel French vanilla on the top, pastel vanilla metallic on the bottom. The Bayville textured vinyl specialty full roof was pastel French vanilla colored. Bodyside accent stripes were dark brown with gold; decklid pin stripes dark brown with the Pucci logo. That Pucci logo in dark brown was also on the front fender, and on the instrument panel. The Givenchy Designer Series had a dual-shade paint treatment with black upper and medium dark pewter metallic lower, black Valino grain coach roof, and choice of pewter cloth or leather seat trim with Givenchy seat buttons. Givenchy also had black bodyside moldings; red and gold dual accent stripes on hood, bodyside and decklid; Givenchy logo on hood and decklid; 'Givenchy' lettering in opera window; an identification plaque on instrument panel; and wire-spoke aluminum wheels.

(LINCOLN) TOWN CAR — V-8 — Only a four-door Town Car was offered for 1982 (sometimes referred to as, simply, "Lincoln"). The two-door model was dropped. New this year was a Cartier Designer Series, joining the former Signature Series. Appearance was the same as 1981. Sole engine was the fuel-injected 302 cid (5.0-liter) V-8, with electronic controls and four-speed overdrive automatic transmission. Town Car had a 3.08:1 rear axle ratio and an 18-gallon fuel tank. Power door locks were now standard, as was a remote-control decklid release (both formerly optional). Thirteen new paint colors were available. A dual exhaust system had joined the option list in mid-year 1981. The Signature Series added a coach roof, and 'Signature Series' script on the rear roof pillar. The new Cartier model featured two-tone paint: light pewter on top and opal on the bottom. It had a light pewter full vinyl roof in Sayville textured vinyl: opal bodyside moldings; opal and pewter in single red bodyside paint stripe; single red decklid paint stripe with Cartier logo in red tape; Cartier Designer logo in rear quarter windows; and turbine-spoke aluminum wheels. The instrument panel also carried the Cartier logo and identification. Cartier's interior was opal leather with light pewter luxury cloth (or leather in the insert area).

I.D. DATA: Lincoln again had a 17-symbol Vehicle Identification Number (VIN), fastened to the instrument panel, visible through the windshield. The first digit three symbols indicate manufacturer, make and vehicle type: '1LN' Lincoln; '1MR' Continental. The fourth symbol ('B') denotes restraint system. Next comes a letter 'P', followed by two digits that indicate body type: '94' 4dr. Town Car; '95' 2dr. Mark VI; '96' 4dr. Mark VI; '98' 4dr. Continental. Symbol eight indicates engine type: 'F' V8-302; '3' V6-232 2Bbl. Next is a check digit. Symbol ten indicates model year ('C' 1982). Symbol eleven is assembly plant ('Y' Wixom, MI). The final six digits make up the sequence number, starting with 600001. A Vehicle Certification Label on the left front door lock face panel or door pillar shows the manufacturer, month and year built, GVW, GAWR, VIN, and codes for body type, color, trim, axle, transmission, and special order information.

CONTINENTAL (V-6/V-8)

Model No.	Body/ Style No.	Body Type & Seating	Factory Price	Shipping Weight	Prod. Total
98	54D	4-dr. Sedan-5P	21302	3512	23,908

1982 Lincoln Continental Givenchy Designer Series sedan. (JG)

Model No.	Body/ Style No.	Body Type & Seating	Factory Price	Shipping Weight	Prod. Total
CONTINENTAL SIGNATURE SERIES (V-6/V-8)					
98/603	54D	4-dr. Sedan 5P	24456	3610	Note 1
CONTINENTAL GIVENCHY DESIGNER SERIES (V-6/V-8)					
98/60M	54D	4-dr. Sedan-5P	24803	3610	Note 1
TOWN CAR (V-8)					
94	54D	4-dr. Sedan-6P	16100	3936	35,069
TOWN CAR SIGNATURE SERIES (V-8)					
94/60U	54D	4-dr. Sedan-6P	17394	3952	Note 1
TOWN CAR CARTIER DESIGNER SERIES (V-8)					
94/605	54D	4-dr. Sedan-6P	18415	3944	Note 1
MARK VI (V-8)					
95	66D	2-dr. Coupe-6P	19452	3879	11,532
96	54D	4-dr. Sedan-6P	19924	3976	14,804
MARK VI SIGNATURE SERIES (V-8)					
95/603	66D	2-dr. Coupe-6P	22252	3888	Note 1
96/603	54D	4-dr. Sedan-6P	22720	3985	Note 1
MARK VI DESIGNER SERIES (V-8)					
95/60M	66D	2-dr. Givenchy-6P	22722	3910	Note 1
95/60N	66D	2-dr. Blass-6P	23594	3910	Note 1
96/60P	54D	4-dr. Pucci-6P	23465	3970	Note 1

NOTE 1: Production of Signature and Designer Series is included in basic model totals.

Model Number Note: Some sources include a prefix 'P' ahead of the two-digit number; e.g., 'P98' for Continental.

ENGINE [Base V-8 (Mark VI, Town Car)]: 90-degree, overhead valve V-8. Cast-iron block and head. Displacement: 302 cid (5.2 liters). Bore & stroke: 4.00 x 3.00 in. Compression ratio: 8.4:1. Brake horsepower: 134 at 3400 rpm. Torque: 232 lbs.-ft. at 2200 rpm. Five main bearings. Hydraulic valve lifters. Electronic fuel injection. VIN Code: F.

ENGINE [Base V-8 (Continental)]: Same as 302 cid V-8 above, but with 2Bbl. variable-venturi carburetor. Brake H.P.: 131 at 3400 rpm. Torque: 229 lbs.-ft. at 1200 rpm.

ENGINE [Optional V-6 (Continental)]: 90-degree, overhead valve V-6. Cast-iron block and head. Displacement: 232 cid (3.8 liters). Bore & stroke: 3.80 x 3.40 in. Compression ratio: 8.7:1. Brake horsepower: 112 at 4000 rpm. Torque: 175 lbs.-ft. at 2600 rpm. Four main bearings. Hydraulic valve lifters. Carburetor: 2Bbl. Motorcraft 2150. VIN Code: 3.

NOTE: Some sources list the V-6 as standard Continental engine, with the V-8 a no-cost option.

1982 Lincoln Continental sedan. (JG)

CHASSIS DATA: Wheelbase: (Continental) 108.7 in.; (Mark 2dr.) 114.3 in.; (Mark/Town 4dr.) 117.3 in. Overall Length: (Cont.) 201.2 in.; (Mark 2dr.) 216.0 in.; (Mark/Town 4dr.) 219.0 in. Height: (Cont.) 55.0 in.; (Mark 2dr.) 55.1 in.; (Mark 4dr.) 56.0 in.; (Town Car) 55.8 in. Width: (Cont.) 73.6 in.; (Mark/Town) 78.1 in. Front Tread: (Cont.) 58.4 in.; (Mark/Town) 62.2 in. Rear Tread: (Cont.) 59.0 in.; (Mark/Town) 62.0 in. Standard Tires: P205/75R15 SBR WSW.

TECHNICAL: Transmission: Four-speed automatic overdrive standard. Gear ratios: (1st) 2.40:1: (2nd) 1.47:1; (3rd) 1.00:1; (4th) 0.67:1; (Rev) 2.00:1. Standard final drive ratio: 3.08:1. Steering: (Continental) rack and pinion; (Mark/Town) recirculating ball; all power-assisted. Suspension: (Continental) modified MacPherson front struts with anti-sway bar, rigid rear axle with upper/lower trailing arms, and gas-pressurized shocks; (others) front control arms w/anti-sway bar, rigid four-link rear axle with lower trailing radius arms and oblique torque arms. Brakes: Front disc and rear drum, power-assisted; except Continental, four-wheel disc brakes. Ignition: Electronic. Body construction: (Continental) unibody; (others) separate body and box-type ladder frame. Fuel Tank: 18 gal. exc. Continental, 22.6 gal.

DRIVETRAIN OPTIONS: Dual exhaust system: Mark/Town ($83) but (NC) w/high-altitude emissions. Traction-Lok differential: Mark/Town ($128). H.D. battery ($28). Engine block heater ($26). Trailer towing pkg. ($223-$306). California emission system ($47). High-altitude emissions (NC).

CONTINENTAL CONVENIENCE/APPEARANCE OPTIONS: Appearance protection group ($47). Keyless entry ($141). Leather-wrapped steering wheel ($59). Dual lighted visor vanity mirrors ($146). Electronic AM/FM radio w/cassette or 8-track ($107). Power glass moonroof ($1259). Color-keyed vinyl bodyside molding ($64). Two-tone paint ($298). Moondust paint ($257). Monotone paint: Signature ($298 credit). Leather interior trim ($535). Wire spoke aluminum wheels ($395).

MARK VI/TOWN CAR CONVENIENCE/APPEARANCE OPTIONS: Option Packages: Headlamp convenience group ($175). Defroster group ($151). Comfort/Convenience: Fingertip speed control: Town ($178). Illuminated entry system ($77). Keyless entry ($141). Twin comfort six-way power seats w/recliners: Mark ($354); w/passenger recliner only ($302). Twin comfort power seats w/passenger recliner: Town Car ($288); dual recliners ($340) exc. ($52) w/Signature Series. Electronic instrument panel: Town ($804); Mark, delete ($804 credit). Garage door opener ($110). Tilt steering wheel: Town ($96). Intermittent wipers: Town ($53). Lighting and Mirrors: Touring lamps: Mark ($78). Right remote mirror: Town ($59). Dual remote mirrors w/lighted left thermometer: Town ($173); Mark ($114). Lighted visor vanity mirrors, pair ($146). Entertainment: Electronic AM/FM stereo radio w/8-track player ($107); w/cassette and Dolby ($107). 40 channel CB radio ($356). Premium sound system ($181). Exterior: Power glass panel moonroof ($1259). Carriage roof: Mark 2dr. ($1057). Full specialty roof: Mark 4dr. ($640) exc. Signature ($368). Specialty coach roof: Mark 2dr. ($1028) exc. Signature ($757). Vinyl coach roof ($272-$357). Moondust paint ($257). Dual-shade paint ($298). Custom accent stripes ($62). Door edge guards ($19-$27). Rocker panel molding delete: Mark ($149 credit). License plate frames: rear ($11); front/rear ($20). Lower bodyside protection ($40). Interior: Leather interior trim: Town ($436-$498); Mark ($535). Floor mats w/carpet inserts: front ($41); rear ($23). Wheels and Tires: Wire wheel covers ($274) exc. Mark Pucci or Town Cartier ($191 credit), or Mark Blass/Givenchy ($586 credit). Wire spoke aluminum wheels ($860) exc. Mark Signature or Town Cartier ($395), or Mark Pucci ($465). Lacy spoke aluminum wheels ($465) exc. Mark Signature ($191), Town Cartier (NC), Mark Givenchy/Blass ($395 credit). Turbine spoke aluminum wheels ($465) exc. Mark Signature ($191) and Mark Givenchy/Pucci ($395 credit). Self-sealing whitewall tires ($129). Conventional spare tire ($52).

HISTORY: Introduced: September 24, 1981, except Continental, Oct. 1, 1981. Model year production: 85,313. Calendar year production: 97,622. Calendar year sales by U.S. dealers: 93,068. Model year sales by U.S. dealers: 81,653.

HISTORY: Lincoln sales climbed more than 25 percent for 1982—just about the same percentage that they'd declined in the previous model year. Of course, there were three models this year, as opposed to only two in 1981. Obviously, some buyers who might otherwise have chosen another model turned to the new Continental instead. In fact, Mark VI sales dropped considerably, from 34,210 down to just 25,386. All Lincolns were built at Wixom, Michigan, a factory that put in considerable overtime to keep up with production. That production total rose sharply in 1982, up to 47,611 from just 26,651 for the prior calendar year. Lincolns had a 36-month, 36,000-mile warranty.

1983 LINCOLN

1983 Lincoln Continental sedan. (OCW)

All three Lincoln models were mainly carryovers this year. Each came in a choice of Designer or Signature Series, as well as base models. Continental lost its short-lived V-6 option, but offered a long list of standard equipment.

CONTINENTAL — V-8 — Bodies of Lincoln's mid-size "bustleback" four-door sedan showed virtually no change this year, except for an 'Electronic Fuel Injection' plaque on the front fender. That space previously held 'Continental' script. Continental now got the fuel-injected (TBI) version of the familiar 302 cid (5.0-liter) V-8, formerly installed only in the big Lincolns. The 3.8-liter V-6 was discontinued. Four-speed automatic overdrive was again the standard transmission, with a lockup torque converter. A heavy-duty 68 ampere-hour battery was now standard. So was a locking fuel filler door with remote release. Digital electronic instruments were standard. Continental's chassis was actually the old rear-drive "Fox" platform, which originated with Fairmont/Zephyr and also appeared (with shorter wheelbase) in this year's new LTD and Marquis. Standard equipment included four-wheel power disc brakes, self-sealing P205/75R15 whitewall tires, tilt steering, power windows and door locks, speed control, tinted glass, intermittent wipers, cornering lamps, dual power heated mirrors (thermometer on driver's side), stereo search radio, and illuminated entry. Six-way power Twin Comfort Lounge seats were upholstered in Radcliffe cloth. An owner's identification kit included two plaques with owner's initials on front doors, and one for his or her signature on the dash. This year's base model was actually a revision of the Signature Series of 1982, leaving no Signature in the lineup. The Givenchy Designer Series returned again in revised form, joined by an all-new Valentino Designer model. Givenchy was painted Midnight Black and Platinum Mist, with tri-color (gray-blue, magenta, and charcoal) accent striping and unique wrapover roof. Twin Comfort Lounge seats had charcoal Radcliffe cloth or leather seating surfaces. Givenchy identification went on the rear pillar, dash, and quarter windows. Valentino came in a dual-shade combination of its own: Walnut Moondust over Golden Mist, with black and gold accent striping and Valentino logo on the bodyside. Gold decklid accent striping included the Valentino logo. Comfort Lounge seats had Desert Tan Radcliffe cloth or leather seating surfaces, both trimmed with walnut straps and buttons. Valentino also had a leather-wrapped steering wheel. Both Designer Series included coach lamps and cast aluminum wire wheels. A dozen new paint colors were offered this year on "ordinary" Continentals, and seven new dual-shade combinations. Standard colors were: Midnight Black, Cameo White, Platinum Mist, Scarlet Red, Aegean Green Mist, Pastel French Vanilla, Desert Tan, Light Desert Tan, Midnight Blue Mist, and Scarlet Mist. Five Moondust colors were optional. Front and rear floor mats were now standard. New options included a three-channel garage door opener, coach lamps, automatic-dimming day/night mirror, and anti-theft alarm system. A bright brushed-aluminum upper bodyside molding option had been added in mid-year 1982.

MARK VI — V-8 — Some shuffling of the Designer Series occurred this year, but otherwise Mark was essentially a carryover with minimal change. Mark had a standard full vinyl roof with opera windows and limousine-style back window, front fender louvers (at the cowl), concealed halogen headlamps, and power vent windows. Standard engine was again the fuel-injected 302 cid (5.0-liter) V-8, with four-speed overdrive automatic. A new all-electronic stereo search radio became standard, while a larger (71 ampere-hour) battery had been standard since mid-year 1982. The Givenchy Designer Series was dropped, as was the four-door specialty roof. But a four-door carriage roof was a new option. Other new options included an automatic dimming day/night mirror, anti-theft alarm, three-channel garage door opener, and locking wire wheel covers. Pucci's Designer Series was now available on both two- and four-door Marks. Body paint was Blue Flannel Mist, with carriage roof in dark blue Cambria cloth. Opera windows were deleted. Inside was a choice of Academy Blue cloth or leather seat trim. Pucci had a wide bright bodyside molding with Midnight Blue vinyl insert, silver sparkle bodyside accent stripes, silver sparkle decklid pin stripe and Pucci logo. 'Emilio Pucci' script went in the rear door quarter window. Pucci's logo also appeared in tape on fender and decklid. Also included: a Mark "star" on rear roof pillar, leather-wrapped steering wheel, and turbine-spoke aluminum wheels. The Bill Blass Designer Series came in two dual-shade combinations: Midnight Black upper and lower, and Light French Vanilla middle, with black Cambria cloth carriage roof; or Light French Vanilla upper/lower and Midnight Black in the middle, with Light French Vanilla Bayville textured vinyl carriage roof. Inside was a choice of French Vanilla cloth or leather seat inserts, with French Vanilla leather bolsters in Signature Series sew style. Midnight Black bodyside moldings, vanilla and black bodyside accent stripes, and vanilla or black decklid accent stripe with the Bill Blass logo were included. (That logo also was on the rear roof pillar and instrument panel.) Bill Blass also had a leather-wrapped steering wheel and wire-spoke aluminum wheels. Rocker panel moldings were deleted. Eleven new paint colors were available on base Marks, and seven new dual-shade combinations. Standard colors were the same as Continental's, except Antique Mahogany Mist replaced Scarlet.

LINCOLN (TOWN CAR) — V-8 — While many sources continued to refer to the traditional big Lincoln sedan as a Town Car, the factory catalog listed it as, simply, "Lincoln." Not much was new, apart from an all-electronic stereo search radio and heavy-duty battery. Eleven new body colors and seven dual-shade combinations were added, along with eight new vinyl roof colors. Sole powertrain was again the fuel-injected 302 cid (5.0-liter) V-8 with four-speed overdrive automatic, the same as Mark VI. Standard equipment included auto-temp air conditioning, power antenna, coach and cornering lamps, power side/vent windows, analog clock, remote decklid release, tinted glass, left remote mirror, and full vinyl roof. The Cartier Designer Series had a new Medium Charcoal Moondust over Platinum Mist dual-shade paint treatment. Up top was a Medium Charcoal Moondust padded full vinyl roof in Valino grain. Also included: silver metallic bodyside moldings, a single red bodyside accent stripe, single red decklid accent stripe with Cartier logo in red tape, Cartier designer logo in rear quarter windows, and turbine-spoke aluminum wheels. Cartier's interior was charcoal luxury cloth or leather. Cartier also had a fingertip speed control, and leather-wrapped steering wheel. 'Signature Series' script on the rear quarter pillar and instrument panel identified that model. Twin Comfort Lounge seats came in distinctively sewn Shubert cloth. The coach roof had a "frenched" backlight. Padded center pillars had lower carpeting.

1983 Lincoln Signature Series Town Car. (OCW)

1983 Lincoln Continental Mark VI coupe. (OCW)

1983 Lincoln Continental Mark VI Pucci Designer Series sedan. (PH)

I.D. DATA: Lincoln again had a 17-symbol Vehicle Identification Number (VIN), fastened to the instrument panel, visible through the windshield. The first three symbols indicate manufacturer, make and vehicle type: '1LN' Lincoln; '1MR' Continental. Symbol four ('B') denotes restraint system. Next comes a letter 'P', followed by two digits that indicate body type: '96' 4dr. Town Car; '97' 4dr. Continental; '98' 2dr. Mark VI; '99' 4dr. Mark VI. Symbol eight indicates engine type: 'F' V8-302 EFI. Next is a check digit. Symbol ten indicates model year ('D' 1983). Symbol eleven is assembly plant ('Y' Wixom, MI). The final six digits make up the sequence number, starting with 600001. A Vehicle Certification Label on the left front door lock face panel or door pillar shows the manufacturer, month and year built, GVW, GAWR, VIN, and codes for body type, color, trim, axle, transmission, and special order data.

Model No.	Body/ Style No.	Body Type & Seating	Factory Price	Shipping Weight	Prod. Total
CONTINENTAL (V-8)					
97	54D	4-dr. Sedan-5P	21201	3719	16,831
CONTINENTAL VALENTINO DESIGNER SERIES (V-8)					
97/60R	54D	4-dr. Sedan-5P	22792	3757	Note 1
CONTINENTAL GIVENCHY DESIGNER SERIES (V-8)					
97/60M	54D	4-dr. Sedan-5P	22792	3757	Note 1
TOWN CAR (V-8)					
96	54D	4-dr. Sedan-6P	17139	4062	53,381
TOWN CAR SIGNATURE SERIES (V-8)					
96/60U	54D	4-dr. Sedan-6P	18481	4078	Note 1
TOWN CAR CARTIER DESIGNER SERIES (V-8)					
96/605	54D	4-dr. Sedan-6P	19817	4070	Note 1
MARK VI (V-8)					
98	66D	2-dr. Coupe-6P	20445	4004	12,743
99	54D	4-dr. Sedan-6P	20933	4105	18,113
MARK VI SIGNATURE SERIES (V-8)					
98/603	66D	2-dr. Coupe-6P	23340	4013	Note 1
99/603	54D	4-dr. Sedan-6P	23828	4114	Note 1
MARK VI DESIGNER SERIES (V-8)					
98/60N	66D	2-dr. Blass-6P	24749	4035	Note 1
98/60P	66D	2-dr. Pucci-6P	24345	N/A	Note 1
99/60P	54D	4-dr. Pucci-6P	24623	4099	Note 1

NOTE 1: Production of Signature and Designer Series is included in basic model totals.

Model Number Note: Model numbers changed slightly this year. Some sources include a prefix 'P' ahead of the two-digit number; e.g., 'P97' for Continental.

ENGINE [Base V-8 (all models)]: 90-degree, overhead valve V-8. Cast-iron block and head. Displacement: 302 cid (5.2 liters). Bore & stroke: 4.00 x 3.00 in. Compression ratio: 8.4:1. Brake horsepower: 130 at 3200 rpm. Torque: 240 lbs.-ft. at 2000 rpm. Five main bearings. Hydraulic valve lifters. Throttle-body (electronic) fuel injection. VIN Code: F.

1983 Lincoln Continental coupe. (OCW)

1983 Lincoln Continental Givenchy Designer Series sedan. (PH)

ENGINE [Optional V-8 (Mark VI)]: Same as 302 cid V-8 above, but Brake H.P.: 145 at 3600 rpm. Torque: 245 lbs.-ft. at 2200 rpm.

CHASSIS DATA: Wheelbase: (Continental) 108.6 in.; (Mark 2dr.) 114.3 in.; (Mark/Town 4dr.) 117.3 in. Overall Length: (Cont.) 201.2 in.; (Mark 2dr.) 216.0 in.; (Mark/Town 4dr.) 219.0 in. Height: (Cont.) 54.8 in.; (Mark 2dr.) 55.2 in.; (Mark 4dr.) 56.1 in.; (Town Car) 55.9 in. Width: (Cont.) 73.6 in.; (Mark/Town) 78.1 in. Front Tread: (Cont.) 58.4 in.; (Mark/Town) 62.2 in. Rear Tread: (Cont.) 59.0 in.; (Mark/Town) 62.0 in. Standard Tires: P205/75R15 SBR WSW (self-sealing on Continental).

TECHNICAL: Transmission: Four-speed automatic overdrive standard. Gear ratios: (1st) 2.40:1; (2nd) 1.47:1; (3rd) 1.00:1; (4th) 0.67:1; (Rev) 2.00:1. Standard final drive ratio: 3.08:1. Steering: (Continental) rack and pinion; (Mark/Town) recirculating ball; all power-assisted. Suspension: (Continental) modified MacPherson strut front with anti-sway bar and gas-pressurized shocks, rigid rear axle w/four links, coil springs and gas-pressurized shocks; (Mark/Town Car) short/long front control arms w/coil springs and anti-sway bar, rigid rear axle with four links and coil springs. Brakes: Front disc and rear drum, power-assisted; except Continental, four-wheel disc brakes. Ignition: Electronic. Body construction: (Continental) unibody; (Mark/Town) separate body and frame. Fuel Tank: 18 gal. exc. Continental, 22.3 gal.

DRIVETRAIN OPTIONS: Dual exhaust system ($83) but (NC) w/high-altitude emissions. Traction-Lok differential ($96-$160). Engine block heater ($26). Trailer towing pkg.: Mark/Town ($210-$306). California emission system ($75). High-altitude emissions (NC).

CONTINENTAL CONVENIENCE/APPEARANCE OPTIONS: Platinum luxury group: scarlet red interior, coach lamps, wire spoke aluminum wheels, brushed-aluminum bodyside moldings and leather-wrapped steering wheel ($656). Keyless entry ($89). Garage door opener ($140). Anti-theft alarm ($185). Leather-wrapped steering wheel ($99). Coach lamps ($88). Dual lighted visor vanity mirrors ($149). Automatic dimming day/night mirror ($89). Electronic AM/FM radio w/cassette or 8 track ($170). Power glass moonroof ($1289). Vinyl-insert bodyside molding ($64). Brushed-aluminum upper bodyside molding ($74). Two-tone paint ($320). Moondust paint ($263). License plate frames: rear ($11); front/rear ($20). Leather interior trim ($551). Wire spoke aluminum wheels ($395). Conventional spare tire ($97).

MARK VI/TOWN CAR CONVENIENCE/APPEARANCE OPTIONS: Option Packages: Appearance protection group ($30-$48). Headlamp convenience group ($178). Defroster group ($160). Comfort/Convenience: Fingertip speed control: Town ($188). Illuminated entry system ($77). Keyless entry ($165). Anti-theft alarm ($185). Twin comfort six-way power seats w/recliners: Mark ($357); w/passenger recliner only ($302). Twin comfort power seats w/passenger recliner: Town Car ($302); dual recliners ($357) exc. ($54) with Signature/Cartier. Electronic instrument panel: Town ($804); Mark, delete ($804 credit). Garage door opener ($140). Leather-wrapped steering wheel ($99). Tilt steering wheel: Town ($96). Interval wipers: Town ($60). Lighting and Mirrors: Touring lamps: Mark ($78). Right remote mirror: Town ($59). Dual power remote mirrors w/lighted left thermometer: Town ($174); Mark ($115). Lighted visor vanity mirrors, pair ($149). Automatic-dimming day/night mirror ($89). Entertainment: Electronic AM/FM stereo radio w/8-track or cassette player ($170). 40 channel CB radio ($356). Premium sound system ($194). Exterior: Power glass panel moonroof ($1289). Carriage roof ($1069-$1102) exc. Signature ($721-$726). Specialty coach roof: Mark 2dr. ($1073) exc. Signature ($779). Vinyl coach roof: Town ($343). Luxury Valino vinyl coach roof: Mark ($294-$381). Moondust paint ($263). Dual-shade paint ($320). Custom accent stripes: Mark ($62). License plate frames: rear ($11); front/rear ($20). Lower bodyside protection ($40). Interior: Leather interior trim ($459-$551) exc. Town Cartier (NC). Floor mats w/carpet inserts: front ($41); rear ($25). Wheels and Tires: Wire wheel covers: Town ($293) exc. Cartier ($145 credit). Locking wire wheel covers ($330) exc. Mark Pucci or Town

Cartier ($142 credit), Mark Blass ($537 credit). Wire spoke aluminum wheels ($867) exc. Mark Pucci or Town Cartier ($395), Mark Signature ($593). Lacy spoke aluminum wheels ($472) exc. Mark Signature ($191), Town Cartier or Mark Pucci (NC), Mark Blass ($395 credit). Turbine spoke aluminum wheels ($472) exc. Mark Signature ($191) and Mark Blass ($395 credit). Self-sealing whitewall tires ($139). Conventional spare tire ($64).

HISTORY: Introduced: October 14, 1982. Model year production: 101,068. Calendar year production: 106,528. Calendar year sales by U.S. dealers: 101,574. Model year sales by U.S. dealers: 105,326. Sales rose sharply for the 1983 model year, reaching a total of 105,326 for the luxury trio (versus 81,653 the year before). Calendar year sales of the bigger Lincolns jumped even more, causing a second shift to be added at the Wixom, Michigan, assembly plant. Continental now offered a 36-month/36,000-mile warranty on maintenance (free for the first year, with $50 deductible later). The full-line factory catalog referred to independent coachbuilders offering special limousine conversions.

1984 LINCOLN

The aero-styled Mark VII was all new for 1984, almost six inches shorter in wheelbase and nearly 400 pounds lighter than before. Aerodynamic features of the Mark VII included a sharply-raked windshield and hidden wipers. Continental alterations were far more modest, focused mainly on the front end. Lincoln added a turbocharged diesel option to both Mark VII and Continental this year, with the engine obtained from BMW. Mark also added an LSC model that combined improved handling with Lincoln's traditional luxury and riding qualities.

CONTINENTAL — SIX/V-8 — A new "aerodynamic" front end gave Continental a more modern look, though not radically different from the 1982-83 version. Rectangular quad headlamps again flanked a grille made up of thin vertical bars. But the front end had a slightly more sloped appearance, and the grille bars were separated into side-by-side sections. Rectangular parking/signal lamps stood immediately below the headlamps, and the wraparound marker lenses (now split into sections) extended farther back on the fender with an angled rear edge. Separate marker lenses below bumper level were no longer used. Two engine types were offered this year: the standard gas 302 cid (5.0-liter) V-8 with fuel injection, or the new 2.4-liter turbo diesel. The V-8 had a 3.08:1 axle ratio; the diesel a 3.73:1. Both were coupled to four-speed overdrive automatic transmissions. Electronic air suspension offered automatic level control. The fully electronic automatic-climate-control system featured a digital display, while the dash held an electronic odometer and digital fuel gauge with multi-color graphics. There was also a low oil level warning light and an overhead console, as well as new sew styles for the cloth and leather seat trim. Cast aluminum wheels were new. Revised instrument and door trim panels had real wood veneer appliqués. Fold-away outside mirrors were used. Continental's Givenchy Designer Series had light blue and Midnight Blue glamour clearcoat metallic paint, with tri-color bodyside accent stripe applied at the break line between the two colors. There was a two-color decklid accent stripe with double-G logo at the center. A rear roof pillar ornament was included. 'Givenchy' script went in the rear quarter window. Twin Comfort Lounge seats came in Admiral Blue luxury cloth (or optional leather at no extra cost). This year's Valentino Designer Series turned to Cabernet wine/medium charcoal glamour clearcoat metallic paint. It had a unique bodyside accent stripe and two-color decklid accent stripe, plus Valentino 'V' logo on the decklid. 'Valentino' script adorned the rear quarter window, and the rear roof pillar held a Valentino ornament. Twin Comfort Lounge seats were charcoal leather and mini-pleated cloth.

1984 Lincoln Continental sedan. (PH)

1984 Lincoln Continental Mark VII LSC coupe. (PH)

MARK VII — SIX/V-8 — Styling on the all-new "contemporary size premium" Lincoln retained traditional Mark cues, but on a dramatically different form. Aerodynamic appearance included aero headlamps, a wedge profile, and sloping back window. Lincoln described the new Mark as "the most airflow-efficient luxury car built in America, with a drag coefficient of 0.38." This edition was over a foot shorter than the Mark VI, mounted on the same chassis as the Continental sedan (downsized two years earlier). Some observers compared Mark VII's new design to Ford Thunderbird (logically enough) and even to Mercedes 380SEC. Mark had electronic air suspension with automatic three-way level control, nitra-cushion gas-pressurized front struts and rear shocks, and four-wheel power disc brakes. An all-new cockpit-style instrument panel had full electronics. The full-length floor console with gearshift lever included a lockable stowage bin in the armrest, while an overhead console held warning lights and dual-intensity courtesy/reading lamps. Base engine was the 302 cid (5.0-liter) V-8 with EFI and EEC-IV, hooked to four-speed automatic overdrive transmission. Mark VII could also be ordered with a new inline turbo diesel with dual exhausts, supplied by BMW-Steyr. Power rack-and-pinion steering replaced the old recirculating-ball system. The modern Mark had integrated, flush-mounted aero headlamps that extended well back onto fenders to form marker lenses; a sharply-sloped windshield; wide color-keyed lower bodyside moldings; bright wheel lip and belt moldings; and large nearly-triangular quarter windows. Full-length upper bodyside dual-band paint stripes were standard. The traditional decklid bulge, shaped as a simulated spare tire housing, was back again. So was an upright grille made up of thin vertical bars. Diesel models had a 'Turbo Diesel' badge on the decklid. Eleven new paint colors and six new interior trim colors were available. Standard equipment included front and rear stabilizer bars, tilt steering, speed control, power windows and door locks, locking gas door with remote release, electric rear defroster, and dual remote-control mirrors. Also standard: tinted glass, auto-temp air conditioning, six-way power driver's seat, electronic AM/FM stereo search radio, and P215/70R15 whitewall tires on cast aluminum wheels with center hub ornament. New options included heated driver and passenger seats, a compass/thermometer group for the header, handling package, and portable CB radio. Aimed at the European luxury coupe market, the new LSC Series had a standard handling package and 3.27:1 axle ratio. LSC had quicker-ratio power steering, high-performance P215/65R15 tires on six-inch aluminum wheels, dark charcoal lower bodyside paint, foglamps, and leather upholstery. There was also a new Versace Designer Series, as well as the popular Bill Blass Designer Series. This year's Blass came in dual-shade clearcoat metallic paint: Goldenrod Glamour with Harvest Wheat. Exterior trim included two-tone cream/dark green bodyside and decklid accent stripes, along with the designer's signature in the quarter window and Bill Blass logo on the decklid. Upholstery was standard two-tone flax and gold ultra-soft leather (or cloth trim at no extra charge). The dash held a Bill Blass logo. Emanating from Gianni Versace of Milan, Italy (a designer of avant-garde clothing), the Mark Versace had a walnut glamour clearcoat metallic body with two-tone tan/bright blue accent stripes on bodyside and decklid, and tan stripes on the hood. Also included: a signature in the quarter window, and Versace logo on the instrument panel. Desert Tan ultra-soft leather went inside, in designer's sew style. Cloth inserts with leather bolster seat trim were available at no extra cost.

1984 Lincoln Continental Mark VII coupe. (JG)

1984 Lincoln Town Car. (PH)

TOWN CAR — V-8 — The traditional long-wheelbase Lincoln sedan kept its same form this year, with little change beyond new nitra-cushion gas-pressurized shocks. Tire size rose a notch, to P215/70R15. The dash held a low oil level warning light and revised electronic radio graphics. Full wheel covers were new. Twelve new paint colors and six new dual-shade combinations were offered. A 100-amp alternator had become optional in mid-year 1983. New this year: an optional power decklid pull-down. The optional power six-way driver's seat had a two-position programmable memory. Town Car came only with the 302 cid (5.0-liter) fuel-injected V-8, four-speed overdrive automatic, and 3.08:1 axle. There was a Town Car Signature Series, and a Cartier Designer Series. The Cartier came in a new dual-shade paint treatment: Arctic White with platinum clearcoat metallic, with a new standard Arctic White coach Valino roof that included a "frenched" backlight, Cartier had premium bodyside moldings with platinum vinyl inserts, platinum and red bodyside tape striping, and a single red paint stripe on the decklid with Cartier logo in red tape. The Cartier logo was also laminated in the rear quarter window. Interiors had a choice of Dove Gray luxury cloth or leather upholstery. Town Car Signature had a coach roof, pleat-pillow upholstery, seatback straps and map pockets, and woodtone accents on doors and quarter trim panels.

I.D. DATA: Lincoln again had a 17-symbol Vehicle Identification Number (VIN), fastened to the instrument panel, visible through the windshield. The first three symbols indicate the manufacturer, make and vehicle type: '1LN' Lincoln; '1MR' Continental. Symbol four ('B') denotes restraint system. Next comes a letter 'P', followed by two digits that indicate body type: '96' 4dr. Town Car; '97' 4dr. Continental; '98' 2dr. Mark VII. Symbol eight indicates engine type: 'F' V8-302 EFI; 'L' turbo diesel L6-146. Next is a check digit. Symbol ten indicates model year ('E' 1984). Symbol eleven is assembly plant ('Y' Wixom, MI). The final six digits make up the sequence number, starting with 600001. A Vehicle Certification Label on the left front door lock face panel or door pillar shows the manufacturer, month and year built, GVW, GAWR, VIN, and codes for such items as body type, color, trim, axle, transmission, and special order data.

Model No.	Body/ Style No.	Body Type & Seating	Factory Price	Shipping Weight	Prod. Total
CONTINENTAL (V-8)					
97	54D	4-dr. Sedan-5P	21769	3719	30,468
CONTINENTAL VALENTINO DESIGNER SERIES (V-8)					
97/60R	54D	4-dr. Sedan-5P	24217	3757	Note 1
CONTINENTAL GIVENCHY DESIGNER SERIES (V-8)					
97/60M	54D	4-dr. Sedan-5P	24242	3757	Note 1
TOWN CAR (V-8)					
96	54D	4-dr. Sedan-6P	18071	4062	93,622
TOWN CAR SIGNATURE SERIES (V-8)					
96/60U	54D	4-dr. Sedan-6P	20040	4078	Note 1
TOWN CAR CARTIER DESIGNER SERIES (V-8)					
96/605	54D	4-dr. Sedan-6P	21706	4070	Note 1
MARK VII (V-8)					
98	63D	2-dr. Coupe-5P	21707	N/A	33,344
MARK VII LSC (V-8)					
98/938	63D	2-dr. Coupe-5P	23706	N/A	Note 1
MARK VII VERSACE DESIGNER SERIES (V-8)					
98/60P	63D	2-dr. Coupe-5P	24406	N/A	Note 1
MARK VII BILL BLASS DESIGNER SERIES (V-8)					
98/60N	63D	2-dr. Coupe-5P	24807	N/A	Note 1

NOTE 1: Production of Signature and Designer Series is included in basic model totals.

Diesel Engine Note: A turbo diesel engine (RPO Code 99L) for Continental or Mark VII cost $1235 extra.

Model Number Note: Some sources include a prefix 'P' ahead of the two-digit number; e.g., 'P97' for Continental.

ENGINE [Base V-8 (all models)]: 90-degree, overhead valve V-8. Cast-iron block and head. Displacement: 302 cid (5.2 liters). Bore & stroke: 4.00 x 3.00 in. Compression ratio: 8.4:1. Brake horsepower: 140 at 3200 rpm. Torque: 250 lbs.-ft. at 1600 rpm. Five main bearings. Hydraulic valve lifters. Throttle-body (electronic) fuel injection. VIN Code: F.

ENGINE [Optional V-8 (Town Car)]: Same as 302 cid V-8 above, with dual exhausts. Brake H.P.: 155 at 3600 rpm. Torque: 265 lbs.-ft. at 2000 rpm.

ENGINE [Optional Turbo Diesel Six (Continental, Mark VII)]: Inline, overhead-cam six-cylinder. Cast-iron block and aluminum head. Displacement: 149 cid (2.4 liters). Bore & stroke: 3.15 x 3.19 in. Compression ratio: 23.0:1. Brake horsepower: 115 at 4800 rpm. Torque: 155 lbs.-ft. at 2400 rpm. Four main bearings. Hydraulic valve lifters. Fuel injection. VIN Code: L.

CHASSIS DATA: Wheelbase: (Continental/Mark) 108.5 in.; (Town Car) 117.3 in. Overall Length: (Cont.) 200.7 in.; (Mark) 202.8 in.; (Town) 219.0 in. Height: (Cont.) 55.5 in.; (Mark) 54.0 in.; (Town) 55.9 in. Width: (Cont.) 73.6 in.; (Mark) 70.9 in.; (Town) 78.1 in. Front Tread: (Cont./Mark) 58.4 in.; (Town) 62.2 in. Rear Tread: (Cont./Mark) 59.0 in.; (Town) 62.0 in. Standard Tires: P215/70R15 SBR WSW exc. Mark LSC, P215/65R15 BSW.

TECHNICAL: Transmission: Four-speed automatic overdrive standard. Gear ratios: (1st) 2.40:1; (2nd) 1.47:1; (3rd) 1.00:1; (4th) 0.67:1; (Rev) 2.00:1. Turbo diesel ratios: (1st) 2.73:1; (2nd) 1.56:1; (3rd) 1.00:1; (4th) 0.73:1; (Rev) 2.09:1. Standard final drive ratio: 3.08:1 exc. turbo diesel, 3.73:1 and Mark VII LSC, 3.27:1. Steering: (Continental/Mark) rack and pinion; (Town Car) recirculating ball; all power-assisted. Suspension: (Continental/Mark) modified MacPherson strut front with anti-sway bar, rigid rear axle w/four links and anti-sway bar, electronically-controlled auto-leveling air springs and gas-pressurized shocks at front and rear; (Town Car) short/long front control arms w/coil springs and anti-sway bar, rigid rear axle with four links and coil springs, gas-pressurized front/rear shocks. Brakes: Four-wheel disc except (Town Car) front disc and rear drum; all power-assisted. Ignition: Electronic. Body construction: Unibody except (Town Car) separate body and frame. Fuel Tank: 22.3 gal. exc. Town Car, 18 gal.

DRIVETRAIN OPTIONS: Dual exhaust system: Town Car LPO ($82) but standard w/high-altitude emissions. Handling pkg.: Mark VII ($243). Traction-Lok differential ($96-$160). 100-amp alternator: Town ($62). Engine block heater ($26). Trailer towing pkg. ($209-$306). California emission system ($99). High-altitude emissions (NC).

CONTINENTAL CONVENIENCE/APPEARANCE OPTIONS: Compass/thermometer group ($191). Keyless entry ($122). Garage door opener ($140). Anti-theft alarm ($190). Power decklid pulldown ($79). Dual heated seats ($159). Dual power recliners ($191). Leather-wrapped steering wheel ($99). Coach lamps ($88). Foglamps ($158). Dual lighted visor vanity mirrors ($156). Automatic-dimming day/night mirror ($89). Electronic AM/FM radio w/cassette or 8-track ($170). Premium sound system ($206). Portable CB radio ($154). Power glass moonroof ($1289). Vinyl-insert bodyside molding ($70). Brushed-aluminum upper bodyside molding ($74). Dual-shade paint ($320). Moondust paint ($263). License plate frames: rear ($11); front/rear ($22). Leather interior trim: Signature ($551): Givenchy (NC). Wire spoke aluminum wheels: Signature ($686). Forged aluminum wheels ($291) exc. Designer ($395 credit). Puncture-sealant tires ($180). Conventional spare tire ($121).

MARK VII/TOWN CAR CONVENIENCE/APPEARANCE OPTIONS: Option Packages: Headlamp/convenience group ($190). Compass/thermometer group: Mark ($191). Defroster group: Town ($165). Comfort/Convenience: Fingertip speed control: Town ($188). Illuminated entry system ($83). Keyless entry ($205). Anti-theft alarm ($190). Power decklid pulldown ($79). Six-way power seats w/dual recliners: Mark ($225); w/power recliners ($416) exc. Designer ($191). Twin comfort power seats w/passenger recliner: Town Car ($320); dual recliners ($374) exc. ($54) with Signature/Cartier. Dual heated seats: Mark ($159). Electronic instrument panel: Town ($804). Garage door opener ($140). Leather-wrapped steering wheel ($99). Tilt steering wheel: Town ($101). Vent windows: Mark ($73). Interval wipers: Town ($60). Lighting and Mirrors: Foglamps: Mark ($158). Right remote mirror: Town ($59). Dual power remote mirrors: Town ($177). Dual heated outside mirrors: Mark ($49). Lighted visor vanity mirrors, pair ($156). Automatic-dimming day/night mirror ($89). Entertainment: Electronic AM/FM stereo radio w/8-track or cassette player ($170). CB radio: Town ($356). Portable CB: Mark ($154). Premium sound system ($206). Exterior: Power glass moonroof ($1289). Carriage roof: Town ($1069) exc. Town Signature ($726). Luxury Valino vinyl coach roof: Town ($343). Moondust paint ($263). Dual-shade paint: Town ($320). License plate frames: rear ($11); front/rear ($22). Interior: Leather interior trim ($459-$551) exc. Town Cartier (NC). Floor mats w/carpet inserts: front ($41); rear ($25). Wheels and Tires: Wire wheel covers: Town ($335) exc. Cartier ($137 credit). Wire spoke aluminum wheels: Town ($867) exc. Cartier ($395), or Signature

($532); Mark ($607-$686). Lacy spoke or turbine spoke aluminum wheels: Town ($472) exc. Signature ($137) or Cartier (NC). Forged aluminum wheels: Mark ($291) exc. Designer ($395 credit). Puncture-sealant whitewall tires ($180). Conventional spare tire: Town ($64); Mark ($121).

HISTORY: Introduced: November 10, 1983, except Town Car, Sept. 22, 1983. Model year production: 157,434. Calendar year production: 168,704. Calendar year sales by U.S. dealers: 151,475. Model year sales by U.S. dealers: 136,753. Lincoln sales rose 31 percent for the 1984 model year, while the all-new aero Mark VII gained a more modest number of customers. Continental, on the other hand, showed a whopping 71 percent sales gain. The new Mark VII design got extensive wind-tunnel testing at the Lockheed facility in Marietta, Georgia. Results were transmitted instantly to Ford engineers at Dearborn, who could then deduce the likely effect of modifications before the next trial. Mark VII's 0.38 drag coefficient was some 25 percent better than its predecessor, suggesting considerable gain in highway fuel economy. The federal government had first opposed the adoption of European-style aero headlamps, but Ford pressed the issue for two years (later joined by Chrysler) until permission was granted. That change in itself accounted for a five percent improvement in aero efficiency, as well as imparting a smooth look to the car's front end. *Ward's Automotive Yearbook* described the restyled Mark as 'an aerodynamic showpiece.'

1985 LINCOLN

1985 Lincoln Continental Mark VII coupe. (JG)

Anti-lock brakes arrived as an option on Continental and Mark VII. The ABS system, supplied by the Teves company of Germany, was the first of its kind to be offered on a domestic automobile. Electronic suspension became available on the Lincoln Town Car, which got a modest face lift. A mobile telephone became optional, anticipating the craze for cellular car phones that would soon arrive.

CONTINENTAL — SIX/V-8 — Biggest news for the four-door Continental was four-wheel anti-lock braking, standard on the two Designer Series with 5.0-liter V-8, and on all West Coast V-8 models. The system used a mini-computer to monitor all four wheels, and control braking pressure to prevent lockup during a hard stop. Otherwise, apart from a new hood ornament, no change was evident. Continental still had quad rectangular headlamps above rectangular parking lights, leading to sectioned wraparound lenses. Vertical tail lamps and the familiar decklid bulge, with 'Continental' lettering around its perimeter and a center emblem, continued as before. Standard engine was the fuel-injected 302 cid (5.0-liter) V-8, with BMW 2.4-liter turbo diesel optional once more (for the last time). A single serpentine accessory drive belt was added to the V-8. Four-speed overdrive automatic was the standard transmission. Standard equipment included auto-temp air conditioning, power four-wheel disc brakes and rack-and-pinion steering, power windows and door locks, electronic AM/FM stereo radio, cast aluminum wheels, overhead console, illuminated entry, tinted glass, and automatic level control. The electronic instrument panel had a message center and systems monitor. Givenchy and Valentino Designer Series were offered again, carrying the same new comfort/convenience package as Mark VII, with seven popular options. Givenchy came in dark rosewood clearcoat metallic paint with special bodyside accent stripe. It had exclusive decklid accent striping with a double-G logo at the center, a rear roof pillar ornament, and 'Givenchy' script in the rear quarter window. Twin Comfort Lounge seats were upholstered in Mulberry Brown leather (or no-cost optional luxury cloth). Valentino was Midnight Black and Burnished Pewter clearcoat metallic. The unique bodyside and decklid accent stripe included a Valentino 'V' logo on the decklid. The designer's badge went on the rear pillar, Valentino's interior held Sand Beige leather and 'vee' cloth seat trim.

1985 Lincoln Continental sedan. (PH)

MARK VII — SIX/V-8 — Like Continental, the Mark VII offered anti-lock braking this year. ABS was standard on the LSC, Bill Blass and Versace Series with 302 cid (5.0-liter) V-8, as well as all V-8s in the five Pacific states. In fact, the two models had become quite similar after Mark's downsizing in 1984 to the Continental-size wheelbase. Mark added a new hood ornament, but not much else in appearance changes. Three engines were offered for Mark VII: the regular fuel-injected 5.0-liter V-8 with 2.73:1 axle; a high-performance V-8 (on LSC only) with 3.27:1 rear axle; and the 2.4-liter turbo diesel with 3.73:1 axle. All engines were coupled to four-speed overdrive automatic. V-8s had the new single serpentine accessory drive belt. The high-performance V-8 had a performance camshaft, tubular exhaust manifolds with dual exhausts, aluminum intake manifolds higher-flow-rate throttle body, and low-restriction air cleaner all giving significant acceleration improvement. LSC also had electronic air suspension with special handling components, including stiffer front and rear stabilizer bars, special struts and shocks, and special air springs. New multi-adjustment, articulated sport seats for passenger and driver, with six-way power adjustments, helped to enhance LSC's driver-oriented image. Leather was used extensively inside. LSC's tires were Goodyear Eagle GT P215/65R15 blackwalls with an 'aggressive' tread pattern. Much of the regular Mark VII's brightwork was replaced with black or dark charcoal accents for the LSC. A 'fluted' dark charcoal full-length lower bodyside molding, with the bodyside painted dark charcoal below the molding, was a distinguishing feature. Also unique to LSC: foglamps and special cast aluminum wheels with exposed lug nuts. Mark's Bill Blass edition came in Silver Sand clearcoat metallic with Burnished Pewter below the lower bodyside moldings. It had two-tone bodyside and decklid accent stripes, designer's name in quarter window, Bill Blass logo on the decklid, and standard Carob Brown leather turn upholstery (or UltraSuede fabric seating surfaces). Either one could have leather designer seat straps to no extra cost. Navy clearcoat metallic was now the color of the Versace Designer Series, with two-tone accent stripes on bodyside and decklid, designer's name in the quarter window, and Admiral Blue ultra-soft leather seats (or at no extra cost, cloth inserts with leather bolster seat trim). A Versace logo went on the dash and floor mats. Standard equipment on the base Mark included power four-wheel disc brakes, power rack-and-pinion steering, front and rear stabilizer bars, tinted glass, digital clock, automatic level control, power windows, cast aluminum wheels, speed control, and electronic AM/FM stereo radio. A new optional comfort/convenience package included eight popular options: power decklid pull-down, keyless entry, illuminated entry, illuminated visor vanity mirrors, six-way power seats (standard on LSC), stereo search radio with cassette, heated remote mirrors, and headlamp convenience system. That package was standard on the Bill Blass and Versace Designer Series.

TOWN CAR — V-8 — 'Senior' Lincolns got a face lift for 1985, keeping the same basic (long wheelbase) body and separate chassis. Restyled wraparound parking/signal lamps were still in the front fender tips, outboard of (and separated from) quad rectangular headlamps. But the new grille texture had a tight crosshatch pattern, dominated by vertical bars. Tail lamps were now angled slightly, each one divided into two side-by-side sections. Flush bumpers also added a more modern look. Body corners were more rounded, at front and rear. Base engine remained the 302 cid (5.0-liter) EFI V-8 with four-speed automatic overdrive transmission. A higher-output version of the V-8 also was announced. Standard equipment now included speed control, tilt steering, manual reclining seats, right remote-control mirror, and intermittent wipers. A single key now operated door locks and ignition. Seat upholstery fabrics and styles were new this year. The horn button returned to the steering wheel from its former turn-signal stalk location. Signature Series and Cartier Designer Series now had standard keyless entry with illuminated entry, stereo search radio with cassette, and Premium Sound System. The Cartier edition was now painted in Arctic White/Platinum clearcoat metallic, with Arctic White coach Valino vinyl roof and 'frenched' backlight. Premium bodyside moldings had light charcoal vinyl inserts. Also included: platinum and red bodyside tape striping, and Cartier logo in red tape on the decklid. Cartier's logo also was laminated in the rear quarter window. Inside was a

choice of gray luxury cloth or leather inserts with Oxford White leather bolsters. New options included an automatic-leveling rear suspension (with electronic sensors and air-adjustable shocks), and hands-free mobile phone. Town Car also offered the comfort/convenience package available on Mark VII, with seven popular options.

I.D. DATA: Lincoln again had a 17-symbol Vehicle Identification Number (VIN) fastened to the instrument panel, visible through the windshield. Coding is similar to 1984. Model year code changed to 'F' for 1985. One engine code was added: 'M' H.O. V8-302 EFI.

Model No.	Body/ Style No.	Body Type & Seating	Factory Price	Shipping Weight	Prod. Total
CONTINENTAL (V-8)					
97/850A	54D	4-dr. Sedan-5P	22573	3719	28,253
CONTINENTAL VALENTINO DESIGNER SERIES (V-8)					
97/865A	54D	4-dr. Sedan-5P	26078	3757	Note 1
CONTINENTAL GIVENCHY DESIGNER SERIES (V-8)					
97/860A	54D	4-dr. Sedan-5P	25783	3757	Note 1
TOWN CAR (V-8)					
96/700A	54D	4-dr. Sedan-6P	19047	4062	119,878
TOWN CAR SIGNATURE SERIES (V-8)					
96/705A	54D	4-dr. Sedan-6P	22130	4078	Note 1
TOWN CAR CARTIER DESIGNER SERIES (V-8)					
96/710A	54D	4-dr. Sedan-6P	23637	4070	Note 1
MARK VII (V-8)					
98/800A	63D	2-dr. Coupe-5P	22399	N/A	18,355
MARK VII LSC (V-8)					
98/805A	63D	2-dr. Coupe-5P	24332	N/A	Note 1
MARK VII VERSACE DESIGNER SERIES (V-8)					

Model No.	Body/ Style No.	Body Type & Seating	Factory Price	Shipping Weight	Prod. Total
98/815A	63D	2-dr. Coupe-5P	26578	N/A	Note 1
MARK VII BILL BLASS DESIGNER SERIES (V-8)					
98/810A	63D	2-dr. Coupe-5P	26659	N/A	Note 1

NOTE 1: Production of LSC, Signature and Designer Series is included in basic model totals.

Diesel Engine Note: A turbo diesel engine (RPO Code 99L) for Continental or Mark VII cost $1234 extra on base models, $772 extra for Designer Series or Mark VII LSC.

Model Number Note: Suffixes changed this year. Some sources include a prefix 'P' ahead of the basic two-digit number; e.g., 'P97' for Continental.

ENGINE [Base V-8 (all models)]: 90-degree, overhead valve V-8. Cast-iron block and head. Displacement: 302 cid (5.2 liters). Bore & stroke: 4.00 x 3.00 in. Compression ratio: 8.4:1. Brake horsepower: 140 at 3200 rpm. Torque: 250 lbs.-ft. at 1600 rpm. Five main bearings. Hydraulic valve lifters. Throttle-body (electronic) fuel injection. VIN Code: F.

ENGINE [Optional V-8 (Town Car)]: Same as 302 cid V-8 above, with dual exhausts. Brake H.P.: 155 at 3600 rpm. Torque: 265 lbs.-ft. at 2000 rpm.

ENGINE [Base V-8 (Mark VII LSC)]: High-output version of 302 cid V-8 above: Compression ratio: 8.3:1. Brake H.P.: 180 at 4200 rpm. Torque: 260 lbs.-ft. at 2600 rpm. VIN Code: M.

1985 Lincoln Continental Mark VII LSC coupe. (PH)

1985 Lincoln Town Car. (PH)

ENGINE [Optional Turbo Diesel Six (Continental, Mark VII)]: Inline, overhead-cam six-cylinder. Cast-iron block and aluminum head. Displacement: 149 cid (2.4 liters). Bore & stroke: 3.15 x 3.19 in. Compression ratio: 23.0:1. Brake horsepower: 115 at 4800 rpm. Torque: 155 lbs.-ft. at 2400 rpm. Four main bearings. Hydraulic valve lifters. Fuel injection. VIN Code: L.

CHASSIS DATA: Wheelbase: (Continental/Mark) 108.5 in.; (Town Car) 117.3 in. Overall Length: (Cont.) 200.7 in.; (Mark) 202.8 in.; (Town) 219.0 in. Height: (Cont.) 55.6 in.; (Mark) 54.2 in.; (Town) 55.9 in. Width: (Cont.) 73.6 in.; (Mark) 70.9 in.; (Town) 78.1 in. Front Tread: (Cont./Mark) 58.4 in.; (Town) 62.2 in. Rear Tread: (Cont./Mark) 59.0 in.; (Town) 62.0 in. Standard Tires: P215/70R15 SBR WSW exc. Mark VII LSC, P215/65R15 BSW.

TECHNICAL: Transmission: Four-speed automatic overdrive standard. Gear ratios: (1st) 2.40:1; (2nd) 1.47:1; (3rd) 1.00:1; (4th) 0.67:1; (Rev) 2.00:1. Turbo diesel ratios: (1st) 2.73:1; (2nd) 1.56:1; (3rd) 1.00:1; (4th) 0.73:1; (Rev) 2.09:1. Standard final drive ratio: 3.08:1 exc. Mark VII, 2.73:1; Mark VII LSC, 3.27:1; and turbo diesel, 3.73:1. Steering/Suspension/Brakes/Body: same as 1984. Fuel Tank: 22.3 gal. exc. Town Car, 18 gal.

DRIVETRAIN OPTIONS: Dual exhaust system: Town Car ($83) but (NC) w/high-altitude emissions. Traction-Lok differential ($96-$160). 100-amp alternator: Town ($62). Engine block heater ($26). Trailer towing pkg.: Town ($223-$306). California emission system ($99). High-altitude emissions (NC).

CONTINENTAL/MARK VII CONVENIENCE/APPEARANCE OPTIONS: Comfort/convenience pkg.: Cont. ($932); Mark ($1293); Mark LSC ($1068). Compass/thermometer group ($191). Anti-theft alarm ($190). Mobile telephone ($2995-$3135). Dual power recliners ($191). Leather-wrapped steering wheel: Mark ($99). Automatic-dimming day/night mirror ($89). Electronic AM/FM radio w/cassette player and premium sound ($389). Power glass moonroof ($1289). Manual vent windows: Mark ($73). Vinyl-insert bodyside molding: Cont. ($70). Brushed-aluminum upper bodyside molding: Cont. ($74). Dual-shade paint: Cont. ($320). Glamour paint ($263). Leather interior trim ($551) exc. Cont. Givenchy (NC). Wire spoke aluminum wheels ($686). Forged or cast aluminum wheels ($291) exc. Designer ($395 credit). Puncture-sealant tires ($180).

TOWN CAR CONVENIENCE/APPEARANCE OPTIONS: Option Packages: Comfort/convenience Pkg. ($607-$821). Headlamp convenience group ($190). Defroster group ($165). Comfort/Convenience: Keyless entry ($205). Anti-theft alarm ($190). Mobile telephone ($2995-$3135). Power decklid pulldown ($79). Twin comfort power seats ($225). Electronic instrument panel ($822). Leather-wrapped steering wheel ($99). Lighting and Mirrors: Dual power remote mirrors ($177). Lighted visor vanity mirrors, pair ($156). Automatic-dimming day/night mirror ($89). Entertainment: Electronic AM/FM stereo radio w/cassette player and premium sound ($389). Exterior: Power glass moonroof ($1289). Carriage roof ($1069) exc. Signature ($726). Luxury Valino vinyl coach roof ($343). Glamour paint

($268). Dual-shade paint ($320). Protective bodyside molding ($70). Interior: Leather interior trim ($459-$521) exc. Cartier (NC). Floor mats w/carpet inserts: front ($41); rear ($25). Wheels and Tires: Wire wheel covers ($335) exc. Cartier ($137 credit). Wire spoke aluminum wheels ($867) exc. Cartier ($395) or Signature ($532). Lacy spoke or turbine spoke aluminum wheels ($472) exc. Signature ($137) or Cartier (NC). Puncture-sealant whitewall tires ($180). Conventional spare tire ($64).

HISTORY: Introduced: October 4, 1984. Model year production: 166,486. Calendar year production: 163,077. Calendar year sales by U.S. dealers: 165,138. Model year sales by U.S. dealers: 165,012.

HISTORY: Customers obviously had a craving for luxury motoring in the traditional style, as sales of Lincoln's Town Car reached a record level. A total of 116,015 found buyers, up a whopping 50 percent from the 1984 figure. The previous record of 94,242 had been set way back in 1978. Continental sales rose only slightly, while the Mark dropped sharply (down to just 20,198, versus 31,502 in the previous model year). The BMW-built turbo diesel found so few buyers that it was discontinued after 1985.

1986 LINCOLN

1986 Lincoln Continental sedan. (JG)

While option prices remained similar to their 1985 levels, the lists (especially for Continental and Mark VII) shrunk considerably. Both models had ample lists of standard equipment. Among other deletions, the slow-selling turbo diesel engine was dropped. Anti-lock braking became standard on all Continentals and Marks. The V-8 engine added sequential fuel injection, fast-burn combustion chambers, low-tension piston rings, and roller tappets, which delivered a boost in compression and horsepower.

CONTINENTAL — V-8 — Lincoln's short-wheelbase, five-passenger luxury four-door sedan showed no appearance change this year. Continental's grille was similar to Mark VII, made up of thin vertical bars with a slightly heavier center bar, and a wide upper header with inset center emblem. Recessed quad rectangular headlamps stood directly above amber-lensed park/signal lamps. The headlamp/park lamp moldings continued around fender tips to surround the large clear/amber marker and cornering lenses, with a molding that angled at the rear. After a couple of years of being branded simply 'Continental,' the mid-size sedan reverted to a 'Lincoln' badge. The standard 302 cid (5.0-liter) V-8 switched from throttle-body to sequential (multi-port) fuel injection, again hooked to four-speed overdrive automatic. The anti-lock, four-wheel disc braking system introduced in 1985 continued this year as standard. Electronic air suspension with level control was also standard. The turbo diesel option was abandoned during the '85 model year. Dropped for 1986 were the mobile phone option and Valentino edition. This year's lineup consisted only of the base Continental and Givenchy Designer Series. Standard equipment included keyless entry (and illuminated entry), power decklid pull-down (and remote release), compass/thermometer group, power remote heated mirrors, rear defroster, tinted glass, power windows and door locks, speed control, gas-pressurized shock absorbers, front and rear stabilizer bars, power steering, and P215/70R15 WSW w/tires on cast aluminum wheels. Also standard: power mini-vent windows, interval wipers, coach lamps, bumper rub strips with argent stripes, dual bodyside and decklid stripes, and electronic instrument panel.

MARK VII — V-8 — 'The car you never expected from Lincoln.' That's how the full-line catalog described Mark VII, now entering its third year in aero-styled shape. No significant changes were evident, other than the required high-mount center stop lamp. Mark's grille consisted of many thin vertical bars, dominated by seven slightly heavier vertical bars, with a heavy bright upper header and side surround molding. Inset into the center of the header was a tiny square emblem. Stretched from the grille edge to fender tips were large aero headlamps with integral parking/signal lamps, which met wraparound marker/cornering lenses. Above the left headlamp was 'Lincoln' lettering. Far below the bumper rub strips were LSC's standard foglamps. Three Marks were offered: base, Bill Blass Designer Series, and handling/performance LSC. The latter was powered by an improved high-output 302 cid (5.0-liter) V-8 with sequential (multi-port) fuel injection. tubular exhaust headers and tuned intake manifold, now delivering 200 horsepower. Other models had a more modest 5.0-liter V-8, also driving a four-speed (overdrive) automatic transmission. All Mark VII models now had a standard anti-lock brake system (ABS), introduced on LSC a year earlier. Electronic air suspension with level control continued as standard. The Versace Designer Series was dropped. Formerly optional equipment that became standard this year included keyless entry, power decklid pull-down, Premium Sound System, and power front seat recliners. LSC added a new analog instrument cluster to replace the former electronic display. Standard equipment on base Marks included auto-temp air conditioning, power steering, tilt wheel, P215/70R15 WSW tires on cast aluminum wheels, compass/thermometer, rear defroster, side window defoggers, power windows and door locks, speed control, tinted glass, interval wipers, and AM/FM stereo with cassette player. LSC added dual exhausts with its high-output engine, a handling suspension, P215/65R15 blackwalls, wide bodyside moldings, lower bodyside accent paint, tachometer, and leather seat trim with perforated leather or cloth inserts. Bill Blass had unique lower bodyside clearcoat paint, two-color bodyside/decklid paint stripes, wire-spoke aluminum wheels, and leather or Ultra Suede seat trim.

TOWN CAR — V-8 — Like its mates, the big four-door Lincoln added sequential fuel injection to its 302 cid (5.0-liter) V-8. That engine also got higher compression, roller tappets, new piston rings, and revised combustion chambers. Town Car's standard equipment list grew, now including the formerly optional dual power remote mirrors, and a defroster group. Three models were fielded again: base Town Car, Signature Series, and Cartier Designer Series. Appearance was the same as 1985. Town Car's classic-look upright grille had a subdued cross-hatch pattern dominated by seven vertical bright divider bars, with a bold and bright upper header bar that continued down the sides. The grille stood forward from the headlamp panel, with the space filled in by its wide, bright surrounding side moldings. Each pair of rectangular headlamps was surrounded by a strong, bright molding. Wraparound amber signal lenses were mounted in the fender extensions, with side marker lenses down below the bodyside moldings. Small 'Lincoln' block letters stood above the left headlamp; tiny 'Town Car' script at the cowl, just ahead of the front door. At the rear were vertical tail lamps, with a horizontal rectangular backup lamp at the center. Standard equipment included power brakes and steering, rear defroster, auto-temp air conditioning, power windows and door locks, power vent windows, tinted glass, gas-pressurized shocks, speed control, tilt steering, P215/70R15 WSW tires, mini spare tire, full vinyl roof, heated power remote mirrors, and a four-speaker AM/FM stereo radio. Town Car Signature and Cartier both added keyless illuminated entry, a conventional spare tire, wide bright lower bodyside moldings, and six-speaker radio with cassette player and premium sound. Signature had two-color hood/bodyside accent paint stripes and wire wheel covers. Cartier featured dual red hood and single red bodyside/decklid paint stripes, and turbine-spoke aluminum wheels. Both had a half coach roof with wrapover molding and "frenched" back window.

I.D. DATA: Lincoln again had a 17-symbol Vehicle Identification Number (VIN), fastened to the instrument panel, visible through the windshield. The first three symbols indicate manufacturer, make and vehicle type: '1LN' Lincoln. Symbol four denotes restraint system. Next comes a letter 'P'. followed by two digits that indicate body type: '96' 4dr. Town Car; '97' 4dr. Continental; '98' 2dr. Mark VII. Symbol eight indicates engine type: 'F' V8-302 EFI; 'M' H.O. V8-302 EFI. Next is a check digit. Symbol ten indicates model year ('G' 1986). Symbol eleven is assembly plant ('Y' Wixom, MI). The final six digits make up the sequence number, starting with 600001. A Vehicle Certification Label on the left front door lock face panel or door pillar shows the manufacturer, month and year built, GVW, GAWR, VIN, and codes for body, color, trim, axle, transmission, and special order data.

1986 Lincoln Continental Mark VII LSC coupe. (JG)

1986 Lincoln "Signature Series" Town Car. (JG)

Model No.	Body/ Style No.	Body Type & Seating	Factory Price	Shipping Weight	Prod. Total
CONTINENTAL (V-8)					
97/850A	54D	4-dr. Sedan-5P	24556	3778	19,012
CONTINENTAL GIVENCHY DESIGNER SERIES (V-8)					
97/860A	54D	4-dr. Sedan-5P	26837	3808	Note 1
TOWN CAR (V-8)					
96/700B	54D	4-dr. Sedan-6P	20764	4038	117,771
TOWN CAR SIGNATURE SERIES (V-8)					
96/705B	54D	4-dr. Sedan-6P	23972	4121	Note 1
TOWN CAR CARTIER DESIGNER SERIES (V-8)					
96/710B	54D	4-dr. Sedan-6P	25235	4093	Note 1
MARK VII (V-8)					
98/800A	63D	2-dr. Coupe-5P	22399	3667	20,056
MARK VII LSC (V-8)					
98/805B	63D	2-dr. Coupe-5P	23857	3718	Note 1
MARK VII BILL BLASS DESIGNER SERIES (V-8)					
98/810B	63D	2-dr. Coupe-5P	23857	3732	Note 1

NOTE 1: Production of LSC, Signature and Designer Series is included in basic model totals.

Model Number Note: Some sources include a prefix 'P' ahead of the basic two-digit number; e.g., 'P97' for Continental. Not all sources include the suffix after the slash.

ENGINE [Base V-8 (all models)]: 90-degree, overhead valve V-8. Cast-iron block and head. Displacement: 302 cid (5.2 liters). Bore & stroke: 4.00 x 3.00 in. Compression ratio: 8.9:1. Brake horsepower: 150 at 3200 rpm. Torque: 270 lbs.-ft. at 2000 rpm. Five main bearings. Hydraulic valve lifters. Sequential port (electronic) fuel injection. VIN Code: F.

ENGINE [Optional V-8 (Town Car)]: Same as 302 cid V-8 above, with dual exhausts. Brake H.P.: 160 at 3400 rpm. Torque: 280 lbs.-ft. at 2200 rpm.

ENGINE [Base V-8 (Mark VII LSC)]: High-output version of 302 cid V-8 above: Compression ratio: 9.2:1. Brake H.P.: 200 at 4000 rpm. Torque: 285 lbs.-ft. at 3000 rpm. VIN Code: M.

CHASSIS DATA: Wheelbase: (Continental/Mark) 108.5 in.; (Town Car) 117.3 in. Overall Length: (Cont.) 200.7 in.; (Mark) 202.8 in.; (Town) 219.0 in. Height: (Cont.) 55.6 in.; (Mark) 54.2 in.; (Town) 55.9 in. Width: (Cont.) 73.6 in.; (Mark) 70.9 in.; (Town) 78.1 in. Front Tread: (Cont./Mark) 58.4 in.; (Town) 62.2 in. Rear Tread: (Cont./Mark) 59.0 in.; (Town) 62.0 in. Standard Tires: P215/70R15 SBR WSW exc. Mark LSC, P215/65R15 BSW.

TECHNICAL: Transmission: Four-speed automatic overdrive standard. Gear ratios: (1st) 2.40:1; (2nd) 1.47:1; (3rd) 1.00:1; (4th) 0.67:1; (Rev) 2.00:1. Standard final drive ratio: 2.73:1 exc. Mark VII LSC, 3.27:1; Town Car Signature/Cartier, 3.08:1. Steering/Suspension/Body: same as 1984-85. Brakes: Four wheel disc except (Town Car) front disc and rear drum; all power-assisted; ABS (anti-lock) standard on Continental/Mark. Fuel Tank: 22.1 gal. exc. Town Car, 18 gal.

DRIVETRAIN OPTIONS: Dual exhaust system: Town Car LPO ($83) but standard w/high-altitude emissions. Traction-Lok differential ($101-$165). 100-amp alternator: Town ($67). Engine block heater ($26). Automatic load leveling: Town ($202). Trailer towing pkg.: Town ($159-$306). California emission system ($99).

CONTINENTAL/MARK VII CONVENIENCE/APPEARANCE OPTIONS: Anti-theft alarm ($200). Automatic-dimming day/night mirror ($89). Power glass moonroof ($1319). Vinyl-insert bodyside molding: Cont. ($70). Brushed-aluminum upper bodyside molding: Cont. ($74). Dual-shade paint: Cont. ($320). Glamour paint ($268). Leather interior trim ($551) exc. Cont. Givenchy (NC). Wire spoke aluminum wheels

($693) exc. Designer (NC). Geometric cast aluminum wheels ($298) exc. Designer ($395 credit). Puncture-sealant tires ($190).

TOWN CAR CONVENIENCE/APPEARANCE OPTIONS: Option Packages: Comfort/ convenience pkg. ($698). Headlamp convenience group ($198). Comfort/Convenience: Keyless illuminated entry ($209). Anti-theft alarm ($200). Power decklid pulldown ($79). Six-way power passenger seat ($235). Electronic instrument panel ($822). Leather-wrapped steering wheel ($105). Lighting/Mirrors: Lighted visor vanity mirrors, pair ($156). Automatic-dimming day/night mirror ($89). Entertainment: Electronic AM/FM stereo radio w/cassette player and premium sound ($389). Exterior: Power glass moonroof ($1319). Carriage roof ($1069) exc. Signature ($726). Luxury Valino vinyl coach roof ($343). Glamour paint ($268). Dual-shade paint ($320). Protective bodyside molding ($70). Interior: Leather interior trim ($459-$521) exc. Cartier (NC). Floor mats w/carpet inserts: front ($43); rear ($25). Wheels and Tires: Wire wheel covers ($341) exc. Cartier ($137 credit) and Signature (NC). Wire spoke aluminum wheels ($873) exc. Cartier ($395) or Signature ($532). Lacy spoke or turbine spoke aluminum wheels ($478) exc. Signature ($137) or Cartier (NC). Puncture-sealant whitewall tires ($190). Conventional spare tire ($64).

HISTORY: Introduced: October 3, 1985. Model year production: 156,839. Calendar year production: 183,035. Calendar year sales by U.S. dealers: 177,584. Model year sales by U.S. dealers: 159,320. Town Car broke its model year sales record for the second year in-a-row, while Continental sales fell 31 percent. Mark VII sold just a trifle better than in 1985. The main reason for buying a Town Car, according to Lincoln, was 'the aura of success it reflects upon its owners.' Lincoln called Town Car 'the roomiest passenger car in America' (not including wagons and vans), and touted its 'regal bearing and formal elegance.'

1987 LINCOLN

1987 Lincoln Continental Givenchy Designer Series sedan. (PH)

Because major reworking was expected soon for both Continental and Mark VII, little changed for the 1987 model year.

CONTINENTAL — V-8 — Essentially a carryover for 1987, the Continental four-door sedan was powered by a 302 cid (5.0 liter) V-8 with overdrive automatic transmission.

MARK VII — V-8 — Only minor equipment changes arrived with the 1987 Mark VII coupe, since a totally reworked version was expected at midyear. The standard 302 cid (5.0-liter) V-8 produced 150 horsepower, but the Mark VII LSC version delivered 200.

1987 Lincoln Mark VII LSC coupe. (PH)

1987 Lincoln Cartier Designer Series Town Car. (PH)

TOWN CAR — V-8 — Continuing as the most popular Lincoln (by far), the full-size Town Car changed little for 1987 except for more extensive use of galvanized metal in the body. A compact-disc player was ready to join the option list, and the Cartier Designer Series got some new body colors and seating fabrics. Powerplant was the same as the Continental and Mark VII: a 5.0-liter V-8 rated at 150 horsepower.

I.D. DATA: Lincoln had a 17-symbol Vehicle Identification Number (VIN) fastened to the instrument panel, visible through the windshield. The first three symbols indicate manufacturer, make, and vehicle type: '1LN' Lincoln. Symbol four denotes restraint system. Next comes a letter 'M', followed by two digits that indicate model number. Symbol eight indicates engine type. Next is a check digit. Symbol ten indicates model year ('H' 1987). Symbol eleven is assembly plant. The final six digits make up the sequence number, starting with 600001.

Model No.	Body/ Style No.	Body Type & Seating	Factory Price	Shipping Weight	Prod. Total
CONTINENTAL (V-8)					
97	54D	4-dr. Sedan-5P	24602	3799	17,597
CONTINENTAL GIVENCHY DESIGNER SERIES (V-8)					
98	54D	4-dr. Sedan-5P	28902	3826	Note 1
TOWN CAR (V-8)					
81	54D	4-dr. Sedan-6P	22549	4051	76,483
TOWN CAR SIGNATURE SERIES (V-8)					
82	54D	4-dr. Sedan-6P	25541	4106	Note 1
TOWN CAR CARTIER DESIGNER SERIES (V-8)					
83	54D	4-dr. Sedan-6P	26868	4086	Note 1
MARK VII (V-8)					
91	63D	2-dr. Coupe-5P	24216	3722	15,286
MARK VII LSC (V-8)					
93	63D	2-dr. Coupe-5P	25863	3772	Note 1
MARK VII BILL BLASS DESIGNER SERIES (V-8)					
92	63D	2-dr. Coupe-5P	25863	3747	Note 1

NOTE 1: Production of LSC, Signature, and Designer Series is included in basic model totals.

ENGINE [Base V-8 (all models)]: 90-degree, overhead valve V-8. Cast-iron block and head. Displacement: 302 cid (5.0 liters). Bore & stroke: 4.00 x 3.00 in. Compression ratio: 8.9:1. Brake horsepower: 150 at 3200 rpm. Torque: 270 lbs.-ft. at 2000 rpm. Five main bearings. Hydraulic valve lifters. Sequential port fuel injection.

ENGINE [Base V-8 (Mark VII LSC)]: High-output version of 302 cid V-8 above except: Compression ratio: 9.2:1. Brake horsepower: 200 at 4000 rpm. Torque: 285 lbs.-ft. at 3000 rpm.

1987 Lincoln "Sail America Commemorative Edition" Town Car. (PH)

CHASSIS DATA: Wheelbase: (Continental/Mark) 108.5 in.; (Town Car) 117.3 in. Overall Length: (Cont.) 200.7 in.; (Mark) 202.8 in.; (Town Car) 219.0 in. Height: (Cont.) 55.6 in.; (Mark) 54.2 in.; (Town) 55.9 in. Width: (Cont.) 73.6 in.; (Mark) 70.9 in.; (Town) 78.1 in. Front Tread: (Cont./Mark) 58.4 in.; (Town) 62.2 in. Rear Tread: (Cont./Mark) 59.0 in.; (Town) 62.0 in. Standard Tires: P215/70R15 SBR WSW exc. Mark LSC, P215/65R15 BSW.

TECHNICAL: Transmission: Four-speed automatic overdrive standard. Steering: (Cont/Mark) rack and pinion; (Town Car) recirculating ball. Front Suspension: (Cont./Mark) modified MacPherson struts with lower control arms, electronically-controlled air springs, automatic leveling and stabilizer bar; (Town Car) upper/lower control arms with coil springs and stabilizer bar. Rear Suspension: (Cont./Mark) rigid four-link axle with air springs, automatic leveling and stabilizer bar; (Town Car) four-link axle with coil springs. Brakes: Four-wheel disc except (Town Car) front disc and rear drum; all power-assisted; ABS (anti-lock) standard on Cont/Mark. Body construction: (Cont/Mark) unibody; (Town) separate body and frame. Fuel Tank: (Mark VII) 22.1 gal.; (Cont.) 20.3 gal.; (Town Car) 18 gal.

DRIVETRAIN OPTIONS: Traction-Lok differential ($101) except ($175) on base Town Car. Automatic load leveling: Town ($202). Trailer towing pkg: Town ($463-$546).

CONTINENTAL CONVENIENCE/APPEARANCE OPTIONS: Puncture sealant tires ($200). Anti-theft alarm system ($200). Automatic day/night mirror ($89). Brushed aluminum upper bodyside molding ($74). Bodyside protection molding ($70). Power glass moonroof ($1319). Glamour paint ($268). Dual-shade paint ($320). Leather seat trim, base ($560). JBL Audio System ($506). Wire spoke aluminum wheels, base ($693). California emission system ($99). Engine block heater ($26).

MARK VII CONVENIENCE/APPEARANCE OPTIONS: Puncture sealant tires ($200). Wire spoke aluminum wheels, base ($693). Anti-theft alarm system ($200). Power glass moonroof ($1319). Automatic day/night mirror ($89). Glamour paint ($268). Leather seat trim ($560). Engine block heater ($26). California emission system ($99).

TOWN CAR CONVENIENCE/APPEARANCE OPTIONS: Puncture sealant tires ($200). Locking wire wheel covers, Cartier ($137 credit). Base ($341). Lacy spoke aluminum wheels, Signature ($137). Others ($478). Turbine spoke aluminum wheels, Cartier ($395). Signature ($532). Base ($873). Electronic instrument panel ($822). Keyless illuminated entry system ($209). Anti-theft alarm system ($200). Power glass moonroof ($1319). Comfort/Convenience Pkg: Power decklid pulldown, illuminated visor mirrors, automatic headlight dimmer, autolamp delay system, dual power seats, rear floor mats ($694). Leather-wrapped steering wheel ($115). Automatic day/night mirror ($89). Bodyside protection molding ($70). Carriage roof, Signature ($726). Others ($1069). Valino luxury coach roof ($343). JBL Audio System ($506). Dual shade paint ($320). Glamour paint ($268). Leather seat trim, Signature ($469). Base ($531). Engine block heater ($26). California emissions system ($99). Dual exhaust system ($83). 100-amp, alternator ($67).

HISTORY: Introduced: October 2, 1986. Model year production: 109,366. Calendar year production: 135,951. Calendar year sales by U.S. dealers: 129,091. Model year sales by U.S. dealers: 180,712. A special, limited production "Sail America Commemorative Edition" Town Car was offered by Lincoln. It came in white with blue carriage roof and white leather interior. The Sail America team, competing to return the America's Cup to the United States, was supported by Ford Motor Co.

A dramatically reworked Continental was the big news at Lincoln for 1988, with front-wheel-drive and a six-cylinder engine—quite a change from the V-12s of the 1940s and the big V-8s since.

CONTINENTAL — V-6 — An all-new front-wheel-drive sedan replaced the former rear drive Continental. Not only was this the first "front driver" from Lincoln, it carried the first engine with fewer than eight cylinders: a 232 cid (3.8-liter) V-6, as used in Thunderbird and Cougar. The 140-horsepower V-6 had a counter-rotating balance shaft inside its block for smoother running, as well as multi-point fuel injection. It drove a four-speed overdrive automatic transmission. Slightly longer in wheelbase (109 inches) than its predecessor, the restyled Continental measured more than four inches longer overall. Though an inch narrower on the outside, the interior offered more room than before, with seating for six. Leather upholstery was standard, with cloth a no-cost option. The short option list included a compact-disc player, InstaClear heated windshield, and power moonroof. Continental's computer-controlled, fully independent suspension included electronic leveling. The four-wheel disc brakes came with a standard anti-lock system. Standard equipment included automatic climate control, tinted glass, power windows/locks, heated power mirrors, power driver's seat, cruise control, stereo radio/cassette and tilt steering. A Signature Series added a power passenger seat, autolamp system, illuminated/keyless entry and alloy wheels.

MARK VII — V-8 — Introduced early in the spring of 1987, the Mark VII coupe carried on with its rear-drive layout and V-8 engine, but added 25 horsepower. The base model was dropped, leaving only the sporty LSC touring coupe and the classy Bill Blass Designer Series. Standard anti-lock braking included a self-diagnostic provision.

TOWN CAR — V-8 — The traditional Lincoln sedan earned a new grille, tail lamps and rear panel this year, for its spring 1987 debut. Interiors wore new fabrics, too. A 150 horsepower, 302 cid (5.0-liter) V-8 with multi-point fuel injection continued to provide the power.

I.D. DATA: Lincoln's 17-symbol Vehicle Identification Number (VIN) was atop the instrument panel, visible through the windshield. The first three symbols indicate manufacturer, make and vehicle type: '1LN' Lincoln. Symbol four denotes restraint system. Next comes a letter 'M', followed by two digits that indicate model number. Symbol eight indicates engine type. Next is a check digit. Symbol ten is for model year ('J' 1988). Symbol eleven is assembly plant. The final six digits make up the sequence number, starting with 600001.

Model No.	Body/ Style No.	Body Type & Seating	Factory Price	Shipping Weight	Prod. Total
CONTINENTAL (V-6)					
97	N/A	4-dr. Sedan-6P	26078	3628	41,287
CONTINENTAL SIGNATURE SERIES (V-6)					
98	N/A	4-dr. Sedan-6P	27944	3618	Note 1
TOWN CAR (V-8)					
81	54D	4-dr. Sedan-6P	23126	4093	201,113
TOWN CAR SIGNATURE SERIES (V-8)					
82	54D	4-dr. Sedan-6P	25990	4119	Note 1
TOWN CAR CARTIER DESIGNER SERIES (V-8)					
83	54D	4-dr. Sedan-6P	27273	4107	Note 1
MARK VII LSC (V-8)					
93	63D	2-dr. Coupe-5P	25016	3772	38,259
MARK VII BILL BLASS DESIGNER SERIES (V-8)					
92	63D	2-dr. Coupe-5P	25016	3747	Note 1

NOTE 1: Production of Signature and Designer Series is included in basic model totals.

1988 LINCOLN

1988 Lincoln Mark VII LSC coupe. (PH)

1988 Lincoln Signature Series Town Car. (PH)

1988 Lincoln Continental sedan. (PH)

ENGINE [Base V-6 (Continental)]: 90-degree, overhead valve V-6. Cast-iron block and aluminum head. Displacement: 232 cid (3.8 liters). Bore & stroke: 3.80 x 3.40 in. Compression ratio: 9.0:1. Brake horsepower: 140 at 3800 rpm. Torque: 215 lbs.-ft. at 2200 rpm. Four main bearings. Hydraulic valve lifters. Multi-point fuel injection.

ENGINE [Base V-8 (Town Car)]: 90-degree, overhead valve V-8. Cast-iron block and head. Displacement: 302 cid (5.0 liters). Bore & stroke: 4.00 x 3.00 in. Compression ratio: 8.9:1. Brake horsepower: 150 at 3200 rpm. Torque: 270 lbs.-ft. at 2000 rpm. Five main bearings. Hydraulic valve lifters. Sequential port fuel injection.

ENGINE [Base V-8 (Mark VII)]: High-output version of 302 cid V-8 above except: Compression ratio: 9.2:1. Horsepower: 225 at 4000 rpm. Torque: 300 lbs.-ft. at 3200 rpm.

CHASSIS DATA: Wheelbase: (Continental) 109 in.; (Mark) 108.5 in.; (Town Car) 117.3 in. Overall length: (Cont.) 205.1 in.; (Mark) 202.8 in.; (Town Car) 219.0 in. Height: (Cont.) 55.6 in.; (Mark) 54.2 in.; (Town) 55.9 in. Width: (Cont.) 72.7 in.; (Mark) 70.9 in.; (Town) 78.1 in. Front Tread: (Cont.) 62.3 in.; (Mark) 58.4 in.; (Town) 62.2 in. Rear Tread: (Cont.) 61.1 in.; (Mark) 59.0 in.; (Town) 62.0 in. Standard Tire: (Cont.) P205/70R15; (Mark LSC) P215/65R15; (Mark Bill Blass/Town Car) P215/70R15.

TECHNICAL: Transmission: Four-speed automatic overdrive standard. Steering: (Cont/Mark) rack and pinion; (Town Car) recirculating ball. Front Suspension: (Cont.) MacPherson struts with integral air springs and two-stage damping; (Mark) modified MacPherson struts with lower control arms, electronically-controlled air springs, automatic leveling and stabilizer bar; (Town Car) upper/lower control arms with coil springs and stabilizer bar. Rear Suspension: (Cont.) MacPherson struts with integral air springs and two-stage damping; (Mark) rigid four-link axle with air springs, automatic leveling and stabilizer bar; (Town Car) four-link axle with coil springs. Brakes: Four-wheel disc except (Town Car) front disc and rear drum; all power-assisted; ABS (anti-lock) standard on Cont/Mark. Body construction: (Cont/Mark) unibody; (Town) separate body and frame. Fuel Tank: (Cont.) 18.6 gal.; (Mark VII) 22.1 gal.; (Town Car) 18.1 gal.

DRIVETRAIN OPTIONS: Traction-Lok differential: Mark/Town ($101). Automatic load leveling: Town ($202). Trailer towing pkg: Town ($463-$546).

CONTINENTAL CONVENIENCE/APPEARANCE OPTIONS: Keyless Illum Entry System ($209). Front License Plate Bracket (NC). Anti-Theft Alarm System ($200). Power Glass Moonroof ($1319). Memory Seat w/Power Lumbar ($301). Leather-Wrapped Strg Wheel ($115). JBL Audio System ($525). Compact Disc Player ($617). InstaClear Heated Windshield ($253). Comfort/Convenience Pkg ($819). Overhead Console Grp ($226). Cloth Seat Trim (NC). Locking Spoke Wheel Covers, Signature ($137). Locking Spoke Wheel Covers ($341). Styled Aluminum Wheels ($478).

MARK VII CONVENIENCE/APPEARANCE OPTIONS: Frt License Plate Bracket (NC). Anti-Theft Alarm System ($200). Pwr Glass Moonroof ($1319). Auto Dim Day/Night Mirror ($89). Eng Block Heater ($26). Calif. Emission System ($99).

TOWN CAR CONVENIENCE/APPEARANCE OPTIONS: Lckng Wire-Styled Wheel Covers, Cartier ($137 credit). Signature ($137 credit). Base ($341). Lacy Spoke Alum Wheels, Cartier (NC). Signature (NC). Base ($478). Turbine Spoke Alum Wheels, Cartier (NC). Signature (NC). Base ($478). Wire Spoke Alum Wheels, Cartier ($395). Signature ($395). Base ($873). Elect. Instrument Panel ($822). Keyless Illum Entry System ($209). Frt License Plate Bracket (NC). Anti-Theft Alarm System ($200). Pwr Glass Moonroof ($1319). Comfort/Convenience Pkg ($694). Leather-Wrapped Strg Wheel ($115). Auto Dim Day/Night Mirror ($89). Bodyside Protection Mldg ($70). Carriage Roof, Signature ($710). Others ($1069). Valino Lux Coach Roof ($359). JBL Audio System ($525). Compact Disc Player ($617). Dual Shade Paint ($320). Cartier Designer Series (NC). Signature Series ($469). Base ($531). Eng Block Heater ($26). Delete Trim Opt, High Alt ($323). Other ($406). Calif. Emission System ($99). Dual Exhaust, w/High Alt (NC). Other ($83). 100 Ampere Alternator ($67). TIRES: WSW Puncture Sealant ($200).

HISTORY: Introduced: March 1987 except (Continental) December 26, 1987. Model year production: 280,659. Calendar year production: 207,230. Calendar year sales by U.S. dealers: 191,624. Model year sales by U.S. dealers: 183,333.

1989 LINCOLN

This was largely a carryover year for the Lincoln luxury trio: two traditional rear-drive models with V-8 engines and one front-drive with a V-6.

CONTINENTAL — V-6 — A year before, Continental became the first Lincoln with front-wheel drive and a V-6 engine. This year, it was the first domestic automobile with standard airbags for both driver and passenger. The left bag fit into the customary spot in the steering wheel hub; its mate was mounted above the glove compartment. Two trim levels were available again, both powered by a 3.8-liter V-6 with four-speed overdrive automatic transmission. An altered final drive ratio improved response. As before, computer-controlled damping adjusted the suspension to changes in the road surface.

MARK VII — V-8 — Little change was evident in the sport/luxury coupes, which cost the same in either LSC or Bill Blass edition. A computer-malfunction warning light, formerly included only on California cars, now came with all models. The sporty LSC had bigger blackwall tires on alloy wheels, plus leather upholstery and quick-ratio power steering. The luxury-oriented Bill Blass Mark VII came with regular power steering, leather or cloth upholstery, and more chrome body trim. Both had automatic climate control, a self-leveling suspension, and six-way power front seats.

TOWN CAR — V-8 — Little changed in the traditional Lincoln sedan. Powerplant remained the 5.0-liter V-8 with 150 horsepower. Standard equipment included power windows and mirrors, automatic climate control, comfort lounge seats, and cruise control. The base model featured a new "Frenched" back window for its standard full vinyl roof. The Signature Series sported a coach roof, while the Cartier came with platinum bodyside moldings and new twin-shade paint.

I.D. DATA: Lincoln's 17-symbol Vehicle Identification Number (VIN) was atop the instrument panel, visible through the windshield. the first three symbols indicate manufacturer, make and vehicle type: 'ILN' Lincoln. Symbol four denotes restraint system. Next comes a letter 'M', followed by two digits that indicate model number. Symbol eight indicates engine type. Next is a check digit. Symbol ten indicates model year ('K' 1989). Symbol eleven is assembly plant. The final six digits make up the sequence number, starting with 600001.

1989 Lincoln Town Car sedan. (OCW)

Model No.	Body/Style No.	Body Type & Seating	Factory Price	Shipping Weight	Prod. Total
CONTINENTAL (V-6)					
97	N/A	4-dr. Sedan-6P	27468	3635	Note 1
CONTINENTAL SIGNATURE SERIES (V-6)					
98	N/A	4-dr. Sedan-6P	29334	3633	Note 1
TOWN CAR (V-8)					
81	54D	4-dr. Sedan-6P	25205	4044	Note 2
TOWN CAR SIGNATURE SERIES (V-8)					
82	43D	4-dr. Sedan-6P	28206	4070	Note 2
TOWN CAR CARTIER DESIGNER SERIES (V-8)					
83	54D	4-dr. Sedan-6P	29352	4059	Note 2
MARK VII LSC (V-8)					
93	63D	2-dr. Coupe-5P	27218	3743	Note 3
MARK VII BILL BLASS DESIGNER SERIES (V-8)					
92	63D	2-dr. Coupe-5P	27218	3783	Note 3

NOTE 1: Production of Continental models totaled 55,083 with no further breakout available.

NOTE 2: Production of Town Car models totaled 123,669 with no further breakout available.

NOTE 3: Production of Mark VII models totaled 28,607 with no further breakout available.

ENGINE [Base V-6 (Continental)]: 90-degree, overhead valve V-6. Cast-iron block and aluminum head. Displacement: 232 cid (3.8 liters). Bore & stroke: 3.80 x 3.40 in. Compression ratio: 9.0:1. Brake horsepower: 140 at 3800 rpm. Torque: 215 lbs.-ft. at 2200 rpm. Four main bearings. Hydraulic valve lifters. Multi-point fuel injection.

ENGINE [Base V-8 (Town Car)]: 90-degree, overhead valve V-8. Cast-iron block and head. Displacement: 302 cid (5.0 liters). Bore & stroke: 4.00 x 3.00 in. Compression ratio: 8.9:1. Brake horsepower: 150 at 3200 rpm. Torque: 270 lbs.-ft. at 2000 rpm. Five main bearings. Hydraulic valve lifters. Sequential port fuel injection.

ENGINE [Base V-8 (Mark VII)]: High-output version of 302 cid V-8 above except: Compression ratio: 9.2:1. Horsepower: 225 at 4000 rpm. Torque: 300 lbs.-ft. at 3200 rpm.

CHASSIS DATA: Wheelbase: (Continental) 109 in.; (Mark) 108.5 in.; (Town Car) 117.3 in. Overall Length: (Cont.) 205.1 in.; (Mark) 202.8 in.; (Town) 219.0 in. Height: (Cont.) 55.6 in.; (Mark) 54.2 in.; (Town) 55.9 in. Width: (Cont.) 72.7 in.; (Mark) 70.9 in.; (Town) 78.1 in. Front Tread: (Cont.) 62.3 in.; (Mark) 58.4 in.; (Town) 62.2 in. Rear Tread: (Cont.) 61.1 in.; (Mark) 59.0 in.; (Town) 62.0 in. Standard Tires: (Cont.) P205/70R15; (Mark LSC) P225/60R16 BSW; (Mark Bill Blass/Town Car) P215/70R15.

TECHNICAL: Transmission: Four-speed overdrive automatic standard. Steering: (Cont/Mark) rack and pinion; (Town Car) recirculating ball. Front Suspension: (Cont.) MacPherson struts with integral air springs and two-stage damping; (Mark) modified MacPherson struts with lower control arms, electronically-controlled air springs, automatic leveling and stabilizer bar: (Town Car) upper/lower control arms with coil springs and stabilizer bar. Rear Suspension: (Cont.) MacPherson struts with integral air springs and two-stage damping; (Mark) rigid four-link axle with air springs, automatic leveling and stabilizer bar; (Town Car) four-link axle with coil springs. Brakes: Four-wheel disc except (Town Car) front disc and rear drum; all power-assisted; ABS (antilock) standard on Cont/Mark. Body construction: (Cont/Mark) unibody; (Town) separate body and frame. Fuel Tank: (Cont.) 18.6 gal.; (Mark VII) 22.1 gal.; (Town Car) 18 gal.

DRIVETRAIN OPTIONS: Traction-Lok differential: Mark/Town ($101). Automatic load leveling: Town ($202). Trailer towing pkg.: Town ($546).

CONTINENTAL CONVENIENCE/APPEARANCE OPTIONS: Styled Alum Wheels ($478). Keyless Illum. Entry System ($209). Frt. Lic. Plate Bracket (NC). Anti-Theft Alarm System ($200). Pwr Glass Moonroof ($1319). Memory Seat w/Pwr Lumbar ($301). Leather-Wrapped Strg Wheel ($115). JBL Audio System ($525). Compact Disc Player ($627). InstaClear Heated Windshield ($253). Comfort/Convenience Grp ($819). Overhead Console Grp ($226). Cloth Seat Trim (NC). Eng Block Heater ($26). Calif. Emission System ($99). TIRES: P205/70R15 WSW (NC).

MARK VII CONVENIENCE/APPEARANCE OPTIONS: Frt Lic Plate bracket (NC). Anti-Theft Alarm System ($200). Pwr Glass Moonroof ($1319). Auto Dim Day/Night Mirror ($89). JBL Audio System ($525). Individual Luxury Seats (NC). Eng Block Heater ($26). Calif. Emission System ($100).

TOWN CAR CONVENIENCE/APPEARANCE OPTIONS: Elect. Instrument Panel ($822). Keyless Illum. Entry System ($225). Frt License Plate Bracket (NC). Anti-Theft Alarm System ($225). Pwr Glass Moonroof ($1420). Comfort/Convenience Grp ($694). Leather-Wrapped Strg Wheel ($120). Auto Dim Day/Night Mirror ($89). Bodyside Protection Mldg ($70). Carriage Roof, Signature ($710). Other ($1069). Valino Lux Coach Roof ($359). JBL Audio System ($525). Compact Disc Player ($617). Leather Seat Trim, Cartier (NC). Signature Series ($509). Base ($570). Eng Block Heater ($26). Delete Trim Opt, High Alt ($323). Other ($406). Calif. Emission System ($100). Dual Exhaust, w/High Alt (NC). Other ($83). 100 Amp Alternator ($67). Lckng Wire-Styled Wheel covers, Cartier ($137 credit). Signature ($137 credit). Base ($341). Lacy Spoke Alum Wheels, Cartier (NC). Signature (NC). Base ($525). Turbine Spoke Alum Wheels, Cartier (NC). Signature (NC). Base ($525). Wire Spoke Alum Wheels, Cartier ($395). Signature ($395). Base ($873).

HISTORY: Introduced: October 6, 1988, except (Continental) December 1988. Model year production: 215,966. Calendar year sales by U.S. dealers: 200,315. Model year sales by U.S. dealers: 203,890.

1990 LINCOLN

1990 Lincoln Continental Signature Series sedan. (OCW)

Dramatically different was the best way to describe the new-for-1990 Town Car, which earned the *Motor Trend* 'Car of the Year' award–the first luxury car to achieve that honor in nearly four decades. Far smoother and more rounded than its forerunners (though similar in size), the new Town Car not only looked modern, it functioned with modern efficiency, slicing through the air with a vastly improved co-efficient of drag. Lincoln's other two models carried on with minimal change.

CONTINENTAL — V-6 — Only a few changes in trim and equipment could be seen in the front-drive Lincoln. Bolder vertical bars made up a revised grille. A new ornament stood atop the hood, and tail lamps gained a slight revision. The power radio antenna now operated automatically, and wire wheel covers left the option list.

MARK VII — V-8 — A restyled grille was the only evident change in Lincoln's two-door coupe duo, but the interior held a new driver's side airbag and rear shoulder belts. The dashboard was new, too. The LSC rode standard BBS alloy wheels, while the luxury oriented Bill Blass Designer Series showed more chrome trim.

TOWN CAR — V-8 — For the first time since its debut a decade earlier, the traditional (and best selling) Lincoln earned a major restyling. Gone was the square look, replaced by gracefully rounded corners (not unlike those in the Continental). Dimensions were similar to its predecessor's, but the car's drag coefficient improved sharply. Still a big luxury automobile, with rear-wheel drive and 5.0-liter V-8 engine. the Town Car continued to sport such extras as opera windows. For safety's sake, twin airbags were installed and anti-lock braking was optional. Aircraft-style doors reached up into the roof. A self-leveling suspension relied upon rear air springs, and power steering was now speed-sensitive. Inside were new seats and a new instrument panel. Dual exhausts were included with the Cartier edition.

1990 Lincoln Town Car sedan. (OCW)

1990 Lincoln Town Car. (OCW)

I.D. DATA: Lincoln's 17-symbol Vehicle Identification Number (VIN) was atop the instrument panel, visible through the windshield. Symbol ten (model year) changed to 'L' for 1990.

Model No.	Body/ Style No.	Body Type & Seating	Factory Price	Shipping Weight	Prod. Total
CONTINENTAL (V-6)					
974	N/A	4-dr. Sedan-6P	29258	3618	Note 1
CONTINENTAL SIGNATURES SERIES (V-6)					
984	N/A	4-dr. Sedan-6P	31181	3628	Note 1
TOWN CAR (V-8)					
81F	N/A	4-dr. Sedan-6P	27315	3936	Note 2
TOWN CAR SIGNATURE SERIES (V-8)					
82F	N/A	4-dr. Sedan-6P	30043	3963	Note 2
TOWN CAR CARTIER DESIGNER SERIES (V-8)					
83F	N/A	4-dr. Sedan-6P	32137	3956	Note 2
MARK VII LSC (V-8)					
93	N/A	2-dr. Coupe-5P	29437	3715	Note 3
MARK VII BILL BLASS DESIGNER SERIES (V-8)					
92	N/A	2-dr. Coupe-5P	29215	3690	Note 3

NOTE 1: Production of Continental models totaled 64,257 with no further breakout available.

NOTE 2: Production of Town Car models totaled 147,160 with no further breakout available.

NOTE 3: Production of Mark VII models totaled 22,313 with no further breakout available.

ENGINE [Base V-6 (Continental)]: 90-degree, overhead valve V-6. Cast-iron block and aluminum head. Displacement: 232 cid (3.8 liters). Bore & stroke: 3.80 x 3.40 in. Compression ratio: 9.0:1. Brake horsepower: 140 at 3800 rpm. Torque: 215 lbs.-ft. at 2200 rpm. Four main bearings. Hydraulic valve lifters. Multi-point fuel injection.

ENGINE [Base V-8 (Town Car)]: 90-degree, overhead valve V-8. Cast-iron block and aluminum head. Displacement: 302 cid (5.0 liters). Bore & stroke: 4.00 x 3.00 in. Compression ratio: 8.9:1. Brake horsepower: 150 at 3200 rpm. Torque: 270 lbs.-ft. at 2000 rpm. Five main bearings. Hydraulic valve lifters. Sequential port fuel injection.

ENGINE [Base V-8 (Mark VII)]: High-output version of 302 cid V-8 above except: Compression ratio: 9.0:1. Horsepower: 225 at 4200 rpm. Torque: 300 lbs.-ft. at 3200 rpm.

CHASSIS DATA: Wheelbase: (Continental) 109 in.; (Mark) 108.5 in.; (Town Car) 117.4 in. Overall Length: (Cont.) 205.1 in.; (Mark) 202.8 in.; (Town) 220.2 in. Height: (Cont.) 55.6 in.; (Mark) 54.2 in.; (Town) 56.7 in. Width: (Cont.) 72.7 in.; (Mark) 70.9 in.; (Town) 78.1 in. Front Tread: (Cont.) 62.3 in.; (Mark) 58.4 in.; (Town) 62.8 in. Rear Tread: (Cont.) 61.1 in.; (Mark) 59.0 in.; (Town) 63.3 in. Standard Tires: (Mark LSC) P225/60R16; (others) P215/70R15.

TECHNICAL: Transmission: Four-speed overdrive automatic standard. Steering: (Cont/Mark) rack and pinion; (Town Car) recirculating ball. Front Suspension: (Cont.) MacPherson struts with integral air springs and two-stage damping; (Mark) modified MacPherson struts with lower control arms, electronically-controlled air springs, automatic leveling and stabilizer bar; (Town Car) upper/lower control arms with coil springs and stabilizer bar. Rear Suspension: (Cont.) MacPherson struts with integral air springs and two-stage damping; (Mark) rigid four-link axle with air springs, automatic leveling and stabilizer bar; (Town Car) four-link axle with coil springs, automatic leveling and stabilizer bar; (Town Car) four-link axle with coil springs. Brakes: Four-wheel disc except (Town Car) front disc and rear drum; all power-assisted; ABS (anti-lock) standard on Cont/Mark. Body construction: (Cont/Mark) unibody; (Town) separate body and frame. Fuel Tank: (Cont.) 18.6 gal.; (Mark VII) 22.1 gal.; (Town Car) 18 gal.

1990 Lincoln Mark VII LSC coupe. (OCW)

DRIVETRAIN OPTIONS: Anti-lock braking: Town ($936). Traction-Lok differential: Mark/Town ($101). Trailer towing pkg.: Town ($335-$417).

CONTINENTAL CONVENIENCE/APPEARANCE OPTIONS: Keyless Illum. Entry System ($225). Frt. Lic. Plate Bracket (NC). Anti-Theft Alarm System ($225). Pwr Moonroof ($1420). Memory Seat w/Pwr Lumbar ($301). Cellular Phone ($926). Leather-Wrapped Strg Wheel ($120). JBL Audio System ($525). Digital Audio Disc Player ($617). InstaClear Heated Windshield ($253). Comfort/Convenience Grp ($819). Overhead Console Grp ($236). Cloth Seat Trim (NC). Eng Block Heater ($26). Calif. Emission System ($100). Styled Alum Wheels, Signature Series (NC). Standard Series ($556). Geometric Spoke Alum Wheels, Signature Series (NC). Standard Series ($556).

MARK VII CONVENIENCE/APPEARANCE OPTIONS: Frt Lic Plate bracket (NC). Anti-Theft Alarm System ($225). Power Moonroof ($1420). Cellular Phone ($926). AM/FM Stereo w/Compact Disc ($299). Auto Day/Night Rearview Mirror ($89). JBL Audio System ($525). Individual Luxury Seats (NC). Eng Block Heater ($26). Calif. Emission System ($100).

TOWN CAR CONVENIENCE/APPEARANCE OPTIONS: Keyless Illum. Entry System ($225). Anti-Theft Alarm System ($225). Pwr Glass Moonroof ($1420). Programmable Memory Seat ($502). Cellular Phone ($926). Leather-Wrapped Strg Wheel ($120). 4-Wheel Anti-Lock Brake System ($936). AM/FM Stereo w/Digital Disc Player ($299). Passenger Side Airbag ($494). Electrochromic Auto Dimming Rr View Mirror ($99). JBL Audio System ($525). InstaClear Windshield ($253). Leather Seat Trim Cartier Designer Series (NC). Signature Series ($570). Base ($570). Comfort/Convenience Grp ($694). Eng Block Heater ($26). Calif. Emission System ($100). Dual Exhaust, w/High Alt (NC). Other ($83). Geometric Spoke Alum Wheels, Cartier (NC). Signature (NC). Base ($556). Turbine Spoke Aluminum Wheels, Cartier (NC). Signature (NC). Base ($556).

HISTORY: Model year production: 226,654. Calendar year sales by U.S. dealers: 231,660. Model year sales by U.S. dealers: 223,596.

1991 LINCOLN

Lincoln implemented the "Lincoln Commitment" program in 1991, which featured a 24-hour toll-free hotline and free emergency roadside service. The lineup remained unchanged from the year previous, but several changes occurred concerning powertrain combinations offered.

TOWN CAR — V-8 — After a complete redesign the year previous, the talk of the Town Car revolved around its new, modular 4.6-liter V-8 that replaced the 5.0-liter V-8 used previously. The new engine featured overhead chain cam drive, steel head gasket, aluminum cylinder heads and sequential electronic fuel injection, and was teamed with the four-speed automatic overdrive transmission. It offered 40 more horsepower than the larger engine it replaced. The 4.6-liter V-8 was available with optional dual exhaust. Town Car was again available in three series: base, Signature and Cartier. Standard equipment for the rear-drive Town Car included speed-sensitive, variable-assist power steering, rear air spring load leveling and automatic temperature control. Town Car offered 22 cubic feet of trunk space. Optional features included InstaClear heated windshield, a cellular phone, JBL audio system, power decklid pulldown and passenger-side airbag. Other improvements to the Town Car for 1991 included a revised front suspension for improved handling, standard four-wheel disc brakes and optional Traction Assist with standard anti-lock brakes. The Town Car's exterior appearance was also refined with redesigned bumpers and bodyside moldings. Inside, analog instrumentation replaced the formerly used electronic instruments.

1991 Lincoln Cartier Designer Series Town Car. (OCW)

CONTINENTAL — V-6 — The Continental was again available in base and Signature series in 1991 with each offering a four-door sedan. The base powerplant used, the 3.8-liter V-6, received several upgrades. A more precise airflow sensor, aluminum alloy pistons and standard dual exhaust all helped to increase the V-6's horsepower rating from 140 to 155. Also new was the AXOD-E electronic four-speed automatic overdrive transaxle. The AXOD-E integrated the transaxle control into the computerized EEC-IV electronic engine control system to achieve optimum economy and performance. Standard equipment for Continental models included four-wheel disc brakes with anti-lock system, driver's-side airbag, speed-sensitive, variable-assist power steering, computer-controlled air suspension, automatic climate control with sunload sensor, power driver's seat, fingertip speed control and tilt steering wheel. In addition, the upscale Signature sedan featured styled aluminum wheels, keyless entry, power passenger seat and power decklid pulldown. The option list for Continental models included a passenger-side airbag, power moonroof, JBL audio system, cellular phone and InstaClear heated windshield.

MARK VII — V-8 — The LSC (Luxury Sport Coupe) and Bill Blass series, each offering a coupe, were again the two Mark VII series available. A Mark VII Special Edition Package was also offered as an option, and featured special monochromatic paint and BBS wheels. Both the LSC and Bill Blass coupes were powered by the 225-hp HO (high output) 5.0-liter V-8, with sequential fuel injection, mated to the four-speed automatic overdrive transmission. Standard features included dual exhaust, four-wheel disc brakes with anti-lock system, electronic air suspension with automatic level control, driver's-side airbag, power antenna, illuminated and keyless entry, electronic climate control and nitrogen gas-pressurized front struts and rear shocks. Optional items included monochromatic paint, JBL audio system, cellular phone, anti-theft system and power moonroof. The Bill Blass coupe received several upgrades (to bring the model more on par with the LSC coupe) including a 3.27 rear axle ratio, constant-rate steering, handling suspension and BBS wheels.

I.D. DATA: Lincoln's 17-symbol Vehicle Identification Number (VIN) was stamped on a metal tab fastened to the instrument panel, visible through the windshield. The first three symbols indicate manufacturer, make and vehicle type. The fourth symbol denotes restraint system. Next comes a letter (usually 'M'), followed by two digits that indicate Model Number, as shown in left column of tables below. (Example: '81' Town Car four-door sedan. Symbol eight indicates engine type. Next is a check digit. Symbol ten indicates model year ('M' 1991). Symbol eleven denotes assembly plant. The final six digits make up the sequence number, starting with 000001.

Model No.	Body/ Style No.	Body Type & Seating	Factory Price	Shipping Weight	Prod. Total
TOWN CAR (V-8)					
M	81	4-dr. Sed-5P	28581	4035	Note 1
M	82	4-dr. Signature Sed-5P	31540	4055	Note 1
M	83	4-dr. Cartier Sed-5P	33627	4072	Note 1

NOTE 1: Production of four-door sedan models totaled 118,982 with no further breakout available.

CONTINENTAL (V-6)					
M	97	4-dr. Sed-5P	30395	3633	Note 1
M	98	4-dr. Signature Sed-5P	32304	3635	Note 1

NOTE 1: Production of four-door sedan models totaled 52,066 with no further breakout available.

1991 Lincoln Continental Signature Series sedan. (OCW)

MARK VII (V-8)					
M	93	2-dr. LSC Cpe-4P	30738	3807	Note 1
M	92	2-dr. Bill Blass Cpe-4P	30862	3782	Note 1

NOTE 1: Production of two-door coupe models totaled 8,880 with no further breakout available.

ENGINE [Base V-6 (Continental)]: 90-degree, overhead valve V-6. Cast-iron block and aluminum head. Displacement: 332 cid (3.8 liters). Bore & stroke: 3.80 x 3.40. Compression ratio: 9.0:1. Brake horsepower: 155 at 4000 RPM. Torque: 220 lbs.-ft. at 2200 RPM. Sequential fuel injection.

ENGINE [Base V-8 (Town Car)]: Modular, overhead cam V-8. Cast-iron block and aluminum head. Displacement: 281 cid (4.6 liters). Bore & stroke: 3.60 x 3.60 in. Compression ratio: 9.0:1. Brake horsepower: 190 at 4200 RPM (210 w/dual exhaust). Torque: 260 lbs.-ft. at 3600 RPM. Sequential fuel injection.

ENGINE [Base V-8 (Mark VII)]: High output 90-degree, overhead valve V-8. Cast-iron block and head. Displacement: 302 cid (5.0 liters). Bore & stroke: 4.00 x 3.00 in. Compression ratio: 9.0:1. Brake horsepower: 225 at 4200 RPM. Torque: 300 lbs.-ft. at 3200 RPM. Sequential fuel injection.

CHASSIS DATA: Wheelbase: (Town Car) 117.4 in.; (Continental) 109.0 in.; (Mark VII) 108.5 in. Overall Length: (Town Car) 218.8 in.; (Continental) 205.1 in.; (Mark VII) 202.8 in. Height: (Town Car) 56.7 in.; (Continental) 55.6 in.; (Mark VII) 54.2 in. Width: (Town Car) 78.1 in.; (Continental) 72.7 in.; (Mark VII) 70.9 in. Front tread: (Town Car) 62.8 in.; (Continental) 62.3 in.; (Mark VII) 58.4 in. Rear tread: (Town Car) 63.3 in.; (Continental) 61.1 in.; (Mark VII) 59.0 in. Standard Tires: (Town Car) P215/70R15; (Continental) P205/70R15; (Mark VII) P225/60R16.

TECHNICAL: Transmission: Four-speed overdrive automatic standard on Town Car, Continental and Mark VII. Drive Axle: (Town Car/Mark VII) rear; (Continental) front. Steering: (Town Car) Speed-sensitive, variable-assist Parallelogram. (Continental/Mark VII) rack/pinion. Front Suspension: (Town Car) Independent short/long arm w/ball joints, coil springs and front stabilizer bar; (Continental/Mark VII) Microprocessor controlled front and rear air springs w/automatic front-to-rear and side-to-side leveling and front and rear stabilizer bars. Rear Suspension: (Town Car) Four-bar link, rubber-coated pivots, rubber-insulated coil springs and direct double-acting shocks; (Continental/Mark VII) see front suspension. Brakes: (All) Front/rear disc (anti-lock system stnd on all). Body construction: (Town Car) separate body and frame; (Continental/Mark VII) unibody. Fuel tank: (Town Car) 20.0 gal.; (Continental) 18.6 gal.; (Mark VII) 21.0 gal.

DRIVETRAIN OPTIONS: Engines: 4.6-liter V-8 equipped w/dual exhaust (Town Car only) ($83). Transmission/Differential: Traction-Assist: Town Car ($222). Traction-Lok Axle: Mark VII ($101). Suspension/Brakes: H.D./handling susp.: Town Car w/High Altitude ($547); w/o ($630). Trailer towing pkg: Town Car w/High Altitude ($335); w/o ($417). Livery Pkg: Town Car w/High Altitude ($335); w/o ($417).

TOWN CAR CONVENIENCE/APPEARANCE OPTIONS: Calif. Emission Syst ($100). Turbine Spoke Alum Whls: Executive ($556), Signature (Std), Cartier (NC). Geometric Spoke Alum Whls: Executive ($556), Signature (NC), Cartier (Std). Leather Twin Comfort Lounge Seats: Executive ($570), Signature ($509), Cartier (NC). Anti-Theft Alarm Syst ($295). Comfort/Convenience Grp incl Rr Carpeted Flr Mats, Headlamp Convenience Grp, 6-Way Pwr Pass Seat, Pwr Decklid Pulldown and Driver Illum Visor Mirrors ($744). Elect Instrumentation ($249). Prog Memory Seat ($502). Electrochromic Auto Dimming Mirror ($111). Pwr Moonroof ($1540). AM/FM Stereo Radio w/Digital Disc Player ($299). JBL Audio Syst ($575). Cellular Phone ($799). Vinyl Roof, Full Padded ($1200). InstaClear Windshield ($309). Frt Lic Plate Bracket (NC). Eng Block Heater ($26). HD Pkg incl HD Cooling Pkg, Aux Trans Fluid Cooler, Unique Frt Stabilizer Bar, HD Shock Absorbers, HD Frt Suspension Lwr Ctrl Arms, Steel Driveshaft w/1330 U-Joint, 3.55 Ratio Traction-Lok HD Axle w/11x2-1/4-inch Rr Brake Drums, Dual Exhaust Syst, Steel Whls w/Lux Whl Cover, P215/70R15 WSW Tires, Full Size Matching Spare Tire w/Steel Whl, 84 Amp Battery, 95 Amp Alt, HD Frame, Std Jack Deleted: High Altitude ($547); Other ($630). Dual Exhaust Syst: w/High Altitude (NC); Other ($83). Trailer Tow Pkg incl HD Cooling, Aux Trans Fluid Cooler, Aux Pwr Strg Fluid Cooler, 1330 U-Joint w/Steel Driveshaft, 3.55 Ratio Axle, Dual Exhaust, Addtl Wiring Harness for Trailer Tail lamps, Stop Lamps, Turn Signals, Electric Brakes & Battery Charging, HD Turn Signals & Flashers, Conventional Size Spare Tire w/Matching Steel Whl, New Upgaged Frt Stabilizer, HD 30mm Shock Absorbers w/Revised Tuning, P215/70R15 Tires, 95 Amp Alt: High Altitude ($335); Other ($417). Livery Pkg incl Aux Trans Fluid Cooler, Aux Pwr Strg Fluid Cooler, 1330 U-Joint w/Steel Driveshaft, 3.27 Ratio Axle, Dual Exhaust, HD 30mm Shock Absorbers, Upgaged Frt Stabilizer Bar, 84 amp HD Battery, 95 Amp Alt, Std Eng Cooling Syst, P215/70R15 tires: High Altitude ($335); Other ($417). Anti-Lock Brake System, 4-Wheel Delete (-$936).

1991 Lincoln Mark VII LSC coupe. (OCW)

CONTINENTAL CONVENIENCE/APPEARANCE OPTIONS: Calif. Emission Syst ($100). Styled Alum Whls: Executive ($556); Signature (Std). Geometric Spoke Alum Whls: Executive ($556); Signature (NC). Anti-Theft Alarm Syst ($295). Comfort/Convenience Grp incl 6-Way Pwr Pass Seat, Dual Illum Visor Mirrors, Headlamp Convenience Grp, Pwr Decklid Pulldown, Rr Flr Mats, Pwr Pass Recline ($828). Overhead Console Grp incl Elect Digital Compass & Electrochromic Auto Dimming Rr View Mirror ($249). Keyless Illum Entry Syst ($225). Memory Seat w/Pwr Lumbar ($301). Pwr Moonroof ($1540). Digital Audio Disc Player ($617). JBL Audio Syst ($575). Leather-Wrapped Strg Whl ($120). Cellular Phone ($799). InstaClear Windshield ($309). Eng Block Heater ($26). Frt Lic Plate Bracket (NC).

MARK VII CONVENIENCE/APPEARANCE OPTIONS: Calif. Emission Syst ($100). Anti-Theft Alarm Syst ($295). Traction-Lok Axle ($101). Electrochromic Auto Dimming Mirror ($111). Pwr Moonroof ($1540). AM/FM Stereo Radio w/Digital Disc Player ($299). JBL Audio Syst ($575). Special Edition Pkg ($680). Cellular Phone ($799). Eng Block Heater ($26). Frt Lic Plate Bracket (NC).

HISTORY: U.S. model year Lincoln production totaled 188,009 for a 3.5 percent industry market share. U.S. calendar year Lincoln sales totaled 178,701.

1992 LINCOLN

Changes to the Lincoln lineup were minimal in 1992 with the formerly unnamed base models for both the Town Car and Continental series being renamed Executive. A passenger-side airbag was also added as standard equipment to the models of those two series.

TOWN CAR — V-8 — The revised 1992 Town Car lineup consisted of Executive (formerly named Town Car), Signature and Cartier series with each offering a four-door sedan. The modular, overhead cam 4.6-liter V-8 and four-speed automatic overdrive transmission again comprised the drivetrain of the Town Car line. New-for-1992 was a Jack Nicklaus Edition Town Car named after the famous professional golfer. It featured either Jewel Green or Arctic White Clearcoat Metallic paint and leather interior trim. A new standard feature of the Town Car was the addition of a passenger-side airbag.

1992 Lincoln Executive Series Town Car. (OCW)

1992 Lincoln Cartier Designer Series Town Car. (OCW)

1992 Lincoln Continental Signature Series sedan. (OCW)

CONTINENTAL — V-6 — Just as the Town Car lineup gained an Executive so, too, did the Continental series. The Executive four-door sedan (formerly named Continental) joined the Signature four-door sedan to round out the 1992 Continental lineup. A passenger-side airbag became standard equipment in all Continentals. Standard engine in the series was again the 3.8-liter V-6 teamed with the AXOD-E electronically controlled four-speed transaxle.

MARK VII — V-8 — The Mark VII series again was comprised of the LSC (Luxury Sport Coupe) and Bill Blass models powered by the HO 5.0-liter V-8 mated to a four-speed automatic transmission. This would be the final year for the Mark VII as a Mark VIII coupe was being readied for release as a 1993 model. The Mark VII Special Edition Package was again optional in 1992.

I.D. DATA: Lincoln's 17-symbol Vehicle Identification Number (VIN) was stamped on a metal tab fastened to the instrument panel, visible through the windshield. The first three symbols indicate manufacturer, make and vehicle type. The fourth symbol denotes restraint system. Next comes a letter (usually 'M'), followed by two digits that indicate Model Number, as shown in left column of tables below. (Example: '81' Town Car Executive four-door sedan). Symbol eight indicates engine type. Next is a check digit. Symbol ten indicates model year ('N' 1992). Symbol eleven denotes assembly plant. The final six digits make up the sequence number, starting with 000001.

Model No.	Body/ Style No.	Body Type & Seating	Factory Price	Shipping Weight	Prod. Total
TOWN CAR (V-8)					
M	81	4-dr. Executive Sed-5P	31211	4024	Note 1
M	82	4-dr. Signature Sed-5P	34252	4025	Note 1
M	83	4-dr. Cartier Sed-5P	36340	4035	Note 1

NOTE 1: Production of four-door sedan models totaled 109,094 with no further breakout available.

Model No.	Body/ Style No.	Body Type & Seating	Factory Price	Shipping Weight	Prod. Total
CONTINENTAL (V-6)					
M	97	4-dr. Executive Sed-5P	32263	3628	Note 1
M	98	4-dr. Signature Sed-5P	34253	3623	Note 1

NOTE 1: Production of four-door sedan models totaled 39,765 with no further breakout available.

Model No.	Body/ Style No.	Body Type & Seating	Factory Price	Shipping Weight	Prod. Total
MARK VII (V-8)					
M	93	2-dr. LSC Cpe-4P	32032	3781	Note 1
M	92	2-dr. Bill Blass Cpe-4P	32156	3768	Note 1

NOTE 1: Production of two-door coupe models totaled 5,439 with no further breakout available.

ENGINE [Base V-6 (Continental)]: 90-degree, overhead valve V-6. Cast-iron block and aluminum head. Displacement: 232 cid (3.8 liters). Bore & stroke: 3.80 x 3.40. Compression ratio: 9.0:1. Brake horsepower: 155 at 4000 RPM. Torque: 220 lbs.-ft. at 2200 RPM. Sequential fuel injection.

1992 Lincoln Continental Executive Series sedan. (OCW)

1992 Lincoln Mark VII Bill Blass Designer Series coupe. (OCW)

ENGINE [Base V-8 (Town Car)]: Modular, overhead cam V-8. Aluminum block and head. Displacement: 281 cid (4.6 liters). Bore & stroke: 3.60 x 3.60 in. Compression ratio: 9.0:1. Brake horsepower: 190 at 4200 RPM (210 at 4600 RPM w/dual exhaust). Torque: 260 lbs.-ft. at 3600 RPM (270 lbs.-ft. at 3400 RPM). Sequential fuel injection.

ENGINE [Base V-8 (Mark VII)]: High output 90-degree, overhead valve V-8. Cast-iron block and head. Displacement: 302 cid (5.0 liters). Bore & stroke: 4.00 x 3.00 in. Compression ratio: 9.0:1. Brake horsepower: 225 at 4200 RPM. Torque: 300 lbs.-ft. at 3200 RPM. Sequential fuel injection.

CHASSIS DATA: Wheelbase: (Town Car) 117.4 in.; (Continental) 109.0 in.; (Mark VII) 108.5 in. Overall Length: (Town Car) 218.9 in.; (Continental) 205.1 in.; (Mark VII) 202.8 in. Height: (Town Car) 56.9 in.; (Continental) 55.6 in.; (Mark VII) 54.2 in. Width: (Town Car) 76.9 in.; (Continental) 72.7 in.: (Mark VII) 70.9 in. Front tread: (Town Car) 62.8 in.; (Continental) 62.3 in.; (Mark VII) 58.4 in. Rear tread: (Town Car) 63.3 in.; (Continental) 61.1 in.; (Mark VII) 59.0 in. Standard Tires: (Town Car) P215/70R15; (Continental) P205/70R15; (Mark VII) P225/60R16.

TECHNICAL: Transmission: Four-speed overdrive automatic standard on Town Car, Continental and Mark VII. Drive Axle: (Town Car/Mark VII) rear; (Continental) front. Steering: (Town Car) Speed-sensitive, variable-assist Parallelogram. (Continental/Mark VII) rack/pinion. Front Suspension: (Town Car) Independent short/long arm w/ball joints, coil springs and front stabilizer bar; (Continental/Mark VII) Microprocessor controlled front and rear air springs w/automatic front-to-rear and side-to-side leveling and front and rear stabilizer bars. Rear Suspension: (Town Car) Four-bar link, rubber-coated pivots, rubber-insulated coil springs and direct double-acting shocks; (Continental/Mark VII) see front suspension. Brakes: (All) Front/rear disc (anti-lock system stnd on all). Body construction: (Town Car) separate body and frame; (Continental/Mark VII) unibody. Fuel tank: (Town Car) 20.0 gal.; (Continental) 18.4 gal.; (Mark VII) 21.0 gal.

DRIVETRAIN OPTIONS: Engines: 4.6-liter V-8 equipped w/dual exhaust (Town Car only) ($83). Transmission/Differential: Traction-Assist: Town Car ($222). Traction-Lok Axle: Mark VII ($101). Suspension/Brakes: H.D./handling susp.: Town Car (N/A Cartier) w/High Altitude ($688); w/o ($770). Trailer towing pkg: Town Car w/High Altitude ($335); w/o ($417). Livery Pkg: Town Car w/High Altitude ($335); w/o ($417).

1992 Lincoln Mark VII LSC coupe. (OCW)

TOWN CAR CONVENIENCE/APPEARANCE OPTIONS: Jack Nicklaus Edition Pref Equip Pkg incl Prog Memory Seat, Monotone Paint Treatment and Leather Interior Trim ($1279). Calif. Emission Syst ($100). Turbine Spoke Alum Whls: Executive ($556); Cartier (NC). Geometric Spoke Alum Whls: Executive ($556); Signature (NC). Leather Twin Comfort Lounge Seats: Executive ($570); Signature ($570); Cartier (NC). Anti-Theft Alarm Syst: Executive ($295). Comfort/Convenience Grp incl Rr Carpeted Flr Mats, Headlamp Convenience Grp, 6-Way Pwr Pass Seat, Pwr Decklid Pulldown and Driver Illum Visor Mirrors: Executive ($658). Elect Instrumentation: Executive ($249). Keyless Illum Entry Syst incl Auto Door Lckng Feature & Ext Lckng Capability: Executive ($225). Prog Memory Seat: Signature ($548). Electrochromic Auto Dimming Mirror ($111). Pwr Moonroof ($1550). Monotone Paint Treatment: Signature (NC). AM/FM Stereo Radio w/CD Changer ($833). JBL Audio Syst ($575). Cellular Phone: Executive ($459). Leather-Wrapped Strg Whl: Executive ($120). Conventional Spare Tire ($86). Traction Assist ($222). Vinyl Roof, Full Padded ($800). InstaClear Windshield ($309). Frt Lic Plate Bracket (NC). Eng Block Heater ($61). HD Pkg incl HD Cooling Pkg, Aux Trans Fluid Cooler, Unique Frt Stabilizer Bar, HD Shock Absorbers, HD Frt Suspension Lwr Ctrl Arms, Steel Driveshaft w/1330 U-Joint, 3.55 Ratio Traction-Lok HD Axle w/11x2-1/4-inch Rr Brake Drums, Dual Exhaust Syst, Steel Whls w/Lux Whl Cover, P215/70R15 WSW Tires, Full Size Matching Spare Tire w/Steel Whl, 84 Amp Battery, 95 Amp Alt, HD Frame, Std Jack Deleted: High Altitude ($688); Other ($770). Dual Exhaust Syst: w/High Altitude (NC); Other ($83). Trailer Tow Pkg incl HD Cooling, Aux Trans Fluid Cooler, Aux Pwr Strg Fluid Cooler, 1330 U-Joint w/Steel Driveshaft, 3.55 Ratio Axle, Dual Exhaust, Addtl Wiring Harness for Trailer Tail lamps, Stop Lamps, Turn Signals, Electric Brakes & Battery Charging, HD Turn Signals & Flashers, Conventional Size Spare Tire w/Matching Steel Whl, New Upgaged Frt Stabilizer, HD 30mm Shock Absorbers w/Revised Tuning, P215/70R15 Tires, 95 Amp Alt: High Altitude ($335); Other ($417). Livery Pkg incl Aux Trans Fluid Cooler, Aux Pwr Strg Fluid Cooler, 1330 U-Joint w/Steel Driveshaft, 3.27 Ratio Axle, Dual Exhaust, HD 30mm Shock Absorbers, Upgaged Frt Stabilizer Bar, 84 amp HD Battery, 95 Amp Alt, Std Eng Cooling Syst, P215/70R15 tires: High Altitude ($335); Other ($417).

CONTINENTAL CONVENIENCE/APPEARANCE OPTIONS: Special Value Pkg 952A incl Comfort/Convenience Grp, Keyless Illum Entry Syst, Leather-Wrapped Strg Whl, Styled Alum Whls (NC). Calif. Emission Syst ($100). Styled Alum Whls: Executive ($556). Geometric Spoke Alum Whls: Executive ($556). Anti-Theft Alarm Syst ($295). Comfort/Convenience Grp incl 6-Way Pwr Pass Seat, Dual Illum Visor Mirrors, Headlamp Convenience Grp, Pwr Decklid Pulldown, Rr Flr Mats, Pwr Pass Recline ($828). Overhead Console Grp incl Elect Digital Compass & Electrochromic Auto Dimming Rr View Mirror ($361). Keyless Illum Entry Syst ($306). Pwr Moonroof ($1550). CD Player ($617). JBL Audio Syst ($575). Leather-Wrapped Strg Whl ($120). Cellular Phone ($495). InstaClear Windshield ($309). Eng Block Heater ($61).

MARK VII CONVENIENCE/APPEARANCE OPTIONS: Special Edition Pkg 413 incl Monochromatic Paint and BBS Whls ($680). Calif. Emission Syst ($100). Anti-Theft Alarm Syst ($295). Traction-Lok Axle ($101). Electrochromic Auto Dimming Mirror ($111). Pwr Moonroof ($1550). Elect AM/FM Stereo Radio w/CD Player ($299). JBL Audio Syst ($575). Cellular Phone ($459). Eng Block Heater ($61).

HISTORY: U.S. model year Lincoln production totaled 160,012 for a 2.83 percent industry market share. U.S. calendar year Lincoln sales totaled 161,648.

1993 LINCOLN

The Mark VIII coupe made its debut later in the 1993 model year than its Town Car and Continental stable mates, and sported its first total redesign since the 1984 Mark VII coupe. It was also a short sales year for the 1993 version of the Continental as the new-design, 1994 models were launched in the spring of 1993.

1993 Lincoln Signature Series Town Car. (OCW)

1993 Lincoln Continental Signature Series sedan. (OCW)

TOWN CAR — V-8 — The Town Car was freshened for 1993 receiving a new grille, geometric-spoke aluminum wheels, new tail lamps and rear safety-reflector bar. New standard equipment included a leather-wrapped steering wheel, electronic instrument cluster, remote-control keyless entry and driver's-side one-touch express-down power windows. Also standard were dual airbags and anti-lock brakes. The line-up again consisted of Executive, Signature and Cartier four-door sedans. The modular, overhead cam 4.6-liter V-8 and electronically assisted four-speed automatic overdrive transmission again provided the power for Town Car models. Optional equipment included traction assist, voice-activated cellular phone, Y-spoke aluminum wheels, JBL audio system and a new handling package. The Jack Nicklaus Town Car Signature Series was again offered.

CONTINENTAL — V-6 — Executive and Signature four-door sedans again comprised the Continental lineup, and for 1993, each offered optional five-passenger seating that included individual seats for driver and front passenger. Other new features included a leather-wrapped steering wheel (standard) and optional hands-free cellular phone. Dual airbags and four-wheel anti-lock disc brakes were also standard. The 3.8-liter V-6 teamed with the AXOD-E electronically controlled four-speed transaxle again powered the Continental. Optional equipment included a power moonroof, JBL audio system and an anti-theft alarm system.

MARK VIII — V-8 — The all-new Mark VIII series was comprised of a single coupe that was much more aerodynamic in styling than its predecessor. The Mark VIII was also a departure from former recent Mark models in that it carried no other identification such as LSC or Bill Blass. Mark VIIIs were powered by the modular, all aluminum DOHC 4.6-liter V-8 teamed with the 4R70W four-speed automatic overdrive transmission. Standard features of the coupe included dual airbags, four-wheel anti-lock disc brakes, leather-wrapped steering wheel, programmable memory driver's seat, dual exhaust and computer-controlled air-spring suspension system with speed-dependent height adjustment.

I.D. DATA: Lincoln's 17-symbol Vehicle Identification Number (VIN) was stamped on a metal tab fastened to the instrument panel, visible through the windshield. The first three symbols indicate manufacturer, make and vehicle type. The fourth symbol denotes restraint system. Next comes a letter (usually 'M'), followed by two digits that indicate Model Number, as shown in left column of tables below. (Example: '81' Town Car Executive four-door sedan). Symbol eight indicates engine type. Next is a check digit. Symbol ten indicates model year ('P' 1993). Symbol eleven denotes assembly plant. The final six digits make up the sequence number, starting with 600001.

Model No.	Body/ Style No.	Body Type & Seating	Factory Price	Shipping Weight	Prod. Total
TOWN CAR (V-8)					
M	81	4-dr. Executive Sed-5P	34190	4050	Note 1
M	82	4-dr. Signature Sed-5P	35494	4050	Note 1
M	83	4-dr. Cartier Sed-5P	37581	4060	Note 1

NOTE 1: Production of four-door sedan models totaled 113,522 with no further breakout available.

1993 Lincoln Mark VIII coupe. (OCW)

Model No.	Body/ Style No.	Body Type & Seating	Factory Price	Shipping Weight	Prod. Total
CONTINENTAL (V-6)					
M	97	4-dr. Executive Sed-5P	33328	3628	Note 1
M	98	4-dr. Signature Sed-5P	35319	3623	Note 1

NOTE 1: Production of four-door sedan models totaled 25,760 with no further breakout available.

Model No.	Body/ Style No.	Body Type & Seating	Factory Price	Shipping Weight	Prod. Total
MARK VIII (V-8)					
M	91	2-dr. Cpe-4P	36640	3741	30,899

ENGINE [Base V-6 (Continental)]: 90-degree, overhead valve V-6. Cast-iron block and aluminum head. Displacement: 232 cid (3.8 liters). Bore & stroke: 3.80 x 3.40. Compression ratio: 9.0:1. Brake horsepower: 160 at 4400 RPM. Torque: 225 lbs.-ft. at 3000 RPM. Sequential fuel injection.

ENGINE [Base V-8 (Town Car)]: Modular, overhead cam V-8. Aluminum block and head. Displacement: 281 cid (4.6 liters). Bore & stroke: 3.60 x 3.60 in. Compression ratio: 9.0:1. Brake horsepower: 190 at 4600 RPM (210 at 4600 RPM w/dual exhaust). Torque: 260 lbs.-ft. at 3200 RPM (270 lbs.-ft. at 3400 RPM w/dual exhaust). Sequential fuel injection.

ENGINE [Base V-8 (Mark VIII)]: Modular, dual-overhead cam V-8. Aluminum block and head. Displacement: 281 cid (4.6 liters). Bore & stroke: 3.60 x 3.60 in. Compression ratio: 9.8:1. Brake horsepower: 280 at 5500 RPM. Torque: 285 lbs.-ft. at 4500 RPM. Sequential fuel injection.

CHASSIS DATA: Wheelbase: (Town Car) 117.4 in.; (Continental) 109.0 in.; (Mark VIII) 113.0 in. Overall Length: (Town Car) 218.9 in.; (Continental) 205.1 in.; (Mark VIII) 206.9 in. Height: (Town Car) 56.9 in.; (Continental) 55.5 in.; (Mark VIII) 53.6 in. Width: (Town Car) 76.9 in.; (Continental) 72.7 in.; (Mark VIII) 73.9 in. Front tread: (Town Car) 62.8 in.; (Continental) 62.3 in.; (Mark VIII) 61.1 in. Rear tread: (Town Car) 63.3 in.; (Continental) 61.1 in.; (Mark VIII) 60.2 in. Standard Tires: (Town Car) P215/70R15; (Continental) P205/70R15; (Mark VIII) P225/60VR16.

TECHNICAL: Transmission: Four-speed overdrive automatic standard on Town Car, Continental and Mark VIII. Drive Axle: (Town Car/Mark VIII) rear; (Continental) front. Steering: (Town Car) Speed-sensitive, variable-assist Parallelogram. (Continental/Mark VIII) rack/pinion. Front Suspension: (Town Car) Independent short/long arm w/ball joints, coil springs and front stabilizer bar; (Continental/Mark VIII) Microprocessor controlled front and rear air springs w/automatic front-to-rear and side-to-side leveling and front and rear stabilizer bars. Rear Suspension: (Town Car) Four-bar link, air suspension springs on axle and direct double-acting shocks; (Continental/Mark VIII) see front suspension. Brakes: (All) Front/rear disc (anti-lock system stnd on all). Body construction: (Town Car) separate body and frame; (Continental/Mark VIII) unibody. Fuel tank: (Town Car) 20.0 gal.; (Continental) 18.4 gal.; (Mark VIII) 18.0 gal.

DRIVETRAIN OPTIONS: Engines: 4.6-liter V-8 equipped w/dual exhaust (Town Car only) ($83). Transmission/Differential: Traction-Assist: Town Car ($222); Mark VIII ($215). Suspension/Brakes: H.D./handling susp.: Town Car ($278). Trailer Tow III pkg: Town Car w/High Altitude ($335); w/o ($417). Livery Pkg: Town Car w/High Altitude ($335); w/o ($417).

TOWN CAR CONVENIENCE/APPEARANCE OPTIONS: Jack Nicklaus Signature Series incl Prog Memory Seat, Monotone Paint Treatment and Leather Interior Trim: Signature ($1279). Calif. Emission Syst ($100). Leather Twin Comfort Lounge Seats: Executive ($570); Signature ($570); Cartier (NC). Anti-Theft Alarm Syst: N/A Executive ($295). Prog Memory Seat: Signature ($548). Electrochromic Auto Dimming Mirror ($111). Pwr Moonroof ($1550). Monotone Paint Treatment: Signature (NC). White Opalescent Clearcoat Metallic Paint ($240). Trunk Mounted CD Changer ($833). JBL Audio Syst ($575). Cellular Phone: N/AExecutive ($706). Conventional Spare Tire ($226). Traction Assist ($222). Vinyl Roof, Full Padded ($1200). Frt Lic Plate Bracket (NC). Eng Block Heater ($61). Dual Exhaust Syst: w/High Altitude (NC); Other ($83). Handling/Suspension Pkg ($278). Trailer Tow Pkg incl HD Cooling, Aux Trans Fluid Cooler, Aux Pwr Strg Fluid Cooler, 1330 U-Joint w/Steel Driveshaft, 3.55 Ratio Axle, Dual Exhaust, Addtl Wiring Harness for Trailer Tail lamps, Stop Lamps, Turn Signals, Electric Brakes & Battery Charging, HD Turn Signals & Flashers, Conventional Size Spare Tire w/Matching Steel Whl, New Upgaged Frt Stabilizer, HD 30mm Shock Absorbers w/Revised Tuning: High Altitude ($335); Other ($417). Livery Pkg incl Aux Trans Fluid Cooler, Aux Pwr Strg Fluid Cooler, 1330 U-Joint w/Steel Driveshaft, Dual Exhaust, HD 30mm Shock Absorbers, Upgaged Frt Stabilizer Bar, P215/70R15 tires: High Altitude ($335); Other ($417).

CONTINENTAL CONVENIENCE/APPEARANCE OPTIONS: Calif. Emission Syst ($100). Styled Alum Whls: Executive (NC). Anti-Theft Alarm Syst ($295). Comfort/Convenience Grp incl 6-Way Pwr Pass Seat, Dual Illum Visor Mirrors, Headlamp Convenience Grp, Pwr Decklid Pulldown, Rr Flr Mats, Pwr Pass Recline ($828). Overhead Console

Grp incl Elect Digital Compass & Electrochromic Auto Dimming Rr View Mirror ($361). Keyless Illum Entry Syst ($306). Pwr Moonroof ($1550). CD Player ($617). JBL Audio Syst ($575). Leather Bucket Seats: Signature ($556). Cellular Phone ($706). Eng Block Heater ($61). White Opalescent Clearcoat Metallic Paint ($240).

MARK VIII CONVENIENCE/APPEARANCE OPTIONS: Electrochromic Auto Dimming Mirror ($215). Elect Traction Assist ($215). Calif. Emission Syst ($100). Pwr Moonroof ($1515). Elect AM/FM Stereo Radio w/CD Player ($290). JBL Audio Syst ($565). Trunk Mounted CD Changer ($815). Cellular Phone ($690). Eng Block Heater ($60). Chrome Directional Wheels ($845).

HISTORY: U.S. model year Lincoln production totaled 280,661 for a 4.02 percent industry market share. U.S. calendar year Lincoln sales totaled 173,644.

1994 LINCOLN

1994 Lincoln Mark VIII coupe. (OCW)

Lincoln experienced a sharp decline in sales of both the new-for-1994 Continental that was launched early in 1993 and the previous year's Town Car. This decline was offset by a more than three-fold increase in sales of the Mark VIII. For 1994, the Lincoln lineup remained unchanged and the Town Car, Continental and Mark VIII underwent minimal change.

TOWN CAR — V-8 — The Town Car lineup again consisted of Executive, Signature and Cartier four-door sedans. The modular, overhead cam 4.6-liter V-8 and electronically assisted four-speed automatic overdrive transmission were again the drivetrain for Town Car models. The 4.6-liter V-8 now breathed through dual exhaust. All Town Cars received solar tinted glass as a standard feature.

CONTINENTAL — V-6 — Executive and Signature four-door sedans again comprised the Continental lineup, the final time these models would be offered as an option, since an all-new, 1995 Continental was being readied for a late 1994 release. Continental models were again powered by the 3.8-liter V-6 and used the AXOD-E electronically controlled four-speed transaxle. The suspension was upgraded and featured front and rear rebound suspension springs. As with the Town Car, Continentals also featured solar tinted glass. An Executive Touring Package was offered as an option and featured five-passenger leather seating and a power moonroof.

MARK VIII — V-8 — The Mark VIII coupe, after its launch the year previous, received only minor revisions including the addition of remote memory recall for seats and mirrors. Again powering the Mark VIII was the modular DOHC 4.6-liter V-8 teamed with the 4R70W four-speed automatic overdrive transmission.

I.D. DATA: Lincoln's 17-symbol Vehicle Identification Number (VIN) was stamped on a metal tab fastened to the instrument panel, visible through the windshield. The first three symbols indicate manufacturer, make and vehicle type. The fourth symbol denotes restraint system. Next comes a letter (usually 'M'), followed by two digits that indicate Model Number, as shown in left column of tables below. (Example: '81' Town Car Executive four-door sedan). Symbol eight indicates engine type. Next is a check digit. Symbol ten indicates model year ('R' 1994). Symbol eleven denotes assembly plant. The final six digits make up the sequence number, starting with 600001.

Model No.	Body/ Style No.	Body Type & Seating	Factory Price	Shipping Weight	Prod. Total
TOWN CAR (V-8)					
M	81	4-dr. Executive Sed-5P	34400	4039	Note 1
M	82	4-dr. Signature Sed-5P	35700	4057	Note 1
M	83	4-dr. Cartier Sed-5P	37800	4095	Note 1

NOTE 1: Production of four-door sedan models totaled 113,008 with no further breakout available.

1994 Lincoln Signature Series Town Car. (OCW)

Model No.	Body/ Style No.	Body Type & Seating	Factory Price	Shipping Weight	Prod. Total
CONTINENTAL (V-6)					
M	97	4-dr. Executive Sed-5P	33850	3576	Note 1
M	98	4-dr. Signature Sed-5P	35750	3613	Note 1

Note 1: Production of four-door sedan models totaled 49,771 with no further breakout available.

Model No.	Body/ Style No.	Body Type & Seating	Factory Price	Shipping Weight	Prod. Total
MARK VIII (V-8)					
M	91	2-dr. Cpe-4P	36890	3768	26,983

ENGINE [Base V-6 (Continental)]: 90-degree, overhead valve V-6. Cast-iron block and aluminum head. Displacement: 232 cid (3.8 liters). Bore & stroke: 3.80 x 3.40. Compression ratio: 9.0:1. Brake horsepower: 160 at 4400 RPM. Torque: 225 lbs.-ft. at 3000 RPM. Sequential fuel injection.

ENGINE [Base V-8 (Town Car)]: Modular, overhead cam V-8. Aluminum block and head. Displacement: 281 cid (4.6 liters). Bore & stroke: 3.60 x 3.60 in. Compression ratio: 9.0:1. Brake horsepower: 210 at 4600 RPM. Torque: 270 lbs.-ft. at 3400 RPM. Sequential fuel injection.

ENGINE [Base V-8 (Mark VIII)]: Modular, dual-overhead cam V-8. Aluminum block and head. Displacement: 281 cid (4.6 liters). Bore & stroke: 3.60 x 3.60 in. Compression ratio: 9.8:1. Brake horsepower: 280 at 5500 RPM. Torque: 285 lbs.-ft. at 4500 RPM. Sequential fuel injection.

CHASSIS DATA: Wheelbase: (Town Car) 117.4 in.; (Continental) 109.0 in.; (Mark VIII) 113.0 in. Overall Length: (Town Car) 218.9 in.; (Continental) 205.6 in.; (Mark VIII) 207.3 in. Height: (Town Car) 56.9 in.; (Continental) 55.5 in.; (Mark VIII) 53.6 in. Width: (Town Car) 76.9 in.; (Continental) 72.7 in.: (Mark VIII) 74.6 in. Front tread: (Town Car) 62.8 in.; (Continental) 62.3 in.; (Mark VIII) 61.1 in. Rear tread: (Town Car) 63.3 in.; (Continental) 61.1 in.; (Mark VIII) 60.2 in. Standard Tires: (Town Car) P215/70R15; (Continental) P205/70R15; (Mark VIII) P225/60VR16.

TECHNICAL: Transmission: Four-speed overdrive automatic standard on Town Car, Continental and Mark VIII. Drive Axle: (Town Car/Mark VIII) rear; (Continental) front. Steering: (Town Car) Speed-sensitive, variable-assist Parallelogram. (Continental/Mark VIII) rack/pinion. Front Suspension: (Town Car) Independent short/long arm w/ball joints, coil springs and front stabilizer bar; (Continental/Mark VIII) Microprocessor controlled front and rear air springs w/automatic front-to-rear and side-to-side leveling and front and rear stabilizer bars. Rear Suspension: (Town Car) Four-bar link, air suspension springs on axle and direct double-acting shocks; (Continental/Mark VIII) see front suspension. Brakes: (All) Front/rear disc (anti-lock system stnd on all). Body construction: (Town Car) separate body and frame; (Continental/Mark VIII) unibody. Fuel tank: (Town Car) 20.0 gal.; (Continental) 18.4 gal.; (Mark VIII) 18.0 gal.

DRIVETRAIN OPTIONS: Transmission/Differential: Elect Traction-Assist: Town Car ($215); Mark VIII ($215). Suspension/Brakes: H.D./handling susp.: Town Car ($805). HD Trailer Tow pkg: Town Car ($465). Ride Control Pkg: Town Car ($285). Livery Pkg: Town Car ($325).

1994 Lincoln Continental Executive Series sedan. (OCW)

TOWN CAR CONVENIENCE/APPEARANCE OPTIONS: Calif. Emission Syst ($100). Leather Twin Comfort Lounge Seats: Executive ($555); Signature ($555); Cartier (NC). Anti-Theft Alarm Syst: ($290). Prog Memory Seat: stnd Cartier ($535). Electrochromic Auto Dimming Mirror ($111). Pwr Moonroof ($1515). Monotone Paint Treatment (NC). White Opalescent Clearcoat Metallic Paint ($235). Trunk Mounted CD Changer ($815). JBL Audio Syst: stnd Cartier ($565). Cellular Phone ($706). Conventional Spare Tire ($220). Elect Traction Assist ($215). Frt Lic Plate Bracket (NC). Eng Block Heater ($61). HD Pkg incl HD Cooling Pkg, Aux Pwr Strg Fluid Cooler, Aux Trans Fluid Cooler, HD Shock Absorbers, Unique Frt Stabilizer Bar, HD Frt Lower Ctrl Arms, Steel Driveshaft w/1330 U-Joint, 3.55 Ratio Traction-Lok HD Axle w/11x2-1/4-inch Rr Brake Drum, P225/75R15 WSW Tires, Y-Spoke Alum Whls, Full-Size Spare Tire, 84-Amp Battery, 130-Amp Alt, HD Frame, Unique Anti-lock Brakes, HD Jack ($805). HD Trailer Tow Pkg incl HD Cooling, Aux Trans Fluid Cooler, Aux Pwr Strg Fluid Cooler, 1330 U-Joint w/Steel Driveshaft, 3.55 Ratio Axle, Addtl Wiring Harness for Trailer Tail lamps, Stop Lamps, Turn Signals, Elect Brakes & Battery Charging, HD Turn Signals & Flashers, Conventional Size Spare Tire w/Matching Steel Whl, New Upgaged Frt Stabilizer, HD 30mm Shock Absorbers w/Revised Tuning ($465). Livery Pkg incl Aux Trans Fluid Cooler, Aux Pwr Strg Fluid Cooler, 1330 U-Joint w/Steel Driveshaft, HD 30mm Shock Absorbers, 84-Amp Battery, 130-Amp Alt, Upgaged Frt Stabilizer Bar, P215/70R15 tires ($325).

CONTINENTAL CONVENIENCE/APPEARANCE OPTIONS: Executive Pref Equip Pkg 953A: Executive Touring Pkg incl 5-Pass Leather Seating and Pwr Moonroof ($1325). Calif. Emission Syst ($100). Styled Alum Whls: Executive (NC). Comfort/Convenience Grp incl 6-Way Pwr Pass Seat, Dual Illum Visor Mirrors, Headlamp Convenience Grp, Pwr Pass Recline ($700). Overhead Console Grp incl Elect Digital Compass, Electrochromic Auto Dimming Rr View Mirror and Electrochromic Driver's O/S Mirror ($350). Keyless Illum Entry Syst ($300). Trunk Mounted Grocery Carrier: N/A Executive ($265). Anti-theft Alarm Syst ($290). Pwr Moonroof ($1515). CD Player ($600). JBL Audio Syst ($565). Leather Bucket Seats ($890). Cellular Phone ($690). Eng Block Heater ($61). White Opalescent Clearcoat Metallic Paint ($235).

MARK VIII CONVENIENCE/APPEARANCE OPTIONS: Electrochromic Auto Dimming Mirror ($215). Elect Traction Assist ($215). Calif. Emission Syst ($100). Pwr Moonroof ($1515). Elect AM/FM Stereo Radio w/CD Player ($290). JBL Audio Syst ($565). Trunk Mounted CD Changer ($815). Cellular Phone ($690). Eng Block Heater ($60). Chrome Directional Wheels ($845).

HISTORY: U.S. model year Lincoln production totaled 196,947 for a 3.27 percent industry market share. U.S. calendar year Lincoln production totaled 180,587. U.S. calendar year Lincoln sales totaled 179,166.

1995 LINCOLN

An all-new single-sedan Continental series debuted late in 1994 as a 1995 model. The new Continental featured a more rounded appearance similar to the Mark VIII and away from its previous squared-off lines similar to the Town Car. The LSC (Luxury Sport Coupe) returned to the Mark series midyear (as a 1996 model) in the capacity of being a limited production option package.

TOWN CAR — V-8 — Executive, Signature and Cartier four-door sedans again comprised the Town Car lineup. Front and rear treatments were slightly revised while inside, seats and the instrument panel received upgrades. The modular, overhead cam 4.6-liter V-8 powering Town Cars was modified to reduce emissions. The electronically assisted four-speed automatic overdrive transmission was used again, and the previously optional anti-theft system became standard equipment. A Signature Spinnaker Edition option package was offered featuring tri-color pearlescent exterior finish, Spinnaker badging and embroidered floor mats and 16-inch aluminum wheels.

1995 Lincoln Signature Series Town Car. (OCW)

CONTINENTAL — V-8 — Gone were the Executive and Signature four-door sedans previously available, replaced by a four-door sedan simply named Continental. The new, aerodynamically-enhanced Continental was powered by the InTech 32-valve, modular DOHC 4.6-liter V-8, rated at 260 hp, and teamed with the AX4N four-speed automatic overdrive transaxle. It was the first Lincoln with the combination of front-wheel drive and V-8 engine. Standard equipment included dual airbags and anti-lock brakes as well as a Memory Profile system that governed three levels of both power steering and suspension damping.

MARK VIII — V-8 — The Mark VIII coupe again was "tweaked" receiving minor interior and exterior modifications including a new delayed accessory-power function that provided 10 minutes of power after the ignition was switched off. The modular DOHC 4.6-liter V-8 teamed with an electronically controlled four-speed automatic overdrive transmission again powered the Mark VIII. Released midyear (as a 1995-1/2/1996 model) was the LSC version of the Mark VIII and offered as a limited production (5,000 available) option package. The LSC featured a monochromatic exterior and aluminum spoke wheels. Its InTech 4.6-liter V-8 delivered 290 hp (10 more than the Mark VIII) and the Luxury Sport Coupe also featured a modified dual exhaust system, a 3.27 axle ratio and sport suspension tuning. The LSC also was the first domestically produced automobile to use high-intensity discharge (HID) headlights, which produce more light and last longer than conventional halogen headlights.

I.D. DATA: Lincoln's 17-symbol Vehicle Identification Number (VIN) was stamped on a metal tab fastened to the instrument panel, visible through the windshield. The first three symbols indicate manufacturer, make and vehicle type. The fourth symbol denotes restraint system. Next comes a letter (usually 'M'), followed by two digits that indicate Model Number, as shown in left column of tables below. (Example: '81' Town Car Executive four-door sedan). Symbol eight indicates engine type. Next is a check digit. Symbol ten indicates model year ('S' 1995). Symbol eleven denotes assembly plant. The final six digits make up the sequence number, starting with 600001.

Model No.	Body/ Style No.	Body Type & Seating	Factory Price	Shipping Weight	Prod. Total
TOWN CAR (V-8)					
M	81	4-dr. Executive Sed-5P	36400	4031	Note 1
M	82	4-dr. Signature Sed-5P	38500	4057	Note 1
M	83	4-dr. Cartier Sed-5P	41200	4095	Note 1

NOTE 1: Production of four-door sedan models totaled 107,700 with no further breakout available.

Model No.	Body/ Style No.	Body Type & Seating	Factory Price	Shipping Weight	Prod. Total
CONTINENTAL (V-8)					
M	97	4-dr. Sed-5P	40750	3972	32,851
MARK VIII (V-8)					
M	91	2-dr. Cpe-4P	38800	3768	20,099

1995 Lincoln Continental sedan. (OCW)

ENGINE [Base V-8 (Town Car)]: Modular, overhead cam V-8. Aluminum block and head. Displacement: 281 cid (4.6 liters). Bore & stroke: 3.60 x 3.60 in. Compression ratio: 9.0:1. Brake horsepower: 210 at 4600 RPM. Torque: 270 lbs.-ft. at 3400 RPM. Sequential fuel injection.

ENGINE [Base V-8 (Continental/Mark VIII)]: Modular, dual-overhead cam V-8. Aluminum block and head. Displacement: 281 cid (4.6 liters). Bore & stroke: 3.60 x 3.60 in. Compression ratio: 9.8:1. Brake horsepower: (Continental) 260 at 5750 RPM; (Mark VIII) 280 at 5500 RPM. Torque: (Continental) 265 lbs.-ft. at 4750 RPM; (Mark VIII) 285 lbs.-ft. at 4500 RPM. Sequential fuel injection.

CHASSIS DATA: Wheelbase: (Town Car) 117.4 in.; (Continental) 109.0 in.; (Mark VIII) 113.0 in. Overall Length: (Town Car) 218.9 in.; (Continental) 206.3 in.; (Mark VIII) 207.3 in. Height: (Town Car) 56.9 in.; (Continental) 55.9 in.; (Mark VIII) 53.6 in. Width: (Town Car) 76.7 in.; (Continental) 73.3 in.; (Mark VIII) 74.8 in. Front tread: (Town Car) 62.8 in.; (Continental) 63.0 in.; (Mark VIII) 61.1 in. Rear tread: (Town Car) 63.3 in.; (Continental) 61.5 in.; (Mark VIII) 60.2 in. Standard Tires: (Town Car) P215/70R15; (Continental) P225/60R16; (Mark VIII) P225/60VR16.

TECHNICAL: Transmission: Four-speed overdrive automatic standard on Town Car, Continental and Mark VIII. Drive Axle: (Town Car/Mark VIII) rear; (Continental) front. Steering: (Town Car) Speed-sensitive, variable-assist Parallelogram. (Continental/Mark VIII) rack/pinion. Front Suspension: (Town Car) Independent short/long arm w/ball joints, coil springs and front stabilizer bar; (Continental/Mark VIII) Microprocessor controlled front and rear air springs w/automatic front-to-rear and side-to-side leveling and front and rear stabilizer bars. Rear Suspension: (Town Car) Four-bar link, air suspension springs on axle and direct double-acting shocks; (Continental/Mark VIII) see front suspension. Brakes: (All) Front/rear disc (anti-lock system stnd on all). Body construction: (Town Car) separate body and frame; (Continental/Mark VIII) unibody. Fuel tank: (Town Car) 20.0 gal.; (Continental) 18.0 gal.; (Mark VIII) 18.0 gal.

DRIVETRAIN OPTIONS: Transmission/Differential: Elect All-Speed Traction Control w/Activation Indicator: Continental ($360). Elect Traction-Assist: Town Car, stnd Cartier ($215); Mark VIII ($215). Suspension/Brakes: Livery/HD Trailer Tow pkg: Town Car ($575). Ride Control Pkg: Town Car, N/A Executive: Signature w/Spinnaker Pkg ($300); Signature w/o ($100); Cartier ($100).

TOWN CAR CONVENIENCE/APPEARANCE OPTIONS: Signature Spinnaker Edition incl Tri-Coat Paint, 16-inch Alum Whls, Spinnaker Badging & Embroidered Flr Mats and Twin Comfort Lounge Seats: w/Tri-Coat Paint ($1260); w/o ($960). Calif. Emission Syst ($100). Leather Seats: Executive ($570); Signature ($570); Cartier (NC). Dual Heated Leather Seats, Signature only ($290). Electrochromic Auto Dimming Mirror w/Compass ($330). Pwr Moonroof, N/A Executive ($1515). Monotone Paint Treatment, Signature only (NC). Tri-Coat Paint, stnd Cartier ($300). Trunk Mounted CD Changer ($815). JBL Audio Syst: stnd Cartier ($565). Cellular Phone ($690). Conventional Spare Tire ($220). Elect Traction Assist, stnd Cartier ($215). Frt Lic Plate Bracket (NC). Eng Block Heater ($61). Livery/HD Trailer Tow Pkg incl HD Cooling, Aux Trans Fluid Cooler, Aux Pwr Strg Fluid Cooler, 1330 U-Joint w/Steel Driveshaft, 3.55 Ratio Axle, Addtl Wiring Harness for Trailer Tail lamps, Stop Lamps, Turn Signals, Elect Brakes & Battery Charging, HD Turn Signals & Flashers, Conventional Size Spare Tire w/Matching Alum Whl, New Upgaged Frt Stabilizer, HD 30mm Shock Absorbers w/Revised Tuning ($575). Ride Control Pkg incl Aux Pwr Strg Cooler, 16-inch Alum Spoke Whls, P225/60R16 WSW Tires, N/A Executive: Signature w/Spinnaker ($300); w/o ($100); Cartier ($100).

CONTINENTAL CONVENIENCE/APPEARANCE OPTIONS: Calif. Emission Syst ($100). Cargo Storage Syst w/Net ($265). Anti-theft Alarm Syst ($290). Pwr Moonroof ($1515). CD Player ($595). JBL Audio Syst ($565). Heated Seats w/5 Temp Settings ($290). Cellular Phone ($690). Eng Block Heater ($61). Electrochromic Auto Dimming Mirror w/Compass ($330). Tri-Coat Paint ($300). Elect All-Speed Traction Control w/Activation Indicator ($360). Chrome Double Window Whls ($845).

MARK VIII CONVENIENCE/APPEARANCE OPTIONS: LSC Pkg incl HID Headlights, Body-Color Fascia & Bodyside Mldgs, Cast Alum Directional Whls, Leather Seats, Spt Susp Tuning, True Dual Exhaust and 3.27 Axle Ratio ($1500). Electrochromic Auto Dimming Mirror, Int & Ext ($215). Elect Traction Assist ($215). Calif. Emission Syst ($100). Pwr Moonroof ($1515). JBL Audio Syst ($565). Trunk Mounted CD Changer ($815). Cellular Phone ($690). Eng Block Heater ($60). Tri-Coat Paint ($300). Cast Alum Directional Whls ($50). Chrome Directional Wheels ($845).

HISTORY: U.S. model year Lincoln production totaled 166,249 for a 2.47 percent industry market share. U.S. calendar year Lincoln production totaled 157,584. U.S. calendar year Lincoln sales totaled 150,814. At the 1995 Chicago Auto Show, the Lincoln L2K (2000) convertible two-passenger sports/concept car was unveiled. The rear-wheel drive sports car was powered by a 3.4-liter V-8 rated at 250 hp, and mated to a four-speed automatic transmission. The L2K weighed 2,900 pounds.

1996 LINCOLN

Lincoln observed its 75th year as an automaker by releasing optional Diamond Anniversary Editions of its Town Car, Continental and Mark VIII. Among the features of the Anniversary Edition Package was a Waterford Crystal and color-coordinated umbrella to go along with the Lincoln purchased. Among the new optional equipment offered was RESCU for Continental buyers. This option was a remote emergency satellite cellular unit that automatically called for roadside assistance in an emergency.

TOWN CAR — V-8 — The Town Car series was again comprised of Executive, Signature and Cartier four-door sedans. For 1996, Lincoln also offered a Diamond Anniversary Edition Town Car as an option package for the Signature model. This Anniversary Edition Signature featured a power moonroof, exterior window badging, leather seats, cellular phone and JBL audio system. The modular 4.6-liter V-8 engine that again powered the Town Car was revised to reduce emissions. Town Cars again used the electronically controlled four-speed automatic overdrive transmission.

CONTINENTAL — V-8 — Available safety and security features were the big news for the Continental four-door sedan buyers in 1996. The previously optional anti-theft system became standard equipment. New optional equipment included the SecuriTire system and RESCU. SecuriTire featured Michelin MXV4-ZP (zero pressure) tires that, even when deflated, could be safely driven up to 50 miles. RESCU (remote emergency satellite cellular unit) used advanced global positioning satellite (GPS) technology and the cellular phone network to track vehicle location and put the Continental's occupants in voice contact with an emergency response center via two buttons located on an overhead console. One button was a tow-truck icon for roadside assistance and the other button an ambulance icon for emergency assistance. The Continental was again powered by the InTech DOHC 4.6-liter V-8 mated to an AX4N four-speed automatic transaxle with non-synchronous shift. Other option packages offered to Continental buyers included the Spinnaker Edition with chrome wheels, the Touring Package with traction control, JBL audio system and power moonroof or the Diamond Anniversary Edition with power moonroof, exterior window badging, leather seats, cellular phone and JBL audio system.

MARK VIII — V-8 — The Mark VIII coupe was again powered by the InTech 4.6-liter V-8 teamed with the electronically controlled four-speed automatic overdrive transmission with 3.07 final drive ratio (including lock-out switch). Option packages available to Mark VIII buyers included the LSC model, debuted midyear in 1995, which featured leather seats, cast aluminum wheels and sport tuned suspension; the Touring Package with electronic traction assist, trunk mounted CD changer and electrochromic mirrors or the Diamond Anniversary Edition with power moonroof, cellular phone and chrome wheels.

1995 Lincoln Mark VIII coupe. (OCW)

1996 Lincoln Signature Series Town Car. (OCW)

1996 Lincoln Mark VIII coupe. (OCW)

I.D. DATA: Lincoln's 17-symbol Vehicle Identification Number (VIN) was stamped on a metal tab fastened to the instrument panel, visible through the windshield. The first three symbols indicate manufacturer, make and vehicle type. The fourth symbol denotes restraint system. Next comes a letter (usually 'M'), followed by two digits that indicate Model Number, as shown in left column of tables below. (Example: '81' Town Car Executive four-door sedan). Symbol eight indicates engine type. Next is a check digit. Symbol ten indicates model year ('T' 1996). Symbol eleven denotes assembly plant. The final six digits make up the sequence number, starting with 600001.

Model No.	Body/ Style No.	Body Type & Seating	Factory Price	Shipping Weight	Prod. Total
TOWN CAR (V-8)					
M	81	4-dr. Executive Sed-5P	36910	4040	Note 1
M	82	4-dr. Signature Sed-5P	38960	4040	Note 1
M	83	4-dr. Cartier Sed-5P	41960	4103	Note 1

NOTE 1: Production of four-door sedan models totaled 90,763 with no further breakout available.

Model No.	Body/ Style No.	Body Type & Seating	Factory Price	Shipping Weight	Prod. Total
CONTINENTAL (V-8)					
M	97	4-dr. Sed-5P	41800	3881	27,851
MARK VIII (V-8)					
M	91	2-dr. Cpe-4P	39650	3767	13,357

ENGINE [Base V-8 (Town Car)]: Modular, overhead cam V-8. Aluminum block and head. Displacement: 281 cid (4.6 liters). Bore & stroke: 3.60 x 3.60 in. Compression ratio: 9.0:1. Brake horsepower: 210 at 4250 RPM. Torque: 275 lbs.-ft. at 3250 RPM. Sequential fuel injection.

ENGINE [Base V-8 (Continental/Mark VIII)]: Modular, dual-overhead cam V-8. Aluminum block and head. Displacement: 281 cid (4.6 liters). Bore & stroke: 3.60 x 3.60 in. Compression ratio: 9.8:1. Brake horsepower: (Continental) 260 at 5570 RPM; (Mark VIII) 280 at 5500 RPM. Torque: (Continental) 265 lbs.-ft. at 4750 RPM; (Mark VIII) 285 lbs.-ft. at 4500 RPM. Sequential fuel injection.

CHASSIS DATA: Wheelbase: (Town Car) 117.4 in.; (Continental) 109.0 in.; (Mark VIII) 113.1 in. Overall Length: (Town Car) 218.9 in.; (Continental) 206.3 in.; (Mark VIII) 207.3 in. Height: (Town Car) 56.9 in.; (Continental) 56.0 in.; (Mark VIII) 53.6 in. Width: (Town Car) 76.7 in.; (Continental) 73.6 in.; (Mark VIII) 74.8 in. Front tread: (Town Car) 62.8 in.; (Continental) 63.0 in.; (Mark VIII) 61.6 in. Rear tread: (Town Car) 63.3 in.; (Continental) 61.5 in.; (Mark VIII) 60.2 in. Standard Tires: (Town Car) P215/70R15; (Continental) P225/60R16; (Mark VIII) P225/60R16.

TECHNICAL: Transmission: Four-speed overdrive automatic standard on Town Car, Continental and Mark VIII. Drive Axle: (Town Car/Mark VIII) rear; (Continental) front. Steering: (Town Car) Speed-sensitive, variable-assist Parallelogram. (Continental/Mark VIII) rack/pinion. Front Suspension: (Town Car) Independent short/long arm w/ball joints, coil springs and front stabilizer bar; (Continental/Mark VIII) Microprocessor controlled front and rear air springs w/automatic front-to-rear and side-to-side leveling and front and rear stabilizer bars. Rear Suspension: (Town Car) Four-bar link, air suspension springs on axle and direct double-acting shocks; (Continental/Mark VIII) see front suspension. Brakes: (All) Front/rear disc (antilock system stnd on all). Body construction: (Town Car) separate body and frame; (Continental/Mark VIII) unibody. Fuel tank: (Town Car) 20.0 gal.; (Continental) 18.0 gal.; (Mark VIII) 18.0 gal.

DRIVETRAIN OPTIONS: Transmission/Differential: Elect All-Speed Traction Control w/Activation Indicator: Continental ($360). Elect Traction-Assist: Town Car, stnd Cartier ($215); Mark VIII ($215). Suspension/Brakes: Livery/HD Trailer Tow pkg: Town Car ($575). Ride Control Pkg: Town Car, N/A Executive: Signature ($300); Cartier ($100). Touring Pkg w/traction control: Continental ($2770); w/elect traction assist: Town Car ($1825); Mark VIII ($450).

TOWN CAR CONVENIENCE/APPEARANCE OPTIONS: Diamond Anniv Edition, Signature only incl Paint Stripe, Leather Seats, Wood Instrmt Panel Trim, Window Badging, Cellular Phone, Pwr Moonroof, JBL Audio Syst, Electrochromic Auto Dimming Mirror and Traction Assist ($1565). Calif. Emission Syst ($100). Leather Seats: Executive ($570); Signature ($570); Cartier (NC). Dual Heated Leather Seats,

Signature only ($290). Electrochromic Auto Dimming Mirror w/Compass, stnd Cartier ($330). Pwr Moonroof, N/A Executive ($1515). Monotone Paint Treatment, Signature only (NC). Tri-Coat Paint, stnd Cartier ($300). Trunk Mounted CD Changer ($815). JBL Audio Syst: stnd Cartier ($565). Cellular Phone, N/A Executive ($690). Conventional Spare Tire ($220); w/Chrome Whl, Signature and Cartier ($430). Elect Traction Assist, stnd Cartier ($215). Frt Lic Plate Bracket (NC). Eng Block Heater ($61). Livery/HD Trailer Tow Pkg incl HD Cooling, Aux Trans Fluid Cooler, Aux Pwr Strg Fluid Cooler, 1330 U-Joint w/Steel Driveshaft, 3.55 Ratio Axle, Addtl Wiring Harness for Trailer Tail lamps, Stop Lamps, Turn Signals, Elect Brakes & Battery Charging, HD Turn Signals & Flashers, Conventional Size Spare Tire w/Matching Alum Whl, 130-Amp Alt w/Increased Pulley Ratio, New Upgaged Frt Stabilizer, HD 30mm Shock Absorbers w/Revised Tuning ($575). Touring Pkg incl Pwr Moonroof, JBL Audio Syst, Electrochromic Mirrors, Aux Pwr Strg Cooler, 16-inch Alum Spoke Whls, P225/60R16 WSW Tires, 28.5mm Frt Stabilizer Bar, Revised Springs & Shocks ($1825). Ride Control Pkg incl Aux Pwr Strg Cooler, 16-inch Alum Spoke Whls, P225/60R16 WSW Tires, 28.5mm Frt Stabilizer Bar, Revised Springs & Shocks, N/A Executive: Signature ($300); Cartier ($100). Chrome 8-Window Whls, Cartier and Signature w/Ride Control Pkg ($845); Signature w/o ($1045).

CONTINENTAL CONVENIENCE/APPEARANCE OPTIONS: Diamond Anniv Edition incl Leather Seats, Cellular Phone, Chrome Whls, Quarter Window Badging, Unique Flr Mats, Waterford Crystal and Color-Coordinated Umbrella ($1750). Spinnaker Edition incl Chrome Whls ($995); w/o ($150). Calif. Emission Syst ($100). Cargo Storage Syst w/Net ($265). Pwr Moonroof ($1515). CD Player ($595). JBL Audio Syst ($565). Heated Seats w/5 Temp Settings ($290). Cellular Phone ($690). Eng Block Heater ($61). Electrochromic Auto Dimming Mirror w/Compass ($330). Tri-Coat Paint ($300). Elect All-Speed Traction Control w/Activation Indicator ($360). Touring Pkg incl Pwr Moonroof, Electrochromic Auto Dimming Mirror, Traction Control, JBL Audio Syst ($2770). Personal Security Pkg incl Cellular Phone, JBL Audio Syst, Zero Pressure Tires and RESCU Syst ($3675). Chrome Double Window Whls ($845).

MARK VIII CONVENIENCE/APPEARANCE OPTIONS: Diamond Anniv Edition incl Cellular Phone, Chrome Whls, Unique Flr Mats, Waterford Crystal, Color-Coordinated Umbrella and Pwr Moonroof ($3285); w/o Pwr Moonroof ($1770). LSC Pkg incl HID Headlights, Body-Color Fascia & Bodyside Mldgs, Cast Alum Directional Whls, Leather Seats, Spt Tuned Susp, True Dual Exhaust and 3.27 Axle Ratio ($1300); w/Chrome Directional Whls ($1800). Electrochromic Auto Dimming Mirror, Int & Ext ($215). Elect Traction Assist ($215). Calif. Emission Syst ($100). Pwr Moonroof ($1515). JBL Audio Syst ($565). Trunk Mounted CD Changer ($815). Cellular Phone ($690). Eng Block Heater ($60). Tri-Coat Paint ($300). Touring Pkg incl JBL Audio Syst, Elect Traction Assist, Trunk Mounted CD Changer and Electrochromic Mirrors ($450). Cast Alum Directional Whls ($50). Chrome Directional Wheels ($845).

HISTORY: U.S. model year Lincoln production totaled 141,080 for a 2.7 percent industry market share. U.S. calendar year Lincoln production totaled 145,035. U.S. calendar year Lincoln sales totaled 141,476.

1996 Lincoln Continental sedan. (OCW)

1997 LINCOLN

The LSC (Luxury Sport Coupe) model was upgraded from an option package to a production Mark VIII offering in 1997. The Mark VIII received a styling revision that included a more prominent hood and modified rear treatment. All-Speed Traction Control became a standard feature on Continentals and Mark VIIIs.

TOWN CAR — V-8 — The Town Car lineup was again comprised of Executive, Signature and Cartier four-door sedans. Town Car models had upgraded steering for 1997 to improve stability and precision. Series designation for the Executive and Signature models was relocated from the rear quarter windows to the front fenders and included new, distinctive graphics while the Cartier nomenclature remained on the quarter window. A new foam-in-place Drysol material replaced cloth on doors for improved soil resistance. Town Cars again used the modular 4.6-liter V-8 engine teamed with the electronically controlled four-speed automatic overdrive transmission for power.

CONTINENTAL — V-8 — The SecuriTire and RESCU safety and security package made available in the year previous was offered in 1997 as two stand-alone optional security packages for Continental buyers. A programmable garage door opener that was offered in each of the SecuriTire and RESCU option packages was also available as a stand-alone item. Other new features of the Continental included a single-key locking system for doors, trunk, ignition and glovebox, and All-Speed Traction Control became standard equipment after several years of being optional. The Continental's suspension was upgraded with steel springs replacing front air springs to reduce harshness and increase ride comfort. Continental's front grille was redesigned to create a more open appearance and chrome door handles added luster to the luxury sedan. The InTech DOHC 4.6-liter V-8 teamed with the AX4N four-speed automatic transaxle with non-synchronous shift again provided power for the Continental. Other new standard features included an extra power point for accessories located in the console of five-passenger models or armrest of six-passenger models as well as an interior auto-dimming, electrochromic rearview mirror with integrated compass.

MARK VIII — V-8 — Mark VIII series' offerings doubled for 1997 with the addition of the LSC model joining the ranks of production Lincolns. As with the Mark VIII, the LSC (Luxury Sport Coupe) was powered by the InTech DOHC 4.6-liter V-8 teamed with the electronically controlled four-speed automatic overdrive transmission. The LSC offered 10 more horsepower and 10 additional pound-feet of torque over the Mark VIII. New features for the Mark VIII included revised frontal styling with a more prominent hood and distinctive grille, exterior mirrors that tilt down when the vehicle is placed in reverse with ground illumination and supplemental turn indicators, revised rear styling with full-width neon lighted appliqué, Luminarc clear-lens headlamps with high-intensity discharge (HID) low beams and halogen high beams, new cornering lamps, power tilt/telescope steering column with memory, Passive Anti-Theft System (PATS) with engine immobilizer, in-glass rear window antenna, center-entry intake manifold and new instrument cluster with integral gear indicator. The LSC model featured a monochromatic appearance with body-colored side and headlamp moldings, tail lamps and decklid appliqué, a unique body-colored grille, unique wheels and LSC badging. Inside, the LSC sported leather seat inserts and LSC embroidered floor mats.

I.D. DATA: Lincoln's 17-symbol Vehicle Identification Number (VIN) was stamped on a metal tab fastened to the instrument panel, visible through the windshield. The first three symbols indicate manufacturer, make and vehicle type. The fourth symbol denotes restraint system. Next comes a letter (usually 'M'), followed by two digits that indicate Model Number, as shown in left column of tables below. (Example: '81' Town Car Executive four-door sedan). Symbol eight indicates engine type. Next is a check digit. Symbol ten indicates model year ('V' 1997). Symbol eleven denotes assembly plant. The final six digits make up the sequence number, starting with 000001.

1997 Lincoln Cartier Designer Series Town Car. (OCW)

1997 Lincoln Mark VIII coupe. (OCW)

Model No.	Body/ Style No.	Body Type & Seating	Factory Price	Shipping Weight	Prod. Total
TOWN CAR (V-8)					
M	81	4-dr. Executive Sed-5P	37280	3997	Note 1
M	82	4-dr. Signature Sed-5P	39640	3977	Note 1
M	83	4-dr. Cartier Sed-5P	43200	3977	Note 1

NOTE 1: Production of four-door sedan models totaled 104,533 with no further breakout available.

Model No.	Body/ Style No.	Body Type & Seating	Factory Price	Shipping Weight	Prod. Total
CONTINENTAL (V-8)					
M	97	4-dr. Sed-5P	37280	3884	32,245
MARK VIII (V-8)					
M	91	2-dr. Cpe-4P	37280	3765	Note 1
M	92	2-dr. LSC Cpe-4P	38880	3785	Note 1

NOTE 1: Production of two-door coupe models totaled 16,365 with no further breakout available.

ENGINE [Base V-8 (Town Car)]: Modular, overhead cam V-8. Aluminum block and head. Displacement: 281 cid (4.6 liters). Bore & stroke: 3.60 x 3.60 in. Compression ratio: 9.0:1. Brake horsepower: 210 at 4250 RPM. Torque: 275 lbs.-ft. at 3250 RPM. Sequential fuel injection.

ENGINE [Base V-8 (Continental/Mark VIII)]: Modular, dual-overhead cam V-8. Aluminum block and head. Displacement: 281 cid (4.6 liters). Bore & stroke: (Mark VIII) 3.60 x 3.60 in.; (Continental) 3.60 x 3.40 in. Compression ratio: 9.9:1. Brake horsepower: (Continental) 260 at 5750 RPM; (Mark VIII) 280 at 5750 RPM; (Mark VIII LSC) 290 at 5750 RPM. Torque: (Continental) 265 lbs.-ft. at 4750 RPM; (Mark VIII) 285 lbs.-ft. at 4500 RPM; (Mark VIII LSC) 295 lbs.-ft. at 4500 RPM. Sequential fuel injection.

CHASSIS DATA: Wheelbase: (Town Car) 117.4 in.; (Continental) 109.0 in.; (Mark VIII) 113.1 in. Overall Length: (Town Car) 218.9 in.; (Continental) 206.3 in.; (Mark VIII) 207.3 in. Height: (Town Car) 56.9 in.; (Continental) 56.0 in.; (Mark VIII) 53.6 in. Width: (Town Car) 76.7 in.; (Continental) 73.6 in.; (Mark VIII) 74.8 in. Front tread: (Town Car) 62.8 in.; (Continental) 63.0 in.; (Mark VIII) 61.6 in. Rear tread: (Town Car) 63.3 in.; (Continental) 61.5 in.; (Mark VIII) 60.2 in. Standard Tires: (Town Car) P215/70R15; (Continental) P225/60R16; (Mark VIII) P225/60R16.

TECHNICAL: Transmission: Four-speed overdrive automatic standard on Town Car, Continental and Mark VIII. Drive Axle: (Town Car/Mark VIII) rear; (Continental) front. Steering: (Town Car) Speed-sensitive, variable-assist Parallelogram. (Continental/Mark VIII) rack/pinion. Front Suspension: (Town Car) Independent short/long arm w/ball joints, coil springs and front stabilizer bar; (Continental) Independent MacPherson strut front drive w/strut-mounted coil springs, stabilizer bar, tension struts, lower control arms and cast knuckles; (Mark VIII) Short/long arm w/combined air springs/shock absorber units and double isolated tension struts. Rear Suspension: (Town Car) Four-bar link, self-leveling air springs on axle, gas-pressurized hydraulic shocks and stabilizer bar; (Continental) Short/long arm independent w/air springs, stabilizer bar, tension struts, upper control arms, parallel lower control arms, cast spindle w/pressed-in forged stem and integrated ball joints. (Mark VIII) Independent, mounted on rubber isolated subframe w/upper control arms and lower H-control arms connected by cast aluminum knuckle and integral with computer-managed air springs. Brakes: (All) Front/rear disc (anti-lock system stnd on all). Body construction: (Town Car) separate body and frame; (Continental/Mark VIII) unibody. Fuel tank: (Town Car) 20.0 gal.; (Continental) 17.8 gal.; (Mark VIII) 18.0 gal.

1997 Lincoln Continental sedan. (OCW)

DRIVETRAIN OPTIONS: Transmission/Differential: Elect Traction Control: Town Car, stnd Cartier ($215). Suspension/Brakes: Livery pkg: Town Car ($360). Ride Control Pkg: Town Car, N/A Executive: Signature ($300); Cartier ($100). Touring Pkg w/traction control: Town Car ($1825).

TOWN CAR CONVENIENCE/APPEARANCE OPTIONS: Special Value Pkg, Signature only incl Traction Control Syst, JBL Audio Syst, Electrochromic Auto Dimming Mirror w/Compass ($610). Calif. Emission Syst ($100). Leather Seats: Executive ($770); Signature ($770); Cartier (NC). Dual Heated Leather Seats, Signature only ($290). Electrochromic Auto Dimming Mirror w/Compass, stnd Cartier ($330). Pwr Moonroof, Signature ($1515). Monotone Paint Treatment, Signature only (NC). Tri-Coat Paint, stnd Cartier, Signature ($300). Trunk Mounted CD Changer ($815). JBL Audio Syst: stnd Cartier, Signature ($565). Cellular Phone, N/A Executive ($690). Conventional Spare Tire ($220); w/Chrome Whl, Signature and Cartier ($430). Elect Traction Control, stnd Cartier ($215). Eng Block Heater ($61). Livery Pkg incl 84-Amp HD Battery, Aux Trans Fluid Cooler, Aux Pwr Strg Fluid Cooler, Single Exhaust, 3.27 Ratio Axle, Conventional Spare Tire w/Match Alum Whl, Upgaged Frt Stabilizer ($360). Touring Pkg incl Pwr Moonroof, Traction Control Syst, JBL Audio Syst, Electrochromic Mirrors, Aux Pwr Strg Cooler, 16-inch Alum Spoke Whls, P225/60R16 WSW Tires, 28.5mm Frt Stabilizer Bar, Revised Springs & Shocks ($1825). Ride Control Pkg incl Aux Pwr Strg Cooler, 16-inch Alum Spoke Whls, P225/60R16 WSW Tires, 3.27 Axle Ratio, 28.5mm Frt Stabilizer Bar, Revised Springs & Shocks, N/A Executive: Signature ($300); Cartier ($100). Trailer Wiring Pkg, Signature ($80). Chrome 8-Window Whls, Cartier and Signature w/Ride Control Pkg ($845); Signature w/o ($1045).

CONTINENTAL CONVENIENCE/APPEARANCE OPTIONS: Calif. Emission Syst ($100). Prog Garage Door Opener ($120). Pwr Moonroof ($1515). CD Player ($595). JBL Audio Syst ($565). Heated Seats w/5 Temp Settings ($290). Cellular Phone ($690). Eng Block Heater ($61). O/S Auto Dimming Mirrors ($110). Tri-Coat Paint ($300). Personal Security Pkg incl SecuriTire Run Flat Tires, Pressure Alert Warning Syst, Prog Garage Door Opener ($750). RESCU Pkg incl Cellular Phone, JBL Audio Syst, Prog Garage Door Opener: w/Personal Security Pkg ($2125); w/o ($2245). Chrome Whls ($845).

MARK VIII CONVENIENCE/APPEARANCE OPTIONS: Calif. Emission Syst ($100). Pwr Moonroof ($1515). Premium Elect AM/FM Stereo Radio w/Cass (NC). Trunk Mounted CD Changer ($670). Cellular Phone ($790). Heated Seats ($290). Eng Block Heater ($60). Tri-Coat Paint ($300). Chrome Octastar Whls ($845).

HISTORY: U.S. model year Lincoln production totaled 153,143. In June 1997, Lincoln introduced its first-ever truck—a 1998 model, luxury sport utility vehicle named Navigator. It was based on Ford's Explorer and was powered by a 5.4-liter V-8.

1998 LINCOLN

Both the Town Car and Continental received new styling, with Lincoln touting the 1998 Continental as having more than 400 improvements over the 1997 version. The lines of the Continental were totally revamped, while among the changes on the Town Car were a re-engineered full perimeter steel frame and body mounting to reduce vibration and noise and the use of Watt's Linkage rear suspension to improve straight-ahead tracking and stability.

TOWN CAR — V-8 — For 1998, Lincoln's flagship luxury sedan, Town Car, featured all-new exterior and interior designs as well as upgrades to its chassis, suspension and brakes. The lineup again consisted of Executive, Signature and Cartier four-door sedans. Functional upgrades to the new-design Town Car included a full-perimeter steel frame and body mounting, the use of Watt's Linkage rear suspension, increased brake rotor size in addition to the use of twin piston calipers

and 40 percent larger strike pad linings, more refined steering gear and improved front lower control arm bushings. Inside, a new 40/20/40 front seat design was used and the instrument panel featured new analog gauges, a revised information center and redesigned controls for easier operation. Outside, the grille was revised and included a new-design "Lincoln Star" emblem in the chrome indent of the grille. Also, the Town Car's beltline was raised, and the traditional C-pillar window was removed for a more flowing design. An optional Touring Package (Signature model only) incorporated new mono-tube shock absorbers for increased firmness and improved handling. Town Car Executive and Signature models again used the modular 4.6-liter V-8 engine teamed with the electronically controlled four-speed automatic overdrive transmission for power. The Cartier and Signature Touring Sedan versions of the Town Car used the dual exhaust version of the 4.6-liter V-8, which delivered 220 hp (vs. 200 for Executive and Signature) and 275 pound-feet of torque (vs. 265).

CONTINENTAL — V-8 — Continental's size remained the same as the previous year's model, but its proportions were changed being shorter at the front center line by two inches and at the corners by four inches. The cowl-forward style of the windshield yielded a sleeker, more aerodynamic look. The rear of the Continental was lengthened by two inches to improve overall design balance as well as trunk layout. The new-look interior featured an instrument panel covered with textured suede for improved durability. Maple wood trim ran across the width of the instrument panel and into the doors. Functional improvements included standard speed-sensitive rack-and-pinion steering that could be adjusted for low-, normal- or high-effort steering. Standard traction control had fewer components and reduced complexity for improved durability. Larger mufflers resulted in a quieter ride. The optional Driver Select System personalized the ride and included semi-active suspension and adjustable ride with choices of firm, normal or plush settings. Spring rates were tuned for precise control of roll, lift and dive characteristics. A Memory Profile System offered storage of 11 settings for up to two drivers. The InTech DOHC 4.6-liter V-8 powering Continental was revised to be more efficient via improved microprocessor electronics that operated 33 percent faster. A revised camshaft delivered improved performance with more torque for additional passing ability. The Continental's four-speed automatic transaxle featured "homesafe," which allowed for the vehicle to travel in second gear (only) in the event that the powertrain control module failed.

MARK VIII — V-8 — The Mark VIII and LSC again comprised the Mark VIII series. Changes were minimal in 1998, contained mainly to the interior including upgraded carpeting and a revised sound system. Both the Mark VIII and LSC (Luxury Sport Coupe) were powered by the InTech DOHC 4.6-liter V-8 teamed with the electronically controlled four-speed automatic overdrive transmission. The LSC delivered 10 more horsepower (290 vs. 280 for Mark VIII) and 10 more pound-feet of torque (295 vs. 285).

I.D. DATA: Lincoln's 17-symbol Vehicle Identification Number (VIN) was stamped on a metal tab fastened to the instrument panel, visible through the windshield. The first three symbols indicate manufacturer, make and vehicle type. The fourth symbol denotes restraint system. Next comes a letter (usually 'M'), followed by two digits that indicate Model Number, as shown in left column of tables below. (Example: '81' Town Car Executive four-door sedan.) Symbol eight indicates engine type. Next is a check digit. Symbol ten indicates model year ('W' 1998). Symbol eleven denotes assembly plant. The final six digits make up the sequence number, starting with 000001.

Model No.	Body/ Style No.	Body Type & Seating	Factory Price	Shipping Weight	Prod. Total
TOWN CAR (V-8)					
M	81	4-dr. Executive Sed-5P	37830	3860	*
M	82	4-dr. Signature Sed-5P	39480	N/A	*
M	83	4-dr. Cartier Sed-5P	41830	N/A	*
CONTINENTAL (V-8)					
M	97	4-dr. Sed-5P	37830	3868	*

1998 Lincoln Cartier Designer Series Town Car. (OCW)

1998 Lincoln Continental sedan. (OCW)

Model No.	Body/ Style No.	Body Type & Seating	Factory Price	Shipping Weight	Prod. Total
MARK VIII (V-8)					
M	91	2-dr. Cpe-4P	37830	3765	*
M	92	2-dr. LSC Cpe-4P	39320	3785	*

*NOTE: Production figures for 1998 Lincoln automobiles were not available when this book went to the printer.

ENGINE [Base V-8 (Town Car)]: Modular, overhead cam V-8. Aluminum block and head. Displacement: 281 cid (4.6 liters). Bore & stroke: 3.60 x 3.60 in. Compression ratio: 9.0:1. Brake horsepower: (Executive/Signature w/single exhaust) 200 at 4500 RPM; (Cartier/Signature Touring Sedan w/dual exhaust) 220 at 4500 RPM. Torque: (Executive/Signature w/single exhaust) 265 lbs.-ft. at 3500 RPM; (Cartier/Signature Touring Sedan w/dual exhaust) 275 lbs.-ft. at 3500 RPM. Sequential fuel injection.

ENGINE [Base V-8 (Continental/Mark VIII)]: Modular, dual-overhead cam V-8. Aluminum block and head. Displacement: 281 cid (4.6 liters). Bore & stroke: (Mark VIII) 3.60 x 3.60 in.; (Continental) 3.60 x 3.40 in. Compression ratio: 9.9:1. Brake horsepower: (Continental) 260 at 5750 RPM; (Mark VIII) 280 at 5750 RPM; (Mark VIII LSC) 290 at 5750 RPM. Torque: (Continental) 270 lbs.-ft. at 3000 RPM; (Mark VIII) 285 lbs.-ft. at 4500 RPM; (Mark VIII LSC) 295 lbs.-ft. at 4500 RPM. Sequential fuel injection.

CHASSIS DATA: Wheelbase: (Town Car) 117.7 in.; (Continental) 109.0 in.; (Mark VIII) 113.0 in. Overall Length: (Town Car) 215.3 in.; (Continental) 207.0 in.; (Mark VIII) 207.2 in. Height: (Town Car) 58.0 in.; (Continental) 56.0 in.; (Mark VIII) 53.6 in. Width: (Town Car) 78.2 in.; (Continental) 73.6 in.; (Mark VIII) 74.8 in. Front tread: (Town Car) 63.4 in.; (Continental) 63.0 in.; (Mark VIII) 61.6 in. Rear tread: (Town Car) 65.3 in.; (Continental) 61.5 in.; (Mark VIII) 60.2 in. Standard Tires: (Town Car) P225/60SR16; (Continental) P225/60R16; (Mark VIII) P225/60R16.

TECHNICAL: Transmission: Four-speed overdrive automatic standard on Town Car, Continental and Mark VIII. Drive Axle: (Town Car/Mark VIII) rear; (Continental) front. Steering: (Town Car) Speed-sensitive, variable-assist Parallelogram. (Continental/Mark VIII) rack/pinion. Front Suspension: (Town Car) Independent short/long arm w/ball joints, coil springs and front stabilizer bar; (Continental) Independent MacPherson strut front drive w/strut-mounted coil springs, stabilizer bar, tension struts, lower control arms and cast knuckles; (Mark VIII) Independent short/long arm w/combined air springs/shock absorber units and double isolated tension struts. Rear Suspension: (Town Car) Four-bar link w/Watt's Linkage, air springs on axle, gas-pressurized hydraulic shocks and stabilizer bar; (Continental) Short/long arm independent w/air springs, stabilizer bar, tension struts, upper control arms, parallel lower control arms, cast spindle w/pressed-in forged stem and integrated ball joints; (Mark VIII) Independent upper and lower control arms w/air springs, automatic front-to-rear and side-to-side load leveling and stabilizer bar. Brakes: (All) Front/rear disc (anti-lock system stnd on all). Body construction: (Town Car) separate body and frame; (Continental/Mark VIII) unibody. Fuel tank: (Town Car) 20.0 gal.; (Continental) 20.0 gal.; (Mark VIII) 18.0 gal.

DRIVETRAIN OPTIONS: Suspension/Brakes, Town Car: Livery pkg: Executive ($170). Touring Pkg: Signature ($500).

TOWN CAR CONVENIENCE/APPEARANCE OPTIONS: Entertainment Pkg, Signature only incl JBL Audio Syst, CD Changer and Pwr Moonroof ($1845); w/o Pwr Moonroof ($845). Premium Pkg, Cartier only incl CD Changer and Pwr Moonroof ($1550). Calif. Emission Syst ($170). Dual Heated Leather Seats, Signature only ($290). Pwr Moonroof, Signature and Cartier ($1515). White Pearlescent Metallic Tri-Coat Paint, Executive and Signature ($365). CD Changer ($585). JBL Audio Syst: stnd Cartier, Signature ($565). Cellular Phone, N/A Executive ($790). Conventional Spare Tire ($120). Eng Block Heater ($61). Livery Pkg incl 78-Amp HD Battery, 3.27 Ratio Axle, Conventional Spare Tire, Upgaged F&R Stabilizer Bars, HD Strg Gear and HD Frt Springs ($170). Touring Pkg incl 16-inch Chrome Alum Whls, P225/60TR16 BSW Tires, Upgraded F&R Stabilizer Bars, Springs & Shocks, Leather Seats, Unique Torque Conv and 3.55 Axle Ratio, Signature ($500). Traction Control Delete, Executive (-$240). Chrome Whls, Cartier ($845).

1998 Lincoln Mark VIII LSC coupe. (OCW)

CONTINENTAL CONVENIENCE/APPEARANCE OPTIONS: Driver Select Syst incl Semi-active Susp, Adjustable Ride Control, Memory Profile Syst, Strg Whl Touch Controls and Auto Day/Nite O/S Mirrors ($595). Calif. Emission Syst ($170). Prog Garage Door Opener ($120). Pwr Moonroof ($1515). CD Changer ($595). JBL Audio Syst ($565). Heated Seats w/5 Temp Settings ($290). Cellular Phone ($790). Eng Block Heater ($61). Tri-Coat Paint ($365). Personal Security Pkg incl SecuriTire Run Flat Tires, Pressure Alert Warning Syst, Prog Garage Door Opener ($750). RESCU Pkg incl Cellular Phone, JBL Audio Syst, Prog Garage Door Opener: w/Personal Security Pkg ($2225); w/o ($2345). Chrome Whls ($845). 16-inch Polished Alum Whls ($350). Painted Alum Whls (NC).

MARK VIII CONVENIENCE/APPEARANCE OPTIONS: Calif. Emission Syst ($170). Prog Garage Door Opener ($120). Pwr Moonroof ($1515). CD Changer ($670). Cellular Phone ($790). Heated Seats ($290). Eng Block Heater ($60). Tri-Coat Paint ($365). Chrome Octastar Whls: Mark VIII ($845); LSC (NC).

HISTORY: Lincoln offered a limited production Collector's Edition of the Mark VIII. Available in either Cordovan or White Pearlescent, the Mark VIII Collector's Edition featured gold badging on side moldings and rear taillamp. A special black Lincoln star adorned the center wheel cap and a Lincoln gold logo was centered on the grille.Wood trim decorated the steering wheel and shift knob, and Collector's Edition badging was inlaid on the wood door trim and embroidered on the floor mats. Buyers of the Collector's Edition also received a set of .999 silver Lincoln ingots.

1999 LINCOLN

TOWN CAR — V-8 — In the what's new department, the 1999 Lincoln Town Car had a short list of changes. Front side impact airbags became standard equipment. An alpine audio system replaced the previous JBL stereo system as Lincoln's premium audio option. A fold-down armrest with cupholders became standard equipment in Executive models.

EXECUTIVE SEDAN: Standard equipment on the Executive series Town Car included a 4.6-liter SOHC V-8, a four-speed electronic overdrive automatic transmission, rear-wheel drive, 16-in. gear tooth aluminum wheel rims, P225/60SR16 all-season black sidewall tires, a mini spare tire on a steel spare wheel, a front independent suspension, four-wheel disc antilock brakes, dual front and side impact airbags, front and rear seat belts, CFC-free air conditioning with automatic temperature control, an automatic blower and sunload sensor, a concealed dual diversity antenna, the Smart Lock antilockout system, the SecuriLock™ passive anti-theft system, a brake/shift interlock feature, an electronic digital clock integrated into the radio, a rear window defroster, delayed accessory power, power door locks, a single outlet exhaust system, Solar-Tinted glass, an analog instrument cluster with electronic message center, an engine temperature gauge, a low engine oil alert lamp, heated and remote-controlled dual outside rearview mirrors, dual lighted visor-vanity mirrors, a premium AM/FM stereo with cassette, a remote keyless entry system, individual 40/20/40 Comfort Lounge front seats with eight-way power and leather trim, two-way front head restraints, dual power seat recliners with driver easy entry/exit feature, fingertip speed control with tap up/tap down feature, a tilt steering column with two-spoke leather-trimmed steering wheel, speed sensitive variable effort rack and pinion steering, one touch power windows and interval windshield wipers.

SIGNATURE SEDAN: Standard equipment on the Signature Edition series Town Car included a 4.6-liter SOHC V-8, a four-speed electronic overdrive automatic transmission, rear-wheel drive, 16-in. snowflake aluminum wheel rims, P225/60SR16 all-season black sidewall tires, a mini spare tire on a steel spare wheel, a front independent suspension, four-wheel disc antilock brakes, dual front and side impact airbags, front and rear seat belts, CFC-free air conditioning with automatic temperature control, an automatic blower and sunload sensor, a concealed dual diversity antenna, the Smart Lock antilockout system, the SecuriLock™ passive anti-theft system, a brake/shift interlock feature, an electronic digital clock integrated into the radio, a rear window defroster, delayed accessory power, power door locks, a single outlet exhaust system, Solar-Tinted glass, an analog instrument cluster with electronic message center, an engine temperature gauge, a low engine oil alert lamp, heated and remote-controlled dual outside rearview mirrors with memory function, dual lighted visor-vanity mirrors, an Alpine AM/FM stereo with digital signal processing, a remote keyless entry system, individual 40/20/40 Comfort Lounge front memory seats with eight-way power and leather trim and power adjustable lumbar support, two-way front head restraints, dual power seat recliners with driver easy entry/exit feature, fingertip speed control with tap up/tap down feature, a tilt steering column and two-spoke leather-trimmed steering wheel with audio and climate controls, speed sensitive variable effort rack and pinion steering, one touch power windows and interval windshield wipers.

CARTIER SEDAN: Standard equipment on the Cartier Edition series Town Car included a 4.6-liter SOHC V-8, a four-speed electronic overdrive automatic transmission, rear-wheel drive, 16-in. Cartier chrome wheel rims, P225/60SR16 all-season black sidewall tires, a mini spare tire on a steel spare wheel, a front independent suspension, four-wheel disc antilock brakes, dual front and side impact airbags, front and rear seat belts, CFC-free air conditioning with automatic temperature control, an automatic blower and sunload sensor, a concealed dual diversity antenna, the Smart Lock antilockout system, the SecuriLock™ passive anti-theft system, a brake/shift interlock feature, a luxury analog clock, a rear window defroster, delayed accessory power, power door locks, a dual outlet exhaust system, Solar-Tinted glass, an analog instrument cluster with electronic message center, an engine temperature gauge, a low engine oil alert lamp, heated and remote-controlled dual outside rearview mirrors with memory function, dual lighted visor-vanity mirrors, an Alpine AM/FM stereo with digital signal processing, a remote keyless entry system, individual 40/20/40 heated Comfort Lounge front memory seats with eight-way power and premium leather trim and power adjustable lumbar support, two-way front head restraints, dual power seat recliners with driver easy entry/exit feature, fingertip speed control with tap up/tap down feature, a tilt steering column and two-spoke leather-trimmed steering wheel with audio and climate controls, speed sensitive variable effort rack and pinion steering, one touch power windows and interval windshield wipers.

I.D. DATA: Lincoln's 17-symbol Vehicle Identification Number (VIN) was stamped on a metal tab fastened to the instrument panel, visible through the windshield. The first symbol indicates country of origin: 1=United States. The second symbol indicates manufacturer: L=Lincoln. The third symbol indicates vehicle type: J=incomplete vehicle; N=passenger car; 1=limousine. The fourth symbol indicates type of restraint system: L=front airbags with active belts in all positions; F=second-generation front airbags with active belts in all positions. The fifth symbol is the designation code: M=Lincoln. The sixth and seventh symbols indicate body type: 81=Executive four-door sedan; 82=Signature four-door sedan; 83=Cartier four-door sedan; 97=Continental four-door sedan. The eighth symbol indicates engine: V=Continental 4.6-liter DOHC V-8 with EFI; W=Town Car 4.6-liter SOHC V-8 with EFI made in Romeo, Mich., engine plant. The ninth symbol is a check digit. The 10th symbol indicated model year: X=1999. The 11th symbol indicates assembly plant and is Y (Wixom, Mich.) for all Lincoln products. The last six symbols are the sequential production number starting with 100001 at each factory.

Model No.	Body/Style No.	Body Type & Seating	Factory Price	Shipping Weight	Prod. Total
TOWN CAR EXECUTIVE SERIES (V-8)					
M	81	4d Sedan-5P	38,995	4,015	Note 1
TOWN CAR SIGNATURE SERIES (V-8)					
M	82	4d Sedan-5P	40,995	4,020	Note 1
TOWN CAR CARTIER SERIES (V-8)					
M	83	4d Sedan-5P	41,695	4,095	Note 1

Note 1: Total model year production of Town Cars was 93,000.

CONTINENTAL — V-8 — The output of the Continental engine was boosted from 260 hp in 1998 to 275 hp in 1999. Driver and passenger side-impact airbags were now standard in the front compartment. Handsome 10-spoke aluminum wheels were another new piece of standard equipment. An Alpine stereo system replaced a JBL system as premium audio equipment. The door lock cylinder on the passenger side door was eliminated. Standard equipment included dual front and side impact air bags, a CFC-free automatic air conditioner with sunload sensor, side window demisters, a concealed antenna in the rear backlight, a flashing LED SecuriLock™ anti-theft system with engine

immobilizer and perimeter protection, power four-wheel disc ABS brakes, a brake/shift interlock feature, a stand-alone analog clock, a heated rear window, a rear window defroster, delayed accessory power, Lincoln's Service Bay Diagnostic System (SBDS), a 4.6-liter DOHC modular Intec V-8, EEC-V electronic engine control, dual exhausts with exposed bright tips, Solar-Tinted glass, backlit glass tinting, a virtual image instrument cluster with dot metrix message center (includes tachometer, temperature gauge, fuel gauge, speedometer warning indicator, antilock braking lamp, service engine soon light, air bag indicator, anti-theft indicator, traction control indicator, brake light, high beam indicator, turn signal indicators, etc.), automatic keyless door locks with door lock confirmation chirp, a Smart Lock antilockout system, childproof rear door locks, a memory seat, dual body-color heated memory-type outside rearview mirrors (mirrors tilt down when car is in reverse), an interior day/night rearview mirror with automatic dimming and compass, a high-level AM/FM audio system with stereo cassette and ETR radio, dual front and rear door radio speakers, five-passenger seating with leather seating surfaces (with six-way power memory driver's seat, two-way power lumbar support for driver and two-way passenger seat) and easy entry/exit, full-length integral door armrests, two fold-down rear seat armrests, seat embroidery with Lincoln star, two-way adjustable front seat headrests, automatic speed control with tap up/tap down feature and backlit controls, driver-adjustable variable assist power steering with leather wrapped tilt steering wheel, cloth covered sun visors with lighted visor-vanity mirrors, an AX4N automatic transmission with non-synchronous shift, P225/60R16 black sidewall all-season tires with 15 x 4-in. mini spare wheel, 16-in. 10-spoke brushed aluminum wheels and power windows with express-down driver's window.

Model No.	Body/Style No.	Body Type & Seating	Factory Price	Shipping Weight	Prod. Total
CONTINENTAL (V-8)					
M	97	4d Sedan-5P	38,995	3,868	28,000

LINCOLN TOWN CAR ENGINE

ENGINE [Standard Executive/Signature SOHC V-8]: Aluminum block and head. Single exhaust. Displacement: 281 cid (4.6 liters). Bore & stroke: 3.55 x 3.54 in. Compression ratio: 10.0:1. Brake horsepower: 200 at 4500 rpm. Torque: 265 lbs.-ft. at 3500 rpm. Sequential multi-port electronic fuel injection. Single exhaust.

ENGINE [Standard Cartier Series SOHC V-8]: Aluminum block and head. Dual exhausts. Displacement: 281 cid (4.6 liters). Bore & stroke: 3.55 x 3.54 in. Compression ratio: 10.0:1. Brake horsepower: 220 at 4500 rpm. Torque: 275 lbs.-ft. at 3500 rpm. Sequential multi-port electronic fuel injection. Dual exhaust.

LINCOLN CONTINENTAL ENGINE

ENGINE [Standard DOHC V-8]: Aluminum block and head. Displacement: 281 cid (4.6 liters). Bore & stroke: 3.55 x 3.54 in. Compression ratio: 9.89:1. Brake horsepower: 260 at 5750 rpm. Torque: 270 lbs.-ft. at 3000 rpm. Sequential multi-port electronic fuel injection.

LINCOLN TOWN CAR CHASSIS: Wheelbase: (all) 117.7 in. Overall Length: (all) 215.3 in. Height: (all) 58.0 in. Width: (all) 78.2 in. Front tread: (all) 63.4 in. Rear tread: (all) 65.3 in.

LINCOLN CONTINENTAL CHASSIS: Wheelbase: 109 in. Overall Length: 208.5 in. Height: 56 in. Width: 73.6 in. Front tread: 63.0 in. Rear tread: 61.5 in.

LINCOLN TOWN CAR TECHNICAL: Transmission: four-speed automatic overdrive. Drive Axle: rear. Steering: speed-sensitive variable-assist rack-and-pinion; ratio 16.4:1, 3.4 turns lock-to-lock, 44.1-ft. curb-to-curb turning circle. Front suspension: Independent unequal length control arms with coil springs ball joints. Rear suspension: Four bar link and Watt's linkage with air springs. Brakes: Front brakes: Power-assisted disc with ABS. Rear brakes: Power-assisted disc with ABS. Gas tank: 19 gallons.

LINCOLN CONTINENTAL TECHNICAL: Transmission: four-speed automatic overdrive. Drive Axle: front. Steering: speed-sensitive variable-assist selectable effort; ratio 16.95:1, 3.4 turns lock-to-lock, 41.1-ft. turning circle. Front suspension: Independent MacPherson struts with aluminum lower control arms, double ball joint stabilizer links and coil springs. Rear suspension: independent unequal-length control arms, double ball joints and rear leveling air springs. Brakes: Front brakes: Power-assisted disc with ABS. Rear brakes: Power-assisted disc with ABS. Gas tank: 20 gallons.

LINCOLN TOWN CAR OPTIONS: 422 California emissions (no cost). 428 high-altitude emissions (no cost). 41H engine block immersion heater ($60). 535 livery package ($125). 61A automatic dimming electrochromatic mirrors with memory and compass ($245). 13B power moonroof ($1,515). 153 front license plate bracket (no cost). Tricoat paint (standard Cartier; $365 on other models). 954 two-tone paint for Signature Edition only ($250). 60P premium package including power moonroof ($1,595). 919 trunk-mounted six-disc CD changer ($605). 467 heated front seats ($290). X perforated leather seating surfaces, Signature only, included in Signature Touring Sedan package (no cost). 663 Signature Touring Sedan package ($700). 518 portable telephone ($790). 508 conventional spare tire ($120). T2A P225/60R16 all-season white sidewall tires ($95 additional; not available with Signature Touring Sedan package).

LINCOLN CONTINENTAL OPTIONS: 153 front license plate bracket (no cost). 667 Driver Select system ($595). 428 high-altitude emissions (no cost). 175 garage door opener ($120). 41H engine block immersion heater ($60). 54A Luxury Appearance package ($1,095). 13B power moonroof ($1,515). Tricoat paint ($365). 675 Personal Security package ($750). 916 Alpine audio system ($565). 919 trunk-mounted six-disc CD changer ($605). 67F RESCU package with programmable garage door opener and cellular phone ($2,225 with Personal Security package or $2,345 otherwise). 467 heated front seats ($290). 516 portable telephone ($790). 64F 16-in. highly-polished aluminum wheels and P225/60VR16 black sidewall tires ($350 additional). 64G 16-in. chrome six-spoke wheels ($845 additional).

HISTORICAL FOOTNOTES: On Jan. 1, 1999, Sir Alex Trotman retired as chairman and chief executive officer of Lincoln's parent, Ford Motor Co. William Clay Ford, Jr., assumed the office of chairman and Jacques Nasser was appointed president and chief executive officer. A new management team took over Ford's leadership. On March 19, 1999 Ford established a new Premier Auto Group consisting of Aston-Martin, Jaguar and Lincoln. Volvo was added to this group later. During the year, Jacques Nasser announced a bold plan to relocate Lincoln-Mercury divisional headquarters to California. An all-new Lincoln LS model was introduced during 1999, but was officially considered a 2000 model. During 1999, Lincoln devised innovative product launches which included using San Francisco's Treasure Island to help launch Lincoln's new LS sedan, *Motor Trend's* 2000 Car of the Year.

2000 LINCOLN

LINCOLN LS — V-8 — Lincoln's entry-level luxury sports sedan was introduced in the spring of 1999 as an all-new 2000 model. It was built on a 114.5-in. wheelbase platform and powered by either a 210-hp V-6 or a 252-hp V-8. The LS was the first Lincoln in 48 years to offer a manual transmission. An optional dual-gate SelectShift transmission gave the driver a choice of manual or automatic gear selection. It featured computerized fuel shutoff to prevent over-revving the engine. Standard features included four-wheel independent suspension, all-speed traction and yaw control, antilock brakes and front and side impact driver and front passenger airbags. There were no major changes to the LS in the fall of 1999, when the other 2000 Lincolns appeared.

V-6 SEDAN: Standard equipment included the 3.0-liter DOHC V-6, a five-speed automatic transmission, rear-wheel drive, 16-in. alloy wheel rims, P21560HR16 all-season tires, a mini spare tire on a steel spare wheel, four-wheel independent suspension, front and rear stabilizer bars, four-wheel ventilated disc antilock brakes, front side mounted airbags, front head airbags, rear door child safety locks, a center rear three-point seat belt, two front headrests, the SecuriLock™ passive anti-theft system with engine immobilizer, dusk-sensing headlamps, automatic delayed-off headlights, front fog lights, variable intermittent windshield wipers, a rear window defogger, five-passenger seating with leather front bucket seats (eight-way power driver's seat with lumbar support and six-way power passenger seat), a split-folding rear seat with center armrest, rear seat heating ducts, remote power door locks, one touch power windows, heated power mirrors, an 80-watt AM/FM cassette stereo, a four-speaker sound system, an element antenna, speed control, speed-proportional power steering, a tilt/telescope steering column, redundant audio and speed controls on the steering wheel, cupholders, front door map pockets, front seatback storage, a 12-volt power outlet, a front console with storage space, retained accessory power, a dual zone climate control system, micron air filtration, front reading lights, dual illuminating visor-vanity mirrors, a leather and wood steering wheel, wood and leather trim on the shift knob, simulated wood trim on the doors, front and rear floor mats, a trunk light, a tachometer, a clock, a low-fuel warning light and a chrome grille.

V-8 SEDAN: Standard equipment included the 3.9-liter DOHC V-8, a five-speed automatic transmission, rear-wheel drive, 16-in. alloy wheel rims, P21560VR16 all-season tires, a mini spare tire on a steel spare wheel, four-wheel independent suspension, front and rear stabilizer bars, four-wheel ventilated disc antilock brakes, traction control, front side mounted airbags, front head airbags, rear door child safety locks, a center rear three-point seat belt, two front headrests, the SecuriLock™ passive anti-theft system with engine immobilizer, dusk-sensing headlamps, automatic delayed-off headlights, front fog lights,

variable intermittent rain-sensing windshield wipers, a rear window defogger, five-passenger seating with leather front bucket seat (eight-way power driver's seat with lumbar support and six-way power passenger seat), memorized seat-steering wheel-mirrors-compass settings, a split-folding rear seat with center armrest, easy-entry rear seat access, rear seat heating ducts, remote power door locks, one touch power windows, heated power mirrors, an auto-dimming inside rearview mirror, an 80-watt AM/FM cassette stereo, a four-speaker sound system, an element antenna, speed control, speed-proportional power steering, a tilt/telescope steering column, redundant audio and speed controls on the steering wheel, cupholders, front door map pockets, front seatback storage, a 12-volt power outlet, a front console with storage space, retained accessory power, a dual zone climate control system, micron air filtration, front reading lights, dual illuminating visor-vanity mirrors, a leather and wood steering wheel, wood and leather trim on the shift knob, simulated wood trim on the doors, front and rear floor mats, a trunk light, a tachometer, a clock, a low-fuel warning, a chrome grille, a universal remote for garage door and security.

I.D. DATA: Lincoln's 17-symbol Vehicle Identification Number (VIN) was stamped on a metal tab fastened to the instrument panel, visible through the windshield. The first symbol indicates country of origin: 1=United States. The second symbol indicates manufacturer: L=Lincoln. The third symbol indicates vehicle type: J=incomplete vehicle; N=passenger car; 1=limousine. The fourth symbol indicates type of restraint system: F=second-generation front airbags with active belts in all positions; H=dual frontal and side impact second-generation airbags for driver and front passenger plus active belts in all positions. The fifth symbol is the designation code: M=Lincoln. The sixth and seventh symbols indicate body type: 81=Executive four-door sedan; 82=Signature four-door sedan; 83=Cartier four-door sedan; 86=LS four-door sedan with V-6; 87=LS four-door sedan with V-8; 97=Continental four-door sedan. The eighth symbol indicates engine: A=Lincoln LS 3.9-liter DOHC V-8 with EFI; S=Lincoln LS 3.0-liter DOHC V-6 with EFI; V=Continental 4.6-liter DOHC V-8 with EFI; W=Town Car 4.6-liter SOHC V-8 with EFI made in the Romeo, Mich., engine plant. The ninth symbol is a check digit. The 10th symbol indicated model year: Y=2000. The 11th symbol indicates assembly plant and is Y (Wixom, Mich.) for all Lincoln products. The last six symbols are the sequential production number starting with 100001 at each factory.

Model No.	Body/ Style No.	Body Type & Seating	Factory Price	Shipping Weight	Prod. Total
LINCOLN LS (V-6 AUTOMATIC)					
M	86	4d Sedan-5P	32,275	3,598	—
LINCOLN LS (V-8 AUTOMATIC)					
M	87	4d Sedan-5P	35,250	3,692	—

TOWN CAR — V-8 — Very modest changes were evident in the 2000 Lincoln Town Car. They included the addition of an inside trunk release, child seat tether anchors, front side impact airbags and all-speed traction control as standard equipment.

EXECUTIVE SEDAN: Standard equipment included a 4.6-liter SOHC V-8, a four-speed automatic transmission, rear-wheel drive, 16-in. alloy wheel rims, P225/60SR16 all-season tires, a mini spare tire on a steel spare wheel, front independent suspension, front and rear stabilizer bars, front disc/rear drum antilock brakes, traction control, front side mounted airbags, front and rear seat belts, rear door child safety locks, child seat anchors, an emergency lock release inside the trunk, a center rear three-point seat belt, two front headrests, the SecuriLock™ passive anti-theft system with an engine immobilizer, dusk-sensing headlamps, auto-delay-off headlights, cornering lights, variable intermittent windshield wipers, a rear window defogger, six-passenger seating with an eight-way power split bench front seat, leather seat upholstery, a rear bench seat with center armrest, rear seat heating ducts, digital keypad remote power door locks, one touch power windows, heated power mirrors, an AM/FM cassette stereo, a diversity antenna, speed control, speed-proportional power steering, a tilt-adjustable steering wheel, audio and speed controls on the steering wheel, climate control, front and rear cupholders, a remote trunk lid release, map pockets, front seatback storage, a front 12-volt power outlet, a front console with storage space, retained accessory power, an auto-dimming inside rearview mirror, front and rear reading lights, dual illuminating visor-vanity mirrors, a leather-wrapped steering wheel, leather trim on the center console, front and rear floor mats, a trunk light, a trip computer, a clock, an external temperature display, a low-fuel warning light and a compass.

SIGNATURE SEDAN: Standard equipment included a 4.6-liter SOHC V-8, a four-speed automatic transmission, rear-wheel drive, 16-in. alloy wheel rims, P225/60SR16 all-season tires, a mini spare tire on a steel spare wheel, front independent suspension, front and rear stabilizer bars, front disc/rear drum antilock brakes, traction control, front side mounted airbags, rear door child safety locks, child seat anchors, an emergency lock release inside the trunk, a center rear three-point seat belt, two front headrests, the SecuriLock™ passive anti-theft system, an engine immobilizer, dusk-sensing headlamps, auto-delay-off headlights, cornering lights, variable intermittent windshield wipers, a rear window defogger, six-passenger seating with an eight-way power split bench front seat with adjustable lumbar support, leather seat upholstery, a rear bench seat with center armrest, easy-entry rear seat access, memorized settings for three drivers, rear seat heating ducts, digital keypad remote power door locks, one touch power windows, heated automatic-dimming electrochromatic power mirrors, a universal remote for garage door and security, an AM/FM cassette stereo, a diversity antenna, speed control, speed-proportional power steering, a tilt-adjustable leather steering wheel, audio and speed controls on the steering wheel, climate control, front and rear cupholders, a remote trunk lid release, map pockets, front seatback storage, a front 12-volt power outlet, a front console with storage space, retained accessory power, an auto-dimming inside rearview mirror, front and rear reading lights, dual illuminating visor-vanity mirrors, a leather-wrapped steering wheel, leather trim on the center console, front and rear floor mats, a trunk light, a trip computer, a clock, an external temperature display, a low-fuel warning light and a compass.

CARTIER SEDAN: Standard equipment included a 4.6-liter 235-hp (instead of standard 220-hp) SOHC V-8, a four-speed automatic transmission, rear-wheel drive, 16-in. chrome alloy wheel rims, P225/60SR16 all-season tires, a mini spare tire on a steel spare wheel, front independent suspension, front and rear stabilizer bars, front disc/rear drum antilock brakes, traction control, front side mounted airbags, front and rear seat belts, rear door child safety locks, child seat anchors, an emergency lock release inside the trunk, a center rear three-point seat belt, two front headrests, two rear seat headrests, the SecuriLock™ passive anti-theft system, an engine immobilizer, dusk-sensing headlamps, auto-delay-off headlights, cornering lights, variable intermittent windshield wipers, a rear window defogger, six-passenger seating with a heated eight-way power split armrest bench front seat with adjustable lumbar support, leather seat upholstery, a rear bench seat with center storage armrest, easy-entry rear seat access, memorized settings for three drivers, rear seat heating ducts, rear seat radio volume controls, rear seat climate controls, front and rear door pockets, digital keypad remote power door locks, one touch power windows, heated automatic-dimming electrochromatic power mirrors, a universal remote for garage door and security, an Alpine premium brand 145-watts stereo system, AM/FM cassette stereo, a diversity antenna, speed control, speed-proportional power steering, a tilt-adjustable leather-wrapped steering wheel, audio and speed controls on the steering wheel, climate control, front and rear cupholders, a remote trunk lid release, front door pockets, front seatback storage, a front 12-volt power outlet, a front console with storage space, retained accessory power, an auto-dimming inside rearview mirror, front and rear reading lights, dual illuminating visor-vanity mirrors, a leather-wrapped steering wheel, leather trim on the center console, front and rear floor mats, a trunk light, a trip computer, a clock, an external temperature display, a low-fuel warning light and a compass.

Model No.	Body/ Style No.	Body Type & Seating	Factory Price	Shipping Weight	Prod. Total
TOWN CAR EXECUTIVE SERIES (V-8)					
M	81	4d Sedan-5P	39,325	4,047	—
TOWN CAR SIGNATURE SERIES (V-8)					
M	82	4d Sedan-5P	41,325	4,047	—
TOWN CAR SIGNATURE SERIES WITH TOURING SEDAN OPTION (V-8)					
M	82	4d Sedan-5P	42,025	4,156	—
TOWN CAR CARTIER SERIES (V-8)					
M	83	4d Sedan-5P	43,825	4,047	—

CONTINENTAL — V-8 — New features for the 2000 Lincoln Continental included an emergency inside trunk release, child seat tether anchors and side impact airbags. Standard equipment included a 4.6-liter 275-hp DOHC V-8, a four-speed automatic transmission, front-wheel drive, 16-in. chrome alloy wheel rims, P225/60HR16 all-season tires, a mini spare tire on a steel spare wheel, four-wheel independent suspension, front and rear stabilizer bars, a self-leveling suspension, front disc/rear drum antilock brakes, traction control, front side mounted airbags, rear door child safety locks, child seat anchors, an emergency lock release inside the trunk, a front center lap belt, a center rear three-point seat belt, two front headrests, a remote anti-theft system with engine immobilizer, dusk-sensing headlamps, auto-delay-off headlights, cornering lights, variable intermittent windshield wipers, a rear window defogger, six-passenger seating with a six-way power front seat with adjustable lumbar support, leather seat upholstery, a rear bench seat, rear seat heating ducts, digital keypad remote power door locks, one touch power windows, heated power mirrors with curbview feature, an AM/FM cassette stereo, a four-speaker sound system, a diversity antenna, adaptive speed control, speed-proportional power steering, a tilt-adjustable leather-wrapped steering wheel, speed controls on the steering wheel, front and rear cupholders, a remote trunk lid release, front door pockets, front seatback storage, a front 12-volt power outlet, a front console with storage space, an overhead console

with storage, a universal remote for garage and security, retained accessory power, easy-entry rear seat access, air conditioning, a micron air filtration system, an auto-dimming inside rearview mirror, front reading lights, dual illuminating visor-vanity mirrors, wood trim on the center console, front and rear floor mats, memorized driver settings for two, a tachometer, a clock, an external temperature display and a low-fuel warning light.

Model No.	Body/ Style No.	Body Type & Seating	Factory Price	Shipping Weight	Prod. Total
CONTINENTAL (V-8)					
M	97	4d Sedan-5P	39,575	3,848	—

LINCOLN LS ENGINES

ENGINE [Standard LS DOHC V-6]: Aluminum block and head. Displacement: 183 cid (3.0 liters). Bore & stroke: 3.5 x 3.13 in. Compression ratio: 10.5:1. Brake horsepower: 210 at 6500 rpm. Torque: 205 lbs.-ft. at 4750 rpm. Sequential multi-port electronic fuel injection.

ENGINE [Optional LS DOHC V-8]: Aluminum block and head. Displacement: 240 cid (3.9 liters). Bore & stroke: 3.39 x 3.35 in. Compression ratio: 10.5:1. Brake horsepower: 252 at 6100 rpm. Torque: 267 lbs.-ft. at 4300 rpm. Sequential multi-port electronic fuel injection.

LINCOLN TOWN CAR ENGINE

ENGINE [Standard Executive/Signature SOHC V-8]: Aluminum block and head. Single exhaust. Displacement: 281 cid (4.6 liters). Bore & stroke: 3.55 x 3.54 in. Compression ratio: 10.0:1. Brake horsepower: 200 at 4500 rpm. Torque: 265 lbs.-ft. at 3500 rpm. Sequential multi-port electronic fuel injection.

ENGINE [Standard Signature w/Touring Sedan Option SOHC V-8]: Aluminum block and head. Dual exhausts. Displacement: 281 cid (4.6 liters). Bore & stroke: 3.55 x 3.54 in. Compression ratio: 10.0:1. Brake horsepower: 215 at 4500 rpm. Torque: 285 lbs.-ft. at 3500 rpm. Sequential multi-port electronic fuel injection.

ENGINE [Optional Cartier Series SOHC V-8]: Aluminum block and head. Dual exhausts. Displacement: 281 cid (4.6 liters). Bore & stroke: 3.55 x 3.54 in. Compression ratio: 9.4:1. Brake horsepower: 235 at 4650 rpm. Torque: 275 lbs.-ft. at 4000 rpm. Sequential multi-port electronic fuel injection.

LINCOLN CONTINENTAL ENGINE

ENGINE [Standard DOHC V-8]: Aluminum block and head. Displacement: 281 cid (4.6 liters). Bore & stroke: 3.55 x 3.54 in. Compression ratio: 9.89:1. Brake horsepower: 275 at 5750 rpm. Torque: 275 lbs.-ft. at 3000 rpm. Sequential multi-port electronic fuel injection.

LINCOLN LS CHASSIS: Wheelbase: 114.5 in. Overall Length: 193.9 in. Height: 56.1 in. Width: 73.2 in. Front tread: 60.5 in. Rear tread: 60.8 in.

LINCOLN TOWN CAR CHASSIS: Wheelbase: (all) 117.7 in. Overall Length: (all) 215.3 in. Height: (all) 58.0 in. Width: (all) 78.2 in. Front tread: (all) 63.4 in. Rear tread: (all) 65.3 in.

LINCOLN CONTINENTAL CHASSIS: Wheelbase: 109 in. Overall Length: 208.5 in. Height: 56 in. Width: 73.6 in. Front tread: 63.0 in. Rear tread: 61.5 in.

LINCOLN LS TECHNICAL: Transmission: five-speed manual overdrive. Drive Axle: rear. Steering: speed-sensitive variable-assist rack-and-pinion; ratio 18.0:1, 3.0 turns lock-to-lock, 38.06-ft. curb-to-curb turning circle. Front suspension: Independent unequal length control arms with coil springs and tubular stabilizer bar. Rear suspension: Independent unequal length control arms with coil springs and solid stabilizer bar mounted on isolated rear sub-frame. Brakes: Front brakes: Power-assisted disc with ABS. Rear brakes: Power-assisted disc with ABS. Gas tank: 18 gallons.

LINCOLN TOWN CAR TECHNICAL: Transmission: four-speed automatic overdrive. Drive Axle: rear. Steering: speed-sensitive variable-assist rack-and-pinion; ratio 16.4:1, 3.4 turns lock-to-lock, 44.1-ft. curb-to-curb turning circle. Front suspension: Independent unequal length control arms with coil springs ball joints. Rear suspension: Four bar link and Watt's linkage with air springs. Brakes: Front brakes: Power-assisted disc with ABS. Rear brakes: Power-assisted disc with ABS. Gas tank: 19 gallons.

LINCOLN CONTINENTAL TECHNICAL: Transmission: four-speed automatic overdrive. Drive Axle: front. Steering: speed-sensitive variable-assist selectable effort; ratio 16.95:1, 3.4 turns lock-to-lock, 41.1-ft. turning circle. Front suspension: Independent MacPherson struts with aluminum lower control arms, double ball joint stabilizer links and coil springs. Rear suspension: Independent unequal-length control arms, double ball joints and rear leveling air springs. Brakes: Front brakes: Power-assisted disc with ABS. Rear brakes: Power-assisted disc with ABS. Gas tank: 20 gallons.

LINCOLN LS OPTIONS: 13B power moonroof ($1,005). 153 front license plate bracket (no cost). 422 California emissions (no cost). 556 AdvanceTrac stability-control system ($735). 58X Six-disc in-dash CD player ($605). 60L V-6 Convenience package ($960). 60N Smart package ($1,385 net price after $605 manufacturer's discount). 632 heated front seats ($400). 64C 17-in. five-spoke chrome aluminum wheel rims ($845). 65L Premium V-6 package ($2,690 net price after $605 manufacturer's discount). 65L Premium V-8 package ($3,090 net price after $605 manufacturer's discount). 916 Alpine audio system ($575). 919 glove box-mounted six-disc CD changer ($605).

LINCOLN TOWN CAR OPTIONS: 153 front license plate bracket (no cost). 422 California emissions (no cost). 467 heated front seats in Signature series sedan ($400). 503 conventional spare tire on Executive series sedan ($114). 54E limited-edition package on Signature series sedan ($995). 60P Cartier/Signature series Premium package ($1,525 net price after $605 manufacturer's discount). 663 Signature Touring Sedan package ($710).

LINCOLN CONTINENTAL OPTIONS: 13B power moonroof ($1,525). 153 front license plate bracket (no cost). 422 California emissions (no cost). 467 heated front seats ($400). 516 cellular phone ($800). 54A Luxury Appearance package ($1,105). 54E limited-edition package ($1,195) 6 individual bucket seats with leather seating surfaces (no cost). 64F 16-in. highly polished aluminum wheel rims ($360). 64G chrome six-spoke wheels ($855). 667 Driver Select system ($605). 675 Personal Security package ($640). 916 Alpine audio system ($575). 919 console-mounted six-disc CD changer ($605). 919 mini console-mounted six-disc CD changer ($605).

HISTORICAL FOOTNOTES: In April 2000, Lincoln announced a multi-year partnership with the United States Tennis Association (USTA) making Lincoln the Official Vehicle of the US Open and Exclusive Sponsor of the Men's Singles Championship. Lincoln said it would partner with the USTA on community outreach programs and become the exclusive vehicle and sponsor of USA League Tennis, the world's largest grass roots tennis league. Lincoln would become the official sponsor of Arthur Ashe Kids' Day and expected to be involved with the USA Tennis NJTL (National Junior Tennis League). "Our partnership with the USTA is a natural fit with Lincoln's American Luxury branding," said Deborah Wahl, Lincoln's marketing communications manager. Lincoln also said it would build a large, interactive pavilion on stadium grounds to, "deliver the American Luxury experience to all attending" the US Open. Lincoln planned to offer a virtual tour of the luxury center via the US Open's Web site www.usopen.org or its own www.lincolnvehicles.com Web site. In August 2000, Lincoln introduced the Blackwood — an auto show concept vehicle brought to life for the 2002 model year — at the US Open as part of the "Lincoln American Luxury Immersion." That was the name of an interactive, multi-media tour of a luxury lifestyle built inside a transformed 8,000 sq. ft. pavilion on the grounds of the US Open. With theatrical designs, dramatic scenery and sounds with the presence of the Blackwood, the Immersion was part Broadway show and part Hollywood sound stage. The Lincoln Blackwood, which was first shown as a concept vehicle at the 1999 Los Angeles Auto Show, would become available in dealerships in the first half of 2001. It marries the dramatic presence of a deep-gloss black Lincoln Navigator SUV with a unique and distinctive pickup box-like trunk with a power-operated tonneau cover. Lincoln also celebrated its 80th anniversary during 2000. "September 14 is a very important date for Lincoln as it signifies the inception of Lincoln's rich heritage and elegant style introduced by Henry Leland 80 years ago today," said division president Mark Hutchins. "With the recent launch of our finest luxury vehicles ever, including the Lincoln Navigator, Lincoln LS and Lincoln Blackwood, we continue to stay focused on producing automobiles that exemplify the unique tradition and uncompromising quality set by Mr. Leland." Lincoln also upped its involvement in its new community in Southern California by becoming active in the business and civic communities and launching both environmental and educational initiatives. From trail clean-ups at Yosemite, to collecting more than 1,000 toys to brighten the holidays for needy local boys and girls, Lincoln team members committed with their hearts, hands and dollars to their new community.

2001 LINCOLN

LINCOLN LS — V-8 — Lincoln's entry-level luxury sedan did a good job of blending American luxury with European-like road manners. Introduced in 2000, the LS became Lincoln's most technically advanced nameplate. Styling characteristics included quad headlights, a swooping grille and a clean-lined hood. A 3.0-liter 210-hp V-6 was standard and a 3.9-liter 252-hp DOHC 32-valve V-8 was available. In the what's new department, traction control became standard with the V-6. All models featured a new glow-in-the-dark manual trunk release and child seat anchors. The sport package featured new 17-in. wheels

and a mini spare tire. Inside there was an added 12-volt outlet or power point, redesigned cupholders, an available six-disc CD changer and an optional rearview mirror with a built-in compass. The height adjustable rear seat headrests were no longer available in cars with the V-8 and automatic transmission. There were four new exterior colors. Also, Lincoln now offered its customers complimentary service for three years or 36,000 miles.

V-6 SEDAN: Standard equipment included the 3.0-liter DOHC V-6, a five-speed automatic transmission, rear-wheel drive, 16-in. alloy wheel rims, P21560HR16 all-season tires, a mini spare tire on a steel spare wheel, four-wheel independent suspension, front and rear stabilizer bars, four-wheel ventilated disc antilock brakes, traction control, front side mounted airbags, front airbags, rear door child safety locks, child seat anchors, an emergency lock release inside the trunk, a center rear three-point seat belt, two front headrests, the SecuriLock™ passive anti-theft system, an engine immobilizer, dusk-sensing headlamps, automatic delayed-off headlights, front fog lights, variable intermittent windshield wipers, a rear window defogger, five-passenger seating with leather front bucket seats (including an eight-way power driver's seat with lumbar support and six-way power passenger seat), a split-folding rear seat with center armrest, rear seat heating ducts, remote power door locks, one touch power windows, heated power mirrors, an 80-watt AM/FM cassette stereo, a four-speaker sound system, an element antenna, speed control, speed-proportional power steering, a tilt/telescope steering column, redundant audio and speed controls on the steering wheel, front and rear cupholders, a remote trunk lid release, front door map pockets, front seatback storage, front and rear 12-volt power outlets, a front console with storage space, retained accessory power, a dual zone climate control system, micron air filtration, front reading lights, dual illuminating visor-vanity mirrors, a leather and wood steering wheel, wood and leather trim on the shift knob, simulated wood trim on the doors, front and rear floor mats, a trunk light, a tachometer, a clock, a low-fuel warning light and a chrome grille.

V-8 SEDAN: Standard equipment included the 3.9-liter DOHC V-8, a five-speed automatic transmission, rear-wheel drive, 16-in. alloy wheel rims, P21560VR16 all-season tires, a mini spare tire on a steel spare wheel, four-wheel independent suspension, front and rear stabilizer bars, four-wheel ventilated disc antilock brakes, traction control, front side mounted airbags, front head airbags, rear door child safety locks, child seat anchors, an emergency lock release inside the trunk, a center rear three-point seat belt, two front headrests, the SecuriLock™ passive anti-theft system, an engine immobilizer, dusk-sensing headlamps, automatic delayed-off headlights, front fog lights, variable intermittent rain-sensing windshield wipers, a rear window defogger, five-passenger seating with a leather front bucket seat (including eight-way power driver's seat with lumbar support and six-way power passenger seat), memorized seat-steering wheel-mirrors-compass settings, a split-folding rear seat with center armrest, easy-entry rear seat access, rear seat heating ducts, remote power door locks, one touch power windows, heated power mirrors, an auto-dimming inside rearview mirror, an 80-watt AM/FM cassette stereo, a four-speaker sound system, an element antenna, speed control, speed-proportional power steering, a tilt/telescope steering column, redundant audio and speed controls on the steering wheel, front and rear cupholders, a remote trunk lid release, front door map pockets, front seatback storage, front and rear 12-volt power outlets, a front console with storage space, retained accessory power, a dual zone climate control system, micron air filtration, front reading lights, dual illuminating visor-vanity mirrors, a leather and wood steering wheel, wood and leather trim on the shift knob, simulated wood trim on the doors, front and rear floor mats, a trunk light, a tachometer, a clock, a low-fuel warning light, a chrome grille, a universal remote for garage door and security.

I.D. DATA: I.D. DATA: Lincoln's 17-symbol Vehicle Identification Number (VIN) was stamped on a metal tab fastened to the instrument panel, visible through the windshield. The first symbol indicates country of origin: 1=United States. The second symbol indicates manufacturer: L=Lincoln. The third symbol indicates vehicle type: J=incomplete vehicle; N=passenger car; 1=limousine. The fourth symbol indicates type of restraint system: F=second-generation front airbags with active belts in all positions; H=dual frontal and side impact second-generation airbags for driver and front passenger plus active belts in all positions. The fifth symbol is the designation code: M=Lincoln. The sixth and seventh symbols indicate body type: 81=Executive four-door sedan, 82=Signature four-door sedan, 83=Cartier four-door sedan, 84=Executive L four-door sedan, 85=Cartier L four-door sedan, 86=LS four-door sedan with V-6 and automatic transmission, 86=LS four-door sedan with V-6 and manual transmission, 87=LS four-door sedan with V-8 and automatic transmission, 97=Continental four-door sedan. The eighth symbol indicates engine: A=Lincoln LS 3.9-liter DOHC V-8 with EFI, S=Lincoln LS 3.0-liter DOHC V-6 with EFI, V=Continental 4.6-liter DOHC V-8 with EFI, W=Town Car 4.6-liter SOHC V-8 with EFI made in the Romeo, Mich., engine plant. The ninth symbol is a check digit. The 10th symbol indicated model year: 1=2001. The 11th symbol indicates assembly plant and is Y (Wixom, Mich.) for all Lincoln products. The last six symbols are the sequential production number starting with 100001 at each factory.

LINCOLN LS (V-6 MANUAL)

Model No.	Body/ Style No.	Body Type & Seating	Factory Price	Shipping Weight	Prod. Total
M	86	4d Sedan-5P	32,900	3,593	-

LINCOLN LS (V-6 AUTOMATIC)

Model No.	Body/ Style No.	Body Type & Seating	Factory Price	Shipping Weight	Prod. Total
M	86	4d Sedan-5P	34,355	3,598	-

LINCOLN LS (V-8)

Model No.	Body/ Style No.	Body Type & Seating	Factory Price	Shipping Weight	Prod. Total
M	87	4d Sedan-5P	36,930	3,692	-

TOWN CAR — V-8 — For 2001, horsepower ratings were increased throughout the Lincoln Town Car model lineup. New features included adjustable control pedals, seat belt pre-tensioners, upgraded map pockets and leather grab handles. Signature Edition models now had a wood trimmed steering wheel as standard equipment. A new piece of standard equipment on the Executive models was seats with power lumbar adjustment. The new three-year/36,000-mile complimentary maintenance program also applied to the Town Car.

EXECUTIVE SEDAN: Standard equipment included a 4.6-liter SOHC V-8, a four-speed automatic transmission, rear-wheel drive, 16-in. alloy wheel rims, P225/60SR16 all-season tires, a mini spare tire on a steel spare wheel, front independent suspension, front and rear stabilizer bars, front disc/rear drum antilock brakes, traction control, front side mounted airbags, front and rear seat belt pre-tensioners, rear door child safety locks, child seat anchors, an emergency lock release inside the trunk, a center rear three-point seat belt, two front headrests, the SecuriLock™ passive anti-theft system, an engine immobilizer, dusk-sensing headlamps, auto-delay-off headlights, cornering lights, variable intermittent windshield wipers, a rear window defogger, six-passenger seating (including an eight-way power split bench front seat with adjustable lumbar support, leather seat upholstery and a rear bench seat with center armrest), rear seat heating ducts, digital keypad remote power door locks, one touch power windows, heated power mirrors, an AM/FM cassette stereo, an diversity antenna, speed control, speed-proportional power steering, a tilt-adjustable steering wheel, audio and speed controls on the steering wheel, height-adjustable pedals, climate control, front and rear cupholders, a remote trunk lid release, front door pockets, front seatback storage, a front 12-volt power outlet, a front console with storage space, retained accessory power, an auto-dimming inside rearview mirror, front and rear reading lights, dual illuminating visor-vanity mirrors, a leather-wrapped steering wheel, leather trim on the center console, front and rear floor mats, a trunk light, a trip computer, a clock, an external temperature display, a low-fuel warning light and a compass.

SIGNATURE SEDAN: Standard equipment included a 4.6-liter SOHC V-8, a four-speed automatic transmission, rear-wheel drive, 16-in. alloy wheel rims, P225/60SR16 all-season tires, a mini spare tire on a steel spare wheel, front independent suspension, front and rear stabilizer bars, front disc/rear drum antilock brakes, traction control, front side mounted airbags, front and rear seat belt pre-tensioners, rear door child safety locks, child seat anchors, an emergency lock release inside the trunk, a center rear three-point seat belt, two front headrests, the SecuriLock™ passive anti-theft system, an engine immobilizer, dusk-sensing headlamps, auto-delay-off headlights, cornering lights, variable intermittent windshield wipers, a rear window defogger, six-passenger seating with an eight-way power split bench front seat with adjustable lumbar support, leather seat upholstery, a rear bench seat with center armrest, easy-entry rear seat access, memorized settings for three drivers, rear seat heating ducts, digital keypad remote power door locks, one touch power windows, heated automatic-dimming electrochromatic power mirrors, a universal remote for garage door and security, an AM/FM cassette stereo, an diversity antenna, speed control, speed-proportional power steering, a tilt-adjustable leather-and-wood steering wheel, audio and speed controls on the steering wheel, height-adjustable pedals, climate control, front and rear cupholders, a remote trunk lid release, front door pockets, front seatback storage, a front 12-volt power outlet, a front console with storage space, retained accessory power, an auto-dimming inside rearview mirror, front and rear reading lights, dual illuminating visor-vanity mirrors, a leather-wrapped steering wheel, leather trim on the center console, front and rear floor mats, a trunk light, a trip computer, a clock, an external temperature display, a low-fuel warning light and a compass.

EXECUTIVE L SEDAN: Standard equipment included a 4.6-liter SOHC V-8, a four-speed automatic transmission, rear-wheel drive, 16-in. alloy wheel rims, P225/70SR16 all-season tires, a mini spare tire on a steel spare wheel, front independent suspension, front and rear stabilizer bars, front disc/rear drum antilock brakes, traction control, front side mounted airbags, front and rear seat belt pre-tensioners, rear door child safety locks, child seat anchors, an emergency lock release inside the trunk, a center rear three-point seat belt, two front headrests, two rear seat headrests, the SecuriLock™ passive anti-theft system, an engine immobilizer, dusk-sensing headlamps, auto-delay-off headlights, cornering lights, variable intermittent windshield wipers, a rear window defogger, six-passenger seating with an eight-way power split bench front seat with adjustable lumbar support, leather seat upholstery, a rear bench seat with center storage armrest, easy-entry rear seat access, memorized settings for three drivers, rear seat heating ducts, rear seat radio volume controls, rear seat climate controls, front and rear door pockets, digital keypad remote power door locks, one touch power windows, heated automatic-dimming electrochromatic power mirrors, a universal remote for garage door and security, an AM/FM cassette stereo, a diversity antenna, speed control, speed-proportional power steering, a tilt-adjustable leather-wrapped steering wheel, audio and speed controls on the steering wheel, height-adjustable pedals, climate control, front and rear cupholders, a remote trunk lid release, front door pockets, front seatback storage, a front 12-volt power outlet, a front console with storage space, retained accessory power, an auto-dimming inside rearview mirror, front and rear reading lights, dual illuminating visor-vanity mirrors, a leather-wrapped steering wheel, leather trim on the center console, front and rear floor mats, a trunk light, a trip computer, a clock, an external temperature display, a low-fuel warning light and a compass.

CARTIER SEDAN: Standard equipment included a 4.6-liter 235-hp (instead of standard 220-hp) SOHC V-8, a four-speed automatic transmission, rear-wheel drive, 16-in. chrome alloy wheel rims, P225/60SR16 all-season tires, a mini spare tire on a steel spare wheel, front independent suspension, front and rear stabilizer bars, front disc/rear drum antilock brakes, traction control, front side mounted airbags, front and rear seat belt pre-tensioners, rear door child safety locks, child seat anchors, an emergency lock release inside the trunk, a center rear three-point seat belt, two front headrests, two rear seat headrests, the SecuriLock™ passive anti-theft system, an engine immobilizer, dusk-sensing headlamps, auto-delay-off headlights, cornering lights, variable intermittent windshield wipers, a rear window defogger, six-passenger seating with a heated eight-way power split armrest bench front seat with adjustable lumbar support, leather seat upholstery, a rear bench seat with center storage armrest, easy-entry rear seat access, memorized settings for three drivers, rear seat heating ducts, rear seat radio volume controls, rear seat climate controls, front and rear door pockets, digital keypad remote power door locks, one touch power windows, heated automatic-dimming electrochromatic power mirrors, a universal remote for garage door and security, an Alpine premium brand 145-watts stereo system, AM/FM cassette stereo, an diversity antenna, speed control, speed-proportional power steering, a tilt-adjustable leather-wrapped steering wheel, audio and speed controls on the steering wheel, height-adjustable pedals, climate control, front and rear cupholders, a remote trunk lid release, front door pockets, front seatback storage, a front 12-volt power outlet, a front console with storage space, retained accessory power, an auto-dimming inside rearview mirror, front and rear reading lights, dual illuminating visor-vanity mirrors, a leather-wrapped steering wheel, leather trim on the center console, front and rear floor mats, a trunk light, a trip computer, a clock, an external temperature display, a low-fuel warning light and a compass.

CARTIER L SEDAN: Standard equipment included a 4.6-liter 235-hp (instead of standard 220-hp) SOHC V-8, a four-speed automatic transmission, rear-wheel drive, 16-in. chrome alloy wheel rims, P225/70SR16 all-season tires, a mini spare tire on a steel spare wheel, front independent suspension, front and rear stabilizer bars, front disc/rear drum antilock brakes, traction control, front side mounted airbags, front and rear seat belt pre-tensioners, rear door child safety locks, child seat anchors, an emergency lock release inside the trunk, a center rear three-point seat belt, two front headrests, two rear seat headrests, the SecuriLock™ passive anti-theft system, an engine immobilizer, dusk-sensing headlamps, auto-delay-off headlights, cornering lights, variable intermittent windshield wipers, a rear window defogger, six-passenger seating with a heated eight-way power split armrest bench front seat with adjustable lumbar support, leather seat upholstery, a heated rear bench seat with folding center storage armrest, easy-entry rear seat access, memorized settings for three drivers, rear seat heating ducts, rear seat radio volume controls, rear seat climate controls, front and rear door pockets, digital keypad remote power door locks, one touch power windows, heated automatic-dimming electrochromatic power mirrors, a universal remote for garage door and security, an Alpine premium brand 145-watts stereo system, AM/FM cassette stereo, an diversity antenna, speed control, speed-proportional power steering, a tilt-adjustable leather-wrapped steering wheel, audio and speed controls on the steering wheel, height-adjustable pedals, climate control, front and rear cupholders, a remote trunk lid release, front door pockets, front seatback storage, a front 12-volt power outlet, a front console with storage space, retained accessory power, an auto-dimming inside rearview mirror, front and rear reading lights, dual illuminating visor-vanity mirrors, a leather-wrapped steering wheel, leather trim on the center console, front and rear floor mats, a trunk light, a trip computer, a clock, an external temperature display, a low-fuel warning light and a compass.

Model No.	Body/Style No.	Body Type & Seating	Factory Price	Shipping Weight	Prod. Total
TOWN CAR EXECUTIVE SERIES (V-8)					
M	81	4d Sedan-5P	40,155	4,047	-
TOWN CAR EXECUTIVE L SERIES (V-8)					
M	84	4d Sedan-5P	43,965	4,156	-
TOWN CAR SIGNATURE SERIES (V-8)					
M	82	4d Sedan-5P	42,325	4,047	-
TOWN CAR CARTIER SERIES (V-8)					
M	83	4d Sedan-5P	44,710	4,121	-
TOWN CAR CARTIER L SERIES (V-8)					
M	85	4d Sedan-5P	49,220	4,156	-

CONTINENTAL — V-8 — Standard equipment included a 4.6-liter 275-hp DOHC V-8, a four-speed automatic transmission, front-wheel drive, 16-in. chrome alloy wheel rims, P225/60HR16 all-season tires, a mini spare tire on a steel spare wheel, four-wheel independent suspension, front and rear stabilizer bars, a self-leveling suspension, front disc/rear drum antilock brakes, traction control, front side mounted airbags, rear door child safety locks, child seat anchors, an emergency lock release inside the trunk, a front center lap belt, a center rear three-point seat belt, two front headrests, a remote anti-theft system, an engine immobilizer, dusk-sensing headlamps, auto-delay-off headlights, cornering lights, variable intermittent windshield wipers, a rear window defogger, six-passenger seating with a six-way power front seat with adjustable lumbar support, leather seat upholstery, a rear bench seat, rear seat heating ducts, digital keypad remote power door locks, one touch power windows, heated power mirrors with curb-view feature, an AM/FM cassette stereo, a four-speaker sound system, a diversity antenna, adaptive speed control, speed-proportional power steering, a tilt-adjustable leather-wrapped steering wheel, speed controls on the steering wheel, front and rear cupholders, a remote trunk lid release, front door pockets, front seatback storage, a front 12-volt power outlet, a front console with storage space, an overhead console with storage, a universal remote for garage and security, retained accessory power, easy-entry rear seat access, air conditioning, a micron air filtration system, an auto-dimming inside rearview mirror, front reading lights, dual illuminating visor-vanity mirrors, wood trim on the center console, front and rear floor mats, memorized driver settings for two, a tachometer, a clock, an external temperature display and a low-fuel warning light.

Model No.	Body/Style No.	Body Type & Seating	Factory Price	Shipping Weight	Prod. Total
CONTINENTAL (V-8)					
M	97	4d Sedan-5P	40,270	3,848	*

LINCOLN LS ENGINES

ENGINE [Standard LS DOHC V-6]: Aluminum block and head. Displacement: 181 cid (3.0 liters). Bore & stroke: 3.5 x 3.13 in. Compression ratio: 10.5:1. Brake horsepower: 210 at 6500 rpm. Torque: 205 lbs.-ft. at 4750 rpm. Sequential multi-port electronic fuel injection.

ENGINE [Optional LS DOHC V-8]: Aluminum block and head. Displacement: 240 cid (3.9 liters). Bore & stroke: 3.39 x 3.35 in. Compression ratio: 10.55:1. Brake horsepower: 252 at 6100 rpm. Torque: 267 lbs.-ft. at 4300 rpm. Sequential multi-port electronic fuel injection.

LINCOLN TOWN CAR ENGINE

ENGINE [Standard SOHC V-8]: Aluminum block and head. Single exhaust. Displacement: 281 cid (4.6 liters). Bore & stroke: 3.55 x 3.54 in. Compression ratio: 9.4:1. Brake horsepower: 220 at 4750 rpm. Torque: 265 lbs.-ft. at 4000 rpm. Sequential multi-port electronic fuel injection.

ENGINE [Optional Cartier Series SOHC V-8]: Aluminum block and head. Dual exhausts. Displacement: 281 cid (4.6 liters). Bore & stroke: 3.55 x 3.54 in. Compression ratio: 9.4:1. Brake horsepower: 235 at 4650 rpm. Torque: 275 lbs.-ft. at 4000 rpm. Sequential multi-port electronic fuel injection.

LINCOLN CONTINENTAL ENGINE

ENGINE [Standard DOHC V-8]: Aluminum block and head. Displacement: 281 cid (4.6 liters). Bore & stroke: 3.55 x 3.54 in. Compression ratio: 9.89:1. Brake horsepower: 275 at 5750 rpm. Torque: 275 lbs.-ft. at 4750 rpm. Sequential multi-port electronic fuel injection.

LINCOLN LS CHASSIS: Wheelbase: 114.5 in. Overall Length: 193.9 in. Height: 56.1 in. Width: 73.2 in. Front tread: 60.5 in. Rear tread: 60.8 in.

LINCOLN TOWN CAR CHASSIS: Wheelbase: (Cartier L) 123.7 in.; (Others) 117.7 in. Overall Length: (Cartier L) 221.3 in.; (others) 215.3 in. Height: (Cartier L) 58.1 in.; (others) 58.1 in. Width: (all) 78.2 in. Front tread: 63.4 in. Rear tread: 65.3 in.

LINCOLN CONTINENTAL CHASSIS: Wheelbase: 109 in. Overall Length: 208.5 in. Height: 56 in. Width: 73.6 in. Front tread: 63.0 in. Rear tread: 61.5 in.

LINCOLN LS TECHNICAL: Transmission: five-speed manual overdrive. Drive Axle: rear. Steering: speed-sensitive variable-assist rack-and-pinion; ratio 18.0:1, 3.0 turns lock-to-lock, 38.06-ft. curb-to-curb turning circle. Front suspension: Independent unequal length control arms with coil springs and tubular stabilizer bar. Rear suspension: Independent unequal length control arms with coil springs and solid stabilizer bar mounted on isolated rear sub-frame. Brakes: Front brakes: Power-assisted disc with ABS. Rear brakes: Power-assisted disc with ABS. Gas tank: 18 gallons.

LINCOLN TOWN CAR TECHNICAL: Transmission: four-speed automatic overdrive. Drive Axle: rear. Steering: speed-sensitive variable-assist rack-and-pinion; ratio 16.4:1, 3.4 turns lock-to-lock, 44.1-ft. curb-to-curb turning circle. Front suspension: Independent unequal length control arms with coil springs ball joints. Rear suspension: Four bar link and Watt's linkage with air springs. Brakes: Front brakes: Power-assisted disc with ABS. Rear brakes: Power-assisted disc with ABS. Gas tank: 19 gallons.

LINCOLN CONTINENTAL TECHNICAL: Transmission: four-speed automatic overdrive. Drive Axle: front. Steering: speed-sensitive variable-assist selectable effort; ratio 16.95:1, 3.4 turns lock-to-lock, 41.1-ft. turning circle. Front suspension: Independent MacPherson struts with aluminum lower control arms, double ball joint stabilizer links and coil springs. Rear suspension: independent unequal-length control arms, double ball joints and rear leveling air springs. Brakes: Front brakes: Power-assisted disc with ABS. Rear brakes: Power-assisted disc with ABS. Gas tank: 20 gallons.

LINCOLN LS OPTIONS: 13B power moonroof ($1,005). 153 front license plate bracket (no cost). 422 California emissions (no cost). 556 AdvanceTrac stability-control system ($735). 58X Six-disc in-dash CD player ($605). 60L V-6 Convenience package ($960). 60N Smart package ($1,385 net price after $605 manufacturer discount). 632 heated front seats ($400). 64C 17-in. five-spoke chrome aluminum wheel rims ($845). 65L Premium V-6 package ($2,690 net price after $605 manufacturer's discount). 65L Premium V-8 package ($3,090 net price after $605 manufacturer's discount). 916 Alpine audio system ($575). 919 glove box-mounted six-disc CD changer ($605).

LINCOLN TOWN CAR OPTIONS: 153 front license plate bracket (no cost). 422 California emissions (no cost). 467 heated front seats in Signature series sedan ($400). 503 conventional spare tire on Executive series sedan ($114). 54E limited-edition package on Signature series sedan ($995) 60P Cartier/Signature series Premium package ($1,525 net price after $605 manufacturer's discount). 663 Signature Touring Sedan package ($710).

LINCOLN CONTINENTAL OPTIONS: 13B power moonroof ($1,525). 153 front license plate bracket (no cost). 422 California emissions (no cost). 467 heated front seats ($400). 516 cellular phone ($800). 54A Luxury Appearance package ($1,105). 54E limited-edition package ($1,195) 6 individual bucket seats with leather seating surfaces (no cost). 64F 16-in. highly polished aluminum wheel rims ($360). 64G chrome six-spoke wheels ($855). 667 Driver Select system ($605). 675 Personal Security package ($640). 916 Alpine audio system ($575). 919 console-mounted six-disc CD changer ($605). 919 mini console-mounted six-disc CD changer ($605).

HISTORICAL FOOTNOTES: On Aug. 27, 2001 Lincoln opened 'Lincoln Innovations,' a dramatically designed pavilion for U.S. Open tennis fans. The company was an Official Sponsor of the 2001 U.S. Open. On Aug. 18, 2001 — following a lengthy and meticulous restoration — a famous Lincoln that served the first president of Israel — Dr. Chaim Weizmann — was shown at the Pebble Beach Concours d'Elegance, in Monterey, Calif., at a Lincoln-sponsored reception of the Automotive Fine Arts Society. On Nov. 9, 2001, Lincoln announced a series of executive changes from its headquarters in Irvine, Calif. Lincoln Mercury Div. president Mark Hutchins said that the key appointments would take effect on December 1. Ann Kalass was appointed marketing communications manager. Ms. Kalass' most recent assignment was Lincoln Mercury Regional Manager for the Orlando (Fla.) Region. Pat Petroske was appointed regional manager for the Orlando Region. Previously, Mr. Petroske held the post of Memphis (Tenn.) Regional Manager. Jennifer Moneagle was appointed Memphis Regional Manager. Ms. Moneagle was previously group brand manager for Mercury. Elena Ford was appointed group brand manager for Mercury. Ms. Ford recently served as director of E-Solutions in Ford Motor Co.'s marketing, sales and service organization. "These changes further strengthen our Lincoln and Mercury leadership teams, both at headquarters and the region," said Hutchins. "In their new roles, this team will help the enterprise focus on its core goal of developing both the Lincoln and Mercury brands and enhancing our relationship with our dealer partners."

2002 LINCOLN

LINCOLN LS — V-8 — Although the 2002 Lincoln LS looked much like the 2001 model, there were a handful of changes in standard equipment and available options. The standard V-6 engine gained 10 hp and 10 ft.-lbs. of torque. Sport arrays (Lincoln's term for "bundled" options) included a no-charge Audiophile system. Premium arrays included a power moonroof at no cost. An All-Season package included heated front seats with the purchase of the AdvanceTrac option, but you could not get these options separately. An in-dash six-CD changer was standard on all Lincoln LS models, along with seven-spoke 16-in. brushed satin aluminum wheels (polished alloy wheels optional). A Vehicle Communication system that required a Sprint PCS airtime plan was optional on all models. It included a hands-free Motorola Timeport phone with Safety and Security Services button, automatic airbag assistance, route guidance and information services. A full Alpine Audiophile sound system was reinstated as a standard Sport package feature. All-Season/AdvanceTrac and heated front seats were available at extra cost on all options arrays. Aspen Green, Silver Birch, and Charcoal Grey clearcoat metallic colors were new and Medium Charcoal Green, Silver Frost and Midnight Grey were deleted.

V-6 SEDAN (MANUAL): Body color bumper treatment (monochromatic appearance with Sport package only), body color door handles, front fascia fog lamps, chrome grille with molded black vertical ribs, complex reflector headlights with clear lenses, dual heated power mirrors, complex reflector taillights, 17-in. super silver aluminum wheels (five-spoke design with Sport package only), new generation dual airbags, front seat side airbags, full-length door armrests, rear center fold-down armrest with two cupholders, 18-oz. "Merino" cut-pile floor carpeting, lower door carpeting, rear window ledge carpeting, electronic alert chimes, electronic digital clock integrated in radio, coat hooks with integrated grab handles, a center front armrest with storage bin, a center front console with power point at rear end, dual front cupholders, wood appearance appliqués on door trim and instrument panel and front ashtray door, carpeted front and rear floor mats, an illuminated and locking glove box, four grab handles with rear seat coat hooks, a cloth covered headlining, adjustable headrests, an analog gauge cluster with tachometer and warning lights, door courtesy lights and integral reflectors, a rear dome light and switch, an instrument panel courtesy lamp, a luggage compartment lamp. Two fixed front map lights, front door map pockets, seatback map pockets, a day/night rearview mirror, visor vanity mirrors, a premium AM/FM radio with a six disc in-dash CD player, safety belts, front and rear scuff plates, leather seating surfaces, individual front bucket seats with power lumbar support, a 60/40 split-folding rear seat with child seat anchors, a leather-wrapped shift knob, a leather-wrapped four-spoke steering wheel, CFC-free automatic air conditioning, a passenger compartment air filtration system, perimeter alarm system with LED, 110-amp. alternator, All-Speed Traction Control, a concealed antenna, a center stack illuminated ashtray with lighter, steering wheel radio controls, a 3.07:1 ratio rear axle, a trunk-mounted 72-amp./hr battery, a battery saver, four-wheel ABS disc brakes, cruise control with fingertip feature on steering wheel, a remote deck lid release, a rear window defroster, delayed accessory power shut off, front and rear door reflectors, function drip rails integrated in doors, electronic engine control, sequential multiport-fuel-injection, an electronic voltage regulator, a 3.0-liter 24-valve DOHC V-6 engine, an engine temperature gauge, a dual exhaust system, a Fail Safe cooling system, a driver's footrest, a fuel filler door release with manual override inside trunk, an 18-gallon fuel tank (premium fuel required), a gas cap tether, Solar-Tinted glass, quad headlights with automatic on/off with delay, a heated wiper park, a dual note horn, a remote keyless entry system, valet keys, lighted switches, a high-mounted rear brake light, an engine oil low alert light, single key locks with Smart Lock and childproof driver's door lock cylinder, dual illuminated vanity mirrors in visor, dual heated power mirrors, three power points, rear seat climate ducts, the SecuriLock™ security system, gas charged twin tube shocks, Smart Lock anti-lockout system, variable-assist power rack-and-pinion, tilt/telescope steering wheel with speed/audio/phone controls, four-wheel independent suspension with rear stabilizer bars, P235/50VR black sidewall all-season high-performance tires, 17-in. aluminum mini spare wheels, five-speed manual transmission, glow-in-the-dark manual trunk release inside trunk, one touch power windows, global remote windows, variable intermittent windshield wipers (with heated park).

V-6 SEDAN (AUTOMATIC): Color-keyed front bumper treatment with chrome inserts, body color door handles, front fascia fog lamps, chrome grille with molded black vertical ribs, complex reflector headlights with clear lenses, dual heated power mirrors, complex reflector taillights, five-spoke 16-in. brushed aluminum five-spoke wheels, new generation dual airbags, front seat side airbags, full-length door armrests, rear center fold-down armrest with two cupholders, 18-oz. "Merino" cut-pile floor carpeting, lower door carpeting, rear window ledge

carpeting, electronic alert chimes, electronic digital clock integrated in radio, coat hooks with integrated grab handles, a center front armrest with storage bin, a center front console with power point at rear end, dual front cupholders, wood appearance appliqués on door trim and instrument panel and front ashtray door, carpeted front and rear floor mats, an illuminated and locking glove box, four grab handles with rear seat coat hooks, a cloth covered headlining, adjustable headrests, an analog gauge cluster with tachometer and warning lights, door courtesy lights and integral reflectors, a rear dome light and switch, an instrument panel courtesy lamp, a luggage compartment lamp. Two fixed front map lights, front door map pockets, seatback map pockets, a day/night rearview mirror, visor vanity mirrors, a premium AM/FM radio with a six disc in-dash CD player, safety belts, front and rear scuff plates, leather seating surfaces, individual front bucket seats with power lumbar support, a 60/40 split-folding rear seat with child seat anchor, a wood shift knob, a wood and leather-wrapped four-spoke steering wheel (without Sport package), CFC-free automatic air conditioning, a passenger compartment air filtration system, perimeter alarm system with LED, 110-amp. alternator, All-Speed Traction Control, a concealed antenna, a center stack illuminated ashtray with lighter, steering wheel radio controls, a 3.58:1 ratio rear axle, a trunk-mounted 72-amp./hr battery, a battery saver, a brake-shift interlock system, four-wheel ABS disc brakes, cruise control with fingertip feature on steering wheel, a remote deck lid release, a rear window defroster, delayed accessory power shut off, front and rear door reflectors, function drip rails integrated in doors, electronic engine control, sequential multiport-fuel-injection, an electronic voltage regulator, a 3.0-liter 24-valve DOHC V-6 engine, an engine temperature gauge, a dual exhaust system, a Fail safe cooling system, a driver's footrest, a fuel filler door release with manual override inside trunk, an 18-gallon fuel tank (premium fuel required), a gas cap tether, Solar-Tinted glass, quad headlights with automatic on/off with delay, a heated wiper park, a dual note horn, a remote keyless entry system, valet keys, lighted switches, a high-mounted rear brake light, an engine oil low alert light, single key locks with Smart Lock and childproof driver's door lock cylinder, dual illuminated vanity mirrors in visor, dual heated power mirrors, three power points, rear seat climate ducts, the SecuriLock™ security system, dash illuminated shift indicator, gas charged twin tube shocks, Smart Lock anti-lockout system, variable-assist power rack-and-pinion, tilt/telescope steering wheel with speed/audio/phone controls, four-wheel independent suspension with rear stabilizer bars, P215/60HR16 black sidewall all-season high-performance tires, 16-in. steel mini spare wheels, five-speed automatic overdrive transmission, glow-in-the-dark manual trunk release inside trunk, one touch power windows, global remote windows, variable intermittent windshield wipers (with heated park).

V-8 SEDAN: Color-keyed front bumper treatment with chrome inserts, body color door handles, front fascia fog lamps, chrome grille with molded black vertical ribs, complex reflector headlights with clear lenses, dual heated power mirrors, complex reflector taillights, five-spoke 16-in. brushed aluminum five-spoke wheels, new generation dual airbags, front seat side airbags, full-length door armrests, rear center fold-down armrest with two cupholders, 18-oz. "Merino" cut-pile floor carpeting, lower door carpeting, rear window ledge carpeting, electronic alert chimes, electronic digital clock integrated in radio, coat hooks with integrated grab handles, a center front armrest with storage bin, a center front console with power point at rear end, dual front cupholders, wood appearance appliqués on door trim and instrument panel and front ashtray door, electronic message center, carpeted front and rear floor mats, an illuminated and locking glove box, four grab handles with rear seat coat hooks, a cloth covered headlining, adjustable headrests, an analog gauge cluster with tachometer and warning lights, door courtesy lights and integral reflectors, a rear dome light and switch, an instrument panel courtesy lamp, a luggage compartment lamp. Two fixed front map lights, front door map pockets, seatback map pockets, electrochromatic interior rearview mirror with compass, visor vanity mirrors, a premium AM/FM radio with a six disc in-dash CD player, safety belts, front and rear scuff plates, leather seating surfaces, individual front bucket seats with power lumbar support (eight-way power driver's seat and six-way power passenger seat with two-way head restraints and manual lumbar support), a 60/40 split-folding rear seat with child seat anchors, a wood shift knob, a wood and leather-wrapped four-spoke steering wheel (without Sport package), CFC-free automatic air conditioning, a passenger compartment air filtration system, perimeter alarm system with LED, 110-amp. alternator, All-Speed Traction Control, a concealed antenna, a center stack illuminated ashtray with lighter, steering wheel radio controls, a 3.31:1 ratio rear axle, a trunk-mounted 72-amp./hr battery, a battery saver, a brake-shift interlock system, four-wheel ABS disc brakes, cruise control with fingertip feature on steering wheel, a remote deck lid release, a rear window defroster, delayed accessory power shut off, front and rear door reflectors, function drip rails integrated in doors, electronic engine control, sequential multiport-fuel-injection, an electronic voltage regulator, a 3.9-liter 24-valve DOHC V-8 engine, an engine temperature gauge, a dual exhaust system, a Fail safe cooling system, a driver's footrest, a fuel filler door release with manual override inside trunk, an 18-gallon fuel tank (premium fuel required), a gas cap tether, Solar-Tinted glass, quad headlights with automatic on/off with delay, a heated wiper park, a dual note horn, a remote keyless entry system, valet keys, lighted switches, a high-mounted rear brake light, an engine oil low alert light, single key locks with Smart Lock and childproof driver's door lock cylinder, dual illuminated vanity mirrors in visor, dual heated power mirrors, three power points, rear seat climate ducts, the SecuriLock™ security system, dash illuminated shift indicator, gas charged twin tube shocks, Smart Lock anti-lockout system, variable-assist power rack-and-pinion, power tilt/telescope steering wheel with memory and speed/audio/phone controls, four-wheel independent suspension with rear stabilizer bars, P215/60HR16 black sidewall all-season high-performance tires, 16-in. steel mini spare wheels, five-speed automatic overdrive transmission, glow-in-the-dark manual trunk release inside trunk, one touch power windows, global remote windows, moisture-sensitive variable intermittent windshield wipers (with heated park).

I.D. DATA: Lincoln's 17-symbol Vehicle Identification Number (VIN) was stamped on a metal tab fastened to the instrument panel, visible through the windshield. The first three symbols indicate manufacturer, make and vehicle type. The fourth symbol denotes restraint system. Next comes a letter (usually 'M'), followed by two digits that indicate Model Number, as shown in left column of tables below. (Example: '81' Town Car Executive four-door sedan). Symbol eight indicates engine type. Next is a check digit. Symbol ten indicates model year (2=2002). Symbol eleven denotes assembly plant. The final six digits make up the sequence number, starting with 000001.

Model No.	Body/Style No.	Body Type & Seating	Factory Price	Shipping Weight	Prod. Total
LINCOLN LS (V-6 MANUAL)					
M	86	4d Sedan-5P	33,655	3,593	—
LINCOLN LS (V-6 AUTOMATIC)					
M	86	4d Sedan-5P	34,840	3,598	—
LINCOLN LS (V-8)					
M	87	4d Sedan-5P	37,830	3,692	—

TOWN CAR — V-8 — With the exception of a new Aspen Green Clearcoat Metallic exterior color (replacing Medium Charcoal Green), the major changes for the 2002 Lincoln Town car were all found on the options list. They included a newly-available vehicle communication system that required a Sprint PCS airtime plan and included a hands-free Motorola Timeport phone with Safety and Security Services button, automatic airbag assistance, route guidance and information services. There were five models (Executive, Signature, Cartier, Executive L and Cartier L) plus the usual wide "array" of optional equipment packages.

EXECUTIVE SEDAN: Standard equipment included bright front and rear bumper inserts, suitcase style chrome pull-away door handles, a bright grille, Lincoln nomenclature on the trunk lid, aero compound reflector headlights, dual remote-control heated power electrochromic mirrors (right-hand convex), bright windshield and rear window moldings, color-keyed body cladding with chrome inserts, complex reflector taillights, 16-in. gear tooth aluminum wheels, dual airbags, full-length door armrests with storage, front center fold-down armrest with storage, rear center fold-down armrest with cupholders, 18-oz. passenger compartment carpeting, rear window ledge carpeting, grey luggage compartment carpeting, grey carpeted deck lid liner, grey carpeted spare tire cover, lower door carpeting, electronic alert chimes, electronic digital clock integrated in radio, coat hooks, front seat ashtray mounted cupholders, an illuminated and locking glove box, four roof rail handles integrated with coat hooks, a cloth covered headlining, an analog instrument cluster with electronic message center, door courtesy lights and integral reflectors, a rear compartment reading lamp, a dual-beam dome and light, an instrument panel courtesy lamp, a luggage compartment lamp, a glove box light, a front ashtray light, front seatback map pockets, electrochromic rearview mirror with compass, dual illuminated visor vanity mirrors, an AM/FM radio with cassette, deluxe color-keyed safety belts, full length door scuff plates, leather seat trim, an individual Comfort Lounge 40/20/40 front seat (eight-way driver's seat) with dual power recliners and lumbar support, two-way front seat head restraints, a leather-wrapped two-spoke tilt steering wheel, door pull straps, adjustable pedals, CFC-free automatic air conditioning, a 120-amp. alternator, All-Speed Traction Control, a concealed dual diversity antenna, a 3.08:1 ratio rear axle, a 72-amp./hr battery, a brake/shift interlock system, four-wheel ABS disc brakes, a compass (located in message center on instrument panel), a coolant recovery system, a remote deck lid release, a rear window defroster, delayed accessory power shut off, functional roof drip rails, an EEC-V malfunction alert light, an EEC-V (electronic engine control) system, sequential multiport-fuel-injection, an electronic voltage regulator, a 4.6-liter SOHC V-8 engine with coil-per-plug ignition, an engine compartment light, an engine temperature gauge, a single exhaust system, a remote fuel filler door release on door trim panel, a 19-gallon fuel tank, a gas cap tether, Solar-Tinted glass, headlights with automatic on/off delay, a dual note horn, a remote keyless entry system, a keyless entry pad, cornering lights, lighted switches, a high-mounted rear brake light, an engine oil low alert light, single key locks

with childproof feature, a valet key for door and ignition, an automatic parking brake release. A 12-volt power point under instrument panel, rear seat air conditioning and heating ducts, a power seat recliner with easy entry and exit feature, the SecuriLock™ security system, nitrogen gas pressurized shock absorbers, the Smart Lock anti-lockout system, soft textured touch zones, fingertip speed control, a tilt steering wheel, short/long arm coil spring front suspension, Watt's linkage rear suspension, P225/60SR16 black sidewall all-season tires, a mini spare tire, electronic automatic overdrive transmission, one touch power windows and interval windshield wipers with steering column control and fluidic washers.

EXCUTIVE L SEDAN: Same as above with six-inch door extension, six-inch wheelbase extension, rear door storage pockets, cigar-sized ashtray in rear door, rear vanity packs with illuminated mirrors, four-way rear seat head restraints, orientation lighting, a rear seat with folding amenities armrest and storage bin and redundant audio/climate controls, a 78-amp/hr battery, a dual exhaust system, and P225/70SR16 tires.

SIGNATURE SEDAN: Standard equipment included bright front and rear bumper inserts, suitcase style chrome pull-away door handles, a bright grille, Lincoln nomenclature on the trunk lid, aero compound reflector headlights, dual remote-control heated power electrochromic mirrors (right-hand convex) with memory, bright windshield and rear window moldings, color-keyed body cladding with chrome inserts, complex reflector taillights, 16-in. snowflake aluminum wheels, dual airbags, full-length door armrests with storage, front center fold-down armrest with storage, rear center fold-down armrest with cupholders, 18-oz. passenger compartment carpeting, rear window ledge carpeting, grey luggage compartment carpeting, grey carpeted deck lid liner, grey carpeted spare tire cover, lower door carpeting, electronic alert chimes, electronic digital clock integrated in radio, coat hooks, front seat ashtray mounted cupholders, an illuminated and locking glove box, four roof rail handles integrated with coat hooks, a cloth covered headlining, an analog instrument cluster with electronic message center, door courtesy lights and integral reflectors, a rear compartment reading lamp, a dual-beam dome and light, an instrument panel courtesy lamp, a luggage compartment lamp, a glove box light, a front ashtray light, front seatback map pockets, electrochromic rearview mirror with compass, dual illuminated visor vanity mirrors, a Lincoln Signature audio system, deluxe color-keyed safety belts, full length door scuff plates, leather seat trim, an individual Comfort Lounge 40/20/40 front memory seat (eight-way driver's seat) with dual power recliners and lumbar support, two-way front seat head restraints, driver easy entry and exit, a wood tilt steering wheel with audio and climate controls, door pull straps, adjustable pedals with memory, CFC-free automatic air conditioning, a 120-amp. alternator, All-Speed Traction Control, a concealed dual diversity antenna, a 3.08:1 ratio rear axle, a 72-amp./hr battery, a brake/shift interlock system, four-wheel ABS disc brakes, a compass (located in message center on instrument panel), a coolant recovery system, a remote deck lid release, a rear window defroster, delayed accessory power shut off, functional roof drip rails, an EEC-V malfunction alert light, an EEC-V (electronic engine control) system, sequential multiport-fuel-injection, an electronic voltage regulator, a 4.6-liter SOHC V-8 engine with coil-per-plug ignition, an engine compartment light, an engine temperature gauge, a single exhaust system, a remote fuel filler door release on door trim panel, a 19-gallon fuel tank, a gas cap tether, Solar-Tinted glass, headlights with automatic on/off delay, a dual note horn, a remote keyless entry system, a keyless entry pad, cornering lights, lighted switches, a high-mounted rear brake light, an engine oil low alert light, single key locks with childproof feature, a valet key for door and ignition, an automatic parking brake release. A 12-volt power point under instrument panel, rear seat air conditioning and heating ducts, a power seat recliner with easy entry and exit feature, the SecuriLock™ security system, nitrogen gas pressurized shock absorbers, the Smart Lock anti-lockout system, soft textured touch zones, fingertip speed control, a tilt steering wheel, short/long arm coil spring front suspension, Watt's linkage rear suspension, P225/60SR16 black sidewall all-season tires, a mini spare tire, electronic automatic overdrive transmission, universal garage door opener, one touch power windows and interval windshield wipers with steering column control and fluidic washers.

CARTIER SEDAN: Standard equipment included bright front and rear bumper inserts, suitcase style chrome pull-away door handles, a gold trim package, a bright grille, Lincoln nomenclature on the trunk lid, aero compound reflector headlights, dual remote-control heated power electrochromic mirrors (right-hand convex) with memory, bright windshield and rear window moldings, color-keyed body cladding with chrome inserts, complex reflector taillights, 16-in. Cartier chrome wheels, dual airbags, full-length door armrests with storage, front center fold-down armrest with storage, rear center fold-down armrest with cupholders, 18-oz. passenger compartment carpeting, rear window ledge carpeting, grey luggage compartment carpeting, grey carpeted deck lid liner, grey carpeted spare tire cover, lower door carpeting, electronic alert chimes, a luxury analog clock, coat hooks, front seat ashtray-mounted cupholders, an illuminated and locking glove box, four roof rail handles integrated with coat hooks, a cloth covered headlining, an analog instrument cluster with electronic message center, door courtesy lights and integral reflectors, a rear compartment reading lamp, a dual-beam dome and light, an instrument panel courtesy lamp, a luggage compartment lamp, a glove box light, a front ashtray light, front seatback map pockets, electrochromic rearview mirror with compass, dual illuminated visor vanity mirrors, an Alpine Audiophile sound system, deluxe color-keyed safety belts, full length door scuff plates, seat trim with premium leather seating surfaces, an individual heated Comfort Lounge 40/20/40 front memory seat (eight-way driver's seat) with dual power recliners and lumbar support, two-way front seat head restraints, driver easy entry and exit, a wood tilt steering wheel with audio and climate controls, door pull straps, adjustable pedals with memory, CFC-free automatic air conditioning, a 120-amp. alternator, All-Speed Traction Control, a concealed dual diversity antenna, a 3.08:1 ratio rear axle, a 72-amp./hr battery, a brake/shift interlock system, four-wheel ABS disc brakes, a compass (located in message center on instrument panel), a coolant recovery system, a remote deck lid release, a rear window defroster, delayed accessory power shut off, functional roof drip rails, an EEC-V malfunction alert light, an EEC-V (electronic engine control) system, sequential multiport-fuel-injection, an electronic voltage regulator, a 4.6-liter SOHC V-8 engine with coil-per-plug ignition, an engine compartment light, an engine temperature gauge, a dual exhaust system, a remote fuel filler door release on door trim panel, a 19-gallon fuel tank, a gas cap tether, Solar-Tinted glass, headlights with automatic on/off delay, a dual note horn, a remote keyless entry system, a keyless entry pad, cornering lights, lighted switches, a high-mounted rear brake light, an engine oil low alert light, single key locks with childproof feature, a valet key for door and ignition, an automatic parking brake release. A 12-volt power point under instrument panel, rear seat air conditioning and heating ducts, a power seat recliner with easy entry and exit feature, the SecuriLock™ security system, nitrogen gas pressurized shock absorbers, the Smart Lock anti-lockout system, soft textured touch zones, fingertip speed control, a tilt steering wheel, short/long arm coil spring front suspension, Watt's linkage rear suspension, P225/60SR16 black sidewall all-season tires, a mini spare tire, electronic automatic overdrive transmission, universal garage door opener, one touch power windows and interval windshield wipers with steering column control and fluidic washers.

CARTIER L SEDAN: Same as above with six-inch door extension, six-inch wheelbase extension, rear door storage pockets, cigar-sized ashtray in rear door, rear vanity packs with illuminated mirrors, four-way rear seat head restraints, orientation lighting, a heated rear seat with folding amenities armrest and storage bin and redundant audio/climate controls, a 78-amp/hr battery, a dual exhaust system, and P225/70SR16 tires.

Model No.	Body/ Style No.	Body Type & Seating	Factory Price	Shipping Weight	Prod. Total
TOWN CAR EXECUTIVE SERIES (V-8)					
M	81	4d Sedan-5P	40,470	4,047	—
TOWN CAR EXECUTIVE L SERIES (V-8)					
M	84	4d Sedan-5P	46,605	4,156	—
TOWN CAR SIGNATURE SERIES (V-8)					
M	82	4d Sedan-5P	42,910	4,047	—
TOWN CAR CARTIER SERIES (V-8)					
M	83	4d Sedan-5P	45,295	4,121	—
TOWN CAR CARTIER L SERIES (V-8)					
M	85	4d Sedan-5P	49,805	4,156	—

CONTINENTAL — V-8 — With the exception of a new Aspen Green Clearcoat Metallic exterior color (replacing Medium Charcoal Green), the major changes for the 2002 Lincoln Continental were all found on the options list. They included a newly-available vehicle communication system that required a Sprint PCS airtime plan and included a hands-free Motorola Timeport phone with Safety and Security Services button, automatic airbag assistance, route guidance and information services. A new bundled option was the Continental Select package, available at no extra charge. It included a power moonroof and an Alpine audio system with a six-disc CD changer. Standard equipment included a radio antenna concealed in the backlight, 5-mph front and rear bumpers, limousine front and rear doors with flush glass, dual exhausts with bright exposed tips, Solar-Tinted glass, unique high-tech complex reflector headlights with wraparound design and cornering lamps. A flexible polycarbonate grille, a keyless entry keypad (to identify the driver), body colored sail mounted heated outside rearview mirrors that tilted down with the car in reverse, body color body side moldings, front and rear fascia moldings with bright chrome inserts, triple door seals, complex reflector taillights, 16-in. 10-spoke brushed aluminum wheels, air extractors behind rear bumper, 18-oz. floor carpet with driver's footrest, stand alone analog clock, dual front/rear cupholders, front and rear floor mats with driver side retention system, right front and dual rear retractable grab handles, illuminated door and window and speed control switches, interior theatre dimming, map lights integrated into overhead console (in rearview mirror if car has moonroof), a fully lined luggage compartment,

automatic dimming inside day/night rearview mirror with compass, six-passenger seating with leather seating surfaces, six-way power front seats, two-way front seat lumbar supports (power on driver's side, automatic driver's seat movement for easy entry and exits, full-length integral door armrest, fold-down rear seat armrest, embroidered Lincoln star, two-way adjustable front seat head restraints, a leather-wrapped steering wheel, a center front seat storage armrest, a large glove box with lock, front door map pockets, cloth covered sun visors with lighted mirrors, CFC-free automatic climate control system with Sunload sensor, 3-microns air filtration system, 125-amp. large-frame alternator with integral rectifier, anti-theft system (with flashing LED when activated), SecuriLock™ system with engine immobilizer, 78-amp/hr battery, battery saver (turns off lights to save battery), four-wheel ABS disc brakes, automatic parking brake release, heated rear window defroster, delayed accessory power, Service Bay Diagnostics System (SBDS), a 3.56:1 final drive ratio, a 4.6-liter DOHC V-8 with EEC, a structural front engine cover for sound control, extendable coat hooks, a 20-gallon fuel tank, an automatic fuel door release on driver's door, front windshield defroster and front and rear seat heat ducts and vents, a center horn-blow pad, a virtual image instrument cluster with analog gauges and dot metrix message center (includes tachometer, temperature indicator, fuel gauge and speedometer), warning indicators, bird's-eye maple real wood trim, ergonomic key fobs for two drivers, a single-key entry system, a valet key, Autolamp lighting. Keyless entry with automatic locks, a locking trunk release on driver's door, a memory seat and memory mirrors, a message center for pre-selects, power points, a high-level audio system with AM/FM stereo cassette and electronically tuned radio, dual front and rear door speakers, dual airbags and safety belt restraints, door bolsters, childproof power door locks, roadside assistance service, speed control, variable-assist power tilt steering, a tilt steering wheel, rear air suspension with automatic load leveling, independent short/long arm rear suspension, All-Speed Traction Control, an AX4N automatic transaxle with non-synchronous shift, a universal remote garage door opener, one touch power windows and interval windshield wipers.

Model No.	Body/ Style No.	Body Type & Seating	Factory Price	Shipping Weight	Prod. Total
CONTINENTAL (V-8)					
M	97	4d Sedan-5P	38,755	3,848	—

LINCOLN LS ENGINES

ENGINE: [STANDARD LS] DOHC V-6. Aluminum block and head. Displacement: 181 cid (3.0 liters). Bore & stroke: 3.5 x 3.13 in. Compression ratio: 10.5:1. Brake horsepower: 220 at 6400 rpm. Torque: 215 lbs.-ft. at 4800 rpm. Sequential multiport electronic fuel injection.

ENGINE: [OPTIONAL LS] DOHC V-8. Aluminum block and head. Displacement: 240 cid (3.9 liters). Bore & stroke: 3.39 x 3.35 in. Compression ratio: 10.55:1. Brake horsepower: 252 at 6100 rpm. Torque: 261 lbs.-ft. at 4300 rpm. Sequential multiport electronic fuel injection.

LINCOLN TOWN CAR ENGINE

ENGINE: [STANDARD] SOHC V-8. Aluminum block and head. Single exhaust. Displacement: 281 cid (4.6 liters). Bore & stroke: 3.55 x 3.54 in. Compression ratio: 9.4:1. Brake horsepower: 220 at 4750 rpm. Torque: 265 lbs.-ft. at 4000 rpm. Sequential multiport electronic fuel injection.

ENGINE: [OPTIONAL CARTIER SERIES] SOHC V-8. Aluminum block and head. Dual exhausts. Displacement: 281 cid (4.6 liters). Bore & stroke: 3.55 x 3.54 in. Compression ratio: 9.4:1. Brake horsepower: 235 at 4650 rpm. Torque: 275 lbs.-ft. at 4000 rpm. Sequential multiport electronic fuel injection.

LINCOLN CONTINENTAL ENGINE

ENGINE: [STANDARD] DOHC V-8. Aluminum block and head. Displacement: 281 cid (4.6 liters). Bore & stroke: 3.55 x 3.54 in. Compression ratio: 9.89:1. Brake horsepower: 275 at 5750 rpm. Torque: 275 lbs.-ft. at 4750 rpm. Sequential multiport electronic fuel injection.

LINCOLN LS CHASSIS: Wheelbase: 114.5 in. Overall Length: 193.9 in. Height: 56.1 in. Width: 73.2 in. Front tread: 60.5 in. Rear tread: 60.8 in.

LINCOLN TOWN CAR CHASSIS: Wheelbase: (Cartier L) 123.7 in.; (Others) 117.7 in. Overall Length: (Cartier L) 221.3 in.; (others) 215.3 in. Height: (Cartier L) 58.1 in.; (others) 58.1 in. Width: (all) 78.2 in. Front tread: 63.4 in. Rear tread: 65.3 in.

LINCOLN CONTINENTAL CHASSIS: Wheelbase: 109 in. Overall Length: 208.5 in. Height: 56 in. Width: 73.6 in. Front tread: 63.0 in. Rear tread: 61.5 in.

LINCOLN LS TECHNICAL: Transmission: five-speed manual overdrive. Drive Axle: rear. Steering: speed-sensitive variable-assist rack-and-pinion; ratio 18.0:1, 3.0 turns lock-to-lock, 38.06-ft. curb-to-curb turning circle. Front suspension: Independent unequal length control arms with coil springs and tubular stabilizer bar. Rear suspension: Independent unequal length control arms with coil springs and solid stabilizer bar mounted on isolated rear sub-frame. Brakes: Front brakes: Power-assisted disc with ABS. Rear brakes: Power-assisted disc with ABS. Gas tank: 18 gallons.

LINCOLN TOWN CAR TECHNICAL: Transmission: four-speed automatic overdrive. Drive Axle: rear. Steering: speed-sensitive variable-assist rack-and-pinion; ratio 16.4:1, 3.4 turns lock-to-lock, 44.1-ft. curb-to-curb turning circle. Front suspension: Independent unequal length control arms with coil springs ball joints. Rear suspension: Four bar link and Watt's linkage with air springs. Brakes: Front brakes: Power-assisted disc with ABS. Rear brakes: Power-assisted disc with ABS. Gas tank: 19 gallons.

LINCOLN CONTINENTAL TECHNICAL: Transmission: four-speed automatic overdrive. Drive Axle: front. Steering: speed-sensitive variable-assist selectable effort; ratio 16.95:1, 3.4 turns lock-to-lock, 41.1-ft. turning circle. Front suspension: Independent MacPherson struts with aluminum lower control arms, double ball joint stabilizer links and coil springs. Rear suspension: independent unequal-length control arms, double ball joints and rear leveling air springs. Brakes: Front brakes: Power-assisted disc with ABS. Rear brakes: Power-assisted disc with ABS. Gas tank: 20 gallons.

LINCOLN LS OPTIONS: [3.0-LITER LS SEDAN] HC Ivory Parchment Clearcoat Metallic Tricoat paint ($375). WF White Pearl Clearcoat Metallic Tricoat paint ($375). 60B All-Season package ($735). 422 California emissions (no cost). 423 California emissions not required (no cost). 93N non-California emissions (no cost). 51C Vehicle Communications System ($1,295). [3.9-LITER LS SEDAN] HC Ivory Parchment Clearcoat Metallic Tricoat paint ($375). WF White Pearl Clearcoat Metallic Tricoat paint ($375). 642 16-in. high-polished seven-spoke aluminum wheels ($405). 60B All-Season package ($735). 916 Alpine Audiophile system ($575). 919 Alpine Audiophile system with cassette ($575). 422 California emissions (no cost). 423 California emissions not required (no cost). 93N non-California emissions (no cost). 51C Vehicle Communications System ($1,295). [3.0-LITER LS CONVENIENCE SEDAN] HC Ivory Parchment Clearcoat Metallic Tricoat paint ($375). WF White Pearl Clearcoat Metallic Tricoat paint ($375). 642 16-in. high-polished seven-spoke aluminum wheels ($405). 60B All-Season package ($735). 916 Alpine Audiophile system ($575). 919 Alpine Audiophile system with cassette ($575). 422 California emissions (no cost). 423 California emissions not required (no cost). 93N non-California emissions (no cost). 13B power moonroof ($1,005). 51C Vehicle Communications System ($1,295). [3.0-LITER LS PREMIUM SEDAN] HC Ivory Parchment Clearcoat Metallic Tricoat paint ($375). WF White Pearl Clearcoat Metallic Tricoat paint ($375). 60B All-Season package ($735). 422 California emissions (no cost). 423 California emissions not required (no cost). 93N non-California emissions (no cost). 13B power moonroof ($1,005). 51C Vehicle Communications System ($1,295). [3.9-LITER LS PREMIUM SEDAN] HC Ivory Parchment Clearcoat Metallic Tricoat paint ($375). WF White Pearl Clearcoat Metallic Tricoat paint ($375). 60B All-Season package ($735). 422 California emissions (no cost). 423 California emissions not required (no cost). 93N non-California emissions (no cost). 13B power moonroof ($1,005). 51C Vehicle Communications System ($1,295). [3.0-LITER LS SPORT SEDAN AUTOMATIC] HC Ivory Parchment Clearcoat Metallic Tricoat paint ($375). WF White Pearl Clearcoat Metallic Tricoat paint ($375). 64C 17-in. chrome aluminum five-spoke wheels ($845). 60B All-Season package ($735). 916 Alpine Audiophile system (no cost). 422 California emissions (no cost). 423 California emissions not required (no cost). LSE Appearance package (no cost). 93N non-California emissions (no cost). 13B power moonroof ($1,005). 51C Vehicle Communications System ($1,295). [3.0-LITER LS SPORT SEDAN MANUAL] HC Ivory Parchment Clearcoat Metallic Tricoat paint ($375). WF White Pearl Clearcoat Metallic Tricoat paint ($375). 64C 17-in. chrome aluminum five-spoke wheels ($845). 60B All-Season package ($735). 916 Alpine Audiophile system (no cost). 422 California emissions (no cost). 423 California emissions not required (no cost). LSE Appearance package (no cost). 93N non-California emissions (no cost). 13B power moonroof ($1,005). 51C Vehicle Communications System ($1,295). [3.9-LITER LS SPORT SEDAN AUTOMATIC] HC Ivory Parchment Clearcoat Metallic Tricoat paint ($375). WF White Pearl Clearcoat Metallic Tricoat paint ($375). 64C 17-in. chrome aluminum five-spoke wheels ($845). 60B All-Season package ($735). 916 Alpine Audiophile system (no cost). 422 California emissions (no cost). 423 California emissions not required (no cost). LSE Appearance package (no cost). 93N non-California emissions (no cost). 13B power moonroof ($1,005). 51C Vehicle Communications System ($1,295).

LINCOLN TOWN CAR OPTIONS: [CARTIER] T2A all-season white sidewall tires ($105 additional). 503 conventional spare tire ($130). 20A early order VCS ($1,172 credit). HC Ivory Parchment Clearcoat Metallic Tricoat paint (no cost). 919 trunk mounted CD changer ($605). 51C Vehicle Communications System ($1,295). WF White Pearl Clearcoat Metallic Tricoat paint (no cost). [CARTIER L] 503 conventional spare tire ($130). 20A early order VCS ($1,295 credit). HC Ivory Parchment Clearcoat Metallic Tricoat paint (no cost). 919

trunk mounted CD changer ($605). 51C Vehicle Communications System ($1,295). WF White Pearl Clearcoat Metallic Tricoat paint (no cost). [PREMIUM CARTIER] T2A all-season white sidewall tires ($105 additional). 503 conventional spare tire ($130). 20A early order VCS ($1,295 credit). B3E Premium Package discount ($2,130 credit). B3E Premium Package discount ($605 credit). 51C Vehicle Communications System ($1,295). [EXECUTIVE] T2A all-season white sidewall tires ($105 additional). 503 conventional spare tire ($130). 20A early order VCS ($1,295 credit). 51C Vehicle Communications System ($1,295). WF White Pearl Clearcoat Metallic Tricoat paint ($375). [PREMIUM TOURING] 503 conventional spare tire ($130). 20A early order VCS ($1,295 credit). 467 heated seats ($400). B3E Premium Package discount ($2,130 credit). B3E Premium Package discount ($605 credit). 51C Vehicle Communications System ($1,295). WF White Pearl Clearcoat Metallic Tricoat paint ($375). [SIGNATURE] T2A all-season white sidewall tires ($105 additional). 503 conventional spare tire ($130). 20A early order VCS ($1,295 credit). 467 heated seats ($400). B3E Premium Package discount ($2,130 credit). B3E Premium Package discount ($605 credit). 51C Vehicle Communications System ($1,295). [PREMIUM SIGNATURE] T2A all-season white sidewall tires ($105 additional). 503 conventional spare tire ($130). 20A early order VCS ($1,295 credit). 467 heated seats ($400). 919 trunk mounted CD changer ($605). 954 two-tone paint ($260). 51C Vehicle Communications System ($1,295). WF White Pearl Clearcoat Metallic Tricoat paint ($375). [SIGNATURE TOURING] 503 conventional spare tire ($130). 20A early order VCS ($1,295 credit). 467 heated seats ($400). 919 trunk mounted CD changer ($605). 51C Vehicle Communications System ($1,295). WF White Pearl Clearcoat Metallic Tricoat paint ($375).

LINCOLN CONTINENTAL OPTIONS: [CONTINENTAL SEDAN] 64G 16-in. six-spoke chrome wheels ($855). 64F 16-in. highly-polished aluminum wheels ($360). 919 Alpine trunk mounted CD changer ($605). 919 Alpine trunk mounted CD changer ($605). 916 Alpine audio system ($575). 153 front license plate bracket (no cost). 467 heated seats ($400). 428 high-altitude package (no cost). HC Ivory Parchment Clearcoat Metallic Tricoat paint ($375). 13B power moonroof ($1,525). 17C Select package (no cost). 51C Vehicle Communications System ($1,295). WF White Pearl Clearcoat Metallic Tricoat paint ($375). [CONTINENTAL DRIVER SELECT SEDAN] 64G 16-in. six-spoke chrome wheels ($855). 64F 16-in. highly-polished aluminum wheels ($360). 919 trunk mounted CD changer ($605). 919 Alpine trunk mounted CD changer ($605). 153 front license plate bracket (no cost). 467 heated seats ($400). 428 high-altitude package (no cost). 6 individual bucket seats with leather seating surfaces (no cost). HC Ivory Parchment Clearcoat Metallic Tricoat paint ($375). 13B power moonroof ($1,525). 17C Select package (no cost). 51C Vehicle Communications System ($1,295). WF White Pearl Clearcoat Metallic Tricoat paint ($375). [CONTINENTAL LUXURY APPEARANCE SEDAN] 919 trunk mounted CD changer ($605). 919 Alpine trunk mounted CD changer ($605). 153 front license plate bracket (no cost). 467 heated seats ($400). 428 high-altitude package (no cost). 6 individual bucket seats with leather seating surfaces (no cost). HC Ivory Parchment Clearcoat Metallic Tricoat paint ($375). 13B power moonroof ($1,525). 17C Select package (no cost). 51C Vehicle Communications System ($1,295). WF White Pearl Clearcoat Metallic Tricoat paint ($375). [CONTINENTAL PERSONAL SECURITY SEDAN] 919 trunk mounted CD changer ($605). 919 Alpine trunk mounted CD changer ($605). 153 front license plate bracket (no cost). 467 heated seats ($400). 428 high-altitude package (no cost). 6 individual bucket seats with leather seating surfaces (no cost). HC Ivory Parchment Clearcoat Metallic Tricoat paint ($375). 13B power moonroof ($1,525). 17C Select package (no cost). 51C Vehicle Communications System ($1,295). WF White Pearl Clearcoat Metallic Tricoat paint ($375).

HISTORICAL FOOTNOTES: On Oct. 30, 2001, Ford Motor Co. Chairman William Clay Ford Jr. forced the resignation of Jacques Nasser, Ford's president and chief executive. Nasser's resignation ended a stormy three-year relationship between he and Henry Ford's 44-year-old great grandson. On Nov. 9, Ford Motor Co. dedicated a new North American Headquarters for its Premier Automotive Group in Southern California. The new facility will house the global headquarters for Lincoln Mercury, as well as the North American headquarters for Aston Martin, Jaguar, Land Rover and Volvo. "California offers a trend-setting, diverse and consumer-focused culture and is the ideal location to plan the growth of our premium brands," said Dr. Wolfgang Reitzle, group vice president, Ford Motor Co, and president, Premier Automotive Group. "The area between the Rocky Mountains and the Pacific comprises the largest luxury vehicle market in the world and it makes terrific sense for us to be at the epicenter." Designed and developed by Ford Motor Land Services Corp., the Premier Automotive Group building integrated several "sustainable design" practices to create an environmentally sound and resource-efficient building. Almost two months after the Sept. 11 World Trade Center tragedy in New York City, Lincoln announced on Nov. 9 that the critical work of the American Red Cross of Greater Chicago was getting a $100,000 grant from Chicago Region Lincoln Mercury dealers.

MERCURY
1939-2003

1960 Mercury Park Lane two-door convertible. (LMD)

"The car that dares to ask 'Why?'" some ads read. Though the question referred to dealt with why a big car couldn't be an economical car too, another question might have been why the Ford Motor Co. hadn't introduced the Mercury sooner? The answer to that one undoubtedly was that it had taken that long for Edsel Ford to convince his father to build it.

The first Mercury was priced in the $1,000 range, several hundred dollars more than the Ford V-8, several hundred less than the Lincoln-Zephyr and about the same as the upper-range Oldsmobiles and Dodges and the lower-range Buicks and Chryslers. It was hoped that sales from all these would be usurped by the new Mercury. Its engine was a 95-hp version of the flathead Ford V-8. Its styling was inspired by the Lincoln-Zephyr. Plus, it had hydraulic brakes from the beginning.

With a 116-in. wheelbase (increased to 118 in 1940) and an overall length of 196 in., the Mercury was a good-sized car and Ford advertised this extensively, together with its up-to-20-mpg performance. "Few cars of any size can equal such economy," the copy said. By 1941, Ford could also headline that "It's made 150,000 owners change cars!" During 1941, another 80,000 Mercurys were produced, plus a total of 4,430 more in 1942. Then production was shut down for the duration of World War II.

Although its prewar history was short, the Mercury had already earned for itself the image of being a fine performer in speed as well as fuel economy. The Mercury's "hot car" image was quite in keeping with its name, which was chosen by Edsel Ford. Mercury had been the fleet-footed messenger of the gods of Roman mythology. The Mercury automobile was strongly identified as an up-market Ford during this period, but in 1945 the Lincoln-Mercury Div. would be established to change that. The division was formed in 1945, but it wasn't until the time that the 1949 Mercurys appeared—in early 1948—that Mercury was able to temporarily shed its "glorified Ford" image.

The 1949-1951 Mercurys became popular with customizers and hot rodders. Actor James Dean, driving one in the classic 1950s youth movie "Rebel Without A Cause," helped assure the car's cult status. The fancy Ford look returned in 1952. Mercury was supposed to have received a new overhead valve V-8 that year, but it wasn't ready in time. So, the flathead V-8 was retained for two more years. The flathead had a reputation as a "hot" engine. This was largely because it was so easy to soup-up.

In addition to an overhead valve V-8, the 1954 Mercury offered one of the most unique cars available that year. Its Sun Valley, like Ford's Skyliner, had a plexiglass section over the front half of the roof. Although not exactly the most practical idea, it did show how innovative Ford Motor Co. was.

1947 Mercury two-door sedan coupe. (LMD)

1950 Mercury two-door convertible. (LMD)

Considering that they were based on Fords, the 1955 and 1956 Mercurys featured distinctive styling. In 1957, the make received its own body, which it shared with no one. That may have been just as well. The man largely responsible for the 1957 Mercury design said, years later, "You could see how we could get the reputation as real hacks and chrome merchants, because looking at those cars, it would be hard to deny."

Ford once again shared a body with Mercury in 1960, when it introduced the successful compact Comet. Full-size Fords and Mercurys also shared bodies in 1961, 1962 and 1963. In addition, the intermediate-size Fairlane and Meteor also shared bodies.

The "Breezeway" roof, with its retractable rear window, which was introduced on the 1957 Mercury Turnpike Cruiser, was revived in 1963. Mercury was the only make to have this unique and useful style roof. Fastback Marauder hardtops were also offered, mainly because their roofline was more aerodynamic and improved the make's chance of winning stock car races.

"It's now in the Lincoln Continental tradition," proclaimed ads for the 1965 Mercury. That same year, Ford group vice-president Lee A. Iacocca was put in charge of a program to improve Lincoln-Mercury sales. He pushed to further identify the make with Lincoln. The results of his efforts are evident in the 1969 and up models.

1957 Mercury Monterey two-door convertible. (LMD)

1962 Mercury Monterey Custom two-door convertible. (LMD)

1965 Mercury Monterey two-door convertible. (LMD)

While full-size Mercurys became plusher, the compact Comet series expanded and certain models —such as the Caliente and Cyclone—began to earn well-deserved reputations as hot street machines. Mid-size Mercurys of the late-1960s and early-1970s were especially potent when equipped with one of several high-powered engines available.

Mercury entered the "pony car" market in 1967. Its Cougar was based on the Mustang, but offered more luxury features and some powerful performance packages during its first several years. However, by 1971, the Comet had become primarily a sporty personal car. Small Mercurys reappeared in the early 1970s. The Comet name was reincarnated and was joined by Bobcat. The mid-size Monarch came on the scene in 1975.

Since its beginning in 1939, Mercury had suffered somewhat of an "identity problem." By 1949, the Mercury and Ford had become two quite different automobiles. As outlined above, that difference faded somewhat later in the 1950s, but a revival began in the next decade. High-powered Cougars of the late 1960s, in particular, renewed Mercury's reputation for performance and, to a lesser extent, for styling that expressed a separate identity. That difference didn't last, however. Through most of the 1976-1986 decade, the Mercury was just—to put it bluntly—a plusher and pricier Ford. Their grilles weren't identical and trim details (even some overall lengths) varied, but down at chassis or engine level and in basic body structure, the Mercury seemed to offer little that was new or original. What Mercury didn't get from Ford—notably styling in the bigger models— came from Lincoln. Style-wise, in fact, Mercury often looked more like a lesser Lincoln, than an upscale Ford.

1969 Mercury Montego MX two-door convertible. (LMD)

1970 Mercury Marquis two-door convertible. (LMD)

1976 Mercury Comet "Custom Option" four-door sedan. (AA)

Much of the change was solidified earlier in the 1970s when Cougar switched from its role as a slightly bigger Mustang and became a mid-size—Thunderbird-like—model. By 1977, the Cougar XR-7 badge lost much of its significance. Rather than a singular sporty offering, the XR-7 model became little more than just another coupe out of a baroquely-trimmed lot styled to resemble Lincoln's "Continental Mark" series. By 1980, the Cougar grew even closer to the Thunderbird became hardly more than a clone of the Ford. It seemed that every other Mercury model had its Ford mate, too. The Bobcat was basically a restyled Pinto, the Monarch was a fancier Granada and the Zephyr was nearly identical to Ford's Fairmont. At the top of the heap, the Marquis and LTD had far more in common than they had differences. This twin-model concept was known as "badge engineering" and Mercury was one of its most adept practitioners.

Actually, the biggest difference between the two makes may have occurred from 1975-1978 when Mercury fielded a German-built Capri instead of turning to a variant of the reduced-size (domestically-built) Mustang II. Even when Mercury finally introduced its version of the all-new Mustang for 1979, it never quite captured the attention of enthusiasts in the same way as Ford's version. That was true even though the chassis and the engines were the same. In fact, just about everything of consequence was similar, if not precisely identical. When Ford V-8s were downsized from 302 cid to 255 cid, so were Mercury's. When Ford models added four-speed overdrive automatics or switched from eight-cylinder to six-cylinder power, so did their Mercury counterparts. When the LTD was downsized in 1979, there was Mercury with its similarly shrunken Marquis.

1978 Mercury Zephyr Z-7 two-door coupe. (LMD)

1979 Mercury Grand Marquis four-door sedan. (LMD)

1983-1/2 Mercury Topaz CS four-door sedan. (LMD)

1986 Mercury Lynx GS four-door station wagon. (LMD)

Mercury was best at turning out mid-size and full-size models that, if not exactly thrilling, at least attracted a regular crop of traditional-minded buyers. Smaller Mercury models never seemed to catch on as well as smaller Fords, but the big and near-big Mercurys didn't fare badly. Perhaps the best example was the two-seater LN7, introduced in 1982. Its corporate twin was the Ford EXP, which didn't exactly set the marketplace ablaze, but Mercury's LN7 sales record was a total disaster.

By 1987, Mercury models included cars made in the United States, Canada, West Germany and Mexico. Qualifying as "genuine" domestic cars were the Cougar built in Lorain, Ohio; the Topaz built in Kansas City, Mo.; the Sable built in Atlanta, Ga., and Chicago, Ill.; the Capri built in Dearborn, Mich. and the Lynx built in Edison, N.J. The Topaz and Grand Marquis were both made in Canadian factories, while Ford's Hermosillo, Mexico, plant manufactured the Mazda-designed Tracer. And the Merkur Scorpio and XR4Ti—part of a planned new line of imported luxury models—were brought in from West Germany.

Mercury and Merkur new car sales for model year 1987 came to 484,845 units, lead by the Sable. Of possible interest to future collectors was an all-wheel-drive system for the Topaz, which also got a GS Sport package with a high-output engine. Cougars received a four-speed automatic transmission and standard air conditioning. Fuel injection was made standard for the Lynx and Sables added a three-liter V-6 base engine.

Standard Marquis were dropped, along with the Capri, although the latter car had almost 2,000 sales in the model year. Likewise, the Lynx and Tracer sales figures were combined while dealers phased out their inventories of Lynx models.

For 1988, sales of Tracer, Topaz, Sable, Cougar, Grand Marquis and Merkur models totaled 499,881 units. Of interest to enthusiasts was the Cougar's new multi-port fuel-injected engine and monochromatic exterior treatments with 16-spoke aluminum wheels for the XR-7. The Topaz had new sheet metal, the Sable got a new engine and the Grand Marquis was made sleeker and given more standard equipment.

1986 Mercury Grand Marquis Colony Park four-door station wagon. (LMD)

1989 Mercury Cougar LS coupe. (OCW)

1989 Mercury Topaz LTS sedan. (OCW)

Mercury's 50th birthday was celebrated in 1989 with a mid-year Grand Marquis Special Anniversary edition. The Cougar had a nine-inch-longer wheelbase, with a supercharged 215-hp intercooled engine for the XR-7. Sables were face-lifted inside and out and all-wheel-drive could now be had on any Topaz. A high-output engine was offered in XR5, LTS and all-wheel-drive Topaz models at extra cost.

Mercury and Merkur sales for the 1989 model year came to 497,150 units, a modest decrease. This was caused, in part, by an extra-long factory changeover needed to prepare for building the larger Cougar. However, the Cougar's sales did increase eight percent by year's end. Another problem was a labor dispute at the Mexican factory, which held down Tracer production. However, it should be pointed out that dealers sold more Lincolns in this period, giving the division a better overall year in both sales and profits.

For 1990, the Merkur Scorpio was dropped due to lackluster sales and production of Tracers, in Mexico, was temporarily halted. Other products were little changed, except for the addition of new options, along with standard equipment upgrades. A new Capri 2+2 convertible—an early launch of a 1991 model—was built in yet another country . . . Australia. It was announced as a new spring model. Mercury sales predictions at the start of 1990 were optimistic. They called for the retailing of 113,000 Grand Marquis, 118,000 Sables, 100,000 Topaz units, 110,000 Cougars and 40,000 Tracers—almost 500,000 cars in all. Falling a bit short of goal, 1990 model year sales for Mercury reached 380,100.

The Mexican-built, Japanese-designed (Mazda Motor Corp.) Tracer was the big news for Mercury in 1991. The all-new-design Tracer series included an LTS notchback four-door sedan powered by a 127-hp DOHC 1.8-liter four-cylinder engine and featuring four-wheel disc brakes and speed control. An all-new 1992 Grand Marquis debuted in 1991, minus the venerable station wagon that had been a cornerstone for that series for many years. The full-size station wagon at FoMoCo had now officially been replaced by the minivan. The Cougar was freshened up a bit cosmetically and the XR7 received a new 200-hp 5.0-liter V-8 to replace the formerly used supercharged 3.8-liter V-6. Sales of the imported Capri—in its first full-year of production—were almost triple the previous year's results (21,200 compared to 8,072).

Cougar observed its 25th Anniversary in 1992 and the occasion was marked by Mercury offering a Cougar LS Anniversary Edition coupe powered by a 5.0-liter V-8. The aforementioned redesigned Grand Marquis, in a sedan-only format, featured the new modular 4.6-liter V-8 as its standard power plant. In Avon Lake, Ohio, the Mercury Villager minivan was being readied for a 1993 release. This minivan was based on a shared platform with the Nissan Quest and used mostly Japanese-designed components.

The Topaz series was thinned considerably in 1993 with the elimination of LS, LTS and XR5 models. This was in advance of the Topaz line going away all together the following year to make way for the all-new Mystique "World Car." Sales of the imported Capri were dwindling with fewer than 10,000 sold in 1993. Cougar was once again—as in 1974 and 1980—known as the Cougar XR7, with no base Cougar model available. Mercury Villager minivans debuted in both GS and LS trim and were priced starting at $16,831. For the first full model year of sales, the Villager attracted 71,567 buyers.

Production of both Topaz and Capri convertibles ended early in 1994. The Capri hatchback ceased production in the fall. Production of the 1995 Mystique began in July 1994 at Mercury assembly plants in Cuautitlan, Mexico and Kansas City, Mo. The addition of safety equipment as standard fare was the sales pitch du jour as Capri (before its termination) and the Cougar XR7 received dual airbags. The Grand Marquis featured improved side impact protection and the Tracer and the Villager offered driver's side airbags. The Cougar XR7 also received the modular 4.6-liter V-8 as its engine option, replacing the 5.0-liter V-8 formerly offered.

In March of 1995, FoMoCo officials announced that assembly of the next-generation Cougar (launched in mid-1998 as a 1999 model) would remain in Lorain, Ohio, with $100 million earmarked for plant upgrades. The all-new Mystique sedan attracted 62,609 buyers in its first full model year of production. Mystiques were powered by either the all-new Zetec 2.0-liter four-cylinder or the Duratec DOHC 2.5-liter V-6. Dual airbags were standard equipment on the Mystique, as well as on the Tracer, for 1995. In late 1995, the all-new 1996 Sable line bowed. It included sedans and station wagons in either GS or LS trim.

Mercury had a banner year for change in 1996. In addition to the aforementioned new Sable, the 1997 Mountaineer—a sport utility vehicle based on the Ford Explorer—was launched amid great fanfare in the spring. The list of standard features of this midsize luxury SUV included dual airbags, antilock brakes, fog lamps and rear reflectors. Also introduced early in 1996 was the all-new 1997 Tracer, which was now being assembled in Wayne, Mich., as well as Hermosillo, Mexico.

Early in 1997, FoMoCo officials announced that the Lorain, Ohio, assembly plant would close, forcing the next-generation Cougar to be built in Flat Rock, Mich., instead. For its final year of production in Lorain a special Cougar XR7 30th Anniversary edition was available. It featured 16-in. aluminum wheels and sport shocks, sport seats with an anniversary logo and commemorative badges and appliqués. The Mystique was offered with a Spree appearance package to attract younger, more fun-loving buyers.

The Villager, Mountaineer and Mystique all received makeovers in 1998, but no Cougar would be offered for this model year. At midyear, the next-generation 1999 Cougar was launched. This four-seat, front-wheel-drive sports coupe had a platform and drive train that it shared with the Mercury Mystique, the Ford Contour and the Ford Mondeo.

The 1999 entry-level Tracer was in its last year of production and had an upgraded interior. The LS featured a standard AM/FM stereo with cassette and new remote keyless entry option. The Mystique got an upgraded front suspension like the European Mondeo, lighter weight seats, a redesigned dash and

1889 Mercury Sable GS sedan. (OCW)

1989 Mercury Grand Marquis LS sedan. (OCW)

1991 Mercury Sable LS station wagon. (OCW)

improved fit and finish. An all-new front-wheel-drive Cougar coupe with "new edge" styling bowed in the spring as a 1999 model. It was based on the Mystique/Contour platform and built by AutoAlliance in Flat Rock, Mich. Engines included a Zetec inline four and Duratec V-6. The Sable GS series got a wagon, five-passenger seating and a rear stabilizer bar in a new 16-in. tire and wheel option package. The Grand Marquis had minimal changes. In January, Lincoln-Mercury announced plans to move its headquarters from Detroit to Irvine, Calif. Division manager, Jim Rogers, promised a "radical change" to push Mercury models further from Fords and Lincolns.

Mark W. Hutchins was president of Lincoln-Mercury Div. in 2000, when the division completed its move to Southern California. There were no major changes in the 2000 Mercury Mystique, which was scheduled to be the last. The Cougar that bowed in the spring of 1998 as a 1999 model had no major changes for 2000. The restyled Sable series was where the action was in 2000. It had new front/rear fascias, new rear-end styling and more power. A new option was an adjustable pedal system. The Grand Marquis received very minimal changes.

The Cougar was heavily revised inside and outside for 2001, but the Sable got only some refinements and Tropic Green Clearcoat paint replaced Spruce Green. The full-size Grand Marquis had a little more power. The interior was also upgraded and the adjustable pedal system became optional. In February, at the Chicago Auto Show, Grand Marquis LSE and Limited models were introduced. Mercury also introduced the Cougar Zn and Cougar C2 models at Chicago, the latest attempt to lure youthful buyers with stylish, energetic coupes. During 2001, the National Highway and Traffic Safety Administration (NHTSA) awarded the Sable, Grand Marquis and Villager its highest double five star safety rating for frontal crashes.

The Cougar sports coupe returned in 2002 with standard speed control, remote keyless entry, illuminated entry and rear wiper/washer, plus new Grabber Green, Light Parchment Gold Red Clearcoat colors. The front-drive Sable was again available in sedan and wagon styles with antilock braking now standard. The Mercury Grand Marquis featured new leather seating options with a small storage pouch sewn into the front seat driver's seat cushion. All Grand Marquis were also equipped with antilock brakes and traction control as standard equipment. The Mercury Marauder—a high performance sedan introduced at the 2001 Chicago Auto Show—was scheduled to go on sale in the U.S. during the summer of 2002. On Nov. 9, 2001 Ford dedicated its new Premier Automotive Group North American Headquarters in Southern California. The new facility housed Lincoln Mercury headquarters. That same day, Lincoln-Mercury Div. announced that the American Red Cross of Greater Chicago would receive a $100,000 grant from Chicago Region Lincoln Mercury dealers.

*(Contributors to the Mercury section of this catalog include James M. Flammang who originally compiled all of the data for the **Standard Catalog of American Cars 1976-1986**, John A. Gunnell who edited the original **Standard Catalog of American Cars 1946-1975**, Beverly Rae Kimes who wrote the prewar histories and compiled the prewar model information for the original **Standard Catalog of American Cars 1805-1942**, Ron Kowalke who edited the second edition of the **Standard Catalog of Fords 1903-1998**, Robert L. Lichty who edited the first edition of the **Standard Catalog of Fords 1903-1990** and Charles Webb who originally compiled the 1946-1975 data for the **Standard Catalog of American Cars 1946-1975**).*

1992 Mercury Topaz XR5 coupe. (OCW)

1992 Mercury Cougar LS coupe. (OCW)

1990 Mercury Grand Marquis LS sedan. (OCW)

1939 MERCURY

1939 Mercury town sedan. (JAC)

1939 Mercury sport convertible. (PH)

1939 Mercury two-door sedan. (OCW)

1939 Mercury coupe. (OCW)

1939 Mercury two-door coupe. (AA)

Series 99A, V-8, 116" wb

Model No.	Body Type & Seating	Factory Price	Shipping Weight	Prod. Total
N/A	2-dr Conv	1018	2995	7,818
N/A	2-dr Cpe	957	3000	8,254
N/A	2-dr Sed	916	2997	13,216
N/A	4-dr Sed	957	3013	39,847

1940 MERCURY

1940 Mercury town sedan. (PH)

1940 Mercury convertible sedan. (PH)

Series 09A, V-8, 116" wb

Model No.	Body Type & Seating	Factory Price	Shipping Weight	Prod. Total
N/A	2-dr Conv	1079	3107	9,741
N/A	4-dr Conv Sed	1212	3249	1,083
N/A	2-dr Cpe	987	3030	16,189
N/A	2-dr Sed	946	3068	16,243
N/A	4-dr Sed	987	3103	42,806

1940 Mercury convertible. (OCW)

1942 Mercury convertible. (OCW)

1941 MERCURY

1941 Mercury town sedan. (AA)

Series 19A, V-8, 118" wb

Model No.	Body Type & Seating	Factory Price	Shipping Weight	Prod. Total
76	2-dr Conv	1100	3222	8,556
77	2-dr Bus Cpe	910	3008	3,313
67	2-dr Cpe-5P	936	3049	1,954
72	2-dr Cpe-6P	977	3118	18,263
70	2-dr Sed	946	3184	20,932
73	4-dr Sed	987	3221	42,984
79	4-dr Sta Wag	1141	3468	2,291

1942 MERCURY

1942 Mercury station wagon. (OCW)

1942 Mercury two-door sedan. (PH)

1942 Mercury town sedan. (PH)

Series 29A, V-8, 118" wb

Model No.	Body Type & Seating	Factory Price	Shipping Weight	Prod. Total
76	2-dr Conv	1215	3288	969
77	2-dr Bus Cpe	995	3073	800
72	2-dr Cpe-6P	1055	3148	5,345
70	2-dr Sed	1030	3228	4,941
73	4-dr Sed	1065	3263	11,784
79	4-dr Sta Wag	1260	3528	857

NOTE: Due to the outbreak of World War II, production of Mercury automobiles was halted on Feb. 10, 1942, after only 24,704 units were assembled.

1946 MERCURY

1946 Mercury two-door sedan. (RLC)

MERCURY SERIES — SERIES 69M — A new grille was the most noticeable difference between the 1942 and 1946 Mercurys. It had thin, vertical bars surrounded by a trim piece painted the same color as the car. The Liquamatic Drive automatic transmission option was also eliminated. The most distinctive new Mercury was the Sportsman convertible. It featured wood body panels.

MERCURY I.D. NUMBERS: Serial numbers were the same as engine numbers. They ranged from 99A50280 to 99A1412707.

MERCURY

Model No.	Body/ Style No.	Body Type & Seating	Factory Price	Shipping Weight	Prod. Total
69M	71	2-dr Sptmn Conv-6P	2209	3407	205
69M	70	2-dr Sed-6P	1448	3240	13,108
69M	72	2-dr Sed Cpe-6P	1495	3190	24,163
69M	73	4-dr Twn Sed-6P	1509	3270	40,280
69M	76	2-dr Conv-6P	1711	3340	6,044
69M	79	4-dr Sta Wag-8P	1729	3540	2,797

ENGINE [V-8]: L-head. Cast-iron block. Displacement: 239.4 cid. Bore and stroke: 3.19 x 3.75 inches. Compression ratio: 6.75:1. Brake hp: 100 at 3800 rpm. Three main bearings. Carburetor: Holley 94 two-barrel.

CHASSIS FEATURES: Wheelbase: 116 inches. Overall length: 201.6 inches. Front tread: 58 inches. Rear tread: 60 inches. Tires: 6.50 x 15.

POWERTRAIN OPTIONS: A three-speed manual transmission was standard.

1946 Mercury two-door convertible, V-8. (OCW)

CONVENIENCE OPTIONS: Radio with foot control. Heater. Fog lamps.

HISTORY: Mercury's model year production for 1946 was 86,603 cars. Sales for the calendar year were counted as 70,955 vehicles. This made the company America's 12th largest automaker. Production difficulties and parts shortages delayed Mercury introductions until Feb. 6, 1946.

1947 MERCURY

1947 Mercury Model 72 club coupe. (OCW)

MERCURY SERIES — SERIES 79M — Styling changes were slight this year. The Mercury name was placed on the side of the hood. Different hubcaps were used. The border around the grille was chrome plated. There was also new trunk trim. More chrome was used on the interior and the dash dial faces were redesigned. The convertible and station wagon came with leather upholstery. The other body styles used fabric.

MERCURY I.D. NUMBERS: Serial numbers were the same as engine numbers. They ranged from 799A1412708 to 799A2002282.

MERCURY

Model No.	Body/ Style No.	Body Type & Seating	Factory Price	Shipping Weight	Prod. Total
79M	70	2-dr Sed-6P	1592	3268	34
79M	72	2-dr Sed Cpe-6P	1645	3218	29,284
79M	73	4-dr Twn Sed-6P	1660	3298	42,281
79M	76	2-dr Conv-6P	2002	3368	10,221
79M	79	4-dr Sta Wag-8P	2207	3571	3,558

ENGINE [V-8]: L-head. Cast-iron block. Displacement: 239.4 cid. Bore and stroke: 3.19 x 3.75 inches. Compression ratio: 6.75:1. Brake hp: 100 at 3800 rpm. Three main bearings. Carburetor: Holley 94 two-barrel.

CHASSIS FEATURES: Wheelbase: 116 inches. Overall length: 201.8 inches. Front tread: 58 inches. Rear tread: 60 inches. Tires: 6.50 x 15.

POWERTRAIN OPTIONS: A three-speed manual transmission was standard.

CONVENIENCE OPTIONS: Radio with foot control. Fog lamps. Heater. Whitewall tires.

HISTORY: The 1947 model year began Jan. 1, 1947. By the time it ended, Mercury produced 86,363 vehicles. Calendar year sales were 124,612 cars. This gave the company ninth rank in the American industry. Technical innovations included a moisture sealed distributor and oil-resistant electrical wiring.

1948 Mercury four-door sedan. (OCW)

1948 Mercury four-door Town Sedan, V-8. (OCW)

MERCURY SERIES — SERIES 89M — If you liked the 1947 Mercurys, you also liked the 1948s. For all practical purposes, they were identical. The major changes consisted of different dial faces and no steering column lock.

MERCURY I.D. NUMBERS: Serial numbers were the same as engine numbers. They ranged from 899A1990957 to 899A2374315.

MERCURY

Model No.	Body/ Style No.	Body Type & Seating	Factory Price	Shipping Weight	Prod. Total
89M	72	2-dr Sed Cpe-6P	1645	3218	16,476
89M	73	4-dr Twn Sed-6P	1660	3298	24,283
89M	76	2-dr Conv-6P	2002	3368	7,586
89M	79	4-dr Sta Wag-8P	2207	3571	1,889

1948 Mercury two-door convertible, V-8. (OCW)

ENGINE [V-8]: L-head. Cast-iron block. Displacement: 239.4 cid. Bore and stroke: 3.19 x 3.75 inches. Compression ratio: 6.75:1. Brake hp: 100 at 3800 rpm. Three main bearings. Carburetor: Mercury two-barrel.

CHASSIS FEATURES: Wheelbase: 118 inches. Overall length: 201.8 inches. Front tread: 58 inches. Rear tread: 60 inches. Tires: 6.50 x 15.

POWERTRAIN OPTIONS: A three-speed manual transmission was standard.

CONVENIENCE OPTIONS: Radio with foot control. Fog lamps. Heater. Whitewall tires.

HISTORY: The new 1948 models bowed in the showrooms on Nov. 1, 1947. During the model year, 50,268 cars were built. This made Mercury 10th in U.S. car sales.

1949 MERCURY

1949 Mercury two-door sedan. (OCW)

1949 Mercury two-door convertible, V-8. (AA)

MERCURY SERIES — SERIES 9CM — The first all-new postwar Mercurys were introduced on April 29, 1948. In a break with tradition they did not look like fancy Fords, but rather, shared Lincoln styling (and basic body shells). The grille resembled a shiny coil divided in the center by a large vertical piece of chrome. A nearly full-length, mid-body chrome spear stretched across the sides. The 1949 Mercury also had wraparound front and rear bumpers. The wood bodied station wagon was replaced by one that used only wood trim. As before, the sedan rear doors opened to the center.

MERCURY I.D. NUMBERS: Serial numbers were the same as engine numbers. They ranged from 9CM101 to 9CM302439.

MERCURY

Model No.	Body/ Style No.	Body Type & Seating	Factory Price	Shipping Weight	Prod. Total
9CM	72	2-dr Cpe-6P	1979	3321	120,616
9CM	74	4-dr Spt Sed-6P	2031	3386	155,882
9CM	76	2-dr Conv-6P	2410	3591	16,765
9CM	79	2-dr Sta Wag-6P	2716	3626	8,044

1949 Mercury two-door station wagon, V-8. (OCW)

ENGINE [V-8]: L-head. Cast-iron block. Displacement: 255.4 cid. Bore and stroke: 3.19 x 4.00 inches. Compression ratio: 6.8:1. Brake hp: 110 at 3600 rpm. Three main bearings. Carburetor: Holley 885FFC two-barrel.

CHASSIS FEATURES: Wheelbase: 118 inches. Overall length: 206.8 inches. Front tread: 58.5 inches. Rear tread: 60 inches. Tires: 7.10 x 15.

POWERTRAIN OPTIONS: A three-speed manual transmission was standard. Touch-O-Matic overdrive was optional.

CONVENIENCE OPTIONS: Radio. Heater. Rear fender shields. Foam rubber seat cushions. Whitewall tires.

HISTORY: The first all-new postwar models were introduced by Mercury on April 29, 1948. Running production changes included early-1949 lever-type door handles being replaced with push-button units as well as a stronger chassis being incorporated to overcome flexing problems associated with the earlier version. Mercury placed ninth in industry sales with 203,339 calendar year deliveries. Model year production for 1949 was 301,319 cars.

1950 MERCURY

1950 Mercury Model OCM convertible. (OCW)

1950 Mercury four-door Sport Sedan, V-8. (OCW)

1950 Mercury two-door station wagon, V-8. (TVB)

MERCURY SERIES — SERIES 0CM — For 1950, the letters of the word Mercury were imbedded in chrome on the front of the hood. The signal lights were chrome encased in a fashion similar to that used on the 1948 Cadillac. The design of the trunk chrome was altered, as was the tip on the side spear. The biggest change was made to the dash. It was completely restyled. Improvements were made to the carburetor, parking brake and steering. To compete with General Motors and Chrysler two-door hardtops, Mercury introduced the Monterey coupe. It featured a padded canvas or vinyl top and custom leather interior.

MERCURY I.D. NUMBERS: Serial numbers were the same as engine numbers. For 1950, they were: 50DA10001M to 50DA79027M; 50LA10001M to 50LA44958M; 50ME10001M to 50ME97749M and 50SL10001M to 50SL110459M. The plant codes were DA = Dearborn, LA = Los Angeles, ME = Metuchen; SL = St. Louis and WA = Wayne.

MERCURY

Model No.	Body/ Style No.	Body Type & Seating	Factory Price	Shipping Weight	Prod. Total
0CM	M-72A	2-dr Cpe-3P	1875	3345	Note 1
0CM	M-72B	2-dr Clb Cpe-6P	1980	3430	Note 1
0CM	M-72C	2-dr Mont Cpe-6P	2146	3626	Note 1
0CM	M-74	4-dr Spt Sed-6P	2032	3470	132,082
0CM	M-76	2-dr Conv-6P	3412	3710	8,341
0CM	M-79	2-dr Sta Wag-8P	2561	3755	1,746

NOTE 1: A total of 151,489 Mercury coupes were made in 1950 with no breakout available.

ENGINE [V-8]: L-head. Cast-iron block. Displacement: 255.4 cid. Bore and stroke: 3.19 x 4.00 inches. Compression ratio: 6.8:1. Brake hp: 110 at 3600 rpm. Three main bearings. Carburetor: Holley 885FFC two-barrel.

CHASSIS FEATURES: Wheelbase: 118 inches. Overall length: (passenger cars) 206.8 inches; (station wagon) 213.5 inches. Front tread: 58.5 inches. Rear tread: 60 inches. Tires: 7.10 x 15.

POWERTRAIN OPTIONS: A three-speed manual transmission was standard. Touch-O-Matic overdrive was optional.

CONVENIENCE OPTIONS: Radio. Power windows (standard in convertible). Power seat. Oil bath air cleaner. Heater. Two-tone paint. Whitewall tires.

HISTORY: The one-millionth Mercury built was a 1950 four-door sedan. Mercurys won two NASCAR Grand National races this year. Mercury was the official pace car at the 1950 Indianapolis 500.

1951 MERCURY

1951 Mercury four-door Sport Sedan, V-8. (TVB)

1951 Mercury two-door convertible, V-8. (OCW)

MERCURY SERIES — SERIES 1CM — A new grille that was integrated with the signal lights appeared in 1951. Vertical taillights replaced the horizontal type found on the 1949 and 1950 Mercurys. New, lower rear quarter panel trim made the wraparound bumper appear to extend even further than before. Chrome gravel shields and rocker panels, a vinyl or canvas roof and custom interior were standard on the Monterey coupe.

MERCURY I.D. NUMBERS: Serial numbers for 1951 were: 51DA10001M to 51DA67910M; 51LA10001M to 51LA46772M; 51ME10001M to 51ME103515M and 51SL10001M to 51SL127830M. The plant codes were DA = Dearborn; LA = Los Angeles; ME = Metuchen; SL = St. Louis and WA = Wayne.

MERCURY

Model No.	Body/ Style No.	Body Type & Seating	Factory Price	Shipping Weight	Prod. Total
1CM	M-72B	2-dr Spt Cpe-6P	1947	3485	Note 1
1CM	M-72C	2-dr Mont Cpe-6P	2314	3485	Notes 1 & 2
1CM	M-74	4-dr Spt Sed-6P	2189	3550	157,648
1CM	M-76	2-dr Conv-6P	2380	3760	6,759
1CM	M-79	2-dr Sta Wag-8P	2530	3800	3,812

NOTE 1: A total of 142,166 Mercury coupes were made in 1951 with no breakout available.

NOTE 2: The higher priced Monterey included a vinyl top covering.

ENGINE [V-8]: L-head. Cast-iron block. Displacement: 255.4 cid. Bore and stroke: 3.19 x 4.00 inches. Compression ratio: 6.8:1. Brake hp: 112 at 3600 rpm. Three main bearings. Carburetor: Holley 885FFC two-barrel.

CHASSIS FEATURES: Wheelbase: 118 inches. Overall length: 206.8 inches; (station wagon) 213.5 inches. Front tread: 58.5 inches. Rear tread: 60 inches. Tires: 7.10 x 15.

POWERTRAIN OPTIONS: A three-speed manual transmission was standard. Overdrive and Merc-O-Matic automatic transmission were optional.

CONVENIENCE OPTIONS: Radio. Fender skirts. Heater. Whitewall tires.

HISTORY: Approximately one in every three 1951 Mercurys were sold with an automatic transmission. In 1951, Mercurys came in first at two NASCAR Grand National races.

1952 MERCURY

1952 Mercury Monterey convertible. (OCW)

1952 Mercury Custom two-door hardtop, V-8. (AA)

CUSTOM SERIES — SERIES 2M — Like all Ford Motor Co. cars, Mercury was completely restyled for 1952. It had frenched headlights; a one-piece curved windshield; wraparound rear window; fake hood scoop; massive integrated bumper/grille; and vertical tail/back-up lights encased in chrome in a manner that made them look like extensions of the rear bumper. The fender level hood line helped give the Custom an aggressive look.

CUSTOM I.D. NUMBERS: Serial numbers for 1952 were: 52SL10001M to 52SL86300M; 52WA10001M to 52WA19422M; 52LA10001M to 52LA38763M and 52ME10001 to 52ME65500M. The plant codes were DA = Dearborn; LA = Los Angeles; ME = Metuchen; SL = St Louis and WA = Wayne.

CUSTOM

Model No.	Body/ Style No.	Body Type & Seating	Factory Price	Shipping Weight	Prod. Total
2M	60E	2-dr Spt Cpe-6P	2100	3435	30,599
2M	70B	2-dr Sed-6P	1987	3335	25,812
2M	73B	4-dr Sed-6P	2040	3390	Note 1
2M	79B	4-dr Sta Wag-6P	2525	3795	Note 1
2M	79D	4-dr Sta Wag-8P	2570	3795	Note 1

NOTE 1: The total production of all 1952 Custom and Monterey four-door sedans was 63,475. The total production of all station wagons was 2,487.

1952 Mercury Custom four-door sedan, V-8. (AA)

1952 Mercury Monterey two-door convertible, V-8. (AA)

ENGINE [Custom V-8]: L-head. Cast-iron block. Displacement: 255.4 cid. Bore and stroke: 3.19 x 4.00 inches. Compression ratio: 7.2:1. Brake hp: 125 at 3700 rpm. Three main bearings. Carburetor: Holley 885FFC two-barrel.

MONTEREY SERIES — SERIES 2M — Except for the chrome rocker panels and fancier wheel covers, exterior styling resembled the lower-priced Custom series. Standard Monterey features included a two-tone paint job and leather and vinyl interior. Suspended pedals were new to both series. The rear doors of Mercury sedans now opened in the conventional manner.

MONTEREY I.D. NUMBERS: Serial numbers for 1952 were: 52SL10001M to 52SL86300M; 52DA10001M to 52DA19422M; 52LA10001M to 52LA38763M and 52ME10001 to 52ME65500M.

MONTEREY

Model No.	Body/ Style No.	Body Type & Seating	Factory Price	Shipping Weight	Prod. Total
2M	60B	2-dr HT Cpe-6P	2225	3520	24,453
2M	73C	4-dr Sed-6P	2115	3375	Note 1
2M	76B	2-dr Conv-6P	2370	3635	5,261

NOTE 1: The total production of all 1952 Custom and Monterey four-door sedans was 63,475.

ENGINE [Monterey V-8]: L-head. Cast-iron block. Displacement: 255.4 cid. Bore and stroke: 3.19 x 4.00 inches. Compression ratio: 7.2:1. Brake hp: 125 at 3700 rpm. Three main bearings. Carburetor: Holley 885FFC two-barrel.

CHASSIS FEATURES: Wheelbase: 118 inches. Overall length: 202.2 inches. Front tread: 58 inches. Rear tread: 56 inches. Tires: 7.10 x 15; (convertible and station wagon) 7.60 x 15.

POWERTRAIN OPTIONS: A three-speed manual transmission was standard. Overdrive and Merc-O-Matic automatic transmission were optional.

CONVENIENCE OPTIONS: Radio. 'Merc-O-Matic' heater. Bumper grille guard. Fender skirts (standard on Monterey). Whitewall tires.

HISTORY: Almost half of all 1952 Mercurys came with automatic transmission and about 33 percent of the manual shift cars were equipped with a three-speed with overdrive. This was the first year for a Mercury two-door hardtop.

1953 MERCURY

1953 Mercury Monterey two-door hardtop. (OCW)

CUSTOM SERIES — SERIES 3M — A major styling change for 1953 was made to the grille. It was still integrated with the bumper, but the bumper guards were now bullet-shaped. The trunk featured a new medallion. Side chrome trim consisted of a full-length mid-body spear and rear fender molding. The doors could stay in position either halfway or fully opened.

CUSTOM I.D. NUMBERS: Serial numbers for 1953 were: 53LA10001M to 53LA50946M; 53WA10001M to 53WA45363M; 53ME10001M and up and 53SL10001M to 53SL14285M. The plant codes were DA = Dearborn; LA = Los Angeles; ME = Metuchen; SL = St. Louis and WA = Wayne.

CUSTOM

Model No.	Body/ Style No.	Body Type & Seating	Factory Price	Shipping Weight	Prod. Total
3M	60E	2-dr Spt Cpe-6P	2117	3465	39,547
3M	70B	2-dr Sed-6P	2004	3405	50,183
3M	73B	4-dr Sed-6P	2057	3450	59,794

ENGINE [Custom V-8]: L-head. Cast-iron block. Displacement: 255.4 cid. Bore and stroke: 3.19 x 4.00 inches. Compression ratio: 7.2:1. Brake hp: 125 at 3800 rpm. Three main bearings. Carburetor: Holley 1901 FFC two-barrel.

MONTEREY SERIES — SERIES 3M — Two-tone paint, fender skirts and chrome rocker panels were standard on Mercury's top-of-the-line series. The Monterey name was placed on the upper front fenders (except on those built early in the model year). The rear side windows of the station wagon featured sliding glass.

MONTEREY I.D. NUMBERS: Serial numbers for 1953 were: 53LA10001M to 53LA50946M; 53WA10001M to 53WA45383M; 53ME10001M and up and 53SL10001M to 53SL14285M. The plant codes were DA = Dearborn; LA = Los Angeles; ME = Metuchen; SL = St. Louis and WA = Wayne.

MONTEREY

Model No.	Body/ Style No.	Body Type & Seating	Factory Price	Shipping Weight	Prod. Total
3M	60B	2-dr HT Cpe-6P	2244	3465	76,119
3M	73C	4-dr Sed-6P	2133	3425	64,038
3M	76B	2-dr Conv-6P	2390	3585	8,463
3M	79B	4-dr Sta Wag-6P	2591	3765	7,719

ENGINE [Monterey V-8]: L-head. Cast-iron block. Displacement: 255.4 cid. Bore and stroke: 3.19 x 4.00 inches. Compression ratio: 7.2:1. Brake hp: 125 at 3800 rpm. Three main bearings. Carburetor: Holley 1901 FFC two-barrel.

CHASSIS FEATURES: Wheelbase: 118 inches. Overall length: 202.2 inches. Front tread: 58 inches. Rear tread: 56 inches. Tires: 7.10 x 15; (convertible and station wagon) 7.60 x 15.

POWERTRAIN OPTIONS: A three-speed manual transmission was standard. Overdrive and Merc-O-Matic automatic transmission were optional.

CONVENIENCE OPTIONS: Wheel covers. Power steering. Power seat. Electric windows. Whitewall tires. Bumper grille guard. Radio. Power brakes.

1953 Mercury Monterey two-door convertible, V-8. (AA)

1953 Mercury Monterey two-door hardtop, V-8. (PH)

HISTORY: An enlarged tailpipe and new, straight-through muffler greatly reduced back pressure. Power brakes were first offered in April of 1953. Fifteen percent of Mercurys were equipped with them. A month later, power steering was introduced. Only eight percent of 1953 Mercurys were sold with this option. The 40-millionth vehicle built by Ford Motor Co. was a 1953 Mercury convertible.

1954 MERCURY

1954 Mercury Monterey two-door hardtop. (OCW)

CUSTOM SERIES — Wraparound vertical taillights were the most noticeable change made for 1954. The grille was modestly restyled but was still integrated with the front bumper. 'Mercury' was written in chrome on the rear fenders above the mid-body spear. New ball joint front suspension improved handling and ride qualities.

CUSTOM I.D. NUMBERS: Serial numbers ranged from 54WA10001M to 54WA75348M. The plant codes were DA = Dearborn; LA = Los Angeles; ME = Metuchen; SL = St Louis and WA = Wayne.

CUSTOM

Model No.	Body/ Style No.	Body Type & Seating	Factory Price	Shipping Weight	Prod. Total
N/A	60E	2-dr HT Cpe-6P	2315	3485	15,234
N/A	70B	2-dr Sed-6P	2194	3435	37,146
N/A	73B	4-dr Sed-6P	2251	3480	32,687

ENGINE [Custom V-8]: Overhead valve. Cast-iron block. Displacement: 256 cid. Bore and stroke: 3.62 x 3.10 inches. Compression ratio: 7.5:1. Brake hp: 162 at 4400 rpm. Carburetor: Holley 2140 four-barrel.

1954 Mercury Monterey Sun Valley two-door hardtop, V-8. (AA)

1954 Mercury Monterey two-door hardtop, V-8. (PH)

MONTEREY SERIES — The Monterey featured its name written in chrome above the side trim on the rear fender. It had a medallion near the tip of the side chrome spear on the front fenders. Chrome rocker panels and fender skirts were standard. The most unique Monterey was the Sun Valley. The front half of its roof contained a green tinted, plexiglass section. As in previous years, the station wagon had simulated wood trim.

MONTEREY I.D. NUMBERS: Serial numbers ranged from 54WA10001M to 54WA75346M. The plant codes were DA = Dearborn; LA = Los Angeles; ME = Metuchen; SL = St Louis and WA = Wayne.

MONTEREY

Model No.	Body/ Style No.	Body Type & Seating	Factory Price	Shipping Weight	Prod. Total
N/A	60B	2-dr HT Cpe-6P	2452	3520	79,533
N/A	60F	2-dr SV HT-6P	2562	3535	9,761
N/A	73C	4-dr Sed-6P	2333	3515	65,995
N/A	76B	2-dr Conv-6P	2610	3620	7,293
N/A	79B	4-dr Sta Wag-6P	2776	3735	11,656

1954 Mercury Monterey four-door sedan, V-8. (PH)

1954 Mercury Monterey two-door convertible, V-8. (OCW)

ENGINE [Monterey V-8]: Overhead valve. Cast-iron block. Displacement: 256 cid. Bore and stroke: 3.62 x 3.10 inches. Compression ratio: 7.5:1. Brake hp: 161 at 4400 rpm. Five main bearings. Carburetor: Holley 2140 four-barrel.

CHASSIS FEATURES: Wheelbase: 118 inches. Overall length: 206.2 inches. Tires 7.10 x 15; (convertible and station wagon) 7.60 x 15.

POWERTRAIN OPTIONS: A three-speed manual transmission was standard. Overdrive and Merc-O-Matic Drive automatic transmission were optional.

CONVENIENCE OPTIONS: Power steering. Power brakes. Four-Way power seat. Radio. Heater. Fender skirts (Custom). Chrome rocker panels (Custom). Whitewall tires. Solex glass.

HISTORY: The 256 cid V-8 was Mercury's first all-new engine since 1939. It featured solid-skirt aluminum alloy pistons, and was rated at 238 lbs.-ft. of torque at 2500 rpm.

1955 MERCURY

1955 Mercury Model 60B Monterey. (OCW)

CUSTOM SERIES — Mercurys were restyled this year. They were longer, lower and wider. Yet they bore a definite resemblance to the 1954 models. The bumper-integrated grille had three heavy vertical bars between the upper and lower bumper. The tall, vertical taillights had a 'chubby cheeks' look. The Custom had slightly different side chrome than the other series. Its rear fender molding was plainer. The Custom station wagon did not have fake wood trim. All 1955 Mercurys featured a wraparound windshield and hooded headlights.

CUSTOM I.D. NUMBERS: Custom serial numbers were: 55WA10001M to 55WA94613M and 55LA10001M to 55LA48892M. The plant codes were DA = Dearborn; LA = Los Angeles; ME = Metuchen; SL = St. Louis and WA = Wayne.

CUSTOM

Model No.	Body/ Style No.	Body Type & Seating	Factory Price	Shipping Weight	Prod. Total
N/A	60E	2-dr HT Cpe-6P	2341	3480	7,040
N/A	70B	2-dr Sed-6P	2218	3395	31,295
N/A	73B	4-dr Sed-6P	2277	3450	21,219
N/A	79B	4-dr Sta Wag-6P	2686	3780	13,134

1955 Mercury Custom two-door sedan, V-8. (OCW)

1955 Mercury Monterey four-door sedan, V-8. (OCW)

ENGINE [Custom V-8]: Overhead valve. Cast-iron block. Displacement: 292 cid. Bore and stroke: 3.75 x 3.30 inches. Compression ratio: 7.6:1. Brake hp: 188 at 4400 rpm. Carburetor: four-barrel.

MONTEREY SERIES — The rear fender trim was lower on the Monterey than on the Custom. It also had chrome rocker panels and a bright band of molding under the windows. 'Monterey' was written in chrome on the front fenders of the sedan and hardtop. The name was placed on the rear doors of the station wagon. A round medallion was placed next to the nameplate.

MONTEREY I.D. NUMBERS: Custom serial numbers were: 55WA10001M to 55WA94613M and 55LA10001M to 55LA46692. The plant codes were: DA = Dearborn; LA = Los Angeles; ME = Metuchen; SL = St. Louis and WA = Wayne.

MONTEREY

Model No.	Body/ Style No.	Body Type & Seating	Factory Price	Shipping Weight	Prod. Total
N/A	60B	2-dr HT Cpe-6P	2465	3510	69,093
N/A	73C	4-dr Sed-6P	2400	3500	70,392
N/A	79C	4-dr Sta Wag-6P	2844	3770	11,968

ENGINE [Monterey V-8]: Overhead valve. Cast-iron block. Displacement: 292 cid. Bore and stroke: 3.75 x 3.30 inches. Compression ratio: 7.6:1. Brake hp: 188 at 4400 rpm. Carburetor: four-barrel.

MONTCLAIR SERIES — In addition to a round medallion and the model name on the front fenders, Montclairs also had a narrow band of chrome under the side windows, which outlined a small panel. They were slightly lower than other Mercurys. The Sun Valley had a tinted plexiglass section over the front half of its roof.

1955 Mercury Montclair four-door sedan, V-8. (OCW)

1955 Mercury Montclair two-door convertible, V-8. (PH)

MONTCLAIR I.D. NUMBERS: Serial numbers were: 55ME10001M to 55ME87345M and 55SL10001M to 55SL13753M. The plant codes were: DA = Dearborn; LA = Los Angeles; ME = Metuchen; SL = St. Louis and WA = Wayne.

MONTCLAIR

Model No.	Body/ Style No.	Body Type & Seating	Factory Price	Shipping Weight	Prod. Total
N/A	58A	4-dr Sed-6P	2685	3600	20,624
N/A	64A	2-dr HT Cpe-6P	2631	3490	71,588
N/A	64B	2-dr SV HT-6P	2712	3560	1,787
N/A	76B	2-dr Conv-6P	2712	3665	10,668

ENGINE [Montclair V-8]: Overhead valve. Cast-iron block. Displacement: 292 cid. Bore and stroke: 3.75 x 3.30 inches. Compression ratio: 8.5:1. Brake hp: 198 at 4400 rpm. Carburetor: four-barrel.

CHASSIS FEATURES: Wheelbase: (passenger car) 119 inches; (station wagon) 118 inches. Overall length: (passenger car) 206.3 inches; (station wagon) 201.7 inches. Overall height: (Montclair) 58.6 inches; (station wagon) 62.45 inches; (others) 61.2 inches. Tires: (convertible) 7.10 x 15; (station wagon) 7.60 x 15.

POWERTRAIN OPTIONS: A three-speed manual transmission was standard. Overdrive and Merc-O-Matic automatic transmission were optional. A 198-hp V-8 was available at extra cost on cars with the automatic.

CONVENIENCE OPTIONS: Power brakes. Power steering. Whitewall tires. Four-Way power seat. Heater. Power windows. Radio. Custom two-tone paint. Custom fender skirts.

HISTORY: Mercury shared honors with Chevrolet as *Motor Trend* magazine's 'Car of the Year'. Part of the credit for this belonged to the Merc's improved, ball-and-socket joint front suspension. Since 1945, Mercury had been under combined management with Lincoln. Both became separate divisions in the spring of 1955.

1956 MERCURY

1956 Mercury Medalist two-door sedan (early trim version), V-8. (OCW)

1956-1/2 Mercury Medalist two-door hardtop, V-8. (PH)

MEDALIST SERIES — The new Medalist was Mercury's low-priced car. A two-door sedan with frugal use of side chrome was introduced in September of 1955. Three additional models—with more elaborate trim—were added to the Medalist lineup when it achieved full series status at midyear. The Medalist lacked the front bumper guards found on the more expensive series. Like all 1956 Mercs, it had a big 'M' medallion on the front of the hood and the word 'Mercury' was spelled out in block letters on the center horizontal grille bar.

MEDALIST I.D. NUMBERS: Medalist serial numbers were: 56WA10001M to 56WA69956M and 56LA10001M to 56LA51292M. The plant codes were: DA = Dearborn; LA = Los Angeles; ME = Metuchen; SL = St. Louis and WA = Wayne.

MEDALIST

Model No.	Body/ Style No.	Body Type & Seating	Factory Price	Shipping Weight	Prod. Total
N/A	57D	4-dr HT Sed-6P	2458	3530	6,685
N/A	64E	2-dr HT Cpe-6P	2389	3545	11,892
N/A	70C	2-dr Sed-6P	2254	3430	20,582
N/A	73D	4-dr Sed-6P	2313	3500	6,653

ENGINE [Medalist V-8]: Overhead valve. Cast-iron block. Displacement: 312 cid. Bore and stroke: 3.80 x 3.44 inches. Compression ratio: 8.0:1. Brake hp: 210 at 4600 rpm. Carburetor: four-barrel.

1956 Mercury Custom four-door sedan, V-8. (PH)

1956 Mercury Custom two-door convertible, V-8. (PH)

CUSTOM SERIES — Chrome window trim was the main styling difference between the Custom and the Medalist (the Medalist two-door sedan also used slightly less side trim).

CUSTOM I.D. NUMBERS: Custom serial numbers were: 56WA10001M to 56WA89958M and 56LA10001M to 56LA51292M. The plant codes were: DA = Dearborn; LA = Los Angeles; ME = Metuchen; SL = St. Louis and WA = Wayne.

CUSTOM

Model No.	Body/ Style No.	Body Type & Seating	Factory Price	Shipping Weight	Prod. Total
N/A	57C	4-dr HT Sed-6P	2555	3550	12,187
N/A	64C	2-dr HT Cpe-6P	2485	3560	20,857
N/A	70B	2-dr Sed-6P	2351	3505	16,343
N/A	73B	4-dr Sed-6P	2410	3520	15,860
N/A	76A	2-dr Conv-6P	2712	3665	2,311
N/A	79B	4-dr Sta Wag-8P	2819	3860	9,292
N/A	79D	4-dr Sta Wag-6P	2722	3790	8,478

ENGINE [Custom V-8]: Overhead valve. Cast-iron block. Displacement: 312 cid. Bore and stroke: 3.80 x 3.44 inches. Compression ratio: 8.0:1. Brake hp: 210 at 4600 rpm. Carburetor: four-barrel.

MONTEREY SERIES — The 1956 Monterey looked a lot like the previous year's model. The hooded headlights, vertical 'chubby cheek' taillights, and bumper-integrated grille were little changed. Montereys featured heavy chrome trim around the side windows and chrome rocker panels. The side body molding made a sort of lightning bolt pattern. 'Monterey' was written in chrome on the front fenders.

MONTEREY I.D. NUMBERS: Monterey serial numbers were: 56ME10001M to 56ME100055M; 56SL10001M to 56SL125006M. The plant codes were: DA = Dearborn; LA = Los Angeles; ME = Metuchen; SL = St. Louis and WA = Wayne.

MONTEREY

Model No.	Body/ Style No.	Body Type & Seating	Factory Price	Shipping Weight	Prod. Total
N/A	57B	4-dr HT Sed-6P	2700	3800	10,726
N/A	58B	4-dr Spt Sed-6P	2652	3550	11,765
N/A	64C	2-dr HT Cpe-6P	2630	3590	42,863
N/A	73C	4-dr Sed-6P	2555	3570	26,735
N/A	79C	4-dr Sta Wag-6P	2977	3885	13,280

ENGINE [Monterey V-8]: Overhead valve. Cast-iron block. Displacement: 312 cid. Bore and stroke: 3.80 x 3.44 inches. Compression ratio: 8.0:1. Brake hp: 210 at 4600 rpm. Carburetor: four-barrel.

1956 Mercury Monterey four-door sedan, V-8. (OCW)

1956 Mercury Monterey two-door hardtop, V-8. (AA)

1956 Mercury Montclair two-door hardtop, V-8. (OCW)

MONTCLAIR SERIES — Top-of-the-line Montclairs had a narrow color panel surrounded by chrome trim below the side windows and chrome rocker panels. A round medallion was placed near the tip of the front fender side trim. 'Montclair' was written, in chrome, on the front fenders. The four-door Sport Sedan was replaced, early in the model year, by a four-door hardtop 'Phaeton' (body/style number 57C).

MONTCLAIR I.D. NUMBERS: Serial numbers were: 56ME10001M to 56ME100055M; 56SL10001M to 56SL125006M. The plant codes were: DA = Dearborn; LA = Los Angeles, ME = Metuchen; SL = St. Louis and WA = Wayne.

MONTCLAIR

Model No.	Body/ Style No.	Body Type & Seating	Factory Price	Shipping Weight	Prod. Total
N/A	57A	4-dr HT Sed-6P	2635	3640	23,493
N/A	58A	4-dr Spt Sed-6P	2766	3610	9,617
N/A	64A	2-dr HT Cpe-6P	2765	3620	50,562
N/A	76B	2-dr Conv-6P	2900	3725	7,762

ENGINE [Montclair V-8]: Overhead valve. Cast-iron block. Displacement: 312 cid. Bore and stroke 3.80 x 3.44 inches. Compression ratio: 8.0:1. Brake hp: 210 at 4600 rpm. Carburetor: four-barrel.

CHASSIS FEATURES: Wheelbase: (passenger car) 119 inches; (station wagon) 118 inches. Overall length: 206.4 inches. Overall width: 76.4 inches. Tires 7.10 x 15; (convertible and station wagon) 7.60 x 15 inches.

POWERTRAIN OPTIONS: A three-speed manual transmission was standard. Overdrive and Merc-O-Matic Drive automatic transmission were optional. Cars equipped with an automatic came with a 312 cid/225-hp V-8 with four-barrel carburetor. In midyear, a new camshaft raised the output in the standard and 225-hp V-8s by 10. Also the M-260 package (two four-barrel carburetors, 260-hp) was offered in all series later in the year.

CONVENIENCE OPTIONS: Power lubrication. Power brakes. Power steering. Four-Way power seat. Air conditioning. Seat belts. Whitewall tires. Radio. Power windows. Padded dash.

HISTORY: Dual exhaust were standard on all Montclairs and Montereys. Almost 90 percent of all 1956 Mercurys were sold with automatic transmission. 78.4 percent had whitewall tires, 88 percent had back-up lights and 96 percent had heaters. Only 11 percent were equipped with an air conditioner. Mercury won five NASCAR Grand National races in 1956.

1957 MERCURY

1957 Mercury convertible cruiser. (OCW)

1957 Mercury Montclair convertible. (OCW)

1957 Mercury Voyager station wagon. (OCW)

MONTEREY SERIES — Mercurys were completely restyled for 1957. For the first time, the marque had bodies that were exclusive to it and not based on Fords or Lincolns. A concave vertical bar grille; front hinged hood; 'V' shaped taillights; upper rear fender and rear deck sculpturing and cowl vent intakes were several of the new features. A chrome 'M' was placed between the grille and bumper. Early models had two headlights; later ones had four.

MONTEREY I.D. NUMBERS: Monterey serial numbers were: 57WA10001M to 57WA90490M and 57LA10001M to 57LA40854M. The plant codes were: DA = Dearborn; LA = Los Angeles; ME = Metuchen; SL = St. Louis and WA = Wayne.

MONTEREY

Model No.	Body/ Style No.	Body Type & Seating	Factory Price	Shipping Weight	Prod. Total
N/A	57A	4-dr HT Sed-6P	2763	3915	22,475
N/A	58A	4-dr Sed-6P	2645	3890	53,839
N/A	63A	2-dr HT Cpe-6P	2693	3870	42,199
N/A	64A	2-dr Sed-6P	2576	3875	33,982
N/A	76A	2-dr Conv-6P	3005	4035	5,003

ENGINE [Monterey V-8]: Overhead valve. Cast-iron block. Displacement: 312 cid. Bore and stroke: 3.80 x 3.44 inches. Compression ratio: 9.7:1. Brake hp: 255 at 4600 rpm. Carburetor: Holley four-barrel.

1957 Mercury Montclair two-door convertible, V-8. (OCW)

1957 Mercury Montclair four-door sedan, V-8. (PH)

MONTCLAIR SERIES — Chrome headlight rims, nameplates on the upper front fenders and an emblem ornament on the rear shelf of sedans and hardtops were the main differences between Montclairs and Montereys. Convertibles in both series had a plexiglass wrap-around rear window.

MONTCLAIR I.D. NUMBERS: Serial numbers were: 57WA10001M to 57WA90490M and 57LA10001M to 57LA40854M. The plant codes were: DA = Dearborn; LA = Los Angeles; ME = Metuchen; SL = St. Louis and WA = Wayne.

MONTCLAIR

Model No.	Body/ Style No.	Body Type & Seating	Factory Price	Shipping Weight	Prod. Total
N/A	57B	4-dr HT Sed-6P	3317	3925	21,156
N/A	58B	4-dr Sed-6P	3188	3905	19,836
N/A	63B	2-dr HT Cpe-6P	3236	3900	30,111
N/A	76B	2-dr Conv-6P	3430	4010	4,248

ENGINE [Montclair V-8]: Overhead valve. Cast-iron block. Displacement: 312 cid. Bore and stroke: 3.80 x 3.44 inches. Compression ratio: 9.7:1. Brake hp: 255 at 4600 rpm. Carburetor: Holley four-barrel.

TURNPIKE CRUISER SERIES — The Turnpike Cruiser was one of the most gadget-laden cars ever built. It was said to have been based on the XM-Turnpike Cruiser, although the opposite is true. All power items were standard. Other special features included: an overhanging roof with retractable rear window; air ducts mounted on top of the

1957 Mercury Turnpike Cruiser two-door hardtop, V-8. (OCW)

1957 Mercury Turnpike Cruiser four-door hardtop, V-8. (OCW)

windshield (with fake aerial sticking out of them); power seat with a memory dial; rubber instrument bezels; special starter button; clock odometer; sliding door locks; and gold anodized insert in the upper rear fender concave section, which led to the taillights.

TURNPIKE CRUISER I.D. NUMBERS: Serial numbers were: 57ME10001M to 57ME65895M and 57SL10001M to 57SL98451M. The plant codes were: DA = Dearborn; LA = Los Angeles; ME = Metuchen; SL = St. Louis and WA = Wayne.

TURNPIKE CRUISER

Model No.	Body/ Style No.	Body Type & Seating	Factory Price	Shipping Weight	Prod. Total
N/A	65A	2-dr HT Cpe-6P	3758	4005	7,291
N/A	75A	4-dr HT Sed-6P	3849	4015	8,305
N/A	76S	2-dr Conv-6P	4103	4100	1,265

ENGINE [Turnpike Cruiser V-8]: Overhead valve. Cast-iron block. Displacement: 368 cid. Bore and stroke: 4.00 x 3.65 inches. Compression ratio: 9.7:1. Brake hp: 290 at 4600 rpm. Five main bearings. Carburetor: Holley four-barrel.

STATION WAGON SERIES — Station wagons were a separate series this year. The top-of-the-line model was the Colony Park. It featured four-door hardtop styling and fake wood trim. The mid-priced wagon was the Voyager. It had a rear vent window like the Colony Park, but did not have wood trim. The lowest priced wagon, the Commuter, looked about the same as the Voyager but lacked a rear vent window.

STATION WAGON I.D. NUMBERS: Serial numbers were: 57WA10001M to 57WA90490M and 57LA10001M to 57LA40654M. The plant codes were: DA = Dearborn; LA = Los Angeles; ME = Metuchen; SL = St. Louis and WA = Wayne.

1957 Mercury Voyager four-door hardtop station wagon, V-8. (OCW)

STATION WAGON

Model No.	Body/ Style No.	Body Type & Seating	Factory Price	Shipping Weight	Prod. Total
N/A	56A	2-dr Comm-6P	2903	4115	4,665
N/A	56B	2-dr Voy-6P	3403	4240	2,283
N/A	77A	4-dr Comm-6P	2973	4195	11,990
N/A	77B	4-dr Col Prk-8P	3677	4240	7,386
N/A	77C	4-dr Comm-8P	3070	4195	5,752
N/A	77D	4-dr Voy-8P	3403	4240	3,716

ENGINE [Station Wagon]: Commuter and Voyager the same as Monterey. Colony Park the same as Turnpike Cruiser.

CHASSIS FEATURES: Wheelbase: 122 inches. Overall length: 211.1 inches. Overall width: 79.1 inches. Tires: 8.00 x 14; (convertible and station wagon) 8.50 x 14.

POWERTRAIN OPTIONS: A three-speed manual transmission was standard in the station wagons and Monterey. Overdrive and Merc-O-Matic automatic transmission were optional. An automatic was standard in the Turnpike Cruiser and Montclair. A 368 cid/290-hp V-8 was optional for the Commuter, Voyager, Montclair and Monterey. The M-335 power package (two four-barrel carbs, 368 cid/335-hp V-8) was optional on Montereys.

CONVENIENCE OPTIONS: Continental kit. Seat-O-Matic. Power steering. Power brakes. Radio. Heater. Whitewall tires. Air conditioning.

HISTORY: With the exception of the Turnpike Cruiser, the early 1957 Mercurys with two headlights had model names at the front of the front fenders, above the side trim. The later models, with four headlights, had model names on the front fenders behind the wheelwells, below the side trim. About one-third (32.6 percent) of 1957 Mercurys came with four headlights. All but 3.9 percent had automatic transmission. Three of the least popular options were air conditioning (1.5 percent), power windows (7.3 percent) and overdrive (1.4 percent). In 1959, *Motor Trend* magazine claimed the 1957 Monterey hardtop was one of the most popular used mid-priced cars. Mercury was the Official Pace Car at the 1957 Indianapolis 500 race.

1958 MERCURY

1958 Mercury two-door sedan (prototype with Medalist script), V-8. (OCW)

MEDALIST SERIES — Only prototype models carried the Medalist script, while the actual production two-door and four-door sedans in this series were referred to as either Mercury or low-priced Mercury. The 1958 Mercury grille was divided into two sections enclosed in the massive bumpers. A chrome 'M' was in the center of the grille. The sculptured rear fenders remained, but the 'V' shaped taillights were altered a bit. There was now a 'projectile' light attached to them. The hood and fenders were new for 1958. Side window trim was painted on the models in this series.

MEDALIST I.D. NUMBERS: Serial numbers were: W500001 to W547046. Plant codes: W = Wayne; J = Los Angeles; T = Metuchen; Z = St Louis.

MEDALIST

Model No.	Body/ Style No.	Body Type & Seating	Factory Price	Shipping Weight	Prod. Total
N/A	58C	4-dr Sed-6P	2617	3875	10,982
N/A	64B	2-dr Sed-6P	2547	3790	7,750

ENGINE [Medalist V-8]: Overhead valve. Cast-iron block. Displacement: 312 cid. Bore and stroke: 3.80 x 3.44 inches. Compression ratio: 9.7:1. Brake hp: 235 at 4600 rpm. Five main bearings. Carburetor: Holley four-barrel.

1958 Mercury Montclair Turnpike Cruiser four-door hardtop, V-8. (OCW)

MONTEREY SERIES — A single full-length chrome strip, which started at the headlights, was used on Monterey station wagons and two-door hardtops. An extra trim piece, running parallel to the first, extended from the front fender to slightly past the front doors on four-door styles. The rear bumper pods contained concave dividers. The Monterey name was on the front fenders.

MONTEREY I.D. NUMBERS: Serial numbers were: W500001 to W547046 and J500001 and up. Plant codes: W = Wayne; J = Los Angeles; T = Metuchen; Z = St Louis.

MONTEREY

Model No.	Body/ Style No.	Body Type & Seating	Factory Price	Shipping Weight	Prod. Total
N/A	57A	4-dr HT Sed-6P	2840	4150	6,909
N/A	58A	4-dr Sed-6P	2721	4160	28,892
N/A	63A	2-dr HT Cpe-6P	2769	4075	13,693
N/A	64A	2-dr Sed-6P	2652	4080	10,526
N/A	76A	2-dr Conv-6P	3081	4225	2,292

ENGINE [Monterey V-8]: Overhead valve. Cast-iron block. Displacement: 383 cid. Bore and stroke: 3.25 x 3.29 inches. Compression ratio: 10.5:1. Brake hp: 312 at 4600 rpm. Five main bearings. Carburetor: Holley four-barrel.

MONTCLAIR SERIES — Distinguishing features of the Montclair were two full-length side chrome strips with silver trim between them, and chrome headlight rims. The Turnpike Cruiser was now part of the Montclair series. It featured an overhanging rear roof, retractable rear window and twin air intakes on the roof above both sides of the windshield.

MONTCLAIR I.D. NUMBERS: Serial numbers were the same as for Montereys plus T500001 and up and, also, Z500001 and up. Plant codes: W = Wayne; J = Los Angeles; T = Metuchen; Z = St Louis.

MONTCLAIR

Model No.	Body/ Style No.	Body Type & Seating	Factory Price	Shipping Weight	Prod. Total
N/A	57B	4-dr HT Sed-6P	3365	4165	3,609
N/A	58B	4-dr Sed-6P	3236	4155	4,801
N/A	63B	2-dr HT Cpe-6P	3284	4085	5,012
N/A	65A	2-dr Tpk Crs-6P	3498	4150	2,864
N/A	85A	4-dr Tpk Crs-6P	3597	4230	3,543
N/A	76B	2-dr Conv-6P	3536	4295	844

ENGINE [Montclair V-8]: Overhead valve. Cast-iron block. Displacement: 383 cid. Bore and stroke: 4.29 x 3.29 inches. Compression ratio: 10.5:1. Brake hp: 330 at 4600 rpm. Five main bearings. Carburetor: Holley four-barrel (standard in Montclair).

1958 Mercury Montclair four-door hardtop, V-8. (PH)

1958 Mercury Park Lane four-door hardtop, V-8. (OCW)

ENGINE [Turnpike Cruiser V-8]: Overhead valve. Cast-iron block. Displacement: 430 cid. Bore and stroke: 4.29 x 3.70 inches. Compression ratio: 10.5:1. Brake hp: 360 at 4600 rpm. Carburetor: Holley four-barrel.

PARK LANE SERIES — The new Park Lane was introduced to compete with Buick's Roadmaster. Front fender ornaments, rear roof panel nameplates, chrome headlight rims and rectangular pattern trim in the rear bumper pods were styling features of the Park Lane. Like the Montclair, the Park Lane convertible had a wraparound rear window.

PARK LANE I.D. NUMBERS: Serial numbers were T500001 and up and, also, Z500001 and up. Plant codes: W = Wayne; J = Los Angeles; T = Metuchen; Z = St. Louis.

PARK LANE

Model No.	Body/ Style No.	Body Type & Seating	Factory Price	Shipping Weight	Prod. Total
N/A	57C	4-dr HT Sed-6P	3944	4390	5,241
N/A	63C	2-dr HT Cpe-6P	3867	4280	3,158
N/A	76C	2-dr Conv-6P	4118	4405	853

ENGINE [Park Lane V-8]: Overhead valve. Cast-iron block. Displacement: 430 cid. Bore and stroke: 4.29 x 3.70 inches. Compression ratio: 10.5:1. Brake hp: 360 at 4600 rpm. Carburetor: Holley four-barrel.

STATION WAGON SERIES — The 1958 Mercury station wagons were based on the Montclair. The Colony Park had simulated wood trim. Like the Voyager and Commuter, it featured a pillarless hardtop look.

STATION WAGON I.D. NUMBERS: See Park Lane I.D. Numbers. Plant codes: W = Wayne; J = Los Angeles; T = Metuchen; Z = St Louis.

STATION WAGON

Model No.	Body/ Style No.	Body Type & Seating	Factory Price	Shipping Weight	Prod. Total
N/A	58A	2-dr Comm-6P	3035	4400	1,912
N/A	56B	2-dr Voy-6P	3535	4435	568
N/A	77A	4-dr Comm-6P	3105	4485	8,601
N/A	77B	4-dr Col Prk-6P	3775	4605	4,474
N/A	77C	4-dr Comm-9P	3201	4525	4,227
N/A	77D	4-dr Voy-6P	3635	4540	2,520

ENGINE [Station Wagon]: Commuter the same as Monterey. Voyager and Colony Park the same as Montclair.

POWERTRAIN OPTIONS: A three-speed manual was standard on station wagons, Medalists and Monterey. Overdrive and Merc-O-Matic automatic transmissions were optional. Merc-O-Matic was standard on the Montclair. Multi-Drive automatic was standard on the Park Lane. A 430 cid/360-hp V-8 was optional on the Montclair. A 430 cid/400-hp V-8 with three two-barrel carburetors was optional on all series. Dual exhaust were a $32.30 option.

1958 Mercury Colony Park four-door hardtop station wagon, V-8. (OCW)

CHASSIS FEATURES: Wheelbase: (Park Lane) 125 inches; (others) 122 inches. Overall length: (station wagon) 214.2 inches; (Park Lane) 220.2 inches; (others) 213.2 inches. Tires: (convertible, Park Lane and station wagon) 8.50 x 14; (others) 8.00 x 14.

CONVENIENCE OPTIONS: Tinted glass ($34.40). Two-tone paint ($17.20). Power lubricator ($43). Power steering ($107.50). Power windows ($107.50). Power brakes ($37.70). Four-Way power seat ($69.90). Seat-O-Matic ($96.80). Radio with electric antenna ($149.50). Push-button radio ($100). Rear speaker ($16.20). Manual heater and defroster ($91.40). Heater and defroster with Climate Control ($109.49). Electric clock ($15.10). Air conditioner and heater ($458.75). Padded instrument panel ($21.50). Power retracting station wagon window ($32.30). Windshield washer ($14). Speed limit safety monitor ($12.90). Wheel covers ($12.90). Nylon four-ply 8.00 x 14 whitewall tires ($67.40); Rayon four-ply 8.00 x 14 whitewall tires ($41). Foam rubber cushions ($21.90).

HISTORY: Only one percent of all 1958 Mercurys came with a manual transmission and overdrive.

1959 MERCURY

1959 Mercury Commuter Country Cruiser station wagon. (OCW)

MONTEREY SERIES — Mercurys once again shared a strong family resemblance with Fords, at least from the front. The bumper-integrated grille of last year was replaced by a separate honeycomb grille and plain, wraparound bumper that contained the signal lights. The concave side body sculpturing now extended almost to the front fenders. The wraparound windshield was larger and curved upward. Glass area size of the back window was also increased. The backlights on four-door and two-door hardtop models curved upward. Four-door and two-door sedans had a unique roof line and a large wraparound rear window. In addition to distinct front fender nameplates, Montereys had a horizontal ribbed rear panel and three chrome bands on the upper rear fenders, in front of the taillights.

MONTEREY I.D. NUMBER: Monterey serial numbers started with: ( )9( )A500001. Code consisted of 10 symbols. The first represented the engine: P = 312 cid two-barrel; N = 383 cid two-barrel; M = 383 cid four-barrel; L = 430 cid four-barrel; K = 430 cid six-barrel. The second symbol stands for the year (9 = 1959). The third symbol represents the assembly plant: J = California; W = Michigan; Z = Missouri and T = New Jersey. The fourth symbol indicates the series: A = Monterey; B = Montclair; C = Park Lane and D = station wagon. The fifth symbol (5) stands for the Mercury Division. The following group of digits is the sequential vehicle production number.

1959 Mercury Monterey two-door hardtop, V-8. (AA)

1959 Mercury Monterey four-door sedan, V-8. (PH)

1959 Mercury Montclair two-door hardtop, V-8. (OCW)

MONTEREY

Model No.	Body/ Style No.	Body Type & Seating	Factory Price	Shipping Weight	Prod. Total
N/A	57A	4-dr HT Sed-6P	2918	4065	11,355
N/A	58A	4-dr Sed-6P	2832	4140	43,570
N/A	63A	2-dr HT Sed-6P	2654	4215	17,232
N/A	64A	2-dr Sed-6P	2768	3975	12,694
N/A	76A	2-dr Conv-6P	3150	4295	4,426

ENGINES [Monterey V-8]: Overhead valve. Cast-iron block. Displacement: 312 cid. Bore and stroke: 3.79 x 3.43 inches. Compression ratio: 8.75:1. Brake hp: 210 at 4400 rpm. Five main bearings. Carburetor: Holley 2300 two-barrel.

MONTCLAIR SERIES — The Montclair had four chrome bands on the upper rear fender, full-length lower body moldings, bright metal 'cubed' grid pattern appliques on the rear panel and special nameplates under the chrome spears on the front fenders. A fabric and vinyl interior, padded dash, windshield washer, electric clock, parking brake, warning light and foam rubber cushions were standard.

MONTCLAIR I.D. NUMBERS: Montclair serial numbers started with: ( )9( )B500001. Code consisted of 10 symbols. The first represented the engine: P = 312 cid two-barrel; N = 383 cid two-barrel; M = 383 cid four-barrel; L = 430 cid four-barrel; K = 430 cid six-barrel. The second symbol stands for the year (9 = 1959). The third symbol represents the assembly plant: J = California; W = Michigan; Z = Missouri and T = New Jersey. The fourth symbol indicates the series: A = Monterey; B = Montclair; C = Park Lane and D = station wagon. The fifth symbol (5) stands for the Mercury Division. The following group of digits is the sequential vehicle production number.

MONTCLAIR

Model No.	Body/ Style No.	Body Type & Seating	Factory Price	Shipping Weight	Prod. Total
N/A	57B	4-dr HT Sed-6P	3437	4275	6,713
N/A	58B	4-dr Sed-6P	3308	4240	9,514
N/A	63B	2-dr HT Cpe-6P	3357	4150	7,375

ENGINE [Montclair V-8]: Overhead valve. Cast-iron block. Displacement: 383 cid. Bore and stroke: 4.30 x 3.30 inches. Compression ratio: 10.0:1. Brake hp: 322 at 4600 rpm. Five main bearings. Carburetor: Mercury four-barrel.

1959 Mercury Park Lane four-door hardtop, V-8. (OCW)

PARK LANE SERIES — Styling distinctions of the Park Lane included chrome-plated projectiles on the rear fender coves, full-length lower body moldings, large aluminum gravel guards on the lower rear quarter panels, bright roof moldings and front fender (instead of hood) ornaments. Rear panel trim was the same as on the Montclair. Once again the Park Lane convertible (like the Monterey) had a wraparound rear window. Park Lanes came equipped with the same items as Montclairs plus power steering, power self-adjusting brakes, dual exhaust, back-up lights, rear center armrest and rear cigarette lighter.

PARK LANE I.D. NUMBERS: Park Lane serial numbers started with ( )9( )C500001. Code consisted of 10 symbols. The first represented the engine: P = 312 cid two-barrel; N = 383 cid two-barrel; M = 383 cid four-barrel; L = 430 cid four-barrel; K = 430 cid six-barrel. The second symbol stands for the year (9 = 1959). The third symbol represents the assembly plant: J = California; W = Michigan; Z = Missouri and T = New Jersey. The fourth symbol indicates the series: A = Monterey; B = Montclair; C = Park Lane and D = station wagon. The fifth symbol (5) stands for the Mercury Division. The following group of digits is the sequential vehicle production number.

PARK LANE

Model No.	Body/ Style No.	Body Type & Seating	Factory Price	Shipping Weight	Prod. Total
N/A	57C	4-dr HT Sed-6P	4031	4445	7,206
N/A	63C	2-dr HT Cpe-6P	3955	4365	4,060
N/A	76C	2-dr Conv-6P	4206	4575	1,257

ENGINE [Park Lane V-8]: Overhead valve. Cast-iron block. Displacement: 430 cid. Bore and stroke: 4.30 x 3.70 inches. Compression ratio: 10.0:1. Brake hp: 345 at 4400 rpm. Five main bearings. Carburetor: AFB-2653S four-barrel.

COUNTRY CRUISER STATION WAGON SERIES — The Commuter station wagons shared trim styling with Montereys. Voyager and Colony Park station wagon trim was like that used on Montclairs, except the Colony Park had simulated wood panels.

COUNTRY CRUISER STATION WAGON I.D. NUMBERS: Country Cruiser serial numbers started with: ( )9( )D500001. Code consisted of 10 symbols. The first represented the engine: P = 312 cid two-barrel; N = 383 cid two-barrel; M = 383 cid four-barrel; L = 430 cid four-barrel; K = 430 cid six-barrel. The second symbol stands for the year (9 = 1959). The third symbol represents the assembly plant: J = California; W = Michigan; Z = Missouri and T = New Jersey. The fourth symbol indicates the series: A = Monterey; B = Montclair; C = Park Lane and D = station wagon. The fifth symbol (5) stands for the Mercury Division. The following group of digits is the sequential vehicle production number.

COUNTRY CRUISER STATION WAGONS

Model No.	Body/ Style No.	Body Type & Seating	Factory Price	Shipping Weight	Prod. Total
N/A	56A	2-dr Comm-6P	3035	4400	1,051
N/A	77A	4-dr Comm-6P	3105	4485	15,122
N/A	77B	4-dr Col Prk-6P	3932	4650	5,959
N/A	77D	4-dr Voy-6P	3793	4565	2,496

PRODUCTION NOTE: A two-door Voyager station wagon may have been built and sold in limited quantities.

ENGINE [Voyager And Colony Park V-8]: Overhead valve. Cast-iron block. Displacement: 383 cid. Bore and stroke: 4.30 x 3.30 inches. Compression ratio: 10.0:1. Brake hp: 322 at 4600 rpm. Five main bearings. Carburetor: Mercury four-barrel.

1959 Mercury Park Lane two-door convertible, V-8. (OCW)

ENGINE [Commuter V-8]: Overhead valve. Cast-iron block. Displacement: 383 cid. Bore and stroke: 4.29 x 3.29 inches. Compression ratio: 10.0:1. Brake hp: 280 at 4400 rpm. Carburetor: four-barrel.

POWERTRAIN OPTIONS: A three-speed manual transmission was standard on Montereys and Commuter station wagons. Merc-O-Matic automatic was standard on Montclair, Colony Park and Voyager station wagons. It was a $173.30 option in Montereys and Commuter station wagons. Multi-Drive Merc-O-Matic was standard in Park Lane and an extra cost option on other series. A 383 cid/280-hp V-8 was optional on the Monterey. A 383 cid/322-hp V-8 with four-barrel carburetor was optional in Montereys. A 430 cid/345-hp V-8 with four-barrel carburetor was optional in Montereys and Montclairs.

CHASSIS FEATURES: Wheelbase: (Park Lane) 128 inches; (others) 126 inches. Overall length: (station wagon) 218.2 inches; (Park Lane) 222.8 inches; (others) 217.8 inches. Tires: (Monterey) 8.00 x 14; (others) 8.50 x 14.

CONVENIENCE OPTIONS: Push-button radio ($68.75). Signal-seeking radio ($90.25). Rear seat radio speaker ($9.30). Electric clock in Monterey and Commuter ($14.20). Windshield washer ($11.75). Tinted glass ($34.90). Tinted windshield ($19.79). Air conditioner with heater ($385). Heater and defroster ($71.15). Heater and defroster with Climate Control ($84.95). Power steering ($83.50). Power brakes ($34.55). Four-Way power seat ($60.40). Seat-O-Matic power seat ($62.20). Power windows ($64.50). Dual exhaust ($25.60). Commuter power tailgate window ($26.80). Safety speed monitor ($12). Padded dash in Monterey and Commuter ($17.10). Back-up lights ($8.90).Courtesy light group ($9.30 Monterey). Whitewall tires ($32.95). Two-tone paint ($14.25). Lower back panel reflector ($10.90). Third seat for station wagons ($90.70). Optional Monterey trim ($30.60). Clear plastic seat covers ($29.95). Undercoating ($15). Outside rearview mirror ($6.95). Seat belts ($12.25 each).

HISTORY: The majority of 1959 Mercurys, 69.7 percent, came with power steering, 47.2 percent had tinted glass and 52.5 percent had power brakes.

1960 MERCURY

1960 Mercury Park Lane convertible. (OCW)

1960 Mercury Comet four-door sedan, 6-cyl. (PH)

COMET SERIES — Mercury introduced its compact Comet in March of 1960. It was the first car of the marque to be powered by a six-cylinder engine. The grille was similar to the one used on full-size Mercurys, but the rear fins and slanting taillights on sedans were distinctive to the Comet. The station wagon used a different rear end style and larger, rounded horizontal taillights. It looked like a dressed-up Falcon. Full-length chrome trim was placed on the bodysides.

COMET I.D. NUMBERS: Serial numbers started at OHO( ) 5800001. Serial number code: The first symbol designates the year. The second symbol designates the assembly plant as follows: R = California; K = Missouri; H = Ohio. The third and fourth symbols designate the body type as follows: four-door sedan = 12 or 02; two-door sedan = 11 or 01; four-door station wagon = 22 or 07; two-door station wagon = 21 or 08. The fifth symbol designates the engine as follows: S = 144 cid six; U = 170 cid six. See Monterey I.D. numbers for V-8s. The last six digits are the sequential vehicle production numbers.

COMET

Model No.	Body/ Style No.	Body Type & Seating	Factory Price	Shipping Weight	Prod. Total
N/A	54A	4-dr Sed-6P	2053	2433	47,416
N/A	59A	2-dr Sta Wag-6P	2310	2548	5,115
N/A	62A	2-dr Sed-6P	1998	2399	45,374
N/A	71A	4-dr Sta Wag-8P	2365	2581	18,426

ENGINE [Comet Six]: Overhead valve. Cast-iron block. Displacement: 144.3 cid. Bore and stroke: 3.50 x 2.50 inches. Compression ratio: 8.7:1. Brake hp: 90 at 4200 rpm. Four main bearings. Carburetor: Holley one-barrel.

CHASSIS FEATURES: Wheelbase: (passenger car) 114 inches; (station wagon) 109.5 inches. Overall length: (passenger car) 194.8 inches; (station wagon) 191.8 inches. Tires: (passenger car) 6.00 x 13; (station wagon) 6.50 x 13.

POWERTRAIN OPTIONS: A three-speed manual transmission was standard. Ford-O-Matic automatic was a $172 option.

CONVENIENCE OPTIONS: Deluxe trim package ($56). Heater and defroster ($74.30). Backup lights ($10.70). Padded instrument panel and visors ($22.40). Two-tone paint ($19.40). Push-button radio ($56.80). Station wagon electric tailgate window ($29.90). Whitewall tires, on sedans ($43.40); on station wagons ($33). Tinted windshield ($10.30). Wheel covers ($16). Windshield washers ($13.70). Two-speed electric windshield wipers ($9.65).

MONTEREY SERIES — The basic body shell was unchanged from 1959, but, except for the windshield and roof treatment, it was hard to see any resemblance. Unlike the previous few models, the new Mercury looked as if the people who designed the front and rear were from the same planet. The four-door sedan featured a wraparound back window. Flared fins and massive vertical taillights integrated into the bumper, highlighted the rear end treatment. Outside of full-length upper side body level moldings, the Monterey was relatively free of stylistic 'doo-dads'. Its rear deck panel had enamel finish.

1960 Mercury Country Cruiser Commuter four-door hardtop station wagon, V-8. (OCW)

MERCURY I.D. NUMBERS: Serial numbers started at 0( ) ( ) ( ) ( ) 500001. Serial number code: The first symbol designates the year: 0 = 1960. The second the assembly plant, as follows: A = Atlanta; B = Oakville, Ontario; E = Mahwah; F = Dearborn; G = Chicago; H = Lorain; J = Los Angeles; K = Kansas City; N = Norfolk; P = Twin Cities; R = San Jose; S = Allen Park; T = Metuchen; U = Louisville; W = Wayne; X = St. Thomas, Ontario; Y = Wixom; Z = St. Louis. The third and fourth numbers designate the body/style number. The fifth symbol designates the engine as follows: Four-cylinder = Y; Six-cylinder: S = 144 cid; T = 200 cid (one-barrel); U = (through 1972) 170 cid (one-barrel); V = (1960 to 1965) 223 cid (one-barrel); (1966) 240 cid (one-barrel); Z = (1975) 170 cid (two-barrel). Eight-cylinder: A = (1960s) 289 cid (four-barrel); (1973-1975) 460 cid (four-barrel); B = (1960s) 406 cid (four-barrel); C = (1966 to 1967) 289 cid (two-barrel); (1970-1971) 429 cid (four-barrel); F = (1960s) 406 cid (three two-barrels); (1970) 'Boss' 302 cid (four-barrel); H = (1970-1975) 351 cid (two-barrel); J = (1971-1972) Ram Air 429 cid (four-barrel); K = (1960s) 289 cid (four-barrel); (1970-1971) 429 cid (two-barrel); L = (1960s) 221 cid; (1970-1975) 250 cid (one-barrel); M = (1966) 410 cid (four-barrel); (1960s) 430 cid; (1970-1971) 351 cid (four-barrel); N = (1960s) 383 cid (two-barrel); (1970-1973) 429 cid (four-barrel); P = (1960s) 312 cid (two-barrel); (1970-1971) 429 cid (four-barrel); Q = (to 1966) 428 cid (four-barrel); (1970) 429 cid (four-barrel); (1972-1974) 351 cid (four-barrel); R = (1960s) 427 cid (dual four-barrel); (1970) Ram Air 429 cid (four-barrel); S = (1970-1975) 400 cid (two-barrel); W = (1960s) 292 cid (two-barrel); (1966) 427 cid (four-barrel); (1970) 351 cid (four-barrel); X = (1960s) 352 cid (two-barrel), (1966) 352 cid (four-barrel); Y = (1960-1970) 390 cid (two-barrel); Z = (1960s) 390 cid (four-barrel); (1970) Boss 429 cid (four-barrel). The last six digits are the sequential vehicle production numbers.

MONTEREY

Model No.	Body/ Style No.	Body Type & Seating	Factory Price	Shipping Weight	Prod. Total
N/A	57A	4-dr HT Sed-6P	2845	4061	9,536
N/A	58A	4-dr Sed-6P	2730	4029	49,594
N/A	63A	2-dr HT Cpe-6P	2781	3984	15,790
N/A	64A	2-dr Sed-6P	2631	3952	21,557
N/A	76A	2-dr Conv-6P	3077	4161	6,062

ENGINE [Monterey V-8]: Overhead valve. Cast-iron block. Displacement: 312 cid. Bore and stroke: 3.80 x 3.44 inches. Compression ratio: 8.9:1. Brake hp: 205 at 4000 rpm. Five main bearings. Carburetor: Holley 2300 two-barrel.

MONTCLAIR SERIES — Montclairs could be identified by their distinctive bright metal horizontal bar pattern, rear deck panel and three vertical chrome bars on the back doors of four-door models and on the panel in front of the rear tires on two-doors. They also had full-length lower body moldings. A model nameplate appeared on the rear fenders. Standard features included: electric clock, wheel covers, padded dash, courtesy light group and back-up lights.

MONTCLAIR

Model No.	Body/ Style No.	Body Type & Seating	Factory Price	Shipping Weight	Prod. Total
N/A	57B	4-dr HT Sed-6P	3394	4330	5,548
N/A	58B	4-dr Sed-6P	3280	4298	8,510
N/A	63B	2-dr HT Cpe-6P	3331	4253	5,756

ENGINE [Montclair V-8]: Overhead valve. Cast-iron block. Displacement: 430 cid. Bore and stroke: 4.30 x 3.70 inches. Compression ratio: 10.0:1. Brake hp: 310 at 4100 rpm. Five main bearings. Carburetor: Carter ABD-2965S two-barrel.

PARK LANE SERIES — The Park Lane had special 'cubed' pattern, bright metal trim between the trunk lid and rear bumper. Chrome also decorated the rocker and rear quarter panels. In addition, five vertical bars of chrome were placed in-a-row on the panel in front of the rear tires. Standard features included those found on the Montclair plus power brakes, power steering, windshield washer and inside non-glare mirror.

PARK LANE

Model No.	Body/ Style No.	Body Type & Seating	Factory Price	Shipping Weight	Prod. Total
N/A	57F	4-dr HT Sed-6P	3858	4421	5,788
N/A	63F	2-dr HT Cpe-6P	3794	4344	2,974
N/A	76D	2-dr Conv-6P	4018	4525	1,525

ENGINE [Park Lane V-8]: Overhead valve. Cast-iron block. Displacement: 430 cid. Bore and stroke: 4.30 x 3.70 inches. Compression ratio: 10.0:1. Brake hp: 310 at 4100 rpm. Five main bearings. Carburetor: Carter ABD-2965S two-barrel.

1960 Mercury Country Cruiser Colony Park four-door hardtop station wagon, V-8. (OCW)

COUNTRY CRUISER STATION WAGON SERIES — The Commuter station wagon was based on the Monterey series. The simulated wood-trimmed Colony Park came with the same standard equipment as Montclair plus a power rear window. Both station wagons had four-door hardtop styling.

COUNTRY CRUISER STATION WAGONS

Model No.	Body/ Style No.	Body Type & Seating	Factory Price	Shipping Weight	Prod. Total
N/A	77A	4-dr Comm-6P	3127	4303	14,949
N/A	77B	4-dr Col Prk-6P	3837	4568	7,411

ENGINE [Country Cruiser Station Wagon]: Commuter engine: see 1960 Monterey series engine data. Colony Park: see 1960 Montclair series engine data.

CHASSIS FEATURES: Wheelbase: 126 inches. Overall length: 219.2 inches. Tires: (Montclair, Colony Park) 6.50 x 14; (Park Lane) 9.00 x 14; (other models) 8.00 x 14.

POWERTRAIN OPTONS: A three-speed manual transmission was standard on Montereys and Commuter station wagons. Merc-O-Matic automatic was standard on Montclairs and Colony Park station wagons. Multi-Drive automatic transmission was standard on Park Lane. Merc-O-Matic transmission was optional on Monterey and Commuter. Multi-Drive was also available but not with the standard engine. Multi-Drive was a $25.50 option on Montclair and Colony Park. A 383 cid/280-hp V-8 (four-barrel) and a 430 cid/310-hp V-8 were optional on Monterey and Commuter.

CONVENIENCE OPTIONS: Tinted glass ($43.10). Air conditioner with heater ($472.10). Electric clock ($17). Heater and defroster ($78.70). Padded instrument panel in Monterey, Commuter ($21.30). Two-tone paint ($17). Power brakes ($43.20). Power rear tailgate window in Commuter ($32). Four-Way power seats ($78.50). Power steering ($106.20). Power windows ($106.20). Rear fender shields ($11.60). Push-button radio ($86). Rear seat radio speaker ($10.70). Tinted windshield ($29). Third seat for station wagons ($113.30). Trim option in Monterey, Commuter ($27.20). Wheel covers, Monterey, Commuter ($19.20). Five Rayon whitewall tires ($43.10). Visual aid group ($57).

HISTORICAL FOOTNOTE: The Comet had originally been planned as the successor to the Edsel. Twenty-four percent of Comets came with tinted glass, four percent had power windows and 62 percent had automatic transmission. Power windows and power seats were relatively unpopular options. Less than eight percent of full-size Mercurys were so-equipped in 1960.

COMET SERIES — A new grille and the addition of three vertical chrome pieces to the front fenders were the main difference between the 1961 Comet and the previous year's model. Mercury considered Comet a 'family-sized' compact. Advertising bragged the Comet was roomier and longer than most of its competition.

COMET/S-22 I.D. NUMBERS: The Vehicle Identification Number is on top surface of left-hand brace to firewall. First symbol: 1 = 1961. Second symbol identifies assembly plant: H = Lorain, Ohio; R = San Jose, Calif. Third and fourth symbols are body code (first two numbers in Body/Style Number in charts below). Fifth symbol identifies engine: S = 144 cid six; D = 144 cid six (low compression); U = 170 cid six; E = 170 cid six (low-compression). Last six symbols are sequential production number starting at 500001. Body plate on front body pillar gives VIN, body code, color, trim, date, engine, transmission and axle codes.

COMET SERIES

Model No.	Body/ Style No.	Body Type & Seating	Factory Price	Shipping Weight	Prod. Total
N/A	54A	4-dr Sed-6P	2053	2411	85,332
N/A	59A	2-dr Sta Wag-6P	2310	2548	4,199
N/A	62A	2-dr Sed-6P	1998	2376	71,563
N/A	71A	4-dr Sta Wag-6P	2353	2581	22,165

S-22 SERIES — The new S-22 coupe was basically a dressed-up Comet two-door sedan. It was introduced in midyear to cash in on the popularity of sporty compacts. Buyers could choose from 10 exterior colors. Standard features included front bucket seats with a vinyl-clad steel console between them, deep-loop yarn carpeting, front and rear armrests, Deluxe steering wheel and horn ring, rear fender medallion, extra insulation and factory-applied undercoating.

S-22 SERIES

Model No.	Body/ Style No.	Body Type & Seating	Factory Price	Shipping Weight	Prod. Total
N/A	62C	2-dr Sed-5P	2282	2432	14,004

METEOR 600 SERIES — Mercurys once again began to look like glamorous Fords. The concave, vertical bar grille housed four chrome rimmed headlights. The unusual roof lines of last year were replaced with square, crisp styling. Meteors had a midbody chrome spear that ran from almost the tip of the rear fender to the front tires. The taillights were small and circular and slightly extended. An ornament was on top of each front fender.

MERCURY I.D. NUMBERS: First symbol: 1 = 1961. Second symbol identifies assembly plant: E = Mahwah, N.J.; H = Lorain, Ohio; J = Los Angeles, Calif.; K = Kansas City, Kan.; R = San Jose, Calif.; W = Wayne, Mich.; Y = Wixom, Mich.; Z = St Louis, Mo. Third and fourth symbols are body code (first two numbers in Body/Style Number in charts below). Fifth symbol identifies engine: (Monterey) V = 223 cid six; W = 292 cid V-8; T = 292 cid V-8 (export); X = 352 cid V-8; (Mercury) same as Meteor, plus Z = 390 cid V-8; R = 390 cid V-8 (export). Last six symbols are sequential production number starting at 500001. Body plate on front body pillar gives VIN, body code, color, trim, date, engine, transmission and axle codes.

METEOR 600

Model No.	Body/ Style No.	Body Type & Seating	Factory Price	Shipping Weight	Prod. Total
N/A	58A	4-dr Sed-6P	2587	3714	Note 1
N/A	64A	2-dr Sed-6P	2533	3647	Note 1

NOTE 1: Total Meteor 600 production was 18,117 with no body style breakout available.

1960 Mercury Monterey two-door hardtop, V-8. (OCW)

1961 Mercury Meteor '600' two-door sedan, V-8. (OCW)

1961 Mercury Meteor '800' two-door hardtop, V-8. (OCW)

METEOR 800 SERIES — Three horizontal chrome bars on the front fenders, rocker panel molding, chromed tailfin tips and more roof panel trim helped distinguish the 800 series from the lower-priced 600 series. Back-up lights and an electric clock were a couple of standard extras.

METEOR 800

Model No.	Body/ Style No.	Body Type & Seating	Factory Price	Shipping Weight	Prod. Total
N/A	54A	4-dr Sed-6P	2765	3762	Note 1
N/A	62A	2-dr Sed-6P	2711	3680	Note 1
N/A	65A	2-dr HT-6P	2772	3694	Note 1
N/A	75A	4-dr HT-6P	2837	3780	Note 1

NOTE 1: Total Meteor 800 production was 35,005 with no body style breakout available.

MONTEREY SERIES — Chrome rear fender stone guards and full-length bodyside moldings were the main exterior styling features of the Monterey. The interior was plusher than the other series and a padded dash was standard.

MONTEREY

Model No.	Body/ Style No.	Body Type & Seating	Factory Price	Shipping Weight	Prod. Total
N/A	54B	4-dr Sed-6P	2869	3777	22,881
N/A	65B	2-dr HT-6P	2876	3709	10,942
N/A	75B	4-dr HT-6P	2941	3795	9,252
N/A	76A	2-dr Conv-6P	3126	3872	7,053

STATION WAGON SERIES — The Commuter station wagon looked like a Meteor. However, it only had two taillights, instead of six, and they were semi-rectangular rather than round. The Colony Park had imitation wood trim and a power tailgate window. It shared the same standard features as the Monterey.

STATION WAGONS

Model No.	Body/ Style No.	Body Type & Seating	Factory Price	Shipping Weight	Prod. Total
N/A	71A	4-dr Comm-6P	2922	4115	8,951
N/A	71B	4-dr Col Prk-6P	3118	4131	7,887

ENGINE [Comet/S-22 Six]: Overhead valve. Cast-iron block. Displacement: 144.3 cid. Bore and stroke: 3.50 x 2.50 inches. Compression ratio: 8.7:1. Brake hp: 85 at 4200 rpm. Four main bearings. Carburetor: Holley 1908 one-barrel.

ENGINE [Meteor Six]: Overhead valve. Cast-iron block. Displacement: 223 cid. Bore and stroke: 3.62 x 3.60 inches. Compression ratio: 8.4:1. Brake hp: 135 at 4000 rpm. Four main bearings. Carburetor: one-barrel.

ENGINE [Monterey V-8]: Overhead valve. Cast-iron block. Displacement: 292 cid. Bore and stroke: 3.75 x 3.30 inches. Compression ratio: 8.8:1. Brake hp: 175 at 4200 rpm. Five main bearings. Carburetor: Mercury two-barrel.

ENGINE [Station Wagon]: Commuter: See 1961 Meteor 600 series engine data. Colony Park: See 1961 Monterey series engine data.

1961 Mercury Monterey two-door hardtop, V-8. (OCW)

1961 Mercury Monterey four-door hardtop, V-8. (PH)

COMET/S-22 CHASSIS FEATURES: Wheelbase: (station wagon) 109.5 inches; (others) 114 inches. Overall length: (station wagon) 191.6 inches; (others) 194.6 inches. Tires: (station wagon) 6.50 x 13; (others) 6.00 x 13.

METEOR/MERCURY CHASSIS FEATURES: Wheelbase: 120 inches. Overall length: (station wagon) 214.4 inches; (others) 214.6 inches. Tires: (convertible and station wagon) 8.00 x 14; (others) 7.50 x 14.

COMET/S-22 OPTIONS: Fashion group interior and exterior trim ($66.90). Heater and defroster ($74.30). Back-up lights ($10.70). Padded instrument panel and visors ($22.40). Two-tone paint ($19.40). Push-button radio ($56.80). Electric tailgate window ($29.90). Whitewall tires, on passenger car ($43.40); on station wagon ($33). Tinted windshield ($10.30). Wheel covers ($16). Windshield washers ($13.70). Two-speed electric windshield wipers ($9.65). A three-speed manual transmission was standard. Ford-O-Matic automatic was optional. A 170 cid/101-hp six with one-barrel carburetor was available at extra cost.

METEOR/MERCURY OPTIONS: Air conditioner with heater ($436). Electric clock ($14.60). Courtesy light group ($13.30). Back-up lights ($10.70). Heater and defroster ($75.10). Padded instrument panel ($21.30). Power brakes ($43.20). Power tailgate window ($32.30 Commuter). Four-Way power seat ($63.60). Two-tone paint ($22). Power steering ($61.70). Power windows ($102.10). Push-button radio ($65). Tinted glass ($43). Station wagon third seat ($70.20). Whitewall tires, on station wagon ($37); on other models ($48). Trim options, on Meteor 800 and Commuter ($27.20). Wheel covers ($19.20). Windshield washer ($13.70). Two-speed windshield wipers ($11.60). A three-speed manual transmission was standard. Overdrive was optional on the Meteor and station wagons. Merc-O-Matic and Multi-Drive automatics were optional. A 292 cid/175-hp V-8 (with two-barrel carburetor) was optional on the Meteor series and Commuter. A 352 cid/220-hp Marauder V-8 (two-barrel), 390 cid/300-hp Marauder V-8 (four-barrel) and a 390 cid/330-hp Marauder V-8 (four-barrel) were optional. A power transfer rear axle was available.

HISTORY: The vast majority of 1961 Mercurys had automatic transmission and power steering. About one in 10 came with air conditioning. Mercury once again shared its body shell with Ford. Most 1961 Comets, 64.7 percent, were equipped with automatic transmission.

1962 MERCURY

1962 Mercury Monterey custom convertible. (OCW)

1962 Mercury Colony Park station wagon. (OCW)

COMET SERIES — A new, fine-patterned, vertical bar grille, round taillights and the repositioning of the Comet nameplates, from rear to front fenders, were the main styling changes for 1962. The model name was now, officially, Mercury Comet. Increased sound insulation, a roomier trunk and easier-to-read instrument panel gauges were among the less obvious improvements.

MERCURY & COMET I.D. NUMBERS: The Vehicle Identification Number is on the left firewall brace of Comets and Meteors and right frame rail, ahead of cowl, on Mercurys. First symbol: 2 = 1962. Second symbol identifies assembly plant: E = Mahwah, N.J.; F = Dearborn, Mich.; H = Lorain, Ohio; J = Los Angeles, Calif.; K = Kansas City, Kan.; R = San Jose, Calif.; S = Pilot Plant; T = Metuchen, N.J.; W = Wayne, Mich.; Y = Wixom, Mich.; Z = St. Louis, Mo. Third and fourth symbols are body code (first two numbers in Body/Style Number in charts below). Fifth symbol identifies engine: (Comet) S = 144 cid six; D = 144 cid six (low compression); U = 170 cid six; E = 170 cid six (low compression); (Monterey) U = 170 cid six; E = 170 cid six (low compression); L = 221 cid V-8; C = 221 cid V-8 (export); F = 260 cid V-8; (Mercury) S = 223 cid six; W = 292 cid V-8; T = 292 cid V-8 (export); X = 352 cid V-8; Z = 390 cid V-8; R = 390 cid V-8 (export); P = 390 cid V-8 (high-performance); B = 406 cid V-8; G = 406 cid V-8 (high-performance). Last six symbols are sequential production number starting at 500001. Body plate on front body pillar gives VIN, body code, color, trim, date, engine, transmission and axle codes).

COMET

Model No.	Body/Style No.	Body Type & Seating	Factory Price	Shipping Weight	Prod. Total
N/A	54A	4-dr Sed-6P	2139	2457	70,227*
N/A	69A	2-dr Sta Wag-6P	2483	2642	2,121*
N/A	62A	2-dr Sed-6P	2084	2420	73,800*
N/A	71A	4-dr Sta Wag-6P	2526	2679	16,759*

NOTE: (*) Production figures include Custom and S-22 series.

COMET CUSTOM SERIES — Outside of the fender nameplates and side window chrome trim, the exterior of the Custom resembled the standard Comet series. However, its interior featured Deluxe upholstery, white steering wheel, bright horn ring, rear seat armrest, carpeting, front door dome light switch and cigarette lighter.

COMET CUSTOM

Model No.	Body/Style No.	Body Type & Seating	Factory Price	Shipping Weight	Prod. Total
N/A	54B	4-dr Sed-6P	2226	2468	Note *
N/A	59B	2-dr Sta Wag-6P	2483	2642	Note *
N/A	62B	2-dr Sed-6P	2171	2431	Note *
N/A	71B	4-dr Sta Wag-6P	2526	2679	Note *

NOTE: (*) See Comet production total.

1962 Mercury Comet Custom four-door sedan, 6-cyl. (OCW)

1962 Mercury Comet Special S-22 two-door sedan, 6-cyl. (PH)

COMET SPECIAL SERIES — The sporty S-22 two-door sedan had six taillights (rather than the four on other Comets), a medallion above the trim on the roof panel and red wheel rims. The all-vinyl interior featured front bucket seats with a storage console between them. Backup lights, whitewall tires and loop-yarn carpeting were among the standard items found on the S-22. The Villager station wagon had simulated wood trim.

COMET SPECIAL

Model No.	Body/Style No.	Body Type & Seating	Factory Price	Shipping Weight	Prod. Total
N/A	62C	2-dr S-22 Sed-5P	2368	2358	Note *
N/A	71C	4-dr Vill Sta Wag-6P	2710	2612	2,318

NOTE: (*) See Comet production total.

METEOR SERIES — The Meteor was now a midsize car. It shared the same basic body as Ford's Fairlane, but featured styling similar to the big Mercurys. Meteors had a wavy, fine pattern vertical bar grille; bumper integrated signal lights; full-length side body moldings (that started above the headlights); a lower chrome spear, which began at the rear bumper and ran about half way across the car (with three thin chrome horizontal bars under it); and cylindrical taillights that stuck out from the tips of the tailfins. Buyers had their choice of 14 solid and 36 two-tone color combinations. The interiors were trimmed in crushed vinyl and cloth.

METEOR

Model No.	Body/Style No.	Body Type & Seating	Factory Price	Shipping Weight	Prod. Total
N/A	54A	4-dr Sed-6P	2340	2877	9,183
N/A	62A	2-dr Sed-6P	2278	2843	3,935

1962 Mercury Meteor two-door sedan, 6-cyl. (PH)

1962 Mercury Meteor Custom two-door sedan, 6-cyl. (OCW)

1962 Mercury Meteor Custom four-door sedan, V-8. (OCW)

METEOR CUSTOM SERIES — Chrome side window trim, rocker panel moldings, lower rear quarter panel, gravel shields and more roof side panel brightwork visually distinguished Meteor Customs from standard Meteors. Interiors were available in cloth and vinyl or all-vinyl. Twisted loop carpeting was standard.

METEOR CUSTOM

Model No.	Body/ Style No.	Body Type & Seating	Factory Price	Shipping Weight	Prod. Total
N/A	54B	4-dr Sed-6P	2428	2885	23,484
N/A	62A	2-dr Sed-6P	2366	2851	9,410

METEOR S-33 SERIES — The S-33 looked like a Meteor Custom two-door sedan. However, it had special wheel covers, a vinyl interior and front bucket seats with a storage console between them.

METEOR S-33

Model No.	Body/ Style No.	Body Type & Seating	Factory Price	Shipping Weight	Prod. Total
N/A	62C	2-dr Sed-5P	2509	2851	5,900

MONTEREY SERIES — The most noticeable styling change was seen in the taillights. They protruded from the tailfins. The new grille had a horizontal bar pattern, with an emblem, at its center, connecting the headlights. Side chrome was at two levels, joined in the middle by a slight chrome arch. The Monterey was one inch lower than the previous year's model.

MONTEREY

Model No.	Body/ Style No.	Body Type & Seating	Factory Price	Shipping Weight	Prod. Total
N/A	54A	4-dr Sed-6P	2726	3721	18,975
N/A	62A	2-dr Sed-6P	2672	3644	5,117
N/A	65A	2-dr HT-6P	2733	3661	5,328
N/A	71A	4-dr Comm Sta Wag-6P	2920	4069	8,389
N/A	75A	4-dr HT-6P	2798	3737	2,691

1962 Mercury Monterey four-door hardtop, V-8. (OCW)

1962 Mercury Monterey Custom two-door convertible, V-8. (PH)

1962 Mercury Monterey Custom Colony Park station wagon, V-8. (PH)

MONTEREY CUSTOM SERIES — Full-length lower body moldings and a large, rectangular chrome trim piece on the forward sides of the front fenders, were found on the Custom. The Colony Park station wagon had imitation wood trim, a power tailgate window, carpeting and either cloth and vinyl or all-vinyl interior.

MONTEREY CUSTOM

Model No.	Body/ Style No.	Body Type & Seating	Factory Price	Shipping Weight	Prod. Total
N/A	54B	4-dr Sed-6P	2965	3836	27,591
N/A	65B	2-dr HT-6P	2972	3772	10,614
N/A	71B	4-dr Col Prk Sta Wag-6P	3219	4186	Note 1
N/A	71D	4-dr Col Prk Sta Wag-9P	3289	4198	Note 1
N/A	75B	4-dr HT-6P	3037	3851	8,932
N/A	76A	2-dr Conv-6P	3222	3936	5,489

NOTE 1: Total Colony Park station wagon production was 9,596 with no breakout between six- and nine-passenger versions.

MONTEREY CUSTOM S-55 SERIES — The S-55 was basically a trim and performance option. Front fender ornaments and special wheel covers were the main exterior differences from a standard Custom. The S-55 had front bucket seats, console, red safety light in the doors, carpeting and a more powerful standard V-8.

MONTEREY CUSTOM S-55

Model No.	Body/ Style No.	Body Type & Seating	Factory Price	Shipping Weight	Prod. Total
N/A	65C	2-dr HT-5P	3488	3772	2,772
N/A	76B	2-dr Conv-5P	3738	3938	1,315

ENGINE [Comet Six]: Overhead valve. Cast-iron block. Displacement: 144.3 cid. Bore and stroke: 3.50 x 2.50 inches. Compression ratio: 8.7:1. Brake hp: 85 at 4200 rpm. Four main bearings. Carburetor: Holley 1909 one-barrel.

ENGINE [Meteor Six]: Overhead valve. Cast-iron block. Displacement: 170 cid. Bore and stroke: 3.50 x 2.94 inches. Compression ratio: 8.7:1. Brake hp: 101 at 4400 rpm. Four main bearings. Carburetor: Holley 1909 one-barrel.

ENGINE [Monterey Six]: Overhead valve. Cast-iron block. Displacement: 223 cid. Bore and stroke: 3.62 x 3.60 inches. Compression ratio: 8.4:1. Brake hp: 138 at 4200 rpm. Four main bearings. Carburetor: Holley one-barrel.

ENGINE [Monterey Custom V-8]: Overhead valve. Cast-iron block. Displacement: 292 cid. Bore and stroke: 3.75 x 3.30 inches. Compression ratio: 8.8:1. Brake hp: 170 at 4200 rpm. Five main bearings. Carburetor: Ford two-barrel.

ENGINE [Monterey Custom S-55 V-8]: Overhead valve. Cast-iron block. Displacement: 390 cid. Bore and stroke: 4.05 x 3.78 inches. Compression ratio: 9.6:1. Brake hp: 300 at 4600 rpm. Carburetor: four-barrel.

COMET CHASSIS FEATURES: Wheelbase: (station wagon) 109.5 inches; (others) 114 inches. Overall length: (station wagon) 191.8 inches; (others) 194.8 inches. Tires: (station wagon) 6.50 x 13; (others) 6.10 x 13.

METEOR CHASSIS FEATURES: Wheelbase: 116.5 inches. Overall length: 203.8 inches. Tires: 6.50 x 14; (7.00 x 14 optional).

MERCURY CHASSIS FEATURES: Wheelbase: 120 inches. Overall length: (station wagon) 121.1 inches; (others) 215.5 inches. Tires: (station wagon and convertible) 8.00 x 14; (others) 7.50 x 14.

COMET OPTIONS: Back-up lights ($10.70). Station wagon luggage rack ($39). Air conditioning ($270.90). Convenience group ($25.80). Padded instrument panel ($16.40). Padded visors ($4.50). Push-button radio

($56.60). Two-tone paint ($19.40). Electric tailgate window ($29.75). Tinted glass ($30.90). Tinted windshield ($12.95). Whitewall tires, on passenger car ($29.90); on station wagon ($33). Wheel covers ($16). Windshield washers ($13.70). Two-speed electric windshield wipers ($9.65). A three-speed manual transmission was standard. Merc-O-Matic automatic transmission was a $171.70 option. A 170 cid/101-hp six was optional at $45.10.

METEOR OPTIONS: Air conditioning ($231.70). Padded instrument panel ($19.95). Outside remote-control rearview mirror ($12). Padded visors ($5.20). Power steering ($61.70). Tinted glass ($40.30). Whitewall tires ($37). Wheel covers ($16.60). Windshield washer ($13.70). Push-button radio ($56.50). Front seat belts ($16.80). Two-tone paint ($22). A three-speed manual transmission was standard. Overdrive and Merc-O-Matic automatic transmission were optional at extra cost. A 221 cid/145-hp V-8 (two-barrel) and a 260 cid/164-hp V-8 were offered.

MERCURY OPTIONS: Air conditioner with heater ($360.90). Electric clock ($14.60). Back-up lights ($10.70). Station wagon luggage rack ($39). Padded dash ($21.30). Padded visors ($5.60). Two-tone paint ($22). Power brakes ($43.20). Power tailgate window in Commuter ($32.30). Power windows ($102.10). Four-Way power seat ($63.80). Power steering ($81.70). Push-button radio ($58.50). Smog reduction system ($5.70). Tinted glass ($43). Tinted windshield ($21.55). Station wagon third seat ($70.20). Wheel covers ($19.20). Windshield washer ($13.70). Two-speed windshield wipers ($7.75). Whitewall tires, on passenger car ($52.60); on station wagon ($37). A three-speed manual transmission was standard. Four-speed manual and Multi-Drive automatic transmissions were optional. A 292 cid/170-hp V-8 (two-barrel) was optional in Montereys. A 352 cid/220-hp V-8 (two-barrel); 390 cid/300-hp V-8 (four-barrel); 390 cid/330-hp V-8 (four-barrel); 406 cid/385-hp V-8 (four-barrel); 406 cid/405-hp V-8 (three two-barrels) and power transfer rear axle were available at extra cost.

HISTORY: Less than five percent of all 1962 Montereys were equipped with a manual transmission. A mere 17 percent were sold with a six-cylinder engine. Mercurys and Checkers were the only medium-priced cars available with a six-cylinder engine in 1962. Most 1962 Comets, 64.7 percent, were equipped with automatic transmission, 47.4 percent had a radio, 3.19 percent had tinted glass and 9 percent had air conditioning. The vast majority of 1962 Meteors came with a V-8 engine and automatic transmission.

1963 MERCURY

1963 Mercury Comet convertible. (OCW)

COMET SERIES — The new Comet looked a lot like the previous year's model. Chrome now outlined the side body sculpturing. The four circular taillights protruded from the rear deck panel. The grille featured a horizontal bar theme and the four headlights had chrome rims.

MERCURY & COMET I.D. NUMBERS: The Vehicle Identification Number is on the left inner fender of Comets and Meteors and right cowl tab on Mercurys. First symbol: 3 = 1963. Second symbol identifies assembly plant: E = Mahwah, N.J.; F = Dearborn, Mich.; H = Lorain, Ohio; J = Los Angeles, Calif.; K = Kansas City, Kan.; R = San Jose, Calif.; S = Pilot Plant; T = Metuchen, N.J.; W = Wayne, Mich.; Y = Wixom, Mich.; Z = St. Louis, Mo. Third and fourth symbols are body code (See Body/Style Number column in charts below). Fifth symbol identifies engine: (Comet) S = 144 cid six; 2 = 144 cid six (export); U = 170 cid six; 4 = 170 cid six (export); F = 260 cid V-8; 8 = 260 cid V-8 (export); (Meteor) U = 170 cid six; 4 = 170 cid six (export); T = 200 cid 'big six'; L = 221 cid V-8; 3 = 221 cid V-8 (export); F = 260 cid V-8; 8 = 260 cid (export); K = 289 cid V-8; (Mercury) Y = 390 cid V-8 2V; Z = 390 cid V-8 4V; 9 = 390 cid V-8 (export); P = 390 cid V-8 (high-

1963 Mercury Comet Special S-22 two-door convertible, 6-cyl. (OCW)

performance); B = 406 cid/385-hp V-8; G = 406 cid/405-hp V-8 (high-performance); Q = 427 cid/410-hp V-8; R = 427 cid/425-hp V-8. Last six symbols are sequential production number starting at 500001. Body plate on front body pillar gives VIN, body code, color, trim, date, engine, transmission and axle codes.

COMET

Model No.	Body/ Style No.	Body Type & Seating	Factory Price	Shipping Weight	Prod. Total
N/A	02	4-dr Sed-6P	2139	2499	24,230
N/A	21	2-dr Sta Wag-6P	2440	2644	623
N/A	01	2-dr Sed-6P	2084	2462	24,351
N/A	22	4-dr Sta Wag-6P	2483	2681	4,419

COMET CUSTOM SERIES — Chrome window trim and three horizontal bars on the rear quarter panel and on front fenders of station wagons, except the Villager, were distinguishing features of the Custom series. The interior came with such items as bright horn ring; rear seat armrests and ashtrays; front door dome light switch; cigarette lighter and carpeting. The Villager station wagon had simulated wood trim and a power tailgate window. Front bucket seats were optional.

COMET CUSTOM

Model No.	Body/ Style No.	Body Type & Seating	Factory Price	Shipping Weight	Prod. Total
N/A	12	4-dr Sed-6P	2226	2508	27,498
N/A	23	2-dr Sta Wag-6P	2527	2659	272
N/A	11	2-dr Sed-6P	2171	2471	11,897
N/A	13	2-dr HT Cpe-6P	2300	2572	9,432
N/A	24	4-dr Sta Wag-6P	2570	2696	5,151
N/A	26	4-dr Villager Sta Wag	2754	2736	1,529
N/A	15	2-dr Conv-6P	2557	2784	7,354

COMET SPECIAL S-22 SERIES — Six taillights made it easy to identify the Special S-22 series from the rear. Outside of the front fender ornaments, they looked about the same as Customs. The Custom interiors featured individually adjustable bucket seats with center console and deep, loop-pile carpeting.

COMET SPECIAL S-22

Model No.	Body/ Style No.	Body Type & Seating	Factory Price	Shipping Weight	Prod. Total
N/A	19	2-dr Sed-5P	2368	2512	6,303
N/A	17	2-dr HT Cpe-5P	2400	2572	5,807
N/A	18	2-dr Conv-5P	2710	2825	5,757

METEOR SERIES — The protruding cone-shaped taillights of 1962 remained on this season's Meteor station wagons, but were replaced on other body types. They now looked like part of the tailfin, rather than an add-on. A slightly sloping full-length chrome spear graced the bodyside. The grille resembled the one used on the 1962 Comet. Once again, bright metal trim was used on the roof quarter panels.

METEOR

Model No.	Body/ Style No.	Body Type & Seating	Factory Price	Shipping Weight	Prod. Total
N/A	32	4-dr Sed-6P	2340	2959	9,183
N/A	31	2-dr Sed-6P	2278	2920	3,935
N/A	38	4-dr Sta Wag-6P	2631	3237	2,359

1963 Mercury Meteor Custom four-door sedan, V-8. (OCW)

METEOR CUSTOM SERIES — Chrome side window trim, full-length lower body moldings and more chrome on the roof quarter panels were features that set the Custom series apart from the standard Meteors. They also had special interiors and carpeting. The Country Cruiser station wagon had simulated wood paneling.

METEOR CUSTOM

Model No.	Body/ Style No.	Body Type & Seating	Factory Price	Shipping Weight	Prod. Total
N/A	42	4-dr Sed-6P	2428	2965	14,498
N/A	41	2-dr Sed-6P	2366	2926	2,704
N/A	43	2-dr HT Cpe-6P	2448	2944	7,565
N/A	49	4-dr Ctry Cr Sta Wag-6P	2886	3253	1,485
N/A	48	4-dr Sta Wag-6P	2719	3245	3,636*

NOTE: (*) Production Total for Meteor Custom station wagon includes optional third-seat/nine-passenger version of which 1,047 were built.

METEOR S-33 SERIES — Triple horizontal chrome bars on the front fenders, rear fender insignia and special medallions on the roof quarter panels were exclusive to the S-33. The interior featured front bucket seats with a center console between them.

METEOR S-33

Model No.	Body/ Style No.	Body Type & Seating	Factory Price	Shipping Weight	Prod. Total
N/A	47	2-dr HT Cpe-6P	2628	2964	4,865

MONTEREY SERIES — Basic Monterey styling seemed more in tune with the 1961 models than the 1962s. Six taillights were (as in 1961) located in the rear deck panel. Side body moldings ran from the taillights to the headlights. Chrome trim was on the roof quarter panels. A concave, vertical bar grille housed four chrome-rimmed headlights. Mercury's fondness for unusual designs surfaced again this year. The Breezeway roof featured a roll-down back window. In midyear, the Marauder two-door hardtop, with fastback styling, was introduced.

MONTEREY

Model No.	Body/ Style No.	Body Type & Seating	Factory Price	Shipping Weight	Prod. Total
N/A	52	4-dr Sed-6P	2887	3994	18,177
N/A	51	2-dr Sed-6P	2834	3854	4,640
N/A	53	2-dr HT Cpe-6P	2930	3869	2,879
N/A	54	4-dr HT Sed-6P	2995	3959	1,692

MONTEREY CUSTOM SERIES — Tire level full-length moldings, three rectangular chrome pieces on the rear fender and front fender nameplates distinguished the Custom from the standard Monterey. All Customs came equipped with back-up lights, courtesy light group, electric clock and two-speed windshield wipers. A fastback model, named the Marauder, was a midyear addition and was developed for use by racers on the big league stock car circuits.

MONTEREY CUSTOM

Model No.	Body/ Style No.	Body Type & Seating	Factory Price	Shipping Weight	Prod. Total
N/A	62	4-dr Sed-6P	3075	3959	39,542

Model No.	Body/ Style No.	Body Type & Seating	Factory Price	Shipping Weight	Prod. Total
N/A	66	2-dr Mar Fsbk Cpe-6P	3083	3887	7,298
N/A	63	2-dr HT Cpe-6P	3083	3881	10,693
N/A	76	4-dr Col Park Sta Wag-6P	3295	4306	6,447
N/A	76	4-dr Col Park Sta Wag-9P	3365	4318	7,529
N/A	64	4-dr HT Sed-6P	3148	3971	8,604
N/A	65	2-dr Conv-6P	3333	4043	3,783

1963 Mercury Monterey four-door hardtop, V-8. (OCW)

MONTEREY S-55 SERIES — The S-55 insignia in front of the rear fender chrome bars and special wheel covers were the most noticeable exterior differences between the S-55 and the Custom. Inside, the S-55 featured vinyl upholstery, front bucket seats with the center console, front and rear armrests and padded dash. Buyers could have an automatic or a four-speed manual transmission at no extra cost.

MONTEREY S-55

Model No.	Body/ Style No.	Body Type & Seating	Factory Price	Shipping Weight	Prod. Total
N/A	68	2-dr Mar Fsbk Cpe-6P	3650	3900	2,317
N/A	67	2-dr HT Cpe-6P	3650	3894	3,863
N/A	60	4-dr HT Sed-6P	3715	3984	1,203
N/A	69	2-dr Conv-5P	3900	4049	1,379

ENGINE [Comet Six]: Overhead valve. Cast-iron block. Displacement: 144.3 cid. Bore and stroke: 3.50 x 2.50 inches. Compression ratio: 8.7:1. Brake hp: 85 at 4200 rpm. Four main bearings. Carburetor: Ford C3GF-9510 one-barrel.

ENGINE [Meteor Six]: Overhead valve. Cast-iron block. Displacement: 170 cid. Bore and stroke: 3.50 x 2.94 inches. Compression ratio: 8 7:1. Brake hp: 101 at 4400 rpm. Four main bearings. Carburetor: Ford C3OF-9510-A one-barrel.

ENGINE [Monterey V-8]: Overhead valve. Cast-iron block. Displacement: 390 cid. Bore and stroke: 4.05 x 3.78 inches. Compression ratio: 8.9:1. Brake hp: 250 at 4400 rpm. Five main bearings. Carburetor: Ford C3MF-9510 two-barrel.

COMET CHASSIS FEATURES: Wheelbase: (station wagon) 109.5 inches; (other models) 114 inches. Overall length: (station wagon) 191.8 inches; (other models) 194.8 inches. Tires: (station wagon and convertible) 6.50 x 13; (other models) 6.00 x 13.

METEOR CHASSIS FEATURES: Wheelbase: (passenger car) 116.5 inches; (station wagon) 115.5 inches. Overall length: (passenger car) 203.8 inches; (station wagon) 202.3 inches. Tires: 6.50 x 14.

MERCURY CHASSIS FEATURES: Wheelbase: 120 inches. Overall length: (passenger car) 215 inches; (station wagon) 212.1 inches. Tires: (passenger car) 7.50 x 14; (station wagon) 8.00 x 14.

COMET OPTIONS: Back-up lights ($10.70). Luggage rack for station wagons ($39). Air conditioning ($270.90). Comet convenience group ($25.60). Padded instrument panel ($16.40). Padded visors ($4.50). Push-button radio ($56.60). Two-tone paint ($19.40). Electric tailgate window for station wagon ($29.75). Tinted glass ($30.90). Tinted windshield ($12.95). Whitewall tires on passenger car ($29.90); on station wagon ($33). Wheel covers ($16). Windshield washers ($13.70). Two-speed electric windshield wipers ($9.65). A three-speed manual transmission was standard. Four-speed manual and Merc-O-Matic automatic transmissions were optional. A 170 cid/101-hp (one-barrel) and a 260 cid/164-hp V-8 (two-barrel) were optional.

1963 Mercury Monterey S-55 two-door convertible, V-8. (OCW)

METEOR OPTIONS: Two-speed windshield wipers ($7.75). Air conditioning ($231.70). Padded instrument panel ($19.95). Outside remote-control rearview mirror ($12). Padded visors ($5.20). Power steering ($61.70). Tinted glass ($40.30). Whitewall tires ($37). Wheel covers ($16.60). Windshield washer ($13.70). Push-button radio ($58.50). Front seat belts ($16.80). Two-tone paint ($22). Station wagon third seat ($43.50). Station wagon power rear window ($32.30). A three-speed manual transmission was standard. Overdrive, four-speed manual and Merc-O-Matic automatic transmissions were optional. A 221 cid/145-hp V-8 (two-barrel) and a 260 cid/164-hp V-8 were available.

MERCURY OPTIONS: Air conditioner with heater ($360.90). Electric clock ($14.60). Back-up lights ($10.70). Station wagon luggage rack ($45.40). Outside remote-control rearview mirror ($12). Padded dash ($21.30). Padded visors ($5.60). Two-tone paint ($22). Power brakes ($43.20). Power driver's bucket seat in S-55 ($92.10). Power steering ($106.20). Power windows ($102.10). Push-button radio ($58.50). AM/FM radio ($129.30). Front seat belts ($16.60). Swing-away steering wheel ($50). Tinted glass ($43). Tinted windshield ($26). Whitewall tires ($52.60). Monterey sedan trim option ($34.60). Wheel covers ($19.20). Windshield washer ($13.70). Courtesy light group ($14.80). Two-speed windshield wipers ($7.75). A three-speed manual transmission was standard on Monterey and Custom series. Multi-Drive automatic or four-speed manual transmissions were standard in the S-55. Automatic transmission was optional on all series. The four-speed manual transmission was available on all, except the Colony Park. A 390 cid/300-hp V-8 (four-barrel); 390 cid/330-hp V-8 (four-barrel); 406 cid/385-hp (four-barrel) and a 406 cid/405-hp V-8 were optional. The last two choices were offered only on cars equipped with a four-speed manual transmission. A 427 cid V-8 was also available in 410-hp and 425-hp formats, with manual transmission only.

HISTORY: Just over 64 percent of 1963 Comets were equipped with an automatic transmission. Most Meteors, 79.6 percent, came with an automatic transmission, 91.4 percent had a V-8 engine, 47 percent had power steering, 68.6 percent had a radio, 46 percent had tinted glass and five percent had air conditioning. The majority of 1963 full-size Mercurys came with automatic transmission, power steering, power brakes, radio and tinted glass. About one in 10 had power windows. Twenty percent were sold with an air conditioner. Mercury won one NASCAR Grand National race in 1963. This was the first year for the 427 cid V-8 in big Mercurys.

1964 MERCURY

1964 Mercury Park Lane Marauder convertible. (OCW)

1964 Mercury Comet Cyclone two-door hardtop, V-8. (OCW)

COMET 202 SERIES — The 1964 Comet had a Lincoln-Continental-style grille. The same theme was repeated on the rear deck panel. A wraparound trim piece was seen on the tips of the front fenders. Three thin, vertical trim slashes were on the sides of the front fenders. The signal lights remained embedded in the front bumper.

MERCURY & COMET I.D. NUMBERS: The Vehicle Identification Number was on the left inner fender of Comets and Meteors and right cowl tab on Mercurys. First symbol: 4 = 1964. Second symbol identifies assembly plant: E = Mahwah, N.J.; F = Dearborn, Mich.; H = Lorain, Ohio; J = Los Angeles, Calif.; K = Kansas City, Kan.; R = San Jose, Calif.; S = Pilot Plant; T = Metuchen, N.J.; W = Wayne, Mich.; Y = Wixom, Mich.; Z = St. Louis, Mo. Third and fourth symbols are body code (See Body/Style Number column in charts below). Fifth symbol identifies engine: (Comet) U = 170 cid six; 4 = 170 cid six (export); F = 260 cid V-8; 6 = 260 cid V-8 (export); D = 289 cid/210-hp V-8; K = 289 cid/271-hp V-8; R = 427 cid/425-hp V-8; (Mercury) Y = 390 cid/250-hp V-8 2V; H = 390 cid/266-hp V-8 2V; Z = 390 cid/300-hp V-8 4V; P = 390 cid/330-hp V-8 4V (high-performance); 9 = 390 cid V-8 (export); Q = 427 cid/410-hp V-8; R = 427 cid/425-hp V-8. Last six symbols are sequential production number starting at 500001. Body plate on front body pillar gives VIN, body code, color, trim, date, engine, transmission and axle codes.

COMET 202

Model No.	Body/Style No.	Body Type & Seating	Factory Price	Shipping Weight	Prod. Total
N/A	02	4-dr Sed-6P	2182	2580	29,147
N/A	01	2-dr Sed-6P	2126	2539	33,824
N/A	32	4-dr Sta Wag-6P	2463	2727	5,504

COMET 404 SERIES — Full-length bodyside moldings were the most obvious exterior difference between the Comet 404 and lower-priced Comet 202. Interior trims were available in cloth and vinyl or all-vinyl. The Villager station wagon featured imitation wood trim.

COMET 404

Model No.	Body/Style No.	Body Type & Seating	Factory Price	Shipping Weight	Prod. Total
N/A	12	4-dr Sed-6P	2269	2588	25,136
N/A	11	2-dr Sed-6P	2213	2551	12,512
N/A	34	4-dr Sta Wag-6P	2550	2741	6,918
N/A	36	4-dr Vill Sta Wag-6P	2734	2745	1,980

CALIENTE SERIES — "Every bit as hot as it looks!", was how sales literature described the Caliente. It had a wide, full-length molding on its sides and a nameplate on the lower front fenders. A padded instrument panel with walnut grain trim and deep-loop carpeting were a couple of standard luxury features. Caliente hardtops and convertibles were available only in solid colors.

1964 Mercury Comet Caliente two-door hardtop, V-8. (OCW)

1964 Mercury Comet Caliente two-door convertible, V-8. (OCW)

CALIENTE

Model No.	Body/ Style No.	Body Type & Seating	Factory Price	Shipping Weight	Prod. Total
N/A	22	4-dr Sed-6P	2350	2668	27,218
N/A	23	2-dr HT Cpe-6P	2375	2688	31,204
N/A	25	2-dr Conv-6P	2636	2861	9,039

CYCLONE SERIES — This two-door hardtop was the first macho Comet. Literature told of "under the hood, a whiplash of surging power" and of the "masculine feel of black vinyl in the instrument panel." As a safety feature the "bucket seats are contoured to hold you more securely in turns." (Apparently, Mercury felt a lot of people were falling out of their bucket seats when driving around corners.) Fender nameplates, full-length lower body moldings, vinyl roof coverings and 'chrome wheel look' wheel covers distinguished the Cyclone. A three-spoke steering wheel, front bucket seats with center console and a tachometer were standard. The engine came with special chromed parts, including air cleaner, dipstick, oil filter, radiator cap and rocker arm covers.

CYCLONE

Model No.	Body/ Style No.	Body Type & Seating	Factory Price	Shipping Weight	Prod. Total
N/A	27	2-dr HT Cpe-6P	2655	2688	7,454

MONTEREY SERIES — Although obviously based on the 1963 models the new full-size Mercurys now seemed closer in styling to Continentals than Fords. The rear end appeared to be influenced by the 1959 Continental Mark IV. Six rectangular tail/back-up lights were set in the rear deck panel. The slightly recessed grille featured bent vertical bars and four chrome rimmed headlights. The signal lights were in the bumper. The unusual Breezeway roof, with its retractable rear window, was offered once again. Full-length upper body moldings and tire level chrome spears decorated the sides.

MONTEREY

Model No.	Body/ Style No.	Body Type & Seating	Factory Price	Shipping Weight	Prod. Total
N/A	42	4-dr Sed-6P	2892	3985	20,234
N/A	48	4-dr HT Fsbk-6P	2957	4017	4,143
N/A	41	2-dr Sed-6P	2819	3895	3,932
N/A	47	2-dr HT Fsbk-6P	2884	3916	8,760
N/A	43	2-dr HT Cpe-6P	2884	3910	2,926
N/A	45	2-dr Conv-6P	3226	4027	2,592

NOTE: Models number 48 and 47, the pillarless fastback styles, were called Marauders.

1964 Mercury Montclair Marauder four-door fastback hardtop, V-8. (PH)

MONTCLAIR SERIES — Montclairs had three horizontal chrome pieces on the front fenders, nameplates on the rear fenders and a wide band of chrome on the rear quarter panel. Buyers had their choice of cloth and vinyl or all-vinyl interiors.

MONTCLAIR

Model No.	Body/ Style No.	Body Type & Seating	Factory Price	Shipping Weight	Prod. Total
N/A	52	4-dr Sed-6P	3116	3996	15,520
N/A	58	4-dr HT Fsbk-6P	3181	4017	8,655
N/A	57	2-dr HT Fsbk-6P	3127	3927	6,459
N/A	53	2-dr HT Cpe-6P	3127	3921	2,329

NOTE: Models number 57 and 58, the pillarless fastback styles, were called Marauders.

PARK LANE SERIES — The Park Lane returned as Mercury's top-of-the-line series. A wide band of tire-level chrome trim, running across the bodysides, set it apart from other Mercurys. Its interior featured nylon face, biscuit-design upholstery and large, walnut-tone door panel inserts. The Park Lane convertible, like the Monterey version, came with a glass rear window.

PARK LANE

Model No.	Body/ Style No.	Body Type & Seating	Factory Price	Shipping Weight	Prod. Total
N/A	62	4-dr Sed-6P	3348	4035	6,230
N/A	68	4-dr HT Fsbk-6P	3413	4056	3,658
N/A	67	2-dr HT Fsbk-5P	3359	3966	2,721
N/A	63	2-dr HT Cpe-6P	3359	3960	1,786
N/A	64	4-dr HT Sed-6P	3413	4050	2,402
N/A	65	2-dr Conv-6P	3549	4066	1,967

NOTE: Models number 67 and 68, the pillarless fastback styles, were called Marauders.

STATION WAGON SERIES — The Commuter station wagon was based on the Monterey. The Colony Park had mahogany-toned side paneling.

STATION WAGONS

Model No.	Body/ Style No.	Body Type & Seating	Factory Price	Shipping Weight	Prod. Total
N/A	72	4-dr Comm-6P	3236	4259	3,484
N/A	76	4-dr Col Prk-6P	3434	4275	4,234
N/A	72	4-dr Comm-9P	3306	4271	1,839
N/A	76	4-dr Col Prk-9P	3504	4287	5,624

ENGINE [Comet Six]: Overhead valve. Cast-iron block. Displacement: 170 cid. Bore and stroke: 3.50 x 2.93 inches. Compression ratio: 8.7:1. Brake hp: 101 at 4400 rpm. Four main bearings. Carburetor: Ford C3YF-9510E one-barrel.

ENGINE [Cyclone V-8]: Overhead valve. Cast-iron block. Displacement: 289 cid. Bore and stroke: 4.00 x 2.37 inches. Compression ratio: 9.0:1. Five main bearings. Brake hp: 210 at 4400 rpm. Carburetor: Ford C5MF-9510A two-barrel.

ENGINE [Mercury V-8]: Overhead valve. Cast-iron block. Displacement: 390 cid. Bore and stroke: 4.05 x 3.78 inches. Compression ratio: 9.4:1. Brake hp: 250 at 4400 rpm. Five main bearings. Carburetor: Ford C4MF-9510D two-barrel.

COMET CHASSIS FEATURES: (passenger car) 114 inches; (station wagon) 109.5 inches. Overall length: (passenger cars) 195.1 inches; (station wagon) 191.8 inches. Tires: (passenger car) 6.50 x 14; (station wagon) 7.00 x 14.

MERCURY CHASSIS FEATURES: Wheelbase: 120 inches. Overall length: (passenger car) 215.5 inches; (station wagon) 210.3 inches. Tires: 8.00 x 14.

1964 Mercury Colony Park station wagon, V-8. (OCW)

COMET OPTIONS: Power steering ($86). Air conditioning ($232). Heavy-duty battery ($7.60). Tinted glass ($27.10). Tinted windshield ($18.10). Station wagon luggage rack ($64.35). Outside remote-control rearview mirror ($12). Padded instrument panel ($18.40). Padded visors ($4.50). Two-tone paint ($19.40). Power brakes ($43.20). Push-button AM radio ($58.50). Tachometer ($43.10). Wheel covers ($19.20). Windshield washer and wipers ($21.80). A three-speed manual transmission was standard. Four-speed manual, Merc-O-Matic and Multi-Drive automatic transmissions were optional. A 200 cid/116-hp six (one-barrel); 260 cid/164-hp V-8 (two-barrel); 289 cid/210-hp V-8 (two-barrel) and a 289 cid/271-hp V-8 (four-barrel) were available. A limited number of Comets with 427 cid/425-hp engines were built as lightweight factory drag racing cars.

MERCURY CONVENIENCE OPTIONS: Air conditioner ($430). Heavy-duty battery ($42.50). Bucket seats ($160.90). Console and tachometer ($88.80). Courtesy light group ($23.20). Electric clock in Monterey ($16.10). Power steering ($106). Tinted glass ($43). Tinted windshield ($26). Station wagon luggage rack ($64.40). Padded dash ($21.30). Two-tone paint ($22). Power brakes ($43.20). Six-Way power seats ($96.50). Power windows ($106.20). Push-button AM radio ($61.10). AM/FM radio ($148.60). Speed control ($92.70). Tilting steering wheel ($43.10). Windshield washer ($13.70). Vinyl roof ($88.80). Wire wheel covers ($45.20). A three-speed manual transmission was standard. Four-speed manual and Multi-Drive automatic transmissions were optional. The four-speed was not available in station wagons. A power transfer rear axle was offered at extra cost. Optional engines included: 390 cid/266-hp V-8 (station wagons only); 390 cid/300-hp V-8 (four-barrel); 390 cid/330-hp V-8 (four-barrel); 427 cid/410-hp V-8 (four-barrel) and 427 cid/425-hp V-8 (dual four-barrel). The last two engines were not available in station wagons.

HISTORY: Most 1964 Comets, 66 percent, had automatic transmissions, 24 percent had power steering and only four percent had power brakes. A team of Comet Calientes, powered by 289 cid/271-hp V-8s, traveled over 100,000 miles at average speeds in excess of 100 mph. Three of the least popular options on full-size Mercurys this year (and their installation rates) were four-speed manual transmission (0.9 percent), locking differential (four percent), and tilting steering wheel (two percent). Marauder was the name given to full-size Mercury fastback two-door and four-door hardtops. Mercurys won five NASCAR Grand National races in 1964. The Comet Boss 427 Dragster, Mercury's counterpart to Ford's Fairlane Thunderbolt, was introduced.

1965 MERCURY

COMET 202 SERIES — The restyled Comet had vertical headlights that made it look more like a Ford than a Mercury. The grille used a horizontal bar theme. Side chrome was limited to the roof quarter panel and three thin horizontal pieces on the front fenders. Wraparound rectangular taillights were used on all body types, except the station wagon, which used square ones. Front seat belts, a heater and defroster and front and rear armrests were standard equipment.

MERCURY & COMET I.D. NUMBERS: The Vehicle Identification Number is on the left inner fender of Comets and Meteors and right cowl tab on Mercurys. First symbol: 5 = 1965. Second symbol identifies assembly plant: E = Mahwah, N.J.; F = Dearborn, Mich.; H = Lorain, Ohio; J = Los Angeles, Calif., K = Kansas City, Kan.; R = San Jose, Calif.; S = Pilot Plant; T = Metuchen, N.J.; W = Wayne, Mich.; Y = Wixom, Mich.; Z = St. Louis, Mo. Third and fourth symbols are body code (See Body/Style Number column in charts below). Fifth symbol identifies engine: (Comet) U = 170 cid six; 4 = 170 cid six (export); F = 260 cid V-8; 6 = 260 cid V-8 (export); D = 289 cid/210-hp V-8; K = 289 cid/271-hp V-8; R = 427 cid/425-hp V-8; (Mercury) Y = 390 cid/250-hp V-8 2V; H = 390 cid/266-hp V-8 2V; Z = 390 cid/300-hp V-8 4V; P = 390 cid/330-hp V-8 4V (high-performance); 9 = 390 cid (export); Q = 427 cid/410-hp V-8; R = 427 cid/425-hp V-8. Last six symbols are sequential production number starting at 500001. Body plate on front body pillar gives VIN, body code, color, trim, date, engine, transmission and axle codes).

1965 Mercury Comet '404' four-door sedan, 6-cyl. (PH)

COMET 202

Model No.	Body/ Style No.	Body Type & Seating	Factory Price	Shipping Weight	Prod. Total
202	01	4-dr Sed-6P	2163	2335	23,501
202	02	2-dr Sed-6P	2108	2295	32,425
202	32	4-dr Sta Wag-6P	2438	2495	4,814

COMET 404 SERIES — Full-length bodyside chrome and side window moldings set the 404 apart from the 202 series. The Villager station wagon had imitation wood paneling and came with a power tailgate window.

COMET 404

Model No.	Body/ Style No.	Body Type & Seating	Factory Price	Shipping Weight	Prod. Total
404	11	4-dr Sed-6P	2248	2340	18,628
404	12	2-dr Sed-6P	2193	2305	10,900
404	34	4-dr Sta Wag-6P	2523	2500	5,226
404	36	4-dr Vill Sta Wag-6P	2703	2500	1,592

CALIENTE SERIES — The most luxurious Comet remained the Caliente. It had a special horizontal chrome bar taillight treatment that blended into the rear deck panel. In addition, it featured a mid-tire level molding. Carpeting, a padded dash and door courtesy lights were among the standard items offered on the Caliente. The convertible had a power top.

1965 Mercury Comet Caliente two-door hardtop, V-8. (PH)

1965 Mercury Comet Caliente two-door convertible, V-8. (PH)

1965 Mercury Comet Cyclone two-door hardtop, V-8. (PH)

1965 Mercury Monterey two-door convertible, V-8. (OCW)

CALIENTE

Model No.	Body/ Style No.	Body Type & Seating	Factory Price	Shipping Weight	Prod. Total
N/A	22	4-dr Sed-6P	2327	2370	20,337
N/A	23	2-dr HT Cpe-6P	2352	2395	29,247
N/A	25	2-dr Conv-6P	2607	2588	6,035

CYCLONE SERIES — A vinyl roof, chrome wheels, curb moldings, distinctive grille design, two hood scoops, bucket seats with console and a tachometer were standard on the Cyclone two-door hardtop.

CYCLONE

Model No.	Body/ Style No.	Body Type & Seating	Factory Price	Shipping Weight	Prod. Total
N/A	27	2-dr HT Cpe-5P	2625	2994	12,347

MONTEREY SERIES — The 1965 Monterey had a horizontal bar grille with the mid-section protruding slightly. Thin vertical signal lights were located at the tips of the front fenders. Outside of the large front fender trim pieces and rocker panel moldings, the Monterey's sides were relatively clean of 'doo-dads'. The taillights were vertical and fully integrated into the bumper and rear fenders. Carpeting, front seat belts and a heater and defroster were among the standard features. The Breezeway sedan, with its retractable rear window, was offered once again.

MONTEREY

Model No.	Body/ Style No.	Body Type & Seating	Factory Price	Shipping Weight	Prod. Total
N/A	44	4-dr Sed-6P	2782	3853	23,363
N/A	43	2-dr Sed-6P	2711	3788	5,775
N/A	47	2-dr HT Fsbk-6P	2843	3823	16,857
N/A	42	4-dr Brzway-6P	2845	3898	19,569
N/A	48	4-dr HT Fsbk-6P	2918	3893	10,047
N/A	45	2-dr Conv-6P	3165	3928	4,762

NOTE: Models number 47 and 48, the pillarless hardtop styles, were called Marauders. Model number 42, the Breezeway, was a sedan with slanting and retractable rear window styling.

MONTCLAIR SERIES — The Montclair had a full-length, chrome middle body spear. Its nameplate was on the rear fenders. As in the Monterey series, the Breezeway model had chrome trim on the roof quarter panels. In addition to the standard items found in Montereys, Montclair buyers received wheel covers, electric clocks and interval selector windshield wipers.

MONTCLAIR

Model No.	Body/ Style No.	Body Type & Seating	Factory Price	Shipping Weight	Prod. Total
N/A	52	4-dr Brzway-6P	3074	3933	18,924
N/A	58	4-dr HT Fsbk-6P	3145	3928	16,977
N/A	57	2-dr HT Fsbk-6P	3072	3848	9,645

1965 Mercury Park Lane Marauder four-door hardtop, V-8. (OCW)

1965 Mercury Park Lane Breezeway four-door sedan, V-8. (PH)

NOTE: Models number 57 and 58, the pillarless hardtop styles, were Marauders. Model number 52, the Breezeway, was a sedan with slanting and retractable rear window styling.

PARK LANE SERIES — Rectangular rear fender nameplates, chrome gravel shields and a band of molding above the rocker panels were three styling features of Park Lanes. They had more luxurious interiors than cars in the other series. Standard equipment included: padded dash, padded visors, courtesy lights, visor-mounted vanity mirrors and a trip odometer.

PARK LANE

Model No.	Body/ Style No.	Body Type & Seating	Factory Price	Shipping Weight	Prod. Total
N/A	62	4-dr Brzway-6P	3301	3988	8,335
N/A	68	4-dr HT Fsbk-6P	3372	3983	14,211
N/A	67	2-dr HT Fsbk-6P	3299	3908	6,853
N/A	65	2-dr Conv-6P	3526	4013	3,008

NOTE: Models number 67 and 68, the pillarless hardtop styles, were called Marauders. Model number 62, the Breezeway, was a sedan with slanting and retractable rear window styling.

STATION WAGONS SERIES — The third seat, in Mercury station wagons equipped with such an option, faced the rear. The rear quarter panels contained wind vanes. The Colony Park had simulated wood paneling.

STATION WAGONS

Model No.	Body/ Style No.	Body Type & Seating	Factory Price	Shipping Weight	Prod. Total
N/A	72	4-dr Comm-6P	3169	4178	8,081
N/A	76	4-dr Col Prk-6P	3364	4213	15,294

ENGINE [Comet Six]: Overhead valve. Cast-iron block. Displacement: 200 cid. Bore and stroke: 3.68 x 3.12 inches. Compression ratio: 9.2:1. Brake hp: 120 at 4400 rpm. Seven main bearings. Carburetor: Ford C5OF-9510E one-barrel.

1965 Mercury Park Lane two-door convertible, V-8. (OCW)

ENGINE [Cyclone V-8]: Overhead valve. Cast-iron block. Displacement: 289 cid. Bore and stroke: 4.00 x 2.87 inches. Compression ratio: 9.3:1. Brake hp: 200 at 4400 rpm. Five main bearings. Carburetor: Ford C5MF-9510A two-barrel.

ENGINE [Monterey V-8]: Overhead valve. Cast-iron block. Displacement: 390 cid. Bore and stroke: 4.05 x 3.78 inches. Compression ratio: 9.4:1. Brake hp: 250 at 4400 rpm. Five main bearings. Carburetor: Ford C5MF-9519A two-barrel.

ENGINE [Park Lane V-8]: Overhead valve. Cast-iron block. Displacement: 390 cid. Bore and stroke: 4.05 x 3.78 inches. Compression ratio: 10.1:1. Brake hp: 300 at 4600 rpm. Five main bearings. Carburetor: Ford C5AF-9510E four-barrel.

COMET CHASSIS FEATURES: Wheelbase: (passenger car) 114 inches; (station wagon) 109.5 inches. Overall length: (passenger car) 195.3 inches; (station wagon) 191.8 inches. Tires: 6.95 x 14.

MERCURY CHASSIS FEATURES: (passenger car) 123 inches; (station wagon) 119 inches. Overall length: (passenger car) 218.4 inches; (station wagon) 214.5 inches. Tires: 8.15 x 15.

COMET OPTIONS: Air conditioner ($257.50). Heavy-duty battery ($7.60). Elapsed-time clock ($20). Courtesy light group ($14.80). Remote-control trunk lid release ($11). Emergency flasher ($12.80). Tinted glass ($27.80). Tinted windshield ($18.10). Back-up lights ($10.70). Station wagon luggage rack ($64.35). Remote-control outside rearview mirror ($12). Curb molding ($16.10). Padded dash ($18.40). Padded visors ($4.50). Two-tone paint ($19.40). Power brakes ($43.20). Power steering ($86.30). Station wagon power tailgate window ($29.75). Push-button AM radio ($56.50). AM/FM radio ($129.30). Rally Pac ($83); same in Cyclone ($40). Retractable front seat belts ($7.10). Front bucket seats with console in Caliente hardtop and convertible ($131.30). Front bucket seats in two-door sedan only ($70.80). Size 6.95 x 14 whitewall tires. Tachometer ($43.10). Vacuum gauge ($20). Wheel covers ($19.20). Wire wheel covers ($64.40); same on Cyclone ($43.20). Windshield washer and wipers ($21.80). Vinyl roof on hardtop ($75.80). A three-speed manual transmission was standard. Four-speed manual and Multi-Drive automatic transmissions were optional. A 289 cid/200-hp Cyclone V-8 (two-barrel) and a 289 cid/225-hp Super Cyclone V-8 (four-barrel) were optional. A performance handling package could be had for $20.80. A power transfer axle cost $38. A power booster fan was $16.10.

MERCURY OPTIONS: Air conditioner ($430). Bucket seats in Monterey hardtop and convertible ($160.90). Reclining passenger side bucket seat in Park Lane ($45.10). Console and tachometer in Monterey ($66.60). Courtesy light group ($23.20). Remote-control trunk lid release ($110). Decor group in Monterey sedans ($34.80); in Monterey hardtops and Commuter ($21.90); in Monterey convertible ($14.20). Power door locks in two-doors ($37.30); in four-doors ($52.80). Speed-actuated rear door locks ($25.80). Electric clock ($16.10). Tinted windshield ($3.00). Tinted glass ($43). Luggage rack ($64.40). Padded dash ($21.30). Padded visors ($5.80). Two-tone paint ($22). Power antenna ($29.60). Power brakes ($43.20). Four-way power bucket seat, driver's side ($92.10). Six-Way power seats ($96.50). Power windows ($106.20). Power vent windows ($52.60). Push-button AM radio ($61.10). AM/FM push-button radio with rear speaker ($146.60). Rear seat speaker ($19.30). Studio-sonic rear speaker ($53.50). Third seat in station wagons ($76.80). Retractable front seat belts ($7.10). Speed control ($92.70). Sports package in Park Lane two-door hardtop and convertible ($423). Tilting steering wheel ($43.10). Whitewall tires ($40.56). All-vinyl Deluxe trim in Monterey hardtops and four-door sedans ($70.80). Leather trim in Park Lanes with bench seats ($98.80). Visibility group in Monterey ($30.80). Trip odometer ($8.90). Wheel covers with spinners on Monterey ($38.40); on Montclair and Park Lane ($19.20). Deluxe wheel covers on Monterey ($19.20). Custom wheel covers on Monterey ($54.10); on Montclair and Park Lane ($34.90). Wire wheel covers on Monterey ($64.40); on Montclair and Park Lane ($45.20). Vinyl roof ($88.80). Windshield washer ($13.70). A three-speed manual transmission was standard. Overdrive, four-speed manual and Multi-Drive Merc-O-Matic automatic transmissions were optional. A 390 cid/255-hp V-8 (two-barrel) was standard on Montclairs and station wagons equipped with automatic. A 390 cid/300-hp V-8 (four-barrel); a 390 cid/330-hp V-8 (four-barrel) and a 427 cid/425-hp V-8 (dual four-barrel) were optional. The latter engine was offered only with cars that had a four-speed manual transmission. It was not available in station wagons. A power transfer axle could be had for $42.50.

HISTORY: Most 1965 Comets, 65.5 percent, had automatic transmissions, 51.3 percent had a six-cylinder engine and only 1.9 percent came with power windows. Just three percent of full-size Mercurys came with a four-speed manual transmission. Other rare options included a tilting steering wheel (6.4 percent) and locking differential (4.5 percent). Mercurys won one NASCAR Grand National race in 1965. The 427 cid single-overhead cam engine was specially available in Comet "Boss" lightweight drag cars/funny cars for 1965.

1966 MERCURY

1966 Mercury Comet '202' two-door sedan, 6-cyl. (OCW)

COMET 202 SERIES — The Comet grew this year, from a compact to an intermediate. A stacked headlight arrangement was continued. The two-level grille consisted of criss-cross pieces. Three bent vertical bars were on the front fenders. A heater and defroster were standard equipment.

MERCURY & COMET I.D. NUMBERS: The Vehicle Identification Number is on the left inner fender of Comets and Meteors and right cowl tab on Mercurys. First symbol: 6 = 1966. Second symbol identifies assembly plant: A = Atlanta, Ga.; B = Oakville, (Canada); D = Dallas, Texas; E = Mahwah, N.J.; F = Dearborn Mich.; G = Chicago, Ill.; H = Lorain, Ohio; J = Los Angeles, Calif.; K = Kansas City, Kan.; N = Norfolk, Va.; P = St. Paul, Minn.; R = San Jose, Calif.; S = Pilot Plant; T = Metuchen, N.J.; W = Wayne, Mich.; Y = Wixom, Mich.; Z = St. Louis, Mo. Third and fourth symbols are body code (See Body/Style Number column in charts below). Fifth symbol identifies engine: (Comet) T = 200 cid six; 2 = 200 cid six (export); C = 289 cid/200-hp V-8; 3 = 289 cid V-8 (export); Y = 390 cid/265-hp V-8; H = 390 cid/275-hp V-8. (Mercury) Y = 390 cid/265-hp V-8 2V; H = 390 cid/275-hp V-8 2V; M = 410 cid/330-hp V-8; Q = 428 cid/360-hp V-8 4V (high-performance); 8 = 428 cid (export); Q = 428 cid/345-hp V-8; R = 427 cid/425-hp V-8. Last six symbols are sequential production number starting at 500001. Body plate on front body pillar gives VIN, body code, color, trim, date, engine, transmission and axle codes.

COMET 202

Model No.	Body/ Style No.	Body Type & Seating	Factory Price	Shipping Weight	Prod. Total
202	01	2-dr Sed-6P	2206	2779	35,964
202	02	4-dr Sed-6P	2263	2823	20,440

COMET CAPRI SERIES — Rocker panel moldings, front fender medallions and chrome side window trim were styling features of the Capri intermediate. Carpeting was standard.

COMET CAPRI

Model No.	Body/ Style No.	Body Type & Seating	Factory Price	Shipping Weight	Prod. Total
N/A	12	4-dr Sed-6P	2378	2844	15,635
N/A	13	2-dr HT Cpe-6P	2400	2876	15,031

1966 Mercury Comet Caliente four-door sedan, 6-cyl. (OCW)

1966 Mercury Comet Caliente two-door convertible, V-8. (PH)

CALIENTE SERIES — Calientes had chrome trimmed wheelwell openings and moldings above the rocker panels. Their interiors were a bit plusher than those on other Comets.

CALIENTE

Model No.	Body/Style No.	Body Type & Seating	Factory Price	Shipping Weight	Prod. Total
N/A	22	4-dr Sed-6P	2453	2846	17,933
N/A	23	2-dr HT Cpe-6P	2475	2882	25,862
N/A	25	2-dr Conv-6P	2735	3143	3,922

1966 Mercury Comet Cyclone two-door hardtop, V-8. (OCW)

1966 Mercury Comet Cyclone 'GT' two-door hardtop, V-8. (OCW)

1966 Mercury Montclair two-door hardtop, V-8. (OCW)

CYCLONE SERIES — A special front fender nameplate, body strips above the rocker panels and a different, horizontal bar grille made it easy to tell a Cyclone from other Comets. Bucket seats and chromed wheels were standard.

CYCLONE

Model No.	Body/Style No.	Body Type & Seating	Factory Price	Shipping Weight	Prod. Total
N/A	27	2-dr HT Cpe-5P	2700	3074	6,889
N/A	29	2-dr Conv-5P	2961	3321	1,305
N/A	26	2-dr GT Conv-5P	3152	3595	2,158
N/A	28	2-dr GT Cpe-5P	2891	3315	13,812

MONTEREY SERIES — The new 1966 Mercury grille consisted of horizontal bars and a thin vertical piece in the center. Small signal lights wrapped around the front fenders. Large chrome ringed tail-lights, at the ends of the rear fenders, appeared to be bumper-integrated. The Mercury name was written on the hood and trunk lid. A Monterey nameplate appeared on the rear fenders. A large, criss-cross pattern trim piece was on the front fenders. Carpeting with fabric and vinyl upholstery was standard, except in the convertible, which had an all-vinyl interior.

MONTEREY

Model No.	Body/Style No.	Body Type & Seating	Factory Price	Shipping Weight	Prod. Total
N/A	42	4-dr Brzway-6P	2917	3966	14,174
N/A	43	2-dr Sed-6P	2783	3835	2,487
N/A	44	4-dr Sed-6P	2854	3903	18,998
N/A	45	2-dr Conv-6P	3237	4039	3,279
N/A	47	2-dr HT Cpe-6P	2915	3885	19,103
N/A	48	4-dr HT Sed-6P	2990	3928	7,647

NOTE: Model number 42, the four-door Breezeway, was a sedan with slanting and retractable rear window styling.

MONTCLAIR SERIES — Fender-to-fender upper body moldings and chrome rocker panels were two styling features of the Montclair. An electric clock, interval selector windshield wipers. Deluxe steering wheel and wheel covers were standard.

MONTCLAIR

Model No.	Body/Style No.	Body Type & Seating	Factory Price	Shipping Weight	Prod. Total
N/A	54	4-dr Sed-6P	3087	3921	11,856
N/A	57	2-dr HT Cpe-6P	3144	3887	11,290
N/A	58	4-dr HT Sed-6P	3217	3971	15,767

PARK LANE SERIES — A wide, full-length molding (at tire level) on the bodysides and rear deck panel trim were distinguishing features of the Park Lane.

1966 Mercury Park Lane Breezeway four-door sedan, V-8. (OCW)

1966 Mercury Park Lane four-door hardtop, V-8. (PH)

1966 Mercury Park Lane two-door convertible, V-8. (OCW)

PARK LANE

Model No.	Body/ Style No.	Body Type & Seating	Factory Price	Shipping Weight	Prod. Total
N/A	62	4-dr Brzway-6P	3389	4051	8,696
N/A	65	2-dr Conv-6P	3608	4148	2,546
N/A	67	2-dr HT Cpe-6P	3387	3971	8,354
N/A	68	4-dr HT Sed-6P	3460	4070	19,204

NOTE: Model number 62, the four-door Breezeway, was a sedan with slanting and retractable rear window styling.

MERCURY S-55 SERIES — The sporty S-55 had full-length mid-body chrome trim, chrome rocker panels and a rear fender medallion. Bucket seats, a center console and dual exhaust were a few of its standard features.

1966 Mercury S-55 two-door convertible, with Super Marauder 428 cid/345-hp V-8. (OCW)

1966 Mercury Comet Villager station wagon, V-8. (OCW)

MERCURY S-55 SERIES

Model No.	Body/ Style No.	Body Type & Seating	Factory Price	Shipping Weight	Prod. Total
N/A	46	2-dr Conv-5P	3614	4148	669
N/A	49	2-dr HT Cpe-5P	3292	4031	2,916

COMET STATION WAGON SERIES — The Voyager was based on the Comet Capri series. The Villager was a bit more luxurious and featured simulated woodgrain body panels.

COMET STATION WAGONS

Model No.	Body/ Style No.	Body Type & Seating	Factory Price	Shipping Weight	Prod. Total
N/A	06	4-dr Voy-6P	2553	3201	7,595
N/A	16	4-dr Vill-6P	2780	3244	3,880

MERCURY STATION WAGON SERIES — Commuters were trimmed like Montclairs and shared the same standard features. The Colony Park had simulated wood panels and Deluxe wheel covers. A power tailgate window was standard in the top-of-the-line station wagon.

MERCURY STATION WAGONS

Model No.	Body/ Style No.	Body Type & Seating	Factory Price	Shipping Weight	Prod. Total
N/A	72	4-dr Comm-6P	3240	4280	6,847
N/A	76	4-dr Col Prk-6P	3502	4332	18,894

ENGINE [Comet Six]: Overhead valve. Cast-iron block. Displacement: 200 cid. Bore and stroke: 3.68 x 3.13 inches. Compression ratio: 9.2:1. Brake hp: 120 at 4400 rpm. Seven main bearings. Carburetor: Ford C3PF-9510-A one-barrel.

ENGINE [Cyclone V-8]: Overhead valve. Cast-iron block. Displacement: 289 cid. Bore and stroke: 4.00 x 2.87 inches. Compression ratio: 9.3:1. Brake hp: 200 at 4400 rpm. Five main bearings. Carburetor: Ford C4OF-9510-AM two-barrel.

ENGINE [Monterey V-8]: Overhead valve. Cast-iron block. Displacement: 390 cid. Bore and stroke: 4.05 x 3.78 inches. Compression ratio: 9.5:1. Brake hp: 265 at 4400 rpm. Five main bearings. Carburetor: Ford C6AF-9510-AM two-barrel.

ENGINE [Park Lane V-8]: Overhead valve. Cast-iron block. Displacement: 410 cid. Bore and stroke: 4.05 x 3.98 inches. Compression ratio: 10.5:1. Brake hp: 330 at 4600 rpm. Carburetor: Ford C6MF-9510-E four-barrel.

ENGINE [S-55 V-8]: Overhead valve. Cast-iron block. Displacement: 428 cid. Bore and stroke: 4.13 x 3.98 inches. Compression ratio:10.5:1. Carburetor: Ford C6AF-9510-AD four-barrel.

ENGINE [Station Wagon Six]: Overhead valve. Cast-iron block. Displacement: 200 cid. Bore and stroke: 3.68 x 3.13 inches. Compression ratio: 9.2:1. Brake hp: 120 at 4400 rpm. Carburetor: Ford C3PF-9510-A one-barrel.

1966 Mercury Colony Park station wagon, V-8. (OCW)

COMET & STATION WAGON CHASSIS FEATURES: Wheelbase: (passenger car) 116 inches; (station wagon) 113 inches. Overall length: (passenger car) 203 inches; (station wagon) 199.9 inches. Tires: (passenger car) 6.95 x 14; (station wagon) 7.75 x 14.

COMET & STATION WAGON OPTIONS: Air conditioner ($257.50). Heavy-duty battery ($7.60). Elapsed-time clock ($20). Courtesy light group ($14.60). Remote-control trunk lid release ($11). Emergency flasher ($12.80). Tinted glass ($27.10). Tinted windshield ($18.10). Backup lights ($10.70). Station wagon luggage rack ($64.35). Remote-control outside rearview mirror ($12). Curb molding ($16.10). Padded dash ($16.40). Padded visors ($4.50). Two-tone paint ($19.40). Power brakes ($43.20). Power steering ($66.30). Power tailgate window ($29.75). Push-button AM radio ($56.50). AM/FM radio ($129.30). Rally Pac, in Cyclone ($40); in other models ($63). Retractable front seat belts ($7.10). Caliente hardtop convertible front bucket seats with console ($131.30). Front bucket seats only in two-door sedan ($79.60). Size 6.95 x 14 whitewall tires. Tachometer ($43.10). Vacuum gauge ($20). Wheel covers ($19.20). Wire wheel covers, in Cyclone ($43.20); in others ($64.40). Windshield washer and wipers ($21.60). Vinyl roof on hardtops ($75.60). A three-speed manual transmission standard. Four-speed manual and Merc-O-Matic transmissions were optional. A 289 cid/200-hp V-8 (two-barrel); 390 cid/265-hp V-8 (two-barrel); 390 cid/275-hp V-8 (four-barrel) and a 390 cid/335-hp V-8 were offered. The last engine was standard with the GT option. It also included twin hood scoops; body strips; distinctive grille; special emblems; heavy-duty suspension; power booster fan and dual exhaust. The Cyclone option was called GTA if ordered with an automatic transmission. A power transfer axle was also available.

MERCURY OPTIONS: Air conditioner ($430). Bucket seats in Monterey hardtop and convertible ($160.90). Reclining passenger side bucket seat in Park Lane ($45.10). Console and tachometer in Monterey ($66.80). Courtesy light group ($23.20). Remote-control trunk lid release ($11). Decor group in Monterey sedans ($34.80); in Monterey hardtop and Commuters ($21.90); in Monterey convertible ($14.20). Power door locks, in two-doors ($37.30); in four-doors ($52.80). Speed actuated rear door locks ($25.80). Electric clock ($16.10). Tinted windshield ($3). Tinted glass ($43). Luggage rack ($64.40). Padded dash ($21.30). Padded visors ($5.60). Two-tone paint ($22). Power antenna ($29.60). Power brakes ($43.20). Four-Way power bucket seat, driver's side ($92.10). Six-Way power seats ($96.50). Power windows ($106.20). Power vent windows ($52.60). Push-button AM radio ($61.10). AM/FM push-button radio with rear speaker ($146.60). Rear seat speaker ($19.30). Studiosonic rear speaker ($53.50). Third seat in station wagons ($75.60). Retractable front seat belts ($7.10). Sports package in Park Lane two-door hardtop and convertible ($423). Tilting steering wheel ($43.10). Whitewall tires ($40.56). All-vinyl Deluxe trim in Monterey hardtops and four-door sedans ($70.60). Leather trim in Park Lane bench seats ($98.80). Visibility group in Monterey ($30.80). Trip odometer ($8.90). Wheel covers with spinners, on Monterey ($38.40); on Montclair and Park Lane ($19.20). Deluxe wheel covers on Monterey ($19.20). Custom wheel covers, on Monterey ($54.10); on Montclair and Park Lane ($34.90). Wire wheel covers on Monterey ($64.40); on Montclair and Park Lane ($45.20). Vinyl roof ($88.80). Windshield washer ($13.70). Cornering lights. A three-speed manual transmission was standard in all but the S-55, which came with either a four-speed manual or Multi-Drive automatic transmission. These transmissions were both optional in the other series, except the four-speed was not available in station wagons. A 390 cid/275-hp V-8 (two-barrel); a 410 cid/330-hp V-8 (four-barrel) and a 428 cid/345-hp V-8 (four-barrel) were offered. A power transfer and a high-performance axle were optional.

HISTORICAL FOOTNOTE: Most 1966 Comets, 72 percent, had automatic transmissions. A V-8 engine was ordered in 63.7 percent of these cars. The one-millionth Comet built was a Caliente four-door sedan. The Cyclone GT was chosen as the official pace car at the 1966 Indianapolis 500 race.

1967 MERCURY

1967 Mercury Cougar. (OCW)

1967 Mercury Comet Caliente four-door sedan, 6-cyl. (PH)

COMET 202 SERIES — Comet styling was close to that of the Ford Fairlane it was based on. The horizontal grille, with a vertical piece in the center, was framed by stacks of two headlights on each fender. The sides were clean except for a '202' nameplate on the front fenders. The vertical taillights were on the ends of the rear fenders. About the only extras not optional on the '202' were a dome light and a cigarette lighter.

MERCURY I.D. NUMBERS: The Vehicle Identification Number is on cowl extension tab below hood and consists of 11 symbols. First symbol: 7 = 1967. Second symbol indicates assembly plant: F = Dearborn, Mich. (Cougar); J = Los Angeles, Calif. (Comet); H = Lorain, Ohio (Comet); W = Wayne, Mich. (Mercury); and Z = St. Louis, Mo. (Mercury). Third and fourth symbols are Body/Style Number in charts below. Fifth symbol identifies engine code. Last six symbols are sequential production number starting at 100001 at each plant. Body Number Plate on left front door lock face panel provides additional information on model year, assembly point, body type, engine, color, trim, axle and transmission.

COMET 202

Model No.	Body/ Style No.	Body Type & Seating	Factory Price	Shipping Weight	Prod. Total
N/A	01	2-dr Sed-6P	2284	2787	14,251
N/A	02	4-dr Sed-6P	2336	2825	10,281

CAPRI SERIES — The Capri had nearly full-length, mid-bodyside moldings and nameplates on the rear quarter panel. Vinyl and fabric or all-vinyl upholstery, deep-loop carpeting and rear armrests were among the standard features.

CAPRI

Model No.	Body/ Style No.	Body Type & Seating	Factory Price	Shipping Weight	Prod. Total
N/A	06	4-dr Sed-6P	2436	2860	9,292
N/A	07	2-dr HT Cpe-6P	2459	2889	11,671

CALIENTE SERIES — Bright fender ornaments, rocker panel and wheel opening moldings and full-length upper-body pin stripes set the Caliente apart from other Comets. Its interior featured woodgrain dash and door panels, luxury armrests and paddle-type door handles.

CALIENTE

Model No.	Body/ Style No.	Body Type & Seating	Factory Price	Shipping Weight	Prod. Total
N/A	10	4-dr Sed-6P	2535	2871	9,153
N/A	11	2-dr HT Cpe-6P	2558	2901	9,966
N/A	12	2-dr Conv-6P	2818	3170	1,539

1967 Mercury Comet Caliente two-door convertible, V-8. (OCW)

1967 Mercury Cyclone 'GT' two-door hardtop, V-8. (OCW)

CYCLONE SERIES — The Cyclone looked about the same as the Caliente, less the fender ornaments. Its grille had fewer horizontal pieces. The rear deck panel was blacked-out and the word Cyclone was spelled out on it. Bucket seats and all-vinyl upholstery were standard.

CYCLONE

Model No.	Body/ Style No.	Body Type & Seating	Factory Price	Shipping Weight	Prod. Total
N/A	15	2-dr HT Cpe-5P	2737	3075	6,101
N/A	16	2-dr Conv-5P	2997	2229	809

COMET STATION WAGON SERIES — The Voyager station wagon had a distinctive elongated U-shaped chrome piece on its front fenders. The Villager featured woodgrain side and tailgate panels. It came with crinkle vinyl upholstery and a dual-action tailgate.

COMET STATION WAGONS

Model No.	Body/ Style No.	Body Type & Seating	Factory Price	Shipping Weight	Prod. Total
N/A	03	4-dr Voy Sta Wag-6P	2604	3230	4,930
N/A	08	4-dr Vill Sta Wag-6P	2841	3252	3,140

COUGAR SERIES — One of America's handsomest 1967 automobiles, the new Cougar was a niche marketing success for Mercury in that it bridged the gap between Ford's Mustang's performance and the Thunderbird's luxury. Cougar featured disappearing headlights, wraparound front and rear fenders and triple taillights (with sequential turn signals). The front and rear end styling were similar. Cougars came equipped with all-vinyl bucket seats, three-spoke 'sport-style' steering wheel, deep-loop carpeting, Deluxe seat belts and floor-mounted three-speed manual transmission.

1967 Mercury Cougar two-door hardtop (with optional GT wheels), V-8.

1967 Mercury Cougar two-door hardtop (with optional GT package), V-8. (PH)

COUGAR

Model No.	Body/ Style No.	Body Type & Seating	Factory Price	Shipping Weight	Prod. Total
N/A	91	2-dr HT Cpe-5P	2851	3005	123,672

COUGAR XR-7 SERIES — The XR-7 was introduced in mid-model year. Except for a medallion on the roof's quarter panel, it looked like the standard Cougar, but it came with a woodgrain dashboard insert and fancier interior.

COUGAR XR-7

Model No.	Body/ Style No.	Body Type & Seating	Factory Price	Shipping Weight	Prod. Total
N/A	93	2-dr HT Cpe-5P	3081	3015	27,221

MONTEREY SERIES — The center section of the horizontal bar grille protruded slightly and the signal lights were now located in the front bumpers. Wheelwell openings had chrome moldings. The only additional side trim on the Monterey was a front fender criss-cross pattern trim piece and the Monterey name on the rear fenders. A fabric and vinyl interior was standard, except in the convertible, which had all-vinyl upholstery. An S-55 Sports Package was optional on the Monterey convertible and two-door hardtop.

MONTEREY

Model No.	Body/ Style No.	Body Type & Seating	Factory Price	Shipping Weight	Prod. Total
N/A	44	4-dr Sed-6P	2904	3798	15,177
N/A	44	4-dr Brzwy-6P	2904	3847	5,910
N/A	45	2-dr Conv-6P	3311	3943	2,673
N/A	47	2-dr HT Cpe-6P	2985	3820	16,910
N/A	48	4-dr HT Sed-6P	3059	3858	8,013

NOTE 1: The Breezeway sedan had a slanting and retractable rear window.

MONTCLAIR SERIES — The Montclair had full-length upper body moldings. A nameplate was located on the rear fenders. Standard features included Deluxe wheel covers, electric clock, Deluxe steering wheel and Deluxe front and rear seat belts with reminder light. Regular equipment was listed as: carpeting; padded dash and visors; two-speed windshield wipers; windshield washers; emergency flasher; courtesy light group and remote-control outside rearview mirror. These same features were also found in Monterey models for 1967.

MONTCLAIR

Model No.	Body/ Style No.	Body Type & Seating	Factory Price	Shipping Weight	Prod. Total
N/A	54	4-dr Sed-6P	3187	3863	5,783
N/A	54	4-dr Brzwy-6P	3187	3881	4,151
N/A	57	2-dr HT Cpe-6P	3244	3848	4,118
N/A	58	4-dr HT Sed-6P	3316	3943	5,870

NOTE 1: The Breezeway sedan had a slanting and retractable rear window.

PARK LANE SERIES — Full-length tire-level moldings, wheelwell chrome trim and front fender emblems were styling features of the Park Lane. Standard equipment included an automatic parking brake release, rear seat armrests, vanity mirror, spare tire cover and power front disc brakes.

1967 Mercury Park Lane Brougham Breezeway four-door sedan, V-8. (PH)

PARK LANE

Model No.	Body/ Style No.	Body Type & Seating	Factory Price	Shipping Weight	Prod. Total
N/A	64	4-dr Brzwy-6P	3736	4011	4,163
N/A	65	2-dr Conv-6P	3984	4114	1,191
N/A	67	2-dr HT Cpe-6P	3752	3947	2,196
N/A	68	4-dr HT Sed-6P	3826	3992	5,412

NOTE 1: The Breezeway sedan had a slanting and retractable rear window.

BROUGHAM SERIES — Broughams were basically similar to the Park Lane models, which they resembled, but were slightly fancier. Extra body insulation, unique interior and exterior ornamentation and woodgrain steering wheel and trim were standard features.

BROUGHAM

Model No.	Body/ Style No.	Body Type & Seating	Factory Price	Shipping Weight	Prod. Total
N/A	61	4-dr Brzwy-6P	3896	3980	3,325
N/A	62	4-dr HT Sed-6P	3986	4000	4,189

NOTE 1: The Breezeway sedan had a slanting and retractable rear window.

MARQUIS SERIES — Two noticeable features of the new Marquis two-door hardtop were a vinyl roof and five, full-length, lower body pin stripes. Power front disc brakes; woodgrain interior trim; Deluxe body insulation; electric clock; courtesy light group; spare tire cover and plush fabric and vinyl upholstery were among the many standard items in the Marquis. The front seats had individual fold-down armrests.

MARQUIS

Model No.	Body/ Style No.	Body Type & Seating	Factory Price	Shipping Weight	Prod. Total
N/A	69	2-dr HT Cpe-6P	3989	3995	6,510

MERCURY STATION WAGON SERIES — The Commuter station wagon had full-length upper body moldings. The Colony Park had woodgrain panels outlined by chrome trim. Both station wagons had a heater and defroster and dual-action tailgate. In addition, the Colony Park came with an electric clock; Deluxe wheel covers; Deluxe steering wheel; power rear tailgate window; power front disc brakes; and all-vinyl or parchment Mosaic fabric interiors.

STATION WAGONS

Model No.	Body/ Style No.	Body Type & Seating	Factory Price	Shipping Weight	Prod. Total
N/A	72	4-dr Comm-6/9P	3269	4178	7,898*
N/A	76	4-dr Col Pk-6/9/10P	3657	4258	18,680*

NOTE: (*) Production Totals are for Commuter and Colony Park station wagons in both six- and nine-passenger (also 10-passenger configuration for Colony Park) versions. The production breakdown is: Commuter-6P (3,447); Commuter-9P (4,451); Colony Park-6P (5,775); Colony Park-9/10P (12,915).

1967 Mercury Marquis two-door hardtop, V-8. (OCW)

ENGINE [(Comet 202/Capri/Comet Station Wagon) Six]: Overhead valve. Cast-iron block. Displacement: 200 cid. Bore and stroke: 3.68 x 3.13 inches. Compression ratio: 9.2:1. Brake hp: 120 at 4400 rpm. Seven main bearings. Carburetor: Autolite C7DF-9510-Z one-barrel (Engine Code T).

ENGINE [(Cyclone/Cougar/XR-7) V-8]: Overhead valve. Cast-iron block. Displacement: 289 cid. Bore and stroke: 4.00 x 2.87 inches. Compression ratio: 9.3:1. Brake hp: 200 at 4400 rpm. Five main bearings. Carburetor: Autolite C7DF-9510-Z two-barrel (Engine Code C).

ENGINE [(Monterey/Montclair/Mercury Station Wagon) V-8]: Overhead valve. Cast-iron block. Displacement: 390 cid. Bore and stroke: 4.05 x 3.78 inches. Compression ratio: 10.5:1. Brake hp: 270 at 4400 rpm. Five main bearings. Carburetor: Holley C7OF-9510-A four-barrel. (Engine Code H).

ENGINE [(Park Lane/Brougham/Marquis) V-8]: Overhead valve. Cast-iron block. Displacement: 410 cid. Bore and stroke: 4.05 x 3.98 inches. Compression ratio: 10.5:1. Brake hp: 330 at 4600 rpm. Carburetor: C7AF-9510-AE four-barrel. (Engine Code M).

CHASSIS FEATURES: Wheelbase: (passenger car) 116 inches; (station wagon) 113 inches. Overall length: (four-doors and convertible) 203.5 inches; (two-doors) 196 inches; (station wagon) 199.9 inches. Tires: (passenger car) 7.35 x 14; (station wagon and Cyclone GT) 7.75 x 14.

COUGAR CHASSIS FEATURES: Wheelbase: 111 inches. Overall length: 190 inches. Tires: 7.35 x 14.

MERCURY CHASSIS FEATURES: Wheelbase: (passenger car) 123 inches; (station wagon) 119 inches. Overall length: (passenger car) 218.5 inches; (station wagon) 213.5 inches. Tires: (passenger car) 8.15 x 15; (station wagon) 8.45 x 15.

COMET OPTIONS: Air conditioning ($355.95). Heavy-duty battery ($7.44). Bright window frames ($17.70). Electric clock ($15.76). Remote-control deck lid release ($12.65). Tinted glass ($26.50). Tinted windshield ($19.50). Luggage rack on station wagons ($66.99). Right-hand side view mirror ($6.95). Outside rearview mirror with remote-control ($9.60). Curb molding ($15.76). Oxford roof ($84.25). Two-tone paint ($27.06). Power brakes ($42.29). Power disc brakes ($84.25). Four-Way power bench seat ($62.45). Power steering ($95). Power windows ($100.10). AM radio with antenna ($60.05). AM/FM radio with antenna ($133.65). Rear seat speaker ($15.60). Deluxe seat belts, front and rear with warning light ($10.40). Station wagon third seat with two belts ($51.31). Shoulder belts ($27.06). Stereo-sonic tape system ($128.50). Dual-action station wagon tailgate ($45.40). Tachometer ($47.30). Vinyl interior for Comet 202 models ($27.47). Wire wheel covers ($69.52). Styled steel wheels ($115.15). Interval selector windshield wipers ($11.59). Courtesy light group ($19.69). Wide oval, whitewall nylon tires ($82.94). A three-speed manual transmission was standard. Four-speed manual and Merc-O-Matic automatic transmissions were optional. A 289 cid/200-hp V-8 (two-barrel); 390 cid/270-hp V-8 (two-barrel) and a 390 cid/320-hp V-8 (four-barrel) were available. The last engine was standard in the Cyclone GT performance package, which also included dual exhaust; racing stripes; wide-oval nylon whitewall tires; heavy-duty suspension; 3.25:1 axle ratio; power booster fan; twin hood scoops and power disc brakes. A performance handling package was offered on cars equipped with the 390 cid/270-hp V-8. It featured higher rate front and rear springs, large diameter stabilizer bar and heavy-duty shocks. Buyers could also order a high-performance or power transfer axle.

COUGAR OPTIONS: Air conditioner ($355.95). Heavy-duty battery ($7.44). Rear bumper guards ($16.85). Electric clock ($15.76). Courtesy light group ($16.85). Door edge guards ($4.40). Tinted glass ($30.25). Tinted windshield ($21.09). Deck lid luggage carrier ($32.45). Oxford roof ($84.25). Two-tone paint ($27.06). Power brakes ($42.29). Power disc brakes ($64.25). Power steering ($95). AM radio ($60.05). AM/FM radio ($133.65). AM radio with Stereo-sonic tape system ($188.50). Front bench seat with center armrest ($24.42). Shoulder belts ($27.06). Speed control ($71.30). Sports console ($57). Tilting steering wheel ($60.05). Comfort-weave vinyl interior ($33.05). Deluxe wheel covers ($16.79). Wire wheel covers ($69.51). Visual check panel ($39.50). Styled steel wheels ($115.15). A three-speed manual transmission was standard except in the XR-7, which came with a four-speed manual transmission. The four-speed was optional in the standard Cougar. Merc-O-Matic SelectShift automatic transmission was optional in both series. A 289 cid/225-hp V-8 (four-barrel) and a 390 cid/320-hp V-8 (four-barrel) were available. The GT performance package included: 390 cid/335-hp V-8; performance handling package; wide-oval white-wall tires; low back pressure exhaust; power disc brakes and medallions. A power transfer axle was available.

MERCURY OPTIONS: Air conditioner ($421.26). Heavy-duty battery ($7.44). Deck lid release with remote control for all passenger cars ($12.65). Door edge guards, in two-doors ($4.40); in four-doors ($6.66). Dual exhaust ($31.52). Electric clock ($15.76). Tinted glass

($42.09). Tinted windshield ($27.41). Automatic headlight dimmer ($41.60). Cornering lights ($33.26). Luggage rack ($62.99). Right-hand side view mirror ($6.95). Remote-control mirror ($9.60). Curb molding ($15.81). Oxford roof, on two-door hardtops ($88.99); on four-door hardtops and sedans ($99.47); on station wagons ($131.65). Two-tone paint ($26.97). Power antenna ($26.97). Power brakes ($42.29). Power door locks, in two-doors ($44.23); in four-doors ($67.62). Power rear windows ($31.62). Six-Way power seats, bucket type ($64.25); bench type ($94.45). Power seat for S-55, bucket type ($166.40); lounge type ($64.25); driver and passenger ($166.40). Power steering ($103.95). Power vent windows ($51.66). Power windows ($103.95). AM push-button radio ($62.15). AM/FM push-button radio ($150.64). AM radio with stereo tape system ($190.65). Deluxe front and rear seat belts ($10.40). Monterey and Commuter shoulder belts ($27.06). Spare tire cover ($3.90). Speed control ($90.74). Tilting steering wheel ($42.19). Station wagon third seat ($95.36). Deluxe interior trim, in Commuter ($69.30); in Colony Park ($77.80). Leather with vinyl trim, in Park Lane and Marquis hardtops ($109.45). Mondero all-vinyl trim in Monterey ($69.30). Visual safety-check panel ($31.42). Deluxe wheel covers on Monterey and Commuter ($18.79). Wheel covers with spinners, in Monterey ($18.79); in Commuter ($37.59). Wire wheel covers, on Monterey ($69.50); on others ($50.75). A three-speed manual transmission was standard in all, but the Park Lane and Brougham. These came with four-speed manual or Merc-O-Matic SelectShift transmission. Both of these transmissions were optional in the other series. The four-speed was not available in station wagons. A 410 cid/330-hp V-8 (four-barrel); 427 cid/345-hp V-8 (four barrel) and a 426 cid/360-hp V-8 (four-barrel) were optional. The 345-hp engine was standard in the S-55 performance package, which also included dual exhaust; engine dress-up kit; heavy-duty battery; power disc brakes; Deluxe wheel covers with spinners; deck lid applique; side paint stripe; door trim panels; bucket seats; sports console; Deluxe steering wheel; Deluxe sound package; and S-55 ornamentation. High-performance and power transfer axles were available.

HISTORY: Three of the most popular Comet options (and their attachment rates) were automatic transmission (82.4 percent), V-8 engine (67.4 percent) and power steering (49.6 percent). A total of 3,419 Cyclone hardtops and 376 convertibles were sold with the GT performance package. Only 7,412 Cougars came with the optional front bench seat. Just 5.3 percent were equipped with a four-speed manual transmission. The most popular options in full-size 1967 Mercurys included: automatic transmission (96.2 percent), power steering (97 percent), tinted glass (69.7 percent) and power brakes (65.6 percent). The Cougar received *Motor Trend* magazine's "Car of the Year" award for 1967. It accounted for nearly half of Mercury's sales this year.

1968 MERCURY

1968 Mercury Montego MX. (OCW)

COMET SERIES — The new Comet was restyled for 1968. It looked like a full-size Mercury that had gone on a diet. The Comet had a horizontal grille, rocker panel moldings, side marker lights and chrome-encased, vertical taillights. Among the standard features were an energy absorbing steering column and steering wheel; front and rear seat belts; shoulder belts; padded dash; padded sun visors; dual brakes with warning light; and two-speed windshield wipers and washers.

MERCURY I.D. NUMBERS: The Vehicle Identification Number is on a tag on top right-hand side of instrument panel, visible through windshield. VIN consists of 11 symbols. First symbol: 8 = 1968. Second symbol indicates assembly plant: F = Dearborn, Mich. (Cougar); J =

San Jose, Calif. (Cougar); H = Lorain, Ohio (Montego/Comet); and Z = St. Louis, Mo. (Mercury). Third and fourth symbols are Body/Style Number in charts below. Fifth symbol identifies engine code. Last six symbols are sequential production number starting at 100001 at each plant. Body Number Plate on left front door lock face panel provides additional information on model year, assembly point, body type, engine, color, trim, axle and transmission.

COMET

Model No.	Body/ Style No.	Body Type & Seating	Factory Price	Shipping Weight	Prod. Total
N/A	01	2-dr HT Cpe-6P	2477	3078	16,693

MONTEGO SERIES — The Montego looked about the same as the Comet. It had the same standard features as well plus curb moldings, cigar lighter and glovebox lock.

MONTEGO

Model No.	Body/ Style No.	Body Type & Seating	Factory Price	Shipping Weight	Prod. Total
N/A	06	4-dr Sed-6P	2504	2982	18,492
N/A	07	2-dr HT Cpe-6P	2552	3057	15,002

MONTEGO MX SERIES — Full-length upper and lower body trim, chrome wheelwell trim and a vinyl top were styling features of the Montego MX. It also had bright metal upper door frames, simulated wood inserts in the lower body molding, woodgrain door trim panel inserts and carpeting.

MONTEGO MX

Model No.	Body/ Style No.	Body Type & Seating	Factory Price	Shipping Weight	Prod. Total
N/A	08	4-dr Sta Wag-6P	2876	3379	9,328
N/A	10	4-dr Sed-6P	2657	3007	15,264
N/A	11	2-dr HT Cpe-6P	2675	3081	25,827
N/A	12	2-dr Conv-6P	2935	3293	3,248

CYCLONE SERIES — Cyclones had a mid-tire-level body tape stripe. Those with the GT option had an upper body level racing stripe; bucket seats; wide tread whitewalls; special wheel covers; all-vinyl interior; and special handling package.

CYCLONE

Model No.	Body/ Style No.	Body Type & Seating	Factory Price	Shipping Weight	Prod. Total
N/A	15	2-dr Fsbk Cpe-6P	2768	3254	12,260
N/A	17	2-dr HT Cpe-6P	2768	3208	1,368

1968 Mercury Montego MX two-door hardtop, V-8. (OCW)

1968 Mercury Cyclone two-door fastback hardtop, V-8. (OCW)

1968 Mercury Cougar two-door hardtop, V-8. (OCW)

1968 Mercury Cougar XR-7 two-door hardtop (GT-E), V-8. (OCW)

COUGAR SERIES — If you liked the 1967 Cougar, you also liked the 1968 version. The biggest change was the addition of side marker lights. Standard equipment included: dual hydraulic brake system with warning light; front and rear seat belts; outside rearview mirror; padded dash; padded sun visors; two-speed windshield wipers and washers; four-way emergency flasher; and back-up lights.

COUGAR

Model No.	Body/ Style No.	Body Type & Seating	Factory Price	Shipping Weight	Prod. Total
N/A	91	2-dr HT Cpe-5P	2933	3094	81,014

COUGAR XR-7 SERIES — Rocker panel moldings, special wheel covers, deck lid medallions and XR-7 plaques on the rear roof pillars set the top-of-the-line Cougar apart from the basic series. Standard equipment included: an overhead console (with map and warning lights); deep-loop carpeting; tachometer; trip odometer; gauges; leather-trimmed vinyl seats and walnut tone instrument panel.

COUGAR XR-7

Model No.	Body/ Style No.	Body Type & Seating	Factory Price	Shipping Weight	Prod. Total
N/A	93	2-dr HT Cpe-5P	3232	3134	32,712

1968-1/2 Mercury Cougar XR7-G two-door hardtop (with optional sunroof), V-8. (PH)

1968 Mercury Monterey two-door convertible, V-8. (OCW)

1968 Mercury Montclair two-door hardtop, V-8. (PH)

MONTEREY SERIES — The Monterey had a new, equal-size horizontal bar grille that protruded at the center. The vertical signal lights wrapped around the front fenders. Rear end treatment resembled the previous year's. As before, the back window on cars with the Breezeway option could be lowered. Standard features included: dual brakes with warning light; energy absorbing steering column and steering wheel; seat belts; padded dash; padded sun visors; outside rearview mirror; side marker lights; heater/defroster; ashtray light; trunk light; four-way emergency flasher; glovebox light and shoulder belts.

MONTEREY

Model No.	Body/ Style No.	Body Type & Seating	Factory Price	Shipping Weight	Prod. Total
N/A	44	4-dr Sed-6P	3052	3798	30,727
N/A	45	2-dr Conv-6P	3436	4114	1,515
N/A	47	2-dr HT Cpe-6P	3133	3820	15,145
N/A	48	4-dr HT Sed-6P	3207	3858	8,927

MONTCLAIR SERIES — Deluxe wheel covers and full-length, tire-level moldings were two exterior differences between the Montclair and the lower-priced Monterey. An electric clock was among the many standard features.

MONTCLAIR

Model No.	Body/ Style No.	Body Type & Seating	Factory Price	Shipping Weight	Prod. Total
N/A	54	4-dr Sed-6P	3331	3863	7,255
N/A	57	2-dr HT Cpe-6P	3387	3848	3,497
N/A	58	4-dr HT Sed-6P	3459	3943	4,008

PARK LANE SERIES — The Park Lane had full-length, tire-level moldings that looked like two thin parallel strips with a narrow band of chrome between them. The wheelwell lips were also chromed and there were three slanted trim pieces on the roof quarter panels. Like all full-size Mercurys for 1968, the Park Lane had a redesigned, clustered dash (i.e.: dash instruments were placed in close proximity to the driver). The electrical system was improved as well. A seldom-ordered Park Lane option was 'yacht paneling', a fancy name for exterior woodgrain appliques on passenger cars.

PARK LANE

Model No.	Body/ Style No.	Body Type & Seating	Factory Price	Shipping Weight	Prod. Total
N/A	64	4-dr Sed-6P	3552	4011	7,008
N/A	65	2-dr Conv-6P	3822	4114	1,112
N/A	67	2-dr HT Cpe-6P	3575	3947	2,584
N/A	68	4-dr HT Sed-6P	3647	3992	10,390

MARQUIS SERIES — The Marquis was trimmed similar to the Montclair, except it came with a vinyl-covered roof. Its interior was also plusher.

MARQUIS

Model No.	Body/ Style No.	Body Type & Seating	Factory Price	Shipping Weight	Prod. Total
N/A	69	2-dr HT Cpe-6P	3685	3995	3,965

1968 Mercury Park Lane Brougham four-door hardtop, V-8. (PH)

1968 Mercury Colony Park station wagon, V-8. (OCW)

STATION WAGON SERIES — Both station wagons had full-length, tire-level moldings and chrome trimmed wheel openings. The Colony Park had plank-style woodgrain applique on its sides. A dual-action tailgate was standard on both.

STATION WAGONS

Model No.	Body/ Style No.	Body Type & Seating	Factory Price	Shipping Weight	Prod. Total
N/A	72	4-dr Comm-6P	3441	4178	8,688
N/A	76	4-dr Col Prk-6P	3760	4258	21,179

NOTE 1: A total of 5,191 Commuter and 15,505 Colony Park station wagons came with either a rear facing or dual-center facing rear seats.

ENGINE [(Comet/Montego/Montego MX) Six]: Overhead valve. Cast-iron block. Displacement: 200 cid. Bore and stroke: 3.66 x 3.13 inches. Compression ratio: 8.8:1. Brake hp: 115 at 3800 rpm. Seven main bearings. Carburetor: Autolite C8OF-9510-E one-barrel. (Engine Code T).

ENGINE [(Cyclone/Cougar/Cougar XR-7) V-8]: Overhead valve. Cast-iron block. Displacement: 302 cid. Bore and stroke: 4.00 x 3.00 inches. Compression ratio: 9.0:1. Brake hp: 210 at 4600 rpm. Carburetor: Autolite C8AF-9510-AF two-barrel. (Engine Code F; released Jan. 1, 1968).

ENGINE [(Monterey/Montclair/Mercury Station Wagon) V-8]: Overhead valve. Cast-iron block. Displacement: 390 cid. Bore and stroke: 4.05 x 3.78 inches. Compression ratio: 9.5:1. Brake hp: 265 at 4400 rpm. Carburetor: Autolite C8AF-9510-M two-barrel. (Engine Code Y).

ENGINE [(Park Lane/Marquis) V-8]: Overhead valve. Cast-iron block. Displacement: 390 cid. Bore and stroke: 4.05 x 3.78 inches. Compression ratio: 10.5:1. Brake hp: 315 at 4600 rpm. Carburetor: Autolite C8AF-9510-B four-barrel. (Engine Code Z).

COMET/MONTEGO CHASSIS FEATURES: Wheelbase: (passenger car) 116 inches; (station wagon) 113 inches. Overall length: (Cyclone fastback) 206.1 inches; (others) 206 inches. Tires: 7.74 x 14.

COUGAR CHASSIS FEATURES: Wheelbase: 111 inches. Overall length: 190.3 inches. Tires: E70-14.

MERCURY CHASSIS FEATURES: Wheelbase: (passenger car) 123 inches; (station wagon) 119 inches. Overall length: (passenger car) 220.1 inches; (station wagon) 215.4 inches. Tires: 8.15 x 15.

COMET/MONTEGO OPTIONS: Brougham interior option includes: exterior 'C' pillar ornament, unique seat and door trim, Brougham script on instrument panel and Deluxe steering wheel for Montego MX four-door sedan and two-door hardtop ($77.80). Appearance protection group includes: vinyl twin front and rear floor mats, door edge guards and license plate frames, for two-doors ($25.28); for four-doors ($29.17). Appearance special equipment group includes: Deluxe wheel covers; whitewall tires; courtesy light group; Comfort Stream ventilation ($64.85). Decor group includes: wheel lip moldings; right upper door frames for four-door only; unique lower back panel applique; Deluxe wheel covers for hardtop only, for hardtop with special appearance equipment group ($42.11); for hardtop without ($60.95); for sedan ($54.45). Light group, includes: two instrument panel lights; glovebox light; ashtray light; luggage compartment light; cargo light on station wagons; rear door jam switches for four-door models ($19.50). Heavy-duty battery ($7.44). Deluxe seat belts and seat belt reminder light includes: Deluxe front seat shoulder belts, Deluxe buckle and color-keyed webbing with black webbing on convertible ($29.61). Front seat shoulder belts includes regular buckle and black webbing; rear seat shoulder belts with regular buckle and black webbing, power disc front brakes, electric clock, Sports console ($50). Rear window defogger ($21.25). Tinted glass ($35.05). Tinted windshield ($21.09). Pair of adjustable head rests ($42.75). Luggage carrier for station wagons only ($62.99). Remote control left-hand mirror ($9.60). Two-tone paint ($30.96). AM radio with antenna ($61.40). AM/FM radio stereo with antenna ($184.95). Reflective tape stripe ($16.65). Oxford roof on two-door hardtop ($94.55); on four-door sedan ($94.55). Bucket seats

($110.15). Third, rear-facing seat in station wagons only ($51.31). Four-Way power bench seat ($62.45). Four-Way power bucket seats ($62.45). Dual rear seat speakers ($26). Power steering ($95). Deluxe steering wheels ($13.90). Tachometer ($46). Dual-action tailgate for station wagons only ($45.40). Comfort weave vinyl bench seat ($24.47). Ventilation system ($15.60). Visual check group, includes: low fuel, parking brake and door ajar warning lights ($32.45). Deluxe wheel covers ($21.29). Deluxe wheel covers with spinners ($20.10). Wheel covers ($41.40). Wire wheel covers with GT group or HT group ($50.75); without ($72.05). Styled steel wheels with GT or HT group ($96.36); without ($117.65). Power rear windows for station wagons ($31.62). Power side windows ($100.10). Two-speed interval selector windshield wipers ($14.19). Heavy-duty three-speed, four-speed manual and Merc-O-Matic SelectShift automatic transmissions were optional. The heavy-duty three-speed transmission was only available with the 390 cid/335-hp V-8. The four-speed manual transmission was not available with the six or 427 cid V-8. A 302 cid/210-hp V-8 (two barrel); 302 cid/230-hp V-8 (four-barrel); 390 cid/265-hp V-8 (two-barrel); 390 cid/335-hp V-8 (four-barrel); 428 cid/335-hp V-8 (four-barrel); and a 427 cid/390-hp V-8 (four-barrel) were optional. The latter two engines were offered only in hardtops. The 390 cid/335-hp V-8 was not available in station wagons. High-performance and power transfer axles were optional. A special handling package was offered on V-8-powered two-door hardtops and convertibles. It included: higher rate front and rear springs, a large diameter stabilizing bar and heavy-duty shocks.

COUGAR OPTIONS: Air conditioner ($360.90). Heavy-duty battery ($7.44). Deluxe seat belt with reminder light ($13.05). Deluxe front seat shoulder belts ($29.61). Deluxe rear seat shoulder belts ($29.61). Front seat shoulder belts ($27.06). Power disc brakes ($64.65). Electric clock ($15.76). Sports console ($57); Sports console for XR-7 only ($72.55). Rear window defogger ($21.25). Tinted glass ($30.25). Tinted windshield ($21.09). Door edge guards ($4.40). Rear bumper guards ($12.95). Adjustable front seat head rests ($42.75). Remote control left-hand mirror ($9.60). Visual-Check panel ($39.50). Two-tone paint ($31.10). AM radio with antenna ($60.90). AM/FM stereo ($21.25). Oxford roof ($41.60). Speed control ($71.30). Power steering ($95). Tilt-away steering wheel ($66.05). Stereo-sonic tape system ($195.15). Three-speed manual transmission ($79). Four-speed manual transmission ($164.02). Four-speed manual transmission with GT group ($105.02). Merc-O-Matic transmission with "302" engine ($206.65). Merc-O-Matic transmission with "390" engine ($226.10). Merc-O-Matic transmission with GT group ($147.10). Deluxe wheel covers ($21.29). Deluxe wheel covers with spinners on XR-7 ($16.79). Deluxe wheel covers, except on XR-7 ($72.05). Styled steel wheels on XR-7 ($96.36). Styled steel wheels ($117.65). Blackwall tubeless tires ($36.35). Whitewall tubeless tires ($36.35-$73.40). Red band tubeless tires ($36.95). SpaceSaver spare tires ($6.55-$19.50). Heavy-duty three-speed, four-speed manual, and SelectShift Merc-O-Matic automatic transmissions were optional. The heavy-duty three-speed transmission was only available with the 325-hp engine. The four-speed manual transmission was not available with the 260-hp or 390-hp V-8s. A 302 cid/230-hp V-8 (four-barrel); 390 cid/280-hp V-8 (two barrel); 390 cid/325-hp V-8 (four-barrel); and a 428 cid/335-hp V-8 (four-barrel) were optional. The 325-hp engine was standard with the GT option. This package also included: stiffer front and rear springs, heavy-duty shocks, low back pressure dual exhaust, power booster fan and a large diameter stabilizer bar. The 427 cid/390-hp V-8 was standard in the 7.0-liter GT-E package. It featured: twin hood scoops; styled steel wheels; quadruple trumpet exhaust; modified grille and taillight design; silver-gray trim on the lower body; extra stiff front and rear springs; heavy-duty shocks; and wide tread radial-ply tires.

1968 Mercury Cyclone GT two-door fastback hardtop, V-8. (OCW)

1968-1/2 Mercury Park Lane two-door convertible (with Colony Park "yacht deck" panel treatment), V-8. (PH)

MERCURY OPTIONS: Appearance and protection group includes: door edge guards, license plate frames, vinyl twin front and rear floor mats in two-doors ($25.30); in four-doors ($29 15). Brougham option includes: exterior Brougham script on 'C' pillar; Brougham script on glovebox; unique door trim panels; dual upper body paint stripes; twin comfort lounge seats; luxury level seat trim; in Park Lane four-door models with Oxford roof ($272.05); without Oxford roof ($172.58). Decor group, for Monterey and Commuter sedans includes: color-keyed interior rear window moldings on vehicles without Breezeway; Deluxe steering wheel; and rear door courtesy switch ($21.49). Decor group for four-door hardtop and Commuter, includes: bright drip moldings, Deluxe steering wheel, rear-door courtesy switch ($21.49). Decor group for two-door hardtop and convertibles includes: Deluxe steering wheel ($13.90). Whisperaire air conditioner ($421.28). Power antenna ($28 97). Heavy-duty battery ($7.44). Deluxe seat belts and seat belt reminder light, includes Deluxe buckle on all six belts and color-keyed webbing ($13.05). Shoulder belts, includes regular buckle and black webbing, front seat ($27.06); back seat ($27.06). Deluxe shoulder belts, includes Deluxe buckle and color-keyed webbing, front seat ($29.61); back seat ($29.61). Power disc brakes ($71.30). Electric clock ($15.76). Spare tire cover ($5.25). Tinted glass ($42.75). Tinted windshield ($27.41). Adjustable front seat head rests ($42.75). Power door locks for two-doors ($45.40); for four-doors ($66 65). Luggage carrier for station wagons only ($62.99). Manual right-hand side view mirror ($6.95). Remote control left-hand mirror ($9.60). Protective bodyside moldings ($45.40). Two-tone paint ($30.96). Visual-Check panel includes door-ajar warning light, seat belt reminder light, low-fuel reminder light and parking brake warning light ($32.45). AM radio with antenna ($63.40). AM/FM radio stereo with antenna ($169.34). Remote control deck lid release ($14). Oxford roof, for two-door ($99.47); for four-door ($99.47); for station wagons ($131.65). Rear-facing third seat in station wagons ($126.11). Dual center-facing seat in station wagons ($95.36). Six-Way power seat, bench ($94.80); driver's seat ($84.25); driver's and passenger's side ($166.40). Twin comfort lounge seats ($77.60). Dual rear seat speakers ($25.90). Speed control ($90.74). Power steering ($115.65). Tilt steering wheel ($42.75). Stereo-sonic tape system/AM radio combination ($197.25). Trim includes: door panels, seat trim and front seat courtesy lights in Colony Park with Deluxe interior ($84.25); in Monterey with Deluxe cloth-and-vinyl, seat interior ($84.25). Breezeway ventilation for sedans ($58.35). Comfort Stream and heating system ventilation ($40.10). Deluxe wheel covers ($21.29). Deluxe wheel covers with medallion for Monterey and Commuter ($40.14); others ($18.79). Wire wheel covers for Monterey and Commuter ($72.05); others ($50.75). Power rear window for Commuter and Colony Park ($31.62). Power side windows ($103.95). Power vent windows ($52.98). Two-speed interval selector windshield wipers ($14.19). A three-speed manual transmission was standard, except in the Park Lane and Marquis. Park Lane/Marquis came with SelectShift Merc-O-Matic transmission. This automatic was optional in the other series. A 390 cid/280-hp V-8 (two-barrel); 390 cid/315-hp V-8 (four-barrel); 390 cid/335-hp V-8 (four-barrel); 428 cid/340-hp V-8 (four-barrel); and 428 cid/360-hp V-8 (four-barrel) were optional. High-performance and power transfer axles were available.

HISTORY: Mercury built a total of 6,105 Cyclone fastbacks and 334 two-door Cyclone hardtops with the Cyclone GT option. Mercurys won seven NASCAR Grand National races in 1968. Only 2.7 percent of all 1968 Cougars were equipped with a four-speed manual transmission, 86.8 percent had an automatic transmission, 87.3 percent had power steering and 38.6 percent had power brakes. An XR-7 'G' was available on special order. It had hood pins, hood scoop, running lights and a vinyl top with sun roof. The vast majority of 1968 full-size Mercurys, 99.6 percent, were equipped with automatic transmission, 99.2 percent had power steering, 42.5 percent had a tilting steering wheel, 59.5 percent had air conditioning and 32.6 percent had power windows.

1969 MERCURY

1969 Mercury Marquis convertible. (OCW)

COMET SERIES — The new Comet had a framed horizontal bar grille. It protruded slightly in the center section, where a Comet emblem was housed. The side marker lights were now at bumper level. Teakwood-toned appliques were used on the instrument panel. The upholstery was cloth and vinyl.

MERCURY I.D. NUMBERS: The Vehicle Identification Number is on a metal tag affixed to left-hand top of dash and viewable through windshield. VIN consists of 11 symbols. First symbol: 9 = 1969. Second symbol indicates assembly plant: F = Dearborn, Mich. (Cougar); H = Lorain, Ohio (Montego); R = San Jose, Calif. (Cougar); and Z = St. Louis, Mo. (Mercury). Third and fourth symbols are Body/Style Number in charts below. Fifth symbol identifies engine code. Last six symbols are sequential production number starting at 100001 at each plant. Body Number Plate on left front door lock face panel provides additional information on model year, assembly point, body type, engine, color, trim, axle and transmission.

COMET

Model No.	Body/ Style No.	Body Type & Seating	Factory Price	Shipping Weight	Prod. Total
N/A	01	2-dr HT Cpe-6P	2515	3087	14,104

MONTEGO SERIES — Montegos had moldings above the rocker panels and trunk lid. There were fender-to-fender upper body twin pin stripes. Carpeting and cloth and vinyl, or all-vinyl upholstery were standard.

MONTEGO

Model No.	Body/ Style No.	Body Type & Seating	Factory Price	Shipping Weight	Prod. Total
N/A	06	4-dr Sed-6P	2538	3060	21,950
N/A	07	2-dr HT Cpe-6P	2588	3074	17,785

MONTEGO MX SERIES — Full-length lower body moldings, chromed wheel lip openings, fender-to-fender upper-body chrome trim, trunk lid appliques and wood-tone appliques on the lower dash panel were features of the Montego MX. The convertible had all-vinyl interior and a power top with glass rear window.

MONTEGO MX

Model No.	Body/ Style No.	Body Type & Seating	Factory Price	Shipping Weight	Prod. Total
N/A	08	4-dr Sta Wag-6P	2962	3458	10,590
N/A	10	4-dr Sed-6P	2701	3094	17,738
N/A	11	2-dr HT Cpe-6P	2719	3106	22,909
N/A	12	2-dr Conv-6P	2979	3356	1,725

1969 Mercury Montego two-door hardtop, V-8. (PH)

1969 Mercury Cougar Eliminator two-door hardtop, with Boss 302 V-8. (PH)

1969-1/2 Mercury Cyclone Spoiler two-door fastback hardtop (available as either Cale Yarborough Special or Dan Gurney Special signature editions), V-8. (PH)

NOTE 1: 3,621 Montego MX station wagons came with woodgrain side trim.

NOTE 2: Brougham option was installed on 1,590 four-door sedans and 1,226 two-door hardtops.

NOTE 3: Only 363 of the convertibles were sold with bucket seats.

CYCLONE SERIES — The sporty Cyclone fastback had rocker panel and wheel lip opening moldings. It also featured twin racing stripes, which ran from the front bumper and across the sides to the end of the rear fenders. Standard items included: carpeting, all-vinyl upholstery, ventless windows, tinted rear window and wood-tone appliques on the instrument cluster and lower dash.

CYCLONE

Model No.	Body/ Style No.	Body Type & Seating	Factory Price	Shipping Weight	Prod. Total
N/A	15	2-dr Fsbk Cpe-6P	2754	3273	5,882

CYCLONE CJ SERIES — A blacked-out grille was framed in chrome and had a single chrome piece in the middle running from each end of the grille. There was also a Cyclone emblem in the center, highlighting the front of the Cyclone CJ. Additional features included wheelwell opening moldings; dual exhaust; a 3.50:1 rear axle; engine dress-up kit; hood tape stripe; and competition handling package.

1969 Mercury Cyclone CJ two-door fastback hardtop, V-8. (PH)

1969 Mercury Cougar two-door hardtop (with optional Ram Air Induction and functional hood scoop), V-8. (PH)

CYCLONE CJ

Model No.	Body/ Style No.	Body Type & Seating	Factory Price	Shipping Weight	Prod. Total
N/A	16	2-dr Fsbk Cpe-6P	3207	3615	3,261

COUGAR SERIES — The Cougar's grille now had horizontal pieces that protruded slightly at the center. Retractable headlights were used again. Rocker panel strips, wheelwell opening moldings and two parallel full-length upper body pin stripes decorated the Cougar's sides. The back-up lights wrapped around the rear fenders and the taillights were trimmed with concave vertical chrome pieces. A vinyl interior with foam-padded bucket seats and carpeting was standard.

COUGAR

Model No.	Body/ Style No.	Body Type & Seating	Factory Price	Shipping Weight	Prod. Total
N/A	65	2-dr HT Cpe-5P	2999	3380	66,331
N/A	76	2-dr Conv-5P	3365	3499	5,796

NOTE 1: 1,615 Cougar hardtops were ordered with optional front bench seats.

COUGAR XR-7 SERIES — The XR-7 looked about the same as the basic Cougar from the outside. Its standard extras included: rim-blow steering wheel; courtesy light group; Visual-Check panel; left-hand remote-control racing mirror; electric clock; Deluxe armrests; walnut-toned instrument panel with tachometer and trip odometer; leather with vinyl upholstery; vinyl door trim panels and special wheel covers.

1969 Mercury Cougar XR-7 two-door convertible (with optional wire wheel covers), V-8. (OCW)

1969 Mercury Marquis Brougham four-door hardtop, V-8. (OCW)

COUGAR XR-7

Model No.	Body/ Style No.	Body Type & Seating	Factory Price	Shipping Weight	Prod. Total
N/A	65	2-dr HT Cpe-5P	3298	3420	23,918
N/A	76	2-dr Conv-5P	3578	3539	4,024

MONTEREY SERIES — The Monterey had a new, horizontal bar grille with a vertical piece in the center. Signal lights wrapped around the front fenders. The concave, rectangular taillights were clustered in the rear deck panel, which was heavily trimmed with vertical chrome pieces. The wheelwell openings, trunk lid and roof quarter panels had moldings. Standard features included: ventless side windows; nylon carpeting; wood-toned dash and door panels; heater and defroster and dome light. The convertible had an all-vinyl interior, while other body types had cloth and vinyl trims.

MONTEREY

Model No.	Body/ Style No.	Body Type & Seating	Factory Price	Shipping Weight	Prod. Total
N/A	44	4-dr Sed-6P	3141	3963	23,009
N/A	45	2-dr Conv-6P	3523	4106	1,297
N/A	47	2-dr HT Cpe-6P	3220	3927	9,865
N/A	48	4-dr HT Sed-6P	3296	3998	6,066
N/A	72	4-dr Sta Wag-6P	3519	4272	5,844

NOTE 1: A total of 3,639 Monterey station wagons came with an optional third seat.

MONTEREY CUSTOM SERIES — Rocker panel moldings and Deluxe wheel covers were two exterior differences between the Custom and the basic Monterey. The Custom also had a Deluxe steering wheel; leather door pulls; woodgrain vinyl appliques; front seat center armrest; bright seat side shields and rear door courtesy light.

MONTEREY CUSTOM

Model No.	Body/ Style No.	Body Type & Seating	Factory Price	Shipping Weight	Prod. Total
N/A	54	4-dr Sed-6P	3360	3968	7,103
N/A	56	2-dr HT Cpe-6P	2442	3959	2,898
N/A	58	4-dr HT Sed-6P	3516	4000	2,827
N/A	74	4-dr Sta Wag-6P	3740	4384	1,920

NOTE 1: A total of 967 Monterey Custom station wagons came with a third seat.

MARQUIS SERIES — The attractive front end styling of the Marquis was influenced by the second generation Continental Mark III. The integrated bumper grille had a horizontal bar theme and a prominent center section. Hidden headlight covers blended into the grille. Dual lower body pin stripes ran above the full-length bright curb moldings. Except for two back-up lights, the rear deck panel was a solid row of concave, rectangular, chrome-accented taillights. The interior featured deep-pile nylon carpeting, burled-walnut vinyl paneling on the dash and doors, front door courtesy lights, electric clock and a steering wheel with wood-toned spokes and rim.

MARQUIS

Model No.	Body/ Style No.	Body Type & Seating	Factory Price	Shipping Weight	Prod. Total
N/A	63	4-dr Sed-6P	3840	4144	31,388
N/A	66	2-dr HT Cpe-6P	3902	3927	18,302
N/A	68	4-dr HT Sed-6P	3973	4184	29,389

Model No.	Body/ Style No.	Body Type & Seating	Factory Price	Shipping Weight	Prod. Total
N/A	65	2-dr Conv-6P	4107	4380	2,319
N/A	76	4-dr Col Prk Sta Wag-6P	3878	4457	25,604

NOTE 1: 16,003 Colony Park station wagons came with the optional third seat.

MARAUDER SERIES — The Marauder had a Marquis front end, special tunneled rear window treatment and twin upper body pin stripes. There was a unique sculptured section with five short, horizontal chrome pieces just behind the doors. The six tail and two back-up lights were embedded in the rear deck panel. Set between them was a blacked-out section with the Marauder name written in chrome. A cloth and vinyl interior was standard.

MARAUDER

Model No.	Body/ Style No.	Body Type & Seating	Factory Price	Shipping Weight	Prod. Total
N/A	60	2-dr HT Cpe-6P	3351	4009	9,031

MARAUDER X-100 SERIES — The Marauder X-100 featured a two-tone paint job; fender skirts; leather with vinyl interior; rim-blow steering wheel; electric clock; glass-belted wide tread tires and styled aluminum wheels.

MARAUDER X-100

Model No.	Body/ Style No.	Body Type & Seating	Factory Price	Shipping Weight	Prod. Total
N/A	61	2-dr HT Cpe-6P	4074	4009	5,635

ENGINE [(Comet/Montego/Montego MX) Six]: Overhead valve. Cast-iron block. Displacement: 250 cid. Bore and stroke: 3.68 x 3.91 inches. Compression ratio: 8.6:1. Brake hp: 155 at 4000 rpm. Carburetor: Autolite C9OF-9510-BD one-barrel. (Engine Code L).

ENGINE [(Cyclone) V-8]: Overhead valve. Cast-iron block. Displacement: 302 cid. Bore and stroke: 4.00 x 3.00 inches. Compression ratio: 9.5:1. Brake hp: 220 at 4400 rpm. Carburetor: Autolite C8AF-9510-B four-barrel. (Engine Code F).

ENGINE [(Cyclone CJ) V-8]: Overhead valve. Cast-iron block. Displacement: 428 cid. Bore and stroke: 4.13 x 3.98 inches. Compression ratio: 10.6:1. Brake hp: 335 at 5200 rpm. Carburetor: Autolite C8AF-9510-B four-barrel. (Engine Code Q).

ENGINE [(Cyclone Spoiler) V-8]: Overhead valve. Cast-iron block. Displacement: 351 cid. Bore and stroke: 4.00 x 3.50 inches. Compression ratio: 10.7:1. Brake hp: 290 at 5200 rpm. Carburetor: Autolite four-barrel. (Engine Code M).

ENGINE [(Cougar/Cougar XR-7) V-8]: Overhead valve. Cast-iron block. Displacement: 351 cid. Bore and stroke: 4.00 x 3.50 inches. Compression ratio: 9.5:1. Brake hp: 250 at 4800 rpm. Carburetor: Autolite two-barrel. (Engine Code H).

ENGINE [(Monterey/Monterey Custom/Marauder) V-8]: Overhead valve. Cast-iron block. Displacement: 390 cid. Bore and stroke: 4.05 x 3.78 inches. Compression ratio: 9.5:1. Brake hp: 265 at 4400 rpm. Carburetor: Autolite C9AF-9510-B two-barrel. (Engine Code Y).

ENGINE [(Marquis/Marquis Brougham) V-8]: Overhead valve. Cast-iron block. Displacement: 429 cid. Bore and stroke: 4.36 x 3.59 inches. Compression ratio: 10.5:1. Brake hp: 320 at 4400 rpm. Carburetor: Autolite C9AF-9510-J two-barrel. (Engine Code K).

1969 Mercury Marauder X-100 two-door hardtop, V-8. (PH)

ENGINE [(Marauder X-100) V-8]: Overhead valve. Cast-iron block. Displacement: 429 cid. Bore and stroke: 4.36 x 3.59 inches. Compression ratio: 10.5:1. Brake hp: 360 at 4600 rpm. Carburetor: four-barrel. (Engine Code N).

COMET/MONTEGO/CYCLONE CHASSIS FEATURES: Wheelbase (passenger car) 116 inches; (station wagon) 113 inches. Overall length: (passenger car) 206.2 inches; (Cyclone and Cyclone CJ) 203.2 inches; (station wagon) 193.6 inches. Tires: (Cyclone) 7.75 x 14; (others) 7.35 x 14.

COUGAR CHASSIS FEATURES: Wheelbase: 111 inches. Overall length: 193.8 inches. Tires: E78-14.

MERCURY CHASSIS FEATURES: (station wagon and Marauder) 121 inches; (others) 124 inches. Overall length: (Marquis) 224.3 inches; (Monterey and Custom) 221.8 inches; (Marauder and X-100) 219.1 inches; (Colony Park) 220.5 inches; (Monterey and Custom station wagon) 218 inches. Tires: (Marquis and station wagon) 8.55 x 15; (X100) H70-15; (others) 8.25 x 15.

COMET/CYCLONE/MONTEGO OPTIONS: Heavy-duty battery ($7.80). Electric clock ($15.60). Courtesy light group includes: twin dash panel lights; glovebox, ashtray and luggage compartment lights; cargo light on station wagon and rear door light switch on sedans ($19.50). Cross-country ride package ($13). Competition handling package ($31.10). Curb moldings ($15.60). Decor group, includes: bright wheel lip moldings; trunk lid applique and bright upper door frames in sedans; Deluxe wheel covers on hardtops and Montego sedan ($54.50); on Montegos with special appearance group ($42.80); on Montego without special appearance group ($60.90). Tinted glass ($35). Front head restraints ($17). Hood lock pins for Cyclone and Cyclone CJ ($7.60). Luggage carrier on MX station wagons ($46.70). Left-hand remote-control racing mirror on Cyclone and Cyclone CJ ($13). Left-hand remote-control mirror ($10.40). Right-hand manual racing mirror ($6.50). MX Brougham, includes: Comfort Stream ventilation; remote-control mirror; rear roof pillar Brougham identification; luxury-level cloth/vinyl interior; vinyl-covered door pull handles; Brougham dash panel nameplate and rim-blow steering wheel for Montego MX hardtop or sedan ($90.70). Two-tone paint ($31.10). Dual paint tape stripes for Cyclone and Cyclone CJ ($31.10). Power disc brakes ($64.60). Four-Way bench seat ($73.90). Power steering ($94.60). Tailgate and power window for MX station wagon ($35). Power windows, except on Comet and Montego ($104.90). AM radio ($60.90). AM/FM stereo with twin speakers ($165.30). Dual rear-seat speakers, except in convertible and station wagon ($25.90). Deluxe seat belts for convertibles, includes a seat belt reminder light ($13). Deluxe front shoulder seat belts, except for convertibles, includes a seat belt reminder light ($15.60). Bucket seats without console for Montego MX, Cyclone hardtops and MX convertible ($110.10). Third seat in MX station wagon ($51.20). Sports console for Montego MX, Cyclone and Cyclone CJ ($155.70). Special appearance group includes: Deluxe wheel covers; whitewall tires; courtesy light group and Comfort Stream ventilation, except Cyclone CJ ($64.80). Sports appearance group includes: bucket seats; remote-control left-hand racing mirror; turbine wheel covers and rim-blow steering wheel for Cyclone CJ ($149). Rim-blow steering wheel ($35). Tachometer ($48). Comfort weave vinyl interior for Montego MX except station wagons and Cyclone ($24.70). Vinyl roof ($99.60). Deluxe wheel covers with spinners over hubs ($41.50); other ($20.60). Styled steel wheels, over hubs ($116.60); other ($95.90). Interval windshield wipers ($16.90). Yacht deck paneling for MX station wagon ($149). A three-speed manual transmission was standard except in the Cyclone CJ, which came with a four-speed manual transmission. Four-speed and SelectShift automatic transmissions were optional in the other series. A 302 cid/220-hp V-8 (two-barrel); 351 cid/250-hp V-8 (two-barrel); 351 cid/290-hp V-8 (four-barrel); 390 cid/320-hp V-8 (four-barrel); 428 cid/335-hp V-8 (four-barrel); 429 cid/360-hp V-8 (four-barrel); and a 427 cid/390-hp V-8 (four-barrel) were optional. High-performance and power transfer axles were available. A special handling package and Traction-Lok differential were optional.

COUGAR OPTIONS: Heavy-duty battery ($7.80). Front bumper guards ($13). Rear window defogger for hardtop ($22.10). Decor group includes: Deluxe wheel covers; curb molding; rim blow steering wheel; custom grade seat; door and quarter trim; door-mounted courtesy lights; rear seat armrests and windshield pillar and roof rail pads ($90.70). Door edge guards ($5.20). Dual exhaust ($31.10). Tinted glass ($29.80). GT appearance group for Cougar, Cyclone, includes: comfort weave vinyl bucket seats; rim-blow steering wheel; remote-control left-hand racing mirror; turbine design wheel covers; GT decal; GT dash nameplate and F70-14 fiberglass belted tires ($168.40). Front head restraints ($17). Hood lock pins ($7.80). Front and rear rubber floor mats ($13). Left-hand remote-control racing mirror ($13). Left-hand remote control mirror ($10.40). Two-tone paint ($31.10). Power steering ($99.80). Sun roof with vinyl roof ($459.80). Power windows ($104.90). AM radio ($60.90). AM/FM stereo with twin speakers ($165.30). AM radio and Stereo-sonic tape system ($195.60). Rear seat speaker ($15.60). Deluxe seat belts in convertibles ($13). Deluxe

front shoulder seat belts, all except convertibles ($15.60). Full-width front seat with center armrest in hardtop ($24.70). Speed control ($71.30). Sports console ($57.10). Tilt-away steering wheel ($68.70). Vinyl roof ($89.40). Visual-Check panel includes: door-ajar, low-fuel warning lights ($25.90). Deluxe wheel covers ($20.80). Deluxe wheel covers, with spinners over hubs ($41.50); other ($20.80). Wire wheel covers, over hubs ($72.60); other ($51.90). Styled steel wheels, over hubs ($95.90); other in hardtops ($16.90). Interval windshield wipers ($16.90). A three-speed manual transmission was standard. Heavy-duty three-speed, four-speed manual and SelectShift automatic transmissions were optional. A 351 cid/290-hp V-8 (four-barrel); 302 cid/290-hp V-8 (four-barrel); 390 cid/320-hp V-8 (four-barrel); 428 cid/335-hp 'CJ' V-8 (four-barrel); and a 429 cid/360-hp V-8 (four-barrel) were available. The 302 cid V-8 was standard in the 'Eliminator' performance package. It featured a two-speed street rear axle; blacked-out grille; ram-air hood scoop; special side body stripe and front and rear spoilers. The 351 cid/290-hp V-8 was standard in the '351' performance package. This option included: competition handling package, dual stripes and a power dome hood. The ram-air induction option came with a 428 cid V-8, hood scoop and F70-14 tires. High-performance rear axles and heavy-duty Traction-Lok differential were optional. Also note that two Cougars were produced with the Boss 429 cid engine.

MERCURY OPTIONS: Air conditioner ($421). Heavy-duty battery ($6.50). Carpeted load floor on station wagons ($15.60). Rear window defogger ($22.10). Electric clock ($15.60). Fender skirts for Marauder ($36.30). Tinted glass ($42.60). Tinted windshield ($27.30). Front head restraints ($17). Luggage-rack carrier for station wagons, with air deflector ($94.60); without air deflector ($73.90). Front and rear rubber floor mats ($13). Outside rearview mirror with remote-control ($10.40). Two-tone paint ($36.30). Two-tone paint, Marauder ($45.40). Power antenna ($31.10). Front disc brakes ($71.30). Power locks, in two-doors ($45.40); in four-doors ($68.70). Rear power window on station wagons ($35). Six-Way bench seat ($99.80). Six-Way twin comfort lounge driver's side ($84.20); driver's and passenger's side ($166.40). Power steering ($115.30). Remote-control trunk release ($14.30). Power windows ($110.10). AM radio with antenna ($63.50). AM/FM radio, stereo with antenna ($190.40). AM radio Stereo-sonic tape system ($198.20). Dual rear speakers ($25.90); automatic ride control ($79.10). Deluxe seat belts with reminder light on all convertibles ($13). Deluxe front and rear shoulder seat belts ($15.60). Bucket seat with console, Marauder ($162). Twin comfort lounge, Marquis ($77.80). Center seat facing rear, station wagons ($91.90). Reclining passenger seat, Marauder and Marquis ($41.50). Twin comfort lounge seats, Marquis ($162). Single-key locking system ($3.90). Speed control ($63.50). Rim-blow steering wheel, Monterey and Marauder ($35); others ($19.50). Tilt steering wheel ($45.40). All-vinyl Deluxe trim, Monterey ($26.50). Leather with vinyl trim, Marquis ($110.10). Visual-Check panel includes: low fuel, door ajar, headlamps-on warning lights, headlamps-on warning buzzer and seat belt reminder light ($32.40). Vinyl roof on passenger cars ($115 30); on station wagons ($142.50). Styled aluminum wheels, Monterey and Marauder ($116.60). Styled aluminum wheels, Monterey and Marquis ($95.90). Deluxe wheel covers ($20.60). Deluxe wheel covers with medallion for Monterey and Marauder ($45.40); for Monterey and Marquis ($24.70). Wire wheels, Marauder ($72.60); others ($51.90). Marauder fender skirts ($20.80). Interval selector windshield wipers ($16.90). Appearance protection group, includes: door edge guards; license plate frames; twin vinyl front and rear floor mats for two-doors except Marauder ($25.90); for four-doors, except Marquis ($29.80). Brougham option for Marquis includes exterior's pillar trim; twin comfort lounge seats; upper body peak molding; luxury-level seat trim; unique door trim panels; rear seat center armrest; and vinyl roof ($212). Decor group, includes: woodgrain rim steering wheel; curb molding and Deluxe wheel covers on Monterey and Monterey station wagons ($57.10). Cooling package ($36). A three-speed manual transmission was standard, except in the Marquis and X-100, both of which came with SelectShift automatic. The automatic transmission was optional in the other models. A 390 cid/260-hp V-8 (two-barrel); 390 cid/320-hp V-8 (four-barrel); 428 cid/335-hp (four-barrel) and a 429 cid/360-hp V-8 (four-barrel) were offered. A competition handling package, which included heavy-duty shocks and larger stabilizer bar, was a $31.10 option on the Marauder and X-100. High-performance and power transfer axles were also offered.

HISTORY: Over five percent of all 1969 Montegos had bucket seats, 26.9 percent had vinyl covered roofs, 1.8 percent had four-speed manual transmissions and about one percent came with power seats. Mercurys won four NASCAR Grand National races in 1969. The vast majority of 1969 Cougars, 92.4 percent, had power steering, 89.4 percent had automatic transmission, 57 percent had tinted glass and 58.9 percent had power brakes. Most full-size 1969 Mercurys, 99.5 percent of Montereys, 99.7 percent of Customs and 99.5 percent of Marauders, were equipped with automatic transmission. Mercury also built the Cyclone Spoiler II, Mercury's equivalent to Ford's NASCAR racer the Torino Talladega.

1970 Mercury Marquis convertible. (OCW)

1970 Mercury Montego MX Brougham four-door hardtop, V-8. (OCW)

MONTEGO SERIES — The protruding hood Mercury had been using for the past few years was carried to extremes on the new Montego. Its grille looked like the front end of a coffin. It had horizontal bars on it and an emblem in the center. The signal lights were placed in the front fenders. Wheelwell and roof drip moldings were used. There were four hooded taillights, each evenly divided into four sections by chrome trim pieces. Standard equipment included concealed wipers; front and rear side markers; cloth and vinyl or all-vinyl interior; wood-tone applique on the dash; and front and rear armrests.

MERCURY I.D. NUMBERS: The Vehicle Identification Number is on a metal tag affixed to left-hand top of dash and viewable through windshield. VIN consists of 11 symbols. First symbol: 0 = 1970. Second symbol indicates assembly plant: F = Dearborn, Mich. (Cougar); H = Lorain, Ohio (Montego); R = San Jose, Calif. (Cougar); and Z = St. Louis, Mo. (Mercury). Third and fourth symbols are Body/Style Number in charts below. Fifth symbol identifies engine code. Last six symbols are sequential production number starting at 100001 at each plant. Body Number Plate on left front door lock face panel provides additional information on model year, assembly point, body type, engine, color, trim, axle and transmission.

MONTEGO

Model No.	Body/ Style No.	Body Type & Seating	Factory Price	Shipping Weight	Prod. Total
N/A	01	2-dr HT-6P	2473	3161	21,298
N/A	02	4-dr Sed-6P	2560	3246	13,988

MONTEGO MX SERIES — The Montego MX had mid-bodyside molding and chrome trim around the trunk lid on all models and the window frames of four-doors. The interior featured loop carpeting, pleated cloth and vinyl or all-vinyl upholstery; and a teakwood applique on the steering wheel.

MONTEGO MX

Model No.	Body/ Style No.	Body Type & Seating	Factory Price	Shipping Weight	Prod. Total
N/A	08	4-dr Sta Wag-6P	2996	3709	5,094
N/A	06	4-dr Sed-6P	2662	3253	16,708
N/A	07	2-dr HT Cpe-6P	2563	3186	31,670

MONTEGO MX BROUGHAM SERIES — Concealed headlights, chrome rocker panels, wheelwell moldings, dual upper body pin stripes, six-pod taillights; and silver or black appliques on the rear deck panel set the Brougham apart from the other Montegos. Standard equipment included a cloth and vinyl interior, nylon loop carpeting and a woodgrain vinyl insert in the steering wheel. The MX station wagon was now called the Villager.

MONTEGO MX BROUGHAM

Model No.	Body/ Style No.	Body Type & Seating	Factory Price	Shipping Weight	Prod. Total
N/A	10	4-dr Sed-6P	2712	3153	3,315
N/A	11	2-dr HT Cpe-6P	2730	3186	8,074
N/A	12	4-dr HT Sed-6P	2844	3206	3,685
N/A	18	4-dr Vill Sta Wag-6P	3090	3624	2,682

CYCLONE SERIES — The protruding center section of the Cyclone grille was outlined by a chrome square. It was equally divided into four pieces, with a chrome circle in the center. Rectangular running lights were embedded in the grille. The lower back panel was either silver or black. Loop carpeting, all-vinyl interior and a competition handling package were standard.

CYCLONE

Model No.	Body/ Style No.	Body Type & Seating	Factory Price	Shipping Weight	Prod. Total
N/A	15	2-dr HT Cpe-6P	3037	3449	1,695

CYCLONE GT SERIES — Concealed headlights, non-functional performance scooped hood, full-length lower bodyside molding, left-hand remote-control and right-hand manual racing mirrors, high-back comfort weave vinyl bucket seats, special door panel trim and a three-spoke Sport-style steering wheel were standard GT features.

CYCLONE GT

Model No.	Body/ Style No.	Body Type & Seating	Factory Price	Shipping Weight	Prod. Total
N/A	16	2-dr HT Cpe-5P	3025	3434	10,170

CYCLONE SPOILER SERIES — The 'Spoiler' was aptly named. It had front and rear spoilers; exposed headlights; mid-bodyside stripes; traction belted tires; scooped hood; dual racing mirrors; competition handling package; and full instrumentation.

CYCLONE SPOILER

Model No.	Body/ Style No.	Body Type & Seating	Factory Price	Shipping Weight	Prod. Total
N/A	17	2-dr HT Cpe-5P	3530	3464	1,631

COUGAR SERIES — The clean Cougar grille of 1969 was replaced by a center hood extension and 'electric shaver' style insert reminiscent of the 1967 and 1968 models. Basic trim was upper body pin stripes, wheel opening and roof moldings and windshield rear window chrome. The interior featured high-back bucket seats, courtesy lights, vinyl headliner and rosewood-toned dash panel. The convertible had comfort weave vinyl interior, door-mounted courtesy lights, three-spoke steering wheel and power top with folding rear glass window.

COUGAR

Model No.	Body/ Style No.	Body Type & Seating	Factory Price	Shipping Weight	Prod. Total
N/A	91	2-dr HT Cpe-5P	2917	3307	49,479
N/A	92	2-dr Conv-5P	3264	3404	2,322

1970 Mercury Cyclone GT two-door hardtop, V-8. (OCW)

1970 Mercury Cougar XR-7 two-door convertible, V-8. (OCW)

COUGAR XR-7 SERIES — The XR-7 had distinctive wheel covers, rocker panel moldings, remote-control racing mirror and an emblem on the rear roof pillar. Interior features included vinyl high-back bucket seats with leather accents; map pockets on the seatbacks; tachometer; trip odometer; rocker switch display; burled walnut vinyl applique on the instrument panel; rear seat armrests; map and courtesy lights; Visual-Check panel; loop yarn nylon carpeting; and an electric clock with elapsed-time indicator.

COUGAR XR-7

Model No.	Body/ Style No.	Body Type & Seating	Factory Price	Shipping Weight	Prod. Total
N/A	93	2-dr HT Cpe-5P	3201	3333	18,565
N/A	94	2-dr Conv-5P	3465	3430	1,977

MONTEREY SERIES — The Monterey grille had thin, bi-level horizontal bars outlined in heavier chrome; a slender vertical emblem in the middle; four recessed chrome rimmed headlights; and large, wraparound signal lights. There were bright moldings on the wheel-well openings, rear roof pillar base and windows. The two large narrow, rectangular deck panel taillights were centrally divided by back-up lamps. The interior featured nylon carpeting; dark teakwood vinyl instrument panel appliques; color-keyed steering wheel; adjustable head restraints; steering column lock; pleated design cloth and vinyl upholstery (all-vinyl in the convertible); and heavy sound insulation.

MONTEREY

Model No.	Body/ Style No.	Body Type & Seating	Factory Price	Shipping Weight	Prod. Total
N/A	44	4-dr Sed-6P	3029	3940	29,432
N/A	47	2-dr HT Cpe-6P	3107	3904	9,359
N/A	48	4-dr HT Sed-6P	3179	3975	5,032
N/A	45	2-dr Conv-6P	3429	4085	581
N/A	72	4-dr Sta Wag-6P	3440	4249	5,164

MONTEREY CUSTOM SERIES — The Custom had full-length, mid-bodyside chrome spears with vinyl inserts, Deluxe wheel covers and curb moldings. On the inside was the cloth and vinyl or all-vinyl upholstery, front seat armrest, teakwood-toned inserts in the steering wheel, vinyl-covered door pull handles and rear courtesy light switches.

MONTEREY CUSTOM

Model No.	Body/ Style No.	Body Type & Seating	Factory Price	Shipping Weight	Prod. Total
N/A	54	4-dr Sed-6P	3288	3945	4,823
N/A	56	2-dr HT Cpe-6P	3365	3936	1,194
N/A	58	4-dr HT Sed-6P	3436	3987	1,357

1970 Mercury Monterey Custom two-door hardtop, V-8. (OCW)

1970 Mercury Marquis four-door hardtop, V-8. (OCW)

MARQUIS SERIES — The Marquis received a modest face lift for 1970. Vertical pieces were added to the bumper-integrated grille and to the signal lights. Dual pin stripes ran from fender to fender at tire level and also above the wheelwell openings outlining them. There were bright and black curb moldings and chrome trim on the lower front fenders. A luxury rim-blow steering wheel, front door courtesy lights and wood-toned door panel inserts graced the Marquis interior.

MARQUIS

Model No.	Body/ Style No.	Body Type & Seating	Factory Price	Shipping Weight	Prod. Total
N/A	40	4-dr Sed-6P	3793	4121	14,384
N/A	41	2-dr HT Cpe-6P	3952	4072	6,229
N/A	42	4-dr HT Sed-6P	3910	4141	8,411
N/A	65	2-dr Conv-6P	4047	4337	1,233
N/A	74	4-dr Sta Wag-6P	3930	4434	2,388
N/A	76	4-dr Col Pk Sta Wag-6P	4123	4480	19,204

NOTE 1: 1,429 Marquis station wagons and 14,549 Colony Parks were sold with third seat.

MARQUIS BROUGHAM SERIES — Instead of pin stripes, the Brougham used upper body moldings that ran from the face of the front fenders to the back of the rear fenders. Also seen on these luxury models were chromed wheel openings and a vinyl roof. The interior featured individually adjustable, twin comfort lounge seats, with two folding armrests. The door trim panels were wood-toned and the door pull handles were covered with vinyl.

MARQUIS BROUGHAM

Model No.	Body/ Style No.	Body Type & Seating	Factory Price	Shipping Weight	Prod. Total
N/A	63	4-dr Sed-6P	4092	4166	14,920
N/A	66	2-dr HT Cpe-6P	4151	4119	7,113
N/A	68	4-dr HT Sed-6P	4219	4182	11,623

MARAUDER SERIES — Except for its name spelled out in chrome on the face of the hood, the Marauder looked the same as the Marquis from the front. Side trim consisted of twin upper body pin stripes, window moldings and a sculptured section with five short horizontal chrome pieces behind the doors. A tunneled rear window remained a Marauder styling highpoint. The same distinctive taillight treatment used the previous year was also found on the 1970 model.

MARAUDER

Model No.	Body/ Style No.	Body Type & Seating	Factory Price	Shipping Weight	Prod. Total
N/A	60	2-dr HT Cpe-6P	3271	3986	3,397

MARAUDER X-100 SERIES — Fender skirts, wheel opening moldings and special wheel covers distinguished the X-100 from the standard Marauder. Interior differences included high-back, all-vinyl bucket seats with center console (or twin comfort lounge seats), luxury steering wheel and bright seat side shields.

MARAUDER X-100

Model No.	Body/ Style No.	Body Type & Seating	Factory Price	Shipping Weight	Prod. Total
N/A	61	2-dr HT Cpe-6P	3873	4128	2,646

ENGINE [(Montego/Montego MX/Montego Brougham) Six]: Overhead valve. Cast-iron block. Displacement: 250 cid. Bore and stroke: 3.68 x 3.91 inches. Compression ratio: 9.0:1. Brake hp: 155 at 4000 rpm. Carburetor: one-barrel. (Engine Code L).

ENGINE [(Cyclone/Marauder X-100) V-8]: Overhead valve. Cast-iron block. Displacement: 429 cid. Bore and stroke: 4.36 x 3.59 inches. Compression ratio: 10.5:1. Brake hp: 360 at 4600 rpm. Carburetor: four-barrel. (Engine Code N).

ENGINE [(Cyclone GT/Cougar/Cougar XR-7) V-8]: Overhead valve. Cast-iron block. Displacement: 351 cid. Bore and stroke: 4.00 x 3.50 inches. Compression ratio: 9.5:1. Brake hp: 250 at 4600 rpm. Carburetor: two-barrel. (Engine Code H).

ENGINE [(Cyclone Spoiler) V-8]: Overhead valve. Cast-iron block. Displacement: 429 cid. Bore and stroke: 4.36 x 3.59 inches. Compression ratio: 11.3:1. Brake hp: 370 at 5400 rpm. Carburetor: four-barrel. (Engine Code N).

ENGINE [(Monterey/Monterey Custom) V-8]: Overhead valve. Cast-iron block. Displacement: 390 cid. Bore and stroke: 4.05 x 3.76 inches. Compression ratio: 9.5:1. Brake hp: 265 at 4400 rpm. Carburetor: two-barrel. (Engine Code Y).

ENGINE [(Marquis/Marquis Brougham/Marauder) V-8]: Overhead valve. Cast-iron block. Displacement: 429 cid. Bore and stroke: 4.36 x 3.59 inches. Compression ratio: 10.5:1. Brake hp: 320 at 4400 rpm. Carburetor: two-barrel. (Engine Code K).

MONTEGO/CYCLONE CHASSIS FEATURES: Wheelbase: (passenger car) 117 inches; (station wagon) 114 inches. Overall length: (passenger car) 209.9 inches; (station wagon) 209 inches. Tires: (Cyclone series) G70-14; (others) E78-14.

COUGAR CHASSIS FEATURES: Wheelbase: 111.1 inches. Overall length: 196.1 inches. Tires: E78-14.

MERCURY CHASSIS FEATURES: Wheelbase: (station wagon, Marauder and X-100) 121 inches; (others) 124 inches. Overall length: (Marquis and Brougham) 224.3 inches; (Marquis station wagon) 220.5 inches; (Monterey and Custom) 221.8 inches; (Monterey station wagon) 218 inches; (Marauder and X-100) 219.1 inches. Tires: (Monterey and Custom) G78-15; (Marquis, Brougham, Marauder) H78-15; (Monterey station wagon) H70-15.

MONTEGO/CYCLONE OPTIONS: Air conditioner ($388.60). Heavy-duty 55 amp alternator ($20.60). Heavy-duty battery ($7.60). Extra cooling ($7.60). Cross-country ride ($9.10). Tinted glass ($36.30). Tinted glass windshield, fleet only ($25.90). Heater and defroster ($22.10). Low gear lockout ($6.50). Luggage carrier with adjustable roof rails for MX station wagon without air deflector ($54.50); with air deflector ($73.90). Left-hand remote-control racing mirror ($13). Front disc brakes ($64.60). Four-Way bench seat ($73.90). Power steering ($104.90). Power windows ($104.90). Protective vinyl bodyside molding ($25.90). AM radio ($60.90). AM/FM stereo radio ($212.50). Dual rear seat speaker ($27.30). Deluxe seat and front shoulder belts ($15.60). Deluxe seat belts with automatic seatback release on two-doors ($38.90). High-back bucket seats with comfort vinyl trim ($119.20). Rear facing third seat, MX station wagon ($63.70). Rim-blow steering wheel ($35). Sun roof, Montego two-door hardtop ($375.70). Upbeat spectrum stripe, MX two-door with bench seats ($32.40). Comfort weave vinyl, MX with bench seats ($32.40). Upbeat watch plaid, MX with bench seats ($32.40). High level ventilation ($15.50). Vinyl roof ($99.60). Deluxe wheel covers ($25.90). Luxury wheel covers ($41.50). Styled wheels ($36.90). Interval windshield wipers ($25.90). Mud and snow tires ($7.80). F78-14 whitewall tires, with '250' or '302' engines ($31.10); with '351' engines ($49.30). G78-14 whitewall tires, with '351' engine ($49.30); with '429' engines ($64.60); with '351' engines ($46.70). F70-14 traction tires, with '250' or '302' engines ($77.80); with '351' engines ($59.60). G70-14 whitewall tires, with '250' or '302' engines ($83); with '351' engines ($64.60). G70-14 traction tires, with '250' or '302' engines ($95.90); with '351' engine ($77.80); with '429' engine ($59.60). Instrumentation group includes: tachometer, oil temperature and ammeter gauges ($77.60). Trailer-towing package includes: '351' two-barrel engine; power disc brakes; competitive handling package; extra-cooling package; heavy-duty alternator; heavy-duty battery, with air conditioner ($151.60); without air conditioner ($159.40). A three-speed manual transmission was standard, except in the Cyclone and Spoiler. Both came with a four-speed manual transmission and Hurst shifter. Four-speed manual and SelectShift automatic transmissions were optional. A 351 cid/220-hp V-8 (two-barrel); 351 cid/250-hp V-8 (two-barrel); 351 cid/300-hp V-8 (four-barrel); 429 cid/360-hp Thunder Jet V-8 (four-barrel); 429 cid/370-hp Cobra Jet V-8 (four-barrel); and a 429 cid/375-hp Super Cobra Jet V-8 (four-barrel) were offered. A limited production Boss 429 cid V-8 (four-barrel) was available on special order. Drag pack, drag pack super and ram-air induction options were offered in the Cyclone, GT and Spoiler series. A higher ratio rear axle and Traction-Lok differential were available at extra cost.

COUGAR OPTIONS: Air conditioner ($375.70). Electric clock ($15.60). Sports console ($57.10). Tinted glass ($32.40). Tinted windshield, fleet only ($22.10). Heater and defroster ($22.10). Left-hand remote-control racing mirror ($13). Two-tone paint ($31.10). Front disc brakes ($64.80). Power steering ($105.90). AM radio ($60.90). AM/FM stereo radio ($212.50). AM radio/Stereo-sonic tape ($195.60). Rear seat speaker ($15.60). Deluxe front seat and shoulder belts ($15.60). Rim-blow steering wheel ($35). Vinyl sun roof ($459.60). Tilt steering wheel ($45.40). Houndstooth cloth and vinyl trim ($32.40). Vinyl roof includes roof and bright roof moldings ($69.40). Deluxe wheel covers ($25.90). Ralley wheel covers, over hubs ($41.50); others ($15.60). Wire wheel covers, over hubs ($74.90); others ($48). Styled steel wheels, over hubs ($116.60); others ($90.70). Internal windshield wipers ($25.90). Mud and snow tires ($760). Tires: E78-14 whitewall wide

tread ($29.80); F70-14 whitewall belted ($63.50); F70-14 traction belted ($76.50). Appearance protection group includes: front bumper guards, door edge guards, rear floor mats ($31.10). Courtesy light group includes: rear roof pillar, trunk, underhood and map lights, head-lamps-on warning buzzer with light ($19.50). Decor group includes: Deluxe wheel covers; curb molding; three spoke rim-blow steering wheel; Custom grade door and quarter trim; door courtesy lights; rear quarter armrests; Comfort weave vinyl high-back bucket seats ($90.70); on Eliminator ($70). Drag-pack option ($207.30). Eliminator option ($129.60). Ram-air induction option includes: ram-air induction system and functional hood scoop in body color; hood stripes (black or argent); color-keyed stripe with Cobra Jet 428 logo ($64.80). Visual-Check panel includes door-ajar, low-fuel warning light ($25.90). A three-speed manual transmission was standard. Four-speed manual and SelectShift automatic transmissions were optional. A 351 cid/300-hp V-8 (four-barrel); 302 cid/290-hp Boss V-8 (four-barrel); 428 cid/335-hp Cobra Jet V-8 (four-barrel); and a 429 cid/375-hp Boss V-8 (four-barrel) were available. The 300-hp engine was standard in the Eliminator performance package. The Boss 302 was only offered in the Eliminator. Drag pack and ram-air induction options could also be ordered. A high-performance rear axle and Traction-Lok differential were available at extra cost.

MERCURY OPTIONS: Air conditioner ($421). Heavy-duty 55 amp alternator ($20.80). Heavy-duty 65 amp alternator ($86.80). Heavy-duty battery ($7.80). Carpeted load floor, station wagons ($19.50). Heavy-duty cooling ($36.30). Cross-county ride ($23.40). Electric rear window defroster ($53.20). Door edge guards in two-doors ($56.50); in four-doors ($10.40). Tinted glass ($36.30). Tinted windshield, fleet only ($27.30). Luggage carrier with adjustable roof rails in station wagons ($73.90); with air deflector ($94.60). Front and rear floor mats ($13). Two-tone paint ($36.30). Two-tone paint, Marauder ($45.40). Power antenna ($31.10). Front disc brakes ($71.30). Power door locks, two-doors ($45.40); four-doors ($68.70); station wagons including power lock for tailgate ($77.80). Automatic seatback release ($25.90, two-doors). Six-Way bench seat ($99.60). Power steering ($115.30). Remote control trunk release ($14.30). Power windows ($110.10). Protective vinyl bodyside moldings in Monterey ($25.90). AM radio ($63.50). AM/FM stereo radio ($239.60). AM radio Stereo-sonic tape ($198.20). Automatic ride control ($28.10). Deluxe front seat and shoulder belts ($15.60). Heavy-duty front seating, fleet only ($33.70). Center-facing rear seats, Mercury station wagons, includes tailgate step pad ($91.90). Single key locking system ($3.90). Speed control ($63.50). Rim-blow steering wheel ($19.50). Tilt steering wheel ($45.40). Deluxe vinyl interior, Monterey and Marauder ($26.50). Vinyl roof ($115.30); station wagons ($142.50). Deluxe wheel covers, Monterey and Marauder ($25.90). Luxury wheel covers ($46.70). Styled aluminum wheels, over hubs ($116.60); over Deluxe ($90.70); Monterey, Marauder X-100 over luxury ($44.10); Monterey over Marauder appearance group ($90.70). Interval windshield wipers ($25.90). Mud and snow tires ($7.60). G78-15 whitewall or blackwall belted Monterey, Monterey Custom, Marauder ($31.10). H78-15 whitewall belted on Mercurys ($33.70); on Marauder, Monterey, Monterey Custom, H70-15 blackwall wide tread ($51.90); on Mercurys ($49.30); on Monterey, Monterey Custom, Marauder ($67.40). Appearance protection group includes: door edge guards; license plate frames; front and rear rubber floor mats, two-door ($25.90); four-door ($29.80). Competition handling group, Marauder ($31.10). Decor group, Monterey, includes: Deluxe steering wheel (with woodgrain spoke accents); curb molding; Deluxe wheel covers ($57.10). Marauder appearance group includes: Marauder wheel covers, fender skirts and wheel opening molding ($57.10). A three-speed manual transmission was standard in Marauder, Monterey and Monterey Custom. SelectShift automatic was standard in Marquis, Brougham and X-100. The automatic was optional in the other series. A 429 cid/320-hp V-8 (two-barrel) and a 429 cid/360-hp V-8 (four-barrel) were optional. A higher ratio rear axle was available.

HISTORY: Most 1970 Montegos, 92.6 percent, were equipped with automatic transmission, 87 percent had a V-8 engine, 49.5 percent had air conditioning, 88.1 percent had power steering, 42.1 percent had disc brakes and one percent had power seats. Mercurys won four NASCAR Grand National races in 1970. The majority of 1970 Cougars, 67.6 percent, were equipped with power brakes, 95.6 percent had power steering, 63.9 percent had tinted glass and 92.2 percent had automatic transmission. A total of 3,507 Monterey station wagons were equipped with the optional third rear-facing seat. Most 1970 Marquis Broughams, 99.6 percent, were equipped with air conditioning. Over 99 percent of all full-size Mercurys that had a three-speed manual transmission listed as standard equipment were sold with an automatic.

1971 MERCURY

1971 Mercury Montego MX. (OCW)

1971 Mercury Cougar XR7. (OCW)

1971 Mercury Comet two-door sedan, 6-cyl. (OCW)

1971 Mercury Comet four-door sedan, 6-cyl. (OCW)

COMET SERIES — Comet returned as a compact this year. It looked basically like a Maverick with makeup. The horizontal bar grille protruded slightly (harmonizing with the 'power dome' hood). The center horizontal bar was chromed. Rectangular signal lights were placed alongside the grille. The two headlights were recessed into a chromed background. Side trim consisted of wheel opening moldings and twin pin stripes, which ran from the tip of the headlights to the door handles. Taillights were of the pod variety used on Montegos. Standard features included: front and rear armrests, carpeting, vinyl headliner, cigar lighter, two-spoke steering wheel and light gray and gold check cloth and vinyl upholstery. A do-it-yourself repair manual was offered to Comet buyers.

MERCURY I.D. NUMBERS: The Vehicle Identification Number is on a metal tag affixed to the left-hand top of dash and viewable through windshield. VIN consists of 11 symbols. First symbol: 1 = 1971. Second symbol indicates assembly plant: F = Dearborn, Mich. (Cougar); H = Lorain, Ohio (Montego); K = Kansas City, Kan. (Comet) and Z = St. Louis, Mo. (Mercury). Third and fourth symbols are Body/Style Number in charts below. Fifth symbol identifies engine code. Last six symbols are sequential production number starting at 100001 at each plant. Vehicle Certification label on left front door lock face panel provides additional information on model year, assembly point, body type, engine, color, trim, axle and transmission.

COMET

Model No.	Body/Style No.	Body Type & Seating	Factory Price	Shipping Weight	Prod. Total
N/A	30	2-dr Sed-4P	2217	2335	54,884
N/A	31	4-dr Sed-4P	2276	2366	28,116

MONTEGO SERIES — The Montegos protruding grille was toned down a bit for 1971. It now had a criss-cross pattern. Side trim consisted of wheel opening and window moldings. The previous year's pod style taillights remained. The instrument panel had woodgrain trim.

MONTEGO

Model No.	Body/Style No.	Body Type & Seating	Factory Price	Shipping Weight	Prod. Total
N/A	01	2-dr HT Cpe-6P	2777	3124	9,623
N/A	02	4-dr Sed-6P	2772	3125	5,718

MONTEGO MX SERIES — The Montego MX had chrome rocker panels and its name written on the rear fenders. Fancier wheel covers and a slightly plusher interior were the main differences between the MX and the basic Montego.

MONTEGO MX

Model No.	Body/Style No.	Body Type & Seating	Factory Price	Shipping Weight	Prod. Total
N/A	06	4-dr Sed-6P	2891	3131	13,559
N/A	07	2-dr HT Cpe-6P	2891	3130	13,719
N/A	06	4-dr Sta Wag-6P	3215	3547	3,698

1971 Mercury Montego MX two-door hardtop, 6-cyl. (OCW)

1971 Mercury Montego MX Brougham four-door hardtop, V-8. (OCW)

MONTEGO MX BROUGHAM SERIES — Upper body twin pin stripes and wheel opening and rocker panel moldings were styling features of the MX Brougham. It also had Deluxe wheel covers. The upholstery was cloth and vinyl or all-vinyl. The door panels had woodgrain vinyl appliques. The Villager station wagon had wood-toned panels framed with chrome trim. A dual action tailgate was standard.

MONTEGO MX BROUGHAM

Model No.	Body/ Style No.	Body Type & Seating	Factory Price	Shipping Weight	Prod. Total
N/A	10	4-dr Sed-6P	3073	3154	1,565
N/A	11	2-dr HT Cpe-6P	3085	3171	2,851
N/A	12	4-dr HT Sed-6P	3157	3198	1,156
N/A	18	4-dr Vill Sta Wag-6P	3456	3483	2,121

MONTEGO CYCLONE SERIES — The new Cyclone looked virtually the same as the previous year's model. It came with a performance hood (having an integral scoop); running lights; cross country ride package; deep-loop carpeting; dual racing mirrors; concealed windshield wipers; and Flow-Thru ventilation.

MONTEGO CYCLONE

Model No.	Body/ Style No.	Body Type & Seating	Factory Price	Shipping Weight	Prod. Total
N/A	15	2-dr HT Cpe-6P	3369	3587	444

MONTEGO CYCLONE GT SERIES — The GT had the same standard equipment as the basic Cyclone, plus high-back bucket seats; Deluxe wheel covers; full instrumentation (tachometer, oil gauge, temperature gauge and ammeter); three-spoke steering wheel and concealed headlights.

MONTEGO CYCLONE GT

Model No.	Body/ Style No.	Body Type & Seating	Factory Price	Shipping Weight	Prod. Total
N/A	16	2-dr HT Cpe-5P	3681	3493	2,287

MONTEGO CYCLONE SPOILER SERIES — Higher positioned side body stripes and a less potent standard engine were the most noticeable changes made to the Spoiler in 1971. It came with front and rear spoilers, hubcaps with bright trim rings and Traction-Lok differential with 3.25:1 gear ratio rear axle.

MONTEGO CYCLONE SPOILER

Model No.	Body/ Style No.	Body Type & Seating	Factory Price	Shipping Weight	Prod. Total
N/A	17	2-dr HT Cpe-5P	3801	3580	353

COUGAR SERIES — The Cougar's front end was restyled. The four headlights were exposed and recessed. The signal lights wrapped around the front fenders. The protruding center grille had vertical bars and was framed in chrome. An ornament was set in its center. Triple, mid-tire level pin stripes ran from fender to fender. There were moldings on the wheelwell openings. The rear bumper was integrated into the rear deck panel, which housed the large rectangular taillights. Standard features included: high-back bucket seats; cigar lighter; concealed windshield wipers; consolette with illuminated ashtray; glovebox and panel courtesy lights; and Flow-Thru ventilation system.

1971 Mercury Cougar XR-7 two-door hardtop, V-8. (OCW)

1971 Mercury Monterey Custom two-door hardtop, V-8. (OCW)

COUGAR

Model No.	Body/ Style No.	Body Type & Seating	Factory Price	Shipping Weight	Prod. Total
N/A	91	2-dr HT Cpe-5P	3289	3285	34,008
N/A	92	2-dr Conv-5P	3681	3415	1,723

COUGAR XR-7 SERIES — The XR-7 had chrome rocker panels, distinctive wheel covers and ornamentation and a unique vinyl covered half-roof. It also provided high-back bucket seats with leather seating surfaces, a fully instrumented dash panel (i.e.: tachometer, trip odometer, toggle switches) and a remote-control left-hand racing mirror. The instrument board and steering wheel had woodgrain appliques. The convertible had a tinted windshield.

COUGAR XR-7

Model No.	Body/ Style No.	Body Type & Seating	Factory Price	Shipping Weight	Prod. Total
N/A	93	2-dr HT Cpe-5P	3629	3314	25,416
N/A	94	2-dr Conv-5P	3877	3454	1,717

MONTEREY SERIES — The Monterey's wraparound grille was a wave of horizontal bars that came to a point at the center. The four chrome-rimmed headlights were recessed into the grille. Signal lights were located in the front bumper. There was no side trim other than the Monterey name written in chrome on the lower quarter panel. The large, rectangular bumper-integrated taillights wrapped around the rear fenders. Standard features included: cloth and vinyl upholstery; carpeting; courtesy and trunk compartment lights; power vent system; recessed outside door handles; dual ashtrays and temperature and braking system warning lights.

MONTEREY

Model No.	Body/ Style No.	Body Type & Seating	Factory Price	Shipping Weight	Prod. Total
N/A	44	4-dr Sed-6P	3423	4028	22,744
N/A	47	2-dr HT Cpe-6P	3465	3958	9,099
N/A	48	4-dr HT Sed-6P	3533	4024	2,483
N/A	72	4-dr Sta Wag-6P	4283	4384	4,160

MONTEREY CUSTOM SERIES — Rocker panel and lower side window moldings plus a full-length, mid-bodyside chrome spear set the Custom apart from the plain Monterey. It also had Deluxe wheel covers and a plusher interior.

MONTEREY CUSTOM

Model No.	Body/ Style No.	Body Type & Seating	Factory Price	Shipping Weight	Prod. Total
N/A	54	4-dr Sed-6P	3958	4105	12,411
N/A	56	2-dr HT Cpe-6P	4141	4028	4,508
N/A	58	4-dr HT Sed-6P	4113	4104	1,397

MARQUIS SERIES — Changes in the Marquis for 1971 were evolutionary, yet noticeable. The word Mercury replaced 'Marquis' on the left headlight door. The protruding-type horizontal bar grille was outlined, at the top, by a larger piece of chrome and was no longer centrally divided by the bumper. A full-length chrome stripe ran at slightly above mid-tire level. There was chrome trim on the front wheel openings and on the standard fender skirts. The taillight treatment was the same as that used on the Monterey, except for the trunk lid molding and distinct center rear deck panel trim.

MARQUIS

Model No.	Body/ Style No.	Body Type & Seating	Factory Price	Shipping Weight	Prod. Total
N/A	40	4-dr Sed-6P	4474	4311	16,030
N/A	41	2-dr HT Cpe-6P	4557	4240	7,726
N/A	42	4-dr HT Sed-6P	4624	4306	5,491
N/A	74	4-dr Sta Wag-6P	4547	4411	2,158
N/A	76	4-dr Col Prk Sta Wag-6P	4806	4471	20,004

1971 Mercury Marquis Brougham four-door hardtop, V-8. (OCW)

MARQUIS BROUGHAM SERIES — The Brougham had full-length, upper body moldings, a vinyl covered roof and color-keyed wheel covers (i.e.: the center hub of the covers was the same color as the car). Like the basic Marquis, it came with most power equipment standard.

MARQUIS BROUGHAM

Model No.	Body/ Style No.	Body Type & Seating	Factory Price	Shipping Weight	Prod. Total
N/A	63	4-dr Sed-6P	4880	4354	25,790
N/A	66	2-dr HT Cpe-6P	4963	4271	14,570
N/A	68	4-dr HT Sed-6P	5033	4341	13,781

CAPRI SERIES — The sporty sub-compact Capri was introduced in April of 1970 as a 1971 model. It was an import, produced by Ford-Werke AG in Germany and sold in the United States through Lincoln-Mercury dealers. The bucket seat-equipped coupe was powered by a British-sourced overhead valve, 71-hp, 1600cc four-cylinder engine coupled to a four-speed manual transmission. A larger engine (German-built 100-hp, two-liter inline four-cylinder) and automatic transmission were optional. The Capri had a 100.8-inch wheelbase and 167.8-inch overall length. Standard equipment included rack-and-pinion steering, all-vinyl interior, power front disc brakes, styled-steel wheels and 165-13 radial tires. Since the Capri was of foreign manufacture, it will not be covered fully in this catalog beyond the data given here.

CAPRI

Model No.	Body/ Style No.	Body Type & Seating	Factory Price	Shipping Weight	Prod. Total
N/A	N/A	2-dr Cpe-4P	2395	N/A	17,300

ENGINE [(Comet) Six]: Cast-iron block. Displacement: 170 cid. Bore and stroke: 3.68 x 3.91 inches. Compression ratio: 9.0:1. Brake hp: 100 at 4200 rpm. Carburetor: one-barrel. [Engine Code U].

ENGINE [(Montego/MX/MX Brougham) Six]: Cast-iron block. Displacement: 250 cid. Bore and stroke: 3.68 x 3.91 inches. Compression ratio: 9.0:1. Brake hp: 145 at 4000 rpm. Carburetor: one-barrel. [Engine Code L].

ENGINE [(Montego Cyclone/Spoiler) V-8]: Overhead valve. Cast-iron block. Displacement: 351 cid. Bore and stroke: 4.00 x 3.50 inches. Compression ratio: 10.7:1. Brake hp: 285 at 5400. Carburetor: two-barrel. [Engine Code H].

ENGINE [(Montego Cyclone GT/Cougar/XR-7/Monterey) V-8]: Overhead valve. Cast-iron block. Displacement: 351 cid. Bore and stroke: 4.00 x 3.50 inches. Compression ratio: 9.0:1. Brake hp: 240 at 4600 rpm. Carburetor: two-barrel. [Engine Code M].

ENGINE [(Monterey Custom) V-8]: Overhead valve. Cast-iron block. Displacement: 400 cid. Bore and stroke: 4.00 x 4.00 inches. Compression ratio: 9.0:1. Brake hp: 260 at 4400 rpm. Carburetor: two-barrel. [Engine Code S].

ENGINE [(Marquis/Marquis Brougham) V-8]: Overhead valve. Cast-iron block. Displacement: 429 cid. Bore and stroke: 4.36 x 3.59 inches. Compression ratio: 10.5:1. Brake hp: 320 at 4400 rpm. Carburetor: two-barrel. [Engine Code K].

COMET CHASSIS FEATURES: Wheelbase: 103 inches. Overall length: 181.7 inches. Tires: 6.45 x 14.

MONTEGO/CYCLONE CHASSIS FEATURES: Wheelbase: (passenger car) 117 inches; (station wagon) 114 inches. Overall length: (passenger car) 209.9 inches; (station wagon) 211.8 inches. Tires: (Montego MX) F78-14; (station wagon and Cyclone GT) G78-14; (Cyclone and Spoiler) G70-14; (other models) E78-14.

COUGAR CHASSIS FEATURES: Wheelbase: 112.1 inches. Overall length: 196.9 inches. Tires: E78-14.

MERCURY CHASSIS FEATURES: Wheelbase (passenger car) 124 inches; (station wagon) 121 inches. Overall length: (passenger car) 224.7 inches; (station wagon) 220.5 inches. Tires: (Monterey) G78-15; (Marquis and station wagon) H78-15.

COMET OPTIONS: GT package includes: black-out grille; dual body tape stripes; high-back bucket seats; wheel trim rings; hood scoop; dual racing mirrors; bright window frames; Deluxe door trim panels; and black instrument panel ($178.80). Heavy-duty battery ($12). Consolette with clock ($41.80). Rear window defogger ($28.60). Tinted glass ($37). Front and rear bumper guards ($23.90). Two-tone paint ($28.60). Power steering ($115.30). AM radio ($60.60). Vinyl roof ($77.50). Floor-mounted shifters, with automatic or three-speed manual transmissions ($13.10). Deluxe trim option ($39.40). Vinyl trim ($17.90). Deluxe wheel covers ($23.90). Convenience group ($26.30). Exterior decor group ($52.50). Air conditioner ($370.60). A three-speed manual transmission was standard, SelectShift automatic was optional for $163. A 200 cid/115-hp six (one-barrel); 200 cid/155-hp six (one-barrel) and a 302 cid/210-hp V-8 (two-barrel) were available at extra cost. A handling and suspension package cost $12 extra.

MONTEGO/CYCLONE OPTIONS: Heavy-duty battery ($13). Electric clock ($18.20). Extra duty cooling package ($7.80). Console ($60.90). Rear window defroster ($48). Tinted glass ($42.80). Luggage carrier on MX station wagon ($59.60); on MX station wagon with air deflector ($79.10). Remote-control left-hand mirror ($13). Bodyside molding ($33.70). Front disc brakes ($70). Four-Way power seat ($77.80). Power windows ($115.30). Power tailgate window ($35). AM radio ($66.10). AM/FM stereo radio ($216.90). Vinyl covered roof ($99.60). Deluxe seat and shoulder belts ($36.90). High-back bucket seats ($132.20). Houndstooth Cyclone interior ($32.40). Third seat for station wagons ($60). Two-tone Comfort weave seats in Montego MX ($32.40). Rim-blow steering wheel ($35). Tilting steering wheel ($45.40). Hubcaps with trim rings in Cyclones ($31.10). Deluxe wheel covers ($25.90). Luxury wheel covers ($16.20). Courtesy light group ($20.80). Instrumentation group ($84.20). Trailer towing package ($120.50). Air conditioner ($408). A three-speed manual transmission was standard in the Montego, MX and MX Brougham. A four-speed manual transmission with Hurst shifter was standard in the Cyclone and Spoiler. The Cyclone GT came with SelectShift automatic. Four-speed and automatic transmissions were optional in the other series. The four-speed was not offered in station wagons. The cross country ride package, which included heavy-duty springs, front stabilizer bar and shocks, cost $16.90. Ram-air induction was available on Cyclones with the 429 cid Cobra Jet V-8 for $64.80. A higher ratio and Traction-Lok axle were optional. The following V-8 engines were available: 302 cid/210-hp (two-barrel); 351 cid/240-hp (two-barrel); 351 cid/285-hp (four-barrel); 429 cid/370-hp Cobra Jet (four-barrel); and 429 cid/370-hp Super Cobra Jet (four-barrel).

COUGAR OPTIONS: Air conditioner ($408). Heavy-duty battery ($13). Sports console with clock ($76.50). Rear window defroster ($46). Tinted glass ($37 60); on convertibles ($15.60). Left-hand remote-control racing mirror ($15.60). Power front disc brakes ($70). Four-Way power driver's seat ($77.80). Power steering ($115.30). Power windows ($115.30). Vinyl roof with power sun roof ($483.10). AM radio ($66.10). AM/FM stereo radio ($218.90). AM radio with stereo tape system ($200.80). Vinyl roof ($89.40). Deluxe wheel covers ($25.90). Wire wheel covers ($84.20). Styled steel wheels ($58.30). Appearance protection group ($32.40). Convenience group on closed cars ($48); on convertibles ($32.40). Decor group ($90.70). A console-mounted three-speed manual transmission was standard. A four-speed manual transmission with Hurst shifter and SelectShift automatic transmission were optional. The following V-8s were available: 351 cid/285-hp (four-barrel) and 429 cid/370-hp Super Cobra Jet (four-barrel). A GT package was offered for $129.60. It featured a high-ratio axle; competition suspension; dual racing mirrors; hood scoop (non-functional except with the 429 Cobra Jet V-8 and Ram-Air); performance cooling package; tachometer; rim-blow steering wheel; F78-14 whitewall tires; hubcaps with bright trim rings; GT fender identification badges and black finished instrument panel. A higher ratio axle cost $13 extra and a competition handling package was a $32.40 option.

MERCURY OPTIONS: Air conditioning ($441.70). Air conditioning with automatic temperature controls ($520.70). Heavy-duty cooling package ($36.30). Rear window defogger ($31.10). Rear window defroster ($63.50). Tinted glass ($51.90). Cornering lamps ($36.30). Automatic load adjuster ($79.10). Luggage carrier with air deflector ($94.60). Luggage carrier with air deflector on Colony Park ($20.60). Metallic paint ($36.90). Power antenna ($32.40). Power front disc brakes ($71.30). Power door locks in two-doors ($45.40); in four-doors ($66.70). Six-Way power seat ($104.90); driver's side power seat ($89.40); both seats power operated ($178.80). Remote-control trunk release ($14.30). Power steering on Monterey sedan and hardtops ($125.70). Power windows ($132.20). AM radio ($66.10). AM/FM stereo radio ($239.60). AM radio with stereo tape system ($200.80). Dual rear-seat speakers ($33.70). Vinyl roof on Monterey ($119.20); on station wagons ($142.50). Vinyl 'Halo' roof on Marquis ($128.30). Deluxe seat and shoulder belts ($15.60). Center-facing third seat on station wagons ($128.60). Reclining passenger seat ($44.10). Twin comfort lounge seats ($77.60). Vinyl interior trim in Monterey ($26.50). Fender skirts in Monterey and Custom ($36.30). Speed control ($68.70). Tilting steering wheel ($45.40). Luxury wheel covers on Monterey ($59.60). Rear window washer on station wagons ($36.90). Convenience group on two-doors ($46.70); on four-doors ($23.40). Appearance protection group ($36.90); same on station wagons ($25.90). Decor group on Monterey ($60.40). Suspension ride package ($23.40). Trailer towing package ($90.70). SelectShift automatic transmission was standard in all, but the basic Monterey sedan and hardtop. They came with a three-speed manual transmission, but could be ordered with the automatic at extra cost. The following V-8 engines were available: 400 cid/260-hp (two-barrel); 429 cid/320-hp (two-barrel); 429 cid/360-hp (four-barrel); and a 429 cid/370-hp (four-barrel). Higher ratio and Traction-Lok axles were optional.

HISTORY: Most 1971 Comets, 61 percent, came with automatic transmission, 61.9 percent had a six-cylinder engine, 46.3 percent had power steering, 33.2 percent had tinted glass and 24.6 percent had air conditioning. Most 1971 Montegos, 97.1 percent, were equipped with automatic transmission, 91.5 percent had a V-8 engine, 94.5 percent had power steering, 49.5 percent had power brakes, 8.5 percent had power windows and 58.3 percent had an air conditioner. Most 1971 Cougars, 96.9 percent, were equipped with automatic transmission, 75 percent had an air conditioner, 98.5 percent had power steering, 77.9 percent had tinted glass, 79.7 percent had disc brakes, 4.6 percent had power seats and 8.9 percent had power windows. Most full-size 1971 Mercurys, 90 percent, were equipped with an air conditioner, 28.5 percent had a tilting steering wheel, 27.6 percent had power windows and 90.4 percent had tinted glass. Mercurys won 11 NASCAR Grand National races in 1971.

1972 MERCURY

1972-1/2 Mercury Comet four-door sedan (with Luxury Edition package), 6-cyl. (PH)

1972 Mercury Comet two-door sedan, V-8. (OCW)

COMET SERIES — Comet's biggest styling change for 1972 was its dual, full-length upper body pin stripes. Aside from that, it looked the same as the previous year's model. Standard features included: locking steering column; two-speed windshield wipers/washers; left-hand outside rearview mirror; padded dash; door-operated courtesy lights; carpeting and heater.

1972 Mercury Montego MX Brougham two-door hardtop, V-8. (OCW)

COMET

Model No.	Body/ Style No.	Body Type & Seating	Factory Price	Shipping Weight	Prod. Total
N/A	30	4-dr Sed-4P	2398	2674	29,092
N/A	31	2-dr Sed-4P	2342	2579	53,267

MONTEGO SERIES — The protruding, chrome-outlined grille of the new Montego featured a criss-cross pattern that was carried over to the headlight panels. Wheelwell opening moldings were about the only side trim used. The four large rectangular taillights were bumper integrated. Interiors were trimmed in either cloth and vinyl or all-vinyl.

MONTEGO

Model No.	Body/ Style No.	Body Type & Seating	Factory Price	Shipping Weight	Prod. Total
N/A	02	4-dr Sed-6P	2843	3454	8,658
N/A	03	2-dr HT Cpe-6P	2848	3390	9,963

MONTEGO MX SERIES: Dual upper body pin stripes running from the front fenders to the rear side windows, and bright rocker panel moldings were two features of the Montego MX. Deluxe sound insulation, carpeting, and, on the station wagon, a three-way tailgate were standard features for the MX line.

MONTEGO MX

Model No.	Body/ Style No.	Body Type & Seating	Factory Price	Shipping Weight	Prod. Total
N/A	04	4-dr Sed-6P	2951	3485	23,387
N/A	07	2-dr HT Cpe-6P	2971	3407	25,802
N/A	08	4-dr Sta Wag-6P	3264	3884	6,268

MONTEGO MX BROUGHAM SERIES — Rocker sill, lower rear quarter panel and upper body moldings were styling features of the Montego MX Brougham, which also came with Deluxe wheel covers; 'flight-bench' folding armrest seats and a woodgrain applique on the steering wheel. The Villager station wagon had woodgrain side body and tailgate paneling.

MONTEGO MX BROUGHAM

Model No.	Body/ Style No.	Body Type & Seating	Factory Price	Shipping Weight	Prod. Total
N/A	10	4-dr Sed-6P	3127	3512	17,540
N/A	11	2-dr HT Cpe-6P	3137	3433	28,417
N/A	18	4-dr Vill Sta Wag-6P	3438	3907	9,237

MONTEGO GT SERIES — The GT had full-length, tire-level bodyside moldings; a performance hood; dual racing mirrors; louvers behind the doors; a tachometer; gauges; and a special black-finished instrument panel.

1972 Mercury Montego MX Brougham four-door sedan, 6-cyl. (OCW)

1972 Mercury Cougar XR-7 two-door hardtop, V-8. (OCW)

MONTEGO GT

Model No.	Body/ Style No.	Body Type & Seating	Factory Price	Shipping Weight	Prod. Total
N/A	16	2-dr HT Fsbk-5P	3346	3517	5,820

COUGAR SERIES — The fine criss-cross pattern on the wraparound front signal lights was replaced by a design of horizontal lines. Otherwise, the 1972 Cougar looked virtually the same as the previous year's model. Among the standard features were: high-back bucket seats; sequential turn signals; locking steering column; back-up lights; consolette with illuminated ashtray; concealed two-speed windshield wipers; dual racing mirrors; two-spoke steering wheel; Deluxe wheel covers; instrument panel courtesy lights; glovebox light; and Flow-Thru ventilation.

COUGAR

Model No.	Body/ Style No.	Body Type & Seating	Factory Price	Shipping Weight	Prod. Total
N/A	91	2-dr HT Cpe-6P	3016	3282	23,731
N/A	92	2-dr Conv-5P	3370	3412	1,240

COUGAR XR-7 SERIES — The XR-7 came with an emblem in the center of the grille; a half vinyl roof; bucket seats with leather seating; tachometer; alternator gauge; oil pressure gauge; and nylon carpeting.

COUGAR XR-7

Model No.	Body/ Style No.	Body Type & Seating	Factory Price	Shipping Weight	Prod. Total
N/A	93	2-dr HT Cpe-5P	3323	3298	26,802
N/A	94	2-dr Conv-5P	3547	3451	1,929

MONTEREY SERIES — A waffle pattern grille was the biggest Monterey styling change for 1972. Standard features included: power steering; simulated Cherrywood instrument cluster; color-keyed two-spoke steering wheel; power front disc brakes; nylon loop carpeting; and cloth and vinyl upholstery.

MONTEREY

Model No.	Body/ Style No.	Body Type & Seating	Factory Price	Shipping Weight	Prod. Total
N/A	44	2-dr Sed-6P	3793	4136	19,012
N/A	46	2-dr HT Cpe-6P	3832	4086	6,731
N/A	48	4-dr HT Sed-6P	3896	4141	1,416
N/A	74	4-dr Sta Wag-6P	4445	4539	4,644

MONTEREY CUSTOM SERIES — Full-length mid-bodyside moldings, Deluxe wheel covers and chrome rocker panels helped distinguish Customs from basic Montereys. The Custom's cloth and vinyl interior was also more luxurious.

1972 Mercury Monterey Custom two-door hardtop, V-8. (OCW)

1972 Mercury Marquis Brougham four-door hardtop, V-8. (OCW)

MONTEREY CUSTOM

Model No.	Body/ Style No.	Body Type & Seating	Factory Price	Shipping Weight	Prod. Total
N/A	54	4-dr Sed-6P	3956	4225	16,879
N/A	56	2-dr HT Cpe-6P	4035	4175	5,910
N/A	58	4-dr HT Sed-6P	4103	4230	1,583

MARQUIS SERIES — A new ice-cube-tray-pattern grille and similar treatment in the center section of the rear deck panel were the main styling changes for 1972. Standard equipment included: power front disc brakes; power steering; Deluxe sound insulation; power ventilation; 100 percent nylon loop carpeting; Deluxe wheel covers; woodgrain instrument panel; electric clock; map light; luggage compartment light; twin ashtrays and courtesy lights.

MARQUIS

Model No.	Body/ Style No.	Body Type & Seating	Factory Price	Shipping Weight	Prod. Total
N/A	63	4-dr Sed-6P	4493	4386	14,122
N/A	66	2-dr HT Cpe-6P	4572	4336	5,507
N/A	68	4-dr HT Sed-6P	4637	4391	1,583
N/A	74	4-dr Sta Wag-6P	4445	4539	2,085

MARQUIS BROUGHAM SERIES — The Brougham had fender-to-fender upper body moldings. In addition to standard Marquis features, it came with a vinyl robe cord; cut-pile nylon carpeting; front door courtesy lights; vanity mirror on the right-hand sun visor; power windows; vinyl roof; color-keyed wheel covers; interior pillar lights; and ashtrays and lighters in the rear seat armrests.

MARQUIS BROUGHAM

Model No.	Body/ Style No.	Body Type & Seating	Factory Price	Shipping Weight	Prod. Total
N/A	62	4-dr Sed-6P	4890	4436	38,242
N/A	64	2-dr HT Cpe-6P	4969	4386	20,064
N/A	67	4-dr HT Sed-6P	5034	4441	12,841
N/A	76	4-dr Sta Wag-6P	4550	4579	20,192

NOTE 1: Model 76 uses same V-8 as Monterey station wagons.

ENGINE [(Comet) Six]: Cast-iron block. Displacement: 170 cid. Bore and stroke: 3.68 x 3.91 inches. Compression ratio: 9.0:1. SAE net hp: 82 at 4400 rpm. Carburetor: one-barrel. [Engine Code U].

ENGINE [(Montego/MX/MX Brougham) Six]: Cast-iron block. Displacement: 250 cid. Bore and stroke: 3.68 x 3.91. Compression ratio: 9.0:1. SAE net hp: 95 at 3500 rpm. Carburetor: one barrel. [Engine Code L].

ENGINE [(Montego GT) V-8]: Overhead valve. Cast-iron block. Displacement: 302 cid. Bore and stroke: 4.00 x 3.00 inches. Compression ratio: 8.5:1. SAE net hp: 140 at 4000 rpm. Carburetor: two barrel. [Engine Code F].

ENGINE [(Cougar/XR-7) V-8]: Overhead valve. Cast-iron block. Displacement: 351 cid. Bore and stroke: 4.00 x 3.50 inches. Compression ratio: 8.6:1. SAE net hp: 163 at 3800 rpm. Carburetor: two-barrel. [Engine Code H].

ENGINE [(Monterey/Monterey Custom Passenger Cars) V-8]: Overhead valve. Cast-iron block. Displacement: 351 cid. Bore and stroke: 4.00 x 3.50 inches. Compression ratio: 8.6:1. SAE net hp: 163 at 3800 rpm. Carburetor: two-barrel. [Engine Code H].

ENGINE [(Monterey/Monterey Custom Station Wagon) V-8]: Overhead valve. Cast-iron block. Displacement: 400 cid. Bore and stroke: 4.00 x 4.00 inches. Compression ratio: 8.4:1. SAE net hp: 172 at 4000 rpm. Carburetor: two-barrel. [Engine Code S].

ENGINE [(Marquis/Marquis Brougham) V-8]: Overhead valve. Cast-iron block. Displacement: 429 cid. Bore and stroke: 4.36 x 3.59 inches. Compression ratio: 8.5:1. SAE net hp: 208 at 4400 rpm. Carburetor: four-barrel. [Engine Code N].

COMET CHASSIS FEATURES: Wheelbase: 110 inches. Overall length: (four-door) 187 inches; (two-door) 182 inches. Tires: 6.45 x 14.

MONTEGO CHASSIS FEATURES: Wheelbase: (four-door) 118 inches; (two-door) 114 inches. Overall length: (four-door) 213 inches; (two-door) 209 inches; (station wagon) 216 inches. Front tread: 62.8 inches. Rear tread: 62.9 inches. Tires: (MX and GT) F78-14; (station wagon) F78-14; (other models) E78-14.

COUGAR CHASSIS FEATURES: Wheelbase: 112.1 inches. Overall length: 196.1 inches. Front tread: 61.5 inches. Rear tread: 61 inches. Tires: E78-14.

MERCURY CHASSIS FEATURES: Wheelbase: (passenger car) 124 inches; (station wagon) 121 inches. Overall length: (passenger car) 225 inches; (station wagon) 221 inches. Front tread: 63.3 inches. Rear tread: 64.3 inches. Tires: H78-15.

COMET OPTIONS: GT package included: high-back bucket seats; Deluxe door trim panels; hood scoop; dual racing mirrors; hubcaps with bright trim rings; bright window frames; dual body tape stripes; black-out grille; headlamp doors and lower back panel paint treatment and black dash panel with bright moldings ($173.34). Air conditioner ($359.59). Front and rear bumper guards ($23.11). Consolette with clock ($40.45). Rear-window defogger ($27.73). Door edge guards on two-doors ($5.78); four-doors ($8.10). Tinted windows ($52.01). Bodyside moldings ($30.05). Two-tone paint ($27.73). Glamour paint ($34.66). Power steering ($92.45). AM radio ($58.94). AM/FM radio ($123.65). Vinyl-covered roof ($72.12). Bucket seats ($72.12). Vinyl trim on two-doors ($17.34). Deluxe trim ($38.14). Trim rings with hubcaps ($27.73). Deluxe wheel covers ($23.11). Convenience group ($25.54). Exterior decor group ($50.84). A three-speed manual transmission was standard. SelectShift automatic was optional. A 200 cid/91-hp six (one-barrel); 250 cid/98-hp six (one-barrel); and a 302 cid/138-hp V-8 (two-barrel) were available at extra cost.

MONTEGO OPTIONS: Air conditioner ($397.91). Front bumper guards ($15.14). Electric clock ($17.67). Console ($59.32). Tinted windows ($41.66). Carpeted load floor in station wagons ($25.24). Dual racing mirrors ($12.62). Left-hand remote-control mirror ($12.62). Glamour paint ($37.86). Power front disc brakes ($68.14). Power door locks in two-doors ($44.17); in four-doors ($66.89); in station wagons ($75.72). Six-Way power bench seat ($102.22). Power steering ($112.33). Power windows ($112.33). Power tailgate window in station wagons ($34.08). AM radio ($58.94). AM/FM stereo radio ($213.29). Vinyl-covered roof ($97.18). High-back bucket seats ($128.72). Rear-facing third seat in station wagons ($75.81). Hubcaps with trim rings ($30.29). Deluxe wheel covers ($25.24). Luxury wheel covers ($17.67). Interval windshield wipers ($25.24). Appearance group on passenger cars ($31.55); on station wagons ($25.54). Convenience group on two-doors ($47.96); on four-doors ($25.24). Instrumentation group ($99.71). Cross country ride package ($16.41). Visibility group ($25.24). A three-speed manual transmission was standard. A four-speed manual transmission (with Hurst shifter) and SelectShift automatic transmission were optional. Buyers of the Cyclone option package (which included: functional dual hood scoop; Traction-Lok differential; wide oval tires; special striping; dual racing mirrors; and three-spoke steering wheel) could choose either four-speed or automatic transmissions. A 302 cid/140-hp V-8 (two-barrel); 351 cid/161-hp V-8 (two-barrel); 351 cid/248-hp Cobra Jet V-8; 400 cid/168-hp V-8 (two-barrel) and 429 cid/201-hp V-8 (four-barrel) were optional. A higher ratio axle cost $12.62. Traction-Lok differential sold for $46.76. A competition handling package was $27.76 extra.

COUGAR OPTIONS: Air conditioning ($364.01). Front bumper guards ($13.87). Sports console with clock ($66.18). Rear window defroster ($42.76). Tinted windows in closed cars ($33.52); in convertibles ($13.87). Dual racing mirrors with left-hand remote-control ($23.11). Protective bodyside molding ($30.05). Glamour paint ($34.66). Power front disc brakes ($62.40). Four-Way power seat ($69.34). Power steering ($102.86). Power sun roof ($431.04). Power windows ($102.66). AM radio ($58.94). AM/FM stereo radio ($195.30). AM radio with stereo tape system ($179.12). Vinyl roof ($79.73). Tilting steering wheel ($40.45). Upbeat stripe cloth trim (no charge with decor group). Deluxe wheel covers ($23.11). Wire wheel covers ($75.12). Interval windshield wipers ($23.11). Appearance protection group ($28.89). Convenience group ($42.76). Exterior decor group ($80.89).

MERCURY OPTIONS: Air conditioner ($430.58); with automatic temperature controls ($507.55). Deluxe seat and shoulder belts ($50.49). Heavy-duty battery ($12.62). Front bumper guards ($8.84). Electric rear window defroster ($61.84). Tinted glass ($50.49). Cornering lamps ($35.34). Automatic load adjuster ($76.99). Luggage carrier with air deflector on station wagons ($92.13). Glamour paint ($37.86). Sure-Track brake system ($189.30). Power

door locks in two-doors ($44.17); in four-doors ($66.89). Six-Way power bench seat ($102.22). Six-Way left- and right-hand power seat ($174.16). Power sun roof ($495.97). Power windows ($128.72). Remote-control trunk release ($13.89). AM radio ($64.37). AM/FM stereo radio ($233.47). AM radio with stereo tape system ($195.62). Vinyl roof, Monterey and Custom ($97.18); Marquis ($124.95). Center-facing third seat ($122.27). Twin comfort lounge seat ($75.72). Speed control ($66.89). Tilting steering ($44.17). Vanity mirror ($3.79). Deluxe wheel covers, Monterey and station wagons ($25.24). Luxury wheel covers ($32.82). Interval windshield wipers ($25.24). Rear windshield washer on station wagon ($37.89). Appearance protection group ($37.36). Convenience group on two-doors ($58.05); on four-doors ($35.34). Cross country ride package ($22.71). Trailer-towing package ($88.34). A three-speed manual transmission was standard. Four-speed manual transmission (with a Hurst shifter) and a SelectShift automatic transmission were offered. A 351 cid/262-hp V-8 (four-barrel) and a 351 cid/266-hp Cobra Jet V-8 were optional. The latter engine came with dual exhaust and competition suspension. The $115.96 GT options package included higher axle ratio; hood scoop; tachometer; performance cooling package; Deluxe steering wheel; trim rings; black instrument panel and dual racing mirrors. A competition handling package was available for $28.89. Higher ratio axles and Traction-Lok differentials were also available. SelectShift automatic transmission was standard. A 400 cid/172-hp V-8 (two-barrel); 429 cid/208-hp V-8 (four-barrel); and a 460 cid/224-hp V-8 were optional.

HISTORY: Most 1972 Comets, 88 percent, were sold with an automatic transmission, 38.3 percent had a V-8 engine, 38.5 percent had tinted glass, 64.8 percent had power steering, 89 percent had radios, 13.6 percent had bucket seats and 36.3 percent had a vinyl roof. Only 3.3 percent of 1972 Montegos came with bucket seats, 60.8 percent had a vinyl roof, 97.1 percent had a radio, 99.2 percent had automatic transmission, 97.2 percent had a V-8 engine, 97.8 percent had power steering and 14.8 percent had power windows. Most full-size 1972 Mercurys, 73.5 percent, came with a vinyl roof. The vast majority of 1972 Cougars, 98.5 percent, were equipped with an automatic transmission, 87.9 percent had power brakes, 98.1 percent had a radio, 78.9 percent had vinyl roofs, 21.9 percent had tilting steering wheels, 5.7 percent had power seats, and 99.1 percent had power steering.

1973 MERCURY

1973 Mercury Comet. (OCW)

COMET SERIES — Comet received a new, criss-cross pattern grille and energy-absorbing bumpers. However, basic styling remained the same as it had since 1971. Standard features included: dual hydraulic brakes with warning light system; blend-air heater; wheel lip moldings; rocker panel moldings; carpeting; front and rear ashtrays and cloth and vinyl upholstery.

COMET

Model No.	Body/ Style No.	Body Type & Seating	Factory Price	Shipping Weight	Prod. Total
N/A	30	4-dr Sed-4P	2389	2904	28,984
N/A	31	2-dr Sed-4P	2432	2813	55,707

1973 Mercury Comet two-door sedan, 6-cyl. (OCW)

MONTEGO SERIES — Larger, energy-absorbing bumpers were the most noticeable change made to Montegos for 1973. The standard interior was vinyl and cloth.

MONTEGO

Model No.	Body/ Style No.	Body Type & Seating	Factory Price	Shipping Weight	Prod. Total
N/A	02	4-dr Sed-6P	2916	3719	7,459
N/A	03	2-dr HT Cpe-6P	2926	3653	7,082

MONTEGO MX SERIES — Like the previous year, rocker panel moldings and dual, upper body pin stripes helped set the MX apart from the basic Montego. It also had Deluxe sound insulation and color-keyed deep loop carpeting.

MONTEGO MX

Model No.	Body/ Style No.	Body Type & Seating	Factory Price	Shipping Weight	Prod. Total
N/A	10	4-dr Sed-6P	3009	3772	25,300
N/A	11	2-dr HT Cpe-6P	3041	3683	27,812
N/A	08	4-dr Sta Wag-6P	3417	4124	7,012

MONTEGO MX BROUGHAM SERIES — Bright upper body moldings and Deluxe wheel covers were two distinguishing exterior features of the Brougham, which came with 'flight bench' seats. These were bench seats with backs that resembled bucket seats and a folding armrest between them. The steering wheel had a woodgrain insert.

MONTEGO MX BROUGHAM

Model No.	Body/ Style No.	Body Type & Seating	Factory Price	Shipping Weight	Prod. Total
N/A	10	4-dr Sed-6P	3189	3813	24,329
N/A	11	2-dr HT Cpe-6P	3209	3706	40,951
N/A	18	4-dr Vill Sta Wag-6P	3606	4167	12,396

MONTEGO GT SERIES — New energy-absorbing bumpers and the placing of the letter 'G' over 'T' on the front fender nameplate were the styling changes made for 1973. Standard features included: Deluxe sound insulation; Deluxe wheel covers; sports-type three-spoke steering wheel; deep loop carpeting; dual racing mirrors and performance hood with nonfunctional dual scoops.

MONTEGO GT

Model No.	Body/ Style No.	Body Type & Seating	Factory Price	Shipping Weight	Prod. Total
N/A	16	2-dr HT Fsbk-6P	3413	3662	4,464

COUGAR SERIES — Styling changes for 1973 consisted mainly of vertical chrome pieces in the headlight panels, a more refined radiator-look grille and vertical trim pieces on the taillights. Standard equipment included: sequential turn signals; high-back bucket seats; wheel lip moldings; two-spoke color-keyed steering wheel; consolette with ashtray and power front disc brakes.

1973 Mercury Montego MX Brougham two-door hardtop, V-8. (OCW)

1973 Mercury Cougar XR-7 two-door hardtop, V-8. (OCW)

COUGAR

Model No.	Body/ Style No.	Body Type & Seating	Factory Price	Shipping Weight	Prod. Total
N/A	91	2-dr HT-6P	3372	3396	21,069
N/A	92	2-dr Conv-5P	3726	3524	1,284

COUGAR XR-7 SERIES — Chrome rocker panels and the XR-7 emblem on top of the grille were two ways to tell the top-of-the-line Cougar from the standard one. In addition to the features offered on the basic Cougar line, XR-7 buyers received special wheel covers; toggle switches; remote-control mirror; vinyl roof; tachometer; trip odometer; alternator gauge; oil pressure gauge and a map light. The high-back bucket seats had leather seating surfaces.

COUGAR XR-7

Model No.	Body/ Style No.	Body Type & Seating	Factory Price	Shipping Weight	Prod. Total
N/A	93	2-dr HT Cpe-5P	3679	3416	35,110
N/A	94	2-dr Conv-5P	3903	3530	3,165

MONTEREY SERIES — The new Monterey was about two inches shorter than the previous year's model, but nobody mistook it for a Comet. Its ice-cube-tray grille was outlined in chrome. The horizontal bars on the recessed headlight panels carried over to the large wraparound signal lights. A full-length, mid-bodyside chrome spear, chrome wheelwell openings and chrome rocker panels graced the Monterey's sides. Six square, chrome trimmed taillights and two back-up lights were located on the rear deck panel. Between them was trim that matched the grille's pattern. All 1973 Montereys came equipped with power steering, nylon loop carpeting, front bumper guards, automatic parking brake release, energy-absorbing bumper and power front disc brakes. A cloth and vinyl interior was standard.

MONTEREY

Model No.	Body/ Style No.	Body Type & Seating	Factory Price	Shipping Weight	Prod. Total
N/A	44	4-dr Sed-6P	3961	4225	16,622
N/A	46	2-dr HT Cpe-6P	4004	4167	6,452
N/A	72	4-dr Sta Wag-6P	4379	4673	4,275

NOTE 1: One Monterey four-door hardtop was made.

MONTEREY CUSTOM SERIES — The Custom was basically a standard Monterey with a plusher interior and a more powerful engine.

MONTEREY CUSTOM

Model No.	Body/ Style No.	Body Type & Seating	Factory Price	Shipping Weight	Prod. Total
N/A	54	4-dr Sed-6P	4124	4295	20,873
N/A	56	2-dr HT Cpe-6P	4207	4239	6,962

NOTE 1: Two Monterey Custom four-door hardtops were made.

MARQUIS SERIES — Changes in the Marquis for 1973 included energy-absorbing bumpers; finger grille squares; wraparound signal lights; a free-standing hood ornament and full-length lower body and wheelwell opening moldings. Automatic parking brake release; fender skirts; electric clock; inside hood latch release; power front disc brakes; and power steering were among the many standard features.

MARQUIS

Model No.	Body/ Style No.	Body Type & Seating	Factory Price	Shipping Weight	Prod. Total
N/A	62	4-dr Sed-6P	5072	4547	15,250
N/A	66	2-dr HT Cpe-6P	4727	4411	5,973
N/A	68	4-dr HT Sed-6P	5206	4565	2,185
N/A	74	4-dr Sta Wag-6P	4608	4695	2,464

1973 Mercury Marquis Brougham four-door sedan, V-8. (OCW)

MARQUIS BROUGHAM SERIES — The Brougham had fender-to-fender upper bodyside moldings; power windows; halo vinyl roof; shag cut-pile carpeting; vanity mirror on right-hand sun visor; rear pillar and luggage compartment lights; and Deluxe wheel covers with inserts. The Colony Park station wagon came with a three-way tailgate, power rear window and Cherry woodgrain yacht deck exterior paneling.

MARQUIS BROUGHAM

Model No.	Body/ Style No.	Body Type & Seating	Factory Price	Shipping Weight	Prod. Total
N/A	62	4-dr Sed-6P	5072	4547	46,624
N/A	64	2-dr HT Cpe-6P	5151	4475	22,770
N/A	67	4-dr HT Sed-6P	5206	4565	10,613
N/A	76	4-dr Col Prk Sta Wag-6P	4713	4730	23,283

ENGINE [(Comet) Six]: Overhead valve. Cast-iron block. Displacement: 200 cid. Bore and stroke: 3.68 x 3.13 inches. Compression ratio: 8.3:1. SAE net hp: 94 at 3800 rpm. Carburetor: one-barrel.

ENGINE [(Montego/MX/MX Brougham) Six]: Overhead valve. Cast-iron block. Displacement: 250 cid. Bore and stroke: 3.68 x 3.91 inches. Compression ratio: 8.0:1. SAE net hp: 92 at 3200 rpm. Carburetor: one-barrel.

ENGINE [(Montego/MX/MX Brougham Station Wagon) V-8]: Overhead valve. Cast-iron block. Displacement: 302 cid. Bore and stroke: 4.00 x 3.00 inches. Compression ratio: 8.0:1. SAE net hp: 137 at 4200 rpm. Carburetor: two-barrel.

ENGINE [(Cougar/XR-7) V-8]: Overhead valve. Cast-iron block. Displacement: 351 cid. Bore and stroke: 4.00 x 3.50 inches. Compression ratio: 8.0:1. SAE net hp: 168 at 4000 rpm. Carburetor: two-barrel.

ENGINE [(Monterey) V-8]: Overhead valve. Cast-iron block. Displacement: 351 cid. Bore and stroke: 4.00 x 3.50 inches. Compression ratio: 8.0:1. SAE net hp: 159 at 4000 rpm. Carburetor: two-barrel.

ENGINE [(Monterey/Marquis/Marquis Brougham Station Wagon) V-8]: Overhead valve. Cast-iron block. Displacement: 400 cid. Bore and stroke: 4.00 x 4.00 inches. Compression ratio: 8.0:1. SAE net hp: 171 at 3600 rpm. Carburetor: two-barrel.

ENGINE [(Marquis/Marquis Brougham) V-8]: Overhead valve. Cast-iron block. Displacement: 429 cid. Bore and stroke: 4.36 x 3.59 inches. Compression ratio: 8.0:1. SAE net hp: 198 at 4400 rpm. Carburetor: four-barrel.

COMET CHASSIS FEATURES: Wheelbase: (two-doors) 103 inches; (four-doors) 109.9 inches. Overall length: (two-doors) 185.4 inches; (four-doors) 192.3 inches. Tires: 6.45 x 14.

MONTEGO CHASSIS FEATURES: Wheelbase: (two-doors) 114 inches; (four-doors and station wagon) 118 inches. Overall length: (two-doors) 211.3 inches; (four-doors) 215.3 inches; (station wagon) 218.5 inches. Tires: (station wagon) F78-14 GT or G78-14; (others) E78-14.

COUGAR CHASSIS FEATURES: Wheelbase: 112.1 inches. Overall length: 199.5 inches. Tires: E78-14.

MERCURY CHASSIS FEATURES: Wheelbase: (passenger car) 124 inches; (station wagon) 121 inches. Overall length: (passenger car) 222.5 inches; (station wagon) 223.4 inches. Tires: (passenger car) HR78-15 steel belted radials; (station wagon) JR78-15 steel-belted radials.

COMET OPTIONS: GT package including high-back bucket seats; Deluxe door trim panels; hood scoop; dual racing mirrors; hubcaps with bright trim rings; bright window frames; dual body tape stripe; blacked-out grille; headlamp door; lower back panel and hood paint treatment and black dash panel with bright moldings ($173.34). Air conditioner ($359.59). Front and rear bumper guards ($23.11). Consolette with clock ($40.45). Rear window defogger ($27.73). Door edge guards, on two-doors ($5.78); on four-doors ($8.10). Tinted windows ($52.01). Bodyside moldings ($30.05). Two-tone paint ($27.73). Glamour paint ($34.66). Power steering ($92.45). AM radio ($58.94). AM/FM radio ($123.65). Vinyl covered roof ($72.12). Bucket seats ($72.12). Vinyl trim, on two-doors ($17.34). Deluxe trim ($38.14). Trim rings with hubcaps ($27.73). Deluxe wheel covers ($23.11). Convenience group ($25.54). Exterior decor group ($50.84). Custom option including Deluxe sound package; grained vinyl roof; radial tires; driver's side remote-control mirror; reclining expanded vinyl bucket seats; mid-side body moldings and distinctive dash ($346). A three-speed manual transmission was standard. SelectShift automatic transmission was optional. A 250 cid/88-hp six (one-barrel) and 302 cid/138-hp V-8 (two-barrel) were available at extra cost.

MONTEGO OPTIONS: Air conditioner ($397.91). Front bumper guards ($15.14). Electric clock ($17.67). Console ($59.32). Tinted windows ($41.66). Carpeted load floor in station wagon ($25.24). Dual racing mirrors ($12.62). Left-hand remote-control mirror ($12.62). Glamour paint ($37.86). Power front disc brakes ($68.14). Power door locks, in two-doors ($44.17); in four-doors ($66.89); in station wagons ($75.72). Six-Way power bench seat ($102.22). Power steering ($112.33). Power window ($121.33). Power tailgate window in station wagons ($34.08). AM radio ($58.94). AM/FM stereo radio ($213.29). Vinyl covered roof ($97.18). High-back bucket seats ($128.72). Rear facing third seat in station wagons ($75.81). Hubcaps with trim rings ($30.92). Deluxe wheel covers ($25.24). Luxury wheel covers ($17.64). Interval windshield wipers ($25.24). Appearance group on station wagons ($25.54); on other models ($31.55). Convenience group on two-doors ($47.96); on four-doors ($25.24). Instrumentation group ($99.71). Cross country ride package ($16.41). Visibility group ($25.24). A three-speed manual transmission was standard. A four-speed manual transmission (with Hurst shifter) and SelectShift automatic transmission were optional. A 302 cid/137-hp V-8 (two-barrel); 351 cid/161-hp V-8 (two-barrel); 351 cid/248-hp Cobra Jet V-8 (four-barrel); 400 cid/168-hp V-8 (two-barrel) and a 429 cid/201-hp V-8 (four-barrel) were optional. A higher ratio axle, Traction-Lok differential and a competition handling package were available.

COUGAR OPTIONS: Air conditioning ($364.01). Front bumper guards ($13.87). Sports console with clock ($68.18). Rear window defroster ($42.76). Tinted windows ($33.52). Tinted windows in convertibles ($13.87). Dual racing mirrors with left-hand remote-control ($23.11). Protective bodyside molding ($30.05). Glamour paint ($34.66). Power front disc brakes ($62.40). Four-Way power seat ($69.34). Power steering ($102.86). Power sun roof ($431.04). Power windows ($102.86). AM radio ($58.94). AM/FM stereo radio ($195.30). AM radio with stereo tape system ($179.12). Vinyl roof ($79.73). Tilting steering wheel ($40.45). Upbeat stripe cloth trim (no charge with decor group). Deluxe wheel covers ($23.11). Wire wheel covers ($75.12). Interval windshield wipers ($23.11). Appearance protection group ($28.89). Convenience group ($42.76). Exterior decor group ($80.89). Select-Shift automatic transmission was standard. A four-speed manual transmission was optional. A 351 cid/264-hp Cobra Jet V-8 was available at extra cost. A higher ratio axle and Traction-Lok differential were also available. Air conditioner ($430.58). Air conditioner with automatic temperature controls ($507.55). Deluxe seat and shoulder belts ($50.49). Heavy-duty battery ($12.62). Front bumper guards ($8.84). Electric rear window defroster ($61.84). Tinted glass ($50.49). Cornering lamps ($35.34). Automatic load adjuster ($75.99). Luggage carrier with air deflector ($92.13). Glamour paint ($37.86). Sure-Track brake system ($189.30). Power door locks, on two-doors ($44.17); on four-doors ($68.99). Six-Way power bench seat ($102.22). Six-Way in left and right-hand power seat ($174.16). Power sun roof ($495.97). Power windows ($128.72). Remote control trunk release ($13.89). AM radio ($64.37). AM/FM stereo radio ($233.47). AM radio with stereo tape system ($195.62). Vinyl roof ($124.95). Center-facing third seat ($122.27). Twin comfort lounge seat ($75.72). Speed control ($66.89). Tilting steering wheel ($44.17). Vanity mirror ($3.79). Luxury wheel covers ($32.82). Interval windshield wipers ($25.24). Rear windshield washer on station wagon ($37.89). Appearance protection group ($37.36). Convenience group, on two-doors ($58.05); on four-doors ($35.34). Cross country ride package ($22.71). Trailer-towing package ($88.34). SelectShift automatic transmission was standard. A 400 cid/171-hp V-8 (two-barrel); 429 cid/198-hp V-8 (four-barrel); and 460 cid/267-hp V-8 (four-barrel) were optional.

HISTORY: Most full-size Mercurys, 75.7 percent, came with a vinyl roof. Most 1973 Comets, 91.82 percent, had radios, 35.2 percent had bucket seats, 37.4 percent had vinyl roofs, 90 percent had automatic transmissions, 45.9 percent had V-8s and 50.4 percent had tinted glass. Just 3.2 percent of 1973 Montegos came with bucket seats, 63.4 percent had vinyl roofs, 97 percent had a radio and 99.2 percent were powered by a V-8 engine. Most 1973 Cougars, 98 percent, had a radio, 94.7 percent had a vinyl roof, 28 percent had a tilting steering wheel, 99.3 percent had automatic transmission and 84.5 percent had air conditioning.

1974 Mercury Montego MX Brougham four-door sedan, V-8. (OCW)

1974 Mercury Montego MX Brougham. (OCW)

COMET SERIES — New front and rear bumpers and slightly different upper and lower body moldings were the biggest Comet styling changes for 1974. Standard features included dual hydraulic brakes with warning light system; Blend-Air heater; windshield washers; locking steering column; cigar lighter; energy-absorbing steering wheel; and two-speed windshield wipers.

COMET

Model No.	Body/ Style No.	Body Type & Seating	Factory Price	Shipping Weight	Prod. Total
N/A	30	4-dr Sed-4P	2489	2904	60,944
N/A	31	2-dr Sed-4P	2432	2813	64,751

MONTEGO SERIES — The slightly protruding, chrome-outlined Montego grille had a criss-cross pattern. The four headlights were nestled in chrome panels. Wheelwell openings and center mid-body moldings were on the sides. Taillights were located on the rear deck panel and wrapped around the fenders. Standard features included: front disc brakes; impact resistant bumpers; locking steering column; concealed windshield wipers; inside hood release and color-keyed deep loop carpeting.

MONTEGO

Model No.	Body/ Style No.	Body Type & Seating	Factory Price	Shipping Weight	Prod. Total
N/A	02	4-dr Sed-6P	3360	4062	5,674
N/A	03	2-dr HT-6P	3327	3977	7,645

MONTEGO MX SERIES — Rocker panel moldings and nameplates on the lower front fenders were two identifying traits of the MX. In addition to a slightly plusher interior than the base Montego, the MX had Deluxe sound insulation.

MONTEGO MX

Model No.	Body/ Style No.	Body Type & Seating	Factory Price	Shipping Weight	Prod. Total
N/A	04	4-dr Sed-6P	3478	4092	19,446
N/A	07	2-dr HT Cpe-6P	3443	3990	20,957
N/A	08	4-dr Sta Wag-6P	4083	4426	4,085

MONTEGO MX BROUGHAM SERIES — Upper body and lower rear quarter panel moldings plus a super sound insulation package and woodgrain applique on the instrument panel were Brougham features. The Villager station wagon had simulated woodgrain bodyside and tailgate paneling, outlined with bright moldings, power tailgate window, flight bench seat with center armrest and imitation Cherrywood instrument and dash panel appliques.

MONTEGO MX BROUGHAM

Model No.	Body/ Style No.	Body Type & Seating	Factory Price	Shipping Weight	Prod. Total
N/A	10	4-dr Sed-6P	3680	4143	13,467
N/A	11	2-dr HT Cpe-6P	3646	4010	20,511
N/A	18	4-dr Vill Sta Wag-6P	4307	4463	6,234

COUGAR XR-7 SERIES — For the first time since its inception in 1967 there was no base Cougar offered for 1974, instead only the upscale XR-7 was produced. Front end styling was similar to the previous year's model, except the grille was wider and had the previous emblem replaced by a hood ornament. Side trim consisted of upper body chrome (running from the tip of the fenders to the rear roof pillars where it connected with a chrome band that went across the roof), full-length upper tire level moldings and a rear roof quarter panel opera window. The rear deck panel taillights wrapped around the fenders. Standard features included: soft vinyl bucket seats or twin comfort lounge seats; steel-belted radial tires; power steering; performance instrumentation; luxury steering wheel; cut-pile carpeting and inside hood release.

COUGAR XR-7

Model No.	Body/ Style No.	Body Type & Seating	Factory Price	Shipping Weight	Prod. Total
N/A	93	2-dr HT Cpe-5P	4706	4255	91,670

MONTEREY SERIES — The Monterey had a squares-within-squares, chrome framed grille. This pattern was carried over to the headlight panels. Signal lights wrapped around the front fenders. Rear quarter pillar nameplate and trim, full-length mid-body spear and wheel opening and rocker panel molding were on the sides. Among the standard features were nylon carpeting; glovebox light; power steering; automatic parking brake release; solid state ignition and cloth and vinyl interior.

MONTEREY

Model No.	Body/ Style No.	Body Type & Seating	Factory Price	Shipping Weight	Prod. Total
N/A	44	4-dr Sed-6P	4367	4559	6,185
N/A	46	2-dr HT Cpe-6P	4410	4506	2,003
N/A	72	4-dr Sta Wag-6P	4731	4916	1,669

MONTEREY CUSTOM SERIES — The Custom series script was on the rear roof quarter panel. Deluxe wheel covers, a Deluxe steering wheel and all-vinyl interior were standard features of the Custom.

1974 Mercury Comet two-door sedan, 6-cyl. (OCW)

1974 Mercury Cougar XR-7 two-door hardtop, V-8. (OCW)

1974 Mercury Marquis Brougham four-door sedan, V-8. (OCW)

MONTEREY CUSTOM

Model No.	Body/ Style No.	Body Type & Seating	Factory Price	Shipping Weight	Prod. Total
N/A	54	4-dr Sed-6P	4480	4561	13,113
N/A	56	2-dr HT Cpe-6P	4523	4504	4,510

MARQUIS SERIES — The Marquis grille had rectangular vertical pieces with slender bars within them. The hidden headlight doors had horizontal bars that extended around the wraparound signal lights. Mercury was spelled out in chrome above the grille. Side trim consisted of full-length, lower body moldings. The six square taillights and two back-up lights were located in the rear deck panel. Standard features on Marquis included: power front disc brakes; power steering; Deluxe sound insulation; loop-pile carpeting; courtesy lights; fender skirts and power ventilation. The interior was cloth and vinyl.

MARQUIS

Model No.	Body/ Style No.	Body Type & Seating	Factory Price	Shipping Weight	Prod. Total
N/A	63	4-dr Sed-6P	5080	4757	6,910
N/A	66	2-dr HT Cpe-6P	5080	4698	2,633
N/A	68	4-dr HT Sed-6P	4080	4753	784
N/A	72	4-dr Sta Wag-6P	4960	4973	1,111

MARQUIS BROUGHAM SERIES — Full-length upper body molding, halo vinyl roof, power windows, door pull straps, left-hand remote-control mirror, Deluxe wheel covers with inserts, pillar lights and lights under the instrument panel were Brougham features.

MARQUIS BROUGHAM

Model No.	Body/ Style No.	Body Type & Seating	Factory Price	Shipping Weight	Prod. Total
N/A	62	4-dr Sed-6P	5519	4833	24,477
N/A	64	2-dr HT Cpe-6P	5519	4762	10,207
N/A	67	4-dr HT Sed-6P	5519	4853	4,189
N/A	76	4-dr Col Prk Sta Wag-6P	5066	5066	10,802

ENGINE [(Comet) Six]: Overhead valve. Cast-iron block. Displacement: 200 cid. Bore and stroke: 3.68 x 3.13 inches. Compression ratio: 8.3:1. SAE net hp: 84 at 3800 rpm. Carburetor: one-barrel.

ENGINE [(Montego/MX/Brougham) V-8]: Overhead valve. Cast-iron block. Displacement: 302 cid. Bore and stroke: 4.00 x 3.00 inches. Compression ratio: 8.0:1. SAE net hp: 140 at 3800 rpm. Carburetor: two-barrel.

ENGINE [(Cougar XR-7) V-8]: Overhead valve. Cast-iron block. Displacement: 351 cid. Bore and stroke: 4.00 x 3.50 inches. Compression ratio: 8.0:1. SAE net hp: 168 at 4000 rpm. Carburetor: two-barrel.

ENGINE [(Monterey/Monterey Custom) V-8]: Overhead valve. Cast-iron block. Displacement: 400 cid. Bore and stroke: 4.00 x 4.00 inches. Compression ratio: 8.0:1. SAE net hp: 170 at 3600 rpm. Carburetor: two-barrel.

ENGINE [(Marquis/Marquis Brougham) V-8]: Overhead valve. Cast-iron block. Displacement: 460 cid. Bore and stroke: 4.36 x 3.85 inches. Compression ratio: 8.0:1. SAE net hp: 195 at 4400 rpm. Carburetor: four-barrel.

COMET CHASSIS FEATURES: Wheelbase: (two-doors) 103 inches; (four-doors) 109 inches. Overall length: (two-doors) 187.7 inches; (four-doors) 196.3 inches. Tires: 6.45 x 14.

MONTEGO CHASSIS FEATURES: Wheelbase: (two-doors) 114 inches; (four-doors and station wagon) 118 inches. Overall length: (two-doors) 215.5 inches; (four-doors) 219.5 inches; (station wagon) 223.1 inches. Tires: (station wagon) H78-14; (Villager station wagon) HR78-14; (others) G78-14.

COUGAR CHASSIS FEATURES: Wheelbase: 114 inches. Overall length: 214.2 inches. Tires: HR78-14.

MERCURY CHASSIS FEATURES: Wheelbase: (passenger car) 124 inches; (station wagon) 121 inches. Overall length: (passenger car) 226.7 inches; (station wagon) 225.6 inches. Tires: (passenger car) HR78-15; (station wagon) JR78-15.

COMET OPTIONS: Air conditioner ($382.70). Heavy-duty battery ($13.60). Manual front disc brakes ($33.90). Rear window defogger ($30). Tinted glass ($37.50). Solid state ignition ($37.80). Left-hand remote-control dual racing mirrors ($25.10). Bodyside moldings ($32.50). Two-tone paint ($30). Glamour paint ($36.50). Power steering ($106.20). Push-button AM radio ($61.40). AM radio with special speakers ($115.50). AM/FM multiplex with dual front door and rear seat speakers ($221.60). AM/FM monaural ($129.10). Embassy roof ($83.20). Bucket seats ($126.40). Floor shifter ($13.80). All-vinyl trim ($13.80). Deluxe interior ($91.30). Deluxe wheel covers ($25.10). Forged aluminum wheels with regular equipment ($153.80); with GT option ($123.80). Appearance protection group including floor mats with carpet inserts; door edge guards; license plate frames and spare tire lock on two-doors ($36.50); on four-doors ($39.10). Bumper protection group including front and rear rubber strips and rear bumper guards on cars without Custom group ($31.32); with Custom group ($23.50). Convenience group including glovebox, trunk, instrument panel courtesy and dual dome lights; day/night mirror; color-keyed seat/shoulder belts; Deluxe and left-hand remote-control racing mirrors, on cars with Deluxe trim or bucket seats ($31.30), with dual racing mirrors ($39.10); with dual racing mirrors and bucket seats or GT option ($23.50). Custom option including: DR78-14 steel-belted whitewall radial tires; Deluxe wheel covers with color-keyed inserts; left-hand remote-control mirror; dual body paint stripe; wheel lip and rocker panel moldings, tan interior; 25-ounce carpeting; higher level NVH package and Odense-grain vinyl roof, on sedans ($408.30); on Villager station wagon ($123.70). GT option including high-back bucket seats; Deluxe sound insulation; leather-wrapped steering wheel; cut-pile carpeting; color-keyed hood scoop; dual racing mirrors; black hubcaps with bright trim rings; black-out hood and black-finished front and lower back panels, on two-doors ($243.70). A three-speed manual transmission was standard. SelectShift automatic transmission was optional. A 250 cid/91-hp six (one-barrel) and 302 cid/140-hp V-8 were available at extra cost.

MONTEGO OPTIONS: Air conditioner ($397.91). Automatic temperature control air conditioner ($507.55). Anti-theft alarm system ($79). Traction-Lok differential axle ($46.70). Deluxe seat belts ($15.14). Load floor carpeting ($25.24). Electric clock ($17.67). Electric rear window defroster in passenger cars ($46.70); in station wagons ($61.84). Heavy-duty electrical system ($27.76). Tinted glass ($41.66). Solid-state ignition ($38.20). Luggage carrier with air deflector for station wagons ($76.99). Dual racing mirrors, left-hand mirror remote-control ($38.20). Illuminated visor vanity mirror ($35.60). Bodyside moldings ($32.82). Front disc brakes for station wagon ($68.14). Power door locks, in two-doors ($44.17); in four-doors ($66.89). Six-Way bench seat ($102.22). Power steering ($112.33). Power windows in two-doors ($85.60); in four-doors ($112.33). AM/FM multiplex with stereo tape ($363.20). AM/FM multiplex with dual front door and rear seat speakers ($213.29). Dual rear speakers with AM radio ($30.29). Vinyl roof ($97.18). Embassy roof ($115.80). Rear facing center seat ($75.81). Automatic speed control ($98.70). Tilt steering wheel ($44.80). Standard wheel covers ($25.24). Deluxe wheel covers on Brougham Villager station wagon ($7.00). Luxury wheel covers ($42.91); same on Brougham Villager station wagon ($17.67). Deluxe wheel covers ($32.90). Styled steel wheels ($117.10); on Brougham Villager station wagon ($92.10). Opera windows on two-doors with vinyl roof ($80.30); interval-selector windshield wipers ($25.24). Appearance protection group including: floor mats with carpet inserts; door edge guards; license plate frames and spare tire lock ($38.20). Brougham Custom trim option including Arden velour seating surfaces; door panel inserts; comfort lounge seats; luxury steering wheel; Cherrywood cluster cover; instrument panel applique with teakwood inlays; super-soft vinyl seat facings and door panels; trunk side lining boards. Deluxe color-keyed wheel covers. Door-pull assist straps; 25-ounce carpet; visor vanity mirror; and Lavant-grain or Odense-grain Embassy vinyl roof ($315.80). Bumper protection group including front and rear rubber strips and rear bumper guards, on passenger car ($35 60); on station wagon ($23.70). Convenience group including remote-control left and visor vanity mirrors; automatic seatback release with two-doors and spare tire extractor on station wagon, two-doors ($51.40); four-doors ($29); station wagon ($31.60). Cross country ride package ($16.41). Sports appearance group including fuel, ammeter, oil pressure and temperature gauges; trip odometer; clock; tachometer; sporty hood; dual racing mirrors; black hubcaps with bright trim rings; lower body tape stripe; G70-14 blackwall tires with raised white letters; lower panel black-out paint; leather-wrapped steering wheel; bright trim pedal pads and H70-14 blackwall tires with raised letters and 460 cid engine in two-doors ($310.29). Trailer-towing package, class II ($32.82); class III ($117.18); station wagon

($80.01). Visibility light group ($29). A three-speed manual transmission was standard. SelectShift automatic transmission was optional. A 351 cid/162-hp V-8 (two-barrel); 351 cid/246-hp Cobra Jet V-8; 400 cid/168-hp V-8 (two-barrel) and 460 cid/244-hp V-8 (four-barrel) were available. The last engine was not offered in station wagons. The 246-hp engine was not available in the MX Brougham series. A high-performance axle and Traction-Lok differential were optional.

COUGAR OPTIONS: Air conditioner ($397.54). Automatic temperature control with air conditioner ($475). Anti-theft alarm system ($79). Traction-Lok differential axle ($46.70). Deluxe seat belts ($15.14). Electric rear window defroster ($61.81). Heavy-duty electrical system ($27.70). Tinted glass ($36.61). Solid-state ignition ($38.20). Left-hand remote-control dual racing mirrors ($38.20). Illuminated visor; vanity mirrors ($35.60). Bodyside moldings ($32.82). Power door locks ($44.80). Six-Way left-hand power seat ($90.80). Electric sun roof ($471.10). Power windows, on two-doors ($85.60); on four-doors ($112.33). AM radio with special speakers ($97.40). AM/FM multiplex with stereo tape ($363.20). AM/FM multiplex with dual front door and rear seat speakers ($213.29). Dual rear speakers with AM radio ($30.30). Vinyl roof ($33.20). Tilt steering wheel ($44.17). Leather-wrapped steering wheel ($6.07). Leather upholstery trim with bucket or twin comfort seats ($167.10). Velour upholstery with twin comfort seats ($77.70). Sporty wheel covers ($61.90). Styled steel wheels ($79). Appearance protection group including floor mats with carpet inserts; door edge guards; license plate frames and spare tire lock ($32.90). Bumper protection group including front and rear rubber strips and rear bumper guards ($35.60). Convenience group including visor vanity mirror; left-hand remote-control mirror and automatic seat-back release, on two-doors, includes Deluxe CC seat belts ($50). Trailer towing package, class II ($32.90); class III ($177.10). Visibility light group ($29). SelectShift automatic was standard. A 351 cid/264-hp Cobra Jet V-8; 400 cid/170-hp V-8 (two-barrel) and 460 cid/220-hp V-8 were optional. A high performance axle and Traction-Lok differential were available at extra cost.

MERCURY OPTIONS: Air conditioner ($430.58). Anti-theft alarm system for station wagons without appearance protection group ($79); with appearance protection group ($73.70); Executive station wagons without appearance protection group ($84.30); with appearance protection group ($78.95). Heavy-duty battery in Monterey and station wagons ($12.62). Deluxe seat and shoulder belts ($15.14). Electric clock in Monterey ($17.67). Digital clock in Monterey ($39.50). Electric rear window defroster ($61.84). Rear fender skirts except Monterey station wagons and Marquis passenger cars ($35.34). Floor mats in Monterey Custom ($23.70). Tinted glass ($50.49). Cornering lights ($35.24). Automatic load adjuster on station wagons ($76.99). Luggage carrier with air deflector on station wagons ($92.13). Visor vanity illuminated mirror on Monterey and Marquis ($35.60). Bodyside molding ($32.82); on Monterey ($14.47). Rocker panel on Monterey Custom ($25). Sure-Track power brakes ($189.30 with 460 cid engine). Six-Way bench seat ($102.22); same on Marquis ($87.08). Six-Way left and right power seat on Marquis ($174.15). Electric power sun roof on Executive station wagons ($495.97). Electric windows ($140.79). Power tailgate window on MX station wagons ($34.08). Power vent windows (four-doors $64.47). Remote-control trunk release on Executive station wagons ($13.89). AM radio with special speakers ($97.40). AM/FM multiplex with stereo tape ($363.20). AM/FM multiplex with dual front-door and rear-seat speakers ($233.47). Dual rear speakers ($32.82). Vinyl roof on Executive station wagons ($116.11); on other station wagons ($138.82). Halo roof on Marquis Executive station wagon ($124.95). Dual-facing third seat on station wagons ($122.27). Twin comfort lounge seats ($75.72). Vinyl bench seat on Monterey ($27.76). Passenger side reclining seat ($42.91). Automatic speed control ($66.89). Tilt steering wheel ($44.17). Storage compartment with locks on station wagon ($32.90). Recreation table on station wagon ($42.11). Trailer brake control ($38.20). Trailer hitch equalizer platform ($88.20). Deluxe cargo area trim, including lockable storage compartment and padded quarter trim on station wagon ($65). Luggage compartment trim on Executive station wagons including carpeting, spare tire cover and side lining board ($40.80). Luxury wheel covers ($32.82). Interval selector wipers ($25.24). Rear tailgate window washer on station wagon ($37.86). Appearance protection group including: floor mats with carpet inserts; door edge guards; license plate frames; spare tire lock; rear mats with carpet inserts and hood lock, on station wagon ($46.10), on Executive station wagons ($47.40). Bumper protection group including front and rear rubber strips and rear bumper guards, on station wagon ($23.68); on Executive station wagons ($35.53). Cross country ride package ($22.71). Decor group including Deluxe steering wheel and wheel covers, wheel lip and rocker panel moldings on Monterey ($63.16). Grand Marquis luxury trim including digital clock; carpeted trunk with side lining boards and flap; hood and deck lid stripes; perforated vinyl headlining with Corinthian grain vinyl covered visors; assist handles; unique head rest and seat trim; dash panel and cluster applique; door and quarter trim panels; dome map/reading lamp; luxury steering wheel; 25-ounce carpeting on Marquis without light group ($325); Marquis with light group ($311.90); station wagon without light group ($390.80); station wagon with light group ($377.70). Lock convenience group

including power door locks; trunk lid release; left-hand remote control mirror; automatic seatback release on two-doors and power tailgate on station wagons, on two-doors with power windows ($82.89); four-doors with power windows ($80.26); station wagon without power windows ($88.16); station wagon with power windows ($75.54); two-doors without power windows ($96.05); four-doors without power windows ($93.42). Marquis Colony Park luxury trim including instrument panel lights; door-pull straps; Brougham wheel covers; Brougham split bench seat and door trim panels; 25-ounce carpeting; visor vanity mirror; Brougham level sound package; front door courtesy lights; rear door armrest; cigar lighters and Brougham trim ($184.21). Trailer towing package, class I ($35.84); class II ($32.82); class III ($88.34). Visibility light group on Monterey ($56.60); on Mercury ($47.40); on Marquis ($39.50). SelectShift automatic transmission was standard. A 460 cid/195-hp V-8 was optional. A high-performance axle and Traction-Lok differential were available at extra cost.

HISTORY: Most 1974 Comets, 82.2 percent, came with a radio, 36.2 percent had a vinyl roof and 24.1 percent had bucket seats. The vast majority of 1974 Montegos, 90.1 percent, had a radio and 65.7 percent came with a vinyl roof. Most Cougar XR-7s, 90.9 percent, were equipped with radio, 38.7 percent had bucket seats, 32.6 percent had a tilting steering wheel and 20.6 percent came with speed control. Seventy-eight percent of all full-size 1974 Mercurys came with a vinyl roof.

1975 MERCURY

1975 Mercury Monarch. (OCW)

1975 Mercury Comet four-door sedan, 6-cyl. (OCW)

COMET SERIES — The styling department must have been in hibernation. The new Comet looked virtually the same as the previous year's model. Standard features included locking steering column, Deluxe sound insulation package, deluxe steering wheel, color-keyed instrument panel with lighted dash, dual hydraulic brake system with warning light and cut-pile carpeting. Buyers had their choice of four colors of cloth and vinyl interior.

MERCURY I.D. NUMBERS: The Vehicle Identification Number was located on left-hand top of dash, viewable through windshield. VIN has 11 symbols. First symbol: 5 = 1975. Second symbol indicates assembly plant: A = Atlanta, Ga. (Cougar); H = Lorain, Ohio (Montego); K = Kansas City, Mo. (Comet) and Z = St. Louis, Mo. (Mercury). Third and fourth symbols are Body/Style Number in second column of charts below. Fifth symbol identifies engine: Previous Engine Codes A, C, F, H, L, Q, S, T available, plus new Y = 139 cid (2.3-liter) four and Z = 169 cid (2.8-liter) four. Final six symbols are sequential production code. Certification Label on rear edge of driver's door indicates manufacturer, build dates (month and year), VIN, body code, color, trim, transmission and axle data.

1975 Mercury Comet two-door sedan (with Custom appearance option), 6-cyl. (OCW)

1975 Mercury Bobcat Runabout two-door hatchback, 4-cyl. (PH)

1975 Mercury Bobcat Villager station wagon, 4-cyl. (PH)

COMET

Model No.	Body/ Style No.	Body Type & Seating	Factory Price	Shipping Weight	Prod. Total
N/A	30	4-dr Sed-4P	3270	3193	31,080
N/A	31	2-dr Sed-4P	3236	3070	22,768

BOBCAT SERIES — The new Bobcat was based on Ford's Pinto. It had an attractive, chrome-framed grille with vertical bars and the word Mercury spelled out above it. Both headlights were recessed into bright moldings. The long, rectangular vertical taillights were placed on the rear deck panel.

BOBCAT

Model No.	Body/ Style No.	Body Type & Seating	Factory Price	Shipping Weight	Prod. Total
N/A	20	2-dr Hatch-4P	3189	N/A	20,651
N/A	21	2-dr Sta Wag-4P	3481	N/A	13,583

NOTE: Model 20, the two-door hatchback coupe, was called a Runabout. Model 21, the two-door station wagon, was called the Villager.

MONARCH SERIES — Mercury called the new Monarch a "precision-size luxury car." It had a chrome-framed grille with vertical bars and Mercury spelled out above it. The two headlights were enclosed in square molding 'boxes' and the signal lights wrapped around the front fenders. Full-length trim (that continued around the rear of the car), wheel lip and window moldings and chrome rocker panels were on the sides. The wraparound rectangular taillights were located on the rear deck panel. The word Mercury was printed in a chrome framed

section between the taillights. Standard equipment included: individually reclining bucket seats, front disc brakes, foot-operated parking brake, solid-state ignition, locking glovebox and inside hood release.

MONARCH

Model No.	Body/ Style No.	Body Type & Seating	Factory Price	Shipping Weight	Prod. Total
N/A	34	4-dr Sed-5P	3822	3284	34,307
N/A	35	2-dr Sed-5P	3764	3234	29,151

MONARCH GHIA SERIES — Wide, full-length upper tire level moldings and upper body pin stripes made it easy to distinguish the Ghia from the basic Monarch. It came with a Deluxe sound insulation package; left-hand remote-control outside mirror; Odense-grain vinyl roof; unique wire spoke wheel covers; carpeted luggage compartment; digital clock and luxury steering wheel.

MONARCH GHIA

Model No.	Body/ Style No.	Body Type & Seating	Factory Price	Shipping Weight	Prod. Total
N/A	37	4-dr Sed-5P	4349	3352	22,723
N/A	38	2-dr Sed-5P	4291	3302	17,755

MONTEGO SERIES — Twin slots in the center of the lower front bumper were the main changes to Montego styling for 1975. Standard features included: power brakes, power steering, solid state ignition, locking steering column, cut-pile carpeting, concealed windshield wipers and front bumper guards. Buyers could choose from a cloth and vinyl or all-vinyl interior in black, tan or blue.

MONTEGO

Model No.	Body/ Style No.	Body Type & Seating	Factory Price	Shipping Weight	Prod. Total
N/A	02	4-dr Sed-6P	4128	4066	4,142
N/A	03	2-dr HT Cpe-6P	4092	4003	4,051

MONTEGO MX SERIES — Upper body pin stripes and rocker panel moldings were distinguishing features on the MX. It also had extra sound insulation and a slightly fancier interior.

MONTEGO MX

Model No.	Body/ Style No.	Body Type & Seating	Factory Price	Shipping Weight	Prod. Total
N/A	04	4-dr Sed-6P	4328	4111	16,033
N/A	07	2-dr HT Cpe-6P	4304	4030	13,666
N/A	08	4-dr Sta Wag-6P	4674	4464	4,508

MONTEGO MX BROUGHAM SERIES — The Brougham had upper body moldings; door-pull assist straps; super-sound insulation package; vinyl roof; woodgrain applique on the steering wheel and wiper mounted windshield washer jets. The Villager station wagon had woodgrain vinyl paneling on its sides and tailgate; power tailgate window; Deluxe steering wheel and flight bench seat with folding center armrest.

1975 Mercury Monarch Ghia four-door sedan, V-8. (OCW)

1975 Mercury Montego MX two-door hardtop, V-8. (OCW)

1975 Mercury Cougar XR-7 two-door hardtop, V-8. (OCW)

MONTEGO MX BROUGHAM

Model No.	Body/ Style No.	Body Type & Seating	Factory Price	Shipping Weight	Prod. Total
N/A	10	4-dr Sed-6P	4498	4130	8,235
N/A	11	2-dr HT Cpe-6P	4453	4054	8,791
N/A	18	4-dr Vill Sta Wag-6P	4909	4522	5,754

COUGAR XR-7 SERIES — Two rectangular openings between the front bumper guards on the lower bumper was the extent of styling changes made to Cougars in 1975. They came with power steering; bucket seats with console (or Twin Comfort lounge seats); luxury steering wheel; deep cut-pile carpeting; passenger assist handle; inside hood release; locking steering column and power front disc brakes.

COUGAR XR-7

Model No.	Body/ Style No.	Body Type & Seating	Factory Price	Shipping Weight	Prod. Total
N/A	93	2-dr HT Cpe-5P	5218	4108	62,987

MARQUIS SERIES — The 1975 Marquis' chrome framed-grille consisted of six rectangular chrome pieces, each containing five vertical bars. A single vertical bar evenly divided the grille in two. The concealed headlight doors looked like music boxes. Both had an emblem in the center. The wraparound signal lights were circled by four thin chrome bands. Side trim consisted of full-length lower body molding and upper body pin stripes. Mercury was spelled out on the center rear deck panel between the wraparound, rectangular taillights. Standard features included: power steering; power front disc brakes; woodgrain applique on instrument panel; left-hand remote-control mirror; power ventilation system; Deluxe wheel covers and cut-pile carpeting.

MARQUIS

Model No.	Body/ Style No.	Body Type & Seating	Factory Price	Shipping Weight	Prod. Total
N/A	63	4-dr Sed-6P	5115	4513	20,058
N/A	66	2-dr HT Cpe-6P	5049	4470	6,807
N/A	74	4-dr Sta Wag-6P	5411	4880	1,904

MARQUIS BROUGHAM SERIES — The Brougham had full-length upper body moldings; vinyl roof; deep cut-pile carpeting; electric clock; power windows; fender skirts; Brougham wheel covers and a visor mounted vanity mirror. The Colony Park station wagon featured simulated Rosewood paneling on the sides and tailgate; flight bench seat with center armrest; door-pull and seatback assist straps; Brougham wheel covers; Deluxe seat and shoulder belts; visor mounted vanity mirror and three-way tailgate.

MARQUIS BROUGHAM

Model No.	Body/ Style No.	Body Type & Seating	Factory Price	Shipping Weight	Prod. Total
N/A	62	4-dr Sed-6P	6037	4799	19,667
N/A	64	2-dr HT Cpe-6P	5972	4747	7,125
N/A	76	4-dr Col Prk Sta Wag-6P	5598	4953	11,652

1975 Mercury Marquis Brougham two-door hardtop, V-8. (OCW)

1975 Mercury Grand Marquis four-door sedan, V-8. (OCW)

GRAND MARQUIS SERIES — A wide upper tire level band of molding across its side set the Grand Marquis apart from the other series. It came with deep, shag cut-pile carpeting; dual map-reading lamps; left-hand remote-control mirror; vinyl roof; carpeted luggage compartment; hood and deck lid paint stripes and passenger assist straps.

GRAND MARQUIS

Model No.	Body/ Style No.	Body Type & Seating	Factory Price	Shipping Weight	Prod. Total
N/A	60	4-dr Sed-6P	6469	4815	12,307
N/A	61	2-dr HT Cpe-6P	6403	4762	4,945

ENGINE [(Bobcat) Four]: Overhead camshaft. Cast-iron block. Displacement: 140 cid. Bore and stroke: 3.78 x 3.13 inches. Compression ratio: 8.4:1. SAE net hp: 83 at 4800 rpm. Carburetor: one-barrel.

ENGINE [(Comet/Monarch) Six]: Overhead valve. Cast-iron block. Displacement: 200 cid. Bore and stroke: 3.68 x 3.13 inches. Compression ratio: 8.3:1. SAE net hp: 75 at 3800 rpm. Carburetor: one-barrel.

ENGINE [(Monarch/Monarch Ghia) Six]: Overhead valve. Cast-iron block. Displacement: 250 cid. Bore and stroke: 3.68 x 3.91 inches. Compression ratio: 8.0:1. SAE net hp: 72 at 2900 rpm. Carburetor: one-barrel.

ENGINE [(Montego/MX/MX Brougham/Cougar XR-7) V-8]: Overhead valve. Cast-iron block. Displacement: 351 cid. Bore and stroke: 4.00 x 3.50 inches. Compression ratio: 8.0:1. SAE net hp: 148 at 3800 rpm. Carburetor: two-barrel.

ENGINE [(Marquis/Marquis Brougham Station Wagon) V-8]: Overhead valve. Cast-iron block. Displacement: 460 cid. Bore and stroke: 4.00 x 4.00 inches. Compression ratio: 8.0:1. SAE net hp: 158 at 3800 rpm. Carburetor: two-barrel.

ENGINE [(Marquis Brougham/Grand Marquis) V-8]: Overhead valve. Cast-iron block. Displacement: 460 cid. Bore and stroke: 4.36 x 3.85. Compression ratio: 8.0:1. SAE net hp: 218 at 4000 rpm. Carburetor: four-barrel.

BOBCAT CHASSIS FEATURES: Wheelbase: (Runabout) 94.5 inches; (Villager) 94.8 inches. Overall length: (Runabout) 169 inches; (Villager) 179 inches. Tires: B78-13.

COMET CHASSIS FEATURES: Wheelbase: (four-doors) 109 inches; (two-doors) 103 inches. Overall length: (four-doors) 196.9 inches; (two-doors) 190 inches. Tires: (four-doors) CR78-14; (two-doors) BR78-14.

MONTEGO CHASSIS FEATURES: Wheelbase (two-doors) 114 inches; (four-doors and station wagon) 118 inches. Overall length: (two-doors) 215.5 inches; (four-doors) 219.5 inches; (station wagon) 224.4 inches. Tires: HR78-14.

MONARCH CHASSIS FEATURES: Wheelbase: 109.9 inches. Overall length: 200 inches. Tires: DR78-14.

COUGAR CHASSIS FEATURES: Wheelbase: 114 inches. Overall length: 215.5 inches. Tires: HR78-14.

MERCURY CHASSIS FEATURES: Wheelbase: (passenger car) 124 inches; (station wagon) 121 inches. Overall length: (passenger car) 229 inches; (station wagon) 227 inches. Tires: (passenger car) JR78-15; (Marquis) HR78-15.

COMET OPTIONS: Air conditioner ($382.70). Heavy-duty battery ($13.60). Manual front disc brakes ($33.90). Rear window defogger ($30). Tinted glass ($37.50). Solid-state ignition ($37.80). Left-hand remote-control dual racing mirrors ($25.10). Bodyside moldings ($32.50). Two-tone paint ($30). Glamour paint ($36.50). Power steering ($106.20). Push-button AM radio ($61.40). AM radio with special speakers ($115.50). AM/FM multiplex with dual front door and rear seat speakers ($221.60). AM/FM monaural ($129.10). Embassy roof ($83.20).

Bucket seats ($126.40). Floor shifter ($13.80). All-vinyl trim ($13.80). Deluxe interior ($91.30). Deluxe wheel covers ($25.10). Forged aluminum wheels ($153.80); same with GT option ($123.80). Appearance protection group including floor mats with carpet inserts; door edge guards; license plate frames and spare tire lock, in two-doors ($36.50); in four-doors ($39.10). Bumper protection group including front and rear rubber strips and rear bumper guards, on models without Custom group ($31.32); on models with Custom group ($23.50). Convenience group including glovebox, trunk, instrument panel courtesy and dual dome lights; day/night mirror; color-keyed seat/shoulder belts; Deluxe and left-hand remote-control racing mirror, on cars with Deluxe bucket seats ($31.30); on cars with dual racing mirrors ($39.10); on cars with dual racing mirrors and bucket seat or GT option ($23.50). Custom option including: DR78-14 steel-belted whitewall radial tires; Deluxe wheel covers with color-keyed inserts; left-hand remote-control mirror; dual body paint stripe; wheel lip and rocker panel moldings; tan interior; 25-ounce carpeting; higher level NVH package and Odense-grain vinyl roof, on sedan ($408.30); on Villager station wagon ($123.70). GT option included: high-back bucket seats; Deluxe sound insulation; leather-wrapped steering wheel; cut-pile carpeting; color-keyed hood scoop; dual racing mirrors; black hubcaps with bright trim rings; black-out hood, front and lower back panel, on two-doors ($243.70). A three-speed manual transmission was standard. SelectShift automatic transmission was optional. A 250 cid/91-hp six and 302 cid/140-hp V-8 (two-barrel) were available at extra cost.

BOBCAT OPTIONS: Air conditioning ($416). Vinyl top on Runabout ($83). Deluxe wheel covers ($25.10). Luggage rack on Villager station wagon ($71). Sun roof ($210). AM radio ($61.40). AM/FM radio ($216). Aluminum wheels ($136). Power steering ($106). Sports accent group ($269). A three-speed manual transmission was standard. SelectShift automatic transmission was optional. A 170 cid/97-hp six was available.

MONARCH OPTIONS: Air conditioning ($416). Vinyl roof ($92). AM radio ($61.40). AM/FM stereo radio ($225). AM/FM stereo radio with tape system ($347). Power seats ($104). Power sun roof ($517). Power windows ($85.60). Power steering ($112.33). Power brakes ($68). Rear window defroster ($46.70). Upholstery with leather seating surfaces. Grand Ghia package. Illuminated visor vanity mirror. Decor package including vinyl seat trim with map pocket and assist rails. A three-speed manual transmission was standard. SelectShift automatic was optional. A 250 cid/72-hp six (one-barrel); 302 cid/129-hp V-8 (two-barrel) and 351 cid/154-hp V-8 (two-barrel) were available.

MONTEGO OPTIONS: Air conditioner ($397.91). Automatic temperature control air conditioning ($507.55). Anti-theft alarm system ($79). Traction-Lok differential axle ($46.70). Deluxe seat belts ($15.14). Load floor carpet ($25.24). Electric clock ($17.67). Electric rear window defroster in passenger car ($46.70); in station wagon ($61.84). Heavy-duty electrical system ($27.76). Tinted glass ($41.66). Solid state ignition ($38.20). Luggage carrier with air deflector ($76.99). Dual racing mirrors with remote control left-hand unit ($38.20). Illuminated visor vanity mirror ($35.60). Bodyside moldings ($32.82). Front disc brakes on station wagon ($68.14). Power door locks, in two-doors ($44.17); four-doors ($66.89). Six-Way bench seat ($124). Power steering ($112.33). Power windows, in two-doors ($85.60); four-doors ($112.33). AM/FM multiplex with stereo tape ($383.20). AM/FM multiplex with dual front door and rear seat speakers ($238.29). Dual rear speakers with AM radio ($30.29). Vinyl roof ($97.18). Embassy roof ($115.80). Rear facing center seat ($86). Automatic speed control ($98.70). Tilt steering wheel ($44.80). Standard wheel covers ($25.24). Deluxe wheel covers for Brougham Villager station wagon ($7.90). Luxury wheel covers ($42.91); same on Brougham Villager station wagon ($17.67). Deluxe wheel covers ($32.90). Styled steel wheels ($117.10); same on Brougham Villager station wagon ($92.10). Opera windows in two-doors with vinyl roof ($80.30). Interval-selector windshield wipers ($25.24). Appearance protection group including floor mats with carpet inserts; door edge guards; license frames and spare tire lock ($38.20). Brougham Custom trim option including: Arden velour seating surfaces; door panel inserts; comfort lounge seats; luxury steering wheel; Cherrywood cluster cover; instrument panel applique with teakwood inlays; super-soft vinyl seat facings and door panels; trunk side lining boards; Deluxe color-keyed wheel covers; door-pull assist straps; 25-ounce carpet; visor vanity mirror and Lavant-grain or Odense-grain Embassy vinyl roof ($384.80). Bumper protection group including front and rear rubber strips and rear bumper guards, on passenger car ($35.60); on station wagon ($23.70). Convenience group including remote-control left-hand and visor vanity mirrors; automatic seatback release with two-doors and spare tire extractor with station wagon, on two-doors ($51.40); on four-doors ($29); on station wagon ($31.60). Cross country ride package ($16.41). Sports appearance group including: fuel, ammeter, oil pressure and temperature gauges; trip odometer; clock; tachometer; sports hood; dual racing mirrors; black hubcaps with bright trim rings; lower body tape stripe; G70-14 blackwall tires with raised white letters (or H70-14 blackwall tires with raised letters and 460 cid engine); lower panel black-out paint; leather-wrapped steering wheel; bright trim pedal pads, for two-doors ($260). Trailer-towing package, class II ($32.82); class III ($117.18); station wagon ($80.01).

Visibility light group ($29). SelectShift automatic was standard. A 400 cid/158-hp V-8 (two-barrel) and 460 cid/216-hp V-8 were optional. A high-performance axle and Traction-Lok differential were available at extra cost.

COUGAR OPTIONS: Air conditioner ($397.54). Automatic temperature control air conditioner ($475). Anti-theft alarm system ($79). Traction-Lok differential axle ($46.70). Deluxe seat belts ($15.14). Electric rear window defroster ($61.81). Heavy-duty electrical system ($27.70). Tinted glass ($38.61). Solid-state ignition ($38.20). Left-hand remote-control dual racing mirrors ($38.20). Illuminated visor vanity mirror ($35.60). Bodyside moldings ($32.82). Power door locks ($44.80). Six-Way left-hand power seat ($124). Electric sun roof ($525). Power windows, on two-doors ($85.60); four-doors ($112.33). AM radio with special speakers ($97.40). AM/FM multiplex with stereo tape ($393.20). AM/FM multiplex with dual front door and rear seat speakers ($213.29). Dual rear speakers with AM radio ($30.30). Vinyl roof ($33.20). Tilt steering wheel ($44.17). Leather-wrapped steering wheel ($6.07). Leather upholstery trim with bucket or twin comfort seats ($167.10). Velour upholstery with twin comfort seats ($77.70). Sporty wheel covers ($61.90). Styled steel wheels ($79). Appearance protection group including floor mats with carpet inserts; door edge guards; license plate frames and spare tire lock ($32.90). Bumper protection group including front and rear rubber strips and rear bumper guards ($35.60). Convenience group including visor vanity mirror; left-hand remote-control mirror; automatic seatback release on two-doors and Deluxe color-coordinated seat belts ($50). Trailer-towing package, class II ($32.90); class III ($117.10). Visibility light group ($29). SelectShift automatic was standard. A 400 cid/158-hp V-8 (two-barrel) and 460 cid/216-hp V-8 (four-barrel) were optional. A high-performance axle and Traction-Lok differential could be ordered.

MERCURY OPTIONS: Air conditioner ($430.58). Anti-theft alarm system, for station wagon, without appearance protection group ($84.30); with appearance protection group ($78.95). Heavy-duty battery, station wagon ($12.62). Deluxe seat and shoulder belts ($15.14). Digital clock ($39.50). Electric rear window defroster ($61.84). Tinted glass ($50.49). Cornering lights ($35.24). Automatic load adjuster, station wagon ($76.99). Luggage carrier with air deflector ($96). Visor vanity illuminated mirror ($35.60). Bodyside molding ($32.82). Sure-Track power brakes with 460 cid V-8 ($189.30). Six-Way bench seat ($124). Six-Way left- and right-hand power seat ($174.16). Electric power sun roof ($495.97). Electric windows ($140.79). Remote control trunk release ($13.89). AM radio with special speakers ($97.40). AM/FM multiplex with stereo tape ($363.20). AM/FM multiplex with dual front door and rear seat speakers ($233.47). Dual rear speakers ($32.82). Vinyl roof ($637). Dual facing third seat, station wagon ($122.27). Twin comfort lounge seats ($75.72). Passenger side reclining seat ($42.91). Automatic speed control ($66.89). Tilt steering wheel ($44.17). Storage compartment with locks, station wagon ($32.90). Recreation table, station wagon ($42.11). Trailer brake control ($38.20). Trailer hitch equalizer platform ($83.20). Deluxe cargo area trim, including lockable storage and padded quarter trim, station wagon ($65). Luggage compartment trim, for station wagon, including: carpeting; spare tire cover and side lining board ($40.80). Luxury wheel covers ($32.82). Interval selector wipers ($25.24). Rear tailgate window washer, station wagon ($37.86). Appearance protection group including: floor mats with carpet inserts; door edge guards; license plate frames; spare tire lock; rear mats with carpet inserts and hood lock, on station wagon ($47.40). Bumper protection group including front and rear rubber bumper strips and rear bumper guards, on station wagon ($23.68); on Executive station wagon ($35.53). Cross country ride package ($22.71). Grand Marquis luxury trim including digital clock; carpeted trunk with side lining boards and flap, hood and deck lid stripes; perforated vinyl headlining with Corinthian-grain vinyl covered visors; assist handles; unique headrest and seat trim; dash panel and cluster applique; door and quarter trim panels; dome map/reading lamp; luxury steering wheel and 25-ounce carpeting, on Marquis without light group ($325); Marquis with light group ($311.90); station wagon without light group ($390.80); station wagon with light group ($377.70). Marquis/Colony Park luxury trim, including instrument panel lights; door-pull straps; Brougham wheel covers; Brougham split bench seat and door trim panels; 25-ounce carpeting; visor vanity mirror; Brougham level sound package; front door courtesy lights; rear door armrest cigar lighters and Brougham trim ($184.21). Trailer-towing package, class I ($36 84); class II ($32.82) and class III ($88.34). Visibility light group ($39.50). SelectShift automatic transmission was standard. A 460 cid/218-hp V-8 (four-barrel) was optional.

HISTORY: Most 1975 Comets, 82.5 percent, were equipped with a radio, 13.2 percent had bucket seats and 39.2 percent came with a vinyl-covered roof. Most 1975 Bobcats, 75 percent, came with radios and 10.5 percent had vinyl roofs. Only 6.3 percent of 1975 Monarchs came with a stereo tape system, 50.6 percent had a vinyl roof and 88.4 percent had a radio. Most 1975 Montegos, 89.1 percent, were equipped with a radio, 59.3 percent had vinyl roofs, 3.7 percent had a stereo tape system and 12.4 percent had a tilting steering wheel. Approximately one in three 1975 full-size Mercurys came with speed control.

1976 Mercury Grand Monarch Ghia. (OCW)

1976 Mercury Marquis Brougham. (OCW)

1976 Mercury Bobcat Runabout. (OCW)

1976-1/2 Mercury Bobcat 'S' Runabout. (PH)

1976 Mercury Bobcat Villager station wagon. (AA)

While the previous model year had brought the longest list of running changes in Lincoln-Mercury history, 1975 was largely a carryover year. The subcompact Bobcat and luxurious Grand Monarch Ghia had been introduced in mid-1975, along with the revised (imported) Capri II. Mercury would not offer a domestic-built cousin to Ford's Mustang until 1979. Otherwise, Mercury offered a model equivalent to each Ford product, typically differing more in body details than basic structure. A number of previously standard items were made optional for 1976 on full-size and luxury models, to keep base prices down. As in the industry generally, fuel economy was a major factor in planning the 1976 lineup. Mercury still offered some 'real' pillarless two-door hardtops, but not for long.

BOBCAT (MPG) — FOUR/V-6 — Bobcat carried on in its first full season with two body styles: the "three-door" (actually two-door with hatch) Runabout, and a Villager station wagon. Bobcat rode a 94.5-inch wheelbase and had a base 140-cid (2.3-liter) four-cylinder engine with four-speed manual gearbox. A 2.8-liter V-6 was optional. As with most Mercury models, Bobcat was essentially a Ford Pinto with a different hood and grille, and a fancier interior. Bobcat's distinctive grille, made up of thin vertical bars (slightly wider center bar) with bright surround molding, along with a domed hood, identified it as a member of the Lincoln-Mercury family. Large 'Mercury' block letters stood above the grille. Small square running/park/signal lamps with crossbar-patterned bright overlay sat between the single round head-lamps and the grille, rather low, just above the bumper. Bodies held front and rear side marker lights, ventless door windows, and fixed quarter windows. Wide, bright wheel lip moldings and bright rocker panel moldings were standard. Also standard: bright windshield, drip rail, side window frame, lower back panel surround, door belt and rear window moldings. At the rear, each wide horizontal three-pod taillamp assembly held a red run/brake/signal light, white backup light and red reflector lens, with bright surround molding. Bright wheel covers were standard (styled steel wheels in California). Inside were all-vinyl high-back front bucket seats with integral head restraints. Villager had simulated rosewood-grain appliqués with bright surround molding on bodyside and liftgate, a front-hinged center side window, and vertical taillamp assembly with integral backup lights and bright surround molding. Bright 'Bobcat' script and 'Villager' block letters went on the liftgate. The full-upswinging liftgate held fixed glass. New standard equipment included high-back bucket seats, revised door trim panels, and regular seatbelts. Deluxe low-back bucket seats became optional. Runabouts had a new optional simulated woodgrain appliqué for side and lower back panels. Woodgrain side panels were standard on the Villager station wagon. Alpine plaid cloth interior trim in four colors replaced polyknit cloth as an interior option. Other new options included an AM radio with stereo tape player, interval-select wipers, sports vinyl roof with optional sports tape stripes, and engine block heater. Bobcat had rack-and-pinion steering, solid-state ignition, electro-coat primer, and unitized body construction. V-6 models came with power brakes.

1976 Mercury Comet "Sports Accent" coupe. (M)

1976 Mercury Monarch Ghia coupe. (M)

1976-1/2 Mercury Monarch 'S' coupe. (PH)

COMET — SIX/V-8 — Introduced in 1971, the compact Comet had only minor changes at the front end and grille this year. New blackout paint went on the grille's vertical bars, and around headlamp doors and parking lamps. The wide, bright protruding horizontal-rib center grille was accompanied by bright framed argent side grille panels with integral run/park/signal lamps. Exposed single headlamps now showed blackout housings. Two-doors had front-hinged rear quarter windows; four-doors, roll-down back windows. Both had ventless door windows, bright rocker panels and upper bodyside molding, and a bright gas cap with L-M crest and 'Comet' block letters. Identification was also provided by bright 'Comet' and 'Mercury' script. Two-pod color-keyed taillamp assemblies held integral backup lights. Inside was a two-pod instrument cluster with recessed instruments and a standard front bench seat. Comet's former GT edition was replaced by a "Sports Accent" Group that included wide lower bodyside moldings, lower body two-tone paint, dual racing mirrors, belt moldings, styled steel wheels with trim rings, and whitewalls. Two-doors could have an optional half-vinyl roof. A Custom option included new bucket seats, door trim and tinted glass. Five new body colors were offered, as well as a revised Custom interior. Alpine plaid was a new cloth seat trim. There was a new double-action foot-operated parking brake, and a new standard two-spoke steering wheel. Base engine was a 200-cid inline six with one-barrel carb (250-cid in California), with three-speed manual shift. A 302-cid V-8 was optional. Comets had unitized body construction and standard bias-ply blackwall tires. Two-doors rode a 103-inch wheelbase; four-doors, 109.9 inches. Comet was a variant of Ford's Maverick.

1976 Mercury Montego MX Brougham sedan. (AA)

1976 Mercury Montego MX coupe. (AA)

MONARCH — SIX/V-8 — Close kin to Ford's Granada, Monarch was described as "precision-size," with 109.9 inch wheelbase. Three models were offered: base, Ghia, and top-rung Grand Monarch Ghia. Little changed this year, except for some engineering improvements that were supposed to improve ride and quiet sound levels inside. Monarch's bright upright grille was made up of thin vertical bars, with a slightly wider center divider bar. Above the grille were 'Mercury' block letters, and a stand-up hood ornament with Monarch 'M' crest and fold-down feature. Single round headlamps sat in color-keyed square frames. Large wraparound park/signal lamps with horizontal ribs were mounted in front fender tips. Bright full-length upper bodyside and decklid moldings were standard. Bright moldings also went on the windshield, full wheel lip, roof drip, and door frame. Full wheel covers displayed a center ornament, composed of three concentric circles on a circular field of red. Two-doors had opera windows. Four-doors included a bright center pillar molding. Three-pod taillamp assemblies included a tri-color lens with white backup lights, and amber-overlay red brake and turn signal light. The textured back panel appliquéd with bright 'Monarch' block lettering had an integral fuel filler door and hidden gas cap, color coordinated with body paint or vinyl roof. 'Mercury' script stood on the decklid. All-vinyl upholstery was standard. Flight bench seats were now standard in Monarch Ghia. Monarch had a standard 200-cid one-barrel six with three-speed manual (fully synchronized) column shift. A 250-cid inline six was optional, along with 302 and 351-cid V-8s. Monarch used unibody construction. Four-leaf semi-elliptic rear springs were nearly five feet long and had stagger-mounted shock absorbers. A new base model had revised standard equipment, including a bench seat, different steering wheel, and revised door trim. Monarch Ghia added a bright driver's side remote mirror, wide Odense grain bodyside molding and partial wheel lip molding, and distinctive Ghia wheel covers with simulated spoke motif and round red center ornament, highlighted by three bright concentric circles. A Ghia ornament adorned the opera window of two-doors, or rear pillar of four-doors. Also on Ghia: hood and decklid contour paint stripes, and a full-length upper bodyside paint stripe. A four-door luxury version (Grand Monarch Ghia) joined the lineup in late spring. That one added power windows, power steering, four-wheel power disc brakes, unique seat and door trim, and a fully padded Normande grain vinyl roof with frenched backlight. Bright 'Grand Monarch' script went on the lower fender. Also included on Grand Monarch: cast aluminum spoked wheels, a Normande grain vinyl center pillar pad, Ghia emblem on rear pillar, digital clock, whitewall tires, and unique tail lamps. The 250-cid six was standard. Buyers had a choice of saddle and white two-tone leather seating, dark red monotone leather, or dark red monotone cloth. (Leather seating had vinyl door trim.) New options were: console with warning lights (standard on Grand Monarch Ghia), power door locks, speed control, tilt steering, and automatic seatback release as part of the convenience group. Monarch's windshield wiper/washer control had moved to the steering column in mid-1975. Other mid-1975 changes included optional Sure-Track brakes, four-wheel disc brakes, and power seats.

MONTEGO — V-8 — This would be the final outing for Mercury's mid-size, offered in three series: Montego, Montego MX, and Montego MX Brougham. In addition to hardtop coupe and sedan models, two station wagons were available, including the simulated woodgrain-sided MX Villager. Five new body colors raised the total to 16. A landau vinyl roof option was available in six colors for two-doors. Another new option: Twin Comfort Lounge seats (with or without reclining feature) available on MX Brougham and Villager. A 351-cid V-8 engine with SelectShift automatic transmission was standard on all Montegos; 400 and 460-cid V-8 available. Quad round headlamps in bright rectangular frames were flanked by large combination run/park/turn signal lamps that followed the inner surface of the fendertip extensions. A rather narrow, forward-protruding grille carried both horizontal and vertical bars, with horizontal theme dominant. A bright 'Mercury' script went on the upper grille panel and decklid; L-M crest on grille panel and fuel filler door; bright 'Montego' script on lower front fender; and 'Montego' block letters on fuel door. Three-pod taillamp assemblies were used. Bright hubcaps were standard. Inside was a standard low-back front bench seat with adjustable head restraint, upholstered in cloth and vinyl. Standard equipment included power steering and brakes. Front bumper guards held rub strips. Montego MX added bright rocker panel moldings, dual upper body paint stripes, 'Montego MX' script on lower front fender, a lower back panel center surround molding, and bright/black 'Montego MX' name on instrument panel. MX Brougham had deluxe wheel covers with L-M crest in the center, over a brushed metal background with simulated spokes on outer circumference. Also on Broughams: bright upper body peak molding, bright plaque with 'Brougham' script on rear pillar, bright lower rear fender molding, and lower back panel box-textured appliqué with blackout paint and bright surround molding. Montego MX station wagons came with bright 'Montego' script and 'Mercury' block letters on the three-way tailgate, a vertical two-pod taillamp assembly, bright roof rear and quarter-window moldings, and bright tailgate belt molding. The top-line Villager wagon added full-length simulated woodgrain bodyside and tailgate paneling, surrounded by bright molding (partially black paint-filled). Also on Villager: bright front and rear partial wheel lip moldings, 'Montego MX' script on lower front fender, with Villager plaque. A power tailgate window was included. Montego also had a police package with choice of V-8 engines: 351-cid, 400-cid 2Bbl., 460-cid 4Bbl., or Police Interceptor 460 4Bbl. V-8 (with mechanical fuel pump, low-restriction air cleaner and exhaust, and engine oil cooler). Montego's front suspension used single lower arm drag struts and a link-type stabilizer bar. At the rear were helical coil springs in a four-link rubber-cushioned system.

COUGAR XR-7 — V-8 — By the mid-1970s, Mercury's Cougar was a far different animal than the version that first appeared in 1967. Mid-size in dimensions, it had a big-car look and styling that emulated the Lincoln Continental Mark IV. Angled horizontal opera windows had been added for 1974, joining the vestigial small quarter windows. The two-door hardtop personal-luxury coupe came with plenty of standard equipment, including a landau vinyl roof and full instrumentation (including tachometer, clock, trip odometer, fuel gauge, ammeter, oil and temp gauges). Standard powerteam was a 351-cid two-barrel V-8 with SelectShift Cruise-O-Matic. 400-cid two-barrel and 460 four-barrel V-8s were optional. Previously standard features, such as a luxury steering wheel, tinted glass, styled steel wheels with trim rings, and bucket seats with console, were made optional this year. New interior options included reclining Twin Comfort Lounge seats, with or without optional velour cloth trim; as well as a cream and gold two-tone interior for the Twin Comfort seats. Other new options: cast aluminum wheels, rocker panel moldings, engine block heater, and AM/FM stereo radio with search feature. A power-operated moonroof had been introduced as an option for 1975, with a sliding panel of tinted one-way glass that could be covered manually by an opaque shade that matched the headliner color and material. Cougar's narrow grille consisted of very thin vertical ribs with a dominant surround molding. Twin side-by-side slots were in the bumper, just below the grille, between the bumper guards. Matching side grilles held quad round headlamps, with parking/turn signal lamps in the front fender extensions. The bright Cougar stand-up hood ornament had a fold-down feature. 'Mercury' script went on both hood and deck. Side marker lights and reflectors were on the front fenders. Horizontal tail lamps had integral backup lights, with bright vertical bars, bright partially black paint-filled surround molding, and red reflex rear center appliqué. Rear side marker lights and reflectors were integral with tail lamps. Lower bodyside moldings held color-keyed vinyl inserts. Side windows were ventless and frameless; quarter windows fixed. Bright Cougar ornaments were embedded in the opera window glass. Luxury wheel covers had an L-M crest and Cougar XR-7 ornament on the center hub.

1976 Mercury Cougar XR-7 Sports Coupe. (M)

1976 Mercury Grand Marquis Ghia sedan. (AA)

1976 Mercury Marquis Brougham hardtop coupe. (M)

MARQUIS — V-8 — Eight models in three series made up the full-size line: Marquis, Marquis Brougham and Grand Marquis. Two wagons were offered, including a simulated woodgrain sided Colony Park. A 400-cid two-barrel V-8 with three-speed SelectShift was standard on all models. Power front disc/rear drum brakes and power steering were standard. Eight new body colors were added. Otherwise, this was basically a carryover year. Half a dozen separate side-by-side "boxes" made up the Marquis grille, each one holding a set of vertical ribs. Fender tips held large wraparound parking/turn signal/side marker lamps with horizontal lens ribbing. Quad headlamps were hidden behind doors with center emblems. The bright wreath stand-up hood ornament had a fold-down feature. 'Mercury' script stood on the upper grille panel; 'Marquis' script on front fender; a Marquis plaque on rear pillar; and 'Mercury' block letters on rear back panel. Two-doors had fixed quarter windows. Bright rocker panel and lower front/rear fender moldings were standard, along with bright wheel lip moldings. Deluxe wheel covers showed the L-M crest. Wraparound tail lamps had horizontal ribs. A textured appliqué between taillamp assemblies was color-keyed to either the optional vinyl roof or the body color. Inside were low-back front bench seats, rear bench seats trimmed in new cloth and vinyl, and a two-spoke color-keyed steering wheel. Four-doors had a fold-down front seat center armrest (dual on two-doors). Simulated baby burl woodgrain adorned the instrument cluster, with a color-keyed appliqué over the glovebox door. Front bumper guards had black vertical protection strips. Marquis Brougham added such extras as a vinyl roof, rear fender skirts with bright lip molding, electric clock, power windows, bright full-length fender peak molding, Brougham plaque on lower front fender, and remote-control driver's mirror. Distinctive Brougham wheel covers had a partially paint-filled Marquis plaque and slots in the outer circumference. The hinged decklid cover showed an L-M crest. Flight bench seats had adjustable low-profile head restraints and a single center folding armrest. Four-doors had rear door courtesy light switches, and a cigar lighter in the back-door armrest ashtrays. Grand Marquis included tinted glass, dual hood and decklid paint stripes, full-length bodyside moldings with wide color-keyed vinyl insert, and gold Marquis crest on rear pillar and headlamp covers. Lower front fenders held 'Grand Marquis' script. Interiors held Twin Comfort lounge seats with dual center armrests and leather (or leather and velour) seating surfaces. A digital clock and dome lamp with dual-beam map lights were standard. Marquis station wagons had three-pod vertical tail lamps, a bright tailgate belt molding, 'Mercury' block letters across the three-way tailgate, bright L-M crest on the tailgate, and a power back window. Seat upho1stery was all vinyl. Rear bumper guards had black vertical rub strips. Colony Park wagons added simulated rosewood-grain paneling on bodyside and tailgate. They were also identified by 'Colony Park' script on lower rear fender, bright full-length fender peak moldings, and Brougham-style wheel covers. Flight bench seats had adjustable low-profile head restraints. New Marquis options included an AM/FM stereo search radio, landau vinyl roof, rocker panel moldings, engine block heater, and forged aluminum wheels. Base Marquis two-doors could get an automatic seatback release. A Tu-Tone group was available on Marquis Brougham and Grand Marquis two-doors. It gave a choice of two distinctive color combinations: tan and dark brown, or cream and gold. Two-tone interior trims in those packages also were available, with colors compatible to the body. The new optional vinyl half-roof for the two-door was offered in a wide range of colors, including two new ones: gold and medium red. There was a full-size Mercury police package, with 460-cid four-barrel V-8 and dual exhausts, automatic transmission with auxiliary oil cooler, 3.00:1 axle ratio, four-wheel power disc brakes, and a list of heavy-duty equipment. It also included a 140 MPH speedometer. Low-gear lockout for the automatic was a limited-production option on the police packages. The packages also were available with other V-8s: 400 2Bbl. (single exhaust); and 460 4Bbl. PI with mechanical fuel pump and dual exhausts.

I.D. DATA: The 11-symbol Vehicle Identification Number (VIN) is stamped on a metal tab fastened to the instrument panel, visible through the windshield. The first digit is a model year code ('6' 1976). The second letter indicates assembly plant: 'A' Atlanta, GA; 'B' Oakville (Canada); 'E' Mahwah, NJ; 'H' Lorain, Ohio; 'K' Kansas City, MO; 'R' San Jose, CA; 'T' Metuchen, NJ; 'W' Wayne, MI; 'Z' St. Louis MO. Digits three and four are the body serial code, which corresponds to the Model Numbers shown in the tables below (e.g., '20' Bobcat 3-dr. Runabout). The fifth digit is an engine code: 'Y' L4-140 2Bbl.; 'Z' V6-170 2Bbl.; 'T' L6-200 1Bbl.; 'L' L6-250 1Bbl.; 'F' V8-302 2Bbl.; 'H' or 'Q' V8-351 2Bbl.; 'S' V8-400 2Bbl.; 'A' V8-460 4Bbl. Finally, digits 6-11 make up the consecutive unit number of cars built at each assembly plant. The number begins with 500001. A Vehicle Certification Label on the left front door lock face panel or door pillar shows the manufacturer, month and year of manufacture, GVW, GAWR, certification statement, VIN, body code, color code, trim code, axle code, transmission code, and domestic (or foreign) special order code.

BOBCAT MPG RUNABOUT (FOUR/V-6)

Model No.	Body/ Style No.	Body Type & Seating	Factory Price	Shipping Weight	Prod. Total
20	64H	3-dr. Hatch-4P	3338/3838	2535/----	28,905

BOBCAT MPG VILLAGER (FOUR/V-6)

| 22 | 73H | 2-dr. Sta Wag-4P | 3643/4143 | 2668/---- | 18,731 |

1976 Mercury Bobcat MPG hatchback coupe. (M)

Model No.	Body/ Style No.	Body Type & Seating	Factory Price	Shipping Weight	Prod. Total
COMET (SIX/V-8)					
31	62B	2-dr. Fast Sed-4P	3250/3398	----/2952	15,068
30	54B	4-dr. Sed-5P	3317/3465	----/3058	21,006
MONARCH (SIX/V-8)					
35	66H	2-dr. Sedan-4P	3773/3927	3111/3294	47,466
34	54H	4-dr. Sedan-5P	3864/4018	3164/3347	56,351
MONARCH GHIA (SIX/V-8)					
38	66K	2-dr. Sedan-4P	4331/4419	3200/3383	14,950
37	54K	4-dr. Sedan-5P	4422/4510	3250/3433	27,056
MONARCH GRAND GHIA (SIX/V-8)					
37	N/A	4-dr. Sedan-5P	5740/5828	3401/3584	Note 1

NOTE 1: Production included in basic Monarch Ghia total above.

Model No.	Body/ Style No.	Body Type & Seating	Factory Price	Shipping Weight	Prod. Total
MONTEGO (V-8)					
03	65B	2-dr. HT-6P	4299	4057	2,287
02	53B	4-dr. HT Sed-6P	4343	4133	3,403
MONTEGO MX (V-8)					
07	65D	2-dr. HT-6P	4465	4085	12,367
04	53D	4-dr. HT Sed-6P	4498	4133	12,666
08	71D	4-dr. Sta Wag-6P	4778	4451	5,012
MONTEGO MX BROUGHAM (V-8)					
11	65K	2-dr. HT-6P	4621	4097	3,905
10	53K	4-dr. HT Sed-6P	4670	4150	5,043
MONTEGO MX VILLAGER (V-8)					
18	71K	4-dr. Sta Wag-6P	5065	4478	6,412
COUGAR XR-7 (V-8)					
93	65F	2-dr. HT Cpe-5P	5125	4168	83,765
MARQUIS (V-8)					
66	65H	2-dr. HT-6P	5063	4436	10,450
63	53H	4-dr. Pill. HT-6P	5063	4460	28,212
74	71H	4-dr. 2S Sta Wag-6P	5275	4796	2,493
74	71H	4-dr. 3S Sta Wag-8P	5401	4824	Note 2
MARQUIS BROUGHAM (V-8)					
64	65K	2-dr. HT-6P	5955	4652	10,431
62	53K	4-dr. Pill. HT-6P	6035	4693	22,411
GRAND MARQUIS (V-8)					

Model No.	Body/ Style No.	Body Type & Seating	Factory Price	Shipping Weight	Prod. Total
61	65L	2-dr. HT-6P	6439	4679	9,207
60	53L	4-dr. Pill. HT-6P	6528	4723	17,650
MARQUIS COLONY PARK (V-8)					
76	71K	4-dr. 2S Sta Wag-6P	5590	4878	15,114
76	71K	4-dr. 3S Sta Wag-8P	5716	4906	Note 2

NOTE 2: Production totals for three-seat station wagons are included in two-seat figures.

1976 Mercury Marquis Brougham pillared hardtop. (AA)

FACTORY PRICE AND WEIGHT NOTE: For Comet and Monarch, prices and weights to left of slash are for six-cylinder, to right for V-8 engine. For Bobcat, prices/weights to left of slash are for four-cylinder, to right for V-6.

ENGINE [Base Four (Bobcat)]: Inline. Overhead cam. Four-cylinder. Cast-iron block and head. Displacement: 140-cid (2.3 liters). Bore & stroke: 3.78 x 3.13 in. Compression ratio: 9.0:1. Brake horsepower: 92 at 5000 rpm. Torque: 121 lbs.-ft. at 3000 rpm. Five main bearings. Hydraulic valve lifters. Carburetor: 2Bbl. Holley-Weber 9510 (D6EE-AA). VIN Code: Y.

ENGINE [Optional V-6 (Bobcat)]: 60-degree, overhead-valve V-6. Cast-iron block and head. Displacement: 170.8-cid (2.8 liters). Bore & stroke: 3.66 x 2.70 in. Compression ratio: 8.7:1. Brake horsepower: 100 at 4600 rpm. Torque: 143 lbs.-ft. at 2600 rpm. Four main bearings. Hydraulic valve lifters. Carburetor: 2Bbl. Motorcraft 9510 (D6ZE-BA). VIN Code: Z.

ENGINE [Base Six (Comet, Monarch)]: Inline. OHV. Six-cylinder. Cast-iron block and head. Displacement: 200-cid (3.3 liters). Bore & stroke: 3.68 x 3.13 in. Compression ratio: 8.3:1. Brake horsepower: 81 at 3400 rpm. Torque: 151 lbs.-ft. at 1700 rpm. Seven main bearings. Hydraulic valve lifters. Carburetor: 1Bbl. Carter YFA 9510 (D6BE-AA). VIN Code: T.

ENGINE [Base Six (Monarch Ghia); Optional (Comet, Monarch)]: Inline. OHV. Six-cylinder. Cast-iron block and head. Displacement: 250-cid (4.1 liters). Bore & stroke: 3.68 x 3.91 in. Compression ratio: 8.0:1. Brake horsepower: 90 at 3000 rpm. (Monarch, 87 at 3000). Torque: 190 lbs.-ft. at 2000 rpm. (Monarch, 187 at 1900). Seven main bearings. Hydraulic valve lifters. Carburetor: 1Bbl. Carter YFA 9510. VIN Code: L.

ENGINE [Optional V-8 (Comet, Monarch)]: 90-degree, overhead valve V-8. Cast-iron block and head. Displacement: 302-cid (5.0 liters). Bore & stroke: 4.00 x 3.00 in. Compression ratio: 8.0:1. Brake horsepower: 138 at 3600 rpm. (Monarch, 134 at 3600). Torque: 245 lbs.-ft. at 2000 rpm. (Monarch, 242 at 2000). Five main bearings. Hydraulic valve lifters. Carburetor: 2Bbl. Ford 2150A 9510 (D5DE-AFA). VIN Code: F.

ENGINE [Base V-8 (Montego, Cougar); Optional (Monarch)]: 90-degree, overhead valve V-8. Cast-iron block and head. Displacement: 351-cid (5.8 liters). Bore & stroke: 4.00 x 3.50 in. Compression ratio: 8.0:1. (Montego, 8.1:1). Brake horsepower: 152 at 3800 rpm. (or 154 at 3400). Torque: 274 lbs.-ft. at 1600 rpm. (or 286 at 1800). Five main bearings. Hydraulic valve lifters. Carburetor: 2Bbl. Ford 2150A 9510. VIN Code: H.

ENGINE [Base V-8 (Marquis); Optional (Cougar, Montego)]: 90-degree, overhead valve V-8. Cast-iron block and head. Displacement: 400-cid (6.6 liters). Bore & stroke: 4.00 x 4.00 in. Compression ratio: 8.0:1. Brake horsepower: 180 at 3800 rpm. Torque: 336 lbs.-ft. at 1800 R.P.M. Five main bearings. Hydraulic valve lifters. Carburetor: 2Bbl. Ford 2150A 9510. VIN Code: S.

ENGINE [Optional V-8 (Cougar, Montego, Marquis)]: 90-degree, overhead valve V-8. Cast-iron block and head. Displacement: 460-cid (7.5 liters). Bore & stroke: 4.36 x 3.85 in. Compression ratio: 8.0:1. Brake horsepower: 202 at 3800 rpm. Torque: 352 lbs.-ft. at 1600 rpm. Five main bearings. Hydraulic valve lifters. Carburetor: 4Bbl. Motorcraft 9510 or Ford 4350A 9510. VIN Code: A.

CHASSIS DATA: Wheelbase: (Bobcat sed) 94.5 in.; (Bobcat wag) 94.8 in.; (Comet 2-dr.) 103.0 in.; (Comet 4-dr.) 109.9 in.; (Monarch) 109.9 in.; (Cougar) 114.0 in.; (Montego) 114.0 in.; (Montego wag) 118.0 in.; (Marquis) 124.0 in.; (Marquis wag) 121.0 in. Overall Length: (Bobcat sed) 169.0 in.; (Bobcat wag) 178.8 in.; (Comet 2-dr.) 189.5 in.; (Comet 4-dr.) 196.4 in.; (Monarch) 197.7 in.; (Cougar) 215.7 in.; (Montego 2-dr.) 215.7 in.; (Montego 4-dr.) 219.7 in.; (Montego wag) 224.4 in.; (Marquis) 229.0 in.; (Marquis wag) 228.3 in. Height: (Bobcat sed) 50.6 in.; (Bobcat wag) 52.0 in.; (Comet) 52.9 in.; (Monarch) 53.2-53.4 in.; (Cougar) 52.6 in.; (Montego 2-dr.) 52.6 in.; (Montego 4-dr.) 53.3 in.; (Montego wag) 54.9 in.; (Marquis 2-dr.) 53.7 in.; (Marquis 4-dr.) 54.7 in.; (Marquis wag) 56.9 in. Width: (Bobcat sed) 69.4 in.; (Bobcat wag) 69.7 in.; (Comet) 70.5 in.; (Monarch 2-dr.) 74.0 in. (exc. Ghia) 74.5 in.; (Monarch 4-dr.) 74.1 in. (exc. Ghia) 75.5 in.; (Cougar) 78.5 in.; (Montego 2-dr.) 78.6 in.; (Montego 4-dr./wag) 79.6 in.; (Marquis) 79.6 in.; (Marquis wag) 79.8 in. Front Tread: (Bobcat) 55.0 in.; (Comet) 56.5 in.; (Monarch) 58.5 in.; (Cougar) 63.4 in.; (Montego) 63.4 in.; (Marquis) 64.1 in. Rear Tread: (Bobcat) 55.8 in.; (Comet) 56.5 in.; (Monarch) 57.7 in.; (Cougar) 63.5 in.; (Montego) 63.5 in.; (Marquis) 64.3 in. Standard Tires: (Bobcat) A78 x 13 exc. V-6/wagon, B78 x 13; (Comet) C78 x 14 exc. V-8, CR78 x 14 or DR78 x 14; (Monarch) DR78 x 14 exc. V8-351, ER78 x 14; (Cougar) HR78 x 14; (Montego) HR78 x 14; (Marquis) HR78 x 15 exc. wagon, JR78 x 15; (Colony Park) LR78 x 15.

TECHNICAL: Transmission: Three-speed manual transmission (column shift) standard on Comet/Monarch six and V8-302. Gear ratios: (1st) 2.99:1; (2nd) 1.75:1; (3rd) 1.00:1; (Rev) 3.17:1. Four-speed floor shift standard on Bobcat. Gear ratios: (1st) 3.65:1; (2nd) 1.97:1; (3rd)

1.37:1; (4th) 1.00:1; (Rev) 3.66:1. Bobcat wagon: (1st) 4.07:1; (2nd) 2.57:1; (3rd) 1.66:1; (4th) 1.00:1; (Rev) 3.95:1. SelectShift three-speed automatic (column lever) standard on Monarch V-8, Cougar, Montego and Marquis; optional on others. Floor lever optional on all except full-size. Bobcat L4-140 automatic gear ratios: (1st) 2.47:1; (2nd) 1.47:1; (3rd) 1.00:1; (Rev) 2.11:1. Bobcat V-6/Comet/Monarch/Cougar V8-351: (1st) 2.46:1; (2nd) 1.46:1; (3rd) 1.00:1; (Rev) 2.20:1. Cougar V8-400/460, Montego, full-size: (1st) 2.46:1; (2nd) 1.46:1; (3rd) 1.00:1; (Rev) 2.18:1. Standard final drive ratio: (Bobcat) 3.18:1 w/four, 3.00:1 w/V-6; (Comet) 2.79:1 w/3spd, 2.79:1 or 3.00:1 w/auto.: (Monarch) 2.79:1 w/3spd and 2.75:1, 3.00:1 or 3.07:1 w/auto.; (Cougar) 2.75:1; (Montego) 2.75:1; (Marquis) 2.75:1. Steering: (Bobcat) rack-and-pinion; (others) recirculating ball. Front Suspension: (Bobcat) coil springs with lower trailing arms, and anti-sway bar on wagon; (Montego) single lower arm drag strut w/coil springs and link-type anti-sway bar; (others) coil springs with short/long arms, lower trailing links and anti-sway bar. Rear Suspension: (Bobcat/Comet/Monarch) rigid axle w/semi-elliptic leaf springs; (Cougar) rigid axle w/lower trailing radius arms, upper oblique torque arms and coil springs; (Montego) four-link rubber-cushioned system w/coil springs; (Marquis) rigid axle w/lower trailing radius arms, upper torque arms and coil springs. Brakes: Front disc, rear drum. Ignition: Electronic. Body construction: (Bobcat/Comet/Monarch) unibody; (others) separate body on perimeter frame; Fuel tank: (Bobcat) 13 gal. exc. wagon, 14 gal.; (Comet) 19.2 gal.; (Monarch) 19.2 gal.; (Cougar) 26.5 gal.; (Montego) 21.3 gal.; (Marquis) 21 gal.

DRIVETRAIN OPTIONS: Engines: 250-cid, 1Bbl. six: Comet/Monarch ($96). 302-cid, 2Bbl. V-8: Monarch ($154); Monarch Ghia ($88). 351-cid, 2Bbl. V-8: Monarch ($200); Monarch Ghia ($134). 400-cid, 2Bbl. V-8: Montego/Cougar ($93). 460-cid, 4Bbl. V-8: Montego/Cougar ($292); Marquis ($212). Transmission/Differential. SelectShift Cruise-O-Matic: Bobcat ($186); Comet/Monarch ($245). Floor shift lever: Comet/Monarch ($27). Traction-Lok differential: Monarch ($48); Montego/Cougar ($53); Marquis ($54). Optional axle ratio: Bobcat/Comet/Monarch ($13); Montego/Cougar/Marquis ($14). Brakes/Steering: Power brakes: Bobcat ($54); Comet ($53); Monarch ($57). Four-wheel power disc brakes: Monarch ($210); Marquis ($170). Sure-Track brakes: Marquis ($217). Power steering: Bobcat ($117); Comet/Monarch ($124). Suspension: H.D susp.: Comet ($17); Monarch ($29). Cross-country susp.: Montego/Cougar ($26). Adjustable air shock absorbers: Marquis ($46). Other: Engine block heater: Bobcat/Comet/Monarch ($17); Montego/Marquis/Cougar ($18). H.D. battery: Comet/Monarch ($14-$16); Marquis ($20). H.D. electrical system: Montego/Cougar ($37). Extended-range fuel tank: Marquis ($99). Trailer towing pkg. (light duty): Monarch ($42); Marquis ($53). Trailer towing pkg. (medium duty): Montego/Cougar ($59); Marquis ($46). Trailer towing pkg. (heavy duty): Montego ($82-$121); Cougar/Marquis ($132). Equalizer hitch: Marquis ($99). High-altitude option: Cougar ($13).

BOBCAT CONVENIENCE/APPEARANCE OPTIONS: Option Packages: Sports accent group ($116-$269). Convenience light group ($92). Appearance protection group ($35). Bumper protection ($64). Comfort/Convenience: Air conditioner ($420). Rear defroster, electric ($67). Tinted glass ($46). Interval wipers ($25). Entertainment: AM radio ($71); w/stereo tape player ($192). AM/FM radio ($128). AM/FM stereo radio ($173). Exterior: Sunroof, manual ($230). Sports vinyl roof ($86). Glamour paint ($54). Sports tape striping ($40). Hinged quarter windows ($34). Wide bodyside moldings ($60); narrow ($35). Rocker panel moldings ($19). Runabout woodgrain ($214). Roof luggage rack ($52-$75). Bumper guards ($34). Interior: Deluxe interior ($139). Alpine plaid seat trim ($30). Deluxe seatbelts ($17). Wheels and Tires: Forged aluminum wheels ($53-$136). Styled steel wheels ($48-$83). A78 x 13 WSW. A70 x 13 RWL. B78 x 13 BSW/WSW. BR78 x 13 SBR BSW/WSW. BR70 x 13 RWL.

COMET CONVENIENCE/APPEARANCE OPTIONS: Option Packages: Sports accent group ($235). Custom decor group ($496). Custom interior decor ($222). Bumper group ($30-$64). Convenience/visibility group ($43-$51). Appearance protection group ($8-$39). Security lock group ($16). Comfort/Convenience: Air cond. ($420). Rear defogger ($43). Tinted glass ($42). Fuel monitor warning light ($18). Interval wipers ($25). Entertainment: AM radio ($71); w/tape player ($192). AM/FM radio ($128). AM/FM stereo radio ($216); w/tape player ($299). Exterior: Vinyl roof ($89). Glamour paint ($54). Lower bodyside paint ($55). Tu-tone paint ($33). Bodyside molding ($35). Rocker panel moldings ($19). Decklid luggage rack ($51). Bumper guards, front ($17). Interior: Reclining bucket seats ($119). Alpine plaid seat trim ($30). Vinyl seat trim ($25). Color-keyed deluxe seatbelts ($17). Wheels and Tires: Forged aluminum wheels ($67-$192). Styled steel wheels ($60-$89). Deluxe wheel covers ($29). C78 x 14 WSW. BR78 x 14 BSW. CR78 x 14 BSW/WSW. DR78 x 14 BSW/WSW. DR70 x 14 RWL. Space-saver spare ($13) except (NC) with radial tires.

MONARCH CONVENIENCE/APPEARANCE OPTIONS: Option Packages: 'S' group ($482). Decor group ($181). Convenience group ($31-$75). Bumper group ($64). Light group ($25-$37). Protection group ($24-$39). Visibility group ($34-$47). Security lock group ($17).

Comfort/Convenience: Air cond. ($437). Rear defogger ($43). Rear defroster, electric ($73). Fingertip speed control ($96). Power windows ($95-$133). Power door locks ($63-$88). Power four-way seat ($119). Tinted glass ($47). Leather-wrapped steering wheel ($14-$33). Luxury steering wheel ($18). Tilt steering wheel ($54). Fuel monitor warning light ($18). Digital clock ($40). Interval wipers ($25). Horns and Mirrors: Dual-note horn ($6). Dual racing mirrors ($29-$42). Lighted visor vanity mirror ($40). Entertainment: AM radio ($71); w/tape player ($192). AM/FM radio ($142). AM/FM stereo radio ($210); w/tape player ($299). Exterior: Power moonroof ($786). Power sunroof ($517). Full or landau vinyl roof ($102). Glamour paint ($54). Bodyside moldings ($35). Rocker panel moldings ($19). Decklid luggage rack ($51). Interior: Console ($65). Reclining bucket seats ($60). Leather seat trim ($181). Luxury cloth seat trim ($88) exc. (NC) w/Grand Ghia. Trunk carpeting ($20). Trunk dress-up ($33). Color-keyed seatbelts ($17). Wheels/Tires: Styled steel wheels ($35-$54); w/trim rings ($70-$89). Spoke aluminum wheels ($112-$201). E78 x 14 BSW/WSW. DR78 x 14 WSW. ER78 x 14 BSW/WSW. FR78 x 14 BSW/WSW. Space-saver spare (NC).

MONTEGO CONVENIENCE/APPEARANCE OPTIONS: Option Packages: Bumper group ($33-$53). Visibility light group ($82). Convenience group ($20-$66). Protection group ($18-$42). Security lock group ($18). Comfort/Convenience: Air cond. ($483); w/auto-temp control ($520). Defroster, electric ($80). Fingertip speed control ($101). Tinted glass ($53). Power windows ($104-$145). Power tailgate window: wag ($43). Power door locks ($68-$109). Electric decklid release ($17). Six-way power seat ($130). Leather-wrapped steering wheel ($36). Luxury steel ring wheel ($20). Tilt steering wheel ($59). Fuel sentry vacuum gauge ($34). Fuel monitor warning light ($20). Electric clock ($20). Interval wipers ($28). Horns and Mirrors: Dual-note horn ($7). Remote driver's mirror ($14). Dual racing mirrors ($36-$50). Entertainment: AM radio ($78). AM/FM stereo radio ($236); w/tape player ($339). Dual rear speakers ($39). Exterior: Full or landau vinyl roof ($112). Opera windows ($50). Rocker panel moldings ($26). Bodyside moldings ($38). Glamour paint ($59). Luggage rack ($82-$97). Interior: Twin comfort lounge seats ($164-$234). Polyknit trim ($50). Vinyl trim ($28). Rear-facing third seat: wag ($108). Trunk trim ($36). Wheels/Tires: Deluxe wheel covers ($32). Luxury wheel covers ($37-$68). Styled wheel ($66-$97). H78 x 14 BSW/WSW. HR78 x 14 BSW/WSW. HR78 x 14C BSW/WSW. JR78 x 14 WSW. Space-saver spare (NC).

COUGAR CONVENIENCE/APPEARANCE OPTIONS: Option Packages: Convenience group ($49-$57). Protection group ($34). Light group ($82). Bumper group ($53). Security lock group ($18). Comfort/Convenience: Air cond. ($483); auto-temp ($520). Rear defroster, electric ($80). Fingertip speed control ($101). Tinted glass ($53). Power seat ($130). Power windows ($104). Power door locks ($68). Electric trunk release ($17). Reclining passenger seat ($70). Leather-wrapped steering wheel ($36). Tilt steering wheel ($59). Fuel monitor warning light ($20). Interval wipers ($28). Driver's remote mirror ($14). Dual racing mirrors ($36-$50). Entertainment: AM radio ($78). AM/FM stereo radio ($236); w/tape player ($339). AM/FM stereo search radio ($386). Dual rear speakers ($39). Exterior: Power moonroof ($859); sunroof ($545). Full vinyl roof ($41). Glamour paint ($59). Bodyside molding ($38). Rocker panel moldings ($26). Interior: Twin comfort lounge seats ($86). Bucket seats w/console ($143). Leather trim ($222). Velour trim ($96). Trunk dress-up ($36). Wheels/Tires: Styled steel wheels ($93). Cast aluminum wheels ($199). HR78 x 14 SBR WSW ($39). HR78 x 15 SBR WSW ($62). HR70 x 15 WSW ($82). Space-saver spare (NC).

MARQUIS CONVENIENCE/APPEARANCE OPTIONS: Option Packages: Grand Marquis option: Colony Park ($305). Tu-tone group ($59-$145). Lock convenience group ($86-$112). Light group ($83-$118). Bumper group ($33-$53). Protection group ($47-$55). Security lock group ($8-$18). Comfort/Convenience: Air cond. ($512); w/auto-temp control ($549). Anti-theft alarm system ($100-$105). Rear defroster, electric ($80). Fingertip speed control ($101). Power windows ($109-$162). Power vent windows ($79). Six-way power driver's seat ($132); driver and passenger ($257). Automatic seatback release ($30). Tinted glass ($66). Deluxe steering wheel ($20). Tilt steering wheel ($59). Fuel monitor warning light ($20). Electric clock ($20). Digital clock ($29-$49). Interval wipers ($28). Lighting and Mirrors: Cornering lamps ($41). Driver's remote mirror ($14). Entertainment: AM radio ($78). AM/FM stereo radio ($236); w/tape player ($339). AM/FM stereo search radio ($386). Dual rear speakers ($39). Power antenna ($39). Exterior: Power sunroof ($632). Full vinyl roof ($126) exc. wagon ($151). Landau vinyl roof ($126). Fender skirts ($41). Glamour metallic paint ($59). Paint stripes ($29). Rocker panel moldings ($26). Vinyl-insert bodyside moldings ($41). Luggage rack: wag ($82-$100). Interior: Twin comfort lounge seats ($86). Reclining passenger seat ($58). Dual-facing rear seats: wagon ($126). Vinyl bench seat ($26). Recreation table: wag ($58). Color-keyed seatbelts ($18). Front/rear mats ($33). Deluxe cargo area ($83-$126). Lockable side stowage compartment: wag ($43). Luggage area trim ($46). Wheels: Brougham wheel covers ($26). Luxury wheel covers ($50-$76). Forged aluminum wheels ($211-$237). Tires: HR78 x 15 WSW. JR78 x 15 BSW/WSW. LR78 x 15B BSW/WSW. LR78 x 15C WSW.

1976 Mercury Colony Park station wagon. (AA)

HISTORY: Introduced: October 3, 1975. Model year production: 482,714. Calendar year production (U.S.): 434,877. Calendar year sales by U.S. dealers: 418,749. Model year sales by U.S. dealers: 428,023.

HISTORY: Lincoln-Mercury sales rose almost 24 percent for the 1976 model year, a far better showing than in 1975, which had posted a significant decline. Showing the strongest increase were Monarch and Marquis, rising by some 60 percent. At the smaller end of the Mercury spectrum, Comet fell by nearly 37 percent, while Montego (in its final season) showed a more moderate decline. Led by Monarch, model year production showed a gain of nearly 17 percent. Although General Motors was ready to downsize its full-size models, Ford/Mercury planned to keep its biggies for two more years, including the massive 400 and 460-cid V-8s.

1977 MERCURY

1977 Mercury Comet. (OCW)

1977 Mercury Bobcat Runabout. (M)

1977 Mercury Comet coupe. (M)

Although the mid-size Montego disappeared, a broad new line of Cougars joined the XR-7. While XR7 competed with Grand Prix, Monte Carlo and Cordoba, the new standard Cougars became rivals to Olds Cutlass and Supreme, Pontiac LeMans, and Buick Century, retaining some of the distinctive sculptured XR-7 styling. Engines had "second generation" DuraSpark electronic ignition that produced higher spark-plug voltage. Monarch added a four-speed gearbox (overdrive fourth gear) as standard equipment. Marquis carried on in full-size form, unlike the downsized GM big cars.

1977-1/2 Mercury Comet Sports Coupe. (PH)

BOBCAT — FOUR/V-6 — Appearance and equipment of Mercury's subcompact changed little this year, except for new colors and trims. Runabouts could have a new optional all-glass third door (hatch). Bumpers were now bright-surfaced, extruded anodized aluminum, which helped cut weight by over 100 pounds. To improve ride/handling, shock absorbers were revalved, and rear-spring front eye bushings stiffened. New Dura-Spark ignition offered higher voltage. Inside, the manual gearshift lever was shortened, while a new wide-ratio four-speed was offered. Rear axle ratios were lowered (numerically) too, to help gas mileage. Joining the option list were: a flip-up removable sunroof, manual four-way bucket seats, Sports Group (handling and instrumentation package), simulated wire wheel covers, and high-altitude option. That Sports Group included a tachometer, ammeter and temperature gauges, new soft-rim sports steering wheel, front stabilizer bar, and higher-rate springs. Bobcats had a domed hood, bright metal vertical-textured grille with surround molding, and clear square park/signal lamps with crosshair bars, positioned between the grille and single round headlamps. Wide-spaced 'Bobcat' block letters stood above the grille. California versions had styled steel wheels, while 49-staters carried deluxe wheel covers. Standard equipment included a lighter, front/rear ashtrays, woodgrain instrument panel appliqué, wide wheel lip and rocker panel moldings, and manual front disc brakes. Bodies also carried bright side window frame and door belt moldings, and center pillar moldings. At the rear were horizontal tri-pod tail lamps with a small backup light in the center of each unit. 'Bobcat' script went in the lower corner of the glass third door. Base engine again was the 140-cid (2.3-liter) four with four-speed floor shift, with 2.8-liter V-6 available. Biasply A78 x 13 blackwalls were standard, except in California which required steel-belted radials. Contoured high-back bucket seats came in all-vinyl or Kirsten cloth and vinyl. An 'S' option group included gold-stripe treatment from hood to back panel, blackout trim, styled steel wheels with gold accents, dual racing mirrors, sports suspension with stabilizer bar, and the new glass third door. A Sports Accent Group included styled steel wheels with trim rings, special paint/tape, leather-wrapped steering wheel, deluxe bucket seats, and sound package.

COMET — SIX/V-8 — Not much changed in the compact Comet, which would not return for 1978. New body and interior colors were offered, along with two new vinyl roof colors. New options included simulated wire wheel covers, two-tone paint, four-way manual bucket seats, high-altitude emissions, and new Decor Groups. The new optional driver's bucket seat adjusted (manually) up and down as well as forward and back. All three engines were modified, including a new variable-venturi carburetor for the California 302-cid V-8. All had improved-response throttle linkage and new Dura-Spark ignition. Drivetrains held a new wide-ratio three-speed manual shift, while the 302 V-8 models had a more efficient torque converter. Comet's grille was peaked forward slightly, made up of thin horizontal bars with a dominant horizontal bar in the center and full-width lower grille molding. Aligned with the grille were surround moldings for the clear rectangular park/signal lenses, framed in argent side panels. Those moldings followed the curve of the single round headlamps at their outer edges. Blackout headlamp frames had argent beads. The entire front end had a full-width look. Amber side marker lenses were just ahead of the front wheels, below the bodyside molding. Front bumpers contained two side-by-side slots in the center. Each taillamp consisted of two separate pods. Two-doors had front-hinged rear quarter windows; four-doors, roll-down back door windows. Bright front/rear wheel lip moldings and rocker panel moldings were used, as well as bright upper bodyside and drip rail moldings. Hubcaps were standard, with C78 x 14 blackwall tires. Bright window frames and belt moldings became part of the optional exterior decor group. Several items, including lighter and rear ashtray, were put into a new interior decor group, which also included a deluxe steering wheel, cloth/vinyl or all-vinyl seat trim, and upgraded sound package. Five colors of vinyl were available in the standard interior. Standard equipment included the 200-cid six, three-speed manual shift (but 250 six with automatic in California), lighted front ashtray, European-type armrests and door handles, glovebox, and dome light. The Custom option included a vinyl roof, whitewalls, bodyside paint stripes, full-length molding with color-keyed vinyl inserts, reclining front bucket seats, tinted glass, and leather-wrapped sports steering wheel. That option was billed as having "a little Cougar in it."

1977 Mercury Monarch Ghia coupe. (M)

1977-1/2 Mercury Monarch Sports Coupe (with louvered opera window appliqués). (PH)

1977 Mercury Monarch Ghia sedan. (OCW)

1977 Mercury Cougar XR-7 Sports Coupe. (M)

MONARCH — SIX/V-8 — "The precision size car with a touch of class." That's how Lincoln-Mercury described Monarch this year. Like other models, it carried a plaque on the dash proclaiming that it was "Ride-Engineered by Lincoln-Mercury." Appearance changed little, however, apart from some new body colors and option choices. New options included four-way manual bucket seats, automatic temperature-control air conditioning, illuminated entry, front cornering lamps, simulated wire wheel covers, white lacy-spoke cast aluminum wheels, wide-band whitewall radial tires, high-altitude emissions, and electric trunk lid release. Several appearance options had debuted in mid-year 1976 and continued this year, including a landau half-vinyl roof, dual racing mirrors, and styled steel wheels. A new standard four-speed manual floor shift had fourth-gear overdrive. California 302-cid V-8s had a new variable-venturi carburetor. Other mechanical changes included an improved-response throttle linkage: new DuraSpark ignition; lower rear axle ratios; and new standard coolant recovery system. Monarch's grille was made up of thin vertical bars with bright surround molding and 'Mercury' block lettering above. Horizontally-ribbed park/signal lamps in front fender extensions turned into amber side marker lenses after wrapping around the fender. Twin side-by-side slots were in the front bumper's center. Single round headlamps were recessed in square bright housings. The unique stand-up hood ornament had seven tiny "knobs" atop a pillar within a circle. 'Monarch' script was on the lower cowl, just above the lower bodyside molding. Backup lenses stood at the inner ends of each square-styled tri-pod wraparound taillamp, with tri-color lenses. Two-doors had opera windows; four-doors, rear quarter windows. The textured back panel appliqué was color-keyed to either the body or vinyl roof. Front and rear full wheel lip moldings, full-length upper bodyside moldings, and bright window frame moldings were standard. Dashboards displayed a simulated burled walnut woodgrain appliqué. Base engine was again the 200-cid inline six. Standard equipment also included front disc brakes, foot parking brake, blackwall SBR tires, full wheel covers, locking glovebox, and lighter. Monarch Ghia moved up to the 250-cid six and added paint striping on hood contours and decklid, a tapered bodyside paint stripe (replacing the usual darts), and Ghia ornament on opera window of two-doors (rear pillar of four-doors). Full-length lower bodyside moldings had wide color-keyed vinyl inserts. Front and rear partial wheel lip moldings replaced the base Monarch's full wheel lip moldings. Ghia also included map pockets, color-keyed wheel covers (or wire wheel covers), carpeted trunk, day/night mirror, remote driver's mirror, inside hood release, and Flight Bench seat. An 'S' option group included a landau vinyl roof (two-door); goldtone paint/tape stripes on bodysides, hood and decklid; rocker panel moldings; dual remote racing mirrors; styled steel wheels with gold-color accents and trim rings; bucket seats; leather-wrapped steering wheel; heavy-duty suspension; and floor lever with optional automatic. Both models could have the optional 302-cid V-8.

COUGAR/XR-7 — V-8 — All-new styling hit Cougar's A-body shell for 1976, as the nameplate expanded to included a set of sedans and wagons as well as the usual XR-7 hardtop coupe. Grille, grille opening panel, quad rectangular headlamps, and combination parking/turn signal lamps were all new. Cougar's rear end had new vertical tail lamps, backup lights, decklid, quarter panel, and deck opening lower panel. Larger side glass and backlight improved visibility. XR-7 had distinctive new wraparound tail lamps, plus a new decklid similar to the Mark V Lincoln. Viewed from the side, the two- and four-door models showed new doors and a straight beltline, as well as a new rear roof (plus optional opera windows). XR-7's profile showed a distinctive large opera window with louvers and a padded landau roof. Base and Villager wagons were offered. Base engine size was reduced from 351 to 302-cid, with new DuraSpark ignition and lower rear axle ratio. Instrument clusters were revised on both Cougars. Air conditioner performance improved with a 40 percent airflow increase. XR-7 had a larger-diameter front stabilizer bar, and an added rear stabilizer bar to improve handling. Appearance of the new models was similar to XR-7, but without the louvered opera windows. tail lamps were different, though: two-section vertical units at quarter panel tips, with small backup lenses at outer ends of a wide red center panel below the decklid. Cougar had a distinctive Continental-type swing-away grille made up of vertical bars, divided into two side-by-side sections (each containing three sections). A heavy surround molding positioned the grille well forward of the headlamps, and it extended slightly below the bumper. No bumper slots were used. Moldings above and below the quad rectangular headlamps continued outward to enclose the large fender-tip wraparound park/signal/marker lenses (which were amber at the rear). Above was a bright stand-up Cougar hood ornament. The red reflective rear center appliqué in the lower back panel had a bright surround molding. Bright rocker panel moldings, full wheel lip moldings, roof drip rail and window frame moldings, and door belt moldings all were standard. Two-doors had rear quarter window moldings. Inside was a standard cloth and vinyl bench seat. Cougar Brougham added a full vinyl roof (on four-door), upper bodyside paint stripe, bright wide door belt molding, deluxe wheel covers, and Flight Bench seat with folding armrest (cloth and vinyl or all vinyl). Opera windows had 'Brougham' script embedded in the glass. Full-length bright bodyside moldings with integral wheel lip moldings replaced the usual full wheel lip and rocker panel moldings. Mercury promoted the XR-7 for its sweeping profile, accentuated by its sculptured rear decklid and accent stripes, calling it "bold" and "aggressive." Cougar XR-7 features included the sport-style roofline, fully padded landau vinyl roof, grille extension below the bumper, hood rear edge molding, full wheel lip and rocker panel moldings, and full wheel covers with unique Cougar center insert. Wide opera windows had a trio of vertical louvers at the forward end. Those were accompanied by a small frameless window just to the rear of the door window, in hardtop style. A Cougar ornament adorned the center pillar, while the rear end held a sculptured simulated-spare-tire decklid with lower molding and paint stripe, and 'Cougar' block lettering. Horizontal wraparound tail lamps were divided into six sections by vertical strips, wrapping around quarter panel tips, with backup lenses in the second section from the inside. 'Mercury' script went just above the right taillamp. Flight Bench seating with decorative accent stripes came in Ashton cloth or Mateao vinyl. Cougar standard equipment included the 302 V-8 and SelectShift, power brakes and steering, HR78 x 14 tires, two-spoke color-keyed steering wheel, day/night mirror, and inside hood release. XR-7 equipment included HR78 x 15 SBR tires, landau vinyl roof, clock, walnut instrument panel appliqués, day/night mirror, dual-note horn, and locking glovebox. Four new XR-7 colors were available. Station wagons had a 351-cid V-8, optional on other models. A 400-cid V-8 also was available. Major new options included opera windows, illuminated entry, day/date clock, sports steering wheel, cornering lamps, monaural AM/FM radio, AM/FM stereo search radio, radio with quadrasonic tape player, wide whitewall radials, wire wheel covers, and (two-doors only) front and rear half-vinyl roof.

MARQUIS — V-8 — New body colors and interior fabrics accounted for most of the changes in Mercury's full-size line. Bright vinyl roof surround moldings replaced color-keyed vinyl moldings on Brougham and Grand Marquis. Grand Marquis had newly styled Twin Comfort lounge seats. New options included a power moonroof, illuminated entry, AM/FM stereo radio with quadrasonic 8-tape player, simulated wire wheel covers, high-altitude emissions, and wide whitewall radials. The improved standard 400-cid V-8 engine had DuraSpark ignition and a new standard coolant recovery system, while the rear axle ratio was lowered (numerically). The Colony Park wagon was now a Brougham-level option package. As before, the upright grille consisted of six side-by-side sections, each with five vertical bars, surrounded by a bright molding. Concealed headlamps stood behind rectangular doors with rectangular trim molding and center crest emblem. 'Mercury' script went above the left headlamp. Horizontally-ribbed park/signal lamps stood at fender tips, wrapping around to amber side marker lenses. Front vertical bumper guards had black inserts. Bright rocker panel moldings included front extensions. Inside was a new "Ride-Engineered by Lincoln-Mercury" dash plaque. Front bench seats came in Ardmore cloth and vinyl, with fold-down center armrest. Standard equipment included three-speed SelectShift, power steering and brakes, and HR78 x 15 blackwall steel belted radials. Marquis Brougham added a full vinyl roof (on four-doors) or landau vinyl roof (two-doors) with bright surround moldings, fender skirts with bright molding, power windows, clock, and full-length upper body peak molding. Decklid lock covers showed the L-M crest. Flight Bench seats came in Wilshire cloth and vinyl with folding center armrest. Two-doors had automatic seatback release. Grand Marquis included the 460 4Bbl. V-8, SelectShift, power windows, tinted glass, vinyl roof, digital clock, automatic parking brake release, fender skirts, Twin Comfort Lounge seats, and hood/decklid paint stripes. The big 460 V-8 was not available in California.

I.D. DATA: As before, Mercury's 11-symbol Vehicle Identification Number (VIN) is stamped on a metal tab fastened to the instrument panel, visible through the windshield. Coding is similar to 1976. Model year code changed to '7' for 1977.

BOBCAT RUNABOUT/WAGON (FOUR/V-6)

Model No.	Body/ Style No.	Body Type & Seating	Factory Price	Shipping Weight	Prod. Total
20	64H	3-dr. Hatch-4P	3438/3739	2369/----	18,405
22	73H	2-dr. Sta Wag-4P	3629/3930	2505/----	Note 1

1977 Mercury Grand Marquis pillared hardtop. (OCW)

1977 Mercury Cougar Brougham sedan. (M)

BOBCAT VILLAGER (FOUR/V-6)

22	73H	2-dr. Sta Wag-4P	3771/4072	N/A	Note 1

NOTE 1: Total station wagon production was 13,047 units. Bobcat Runabout and wagon totals include 3,616 vehicles produced in 1978 but sold as 1977 models.

COMET (SIX/V-8)

31	62B	2-dr. Fast Sed-4P	3392/3544	----/2960	9,109
30	548	4-dr. Sed-5P	3465/3617	----/3065	12,436

MONARCH (SIX/V-8)

35	66H	2-dr. Sedan-4P	4092/4279	3123/3277	44,509
34	54H	4-dr. Sedan-5P	4188/4375	3173/3327	55,592

MONARCH GHIA (SIX/V-8)

38	66K	2-dr. Sedan-4P	4659/4749	3244/3398	11,051
37	54K	4-dr. Sedan-5P	4755/4850	3305/3459	16,545

COUGAR (V-8)

91	65D	2-dr. HT Cpe-6P	4700	3811	15,910
90	53D	4-dr. Pill. HT-6P	4832	3893	15,256
92	71D	4-dr. Sta Wag-6P	5104	4434	4,951

COUGAR BROUGHAM (V-8)

95	65K	2-dr. HT Cpe-6P	4990	3852	8,392
94	53K	4-dr. Pill. HT-6P	5230	3946	16,946

COUGAR VILLAGER (V-8)

96	71K	4-dr. Sta Wag-6P	5363	4482	8,569

COUGAR XR-7 (V-8)

93	65L	2-dr. HT Cpe-6P	5274	3909	124,799

MARQUIS (V-8)

66	65H	2-dr. HT-6P	5496	4293	13,242
63	53H	4-dr. Pill. HT-6P	5496	4326	36,103
74	71H	4-dr. 2S Sta Wag-6P	5631	4628	20,363
74	71H	4-dr. 3S Sta Wag-8P	5794	N/A	Note 2

NOTE 2: Production total for three-seat station wagon is included in two-seat figure.

MARQUIS BROUGHAM (V-8)

Model No.	Body/ Style No.	Body Type & Seating	Factory Price	Shipping Weight	Prod. Total
64	65K	2-dr. HT-6P	6229	4350	12,237
62	53K	4-dr. Pill. HT-6P	6324	4408	29,411

GRAND MARQUIS (V-8)

61	65L	2-dr. HT-6P	6880	4516	13,445
60	53L	4-dr. Pill. HT-6P	6975	4572	31,231

FACTORY PRICE AND WEIGHT NOTE: For Comet and Monarch, prices and weights to left of slash are for six-cylinder, to right for V-8 engine. For Bobcat, prices/weights to left of slash are for four-cylinder, to right for V-6.

ENGINE [Base Four (Bobcat)]: Inline. Overhead cam. Four-cylinder. Cast-iron block and head. Displacement: 140-cid (2.3 liters). Bore & stroke: 3.78 x 3.13 in. Compression ratio: 9.0:1. Brake horsepower: 89 at 4800 rpm. Torque: 120 lbs.-ft. at 3000 rpm. Five main bearings. Hydraulic valve lifters. Carburetor: 2Bbl. Motorcraft 5200. VIN Code: Y.

ENGINE [Optional V-6 (Bobcat)]: 60-degree, overhead-valve V-6. Cast-iron block and head. Displacement: 170.8-cid (2.8 liters). Bore & stroke: 3.66 x 2.70 in. Compression ratio: 8.7:1. Brake horsepower: 90-93 at 4200 rpm. Torque: 139-140 lbs.-ft. at 2600 rpm. Four main bearings. Hydraulic valve lifters. Carburetor: 2Bbl. Motorcraft 2150. VIN Code: Z.

ENGINE [Base Six (Comet, Monarch)]: Inline. OHV. Six-cylinder. Cast-iron block and head. Displacement: 200-cid (3.3 liters). Bore & stroke: 3.68 x 3.13 in. Compression ratio: 8.5:1. Brake horsepower: 96 at 4400 rpm. Torque: 151 lbs.-ft. at 2000 rpm. Seven main bearings. Hydraulic valve lifters. Carburetor: 1Bbl. Carter YFA. VIN Code: T.

ENGINE [Base Six (Monarch Ghia); Optional (Comet, Monarch)]: Inline. OHV. Six-cylinder. Cast-iron block and head. Displacement: 250-cid (4.1 liters). Bore & stroke: 3.68 x 3.91 in. Compression ratio: 8.0:1. Brake horsepower: 98 at 3400 rpm. Torque: 182 lbs.-ft. at 1800 rpm. Seven main bearings. Hydraulic valve lifters. Carburetor: 1Bbl. Carter YFA. VIN Code: L.

ENGINE [Base V-8 (Cougar); Optional (Comet, Monarch)]: 90-degree, overhead valve V-8. Cast-iron block and head. Displacement: 302-cid (5.0 liters). Bore & stroke: 4.00 x 3.00 in. Compression ratio: 8.4:1. Brake horsepower: 130-137 at 3400-3600 rpm. (some Monarchs, 122 at 3200). Torque: 242-245 lbs.-ft. at 1600-1800 rpm. (some Monarchs, 237 at 1600). Five main bearings. Hydraulic valve lifters. Carburetor: 2Bbl. Motorcraft 2150. VIN Code: F.

ENGINE [Optional V-8 (Cougar, Monarch)]: 90-degree, overhead valve V-8. Cast-iron block and head. Displacement: 351-cid (5.8 liters). Bore & stroke: 4.00 x 3.50 in. Compression ratio: 8.3:1. Brake horsepower: 149 at 3200 rpm. Torque: 291 lbs.-ft.. at 1600 rpm. Five main bearings. Hydraulic valve lifters. Carburetor: 2Bbl. Motorcraft 2150. Windsor engine. VIN Code: H.

ENGINE [Optional V-8 (Monarch Ghia):] Same as 351-cid V-8 above, but Horsepower: 135 at 3200 rpm. Torque: 275 lbs.-ft. at 1600 rpm.

ENGINE [Base V-8 (Cougar wagon); Optional (Cougar)]: Same as 351-cid V-8 above, but Compression ratio: 8.0:1. Horsepower: 161 at 3600 rpm. Torque: 285 lbs.-ft. at 1800 rpm. VIN Code: Q.

ENGINE [Base V-8 (Marquis); Optional (Cougar)]: 90-degree, overhead valve V-8. Cast-iron block and head. Displacement: 400-cid (6.6 liters). Bore & stroke: 4.00 x 4.00 in. Compression ratio: 8.0:1. Brake horsepower: 173 at 3800 rpm. Torque: 328 lbs.-ft. at 1600 rpm. Five main bearings. Hydraulic valve lifters. Carburetor: 2Bbl. Motorcraft 2150. VIN Code: S.

ENGINE [Base V-8 (Grand Marquis); Optional (Marquis)]: 90-degree, overhead valve V-8. Cast-iron block and head. Displacement: 460-cid (7.5 liters). Bore & stroke: 4.36 x 3.85 in. Compression ratio: 8.0:1. Brake horsepower: 197 at 4000 rpm. Torque: 353 lbs.-ft. at 2000 rpm. Five main bearings. Hydraulic valve lifters. Carburetor: 4Bbl. Motorcraft 4350. VIN Code: A.

CHASSIS DATA: Wheelbase: (Bobcat sed) 94.5 in.; (Bobcat wag) 94.8 in.; (Comet 2-dr.) 103.0 in.; (Comet 4-dr.) 109.9 in.; (Monarch) 109.9 in.; (Cougar 2-dr.) 114.0 in.; (Cougar 4-dr.) 118.0 in.; (Marquis) 124.0 in.; (Marquis wag) 121.0 in. Overall Length: (Bobcat sed) 169.0 in.: (Bobcat wag) 179.1 in.; (Comet 2-dr.) 189.4 in.; (Comet 4-dr.) 196.3 in.; (Monarch) 197.7 in.; (Cougar 2-dr.) 215.5 in.; (Cougar 4-dr.) 219.5 in.; (Cougar wag) 223.1 in.; (Marquis) 229.0 in.; (Marquis wag) 228.3 in. Height: (Bobcat sed) 50.6 in.; (Bobcat wag) 52.1 in.; (Comet) 52.9 in.; (Monarch) 53.2-53.3 in.; (Cougar) 52.6 in.; (Cougar 4-dr.) 53.3 in.; (XR-7) 53.0 in.; (Marquis 2-dr.) 53.7-53.8 in.; (Marquis 4-dr.) 54.7-54.8 in.; (Marquis wag) 56.9 in. Width: (Bobcat sed) 69.4 in.; (Bobcat wag) 69.7 in.; (Comet) 70.5 in.; (Monarch 2-dr.) 74.0 in. exc. Ghia, 74.5 in.; (Monarch 4-dr.) 74.1 in. exc. Ghia, 75.5 in.; (Cougar) 78.0 in.; (Marquis) 79.6 in.; (Marquis wag) 79.8 in. Front Tread: (Bobcat) 55.0 in.; (Comet) 56.5 in.; (Monarch) 59.0 in.; (Cougar) 63.6 in.; (Marquis) 64.1 in. Rear Tread: (Bobcat) 55.8 in.; (Comet) 56.5 in.; (Monarch) 57.7 in.; (Cougar) 63.5 in.; (Marquis) 64.3 in. Standard Tires: (Bobcat) A78 x 13 BSW exc. B78 x 14 w/V-6; (Comet) C78 x 14 BSW; (Monarch) DR78 x 14 BSW; (Cougar) HR78 x 14 BSW; (XR-7) HR78 x 15 BSW; (Marquis) HR78 x 15; (Marquis wag) JR78 x 15.

TECHNICAL: Transmission: Three-speed manual transmission (column shift) standard on Comet six. Gear ratios: (1st) 3.56:1; (2nd) 1.90:1; (3rd) 1.00:1; (Rev) 3.78:1. Four-speed overdrive floor shift standard on Monarch: (1st) 3.29:1; (2nd) 1.84:1; (3rd) 1.00:1; (4th) 0.81:1; (Rev) 3.29:1. Four-speed floor shift standard on Bobcat sedan: (1st) 3.98:1; (2nd) 2.14:1; (3rd) 1.42:1; (4th) 1.00:1; (Rev) 3.99:1. Bobcat wagon: (1st) 3.65:1; (2nd) 1.97:1; (3rd) 1.37:1; (4th) 1.00:1; (Rev) 3.66:1. SelectShift three-speed automatic (column lever) standard on Cougar and Marquis, optional on others. Bobcat L4-140 automatic gear ratios: (1st) 2.47:1; (2nd) 1.47:1; (3rd) 1.00:1; (Rev) 2.11:1. Bobcat V-6/Comet/Monarch/Cougar/Marquis: (1st) 2.46:1; (2nd) 1.46:1; (3rd) 1.00:1; (Rev) 2.14:1 to 2.19:1. Some Cougar/Marquis: (1st) 2.40:1; (2nd) 1.47:1; (3rd) 1.00:1; (Rev) 2.00:1. Standard final drive ratio: (Bobcat) 2.73:1 w/4spd, 3.18:1 w/auto.; (Bobcat V-6) 3.00:1; (Comet) 3.00:1 w/3spd, 2.79:1 w/250 six and 3spd or any auto.; (Monarch) 3.40:1 w/200 six, 3.00:1 w/250 six or V-8, 2.47:1 w/auto.; (Cougar) 2.50:1 or 2.75:1; (Marquis) 2.47:1 w/V8-400, 2.50:1 w/V8-460. Steering: (Bobcat) rack-and-pinion; (others) recirculating ball. Front Suspension: (Bobcat) coil springs with short/long control arms, lower leading arms, and anti-sway bar on wagon; (Comet/Monarch/Cougar) coil springs with short/long arms, lower trailing links and anti-sway bar; (XR-7/Marquis) coil springs w/single lower control arms, lower trailing links, strut bar and anti-sway bar. Rear Suspension: (Bobcat/Comet/Monarch) rigid axle w/semi-elliptic leaf springs; (Cougar) rigid axle w/lower trailing radius arms, upper oblique torque arms and coil springs; (Marquis) rigid axle with upper/lower control arms and coil springs. Brakes: Front disc, rear drum. Ignition: Electronic. Body construction: (Bobcat/Comet/Monarch) unibody; (others) separate body on perimeter frame; Fuel tank: (Bobcat) 13 gal. exc. wagon, 14 gal.; (Comet) 19.2 gal.; (Monarch) 19.2 gal.; (Cougar) 26.0 gal.; (Marquis) 24.2 gal.

DRIVETRAIN OPTIONS: Engines: 170-cid V-6: Bobcat ($301). 250-cid, 1Bbl. six: Comet/Monarch ($102). 302-cid, 2Bbl. V-8: Comet (N/A); Monarch ($93-$163). 351-cid, 2Bbl. V-8: Monarch ($142); Cougar ($66). 400-cid, 2Bbl. V-8: Cougar ($132); Cougar wag ($66); Marquis (NC). 460-cid, 4Bbl. V-8: Marquis ($225). Transmission/Differential: SelectShift Cruise-O-Matic: Bobcat ($197); Comet/Monarch ($259). Floor shift lever: Monarch ($28). Traction-Lok differential: Marquis ($57); Cougar ($54). Optional axle

ratio: Cougar ($16); Marquis ($15). Brakes/Steering: Power brakes: Bobcat ($57); Comet ($56); Monarch ($60). Four-wheel power disc brakes: Monarch ($273); Marquis ($180). Power steering: Bobcat ($124); Comet/Monarch ($132). Suspension: H.D. susp.: Monarch ($31). Cross country pkg.: Cougar XR-7/wag, Marquis ($27). Other: H.D. battery: Bobcat ($15); Comet ($17); Cougar ($18); Marquis ($21). H.D. alternator: Cougar/Marquis ($45). Engine block heater: Bobcat/Monarch ($18); Marquis ($20). Trailer towing pkg. (heavy duty): Cougar ($117-$157); Marquis ($188). California emission system: Bobcat ($52); Comet/Monarch ($49); Marquis ($53). High-altitude option: Bobcat/Monarch ($38); Marquis ($42).

BOBCAT CONVENIENCE/APPEARANCE OPTIONS: Option Packages: 'S' group ($115). Sports accent group ($285-$308). Sports instrument/handling group ($77-$89). Convenience light group ($68-$125). Bumper group ($68). Protection group ($37). Comfort/Convenience: Air conditioner ($446). Rear defroster, electric ($72). Tinted glass ($49). Driver's remote mirror ($14). Entertainment: AM radio ($75); w/stereo tape player ($203). AM/FM radio ($135). AM/FM stereo radio ($184). Exterior: Sunroof, manual ($244). Flip-up/removable moonroof ($147). Sports vinyl roof ($133). Glass third door ($13). Hinged quarter windows ($36). Glamour paint ($57). Narrow bodyside moldings ($37). Wide color-keyed bodyside moldings ($64). Roof luggage rack ($79). Rocker panel moldings ($20). Interior: Four-way bucket seat ($32). Plaid seat trim ($32). Deluxe interior trim ($147). Load floor carpet ($23). Cargo area cover ($34). Deluxe seatbelts ($18). Wheels/Tires: Wire wheel covers ($86). Forged aluminum wheels ($56-$144). Styled steel wheels ($88). Trim rings ($32). A78 x 13 WSW. B78 x 13 BSW/WSW. BR78 x 13 BSW/WSW. BR70 x 13 RWL.

COMET CONVENIENCE/APPEARANCE OPTIONS: Option Packages: Custom group ($609). Sports accent group ($249). Exterior decor group ($64). Interior decor group ($112). Custom interior ($296). Bumper group ($32-$68). Convenience/visibility group ($65-$80). Protection group ($9-$41). Comfort/Convenience: Air cond. ($46). Electric rear defogger ($46). Tinted window glass ($47). Dual racing mirrors ($14-$28). Entertainment: AM radio ($75), w/tape player ($203). AM/FM radio ($135). AM/FM stereo radio ($229); w/tape player ($317). Exterior: Vinyl roof ($95). Glamour paint ($57). Tu-tone paint ($59). Bodyside moldings ($37). Rocker panel moldings ($20). Interior: Four-way seat ($32). Reclining vinyl bucket seats ($156). Vinyl seat trim ($27). Plaid seat trim ($32). Deluxe seatbelts ($18). Wheels/Tires: Deluxe wheel covers ($31). Wire wheel covers ($22-$116). Cast aluminum wheels ($138-$233). Styled steel wheels ($64-$95). C78 x 14 WSW ($32). CR78 x 14 SBR BSW ($57-$89). CR78 x 14 SBR WSW ($89-$121). DR78 x 14 SBR BSW ($57-$112). DR78 x 14 SBR WSW ($89-$144). Space-saver spare ($14) except (NC) with radial tires.

MONARCH CONVENIENCE/APPEARANCE OPTIONS: Option Packages: 'S' group ($483-$511). Interior decor group ($192). Convenience group ($27-$79). Bumper group ($68). Light group ($40). Cold weather group ($18-$51). Heavy-duty group ($26-$51). Protection group ($26-$41). Visibility group ($4-$50). Comfort/Convenience: Air cond. ($464); auto-temp ($499). Rear defogger ($46). Rear defroster, electric ($78). Fingertip speed control ($98). Illuminated entry system ($50). Power windows ($101-$140). Power door locks ($66-$93). Power decklid release ($17). Power four-way seat ($126). Tinted glass ($50). Tilt steering wheel ($57). Digital clock ($42). Lighting and Mirrors: Cornering lamps ($40). Dual racing mirrors ($31-$45). Lighted right visor vanity mirror ($42). Entertainment: AM radio ($75); w/tape player, ($203). AM/FM radio ($151). AM/FM stereo radio ($222); w/tape player ($317). Exterior: Power moonroof ($833). Full or landau vinyl roof ($109). Glamour paint ($57). Bodyside moldings ($37). Rocker panel moldings ($20). Decklid luggage rack ($54). Interior: Console ($69). Four-way seat ($32). Reclining bucket seats ($64). Leather seat trim ($192). Barletta cloth seat ($12). Luxury cloth trim ($93). Color-keyed seatbelts ($18). Wheels/Tires: Deluxe wheel covers ($31) exc. Ghia (NC). Wire wheel covers ($77-$86). Styled steel wheels w/trim rings ($74-$95). Cast aluminum wheels ($118-$213). White aluminum wheels ($138-$232). DR78 x 14 SBR WSW. ER78 x 14 SBR BSW/WSW. FR78 x 14 SBR BSW/WSW/wide WSW.

1977 Mercury Marquis pillared hardtop. (M)

COUGAR CONVENIENCE/APPEARANCE OPTIONS: Option Packages: Sports instrumentation group ($130-$151). Appearance protection group ($42-$50). Bumper group ($68). Convenience group ($53-$130). Power lock group ($92-$121). Comfort/Convenience: Air cond. ($505); w/auto-temp control ($551). Rear defroster, electric ($82). Fingertip speed control ($78-$97). Illuminated entry system ($51). Tinted glass ($57). Power windows ($114-$158). Power tailgate window: wag ($47). Six-way power seat ($143). Leather-wrapped steering wheel ($61). Tilt steering wheel ($63). Day/date clock ($21-$42). Lighting and Mirrors: Cornering lamps ($50). Remote driver's mirror ($14). Dual racing mirrors ($51). Lighted visor vanity mirror ($42). Entertainment: AM radio ($79). AM/FM radio ($132). AM/FM stereo radio ($192); w/tape player ($266); w/quadrasonic tape player ($399). AM/FM stereo search radio ($349). Dual rear speakers ($42). Exterior: Power moonroof: XR-7 ($934). Full vinyl roof ($111-$161). Opera vinyl roof ($111). Opera windows ($50). Bodyside moldings ($42). Rocker panel moldings ($26). Glamour paint ($63). Two-tone paint ($45-$66). Paint stripes ($33). Luggage rack: wag ($100). Interior: Twin comfort seats: XR-7 ($141). Flight Bench seat: wag ($66). Leather seat trim: XR-7 ($241). Bucket seats w/console ($141-$207). Rear-facing third seat: wag ($113). Vinyl seat trim ($28). Color-keyed seatbelts ($18). Wheels/Tires: Deluxe wheel covers ($29). Luxury wheel covers ($32-$61). Wire wheel covers ($100-$129). Cast aluminum wheels ($211-$239). Styled wheels: XR-7 ($146). Styled wheels w/trim rings ($72-$101). HR78 x 14 SBR WSW ($41-$68). HR78 x 14 wide-band WSW ($55). JR78 x 14 SBR WSW ($68). XR-7 Tires: HR78 x 15 WSW ($46-$61). HR70 x 15 WSW ($67).

MARQUIS CONVENIENCE/APPEARANCE OPTIONS: Option Packages: Grand Marquis decor ($543). Colony Park option ($315). Tu-tone group ($63-$215). Lock/convenience group ($91-$134). Visibility light group ($46-$86). Protection group ($56). Comfort/Convenience: Air cond. ($543); w/auto-temp control ($582). Rear defroster, electric ($85). Fingertip speed control ($86-$107). Illuminated entry system ($54). Power windows ($116-$172). Power vent windows ($84). Six-way power driver's seat ($139); driver and passenger ($272). Tinted glass ($70). Tilt steering wheel ($63). Digital clock ($31-$52). Interval wipers ($29). Lighting and Mirrors: Cornering lamps ($43). Driver's remote mirror ($15). Lighted visor vanity mirror ($46). Entertainment: AM radio ($82). AM/FM radio (N/A). AM/FM stereo radio ($250); w/tape player ($360); w/quadrasonic tape player ($499). AM/FM stereo search radio ($409). Dual rear speakers ($42). Power antenna ($81). Exterior: Power moonroof ($926). Full vinyl roof ($134). Landau vinyl roof ($134). Fender skirts ($43). Glamour paint ($63). Paint stripes ($31). Rocker panel moldings ($28). Bodyside moldings ($40). Door edge guards ($8-$17). Rear bumper guards ($20). Luggage rack ($106). Interior: Dual-facing rear seats: wagon ($134). Twin comfort seats ($152). Vinyl seat trim ($28). Floor mats ($10). Deluxe seatbelts ($20). Lockable side stowage compartment ($46). Wheels/Tires: Luxury wheel covers ($81). Wire wheel covers ($105). Forged aluminum wheels ($251). HR78 x 15 SBR WSW. JR78 x 15 SBR BSW/WSW/wide WSW. LR78 x 15 SBR WSW.

HISTORY: Introduced: October 1, 1976. Model year production: 531,549 (including 3,616 Bobcats produced as 1978 models but sold as 1977s, but not incl. Canadian Bobcats). Calendar year production (U.S.): 583,055. Calendar year sales by U.S. dealers: 508,132. Model year sales by U.S. dealers: 475,211.

HISTORY: Full-size and luxury models demonstrated a strong sales rise for the 1977 model year, while subcompacts (Bobcat and the imported Capri) declined by nearly 15 percent. That's how it was throughout the industry, though, as customers still craved big cars. The compact Comet and Monarch both declined substantially, while the full-size Marquis found 21 percent more buyers this year, leading the Lincoln-Mercury division in sales. Sales of the specialty Cougar XR-7 jumped by 53 percent, from 78,497 in 1976 to an impressive 120,044 this season. The new Cougar models did better than the Montegos they replaced, showing an 18 percent sales rise. Fleet sales were becoming more significant for the Lincoln-Mercury division in the mid-1970s, as dealers pushed harder in their leasing/rental departments.

1978 MERCURY

1978 Mercury Bobcat Villager station wagon. (M)

1978 Mercury Zephyr sedan (with Luxury Exterior Decor Group). (OCW)

1978 Mercury Zephyr Z-7 coupe. (PH)

1978 Mercury Zephyr sedan with ES option. (M)

Comet was gone, replaced by the new Zephyr—close relative of Ford's Fairmont. Based on the "Fox" platform, its chassis would serve as the basis for a variety of FoMoCo products in the coming years. Among its mechanical features were MacPherson struts in the front suspension. Mercury's German-import Capri was in its final season, soon to be replaced by a domestic version based on Mustang. Monarch enjoyed a modest restyle, while the big Marquis continued in its large-scale form for one more year.

BOBCAT — FOUR/V-6 — Subcompact appearance and equipment changed little this year, except for new body and interior colors. New options included white-painted aluminum wheels and a stripe treatment in four color combinations. The optional 2.8-liter V-6 had a new lightweight plastic fan. Optional power rack-and-pinion steering had a new variable-ratio system similar to Fairmont/Zephyr. Bobcat again had a domed hood, vertical-textured grille with surround moldings, bright-framed round headlamps, and aluminum bumpers. Combination park/signal lamps sat between the grille and headlamps. High-back front bucket seats came in all-vinyl or cloth and vinyl. The rear bench seat had new split bucket-style cushions. Runabout, station wagon and Villager models were offered. Standard equipment included the 140-cid (2.3-liter) OHC four, four-speed manual gearbox, A78 x 13 BSW tires, full fender splash shields, front bucket seats, lighter, front/rear ashtrays, wide wheel lip and rocker panel moldings, wheel covers, and simulated woodgrain instrument panel appliqué. Power brakes and tinted glass became standard later. Wagons had a liftgate-open warning, high-back bucket seats, three-pod vertical tail lamps, hinged rear-quarter windows, cargo area light, wheel lip and rocker panel moldings, and door-operated courtesy lights. Villager wagons added simulated rosewood appliqués on bodyside and liftgate, and load floor carpeting.

1978 Mercury Monarch sedan. (M)

ZEPHYR — FOUR/SIX/V-8 — Weighing some 300 pounds less than the Comet it replaced, the new Zephyr (and similar Ford Fairmont) came in two-door and four-door sedan form, along with a station wagon. Base engine was a 140-cid (2.3-liter) four with four-speed manual gearbox. Options included both an inline six and small-block V-8. Sixes had three-speed shift. Zephyr had MacPherson strut front suspension with lower control arms, and four-link rear suspension with coil springs. Rack-and-pinion steering was used, and the body was unitized. A total of 13 body colors were available, as well as European-style trim. Quad rectangular headlamps stood directly above quad clear-lensed park/signal lamps, in a clean front-end style that would become typical. Bright frames surrounded the headlamps and parking lamps. Zephyr's vertical-theme grille consisted of many very thin vertical bars, with 'Mercury' lettering on the driver's side. Bumpers were bright anodized aluminum. Body features also included a bright windshield molding, stand-up hood ornament, and upper bodyside dual accent paint stripes. Twin vertical front fender louvers decorated the cowl. Bright wheel lip, rocker panel, door belt and roof drip moldings were used. Wide horizontally-ribbed tail lamps (five ribbed segments) had vertical backup lenses inside, adjoining the license plate recess. Two- and four-door sedans had a wide louver-like design at the rear of the quarter windows or rear door. Doors displayed a thin-line appearance. Low-back bucket seats were upholstered in Colton all-vinyl trim. Steering-column mounted controls operated the wiper/washer, horn, signals and dimmer. Standard equipment included the 2.3-liter OHC four, four-speed manual transmission, high/low ram air ventilation, front disc brakes, foot parking brake, low-back bucket seats (with four-cylinder), bench seats (other engines), woodtone cluster appliqués, header-mounted dome lamp, and deluxe wheel covers. Four-doors and wagons had movable quarter windows. B78 x 14 blackwalls were standard except with V-8 engine, which required CR78 x 14. Zephyr's ES option displayed a different front-end look with blackout grille, black rear hood grille, and no hood ornament. ES also had black window frames and rear window ventilation louver, bright full-length lower bodyside moldings, black lower back panel, and styled wheel covers. Inside was a black three-spoke sports steering wheel, black instrument panel and pad, and full-width gunmetal gray instrument panel appliqué. Dual black outside mirrors were standard. The ES handling suspension included a rear stabilizer bar as well as modified spring rates and shock valving. Rocker panel moldings and upper bodyside paint stripes were deleted. Yet another form was evident on the Zephyr Z-7 sport coupe (kin to Fairmont's Futura Coupe). Most notable was the contemporary wrapover roof design, with very wide B-pillar that held a Z-7 ornament. Z-7 also included hood tape stripes, upper bodyside tape stripes, full-length lower bodyside molding, bright window frames, and wraparound tail lamps. Rocker panel moldings were deleted. Interiors contained pleated Corinthian vinyl seat trim and a woodtone dash appliqué. The Villager station wagon had woodtone bodyside/tailgate appliqués in medium cherry, with bright surround moldings and woodtone inserts. A Luxury Exterior Decor Group included dual accent hood paint stripes, deluxe bodyside protective molding, bright door frame and quarter window moldings, and dual mirrors (driver's remote).

MONARCH — SIX/V-8 — Both Monarch and the closely related Ford Granada entered 1978 with a new look, including new grille, rectangular headlamps, parking lamps, front bumper air spoiler, wide wheel lip moldings, and lower back panel appliqués. Two-doors also sported new "twindow" opera windows (two narrow side-by-side windows in the space one would ordinarily occupy). A new ESS option included black vertical grille texture, rocker panels, door frames and bodyside molding; black rubber bumper guards and wide rub strips; and a unique interior. Also optional: AM/FM stereo with cassette tape player and 40-channel CB. Monarch's spoiler and hood-to-grille-opening panel seal, and revised decklid surface, helped reduce aerodynamic drag. The 302-cid V-8 with variable-venturi carburetor was now available. Single rectangular headlamps stood directly above large clear rectangular park/signal lamps, surrounded by a single bright molding. The vertical-bar grille was similar to 1977, but with a heavier upper header bar that reached to the hood top, with no block lettering above. 'Mercury' script went on the side of the grille, with 'Monarch' script again at the cowl area of front fenders. Narrow amber reflector lenses were set back from the front fender tips. Monarch's hood ornament consisted of a castle-like shape within a circle, with seven tiny "knobs" atop the inner segment. Bright front/rear full wheel lip moldings were used, along with a full-length upper bodyside molding. New full-width wraparound tail lamps were three-pod design. The red reflective back panel appliqué held 'Monarch' lettering. Inside was an all-vinyl Flight Bench seat. Under the hood, a standard 250-cid (4.1-liter) inline six and four-speed manual overdrive gearbox with floor shift lever. Full wheel covers were

standard, along with SBR blackwall tires, an inflatable spare tire, foot parking brake, column-mounted wiper/washer control, and buried woodtone instrument cluster. Monarch Ghia added wire wheel covers, paint stripes on hood and decklid contours, tapered bodyside paint stripes, remote-control driver's mirror, and Ghia ornament on two-door's front quarter panel (or four-door's rear pillar). Ghia's full-length lower bodyside molding had a wide Odense grain color-keyed vinyl insert. Burled walnut woodtone accents went on the deluxe steering wheel and door trim panel. Extra conveniences included seatback map pockets, and rear door courtesy lamp switches on the four-door. Ghia also included a dual-note horn, padded door trim with lower carpeting, and driver's remote mirror. The new ESS (Euro-style) option package included a blackout grille, black wipers, black hood paint stripes, and front/rear bumper guards with horizontal rub strip. Also on ESS: bright wide wheel lip moldings, dual racing mirrors, color-keyed wheel covers, black/argent lower back appliqués, black bodyside molding with bright mylar insert, black rocker panel paint treatment, and black side window surround moldings. Two-doors had a louvered opera window appliqué. ESS equipment included a leather-wrapped three-spoke sport steering wheel, day/night mirror, dual-note horn, Flight Bench seat, FR78 x 14 BSW tires, and heavy-duty suspension.

COUGAR/XR-7 — V-8 — After just one year of availability, station wagons left the Cougar lineup, since the new Zephyr came in wagon form. Little appearance change was evident either on the basic or XR-7 models. Brougham became an option package this year. A 40-channel CB transceiver became optional. A new front bumper air spoiler, hood-to-grille-opening panel seal and other alterations were supposed to reduce XR-7 aerodynamic drag, thus improve gas mileage. A revised low-restriction fresh-air intake went on the 302 and larger V-8s. A new mechanical spark control system hit the 351 and 400-cid V-8 engines. Basic Cougars were related to Ford's LTD II, while Cougar shared structural details with Thunderbird. As in 1977, Cougar's Continental-style grille extended slightly below the front bumper. Atop the hood was a bright new stand-up Cougar-head ornament. Signal/marker lamps in front fender extensions were said to "emphasize the wide stance and clean look." The twin-pod vertical tail-lamp assembly held integral side marker lights. A bright molding surrounded the red reflective rear center appliqué in the lower back panel. Standard Cougar equipment included the 302-cid V-8 and SelectShift three-speed automatic transmission, power brakes/steering, blackwall SBR tires, two-speed wipers, cloth/vinyl bench seat, simulated rosewood dash appliqué, full wheel lip moldings, bright backlight and windshield moldings, bright taillamp bezels with ornament, and Cougar decklight, script. Cougar Brougham added a full vinyl roof (on four-doors), full-length bright bodyside molding with integral wheel lip moldings, and opera windows with 'Brougham' script embedded in the glass. Also on Brougham: upper bodyside paint stripes, bright wide door belt moldings, electric clock, deluxe wheel covers, and Flight Bench seat with folding center armrest. Cougar XR-7 had a grille extension below the bumper, a hood rear edge molding, sport-style roofline with opera window and louvers, and fully padded landau vinyl roof. Its Flight Bench seat came in a new sew style, with accent stripes in Rossano cloth or Mateao vinyl. XR-7 had a rear stabilizer bar and 15 in. wheels. 'Cougar' block lettering went on the "sculptured" simulated-spare portion of the decklid. Horizontal wraparound tail lamps were divided into five segments, three of them on the back panel with an integral backup lamp in one. Standard XR-7 equipment included the 302-cid V-8, SelectShift, power brakes/steering, baby burl walnut woodtone instrument panel appliqués, and day/night mirror. An XR-7 Decor Option included styled wheels, full-length bodyside molding with color-keyed vinyl inserts, color-keyed remote mirrors, Twin Comfort Lounge seats with recliner (or bucket seats with console), and hood stripes. A Midnight/Chamois Decor Option (available later) for XR-7 offered a half vinyl roof with vinyl crossover strap, padded 'Continental' type rear deck, and straight-through paint stripes; plus Midnight Blue and Chamois interior, with Tiffany carpeting.

1978 Mercury Cougar XR-7 "Midnight/Chamois Decor" coupe. (AA)

1978 Mercury Marquis pillared hardtop. (M)

1978 Mercury Grand Marquis pillared hardtop. (M)

MARQUIS — V-8 — Full-size models were carryovers, with new body colors but little other change. Station wagons could now have optional removable auxiliary dual seat cushions. As before, they came in pillarless-look two-door hardtop style, and a narrow-pillar four-door. Standard equipment included the 351-cid (5.8-liter) 2Bbl. V-8 (400-cid engine in California and high-altitude areas), SelectShift three-speed automatic, power brakes/steering, HR78 x 15 SBR tires, bench seat in Althea cloth/vinyl, and fold-down center armrest. Marquis again featured a bright vertical box-textured grille, flanked by concealed headlamps with body-color textured pad and Marquis crest. The front end also displayed integral parking/signal/side marker lights, concealed wipers, and a bright stand-up hood ornament. Vertical front bumper guards had black inserts. Rear pillars held a Marquis plaque. Full wheel lip moldings and bright rocker panel moldings with front extensions were standard. Wraparound horizontal-ribbed tail lamps had integral rear side marker lights, while the textured color-keyed rear center appliqué below the decklid had 'Mercury' block letters and little backup lamps at its ends. Marquis Brougham added a landau vinyl roof (two-door) or full vinyl roof (four-door), both with bright surround molding. The full vinyl roof was also available as a no-cost option on two-doors. Brougham also had power windows, fender skirts with bright molding, full-length upper body peak molding, and a decklid lock cover with L-M crest. Brougham wheel covers displayed slots around the circumference and a center crest emblem. Flight Bench seats had a folding center armrest and automatic seatback release (on two-door). Moving all the way up, Grand Marquis had a vinyl roof, fender skirts, hood and decklid paint stripes, and a gold Marquis crest on the headlamp cover and the rear pillar. Full-length wide bodyside moldings had color-keyed vinyl inserts; rocker panel extensions and wheel lip moldings were deleted. 'Grand Marquis' script highlighted the decklid. Standard features included tinted glass, a digital clock, dual-beam dome/map light, and Twin Comfort lounge seats in Media velour with dual center folding armrests and headrests with vinyl welts.

I.D. DATA: As before, Mercury's 11-symbol Vehicle Identification Number (VIN) is stamped on a metal tab fastened to the instrument panel, visible through the windshield. Coding is similar to 1976-77. Model year code changed to '8' for 1978. One Canadian assembly plant was added: 'X' St. Thomas, Ontario.

BOBCAT RUNABOUT/WAGON (FOUR/V-6)

Model No.	Body/ Style No.	Body Type & Seating	Factory Price	Shipping Weight	Prod. Total
20	64H	3-dr. Hatch-4P	3537/3810	2389/----	23,428
22	73H	2-dr. Sta Wag-4P	3878/4151	2532/----	Note 1

BOBCAT VILLAGER (FOUR/V-6)

22	73H	2-dr. Sta Wag-4P	4010/4283	N/A	Note 1

NOTE 1: Total station wagon production was 8,840 units.

ZEPHYR (FOUR/SIX)

31	66D	2-dr. Sed-5P	3742/3862	2572/2615	27,673
32	54D	4-dr. Sed-5P	3816/3936	2614/2657	47,334
36	74D	4-dr. Sta Wag-5P	4184/4304	2722/2765	32,596

ZEPHYR Z-7 (FOUR/SIX)

35	36R	2-dr. Spt Cpe-5P	4095/4215	2609/2652	44,569

Zephyr Engine Note: A V-8 engine cost $199 more than the six.

MONARCH (SIX/V-8)

35	66H	2-dr. Sedan-5P	4330/4511	3058/3130	38,939
34	54H	4-dr. Sedan-5P	4409/4590	3102/3174	52,775

COUGAR (V-8)

91	65D	2-dr. HT Cpe-6P	5009	3761	21,398
92	53D	4-dr. Pill. HT-6P	5126	3848	25,364

COUGAR XR-7 (V-8)

93	65L	2-dr. HT Cpe-6P	5603	3865	166,508

MARQUIS (V-8)

61	65H	2-dr. HT-6P	5764	4296	11,176
62	53H	4-dr. Pill. HT-6P	5806	4328	27,793
74	71K	4-dr. 2S Sta Wag-6P	5958	4578	16,883
74	71K	4-dr. 3S Sta Wag-8P	N/A	4606	Note 2

NOTE 2: Production total for three-seat station wagon is included in two-seat figure.

MARQUIS BROUGHAM (V-8)

63	65K	2-dr. HT-6P	6380	4317	10,368
64	53K	4-dr. Pill. HT-6P	6480	4346	26,030

GRAND MARQUIS (V-8)

Model No.	Body/ Style No.	Body Type & Seating	Factory Price	Shipping Weight	Prod. Total
65	65L	2-dr. HT-6P	7132	4342	15,624
66	53L	4-dr. Pill. HT-6P	7232	4414	37,753

FACTORY PRICE AND WEIGHT NOTE: Monarch prices and weights to left of slash are for six-cylinder, to right for V-8 engine. For Bobcat and Zephyr, prices/weights to left of slash are for four-cylinder, to right for V-6.

ENGINE [Base Four (Bobcat, Zephyr)]: Inline. Overhead cam. Four-cylinder. Cast-iron block and head. Displacement: 140-cid (2.3 liters). Bore & stroke: 3.78 x 3.13 in. Compression ratio: 9.0:1. Brake horsepower: 88 at 4800 rpm. Torque: 118 lbs.-ft. at 2800 rpm. Five main bearings. Hydraulic valve lifters. Carburetor: 2Bbl. Motorcraft 5200. VIN Code: Y.

ENGINE [Optional V-6 (Bobcat)]: 60-degree, overhead-valve V-6. Cast-iron block and head. Displacement: 170.8-cid (2.8 liters). Bore & stroke: 3.66 x 2.70 in. Compression ratio: 8.7:1. Brake horsepower: 90 at 4200 rpm. Torque: 143 lbs.-ft. at 2200 rpm. Four main bearings. Hydraulic valve lifters. Carburetor: 2Bbl. Motorcraft 2150. VIN Code: Z.

ENGINE [Optional Six (Zephyr)]: Inline. OHV. Six-cylinder. Cast-iron block and head. Displacement: 200-cid (3.3 liters). Bore & stroke: 3.68 x 3.13 in. Compression ratio: 8.5:1. Brake horsepower: 85 at 3600 rpm. Torque: 154 lbs.-ft. at 1600 rpm. Seven main bearings. Hydraulic valve lifters. Carburetor: 1Bbl. Carter YFA. VIN Code: T.

ENGINE [Base Six (Monarch)]: Inline. OHV. Six-cylinder. Cast-iron block and head. Displacement: 250-cid (4.1 liters). Bore & stroke: 3.68 x 3.91 in. Compression ratio: 8.5:1. Brake horsepower: 97 at 3200 rpm. Torque: 210 lbs.-ft. at 1400 rpm. Seven main bearings. Hydraulic valve lifters. Carburetor: 1Bbl. Carter YFA or Holley 1946. VIN Code: L.

ENGINE [Base V-8 (Cougar); Optional (Zephyr, Monarch)]: 90-degree, overhead valve V-8. Cast-iron block and head. Displacement: 302-cid (5.0 liters). Bore & stroke: 4.00 x 3.00 in. Compression ratio: 8.4:1. Brake horsepower: 134-139 at 3400-3600 rpm. Torque: 248-250 lbs.-ft. at 1600 rpm. Five main bearings. Hydraulic valve lifters. Carburetor: 2Bbl. Motorcraft 2150. VIN Code: F.

ENGINE [Base V-8 (Marquis); Optional (Cougar)]: 90-degree, overhead valve V-8. Cast-iron block and head. Displacement: 351-cid (5.8 liters). Bore & stroke: 4.00 x 3.50 in. Compression ratio: 8.3:1. Brake horsepower: 145-152 at 3400-3600 rpm. Torque: 273-278 lbs.-ft. at 1800 rpm. Five main bearings. Hydraulic valve lifters. Carburetor: 2Bbl. Motorcraft 2150. Windsor engine. VIN Code: H.

ENGINE [Optional V-8 (Cougar/Marquis)]: 90-degree, overhead valve V-8. Cast-iron block and head. Displacement: 400-cid (6.6 liters). Bore & stroke: 4.00 x 4.00 in. Compression ratio: 8.0:1. Brake horsepower: 160-166 at 3800 rpm. Torque: 314-319 lbs.-ft. at 1800 rpm. Five main bearings. Hydraulic valve lifters. Carburetor: 2Bbl. Motorcraft 2150. VIN Code: S.

ENGINE [Base V-8 (Grand Marquis); Optional (Marquis)]: 90-degree, overhead valve V-8. Cast-iron block and head. Displacement: 460-cid (7.5 liters). Bore & stroke: 4.36 x 3.85 in. Compression ratio:

8.0:1. Brake horsepower: 202 at 4000 rpm. Torque: 348 lbs.-ft. at 2000 rpm. Five main bearings. Hydraulic valve lifters. Carburetor: 4Bbl. Motorcraft 4350. VIN Code: A.

CHASSIS DATA: Wheelbase: (Bobcat sed) 94.5 in.; (Bobcat wag) 94.8 in.; (Zephyr) 105.5 in.; (Monarch) 109.9 in.; (Cougar 2-dr.) 114.0 in.; (Cougar 4-dr.) 118.0 in.; (Marquis) 124.0 in.; (Marquis wag) 121.0 in. Overall Length: (Bobcat sed) 169.3 in.; (Bobcat wag) 179.8 in.; (Zephyr) 193.8 in.; (Z-7) 195.8 in.; (Monarch) 197.7 in.; (Cougar 2-dr.) 215.5 in.; (Cougar 4-dr.) 219.5 in.; (Marquis) 229.0 in.; (Marquis wag) 227.1 in. Height: (Bobcat sed) 50.6 in.; (Bobcat wag) 52.1 in.; (Zephyr) 53.5 in.; (Zephyr wag) 54.7 in.; (Z-7) 52.2 in.; (Monarch) 53.2-53.3 in.; (Cougar 2-dr.) 52.6 in.; (Cougar 4-dr.) 53.3 in.; (XR-7) 52.9 in.; (Marquis 2-dr.) 53.7-53.8 in.; (Marquis 4-dr.) 54.7-54.8 in.; (Marquis wag) 56.9 in. Width: (Bobcat sed) 69.4 in.; (Bobcat wag) 69.7 in.; (Zephyr) 70.2 in.; (Monarch) 74.0 in.; (Cougar) 78.6 in.; (Marquis) 79.6-79.7 in. Front Tread: (Bobcat) 55.0 in.; (Zephyr) 56.6 in.; (Monarch) 59.0 in.; (Cougar) 63.6 in.; (XR-7) 63.2 in.; (Marquis) 64.1 in. Rear Tread: (Bobcat) 55.8 in.; (Zephyr) 57.0 in.; (Monarch) 57.7 in.; (Cougar) 63.5 in.; (XR-7) 63.1 in.; (Marquis) 64.3 in. Standard Tires: (Bobcat) A78 x 13 BSW; (Zephyr) B78 x 14 BSW; (Zephyr V-8) CR78 x 14; (Monarch) DR78 x 14 BSW; (Cougar) HR78 x 14 BSW; (XR-7) HR78 x 15 BSW; (Marquis) HR78 x 15; (Marquis wag) JR78 x 15.

TECHNICAL: Transmission: Three-speed manual transmission (column shift) standard on Zephyr six. Gear ratios: (1st) 3.56:1; (2nd) 1.90:1; (3rd) 1.00:1; (Rev) 3.78:1. Four-speed overdrive floor shift standard on Monarch: (1st) 3.29:1; (2nd) 1.84:1; (3rd) 1.00:1; (4th) 0.81:1; (Rev) 3.29:1. Four-speed floor shift standard on Bobcat/Zephyr four: (1st) 3.98:1; (2nd) 2.14:1; (3rd) 1.42:1; (4th) 1.00:1; (Rev) 3.99:1. SelectShift three-speed automatic (column lever) standard on Cougar and Marquis, optional on others. Bobcat L4-140 automatic gear ratios: (1st) 2.47:1; (2nd) 1.47:1; (3rd) 1.00:1; (Rev) 2.11:1. Cougar/Marquis with V8-351: (1st) 2.40:1; (2nd) 1.47:1; (3rd) 1.00:1; (Rev) 2.00:1. Other automatics: (1st) 2.46:1; (2nd) 1.46:1; (3rd) 1.00:1; (Rev) 2.18:1 to 2.20:1. Standard final drive ratio: (Bobcat) 2.73:1 w/four, 3.40:1 w/V-6; (Zephyr) 3.08:1 w/four, 2.73:1 w/six and 2.47:1 w/V-8; (Monarch) 3.00:1 w/six and 4-spd, 2.47:1 w/auto.; (Cougar) 2.75:1 w/V8-302, 2.50:1 w/V8-351/400. (Marquis) 2.47:1 w/V8-400, 2.50:1 w/V8-460. Steering: (Bobcat/Zephyr) rack-and-pinion; (others) recirculating ball. Front Suspension: (Bobcat) coil springs with short/long control arms, lower leading arms, and anti-sway bar on wagon; (Zephyr) MacPherson struts w/coil springs mounted on lower control arm; (others) coil springs w/lower trailing links and anti-sway bar. Rear Suspension: (Bobcat/Monarch) rigid axle w/semi-elliptic leaf springs; (Zephyr) four-link w/coil springs; (Cougar/Marquis) rigid axle with upper/lower control arms and coil springs. Brakes: Front disc, rear drum. Ignition: Electronic. Body construction: (Bobcat/Zephyr/Monarch) unibody; (others) separate body on perimeter frame; Fuel tank: (Bobcat) 11.7 or 13 gal. exc. wagon, 14 gal.; (Zephyr) 16.0 gal.; (Monarch) 18.0 gal.; (Cougar) 21.0 gal.; (Marquis) 24.2 gal. exc. wagon. 21 gal.

DRIVETRAIN OPTIONS: Engines: 170-cid V-6: Bobcat ($273). 200-cid, 1Bbl. six: Zephyr ($120). 302-cid, 2Bbl. V-8: Monarch ($181). 351-cid, 2Bbl. V-8: Cougar ($157). 400-cid, 2Bbl. V-8: Cougar ($283); Marquis ($126). 460-cid, 4Bbl. V-8: Marquis ($271). Transmission/Differential: SelectShift Cruise-O-Matic: Bobcat/Zephyr ($281); Monarch ($193). Floor shift lever: Zephyr/Monarch ($30). First-gear lockout: Zephyr (NC). Traction-Lok differential: Cougar ($59); Marquis ($63). Optional axle ratio: Bobcat ($13); Marquis ($14). Brakes & Steering: Power brakes: Bobcat (N/A); Zephyr/Monarch ($63). Four-wheel power disc brakes: Monarch ($300); Marquis ($197). Power steering: Bobcat ($131); Zephyr ($140); Monarch ($148). Suspension: H.D. susp.: Monarch ($27). Handling susp.: Zephyr ($30). Cross-country susp.: Cougar ($20); Marquis ($26). Other: H.D. battery: Zephyr ($18); Cougar/Marquis ($20). H.D. alternator: Cougar/Marquis ($49). Engine block heater: Bobcat/Zephyr/Monarch ($12); Cougar ($13); Marquis ($21). Trailer towing pkg. (heavy duty): Cougar ($184); Marquis ($138). California emission system: Bobcat/Zephyr/Monarch ($69); Cougar/Marquis ($75). High-altitude option (NC).

BOBCAT CONVENIENCE/APPEARANCE OPTIONS: Option Packages: Sports accent group ($212-$235). Sports instrument/handling group ($90). Sports pkg. ($108). Convenience/light group ($72-$137). Bumper group ($70). Protection group ($40). Comfort/Convenience: Air conditioner ($459). Rear defroster, electric ($77). Tinted glass (NC). Driver's remote mirror ($14). Day/night mirror ($7). Entertainment: AM radio ($72); w/digital clock ($119); w/stereo tape player ($192). AM/FM radio ($120). AM/FM stereo radio ($161). Exterior: Flip-up/removable moonroof ($167). Sunroof ($259). Sports vinyl roof ($145). Glass third door ($25). Hinged quarter windows ($41). Glamour paint ($40). Narrow bodyside moldings ($39); wide ($67). Roof luggage rack ($59). Rocker panel moldings ($22). Lower bodyside protection ($30). Interior: Four-way bucket seat ($33). Load floor carpet ($23). Cargo area cover ($25). Deluxe interior ($158-$181). Deluxe seatbelts ($18). Wheels/Tires: Wire wheel covers ($20). Forged aluminum wheels ($128); white ($141). Styled steel wheels (NC). Trim rings ($34). BR78 x 13 WSW ($42). BR70 x 13 RWL ($77).

ZEPHYR CONVENIENCE/APPEARANCE OPTIONS: Option Packages: ES option ($180). Villager option ($169). Exterior decor group ($96). Interior decor group ($72). Luxury interior ($199-$289). Bumper protection group ($70). Convenience group ($36). Appearance protection group ($36-$43). Light group ($36-$40). Comfort/Convenience: Air cond. ($465). Rear defogger ($47). Rear defroster, electric ($84). Tinted glass ($52). Sport steering wheel ($36). Electric clock ($20). Cigar lighter ($6). Interval wipers ($29). Liftgate wiper/washer: wag ($78). Map light ($16). Trunk light ($6). Left remote mirror ($14). Dual mirrors ($14-$30). Day/night mirror ($7). Entertainment: AM radio ($72); w/8-track tape player ($192). AM/FM radio ($120). AM/FM stereo radio ($176); w/8-track or cassette player ($243). Exterior: Vinyl roof ($89). Glamour paint ($46). Two-tone paint ($42). Pivoting front vent windows ($54). Rear vent louvers ($33). Bodyside moldings ($39). Rocker panel moldings ($24-$29). Bright window frames ($24-$29). Bumper guards, front and rear ($37). Luggage rack ($72). Lower bodyside protection ($30-$42). Interior: Bucket seats ($72). Cloth seat trim ($19-$37). Lockable side storage box ($19). H.D. mats ($8). Wheels/Tires: Styled wheel covers ($33). Wire wheel covers ($81). Aluminum wheels ($242). B78 x 14 WSW. BR78 x 14 BSW/WSW. C78 x 14 BSW/WSW. CR78 x 14 BSW/WSW. DR78 x 14 SBR BSW/WSW/RWL.

MONARCH CONVENIENCE/APPEARANCE OPTIONS: Option Packages: ESS option ($524). Ghia option ($426). Interior decor group ($211). Convenience group ($33-$89). Bumper protection group ($70). Light group ($43). Cold weather group ($36-$54). Heavy-duty group ($36-$54). Protection group ($29-$43). Visibility group ($7-$58). Comfort/Convenience: Air cond. ($494); auto-temp ($535). Rear defogger ($47). Rear defroster, electric ($84). Fingertip speed control ($102). Illuminated entry system ($49). Power windows ($116-$160). Power door locks ($76-$104). Power decklid release ($19). Auto. parking brake release ($8). Power four-way seat ($90). Tinted glass ($54). Tilt steering wheel ($58). Digital clock ($42). Lighting and Mirrors: Cornering lamps ($42). Trunk light ($6). Left remote mirror ($14). Right remote mirror ($31). Dual racing mirrors ($39-$53). Day/night mirror ($7). Lighted right visor vanity mirror ($34). Entertainment: AM radio ($72); w/tape player ($192). AM/FM radio ($135). AM/FM stereo radio ($176); w/8-track or cassette player ($243); w/quadrasonic tape ($365). AM/FM stereo search radio ($319). CB radio ($270). Exterior: Power moonroof ($820). Full or landau vinyl roof ($102). Glamour paint ($46). Bodyside moldings ($39). Rocker panel moldings ($23). Lower bodyside protection ($30). Interior: Console ($75). Four-way seat ($33). Reclining bucket seats ($84). Leather seat trim ($271). Barletta cloth seat ($54). Luxury cloth seat/door trim ($99). Deluxe seatbelts ($19). Wheels: Deluxe wheel covers ($37) exc. Ghia/ESS (NC). Wire wheel covers ($59-$96). Styled steel wheels w/trim rings ($59-$96). Cast aluminum wheels ($146-$242): white ($159-$255). Tires: DR78 x 14 SBR WSW. ER78 x 14 SBR BSW/WSW. FR78 x 14 SBR BSW/WSW/wide WSW.

COUGAR CONVENIENCE/APPEARANCE OPTIONS: Option Packages: Brougham option ($271-$383). Midnight/chamois decor group: XR-7 ($592). Sports instrumentation group ($100-$138). Decor group ($211-$461). Bumper protection group ($76). Light group ($51). Convenience group ($58-$139). Power lock group ($100-$132). Appearance protection group ($45-$53). Comfort/Convenience: Air cond. ($543); w/auto-temp control ($588). Rear defroster, electric ($93). Fingertip speed control ($99-$117). Illuminated entry system ($54). Tinted glass ($66). Power windows ($126-$175). Power seat ($149). Auto. parking brake release ($9). Leather-wrapped steering wheel ($64). Tilt steering wheel ($70). Day/date clock ($22-$42). Lighting, Horns and Mirrors: Cornering lamps ($46). Trunk light ($7). Dual-note horn ($7). Remote driver's mirror ($16). Dual racing mirrors ($58). Lighted visor vanity mirror ($37). Entertainment: AM radio ($79). AM/FM radio ($132). AM/FM stereo radio ($192); w/tape player ($266); w/quadrasonic tape player ($399). AM/FM stereo search radio ($349). CB radio ($295). Upgraded sound ($29). Dual rear speakers ($46). Power antenna: XR-7 ($42). Exterior: Power moonroof ($789). Front/landau vinyl roof ($112). Full vinyl roof ($112-$163). Opera windows ($51). Bodyside moldings ($42). Wide bodyside moldings: XR-7 ($55). Rocker panel moldings: Brghm ($29). Glamour paint ($62). Two-tone paint ($41-$95). Paint striping ($33). Bumper guards ($49). Lower body side protection ($33). Interior: Twin comfort seats w/passenger recliner: XR-7 ($175). Bucket seats w/console ($175-$247). Vinyl bench seat ($28). Leather seat: XR-7 ($296). Trunk trim ($39). Color-keyed seatbelts ($27). Wheels/Tires: Deluxe wheel covers ($38). Luxury wheel covers ($30-$68). 15 in. wheel covers ($38). Wire wheel covers ($105-$143). Cast aluminum wheels ($118-$303). Styled wheels ($146). Styled wheels w/trim rings ($105-$143) exc. XR-7. HR78 x 14 SBR WSW ($46). HR78 x 14 wide-band WSW ($66). HR78 x 15 SBR WSW ($68).

MARQUIS CONVENIENCE/APPEARANCE OPTIONS: Option Packages: Colony Park option ($547). Grand Marquis decor: wag ($559). Tu-tone group ($72-$151). Lock convenience group ($108-$161). Bumper protection group ($59). Appearance protection group ($50-$58). Visibility light group ($47-$96). Comfort/Convenience: Air cond. ($583); w/auto-temp control ($628). Rear defroster, electric ($84). Fingertip speed control ($101-$120). Illuminated entry system ($54). Power windows ($129-$188). Six-way power driver's seat ($149); driver and passenger ($297). Tinted glass ($75); windshield only ($36). Tilt steering wheel ($72). Digital clock ($26-$49). Interval wipers ($32). Lighting and Mirrors: Cornering lamps ($46). Driver's remote mirror ($16). Lighted visor vanity mirror ($33-$37). Entertainment: AM radio ($79). AM/FM stereo radio ($192); w/tape player ($266); w/quadrasonic tape player ($399). AM/FM stereo search radio ($349). Dual rear speakers ($46). Power antenna ($42). Exterior: Power moonroof ($896). Full or landau vinyl roof ($141). Fender skirts ($50). Glamour metallic paint ($62). Paint stripes ($34). Rocker panel moldings ($29). Narrow bodyside moldings ($42). Rear bumper guards: wag ($22). Luggage rack: wag ($80). Lower bodyside protection ($33). Interior: Dual-facing rear seats: wagon ($186). Twin comfort seats ($97); w/passenger recliner ($149). Reclining passenger seat ($63). Vinyl bench seat trim ($29). Deluxe floor mats ($36). Deluxe seatbelts ($21). Lockable side storage compartment: wag ($49). Wheels/Tires: Luxury wheel covers ($55-$84). Wire wheel covers ($30-$109). Forged aluminum wheels ($236-$264). HR78 x 15 SBR WSW. JR78 x 15 SBR BSW/WSW/wide WSW. LR78 x 15 SBR WSW.

HISTORY: Introduced: October 7, 1977. Model year production: 635,051. Calendar year production (U.S.): 624,229. Calendar year sales by U.S. dealers: 579,498 (incl. 18,035 Capris). Model year sales by U.S. dealers: 571,118.

HISTORY: Model year sales for Lincoln-Mercury division climbed 15 percent, led by Cougar's XR-7, setting a new record for the second year in-a-row. This put L-M surprisingly close to Buick in the sales race. A total of 152,591 Cougar XR-7 models found buyers. Second best seller was the full-size Marquis, again demonstrating the continued appeal of big cars. Some of the sales, though, may well have been due to the fact that downsizing was expected for 1979, so this would be the last chance for big-car fans. The new compact Zephyr sold far better than had Comet in its final (1977) year. This was the final year for the imported Capri, as a domestic Mercury of that name (closely related to the Ford Mustang) was being readied for the '79 model year.

1979 MERCURY

1979 Mercury Capri two-door hatchback. (OCW)

1979 Mercury Grand Marquis. (OCW)

Two all-new vehicles entered the Mercury stable for 1979: Capri and Marquis. The Capri nameplate moved from a German-made model to a clone of Ford's Mustang. The full-size Marquis was sharply downsized, losing some 800 pounds and 17 inches of overall length. A second generation of electronic controls (EEC-II) was now standard on Marquis with the optional 351W V-8. Bobcat got a significant styling change, with new front/rear appearance. Option availability expanded considerably, especially in Capri and Zephyr, which offered many more options than their predecessors, including speed control (available for first time with manual shift) and tilt steering. AM/FM stereo radios with cassette tape players, formerly offered only on Zephyr and Monarch, were now available in all models. Various engines had a new electronic voltage regulator.

1979 Mercury Marquis Colony Park station wagon. (OCW)

1979 Mercury Bobcat "Sports Option" hatchback coupe. (M)

BOBCAT — FOUR/V-6 — Rectangular headlamps and a new rakishly sloped, fine-patterned grille dominated by vertical bars gave Mercury's subcompact a fresh front-end look. The hood and front fenders also sloped more than before. Vertical-styled park/signal lamps were inboard of the single headlamps, in the same recessed housings. New front side marker lamps had no surround moldings. A new rear-end appearance on the Runabout included unique horizontal tail lamps and exposed black third-door hinges; but the wagon retained its three-pod vertical configuration with integrated backup lights. Bright extruded aluminum bumpers had black rubber end caps. Villager wagons added new rosewood-grain bodyside appliqués with simulated wood surround moldings. Inside was a new rectangular instrument cluster, with miles/kilometer speedometer. This was the first Bobcat restyle since its 1975 debut. Five new paint colors were offered. The optional V-6 had a higher-performance camshaft this year, and engines had a new electronic voltage regulator. Standard tires grew to BR78 x 13 steel-belted radials.

1979 Mercury Capri RS hatchback coupe. (M)

1979 Mercury Capri hatchback coupe. (PH)

CAPRI — FOUR/V-6/V-8 — No longer did Mercury have to do without a domestically built equivalent to Ford's Mustang. Capri differed mainly in grille pattern and body details from the Ford pony car. Unlike Mustang, though, the Mercury version came only in three-door hatchback body style. The company described the shape as a "linear, flowing look highlighted by a sloping roof, soft front and rear bumper coverings, and standard wide bodyside moldings... to create a wraparound effect." Two models were offered: base and Ghia, plus an R/S and Turbo R/S option. The latter included a turbocharged turbo four and TRX tires and suspension. TRX was one of three specially-tuned variants of the Zephyr-type suspension system. It came with new low-profile wide-aspect Michelin 190/65R390 TRX tires. Base engine was a 140-cid (2.3-liter) four. Capri could also have a 2.8-liter V-6 or 302-cid (5.0-liter) V-8. Only on Capri did the optional V-8 have a single belt accessory drive system. That engine also hooked to a four-speed manual overdrive transmission with new single-rail shift design, standard on all Capris. Capri featured a horizontal-bar black and bright grille, flanked by quad rectangular headlamps in bright frames. A sloping hood held color-keyed simulated (non-working) louvers. Wide black bodyside moldings with dual color-keyed center stripe accompanied partial wheel lip moldings. Body trim included upper bodyside paint stripes: black window frame moldings with black frames; black belt and cowl moldings; bright windshield, rear window and drip moldings; black wiper arms; and a black window-frame-mounted remote-control driver's mirror. Soft bumpers were color-keyed. Steel wheels came with hub covers and lug nuts. Large horizontal wraparound tail lamps carried integral backup lights. On the mechanical front, Capri had a strut-type coil-spring front suspension with stabilizer, four-bar link coil-spring rear suspension, unitized body, and rack-and-pinion steering. Front high-back bucket seats carried pleated trim. Dashboards held a tachometer and gauges in woodtone cluster appliqué, with European ISO style identification symbols on controls. A three-spoke sport steering wheel was standard. Capri rode a 100.4-inch wheelbase and measured 179.1 inches in length. Standard tires were B78 x 13. Among Capri's new options were tilt steering and speed control (offered for the first time on a FoMoCo car with floor-shift automatic or manual). Capri Ghia came with BR78 x 14 radial tires, dual black remote-control outside mirrors, argent sport wheel covers, a light group, soft-rim sport steering wheel, low-back bucket seats with European headrests, door map pockets, and passenger assist handle on roof rail. Capri R/S option equipment included BR78 x 14 RWL tires and handling suspension; black grille, headlamp housings and quarter louvers; argent sport wheel covers: black greenhouse moldings: hood scoop; dual black window-frame-mounted remote mirrors; and bright tailpipe extension. Tape treatment on bodysides (over the wheels) substituted for the usual pin stripes. inside were engine-turned instrument panel appliqués and Ghia soft door trim panels. In addition to the turbo-charged engine and TRX suspension, the Turbo R/S option included a sport-tuned exhaust and tailpipe extension, three-spoke TRX aluminum wheels, and low-back bucket seats with European headrests. Turbo models came only with four-speed manual.

1979 Mercury Zephyr sedan. (M)

1979 Mercury Zephyr coupe (with Exterior Decor Group). (OCW)

ZEPHYR — FOUR/SIX/V-8 — For its second year in Mercury's lineup, Zephyr looked the same but enjoyed a few mechanical improvements and extra options. Four-speed overdrive manual shift became standard this year for both the 200-cid (3.3-liter) V-6 and 302-cid (5.0-liter) V-8 engines. A new single-rail shift mechanism with enclosed linkage was supposed to eliminate the need for adjustments. California station wagons could now get the 3.3-liter six. The 302 V-8 with SelectShift had reduced rear axle ratio, now 2.26:1. Options added to Zephyr during the 1978 model year included power seats, windows and door locks; plus a flip-up removable moonroof. New options this year included speed control, tilt steering, performance instruments, and electric trunk lid release. Eight body colors were new. A revised tone-on-tone paint treatment was available on sedans, and on Z-7 (except ES type, which had its own unique paint treatment). Zephyr police and taxi packages had been introduced during the 1978 model year. Zephyr had a vertical-design grille, quad rectangular headlamps in bright frames, bright rocker panel and wheel lip moldings, deluxe wheel covers, and upper bodyside dual paint stripes. Front bucket seats came with four-cylinder models, but bench seating with six/V-8. In addition to its unique wrapover roof design with wide center pillar, the Z-7 sport coupe added tinted rear window glass, large wraparound tail lamps, special hood and bodyside tape stripes, full-length vinyl-insert bodyside molding, bright window frames, and pleated vinyl seat trim. Z-7 deleted the base model's rocker panel moldings. Zephyr wagons had tinted liftgate glass and a cargo area light. Villager wagons added woodtone bodyside and tailgate appliqués in medium cherry color, with woodtone-insert bright surround moldings. On the option list, Zephyr ES added a handling suspension and bumper protection group; blackout grille treatment; dual black mirrors (driver's remote); and black cowl grille that was almost full hood width. ES also sported black window frames and rear window ventilation louvers, full-length bright lower bodyside molding, black lower back panel, styled wheel covers with unique all-bright treatment, and gray engine-turned instrument panel and cluster appliqués. ES deleted the usual hood ornament, paint stripes, rocker panel and wheel lip moldings.

MONARCH — SIX/V-8 — Blackout paint treatment on the vertical-theme grille was Monarch's major body change this year. Bright vinyl roof moldings replaced the former color-keyed moldings. Engines had new electronic voltage regulators. A new single-rail shift four-speed manual overdrive transmission came in an aluminum case, and a new lightweight aluminum intake manifold went on the 302-cid V-8 (installed in four-doors). Options dropped included four-wheel power disc brakes, and Traction-Lok. Monarchs had single rectangular headlamps, a stand-up hood ornament, bright upper bodyside and wheel lip moldings, full wheel covers, and red reflectorized back panel appliqué with integral fuel filler door. Base engine was the 250-cid inline six; standard tires, DR78 x 14 blackwall steel-belted radials. All-vinyl Flight Bench seating was standard, as was a burled woodtone instrument cluster. In addition to the base model, Ghia and ES option groups were available. The Ghia option group included a dual-note horn; day/night mirror; paint stripes on hood, upper bodyside and decklid; wire wheel covers; and wide Odense grain vinyl bodyside moldings and partial wheel lip moldings. Lettering on the cowl read 'ESS Monarch' (formerly 'Monarch ESS') when that package was installed. The ESS group included FR78 x 14 blackwalls; black wipers and rocker panel treatment; black bodyside moldings with bright inserts; black window frames and center roof pillar; black hood and decklid paint stripes; and louvered opera window appliqués (on two-door). Wide wheel lip moldings and color-keyed wheel covers also were included. Four-doors had a black division bar on the back door window. ESS did not have the standard upper bodyside moldings, and offered a choice of all-vinyl Flight Bench seat or carryover bucket seats. A leather-wrapped sport steering wheel was standard.

COUGAR/XR-7 — V-8 — As before, two types of Cougars were available: basic two- and four-door pillared-hardtop models (in base or Brougham trim), and the personal-luxury XR-7. Under Cougar's hood was a new electronic voltage regulator, plastic battery tray, and modified carburetor. Base engine was the 302-cid (5.0-liter) V-8. Aerodynamic improvements included a modified under-the-front-bumper spoiler. XR-7 had a new black/bright accented grille with body-color tape stripes and new horizontal-style wraparound tail lamps (each with two horizontal chrome trim strips). Once again, the XR-7 grille included a lower extension below the front bumper. Other models kept their 1978 styling. New color fabric was available for the XR-7 Chamois Decor Group. An extended-range fuel tank became optional. Standard Cougars had a vertical swing-away grille, quad rectangular headlamps, wraparound amber parking lamps with integral side markers, stand-up hood ornament, full wheel lip moldings, and rocker panel moldings. Vertical tail lamps had bright bezels and integral side markers. Equipment included SelectShift three-speed automatic, HR78 x 14 tires, power steering and brakes, and rear bumper guards. Cougar Brougham added opera windows: a full vinyl roof (on four-door); upper bodyside paint stripes; deluxe wheel covers; full-length bright bodyside molding with integral wheel lip moldings; wide bright door belt moldings; and Flight Bench seat with folding center armrest. Cougar XR-7 rode on 15 inch wheels with GR78 x 15 BSW tires and carried a rear stabilizer bar. Also included; a dual-note horn; special wheel covers with Cougar insert; hood rear edge molding; unique C-pillar treatment and ornament; padded landau vinyl roof with louvered opera window; and the typical sculptured spare-tire decklid design with lower molding. Full wheel lip and rocker panel moldings replaced the usual full-length bright bodyside molding. Dashboards held a simulated walnut instrument cluster faceplate.

1979 Mercury Zephyr Z-7 coupe. (PH)

1979 Mercury Zephyr ES coupe. (OCW)

MARQUIS — V-8 — Two years later than equivalent GM models, the full-size Mercury got its awaited downsizing, losing some 17 inches and over 800 pounds. The new aerodynamically-influenced body came in two- and four-door sedan form, along with station wagons. Underneath was a new long/short A-arm coil-spring front suspension and four-link coil-spring rear suspension. Standard powerplant was now a 302-cid V-8 with variable-venturi carburetor (except wagons with California emissions, a 351 V-8). The big 400 and 460 V-8 engines were gone. Four-wheel disc brakes and Traction-Lok axle also left the option list, along with the power moonroof. Newly optional was an electronic AM/FM stereo search radio with quadrasonic 8-tape player and premium sound system. Also joining the option list: an analog clock, digital clock with day/date and elapsed time, AM/FM stereo with cassette, 40-channel CB, and Grand Marquis package. Speed control included a 'resume' feature. This smaller Marquis had a lower hood, cowl and beltline. The new vertical-theme grille consisted of six separate side-by-side box sections. Concealed headlamps were replaced by exposed quad rectangular headlamps, which led into wraparound park/signal/marker lenses. A new chrome trim strip appeared along the mid-bodyside. So did front fender louvers. At the rear were large horizontal wraparound tail lamps with integral side marker lights. Vertical backup lamps were adjacent to the recessed rear license plate bracket. Four-doors had a bright rear door window divider bar. Bright rocker panel, belt, wheel lip, roof drip, windshield, rear window and hood rear edge moldings were standard. Doors were thinner and armrests smaller, adding interior space. A mini spare tire was now used. Under the hood, a new EEC-II electronic engine control system monitored six functions. Inside was a new four-spoke steering wheel. Flight Bench seats were trimmed in Fontainne cloth or optional Ruffino vinyl. Marquis still had a separate body on perimeter frame. Standard equipment included three-speed automatic transmission, power steering and brakes, dual-note horn, bright full wheel covers, stand-up hood ornament, rear roof pillar louvers, and FR78 x 14 SBR blackwall tires. Marquis Brougham added power windows, a full vinyl roof (on four-door) or landau vinyl roof (two-door), bright door frames, hood and decklid paint stripes, deluxe wheel covers, analog clock, and remote driver's mirror. Wide bright lower bodyside moldings included the quarter panels. Two-door Broughams could have the full vinyl roof at no extra cost. The Grand Marquis option added tinted glass, coach lamps, bodyside paint stripes, and wide bright/black lower bodyside moldings. Twin Comfort lounge seats with dual center armrests and reclining passenger seat were upholstered in Kinvara cloth or optional leather and vinyl. Also included: a right visor vanity mirror, dome/dual-beam map light, and pull straps. Marquis wagons had a three-way tailgate and power tailgate window. The Colony Park wagon added full-length bodyside and tailgate rosewood woodtone appliqués with bright and woodtone rails, remote driver's mirror, coach lamps, bright door frames, and deluxe wheel covers. Rocker panel and wheel lip moldings were deleted.

I.D. DATA: Mercury's 11-symbol Vehicle Identification Number (VIN) is stamped on a metal tab fastened to the instrument panel, visible through the windshield. The first digit is a model year code ('9' 1979). The second letter indicates assembly plant: 'E' Mahwah, NJ: 'F' Dearborn, MI: 'H' Lorain, Ohio; 'R' San Jose, CA; 'K' Kansas City, MO; 'S' St. Thomas, Ontario; 'T' Metuchen, NJ; 'Z' St. Louis, MO; 'W' Wayne, MI. Digits three and four are the body serial code, which corresponds to the Model Numbers shown in the tables below (e.g., '20' Bobcat hatchback Runabout). The fifth symbol is an engine code: 'Y' L4-140 2Bbl.; 'W' Turbo L4-140 2Bbl.; 'Z' V6-170 2Bbl.; 'T' L6-200 1Bbl.; 'L' L6-250 1Bbl.; 'F' V8-302 2Bbl.; 'H' V8-351 2Bbl. Finally, digits 6-11 make up the consecutive unit number of cars built at each assembly plant. The number begins with 600001. A Vehicle Certification Label on the left front door lock face panel or door pillar shows the manufacturer, month and year of manufacture, GVW, GAWR, certification statement, VIN, body code, color code, trim code, axle code, transmission code, and special order code.

BOBCAT RUNABOUT/WAGON (FOUR/V-6)

Model No.	Body/Style No.	Body Type & Seating	Factory Price	Shipping Weight	Prod. Total
20	64H	3-dr. Hatch-4P	3797/4070	2474/----	35,667
22	73H	2-dr. Sta Wag-4P	4099/4372	2565/----	Note 1

BOBCAT VILLAGER (FOUR/V-6)

22	73H	2-dr. Sta Wag-4P	4212/4485	N/A	Note 1

NOTE 1: Total station wagon production was 9,119 units.

Engine Note: An automatic transmission was required with Bobcat V-6 engine, at a cost of $307 more.

CAPRI (FOUR/V-6)

14	61D	3-dr. Fastbk-4P	4481/4754	2548/----	92,432

CAPRI GHIA (FOUR/V-6)

16	61H	3-dr. Fastbk-4P	4845/5118	2645/----	17,712

Capri Engine Note: A V-8 engine cost $241 more than the V-6.

ZEPHYR (FOUR/SIX)

31	66H	2-dr. Sed-5P	3870/4111	2516/2519	15,920
32	54D	4-dr. Sed-5P	3970/4211	2580/2583	41,316
36	740	4-dr. Sta Wag-5P	4317/4558	2681/2684	25,218

ZEPHYR Z-7 (FOUR/SIX)

35	36R	2-dr. Spt Cpe-5P	4122/4363	2551/2554	42,923

Zephyr Engine Note: A V-8 engine cost $283 more than the six.

MONARCH (SIX/V-8)

33	66H	2-dr. Sedan-5P	4412/4695	3070/3150	28,285
34	54H	4-dr. Sedan-5P	4515/4798	3111/3191	47,594

COUGAR (V-8)

91	65D	2-dr. HT Cpe-6P	5379	3792	2,831
92	53D	4-dr. Pill. HT-6P	5524	3843	5,605

COUGAR XR-7 (V-8)

93	65L	2-dr. HT Cpe-6P	5994	3883	163,716

MARQUIS (V-8)

61	66H	2-dr. Sedan-6P	5984	3507	10,035
62	54H	4-dr. Sedan-6P	6079	3557	32,289
74	74H	4-dr. 2S Sta Wag-6P	6315	3775	5,994

MARQUIS COLONY PARK (V-8)

74	74H	4-dr. 2S Sta Wag-6P	7100	3800	13,758

Station Wagon Note: Dual facing rear seats for the base Marquis or Colony Park wagon were available for $193.

MARQUIS BROUGHAM (V-8)

63	66K	2-dr. Sedan-6P	6643	3540	10,627
64	54K	4-dr. Sedan-6P	6831	3605	24,682

GRAND MARQUIS (V-8)

65	66L	2-dr. Sedan-6P	7321	3592	11,066
66	54L	4-dr. Sedan-6P	7510	3659	32,349

FACTORY PRICE AND WEIGHT NOTE: Monarch prices and weights to left of slash are for six-cylinder, to right for V-8 engine. For Bobcat and Zephyr, prices/weights to left of slash are for four-cylinder, to right for V-6.

ENGINE [Base Four (Bobcat, Capri, Zephyr)]: Inline. Overhead cam. Four-cylinder. Cast-iron block and head. Displacement: 140-cid (2.3 liters). Bore & stroke: 3.78 x 3.13 in. Compression ratio: 9.0:1. Brake horsepower: 88 at 4800 rpm. Torque: 118 lbs.-ft. at 2800 rpm. Five main bearings. Hydraulic valve lifters. Carburetor: 2Bbl. Motorcraft 5200. VIN Code: Y.

ENGINE [Optional Turbocharged Four (Capri)]: Same as 140-cid four above, but with turbocharger. Horsepower: 140 at 4800 rpm. Torque: N/A. Carburetor: 2Bbl. Holley 6500. VIN Code: W.

ENGINE [Optional V-6 (Bobcat, Capri)]: 60-degree, overhead-valve V-6. Cast-iron block and head. Displacement: 170.8-cid (2.8 liters). Bore & stroke: 3.66 x 2.70 in. Compression ratio: 8.7:1. Brake horsepower: 102 at 4400 rpm. (Capri, 109 at 4800). Torque: 138 lbs.-ft. at 3200 rpm.

1979 Mercury Monarch Ghia sedan. (M)

1979 Mercury Cougar XR-7 Sports Coupe. (M)

(Capri, 142 at 2800). Four main bearings. Hydraulic valve lifters. Carburetor: 2Bbl. Motorcraft 2150 or 2700VV. VIN Code: Z.

ENGINE [Optional Six (Zephyr)]: Inline. OHV. Six-cylinder. Cast-iron block and head. Displacement: 200-cid (3.3 liters). Bore & stroke: 3.68 x 3.13 in. Compression ratio: 8.5:1. Brake horsepower: 85 at 3600 rpm. Torque: 154 lbs.-ft. at 1600 rpm. Seven main bearings. Hydraulic valve lifters. Carburetor: 1Bbl. Carter YFA or Holley 1946. VIN Code: T.

ENGINE [Base Six (Monarch)]: Inline. OHV. Six-cylinder. Cast-iron block and head. Displacement: 250-cid (4.1 liters). Bore & stroke: 3.68 x 3.91 in. Compression ratio: 8.6:1. Brake horsepower: 97 at 3200 rpm. Torque: 210 lbs.-ft. at 1400 rpm. Seven main bearings. Hydraulic valve lifters. Carburetor: 1Bbl. Carter YFA. VIN Code: L.

ENGINE [Base V-8 (Cougar, Marquis); Optional (Capri, Zephyr, Monarch)]: 90-degree, overhead valve V-8. Cast-iron block and head. Displacement: 302-cid (5.0 liters). Bore & stroke: 4.00 x 3.00 in. Compression ratio: 8.4:1. Brake horsepower: 129-140 at 3400-3600 rpm. Torque: 223-250 lbs.-ft. at 1600-2600 rpm. Five main bearings. Hydraulic valve lifters. Carburetor: 2Bbl. Motorcraft 2150 or 2700VV. VIN Code: F.

ENGINE [Optional V-8 (Cougar, Marquis)]: 90-degree, overhead valve V-8. Cast-iron block and head. Displacement: 351-cid (5.8 liters). Bore & stroke: 4.00 x 3.50 in. Compression ratio: 8.3:1. Brake horsepower: 135-138 at 3200 rpm. Torque: 260-288 lbs.-ft. at 1400-2200 rpm. Five main bearings. Hydraulic valve lifters. Carburetor: 2Bbl. Motorcraft 7200VV, Windsor engine. VIN Code: H.

ENGINE [Optional V-8 (Cougar)]: Modified version of 351-cid V-8 above: Compression ratio: 8.0:1. Horsepower: 151 at 3600 rpm. Torque: 270 lbs.-ft. at 2200 rpm. Carburetor: 2Bbl. Motorcraft 2150.

CHASSIS DATA: Wheelbase: (Bobcat) 94.5 in.; (Bobcat wag) 94.8 in.; (Capri) 100.4 in.; (Zephyr) 105.5 in.; (Monarch) 109.9 in.; (Cougar 2-dr.) 114.0 in.; (Cougar 4-dr.) 118.0 in.; (Marquis) 114.4 in. Overall Length: (Bobcat) 169.3 in.; (Bobcat wag) 179.8 in.; (Capri) 179.1 in.; (Zephyr) 193.8 in.; (Z-7) 195.8 in.; (Monarch) 197.7 in.; (Cougar 2-dr.) 215.5 in.; (Cougar 4-dr.) 219.5 in. (Marquis) 212.0 in.; (Marquis wag) 217.7 in. Height: (Bobcat) 50.6 in.; (Bobcat wag) 52.1 in.; (Capri) 51.5 in.; (Zephyr) 53.5 in.; (Zephyr wag) 54.7 in.; (Z-7) 52.2 in.; (Monarch) 53.2-53.3 in.; (Cougar 2-dr.) 52.6 in.; (Cougar 4-dr.) 53.3 in.; (XR-7) 53.0 in.; (Marquis) 54.5 in.; (Marquis wag) 56.8 in. Width: (Bobcat) 69.4 in.; (Bobcat wag) 69.7 in.; (Capri) 69.1 in.; (Zephyr) 71.0 in.; (Monarch) 74.5 in.; (Cougar) 78.6 in.; (Marquis) 77.5 in.; (Marquis wag) 79.3 in. Front Tread: (Bobcat) 55.0 in.; (Capri) 56.6 in.; (Zephyr) 56.6 in.; (Monarch) 59.0 in.; (Cougar) 63.6 in.; (XR-7) 63.2 in.; (Marquis) 62.2 in. Rear Tread: (Bobcat) 55.8 in.; (Capri) 57.0 in.; (Zephyr) 57.0 in.; (Monarch) 57.7 in.; (Cougar) 63.5 in.; (XR-7) 63.1 in.; (Marquis) 62.0 in. Standard Tires: (Bobcat) BR78 x 13 SBR; (Capri) B78 x 13; (Capri Ghia) BR78 x 14; (Zephyr) B78 x 14 BSW; (Monarch) DR78 x 14; (Cougar) HR78 x 14; (XR-7) GR78 x 15; (Marquis) FR78 x 14; (Marquis wag) GR78 x 14.

1979 Mercury Marquis Brougham coupe. (OCW)

TECHNICAL: Transmission: Four-speed manual transmission standard on Capri; automatic optional (gear ratios N/A). Four-speed overdrive floor shift standard on Zephyr/Monarch six: (1st) 3.29:1; (2nd) 1.84:1; (3rd) 1.00:1; (4th) 0.81:1; (Rev) 3.29:1. Zephyr/Monarch V-8: (1st) 3.07:1; (2nd) 1.72:1; (3rd) 1.00:1; (4th) 0.70:1; (Rev) 3.07:1. Four-speed floor shift standard on Bobcat/Zephyr four: (1st) 3.98:1; (2nd) 2.14:1; (3rd) 1.42:1; (4th) 1.00:1; (Rev) 3.99:1. SelectShift three-speed automatic (column lever) standard on Cougar and Marquis, optional on others. Bobcat/Zephyr automatic gear ratios: (1st) 2.47:1; (2nd) 1.47:1; (3rd) 1.00:1; (Rev) 2.11:1. Other automatics: (1st) 2.46:1; (2nd) 1.46:1; (3rd) 1.00:1; (Rev) 2.18:1 to 2.20:1. Standard final drive ratio: (Bobcat) 2.73:1 w/4spd, 3.40:1 w/others; (Capri) 3.08:1 w/four or V-6, 3.45:1 w/turbo, 2.47:1 w/V-8 and auto.; (Zephyr) 3.08:1 exc. 2.73:1 w/six and auto., 2.26:1 w/V-8 and auto.; (Monarch) 3.00:1 w/4spd, 2.79:1 w/auto.; (Cougar) 2.75:1 w/V8-302, 2.47:1 w/V8-351. (Marquis) 2.26:1 exc. wagon, 2.73:1. Steering: (Bobcat/Capri/Zephyr) rack-and-pinion; (others) recirculating ball. Front Suspension: (Bobcat) coil springs with short/long control arms, lower leading arms, and anti-sway bar w/V-6; (Capri) modified MacPherson struts w/coil springs and anti-sway bar; (Zephyr) MacPherson struts w/coil springs mounted on lower control arm; (others) coil springs with long/short A arms and anti-sway bar. Rear Suspension: (Bobcat/Monarch) rigid axle w/semi-elliptic leaf springs; (Capri/Zephyr/Cougar) four-link w/coil springs; (Marquis) rigid axle with upper/lower control arms and coil springs. Brakes: Front disc, rear drum. Ignition: Electronic. Body construction: (Bobcat/Capri/Zephyr/Monarch) unibody; (others) separate body on perimeter frame; Fuel tank: (Bobcat) 11.7 gal. exc. 13 gal. w/V-6 and wagon 14 gal.; (Capri) 11.5 gal. w/four, others 12.5 gal.; (Zephyr) 16.0 gal.; (Monarch) 18.0 gal.; (Cougar) 21.0 gal.; (Marquis) 19 gal. exc. wagon, 20 gal.

DRIVETRAIN OPTIONS: Engines: Turbo 140-cid four: Capri ($542). 170-cid V-6: Bobcat/Capri ($273). 200-cid, 1Bbl. six: Zephyr ($241). 302-cid, 2Bbl. V-8: Capri ($514); Zephyr ($524); Monarch ($283). 351-cid, 2Bbl. V-8: Cougar/Marquis ($263). Sport-tuned exhaust: Capri ($34). Transmission/Differential: SelectShift Cruise-O-Matic: Bobcat/Capri/Monarch ($307); Zephyr ($307-$398). Floor shift lever: Zephyr/Monarch ($31). Traction-Lok differential: Cougar ($64). Optional axle ratio: Bobcat/Capri ($13); Marquis ($16). Brakes & Steering: Power brakes: Bobcat/Capri/Zephyr/Monarch ($70). Power steering: Bobcat/Capri ($141); Zephyr/Monarch ($149). Suspension: H.D. susp.: Monarch ($27); Marquis ($22). Sport handling susp.: Zephyr ($34). Handling pkg.: Marquis ($51). Cross-country susp.: Cougar ($22-$36). Radial sport susp.: Capri ($33). Load levelers: Marquis ($53-$67). Other: H.D. battery ($18-$21). Engine block heater ($13-$14) exc. Marquis ($21). Extended-range fuel tank: Cougar ($33). Trailer towing pkg. (heavy duty): Marquis ($146). California emission system ($76-$83). High-altitude option ($31-$36).

BOBCAT CONVENIENCE/APPEARANCE OPTIONS: Option Packages: Sports accent group ($223-$247). Sports instrument group ($94). Sport pkg. ($72). Deluxe interior ($158-$182). Interior accent group ($42). Convenience group ($55-$96). Appearance protection group ($41-$49). Light group ($33). Comfort/Convenience: Air conditioner ($484). Dual racing mirrors ($36-$52). Day/night mirror ($8). Entertainment: AM radio w/digital clock ($47). AM/FM radio ($48). AM/FM stereo radio ($89); w/tape player ($119); w/cassette player ($157). Radio flexibility option ($90). AM radio delete ($72 credit). Exterior: Flip-up/removable moonroof ($199). Glass third door ($25). Glamour paint ($41). Narrow bodyside moldings ($41). Deluxe bodyside moldings ($51). Rocker panel moldings ($24). Roof luggage rack: wag ($63). Mud/stone deflectors ($22). Lower bodyside protection ($30). Interior: Four-way bucket seat ($35). Load floor carpet ($24). Cargo area cover ($28). Wheels/Tires: Wire wheel covers ($33). Forged or cast aluminum wheels ($164); white forged ($177). BR78 x 13 ($43). BR70 x 13 RWL ($79).

CAPRI CONVENIENCE/APPEARANCE OPTIONS: Option Packages: RS option ($249). Turbo RS option ($1186). Interior accent group ($42-$108). Light group ($16-$28). Appearance protection group ($41-$45). Power lock group ($99). Comfort/Convenience: Air cond. ($484). Rear defroster, electric ($84). Fingertip speed control ($104). Tinted glass ($59); windshield only ($27). Leather-wrapped steering wheel ($36). Tilt steering wheel ($69). Interval wipers ($35). Rear wiper/washer ($63). Right remote mirror ($30). Entertainment: AM radio ($72): w/digital clock ($119). AM/FM radio ($120). AM/FM stereo

1979 Mercury Grand Marquis coupe. (M)

1979 Mercury Marquis Colony Park station wagon. (OCW)

radio ($176); w/8-track or cassette tape player ($243). Premium sound system ($67). Dual rear speakers ($43). Radio flexibility option ($93). Exterior: Flip-up/removable moonroof ($199). Glamour paint ($41). Two-tone paint, black ($48). Rocker panel moldings ($24). Mud/stone deflectors ($22). Lower bodyside protection ($30). Interior: Console ($127). Four-way driver's seat ($35). Danbury or Bradford cloth w/vinyl seat trim ($20). Leather seat trim ($283). Color-keyed deluxe seatbelts ($20). Wheels and Tires: Wire wheel covers ($64). TRX or cast aluminum wheels ($240). Styled steel wheels w/trim rings ($65). B78 x 13 WSW ($43). C78 x 13 BSW ($22); WSW ($65). B78 x 14 WSW ($65). BR78 x 14 BSW ($125); WSW ($43-$168). CR78 x 14 WSW ($65-$190); RWL ($14-$204). TRX 190/65R390 Michelin BSW ($51-$241).

ZEPHYR CONVENIENCE/APPEARANCE OPTIONS: Option Packages: ES option ($237). Ghia option ($211-$428). Villager option ($195). Sports instrument group ($78). Exterior decor group ($102). Interior decor group ($72-$108). Luxury interior ($208-$323). Bumper protection group ($58). Convenience group ($31-$51). Appearance protection group ($48-$54). Light group ($35-$41). Comfort/Convenience: Air cond. ($484). Rear defogger ($51). Rear defroster, electric ($90). Speed control ($83-$104). Tinted glass ($59). Power windows ($116-$163). Power door locks ($78-$107). Power, four-way ($94). Electric trunk release ($22). Sport steering wheel ($39). Tilt steering ($48-$69). Electric clock ($20). Cigar lighter ($6). Interval wipers ($35). Liftgate wiper/washer: wag ($80). Lighting and Mirrors: Trunk light ($7). Left remote mirror ($17). Dual mirrors ($35). Day/night mirror ($8). Entertainment: AM radio ($72); w/8-track tape player ($192). AM/FM radio ($120). AM/FM stereo radio ($176); w/8-track or cassette player ($243). Premium sound ($67). Radio flexibility ($93). Exterior: Flip-up/removable moonroof ($199). Vinyl roof ($90). Glamour paint ($48). Two-tone paint ($81-$96). Pivoting front vent windows ($41). Rear vent louvers ($35). Bodyside moldings ($41). Deluxe wide bodyside moldings ($53). Rocker panel moldings ($24). Bright window frames ($25-$30). Bumper guards, rear ($20). Mud/stone deflectors ($22). Roof luggage rack ($76). Lower bodyside protection ($30-$42). Interior: Bucket seats ($72). Ardmore or Brodie cloth seat trim ($39). Kirsten cloth trim ($20). Lockable side storage box ($20). Wheels/Tires: Styled wheel covers ($41). Wire wheel covers ($52-$93). Aluminum wheels ($237-$278). Styled wheels ($54-$95). B78 x 14 WSW. BR78 x 14 BSW/WSW. C78 x 14 BSW/WSW. CR78 x 14 BSW/WSW. DR78 x 14 SBR BSW/WSW/ RWL.

MONARCH CONVENIENCE/APPEARANCE OPTIONS: Option Packages: ESS option ($524). Ghia option ($425). Interior decor group ($211). Convenience group ($36-$94). Bumper protection group ($78). Light group ($46). Cold weather group ($57). Heavy-duty group ($57). Appearance protection group ($33-$51). Visibility group ($8-$64). Comfort/Convenience: Air cond. ($514); auto-temp ($555). Rear defogger ($51). Rear defroster, electric ($90). Fingertip speed control ($104). Illuminated entry system ($52). Power windows ($116-$163). Power door locks ($78-$107). Power decklid release ($22). Auto. parking brake release ($8). Power four-way seat ($94). Tinted glass ($64). Tilt steering wheel ($69). Digital clock ($45). Lighting and Mirrors: Cornering lamps ($45). Trunk light ($7). Dual racing mirrors ($42-$59). Lighted right visor vanity mirror ($37). Entertainment: AM radio ($72); w/tape player ($192). AM/FM radio ($135). AM/FM stereo radio ($176); w/8-track or cassette player ($243); w/quadrasonic tape ($365). AM/FM stereo search radio ($319). CB radio ($270). Radio flexibility ($93). Exterior: Power moonroof ($849). Full or landau vinyl roof ($106). Glamour paint ($48). Tone-on-tone ($123). Bodyside moldings ($41). Rocker panel moldings ($24). Mud/stone deflectors ($22). Lower bodyside protection ($30). Interior: Console ($84). Four-way seat ($34). Leather seat trim ($283). Rossano cloth seat ($54). Wilshire cloth trim ($104). Deluxe seatbelts ($20). Wheels/Tires: Deluxe wheel covers ($40) exc. Ghia/ESS (NC). Wire wheel covers ($69-$108). Styled steel wheels w/trim rings ($75-$114). Cast aluminum wheels ($170-$278). DR78 x 14 SBR WSW. ER78 x 14 SBR BSW/WSW. FR78 x 14 SBR BSW/WSW/wide WSW.

COUGAR CONVENIENCE/APPEARANCE OPTIONS: Option Packages: Brougham option ($266-$382). Brougham decor ($221). Chamois decor group: XR-7 ($625). XR-7 decor ($487). Sports instrumentation group ($105-$149). Bumper protection group ($63). Light group ($54). Convenience group ($62-$147). Power lock group ($111-$143). Appearance protection group ($66-$76). Comfort/Convenience: Air cond. ($562); w/auto-temp control ($607). Rear defroster, electric ($99). Fingertip speed control ($105-$125). Illuminated entry system ($57). Tinted glass ($70). Power windows ($132-$187). Six-way power seat ($153). Tilt steering wheel ($75). Day/date clock ($22-$46). Seatbelt chime: XR-7 ($22). Lighting and Mirrors: Cornering lamps ($49). Remote driver's mirror ($18). Dual racing mirrors ($64). Lighted visor vanity mirror ($39). Entertainment: AM radio ($79). AM/FM radio ($132). AM/FM stereo radio ($192); w/tape or cassette player ($266); w/quadrasonic tape player ($399). AM/FM stereo search radio ($349). CB radio ($295). Upgraded sound: XR-7 ($30). Dual rear speakers ($47). Power antenna: XR-7 ($47). Radio flexibility ($105). Exterior: Power moonroof ($789). Landau vinyl roof ($116). Full vinyl roof ($170). Opera windows: base ($54). Glamour paint ($64). Two-tone paint ($74-$128). Paint striping ($36). Narrow bodyside moldings ($45). Wide bodyside moldings ($58). Rocker panel moldings: Brghm ($29). Mud/stone deflectors ($24). Lower bodyside protection ($33). Interior: Twin comfort seats w/passenger recliner: XR-7/Brghm ($184). Bucket seats w/console ($184-$259). Vinyl bench seat ($30). Flight Bench seat ($75). Velour trim: XR-7 ($208). Leather seat: XR-7 ($309). Trunk trim ($42). Color-keyed seatbelts ($22). Wheels/Tires: Deluxe wheel covers ($43). Luxury wheel covers ($34-$78). Wire wheel covers ($118-$162). Cast aluminum wheels ($136-$345). Styled wheels: XR-7 ($166). Styled wheels w/trim rings ($120-$163) exc. XR-7. HR78 x 14 SBR WSW ($47). GR78 x 15 WSW ($47). HR78 x 15 SBR WSW ($71).

MARQUIS CONVENIENCE/APPEARANCE OPTIONS: Option Packages: Grand Marquis decor: Colony Park ($586). Convenience group ($78-$93). Lock convenience group ($91-$154). Visibility light group ($18-$47). Appearance protection group ($61-$71). Comfort/Convenience: Air cond. ($597); w/auto-temp control ($642). Rear defroster, electric ($100). Fingertip speed control ($111-$130). Illuminated entry system ($57). Power windows ($137-$203). Six-way power seat ($164); driver and passenger ($329). Tinted glass ($83). Tilt steering wheel ($76). Electric clock ($24). Digital clock ($36-$59). Seatbelt chimes ($22). Lighting and Mirrors: Cornering lamps ($49). Driver's remote mirror ($18). Right remote mirror ($38). Lighted visor vanity mirror ($41). Entertainment: AM radio ($79). AM/FM radio ($132). AM/FM stereo radio ($192); w/tape or cassette player ($266). CB radio ($295). Power antenna ($45). Dual rear speakers ($47). Premium sound system ($74-$158). Radio flexibility ($105). Exterior: Full or landau vinyl roof ($143). Glamour metallic paint ($64). Two-tone paint ($99-$129). Paint striping ($36). Hood striping: Colony Park ($20). Rocker panel moldings: Colony Park ($29). Narrow bodyside moldings ($45). Window frame moldings ($34-$39). Bumper guards, front or rear ($22). Bumper rub strips ($41). Luggage rack: wag ($86). Lower bodyside protection ($33). Interior: Dual-facing rear seats: wag ($193). Twin comfort seats: Brghm/Colony ($89). Dual seat recliners ($89). Cloth seat trim: Colony ($42). Vinyl seat trim ($34). Polyknit Flight Bench seat trim: wag ($53). Leather twin comfort seat trim, Grand Marquis/Colony ($261). Trunk trim ($45). Spare tire cover ($13). Deluxe seatbelts ($24). Wheels/Tires: Luxury wheel covers ($64-$93). Wire wheel covers ($89-$118). FR78 x 14 WSW ($47). GR78 x 14 BSW ($23). GR78 x 14 WSW ($47-$71). HR78 x 14 (wagon): BSW ($23); WSW ($71). Conventional spare ($13).

HISTORY: Introduced: October 6, 1978. Model year production: 669,138. Calendar year production (U.S.): 509,450. Calendar year sales by U.S. dealers: 509,999. Model year sales by U.S. dealers: 540,526.

HISTORY: Sales for the '79 model year fell by close to 10 percent for the Lincoln-Mercury division, as motorists worried more about gas mileage. The shrunken Marquis sold far fewer copies than its full-size predecessor of 1978. Model year production rose, however, partly as a result of the new domestically-built Capri; but calendar year production was down considerably. The turbocharger option in the new Capri was supposed to give Mercury a "sporty" image to add to its luxury role.

1980 MERCURY

1980 Mercury Bobcat "Sport Option" hatchback coupe. (M)

1980 Mercury Capri hatchback coupe. (M)

A new four-speed overdrive automatic transmission, and some weight reductions in the engines, helped give Lincoln-Mercury models considerably better gas mileage. A turbo option was announced for Zephyr as a mid-year addition, but failed to materialize. Capri got a new five-speed gearbox option. Also arriving this year was a new (smaller) Cougar XR-7 model. A new powerplant appeared: the 255-cid V-8, replacing the 302 in some models.

BOBCAT — FOUR — Since the front-drive subcompact Lynx would appear for 1981, this would be Bobcat's final year. Little changed in appearance or equipment, apart from a new optional two-tone paint treatment and new sport option. Standard front/rear bumper guards moved inward by four inches. Five new paint colors were available. Bobcat again displayed a rakishly-angled, vertical-textured grille with single rectangular headlamps and vertical park/signal lamps in the same recessed housings. Styled steel wheels came with trim rings. Bodies held bright wide wheel lip moldings; bright rocker panel, side window frame and door belt moldings; and ventless front side windows. Horizontal tail lamps had integral backup lights. Aluminum bumpers had black rubber end caps. High-back front bucket seats were standard. Equipment also included the 140-cid (2.3-liter) four with four-speed manual shift; BR78 x 13 BSW tires; an AM radio (which could be deleted); tinted glass; rear window defroster; front and rear bumper guards with rub strips; and choice of all-vinyl or cloth and vinyl interior. Manual-shift models had a woodgrain shift knob. Two wagons were available again: base and Villager (with full-length rosewood woodtone bodyside appliqué). New options included mud/stone deflectors (introduced in late 1979). The new Sport option included a front air dam, rear spoiler, and special paint/tape treatment. It included large Bobcat decal lettering on the door as part of the wide stripe treatment. No V-6 engine was offered in this final season.

CAPRI — FOUR/SIX/V-8 — Introduced for 1979, Mercury's equivalent to the Ford Mustang looked the same this year, but enjoyed a few mechanical changes. After the new model year began, the turbo engine was to be available with optional automatic as well as the standard four-speed manual shift. A new 255-cid (4.2-liter) V-8 replaced the optional 302. An inline 200-cid six became available late in the model year, replacing the former V-6 as first choice above the base 140-cid (2.3-liter) four. Five-

speed shifting became optional with the four at mid-year. New standard equipment included halogen headlamps and metric-size (P185/80R13) steel-belted radials. An AM radio was also made standard later. Wide-aspect, low-profile Michelin TRX tires were again optional. New options included a roof luggage carrier, concealed cargo compartment cover, tri-tone accent tape stripe, and Recaro bucket seats. Capris carried a black/bright horizontal-bar grille and quad rectangular headlamps in bright frames. Color-keyed louvers decorated the hood; black louvers went on the cowl. Semi-styled 13 inch steel wheels had trim rings. Extra-wide wraparound black bodyside moldings held dual color-keyed center stripes. The swing-up hatch had a bright window molding. High-back bucket seats wore pleated all-vinyl trim. Standard equipment included the 2.3-liter four with four-speed manual, inside hood release, front stabilizer bar, color-keyed bumpers, full fender splash shields, woodgrain instrument panel appliqué, full instrumentation (including tachometer), lighter, trip odometer, sport steering wheel, locking glovebox, day/night mirror, and a remote driver's mirror. Ghia added P175/75R14 SBR tires on 14 inch wheels, sport wheel covers, dual black remote mirrors, a Ghia badge, low-back bucket seats with European-style headrests, four-spoke steering wheel with woodtone insert, and a light group. Capri RS included a rear spoiler; non-functional hood scoop; black grille; black right-hand remote mirror; sport wheel covers; and upper bodyside dual accent paint striping. 'RS' tape identification went on the front fender, at the cowl. Blackout headlamp frames, windshield molding, window frame moldings, and third door window molding were RS standards. So was a simulated engine-turned instrument panel. P175/75R14 tires rode 14 inch wheels, with a radial sport suspension. Topping the line, the Turbo RS model had 'Turbo RS' tape identification on the front fender (at cowl); a bright 'Turbo' plaque on the hood scoop; sport-tuned exhaust; three-spoke 15.3 inch forged aluminum wheels; Michelin TRX 190/65R390 low-profile tires; 8000 rpm. tachometer; turbo function indicator lights on dash; and rally suspension. Low-back bucket seats had European-style headrests. Turbo engines had a dual bright tailpipe extension (optional with V-8).

ZEPHYR — FOUR/SIX/V-8 — Biggest news for Zephyr was to be the availability of a turbocharged four-cylinder engine, but that prospect faded away. However, a new 255-cid (4.2-liter) V-8 replaced the former 302. Zephyrs now had high-pressure P-metric SBR tires (P175/75R14) and new quad rectangular halogen headlamps. Manual-shift models had a new self-adjusting clutch. Standard front bumper guards were moved inward a little over three inches, but Zephyr was otherwise little changed. Styling features included bright frames around quad headlamp and quad park/signal lamps; a thin-vertical-bar grille; aluminum bumper (with front guards); upper bodyside dual accent stripes; dual front fender louvers; and deluxe wheel covers. Horizontal tail lamps had integral backup lenses and bright bezels. Zephyrs had bright wheel lip and rocker panel moldings, bright door belt and roof drip moldings, and all-vinyl low-back bucket seats. Standard equipment included the 140-cid (2.3-liter) four with four-speed manual shift, inside hood release, front stabilizer bar, woodgrain instrument cluster appliqué, Euro-style front door armrest, and a stand-up hood ornament. Zephyr's Z-7 sport coupe was noted for its contemporary wrapover roof design with upper bodyside accent stripe treatment that continued over the roof. Also standard on Z-7: lower bodyside molding with black vinyl insert; bright wheel lip moldings and window frames; Z-7 ornament on wide center pillar; wraparound tail lamps; pleated vinyl seat trim; and tinted rear window glass. The Villager station wagon had woodtone bodyside paneling appliqués. There was also a standard wagon. Ghia packages were available an all models, but the ES option was abandoned.

MONARCH — SIX/V-8 — Styling remained the same as 1979, but eight new paint colors and three new tone-on-tone combinations were offered. New electronic chimes replaced the buzzer warning system. A new full-width aluminum lower back panel appliqué with black center replaced the former red reflective appliqué. Three new vinyl roof colors were available. Again, there was a base model, Ghia option group, and sporty ESS option group. Standard Monarchs had Flight Bench seating with fold-down center armrest. Ghia and ESS had a choice of special sculptured Flight Bench or bucket seats. Standard equipment included a 250-cid (4.1-liter) inline six with four-speed manual overdrive and floor lever (automatics had column shift), DR78 x 14 BSW SBR tires, inside hood release, vinyl seat trim, lighter, buried woodgrain instrument cluster, locking glovebox, stand-up hood ornament, and full wheel covers. Moldings were included for windshield, wheel lip, backlight, drip, belt, door frame and decklid. Two-doors had opera windows. The optional 302-cid (5.0-liter) V-8 was required in California. Monarch's Ghia option group included accent stripes on hood contours, tapered bodyside accent stripes, wire wheel covers, full-length lower bodyside molding with wide color-keyed vinyl insert, bright driver's remote mirror, accent stripes on decklid and decklid contours, and Ghia decklid ornament. Ghias rode on ER78 x 14 tires and carried a dual-note horn, rear door courtesy light switches, vinyl seats, seatback map pockets, and day/night mirror. The ESS option group had black wipers, black hood accent stripes, front/rear bumper guards and horizontal rub strip, bright wide wheel lip moldings, dual racing mirrors, and color-keyed wheel covers. Also on ESS: black bodyside molding with bright mylar insert; black rocker panel paint; black side window surround moldings; louvered opera window appliqué (two-doors); black rear window division bar (four-doors); black decklid accent stripes; and FR78 x 14 tires. 'ESS' block lettering on front fenders (at cowl) replaced the former 'ESS Monarch' label.

1980 Mercury Capri RS hatchback coupe. (PH)

COUGAR XR-7 — V-8 — Aerodynamic styling on an all-new and smaller unitized body changed Cougar substantially. So did a new standard 255-cid (4.1-liter) V-8 instead of the former 302 (which was now optional). Also optional this year was new four-speed automatic overdrive transmission. The new Cougar weighed 700 pounds less than the old, and rode a shorter 108.4-inch wheelbase. More important, the base models were dropped, leaving only the XR-7. Cougar now had a strut-type front suspension, four-bar link coil-spring rear suspension, standard variable-ratio power rack-and-pinion steering, sealed-beam halogen headlamps, and P-metric SBR tires (P185/75R14 BSW). Keyless entry was a new option, using door-mounted push buttons to activate the door locks and trunk lid. Bodies featured distinctive deep bodyside sculpturing, color-keyed soft front/rear bumper coverings, new vertical-theme tail lamps, a padded half-vinyl roof, quarter window louvers, all-new wheels and wheel covers. Passenger capacity dropped to four. Standard equipment included three-speed automatic transmission, power steering and brakes, dual-note horn, front and rear stabilizer bars, brake failure warning light, Flight Bench seat, woodgrain instrument panel appliqué, trip odometer, front/rear center seat dividers, ashtray and glovebox lights, four-spoke steering wheel, analog clock, soft color-keyed bumpers, and quarter-window louvers. Cougar's upright vertical-bar grille with bright surround molding had its pattern repeated in a lower bumper grille opening. Quad rectangular halogen headlamps in bright housings led into wraparound marker lenses. Turn signals were bumper-mounted. Styling touches included a stand-up hood ornament, wide rocker moldings, wheel lip moldings, "frenched" rear window, and dual bodyside accent stripes. Black door and quarter window frames had bright moldings. An optional Decor Group included such items as full-length wide bodyside moldings (with vinyl inserts to match the roof), hood and decklid accent stripes, bright sail-mount dual remote mirrors, and Twin Comfort lounge seats. A Sports Group (available later) had a striking two-tone treatment and low-profile TR type tires on cast aluminum wheels, with special suspension tuning. The Sports model also had Recaro bucket seats with cloth trim and lumbar/depth/shoulder support adjustment, and power windows. The Luxury Group added such extras as Michelin TRX whitewall tires on cast aluminum wheels, a 5.0-liter V-8, luxury half-vinyl roof, automatic overdrive transmission, split bench seat, electronic instruments, diagnostic warning light module, power windows, lighted visor mirror, quarter courtesy lamp, and hood/decklid paint stripes.

MARQUIS — V-8 — Downsized in 1979 to almost full-size, Marquis changed only slightly in appearance this year with new taillamp and lower back panel moldings. New paint combinations put the darker color on top. Halogen headlamps and P-metric (P205/75R14) radial tires were new. So were front bumper guards. Both the base 302-cid (5.0-liter) V-8 and optional 351-cid (5.8-liter) could have four-speed automatic overdrive transmission instead of the standard three-speed automatic. An improved EEC-III system was standard on 351 V-8s. and California 302s. The Traction-Lok option reappeared. Two new versions of the electronic AM/FM stereo search radio, introduced on the '79 Marquis, were offered: plain or with cassette and Dolby. A mid-year 1979 option had been pivoting front vent windows. Joining the option list: turbine-spoke cast aluminum wheels. Again, two and four-door sedans in base, Brougham and Grand Marquis trim were offered, along with base and Colony Park wagons. A bright Marquis crest or 'Grand Marquis' script replaced the former louvers on rear roof pillar. Accent stripes were added to the fender louvers on Grand Marquis. Bodies had bright decklid edge and taillamp surround moldings, bright window frame and lower quarter extension moldings, and wraparound parking lamps with integral side marker lights. Fender louvers and a wide center pillar were standard. Four-doors had a rear door window divider bar; two-doors, a fixed quarter window. At the back was a black lower back panel, bright rear window molding, horizontal wraparound tail lamps with integral side marker lights, and bright decklid lower edge and taillamp surround molding. Flight Bench seats had a fold-down center armrest and cloth and vinyl upholstery. Electronic chimes replaced the buzzer as seatbelt warning on Brougham, Grand Marquis

and Colony Park. All steering wheels had a woodgrain insert. Two new luxury half-vinyl roofs were available: the standard coach roof on all Grand Marquis models (optional on Brougham); and a formal coach roof optional only on four-door Grand Marquis. Vinyl roofs later switched to smooth French seams and color-keyed back window moldings. Base Marquis standard equipment included power brakes and steering, dual-note horn, four-spoke steering wheel, woodgrain instrument panel appliqué, day/night mirror, front bumper guards and rub strips, and hood ornament. Brougham added hood accent stripes; full vinyl roof (four-door) or landau vinyl roof (two-door); driver's remote mirror; deluxe wheel covers; wide bright lower bodyside molding with quarter panel extensions; decklid accent stripes; power windows; dash and trunk courtesy lights; and 'Brougham' nameplate on decklid. Grand Marquis included coach lamps, wide bright/black lower bodyside moldings, upper bodyside accent stripes, black painted rocker panel flange, 'Grand Marquis' script on rear roof pillar, and 'Grand Marquis' decklid nameplate. Grand Marquis had standard tinted glass and Twin Comfort lounge seats with dual center folding armrests. Colony Park wagons had full-length bodyside rosewood woodtone appliqués, with bright and woodtone rails; plus 'Colony Park' script on quarter panel. Both wagons carried P215/75R14 tires.

I.D. DATA: Mercury's 11-symbol Vehicle Identification Number (VIN) is stamped on a metal tab fastened to the instrument panel, visible through the windshield. Coding is the same as 1979, except engine codes (symbol five) changed as follows: 'A' L4-140 2Bbl.; 'A' Turbo L4-140 2Bbl.; 'B' or 'T' L6-200 1Bbl.; 'C' L6-250 1Bbl.; 'D' V8-255 2Bbl.; 'F' V8-302 2Bbl.; 'G' V8-351 2Bbl. Model year code changed to 'O' for 1980.

BOBCAT RUNABOUT/WAGON (FOUR)

Model No.	Body/ Style No.	Body Type & Seating	Factory Price	Shipping Weight	Prod. Total
20	64H	3-dr. Hatch-4P	4384	2445	28,103
22	73H	2-dr. Sta Wag-4P	4690	2573	Note 1

BOBCAT VILLAGER (FOUR)

Model No.	Body/ Style No.	Body Type & Seating	Factory Price	Shipping Weight	Prod. Total
22	73H	2-dr. Sta Wag-4P	4803	N/A	Note 1

NOTE 1: Total station wagon production was 5,547 units.

CAPRI (FOUR/SIX)

Model No.	Body/ Style No.	Body Type & Seating	Factory Price	Shipping Weight	Prod. Total
14	61D	3-dr. Fastbk-4P	5250/5469	2547/2585	72,009

CAPRI GHIA (FOUR/SIX)

Model No.	Body/ Style No.	Body Type & Seating	Factory Price	Shipping Weight	Prod. Total
16	61H	3-dr. Fastbk-4P	5545/5764	2632/2670	7,975

Capri Engine Note: A V-8 engine cost $119 more than the six.

ZEPHYR (FOUR/SIX)

Model No.	Body/ Style No.	Body Type & Seating	Factory Price	Shipping Weight	Prod. Total
31	66D	2-dr. Sed-5P	4582/4751	2605/2608	10,977
32	54D	4-dr. Sed-5P	4700/4869	2647/2650	40,399
36	74D	4-dr. Sta Wag-5P	4870/5039	2769/2772	20,341

ZEPHYR Z-7 (FOUR/SIX)

Model No.	Body/ Style No.	Body Type & Seating	Factory Price	Shipping Weight	Prod. Total
35	36R	2-dr.Spt Cpe-5P	4876/5045	2644/2647	19,486

Zephyr Engine Note: A V-8 engine cost $119 more than the six.

MONARCH (SIX/V-8)

Model No.	Body/ Style No.	Body Type & Seating	Factory Price	Shipping Weight	Prod. Total
33	66H	2-dr. Sedan-5P	5074/5262	3093/3160	8,772
34	54H	4-dr. Sedan-5P	5194/5382	3134/3227	21,746

Monarch Engine Note: Prices are for 302-cid V-8; a 255 V-8 cost only $38 more than the six.

COUGAR XR-7 (V-8)

Model No.	Body/ Style No.	Body Type & Seating	Factory Price	Shipping Weight	Prod. Total
93	66D	2-dr. HT Cpe-4P	6569	3191	58,028

Cougar Engine Note: Price shown is for 255-cid V-8; a 302 V-8 cost $150 more.

MARQUIS (V-8)

Model No.	Body/ Style No.	Body Type & Seating	Factory Price	Shipping Weight	Prod. Total
61	66H	2-dr. Sedan-6P	6134	3450	2,521
62	54H	4-dr. Sedan-6P	6722	3488	13,018
74	74H	4-dr. 2S Sta Wag-6P	7071	3697	2,407

1980 Mercury Zephyr Z-7 Sports Coupe. (AA)

1980 Mercury Monarch Ghia sedan. (AA)

MARQUIS BROUGHAM (V-8)

63	66K	2-dr. Sedan-6P	7298	3476	2,353
64	54K	4-dr. Sedan-6P	7490	3528	8,819

MARQUIS COLONY PARK (V-8)

76	74K	4-dr. 2S Sta Wag-6P	7858	3743	5,781

GRAND MARQUIS (V-8)

65	66L	2-dr. Sedan-6P	8075	3504	3,434
66	54L	4-dr. Sedan-6P	8265	3519	15,995

FACTORY PRICE AND WEIGHT NOTE: Monarch prices and weights to left of slash are for six-cylinder, to right for V-8 engine. For Capri and Zephyr, prices/weights to left of slash are for four-cylinder, to right for V-6.

ENGINE [Base Four (Bobcat, Capri, Zephyr)]: Inline. Overhead cam. Four-cylinder. Cast-iron block and head. Displacement: 140-cid (2.3 liters). Bore & stroke: 3.78 x 3.13 in. Compression ratio: 9.0:1. Brake horsepower: 88 at 4600 rpm. Torque: 119 lbs.-ft. at 2600 rpm. Five main bearings. Hydraulic valve lifters. Carburetor: 2Bbl. Motorcraft 5200. VIN Code: A.

ENGINE [Optional Turbocharged Four (Capri)]: Same as 140-cid four above, but with turbocharger. Horsepower: 150 at 4800 rpm. Torque: N/A. Carburetor; 2Bbl. Holley 6500. VIN Code: A.

ENGINE [Optional Six (Capri, Zephyr)]: Inline. OHV. Six-cylinder. Cast-iron block and head. Displacement: 200-cid (3.3 liters). Bore & stroke: 3.68 x 3.13 in. Compression ratio: 8.6:1. Brake horsepower: 91 at 3800 rpm. Torque: 160 lbs.-ft. at 1600 rpm. Seven main bearings. Hydraulic valve lifters. Carburetor: 1Bbl. Holley 1946. VIN Code: B.

ENGINE [Base Six (Monarch)]: Inline. OHV. Six-cylinder. Cast-iron block and head. Displacement: 250-cid (4.1 liters). Bore & stroke: 3.68 x 3.91 in. Compression ratio: 8.6:1. Brake horsepower: 90 at 3200 rpm. Torque: 194 lbs.-ft. at 1660 rpm. Seven main bearings. Hydraulic valve lifters. Carburetor: 1Bbl. Carter YFA. VIN Code: C.

ENGINE [Base V-8 (Cougar); Optional (Capri, Zephyr)]: 90-degree, overhead valve V-8. Cast-iron block and head. Displacement: 255-cid (4.2 liters). Bore & stroke: 3.68 x 3.00 in. Compression ratio: 8.8:1. Brake horsepower: 115-119 at 3800 rpm. Torque: 191-194 lbs.-ft. at 2200 rpm. Five main bearings. Hydraulic valve lifters. Carburetor: 2Bbl. Motorcraft 2150. VIN Code: D.

ENGINE [Base V-8 (Marquis); Optional (Cougar, Monarch)]: 90-degree, overhead valve V-8. Cast-iron block and head. Displacement: 302-cid (5.0 liters). Bore & stroke: 4.00 x 3.00 in. Compression ratio: 8.4:1. Brake horsepower: 130-134 at 3600 rpm. Torque: 230-232 lbs.-ft. at 1600 rpm. Five main bearings. Hydraulic valve lifters. Carburetor: 2Bbl. Motorcraft 2150 or 27OOVV. VIN Code: F.

ENGINE [Optional V-8 (Marquis)]: 90-degree, overhead valve V-8. Cast-iron block and head. Displacement: 351-cid (5.8 liters). Bore & stroke: 4.00 x 3.50 in. Compression ratio: 8.3:1. Brake horsepower: 140 at 3400 rpm. Torque: 265 lbs.-ft. at 2000 rpm. Five main bearings. Hydraulic valve lifters. Carburetor: 2Bbl. Motorcraft 72OOVV. VIN Code: G.

CHASSIS DATA: Wheelbase: (Bobcat) 94.5 in.; (Bobcat wag) 94.8 in.; (Capri) 100.4 in.: (Zephyr) 105.5 in.; (Monarch) 109.9 in.; (Cougar) 108.4 in.; (Marquis) 114.3 in. Overall Length: (Bobcat) 170.8 in.; (Bobcat wag) 180.6 in.; (Capri) 179.1 in.; (Zephyr) 195.5 in.; (Z-7) 197.4 in.; (Monarch) 199.7 in.; (Cougar) 200.4 in.; (Marquis) 212.3 in.; (Marquis wag) 218.0 in. Height: (Bobcat) 50.5 in.; (Bobcat wag) 52.0 in.; (Capri) 51.4 in.; (Zephyr) 52.9 in.; (Zephyr wag) 54.2 in.; (Z-7) 51.7 in.; (Monarch) 53.2-53.3 in.; (Cougar) 53.0 in.; (Marquis) 54.7 in.; (Marquis wag) 57.4 in. Width: (Bobcat) 69.4 in.; (Bobcat wag) 69.7 in.; (Capri) 69.1 in.; (Zephyr) 71.0 in.; (Monarch) 74.5 in.; (Cougar) 74.1 in.; (Marquis) 77.5 in. (Marquis wag) 79.3 in. Front Tread: (Bobcat) 55.0 in.; (Capri) 56.6 in.; (Zephyr) 56.6 in.; (Monarch) 59.0 in.; (Cougar) 58.1 in.; (Marquis) 62.2 in. Rear Tread: (Bobcat) 55.8 in.; (Capri) 57.0 in.; (Zephyr) 57.0 in.; (Monarch) 57.7 in.; (Cougar) 57.0 in.; (Marquis) 62.0 in. Standard Tires: (Bobcat) BR78 x 13 SBR BSW; (Capri) P185/80R13 SBR; (Capri Ghia) P175/75R14; (Capri turbo) TRX 190/65R390. (Zephyr) P175/75R14 SBR; (Monarch) DR78 x 14 exc. Ghia, ER78 x 14; (Cougar) P184/75R14 SBR BSW; (Marquis) P205/75R14 SBR; (Marquis wag) P215/75R14.

TECHNICAL: Transmission: Four-speed overdrive floor shift standard on Capri/Zephyr/Monarch six: (1st) 3.29:1; (2nd) 1.84:1; (3rd) 1.00:1; (4th) 0.81:1; (Rev) 3.29:1. Four-speed floor shift standard on Bobcat/Capri/Zephyr four: (1st) 3.98:1; (2nd) 2.14:1; (3rd) 1.42:1; (4th) 1.00:1; (Rev) 3.99:1. Capri turbo: (1st) 4.07:1; (2nd) 2.57:1; (3rd) 1.66:1; (4th) 1.00:1; (Rev) 3.95:1. SelectShift three-speed automatic standard on Cougar and Marquis, optional on others. Bobcat/Capri/Zephyr automatic gear ratios: (1st) 2.47:1; (2nd) 1.47:1; (3rd) 1.00:1; (Rev) 2.11:1. Other automatics: (1st) 2.46:1; (2nd) 1.46:1; (3rd) 1.00:1; (Rev) 2.18:1 to 2.20:1. Four-speed overdrive automatic standard on Cougar w/V8-302: (1st) 2.47:1; (2nd) 1.47:1; (3rd) 1.00:1; (4th) 0.67:1; (Rev) 2.00:1. Standard final drive ratio: (Bobcat) 2.73:1 or 2.79:1 w/4spd, exc. 3.08:1 or 3.00:1 for wagon or either model with auto.; (Capri) 2.73:1 w/four and 4spd, 3.08:1 w/four and auto., 3.08:1 w/six and 4spd, 2.73:1 w/six and auto., 2.26:1 w/V-8 and auto., 3.45:1 w/turbo; (Zephyr) 3.08:1 exc. 2.73:1 w/six and auto., 2.26:1 w/V-8 and auto.; (Monarch) 3.00:1 w/4spd, 2.79:1 w/auto.; (Cougar) 2.26:1 exc. 3.08:1 w/V8-302 and overdrive auto.; (Marquis) 2.26:1 exc. 3.08:1 w/V8-302 and overdrive auto., 2.73:1 w/V8-351; (Marquis wagon) 2.73:1 w/V8-302. Steering: (Marquis) recirculating ball; (others) rack and pinion. Front Suspension: (Bobcat) coil springs with short/long control arms and lower leading arms; (Capri) modified MacPherson struts w/coil springs and anti-sway bar; (Zephyr) MacPherson struts w/coil springs mounted on lower control arm; (Cougar) MacPherson struts with anti-sway bar; (Marquis) coil springs with long/short A-arms and anti-sway bar. Rear Suspension: (Bobcat/Monarch) rigid axle w/semi-elliptic leaf springs; (Capri/Zephyr/Marquis) four-link w/coil springs; (Cougar) four-link with coil springs and anti-sway bar. Brakes: Front disc, rear drum. Ignition: Electronic. Body construction: (Marquis) separate body and frame; (others) unibody. Fuel tank: (Bobcat) 13 gal. exc. wagon, 14 gal.; (Capri) 11.5 gal. w/four, 11.9 w/turbo, others 12.5 gal.; (Zephyr) 14 or 16 gal.; (Monarch) 18.0 gal.; (Cougar) 17.5 gal.; (Marquis) 19 gal. exc. wagon, 20 gal.

DRIVETRAIN OPTIONS: Engines: Turbo 140-cid four: Capri ($481). 200-cid six: Capri ($219); Zephyr ($169). 255-cid V-8: Capri ($338); Zephyr ($288); Monarch ($38). 302-cid V-8: Monarch ($188); Cougar ($150). 351-cid V-8: Marquis ($150). Sport-tuned exhaust: Capri ($38). Transmission/Differential: Five-speed manual trans.: Capri ($156). SelectShift auto. trans.: Bobcat/Capri/Zephyr/Monarch ($340). Four-speed overdrive automatic trans.: Marquis/Cougar ($138). Floor shift lever: Zephyr/Monarch ($138). Traction-Lok differential: Marquis ($106). Optional axle ratio: Bobcat/Capri/Zephyr/Marquis ($15). Brakes & Steering: Power brakes: Bobcat/Capri/Zephyr/Monarch ($78). Power steering: Bobcat/Capri ($160); Zephyr/Monarch ($165). Suspension: H.D. susp.: Monarch ($29); Cougar/Marquis ($23). Handling susp.: Capri/Zephyr ($35). Marquis ($51). Adjustable air shock absorbers: Marquis ($55). Other: H.D. battery ($19-$21). Engine block heater ($15). Trailer towing pkg., heavy: Marquis ($131-$168). California emission system ($238). High-altitude option ($36).

BOBCAT CONVENIENCE/APPEARANCE OPTIONS: Option Packages: Sport pkg. ($206). Sports accent group ($235-$263). Sports instrument group ($80-$111). Deluxe interior ($173-$200). Interior decor group ($50). Convenience group ($69-$111). Appearance protection group ($38-$41). Light group ($24-$36). Comfort/Convenience: Air conditioner ($538). Dual racing mirrors ($43-$60). Day/night mirror ($10). Entertainment: AM/FM radio ($65). AM/FM stereo radio ($103); w/cassette player ($191). AM radio delete ($76 credit). Exterior: Flip-up/removable moon roof ($219). Glass third door ($31). Glamour paint ($45). Tu-tone paint ($113). Narrow vinyl-insert bodyside moldings ($44). Wide black bodyside moldings ($54). Rocker panel moldings ($28). Roof luggage rack: wag ($71). Mud/stone deflectors ($25). Lower bodyside protection ($31). Interior: Four-way driver's seat ($38). Load floor carpet ($28). Cargo area cover ($30). Front floor mats ($19). Wheels/Tires: Wire wheel covers ($40). Forged or cast aluminum wheels ($185): white forged ($200). BR78 x 13 WSW ($50). BR70 x 13 RWL ($89).

1980 Mercury Cougar XR-7 Sports Coupe. (AA)

1980 Mercury Grand Marquis "Coach Roof" sedan. (AA)

CAPRI CONVENIENCE/APPEARANCE OPTIONS: Option Packages: RS option ($204). Turbo RS option ($1185). Interior accent group ($50-$120). Light group ($20-$33). Appearance protection group ($38-$41). Comfort/Convenience: Air cond. ($538). Rear defroster, electric ($96). Fingertip speed control ($129). Tinted glass ($65). Power door locks ($113). Leather-wrapped steering wheel ($44). Tilt steering wheel ($78). Interval wipers ($39). Rear wiper/washer ($76). Right remote mirror ($36). Entertainment: AM radio ($93). AM/FM radio ($145). AM/FM stereo radio ($183); w/8-track tape player ($259); w/cassette player ($271). Premium sound system ($94). Dual rear speakers ($38). Exterior: Flip-up/removable moonroof ($219). Glamour glow paint ($46). Black lower Tu-tone paint ($56). Accent tape stripes: base ($53). Backlight louvers ($141). Rocker panel moldings ($28). Roof luggage rack ($86). Mud/stone deflectors ($25). Lower bodyside protection ($31). Interior: Console ($156). Four-way driver's seat ($38). Recaro bucket seats ($531). Cloth/vinyl bucket seats ($21). Accent cloth/vinyl seat trim ($21). Leather/vinyl bucket seats ($313). Cargo area cover ($34). Color-keyed seatbelts ($24). Wheels and Tires: Wire wheel covers ($89). Forged aluminum wheels ($279). Cast aluminum wheels ($279). Styled steel wheels w/trim rings ($68). P185/80R13 WSW ($50). P175/75R14 BSW (NC); WSW ($50). P185/75R14 BSW ($24); WSW ($74); RWL ($89). TRX 190/65 390 BSW ($150).

ZEPHYR CONVENIENCE/APPEARANCE OPTIONS: Option Packages: Ghia pkg.: Z-7 ($254); sedan ($499); Villager ($373). Villager option ($226). Luxury exterior decor group ($126). Luxury interior group ($370). Interior accent group ($100). Sports instrument group ($85). Convenience group ($31-$55). Appearance protection group ($43-$53). Light group ($40-$48). Comfort/Convenience: Air cond. ($571). Rear defroster, electric ($101). Fingertip speed control ($108-$129). Power windows ($135-$191). Power door locks ($88-$125). Power decklid release ($25). Power seat ($111). Tinted glass ($71). Sport steering wheel ($43). Leather-wrapped steering wheel ($44). Tilt steering ($78-$99). Electric clock ($24). Cigar lighter ($6). Interval wipers ($39). Rear wiper/washer: wag ($91). Trunk light ($8). Dual bright sculptured remote mirrors ($60). Entertainment: AM radio ($93). AM/FM radio ($145). AM/FM stereo radio ($183); w/8-track player ($259); w/cassette player ($271). Premium sound system ($94). Exterior: Flip-up/removable moonroof ($219). Vinyl roof ($118). Glamour paint ($54). Tu-tone paint ($88-$106). Pivoting front vent windows ($50). Rear window vent louvers ($41). Narrow vinyl-insert bodyside moldings ($44); wide black vinyl ($56). Rocker panel moldings ($28). Bright window frames ($24). Bumper guards, rear ($24). Bumper rub strips ($41). Luggage rack: wag ($86). Liftgate assist handle: wag ($13). Mud/stone deflectors ($25). Lower bodyside protection ($31-$44). Interior: Non-reclining bucket seats ($31-$50). Bench seat ($50 credit). Accent cloth seat trim ($40). Base cloth seat trim ($28). Lockable side storage box ($23). Wheels/Tires: Deluxe wheel covers ($41). Styled wheel covers ($46). Wire wheel covers ($120). Styled steel wheels ($99). Cast aluminum wheels ($310). P175/75R14 WSW ($50). P185/75R14 BSW ($24); WSW ($50-$74); RWL ($65-$89). Conventional spare ($37).

MONARCH CONVENIENCE/APPEARANCE OPTIONS: Option Packages: ESS group ($516). Ghia group ($476). Interior decor group ($234). Convenience group ($40). Light group ($51). Cold weather group ($65). Heavy-duty group ($65). Appearance protection group ($30-$53). Visibility group ($71). Comfort/Convenience: Air cond. ($571); auto-temp ($634). Rear defroster, electric ($101). Fingertip speed control ($129). Illuminated entry system ($58). Power windows ($136-$193). Power door locks ($89-$125). Power decklid release ($25). Power four-way seat ($111). Tinted glass ($71). Tilt steering wheel ($78). Auto. parking brake release ($10). Digital clock ($51). Lighting and Mirrors: Cornering lamps ($50). Dual racing mirrors ($49-$68). Lighted right visor vanity mirror ($41). Entertainment: AM radio ($93). AM/FM radio ($145). AM/FM stereo radio ($183); w/8-track player ($259); w/cassette ($271). AM/FM stereo search radio ($333); w/8-track ($409); w/cassette and Dolby ($421). CB radio ($313). Exterior: Power moonroof ($923). Full or landau vinyl roof ($118). Glamour paint ($54). Tone-on-tone paint ($138). Bodyside moldings ($44). Rocker panel moldings ($28). Bumper rub strips ($41). Mud/stone deflectors ($25). Lower bodyside protection ($31). Interior: Console ($93). Four-way driver's seat ($38). Reclining bucket seats (NC). Luxury cloth seat ($108). Base cloth flight bench seat trim ($60). Leather seat trim ($313). Color-keyed seatbelts ($24). Wheels/Tires: Luxury wheel covers ($46) exc. Ghia/ESS (NC). Wire wheel covers ($74-$120). Styled steel wheels w/trim rings ($79-$125). Cast aluminum wheels ($190-$310). DR78 x 14 SBR WSW. ER78 x 14 SBR BSW/WSW. FR78 x 14 SBR BSW/WSW/wide WSW.

COUGAR XR-7 CONVENIENCE/APPEARANCE OPTIONS: Option Packages: Luxury group ($1987). Sports group ($1687). Decor group ($516). Appearance protection group ($43-$46). Light group ($35). Power lock group ($113). Comfort/Convenience: Air cond. ($571); auto-temp ($634). Rear defroster ($101). Fingertip speed control ($108-$129). Illuminated entry system ($58). Keyless entry ($231). Garage door opener w/lighted vanity mirrors ($171). Autolamp on/off delay ($63). Tinted glass ($71). Power windows ($136). Four-way power seat ($111). Six-way power driver's seat ($166). Auto. parking brake release ($10). Leather-wrapped steering wheel ($44). Tilt steering wheel ($78). Electronic instrument cluster ($313). Diagnostic warning lights ($50). Digital clock ($38). Seatbelt chimes ($23). Interval wipers ($39). Lighting and Mirrors: Cornering lamps ($50). Driver's remote mirror ($19). Dual remote mirrors ($60). Lighted right visor vanity mirror ($41). Entertainment: AM radio ($93). AM/FM radio ($145). AM/FM stereo radio ($183); w/8-track player ($259); w/cassette ($271). AM/FM stereo search radio ($333); w/8-track ($409); w/cassette ($421). CB radio ($313). Power antenna ($49). Dual rear speakers ($38). Premium sound system ($119-$150). Exterior: Flip-up/removable moonroof ($219). Luxury half vinyl roof ($125). Vinyl roof delete ($156 credit). Glamour paint ($65). Tu-tone paint ($96-$119). Hood/decklid stripes ($24). Manual vent windows ($50). Wide vinyl-insert bodyside moldings ($56). Rocker panel moldings ($28). Mud/stone deflectors ($25). Lower bodyside protection ($31-$44). Interior: Twin comfort lounge seats ($209). Bucket seats w/console ($176) exc. (NC) w/decor group. Leather seat trim ($303). Trunk trim ($43). Color-keyed seatbelts ($24). Wheels/Tires: Wire wheel covers ($50-$138). Luxury wheel covers ($88). P195/75R14 BSW ($24); WSW ($50). TR220/55R390 WSW tires on alum. wheels: base ($442-$530). Conventional spare ($37).

MARQUIS CONVENIENCE/APPEARANCE OPTIONS: Option Packages: Grand Marquis decor: Colony Park ($581). Convenience group ($80-$98). Power lock group ($90-$164). Visibility light group ($19-$48). Appearance protection group ($51-$61). Comfort/Convenience: Air cond. ($606); w/auto-temp control ($669). Rear defroster, electric ($103). Fingertip speed control ($111-$133). Illuminated entry system ($58). Power windows ($140-$208). Six-way power driver's or bench seat ($168); driver and passenger ($335). Tinted glass ($85). Autolamp on/off delay ($63). Leather-wrapped steering wheel ($44). Tilt steering wheel ($78). Auto. parking brake release ($10). Electric clock ($25). Digital clock ($38-$63). Seatbelt chime ($23). Lighting and Mirrors: Cornering lamps ($50). Driver's remote mirror ($19); passenger's ($41). Lighted right visor vanity mirror ($35-$43). Entertainment: AM radio ($93). AM/FM stereo radio ($183); w/8-track tape player ($259); w/cassette ($271). AM/FM stereo search radio ($333); w/8-track ($409); w/cassette ($421). CB radio ($313). Power antenna ($49). Dual rear speakers ($38). Premium sound system ($94). Exterior: Full or landau vinyl roof ($145). Coach vinyl roof ($130). Glamour paint ($65). Tu-tone paint ($103-$131). Upper bodyside paint stripes ($36). Hood striping ($14). Hood/decklid paint stripes: base ($23). Pivoting front vent windows ($50). Rocker panel moldings: Colony Park ($29). Narrow bodyside moldings ($44). Bumper guards, rear ($24). Bumper rub strips ($41). Luggage rack: wag ($86-$118). Lower bodyside protection ($31-$44). Interior: Dual-facing rear seats: wag ($199). Twin comfort seats ($104-$130). Leather seating ($303). Dual seat recliners ($56). All-vinyl seat trim ($34). Cloth trim: wag ($40). Duraweave vinyl trim: wag ($50). Trunk trim ($46). Trunk mat ($14). Color-keyed seatbelts ($25). Wheels/Tires: Luxury wheel covers ($66-$94). Wire wheel covers ($110-$138). Turbine-spoke cast aluminum wheels ($283-$310). P205/75R14 WSW. P215/75R14 BSW/WSW. P225/75R14 WSW. P205/75R15WSW.

HISTORY: Introduced: October 12, 1979. Model year production: 347,711. Calendar year production (U.S.): 324,518. Calendar year sales by U.S. dealers: 330,852. Model year sales by U.S. dealers: 345,111.

HISTORY: Lincoln-Mercury sales plunged 37 percent for the 1980 model year, drastically below predictions. This would be the final season for Bobcat and Monarch, which would be replaced by the new Lynx and revised Cougar. Bobcat was the slowest-selling Mercury model this year, with Monarch a close second. Sales of both dropped substantially. Plenty of leftover Monarchs remained when the new model year began. Best seller this year was the Zephyr, which found 85,946 buyers. Both sales and production fell sharply for the calendar year, down around 40 percent. Only four Mercury models were expected to reach or exceed the EPA's gas mileage standard, now 20 MPG. Mercury was still perceived as a big, heavy car, at a time when small, lightweight cars were taking over the market.

1981 Mercury Lynx three-door hatchback. (OCW)

1981 Mercury Cougar GS. (OCW)

1981 Mercury Lynx GS hatchback coupe. (M)

The new Lynx and Cougar replaced Bobcat and Monarch, both of which had been selling poorly. Like Ford's Escort, Lynx was billed as a "world car." Two models got smaller base engines this year. Cougar XR-7 dropped from the 255-cid (4.2-liter) V-8 to a 200-cid (3.3-liter) inline six, while Marquis went from a 5.0-liter V-8 down to 4.2 liters.

1981 Mercury Lynx Villager liftgate station wagon. (OCW)

1981 Mercury Lynx RS liftgate station wagon. (OCW)

LYNX — FOUR — Heralding the coming trend toward front-wheel-drive was Mercury's new subcompact "world car," a close twin to Ford Escort. Lynx came in two models and five series: three-door hatchback and four-door liftgate wagon in standard, GL, GS or sporty RS; and with the Villager woodgrain option. The hatchback also came in a fifth, top-of-the-line LS series (a Lincoln-Mercury exclusive). Lynx had four-wheel fully independent suspension, a 97.6-cid (1.6-liter) CVH (Compound Valve Hemispherical) engine, fully synchronized four-speed manual transaxle, and rack-and-pinion steering. Optional: a split-torque three-speed automatic transaxle. A smaller 1.3-liter engine was planned but abandoned. Front suspension consisted of MacPherson struts with strut-mounted coil springs, forged lower control arms, cast steering knuckle, and stabilizer bar. At the rear was an independent trailing-arm suspension with modified MacPherson struts and coil springs on stamped lower control arms. Both Escort and Lynx were designed for easy (and minimal) servicing. Many parts were secured with simple fasteners, including the radiator, fan shroud, oil pan, front fenders, bumpers, grilles, and doors. It was supposed to be easy to replace the battery, headlamps, and exhaust system. Fuses and most bulbs could be replaced without tools. The tight crosshatch-patterned grille was divided into six side-by-side sections by bright vertical bars. Clear wraparound park/signal lamps were outboard of the single rectangular halogen headlamps, which sat within argent housings. Styling included long black front/rear bumper end caps, standard semi-styled steel wheels with white trim rings, bodyside accent striping, and matte black rocker panel paint. Three-doors had high-gloss black center roof pillar appliqués and wraparound horizontal tail lamps. Four-doors had brushed aluminum center roof pillar appliqués. Standard Lynx models had bright wheel lip, window frame, beltline and drip moldings; forward-folding rear bench seat; lighter; day/night mirror; AM radio; and P155/80R13 SBR blackwall tires with European-type wraparound tread patterns. Standard high back front bucket seats had vinyl upholstery. Options included reclining high or low-back bucket seats, console with graphic warning display, speed control, premium sound, digital clock, manual pivoting front vent windows, rear wiper/washer, and cast aluminum spoked wheels. Lynx GL added a black air dam, black bumper rub strips with argent accent stripe (front and rear), wide bodyside molding with argent accent stripe, GL badge on hatch or liftgate, and reclining high-back front bucket seats. Lynx GL three-door hatchbacks had a black lower back panel surround molding, and both models deleted the matte black rocker panel paint. Lynx GS had front and rear black rubber bumper guards and rub strips, reclining low-back bucket seats, cloth/vinyl seat trim, console with graphic warning display, full instrumentation, GS badge on hatch or liftgate, P165/80R13 SBR BSW tires, intermittent wipers, headlamps-on warning buzzer, and glovebox lock. Two-color upper bodyside accent striping replaced the standard single color. GS also had fully styled steel wheels with bright trim rings, argent hub covers and bright wheel nuts, and dual color-keyed remote mirrors. Lynx RS had a blackout grille with bright 'Mercury' plaque, black bumpers with black rub strip and argent accent stripe, black headlamp housings and windshield molding, and black air dam. Special RS accent stripe/decal treatment replaced the standard upper bodyside accent stripe. RS also had black dual remote mirrors, and blackout treatment on the 'B' pillar appliqué, 'C' pillar appliqué, drip and belt moldings, wheel lip moldings, door window frame and quarter window moldings. An RS badge went on the hatch or liftgate. RS also included a handling suspension with larger front stabilizer bar, heavy-duty shocks and stiffer springs, plus P165/80R13 blackwalls. Inside were high-back reclining front bucket seats and a console with graphic warning display. Topline LS hatchbacks offered all the GS features, plus two-tone paint (four combinations available), hatch accent stripe, pleated velour seat trim, electric rear defroster, AM/FM stereo radio, and burled walnut woodtone appliqués on the dash, radio panel and console.

CAPRI — FOUR/SIX/V-8 — Five possibilities greeted Capri customers this year: the base or GS model, RS option, Turbo RS, and Black Magic option. GS replaced the former Ghia. Five-speed manual overdrive became available with either the standard or turbo four-cylinder engine. For 1981, the 200-cid inline six was available with standard four-speed manual overdrive transmission, as well as the optional automatic. Power brakes were now standard, along with 14 inch tires and wheels, and turbine wheel covers. Sport wheel covers were a no-cost option. An AM radio also was standard. New options included a Traction-Lok rear axle and power windows. An optional T-Roof came with two removable tinted glass panels. Capri again displayed a black and bright horizontal grille theme with bright headlamp frames, color-keyed hood louvers, black cowl louvers, and black wiper arms. Standard equipment included the 140-cid (2.3-liter) four and four-speed manual shift, and P175/75R14 SBR BSW tires. Powertrain choices included an inline 200-cid (3.3-liter) six, and 255-cid (4.2-liter) V-8, along with the turbo four. Turbos came only with manual shift, V-8s only with automatic. Both the V-8 and turbo had a dual bright tailpipe extension. Capri GS added black dual remote control mirrors, a light group, door map pocket, and four-spoke steering wheel with woodtone insert and GS badge. RS had a large (nonfunctional) hood scoop; black grille; black headlamp frames and windshield molding: dual black remote mirrors: upper bodyside dual accent stripe (which meant deleting the customary pin stripes): black window frame moldings: and black rear spoiler. RS also included a handling suspension, leather-wrapped steering wheel, and simulated engine-turned instrument panel. Turbo RS models were identified by 'Turbo RS' tape on the front fender, and a bright Turbo plaque on the hood scoop. They also featured a sport-tuned exhaust, three-spoke 15.3 inch forged aluminum wheels, 8000 rpm. tachometer, and Rally suspension. Black Magic sported black or white paint with gold accents. The option package included a smallish body-color hood scoop, gold paint on the grille's leading edge, body-color rear spoiler, and Rally suspension. Gold bodyside accent stripes replaced the standard upper bodyside pinstripes. Also included: black bodyside moldings with gold accent stripes; blackout window frame moldings; spoiler; and gold license plate frames. White cars with this option had white taillamp accents and quarter louvers. Black Magic also had Michelin TRX low-profile tires and three-spoke 15.3 inch forged metric aluminum wheels with gold-color finish. Inside were black engine-turned cluster, radio and right-hand appliqués. Black vinyl seat trim had gold-color cloth inserts. Black Magic and Turbo models carried TRX 190/65R390 tires.

1981 Mercury Capri 'Black Magic' T-top coupe. (OCW)

1981 Mercury Zephyr Z-7 Sports Coupe. (M)

ZEPHYR — FOUR/SIX/V-8 — Not much changed in Zephyr's appearance, but new standard equipment included power (front disc/rear drum) brakes, narrow protective bodyside moldings, and deluxe sound insulation. A new GS option replaced the former Ghia, available on all except the base wagon. Traction-Lok was now available with the V-8. Inline sixes now required automatic. Also made standard: a glovebox lock and dual-note horn. Zephyr's gas tank grew to 16 gallons except for the four-cylinder, which stayed at 14. Low-back front bucket seats with pleated vinyl trim were standard on all models. Also standard: AM radio, day/night inside mirror, cigar lighter, rear ashtray, and right-hand visor vanity mirror. New options included a console, illuminated entry, and Michelin TRX tires on forged aluminum wheels. Base Zephyr sedans had dual front fender louvers, bright lower bodyside moldings with black vinyl insert, upper bodyside dual accent stripes, and front bumper guards. The vertical-theme grille was made up of thin vertical bars in a uniform pattern (no wider divider bar at any point). Quad rectangular headlamps stood over amber quad rectangular parking lamps. Low-back bucket seats had pleated vinyl trim. Zephyr's Z-7 Sport Coupe retained its contemporary wrapover roof design, wraparound tail lamps, and upper bodyside accent striping that continued over the roof. A Z-7 ornament was on the center pillar. It had no rocker panel moldings. Standard equipment included tinted rear window glass. Zephyr's GS option added dual accent stripes on the hood, rear quarter window moldings, protective bodyside moldings with integral partial wheel lip moldings, dual bright remote mirrors, and GS decklid badge. Both police and taxi packages were available.

1981 Mercury Cougar GS sedan. (M)

1981 Mercury Cougar GS coupe. (PH)

1981 Mercury Cougar XR-7 Sports Coupe. (M)

COUGAR — FOUR/SIX/V-8 — Whereas the 1980 lineup had included only a Cougar XR-7, basic Cougars returned this year in the form of a new mid-size five-passenger model, to replace the former Monarch. Two- and four-door sedans were offered, over 3.5 inches narrower than Monarch, but with more hip room in front and rear. Three trim levels were available: base, GS and LS (the latter actually option packages, not separate models). Base engine was now a 140 cu. in (2.3-liter) four with four-speed manual gearbox. Standard tires: P175/75R14 SBR. The hybrid MacPherson strut front suspension placed the coil spring on the lower arm. At the rear: a four-bar link coil spring system. Rack-and-pinion steering with variable-ratio power assist was standard. Manual gearboxes had a self-adjusting clutch. Four-cylinder powered, the new Cougar managed an EPA estimate of 23 MPG (city), as opposed to just 19 for the six-cylinder Monarch it replaced. It also displayed a bit more aerodynamic styling. Cougar sedans had a bright grille with surround molding, made up of thin vertical bars and a wider center bar, plus three subdued horizontal strips. Quad rectangular halogen headlamps stood in bright housings. Park/turn signal lamps were bumper-mounted. Body features included a Cougar hood ornament, bright bumper with flexible black end caps (front guards standard), bright windshield molding, wide lower bodyside molding with black tape insert and integral partial wheel lip moldings, and full-width wraparound tail lamps with integral backups. A Cougar medallion went on the roof pillar, and there was a brushed center pillar appliqué as well as a color-keyed rear pillar louver appliqué. Low-back bucket seats wore all-vinyl upholstery. A four-spoke color-keyed steering wheel and AM radio were standard. Basic equipment also included interval wipers, power brakes, dual-note horn, locking glovebox, visor vanity mirror, lighter, trunk mat, hood ornament, full wheel covers, and driver's remote mirror. A 200-cid (3.3-liter) inline six and 255-cid (4.2-liter) V-8 were optional, as was automatic transmission. Cougar GS added such items as hood/bodyside accent stripes, bumper rub strips with white accent stripes, lower bodyside molding with color-keyed vinyl insert, GS badge on front fender, rear bumper guards, upgraded vinyl bucket seat trim, and four-spoke steering wheel with woodtone insert. Cougar LS was available only as a four-door, including ribbed vinyl-insert color-keyed bodyside moldings, a rear half-vinyl roof with color-keyed back window molding, and special bright wheel lip moldings. Also on LS: special bodyside accent stripe, luxury wheel covers, bright passenger remote mirror, LS fender badge, Twin Comfort lounge front seats, cornering lamps, and a light group.

COUGAR XR-7 — SIX/V-8 — After years of V-8 power, XR-7 dropped down to an inline six as standard engine. Both 255-cid and 302-cid V-8s remained optional, however. Automatic overdrive transmission (introduced in 1980) was now available with both V-8s. The gas tank grew to 18 gallons. New options included puncture-resistant self-sealing tires, Traction-Lok, and pivoting vent windows. Options also included a flip-up removable glass moonroof and keyless entry. Appearance changes included a standard wide bodyside molding with color-keyed vinyl insert, and a wide bright/black belt molding that framed the lower edge of the door and quarter glass. The accent stripe was raised to belt level. Quarter window louvers were removed. The grille and bumper were revised, but still a vertical-bar grille style with bright surround molding. The color-keyed soft bumper covering had a bright insert. Bright rear moldings replaced the "frenched" window design. At the rear was a new standard decklid stripe, plus revised large vertical-theme tail lamps (with integral backup lenses) and ornamentation. Later in the season, the vinyl roof wrapover molding was moved forward. New standard equipment included power brakes and variable-ratio power steering. Also standard: the 200-cid (3.3-liter) inline six with automatic transmission, P195/75R14 SBR BSW tires, AM radio, dual-note horn, mini spare tire, halogen headlamps, stand-up hood ornament, upper bodyside paint stripe, analog clock, and half-vinyl roof with black belt molding. XR-7's GS option included hood accent stripes, bright right-hand remote mirror, Twin Comfort lounge seats, woodgrain steering wheel, and luxury wheel covers. LS added power windows and luxury interior trim, as well as door pull straps and electronic seatbelt warning chimes.

MARQUIS — V-8 — A new 255-cid (4.2-liter) V-8, derived from the 302, was standard on base and Brougham Marquis this year. The 302 remained standard on Grand Marquis and on both wagons. The 255 came with automatic overdrive transmission, introduced for 1980 and made standard on all Marquis models for '81. Nine new paint colors were offered, with five new two-tones and three new vinyl roof colors. Among the new options were puncture-resistant self-sealing tires. The optional premium sound system added two more door-mount speakers, making six in all. A high-output 351-cid (5.8-liter) V-8 was available with optional trailer towing or police packages. Tinted glass had become standard on the wagon's tailgate window in mid-year 1980. So had an AM radio on the base sedan and wagon; AM/FM on Brougham, Grand Marquis and Colony Park. For 1981, P205/75R14 SBR whitewalls were standard on all Marquis, and a coach roof on Brougham and Grand Marquis. Rear bumper guards were now standard on Grand Marquis. Appearance was similar to 1980, with a bright vertical-bar grille and quad rectangular halogen headlamps within bright headlamp/parking lamp surround moldings. Front bumper guards and a stand-up hood ornament were standard. Wraparound parking lamps had integral side markers, as did the horizontal wraparound tail lamps. Twin fender louvers decorated each side of the car. Marquis Brougham added hood accent stripes, a coach vinyl roof, coach lamps, Brougham decklid nameplate, wide bright lower bodyside molding with quarter panel extensions, deluxe wheel covers, and power windows. The AM/FM stereo had two rear speakers. Twin Comfort lounge seats came in Brougham cloth and vinyl trim. Grand Marquis included tinted glass, wide bright/black lower bodyside molding, upper bodyside accent stripes, black rocker panel flanges, accent stripes on fender louvers, and rear bumper guards. Twin Comfort lounge seats were luxury cloth with dual center folding armrests. The Grand Marquis nameplate went on the rear roof pillar and decklid.

I.D. DATA: Mercury had a new 17-symbol Vehicle Identification Number (VIN), again stamped on a metal tab fastened to the instrument panel, visible through the windshield. Symbols one to three indicates manufacturer, make and vehicle type: '1ME' Mercury passenger car. The fourth symbol ('B') denotes restraint system. Next comes a letter 'P', followed by two digits that indicate body type: Model Number, as shown in left column of tables below. (Example: '31' Zephyr two-door sedan.) Symbol eight indicates engine type: '2' L4-98 2Bbl.; 'A' L4-140 2Bbl.; 'B' or 'T' L6-200 1Bbl.; 'D' V8-255 2Bbl.; 'F' V8-302 2Bbl.; 'G' V8-351 2Bbl. Next is a check digit. Symbol ten indicates model year ('B' 1981). Symbol eleven is assembly plant: 'A' Atlanta, GA; 'F' Dearborn, MI; 'R' San Jose, CA; 'G' Chicago; 'H' Lorain, Ohio; 'K' Kansas City, MO; 'X' St. Thomas, Ontario; 'T' Metuchen, NJ; 'Z' St. Louis, MO; 'W' Wayne, MI. The final six digits make up the sequence number, starting with 600001. A Vehicle Certification Label on the left front door lock face panel or door pillar shows the manufacturer, month and year of manufacture, GVW, GAWR, certification statement, VIN, and codes for such items as body type, color, trim, axle, transmission, and special order information.

LYNX (FOUR)

Model No.	Body/ Style No.	Body Type & Seating	Factory Price	Shipping Weight	Prod. Total
63	61D	3-dr. Hatch-4P	5603	N/A	Note 1
65	74D	4-dr. Lift-4P	5931	N/A	Note 1
63	61D	3-dr. L Hatch-4P	5665	1935	Note 1
65	74D	4-dr. L Lift-4P	6070	2059	Note 1
63/60Z	61D	3-dr. GL Hatch-4P	5903	1957	Note 1
65/60Z	74D	4-dr. GL Lift-4P	6235	2074	Note 1
63/602	61D	3-dr. GS Hatch-4P	6642	1996	Note 1
65/602	74D	4-dr. GS Lift-4P	6914	2114	Note 1
63/603	61D	3-dr. LS Hatch-4P	7127	2004	Note 1
63/936	61D	3-dr. RS Hatch-4P	6223	1980	Note 1
65/936	74D	4-dr. RS Lift-4P	6563	2098	Note 1

NOTE 1: Total Lynx production, 72,786 three-door hatchbacks and 39,192 four-door liftgate models.

CAPRI (FOUR/SIX)

67	61D	3-dr. Fastbk-4P	6685/6898	2576/2603	51,786

CAPRI GS (FOUR/SIX)

68	61H	3-dr. Fastbk-4P	6867/7080	2623/2650	7,160

Capri Engine Note: A V-8 engine cost $50 more than the six.

ZEPHYR (FOUR/SIX)

70	66D	2-dr. Sed-5P	6103/6316	2532/2585	5,814
N/A	66D	2-dr. S Sed-5P	5769/5982	N/A	N/A
71	54D	4-dr. Sed-5P	6222/6435	2597/2650	34,334
73	74D	4-dr. Sta Wag-5P	6458/6671	2672/2725	16,283

ZEPHYR Z-7 (FOUR/SIX)

72	36R	2-dr. Spt Cpe-5P	6252/6465	2584/2637	10,078

COUGAR (FOUR/SIX)

76	66D	2-dr. Sedan-5P	6535/6748	2682/2772	10,793
77	54D	4-dr. Sedan-5P	6694/6907	2726/2816	42,860

Zephyr/Cougar Engine Note: A 255-cid V-8 engine cost $50 more than the six.

1981 Mercury Grand Marquis sedan. (AA)

Model No.	Body/ Style No.	Body Type & Seating	Factory Price	Shipping Weight	Prod. Total
COUGAR XR-7 (SIX/V-8)					
90	66D	2-dr. HT Cpe-4P	7799/7849	3000/3137	37,275

XR-7 Engine Note: Price shown is for 255-cid V-8; a 302 V-8 cost $41 more.

Model No.	Body/ Style No.	Body Type & Seating	Factory Price	Shipping Weight	Prod. Total
MARQUIS (V-8)					
81	54H	4-dr. Sedan-6P	7811	3493	10,392
87	74H	4-dr. 2S Sta Wag-6P	8309	3745	2,219
MARQUIS BROUGHAM (V-8)					
82	66K	2-dr. Sedan-6P	8601	3513	2,942
83	54K	4-dr. Sedan-6P	8800	3564	11,744
MARQUIS COLONY PARK (V-8)					
88	74K	4-dr. 2S Sta Wag-6P	9304	3800	6,293
GRAND MARQUIS (V-8)					
84	66L	2-dr. Sedan-6P	9228	3533	4,268
85	54L	4-dr. Sedan-6P	9459	3564	23,780

FACTORY PRICE AND WEIGHT NOTE: Cougar XR-7 prices and weights to left of slash are for six-cylinder, to right for V-8 engine. For Capri, Zephyr and Cougar, prices/weights to left of slash are for four-cylinder, to right for V-6.

ENGINE [Base Four (Lynx)]: Inline. Overhead cam. Four-cylinder. Cast-iron block and aluminum head. Displacement: 97.6-cid (1.6 liters). Bore & stroke: 3.15 x 3.13 in. Compression ratio: 8.8:1. Brake horsepower: 65 at 5200 rpm. Torque: 85 lbs.-ft. at 3000 rpm. Five main bearings. Hydraulic valve lifters. Carburetor: 2Bbl. Holley-Weber 5740. VIN Code: 2.

ENGINE [Base Four (Capri, Zephyr, Cougar)]: Inline. Overhead cam. Four-cylinder. Cast-iron block and head. Displacement: 140-cid (2.3 liters). Bore & stroke: 3.78 x 3.13 in. Compression ratio: 9.0:1. Brake horsepower: 88 at 4600 rpm. Torque: 118 lbs.-ft. at 2600 rpm. Five main bearings. Hydraulic valve lifters. Carburetor: 2Bbl. Holley 6500. VIN Code: A.

ENGINE [Optional Turbocharged Four (Capri)]: Same as 140-cid four above, but with turbocharger: Horsepower: N/A. Torque: N/A. Carburetor: 2Bbl. VIN Code: A.

ENGINE [Base Six (XR-7); Optional (Capri, Zephyr, Cougar)]: Inline. OHV. Six-cylinder. Cast-iron block and head. Displacement: 200-cid (3.3 liters). Bore & stroke: 3.68 x 3.13 in. Compression ratio: 8.6:1. Brake horsepower: 88-94 at 3800-4000 rpm. Torque: 154-158 lbs.-ft. at 1400 rpm. Seven main bearings. Hydraulic valve lifters. Carburetor: 1Bbl. Holley 1946. VIN Code: B or T.

ENGINE [Base V-8 (Marquis); Optional (Capri, Zephyr, Cougar)]: 90-degree, overhead valve V-8. Cast-iron block and head. Displacement: 255-cid (4.2 liters). Bore & stroke: 3.68 x 3.00 in. Compression ratio: 8.8:1. Brake horsepower: 115-120 at 3100-3400 rpm. Torque: 195-205 lbs.-ft. at 2000-2600 rpm. Five main bearings. Hydraulic valve lifters. Carburetor: 2Bbl. Motorcraft 2150 or 7200VV. VIN Code: D.

ENGINE [Optional V-8 (XR-7, Marquis)]: 90-degree, overhead valve V-8. Cast-iron block and head. Displacement: 302-cid (5.0 liters). Bore & stroke: 4.00 x 3.00 in. Compression ratio: 8.4:1. Brake horsepower: 130 at 3400 rpm. Torque: 235 lbs.-ft. at 1600 rpm. Five main bearings. Hydraulic valve lifters. Carburetor: 2Bbl. Motorcraft 2150 or 2700VV. VIN Code: F.

ENGINE [Optional V-8 (Marquis)]: 90-degree, overhead valve V-8. Cast-iron block and head. Displacement: 351-cid (5.8 liters). Bore & stroke: 4.00 x 3.50 in. Compression ratio: 8.3:1. Brake horsepower: 145 at 3200 rpm. Torque: 270 lbs.-ft. at 1800 rpm. Five main bearings. Hydraulic valve lifters. Carburetor: 2Bbl. Motorcraft 7200VV. VIN Code: G.

NOTE: A police version of the 351 V-8 was available, rated 165 horsepower at 3600 rpm. and 285 lbs.-ft. at 2200 rpm.

CHASSIS DATA: Wheelbase: (Lynx) 94.2 in.; (Capri) 100.4 in.; (Zephyr) 105.5 in.; (Cougar) 105.5 in.; (XR-7) 108.4 in.; (Marquis) 114.3 in. Overall Length: (Lynx) 163.9 in.; (Lynx lift) 165.0 in.; (Capri) 179.1 in.; (Zephyr) 195.5 in.; (Z-7) 197.4 in.; (Cougar) 196.5 in.; (XR-7) 200.4 in.; (Marquis) 212.3 in.; (Marquis wag) 218.0 in. Height: (Lynx) 53.3 in.; (Capri) 51.4 in.; (Zephyr) 52.9 in.; (Zephyr wag) 54.2 in.; (Z-7) 51.7 in.; (Cougar) 53.0 in.; (XR-7) 53.2 in.; (Marquis) 54.7 in.; (Marquis wag) 57.4 in. Width: (Lynx) 65.9 in.; (Capri) 69.1 in.; (Zephyr) 71.0 in.; (Cougar) 68.7 in.; (XR-7) 74.1 in.; (Marquis) 77.5 in.; (Marquis wag) 79.3 in. Front Tread: (Lynx) 54.7 in.; (Capri) 56.6 in.; (Zephyr/Cougar) 56.6 in.; (XR-7) 58.1 in.; (Marquis) 62.2 in. Rear Tread: (Lynx) 56.0 in.; (Capri) 57.0 in.; (Zephyr/Cougar) 57.0 in.; (XR-7) 57.0 in.; (Marquis) 62.0 in. Standard Tires: (Lynx) P155/80R13; (Capri) P175/75R14; (Capri turbo) TRX190/65R390. (Zephyr/Cougar) P175/75R14 SBR; (XR7) P195/75R14 SBR BSW; (Marquis) P205/75R14 SBR: (Marquis wag) P215/75R14.

TECHNICAL: Transmission: Four-speed manual standard on Lynx. Gear ratios: (1st) 3.58:1. (2nd) 2.05:1. (3rd) 1.21:1. (4th) 0.81:1. (Rev) 3.46:1. Four-speed floor shift standard on Capri/Zephyr/Cougar four: (1st) 3.98:1. (2nd) 2.14:1. (3rd) 1.42:1. (4th) 1.00:1. (Rev) 3.99:1. Four-speed overdrive floor shift standard on Capri six: (1st) 3.29:1. (2nd) 1.84:1. (3rd) 1.00:1. (4th) 0.81:1. (Rev) 3.29:1. Capri turbo four-speed: (1st) 4.07:1. (2nd) 2.57:1. (3rd) 1.66:1. (4th) 1.00:1. (Rev) 3.95:1. Capri five-speed: (1st) 4.05:1. (2nd) 2.43:1. (3rd) 1.48:1. (4th) 1.00:1. (5th) 0.82:1. (Rev) 3.90:1. Capri turbo five-speed: (1st) 3.72:1. (2nd) 2.23:1. (3rd) 1.48:1. (4th) 1.00:1. (5th) 0.76:1. (Rev) 3.59:1. SelectShift three-speed automatic standard on XR-7, optional on others. Gear ratios: (1st) 2.46:1 or 2.47:1. (2nd) 1.46:1 or 1.47:1. (3rd) 1.00:1. (Rev) 2.11:1 to 2.19:1. Lynx three-speed automatic: (1st) 2.80:1. (2nd) 1.60:1. (3rd) 1.00:1. (Rev) 1.97:1. Four-speed overdrive automatic on XR-7/Marquis: (1st) 2.40:1. (2nd) 1.47:1. (3rd) 1.00:1. (4th) 0.67:1. (Rev) 2.00:1. Standard final drive ratio: (Lynx) 3.59:1 w/4spd, 3.31:1 w/auto.; (Capri four/turbo) 3.08:1 w/4spd, 3.45:1 w/5spd; (Capri six) 3.08:1 w/4spd, 2.73:1 w/5spd; (Capri V-8) 2.26:1; (Zephyr/Cougar) 2.73:1 w/six, 2.26:1 w/V-8; (Cougar) 2.73:1 w/six, 2.26:1 w/V8-255 and auto., 3.08:1 w/V-8 and 4spd auto.; (Marquis) 3.08:1 exc. 2.73:1 w/high-output 351 V-8 and 4spd auto. Steering: (Marquis) recirculating ball; (others) rack-and-pinion. Front Suspension: (Lynx) MacPherson strut-mounted coil springs w/lower control arms and stabilizer bar; (Capri) modified MacPherson struts w/coil springs and anti-sway bar; (Zephyr/Cougar) MacPherson struts w/coil springs mounted on lower control arm and anti-sway bar; (Marquis) coil springs with long/short A-arms and anti-sway bar. Rear Suspension: (Lynx) independent trailing arms w/modified MacPherson struts and coil springs on lower control arms; (Capri/Zephyr/Cougar/Marquis) four-link w/coil springs; (XR-7) four-link with coil springs and anti-sway bar. Brakes: Front disc, rear drum. Ignition: Electronic. Body construction: (Marquis) separate body and frame; (others) unibody. Fuel tank: (Lynx) 10 gal.; (Capri) 12.5 gal.; (Zephyr) 16 gal. exc. 14 gal. w/four; (Cougar) 16 gal.; (XR-7) 18 gal.; (Marquis) 19 gal. exc. wagon, 20 gal.

DRIVETRAIN OPTIONS: Engines: Turbo 140-cid four: Capri ($610). 200-cid six: Capri/Zephyr/Cougar ($213). 255-cid V-8: Capri/Zephyr/Cougar ($263). 302-cid V-8: Cougar XR-7 ($91). Marquis ($41). 351-cid V-8: Marquis ($83); Grand Marquis 4-dr., wagon ($41). H.O. 351-cid V-8: Marquis ($139-$180). Sport-tuned exhaust: Capri ($39). Transmission/Differential: Five-speed manual trans.: Capri ($152). Automatic transaxle: Lynx ($344). SelectShift auto. trans.: Capri/Zephyr/Cougar ($349). Four-speed overdrive automatic trans.: Cougar XR-7 ($162). Floor shift lever: Zephyr/Cougar ($43). Traction-Lok differential: Capri/Zephyr/Cougar/XR-7 ($67); Marquis ($71). Brakes & Steering: Power brakes: Lynx ($79). Power steering: Lynx/Capri ($163); Zephyr ($168); Cougar ($161). Suspension: H.D.

susp.: Marquis ($22); Cougar XR-7 ($23). Handling susp.: Lynx ($37); Zephyr ($45); Capri/Marquis ($43). Load revelers: Marquis ($57). Other: H.D. battery ($20). Extended-range gas tank: Lynx ($32). Engine block heater ($16). Trailer towing pkg., heavy duty: Marquis ($176-$206). California emission system ($46). High-altitude option ($35-$36).

LYNX CONVENIENCE/APPEARANCE OPTIONS: Option Packages: Villager woodtone option: GL/GS ($224). Appearance protection group ($49). Light group ($39). Comfort/Convenience: Air conditioner ($530). Rear defroster, electric ($102). Fingertip speed control ($132). Tinted glass ($70); windshield only ($28). Digital clock ($52). Intermittent wipers ($41). Rear wiper/washer ($100). Dual remote sport mirrors ($56). Entertainment: AM/FM radio ($63). AM/FM stereo radio ($100); w/cassette player ($87-$187). Dual rear speakers ($37). Premium sound ($91). AM radio delete ($61 credit). Exterior: Flip-up/open air roof ($154-$228). Glamour paint ($45). Tu-tone paint ($91). Front vent windows, pivoting ($55). Vinyl-insert bodyside moldings ($41). Bumper guards, front or rear ($23). Bumper rub strips ($34). Roof luggage rack ($74). Roof air deflector ($26). Lower bodyside protection ($60). Interior: Console ($98). Low-back reclining bucket seats ($30). Reclining front seatbacks ($55). Cloth/vinyl seat trim ($28); vinyl (NC). Deluxe seatbelts ($23). Wheels/Tires: Cast aluminum spoke wheels ($193-$279). P155/80R13 WSW ($55). P165/80R13 BSW ($19); WSW ($55-$74).

CAPRI CONVENIENCE/APPEARANCE OPTIONS: Option Packages: Black magic option ($644). RS option ($234). Turbo RS option ($1191). Light group ($43). Appearance protection group ($41). Comfort/Convenience: Air cond. ($560). Rear defroster, electric ($107). Fingertip speed control ($132). Power windows ($140). Power door locks ($93). Tinted glass ($76). Leather-wrapped steering wheel ($49). Tilt steering wheel ($80-$93). Interval wipers ($41). Rear wiper/washer ($85). Right remote mirror ($37). Entertainment: AM/FM radio ($51). AM/FM stereo radio ($88); w/8-track tape player ($162); w/cassette player ($174). Premium sound system ($91). Dual rear speakers ($37). Radio flexibility option ($61). AM radio delete ($61 credit). Exterior: T-Roof ($874). Flip-up/open air roof ($213-$228). Glamour paint ($48). Tu-tone paint ($57-$110). Gold accent stripes ($54). Liftgate louvers ($145). Rocker panel moldings ($30). Roof luggage rack ($90). Mud/stone deflectors ($26). Lower bodyside protection ($37). Interior: Console ($168). Recaro bucket seats ($610). Accent cloth/vinyl seat trim ($22). Leather/vinyl seat trim ($359). Front floor mats ($18). Wheels and Tires: Wire wheel covers ($80). Sport wheel covers (NC). Forged metric aluminum wheels ($340). Cast aluminum wheels ($305). Styled steel wheels w/trim rings ($63). P175/75R14 WSW ($55). P185/75R14 BSW (N/A); WSW ($82); RWL ($102). TR190/65R390 BSW ($128).

ZEPHYR CONVENIENCE/APPEARANCE OPTIONS: Option Packages: Villager option ($229). GS option ($327-$383). Instrument cluster ($88). Appearance protection group ($50). Light group ($43). Comfort/Convenience: Air cond. ($585). Rear defroster, electric ($107). Fingertip speed control (N/A). Illuminated entry ($60). Power windows ($140-$195). Power door locks ($93-$132). Remote decklid release ($27). Power seat ($122). Tinted glass ($76). Leather-wrapped steering wheel ($49). Tilt steering ($80-$93). Electric clock ($23). Interval wipers ($41). Rear wiper/washer: wag ($110). Lighting and Mirrors: Dual-beam map light ($13). Trunk light ($6). Left remote mirror ($15). Dual remote mirrors ($55). Lighted visor vanity mirror ($43). Entertainment: AM/FM radio ($51). AM/FM stereo radio ($88); w/8-track player ($162); w/cassette player ($174). Twin rear speakers ($37). Premium sound system ($91). Radio flexibility ($61). AM radio delete ($61 credit). Exterior: Flip-up/open air roof (N/A). Full vinyl roof ($115). Glamour paint ($55). Tu-tone paint ($90-$110). Pivoting front vent windows ($55). Tailgate assist handle: wag ($16). Wide vinyl bodyside moldings: Z-7 ($55). Rocker panel moldings ($30). Bumper guards, rear ($23). Bumper rub strips ($43). Luggage rack: wagon ($90). Lower bodyside protection ($37-$49). Interior: Console ($168). Bench seat ($24 credit). Cloth/vinyl seat trim ($28). Vinyl trim: Z-7 ($26). Front floor mats ($18). Locking storage box ($24). Deluxe seatbelts ($23). Wheels/Tires: Wire wheel covers ($117). Styled steel wheels ($48); w/trim rings ($94). P175/75R14 WSW ($55). P185/75R14 WSW ($86). TR190/65R390 BSW on TRX alum. wheels ($512). Conventional spare ($39).

COUGAR CONVENIENCE/APPEARANCE OPTIONS: Option Packages: GS option ($371). LS option ($972). Light group ($45). Cold weather group ($67). Appearance protection group ($45). Comfort/Convenience: Air cond. ($585). Rear defroster ($107). Fingertip speed control ($126). Illuminated entry system ($60). Six-way power twin comfort seats ($162). Four-way power Flight Bench seat ($122). Power windows ($140-$195). Power door locks ($93-$132). Remote decklid release ($27). Tinted glass ($76). Tilt steering wheel ($96). Electric clock ($23). Interval wipers ($41). Lighting and Mirrors: Cornering lamps ($51). Lighted right visor vanity mirror ($43). Entertainment: AM/FM radio ($51). AM/FM stereo radio ($88); w/8-track player ($162); w/cassette ($174). Premium sound ($91). Dual rear speakers

($37). Radio flexibility ($61). AM radio delete ($61 credit). Exterior: Flip-up/open air roof ($228). Full or landau vinyl roof ($115). Glamour paint ($55). Tu-tone paint ($66-$162). Bodyside moldings ($45). Bumper rub strips ($41). Mud/stone deflectors ($26). Lower bodyside protection ($37). Interior: Console ($168). Twin comfort seats ($168). Cloth seat trim ($45-$62). Leather seat trim ($340). Deluxe seatbelts ($22). Wheels/Tires: Luxury wheel covers: base ($43). Wire wheel covers ($80-$124). Aluminum wheels ($306-$350). P175/75R14 WSW. P185/75R14 BSW/WSW/RWL. TR on aluminum wheels. Conventional spare ($39).

COUGAR XR-7 CONVENIENCE/APPEARANCE OPTIONS: Option Packages: LS option ($715). GS option ($320) exc. ($96) w/LS option. Appearance protection group ($45). Light group ($30). Power lock group ($120). Comfort/Convenience: Air cond. ($585); auto-temp ($652). Rear defroster ($107). Fingertip speed control ($105-$132). Illuminated entry system ($60). Keyless entry ($227). Garage door opener w/lighted vanity mirrors ($177). Autolamp on/off delay ($65). Tinted glass ($76). Power windows ($140). Four-way power seat ($122). Six-way power driver's seat ($173). Auto. parking brake release ($10). Leather-wrapped steering wheel ($45). Tilt steering wheel ($80). Electronic instrument cluster ($322). Diagnostic warning lights ($51). Seatbelt chimes ($23). Digital clock ($40). Interval wipers ($41). Lighting and Mirrors: Cornering lamps ($51). Remote right mirror ($52). Lighted right visor vanity mirror ($41). Entertainment: AM/FM radio ($51). AM/FM stereo radio ($88); w/8-track player ($162); w/cassette ($174). AM/FM stereo search radio ($234); w/8-track ($309); w/cassette ($321). Power antenna ($48). Dual rear speakers ($37). Premium sound system ($116-$146). Radio flexibility ($65). AM radio delete ($61 credit). Exterior: Carriage roof ($772). Flip-up/open air roof ($228). Luxury rear vinyl half roof ($165). Vinyl roof delete ($130 credit). Glamour paint ($70). Tu-tone paint ($99). Hood paint stripes ($16). Pivoting front vent windows ($55). Rocker panel moldings ($30). Mud/stone deflectors ($26). Lower bodyside protection ($48). Interior: Bucket seats w/console ($182) exc. (NC) with GS/LS. Recaro bucket seats ($528). Twin comfort lounge seats w/recliners ($215). Leather seat trim ($359). Vinyl seat trim ($28). Front floor mats ($13). Trunk trim ($44). Wheels: Wire wheel covers ($93). Luxury wheel covers ($43).

MARQUIS CONVENIENCE/APPEARANCE OPTIONS: Option Packages: Grand Marquis decor: Colony Park ($491). Convenience group ($70-$101). Power lock group ($93-$176). Light group ($22-$37). Appearance protection group ($57). Comfort/Convenience: Air cond. ($624); w/auto-temp control ($687). Rear defroster, electric ($107). Fingertip speed control ($135). Illuminated entry system ($59). Power windows: base 4-dr. ($211). Power seat ($173). Six-way power seats w/recliners ($229). Power twin comfort seats: base ($402). Tinted glass ($87). Autolamp on/off delay ($65). Leather-wrapped steering wheel ($45). Tilt steering wheel ($80). Electric clock ($23). Digital clock ($40-$63). Seatbelt chime ($23). Lighting and Mirrors: Cornering lamps ($49). Remote right mirror ($39). Lighted right visor vanity mirror ($38). Entertainment: AM/FM stereo radio ($88); w/8-track tape player ($74) exc. base ($162); w/cassette ($87) exc. base ($174). AM/FM stereo search radio ($146) exc. base ($234); w/tape player ($233-$321). CB radio ($305). Power antenna ($48). Dual rear speakers ($37). Premium sound system ($116). Radio flexibility ($65). AM radio delete ($61 credit). Exterior: Coach vinyl roof: Brghm ($567). Full vinyl roof: base sed ($141). Glamour paint ($67). Tu-tone paint ($100-$134). Paint stripes ($34). Hood striping ($15). Pivoting front vent windows ($55). Rocker panel moldings: Colony Park ($27). Bodyside moldings ($44). Bumper rub strips ($46). Luggage rack: wag ($84). Lower bodyside protection ($46). Interior: Dual-facing rear seats: wag ($146). Cloth twin comfort seats: wag ($39). Leather twin comfort seating ($361). Duraweave flight bench seats: wag ($54). Vinyl seat trim ($28). Deluxe seatbelts ($24). Trunk trim ($45). Wheels/Tires: Luxury wheel covers ($45-$72). Wire wheel covers ($112-$139). P215/75R14 WSW. P225/75R14 WSW. P205/75R15 WSW/puncture-resistant. Conventional spare ($39).

1981 Mercury Zephyr Villager station wagon. (JG)

HISTORY: Introduced: October 3, 1980. Model year production: 389,999. Calendar year production (U.S.): 363,970. Calendar year sales by U.S. dealers: 339,550. Model year sales by U.S. dealers: 354,335 (including 5,730 leftover Bobcats and 13,954 early '82 LN7 models). After a terrible 1980, the Lynx arrived to give Mercury new hope. First-year sales were heartening, totaling the highest figure since the Comet appeared back in 1960. Model year sales fell only slightly, as a result of the Lynx success. Calendar year sales and production both rose, as did model year production. Cougar XR-7 scored far weaker and well below expectations, but the new smaller standard Cougar did better, finding many more buyers than it had a year earlier wearing a Monarch badge. Sales of the full-size Marquis fell, but not drastically. The new LN7, kin to Ford's EXP, debuted in April 1981 but as an early '82 model.

1982 MERCURY

1982 Mercury Lynx GL Villager station wagon. (JG)

A new four-door Lynx was introduced this year. So was a close-ratio manual transaxle option for both Lynx and the new LN7 two-seater, which arrived in April 1981. Cougar added a station wagon model, and an optional lightweight 232-cid (3.8-liter) V-6 with aluminum heads and plastic rocker arms. Several models had a new lockup torque converter in the SelectShift automatic transmission. A high-output 302-cid (5.0-liter) V-8 became standard on the Capri RS, optional on other Capris.

LYNX — FOUR — A new five-door (actually four "people" doors) hatchback model joined the original two-door hatchback and four-door wagon, but appearance was the same as the original 1981 version. Lynx had quickly become Mercury's best seller. As for mileage, the EPA rating with the base 97.6-cid (1.6-liter) four was 31 city and 47 highway. That CVH engine got a new reduced-restriction exhaust system. The gas tank grew to 11.3 gallons this year, and P165/80R13 tires replaced the former P155 size, but not much else changed. Not until mid-year, at any rate, when a number of mechanical improvements were announced. A high-output 1.6-liter engine was added to the option list in mid-year. So was a new sport close-ratio manual transaxle with higher numerical gear ratios in third and fourth gear, and smaller steps between second and third, and third and fourth. The H.O. powerplant had a higher-lift cam, less-restrictive muffler, stainless steel tubular exhaust header, less-restrictive air intake system, and larger carburetor venturi. Both engines came with a 3.59:1 drive axle ratio (3.31:1 with three-speed automatic).

1982 Mercury Lynx LN7 hatchback coupe. (PH)

LN7 — FOUR — Even though Lynx was essentially a carryover this year, the two-seater derived from its basic chassis was brand new. Wearing a "bubbleback" third-door treatment, the LN7 coupe displayed an aerodynamic design with 0.34 drag coefficient. The front-wheel drive chassis had four-wheel, fully independent suspension. Powertrain was the same as Lynx: 1.6-liter Compound Valve Hemi-spherical (CVH) OHC engine with four-speed manual transaxle (overdrive fourth). Mechanically, LN7 was identical to Ford's new EXP. Mercury's version was considered the more radical of the pair, though, as a result of its large wraparound "bubbleback" back window. Both EXP and LN7 had sizable wheel lips, wide bodyside moldings, and steep windshield angle. Large sloped tail lamps wrapped around to a point on each quarter panel. Single rectangular halogen headlamps sat in black "eyebrow" housings. Park/signal lamps were mounted below the bumper strip. The LN7 grille consisted of 10 small slots (in two rows) in a sloping body-color panel, versus just two on EXP. Wide black bodyside moldings had argent accent striping. So did the soft black front and rear bumpers. LN7 had dual black door-mounted remote sport mirrors, and a single-color dual bodyside paint stripe. The slotted front fascia held a cat-head ornament, while rear pillars were vertically-louvered. Black paint treatment went on the front pillar, quarter window frame, door frame, and rocker panels. An ample standard equipment list included power brakes, electric rear defroster, AM radio, full performance instrumentation, power liftgate release, self-adjusting clutch linkage, throaty tuned exhaust (with manual shift), interval wipers, and full tinted glass. LN7 also had bright exposed dual exhausts, reclining low-back bucket seats with vinyl trim, tachometer, trip odometer, and temperature gauge. A console held the ammeter, oil pressure gauge and other indicators. Tires were P165/80R13 blackwall steel-belted radials with European-type wraparound tread pattern, on styled steel wheels with trim rings.

1982 Mercury Lynx LS hatchback sedan. (M)

1982 Mercury Capri L hatchback coupe. (CP)

1982 Mercury Capri RS hatchback coupe (with 5.0-liter V-8). (PH)

1982 Mercury Zephyr sedan. (CP)

CAPRI — FOUR/SIX/V-8 — Changes in Mercury's variant of Mustang were mainly mechanical this year. Both the optional 200-cid (3.3-liter) inline six with SelectShift automatic, and 255-cid (4.2-liter) V-8, had a new lockup torque converter for the automatic transmission. A new powerteam also was available: the 302-cid (5.0-liter) V-8 with four-speed manual overdrive. That high-output 5.0-liter V-8 had new camshaft timing, low-restriction air cleaner with dual air inlets, large-venturi carburetor, and low-restriction sporty-tuned exhaust. Five-speed manual overdrive with the base 140-cid (2.3-liter) four-cylinder engine later became optional in 45 states. A new base series was added, so the prior base model with console became now Capri L. Selection consisted of base, L, GS, RS, and Black Magic models. This year's gas tank held 15.4 gallons. Flash-to-pass was added to the stalk, and the new screw-on gas cap had a tether. Rear pillar louvers were now body-colored, except for the RS, which had black ones. A console with graphic warning display was now standard on all except the base model. Base Capris had a black and bright horizontal-style grille, front and rear bumpers with color-keyed soft urethane cover, extra-wide wraparound black bodyside molding with dual color-keyed center stripes, turbine wheel covers, upper bodyside pin stripes, black driver's side remote mirror, black and bright window frames, black cowl louver, and color-keyed hood louvers. High-back bucket seats had reclining seatbacks and pleated vinyl trim. Tires were P175/75R14SBR blackwalls. Capri L had low-back bucket seats, a passenger-side visor vanity mirror, upgraded door trim, console with graphic warning display, and 'L' badge. GS included dual black remote mirrors, 'GS' badge, light group, four-spoke steering wheel with woodtone insert, and driver's door map pocket. Capri RS had a large non-functional hood scoop, black grille, black headlamp frames and windshield molding, dual black remote mirrors, upper bodyside dual accent tape striping, 'RS' identification on front fender, black window frame moldings, rear spoiler, and black "third door" window molding. Several revisions hit the RS later on, including a '5.0' badge on the side, dual bright tailpipe outlets, and Rallye suspension with TR performance package replacing the original handling suspension. It also came with Traction-Lok axle, P185/75R14 blackwalls, and power steering. Capri's Black Magic was offered again, with either black or white body color and gold accents. It had a small body-color hood scoop, gold paint on leading edge of grille, and other gold and black trim. Black Magic included a gold cat's head on the fender, and gold license plate frame at the back. Also included: a body-color rear spoiler, Michelin TRX tires on forged metric aluminum wheels with gold-color finish, and rallye suspension. A fuel economy calibration option (with four-cylinder) was added, to attract the economy-minded buyer. It had a feedback fuel system, four-speed manual shift, and 2.73:1 axle (to replace the standard 3.08:1).

ZEPHYR — FOUR/SIX/V-8 — Not much was new on the Zephyr compact, but the two-door sedan and station wagon were dropped. That left only a two-door (Z-7) sport coupe and four-door sedan. Both came in base or GS trim. A new locking torque converter was added to the automatic transmission with optional inline six and 255-cid (4.2-liter) V-8. That V-8 was available only with police and taxi packages. There was a new tethered gas cap and new deep-well trunk design. Tires were P175/75R14 blackwalls. Sedan interiors were upgraded to Z-7 level by adding luxury door trim panels, high-gloss woodtone instrument panel appliqués, and color-keyed seatbelts. A fuel economy calibration version of the base 140-cid (2.3-liter) four replaced the standard 3.08:1 axle with a 2.73:1, as a no-extra-cost option with restricted options list. It was supposed to deliver 40 MPG on the highway, 25 overall in EPA estimates. Z-7 again had the wrapover roof design with broad center pillar and thin rear pillar, no rocker panel moldings, Z-7 ornament on the center pillar, and wraparound tail lamps. Also standard: tinted rear window glass. GS models had dual accent stripes on the hood, protective bodyside moldings with integral partial wheel lip moldings, a 'GS' badge on the decklid, and dual bright remote mirrors. Rocker panel moldings were deleted from the four-door sedan with GS option.

COUGAR — SIX/V-6 — For its second season in this Monarch-based body style, Cougar added a new station wagon model and lost the prospect of V-8 power. Wagons came in either GS or Villager form; sedans were either GS or LS. GS was now the basic level. Passenger capacity increased from five to six, because of the new standard Flight Bench seat. Base engine was now the 200-cid (3.3-liter) inline six. SelectShift automatic with locking torque converter was now standard. Manual shift was dropped. An AM radio with dual speakers was now standard. A tether was added to the gas cap, and the tank grew to 16 gallons. Flash-to-pass was added later to the steering column stalk control, while 'GS' badges went on fenders. A rear bumper sight shield was added. Hood and bodyside accent stripes were now standard, along with color-keyed vinyl-insert bodyside moldings. Cougar had a unitized body, strut-type front suspension with spring on lower arm, variable-ratio power-assist rack-and-pinion steering, and four-bar link rear suspension. Cougar LS added unique hood accent stripes that extended across the grille opening panel; bumper rub strips with white accent stripes; ribbed vinyl color-keyed bodyside molding; special bright wheel lip moldings; rear bumper guards; and luxury wheel covers with cat's head center insert. 'LS' badges went on front fenders. LS also added Twin Comfort lounge seats, whereas the GS had a Flight Bench seat. The GS station wagon had a bodyside paint stripe in a straight-through design with no kickup, which did not extend onto the liftgate. The Villager wagon deleted the hood accent stripes and had medium rosewood woodtone bodyside paneling appliqués. 'Villager' script went on the liftgate and the 'GS' badge was deleted from front fenders. Options included an all-new 232-cid (3.8-liter) V-6, power lock group, and extended-range fuel tank. Options dropped: the floor shifter, console, mud/stone deflectors, and radio flexibility.

COUGAR XR-7 — SIX/V-6/V-8 — No longer available on this year's personal-luxury XR-7 was the 302-cid V-8 engine. Three choices were offered, though: base 200-cid (3.3-liter) inline six, new optional aluminum-head 232-cid (3.8-liter) V-6, and 255-cid (4.2-liter) V-8. The two-door hardtop body came in GS and upscale LS form, as the former base model dropped out. Gas tanks grew from 18 to 21 gallons. Four-speed automatic overdrive transmission was standard with the V-6 or V-8, while the base inline six had SelectShift three-speed automatic with a lockup torque converter clutch. Looking at appearance changes, black vinyl-insert bodyside moldings replaced the former color-keyed moldings. Black bumper strips with white accent stripes replaced bright rub strips. A new half-vinyl roof design with wide black accent and wrapover molding arrived this year. That molding blended into the door belt moldings to give a unified look. The analog clock was now quartz-type. New options included a Tripminder computer. XR-7 GS had a vertical-bar grille with bright surround molding, color-keyed soft bumper covering with black rub strips (including white accent stripes), quad rectangular halogen headlamps, amber wraparound park/signal lamps, hood/decklid accent stripes, and upper bodyside paint stripe. Large vertical-theme tail lamps had integral backup lenses. Twin Comfort lounge seats had fold-down center armrests and dual recliners. Power brakes and variable-ratio rack-and-pinion steering were standard. Also standard: AM radio, halogen headlamps, and P195/75R14 SBR whitewalls. LS added dual bright remote window-frame-mounted mirrors and luxury wheel covers, plus power windows and tinted glass.

MARQUIS — V-8 — Full-size Mercury models didn't look much different, but dropped their fender louvers. The former bumper-slot grille extensions were deleted too, replaced by slotless bumpers. Decklid lock covers were replaced with a bezel and ornament. A 302-cid (5.0-liter) V-8 became standard on the Brougham and Grand Marquis four-door this year. Base engine on other models was the 255-cid (4.2-liter) V-8. The 351-cid high-output V-8 was now available only with the police package. All models had four-speed automatic overdrive transmission. AM radios now included two instrument-panel speakers. Electric clocks became quartz. The CB radio option was deleted, as were the radio flexibility option and manual load levelers. One noteworthy new option was a Tripminder computer, which had a multi-function digital clock. It could also compute and display such trip-related information as distance traveled, average speed, instantaneous and trip-average fuel economy, and gallons of fuel consumed. Also joining the option list: a Class II Trailer Towing package, rated up to 3,500 pounds. As before, Marquis had a bright vertical-bar theme grille, front bumper guards, quad rectangular halogen headlamps with

1982 Mercury Cougar LS sedan. (CP)

bright headlamp/parking lamp surround moldings, and stand-up hood ornament. Wraparound front parking lamps had integral side markers. Bodies also showed a wide center pillar, rear door window divider bar, black lower back panel with vertical backup lamps adjacent to the recessed license plate bracket, and horizontal wraparound tail lamps with integral side marker lights. Marquis rode P205/75R14 steel-belted radial whitewalls and carried a mini spare tire. Marquis Brougham added a rear half vinyl roof, coach lamps, hood accent stripes, 'Brougham' decklid nameplate, deluxe wheel covers, and wide bright lower bodyside molding with quarter panel extensions. Inside were Twin Comfort lounge seats in cloth/vinyl. Four-door Broughams had a standard 302 V-8 with variable venturi carburetor. Also standard: an AM/FM stereo radio and power windows. Grand Marquis had upper bodyside accent stripes, wide bright/black lower bodyside molding, black painted rocker panel flange, nameplate on rear roof pillar and decklid, rear bumper guards, tinted glass, dual-beam dome light, and Twin Comfort seats in luxury cloth. Grand Marquis four-doors carried the 302 V-8. There was still a base Marquis station wagon, and a Colony Park wagon with full-length bodyside rosewood woodtone appliqué. Wagons had the 302 V-8 and P215/75R14 SBR whitewalls.

I.D. DATA: Mercury's 17-symbol Vehicle Identification Number (VIN) was stamped on a metal tab fastened to the instrument panel, visible through the windshield. Symbols one to three indicates manufacturer, make and vehicle type: '1ME' Mercury passenger car. The fourth symbol ('B') denotes restraint system. Next comes a letter 'P', followed by two digits that indicate body type: Model Number, as shown in left column of tables below. (Example: '71' Zephyr four-door sedan.) Symbol eight indicates engine type: '2' L4-98 2Bbl.; 'A' L4-140 2Bbl.; 'B' or 'T' L6-200 1Bbl.; '3' V6-232 2Bbl.; 'D' V8-255 2Bbl.; 'F' V8-302 2Bbl.; 'G' V8-351 2Bbl. Next is a check digit. Symbol ten indicates model year ('C' 1982). Symbol eleven is assembly plant: 'A' Atlanta, GA; 'F' Dearborn, MI; 'R' San Jose, CA; 'G' Chicago; 'H' Lorain, Ohio; 'K' Kansas City, MO; 'X' St. Thomas, Ontario; 'Z' St. Louis, MO; 'W' Wayne, MI; or Edison, NJ. The final six digits make up the sequence number, starting with 600001. A Vehicle Certification Label on the left front door lock face panel or door pillar shows the manufacturer, month and year of manufacture, GVW, GAWR, certification statement, VIN, and codes for such items as body type, color, trim, axle, transmission, and special order information.

LYNX (FOUR)

Model No.	Body/ Style No.	Body Type & Seating	Factory Price	Shipping Weight	Prod. Total
63	61D	3-dr. Hatch-4P	5502	1924	Note 1
64	58D	5-dr. Hatch-4P	5709	1986	Note 1
63	61D	3-dr. L Hatch-4P	6159	1932	Note 1
64	58D	5-dr. L Hatch-4P	6376	1994	Note 1
65	74D	4-dr. L Sta Wag-4P	6581	2040	Note 1
63/60Z	61D	3-dr. GL Hatch-4P	6471	1927	Note 1
64/60Z	58D	5-dr. GL Hatch-4P	6688	1989	Note 1
65/60Z	74D	4-dr. GL Sta Wag-4P	6899	2040	Note 1
63/602	61D	3-dr. GS Hatch-4P	7257	1963	Note 1
64/602	58D	5-dr. GS Hatch-4P	7474	2025	Note 1
65/602	74D	4-dr. GS Sta Wag-4P	7594	2062	Note 1
63/603	61D	3-dr. LS Hatch-4P	7762	1952	Note 1
64/603	58D	5-dr. LS Hatch-4P	7978	2014	Note 1
65/603	74D	4-dr. LS Sta Wag-4P	8099	2052	Note 1
63/936	61D	3-dr. RS Hatch-4P	6790	1961	Note 1

NOTE 1: Total Lynx production, 54,611 three-door hatchbacks, 40,713 five-door hatchbacks, and 23,835 four-door liftgate station wagons.

LN7 (FOUR)

61	67D	3-dr. Hatch Cpe-2P	7787	2059	35,147

CAPRI (FOUR/SIX)

67	61D	3-dr. Fastbk-4P	6711/7245	N/A	Note 2
67	61D	3-dr. L Fastbk-4P	7245/7869	2591/----	Note 2

CAPRI BLACK MAGIC (FOUR/SIX)

67	61D	3-dr. Fastbk-4P	7946/8570	2562/2676	Note 2

CAPRI RS (V-8)

67	61D	3-dr. Fastbk-4P	8107	2830	Note 2

CAPRI GS (FOUR/SIX)

68	61H	3-dr. Fastbk-4P	7432/8056	2590/2704	Note 2

NOTE 2: Total Capri production was 31,525, plus 4,609 GS-level models.

Capri Engine Note: Six-cylinder prices include cost of the required automatic transmission. A 255-cid V-8 engine cost $70 more than the six; a 302 V-8, $189-$239 more.

ZEPHYR (FOUR/SIX)

71	54D	4-dr. Sed-5P	6411/7035	2630/2750	31,698
71/602	54D	4-dr. GS Sed-5P	6734/7358	2643/2763	Note 3

ZEPHYR Z-7 (FOUR/SIX)

72	36R	2-dr. Spt Cpe-5P	6319/6943	2627/2747	7,394
72/602	36R	2-dr. GS Cpe-5P	6670/7294	2637/2757	Note 3

NOTE 3: Production of GS models is included in basic totals.

Zephyr Engine Note: Six-cylinder prices include cost of the required automatic transmission. A V-8 cost $70 more than the six.

COUGAR (SIX/V-6)

Model No.	Body/ Style No.	Body Type & Seating	Factory Price	Shipping Weight	Prod. Total
76	66D	2-dr. GS Sed-6P	7983/8053	2937/2941	6,984
77	54D	4-dr. GS Sed-6P	8158/8228	2980/2983	30,672
78	74D	4-dr. GS Wag-6P	8216/8286	3113/3116	19,294
76	66D	2-dr. LS Sed-6P	8415/8485	2973/2976	Note 4
77	54D	4-dr. LS Sed-6P	8587/8657	3022/3025	Note 4

Cougar Engine Note: V-6 engine required power steering (not incl. in above prices).

COUGAR XR-7 (SIX/V-8)

90	66D	2-dr. GS Cpe-4P	9094/9235	3152/3289	16,867
90/60H	66D	2-dr. LS Cpe-4P	9606/9847	3161/3298	Note 4

NOTE 4: Production of LS models is included in GS totals.

XR-7 Engine Note: A V-6 cost the same as a V-8 under XR-7 hoods.

MARQUIS (V-8)

81	54H	4-dr. Sedan-6P	8674	3734	9,454
87	74H	4-dr. 2S Sta Wag-6P	9198	3880	2,487

MARQUIS BROUGHAM (V-8)

82	66K	2-dr. Sedan-6P	9490	3693	2,833
83	54K	4-dr. Sedan-6P	9767	3776	15,312

MARQUIS COLONY PARK (V-8)

88	74K	4-dr. 2S Sta Wag-6P	10252	3890	8,004

GRAND MARQUIS (V-8)

84	66L	2-dr. Sedan-6P	10188	3724	6,149
85	54L	4-dr. Sedan-6P	10456	3809	32,918

FACTORY PRICE AND WEIGHT NOTE: Cougar prices and weights to left of slash are for inline six-cylinder, to right for V-6 engine. For Capri/Zephyr, prices/weights to left of slash are for four-cylinder, to right for V-6.

ENGINE [Base Four (Lynx, LN7)]: Inline. Overhead cam. Four-cylinder. Cast-iron block and aluminum head. Displacement: 97.6-cid (1.6 liters). Bore & stroke: 3.15 x 3.13 in. Compression ratio: 8.8:1. Brake horsepower: 70 at 4600 rpm. Torque: 89 lbs.-ft. at 3000 rpm. Five main bearings. Hydraulic valve lifters. Carburetor: 2Bbl. Motorcraft 740. VIN Code: 2.

ENGINE [Base Four (Capri, Zephyr)]: Inline. Overhead cam. Four-cylinder. Cast-iron block and head. Displacement: 140-cid (2.3 liters). Bore & stroke: 3.78 x 3.13 in. Compression ratio: 9.0:1. Brake horsepower: 86 at 4600 rpm. Torque: 117 lbs.-ft. at 2600 rpm. Five main bearings. Hydraulic valve lifters. Carburetor: 2Bbl. Holley 6500 or Motorcraft 5200. VIN Code: A.

ENGINE [Base Six (Cougar, XR-7); Optional (Capri, Zephyr)]: Inline. OHV. Six-cylinder. Cast-iron block and head. Displacement: 200-cid (3.3 liters). Bore & stroke: 3.68 x 3.13 in. Compression ratio: 8.6:1. Brake horsepower: 87 at 3800 rpm. Torque: 151-154 lbs.-ft. at 1400 rpm. Seven main bearings. Hydraulic valve lifters. Carburetor: 1Bbl. Holley 1946. VIN Code: B or T.

ENGINE [Optional V-6 (Cougar, XR-7)]: 90-degree, overhead valve V-6. Cast-iron block and aluminum head. Displacement: 232-cid (3.8 liters). Bore & stroke: 3.80 x 3.40 in. Compression ratio: 8.65:1. Brake horsepower: 112 at 4000 rpm. Torque: 175 lbs.-ft. at 2000 rpm. Four main bearings. Hydraulic valve lifters. Carburetor: 2Bbl. Motorcraft 2150. VIN Code: 3.

ENGINE [Base V-8 (Marquis); Optional (Capri, Zephyr, XR-7)]: 90-degree, overhead valve V-8. Cast-iron block and head. Displacement:

255-cid (4.2 liters). Bore & stroke: 3.68 x 3.00 in. Compression ratio: 8.2:1. Brake horsepower: 120-122 at 3400 rpm. Torque: 205-209 lbs.-ft. at 1600-2400 rpm. Five main bearings. Hydraulic valve lifters. Carburetor: 2Bbl. Motorcraft 2150 or 7200VV. VIN Code: D.

ENGINE [Base V-8 (Marquis Brougham, Grand Marquis 4-dr.); Optional (Marquis)]: 90-degree, overhead valve V-8. Cast-iron block and head. Displacement: 302-cid (5.0 liters). Bore & stroke: 4.00 x 3.00 in. Compression ratio: 8.4:1. Brake horsepower: 132 at 3400 rpm. Torque: 236 lbs.-ft. at 1800 rpm. Five main bearings. Hydraulic valve lifters. Carburetor: 2Bbl. Motorcraft 2150A or 7200VV. VIN Code: F.

ENGINE [Optional V-8 (Capri)]: High-output version of 302-cid V-8 above: Compression ratio: 8.3:1. Horsepower: 157 at 4200 rpm. Torque: 240 lbs.-ft. at 2400 rpm.

ENGINE [Police V-8 (Marquis)]: 90-degree, overhead valve V-8. Cast-iron block and head. Displacement: 351-cid (5.8 liters). Bore & stroke: 4.00 x 3.50 in. Compression ratio: 8.3:1. Brake horsepower: 165 at 3600 rpm. Torque: 285 lbs.-ft. at 2200 rpm. Five main bearings. Hydraulic valve lifters. Carburetor: VV. VIN Code: G.

CHASSIS DATA: Wheelbase: (Lynx/LN7) 94.2 in.; (Capri) 100.4 in.; (Zephyr) 105.5 in.; (Cougar) 105.5 in.; (XR-7) 108.4 in.; (Marquis) 114.3 in. Overall Length: (Lynx) 163.9 in.; (Lynx lift) 165.0 in.; (LN7) 170.3 in.; (Capri) 179.1 in.; (Zephyr) 195.5 in.: (Z-7) 197.4 in.; (Cougar) 196.5 in.; (XR-7) 200.4 in.; (Marquis) 212.3 in.; (Marquis wag) 218.0 in. Height: (Lynx) 53.3 in.; (LN7) 50.5 in.; (Capri) 51.4 in.; (Zephyr) 52.9 in.; (Z-7) 51.7 in.; (Cougar) 53.0 in.; (Cougar wag) 54.3 in.; (XR-7) 53.2 in.; (Marquis) 55.1 in.; (Marquis wag) 57.2 in. Width: (Lynx/LN7) 65.9 in.; (Capri) 69.1 in.; (Zephyr) 71.0 in.; (Cougar) 71.0 in.; (XR-7) 74.1 in.; (Marquis) 77.5 in.; (Marquis wag) 79.3 in. Front Tread: (Lynx/LN7) 54.7 in.; (Capri) 56.6 in.; (Zephyr/Cougar) 56.6 in.; (XR-7) 58.1 in.; (Marquis) 62.2 in. Rear Tread: (Lynx/LN7) 56.0 in.; (Capri) 57.0 in.; (Zephyr/Cougar) 57.0 in.; (XR-7) 57.0 in.; (Marquis) 62.0 in. Standard Tires: (Lynx/LN7) P165/80R13; (Capri) P175/75R14; (Zephyr/Cougar) P175/75R14 SBR; (XR-7) P195/75R14 SBR WSW; (Marquis) P205/75R14 SBR; (Marquis wag) P215/75R14.

TECHNICAL: Transmission: Four-speed manual standard on Lynx. Gear ratios: (1st) 3.58:1; (2nd) 2.05:1; (3rd) 1.21:1 or 1.36:1; (4th) 0.81:1 or 0.95:1; (Rev) 3.46:1. Four-speed floor shift standard on Capri/Zephyr four: (1st) 3.98:1; (2nd) 2.14:1; (3rd) 1.42:1; (4th) 1.00:1; (Rev) 3.99:1. Four-speed overdrive floor shift standard on Capri V-8: (1st) 3.07:1; (2nd) 1.72:1; (3rd) 1.00:1; (4th) 0.70:1; (Rev) 3.07:1. Capri four-cylinder five-speed: (1st) 3.72:1; (2nd) 2.23:1; (3rd) 1.48:1; (4th) 1.00:1; (5th) 0.76:1; (Rev) 3.59:1. SelectShift three-speed automatic standard on Cougar and XR-7 six, optional on others. Gear ratios: (1st) 2.46:1 or 2.47:1; (2nd) 1.46:1 or 1.47:1; (3rd) 1.00:1; (Rev) 2.11:1 to 2.19:1. Lynx three-speed automatic: (1st) 2.79:1; (2nd) 1.61:1; (3rd) 1.00:1; (Rev) 1.97:1. Four-speed overdrive automatic on XR-7/Marquis: (1st) 2.40:1; (2nd) 1.47:1; (3rd) 1.00:1; (4th) 0.67:1; (Rev) 2.00:1. Standard-final drive ratio: (Lynx/LN7) 3.59:1 w/4spd, 3.31:1 w/auto.; (Capri four) 3.08:1 w/4spd or auto., 3.45:1 w/5spd; (Capri six/V-8) 2.73:1; (Capri V-8 w/4spd auto.) 3.08:1; (Zephyr) 3.08:1 exc. 2.73:1 w/six or V-8; (Cougar) 2.73:1 w/six, 2.47:1 with V-6; (XR-7) 2.73:1 w/six, 3.08:1 with V-6/V-8. (Marquis) 3.08:1 exc. 2.73:1 w/police 351 V-8. Steering: (Marquis) recirculating ball; (others) rack-and-pinion. Front Suspension: (Lynx/LN7) MacPherson strut-mounted coil springs w/lower control arms and stabilizer bar; (Capri) modified MacPherson struts w/coil springs and anti-sway bar; (Zephyr/Cougar) MacPherson struts w/coil springs mounted on lower control arm and anti-sway bar; (Marquis) coil springs with long/short A-arms and anti-sway bar. Rear Suspension: (Lynx/LN7) independent trailing arms w/modified MacPherson struts and coil springs on lower control arms; (Capri/Zephyr/Cougar/Marquis) four-link w/coil springs; (XR-7) four-link with coil springs and anti-sway bar. Brakes: Front disc, rear drum. Ignition: Electronic. Body construction: (Marquis) separate body and frame; (others) unibody. Fuel tank: (Lynx/LN7) 11.3 gal.; (Capri) 15.4 gal.; (Zephyr) 16 gal.; (Cougar) 16 gal.; (XR-7) 21 gal.; (Marquis) 20 gal.

DRIVETRAIN OPTIONS: Engines: 200-cid six: Capri/Zephyr ($213). 232-cid V-6: Cougar ($70); Cougar XR-7 ($241). 255-cid V-8: Capri/Zephyr ($283); Capri RS ($57 credit): Cougar XR-7 ($241). 302 cu. in, V-8: Capri ($402-$452); Marquis sedan ($59). Transmission/Differential: Five-speed manual trans.: Capri ($196). Automatic transaxle: Lynx/LN7 ($411). Auto. transmission.: Capri/Zephyr ($411). Floor shift lever: Zephyr ($49). Traction-Lok differential: Capri/Zephyr/Cougar/XR-7 ($76); Marquis ($80). Optional axle ratio: Lynx/LN7/Capri/Zephyr (NC). Brakes & Steering: Power brakes: Lynx ($93). Power steering: Lynx/LN7/Capri ($190); Zephyr/Cougar ($195). Suspension: H.D. susp.: Zephyr/Cougar ($24); Marquis/Cougar XR-7 ($26). Handling susp.: Lynx ($41); Capri ($50); Zephyr ($52); Marquis ($49). Other: H.D. battery ($24-$26). H.D. alternator: LN7 ($27). Extended-range gas tank Zephyr/Cougar ($46). Engine block heater ($17-$18). Trailer towing pkg., medium duty: Marquis ($200-$251). California emission system ($46-$65). High-altitude emissions (NC).

LYNX CONVENIENCE/APPEARANCE OPTIONS: Option Packages: Villager woodtone pkg.: GL/GS/RS wag ($259). Instrument group ($87).

1982 Mercury Cougar XR-7 Sports Coupe. (CP)

Appearance protection group ($55). Light group ($43). Comfort/Convenience: Air conditioner ($611). Speed control ($151). Remote liftgate release ($30). Tinted glass ($82); windshield only ($32). Digital clock ($57). Interval wiper, ($48). Rear wiper/washer ($117). Dual remote sport mirrors ($66). Entertainment: AM radio delete ($61 credit). AM/FM radio ($76). AM/FM stereo radio ($106); w/cassette or 8-track player ($184) exc. LS ($78). Premium sound ($105). Dual rear speakers ($39). Exterior: Flip-up/open air roof ($183-$276). Glamour paint ($61) exc. RS. Tu-tone paint ($122) exc. RS. Front vent windows ($60). Narrow bodyside moldings ($45). Bumper guards, front or rear ($26). Bumper rub strips: base/L ($41). Luggage rack ($93). Roof air deflector ($29). Lower bodyside protection ($68). Interior: Console ($111). Low-back reclining bucket seats ($33-$98). High-back reclining bucket seats ($65). Cloth/vinyl seat trim ($29). Vinyl trim GS (NC). Shearling/leather seat trim ($59-$138). Deluxe seatbelts ($24). Wheels/Tires: Aluminum wheels ($232-$329). P165/80R13 WSW ($58).

LN7 CONVENIENCE/APPEARANCE OPTIONS: Comfort/Convenience: Appearance protection group ($48). Air conditioner ($611). Fingertip speed control ($151). Entertainment: AM/FM radio ($76). AM/FM stereo radio ($106): w/cassette or 8-track player ($184). Premium sound ($105). AM radio delete ($37 credit). Exterior: Flip-up/open air roof ($276). Glamour paint ($51). Tu-tone paint ($122). Luggage rack ($93). Lower bodyside protection ($68). Interior: Vinyl high-back reclining seats (NC). Cloth/vinyl seat trim ($29). Leather seat trim ($138). Shearling/leather seat trim ($138). Wheels/Tires: Cast aluminum spoke wheels ($232). P165/80R13 RWL ($72).

CAPRI CONVENIENCE/APPEARANCE OPTIONS: Option Packages: TR performance pkg. ($483-$533). Light group ($49). Appearance protection group ($48). Power lock group ($139). Comfort/Convenience: Air cond. ($676). Rear defroster, electric ($124). Fingertip speed control ($155). Power windows ($165). Tinted glass ($88). Leather-wrapped steering wheel ($55). Tilt steering wheel ($95). Interval wipers ($48). Rear wiper/washer ($101). Remote right mirror ($41). Entertainment: AM/FM radio ($76). AM/FM stereo radio ($106): w/8-track or cassette player ($184). Premium sound system ($105). Dual rear speakers ($39). AM radio delete ($61 credit). Exterior: T-Roof ($1021). Flip-up/open air roof ($276). Carriage roof ($734). Full vinyl roof ($137). Glamour paint ($54). Tu-tone paint ($66-$124). Gold accent stripes ($62). Hood scoop ($72). Liftgate louvers ($165). Rocker panel moldings ($33). Lower bodyside protection ($41). Interior: Recaro bucket seats ($834). Cloth/vinyl seats: base ($23). Cloth/vinyl accent trim: L/RS ($34). Leather/vinyl seats ($409). Wheels and Tires: Wire wheel covers ($91). Cast aluminum wheels ($348). Styled steel wheels w/trim rings ($72). P175/75R14 WSW ($66). P185/75R14 BSW ($30); WSW ($66-$96); RWL ($85-$116).

ZEPHYR/COUGAR CONVENIENCE/APPEARANCE OPTIONS: Option Packages: Cougar Villager option: wag ($282). Power lock group: Cougar ($138-$184). Instrument cluster: Zephyr ($100). Cold weather group: Cougar ($77). Appearance protection group ($57-$59). Light group ($49-$51). Comfort/Convenience: Air cond. ($676). Rear defroster, electric ($124). Fingertip speed control ($155). Illuminated entry ($68). Power windows ($165-$235). Power door locks: Cougar ($106-$152). Four-way power seat ($139). Six-way power seats: Cougar ($196). Remote decklid release: Zephyr ($32). Tinted glass ($88). Leather-wrapped steering wheel: Cougar ($55). Tilt steering ($95). Quartz clock ($32). Interval wipers ($48). Liftgate wiper/washer: wag ($99). Lighting and Mirrors: Cornering lamps: Cougar ($59). Map light: Cougar ($15). Trunk light: Zephyr ($7). Left remote mirror: Zephyr ($22). Dual bright remote mirrors: Zephyr ($65). Right remote mirror: Cougar ($60). Lighted right visor vanity mirror ($46); pair ($72). Entertainment: AM/FM radio ($54). AM/FM stereo radio ($85); w/8-track or cassette player ($172). Twin rear speakers: Zephyr ($39). Premium sound system ($105). AM radio delete ($61 credit). Exterior: Flip-up/open air roof ($276). Full or half vinyl roof ($137-$140). Glamour paint ($63). Tu-tone paint ($82-$105). Pivoting front vent windows ($63). Two-way liftgate: wag ($105). Rocker panel moldings: Zephyr Z-7/GS ($33). Protective bodyside moldings: Cougar ($49). Wide bodyside moldings: Zephyr Z-7 ($59). Bumper guards, rear ($28). Bumper rub strips ($50). Luggage rack: wag ($115). Lower bodyside protection ($41). Interior: Console: Zephyr ($191). Twin comfort seats: Cougar ($204). Cloth/vinyl seat trim:

1982 Mercury Marquis Brougham sedan. (CP)

Zephyr ($29). Vinyl seat trim ($29). Leather trim: Cougar LS ($409). Flight Bench seat: Zephyr (NC). Floor mats: Zephyr ($13). Wheels/Tires: Luxury wheel covers: Cougar ($49). Wire wheel covers ($104-$152). Styled steel wheels: Zephyr ($54); w/trim rings ($107). Cast aluminum wheels: Cougar ($348-$396). P175/75R14 WSW ($66). P185/75R14 BSW: Cougar ($38). P185/75R14 WSW ($104) exc. wagon ($66). P185/75R14 RWL: Cougar ($121) exc. wagon ($83). TR BSW on alum. wheels ($534-$583). Conventional spare ($51).

COUGAR XR-7 CONVENIENCE/APPEARANCE OPTIONS: Option Packages: Appearance protection group ($51). Light group ($35). Power lock group ($138). Comfort/Convenience: Air cond. ($676); auto-temp ($754). Rear defroster ($126). Fingertip speed control ($155). Illuminated entry system ($68). Keyless entry ($277). Tripminder computer ($215-$261). Autolamp on/off delay ($73). Tinted glass ($88). Power windows ($165). Six-way power driver's seat ($198). Auto. parking brake release ($12). Leather-wrapped steering wheel ($51). Tilt steering wheel ($95). Electronic instrument cluster ($367). Diagnostic warning lights ($59). Seatbelt chimes ($27). Digital clock ($46). Interval wipers ($48). Lighting and Mirrors: Cornering lamps ($59). Remote right mirror ($60). Lighted right visor vanity mirrors ($91). Entertainment: AM/FM radio ($54). AM/FM stereo radio ($85); w/8-track or cassette player ($172). AM/FM stereo search radio ($232); w/8-track or cassette ($318). Power antenna ($55). Dual rear speakers ($39). Premium sound system ($133-$167). AM radio delete ($61 credit). Exterior: Carriage roof ($885). Flip-up/open-air roof ($276). Vinyl rear half roof ($187). Vinyl roof delete ($156 credit). Glamour paint ($80). Tu-tone paint ($112). Pivoting front vent windows ($63). Rocker panel moldings ($33). Lower bodyside protection ($54). Interior: Bucket seats w/console (NC). Recaro bucket seats w/console ($523). Leather seat trim ($409). Vinyl seat trim ($28). Trunk trim ($48). Wheels/Tires: Wire wheel covers ($99-$152). Luxury wheel covers: GS ($54). Self-sealing tires ($106). TR tires on aluminum wheels ($589-$643). Conventional spare ($51).

MARQUIS CONVENIENCE/APPEARANCE OPTIONS: Option Packages: Grand Marquis decor: Colony Park ($555). Convenience group ($90-$116). Power lock group ($106-$201). Light group ($27-$43). Appearance protection group ($67). Comfort/Convenience: Air cond. ($695); w/auto-temp control ($761). Rear defroster, electric ($124). Fingertip speed control ($155). Illuminated entry system ($68). Power windows ($240). Six-way power Flight Bench seat: base ($198); reclining ($262). Six-way power twin comfort driver's seat w/recliner ($262); driver and passenger ($460). Tinted glass ($102). Autolamp on/off delay ($73). Leather-wrapped steering wheel ($51). Tilt steering wheel ($95). Tripminder computer ($215-$293). Quartz clock ($32). Digital clock ($46-$78). Seatbelt chime ($27). Lighting and Mirrors: Cornering lamps ($55). Remote right mirror ($43). Lighted right visor vanity mirrors ($91). Entertainment: AM/FM stereo radio ($85-$172); w/8-track or cassette tape player ($87-$172). AM/FM stereo search radio ($146-$232); w/8-track or cassette ($233-$318). Power antenna ($55). Dual rear speakers ($41). Premium sound system ($133-$167). AM radio delete ($61 credit). AM/FM radio delete ($152 credit). Exterior: Formal vinyl coach roof: Brghm/Grand 4-dr. ($638). Full vinyl roof: base sed ($165). Vinyl roof delete ($71 credit). Glamour paint ($77). Tu-tone paint ($117-$156). Dual accent bodyside stripes ($39). Hood striping ($17). Pivoting front vent windows ($63). Rocker panel moldings ($32). Vinyl-insert bodyside moldings ($51). Bumper guards, rear ($30). Bumper rub strips ($52). Luggage rack ($104). Lower bodyside protection ($39-$52). Interior: Dual-facing rear seats: wagon ($167). Twin comfort lounge seats: base ($139). All-vinyl seat trim: base ($28). Cloth seat trim: wag ($41). Duraweave trim: wag ($62). Leather seating: Grand Marquis ($412). Dual seatback recliners ($65). Trunk trim ($49). Wheels/Tires: Luxury wheel covers ($52-$82). Wire wheel covers ($123-$152). Cast aluminum wheels ($355-$384). P215/75R14 WSW ($36). P225/75R14 WSW ($36-$73). P205/75R15 WSW ($11-$47); puncture-resistant ($112-$148). Conventional spare ($51).

HISTORY: Introduction: September 24, 1981, except LN7, April 9, 1981. Production: 380,506. Calendar year production (U.S.): 315,798.

Calendar year sales by U.S. dealers: 327,140. Model year sales by U.S. dealers: 319,697 (not including 13,954 early '82 LN7 models sold during 1981 model year).

HISTORY: Sales slumped again this model year, but not so dramatically as in 1981. Mercury's 6.6 percent decline was well under the 16 percent plunge experienced by the domestic auto industry as a whole. The full-size Marquis found more buyers this year, up by almost one-third. Lynx sales proved disappointing, falling well behind the slow-moving EXP, even when the new high-output engine became available. Some observers felt the two-seater's performance didn't match its sporty looks, accounting for lack of buyer interest. In a *Road & Track* test, LN7 took 15 seconds to hit 60 MPH, which wasn't quite sparkling performance for a sporty lightweight. Zephyr and XR-7 sales fell sharply, while the standard Cougar gained a little. Lynx production dropped quite a bit, causing Ford to plan a shutdown of its San Jose, California, plant in 1983.

1983 MERCURY

1983 Mercury Lynx RS hatchback coupe. (OCW)

A total restyle hit XR-7, which changed its name to, simply, Cougar. Its aerodynamic design managed a 0.40 drag coefficient. A bubble-back hatchback was added to Capri, along with more engine choices. Two vehicles now carried the Marquis badge: a derivation of the former four-door Cougar on 105.5 inch wheelbase, and Grand Marquis with a 114.3 in. wheelbase. The smaller one had nitrogen-pressurized gas shocks and new sheetmetal. The new front-drive Topaz, replacing the Zephyr, arrived in spring 1983 as an early '84 model.

LYNX — FOUR — Mercury's best seller took on a new grille and striping this year, offering a broader selection of engines. The powertrain list included the base 1.6-liter carbureted four with four-speed manual or three-speed automatic; a fuel-injected 1.6; or high-output 1.6. A simplified model lineup included L, GS and LS. Base models and GL were dropped. The new grille had thin vertical bars, as before, but only two wider vertical divider bars (formerly five). The grille emblem moved from the side to the center. Otherwise, appearance was similar to 1982. Interiors were revised, with standard full-width cloth seat trim. Hatchbacks had a removable rear package shelf. Manual-shift models added an upshift indicator light. A high-mileage model (with economy gearing) was available everywhere except California. All except L now had a standard remote-locking fuel filler door. The fuel tank grew to 13 gallons. Standard equipment on Lynx L included four-speed manual shift, P165/80R13 SBR BSW tires on semi-styled steel wheels, four-spoke color-keyed steering wheel, compact spare tire, cloth/vinyl high-back bucket front seats (folding rear bench seat), four-speed heater/defroster, consolette, cargo area cover, and dome lamp. Bright bumpers showed black end caps, Wagons had power brakes. Lynx GS added a black front air dam, AM radio, passenger assist handles, carpeted lower door trim panels, locking gas filler door, power hatch release, dual visor vanity mirrors, two-color upper bodyside accent paint stripes, reclining cloth/vinyl low-back bucket seats with head restraints, and wide bodyside moldings with argent accent stripe. Rocker panel moldings were deleted. Black bumper end caps and rub strips had argent accent stripes. Lynx LS included styled steel wheels, an AM/FM stereo radio, dual remote sport mirrors, velour cloth low-back bucket seats, buried walnut appliqués, digital clock, console with graphic warning display, electric back window defroster, and instrument group. The three-door RS now carried a fuel-injected four- and five-speed gearbox, plus TR sport suspension and wheels, and Michelin P165/70R365 blackwall TRX tires. Also included with RS: an AM radio, black wheel spats, tape decals, front/rear spoilers, dual black remote sport mirrors, cloth reclining sport bucket seats, black console, foglamps, locking fuel filler door, instrument group, and black steering wheel. Wide black bodyside moldings had argent accent stripes. Black moldings were used on the rocker panels, drip belt, wheel lip, windshield, windows, and lower back panel surround. Blackout treatment extended to the grille, louvered center pillar appliqué, front roof pillar, wheel housings, dash and license plate area.

LN7 — FOUR — In an attempt to defeat claims of substandard performance, the two-passenger LN7 could now have a high-output version of the CVH 1.6-liter four, hooked to a five-speed manual gearbox. A multi-port fuel-injected four also was available, to improve idling and low-end torque. New options included a four-way adjustable driver's seat and shift indicator light. The gas tank was now 13 gallons. Standard LN7 equipment included the basic 98-cid four with five-speed manual shift. P165/80R13 SBR BSW tires, power brakes, AM radio, C-pillar louvers, black sport steering wheel, interval wipers, digital clock, and electric rear defroster. Also standard: a console, cargo area cover, remote-lock fuel filler door, tachometer, tinted glass, power liftgate release, dual remote black mirrors, and color-keyed scuff plates. Black windshield surround, backlight and wide bodyside moldings were used. Black bumpers had argent stripe and soft fascia. Black paint treatment was evident on the A-pillar, quarter windows, door frames, rocker panels, and back license plate area. Sport models had an AM/FM stereo radio; Grand Sport and RS, an AM/FM stereo with cassette player. Models with the TR package had P165/70R365 Michelin BSW tires.

CAPRI — FOUR/V-6/V-8 — Mercury's version of the pony car distanced itself from Mustang with a new "bubbleback" hatchback design. This year's grille used only one bright horizontal divider bar to separate the pattern into an upper and lower section, unlike the previous multi-bar form. Wraparound tail lamps now reached the license plate recess. New standard equipment included a cargo cover. Instruments got more legible graphics. Under Capri hoods, the high-output 302-cid (5.0-liter) V-8 switched from a two- to a four-barrel carburetor and added horsepower. A Borg-Warner five-speed was to be offered with the H.O. engine later in the model year. First step-up engine above the base 140-cid (2.3-liter) four was now the "Essex" 232-cid (3.8-liter) V-6. The base engine changed from a two-barrel to one-barrel carb. A turbo four was announced for spring 1983 arrival (similar to the turbo offered in 1979-81, but fuel-injected). Manual-shift models now had an upshift indicator light. Standard tires grew one size and took on all-season tread. RS tires grew two sizes. Standard Capri equipment included the 140-cid (2.3-liter) four with four-speed manual shift, P185/75R14 SBR BSW tires, power brakes, AM radio, tachometer, trip odometer, aero wheel covers, black bumper rub strips, cargo area cover, black remote driver's mirror, day/night mirror, and halogen headlamps. Extra-wide wrap-around black bodyside moldings had dual color-keyed stripes. Bright moldings went on the windshield and roof drip; black molding on the back window; black/bright on window frames. Interiors held high-back vinyl bucket seats with reclining seatbacks (fold-down rear seat), black sport steering wheel, and woodtone dash appliqué. Capri L added a digital clock, console with graphic warning display, center armrest, low-back bucket seats, and right visor vanity mirror. GS included a wood-tone-insert four-spoke steering wheel, black right-hand remote mirror, luxury cloth seats, map pocket, and light group. Capri RS added a Traction-Lok axle, P205/70R14 SBR BSW tires, power steering, leather-wrapped steering wheel, handling suspension, upper bodyside dual accent stripes, tape striping, black windshield and window frame moldings, black right hand remote mirror, non-working hood scoop, black grille, and black brushed instrument panel. Black Magic came with P220/55R390 Michelin TRX tires on gold 15.3 inch forged metric aluminum wheels, a handling suspension, black leather-wrapped steering wheel, power steering, black hood scoop, black bodyside and window frame moldings, and black right-hand remote mirror. Reclining black vinyl low-back bucket seats had gold cloth inserts. Styling features included gold-accent bodyside taping, and gold accents on fender, grille edge, hood and license frames. Crimson Cat added TR cast aluminum wheels, 'Crimson Cat' tape treatment, sport steering wheel, and dual remote mirrors.

ZEPHYR — FOUR/SIX — Facing its last year in the lineup, Zephyr changed little. The base 140 cu. in (2.3-liter) four now had a one-barrel carburetor instead of two barrels. Manual-shift models had an optional upshift indicator light. The 4.2-liter V-8 was dropped, but Zephyrs could still have a 200-cid (3.3-liter) inline six with locking torque converter in the automatic transmission. The optional Traction-Lok differential could now be ordered with TR-type tires. As in 1982, two trim levels were offered: base and GS, in four-door sedan or sporty coupe form. The Fairmont/Zephyr chassis/body design would continue as the downsized Ford LTD/Mercury Marquis (introduced this year). Zephyr standard equipment included the 2.3-liter four with four-speed manual gearbox, power brakes, deluxe wheel covers, P175/75R14 SBR BSW tires, AM radio, day/night mirror, vinyl low-back bucket seats, two-spoke color-keyed steering wheel, dual upper bodyside accent stripes, front bumper guards, dome lamp, and trunk mat. Bright moldings went on the windshield, back window, roof drip, wheel lip, door belt, rocker panels, and side window frames. Narrow lower bodyside moldings had black inserts. Zephyr's Z-7 Sport Coupe added tinted rear window glass, and deleted rocker panel moldings. GS models (Z-7 or sedan) included dual hood

1983 Mercury Marquis Brougham sedan. (OCW)

accent stripes, four-spoke steering wheel, luxury cloth Flight Bench seating, dual bright remote mirrors, and protective bodyside and integral partial wheel lip moldings (no rocker panel moldings).

MARQUIS — FOUR/SIX/V-6 — Mercury borrowed the rear-drive "Fox" platform to create a new mid-size model bearing the Marquis badge. To avoid confusion, the big one was now called Grand Marquis. This smaller Marquis was basically the former Cougar sedan (and wagon), but with new sheetmetal and redone interior, and a more aero look. It was a six-window design, offered in Two trim levels: base and Brougham. Marquis was closely related to Ford's new LTD, but with a different grille and tail lamps. The sloped grille was made up of thin vertical bars with a wider center bar, heavy bright surround molding, and nameplate on the lower driver's side. Quad rectangular headlamps were used, with park/signal lamps mounted in the bumper. Wide tail lamps had horizontal ribbing, and the profile showed a 60-degree backlight angle. Marquis used the same drivetrains as LTD, including an optional propane four. Nitrogen gas-pressurized front struts and rear shocks were used. Front suspension had modified MacPherson struts; rear, a four-bar link arrangement. Standard tires were one size bigger than the '82 Cougar. A tethered gas cap was new. A contoured split-front bench seat with individual recliners was standard on automatic-transmission models. New options included an electronic instrument cluster, six-way power seats, and locking wire wheel covers. A sunroof and extended-range gas tank also were offered. Standard Marquis equipment included a 140-cid (2.3-liter) four with four-speed manual gearbox, AM radio, power brakes, deluxe full wheel covers, P185/75R14 BSW tires, black front bumper guards, lighter, locking glovebox, three-speed heater/defroster, dual-note horn, and trunk mat. A bright remote driver's mirror, day/night mirror, and right visor vanity mirror were standard. Cloth-upholstered Twin Comfort Lounge seats came with seatback recliners. Also included: a mini spare tire and luxury steering wheel with woodtone insert. Dual accent stripes went on hood and upper bodysides. Moldings appeared on window frames, wheel lip, belt, back window, license plate bracket, roof drip and windshield. Bodyside moldings were color-keyed vinyl. Wagons came with the inline 200-cid (3.3-liter) six and automatic shift, tinted liftgate glass, cargo area light, and fold-down rear seat. Marquis Brougham added an illuminated passenger visor vanity mirror, digital clock, electronic warning chimes, full-length armrest, trunk carpeting, and extra interior lights.

COUGAR — V-6/V-8 — Like the closely related Thunderbird, Cougar enjoyed a major restyle. Foremost difference between the two was Cougar's notchback formal appearance with upright backlight and upswept quarter-window shape. T-bird had a rounded backlight. Cougar also had a different grille design made up of thin vertical bars. Otherwise, Cougar (no longer called XR-7) looked much like its mate, with rounded contours, sloping front end and raked windshield, and an aero drag coefficient not too much worse than Thunderbird's. Extended-height doors curved inward at the top. Wipers and body moldings were concealed. Body dimensions dropped a bit, as did Cougar's weight. Cougar's rear-drive "Fox" chassis had coil springs all around. New this year were gas-pressurized shock absorbers. Only two engine choices were offered: base 232-cid (3.8-liter) V-6 or (later) the 302-cid V-8 with throttle-body fuel injection. Four-speed overdrive automatic transmission was optional. Standard Cougar equipment included three-speed automatic transmission, power brakes and steering, AM radio, bumper rub strips, center pillar appliqué, console with storage bin, analog clock, locking glovebox, hood ornament, brushed instrument panel, and driver's remote mirror. Sport cloth bucket seats included reclining seatbacks. Also standard: a mini spare tire, decklid and bodyside accent stripes, deluxe wheel covers, and P195/75R14 WSW SBR tires. Bright moldings went on the grille surround, concealed drip, door frames, windshield, backlight, and belt. Charcoal lower bodyside moldings had bright accents. Cougar LS added a woodtone instrument panel appliqué, 'LS' fender badge, tinted glass, coach lamps, dual power remote mirrors, bright rocker panel moldings, luxury cloth seat trim, power windows, luxury wheel covers, hood accent stripes, steering wheel with woodtone insert, and luxury door trim. New options included an anti-theft alarm, emergency kit, and locking fuel filler door. Articulated sport seats and a voice-alert system also joined the option selection.

GRAND MARQUIS — V-8 — Still selling well, the biggest Mercury carried on with a revised nameplate and modified grille style. This version, shaped similar to its predecessor, consisted of rather heavy bright vertical bars and a wider center bar, with bright surround molding. Sedans also carried new full-width wraparound tail lamps with horizontal ribbing. Backup lenses adjoined the license plate opening, at the inner ends of each taillamp. Grand Marquis came in base and LS trim, in the same three bodies as before: two- and four-door sedan, and four-door Colony Park wagon. Sole engine was the 302-cid (5.0-liter) V-8, now with throttle-body fuel injection. Four-speed overdrive automatic transmission was standard. Sedan tires grew one size. New options included a remote locking fuel filler door and locking wire wheel covers. Marquis was similar to Ford's similarly renamed LTD Crown Victoria, sharing drivetrains and suspension. Standard Grand Marquis equipment included a coach vinyl roof, coach lamps, power windows, power brakes and steering, AM/FM stereo radio, cloth/vinyl Twin Comfort Lounge seats, mini spare tire with cover, color-keyed steering wheel, bright wheel covers, bumper guards, analog clock, and dual-note horn. The instrument panel was argent with woodtone appliqué. Bright moldings went on rocker panels, belt, window frames, wheel lips, tail lamps, hood rear edge, windshield, roof drip, grille and parking lamp surround. Wide lower bodyside moldings were used, with color-keyed quarter and rear window moldings. Accent stripes went on the hood and upper bodyside. Grand Marquis LS added tinted glass, luxury cloth Twin Comfort seats, full-length armrests, door pull straps, woodtone appliqué on door trim panels, front seatback map pocket, dual-beam dome lamp, and a right visor vanity mirror. Colony Park wagons had a three-way tailgate with power tinted window, vinyl-trimmed Twin Comfort seats, conventional spare tire, lockable stowage compartment, woodtone appliqué on bodyside and tailgate, bumper step pad, bright/black tailgate window moldings, and bright/woodtone bodyside appliqué surround moldings. Wagons had no rocker panel, lower bodyside or wheel lip moldings.

I.D. DATA: Mercury's 17-symbol Vehicle Identification Number (VIN) was stamped on a metal tab fastened to the instrument panel, visible through the windshield. Symbols one to three indicates manufacturer, make and vehicle type: '1ME' Mercury passenger car. The fourth symbol ('B') denotes restraint system. Next came a letter 'P', followed by two digits that indicate body type: Model Number, as shown in left column of tables below. (Example: '86' Zephyr four-door sedan.) Symbol eight indicates engine type: '2' L4-98 2Bbl.; '4' H.O. L4-98 2Bbl.; '5' L4-98 FI; 'A' L4-140 2Bbl.; 'D' Turbo L4-140 2Bbl.; 'X' L6-200 1Bbl.; '3' V6-232 2Bbl.; 'F' V8-302 2Bbl.; 'G' V8-351 2Bbl. Next is a check digit. Symbol ten indicates model year ('D' 1983). Symbol eleven is assembly plant: 'A' Atlanta, GA; 'F' Dearborn, MI; 'G' Chicago; 'H' Lorain, OH; 'K' Kansas City, MO; 'R' San Jose, CA; 'W' Wayne, MI; 'X' St. Thomas, Ontario; 'Z' St. Louis, MO; and Edison, NJ. The final six digits make up the sequence number, starting with 600001. A Vehicle Certification Label on the left front door face panel or door pillar shows the manufacturer, month and year of manufacture, GVW, GAWR, certification statement, VIN, and codes for such items as body type, color, trim, axle, transmission, and special order information.

LYNX (FOUR)

Model No.	Body/Style No.	Body Type & Seating	Factory Price	Shipping Weight	Prod. Total
54	61D	3-dr. L Hatch-4P	5751	1922	Note 1
55	58D	5-dr. L Hatch-4P	5958	1984	Note 1
60	74D	4-dr. L Sta Wag-4P	6166	2026	Note 1
55	61D	3-dr. GS Hatch-4P	6476	1948	Note 1
66	58D	5-dr. GS Hatch-4P	6693	2010	Note 1
61	74D	4-dr. GS Sta Wag-4P	6872	2050	Note 1
58	61D	3-dr. LS Hatch-4P	7529	1950	Note 1
68	58D	5-dr. LS Hatch-4P	7746	2012	Note 1
63	74D	4-dr. LS Sta Wag-4P	7909	2050	Note 1
57	61D	3-dr. RS Hatch-4P	7370	1997	Note 1
65/934	58D	5-dr. LTS Hatch-4P	7334	1920	Note 1

NOTE 1: Total Lynx production, 40,142 three-door hatchbacks, 28,461 five-door hatchbacks, and 19,192 four-door liftgate station wagons.

LN7 (FOUR)

51/A80	67D	3-dr. Hatch Cpe-2P	7398	2076	4,528
51/A8C	67D	3-dr. RS Hatch-2P	8765	N/A	Note 2

LN7 SPORT (FOUR)

51/A8A	67D	3-dr. Hatch Cpe-2P	8084	N/A	Note 2

LN7 GRAND SPORT (FOUR)

51/A8B	67D	3-dr. Hatch Cpe-2P	8465	N/A	Note 2

NOTE 2: Total LN7 production is included in figure above.

1983 Mercury Cougar Sports Coupe. (JG)

CAPRI (FOUR/V-6)

79/41P	61D	3-dr. Fastbk-4P	7156/7465	2589/2697	Note 3
79	61D	3-dr. L Fastbk-4P	7711/8020	2615/2723	Note 3

CAPRI CRIMSON CAT (FOUR/V-6)

79	61D	3-dr. Fastbk-4P	8525/8834	N/A	Note 3

CAPRI BLACK MAGIC (FOUR/SIX)

79/932	61D	3-dr. Fastbk-4P	8629/8938	2597/2705	Note 3

CAPRI GS (FOUR/SIX)

79/602	61H	3-dr. Fastbk-4P	7914/8223	N/A	Note 3

CAPRI RS (V-8)

79	61D	3-dr. Fastbk-4P	9241	2894	Note 3

NOTE 3: Total Capri production was 25,376.

Capri Engine Note: Six-cylinder prices do not include cost of the required automatic transmission ($439). A high-output 302-cid V-8 engine cost $1034 more than the V-6 on L or GS: $866 more on Black Magic.

ZEPHYR (FOUR/SIX)

86	54D	4-dr. Sed-5P	6545/6774	2630/2750	21,732
86/602	54D	4-dr. GS Sed-5P	7311/7550	2696/2881	Note 4

ZEPHYR Z-7 (FOUR/SIX)

87	36R	2-dr. Spt Cpe-5P	6442/6681	2627/2747	3,471
87/602	36R	2-dr. GS Cpe-5P	7247/7486	2690/2810	Note 4

Zephyr Price Note: Six-cylinder prices do not include cost of the required automatic transmission ($439).

MARQUIS (FOUR/SIX)

Model No.	Body/Style No.	Body Type & Seating	Factory Price	Shipping Weight	Prod. Total
89	54D	4-dr. Sedan-5P	7893/8132	N/A	50,169
90	74D	4-dr. Sta Wag-5P	----/8693	N/A	17,189

MARQUIS BROUGHAM (FOUR/SIX)

89	54D	4-dr. Sedan-5P	8202/8441	N/A	Note 4
90	74D	4-dr. Sta Wag-5P	----/8974	N/A	Note 4

NOTE 4: Brougham production is included in basic totals above.

Marquis Engine Note: A V-6 engine cost $70 more than the inline six on sedan.

COUGAR (V-6/V-8)

Model No.	Body/Style No.	Body Type & Seating	Factory Price	Shipping Weight	Prod. Total
92	66D	2-dr. Cpe-4P	9521/9809	29111	75,743
92/603	66D	2-dr. LS Cpe-4P	10850/11138	29111	Note 5

NOTE 5: Production of LS models is included in base or GS totals.

GRAND MARQUIS (V-8)

93	66K	2-dr. Sedan-6P	10654	3607	11,117
95	54K	4-dr. Sedan-6P	10718	3761	72,207
93/60H	66K	2-dr. LS Sed-6P	11209	3607	Note 6
95/60H	54K	4-dr. LS Sed-6P	11273	3761	Note 6

1983 Mercury Grand Marquis Colony Park LS station wagon. (OCW)

GRAND MARQUIS COLONY PARK (V-8)

| 94 | 74K | 4-dr. 2S Sta Wag-6P | 10896 | 3788 | 12,394 |

NOTE 6: LS production is included in basic Grand Marquis totals.

FACTORY PRICE AND WEIGHT NOTE: Cougar prices and weights to left of slash are for V-6, to right for V-8 engine. For Capri/Zephyr/Marquis, prices/weights to left of slash are for four-cylinder, to right for inline six (or V-6).

ENGINE [Base Four (Lynx, LN7)]: Inline. Overhead cam. Four-cylinder. Cast-iron block and aluminum head. Displacement: 97.6-cid (1.6 liters). Bore & stroke: 3.15 x 3.13 in. Compression ratio: 8.8:1. Brake horsepower: 70 at 4600 rpm. Torque: 88 lbs.-ft. at 2600 rpm. Five main bearings. Hydraulic valve lifters. Carburetor: 2Bbl. Motorcraft 740. VIN Code: 2.

ENGINE [Optional Four (Lynx, LN7)]: High-output version of 1.6-liter engine above. Horsepower: 80 at 5400 rpm. Torque: 88 lbs.-ft. at 3000 rpm. VIN Code: 4.

ENGINE [Optional Four (Lynx, LN7)]: Fuel-injected version of 1.6-liter engine above. Compression ratio: 9.5:1. Horsepower: 88 at 5400 rpm. Torque: 94 lb.-ft. at 4200 rpm. VIN Code: 5.

ENGINE [Base Four (Capri, Zephyr, Marquis)]: Inline. Overhead cam. Four-cylinder. Cast-iron block and head. Displacement: 140-cid (2.3 liters). Bore & stroke: 3.78 x 3.13 in. Compression ratio: 9.0:1. Brake horsepower: 90 at 4600 rpm. Torque: 122 lbs.-ft. at 2600 rpm. Five main bearings. Hydraulic valve lifters. Carburetor: 1Bbl. Carter YFA. VIN Code: A.

ENGINE [Optional Turbocharged Four (Capri)]: Same as 140-cid four above, but with turbocharger. Compression ratio: 8.0:1. Horsepower: 142 at 5000 rpm. Torque: 172 lbs.-ft. at 3800 rpm. VIN Code: D.

NOTE: Propane four was available for Marquis.

ENGINE [Optional Six (Zephyr, Marquis)]: Inline. OHV. Six-cylinder. Cast-iron block and head. Displacement: 200-cid (3.3 liters). Bore & stroke: 3.68 x 3.13 in. Compression ratio: 8.6:1. Brake horsepower: 92 at 3800 rpm. Torque: 156 lbs.-ft. at 1400 rpm. Seven main bearings. Hydraulic valve lifters. Carburetor: 1Bbl. Holley 1946. VIN Code: X.

ENGINE [Base V-6 (Cougar); Optional (Marquis)]: 90-degree, overhead valve V-6. Cast-iron block and aluminum head. Displacement: 232-cid (3.8 liters). Bore & stroke: 3.80 x 3.40 in. Compression ratio: 8.65:1. Brake horsepower: 110-112 at 3800-4000 rpm. Torque: 175 lbs.-ft. at 2200-2600 rpm. Four main bearings. Hydraulic valve lifters. Carburetor: 2Bbl. Motorcraft 2150 or 7200VV. VIN Code: 3.

ENGINE [Base V-8 (Grand Marquis); Optional (Cougar)]: 90-degree, overhead valve V-8. Cast-iron block and head. Displacement: 302-cid (5.0 liters). Bore & stroke: 4.00 x 3.00 in. Compression ratio: 8.4:1. Brake horsepower: 130 at 3200 rpm. Torque: 240 lbs.-ft. at 2000 rpm. Five main bearings. Hydraulic valve lifters. Fuel injection. VIN Code: F.

ENGINE [Optional V-8 (Grand Marquis)]: Carbureted version of 302-cid V-8 above: Compression ratio: 8.4:1. Horsepower: 145 at 3800 rpm. Torque: 245 lbs.-ft. at 2200 rpm.

ENGINE [Optional V-8 (Capri)]: High-output version of 302-cid V-8 above: Compression ratio: 8.3:1. Horsepower: 175 at 4000 rpm. Torque: 245 lbs.-ft. at 2400 rpm. Carburetor: 4Bbl. Holley 4180.

ENGINE [Police V-8 (Grand Marquis)]: 90-degree, overhead valve V-8. Cast-iron block and head. Displacement: 351-cid (5.8 liters). Bore & stroke: 4.00 x 3.50 in. Compression ratio: 8.3:1. Brake horse-

power: 165 at 3600 rpm. Torque: 290 lbs.-ft. at 2200 rpm. Five main bearings. Hydraulic valve lifters. Carburetor: 2Bbl. VV. VIN Code: G.

CHASSIS DATA: Wheelbase: (Lynx/LN7) 94.2 in.; (Capri) 100.4 in.; (Zephyr/Marquis) 105.5 in.; (Cougar) 104.0 in.; (Grand Marquis) 114.3 in. Overall Length: (Lynx) 163.9 in.; (Lynx lift) 165.0 in.; (LN7) 170.3 in.; (Capri) 179.1 in.; (Zephyr) 195.5 in.; (Z-7) 197.4 in.; (Marquis) 196.5 in.; (Cougar) 197.6 in.; (Grand Marquis) 214.0 in.; (Grand Marquis wag) 218.0 in. Height: (Lynx) 53.3 in.; (LN7) 50.5 in.; (Capri) 51.9 in.; (Zephyr) 52.9 in.; (Z-7) 51.7 in.; (Marquis) 53.6 in.; (Marquis wag) 54.3 in.; (Cougar) 53.4 in.; (Grand Marquis) 55.2 in.; (Grand Marquis wag) 56.8 in. Width: (Lynx/LN7) 65.9 in.; (Capri) 69.1 in.; (Zephyr/Marquis) 71.0 in.; (Cougar) 71.1 in.; (Grand Marquis) 77.5 in.; (Grand Marquis wag) 79.3 in. Front Tread: (Lynx/LN7) 54.7 in.; (Capri) 56.6 in.; (Zephyr/Marquis) 56.6 in.; (Cougar) 58.1 in.; (Grand Marquis) 62.0 in. Rear Tread: (Lynx/LN7) 56.0 in.; (Capri) 57.0 in.; (Zephyr/Marquis) 57.0 in.; (Cougar) 58.5 in.; (Grand Marquis) 62.0 in. Standard Tires: (Lynx/LN7) P165/80R13; (Capri) P185/75R14; (Capri RS) P205/70R14; (Zephyr) P175/75R14 SBR; (Marquis) P185/75R14; (Cougar) N/A; (Grand Marquis) P215/75R14 SBR.

TECHNICAL: Transmission: Four-speed manual standard on Lynx. Gear ratios: (1st) 3.58:1; (2nd) 2.05:1; (3rd) 1.23:1 or 1.36:1; (4th) 0.81:1 or 0.95:1; (Rev) 3.46:1. Alternate Lynx four-speed: (1st) 3.23:1; (2nd) 1.90:1; (3rd) 1.23:1; (4th) 0.81:1; (Rev) 3.46:1. Four-speed floor shift standard on Capri/Marquis four: (1st) 3.98:1; (2nd) 2.14:1; (3rd) 1.42:1 or 1.49:1; (4th) 1.00:1; (Rev) 3.99:1. Four-speed standard on Capri V-8: (1st) 3.07:1; (2nd) 1.72:1; (3rd) 1.00:1; (4th) 0.70:1; (Rev) 3.07:1. Lynx/LN7 five-speed manual: (1st) 3.60:1; (2nd) 2.12:1; (3rd) 1.39:1; (4th) 1.02:1; (5th) 1.02:1; (Rev) 3.62:1. Capri four-cylinder five-speed: (1st) 3.72:1; (2nd) 2.23:1; (3rd) 1.48:1; (4th) 1.00:1; (5th) 0.76:1; (Rev) 3.59:1. Capri V-8 five-speed manual: (1st) 2.95:1; (2nd) 1.94:1; (3rd) 1.34:1; (4th) 1.00:1; (5th) 0.73:1; (Rev) 2.76:1. Capri turbo five-speed manual: (1st) 4.03:1; (2nd) 2.37:1; (3rd) 1.50:1; (4th) 1.00:1; (5th) 0.86:1; (Rev) 3.76:1. Alternate Capri turbo five-speed manual: (1st) 3.76:1; (2nd) 2.18:1; (3rd) 1.36:1; (4th) 1.00:1; (5th) 0.86:1; (Rev) 3.76:1. SelectShift three-speed automatic standard on Capri/Cougar/Marquis six, optional on others. Gear ratios: (1st) 2.46:1 or 2.47:1; (2nd) 1.46:1 or 1.47:1; (3rd) 1.00:1; (Rev) 2.11:1 to 2.19:1. Lynx three-speed automatic: (1st) 2.79:1; (2nd) 1.61:1; (3rd) 1.00:1; (Rev) 1.97:1. Four-speed overdrive automatic on Cougar/Marquis/Grand Marquis: (1st) 2.40:1; (2nd) 1.47:1; (3rd) 1.00:1; (4th) 0.67:1; (Rev) 2.00:1. Standard final drive ratio: (Lynx/LN7) 3.59:1 w/4spd, 3.73:1 w/5spd, 3.31:1 w/auto.; (Capri four) 3.08:1 w/4spd or auto., 3.45:1 w/5spd; (Capri V-6) 2.73:1; (Capri V-8) 3.08:1 w/4spd; (Capri turbo) 3.45:1; (Zephyr four) 3.08:1; (Zephyr six) 2.73:1; (Marquis) 3.45:1 w/four, 2.73:1 w/six, 3.08:1 w/V-8; (Cougar) 2.47:1 w/3spd auto., 3.08:1 with 4spd auto.; (Grand Marquis) 3.08:1. Steering: (Grand Marquis) recirculating ball; (others) rack-and-pinion. Front suspension: (Lynx/LN7) MacPherson strut-mounted coil springs w/lower control arms and stabilizer bar; (Capri/Zephyr/Cougar/Marquis) modified MacPherson struts w/coil springs and anti-sway bar; (Grand Marquis) coil springs with long/short A-arms and anti-sway bar. Rear Suspension: (Lynx/LN7) independent trailing arms w/modified MacPherson struts and coil springs on lower control arms; (Capri/Zephyr/Cougar/Marquis/Grand Marquis) four-link w/coil springs. Brakes: Front disc, rear drum. Ignition: Electronic. Body construction: (Grand Marquis) separate body and frame; (others) unibody. Fuel tank: (Lynx/LN7) 13 gal.; (Capri) 15.4 gal.; (Zephyr) 16 gal.; (Marquis) 16 gal.; (Cougar) 21 gal.; (Grand Marquis) 18 gal.; (Grand Marquis wag) 18.5 gal.

DRIVETRAIN OPTIONS: Engines: H.O. 1.6-liter four: Lynx ($70-$73); LN7 RS ($70). Fuel-injected 1.6-liter four: Lynx LS ($367); Lynx LTS ($294). Propane 140-cid four: Marquis ($896). 200-cid six: Zephyr/Marquis ($239). 232-cid V-6: Capri/Marquis ($309) exc. wagon ($70). 302-cid V-8: Capri L/GS ($1343); Capri Black Magic ($866); Capri Redline ($1118); Cougar ($288). Transmission/Differential: Close-ratio four-speed trans.: Lynx (NC). Five-speed manual trans.: Lynx ($76). Automatic transaxle: Lynx ($439) exc. LTS/RS ($363); LN7 ($363). SelectShift auto. transmission.: Capri/Zephyr/Marquis ($439). Overdrive auto. trans.: Marquis ($615) exc. wagon ($176); Cougar ($176). Floor shift lever: Zephyr/Marquis ($49). First-gear lock-out delete: Zephyr ($9). Traction-Lok differential: Capri/Zephyr/Marquis/Grand Marquis/Cougar ($95). Optional axle ratio: Capri/Zephyr (NC). Brakes & Steering: Power brakes: Lynx ($95). Power steering: Lynx/LN7 ($210); Capri ($202); Zephyr/Marquis ($218). Suspension: H.D. susp.: Zephyr/Marquis ($24); Grand Marquis/Cougar ($26). Handling susp.: Lynx L/GS ($145); Lynx LS ($41); Zephyr ($52); Grand Marquis ($49). Handling susp. pkg.: Capri ($252). TR performance susp.: Lynx ($41). TR sport susp.: LN7 ($41). Other: H.D. battery ($26). H.D. alternator: LN7 ($27). Extended-range gas tank: Zephyr/Marquis ($46). Engine block heater ($17-$18). Trailer towing pkg., medium duty: Grand Marquis ($200-$251); heavy duty: ($251-$302). Trailer towing pkg.: Cougar ($251). California emission system ($46-$76). High-altitude emissions (NC).

LYNX CONVENIENCE/APPEARANCE OPTIONS: Option Packages: TR performance pkg. ($185-$515). Villager woodtone pkg. ($316). Instrument group ($87). Light group ($43). Comfort/Convenience: Air conditioner ($624). Rear defroster, electric ($124). Fingertip speed control ($170). Tinted glass ($90); windshield only ($38). Digital clock ($57). Interval wipers ($49). Rear wiper/washer ($117). Dual remote sport mirrors ($67). Entertainment: AM radio ($61). AM/FM radio ($82) exc. L ($143). AM/FM stereo radio ($109) exc. L ($170); w/cassette or 8-track player ($199) exc. L ($260), LS ($90). Premium sound ($117). Exterior: Flip-up/open air roof ($217-$310). Clearcoat metallic paint: RS ($305). Glamour paint ($51). Tu-tone paint ($134-$173). Dual bodyside paint stripes ($39). Front vent windows, pivoting ($60). Remote quarter windows ($109). Vinyl-insert bodyside moldings ($45). Bumper guards, front or rear ($28). Bumper rub strips ($48). Luggage rack ($93). Lower bodyside protection ($68). Interior: Console ($111). Fold-down center armrest ($55). Low-back reclining bucket seats ($98). High-back reclining bucket seats ($65). Vinyl seats ($24). Wheels and Tires: Cast aluminum wheels ($226-$329). P165/80R13 SBR WSW ($59).

LN7 CONVENIENCE/APPEARANCE OPTIONS: Comfort/Convenience: Air conditioner ($624). Entertainment: AM/FM radio ($82). AM/FM stereo radio ($109); w/cassette or 8-track player ($199) exc. Sport ($90). Premium sound ($117). AM radio delete ($37 credit). AM/FM stereo delete ($145 credit). AM/FM stereo/cassette delete ($352 credit). Exterior: Flip-up/open air roof ($310). Glamour paint ($51). Two-tone paint/tape ($146). Sport tape stripe ($41). Lower bodyside protection ($68). Interior: Cloth, sport cloth or knit vinyl bucket seats (NC). Sport seats ($173). Leather low-back seat trim ($144). Shearling low-back bucket seats ($227).

CAPRI CONVENIENCE/APPEARANCE OPTIONS: Option Packages: Light group ($55). Appearance protection group ($60). Power lock group ($160). Comfort/Convenience: Air cond. ($724). Rear defroster, electric ($135). Fingertip speed control ($170). Power windows ($180). Tinted glass ($105); windshield only ($38). Leather-wrapped steering wheel ($59). Tilt steering wheel ($105). Interval wipers ($49). Remote right mirror ($44). Entertainment: AM/FM radio ($82). AM/FM stereo radio ($109); w/8-track or cassette player ($199). Premium sound system ($117). AM radio delete ($61 credit). Exterior: T-Roof ($1055). Flip-up/open air roof ($310). Glamour paint ($54). Two-tone paint ($78-$137). Rocker panel moldings ($33). Lower bodyside protection ($41). Interior: Console ($191). Cloth/vinyl seats ($29-$40). Leather/vinyl seats ($415). Sport seats ($196). Front floor mats, carpeted ($22). Wheels and Tires: Wire wheel covers ($98). Turbine wheel covers (NC). Cast aluminum wheels ($345). Styled steel wheels w/trim rings ($78). P185/75R14 WSW ($72). P195/75R14 WSW ($108). P205/75R14 BSW ($224). TRX P220/55R390 BSW ($327-$551).

ZEPHYR CONVENIENCE/APPEARANCE OPTIONS: Option Packages: Instrument cluster ($100). Appearance protection group ($32-$60). Light group ($55). Comfort/Convenience: Air cond. ($724). Rear defroster, electric ($135). Fingertip speed control ($170). Illuminated entry ($82). Power windows ($180-$255). Power door locks ($120-$170). Remote decklid release ($40). Four-way power seat ($139). Tinted glass ($105). Tinted windshield ($38). Tilt steering ($105). Quartz clock ($35). Interval wipers ($49). Lighting and Mirrors: Map light ($10). Trunk light ($7). Left remote mirror ($22). Dual bright remote mirrors ($68). Lighted visor vanity mirrors, pair ($106). Entertainment: AM/FM radio ($59). AM/FM stereo radio ($109); w/8-track or cassette player ($199). Premium sound system ($117). AM radio delete ($61 credit). Exterior: Flip-up/open air roof ($310). Full or half vinyl roof ($152). Glamour paint ($63). Two-tone paint ($117). Pivoting front vent windows ($63). Wide bodyside moldings ($59). Rocker panel moldings ($39). Bumper guards, rear ($28). Bumper rub strips ($50). Lower bodyside protection ($41). Interior: Console ($191). Bucket seats ($21). Cloth/vinyl seat trim ($35). Bench seat (NC). Front floor mats, carpeted ($24). Front/rear rubber mats ($15). Wheels and Tires: Wire wheel covers ($152). Styled steel wheels ($66). Styled steel wheels w/trim rings ($126). Steel wheels, 5.5 in. ($18); H.D. ($74). P175/75R14 SBR WSW ($72). P185/75R14 WSW ($116). TR BSW on aluminum wheels ($601). Conventional spare ($63).

MARQUIS CONVENIENCE/APPEARANCE OPTIONS: Option Packages: Woodtone option ($282). Heavy-duty pkg. ($210). Power lock group ($170-$210). Cold weather group ($77). Appearance protection group ($60). Light group ($38). Comfort/Convenience: Air cond. ($724); auto-temp ($802). Rear defroster, electric ($135). Fingertip speed control ($170). Illuminated entry ($76). Autolamp on-off delay ($73). Power windows ($255). Six-way power driver's seat ($207); dual ($415). Tinted glass ($105). Tinted windshield ($38). Leather-wrapped steering wheel ($59). Tilt steering ($105). Electronic instrument cluster ($289-$367). Tripminder computer ($215-$293). Digital clock ($78). Diagnostic warning lights ($59). Auto. parking brake release ($12). Interval wipers ($49). Liftgate wiper/washer: wagon ($99). Lighting and Mirrors: Cornering lamps ($60). Map light ($15). Right remote convex mirror ($60). Lighted visor vanity mirrors ($51-$100). Entertainment: AM/FM radio ($59). AM/FM stereo radio ($109); w/8-track or cassette player ($199). Electronic-tuning AM/FM stereo radio ($252); w/cassette ($396). Premium sound system ($117-$151). AM radio delete ($61 credit). Exterior: Flip-up/open air roof ($310). Full vinyl roof ($152). Glamour paint ($63). Two-tone paint ($117). Pivoting

1983 Mercury Grand Marquis LS sedan. (JG)

front vent windows (N/A). Two-way liftgate: wag ($105). Protective bodyside moldings (N/A). Bumper guards, rear ($28). Bumper rub strips ($56). Luggage rack: wag ($126). Lower bodyside protection ($41). Interior: Console ($100). Vinyl seat trim ($35). Individual seats w/console ($61). Leather seat trim ($415). Front floor mats ($23). Wheels and Tires: Luxury wheel covers ($55). Wire wheel covers ($159); locking ($198). Styled wheels w/trim rings ($54). Cast aluminum wheels ($402). P185/75R14 BSW ($38); WSW ($72). P195/75R14 WSW ($72-$116). Puncture-sealant P195/75R14 WSW ($240). Conventional spare ($63).

COUGAR CONVENIENCE/APPEARANCE OPTIONS: Option Packages: Luxury carpet group ($72). Traveler's assistance kit ($65). Light group ($35). Power lock group ($172). Comfort/Convenience: Air cond. ($737); auto-temp ($802). Rear defroster ($135). Fingertip speed control ($170). Illuminated entry system ($82). Keyless entry ($163). Anti-theft system ($159). Remote fuel door lock ($26). Tripminder computer ($215-$276). Autolamp on/off delay ($73). Tinted glass ($105); windshield only ($38). Power windows ($193). Six-way power driver's seat ($222); dual ($444). Auto. parking brake release ($12). Leather-wrapped steering wheel ($59). Tilt steering wheel ($105). Electronic instrument cluster ($382). Electronic voice alert ($67). Diagnostic warning lights ($59). Digital clock ($61). Interval wipers ($49). Lighting and Mirrors: Cornering lamps ($68). Electro-luminescent coach lamps ($84). Dual electric remote mirrors ($94). Electronic-dimming day/night mirror ($77). Lighted visor vanity mirrors, pair ($106). Entertainment: AM/FM stereo radio ($109); w/8-track or cassette player ($199). Electronic-tuning AM/FM stereo search radio ($252); w/cassette ($396). Power antenna ($66). Premium sound system ($179). AM radio delete ($61 credit). Exterior: Flip-up/open air roof ($310). Luxury vinyl rear half roof ($240). Clearcoat metallic paint ($152). Two-tone paint: LS ($148-$163). Hood striping ($16). Pivoting front vent windows ($76). Rocker panel moldings ($39). License frames ($9). Lower bodyside protection ($39-$54). Interior: Articulated sport seats ($427) exc. LS ($183). Leather seat trim ($415-$659). Vinyl seat trim ($34). Front floor mats, carpeted ($22). Wheels and Tires: Wire wheel covers, locking ($84-$198). Luxury wheel covers ($113). Puncture-sealing tires ($124). P205/70R14 WSW ($62). P205/70HR14 performance BSW ($152). 220/55R390 TRX performance tires on aluminum wheels ($499-$649). Conventional spare ($63).

GRAND MARQUIS CONVENIENCE/APPEARANCE OPTIONS: Option Packages: Grand Marquis LS decor ($616). Convenience group ($95-$116). Power lock group ($123-$220). Light group ($30-$48). Comfort/Convenience: Air cond. ($724); w/auto-temp control ($802). Rear defroster, electric ($135). Fingertip speed control ($170). Illuminated entry system ($76). Power driver's seat ($210); driver and passenger ($420). Remote fuel door lock ($24). Tinted glass ($105); windshield only ($38). Autolamp on/off delay ($73). Leather-wrapped steering wheel ($59). Tilt steering wheel ($105). Tripminder computer ($261). Digital clock ($61). Lighting and Mirrors: Cornering lamps ($60). Remote right mirror ($43). Lighted visor vanity mirrors ($100). Entertainment: AM/FM stereo radio w/8-track or cassette tape player ($112). AM/FM stereo search radio ($166); w/8-track or cassette ($310). Power antenna ($60). Premium sound system ($145-$179). AM/FM delete ($152 credit). Exterior: Formal coach vinyl roof ($650). Glamour paint ($77). Two-tone paint ($129). Pivoting front vent windows (N/A). Rocker panel moldings ($32). Vinyl-insert bodyside moldings ($55). Bumper rub strips ($52). Luggage rack ($110). Lower bodyside protection ($39-$52). Interior: Dual-facing rear seats: wag ($167). Cloth trim ($48). Leather seat trim ($418). Duraweave vinyl seat trim ($96). Carpeted front floor mats ($21). Wheels and Tires: Luxury wheel covers ($55). Wire wheel covers ($129); locking ($168). Cast aluminum wheels ($361). P225/75R14 WSW ($42-$43). P205/75R15 WSW ($17); Puncture-resistant ($130). Conventional spare ($63).

HISTORY: Introduced: September 23, 1982, or October 14, 1982, except Cougar, February 17, 1983. Model year production: 381,721. Calendar year production (U.S.): 432,353. Calendar year sales by U.S. dealers: 409,433. Model year sales by U.S. dealers: 357,617 (not incl. 21,745 early '84 Topaz models). Grand Marquis was Mercury's best seller for the '83 model year, taking over that spot from the subcompact Lynx. Model year sales jumped nearly 40 percent for the big full-size model. The two-seater LN7 never had found an adequate number of customers, and dropped out after 1983. Ford's similar EXP hung on longer. Capri sales declined a bit, but remained strong enough to carry on. Only about 30 percent of Capris had V-8 power. Topaz, introduced spring as an early '84, found 21,745 buyers in just the few months before the full model year began. Sales were helped by Hertz, which bought 15,200 Tempo/Topaz models for its rental fleet. Cougar sold quite well with its new "reverse-curve" back window styling, though analysts thought the design inferior to Thunderbird's aero-look. Mercury discovered that 40 percent of them were bought by women. Production of Marquis and Grand Marquis rose sharply, adding jobs at the Chicago and St. Louis plants. For the first time, both large and small cars (front-drive Escort/Lynx and rear-drive Grand Marquis) were produced on the same assembly (at St. Thomas, Ontario). Mercury's market share rose from 5.5 percent to 6.1 percent in two years, with credit taken by Lincoln-Mercury General Manager Gordon B. MacKenzie, who took over in 1981. However, MacKenzie soon left Mercury to return to his former spot at Ford of Europe. The new General Manager was Robert L. Rewey, Jr.

1984 MERCURY

1984 Mercury Lynx GS hatchback coupe. (JG)

Mercury's factory sales catalog promised "a new direction in automotive technology." That meant cars that were exciting to drive, pleasing to the eye, "combining innovative design, aerodynamic styling and meticulous engineering." Highlight of the year was the arrival of the front-wheel-drive Tempo compact, which actually emerged as an early '84 model. A diesel four-cylinder engine was available on Lynx and Topaz. Turbos were optional on Lynx and Capri, and standard on the revived Cougar XR-7. Due to sluggish sales, the two-seater LN7 was abandoned.

LYNX — FOUR — "The quality-built small car." So went Mercury's claim for the subcompact Lynx, now in its fourth season. Three-door, five-door and wagon bodies were offered again, with little appearance change. Wraparound tail lamps with two horizontal ribs came to a point at their forward limit on the rear quarter panel. Trim levels ran from base and L to GS, sporty RS, RS Turbo, and top-rung LTS (five-door only). Base engine remained the 1.6-liter CVH four, with four-speed manual transaxle. New this year: an optional 2.0-liter diesel engine with five-speed transaxle. Lynx had a "lubed-for-life" chassis, self-adjusting brakes and clutch, rack-and-pinion steering, fully independent suspension, and maintenance-free battery. A new full-width, flat-folding rear seat went into L models; new split-folding rear seat on others. Instrument panels and interiors were revised, including new side-window defoggers. The RS Turbo had a fuel-injected turbocharged engine, five-speed manual overdrive transaxle, special suspension with Koni shocks and TR sport cast aluminum wheels with Michelin 185/60R365 TRX traction compound tires, plus power steering and brakes. New options included a tilt steering wheel, power door locks, overhead console with digital clock and map lights, electronic stereo search radio, and graphic equalizer. Also available: air conditioning, electric rear window defroster, flip-up/open air roof, tinted glass, and Premium Sound System.

1984 Mercury Capri GS hatchback coupe. (JG)

CAPRI — FOUR/V-6/V-8 — A simplified Capri model lineup included the base GS, high-performance RS, and RS Turbo. Base, L, Black Magic, and Crimson Cat models were dropped. Promoting the Capri turbo, Mercury's factory catalog insisted that "automotive technology didn't became less exhilarating with the passing of the old muscle cars—it merely became more intelligent." The turbocharged four, introduced in 1983 on Mustang GT and T-bird Turbo Coupe, produced 145 horsepower at 4600 rpm. (60 percent more than standard four). It was hooked to a five-speed manual overdrive transmission and Traction-Lok axle. Capri RS or GS could have a High Output 302-cid (5.0-liter) V-8 with either fuel injection or four-barrel. The four-barrel version (on RS) had a 2.5 inch diameter exhaust and dual outlets, cast aluminum rocker arm covers, and high-lift camshaft. The fuel-injected V-8 now came with automatic overdrive transmission. Fuel injection was added to the 232-cid (3.8-liter) V-6, optional on GS. All Capris had a split rear seatback, with each side folding separately. Instrument panels were revised, now with red backlighting. New steering wheels put the horn button on the hub rather than the column stalk. Gas-pressurized shocks were used at front and rear. Bodies had extra-wide wraparound black bodyside moldings with dual color-keyed stripes, bright roof drip and windshield moldings, black rear window molding, and black/bright window frame moldings. Wrap-around horizontally-ribbed tail lamps were used, and the rear license plate fit in a recessed opening. Standard front seats were cloth/vinyl reclining low-back buckets. Capri had color-keyed hood and rear pillar louvers, and black cowl louvers. The instrument panel was gray suede painted, with appliqué. Bumpers had integral black rub strips. GS standard equipment included four-speed manual shift, power brakes, turbine wheel covers, trip odometer, tachometer, three-oval black sport steering wheel, integral rear spoiler, AM radio, black left remote mirror, day/night mirror, and dual visor vanity mirrors. Also standard: a dual-note horn, halogen headlamps, locking glovebox, temp/amp/oil gauges, lighter, digital clock, cargo area cover, and console with graphic warning display and stowage bin. Capri RS added a front air dam, power steering, wrapped steering wheel, five-speed manual gearbox, handling suspension, Traction-Lok axle, foglamps, and locking fuel filler door. Styling features included a black right remote mirror, black grille, black rear pillar louver, and tu-tone black/gray instrument panel. RS had black windshield, roof drip and window frame moldings. Turbo RS added identifying decals on fenders and decklid, sport-tuned exhaust with bright tailpipe extension, a hood scoop, cast aluminum valve covers, and heavy-duty battery.

TOPAZ — FOUR — Taking up the rising tide toward front-wheel-drive, Mercury introduced its second model, the compact Topaz, closely tied to Ford's Tempo. Two- and four-door sedans, replacements for the departed Zephyr, carried five passengers. Riding a wheelbase under 100 inches (actually a stretched Lynx platform), Topaz tipped the scales at about 2,200 pounds. The aerodynamically-styled body had a horizontal-bar grille with center emblem. Single rectangular headlamps met amber wraparound front side marker lenses. Euro-style wraparound tail lamps tapered downward on each quarter panel. Two-doors had decklid stripes and dual bodyside accent stripes, and a black B-pillar molding. Both bodies had a lower back panel appliqué with argent accents. Two trim levels were offered: GS and LS. Both had standard lower bodyside protection. Color-keyed bodyside moldings were wide in Pacific states, narrow elsewhere. Standard GS features included bright upper/lower grille bars, and window frame, belt, rear window surround and windshield moldings. Bumpers had color-keyed end caps and rub strips. Base engine was a 140-cid (2.3-liter) 2300 HSC (High Swirl Combustion) four with EEC-IV. Displacement was the same as the four that had been around for some years, but bore and stroke were not. This was a different design, derived from the inline six. The standard four-speed manual overdrive transaxle (five-speed in Pacific states) had a self-adjusting clutch. A 2.0-liter diesel also was offered, with five-speed transaxle. Topaz had rack-and-pinion steering and a parallel four-bar-link independent rear suspension. A firm-handling suspension was standard. Interiors held contoured front seats, a locking glovebox, and a color-keyed consolette. Door trim panels were carpeted on the lower section, with built-in storage bins. Cloth/vinyl low-back bucket seats were standard. Standard GS equipment included polycast wheels, two-speed wiper/washer, AM radio (AM/FM in Pacific states), power brakes, lighter, temp gauge, ammeter, locking glovebox, dual-note horn, four-speed heater/defroster, halogen headlamps, color-keyed instrument panel appliqué, dual color-keyed remote mirrors, day/night mirror, and dual visor vanity mirrors. The radio could be deleted for credit. Topaz LS added passenger assist handles, a swivel map light, interval wipers, dual color bodyside accent stripes, color-keyed wide bodyside moldings, decklid moldings (four-door), comfort/convenience group, digital clock, and color-keyed bumper end cap extensions. Pacific-state models also had power steering, power door locks, power windows, dual lighted visor vanity mirrors, console with graphic warning display, and illuminated entry. The special Western State Package, adding standard equipment, was offered only in California, Oregon, Washington, Alaska and Hawaii.

1984 Mercury Topaz LS coupe (left) and sedan (right). (PH)

1984 Mercury Marquis station wagon (with woodtone option). (OCW)

MARQUIS — FOUR/V-6 — Descended from the old Cougar, the rear-drive Marquis changed little for its second season. Three-speed Select-Shift automatic was now the standard transmission, and the inline six option was dropped. A fuel-injected 232-cid (3.8-liter) V-6 was standard in wagons, optional in sedans. Power steering became standard, and the horn button returned to the center hub of the steering wheel. Gas-pressurized shocks were standard. Thin vertical bars made up the Marquis grille. Angled clear/amber side marker lenses continued back from the housing that contained the quad rectangular headlamps. Amber parking lamps were built into the bumper. Separate clear horizontal rectangular marker lenses were below the bodyside molding, just ahead of the front wheel. At the rear were wraparound tail lamps. Front seatbacks had individual recliners. An extra-cost front bench seat expanded capacity to six passengers. Marquis Brougham had Twin Comfort Lounge seats with dual recliners and individual fold-down center armrests. Cloth upholstery was standard; vinyl or leather seating surfaces optional. Options included an Electronic Instrument Cluster with Tripminder computer, auto-temp air conditioner, power lock group, and Premium Sound System. Marquis wagons had a standard liftgate-open warning light and cargo area lamp.

COUGAR/XR-7 — FOUR/V-6/V-8 — Following a year out of the line-up, the XR-7 name returned this year on a turbocharged Cougar-Mercury's version of the Thunderbird Turbo Coupe. XR-7 had a standard five-speed manual or optional (extra cost) three-speed automatic transmission, along with a handling suspension, high-performance tires, and a tachometer. Turbo models featured Quadra-Shock rear suspension, with two horizontal dampers. Fuel injection went on the basic Cougar's 232-cid (3.8-liter) base V-6 engine. Standard automatic transmissions had a lock-up torque converter. The 302-cid (5.0-liter) V-8 was optional. All engines now had EEC-IV electronic controls. The horn button moved to the center hub of the new steering wheel. Nitrogen gas-pressurized front struts and rear shocks were standard. So was variable-ratio power rack-and-pinion steering. Appearance was similar to 1983, with upswept quarter-window design and wide rear pillars with round emblem. Cougars had deeply recessed quad rectangular headlamps. Wraparound amber side marker lenses extended from the same housing. An optional Electronic Instrument Cluster contained a digital speedometer, graphic fuel gauge, and digital clock. Base Cougars came with automatic transmission, AM radio, bright wheel covers, power brakes and steering, driver's remote mirror, reminder chimes, analog clock, lighter, full console with padded lid, and mini spare tire. Bright moldings went on the grille surround, belt, concealed drip, quarter and back windows, door frames, windshield, and bodyside (with charcoal vinyl insert). Bodies displayed a center pillar appliqué, charcoal bumper rub strips with extensions, and decklid and upper bodyside accent stripes. Cougar LS added a woodtone appliqué instrument panel, tinted glass, coach lamps, dual black power remote mirrors, bright rocker panel moldings, power windows, and hood accent stripes. LS also had standard luxury cloth 40/40 seats

and a passenger visor vanity mirror. In addition to the turbo engine, Cougar XR-7 had a Traction-Lok axle, tachometer, heavy-duty (54-amp) battery, charcoal floor console with Oxford Gray armrest pad, Oxford Gray headliner, charcoal instrument panel, power windows, and silver metallic polycast wheels. Also on XR-7: Oxford Gray tri-band lower tape striping, black leather-wrapped four-spoke steering wheel, clearcoat metallic paint with lower accent, and color-keyed rear window moldings. Seats were Oxford Gray cloth sport buckets.

GRAND MARQUIS — V-8 — Immodestly described as an "American classic," the full-size (by modern standards, at any rate) Grand Marquis continued with little change, carrying six passengers. Sole engine was the 302-cid (5.0-liter) V-8 with EFI and EEC-IV, coupled to four-speed automatic overdrive. Base and LS trim levels were available in the two- and four-door sedans. LS had Twin Comfort Lounge seats in luxury cloth or optional leather. As before, the upright grille was made up of six vertical bars on each side of a slightly wider center divider bar. Surround moldings of the recessed quad headlamps continued to meet clear park/signal lights at the fender tips, which wrapped around the fenders to a narrow amber lens at the rear. Wraparound horizontally-ribbed tail lamps were used. Colony Park and Colony Park LS wagons both had a three-way tailgate with power window, locking stowage compartment, and load floor carpeting. Twin Comfort Lounge seats had standard vinyl upholstery, with cloth and knitted vinyl optional; cloth standard on Colony Park LS. Dual-facing optional rear seats held two passengers (for a total of eight). A heavy-duty suspension package included bigger front stabilizer bar, heavy-duty springs and revalved shocks. The heavy-duty (Class III) Trailer Towing Package that could haul 5,000 pounds included a heavy-duty radiator, auxiliary power steering and transmission oil coolers.

I.D. DATA: Mercury's 17-symbol Vehicle Identification Number (VIN) was stamped on a metal tab fastened to the instrument panel, visible through the windshield. Symbols one to three indicate manufacturer, make and vehicle type: '1ME' Mercury passenger car. The fourth symbol ('B') denotes restraint system. Next comes a letter 'P', followed by two digits that indicate body type: Model Number, as shown in left column of tables below. (Example: '54' base Lynx three-door hatchback.) Symbol eight indicates engine type: '2' L4-98 2Bbl.; '4' H.O. L4-98 2Bbl.; '5' L4-98 EFI; '8' Turbo L4-98 FI; 'H' Diesel L4-121; 'A' L4-140 1Bbl.; 'R' or 'J' HSC L4-140 1Bbl.; '6' Propane L4-140; 'W' Turbo L4-140 EFI; '3' V6-232 2Bbl. or FI; 'F' V8-302 2Bbl. or FI; 'M' V8-302 4Bbl.; 'G' V8-351 2Bbl. Next is a check digit. Symbol ten indicates model year ('E' 1984). Symbol eleven is assembly plant: 'A' Atlanta, GA; 'B' Oakville, Ontario (Canada); 'F' Dearborn, MI; 'G' Chicago, IL; 'H' Lorain, OH; 'K' Kansas City, MO; 'W' Wayne, MI; 'X' St. Thomas, Ontario (Canada); 'Z' St. Louis, MO; and Edison, NJ. The final six digits make up the sequence number, starting with 600001. A Vehicle Certification Label on the left front door lock face panel or door pillar shows the month and year of manufacture, GVW, GAWR, VIN, and codes for such items as body type, color, trim, axle, transmission, and special order information.

LYNX (FOUR)

Model No.	Body/ Style No.	Body Type & Seating	Factory Price	Shipping Weight	Prod. Total
54	61D	3-dr. Hatch-4P	5758	1928	Note 1
65	58D	5-dr. Hatch-4P	5965	1984	Note 1
54	61D	3-dr. L Hatch-4P	6019	1922	Note 1
65	58D	5-dr. L Hatch-4P	6233	N/A	Note 1
60	74D	4-dr. L Sta Wag-4P	6448	N/A	Note 1
55	61D	3-dr. GS Hatch-4P	6495	1948	Note 1
66	58D	5-dr. GS Hatch-4P	6709	N/A	Note 1
61	74D	4-dr. GS Sta Wag-4P	6887	N/A	Note 1
57	61D	3-dr. RS Hatch-4P	7641	N/A	Note 1
68/934	58D	5-dr. LTS Hatch-4P	7879	1920	Note 1

LYNX TURBO (FOUR)

Model No.	Body/ Style No.	Body Type & Seating	Factory Price	Shipping Weight	Prod. Total
57	61D	3-dr. RS Hatch-4P	8728	1997	Note 1

NOTE 1: Total Lynx production, 38,208 three-door hatchbacks, 21,090 five-door hatchbacks, and 16,142 four-door liftgate station wagons.

1984 Mercury Cougar XR-7 Sports Coupe. (JG)

1984 Mercury Marquis Brougham sedan. (JG)

CAPRI GS (FOUR/V-6)

Model No.	Body/Style No.	Body Type & Seating	Factory Price	Shipping Weight	Prod. Total
79	61D	3-dr. Fastbk-4P	7758/8167	2615/2723	Note 2

Capri Engine Note: Six-cylinder price does not include cost of the required automatic transmission ($439). The high-output 302-cid V-8 engine cost $1165 more than the V-6.

CAPRI RS TURBO (FOUR)

79	61D	3-dr. Fastbk-4P	9822	2894	Note 2

CAPRI RS (V-8)

79	61D	3-dr. Fastbk-4P	9638	2894	Note 2

NOTE 2: Total Capri production was 20,642.

TOPAZ (FOUR)

72	66D	2-dr. GS Sedan-5P	7469	2329	32,749
75	54D	4-dr. GS Sedan-5P	7469	2413	96,505
73	66D	2-dr. LS Sedan-5P	7872	2353	Note 3
76	54D	4-dr. LS Sedan-5P	7872	2434	Note 3

NOTE 3: Production of LS models is included in GS totals.

Diesel Engine Note: A diesel model Topaz cost $8027 (GS) or $8429 (LS).

MARQUIS (FOUR/V-6)

89	54D	4-dr. Sedan-5P	8727/9136	2796/----	91,808
90	74D	4-dr. Sta Wag-5P	----/9224	----/2996	16,004

MARQUIS BROUGHAM (FOUR/V-6)

89	54D	4-dr. Sedan-5P	9030/9439	2796/----	Note 4
90	74D	4-dr. Sta Wag-5P	----/9498	N/A	Note 4

NOTE 4: Brougham production is included in basic totals above.

COUGAR (V-6/V-8)

92	66D	2-dr. Cpe-4P	9978/10361	2912/----	131,190
92/603	66D	2-dr. LS Cpe-4P	11265/11648	2941/----	Note 5

Cougar Engine Note: The V-8 engine required a four-speed automatic transmission at $237 extra.

COUGAR XR-7 (TURBO FOUR)

92/934	66D	2-dr. Cpe-4P	13065	2900	Note 5

NOTE 5: Production of LS and XR-7 is included in basic total above.

GRAND MARQUIS (V-8)

93	66K	2-dr. Sedan-6P	11576	3607	13,657
95	54K	4-dr. Sedan-6P	11640	3761	117,739
93/60H	66K	2-dr. LS Sed-6P	12131	3607	Note 6
95/60H	54K	4-dr. LS Sed-6P	12195	3761	Note 6

GRAND MARQUIS COLONY PARK (V-8)

94	74K	4-dr. Sta Wag-6P	11816	3788	17,421

NOTE 6: LS production is included in basic Grand Marquis totals.

FACTORY PRICE AND WEIGHT NOTE: Cougar prices and weights to left of slash are for V-6, to right for V-8 engine. For Capri/Marquis, prices/weights to left of slash are for four-cylinder, to right for V-6.

ENGINE [Base Four (Lynx)]: Inline. Overhead cam. Four-cylinder. Cast-iron block and aluminum head. Displacement: 97.6-cid (1.6-liters). Bore & stroke: 3.15 x 3.13 in. Compression ratio: 9.0:1. Brake horsepower: 70 at 4600 rpm. Torque: 88 lbs.-ft. at 2600 rpm. Five main bearings. Hydraulic valve lifters. Carburetor: 2Bbl. Motorcraft 740. VIN Code: 2.

ENGINE [Optional Four (Lynx)]: High-output version of 1.6-liter engine above: Horsepower: 80 at 5400 rpm. Torque: 88 lbs.-ft. at 3000 rpm. VIN Code: 4.

ENGINE [Optional Four (Lynx)]: Fuel-injected version of 1.6-liter engine above: Compression ratio: 9.5:1. Horsepower: 84 at 5200 rpm. Torque: 90 lbs.-ft. at 2800 rpm. VIN Code: 5.

ENGINE [Turbo Four (Lynx)]: Same as 1.6-liter four above, with fuel injection and turbocharger. Compression ratio: 8.0:1. Horsepower: 120 at 5200 rpm. Torque: 120 lbs.-ft. at 3400 rpm. VIN Code: 8.

ENGINE [Diesel Four (Lynx, Topaz)]: Inline. Overhead cam. Four-cylinder. Cast-iron block and aluminum head. Displacement: 121.-cid (2.0-liters). Bore & stroke: 3.39 x 3.39 in. Compression ratio: 22.5:1. Brake horsepower: 52 at 4000 rpm. Torque: 82 lbs.-ft. at 2400 rpm. Five main bearings. Solid valve lifters. Fuel injection. VIN Code: H.

ENGINE [Base Four (Topaz)]: Inline. Overhead valve. Four-cylinder. Cast-iron block and head. Displacement: 140-cid (2.3-liters). Bore & stroke: 3.70 x 3.30 in. Compression ratio: 9.0:1. Brake horsepower: 84 at 4400 rpm. Torque: 118 lbs.-ft. at 2600 rpm. Five main bearings. Hydraulic valve lifters. Carburetor: 1Bbl. Holley 6149. High Swirl Combustion (HSC) design. VIN Code: R (U.S.) or J (Mexico).

ENGINE [Base Four (Capri, Marquis)]: Inline. Overhead cam. Four-cylinder. Cast-iron block and head. Displacement: 140-cid (2.3-liters). Bore & stroke: 3.78 x 3.13 in. Compression ratio: 9.0:1. Brake horsepower: 88 at 4000 rpm. Torque: 122 lbs.-ft. at 2400 rpm. Five main bearings. Hydraulic valve lifters. Carburetor: 1Bbl. Carter YFA. VIN Code: A.

ENGINE [Base Turbo Four (Cougar XR-7); Optional (Capri)]: Same as 140-cid four above, but with turbocharger. Compression ratio: 8.0:1. Horsepower: 145 at 4600 rpm. (Capri, 175 at 4400 rpm.). Torque: 180 lbs.-ft. at 3800 rpm. (Capri, N/A). VIN Code: W.

NOTE: Propane four was available for Marquis.

ENGINE [Base V-6 (Cougar); Optional (Capri, Marquis)]: 90-degree, overhead valve V-6. Cast-iron block and aluminum head. Displacement: 232-cid (3.8-liters). Bore & stroke: 3.80 x 3.40 in. Compression ratio: 8.65:1. Brake horsepower: 120 at 3600 rpm. Torque: 205 lbs.-ft. at 1600 rpm. Four main bearings. Hydraulic valve lifters. Carburetor: 2Bbl. (or fuel-injected). VIN Code: 3.

ENGINE [Base V-8 (Grand Marquis); Optional (Cougar)]: 90-degree, overhead valve V-8. Cast-iron block and head. Displacement: 302-cid (5.0-liters). Bore & stroke: 4.00 x 3.00 in. Compression ratio: 8.4:1. Brake horsepower: 140 at 3200 rpm. Torque: 250 lbs.-ft. at 1600 rpm. Five main bearings. Hydraulic valve lifters. Fuel injection. VIN Code: F.

ENGINE [Optional V-8 (Grand Marquis)]: Carbureted version of 302-cid V-8 above: Compression ratio: 8.4:1. Horsepower: 155 at 3600 rpm. Torque: 265 lbs.-ft. at 2000 rpm.

ENGINE [Optional V-8 (Capri)]: Fuel-injected version of 302-cid V-8 above. Compression ratio: 8.3:1. Horsepower: 165 at 4000 rpm. Torque: 245 lbs.-ft. at 2200 rpm.

ENGINE [Optional V-8 (Capri)]: High-output version of 302-cid V-8 above: Compression ratio: 8.3:1. Horsepower: 175 at 4000 rpm. Torque: 245 lbs.-ft. at 2200 rpm. Carburetor: 4Bbl. Holley 4180C. VIN Code: M.

NOTE: High-output version rated 205 H.P. was announced but delayed.

ENGINE [Police V-8 (Grand Marquis)]: 90-degree, overhead valve V-8. Cast-iron block and head. Displacement: 351-cid (5.8 liters). Bore & stroke: 4.00 x 3.50 in. Compression ratio: 8.3:1. Brake horsepower: 180 at 3600 rpm. Torque: 285 lbs.-ft. at 2400 rpm. Five main bearings. Hydraulic valve lifters. Carburetor: 2Bbl. VV. VIN Code: G.

CHASSIS DATA: Wheelbase: (Lynx) 94.2 in.; (Capri) 100.5 in.; (Topaz) 99.9 in.; (Marquis) 105.6 in.; (Cougar) 104.0 in.; (Grand Marquis) 114.3 in. Overall Length: (Lynx) 163.9 in.; (Capri) 179.1 in.; (Topaz) 176.5 in.; (Marquis) 196.5 in.; (Cougar) 197.6 in.; (Grand Marquis) 214.0 in.; (Grand Marquis wag) 218.0 in. Height: (Lynx) 53.3 in.; (Capri) 51.9 in.; (Topaz 2-dr.) 52.5 in.; (Topaz 4-dr.) 52.7 in.; (Marquis) 53.6 in.; (Marquis wag) 54.3 in.; (Cougar) 53.4 in.; (Grand Marquis) 55.2 in.; (Grand Marquis wag) 56.8 in. Width: (Lynx) 65.9 in.; (Capri) 69.1 in.; (Topaz) 66.2 in.; (Marquis) 71.0 in.; (Cougar) 71.1 in.; (Grand Marquis) 77.5 in.; (Grand Marquis wag) 79.3 in. Front Tread: (Lynx) 54.7 in.; (Capri) 56.6 in.; (Topaz) 54.7 in.; (Marquis) 56.6 in.; (Cougar) 58.1 in.; (Grand Marquis) 62.2 in. Rear Tread: (Lynx) 56.0 in.; (Capri/Marquis) 57.0 in.; (Topaz) 57.6 in.; (Grand Marquis) 58.5 in.; (Cougar) 62.0 in. Standard Tires: (Lynx) P165/80R13; (Lynx RS/LTS) 165/70R365 Michelin TRX; (Capri) P185/75R14; (Capri RS) P205/70R14; (Topaz) P175/80R13; (Marquis) P185/75R14; (Cougar) P185/75R14; (XR7) P205/70HR14; (Grand Marquis) P215/75R14 SBR WSW.

TECHNICAL: Transmission: Four-speed manual standard on Lynx/Topaz; five-speed manual or three-speed automatic optional. Four-speed manual standard on Capri; five-speed manual, three- or four-speed automatic optional. SelectShift three-speed automatic standard on Cougar/Marquis; four-speed overdrive optional. Five-speed manual standard on Cougar XR-7. Four-speed overdrive automatic standard on Grand Marquis. Gear ratios same as equivalent Ford models; see

Ford/Mustang listings. Standard final drive ratio: (Lynx) 3.59:1 w/4spd, 3.73:1 w/5spd, 3.31:1 w/auto., 3.52:1 w/diesel; (Capri four) 3.08:1 w/4spd, 3.27:1 w/auto.; (Capri V-6) 3.08:1; (Capri V-8) 3.08:1 w/5spd, 2.73:1 w/auto., 3.27:1 w/4spd auto.; (Capri turbo) 3.45:1; (Topaz) 3.04:1 w/4spd, 3.23:1 w/5spd or auto., 3.73:1 w/diesel; (Marquis) 3.08:1, 3.27:1 or 2.73:1; (Cougar V-6) 2.73:1 w/3spd auto., 3.27:1 with 4spd auto.; (Cougar V-8) 3.08:1; (Cougar XR-7 turbo) 3.45:1 w/5spd, 3.73:1 w/auto.; (Grand Marquis) 3.08:1. Steering: (Grand Marquis) recirculating ball; (others) rack-and-pinion. Front Suspension: (Lynx) MacPherson strut-mounted coil springs w/lower control arms and stabilizer bar; (Topaz) MacPherson struts w/stabilizer bar; (Capri/Cougar/Marquis) modified MacPherson struts w/coil springs and anti-sway bar; (Grand Marquis) coil springs with long/short A-arms and anti-sway bar. Rear Suspension: (Lynx) independent trailing arms w/modified MacPherson struts and coil springs on lower control arms; (Topaz) fully independent quadra-link w/MacPherson struts; (Capri/Cougar/Marquis/Grand Marquis) four-link w/coil springs. Brakes: Front disc, rear drum. Ignition: Electronic. Body construction: (Grand Marquis) separate body and frame; (others) unibody. Fuel tank: (Lynx) 13 gal.; (Capri) 15.4 gal.; (Topaz) 15.2 gal.; (Marquis) 16 gal.; (Cougar) 20.6 gal.; (Grand Marquis) 18 gal.; (Grand Marquis wag) 18.5 gal.

DRIVETRAIN OPTIONS: Engines: Fuel-saver 1.6-liter four: Lynx (NC). H.O. 1.6-liter four: Lynx ($73). Propane 140-cid four: Marquis ($896). 232-cid V-6: Capri/Marquis ($409). 302-cid V-8: Capri ($1372-$1574); Cougar ($383). Transmission/Differential: Five-speed manual trans.: Lynx/Topaz ($76). Automatic transaxle: Lynx ($439) exc. LTS/RS ($363); Topaz ($439). Auto. transmission: Capri ($439). Overdrive auto. trans.: Capri ($551); Marquis/Cougar ($237). Traction-Lok differential: Capri/Marquis/Grand Marquis/Cougar ($95). Brakes & Steering: Power brakes: Lynx ($95). Power steering: Lynx ($215); Capri ($202); Topaz ($223); Suspension: H.D. susp.: Topaz (NC); Marquis ($43); Grand Marquis/Cougar ($26). Handling susp.: Lynx L ($145); Lynx GS ($41); Grand Marquis ($49). Handling susp. pkg.: Capri ($252) exc. w/VIP pkg. ($50). Soft ride susp. pkg.: Topaz (NC). Other: H.D. battery ($27). Engine block heater ($18). Trailer towing pkg.: Grand Marquis ($200-$302); Cougar ($251). California emission system: Lynx ($46); others ($99). High-altitude emissions (NC).

LYNX CONVENIENCE/APPEARANCE OPTIONS: Option Packages: Villager woodtone pkg. ($339). Instrument group ($87). Power door lock group ($124-$176). Light group ($67). Comfort/Convenience: Air conditioner ($643). Rear defroster, electric ($130). Fingertip speed control ($176). Tinted glass ($95); windshield only ($48). Tilt steering ($104). Overhead console w/digital clock ($82). Interval wipers ($50). Rear wiper/washer ($120). Dual remote sport mirrors ($68). Entertainment: AM radio ($39). AM/FM stereo radio ($109) exc. L ($148); w/cassette player ($204) exc. L ($243). Electronic-tuning AM/FM stereo w/cassette ($396-$435). Premium sound ($117). Radio delete ($39 credit). Exterior: Flip-up/open air roof ($315) exc. Villager ($215). Clearcoat metallic paint (NC). Glamour paint ($51). Dual bodyside paint stripes ($39). Front vent windows, pivoting ($63). Vinyl-insert bodyside moldings ($45). Bumper guards, front or rear ($28). Bumper rub strips ($48). Luggage rack ($100). Lower bodyside protection ($68). Interior: Console ($111). Vinyl seat trim ($24). Wheels and Tires: Wheel trim rings ($54). TR aluminum wheels: LTS/RS ($201). Styled steel wheels ($104 credit). P165/80R13 SBR WSW ($59). P175/80R13 SBR BSW (NC).

CAPRI CONVENIENCE/APPEARANCE OPTIONS: Option Packages: Light group ($55-$88). Power lock group ($177). Comfort/Convenience: Air cond. ($743). Rear defroster, electric ($140). Fingertip speed control ($176). Power windows ($198). Tinted glass ($110). Tilt steering wheel ($110). Interval wipers ($50). Remote right mirror ($46). Entertainment: AM/FM stereo radio ($109); w/cassette player ($222) exc. w/VIP pkg. ($113). Premium sound system ($151). AM radio delete ($39 credit); AM/FM ($148 credit). Exterior: T-Roof ($874-$1074). Flip-up/open air roof ($315). Glamour paint ($54). Lower bodyside protection ($41). Interior: Sport seats ($196). Vinyl low-back seats ($29). Wheels and Tires: Wire wheel covers ($98). P195/75R14 WSW ($108). P205/70HR14 BSW ($224). TRX 220/55R390 BSW in performance pkg. ($327-$551).

TOPAZ CONVENIENCE/APPEARANCE OPTIONS: Option Packages: TR performance pkg. w/aluminum wheels ($293). Power lock group ($202-$254). Appearance protection group ($71). Light/convenience group ($50-$70). Comfort/Convenience: Air cond. ($743). Rear defroster, electric ($140). Fingertip speed control ($176). Illuminated entry ($82). Anti-theft system ($159). Power windows ($272). Power decklid release ($40). Six-way power seat ($224). Tinted glass ($110); windshield ($48). Tilt steering ($110). Digital clock ($61). Interval wipers ($50). Lighted visor vanity mirrors, pair ($100). Entertainment: AM/FM stereo radio ($109) w/cassette player ($204). Electronic-tuning AM/FM stereo ($252); w/cassette ($396). Premium sound system ($117). AM radio delete ($39 credit). Exterior: Flip-up/open air roof ($315). Metallic glamour glow paint ($63). Black lower body accent paint ($78-$133). Bumper guards, front/rear ($56). Interior: Console ($111). Fold-down front armrest ($55). Vinyl seat trim ($35). Carpeted front floor mats ($13). Trunk trim ($30). Tires: P175/80R13 WSW ($72).

1984 Mercury Grand Marquis LS sedan. (JG)

MARQUIS CONVENIENCE/APPEARANCE OPTIONS: Option Packages: Woodtone option ($282). Power lock group ($213-$254). Cold weather group ($77). Light group ($38). Police pkg. ($859-$1387). H.D. pkg. ($210). Comfort/Convenience: Air cond. ($743): auto-temp ($809). Rear defroster, electric ($140). Fingertip speed control ($176). Illuminated entry ($82). Autolamp on-off delay ($73). Power windows ($272). Six-way power driver's seat ($224); dual ($449). Tinted glass ($110). Tinted windshield ($48). Leather-wrapped steering wheel ($59). Tilt steering ($110). Electronic instrument cluster ($289-$367). Tripminder computer ($215-$293). Digital clock ($78). Diagnostic warning lights ($89). Auto. parking brake release ($12). Interval wipers ($50). Liftgate wiper/washer: wag ($99). Lighting and Mirrors: Cornering lamps ($68). Right remote convex mirror ($61). Lighted visor vanity mirrors ($57-$106). Entertainment: AM/FM stereo radio ($109); w/cassette player ($204). Electronic-tuning AM/FM stereo radio w/cassette ($396). Premium sound system ($117-$151). AM radio delete ($39 credit). Exterior: Carriage roof ($848). Full vinyl roof ($152). Glamour paint ($63). Two-tone paint ($117). Pivoting front vent windows ($79). Two-way liftgate: wag ($105). Protective bodyside moldings ($55). Bumper guards, rear ($28). Bumper rub strips ($56). Luggage rack: wagon ($126). Lower bodyside protection ($41). Interior: Vinyl seat trim ($35). Individual seats w/console ($61). Leather seat trim ($415). Front floor mats, carpeted ($23). Wheels and Tires: Luxury wheel covers ($55). Wire wheel covers, locking ($204). Polycast wheels ($178). Styled steel wheels w/trim rings ($54). P185/75R14 WSW ($72). P195/75R14 BSW ($38); WSW ($116). Puncture-sealant P195/75R14 WSW ($240). Conventional spare ($63).

COUGAR CONVENIENCE/APPEARANCE OPTIONS: Option Packages: Luxury carpet group ($72). Traveler's assistance kit ($65). Light group ($35). Power lock group ($177). Comfort/Convenience: Air cond. ($743); auto-temp ($809). Rear defroster ($140). Fingertip speed control ($176). Illuminated entry system ($82). Keyless entry ($198). Anti-theft system ($159). Remote fuel door lock ($37). Tripminder computer ($215-$276). Autolamp on/off delay ($73). Tinted glass ($110); windshield only ($48). Power windows ($198). Six-way power driver's seat ($227); dual ($454). Auto. parking brake release ($12). Leather-wrapped steering wheel ($59). Tilt steering wheel ($110). Electronic instrument cluster ($382). Diagnostic warning lights ($89). Digital clock ($61). Interval wipers ($49). Lighting and Mirrors: Cornering lamps ($68). Electro-luminescent coach lamps ($84). Dual electric remote mirrors ($96). Electronic-dimming day/night mirror ($77). Lighted visor vanity mirrors, pair ($106). Entertainment: AM/FM stereo radio ($109); w/cassette player ($204). Electronic-tuning AM/FM stereo search radio ($252); w/cassette ($396). Power antenna ($66). Premium sound system ($179). AM radio delete ($39 credit). Exterior: Luxury vinyl half rear roof ($245). Flip-up/open-air roof ($315). Metallic clearcoat paint ($183). Hood accent striping ($16). Pivoting front vent windows ($79). Rocker panel moldings ($39). License frames ($9). Lower bodyside protection ($39-$54). Interior: Articulated seats ($183-$427). Leather seat trim ($415). Vinyl seat trim ($37). Front floor mats, carpeted ($22). Wheels/Tires: Wire wheel covers, locking ($90-$204). Luxury wheel covers ($113). Polycast wheels ($65-$178). P195/75R14 puncture-sealing tires ($124). P205/70R14 BSW (NC). P205/70R14 WSW ($62). P205/70HR14 performance BSW ($152). Cast aluminum TRX wheels w/BSW performance tires ($535-$649) exc. XR-7 ($318).

GRAND MARQUIS CONVENIENCE/APPEARANCE OPTIONS: Option Packages: LS decor: Colony Park ($621). Convenience group ($109-$134). Power lock group ($140-$238). Light group ($30-$48). Comfort/Convenience: Air cond. ($743); w/auto-temp control ($809). Rear defroster, electric ($140). Fingertip speed control ($176). Illuminated entry system ($82). Power driver's seat ($227); driver and passenger ($454). Remote fuel door lock ($35). Tinted glass ($110); windshield only ($48). Autolamp on/off delay ($73). Leather-wrapped steering wheel ($59). Tilt steering wheel ($110). Tripminder computer ($261). Digital clock ($61). Interval wipers ($50). Lighting and Mirrors: Cornering lamps ($68). Remote right mirror ($44). Lighted visor vanity mirrors ($106). Entertainment: Electronic-tuning AM/FM stereo radio w/cassette ($166). Power antenna ($66). Premium sound system ($151-$179). Radio delete ($148 credit). Exterior: Formal vinyl coach roof: 4-dr. ($650). Glamour paint ($77). Two-tone paint ($129). Pivoting front vent windows ($79). Rocker panel moldings ($18-$38). Vinyl-insert bodyside moldings ($61). Bumper rub strips ($59). Luggage rack ($104). Lower bodyside protection ($39-$52). Interior: Dual-facing rear seats: wagon ($167). Cloth twin comfort seats ($48). All-vinyl seat trim ($418). Leather seat trim ($418). All-vinyl seat trim ($34); Duraweave vinyl ($96). Carpeted front floor mats ($21). Wheels/Tires: Wire wheel covers, locking ($174). Cast aluminum wheels ($361). P225/75R14 WSW ($42-$43). P205/75R15 WSW ($17); puncture-sealant ($178). P215/75R14 BSW ($66 credit). Conventional spare ($63).

NOTE: Many value option packages were offered for each Mercury model.

HISTORY: Introduced: September 22, 1983, except Topaz, April 1983. Model year production: 613,155. Calendar year production (U.S.): 461,504. Calendar year sales by U.S. dealers: 527,198. Model year sales by U.S. dealers: 529,300 (including early '84 Topaz models). A giant sales leap highlighted the 1984 model year, up about one-third from 484,688 (including 21,745 early Topaz models) to 644,308. Marquis sales rose dramatically, and Cougar wasn't so far from doubling (up 82 percent). Big and luxury models seemed to be doing well, as was the case in the industry as a whole, while Lynx and Capri sales slipped notably, though not drastically. LN7 was dropped in 1984, as it had never found a significant number of buyers. Only a few leftovers were sold during the 1984 model year. Lincoln-Mercury now had its own import: the sporty Merkur XR4Ti, from Ford Werke AG in West Germany, rivaling BMW, Audi and Volvo. It was actually sold under a separate franchise.

1985 MERCURY

1985-1/2 Mercury Lynx hatchback sedan. (CP)

1985 Mercury Lynx GS liftgate station wagon. (PH)

Cougar got a modest face lift this year, including grille, tail lamps and dash. Grand Marquis offered an electronic suspension system. A fuel-injected four-cylinder engine and five-speed manual transaxle were made standard on Topaz. Lynx was a carryover at introduction time, but a Second Series arrived at mid-year, with a larger (1.9-liter) engine under the hood.

1985 Mercury Capri GS hatchback coupe. (CP)

1985 Mercury Capri RS hatchback coupe (with 5.0-liter V-8). (PH)

LYNX — FOUR — Since a Second Series Lynx with larger (1.9-liter) CVH four-cylinder engine would arrive as a 1985.5 model, the early carryover version continued with fewer models and engine possibilities. Only the three-door base model survived, along with GS and LS editions. The RS (three-door) and LTS (five-door) were dropped. Also dropped was the port fuel-injected 1.6 engine, leaving only the carbureted version. A new shift pattern for the five-speed transaxle put reverse below fifth gear, instead of by itself at the upper left. All except the base three-door now had power brakes. An AM/FM stereo radio was now standard on GS. The 2.0-liter diesel engine was available again, but turbos faded away. Base Lynx standard equipment included the two-barrel four-cylinder engine, four-speed manual transaxle, P165/80R13 SBR BSW tires on semi-styled steel wheels with bright trim rings, color-keyed door scuff plates, compact spare tire, cargo area cover, consolette, side window demisters, dome light, and day/night mirror. Bright bumpers had black end caps. Cloth reclining high-backbucket seats were standard. So was a 10-gallon fuel tank. Lynx L added power brakes, an AM radio, black carpeting, 13-gallon fuel tank, black rocker panel paint, and cloth reclining low-back bucket seats. Pacific state models had a five-speed manual transaxle, AM/FM stereo and an instrument group. GS models included a black front air dam, AM/FM stereo radio, styled steel wheels, high-output engine, five-speed transaxle, dual-color upper bodyside accent paint stripes, assist handles, bumper rub strips with argent accent stripe, and color-keyed lower back panel carpeting. Also on GS: a locking glovebox, remote fuel filler door lock/release, and power hatch release. Wide bodyside moldings had argent accent striping, and rocker panels had no black paint. See 1986 listing for description of the Second Series Lynx.

CAPRI — FOUR/V-6/V-8 — Appearance of Mercury's Mustang clone was similar to 1984. As usual, Capri had a different grille than Mustang, and horizontal louvers at the rear of the quarter window rather than vertical. Biggest styling difference, though, was the "bubbleback" glass hatch. Roller tappets were added to the 302-cid (5.0-liter) V-8, standard in the RS (later changed to 5.0L name), along with a higher-performance camshaft and two-speed accessory drive. The five-speed manual gearbox got tighter gear ratios and shorter lever travel. Capri GS continued with a standard 140-cid (2.3-liter) four. Other choices included the 232-cid (3.8-liter) V-6, and fuel-injected or four-barrel V-8. The turbo four was scheduled to reappear, but didn't make it. Both the V-6 and V-8 had a low oil level warning light. Bodies now had charcoal highlights. Standard equipment was added, including an electric rear-window defroster, tinted glass, power steering, interval wipers, and tilt steering. Capri GS standard equipment included the 140-cid four with four-speed manual gearbox, P195/75R14 SBR BSW tires, turbine wheel covers, power windows, tachometer, integral rear spoiler, power brakes, charcoal bumper rub strips, digital clock, console with graphic warning display, and charcoal dual remote mirrors. Capri's charcoal grille had bright edges. Extra-wide wraparound charcoal bodyside moldings were used. Bodies also had dual fender and quarter panel pinstripes, lower bodyside protection, and color-keyed bumpers. Color-keyed louvers went on the hood, rear pillar and quarter panel; charcoal louvers on the cowl. Capri 5.0L included the V-8 engine, P205/70R14 tires, five-speed gearbox, cast aluminum wheels, handling suspension, three-oval black sport steering wheel, foglamps, locking remote gas filler door, front air dam, Traction-Lok, and dual exhausts. Bodies featured a charcoal lower bodyside paint treatment, charcoal moldings and grille, and charcoal rear pillar and quarter panel louvers. Tu-tone articulated sport seats offered adjustable thigh support.

1985 Mercury Topaz LS sedan. (CP)

1985 Mercury Topaz GS Sports Sedan. (PH)

TOPAZ — FOUR — Changes to the front-drive compact in its second year were mainly mechanical. Throttle-body fuel injection was added to the standard 140-cid (2.3-liter) four. A new expanded option, the GS Sports Group, included a high-output four with new cylinder head and intake manifold, offered only with manual shift. All manual transaxles were now five-speed, with a new shift pattern (reverse moved from upper left to lower right position). Standard equipment now included power steering, tinted glass, and AM/FM stereo, leaving fewer items on the option list. A restyled instrument panel included a package tray and side window defoggers. Child-proof rear door locks were new. Joining the option list: leather seat trim, and a graphic equalizer for audio fans. Topaz had more standard equipment than Tempo—and more yet in Western states. Another difference between the two was Topaz's vertical-style wraparound tail lamps, which connected with a full-width ribbed horizontal panel. Topaz GS standard equipment included the five-speed manual transaxle, P175/80R13 SBR BSW tires on polycast aluminum wheels, handling suspension, and tachometer. Styling features included dual bodyside accent stripes, decklid stripes (two-door), dual sport remote mirrors, color-keyed bumper end caps and rub strips, and a black grille. Wide bodyside moldings were color-keyed. Cloth/vinyl low-back reclining bucket seats were standard, along with vinyl lower bodyside protection, consolette, side window demisters, and power brakes. Topaz LS equipment included AM/FM stereo with cassette player, power windows, interval wipers, dual lighted visor vanity mirrors, and tilt steering. LS also had three assist handles, a digital clock, console, remote decklid release, electric rear window defroster, power door locks, illuminated entry, and remote gas filler door lock/release. New optional leather seat trim came only in charcoal.

MARQUIS — FOUR/V-6 — Apart from a revised grille, little change was evident on Mercury's rear-drive mid-size (nearly identical to Ford LTD), redesigned in 1983 on the former Cougar platform. This year's grille had fewer (and wider) vertical bars, and a center bar that was wider yet. New wide wraparound tail lamps had horizontal ribbing in a two-tiered, all-red design. The base 140-cid (2.3-liter) four added low-friction rings and gained compression. Standard tires increased to P195/75R14 size, with P205/70R14 newly optional. A high-output V-8 package also was announced, equivalent to LTD's LX model, but failed to appear. A four-door sedan and wagon came in base or Brougham trim. Wagons had a standard 232-cid (3.8-liter) V-6. Standard Marquis equipment included automatic transmission, AM radio, cloth reclining Twin Comfort lounge seats, black front bumper guards, remote driver's mirror, power brakes and steering, and a mini spare tire. Dual hood and upper bodyside accent stripes were used. Wide color-keyed vinyl bodyside moldings had argent striping. Marquis Brougham added a digital clock, lighted passenger visor vanity mirror, luxury cloth reclining Twin Comfort seats, light group, and luxury interior touches. New options included rocker panel moldings, dual power remote mirrors, and Brougham Flight Bench seating.

1985 Mercury Marquis sedan. (CP)

COUGAR — FOUR/V-6/V-8 — Two years after its massive restyling, Cougar got a modest face lift. The new grille, styled a la Mercedes, had two horizontal bars and one vertical bar. Its basic shape, though, wasn't much different than before. tail lamps also were revised. A restyled instrument cluster contained a digital speedometer, plus analog fuel and temperature gauges. A full electronic display was optional. XR-7 carried an all-analog cluster, and switched to 15 inch wheels. The 60/40 split bench front seat came with a consolette (not full console). Flatter back seat cushions now held three people. A soft-feel dashboard held side-window defoggers. The turbocharged four-cylinder engine in XR-7 was modified for smoother, quiet running, and added horsepower. Five-speed gearboxes got a tighter shift pattern. New standard tires were P205/70R14 on basic models, P225/60VR15 for the XR-7. Base models had a standard 232-cid (3.8-liter) V-6 with SelectShift three-speed automatic (four-speed available); or optional 302 V-8 with four-speed overdrive automatic. Standard equipment also included power brakes and steering, four-speaker AM/FM stereo radio, cloth/vinyl reclining Twin Comfort lounge seats, bumper rub strips with extensions, analog clock, side defoggers, and dual-note horn. Upper bodyside accent stripes were standard. Bright moldings went on belt, drip, door frame, quarter and back windows, and windshield. Lower bodyside moldings had charcoal vinyl inserts. Cougar LS added power windows, hood accent stripes, cloth seat trim, bright rocker panel moldings, dual power remote mirrors, tinted glass, coach lamps, and trunk carpeting. XR-7 included the turbocharged four with five-speed gearbox, P225/60VR15 performance Goodyear Gatorback BSW tires on cast aluminum wheels, handling suspension, Traction-Lok axle, front air dam, foglamps, and color-keyed dual power remote mirrors. Inside were Oxford Gray cloth sport bucket seats, a black sport steering wheel, digital clock, and charcoal console. Oxford Gray tri-band lower tape stripes, tinted glass, and charcoal moldings were standard on XR-7.

1985 Mercury Cougar XR-7 coupe. (CP)

1985 Mercury Cougar LS coupe. (PH)

1985 Mercury Grand Marquis sedan. (CP)

GRAND MARQUIS — V-8 — Full-size rear-drives didn't have to change much each year to attract buyers. This year was no exception. Gas-pressurized front struts and rear shocks became standard. The horn button moved from the steering-column stalk to the hub, and a flash-to-pass feature was added. One key now worked both ignition and door locks. An ignition diagnostic monitor was added to EEC-IV engine control. Lower bodysides added chip-resistant urethane coating. Late in the model year, electronic rear leveling was to be made optional. As before, the full-size selection included a two- and four-door sedan, and four-door wagon. Standard equipment included the 302-cid (5.0-liter) V-8 with automatic overdrive transmission, P215/75R14 SBR WSW tires, power brakes/steering, power windows, analog quartz clock, driver's remote mirror, and AM/FM stereo radio. Body features included upper bodyside accent stripes, a coach vinyl roof, bumper guards, and coach lamps. Color-keyed moldings went on quarter windows and roof wraparound of two-doors, and on the rear window; other moldings were bright, including wide lower bodyside moldings. Cloth reclining Twin Comfort lounge seats were standard. Grand Marquis LS added luxury cloth Twin Comfort seats, tinted glass, a folding center rear armrest, dual-beam dome light, and woodtone appliqué door trim panels. Colony Park wagons had P215/75R14 WSW tires, conventional spare tire, three-way tailgate with power window, full-length bodyside/rail/tailgate woodtone appliqué, and vinyl Twin Comfort seats.

I.D. DATA: Mercury's 17-symbol Vehicle Identification Number (VIN) was stamped on a metal tab fastened to the instrument panel, visible through the windshield. Symbols one to three indicates manufacturer, make and vehicle type: '1ME' Mercury passenger car. The fourth symbol ('B') denotes restraint system. Next comes a letter 'P', followed by two digits that indicate body type: Model Number, as shown in left column of tables below. (Example: '72' Topaz GS two-door sedan.) Symbol eight indicates engine type: '2' L4-98 2Bbl.; '4' H.O. L4-98 2Bbl.; 'H' Diesel L4-121; 'A' L4-140 1Bbl.; 'X' HSC L4-140 1Bbl.; 'S' H.O. L4-140 FI; 'W' Turbo L4-140 EFI; '3' V6-232 FI; 'F' V8-302 2Bbl. or FI; 'M' V8-302 4Bbl.; 'G' V8-351 2Bbl. FI. Next is a check digit. Symbol ten indicates model year ('F' 1985). Symbol eleven is assembly plant: 'A' Atlanta, GA; 'B' Oakville, Ontario (Canada); 'F' Dearborn, MI; 'G' Chicago, IL; 'H' Lorain, OH; 'K' Kansas City, MO; 'W' Wayne, MI; 'X' St. Thomas, Ontario (Canada); 'Z' St. Louis, MO; and Edison, NJ. The final six digits make up the sequence number, starting with 600001. A Vehicle Certification Label on the left front door lock face panel or door pillar shows the manufacturer, month and year of manufacture, GVW, GAWR, certification statement, VIN, and codes for such items as body type, color, trim, axle, transmission, and special order information.

LYNX (FOUR)

Model No.	Body/ Style No.	Body Type & Seating	Factory Price	Shipping Weight	Prod. Total
54/41P	61D	3-dr. Hatch-4P	5750	1922	Note 1
54	61D	3-dr. L Hatch-4P	6170	1985	Note 1
65	58D	5-dr. L Hatch-4P	6384	2050	Note 1
60	74D	4-dr. L Sta Wag-4P	6508	2076	Note 1
55	61D	3-dr. GS Hatch-4P	6707	2054	Note 1
66	58D	5-dr. GS Hatch-4P	6921	2121	Note 1
61	74D	4-dr. GS Sta Wag-4P	6973	2137	Note 1

Diesel Engine Note: Lynx diesel models cost $558 more (L) or $415 more (GS).

1985.5 LYNX (FOUR)

Model No.	Body/ Style No.	Body Type & Seating	Factory Price	Shipping Weight	Prod. Total
51	61D	3-dr. Hatch-4P	5986	2060	Note 1
51	61D	3-dr. L Hatch-4P	6272	2060	Note 1
63	58D	5-dr. L Hatch-4P	6486	2106	Note 1
58	74D	4-dr. L Sta Wag-4P	6767	2141	Note 1
52	61D	3-dr. GS Hatch-4P	6902	2149	Note 1
64	58D	5-dr. GS Hatch-4P	7176	2192	Note 1
59	74D	4-dr. GS Sta Wag-4P	7457	2215	Note 1

NOTE 1: Total Lynx production for the 1985.5 model year, 20,515 three-door hatchbacks, 11,297 five-door hatchbacks, and 6,721 four-door liftgate station wagons. Further information not available.

CAPRI GS (FOUR/V-6)

Model No.	Body/ Style No.	Body Type & Seating	Factory Price	Shipping Weight	Prod. Total
79	61D	3-dr. Fastbk-4P	7944/8383	2615/2723	Note 2

Capri Engine Note: Six-cylinder price does not include cost of the required automatic transmission ($439). The high-output 302-cid V-8 engine cost $799 more than the V-6.

CAPRI RS/5.0L (V-8)

79	61D	3-dr. Fastbk-4P	10223	N/A	Note 2

NOTE 2: Total Capri production was 18,657.

TOPAZ (FOUR)

72	66D	2-dr. GS Sedan-5P	7767	2313	18,990
75	54D	4-dr. GS Sedan-5P	7767	2368	82,366
73	66D	2-dr. LS Sedan-5P	8931	2335	Note 3
76	54D	4-dr. LS Sedan-5P	8980	2390	Note 3

NOTE 3: Production of LS models is included in GS totals.

Diesel Engine Note: A diesel model Topaz cost $8246 (GS) or $9410-$9459 (LS).

MARQUIS (FOUR/V-6)

89	54D	4-dr. Sedan-5P	8996/9414	2755/----	91,465
90	74D	4-dr. Sta Wag-5P	----/9506	----/2978	12,733

MARQUIS BROUGHAM (FOUR/V-6)

89/60H	54D	4-dr. Sedan-5P	9323/9741	2849/----	Note 4
90/60H	74D	4-dr. Sta Wag-5P	----/9805	N/A	Note 4

NOTE 4: Brougham production is included in basic totals above.

COUGAR (V-6/V-8)

92	66D	2-dr. Cpe-5P	10650/11048	2931/----	117,274
92/603	66D	2-dr. LS Cpe-5P	11850/12248	2961/----	Note 5

Cougar Engine Note: The V-8 engine required a four-speed automatic transmission at $237 extra.

COUGAR XR-7 (TURBO FOUR)

92/934	66D	2-dr. Cpe-5P	13599	2947	Note 5

NOTE 5: Production of LS and XR-7 is included in basic total above.

GRAND MARQUIS (V-8)

93	66K	2-dr. Sedan-6P	12240	3607	10,900
95	54K	4-dr. Sedan-6P	12305	3761	136,239
93/60H	66K	2-dr. LS Sed-6P	12789	3607	Note 6
95/60H	54K	4-dr. LS Sed-6P	12854	3761	Note 6

GRAND MARQUIS COLONY PARK (V-8)

94	74K	4-dr. Sta Wag-6P	12511	3788	14,119

NOTE 6: LS production is included in basic Grand Marquis totals.

FACTORY PRICE AND WEIGHT NOTE: Cougar prices and weights to left of slash are for V-6, to right for V-8 engine. For Capri/Marquis, prices/weights to left of slash are for four-cylinder, to right for V-6.

ENGINE [Base Four (Lynx)]: Inline. Overhead cam. Four-cylinder. Cast-iron block and aluminum head. Displacement: 97.6-cid (1.6-liters). Bore & stroke: 3.15 x 3.13 in. Compression ratio: 9.0:1. Brake horsepower: 70 at 4600 rpm. Torque: 88 lbs.-ft. at 2600 rpm. Five main bearings. Hydraulic valve lifters. Carburetor: 2Bbl. Holley 740. VIN Code: 2.

NOTE: Second Series Lynx, introduced at mid-year, used a new 1.9-liter four; see 1986 listing for specifications.

ENGINE [Optional Four (Lynx)]: High-output version of 1.6-liter engine above: Horsepower: 80 at 5400 rpm. Torque: 88 lbs.-ft. at 2600 rpm. VIN Code: 4.

ENGINE [Diesel Four (Lynx, Topaz)]: Inline. Overhead cam. Four-cylinder. Cast-iron block and aluminum head. Displacement: 121-cid (2.0 liters). Bore & stroke: 3.39 x 3.39 in. Compression ratio: 22.5:1. Brake horsepower: 52 at 4000 rpm. Torque: 82 lbs.-ft. at 2400 rpm. Five main bearings. Solid valve lifters. Fuel injection. VIN Code: H.

ENGINE [Base Four (Topaz)]: Inline. Overhead valve. Four-cylinder. Cast-iron block and head. Displacement: 140-cid (2.3-liters). Bore & stroke: 3.70 x 3.30 in. Compression ratio: 9.0:1. Brake horsepower: 86 at 4000 rpm. Torque: 122 lbs.-ft. at 2800 rpm. Five main bearings. Hydraulic valve lifters. Fuel injection (TBI). High Swirl Combustion (HSC) design. VIN Code: X.

ENGINE [Optional Four (Topaz)]: High-output version of 140-cid HSC four above. Horsepower: 100 at 4600 rpm. Torque: 125 lbs.-ft. at 3200 rpm. VIN Code: S.

ENGINE [Base Four (Capri, Marquis)]: Inline. Overhead cam. Four-cylinder. Cast-iron block and head. Displacement: 140-cid (2.3 liters). Bore & stroke: 3.78 x 3.13 in. Compression ratio: 9.0:1, Brake horsepower: 88 at 4200 rpm. Torque: 122 lbs.-ft. at 2600 rpm. Five main bearings. Hydraulic valve lifters. Carburetor: 1Bbl. Carter YFA. VIN Code: A.

ENGINE [Base Turbo Four (Cougar XR-7)]: Same as 140-cid four above, but with turbocharger. Compression ratio: 8.0:1. Brake horsepower: 155 at 4600 rpm. Torque: 190 lbs.-ft. at 2800 rpm. VIN Code: W.

ENGINE [Base V-6 (Cougar); Optional (Capri, Marquis)]: 90-degree, overhead valve V-6. Cast-iron block and aluminum head. Displacement: 232-cid (3.8-liters). Bore & stroke: 3.80 x 3.40 in. Compression ratio: 8.65:1. Brake horsepower: 120 at 3600 rpm. Torque: 205 lbs.-ft. at 1600 rpm. Four main bearings. Hydraulic valve lifters. Fuel-injected. VIN Code: 3.

ENGINE [Base V-8 (Grand Marquis); Optional (Cougar)]: 90-degree, overhead valve V-8. Cast-iron block and head. Displacement: 302-cid (5.0 liters). Bore & stroke: 4.00 x 3.00 in. Compression ratio: 8.4:1. Brake horsepower: 140 at 3200 rpm. Torque: 250 lbs.-ft. at 1600 rpm. Five main bearings. Hydraulic valve lifters. Fuel injection. VIN Code: F.

ENGINE [Optional V-8 (Grand Marquis)]: High-output version of 302-cid V-8 above: Compression ratio: 8.4:1. Horsepower: 155 at 3600 rpm. Torque: 265 lbs.-ft. at 2000 rpm.

ENGINE [Optional V-8 (Capri)]: High-output version of 302-cid V-8 above: Compression ratio: 8.3:1. Horsepower: 180 at 4200 rpm. Torque: 260 lbs.-ft. at 2600 rpm.

ENGINE [Optional V-8 (Capri)]: High-output version of 302-cid V-8 above: Compression ratio: 8.3:1. Horsepower: 210 at 4400 rpm. Torque: 270 lbs.-ft. at 3200 rpm. Carburetor: 4Bbl. Holley. VIN Code: M.

NOTE: Police 351-cid V-8 remained available for Grand Marquis.

CHASSIS DATA: Wheelbase: (Lynx) 94.2 in.; (Capri) 100.5 in.; (Topaz) 99.9 in.; (Marquis) 105.6 in.; (Cougar) 104.0 in.; (Grand Marquis) 114.3 in. Overall Length: (Lynx) 163.9 in.; (Lynx wag) 165.0 in.; (Capri) 179.3 in.; (Topaz) 176.5 in.; (Marquis) 196.5 in.; (Cougar) 197.6 in.; (Grand Marquis) 211.0 in.; (Grand Marquis wag) 215.0 in. Height: (Lynx) 53.3-53.4 in.; (Capri) 52.1 in.; (Topaz) 52.7 in.; (Marquis) 53.8 in.; (Marquis wag) 54.4 in.; (Cougar) 53.4 in.; (Grand Marquis) 55.2 in.; (Grand Marquis wag) 56.8 in. Width: (Lynx) 65.9 in.; (Capri) 69.1 in.; (Topaz) 68.3 in.; (Marquis) 71.0 in.; (Cougar) 71.1 in.; (Grand Marquis) 77.5 in.; (Grand Marquis wag) 79.3 in. Front Tread: (Lynx) 54.7 in.; (Capri) 56.6 in.; (Topaz) 54.7 in.; (Marquis) 56.6 in.; (Cougar) 58.1 in.; (Grand Marquis) 62.2 in. Rear Tread: (Lynx) 56.0 in.; (Capri/Marquis) 57.0 in.; (Topaz) 57.6 in.; (Cougar) 58.5 in.; (Grand Marquis) 62.0 in. Standard Tires: (Lynx) P165/80R13; (Capri) P195/75R14; (Capri 5.0L) P225/60VR15; (Topaz) P175/80R13; (Marquis) P195/75R14; (Cougar) P205/75R14; (XR-7) P225/60VR15; (Grand Marquis) P215/75R14 SBR WSW.

TECHNICAL: Transmission: Four-speed manual standard on Lynx; five-speed manual or three-speed automatic optional. Four-speed manual standard on Capri; five-speed manual standard on Capri 5.0L; three-speed or four-speed automatic optional. Five-speed manual standard on Topaz; three-speed automatic optional. SelectShift three-speed automatic standard on Cougar/Marquis; four-speed overdrive optional. Five-speed manual standard on Cougar XR-7. Four-speed overdrive automatic standard on Grand Marquis. Gear ratios same as equivalent Ford models; see Ford/Mustang listings. Standard final drive ratio: (Lynx) 3.59:1 w/4spd, 3.73:1 w/5spd, 3.31:1 w/auto., 3.52:1 w/diesel; (Capri-four) 3.08:1 w/4spd, 3.27:1 w/auto.; (Capri V-6) 2.73:1; (Capri V-8) 2.73:1 w/5spd or auto., 3.27:1 w/4spd auto.; (Capri turbo) 3.45:1; (Topaz) 3.33:1 w/5spd, 3.23:1 w/auto., 3.73:1 w/diesel or FI four; (Marquis) 3.27:1 or 2.73:1; (Cougar V-6) 2.73:1 w/3spd auto., 3.27:1 with 4spd auto.; (Cougar V-8) 3.08:1; (Cougar XR-7 turbo) 3.45:1; (Grand Marquis) 3.08:1. Steering: (Grand Marquis) recirculating ball; (others) rack-and-pinion. Front Suspension: (Lynx/Topaz) MacPherson strut-mounted coil springs

w/lower control arms and stabilizer bar; (Capri/Cougar/Marquis) modified MacPherson struts w/lower control arms, coil springs and anti-sway bar; (Grand Marquis) coil springs with long/short A-arms and anti-sway bar. Rear Suspension: (Lynx) independent trailing arms w/modified MacPherson struts and coil springs on lower control arms; (Topaz) fully independent quadra-link w/MacPherson struts; (Capri/Cougar/Marquis/Grand Marquis) four-link w/coil springs. Brakes: Front disc, rear drum. Ignition: Electronic. Body construction: (Grand Marquis) separate body and frame; (others) unibody. Fuel tank: (Lynx) 10 gal., exc. wag, 13 gal.; (Capri) 15.4 gal.; (Topaz) 15.2 gal.; (Marquis) 16 gal.; (Cougar) 20.6 gal.; (Grand Marquis) 18 gal.; (Grand Marquis wag) 18.5 gal.

DRIVETRAIN OPTIONS: Engines: H.O. 1.6-liter four: Lynx ($73). 232-cid V-6: Capri ($439); Marquis sedan ($418). 302-cid V-8: Capri ($1238); Cougar ($398). Transmission/Differential: Five-speed manual trans.: Lynx L ($76); Capri GS w/V-8 (NC). Automatic transaxle: Lynx L ($439); Lynx GS ($363); Topaz ($363). SelectShift auto. trans.: Capri ($439); Cougar XR-7 ($315). Overdrive auto. trans.: Capri ($551-$676); Cougar ($237). Traction-Lok differential: Marquis/Grand Marquis/Cougar ($95). Brakes & Steering: Power brakes: Lynx ($95). Power steering: Lynx ($215). Suspension: H.D. susp.: Cougar base/LS, Grand Marquis ($26); Marquis LPO ($43). Auto. load leveling: Grand Marquis ($200). Other: H.D. battery ($27). Extended-range gas tank: Marquis sedan ($46). Engine block heater ($18). Trailer towing pkg.: Grand Marquis ($251-$302); Cougar ($251) exc. XR-7. California emission system: Lynx ($46); others ($99). High-altitude emissions (NC).

LYNX CONVENIENCE/APPEARANCE OPTIONS: Option Packages: Comfort/convenience group ($259-$384). Comfort/Convenience: Air conditioner ($643). Rear defroster, electric ($130). Fingertip speed control ($176). Power door locks ($124-$176). Tinted glass ($95). Tilt steering ($104). Console w/graphic warning display ($111). Rear wiper/washer ($120). Entertainment: AM/FM stereo radio ($109) exc. base ($148); w/cassette player ($148-$295). Graphic equalizer ($218). Exterior: Clearcoat metallic paint ($91). Two-tone paint ($134-$173). Dual bodyside stripes: L ($39). Black vinyl-insert bodyside moldings ($45). Bumper guards, front or rear ($28). Bumper rub strips ($48) exc. base. Luggage rack: wag ($100). Interior: Vinyl seat trim ($24). Tires: P165/80R13 SBR WSW ($59).

NOTE: Many options were not available on base Lynx.

CAPRI CONVENIENCE/APPEARANCE OPTIONS: Option Packages: TR performance pkg. P220/55VR390 TRX tires on aluminum wheels w/handling suspension: GS ($565) exc. w/V-8 ($377). Power lock group ($177). Comfort/Convenience: Air cond. ($743). Fingertip speed control ($176). Entertainment: Electronic AM/FM stereo radio w/cassette ($300). Premium sound system ($138). Radio delete ($148 credit). Exterior: T-Roof ($1074). Flip-up open air roof ($315). Interior: Low-back vinyl bucket seats: GS ($29). GS Wheels and Tires: Wire wheel covers ($98). Polycast steel wheels ($178). P205/75R14 WSW ($109).

TOPAZ CONVENIENCE/APPEARANCE OPTIONS: Option Packages: Sports group: GS ($439). Comfort/convenience pkg.: GS ($320-$706). TR performance pkg.: P185/65R365 Michelin TRX tires on cast aluminum wheels w/handling suspension ($293). Power lock group ($188-$254). Comfort/Convenience: Air cond. ($743). Rear defroster, electric ($140). Fingertip speed control ($176). Power windows: GS LPO ($272). Six-way power driver's seat LPO ($224). Tilt steering: GS ($110). Entertainment AM/FM stereo radio w/cassette player: GS ($148). Electronic-tuning AM/FM stereo w/cassette ($78-$300). Graphic equalizer ($218). Exterior: Clearcoat paint ($91). Lower body accent paint ($78). Interior: Vinyl reclining bucket seat trim LPO ($35). Leather seat trim ($300). Wheels/Tires: Styled wheels: GS LPO ($59). P175/80R13 WSW ($72). Conventional spare ($63).

MARQUIS CONVENIENCE/APPEARANCE OPTIONS: Option Packages: Woodtone option: wagon ($282). Power lock group ($213-$254). Light group: base ($38). Comfort/Convenience: Air cond. ($743). Rear defroster ($140). Fingertip speed control ($176). Illuminated entry ($82). Autolamp on-off delay ($73). Power windows ($272). Six-way power driver's seat ($224). Tinted glass ($110). Leather-wrapped steering wheel ($59). Tilt steering ($110). Digital clock: base ($78). Auto. parking brake release LPO ($12). Interval wipers ($50). Lighting and Mirrors: Cornering lamps ($68). Right remote convex mirror ($61). Dual electric remote mirrors ($96). Lighted visor vanity mirrors ($57-$106). Entertainment: AM/FM stereo radio ($109); w/cassette player ($256). Electronic-tuning AM/FM stereo radio w/cassette ($409). AM radio delete ($39 credit). Exterior: Full vinyl roof ($152). Two-tone paint ($117). Pivoting front vent windows ($79). Two-way liftgate: wag ($105). Rocker panel moldings ($40). Bumper guards, rear ($28). Black bumper rub strips w/argent stripe ($56). Luggage rack: wagon ($126). Interior: Vinyl seat trim ($35). Flight Bench seat: base (NC). Front floor mats, carpeted ($23). Wheels/Tires: Luxury wheel covers ($55). Wire wheel covers, locking ($204). Polycast wheels ($178). Styled steel wheels w/trim rings fleet ($54). P195/75R14 WSW ($72). P205/70R14 WSW ($134). Conventional spare LPO fleet ($63).

COUGAR CONVENIENCE/APPEARANCE OPTIONS: Option Packages: Headlamp convenience group ($176). Light group ($35). Power lock group ($213). Comfort/Convenience: Air cond. ($743); auto-temp ($905). Rear defroster ($140). Fingertip speed control ($176). Illuminated entry system ($82). Keyless entry ($198). Tinted glass: base ($110). Power windows: base ($198). Six-way power driver's seat ($227): dual ($454). Dual power seat recliners: base/LS ($189). Auto. parking brake release: base/LS ($12). Leather-wrapped steering wheel ($59). Tilt steering wheel ($110). Electronic instrument cluster ($330); N/A XR-7. Diagnostic warning lights ($89). Low oil warning light LPO ($24). Digital clock ($61). Interval wipers ($50). Lighting and Mirrors: Cornering lamps ($68). Dual electric remote mirrors: base ($96). Lighted visor vanity mirrors, pair ($106). Entertainment: AM/FM stereo radio w/cassette player ($148). Electronic-tuning AM/FM stereo search radio w/cassette ($300). Power antenna ($66). Graphic equalizer ($252). Premium sound system ($168). AM/FM radio delete ($148 credit). Exterior: Padded half vinyl roof: base/LS ($245). Metallic clearcoat paint ($183). Two-tone paint/tape: base ($163). Hood accent stripe: base ($16). Pivoting front vent windows ($79). Interior: Heated seats ($157). Leather/vinyl seat trim ($415). Vinyl seat trim: base ($37). Front floor mats, carpeted ($22). Wheels/Tires (except XR-7): Wire wheel covers. locking ($204). Polycast wheels ($178). P205/70R14 BSW ($62 credit). P215/70R14 WSW ($37). P215/70HR14 performance BSW ($152). Conventional spare ($63).

GRAND MARQUIS CONVENIENCE/APPEARANCE OPTIONS: Option Packages: LS decor: Colony Park ($621). Convenience group ($109-$134). Power lock group ($176-$273). Light group ($30-$48). Comfort/Convenience: Air cond. ($743); w/auto-temp control ($809). Rear defroster, electric ($140). Fingertip speed control ($176). Illuminated entry system ($82). Power driver's seat ($227); driver and passenger ($454). Tinted glass ($110). Autolamp on-off delay ($73). Leather-wrapped steering wheel ($59). Tilt steering wheel ($110). Tripminder computer ($261). Digital clock ($61). Lighting and Mirrors: Cornering lamps ($68). Remote right convex mirror ($46). Lighted visor vanity mirrors ($106). Entertainment: AM/FM stereo radio w/cassette tape player ($148). Electronic-tuning AM/FM stereo radio w/cassette ($300). Power antenna ($66). Premium sound system ($168). AM/FM radio delete ($148 credit). Exterior: Formal coach vinyl roof ($650). Two-tone paint/tape ($129). Hood accent stripes ($18). Pivoting front vent windows ($79). Rocker panel moldings ($18-$38). Narrow vinyl-insert bodyside moldings ($61). Bumper rub strips ($59). Luggage rack: wagon ($110). License frames ($9). Interior: Dual-facing rear seats: wagon ($167). Leather seat trim: LS ($418). All-vinyl seat trim ($34). Cloth trim: wagon ($48). Carpeted front/rear floor mats LPO fleet ($33). Wheels/Tires: Wire wheel covers, locking ($174). Turbine spoke cast aluminum wheels ($361). P205/75R15 WSW ($17); puncture-sealant ($178). P215/70R15 WSW ($79). Conventional spare ($63).

HISTORY: Introduced: October 4, 1984. Model year production: 541,276 (including only mid-year Lynx models). Calendar year production (U.S.): 374,535. Calendar year sales by U.S. dealers: 519,059. Model year sales by U.S. dealers: 555,021.

HISTORY: Grand Marquis sold the best since record-setting 1978, reaching 145,242 buyers (up from 131,515 in 1984). Cougar sales rose about 13 percent; Topaz a bit; Marquis down just a hair. Capri was not doing at all well, finding only 16,829 customers. The imported Merkur wasn't strong either, in its first (short) season. Front-drive may have been the wave of the future by the mid-1980s, but Lincoln-Mercury's rear-drives were doing quite well, not yet ready for retirement.

1986 MERCURY

1986 Mercury Cougar LS coupe. (OCW)

1986 Mercury Lynx XR3 hatchback coupe. (JG)

A new aero-styled Sable, close kin to Ford Taurus suffered a delayed introduction but replaced the old Marquis (which hung on for this model year). Lynx added a sporty equivalent to Escort's GT. All Lynx models now carried the 1.9-liter engine.

LYNX — FOUR — A sporty new XR3 hatchback, similar to Ford's Escort GT, joined the Lynx line, which had arrived in revised form at mid-year 1985. The former 1.6-liter CVH engine had been reworked to reach 1.9-liter displacement. XR3 carried a standard high-output version with multi-port fuel injection, plus 15 inch performance radial tires on aluminum wheels, an asymmetrical grille (again like Escort), foglamps, wheel spats, rocker panel moldings, rear spoiler, and front air dam. Standard five-speed manual or optional three-speed automatic were the two transmission choices. Base, L and GS models were offered, in three- or five-door (actually two and four) hatchback or wagon body styles. The diesel engine option returned (with five-speed gearbox). Lynx carried a new four-spoke steering wheel and new wraparound bumper end treatment, as well as a larger-diameter front stabilizer bar. The 1985.5 Lynx restyle had incorporated new front-end styling and headlamps, along with a revised rear end. Aero headlamps extended outward from the squat angled grille, made up of thin vertical bars with a round center emblem. Above the grille on the driver's side was 'Mercury' block lettering. The headlamps met wraparound park/signal/marker lenses that were amber colored. Horizontally-ribbed, wraparound full-width tail lamps extended outward from the recessed rear license plate opening. Small integral, squarish backup lenses were part of each assembly. 'Lynx' lettering (and model identification) went above the left tail lamps; 'Mercury' lettering above the right one. Standard Lynx equipment included the 1.9-liter OHC four-cylinder engine, four-speed manual transaxle, power brakes, P175/80R13 BSW SBR tires, semi-styled steel wheels with bright trim rings and argent hub covers with black lug nuts, high-mount rear stoplamp, and black driver's mirror. Bumper end caps extended to wheel openings. Interiors contained low-back reclining front seats with cloth upholstery, a flat-folding rear seat, soft-feel instrument panel, and grained-finish glovebox with coin slots. Lynx L added an AM radio (which could be deleted for credit), bright hood molding, bright hub covers and lug nuts, matte black rocker panel paint, and dual bodyside paint stripes. GS added a five-speed manual transaxle, AM/FM stereo radio, locking fuel filler door with remote release, body-color rocker panels, styled steel wheels, bumper rub strips, wide bodyside molding, roof grab handles, dual visor vanity mirrors, and fold-down front center armrest. XR3's minimalist grille consisted of two slots, one above the other, occupying just two-thirds of the body-color front panel, with 'XR3' identification on the other side. XR3 also had an aerodynamic front air dam with built-in foglamps. Equipment included the high-output engine, P195/60HR15 BSW SBR Goodyear Eagle unidirectional tires on cast aluminum wheels, power steering, overhead console with digital clock, foglamps, full console with graphic warning display, and an instrument group (including tachometer). Also part of XR3: a leather-wrapped steering wheel, cloth sport seats, dual remote mirrors, blackout greenhouse treatment, Midnight Smoke lower bodyside treatment, body-color spoiler, and narrow bodyside moldings.

CAPRI — FOUR/V-6/V-8 — Changes to Mercury's pony car went mostly under the hood for 1986. The 302-cid (5.0-liter) V-8 added sequential fuel injection, along with roller tappets, new rings, a knock sensor, and tuned intake/exhaust manifolds. Carbureted V-8s were gone. So was the turbo four, which hadn't even arrived for 1985, though it had been announced. Capri's simple model lineup was the same this year: just GS and 5.0L, the latter signifying V-8 power. Capri's ample standard equipment list meant few options were available. Standard equipment included the 140-cid (2.3-liter) four with four-speed manual gearbox, power brakes/steering, tinted glass, interval wipers, electric back window defroster, AM/FM stereo radio, tilt steering, and power windows. GS also had aero wheel covers, upper bodyside paint stripes, a black remote driver's mirror, tachometer and trip odometer, console with graphic warning display, digital clock, and passenger visor vanity mirror. Low-back front bucket seats had cloth upholstery. Options included the 232-cid (3.8-liter) V-6 and three-speed automatic. Capri 5.0 added the 302-cid V-8 and five-speed overdrive manual gearbox, P225/60VR15 tires, hood scoop (non-working), Traction-Lok differential, handling suspension, black brushed-finish dash appliqué, black remote passenger mirror, upper bodyside dual accent tape stripes, blackout body trim, and twin bright tailpipe outlets.

1986 Mercury Capri hatchback coupe. (JG)

1986 Mercury Topaz sedan. (JG)

TOPAZ — FOUR — Two years after its debut, the front-drive Topaz deserved a change or two. They came in the form of revised front-end styling with aero headlamps, a new grille, and body-color bumpers. Standard tires grew to P185/70R14 size with all-season tread, on 14 inch wheels. Four-way adjustable head restraints were new. The base GS model also got a new standard touring suspension with gas-filled struts. A push/pull headlamp switch replaced the rocker switch, and the wiper/washer control moved from the stalk to the instrument panel. The Sport Group option included new six inch aluminum wheels with 15 inch tires, and its high-output engine came only with five-speed manual. Diesel power remained available. The new aerodynamic body featured softly rounded edges and aircraft-inspired doors, with windshield and back window slanted nearly 60 degrees. The sloping front panel contained a single air intake slot, below a bright, horizontally-ribbed upper panel with center round emblem and 'Mercury' lettering on the driver's side. A series of six air intake slots went below the bumper strip. Aero headlamps extended outward to meet wraparound park/signal lenses and amber side markers. At the rear were tall wraparound tail lamps. A drag coefficient of 0.36 was recorded for the four-door. Inside was a new four-spoke steering wheel; outside, sail-mounted dual power remote mirrors. Front suspension again used MacPherson struts, with a parallel four-bar arrangement at the back. Standard GS equipment included the HSC 1.3-liter four, five-speed manual transaxle, power brakes and steering, blackwall tires with full wheel covers, low-back cloth reclining front seats, tachometer, AM/FM stereo radio (which could be deleted), side-window demisters, and color-keyed consolette. Dark Smoke bumper rub strips had bright inserts. Other body features: an acrylic grille appliqué with bright/argent accents, Dark Smoke cowl grille, bright windshield moldings, and black wiper arms. The optional GS Sport Group added Michelin TRX BSW tires on TR cast aluminum wheels with locking lug nuts, and special handling components, along with a high specific output (HSO) version of the 2.3-liter four. A revised intake manifold, higher-lift camshaft, larger cylinder head and other modifications boosted horsepower by 16 percent over the standard engine. It also got a new cast aluminum rocker cover. GS Sport Group also included a graphic display alert module, red inserts in bodyside moldings and bumper rub strips, Dark Smoke greenhouse moldings, and black leather-wrapped steering wheel. Topaz LS included a Touring suspension with gas-filled struts, full console, power windows and door locks, dual-lighted visor vanity mirrors, dual-color accent stripes, argent lower taillamp molding, woodgrain instrument cluster accents, and illuminated entry.

1986 Mercury Sable LS wagon. (JG)

1986 Mercury Sable LS sedan. (PH)

SABLE — FOUR/V-6 — Like Ford's new mid-size Taurus, the closely-related Sable lacked a conventional grille. Unlike Taurus with its mostly solid "grille" panel, Sable sported an illuminated plastic light bar between flush headlamps. Those headlamps extended outward to meet park/signal lamps, and wraparound the fenders into side marker lenses. Below the front bumper rub strip was a set of many vertical slots, arranged in four sections. Bodyside moldings followed a straight line from front to back, above horizontal ribbing in the center segment. At the rear were wide wraparound tail lamps (wider than Taurus). Surprisingly, sedans shared no sheetmetal at all. Wagons shared body parts only to the rear of the windshield. The first Sables came only with 181-cid (3.0-liter) fuel-injected V-6 and four-speed overdrive automatic, but a 151-cid (2.5-liter) four- and new three-speed automatic would become standard later. Sable's standard cluster included a tachometer and temp gauge. Gas shock absorbers were used in the fully independent suspension. Sable offered seating for six. Two trim levels were offered, GS and LS, in four-door sedan and station wagon form. Standard GS equipment included the 2.5-liter four- and three-speed automatic, power brakes/steering, cornering lamps, bumper rub strips, driver's remote mirror, side-window defoggers, passenger assist handles, tachometer, trip odometer, P205/70R14 tires, and a day/night mirror. Wagons had the 3.0-liter V-6 engine and four-speed automatic. Interiors contained a cloth Flight Bench seat with driver's side recliner, and fold-down center front armrest. Sable LS added the V-6 engine and four-speed automatic, power windows, remote decklid release, remote gas door release, digital clock, intermittent wipers, dual power remote mirrors, diagnostic warning lights, and AM/FM stereo radio. Twin Comfort lounge seats had dual recliners and power lumbar support adjusters. Urethane lower door and rocker panel coating was included. Taurus/Sable came from a $3 billion development program that began in 1980. In early tests, Sable demonstrated an even lower coefficient of drag than Taurus: 0.29 versus 0.32, partly because Sable had two inches more rear overhang.

MARQUIS — FOUR/V-6 — With the new Sable getting all the attention, the car it replaced was almost overlooked. In fact, quite a few examples were sold in this, its final season. The holdover rear-drive mid-size came with a base 140-cid (2.3-liter) four or optional 232-cid (3.8-liter) V-6. Appearance was the same as 1985.

1986 Mercury Marquis sedan. (JG)

1986 Mercury Cougar XR-7 coupe. (JG)

COUGAR — FOUR/V-6/V-8 — Mercury's two-door personal-luxury coupe again came in three levels: GS, LS, and the turbocharged XR-7. Appearance was similar to 1985. Cougar still displayed an upswept quarter-window design, which was its most notable difference from the closely-related Thunderbird. Base powerplant was the 232-cid (3.8-liter) V-6, with three-speed automatic. The optional 302-cid (5.0-liter) V-8 had new sequential (multi-point) fuel injection and other improvements. Standard tires grew wider, to P215/70R14 size. For the third year in-a-row, counterbalanced hood springs were promised to replace the prop rod. A standard electronic-tuning stereo radio replaced the manual-tuning version. New options included a power moonroof (arriving later), seven-band graphic equalizer, and inflatable spare tire (complete with air compressor). Standard equipment included power steering/brakes, halogen headlamps, AM/FM stereo, driver's remote mirror, bodyside/decklid accent stripes, vinyl-insert bodyside moldings, analog quartz clock, console, four-spoke steering wheel, and brushed instrument panel appliqué. Individual cloth/vinyl front seats came with recliners. Cougar LS added tinted glass, power windows, remote passenger mirror, rocker panel moldings, hood accent striping, digital clock, velour upholstery, lighted right visor vanity mirror, and woodtone dash appliqué. Cougar XR-7 included the turbo four with five-speed manual, handling suspension, P205/70HR14 BSW tires on polycast wheels, leather-wrapped steering wheel, tinted glass, and Traction-Lok differential.

GRAND MARQUIS — V-8 — Mercury's most popular model, the big rear-drive sedan (and wagon) enjoyed mostly mechanical changes for 1986. The standard 302-cid (5.0-liter) V-8 gained sequential port fuel injection and other internal changes, including roller lifters and tuned intake manifold, with low-tension rings and higher compression ratio. Standard tires grew from 14 to 15 inch diameter. Wagons now had a compact spare tire (conventional optional). Gas caps were tethered. Standard equipment included four-speed overdrive automatic, P215/75R15 whitewalls, AM/FM stereo, wide lower bodyside moldings, power windows, vinyl roof, power brakes/steering, rocker panel and wheel lip moldings, Flight Bench seat, gas-filled shocks, hood/decklid paint stripes, and an analog clock. Grand Marquis LS added a visor vanity mirror and luxury interior touches. Colony Park wagons had the woodgrain bodyside and tailgate appliqué, three-way tailgate with power window, fold-down rear seat, and conventional spare tire.

I.D. DATA: Mercury's 17-symbol Vehicle Identification Number (VIN) was stamped on a metal tab fastened to the instrument panel, visible through the windshield. Symbols one to three indicates manufacturer, make and vehicle type: '1 ME' Mercury passenger car. The fourth symbol ('B') denotes restraint system. Next comes a letter 'P', followed by two digits that indicate body type: Model Number, as shown in left column of tables below. (Example: '72' Topaz GS two-door sedan.) Symbol eight indicates engine type: '9' L4-113 2Bbl.; 'J' H.O. L4-113 MFI; 'H' Diesel L4-121; 'A' L4-140 1Bbl.; 'X' HSC L4-140 FI; 'S' H.O. L4-140 FI; 'W' Turbo L4-140 EFI; 'D' L4-153 FI; '3' V6-232 FI; 'U' V6-183 FI; 'F' V8-302 FI; 'M' H.O. V8-302 FI; 'G' Police V8-351 2Bbl. Next is a check digit. Symbol ten indicates model year ('G' 1986). Symbol eleven is assembly plant: 'A' Atlanta, GA; 'B' Oakville, Ontario (Canada); 'F' Dearborn, MI; 'G' Chicago, IL; 'H' Lorain, Ohio; 'K' Kansas City, MO; 'W' Wayne, MI; 'X' St. Thomas, Ontario (Canada); and Edison, NJ. The final six digits make up the sequence number, starting with 600001. A Vehicle Certification Label on the left front door lock face panel or door pillar shows the manufacturer, month and year of manufacture, GVW, GAWR, certification statement, VIN, and codes for such items as body type, color, trim, axle, transmission, and special order information.

LYNX (FOUR)

51	61D	3-dr. Hatch-4P	6182	2060	Note 1
51	61D	3-dr. L Hatch-4P	6472	2060	Note 1
63	58D	5-dr. L Hatch-4P	6886	2106	Note 1
58	74D	4-dr. L Sta Wag-4P	6987	2141	Note 1
52	61D	3-dr. GS Hatch-4P	7162	2149	Note 1
64	58D	5-dr. GS Hatch-4P	7376	2192	Note 1
59	74D	4-dr. GS Sta Wag-4P	7657	2215	Note 1
53	61D	3-dr. XR3 Hatch-4P	8193	2277	Note 1

NOTE 1: Total Lynx production, 45,880 three-door hatchbacks, 26,512 five-door hatchbacks, and 13,580 four-door liftgate station wagons.

1986 Mercury Grand Marquis LS sedan. (JG)

1986 Mercury Topaz coupe. (JG)

Diesel Engine Note: Lynx diesel models cost $591-$667 more than a gas engine.

CAPRI GS (FOUR/V-6)

79	61D	3-dr. Fastbk-4P	8331/8785	2692/2808	Note 2

Capri Engine Note: Six-cylinder price does not include cost of the required automatic transmission ($510). The high-output 302-cid V-8 engine cost $1330 more than the V-6.

CAPRI 5.0L (V-8)

79	61D	3-dr. Fastbk-4P	10950	3055	Note 2

NOTE 2: Total Capri production was 20,869.

TOPAZ (FOUR)

Model No.	Body/ Style No.	Body Type & Seating	Factory Price	Shipping Weight	Prod. Total
72	66D	2-dr. GS Sedan-5P	8085	2313	15,757
75	54D	4-dr. GS Sedan-5P	8235	2368	62,640
73	66D	2-dr. LS Sedan-5P	9224	2335	Note 3
76	54D	4-dr. LS Sedan-5P	9494	2390	Note 3

Diesel Engine Note: A diesel engine cost $509 more than the gasoline-powered Topaz.

SABLE GS (FOUR/V-6)

87	54D	4-dr. Sedan-6P	10700/11311	2812/2812	71,707
88	74D	4-dr. Sta Wag-6P	-----/12574	----/3092	23,931

SABLE LS (V-6)

87	54D	4-dr. Sedan-6P	11776	2812	Note 3
88	74D	4-dr. Sta Wag-6P	13068	3092	Note 3

NOTE 3: Production of Topaz and Sable LS models is included in GS totals.

MARQUIS (FOUR/V-6)

89	54D	4-dr. Sedan-6P	9660/10154	2883/2935	24,121
90	74D	4-dr. Sta Wag-6P	----/10254	----/2987	4,461

MARQUIS BROUGHAM (FOUR/V-6)

89/60H	54D	4-dr. Sedan-6P	10048/10542	2895/2947	Note 4
90/60H	74D	4-dr. Sta Wag-6P	-----/10613	----/2999	Note 4

NOTE 4: Brougham production is included in basic totals above.

COUGAR (V-6/V-8)

Model No.	Body/ Style No.	Body Type & Seating	Factory Price	Shipping Weight	Prod. Total
92	66D	2-dr. Cpe-4P	11421/11969	2918/3096	135,909
92	66D	2-dr. LS Cpe-4P	12757/13305	2918/3096	Note 5

Cougar Engine Note: The V-8 engine required a four-speed automatic transmission at $237 extra.

COUGAR XR-7 (TURBO FOUR)

92	66D	2-dr. Cpe-4P	14377	3015	Note 5

1986 Mercury Cougar LS coupe. (JG)

NOTE 5: Production of LS and XR-7 is included in basic total above.

GRAND MARQUIS (V-8)

93	66K	2-dr. Sedan-6P	13480	3730	5,610
95	54K	4-dr. Sedan-6P	13504	3672	93,919
93/60H	66K	2-dr. LS Sed-6P	13929	3730	Note 6
95/60H	54K	4-dr. LS Sed-6P	13952	3672	Note 6

GRAND MARQUIS COLONY PARK (V-8)

94	74K	4-dr. Sta Wag-6P	13724	3851	9,891

NOTE 6: LS production is included in basic Grand Marquis totals.

FACTORY PRICE AND WEIGHT NOTE: Cougar prices and weights to left of slash are for V-6, to right for V-8 engine. For Capri/Marquis/Sable, prices/weights to left of slash are for four-cylinder, to right for V-6.

ENGINE [Base Four (Lynx)]: Inline. Overhead cam. Four-cylinder. Cast-iron block and aluminum head. Displacement: 113-cid (1.9-liters). Bore & stroke: 3.23 x 3.46 in. Compression ratio: 9.0:1. Brake horsepower: 86 at 4800 rpm. Torque: 100 lbs.-ft. at 3000 rpm. Five main bearings. Hydraulic valve lifters. Carburetor: 2Bbl. Holley 740. VIN Code: 9.

ENGINE [Optional Four (Lynx)]: High-output, multi-port fuel injected version of 1.9-liter engine above: Horsepower: 108 at 5200 rpm. Torque: 114 lbs.-ft. at 4000 rpm. VIN Code: J.

ENGINE [Diesel Four (Lynx, Topaz)]: Inline. Overhead cam. Four-cylinder. Cast-iron block and aluminum head. Displacement: 121-cid (2.0 liters). Bore & stroke: 3.39 x 3.39 in. Compression ratio: 22.7:1. Brake horsepower: 52 at 4000 rpm. Torque: 82 lbs.-ft. at 2400 rpm. Five main bearings. Solid valve lifters. Fuel injection. VIN Code: H.

ENGINE [Base Four (Topaz)]: Inline. Overhead valve. Four-cylinder. Cast-iron block and head. Displacement: 140-cid (2.3-liters). Bore & stroke: 3.70 x 3.30 in. Compression ratio: 9.0:1. Brake horsepower: 86 at 4000 rpm. Torque: 124 lbs.-ft. at 2800 rpm. Five main bearings. Hydraulic valve lifters. Fuel injection (TBI). High Swirl Combustion (HSC) design. VIN Code: X.

ENGINE [Optional Four (Topaz)]: High-output version of 140-cid HSC four above: Horsepower: 100 at 4600 rpm. Torque: 125 lbs.-ft. at 3200 rpm. VIN Code: S.

ENGINE [Base Four (Capri, Marquis)]: Inline. Overhead cam. Four-cylinder. Cast-iron block and head. Displacement: 140-cid (2.3-liters). Bore & stroke: 3.78 x 3.13 in. Compression ratio: 9.5:1. Brake horsepower: 88 at 4200 rpm. Torque: 122 lbs.-ft. at 2600 rpm. Five main bearings. Hydraulic valve lifters. Carburetor: 1Bbl. Carter YFA. VIN Code: A.

ENGINE [Base Turbo Four (Cougar XR-7)]: Same as 140-cid four above, but with turbocharger. Compression ratio: 8.0:1. Horsepower: 155 at 4600 rpm. (145 at 4400 with automatic). Torque: 190 lbs.-ft. at 2800 rpm. (180 at 3000 w/automatic). VIN Code: W.

ENGINE [Base Four (Sable)]: Inline. Overhead valve. Four-cylinder. Cast-iron block and head. Displacement: 153-cid (2.5-liters). Bore & stroke: 3.70 x 3.60 in. Compression ratio: 9.0:1. Brake horsepower: 88 at 4600 rpm. Torque: 130 lbs.-ft. at 2800 rpm. Five main bearings. Hydraulic valve lifters. Fuel injection (TBI). VIN Code: D.

ENGINE [Base V-6 (Sable LS, wagon); Optional (Sable)]: 60-degree, overhead valve V-6. Cast-iron block and head. Displacement: 183-cid (3.0-liters). Bore & stroke: 3.50 x 3.10 in. Compression ratio: 9.25:1. Brake horsepower: 140 at 4800 rpm. Torque: 160 lbs.-ft. at 3000 rpm. Four main bearings. Hydraulic valve lifters. Multi-port fuel injection. VIN Code: U.

ENGINE [Base V-6 (Cougar); Optional (Capri, Marquis)]: 90-degree, overhead valve V-6. Cast-iron block and aluminum head. Displacement: 232-cid (3.8-liters). Bore & stroke: 3.80 x 3.40 in. Compression ratio: 8.7:1. Brake horsepower: 120 at 3600 rpm. Torque: 205 lbs.-ft. at 1600 rpm. Four main bearings. Hydraulic valve lifters. Fuel-injected. VIN Code: 3.

ENGINE [Base V-8 (Grand Marquis); Optional (Cougar)]: 90-degree, overhead valve V-8. Cast-iron block and head. Displacement: 302-cid (5.0-liters). Bore & stroke: 4.00 x 3.00 in. Compression ratio: 8.9:1. Brake horsepower: 150 at 3200 rpm. Torque: 270 lbs.-ft. at 2000 rpm. Five main bearings. Hydraulic valve lifters. Sequential fuel injection. VIN Code: F.

ENGINE [Optional V-8 (Capri)]: High-output version of 302-cid V-8 above. Compression ratio: 9.2:1. Horsepower: 200 at 4000 rpm. Torque: 285 lbs.-ft. at 3000 rpm. VIN Code: M.

NOTE: Police 351-cid V-8 remained available for Grand Marquis, rated 180 horsepower at 3600 rpm., 285 lbs.-ft. at 2400 rpm.

CHASSIS DATA: Wheelbase: (Lynx) 94.2 in.; (Capri) 100.5 in.; (Topaz) 99.9 in.; (Sable) 106.0 in.; (Marquis) 105.6 in.; (Cougar) 104.0 in.; (Grand Marquis) 114.3 in. Overall Length: (Lynx) 166.9 in.; (Lynx wag) 168.0 in.; (Capri) 179.3 in.; (Topaz) 176.2 in.; (Sable) 190.9 in.; (Sable wag) 191.9 in.; (Marquis) 196.5 in.; (Cougar) 197.6 in.; (Grand Marquis) 214.0 in.; (Grand Marquis wag) 218.0 in. Height: (Lynx) 53.3-53.5 in.; (Capri) 52.1 in.; (Topaz) 52.7 in.; (Sable) 54.2 in.; (Sable wag) 55.1 in.; (Marquis) 53.8 in.; (Marquis wag) 54.4 in.; (Cougar) 53.4 in.; (Grand Marquis) 55.2 in.; (Grand Marquis wag) 56.8 in. Width: (Lynx) 65.9 in.; (Capri) 69.1 in.; (Topaz) 68.3 in.; (Sable) 70.7 in.; (Marquis) 71.0 in.; (Cougar) 71.1 in.; (Grand Marquis) 77.5 in.; (Grand Marquis wag) 79.3 in. Front Tread: (Lynx) 54.7 in.; (Capri) 56.6 in.; (Topaz) 54.7 in.; (Sable) 61.6 in.; (Marquis) 56.6 in.; (Cougar) 58.1 in.; (Grand Marquis) 62.2 in. Rear Tread: (Lynx) 56.0 in.; (Capri/Marquis) 57.0 in.; (Topaz) 57.6 in.; (Sable) 60.5 in.; (Sable wag) 59.9 in.; (Cougar) 58.5 in.; (Grand Marquis) 62.0 in. Standard Tires: (Lynx) P165/80R13; (XR3) P195/60HR15; (Capri) P195/75R14; (Capri 5.0L) P225/60VR15; (Topaz) P185/70R14; (Sable) P205/70R14; (Marquis) P195/75R14; (Cougar) P215/70R14; (XR-7) P225/60VR15 Goodyear Gatorback; (Grand Marquis) P205/75R15 SBR WSW.

TECHNICAL: Transmission: Four-speed manual standard on Lynx; five-speed manual or three-speed automatic optional. Four-speed manual standard on Capri; five-speed manual standard on Capri 5.0L; three- or four-speed automatic optional. Five-speed manual standard on Topaz; three-speed automatic optional. SelectShift three-speed automatic standard on Cougar/Marquis; four-speed overdrive optional (standard on Cougar V-8). Three-speed automatic standard on Sable four; four-speed on Sable V-6. Five-speed manual standard on Cougar XR-7. Four-speed overdrive automatic standard on Grand Marquis. Gear ratios same as equivalent Ford models; see Ford/Mustang listings. Standard final drive ratio: (Lynx) 3.52:1 w/4spd, 3.73:1 w/5spd, 3.23:1 w/auto., 3.52:1 w/diesel; (Capri four) 3.08:1 w/4spd, 3.27:1 w/auto.; (Capri V-6) 2.73:1; (Capri V-8) 2.73:1 w/5spd or auto., 3.27:1 w/4spd auto.; (Topaz) 3.33:1 w/5spd, 3.23:1 w/auto., 3.73:1 w/diesel or FI four; (Sable) 3.23:1 w/four, 3.37:1 w/V-6; (Marquis) 3.27:1 or 2.73:1; (Cougar V-6) 2.73:1 w/3spd auto., 3.27:1 with 4spd auto.; (Cougar V-8) 3.08:1: (Cougar XR-7 turbo) 3.45:1; (Grand Marquis) 2,73:1. Steering: (Grand Marquis) recirculating ball; (others) rack-and-pinion. Front Suspension: (Lynx/Topaz) MacPherson strut-mounted coil springs w/lower control arms and stabilizer bar; (Capri/Cougar/Marquis) modified MacPherson struts w/lower control arms, coil springs and anti-sway bar; (Sable) MacPherson struts w/control arm, coil springs and anti-sway bar; (Grand Marquis) coil springs with long/short A-arms and anti-sway bar. Rear Suspension: (Lynx) independent trailing arms w/modified MacPherson struts and coil springs on lower control arms; (Topaz) fully independent quadra-link w/MacPherson struts; (Sable) MacPherson struts w/coil springs, parallel suspension arms and anti-sway bar; (Capri/Cougar/Marquis/Grand Marquis) four-link w/coil springs. Brakes: Front disc, rear drum. Ignition: Electronic. Body construction: (Grand Marquis) separate body and frame; (others) unibody. Fuel tank: (Lynx) 10 gal., exc. wag, 13 gal.; (Capri) 15.4 gal.; (Topaz) 15.2 gal.; (Sable) 16 gal.; (Marquis) 16 gal.; (Cougar) 20.6 gal.; (Grand Marquis) 18 gal.; (Grand Marquis wag) 18.5 gal.

DRIVETRAIN OPTIONS: Engines: Diesel 2.0-liter four: Lynx ($591); Topaz ($509). 182-cid V-6: Sable (N/A). 232-cid V-6: Capri ($454); Marquis ($494). 302-cid V-8: Capri ($1784); Cougar ($548). Transmission/Differential: Five-speed manual trans.: Lynx ($76). Automatic transaxle: Lynx L ($466); Lynx GS ($390); Topaz ($448) exc. w/GS sport group ($350). Three-speed auto. transmission.: Capri ($510); Cougar XR-7 ($315). Floor shift lever: Sable sedan (NC). Overdrive auto. trans.: Capri GS ($746); Capri 5.0L ($622); Sable GS ($611); Cougar/Marquis ($237). Traction-Lok differential: Marquis/Grand Marquis/Cougar ($100). Steering/Suspension: Power steering: Lynx ($226). H.D. susp.: Lynx/Sable/Grand Marquis ($26); Sable LPO ($26); Marquis ($43). Auto. load leveling: Grand Marquis ($200). Other: H.D. battery ($27). H.D. alternator: Lynx ($27). Extended-range gas tank: Sable/Marquis ($46). Engine block heater ($18). Trailer towing pkg.: Grand Marquis ($377-$389). California emission system: Lynx/EXP ($46); others ($99). High-altitude emissions (NC).

LYNX CONVENIENCE/APPEARANCE OPTIONS: Option Packages: Comfort/convenience pkg. ($298) exc. XR3 ($117) and diesel ($211). Climate control group ($791-$818). Comfort/Convenience: Air conditioner ($657). Rear defroster, electric ($135). Fingertip speed control ($176). Tinted glass ($99). Tilt steering ($115). Console w/graphic systems monitor ($111). Rear wiper/washer ($126). Dual remote mirrors ($68). Entertainment: AM/FM stereo radio: L ($109); base ($148). AM/FM stereo w/cassette player: L ($256); base ($295); GS/XR3 ($148). Radio delete: AM ($39 credit); AM/FM ($148 credit). Premium sound ($138). Exterior: Clearcoat paint ($91). Two-tone paint ($156). Wide vinyl bodyside moldings ($45). Bumper guards, front/rear ($56). Bumper rub strips ($48). Luggage rack: wag ($100). Interior: Vinyl seat trim ($24). Wheels/Tires: Styled wheels ($128). P165/80R13 SBR WSW ($59). Full-size spare ($63).

CAPRI CONVENIENCE/APPEARANCE OPTIONS: Option Packages: Power lock group ($182). Comfort/Convenience: Air cond. ($762). Fingertip speed control ($176). Entertainment: Electronic seek/scan AM/FM stereo w/cassette ($300). Premium sound system ($138). Radio delete ($148 credit). Exterior: T-Roof ($1100). Flip-up open air roof ($315). Interior: Vinyl bucket seats ($29). Wheels and Tires: Wire wheel covers ($98). Polycast wheels ($178). P205/70R14 WSW ($112).

TOPAZ CONVENIENCE/APPEARANCE OPTIONS: Option Packages: GS sport group ($610). Comfort/Convenience pkg. ($330). Convenience group ($246). Power lock group ($141-$259). Comfort/Convenience: Air bag restraint system ($815). Air cond. ($743). Rear defroster, electric ($145). Fingertip speed control ($176). Power windows ($207-$282). Six-way power driver's seat ($234). Tilt steering ($115). Entertainment: AM/FM stereo radio w/cassette player ($148). Electronic-tuning AM/FM stereo w/cassette ($161-$309). Premium sound ($138). Radio delete ($148-$295 credit). Exterior: Clearcoat metallic paint ($91). Lower body accent paint ($78-$118). Interior: Vinyl seat trim ($35). Leather seat trim ($300). Wheels/Tires: Polycast wheels ($178). P185/70R14 WSW ($72).

SABLE CONVENIENCE/APPEARANCE OPTIONS: Option Packages: Power lock group ($186-$257). Light group ($48-$51). Comfort/Convenience: Air cond. ($762). Electronic climate control air cond. ($945). Rear defroster ($145). Heated windshield ($250). Fingertip speed control ($176). Keyless entry ($202). Power windows ($282). Six-way power driver's seat ($237); dual ($473). Tinted glass ($115); windshield only LPO ($48). Leather-wrapped steering wheel ($59). Tilt steering ($115). Electronic instrument cluster ($305). Autolamp on/off delay ($73). Auto. parking brake release: GS ($12). Digital clock: GS ($78). Interval wipers ($50). Rear wiper/washer: wag ($124). Dual lighted visor vanity mirrors: GS ($99). Entertainment: AM/FM stereo w/cassette ($127). Power antenna ($71). Premium sound system ($168), Radio delete LPO ($196 credit). Exterior: Power moonroof ($701). Vent windows ($79). Clearcoat paint ($183). Bodyside accent paint ($57). Luggage rack delete: wag LPO ($105 credit). Interior: Cloth twin comfort reclining seats: GS ($195). Vinyl seat trim: GS ($39). Leather seat trim: LS ($415). Rear-facing third seat: wag ($155). Reclining passenger seat: GS ($45). Picnic tray: wagon ($66). Carpeted floor mats ($43). Wheels/Tires: Polycast wheels ($64). Aluminum wheels ($335). P205/70R14 WSW ($72). P205/65R15 BSW ($46); WSW ($124). Conventional spare ($63).

MARQUIS CONVENIENCE/APPEARANCE OPTIONS: Option Packages: Woodtone option ($282). Interior luxury group ($388). Power lock group ($218-$259). Light group ($38). Comfort/Convenience: Air cond. ($762). Rear defroster ($145). Fingertip speed control ($176). Autolamp on-off delay ($73). Power windows ($282). Six-way power driver's seat ($234). Tinted glass ($115). Leather-wrapped steering wheel ($59). Tilt steering ($115). Digital clock ($78). Auto. parking brake release ($12). Lighting and Mirrors: Cornering lamps ($68). Right remote convex mirror ($61). Dual electric remote mirrors ($96). Lighted visor vanity mirrors ($57-$106). Entertainment: AM/FM stereo radio ($109); w/cassette player ($256). AM radio delete ($39 credit). Exterior: Full vinyl roof ($152). Clearcoat metallic paint ($183). Two-tone paint w/tape stripe ($117). Pivoting front vent windows ($79). Two-way liftgate: wag ($105). Rocker panel moldings ($40). Bumper guards, rear ($28). Bumper rub strips ($56). Luggage rack: wagon ($126). Interior: Vinyl seat trim ($35). Flight Bench seat (NC). Front floor mats, carpeted ($23). Wheels/Tires: Luxury wheel covers ($55). Wire wheel covers, locking ($212). Polycast wheels ($178). Styled steel wheels w/trim rings ($54). P195/75R14 WSW ($72). P205/70R14 WSW ($134). Conventional spare ($63).

1986 Mercury Capri 5.0L hatchback coupe. (JG)

1986 Mercury Marquis Brougham Villager wagon. (JG)

COUGAR CONVENIENCE/APPEARANCE OPTIONS: Option Packages: Headlamp convenience group ($176). Light group ($35). Power lock group ($220). Comfort/Convenience: Air cond. ($762); auto-temp ($924). Rear defroster ($145). Fingertip speed control ($176). Illuminated entry system ($82). Keyless entry ($198). Tinted glass ($115). Power windows ($207). Six-way power driver's seat ($238); dual ($476). Dual power seat recliners ($189). Leather-wrapped steering wheel ($59). Tilt steering wheel ($115). Electronic instrument cluster ($330). Diagnostic warning lights ($89). Low-oil alert ($24). Digital clock ($61). Auto. parking brake release ($12). Interval wipers ($50). Lighting and Mirrors: Cornering lamps ($68). Dual electric remote mirrors ($96). Lighted visor vanity mirrors, pair ($106). Entertainment: Electronic-tuning AM/FM stereo w/cassette ($127). Power antenna ($71). Graphic equalizer ($218). Premium sound system ($168). AM/FM radio delete ($196 credit). Exterior: Power moonroof ($701). Luxury vinyl rear half roof ($245). Metallic clearcoat paint ($183). Two-tone paint ($163). Hood accent stripes ($16). Pivoting front vent windows ($79). Interior: Leather seat trim ($415). Vinyl seat trim ($37). Front floor mats, carpeted ($22). Wheels/Tires: Wire wheel covers, locking: base ($212), LS ($90). TRX cast aluminum wheels: base ($612); LS ($490). Polycast wheels: base ($178); LS ($56). P215/70R14 BSW ($62 credit). P215/70HR14 performance BSW ($116). Conventional spare ($63). Inflatable spare ($122).

GRAND MARQUIS CONVENIENCE/APPEARANCE OPTIONS: Option Packages: LS decor ($521). Convenience group ($109-$134). Power lock group ($178-$278). Light group ($30-$48). Comfort/Convenience: Air cond. ($762); w/auto-temp control ($828). Rear defroster, electric ($145). Fingertip speed control ($176). Illuminated entry system ($82). Power six-way driver's seat ($237); driver and passenger ($473). Tinted glass ($118). Auto-lamp on-off delay ($73). Leather-wrapped steering wheel ($59). Tilt steering wheel ($115). Tripminder computer ($261). Digital clock ($61). Lighting and Mirrors: Cornering lamps ($68). Dual electric remote mirrors ($100). Lighted visor vanity mirrors ($109). Entertainment: AM/FM stereo radio w/cassette tape player ($148). Electronic-tuning AM/FM stereo radio w/cassette ($300). Power antenna ($71). Premium sound system ($168). AM/FM radio delete ($148 credit). Exterior: Formal coach vinyl roof ($650). Two-tone paint/tape ($129). Hood accent stripes ($18). Pivoting front vent windows ($79). Rocker panel moldings ($18-$38). Narrow vinyl-insert bodyside moldings ($61). Bumper rub strips ($59). License frames ($9). Luggage rack: wagon ($110). Interior: Dual-facing rear seats: wagon ($167). Cloth seat trim ($54). All-vinyl seat trim ($34). Leather seat trim ($418). Carpeted front floor mats ($21); front/rear ($33). Wheels/Tires: Wire wheel covers, locking ($176). Turbine spoke cast aluminum wheels ($361). P205/75R15 puncture-sealant ($161). P215/70R15 WSW ($62). Conventional spare ($63).

HISTORY: Introduced: October 3, 1985. Model year production: 791,149. Calendar year production (U.S.): 359,002. Calendar year sales by U.S. dealers: 491,782. Model year sales by U.S. dealers: 474,612. Every model in the Mercury lineup slipped in the sales race this year. Availability of the new Sable was limited at first, and production flaws (later recalls) were a problem. Rear-drive luxury was still promoted, despite the new front-drive models. Cougar was Lincoln-Mercury's number one seller, and Capri finally dropped out.

1987 MERCURY

Capri, the Mustang clone with a Mercury badge, dropped out of the lineup for 1987. So did the Marquis, like its Ford LTD twin, both replaced by the popular aero-styled Taurus/Sable duo.

1987 Mercury Lynx GS station wagon. (OCW)

1987 Mercury Sable GS station wagon. (OCW)

1987 Mercury Lynx GS hatchback sedan. (PH)

LYNX — FOUR — Biggest news for Mercury's subcompact was the addition of standard fuel injection to replace carburetors on the 1.9-liter four-cylinder engine. This would be Lynx's final year, though the comparable Ford Escort would continue as a top seller. The diesel engine was still available, at no extra charge, except on the sporty XR3.

TOPAZ — FOUR — Nitrogen-filled shock absorbers went into the Topaz suspension for 1987, to help ride/handling a bit. Two notable options joined the list: a new three-speed automatic with fluid-linked torque converter, and a part-time four-wheel-drive system. 4WD was available only with automatic and the high-output engine. A driver's side airbag, available only in limited quantities in 1986, became a regular production option this year.

1987 Mercury Sable LS sedan. (PH)

1987 Mercury Sable LS station wagon. (PH)

SABLE — V-6 — Little change was evident on the Mercury version of the hot-selling aero-styled Ford Taurus, as both models entered their second season. Air conditioning became standard on the top-rung LS models. Ford's four-cylinder engine was not offered on Sable, though it continued as a Taurus staple. Instead, Sables had a 3.0-liter V-6 with four-speed overdrive automatic transmission.

1987 Mercury Topaz LS sedan. (OCW)

1987 Mercury Cougar XR-7 coupe. (OCW)

1987 Mercury Topaz GS Sport coupe. (PH)

1987 Mercury Cougar LS coupe. (PH)

1987 Mercury Grand Marquis Colony Park station wagon. (OCW)

1987 Mercury Grand Marquis sedan. (PH)

COUGAR — V-6/V-8 — Mercury's mid-size Thunderbird cousin got a restyle for 1987, including a new greenhouse profile, aero headlamp, flush-fit glass, and full-width tail lamps. The sporty XR-7 switched from the former turbocharged four to a 5.0-liter V-8. All models now came with standard four-speed overdrive automatic transmission, as manual shifts dropped out of the lineup. The base GS model also disappeared. Both Cougar models came with standard air conditioning and tinted glass. Late in the year, *Motor Trend* tested a special 20th Anniversary edition.

GRAND MARQUIS — V-8 — Except for the addition of air conditioning as standard equipment, the full-size Mercury (close kin to Ford's LTD Crown Victoria) changed little for 1987. New standard equipment also included an electronic-tuning radio, replacing the former manual version.

I.D. DATA: Mercury's 17-symbol Vehicle Identification Number (VIN) was stamped on a metal tab fastened to the instrument panel, visible through the windshield, Symbols one to three indicate manufacturer, make and vehicle type. The fourth symbol ('B') denotes restraint system. Next comes a letter 'M' (for series), followed by two digits that indicate body type: Model Number, as shown in left column of tables below. (Example: '31' Topaz GS two-door sedan.) Symbol eight indicates engine type. Next is a check digit. Symbol ten indicates model year ('H' 1987). Symbol eleven denotes assembly plant. The final six digits make up the production sequence number, starting with 600001.

LYNX (FOUR)

Model No.	Body/ Style No.	Body Type & Seating	Factory Price	Shipping Weight	Prod. Total
20	61D	3-dr. L Hatch-4P	6569	2183	Note 1
21	61D	3-dr. GS Hatch-4P	6951	2202	Note 1
25	58D	5-dr. GS Hatch-4P	7172	2258	12,124
28	74D	4-dr. GS Sta Wag-4P	7462	2277	5,985
23	61D	3-dr. XR3 Hatch-4P	8808	2395	Note 1

NOTE 1: Total Lynx production, 20,930 three-door hatchbacks.

TOPAZ (FOUR)

31	66D	2-dr. GS Sedan-5P	8562	2503	Note 2
33	66D	2-dr. GS Spt Sed-5P	9308	2565	Note 2
36	54D	4-dr. GS Sedan-5P	8716	2557	Note 3
38	54D	4-dr. GS Spt Sed-5P	9463	2621	Note 3
76	54D	4-dr. LS Sedan-5P	10213	2631	Note 3

NOTE 2: A total of 19,738 two-door sedans were produced.

NOTE 3: A total of 78,692 four-door sedans were produced.

SABLE GS (V-6)

50	54D	4-dr. Sedan-6P	12240	3054	Note 4
55	74D	4-dr. Sta Wag-6P	12793	3228	Note 5

SABLE LS (V-6)

53	54D	4-dr. Sedan-6P	14522	3138	Note 4
58	74D	4-dr. Sta Wag-6P	15054	3311	Note 5

NOTE 4: A total of 91,001 Sable sedans were built.

NOTE 5: A total of 30,312 Sable wagons were built.

COUGAR (V-6/V-8)

60	66D	2-dr. LS Cpe-5P	13595/14234	3133/3272	104,526

COUGAR XR-7 (V-8)

62	66D	2-dr. Cpe-5P	15832	3355	Note 6

NOTE 6: Production of XR-7 is included in basic Cougar total above.

GRAND MARQUIS (V-8)

72	66K	2-dr. LS Sed-6P	15323	3764	4,904
74	54K	4-dr. GS Sed-6P	15198	3794	115,599
75	54K	4-dr. LS Sed-6P	15672	3803	Note 7

GRAND MARQUIS COLONY PARK WAGON (V-8)

78	74K	4-dr. Sta Wag-6P	15462	3975	10,691
79	74K	4-dr. LS Sta Wag-6P	16010	4015	Note 7

NOTE 7: LS production is included in basic Grand Marquis totals.

FACTORY PRICE AND WEIGHT NOTE: Cougar prices and weights to left of slash are for V-6. to right for V-8 engine.

ENGINE [Base Four (Lynx)]: Inline. Overhead cam. Four-cylinder. Cast-iron block and aluminum head. Displacement: 113 cid (1.9-liters). Bore & stroke: 3.23 x 3.46 in. Compression ratio: 9.0:1. Brake horsepower: 90 at 4600 rpm. Torque: 106 lbs.-ft. at 3400 rpm. Five main bearings. Hydraulic valve lifters. Fuel injection.

ENGINE [Optional Four (Lynx)]: High-output, multi-port fuel injected version of 1.9-liter engine above. Horsepower: 115 at 5200 rpm. Torque: 120 lbs.-ft. at 4400 rpm.

ENGINE [Diesel Four (Lynx)]: Inline. Overhead cam. Four-cylinder. Cast-iron block and aluminum head. Displacement: 121 cid (2.0-liters). Bore & stroke: 3.39 x 3.39 in. Compression ratio: 22.7:1. Brake horsepower: 58 at 3600 rpm. Torque: 84 lbs.-ft. at 3000 rpm. Five main bearings. Solid valve lifters. Fuel injection.

ENGINE [Base Four (Topaz)]: Inline. Overhead valve. Four-cylinder. Cast-iron block and head. Displacement: 140 cid (2.3-liters). Bore & stroke: 3.70 x 3.30 in. Compression ratio: 9.0:1. Brake horsepower: 86 at 3800 rpm. Torque: 120 lbs.-ft. at 3200 rpm. Five main bearings. Hydraulic valve lifters. Fuel injection (TBI). High Swirl Combustion (HSC) design.

ENGINE [Optional Four (Topaz)]: High-output version of 140 cid HSC four above. Horsepower: 94 at 4000 rpm. Torque: 126 lbs.-ft. at 3200 rpm.

ENGINE [Base V-6 (Sable)]: 60-degree, overhead valve V-6. Cast-iron block and head. Displacement: 182 cid (3.0-liters). Bore & stroke: 3.50 x 3.10 in. Compression ratio: 9.3:1. Brake horsepower: 140 at 4800 rpm. Torque: 160 lbs.-ft. at 3000 rpm. Four main bearings. Hydraulic valve lifters. Multi-port fuel injection.

ENGINE [Base V-6 (Cougar)]: 90-degree, overhead valve V-6. Cast-iron block and aluminum head. Displacement: 232 cid (3.8-liters). Bore & stroke: 3.80 x 3.40 in. Compression ratio: 8.7:1. Brake horsepower: 120 at 3600 rpm. Torque: 205 lbs.-ft. at 1600 rpm. Four main bearings. Hydraulic valve lifters. Multi-port fuel-injected.

ENGINE [Base V-8 (Grand Marquis); Optional (Cougar)]: 90-degree, overhead valve V-8. Cast-iron block and head. Displacement: 302 cid (5.0-liters). Bore & stroke: 4.00 x 3.00 in. Compression ratio: 8.9:1. Brake horsepower: 150 at 3200 rpm. Torque: 270 lbs.-ft. at 2000 rpm. Five main bearings. Hydraulic valve lifters. Sequential fuel injection.

CHASSIS DATA: Wheelbase: (Lynx) 94.2 in.; (Topaz) 99.9 in.; (Sable) 106.0 in.; (Cougar) 104.2 in.; (Grand Marquis) 114.3 in. Overall Length: (Lynx) 166.9 in.; (Lynx wag) 168.0 in.; (Topaz) 177.0 in.; (Sable) 190.0 in.; (Sable wag) 191.9 in.; (Cougar) 200.8 in.; (Grand Marquis) 214.0 in.; (Grand Marquis wag) 218.0 in. Height: (Lynx) 53.1-53.3 in.; (Topaz) 52.7 in.; (Sable) 54.3 in.; (Sable wag) 55.1 in.; (Cougar) 53.8 in.; (Grand Marquis) 55.5 in.; (Grand Marquis wag) 57.1 in. Width: (Lynx) 65.9 in.; (Topaz) 68.3 in.; (Sable) 70.8 in.; (Cougar) 71.1 in.; (Grand Marquis) 77.5 in.; (Grand Marquis wag) 79.3 in. Front Tread: (Lynx) 54.7 in.; (Topaz) 54.9 in.; (Sable) 61.6 in.; (Cougar) 58.1 in.; (Grand Marquis) 62.2 in. Rear Tread: (Lynx) 56.0 in.; (Topaz) 57.6 in.; (Sable) 60.5 in.; (Sable wag) 59.9 in.; (Cougar) 58.5 in.; (Grand Marquis) 62.0 in. Standard Tires: (Lynx) P165/80R13; (XR3) P195/60HR15; (Topaz) P185/70R14; (Topaz GS Sport) P185/65R365: (Sable) P205/70R14; (Cougar) P215/70R14; (XR-7) P205/70HR14; (Grand Marquis) P215/75R15 SBR WSW.

TECHNICAL: Transmission: Four-speed manual standard on Lynx; five-speed manual or three-speed manual optional. Five-speed manual standard on Topaz; three-speed automatic optional. Four-speed overdrive automatic standard on Sable, Cougar and Grand Marquis. Steering: (Grand Marquis) recirculating ball: (others) rack-and-pinion. Front Suspension:

(Lynx/Topaz) MacPherson strut-mounted coil springs w/lower control arms and stabilizer bar; (Cougar) modified MacPherson struts w/lower control arms, coil springs and anti-sway bar; (Sable) MacPherson struts w/control arm, coil springs and anti-sway bar; (Grand Marquis) coil springs with long/short A-arms and anti-sway bar. Rear Suspension: (Lynx) independent trailing arms w/modified MacPherson struts and coil springs on lower control arms; (Topaz) independent quadralink w/MacPherson struts; (Sable) MacPherson struts w/coil springs, parallel suspension arms and anti-sway bar; (Cougar/Grand Marquis) four-link w/coil springs. Brakes: Front disc, rear drum. Body construction: (Grand Marquis) separate body and frame; (others) unibody. Fuel tank: (Lynx) 13 gal.; (Topaz) 15.4 gal.; (Topaz 4WD) 13.7 gal.; (Sable) 16 gal.; (Cougar) 22.1 gal.; (Grand Marquis) 18 gal.

DRIVETRAIN OPTIONS: Engines: Diesel four: Lynx (NC). 302 cid V-8: Cougar ($639). Transmission/Differential: Five-speed manual trans.: Lynx L/GS ($76). Automatic transaxle: Lynx GS ($490); Topaz ($482). Traction-Lok: Grand Marquis ($100). Steering/Suspension: Power steering: Lynx ($235). H.D. suspension: Grand Marquis ($26). Trailer towing pkg. Grand Marquis ($387-399).

LYNX CONVENIENCE/APPEARANCE OPTIONS: Climate control group, GS ($865). XR3 ($838). Comfort/Convenience Group: overhead console w/digital clock, intermittent wipers, trip odometer, tachometer, temperature gauge, GS ($327). Air conditioning ($688). Bumper guards ($56). Bumper rub strips ($48). Rear defogger ($145). Tinted glass ($105). Dual-power mirrors ($88). Wide vinyl bodyside molding ($50). Clearcoat metallic paint ($91). Two-tone paint ($156). AM/FM Stereo: L ($159). GS($120). AM/FM Stereo with cassette: GS($267). XR3 ($148). Premium sound system ($138). Speed control ($176). Tilt steering ($179) w/Comfort/Conv ($124). Split fold-down rear seatback ($49). Front center armrest ($55). Polycast wheels ($128). Vinyl seat trim ($24). Heavy-duty battery ($27). Rear wiper/washer ($126). Engine block heater ($18). Deluxe luggage rack ($110). AM radio delete, GS ($39 credit). AM/FM stereo delete, XR ($159 credit). Vinyl seat trim, L ($24).

TOPAZ CONVENIENCE/APPEARANCE OPTIONS: Comfort/Convenience Pkg: Fold-down center armrest, intermittent wipers, digital clock, light group, remote fuel filler & decklid releases: GS ($409). GS Sport ($368). All-Wheel-Drive Pkg: Four-wheel-drive, high-output engine, GS & GS Sport and LS ($800). Air conditioning ($773). Rear defogger ($145). Clearcoat metallic paint ($91). Power lock group (stnd LS), 2-dr ($237). 4-dr ($288). 2-dr w/Comfort/Conv Pkg ($156). 4-dr w/Comfort/Conv Pkg ($207). Lower bodyside accent paint: GS ($78). GS Sport & LS ($118). Premium sound system ($138). Speed control ($176). Tilt strg column ($124). Styled wheels ($178). Decklid luggage rack ($115). Pwr windows: 2-dr ($222). 4-dr ($296). Airbag: GS ($815). GS w/Comfort/Conv., LS ($751). AM/FM stereo delete, GS & GS Sport ($157 credit). AM/FM cassette delete, LS ($315 credit). AM/FM stereo elect tuning cassette, GS ($157). Heavy-duty battery ($27). Engine block heater ($18). Pwr driver's seat ($251). Calif. emission pkg ($99). Vinyl seat trim ($35).

SABLE CONVENIENCE/APPEARANCE OPTIONS: Conventional spare tire ($73). Automatic air cond ($945). Manual air cond ($788). Autolamp System ($73). Automatic parking brake release ($12). Digital clock ($78). Dual illum visor mirrors ($99). Elect instrument cluster ($351) InstaClear heated windshield ($250). Intermittent wipers ($55). Keyless entry system ($202). Pwr moonroof ($741). Rear defogger ($145). Sliding vent windows ($79). Cruise control ($176). Tilt steering column ($124). Tinted glass ($120). Light group: GS sed ($48). GS sta wag ($52). Heavy-duty battery ($27). Heavy-duty susp ($26). Ext range fuel tank ($46). Power antenna ($76). Pwr door locks: GS sed ($285). GS sta wag ($237). LS ($195). 6-way pwr driver's seat ($251). Dual pwr seats ($502). Pwr windows ($296). AM/FM stereo elect tuning cassette ($137). Premium sound system ($168). AM/FM stereo, delete ($206 credit). Clearcoat paint ($183). Cast alum wheels ($335). Locking wire wheel covers ($150). Polycast wheels ($123). Leather-wrapped strg wheel ($59). Leather trim ($415). Vinyl trim ($39). Twin comfort seats, GS ($195). Bucket seats, GS ($195). Picnic tray, sta wag ($66). Rear facing third seat, sta wag ($155). Rear window wiper/washer, sta wag ($126). Luggage rack delete, sta wag ($115 credit). Engine block heater ($18).

COUGAR CONVENIENCE/APPEARANCE OPTIONS: Conventional spare tire ($73). Locking wire wheel covers ($212). Polycast wheels, LS ($178). Pwr lock group ($249). Pwr windows ($222). Pwr moonroof ($841). Pwr driver's seat ($251). Dual pwr seats: LS ($554). XR-7 ($502). AM/FM stereo elect tuning w/cassette ($137). AM/FM stereo elect tuning delete ($206 credit). Premium sound system ($168). Pwr antenna ($71). Graphic equalizer ($218). Clearcoat metallic paint ($183). Two-tone paint ($163). Rear half luxury vinyl roof ($260). Leather seat trim ($415). Automatic air cond ($162). Heavy-duty battery ($27). Eng block heater ($18). Rear defogger ($145). Intermittent wipers ($55). Headlamp Convenience Grp: Automatic dimmer, Autolamp delay system ($176). Keyless entry system ($202). Cornering lamps ($68). Light grp ($35). Dual illum visor mirrors ($100). Speed control ($176). Leather-wrapped strg wheel, LS ($59). Elect digital clock ($61). Illum entry system ($82). Elect instrument cluster ($330). Tilt strg column ($124).

GRAND MARQUIS CONVENIENCE/APPEARANCE OPTIONS: Automatic climate control ($211). Pwr antenna ($76). Autolamp delay system ($73). Digital clock ($61). Convenience Grp: intermittent wipers, pwr decklid/tailgate release, trip odometer, low fuel, oil & washer fluid warning lights ($135), w/Power lock grp ($85). Cornering lamps ($68). Rear defogger ($145). Illum entry system ($82). Light grp ($48). Pwr lock grp, incl remote fuel filler & trunk releases: 2-dr ($207). 4-dr, sta wag ($257). Deluxe luggage rack ($115). Dual illum visor mirrors ($109). Bodyside protection moldings ($66). Two-tone paint w/tape stripes ($129). AM/FM stereo radio w/cass ($137). AM/FM stereo elect tuning delete ($206 credit). Premium sound system ($168). Formal coach vinyl roof ($665). Pwr driver's seat ($251). Dual pwr seats ($502). Dual facing rear seats, sta wag ($173). Speed control ($176). Leather-wrapped strg wheel ($59). Tilt strg column ($124). Leather seat trim ($418). Tripminder computer ($261). Pivoting front vent windows ($79). Locking wire wheel covers ($183). Cast alum wheels ($361). P215/70R15 tires ($72). Conventional spare tire ($73).

HISTORY: Introduced: October 2, 1986. Model year production: 494,502 (total). Calendar year production (U.S.): 328,509. Calendar year sales by U.S. dealers: 463,860. Model year sales by U.S. dealers: 470,644.

1988 Mercury Topaz LTS sedan. (PH)

1988 Mercury Topaz XR5 coupe. (PH)

The Lynx subcompact bit the dust this year, while the full-size Grand Marquis and compact Topaz enjoyed a restyling. The aero-look Sable added a larger, more potent powerplant option.

TOPAZ — FOUR — Both four-cylinder engines added power this year, as Mercury's compact took on new sheetmetal. Two sporty models (an XR5 two-door and LS Sport four-door) replaced the former GS Sport edition. The Topaz grille had a vertical-bar pattern, quite different from the related Ford Tempo with its twin-slot grille. Bumpers were now integrated into the body. Wraparound signal/marker lamps flanked aero headlamps. At the rear were full-width wraparound tail lamps. Under Topaz hoods, multi-point fuel injection replaced the former single-point system. A new analog instrument cluster contained a tachometer. Motorized automatic front shoulder belts became standard. Front-drive models came with standard five-speed manual shift (automatic optional), but the four-wheel-drive version could only have automatic.

SABLE — V-6 — Performance fans could order this year's Sable with a new 3.8-liter V-6 option, instead of the standard 3.0-liter. That engine had a counter-rotating balance shaft for smoother running, as well as multi-point fuel injection. Both engines produced 140 horsepower, but the 3.8 delivered considerably more torque. Both air conditioning and tinted glass became standard in all Sables (but could be deleted on the GS). The GS added other formerly-optional items as standard this year: intermittent wipers, separate front seats, digital clock, and a cargo net. Whitewall tires were optional only with the standard steel wheels, not the optional cast aluminum or polycast wheels.

COUGAR — V-6/V-8 — Engine modifications gave Cougar's base V-6 engine an extra 20 horsepower for 1987, and a new balance shaft gave it smoother running. Multi-point fuel injection replaced the former throttle-body (single-point) system. Dual exhaust became standard with the optional V-8, while blackwall tires went on the base LS model. The sporty XR-7 (V-8 engine only) added body-colored bumpers on both ends, plus a body-color grille, bodyside moldings and mirrors, for a monochromatic look. New 16-spoke cast aluminum wheels came in either argent or body color. Analog instruments replaced the former electronic cluster in the XR-7 dashboard (but the electronic version remained optional). The XR-7 final drive ratio switched from 2.73:1 to 3.08:1 to boost acceleration. Aluminum wheels held 225/60VR15 tires.

1988 Mercury Sable LS sedan. (PH)

1988 Mercury Cougar XR-7 coupe. (PH)

1988 Mercury Grand Marquis LS sedan. (PH)

1988 Mercury Grand Marquis Colony Park LS station wagon. (PH)

GRAND MARQUIS — V-8 — Revised front/rear styling gave the full-size, rear-drive Mercury a new look, as the lineup dropped to four-door sedans and station wagons only. The two-door model was gone. This year's bumpers had an integrated appearance, while wraparound tail lamps highlighted the rear. Wide lower bodyside moldings were standard on both the GS and LS models. Sedans added a half-vinyl roof (rear only). Whitewall P215/75R15 tires became standard on all models. An automatic headlamp on-off warning system also was standard. Joining the option list: an InstaClear heated windshield.

I.D. DATA: Mercury's 17-symbol Vehicle Identification Number (VIN) was stamped on a metal tab fastened to the instrument panel, visible through the windshield. Symbols one to three indicate manufacturer, make and vehicle type. The fourth symbol denotes restraint system. Next comes a letter 'M' (for series), followed by two digits that indicate body type: Model Number, as shown in left column of tables below. (Example: '31' Topaz GS two-door sedan.) Symbol eight indicates engine type. Next is a check digit. Symbol ten indicates model year ('J' 1988). Symbol eleven denotes assembly plant. The final six digits make up the production sequence number, starting with 600001.

TOPAZ (FOUR)

Model No.	Body/ Style No.	Body Type & Seating	Factory Price	Shipping Weight	Prod. Total
31	66D	2-dr. GS Sedan-5P	9166	2565	Note 1
33	66D	2-dr. XR5 Sed-5P	10058	2560	Note 1
36	54D	4-dr. GS Sedan-5P	9323	2608	Note 1
37	54D	4-dr. LS Sedan-5P	10591	2651	Note 1
38	54D	4-dr. LTS Sed-5P	11541	2660	Note 1

NOTE 1: A total of 111,886 Topaz models were produced (16,001 two-door and 95,885 four-door).

SABLE (V-6)

Model No.	Body/ Style No.	Body Type & Seating	Factory Price	Shipping Weight	Prod. Total
50	54D	4-dr. GS Sed-6P	14145	3097	94,694
53	54D	4-dr. LS Sed-6P	15138	3165	Note 2
55	74D	4-dr. GS Sta Wag-6P	14665	3208	26,591
58	74D	4-dr. LS Sta Wag-6P	15683	3268	Note 2

NOTE 2: LS production is included in GS totals.

COUGAR (V-6/V-8)

60	66D	2-dr. LS Cpe-5P	14134/14855	3237/3392	119,162

COUGAR XR-7 (V-8)

62	66D	2-dr. Cpe-5P	16266	3485	Note 3

NOTE 3: Production of XR-7 is included in basic Cougar total above.

GRAND MARQUIS (V-8)

74	54K	4-dr. GS Sed-6P	16100	3828	111,611
75	54K	4-dr. LS Sed-6P	16612	3839	Note 4

GRAND MARQUIS COLONY PARK WAGON (V-8)

78	74K	4-dr. GS Sta Wag-6P	16341	4019	9,456
79	74K	4-dr. LS Sta Wag-6P	16926	4025	Note 4

NOTE 4: LS production is included in GS totals.

FACTORY PRICE AND WEIGHT NOTE: Cougar price and weight to left of slash is for V-6, to right for V-8 engine.

ENGINE [Base Four (Topaz)]: Inline. Overhead valve. Four-cylinder. Cast-iron block and head. Displacement: 140 cid (2.3-liters). Bore & stroke: 3.70 x 3.30 in. Compression ratio: 9.0:1. Brake horsepower: 98 at 4400 rpm. Torque: 124 lbs.-ft. at 2200 rpm. Five main bearings. Hydraulic valve lifters. Multi-point fuel injection.

ENGINE [Base Four (Topaz XR5, LS Sport and AWD)]: High-output version of 140 cid four above: Horsepower: 100 at 4400 rpm. Torque: 130 lbs.-ft. at 2600 rpm.

ENGINE [Base V-6 (Sable)]: 60-degree, overhead valve V-6. Cast-iron block and head. Displacement: 182 cid (3.0-liters). Bore & stroke: 3.50 x 3.10 in. Compression ratio: 9.3:1. Brake horsepower: 140 at 4800 rpm. Torque: 160 lbs.-ft. at 3000 rpm. Four main bearings. Hydraulic valve lifters. Multi-port fuel injection.

ENGINE [Base V-6 (Cougar); Optional (Sable)]: 90-degree, overhead valve V-6. Cast-iron block and aluminum head. Displacement: 232 cid (3.8-liters). Bore & stroke: 3.80 x 3.40 in. Compression ratio: 9.0:1. Brake horsepower: (Cougar) 140 at 3800 RPM; (Sable) 140 at 4800. Torque: (Cougar) 215 lbs.-ft. at 2400 RPM; (Sable) 215 at 2200. Four main bearings. Hydraulic valve lifters. Multi-point fuel injection.

ENGINE [Base V-8 (Grand Marquis); Optional (Cougar)]: 90-degree, overhead valve V-8. Cast-iron block and head. Displacement: 302 cid (5.0 liters). Bore & stroke: 4.00 x 3.00 in. Compression ratio: 8.9:1. Brake horsepower: (Cougar) 155 at 3400 RPM; (Grand Marquis) 150 at 3200. Torque: (Cougar) 265 lbs.-ft. at 2200 RPM; (Grand Marquis) 270 at 2000. Five main bearings. Hydraulic valve lifters. Sequential fuel injection.

CHASSIS DATA: Wheelbase: (Topaz) 99.9 in.; (Sable) 106.0 in.; (Cougar) 104.2 in.; (Grand Marquis) 114.3 in. Overall Length: (Topaz 2-dr) 176.7 in.; (Topaz 4-dr) 177.0 in.; (Sable) 190.9 in.; (Sable wag) 191.9 in.; (Cougar) 200.8 in.; (Grand Marquis) 213.5 in.; (Grand Marquis wag) 218.3 in. Height: (Topaz) 52.8 in.; (Sable) 54.3 in.; (Sable wag) 55.1 in.; (Cougar) 53.8 in.; (Grand Marquis) 55.4 in.; (Grand Marquis wag) 57.0 in. Width: (Topaz 2-dr) 68.3 in.; (Topaz 4-dr) 66.8 in.; (Sable) 70.8 in.; (Cougar) 71.1 in.; (Grand Marquis) 77.5 in.; (Grand Marquis wag) 79.3 in. Front Tread: (Topaz) 54.9 in.; (Sable) 61.6 in.; (Cougar) 58 1 in.; (Grand Marquis) 62.2 in. Rear Tread: (Topaz) 57.6 in.; (Sable) 60.5 in.; (Sable wag) 59.9 in.; (Cougar) 58.5 in.; (Grand Marquis) 62.0 in. Standard Tires: (Topaz) P185/70R14: (Sable) P205/70R14; (Cougar) P215/70R14; (XR-7) P225/60VR15; (Grand Marquis) P215/70R15 SBR WSW.

TECHNICAL: Transmission: Five-speed manual standard on Topaz; three-speed automatic optional. Four-speed overdrive automatic standard on Sable, Cougar and Grand Marquis. Steering: (Grand Marquis) recirculating ball; (others) rack-and-pinion. Front Suspension: (Topaz) MacPherson strut-mounted coil springs w/lower control arms and stabilizer bar; (Cougar) modified MacPherson struts w/lower control arms, coil springs and anti-sway bar; (Sable) MacPherson struts w/control arm, coil springs and anti-sway bar; (Grand Marquis) coil springs with long/short A-arms and anti-sway bar. Rear Suspension: (Topaz) independent quadralink w/MacPherson struts; (Sable) MacPherson struts w/coil springs, parallel suspension arms and anti-sway bar; (Cougar/Grand Marquis) four-link w/coil springs. Brakes: Front disc, rear drums. Body construction: (Grand Marquis) separate body and frame; (others) unibody. Fuel tank: (Topaz) 15.4 gal.; (Topaz 4WD) 13.7 gal.; (Sable) 16 gal.; (Cougar) 22.1 gal.; (Grand Marquis) 18 gal.

DRIVETRAIN OPTIONS: Engines: 3.8-liter V-6: Sable ($396). 5.0-liter V-8: Cougar ($721). Transmission/Differential: Automatic transaxle: Topaz ($482). All-Wheel-Drive: Topaz ($1257-$1409). Traction-Lok: Cougar/Grand Marquis ($100). Suspension: Automatic leveling: Grand Marquis ($195). H.D. suspension: Grand Marquis ($26). Trailer towing pkg: Grand Marquis ($389-$399).

TOPAZ CONVENIENCE/APPEARANCE OPTIONS: GS Supplemental Restraint System Pkg ($1180). LS Supplemental Restraint System Pkg ($880). Manual Control Air Cond ($773). Comfort/Convenience Grp, GS ($179). Rear Window Defroster ($145). Pwr Lock Grp: 2-dr GS ($237). 2-dr XR5 ($156). 4-dr ($288). 2-dr GS w/Comf/Conv Grp ($156). 4-dr GS w/Comf/Conv Grp ($207). Clearcoat Metallic Paint ($91). Premium Sound System ($138). Speed Control ($182). Tilt Steering Wheel ($124). Polycast Wheels ($178). Decklid Luggage Rack ($115). Power Windows, 4-dr ($296). All-Wheel-Drive: GS ($1409). XR5, LTS ($1257). LS ($1274). Elect AM/FM Stereo Radio w/Cass & Clock, GS ($141). GS Driver's Side Airbag ($815). LS Driver's Side Airbag ($622). 6-Way Pwr Driver's Seat ($251). Locking Spoke Wheel Covers ($212). Calif. Emission System ($99). Frt License Plate Bracket (NC). Eng Block Heater ($18). Vinyl Seat Trim ($37). TIRES: P185/70R14 WSW ($82). P185/70R14 Perf WSW ($82).

SABLE CONVENIENCE/APPEARANCE OPTIONS: Air Cond Man Temp Control, delete (credit). Auto Air Cond ($183). Auto Lamp System ($73). Auto Parking Brake Release ($12). Dual Illum Visor Mirrors ($99). Elect Instrument Cluster ($351). InstaClear Heated Windshield ($250). Keyless Entry System ($202). Pwr Moonroof ($741). Rear Window Defroster ($145). Fingertip Speed Control ($182). Tilt Strg Wheel ($124). Light Group, GS ($59). H.D. Battery ($27). H.D. Suspension ($26). Ext Range Fuel Tank ($46). Calif. Emission System ($99). Pwr Lock Grp: GS sed ($287). GS sta wag ($237). LS ($195). 6-Way Pwr Driver's Seat ($251). 6-Way Pwr Driver & Pass Seat ($502). Pwr Side Windows ($296). AM/FM Radio w/Cass Player ($137). Premium Sound System ($168). Premium Elect AM/FM Stereo ($472). Pwr Antenna ($76). Clearcoat Paint ($183). Frt License Plate Bracket (NC). Paint Stripe ($57). F&R Floor Mats ($43). Leather-Wrapped Strg Wheel ($59). Leather Seat Trim ($415). All Vinyl Trim

($37). Individual Bucket Seats, GS (NC). Picnic Tray, sta wag ($66). Rear Facing Third Seat, sta wag ($155). Liftgate Window Washer/Wiper ($126). Cargo Area Cover ($66). Eng Block Heater ($18). AM/FM Radio Delete (credit). Conventional Spare Tire ($73). Cast Alum Wheels ($172). Radial Design Wheel Covers ($157). Polycast Wheels ($123). TIRES: P205/70R14 WSW ($82). P205/65R15 BSW ($65). P205/65R15 WSW ($146). P205/65R15 WSW ($82).

COUGAR CONVENIENCE/APPEARANCE OPTIONS: Pwr Lock Grp ($237). Pwr Windows ($222). Lux Light Grp ($741). Pwr Moonroof ($841). 6-Way Pwr Driver's Seat ($251). Dual 6-Way Pwr Seats: ($302). LS ($554). XR-7 ($502). Elect AM/FM Stereo Radio w/Cass ($137). Premium Sound System ($168). Pwr Antenna ($76). Graphic Equalizer ($218). Hood Accent Paint Stripes ($16). Clearcoat Metallic Paint ($183). Two-Tone Paint ($159). Leather Seat Trim ($415). Auto Climate Air Cond ($162). H.D. Battery ($27). Eng Block Heater ($18). Elect Rear Window Defroster ($145). Interval Wipers ($55). Auto Park Brake Release ($12). Lux Lamp Grp: XR-7 ($176). LS ($244). Keyless Entry System ($202). w/Lux Light Grp, Illum Entry ($121). Speed Control ($182). Leather-Wrapped Strg Wheel ($59). Lux Light Grp ($228). Frt Floor Mats ($33). Illum Entry System ($82). Elect Instrument Cluster ($270). Tilt Strg Wheel ($124). Frt License Plate Bracket (NC). Calif. Emission System ($99). TIRES: P215/70R14 WSW ($73). Conventional Spare Tire ($73). Lckg Wire Style Wheel Covers ($212). Polycast Wheels ($178).

GRAND MARQUIS CONVENIENCE/APPEARANCE OPTIONS: Conventional Spare Tire ($73). Automatic Climate Control ($211). Elect Rear Window Defroster ($145). InstaClear Heated Windshield ($250). Pwr Lock Grp ($245). Pwr Decklid Release ($50). 6-Way Pwr Driver's Seat ($251). Dual 6-Way Pwr Seats ($502). w/Pkgs Containing 6-Way Pwr Driver's Seat ($251). Elect AM/FM Stereo Radio w/Cass ($137). High Level Audio System ($472). Premium Sound System ($168). Pwr Antenna ($76). Frt License Plate Bracket (NC). License Plate Frames ($9). Dlx Luggage Rack ($115). Cornering Lamp ($68). Bodyside Protection Moldings ($66). Two-Tone Paint w/Tape Stripes ($159). Formal Coach Vinyl Roof ($665). Hood Accent Paint Stripes ($18). Leather-Wrapped Strg Wheel ($59). F&R Floor Mats ($43). Fingertip Spd Control ($182). Tilt Strg Wheel ($124). Illum Entry System ($82). Light Grp ($46). Dual Illum Visor Mirrors ($109). Tripminder Computer ($215). Pivoting Frt Vent Windows ($79). Dual Facing Rear Seats, sta wag ($173). Cloth Seat Trim, sta wag ($54). Vinyl Seat Trim, sed ($37). Leather Seat Trim ($415). Lckg Wire-Styled Wheel Covers ($183). Turbine Spoke Alum Wheels ($361). Calif. Emission System ($99). Frt Carpet Floor Mats ($26). Eng Block Heater ($18).

HISTORY: Introduced: October 1, 1987, except (Topaz) November 1987. Model year production: 473,400 (total). Calendar year production (U.S.): 293,689. Calendar year sales by U.S. dealers: 486,208 (incl. Tracer). Model year sales by U.S. dealers: 485,613.

1989 MERCURY

Cougar got nearly all the attention for 1989, appearing in a completely new form; and with a supercharged V-6 engine under the hood of the sporty XR-7.

1989 Mercury Topaz GS sedan. (OCW)

1989 Mercury Topaz LTS sedan. (OCW)

1989 Mercury Sable GS sedan. (OCW)

1989 Mercury Sable LS sedan. (OCW)

1989 Mercury Sable LS station wagon. (OCW)

TOPAZ — FOUR — Little changed in Mercury's compact sedans, which got a moderate restyle for 1988. A driver's side airbag was now available in all except the sporty XR5 two-door.

SABLE — V-6 — Modest revision of Sable's front end included new headlamps and park/signal lamps, as well as full-width illumination of the panel between the headlamps. Sedans changed their taillamp design. The optional 3.8-liter V-6 turned to sequential fuel injection this year.

COUGAR — V-6 — An all-new Cougar coupe arrived for 1989, again closely related to the Ford Thunderbird. Though roomier inside than its predecessor, the new edition was smaller outside, but tipped the scales at some 400 pounds more. Wheelbase grew by almost nine inches. Again rear-drive, the Cougar now had four-wheel independent suspension. As before, a formal-style roofline was the main difference from its Thunderbird cousin. Model availability was the same as the previous edition: a base LS and sporty XR-7. But while the LS came with the standard 3.8-liter V-6 (lacking the former balance shaft) and four-speed overdrive automatic transmission, the XR-7 contained a supercharged/intercooled V-6 that developed 210 horsepower. A five-speed manual gearbox was standard in the XR-7, with automatic optional. No V-8 engine was available. LS Cougars now rode on 15-inch tires, while the XR-7 used 16-inch performance tires. Standard equipment included: air conditioning, tinted glass, electronic instruments, power windows/mirrors, and AM/FM stereo radio. Styling features of the XR-7 included monochromatic body treatment and alloy wheels. Anti-lock braking was standard on XR-7, which used four-wheel disc brakes rather than the disc/drum arrangement on the LS. Adjustable shock-absorber damping allowed the selection of a soft or firm ride. Extras on the XR-7 included a handling suspension, Traction-Lok axle, sport seats with power bolsters, and analog gauges.

GRAND MARQUIS — V-8 — Little changed in the full-size Mercury, except that clearcoat metallic paint joined the option list this year.

I.D. DATA: Mercury's 17-symbol Vehicle Identification Number (VIN) was stamped on a metal tab fastened to the instrument panel, visible through the windshield. Symbols one to three indicate manufacturer, make and vehicle type. The fourth symbol denotes restraint system. Next comes a letter 'M' (for series), followed by two digits that indicate body type: Model Number, as shown in left column of tables below. (Example: '31' Topaz GS two-door sedan.) Symbol eight indicates engine type. Next is a check digit. Symbol ten indicates model year ('K' 1989). Symbol eleven denotes assembly plant. The final six digits make up the production sequence number, starting with 600001.

1989 Mercury Cougar LS coupe. (OCW)

TOPAZ (FOUR)

Model No.	Body/ Style No.	Body Type & Seating	Factory Price	Shipping Weight	Prod. Total
31	66D	2-dr. GS Sedan-5P	9577	2567	Note 1
33	66D	2-dr. XR5 Sedan-5P	10498	2544	Note 1
36	54D	4-dr. GS Sedan-5P	9734	2608	Note 2
37	54D	4-dr. LS Sedan-5P	11030	2647	Note 2
38	54D	4-dr. LTS Sedan-5P	11980	2706	Note 2

NOTE 1: Production of two-door sedans totaled 7,705 with no further breakout available.

NOTE 2: Production of four-door sedans totaled 85,812 with no further breakout available.

SABLE (V-6)

50	54D	4-dr. GS Sed-6P	14101	3054	Note 1
53	54D	4-dr. LS Sed-6P	15094	3168	Note 1
55	74D	4-dr. GS Sta Wag-6P	14804	3228	Note 2
58	74D	4-dr. LS Sta Wag-6P	15872	3252	Note 2

NOTE 1: Production of four-door sedans totaled 93,052 with no further breakout available.

NOTE 2: Production of station wagons totaled 25,998 with no further breakout available.

COUGAR (V-6)

60	66D	2-dr. LS Cpe-5P	15448	3553	Note 1
62	66D	2-dr. XR-7 Cpe-5P	19650	3710	Note 1

NOTE 1: Production of two-door coupes totaled 92,702 with no further breakout available.

GRAND MARQUIS (V-8)

74	54K	4-dr. GS Sed-6P	16701	3763	Note 1
75	54KK	4-dr. LS Sed-6P	17213	3774	Note 1

NOTE 1: Production of four-door sedans totaled 118,979 with no further breakout available.

GRAND MARQUIS COLONY PARK WAGON (V-8)

78	74K	4-dr. GS Sta Wag-6P	17338	3995	Note 1
79	74K	4-dr. LS Sta Wag-6P	17922	3913	Note 1

NOTE 1: Production of station wagons totaled 8,173 with no further breakout available.

ENGINE [Base Four (Topaz)]: Inline. Overhead valve. Four-cylinder. Cast-iron block and head. Displacement: 140 cid (2.3-liters). Bore & stroke: 3.70 x 3.30 in. Compression ratio: 9.0:1. Brake horsepower: 98 at 4400 rpm. Torque: 124 lbs.-ft. at 2200 rpm. Five main bearings. Hydraulic valve lifters. Multi-point fuel injection.

ENGINE [Base Four (Topaz XR5, LTS and 4WD)]: High-output version of 140 cid four above: Horsepower: 100 at 4400 rpm. Torque: 130 lbs.-ft. at 2600 rpm.

ENGINE [Base V-6 (Sable)]: 60-degree, overhead valve V-6. Cast-iron block and head. Displacement: 182 cid (3.0-liters). Bore & stroke: 3.50 x 3.10 in. Compression ratio: 9.3:1. Brake horsepower: 140 at 4800 rpm. Torque: 160 lbs.-ft. at 3000 rpm. Four main bearings. Hydraulic valve lifters. Multi-port fuel injection.

ENGINE [Base V-6 (Cougar); Optional (Sable)]: 90-degree, overhead valve V-6. Cast-iron block and aluminum head. Displacement: 232 cid (3.8-liters). Bore & stroke: 3.80 x 3.40 in. Compression ratio: 9.0:1. Brake horsepower: 140 at 3800 rpm. Torque: (Cougar) 215 lbs.-ft. at 2400 RPM; (Sable) 215 at 2200. Four main bearings. Hydraulic valve lifters. Multi-point fuel injection.

1989 Mercury Cougar XR-7 coupe. (OCW)

1989 Mercury Grand Marquis LS sedan. (OCW)

ENGINE [Supercharged V-6 (Cougar XR-7)]: 90-degree, overhead valve V-6. Cast-iron block and aluminum head. Displacement: 232 cid (3.8-liters). Bore & stroke: 3.80 x 3.40 in. Compression ratio: 8.2:1. Brake horsepower: 210 at 4000 rpm. Torque: 315 lbs.-ft. at 2600 rpm. Four main bearings. Hydraulic valve lifters. Multi-point fuel injection.

ENGINE [Base V-8 (Grand Marquis)]: 90-degree, overhead valve V-8. Cast-iron block and head. Displacement: 302 cid (5.0-liters). Bore & stroke: 4.00 x 3.00 in. Compression ratio: 8.9:1. Brake horsepower: 150 at 3200 rpm. Torque: 270 lbs.-ft. at 2000 rpm. Five main bearings. Hydraulic valve lifters. Sequential fuel injection.

CHASSIS DATA: Wheelbase: (Topaz) 99.9 in.; (Sable) 106.0 in.; (Cougar) 113.0 in.; (Grand Marquis) 114.3 in. Overall Length: (Topaz 2-dr) 176.7 in.; (Topaz 4-dr) 177.0 in.; (Sable) 190.9 in.; (Sable wag) 191.9 in.; (Cougar) 198.7 in.; (Grand Marquis) 213.5 in.; (Grand Marquis wag) 218.3 in. Height: (Topaz) 52.8 in.; (Sable) 54.3 in.; (Sable wag) 55.1 in.; (Cougar) 52.7 in.; (Grand Marquis) 55.4 in.; (Grand Marquis wag) 57.0 in. Width: (Topaz 2-dr) 68.3 in.; (Topaz 4-dr) 66.8 in.; (Sable) 70.8 in.; (Cougar) 72.7 in.; (Grand Marquis) 77.5 in.; (Grand Marquis wag) 79.3 in. Front Tread: (Topaz) 54.9 in.; (Sable) 61.6 in.; (Cougar) 61.4 in.; (Grand Marquis) 62.2 in. Rear Tread: (Topaz) 57.6 in.; (Sable) 60.5 in.; (Sable wag) 59.9 in.; (Cougar) 61.2 in.; (Grand Marquis) 62.0 in. Standard Tires: (Topaz) P185/70R14; (Sable) P205/70R14; (Cougar) P205/70R15; (XR-7) P225/60VR15; (Grand Marquis) P215/70R15 SBR WSW.

TECHNICAL: Transmission: Five-speed manual standard on Topaz; three-speed automatic optional. Five-speed manual standard on Cougar XR-7; four-speed automatic optional. Four-speed overdrive automatic standard on Sable, Cougar LS and Grand Marquis. Steering: (Grand Marquis) recirculating ball; (others) rack-and-pinion. Front Suspension: (Topaz) MacPherson strut-mounted coil springs w/lower control arms and stabilizer bar; (Cougar) long spindle SLA with coil springs, gas shocks, upper A-arm, lower arm, tension strut and stabilizer bar; (Sable) MacPherson struts w/control arm, coil springs and anti-sway bar; (Grand Marquis) coil springs with long/short A-arms and anti-sway bar. Rear Suspension: (Topaz) independent quadralink w/MacPherson struts; (Cougar) independent with coil springs, gas shocks, lower 'H' arm, upper arm and stabilizer bar; (Sable) MacPherson struts w/coil springs, parallel suspension arms and anti-sway bar; (Grand Marquis) four-link w/coil springs. Brakes: Front disc, rear drum except (Cougar XR-7) front/rear discs with anti-lock. Body construction: (Grand Marquis) separate body and frame; (others) unibody. Fuel tank: (Topaz) 15.4 gal.; (Topaz 4WD) 14.7 gal.; (Sable) 16 gal.; (Cougar) 19.0 gal.; (Grand Marquis) 18 gal.

DRIVETRAIN OPTIONS: Engines: 3.8-liter V-6: Sable ($400). Transmission/Differential: Automatic transaxle: Topaz ($515). All-Wheel-Drive: Topaz ($915-$1441). Automatic transmission: XR-7 ($539). Traction-Lok: Cougar/Grand Marquis ($100). Suspension/Brakes: Anti-lock brakes: Cougar ($985). Automatic leveling: Grand Marquis ($195). H.D. suspension: Sable/Grand Marquis ($26). Trailer towing pkg.: Grand Marquis ($405).

TOPAZ CONVENIENCE/APPEARANCE OPTIONS: GS Special Value Pkg 361A ($460). GS Special Value Pkg 363A ($799). GS Supplemental Restraint System, 4-dr ($1172). XR5 Model Special Value Pkg 371A ($456). LS Model Special Value Pkg 365A (NC). LS Supplemental Restraint System Pkg 366A ($939). LTS Supplemental Restraint System Pkg 376A ($646). Man Control Air Cond ($788). Comfort/Convenience Grp, GS ($179). Rear Window Defroster ($145). Pwr Lock Grp: GS 2-dr ($237). XR5 2-dr ($156). GS 4-dr ($288). GS 2-dr w/Comf/Conv Grp ($156). GS 4-dr w/Comf/Conv Grp ($207). Clearcoat Metallic Paint ($91). Premium Sound System ($138). Speed Control ($182). Tilt Steering Wheel ($124). Polycast Wheels ($178). Decklid Luggage Rack ($115). Power Windows, 4-dr ($296). All-Wheel-Drive: GS ($1441). LTS ($1332). LS ($1429). Elect AM/FM Stereo Radio w/Cass & Clock, GS ($137). Elect AM/FM Stereo Radio Delete ($245 credit). Elect AM/FM Cass Delete: XR5, LS, LTS ($382 credit). GS Driver's Side Airbag ($815). LS & LTS Driver's Side Airbag ($622). 6-Way Pwr Driver's Seat ($251). Lckg Spoke Wheel Covers ($212). Calif. Emission System ($100). Frt License Plate Bracket (NC). Eng Block Heater ($20). Vinyl Seat Trim ($37). TIRES: P185/70R14 WSW ($82).

SABLE CONVENIENCE/APPEARANCE OPTIONS: Air Cond, Man. Temp Control Delete, GS only ($807 credit). Auto Air Cond ($183). Auto Lamp System ($73). Auto Parking Brake Release ($12). Dual-Illum Visor Mirrors ($100). Elect Instrument Cluster ($351). InstaClear Heated Windshield ($250). Keyless Entry System ($218). Pwr Moonroof ($741). Rear Window Defroster ($150). Fingertip Speed Control ($191). Tilt Steering Wheel ($124). Light Group, GS ($59). H.D. Battery ($27). Ext Range Fuel Tank ($46). Calif. Emission System ($100). Pwr Lock Grp: GS ($287). LS ($195). 6-Way Pwr Driver's Seat ($251). 6-Way Pwr Driver & Pass. Seat ($502). Power Windows ($296). AM/FM Stereo Radio w/Cass Player ($137). Premium Sound System ($168). High Level Audio System ($472). Pwr Antenna ($76). Clearcoat Paint ($183). Frt. License Plate Bracket (NC). Paint Stripe ($61). F&R Floor Mats ($43). Leather-Wrapped Strg Wheel ($59). Leather Seat Trim ($415). All Vinyl Trim ($37). Picnic Tray, sta wag ($66). Rear Facing Third Seat, sta wag ($155). Liftgate Window Washer/Wiper, sta wag ($126). Cargo Area Cover, sta wag ($66). Eng Block Heater ($20). AM/FM Radio Delete ($206 credit). TIRES: P205/70R14 WSW ($82). P205/65R15 BSW ($65). P205/65R15 WSW ($146). P205/65R15 WSW ($82). Conventional Spare Tire ($73). Cast Alum Wheels ($224). Polycast Wheels ($138).

COUGAR CONVENIENCE/APPEARANCE OPTIONS: Cold Weather Grp: elect rear window defroster, eng block heater, H.D. battery, H.D. alternator ($195). XR-7 ($168). Pwr Lock Grp: pwr door locks, pwr decklid release, remote-release fuel filler door, LS ($216). Luxury Lamp Grp: auto headlamp dimmer, autolamp on-off delay system, frt cornering lamps, LS ($244). Luxury Light Grp: underhood light, dual beam dome-map light, instrument panel courtesy lights, dual illum visor vanity mirrors, illum entry system ($228). Preferred Equipment Pkg: tilt strg column, cruise control, elect rear window defroster, and Pwr Lock Grp, LS ($636). Preferred Equip Pkg: P215/70R15 blackwall tires, frt carpeted floor mats, tilt strg column, leather-wrapped strg wheel, cruise control, 6-way pwr driver's seat, elect rear window defroster, Elect AM/FM stereo radio w/cass, Lux Light Grp, cast alum wheels, Pwr Lock Grp ($1081). Preferred Equip Pkg: P215/70R15 blackwall tires, frt carpeted floor mats, keyless entry system, diagnostic maintenance monitor, tilt strg column, leather-wrapped strg wheel, cruise control, dual 6-way pwr seats, elect rear window defroster, high-level elect AM/FM stereo radio w/cass, Lux Light Grp, Luxury Lamp Grp, cast alum wheels, pwr antenna, pwr lock grp ($1814). Preferred Equip Pkg: tilt strg column, cruise control, 6-way pwr driver's seat, elect rear window defroster, elect AM/FM stereo radio w/cass, Pwr Lock Grp, XR-7 (NC). Preferred Equip Pkg: color-keyed frt carpeted floor mats, keyless entry system, tilt strg column, cruise control, 6-way pwr driver's seat, elect rear window defroster, high-level elect AM/FM stereo radio w/cass, Luxury Light Grp, Luxury Lamp Grp, pwr antenna, Pwr Lock Grp, XR-7 ($862). Pwr Antenna ($76). Anti-Theft System ($183). Diagnostic Maintenance Monitor ($89). Elect Rear Window Defroster ($150). Calif. Emission System ($100). Keyless Entry System ($218). Speed Control ($191). Frt Carpeted Color-Keyed Floor Mats ($33). Elect AM/FM Stereo Radio w/Cass & Clock ($137). High-Level Elect AM/FM Stereo Radio w/Cass ($441). JBL Sound System ($488). Digital Audio Disc Player ($491). Pwr Moonroof incl dual reading lights, pop-up air deflector, sliding sun shade, rear tilt-up ($741). Pwr 6-way driver's seat ($261). Dual 6-way pwr seats ($522). Leather-Wrapped Steering Wheel ($63). Split Fold-Down Rear Seat ($133). Tilt Wheel ($124). Leather Seat Trim, LS ($489). Leather Seat Trim, XR-7 ($489). Diagnostic Maintenance Monitor Warning Lights (warning lights for low fuel, low oil, low coolant & low washer fluid, adaptive oil change indicator), LS ($89). Frt License Plate Bracket (NC). Locking Radial Spoke Wheel Covers ($228). Styled Sport Wheel Covers ($85). Cast Aluminum 15-inch Wheels ($299). TIRES: P205/70R15 WSW ($73). P225/60VR16 BSW All-Season Perf Tires ($73). Conventional Spare Tire ($73).

1989 Mercury Grand Marquis Colony Park LS station wagon. (OCW)

GRAND MARQUIS CONVENIENCE/APPEARANCE OPTIONS: Preferred Equip. Pkgs: GS 4-dr sed (157A) w/locking Wire Style Wheel Covers ILO Turbine Spoke Alum Wheels ($1101). Colony Park GS (192A) Auto OD Trans; Conv. Axle, P215/70R15 All-Season WSW Tires; Illum Entry System; Frt Cornering Lamps; Tilt Strg Wheel; Fingertip Spd Control; 6-Way Pwr Driver's Seat; Dual Inboard Facing Rear Seats; Elect Rear Window Defroster; Turbine Spoke Alum Wheels; Bodyside Protection Mldg; Light Grp; Pwr Lock Group ($1256). (193A) all 192A plus Leather-Wrapped Strg Wheel; Dual Illum Visor Mirrors; Pwr Antenna; Premium Sound System; Elect AM/FM Stereo Radio w/Cass ($1509). Colony Park LS (192A) same as GS ($1210). Conventional Spare Tire ($85). Auto Climate Cntrl Air Cond ($216). Elect Rear Window Defroster ($150). InstaClear Heated Windshield ($250). H.D. Battery ($27). Pwr Lock Grp ($255). Pwr Decklid Release ($50). 6-Way Pwr Driver's Seat ($261). Dual 6-Way Pwr Seats ($522). w/Pkgs containing 6-Way Pwr Driver's Seat ($261). Elect AM/FM Stereo Radio w/Cass ($137). High Level Audio System ($472). Premium Sound System ($168). Power Antenna ($76). Frt Lic Plate Bracket (NC). Lic Plate Frames ($9). Cornering Lamps ($68). Bodyside Protection Mldgs ($66). Tu-Tone Paint w/Tape Stripes ($159). Formal Coach Vinyl Roof ($665). Clearcoat Paint ($226). Hood Accent Paint Stripes ($18). Leather-Wrapped Strg Wheel ($63). Floor Mats F&R ($43). Fingertip Spd Control ($191). Tilt Wheel ($124). Illum Entry System ($82). Light Grp ($46). Dual Illum Visor Mirrors ($109). Tripminder Computer ($215). Pivoting Frt Vent Windows ($79). Dual Facing Rear Seats ($173). Cloth Seat Trim, sta wag ($54). Vinyl Seat Trim, sed ($37). Leather Seat Trim ($489). Lckg Wire-Styled Wheel Covers ($228). Turbine Spoke Alum Wheels ($440). Pkgs containing Lckg Wire-Style Wheels ($212). Calif. Emission System ($100). Frt Carpet Flr Mats ($26). Eng Block Heater ($20).

HISTORY: Introduced: October 6, 1988, except (Cougar) December 26, 1988. Model year production: 294,899 (U.S.); 495,017 (total). Calendar year sales by U.S. dealers: 465,908 (incl Tracer). Model year sales by U.S. dealers: 485,357.

1990 MERCURY

1990 Mercury Topaz four-door sedan. (OCW)

This was essentially a carryover year for Mercury, and all Mercury models remained closely related to a model in the Ford lineup. In addition to the four domestically-built models, Mercury dealers had been selling a Mexican-built Tracer, but production halted for 1990, awaiting a revised version for 1991. Also, an Australian-built 1991 Capri 2+2 convertible was launched in the summer of 1990, but because this Mercury was imported into the United States it is not in the scope of this catalog and will not be covered in detail.

TOPAZ — FOUR — Shoulder belts added to rear seats were the only notable change for the Mercury compact. Trunk and footwell lights became standard; as did floor mats. Wire wheel covers left the option list. As before, both the standard and high-output 2.3-liter four-cylinder engines were available, the latter standard in the XR5, LTS and four-wheel-drive models.

1990 Mercury Topaz LTS sedan. (OCW)

1990 Mercury Sable LS sedan. (OCW)

1990 Mercury Sable LS station wagon. (OCW)

1990 Mercury Cougar LS coupe. (OCW)

1990 Mercury Cougar XR-7 coupe. (OCW)

SABLE — V-6 — Except for the addition of a standard driver's side airbag and optional anti-lock braking (on sedans only), the midsize Sable sedan and station wagons were a carryover for 1990. Inside was a new instrument cluster, with slide-out coin and cupholder trays. Tilt steering became standard; a compact-disc player a new option. Variable-assist power steering now came with the optional 3.8-liter V-6 engine.

COUGAR — V-6 — Not much changed for 1990 on the Mercury midsize coupe, which enjoyed a full restyling for 1989, beyond the addition of contoured head restraints and a few option adjustments.

1990 Mercury Grand Marquis Colony Park LS station wagon. (OCW)

1990 Mercury Grand Marquis LS sedan. (OCW)

GRAND MARQUIS — V-8 — Nearly all the changes for the Mercury full-size sedans and station wagons went inside: a driver's airbag, new instrument panel, rear shoulder belts, and standard tilt steering. As before, the station wagons could get optional third rear seats for eight-passenger seating. Sedans no longer had standard bumper guards, but they remained on the option list. Rear track width grew by 1.3 inches, because of a different rear axle. A single key now operated doors and ignition.

I.D. DATA: Mercury's 17-symbol Vehicle Identification Number (VIN) was stamped on a metal tab fastened to the instrument panel, visible through the windshield. Symbols one to three indicate manufacturer, make and vehicle type. The fourth symbol denotes restraint system. Next comes a letter 'M' (for series), followed by two digits that indicate body type: Model Number, as shown in left column of tables below. (Example: '31' Topaz GS two-door sedan.) Symbol eight indicates engine type. Next is a check digit. Symbol ten indicates model year ('L' 1990). Symbol eleven denotes assembly plant. The final six digits make up the production sequence number, starting with 600001.

TOPAZ (FOUR)

Model No.	Body/ Style No.	Body Type & Seating	Factory Price	Shipping Weight	Prod. Total
31	66D	2-dr. GS Sedan-5P	10027	2447	Note 1
33	66D	2-dr. XR5 Sedan-5P	10988	2442	Note 1
36	54D	4-dr. GS Sedan-5P	10184	2490	Note 2
37	54D	4-dr. LS Sedan-5P	11507	2533	Note 2
38	54D	4-dr. LTS Sedan-5P	12514	2542	Note 2

NOTE 1: Production of two-door sedans totaled 7,705 with no further breakout available.

NOTE 2: Production of four-door sedans totaled 85,812 with no further breakout available.

SABLE (V-6)

50	54D	4-dr. GS Sed-6P	15009	2977	Note 1
53	54D	4-dr. LS Sed-6P	16011	3045	Note 1
55	74D	4-dr. GS Sta Wag-6P	15711	3088	Note 2
58	74D	4-dr. LS Sta Wag-6P	16789	3148	Note 2

NOTE 1: Production of four-door sedans totaled 69,355 with no further breakout available.

NOTE 2: Production of station wagons totaled 23,614 with no further breakout available.

COUGAR (V-6)

60	66D	2-dr. LS Cpe-5P	15911	3314	Note 1
62	66D	2-dr. XR-7 Cpe-5P	20217	3562	Note 1

NOTE 1: Production of two-door coupes totaled 76,467 with no further breakout available.

GRAND MARQUIS (V-8)

74	54K	4-dr. GS Sed-6P	17633	3685	N/A
75	54K	4-dr. LS Sed-6P	18133	3696	N/A

GRAND MARQUIS COLONY PARK WAGON (V-8)

78	74K	4-dr. GS Sta Wag-6P	18348	3876	N/A
79	74K	4-dr. LS Sta Wag-6P	18920	3882	N/A

ENGINE [Base Four (Topaz)]: Inline. Overhead valve. Four-cylinder. Cast-iron block and head. Displacement: 140 cid (2.3-liters). Bore & stroke: 3.70 x 3.30 in. Compression ratio: 9.0:1. Brake horsepower: 98 at 4400 rpm. Torque: 124 lbs.-ft. at 2200 rpm. Five main bearings. Hydraulic valve lifters. Multi-point fuel injection.

ENGINE [Base Four (Topaz XR5, LTS and 4WD)]: High-output version of 140 cid four above: Horsepower: 100 at 4400 rpm. Torque: 130 lbs.-ft. at 2600 rpm.

ENGINE [Base V-6 (Sable)]: 60-degree, overhead valve V-6. Cast-iron block and head. Displacement: 182 cid (3.0-liters). Bore & stroke: 3.50 x 3.10 in. Compression ratio: 9.3:1. Brake horsepower: 140 at 4800 rpm. Torque: 160 lbs.-ft. at 3000 rpm. Four main bearings. Hydraulic valve lifters. Multi-port fuel injection.

ENGINE [Base V-6 (Cougar); Optional (Sable)]: 90-degree, overhead valve V-6. Cast-iron block and aluminum head. Displacement: 232 cid (3.8-liters). Bore & stroke: 3.80x 3.40 in. Compression ratio: 9.0:1. Brake horsepower: 140 at 3800 rpm. Torque: (Cougar) 215 lbs.-ft. at 2400 RPM; (Sable) 215 at 2200. Four main bearings. Hydraulic valve lifters. Multi-point fuel injection.

ENGINE [Supercharged V-6 (Cougar XR-7)]: 90-degree, overhead valve V-6. Cast-iron block and aluminum head. Displacement: 232 cid (3.8-liters). Bore & stroke: 3.80 x 3.40 in. Compression ratio: 8.2:1. Brake horsepower: 210 at 4000 rpm. Torque: 315 lbs.-ft. at 2600 rpm. Four main bearings. Hydraulic valve lifters. Multi-point fuel injection.

ENGINE [Base V-8 (Grand Marquis)]: 90-degree, overhead valve V-8. Cast-iron block and head. Displacement: 302 cid (5.0-liters). Bore & stroke: 4.00 x 3.00 in. Compression ratio: 8.9:1. Brake horsepower: 150 at 3200 rpm. Torque: 270 lbs.-ft. at 2000 rpm. Five main bearings. Hydraulic valve lifters. Sequential fuel injection.

CHASSIS DATA: Wheelbase: (Topaz) 99.9 in.; (Sable) 106.0 in.; (Cougar) 113.0 in.; (Grand Marquis) 114.3 in. Overall Length: (Topaz 2-dr) 176.7 in.; (Topaz 4-dr) 177.0 in.; (Sable) 192.2 in.; (Sable wag) 193.2 in.; (Cougar) 198.7 in.; (Grand Marquis) 213.6 in.; (Grand Marquis wag) 218.0 in. Height: (Topaz) 52.8 in.; (Sable) 54.3 in.; (Cougar) 55.1 in.; (Cougar) 52.7 in.; (Grand Marquis) 55.6 in.; (Grand Marquis wag) 56.5 in. Width: (Topaz) 68.3 in.; (Sable) 70.8 in.; (Cougar) 72.7 in.; (Grand Marquis) 77.5 in.; (Grand Marquis wag) 79.3 in. Front Tread: (Topaz) 54.9 in.; (Sable) 61.6 in.; (Cougar) 61.6 in.; (Grand Marquis) 62.2 in. Rear Tread: (Topaz) 57.6 in.; (Sable) 60.5 in.; (Sable wag) 59.9 in.; (Cougar) 60.2 in.; (Grand Marquis) 63.3 in. Standard Tires: (Topaz) 185/70R14; (Sable) 205/70R14; (Cougar) 205/70R15; (XR-7) 225/60VR16; (Grand Marquis) P215/70R15 SBR WSW.

TECHNICAL: Transmission: Five-speed manual standard on Topaz; three-speed automatic optional. Five-speed manual standard on Cougar XR-7; four-speed automatic optional. Four-speed overdrive automatic standard on Sable, Cougar LS and Grand Marquis. Steering: (Grand Marquis) recirculating ball; (others) rack-and-pinion. Front Suspension: (Topaz) MacPherson strut-mounted coil springs w/lower control arms and stabilizer bar; (Cougar) long spindle SLA with coil springs, gas shocks, upper A-arm, lower arm, tension strut and stabilizer bar; (Sable) MacPherson struts w/control arm, coil springs and anti-sway bar; (Grand Marquis) coil springs with long/short A-arms and anti-sway bar. Rear Suspension: (Topaz) independent quadralink w/MacPherson struts; (Cougar) independent with coil springs, gas shocks, lower 'H' arm, upper arm and stabilizer bar; (Sable) MacPherson struts w/coil springs, parallel suspension arms and anti-sway bar; (Grand Marquis) four-link w/coil springs. Brakes: Front disc, rear drum except (Cougar XR-7) front/rear discs with anti-lock; anti-locking available on Sable sedan. Body construction: (Grand Marquis) separate body and frame; (others) unibody. Fuel tank: (Topaz) 15.9 gal.; (Topaz 4WD) 14.7 gal.; (Sable) 16 gal.; (Cougar) 19.0 gal.; (Grand Marquis) 18 gal.

DRIVETRAIN OPTIONS: Engines: 3.8-liter V-6: Sable ($400). Transmission/Differential: Automatic transaxle: Topaz ($539). All-Wheel-Drive: Topaz ($915-$1466). Automatic trans: XR-7 ($539). Traction-Lok: Cougar/Grand Marquis ($100). Steering/Suspension/Brakes: Variable-assist power steering: Sable ($104). Automatic leveling: Grand Marquis ($195). H.D. Suspension: Sable/Grand Marquis ($26). Trailer towing pkg.: Grand Marquis ($405). Anti-lock braking: Sable sedan/Cougar ($985).

1990 Mercury Topaz GS sedan. (OCW)

TOPAZ CONVENIENCE/APPEARANCE OPTIONS: GS Models Special Value Pkg 361A ($454). Special Value Pkg 363A ($793). XR5 Model Special Value Pkg 371A ($456). LS Model Special Value Pkg 365A (NC). Polycast Wheels ($193). Decklid Luggage Rack ($115). Pwr Windows, 4-dr ($306). 6-Way Pwr Driver's Seat ($261). Driver-Side Airbag: GS ($815). LS or LTS ($622). All-Wheel-Drive: GS ($1466). LTS ($1356). LS ($1454). Elect AM/FM Stereo Radio w/Cass & Clock, GS ($137). Calif. Emission System ($100). Frt. License Plate Bracket (NC). Eng Block Heater ($20). Lower Accent Paint Treatment ($159). Vinyl Seat Trim ($37). Manual Control Air Cond ($807). Comfort/Convenience Grp, GS ($173). Rear Window Defroster ($150). Pwr Lock Grp: 2-dr GS ($246). 2-dr XR5 ($166). 4-dr GS ($298). 2-dr GS w/Comf/Conv Grp ($166). 4-dr GS w/Comf/Conv Grp ($217). Clearcoat Metallic Paint ($91). Premium Sound System ($138). Speed Control ($191). Tilt Strg Wheel ($124). TIRES: P185/70R14 WSW ($82).

SABLE CONVENIENCE/APPEARANCE OPTIONS: Auto. Air Cond ($183). Auto Lamp System ($73). Dual Illum Visor Mirrors ($100). Elect Instrument Cluster ($351). InstaClear Windshield ($250). Keyless Entry System ($218). Pwr Moonroof ($741). Rear Window Defroster ($150). Fingertip Speed Control ($191). Luxury Touring Pkg (LS sed): Anti-lock Brakes, Moonroof, Leather Bucket Seats ($2015). Light Grp, GS ($59). H.D. Battery ($27). Ext Range Fuel Tank ($46). Calif. Emission System ($100). Pwr Lock Grp: GS sed ($296). GS sta wag ($244). LS sed ($205). 6-Way Pwr Driver's Seat ($261). 6-Way Pwr Driver & Pass. Seats ($522). Pwr Windows ($306). AM/FM Stereo Radio w/Cass ($137). Premium Sound System ($168). High Level AM/FM Stereo w/Cass Audio System ($472). JBL Sound System ($488). Digital Compact Disc Player ($491). Pwr Radio Antenna ($76). Clearcoat Paint ($189). Frt. License Plate Bracket (NC). Bodyside Accent Stripes ($61). F&R Floor Mats ($43). Leather-Wrapped Strg. Wheel ($63). Leather Seat Trim ($489). All Vinyl Trim ($37). Picnic Tray, sta wag ($66). Rear Facing Third Seat, sta wag ($155). Rear Window Wiper/Washer, sta wag ($126). Cargo Area Cover, sta wag ($66). Eng Block Heater ($20). TIRES: P205/70R14 WSW ($82). P205/65R15 BSW ($65). P205/65R15 WSW ($82-$146). Conventional Spare Tire ($73). Cast Alum Wheels ($224). Polycast Wheels ($138).

COUGAR CONVENIENCE/APPEARANCE OPTIONS: Pwr Lock Group ($246). Diagnostic Maintenance Monitor ($89). Pwr Moonroof ($741). 6-Way Pwr Driver's Seat ($261). Dual 6-Way Pwr Seats ($522). Elect AM/FM Stereo Radio w/Cass & Clock ($137). High Level Audio AM/FM w/Cass & Clock ($441). JBL Sound System ($488). Compact Disc Player ($491). Pwr Antenna ($76). Clearcoat Metallic Paint: LS ($188), XR-7 ($188). Leather Seat Trim: LS ($489). XR-7 ($489). Split Fold-Down Rear Seat ($133). Cold Weather Grp: LS, XR-7 w/MTX ($195). XR-7, w/ATX ($168). Elect Rear Window Defroster ($150). Light Grp ($46). Dual Illum Visor Vanity Mirrors ($100). Illum Entry ($82). Lux Lamp Grp ($244). Headlamp Convenience Grp ($176). Frt Cornering Lamps ($68). Keyless Entry System ($219). Speed Control ($191). Tilt Strg Wheel ($124). Leather-Wrapped Strg Wheel ($63). Frt Carpeted Floor Mats ($33). Anti-Theft Alarm System ($183). Frt License Plate Bracket (NC). Calif. Emission System ($100). TIRES: P205/70R15 WSW ($73). P225/60VR16 BSW All-Season Perf ($73). Conventional Spare Tire ($73). Lckg Radial Spoke Wheel Covers ($228). 15-inch Cast Aluminum Wheels ($298). Styled Sport Wheel Covers ($85).

GRAND MARQUIS CONVENIENCE/APPEARANCE OPTIONS: GS 4-dr sed Preferred Equipment Pkg 157A ($1021). LS 4-dr sed Preferred Equipment Pkg 172A ($1253). Colony Park GS Preferred Equipment Pkg 192A ($1132). Colony Park GS Preferred Equipment Pkg 193A ($1385). Colony Park LS Preferred Equipment Pkg 192A ($1086). Colony Park LS Preferred Equipment Pkg 193A ($1339). Auto Climate Control ($216). Elect Rear Window Defroster ($150). InstaClear Heated Windshield ($250). H.D. Battery ($27). Pwr Lock Grp ($255). Power Decklid Release ($50). 6-Way Pwr Driver's Seat ($261). Dual 6-Way Pwr Seats ($522). w/Pkgs containing 6-Way Pwr Driver's Seat ($261). Elect AM/FM Stereo Radio w/Cass ($137). High Level Audio System ($472). Premium Sound System ($168). Pwr Antenna ($76). Frt License Plate Bracket (NC). License Plate Frames ($9). Frt Cornering Lamps ($68). Bodyside Protection Moldings, sta wag ($66). Tu-Tone Paint w/Tape Stripes ($159). Formal Coach Vinyl Roof ($665). Clearcoat Paint ($230). Frt Bumper Guards ($38). Rear Bumper Guards ($24). Leather-Wrapped Strg Wheel ($63). F&R Floor Mats ($43). Fingertip Speed Control ($191). Illum Entry System ($82). Light Grp ($46). Dual Illum Visor Mirrors ($109). Dual Inboard Facing Rear Seats, sta wag ($173). Cloth Seat Trim, GS sta wag ($54). Vinyl Seat Trim, GS sed ($37). Leather Seat Trim, LS sed and sta wag ($489). Calif. Emission System ($100). Frt Carpet Flr Mats ($26). Eng Block Heater ($20). Lckg Wire Styled Wheel Covers ($228). Turbine Spoke Alum Wheels ($440). In Pkgs containing Locking Wire Style Wheels ($212). Conventional Spare Tire ($85).

HISTORY: U.S. model year production: 353,086 (includes 1991 Grand Marquis models introduced early in 1990).

1991 Mercury Topaz GS sedan. (OCW)

Cougar got a new look for 1991 with a redesigned front end as well as a new High Output 5.0-liter V-8 as standard engine in the XR7 and optional in Cougar LS models. The Grand Marquis was essentially a carry-over model from the year previous as the all-new, 1992 model was scheduled for introduction in the spring of 1991. Mercury's built-in-Mexico Tracer was also an all-new design for 1991, but is beyond the scope of this catalog. Also, Mercury launched its new-for-1991 Capri 2+2 convertible in the summer of 1990. Built in Australia and imported into the United States, the Capri is also beyond the scope of this catalog and will not be discussed further.

TOPAZ -- FOUR — The Topaz lineup returned unchanged from the year previous with two-door sedans offered in GS and XR5 trim and four-door sedans available in GS, LS and LTS trim. All Topaz models received minor structural upgrades to reduce noise and vibration. Standard powerplant for Topaz GS and LS models was the 2.3-liter high swirl combustion (HSC) four-cylinder engine. LTS and XR5 models used the higher specific output (HSO) version of the same engine. The five-speed manual transaxle was the standard unit while the three-speed automatic was optional. Other optional equipment for Topaz included a four-wheel-drive model (previously called all-wheel-drive) and a driver's side airbag.

SABLE — V-6 — Sable was again offered in GS and LS versions, each offering a four-door sedan and station wagon. For 1991, sequential port fuel injection was added to Sable's standard 3.0-liter V-6 which was mated to a new electronic four-speed automatic transaxle. The 3.8-liter V-6 was the option engine. Four-wheel anti-lock disc brakes, offered previously on Sable sedans, were now also optional on station wagons. Also optional equipment on the Sable station wagon was a moonroof. Upgrades to Sable included new hydraulic engine mounts, isolated valve covers and double-isolated strut mounts.

1991 Mercury Sable GS sedan. (OCW)

1991 Mercury Sable LS station wagon. (OCW)

1991 Mercury Cougar XR7 coupe. (OCW)

COUGAR — V-6/V-8 — Cougar received a face lift for 1991 including an updated fascia, hood, grille and headlamps as well as revised bodyside moldings and updated tail lamps. Available as a two-door coupe in either the LS or XR7 series, Cougar upgrades included an analog instrument cluster as standard equipment and electronic temperature control system, compact digital disc player, power moonroof and keyless entry system as options. The XR7 received a new High Output, 200-hp 5.0-liter V-8 with sequential port fuel injection as standard engine, which was optional for the LS model. It replaced the supercharged version of the 3.8-liter V-6 offered previously. The LS used the 3.8-liter V-6 with sequential port fuel injection. Both series used the four-speed automatic overdrive transmission.

GRAND MARQUIS — V-8 — Aside from a blacked-out grille treatment and the addition of clearcoat paint, the Grand Marquis was essentially a carry-over version of the previous year's model. Again offered in GS and LS four-door sedans and GS and LS Colony Park station wagons, 1991 was the final year for the wagons. It was a short year for all 1991 Grand Marquis models as the all-new-design 1992 models were introduced in the spring of 1991. Grand Marquis was again powered by the 5.0-liter V-8 coupled to a four-speed automatic overdrive transmission. A slightly more powerful version of this engine equipped with dual exhaust was optional.

I.D. DATA: Mercury's 17-symbol Vehicle Identification Number (VIN) was stamped on a metal tab fastened to the instrument panel, visible through the windshield. The first three symbols indicate manufacturer, make and vehicle type. The fourth symbol denotes restraint system. Next comes a letter (usually 'M'), followed by two digits that indicate Model Number, as shown in left column of tables below. (Example: '31' Topaz GS two-door sedan). Symbol eight indicates engine type. Next is a check digit. Symbol ten indicates model year ('M' - 1991). Symbol eleven denotes assembly plant. The final six digits make up the sequence number, starting with 000001.

TOPAZ (FOUR)

Model No.	Body/ Style No.	Body Type & Seating	Factory Price	Shipping Weight	Prod. Total
M	31	2-dr. GS Sed-5P	10448	2546	Note 1
M	36	4-dr. GS Sed-5P	10605	2602	Note 2
M	37	4-dr. LS Sed-5P	11984	2647	Note 2
M	38	4-dr. LTS Sed-5P	13008	2708	Note 2
M	33	2-dr. XR5 Sed-5P	11447	2545	Note 1

1991 Mercury Grand Marquis LS sedan. (OCW)

1991 Mercury Grand Marquis Colony Park LS station wagon. (OCW)

NOTE 1: Production of two-door sedans totaled 531 with no further breakout available.

NOTE 2: Production of four-door sedans totaled 55,068 with no further breakout available.

SABLE (V-6)

M	50	4-dr. GS Sed-5P	15821	3174	Note 1
M	55	4-dr. GS Sta Wag-5P	16766	3311	Note 2
M	53	4-dr. LS Sed-5P	16823	3225	Note 1
M	58	4-dr. LS Sta Wag-5P	17794	3366	Note 2

NOTE 1: Production of four-door sedans totaled 72,055 with no further breakout available.

NOTE 2: Production of station wagons totaled 17,217 with no further breakout available.

COUGAR (V-6/V-8)

M	60	2-dr. LS Cpe-4P	16094/17278	3587/3753	Note 1
M	62	2-dr. XR7 Cpe-4P	-----/21139	----/3800	Note 1

NOTE: Figures to left of slash for V-6, right for V-8.

NOTE 1: Production of two-door coupes totaled 60,564 with no further breakout available.

GRAND MARQUIS (V-8)

M	74	4-dr. GS Sed-6P	18199	3836	Note 1
M	78	4-dr. GS Clny Park Sta Wag-6P	18918	4032	Note 2
M	75	4-dr. LS Sed-6P	18699	3794	Note 1
M	79	4-dr. LS Clny Park Sta Wag-6P	19490	4012	Note 2

NOTE 1: Production of four-door sedans totaled 132,192 with no further breakout available.

NOTE 2: Production of station wagons totaled 2,947 with no further breakout available.

ENGINE [Base Four (Topaz)]: Inline. Overhead cam. Four-cylinder. Cast-iron block and aluminum head. Displacement: 141 cid (2.3 liters). Bore & stroke: 3.70 x 3.30 in. Compression ratio: 9.0:1. Brake horsepower: (GS and LS) 98 at 4400 RPM; (LTS and XR5) 100 at 4400 rpm. Torque: (GS and LS) 124 lbs.-ft. at 2200 RPM; (LTS and XR5) 130 lbs.-ft. at 2600 rpm. Multi-port fuel injection.

ENGINE [Base V-6 (Sable)]: 60-degree, overhead valve V-6. Cast-iron block and head. Displacement: 182 cid (3.0 liters). Bore & stroke: 3.50 x 3.10 in. Compression ratio: 9.3:1. Brake horsepower: 140 at 4800 rpm. Torque: 160 lbs.-ft. at 3000 rpm. Sequential fuel injection.

ENGINE [Base V-6 (Cougar LS); Optional (Sable)]: Overhead valve V-6. Cast-iron block and head. Displacement: 302 cid (3.8 liters). Bore & stroke: 3.80 x 3.40 in. Compression ratio: 9.0:1. Brake horsepower: 140 at 3800 rpm. Torque: 215 lbs.-ft. at 2400 rpm. Sequential fuel injection.

ENGINE [Base V-8 (Cougar XR-7); Optional (Cougar LS)]: High Output, 90-degree, overhead valve V-8. Cast-iron block and head. Displacement: 302 cid (5.0 liters). Bore & stroke: 4.00 x 3.00 in. Compression ratio: 9.0:1. Brake horsepower: 225 at 4200 rpm. Torque: 275 lbs.-ft. at 3000. Sequential fuel injection.

ENGINE [Base V-8 (Grand Marquis)]: 90-degree, overhead valve V-8. Cast-iron block and head. Displacement: 302 cid (5.0-liter). Bore & stroke: 4.00 x 3.00 in. Compression ratio: 8.9:1. Brake horsepower: 150 at 3200 rpm. Torque: 270 lbs.-ft. at 2000 rpm. Sequential fuel injection.

ENGINE [Optional V-8 (Grand Marquis)]: same as Grand Marquis 5.0-liter V-8 above except - Brake horsepower: 160 at 3400 rpm. Torque: 280 lbs.-ft. at 2200 rpm. Dual exhaust.

CHASSIS DATA: Wheelbase: (Topaz) 99.9 in.; (Sable) 106.0 in.; (Cougar) 113.0 in.; (Grand Marquis) 114.3 in. Overall Length: (Topaz two-door sed) 176.7 in.; (Topaz four-door sed) 177.0 in.; (Sable) 193.2 in.; (Cougar) 199.9 in.; (Grand Marquis sed) 213.6 in.; (Grand Marquis sta wag) 218.0 in. Height: (Topaz two-door sed) 52.8 in.; (Topaz four-door sed) 52.9 in.; (Sable sed) 54.3 in.; (Sable sta wag) 55.1 in.; (Cougar) 52.7 in.; (Grand Marquis sed) 55.5 in.; (Grand Marquis sta wag) 56.5 in. Width: (Topaz) 68.3 in.; (Sable) 70.8 in.; (Cougar) 72.7 in.; (Grand Marquis) 77.5 in.; (Grand Marquis sta wag) 79.3 in. Front Tread: (Topaz) 54.9 in.; (Sable) 61.6 in.; (Cougar) 61.6 in.; (Grand Marquis) 62.2 in. Rear Tread: (Topaz) 57.6 in.; (Sable sed) 60.4 in.; (Grand Marquis sta wag) 59.9 in.; (Cougar) 60.2 in.; (Grand Marquis) 63.3 in. Standard Tires: (Topaz) P185/70R14; (Sable) P205/70R14; (Cougar) P205/70R15; (Grand Marquis) P215/70R15.

TECHNICAL: Transmission: Five-speed manual transaxle standard on Topaz. Four-speed automatic overdrive standard on Sable, Cougar and Grand Marquis/Colony Park. Drive Axle: (Cougar/Grand Marquis/Colony Park) rear; (others) front. Steering: (Grand Marquis/Colony Park) recirculating ball; (others) rack/pinion. Front Suspension: (Topaz) Independent MacPherson strut w/coil springs and nitrogen gas-pressurized shocks; (Sable) Independent MacPherson strut w/coil springs and hydraulic/telescoping/double-acting shocks; (Cougar) Long spindle SLA (short and long arm) w/upper 'A' arm, lower arm, tension strut and stabilizer bar; (Grand Marquis/Colony Park) Independent SLA w/ball joints, coil springs, gas-pressurized/hydraulic/telescoping shocks and stabilizer bar. Rear Suspension: (Topaz) Parallel four-bar fully independent MacPherson strut w/coil springs and nitrogen gas-pressurized shocks; (Sable sed) Fully independent MacPherson strut w/coil spring on shock strut and hydraulic/telescoping/double-acting shocks; (Sable sta wag) SLA independent w/coil springs and nitrogen gas-pressurized shocks; (Cougar) Independent w/lower 'H' arm, upper arm, stabilizer bar, variable rate coil springs and nitrogen gas-pressurized hydraulic shocks (automatic adjustable on XR7); (Grand Marquis/Colony Park) Four-bar link, coil springs w/rubber insulators and gas-pressurized/hydraulic/telescoping shocks. Brakes: Front disc, rear drum (power assisted) except (Cougar XR7) front/rear disc w/anti-lock system. Body construction: (Grand Marquis/Colony Park) separate body and frame; (others) unibody. Fuel tank: (Topaz) 15.9 gal.; (Topaz 4WD) 14.2 gal.; (Sable) 16.0 gal.; (Cougar) 19.0 gal.; (Grand Marquis/Colony Park) 18.0 gal.

DRIVETRAIN OPTIONS: Engines: 3.8-liter V-6: Sable ($555). High Output 5.0-liter V-8: Cougar LS ($1184). Transmission/Differential: Three-speed automatic transaxle: Topaz (except stnd in 4WD) ($563). Traction-Lok differential: Cougar LS/Grand Marquis/Colony Park ($100). Suspension/Brakes: Rear Air Suspension: Grand Marquis/Colony Park ($285). HD Suspension: Sable ($26). Trailer towing pkg: Grand Marquis/Colony Park ($405). Anti-lock brakes: Sable/Cougar LS ($985); Grand Marquis/Colony Park (includes Traction-Lok) ($1085).

TOPAZ CONVENIENCE/APPEARANCE OPTIONS: Preferred Equip Pkgs (Topaz GS 361A): Incl Comfort Convenience Grp, Tilt Strg Whl, Electric Rr Window Defroster and Man Air Cond ($485). (Topaz GS four-door 362A) Auto Trans, Comfort Convenience Grp, Electric Rr Window Defroster, Man Air Cond, Elect AM/FM Stereo Cass w/Integral Clock and Driver's Side Air Bag ($1228). (Topaz GS 363A): same as 361A plus Auto Trans ($848). (Topaz GS four-door 364A): same as 363A plus Pwr Side Windows, Spd Ctrl and Polycast Whls ($1216). (Topaz GS four-door 368B): Auto Trans, Comfort Convenience Grp, Tilt Strg Whl, Decklid Luggage Rack, Rr Window Defroster, Man Air Cond and Tu-Tone Paint ($957). (Topaz LS 365A): Man Trans, Conventional Axle and P195/70R14 BSW Tires (NC). Topaz XR5 371A): Incl 6-Way Pwr Driver's Seat, Spd Ctrl, Pwr Lock Grp and Premium Sound Syst ($533). Calif. Emission Syst ($100). Man Air Cond ($817). Comfort Convenience Grp Incl Frt Center Armrest, Elect Decklid & Fuel Filler Dr Releases and Light Grp ($173). Elect Rr Window Defroster ($160). 4WD (four-door only): GS ($1490); LS ($1478); LTS ($1380). Pwr Lock Grp Incl Pwr Dr Locks w/Switch Located on Dr Trim Panel, Elect Decklid & Fuel Filler Dr Release w/Switches Located in Glove Box: GS two-door ($276); XR5 ($195); GS four-door ($318). Luggage Rack, Decklid ($115). Clearcoat Paint ($91). Tu-Tone Paint ($159). AM/FM Stereo Radio w/Cass (GS only) ($155). Premium Sound System ($138). 6-Way Pwr Driver's Seat ($290). Spd Ctrl ($210). Tilt Strg Whl ($135). Driver's Side Airbag: GS ($815); LS or LTS ($622). Polycast Whls ($193). Pwr Side Windows (four-door only) ($315). Eng Block Heater ($20). TIRES: P185/70R14 WSW ($82).

SABLE CONVENIENCE/APPEARANCE OPTIONS: Preferred Equip Pkgs (Sable GS 450A): Incl Pwr Side Windows, Spd Ctrl, Elect Rr Window Defroster and Pwr Lock Grp ($802). (Sable GS 451A): same as 450A plus Carpeted Flr Mats F&R, 6-Way Pwr Driver's Seat, Elect AM/FM Stereo Radio w/Cass, P205/65R15 BSW Tires, Alum Whls and Light Grp ($1138). (Sable LS 461A): Carpeted Flr Mats F&R, 6-Way Pwr Driver's Seat, Leather-Wrapped Strg Whl, Spd Ctrl, Elect Rr Window Defroster, Elect AM/FM Stereo Radio w/Cass, P205/65R15 BSW Tires, Alum Whls, Pwr Lock Grp, Premium Sound Syst, Pwr Radio Antenna, Bodyside Accent Stripes and 3.8-liter EFI V-6 ($1502). (Sable LS 462A): same as 461A plus Keyless Entry Syst, Elect Instrument Cluster, Autolamp On/Off Delay Syst, Auto Air Cond and High Level Elect AM/FM Stereo Radio w/Cass Audio System ($2294). Calif. Emission Syst ($100). Auto Air Cond ($183). Anti-Lock Brake Syst ($985). Autolamp On/Off Delay System ($73). HD Battery (3.0-liter Eng only) ($27). Cargo Area Cover ($66). Elect Rr Window Defroster ($160). Carpeted Flr Mats F&R ($43). Fuel Tank, Extd Range ($46). Elect Instrument Cluster (Incl Extd Range Fuel Tank) ($351). Keyless Entry System (Incl Illum Entry Syst) ($218). Light Grp (GS): Incl Eng Comp Light, Dual Beam Dome Lamp, Instrument Panel Courtesy Light and Headlamp-on Reminder Chime ($59). Pwr Lock Grp Incl Pwr Dr Locks, Remote Decklid Release, Remote Fuel Filler Dr, Remote Liftgate Release (sta wag only): GS sed ($317); GS sta wag ($267); LS sed & sta wag ($226). Lux Trip Opt Incl Lux Cloth & Leather Seat & Dr Trim, 18 oz Carpet & Flr Mats, Unique Ext Paint Scheme, Unique Alum Whls and Tu-tone Paint (LS sed only) ($600). Monochrome Paint (LS sed only) ($539). Lux Touring Pkg Incl Anti-Lock Brakes, Pwr Moonroof and Leather Individual Seats (LS sed only) ($2050). Dual Illum Visor Mirrors ($100). Pwr Moonroof ($776). Clearcoat Paint ($188). Picnic Tray Load Flr Ext ($90). AM/FM Stereo Radio w/Cass ($155). High-level Audio Syst ($490). Digital CD (w/High-Level Audio Syst only) ($491). JBL Sound Syst (sed only) ($526). Premium Sound Syst ($168). Pwr Antenna ($82).

Rr Facing Third Seat (NA w/Conventional Spare Tire) ($155). 6-Way Pwr Driver's Seat ($290). 6-Way Dual Pwr Seats ($580). Leather Twin Comfort Seat Trim (LS only) ($489). Leather Individual Seat Trim (LS only) ($489). Vinyl Seat Trim (GS sta wag only) ($37). Spd Ctrl (w/Leather-Wrapped Strg Whl only) ($210). Variable Assist Pwr Strg ($104). Leather-Wrapped Strg Whl ($63). Bodyside Accent Stripes ($61). HD Suspension ($26). Rr Window Washer/Wiper ($126). Alum Whls ($224). Polycast Whls ($138). Pwr Side Windows ($315). Insta-Clear Windshield ($305). Eng Block Heater ($20). TIRES: P205/70R14 WSW ($82); P205/65R15 BSW ($65); P205/65R15 WSW ($146). Dlx Whl Covers ($82). Conventional Spare Tire ($73).

COUGAR CONVENIENCE/APPEARANCE OPTIONS: Preferred Equip Pkgs (Cougar LS 261A): Incl Tilt Strg Whl, Spd Ctrl, Electric Rr Window Defroster and Styled Spt Whl Covers ($460). (Cougar LS 262A): same as 261A exc Styled Spt Whl Covers plus Frt Carpeted Flr Mats, 6-Way Pwr Driver's Seat, Lux Trim Opt, Illum Entry Syst, Leather-Wrapped Strg Whl, Elect AM/FM Stereo Radio w/Cass, Cast Alum Whls, P215/70R14 BSW Tires, Dual Illum Visor Mirrors, Pwr Lock Grp and Light Grp ($1673). (Cougar LS 263A) same as 262A exc 6-Way Pwr Driver's Seat, Illum Entry Syst, Elect AM/FM Stereo Radio w/Cass plus Keyless Entry Syst, Diagnostic Maintenance Monitor, 6-Way Dual Pwr Seats, High Level Elect AM/FM Stereo Radio w/Cass, Lux Lamp Grp and Pwr Antenna ($2772). (Cougar XR7 265A): Incl 6-Way Pwr Driver's Seat, Tilt Strg Whl, Spd Ctrl, Elect Rr Window Defroster, Elect AM/FM Stereo Radio w/Cass and Pwr Lock Grp (NC). (Cougar XR7 266A): same as 265A exc Elect AM/FM Stereo Radio w/Cass plus Frt Carpeted Flr Mats, Keyless Entry System, Diagnostic Maintenance Monitor, High Level Elect AM/FM Stereo Radio w/Cass, Lux Lamp Grp, Dual Illum Visor Mirrors, Pwr Antenna and Light Grp ($1124). Calif. Emission Syst ($100). Traction-Lock Axle ($100). Anti-Lock Brake Syst ($985). Anti-Theft Alarm Syst ($245). Cold Weather Grp Incl Elect Rr Window Defroster, Eng Block Heater and HD Battery: LS ($205). XR7 ($178). Frt Cornering Lamps ($68). Rr Window Defroster ($160). Diagnostic Maintenance Monitor ($89). Frt Carpeted Flr Mats ($33). Headlamp Convenience Grp ($176). Illum Entry Syst ($82). Elect Instrument Cluster ($270). Keyless Entry Syst ($219). Lux Lamp Grp Incl Headlamp Convenience Grp & Auto Day/Night Rr View Mirror (deleted when Pwr Moonroof is ordered) and Frt Cornering Lamps ($244). Light Grp Incl Comp Light, Dual Beam Dome/Map Light and Instrument Panel Courtesy Lights ($46). Pwr Lock Grp Incl Pwr Dr Locks, Pwr Decklid Release and Remote Fuel Filler Dr ($276). Lux Trip Opt Incl Spt Analog Cluster w/Tach, 24 oz Carpeting in lieu of 16 oz, Lux Cloth & Leather Seat Trim and Woodgrain Instrument Panel Appliqué ($674). Dual Illum Visor Mirrors ($100). Pwr Moonroof Incl Dual Reading Lamps, Pop-up Air Deflector and Sliding Sunshade ($776). Elect AM/FM Stereo Radio w/Cass & Clock ($155). High-level AM/FM Stereo Radio w/Cass & Clock ($460). JBL Sound Syst ($526). Compact Disc Player ($491). Pwr Antenna ($82). 6-Way Pwr Driver's Seat ($290). Dual 6-Way Pwr Seats in Pkgs w/6-Way Pwr Driver's Seat ($290); Dual 6-Way Pwr Seats ($580). Split Fold-down Rr Seat ($133). Leather Seat Trim: LS ($489); XR7 ($489). Spd Ctrl ($210). Leather-Wrapped Strg Whl ($63). Elect Auto Temp Ctrl ($162). Tilt Strg Whl ($135). Styled Spt Whl Covers ($85). Locking Radial Spoke Whl Covers ($228). (NC). 15-inch Cast Alum Whls (LS only) ($299). TIRES: P205/70R15 WSW (LS only) ($73). Conventional Spare Tire (LS only) ($73).

GRAND MARQUIS CONVENIENCE/APPEARANCE OPTIONS: refer to 1990 Grand Marquis options list (1992 Grand Marquis introduced in spring of 1991—see 1992 Grand Marquis options list for that model).

HISTORY: U.S. model year Mercury production totaled 340,574. U.S. calendar year Mercury production totaled 211,404 for 3.9 percent of industry market share.

1992 Mercury Grand Marquis four-door sedan. (OCW)

The full-size station wagon was history within the Mercury division as the Colony Park wagon offered previously was discontinued for 1992. This was the only significant lineup change for Mercury in that year. To observe Cougar's 25th Anniversary, a special LS coupe with a 5.0-liter V-8 was offered. The Grand Marquis, now trimmed to two four-door sedan models, was all-new (introduced early in 1991 as a 1992 model), and featured an all-new 4.6-liter V-8 for power. The Topaz received a face lift as well as a new 3.0-liter V-6 as the standard engine for LTS and XR5 models.

TOPAZ — FOUR/V-6 — The Topaz lineup remained unchanged from the year previous with two-door coupes offered in GS and XR5 series and four-door sedans available in GS, LS and LTS series. The 1992 Topaz received a moderate redesign externally. Under the hood, a new 3.0-liter V-6 was the standard powerplant in the LTS and XR5 models. This was also the option engine for GS and LS models. The 2.3-liter four-cylinder engine that was standard in those two series received sequential fuel injection as an upgrade. The five-speed manual transaxle was again the base unit for Topaz with the three-speed automatic optional equipment.

1992 Mercury Topaz LS sedan. (OCW)

1992 Mercury Topaz LTS sedan. (OCW)

1992 Mercury Topaz XR5 coupe. (OCW)

1992 Mercury Sable GS sedan. (OCW)

1992 Mercury Sable LS sedan. (OCW)

1992 Mercury Sable LS station wagon. (OCW)

SABLE — V-6 — The Sable was slightly revised from the year previous including the addition of composite headlamps that had a longer, narrower appearance. Inside, upholstery was new and amber-colored switch illumination was added to the instrument panel. New optional equipment included a passenger side airbag. Four-door sedans and station wagons in either GS or LS trim again comprised the lineup. The 135-hp 3.0-liter V-6 mated to a four-speed automatic overdrive transaxle was standard equipment while the 140-hp 3.8-liter V-6 was again optional.

1992 Mercury Cougar LS coupe. (OCW)

1992 Mercury Cougar XR7 coupe. (OCW)

COUGAR –V-6/V-8 — Cougar marked its 25th Anniversary in 1992 and this special occasion was observed with a limited-edition LS coupe equipped with the High Output 5.0-liter V-8, monochromatic paint, BBS alloy wheels and special trim. Cougar was also again offered as an XR7 coupe. The non-anniversary LS model was powered by the 3.8-liter V-6 while the XR7 again used the High Output 5.0-liter V-8, which was optional in the LS coupe. The four-speed automatic overdrive transmission was again the only transmission offered.

GRAND MARQUIS — V-8 — The all-new-design 1992 Grand Marquis was offered as a four-door sedan in either GS or LS trim. Launched in the spring of 1991, the new Grand Marquis lineup no longer offered a station wagon with the discontinuation of the Colony Park. The new Grand Marquis was sleeker than its predecessor with a Cd (coefficient of drag) of 0.36 compared to the former model's 0.45. Enhanced aerodynamics both improved fuel economy and reduced wind noise. An all-new 4.6-liter V-8 coupled to a four-speed automatic overdrive transmission was the standard drivetrain. The new V-8 featured overhead chain cam drive, aluminum cylinder heads and sequential fuel injection. Horsepower was increased by 40 over the previous model's engine. Equipped with optional dual exhaust, the 4.6-liter V-8 generated 210 hp at 4600 rpm. Other functional improvements included standard four-wheel disc brakes, speed-sensitive variable-assist power steering, 20-gallon fuel tank, childproof rear door locks, improved front suspension and the addition of a rear stabilizer bar. New optional equipment included an anti-lock brake system with Electronic Traction Assist, rear air spring suspension, passenger's side airbag, JBL Sound System, Keyless Entry System, Electronic Instrument Cluster with Trip Computer, dual power seats and a performance and handling package.

I.D. DATA: Mercury's 17-symbol Vehicle Identification Number (VIN) was stamped on a metal tab fastened to the instrument panel, visible through the windshield. The first three symbols indicate manufacturer, make and vehicle type. The fourth symbol denotes restraint system. Next comes a letter (usually 'M'), followed by two digits that indicate Model Number, as shown in left column of tables below. (Example: '31' Topaz GS two-door sedan). Symbol eight indicates engine type. Next is a check digit. Symbol ten indicates model year ('N' - 1992). Symbol eleven denotes assembly plant. The final six digits make up the sequence number, starting with 000001.

TOPAZ (FOUR/V-6)

Model No.	Body/ Style No.	Body Type & Seating	Factory Price	Shipping Weight	Prod. Total
M	31	2-dr. GS Sed-5P	10512	2544	Note 1
M	36	4-dr. GS Sed-5P	10678	2600	Note 2
M	37	4-dr. LS Sed-5P	12057	2625	Note 2
M	38	4-dr. LTS Sed-5P	14244	2763	Note 2
M	33	2-dr. XR5 Sed-5P	13452	2608	Note 1

NOTE: GS and LS series used four-cylinder power, LTS and XR5 series used V-6 power.

NOTE 1: Production of two-door sedans totaled 18,586 with no further breakout available.

NOTE 2: Production of four-door sedans totaled 58,112 with no further breakout available.

SABLE (V-6)

M	50	4-dr. GS Sed-5P	16418	3147	Note 1
M	55	4-dr. GS Sta Wag-5P	17396	3292	Note 2
M	53	4-dr. LS Sed-5P	17368	3168	Note 1
M	58	4-dr. LS Sta Wag-5P	18395	3331	Note 2

NOTE 1: Production of four-door sedans totaled 96,223 with no further breakout available.

NOTE 2: Production of station wagons totaled 21,975 with no further breakout available.

COUGAR (V-6/V-8)

M	60	2-dr. LS Cpe-4P	16460/17540	3587/3753	Note 1
M	62	2-dr. XR7 Cpe-4P	-----/22054	----/3800	Note 1

NOTE: Figures to left of slash for V-6, to right for V-8.

NOTE 1: Production of two-door coupes totaled 46,982 with no further breakout available.

GRAND MARQUIS (V-8)

M	74	4-dr. GS Sed-6P	20216	3768	Note 1
M	75	4-dr. LS Sed-6P	20644	3780	Note 1

NOTE 1: Production of four-door sedans totaled 146,370 with no further breakout available.

ENGINE [Base Four (Topaz GS and LS)]: Inline. Overhead cam. Four-cylinder. Cast-iron block and aluminum head. Displacement: 141 cid (2.3 liters). Bore & stroke: 3.70 x 3.30 in. Compression ratio: 9.0:1. Brake horsepower: 96 at 4400 rpm. Torque: 128 lbs.-ft. at 2600 rpm. Sequential fuel injection.

ENGINE [Base V-6 (Topaz LTS and XR5); Optional (Topaz GS and LS)]: 60-degree, overhead valve V-6. Cast-iron block and head. Displacement: 182 cid (3.0 liters). Bore & stroke: 3.50 x 3.10 in. Compression ratio: 9.3:1. Brake horsepower: 135 at 5500 rpm. Torque: 150 lbs.-ft. at 3250 rpm. Sequential fuel injection.

ENGINE [Base V-6 (Sable)]: 60-degree, overhead valve V-6. Cast-iron block and head. Displacement: 182 cid (3.0 liters). Bore & stroke: 3.50 x 3.10 in. Compression ratio: 9.3:1. Brake horsepower: 135 at 4800 rpm. Torque: 165 lbs.-ft. at 3000 rpm. Sequential fuel injection.

ENGINE [Base V-6 (Cougar LS); Optional (Sable)]: 60-degree, overhead valve V-6. Cast-iron block and head. Displacement: 232 cid (3.8 liters). Bore & stroke: 3.80 x 3.40 in. Compression ratio: 9.0:1. Brake horsepower: 140 at 3800 rpm. Torque: 215 lbs.-ft. at 2400 rpm. Sequential fuel injection.

ENGINE [Base V-8 (Cougar XR7); Optional (Cougar LS and 25th Anniversary Edition)]: High Output 90-degree, overhead valve V-8. Cast-iron block and head. Displacement: 302 cid (5.0 liters). Bore & stroke: 4.00 x 3.00 in. Compression ratio: 9.0:1. Brake horsepower: 225 at 4200 rpm. Torque: 275 lbs.-ft. at 3000. Sequential fuel injection.

ENGINE [Base V-8 (Grand Marquis)]: 90-degree, overhead cam V-8. Cast-iron block and aluminum head. Displacement: 281 cid (4.6-liter). Bore & stroke: 3.60 x 3.60 in. Compression ratio: 9.0:1. Brake horsepower: 190 at 4200 rpm. Torque: 260 lbs.-ft. at 3200 rpm.

ENGINE [Optional V-8 (Grand Marquis)]: same as 4.6-liter V-8 above except - Brake horsepower: 210 at 4600 rpm. Torque: 270 lbs.-ft. at 3400 rpm. Equipped with dual exhaust.

CHASSIS DATA: Wheelbase: (Topaz) 99.9 in.; (Sable) 106.0 in.; (Cougar) 113.0 in.; (Grand Marquis) 114.4 in. Overall Length: (Topaz two-door) 176.7 in.; (Topaz four-door) 177.0 in.; (Sable sed) 192.2 in.; (Sable sta wag) 193.3 in.; (Cougar) 199.9 in.; (Grand Marquis) 212.4 in. Height: (Topaz two-door) 52.8 in.; (Topaz four-door) 52.9 in.; (Sable sed) 54.4 in.; (Sable sta wag) 55.1 in.; (Cougar) 52.7 in.; (Grand Marquis) 56.9 in. Width: (Topaz) 68.3 in.; (Sable) 71.2 in.; (Cougar) 72.7 in.; (Grand Marquis) 77.8 in. Front Tread: (Topaz) 54.9 in.; (Sable) 61.6 in.; (Cougar) 61.6 in.; (Grand Marquis) 62.8 in. Rear Tread: (Topaz) 57.6 in.; (Sable sed) 60.5 in.; (Sable sta wag) 59.9 in.; (Cougar) 60.2 in.; (Grand Marquis) 63.3 in. Standard Tires: (Topaz) P185/70R14; (Sable) P205/65R15; (Cougar) P205/70R15; (Grand Marquis) P215/70R15.

TECHNICAL: Transmission: Five-speed manual transaxle standard on Topaz. Four-speed automatic overdrive standard on Sable, Cougar and Grand Marquis. Drive Axle: (Cougar/Grand Marquis) rear; (others) front. Steering: (Grand Marquis) recirculating ball; (others) rack/pinion. Front Suspension: (Topaz) Independent MacPherson strut w/coil springs and nitrogen gas-pressurized shocks; (Sable) Independent MacPherson strut w/coil springs and hydraulic/telescoping/double-acting shocks; (Cougar) Long spindle SLA (short and long arm) w/upper 'A' arm, lower arm, tension strut and stabilizer bar; (Grand Marquis) Independent SLA w/ball joints, coil springs and gas-pressurized/hydraulic/telescoping shocks. Rear Suspension: (Topaz) Parallel four-bar fully independent

MacPherson strut w/coil springs and nitrogen gas-pressurized shocks; (Sable sed) Fully independent MacPherson strut w/coil spring on shock strut and hydraulic/telescoping/double-acting shocks; (Sable sta wag) SLA independent w/coil springs and nitrogen gas-pressurized shocks; (Cougar) Independent w/lower 'H' arm, upper arm, stabilizer bar, variable rate coil springs and nitrogen gas-pressurized hydraulic shocks (automatic adjustable on XR7); (Grand Marquis) Four-bar link, coil springs w/rubber insulators and gas-pressurized/hydraulic/telescoping shocks. Brakes: Front disc, rear drum (power assisted) except (Cougar XR7 and Grand Marquis) front/rear disc (XR7 equipped w/anti-lock brake system). Body construction: (Grand Marquis) separate body and frame; (others) unibody. Fuel tank: (Topaz) 15.9 gal.; (Sable) 16.0 gal.; (Cougar) 18.0 gal.; (Grand Marquis) 20.0 gal.

DRIVETRAIN OPTIONS: Engines: 3.0-liter V-6: Topaz GS and LS ($685). 3.8-liter V-6: Sable ($555). High Output 5.0-liter V-8: Cougar LS ($1184). Transmission/Differential: Three-speed automatic transaxle: Tempo ($563). Traction-Lok differential: Cougar LS ($100). Suspension/Brakes: HD Suspension: Sable ($26). Rear Air Suspension: Grand Marquis ($285). Trailer Towing Pkg: Grand Marquis ($490). Anti-lock Brakes: Sable ($595); Cougar LS (w/Traction-Lok Axle) ($695). Grand Marquis (w/Elect Traction Assist) ($695).

TOPAZ CONVENIENCE/APPEARANCE OPTIONS: Preferred Equip Pkgs (Topaz GS Pkg 352A): Auto Trans, Comfort Convenience Grp, Elect Rr Window Defroster and Man Air Cond: two-door ($875); four-door ($915). (Topaz GS 353A): same as 352A plus Pwr Side Windows, Tilt Strg Whl, Spd Ctrl and AM/FM Stereo Radio w/Cass ($1302). (Topaz LS 365A): w/Auto Trans (NC), w/Man Trans (NC). (Topaz XR5 371A): Spd Ctrl, Pwr Lock Grp, Premium Sound Syst ($272). Calif. Emission Syst ($100). Man Air Cond ($817). Comfort Convenience Grp Incl Frt Center Armrest, Elect Decklid & Fuel Filler Dr Releases and Light Grp ($198). Elect Rr Window Defroster ($170). Pwr Lock Grp Incl Pwr Dr Locks w/Switch on Dr Trim Panel, Elect Decklid & Fuel Filler Dr Releases w/Switches in Glovebox: GS two-door w/o Comfort/Convenience Grp ($311); w/Comfort/Convenience Grp ($210); GS four-door w/o Comfort/Convenience Grp ($351); w/Comfort Convenience Grp ($250). Decklid Luggage Rack (GS only) (w/Clearcoat Paint) ($115); w/o Clearcoat Paint (NC). Clearcoat Paint ($91). Tu-Tone Paint ($159). AM/FM Stereo Radio w/Cass ($155). Premium Sound System ($138). 6-Way Pwr Driver's Seat ($305). Spd Ctrl ($224). Tilt Strg Whl ($145). Driver's Side Airbag: GS ($369); LS (NC). Polycast Whls ($193). 14-inch Alum Whls ($278). Pwr Side Windows (four-door only) ($330). Eng Block Heater ($20). TIRES: P185/70R14 WSW ($82); P185/70R14 Perf WSW ($82).

SABLE CONVENIENCE/APPEARANCE OPTIONS: Preferred Equip Pkgs (Sable GS 450B): Pwr Side Windows, Spd Ctrl, Elect Rr Window Defroster, Pwr Lock Grp and Bodyside Accent Stripe ($899). (Sable GS 451B): same as 450B plus F&R Carpeted Flr Mats, 6-Way Pwr Driver's Seat, Elect AM/FM Stereo Radio w/Cass, Alum Whls and Light Grp ($1319). (Sable LS 461B): F&R Carpeted Flr Mats, 6-Way Pwr Driver's Seat, Leather-Wrapped Strg Whl, Spd Ctrl, Elect Rr Window Defroster, Elect AM/FM Stereo Radio w/Cass, Alum Whls, Pwr Lock Grp, Premium Sound Syst, Pwr Radio Antenna, Bodyside Accent Stripes, 3.8-liter V-6 and Ext Range Fuel Tank ($1505). (Sable LS 462B): same as 461B exc Elect AM/FM Stereo Radio w/Cass & Premium Sound Syst plus Keyless Entry Syst, Elect Instrument Cluster, Autolamp On/Off Delay Syst, Auto Air Cond and High Level Elect AM/FM Stereo Radio w/Cass Audio Syst ($2247). Calif. Emission Syst ($100). Conventional Spare ($73). Auto Air Cond ($183). Pass Side Airbag ($488). Anti-Lock Pwr 4-Whl Disc Brakes ($595). Autolamp On/Off Delay Syst Incl Headlights On/Off Feature and Variable Headlight Turn-Off Delay ($73). HD Battery (3.0-liter V-6 only) ($27). Cargo Area Cover ($66). Elect Rr Window Defroster (w/Rr Window Washer/Wiper) ($170). Carpeted Flr Mats F&R ($45). Fuel Tank, Ext Range ($46). Digital Instrument Cluster Incl Elect Tach w/On-Off Switch, Speedometer, Odometer & Trip Odometer, Fuel Computer, Diagnostic Functions and Ext Range Fuel Tank ($351). Keyless Entry System Incl Illum Entry Syst ($228). Light Grp Incl Eng Comp Light, Dual Beam Dome Lamp (exc w/Pwr Moonroof), Instrument Panel Courtesy Light and Headlamp-on Reminder Chime (GS only) ($59). Pwr Lock Grp Incl Pwr Dr Locks, Remote Decklid Release (sed), Remote Fuel Filler Dr and Remote Liftgate Release (sta wag): GS sed and sta wag ($358); LS sed & sta wag (w/Keyless Entry & Pwr Side Windows) ($257). Pwr Moonroof Incl Pop-up Air Deflector, Dual Outboard/Dome Lights, Sliding Sunshade (LS only) ($776). Picnic Tray Load Flr Ext ($90). Safety Plus Opt Grp Incl Anti-lock Brakes w/Traction Assist, Pass Side Airbag ($1083). Rr Facing Third Seat Incl D-Pillar Assist Handle, Vinyl Trim and Seatbelts w/Retractors (sta wag only) ($155). 6-Way Pwr Driver's Seat ($305). 6-Way Dual Pwr Seats ($610). UPHOLSTERY: Leather Twin Comfort ($515); Leather Individual ($515); Vinyl ($37). Spd Ctrl (w/Leather-Wrapped Strg Whl) ($224). Leather-Wrapped Strg Whl ($96). HD Suspension Incl HD Frt Stabilizer Bar, Heavier Springs, Unique Valving on MacPherson Struts ($26). Rr Window Washer/Wiper ($135). Alum Whls ($270). Pwr Side Windows ($356). AM/FM Stereo Radio w/Cass ($171). High-level Audio System ($502); GS ($332); LS ($163). Digital CD (w/High-Level Audio System) ($491). JBL Sound Syst (w/High Level Audio or CD Available) (sed only) ($526). Premium Sound Syst ($168). Pwr Antenna ($102). Eng Block Heater ($20).

1992 Mercury Grand Marquis LS sedan. (OCW)

COUGAR CONVENIENCE/APPEARANCE OPTIONS: Preferred Equip Pkgs (Cougar LS 260B): P215/70R15 BSW Tires, 6-Way Pwr Driver's Seat, Tilt Strg Whl, Spd Ctrl, Electric Rr Window Defroster, Elect AM/FM Stereo Radio w/Cass, Cast Alum Whls, Pwr Lock Grp and Light Grp ($1345). (Cougar LS 262A): same as 260A plus Frt Carpet Flr Mats, Lux Trim Opt, Illum Entry Syst and Leather-Wrapped Strg Whl ($1947). (Cougar LS 263A): same as 262A exc 6-Way Pwr Driver's Seat, Elect AM/FM Stereo Radio w/Cass plus Keyless Entry Syst, Diagnostic Maintenance Monitor, 6-Way Dual Pwr Seats, High-Level Elect AM/FM Stereo Radio w/Cass, Lux Lamp Grp and Pwr Antenna ($2953). (Cougar XR7 265A): 6-Way Pwr Driver's Seat, Tilt Strg Whl, Spd Ctrl, Electric Rr Window Defroster, Elect AM/FM Stereo Radio w/Cass and Pwr Lock Grp (NC). (Cougar XR7 266A): same as 265A exc AM/FM Stereo Radio w/Cass plus Frt Carpeted Flr Mats, Keyless Entry Syst, Diagnostic Maintenance Monitor, High-Level Elect AM/FM Stereo Radio w/Cass, Lux Lamp Grp, Pwr Antenna and Light Grp ($1237). Calif. Emission Syst ($100). Traction-Lok Axle ($100). Anti-Lock Brake Syst (w/Traction-Lok Axle) ($695). Anti-Theft Alarm Syst ($245). Cold Weather Grp Incl Elect Rr Window Defroster, Eng Block Heater, HD Battery: LS ($215); XR7 ($188). Rr Window Defroster ($170). Diagnostic Warning Lights Incl for Low Fuel, Oil Coolant & Washer Fluid, Adaptive Oil Change Indicator ($89). Carpeted Frt Flr Mats ($33). Headlamp Convenience Grp ($176). Illum Entry Syst ($82). Keyless Entry Syst: LS ($228); XR7 ($146). Elect Instrument Cluster ($270). Lux Lamp Grp Incl Headlamp Convenience Grp & Auto Day/Night Rr View Mirror (deleted when Pwr Moonroof ordered) and Frt Cornering Lamps ($261). Light Grp Incl Underhood Light, Instrument Panel Courtesy Lights and Dual Illum Visor Vanity Mirrors ($146). Pwr Lock Grp Incl Pwr Dr Locks, Pwr Decklid Release and Remote Fuel Filler Dr Release ($311). Lux Trip Opt Incl Spt Analog Cluster w/Tach, 24 oz Carpeting in lieu of 16 oz and Lux Cloth & Leather Seat Trim ($674). Pwr Moonroof Incl Dual Reading Lamps, Pop-up Air Deflector, Sliding Sunshade (w/Light Grp) ($776). Elect AM/FM Stereo Radio w/Cass ($155). High-level AM/FM Stereo Radio w/Cass & Clock ($460). JBL Sound Syst ($526). Compact Disc Player ($491). Pwr Antenna ($85). 6-Way Pwr Driver's Seat ($305). Dual 6-Way Pwr Seats (w/6-Way Pwr Driver's Seat pkg) ($305); w/o 6-Way Pwr Driver's Seat pkg ($610). Split Fold-down Rr Seat ($133). Leather Seat Trim ($515). Spd Ctrl ($224). Leather-Wrapped Strg Whl ($96). Auto Air Cond ($162). Tilt Strg Whl ($145). Styled Spt Whl Covers ($85). 15-inch Cast Alum Whls Incl P215/70R15 BSW Tires (LS only) ($306).

GRAND MARQUIS CONVENIENCE/APPEARANCE OPTIONS: Preferred Equip Pkgs (Grand Marquis GS 156A): Incl P215/70R15 All Season WSW Tires, Carpeted Flr Mats F&R, 6-way Pwr Driver's Seat, Illum Entry Syst, Spd Ctrl, Elect Rr Window Defroster, Pwr Lock Grp, Lux Light Grp and Bodyside Paint Stripe ($1159). (Grand Marquis GS 157A): same as 156A plus Elect AM/FM Stereo Radio w/Cass and Lckg Radial Spoked Whl Covers ($1425). (Grand Marquis LS 172A): same as 156A plus Lic Plate Frame, Frt Corning Lamps, Leather-Wrapped Strg Whl, Cast Alum Whls and Pwr Antenna ($1662). Calif. Emission Syst ($100). Anti-Lock Brakes w/Elect Traction Assist ($695). HD Battery, 72-Amp ($27). Elect Rr Window Defroster ($170). Elect Grp Incl Auto Air Cond w/OS Temp Readout, Elect Digital Instrumentation and Tripminder Computer (w/Elect Rr Window Defroster) ($516). Cornering Lamps ($68). Color-Keyed Carpeted Flr Mats F&R ($46). Lic Plate Frames ($9). Eng Block Heater ($26). Illum Entry Syst ($82). Keyless Entry Syst

($146). Lux Light Grp Incl Dual Illum Visor Mirrors, Dual Beam Dome/Map Lights, Eng Comp Light and Rr Seat Reading Lamps ($179). Pwr Lock Grp Incl Pwr Dr Locks and Pwr Decklid Release ($310). Bodyside Paint Stripe ($61). Pass Side Airbag ($488). 41G Perf & Handling Pkg Incl 3.27 Axle, Anti-lock Braking Syst w/Traction Assist, Upsized F&R Stabilizer Bars, P225/70HR15 BSW Tires, Rr Air Suspension w/Unique Springs, Unique Tuned Suspension Shocks, Springs Rates, Unique Strg Gear, Cast Alum Whls and Dual Exhaust ($1612). Safety Plus Opt Grp Incl Anti-Lock Brakes w/Traction Assist, Pass Side Airbag ($1183). Elect AM/FM Stereo Radio w/Cass ($155). High Level Elect AM/FM Stereo Radio w/Cass Audio Syst Incl Premium Elect AM/FM Stereo Radio w/Cass, Radio/Tape Scan, AM Stereo, Pop-out Tuning Ctrls, Unique 4-Channel Premium Amplifier w/80 Total Watts RMS, 6 Upgraded Spkrs ($490). JBL Sound Syst ($562). Pwr Antenna ($85). Leather Trim Opt ($555). 6-Way Pwr Driver's Seat ($305). 6-Way Pwr Driver & Pass Seats w/Pwr Lumbar Support & Pwr Recline ($809). Spd Ctrl ($224). Leather-Wrapped Strg Whl ($96). Rr Air Suspension ($285). Trailer Tow III Pkg (5,000-lb. Cap) Incl Rr Air Spring Suspension, HD Battery, HD Cooling, Dual Exhaust, Trailer Wiring Harness, Pwr Strg Oil Cooler, Trans Oil Cooler, HD Flashers, Conventional Spare Tire, HD U-joints and 3.55 Traction-Lok Axle ($490). Lckg Radial Spoked Whl Covers ($311). Cast Alum Whls Incl Anti-Theft Lckg Lug Nuts ($440). Vinyl Roof ($1185). Insta-Clear Windshield Incl 84-Amp HD Battery ($305). TIRES: P215/70R15 All-Season WSW Radials ($82). Conventional Spare Tire ($85).

HISTORY: U.S. model year Mercury production totaled 388,248. U.S. calendar year Mercury production totaled 242,534 for 4.3 percent of industry market share.

1993 MERCURY

1993 Mercury Topaz GS sedan. (OCW)

The Mercury lineup was trimmed for 1993 with the Topaz series offering just two models and the newly renamed Cougar XR7 series offering a single coupe. Launched in 1967, the quarter-century-old Cougar series name was no longer used, as Mercury now referred to its one-model 1993 series as the Cougar XR7 (as it also did in 1974-76 and 1980). The realigned Topaz series was thinned to just a GS series comprised of a two-door sedan and four-door sedan. On the Sable and Grand Marquis, a passenger's side airbag was made standard equipment.

TOPAZ — FOUR/V-6 — The LS, LTS and XR5 models offered previously were discontinued for 1993. The revised Topaz lineup consisted of a two-door sedan and four-door sedan in the GS series. Standard equipment on the front-drive, five-passenger Topaz GS included an electronic AM/FM stereo radio with clock, fully independent suspension, power rack-and-pinion steering and a five-speed manual transaxle. Optional was a driver's side airbag, premium sound system, six-way power driver's seat, air conditioning and rear window defroster. The 2.3-liter four-cylinder engine remained as the base powerplant while the 3.0-liter V-6 was the option engine. The three-speed automatic transaxle again was optional.

1993 Mercury Sable GS sedan. (OCW)

SABLE — V-6 — Sable again offered four-door sedan and station wagon models in either GS or LS trim. New standard features for 1993 included both driver's- and passenger's-side airbags, integrated console and floor shift with individual front seats, new seat fabrics, dual illuminated mirrors and a new clock. Options included anti-lock brakes, JBL Audio System, compact disc player, fingertip speed control, automatic air conditioning system, power moonroof, six-way dual power seats and keyless entry system. Standard engine in the Sable was the 3.0-liter V-6 with electronic fuel injection. The 3.8-liter V-6 was the option engine. All Sables used the electronic four-speed automatic overdrive transaxle.

COUGAR XR7 –V-6/V-8 — A revised series name and just one model offered were the sweeping changes to Mercury's long-running Cougar (now XR7) series for 1993. The LS coupe previously offered was discontinued with the XR7 coupe now the only choice for buyers. Standard features new to the XR7 included a sport instrument cluster, leather-wrapped shift knob, color-keyed steering wheel and column, new wheel covers and color-keyed roof moldings. Optional equipment included anti-lock brakes (which, oddly, were previously standard on the XR7), JBL Audio System, compact disc player, electric rear window defroster, tilt steering wheel, power door locks, six-way dual power seats, speed control, electronic temperature control and remote keyless entry system. The base drivetrain on the XR7 was the 3.8-liter V-6 teamed with the four-speed automatic overdrive transmission. Performance enthusiasts could order the optional High Output 5.0-liter V-8 that generated 200 hp.

GRAND MARQUIS — V-8 — The Grand Marquis four-door sedan again was available in either GS or LS versions. New standard features for 1993 included both driver's- and passenger's-side airbags, one-touch express-down driver's power window, a new clock, color-keyed bodyside moldings and bumper strips and several new electronic stereo radios with larger display and controls. Options included an electronic instrument cluster, electric rear window defroster, keyless entry system, six-way dual power seats and aluminum wheels. The Grand Marquis again featured power four-wheel disc brakes that were introduced on the previous year's model. An anti-lock brake system with traction assist was again offered as optional equipment. The 4.6-liter V-8 engine coupled to an electronically controlled four-speed automatic overdrive transmission remained as the standard powertrain.

I.D. DATA: Mercury's 17-symbol Vehicle Identification Number (VIN) was stamped on a metal tab fastened to the instrument panel, visible through the windshield. The first three symbols indicate manufacturer, make and vehicle type. The fourth symbol denotes restraint system. Next comes a letter (usually 'M'), followed by two digits that indicate Model Number, as shown in left column of tables below. (Example: '31' Topaz two-door sedan.) Symbol eight indicates engine type. Next is a check digit. Symbol ten indicates model year ('P' - 1993). Symbol eleven denotes assembly plant. The final six digits make up the sequence number, starting with 600001.

TOPAZ (FOUR/V-6)

Model No.	Body/ Style No.	Body Type & Seating	Factory Price	Shipping Weight	Prod. Total
M	31	2-dr. GS Sed-5P	10809/11494	2546/NA	16,989
M	36	4-dr. GS Sed-5P	10976/11661	2602/NA	58,594

NOTE: Figure to left of slash for four-cylinder, to right for V-6.

SABLE (V-6)

Model No.	Body/ Style No.	Body Type & Seating	Factory Price	Shipping Weight	Prod. Total
M	50	4-dr. GS Sed-5P	17480	3122	Note 1
M	55	4-dr. GS Sta Wag-5P	18459	3271	Note 2
M	53	4-dr. LS Sed-5P	18430	3165	Note 1
M	58	4-dr. LS Sta Wag-5P	19457	3314	Note 2

NOTE 1: Production of four-door sedans totaled 106,585 with no further breakout available.

NOTE 2: Production of station wagons totaled 20,677 with no further breakout available.

COUGAR XR7 (V-6/V-8)

Model No.	Body/ Style No.	Body Type & Seating	Factory Price	Shipping Weight	Prod. Total
M	62	2-dr. XR7 Cpe-4P	14855/16045	3548/3701	79,700

NOTE: Figures to left of slash for V-6, to right for V-8.

GRAND MARQUIS (V-8)

Model No.	Body/ Style No.	Body Type & Seating	Factory Price	Shipping Weight	Prod. Total
M	74	4-dr. GS Sed-6P	22082	3784	Note 1
M	75	4-dr. LS Sed-6P	22609	3796	Note 1

NOTE 1: Production of four-door sedans totaled 82,976 with no further breakout available.

1993 Mercury Cougar XR7 coupe. (OCW)

ENGINE [Base Four (Topaz)]: Inline. Overhead valve. Four-cylinder. Cast-iron block and aluminum head. Displacement: 141 cid (2.3 liters). Bore & stroke: 3.70 x 3.30 in. Compression ratio: 9.0:1. Brake horsepower: 96 at 4200 rpm. Torque: 126 lbs.-ft. at 2600 rpm. Sequential fuel injection.

ENGINE [Base V-6 (Sable); Optional (Topaz)]: 60-degree, overhead valve V-6. Cast-iron block and head. Displacement: 182 cid (3.0 liters). Bore & stroke: 3.50 x 3.10 in. Compression ratio: 9.3:1. Brake horsepower: 135 at 4800 rpm. Torque: (Sable sed) 165 lbs.-ft. at 3250 RPM; (Sable sta wag) 165 lbs.-ft. at 3000 rpm. Sequential fuel injection.

ENGINE [Base V-6 (Cougar XR7); Optional (Sable)]: 60-degree, overhead valve V-6. Cast-iron block and head. Displacement: 232 cid (3.8 liters). Bore & stroke: 3.80 x 3.40 in. Compression ratio: 9.0:1. Brake horsepower: 140 at 3800 rpm. Torque: 215 lbs.-ft. at 2400 rpm. Sequential fuel injection.

ENGINE [Base V-8 (Cougar XR-7)]: High Output 90-degree, overhead valve V-8. Cast-iron block and aluminum head. Displacement: 302 cid (5.0 liters). Bore & stroke: 4.00 x 3.00 in. Compression ratio: 9.0:1. Brake horsepower: 200 at 4000 rpm. Torque: 275 lbs.-ft. at 3000 rpm. Sequential fuel injection.

ENGINE [Base V-8 (Grand Marquis)]: 90-degree, overhead cam V-8. Displacement: 281 cid (4.6-liter). Bore & stroke: 3.60 x 3.60 in. Compression ratio: 9.0:1. Brake horsepower: 190 at 4200 rpm. Torque: 260 lbs.-ft. at 3200 rpm. Sequential fuel injection.

ENGINE [Optional V-8 (Grand Marquis)]: same as 4.6-liter V-8 above except - Brake horsepower: 210 at 4600 rpm. Torque: 270 lbs.-ft. at 3400 rpm. Equipped w/dual exhaust.

CHASSIS DATA: Wheelbase: (Topaz) 99.9 in.; (Sable) 106.0 in.; (Cougar) 113.0 in.; (Grand Marquis) 114.4 in. Overall Length: (Topaz two-door) 176.7 in.; (Topaz four-door) 177.0 in.; (Sable sed) 192.2 in.; (Sable sta wag) 193.3 in.; (Cougar) 199.9 in.; (Grand Marquis) 212.4 in. Height: (Topaz two-door) 52.8 in.; (Topaz four-door) 52.9 in.; (Sable sed) 54.4 in.; (Sable sta wag) 61.6 in.; (Cougar) 52.5 in.; (Grand Marquis) 56.8 in. Width: (Topaz) 68.3 in.; (Sable) 71.2 in.; (Cougar) 72.7 in.; (Grand Marquis) 77.8 in. Front Tread: (Topaz) 54.9 in.; (Sable) 61.6 in.; (Cougar) 61.6 in.; (Grand Marquis) 62.8 in. Rear Tread: (Topaz) 57.6 in.; (Sable sed) 60.5 in.; (Sable sta wag) 59.9 in.; (Cougar) 60.2 in.; (Grand Marquis) 63.3 in. Standard Tires: (Topaz) P185/70R14; (Sable) P205/65R15; (Cougar) P205/70R15; (Grand Marquis) P215/70R15.

TECHNICAL: Transmission: Five-speed manual transaxle standard on Topaz. Four-speed automatic overdrive standard on Sable, Cougar and Grand Marquis. Drive Axle: (Cougar/Grand Marquis) rear; (others) front. Steering: (Grand Marquis) recirculating ball; (others) rack/pinion. Front Suspension: (Topaz) Independent MacPherson strut w/strut-mounted coil spring, forged lower control arm and cast steering knuckle; (Sable) Independent MacPherson strut w/strut-mounted coil spring, stabilizer bar, tension strut, lower control arm and cast steering knuckle; (Cougar) Short/long arm (SLA) w/double isolated tension strut, variable rate coil spring and stabilizer bar; (Grand Marquis) Independent SLA w/ball joints and coil springs and stabilizer bar. Rear Suspension: (Topaz) Parallel four-bar, fully independent MacPherson strut w/coil springs offset on shock strut; parallel suspension arms and tension strut; (Sable sed) Independent MacPherson strut w/coil spring on shock strut, stabilizer bar, tension strut, parallel control arms and two-piece cast forged spindle; (Sable sta wag) SLA independent w/variable rate spring on lower control arm, stabilizer bar, stamped tension strut with two-piece cast spindle w/forged stem; (Cougar) H-arm independent, variable rate coil springs and stabilizer bar; (Grand Marquis) Four-bar link w/rubber insulated coil spring on axle and stabilizer bar. Brakes: Front disc, rear drum (power assisted) except (Cougar XR7 and Grand Marquis) front/rear disc. Body construction: (Grand Marquis) separate body and frame; (others) unibody. Fuel tank: (Topaz) 15.9 gal.; (Sable) 16.0 gal.; (Cougar) 18.0 gal.; (Grand Marquis) 18.0 gal.

DRIVETRAIN OPTIONS: Engines: 3.0-liter V-6: Topaz ($685). 3.8-liter V-6: Sable ($555). High Output 5.0-liter V-8: Cougar XR7 ($1184). Transmission/Differential: Three-speed automatic transaxle: Topaz ($563). Traction-Lok differential: Cougar XR7 ($100). Suspension/Brakes: HD Suspension: Sable ($26). Rear Air Suspension: Grand Marquis LS ($285). Anti-lock Brakes: Sable ($595); Cougar XR7 w/Traction-Lok Axle ($565); Grand Marquis w/Traction Assist ($695). Trailer towing pkg: Grand Marquis LS ($585). 41G Perf & Handling Pkg: Grand Marquis LS ($1530).

TOPAZ CONVENIENCE/APPEARANCE OPTIONS: Preferred Equip Pkgs (Topaz 352A): Auto Trans, Comfort Convenience Grp, Elect Rr Window Defroster, Man Air Cond and Pwr Dr Locks ($915). (Topaz 353A): same as 352A plus Pwr Windows, Tilt Strg Whl, Cruise Ctrl and Elect AM/FM Stereo Radio w/Cass & Clock ($1302). (Topaz 354A): Man Air Cond, Comfort Convenience Grp, Elect Rr Window Defroster, Dlx Luggage Rack, AM/FM Stereo Radio w/Cass & Clock, Tilt Strg Whl and 7-Spoke Alum Whls ($867). Calif. Emission Syst ($100). Driver's Side Airbag ($369). Man Air Cond ($817). Comfort Convenience Grp incl Frt Center Armrest, Elect Decklid & Fuel Filler Dr Releases, Light Grp w/Ashtray, Glovebox & Eng Comp Lights, Rr Dr Courtesy Light Switches and Headlights-On Warning Chime ($198). Elect Rr Window Defroster ($170). Pwr Lock Grp incl Pwr Dr Locks w/Switch on Dr Trim Panel, Elect Decklid & Fuel Filler Dr Release w/Switches in Glovebox: GS two-door w/Comfort Convenience Grp ($210); w/o Comfort Convenience Grp ($311); GS four-door w/Comfort Convenience Grp ($250); w/o Comfort Convenience Grp ($351). Dlx Luggage Rack ($115). AM/FM Stereo Radio w/Cass & Clock ($155). Premium Sound Syst ($138). Clearcoat Paint ($91). Tu-Tone Paint ($159). 6-Way Pwr Driver's Seat ($305). Spd Ctrl ($224). Tilt Strg Whl ($145). Polycast Whls ($193). 14-inch Cast Alum Whls ($278). Pwr Side Windows (four-door only) ($330). Eng Block Heater ($20). TIRES: P185/70R14 Perf WSW ($82).

SABLE CONVENIENCE/APPEARANCE OPTIONS: Preferred Equip Pkgs (Sable GS 450A): Pwr Windows, Spd Ctrl, Rr Window Defroster, Pwr Lock Grp and Bodyside Accent Stripe ($899). (Sable GS 451A): same as 450A plus F&R Carpeted Flr Mats, 6-Way Pwr Driver's Seat, Elect AM/FM Stereo Radio w/Cass, Alum Whls and Light Grp ($1319). (Sable LS 461A): incl 3.8-liter V-6 in Place of 3.0-liter V-6, F&R Carpeted Flr Mats, 6-Way Pwr Driver's Seat, Leather-Wrapped Strg Whl, Spd Ctrl, Rr Window Defroster, AM/FM Stereo Radio w/Cass, Alum Whls, Pwr Lock Grp, Premium Sound Syst, Pwr Antenna and Bodyside Accent Stripes ($1459). (Sable LS 462A): same as 461A plus Keyless Entry Syst, Elect Instrument Cluster, Autolamp On/Off Delay Syst, Auto Air Cond, High Level Elect AM/FM Stereo Radio w/Cass Audio Syst ($2247). Calif. Emission Syst ($100). Conventional Spare Tire ($73). Leather Twin Comfort Seat Trim (LS only) ($515). Leather Individual Seat Trim (LS only) ($515). Auto Air Cond ($183). Anti-Lock Brake Syst ($595). Autolamp On/Off Delay Syst ($73). Body Accent Stripe ($61). HD Battery (3.0-liter V-6 only) ($27). Cargo Area Cover ($66). Elect Rr Window Defroster ($170). Carpeted Flr Mats F&R ($45). Fuel Tank, Ext Range ($46). Elect Instrument Cluster ($305). Remote Keyless Entry Syst incl Illum Entry Syst, Hand-held Transmitter and Dr Mounted Keypad ($247). Light Grp incl Eng Comp Light, Dual Beam Dome Lamp exc w/Pwr Sunroof, Instrument Panel Courtesy Light and Headlamp-on Reminder Chime ($59). Picnic Tray Load Flr Ext (sta wag only) ($90). Pwr Lock Grp: GS sed and sta wag ($359); LS sed and sta wag ($257). Pwr Moonroof ($776). AM/FM Stereo Radio w/Cass ($171). High-level Audio Syst, AM/FM w/Cass ($502). Premium Sound Syst ($168). JBL Sound Syst (NA sta wag) ($526). Digital CD (w/High-Level Audio Syst) ($491). Pwr Antenna ($102). Rr Facing Third Seat (sta wag only) ($155). 6-Way Pwr Driver's Seat ($305). 6-Way Dual Pwr Seats ($610). Spd Ctrl ($224). Leather-Wrapped Strg Whl ($96). HD Suspension incl HD Stabilizer Bar, Heavier Springs & Unique Valving on Struts ($26). Rr Window Washer/Wiper ($135). Alum Whls incl Lckg Lug Nuts ($270). Pwr Side Windows ($356). Eng Block Heater ($20).

COUGAR CONVENIENCE/APPEARANCE OPTIONS: See 1994 Cougar Convenience/Appearance Options list (1994 prices higher than 1993 in some cases).

1993 Mercury Grand Marquis LS sedan. (OCW)

GRAND MARQUIS CONVENIENCE/APPEARANCE OPTIONS: Preferred Equip Pkgs (Grand Marquis GS 157A): Elect Rr Window Defroster, Carpeted Flr Mats F&R, Illum Entry Syst, Pwr Lock Grp, Lux Light Grp, Bodyside Paint Stripe, Spd Ctrl and Spoked Lckg Whl Covers ($902). (Grand Marquis LS 172A): Elect Rr Window Defroster, Carpeted Flr Mats F&R, Illum Entry Syst, Pwr Lock Grp, Lux Light Grp, Bodyside Paint Stripe, Spd Ctrl, Frt Cornering Lamps, Rr Lic Plate Frame, Leather-Wrapped Strg Whl, Cast Alum Whls and Pwr Antenna ($1139). Calif. Emission Syst ($100). Conventional Spare Tire ($180). Leather Twin Comfort Seat Trim (LS only) ($555). Anti-Lock Brakes w/Elect Traction Assist ($695). Frt Cornering Lamps ($68). Elect Rr Window Defroster ($170). Elect Grp incl Elect Cluster, Tripminder Computer, Auto Temp Ctrl Air Cond, 20 gal Fuel Tank and 72 Amp Battery ($543). Carpeted Flr Mats F&R ($46). Formal Coach Vinyl Roof ($1185). Eng Block Heater ($26). Illum Entry Syst ($82). Keyless Entry Syst ($137). Rr Lic Plate Frame ($9). Pwr Lock Grp (w/Pwr Decklid Release) ($310). Light Grp incl Eng Comp Light, Dual Illum Visor Mirrors w/Dual Secondary Sun Visors, Dual Beam Dome/Map Lights and Rr Seat Reading Lamps ($198). Bodyside Paint Stripe ($61). Perf & Handling Pkg incl 3.27 Axle, Anti-lock Braking Syst, Upsized F&R Stabilizer Bars, P225/70HR15 BSW Tires, Cast Alum Whls, Rr Air Suspension and Unique Strg Gear ($1530). Pwr Antenna ($85). High Level Elect AM/FM Stereo Radio w/Cass (LS only) ($332). 6-Way Pwr Driver & Pass Seats w/Pwr Lumbar Support & Pwr Recline (LS only) ($405). Spd Ctrl ($224). Leather-Wrapped Strg Whl ($96). Rr Air Suspension (LS only) ($285). Trailer Tow Pkg Class III HD, incl Rr Air Spring Suspension, HD Battery, Wiring Harness, Trans Oil Cooler, Dual Exhaust, Pwr Strg Oil Cooler, HD Flashers, Conventional Spare Tire, HD U-joints and 3.55 Traction-Lok Axle (LS Only) ($585). Lckg Radial Spoked Whl Covers ($311). Cast Alum Whls ($440).

HISTORY: U.S. model year Mercury production totaled 365,521. U.S. calendar year Mercury production totaled 278,958 for 4.7 percent of industry market share.

1994 MERCURY

1994 Mercury Topaz GS sedan. (OCW)

Mercury returned in 1994 with an identical lineup from the year previous. The biggest news was that the Topaz had a short model year as production ended in the spring of 1994 to make way for its replacement, the 1995 Mercury Mystique. Other major changes included the discontinuation of Cougar XR7's High Output 5.0-liter V-8 option engine. It was replaced with a 4.6-liter V-8. On the safety front, the Grand Marquis sedans received beefed-up front- and rear-door side impact protection while the Cougar XR7 now offered both driver- and passenger-side airbags as well as three-point seatbelts as standard equipment.

TOPAZ — FOUR/V-6 — The Topaz was essentially a carry-over model from the previous year as production was halted in the spring of 1994 after 11 years of production (introduced in the spring of 1983 as a 1984 model). Again offered were a two-door sedan and four-door sedan in the GS series. Base powerplant was again the 2.3-liter four-cylinder engine while the 3.0-liter V-6 was optional. The five-speed manual transaxle was standard while the three-speed automatic transaxle was the option unit.

1994 Mercury Sable GS sedan. (OCW)

SABLE — V-6 — The GS and LS series again comprised the Sable lineup with each offering a four-door sedan and station wagon. New standard equipment included a rear window wiper on station wagon models. The 3.0-liter V-6 was again the standard powerplant with the 3.8-liter V-6 the option engine. The four-speed automatic overdrive transaxle was the only unit offered on Sable models.

COUGAR XR7 — V-6/V-8 — The Cougar XR7 two-door coupe was again the only offering in the Cougar XR7 series. Driver's and passenger's airbags were now standard equipment as three-point-style seatbelts. The XR7's grille and interior were both revised. The High Output 5.0-liter V-8 that was previously offered as the option engine was discontinued for 1994. In its place was the modular 4.6-liter V-8 while the 3.8-liter V-6 continued as the base powerplant. The four-speed automatic overdrive transmission was used on all XR7 coupes.

GRAND MARQUIS — V-8 — All Grand Marquis GS and LS series four-door sedans received improved side impact protection for 1994. The modular 4.6-liter V-8 teamed with the four-speed automatic overdrive transmission was again the standard powertrain.

I.D. DATA: Mercury's 17-symbol Vehicle Identification Number (VIN) was stamped on a metal tab fastened to the instrument panel, visible through the windshield. The first three symbols indicate manufacturer, make and vehicle type. The fourth symbol denotes restraint system. Next comes a letter (usually 'M'), followed by two digits that indicate Model Number, as shown in left column of tables below. (Example: '31' Topaz GS two-door sedan). Symbol eight indicates engine type. Next is a check digit. Symbol ten indicates model year ('R' - 1994). Symbol eleven denotes assembly plant. The final six digits make up the sequence number, starting with 600001.

TOPAZ (FOUR/V-6)

Model No.	Body/ Style No.	Body Type & Seating	Factory Price	Shipping Weight	Prod. Total
M	31	2-dr. GS Sed-5P	10900/11555	2531/NA	9,576
M	36	4-dr. GS Sed-5P	10900/11555	2588/NA	40,822

NOTE: Figures to left of slash for four-cylinder engine, to right for V-6.

SABLE (V-6)

Model No.	Body/ Style No.	Body Type & Seating	Factory Price	Shipping Weight	Prod. Total
M	50	4-dr. GS Sed-5P	17460	3126	Note 1
M	55	4-dr. GS Sta Wag-5P	18570	3275	Note 2
M	53	4-dr. LS Sed-5P	18540	3169	Note 1
M	58	4-dr. LS Sta Wag-5P	19570	3318	Note 2

NOTE 1: Production of four-door sedan models totaled 88,550 with no further breakout available.

NOTE 2: Production of four-door station wagon models totaled 14,416 with no further breakout available.

COUGAR XR7 (V-6/V-8)

Model No.	Body/ Style No.	Body Type & Seating	Factory Price	Shipping Weight	Prod. Total
M	62	2-dr. XR7 Cpe-4P	14855/16045	3564/3726	71,026

NOTE: Figures to left of slash for V-6, to right for V-8.

GRAND MARQUIS (V-8)

Model No.	Body/ Style No.	Body Type & Seating	Factory Price	Shipping Weight	Prod. Total
M	74	4-dr. GS Sed-6P	22130	3787	Note 1
M	75	4-dr. LS Sed-6P	22690	3796	Note 1

NOTE 1: Production of four-door sedan models totaled 95,075 with no further breakout available.

ENGINE [Base Four (Topaz)]: Inline. Overhead valve. Four-cylinder. Cast-iron block and aluminum head. Displacement: 141 cid (2.3 liters). Bore & stroke: 3.70 x 3.30 in. Compression ratio: 9.0:1. Brake horsepower: 96 at 4200 rpm. Torque: 126 lbs.-ft. at 2600 rpm. Sequential fuel injection.

ENGINE [Base V-6 (Sable); Optional (Topaz)]: 60-degree, overhead valve V-6. Cast-iron block and head. Displacement: 182 cid (3.0 liters). Bore & stroke: 3.50 x 3.10 in. Compression ratio: 9.3:1. Brake horsepower: 140 at 4800 rpm. Torque: 165 lbs.-ft. at 3250 rpm. Sequential fuel injection.

ENGINE [Base V-6 (Cougar XR7); Optional (Sable)]: 60-degree, overhead valve V-6. Cast-iron block and head. Displacement: 232 cid (3.8 liters). Bore & stroke: 3.80 x 3.40 in. Compression ratio: 9.0:1. Brake horsepower: 140 at 3800 rpm. Torque: 215 lbs.-ft. at 2400 rpm. Sequential fuel injection.

ENGINE [Base V-8 (Grand Marquis); Optional (Cougar XR7)]: Modular, overhead cam V-8. Displacement: 281 cid (4.6-liter). Bore & stroke: 3.60 x 3.60 in. Compression ratio: 9.0:1. Brake horsepower: (Cougar XR7) 205 at 4500 RPM; (Grand Marquis) 190 at 4600 rpm. Torque: (Cougar XR7) 265 lbs.-ft. at 3200 RPM. (Grand Marquis) 260 lbs.-ft. at 3200 rpm.

1994 Mercury Cougar XR7 coupe. (OCW)

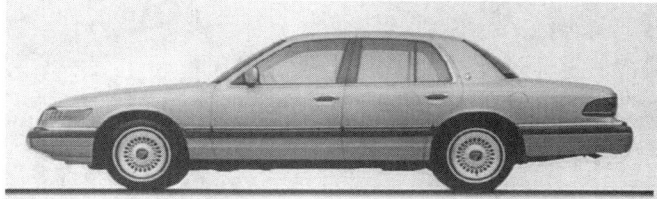

1994 Mercury Grand Marquis GS sedan. (OCW)

CHASSIS DATA: Wheelbase: (Topaz) 99.9 in.; (Sable) 106.0 in.; (Cougar) 113.0 in.; (Grand Marquis) 114.4 in. Overall Length: (Topaz two-door) 176.7 in; (Topaz four-door) 177.0 in.; (Sable sed) 192.2 in.; (Sable sta wag) 193.3 in.; (Cougar) 199.9 in.; (Grand Marquis) 212.4 in. Height: (Topaz two-door) 52.8 in.; (Topaz four-door) 52.9 in.; (Sable sed) 54.1 in.; (Sable sta wag) 55.5 in.; (Cougar) 52.5 in.; (Grand Marquis) 56.8 in. Width: (Topaz) 68.3 in.; (Sable) 70.9 in.; (Cougar) 72.7 in.; (Grand Marquis) 77.8 in. Front Tread: (Topaz) 54.9 in.; (Sable) 61.6 in.; (Cougar) 61.6 in.; (Grand Marquis) 62.8 in. Rear Tread: (Topaz) 57.6 in.; (Sable sed) 60.5 in.; (Sable sta wag) 59.9 in.; (Cougar) 60.2 in.; (Grand Marquis) 63.3 in. Standard Tires: (Topaz) P185/70R14; (Sable) P205/65R15; (Cougar) P205/70R15; (Grand Marquis) P215/70R15.

TECHNICAL: Transmission: Five-speed manual transaxle standard on Topaz. Four-speed automatic overdrive standard on Sable, Cougar XR7 and Grand Marquis. Drive Axle: (Cougar XR7/Grand Marquis) rear; (others) front. Steering: (Grand Marquis) recirculating ball; (others) rack/pinion. Front Suspension: (Topaz) Independent MacPherson strut w/strut-mounted coil spring, forged lower control arm and cast steering knuckle; (Sable) Independent MacPherson strut w/strut-mounted coil spring, stabilizer bar, tension strut, lower control arm and cast steering knuckle; (Cougar) Short/long arm (SLA) w/double isolated tension strut, variable rate coil springs and stabilizer bar; (Grand Marquis) Independent SLA w/ball joints and coil springs and stabilizer bar. Rear Suspension: (Topaz) Parallel four-bar, fully independent MacPherson strut w/coil springs offset on shock strut, parallel suspension arms and tension strut; (Sable sed) Independent MacPherson strut w/coil spring on shock strut, stabilizer bar, tension strut, parallel control arms and two-piece cast forged spindle; (Sable sta wag) SLA independent w/variable rate spring on lower control arm, stabilizer bar, stamped tension strut with two-piece cast spindle w/forged stem; (Cougar) H-arm independent, variable rate coil springs and stabilizer bar; (Grand Marquis) Four-bar link w/rubber-insulated coil spring on axle and stabilizer bar. Brakes: Front disc, rear drum (power assisted) except (Cougar XR7 and Grand Marquis) front/rear disc. Body construction: (Grand Marquis) separate body and frame; (others) unibody. Fuel tank: (Topaz) 15.9 gal.; (Sable) 16.0 gal.; (Cougar) 18.0 gal.; (Grand Marquis) 20.0 gal.

DRIVETRAIN OPTIONS: Engines: 3.0-liter V-6: Topaz ($655). 3.8-liter V-6: Sable ($630). 4.6-liter V-8: Cougar XR7 ($615). Transmission/Differential: Three-speed automatic transaxle: Topaz ($535). Elect Traction Assist: Cougar XR7 ($210). Suspension/Brakes: HD Suspension: Sable ($25). Rear Air Suspension: Grand Marquis LS ($270). Trailer towing pkg: Grand Marquis LS ($785). Anti-lock brakes: Sable ($565); Cougar XR7 ($565); Grand Marquis (w/Elect Traction Assist) ($665). 41G Handling Pkg: Grand Marquis GS ($1485); Grand Marquis LS ($1065).

TOPAZ CONVENIENCE/APPEARANCE OPTIONS: Preferred Equip Pkgs (Topaz GS 352A): Man Air Cond, Comfort Convenience Grp, Elect Rr Window Defroster, Pwr Lock Grp, Auto Trans: two-door ($830); four-door ($870). (Topaz GS 343A): same as 352A plus Cruise Ctrl, Tilt Strg Whl, Pwr Windows, Elect AM/FM Stereo Radio w/Cass ($1245). (Topaz GS 354A): Man Air Cond, Comfort Convenience Grp, Elect Rr Window Defroster, AM/FM Stereo Radio w/Cass, Dlx Luggage Rack, 7-Spoke Alum Whls ($830). Calif. Emission Syst ($95). Driver's Side Airbag ($465). Man Air Cond ($780). Comfort Convenience Grp incl Frt Center Armrest, Elect Decklid & Fuel Filler Dr Releases and Light Grp ($190). Elect Rr Window Defroster ($160). Pwr Lock Grp incl Pwr Dr Locks w/Switch on Dr Trim Panel, Elect Decklid & Fuel Filler Dr Release w/Switches in Glovebox: GS two-door w/Comfort Convenience Grp ($200); w/o Comfort Convenience Grp ($295); GS four-door w/Comfort Convenience Grp ($240); w/o Comfort Convenience Grp ($335). Max Ed Opt Grp (GS four-door only) ($290). AM/FM Stereo Radio w/Cass ($150). Clearcoat Paint ($85). Tu-Tone Paint ($150). 6-Way Pwr Driver's Seat ($290). Spd Ctrl ($215). Tilt Strg Whl ($140). Polycast Whls ($185). 14-inch Cast Alum Whls ($265). Pwr Side Windows (four-door only) ($315). Eng Block Heater ($20). TIRES: P185/70R14 Perf WSW ($80).

SABLE CONVENIENCE/APPEARANCE OPTIONS: Preferred Equip Pkgs (Sable GS 450A): Pwr Windows, Spd Ctrl, Light Grp, F&R Carpeted Flr Mats, Pwr Lock Grp and Bodyside Accent Stripe ($800). (Sable GS 451A): same as 450A plus 6-Way Pwr Driver's Seat, Elect AM/FM Stereo Radio w/Cass and Alum Whls ($1100). (Sable LS 461B): incl 450A plus Leather-Wrapped Strg Whl, High Level Cass, Pwr Antenna and Keyless Entry ($445). (Sable LS 462B): same as 461A plus Elect Instrument Cluster, Autolamp On/Off Delay Syst, Auto Air Cond, Elect Auto Temp Ctrl ($780). Calif. Emission Syst ($95). Conventional Spare Tire ($70). Leather Twin Comfort Seats (LS only) ($495). Leather Individual Seats (LS only) ($495). Auto Air Cond ($175). Anti-Lock Brake Syst ($565). HD Battery ($30). Cargo Area Cover ($65). Cellular Telephone ($500). Fuel Tank, Ext Range ($45). Keyless Entry Syst ($295). Pwr Moonroof ($740). AM/FM Stereo Radio w/Cass ($165). Digital CD ($470). Rr Facing Third Seat (sta wag only) ($150). 6-Way Pwr Driver's Seat ($290). 6-Way Dual Pwr Seats ($580). Leather-Wrapped Strg Whl ($90). HD Suspension ($25). Alum Whls ($255). Eng Block Heater ($20).

COUGAR XR7 CONVENIENCE/APPEARANCE OPTIONS: Preferred Equip Pkgs (Cougar XR7 260A): P215/70R15 BSW Tires, 6-Way Pwr Driver's Seat, Spd Ctrl, Elect Rr Window Defroster, Cast Alum Whls, Pwr Lock Grp, Light Grp w/Dual Illum Visors, Illum Entry, Frt Flr Mats and Leather-Wrapped Strg Whl ($990). Calif. Emission Syst ($95). Elect Auto Temp Ctrl Air Cond ($155). Auto Lamp Grp ($70). Anti-Lock Brake Syst ($565). Keyless Entry Syst ($215). Pwr Moonroof ($740). Dual 6-Way Pwr Seats ($290). Tri-coat Paint ($225). JBL Sound Syst ($500). CD Changer, Trunk Mounted ($785). Elect AM/FM Stereo Radio w/Cass (w/Pwr Antenna) ($370). Cold Weather Grp incl Elect Rr Window Defroster, Eng Block Heater and HD Battery ($140); w/4.6-liter V-8 ($115); w/Traction Assist ($45); w/4.6-liter V-8 and Traction Assist ($20). Cellular Phone ($530).

GRAND MARQUIS CONVENIENCE/APPEARANCE OPTIONS: Preferred Equip Pkgs (Grand Marquis GS 157A): Elect Rr Window Defroster, Carpeted Flr Mats F&R, Pwr Lock Grp and Spd Ctrl ($225). (Grand Marquis LS 172A): incl 157A plus Lux Light Grp, Bodyside Paint Stripe, Illum Entry Syst, Cornering Lamps, Rr Lic Plate Frame, Leather-Wrapped Strg Whl, Cast Alum Whls and Pwr Antenna ($1056). Calif. Emission Syst ($95). Conventional Spare Tire ($185). Leather Twin Comfort Seats (LS only) ($530). Anti-Lock Brakes (w/Elect Traction Assist) ($665). Elect Grp incl Elect Instrument Cluster, Tripminder Computer, Auto Temp Ctrl and 72 Amp Battery ($515). 41G Handling Pkg incl 3.27 Axle, Anti-lock Brakes w/Traction Assist, Upsized F&R Stabilizer Bar, P225/70R15 WSW Tires, Rr Air Suspension w/Unique Springs, Unique Tuned Suspension, Unique Strg Gear, Alum Whls and Dual Exhaust: LS ($1065); GS ($1485). Illum Entry Syst ($80). Keyless Entry Syst ($215). Frt Cornering Lamps ($65). Rr License Plate Frame ($10). Lux Light Grp incl Dual Illum Visor Mirrors, Dual Beam Dome/Map Lights, Eng Comp Light, Rr Seat Reading Lamps and Dual Secondary Sunvisors for Frt/Side Coverage ($190). Bodyside Paint Stripe ($60). 6-Way Pwr Pass Seat w/Pwr Lumbar Support and Pwr Recline (LS only) ($385). Leather-Wrapped Strg Whl ($90). Rr Air Suspension (LS only) ($270). Trailer Tow III Pkg incl 5000 lbs Cap, Rr Air Spring Suspension, 72-Amp HD Battery, Wiring Harness, Trans Oil Cooler, Dual Exhaust, Pwr Strg Oil Cooler, HD Flashers, Conventional Spare Tire, HD U-joints and 3.27 Traction-Lok Axle (LS only) ($785). Formal Coach Vinyl Roof ($1185). Lckg Radial Spoked Whl Covers (GS only) ($295). Cast Alum Whls (LS only) ($420). Premium Elect AM/FM Stereo Radio w/Cass (LS only) ($315). Pwr Antenna ($80). Eng Block Heater ($25).

HISTORY: U.S. model year Mercury production totaled 319,465. U.S. calendar year Mercury production totaled 260,251 for 3.9 percent of industry market share.

1995 MERCURY

After 11 years of production, the Topaz was discontinued in 1995 and replaced by FoMoCo's initial "World Car" called the Mercury Mystique four-door sedan (built on the same platform as the Ford Contour and the European Ford Mondeo). Mystique was assembled in Ford plants

1995 Mercury Mystique LS sedan. (OCW)

in both Kansas City, Missouri, as well as Cuautitlan, Mexico. Also discontinued was the Australian-built Mercury Capri, a foreign-built import not in the scope of this catalog. Sable added an LTS four-door sedan to its lineup, with an all-new design Sable to follow for 1996. Cougar XR7 was offered with the Sports Appearance package. The Grand Marquis underwent several changes including new-design front and rear treatments as well as a restyling of its interior including new seats and instrument panel.

MYSTIQUE — FOUR/V-6 — One of the trio of FoMoCo's global car platform (along with Contour and Mondeo), the all-new Mystique debuted in two series, GS and LS, each offering a mid-sized, front-wheel-drive four-door sedan with five-passenger capacity. The Mystique featured a safety cell body structure with high-tensile boron steel door beams, a cross-car beam running between the windshield pillars and a reinforced subframe. Its aerodynamic body allowed for a Cd (coefficient of drag) of 0.31, and featured a low cowl and hood. Inside, the Mystique offered a six-way power driver's seat in the GS sedan while an eight-way power driver's seat was standard in the LS sedan. Both models used solar-reflective glass throughout to reduce interior heat build-up. Optional on the Mystique was an "All-Speed" full traction control system and MicronAir filtration system to purify passenger compartment air. The Mystique came standard with the Zetec DOHC 2.0-liter four-cylinder engine rated at 125 hp. Optional was the all-aluminum, modular Duratec DOHC 2.5-liter V-6 rated at 165 hp. Base transaxle was the MTX75 five-speed manual unit with the CD4E electronically controlled four-speed automatic transaxle the option unit. Both the Zetec and Duratec engines were controlled by the EEC-IV electronic engine controller and featured distributorless ignition and sequential fuel injection.

SABLE — V-6 — Sable's lineup of GS and LS sedans and station wagons was increased for 1995 with the addition of an LTS four-door sedan. This upscale Sable featured six-way power leather sport bucket seats, leather-wrapped steering wheel and shift handle, cast aluminum wheels and LTS bodyside cladding and embossed floor mats. Sable's base engine, the 3.0-liter V-6, was modified to make it lighter as well as to reduce emissions and improve cooling. The suspension and body of the Sable also received revisions to enhance ride quality and aerodynamics. A new standard feature was solar tinted glass. The optional engine for all Sables was again the 3.8-liter V-6 and all Sables again used the four-speed automatic overdrive transaxle. An all-new design, 1996 Sable was launched in June of 1995.

1995 Mercury Sable LS sedan. (OCW)

1995 Mercury Sable LS station wagon. (OCW)

COUGAR XR7 –V-6/V-8 — The Cougar XR7 series again consisted of a single two-door coupe. A Sports Appearance package was optional. Standard powerplant was again the 3.8-liter V-6 with the 4.6-liter V-8 again the option engine. The four-speed automatic overdrive transmission was the only unit used in the Cougar XR7.

GRAND MARQUIS — V-8 — The Grand Marquis lineup again consisted of the GS and LS series, each offering a four-door sedan. The Grand Marquis received revised front and rear styling as well as a redesigned interior including new seats and a new instrument panel. New standard features included solar tinted glass, rear window defroster, heated rearview mirror and battery saver. Standard powertrain for all Grand Marquis models was the modular 4.6-liter V-8 teamed with the four-speed automatic overdrive transmission.

I.D. DATA: Mercury's 17-symbol Vehicle Identification Number (VIN) was stamped on a metal tab fastened to the instrument panel, visible through the windshield. The first three symbols indicate manufacturer, make and vehicle type. The fourth symbol denotes restraint system. Next comes a letter (usually 'M'), followed by two digits that indicate Model Number, as shown in left column of tables below. (Example: '65' Mystique GS four-door sedan). Symbol eight indicates engine type. Next is a check digit. Symbol ten indicates model year ('S' - 1995). Symbol eleven denotes assembly plant. The final six digits make up the sequence number, starting with 600001.

MYSTIQUE (FOUR/V-6)

Model No.	Body/ Style No.	Body Type & Seating	Factory Price	Shipping Weight	Prod. Total
M	65	4-dr. GS Sed-5P	13855/14900	2824/NA	Note 1
M	66	4-dr. LS Sed-5P	15230/16220	2873/2959	Note 1

NOTE: Figures to left of slash for four-cylinder engine, to right for V-6.

NOTE 1: Production of four-door sedans totaled 66,742 with no further breakout available.

SABLE (V-6)

M	50	4-dr. GS Sed-5P	18210	3144	Note 1
M	55	4-dr. GS Sta Wag-5P	19360	3292	Note 2
M	53	4-dr. LS Sed-5P	20470	3188	Note 1
M	58	4-dr. LS Sta Wag-5P	21570	3336	Note 2
M	53	4-dr. LTS Sed-5P	21715	3188	Note 1

NOTE 1: Production of four-door sedans totaled 90,197 with no further breakout available.

NOTE 2: Production of station wagons totaled 12,300 with no further breakout available.

COUGAR XR7 (V-6/V-8)

M	62	2-dr. XR7 Cpe-4P	16860/17305	3533/3673	60,201

NOTE: Figures to left of slash for V-6, to right for V-8.

GRAND MARQUIS (V-8)

M	74	4-dr. GS Sed-6P	21270	3761	Note 1
M	75	4-dr. LS Sed-6P	22690	3796	Note 1

NOTE 1: Production of four-door sedans totaled 94,202 with no further breakout available.

ENGINE [Base Four (Mystique)]: Inline. Dual overhead cam. Four-cylinder. Cast-iron block and aluminum head. Displacement: 121 cid (2.0 liters). Bore & stroke: 3.34 x 3.46 in. Compression ratio: 9.6:1. Brake horsepower: 125 at 5500 rpm. Torque: 125 lbs.-ft. at 4500 rpm. Sequential fuel injection.

ENGINE [Optional V-6 (Mystique)]: Modular, dual overhead cam V-6. Aluminum block and head. Displacement: 155 cid (2.5 liters). Bore & stroke: 3.24 x 3.13 in. Compression ratio: 9.7:1. Brake horsepower: 170 at 6200 rpm. Torque: 165 lbs.-ft. at 5000 rpm. Sequential fuel injection.

ENGINE [Base V-6 (Sable)]: 60-degree, overhead valve V-6. Cast-iron block and head. Displacement: 182 cid (3.0 liters). Bore & stroke: 3.50 x 3.15 in. Compression ratio: 9.3:1. Brake horsepower: 140 at 4800 rpm. Torque: 165 lbs.-ft. at 3250 rpm. Sequential fuel injection.

1995 Mercury Cougar XR7 coupe. (OCW)

ENGINE [Base V-6 (Cougar XR7); Optional (Sable)]: 60-degree, overhead valve V-6. Cast-iron block and head. Displacement: 232 cid (3.8 liters). Bore & stroke: 3.80 x 3.40 in. Compression ratio: 9.0:1. Brake horsepower: 140 at 3800 rpm. Torque: 215 lbs.-ft. at 2400 rpm. Sequential fuel injection.

ENGINE [Base V-8 (Grand Marquis); Optional (Cougar XR7)]: Modular, overhead cam V-8. Displacement: 281 cid (4.6-liter). Bore & stroke: 3.60 x 3.60 in. Compression ratio: 9.0:1. Brake horsepower: (Cougar XR7) 205 at 4500 RPM; (Grand Marquis) 190 at 4250 rpm. Torque: (Cougar XR7) 265 lbs.-ft. at 3200 RPM; (Grand Marquis) 260 lbs.-ft. at 3200 rpm. Sequential fuel injection.

CHASSIS DATA: Wheelbase: (Mystique) 106.5 in.; (Sable) 106.0 in.; (Cougar) 113.0 in.; (Grand Marquis) 114.4 in. Overall Length: (Mystique) 183.9 in.; (Sable sed) 192.2 in.; (Sable sta wag) 193.3 in.; (Cougar) 199.9 in.; (Grand Marquis) 211.8 in. Height: (Mystique) 54.5 in.; (Sable sed) 54.1 in.; (Sable sta wag) 55.5 in.; (Cougar) 52.5 in.; (Grand Marquis) 56.8 in. Width: (Mystique) 69.1 in.; (Sable) 71.2 in.; (Cougar) 72.7 in.; (Grand Marquis) 77.8 in. Front Tread: (Mystique) 59.2 in.; (Sable) 61.6 in.; (Cougar) 61.6 in.; (Grand Marquis) 62.8 in. Rear Tread: (Mystique) 58.5 in.; (Sable sed) 60.5 in.; (Sable sta wag) 59.9 in.; (Cougar) 60.2 in.; (Grand Marquis) 63.3 in. Standard Tires: (Mystique GS) P185/70R14; (Mystique LS) P205/60R15; (Sable) P205/65R15; (Cougar) P205/70R15; (Grand Marquis) P215/70R15.

TECHNICAL: Transmission: Five-speed manual transaxle standard on Mystique. Four-speed automatic overdrive standard on Sable, Cougar XR7 and Grand Marquis. Drive Axle: (Cougar/Grand Marquis) rear; (others) front. Steering: (Grand Marquis) recirculating ball; (others) rack/pinion. Front Suspension: (Mystique) Independent subframe-mounted MacPherson strut; (Sable) Independent MacPherson strut w/strut-mounted coil spring, stabilizer bar, tension strut, lower control arm and cast steering knuckle; (Cougar) Short/long arm (SLA) w/double isolated tension strut, variable rate coil springs and stabilizer bar; (Grand Marquis) Independent SLA w/ball joints, coil springs and stabilizer bar. Rear Suspension: (Mystique) Quadralink independent w/passive rear wheel steering (compliance understeer); (Sable sed) Independent MacPherson strut w/coil spring on shock strut, stabilizer bar, tension strut, parallel control arms and two-piece cast forged spindle. (Sable sta wag) SLA independent w/variable rate spring on lower control arm, stabilizer bar, stamped tension strut with two-piece cast spindle w/forged stem; (Cougar) H-arm independent, variable rate coil springs and stabilizer bar; (Grand Marquis) Four-bar link w/rubber-insulated coil spring on axle and stabilizer bar. Brakes: Front disc, rear drum (power assisted) except (Mystique w/V-6, Sable LS, Sable LTS, Cougar XR7 and Grand Marquis) front/rear disc. Body construction: (Grand Marquis) separate body and frame; (others) unibody. Fuel tank: (Mystique) 15.0 gal.; (Sable) 16.0 gal.; (Cougar) 18.0 gal.; (Grand Marquis) 20.0 gal.

DRIVETRAIN OPTIONS: Engines: 2.5-liter V-6: Mystique GS ($1045); Mystique LS ($900). 3.8-liter V-6: Sable ($630). 4.6-liter V-8: Cougar XR7 ($615). Transmission/Differential: Four-speed automatic transaxle: Mystique ($815). All-Speed Traction Control: Mystique w/Anti-lock Brakes ($800). Traction-Lok Axle: Cougar XR7 (NA w/Traction Assist) ($95). Traction Assist: Cougar XR7 w/Anti-lock Brakes ($210). Suspension/Brakes: HD Suspension: Sable ($25). Rear Air Suspension: Grand Marquis LS ($270). Trailer towing pkg: Grand Marquis LS ($900). Anti-lock brakes: Mystique ($565); Sable GS ($565); Cougar XR7 ($565); Grand Marquis (w/Traction Assist) ($665). 41G Handling Pkg: Grand Marquis LS ($1020).

MYSTIQUE CONVENIENCE/APPEARANCE OPTIONS: Preferred Equip Pkgs (Mystique GS 370A): Elect Rr Window Defroster, Heated Ext Mirrors, Man Air Cond, AM/FM Stereo Radio w/Cass and Pwr Antenna ($895). (Mystique GS 371A): same as 370A plus Pwr Windows & Pwr Dr Locks/Light Grp w/Dual Illum Visor Mirrors, Trunk & Eng Comp Lights, Frt Map/Reading Lights, Illum Entry Syst, Illum Inside Dr Handles and Spd Ctrl ($1485). (Mystique GS 372A): same as 371A plus 2.5-liter DOHC 24-Valve V-6, 4-Whl Disc Brakes, P195/65R14 Tire Upgrade and Perf Tuned Strg & Suspension

($2430). (Mystique LS 380A): Air Cond, Pwr Windows, Remote Lckg Feature & Pwr Locks/Light Grp w/Dual Illum Visor Mirrors, Trunk & Eng Comp Lights, Frt Map/Reading Lights, Illum Entry Syst and Illum Inside Dr Handles ($1380). (Mystique LS 381A): same as 380A plus 2.5-liter DOHC 24-Valve V-6, 4-Whl Disc Brakes, P205/60R15 Tire Upgrade and Perf Tuned Strg & Suspension ($2220). Dr Locks/Light Grp incl Pwr Dr Locks, Dual Illum Visor Mirrors, Trunk & Eng Comp Lights, Frt Map/Reading Lights, Illum Entry Syst and Illum Inside Dr Handles ($335). Remote Keyless Lock Syst ($160). Pwr Moonroof ($595). 10-Way Pwr Driver's Seat ($330). Elect AM/FM Stereo Radio, Premium Sound w/Cass, Amplifier & Upgraded Spkrs: GS w/Cass ($130); GS w/o Cass ($295); LS ($130). Elect AM/FM Stereo Radio, Premium Sound w/CD Player, Amplifier & Upgraded Spkrs: GS w/AM/FM & Cass ($130); GS w/o Cass ($295); LS ($130). Anti-Lock Braking Syst ($565). Man Air Cond ($780). Elect Rr Window Defroster incl Heated Ext Mirrors ($160). Calif. Emission Syst ($95). Flr Mats F&R ($45). Eng Block Heater ($20). Leather Bucket Seats (LS only) ($595). Spd Ctrl ($215). 14-inch Cast Alum Whls (GS only) ($265).

SABLE CONVENIENCE/APPEARANCE OPTIONS: Preferred Equip Pkgs (Sable GS 450A): Pwr Windows, Spd Ctrl, Light Grp, F&R Carpeted Flr Mats, Pwr Lock Grp and Bodyside Accent Stripe ($800). (Sable GS 451A): same as 450A plus 6-Way Pwr Driver's Seat, Elect AM/FM Stereo Radio w/Cass and Alum Whls: w/3.0-liter V-6 ($765); w/3.8-liter V-6 ($1265). (Sable LS 461A): F&R Carpeted Flr Mats, Leather-Wrapped Strg Whl, Spd Ctrl, Keyless Entry w/Dual Remote Transmitters, High Level Cass, Pwr Lock Grp, Pwr Antenna and Bodyside Accent Stripe ($445). (Sable LS 462A): same as 461A plus Elect Instrument Cluster, Autolamp On/Off Delay Syst and Auto Air Cond ($780). (Sable LTS 470A): F&R Carpeted Flr Mats, Pwr Lock Grp, Spd Ctrl, Leather-Wrapped Strg Whl, Pwr Radio Antenna, High-Level AM/FM Stereo Radio w/Cass, Keyless Entry Syst, Leather Spt Bucket Seats, 6-Way Dual Pwr Seats, LTS Bodyside Cladding, Leather-Wrapped Shift Handle, Luxury Pile Carpeting, Unique Cast Alum Whls and Unique LTS Flr Mats ($1245). Keyless Entry Syst incl Illum Entry and Remote Feature ($295). Pwr Moonroof incl Sliding Sunshade and Pop-Up Air Deflector ($740). 6-Way Pwr Driver's Seat ($290). 6-Way Dual Pwr Seats ($580). AM/FM Stereo Radio w/Cass ($165). Digital CD Player incl Auto Music Search, Scan Feature and Instant Return Feature ($375). Auto Air Cond ($175). Anti-Lock Brake Syst incl 4 Whl Disc Brakes ($565). HD Battery ($30). Cargo Area Cover (sta wag only) ($65). Cellular Phone ($500). Fuel Tank, Ext Range ($45). Eng Block Heater ($20). Calif. Emission Syst ($95). LTS Decor Grp incl Leather Spt Bucket Seats, LTS Bodyside Cladding, 6-Way Dual Pwr Seats, Leather-Wrapped Shift Handle, Luxury Pile Carpeting, Unique Cast Alum Whls, Unique LTS Flr Mats and Paint Stripe ($1150). Rr Facing Third Seat (sta wag only) ($150). Leather Individual Bucket Seats w/Console (LS only) ($495). Leather Twin Comfort Seats (LS only) ($495). HD Suspension incl HD Stabilizer Bar, Heavier Spring and Unique Valving on Struts ($25). Alum Whls w/Lckg Lug Nuts ($225). Chrome Whls ($580). Conventional Spare Tire ($70).

COUGAR CONVENIENCE/APPEARANCE OPTIONS: Preferred Equip Pkgs (Cougar XR7 260A): Elect Rr Window Defroster, Illum Entry, 6-Way Pwr Driver's Seat, Spd Ctrl, Leather-Wrapped Strg Whl, Pwr Lock Grp, P215/70R15 BSW Tires, Frt Flr Mats and Cast Alum Whls ($990). Keyless Entry Syst ($215). Pwr Moonroof incl Dual Reading Lamps, Pop-Up Air Deflector, Sliding Sunshade and Rr Tilt-Up ($740). 6-Way Dual Pwr Seats ($290). Elect AM/FM Stereo Radio w/Cass ($370). Premium Elect AM/FM Stereo Radio w/CD Player incl 80-Watt Amp and Premium Spkrs ($430). Elect Auto Temp Ctrl Air Cond ($155). Anti-Lock Brake Syst ($565). Auto Lamp ($70). Traction-Lok Axle, 3.27 Ratio ($95). HD Battery ($25). Calif. Emission Syst ($95). Luxury Light Grp incl Dual Illum Visor Mirrors, Pass Side Footwell Courtesy Light and Eng Comp Light ($140). Tri-coat Paint ($225). Leather Seat Trim ($490). Spts Appearance Grp incl BBS Whls and Non-Functional Luggage Rack ($115). Elect Traction Assist ($210).

1995 Mercury Grand Marquis LS sedan. (OCW)

GRAND MARQUIS CONVENIENCE/APPEARANCE OPTIONS: Preferred Equip Pkgs (Grand Marquis GS 157A): Carpeted Flr Mats F&R, Pwr Lock Grp, Spd Ctrl, Illum Entry Syst and Lckg Radial-Spoke Whl Covers (-$855) (Grand Marquis LS 172A): same as 157A plus Lux Light Grp, Bodyside Paint Stripe, Cornering Lamps, Leather-Wrapped Strg Whl, 12-Spoke Alum Whls and Keyless Entry Syst (-$70). Keyless Entry Syst incl Dual Remote Transmitters ($215). 6-Way Pwr Pass Seat w/Pwr Recline (LS only) ($360). Premium Elect AM/FM Stereo Radio w/Cass incl Radio/Tape Scan, AM Stereo, Auto Memory Set, 4 Channel Amp w/80 Watts and DNR 4 Tape Storage Feature (LS only) ($360). Elect Auto Temp Ctrl Air Cond incl O/S Temp Display (LS only) ($175). Elect Grp incl Elect Cluster, Tripminder Computer and 72 Amp Battery (LS only) ($455). Calif. Emission Syst ($95). 41G Handling Pkg incl Pwr Steering Cooler, Up-Sized F&R Stabilizer Bars, 3.27 Axle, 16-inch Alum Whls, Rr Air Suspension w/Unique Springs, Unique Tuned Suspension, Unique Strg Gear and Dual Exhaust: LS ($600); GS ($1020). Eng Block Heater ($25). Lux Light Grp incl Eng Comp Light, Dual Illum Visor Mirrors, Dual Beam Dome/Map Lights, Rr Seat Reading Lamps and Dual Secondary Sunvisors for Frt/Side Coverage ($190). Bodyside Paint Stripe ($60). Rr Air Suspension (LS only) ($270). Trailer Tow III incl 5000 lbs Cap, Rr Air Spring Suspension, HD Battery, Wiring Harness, Trans Oil Cooler, Dual Exhaust, Pwr Strg Oil Cooler, Conventional Spare Tire and 3.27 Traction-Lok Axle (LS only) ($900). Leather Seat Trim (LS only) ($645). Conventional Spare Tire (LS only): w/Handling Pkg ($240); w/o Handling Pkg ($185).

HISTORY: U.S. model year Mercury production totaled 323,642. U.S. calendar year Mercury production totaled 227,121 for a 3.6 percent industry market share. Mercury offered a special-edition Mystique model called the "Young America" to commemorate the 1995 America's Cup sailboat race. The limited-edition Mystique featured an all-white exterior, including grille and 15-inch wheels, and Atlantic blue leather interior trim with white leather inserts. The big news in the Mercury camp for 1996 was the all-new-design Sable, which was launched in September of 1995. The new Sable lineup consisted of a base G-series four-door sedan and GS and LS series each offering a four-door sedan and station wagon. The Sable LTS sedan offered previously was discontinued. The Sable G and GS series utilized the Vulcan 3.0-liter V-6 while the Sable LS series used the more potent Duratec DOHC 3.0-liter V-6. The Cougar XR7 received revised front and rear styling as well as upgrades in both its standard 3.8-liter V-6 and optional 4.6-liter V-8. Mercury Tracer, previously only produced in Hermosillo, Mexico, and not in the scope of this book, had its all-new-design 1997 model production expanded to include an assembly plant in Wayne, Michigan. Production of the 1997 Tracer began in the spring of 1996 and will be covered in-depth as a domestically produced automobile beginning with the 1997 Mercury listings.

1996 MERCURY

1996 Mercury Sable LS sedan. (OCW)

MYSTIQUE — FOUR/V-6 — After its debut the year previous, the Mystique returned with minor changes, the most significant being new additions to the options list. Available in 1996 on all Mystique models was a dealer-installed spoiler and on GS models the Sports Appearance Package. The Zetec DOHC 2.0-liter four-cylinder engine was again the base powerplant with the Duratec DOHC 2.5-liter V-6 again the option engine. Standard transaxle was again the five-speed manual with the electronically controlled four-speed automatic the option unit.

1996 Mercury Sable LS station wagon. (OCW)

SABLE — V-6 — The all-new-design 1996 Sable debuted in three series: base G, GS and LS. All three series offered a four-door sedan while the GS and LS series each also offered a station wagon. The totally redesigned front-wheel-drive Sable sedan and station wagon models were longer, wider and featured a more rounded body than previous Sables as well as a safety cell structural design that integrated a network of steel beams into a protective, impact-absorbing system. Standard features included four-wheel disc brakes, dual airbags, anti-theft system (LS only) and air filtration system. The G and GS series were powered by the Vulcan 3.0-liter V-6 rated at 145 hp. The LS models used the Duratec DOHC 3.0-liter V-6 rated at 200 hp. The electronically controlled four-speed automatic overdrive transaxle was the only unit offered on Sable models. Inside, Sable sedan models offered either five- or six-passenger seating. The five-passenger version featured a unique instrument panel with an integrated full-length console. A three-way console/seat system was offered on Sable sedans with six-passenger seating. The center front-seating position could be converted to an armrest or, with another downward flip, a console with small storage compartments.

COUGAR XR7 — V-6/V-8 — The Cougar XR7 two-door coupe again comprised the Cougar XR7 series for 1996. The latest version of the XR7 featured restyled front and rear treatments and offered an anti-theft system as a new option. Standard engine for the XR7 was again the 3.8-liter V-6 while the modular 4.6-liter V-8 was again the option unit. Both engines received upgrades to improve fuel mileage and extend the timeframe for scheduled maintenance. The Cougar XR7 used the electronically controlled four-speed automatic overdrive transmission.

GRAND MARQUIS — V-8 — Grand Marquis was again represented by a GS and LS series, each offering a four-door sedan. For 1996, an LS Feature Decor edition model was offered, which had embroidered front seat backs and floor mats, leather seat trim and six-way power passenger seat. The LS model's option list also offered new dual plane cast aluminum wheels in place of the standard 12-spoke versions. Powertrain for the Grand Marquis was the upgraded modular 4.6-liter V-8 teamed with the electronically controlled four-speed automatic overdrive transmission.

I.D. DATA: Mercury's 17-symbol Vehicle Identification Number (VIN) was stamped on a metal tab fastened to the instrument panel, visible through the windshield. The first three symbols indicate manufacturer, make and vehicle type. The fourth symbol denotes restraint system. Next comes a letter (usually 'M'), followed by two digits that indicate Model Number, as shown in left column of tables below. (Example: '65' Mystique GS four-door sedan). Symbol eight indicates engine type. Next is a check digit. Symbol ten indicates model year ('T' - 1996). Symbol eleven denotes assembly plant. The final six digits make up the sequence number, starting with 600001.

MYSTIQUE (FOUR/V-6)

Model No.	Body/ Style No.	Body Type & Seating	Factory Price	Shipping Weight	Prod. Total
M	65	4-dr. GS Sed-5P	14330/15375	2833/2946	Note 1
M	66	4-dr. LS Sed-5P	15705/16695	2855/2952	Note 1

NOTE: Figures to left of slash for four-cylinder engine, to right for V-6.

NOTE 1: Production of four-door sedans totaled 51,677 with no further breakout available.

SABLE (V-6)

Model No.	Body/ Style No.	Body Type & Seating	Factory Price	Shipping Weight	Prod. Total
M	51	4-dr. G Sed-5P	18360	NA	Note 1
M	50	4-dr. GS Sed-5P	18995	3358	Note 1
M	55	4-dr. GS Sta Wag-5P	20015	3502	Note 2
M	53	4-dr. LS Sed-5P	21295	3359	Note 1
M	58	4-dr. LS Sta Wag-5P	22355	3525	Note 2

NOTE 1: Production of four-door sedans totaled 109,866 with no further breakout available.

NOTE 2: Production of station wagons totaled 13,578 with no further breakout available.

COUGAR XR7 (V-6/V-8)

M	62	2-dr. XR7 Cpe-4P	17430/18560	3559/3687	38,929

NOTE: Figures to left of slash for V-6, to right for V-8.

GRAND MARQUIS (V-8)

M	74	4-dr. GS Sed-6P	21975	3796	Note 1
M	75	4-dr. LS Sed-6P	23385	3796	Note 1

NOTE 1: Production of four-door sedans totaled 95,030 with no further breakout available.

ENGINE [Base Four (Mystique)]: Inline. Dual overhead cam. Four-cylinder. Cast-iron block and aluminum head. Displacement: 121 cid (2.0 liters). Bore & stroke: 3.34 x 3.46 in. Compression ratio: 9.6:1. Brake horsepower: 125 at 5500 rpm. Torque: 125 lbs.-ft. at 4500 rpm. Sequential fuel injection.

ENGINE [Optional V-6 (Mystique)]: Modular, dual overhead cam V-6. Aluminum block and head. Displacement: 155 cid (2.5 liters). Bore & stroke: 3.24 x 3.13 in. Compression ratio: 9.7:1. Brake horsepower: 170 at 6250 rpm. Torque: 165 lbs.-ft. at 5000 rpm. Sequential fuel injection.

ENGINE [Base V-6 (Sable GS)]: 60-degree, overhead valve V-6. Cast-iron block and head. Displacement: 182 cid (3.0 liters). Bore & stroke: 3.50 x 3.15 in. Compression ratio: 9.3:1. Brake horsepower: 145 at 5250 rpm. Torque: 170 lbs.-ft. at 3250 rpm. Sequential fuel injection.

ENGINE [Base V-6 (Sable LS)]: same as 3.0-liter V-6 mentioned above except - DOHC V-6. Brake horsepower: 200 at 5750 rpm. Torque: 200 lbs.-ft. at 4500 rpm.

ENGINE [Base V-6 (Cougar XR7)]: 60-degree, overhead valve V-6. Cast-iron block and head. Displacement: 232 cid (3.8 liters). Bore & stroke: 3.80 x 3.40 in. Compression ratio: 9.0:1. Brake horsepower: 145 at 4000 rpm. Torque: 215 lbs.-ft. at 2750 rpm. Sequential fuel injection.

ENGINE [Base V-8 (Grand Marquis); Optional (Cougar XR7)]: Modular, overhead cam V-8. Displacement: 281 cid (4.6-liter). Bore & stroke: 3.60 x 3.60 in. Compression ratio: 9.0:1. Brake horsepower: (Cougar XR7) 205 at 4250 RPM; (Grand Marquis) 190 at 4250 rpm. Torque: (Cougar XR7) 280 lbs.-ft. at 3000 RPM; (Grand Marquis) 265 lbs.-ft. at 3250 rpm. Sequential fuel injection.

CHASSIS DATA: Wheelbase: (Mystique) 106.5 in.; (Sable) 108.5 in.; (Cougar) 113.0 in.; (Grand Marquis) 114.4 in. Overall Length: (Mystique) 183.5 in.; (Sable) 197.5 in.; (Cougar) 199.9 in.; (Grand Marquis) 211.8 in. Height: (Mystique) 54.5 in.; (Sable) 55.1 in.; (Cougar) 52.5 in.; (Grand Marquis) 56.8 in. Width: (Mystique) 69.1 in.; (Sable) 73.0 in.; (Cougar) 72.7 in.; (Grand Marquis) 77.8 in. Front Tread: (Mystique) 59.2 in.; (Sable) 61.6 in.; (Cougar) 61.6 in.; (Grand Marquis) 62.8 in. Rear Tread: (Mystique) 58.5 in.; (Sable sed) 61.4 in.; (Sable sta wag) 61.8 in.; (Cougar) 60.2 in.; (Grand Marquis) 63.3 in. Standard Tires: (Mystique GS) P185/70R14; (Mystique LS) P205/60R15; (Sable) P205/65R15; (Cougar XR7) P205/70R15; (Grand Marquis) P215/70R15.

TECHNICAL: Transmission: Five-speed manual transaxle standard on Mystique. Four-speed automatic overdrive standard on Sable, Cougar XR7 and Grand Marquis. Drive Axle: (Cougar/Grand Marquis) rear; (others) front. Steering: (Grand Marquis) recirculating ball; (others) rack/pinion. Front Suspension: (Mystique) Independent subframe-mounted MacPherson strut; (Sable) Independent MacPherson strut w/strut-mounted coil spring, stabilizer bar, tension strut, lower control arm and cast steering knuckle; (Cougar XR7) Short/long arm (SLA) w/double-isolated tension strut, variable rate coil springs and stabilizer bar; (Grand Marquis) Independent SLA w/ball joints, coil springs and stabilizer bar. Rear Suspension: (Mystique) Quadralink independent w/passive rear wheel steering (compliance understeer); (Sable sed) Independent Quadralink w/coil spring on shock strut, stabilizer bar, tension strut, parallel control arms and cast spindle w/pressed-in forged stem; (Sable sta wag) SLA independent w/variable rate coil spring on lower control arm, stabilizer bar, tension strut and cast spindle w/pressed-in forged stem; (Cougar) H-arm independent, variable rate coil springs and stabilizer bar; (Grand Marquis) Four-bar link w/rubber-insulated coil spring on axle and stabilizer bar. Brakes: (Mystique w/o V-6) front disc, rear drum (power assisted); (others) front/rear disc. Body construction: (Grand Marquis) separate body and frame; (others) unibody. Fuel tank: (Mystique) 15.0 gal.; (Sable) 16.0 gal.; (Cougar) 18.0 gal.; (Grand Marquis) 20.0 gal.

DRIVETRAIN OPTIONS: Engines: 2.5-liter V-6: Mystique GS ($1045); Mystique LS ($990). 4.6-liter V-8: Cougar XR7 ($1130). Transmission/Differential: Four-speed automatic transaxle: Mystique ($815). All-Speed Traction Control: Mystique w/Anti-lock Brakes ($805). Traction-Lok Axle: Cougar XR7 (NA w/Traction Assist) ($95). Traction Assist: Cougar XR7 w/Anti-lock Brakes ($210). Suspension/Brakes: Rear Air Suspension: Grand Marquis LS ($270). Trailer towing pkg: Grand Marquis LS ($900). Anti-lock brakes: Mystique ($570); Sable G/Sable GS ($570); Cougar XR7 ($570); Grand Marquis (w/Traction Assist) ($670). 41G Handling Pkg: Grand Marquis LS ($1020).

MYSTIQUE CONVENIENCE/APPEARANCE OPTIONS: Preferred Equip Pkgs (Mystique GS 370A): Elect Rr Window Defroster, Heated Ext Mirrors, Man Air Cond and AM/FM Stereo Radio w/Cass & Pwr Antenna ($915). (Mystique GS 371A): same as 370A plus Pwr Windows & Pwr Dr Locks/Light Grp w/Dual Illum Visor Mirrors, Trunk & Eng Comp Lights, Frt Map/Reading Lights, Illum Entry Syst, Illum Inside Dr Handles and Spd Ctrl ($1505). (Mystique GS 372A): same as 371A plus 2.5-liter DOHC Duratec V-6 ($2450). (Mystique LS 381A): 2.5-liter DOHC Duratec V-6, Air Cond, Pwr Windows, Pwr Locks w/Remote Lckg Feature, Leather-Wrapped Strg Whl, Light Grp w/RH Illum Visor Mirror, Trunk Comp Light, Frt Map/Reading Lights, Illum Entry Syst and Illum Inside Dr Handles ($2250). Calif. Emission Syst ($100). 15-inch Cast Alum Whls (GS only) ($425). 10-Way Pwr Driver's Side Seat ($330). Leather Bucket Seats (LS only) ($595). All-Spd Traction Ctrl incl Anti-Lock Braking Syst ($805). Anti-Lock Braking Syst ($570). Flr Mats F&R ($45). Pwr Moonroof ($595). Dr Locks/Light Grp incl Pwr Dr Locks, RH Illum Visor Mirrors, Trunk Comp Light, Frt Map/Reading Lights, Illum Entry Syst and Illum Inside Dr Handles ($335). Remote Keyless Lock Syst ($190). Spd Ctrl ($215). Rr Decklid Spoiler ($345). Spts Appearance Pkg incl 15-inch Cast Alum Whls and Rr Spoiler (GS Only) ($675). Elect AM/FM Stereo Radio w/Cass, Premium Sound, Amplifier & Upgraded Spkrs: GS w/Cass ($130); GS w/o Cass ($295); LS ($130). Elect AM/FM Stereo Radio, Premium Sound w/CD Player, Amplifier & Upgraded Spkrs: GS w/AM/FM & Cass ($270); GS w/o Cass ($435); LS ($270). Man Air Cond ($780). Elect Rr Window Defroster incl Heated Ext Mirrors ($170). Eng Block Heater ($20).

SABLE CONVENIENCE/APPEARANCE OPTIONS: Preferred Equip Pkgs (Sable GS 450A): Spd Ctrl, F&R Carpeted Flr Mats, Pwr Lock Grp and AM/FM Stereo Radio w/Cass ($210). (Sable GS 451A): same as 450A plus 6-Way Pwr Driver's Seat, Light Grp and Alum Whls ($810). (Sable LS 460A): F&R Flr Mats and Spd Ctrl ($150). (Sable LS 461A): same as 460A plus Keyless Entry w/Dual Remote Transmitters w/Perimeter Anti-theft and Anti-Lock Brakes ($860). (Sable LS 462A): same as 461A plus Auto Air Cond, Elect Temp Ctrl, JBL Audio Syst and Chrome Alum Whls: sed ($1915); sta wag ($1730). Calif. Emission Syst ($95). Alum Whls ($315). Chrome Whls ($580). Conventional Spare Tire ($125). Leather Bucket Seats (LS five-pass only) ($990). Integrated Rr Child's Seat (sta wag only) ($135). Rr Facing Third Seat (sta wag only) ($200). 6-Way Pwr Driver's Seat ($340). Auto Air Cond ($175). Anti-Lock Brake Syst incl 4 Whl Disc Brakes ($570). Cargo Tie-down Net (sta wag only) ($40). Cellular Phone ($650). Remote Keyless Entry Syst (GS only) ($190). Remote Keyless Entry Syst w/Perimeter Anti-Theft (LS only) ($440). Pwr Moonroof incl Unique Map Lamps in OH Console (LS only) ($740). AM/FM Stereo Radio w/Cass & Premium Sound (LS sta wag only) ($315). JBL Audio Syst (LS sed only) ($500). CD Changer ($595). Elect AM/FM Stereo Radio w/Cass (G only) ($175). Daytime Running Lights ($40). Eng Block Heater ($35). Light Grp incl Dual Courtesy Lights, Under Instrument Panel Map Lights and Dual Beam Reading & Dome ($45).

COUGAR CONVENIENCE/APPEARANCE OPTIONS: Preferred Equip Pkgs (Cougar XR7 260A): Elect Rr Window Defroster, Spd Ctrl, Pwr Lock Grp, P215/70R15 BSW Tires, Frt Flr Mats and Cast Alum Whls ($505). (Cougar XR7 262A): same as 260A plus 4.6-liter V-8, Illum Entry Syst, 6-Way Pwr Driver's Seat and Leather-Wrapped Strg Whl ($1340). Calif. Emission Syst ($100). Chrome Whls ($580). Individual Seats w/Leather Seating Surfaces ($490). 6-Way Pwr Driver's Seat ($290). 6-Way Pwr Pass Seat ($290). Elect Auto Temp Ctrl Air Cond ($155). Anti-Lock Brake Syst incl 4-Whl Disc Brakes ($570). Anti-Theft Alarm Syst ($145). Auto Lamp Grp ($70). Luxury Light Grp incl Dual Illum Visor Mirrors, Pass Side Footwell Courtesy Light, Eng Comp Light, Traction Assist Lamp & Warning Indicator Lamps for Dr Ajar, Low Fuel, Low Coolant, & Low Washer Fluid ($200). Pwr Moonroof incl Dual Reading Lamps, Pop-Up Air Deflector, Sliding Sunshade and Rr Tilt-Up ($740). Remote Keyless Entry Syst ($270). Spts Appearance Grp incl Geometric Spoke Whls and Non-Functional Luggage Rack ($115). Leather-Wrapped Strg Whl ($90). Elect Traction Assist ($210). Tri-coat Paint ($225). Pwr Antenna ($85). Elect AM/FM Stereo Radio w/Cass incl 8-Watt Amp & Premium Spkrs ($290). Premium Elect AM/FM Stereo Radio w/CD Player incl 80-Watt Amp & Premium Spkrs ($430). Traction-Lok Axle, 3.27 Ratio ($95). HD Battery ($25). Eng Block Heater ($20).

GRAND MARQUIS CONVENIENCE/APPEARANCE OPTIONS: Preferred Equip Pkgs (Grand Marquis 157A): Carpeted Flr Mats F&R, Pwr Lock Grp, Spd Ctrl, Illum Entry Syst and Lckg Radial-Spoke Whl Covers ($40). (Grand Marquis LS 172A): F&R Carpeted Flr Mats, Illum Entry Syst, Pwr Lock Grp, Lux Light Grp, Bodyside Paint Stripe, Spd Ctrl, Frt Cornering Lamps, Leather-Wrapped Strg Whl, 12-Spoke Alum Whls and Keyless Entry Syst ($820). (Grand Marquis LS 173A): same as 172A plus Anti-Lock Brakes w/Traction Assist, Elect Grp, Elect Auto Temp Ctrl, Pwr Pass Seat, AM/FM Stereo Radio w/Cass and Elect Auto Dim Mirror ($2780). Calif. Emission Syst ($95). Leather Seat Trim (LS only) ($645). 6-Way Pwr Pass Seat w/Pwr Recliner (LS only) ($360). Anti-Lock Brakes w/Traction Assist (LS only) ($670). Elect Grp incl Elect Cluster, Tripminder Computer and Battery Upgrade (LS only) ($455). Elect Auto Temp Ctrl Air Cond incl O/S Temp Display (LS only) ($175). 41G Handling Pkg incl Pwr Steering Cooler, Upsized F&R Stabilizer Bars, 3.27 Axle, P225/60R16 BSW Tires, 16-inch Alum Whls, Rr Air Suspension w/Unique Springs, Unique Tuned Suspension, Unique Strg Gear and Dual Exhaust ($1020). Remote Keyless Entry Syst w/Dual Transmitters ($240). Lux Light Grp incl Dual Illum Visor Mirrors, w/Secondary Sunvisors, Dual

Beam Dome/Map Lights and Rr Seat Reading Lamps ($190). Bodyside Paint Stripe ($60). Rr Air Suspension (LS only) ($270). Premium Elect AM/FM Stereo Radio w/Cass incl Radio/Tape Scan, AM Stereo, Auto Memory Set, 4 Channel Amp w/80 Watts, DNR and Tape Storage Feature (LS only) ($360). Trailer Towing Pkg III incl 5000 lbs Cap, Rr Air Suspension, HD Battery, Wiring Harness, Eng Oil & Trans Oil Cooler, Dual Exhaust, Pwr Strg Oil Cooler, Conventional Spare Tire and 3.27 Traction-Lok Axle (LS only) ($900). Eng Block Heater ($25). Conventional Spare Tire (LS only): w/Handling Pkg ($240); w/o Handling Pkg ($185).

HISTORY: U.S. model year Mercury production totaled 322,280. U.S. calendar year Mercury production totaled 244,676 for 4.0 percent of industry market share.

1997 MERCURY

1997 Mercury Tracer Trio sedan. (OCW)

After 11 years of being assembled only in Mexico, the Mercury Tracer—in its all-new, 1997 design—began production in Wayne, Michigan, and from this point on will be covered in-depth as a domestically produced automobile. Launched as an all-new design in the spring of 1996, the 1997 Tracer was available as a four-door sedan in GS and LS versions as well as a station wagon in LS trim (an appearance package version of the LS sedan called the "Trio" was also marketed). The Mystique series added a base sedan as well as offering the GS four-door sedan with an appearance package called "Spree," which included decklid badging and a unique Dark Pumice interior. The Cougar (XR7) had reached its 30th Anniversary in 1997 and to mark the occasion, Mercury offered a 30th Anniversary Edition of the Cougar XR7 coupe complete with commemorative badges and appliqués as well as embroidered seats.

1997 Mercury Tracer sedan. (OCW)

1997 Mercury Tracer LS station wagon. (OCW)

1997 Mercury Mystique GS sedan. (OCW)

TRACER — FOUR — Totally redesigned for 1997, the front-wheel-drive Tracer was now four inches longer than its predecessor. Tracer featured one-piece bodyside construction that smoothed-out exterior appearance and increased torsional stiffness by 25 percent over the 1996 version. Offered as a four-door sedan in both the GS and LS series or station wagon in LS trim, the Tracer LS sedan could also be ordered with the Trio appearance package that included 14-inch aluminum wheels, foglamps, Trio graphics and rear decklid spoiler. The new 2.0-liter four-cylinder engine with Split Port Induction that powered all Tracers qualified the Tracer as a low-emission vehicle (LEV) by the California Air Resources Board. It was rated at 110 hp. Tracers used a five-speed manual transaxle as standard equipment while the electronically controlled four-speed automatic overdrive transaxle was optional. Standard features of the Tracer included dual airbags, child safety door locks, solar tinted glass and intermittent wipers. Inside, the Tracer featured a new Integrated Control Panel that placed climate control, clock and audio system controls within easy reach in one central location.

MYSTIQUE — FOUR/V-6 — A year away from undergoing a redesign by Mercury engineers, a base Mystique four-door sedan joined the GS and LS series' four-door sedans for 1997. In addition, the GS sedan could be ordered with the Spree appearance package that included 15-inch aluminum wheels, foglamps, leather-wrapped steering wheel and shift handle, Spree decklid badging and a unique Dark Pumice jigsaw fabric interior. A Sports Appearance Package was also offered to Mystique GS buyers and included 15-inch aluminum wheels with P205/60R15 BSW tires and a rear decklid spoiler. Standard equipment on the Mystique included dual airbags, child safety door locks, solar tinted glass and tilt steering column. Mystique's standard powerplant for the base and GS series was the Zetec DOHC 2.0-liter four-cylinder rated at 125 hp. The LS series used the modular Duratec DOHC 2.5-liter V-6 rated at 170 hp, which was optional in the GS. Both engines were mated to the five-speed manual transaxle or could be ordered with the optional four-speed automatic overdrive transaxle.

1997 Mercury Sable GS sedan. (OCW)

1997 Mercury Sable LS station wagon. (OCW)

SABLE — V-6 — After undergoing a total revamp the previous year, Sable returned for 1997 with its lineup unchanged but with several new features. Offering both a four-door sedan and station wagon in each of its GS and LS series, Sable was Mercury's best-selling vehicle. New-for-1997 was the use of submersible connectors, which extended the life of Sable components such as the brake fluid switch, engine coolant temperature sensor and washer pump motor. The LS series offered a new, optional Mach Audio System as well as standard features including an anti-theft system with non-driveaway coded key, power central door locking system and five-spoke aluminum wheels. Again, the Vulcan 3.0-liter V-6, rated at 145 hp, powered the GS series while the LS series used the Duratec DOHC 3.0-liter V-6, rated at 200 hp. The AX4N electronically controlled four-speed automatic overdrive transaxle was used with both powerplants. In addition to a new mass airflow sensor to improve efficiency at extreme temperatures, the Vulcan engine featured a Cast-iron cylinder block and a nodular, Cast-iron crankshaft. Hydraulic, roller-tipped valve lifters reduced friction and heat build-up while hollow valve stems and lightweight valve springs and retainers helped control high rpm engine noise. Cast aluminum pistons resulted in lower friction and reduced hydrocarbon emissions. The all-aluminum Duratec V-6 received revisions to its powertrain control module for enhanced responsiveness, and featured reduced-distortion cylinder bores with cast-in iron liners for low oil use and longer engine life. Both engines offered 100,000-mile tune-up intervals under normal driving conditions.

COUGAR XR7 –V-6/V-8 — Mercury observed three decades of selling Cougar models by offering a 30th Anniversary Edition of the XR7 coupe. Finished in Dark Toreador red, the special edition XR7 featured anniversary emblem appliqués on its rear pillars, 16-inch blackwall tires and lacy spoked wheels and sport shocks. Models ordered with the XR7's optional 4.6-liter V-8 also received a sport suspension package. The interior of the anniversary XR7 featured unique front sport seats with power lumbar support and side bolsters. Available in cloth or optional leather-trim, the seats had a 30th Anniversary logo embroidered into the front of the seat backs. An electrochromic rearview mirror and 30th Anniversary floor mats were also standard. New features of the non-anniversary edition coupe included new seat trim, easier-to-read instrument cluster, redesigned center console and the addition of a passenger-side footwell light. New optional equipment included a power moonroof with one-touch open feature, decklid spoiler with integrated stoplight and leather-wrapped steering wheel and shifter handle. A Sport Edition package was also available to XR7 buyers and included a decklid spoiler, sport suspension and 16-inch/seven-spoke wheels. The 3.8-liter V-6 was again the standard engine for the XR7. Both it and the aforementioned optional 4.6-liter V-8 used the 4R70W electronically controlled four-speed automatic overdrive transmission, which was upgraded to improve reliability.

1997 Mercury Cougar XR7 coupe. (OCW)

GRAND MARQUIS — V-8 — The rear-wheel-drive Grand Marquis four-door sedan again could be ordered from either the GS or LS series. New-for-1997 was the revision of the Grand Marquis' steering gear and related components to reduce friction and increase precision as well as quiet hydraulic performance and improve durability. The modular 4.6-liter V-8 teamed with the electronically controlled four-speed automatic overdrive transmission was again the standard powertrain for all Grand Marquis models.

I.D. DATA: Mercury's 17-symbol Vehicle Identification Number (VIN) was stamped on a metal tab fastened to the instrument panel, visible through the windshield. The first three symbols indicate manufacturer, make and vehicle type. The fourth symbol denotes restraint system. Next comes a letter (usually 'M'), followed by two digits that indicate Model Number, as shown in left column of tables below. (Example: '10' Tracer GS four-door sedan). Symbol eight indicates engine type. Next is a check digit. Symbol ten indicates model year ('V' - 1997). Symbol eleven denotes assembly plant. The final six digits make up the sequence number, starting with 000001.

TRACER (FOUR)

Model No.	Body/ Style No.	Body Type & Seating	Factory Price	Shipping Weight	Prod. Total
M	10	4-dr. GS Sed-4P	11145	2457	Note 1
M	13	4-dr. LS Sed-4P	11670	2503	Note 1
M	15	4-dr. LS Sta Wgn-4P	12220	2569	7,250

NOTE 1: Production of four-door sedans totaled 58,662 with no further breakout available.

MYSTIQUE (FOUR/V-6)

M	65	4-dr. Sed-5P	13960/-----	NA/----	Note 1
M	65	4-dr. GS Sed-5P	14775/15975	2861/NA	Note 1
M	66	4-dr. LS Sed-5P	16150/17295	2884/NA	Note 1

NOTE: Figures to left of slash for four-cylinder engine, to right for V-6.

NOTE 1: Production of four-door sedans totaled 23,321 with no further breakout available.

SABLE (V-6)

M	51	4-dr. G Sed-5P	18505	NA	Note 1
M	50	4-dr. GS Sed-5P	19495	3333	Note 1
M	55	4-dr. GS Sta Wag-5P	19495	3476	Note 2
M	53	4-dr. LS Sed-5P	22080	3360	Note 1
M	58	4-dr. LS Sta Wag-5P	22080	3502	Note 2

NOTE 1: Production of four-door sedans totaled 89,108 with no further breakout available.

NOTE 2: Production of station wagons totaled 25,132 with no further breakout available.

COUGAR XR7 (V-6/V-8)

Model No.	Body/ Style No.	Body Type & Seating	Factory Price	Shipping Weight	Prod. Total
M	62	2-dr. XR7 Cpe-4P	17830/18960	3528/3666	35,267

NOTE: Figures to left of slash for V-6, to right for V-8.

GRAND MARQUIS (V-8)

M	74	4-dr. GS Sed-6P	22495	3792	Note 1
M	75	4-dr. LS Sed-6P	23905	3796	Note 1

NOTE 1: Production of four-door sedans totaled 127,949 with no further breakout available.

ENGINE [Base Four (Tracer)]: Inline. Overhead cam. Four-cylinder. Cast-iron block and aluminum head. Displacement: 122 cid (2.0 liters). Bore & stroke: 3.33 x 3.46 in. Compression ratio: 9.2:1. Brake horsepower: 110 at 5000 rpm. Torque: 125 lbs.-ft. at 3750 rpm. Split Port Induction.

ENGINE [Base Four (Mystique/Mystique GS)]: Inline. Dual overhead cam. Four-cylinder. Cast-iron block and aluminum head. Displacement: 121 cid (2.0 liters). Bore & stroke: 3.34 x 3.46 in. Compression ratio: 9.6:1. Brake horsepower: 125 at 5500 rpm. Torque: 130 lbs.-ft. at 4000 rpm. Sequential fuel injection.

ENGINE [Base V-6 (Mystique LS); Optional (Mystique GS)]: Modular, Dual overhead cam V-6. Aluminum block and head. Displacement: 155 cid (2.5 liters). Bore & stroke: 3.24 x 3.13 in. Compression ratio: 9.7:1. Brake horsepower: 170 at 6250 rpm. Torque: 165 lbs.-ft. at 4250 rpm. Sequential fuel injection.

ENGINE [Base V-6 (Sable GS)]: 60-degree, overhead valve V-6. Cast-iron block and head. Displacement: 182 cid (3.0 liters). Bore & stroke: 3.50 x 3.15 in. Compression ratio: 9.3:1. Brake horsepower: 145 at 5250 rpm. Torque: 170 lbs.-ft. at 3250 rpm. Sequential fuel injection.

ENGINE [Base V-6 (Sable LS)]: same as 3.0-liter V-6 above except - DOHC V-6. Brake horsepower: 200 at 5750 rpm. Torque: 200 lbs.-ft. at 4500 rpm. Sequential fuel injection.

1997 Mercury Grand Marquis LS sedan. (OCW)

ENGINE [Base V-6 (Cougar XR7)]: 60-degree, overhead valve V-6. Cast-iron block and head. Displacement: 232 cid (3.8 liters). Bore & stroke: 3.80 x 3.40 in. Compression ratio: 9.0:1. Brake horsepower: 145 at 4000 rpm. Torque: 215 lbs.-ft. at 2750 rpm. Sequential fuel injection.

ENGINE [Base V-8 (Grand Marquis); Optional (Cougar XR7)]: Modular, overhead cam V-8. Displacement: 281 cid (4.6-liter). Bore & stroke: 3.60 x 3.60 in. Compression ratio: 9.0:1. Brake horsepower: (Cougar XR7) 205 at 4250 RPM; (Grand Marquis) 190 at 4250 rpm. Torque: (Cougar XR7) 280 lbs.-ft. at 3000 RPM; (Grand Marquis) 265 lbs.-ft. at 3250 rpm. Sequential fuel injection.

CHASSIS DATA: Wheelbase: (Tracer) 98.4 in.; (Mystique) 106.5 in.; (Sable) 106.0 in.; (Cougar) 113.0 in.; (Grand Marquis) 114.4 in. Overall Length: (Tracer sta wag) 172.7 in.; (Tracer sed) 174.7 in.; (Mystique) 183.5 in.; (Sable) 199.7 in.; (Cougar) 199.9 in.; (Grand Marquis) 211.8 in. Height: (Tracer sed) 53.3 in.; (Tracer sta wag) 53.9 in.; (Mystique) 54.5 in.; (Sable sed) 55.4 in.; (Sable sta wag) 57.6 in.; (Cougar) 52.5 in.; (Grand Marquis) 56.8 in.; Width: (Tracer) 67.0 in.; (Mystique) 69.1 in.; (Sable) 73.0 in.; (Cougar) 72.7 in.; (Grand Marquis) 77.8 in. Front Tread: (Tracer) 56.5 in.; (Mystique) 59.2 in.; (Sable) 61.6 in.; (Cougar) 61.6 in.; (Grand Marquis) 62.8 in. Rear Tread: (Tracer) 56.5 in.; (Mystique) 58.5 in.; (Sable sed) 61.4 in.; (Sable sta wag) 61.8 in.; (Cougar) 60.2 in.; (Grand Marquis) 63.3 in. Standard Tires: (Tracer) P185/55R14; (Mystique/Mystique GS) P185/70R14; (Mystique LS) P205/60R15; (Sable) P205/65R15; (Cougar) P205/70R15; (Grand Marquis) P215/70R15.

TECHNICAL: Transmission: Five-speed manual transaxle standard on Tracer and Mystique. Four-speed automatic overdrive standard on Sable, Cougar XR7 and Grand Marquis. Drive Axle: (Cougar XR7/Grand Marquis) rear; (others) front. Steering: (Grand Marquis) recirculating ball; (others) rack/pinion. Front Suspension: (Tracer) Independent MacPherson strut w/strut-mounted coil springs and stabilizer bar; (Mystique) Independent strut-type w/strut-mounted coil springs, lower control A-arm and cast steering knuckle connected to rubber-mounted subframe; (Sable) Independent MacPherson strut w/strut-mounted coil spring, stabilizer bar, tension strut, lower control arm and cast steering knuckle; (Cougar) Short and long arm (SLA) w/double-isolated tension strut, variable rate coil springs and stabilizer bar; (Grand Marquis) Independent SLA w/ball joints, coil springs and stabilizer bar. Rear Suspension: (Tracer) Independent, Quadralink w/coil springs and stabilizer bar; (Mystique) Quadralink strut w/coil spring on shock strut; mounted to rigid subframe and w/stabilizer bar; (Sable sed) Independent Quadralink w/coil spring on shock strut, stabilizer bar, tension strut, parallel control arms and cast spindle w/pressed-in forged stem; (Sable sta wag) SLA independent w/variable-rate coil spring on lower control arm, stabilizer bar, tension strut and cast spindle w/pressed-in forged stem; (Cougar) H-arm independent w/variable-rate coil springs and stabilizer bar; (Grand Marquis) Four-bar link w/rubber-insulated coil springs on axle and stabilizer bar. Brakes: (Tracer/Mystique w/o V-6) front disc, rear drum (power assisted); (others) front/rear disc. Body construction: (Grand Marquis) separate body and frame; (others) unibody. Fuel tank: (Tracer) 12.7 gal.; (Mystique) 14.5 gal.; (Sable) 16.0 gal.; (Cougar) 18.0 gal.; (Grand Marquis) 20.0 gal.

DRIVETRAIN OPTIONS: Engines: 2.5-liter V-6: Mystique GS ($1200). 4.6-liter V-8: Cougar XR7 ($1130). Transmission/Differential: Four-speed automatic transaxle: Tracer ($815). Mystique ($815). Traction-Lok Axle: Cougar XR7 ($95). Elect Traction Control w/Antilock Brakes: Cougar XR7 ($210). Suspension/Brakes: HD Suspension: Sable sta wag ($25). Rear Air Suspension: Grand Marquis ($270). Anti-lock brakes: Tracer ($570); Mystique ($570); Sable ($600); Cougar XR7 ($570); Grand Marquis w/Traction Control System ($670). 41G Handling Pkg: Grand Marquis GS ($1020); Grand Marquis LS ($600).

TRACER CONVENIENCE/APPEARANCE OPTIONS: Preferred Equip Pkgs (Tracer LS 541A): Rr Window Defroster, Dual Pwr Mirrors, Air Cond and Driver's Dr Remote Entry Syst ($835). (Tracer LS 542A): same as 541A plus AM/FM Stereo Radio w/Cass, Pwr Windows and Pwr Locks w/Anti-Theft ($1530). Calif. Emission Syst ($100). Alum Geometric Whls (LS only) ($265); w/Trio Pkg (NC). Integrated Child's Seat ($135). Man Air Cond ($795). Anti-Lock Braking Syst ($570). Convenience Grp incl Tilt Strg, Spd Ctrl, Dual Map Lights, Dual Vanity Mirrors and F&R Flr Mats (LS only) ($435). F&R Flr Mats ($45). Trio Pkg incl 14-inch Alum Whls, Bright-Tip Exhaust, Foglamps, Unique Seat Trim, Trio Nomenclature and Rr Decklid Spoiler (LS only) ($495). Eng Block Heater ($20). Wagon Grp incl Luggage Rack and Dlx Rr Window Wiper/Washer ($240). AM/FM Stereo Radio w/Cass ($165). Elect AM/FM Stereo Radio w/Cass, Premium Sound w/6-Disc Compact Changer (LS only) ($350).

MYSTIQUE CONVENIENCE/APPEARANCE OPTIONS: Preferred Equip Pkgs (Mystique GS 371A): Man Air Cond, Elect Rr Window Defroster, AM/FM Stereo Radio w/Cass, Heated Ext Mirrors, Pwr Windows w/Driver's Side Express Down, Rr Window Lockout, Pwr Dr Locks, Illum Switches on all Drs, Right Illum Visor Vanity Mirror, Frt Map Reading Lights & Illum Entry, Illum Inside Dr Handles and Spd Ctrl ($1480). (Mystique GS 372A): same as 371A plus 2.5-liter DOHC Duratec V-6, P195/65R14 Perf BSW Tires, Perf-Tuned Strg & Suspension and 100,000-Mile Service Interval ($2580). (Mystique LS 381A): Air Cond, Rr Window Defroster, Pwr Dr Locks, Pwr Windows w/Driver's Side Express Down, Rr Window Lockout, Illum Switches on All Drs, Right Illum Visor Vanity Mirror, Frt Map Reading Lights & Illum Entry Syst, Remote Lckg, Cruise Ctrl, Leather-Wrapped Strg Whl, 2.5-liter Duratec V-6, P205/60R15 Perf BSW Tires, Perf-Tuned Strg & Suspension and 100,000-Mile Service Interval ($2420). Man Air Cond ($795). Pwr Antenna (GS only) ($80). Anti-Lock Brakes ($570). Cruise Ctrl ($215). Elect Rr Window Defroster (base and GS only) ($190). Calif. Emission Syst ($100). Eng Block Heater ($20). Lckg Remote ($190). F&R Carpeted Flr Mats (GS only) ($45). Spt Appearance Pkg incl 15-inch Alum Whls, Rr Spoiler and P205/60R15 BSW Tires ($675). Spree Pkg incl 15-inch Alum Whls, Unique Flr Mats, Leather-Wrapped Strg Whl, Foglamps and Unique Interior Trim (GS only) ($495). AM/FM Stereo Radio, Premium Sound w/Cass, Amplifier: LS ($270); base and GS ($315). AM/FM Stereo Radio, Premium Sound w/CD Player, Amplifier: GS ($455); LS ($270). Pwr Moonroof ($595). 10-Way Pwr Driver's Side Seat ($330). Rr Decklid Spoiler ($345). Leather Seating Surface Upholstery (LS only) ($595). 15-inch Cast Alum Whls incl P205/60R15 BSW Tires (GS only) ($425).

SABLE CONVENIENCE/APPEARANCE OPTIONS: Preferred Equip Pkgs (Sable GS 450A): Spd Ctrl, F&R Carpeted Flr Mats, Particulate Air Filtration Syst, Pwr Dr Locks and AM/FM Stereo Radio w/Cass ($250). (Sable GS 451A): same as 450A plus 6-Way Pwr Driver's Seat, Light Grp and Alum Whls ($850). (Sable LS 461A): F&R Carpeted Flr Mats, Spd Ctrl, Particulate Air Filtration Syst, Keyless Entry w/Dual Remote Transmitters w/Perimeter Anti-theft and Anti-Lock Brakes ($720). (Sable LS 462A): same as 461A plus Auto Air Cond, MACH Audio Syst and Chrome Alum Whls ($1710). Auto Air Cond incl Dual Heated Pwr Mirrors ($210). Anti-Lock Brake Syst incl 4 Whl Disc Brakes ($600). CD Changer incl 6-Disc Changer (LS only) ($595). Calif. Emission Syst ($100). Remote Keyless Entry Syst (GS only) ($190). Remote Keyless Entry Syst w/Perimeter Anti-Theft (LS only) ($440). Eng Block Heater ($35). Daytime Running Lights ($40). Light Grp incl Dual Courtesy Lights Under Instrument Panel, Map Lights and Dual Beam Reading & Dome (GS only) ($45). Wagon Grp incl Cargo Area Cover, Rr Window Wiper/Washer and Cargo Convenience Net ($295). MACH Audio Syst ($400). Pwr Moonroof incl Unique Map Lights in OH Console (LS only) ($740). Vinyl Rr Facing Third Seat (sta wag only) ($200). Leather Bucket Seats (LS 5-Pass only) ($990). HD Suspension (sta wag only) ($25). Cellular Phone incl Voice Activation ($650). Conventional Spare Tire (sed only) ($125). Alum Whls ($315). Chrome Alum Whls incl Lckg Lug Nuts ($580).

COUGAR CONVENIENCE/APPEARANCE OPTIONS: Preferred Equip Pkgs (Cougar XR7 260A): Elect Rr Window Defroster, Spd Ctrl, 15-inch 21-Spoke Cast Alum Whls, Pwr Lock Grp, P215/70R15 BSW Tires and Frt Flr Mats ($505). (Cougar XR7 262A): same as 260A plus 4.6-liter V-8, Illum Entry, 6-Way Pwr Driver's Seat and Leather-Wrapped Strg Whl & Shift Knob ($1345). Semi-Auto Air Cond ($155). Anti-Theft Alarm Syst ($145). Autolamp Syst ($70). Pwr Antenna ($85). Traction-Lok Axle ($95). HD Battery ($25). Anti-Lock Brake Syst incl 4-Whl Disc Brakes ($570). Calif. Emission Syst ($100). Remote Keyless Entry Syst, Illum, incl Remote Hand-Held Transmitter, Ext Lckg Capability ($270). Eng Block Heater ($20). Dual Illum Visor Vanity Mirrors ($95). Tri-Coat Paint ($225). 30th Anniv Special Edition incl Dark Toreador Red Unique Ext Color, Seat Trim Embroidered w/30th Anniv Logo, Unique Frt Bucket Seats w/Pwr Driver Lumbar Support & Side Bolsters, Frt Flr Mats Embroidered w/30th Anniv Logo, 30th Anniv C-Pillar Badges, Auto Dimming Day/Night Rearview Mirror, Unique 16-inch Whls, P225/60R16 Tires, Larger Frt Disc Brake Rotors, Spt-Tuned Suspension (w/V-8 only), Merchandising Kit incl Certificate, Maglight, Desk Plate, Key Chain, Umbrella, Pen and Presentation Book ($495). Lux Appearance Grp incl Geometric Spoke Whls and Non-Functional Luggage Rack ($115). Sport Edition incl Color-Keyed

Decklid Spoiler w/Integrated Stop Light, 16-inch 7-Spoke Alum Whls, P225/60R16 Touring Tires, Larger Frt Disc Brake Rotors, Spt-Tuned Suspension, F&R Spt-Tuned Shocks (models w/V-8 also incl Firmer Springs, Revised Frt Lwr Arm Bushings and Larger Rr Stabilizer Bar ($450). Premium AM/FM Stereo Radio w/Cass incl 8-Watt Amp & Premium Spkrs ($290). Elect AM/FM Stereo Radio w/CD Player incl 8-Watt Amp & Premium Spkrs ($430). Pwr Moonroof incl One-Touch Open Feature, Dual Reading Lamps, Pop-Up Air Deflector, Sliding Sunshade and Rr Tilt-Up ($740). 6-Way Pwr Driver's Seat ($290). 6-Way Pwr Pass Seat ($290). Individual Bucket Seats w/Leather Seating Surfaces ($490). Decklid Spoiler ($250). Leather-Wrapped Strg Whl incl Leather-Wrapped Gear Shift Knob ($90). Elect Traction Ctrl ($210).

GRAND MARQUIS CONVENIENCE/APPEARANCE OPTIONS: Preferred Equip Pkgs (Grand Marquis GS 157A): Carpeted Flr Mats F&R, Pwr Lock Grp, Spd Ctrl, Illum Entry Syst, Lckg Radial-Spoke Whl Covers ($40). (Grand Marquis LS 172A): F&R Carpeted Flr Mats, Pwr Lock Grp, Illum Entry Syst, Lux Light Grp, Bodyside Paint Stripe, Spd Ctrl, Frt Cornering Lamps, Leather-Wrapped Strg Whl, 12-Spoke Alum Whls and Remote Keyless Entry Syst ($820). (Grand Marquis LS 173A): same as 172A plus Anti-Lock Brakes w/Traction Assist, Elect Grp, Elect Auto Air Cond, 6-Way Pwr Pass Seat, AM/FM Stereo Radio w/Cass and Elect Auto Dim Mirror ($2780). Auto Air Cond incl O/S Temp Display (LS only) ($175). Anti-Lock Brakes w/Traction Ctrl Syst ($670). Calif. Emission Syst ($100). Remote Keyless Entry Syst incl Dual Remote Transmitters and Keypad (GS only) ($240). Eng Block Heater ($25). 41G Handling Pkg incl Pwr Steering Cooler, Upsized F&R Stabilizer Bars, 3.27 Axle, P225/60R16 BSW Tires, 16-inch Lacy-Spoke Alum Whls, Rr Air Suspension w/Unique Springs, Unique Tuned Suspension, Unique Strg Gear and Dual Exhaust: LS ($600); GS ($1020). Lux Light Grp incl Dual Illum Visor Mirrors, Dual Beam Dome/Map Lights and Rr Seat Reading Lamps ($190). Premium Elect AM/FM Stereo Radio w/Cass incl Radio/Tape Scan, AM Stereo, Auto Memory Set, 4 Channel Amp w/80 Watts, Auto Dynamic Noise Reduction on FM, CrO2 Tape Capability and Premium Spkrs (LS only) ($360). Pass 6-Way Pwr Seat w/Pwr Recliner (LS only) ($360). Leather Twin Comfort Lounge Seats (LS only) ($645). Bodyside Paint Stripe (GS only) ($60). Conventional Spare Tire (LS only): w/Handling Package ($240); w/o Handling Pkg ($185).

HISTORY: U.S. model year Mercury production totaled 366,689.

1998 MERCURY

1998 Mercury Tracer Trio sedan. (OCW)

While there was much that was new for 1998 at Mercury, the big news was what there was not—namely a Cougar. Produced continuously since 1967, the Cougar was discontinued for 1998 awaiting its return midyear as a 1999 model in next-generation form (see sidebar story following 1998 Mercury text), and produced at Flat Rock, Mich., instead of its longtime Lorain, Ohio, assembly plant, which was closed. Also discontinued were the base Mystique sedan and Sable G sedan and GS station wagon. The Mystique and Grand Marquis were restyled as well as receiving chassis upgrades while the Sable LS series now used the Vulcan 3.0-liter V-6 as standard powerplant while its previously standard Duratec 3.0-liter V-6 became optional.

TRACER — FOUR — Tracer's lineup returned intact, again comprised of GS and LS four-door sedans and an LS station wagon. The GS sedan could be ordered with the Trio Appearance Group including chrome wheel covers, leather-wrapped steering wheel and rear decklid spoiler. New equipment on the GS sedan included a 60/40 split-fold bench seat, upgraded interior trim and expanded exterior color selection. The LS models' list of new standard features included air conditioning, rear window defroster, dual power mirrors and driver's door remote entry system. The LS station wagon added a cargo cover, luggage rack and rear window wiper/washer. In addition, buyers of LS models could choose from three specific option groups to simplify selection: Power Group, Comfort Group or Sport Group. The Tracer was again powered by the overhead cam

2.0-liter four-cylinder engine mated to a five-speed manual transaxle. A sensor was added to the engine to reduce knocking during high-load operation. The optional electronically controlled four-speed automatic transaxle was also upgraded to improve shifting smoothness and offer a crisper response. To make the Tracer more visible in traffic, side marker lamps were revamped to flash in synch with front turn signals.

MYSTIQUE — FOUR/V-6 — The streamlined Mystique lineup offered a four-door sedan in two separate trim levels for 1998: GS and LS. Gone after only one year of availability was the base sedan. Mystique's exterior styling was revised including headlamps with integrated high/low beams with park and turn signals under one lens. New features included power windows as standard and a low-fuel warning lamp added to the instrument cluster. Recontoured rear seat cushions allowed for more knee room in back. The GS sedan was powered by the Zetec 2.0-liter four-cylinder engine while the LS sedan used the Duratec 2.5-liter V-6. Both series again had the five-speed manual transaxle as standard with the four-speed automatic overdrive unit as optional. The manual unit's shift linkage now used cables, instead of the rods formerly employed, to reduce vibration. The Zetec powerplant underwent significant revision to also reduce noise and vibration. The engine's cylinder block was bolstered with a "ladderframe" lower reinforcement. In addition, internal components were lightened and engine efficiency was improved via a new variable-valve timing system. The LS sedan's new standard equipment included leather seats, foglamps and SecuriLock anti-theft system. The GS sedan could be ordered with a new, optional Sport Package that included leather-wrapped steering wheel and shift knob, foglamps, rear decklid spoiler and embroidered floor mats and special exterior badging.

SABLE — V-6 — The Sable offerings were also thinned as the G sedan and GS station wagon offered previously were not continued for 1998. The revised lineup consisted of a GS four-door sedan and LS four-door sedan and station wagon. Standard engine for both GS and LS models was the Vulcan 3.0-liter V-6 rated at 145 hp. Optional for both was the Duratec DOHC 3.0-liter V-6 rated at 200 hp—the engine that formerly standard in LS models. Both engines featured 100,000 mile tune-up intervals. Throttle response of the Duratec V-6 was improved via a higher stall speed torque converter and new axle ratio that accelerated the climb to cruising speed. SecuriLock anti-theft system was included when the Duratec engine option was ordered. The AX4N electronically controlled four-speed automatic overdrive transaxle was the only unit used in Sables. Sable's safety features included standard reinforced side-door guard beams, five mph bumpers and second-generation dual airbags. For 1998, a new single-point sensor was used to trigger the airbags. Anti-lock brakes were optional. The Sable LS could be ordered with the optional Premium Group that included the Duratec V-6, electronic automatic temperature control, dual illuminated visor vanity mirrors, power antenna and remote keyless entry.

1998 Mercury Mystique LS sedan. (OCW)

1998 Mercury Sable LS station wagon. (OCW)

1998 Mercury Grand Marquis LS sedan. (OCW)

GRAND MARQUIS — V-8 — The Grand Marquis received a design "freshening" to give the rear-drive four-door sedan—available in GS or LS trim levels—a more contemporary look. Among the revisions were a new front fascia and bumper, six-section grille flanked by larger headlamps and a chrome strip topping the grille, which houses the Mercury emblem. The hood and fenders were also revised, and new cornering lamps were now standard equipment. The sides of the Grand Marquis were also revamped with the addition of a wide chrome body strip, aerodynamic mirrors and new wheel covers. Tail lamps were more prominent and were accented with chrome. The interior of the Grand Marquis was also upgraded with a new, two-spoke steering wheel and green backlighting of the instrument panel. Upgrades in the chassis included the use of Watt's Linkage rear suspension for straighter tracking, larger brake rotors and linings and new 16-inch wheels and tires. All-Speed Traction Control was optional as was air suspension and handling packages. The 4.6-liter V-8 was again the standard (and only) engine, but it was also upgraded to deliver 200 hp (vs. 190 the year previous). A dual-speed electric fan replaced the engine-driven fan used previously, which resulted in less engine noise and improved air conditioning operation at idle. Grand Marquis buyers who ordered the optional handling package also received 15 extra hp (215) and 10 more pound-feet of torque (275). The handling package included a 3.27 axle ratio (compared to the 2.73 standard ratio), dual exhaust, performance tires, rear air suspension and heavier stabilizer bars. Grand Marquis again used the electronically controlled four-speed automatic overdrive transmission.

I.D. DATA: Mercury's 17-symbol Vehicle Identification Number (VIN) was stamped on a metal tab fastened to the instrument panel, visible through the windshield. The first three symbols indicate manufacturer, make and vehicle type. The fourth symbol denotes restraint system. Next comes a letter (usually 'M'), followed by two digits that indicate Model Number, as shown in left column of tables below. (Example: '10' Tracer GS four-door sedan). Symbol eight indicates engine type. Next is a check digit. Symbol ten indicates model year ('W' - 1998). Symbol eleven denotes assembly plant. The final six digits make up the sequence number, starting with 000001.

TRACER (FOUR)

Model No.	Body/ Style No.	Body Type & Seating	Factory Price	Shipping Weight	Prod. Total
M	10	4-dr. GS Sed-4P	11355	2469	*
M	13	4-dr. LS Sed-4P	12710	2469	*
M	15	4-dr. LS Sta Wgn-4P	14205	2532	*

MYSTIQUE (FOUR/V-6)

Model No.	Body/ Style No.	Body Type & Seating	Factory Price	Shipping Weight	Prod. Total
M	65	4-dr. GS Sed-5P	16235/NA	2808/NA	*
M	66	4-dr. LS Sed-5P	17645/NA	2808/NA	*

NOTE: Figures to left of slash for four-cylinder engine, to right for V-6.

SABLE (V-6)

Model No.	Body/ Style No.	Body Type & Seating	Factory Price	Shipping Weight	Prod. Total
M	50	4-dr. GS Sed-5P	19445	3299	*
M	50/60L	4-dr. LS Sed-5P	20445	3299	*
M	55	4-dr. LS Sta Wag-5P	22285	3462	*

GRAND MARQUIS (V-8)

Model No.	Body/ Style No.	Body Type & Seating	Factory Price	Shipping Weight	Prod. Total
M	74	4-dr. GS Sed-6P	21890	3917	*
M	75	4-dr. LS Sed-6P	23790	3922	*

*NOTE: Production figures for 1998 Mercury automobiles were not available when this book went to the printer.

ENGINE [Base Four (Tracer)]: Inline. Overhead cam. Four-cylinder. Cast-iron block and aluminum head. Displacement: 122 cid (2.0 liters). Bore & stroke: 3.33 x 3.46 in. Compression ratio: 9.2:1. Brake horsepower: 110 at 5000 rpm. Torque: 125 lbs.-ft. at 3750 rpm. Split Port Induction.

ENGINE [Base Four (Mystique GS)]: Inline. Dual overhead cam. Four-cylinder. Cast-iron block and aluminum head. Displacement: 121 cid (2.0 liters). Bore & stroke: 3.34 x 3.46 in. Compression ratio: 9.6:1. Brake horsepower: 125 at 5500 rpm. Torque: 130 lbs.-ft. at 4000 rpm. Sequential fuel injection.

ENGINE [Base V-6 (Mystique LS)]: Modular, dual overhead cam V-6. Aluminum block and head. Displacement: 155 cid (2.5 liters). Bore & stroke: 3.24 x 3.13 in. Compression ratio: 9.7:1. Brake horsepower: 170 at 6250 rpm. Torque: 165 lbs.-ft. at 4250 rpm. Sequential fuel injection.

ENGINE [Base V-6 (Sable GS/Sable LS)]: 60-degree, overhead valve V-6. Cast-iron block and head. Displacement: 182 cid (3.0 liters). Bore & stroke: 3.50 x 3.15 in. Compression ratio: 9.3:1. Brake horsepower: 145 at 5250 rpm. Torque: 170 lbs.-ft. at 3250 rpm. Sequential fuel injection.

ENGINE [Optional V-6 (Sable GS/Sable LS)]: same as 3.0-liter V-6 above except - DOHC V-6. Brake horsepower: 200 at 5750 rpm. Torque: 200 lbs.-ft. at 4500 rpm. Sequential fuel injection.

ENGINE [Base V-8 (Grand Marquis)]: Modular, overhead cam V-8. Displacement: 281 cid (4.6-liter). Bore & stroke: 3.60 x 3.60 in. Compression ratio: 9.0:1. Brake horsepower: 200 at 4250 rpm. Torque: 265 lbs.-ft. at 3000 rpm. Sequential fuel injection.

CHASSIS DATA: Wheelbase: (Tracer) 98.4 in.; (Mystique) 106.5 in.; (Sable) 108.5 in.; (Grand Marquis) 114.4 in. Overall Length: (Tracer sta wag) 172.7 in.; (Tracer sed) 174.7 in.; (Mystique) 184.8 in.; (Sable sta wag) 199.1 in.; (Sable sed) 199.7 in.; (Grand Marquis) 211.8 in. Height: (Tracer sed) 53.3 in.; (Tracer sta wag) 53.9 in.; (Mystique) 54.5 in.; (Sable sed) 55.4 in.; (Sable sta wag) 57.6 in.; (Grand Marquis) 56.8 in. Width: (Tracer) 67.0 in.; (Mystique) 69.1 in.; (Sable) 73.0 in.; (Grand Marquis) 77.8 in. Front Tread: (Tracer) 56.5 in.; (Mystique) 59.2 in.; (Sable) 61.6 in.; (Grand Marquis) 62.8 in. Rear Tread: (Tracer) 56.5 in.; (Mystique) 58.5 in.; (Sable sed) 61.4 in.; (Sable sta wag) 61.8 in.; (Grand Marquis) 63.3 in. Standard Tires: (Tracer) P185/65R14; (Mystique GS) P185/70R14; (Mystique LS) P205/60R15; (Sable) P205/65R15; (Grand Marquis) P225/60R16.

TECHNICAL: Transmission: Five-speed manual transaxle standard on Tracer and Mystique. Four-speed automatic overdrive standard on Sable and Grand Marquis. Drive Axle: (Grand Marquis) rear; (others) front. Steering: (Grand Marquis) recirculating ball; (others) rack/pinion. Front Suspension: (Tracer) Independent MacPherson strut w/strut-mounted coil springs and stabilizer bar; (Mystique) Independent strut-type w/strut-mounted coil springs, lower control A-arm and cast steering knuckle connected to rubber-mounted subframe; (Sable) Independent MacPherson strut w/strut-mounted coil spring, stabilizer bar, tension strut, lower control arm and cast aluminum knuckle w/integral ball joint; (Grand Marquis) Independent SLA w/ball joints, coil springs and stabilizer bar. Rear Suspension: (Tracer) Independent, Quadralink w/coil springs and stabilizer bar; (Mystique) Quadralink strut w/coil spring on shock strut; mounted to rigid subframe and w/stabilizer bar; (Sable sed) Independent Quadralink w/coil spring on shock strut, stabilizer bar, tension strut, parallel control arms and cast spindle w/pressed-in forged stem; (Sable sta wag) SLA independent w/variable-rate coil spring on lower control arm, stabilizer bar, tension strut and cast spindle w/pressed-in forged stem and integrated ball joint; (Grand Marquis) Four-bar link w/Watt's Linkage, air suspension springs on axle and stabilizer bar. Brakes: (Tracer/Mystique w/auto trans/Sable sed) front disc, rear drum (power assisted); (others) front/rear disc. Body construction: (Grand Marquis) separate body and frame; (others) unibody. Fuel tank: (Tracer) 12.8 gal.; (Mystique) 14.5 gal.; (Sable) 16.0 gal.; (Grand Marquis) 20.0 gal.

DRIVETRAIN OPTIONS: Engines: Duratec 3.0-liter V-6: Sable GS/Sable LS ($495). Transmission/Differential: Four-speed automatic transaxle: Tracer ($815). Mystique ($815). Suspension/Brakes: Rear Air Suspension: Grand Marquis LS only ($270). Anti-lock brakes: Tracer ($400); Mystique ($500); Sable ($600); Grand Marquis w/Traction Control System ($775). 41G Handling Pkg: Grand Marquis ($855). Ultimate Pkg w/All-Speed Traction Control: Grand Marquis LS only ($2400).

TRACER CONVENIENCE/APPEARANCE OPTIONS: Man Air Cond ($795). Anti-Lock Braking Syst ($400). Comfort Grp incl Flr Mats, Dual Visor Vanity Mirrors, Reading Lights, Spd Ctrl and Tilt Strg Whl ($365). Rr Window Defroster ($190). Calif. Emission Syst ($170). Driver Keyless Remote Ctrl Entry Syst ($135). F&R Flr Mats ($55). Eng Block Heater ($20). Dual Pwr Mirrors ($95). Pwr Grp incl All Dr Keyless Remote Ctrl Entry Syst, Pwr Locks and Pwr Windows ($395). AM/FM Stereo Radio w/Cass ($185); GS and LS sed ($255). Elect

AM/FM Stereo Radio w/Cass incl 6-Disc CD Changer ($515). Integrated Child Seat ($135). Smoker's Pkg incl Ashtray & Cigarette Lighter ($15). Spt Grp incl Foglights, Bright Tip Exhaust, Rr Spoiler, Alum Whls, Leather-Wrapped Strg Whl, Cloth Spt Bucket Seats and Badging ($515). Trio Opt Pkg incl Leather-Wrapped Strg Whl, Rr Decklid Spoiler, Badging and Chrome Whl Covers ($260). Alum Whls ($265).

MYSTIQUE CONVENIENCE/APPEARANCE OPTIONS: Pwr Antenna ($95). Anti-Lock Braking Syst ($500). Calif. Emission Syst ($170). Keyless Remote Ctrl Entry Syst ($190). F&R Flr Mats ($55). Eng Block Heater ($20). Pwr Moonroof ($595). AM/FM Stereo CD incl Premium Sound ($275). AM/FM Stereo Radio w/Cass incl Premium Sound ($135). Integrated Child Seat ($135). 10-Way Adjustable Pwr Driver's Seat ($350). Smoker's Pkg incl Ashtray & Cigarette Lighter ($15). Rr Spoiler ($245). Spt Grp incl Rr Spoiler, Leather-Wrapped Strg Whl, Fog Lights, Spt Flr Mats and Badging ($395). Spree Pkg incl Polished Mach Alloy Whls, Fog Lights, Leather-Wrapped Strg Whl and Unique Flr Mats ($525). Polished Mach Alloy Whls incl P205/60R15 Perf BSW Tires ($475).

SABLE CONVENIENCE/APPEARANCE OPTIONS: Air Filtration Syst, Ltd Production Opt ($30). Anti-Lock Braking Syst incl F&R Disc Brakes ($600). Calif. Emission Syst ($170). Keyless Remote Ctrl Entry Syst ($190). F&R Flr Mats ($55). Eng Block Heater ($35). Light Grp incl Map & Reading Lights ($45). Daytime Running Lights incl 72-Amp Battery ($40). Dual Heated Mirrors ($35). Pwr Moonroof incl Map Lights ($740). Premium Grp incl 3.0-liter V-6, Auto Air Cond, Auto Headlamps, Dual Illum Visor Vanity Mirrors, Pwr Antenna, Keyless Remote Ctrl Sys w/Keypad & Alarm Syst: LS sed ($825); LS sta wag ($675). 6-Disc CD Changer ($350). MACH Audio Syst incl Pwr Antenna: LS w/o Prem Grp ($400); w/Prem Grp ($320). 6-Way Adjustable Pwr Pass Seat ($350). Leather Bucket Seats (LS only) ($895). Integrated Child Seat (LS sta wag) ($135). Vinyl Rr Facing Third Seat (LS sta wag) ($200). Conventional Spare Tire ($125). Wagon Grp incl Cargo Cover and Cargo Net (LS sta wag) ($140). Painted Alum Whls ($315). Chrome Alum Whls ($580).

GRAND MARQUIS CONVENIENCE/APPEARANCE OPTIONS: Anti-Lock Brakes w/Traction Ctrl ($775). Elect Auto Temp Ctrl (LS only) ($175). Elect Instrumentation (LS only) ($425). Calif. Emission Syst ($170). Eng Block Heater ($25). Handling Pkg: Upgrade From Steel Whls w/Whl Covers ($855); Upgrade from Teardrop Alum Whls ($535). Luxury Light Grp ($190). Bodyside Paint Stripe ($60). Premium Pkg incl Teardrop Alum Whls, Leather-Wrapped Strg Whl, Elect Auto Temp Ctrl, Pwr Pass Seat and Auto Dim Mirror w/Compass (LS only) ($1000). Sgl Disc CD Player (GS only) ($140). 6-Disc CD Changer ($350). Remote Keyless Entry Syst ($240). Leather Twin Comfort Seats ($735). Conventional Spare Tire (LS only) w/Handling Package ($120); all other ($105). Rear Air Susp (LS only) ($270). Ultimate Pkg incl Prem Pkg plus Anti-lock Brakes w/All-Spd Traction Ctrl, Elect Instrumentation, Prem Elect AM/FM Radio w/Cass (LS only) ($2400). Universal Garage Dr Opener (LS only) ($115). 16-inch Teardrop Alum Whls (LS only) ($320).

HISTORY: The all-new-design, 1999 Cougar returned after a one-year hiatus, launched in midyear 1998. (See next page).

1999 MERCURY

1999 Mercury Tracer four-door wagon. (FMC)

TRACER – FOUR – The Tracer was Mercury's entry-level model and was in its last year of production. New for 1999 was an upgraded interior. An AM/FM stereo with cassette was now standard on the LS model, which also had a new option — a remote keyless entry system that operated the locks on all of the doors.

1999 Mercury Tracer four-door sedan. (FMC)

TRACER GS: Standard equipment included dual second-generation (de-powered) airbags, power front disc/rear drum brakes, side window demisters, rear door child safety locks, a 2.0-liter split port injected four-cylinder engine, a single tip exhaust pipe, Solar-Tinted glass, an instrument panel with climate and audio control panel and a storage bin and clock, dual black manual outside rearview mirrors, a day/night inside rearview mirror, dual visor-vanity mirrors, a series II onboard diagnostic system, an electronic AM/FM stereo with cassette and four speakers, cloth and vinyl low-back bucket seats, a 60/40 split-folding rear seat with dual release handles, a tilt steering column, a four-spoke steering wheel, power rack-and-pinion steering, P185/65R14 black sidewall tires, a mini spare tire, a five-speed manual transmission, a trip odometer, two-speed interval windshield wipers and full wheel covers.

TRACER LS: Standard equipment included dual second-generation (de-powered) airbags, power front disc/rear drum brakes, side window demisters, rear door child safety locks, a 2.0-liter split port injected four-cylinder engine, a single tip exhaust pipe, Solar-Tinted glass, an instrument panel with climate and audio control panel and a storage bin and clock, air conditioning, dual power outside rearview mirrors, a day/night inside rearview mirror, dual visor-vanity mirrors, a series II onboard diagnostic system, an electronic AM/FM stereo with cassette and four speakers (two premium), remote keyless entry, an all-door perimeter anti-theft system, speed control, cloth and vinyl low-back bucket seats, a 60/40 split-folding rear seat with dual release handles, a tilt steering column, a color-keyed steering wheel, speed control, a tachometer, power rack-and-pinion steering, P185/65R14 black sidewall tires, a mini spare tire, a five-speed manual transmission, a trip odometer, two-speed interval windshield wipers and full wheel covers. The LS station wagon also included a removable shade and cargo area cover, a deluxe luggage rack, a rear window wiper/washer and luxury bolt-on wheel covers.

I.D. DATA: Mercury's 17-symbol Vehicle Identification Number (VIN) was stamped on a metal tab fastened to the instrument panel, visible through the windshield. The first symbol indicates the nation of origin: 1=United States; 2=Canada; 3=Mexico. The second symbol indicates manufacturer: M=Mercury Division, Ford Motor Co.; Z=Mercury Division, Ford Motor Co. The third symbol indicates vehicle type: E=passenger car; H=incomplete vehicle; W=Cougar. The fourth symbol indicates type of restraint system: B=driver and passenger airbags and active belts (except Escort ZX2 coupe); F=driver and passenger airbags and active belts; H= driver and passenger front and side airbags and active belts in all outboard positions; L= driver and passenger airbags and front passive belts, rear active belts. The fifth symbol indicates designation: M=Mercury; T=Imported from outside North America or non-Ford car marketed by Ford in North America. The sixth and seventh symbols indicate body type: 10=Tracer GS four-door sedan; 13=Tracer LS four-door sedan; 15=Tracer LS four-door station wagon; 50=Sable GS four-door sedan; 53=Sable LS four-door sedan; 55=Sable LS premium sedan; 58=Sable LS four-door station wagon; 60=Cougar three-door coupe with I-4; 61=Cougar three-door coupe with V-6; 65=Mystique GS four-door sedan; 66=Mystique LS four-door sedan; 74=Grand Marquis GS four-door sedan; 75=Grand Marquis LS four-door sedan. The eighth symbol indicates engine: L= Cougar 2.5-liter DOHC V-6 with EFI; 3=Cougar 2.0-liter DOHC I-4 with EFI; P=Tracer 2.0-liter I-4 with EFI; L=Mystique 2.5-liter DOHC V-6 with EFI; 3=Mystique 2.0-liter DOHC I-4 with EFI; S=Sable 3.0-liter DOHC V-6 with EFI; U=Sable 3.0-liter V-6 with EFI; W=Grand Marquis 4.6-liter SOHC V-8 with EFI (Romeo engine plant). The ninth symbol is a check digit. The 10th symbol indicates model year: X=1999. The 11th symbol indicates assembly plant: A=Hapeville (Atlanta), Ga.; G=Chicago, Ill.; K=Claycomo (Kansas City), Mo.; M=Cuautitlan, Mexico; R=Hermosillo, Mexico; X=Talbotville (St. Thomas), Ontario, Canada; 5=AAI: Flat Rock, Mich. The last six symbols are the sequential production number starting at 100001 at each factory.

1999 Mercury Mystique four-door sedan. (FMC)

Model No.	Body/ Style No.	Body Type & Seating	Factory Price	Shipping Weight	Prod. Total
TRACER GS (FOUR)					
M	10	4d Sedan-4P	11,945	2,469	Note 1
TRACER LS (FOUR)					
M	13	4d Sedan-4P	13,485	2,469	Note 1
M	15	4d Wagon-4P	14,690	2,523	Note 1

Note 1: Total model year production was 25,981.

MYSTIQUE – FOUR/V-6 – The Mystique front suspension was upgraded in 1999. It now matched that of the European Mondeo, on which the Mystique was based. New seats were used that weighed less and provided more rear passenger legroom. A redesigned instrument panel also weighed less and featured improved fit and finish. There was no more "base" model, but the GS and LS editions remained. Other new-for-1999 features included de-powered second-generation airbags, throttle-type traction control and redesigned brake calipers (actually a late-1998 improvement).

MYSTIQUE GS: Standard equipment included dual second generation airbags, a fixed antenna mounted on the rear quarter panel, power front disc and rear drum brakes, an electric digital clock, child proof rear door locks, the 2.0-liter DOHC Zetec 16-valve I-4, semi flush exterior glass with Solar-Tint, a heater and defroster with a four-speed blower control, a soft touch dashboard with knee bolsters and four positive shutoff registers, a backlit cluster with 130-mph speedometer, analog gauges (including a trip odometer, a fuel gauge, a high-beam warning light, a coolant temperature gauge and a low-oil-pressure light, turn signal indicator lights, a handbrake-on warning light, a catalyst malfunction light and a seat belt reminder light), left- and right-hand body-color exterior mirrors, a day/night rearview mirror, an AM/FM stereo, individual manual two-way adjustable front bucket seats with reclining seat backs and cloth trim and a driver's side armrest attached to the seat, a tilt steering column, a soft touch steering wheel with center horn control, power rack-and-pinion steering, a driver's side covered visor mirror and passenger side uncovered visor mirror, P185/70R14S black sidewall radial tires, a five-speed manual transmission with overdrive, single-speed windshield wipers with intermittent feature and fluidic washers and 14-in. wheel covers with full bolt-on appearance.

MYSTIQUE LS: Standard equipment included dual second generation airbags, air conditioning, a fixed antenna mounted on the rear quarter panel, power front disc and rear drum brakes, an electric digital clock, child proof rear door locks, the 2.0-liter DOHC Zetec 16-valve I-4, semi flush exterior glass with Solar-Tint, a heater and defroster with a four-speed blower control, a soft touch dashboard with knee bolsters and four positive shutoff registers, a backlit cluster with 130-mph speedometer, analog gauges (including a trip odometer, a fuel gauge, a tachometer, a high-beam warning light, a coolant temperature gauge and a low-oil-pressure light, turn signal indicator lights, a handbrake-on warning light, a catalyst malfunction light and a seat belt reminder light), left- and right-hand power body-color exterior mirrors, remote keyless entry, all-door and perimeter anti-theft system, speed control, a day/night rearview mirror, an electronic AM/FM stereo and cassette with two premium speakers and two standard speakers, individual manual two-way adjustable front bucket seats with reclining seat backs and cloth trim and a driver's side armrest attached to the seat, a tilt steering column, a color-keyed steering wheel with center horn control, power rack-and-pinion steering, a driver's side covered visor mirror and passenger side uncovered visor mirror, P185/70R14S black sidewall radial tires, a five-speed manual transmission with overdrive, single-speed windshield wipers with intermittent feature and fluidic washers and 14-in. wheel covers with full bolt-on appearance. The wagon also featured a removable shade and cargo cover, a deluxe luggage rack, a rear window washer/wiper and luxury bolt-on wheel covers.

Model No.	Body/ Style No.	Body Type & Seating	Factory Price	Shipping Weight	Prod. Total
MYSTIQUE GS (FOUR)					
M	65	4d Sedan-5P	16,845	2,808	Note 2
MYSTIQUE LS (V-6)					
M	66	4d Sedan-5P	18,180	2,808	Note 2

Note 2: Total model year production was 40,947.

COUGAR – FOUR/V-6 – An all-new front-wheel-drive coupe that bowed in the spring of 1998 as a 1999 model put the Cougar name back in Mercury's model lineup after a short absence. The new car was based on the Mystique/Contour platform and built by Ford's AutoAlliance arm in Flat Rock, Mich. It featured so-called "new-edge" styling aimed at the youth market. Power options included the 2.0-liter Zetec inline four and the 2.5-liter Duratec V-6 also used in Mercury's mid-sized sedans.

COUGAR FOUR: Standard equipment included dual airbags, air conditioning, the SecuriLock™ passive anti-theft system, power front disc/rear drum brakes, an electronic digital clock located in the instrument cluster, a rear window defroster, side window demisters, power door locks, full coverage door trim with an armrest, cloth insert and storage bin, 2.0-liter 16-valve DOHC Zetec I-4 engine, Solar-Tinted glass, a soft feel instrument panel (with tachometer, odometer, trip odometer, fuel and temperature gauges, low fuel warning light and integrated trip computer with external temperature display), Micronair air filtration system, dual body-color heated outside rearview mirrors, dual visor-vanity mirrors (driver's side covered), a day/night inside rearview mirror, a midline AM/FM stereo with cassette and four speakers, a fixed radio antenna, reclining front bucket seats with cloth trim, a 50/50 split folding rear seat, a four-spoke comfort steering wheel with manual tilting column, power rack-and-pinion steering, P205/60R15 all-season black sidewall tires with mini spare, a five-speed manual transmission, two-speed variable intermittent windshield wipers, 15-in. aluminum alloy wheels and one touch power windows with illuminated switches.

COUGAR V-6: Standard equipment included dual airbags, air conditioning, the SecuriLock™ passive anti-theft system, power four-wheel disc brakes, an electronic digital clock located in the instrument cluster, a rear window defroster, side window demisters, power door locks, full coverage door trim with an armrest, cloth insert and storage bin, 2.5-liter 24-valve DOHC Duratec V-6 engine, brushed finish exhaust tips, Solar-Tinted glass, a soft feel instrument panel (with tachometer, odometer, trip odometer, fuel and temperature gauges, low fuel warning light and integrated trip computer with external temperature display), Micronair air filtration system, dual body-color heated outside rearview mirrors, dual visor-vanity mirrors (driver's side covered), a day/night inside rearview mirror, a midline AM/FM stereo with cassette and four speakers, a fixed radio antenna, reclining front bucket seats with high series cloth trim and manually adjustable driver's side lumbar support and height adjustment, seatback map pockets, height-adjustable headrests, a 50/50 split folding rear seat, a leather-wrapped four-spoke comfort steering wheel with manual tilting column, a leather-wrapped shift knob, power rack-and-pinion steering, P215/50R16 all-season black sidewall tires with mini spare, a five-speed manual transmission, two-speed variable intermittent windshield wipers, 16-in. aluminum alloy wheels and one touch power windows with illuminated switches.

Model No.	Body/ Style No.	Body Type & Seating	Factory Price	Shipping Weight	Prod. Total
COUGAR (FOUR)					
M	60	2d Coupe-5P	16,595	2,829	Note 3

Model No.	Body/ Style No.	Body Type & Seating	Factory Price	Shipping Weight	Prod. Total
COUGAR (V-6)					
M	61	2d Coupe-5P	17,095	2,929	Note 3

1999 Mercury Cougar two-door coupe. (FMC)

COUGAR SPORT (V-6)

M	62	2d Coupe-5P	17,870	2,941	Note 3

Note 3: Total model year production was 88,288.

SABLE – V-6 – A station wagon was added to the lower level Sable GS series. Five-passenger seating became standard equipment, while six-passenger seating was made a no-cost option. A rear stabilizer bar, previously offered on sedans, became a part of a new 16-in. tire and wheel option package. Mercury also made an air filtration system a dealer-installed option.

SABLE GS: Standard equipment included dual second generation airbags, CFC-free manual temperature control air conditioning, a fixed whip antenna mounted on the rear quarter panel, power front disc/rear drum brakes, an electric digital clock with dimming feature, a rear window defroster and defogger, the 3.0-liter Vulcan two-valve six-cylinder engine, complete Solar-Tinted glass, a backlit instrument panel cluster with positive shut-off climate control registers, a full-width windshield defroster and side window demisters, a dual grain instrument panel finish for reduced glare, a temperature gauge, a fuel gauge, an electronic 120-mph speedometer, a warning light for low brake, a "fluids-low" alert light, a million mile odometer, a tachometer, an integrated control panel (with radio and climate controls, rear defroster control and clock controls), rear door child safety locks, black exterior mirrors, an interior day/night mirror, an electronic AM/FM stereo radio, five-passenger seating with dual recliners, front armrests and front seat map pockets, two-way headrests, a mini console, a fixed rear seat back, a tilt steering column, a color-keyed four-spoke soft feel steering wheel with center horn engagement, power rack-and-pinion steering with variable assist, cloth covered sun visors with covered vanity mirrors, P205/65R15 all-season tires, an electronic four-speed automatic transmission with overdrive, two-speed intermittent windshield wipers, deluxe five-bolt full wheel covers, illuminated power side windows with lockout switch and driver's side express down and accessory delay.

SABLE LS: Standard equipment included dual second generation airbags, CFC-free manual temperature control air conditioning, a fixed whip antenna mounted on the rear quarter panel, power front disc/rear drum brakes, an electric digital clock with dimming feature, a rear window defroster and defogger, the 3.0-liter two-valve six-cylinder engine, complete Solar-Tinted glass, a backlit instrument panel cluster with positive shut-off climate control registers, a full-width windshield defroster and side window demisters, a dual grain instrument panel finish for reduced glare, a temperature gauge, a fuel gauge, a 110-mph speedometer (120-mph with Duratec V-6 or 150-mph in SHO), a warning light for low brake, a "fluids-low" alert light, a million mile odometer, a tachometer, an integrated control panel (with radio and climate controls, rear defroster control and clock controls), rear door child safety locks, remote keyless entry, illuminated door controls for power accessories, colored-keyed remote-control outside mirrors, an interior day/night mirror, an electronic AM/FM stereo with full logic stereo cassette player and four speakers, five-passenger seating with dual recliners, front armrests and front seat map pockets, two-way headrests, a mini console, a 60/40 split-folding rear seat, a tilt steering column, a color-keyed four-spoke soft feel steering wheel with center horn engagement, power rack-and-pinion steering with variable assist, cloth covered sun visors with covered vanity mirrors, P205/65R15 all-season tires, an electronic four-speed automatic transmission with overdrive, two-speed intermittent windshield wipers, 15 x 6-in. bright aluminum wheels, illuminated power side windows with lockout switch and driver's side express down and accessory delay. In addition, the LS wagon only featured a power antenna, four-wheel disc brakes, a unique liftgate latch and a rear washer/wiper.

Model No.	Body/ Style No.	Body Type & Seating	Factory Price	Shipping Weight	Prod. Total
SABLE GS (V-6)					
M	50	4d Sedan-5P	18,995	3,388	Note 4
SABLE LS (V-6)					
M	53	4d Sedan-5P	20,095	3,388	Note 4

1999 Mercury Sable four-door sedan. (FMC)

1999 Mercury Grand Marquis four-door sedan. (FMC)

SABLE LS (DOHC V-6)					
M	55	4d Sedan-5P	20,650	3,388	Note 4
SABLE LS (V-6)					
M	58	4d Wagon-5P	21,195	3,536	Note 4
SABLE LS (DOHC V-6)					
M	59	4d Wagon-5P	21,750	3,536	Note 4

Note 4: Total model year production was 120,117.

GRAND MARQUIS – V-8 – The Grand Marquis received very minimal changes. Antilock brakes and traction control became available as separate options.

GRAND MARQUIS GS: Standard equipment included dual airbags, manual air conditioning with positive shut-off registers, a radio antenna hidden in the rear window defroster, the SecuriLock™ passive anti-theft system, a brake/shift interlock, power four-wheel disc antilock brakes, rear seat child safety latches, an electric digital clock with dimming feature, a rear window defroster, the 4.6-liter OHC sequential fuel-injected V-8, a stainless steel exhaust system, a gauge cluster with analog gauges (voltmeter, oil pressure, water temperature and fuel), full Solar-Tinted glass, woodgrain instrument panel appliqués, side window demisters, power door locks, dual remote-control fold-away power exterior mirrors with color-keyed finish, a day/night inside rearview mirror, an electronic AM/FM stereo with cassette and door-mounted speakers, a cloth trimmed split bench front seat with center fold-down armrest and reclining seatbacks (two-way manual adjusting type with 10-in. track travel), a sound insulation package, speed control, a color-keyed steering wheel with center horn blow, speed sensitive variable-assist power steering (not available in cars with the natural gas engine), cloth covered sun visors with retention clips, a tilt steering column with stalk-mounted controls, P225/60R16 white sidewall Michelin tires, an ECT automatic transmission with overdrive lockout, a trip odometer, concealed two-speed interval windshield wipers, 16-in. steel wheel rims with locking GS chrome wheel covers and power windows with driver side express down.

GRAND MARQUIS LS: Standard equipment included dual airbags, manual air conditioning with positive shut-off registers, a radio antenna hidden in the rear window defroster, the SecuriLock™ passive anti-theft system, a brake/shift interlock, power four-wheel disc antilock brakes, rear seat child safety latches, remote keyless entry, an electric digital clock with dimming feature, a rear window defroster, the 4.6-liter OHC sequential fuel-injected V-8, a stainless steel exhaust system, a gauge cluster with analog gauges (voltmeter, oil pressure, water temperature and fuel), full Solar-Tinted glass, woodgrain instrument panel appliqués, side window demisters, power door locks, dual remote-control fold-away power exterior mirrors with color-keyed finish, a day/night inside rearview mirror, an electronic AM/FM stereo with cassette and door-mounted speakers, a split bench seat with fold-down center armrest trimmed in luxury cloth (with power lumbar adjustment and six-way power adjustment on the driver's side, plus a power back recliner), a sound insulation package, speed control, a color-keyed steering wheel with center horn blow, speed sensitive variable-assist power steering (not available in cars with the natural gas engine), cloth covered sun visors with retention clips, a tilt steering column with stalk-mounted controls, P225/60R16 white sidewall Michelin tires, an ECT automatic transmission with overdrive lockout, a trip odometer, concealed two-speed interval windshield wipers, chrome-plated, locking cross-spoke wheel covers, 16-in. steel wheel rims with locking LS luxury chrome wheel covers and power windows with driver side express down.

Model No.	Body/ Style No.	Body Type & Seating	Factory Price	Shipping Weight	Prod. Total
GRAND MARQUIS GS (V-8)					
M	74	4d Sedan-6P	22,825	3,920	Note 5
GRAND MARQUIS LS (V-8)					
M	75	4d Sedan-6P	24,725	3,922	Note 5

Note 5: Total model year production was 122,582.

TRACER ENGINE

ENGINE: [BASE LX/SE] Inline. Overhead cam. Four-cylinder. Cast-iron block and aluminum head. Displacement: 122 cid (2.0 liters). Bore & stroke: 3.33 x 3.46 in. Compression ratio: 9.2:1. Brake horsepower: 110 at 5000 rpm. Torque: 125 lbs.-ft. at 3750 rpm. Split Port induction. VIN code P.

MYSTIQUE ENGINES

ENGINE [BASE GS]: Inline. Double overhead cam. Four-cylinder. Cast-iron block and aluminum head. Displacement: 121 cid (2.0 liters). Bore & stroke: 3.34 x 3.46 in. Compression ratio: 9.6:1. Brake horsepower: 125 at 5500 rpm. Torque: 130 lbs.-ft. at 4000 rpm. Sequential fuel injection. VIN code 3.

ENGINE [BASE LS]: Modular, double overhead cam V-6. Aluminum block and head. Displacement: 155 cid (2.5 liters). Bore & stroke: 3.24 x 3.13 in. Compression ratio: 9.7:1. Brake horsepower: 170 at 6250 rpm. Torque: 165 lbs.-ft. at 4250 rpm. Sequential fuel injection. VIN code L.

COUGAR ENGINES

ENGINE [BASE FOUR]: Inline. Double overhead cam. Four-cylinder. Cast-iron block and aluminum head. Displacement: 121 cid (2.0 liters). Bore & stroke: 3.34 x 3.46 in. Compression ratio: 9.6:1. Brake horsepower: 125 at 5500 rpm. Torque: 130 lbs.-ft. at 4000 rpm. Sequential fuel injection. VIN code 3.

ENGINE [BASE V-6]: Modular, double overhead cam V-6. Aluminum block and head. Displacement: 155 cid (2.5 liters). Bore & stroke: 3.24 x 3.13 in. Compression ratio: 9.7:1. Brake horsepower: 170 at 6250 rpm. Torque: 165 lbs.-ft. at 4250 rpm. Sequential fuel injection. VIN code L.

SABLE ENGINES

ENGINE [BASE GS/LS]: Overhead valve V-6. Cast-iron block and head. Displacement: 182 cid (3.0 liters). Bore & stroke: 3.50 x 3.15 in. Compression ratio: 9.3:1. Brake horsepower: 145 at 5250 rpm. Torque: 170 lbs.-ft. at 3250 rpm. Sequential fuel injection. VIN code U.

ENGINE [OPTIONAL LS]: Double overhead cam V-6. Aluminum block and head. Displacement: 182 cid (3.0 liters). Bore & stroke: 3.50 x 3.15 in. Compression ratio: 10.0:1. Brake horsepower: 200 at 5750 rpm. Torque: 200 lbs.-ft. at 4500 rpm. Sequential fuel injection. VIN code S.

GRAND MARQUIS ENGINE

ENGINE [BASE]: Modular, overhead valve V-8. Displacement: 281 cid (4.6 liters). Bore & stroke: 3.60 x 3.60. Compression ratio: 9.0:1. Brake horsepower: 200 at 4250 rpm. Torque: 275 lbs.-ft. at 3000 rpm. Sequential fuel injection. VIN code W.

TRACER CHASSIS: Wheelbase: (all) 98.4 in. Overall length: (GS/LS sedan) 174.7 in.; (LS wagon) 172.7 in. Overall width: (all) 67 in. Overall height: (GS/LS sedan) 53.3 in.; (LS wagon) 53.9 in. Front tread: (all) 56.5 in. Rear tread: (all) 56.5 in.

MYSTIQUE CHASSIS: Wheelbase (all) 106.5 in.; Overall length: (all) 184.7 in. Overall width: (all) 69.1 in.; Overall height: (all) 54.5 in. Front tread: (all) 59.2 in. Rear tread: (all) 58.5 in.

COUGAR CHASSIS: Wheelbase: (all) 106.5 in.; Overall length: (all) 185 in. Overall width: (all) 69.6 in.; Overall height: (all) 52.2 in. Front tread: (all) 59.2 in. Rear tread: (all) 58.5 in.

SABLE CHASSIS: Wheelbase: (all) 108.5 in. Overall length: (sedan) 199.7 in.; (wagon) 199.1 in. Overall width: (all) 73 in. Overall height: (sedan) 55.4 in.; (wagon) 57.6 in. Front tread: 61.6 in. Rear tread: 61.4 in.

GRAND MARQUIS CHASSIS: Wheelbase: (all) 114.4 in. Overall Length: (all) 212 in. Overall width: (all) 78.2 in. Overall height: (all) 56.8 in. Front Tread: (all) 62.8 in. Rear Tread: (all) 63.3 in.

TRACER TECHNICAL: Standard transmission: five-speed manual transaxle. Drive axle: front. Steering: rack-and-pinion. Front suspension: independent MacPherson strut with strut-mounted coil springs. Rear suspension: independent, Quadra-link with stabilizer bar. Brakes: front disc/rear drum (power assisted). Body construction: unibody. Fuel tank: 12.7 gallons.

MYSTIQUE TECHNICAL: Standard transmission: five-speed manual transaxle. Drive axle: front. Steering: rack-and-pinion. Front suspension: independent, subframe rubber mounted MacPherson strut with strut-mounted coil springs, lower control A-arms and cast steering knuckles. Rear suspension: independent, Quadra-link strut with coil spring on shock strut, mounted to rigid subframe. Brakes: front disc/rear drum (power assisted). Body construction: unibody. Fuel tank: 14.5 gallons.

COUGAR TECHNICAL: Standard transmission: five-speed manual transaxle. Drive axle: front. Steering: rack-and-pinion. Front suspension: independent, subframe rubber mounted MacPherson strut with strut-mounted coil springs, lower control A-arms and cast steering knuckles. Rear suspension: independent Quadra-link design, coil springs, tube shock dampers and stabilizer bar. Brakes: (four) front disc/rear drum; (V-6) four-wheel discs. Body construction: unibody. Fuel tank: 14.5 gallons.

SABLE TECHNICAL: Standard transmission: Four-speed overdrive automatic. Drive axle: front. Steering: rack-and-pinion. Front suspension: independent MacPherson strut front drive with strut-mounted coil springs, stabilizer bar, lower control arm and cast aluminum knuckle with integral ball joint. Rear suspension: (sedan) independent Quadra-link with coil spring on shock strut, stabilizer bar, tension strut, parallel suspension arms and two-piece cast spindle with forged stem; (wagon) Independent short/long arm with spring on lower control arm, stabilizer bar, tension strut and cast spindle with pressed-in forged stem and integrated ball joints. Brakes: front disc/rear drum (power assisted) except wagon has four-wheel discs. Body construction: unibody. Fuel tank: 16.0 gallons.

GRAND MARQUIS TECHNICAL: Standard transmission: four-speed overdrive automatic. Drive axle: rear. Steering: re-circulating ball. Front suspension: independent short/long arm with ball joints, coil springs and stabilizer bar. Rear suspension: Watt's linkage. Brakes: four-wheel disc. Body construction: separate body and frame. Fuel tank: 20.0 gallons.

TRACER OPTIONS: 572 air conditioning, standard in SE ($795). 552 antilock braking system ($400). 57Q rear window defroster, standard in LS ($190). 422 California emissions (no cost). 60A GS Trio Appearance group ($260). 41H engine block heater ($20). 60B LS Comfort group ($365). 65A LS Power group ($345). 68S LS Sport group ($515). LS sedan leather trim ($795). LS Wagon group available only with leather trim ($495). 12Y front and rear floor mats ($55). 54J dual electric remote-control mirrors ($95). 58H AM/FM stereo with cassette ($185). 919 AM/FM stereo cassette with premium sound and six disc CD changer ($295). R unique leather sport bucket seats in LS wagon (no cost). 44T four-speed automatic overdrive transmission with 16-valve Zetec 2.0-liter DOHC engine, ZX2 only ($815).

MYSTIQUE OPTIONS: 153 front license plate bracket (no cost). 552 antilock braking system, standard on SVT ($500). 422 California emissions system (no cost). 428 high-altitude emissions system (no cost). 53G GS Sport group, includes rear spoiler, leather wheel and shift knob, fog lamps, sport logo floor mats and sport badge ($195). 41H engine block heater ($20). 12Y floor mats, front and rear ($55). 13B moonroof SE ($595). 585 ETR AM/FM stereo with CD player and premium sound, in SE ($275). 58P premium sound with electronic AM/FM stereo cassette ($135). 91H power antenna ($95). 143 remote keyless entry, includes illuminated entry system ($190). 219 60/40 split folding rear seat in SE ($205). 21A six-way power driver's seat, in GS ($350). 63B smoker's package ($15). 13K raised wing spoiler, LS only ($245). 553 traction control, requires antilock brakes ($175). 44T ECT automatic transmission ($815). 64Y 15-in. Mach alloy seven-hole wheels, includes P205/60R15 black sidewall tires, on GS ($475). 64M 15-in. polished Mach alloy six-spoke wheels, includes P205/60R15 black sidewall tires, on GS ($475).

COUGAR OPTIONS: 59M side airbags ($375). 552 antilock brakes ($500). 94A convenience group ($615). 60L V-6 group ($720). 422 California emissions (no cost). 428 high-altitude emissions (no cost). 153 front license plate bracket (no cost). 41H engine block imersion heater ($20). 98G body side moldings ($50). 582 premium AM/FM stereo cassette with four speakers ($130). 583 AM/FM ETR stereo with CD and premium four-speaker sound system ($140). 919 trunk-mounted remote CD player ($350). 21A six-way power driver's seat ($235). 8 leather seat trim ($895). 13K rear deck lid spoiler ($235). 433 spoiler delete, requires sport package ($235 credit). 97S V-6 sport package ($815). 13E power tilt/slide sunroof ($615). 533 traction control ($235). 44T ECT four-speed electronic automatic transmission, with V-6 only ($815). 645N 16-in. polished aluminum wheels, V-6 only, requires sport group ($250).

SABLE OPTIONS: 59B air filtration system ($30). 552 antilock braking system ($600). 942 daytime running lights ($40). 422 California emissions system (no cost). 428 high-altitude emissions system (no cost). 99S 3.0-liter Duratec V-6 ($555). 41H engine block heater ($35). 60L LS Premium group, includes 3.0-liter four, overdrive automatic transmission, electronic temperature control air conditioning, automatic headlamps, remote entry with keypad and perimeter anti-theft, light group, illuminated visor mirrors ($1,200). 943 light group ($45). 12Y floor mats, front and rear ($55). 54P heated exterior mirrors ($35). 13B power moonroof, includes unique map lamps in overhead console, LS only ($740). 916 Ford Mach audio system with six speakers in SE ($320). 919 trunk-mounted six-disc CD changer ($350).

143 remote keyless entry ($190). Q leather bucket seats, requires 21A power seat ($895). 21J dual power seats in LS ($350). 47B power side window delete, wagon only ($350 credit). 214 rear facing vinyl third seat in wagon ($200). 46S 60/40 split-folding rear seat ($175). 508 conventional spare tire ($125). 96W wagon group, includes cargo net and cargo area cover ($140). 64G bright aluminum GS wheels ($395). 64V 16-in. chrome alloy wheels ($580).

GRAND MARQUIS OPTIONS: 573 electronic automatic temperature control air conditioning ($175). 552 antilock brakes ($600). 553 antilock brakes with all-speed traction control ($775). 155 electronic instrumentation ($425). 175 garage door opener ($115). 41G Handling and Performance package, includes revised springs, shocks and stabilizer bar, P225/60R16 black sidewall touring tires, 16-in. lacy-spoke wheels, rear air suspension, dual exhausts with 215-hp/275-ft.-lbs. rating and 3.27:1 axle ($855); same with upgrade from teardrop aluminum wheels ($535). 41H engine block immersion heater ($25). 144 remote keyless entry ($240). 153 front license plate bracket (no cost). 144 remote keyless entry with keypad ($240). 943 light group ($190). 54F Ltd feature car package, includes gold-plated 16-in. aluminum wheels, rear seat center armrest with cupholders, dual front seat storage armrests, embroideredd logo on front and rear seats, exclusive graystone leather trim, unique front and rear floor mats, special gold exterior trim package, on LS only ($460). 972 body side paint stripe on LS ($60). 68E premium package includes 16-in. teardrop aluminum wheels, a leather-wrapped steering wheel, automatic temperature control air conditioning, an eight-way power passenger seat with power lumbar support adjustment and an automatic dimming inside rearview mirror with compass ($1,000). 586 premium sound system ($360). 919 trunk-mounted six-disc CD changer ($350). 585 single CD player replacing cassette ($140). J leather seat trim, requires power passenger seat, LS only ($735). 66B rear air suspension, LS only ($270). 508 conventional spare tire ($120). 68F Ultimate package, includes all contents of 68E premium package plus antilock brakes with traction control, electronic instrumentation and 586 radio upgrade ($2,400). 64R 16-in. teardrop wheels, LS only ($320).

HISTORICAL FOOTNOTES: Jack Nasser, a 30-year FoMoCo veteran and former president of Ford Automotive Operations took over as corporate president and chief executive officer on Jan. 1, 1999. January was also the month that Lincoln-Mercury Div. announced plans to move its headquarters from Detroit to Irvine, Calif. This move was said to be aimed at enhancing "brand equity" by increasing product differentiation vis-à-vis Ford Div. The move was scheduled to be completed by September of 1999. Division manager, Jim Rogers, promised a "radical change" for Mercury and said it would push Mercury models further from their Ford and Lincoln cousins. "In the past, Mercury was a re-badged Ford with a few more features at a higher price. We need to establish Mercury as a marque that stands for something. It will take time," Rogers said. "But, we have an aggressive plan for the future and the new Cougar is just the first of our plans." The launch of the 1999 Cougar, in the spring of 1998, took place in March. That was a month later than originally scheduled. It was built at the AutoAlliance International plant in Flat Rock, Mich. At about the same time, William Boddie, Ford's vice president for small and medium cars, confirmed that the Escort-based Mercury Tracer was on its way out and that the Mystique would become Mercury's small car once the Tracer was gone.

2000 MERCURY

2000 Mercury Mystique four-door sedan. (FMC)

MYSTIQUE – FOUR/V-6 – There were no major changes in the 2000 Mercury Mystique, which was scheduled to be the last in the series. It was built in Mercury factories in Kansas City, Mo., and Cuautitlan, Mexico.

MYSTIQUE GS: Standard equipment included dual second generation air bags, air conditioning, a fixed antenna mounted on the rear quarter panel, power front disc/rear drum brakes, an electric digital clock, child proof rear door locks, the 2.0-liter DOHC Zetec 16-valve I-4, semi flush exterior glass with Solar-Tint, a heater and defroster with a four-speed blower control, a soft touch dashboard with knee bolsters and four positive shutoff registers, a backlit cluster with 130-mph speedometer, analog gauges (including a trip odometer, a fuel gauge, a high-beam warning light, a coolant temperature gauge and a low-oil-pressure light, turn signal indicator lights, a handbrake-on warning light, a catalyst malfunction light and a seat belt reminder light), left- and right-hand power body-color exterior mirrors, a day/night rearview mirror, an AM/FM stereo, individual manual two-way adjustable front bucket seats with reclining seat backs and cloth trim and a driver's side armrest attached to the seat, a tilt steering column, a soft touch steering wheel with center horn control, power rack-and-pinion steering, a driver's side covered visor mirror and passenger side uncovered visor mirror, P185/70R14S black sidewall radial tires, a five-speed manual transmission with overdrive, single-speed windshield wipers with intermittent feature and fluidic washers and 14-in. wheel covers with full bolt-on appearance.

MYSTIQUE LS: Standard equipment included dual second generation airbags, air conditioning, a fixed antenna mounted on the rear quarter panel, power front disc and rear drum brakes, an electric digital clock, child proof rear door locks, the 2.0-liter DOHC Zetec 16-valve I-4, semi flush exterior glass with Solar-Tint, a heater and defroster with a four-speed blower control, a soft touch dashboard with knee bolsters and four positive shutoff registers, a backlit cluster with 130-mph speedometer, analog gauges (including a trip odometer, a fuel gauge, a tachometer, a high-beam warning light, a coolant temperature gauge and a low-oil-pressure light, turn signal indicator lights, a handbrake-on warning light, a catalyst malfunction light and a seat belt reminder light), left- and right-hand power body-color exterior mirrors, remote keyless entry, all-door and perimeter anti-theft system, speed control, a day/night rearview mirror, an electronic AM/FM stereo and cassette with two premium speakers and two standard speakers, individual manual two-way adjustable front bucket seats with reclining seat backs and cloth trim and a driver's side armrest attached to the seat, a tilt steering column, a color-keyed steering wheel with center horn control, power rack-and-pinion steering, a driver's side covered visor mirror and passenger side uncovered visor mirror, P185/70R14S black sidewall radial tires, a five-speed manual transmission with overdrive, single-speed windshield wipers with intermittent feature and fluidic washers and 14-in. wheel covers with full bolt-on appearance. The wagon also featured a removable shade and cargo cover, a deluxe luggage rack, a rear window washer/wiper and luxury bolt-on wheel covers.

I.D. DATA: Mercury's 17-symbol Vehicle Identification Number (VIN) was stamped on a metal tab fastened to the instrument panel, visible through the windshield. The first symbol indicates the nation of origin: 1=United States; 2=Canada; 3=Mexico. The second symbol indicates manufacturer: M=Mercury Division, Ford Motor Co.; Z=Mercury Division, Ford Motor Co. The third symbol indicates vehicle type: E=passenger car; H=incomplete vehicle; W=Cougar. The fourth symbol indicates type of restraint system: B=driver and passenger air bags and active belts (except Escort ZX2 coupe); F=driver and passenger air bags and active belts; H= driver and passenger front and side airbags and active belts in all outboard positions. The fifth symbol indicates designation: M=Mercury; T=Imported from outside North America or non-Ford car marketed by Ford in North America. The sixth and seventh symbols indicate body type: 50=Sable GS four-door sedan; 53=Sable LS four-door sedan; 55=Sable LS premium sedan; 58=Sable GS four-door station wagon; 59=Sable LS premium four-door station wagon; 60=Cougar three-door coupe with I-4; 61=Cougar three-door coupe with V-6; 62=Cougar three-door coupe with V-6; 65=Mystique GS four-door sedan; 66=Mystique LS four-door sedan; 74=Grand Marquis GS four-door sedan; 75=Grand Marquis LS four-door sedan. The eighth symbol indicates engine: L= Cougar 2.5-liter DOHC V-6 with EFI; 3=Cougar 2.0-liter DOHC I-4 with EFI; L=Mystique 2.5-liter DOHC V-6 with EFI; 3=Mystique 2.0-liter DOHC I-4 with EFI; S=Sable 3.0-liter DOHC V-6 with EFI; U=Sable 3.0-liter V-6 with EFI; W=Grand Marquis 4.6-liter SOHC V-8 with EFI (Romeo engine plant). The ninth symbol is a check digit. The 10th symbol indicates model year: Y=2000. The 11th symbol indicates assembly plant: A=Hapeville (Atlanta), Ga.; G=Chicago, Ill.; K=Claycomo (Kansas City), Mo.; M=Cuautitlan, Mexico; X=Talbotville (St. Thomas), Ontario, Canada; 5=AAI: Flat Rock, Mich. The last six symbols are the sequential production number starting at 100001 at each factory.

Model No.	Body/ Style No.	Body Type & Seating	Factory Price	Shipping Weight	Prod. Total
MYSTIQUE GS (FOUR)					
M	65	4d Sedan-5P	16,705	2,805	—
MYSTIQUE LS (V-6)					
M	66	4d Sedan-5P	18,005	2,824	—

COUGAR – FOUR/V-6 – The Cougar bowed in the spring of 1998 as a 1999 model and had no major changes for 2000. The sole factory producing it was the AutoAlliance facility in Flat Rock, Mich.

COUGAR FOUR: Standard equipment included dual airbags, air conditioning, the SecuriLock™ passive anti-theft system, power front disc/rear drum brakes, an electronic digital clock located in the instrument cluster, a rear window defroster, side window demisters, power door locks, full coverage door trim with an armrest, cloth insert and storage bin, 2.0-liter 16-valve DOHC Zetec I-4 engine, Solar-Tinted glass, a soft feel instrument panel with tachometer (with tachometer, odometer, trip odometer, fuel and temperature gauges, low fuel warning light and integrated trip computer with external temperature display), Micronair air filtration system, dual body-color heated outside rearview mirrors, dual visor-vanity mirrors (driver's side covered), a day/night inside rearview mirror, a midline AM/FM stereo with cassette and four speakers, a fixed radio antenna, reclining front bucket seats with cloth trim, a 50/50 split folding rear seat, a four-spoke comfort steering wheel with manual tilting column, power rack-and-pinion steering, P205/60R15 all-season black sidewall tires with mini spare, a five-speed manual transmission, two-speed variable intermittent windshield wipers, 15-in. aluminum alloy wheels and one touch power windows with illuminated switches.

COUGAR V-6: Standard equipment included dual airbags, air conditioning, the SecuriLock™ passive anti-theft system, power four-wheel disc brakes, an electronic digital clock located in the instrument cluster, a rear window defroster, side window demisters, power door locks, full coverage door trim with an armrest, cloth insert and storage bin, 2.5-liter 24-valve DOHC Duratec V-6 engine, brushed finish exhaust tips, Solar-Tinted glass, a soft feel instrument panel with tachometer (with tachometer, odometer, trip odometer, fuel and temperature gauges, low fuel warning light and integrated trip computer with external temperature display), Micronair air filtration system, dual body-color heated outside rearview mirrors, dual visor-vanity mirrors (driver's side covered), a day/night inside rearview mirror, a midline AM/FM stereo with cassette and four speakers, a fixed radio antenna, reclining front bucket seats with high series cloth trim and manually adjustable driver's side lumbar support and height adjustment, seatback map pockets, height-adjustable headrests, a 50/50 split folding rear seat, a leather-wrapped four-spoke comfort steering wheel with manual tilting column, a leather-wrapped shift knob, power rack-and-pinion steering, P215/50R16 all-season black sidewall tires with mini spare, a five-speed manual transmission, two-speed variable intermittent windshield wipers, 16-in. aluminum alloy wheels and one touch power windows with illuminated switches.

Model No.	Body/ Style No.	Body Type & Seating	Factory Price	Shipping Weight	Prod. Total
COUGAR (FOUR)					
M	60	2d Coupe-5P	16,820	2,829	—
COUGAR (V-6)					
M	61	2d Coupe-5P	17,370	2,941	—

SABLE – V-6 – The Sable series was where the Mercury action was in model-year 2000. It was totally restyled with new front and rear fascias on the sedan and a new front fascia for the station wagon. The new rear-end styling gave the sedan more trunk space. Engine power and torque were increased for better performance. A new option was an adjustable pedal system that allowed the driver to move the accelerator and brake pedal forward or backward for comfort. Dual-stage front airbags increased the driver safety level, as did the addition of crash severity sensors, safety belt usage sensors and a driver's seat position sensor. Child seat tether anchors and a passive anti-theft system are other new features, front side-impact airbags were optional and all-speed traction control was available teamed with antilock brakes. The lowest-priced station wagon became a GS instead of an LS, but an LS premium wagon was added along with an LS premium sedan.

SABLE GS: Standard equipment included a V-6 engine, a four-speed automatic transmission, P215/60R16 all-season tires, a space saver spare, full wheel covers, a four-wheel independent suspension, a front stabilizer bar, front and rear solid disc brakes, front seat belt pre-tensioners, rear door child safety locks, child seat anchors, an emergency release in the trunk, two front headrests, variable intermittent windshield wipers, a rear defogger, five-passenger seating with cloth upholstered bucket front seats and a rear bench seat, rear seat heating ducts, power door locks, one-touch power windows, power mirrors, an AM/FM stereo system with four speakers, a mast antenna, speed-proportional power steering, a tilt-adjustable steering wheel, front cupholders, a remote trunk lid release, front seatback storage, a front 12-volt power outlet, a front console with storage space, retained accessory power, air conditioning, front reading lights, dual visor-vanity mirrors, a trunk light, a tachometer, a clock and a low-fuel warning indicator. The wagon featured six-passenger seating with a split front bench seat and a split-folding rear seat, remote power door locks, cargo area lighting and cargo tie downs.

SABLE LS: Standard equipment included a V-6 engine, a four-speed automatic transmission, P215/60R16 all-season tires, a space saver spare, full wheel covers, a four-wheel independent suspension, a front stabilizer bar, front and rear solid disc ABS brakes, front seat belt pre-tensioners, rear door child safety locks, child seat anchors, an emergency release in the trunk, two front headrests, variable intermittent windshield wipers, a rear defogger, five-passenger seating with cloth upholstered bucket front seats and a rear bench seat, rear seat heating ducts, power door locks, one-touch power windows, power mirrors, an AM/FM stereo system with four speakers, a mast antenna, speed-proportional power steering, a tilt-adjustable steering wheel, front cupholders, a remote trunk lid release, front seatback storage, a front 12-volt power outlet, a front console with storage space, retained accessory power, air conditioning, front reading lights, dual visor-vanity mirrors, a trunk light, a tachometer, a clock, a low-fuel warning indicator, alloy rims, remote power door locks, and AM/FM cassette stereo system and cruise control. The wagon featured alloy rims, front and rear stabilizer bars, front disc/rear drum brakes, a front center lap belt, a roof rack, rear window wipers, six-passenger seating with a split front bench seat and a split folding rear seat, remote power door locks, an AM/FM cassette sound system, a power radio antenna, cargo area lighting and cargo tie downs.

Model No.	Body/ Style No.	Body Type & Seating	Factory Price	Shipping Weight	Prod. Total
SABLE GS (V-6)					
M	50	4d Sedan-5P	19,395	3,379	—
SABLE LS (V-6)					
M	53	4d Sedan-5P	20,495	3,325	—
SABLE LS (DOHC V-6)					
M	55	4d Sedan-5P	21,190	3,388	—
SABLE GS (V-6)					
M	58	4d Wagon-5P	21,195	3,544	—
SABLE LS PREMIUM (DOHC V-6)					
M	55	4d Sedan-5P	21,795	3,325	—
SABLE LS PREMIUM (DOHC V-6)					
M	59	4d Wagon-5P	22,895	3,473	—

2000 Mercury Cougar two-door coupe. (FMC)

2000 Mercury Sable four-door sedan. (FMC)

GRAND MARQUIS – V-8 – The Grand Marquis received very minimal changes. Safety provisions were enhanced by the addition of an inside-the-trunk emergency release handle and rear seat child seat tethers.

GRAND MARQUIS GS: Standard equipment included dual air bags, manual air conditioning with positive shut-off registers, a radio antenna hidden in the rear window defroster, the SecuriLock™ passive anti-theft system, a brake/shift interlock, power four-wheel disc antilock brakes, rear seat child safety latches, an electric digital clock with dimming feature, a rear window defroster, the 4.6-liter OHC sequential fuel-injected V-8, a stainless steel exhaust system, a gauge cluster with analog gauges (voltmeter, oil pressure, water temperature and fuel), full Solar-Tinted glass, woodgrain instrument panel appliqués, side window demisters, power door locks, dual remote-control fold-away power exterior mirrors with color-keyed finish, a day/night inside rearview mirror, an electronic AM/FM stereo with cassette and door-mounted speakers, a cloth trimmed split bench front seat with center fold-down armrest and reclining seatbacks (two-way manual adjusting type with 10-in. track travel), a sound insulation package, speed control, a color-keyed steering wheel with center horn blow, speed sensitive variable-assist power steering (not available in cars with the natural gas engine), cloth covered sun visors with retention clips, a tilt steering column with stalk-mounted controls, P225/60R16 white sidewall Michelin tires, an ECT automatic transmission with overdrive lockout, a trip odometer, concealed two-speed interval windshield wipers, 16-in. steel wheel rims with locking GS chrome wheel covers and power windows with driver side express down.

GRAND MARQUIS LS: Standard equipment included dual air bags, manual air conditioning with positive shut-off registers, a radio antenna hidden in the rear window defroster, the SecuriLock™ passive anti-theft system, a brake/shift interlock, power four-wheel disc antilock brakes, rear seat child safety latches, remote keyless entry, an electric digital clock with dimming feature, a rear window defroster, the 4.6-liter OHC sequential fuel-injected V-8, a stainless steel exhaust system, a gauge cluster with analog gauges (voltmeter, oil pressure, water temperature and fuel), full Solar-Tinted glass, woodgrain instrument panel appliqués, side window demisters, power door locks, dual remote-control fold-away power exterior mirrors with color-keyed finish, a day/night inside rearview mirror, an electronic AM/FM stereo with cassette and door-mounted speakers, a split bench seat with fold-down center armrest trimmed in luxury cloth (with power lumbar adjustment and six-way power adjustment on the driver's side, plus a power back recliner), a sound insulation package, speed control, a color-keyed steering wheel with center horn blow, speed sensitive variable-assist power steering (not available in cars with the natural gas engine), cloth covered sun visors with retention clips, a tilt steering column with stalk-mounted controls, P225/60R16 white sidewall Michelin tires, an ECT automatic transmission with overdrive lockout, a trip odometer, concealed two-speed interval windshield wipers, chrome-plated, locking cross-spoke wheel covers, 16-in. steel wheel rims with locking LS luxury chrome wheel covers and power windows with driver side express down.

Model No.	Body/ Style No.	Body Type & Seating	Factory Price	Shipping Weight	Prod. Total
GRAND MARQUIS GS (V-8)					
M	74	4d Sedan-6P	23,045	3,958	—
GRAND MARQUIS LS (V-8)					
M	75	4d Sedan-6P	24,945	3,973	—

MYSTIQUE ENGINES

ENGINE [BASE GS]: Inline. Double overhead cam. Four-cylinder. Cast-iron block and aluminum head. Displacement: 121 cid (2.0 liters). Bore & stroke: 3.34 x 3.46 in. Compression ratio: 9.6:1. Brake horsepower: 125 at 5500 rpm. Torque: 130 lbs.-ft. at 4000 rpm. Sequential fuel injection. VIN code 3.

ENGINE [BASE LS]: Modular, double overhead cam V-6. Aluminum block and head. Displacement: 155 cid (2.5 liters). Bore & stroke: 3.24 x 3.13 in. Compression ratio: 9.7:1. Brake horsepower: 170 at 6250 rpm. Torque: 165 lbs.-ft. at 4250 rpm. Sequential fuel injection. VIN code L.

COUGAR ENGINES

ENGINE [BASE FOUR]: Inline. Double overhead cam. Four-cylinder. Cast-iron block and aluminum head. Displacement: 121 cid (2.0 liters). Bore & stroke: 3.34 x 3.46 in. Compression ratio: 9.6:1. Brake horsepower: 125 at 5500 rpm. Torque: 130 lbs.-ft. at 4000 rpm. Sequential fuel injection. VIN code 3.

ENGINE [BASE V-6]: Modular, double overhead cam V-6. Aluminum block and head. Displacement: 155 cid (2.5 liters). Bore & stroke: 3.24 x 3.13 in. Compression ratio: 9.7:1. Brake horsepower: 170 at 6250 rpm. Torque: 165 lbs.-ft. at 4250 rpm. Sequential fuel injection. VIN code L.

2000 Mercury Marquis four-door sedan. (FMC)

SABLE ENGINES

ENGINE [BASE GS/LS]: Overhead valve V-6. Cast-iron block and head. Displacement: 182 cid (3.0 liters). Bore & stroke: 3.50 x 3.15 in. Compression ratio: 9.3:1. Brake horsepower: 155 at 4900 rpm. Torque: 185 lbs.-ft. at 3950 rpm. Sequential fuel injection. VIN code U.

ENGINE [OPTIONAL LS]: Double overhead cam V-6. Aluminum block and head. Displacement: 182 cid (3.0 liters). Bore & stroke: 3.50 x 3.15 in. Compression ratio: 10.0:1. Brake horsepower: 200 at 5750 rpm. Torque: 200 lbs.-ft. at 4500 rpm. Sequential fuel injection. VIN code S.

GRAND MARQUIS ENGINE

ENGINE [BASE]: Modular, overhead valve V-8. Displacement: 281 cid (4.6 liters). Bore & stroke: 3.60 x 3.60. Compression ratio: 9.0:1. Brake horsepower: 200 at 4250 rpm. Torque: 275 lbs.-ft. at 3000 rpm. Sequential fuel injection. VIN code W.

MYSTIQUE CHASSIS: Wheelbase (all) 106.5 in.; Overall length: (all) 184.7 in. Overall width: (all) 69.1 in.; Overall height: (all) 54.5 in. Front tread: (all) 59.2 in. Rear tread: (all) 58.5 in.

COUGAR CHASSIS: Wheelbase (all) 106.5 in.; Overall length: (all) 185 in. Overall width: (all) 69.6 in.; Overall height: (all) 52.2 in. Front tread: (all) 59.2 in. Rear tread: (all) 58.5 in.

SABLE CHASSIS: Wheelbase: (all) 108.5 in. Overall length: (sedan) 199.7 in.; (wagon) 199.1 in. Overall width: (all) 73 in. Overall height: (sedan) 55.4 in.; (wagon) 57.6 in. Front tread: 61.6 in. Rear tread: 61.4 in.

GRAND MARQUIS CHASSIS: Wheelbase: (all) 114.4 in. Overall Length: (all) 212 in. Overall width: (all) 78.2 in. Overall height: (all) 56.8 in. Front Tread: (all) 62.8 in. Rear Tread: (all) 63.3 in.

MYSTIQUE TECHNICAL: Standard transmission: five-speed manual transaxle. Drive axle: front. Steering: rack-and-pinion. Front suspension: independent, subframe rubber mounted MacPherson strut with strut-mounted coil springs, lower control A-arms and cast steering knuckles. Rear suspension: independent, Quadra-link strut with coil spring on shock strut, mounted to rigid subframe. Brakes: front disc/rear drum (power assisted). Body construction: unibody. Fuel tank: 14.5 gallons.

COUGAR TECHNICAL: Standard transmission: five-speed manual transaxle. Drive axle: front. Steering: rack-and-pinion. Front suspension: independent, subframe rubber mounted MacPherson strut with strut-mounted coil springs, lower control A-arms and cast steering knuckles. Rear suspension: independent Quadra-link design, coil springs, tube shock dampers and stabilizer bar. Brakes: (four) front disc/rear drum; (V-6) four-wheel discs. Body construction: unibody. Fuel tank: 14.5 gallons.

SABLE TECHNICAL: Standard transmission: Four-speed overdrive automatic. Drive axle: front. Steering: rack-and-pinion. Front suspension: independent MacPherson strut front drive with strut-mounted coil springs, stabilizer bar, lower control arm and cast aluminum knuckle with integral ball joint. Rear suspension: (sedan) independent Quadra-link with coil spring on shock strut, stabilizer bar, tension strut, parallel suspension arms and two-piece cast spindle with forged stem; (wagon) independent short/long arm with spring on lower control arm, stabilizer bar, tension strut and cast spindle with pressed-in forged stem and integrated ball joints. Brakes: front disc/rear drum (power assisted) except wagon has four-wheel discs. Body construction: unibody. Fuel tank: 16.0 gallons.

GRAND MARQUIS TECHNICAL: Standard transmission: four-speed overdrive automatic. Drive axle: rear. Steering: re-circulating ball. Front suspension: independent short/long arm with ball joints, coil springs and stabilizer bar. Rear suspension: Watt's linkage. Brakes: four-wheel disc. Body construction: separate body and frame. Fuel tank: 20.0 gallons.

MYSTIQUE OPTIONS: 153 front license plate bracket (no cost). 552 antilock braking system, standard on SVT ($500). 422 California emissions system (no cost). 428 high-altitude emissions system (no cost). 53G GS Sport group, includes rear spoiler, leather wheel and shift knob, fog lamps, sport logo floor mats and sport badge ($195). 41H engine block heater ($20). 12Y floor mats, front and rear ($55). 13B moonroof SE ($595). 585 ETR AM/FM stereo with CD player and premium sound, in SE ($275). 58P premium sound with electronic AM/FM stereo cassette ($135). 91H power antenna ($95). 143 remote keyless entry, includes illuminated entry system ($190). 219 60/40 split folding rear seat in SE ($205). 21A six-way power driver's seat, in GS ($350). 63B smoker's package ($15). 13K raised wing spoiler, LS only ($245). 553 traction control, requires antilock brakes ($175). 44T ECT automatic transmission ($815). 64Y 15-in. Mach alloy seven-hole wheels, includes P205/60R15 black sidewall tires, on GS ($475). 64M 15-in. polished Mach alloy six-spoke wheels, includes P205/60R15 black sidewall tires, on GS ($475).

COUGAR OPTIONS: 59M side airbags ($375). 552 antilock brakes ($500). 94A convenience group ($615). 60L V-6 group ($720). 422 California emissions (no cost). 428 high-altitude emissions (no cost). 153 front license plate bracket (no cost). 41H engine block imersion heater ($20). 98G body side moldings ($50). 582 premium AM/FM stereo cassette with four speakers ($130). 583 AM/FM ETR stereo with CD and premium four-speaker sound system ($140). 919 trunk-mounted remote CD player ($350). 21A six-way power driver's seat ($235). 8 leather seat trim ($895). 13K rear deck lid spoiler ($235). 433 spoiler delete, requires sport package ($235 credit). 97S V-6 sport package ($815). 13E power tilt/slide sunroof ($615). 533 traction control ($235). 44T ECT four-speed electronic automatic transmission, with V-6 only ($815). 645N 16-in. polished aluminum wheels, V-6 only, requires sport group ($250).

SABLE OPTIONS: 59B air filtration system ($30). 552 antilock braking system ($600). 942 daytime running lights ($40). 422 California emissions system (no cost). 428 high-altitude emissions system (no cost). 99S 3.0-liter Duratec V-6 ($555). 41H engine block heater ($35). 60L LS Premium group, includes 3.0-liter four, overdrive automatic transmission, electronic temperature control air conditioning, automatic headlamps, remote entry with keypad and perimeter anti-theft, light group, illuminated visor mirrors ($1,200). 943 light group ($45). 12Y floor mats, front and rear ($55). 54P heated exterior mirrors ($35). 13B power moonroof, includes unique map lamps in overhead console, LS only ($740). 916 Ford Mach audio system with six speakers in SE ($320). 919 trunk-mounted six-disc CD changer ($350). 143 remote keyless entry ($190). Q leather bucket seats, requires 21A power seat ($895). 21J dual power seats in LS ($350). 47B power side window delete, wagon only ($350 credit). 214 rear facing vinyl third seat in wagon ($200). 46S 60/40 split-folding rear seat ($175). 508 conventional spare tire ($125). 96W wagon group, includes cargo net and cargo area cover ($140). 64G bright aluminum GS wheels ($395). 64V 16-in. chrome alloy wheels ($580).

GRAND MARQUIS OPTIONS: 573 electronic automatic temperature control air conditioning ($175). 552 antilock brakes ($600). 553 antilock brakes with all-speed traction control ($775). 155 electronic instrumentation ($425). 175 garage door opener ($115). 41G handling and performance package includes revised springs, shocks and stabilizer bar, P225/60R16 black sidewall touring tires, 16-in. lacy-spoke wheels, rear air suspension, dual exhausts with 215-hp/275-ft.-lbs. rating and 3.27:1 axle ($855); same with upgrade from teardrop aluminum wheels ($535). 41H engine block immersion heater ($25). 144 remote keyless entry ($240). 153 front license plate bracket (no cost). 144 remote keyless entry with keypad ($240). 943 light group ($190). 54F Ltd feature car package, includes gold-plated 16-in. aluminum wheels, rear seat center armrest with cupholders, dual front seat storage armrests, embroideredd logo on front and rear seats, exclusive graystone leather trim, unique front and rear floor mats, special gold exterior trim package, on LS only ($460). 972 body side paint stripe on LS ($60). 68E Premium package includes 16-in. teardrop aluminum wheels, a leather-wrapped steering wheel, automatic temperature control air conditioning, an eight-way power passenger seat with power lumbar support adjustment and an automatic dimming inside rearview mirror with compass ($1,000). 586 premium sound system ($360). 919 trunk-mounted six-disc CD changer ($350). 585 single CD player replacing cassette ($140). J leather seat trim, requires power passenger seat, LS only ($735). 66B rear air suspension, LS only ($270). 508 conventional spare tire ($120). 68F Ultimate package includes all contents of 68E Premium package plus antilock brakes with traction control, electronic instrumentation and 586 radio upgrade ($2,400). 64R 16-in. teardrop wheels, LS only ($320).

HISTORICAL FOOTNOTES: Mark W. Hutchins continued as president of Lincoln-Mercury Div. in 2000. The division completed its relocation to Southern California.

2001 Mercury Cougar two-door coupe. (FMC)

Edge" look combined rounded body feature lines with straight-edged creases. Changes included redesigned fascias at the front and rear, new cat's-eye headlights with a projector and reflector system, a new grille, a redesigned rear deck lid spoiler, new front fog lights and a choice of two new types of wheels: 16-in. painted or 17-in. machined aluminum. Dark Shadow Grey, Tropic Green, French Blue and Sunburst Gold joined the Cougar's color palette.

COUGAR FOUR: Standard equipment included dual airbags, the SecuriLock™ passive anti-theft system with engine immobilizer, power front disc/rear drum brakes, front door pockets, a 2.0-liter 16-valve DOHC Zetec I-4 engine, a front 12-volt power point, air conditioning, a micron air filtration system, heated power outside rearview mirrors, a driver's visor-vanity mirror, an AM/FM CD stereo with four speakers, a mast radio antenna, reclining front bucket seats with cloth trim and a two-way power driver's seat, dual front headrests, front cupholders, a front console with storage, front floor mats, an easy-entry split folding rear seat, rear child seat tether anchors, rear seat heating ducts, a tilt-adjustable steering wheel, speed-proportional power rack-and-pinion steering, P205/60R15 all-season black sidewall tires with a mini spare tire, a five-speed manual transmission, variable intermittent windshield wipers, 15-in. aluminum alloy wheels, one touch power windows with illuminated switches, power door locks, a rear window defogger, front-wheel drive, four-wheel independent suspension with front and rear stabilizer bars, a trunk light, a remote trunk release and an inside the trunk emergency deck lid release.

COUGAR V-6: Standard equipment included dual airbags, the SecuriLock™ passive anti-theft system with engine immobilizer, power front disc/rear drum brakes, front door pockets, a 2.5-liter DOHC 24-valve V-6 engine, a front 12-volt power point, air conditioning, a micron air filtration system, heated power outside rearview mirrors, a driver's visor-vanity mirror, an AM/FM CD stereo with four speakers, a mast radio antenna, reclining front bucket seats with cloth trim and a two-way power driver's seat, dual front headrests, front cupholders, a front console with storage, front floor mats, an easy-entry split folding rear seat, rear child seat tether anchors, rear seat heating ducts, a tilt-adjustable steering wheel, speed-proportional power rack-and-pinion steering, P205/60R15 all-season black sidewall tires with a mini spare tire, a five-speed manual transmission, variable intermittent windshield wipers, 15-in. aluminum alloy wheels, one touch power windows with illuminated switches, power door locks, a rear window defogger, front-wheel drive, four-wheel independent suspension with front and rear stabilizer bars, a trunk light, a remote trunk release and an inside the trunk emergency deck lid release.

COUGAR C2: The Cougar C2 blended unique styling features with a one-of-a-kind French Blue paint. In addition, a French Blue instrument panel and color-keyed spoiler, as well as machined aluminum wheels with French Blue center caps were also offered. The Cougar C2 was also available in Silver Frost, Vibrant White and Black. The C2 also featured midnight black diamond-patterned sport cloth bucket seats. Midnight black leather seats were also available, as well as dark graphite floor mats. Both the dark graphite floor mats and the midnight black leather seats included French Blue Cougar logo badging. In addition, an electronic AM/FM stereo with an in-dash six-disc compact disc changer/player was standard on all C2s.

COUGAR ZN: The 2001 Cougar Zn was an eye-catching vehicle with new features and distinctive styling, including unique Zinc Yellow (Zn) clearcoat paint. With a Zinc Yellow hood scoop and spoiler, the Cougar Zn introduced standard 17-in. machined aluminum wheels with ebony accents and center caps. The Cougar logo appeared in the back-glass blackout. The Zn used the standard Cougar engine and came with either an automatic or manual transmission. It also featured midnight black diamond-patterned sport cloth bucket seats. Midnight black leather seats were also available, as well as dark graphite floor mats. Both the dark graphite floor mats and the midnight black leather seats included Zinc Yellow Cougar logo badging. In addition, an electronic AM/FM stereo with an in-dash six-disc compact disc changer/player was standard on all Zns.

2001 MERCURY

COUGAR – FOUR/V-6 – The distinctive, youth-oriented Mercury Cougar was heavily revised inside and outside for model year 2001. Its "New

2001 Mercury Sable four-door sedan. (FMC)

I.D. DATA: Mercury's 17-symbol Vehicle Identification Number (VIN) was stamped on a metal tab fastened to the instrument panel, visible through the windshield. The first symbol indicates the nation of origin: 1=United States; 2=Canada; 3=Mexico. The second symbol indicates manufacturer: M=Mercury Division, Ford Motor Co.; Z=Mercury Division, Ford Motor Co. The third symbol indicates vehicle type: M=passenger car; H=incomplete vehicle; W=Cougar. The fourth symbol indicates type of restraint system: B=driver and passenger air bags and active belts; F=driver and passenger air bags and active belts; H= driver and passenger front and side airbags and active belts in all outboard positions. The fifth symbol indicates designation: M=Mercury; T=Imported from outside North America or non-Ford car marketed by Ford in North America. The sixth and seventh symbols indicate body type: 50=Sable GS four-door sedan; 53=Sable LS four-door sedan; 55=Sable LS premium sedan; 58=Sable GS our-door station wagon; 59=Sable LS premium four-door station wagon; 60=Cougar three-door coupe with I-4; 61=Cougar three-door coupe with V-6; 74=Grand Marquis GS four-door sedan; 75=Grand Marquis LS four-door sedan. The eighth symbol indicates engine: L= Cougar 2.5-liter DOHC V-6 with EFI; 3=Cougar 2.0-liter DOHC I-4 with EFI; S=Sable 3.0-liter DOHC V-6 with EFI; U=Sable 3.0-liter V-6 with EFI; W=Grand Marquis 4.6-liter SOHC V-8 with EFI (Romeo engine plant). The ninth symbol is a check digit. The 10th symbol indicates model year: 1=2001. The 11th symbol indicates assembly plant: A=Hapeville (Atlanta), Ga.; G=Chicago, Ill.; K=Claycomo (Kansas City), Mo.; M=Cuautitlan, Mexico; X=Talbotville (St. Thomas), Ontario, Canada; 5=AAI: Flat Rock, Mich. The last six symbols are the sequential production number starting at 100001 at each factory.

Model No.	Body/ Style No.	Body Type & Seating	Factory Price	Shipping Weight	Prod. Total
COUGAR (FOUR)					
M	60	2d Coupe-5P	17,175	2,861	—
COUGAR C2 (FOUR)					
M	60	2d Coupe-5P	19,715	2,861	—
COUGAR Zn (FOUR)					
M	60	2d Coupe-5P	20,595	2,861	—
COUGAR (V-6)					
M	61	2d Coupe-5P	17,675	3,013	—

SABLE – V-6 – After its major revision in 2000, the Sable got some refinements for 2001. A new child safety seat tether/anchor system was introduced. A larger 18-gallon fuel tank was added. Tropic Green Clearcoat paint replaced Spruce Green. And that was about it.

SABLE GS SEDAN: Standard equipment included a 3.0-liter SOHC 12-valve V-6 engine, a four-speed automatic transmission, front-wheel drive, P215/60TR16 all-season tires, 16-in. steel wheel rims, a space saver spare tire, full wheel covers, a four-wheel independent suspension, front and rear stabilizer bars, front and rear solid disc brakes, front seat belt pre-tensioners, rear door child safety locks, child seat anchors, an emergency release in the trunk, a rear center lap belt, two front headrests, a security system engine immobilizer, variable intermittent windshield wipers, a rear defogger, six-passenger seating (with a cloth upholstered split-bench front seat and a rear bench seat), rear seat heating ducts, remote power door locks, one-touch power windows, power mirrors, an AM/FM cassette stereo system with four speakers, a mast antenna, cruise control, speed-proportional power steering, a tilt-adjustable steering wheel with cruise controls, front and rear cupholders, a remote trunk lid release, front and rear door pockets, front seatback storage, front and rear 12-volt power outlets, air conditioning, a micron air filtration system, dual visor-vanity mirrors, a tachometer, a clock, a low-fuel warning indicator and cargo tie downs.

SABLE GS WAGON: Standard equipment included a 3.0-liter DOHC 24-valve V-6 engine, a four-speed automatic transmission, front-wheel drive, P215/60TR16 all-season tires, 16-in. steel wheel rims, a space saver spare tire, full wheel covers, a four-wheel independent suspension, front and rear stabilizer bars, front disc/rear drum brakes, front seat belt pre-tensioners, rear door child safety locks, child seat anchors, an emergency release in the trunk, a rear center lap belt, two front headrests, a security system engine immobilizer, variable intermittent windshield wipers, a rear defogger, eight-passenger seating (with a cloth upholstered split-bench front seat, a rear bench seat and a fold-flat third row seat), rear seat heating ducts, remote power door locks, one-touch power windows, power mirrors, an AM/FM cassette stereo system with four speakers, a power antenna, cruise control, speed-proportional power steering, a tilt-adjustable steering wheel with cruise controls, front and rear cupholders, a remote trunk lid release, front and rear door pockets, front seatback storage, front and rear 12-volt power outlets, air conditioning, a micron air filtration system, dual visor-vanity mirrors, front reading lights, a roof rack, a tachometer, a clock, a low-fuel warning indicator and cargo tie downs.

SABLE LS SEDAN: Standard equipment included a 3.0-liter SOHC 12-valve V-6 engine, a four-speed automatic transmission, front-wheel drive, P215/60TR16 all-season tires, 16-in. alloy wheel rims, a space saver spare tire, full wheel covers, a four-wheel independent suspension, front and rear stabilizer bars, front and rear solid disc brakes, front seat belt pre-tensioners, rear door child safety locks, child seat anchors, an emergency release in the trunk, a rear center lap belt, two front headrests, a security system engine immobilizer, variable intermittent windshield wipers, a rear defogger, five-passenger seating (with cloth upholstered front bucket seats including a six-way power driver's seat with adjustable lumbar support and a split-folding rear bench seat), a front console with storage, rear seat heating ducts, remote power door locks, one-touch power windows, heated power mirrors, height-adjustable pedals, an AM/FM cassette stereo system with four speakers, a mast antenna, cruise control, speed-proportional power steering, a leather-wrapped tilt-adjustable steering wheel with cruise controls, front and rear cupholders, a remote trunk lid release, front and rear door pockets, front seatback storage, front and rear 12-volt power outlets, air conditioning, a micron air filtration system, dual visor-vanity mirrors, a tachometer, a clock and a low-fuel warning indicator. The wagon also featured cargo tie downs.

SABLE LS PREMIUM SEDAN: Standard equipment included a 3.0-liter SOHC 12-valve V-6 engine, a four-speed automatic transmission, front-wheel drive, P215/60TR16 all-season tires, 16-in. alloy wheel rims, a space saver spare tire, full wheel covers, a four-wheel independent suspension, front and rear stabilizer bars, front and rear solid disc brakes, front seat belt pre-tensioners, rear door child safety locks, child seat anchors, an emergency release in the trunk, a remote vehicle anti-theft system, dusk-sensing headlights, front fog lights, digital keyboard door locks, a rear center lap belt, two front headrests, a security system engine immobilizer, variable intermittent windshield wipers, a rear defogger, five-passenger seating (with cloth upholstered front bucket seats including a six-way power driver's seat with adjustable lumbar support and a split-folding rear bench seat), a front console with storage, rear seat heating ducts, one-touch power windows, heated power mirrors, dual illuminating visor-vanity mirrors, height-adjustable pedals, an AM/FM cassette stereo system with four speakers, a mast antenna, cruise control, speed-proportional power steering, a leather-wrapped tilt-adjustable steering wheel with cruise controls, front and rear cupholders, a remote trunk lid release, front and rear door pockets, front seatback storage, front and rear 12-volt power outlets, air conditioning, a micron air filtration system, dual visor-vanity mirrors, a tachometer, a clock and a low-fuel warning indicator. The wagon also featured cargo tie downs.

SABLE LS PREMIUM WAGON: Standard equipment included a 3.0-liter DOHC 24-valve V-6 engine, a four-speed automatic transmission, front-wheel drive, P215/60TR16 all-season tires, 16-in. steel wheel rims, a space saver spare tire, full wheel covers, a four-wheel independent suspension, front and rear stabilizer bars, front disc/rear drum brakes, front seat belt pre-tensioners, rear door child safety locks, child seat anchors, an emergency release in the trunk, a remote vehicle anti-theft system, dusk-sensing headlights, front fog lights, a rear center lap belt, two front headrests, a security system engine immobilizer, variable intermittent windshield wipers, a rear defogger, seven-passenger seating (with cloth upholstered bucket front seats including a six-way power driver's seat with adjustable lumbar support, a rear bench seat and a fold-flat third row seat), a front console with storage, rear seat heating ducts, digital keyboard power door locks, one-touch power windows, heated power mirrors, height-adjustable pedals, an AM/FM cassette stereo system with four speakers, a power antenna, cruise control, speed-proportional power steering, a leather-wrapped tilt-adjustable steering wheel with cruise controls, front and rear cupholders, a remote hatch lid release, front and rear door pockets, front seatback storage, front and rear 12-volt power outlets, air conditioning, a micron air filtration system, dual illuminating visor-vanity mirrors, front reading lights, a roof rack, a tachometer, a clock, a low-fuel warning indicator and cargo tie downs.

Model No.	Body/ Style No.	Body Type & Seating	Factory Price	Shipping Weight	Prod. Total
SABLE GS (V-6)					
M	50	4d Sedan-5P	20,110	3,369	—
SABLE LS (V-6)					
M	53	4d Sedan-5P	21,210	3,325	—
SABLE GS (V-6)					
M	58	4d Wagon-5P	21,910	3,544	—

SABLE LSPREMIUM (DOHC V-6)

M	55	4d Sedan-5P	22,510	3,325	—

SABLE LS PREMIUM (DOHC V-6)

M	59	4d Wagon-5P	23,610	3,473	—

GRAND MARQUIS – V-8 – The Mercury Marquis soldiered on as a big full-size car with plenty of get-up-and-go and a great safety record. It was a premium-level, full-size, rear-wheel drive family sedan. Mercury gave the Grand Marquis a little more power for 2001. The interior was also upgraded and the adjustable pedal system became optional. For safety's sake, Mercury added a crash severity sensing device, safety belt pre-tensioners, next-generation dual-stage airbags and seat position sensors.

GRAND MARQUIS GS: Standard equipment included dual airbags, front seat belt pre-tensioners, a front center lap belt, a rear center lap belt, air conditioning, front independent suspension, front and rear stabilizer bars, power front disc/rear drum brakes, rear seat child safety locks, child seat anchors, and emergency deck lid release inside the trunk, a clock, a rear window defogger, the 4.6-liter SOHC 16-valve sequential fuel-injected V-8, a stainless steel exhaust system, a gauge cluster with analog gauges (voltmeter, oil pressure, water temperature and fuel), automatic delay-off headlights, cornering lights, full Solar-Tinted glass, side window demisters, power door locks, a day/night inside rearview mirror, power outside rearview mirrors, an AM/FM stereo with cassette and four speakers, an element radio antenna, six-passenger seating (with a premium cloth upholstered split bench front seat including eight-way power driver's seat with adjustable lumbar support and a rear bench seat with folding center armrest), front seatback storage, two front headrests, front cupholders, a remote trunk release, an anti-theft system with engine immobilizer, simulated wood trim on the dashboard, simulated wood trim on the doors, front and rear floor mats, a trunk light, a sound insulation package, a color-keyed steering wheel with center horn blow, speed proportional power steering, cruise control, cloth covered sun visors with retention clips, dual visor-vanity mirrors, a tilt steering column with stalk-mounted controls, P225/60R16 all-season tires, a four-speed ECT automatic transmission with overdrive lockout, rear-wheel-drive, a trip odometer, intermittent windshield wipers, 16-in. steel wheel rims, full wheel covers and one touch power windows with driver side express down.

GRAND MARQUIS LS: Standard equipment included dual airbags, front seat belt pre-tensioners, a front center lap belt, a rear center lap belt, air conditioning, front independent suspension, front and rear stabilizer bars, power front disc/rear drum brakes, rear seat child safety locks, child seat anchors, and emergency deck lid release inside the trunk, a clock, a rear window defogger, the 4.6-liter SOHC 16-valve sequential fuel-injected V-8, a stainless steel exhaust system, a gauge cluster with analog gauges (voltmeter, oil pressure, water temperature and fuel), automatic delay-off headlights, cornering lights, full Solar-Tinted glass, side window demisters, digital keypad power door locks, a day/night inside rearview mirror, front and rear reading lights, power outside rearview mirrors, an AM/FM stereo with cassette and four speakers, an element radio antenna, six-passenger seating (with a premium cloth upholstered split bench front seat including eight-way power driver's seat with adjustable lumbar support and a rear bench seat with folding center armrest), front seatback storage, two front headrests, front cupholders, a remote trunk release, an anti-theft system with engine immobilizer, simulated wood trim on the dashboard, simulated wood trim on the doors, front and rear floor mats, a trunk light, a sound insulation package, a color-keyed steering wheel with center horn blow, speed proportional power steering, cruise control, cloth covered sun visors with retention clips, dual illuminating visor-vanity mirrors, a tilt steering column with stalk-mounted controls, P225/60R16 all-season tires, a four-speed ECT automatic transmission with overdrive lockout, rear-wheel-drive, a trip odometer, intermittent windshield wipers, 16-in. steel wheel rims, full wheel covers and one touch power windows with driver side express down.

GRAND MARQUIS LSE: The Grand Marquis LSE package was introduced at the Chicago Auto Show in February. It combined a finely-tuned suspension, 16-in. lacy-spoke wheels and a new five passenger-seating configuration with center console. The LSE offered exceptional handling and stability, sports styling details and amenities. It had a 235-horsepower V-8 and a specially tuned, firmer suspension. Other features of the LSE included five-passenger leather seating with dual eight-way power seats (including lumbar and power reclining functions), electronic automatic temperature control, a leather-wrapped steering wheel with radio, temperature and speed controls and a leather-wrapped floor shifter mounted in a custom center console (with a large storage bin, padded armrest, concealed power point, dual cupholders and center stack mini-storage bin with cigar lighter). A rear armrest with dual cupholders also was standard. The Grand Marquis provided agile road manners, improved off-the-line acceleration and excellent cornering thanks to a dual exhaust system (that increased engine power), revised shocks and spring rates, stabilizer bars, rear load leveling air spring suspension and a 3.27:1 rear axle ratio. The 16-in. lacy-spoke aluminum wheels were shod with P225/60TR16 black sidewall "handling" tires that provided extra road grip in the corners.

GRAND MARQUIS LIMITED: Finely crafted amenities highlighted the Grand Marquis Limited sedan. Mounted on an elegant wood-and-leather-wrapped steering wheel were convenient audio, climate and speed controls right at the driver's fingertips. The electronic automatic temperature control system fine-tuned the luxurious car's interior environment. Distinctive light parchment leather seating and floor mats featured an embroidered "Limited" designation. Dual front storage armrests and a rear center armrest with dual cupholders rounded out the interior. Under the hood, the Grand Marquis Limited showcased a SOHC 4.6L V-8 with a rear-wheel-drive power train and PrecisionTrac™ suspension system. Sixteen-inch aluminum wheels were standard. Also, an understated touch of gold trim adorned the exterior. The Grand Marquis Limited edition package was a $555 option.

Model No.	Body/ Style No.	Body Type & Seating	Factory Price	Shipping Weight	Prod. Total
GRAND MARQUIS GS (V-8)					
M	74	4d Sedan-6P	23,785	3,958	—
GRAND MARQUIS LS (V-8)					
M	75	4d Sedan-6P	25,685	3,973	—
GRAND MARQUIS LSE (V-8)					
M	75	4d Sedan-6P	28,975	3,973	—

COUGAR ENGINES

ENGINE [BASE FOUR]: Inline. Double overhead cam. Four-cylinder. Cast-iron block and aluminum head. Displacement: 121 cid (2.0 liters). Bore & stroke: 3.34 x 3.46 in. Compression ratio: 9.6:1. Brake horsepower: 125 at 5500 rpm. Torque: 130 lbs.-ft. at 4000 rpm. Sequential fuel injection. VIN code 3.

ENGINE [BASE V-6]: Modular, double overhead cam V-6. Aluminum block and head. Displacement: 155 cid (2.5 liters). Bore & stroke: 3.24 x 3.13 in. Compression ratio: 9.7:1. Brake horsepower: 170 at 6250 rpm. Torque: 165 lbs.-ft. at 4250 rpm. Sequential fuel injection. VIN code L.

SABLE ENGINES

ENGINE [BASE GS/LS]: Overhead valve V-6. Cast-iron block and head. Displacement: 182 cid (3.0 liters). Bore & stroke: 3.50 x 3.15 in. Compression ratio: 9.3:1. Brake horsepower: 155 at 4900 rpm. Torque: 185 lbs.-ft. at 3950 rpm. Sequential fuel injection. VIN code U.

ENGINE [OPTIONAL LS]: Double overhead cam V-6. Aluminum block and head. Displacement: 182 cid (3.0 liters). Bore & stroke: 3.50 x 3.15 in. Compression ratio: 10.0:1. Brake horsepower: 200 at 5750 rpm. Torque: 200 lbs.-ft. at 4500 rpm. Sequential fuel injection. VIN code S.

GRAND MARQUIS ENGINE

ENGINE [BASE]: Modular, overhead valve V-8. Displacement: 281 cid (4.6 liters). Bore & stroke: 3.60 x 3.60. Compression ratio: 9.0:1. Brake horsepower: 220 at 4750 rpm. Torque: 265 lbs.-ft. at 4000 rpm. Sequential fuel injection. VIN code W.

COUGAR CHASSIS: Wheelbase (all) 106.4 in.; Overall length: (all) 185 in. Overall width: (all) 69.6 in.; Overall height: (all) 52.2 in. Front tread: (all) 59.2 in. Rear tread: (all) 58.5 in.

SABLE CHASSIS: Wheelbase: (all) 108.5 in. Overall length: (sedan) 199.8 in.; (wagon) 197.8 in. Overall width: (all) 73 in. Overall height: (sedan) 55.5 in.; (wagon) 59.8 in. Front tread: 61.6 in. Rear tread: 61.4 in.

GRAND MARQUIS CHASSIS: Wheelbase: (all) 114.7 in. Overall Length: (all) 211.9 in. Overall width: (all) 78.2 in. Overall height: (all) 56.8 in. Front Tread: (all) 62.8 in. Rear Tread: (all) 63.3 in.

COUGAR TECHNICAL: Standard transmission: five-speed manual transaxle. Drive axle: front. Steering: rack-and-pinion. Front suspension: independent, subframe rubber mounted MacPherson strut with strut-mounted coil springs, lower control A-arms, cast steering knuckles and stabilizer bar. Rear suspension: independent Quadra-link design, coil springs, tube shock dampers and stabilizer bar. Brakes: (four) front disc/rear drum; (V-6) four-wheel discs. Body construction: unibody. Fuel tank: 15.5 gallons.

SABLE TECHNICAL: Standard transmission: Four-speed overdrive automatic. Drive axle: front. Steering: rack-and-pinion. Front suspension: independent MacPherson strut front drive with strut-mounted coil springs, stabilizer bar, lower control arm and cast aluminum knuckle with integral ball joint. Rear suspension: (sedan) independent Quadra-link with coil spring on shock strut, stabilizer bar, tension strut, parallel suspension arms and two-piece cast spindle with forged stem; (wagon) Independent short/long arm with spring on lower control arm, stabilizer bar, tension strut and cast spindle with pressed-in forged stem and integrated ball joints. Brakes: front disc, rear drum (power assisted) except wagon has four-wheel discs. Body construction: unibody. Fuel tank: 18 gallons.

2001 Mercury Grand Marquis four-door sedan. (FMC)

GRAND MARQUIS TECHNICAL: Standard transmission: four-speed overdrive automatic. Drive axle: rear. Steering: re-circulating ball. Front suspension: independent short/long arm with ball joints, coil springs and stabilizer bar. Rear suspension: Watt's linkage with stabilizer bar. Brakes: four-wheel disc. Body construction: separate body and frame. Fuel tank: 19 gallons.

COUGAR OPTIONS: 59M side airbags ($390). 552 antilock brakes ($500). 60L V-6 convenience group ($660). 422 California emissions (no cost). 153 front license plate bracket (no cost). 41H engine block imersion heater ($20). 96G body side moldings ($50). 58K AM/FM stereo cassette and CD player ($80). 586 in-dash CD changer ($130). 586 in-dash CD changer ($210). 21A six-way power driver's seat ($235). 8 leather seat trim ($895). T unique black leather sport bucket seats ($895). 13K rear deck lid spoiler ($235). 97S V-6 sport package ($865). 13E power tilt/slide sunroof ($615). 533 traction control ($235). 44T ECT four-speed electronic automatic transmission, with V-6 only ($815). 63B smoker's package ($15). 94A convenience group with speed control, remote keyless entry, illuminated entry and rear window wiper/washer ($615). 90C C2 feature vehicle group ($4515). 90Z feature vehicle group ($1,395).

SABLE OPTIONS: 552 antilock braking system (no cost). 422 California emissions system (no cost). 13B power moonroof, includes unique map lamps in overhead console, LS only ($890). 21J dual power seats in LS ($350). 184 six-passenger seating with flip-fold center console in LS Premium sedan/wagon (no cost). 186 five-passenger seating with floor console and floor shifter in GS sedan ($105). 21A six-way power driver seat, GS sedan and wagon ($395). 53A audio group ($670). 553 all-speed traction control ($175). 585 AM/FM stereo and single CD player ($140). 59C power adjustable pedals ($140). 61B side impact airbags ($390). 64N seven-spoke alloy wheels ($395). 64W Chrometec wheels ($295). 85R Secure group, includes side impact airbags, all-speed traction control and antilock braking system ($565). 93N non-California emissions (no cost). 99S 3.0-liter Duratec V-6 ($695).

GRAND MARQUIS OPTIONS: 422 California emissions (no cost). 552 antilock brakes ($600). 553 antilock brakes with all-speed traction control ($775). 41G Handling and Performance package, includes revised springs, shocks and stabilizer bar, P225/60R16 black sidewall touring tires, 16-in. lacy-spoke wheels, rear air suspension, dual exhausts with 215-hp/275-ft.-lbs. rating and 3.27:1 axle ($855); same with upgrade from teardrop aluminum wheels ($535). 153 front license plate bracket (no cost). 144 remote keyless entry with keypad ($240). 155 electronic instrumentation ($425). 175 HomeLink universal garage door opener ($115). 943 luxury light group ($190). 54E limited-edition package ($555). 972 body side paint stripe on LS ($60). 68E premium package includes 16-in. teardrop aluminum wheels, a leather-wrapped steering wheel, automatic temperature control air conditioning, an eight-way power passenger seat with power lumbar support adjustment and an automatic dimming inside rearview mirror with compass ($1,120). 586 premium sound system ($360). 919 trunk-mounted six-disc CD changer ($360). 585 single CD player replacing cassette ($140). J leather seat trim, requires power passenger seat, LS only ($795). 66B rear air suspension, LS only ($270). 508 conventional spare tire ($105). 508 conventional spare tire ($120). 68F Ultimate package, includes all contents of 68E premium package plus antilock brakes with traction control, electronic instrumentation and 586 radio upgrade ($2,520). 64R 16-in. teardrop wheels, LS only ($320). 59C power adjustable pedals ($120). 652 LSE package ($895). 919 trunk mounted six-disc CD changer ($350). 93N non-California emissions (no cost).

HISTORICAL FOOTNOTES: Mercury introduced the 2001 Grand Marquis LSE and the 2001 Grand Marquis Limited at the Chicago Auto Show today on Feb. 8, 2001. "Building on an already successful platform, the Grand Marquis LSE offers both performance and classic refinement," said Tony Picarello, brand manager for Mercury Grand Marquis. "The size, power, comfort, convenience and luxury of the LSE are remarkable attributes, especially considering its price tag of $28,295 MSRP. I believe this package makes it one of the best values in its class." "In addition to the Grand Marquis' impressive list of standard equipment, the Limited package features a selection of interior and exterior refinements," said Jennifer Moneagle, Mercury Group brand manager. "And it's more than just a pretty face — the Grand Marquis

delivers a smooth, responsiveness driving performance traditional luxury car owners expect." Building on the dynamic appeal of the sporty Cougar line, Mercury also introduced the 2001 Cougar Zn and Cougar C2 models at the 2001 Chicago Auto Show. They represented Mercury's latest attempt to lure the more youthful consumer with new, stylish and energetic coupes. By expanding the current Cougar line, the Cougar Zn and C2 continued to embody the "break-the-mold" look Mercury had been defining since it introduced the Cougar three years earlier. Also during 2001, the National Highway and Traffic Safety Administration (NHTSA) awarded the 2001 Mercury Sable, Mercury Grand Marquis and Mercury Villager the federal government's highest safety rating for frontal crashes — double five-star ratings for both driver and passenger.

2002 MERCURY

COUGAR – FOUR/V-6 – Introduced in 1999 to appeal to younger drivers and attract new consumers to the Mercury brand, the Cougar sports coupe returned in 2002. Mercury hoped to build on the key elements of its bold exterior and interior styling, which was updated for 2001. The base Cougar was offered as a four-cylinder sports coupe with a five-speed manual transmission and as a V-6 coupe with either a five-speed manual or four-speed automatic transmission. The Cougar continued to be manufactured at Ford's AutoAlliance facility in Flat Rock, Mich. In the what's new department, a convenience group, which included speed control, remote keyless entry, illuminated entry and a rear wiper/washer, was now standard. New colors for 2002 were Grabber Green Clearcoat Metallic, Light Parchment Gold Clearcoat Metallic and Red Clearcoat. The Cougar retained many elements of its distinctive "New Edge" design, which emphasized sharp creases and flowing lines. The front and rear fascias and grille flowed into the body lines. Amber repeater signal lamps in the front fenders provided a European design cue. The frameless door glass provided a flush, clean appearance, while the rear, color-keyed spoiler suggested performance. Inside, the instrument panel had a satin aluminum face with sharp graphics, satin aluminum surround rings and gauge pointers. For 2002, V-6 powered Cougars were offered in base and Sport series. The Sport models were offered in Sport, Sport Premium and Sport Ultimate packages. The Sport packages made a number of comfort, convenience and performance features available as standard equipment, including 16-in. wheels and tires and unique items such as aluminum accelerator, brake and clutch pedals. The Cougar's comfort and versatility made it a perfect fit for buyers with active lifestyles. The seats combined comfort, practicality and a sporty appearance. The seats were placed lower than conventional designs, making them closer to the center of gravity. This gave a greater feeling of control while accelerating into turns and a feeling of being connected with the vehicle. The "bucket" design of the rear seat provided supportive comfort. The front passenger seat had a tip/slide feature with memory for easy access to the rear seats. The driver's seat featured power height adjustment. The 50/50 split-folding rear seatbacks folded flat for cargo-carrying flexibility. The Cougar's luggage compartment of 14.5 cu. ft, expanded to 24 cu. ft. when the rear seatbacks were folded down. Cougar's door openings and floor structures were designed to resist side-impact forces. The Cougar V-6 Sport Ultimate featured standard driver and front passenger side-impact airbags that deployed from the sides of the front seatbacks, protecting the driver's and front passenger's head and chest.

COUGAR FOUR: Standard equipment included a fixed center roof antenna, body color door handles, color-coordinated 5-mph bumpers, projector and reflector headlamp system, dual body-color heated power mirrors, side moldings, side repeat turn indicators, 15-in. aluminum alloy wheels, one touch power windows with illuminated switches, Solar-Tinted glass, dual front airbags, black carpet, an electronic clock in the center of the instrument cluster, child seat tethers, a full-length center console (with stowage bin, cupholder and power point), a courtesy light delay function, side window demisters, molded full coverage door trim with armrest and cloth insert, front floor mats, a driver's footrest, front door bins, a non-locking glove box, a cloth covered headliner, fixed head restraints, rear seat heat ducts, a soft feel instrument panel (with speedometer, odometer, trip odometer, tachometer, fuel and water temperature gauges, a low-fuel warning light and an integrated trip computer with external temperature display), a front header mounted interior courtesy light, an illuminated rotary master light switch, illuminated switches and heater controls, a fully trimmed lighted load compartment, the Micronair filtration system, a day/night inside rearview mirror, a driver vanity mirror, an AM/FM stereo CD player with premium sound and four speakers, rear coat hooks, a removable rear package tray, individual bucket seats with cloth trim (driver's seat with manual recliner and fore/aft power height adjustment; passenger seat with manual recliner and fore/aft –tip/slide mechanism), a 50/50 split-folding rear seat, three-point seat belts with warning indicator, manual tilt steering, a four-spoke comfort steering wheel, cloth covered sun visors, a warning chime system (for ignition key, lights on and seat belts), a warning light system (for parking brake, brake, safety belts, airbags, high beam, check engine, low oil pressure, ignition on and lights on), air conditioning, a 105-amp alternator, the SecuriLock™

passive anti-theft system, a maintenance free battery, power front disc/rear drum brakes, a remote electric trunk lid release, a rear window defroster, power door locks, a 2.0-liter Zetec DOHC 16-valve four-cylinder engine, a 15.5-gal. Fuel tank with tethered cap, remote keyless entry with illuminated entry, a' rear wiper/washer, a single ignition and door key, speed control, power rack-and-pinion steering, a MacPherson strut front suspension, a quadra-link rear suspension with anti-roll bar, P20560R15 tires, a five-speed manual transaxle a two-speed variable intermittent windshield wipers.

COUGAR V-6: Standard equipment included a fixed center roof antenna, body color door handles, brushed aluminum exhaust tips, color-coordinated 5-mph bumpers, projector and reflector headlamp system, dual body-color heated power mirrors, side moldings, side repeat turn indicators, 15-in. aluminum alloy wheels, one touch power windows with illuminated switches, Solar-Tinted glass, dual front airbags, black carpet, an electronic clock in the center of the instrument cluster, child seat tethers, a full-length center console (with stowage bin, cupholder and power point), a courtesy light delay function, side window demisters, molded full coverage door trim with armrest and cloth insert, front floor mats, a driver's footrest, front door bins, a non-locking glove box, a cloth covered headliner, fixed head restraints, rear seat heat ducts, a soft feel instrument panel (with speedometer, odometer, trip odometer, tachometer, fuel and water temperature gauges, a low-fuel warning light and an integrated trip computer with external temperature display), a front header mounted interior courtesy light, an illuminated rotary master light switch, illuminated switches and heater controls, a fully trimmed lighted load compartment, the Micronair filtration system, a day/night inside rearview mirror, a driver vanity mirror, an AM/FM stereo CD player with premium sound and four speakers, rear coat hooks, a removable rear package tray, individual bucket seats with cloth trim (driver's seat with manual recliner and fore/aft power height adjustment; passenger seat with manual recliner and fore/aft-tip/slide mechanism), a 50/50 split-folding rear seat, three-point seat belts with warning indicator, manual tilt steering, a four-spoke comfort steering wheel, cloth covered sun visors, a warning chime system (for ignition key, lights on and seat belts), a warning light system (for parking brake, brake, safety belts, airbags, high beam, check engine, low oil pressure, ignition on and lights on), air conditioning, a 130-amp alternator, the SecuriLock™ passive anti-theft system, a maintenance free battery, power front disc/rear drum brakes, a remote electric trunk lid release, a rear window defroster, power door locks, a 2.5-liter Duratec DOHC 24-valve V-6 engine, a 15.5-gal. Fuel tank with tethered cap, remote keyless entry with illuminated entry, a rear wiper/washer, a single ignition and door key, speed control, power rack-and-pinion steering, a MacPherson strut front suspension, a quadra-link rear suspension with anti-roll bar, P20560R15 tires, a five-speed manual transaxle a two-speed variable intermittent windshield wipers.

COUGAR V-6 SPORT: Standard equipment included a fixed center roof antenna, body color door handles, brushed aluminum exhaust tips, color-coordinated 5-mph bumpers, front fog lamps, projector and reflector headlamp system, dual body-color heated power mirrors, side moldings, side repeat turn indicators, a color-keyed rear deck lid spoiler, 16-in. aluminum alloy wheels, one touch power windows with illuminated switches, Solar-Tinted glass, dual front airbags, black carpet, an electronic clock in the center of the instrument cluster, child seat tethers, a full-length center console (with stowage bin, cupholder, power point, armest and rear storage tray), a courtesy light delay function, side window demisters, bright door sill plates, molded full coverage door trim with armrest and cloth insert, front floor mats, a driver's footrest, front door bins, a non-locking glove box, a cloth covered headliner, two-way height adjustable head restraints, rear seat heat ducts, a soft feel instrument panel (with speedometer, odometer, trip odometer, tachometer, fuel and water temperature gauges, a low-fuel warning light and an integrated trip computer with external temperature display), a front header mounted interior courtesy light, an illuminated rotary master light switch, illuminated switches and heater controls, a fully trimmed lighted load compartment, the Micronair filtration system, a day/night inside rearview mirror, dual illuminated vanity mirrors, aluminum pedals, an AM/FM stereo CD player with premium sound and four speakers, rear coat hooks, a removable rear package tray, individual sport bucket seats with cloth trim (six-way power driver's seat with manual recliner, fore/aft power height adjustment and lumbar support, driver and passenger seat map pockets, passenger seat with manual recliner and fore/aft –tip/slide mechanism), a 50/50 split-folding rear seat, three-point seat belts with warning indicator, manual tilt steering, a leather-wrapped steering wheel and shift knob, cloth covered sun visors, a warning chime system (for ignition key, lights on and seat belts), a warning light system (for parking brake, brake, safety belts, airbags, high beam, check engine, low oil pressure, ignition on and lights on), air conditioning, a 130-amp alternator, the SecuriLock™ passive anti-theft system, a maintenance free battery, power four-wheel disc brakes, a remote electric trunk lid release, a rear window defroster, power door locks, a 2.5-liter Duratec DOHC 24-valve V-6 engine, a 15.5-gal. Fuel tank with tethered cap, remote keyless entry with illuminated entry, a rear wiper/washer, a single ignition and door key, speed control, power rack-and-pinion steering, an upraded MacPherson strut front suspension, an upgraded quadra-link rear suspension with anti-roll bar, P21550R16 tires, a five-speed manual transaxle a two-speed variable intermittent windshield wipers.

COUGAR C2 V-6: The Cougar C2 package (introduced in 2001) was available on V-6 powered vehicles equipped with a Sport package. The body, spoiler and the center caps of the machined aluminum wheels of the Cougar C2 were painted French Blue. (The Cougar C2 was also available in Silver Frost, Vibrant White and Black.) Inside, French Blue adorned the faceplate of the in-dash six-disc CD changer, the speedometer cluster background, the diamond-patterned cloth bucket seats and the Cougar C2 logo on the floor mats. When fitted with the optional black leather-trimmed seats, the logo badge was also embroidered in French Blue.

COUGAR XR V-6: The Cougar XR was offered in red or black clearcoat with a color-keyed hood scoop and spoiler. The Cougar XR's unique 17-in. wheels were partially painted black with red center caps. The Cougar logo was emblazoned on the car's front and the back glass. Cloth seats with black bolsters in midnight black or dark graphite were standard. Midnight black leather-trimmed seats with black bolsters and red inserts were optional.

I.D. DATA: Mercury's 17-symbol Vehicle Identification Number (VIN) was stamped on a metal tab fastened to the instrument panel, visible through the windshield. The first symbol indicates the nation of origin: 1=United States; 2=Canada; 3=Mexico. The second symbol indicates manufacturer: M=Mercury Division, Ford Motor Co.; Z=Mercury Division, Ford Motor Co. The third symbol indicates vehicle type: E=passenger car; H=incomplete vehicle; W=Cougar. The fourth symbol indicates type of restraint system: B=driver and passenger air bags and active belts (except Escort ZX2 coupe); F=driver and passenger air bags and active belts; H= driver and passenger front and side airbags and active belts in all outboard positions. The fifth symbol indicates designation: M=Mercury; T=Imported from outside North America or non-Ford car marketed by Ford in North America. The sixth and seventh symbols indicate body type: 50=Sable GS four-door sedan; 53=Sable LS four-door sedan; 55=Sable LS premium sedan; 58=Sable GS our-door station wagon; 59=Sable LS premium four-door station wagon; 60=Cougar three-door coupe with I-4; 61=Cougar three-dor coupe with V-6; 62=Cougar three-door coupe with V-6; 74=Grand Marquis GS four-door sedan; 75=Grand Marquis LS four-door sedan. The eigth symbol indicates engine: L= Cougar 2.5-liter DOHC V-6 with EFI; 3=Cougar 2.0-liter DOHC I-4 with EFI; S=Sable 3.0-liter DOHC V-6 with EFI; U=Sable 3.0-liter V-6 with EFI; W=Grand Marquis 4.6-liter SOHC V-8 with EFI (Romeo engine plant). The ninth symbol is a check digit. The 10th symbol indicates model year: 2=2002. The 11th symbol indicates assembly plant: A=Hapeville (Atlanta), Ga.; G=Chicago, Ill.; K=Claycomo (Kansas City), Mo.; M=Cuautitlan Mexico; X=Talbotville (St. Thomas), Ontario Canada; 5=AAI: Flat Rock, Mich. The last six symbols are the sequential production number starting at 100001 at each factory.

Model No.	Body/ Style No.	Body Type & Seating	Factory Price	Shipping Weight	Prod. Total
COUGAR (FOUR)					
T	60	2d Coupe-5P	16,995	2,861	Note 1
COUGAR (V-6)					
T	61	2d Coupe-5P	17,495	3,013	Note 1
COUGAR SPORT (V-6)					
T	61	2d Coupe-5P	17,995	3,200	Note 1
COUGAR SPORT PREMIUM (V-6)					
T	61	2d Coupe-5P	18,995	3,200	Note 1
COUGAR SPORT ULTIMATE (V-6)					
T	61	2d Coupe-5P	20,395	3,200	Note 1

Note 1: Production total not available at publication date.

SABLE – V-6 – The front-wheel drive Mercury Sable was again available in four-door sedan and four-door station wagon body styles. The Sable had delivered a combination of style, comfort and practicality since its debut in 1986. For 2002, the Sable built on its reputation for safety by offering an antilock braking system at no-charge. Mercury also added new security and convenience features to the Sable, such as security approach lighting. The company poured some heavy promotion into the fact that the Sable had earned double five-star crash safety ratings from the National Highway Transportation Safety Administration for three straight years. New-for-2002 features included an LED rear center-high-mounted stoplight on all series. An auto-dimming rearview mirror with compass was made available on the GS Plus and LS Premium models. Mercury also simplified the Sable's packaging and series lineups. Both body styles were available in GS, GS Plus and highline LS Premium configurations. All Sables came equipped with standard four-wheel antilock brakes for the first time. Security approach lightning, built into the outside rearview mirror housings, was now made standard equipment on all Sables. The Sable LS Premium sedan and wagon also offered leather seating surfaces as a no-charge option. New colors included Matador Red Clearcoat Metallic, Dark Shadow Grey Clearcoat Metallic, Arizona Beige Clearcoat Metallic and Medium True Blue Clearcoat Metallic.

SABLE GS SEDAN: Standard equipment included a 3.0-liter 12-valve V-6 engine, a four-speed automatic transmission, front-wheel drive, four-wheel independent suspension, a front stabilizer bar, a tachometer, a clock, a low-fuel level warning indicator, a tachometer, a clock, a low-fuel level warning indicator, 16-in. steel wheel rims, P215/60R16 tires, a space saver spare tire, a steel spare wheel, full wheel covers, variable intermittent windshield wipers, a rear window defogger, ventilated front disc/rear drum brakes, front seat belt pretensioners, rear door child safety locks, child seat anchors, an inside-the-trunk emergency rear deck lid release, a front center lap belt, a rear center three-point seat belt, dual front seat headrests, an anti-theft system, remote power door locks, one touch power windows, power mirrors, adaptive cruise control, speed-proportional power steering, a tilt-adjustable steering wheel with hub-mounted cruise controls, front cupholders, front door pockets, front seatback storage, a front 12-volt power point, a front console with storage provisions, retained accessory power, six-passenger total seating with a split-bench front seat and split-folding rear bench seat, cloth upholstery, rear seat heating ducts, air conditioning, dual visor-vanity mirrors, a micron air filtration system, an AM/FM cassette stereo with four-speaker sound system and a mast antenna.

SABLE GS PLUS SEDAN: Standard equipment included a 3.0-liter 12-valve V-6 engine, a four-speed automatic transmission, front-wheel drive, four-wheel independent suspension, a front stabilizer bar, a tachometer, a clock, a low-fuel level warning indicator, a compass, 16-in. steel wheel rims, P215/60R16 all-season tires, a space saver spare tire, a steel spare wheel, full wheel covers, variable intermittent windshield wipers, a rear window defogger, ventilated front disc/rear drum brakes, front seat belt pre-tensioners, rear door child safety locks, child seat anchors, an inside-the-trunk emergency rear deck lid release, a front center lap belt, a rear center three-point seat belt, dual front seat headrests, an anti-theft system, remote power door locks, one touch power windows, power mirrors, adaptive cruise control, speed-proportional power steering, a tilt-adjustable steering wheel with hub-mounted cruise controls, height-adjustable pedals, front cupholders, front door pockets, front seatback storage, a front 12-volt power point, a front console with storage provisions, retained accessory power, six-passenger total seating with a split-bench front seat (six-way power and adjustable lumbar support on driver's side seat) and split-folding rear bench seat, cloth upholstery, rear seat heating ducts, air conditioning, an automatic dimming inside rearview mirror, dual visor-vanity mirrors, a micron air filtration system, an AM/FM CD stereo with four-speaker sound system and a mast antenna.

SABLE LS PREMIUM SEDAN: Standard equipment included a 3.0-liter 12-valve V-6 engine, a four-speed automatic transmission, front-wheel drive, four-wheel independent suspension, a front stabilizer bar, a tachometer, a clock, a low-fuel level warning indicator, a compass, 16-in. alloy wheel rims, P215/60R16 all-season tires, a space saver spare tire, a steel spare wheel, variable intermittent windshield wipers, a rear window defogger, ventilated front disc/rear drum brakes, front seat belt pre-tensioners, rear door child safety locks, child seat anchors, an inside-the-trunk emergency rear deck lid release, a front center lap belt, a rear center three-point seat belt, dual front seat headrests, an anti-theft system, dusk-sensing headlights, front fog lights, remote power door locks, one touch power windows, power mirrors, adaptive cruise control, speed-proportional power steering, a tilt-adjustable steering wheel with hub-mounted cruise controls, height-adjustable pedals, front cupholders, front door pockets, front seatback storage, a cargo net, a front 12-volt power point, a front console with storage provisions, retained accessory power, five-passenger seating with a split-bench front seat (six-way power and adjustable lumbar support on driver's side seat) and split-folding rear bench seat, cloth upholstery, rear seat heating ducts, a climate control system, an automatic dimming inside rearview mirror, dual illuminating visor-vanity mirrors, a leather-wrapped steering wheel, an AM/FM CD stereo with four-speaker sound system and a mast antenna.

SABLE GS WAGON: Standard equipment included a 3.0-liter 12-valve V-6 engine, a four-speed automatic transmission, front-wheel drive, four-wheel independent suspension, a front stabilizer bar, a tachometer, a clock, a low-fuel level warning indicator, 16-in. steel wheel rims, P215/60R16 all-season tires, a space saver spare tire, a steel spare wheel, full wheel covers, variable intermittent windshield wipers, a roof rack, a rear window defogger, a rear window wiper, ventilated front disc/solid rear disc brakes, front seat belt pre-tensioners, rear door child safety locks, child seat anchors, a front center lap belt, a rear center three-point seat belt, dual front seat headrests, an anti-theft system, remote power door locks, one touch power windows, power mirrors, adaptive cruise control, speed-proportional power steering, a tilt-adjustable steering wheel with hub-mounted cruise controls, front cupholders, front door pockets, front seatback storage, a front 12-volt power point, a front console with storage provisions, retained accessory power, six-passenger total seating with a split-bench front seat and split-folding rear bench seat, cloth upholstery, rear seat heating ducts, third row bench seating, air conditioning, dual visor-vanity mirrors, a micron air filtration system, front reading lights, a cargo area light, an AM/FM cassette stereo with four-speaker sound system and a power antenna.

SABLE GS PLUS WAGON: Standard equipment included a 3.0-liter 12-valve V-6 engine, a four-speed automatic transmission, front-wheel drive, four-wheel independent suspension, a front stabilizer bar, a

tachometer, a clock, a low-fuel level warning indicator, a compass, 16-in. steel wheel rims, P215/60R16 all-season tires, a space saver spare tire, a steel spare wheel, full wheel covers, variable intermittent windshield wipers, a roof rack, a rear window defogger, a rear window wiper, ventilated front disc/solid rear disc brakes, front seat belt pre-tensioners, rear door child safety locks, child seat anchors, a front center lap belt, a rear center three-point seat belt, dual front seat headrests, an anti-theft system, remote power door locks, one touch power windows, power mirrors, adaptive cruise control, speed-proportional power steering, a tilt-adjustable steering wheel with hub-mounted cruise controls, height-adjustable pedals, front cupholders, front door pockets, front seatback storage, a front 12-volt power point, a front console with storage provisions, retained accessory power, six-passenger total seating with a split-bench front seat (six-way power and adjustable lumbar support on driver's side seat) and split-folding rear bench seat, cloth upholstery, rear seat heating ducts, third row bench seating, air conditioning, dual illuminating visor-vanity mirrors, a micron air filtration system, an automatically dimming inside rearview mirror, front reading lights, a cargo area light, an AM/FM cassette stereo with four-speaker sound system and a power antenna.

SABLE GS PREMIUM WAGON: Standard equipment included a 3.0-liter 12-valve V-6 engine, a four-speed automatic transmission, front-wheel drive, four-wheel independent suspension, a front stabilizer bar, a tachometer, a clock, a low-fuel level warning indicator, a compass, 16-in. alloy wheel rims, P215/60R16 all-season tires, a space saver spare tire, a steel spare wheel, variable intermittent windshield wipers, a roof rack, a rear window defogger, a rear window wiper, ventilated front disc/solid rear disc brakes, front seat belt pre-tensioners, rear door child safety locks, child seat anchors, a front center lap belt, a rear center three-point seat belt, dual front seat headrests, an anti-theft system, dusk-sensing headlights, front fog lights, remote power door locks, one touch power windows, power mirrors, adaptive cruise control, speed-proportional power steering, a leather-wrapped tilt-adjustable steering wheel with hub-mounted cruise controls, height-adjustable pedals, front cupholders, front door pockets, front seatback storage, a front 12-volt power point, a front console with storage provisions, retained accessory power, five-passenger total seating with a split-bench front seat (six-way power and adjustable lumbar support on driver's side seat) and split-folding rear bench seat, cloth upholstery, rear seat heating ducts, third row bench seating, a climate control system, dual illuminating visor-vanity mirrors, a micron air filtration system, an automatically dimming inside rearview mirror, front reading lights, a cargo area light, an AM/FM cassette stereo with four-speaker sound system and a power antenna.

SABLE LS PLATINUM EDITION: Enhancing the look of the 2002 Sable, the Platinum Edition package was offered for both the sedan and the wagon. It featured unique front and rear perforated leather seating, "Platinum Edition" fender badge and aluminum wheels featuring a satin aluminum Mercury logo on the center cap. The interior of the Platinum incorporated the use of real satin aluminum on the center floor console and the instrument panel center stack. The instrument cluster bezel was painted to match. The front grille and deck lid appliqués also had a satin aluminum finish. The Sable Platinum was offered in seven exterior colors, with medium graphite leather interior. It hit Mercury dealer showroom floors in January 2002 with production to be limited to 3,500 units.

Model No.	Body/ Style No.	Body Type & Seating	Factory Price	Shipping Weight	Prod. Total
SABLE GS (V-6)					
M	50	4d Sedan-5P	20,255	3,379	—
SABLE GS PLUS (V-6)					
M	50	4d Sedan-5P	21,315	3,379	—
SABLE GS FLEET (V-6)					
M	50	4d Sedan-5P	20,540	3,379	—
SABLE GS FLEET PLUS (V-6)					
M	50	4d Sedan-5P	21,595	3,379	—
SABLE LS PREMIUM (V-6)					
M	55	4d Sedan-5P	22,680	3,325	—
SABLE LS PLATINUM EDITION (V-6)					
M	55	4d Sedan-5P	23,275	3,325	—
SABLE GS (V-6)					
M	58	4d Wagon-5P	21,665	3,544	—
SABLE GS PLUS (V-6)					
M	58	4d Wagon-5P	22,555	3,544	—
SABLE GS FLEET (V-6)					
M	58	4d Wagon-5P	21,945	3,544	—
SABLE GS PLUS FLEET (V-6)					
M	58	4d Wagon-5P	22,835	3,325	—

SABLE LS PREMIUM (V-6)
M 59 4d Wagon-5P 23,845 3,473 —

SABLE LS PLATINUM EDITION (V-6)
M 59 4d Wagon-5P 24,440 3,473 —

GRAND MARQUIS – V-8 – The 2002 Mercury Grand Marquis projected a classic and enduring design. Its distinctive appearance featured a bright, vertical-rail chrome grille and jeweled headlamps with integrated parking lamps and cornering lamps. The Grand Marquis was huge. It offered 109.3 cu. ft. of passenger volume, with seating for six adults in the Grand Marquis GS, GS Convenience, LS Premium and LS Ultimate. The five-passenger Grand Marquis LSE featured leather-trimmed front bucket seats. Also in the LSE, the standard column shift was replaced with a leather-wrapped floor shifter mounted in a custom center console. The center console included a large storage bin, a padded armrest, a concealed 12-volt power point, dual cupholders and a center stack mini-storage bin with cigar lighter. The trunk of the Mercury Grand Marquis was the largest in its class, with 20.6 cu. ft of space. The trunk's low liftover height of 26.6 in. made loading and unloading easier. A remote trunk lid opener on the driver's door panel allowed convenient cargo access. A trunk organizer was available in all models. An eight-way power driver's seat with power-adjustable lumbar support was standard on all Grand Marquis models. The Grand Marquis LS Premium, LSE and LS Ultimate also featured a standard eight-way power passenger's seat. New for 2002, leather seating surfaces were a no-charge option on the LS Premium, LSE and LS Ultimate. Also new in all models was a small storage pouch sewn into the front seat driver's seat cushion. All Grand Marquis models, except the GS model, had standard power adjustable accelerator and brake pedals that allowed drivers to establish their optimum steering wheel-to-pedal relationship. A 4.6-liter SOHC V-8 engine powered the Mercury Grand Marquis GS, GS Convenience, LS Premium and LS Ultimate models. It produced 220 hp and 265 ft.-lbs. of torque at 4,000 rpm. All 2002 Mercury Grand Marquis models were equipped with antilock brakes and traction control as standard equipment. All models were also equipped with dual fold-away, power-adjustable and heated side-view mirrors. Redundant audio/climate controls on the steering wheel became standard on the Grand Marquis LS Ultimate and LSE. The 2002 Grand Marquis LS Premium, Ultimate and LSE now offered no-charge leather seating surfaces. Leather-trimmed seats were made available on the Grand Marquis GS Convenience. Other interior changes included a front seat pouch sewn into the driver's seat. A trunk cargo organizer became optional on all Grand Marquis models this year. Three new colors were offered, Matador Red Clearcoat Metallic, Aspen Green Clearcoat Metallic and Light Ice Blue Clearcoat Metallic.

GRAND MARQUIS GS: Standard equipment included a 4.6-liter SOHC V-8, a four-speed automatic transmission, rear-wheel drive, a front independent suspension, a front stabilizer bar, a clock, 16-in. steel wheel rims, P225/60SR16 all-season tires, a space saver spare tire, a steel spare wheel, full wheel covers, intermittent windshield wipers, a rear window defogger, ventilated front disc/rear drum antilock brakes, all-speed traction control, front seat belt pre-tensioners, rear door child safety locks, child seat belt anchors, a front center lap belt, a rear center lap belt, an engine immobilizer, dusk-sensing headlights, auto-delay off headlights, cornering lights, power door locks, one touch power windows, heated power outside rearview mirrors, cruise control, speed-proportional power steering, a tilt-adjustable steering wheel with cruise controls on center hub, front cupholders, an inside-the-trunk remote deck lid release, front seatback storage, a cargo net, six-passenger seating with a split-bench front seat (driver/passenger eight-way power and adjustable lumbar support), a rear bench seat with folding center armrest, cloth upholstery, rear seat heating ducts, air conditioning, front reading lights, a passenger visor-vanity mirror, simulated wood trim on the dashboard and door panels, front floor mats, rear floor mats, a luggage compartment light, an AM/FM cassette stereo with four speaker sound system and an element radio antenna.

GRAND MARQUIS GS CONVENIENCE: Standard equipment included a 4.6-liter SOHC V-8, a four-speed automatic transmission, rear-wheel drive, a front independent suspension, a front stabilizer bar, a clock, 16-in. steel wheel rims, P225/60SR16 all-season tires, a space saver spare tire, a steel spare wheel, full wheel covers, intermittent windshield wipers, a rear window defogger, ventilated front disc/rear drum antilock brakes, all-speed traction control, front seat belt pre-tensioners, rear door child safety locks, child seat belt anchors, a front center lap belt, a rear center lap belt, an engine immobilizer, dusk-sensing headlights, auto-delay off headlights, cornering lights, remote power door locks, one touch power windows, heated power outside rearview mirrors, cruise control, speed-proportional power steering, a tilt-adjustable steering wheel with cruise controls on center hub, height adjustable pedals, front cupholders, an inside-the-trunk remote deck lid release, front seatback storage, a cargo net, a 12-volt power point, six-passenger seating with a split-bench front seat (driver/passenger eight-way power and adjustable lumbar support), a rear bench seat with folding center armrest, cloth upholstery, rear seat heating ducts, air conditioning, front reading lights, a passenger visor-vanity mirror, simulated wood trim on the dashboard and door panels, front floor mats, rear floor mats, a luggage compartment light, an AM/FM cassette stereo with four speaker sound system and an element radio antenna.

GRAND MARQUIS LS PREMIUM: Standard equipment included a 4.6-liter SOHC V-8, a four-speed automatic transmission, rear-wheel drive, a front independent suspension, a front stabilizer bar, a clock, a compass, 16-in. alloy wheel rims, P225/60SR16 all-season tires, a space saver spare tire, a steel spare wheel, intermittent windshield wipers, a rear window defogger, ventilated front disc/rear drum antilock brakes, all-speed traction control, front seat belt pre-tensioners, rear door child safety locks, child seat belt anchors, a front center lap belt, a rear center lap belt, an engine immobilizer, dusk-sensing headlights, auto-delay off headlights, cornering lights, remote power door locks, one touch power windows, heated power outside rearview mirrors, cruise control, speed-proportional power steering, a leather-wrapped tilt-adjustable steering wheel with cruise controls on center hub, height adjustable pedals, front and rear cupholders, an inside-the-trunk remote deck lid release, front seatback storage, a cargo net, a 12-volt power point, a universal remote for garage door opening and security system operation, six-passenger seating with a split-bench front seat (driver/passenger eight-way power and adjustable lumbar support), a rear bench seat with folding center armrest, cloth upholstery, rear seat heating ducts, a climate control system, an automatically-dimming inside rearview mirror, front and rear reading lights, dual illuminating visor-vanity mirrors, simulated wood trim on the dashboard and door panels, front floor mats, rear floor mats, a luggage compartment light, an AM/FM cassette stereo with four speaker sound system and an element radio antenna.

GRAND MARQUIS LS ULTIMATE: Standard equipment included a 4.6-liter SOHC V-8, a four-speed automatic transmission, rear-wheel drive, a front independent suspension, a front stabilizer bar, a self-leveling rear suspension, a clock, a compass, 16-in. alloy wheel rims, P225/60SR16 all-season tires, a space saver spare tire, a steel spare wheel, intermittent windshield wipers, a rear window defogger, ventilated front disc/rear drum antilock brakes, all-speed traction control, front seat belt pre-tensioners, rear door child safety locks, child seat belt anchors, a front center lap belt, a rear center lap belt, an engine immobilizer, dusk-sensing headlights, auto-delay off headlights, cornering lights, remote power door locks, one touch power windows, heated power outside rearview mirrors, cruise control, speed-proportional power steering, a leather-and-wood tilt-adjustable steering wheel with cruise/audio controls on center hub, height adjustable pedals, front and rear cupholders, an inside-the-trunk remote deck lid release, front seatback storage, a cargo net, a 12-volt power point, a universal remote for garage door opening and security system operation, six-passenger seating with a split-bench front seat (driver/passenger eight-way power and adjustable lumbar support), a rear bench seat with folding center armrest, cloth upholstery, rear seat heating ducts, a climate control system, an automatically-dimming inside rearview mirror, front and rear reading lights, dual illuminating visor-vanity mirrors, simulated wood trim on the dashboard and door panels, front floor mats, rear floor mats, a luggage compartment light, an AM/FM cassette stereo with four speaker sound system and an element radio antenna.

GRAND MARQUIS LSE: Standard equipment included a 4.6-liter SOHC V-8 with a dual exhaust system, a four-speed automatic transmission, rear-wheel drive, a front independent suspension, a front stabilizer bar, a rear stabilizer bar, a clock, a compass, 16-in. alloy wheel rims, P225/60TR16 all-season tires, a space saver spare tire, a steel spare wheel, intermittent windshield wipers, a rear window defogger, ventilated front disc/rear drum antilock brakes, all-speed traction control, front seat belt pre-tensioners, rear door child safety locks, child seat belt anchors, a rear center lap belt, an engine immobilizer, dusk-sensing headlights, auto-delay off headlights, cornering lights, remote power door locks, one touch power windows, heated power outside rearview mirrors, cruise control, speed-proportional power steering, a leather-wrapped tilt-adjustable steering wheel with cruise/audio controls on center hub, height adjustable pedals, front and rear cupholders, an inside-the-trunk remote deck lid release, front seatback storage, a cargo net, a 12-volt power point, a universal remote for garage door opening and security system operation, five-passenger seating with bucket front seats (driver/passenger eight-way power and adjustable lumbar support), a rear bench seat with folding center armrest, cloth upholstery, rear seat heating ducts, a climate control system, an automatically-dimming inside rearview mirror, front and rear reading lights, dual illuminating visor-vanity mirrors, simulated wood trim on the dashboard and door panels, front floor mats, rear floor mats, a luggage compartment light, an AM/FM cassette stereo with four speaker sound system and an element radio antenna.

Model No.	Body/Style No.	Body Type & Seating	Factory Price	Shipping Weight	Prod. Total
GRAND MARQUIS GS (V-8)					
M	74	4d Sedan-6P	24,325	3,958	—
GRAND MARQUIS GS CONVENIENCE (V-8)					
M	74	4d Sedan-6P	24,745	3,958	—
GRAND MARQUIS LS PREMIUM (V-8)					
M	75	4d Sedan-6P	27,800	3,973	—
GRAND MARQUIS LSE (V-8)					
M	75	4d Sedan-5P	29,305	3,973	—

GRAND MARQUIS LS ULTIMATE (V-8)

M	75	4d Sedan-6P	28,980	3,973	—

COUGAR ENGINES

ENGINE [BASE FOUR]: Inline. Double overhead cam. Four-cylinder. Cast-iron block and aluminum head. Displacement: 121 cid (2.0 liters). Bore & stroke: 3.34 x 3.46 in. Compression ratio: 9.6:1. Brake horsepower: 125 at 5500 rpm. Torque: 130 lbs.-ft. at 4000 rpm. Sequential fuel injection. VIN code 3.

ENGINE [BASE V-6]: Modular, double overhead cam V-6. Aluminum block and head. Displacement: 155 cid (2.5 liters). Bore & stroke: 3.24 x 3.13 in. Compression ratio: 9.7:1. Brake horsepower: 170 at 6250 rpm. Torque: 165 lbs.-ft. at 4250 rpm. Sequential fuel injection. VIN code L.

SABLE ENGINES

ENGINE [BASE GS/LS]: Overhead valve V-6. Cast-iron block and head. Displacement: 182 cid (3.0 liters). Bore & stroke: 3.50 x 3.15 in. Compression ratio: 9.7:1. Brake horsepower: 155 at 4900 rpm. Torque: 185 lbs.-ft. at 3900 rpm. Sequential fuel injection. VIN code U.

ENGINE [OPTIONAL LS]: Double overhead cam V-6. Aluminum block and head. Displacement: 182 cid (3.0 liters). Bore & stroke: 3.50 x 3.15 in. Compression ratio: 10.0:1. Brake horsepower: 200 at 5650 rpm. Torque: 200 lbs.-ft. at 4400 rpm. Sequential fuel injection. VIN code S.

GRAND MARQUIS ENGINE

ENGINE [BASE]: Modular, overhead valve V-8. Displacement: 281 cid (4.6 liters). Bore & stroke: 3.60 x 3.60. Compression ratio: 9.4:1. Brake horsepower: 200 at 4250 rpm. Torque: 265 lbs.-ft. at 3000 rpm. Sequential fuel injection. Single exhausts. VIN code W.

ENGINE [LSE]: Modular, overhead valve V-8. Displacement: 281 cid (4.6 liters). Bore & stroke: 3.60 x 3.60. Compression ratio: 9.4:1. Brake horsepower: 235 at 4750 rpm. Torque: 275 lbs.-ft. at 4000 rpm. Sequential fuel injection. Dual exhausts. VIN code W.

COUGAR CHASSIS: Wheelbase (all) 106.4 in.; Overall length: (all) 185 in. Overall width: (all) 69.6 in.; Overall height: (all) 52.2 in. Front tread: (all) 59.3 in. Rear tread: (all) 58.7 in.

SABLE CHASSIS: Wheelbase: (all) 108.5 in. Overall length: (sedan) 199.8 in.; (wagon) 197.8 in. Overall width: (all) 73 in. Overall height: (sedan) 55.5 in.; (wagon) 57.8 in. Front tread: 61.6 in. Rear tread: 62.1 in.

GRAND MARQUIS CHASSIS: Wheelbase: (all) 114.7 in. Overall Length: (all) 211.9 in. Overall width: (all) 78.2 in. Overall height: (all) 56.8 in. Front Tread: (all) 63.4 in. Rear Tread: (all) 65.3 in.

COUGAR TECHNICAL: Standard transmission: five-speed manual transaxle. Drive axle: front. Steering: Power assisted rack-and-pinion. Front suspension: Independent, MacPherson struts, coil springs, lower A-arms. Rear suspension: independent Quadra-link design, coil springs and stabilizer bar. Brakes: Power front disc/rear drum; ABS optional. Body construction: unibody. Fuel tank: 14.5 gallons.

SABLE TECHNICAL: Standard transmission: Four-speed overdrive automatic. Drive axle: front. Steering: Power rack-and-pinion with engine-sensitive power assist. Front suspension: independent MacPherson strut front drive with strut-mounted coil springs, stabilizer bar, tension strut, lower control arm and cast aluminum knuckle with integral ball joint. Rear suspension: (sedan) independent MacPherson strut with strut-mounted coil springs, tension strut, parallel control arms, stabilizer bar and two-piece cast spindle with forged stem; (wagon) Independent short/long arm with variable-rate coil spring on lower control arms, upper control bars, stabilizer bar, shock absorbers and tension strut. Front brakes: (All) Power front disc, optional ABS. Rear brakes: (sedan) power rear drum; (wagon) power disc, optional ABS. Body construction: unibody. Fuel tank: 18 gallons.

GRAND MARQUIS TECHNICAL: Standard transmission: four-speed overdrive automatic. Drive axle: rear. Steering: re-circulating ball and nut, speed-sensitive, power-assisted. Front suspension: independent short/long arm with ball joints, coil springs and stabilizer bar. Rear suspension: Four-bar link with coil on axle and Watt's linkage. Brakes: Four-wheel power disc with dual-action front calipers and ABS. Body construction: separate body and frame. Fuel tank: 19 gallons.

COUGAR FOUR: [COUGAR FOUR] 58K AM/FM radio with CD player and cassette deck ($74). 422 California emissions requirements (no cost). 13E power tilt and sliding sunroof ($568). 13K rear spoiler ($217). [COUGAR V-6] 44T four-speed automatic transmission with overdrive ($920). 552 four-wheel antilock brakes ($462). 422 California emissions requirements (no cost). 586 in-dash six-disc CD player ($120). 13E power tilt and sliding sunroof ($568). 13K rear spoiler ($217). [COUGAR SPORT V-6] 90C C2 feature vehicle package ($476). 90X XR feature vehicle package ($878). 44T four-speed automatic transmission with overdrive ($920). 552 four-wheel antilock brakes ($462). 422 California emissions requirements (no cost). 586 in-dash six-disc CD player ($120). 13E power tilt and sliding sunroof ($568). [COUGAR SPORT PREMIUM V-6] 90C C2 feature vehicle package ($476). 90X XR feature vehicle

package ($878). 646 16-in. machined-look aluminum wheels ($231). 44T four-speed automatic transmission with overdrive ($920). 552 four-wheel antilock brakes ($462). 422 California emissions requirements (no cost). 586 in-dash six-disc CD player ($120). 8 leather sport bucket seats ($827). 553 traction control ($217). [COUGAR SPORT ULTIMATE] 90C C2 feature vehicle package ($245). 90X XR feature vehicle package ($877). 44T four-speed automatic transmission with overdrive ($920). 422 California emissions requirements (no cost). 8 leather sport bucket seats (no charge).

SABLE OPTIONS: [GS SEDAN] 186 bucket seats ($96). 64N seven-spoke alloy wheels ($364). 552 antilock braking system (included in package). 422 California emissions (no cost). 423 California emissions not required (no cost). 428 high-altitude emissions (no cost). 85R Secure package ($521). [GS PLUS SEDAN] 186 bucket seats ($96). 64N seven-spoke alloy wheels ($364). 552 antilock braking system (included in package). 422 California emissions (no cost). 423 California emissions not required (no cost). 428 high-altitude emissions (no cost). 93N non-California emissions (no cost). 85R Secure package ($521). [LS PREMIUM SEDAN] 186 bucket seats (no cost). 184 six-passenger leather seating with flip-fold center console (no cost). 21J six-way power passenger seat ($323). 552 antilock braking system (included in package). 422 California emissions (no cost). 423 California emissions not required (no cost). 64W Chrometec wheels ($272). 428 high-altitude emissions (no cost). 916 Mach audio group ($617). 93N non-California emissions (no cost). B3B power moonroof (no cost). 13B power moonroof ($819). 85R Secure package ($521). [GS SEDAN] 64N seven-spoke alloy wheels ($364). 552 antilock braking system (included in package). 422 California emissions (no cost). 423 California emissions not required (no cost). 428 high-altitude emissions (no cost). 93N non-California emissions (no cost). 85R Secure package ($521). [GS PLUS WAGON] 64N seven-spoke alloy wheels ($364). 552 antilock braking system (included in package). 422 California emissions (no cost). 423 California emissions not required (no cost). 93N non-California emissions (no cost). 85R Secure package ($521). [LS PREMIUM WAGON] 186 bucket seats (no cost). 184 six-passenger leather seating with flip-fold center console (no cost). 21J six-way power passenger seat ($323). 552 antilock braking system (included in package). 422 California emissions (no cost). 423 California emissions not required (no cost). 64W Chrometec wheels ($272). 428 high-altitude emissions (no cost). 916 Mach audio group ($617). 93N non-California emissions (no cost). 13B power moonroof ($819). 85R Secure package ($521).

GRAND MARQUIS OPTIONS: [GS] 972 body side paint stripe ($57). 422 California emissions requirements (no cost). 508 conventional spare tire ($113). 153 front license plate bracket (no cost). 585 single-disc CD player ($131). 13C trunk organizer ($187). [GS CONVENIENCE] 422 California emissions requirements (no cost). 508 conventional spare tire ($113). 153 front license plate bracket (no cost). J Twin Comfort split bench seat with leather seating surfaces ($933). Regional vehicle discount ($19 credit). 585 single-disc CD player ($131). 13C trunk organizer ($187). [LS PREMIUM] 422 California emissions requirements (no cost). 508 conventional spare tire ($113). 153 front license plate bracket (no cost). 64P 16-in. lacy-spoke alloy wheels ($346). J Twin Comfort split bench seat with leather seating surfaces (no cost). 586 premium electronic six-disc CD changer ($328). 13C trunk organizer ($187). [LS ULTIMATE] 422 California emissions requirements (no cost). 508 conventional spare tire ($113). 153 front license plate bracket (no cost). J Twin Comfort split bench seat with leather seating surfaces (no cost). Regional vehicle discount ($1,409 credit). 919 trunk-mounted six-disc CD changer ($328). 13C trunk organizer ($187). [LSE] 422 California emissions requirements (no cost). 508 conventional spare tire ($113). 153 front license plate bracket (no cost). Regional vehicle discount ($1,414 credit). 919 trunk-mounted six-disc CD changer ($328). 13C trunk organizer ($187).

HISTORICAL FOOTNOTES: On Feb. 8, 2001 Ford of Canada's St. Thomas Assembly Plant, located near London, Ont., was selected to build the Mercury Marauder — a high performance sedan scheduled to go on sale in the U.S. during the summer of 2002. On Feb. 14, the National Highway and Traffic Safety Administration (NHTSA) gave Mercury a Valentine's Day present by awarding the 2001 Mercury Sable, Mercury Grand Marquis and Mercury Villager the federal government's highest safety rating for frontal crashes. All of the models got double five-star ratings for both driver and passenger. As part of its ongoing commitment to cycling, Mercury signed on as the Official Vehicle and Exclusive Automotive Sponsor of the 2001 and 2002 Pro Cycling Tour, the nation's premier cycling series. The Tour includes 14 of the top professional road cycling events across the United States from March through October. In July, more than 230 energetic Mercury Cougar owners from all over the country tuned up their vehicles for a trip to the third annual Cougar Fest in Flat Rock and Dearborn, Mich. The two-day event was a unique way for Mercury to interact with its customers face-to-face in a casual and fun setting while Cougar owners got a chance to show off their own vehicles. On Nov. 9, 2001 Ford dedicated a new North American Headquarters for its Premier Automotive Group in Southern California. The new facility housed Lincoln Mercury headquarters. That same day, Lincoln-Mercury Div. announced that the American Red Cross of Greater Chicago would receive a $100,000 grant from Chicago Region Lincoln Mercury dealers.

1941 Mercury Convertible. (OCW)

1957 Mercury Montclair 76B 2dr. Convertible. (OCW)

MUSTANG
1964-2002

1964-1/2 Ford Mustang 2+2 two-door fastback. (FMC)

What a coup! To produce an extremely popular car, with virtually no competition. That is exactly what Ford did when it began marketing the Mustang in April 1964. After the record-breaking success of the compact Falcon, Ford saw the need for a small sporty car in the lower price range—a working man's Thunderbird, perhaps. So, with relatively little effort, a new car was concocted using the Falcon's chassis and many of its components. This *Mustang* was introduced in mid-1964. The best time to introduce a new car is in the spring. Interest in new cars peaks then. Unlike the fall, there is not a profusion of new models.

The 1964-1/2 Mustang—officially considered an early 1965 model—came in a spunky-looking little hardtop coupe and convertible. Its wheelbase was 108 in., overall length was 181.6 in. and its weight was just under 2,500 lbs. The base price was $2,368 for the hardtop.

The closest competition already on the market was the Corvair Monza Spyder priced at $2,599. The Mustang's standard power plant was a 170 cid 101-hp six. Admittedly, that was anemic compared to the Spyder's 150 hp, but for just a few bucks extra, a 289 cid 195-hp V-8 was optional in the Mustang. That was where Ford had the drop on Chevrolet. Virtually any Ford-built engine (except the FE series blocks that had shock clearance problems) could be slipped under the early Mustang hood. The Corvair had no such possibilities, because of its flat-six engine and its rear engine configuration.

The Mustang was an instant hit. So great was its popularity, that the Dearborn factory (shared by Falcon) was not sufficient to meet the demand for new Mustangs. In July, additional production started at Ford's San Jose, Calif., plant. Soon after that, the Falcon assembly line at Metuchen, N.J., was switched over to Mustang production as well. History books are filled with instances where cars were extremely popular on introduction, but lack of finances and/or production capacity cooled public interest. When the problems were eventually overcome, the buyers were gone. The Mustang is the most outstanding exception to that sad fate.

By the end of 1964, the Mustang had scored 263,434 sales. Despite its late start, the Mustang was outsold in the calendar year only by the Impala, the Galaxie 500, the Bel Air and the Chevelle. Its sales even surpassed those of the Falcon, from which it was derived.

When the other Ford lines were altered for 1965, practically no changes were made to the Mustang. The standard six-cylinder engine became the larger 200 cid 120-hp engine. Almost 27 percent of 1964-1/2 Mustangs had the six, which grew to over 35 percent popularity in the 1965 models. The rest, of course, were V-8s. The standard V-8 was the 200-hp edition of the 289 cid V-8. Engine options included 225-hp and 271-hp versions of the same engine.

A fastback model—originally called the 2+2—was added to the hardtop and convertible choices. The 2+2 was not a hardtop in the sense of having pillarless styling, because it had no rear side windows. In the area where such windows are normally expected there was a set of louvers that were used as the outlet for the flow-through ventilation.

Mustangs could be loaded with all the popular power accessories. Automatic or four-speed stick shift transmissions were on the option list, as well as power brakes, power steering and air conditioning.

1965 Ford Mustang two-door hardtop. (FMC)

1965 Ford Mustang 2+2 two-door fastback. (FMC)

1965 Ford Mustang GT two-door convertible. (FMC)

On April 17, 1965, the Mustang celebrated its first birthday. It took the cake by setting a new world record of over 418,000 sales in its first year on the market for a new model. It exceeded the previous record set by the Falcon by about 1,000 units. It is good to remember that both these achievements came from the same company that, just a few years earlier, misjudged the market with the Edsel. During calendar year 1965, the Mustang racked up a total of 518,252 registrations. It was second only to the Chevrolet Impala and almost equaled all models of Dodge combined.

Again in 1966, little change was made to the new Mustang. A revised instrument panel, less like the Falcon's, was used. The grille was still the same shape, but used horizontal bars. The bright accents were about the same, except for a strip on Mustangs with the $152 GT option. That accessory package (it was not a model) included clear lens fog lights mounted in the outer ends of the grille. The GT also featured racing stripes along the body sills. Only the 225-hp or 271-hp engines were available with the GT package. Faster steering, stiffer suspension and front disc brakes were mechanical features standard on the GT. Despite a general industry trend towards more V-8s, Ford heavily promoted sales of six-cylinder Mustangs in 1966. Thus, only 58 percent of the "pony cars" were V-8 powered. That was the lowest percentage in marque history. Production of the 1966 Mustang reached an all-time peak of 607,568. By model year's end, there had been a total of 1,288,556 Mustangs made.

For 1967, competition in the so-called pony car market was noticeably stiffer. The Mustang had caught other companies unprepared. Only the Plymouth Barracuda (which had been introduced almost simultaneously with the Mustang) could be considered, more or less, in the same class as Mustang. The Dodge Charger, though of the same sports/personal character,

1967 Ford Mustang two-door convertible. (FMC)

was bigger and heavier and could not be classed as a pony car. Mercury introduced its version of the pony car—the Cougar—for 1967. Chevrolet made no attempt to respond to the Mustang with the Corvair Monza Spyder, choosing instead to develop an entirely new car for 1967. It was the Camaro. The Firebird was Pontiac's version of the Camaro, brought out in mid-1967.

An all-new body was used on the 1967 Mustang. It was said that the original dies were worn-out after making nearly 1.3 million copies, but competition, no doubt, was a major factor in the redesign. Styling, however, stayed almost the same. That was a wise move, because a big change in appearance could have hurt the Mustang's obvious appeal when there were other ponies to pick from. The same three body types remained and the same engine choices were also offered, along with a big 390 cid 320-hp version of the Thunderbird V-8. The GT option was obtainable with any V-8-powered Mustang, which meant some 70 percent of all 1967 editions. Nearly 16 percent of the Mustangs that year had factory air conditioning.

Production of the 1967 models dropped over 22 percent to 472,121 units. This was due to a smaller total Ford production that year . . . and increased competition. However, the Mustang accounted for 6.2 percent of all 1967 cars built in the United States. Mustang production amounted to slightly more than twice American Motors' total production that year. In the pony car market, Mustang corralled 42.5 percent.

Only subtle appearance changes were made to the 1968 Mustang. The GT option included a choice of stripes. A choice of rocker panel stripes or a reflecting "C" stripe was offered. The latter widened along the front fender ridge, crossed the door to the rear quarter panel, then swept around the depression ahead of the rear wheel and tapered along the bottom of the door. Some new engine options were offered in 1968. The six and standard V-8 remained, but dropped down to 115 and 195 hp, respectively. Optional V-8s included a 302 cid V-8 rated at 230 hp and a 390 cid V-8 developing 280 or 325 hp. The legendary 427 cid 390-hp V-8 was offered for just a short while, then replaced with a 428 cid 335-hp V-8. Seven power plant possibilities were offered in total.

Mustang production fell again in 1968, dropping to 317,404 units. Mustangs accounted for only 3.8 percent of the industry total. The Mustang had slipped from second place in production for 1965 to seventh rank for 1967. However, it still remained leader of the pony car pack.

1969 Ford Mustang two-door Sportsroof fastback. (FMC)

The body on 1969 Mustangs was altogether different than the 1968 design and reflected a major restyling of the five-year-old line. It kept the overall Mustang image. Dual headlights were used, with the outer pair in the fenders. The inboard high-beam headlights were located in the grille ends. Two new models were added. The Grande was a dressed-up edition of the hard-top. A vinyl roof and plush interior were two of its standard features. It was priced $231 above a normal hardtop with comparable equipment. The Mach I was a variation of the fast-back, which was now called the Sportsroof. Beginning with the 1969 models, the Mustang fastbacks were true hardtops. The rear quarter louvers of the original 2+2 model were gone and there was more glass area, by way of a small window that abutted the door window. The Mach I was identifiable by special paint stripes along the sides and across the integral rear spoiler. Only the five optional V-8s were obtainable in the Mach I. They were the 250-hp and 290-hp versions of the 351 cid V-8; the 390 cid 320-hp V-8 and the 428 cid 335-hp Cobra-Jet Ram Air engine with cold air induction. The 428CJ option was quite evident, even in a parked Mustang. Its air intake protruded through a large hole in the so-called "shaker" hood.

At the tame end of the engine options, it should be noted that Ford's 250 cid 155-hp six-cylinder engine was available for the first time in the Mustang. The standard six, optional six and standard 302 cid 220-hp V-8 could not be had in the Mach I. V-8 power was installed in 81.5 percent of the 1969 Mustangs. Automatic transmission installations were running just over 71 percent, but the four-speed stick shift options (a choice of a wide- or close-ratio) were found in nearly 11 percent—a record high for Mustang. Power disc brakes were featured on 28 percent and power steering on nearly 66 percent of the 1969 Mustangs, with both options showing increased acceptance. Nevertheless, total production was down.

The most potent power plant for the 1970 Mustang was the 429 cid 375-hp V-8. Imagine 375 horses to pull a 3,000-lb. car! Mustang was extending itself from the fancy little runabout to an all-out performance machine. Oh yes, the sedate sixes were still available, but the Mustang also stressed "GO!" The hot Boss 302 listed for $3,720, which was only $999 more than the base two-door hatchback hardtop.

A 1971 Mustang restyling featured a more European look. The cars were now longer, wider and heavier and seemed more like a mid-sized car than a pony car. The body was slightly lower

1970 Ford Mustang two-door convertible. (FMC)

1972 Ford Mustang Sprint two-door hardtop coupe. (FMC)

1973 Ford Mustang Mach 1 two-door Sportsroof fastback. (FMC)

because of a flatter roof shape. Six models were available again, but the Boss 302 was renamed Boss 351 because it now had a 351 cid 330-hp engine. Further emphasis on performance was evident by the omission of the 200 cid six. The standard engine became the 250 cid 145-hp six and the base V-8 was the 302 cid 210-hp version. Optional were 240-hp, 285-hp and 330-hp versions of the 351 cid V-8 and the 429 Cobra Jet/429 Super Cobra Jet V-8s, the latter pair rated at 370 hp and 375 hp, respectively.

For 1973, the convertible, which had been in the Mustang line since the start, was to become noteworthy as the final (for a while) convertible to bear the Ford name. There were 16,302 Mustang ragtops built that model year. Total 1973 Mustang production was up nearly eight percent to 134,867.

During the Mustang's first 10 model years (not lumping 1964 with 1965) nearly three million cars were built in an interesting variety, from adequate coupes to road-scorching racers. For collectors interested in Ford or specialty-type cars, the early Mustangs are still around and awaiting a good home. They can be had with virtually any degree of engine potency, in hardtop, convertible or fastback models, with just about any contemporary power accessory. (At the last, over 56 percent of them had factory air conditioning, nearly 78 percent had power disc brakes and almost 93 percent had power steering.) Luxury at an affordable price helped make the Mustang so phenomenally popular with the new car buyer. That will probably also hold true for the collector, now, and for some time to come.

Disappointment was doubtless a common reaction among pony car fans when the Mustang II replaced the former edition for 1974. Ford's claim that it was the "right car at the right time" may well have been accurate, especially in view of the gas crisis. Yet it was far removed from the original concept of a decade past and farther yet from the scorching performance versions that greeted the early 1970s. Still, the new and smaller Mustang sold a lot better than its ample predecessor. Sales fell after the opening year, but remained well above the levels of 1971-1973.

As 1976 rolled around, Mustang came with a four, a German-made V-6 or a small-block (302 cid) V-8. The two-door hardtop had a restrained look, while the 2+2 hatchback showed more sporty lines. The Ghia coupe was the luxury edition, while the Mach 1 sounded a lot more exciting than it really was. A silver Stallion appearance group added few thrills and even the new blackout-trimmed Cobra II package was stronger on bold looks than performance.

1976 Ford Mustang Cobra II 2 + 2 two-door fastback. (FMC)

The Cobra II became more colorful by 1977 and a T-top roof became available. However, the sporty Mustang was not much changed otherwise. For its next and final season, the Mustang II added the V-8 powered King Cobra model with giant snake on the hood. Though ranking with collectible Mustangs, the King added little to Mustang's performance capability.

Customers eagerly awaited the next Mustang, which took on a far different form—a design that was destined for long life. Notchback (two-door) and hatchback (three-door) bodies were offered again, but the new aero wedge shape could hardly be compared with Mustang II. By year's end, five different engines had been installed under the hoods of the new Mustang: a base in-line four-cylinder job, a carryover V-6, a replacement in-line six, a 302 cid V-8 and a new turbocharged four. Both the turbo and the V-8 produced 140 hp. The Cobra option package could have either engine. Sport and TRX packages helped the Mustang's handling. To tempt contemporary customers and later collectors, about 6,000 Indy Pace Car replicas were produced. Sales zoomed upward for the model year, but slipped back close to pre-1979 levels later.

The Cobra for 1980 adopted some styling touches from the Indy Pace Car. They included a slat-style grille, fog lamps and a hood scoop. While the power of the turbo four went up, the 302 cid V-8 temporarily disappeared and was replaced by a 255 cid V-8. A new carriage roof was designed to resemble a convertible top, but the real thing would arrive a couple of years later. Not much changed for 1981 except for the availability of a new five-speed gearbox. But a year later the Boss 302 V-8 was back stronger than before (while the turbo took a breather for one season). Mustang's revised model lineup now included a GT, instead of the old Cobra option, but sales declined for the third year in a row.

The long-awaited convertible Mustang arrived for 1983, along with restyled front and rear ends. Ford replaced the V-8's two-barrel carburetor with a four-barrel that boosted horsepower up to 175. At the other end, the base four's carburetor switched from two barrels to one. When the turbo emerged again, it had new multi-port fuel injection. Borg-Warner's close-ratio five-speed transmission could help Mustang GTs hit 60 mph in the seven-second neighborhood.

1980 Ford Mustang "Carriage Roof" two-door coupe. (FMC)

1982 Ford Mustang 5.0L two-door coupe. (FMC)

1984 Ford Mustang SVO two-door coupe. (FMC)

1984-1/2 Ford Mustang GT-350 20th Anniversary two-door convertible. (FMC)

Several years earlier, Ford had formed a Special Vehicle Operations Department to oversee racing and limited-edition production. The first regular-production fruit of their labor appeared for 1984: the Mustang SVO. It featured an air-to-air intercooler on its turbocharged four-cylinder engine. The SVO's five-speed transmission had a Hurst shift linkage, its wheels held big 16-in. tires and it stopped with disc brakes on all wheels. A non-intercooled turbo went into GT models. Sales edged upward again in 1984 and further yet in the next two years.

All Mustangs for 1985 sported a single-slot grille similar to the SVO. Roller tappets and a performance camshaft gave the GT's carbureted 302 cid V-8 a 210-hp rating, 30 more than the fuel-injected V-8. Sequential fuel injection went into V-8s for 1986, adding 20 hp, but the four-barrel version faded away. SVO turbos now managed to produce 200 hp and were ready for the Hurst-shifted five-speed gear box.

Expensive when new, the SVO is surely a Mustang that's worth hanging onto. Far more exotic would be the McLaren Mustang, but only 250 were produced in 1981. A mid-1980s GT wouldn't be a bad choice either, with so many more available. Quite a few of the 1979 Pace Car replicas went on sale, too, and might be worth a look. The King Cobras of 1978 have attracted some interest, as have some of the "ordinary" Cobra versions. Of course, some people considering just about every Mustang to be worth owning, if not exactly collectible.

By 1984, the Mustang was again emphasizing high performance in the GT model, which came in both convertible and hatchback styles. When Ford threatened to discontinue the traditional Mustang in favor of the Mazda-based Probe, a flood of letters from high-performance V-8 fans urged Ford to produce both cars.

The Mustang entered 1987 as a rear-drive hatchback model. All 1987 Mustangs were made at the Dearborn assembly plant between Sept. 30, 1986 and Oct. 13, 1987. The factory operated two shifts and built an average of 45.9 Mustangs per hour or a total of 163,392 for the model year. Gone this season was the SVO (Special Vehicle Operations) version of the Mustang. The horsepower generated by the GT's 5.0-liter engine rose to 225. The new GT also featured an aero ground-effects package, fog lamps and a unique taillight treatment on both convertibles and hatchbacks. LX Mustangs came in sedan, convertible and hatchback styles stressing luxury. New for the year were a redesigned instrument panel, pod-mounted headlamp switches and a console. The standard transmission was now a five-speed manual gear box and a four-speed automatic was also introduced.

Industry analysts had expected the Mustang's popularity to wane when the Mazda-made Probe bowed in mid-1988, but they predicted wrong. Instead, Mustang sales leaped to 170,601, more than 40,000 cars above the goal set in the fall. Workers on two shifts at Dearborn built 46 Mustangs per hour between July 31, 1987 and Aug. 3, 1988. There was little change in the cars, except for higher sticker prices. The least expensive Mustang listed for $9,209 versus $8,645 the previous year. Ford executives must have been happy with a 4.4 percent sales increase in spite of $600 higher prices. In fact, they even made plans to modernize the factory and keep the Mustang alive through the 1990s.

The 25th anniversary of the Mustang was highlighted in 1989, when a new LX 5.0-liter series was introduced. Model year sales increased to 172,218 units and the pony car's market share held steady at 2.3 percent. Production of Mustangs built to 1989 specifications began Aug. 31, 1988, and ended Sept. 5, 1989. An average of 46 units per hour was maintained at the factory in Dearborn. This pushed the nameplate's all-time sales total over six million cars since April 1, 1964, when it bowed at the New York World's Fair.

Mustang collectors whispered of a 1984 Silver Anniversary edition GT with a 351 cid V-8, twin turbos and 400 hp being sourced from race car builder Jack Roush, but with sales galloping, Ford insisted that the first 1964-1/2 model was originally planned as a 1965 Mustang, meaning that the 25th anniversary would come in 1990. It's likely that Ford management saw some sense in waiting a year, as a limited-edition car could be a good sales motivator in a slacker market.

When the 1990 models appeared, there was little change obvious in the Mustang lineup. Sedans, hatchbacks and ragtops again came in the LX and LX 5.0-liter series, with hatchbacks and convertibles available as GTs. A 2.3-liter four remained the LX engine with the 220-hp 5.0-liter H.O. V-8 reserved for LX 5.0-liter and GT versions. A limited-edition metallic emerald green convertible with a white interior was announced for release in the spring. The rumored 351-powered 25-year edition was deemed too costly to produce, according to knowledgeable sources.

Mustang stayed the course through 1991 and 1992, but during that latter year, Ford's engineering Special Vehicle Team (SVT) was designing the Cobra—a high-performance version of the Mustang GT set to debut in 1993. Advanced publicity called for 5,000 Cobras to be produced annually, guaranteeing them instant collector car status.

The Mustang received an entirely new design—its first major overhaul since 1979—for its 30th anniversary in 1994. The LX series was dropped, as was the four-cylinder power plant and the hatchback body style. Mustangs were now available as either a coupe or convertible in base, GT and Cobra trim levels and included convertibles that were assembled in-house at the Ford factory. The limited-edition (5,000 produced) Cobra was powered by a "tweaked" 230-hp version of the 5.0-liter V-8 and featured 17-in. wheels, a rear spoiler and ground-effects trim. The base engine for the new-design Mustang was a 3.8-liter V-6, while Mustang GT models continued to be powered by the 215-hp 5.0-liter V-8.

A GTS coupe joined the Mustang lineup in 1995, but was dropped after one year of availability. In 1996, a 4.6-liter V-8 replaced the 5.0-liter version in both the GT and Cobra series. The Mustang GT used the 215-hp version, while the Cobra received the more potent 305-hp power plant. The five-speed manual transmission standard in Mustangs—called the T-45—was also new. The Cobra was available with an experimental

(one-year only) Mystic Clearcoat Metallic finish that changed hues depending upon the angle from which the car was viewed. A Cobra SVT convertible bowed in February 1996 and it, too, was a limited-edition (2,500 produced) model powered by the 305-hp 4.6-liter V-8.

A coupe version of the Cobra SVT joined the convertible for 1997. Base price for the hardtop was $25,860, while the ragtop started at $28,660. Production was limited to 10,000 units with the breakdown being 7,475 coupes and 2,525 convertibles. Color choices for Mustang Cobra SVTs were the new Pacific Green Clearcoat Metallic, Rio Red Tinted Clearcoat, Crystal White Clearcoat and Black Clearcoat. All Mustangs in 1997 used an encoded ignition key containing a radio transponder as part of a Passive Anti-Theft System (PATS) that was standard equipment. With the discontinuation of both the Probe and Thunderbird in 1998, the Mustang was Ford's standard-bearer of its traditional sporty set.

All 1999 Mustangs wore beautiful 35th Anniversary wreath design emblems on their front fenders and got a "body builder" remake with strong creases, straighter feature lines and the tallest-ever hood scoop. The headlights took on a more sinister appearance and the taillights received a harder, harsher look. Thanks to a higher-lift cam, a coil-on-plug ignition system, bigger valves and a new intake manifold, V-8s had a big power increase since 1987. Despite these improvements, sales dropped to 133,637. Model year production hit 126,067 units. A pair of 415-hp FR500 prototype Mustangs was built by the Ford Racing Technology Group. They could do 0-60 mph in 4.5 sec.

For 2000, new Sunburst Gold, Performance Red and Amazon Gold finish was about the extent of change to the Mustang. In the spring, the third in a series of Cobra R models bowed. Mustang production climbed more than 70 percent from 1999. Ford had plans to market a 2000 SVT Cobra coupe and convertible with a single overhead cam (SOHC) V-8, but due to heavy recalls on 1999 Cobras with the 4.6-liter DOHC V-8, the SVT Cobra was not produced. Instead, a Cobra R with a bigger DOHC V-8 based on a 5.4-liter Ford truck engine arrived. The Bullitt Mustang GT concept car made waves at the 2000 Los Angeles Auto Show. It paid homage to the 1968 Mustang GT featured in the 1968 Steve McQueen movie. It featured special front and rear styling, a new hood, front and rear lamps, five-spoke 18-in. aluminum wheels, unique gauges, racing-inspired seats and Pursuit Green paint.

The 2001 Mustang incorporated classic Mustang design elements. All models had new blacked out headlights and spoilers. A new "value leader" V-6 was offered. A version of the 2000 Bullitt show car appeared in showrooms and 5,532 copies were built. Ford's SVT dealer network also announced a SVT Premium Service plan to give Cobra buyers a "special" ownership experience. It provided a 2001 loaner vehicle while their Cobra was in the shop.

For 2002, Ford refreshed the base V-6 Mustang inside and out and added new audio options. A new tape stripe was included in the V-6 Sport Appearance group. Sixteen-inch wheels and tires were made standard on base and deluxe V-6 coupes. A new speed-sensitive radio was now part of the Mach 1000 and Mach 460 audio systems. Also new was a four-piece two-tone leather steering wheel, a new storage net in coupes and optional Nudo leather-trimmed seats.

*(Contributors to the Mustang section of this catalog include R. Perry Zavitz and John R. Smith, who originally compiled the technical data and tables for the 1964-1975 Mustang section of the **Standard Catalog of American Cars 1946-1975**, James M. Flammang who originally compiled all of the 1976-1986 data for the **Standard Catalog of American Cars 1976-1986**, John A. Gunnell who edited the original **Standard Catalog of American Cars** series, Ron Kowalke who edited the second edition of the **Standard Catalog of Ford 1903-1998** and Brad Bowling who recently edited the **Standard Catalog of Mustangs 1964-2000**).*

1964-1/2 MUSTANG

1964-1/2 Ford Mustang GT convertible. (OCW)

1964-1/2 Ford Mustang. (OCW)

1964-1/2 MUSTANG — (6-CYL) — The biggest news for 1964 was not the restyled Galaxie, Fairlane, Falcon or Thunderbird, but, rather, the later introduction of a small, sporty Ford Mustang, which caught the rest of the automotive industry totally off guard as well as catching the hearts of the American car buying public. The Mustang was the midyear model that set records, which have yet to be broken. It combined sporty looks, economy and brisk performance in a package that had a base price of $2,368. Mustangs could be equipped to be anything from absolute economy cars to luxury sports cars. The Mustang, with its extended hood, shortened rear deck, sculptured body panels and sporty bucket seats provided a family-size sedan for grocery-getting mothers; an appearance for those people who yearned for another two-seat Thunderbird and plenty of power and handling options for the performance Ford enthusiast. So successful was the Mustang that a whole assortment of similar cars, by competing manufacturers, came to be known as 'pony cars' or, in other words, cars in the original Mustang image. Mustangs came powered by everything from the tame 170 cid/101 hp six-cylinder engine to a wild, solid-lifter high-performance 289 cid/271 hp V-8 (and available only with the four-speed manual transmission). The basic standard equipment package found on all 1964-1/2 Mustangs included three-speed manual transmission with floor lever controls; front bucket seats; padded instrument panel; full wheel covers; cloth and vinyl (hardtop) or all-vinyl upholstery; color-keyed carpeting; Sports steering wheel; cigarette lighter; door courtesy lights; glovebox light; and heater and defroster. The original base powerplants were the 170 cid six or the 260 cid V-8. In the fall of 1964, the 200 cid six or the 289 cid V-8 became the standard powerplants in the six- and eight-cylinder Mustang lines, respectively.

1964-1/2 Ford Mustang two-door convertible, V-8. (IMS)

MUSTANG I.D. NUMBERS: Vehicle Identification Numbers and other important encoded information is found on the Ford Motor Co. data plate, located on the rear edge of the left front door. The data plate contains an upper row of codes that reveal body and trim information plus (at center level) a Vehicle Warranty Number that reveals other important data. In the upper row, the first three symbols are a body code with '65A' designating hardtop coupe and '76A' designating convertible. The fourth symbol is the paint code, as follows: 'A' = Raven Black; 'B' = Pagoda Green; 'D' = Dynasty Green; 'F' = Guardsman Blue; 'J' = Rangoon Red; 'K' = Silversmoke Gray, 'M' = Wimbeldon White; 'P' = Prairie Bronze; 'S' = Cascade Green, 'V' = Sunlight Yellow; 'X' = Vintage Burgundy; 'Y' = Skylight Blue; 'Z' = Chantilly Beige and '3' = Poppy Red. The next pair of symbols are the trim code. Many different interior trims, too numerous to catalog here, were available. The next group of symbols consisted of two numbers and a letter, which represent the assembly date code. The numbers give the day (i.e.: '01' = first day) and the letter designates month of year, following normal progression (i.e.: 'A' = January; 'B' = February, etc.), except that the letter 'I' is skipped. The next group of symbols is the DSO (district sales office) code, which is relatively unimportant to collectors. This is followed by a number or letter designating the axle ratio code. A number indicates conventional axle and a letter indicates EquaLock. The codes are as follows: '1' or 'A' = 3.00:1; '3' or 'C' = 3.20:1; '4' or 'D' = 3.25:1; '5' or 'E' = 3.50:1; '6' or 'F' = 2.80:1; '7' or 'G' = 3.80:1; '8' or 'H' = 3.89:1 and '9' or '1' = 4.11:1. The final code on the top row of symbols is a transmission code, as follows: 'I' = three-speed manual, '5' = four-speed manual and '6' = C-4 Dual-Range automatic. The first symbol in the Vehicle Warranty Number is a '5' designating 1965 model year (all 1964-1/2 Mustangs were considered 1965 models). The second symbol is a letter designating the assembly point, as follows: Atlanta (A); Dallas (D); Mahwah (E); Dearborn (F); Chicago (G); Lorain (H); Los Angeles (J); Kansas City (K); Michigan Truck (L); Norfolk (N); Twin Cities (P); San Jose (R); Pilot Plant (S); Metuchen (T); Louisville (U); Wayne (W); Wixom (Y) and St. Louis (Z). The next two symbols are the body serial number and agree with the numbers listed in the second column of the specifications charts below (i.e. '07' = two-door hardtop). The fifth symbol is an engine code, which is listed with the engine specifications below. The next group of symbols is the consecutive unit number, beginning with 100001 and up at each factory.

MUSTANG SERIES

Model No.	Body/ Style No.	Body Type & Seating	Factory Price	Shipping Weight	Prod. Total
N/A	07	2-dr HT Cpe-4P	2368	2449	97,705
N/A	08	2-dr Conv-4P	2614	2615	28,833

NOTE 1: Total series output was 126,538 units. In rounded off figures, 32,900 were sixes and 93,600 were V-8s.

ENGINE [Inline Six]: Overhead valve. Cast-iron block. Displacement: 170 cid. Bore and stroke: 3.50 x 2.94 inches. Compression ratio: 8.7:1. Brake hp: 101 at 4400 rpm. Seven main bearings. Hydraulic valve lifters. Carburetor: Ford (Autolite) one-barrel Model C30F-9510-G. Serial number code 'U.'

ENGINE [V-8]: Overhead valve. Cast-iron block. Displacement: 260 cid. Bore and stroke: 3.80 x 2.87 inches. Compression ratio: 8.8:1. Brake hp: 164 at 4400 rpm. Five main bearings. Hydraulic valve lifters. Carburetor: Ford (Autolite) two-barrel Model C40F-9510E. Serial number code 'F.'

ENGINE [Challenger V-8]: Overhead valve. Cast-iron block. Displacement: 289 cid. Bore and stroke: 4.00 x 2.87 inches. Compression ratio: 9.0:1. Brake hp: 210 at 4400 rpm. Five main bearings. Hydraulic valve lifters. Carburetor: Ford (Autolite) four-barrel Model C4AF-9510-B. Serial number code 'D.'

ENGINE [Challenger High-Performance V-8]: Overhead valve. Cast-iron block. Displacement: 289 cid. Bore and stroke: 4.00 x 2.87 inches. Compression ratio: 10.5:1. Brake hp: 271 at 6000 rpm. Five main bearings. Solid valve lifters. Carburetor: Ford (Autolite) four-barrel Model C4OF-9510-AL. Serial number code 'K.'

CHASSIS FEATURES: Wheelbase: 108 inches. Overall length: 181.6 inches. Tires: (with V-8) 7.00 x 13 four-ply tubeless; (with high-performance '289' V-8) 7.00 x 14 four-ply tubeless blackwall; (other models) 6.50 x 13 four-ply tubeless blackwall.

OPTIONS: Accent Group ($27.70). Ford air conditioner ($283.20). Heavy-duty battery ($7.60). Front disc brakes ($58). Full-length center console ($51.50). Console with air conditioning ($32.20). Equa-Lock limited slip differential ($42.50). California-type closed emissions system ($5.30). Challenger V-8 ($108). Challenger four-barrel V-8 engine ($162). Challenger high-performance four-barrel V-8 ($442.60). Early year only, 260 cid V-8 ($75). Emergency flashers ($19.60). Tinted glass with banded windshield ($30.90). Banded, tinted windshield only ($21.55). Back-up lights ($10.70). Rocker panel moldings ($16.10). Power brakes ($43.20). Power steering ($86.30). Power convertible top ($54.10). Push-button radio with antenna

($58.50). Rally-Pac instrumentation with clock and tachometer ($70.80). Deluxe retractable front seat safety belts ($7.55). Special Handling Package ($31.30). Padded sun visors ($5.70). Cruise-O-Matic transmission, with six ($179.80); with 200-hp and 225-hp V-8s ($189.60). Four-speed manual transmission with six ($115.90); with V-8 ($75.80). Hardtop vinyl roof ($75.80). Visibility Group including remote-control mirror; day/nite mirror; two-speed electric wipers and windshield washers ($36). Wheel covers with simulated knock-off hubs ($18.20). Wire wheel covers, 14 inch ($45.80). Styled steel wheels, 14 inch ($122.30). NOTE: The MagicAire heater ($32.20 credit) and front seat belts ($11 credit) were 'delete options.' Size 6.50 x 13 whitewalls with six ($33.90). Size 6.95 x 14 tires, blackwall with six ($7.40); whitewall with six ($41.30); whitewall with V-8s, except high-performance type ($33.90); black nylon, except with high-performance V-8 ($15.80); Red Band nylon with V-8s except high-performance V-8 ($49.60); Black nylon or white sidewall nylon with high-performance V-8 (no charge).

HISTORY: Mustang was introduced April 17, 1964. Model year production peaked at 121,538 units. Lee Iacocca headed an eight-man committee that conceived the idea for the new car. Stylists Joe Oros, Gail Halderman and David Ash designed the car. So cleanly styled was the new Mustang that it was awarded the Tiffany Award for Excellence in American Design, the first and only automobile ever to be so honored by Tiffany & Co. Not only did the design purists like the new Mustang, so did the public. More than 100,000 were sold in the first four months of production, followed by 500,000 more in the next 12 months. More than 1,000,000 found buyers in less than 24 months. This set an automotive industry sales record that has yet to be equalled or eclipsed. A 1964-1/2 Mustang convertible was also selected as the Indianapolis 500 pace car. Out of all the Mustangs built in the 1964 model run, some 49.2 percent featured an automatic transmission; 19.3 percent four-speed manual transmission; 73.1 percent V-8 engines; 26.9 percent six-cylinder engines; 77.8 percent radio; 99:1 percent heater; 30.9 percent power steering; 7.7 percent power brakes; 88.2 percent whitewalls; 48.3 percent windshield washers; 22.4 percent tinted windshields only and 8.0 percent all tinted glass; 44.6 percent back-up lights and 6.4 percent air conditioning.

1965 Ford Mustang GT. (OCW)

1965 Ford Mustang two-door hardtop coupe, V-8. (OCW)

1965 MUSTANG — (6-CYL/V-8) — One brand-new model and a number of minor revisions were seen in the 1965 Mustang lineup. A 2+2 fastback body joined the hardtop and convertible, creating an expanded

'stable' of three pony cars. Perhaps the most significant change for 1965 was the use of an alternator in the place of the previously used generator. Engine choices remained the same as in late 1964, with one exception. The old workhorse I-block, 170 cid engine was replaced by the 200 cid version as base six-cylinder powerplant. A number of small changes and some new options were seen on the 1965 models. While interior door handles on the earliest Mustangs were secured by 'C' type clips, Allen screw attachments were a running production change adopted for later cars. Also, the spacing between the letters in the lower bodyside nameplates was modified, giving them a five-inch measurement or about one-quarter-inch longer than before. The push-down door lock buttons were chrome plated, in contrast to the 1964-1/2 type, which were colored to match the interior. Front disc brakes were one new option. So was the GT Package, racing stripes as a standard, but deleteable, feature. The standard equipment list for 1965 was much the same as before, including heater and defroster; dual sun visors; Sports-type front bumpers; full wheel covers; vinyl upholstery; seat belts; padded instrument panel; automatic courtesy lights; cigarette lighter; front and rear carpets; foam-padded front bucket seats; self-adjusting brakes; Sports steering wheel; five 6.50 x 13 four-ply tubeless black sidewall tires; and the 200 cid/120 hp six. The '289' V-8 and 6.95 x 14 size tires were standard in the Mustang V-8 series.

MUSTANG I.D. NUMBERS: The numbering system and code locations were the same as on previous models. Several additions and deletions in exterior colors were seen. New codes and colors included: Code 'C' = Honey Gold; Code 'I' = Champagne Beige; Code 'O' = Tropical Turquoise and Code 'R' = Ivy Green. Colors deleted were Guardsman Blue (Code 'H'); Cascade Green (Code 'S') and Chantilly Beige (Code 'Z'). The 1965 date codes were changed in regards to the letter used to designate a specific month. Code 'N' designated January. Code 'O' was not used and the remaining months ran in normal alphabetical progression from Code 'P' (for February) through Code 'Z' (for December). The body serial number code for the new two-door fastback was '09.' The 1965 engine serial number codes are indicated in the engine date charts below. All other codes were the same as those used on 1964-1/2 models, except for interior trim codes, which are not included in this catalog.

MUSTANG SERIES

Model No.	Body/ Style No.	Body Type & Seating	Factory Price	Shipping Weight	Prod. Total
N/A	65A (07)	2-dr HT Cpe-4P	2372	2465	409,260
N/A	63A (09)	2-dr FsBk Cpe-4P	2589	2515	77,079
N/A	76A (08)	2-dr Conv-4P	2614	2650	73,112

NOTE 1: Total model year output was 559,451 units. This figure includes 5,776 Luxury fastbacks; 22,232 Luxury hardtops; 14,905 bench seat-equipped hardtops; 5,338 Luxury convertibles and 2,111 convertibles equipped with bench seats.

NOTE 2: In figures rounded off to the nearest 100 units, the total included 198,900 sixes and 360,600 V-8s.

1965 Ford Mustang two-door convertible, V-8. (OCW)

1965 MUSTANG

1965 Ford Mustang 2+2 two-door fastback coupe, V-8. (PH)

ENGINE [Inline Six]: Overhead valve. Cast-iron block. Displacement: 200 cid. Bore and stroke: 3.68 x 3.13 inches. Compression ratio: 9.2:1. Brake hp: 120 at 4400 rpm. Seven main bearings. Hydraulic valve lifters. Carburetor: Ford (Autolite) two-barrel Model C5OF-9510-E. Serial number code 'T.'

ENGINE [Challenger V-8]: Overhead valve. Cast-iron block. Displacement: 289 cid. Bore and stroke: 4.00 x 2.87 inches. Compression ratio: 9.3:1. Brake hp: 200 at 4400 rpm. Five main bearings. Hydraulic valve lifters. Carburetor: Ford (Autolite) two-barrel Model C5ZF-9510-A. Serial number code 'C.'

ENGINE [Challenger Four-Barrel V-8]: Overhead valve. Cast-iron block. Displacement: 289 cid. Bore and stroke: 4.00 x 2.87 inches. Compression ratio: 10.0:1. Brake hp: 225 at 4800 rpm. Five main bearings. Hydraulic valve lifters. Carburetor: Ford (Autolite) four-barrel Model C5ZF-9510-C. Serial number code 'A.'

ENGINE [Challenger High-Performance V-8]: Overhead valve. Cast-iron block. Displacement: 289 cid. Bore and stroke: 4.00 x 2.87 inches. Compression ratio: 10.5:1. Brake hp: 271 at 6000 rpm. Five main bearings. Solid valve lifters. Carburetor: Ford (Autolite) four-barrel Model C4OF-9510-AL. Serial number code 'K.'

CHASSIS FEATURES: Wheelbase: 108 inches. Overall length: 181.6 inches. Tires: (V-8) 7.00 x 13 four-ply tubeless blackwalls; (high-performance '289' V-8) 7.00 x 14 four-ply tubeless blackwall; (other models) 6.50 x 13 four-ply tubeless blackwall.

OPTIONS: Accent Group, on hardtop and convertible ($27.70); on fastback coupe ($14.20). Ford air conditioner ($283.20). Heavy-duty battery ($7.60). Front disc brakes with V-8 and manual brakes only ($58). Full-length center console ($51.50). Console for use with air conditioner ($32.20). Equa-Lock limited-slip differential ($42.50). California-type closed emissions system ($5.30). Challenger 200-hp V-8 ($108). Challenger four-barrel 225-hp V-8 ($162). Challenger 271-hp high-performance V-8 including Special Handling Package and 6.95 x 14 nylon tires ($442.60). Emergency flashers ($19.60). Tinted glass with banded windshield ($30.90). Tinted-banded windshield glass ($21.55). Back-up lights ($10.70). Rocker panel moldings, except fastback coupe ($16.10). Power brakes ($43.20). Power steering ($86.30). Power convertible top ($54.10). Push-button radio with antenna ($58.50). Rally-Pac instrumentation with clock and tachometer ($70.80). Deluxe retractable front seat safety belts ($7.55). Special Handling package, with 200-hp or 225-hp V-8s ($31.30). Padded sun visors ($5.70). Cruise-O-Matic transmission, with six ($179.80); with 200-hp and 225-hp V-8s ($189.60). Four-speed manual transmission, with six ($115.90); with V-8 ($188). Vinyl roof, on two-door hardtop only ($75.80). Visibility Group, includes remote-control outside rearview mirror; day/nite inside rearview mirror, two-speed electric wipers and windshield washers ($36). Wheel covers with knock-off hubs ($18.20). Fourteen-inch wire wheel covers ($45.80). Fourteen-inch styled steel wheels ($122.30).

NOTE: Delete options and tire options same as 1964-1/2 models.

HISTORY: The 1965 Mustang was officially introduced on Oct. 1, 1964. Model year production peaked at 559,451 cars. Of these, 53.6 percent were equipped with automatic transmission; 14.5 percent with four-speed manual transmissions; 64.4 percent with V-8 engines, 35.6 percent with sixes; 78.9 percent with radio; 98.9 percent with heaters; 24.9 percent with power steering; 4.3 percent with power brakes; 97 percent with bucket seats; 100 percent with front seat safety belts; 83.6 percent with white sidewall tires; 47.3 percent with windshield washers; 24.8 percent with tinted windshields; 9 percent with all-tinted glass; 38.6 percent with back-up lights; 9.1 percent with air conditioning; 3.9 percent with dual exhaust and two percent with limited-slip differential. A total of 1.3 percent of all 1965 Mustangs or 6,996 cars, were sold with the 271-hp V-8 (Code 'K') and all of these units had four-speed manual transmission. An interesting historical point is that Mustangs made in

Germany were called Ford T-5 models, since the right to the Mustang name in that country belonged to another manufacturer.

1966 MUSTANG

1966 Ford Mustang convertible. (OCW)

1966 Ford Mustang convertible. (OCW)

1966 Shelby GT 350 coupe. (OCW)

1966 Ford Mustang two-door hardtop coupe, V-8. (PH)

1966 Ford Mustang two-door convertible, V-8. (OCW)

1966 MUSTANG — (6-CYL/V-8) — The 1966 Mustang continued to sell like 'hot cakes,' in spite of only minor restyling in the trim department. The grille featured a floating Mustang emblem in the center, with no horizontal or vertical dividing bars. Brand new trim, on the rear fender, featured three chrome steps leading into the simulated scoop. This was the first year of federally mandated safety standards and all 1966 Fords included front and rear seat belts; padded instrument panel; emergency flashers; electric wipers; and windshield washers as standard equipment. In addition, the list of regular Mustang features was comprised of the following: front bucket seats; pleated vinyl upholstery and interior trim; Sports-type steering wheel; five dial instrument cluster; full carpeting; heater and defroster; left-hand door outside rearview mirror; back-up lamps; door courtesy lights; rocker panel moldings; full wheel covers; three-speed manual transmission with floor lever control; and 200 cid/120 hp six-cylinder engine. The fastback coupe also came with special Silent-Flo ventilation and the base V-8 engine was the 200-hp version of the '289.'

MUSTANG I.D. NUMBERS: The numbering system and code location was the same as on previous models, although the size and color of the data plate itself was changed. The plate was narrower and the warranty number (formerly on the lower row) was now at the top left-hand corner of the plate. The data on the upper row of codes (body code, color code, trim code, etc.) was moved to a narrow, unfinished band that crossed the data plate, horizontally, nearly at its center. Another change was that, previously, data plates finished in black had indicated cars painted in conventional enamel, while gray finish indicated cars done in acrylic enamel. This color-coding system was reversed for 1966. Reading along the top row of codes, the first symbol became a '6' to indicate 1966 model year. The next symbol was a letter designating the assembly plant (with the same codes as previously used). The next two symbols were the Body Serial Code ('07' = hardtop coupe; '09' = fastback coupe; '08' = convertible). The fifth symbol was a letter designating the type of engine, as indicated in the engine data listings below. The next six symbols in the upper row of codes were the consecutive unit number. The first three symbols in the lower row of codes represented the Body/Style Number, as indicated in the second column of the charts below. The fourth symbol was a letter indicating the exterior color, as follows: Code 'A' Raven Black, Code 'F' Light Blue, Code 'H' Light Beige, Code 'K' Dark Blue Metallic, Code 'M' Wimbledon White, Code 'P' Medium Palomino Metallic, Code 'R' Dark Green Metallic, Code 'T' Sandy Apple Red, Code 'U' Medium Turquoise Metallic, Code 'V' Emberglo Metallic, Code 'X' Maroon Metallic, Code 'Y' Light Blue Metallic, Code 'Z' Medium Sage Metallic, Code '4' Medium Silver Metallic, Code '5' Signal Flare Red and Code '8' Springtime Yellow. The fifth and sixth symbols were the interior trim code (not cataloged here). The next three symbols were the assembly date code, following the system used in 1964 (i.e.: 21A = 21st day of January). The 10th and 11th symbols were numbers designating the District Sales Office code. The next symbol was a number designating the type of axle and the last (13th) symbol on the lower row was the transmission code. Axle codes and transmission codes are the same as those listed in the 1964 Mustang I.D. Number section.

MUSTANG SERIES

Model No.	Body/Style No.	Body Type & Seating	Factory Price	Shipping Weight	Prod. Total
N/A	65A (07)	2-dr HT Cpe-4P	2416	2488	499,751
N/A	63A (09)	2-dr FsBk Cpe-4P	2607	2519	35,698
N/A	76A (08)	2-dr Conv-4P	2653	2650	72,119

NOTE 1: Total series output was 607,568 units. This figure included 7,889 Luxury fastbacks; 55,938 Luxury hardtops; 21,397 hardtops equipped with bench seats; 12,520 Luxury convertibles and 3,190 convertibles equipped with bench seats.

NOTE 2: In figures rounded off to the nearest 100 units, the total included 253,200 sixes and 354,400 V-8s.

1966 Ford Mustang GT two-door fastback coupe, V-8. (OCW)

ENGINE [Inline Six]: Overhead valve. Cast-iron block. Displacement: 200 cid. Bore and stroke: 3.68 x 3.12 inches. Compression ratio: 9.2:1. Brake hp: 120 at 4400 rpm. Seven main bearings. Hydraulic valve lifters. Carburetor: Ford (Autolite) one-barrel Model C6OF-9510-AD. Serial number code 'T.'

ENGINE [Challenger V-8]: Overhead valve. Cast-iron block. Displacement: 289 cid. Bore and stroke: 4.00 x 2.87 inches. Compression: 9.3:1. Brake hp: 200 at 4400 rpm. Five main bearings. Hydraulic valve lifters. Carburetor: Ford (Autolite) two-barrel Model C6DF-9510-A. Serial number code 'C.'

ENGINE [Challenger Four-Barrel V-8]: Overhead valve. Cast-iron block. Displacement: 289 cid. Bore and stroke: 4.00 x 2.87 inches. Compression: 10.1:1. Brake hp: 225 at 4800 rpm. Five main bearings. Hydraulic valve lifters. Carburetor: Ford (Autolite) four-barrel Model C6ZF-9510-A. Serial number code 'A.'

ENGINE [Challenger High-Performance V-8]: Overhead valve. Cast-iron block. Displacement: 289 cid. Bore and stroke: 4.00 x 2.875 inches. Compression ratio: 10.5:1. Brake hp: 271 at 6000 rpm. Five main bearings. Solid valve lifters. Carburetor: Ford (Autolite) four-barrel Model C6OF-9510-C. Serial number code 'K.'

CHASSIS FEATURES: Wheelbase: 108 inches. Overall length: 181.6 inches. Tires: 6.95 x 14 four-ply tubeless blackwall; (high-performance V-8) 7.00 x 14 four-ply tubeless blackwall.

OPTIONS: Challenger 289 cid V-8 ($105.63). Challenger four-barrel 289 cid/225 hp V-8 ($158.48). High-performance 289 cid/271 hp V-8, in standard Mustang ($433.55); in Mustang GT ($381.97). NOTE: The total cost of the high-performance engine was $327.92 on regular Mustangs and $276.34 on Mustang GTs, plus the cost of the base V-8 attachment over the six (which was $105.63). Cruise-O-Matic automatic transmission with six ($175.80); with standard V-8s ($185.39); with high-performance V-8 ($216.27). Four-speed manual floor shift transmission, with six ($113.45); with all V-8s ($184.02). Power brakes ($42.29). Power steering ($84.47). Power convertible top ($52.95). Heavy-duty 55-amp battery ($7.44). Manual disc brakes, with V-8 only ($56.77). GT Equipment group, with high-performance V-8 only, includes: dual exhaust; fog lamps; special ornamentation; disc brakes; GT racing stripes (rocker panel moldings deleted); and Handling Package components ($152.20). Limited-slip differential ($41.60). Rally-Pack instrumentation, includes clock and tachometer ($69.52). Special Handling Package, with 200-hp and 225-hp V-8 engines, includes increased rate front and rear springs, larger front and rear shocks; 22:1 overall steering ratio and large diameter stabilizer bar ($30.84). Fourteen-inch styled steel wheels, on V-8 models only ($93.84). Two-speed electric windshield wipers ($12.95). Tinted-banded windshield only ($21.09). All glass tinted with banded windshield ($30.25). Deluxe, retractable front seat safety belts and warning lamp ($14.53). Visibility Group, includes remote-control outside rearview mirror; day/nite inside mirror and two-speed electric wipers ($29.81). Ford air conditioner ($310.90). Stereo tape player, AM radio mandatory ($128.49). Full-width front seat with armrest for Styles 65A and 76A only ($24.42). Rear deck luggage rack, except fastback ($32.44). Radio and antenna ($57.51). Accent striping, less rear quarter ornamentation ($13.90). Full-length center console ($50.41). Console for use with air conditioning ($31.52). Deluxe steering wheel with simulated woodgrain rim ($31.52). Interior Decor Group, includes special interior trim; Deluxe woodgrain steering wheel; rear window door courtesy lights and pistol grip door handles ($94.13). Vinyl top, on hardtop ($74.36). Simulated wire wheel covers ($58.24). Wheel covers with simulated knock-off hubs ($19.48). Closed crankcase emissions system, except with high-performance V-8 ($519). Exhaust emissions control system, except with high-performance V-8 ($45.45). Tire options, exchange prices listed indicate cost above base equipment: 6.95 x 14 four-ply rated whitewall ($33.31); nylon blackwall ($15.67); nylon whitewall ($48.89); nylon with dual red band design, on cars with high-performance V-8 (no charge); all other

($48.97). No charge for substitution of nylon blackwalls or whitewalls on cars with high-performance V-8. MagicAire heater could be deleted for $45.45 credit. Air conditioning, three-speed manual transmission, power steering and U.S. Royal tires not available in combination with high-performance V-8. Power brakes and accent striping not available with GT Equipment Group. Full-width front seat not available in cars with Interior Decor Group, or Model 63A or cars with console options.

HISTORY: The 1966 Mustangs were introduced Oct. 1, 1965, the same day as all other Fords. Model year production hit 607,568 Mustangs with the little 'pony' pulling down a significant 7.1 percent share of all American car sales. Of all Mustangs built during the 1966 model run, only 7.1 percent had four-speed transmissions; 62.8 percent automatic transmission; 58.3 percent V-8 engines; 79.3 percent radio; 98.8 percent heater, 28.9 percent power steering; 3.3 percent power brakes; 9.5 percent vinyl tops; 29.1 percent tinted windshields; 7.3 percent all tinted glass; 6.7 percent disc brakes; 5 percent dual exhaust; 2.6 percent limited-slip differential; 17.9 percent a non-glare inside rearview mirror; 85.3 percent whitewalls and 9.5 percent air conditioning. Henny Ford II was Ford Motor Co. board chairman and Arjay Miller was the president. The Ford Division, which was actually responsible for Mustang sales, was headed by M.S. McLaughlin who had the titles of vice-president and general manager. For 1966, Mustang was the third best-selling individual nameplate in the American industry, an outstanding achievement for a car only three model years old.

1967 MUSTANG

1967 Ford Mustang convertible. (OCW)

1967 Ford Mustang GTA 2+2 two-door fastback coupe, V-8. (OCW)

MUSTANG SERIES — (6-CYL/V-8) — For the first time since its mid-1964 introduction the Mustang was significantly changed. The styling was similar to the original in its theme, but everything was larger. The grille featured a larger opening. The feature lines on the side led to a larger simulated scoop. The taillights took the form of three vertical lenses on each side of a concave indentation panel, with a centrally located gas cap. Standard equipment included all Ford Motor Co. safety features plus front bucket seats; full carpeting; floor-mounted shift; vinyl interior trim; heater; wheel covers and cigarette lighter. The fastback came with wheel covers; special emblems; and rocker panel moldings. There were five engine choices ranging from a 200 cid/120 hp six to a 390 cid/320 hp V-8. New options available included SelectShift Cruise-O-Matic.

1967 Ford Mustang two-door hardtop coupe, V-8. (PH)

MUSTANG I.D. NUMBERS: The Vehicle Identification Number is stamped on top upper flange of left front fender apron. First symbol: 7 = 1967. Second symbol indicates assembly plant: F=Dearborn, Mich; R=San Jose, Calif.; T=Metuchen, N.J. Third and fourth symbols equated to Body/Style Number: 63A=bucket seat fastback; 65A=bucket seat hardtop; 76A=bucket seat convertible; 63B=bucket seat luxury fastback; 65B=bucket seat luxury hardtop; 76B=bucket seat luxury convertible; 65C=bench seat hardtop and 76C=bench seat convertible. Fifth symbol indicates engine: T=200 cid/120 hp six; 2=200 cid six export; C=289 cid/200 hp V-8; 3=289 cid V-8 export; A=289 cid/225 hp V-8; K=289 cid/271 hp V-8; S=390 cid/320 hp V-8. The next six symbols are the sequential production number beginning at 100001 for each series at each factory. Body Number Plate located on left front door lock face indicates serial number, Body/Style Number, color, trim, District Code, DSO Number, axle and transmission.

MUSTANG SERIES

Model No.	Body/ Style No.	Body Type & Seating	Factory Price	Shipping Weight	Prod. Total
N/A	07	2-dr HT Cpe-4P	2461	2578	356,271
N/A	09	2-dr FsBk Cpe-4P	2592	2605	71,042
N/A	08	2-dr Conv-4P	2698	2738	44,808

NOTE 1: Total series output was 472,121 units including both sixes and V-8s.

NOTE 2: Series output includes 22,228 Luxury hardtops; 8,190 hardtops with bench seats; 17,391 Luxury fastbacks; 4,848 Luxury convertibles and 1,209 convertibles equipped with bench seats.

NOTE 3: In figures rounded off to the nearest 100, the model year output of 1967 Mustangs included 141,500 sixes and 330,600 V-8s.

ENGINE [Mustang Six-Cylinder]: Overhead valve. Cast-iron block. Displacement: 200 cid. Bore and stroke: 3.68 x 3.13 inches. Compression ratio: 9.2:1. Brake hp: 120 at 4400 rpm. Carburetor: Holley one-barrel. Seven main bearings. Serial number code 'T.'

ENGINE [Challenger 289 V-8]: Overhead valve. Cast-iron block. Displacement: 289 cid. Bore and stroke: 4.00 x 2.87 inches. Compression ratio: 9.3:1. Brake hp: 200 at 4400 rpm. Carburetor: Holley two-barrel. Five main bearings. Serial number code 'C.'

ENGINE [Challenger 289 V-8]: Overhead valve. Cast-iron block. Displacement: 289 cid. Bore and stroke: 4.00 x 2.87 inches. Compression ratio: 9.8:1. Brake hp: 225 at 4800 rpm. Carburetor: Holley four-barrel. Five main bearings. Serial number code 'A.'

1967 Ford Mustang two-door convertible, V-8. (OCW)

ENGINE [High-Performance 289 V-8]: Overhead valve. Cast-iron block. Displacement: 289 cid. Bore and stroke: 4.00 x 2.87 inches. Compression ratio: 10.5:1. Brake hp: 271 at 6000 rpm. Carburetor: Holley four-barrel. Five main bearings. Serial number code 'K.'

ENGINE [Four-Barrel V-8]: Overhead valve. Cast-iron block. Displacement: 390 cid. Bore and stroke: 4.05 x 3.78 inches. Compression ratio: 10.5:1. Brake hp: 320 at 4600 rpm. Carburetor: Holley four-barrel. Five main bearings. Serial number code 'Z.'

CHASSIS FEATURES: Wheelbase: 108 inches. Overall length: 183.6 inches. Tires: 6.95 x 14 four-ply tubeless blackwall.

OPTIONS: 200-hp V-8 ($106). 225-hp V-8 ($158). 271-hp V-8, included with GT Equipment Group ($434). 320-hp V-8 ($264). Cruise-O-Matic three-speed automatic transmission with six-cylinder ($188); with 200-hp and 225-hp V-8s ($198); with 271-hp and 320-hp V-8s ($232). Four-speed manual transmission, with six-cylinder or 225-hp V-8 ($184); with other V-8s ($233). Heavy-duty three-speed manual, required with 390 cid V-8 ($79). Power front disc brakes ($65). Power steering ($84). Power top, convertible ($53). GT Equipment Group, V-8s only ($205). Limited-slip differential ($42). Competition Handling Package, with GT Group only ($62). Styled steel wheels, 2+2 ($94); other models ($115). Tinted windows and windshield ($30). Convenience control panel ($40). Fingertip speed control, V-8 and Cruise-O-Matic required ($71). Remote-control left door mirror, standard 2+2 ($10). Safety-glass rear window, convertible ($32). Select-Aire conditioning ($356). Push-button AM radio ($58). Push-button AM/FM radio ($134). Stereo-Sonic tape system, AM radio required ($128). "Sport Deck" option with folding rear seat and access door for 2+2 ($65). Full-width front seat, not available with 2+2 ($24). Tilt-Away steering wheel ($60). Deck lid luggage rack not available on 2+2 ($32). Comfort-weave vinyl trim, not available on convertible ($25). Center console, radio required ($50). Deluxe steering wheel ($32). Exterior Decor Group ($39). Lower back panel grille ($19). Interior Decor Group for convertible ($95); for other models ($108). Two-tone paint, lower back grille ($13). Accent stripe ($14). Vinyl roof, hardtop ($74). Wheel covers, standard on 2+2 ($21). Wire wheel covers, 2+2 ($58); other models ($80). Typical whitewall tire option ($33). Rocker panel moldings, standard on 2+2 ($16). Magic-Aire heater delete option ($32 credit).

HISTORY: The 1967 Mustang was introduced Sept. 30, 1966. Model year output peaked at 472,121 units. Dealer sales totaled 377,827 units, a 31.2 percent decline due to increased competition in the sports/personal car market, plus a strike in the final business quarter. Henry Ford II was chairman of Ford Motor Co. Mustang's creator, Lee Iacocca, was an executive vice-president in charge of North American Operations and was definitely on his way up the corporate ladder, thanks to the success his 'pony car' had seen. About seven percent of all 1967 Mustangs had four-speed manual transmissions; 98 percent had bucket seats; nearly 15 percent vinyl tops and some 16 percent air conditioning. A rare feature was dual exhaust, found only on about 25,000 cars.

1968 MUSTANG

1968 Ford Mustang GT 2+2. (FMC)

MUSTANG SERIES — (6-CYL/V-8) — The 1968 Mustang continued to use the same body shell introduced the previous year, with minor trim changes. The Mustang emblem appeared to float in the center of the grille, with no horizontal or vertical bars attached to the emblem. Also, the side scoop had much cleaner chrome trim than the previous year, with no horizontal stripes connected to it.

1968 Ford Mustang two-door convertible, V-8. (OCW)

MUSTANG I.D. NUMBERS: The Vehicle Identification Number is stamped on aluminum tab on instrument panel, viewable through windshield. First symbol: 8=1968. Second symbol indicates assembly plant: F=Dearborn, Mich.; R=San Jose, Calif.; T=Metuchen, N.J. Third and fourth symbols equated to Body/Style Number: 63A=bucket seat fastback; 65A=bucket seat hardtop; 76A=bucket seat convertible; 63B=bucket or bench seat luxury fastback; 65B=bucket seat luxury hardtop; 76B=bucket or bench seat luxury convertible; 63C=bench seat fastback; 65C=bench seat hardtop; 65D=bench seat luxury hardtop; and 63D=bench seat luxury fastback. Fifth symbol indicates engine: T=200 cid/115 hp six; 2=200 cid six export; C=289 cid/195 hp V-8; J=302 cid/230 hp V-8; X=390 cid/280 hp V-8; S=390 cid/325 hp V-8; W=427 cid/390 hp V-8; G=302 cid/306 hp V-8; R=428 cid/335 hp Cobra-Jet V-8. The next six symbols are the sequential production number beginning at 100001 for each series at each factory. Body Number Plate located on left front door lock face indicates serial number, Body/Style Number, color, trim, District Code, DSO Number, axle and transmission.

MUSTANG SERIES

Model No.	Body/ Style No.	Body Type & Seating	Factory Price	Shipping Weight	Prod. Total
N/A	65A	2-dr HT Cpe-4P	2602	2635	249,447
N/A	63A	2-dr FsBk Cpe-4P	2712	2659	42,325
N/A	76A	2-dr Conv-4P	2814	2745	25,376

NOTE 1: Total series output was 317,148 units. This figure included 9,009 Deluxe hardtops; 6,113 hardtops equipped with bench seats; 7,661 Deluxe fastbacks; 256 fastbacks equipped with bench seats; 853 Deluxe hardtops equipped with bench seats and 3,339 Deluxe convertibles.

ENGINE [Mustang Six-Cylinder]: Overhead valve. Cast-iron block. Displacement: 200 cid. Bore and stroke: 3.68 x 3.13 inches. Compression ratio: 8.8:1. Brake hp: 115 at 3800 rpm. Carburetor: Autolite Model C8OF-9510-E one-barrel. Seven main bearings. Serial number code 'T.'

ENGINE [Challenger 289 V-8]: Overhead valve. Cast-iron block. Displacement: 289 cid. Bore and stroke: 4.00 x 2.87 inches. Compression ratio: 8.7:1. Brake hp: 195 at 4600 rpm. Carburetor: Autolite Model C8AF-9510-AF two-barrel. Five main bearings. Serial number code 'C.'

ENGINE [302 Four-Barrel V-8]: Overhead valve. Cast-iron block. Displacement: 302 cid. Bore and stroke: 4.00 x 3.00 inches. Compression ratio: 10.0:1. Brake hp: 230 at 4800 rpm. Carburetor: Motorcraft four-barrel. Five main bearings. Serial number code 'J.'

1968 Ford Mustang two-door hardtop coupe, V-8. (OCW)

1968 Ford Mustang GT two-door fastback coupe, V-8. (OCW)

ENGINE [390 V-8]: Overhead valve. Cast-iron block. Displacement: 390 cid. Bore and stroke: 4.05 x 3.78 inches. Compression ratio: 10.5:1. Brake hp: 280 at 4800 rpm. Carburetor: Holley four-barrel. Five main bearings. Serial number code 'X.'

ENGINE [GT 390 V-8]: Overhead valve. Cast-iron block. Displacement: 390 cid. Bore and stroke: 4.05 x 3.78 inches. Compression ratio: 10.5:1. Brake hp: 325 at 4800 rpm. Carburetor: Holley four-barrel. Five main bearings. Serial number code 'S.'

ENGINE [High-Performance V-8]: Overhead valve. Cast-iron block. Displacement: 427 cid. Bore and stroke: 4.23 x 3.78 inches. Compression ratio: 10.9:1. Brake hp: 390 at 4600 rpm. Carburetor: Motorcraft four-barrel. Five main bearings. Serial number code 'W.'

ENGINE [Cobra Jet 428 V-8]: Overhead valve. Cast-iron block. Displacement: 428 cid. Bore and stroke: 4.13 x 3.98 inches. Compression ratio: 10.7:1. Brake hp: 335 at 5600 rpm. Carburetor: Holley four-barrel. Five main bearings. Serial number code 'R.'

CHASSIS FEATURES: Wheelbase: 108 inches. Overall length: 183.6 inches. Tires: 6.95 x 14 four-ply tubeless blackwall (E70-14 four-ply tubeless blackwall, with Wide-Oval Sport tire option).

OPTIONS: 289 cid/195 hp two-barrel V-8 ($106). 302 cid/230 hp four-barrel ($172). 390 cid/325 hp four-barrel V-8 ($158). 427 cid/390 hp four-barrel V-8 ($775). 428 cid/335 hp four-barrel Cobra-Jet V-8 ($245). SelectShift Cruise-O-Matic three-speed automatic with six-cylinder ($19); with '289' V-8 ($201); with '390' V-8 ($233). Four-speed manual, not available with six-cylinder; with '289' V-8 ($184); with '390' V-8 ($233). Power front disc brakes, V-8s only, required with '390' V-8 or GT Equipment Group ($54). Power steering ($84). Power top, convertible ($53). GT Equipment Group, 230-hp or 325-hp V-8s with power brakes not available with Sports Trim Group of optional wheel covers ($147). Tachometer, V-8s only ($54). Limited-slip differential, V-8s only ($79). Glass backlight, convertible ($39). Tinted glass ($30). Convenience Group, console required with Select-Aire ($32). Fingertip speed control, V-8 and SelectShift required ($74). Remote-control left door mirror ($10). Select-Aire conditioner ($360). Push-button AM radio ($360). AM/FM stereo radio ($61). Stereo-Sonic Tape System, AM radio required ($181). Sport deck rear seat, 2+2 only ($65). Full-width front seat, hardtop and 2+2 only, not available with console ($32). Tilt-Away steering wheel ($66). Center console, radio required ($54). Interior Decor Group in convertibles and models with full-width front seat ($110); in others without full-width front seat ($124). Two-tone hood paint ($19). Accent paint stripe ($14). Vinyl roof, hardtop ($74). Wheel covers, not available with GT or V-8 Sports Trim Group ($34). Whitewall tires ($33).

HISTORY: The 1968 Mustangs were introduced in September 1967. Model year production peaked at 317,148 units. The 427-powered Mustang was capable of moving from 0-to-60 mph in around six seconds. The price for this engine was $775 above that of the base

Mustang V-8. The 427 was rare, but 428 V-8s were installed in 2,854 Mustangs built this model year. Side marker lights and other new federally mandated safety features were required on all Mustangs built this year. Ford went through a 60-day strike from late September to late November 1967. This had a negative effect on sales and production. A collectible model-option produced this year was the highly sought after "California Special," a variant of the coupe with special features such as Shelby-type taillights. There was also the "High-Country Special," a similar regional edition model, produced for the Colorado Sales Zone.

1969 MUSTANG

1969 Ford Mustang Mach 1. (OCW)

1969 Shelby GT-500 convertible. (OCW)

1969 Ford Mustang two-door hardtop coupe, 6-cyl. (OCW)

MUSTANG SERIES — (6-CYL/V-8) — The Mustang was different for 1969. It was enlarged considerably and significantly restyled for the new year. For the first time, Mustangs had quad headlights, the outboard units being mounted in deeply recessed openings at the outer edges of the fenders. The inboard units were mounted inside the grille opening. The side scoop was now located high on the rear fenders of fastback models. It was in the same location as before on the hardtops and convertibles but now faced rearward. High-performance was the theme for Ford in 1969 and the hot new Mustangs were in the spotlight. The sizzling Mach I came with a 351 cid V-8 as standard equipment. The 390 cid V-8 and '428' Cobra Jet V-8 engines were optional. Trans-Am road racing was popular at this time. To compete with the Chevrolet Camaro race cars Ford introduced the famous and powerful Boss 302 Mustang. The top engine option for 1969 Mustangs became the huge Boss 429. Even though these monsters came with a factory horse-power rating of 375, actual output was much higher. They were definitely not machines for the weak-spirited individual.

1969 Ford Mustang two-door convertible, 6-cyl. (OCW)

1969 Ford Mustang two-door Sportsroof coupe, V-8. (OCW)

MUSTANG I.D. NUMBERS: The Vehicle Identification Number is stamped on aluminum tab on instrument panel, viewable through windshield. First symbol: 9=1969. Second symbol indicates assembly plant: F=Dearborn, Mich.; R=San Jose, Calif.; T=Metuchen, N.J. Third and fourth symbols equated to Body/Style Number: 63A=bucket or high-back bucket seat fastback; 65A=bucket seat or high-back bucket seat hardtop; 76A=bucket or high-back bucket seat convertible; 63B=bucket or high-back bucket seat luxury fastback; 65B=bucket seat or high-back bucket seat luxury hardtop; 76B=bucket or high-back bucket seat luxury convertible; 63C=high-back bucket seat Mach I; 65C=bench seat luxury hardtop; 65D=bench seat luxury hardtop; and 65E=bucket seat Grande hardtop. Fifth symbol indicates engine: T=200 cid/119 hp six; 2=200 cid six export; F=302 cid/220 hp V-8; 6=302 cid export V-8; H=351 cid/250 hp V-8; M=351 cid/290 hp V-8; S=390 cid/320 hp V-8; Q=428 cid/335 hp CJ V-8; R=428 cid/335 hp SCJ Ram-Air V-8; G=Boss 302 cid/290 hp V-8; and Z=429 cid/370 hp V-8. The next six symbols are the sequential production number beginning at 100001 for each series at each factory. Body Number Plate located on left front door lock face indicates serial number, Body/Style Number, color, trim, District Code, DSO Number, axle and transmission.

MUSTANG SERIES

Model No.	Body/ Style No.	Body Type & Seating	Factory Price	Shipping Weight	Prod. Total
N/A	65A	2-dr HT Cpe-4P	2618/2723	2690	127,954
N/A	63A	2-dr FsBk Cpe-4P	2618/2723	2713	61,980
N/A	76A	2-dr Conv-4P	2832/2937	2800	14,746
N/A	65E	2-dr Grande HT-4P	2849/2954	2981	22,182
N/A	63C	2-dr Mach I FsBk-4P	3122	3175	72,458

1969 Ford Mustang Grande two-door hardtop coupe, V-8. (OCW)

1969 Ford Mustang Mach 1 two-door Sportsroof coupe, V-8. (PH)

NOTE 1: Total series output was 299,824 units.

NOTE 2: Data above slash for six/below slash for V-8.

NOTE 3: Series output included 5,210 Deluxe hardtops; 4,131 hardtops equipped with bench seats; 5,958 Deluxe fastbacks; 504 Deluxe hardtops equipped with bench seats and 3,439 Deluxe convertibles.

ENGINE [Mustang Six-Cylinder]: Overhead valve. Cast-iron block. Displacement: 200 cid. Bore and stroke: 3.68 x 3.13 inches. Compression ratio: 8.8:1. Brake hp: 115 at 3800 rpm. Carburetor: Motorcraft one-barrel. Seven main bearings. Serial number code 'T.'

ENGINE [302 V-8]: Overhead valve. Cast-iron block. Displacement: 302 cid. Bore and stroke: 4.00 x 3.00 inches. Compression ratio: 9.5:1. Brake hp: 220 at 4600 rpm. Carburetor: Motorcraft two-barrel. Five main bearings. Serial number code 'F.'

ENGINE [302 V-8]: Overhead valve. Cast-iron block. Displacement: 302 cid. Bore and stroke: 4.00 x 3.00 inches. Compression ratio: 10.5:1. Brake hp: 290 at 5000 rpm. Carburetor: Motorcraft four-barrel. Five main bearings. Serial number code 'G.'

ENGINE [351 V-8]: Overhead valve. Cast-iron block. Displacement: 351 cid. Bore and stroke: 4.00 x 3.50 inches. Compression ratio: 9.5:1. Brake hp: 250 at 4600 rpm. Carburetor: Motorcraft two-barrel. Five main bearings. Serial number code 'H.'

ENGINE [351 Four-Barrel V-8]: Overhead valve. Cast-iron block. Displacement: 351 cid. Bore and stroke: 4.00 x 3.50 inches. Compression ratio: 10.7:1. Brake hp: 290 at 4800 rpm. Carburetor: Motorcraft four-barrel. Five main bearings. Serial number code 'M.'

ENGINE [390 GT V-8]: Overhead valve. Cast-iron block. Displacement: 390 cid. Bore and stroke: 4.05 x 3.78 inches. Compression ratio: 10.5:1. Brake hp: 320 at 4600 rpm. Carburetor: Holley four-barrel. Five main bearings. Serial number code 'S.'

1969 Ford Mustang 'Boss 302' two-door Sportsroof coupe, V-8. (PH)

1969 Ford Mustang 'Boss 429' two-door Sportsroof coupe, V-8. (PH)

ENGINE [Cobra Jet 428 V-8]: Overhead valve. Cast-iron block. Displacement: 428 cid. Bore and stroke: 4.13 x 3.98 inches. Compression ratio: 10.6:1. Brake hp: 335 at 5200 rpm. Carburetor: Holley four-barrel. Five main bearings. Serial number code 'Q.'

ENGINE [Super Cobra Jet 428 V-8]: Overhead valve. Cast-iron block. Displacement: 428 cid. Bore and stroke: 4.13 x 3.98 inches. Compression ratio: 10.5:1. Brake hp: 360 at 5400 rpm. Carburetor: Holley four-barrel. Ram-Air induction. Five main bearings. Serial number code 'R.'

ENGINE [Boss 429 V-8]: Overhead valve. Cast-iron block. Displacement: 429 cid. Bore and stroke: 4.36 x 3.59 inches. Compression ratio: 11.3:1. Brake hp: 370 at 5600 rpm. Carburetor: Holley four-barrel. Five main bearings. Serial number code 'Z.'

CHASSIS FEATURES: Wheelbase: 108 inches. Overall length: 187.4 inches. Tires: C78-14 four-ply tubeless blackwall (E78-14 four-ply on small V-8-equipped models and F70-14 four-ply on large V-8-equipped models).

OPTIONS: 302 cid/220 hp two-barrel V-8, not available in Mach I ($105). 351 cid/250 hp two-barrel V-8, standard in Mach I ($163 in other models). 351 cid/290 hp four-barrel V-8, in Mach I ($26); in other models ($189). 390 cid/320 hp four-barrel V-8, in Mach I ($100); in other models ($158). 428 cid/335 hp four-barrel V-8, in Mach I ($224); in other models ($288). 428 cid four-barrel Cobra Jet V-8 including Ram Air, in Mach I ($357); in other models ($421). SelectShift Cruise-O-Matic transmission; six-cylinder engines ($191); '302' and '351' V-8s ($201); '390' and '428' V-8s ($222). Four-speed manual; '302' and '351' V-8s ($205); '390' and '428' V-8s ($254). Power disc brakes, not available with 200 cid inline six ($65). Power steering ($95). Power top convertible ($53). GT Equipment Group, not available on Grande or with six-cylinder or 302 cid V-8, ($147). Tachometer, V-8s only ($54). Handling suspension, not available on Grande or with six-cylinder and '428' V-8 engines ($31). Competition suspension, standard on Mach I and GT; '428' V-8 required ($31). Glass backlight, convertible ($39). Limited slip differential, '250' inline six and '302' V-8 ($42). Traction-Lok differential, not available on sixes and '302' V-8s ($64). Intermittent windshield wipers ($17). High-back front bucket seats, not available in Grande ($85). Color-keyed dual racing mirrors, standard in Mach I and Grande, ($19). Power ventilation, not available with Select-Aire ($40). Electric clock, standard in Mach I and Grande ($16). Tinted windows and windshield ($32). Speed control, V-8 and automatic transmission required ($74). Remote-control left door mirror ($13). Select-Aire conditioner, not available with '200' inline six or '428' V-8 with four-speed ($380). Push-button AM radio ($61). AM/FM stereo radio ($181). Stereo-Sonic tape system, AM radio required ($134). Rear seat speaker, hardtop and Grande ($13). Rear seat deck, Sportsroof and Mach I ($97). Full-width front seat, hardtop, not available with console ($32). Tilt-Away steering wheel ($66). RimBlow Deluxe steering wheel ($36). Console ($54). Interior Decor Group, not available on Mach I and Grande ($101); with dual racing mirrors ($88). Deluxe Interior Decor Group, Sportsroof and convertible ($133); with dual racing mirrors ($120). Deluxe seat belts with reminder light ($16). Vinyl roof, hardtop ($84). Wheel covers, not available on Mach I, Mustang GT or Grande, but included with exterior Decor Group ($21). Wire wheel covers, not available with Mach I and Mustang GT; standard on Grande, with Exterior Decor Group ($58); without Exterior Decor Group ($80). Exterior Decor Group, not available on Mach I and Grande, ($32). Chrome styled steel wheels, standard on Mach I; not available on Grande or with '200' inline six ($117); with GT Equipment Group ($78); with Exterior Decor Group ($95). Adjustable head restraints, not available on Mach I ($17).

HISTORY: The 1969 Mustangs were introduced in September 1968. Model year production peaked at 299,824 units. The new fastback styling was called the "Sportsroof" treatment. The fantastic Boss 302 Mustang was styled and detailed by Larry Shinoda. Its standard equipment included the special competition engine; staggered shock

absorbers; heavy-duty springs; CJ four-speed gearbox; power front disc brakes; heavy-duty rear drums; special ignition system (with high rpm cut-out feature); and F60-15 Goodyear Polyglas tires. A total of 1,934 Boss 302 Mustangs were built, almost twice as many as needed to qualify the model for Trans-Am racing. Bunkie Knudsen was the chief executive officer of the company this year, but was in his last year at the helm. Ford Motor Co. chairman Henry Ford II fired Knudsen in August. Knudsen, of course, was famous for creating Pontiac's 'performance image' in the early 1960s. Part of his problem at FoMoCo was that auto sales were becoming less relative to high-performance marketing techniques in the early 1970s. Others, however, suggested that Knudsen was the victim of Ford's traditional family controlled management system. He had tried to overstep the limits of his power and, for doing this, was dismissed on short notice.

1970 MUSTANG

1970 Ford Mustang 'Boss 302' two-door Sportsroof coupe, V-8. (OCW)

MUSTANG SERIES — (6-CYL/V-8) — For 1970, Mustangs were slightly revised versions of the 1969 models. The biggest change was the return to single headlights. They were located inside the new, larger grille opening. Simulated air intakes were seen where the outboard lights were on the 1969 models. The rear was also slightly restyled. There were flat taillight moldings and a flat escutcheon panel, taking the place of the concave panel and lights used in 1969. The year 1970 saw the introduction of the famous 351 cid 'Cleveland' V-8 engine, in two-barrel and four-barrel configurations. Standard equipment in Mustangs included vinyl high-back bucket seats; carpeting; floor-mounted shift lever; instrument gauges; E78-15 tires; and either the '200' six or the '302' V-8. The Grande came with all the above plus Deluxe two-spoke steering wheel; color-keyed racing mirrors; wheel covers; electric clock; bright exterior moldings; dual outside paint stripes; and luxury trim bucket seats. Convertibles had power-operated tops. The Mach I featured vinyl buckets; hood scoop; competition suspension; color-keyed racing mirrors; console-mounted shift controls; Deluxe steering wheel with rim-blow feature; rocker panel moldings; rear deck lid tape stripe; deep-dish sport wheel covers; carpeting; E70-15 fiberglass-belted whitewall tires; and the 351 cid/250 hp two-barrel V-8. The Mustang Boss 302 had, in addition to the above, quick-ratio steering, functional front spoiler and Space Saver spare tire.

MUSTANG I.D. NUMBERS: The Vehicle Identification Number is stamped on top of dash on driver's side, viewable through windshield. First symbol: 0=1970. Second symbol indicates assembly plant: F=Dearborn Mich.; R=San Jose, Calif.; T=Metuchen, N.J. Third and fourth symbols equated to Body/Style Number: 63A=bucket seat Sportsroof; 65A=bucket seat hardtop; 76A=bucket seat convertible; 63C=Mach I Sportsroof; 65E=bucket seat Grande hardtop. Fifth symbol indicates engine (See engine list below). The next six symbols are the sequential production number beginning at 100001 for each series at each factory. Vehicle Certification Label attached to driver's door has VIN, body code, color code, trim code, transmission code, rear axle code and special equipment codes.

MUSTANG SERIES

Model No.	Body/ Style No.	Body Type & Seating	Factory Price	Shipping Weight	Prod. Total
N/A	65B	2-dr HT Cpe-4P	2721/2822	2721/2923	82,569
N/A	63B	2-dr FsBk-4P	2771/2872	2745/2947	45,934
N/A	76B	2-dr Conv-4P	3025/3126	2831/3033	7,673
N/A	65E	2-dr Grande-4P	2926/3028	2806/3008	13,581
N/A	63C	2-dr Mach I-4P	3271	3240	40,970
N/A	63	2-dr Boss 302-4P	3720	3227	6,318

NOTE 1: Total series output was 197,045.

NOTE 2: Data above slash for six/below slash for V-8.

1970 Ford Mustang two-door Sportsroof coupe, 6-cyl. (OCW)

1970 Ford Mustang Grande two-door hardtop coupe, V-8. (PH)

ENGINE [Mustang Six-Cylinder]: Overhead valve. Cast-iron block. Displacement: 200 cid. Bore and stroke: 3.68 x 3.13 inches. Compression ratio: 8.8:1. Brake hp: 115 at 3800 rpm. Carburetor: Motorcraft one-barrel. Seven main bearings. Serial number code 'T.'

ENGINE [Ford Six-Cylinder]: Overhead valve. Cast-iron block. Displacement: 250 cid. Bore and stroke: 3.68 x 3.91 inches. Compression ratio: 9.0:1. Brake hp: 155 at 4400 rpm. Carburetor: Motorcraft one-barrel. Seven main bearings. Serial number code 'L.'

ENGINE [302 V-8]: Overhead valve. Cast-iron block. Displacement: 302 cid. Bore and stroke: 4.00 x 3.00 inches. Compression ratio: 9.5:1. Brake hp: 220 at 4600 rpm. Carburetor: Motorcraft two-barrel. Five main bearings. Serial number code 'F.'

ENGINE [Boss 302 V-8]: Overhead valve. Cast-iron block. Displacement: 302 cid. Bore and stroke: 4.00 x 3.00 inches. Compression ratio: 10.6:1. Brake hp: 290 at 5800 rpm. Carburetor: Holley four-barrel. Five main bearings. Serial number code 'G.'

ENGINE [351 V-8]: Overhead valve. Cast-iron block. Displacement: 351 cid. Bore and stroke: 4.00 x 3.50 inches. Compression ratio: 9.5:1. Brake hp: 250 at 4600 rpm. Carburetor: Motorcraft two-barrel. Five main bearings. Serial number code 'H.'

1970 Ford Mustang Mach 1 two-door Sportsroof coupe, V-8. (PH)

ENGINE [351 Four-Barrel V-8]: Overhead valve. Cast-iron block. Displacement: 351 cid. Bore and stroke: 4.00 x 3.50 inches. Compression ratio: 11.0:1. Brake hp: 300 at 5400 rpm. Carburetor: Motorcraft four-barrel. Five main bearings. Serial number code 'M.'

ENGINE [Cobra Jet 428 V-8]: Overhead valve. Cast-iron block. Displacement: 428 cid. Bore and stroke: 4.13 x 3.98 inches. Compression ratio: 10.6:1. Brake hp: 335 at 5400 rpm. Carburetor: Holley four-barrel. Five main bearings.

ENGINE [Super Cobra Jet 428 V-8]: Overhead valve. Cast-iron block. Displacement: 428 cid. Bore and stroke: 4.13 x 3.98 inches. Compression ratio: 10.5:1. Brake hp: 360 at 5400 rpm. Carburetor: Holley four-barrel. Five main bearings. Serial number code 'R.'

ENGINE [Boss 429 V-8]: Overhead valve. Cast-iron block. Displacement: 429 cid. Bore and stroke: 4.36 x 3.59 inches. Compression ratio: 11.3:1. Brake hp: 375 at 5600 rpm. Carburetor: Holley four-barrel. Five main bearings. Serial number code 'Z.'

CHASSIS FEATURES: Wheelbase: 108 inches. Overall length: 187.4 inches. Tires: C78-14 four-ply tubeless blackwall (E78-14 four-ply on cars equipped with small V-8s and F70-14 four-ply on those with large V-8s). Boss 302s and Boss 429s used F70-15 tires.

OPTIONS: 351 cid/250 hp V-8, in Mach I (standard); in other Mustangs ($45). 351 cid/300 hp V-8 in Mach I ($48); in other Mustangs ($93). 428 cid/335 hp Cobra Jet V-8 engine with Ram Air induction, in Mach I ($376); in other Mustangs ($421). Cruise-O-Matic automatic transmission ($222). Four-speed manual transmission ($205). Power steering ($95). Power front disc brakes ($65). Limited slip differential ($43). Styled steel wheels ($58). Magnum 500 chrome wheels ($129). AM radio ($61). AM/FM stereo radio ($214). AM/8-track stereo ($134). Center console ($54). Tilt steering wheel ($45). Exterior Decor Group ($78). Vinyl roof ($84); on Grande ($26). Wheel covers ($26). Rocker panel moldings ($16).

HISTORY: The 1970 Mustangs were introduced in September 1969. Model year production peaked at 190,727 units. Ford ceased its official racing activities late in the 1970 calendar year. Before getting out of racing, Ford captured the 1970 Trans-Am title with the Mustang.

1971 MUSTANG

1971 Ford Mustang Boss 351 SportsRoof. (OCW)

1971 Ford Mustang Mach 1. (OCW)

MUSTANG SERIES — (6-CYL/V-8)

MUSTANG SERIES — (6-CYL/V-8) — The 1971 Mustangs were completely restyled. They were over two inches longer and had a new hood and concealed windshield wipers. The styling left little doubt that the cars were Mustangs, but they were lower, wider and heavier than any previous models. A full-width grille, incorporating the head-lights within its opening, was used. The Mustang corral was again seen in the center. The roof had a thinner appearance. New door handles fit flush to the body. New on the options list were the Special Instrumentation Group package; electric rear window defogger; and a Body Protection Group package that included side moldings and front bumper guards. The fastback-styled 'Sportsroof' was now available dressed in a vinyl top. Sadly, two of the most exotic engines were gone. The Boss 302 and Boss 429 powerplants bit the dust. Although rumors persist that five cars were assembled with the 'Boss 429,' they are unconfirmed. There was a new Boss 351 Mustang that provided a more refined package, with a better weight distribution layout than the front-heavy Boss 429. Standard equipment on base Mustangs included color-keyed nylon carpeting; floor-shift; high-back bucket seats; steel guardrail door construction; DirectAire ventilation system; concealed windshield wipers with cowl air inlets; mini console with ashtray; armrests; courtesy lights; cigar lighter; heater and de-froster; all-vinyl interior; glovebox; E78-14 belted black sidewall tires; power convertible top and either the 250 cid six or 302 cid V-8. The Mustang Grande coupe had the same basic features plus bright pedal pads; Deluxe high-back bucket seats in cloth trim; Deluxe instrument panel; Deluxe two-spoke steering wheel; electric clock; molded trim panels with integral pull handles and armrests; right rear quarter panel trim with ashtray; dual paint accent stripes; dual color-keyed racing mirrors (left remote-control); rocker panel moldings; vinyl roof; wheel covers; and wheel lip moldings. The Mustang Mach I had all of the basic equipment plus color-keyed spoiler; hood moldings; fender moldings; and racing mirrors; a unique grille with Sportlamps; competition suspension; trim rings and hubcaps; high-back bucket seats; honeycomb texture back panel applique; pop open gas cap; deck lid paint stripe; black or Argent Silver finish on lower bodysides (with bright molding at upper edge); E70-14 whitewalls; and the two-barrel 302 cid V-8. A NASA-styled hood scoop treatment was a no-cost option. The Mustang Boss 351 had even more extras. In addition to the basic equipment, this model featured a functional NASA hood scoop; black or Argent Silver painted hood; hood lock pins; Ram-Air engine call-outs; color-keyed racing mirrors (left remote-controlled); unique grille with Sportslamps; hubcaps with trim rings; bodyside tape stripes in black or Argent Silver; color-keyed hood and front fender moldings; Boss 351 call-out nomenclature; dual exhaust; power disc brakes; Space Saver spare tire; competition suspension with stag-gered rear shocks; 3.91:1 rear axle gear ratio with TractionLok dif-ferential; electronic rpm limiter; functional front spoiler (finished in black and shipped 'knocked-down'); 80-ampere battery; Instrumen-tation Group; F60-15 raised white letter tires; High-Output 351 cid/330 hp V-8 with four-barrel carburetion; special cooling package; and wide ratio four-speed manual gearbox with Hurst shifter.

MUSTANG I.D. NUMBERS: The Vehicle Identification Number is stamped on top of dash on driver's side, viewable through windshield. First symbol: 1=1971. Second symbol indicates assembly plant: F=Dearborn, Mich.; T=Metuchen, N.J. Third and fourth symbols equat-ed to Body/Style Number: 65D=standard two-door hardtop; 63D=stan-dard two-door Sportsroof; 76D=standard convertible; 65F=Grande hardtop; 63R=Mach I Sportsroof. Fifth symbol indicates engine (see engine list below). The next six symbols are the sequential production number beginning at 100001 for each series at each factory. Vehicle Certification Label attached to driver's door has VIN, body code, color code, trim code, transmission code, rear axle code and special equip-ment codes.

1971 Ford Mustang 'Boss 351' two-door Sportsroof coupe, V-8. (OCW)

MUSTANG SERIES

Model No.	Body/Style No.	Body Type & Seating	Factory Price	Shipping Weight	Prod. Total
N/A	65D	2-dr HT Cpe-4P	2911/3006	2937/3026	65,696
N/A	63D	2-dr FsBk-4P	2973/3068	2907/2993	23,956
N/A	76D	2-dr Conv-4P	3227/3322	3059/3145	6,121
N/A	65F	2-dr Grande-4P	3117/3212	2963/3049	17,406
N/A	63	2-dr Boss 351-4P	4124	3281	1,800
N/A	63R	2-dr Mach I-4P	3268	3220	36,449

NOTE 1: Total series output was 149,678 units.

NOTE 2: Data above slash for six/below slash for V-8.

ENGINE [Mustang Six-Cylinder]: Overhead valve. Cast-iron block. Displacement: 250 cid. Bore and stroke: 3.68 x 3.91 inches. Com-pression ratio: 9.0:1. Brake hp: 145 at 4000 rpm. Carburetor: Motor-craft one-barrel. Seven main bearings. Serial number code 'L.'

1971 Ford Mustang two-door hardtop coupe, 6-cyl. (OCW)

1971-1/2 Ford Mustang two-door hardtop coupe (with optional sport appearance package), V-8. (PH)

1971 Ford Mustang two-door Sportsroof coupe, V-8. (PH)

ENGINE [302 V-8]: Overhead valve. Cast-iron block. Displacement: 302 cid. Bore and stroke: 4.00 x 3.00 inches. Compression ratio: 9.0:1. Brake hp: 210 at 4600 rpm. Carburetor: Motorcraft two-barrel. Five main bearings. Serial number code 'F.'

ENGINE [351 V-8]: Overhead valve. Cast-iron block. Displacement: 351 cid. Bore and stroke: 4.00 x 3.50 inches. Compression ratio: 9.0:1. Brake hp: 240 at 4600 rpm. Carburetor: Motorcraft two-barrel. Five main bearings. Serial number code 'H.'

ENGINE [351 'Cleveland' Four-Barrel V-8]: Overhead valve. Cast-iron block. Displacement: 351 cid. Bore and stroke: 4.00 x 3.50 inches. Compression ratio: 10.7:1. Brake hp: 285 at 5400 rpm. Carburetor: Holley four-barrel. Five main bearings. Serial number code 'M.'

ENGINE [Boss 351 V-8]: Overhead valve. Cast-iron block. Displacement: 351 cid. Bore and stroke: 4.00 x 3.50 inches. Compression ratio: 11.1:1. Brake hp: 330 at 5400 rpm. Carburetor: Holley four-barrel. Five main bearings. Serial number code 'Q.'

ENGINE [Cobra Jet 429 V-8]: Overhead valve. Cast-iron block. Displacement: 429 cid. Bore and stroke: 4.36 x 3.59 inches. Compression ratio: 11.3:1. Brake hp: 370 at 5400 rpm. Carburetor: Holley four-barrel. Five main bearings. Serial number code 'C.'

ENGINE [Super Cobra Jet 429 V-8]: Overhead valve. Cast-iron block. Displacement: 429 cid. Bore and stroke: 4.36 x 3.59 inches. Compression ratio: 11.5:1. Brake hp: 375 at 5600 rpm. Carburetor: Holley four-barrel (with Ram-Air induction). Five main bearings. Serial number code 'J.'

CHASSIS FEATURES: Wheelbase: 109 inches. Overall length: 189.5 inches. Width: 75 inches. Tires: E78-14 belted blackwall.

1971 Ford Mustang Grande two-door hardtop coupe, V-8. (PH)

1971 Ford Mustang Mach 1 two-door Sportsroof coupe, V-8. (OCW)

OPTIONS: 351 cid/240 hp V-8 engine ($45). 351 cid/285 hp 'Cleveland' V-8 engine ($93). 429 cid/370 hp Cobra Jet V-8 engine ($372). Cruise-O-Matic automatic transmission ($217-$238). Four-speed manual transmission ($216). Power steering ($115). Power front disc brakes ($70). Limited-slip differential ($48). Magnum 500 chrome wheels ($129). Am radio ($66). AM/FM stereo radio ($214). AM/8-track stereo ($129). Center console ($60). Electric rear window defogger ($48). NASA-style hood scoops (no charge). Drag-Pac rear axle 3.91:1 ratio ($155); 4.11:1 ratio ($207). Vinyl roof ($26). White sidewall tires ($34).

HISTORY: The 1971 Mustangs were introduced Sept. 19, 1970. Model year production peaked at 149,678 units. Calendar year sales of 127,062 cars were recorded. J.B. Naughton was the chief executive officer of the Ford Division this year. This branch of the corporation was also known as Ford Marketing Corp. Of all Mustangs built in the model year 1971, some 5.3 percent had four-speed manual transmissions; 5.6 percent had stereo eight-track tape players; 1.9 percent had power windows and 29 percent had vinyl roofs.

1972 MUSTANG

1972 Ford Mustang convertible. (OCW)

MUSTANG SERIES — (6-CYL/V-8) — The Mustang was a versatile package. The original of 1964-1/2 was promoted as a sports/personal car. Later, the Mustang became a luxury automobile and, then, a high-performance machine. Actually the basic car itself was changed very little in overall concept. Yet, for 1972, it was suddenly being called Ford's "Sports Compact." It came in five two-door styles, two hardtops, two Sportsroofs (fastbacks) and a convertible. Styling was generally unaltered, the only appearance refinements being a color-keyed front bumper and redesigned deck latch panel nameplate. The color-keyed bumper was standard on Mach Is, while other models continued to use chrome front bumpers as standard equipment. A lot of customers ordered the monochromatic bumpers at slight extra-cost. Instead of spelling Mustang in block letters on the rear, a chrome signature script was used. The powerful 429 cid V-8 was no longer offered. The Cleveland 351 cid four-barrel carbureted V-8 was the hairiest powerplant around. Standard equipment in all body styles included concealed wipers; rocker panel and wheel lip moldings; lower back panel applique with bright moldings; color-keyed dual racing mirrors; recessed exterior door handles; wheel covers; DirectAire ventilation; heater and defroster; high-back bucket seats; and bonded door trim panels with pull-type handles and armrests. At this point, the specific equipment in different styles varied. The hardtop and Sportsroof featured carpeting, mini-consoles, courtesy lights, Deluxe two-spoke steering wheel with wood-toned inserts, three-speed floor shift, E78-14 black belted tires, and a base 250 cid six. In addition to all of this, the Sportsroof also featured fixed rear quarter windows (except with power lifts) and a tinted backlight. The Mustang convertible also had a five-ply power-operated top; color-keyed top boot; tinted windshield and glass backlight; bright, upper back panel moldings; knitted vinyl seat trim; molded door handles; and black instrument panel appliques. The Mustang Grande featured — in addition to the above — a vinyl top with Grande script nameplates; unique bodyside tape stripes; unique wheel covers; floor mat in trunk; Lambeth cloth and vinyl interior trim; bright pedal moldings; Deluxe camera grain instrument panel with wood-toned appliques; panel-mounted electric clock and rear ashtrays. The Mach I Sportsroof featured the following standard extras: competition suspension; NASA-type hood scoops (listed as a no-cost option on all Mach Is, but essentially standard for the model); front spoiler-type bumper; color-keyed hood and rear fender moldings; black grille with integral Sportslamps; back panel applique; black or Argent Silver painted lower body, front and rear valance panels; rear tape stripes with Mach I decals; wheel trim rings and hubcaps; E70-14 bias-belted whitewall tires; and '302' two-barrel carbureted V-8.

MUSTANG I.D. NUMBERS: The Vehicle Identification Number is stamped on top of dash on driver's side, viewable through windshield. First symbol: 2=1972. Second symbol indicates assembly plant: F=Dearborn, Mich. Third and fourth symbols equated to Body/Style Number: 65D=standard two-door hardtop; 63D=standard two-door Sportsroof; 76D=standard convertible; 65F=Grande hardtop; 63R=Mach I Sportsroof. Fifth symbol indicates engine (see engine list below). The next six symbols are the sequential production number beginning at 100001 for each series at each factory. Vehicle Certification Label attached to driver's door has VIN, body code, color code, trim code, transmission code, rear axle code and special equipment codes.

MUSTANG SERIES

Model No.	Body/ Style No.	Body Type & Seating	Factory Price	Shipping Weight	Prod. Total
N/A	65D	2-dr HT Cpe-4P	2729/2816	2941/3025	57,350
N/A	63D	2-dr FsBk-4P	2786/2873	2909/2995	15,622
N/A	76D	2-dr Conv-4P	3015/3101	3061/3147	6,401
N/A	65F	2-dr Grande-4P	2915/3002	2965/3051	18,045
N/A	63R	2-dr Mach I-4P	3053	3046	27,675

NOTE 1: Total series output was 125,405 units.

NOTE 2: Data above slash for six/below slash for V-8.

1972 Ford Mustang two-door hardtop coupe, V-8. (OCW)

1972 Ford Mustang two-door convertible, V-8. (PH)

1972 Ford Mustang Grande two-door hardtop coupe, V-8. (OCW)

ENGINE [Mustang Six-Cylinder]: Overhead valve. Displacement: 250 cid. Bore and stroke: 3.68 x 3.91 inches. Compression ratio: 8.0:1. Net hp: 98 at 3400 rpm. Carburetor: Motorcraft one-barrel. Seven main bearings. Serial number code 'L.'

ENGINE [302 V-8]: Overhead valve. Cast-iron block. Displacement: 302 cid. Bore and stroke: 4.00 x 3.00 inches. Compression ratio: 8.5:1. Net hp: 140 at 4000 rpm. Carburetor: Motorcraft two-barrel. Five main bearings. Serial number code 'F.'

ENGINE [351 'Cleveland' V-8]: Overhead valve. Cast-iron block. Displacement: 351 cid. Bore and stroke: 4.00 x 3.50 inches. Compression ratio: 8.6:1. Net hp: 163 at 3800 rpm. Carburetor: Motorcraft two-barrel. Five main bearings. Serial number code 'H.'

ENGINE [351 'Cleveland' Four-Barrel V-8]: Overhead valve. Cast-iron block. Displacement: 351 cid. Bore and stroke: 4.00 x 3.50 inches. Compression ratio: 8.6:1. Net hp: 248 at 5400 rpm. Carburetor: Holley four-barrel. Five main bearings.

ENGINE [351 Ho 'Cleveland' V-8]: Overhead valve. Cast-iron block. Displacement: 351 cid. Bore and stroke: 4.00 x 3.50 inches. Compression ratio: 8 6:1 Net hp: 266 at 5400 rpm. Carbretion: Holley four-barrel. Five main bearings. Serial number code 'Q.'

CHASSIS FEATURES: Wheelbase: 109 inches. Overall length: 189.5 inches. Width: 75 inches. Tires: E78-14. (Note: Additional tire sizes are noted in text when used as standard equipment on specific models.)

1972 Ford Mustang Mach 1 two-door Sportsroof coupe, V-8. (PH)

OPTIONS: 351 cid/177 hp 'Cleveland' V-8 ($41). 351 cid/266 hp 'Cleveland' V-8 engine ($115). 351 cid/275 hp High-Output V-8 with four-barrel carburetion ($841-$870). Cruise-O-Matic transmission ($204). Four-speed manual transmission ($193). Power steering ($103). Power front disc brakes ($62). Limited-slip differential ($43). Magnum 500 chrome wheels ($108-$139). Center console ($53-$97). Vinyl roof ($79). White sidewall tires ($34).

HISTORY: The 1972 Mustangs were introduced Sept. 24, 1971. Calendar year sales by United States dealers stopped at 120,589 units, a decline from the previous season. Ford had already stopped building Mustangs in San Jose, Calif., in 1971. Now, the Metuchen, N.J., factory was converted to Pinto production, leaving the sole Mustang assembly line in Dearborn. This would not last long, though. Sales took a sudden leap from 127,062 to 238,077 units and Mustang II production was soon resumed at San Jose, Calif. Model year production stopped at 111,015 cars. Of these, 27 percent had a four-speed manual transmission, 3.9 percent had Tilt-Telescope steering, 6.2 percent wore optional styled wheels and 32.3 percent had vinyl tops. There were no changes in top Ford management, although B.E. Bidwell would soon be elected vice-president and general manager of Ford Marketing Corp.

1973 MUSTANG

1973 Ford Mustang two-door convertible, V-8. (OCW)

MUSTANG SERIES — (6-CYL/V-8) — The 1973 Mustangs were virtually the same as the 1972 models. The Mustang convertible was the only car of that body style still offered by Ford as well as one of the few remaining ragtops in the entire industry. All Mustangs featured a high-impact molded urethane front bumper that was color-keyed to the body. One design change for the new season was a revised cross-hatch design in the grille. New Mustang exterior colors and interior trims were provided. New options included forged aluminum wheels and steel-belted radial-ply tires. Headlights, still of single-unit design, were housed inside square panels that flanked the grille on each side. New features of the grille itself included a 'floating' pony badge at the center and an eggcrate-style insert with vertical parking lights in the outboard segments. A new front valance panel was of an unslotted design. Standard equipment included the 250 cid six or 302 cid V-8; three-speed manual transmission; floor-mounted shift control; E78-14 black sidewall tires; rocker panel and wheel lip moldings; lower back panel applique with bright molding; chrome, rectangular left-hand door mirror; all-vinyl upholstery and door trim; mini front console; color-keyed loop-pile carpets; Deluxe two-spoke steering wheel (with wood-tone insert); cigarette lighter; seat belt reminder system; and door courtesy lamps. The Sportsroof style also included a tinted back window and fixed rear quarter windows. The convertible added under-dash courtesy lights; power-operated vinyl top; glass backlight; knit-vinyl seat trim; and power front disc brakes. Standard extras on the Mustang Grande, in addition to base equipment, was comprised of dual, color-keyed racing mirrors; vinyl roof; bodyside tape striping; special wheel covers; trunk mat; Lambeth cloth and vinyl seat trim; molded door panels with integral armrests; bright pedal pads; Deluxe instrument panel; and electric clock. Also available was the Mustang Mach I, which came with all of the following: competition suspension package; choice of two hood designs (one with NASA-type hood scoops); size E70-14 whitewall tires of bias-belted wide-oval construction; color-keyed dual racing mirrors; black grille and back panel appliques; back panel tape stripe; wheel trim rings and hubcaps; tinted back window; all-vinyl upholstery and trim (with high-back bucket seats) and the 136 SAE nhp version of the two-barrel carbureted 302 cid V-8.

MUSTANG I.D. NUMBERS: The Vehicle Identification Number is stamped on top of dash on driver's side, viewable through windshield).

1973 Ford Mustang Grande two-door hardtop coupe, V-8. (OCW

First symbol: 3=1973. Second symbol indicates assembly plant: F=Dearborn Mich.; R=San Jose, Calif. Third and fourth symbols equate to Body/Style Number: 65D=standard two-door hardtop; 63D=standard two-door Sportsroof; 76D=standard convertible; 65F=Grande hardtop; 63R=Mach I Sportsroof. Fifth symbol indicates engine (see engine list below). The next six symbols are the sequential production number beginning at 100001 for each series at each factory. Vehicle Certification Label attached to driver's door has VIN, body code, color code, trim code, transmission code, rear axle code and special equipment codes.

MUSTANG SERIES

Model No.	Body/ Style No.	Body Type & Seating	Factory Price	Shipping Weight	Prod. Total
N/A	65D	2-dr HT Cpe-4P	2760/2847	2984/3076	51,430
N/A	63D	2-dr FsBk-4P	2820/2907	2991/3083	10,820
N/A	76D	2-dr Conv-4P	3102/3189	3106/3198	11,853
N/A	65F	2-dr Grande-4P	2946/3033	2982/3074	25,274
N/A	63R	2-dr Mach I-4P	3088	3090	35,440

NOTE 1: Total series output was 134,867 units.

NOTE 2: Data above slash for six/below slash for V-8.

NOTE 3: This year the Mach I could be had with a 250 cid six.

ENGINE [Mustang Six-Cylinder]: Overhead valve. Cast-iron block. Displacement: 250 cid. Bore and stroke: 3.68 x 3.91 inches. Compression ratio: 8.0:1. Net hp: 88 at 3200 rpm. Carburetor: Motorcraft single-barrel. Seven main bearings. Serial number code 'L.'

ENGINE [302 V-8]: Overhead valve. Cast-iron block. Displacement: 302 cid. Bore and stroke: 4.00 x 3.00 inches. Compression ratio: 8.0:1. Net hp: 135 at 4200 rpm. Carburetor: Motorcraft two-barrel. Five main bearings. Serial number code 'F.'

ENGINE [351 'Windsor' V-8]: Overhead valve. Cast-iron block. Displacement: 351 cid. Bore and stroke: 4.00 x 3.50 inches. Compression ratio: 8.0:1. Net hp: 156 at 3800 rpm. Carburetor: Motorcraft two-barrel. Five main bearings. Serial number code 'H.'

ENGINE [351 'Cleveland' V-8]: Overhead valve. Cast-iron block. Displacement: 351 cid. Bore and stroke: 4.00 x 3.50 inches. Compression ratio: 8.0:1. Net hp 154 at 4000 rpm. Carburetor: Motorcraft two-barrel. Five main bearings. Serial number code 'H.'

CHASSIS FEATURES: Wheelbase: 109 inches. Overall length: 189.5 inches. Width: 75 inches. Tires: E78-14. (Note: Additional tire sizes are noted in text when used as standard equipment on specific models.)

OPTIONS: 302 cid two-barrel V-8 standard in Mach I, in other models ($87). 351 cid two-barrel V-8 ($128). 351 cid four-barrel V-8, including 55-amp alternator; heavy-duty 55-amp battery; special intake manifold; special valve springs and dampers; large-capacity 4300-D carburetor; 25-inch diameter dual exhaust outlets; modified camshaft and four-bolt main bearing caps. Requires Cruise-O-Matic 3.25:1 axle ratio or four-speed manual transmission, 3.50:1 axle combination, power front disc brakes and competition suspension ($194). California emission testing ($14). SelectShift Cruise-O-Matic transmission ($204). Four-speed manual transmission with Hurst shifter, not available with six-cylinder ($193). Power front disc brakes, standard on convertible; required with '351' V-8 ($62). Power windows ($113). Power steering, required with Tilt-Away steering wheel ($103). SelectAire conditioning, including extra cooling package; not available on six-cylinder with three-speed manual transmission ($368). Console, in Grande ($53); in other models ($68). Convenience Group, including trunk light; glove compartment light; map light; underhood light; 'lights-on' warning buzzer; automatic seatback releases; under-dash courtesy lights (standard on convertible); parking brake warning light; and glove compartment lock ($46). Electric rear window defroster, not available with convertible or six-cylinder ($57). Tinted glass, convertible ($14); others ($36). Instrumentation Group, including tachometer, trip odometer and oil pressure, ammeter and temperature gauges; included with Mach I Sports Interior, not available on six-cylinder; in Grande without console ($55); in other models ($71). Color-keyed dual racing mirrors, standard on Grande, Mach I ($23). AM radio ($59). AM/FM stereo radio ($191). Sport deck rear seat Sportsroof, Mach I only ($86). Deluxe three-spoke Rim-Blow steering wheel ($35). Tilt-Away steering wheel, power steering required ($41). Deluxe leather-wrapped two-spoke steering wheel ($23). Stereo-Sonic Tape System, AM radio required ($120). Intermittent windshield wipers ($23). Optional axle ratios ($12). Traction-Lok differential ($43). Heavy-duty 70-amp hour battery, standard hardtop and convertible with '351' two-barrel in combination with Instrument Group or SelectAire ($14). Extra cooling package, standard with SelectAire, not available on six-cylinder ($13). Dual Ram Induction, '351' two-barrel V-8, including functional NASA-type hood with black or argent two-tone paint, hood lock pins, 'Ram-Air' engine decals ($58). Rear deck spoiler, with Sportsroof or Mach I only ($29). Competition suspension, including extra heavy-duty front and rear springs, extra heavy-duty front and rear shock absorbers, standard with Mach I and not available with six-cylinder ($28). Deluxe seat and shoulder belts package, standard without shoulder belts in convertible ($15). Deluxe Bumper Group including rear rubber bumper inserts and full-width horizontal strip ($25). Rear bumper guards ($14). Decor Group, including black or argent lower bodyside paint with bright upper edge moldings, unique grille with Sportslamps; trim rings with hubcaps [deletes rocker panel and wheel lip moldings with Decor Group] ($51). Door edge guards, included with Protection Group ($6). Color-keyed front floor mats ($13). Metallic Glow paint ($35). Two-tone hood paint, for Mach I ($18); for other models ($34). Protection Group including vinyl-insert bodyside moldings; spare tire lock; door edge guards [deletes bodyside tape stripe] on Grande ($23); on other models ($36), but not available on Mach I or Mustangs with Decor Group. Vinyl roof on hardtops, including C-pillar tri-color ornament [standard on Grande] ($80). Three-quarter vinyl roof for Sportsroofs only ($52). Mach I Sports Interior, for Mach I and V-8 Sportsroof only, including knitted vinyl trim; high-back bucket seats with accent stripes; Instrumentation Group; door trim panels with integral pull handles and armrests; color-accented, deep-embossed carpet runners; Deluxe black instrument panel applique with wood-tone center section; bright pedal pads and rear seat ashtray ($115). Black or argent bodyside stripes, with Decor Group only ($23). Trim rings with hubcaps [standard on Mach I and Mustangs with Decor Group], for Grande ($8); for other models ($31). Sports wheel covers on Grande ($56); on Mach I or Mustangs with Decor Group ($48); on other models ($79). Forged aluminum wheels on Grande ($119); on Mach I or Mustangs with Decor Group ($111); on other models ($142).

HISTORY: Most 1973 Mustangs, 90.4 percent were equipped with the automatic, 6.7 percent had the three-speed manual, 2.9 percent had the four-speed manual, 92.9 percent had power steering, 77.9 percent had power brakes, 5.6 percent had a tilting steering wheel, 62.8 percent had tinted glass, 3.2 percent had power windows and 56.2 percent were sold with an air conditioner.

1974 MUSTANG

1974 Ford Mustang II two-door hatchback coupe, 4-cyl. (OCW)

MUSTANG II SERIES — (4-CYL/V-6) — Ford Motor Co. introduced its all-new Mustang II in 1974. It was billed as the 'right car at the right time.' The new pony measured seven inches shorter than the original 1964-1/2 Mustang and was a full 13 inches shorter than the 1973 model. Sales of the new entry were sluggish at first, since the company loaded most cars in the early mix with a lot of optional equipment. It didn't take long, however, for the marketing men to see that the car had its greatest appeal as an economy model. The Mustang II was a combination of design motifs derived from both sides of the Atlantic. The Italian coach building firm of Ghia, recently acquired by Ford Motor Co., did some of the primary design work. Other ingredients came straight from the Ford/Mercury/Lincoln styling studios. Four models were available: the notch back coupe, three-door fastback, Ghia notch back coupe and fastback Mach I. Standard equipment included a 2.3-liter four; four-speed manual transmission with floor shifter; solid state ignition; front disc brakes; tachometer; steel-belted whitewalls; low-back front bucket seats; vinyl upholstery and door trim; color-keyed carpeting; wood-tone instrument panel applique; European-type armrests; and full wheel covers. The 2+2 model added a fold-down rear seat and styled steel wheels. The Ghia notch back coupe also had, in addition to the base equipment, color-keyed Deluxe seat trim; dual color-keyed remote-control door mirrors; Super Sound Package; shag carpeting; wood-tone door panel accents; digital clock; supersoft vinyl or Westminster cloth interior trim; color-keyed vinyl roof; and spoke-style wheel covers. The Mach I had all 2+2 equipment plus 2.8-liter V-6 engine; dual color-keyed remote control door mirrors; Wide-Oval steel-belted black sidewall radial tires; black lower bodyside paint; deck lid striping; and styled steel wheels with trim rings.

MUSTANG I.D. NUMBERS: The Vehicle Identification Number is on top of dash, driver's side, viewable through windshield and prefixed and suffixed with 'F' for Ford. First symbol of actual VIN is 4=1974. Second symbol identifies assembly plant: F=Dearborn, Mich.; R=San Jose, Calif. Third/fourth symbols indicate body: 02=notch back; 03=hatchback; 04=Ghia notch back; 05=Mach I notch back. Fifth symbol is the engine code (see Engine section below). Last six digits are sequential production number starting at 100001 at each plant. Vehicle Certification Label attached to driver's door has VIN, body code, color code, trim code, transmission code, rear axle code and special equipment codes.

MUSTANG II SERIES

Model No.	Body/ Style No.	Body Type & Seating	Factory Price	Shipping Weight	Prod. Total
N/A	60F	2-dr HT Cpe-4P	3081	2620	177,671
N/A	69F	3-dr FsBk-4P	3275	2699	74,799
N/A	60H	2-dr Ghia-4P	3427	2866	89,477
N/A	69R	2-dr Mach I-4P	3621	2778	44,046

NOTE 1: Total series output was 385,993 units.

1974 Ford Mustang II 2+2 two-door hatchback coupe, 4-cyl. (PH)

1974 Ford Mustang II Ghia two-door hardtop coupe, 4-cyl. (PH)

ENGINE [Mustang Four-Cylinder]: Overhead cam. Cast-iron block. Displacement: 140 cid. Bore and stroke: 3.78 x 3.13 inches. Compression ratio: 8.4:1. SAE Net hp: 85. Carburetor: Motorcraft two-barrel. Five main bearings. Serial number code 'Y.'

ENGINE [Mustang V-6]: Overhead valve. Cast-iron block. Displacement: 169 cid. Bore and stroke: 3.66 x 2.70 inches. Compression ratio: 8.0:1. SAE Net hp: 105. Carburetor: two-barrel. Serial number code 'Z.'

ENGINE [Mustang 'Mach I' V-6]: Overhead valve. Cast-iron block. Displacement: 171 cid. Bore and stroke: 3.66 x 2.70 inches. Compression ratio: 8.7:1. SAE Net hp: 109. Carburetor: two-barrel.

CHASSIS FEATURES: Wheelbase: 96.2 inches. Overall length: 175 inches. Width: 70.2 inches. Tires: B78-13 belted blackwall (BR78-13 on Ghia model).

OPTIONS: 2.8-liter (171 cid/109 hp) V-6, standard in Mach I; in other Mustang IIs ($299). SelectShift Cruise-O-Matic ($212). Convenience Group includes: dual color-keyed remote control door mirrors; right visor vanity mirror; inside day/night mirror; parking brake boot and rear ashtray, on Mustangs with Luxury Interior Group ($41); on Mach I or Mustangs with Rallye Package ($21); on other Mustangs ($57). Light Group includes: underhood, glovebox, map, ashtray and instrument panel courtesy lights, plus trunk or cargo area courtesy light and warning lamps for parking brake, 'door ajar' and 'headlamps-on' ($44). Luxury Interior Group includes: super-soft vinyl upholstery; Deluxe door panels with large armrests and wood-tone accents; Deluxe rear quarter trim; 25-ounce cut-pile carpeting; sound package; parking brake boot; door courtesy lamps; rear ashtray; standard in Ghia, in other Mustangs ($100). Maintenance Group includes: shop manual; spare bulbs; fire extinguisher; flares; warning flag; fuses; tire gauge; bungee cord; lube kit; trouble light; pliers; screwdriver and crescent wrench ($44). Rallye Package, 2.8-liter V-8 required [not available on Ghia], includes Traction-Lok differential; steel-belted raised white letter tires; extra-cooling package; competition suspension; dual color-keyed remote-control door mirrors; styled steel wheels; Sport exhaust system; digital clock and leather-wrapped steering wheel; on Mach I ($150); on 2+2 ($284); on others ($328). SelectAire conditioning ($383). Anti-theft alarm system ($75). Traction-Lok differential ($45). Heavy-duty battery ($14). Color-keyed Deluxe seat belts, standard in Ghia, in others ($17). Front and rear bumper guards ($37). Digital clock, standard in Ghia, in others ($36). Console ($43). Electric rear window defroster ($59). California emission equipment ($19). Full tinted glass ($37). Dual color-keyed door mirrors, standard in Ghia and Mach I, in others ($36). Rocker panel moldings ($14). Vinyl-insert bodyside moldings ($50). Glamour paint ($36). Pin stripes ($14). Power brakes ($45). Power steering ($106). Radios, AM ($61); AM/FM monaural ($124); AM/FM stereo ($222); AM/FM stereo with tape player ($346). Competition suspension, including heavy-duty springs; adjustable shocks; rear anti-roll bar and 195/70 BWL tires ($37). Flip-out quarter windows, for 2+2 and Mach I fastbacks only ($29). Vinyl roof, hardtop only, standard on Ghia; on other models ($83). Fold-down rear seat ($61). Super Sound Package, standard in Ghia; in others ($22). Leather-wrapped steering wheel ($30). Sun roof ($149). Luggage compartment trim ($28). Picardy velour cloth trim, Ghia ($62). Wheel trim rings, standard on Ghia; on others ($32).

HISTORY: The new Mustang II was initially released as a luxury subcompact in mid-1973 and by the end of model year 1974 had recorded an impressive record of 338,136 assemblies, which compared to only 193,129 sales of the 'big' Mustangs the previous model year.

1975 MUSTANG

1975 Ford Mustang II Ghia two-door coupe, 4-cyl. (OCW)

MUSTANG II — (4-CYL/V-6/V-8) — SERIES O — Throughout its five years of availability, the Mustang II would see little change. A 'moon roof' option and extra-cost V-8 engine were the major revisions for

1975. The design of the steering wheel was modified. A two-spoke-type was used again, but the spokes bent downward at each end instead of running nearly straight across as in the 1974 models. Ghia models had a new roofline with thicker, 'blind' rear quarters. This made the opera windows somewhat smaller. Another Ghia addition was a stand-up hood ornament. New hubcaps were featured with most decor-levels and, on cars with catalytic converters, unleaded fuel decals were affixed to the gas filler cap. In midyear, several changes took effect. The first was a slightly plainer Ghia coupe with restyled hubcaps and no hood ornament. The second was the Mustang II MPG, an economy leader that gave 26-28 highway miles per gallon. Standard equipment on the basic notch back hardtop included solid state ignition; front disc brakes; tachometer; steel-belted BR78-13 black sidewall tires; low-back front bucket seats; vinyl upholstery and trim; woodgrained dash appliques; armrests; full wheel covers; four-speed manual transmission with floor shift; and the 2.3-liter four. The standard 2+2 fastback added a fold-down rear seat and styled steel wheels. The Ghia coupe had all base equipment plus Deluxe color-keyed seat belts; dual color-keyed, remote controlled outside rearview door mirrors; radial whitewalls; Super Sound package; shag carpeting; woodgrained door accent panels; digital clock; choice of Westminster cloth or super-soft vinyl trim; color-keyed vinyl roof; and spoke-style wheel covers. The Mach I fastback model had all equipment used on the 2+2 plus color-keyed remote-control outside rearview door mirrors; steel-belted BR70-13 wide oval tires; black lower bodyside paint; specific rear deck lid striping; styled steel wheels with trim rings; and the 2.8-liter V-6 engine.

MUSTANG I.D. NUMBERS: Vehicle Identification Numbers were located on the top left-hand surface of the instrument panel and had 11 symbols. The first symbol '5' designated the 1975 model year. The second symbol designated the assembly plant: F=Dearborn, Mich.; R=San Jose, Calif. The third symbol 'O' designated Mustang. The fourth symbol designated the Body/Style Number as follows: '2' = two-door notch back coupe; '3' = three-door fastback coupe; '4' = two-door Ghia notch back coupe and '5' = two-door fastback Mach I coupe. The fifth symbol designated the engine (see Engine listings below). The last six symbols were the sequential unit number beginning at 100001 and up. The third and fourth symbols in the VIN (first and second columns of the chart below) were the same as the Ford Model Number.

MUSTANG II SERIES

Model No.	Body/ Style No.	Body Type & Seating	Factory Price	Shipping Weight	Prod. Total
MUSTANG II LINE					
O	2	2-dr Cpe-4P	3529/3801	2660/2775	85,155
O	3	3-dr FsBk Cpe-4P	3818/4090	2697/2812	30,038
O	4	2-dr Ghia Cpe-4P	3938/4210	2704/2819	52,320
MUSTANG II MACH I LINE					
O	5	3-dr FsBk Cpe-4P	4188	2879	21,062

NOTE 1: Total series output was 188,575.

NOTE 2: Data above slash for four-cylinder/below slash for V-6.

ENGINE [2.3-Liter Four]: Inline four. Overhead valve and camshaft. Cast-iron block. Displacement: 140 cid. Bore and stroke: 3.78 x 3.13 inches. Compression ratio: 8.4:1. SAE Net hp: 83. Hydraulic valve lifters. Carburetor: Motorcraft two-barrel Model 5200. Serial number code 'Y.'

ENGINE [2.8-Liter V-6]: Overhead valve and camshaft. Cast-iron block. Displacement: 171 inches. Bore and stroke: 3.66 x 2.70 inches. Compression ratio: 8.7:1. SAE Net hp: 97. Carburetor: Motorcraft two-barrel Model 5200. Serial number code 'Z.'

ENGINE [Optional 5.0-Liter V-8]: Overhead valve. Cast-iron block. Displacement: 302 cid. Bore and stroke: 4.00 x 3.00 inches. Compression ratio: 8.0:1. SAE Net hp: 122. Carburetor: Motorcraft two-barrel Model 2150. Serial number code 'F.'

CHASSIS FEATURES: Wheelbase: 96.2 inches. Overall length: 175 inches. Front tread: 55.6 inches. Rear tread: 55.8 inches. Tires: Refer to text.

OPTIONS: Exterior Accent Group ($151). Select-Aire conditioning ($401). Anti-Theft alarm system ($71). Deluxe color-keyed seat belts in Ghia (standard); in other models ($51). Front and rear bumper guards ($31). Digital quartz electric clock ($37). Console ($63). Electric rear window defroster ($59). California emissions equipment ($41). Fuel monitor warning light ($14). Deck lid luggage rack ($43). Dual color-keyed outside rearview door mirrors, standard Ghia/Mach I, on others ($36). Rocker panel moldings ($14). Color-keyed vinyl insert type bodyside moldings ($51). Power steering ($111). Glass moon roof ($422). Radio, AM ($63); AM/FM ($124); AM/FM stereo ($213); same with 8-track ($333). Glamour paint ($43). Vinyl roof for hardtop coupe, standard with Ghia, on others ($83). Fold-down rear seat, standard in fastbacks, on others ($61). Leather-wrapped steering wheel

($30). Pin striping ($18). Sun roof ($195). Competition suspension, includes heavy-duty springs; adjustable shock absorbers; rear anti-roll bar; and 195/70 blackwall or White Line tires on Ghia or others with Exterior Accent Group ($43); on Mach I ($25); on others ($55). Velour cloth interior trim ($63). Flip-out rear quarter windows on fastbacks ($31). Four-speed manual transmission with floor shift (standard); Select-Shift Cruise-O-Matic ($227). Mach I 2.8-liter/171 cid V-6 engine, in Mach I (no charge); in other models ($253). 5.0-liter/302 cid V-8 engine, in Mach I ($172); in other models ($199). Traction-Lok differential ($46). Heavy-duty battery ($14). Extended range fuel tank ($18).

OPTION PACKAGES: Convenience-Group, includes dual, color-keyed, remote-controlled outside rearview door mirrors; right-hand visor/vanity mirror; inside day/night mirror; parking brake boot; and rear ashtray, with Luxury Interior Group ($48); on Mach I or models with Rallye Package or Exterior Accent Group ($29); on other models ($65). Light Group, includes underhood glovebox; ashtray; dashboard courtesy lights; plus map, 'door ajar' and 'headlamps-on' warning lights ($33). Security Lock Group, includes locking gas cap; inside hood release lock and spare tire lock ($14). Luxury Interior Group, includes Super-Soft vinyl seats; door trim with large armrests; Deluxe rear quarter trim; door courtesy lights; color-keyed seat belts; shag carpets; parking brake boot; rear ashtray and Super-Sound package ($100). Ghia Silver Luxury Group (for Ghia coupe only), includes Silver metallic paint; silver Nommande-grain half vinyl roof; stand-up hood ornament; Cranberry striping; Silver bodyside moldings; all-Cranberry interior in Media velour cloth; color-keyed sun visors and headliner, plus center console ($151). Maintenance Group, includes shop manual; bulbs; fire extinguisher; flares; warning flag; fuses; tire gauge; bungee cord; lube kit; trouble light; pliers; screwdriver; and crescent wrench ($45). Rallye Package, includes Traction-Lok differential; 195/70 raised white letter tires; extra-cooling package; bright exhaust tips; competition suspension package; dual color-keyed, remote-control outside rearview door mirrors; leather-wrapped steering wheel; and styled steel wheels with trim rings, on Mach I ($168); on 2+2 ($218); on other models ($262). Protection Group, includes door edge guards; front floor mats; and license plate frames; on Mach I ($19); on others ($27).

HISTORY: The 1975 Mustang II lineup was introduced in September 1974, with the plainer Ghia coupe and Mustang II MPG bowing at midyear. Model year production of 188,575 cars was recorded. Lee Iacocca was chief executive officer of the company this year. The new Mustang II V-8 was capable of a top speed above 105 mph and could cover the standing-start quarter-mile in 17.9 seconds with a terminal speed of 77 mph.

1976 MUSTANG

1976 Ford Mustang Cobra II 2+2 coupe. (OCW)

MUSTANG II — FOUR/V-6/V-8 — Restyled in a new smaller size in 1974, Mustang came in two basic body styles; a two-door hardtop and three-door 2+2 hatchback. The two-door was commonly referred to by Ford as a sedan rather than a coupe, which distinguished it from the old (larger) coupe design. The "three-door" model had only two doors for people, and was designated either a hatchback or fastback, both terms accurately describing the sloping lift-up rear design. Two-doors came in base or Ghia trim; fastbacks in base or Mach 1 form. Fastbacks had fold-down rear seats, while the hardtops displayed a formal-look roofline. An MPG series, carrying fewer standard items and a smaller price tag, had joined the Mustang lineup for mid-year 1975 and continued in 1976. This year's highlights include significant fuel economy gains, some new options, and a new sport exterior dress-

up package for the 2+2 and Mach 1. The former horizontal stainless steel bumper inserts were replaced by black bumper rub strips with white stripes. The wiper/washer control had moved to the turn signal lever in mid-year 1975, and continued there this year. To improve economy, Mustang II got a lower optional 2.79:1 axle ratio. An optional wide-ratio transmission was available with that rear-end ratio. New options included sporty plaid trim on seating surfaces; expanded availability of Ghia luxury coupe colors; whitewall tires; and an AM radio with stereo tape player. Styling was similar to 1975, except for a new air scoop below the front bumper. Rectangular parking/signal lamps were inset right into the forward-slanting grille, which had a 14 x 6 hole crosshatch pattern. The grille was narrower at the top than at the base, with a traditional Mustang (horse) emblem in its center. Separate 'Ford' block letters stood above the grille, facing upward. Single round headlamps were recessed into squarish housings. The front bumper protruded forward in the center, matching the width of the grille. Rub strips wrapped only slightly onto the bumper sides. Door sheetmetal had a sculptured, depressed area that began near the back and extended for a short distance on the quarter panel, following the contour of the wheel opening. The curvaceous bodyside crease ran below the door handle. Two-doors had a 'B' pillar and conventional quarter window. Fastbacks had sharply tapered quarter windows that came to a point at the rear. Each European-style taillamp consisted of three side-by-side sections, with a small backup lens at the end of each center section and larger amber turn signal lenses. Large 'Ford' block letters stood on the panel between the tail lamps, above the license plate housing. Bodies had a one-piece fiberglass-reinforced front end and color-keyed urethane-coated bumpers. Standard features included wheel lip moldings, side marker lights with die-cast bezels, recessed door handles, and slim high-luster exterior trim moldings. Inside were low-back all-vinyl front bucket seats with full-width head restraints, tachometer, speedometer, ammeter, fuel and temperature gauges, European-type armrests with integral pull handles, a two-spoke steering wheel, and lockable glovebox. Simulated burled walnut woodtone accents went on the instrument panel and shift knob. Mustang had a unitized body and chassis with front isolated mini-frame, Hotchkiss-type rear suspension, and rack-and-pinion steering. The rear suspension consisted of longitudinal semi-elliptic leaf springs (four leaves), while the independent front suspension used ball joints, a stabilizer bar, and compression-type struts. Standard engine was a 140 cu. in. (2.3-liter) four with four-speed floor shift. Optional: a 302 cu. in. (5.0-liter) V-8 with Cruise-O-Matic, or 171 cu. in. (2.8-liter) V-6 with four-speed manual. Mach 1 had the V-6 as standard. A four-speed manual gearbox became available with the V-8 later in the season. Front disc brakes were standard; power brakes (and steering) optional. Ghias included a quartz design clock, bodyside molding. BR78 x 13 steel-belted radial whitewalls, padded half or full vinyl roof, hood ornament, dual remote mirrors, crushed velour seats surfaces, full console, and bodyside paint stripes. Mach 1 added the 2.8-liter V-6, dual remote racing mirrors, BR70 x 13 raised-white-letter tires on styled steel wheels, and rear tape and fender decals. Black paint went on lower bumpers; lower bodyside; and between rear tail lamps. Ghias had wire-type wheel covers; Mach 1 included wheel trim rings. Three Luxury Groups were available: Silver, Tan Glow, and Silver Blue Glow (the latter two colors new this year). Two special option packages were offered: a new Stallion group intended to appeal to youthful buyers, and the more notorious Cobra II. The sporty silver Stallion package featured a two-tone paint and tape treatment (on fastback models); a large Stallion decal on front fenders (at the cowl); dual racing mirrors; styled steel wheels with raised-white-letter tires; and a competition suspension. Black paint highlighted the greenhouse, lower body, hood, grille, decklid, and lower back panel. On the ultimate option, large 'Cobra II' decal lettering at the door bottoms was easy to spot from a distance. Cobra II sported a black grille with cobra emblem, front air dam, simulated hood scoop, rear spoiler, and rocker-panel racing stripes. Dual wide stripes ran from the grille, over the hood and roof, onto the deck area. Front fenders displayed large cobra (snake) decals. Louvers covered the triangular flip-out quarter windows. Inside was a sport steering wheel and brushed-aluminum trim on dash and door panels, plus dual remote-control mirrors. Cobra II carried a standard V-6 engine and four-speed, with raised-white-letter tires on styled steel wheels. Only one body color scheme was offered at first: white with blue striping.

I.D. DATA: Mustang's 11-symbol Vehicle Identification Number (VIN) is stamped on a metal tab fastened to the instrument panel, visible through the windshield. The first digit is a model year code ('6' 1976). The second letter indicates assembly plant: 'F' Dearborn, MI; 'R' San Jose, CA. Digits three and four are the body serial code, which corresponds to the Model Numbers shown in the tables below: '02' 2-dr. HT; '03' 3-dr. 2+2 hatchback; '04' Ghia 2-dr HT; '05' Mach 1 3-dr 2+2 hatchback. The fifth digit is an engine code: 'Y' L4-140 2Bbl.; 'Z' V6-170 2Bbl.; 'F' V8-302 2Bbl. Finally, digits 6-11 make up the consecutive unit number, starting with 100001. A Vehicle Certification Label on the left front door lock face panel or door pillar shows the manufacturer, month and year of manufacture. GVW, GAWR, certification statement, VIN, body code, color code, trim code, axle code, transmission code, and domestic (or foreign) special order code.

1976 Ford Mustang II Stallion 2+2 coupe. (F)

1976 Ford Mustang II Ghia coupe. (F)

MUSTANG II (FOUR/V-6)

Model No.	Body/ Style No.	Body Type & Seating	Factory Price	Shipping Weight	Prod. Total
02	60F	2-dr. Notch Cpe-4P	3525/3791	2678/2756	78,508
03	69F	3-dr. 2+2 Hatch-4P	3781/4047	2706/2784	62,312

MUSTANG GHIA (FOUR/V-6)

04	60H	2-dr. Notch Cpe-4P	3859/4125	2729/2807	37,515

MUSTANG MACH 1 (V-6/V-8)

05	69R	3-dr. 2+2 Hatch-4P	4209/4154	2822/N/A	9,232

FACTORY PRICE/WEIGHT NOTE: Figures to left of slash are for four-cylinder engine, to right of slash for V-6 engine (Mach 1, V-6 and V-8). A V-8 engine on base or Ghia initially was priced $212 higher than the V-6, but later cost $54 less than a V-6.

ENGINE [Base Four]: Inline, overhead cam, four-cylinder. Cast-iron block and head. Displacement: 140 cid (2.3 liters). Bore & stroke: 3.78 x 3.13 in. Compression ratio: 9.0:1. Brake horsepower: 92 at 5000 rpm. Torque: 121 lbs.-ft. at 3000 rpm. Five main bearings. Hydraulic valve lifters. Carburetor: 2Bbl. Holley-Weber 9510. VIN Code: Y.

ENGINE [Optional V-6]: 60-degree, overhead valve V-6. Cast-iron block and head. Displacement: 170.8 cid (2.8 liters). Bore & stroke: 3.66 x 2.70 in. Compression ratio: 8.7:1. Brake horsepower: 103 at 4400 rpm. Torque: 149 lbs.-ft. at 2800 rpm. Four main bearings. Solid valve lifters. Carburetor: 2Bbl. Holley-Weber 9510. German-built. VIN Code: Z.

ENGINE [Optional V-8]: 90-degree, overhead valve V-8. Cast-iron block and head. Displacement: 302 cid (5.0 liters). Bore & stroke: 4.00 x 3.00 in. Compression ratio: 8.0:1. Brake horsepower: 134 at 3600 rpm. Torque: 247 lbs.-ft. at 1800 rpm. Five main bearings. Hydraulic valve lifters. Carburetor: 2Bbl. Motorcraft 9510. VIN Code: F.

CHASSIS DATA: Wheelbase: 96.2 in. Overall length: 175.0 in. Height: (Notch cpe) 50.0 in.; (Hatch) 49.7 in. Width: 70.2 in. Front Tread: 55.6 in. Rear Tread: 55.8 in. Wheel Size: 13 x 5 in. Standard Tires: B78 x 13 exc. (Ghia) BR78 x 13: (Mach 1) BR70 x 13 RWL SBR. Sizes CR70 x 13 and 195/70R13 were available.

TECHNICAL: Transmissions: Four-speed manual transmission (floor shift) standard. Gear ratios: (1st) 4.07:1; (2nd) 2.57:1; (3rd) 1.66:1; (4th) 1.00:1; (Rev) 3.95:1. Four-cylinder four-speed; (1st) 3.50:1; (2nd) 2.21:3; (3rd) 1.43:1; (4th) 1.00:1; (Rev) 3.38:1. Select-Shift three-speed automatic optional (initially standard on V-8). Four-cylinder: (1st) 2.47:1; (2nd) 1.47:1; (3rd) 1.00:1; (Rev) 2.11:1. V-6/V-8 automatic: (1st) 2.46:1; (2nd) 1.46:1; (3rd) 1.00:1; (Rev) 2.20:1. Standard final drive ratio: 2.79:1 w/4spd, 3.18:1 w/auto.; (V-6) 3.00:1; (V-8) 2.79:1; Steering: Rack and pinion. Front Suspension: Compression strut with lower trailing links, stabilizer bar and coil springs. Rear Suspension: Hotchkiss rigid axle w/semi-elliptic leaf springs (four leaves) and anti-sway bar. Brakes: Front disc, rear drum. Disc dia.: 9.3 in. outer, 6.2 in. inner. Drum dia.: 9.0 in. Ignition. Electronic. Body construction: Unibody w/front isolated mini-frame. Fuel tank: 13 gal.

DRIVETRAIN OPTIONS: Engines: 1.40 cid four ($272 credit from base V-6 price). Transmission/Differential: Cruise-O-Matic trans. ($239). Optional axle ratio ($13). Traction-Lok differential ($48). Brakes/Steering/Suspension: Power brakes ($54). Power steering ($117). Competition suspension ($29-$191). Other: H.D. 53-amp battery ($14). Extended-range fuel tank ($24). Engine block heater ($17). California emission system ($49).

CONVENIENCE/APPEARANCE OPTIONS: Option Packages: Cobra II pkg. ($325). Cobra II modification pkg. ($287). Rallye package: Mach 1 ($163); 22/hardtop ($267-$399). Ghia luxury group ($177). Stallion option ($72). Exterior accent group ($169). Luxury interior group ($117). Convenience group ($35). Light group ($28-$41). Protection group ($36-$43). Comfort/Convenience: Air cond. ($420). Rear defroster, electric ($70). Tinted glass ($46). Leather-wrapped steering wheel ($33). Electric clock ($17). Digital clock ($40). Fuel monitor warning light ($18). Anti-theft alarm ($83). Security lock group ($16). Horns and Mirrors: Dual-note horn ($6). Color-keyed mirrors ($42). Entertainment: AM radio ($71); w/tape player ($192). AM/FM radio ($128). AM/FM stereo radio ($173); w/tape player ($299). Exterior: Glass moonroof ($470). Manual sunroof ($230). Vinyl roof ($86). Half-vinyl roof: Ghia (NC). Glamour paint ($54). Two-tone paint/tape ($84). Pinstriping ($27). Bumper guards, front/rear ($34). color-keyed vinyl-insert bodyside molding ($60). Rocker panel moldings ($19). Pivoting rear quarter windows ($33). Decklid luggage rack ($51). Interior: Console ($71). Fold-down rear seat ($72). Velour cloth trim ($99). Color-keyed deluxe seatbelts ($17). Wheels and Tires: Cast aluminum spoke wheels ($96-$182). Forged aluminum wheels ($96-$182). Styled steel wheels: 2+2/HT ($51); Ghia (NC). Trim rings ($35). B78 x 13 BSW ($84). B78 x 13 WSW ($33-$52). BR78 x 13 BSW ($97). BR78 x 13 WSW ($33-$130). BR70 x 13 RWL ($30-$160). CR70 x 13 WSW ($10-$169). 195/70R13 WSW ($22-$191). 195/70R13 RWL ($12-$203). 195/70R13 wide WSW ($5-$208).

HISTORY: Introduced: October 3, 1975. Model year production (U.S.): 187,567. Total production for the U.S. market of 172,365 included 91,880 four-cylinder, 50,124 V-6, and 30,361 V-8 Mustangs. Calendar year production (U.S.): 183,369. Calendar year sales: 167,201. Model year sales by U.S. dealers: N/A.

HISTORY: Mustang, America's best selling small specialty car, had been outselling Monza, Starfire and Skyhawk combined. The optional V-6, also used on the imported Mercury Capri, was made in Germany. A V-8 powered Cobra II could do 0-60 MPH in around 9 seconds.

1977 MUSTANG

MUSTANG II — FOUR/V-6/V-8 — No significant styling changes were evident on Mustang for 1977, though new colors were offered and both four and V-6 engines lost power. As before, hardtop (notchback) and three-door fastback models were available. Simulated pecan replaced the burled walnut woodgrain interior appliqués. California models used a variable-venturi carburetor. Joining the option list were simulated wire wheel covers, painted cast aluminum spoke wheels, a flip-up removable sunroof, four-way manual bucket seats, and high-altitude option. The bronze-tinted glass sunroof panels could either be propped partly open, or removed completely for storage in the trunk. That T-Bar roof package included a wide black band across the top (except with the Cobra II).

Mustang's engine/transmission selection continued as before. Neither a V-6, nor a V-8 with four-speed manual gearbox was offered in California. The basic two-door hardtop carried a standard 140 cid (2.3-liter) four-cylinder engine with Dura-Spark ignition, four-speed manual gearbox, front disc brakes. color-keyed urethane bumpers, low-back bucket seats with vinyl trim, B78 x 13 tires, and full wheel covers. Bright moldings highlighted the windshield, drip rail, belt, back window and center pillar. Mustang 2+2 hatchbacks included a front spoiler at no extra cost (which could be deleted), along with a sport steering wheel, styled steel wheels, B78 x 13 bias-belted raised-white-letter or 195R/70 whitewall tires, black-out grille, and brushed aluminum instrument panel appliqués. Ghia added a half-vinyl roof, pinstripes, unique wheel covers, and bodyside moldings with color-keyed vinyl inserts. Ghia interiors could have Media Velour cloth with large armrests. Stepping up another notch, Mach 1 carried a standard 2.8-liter V-6 and sported a black paint treatment on lower bodyside and back panel. Also included: dual Mach 1 emblem, and raised-white-letter BR70 x 13 (or 195R/70) steel-belted radial tires on styled steel wheels with trim rings. Cobra II changed its look after the model year began. Big new tri-color tape stripes went on the full bodyside and front spoiler, front bumper, hood, hood scoop, decklid and rear spoiler. 'Cobra II' block lettering was low on the doors at first, later halfway up as part of the huge center bodyside tape stripe. The decklid spoiler displayed a Cobra snake decal, and another snake highlighted the black grille. Early Cobras also had snake cowl decals. Flat black greenhouse moldings, vertical-style quarter-window louvers (without the snake) and rear-window louvers also became standard. So was a narrow band of flat black along the upper doors. Cobra II equipment also included dual black sport mirrors, rear-opening hood scoop, BR70 or 195/R70 x 13 RWL tires, and brushed aluminum door trim inserts. The required power brakes cost extra. Cobra II was now offered in four color choices, not just the original white with blue striping. Selections were white body with red, blue or green stripes; or black with gold stripes. A new Rallye package included dual racing mirrors, heavy-duty springs and cooling, adjustable shocks, and rear stabilizer bar. Mustang's Sports Performance package included a 302 cid V-8 with two-barrel carb, heavy-duty four-speed manual gearbox, power steering and brakes, and P195R/70 radial tires. Ghia's Sports Group was available with black or tan body, including a vinyl roof and many color-coordinated components in black or chamois color. Also included was a three-spoke sports steering wheel, cast aluminum wheels with chamois-color spokes, and trunk luggage rack with straps and buckles. The later-arriving 2+2 Rallye Appearance Package replaced the Stallion option. It included dual gold accent stripes on hood and bodysides; flat black wiper arms, door handles, lock cylinders, and antenna; dual black sport mirrors; and argent styled steel wheels with trim rings. A gold-color surround molding highlighted the black grille (which lost its horse emblem). Also included: gold tail lamp accent moldings and dual gold accent stripes in bumper rub strips. A black front spoiler was a no-cost option. Black and Polar White body colors were offered with the package. Inside were black or white vinyl seats with gold ribbed velour Touraine cloth inserts and gold welting, and gold accent moldings on door panels.

1977 Ford Mustang II Ghia coupe. (F)

1977 Ford Mustang Cobra II 2+2 coupe. (F)

I.D. DATA: As before, Mustang's 11-symbol Vehicle Identification Number (VIN) is stamped on a metal tab fastened to the instrument panel, visible through the windshield. Coding is similar to 1976. Model year code changed to '7' for 1977.

MUSTANG II (FOUR/V-6)

Model No.	Body/Style No.	Body Type & Seating	Factory Price	Shipping Weight	Prod. Total
02	60F	2-dr. Notch Cpe-4P	3702/3984	2627/2750	67,783
03	69F	3-dr. 2+2 Hatch-4P	3901/4183	2672/2795	49,161

MUSTANG GHIA (FOUR/V-6)

04	60H	2-dr. Notch Cpe-4P	4119/4401	2667/2790	29,510

MUSTANG MACH 1 (V-6/V-8)

05	69R	3-dr. 2+2 Hatch 4P	4332/4284	2785/----	6,719

FACTORY PRICE/WEIGHT NOTE: Figures to left of slash are for four-cylinder engine, to right of slash for V-6 engine (Mach 1, V-6 and V-8). A V-8 engine on base or Ghia initially was priced $234 higher than the V-6.

PRODUCTION NOTE: Totals shown include 20,937 Mustangs produced as 1978 models. but sold as 1977 models (9,826 model 02, 7,019 model 03, 3,209 Ghia, and 883 Mach 1).

ENGINE [Base Four]: Inline, overhead cam, four-cylinder. Cast-iron block and head. Displacement: 140 cid (2.3 liters). Bore & stroke: 3.78 x 3.13 in. Compression ratio: 9.0:1. Brake horsepower: 89 at 4800 rpm. Torque: 120 lbs.-ft. at 3000 rpm. Five main bearings. Hydraulic valve lifters. Carburetor: 2Bbl. Motorcraft 5200. VIN Code: Y.

ENGINE [Optional V-6]: 60-degree, overhead valve V-6. Cast-iron block and head. Displacement: 170.8 cid (2.8 liters). Bore & stroke: 3.66 x 2.70 in. Compression ratio: 8.7:1. Brake horsepower: 93 at 4200 rpm. Torque: 140 lbs.-ft. at 2600 rpm. Four main bearings. Solid valve lifters. Carburetor: 2Bbl. Motorcraft 2150. German-built. VIN Code: Z.

ENGINE [Optional V-8]: 90-degree, overhead valve V-8. Cast-iron block and head. Displacement: 302 cid (5.0 liters). Bore & stroke: 4.00 x 3.00 in. Compression ratio: 8.4:1. Brake horsepower: 139 at 3600 rpm. Torque: 247 lbs.-ft. at 1800 rpm. Five main bearings. Hydraulic valve lifters. Carburetor: 2Bbl. Motorcraft 2150. VIN Code: F.

CHASSIS DATA: Wheelbase: 96.2 in. Overall length: 175.0 in. Height: (Notch cpe) 50.3 in.; (Hatch) 50.0 in. Width: 70.2 in. Front Tread: 55.6 in. Rear Tread: 55.8 in. Standard Tires: B78 x 13 exc. (Ghia) BR78 x 13; (Mach 1) BR70 x 13.

TECHNICAL: Transmission: Four-speed manual transmission (floor shift) standard. V-8 gear ratios: (1st) 2.64:1; (2nd) 1.89:1; (3rd) 1.34:1; (4th) 1.00:1; (Rev) 2.56:1. Four/V-6 four-speed: (1st) 3.50:1; (2nd) 2.21:1; (3rd) 1.43:1; (4th) 1.00:1; (Rev) 3.38:1. Select-Shift three-speed automatic optional. Four-cylinder: (1st) 2.47:1; (2nd) 1.47:1; (3rd) 1.00:1 (Rev) 2.11:1. V-8 automatic: (1st) 2.46:1; (2nd) 1.46:1; (3rd) 1.00:1; (Rev) 2.19:1. Standard final drive ratio: (four) 3.18:1; (V-6/V-8) 3.00:1. Steering/suspension/brakes/body: same as 1976. Fuel tank: 13 gal. exc. w/V-8, 16.5 gal.

DRIVETRAIN OPTIONS: Engines: 140 cid four ($289 credit from base V-6 price). 170 cid V-6 ($289). 302 cid V-8 ($230). Other: Cruise-O-Matic trans. ($253). Power brakes ($58). Power steering ($124). H.D. battery ($16). California emission system ($52). High-altitude emissions ($39).

CONVENIENCE/APPEARANCE OPTIONS: Option Packages: Cobra II pkg. ($535). Sports performance pkg. ($451-$607) exc. Mach 1 ($163). Rallye package ($43-$88). Ghia sports group ($422). Exterior accent group ($216). Appearance decor group ($96-$152). Luxury interior group ($124). Convenience group ($37-$71). Light group ($29-$43). Protection group ($39-$46). Comfort/Convenience: Air cond. ($446). Rear defroster, electric ($73). Tinted glass ($48). Leather-wrapped steering wheel ($35-$49). Digital clock ($42). Dual sport mirrors ($45). Entertainment: AM radio ($76); w/tape player ($204). AM/FM radio ($135). AM/FM stereo radio ($184): w/tape player ($317). Exterior: Flip-up open air roof ($147). Manual sunroof ($243). Full vinyl roof ($90). Front spoiler (NC). Metallic glow paint ($58). Pinstriping ($28). Color-keyed vinyl-insert bodyside moldings ($64). Rocker panel moldings ($20). Decklid luggage rack ($54). Interior: Console ($76). Four-way driver's seat ($33). Fold down rear seat ($77). Media velour cloth trim ($105). Color-keyed deluxe seatbelts ($18). Wheels and Tires: Wire wheel covers ($33-$86). Forged aluminum wheels ($102-$193). Lacy spoke aluminum wheels ($102-$193); white ($153-$243). Styled steel wheels ($37-$90). Trim rings ($37). B78 x 13 BSW/WSW. BR78 x 13 BSW/WSW. BR70 x 13 RWL. 195/70R13 WSW/wide WSW/RWL.

HISTORY: Introduced: October 1, 1976. Model year production (U.S.): 153,173. Total production for the U.S. market of 141,212 included 71,736 four-cylinder. 33,326 V-6. and 36,150 V-8 Mustangs. Calendar year production (U.S.): 170,315. Calendar year sales: 170,659. Model year sales by U.S. dealers: 161,513.

HISTORY: After a strong showing following the 1974 restyle, Mustang sales had begun to sag somewhat in 1975 and '76. The Cobra packages looked dramatic, and performed well enough with a V-8, but Mustang couldn't find enough customers in this form. Production declined significantly this year. A four-cylinder Mustang with manual four-speed managed a 26 MPG city/highway rating in EPA estimates.

1978 MUSTANG

1978 Ford Mustang King Cobra. (OCW)

1978 Ford Mustang coupe. (JG)

1978 Ford Mustang Cobra II 2+2 coupe. (PH)

1978-1/2 Ford Mustang II "King Cobra" coupe. (PH)

MUSTANG II — FOUR/V-6/V-8 — New colors and interior trims made up most of the changes for 1978. The 2.8-liter V-6 got a plastic cooling fan. A new electronic voltage regulator gave longer-life reliability than the old electromechanical version. New this year was optional variable-ratio power steering, first introduced on the Fairmont. New inside touches included separate back-seat cushions, revised door and seat trim, new carpeting, and new tangerine color. Six new body colors added late in the 1977 model year were carried over this time. As before, clear rectangular horizontal parking lamps were set into the crosshatch black grille. Angled outward at its base, that grille had a 14 x 6 hole pattern, with Mustang (horse) badge in the center. Separate 'Ford' letters stood above the grille. Single round headlamps continued this year. Engine choices were the same as in 1977. So were the two body styles: two-door hardtop (notchback) or 'three-door' 22 fastback (hatchback). Base and Ghia notchback models were offered; base and Mach 1 hatchbacks. Standard equipment included the 140 cid (2.3-liter) four-cylinder engine with electronic ignition, four-speed transmission, front disc brakes, rack-and-pinion steering, tachometer, and ammeter. Mustang's Cobra II package (for hatchback only) continued in the form introduced at mid-year in 1977. Tri-color tape stripes decorated bodysides and front spoiler, front bumper, hood, hood scoop, roof, decklid and rear spoiler. Huge 'Cobra' block letters went on the center bodyside tape stripe and decklid spoiler; a Cobra decal on the back spoiler; and Cobra II snake emblem on the black grille. The package also included flat black greenhouse moldings, black quarter-window and backlight louvers, black rocker panels and dual racing mirrors, a narrow black band along upper doors, rear-opening hood scoop. Rallye package, and flipper quarter windows (except with T-Roof option). Styled steel wheels with trim rings held BR70 RWL tires (195/70R with V-8, or with V-6 engine and air conditioner). King Cobra, new this year, might be viewed as a regular Cobra and more of the same, with plenty of striping and lettering. The King did without the customary bodyside striping, but sported a unique tape treatment including a giant snake decal on the hood and pinstriping on the greenhouse, decklid, wheel lips, rocker panels, belt, over-the-roof area, and around the side windows. Up front was a tough-looking spoiler. The 302 cid (5.0-liter) V-8 was standard on the King. with four-speed transmission and power brakes/steering. A 'King Cobra' nameplate went on each door and the back spoiler; '5.0L' badge on the front hood scoop. King Cobra also had rear quarter flares, a black grille and moldings, and color-keyed dual sport mirrors. Raised-white-letter tires rode lacy spoke aluminum wheels with twin rings and Cobra symbol on the hubs. A Fashion Accessory Group, aimed at women, consisted of a four-way adjustable driver's seat, striped cloth seat inserts, illuminated entry, lighted driver's vanity visor mirror, coin tray, and door pockets. It came in nine body colors. The simulated convertible T-Roof, with dual removable tinted glass panels, was now entering its first full model year as an option on the 2+2 and Mach 1 hatchbacks. Mustang's Ghia sports group came with black, blue or chamois body paint and a chamois or black vinyl half-roof, along with vinyl-insert bodyside moldings and pinstripes. Aluminum wheels had chamois-color lacy spokes. Inside was all-vinyl chamois or black seat trim, black "engine-turned" dash appliqués, and a leather-wrapped steering wheel.

I.D. DATA: As before, Mustang's 11-symbol Vehicle Identification Number (VIN) is stamped on a metal tab fastened to the instrument panel, visible through the windshield. Coding is similar to 1976-77. Model year code changed to '8' for 1978.

MUSTANG II (FOUR/V-6)

Model No.	Body/ Style No.	Body Type & Seating	Factory Price	Shipping Weight	Prod. Total
02	60F	2-dr. Notch Cpe-4P	3555/3768	2608/2705	81,304
03	69F	3-dr. 2+2 Hatch-4P	3798/4011	2654/2751	68,408

MUSTANG GHIA (FOUR/V-6)

04	60H	2-dr. Notch Cpe-4P	3972/4185	2646/2743	34,730

MUSTANG MACH 1 (V-6/V-8)

Model No.	Body/ Style No.	Body Type & Seating	Factory Price	Shipping Weight	Prod. Total
05	69R	3-dr. 2+2 Hatch-4P	4253/4401	2733/----	7,968

FACTORY PRICE/WEIGHT NOTE: Figures to left of slash are for four-cylinder engine, to right of slash for V-6 engine (Mach 1, V-6 and V-8). A V-8 engine on base or Ghia initially was priced $148 higher than the V-6.

PRODUCTION NOTE: Totals shown do not include 20,937 Mustangs produced as 1978 models, but sold as 1977 models (see note with 1977 listing).

ENGINE [Base Four]: Inline, overhead cam, four-cylinder. Cast-iron block and head. Displacement: 140 cid (2.3 liters). Bore & stroke: 3.78 x 3.13 in. Compression ratio: 9.0:1. Brake horsepower: 88 at 4800 rpm. Torque: 118 lbs.-ft. at 2800 rpm. Five main bearings. Hydraulic valve lifters. Carburetor: 2Bbl. Motorcraft 5200. VIN Code: Y.

ENGINE [Optional V-6]: 60-degree, overhead valve V-6. Cast-iron block and head. Displacement: 170.8 cid (2.8 liters). Bore & stroke: 3.66 x 2.70 in. Compression ratio: 8.7:1. Brake horsepower: 90 at 4200 rpm. Torque: 143 lbs.-ft. at 2200 rpm. Four main bearings. Solid valve lifters. Carburetor: 2Bbl. Motorcraft 2150. German-built. VIN Code: Z.

ENGINE [Optional V-8]: 90-degree, overhead valve V-8. Cast-iron block and head. Displacement: 302 cid (5.0 liters). Bore & stroke: 4.00 x 3.00 in. Compression ratio: 8.4:1. Brake horsepower: 139 at 3600 rpm. Torque: 250 lbs.-ft. at 1600 rpm. Five main bearings. Hydraulic valve lifters. Carburetor: 2Bbl. Motorcraft 2150. VIN Code: F.

CHASSIS DATA: Wheelbase: 96.2 in. Overall length: 175.0 in. Height: (Notch cpe) 50.3 in.; (Hatch) 50.0 in. Width: 70.2 in. Front Tread: 55.6 in. Rear Tread: 55.8 in. Standard Tires: B78 x 13 exc. (Ghia) BR78 x 13 SBR; (Mach 1) BR70 x 13 SBR RWL.

TECHNICAL: Transmission: Four-speed manual transmission (floor shift) standard. V-8 gear ratios: (1st) 2.64:1; (2nd) 1.89:1; (3rd) 1.34:1; (4th) 1.00:1; (Rev) 2.56:1. Four-cylinder four-speed: (1st) 3.50:1; (2nd) 2.21:1; (3rd) 1.43:1; (4th) 1.00:1; (Rev) 3.38:1. V-6 four-speed: (1st) 4.07:1; (2nd) 2.57:1; (3rd) 1.66:1; (4th) 1.00:1; (Rev) 3.95:1. Select-Shift three-speed automatic optional. Four-cylinder: (1st) 2.47:1; (2nd) 1.47:1; (3rd) 1.00:1; (Rev) 2.11:1. V-6/V-8 automatic: (1st) 2.46:1; (2nd) 1.46:1; (3rd) 1.00:1; (Rev) 2.19:1. Standard final drive ratio: (four) 3.18:1 (V-6) 3.00:1 w/4spd, 3.40:1 w/auto.; (V-8) 2.79:1. Steering/suspension/brakes/body: same as 1976-77. Fuel tank: 13 gal. exc. w/V-8 engine, 16.5 gal.

DRIVETRAIN OPTIONS: Engine/Transmission: 140 cid four ($213 credit from base V-6 price). 170 cid V-6 ($213). 302 cid V-8 ($361) exc. Mach 1 ($148). Cruise-O-Matic trans. ($281). Brakes/Steering: Power brakes ($64). Power steering ($131). Other: Engine block heater ($12). California emission system ($69). High-altitude emissions (NC).

CONVENIENCE/APPEARANCE OPTIONS: Option Packages: Cobra II pkg.: hatch ($677-$700). King Cobra pkg.: hatch ($1253). Fashion accessory pkg.: 2-dr. ($207). Rally package ($43-$93). Rally appearance pkg. ($163). Ghia sports group ($361). Exterior accent group: pinstripes, wide bodyside moldings, dual remote sport mirrors, and whitewalls on styled wheels ($163-$245). Appearance decor group: lower body two-tone, pinstripes, styled wheels, brushed aluminum dash appliqué ($128-$167). Luxury interior group ($149-$155). Convenience group: interval wipers, vanity and day/night mirrors, and pivoting rear quarter windows on hatchback ($34-$81). Light group ($40-$52). Appearance protection group ($24-$36). Comfort/Convenience: Air cond. ($459). Rear defroster, electric ($77). Tinted glass ($53). Leather-wrapped steering wheel ($34-$49). Digital clock ($43). Lighting and Mirrors: Trunk light ($4). Color-keyed driver's sport mirror ($16). Dual sport mirrors ($49). Day/night mirror ($7) Entertainment: AM radio ($72); w/tape player ($192). AM/FM radio ($120). AM/FM stereo radio ($161); w/8 track or cassette tape player ($229). Exterior: T-Roof 'convertible' option ($587-$629). Flip-up open air roof ($167). Full vinyl roof ($99). Front spoiler ($8). Metallic glow paint ($40). Pinstriping ($30). Color-keyed bodyside moldings ($66). Rocker panel moldings ($22). Bumper guards, front and rear ($37). Lower bodyside protection ($30). Interior: Console ($75). Four-way driver's seat ($33). Fold-down rear seat ($90). Wilshire cloth trim ($100). Ashton cloth/vinyl trim ($12). Color-keyed deluxe seatbelts ($18). Wheels and Tires: Rear wheel covers ($12-$90). Forged aluminum wheels ($173-$252); white ($187-$265). Lacy spoke aluminum wheels ($173-$252); white ($187-$265). Styled steel wheels ($59-$78). Trim rings ($39). B78 x 13 WSW. BR78 x 13 BSW/WSW. BR70 x 13 RWL. 195/70R13 WSW/wide WSW/RWL.

HISTORY: Introduced: October 7, 1977. Model year production: 192,410. Total production for the U.S. market of 173,423 units included 85,312 four-cylinder, 57,060 V-6, and 31,051 V-8 Mustangs. Calendar year production: 240,162. Calendar year sales by U.S. dealers: 199,760. Model year sales by U.S. dealers: 179,039.

HISTORY: This would be the final year for Mustang II, as an all-new Mustang was planned for 1979. Although plenty of Mustangs were built during the 1974-78 period, Cobra II production was modest. King Cobra, offered only for 1978, is the rarest of the lot.

1979 MUSTANG

1979 Ford Mustang Cobra. (OCW)

1979 Ford Mustang 5.0L Sport Option coupe. (F)

MUSTANG — FOUR/V-6/SIX/V-8 — All-new sheetmetal created what appeared to be an all-new Mustang for 1979. Its chassis came from Fairmont, though, shortened and modified to hold the new body metal. The familiar curved crease in the bodyside was gone. At a time when most cars were shrinking, the new Mustang managed to gain 4 inches in length and 20 percent more passenger space. Soft urethane bumpers added to the illusion of length. Weight was down by some 200 pounds, however. The aerodynamic wedge design featured a sloping front and hood, and sculptured roofline. A lowered window line gave Mustang large glass area for improved visibility. As in the prior version, two door notchback and three door hatchback bodies were offered in base and Ghia levels. There was also a Sport package, and a high-performance TRX package. As before Ford generally referred to the two door as a sedan while the third door of the "three door" was a hatch rather than an entry for people. The new hatchback did not have the sharply-angled fastback shape of the former Mustang. The notchback two-door did look more like a sedan than its predecessor, though enthusiasts still tend to view it as a coupe (especially since a convertible would appear on that body a few years later). Mercury Capri was similar but offered only in hatchback form. Both bodies had sail-shaped quarter windows that were wider at the base, but the hatchback's were much narrower at the top, almost triangle-shaped. Both models had a set of tall louver-like ribs formed in a tapered panel on the 'C' pillar. angled to match the quarter window's rear edge, but the hatchback had one more of them. Staggered, recessed quad rectangular headlamps replaced the former single round units. The outer units sat a little farther back than the inner pair. The new black crosshatch grille (with 10 x 5 hole pattern) angled forward at the base and no longer held a Mustang badge. It did have 'Ford' lettering at the driver's side. Rectangular amber parking/signal lamps were mounted in the bumper, just below the outboard headlamps. Narrow amber front side marker lenses followed the angle of front fender tips. Well below the front bumper was an air scoop with five holes. On the hood, above the grille, was a round tri-color Mustang emblem. A '2.8' or '5.0' badge on front fenders, at the cowl ahead of the door, denoted a V-6 or V-8 engine under the hood. Tail lamps were wider than before, now wrapping around each quarter panel. In addition to the German-built 170 cid (2.8-liter) V-6 and 302 cid (5.0-liter) V-8. both carried over from 1978, there was a new engine option: a turbocharged 140 cid (2.3-liter) four. Base engine remained a non-turbo four. Later in the year, Ford's inline six replaced the V-6 as first option above the base model. The turbo was also optional in other Mustangs. A V-8 model could have a new four-speed manual overdrive transmission, with "peppy" 3.07:1 first gear and 0.70:1 overdrive. A single (serpentine) belt now drove engine accessories. Mustangs new front suspension used a hydraulic shock strut to replace the conventional upper arm. Rear suspension was a new four-bar link-and-coil system, replacing the old leaf-

1979 Ford Mustang hatchback coupe. (OCW)

1979 Ford Mustang notchback. (OCW)

spring Hotchkiss design. Two handling/suspension options were offered. The basic handling suspension with 14-inch radial tires included different spring rates and shock valving, stiffer bushings in front suspension and upper arm in the rear, and a special rear stabilizer bar. The second level package came with a Michelin TRX tire option, an ultra-low aspect ratio tire (390 MM) introduced on the European Granada. Its 15.35 inch size demanded special metric wheels. That package also included unique shock valving, increased spring rates, and wider front/rear stabilizer bars. All Mustangs had full instruments including tachometer, trip odometer, and gauges for fuel, oil pressure, alternator and temperature, Mustangs also had bucket seats, simulated woodgrain instrument panel appliqué, and stalk-mounted controls for horn, headlamp dimmer, and wiper/washer. At the chassis, standard equipment included rack-and-pinion steering, manual front disc brakes, and a front stabilizer bar. Also standard: vinyl door trim with carpeted lower panel, squeeze-open lockable glovebox, day/night mirror, lighter, black remote driver's mirror, and full wheel covers. Fastbacks had black rocker panel moldings, full wraparound bodyside moldings with dual accent stripe insert, and semi-styled wheels with black sport hub covers and trim rings. Quite a few options joined the list, including a sport-tuned exhaust, cruise control, tilt steering, leather seat trim, and interval windshield wipers. Ghia Mustangs used many color-keyed components including dual remote-control mirrors, quarter louvers, and bodyside molding inserts. Ghia also had turbine-style wheel covers, BR78 x 14 radial tires, pin stripes, body-color window frames, a 'Ghia' badge on decklid or hatch, low-back bucket seats with European-type headrests, and convenience pockets in color-keyed door panels. Interiors came in six leather colors and five of soft cloth. The costly ($1173) Cobra package included a 2.3-liter turbocharged four, turbo hood scoop with 'Turbo' nameplate, 190/65R x 390 TRX tires on metric forged aluminum wheels, and special suspension. A 302 cid V-8 was available instead of the turbo. Cobras had blacked-out greenhouse trim, black lower bodyside tape treatment, and wraparound bodyside moldings with dual color-keyed inserts. Also included: color-keyed grille and quarter louvers, dual sport mirrors, black bumper rub strips with dual color-keyed inserts,

an 8000 rpm. tachometer, engine-turned instrument cluster panel, sport-tuned exhaust, and bright tailpipe extension. Rocker panel moldings were deleted. Optional hood graphics cost $78 extra.

I.D. DATA: Mustang's 11-symbol Vehicle Identification Number (VIN) is stamped on a metal tab fastened to the instrument panel, visible through the windshield. The first digit is a model year code ('9' 1979). The second letter indicates assembly plant: 'F' Dearborn, MI; 'R' San Jose, CA. Digits three and four are the body serial code, which corresponds to the Model Numbers shown in the tables below: '02' 2-dr. notchback; '03' 3-dr. hatchback; '04' Ghia 2-dr. notchback; '05' Ghia 3-dr. hatchback. The fifth digit is an engine code 'Y' L4-140 2Bbl.; 'W' turbo L4-140 2Bbl.; 'Z' V6-170 2Bbl.; 'T' L6-200 (late); 'F' V8-302 2Bbl. Finally, digits 6-11 make up the consecutive unit number, starting with 100001. A Vehicle Certification Label on the left front door lock face panel or door pillar shows the manufacturer, month and year of manufacture, GVW, GAWR, certification statement, VIN, and codes for body type, color. trim, axle, transmission, and special order data.

MUSTANG (FOUR/V-6)

Model No.	Body/ Style No.	Body Type & Seating	Factory Price	Shipping Weight	Prod. Total
02	66B	2-dr. Notch-4P	4071/4344	2431/2511	156,666
03	61R	3-dr. Hatch-4P	4436/4709	2451/2531	120.535

MUSTANG GHIA (FOUR/V-6)

Model No.	Body/ Style No.	Body Type & Seating	Factory Price	Shipping Weight	Prod. Total
04	66H	2-dr. Notch-4P	4642/4915	2539/2619	56,351
05	61H	3-dr. Hatch-4P	4824/5097	2548/2628	36,384

PRODUCTION NOTE: Approximately 6,000 Indy Pace Car Replicas were built, offered for sale at mid-year.

FACTORY PRICE/WEIGHT NOTE: Figures to left of slash are for four-cylinder engine, to right of slash for V-6 engine. A V-8 engine was priced $241 higher than the V-6.

ENGINE [Base Four]: Inline, overhead cam, four-cylinder. Cast-iron block and head. Displacement: 140 cid (2.3 liters). Bore & stroke: 3.78 x 3.13 in. Compression ratio: 9.0:1 Brake horsepower: 88 at 4800 rpm. Torque: 118 lbs.-ft. at 2800 rpm. Five main bearings. Hydraulic valve lifters. Carburetor: 2Bbl. Motorcraft 5200. VIN Code: Y.

ENGINE [Turbo Four]: Same as 140 cid four above, but with turbocharger Brake H.P.: 140 at 4800 rpm. Torque: N/A. Carburetor: 2Bbl. Holley 6500. VIN Code: W

1979 Ford Mustang "Pace Car Replica" coupe. (PH)

1979 Ford Mustang Cobra hatchback coupe (turbocharged). (OCW)

ENGINE [Optional V-6]: 60-degree, overhead valve V-6. Cast-iron block and head. Displacement: 170.8 cid (2.8 liters). Bore & stroke: 3.66 x 2.70 in. Compression ratio: 8.7:1. Brake horsepower 109 at 4800 rpm. Torque: 142 lbs.-ft. at 2800 rpm. Four main bearings. Solid valve lifters. Carburetor: 2Bbl. Ford 2150 or Motorcraft 2700VV. German-built. VIN Code: Z.

NOTE: A 200 cid inline six became optional late in the model year; see 1980 listing for specifications.

ENGINE [Optional V-8]: 90-degree. overhead valve V 8. Cast-iron block and head. Displacement: 302 cid (5.0 liters). Bore & stroke: 4.00 x 3.00 in. Compression ratio: 8.4:1. Brake horsepower 140 at 3600 rpm. Torque: 250 lbs.-ft. at 1800 rpm. Five main bearings. Hydraulic valve lifters. Carburetor: 2Bbl. Motorcraft 2150. VIN Code: F.

CHASSIS DATA: Wheelbase: 100.4 in. Overall length: 179.1 in. Height: 51.8 in. Width 69.1 in. Front Tread: 56.6 in. Rear Tread: 57.0 in. Standard Tires: B78 x 13 BSW exc. (Ghia) BR78 x 14 SBR BSW.

TECHNICAL: Transmission: Four-speed manual (floor shift) standard on four-cylinder. Gear ratios: (1st) 3.98:1; (2nd) 2.14:1; (3rd) 1.42:1; (4th) 1.00:1; (Rev) 3.99:1. Turbo four speed: (1st) 4.07:1; (2nd) 2.57:1; (3rd) 1.66:1; (4th) 1.00:1; (Rev) 3.95:1. Four-speed overdrive manual transmission standard on V-8. Gear ratios: (1st) 3.07:1; (2nd) 1.72:1; (3rd) 1.00:1; (4th) 0.70:1; (Rev) 3.07:1. SelectShift three-speed automatic optional. Four cylinder: (1st) 2.47:1; (2nd) 1.47:1; (3rd) 1.00:1; (Rev) 2.11:1. V-6/V-8 automatic: (1st) 2.46:1; (2nd) 1.46:1; (3rd) 1.00:1; (Rev) 2.18:1 or 2.19:1. Standard final drive ratio: 308:1 except 3.45:1 w/turbo, 2.47:1 w/V-8 and auto. (early models differed). Steering: Rack and pinion. Front Suspension: Modified MacPherson hydraulic shock struts with coil springs and stabilizer bar. Rear Suspension: Four-bar link and coil spring system: anti-sway bar with V-8. Brakes: Front disc, rear drum. Disc dia.: 9.3 in. (10.4 in. w/V-8). Rear drum dia.: 9 in. Ignition: Electronic. Body construction: unibody w/front isolated mini-frame. Fuel tank 11.5 gal. exc with V-6/V-8 engine, 12.5 gal.

DRIVETRAIN OPTIONS: Engine/Transmission Turbo 140 cid four ($542). 170 cu. in V-6 ($273). 302 cid V-8 ($514). Sport-tuned exhaust ($34). Automatic trans. ($307). Brakes & Steering: Power brakes ($70). Variable-ratio power steering ($141) Other: Handling suspension ($33). Engine block heater ($13). H.D. battery ($18). California emission system ($76). High-altitude emissions ($33).

CONVENIENCE/APPEARANCE OPTIONS: Option Packages: Cobra pkg. ($1173). Cobra hood graphics ($78), Sport option ($175). Exterior accent group ($72). Interior accent group ($108-$120). Light group ($25-$37). Protection group ($33-$36). Power lock group ($99). Comfort/Convenience: Air cond. ($484). Rear defroster, electric ($84) Fingertip speed control ($104-$116). Tinted glass ($59); windshield only ($25). Leather wrapped steering wheel ($41-$53). Tilt steering wheel ($69-$81). Interval wipers ($35). Rear wiper/washer ($63). Lighting and Mirrors: Trunk light ($5). Driver's remote mirror ($18). Dual remote mirrors ($52). Entertainment: AM radio ($72); w/digital clock ($119); w/tape player ($192). AM/FM radio ($120). AM/FM stereo radio ($176): w/8 track or cassette tape player ($243). Premium sound system ($67). Dual rear speakers ($42) Radio flexibility option ($90). Exterior: Flip-up open air roof ($199). Full vinyl roof ($102). Metallic glow paint ($41). Lower two-tone paint ($78). Bodyside/decklid pinstripes ($30). Wide bodyside moldings ($66). Narrow vinyl-insert bodyside moldings ($39). Rocker panel moldings ($24). Mud/stone deflectors ($23). Lower bodyside protection ($30). Interior: Console ($140). Four-way driver's seat ($35). Cloth seat trim ($20). Ghia cloth seat trim ($42). Accent cloth seat trim ($29). Leather seat trim ($282). Front floor mats ($18). Color-keyed deluxe seatbelts ($26). Wheels and Tires: Wire wheel covers ($60-$99). Turbine wheel covers ($10-$39). Forged metric aluminum wheels ($259-$298). Cast aluminum wheels ($251-$289). Styled steel wheels w/trim rings ($55-$94). B78 x 13 WSW ($43). C78 x 13 BSW ($25): WSW ($69). B78 x 14 WSW ($66). C78 x 14 BSW ($48). BR78 x 14 BSW ($124); WSW ($43 $167). CR78 x 14 WSW ($69-$192); RWL ($86-$209). TRX 190/65R 390 Michelin BSW ($117-$241). Tire Note: Lower prices are for Mustang Ghia.

HISTORY: Introduced; October 6, 1978. Model year production: 369,936 Total production for the U.S. market of 332,024 units included 181,066 four-cylinder (29,242 with turbocharger), 103,390 sixes, and 47,568 V-8 Mustangs. Calendar year production; 365,357. Calendar year sales by U.S. dealers: 304,053. Model year sales by U.S. dealers: 302,309.

HISTORY: If the second-generation Mustang had lacked some of the pizzazz of the original pony car, the "new breed" third-generation edition offered a chance to boost the car's image. The optional turbocharged 2.3-liter four was said to offer "V-8 performance without sacrificing fuel economy." In Ford tests, the Mustang turbo went 0-55 MPH in just over 8 seconds (a little quicker than a V-8). Gas mileage reached well into the 20s. A V-8 version was named pace car for the Indy 500, prompting the production of a Pace Car Replica later in the year. Ready for the 1980s, Mustang now offered a pleasing blend of American and European design. Of many styling proposals, the final one came from a team led by Jack Telnack of the Light Truck and Car Design Group. Plastic

and aluminum components helped cut down the car's weight, and it was considerably roomier inside than the former Mustang II. Drag coefficient of 0.44 (for the fastback) was the best Ford had ever achieved. Customers must have liked the new version, as Mustang leaped from No. 22 to No. 7 in the sales race.

1980 MUSTANG

1980 Ford Mustang carriage top. (FMC)

1980 Ford Mustang Sport Option coupe. (JG)

1980 Ford Mustang Cobra hatchback coupe (turbocharged). (PH)

MUSTANG — FOUR/SIX/V-8 — Appearance of the modern, resized Mustang changed little in its second season, except for a new front/rear look on the sporty Cobra model. Two-door notchbacks also had an aerodynamic revision to their decklids. Mustang's tail lamps consisted of five sections on each side, plus a backup lens section inboard (toward the license plate). A larger section at the outside wrapped around onto each quarter panel. Decklids held 'Ford' and 'Mustang' lettering. Bodyside moldings stretched all the way around the car, meeting bumper strips. Body striping came down ahead of the front marker lenses. Four-cylinder models had no fender identifier; others were marked with a liter figure. Base and Ghia models were offered again, in notchback or hatchback form. Base notchbacks had black bumper rub strips; hatchback bumpers had dual argent stripe inserts. Hatchbacks also had full wraparound. wide black bodyside moldings with dual argent inserts. Both models carried high-back vinyl bucket seats. Notchback rear pillar louvers were color-keyed, while the hatchback's were black. Ghia added low-back bucket seats with Euro-style headrests, a roof assist handle, color-keyed window frames, dual remote mirrors, pin striping, 14-inch tires, turbine wheel covers, and Ghia insignia on decklid or hatch. Available again was the Cobra option, raised in price to $1482. Cobra's slat-style three-hole grille, hood scoop (with simulated rear opening), front air dam (with built-in foglamps) and rear spoiler were restyled with the '79 Indy Pace Car replica in mind. Cobra's tape treatment was also revised, and it carried the TRX suspension. Features included black lower Tu-Tone treatment, special bodyside and quarter window taping, dual black sport mirrors, sport-tuned exhaust with bright tailpipe extension, black bumper rub strips. 190/65R x 390 TRX tires on forged metric aluminum wheels, engine-turned instrument cluster panel with Cobra medallion, bodyside molding with dual color-keyed accent stripes, 8000 rpm. tach and the turbo engine. 'Cobra' lettering went on quarter windows. A 255 cid (4.2-liter) V-8 replaced the former 302, but engines were otherwise the same as before. The 200 cid (3.3-liter) inline six had replaced the former V-6 as a powerplant option during 1979. Both the non-turbocharged 2.3-liter four and inline six could have a four-speed manual gearbox (overdrive fourth with the six), while all engines could have automatic. All models now had high-pressure P-metric radial tires and halogen headlamps. Maintenance-free batteries were standard, and radios added a Travelers' Advisory Band. Semi-metallic front disc brake pads were included with optional engines. Two suspension options were available: The standard package and a modified "Special Suspension System" that included Michelin TRX tires on special forged aluminum wheels. A new Carriage Roof option for the notchback model was supposed to resemble a convertible, even though the car had a solid 'B' pillar. It used diamond-grain vinyl. Other new options included a roof luggage rack, cargo area cover (hatchback), liftback window louvers, and Recaro adjustable seatback bucket seats with improved thigh support. Inside door handles were relocated to the upper door.

I.D. DATA: As before, Mustang's 11-symbol Vehicle Identification Number (VIN) is stamped on a metal tab fastened to the instrument panel, visible through the windshield. Engine codes changed this year. The first digit is a model year code ('O' 1980). The second letter indicates assembly plant: 'F' Dearborn, MI; 'R' San Jose, CA. Digits three and four are the body serial code, which corresponds to the Model Numbers shown in the tables below: '02' 2-dr. notchback; '03' 3-dr. hatchback; '04' Ghia 2-dr. notchback; '05' Ghia 3-dr. hatchback. The fifth digit is an engine code: 'A' L4-140 2Bbl.; 'A' turbo L4-140 2Bbl.; 'T' L6-200 1Bbl.; 'D' V8-255 2Bbl. Finally, digits 6-11 make up the consecutive unit number, starting with 100001. A Vehicle Certification Label on the left front door lock face panel or door pillar shows the manufacturer, month and year of manufacture, GVW, GAWR, certification statement, VIN, and codes for body type and color, trim, axle, transmission, and special order information.

MUSTANG (FOUR/SIX)

Model No.	Body/ Style No.	Body Type & Seating	Factory Price	Shipping Weight	Prod. Total
02	66B	2-dr. Notch-4P	4884/5103	2497/2532	128,893
03	61R	3-dr. Spt Hatch-4P	5194/5413	2531/2566	98,497

MUSTANG GHIA (FOUR/SIX)

04	66H	2-dr. Notch-4P	5369/5588	2565/2600	23,647
05	61H	3-dr. Hatch-4P	5512/5731	2588/2623	20,285

FACTORY PRICE/WEIGHT NOTE: Figures to left of slash are for four-cylinder engine, to right of slash for six-cylinder. A V-8 engine cost $119 more than the six.

ENGINE [Base Four]: Inline, overhead cam, four-cylinder. Cast-iron block and head. Displacement: 140 cid (2.3 liters). Bore & stroke: 3.78 x 3.13 in. Compression ratio: 9.0:1. Brake horsepower: 88 at 4600 rpm. Torque: 119 lbs.-ft. at 2600 rpm. Five main bearings. Hydraulic valve lifters. Carburetor: 2Bbl. Motorcraft 5200. VIN Code: A.

ENGINE [Turbo Four]: Same as 140 cid four above, but with turbocharger. Brake H.P.: 150 at 4800 rpm. Torque: N/A. Carburetor: 2Bbl. Holley 6500.

ENGINE [Optional Six]: Inline, overhead valve six-cylinder. Cast-iron block and head. Displacement: 200 cid (3.3 liters). Bore & stroke: 3.68 x 3.13 in. Compression ratio: 8.6:1. Brake horsepower: N/A. Torque: N/A. Seven main bearings. Hydraulic valve lifters. Carburetor: 2Bbl. Holley 1946. VIN Code: T.

ENGINE [Optional V-8]: 90-degree, overhead valve V-8. Cast-iron block and head. Displacement: 255 cid (4.2 liters). Bore & stroke: 3.68 x 3.00 in. Compression ratio: 8.8:1. Brake horsepower: 119 at 3800 rpm. Torque: 194 lbs.-ft. at 2200 rpm. Five main bearings. Hydraulic valve lifters. Carburetor: 2Bbl. Motorcraft 2150. VIN Code: D.

CHASSIS DATA: Wheelbase: 100.4 in. Overall length: 179.1 in. Height: 51.4 in. Width: 69.1 in. Front Tread: 56.6 in. Rear Tread: 57.0 in. Standard Tires: P185/80R13 BSW exc. (Ghia) P175/75R14.

TECHNICAL: Transmission: Four-speed manual (floor shift) standard on four-cylinder. Gear ratios: (1st) 3.98:1. (2nd) 2.14:1; (3rd) 1.42:1; (4th) 1.00:1; (Rev) 3.99:1. Turbo four-speed: (1st) 4.07:1; (2nd) 2.57:1; (3rd) 1.66:1; (4th) 1.00:1; (Rev) 3.95:1. Four-speed overdrive manual transmission standard on six. Gear ratios: (1st) 3.29:1; (2nd) 1.84:1; (3rd) 1.00:1;

(4th) 0.81:1; (Rev) 3.29:1. SelectShift three-speed automatic optional. Four-cylinder: (1st) 2.47:1; (2nd) 1.47:1; (3rd) 1.00:1; (Rev) 2.11:1. Turbo/six/V-8 automatic: (1st) 2.46:1; (2nd) 1.46:1; (3rd) 1.00:1; (Rev) 2.19:1. Standard final drive ratio: 3.08:1 w/four, 2.26:1 w/V-8 and auto., 3.45:1 w/turbo; Steering: Rack and pinion. Front Suspension: Modified MacPherson hydraulic shock struts with coil springs and stabilizer bar. Rear Suspension: Four-bar link and coil spring system. Brakes: Front disc, rear drum. Ignition: Electronic. Body construction: Unibody w/front isolated mini-frame. Fuel tank: 11.5 gal. exc. w/V-8 engine, 12.5 gal.

DRIVETRAIN OPTIONS: Engine/Transmission: Turbo 140 cid four ($481). 200 cid six ($219). 255 cid V-8 ($338) exc. w/Cobra pkg. ($144 credit). Sport-tuned exhaust: V-8 ($38). Select Shift automatic trans. ($340). Optional axle ratio ($18). Brakes & Steering: Power brakes ($78). Power steering ($160). Other: Handling suspension ($35). Engine block heater ($15). H.D. battery ($20). California emission system ($253). High-altitude emissions ($36).

CONVENIENCE/APPEARANCE OPTIONS: Option Packages: Cobra pkg. ($1482). Cobra hood graphics ($88). Sport option: black rocker/belt moldings and door/window frames, full wraparound bodyside molding with dual argent stripe insert, sport wheel trim rings and steering wheel ($168-$186). Exterior accent group ($63). Interior accent group ($120-$134). Light group ($41). Appearance protection group ($38-$41). Power lock group ($113). Comfort/Convenience: Air cond. ($583). Rear defroster, electric ($96). Fingertip speed control ($116-$129). Tinted glass ($65); windshield only ($29). Leather-wrapped steering wheel ($44-$56). Tilt steering wheel ($78-$90). Interval wipers ($39). Rear wiper/washer ($79). Lighting and Mirrors: Trunk light ($5). Driver's remote mirror ($19). Dual remote mirrors ($58). Entertainment: AM radio ($93). AM/FM radio ($145). AM/FM stereo radio ($183); w/8 track tape player ($259); w/cassette player ($271). Premium sound system ($94). Dual rear speakers ($38). Radio flexibility option ($63). Exterior: Flip-up open air roof ($204-$219). Carriage roof ($625). Full vinyl roof ($118). Metallic glow paint ($46). Lower two-tone paint ($88). Bodyside/decklid pinstripes ($34). Accent tape stripes ($19-$53). Hood scoop ($31). Liftgate louvers ($141). Narrow vinyl-insert bodyside moldings ($43); wide ($74). Rocker panel moldings ($30). Roof luggage rack ($86). Mud/stone deflectors ($25). Lower bodyside protection ($34). Interior: Console ($166). Four-way driver's seat ($38). Recaro high-back bucket seats ($531). Cloth/vinyl bucket seats ($21-$46). Vinyl low-back bucket seats (NC). Accent cloth/vinyl seat trim ($30). Leather low-back bucket seats ($345). Cargo area cover ($44). Front floor mats ($19). Color-keyed seatbelts ($23). Wheels and Tires: Wire wheel covers ($79-$121). Turbine wheel covers ($10-$43). Forged aluminum wheels ($313-$355). Cast aluminum wheels ($279-$321). Styled steel wheels w/trim rings ($61-$104). P185/80R13 WSW ($50). P175/75R14 BSW ($25); WSW ($50-$75). P185/75R14 BSW ($25-$49); WSW ($75-$100); RWL ($92-$117). TRX 190/65 390 BSW ($125-$250).

HISTORY: Introduced: October 12, 1979. Model year production: 271,322. Total production for the U.S. market of 241,064 units included 162,959 four-cylinder (12,052 with turbocharger), 71,597 sixes, and 6,508 V-8 Mustangs. Calendar year production: 232,517. Calendar year sales by U.S. dealers: 225,290. Model year sales by U.S. dealers: 246,008.

HISTORY: Mustang's base 2.3-liter four-cylinder engine was said to deliver an ample boost in gas mileage this year. Short supplies of the German-made V-6 had prompted Ford to switch to the familiar inline six during the 1979 model year. After a whopping sales increase for 1979, Mustang slackened this year. Still, most observers felt the new model showed a vast improvement over the Mustang II and would give Ford another strong hold on the pony car market.

1981 MUSTANG

1981 Ford Mustang T-top coupe. (F)

1981 Ford Mustang notchback. (PH)

1981 Ford Mustang hatchback coupe (with "air roof" option). (PH)

MUSTANG (FOUR/SIX)

Model No.	Body/ Style No.	Body Type & Seating	Factory Price	Shipping Weight	Prod. Total
10	66B	2-dr. Notch-4P	6171/6384	2524/2551	77,458
15	61R	3-dr. Spt Hatch-4P	6408/6621	2544/2571	77,399

MUSTANG GHIA (FOUR/SIX)

12	66H	2-dr. Notch-4P	6645/6858	2558/2585	13,422
13	61H	3-dr. Hatch-4P	6729/6942	2593/2620	14,273

FACTORY PRICE/WEIGHT NOTE: Figures to left of slash are for four-cylinder engine, to right of slash for six-cylinder engine. A V-8 engine was priced $50 higher than the six.

ENGINE [Base Four]: Inline, overhead cam, four-cylinder. Cast-iron block and head. Displacement: 140 cid (2.3 liters). Bore & stroke: 3.78 x 3.13 in. Compression ratio: 9.0:1. Brake horsepower: 88 at 4600 rpm. Torque: 118 lbs.-ft. at 2600 rpm. Five main bearings. Hydraulic valve lifters. Carburetor: 2Bbl. Motorcraft 5200 or Holley 6500. VIN Code: A.

ENGINE [Turbo Four]: Same as 140 cid four above, but with turbocharger Brake H.P.: N/A. Torque: N/A.

ENGINE [Optional Six]: Inline, overhead valve six-cylinder. Cast-iron block and head. Displacement: 200 cid (3.3 liters). Bore & stroke: 3.68 x 3.13 in. Compression ratio: 8.6:1. Brake horsepower: 94 at 4000 rpm. Torque: 158 lbs.-ft. at 1400 rpm. Seven main bearings. Hydraulic valve lifters. Carburetor: 2Bbl. Holley 1946. VIN Code: T.

ENGINE [Optional V-8]: 90-degree, overhead valve V-8. Cast-iron block and head. Displacement: 255 cid (4.2 liters). Bore & stroke: 3.68 x 3.00 in. Compression ratio: 8.2:1. Brake horsepower: 115 at 3400 rpm. Torque: 195 lbs.-ft. at 2200 rpm. Five main bearings. Hydraulic valve lifters. Carburetor: 2Bbl. Motorcraft 7200VV or 2150. VIN Code: D.

CHASSIS DATA: same as 1980.

TECHNICAL: Transmission: Four-speed manual (floor shift) standard on four-cylinder. Gear ratios: (1st) 3.98:1; (2nd) 2.14:1; (3rd) 1.42:1; (4th) 1.00:1; (Rev) 3.99:1. Turbo four-speed: (1st) 4.07:1; (2nd) 2.57:1; (3rd) 1.66:1; (4th) 1.00:1; (Rev) 3.95:1. Four-speed overdrive manual transmission standard on six. Gear ratios: (1st) 3.29:1; (2nd) 1.84:1; (3rd) 1.00:1; (4th) 0.81:1; (Rev) 3.29:1. Other models: (1st) 3.98:1; (2nd) 2.14:1; (3rd) 1.42:1; (4th) 1.00:1; (Rev) 3.99:1. Five-speed manual overdrive optional: (1st) 4.05:1; (2nd) 2.43:1; (3rd) 1.48:1; (4th) 1.00:1; (5th) 0.82:1; (Rev) 3.90:1. Turbo five-speed: (1st) 3.72:1; (2nd) 2.23:1; (3rd) 1.48:1; (4th) 1.00:1; (5th) 0.76:1; (Rev) 3.59:1. Select Shift three-speed automatic optional: (1st) 2.46:1 or 2.47:1; (2nd) 1.46:1 or 1.47:1; (3rd) 1.00:1; (Rev) 2.11:1 or 2.19:1. Standard final drive ratio: (four) 3.08:1 exc. 3.45:1 w/5spd; (six) 3.45:1 w/4spd, 2.73:1 w/auto.; (V-8) 2.26:1. Steering: Rack and pinion. Front Suspension: Modified MacPherson struts with lower control arms, coil springs and stabilizer bar. Rear Suspension: Four-bar link and coil spring system with lower trailing arms and transverse linkage bar. Brakes: Front disc, rear drum. Ignition: Electronic. Body construction: Unibody. Fuel tank: 12.5 gal.

DRIVETRAIN OPTIONS: Engine/Transmission: Turbo 140 cid four ($610). 200 cid six ($213). 255 cid V-8 ($263) exc. w/Cobra pkg. ($346 credit). Sport-tuned exhaust: V-8 ($39); w/turbo and auto. (NC). Five-speed manual trans. ($152). Select Shift automatic trans. ($349). Traction-Lok differential ($63). Optional axle ratio ($20). Brakes & Steering: Power brakes ($76). Power steering ($163). Other: Handling suspension ($43). Engine block heater ($16). H.D. battery ($20). California emission system ($46). High-altitude emissions ($38).

CONVENIENCE/APPEARANCE OPTIONS: Option Packages: Cobra pkg. ($1588); tape delete ($65 credit). Cobra hood graphics ($90). Sport option ($52-$72). Interior accent group ($126-$139). Light group ($43). Appearance protection group ($41). Power lock group ($93-$120). Comfort/Convenience: Air cond. ($560). Rear defroster, electric ($107). Fingertip speed control ($132). Power windows ($140). Tinted glass ($76); windshield only ($29). Leather-wrapped steering wheel ($49-$61). Tilt steering wheel ($80-$93). Interval wipers ($41). Rear wiper/washer ($85). Lighting and Mirrors: Trunk light ($6). Driver's remote mirror ($20). Dual remote mirrors ($56). Entertainment: AM/FM radio ($51). AM/FM stereo radio ($88); w/8 track tape player ($162); w/cassette player ($174). Premium sound system ($91). Dual rear speakers ($37). Radio flexibility option ($61). AM radio delete ($61 credit). Exterior: T-Roof ($874). Flip-up open air roof ($213-$228). Carriage roof ($644). Full vinyl roof ($115). Metallic glow paint ($48). Two-tone paint ($121-$155). Lower two-tone paint ($90). Pin striping ($34). Accent tape stripes ($54). Hood scoop ($32). Liftgate louvers ($145). Rocker panel moldings ($30). Roof luggage rack ($90). Mud/stone deflectors ($26). Lower bodyside protection ($37). Interior: Console ($168). Recaro high-back bucket seats ($732). Cloth/vinyl bucket seats ($22-$48). Accent cloth/vinyl seat trim ($30). Leather low-back bucket seats ($359). Cargo area cover: hatch ($45). Front floor mats ($18-$20). Color-keyed seatbelts ($23). Wheels and Tires: Wire wheel covers ($77-$118). Turbine wheel covers ($10-$41). Forged metric aluminum wheels ($340). Cast aluminum wheels ($305). Styled steel wheels w/trim rings ($60-$101).

MUSTANG — FOUR/SIX/V-8 — For Mustang's third season in this form, little change was evident. A variety of manual transmission ratios was offered, both four-speed and new five-speed. First offered only on four-cylinder models (standard or turbocharged), the five-speed cost an extra $152. Its fifth gear was an overdrive ratio, but the lower four did not offer close-ratio gearing. Some critics found fault with the five-speed's shift pattern, which put fifth gear right next to fourth. The standard 140 cid (2.3-liter) four-cylinder overhead-camshaft engine was rated at 23 MPG city (34 highway) with four-speed manual gearbox. Two other engines (inline six and 255 cid V-8) were optional, along with a total of seven transmissions. Turbocharged models no longer came with automatic shift. For identification, both 'Ford' and 'Mustang' block lettering stood on the hatch or decklid. As usual, Ford tended to describe the notchback two-door model as a 'sedan,' though most observers call it a coupe. Joining the option list was a T-Roof with twin removable tinted glass panels, offered on either the two-door notchback or three-door hatchback. Other new options included reclining bucket seats (either high- or low-back), power windows, and remote right convex mirror. An optional console included a graphic display module that contained a digital clock with elapsed time, and warned of low fuel or washer level as well as inoperative lights. Mustangs could also get a Traction-Lok rear axle. Ghia was a separate model again, while Cobra was a $1588 option package. Cobra equipment was similar to 1979-80, including 190/65R 390 TRX tires on forged metric aluminum wheel, an 8000 rpm. tachometer, lower two-tone paint, 'Cobra' tape treatment, hood scoop, sport-tuned exhaust, dual black sport mirrors, black bumper rub strips, bodyside moldings with dual accent stripes. and black greenhouse moldings. Cobra had a built-in front spoiler, black quarter-window louvers, Cobra medallion on dash and door trim, and a handling suspension. A V-8 engine could replace the standard turbo four, for a $346 credit. Taping could be deleted from the Cobra package, if desired, knocking $65 off the price; but the bold hood decal cost $85 extra. Offered late in 1980 was the limited-production, much-modified McLaren Mustang, similar in appearance to the IMSA show car. McLaren had no grille, a low (and large) front spoiler, working hood scoops, prominent fender flares, and Firestone HPR radial tires on BBS alloy wheels. The variable-boost turbo engine produced 175 horsepower. A total of 250 McLarens were built, priced at $25,000.

I.D. DATA: Like other Ford products, Mustang had a new 17-symbol Vehicle Identification Number (VIN), again stamped on a metal tab fastened to the instrument panel, visible through the windshield. The first three symbols specify manufacturer, make and vehicle type: '1FA' Ford passenger car. Symbol four ('B') denotes restraint system. Next come a letter 'P', followed by two digits that indicate body type: '10' 2-dr. notchback; '15' 3-dr. hatchback; '12' Ghia 2-dr. notchback; '13' Ghia 3-dr. hatchback. Symbol eight indicates engine type: 'A' L4-140 2Bbl.; 'A' turbo L4-140 2Bbl.; 'T' L6-200 1Bbl.; 'D' V8-255 2Bbl. Next is a check digit. Symbol ten indicates model year ('B' 1981). Symbol eleven is assembly plant: 'F' Dearborn, MI; 'R' San Jose, CA. The final six digits make up the sequence number, starting with 100001. A Vehicle Certification Label on the left front door lock face panel or door pillar shows the month and year of manufacture, GVW, GAWR, VIN, and codes for body type and color, trim, axle, transmission, accessories, and special order information.

P185/80R13 WSW ($49). P175/75R14 BSW ($24); WSW ($49-$73). P185/75R14 BSW ($24-$49); WSW ($73-$97); RWL ($90-$114). TRX 190/65R 390 BSW ($122-$146).

HISTORY: Introduced: October 3, 1980. Model year production: 182,552. Total production for the U.S. market of 162,593 Mustangs included 101,860 four-cylinder, 55,406 sixes, and only 5,327 V-8 engines. Calendar year production: 153,719. Calendar year sales by U.S. dealers: 154,985. Model year sales by U.S. dealers: 173,329.

HISTORY: Mustang prices rose sharply this year, as did those of other Ford products. The new T-Roof met all federal body structure regulations, as a result of body modifications that included the use of H-shaped reinforcements. Both production and sales slipped considerably, but this was a weak period for the industry as a whole. Ford's Special Vehicle Operations department started up in September 1980, headed by Michael Kranefuss. Its goal: limited production performance cars and motorsports activities. Several racing Mustangs got factory assistance, including a turbo model driven in IMSA GT events and a Trans Am model. A turbo-powered IMSA 'concept car' with big Pirelli tires and huge fender flares toured the auto show circuit.

1982 MUSTANG

1982 Ford Mustang 5.0L Sport Option coupe. (JG)

MUSTANG — FOUR/SIX/V-8 — 'The Boss is Back!' declared Ford ads. Biggest news of the year was indeed the return of the 302 cid (5.0-liter) V-8, coupled with the temporary disappearance of the turbo four. Performance-oriented Mustangs could have a high-output 302 with four-speed manual overdrive transmission, a combination that had last been offered in 1979. This year's 302 V-8 had a bigger (356 CFM) two-barrel carburetor, larger-diameter (freer-flowing) exhaust system, and low-restriction air cleaner with dual inlets. That setup delivered considerably faster acceleration than the '79 version, able to hit 60 MPH in less than 8 seconds. Base engine was the 140 cid (2.3-liter) four; also optional, a 255 cid (4.2-liter) V-8, and 200 cid inline six. A lockup torque converter (all three gears) was included on automatics with the inline six or small V-8 engine. A high-altitude emissions system was available with all engines. Appearance changed little for 1981, but model designations were revised. The new lineup included an L, GL and GLX, as well as a GT that replaced the former Cobra option. Mustang L was the new base model, with full wheel covers, full wraparound bodyside moldings, and an AM radio. New standard equipment included seatbelts with tension relievers, a remote-control left-hand mirror, new flash-to-pass headlamp feature, and new screw-on gas cap tethered to the filler neck. There was also a switch to 14-inch wheels with P-metric (P175/75R14) steel-belted radial tires. Four-cylinder Mustangs with air conditioning had an electro-drive cooling fan. Radios had dual front speakers plus wiring for two more. Mustang's GT (first designated an SS) added P185/75R14 blackwall steel-belted radials on cast aluminum wheels, a handling suspension, dual black remote mirrors, and built-in foglamps. Styling features included body-colored front fascia with integral spoiler and air dam, three-slot grille, color-keyed rear spoiler, and body-color cowl grille. 'GT' identification went on the liftgate. Body-color headlamp frames replaced the black doors on other models. Black bodyside moldings had a black plastic insert and aluminum end caps. Equipment included a Traction-Lok differential, power brakes and steering, and a console with digital clock and diagnostic warning module. Blackout treatment continued on interior components. An optional TR performance package could enhance the handling qualities of all Mustang models. It included Michelin TRX tires on forged metric aluminum wheels, and a handling suspension with rear stabilizer bar.

I.D. DATA: Mustang's 17-symbol Vehicle Identification Number (VIN), stamped on a metal tab fastened to the instrument panel, is visible through the windshield. The first three symbols specify manufacturer, make and

vehicle type: '1FA' Ford passenger car. Symbol four ('B') denotes restraint system. Next comes a letter 'P', followed by two digits that indicate body type: '10' 2-dr. notchback sedan; '16' 3-dr. hatchback; '12' GLX 2-dr. notchback; '13' GLX 3-dr. hatchback. Symbol eight indicates engine type: 'A' L4-140 2Bbl.; 'B' L6-200 1Bbl.; 'D' V8-255 2Bbl,; 'F' V8-302 2Bbl. Next is a check digit. Symbol ten indicates model year ('C' 1982). Symbol eleven is assembly plant: 'F' Dearborn, MI. The final six digits make up the sequence number, starting with 100001. A Vehicle Certification Label on the left front door lock face panel or door pillar shows the month and year of manufacture, VIN, and codes for body type and color, trim, axle ratio, transmission, and special order information.

MUSTANG (FOUR/SIX)

Model No.	Body/ Style No.	Body Type & Seating	Factory Price	Shipping Weight	Prod. Total
10	N/A	2-dr. L Notch-4P	6345/7062	2511/2635	Note 1
10	66B	2-dr. GL Notch-4P	6844/7468	2528/2652	45,316
16	61B	3-dr. GL Hatch-4P	6979/7390	2565/2689	69,348
12	66H	2-dr. GLX Notch-4P	6980/7604	2543/2667	5,828
13	61H	3-dr. GLX Hatch-4P	7101/7725	2579/2703	9,926

MUSTANG GT (V-8)
16	N/A	3-dr. Hatch-4P	----/8308	----/2629	Note 2

NOTE 1: Production of L model is included in GL total.

NOTE 2: Ford figures include GT production in GL hatchback total above. Other industry sources report a total of 23,447 GT models produced.

FACTORY PRICE/WEIGHT NOTE: Figures to left of slash are for four-cylinder engine, to right of slash for six-cylinder. (The higher amount includes the cost of an automatic transmission.) A 255 cid V-8 engine was priced $70 higher than the six; a 302 V-8 was $189 higher.

ENGINE [Base Four]: Inline, overhead cam, four-cylinder. Cast-iron block and head. Displacement: 140 cid (2.3 liters). Bore & stroke: 3.78 x 3.13 in. Compression ratio: 9.0:1. Brake horsepower: 86 at 4600 rpm. Torque: 117 lbs.-ft. at 2600 rpm. Five main bearings. Hydraulic valve lifters. Carburetor: 2Bbl. Motorcraft 5200 or Holley 6500. VIN Code: A.

ENGINE [Optional Six]: Inline, overhead valve six-cylinder. Cast-iron block and head. Displacement: 200 cid (3.3 liters). Bore & stroke: 3.68 x 3.13 in. Compression ratio: 8.6:1. Brake horsepower: 87 at 3800 rpm. Torque: 154 lbs.-ft. at 1400 rpm. Seven main bearings. Hydraulic valve lifters. Carburetor: 2Bbl. Holley 1946. VIN Code: B.

ENGINE [Optional V-8]: 90-degree, overhead valve V-8. Cast-iron block and head. Displacement: 255 cid (4.2 liters). Bore & stroke: 3.68 x 3.00 in. Compression ratio: 8.2:1. Brake horsepower: 120 at 3400 rpm. Torque: 205 lbs.-ft. at 1600 rpm. Five main bearings. Hydraulic valve lifters. Carburetor: 2Bbl. Motorcraft 2150 or 7200VV. VIN Code: D.

ENGINE [Optional High-Output V-8]: 90-degree, overhead valve V-8. Cast-iron block and head. Displacement: 302 cid (5.0 liters). Bore & stroke: 4.00 x 3.00 in. Compression ratio: 8.3:1. Brake horsepower: 157 at 4200 rpm. Torque: 240 lbs.-ft. at 2400 rpm. Five main bearings. Hydraulic valve lifters. Carburetor: 2Bbl. Motorcraft 2150A. VIN Code: F.

CHASSIS DATA: Wheelbase: 100.4 in. Overall length: 179.1 in. Height: 51.4 in. Width: 69.1 in. Front Tread: 56.6 in. Rear Tread: 57.0 in. Standard Tires: P175/75R14 BSW exc. GT, P185/75R14.

TECHNICAL: Transmission: Four-speed manual (floor shift) standard on four-cylinder. Gear ratios: (1st) 3.98:1; (2nd) 2.14:1; (3rd) 1.49:1; (4th) 1.00:1; (Rev) 3.99:1. Four-speed overdrive manual transmission standard on V-8. Gear ratios: (1st) 3.07:1; (2nd) 1.72:1; (3rd) 1.00:1; (4th) 0.70:1; (Rev) 3.07:1. Five-speed manual overdrive optional: (1st) 3.72:1; (2nd) 2.23:1; (3rd) 1.48:1; (4th) 1.00:1; (5th) 0.76:1; (Rev) 3.59:1. Select-Shift three-speed automatic optional on four-cylinder, standard on six: (1st) 2.47:1; (2nd) 1.47:1; (3rd) 1.00:1; (Rev) 2.11:1. Converter clutch automatic available with six/V-8: (1st) 2.46:1; (2nd) 1.46:1; (3rd) 1.00:1; (Rev) 2.19:1. Standard final drive ratio: 2.73:1 except four w/5spd, 3.45:1; four w/auto. or 302 V-8 w/4spd, 3.08:1. Steering/Suspension/Brakes: same as 1981. Body construction: unibody. Fuel tank: 15.4 gal.

DRIVETRAIN OPTIONS: Engine/Transmission: 200 cid six ($213). 255 cid V-8 ($263) exc. w/GT ($57 credit). 302 cid V-8 ($452) exc. w/TR performance pkg. ($402). Five-speed manual trans. ($196). SelectShift automatic trans. ($411). Traction-Lok differential ($76). Optional axle ratio (NC). Brakes/Steering/Suspension: Power brakes ($93). Power steering ($190). TR performance suspension pkg. ($533-$583) exc. GT ($105). Handling suspension ($50). Other: Engine block heater ($17). H.D. battery ($24). California emission system ($46). High-altitude emissions (NC).

CONVENIENCE/APPEARANCE OPTIONS: Option Packages: Light group ($49). Appearance protection group ($48). Power lock group ($139). Comfort/Convenience: Air cond. ($676). Rear defroster, electric ($124). Fingertip speed control ($155). Power windows ($165). Tinted glass ($88): windshield only ($32). Leather-wrapped steering wheel

($55). Tilt steering wheel ($95). Interval wipers ($48). Rear wiper/washer ($101). Lighting and Mirrors: Trunk light ($7). Remote right mirror ($41). Entertainment: AM/FM radio ($76). AM/FM stereo radio ($106); w/8-track or cassette player ($184). Premium sound system ($105). Dual rear speakers ($39). AM radio delete ($61 credit). Exterior: T-Roof ($1021). Flip-up open air roof ($276). Carriage roof ($734). Full vinyl roof ($137). Metallic glow paint ($54). Two-tone paint ($138-$177). Lower two-tone paint ($104). Accent tape stripes ($62). Hood scoop ($38). Liftgate louvers ($165). Black rocker panel moldings ($33). Lower bodyside protection ($41). Interior: Console ($191). Recaro high-back bucket seats ($834). Cloth/vinyl seats ($23-$51). Leather low-back bucket seats ($409). Front floor mats, carpeted ($22). Wheels and Tires: Wire wheel covers ($91-$141). Cast aluminum wheels ($348-$398). Styled steel wheels w/trim rings ($72-$122). P175/75R14 WSW ($66). P185/75R14 BSW ($30); WSW ($66-$96); RWL ($85-$116).

HISTORY: Introduced: September 24, 1981. Model year production: 130,418. Total production for the U.S. market of 119,314 Mustangs included 54,444 four-cylinder, 37,734 sixes, and 27,136 V-8 engines. Calendar year production: 127,370. Calendar year sales by U.S. dealers: 119,526. Model year sales by U.S. dealers: 116,804.

HISTORY: Option prices rose sharply this year, by around 20 percent on the average. Production of V-8 engines also rose sharply, with five times as many coming off the line as in 1981. Mustang sales declined by almost one-third this year. A convertible model was announced, but it didn't appear until the 1983 model year.

1983 MUSTANG

1983 Ford Mustang convertible. (OCW)

1983 Ford Mustang. (OCW)

MUSTANG — FOUR/V-6/V-8 — A restyled nose and rear end improved Mustang's aerodynamics, but the model was otherwise essentially a carryover for 1983. All Mustangs had a new angled-forward front end and new front fascia, with deeply recessed headlamp housings. A narrower grille design tapered inward slightly at the base, with a Ford oval in its center. Rectangular parking lamps stood at bumper level, as before. below the outboard headlamps. Tail lamps continued the wraparound design, but in restyled form. The use of galvanized and zincrometal coatings was expanded. The high output 302 cid V-8 edition displayed a new hood scoop design. Most noteworthy, though, was the return of the ragtop. A new convertible (part of the GLX series) came

with any powertrain except the 2.3-liter four with automatic. Unlike the Chrysler LeBaron, Mustang convertibles had a glass backlight and roll-down quarter windows, along with a power top. Engine choices changed considerably for (and during) 1983. A 232 cid (3.8-liter) 'Essex' V-6, offered in Mustang for the first time, delivered a 2-second improvement in 0-60 mph time over the previous 3.3-liter inline six. The high-output 302 cid (5.0-liter) V-8 with four-speed manual continued this year, but a four-barrel carburetor replaced the former two-barrel. Horsepower jumped to 175 (formerly 157). The V-8 also got an aluminum intake manifold and freer exhaust flow. It was standard on the GT. The base 140 cid (2.3-liter) four switched from two-barrel to single-barrel carburetion. Later in the season, a new 140 cid OHC turbo arrived, with multiport fuel injection. The last previous turbo four, in 1981, had been carbureted. Turbo models could not have air conditioning. Both the inline six and 255 cid (4.2-liter) V-8 were dropped. A new manual five-speed gearbox, optional with the four, had Ford's U-shaped shift motion between fourth and fifth gear. A Borg-Warner T5 close-ratio five-speed arrived later for the GT's high-output 5.0-liter V-8, hooked to a 3.27:1 final drive. An upshift indicator light option (with manual transmission) was available, to show the most fuel-efficient shift points. All Mustang tires increased by at least one size, while the optional handling suspension got tougher anti-sway bars and retuned springs/shocks. It was now available without the formerly-required Michelin TRX tires. Joining the option list were: cloth sport performance low back bucket seats; turbine wheel covers; restyled wire wheel covers; convex right hand mirror; new special two-tone paint and tape treatment; and TRX tires and wheels without the TR performance suspension. Several options were deleted, including the rear wiper/washer, dual rear speakers, carriage roof, liftgate louvers, accent tape stripe, and Recaro seats. Standard equipment on the L (base) Mustang included black bumper rub strips, halogen headlamps, three-speed heater/defroster, woodtone instrument panel appliqué, quarter-window louvers, black remote left mirror, AM radio, and four-spoke steering wheel with woodgrain insert. Also standard: four-speed manual gearbox, full wheel covers, argent accent striping, cigarette lighter, and high-back reclining bucket seats with vinyl upholstery. Mustang GL added black rocker panel, door and window frame moldings; dual accent bodyside pinstripes; a black sport steering wheel; lower-carpeted door trim panels; right visor vanity mirror; and low-back bucket seats. Mustang GLX came with dual bright remote-control mirrors, woodgrain-insert four-spoke steering wheel, bright rocker panel moldings, map pockets in the driver's door trim panel. and a light group. The GLX convertible included power brakes, tinted glass, dual black remote-control mirrors, black rocker moldings, and automatic transmission. Mustang GT carried a standard Traction-Lok rear axle, power brakes and steering, black grille, rear spoiler, black hood scoop, handling suspension, and five-speed manual gearbox. GT models could have Michelin TRX tires on cast aluminum wheels and a console with digital clock and diagnostic module, but no dual accent bodyside pin striping. Black windshield, window and door frames completed the GT's appearance.

I.D. DATA: As before, Mustang's 17-symbol Vehicle Identification Number (VIN) was stamped on a metal tab fastened to the instrument panel,

1983 Ford Mustang GLX convertible (with 5.0L V-8). (OCW)

visible through the windshield. Symbols one to three specify manufacturer, make and vehicle type: '1FA' Ford passenger car. Symbol four ('B') denotes restraint system. Next comes a letter 'P', followed by two digits that indicate body type: '26' 2-dr. notchback sedan; '28' 3-dr. hatchback; '27' 2-dr. convertible. Symbol eight indicates engine type: 'A' L4-140 1Bbl.; 'D' turbo L4-140 FI; '3' V6-232 2Bbl.; 'F' V8-302 4Bbl. Next is a check digit. Symbol ten indicates model year ('D' 1983). Symbol eleven is assembly plant: 'F' Dearborn, MI. The final six digits make up the sequence number, starting with 100001. A Vehicle Certification Label on the left front door lock face panel or door pillar shows the manufacturer, month and year of manufacture, GVW, GAWR, certification statement, VIN, and codes for body type, color. trim, axle, transmission, and special order information

MUSTANG (FOUR/V-6)

Model No.	Body/ Style No.	Body Type & Seating	Factory Price	Shipping Weight	Prod. Total
26	66B	2-dr. L Notch-4P	6727/7036	2532/2621	Note 1
26/60C	66B	2-dr. GL Notch-4P	7264/7573	2549/2638	Note 1
28/60C	61B	3-dr. GL Hatch-4P	7439/7748	2584/2673	Note 1
26/602	66B	2-dr. GLX Notch-4P	7398/7707	2552/2641	Note 1
28/602	61B	3-dr. GLX Hatch-4P	7557/7866	2587/2676	Note 1
27/602	N/A	2-dr. GLX Conv.-4P	----/9449	----/2759	Note 1

MUSTANG GT (V-8)

Model No.	Body/ Style No.	Body Type & Seating	Factory Price	Shipping Weight	Prod. Total
28/932	61B	3-dr. Hatch 4P	----/9328	----/2891	Note 1
27/932	N/A	2 dr. Conv.-4P	----/13479	N/A	Note 1

MUSTANG TURBO GT (FOUR)

Model No.	Body/ Style No.	Body Type & Seating	Factory Price	Shipping Weight	Prod. Total
28/932	61B	3-dr. Hatch-4P	9714/----	N/A	Note 1

NOTE 1: Ford reports total production of 33,201 two-doors, 64,234 hatchbacks, and 23,438 convertibles.

FACTORY PRICE/WEIGHT NOTE: Figures to left of slash are for four cylinder engine, to right of slash for V-6. A 4Bbl. 302 cid V-8 engine cost $1044 more than the V-6 ($595 more on the GLX convertible). The price of the GLX convertible jumped sharply after the model year began, to $12,467.

ENGINE [Base Four]: Inline, overhead cam, four-cylinder. Cast-iron block and head. Displacement: 140 cid (2.3 liters). Bore & stroke: 3.78 x 3.13 in. Compression ratio: 9.0:1. Brake horsepower: 90 at 4600 rpm. Torque: 122 lbs.-ft. at 2600 rpm. Five main bearings. Hydraulic valve lifters. Carburetor: 1Bbl. Carter YFA. VIN Code: A.

ENGINE [Optional Turbo Four]: Same as 140 cid four above, but with turbocharger and electronic fuel injection. Compression ratio: 8.0:1. Brake H.P.: 142 at 5000 rpm. Torque 172 lbs.-ft. at 3800 rpm. VIN Code: D.

ENGINE [Optional V-6]: 90 degree, overhead valve V-6. Cast-iron block and aluminum head. Displacement: 232 cid (3.8 liters). Bore & stroke: 3.80 x 3.40 in. Compression ratio: 8.7:1. Brake horsepower: 112 at 4000 rpm. Torque: 175 lbs.-ft. at 2600 rpm. Four main bearings. Hydraulic valve lifters. Carburetor: 2Bbl. Motorcraft 2150. VIN Code: 3.

ENGINE [Optional V-8]: 90-degree, overhead valve V-8. Cast-iron block and head. Displacement: 302 cid (5.0 liters). Bore & stroke: 4.00 x 3.00 in. Compression ratio: 8.3:1. Brake horsepower: 175 at 4000 rpm. Torque: 245 lbs.-ft. at 2400 rpm. Five main bearings. Hydraulic valve lifters. Carburetor: 4Bbl. Holley 4180. VIN Code: F.

CHASSIS DATA: Wheelbase: 100.4 in. Overall length: 179.1 in. Height: 51.9 in. Width: 69.1 in. Front Tread: 56.6 in. Rear Tread: 57.0 in. Standard Tires: P185/75R14 SBR BSW exc. GT, P205/70HR14 or Michelin P220/55R390 TRX.

TECHNICAL: Transmission: Four-speed manual (floor shift) standard on four-cylinder. Gear ratios: (1st) 3.98:1; (2nd) 2.14:1; (3rd) 1.49:1; (4th) 1.00:1; (Rev) 3.99:1. Four-speed overdrive manual transmission standard on V-8. Gear ratios: (1st) 3.07:1; (2nd) 1.72:1; (3rd) 1.00:1; (4th) 0.70:1; (Rev) 3.07:1. Five-speed manual overdrive optional: (1st) 3.72:1; (2nd) 2.23:1; (3rd) 1.48:1; (4th) 1.00:1; (5th) 0.76:1; (Rev) 3.59:1. Turbo five-speed: (1st) 4.03:1; (2nd) 2.37:1; (3rd) 1.50:1; (4th) 1.00:1; (5th) 0.86:1; (Rev) 3.76:1. Alternate turbo five-speed: (1st) 3.76:1; (2nd) 2.18:1; (3rd) 1.36:1; (4th) 1.00:1; (5th) 0.86:1; (Rev) 3.76:1. V-8 five-speed: (1st) 2.95:1; (2nd) 1.94:1; (3rd) 1.34:1; (4th) 1.00:1; (5th) 0.73:1; (Rev) 2.76:1. SelectShift three-speed automatic optional on four-cylinder, standard on six: (1st) 2.47:1; (2nd) 1.47:1; (3rd) 1.00:1; (Rev) 2.11:1. V-6 ratios: (1st) 2.46:1; (2nd) 1.46:1; (3rd) 1.00:1; (Rev) 2.19:1. Standard final drive ratio: 3.08:1 w/4spd, 3.45:1 w/5spd, 3.08:1 or 2.73:1 w/auto. Steering: Rack and pinion. Front Suspension: Modified MacPherson struts with lower control arms and stabilizer bar. Rear Suspension: Rigid axle w/four-bar link and coil springs. Brakes: Front disc, rear drum. Ignition: Electronic. Body construction: Unibody. Fuel tank: 15.4 gal.

DRIVETRAIN OPTIONS: Engine/Transmission: 232 cid V-6 ($309). 302 cid V-8 ($1343) exc. conv. ($595). Five-speed manual trans. ($124). Select-shift automatic trans. ($439). Traction-Lok differential ($95). Optional axle ratio (NC). Brakes/Steering/Suspension: Power brakes ($93). Power steering ($202). Handling suspension ($252). Other: Engine block heater ($17). H.D. battery ($26). California emission system ($76). High-altitude emissions (NC)

CONVENIENCE/APPEARANCE OPTIONS: Option Packages Sport performance pkg. ($196). Light group ($55). Appearance protection group ($60). Power lock group ($160). Comfort/Convenience: Air cond. ($724). Rear defroster, electric ($135). Fingertip speed control ($170). Power windows ($180). Tinted glass ($105); windshield only ($38). Leather-wrapped steering wheel ($59). Tilt steering wheel ($105). Interval wipers ($49). Remote right mirror ($44). Entertainment: AM/FM radio ($82) AM/FM stereo radio ($109); w/8-track or cassette player ($199). Premium sound system ($117). AM radio delete ($61 credit). Exterior: T-Roof ($1055). Flip-up open-air roof ($310). Metallic glow paint ($54). Two-tone paint ($150-$189). Liftgate louvers: hatch ($171). Rocker panel moldings ($33). Lower bodyside protection ($41). Interior: Console ($191). Cloth/vinyl seats ($29-$57). Leather low back bucket seats ($415). Front floor mats, carpeted ($22). Wheels and Tires: Wire wheel covers ($98-$148). Turbine wheel covers (NC). Cast aluminum wheels ($354-$404). Styled steel wheels w/trim rings ($78-$128). P185/75R14 WSW ($72). P195/75R14 WSW ($108). P205/75R14 BSW ($224). TRX P220/55R390 BSW ($327-$551).

HISTORY: Introduced: October 14, 1982, except convertible, November 5, 1982. Model year production: 108,438 Total production for the U.S. market of 108,438 Mustangs included 27,825 four-cylinder, 47,766 sixes, and 32,847 V-8 engines. Calendar year production: 124,225. Calendar year sales by U.S. dealers: 116,976. Model year sales by U.S. dealers: 116,120.

HISTORY: Mustang's convertible actually began life as a steel-topped notchback, modified by an outside contractor. The car itself was assembled at Dearborn, then sent to Cars & Concepts in Brighton, Michigan, for installation of the top and interior trim. Mustang GT was said to deliver a seven-second 0-60 mph time (quickest of any standard domestic model), as well as cornering that matched exotic cars. All that plus fuel economy in the mid-20s.

1984 MUSTANG

1984 Ford Mustang SVO. (OCW)

MUSTANG — FOUR/V-6/V-8 — Performance-minded Mustangers enjoyed fresh temptation this year in the new SVO. Developed by Ford's Special Vehicle Operations department, SVO carried an air-to-air intercooler on its 140 cid (2.3-liter) turbocharged, fuel-injected four-cylinder engine. That helped boost horsepower up to 175, and improve low-end performance. The SVO package included a Borg-Warner T5 five-speed manual gearbox with Hurst linkage, four-wheel disc brakes, performance suspension with adjustable Koni gas-filled shocks, P225/50VR16 Goodyear NCT tires on cast aluminum 16 x 7 in. wheels, and functional hood scoop. SVO could, according to Ford, hit 134 MPH and get to 60 MPH in just 7.5 seconds. Inside were multi-adjustable articulated leather bucket seats. SVO's shock absorbers and struts had three settings: cross-country (for front and rear), GT (front only), and competition (front and rear). Four-wheel disc brakes were standard. SVO had a much different front-end look than the standard Mustang,

1984 Ford Mustang SVO coupe. (JG)

1984 Ford Mustang GT 5.0L HO Sport Coupe. (JG)

with a 'grille-less' front fascia and integrated foglamps. Just a single slot stood below the hood panel, which contained a Ford oval. Large single rectangular headlamps were deeply recessed, flanked by large wraparound lenses. A polycarbonate dual-wing rear spoiler was meant to increase rear-wheel traction, while rear-wheel 'spats' directed airflow around the wheel wells. SVO's price tag was more than double that of a base Mustang. Offered in 'three-door' hatchback form, SVO came only in black, silver metallic, dark charcoal metallic, or red metallic. Interiors were all charcoal. Only six major options were available for SVO, because it had so much standard equipment. Those were: air conditioning, power windows. power door locks, cassette player, flip-up sunroof, and leather seat trim. Standard SVO equipment included an 8000 rpm. tachometer; quick-ratio power steering; Traction-Lok rear axle; leather-wrapped steering wheel, shift knob and brake handle; unique instrument panel appliqués; narrow bodyside moldings; and unique C-pillar and tail lamp treatments. A premium/regular fuel switch recalibrated the ignition instantly. Revised pedal positioning allowed 'heel and toe' downshifting, and had a footrest for the left foot during hard cornering. Standard models looked the same as in 1983. Through-out the line were new steering wheels with center horn, new instrument panel appliqués, and split folding rear seats. All manual transmissions now had a clutch/starter interlock, so the engine couldn't start unless the clutch was depressed. Mustang instrument panels had red lighting this year. Buyers could also select a more modest turbo model, without the intercooler. Mustang's GT Turbo had been introduced in spring 1983, and continued for '84. GT customers also had a choice of V-8 engines, and an available overdrive automatic transmission. The series lineup was simplified this year. The L series, previously two-door notch-back only, was now also available in 'three-door' hatchback form. GL and GLX models of 1983 were gone, replaced by a single LX series. A convertible was offered again this year, in both LX and GT form. The GT series displayed a new front air dam, with road lamps available. GT also added gas-filled shock absorbers and a handling suspension. Else-where on the powerplant front, the optional 232 cid (3.8-liter) V-6 switched to throttle-body fuel injection and gained some horsepower. A fuel-injected high-output 5.0-liter V-8 came with automatic overdrive transmission. A higher-output version of the four-barrel V-8, producing 205 horsepower, was announced for December arrival but delayed.

I.D. DATA: Mustang's 17-symbol Vehicle Identification Number (VIN) again was stamped on a metal tab fastened to the instrument panel, visible through the windshield. The first three symbols specify manu-facturer, make and vehicle type: '1FA' Ford passenger car. Symbol four ('B') denotes restraint system. Next comes a letter 'P', followed by two digits that indicate body type: '26' 2-dr. notchback sedan; '28' 3-dr. hatchback; '27' 2-dr. convertible. Symbol eight indicates engine type:

'A' L4-140 1Bbl.; 'W' turbo L4-140 FI; '3' V6-232 FI; 'F' V8-302 FI; 'M' V8-302 4Bbl. Next is a check digit. Symbol ten indicates model year ('E' 1984). Symbol eleven is assembly plant: 'F' Dearborn, MI. The final six digits make up the sequence number, starting with 100001. A Vehicle Certification Label on the left front door lock face panel or door pillar shows the manufacturer, month and year of manufacture, GVW, GAWR, certification statement, VIN, and codes for body type and color, trim, axle, transmission, and special order information.

MUSTANG (FOUR/V-6)

Model No.	Body/ Style No.	Body Type & Seating	Factory Price	Shipping Weight	Prod. Total
26	66B	2-dr. L Notch-4P	7098/7507	2538/2646	Note 1
28	61B	3-dr. L Hatch-4P	7269/7678	2584/2692	Note 1
26/602	66B	2-dr. LX Notch-4P	7290/7699	2559/2667	Note 1
28/602	61B	3-dr. LX Hatch-4P	7496/7905	2605/2713	Note 1
27/602	66B	2-dr. LX Conv.-4P	----/11849	----/2873	Note 1

L/LX Price/Weight Note: Figures to left of slash are for four-cylinder engine, to right of slash for V-6. A 4Bbl. 302 cid V-8 engine cost $1165 more than the V-6 ($318 more on the LX convertible).

MUSTANG GT (TURBO FOUR/V-8)

| 28/932 | 61B | 3-dr. Hatch-4P | 9762/9578 | 2753/2899 | Note 1 |
| 27/932 | 66B | 2-dr. Conv.-4P | 13245/13051 | 2921/3043 | Note 1 |

GT Price and Weight Note: Figures to left of slash are for turbo four, to right for V-8.

MUSTANG SVO (TURBO FOUR)

Model No.	Body/ Style No.	Body Type & Seating	Factory Price	Shipping Weight	Prod. Total
28/939	61B	3-dr. Hatch-4P	15596	2881	Note 1

NOTE 1: Ford reports total production of 37,680 two-doors, 86,200 hatchbacks and 17,600 convertibles.

ENGINE [Base Four]: Inline, overhead cam, four-cylinder. Cast-iron block and head. Displacement: 140 cid (2.3 liters). Bore & stroke: 3.78 x 3.13 in. Compression ratio: 9.0:1. Brake horsepower: 88 at 4000 rpm. Torque: 122 lbs.-ft. at 2400 rpm. Five main bearings. Hydraulic valve lifters. Carburetor: 1Bbl. Carter YFA. VIN Code: A.

ENGINE [Optional Turbo Four]: Same as 140 cid four above, but with turbocharger and electronic fuel injection. Compression ratio: 8.0:1. Brake H.P.: 145 at 4600 rpm. Torque: 180 lbs.-ft. at 3600 rpm. VIN Code: W.

ENGINE [Svo Turbo Four]: Same as standard turbo four above, ex-cept: Brake H.P.: 175 at 4400 rpm. Torque: 210 lbs.-ft. at 3000 rpm.

ENGINE [Optional V-6]: 90-degree, overhead valve V-6. Cast-iron block and aluminum head. Displacement: 232 cid (3.8 liters). Bore & stroke: 3.80 x 3.40 in. Compression ratio: 8.7:1. Brake horsepower: 120 at 3600 rpm. Torque: 205 lbs.-ft. at 1600 rpm. Four main bearings. Hydraulic valve lifters. Electronic fuel injection (TBI). VIN Code: 3.

ENGINE [Optional V-8]: 90-degree, overhead valve V-8. Cast-iron block and head. Displacement: 302 cid (5.0 liters). Bore & stroke: 4.00 x 3.00 in. Compression ratio: 8.3:1. Brake horsepower: 175 at 4000 rpm. Torque: 245 lbs.-ft. at 2200 rpm. Five main bearings. Hydraulic valve lifters. Carburetor: 4Bbl. Holley 4180C. VIN Code: M.

ENGINE [Optional V-8]: Fuel injected version of 302 cid V-8 above except: Brake H.P.: 165 at 3800 rpm. Torque: 245 lbs.-ft. at 2000 rpm. VIN Code: F.

1984-1/2 Ford Mustang GT-350 20th Anniversary convertible. (F)

NOTE: A high-output version of the carbureted V-8, rated 205 horsepower at 4400 rpm. was announced but delayed.

CHASSIS DATA: Wheelbase: 100.5 in. Overall length: 179.1 in. except SVO, 181.0 in. Height: 51.9 in. Width: 69.1 in. Front Tread: 56.6 in. except SVO, 57.8 in. Rear Tread: 57.0 in. except SVO, 58.3 in. Standard Tires: P185/75R14 SBR BSW exc. GT, P205/70HR14.

TECHNICAL: Transmission: Four-speed manual (floor shift) standard on four-cylinder. Gear ratios: (1st) 3.98:1; (2nd) 2.14:1; (3rd) 1.49:1; (4th) 1.00:1; (Rev) 3.99:1. Standard turbo five-speed: (1st) 4.03:1; (2nd) 2.37:1; (3rd) 1.50:1; (4th) 1.00:1; (5th) 0.86:1; (Rev) 3.76:1. Standard V-8 five-speed: (1st) 2.95:1; (2nd) 1.94:1; (3rd) 1.34:1; (4th) 1.00:1; (5th) 0.63:1; (Rev) 2.76:1. SelectShift three-speed automatic optional on four-cylinder: (1st) 2.47:1; (2nd) 1.47:1; (3rd) 1.00:1; (Rev) 2.11:1. Four-speed overdrive automatic standard on V-6: (1st) 2.40:1; (2nd) 1.47:1; (3rd) 1.00:1; (4th) 0.67:1; (Rev) 2.00:1. Standard final drive ratio: (four) 3.08:1 w/4spd, 3.27:1 w/auto.; (V-6) 3.08:1; (V-8) 3.08:1 w/5spd, 2.73:1 w/3spd auto., 3.27:1 w/4spd auto.; (turbo) 3.45:1. Steering: Rack and pinion. Front Suspension: Modified MacPherson struts with lower control arms and stabilizer bar; SVO added adjustable gas-pressurized shocks. Rear Suspension: Rigid axle w/four-bar link and coil springs; SVO and GT Turbo added an anti-sway bar. Brakes: Front disc, rear drum except SVO, four-wheel disc brakes. Ignition: Electronic. Body construction: Unibody. Fuel tank: 15.4 gal.

DRIVETRAIN OPTIONS: Engine/Transmission: 232 cid V-6 ($409). 302 cid V-8 pkg. ($1574) exc. LX conv. ($727). Five-speed manual trans. (NC). Three-speed automatic trans. ($439). Four-speed overdrive auto. trans. ($551). Traction-Lok differential ($95). Optional axle ratio (NC). Brakes/Steering/Suspension: Power brakes ($93). Power steering ($202). Handling suspension ($252) exc. w/VIP pkg. ($50). Other: Engine block heater ($18). H.D. battery ($27). California emission system ($99). High-altitude option (NC).

CONVENIENCE/APPEARANCE OPTIONS: Option Packages: SVO competition preparation pkg.: delete air cond., power locks. AM/FM/cassette and power windows ($1253 credit). VIP pkg. for L/LX with AM/FM stereo or tilt wheel ($93); both ($196). VIP pkg. for GT ($110). 20th anniversary VIP pkg.: GT ($25-$144). Light/convenience group ($55-$88). Power lock group ($177). Comfort/Convenience: Air cond. ($743). Rear defroster, electric ($140). Fingertip speed control ($176). Power windows ($198). Tinted glass ($110). Tilt steering wheel ($110). Interval wipers ($50). Remote right mirror ($46). Entertainment: AM/FM stereo radio ($109); w/cassette player ($222) exc. SVO or w/VIP pkg. ($113). Premium sound system ($151). AM radio delete ($39 credit). Exterior: T-Roof ($1074) exc. w/VIP pkg. ($760). Flip-up open air roof ($315). Metallic glow paint ($54). Two-tone paint: L/LX ($150-$189). Lower two-tone paint ($116). Liftgate louvers: hatch ($171). Rocker panel moldings ($39). Lower bodyside protection ($41). Interior: Console ($191). Articulated sport seats ($196). High-back vinyl bucket seats: L ($29); low-back, LX/GT ($29). Leather bucket seats ($189). Front floor mats, carpeted ($22). Wheels and Tires: Wire wheel covers ($98). Cast aluminum wheels ($354). Styled steel wheels w/trim rings ($78). P185/75R14 WSW ($72). P195/75R14 WSW ($108). P205/75R14 BSW ($224). TRX P220/55R390 BSW ($327-$551) exc. GT ($27 credit).

HISTORY: Introduced: September 22, 1983. Model year production: 141,480. Total production for the U.S. market of 129,621 Mustangs included 46,414 four-cylinder, 47,169 sixes, and 36,038 V-8 engines. Calendar year production: 140,338. Calendar year sales by U.S. dealers: 138,296. Model year sales by U.S. dealers: 131,762.

HISTORY: Ford's Special Vehicle Operations Department had been formed in 1981 to supervise the company's renewed involvement in motorsports (among other duties), and to develop special limited-edition high-performance vehicles. SVO was the first of those offered as a production model. *Motor Trend* called SVO "the best driving street Mustang the factory has ever produced." *Road & Track* claimed that SVO 'outruns the Datsun 280ZX, outhandles the Ferrari 308 and Porsche 944 ... and it's affordable.' Its hefty price tag meant SVO was targeted toward more affluent, car-conscious consumers.

1985 MUSTANG

MUSTANG — FOUR/V-6/V-8 — Changes for 1985 focused mainly on Mustang's front end and mechanical matters. All models wore a new front-end look with a four-hole integral air dam below the bumper, flanked by low rectangular parking lamps. GT also had integral foglamps. A 'grille' similar to SVO-essentially one wide slot with angled sides in a sloping front panel-appeared on all Mustangs. That panel displayed a Ford oval. Tail lamps were full-width (except for the license plate opening), with backup lenses at the upper portion of each inner section. A Ford script oval stood above the right tail

1985 Ford Mustang GT hatchback coupe (with 5.0L V-8). (PH)

lamp. Most Mustang exterior trim and accents switched from black to a softer charcoal shade. All models had new charcoal front and rear bumper rub strips and bodyside moldings. Also new: charcoal hood paint/tape treatment, a revised decklid decal, and GT nomenclature (where applicable) molded into the bodyside molding. The base L series was dropped, making LX the bottom-level Mustang. Standard LX equipment now included power brakes and steering, remote-control right-side mirror, dual-note horn, interval windshield wipers, and an AM/FM stereo radio. Also available were the GT and SVO, as well as LX and GT convertibles. As before, both notchback and hatchback bodies were offered. New standard interior features included a console, low-back bucket seats (on LX), articulated sport seats (on GT), luxury door trim panels, and covered visor mirrors. The convertible's quarter trim panels were revised to accommodate a refined seatbelt system. Mechanical radio faces switched to a contemporary flat design. All Mustangs had larger tires this year, and added urethane lower bodyside protection. New GT tires were P225/60VR15 Goodyear Eagleunidirectional 'Gatorbacks' on 15 x 7 in. cast aluminum wheels. Added to the option list: a new electronic AM/FM stereo radio with cassette player. The 140 cid (2.3-liter) four remained standard, but buyers had quite a choice of other powerplants, as usual. Mustang GT's high-output carbureted 302 cid (5.0-liter) V-8 gained a high-performance camshaft, plus roller tappets and a two-speed accessory drive system. That engine now produced 210 horsepower, while its mating five-speed manual gearbox had a tighter shift pattern and new gear ratios. The high-output, fuel-injected V-8 also gained strength, reaching 180 horsepower. The turbocharged SVO returned a little late, now wearing Eagle 50-series tires on 16-inch wheels. Both the 3.8-liter V-6 and 5.0-liter V-8 had a new oil warning light.

I.D. DATA: Mustang's 17-symbol Vehicle Identification Number (VIN) again was stamped on a metal tab fastened to the instrument panel, visible through the windshield. Coding was similar to 1984. Model year code changed to 'F' for 1985. Coding for the SVO turbocharged four changed to 'T'.

1985 Ford Mustang SVO coupe. (JG)

MUSTANG LX (FOUR/V-6)

Model No.	Body/Style No.	Body Type & Seating	Factory Price	Shipping Weight	Prod. Total
26/602	66B	2-dr. Notch-4P	6885/8017	2559/2667	Note 1
28/602	61B	3-dr. Hatch-4P	7345/8477	2605/2713	Note 1
27/602	66B	2-dr. Conv.-4P	----/11985	----/2873	Note 1

LX Price/Weight Note: Figures to left of slash are for four-cylinder engine, to right of slash for V-6 (including the price of the required automatic transmission). A 4Bbl. 302 cid V-8 engine cost $561 more than the V-6 ($152 more on the LX convertible).

MUSTANG GT (V-8)

Model No.	Body/Style No.	Body Type & Seating	Factory Price	Shipping Weight	Prod. Total
28/932	61B	3-dr. Hatch-4P	9885	2899	Note 1
27/932	66B	2-dr. Conv.-4P	13585	3043	Note 1

MUSTANG SVO (TURBO FOUR)

28/939	61B	3 dr. Hatch-4P	14521	2881	Note 1

NOTE 1: Ford reports total production of 56,781 two-doors, 84,623 hatchbacks and 15,110 convertibles.

ENGINE [Base Four]: Inline, overhead cam, four-cylinder. Cast-iron block and head. Displacement: 140 cid (2.3 liters). Bore & stroke: 3.78 x 3.13 in. Compression ratio: 9.0:1. Brake horsepower: 88 at 4000 rpm. Torque: 122 lbs.-ft. at 2600 rpm. Five main bearings. Hydraulic valve lifters. Carburetor: 1Bbl. Carter YFA. VIN Code: A.

ENGINE [SVO Turbo Four]: Same as 140 cid four above, but with turbocharger and electronic fuel injection Compression ratio: 8.0:1. Brake H.P.: 175 at 4400 rpm. Torque: 210 lbs.-ft. at 3000 rpm. VIN Code: T.

ENGINE [Optional V-6]: 90-degree, overhead valve V-6. Cast-iron block and aluminum head. Displacement 232 cid (3.8 liters). Bore & stroke: 3.80 x 3.40 in. Compression ratio: 8.7:1. Brake horsepower: 120 at 3600 rpm. Torque: 205 lbs.-ft. at 1600 rpm. Four main bearings. Hydraulic valve lifters. Electronic fuel injection (TBI). VIN Code: 3.

ENGINE [Optional V-8]: 90-degree, overhead valve V-8. Cast-iron block and head. Displacement: 302 cid (5.0 liters). Bore & stroke: 4.00 x 3.00 in. Compression ratio: 8.3:1. Brake horsepower: 180 at 4200 rpm. Torque: 260 lbs.-ft. at 2600 rpm. Five main bearings. Hydraulic valve lifters. Electronic fuel injection. VIN Code: F.

ENGINE [Optional High-Output V-8]: Same as 302 cid V-8 above, but with Holley 4Bbl. carburetor. Brake H.P.: 210 at 4400 rpm. Torque: 270 lbs.-ft. at 3200 rpm. VIN Code: M.

CHASSIS DATA: Wheelbase: 100.5 in. Overall length: 179.3 in. except SVO, 180.8 in. Height: 52.1 in. Width: 69.1 in. Front Tread: 56.6 in. except SVO, 57.8 in. Rear Tread: 57.0 in. except SVO, 58.3 in. Standard Tires: P195/75R14 SBR WSW exc. GT, P225/60VR15 SBR BSW; and SVO, P225/50VR16 Eagle BSW.

TECHNICAL: Transmission: Four-speed manual (floor shift) standard on four-cylinder. Gear ratios: (1st) 3.98:1; (2nd) 2.14:1; (3rd) 1.42:1; (4th) 1.00:1; (Rev) 3.99:1. SVO turbo five-speed: (1st) 3.50:1; (2nd) 2.14:1; (3rd) 1.36:1; (4th) 1.00:1; (5th) 0.78:1; (Rev) 3.39:1. Standard V-8 five-speed: (1st) 3.35:1; (2nd) 1.93:1; (3rd) 1.29:1; (4th) 1.00:1; (5th) 0.68:1; (Rev) 3.15:1. SelectShift three-speed automatic optional on four-cylinder: (1st) 2.47:1; (2nd) 1.47:1; (3rd) 1.00:1; (Rev) 2.11:1. V-6 three-speed automatic: (1st) 2.46:1; (2nd) 1.46:1; (3rd) 1.00:1; (Rev) 2.19:1. Four-speed overdrive automatic standard on V-8: (1st) 2.40:1; (2nd) 1.47:1; (3rd) 1.00:1; (4th) 0.67:1; (Rev) 2.00:1. Standard final drive ratio: (four) 3.08:1 w/4spd, 3.27:1 w/auto.; (V-6) 2.73:1; (V-8) 3.08:1 w/5spd, 3.27:1 w/4spd auto.; (turbo) 3.45:1. Steering: Rack and pinion, power-assisted. Front Suspension: Modified MacPherson struts with lower control arms and stabilizer bar; SVO added adjustable gas-pressurized shocks. Rear Suspension: Rigid axle w/four-bar link and coil springs; GT/SVO added an anti-sway bar. Brakes: Front disc, rear drum (power-assisted) except SVO, four-wheel discs. Ignition: Electronic. Body construction: Unibody. Fuel tank: 15.4 gal.

DRIVETRAIN OPTIONS: Engine/Transmission/Suspension: 232 cid V-6: LX ($439). 302 cid V-8 pkg. ($1000) exc. LX conv. ($152). Five-speed manual trans.: LX ($124). Three-speed automatic trans.: LX ($439). Four-speed overdrive auto trans.: LX ($676); GT ($551). Traction-Lok differential ($95). Optional axle ratio (NC). Handling suspension: LX ($258). Engine block heater ($18). H.D. battery ($27). California emission system ($99). High-altitude option (NC).

CONVENIENCE/APPEARANCE OPTIONS: Option Packages: SVO competition preparation pkg.: delete air cond., power locks, AM/FM stereo/cassette and power windows ($1417 credit). Light/convenience group ($55). Power lock group ($177-$210). Comfort/Convenience: Air cond. ($743). Rear defroster, electric ($140). Fingertip

speed control ($176). Power windows ($198) exc. conv. ($272). Tinted glass ($110). Tilt steering wheel: LX ($110). Entertainment: AM/FM stereo radio w/cassette player: LX/GT ($148). Electronic AM/FM stereo w/cassette: LX/GT ($300). Premium sound system: LX/GT ($138). Radio delete ($148 credit). Exterior: T-Roof: hatch ($1074). Flip-up open air roof: hatch ($315). Lower two-tone paint ($116). Single wing spoiler: SVO (NC). Interior: Console ($191). Low-back vinyl bucket seats: LX ($29). Leather sport performance bucket seats: LX conv. ($780); GT conv. ($415); SVO ($189). LX Wheels and Tires: Wire wheel covers ($98). Styled steel wheels ($178). P205/75R14 WSW ($109). P205/70VR14 BSW ($238). P225/60VR15 SBR BSW ($665).

HISTORY: Introduced: October 4, 1984. Model year production: 156,514. Total production for the U.S. market of 143,682 Mustangs included 79,885 four-cylinder, 18,334 sixes, and 45,463 V-8 engines. Calendar year production: 187,773. Calendar year sales by U.S. dealers: 157,821. Model year sales by U.S. dealers: 159,741.

HISTORY: This year's GT proved that the V-8 had a future under Mustang hoods, even with the turbocharged SVO available. For one thing, the GT was a lot cheaper. It also performed more sedately than a turbo under ordinary conditions, yet was able to deliver impressive performance whenever needed. *Motor Trend* applauded the arrival of the potent 210-horsepower V-8 for delivering 'lovely axle-creaking torque reminiscent of another time.'

1986 MUSTANG

1986 Ford Mustang GT convertible. (JG)

1986 Ford Mustang GT hatchback coupe (with 5.0L V-8). (PH)

MUSTANG — FOUR/V-6/V-8 — Model lineup was the same as in 1985: LX two-door sedan or hatchback (and convertible), GT hatchback and convertible, and SVO. LX had full bodyside striping, power brakes and steering, and such extras as interval wipers, luxury sound package, and an AM/FM stereo radio (which could be deleted for credit). Base engine remained the 140 cid (2.3-liter) OHC four, with four-speed manual gearbox. V-8 engines now had sequential port fuel injection. The 232 cid (3.8-liter) V-6 with throttle-body injection also was optional again, and standard on the LX convertible. Appearance was essentially the same as in 1985. The sloping center front-end panel held a Ford oval at the top, and a single wide opening below. Quad rectangular headlamps were deeply recessed. Parking lamps stood far down on the front end. Side marker lenses were angled to match the front fender tips. Tail lamps were distinctly divided into upper and lower sections by a full-width divider bar. 'Mustang' lettering stood above the left tail lamp, a Ford oval above the right. Three new body colors were offered. Turbine wheel covers switched from bright/argent to bright/black. Mustang's rear axle was upgraded to 8.7 inches with the standard 2.73:1 axle ratio (8.8 inch with others), for use with the 5.0-liter V-8. Viscous engine mounts were added on the 3.8-liter V-6 and the V-8, as used on the turbo four starting in mid-year 1985. One key now operated door locks and ignition. The two-door LX notchback had its high mount brake lamp added to the package tray; GT and SVO were modified to take it on the spoilers. Hatchback LX models added a spoiler to house that brake lamp, while LX and GT convertibles installed a luggage rack with integrated brake lamp. Preferred Equipment Packages included such items as air conditioning, styled wheels, and Premium Sound System. Mustang GT carried a new high-output 302 cid (5.0-liter) V-8 with multi-port fuel injection. Rated 200 horsepower, with EEC-IV electronic engine controls, it was hooked to a five-speed manual (overdrive) transmission, or automatic overdrive. GT included a special suspension, Goodyear Eagle VR performance tires, quick-ratio power steering, and articulated front sport seats. The four-barrel V-8 was abandoned. All Mustang V-8s with five-speed manual also added an upshift indicator light. SVO, the 'Ultimate Mustang,' carried a computer-controlled 200-horsepower 2.3-liter four with intercooled turbocharger and multiport fuel injection. A five speed transmission, with Hurst shifter that offered short, quick throws, was standard. So were disc brakes all around.

I.D. DATA: Mustang's 17 symbol Vehicle Identification Number (VIN) again was stamped on a metal tab fastened to the instrument panel, visible through the windshield. Coding was similar to 1984-85. Model year code changed to 'G' for 1986.

MUSTANG LX (FOUR/V-6)

Model No.	Body/ Style No.	Body Type & Seating	Factory Price	Shipping Weight	Prod. Total
26	66B	2-dr. Notch-4P	7189/8153	2601/2722	Note 1
28	61B	3-dr. Hatch-4P	7744/8708	2661/2782	Note 1
27	66B	2-dr. Conv. 4P	----/12821	----/2908	Note 1

LX Price/Weight Note: Figures to left of slash are for four-cylinder engine, to right of slash for V-6 (including the price of the required automatic transmission). A 302 cid V-8 engine cost $1120 more than the four ($106 more on the LX convertible).

MUSTANG GT (V-8)

Model No.	Body/ Style No.	Body Type & Seating	Factory Price	Shipping Weight	Prod. Total
28	61B	3-dr. Hatch-4P	10691	2976	Note 1
27	66B	2-dr. Conv.-4P	14523	3103	Note 1

MUSTANG SVO (TURBO FOUR)

28/937	618	3-dr. Hatch-4P	15272	3028	Note 1

NOTE 1: Ford reports total production of 106,720 two-doors (including convertibles) and 117,690 hatchbacks.

ENGINE [Base Four]: Inline, overhead cam, four-cylinder. Cast-iron block and head. Displacement: 140 cid (2.3 liters). Bore & stroke: 3.78 x 3.13 in. Compression ratio: 9.5:1. Brake horsepower: 88 at 4200 rpm. Torque: 122 lbs.-ft. at 2600 rpm. Five main bearings. Hydraulic valve lifters. Carburetor: 1Bbl. Carter YFA. VIN Code: A.

ENGINE [SVO Turbo Four]: Same as 140 cid four above, but with turbocharger and electronic fuel injection. Compression ratio: 8.0:1. Brake H.P.: 200 at 5000 rpm. Torque: 240 lbs.-ft. at 3200 rpm. VIN Code: T.

ENGINE [Optional V-6]: 90-degree, overhead valve V-6. Cast-iron block and aluminum head. Displacement: 232 cid (3.8 liters). Bore & stroke: 3.80 x 3.40 in. Compression ratio: 8.7:1. Brake horsepower: 120 at 3600 rpm. Torque: 205 lbs.-ft. at 1600 rpm. Four main bearings. Hydraulic valve lifters. Electronic fuel injection (TBI). VIN Code: 3.

ENGINE [Optional V-8]: 90-degree, overhead valve V-8. Cast-iron block and head. Displacement: 302 cid (5.0 liters). Bore & stroke: 4.00 x 3.00 in. Compression ratio: 9.2:1. Brake horsepower: 200 at 4000 rpm. Torque: 285 lbs.-ft. at 3000 rpm. Five main bearings. Hydraulic valve lifters. Sequential fuel injection. VIN Code: M.

CHASSIS DATA: Wheelbase: 100.5 in. Overall length: 179.3 in. except SVO, 180.8 in. Height: 52.1 in. exc. conv., 51.9 in. Width: 69.1 in. Front Tread: 56.6 in. except SVO, 57.8 in. Rear Tread: 57.0 in. except SVO, 58.3 in. Standard Tires: P195/75R14 SBR WSW exc. GT, P225/60VR15 SBR BSW, P225/50VR16 'Gatorback' BSW.

TECHNICAL: Transmission: Four-speed manual (floor shift) standard on four-cylinder. Five-speed manual standard on turbo and V-8. Gear ratios N/A. SelectShift three-speed automatic optional on four-cylinder, standard on V-6. Gear ratios: (1st) 2.47:1; (2nd) 1.47:1; (3rd) 1.00:1; (Rev) 2.11:1. V-6 three-speed automatic: (1st) 2.46:1; (2nd) 1.46:1; (3rd) 1.00:1; (Rev) 2.19:1. Four-speed overdrive automatic available with V-8: (1st) 2.40:1; (2nd) 1.47:1; (3rd) 1.00:1; (4th) 0.67:1; (Rev) 2.00:1. Standard final drive ratio: (four) 3.08:1 w/4spd, 3.27:1 w/auto.;

(V-6) 2.73:1; (V-8) 2.73:1 w/5spd, 3.27:1 w/4spd auto.; (turbo) 3.73:1. Steering: Rack and pinion, power-assisted. Front Suspension: Modified MacPherson struts with lower control arms and stabilizer bar; SVO added adjustable gas-pressurized shocks. Rear Suspension: Rigid axle w/four-bar link and coil springs; GT/SVO added an anti-sway bar and dual shocks on each side. Brakes: Front disc, rear drum (power-assisted) except SVO, four-wheel disc brakes. Ignition: Electronic. Body construction: Unibody. Fuel tank: 15.4 gal.

DRIVETRAIN OPTIONS: Engine/Transmission/Suspension: 232 cid V-6: LX ($454). 302 cid V-8 pkg. ($1120) exc. LX conv. ($106). Five-speed manual trans.: LX ($124). Three-speed automatic trans.: LX ($510); std. on conv. Four-speed overdrive auto trans.: LX ($746); GT ($622). Engine block heater ($18). H.D. battery ($27). California emission system ($102). High-altitude option (NC).

CONVENIENCE/APPEARANCE OPTIONS: Option Packages: SVO competition preparation pkg.: equipment deleted ($1451 credit). Light/convenience group ($55). Power lock group ($182-$215). Comfort/Convenience: Air cond. ($762). Rear defroster, electric ($145). Fingertip speed control ($176). Power windows ($207) exc. conv. ($282). Tinted glass ($115). Tilt steering wheel: LX ($115). Entertainment: AM/FM stereo radio w/cassette player: LX/GT ($148). Electronic seek/scan AM/FM stereo w/cassette: LX/GT ($300). Premium sound system ($138). Radio delete ($148 credit). Exterior: T-Roof: hatch ($1100). Flip-up open air roof: hatch ($315). Lower charcoal accent paint ($116). Single wing spoiler: SVO (NC). Interior: Console w/clock and systems monitor ($191). Vinyl bucket seats: LX ($29). Articulated leather sport bucket seats: LX conv. ($807): GT conv. ($429). Leather seat upholstery: SVO ($189). LX Wheels and Tires Wire wheel covers ($98). Styled steel wheels ($178). P205/75R14 WSW ($109) P225/60VR15 on cast aluminum wheels ($665).

HISTORY: Introduced: October 3, 1985. Model year production: 224,410. Total production for the U.S. market of 198,358 Mustangs included 107,340 four-cylinder, 38,422 sixes and 52,596 V-8 engines. Calendar year production: 177,737. Calendar year sales by U.S. dealers: 167,699. Model year sales by U.S. dealers: 175,598.

HISTORY: Mustang was the only Ford model to show a sales increase for 1986 Mercury's similar Capri would not return for another year, but Mustang was prepared to carry on in ordinary and high-performance trim. Turbocharging forced a hefty amount of horsepower out of SVO's small four-cylinder engine, delivering acceleration that rivaled big old V-8s.

1987 MUSTANG

1987 Ford Mustang GT hatchback coupe. (OCW)

1987 Ford Mustang LX notchback (with 5.0L V-8). (PH)

Mercury's Capri was out of the lineup after 1986, leaving Mustang as Ford's sole pony car. The turbocharged SVO Mustang also departed, leaving only an LX and GT model. Also gone: the V-6 engine.

1987 Ford Mustang GT convertible (with 5.0L V-8). (PH)

MUSTANG - FOUR/V-8 - Ford's pony car got a fresh look for 1987 with a significant restyling -- the first one since its debut for 1979. Changes included new front and rear fascias, a switch to aero headlamps, and the addition of substantial lower bodyside moldings. The GT had a lower air dam with integrated foglamps and air scoops, as well as 'Mustang GT' lettering formed into its flared rocker panel moldings and rear fascia. The GT hatchback also had a large spoiler that held the required high-mount stop lamp. Wide tail lamps on the GT were covered by a louver-like slotted appliqué. Inside all Mustangs was a new instrument panel that showed a more European took, accompanied by a two-spoke steering wheel. Multi-point fuel injection replaced the former carburetor on the base four-cylinder engine. while the V-8 got a boost from 200 to 225 horsepower. A five-speed manual gearbox was now standard, with four-speed overdrive automatic optional.

I.D. DATA: Mustang's 17-symbol Vehicle Identification Number (VIN) again was stamped on a metal tab fastened to the instrument panel, visible through the windshield. Coding was similar to 1984-86. Model year code (symbol ten) changed to 'H' for 1987.

MUSTANG LX (FOUR/V-8)

Model No.	Body/ Style No.	Body Type & Seating	Factory Price	Shipping Weight	Prod. Total
40	66B	2-dr. Notch-4P	8043/9928	2724/3000	Note 1
41	61B	3-dr. Hatch-4P	8474/10359	2782/3058	Note 1
44	66B	2-dr. Conv.-4P	12840/14725	2921/3197	Note 1

LX Price/Weight Note: Figures to left of slash are for four-cylinder engine, to right of slash for V-8.

MUSTANG GT (V-8)

42	61B	3-dr. Hatch-4P	11835	3080	Note 1
45	66B	2-dr. Conv.-4P	15724	3214	Note 1

NOTE 1: Ford reports total production of 64,704 two-doors (including convertibles) and 94,441 hatchbacks. Other sources claim totals of 58,100 two-doors, 80,717 hatchbacks, and 20,328 convertibles.

ENGINE [Base Four (LX)]: Inline, overhead cam, four-cylinder. Cast-iron block and head. Displacement: 140 cid (2.3 liters). Bore & stroke: 3.78 x 3.13 in. Compression ratio: 9.5:1. Brake horsepower: 90 at 3800 rpm. Torque: 130 lbs.-ft. at 2800 rpm. Five main bearings. Hydraulic valve lifters. Port fuel injection.

ENGINE [Base V-8 (GT); Optional (LX)]: 90-degree, overhead valve V-8. Cast-iron block and head. Displacement: 302 cid (5.0 liters). Bore & stroke: 4.00 x 3.00 in. Compression ratio: 9.2:1. Brake horsepower: 225 at 4000 rpm. Torque: 300 lbs.-ft. at 3200 rpm. Five main bearings. Hydraulic valve lifters. Sequential fuel injection.

CHASSIS DATA: Wheelbase: 100.5 in. Overall length: 179.6 in. Height: 52.1 in. exc. conv., 51.9 in. Width: 69.1 in. Front Tread: 56.6 in. Rear Tread: 57.0 in. Standard Tires: P195/75R14 except GT, P225/60VR16 Goodyear Eagle GT Gatorback.

TECHNICAL: Transmission: Five-speed manual (floor shift) standard. Four-speed overdrive automatic available. Steering: Rack and pinion, power-assisted. Front suspension: Modified MacPherson struts with lower control arms and stabilizer bar (gas shocks on GT). Rear Suspension: Rigid axle w/four links and coil springs (stabilizer bar on GT). Brakes: Front disc, rear drum (power-assisted). Body construction: Unibody. Fuel tank: 15.4 gal.

DRIVETRAIN OPTIONS: Engine/Transmission/Suspension: 5.0-liter V-8 pkg.: LX ($1885). Four-speed overdrive auto trans. ($515).

CONVENIENCE/APPEARANCE OPTIONS: Climate Control Group (Air conditioning, heavy-duty battery, rear defogger, tinted glass), LX coupe w/four ($1005); LX coupe w/V-8 ($978); LX conv. w/four ($740); LX coupe w/V-8 ($713); GT coupe ($858); GT conv. ($713). Air conditioning ($788). Heavy-duty battery ($27). Tinted glass ($120). Climate Control Group w/Premium Sound instead of rear defogger, LX coupes w/four ($1028); LX coupes w/V-8 ($1001); LX conv. w/four ($908); LX conv. w/V-8 GT ($881). Climate Control Group w/Custom Equipment

Group and Premium Sound instead of rear defogger, LX coupes w/four ($860); LX coupes w/V-8 ($833); LX conv. w/four ($740); LX conv. w/V-8, GT ($713). Custom Equipment Group (Graphic Equalizer, dual power mirrors, lighted visor mirrors, tilt steering column, power windows), LX coupes ($624); LX conv. ($538); GT coupe ($500); GT conv. ($414). Graphic Equalizer ($218). Dual power mirrors ($60). Lighted visor mirrors ($100). Tilt steering column, LX ($124). Power windows, coupes ($222); convertibles ($296). Special Value Group: Power Lock Group (includes remote fuel filler & decklid/hatch releases), AM/FM radio w/cass, speed control, styled road wheels), LX w/V-8 ($735); GT ($519). Power Lock Group, LX ($244); GT ($206). AM/FM Stereo Radio w/cass ($137). Speed control ($176). Styled road wheels, LX ($178). Bodyside molding insert stripe ($49). AM/FM Stereo delete ($206 credit). Flip-up/open-air sunroof ($355). T-Roof, LX ($1737); LX w/Climate Control Group ($1667); LX w/Special Value Group ($1543); LX w/Custom Equipment Group ($1505); GT ($1608); GT w/Special Value Group ($1401); GT w/Custom Equipment Group ($1341). Premium Sound System ($168). Wire wheel covers, LX ($98). Leather articulated sport seats, LX conv. ($780); GT conv. ($415).

HISTORY: Introduced: October 2, 1986. Model year production: 159,145. Calendar year production: 214,153. Calendar year sales by U.S. dealers: 172,602. Model year sales by U.S. dealers: 163,392.

1988 MUSTANG

1988 Ford Mustang GT hatchback coupe. (OCW)

1988 Ford Mustang GT convertible (with 5.0L V-8). (OCW)

In the wake of the 1987 restyling, Mustang entered this model year with minimal change.

MUSTANG - FOUR/V-8 - As in 1987, two powerplants were available for the Ford pony car: a 2.3-liter four-cylinder engine rated 90 horsepower, or a 225-horsepower V-8 (standard on the GT). A five-speed manual floor shift was standard, with four-speed overdrive automatic optional.

I.D. DATA: Mustang's 17-symbol Vehicle Identification Number (VIN) again was stamped on a metal tab fastened to the instrument panel, visible through the windshield. Coding was similar to 1984-87. Model year code (symbol ten) changed to 'J' for 1988.

1988 Ford Mustang convertible. (PH)

MUSTANG LX (FOUR/V-8)

Model No.	Body/ Style No.	Body Type & Seating	Factory Price	Shipping Weight	Prod. Total
40	66B	2-dr. Notch-4P	8726/10611	2751/3037	Note 1
41	61B	3-dr. Hatch-4P	9221/11106	2818/3105	Note 1
44	66B	2-dr. Conv.-4P	13702/15587	2953/3209	Note 1

LX Price/Weight Note: Figures to left of slash are for four-cylinder engine, to right of slash for V-8.

MUSTANG GT (V-8)

Model No.	Body/ Style No.	Body Type & Seating	Factory Price	Shipping Weight	Prod. Total
42	61B	3-dr. Hatch-4P	12745	3193	Note 1
45	66B	2-dr. Conv.-4P	16610	3341	Note 1

NOTE 1: A total of 179,565 Mustangs were produced for the U.S. market (71,890 two-doors, 74,331 hatchbacks, and 33,344 convertibles).

ENGINE [Base Four (LX)]: Inline, overhead cam, four-cylinder. Cast-iron block and head. Displacement: 140 cid (2.3 liters). Bore & stroke: 3.78 x 3.13 in. Compression ratio: 9.5:1. Brake horsepower: 90 at 3800 rpm. Torque: 130 lbs.-ft. at 2800 rpm. Five main bearings. Hydraulic valve lifters. Port fuel injection.

ENGINE [Base V-8 (GT); Optional (LX)]: 90-degree, overhead valve V-8. Cast-iron block and head. Displacement: 302 cid (5.0 liters). Bore & stroke: 4.00 x 3.00 in. Compression ratio: 9.5:1. Brake horsepower: 225 at 4200 rpm. Torque: 300 lbs.-ft. at 3200 rpm. Five main bearings. Hydraulic valve lifters. Sequential fuel injection.

CHASSIS DATA: Wheelbase: 100.5 in. Overall length: 179.6 in. Height: 52.1 in. exc. conv., 51.9 in. Width: 69.1 in. Front Tread: 56.6 in. Rear Tread: 57.0 in. Standard Tires: P195/75R14 except (GT) P225/60VR16 Goodyear Eagle GT Gatorback.

TECHNICAL: Transmission: Five-speed manual (floor shift) standard. Four-speed overdrive automatic available. Steering: Rack and pinion, power-assisted. Front Suspension: Modified MacPherson struts with lower control arms and stabilizer bar (gas shocks on GT). Rear Suspension: Rigid axle w/four links and coil springs (stabilizer bar on GT). Brakes: Front disc, rear drum (power-assisted). Front disc, rear drum (power-assisted). Body construction: Unibody. Fuel tank: 15.4 gal.

DRIVETRAIN OPTIONS: 5.0-liter V-8 pkg.: LX ($1885). Four-speed overdrive auto trans. ($515).

CONVENIENCE/APPEARANCE OPTIONS: Preferred Equip. Pkgs., LX Sdn or hatchback w/four (NC); LX Sdn or hatchback w/V-8 ($615); LX convertible w/four (NC); LX Convertible w/V-8 ($555); GT Hatchback ($615); GT Convertible ($555). Manual Control Air Cond ($788). Pwr Side Windows ($222). Tilt Strg Wheel ($124). Dual Illum. Visor Mirrors ($100). Custom Equipment Group, LX ($1034); LX Convertible ($934); GT ($910); GT Convertible ($810). Bodyside Mldg. Insert Stripe ($49). Rr Window Defroster ($145). Graphic Equalizer ($218). Pwr Lock Grp. ($237). Dual Elect. Remote Mirrors ($60). Elect. AM/FM Radio w/Cass ($137). Flip-Up Open Air Roof ($355). T-Roof, LX ($1800); w/Preferred Equip. Pkg. ($1505); w/Custom Equip. Grp. ($1459); w/Custom Equip. Grp & Preferred Equip. Pkg. ($1163); GT ($1659); w/Preferred Equip. Pkg. ($1363); w/Custom Equip. Grp. ($1437); w/Custom Equip. Grp. & Preferred Equip. Pkg. ($1141). Premium Sound System ($168). Speed Control ($182). Wire Style Wheel Covers ($178). Styled Road Wheels ($178). Frt. Lic. Plate Bracket (NC). Eng. Block Heater ($18). Calif. Emission System ($99). High Alt. Emissions System (NC). Lower Titanium Accent Treatment Ext. Paint, GT (NC). Leather Articulated Spt Seats, LX Conv. ($780); GT Conv. ($415). Vinyl Seat Trim ($37). P195/75R14 WSW Tires ($82).

HISTORY: Introduced: October 1, 1987. Model year production: 211,225 (total). Calendar year production: 200,089. Calendar year sales by U.S. dealers: 170,080. Model year sales by U.S. dealers: 170,601.

1989 Ford Mustang GT. (OCW)

Ford's pony car entered the 1989 marketplace with little change, except that the LX, when equipped with an available V-8 engine, was now called "LX 5.0L Sport."

MUSTANG - FOUR/V-8 - Once again, two powerplants were available for Ford's pony car: a 90-horsepower four or 225-horsepower V-8. Standard on the GT, the V-8 was optional in LX Mustangs. When installed in an LX, the V-8 package included articulated sport seats (as in the GT). Both convertible models now had standard power windows and door locks.

I.D. DATA: Mustang's 17-symbol Vehicle Identification Number (VIN) again was stamped on a metal tab fastened to the instrument panel, visible through the windshield. Coding was similar to 1984-88. Model year code (symbol ten) changed to 'K' for 1989.

MUSTANG LX (FOUR/V-8)

Model No.	Body/ Style No.	Body Type & Seating	Factory Price	Shipping Weight	Prod. Total
40	66B	2-dr. Notch-4P	9050/11410	2754/3045	42,349
41	61B	3-dr. Hatch-4P	9556/12265	2819/3110	Note 1
44	66B	2-dr. Conv.-4P	14140/17001	2966/3257	Note 2

LX Price/Weight Note: Figures to left of slash are for four-cylinder engine, to right of slash for V-8.

MUSTANG GT (V-8)

42	61B	3-dr. Hatch-4P	13272	3194	Note 1
45	66B	2-dr. Conv.-4P	17512	3333	Note 2

NOTE 1: Production of LX and GT hatchbacks totaled 105,692 with no further breakout available.

1989 Ford Mustang LX 5.0L Sport hatchback coupe. (OCW)

1989 Ford Mustang LX notchback (with 5.0L V-8). (OCW)

NOTE 2: Production of LX and GT convertibles totaled 40,518 with no further breakout available.

ENGINE [Base Four (LX)]: Inline, overhead cam, four-cylinder. Cast-iron block and head. Displacement: 140 cid (2.3 liters). Bore & stroke: 3.78 x 3.13 in. Compression ratio: 9.5:1. Brake horsepower: 90 at 3800 rpm. Torque: 130 lbs.-ft. at 2800 rpm. Five main bearings. Hydraulic valve lifters. Port fuel injection.

ENGINE [Base V-8 (GT); Optional (LX)]: 90-degree, overhead valve V-8. Cast-iron block and head. Displacement: 302 cid (5.0 liters). Bore & stroke: 4.00 x 3.00 in. Compression ratio: 9.2:1. Brake horsepower: 225 at 4200 rpm. Torque: 300 lbs.-ft. at 3200 rpm. Five main bearings. Hydraulic valve lifters. Sequential fuel injection.

CHASSIS DATA: Wheelbase: 100.5 in. Overall length: 179.6 in. Height: 52.1 in. exc. conv., 51.9 in. Width: 69.1 in. Front Tread: 56.6 in. Rear Tread: 57.0 in. Standard Tires: P195/70R14 except (LX 5.0L Sport and GT) P225/60VR15.

TECHNICAL: Transmission: Five-speed manual (floor shift) standard. Four-speed overdrive automatic available. Steering: Rack and pinion, power-assisted. Front Suspension: Modified MacPherson struts with lower control arms and stabilizer bar (gas shocks on GT). Rear Suspension: Rigid axle w/four links and coil springs (stabilizer bar on GT). Brakes: Front disc, rear drum (power-assisted). Body construction: Unibody. Fuel tank: 15.4 gal.

DRIVETRAIN OPTIONS: Four-speed overdrive auto trans. ($515).

CONVENIENCE/APPEARANCE OPTIONS: Preferred Equip. Pkgs., LX w/four, Special Value Grp, Pwr Lock Grp, Dual Elect. Remote Mirrors, Elect. AM/FM Radio w/Cass Player & Clock, Speed Control, Styled Road Wheels, Pwr Side Windows, LX Sdn or hatchback (NC); LX Conv. (NC). LX V-8 Sport GT, Special Value Grp, Pwr Lock Grp, Dual Elect. Remote Mirrors, Elect. AM/FM Radio w/Cass Player & Clock, Spd Control, Power Windows, Custom Equipment Grp, Man Control Air Cond, Dual Illum Visor Mirrors, Tilt Wheel, Premium Sound System, Sedan or Hatchback ($1006); Conv. ($487). Group Opts. Custom Equipment Group (four LX Series only) Manual Control, Dual Illum Visor Mirrors, Tilt Wheel, Premium Sound System, LX Sdn & Hatchback ($1180); LX Conv. ($1080). Bodyside Molding Insert Stripe ($61). Rear Window Defroster ($150). Flip-Up Open Air Roof ($355). Wire Style Wheel Covers ($193). Calif. Emission System ($100). High Alt. Emissions System (NC). Lower Titanium Accent Treatment Ext. Paint, GT (NC). Leather Articulated Sport Seats, LX Conv. ($855); LX V-8 Sport Conv. or GT Conv. ($489). Vinyl Seat Trim ($37). Frt. License Plate Bracket (NC). P195/75R14 WSW Tires ($82).

HISTORY: Introduced: October 6, 1988. Model year production: 209,769. Calendar year sales by U.S. dealers: 161,148. Model year sales by U.S. dealers: 172,218.

1990 MUSTANG

1990 Ford Mustang GT convertible. (OCW)

Safety led Mustang into 1990, as a driver's airbag and rear shoulder belts became standard. Otherwise, the familiar rear-drive pony car continued as before, for its twelfth season in this form.

1990 Ford Mustang LX 5.0L two-door hatchback. (OCW)

1990 Ford Mustang GT hatchback coupe (with 5.0L V-8). (OCW)

MUSTANG - FOUR/V-8 - Body styles and powertrains were the same as prior years: coupe, hatchback, and convertible, with 2.3-liter four or 5.0-liter V-8. No longer did Mustang's interior hold a tilt steering column or console armrest, but door panels now held map pockets. The LX 5.0L, with V-8 engine, came with the heftier suspension and bigger tires from the GT, but without the GT's spoilers and air dams. Clearcoat paint was now optional, as was leather interior trim for the V-8 hatchbacks.

I.D. DATA: Mustang's 17-symbol Vehicle Identification Number (VIN) again was stamped on a metal tab fastened to the instrument panel, visible through the windshield. Coding was similar to 1984-89. Model year code (symbol ten) changed to 'L' for 1990.

MUSTANG LX (FOUR/V-8)

Model No.	Body/ Style No.	Body Type & Seating	Factory Price	Shipping Weight	Prod. Total
40	66B	2-dr. Notch-4P	9638/12107	2634/2715	17,808
41	61B	3-dr. Hatch-4P	10144/12950	2634/2715	Note 1
44	66B	2-dr. Conv.-4P	14495/17681	2871/2952	Note 2

LX Price/Weight Note: Figures to left of slash are for four-cylinder engine, to right of slash for LX 5.0L Sport V-8.

MUSTANG GT (V-8)

Model No.	Body/ Style No.	Body Type & Seating	Factory Price	Shipping Weight	Prod. Total
42	61B	3-dr. Hatch-4P	13929	3065	Note 1
45	66B	2-dr. Conv.-4P	18303	3213	Note 2

NOTE 1: Production of LX and GT hatchbacks totaled 71,798 with no further breakout available.

NOTE 2: Production of LX and GT convertibles totaled 25,624 with no further breakout available.

ENGINE [Base Four (LX)]: Inline, overhead cam, four-cylinder. Cast-iron block and head. Displacement: 140 cid (2.3 liters). Bore & stroke: 3.78 x 3.13 in. Compression ratio: 9.5:1. Brake horsepower: 88 at 4000 rpm. Torque: 132 lbs.-ft. at 2600 rpm. Five main bearings. Hydraulic valve lifters. Port fuel injection.

ENGINE [Base V-8 (GT); Optional (LX)]: 90-degree, overhead valve V-8. Cast-iron block and head. Displacement: 302 cid (5.0 liters). Bore & stroke: 4.00 x 3.00 in. Compression ratio: 9.0:1. Brake horsepower: 225 at 4200 rpm. Torque: 300 lbs.-ft. at 3200 rpm. Five main bearings. Hydraulic valve lifters. Sequential fuel injection.

CHASSIS DATA: Wheelbase: 100.5 in. Overall length: 179.6 in. Height: 52.1 in. Width: 68.3 in. Front Tread: 56.6 in. Rear Tread: 57.0 in. Standard Tires: P195/75R14 exc. (LX 5.0L Sport and GT) P225/60VR15.

TECHNICAL: Transmission: Five-speed manual (floor shift) standard. Four-speed overdrive automatic available. Steering: Rack and pinion, power-assisted. Front Suspension: Modified MacPherson struts with lower control arms and stabilizer bar (gas shocks on GT). Rear Suspension: Rigid axle w/four links and coil springs (stabilizer bar on GT). Brakes: Front disc, rear drum (power-assisted). Body construction: Unibody. Fuel tank: 15.4 gal.

DRIVETRAIN OPTIONS: Four-speed overdrive auto trans. ($539).

1990 Ford Mustang LX 5.0L convertible. (OCW)

CONVENIENCE/APPEARANCE OPTIONS: Preferred Equip Pkgs., LX w/four Special Value Grp, Pwr Equipment Grp, Pwr Lock Grp, Dual Elect. Remote Mirrors, Pwr Side Windows, Spd Cntrl, Elect. AM/FM Radio w/Cass Player & Clock, LX Sdn or Hatchback (NC); LX Conv. (NC). LX V-8 Sport GT Special Value Grp, Pwr Equipment Grp, Pwr Lock Grp, Dual Elect. Remote Mirrors, Power Windows, Elect. AM/FM Radio w/Cass Player & Clock, Spd Control, Custom Equip. Grp, Air Conditioner, Dual Illum Visor Mirrors, Premium Sound System, Sedan or Hatchback ($1003); Conv. ($496). Custom Equipment Grp (four LX Series only), Air Conditioner, Dual Illum Visor Mirrors, LX Sdn & Hatchback ($907); LX Conv. ($807). Rr Window Defroster ($150). Flip-Up Open Air Roof ($355). Wire Style Wheel Covers ($193). Premium Sound System, incl 6 premium spkrs & 4 channel amplifier 80 watts ($168). Calif. Emission System ($100). High Alt Emissions (NC). Clearcoat Exterior Paint ($91). Lower Titanium Accent Treatment, GT ($159). Leather Seating Surfaces on Articulated Spt Seats ($489). Vinyl Seat Trim ($37). Frt License Plate Bracket (NC). Eng Block Heater ($20). P195/75R14 WSW Tires ($82).

HISTORY: Model year production: 128,189. Calendar year sales by U.S. dealers: 124,135. Model year sales by U.S. dealers: 120,486.

1991 MUSTANG

1991 Ford Mustang LX convertible (with 5.0L V-8). (PH)

MUSTANG — (4-CYL/V-8) — SERIES P — Mustang was available in three series: Mustang LX and 5.0-liter Mustang LX (both comprised of two-door sedan, three-door hatchback and two-door convertible) and Mustang GT (two-door hatchback and convertible). A new twin-plug version of the 2.3-liter engine improved base Mustang horsepower from 86 to 105 for heightened performance. Powertrain availability included a 2.3-liter electronically fuel-injected engine and the 5.0-liter HO (High Output) engine. Both were available with either five-speed manual (standard) or four-speed automatic (optional) transmissions. GT and LX 5.0-liter models got new, upsized 16-inch five-spoke aluminum wheels. New P225/55ZR16 all-season performance tires were made standard on LX 5.0-liter, and optional on GT. The convertible received a lowered top-down stack height for a cleaner, more attractive appearance. For interior changes, new cloth seat materials on the 2.3-liter LX models were added. Other improvements included vinyl door trim panel inserts added to power window-equipped units, and an articulated sport

1991 Ford Mustang GT convertible (with 5.0L V-8). (OCW)

seat was made standard on the LX 5.0-liter sedan. Options added for 1991 included: cargo tie down net, front floor mats, graphic equalizer, 15-inch cast aluminum wheels with P205/65R15 BSW tires (2.3-liter LX), and 14-inch styled road wheels. A driver's-side airbag supplemental restraint system and rear-passenger manual lap/shoulder belts were now included as standard equipment.

I.D. DATA: Mustang's 17-symbol Vehicle Identification Number (VIN) again was stamped on a metal tab fastened to the instrument panel, visible through the windshield. Coding was similar to 1984-1990. Model year code (symbol ten) changed to 'M' for 1991.

MUSTANG SERIES

MUSTANG LX (FOUR/V-8)

Model No.	Body/ Style No.	Body Type & Seating	Factory Price	Shipping Weight	Prod. Total
P	40	2-dr Cpe-4P	10157/13270	2759/3037	16,846
P	41	3-dr Hatch-4P	10663/14055	2824/3102	Note 1
P	44	2-dr Conv-4P	16222/19242	2960/3238	Note 2

LX Price/Weight Note: Figures to left of slash for four-cylinder, to right for V-8.

MUSTANG GT (V-8)

P	42	3-dr Hatch-4P	15034	3191	Note 1
P	45	2-dr Conv-4P	19864	3327	Note 2

NOTE 1: Production of hatchbacks totaled 53,358 with no further breakout available.

NOTE 2: Production of convertibles totaled 20,181 with no further breakout available.

ENGINE [Base Four (LX)]: Inline, overhead cam, four-cylinder. Cast-iron block and head. Displacement: 140 cid (2.3 liters). Bore & stroke: 3.78 x 3.12 in. Compression ratio: 9.5:1. Brake horsepower: 105 at 4600 rpm. Torque: 135 lbs.-ft. at 2600 rpm. Five main bearings. Hydraulic valve lifters. Multi-port fuel injection.

ENGINE [Base V-8 (GT); Optional (LX)]: 90-degree, overhead valve V-8. Cast-iron block and head. Displacement: 302 cid (5.0 liters). Bore & stroke: 4.00 x 3.00 in. Compression ratio: 9.0:1. Brake horsepower: 225 at 4200 rpm. Torque: 300 lbs.-ft. at 3200 rpm. Five main bearings. Hydraulic valve lifters. Sequential fuel injection.

CHASSIS DATA: Wheelbase: 100.5 in. Overall length: 179.6 in. Height: 52.1 in. Width: 68.3 in. Front Tread: 56.6 in. Rear Tread: 57.0 in. Standard Tires: P195/75R14 except (LX 5.0L and GT) P225/55ZR16.

TECHNICAL: Transmission: Five-speed manual (floor shift) standard. Four-speed overdrive automatic available. Steering: Rack and pinion, power-assisted. Front Suspension: Modified MacPherson struts with lower control arms and stabilizer bar. Rear Suspension: Rigid axle w/four links and coil springs (stabilizer bar on GT). Brakes: Front disc, rear drum (power-assisted). Body construction: Unibody. Fuel tank: 15.4 gal.

DRIVETRAIN OPTIONS: Four-speed automatic overdrive transmission ($595).

CONVENIENCE/APPEARANCE OPTIONS: Preferred Equip Pkgs (LX Sdn & HB): Pwr Equip Grp incl Dual Elect Remote Ctrl Mirrors, Pwr Side Windows, Pwr Lock Grp, Cargo Tie-Down Net, Frt Flr Mats, Spd Ctrl, Elect AM/FM Radio w/Cass Player & Clock, Styled Road Whls ($222); LX Conv ($207). LX 5.0L Sdn & HB: incl same as LX Sdn & HB except Whls plus Prem Sound Syst, Custom Equip Grp incl Man Ctrl Air Cond, Dual Illum Visor Mirrors ($1314); LX 5.0L Conv ($749). GT HB ($1314); GT Conv ($749). Calif. Emission Syst ($100). LX: Vinyl Low Back Seats ($37). LX 5.0L & GT: Leather Seating Surfaces Articulated Spt ($489). Cargo Tie-Down Net ($66). Custom Equip Grp: LX Sdn & HB ($917). Rr Window Defroster (NA Conv) ($160). Flr Mats, Frt ($33). Graphic Equalizer incl Premium Sound ($139). Clearcoat Paint

($91). Pwr Equip Grp (stnd on Conv) ($565). Premium Sound Syst ($168). Elect AM/FM Stereo Radio w/Cass ($155). Roof, Flip-Up Open Air (HB Mdls only) ($355). Spd Ctrl ($210). Titanium Lower Bodyside Accent Treatment (GT only) ($159). Wire Whl Covers (LX only) (NC); other Mdls ($193). Cast Alum Whls w/Upsized P205/65R15 BSW Tires (LX only) ($167); other Mdls ($360). Styled Road Whls (LX only) ($193). Eng Block Heater ($20).

HISTORY: U.S. model year Mustang production totaled 98,737. U.S. calendar year Mustang production totaled 81,558. In 1991, Ford's new engineering offshoot, called the Special Vehicle Team, began work on the Mustang Cobra—a higher performance version of the Mustang GT—tentatively scheduled for release in 1993.

1992 MUSTANG

1992 Ford Mustang convertible (with 5.0L V-8). (OCW)

1992 Ford Mustang GT hatchback coupe (with 5.0L V-8). (OCW)

MUSTANG—(4-CYL/V-8)—SERIES P—The 1992 Mustang received several body enhancements including color-keyed bodyside molding,

bumper strips, a four-way power driver's seat option and two new colors: Bimini blue and Calypso green. Powertrain availability again included a 2.3-liter four-cylinder engine with electronic fuel-injection and a 5.0-liter HO (High Output) V-8 engine. Both were available with either five-speed manual (standard) or four-speed automatic overdrive (optional) transmissions. Standard equipment for Mustang included a driver's side airbag, power front disc brakes, front- and rear-passenger shoulder seat belts, a modified MacPherson-strut rear suspension, rear spoiler, low-back reclining bucket seats with headrests and an electronic AM/FM stereo radio with four speakers.

I.D. DATA: Mustang's 17-symbol Vehicle Identification Number (VIN) again was stamped on a metal tab fastened to the instrument panel, visible through the windshield. Coding was similar to 1984-1991. Model year code (symbol ten) changed to 'N' for 1992.

MUSTANG SERIES

MUSTANG LX (FOUR/V-8)

Model No.	Body/ Style No.	Body Type & Seating	Factory Price	Shipping Weight	Prod. Total
P	40	2-dr Cpe-4P	10215/13422	2775/3010	13,836
P	41	3-dr Hatch-4P	10721/14207	2834/3069	Note 1
P	44	2-dr Conv-4P	16899/19644	2996/3231	Note 2

Note: Figures to left of slash for four-cylinder engine, to right for V-8.

MUSTANG GT (V-8)

P	42	3-dr Hatch-4P	15243	3144	Note 1
P	45	2-dr Conv-4P	20199	3365	Note 2

NOTE 1: Production of hatchbacks totaled 36,818 with no further breakout available.

NOTE 2: Production of convertibles totaled 22,546 with no further breakout available.

ENGINE [Base Four (LX)]: Inline, overhead cam, four-cylinder. Cast-iron block and head. Displacement: 140 cid (2.3 liters). Bore & stroke: 3.78 x 3.12 in. Compression ratio: 9.5:1. Brake horsepower: 105 at 4600 rpm. Torque: 135 lbs.-ft. at 2600 rpm. Five main bearings. Hydraulic valve lifters. Multi-port fuel injection.

ENGINE [Base V-8 (GT); Optional (LX)]: 90-degree, overhead valve V-8. Cast-iron block and head. Displacement: 302 cid (5.0 liters). Bore & stroke: 4.00 x 3.00 in. Compression ratio: 9.0:1. Brake horsepower: 225 at 4200 rpm. Torque: 300 lbs.-ft. at 3200 rpm. Five main bearings. Hydraulic valve lifters. Sequential fuel injection.

CHASSIS DATA: Wheelbase: 100.5 in. Overall length: 179.6 in. Height: 52.1 in. Width: 68.3 in. Front Tread: 56.6 in. Rear Tread: 57.0 in. Standard Tires: P195/75R14 except (LX 5.0L and GT) P225/55ZR16.

TECHNICAL: Transmission: Five-speed manual (floor shift) standard. Four-speed overdrive automatic available. Steering: Rack and pinion, power-assisted. Front Suspension: Modified MacPherson strut with separate spring on lower arm, both strut and arm rubber bushed at attachment points. Rear Suspension: Four bar link (upper, leading; lower, arm) (unique Quadra-shock on LX 5.0L and GT). Brakes: Front disc, rear drum (power-assisted). Body construction: Unibody. Fuel tank: 15.4 gal.

DRIVETRAIN OPTIONS: Four-speed automatic overdrive transmission ($595).

CONVENIENCE/APPEARANCE OPTIONS: Preferred Equip Pkgs (LX Sdn & HB): Pwr Equip Grp incl Dual Electric Remote Ctrl Mirrors, Pwr Side Windows, Pwr Lock Grp, Spd Ctrl, Elect AM/FM Stereo Radio w/Cass Player & Clock, Dual Illum Visor Mirrors, Styled Road Whls ($276); LX Conv ($122). (LX 5.0L Sdn & HB): incl same as LX Sdn & HB except Whls, Dual Illum Visor Mirrors are stnd; plus Premium Sound Syst ($551); LX 5.0L Conv (NC). (GT HB): incl same as LX 5.0L Conv plus Man Air Cond, Convenience Grp incl Cargo Tie-Down Net, Frt Flr Mats ($1367); GT Conv ($763). Calif. Emission Syst ($100). (LX) Vinyl Low Back Seats ($76). (LX 5.0L & GT) Leather Seating Surfaces Articulated Spt ($523). Man Air Cond ($817). Convenience Grp incl Cargo Tie-Down Net, Frt Flr Mats ($99). Rr Window Defroster (NA/Conv) ($170). Premium Sound Syst incl 6 Premium Spkrs, 4-Channel Amplifier ($168). Premium Sound Syst w/Graphic Equalizer ($307). Clearcoat Paint ($91). Titanium Lower Bodyside Accent Treatment (GT) ($159). Pwr Equip Grp incl Pwr Dr Locks, Pwr Decklid/Liftgate, Dual Elect Remote Ctrl Mirrors, Pwr Side Windows ($604). Elect AM/FM Stereo Radio w/Cass ($155). Flip-Up Open Air Roof (HB Mdls only) ($355). 4-Way Pwr Driver's Seat ($183). Spd Ctrl ($224). Cast Alum Whls w/Upsized P205/65R15 SBR BSW Tires (LX only): LX Conv ($208); LX ($401). Styled Road Whls (LX only) ($193). Eng Block Heater ($20).

HISTORY: U.S. model year Mustang production totaled 79,280. U.S. calendar year Mustang production totaled 88,568.

1993 MUSTANG

1993 Ford Mustang LX. (OCW)

1993 Ford Mustang GT hatchback coupe (with 5.0L V-8). (OCW)

MUSTANG — (4-CYL/V-8) — SERIES P — The aging Mustang lineup received a limited edition Cobra model in 1993 to go along with its LX and GT series. This specialty model featured a "tweaked" 230-hp version of the GT's 5.0-liter V-8, five-speed manual transmission, 17-inch aluminum wheels, rear spoiler and ground-effects trim. The remainder of the Mustang lineup was again comprised of three distinct body styles within the aforementioned two series. These included coupe, hatchback and convertible in the LX series and hatchback and convertible in the GT series. The LX again used the 2.3-liter four-cylinder engine with electronic fuel injection, while the LX 5.0 models used a High Output 5.0-liter V-8 with sequential electronic fuel injection (SEFI). The GT was also powered by the 5.0-liter SEFI V-8 engine. All models included a higher wattage radio with an easy-to-read display. The convertible had a new headliner. There were seven new exterior colors. New options included a compact disc player and an electronic premium cassette radio. The GT had cast aluminum 16-inch wheels and performance tires.

I.D. DATA: Mustang's 17-symbol Vehicle Identification Number (VIN) again was stamped on a metal tab fastened to the instrument panel, visible through the windshield. Coding was similar to 1984-1992. Model year code (symbol ten) changed to 'P' for 1993.

MUSTANG SERIES

MUSTANG LX (FOUR/V-8)

Model No.	Body/ Style No.	Body Type & Seating	Factory Price	Shipping Weight	Prod. Total
P	40	2-dr Cpe-4P	10719/13926	2751/3035	23,579
P	41	3-dr Hatch-4P	11224/14710	2812/3096	Note 1
P	44	2-dr Conv-4P	17548/20293	2973/3259	Note 2

NOTE: Figures to left of slash for four-cylinder engine, to right for V-8.

MUSTANG GT (V-8)

P	42	3-dr Hatch-4P	15747/18247	3144	Note 1
P	45	2-dr Conv-4P	20848	3365	Note 2

COBRA (V-8)

P	42	3-dr Hatch-4P	18247	NA	4,993

NOTE 1: Production of hatchbacks totaled 60,227 with no further breakout available.

NOTE 2: Production of convertibles totaled 26,560 with no futher breakout available.

ENGINE [Base Four (LX)]: Inline, overhead cam, four-cylinder. Cast-iron block and head. Displacement: 140 cid (2.3 liters). Bore & stroke: 3.78 x 3.12 in. Compression ratio: 9.5:1. Brake horsepower: 105 at 4600 rpm. Torque: 135 lbs.-ft. at 2600 rpm. Five main bearings. Hydraulic valve lifters. Multi-port fuel injection.

ENGINE [Base V-8 (GT); Optional (LX)]: 90-degree, overhead valve V-8. Cast-iron block and head. Displacement: 302 cid (5.0 liters). Bore & stroke: 4.00 x 3.00 in. Compression ratio: 9.0:1. Brake horsepower: 205 at 4200 rpm. Torque: 275 lbs.-ft. at 3000 rpm. Five main bearings. Hydraulic valve lifters. Sequential fuel injection.

ENGINE [Base V-8 (Cobra)]: 90-degree, overhead valve V-8. Cast-iron block and head. Displacement: 302 cid (5.0 liters). Bore & stroke: 4.00 x 3.00 in. Compression ratio: 9.0:1. Brake horsepower: 230 at 4200 rpm. Torque: NA. Five main bearings. Hydraulic valve lifters. Sequential fuel injection.

CHASSIS DATA: Wheelbase: 100.5 in. Overall length: 179.6 in. **Height:** 52.1 in. Width: 68.3 in. Front Tread: 56.6 in. Rear Tread: 57.0 in. Standard Tires: P195/75R14 except (LX 5.0L and GT) P225/55ZR16.

TECHNICAL: Transmission: Five-speed manual (floor shift) standard. Four-speed overdrive automatic available except Cobra. Steering: Rack and pinion, power-assisted. Front Suspension: Modified MacPherson strut with separate spring on lower arm, both strut and arm rubber bushed at attachment points. Rear Suspension: Four bar link (upper, leading; lower, arm) (Unique Quadra-shock on LX 5.0L and GT). Brakes: Front disc, rear drum (power-assisted). Body construction: Unibody. Fuel tank: 15.4 gal.

DRIVETRAIN OPTIONS: Four-speed automatic overdrive transmission ($595).

CONVENIENCE/APPEARANCE OPTIONS: Preferred Equip Pkgs (LX): Pwr Equip Grp, Elect AM/FM Stereo Radio w/Cass & Premium Sound, Spd Ctrl, Dual Illum Visor Mirrors and Styled Road Whls ($276); LX Conv ($306). (LX 5.0L): incl Pwr Equip Grp, Elect AM/FM Stereo Radio w/Cass & Premium Sound and Spd Ctrl ($567); LX 5.0L Conv (NC). (GT): incl same as LX 5.0L Conv plus Man Air Cond and Convenience Grp ($1383); GT Conv ($779). Calif. Emission Syst ($100). Leather Seating Surfaces Articulated Spt (LX 5.0L and GT) ($523). Man Air Cond ($817). Convenience Grp incl Cargo Tie-Down Net, Frt Fir Mats ($99). Rr Window Defroster (NA Conv) ($170). Eng Block Heater ($20). Dual Illum Visor Mirrors ($100). Clearcoat Paint ($91). Titanium Lower Bodyside Accent Treatment (GT only) ($159). Pwr Equip Grp incl Dual Electric Remote Ctrl Mirrors and Pwr Side Windows ($604). Flip-Up Open Air Roof (HB Mdls only) ($355). 4-Way Pwr Driver's Seat ($183). Spd Ctrl ($224). Cast Alum Whls w/Upsized P205/65R15 SBR BSW Tires (LX only): LX Conv ($208); LX Conv ($401). Styled Road Whls (LX only) ($193). Elect AM/FM Stereo Radio w/CD Player ($629). Elect AM/FM Stereo Radio w/Cass, Auto Reverse & Premium Sound ($339).

HISTORY: U.S. model year Mustang production totaled 114,412. U.S. calendar year Mustang production totaled 106,238. The Special Vehicle Team produced 107 Mustang Cobra R models, built for competition.

1994 MUSTANG

1994 Ford Mustang GT convertible. (JAG)

1994 Ford Mustang convertible. (PH)

MUSTANG — (V-6/V-8) — SERIES P — In its 30th Anniversary year, the next-generation Mustang was unveiled in two body styles—coupe and convertible—and three series: base, GT and Cobra. Gone was the three-door hatchback previously offered, as well as the LX series. Also discontinued was four-cylinder power in Mustangs as engine choices were now either the 3.8-liter V-6 (base models) or 5.0-liter V-8 (GT and Cobra models). The Cobra's sequentially fuel-injected V-8 was modified through the use of GT-40 cylinder heads, roller rockers, stronger valve springs and a tuned-length cast-aluminum upper intake manifold. Other changes included an oil cooler and a lightened flywheel. The gears in the Cobra's T5OD five-speed manual transmission were phosphate-coated to better handle the engine's 240 hp. The Cobra's springs, shocks and stabilizer bars were upgraded and recalibrated, while the 8 x 17-inch wheels carried all-weather P255/45ZR17 performance tires. The Cobra's 13-inch front discs were clamped by twin-piston calipers, and the rotors featured curved-vane ventilation to help dissipate heat. Anti-lock braking was standard on the Cobra. Standard equipment in all Mustangs included dual airbags. The limited edition Cobra was created by Ford's Special Vehicle Team and was based on the Mustang GT chassis. Production was limited to 1,000 convertibles and 5,000 coupes for 1994. Exterior differences between Cobra and the Mustang GT included a front fascia and air dam incorporating fog lights, unique headlights, a rear spoiler with integral LED stoplamp, and Cobra badging.

I.D. DATA: Mustang's 17-symbol Vehicle Identification Number (VIN) again was stamped on a metal tab fastened to the instrument panel, visible through the windshield. Coding was similar to 1984-1993. Model year code (symbol ten) changed to 'R' for 1994.

MUSTANG SERIES

MUSTANG (V-6)

Model No.	Body/ Style No.	Body Type & Seating	Factory Price	Shipping Weight	Prod. Total
P	40	2-dr Cpe-4P	13355	3055	Note 1
P	44	2-dr Conv-4P	20150	3193	Note 2

MUSTANG GT (V-8)

Model No.	Body/ Style No.	Body Type & Seating	Factory Price	Shipping Weight	Prod. Total
P	42	2-dr Cpe-4P	17270	3258	Note 1
P	45	2-dr Conv-4P	21960	3414	Note 2

MUSTANG COBRA (V-8)

Model No.	Body/ Style No.	Body Type & Seating	Factory Price	Shipping Weight	Prod. Total
P	42	2-dr Cpe-4P	20765	NA	5,009
P	45	2-dr Conv-4P	23535	NA	1,000

NOTE 1: Production of two-door coupes totaled 78,480 with no further breakout available.

NOTE 2: Production of convertibles totaled 44,713 with no further breakout available.

1994 Ford Mustang GT coupe (with 5.0L V-8). (PH)

1994 Ford Mustang Cobra coupe (with 5.0L V-8). (OCW)

ENGINE [Base V-6 (Mustang)]: Overhead valve V-6. Cast-iron block and head. Displacement: 232 cid (3.8 liters). Bore & stroke: 3.80 x 3.40 in. Compression ratio: 9.0:1. Brake horsepower: 145 at 4000 rpm. Torque: 215 lbs.-ft. at 2500 rpm. Sequential fuel injection.

ENGINE [Base V-8 (GT)]: 90-degree, overhead valve V-8. Cast-iron block and head. Displacement: 302 cid (5.0 liters). Bore & stroke: 4.00 x 3.00 in. Compression ratio: 9.0:1. Brake horsepower: 215 at 4200 rpm. Torque: 285 lbs.-ft. at 3400 rpm. Sequential fuel injection.

ENGINE [Base V-8 (Cobra)]: 90-degree, overhead valve V-8. Cast-iron block and head. Displacement: 302 cid (5.0 liters). Bore & stroke: 4.00 x 3.00 in. Compression ratio: 9.0:1. Brake horsepower: 240 at 4800 rpm. Torque: 285 lbs.-ft. at 4000 rpm. Sequential fuel injection.

CHASSIS DATA: Wheelbase: 101.3 in. Overall length: 181.5 in. Height: (conv) 52.8 in.; (cpe) 52.9 in. Width: 71.8 in. Front Tread: 60.6 in. Rear Tread: 59.1 in. Standard Tires: (Mustang) P205/65R15; (GT) P225/55R16; (Cobra) P255/45ZR17.

TECHNICAL: Transmission: Five-speed manual (floor shift) standard. Four-speed overdrive automatic available except Cobra. Steering: Rack and pinion, power-assisted. Front Suspension: Modified MacPherson gas-pressurized struts and stabilizer bar. Rear Suspension: Rigid axle w/four links and coil springs and gas shocks. Brakes: Four-wheel disc (anti-lock stnd on Cobra). Body construction: Unibody. Fuel tank: 15.4 gal.

DRIVETRAIN OPTIONS: Four-speed automatic overdrive transmission (NA Cobra) ($790).

CONVENIENCE/APPEARANCE OPTIONS: Preferred Equip Pkgs (Mustang 241A): Air Cond and Elect AM/FM Stereo Radio w/Cass ($565). (Mustang 243A): Air Cond, Pwr Side Windows, Pwr Door Locks, Pwr Decklid Release, Spd Ctrl, Dual Illum Visor Mirrors, 15-inch Alum Whls, Elect AM/FM Stereo Radio w/Cass & Premium Sound, Remote Keyless Illum Entry and Cargo Net ($1825); Conv ($1415). (GT): Air Cond, Spd Ctrl, Dual Illum Visor Mirrors, 15-inch Alum Whls and Elect AM/FM Stereo Radio w/Cass & Premium Sound ($1405); GT Conv ($1405). (Cobra Cpe 250A): Air Cond, Rr Window Defroster, Frt Flr Mats and Spd Ctrl ($1185). (Cobra Conv 250P): Air Cond, Rr Window Defroster, Frt Flr Mats, Spd Ctrl, Remote Keyless Illum Entry, CD Player & Mach 460 Stereo Syst ($2835). Calif. Emission Syst ($95). 15-inch Alum Whls (NA GT or Cobra) ($265). 17-inch Alum Whls (GT only) ($380). Leather Spt Bucket Seats: Mustang Conv only ($500); Mustang GT ($500); Cobra Cpe only ($500). Man Air Cond ($780). Anti-Lock Braking Syst (stnd Cobra) ($565). Anti-Theft Syst ($235). Conv Hardtop ($1545). Rr Window Defroster ($160). Frt Flr Mats ($30). Eng Block Heater (NA Cobra) ($20). Bodyside Mldgs ($50). Elect AM/FM Stereo Radio w/Cass & Premium Sound (stnd/Cobra, NA w/Mustang Cpe) ($165). Mach 460 AM/FM Stereo Radio w/Cass, Seek & Scan, 60-Watt Equalizer, Upgraded Spkrs & Amplifiers & CD Changer ($375). CD Player (NA w/Mustang Cpe) ($475).

HISTORY: In Mustang's 30th Anniversary year, a Ford Mustang Cobra convertible paced the 1994 Indianapolis 500. The 1994 Mustang also had the distinction of being named *Motor Trend* magazine's "Car of the Year." U.S. model year Mustang production totaled 137,074. U.S. calendar year Mustang production totaled 199,048.

1995 MUSTANG

MUSTANG — (V-6/V-8) — SERIES P — After a all-new-design debut the year previous, the big change for Mustang in 1995 was the addition of a GTS coupe positioned between the base Mustang and Mustang GT. The GTS coupe was powered by the 5.0-liter HO (High Output) V-8 and featured 16-inch/five-spoke cast aluminum wheels and stainless steel dual exhaust. Buyers of Mustang convertibles again could order the removable hardtop that was introduced midyear in 1994. Base models were again powered by the 3.8-liter V-6 while GTS, GT and Cobra models all used a version of the 5.0-liter V-8. The five-speed manual transmission was the standard unit and all but the Cobra series offered an AX4N electronically controlled automatic overdrive transmission as optional equipment.

I.D. DATA: Mustang's 17-symbol Vehicle Identification Number (VIN) again was stamped on a metal tab fastened to the instrument panel, visible through the windshield. Coding was similar to 1984-1994. Model year code (symbol ten) changed to 'S' for 1995.

MUSTANG SERIES

MUSTANG (V-6)

Model No.	Body/ Style No.	Body Type & Seating	Factory Price	Shipping Weight	Prod. Total
P	40	2-dr Cpe-4P	14330	3077	Note 1
P	44	2-dr Conv-4P	20795	3257	Note 2

MUSTANG GT (V-8)

P	42	2-dr Cpe-4P	17905	3280	Note 1
P	45	2-dr Conv-4P	22595	3451	Note 2

MUSTANG GTS (V-8)

P	42	2-dr Cpe-4P	16910	3246	Note 1

COBRA (V-8)

P	42	2-dr Cpe-4P	21300	3354	4,005
P	45	2-dr Conv-4P	24070	3524	1,003

NOTE 1: Production of coupes totaled 120,432 with no further breakout available.

NOTE 2: Production of convertibles totaled 44,593 with no further breakout available.

ENGINE [Base V-6]: Overhead valve V-6. Cast-iron block and head. Displacement: 232 cid (3.8 liters). Bore & stroke: 3.80 x 3.40 in. Compression ratio: 9.0:1. Brake horsepower: 145 at 4000 rpm. Torque: 215 lbs.-ft. at 2500 rpm. Sequential fuel injection.

ENGINE [Base V-8 (GTS)]: 90-degree, overhead valve V-8. Cast-iron block and head. Displacement: 302 cid (5.0 liters). Bore & stroke: 4.00 x 3.00 in. Compression ratio: 9.0:1. Brake horsepower: 215 at 4000 rpm. Torque: 285 lbs.-ft. at 3400 rpm. Sequential fuel injection.

ENGINE [Base V-8 (GT)]: 90-degree, overhead valve V-8. Cast-iron block and head. Displacement: 302 cid (5.0 liters). Bore & stroke: 4.00 x 3.00 in. Compression ratio: 9.0:1. Brake horsepower: 215 at 4000 rpm. Torque: 285 lbs.-ft. at 3400 rpm. Sequential fuel injection.

ENGINE [Base V-8 (Cobra)]: 90-degree, overhead valve V-8. Cast-iron block and head. Displacement: 302 cid (5.0 liters). Bore & stroke: 4.00 x 3.00 in. Compression ratio: 9.0:1. Brake horsepower: 240 at 4800 rpm. Torque: 285 lbs.-ft. at 4000 rpm. Sequential fuel injection.

CHASSIS DATA: Wheelbase: 101.3 in. Overall length: 181.5 in. Height: (cpe) 53.0 in.; (conv) 53.2 in. Width: 71.8 in. Front Tread: 60.6 in. Rear Tread: 59.1 in. Standard Tires: (Mustang) P205/65R15; (GTS and GT) P225/55ZR16; (Cobra) P255/45ZR17.

TECHNICAL: Transmission: Five-speed manual (floor shift) standard. Four-speed automatic overdrive available except Cobra. Steering: Rack and pinion, power-assisted. Front Suspension: Modified MacPherson gas-pressurized struts and stabilizer bar. Rear Suspension: Rigid axle w/four links and coil springs and gas shocks. Brakes: Four-wheel disc (anti-lock stnd on Cobra). Body construction: Unibody. Fuel tank: 15.4 gal.

DRIVETRAIN OPTIONS: Four-speed automatic overdrive transmission (NA Cobra) ($815).

CONVENIENCE/APPEARANCE OPTIONS: Preferred Equip Pkgs (Mustang 214A): Air Cond, Elect AM/FM Stereo Radio w/Cass ($565). (Mustang Cpe 243A): Man Air Cond, Pwr Driver's Seat, Pwr Side Windows, Pwr Door Locks, Pwr Decklid Release, Dual Illum Visor Mirrors, Spd Ctrl, Elect AM/FM Stereo Radio w/Cass & Premium Sound, 15-inch Alum Whls, Remote Keyless Illum Entry and Cargo Net ($2030). (Mustang Conv 243C): Man Air Cond, Dual Illum Visor Mirrors, Spd Ctrl, Elect AM/FM Stereo Radio w/Cass & Premium Sound, 15-inch Alum Whls, Remote Keyless Illum Entry and Cargo Net ($1625). (GTS 248A): Man Air Cond and Elect AM/FM Stereo Radio w/Cass ($640). (GT 249A): Man Air Cond, Pwr Driver's Seat, Dual Illum Visor Mirrors, Spd Ctrl, Elect AM/FM Stereo Radio w/Cass & Premium Sound and 15-inch Alum Whls ($1615). (Cobra Cpe 250A): Man Air Cond, Rr Window Defroster, Frt Flr Mats and Cruise Ctrl ($1260). (Cobra Conv 250C): Man Air Cond, Rr Window Defroster, Frt Flr Mats, Cruise Ctrl, Remote Keyless Illum Entry, Elect AM/FM Stereo MACH 460 Radio w/Cass, CD Player and Spt Leather Bucket Seats ($2755). Calif. Emission Syst ($95). 15-inch Alum Whls (base only) ($265). 17-inch Alum Whls (GT only) ($380). Spt Leather Bucket Seats: base Conv ($500); GT and Cobra ($500). Pwr Driver's Seat (NA Cobra) ($175). Man Air Cond ($855). Anti-Lock Braking Syst (stnd Cobra) ($565). Anti-Theft Syst ($145). Opt Axle Ratio (GTS and GT) ($45). Conv Hardtop ($1825). Elect Rr Window Defroster ($160). Frt Flr Mats ($30). Bodyside Mldgs (base and GT) ($50). Spd Ctrl ($215). CD Player (NA GTS) ($375). Elect AM/FM Stereo Radio w/Cass (Base and GTS) ($165). Elect AM/FM Stereo MACH 460 Radio w/Cass: Cobra ($375); base and GT ($670). Elect AM/FM Stereo Radio w/CD Player & Premium Sound: Cobra ($140); base, GTS and GT ($435). MACH 460 Sound Syst (GTS and Cobra Conv) ($375). Eng Block Heater (NA Cobra) ($20).

HISTORY: U.S. model year Mustang production totaled 174,924. U.S. calendar year Mustang production totaled 143,947. Ford's Special Vehicle Team produced 250 Mustang Cobra R models, built for competition.

1996 MUSTANG

1995 Ford Mustang convertible. (OCW)

1995 Ford Mustang GT coupe. (OCW)

1996 Ford Mustang Cobra coupe. (OCW)

1996 Ford Mustang Cobra convertible. (OCW)

MUSTANG — (V-6/V-8) — SERIES P — The base, GT and Cobra Mustang series all returned for 1996, but after only one year of availability in 1995 the GTS coupe was discontinued. Ford's Special Vehicle Team's Cobra convertible was not put into production until the spring of 1996 while the coupe was available at the beginning of the model year (October 1995). Under the hood of the Mustang was where major changes occured. The base models' 3.8-liter V-6 was refined. The 5.0-liter V-8 offered previously in the GT and Cobra Mustangs was discontinued and replaced by a modular 4.6-liter V-8. The Cobra also used a new T45 five-speed manual transmission, which replaced its predecessor T5 unit. Also new in the Cobra was a 3.27:1 rear axle ratio. Standard equipment on all V-8-powered Mustangs included the Passive Anti-theft System.

I.D. DATA: Mustang's 17-symbol Vehicle Identification Number (VIN) again was stamped on a metal tab fastened to the instrument panel, visible through the windshield. Coding was similar to 1984-1995. Model year code (symbol ten) changed to 'T' for 1996.

MUSTANG SERIES

MUSTANG (V-6)

Model No.	Body/ Style No.	Body Type & Seating	Factory Price	Shipping Weight	Prod. Total
P	40	2-dr Cpe-4P	15180	3057	Note 1
P	44	2-dr Conv-4P	21060	3269	Note 2

MUSTANG GT (V-8)

P	42	2-dr Cpe-4P	17610	3279	Note 1
P	45	2-dr Conv-4P	23495	3468	Note 2

MUSTANG COBRA (V-8)

P	47	2-dr Cpe-4P	24810	3401	5,496
P	46	2-dr Conv-4P	27580	3566	2,510

NOTE 1: Production of coupes totaled 92,655 with no further breakout available.

NOTE 2: Production of convertibles totaled 33,781 with no further breakout available.

ENGINE [Base V-6]: Overhead valve V-6. Cast-iron block and head. Displacement: 232 cid (3.8 liters). Bore & stroke: 3.80 x 3.40 in. Compression ratio: 9.0:1. Brake horsepower: 145 at 4000 rpm. Torque: 215 lbs.-ft. at 2500 rpm. Sequential fuel injection.

ENGINE [Base V-8 (GT)]: 90-degree, overhead valve V-8. Cast-iron block and head. Displacement: 281 cid (4.6 liters). Bore & stroke: 3.60 x 3.60 in. Compression ratio: 9.0:1. Brake horsepower: 215 at 4400 rpm. Torque: 285 lbs.-ft. at 4800 rpm. Sequential fuel injection.

ENGINE [Base V-8 (Cobra)]: 90-degree, dual overhead cam V-8. Cast aluminum block and head. Displacement: 281 cid (4.6 liters). Bore & stroke: 3.60 x 3.60 in. Compression ratio: 9.85:1. Brake horsepower: 305 at 5800 rpm. Torque: 300 lbs.-ft. at 4800 rpm. Sequential fuel injection.

CHASSIS DATA: Wheelbase: 101.3 in. Overall length: (Mustang and GT) 181.5 in.; (Cobra) 182.5 in. Height: (cpe) 53.2 in.; (conv) 53.4 in. Width: 71.8 in. Front Tread: 60.6 in. Rear Tread: 59.1 in. Standard Tires: (Mustang) P205/65R15; (GT) P225/55ZR16; (Cobra) P245/45ZR17.

TECHNICAL: Transmission: Five-speed manual (floor shift) standard. Four-speed automatic overdrive available except Cobra. Steering: Rack and pinion, power-assisted. Front Suspension: Modified MacPherson strut, w/separate spring on lower arm, variable rate coil springs and stabilizer bar. Rear Suspension: Rigid axle w/four links (two leading hydraulic), variable rate coil springs and stabilizer bar. Brakes: Four-wheel disc (anti-lock stnd on Cobra). Body construction: Unibody. Fuel tank: 15.4 gal.

DRIVETRAIN OPTIONS: Four-speed automatic overdrive transmission (NA Cobra) ($815).

CONVENIENCE/APPEARANCE OPTIONS: Preferred Equip Pkgs (Mustang 241A): Man Air Cond and Elect AM/FM Stereo Radio w/Cass ($670). (Mustang 243A) Man Air Cond, Dual Illum Visor Mirrors, Remote Keyless Illum Entry, Pwr Driver's Seat, Pwr Side Windows, Pwr Door Locks, Pwr Decklid Release, Spd Ctrl, 15-inch Alum Whls and Elect AM/FM Stereo Radio w/Cass & Premium Sound: Cpe ($2020); Conv ($1590). (GT 248A): Man Air Cond and Elect AM/FM Stereo Radio w/Cass ($670). (GT Cpe 249A): Anti-Lock Brakes, GT Spt Seats, Leather-wrapped Strg Whl, Rr Spoiler, Dual Illum Visor Mirrors, Man Air Cond, Pwr Driver's Seat, Pwr Windows, Pwr Door Locks, Pwr Decklid Release, Spd Ctrl, Cast Alum Whls and Elect AM/FM Stereo Radio w/Cass & Premium Sound ($2845). (GT Conv 249C): Anti-Lock Brakes, Man Air Cond, Spd Ctrl, Cast Alum Whls, Pwr Driver's Seat and Elect AM/FM Stereo Radio w/Cass & Premium Sound ($1650). (Cobra 250A): CD Player, MACH 460 Radio, Anti-Theft Syst and Leather Seats ($1335). Calif. Emission Syst ($100). Man Air Cond ($895). Anti-Theft Syst ($145). Opt Axle Ratio (GT only) ($200). Anti-Lock Braking Syst (stnd Cobra) ($570). Elect Rr Window Defroster (stnd Cobra) ($170). Flr Mats (stnd Cobra) ($30). Eng Block Heater (NA Cobra) ($20). Remote Keyless Illum Entry Syst (stnd Cobra) ($270). Dual Illum Visor Mirrors ($95). Bodyside Mldgs ($60). Elect AM/FM Stereo Radio w/Cass & Premium Sound ($165). Elect AM/FM Stereo Radio w/Cass & Premium Sound ($295). MACH 460 AM/FM Stereo Radio w/Cass, Seek & Scan, 60-watt Equalizer and CD Changer ($690). CD Player ($295). Pwr Driver's Seat (stnd Cobra) ($175). Leather Spt Bucket Seats: Mustang Conv ($500); GT ($500). Spd Ctrl (stnd Cobra) ($215). Spoiler ($195). 15-inch Alum Whls (base only) ($265). 17-inch Alum Whls incl P245/45ZR17 BSW Tires ($400).

HISTORY: U.S. model year Mustang production totaled 124,698. U.S. calendar year Mustang production totaled 130,488. 2,000 of the 5,496 1996 Cobra coupes produced were finished in light-refracting Mystic Clearcoat paint, which changed hue based on light intensity and from what angle it was viewed. The Mystic finish was an $815 option available only in 1996 and only on the Cobra coupe.

1997 MUSTANG

1997 Ford Mustang convertible. (OCW)

MUSTANG — (V-6/V-8) — SERIES P — Mustang series offered for 1997 remained the base, GT and limited-production Cobra from Ford's Special Vehicle Team. Each series again was comprised of coupe and convertible. The Mustang's 3.8-liter V-6 delivered 150-hp performance. The GT was powered by a 215-hp SOHC 4.6-liter V-8, and the Cobra used an all-aluminum alloy, 305-hp, 32-valve DOHC version of the 4.6-liter V-8. The Cobra's engine was hand-assembled and signed by its builders. The GT featured a new flecked seat fabric pattern. The Mustang convertible had new gray leather seating surfaces instead of white. Pacific green clearcoat metallic was a new color available on the Cobra. A thicker, firmer and more ergonomic shift handle with an overdrive button on the knob was included with the four-speed automatic transmission, which was optional on all Mustangs except the Cobra (NA). Mustang's instrument panel retained its two-tone appearance. New diamond-cut, brightly machined 17-inch cast-aluminum wheels with a dark gray metallic center were available on the GT. Installation of Passive Anti-Theft System (PATS) was made standard on all models. PATS used an encoded ignition key with a transponder to electronically disable the engine if the transponder code did not match a preset code in the Electronic Engine Control System.

1997 Ford Mustang GT coupe. (OCW)

1997 Ford Mustang Cobra coupe. (OCW)

I.D. DATA: Mustang's 17-symbol Vehicle Identification Number (VIN) again was stamped on a metal tab fastened to the instrument panel, visible through the windshield. Coding was similar to 1984-1996. Model year code (symbol ten) changed to 'V' for 1997.

MUSTANG SERIES

MUSTANG (V-6)

Model No.	Body/ Style No.	Body Type & Seating	Factory Price	Shipping Weight	Prod. Total
P	40	2-dr Cpe-4P	15355	3084	Note 1
P	44	2-dr Conv-4P	20755	3264	Note 2

MUSTANG GT (V-8)

P	42	2-dr Cpe-4P	18000	3288	Note 1
P	45	2-dr Conv-4P	23985	3422	Note 2

MUSTANG COBRA (V-8)

P	47	2-dr Cpe-4P	25335	3404	7,475
P	46	2-dr Conv-4P	28135	3540	2,525

NOTE: Production figures for Cobra series are estimates based on Ford's Special Vehicle Team's announced annual production of Cobras.

NOTE 1: Production of coupes totaled 75,760 with no further breakout available.

NOTE 2: Production of convertibles totaled 24,490 with no further breakout available.

ENGINE [Base V-6]: Overhead valve V-6. Cast-iron block and head. Displacement: 232 cid (3.8 liters). Bore & stroke: 3.80 x 3.40 in. Compression ratio: 9.0:1. Brake horsepower: 150 at 4000 rpm. Torque: 215 lbs.-ft. at 2750 rpm. Sequential fuel injection.

ENGINE [Base V-8 (GT)]: 90-degree, overhead cam V-8. Cast-iron block and head. Displacement: 281 cid (4.6 liters). Bore & stroke: 3.60 x 3.60 in. Compression ratio: 9.0:1. Brake horsepower: 215 at 5000 rpm. Torque: 285 lbs.-ft. at 4800 rpm. Sequential fuel injection.

ENGINE [Base V-8 (Cobra)]: 90-degree, dual overhead cam V-8. Cast aluminum block and head. Displacement: 281 cid (4.6 liters). Bore & stroke: 3.60 x 3.60 in. Compression ratio: 9.85:1. Brake horsepower: 305 at 5800 rpm. Torque: 300 lbs.-ft. at 4800 rpm. Sequential fuel injection.

1997 Ford Mustang Cobra convertible. (OCW)

CHASSIS DATA: Wheelbase: 101.3 in. Overall length: (base and GT) 181.5 in.; (Cobra) 182.5 in. Height: 53.2 in. Width: 71.8 in. Front Tread: 60.5 in. Rear Tread: 59.2 in. Standard Tires: (base) P205/65TR15; (GT) P225/55ZR16; (Cobra) P245/45ZR17.

TECHNICAL: Transmission: Five-speed manual (floor shift) standard. Four-speed automatic overdrive available except Cobra. Steering: Rack and pinion, power-assisted. Front Suspension: Modified MacPherson strut with separate spring on lower arm, variable rate coil springs and stabilizer bar. Rear Suspension: Rigid axle w/four links (two leading hydraulic), variable rate coil springs and stabilizer bar. Brakes: Four-wheel disc (anti-lock stnd on GT Conv and Cobra). Body construction: Unibody. Fuel tank: 15.4 gal.

DRIVETRAIN OPTIONS: Four-speed automatic overdrive transmission (NA Cobra) ($815).

CONVENIENCE/APPEARANCE OPTIONS: Preferred Equip Pkgs (Mustang 241A): Man Air Cond and Elect AM/FM Stereo Radio w/Cass ($615). (Mustang 243A): Man Air Cond, Dual Illum Visor Mirrors, Remote Keyless Illum Entry, Pwr Driver's Seat, Pwr Side Windows, Pwr Door Locks, Pwr Decklid Release, Spd Ctrl, Elect AM/FM Stereo Radio w/Cass & Premium Sound and 15-inch Alum Whls: Cpe ($2115); Conv ($1615). (GT 248A): Man Air Cond and Elect AM/FM Stereo Radio w/Cass ($670). (GT 249A): Man Air Cond, Pwr Driver's Seat, Pwr Side Windows, Pwr Door Locks, Pwr Decklid Release, Spd Ctrl, Elect AM/FM Stereo Radio w/Cass & Premium Sound and 15-inch Alum Whls: Cpe ($2940); Conv ($1685). (Cobra 250A): CD Player, MACH 460 Radio, Anti-Theft Syst and Leather Seats ($1335). Calif. Emission Syst ($170). Cast Alum Whls w/P205/65TR15 BSW Tires (base only) ($265). Polished Alum Whls w/P245/45ZR17 BSW Tires ($500). Leather Spt Bucket Seats: base ($500); GT ($500). Pwr Driver's Seat ($210). Man Air Cond ($895). Spt Appearance Grp incl Rr Decklid Spoiler, 15-inch Alum Whls, Leather-wrapped Strg Whl, Lower Bodyside Accent Stripe ($345). Anti-Lock Braking Syst (stnd GT Conv and Cobra) ($570). Anti-Theft Syst ($145). Opt Axle Ratio (NA base) ($200). Elect Rr Window Defroster ($190). Dual Illum Visor Mirrors ($95). Frt Flr Mats ($30). Rr Decklid Spoiler (stnd GT Conv) ($195). Remote Keyless Illum Entry Syst (GT only) ($270). Spd Ctrl (GT only) ($215). CD Player ($295). Elect AM/FM Stereo Radio w/Cass ($165). Elect AM/FM Stereo Radio w/Cass & Premium Sound ($295). MACH 460 AM/FM Stereo Radio w/Cass ($690). Eng Block Heater ($20).

HISTORY: Tommy Kendall, driving a Ford Mustang Cobra in the Trans-Am series, set a record for consecutive race victories (11) en route to winning the 1997 Trans-Am championship.

1998 MUSTANG

MUSTANG — (V-6/V-8) — SERIES P — Base, GT and Cobra again comprised the Mustang lineup for 1998 and body styles available were again the coupe and convertible. The 3.8-liter V-6 (base Mustangs) and 4.6-liter V-8 (GT and Cobra models) were again the engines used, with the GT's powerplant rated at 10 hp more (from 215 to 225 hp). Improvements to the Mustang for 1998 included polished aluminum wheels and a premium sound system with cassette and CD play capability added as standard equipment on the base coupe and convertible. Other items added as standard equipment included air conditioning, power windows, power door locks, power decklid release and remote keyless illuminated entry. In addition, the GT received a sound system upgrade, spoiler and sport seats. The power receptacle was relocated inside the console storage box. Ford's SecuriLock anti-theft system was standard on the Mustang. The limited-production SVT Cobra received new five-spoke alloy wheels. Mustangs equipped with the four-speed automatic transmission qualified as Low Emission Vehicles (LEV) in four states that posted tighter emissions standards: California, New York, Massachusetts and Connecticut.

I.D. DATA: Mustang's 17-symbol Vehicle Identification Number (VIN) again was stamped on a metal tab fastened to the instrument panel, visible through the windshield. Coding was similar to 1984-1997. Model year code (symbol ten) changed to 'W' for 1998.

MUSTANG SERIES

Model No.	Body/ Style No.	Body Type & Seating	Factory Price	Shipping Weight	Prod. Total
MUSTANG (V-6)					
P	40	2-dr Cpe-4P	15970	3065	*
P	44	2-dr Conv-4P	20470	3210	*
MUSTANG GT (V-8)					
P	42	2-dr Cpe-4P	19970	3227	*
P	45	2-dr Conv-4P	23970	3400	*
MUSTANG COBRA (V-8)					
P	47	2-dr Cpe-4P	26,400	3364	*
P	46	2-dr Conv-4P	30,200	3506	*

*NOTE: Production figures were not available at the time this book went to the printer.

ENGINE [Base V-6]: Overhead valve V-6. Cast-iron block and head. Displacement: 232 cid (3.8 liters). Bore & stroke: 3.80 x 3.40 in. Compression ratio: 9.0:1. Brake horsepower: 150 at 4000 rpm. Torque: 215 lbs.-ft. at 2750 rpm. Sequential fuel injection.

ENGINE [Base V-8 (GT)]: 90-degree, overhead cam V-8. Cast-iron block and head. Displacement: 281 cid (4.6 liters). Bore & stroke: 3.60 x 3.60 in. Compression ratio: 9.0:1. Brake horsepower: 225 at 4750 rpm. Torque: 290 lbs.-ft. at 3500 rpm. Sequential fuel injection.

ENGINE [Base V-8 (Cobra)]: 90-degree, dual overhead cam V-8. Cast aluminum block and head. Displacement: 281 cid (4.6 liters). Bore & stroke: 3.60 x 3.60 in. Compression ratio: 9.85:1. Brake horsepower: 305 at 5800 rpm. Torque: 300 lbs.-ft. at 4800 rpm. Sequential fuel injection.

CHASSIS DATA: Wheelbase: 101.3 in. Overall length: 181.5 in. Height: (cpe) 53.2 in.; (conv) 53.4 in. Width: 71.8 in. Front Tread: 60.5 in. Rear Tread: 59.2 in. Standard Tires: (base) P205/65TR15; (GT) P225/55HR16; (Cobra) P245/45ZR17.

TECHNICAL: Transmission: Five-speed manual (floor shift) standard. Four-speed automatic overdrive available except Cobra. Steering: Rack and pinion, power-assisted. Front Suspension: Modified MacPherson strut with separate spring on lower arm, both strut and arm rubber bushed at attachment points, and stabilizer tube. Rear Suspension: Rigid axle w/four links (two upper arms and two lower arms), and variable rate coil springs. Brakes: Four-wheel disc (anti-lock stnd on GT Conv and Cobra). Body construction: Unibody. Fuel tank: 15.7 gal.

1998 Ford Mustang GT convertible. (OCW)

DRIVETRAIN OPTIONS: Four-speed automatic overdrive transmission (NA Cobra) ($815).

CONVENIENCE/APPEARANCE OPTIONS: Anti-Theft Syst ($145). Opt Axle Ratio (GT only) ($200). Anti-Lock Braking Syst ($500). Convenience Grp incl Frt Flr Mats, Rr Window Defroster, Spd Ctrl and Pwr Driver's Seat (stnd GT): base ($495); GT ($295). Elect Rr Window Defroster ($190). Dual Illum Visor Mirrors (stnd Conv) ($95). Eng Block Heater ($20). Color-Keyed Bodyside Mldgs ($60). MACH 460 AM/FM Stereo Radio w/Cass & CD Changer Compatibility ($395). Calif. Emission Syst ($170). Leather Bucket Seats (base and GT only) ($500). Rr Decklid Spoiler (stnd GT) ($195). 17-inch Alum Whls w/P245/45ZR15 BSW Tires (GT only) ($500).

1999 MUSTANG

1999 Ford Mustang two-door coupe. (FMC)

MUSTANG – V-6 – SERIES P – Remembering how badly it had been criticized in the press for "forgetting" the Mustang's 25th anniversary, Ford gave fans of the marque a year-long surprise party in 1999. All Mustangs (whether powered by the V-6 or V-8) wore beautiful wreath design emblems on their front fenders that featured a solid ring encircling the classic running horse and tricolor bar. Not content to merely spruce up a six-year-old design with fender jewelry, Ford's designers went on to give the line a much-appreciated facelift and tummy tuck, while prescribing some steroid therapy. The smooth, mostly feminine, curves of the 1994-1998 Mustang were replaced with strong creases and straight lines. The sides of the car took on a more vertical angle and the tallest scoop ever to grace a Mustang was installed just behind the door. This "pumping up" of the previous design reminded many Mustang fans of the changes that had given the original 1965 a "body builder" look in 1967. Up front, the Mustang's headlights took on a sinister appearance. Taillights received the same treatment as the rest of the car, going from soft and rounded to hard and harsh. Looking for ways to reduce weight at every turn, designers created a new deck lid made from a sheet molded compound. While the exterior improvements were enough to bring new customers, there were refinements in areas that couldn't be seen so easily, such as the revised floor pan sealing and foam-packed rocker panels — both of which reduced road noise. Engineers reduced a troublesome "mid-car shake" on the convertible models through the use of sub-frame connectors and gained a tiny bit of rear suspension travel on all models by raising the drive tunnel 1.5 inches. As the Mustang drew nearer to the end of the century, it received new technology provided in the form of an optional all-speed traction control system (TCS), a $230 option that worked in harmony with the also-optional (on base models) ABS to reduce tire spin in slippery conditions. Taller *Mustangers* no doubt appreciated the extra inch of travel built into the driver's seat for 1999. Thanks to a higher-lift camshaft, coil-on-plug ignition, bigger valves and a revised intake manifold, the V-8 Mustang received its biggest power increase since 1987.

BASE MUSTANG: Standard equipment included dual second-generation airbags, manual control air conditioning, the SecuriLock™ passive anti-theft system, power four-wheel disc brakes with new front calipers, a CD player, a clock integrated into the radio, side window demisters, power door locks, a 3.8-liter EFI V-6 engine, a stainless steel exhaust system, Solar-Tinted glass, a power ventilation system with four instrument panel registers with positive shutoffs, an analog instrument cluster (with tachometer, trip odometer, voltmeter, temperature gauge, fuel gauge, oil pressure gauge and overdrive-off indicator with automatic transmission), remote keyless entry, dual electric remote-control outside rearview mirrors (right-hand convex), dual visor-vanity mirrors with covers (and illumination on convertible), ETR AM/FM stereo with cassette tape player, premium sound system with premium speakers and 80-watt amplifier, reclining cloth bucket seats with cloth head restraints, a bench rear

1999 Ford Mustang GT two-door coupe. (FMC)

seat with split-folding seatback, a tilt steering wheel with center horn, power rack-and-pinion steering, P205/65R15 black sidewall all-season tires, a five-speed manual overdrive transmission, interval windshield wipers, 15-in. six-spoke cast aluminum wheels with ornaments and power side windows with driver's side "express down" feature. The convertible also had a power folding top and power rear quarter windows.

I.D. DATA: A 17-character Vehicle Identification Number is stamped on an aluminum tab on the instrument panel, viewable through the windshield. A vehicle certification label is found on the body side of where the driver's door closes. The first symbol indicates the nation of origin: 1=United States of America. The second symbol indicates the manufacturer: F=Ford Motor Co. The third symbol indicates vehicle type: A=passenger car. The fourth symbol indicates type of restraint system: L= driver and front passenger airbags with passive front belts and active rear belts. The fifth symbol is the designation number: P=passenger car. The sixth and seventh symbols indicate car line and body type: 40=two-door coupe; 42=two-door GT coupe; 44=two-door convertible; 45=two-door GT convertible; 46=two-door Cobra convertible; 47=two-door Cobra or Cobra R coupe. The eighth symbol indicates engine type: 4=232 cid (3.8-liter) EFI V-6; X=281 cid (4.6-liter) EFI SOHC V-8; V=281 cid (4.6-liter) EFI DOHC V-8. The ninth symbol is a check digit. The 10th symbol indicates model year: X=1999. The 11th symbol indicates assembly plant: F=Dearborn, Mich. The last six symbols are the consecutive unit production number staring at 100001 at each factory. Paint Codes: BZ=Chrome Yellow, ES=Performance Red, E8=Rio Red, E9=Laser Red, FU=Dark Green Satin, K6=Atlantic Blue, K7=Bright Atlantic Blue; SW=Electric Green, UA=Black, YN=Silver and ZR=Crystal White.

Model No.	Body/ Style No.	Body Type & Seating	Factory Price	Shipping Weight	Prod. Total
BASE MUSTANG (V-6)					
P	40	2d Coupe-4P	16,995	3,069	73,180
P	44	2d Convertible-4P	21,595	3,211	19,299

Note 1: Prices include dealer destination charges.

MUSTANG GT: On GT models the hood grew a simulated recessed scoop that recalled the air-grabber that the 1968 sported when it received its first 428 cid V-8. GT exhaust tips also were enlarged slightly, from 2.75 inches to three inches. The GT's 4.6-liter was boosted to 260 hp and the base 3.8-liter V-6 jumped to 190 hp. Standard GT equipment included dual second-generation airbags, manual control air conditioning, the SecuriLock™ passive anti-theft system, power four-wheel disc antilock brakes with new front calipers, a CD player, a clock integrated into the radio, side window demisters, power door locks, a 4.6-liter SOHC V-8 engine, a stainless steel dual exhaust system, Solar-Tinted glass, a power ventilation system with four instrument panel registers with positive shutoffs, an analog instrument cluster (with tachometer, trip odometer, voltmeter, temperature gauge, fuel gauge, oil pressure gauge and overdrive-off indicator with automatic transmission), remote keyless entry, dual electric remote-control outside rearview mirrors (right-hand convex), dual visor-vanity mirrors with covers (and illumination on convertible), ETR AM/FM stereo with cassette tape player, premium sound system with premium speakers and 80-watt amplifier, GT Sport two-tone cloth trim bucket seats, a 150-mph speedometer, a bench rear seat with split-folding seatback, a leather-wrapped tilt steering wheel with center horn (two-toned when combined with Medium Graphite and Medium Parchment interior), power rack-and-pinion steering, P225/55R16 black sidewall all-season tires, a five-speed manual overdrive transmission, interval windshield wipers, 16-in. six-spoke forged aluminum wheels with carryover ornaments and power side windows with driver's side "express down" feature. The convertible also had a power folding top and power rear quarter windows.

1999 Ford Mustang GT two-door convertible. (FMC)

MUSTANG GT (V-8)

P	42	2d Coupe-4P	16,995	3,242	17,316
P	45	2d Convertible-4P	21,595	3,386	11,383

Note 2: Prices include dealer destination charges.

35th ANNIVERSARY MUSTANG GT: To commemorate the Mustang's 35th anniversary in grand style, Ford produced a special run of Limited Edition models that stickered for $2,695 above the cost of a GT. Originally, it was announced that 5,000 of these cars were scheduled to be built, but actual production came to 4,628 units. Features included a special, raised hood scoop (at the end of a wide black stripe), a rear deck wing, stand-out side scoops, a black honeycomb deck lid appliqué, body color rocker moldings; a Midnight Black GT leather interior with silver leather inserts, special floor mats with a 35th Anniversary script and a special aluminum shift knob (in cars with the five-speed transmission only). Exterior colors were limited to Black, Silver, Crystal White and Performance Red. Mustangers did not realize it at the time, but the Limited Edition model incorporated many of the cosmetic upgrades that would become standard with the 2001 model. Standard 35th Anniversary equipment included: Aerodynamic halogen headlamps, front fog lamps, a hood scoop, a black appliqué on the hood, body side scoops, rocker panel moldings, dual electric control outside rearview mirrors, a power retractable convertible top with semi-hard boot (on convertibles only, of course), a rear deck lid spoiler, a black deck lid appliqué between the taillights, 17 x 8-in. bright machined five-spoke aluminum wheels, Midnight Black leather-and-vinyl seats with silver leather inserts and a pony logo, a split/fold-down rear seat (coupe only), air conditioning, a console with an armrest and integral storage bin and dual cupholders, an auxiliary 12-volt power point, an 80-watt premium sound system with cassette and CD players, a leather-wrapped tilt steering wheel, a driver's footrest, an instrument cluster with gray mask and 35th Anniversary script (with speedometer, tachometer, voltmeter, engine temperature gauge, fuel gauge and oil pressure gauge), stalk-mounted controls (for turn signals, wiper-washer, high beams and flash-to-pass feature), courtesy lamps, a dome with side-door-ajar switches, a luggage compartment lamp, power door locks, one touch power windows, a deck lid release, Midnight Black carpeted floor mats with the 35th Anniversary logo, silver leather door trim inserts, an aluminum shift knob (manual transmission), second-generation driver and front passenger airbags, three-point lap/shoulder safety belts, high-strength side door intrusion beams, interval windshield wipers, the SecuriLock™ passive anti-theft system, remote keyless entry system and antilock brakes.

35th ANNIVERSARY MUSTANG GT (V-8)

P	42	2d Coupe-4P	21,395	3,069	2,318
P	45	2d Convertible-4P	25,395	3,211	2,310

Note 3: Prices include dealer destination charges.

Note 4: Total production of 4,628 limited-edition 35th anniversary models was imbedded in GT production totals.

Note 5: 35th Anniversary production included 1,555 red cars; 1,299 black cars; 1,259 silver cars and 515 white cars.

MUSTANG SVT COBRA: The SVT Cobra was based on the GT. Standard SVT Cobra equipment included dual second-generation airbags, manual control air conditioning, the SecuriLock™ passive anti-theft system, power four-wheel disc antilock brakes with new front calipers, a CD player, a clock integrated into the radio, side window demisters, rear window defroster, power door locks, a 4.6-liter DOHC V-8 engine, a stainless steel dual exhaust system, Solar-Tinted glass, a power ventilation system with four instrument panel registers with positive shutoffs, an analog instrument cluster (with tachometer, trip odometer, voltmeter, temperature gauge, fuel gauge, oil pressure gauge and overdrive-off indicator with

1999 Ford Mustang SVT Cobra two-door convertible. (FMC)

automatic transmission), remote keyless entry, dual electric remote-control outside rearview mirrors (right-hand convex), dual illuminated visor-vanity mirrors, ETR AM/FM stereo with cassette tape player, premium sound system with premium speakers and 80-watt amplifier, sport bucket seats with leather trim and six-way power on driver's seat, color-keyed sun visors, a 150-mph speedometer, speed control, a bench rear seat with split-folding seatback, a leather-wrapped tilt steering wheel with center horn (two-toned when combined with Medium Graphite and Medium Parchment interior), power rack-and-pinion steering, P245/45ZR17 black sidewall performance tires, a five-speed manual overdrive transmission, interval windshield wipers, 17-in. five-spoke forged aluminum wheels, power side windows with driver's side "express down" feature, power door locks and a power deck lid release. The convertible also had a power folding top and power rear quarter windows.

MUSTANG SVT COBRA (V-8)

P	47	2d Coupe-4P	27,995	3,240	4,040
P	46	2d Convertible-4P	31,995	3,384	4,055

Note 6: Prices include dealer destination charges.

Note 7: SVT Cobra coupe production by color was: (Black) 1,619; (Red) 1,219; (White) 794 and (Green) 408.

Note 8: SVT Cobra convertible production by color was: (Black) 1,755; (Red) 1,251; (White) 731 and (Green) 318.

MUSTANG ENGINES

ENGINE [BASE]: Overhead valve V-6. Cast-iron block. Hydraulic valve lifters. Four main bearings. Displacement: 232 cid (3.8 liters). Bore & stroke: 3.80 x 3.40 in. Compression ratio: 9.36:1. Brake horsepower: 190 at 5250 rpm. Torque: 220 lbs.-ft. at 2750 rpm. Sequential electronic fuel injection. VIN code 4.

ENGINE [GT]: Single overhead camshaft V-8. Cast-iron block. Hydraulic valve lifters. Displacement: 281 cid (4.6 liters). Bore & stroke: 3.60 x 3.60 in. Compression ratio: 9.0:1. Brake horsepower: 260 at 5250 rpm. Torque: 302 lbs.-ft. at 4000 rpm. Sequential electronic fuel injection. VIN code W.

ENGINE [SVT COBRA]: Double overhead camshaft V-8. Aluminum block. Hydraulic valve lifters. Displacement: 281 cid (4.6 liters). Bore & stroke: 3.60 x 3.60 in. Compression ratio: 9.85:1. Brake horsepower: 320 at 6000 rpm. Torque: 315 lbs.-ft. at 4000 rpm. Sequential electronic fuel injection. VIN code V.

CHASSIS: Wheelbase: 101.3 in. Overall length: 183.5 inches. Height 53.2 in. Width 73.1 in. Front tread: 59.9 in. Rear tread: 59.9 inches

TECHNICAL: Standard transmission: five-speed manual overdrive. Drive axle: rear. Steering: Power assisted rack-and-pinion. Front suspension: modified MacPherson gas-pressurized shock struts with coil springs and stabilizer bar. Rear suspension: four-bar link and coil spring system, gas shocks. Front brakes: power assisted discs. Rear brakes: power assisted discs. Ignition: electronic. Body construction: unibody with front isolated mini-frame. Fuel tank: 15.4 gal.

OPTIONS: 44U four-speed automatic overdrive transmission, not available on Cobra ($815). 552 antilock braking system ($500). 60C convenience group including front floor mats, rear window defroster, speed control and power driver's seat ($550). GT Sport group includes 17-in. five-spoke aluminum wheels, hood stripe and wraparound fender stripes, leather-wrapped shift knob and engine oil cooler ($595). V6

Sport Appearance group includes 15-in. cast aluminum wheels, rear spoiler, leather-wrapped steering wheel, lower body side accent stripe, base model only ($310). 35th Anniversary Limited Edition package, includes 17-in. five-spoke aluminum wheels, black appliqué on hood, side scoops, rocker panel moldings, rear spoiler, taillight appliqué, black and silver leather seats, silver door trim inserts, silver and black floor mats with 35th Anniversary logo and aluminum shifter knob, GT only ($2,695). 57Q Electric rear window defroster ($190). 677 dual illuminated visor mirrors, standard on convertible ($95). Color-keyed body side moldings ($60). 588 Mach 460 AM/FM stereo radio with cassette and CD changer compatibility ($395). 13K single wing rear spoiler, standard on GT ($195). 422 California emissions system (no cost). 428 high altitude emissions (no cost). T leather front bucket seats with vinyl trim, base and GT only ($500). X leather front sport bucket seats, GT only ($500). 41H engine block immersion heater ($20). 63B smoker's package including ashtray and lighter ($15). 553 all-speed traction control, requires antilock brakes, standard on Cobra ($230). 64X 17-in. forged aluminum wheels with P245/45ZR17 black sidewall tires and locking lug nuts, GT only ($500).

HISTORICAL FOOTNOTES: The heavily face-lifted 1999 model, despite positive reviews from the motor press, saw a decline in sales from the previous year, at 133,637 total. Model year production included 91,847 coupes and 34,220 convertibles for a grand total of 126,067 Mustangs. The four-speed automatic transmission was used in 61.8 percent of production. The five-speed manual transmission was used in 38.2 percent. Four-wheel power disc brakes were installed on 52.5 percent and 48.3 percent had ABS braking. Leather seats were installed in 29.8 percent. The V-6 was used in 70.2 percent of all 1999 Mustangs, 23.6 percent had the SOHC V-8 and 6.2 percent had the DOHC V-8. A pair of Mustang FR500 prototypes was built by the Ford Racing Technology Group. These awesome cars had a 415-hp engine attached to a six-speed manual transmission. They could go from 0-60 mph in 4.5 seconds. For additional facts about 35th Anniversary Mustang GTs visit www.mustang35th.com. A good Web site to visit for 1987-2002 Cobra information is www.2stylin.stangnet.com.

2000 MUSTANG

2000 Ford Mustang Cobra R two-door coupe. (FMC)

MUSTANG – V-6 – SERIES P – Three new Mustang colors called Sunburst Gold, Performance Red and Amazon Gold, replaced Chrome Yellow, Rio Red and Dark Green Satin. That was about it for the obvious changes to the 2000 model. Two new safety features were added. First, child seat tether anchor brackets were added to the rear seating areas of all Mustangs. Second, an inside-the-trunk deck lid release with glow-in-the-dark illumination became standard equipment after news reports of carjacking victims being locked in the trunks of their cars. In the spring, a new 2000 model became the third in a series of Cobra R models. This new, limited-edition racing car followed the tradition of the 1993 and 1995 Cobra R Mustangs.

BASE MUSTANG: Standard equipment included dual second-generation airbags, manual control air conditioning, the SecuriLock™ passive anti-theft system, power four-wheel disc brakes with new front calipers, a CD player, a clock integrated into the radio, side window demisters, power door locks, a 3.8-liter EFI V-6 engine, a stainless steel exhaust system, Solar-Tinted glass, a power ventilation system with four instrument panel registers with positive shutoffs, an analog instrument cluster (with tachometer, trip odometer, voltmeter, temperature gauge, fuel gauge, oil pressure gauge and overdrive-off indicator with automatic transmission), remote keyless entry, dual electric remote-control outside rearview mirrors (right-hand convex), dual visor-vanity mirrors with covers (and illumination on convertible), ETR AM/FM stereo with cassette tape player, premium sound system with premium speakers and 80-watt amplifier, reclining cloth bucket seats with cloth head restraints, a bench rear seat with split-folding seatback, child seat tether anchors, a tilt steering wheel with center horn, power rack-and-pinion steering, P205/65R15 black sidewall all-season tires, a five-speed manual overdrive transmission, interval windshield wipers, 15-in. six-spoke cast aluminum wheels with ornaments, an inside-the-trunk deck lid release and power side windows with driver's side "express down" feature. The convertible also had a power folding top and power rear quarter windows.

I.D. DATA: A 17-character Vehicle Identification Number is stamped on an aluminum tab on the instrument panel, viewable through the windshield. A vehicle certification label is found on the body side of where the driver's door closes. The first symbol indicates the nation of origin: 1=United States of America. The second symbol indicates the manufacturer: F=Ford Motor Co. The third symbol indicates vehicle type: A=passenger car. The fourth symbol indicates type of restraint system: L= driver and front passenger airbags with passive front belts and active rear belts. The fifth symbol is the designation number: P=passenger car. The sixth and seventh symbols indicate car line and body type: 40=two-door coupe; 42=two-door GT coupe; 44=two-door convertible; 45=two-door GT convertible; 46=two-door Cobra convertible; 47=two-door Cobra/Cobra R coupe. The eighth symbol indicates engine type: 4=232 cid (3.8-liter) EFI V-6; X=281 cid (4.6-liter) EFI SOHC V-8. The ninth symbol is a check digit. The 10th symbol indicates model year: Y=2000. The 11th symbol indicates assembly plant: F=Dearborn, Mich. The last six symbols are the consecutive unit production number staring at 100001 at each factory. Paint Codes: BP=Sunburst Gold, ES=Performance Red, E9=Laser Red, K6=Atlantic Blue, K7=Bright Atlantic Blue, SU=Amazon Green, SW=Electric Green, UA=Black, YN=Silver and ZR=Crystal White.

Model No.	Body/ Style No.	Body Type & Seating	Factory Price	Shipping Weight	Prod. Total
BASE MUSTANG (V-6)					
P	40	2d Coupe-4P	17,070	3,069	Note 2
P	44	2d Convertible-4P	21,920	3,111	Note 2

Note 1: Prices include dealer destination charges.

Note 2: Total production of all models was 218,525. This included Base V-6 and GT models.

MUSTANG GT - V-8 - SERIES P - On GT models the hood grew a simulated recessed scoop that recalled the air-grabber that the 1968 sported when it received its first 428 cid V-8. GT exhaust tips also were enlarged slightly, from 2.75 inches to three inches. The GT's 4.6-liter was boosted to 260 hp and the base 3.8-liter V-6 jumped to 190 hp. Standard GT equipment included dual second-generation airbags, manual control air conditioning, the SecuriLock™ passive anti-theft system, power four-wheel disc antilock brakes with new front calipers, a CD player, a clock integrated into the radio, side window demisters, power door locks, a 4.6-liter SOHC V-8 engine, a stainless steel dual exhaust system, Solar-Tinted glass, a power ventilation system with four instrument panel registers with positive shutoffs, an analog instrument cluster (with tachometer, trip odometer, voltmeter, temperature gauge, fuel gauge, oil pressure gauge and overdrive-off indicator with automatic transmission), remote keyless entry, dual electric remote-control outside rearview mirrors (right-hand convex), dual visor-vanity mirrors with covers (and illumination on convertible), ETR AM/FM stereo with cassette tape player, premium sound system with premium speakers and 80-watt amplifier, GT Sport two-tone cloth trim bucket seats, a 150-mph speedometer, a bench rear seat with split-folding seatback, child seat tether anchors, a leather-wrapped tilt steering wheel with center horn (two-toned when combined with Medium Graphite and Medium Parchment interior), power rack-and-pinion steering, P225/55R16 black sidewall all-season tires, a five-speed manual overdrive transmission, interval windshield wipers, 16-in. six-spoke forged aluminum wheels with carryover ornaments, an inside-the-trunk deck lid release and power side windows with driver's side "express down" feature. The convertible also had a power folding top and power rear quarter windows.

MUSTANG GT (V-8)					
P	42	2d Coupe-4P	21,565	3,242	Note 4
P	45	2d Convertible-4P	25,820	3,386	Note 4

Note 3: Prices include dealer destination charges.

Note 4: Total production of all models was 218,525. This included Base V-6 and GT models. About 30 percent were GTs.

MUSTANG SVT COBRA R – V-8 – SERIES P - Ford called the 2000 SVT Cobra R the "fastest and best-handling Mustang ever." A total of 300 Mustang Cobra R models rolled off the Dearborn, Mich. production line in May 2000. These cars were offered by certified SVT dealers. The Cobra R was a limited production street legal race-prepped version of the Mustang. Built with the racetrack in mind, it featured a 5.4L DOHC modular V-8 that produced 385 hp and 385 ft.-lbs. of torque. The new

Cobra R also featured exterior enhancements including a front air-splitter and tall rear deck spoiler (designed to create a downforce that promoted increased stability at track speeds). Other distinctions of the Cobra R included a "power dome" hood with a rear air extractor for improved engine cooling, 18-in. wheels, BF Goodrich g-Force KD tires and a lowered suspension for enhanced handling. Interior enhancements included Recaro sport bucket seats and the deletion of a radio, air-conditioner and back seat to save weight. A number of approved aftermarket performance parts suppliers worked with Ford's Special Vehicles Team (SVT) to develop the Cobra R. They contributed the Brembo brake rotors and calipers, Tremec transmission, Eibach and Bilstein suspension components and Borla exhaust system.

MUSTANG SVT COBRA (V-8)					
P	47	2d Coupe-4P	54,995	3,590	300

Note 5: Prices include dealer destination charges.

Note 6: Total production of all models was 218,525. This included 300 Cobra R models.

MUSTANG ENGINES

ENGINE [BASE]: Overhead valve V-6. Cast-iron block. Hydraulic valve lifters. Four main bearings. Displacement: 232 cid (3.8 liters). Bore & stroke: 3.80 x 3.40 in. Compression ratio: 9.36:1. Brake horsepower: 190 at 5250 rpm. Torque: 220 lbs.-ft. at 2750 rpm. Sequential electronic fuel injection. VIN code 4.

ENGINE [GT]: Single overhead camshaft V-8. Cast-iron block. Hydraulic valve lifters. Displacement: 281 cid (4.6 liters). Bore & stroke: 3.60 x 3.60 in. Compression ratio: 9.0:1. Brake horsepower: 260 at 5250 rpm. Torque: 302 lbs.-ft. at 4000 rpm. Sequential electronic fuel injection. VIN code W.

ENGINE [COBRA R]: Double overhead camshaft V-8. Cast-iron block. Aluminum heads. Hydraulic valve lifters. Displacement: 330 cid (5.4 liters). Bore & stroke: 3.55 x 4.15 in. Compression ratio: 9.6:1. Brake horsepower: 385 at 6250 rpm. Torque: 385 lbs.-ft. at 4250 rpm. Sequential electronic fuel injection. VIN code H.

CHASSIS: Wheelbase: 101.3 in. Overall length: 183.2 inches. Height: (Cobra R Coupe) 52.2 in.; (all other models) 53.3 in. Width 73.1 in. Front tread: 60.4 in. Rear tread: 60.6 inches

TECHNICAL: [BASE V-6/GT] Standard transmission: five-speed manual overdrive. Drive axle: rear. Steering: Power assisted rack-and-pinion. Front suspension: modified MacPherson gas-pressurized shock struts with coil springs and stabilizer bar. Rear suspension: four-bar link and coil spring system, gas shocks. Front brakes: power assisted discs. Rear brakes: power assisted discs. Ignition: electronic. Body construction: unibody with front isolated mini-frame. Fuel tank: 15.4 gal.

TECHNICAL: [COBRA R] Standard transmission: five-speed manual overdrive. Drive axle: rear. Steering: Power assisted rack-and-pinion. Front suspension: modified MacPherson gas-pressurized shock struts with coil springs and stabilizer bar; lowered for enhanced handling. Rear suspension: four-bar link and coil spring system, gas shocks; lowered for enhanced handling. Brakes: power assisted four-wheel disc brakes with Brembo rotors and calipers. Ignition: electronic. Body construction: unibody with front isolated mini-frame. Fuel tank: 15.4 gal.

OPTIONS: 44U four-speed automatic overdrive transmission ($815). 552 antilock braking system ($500). 553 all-speed traction control, requires antilock brakes ($230). 60C convenience group including front floor mats, rear window defroster, speed control and power driver's seat ($550). GT Sport group includes 17-in. five-spoke aluminum wheels, hood stripe and wraparound fender stripes, leather-wrapped shift knob and engine oil cooler ($595). V6 Sport Appearance group includes 15-in. cast aluminum wheels, rear spoiler, leather-wrapped steering wheel, lower body side accent stripe, base model only ($310). 57Q Electric rear window defroster ($190). 677 dual illuminated visor mirrors, standard on convertible ($95). Color-keyed body side moldings ($60). 588 Mach 460 AM/FM stereo radio with cassette and CD changer compatibility ($395). 13K single wing rear spoiler, standard on GT ($195). 422 California emissions system (no cost). T Leather front bucket seats with vinyl trim, base and GT only ($500). X Leather front sport bucket seats, GT only ($500). 41H engine block immersion heater ($20). 63B smoker's package including ashtray and lighter ($15). 64X 17-in. forged aluminum wheels with P245/45ZR17 black sidewall tires and locking lug nuts, GT only ($500).

HISTORICAL FOOTNOTES: Mustang production climbed more than 70 percent from 1999. The total included 39,791 Black cars; 37,617 Silver cars; 33,804 Laser Red cars; 32,606 Crystal White cars; 17,764 Performance Red cars; 13,262 Amazon Tropic Green cars; 11,873 Atlantic Blue cars; 5,206 Electric Green cars; 5,171 Sunburst Gold cars; 4,979 Bright Atlantic Blue cars and 917 Zinc Yellow spring feature cars. For more information about yellow Mustangs visit www.2stylin.stangenet.com. Ford had planned to market a 2000 SVT Cobra coupe and convertible with a single overhead cam (SOHC) V-8 with introductory prices of $28,155 for the coupe and $32,155 for the convertible. The National Insurance Crime Bureau's *2000 Passenger Vehicle Identification Manual* showed body code numbers for these models. However, due to heavy recalls on 1999 models with the 4.6-liter DOHC V-8, the 2000 SVT Cobra was not produced. Instead the Cobra R bowed in the spring with a bigger DOHC V-8 based on a heavily-modified 5.4-liter Ford truck engine. Ford's newest concept car — the 2000 Bullitt Mustang GT — made its world debut at the 2000 Los Angeles Auto Show. The car was designed with all the excitement of its namesake classic Hollywood film in mind and paid homage to the 1968 fastback Mustang GT featured in the edge-of-your-seat police thriller, the 1968 Warner Brothers film "Bullitt" with Steve McQueen. Many of the 2000 Bullitt Mustang's styling cues are based on the original Mustang featured in one of cinema history's most memorable car chases, which depicted Det. Frank Bullitt (Steve McQueen) in hot pursuit of bad guys through the challenging streets of San Francisco. "With the Bullitt concept, we have visually and emotionally recreated the excitement of one of the greatest movie car chase scenes," said J. Mays, Ford Motor Co. vice president of design. "Still as popular today as it was when it was introduced in 1964, the Mustang and the Bullitt concept show the possibilities for customizing this car and keeping the excitement alive as ever." The Bullitt concept was a 2000 Mustang GT that had been modified to resemble the Mustang used in the film. It featured new front and rear fascias, a new hood, front and rear lamps, five-spoke 18-in. aluminum wheels reminiscent of the originals, unique gauges on the instrument panel and racing-inspired seats. The exterior body panels were finished in pursuit green.

2001 MUSTANG

2001 Ford Mustang two-door convertible. (FMC)

MUSTANG – V-6 – SERIES P – The 2001 Mustang still retained some of the original styling cues that first turned heads more than three decades ago, but remained a highly contemporary looking automobile befitting its performance image. The exterior profile reinforced its sports car heritage with an overall ground-hugging appearance that emphasized an agile, aggressive stance. The hood scoop, side scoop and pony emblem in chrome "corral" brand incorporated classic Mustang design elements. All models had new blacked out headlights and spoilers. Inside, the dual cockpit shape was reminiscent of the original Mustang; yet, its wraparound design was modern and user-friendly. The headliner, rear package tray and A- and C-pillar moldings were color-keyed to the rest of the interior. The Mustang convertible provided a fun-to-drive experience, but had a practical and easy-to-use design. The power retractable convertible top came with a semi-hard boot that protected the top from dust when lowered and enhanced the exterior appearance. A hydraulic system allowed quick raising and lowering of the top. The rear window was made of scratch-resistant glass. A new "value leader" V-6 coupe was made available in the 2001 Mustang lineup. This year's base Mustang got a new console with a larger rear cupholder, a repositioned front cupholder, a 12-volt power point, a tissue holder and a parking brake boot. A rear-window defroster became standard on all models. A new six-disc in-dash CD player was available with the Mach® 460 Sound System. New colors for the year were Mineral Grey Clearcoat Metallic, True Blue Clearcoat Metallic, Zinc Yellow Clearcoat and Oxford White Clearcoat. Never one to shy away from a limited-production "special" model, Ford brought to showrooms in 2001 a version of its 2000 Bullitt show car. Some sources say that production of the Bullitt Mustang was set at 5,000 units and some say 6,000 units. The actual production fell between the two numbers at 5,532.

BASE MUSTANG COUPE: Standard equipment included body color front and rear fascias with Mustang nomenclature, a composite hood with scoop, complex reflector halogen headlights with integral turn/park lamps, three-tiered taillights, dual electric remote-control outside rearview mirrors (right-hand with convex glass), clearcoat paint, color-keyed

rocker panel moldings, 15 x 7-in six-spoke cast-aluminum wheels, a steel mini spare and 15-in. temporary tire, second generation driver and front passenger airbags, a three-point active restraint system, deluxe carpets, child seat tether anchor brackets on the package tray, a cigarette lighter port and auxiliary power point, a clock integrated with the radio, a console (with armrest, integral storage bin, tissue holder, dual cupholders and parking brake boot), a power-operated inside-the-trunk deck lid release with glow-in-the-dark handle, a driver's footrest, a locking glove box, an analog instrument cluster (including a tachometer, a trip odometer, a voltmeter, a temperature gauge, a fuel gauge, an oil pressure gauge and an "overdrive-off" indicator with automatic transmission), a light group (with lamps in dome, front "door ajar" switches and a "headlamps on" chime), luggage compartment trim and carpeting, dual visor-vanity mirrors, reclining cloth bucket seats with cloth head restraints, a split-folding rear seat, stalk-mounted controls, a tilt steering wheel with center horn, monochromatic full wrapover door trim, soft flow-through door panels with full-length armrests and vinyl inserts, color-keyed upper instrument panel finish, a color keyed headliner, color-keyed safety belts, a color-keyed shifter bezel, color-keyed A and C pillar appliqués, color-keyed instrument cluster finish, manual control air conditioning, a heavy-duty 130-amp alternator, a 58-amp/hr heavy-duty maintenance-free battery, four-wheel power disc brakes, side window demisters, power door locks, an electrodrive cooling fan, EEC-V electronic engine controls, a 3.8-liter SEFI V-6, a stainless steel exhaust system, a fuel pump inertia shutoff switch, a 15.5-gal. fuel tank with tethered cap, complete Solar-Tinted glass, power ventilation with four instrument panel registers and positive shutoff, a dual note horn, a tunnel mounted parking brake with integral boot, an electronic AM/FM stereo cassette tape player with single disc CD and premium speakers and 80-watt integrated amplifier, the SecuriLock™ passive anti-theft system, remote keyless entry, power rack-and-pinion steering, a modified MacPherson strut front suspension with front stabilizer bar, a rear coil spring four-bar-link suspension with increased travel for smoother ride, gas pressurized front struts and rear shock absorbers, P205/65R15 all-season black sidewall tires, a rear window defroster, a five-speed manual overdrive transmission, interval windshield wipers and one touch power windows.

BASE MUSTANG CONVERTIBLE: Standard equipment included body color front and rear fascias with Mustang nomenclature, a power retractable convertible top with semi-hard boot, a composite hood with scoop, complex reflector halogen headlights with integral turn/park lamps, three-tiered taillights, dual electric remote-control outside rearview mirrors (right-hand with convex glass), clearcoat paint, color-keyed rocker panel moldings, 16 x 7-in cast-aluminum wheels, a steel mini spare and 15-in. temporary tire, second generation driver and front passenger airbags, a three-point active restraint system, deluxe carpets, child seat tether anchor brackets on the seatbacks, a cigarette lighter port and auxiliary power point, a clock integrated with the radio, a console (with armrest, integral storage bin, tissue holder, dual cupholders and parking brake boot), a power-operated inside-the-trunk deck lid release with glow-in-the-dark handle, a driver's footrest, a locking glove box, an analog instrument cluster (including a tachometer, a trip odometer, a voltmeter, a temperature gauge, a fuel gauge, an oil pressure gauge and an "overdrive-off" indicator with automatic transmission), a light group (with dome lamps integrated in mirror, front "door ajar" switches and a "headlamps on" chime), luggage compartment trim and carpeting, dual illuminated visor-vanity mirrors, reclining cloth bucket seats with cloth head restraints, a split-folding rear seat, stalk-mounted controls, a tilt steering wheel with center horn, monochromatic full wrapover door trim, soft flow-through door panels with full-length armrests and vinyl inserts, color-keyed upper instrument panel finish, a color keyed headliner, color-keyed safety belts, a color-keyed shifter bezel, color-keyed A and C pillar appliqués, color-keyed instrument cluster finish, manual control air conditioning, a heavy-duty 130-amp alternator, a 58-amp/hr heavy-duty maintenance-free battery, four-wheel power disc brakes, side window demisters, power door locks, an electrodrive cooling fan, EEC-V electronic engine controls, a 3.8-liter SEFI V-6, a stainless steel exhaust system, a fuel pump inertia shutoff switch, a 15.5-gal. fuel tank with tethered cap, complete Solar-Tinted glass, power ventilation with four instrument panel registers and positive shutoff, a dual note horn, a tunnel mounted parking brake with integral boot, an electronic AM/FM stereo cassette tape player with single disc CD and premium speakers and 80-watt integrated amplifier, the SecuriLock™ passive anti-theft system, remote keyless entry, power rack-and-pinion steering, a modified MacPherson strut front suspension with front stabilizer bar, a rear coil spring four-bar-link suspension with increased travel for smoother ride, gas pressurized front struts and rear shock absorbers, P205/65R16 all-season black sidewall tires, a five-speed manual overdrive transmission, a rear window defroster, interval windshield wipers, one touch power windows and power rear quarter windows.

I.D. DATA: A 17-character Vehicle Identification Number is stamped on an aluminum tab on the instrument panel, viewable through the windshield. A vehicle certification label is found on the body side of where the driver's door closes. The first symbol indicates the nation of origin: 1=United States of America. The second symbol indicates the manufacturer: F=Ford Motor Co. The third symbol indicates vehicle type:

A=passenger car. The fourth symbol indicates type of restraint system: L= driver and front passenger airbags with passive front belts and active rear belts. The fifth symbol is the designation number: P=passenger car. The sixth and seventh symbols indicate car line and body type: 40=two-door coupe; 42=two-door GT coupe; 44=two-door convertible; 45=two-door GT convertible; 46=two-door SVT Cobra convertible; 47=two-door SVT Cobra coupe. The eighth symbol indicates engine type: 4=232 cid (3.8-liter) EFI V-6; X=281 cid (4.6-liter) EFI SOHC V-8; W=281 cid (4.6-liter) EFI SOHC "Bullitt" V-8; V=281 cid (4.6-liter) EFI DOHC V-8. The ninth symbol is a check digit. The 10th symbol indicates model year: 1=2001. The 11th symbol indicates assembly plant: F=Dearborn, Mich. The last six symbols are the consecutive unit production number staring at 100001 at each factory. Paint Codes: B7=Zinc Yellow; ES=Performance Red, E9=Laser Red, L2=True Blue, PY=Bullitt Green, SU=Amazon Green, SW=Electric Green, TK=Mineral Gray; YN=Silver and Z1=Oxford White

Model No.	Body/ Style No.	Body Type & Seating	Factory Price	Shipping Weight	Prod. Total
MUSTANG VALUE LEADER (V-6)					
P	40	2d Coupe-4P	17,695	3,069	Note 2
MUSTANG DELUXE (V-6)					
P	40	2d Coupe-4P	18,260	3,069	Note 2
P	44	2d Convertible-4P	23,110	3,111	Note 2
MUSTANG PREMIUM (V-6)					
P	40	2d Coupe-4P	19,490	3,069	Note 2
P	44	2d Convertible-4P	25,675	3,111	Note 2

Note 1: Prices include dealer destination charges.

Note 2: Production totals not available at publishing date.

MUSTANG GT - V-8 - SERIES P - The Mustang became even more of a 1960s muscle car throwback with the 2001 GT model when the pumped-up body gained a tall (though non-functional) hood scoop and side scoops that were designed to set it more apart from the V-6 series. New 17-in. premium aluminum heavier spoke wheels with bright flanges were available with the GT Premium option group.

MUSTANG GT COUPE: Standard equipment included body color front and rear fascias with Mustang nomenclature and dual tailpipe outlets at rear, a GT hood and side scoop, complex reflector halogen headlights with integral turn/park lamps, front fog lamps, three-tiered taillights, dual electric remote-control outside rearview mirrors (right-hand with convex glass), a single-wing rear deck lid spoiler, clearcoat paint, color-keyed rocker panel moldings, 17 x 8-in six-spoke forged aluminum wheels with carryover ornaments, an aluminum spare wheel and 15-in. mini spare tire, second generation driver and front passenger airbags, a three-point active restraint system, deluxe carpets, child seat tether anchor brackets on the package tray, a cigarette lighter port and auxiliary power point, a clock integrated with the radio, a console (with armrest, integral storage bin, tissue holder, dual cupholders and parking brake boot), a power-operated inside-the-trunk deck lid release with glow-in-the-dark handle, a driver's footrest, a locking glove box, an analog instrument cluster (including a tachometer, a trip odometer, a voltmeter, a temperature gauge, a fuel gauge, an oil pressure gauge and an "overdrive-off" indicator with automatic transmission), a 150-mph speedometer, a light group (with lamps in dome, front "door ajar" switches and a "headlamps on" chime), luggage compartment trim and carpeting, dual visor-vanity mirrors, reclining two-tone cloth GT sport seats with cloth head restraints, a split-folding rear seat, stalk-mounted controls, a leather-wrapped tilt steering wheel with center horn (two-tone in combination with Medium Graphite and Medium Parchment interior), monochromatic full wrapover door trim, soft flow-through door panels with full-length armrests and vinyl inserts, color-keyed upper instrument panel finish, a color keyed headliner, color-keyed safety belts, a color-keyed shifter bezel, color-keyed A and C pillar appliqués, color-keyed instrument cluster finish, manual control air conditioning, a heavy-duty 130-amp alternator, a Traction-Loc rear axle, a 58-amp/hr heavy-duty maintenance-free battery, four-wheel power ABS disc brakes, side window demisters, power door locks, an electrodrive cooling fan, EEC-V electronic engine controls, a 4.6-liter SOHC two-valve V-8, a dual stainless steel exhaust system, a fuel pump inertia shutoff switch, a 15.5-gal. fuel tank with tethered cap, complete Solar-Tinted glass, power ventilation with four instrument panel registers and positive shutoff, a dual note horn, a tunnel mounted parking brake with integral boot, an electronic AM/FM stereo cassette tape player with single disc CD and premium speakers and 80-watt integrated amplifier, the SecuriLock™ passive anti-theft system, remote keyless entry, power rack-and-pinion steering, a modified MacPherson strut front suspension with front stabilizer bar, a rear coil spring four-bar-link suspension with increased travel for smoother ride, gas pressurized front struts and rear shock absorbers with unique GT calibrations, a GT suspension package with variable rate coil springs and a quadra-link-shock rear suspension, P245/45ZR17 sidewall performance tires, a rear window defroster, a five-speed manual overdrive transmission, interval windshield wipers and one touch power windows.

2001 Ford Mustang GT two-door coupe. (FMC)

MUSTANG GT CONVERTIBLE: Standard equipment included body color front and rear fascias with Mustang nomenclature and dual tailpipe outlets at rear, a power retractable convertible top with semi-hard boot, a GT hood and side scoop, complex reflector halogen headlights with integral turn/park lamps, front fog lamps, three-tiered taillights, dual electric remote-control outside rearview mirrors (right-hand with convex glass), a single-wing rear deck lid spoiler, clearcoat paint, color-keyed rocker panel moldings, 16 x 7-in cast-aluminum wheels, a steel mini spare and 15-in. temporary tire, second generation driver and front passenger airbags, a three-point active restraint system, deluxe carpets, child seat tether anchor brackets on the seatbacks, a cigarette lighter port and auxiliary power point, a clock integrated with the radio, a console (with armrest, integral storage bin, tissue holder, dual cupholders and parking brake boot), a power-operated inside-the-trunk deck lid release with glow-in-the-dark handle, a driver's footrest, a locking glove box, an analog instrument cluster (including a tachometer, a trip odometer, a voltmeter, a temperature gauge, a fuel gauge, an oil pressure gauge and an "overdrive-off" indicator with automatic transmission), a 150-mph speedometer, a light group (with dome lamps integrated in mirror, front "door ajar" switches and a "headlamps on" chime), luggage compartment trim and carpeting, dual illuminated visor-vanity mirrors, reclining two-tone cloth GT sport seats with cloth head restraints, a split-folding rear seat, stalk-mounted controls, a leather-wrapped tilt steering wheel with center horn (two-tone in combination with Medium Graphite and Medium Parchment interior), monochromatic full wrapover door trim, soft flow-through door panels with full-length armrests and and vinyl inserts, color-keyed upper instrument panel finish, a color keyed headliner, color-keyed safety belts, a color-keyed shifter bezel, color-keyed A and C pillar appliqués, color-keyed instrument cluster finish, manual control air conditioning, a Traction-Loc rear axle, a heavy-duty 130-amp alternator, a 58-amp/hr heavy-duty maintenance-free battery, four-wheel power ABS disc brakes,, side window demisters, power door locks, an electrodrive cooling fan, EEC-V electronic engine controls, a 4.6-liter SOHC two-valve V-8, a dual stainless steel exhaust system, a fuel pump inertia shutoff switch, a 15.5-gal. fuel tank with tethered cap, complete Solar-Tinted glass, power ventilation with four instrument panel registers and positive shutoff, a dual note horn, a tunnel mounted parking brake with integral boot, an electronic AM/FM stereo cassette tape player with single disc CD and premium speakers and 80-watt integrated amplifier, the SecuriLock™ passive anti-theft system, remote keyless entry, power rack-and-pinion steering, a modified MacPherson strut front suspension with front stabilizer bar, a rear coil spring four-bar-link suspension with increased travel for smoother ride, gas pressurized front struts and rear shock absorbers with unique GT calibrations, a GT suspension package with variable rate coil springs and a quadra-link shock rear suspension, P245/45ZR17 black sidewall performance tires, a five-speed manual overdrive transmission, a rear window defroster, interval windshield wipers, one touch power windows and power rear quarter windows.

MUSTANG GT DELUXE (V-8)					
P	42	2d Coupe-4P	23,330	3,242	Note 4
P	45	2d Convertible-4P	27,585	3,386	Note 4
MUSTANG GT PREMIUM (V-8)					
P	42	2d Coupe-4P	24,480	3,242	Note 4
P	45	2d Convertible-4P	28,735	3,386	Note 4

MUSTANG GT BULLITT COUPE: Based on the 1968 fastback driven by Steve McQueen in the gritty detective drama *Bullitt*, this coupe-only model featured exterior enhancements that visually and emotionally connected it to the classic film's famous chase scene. Modifications to the Bullitt Mustang included unique side scoops, a set of 17-in. American Racing aluminum wheels, a lowered suspension, modified C pillars and a quarter panel molding that set the car apart from a stock GT. Rocker panel moldings enhanced the car's lowered appearance. A bold, brushed aluminum fuel filler door was prominently placed on the quarter panel. Special Bullitt badging and polished-rolled tailpipe tips further distinguished the car. The Bullitt Mustang was available in Dark Highland Green, True Blue and Black. Providing 270 hp was a mildly modified 4.6-liter V-8 with a twin 57mm diameter throttle body, a cast aluminum

2001 Ford Mustang "Bullit" GT two-door coupe. (FMC)

intake manifold and high-flow mufflers. Re-valved Tokico™ struts and shocks, unique stabilizer bars (at the front and rear), frame rail connectors, 13-in. Brembo™ front brake rotors and Brembo™ performance brake calipers made up a unique suspension for this special Mustang model. Other standard Bullitt Mustang features included unique leather-surfaced seat trim, a "Heritage" instrument cluster, underhood clearcoat paint (in UA Black or PY Green), a charcoal interior and serialized special edition identification.

MUSTANG GT BULLITT (V-8)

P	42	2d Coupe-4P	26,830	3,242	5,532

Note 3: Prices include dealer destination charges.

Note 4: Production totals not available at publishing date.

MUSTANG SVT COBRA COUPE – V-8 – SERIES P – As always, the SVT Cobra was distinguished from other Mustangs by a number of visual signatures. They included a unique hood design, a front fascia incorporating round driving lights and a deep intake that forced air through the cooling system. Cobra badges decorated the front fenders. At the rear, tri-color taillights, polished three-inch diameter exhaust tips, an SVT badge, the word "Cobra" across the rear fascia and an optional low-drag spoiler set the SVT Cobra apart. Both the hood and the rear deck were constructed of lightweight composite materials. The 2001 model was scheduled for release in May of the year, with deliveries starting in the summer. When it arrived it had minor exterior and interior changes. External revisions included the use of five of the year's new exterior colors on the Cobra. They were True Blue, Zinc Yellow, Mineral Gray, Performance Red and Laser Red. The Cobra interior received all-new seats with added support and a six-disc in-dash CD player. The engine used was the 4.6-liter 90-degree 32-vale DOHC V-8 rated for 320 hp at 6000 rpm. and 317 ft.-lbs. of torque at 4750 rpm.

MUSTANG SVT COBRA COUPE: Standard coupe equipment included the 4.6-liter DOHC V-8, a five-speed manual transmission, rear-wheel drive, a rear limited-slip differential, a modified MacPherson strut front suspension with stabilizer bar and 500 lb./in. coil springs, an independent rear suspension with steel upper and aluminum lower control arms and 470 lb./in. coil springs, front ABS brakes with 13-in. vented Brembo™ discs and PBR™ twin-piston caliper, rear ABS brakes with 11.65-in. vented discs and single-piston calipers, 17 x 8-in. five-spoke cast aluminum alloy wheel rims with painted surfaces, P245/45ZR17 black sidewall performance tires, an alloy spare wheel with mini spare tire, variable intermittent windshield wipers, all-speed traction control, a rear defogger, a tachometer, a clock, a rear deck lid spoiler, the SecuriLock™ anti-theft system with engine immobilizer, an inside-the-trunk emergency deck lid release, remote power door locks, one touch power windows, dual power outside rearview mirrors, cruise control, a leather-wrapped tilt-adjustable steering wheel, power steering, front door pockets, a front console with storage provisions, sport front bucket seats with six-way power driver's seat and front seat adjustable lumbar support, a remote trunk release, a rear split-folding bench seat, air conditioning, dual illuminated visor-vanity mirrors, a leather-trimmed gearshift knob, front and rear floor mats, an AM/FM stereo cassette with six-disc in-dash multi-CD player and 460-watts speakers.

MUSTANG SVT COBRA CONVERTIBLE: Standard convertible equipment included the 4.6-liter DOHC V-8, included a five-speed manual transmission, rear-wheel drive, a rear limited-slip differential, a modified MacPherson strut front suspension with stabilizer bar and 500 lb./in. coil springs, an independent rear suspension with steel upper and aluminum lower control arms and 470 lb./in. coil springs, front ABS brakes with 13-in. vented Brembo™ discs and PBR™ twin-piston caliper, rear ABS brakes with 11.65-in. vented discs and single-piston calipers, 17 x 8-in. five-spoke cast aluminum alloy wheel rims with painted surfaces, P245/45ZR17 black sidewall performance tires, an alloy spare wheel with mini spare tire, variable intermittent windshield wipers, a power convertible roof, a glass rear window, all-speed traction control, a rear defogger, a tachometer, a clock, a rear deck lid spoiler, the SecuriLock™ anti-theft system with engine immobilizer, an inside-the-trunk emergency deck lid release, remote power door locks, one touch power windows, dual power outside rearview mirrors, cruise control, a leather-wrapped tilt-adjustable steering wheel, power steering, front door pockets, a front console with storage provisions, sport front bucket seats with six-way power driver's seat and front seat adjustable lumbar support, a remote trunk release, a rear bench seat, air conditioning, dual illuminated visor-vanity mirrors, a leather-trimmed gearshift knob, front and rear floor mats, an AM/FM stereo cassette with six-disc in-dash multi-CD player and 460-watts speakers.

MUSTANG SVT COBRA (V-8)

P	47	2d Coupe-4P	29,205	3,242	3,867
P	46	2d Convertible-4P	33,205	3,386	3,384

Note 5: Prices include dealer destination charges.

MUSTANG ENGINES

ENGINE [BASE]: Overhead valve V-6. Cast-iron block. Hydraulic valve lifters. Four main bearings. Displacement: 232 cid (3.8 liters). Bore & stroke: 3.80 x 3.40 in. Compression ratio: 9.36:1. Brake horsepower: 190 at 5250 rpm. Torque: 220 lbs.-ft. at 2750 rpm. Sequential electronic fuel injection. VIN code 4.

ENGINE [GT]: Single overhead camshaft V-8. Cast-iron block. Hydraulic valve lifters. Displacement: 281 cid (4.6 liters). Bore & stroke: 3.60 x 3.60 in. Compression ratio: 9.0:1. Brake horsepower: 260 at 5250 rpm. Torque: 302 lbs.-ft. at 4000 rpm. Sequential electronic fuel injection. VIN code W.

ENGINE [BULLITT GT]: Single overhead camshaft V-8. Cast-iron block. Hydraulic valve lifters. Displacement: 281 cid (4.6 liters). Bore & stroke: 3.60 x 3.60 in. Compression ratio: 9.0:1. Brake horsepower: 265 at 5250 rpm. Torque: 305 lbs.-ft. at 4000 rpm. Sequential electronic fuel injection. VIN code X.

ENGINE [SVT COBRA]: Double overhead camshaft V-8. Aluminum block. Aluminum heads. Hydraulic valve lifters. Displacement: 330 cid (5.4 liters). Bore & stroke: 3.55 x 4.15 in. Compression ratio: 9.85:1. Brake horsepower: 320 at 6000 rpm. Torque: 317 lbs.-ft. at 4750 rpm. Sequential electronic fuel injection. VIN code V.

CHASSIS: Wheelbase: 101.3 in. Overall length: 183.2 inches. Height: (coupe) 53.1 in.; (convertible) 53.2 in. Width 73.1 in. Front tread: 60.2 in. Rear tread: 60.6 inches

TECHNICAL: [BASE V-6] Standard transmission: five-speed manual overdrive. Drive axle: rear. Steering: Power assisted rack-and-pinion. Front suspension: modified MacPherson gas-pressurized shock struts with coil springs and stabilizer bar. Rear suspension: four-bar link and coil spring system, gas shocks. Front brakes: power assisted discs. Rear brakes: power assisted discs. Ignition: electronic. Body construction: unibody with front isolated mini-frame. Fuel tank: 15.5 gal.

TECHNICAL: [GT] Standard transmission: five-speed manual overdrive. Drive axle: rear. Steering: Power assisted rack-and-pinion. Front suspension: modified MacPherson gas-pressurized shock struts with unique GT calibrations and coil springs and stabilizer bar. Rear suspension: four-bar link and GT-specific variable-rate coil springs, and quadra-link shocks. Front brakes: power assisted discs. Rear brakes: power assisted discs. Ignition: electronic. Body construction: unibody with front isolated mini-frame. Fuel tank: 15.7 gal.

2001 Ford Mustang SVT Cobra two-door convertible. (FMC)

2001 Ford Mustang SVT Cobra two-door coupe. (FMC)

TECHNICAL: [BULLITT GT] Standard transmission: five-speed manual overdrive. Drive axle: rear. Steering: Power assisted rack-and-pinion. Front suspension: modified MacPherson strut with Tokico™ struts, coil springs and a unique stabilizer bar. Rear suspension: four-bar link and coil spring system, with Tokico™ shocks, unique stabilizer bar and frame rail connectors. Front brakes: power assisted discs with 13-in. Brembo™ front brake rotors and Brembo™ performance brake calipers. Rear brakes: power assisted discs with Brembo™ front brake rotors and Brembo™ performance brake calipers. Ignition: electronic. Body construction: unibody with front isolated mini-frame. Fuel tank: 15.5 gal.

TECHNICAL: [COBRA SVT] Standard transmission: five-speed manual overdrive. Drive axle: rear. Steering: Power assisted rack-and-pinion. Front suspension: modified MacPherson gas-pressurized shock struts with coil springs and stabilizer bar; lowered for enhanced handling. Rear suspension: four-bar link and coil spring system, gas shocks; lowered for enhanced handling. Brakes: power assisted four-wheel disc brakes with Brembo™ rotors and calipers. Ignition: electronic. Body construction: unibody with front isolated mini-frame. Fuel tank: 15.5 gal.

OPTIONS: [V-6 VALUE LEADER COUPE] 422 California emissions system (no cost). 44U four-speed automatic overdrive transmission ($815). 428 high-altitude emissions (no cost). 93N non-California emissions (no cost).

OPTIONS: [V-6 DELUXE COUPE] 552 antilock braking system with all-speed traction control ($730). 422 California emissions system (no cost). 44U four-speed automatic overdrive transmission ($815). 428 high-altitude emissions (no cost). 58M Mach 460 stereo system ($550). 93N non-California emissions (no cost). 54V Sport Appearance package ($250).

OPTIONS: [V-6 DELUXE CONVERTIBLE] 552 antilock braking system with all-speed traction control ($730). 422 California emissions system (no cost). 44U four-speed automatic overdrive transmission ($815). 428 high-altitude emissions (no cost). T Leather front bucket seats ($500). 58M Mach 460 stereo system ($550). 93N non-California emissions (no cost).

OPTIONS: [V-6 PREMIUM COUPE] 422 California emissions system (no cost). 44U four-speed automatic overdrive transmission ($815). 428 high-altitude emissions (no cost). T Leather front bucket seats ($500). 93N non-California emissions (no cost).

OPTIONS: [V-6 PREMIUM CONVERTIBLE] 422 California emissions system (no cost). 428 high-altitude emissions (no cost). 93N non-California emissions (no cost).

OPTIONS: [V-6 GT DELUXE COUPE] 422 California emissions system (no cost). 44U four-speed automatic overdrive transmission ($815). 428 high-altitude emissions (no cost). X Leather front sport bucket seats ($500). 58M Mach 460 stereo system ($550). 93N non-California emissions (no cost).

OPTIONS: [GT DELUXE CONVERTIBLE] 422 California emissions system (no cost). 44U four-speed automatic overdrive transmission ($815). 428 high-altitude emissions (no cost). X Leather front sport bucket seats ($500). 58M Mach 460 stereo system ($550). 93N non-California emissions (no cost).

OPTIONS: [GT PREMIUM COUPE] 422 California emissions system (no cost). 44U four-speed automatic overdrive transmission ($815). 428 high-altitude emissions (no cost). 93N non-California emissions (no cost).

OPTIONS: [GT PREMIUM CONVERTIBLE] 422 California emissions system (no cost). 44U four-speed automatic overdrive transmission ($815). 428 high-altitude emissions (no cost). 93N non-California emissions (no cost).

OPTIONS: [GT BULLITT COUPE] 422 California emissions system (no cost). 428 high-altitude emissions (no cost). 58M Mach 460 stereo system ($550). 93N non-California emissions (no cost).

OPTIONS: [SVT COBRA COUPE] 64W 17 x 8 polished forged aluminum wheels ($395) 422 California emissions system (no cost). 12H front floor mats ($30). 428 high-altitude emissions (no cost). 93N non-California emissions (no cost). 13K rear spoiler ($195).

OPTIONS: [SVT COBRA CONVERTIBLE] 64W 17 x 8 polished forged aluminum wheels ($395) 422 California emissions system (no cost). 12H front floor mats ($30). 428 high-altitude emissions (no cost). 93N non-California emissions (no cost). 13K rear spoiler ($195).

HISTORICAL FOOTNOTES: The Ford Special Vehicle Team and the 623 Ford dealers in North America who sell and service SVT's compelling line of high-performance vehicles proudly announced a SVT Premium Service plan during 2001. Every 2001 SVT vehicle was part of this enhancement to SVT ownership. SVT Premium Service provided SVT Mustang Cobra owners with subtle touches that gave them a special ownership experience. It provided a 2001 loaner vehicle while their Cobra was at a certified SVT dealer's service department. The loaner was available from the time the vehicle was dropped off until it was picked up and the cost was covered. In addition, the customer's 2001 Cobra was returned washed and vacuumed as a part of the program. Every SVT dealer was required to participate in special training courses designed to teach each dealership employee the expectations and demands of SVT vehicle owners. "They are given the training and tools to not only meet these needs, but exceed them," said Ford.

2002 MUSTANG

MUSTANG – V-6 – SERIES P – For 2002, Ford refreshed the exterior and interior of the base V-6 models and added new audio options. Two new colors, Satin Silver Clearcoat and Torch Red Clearcoat replaced Silver Metallic and Performance Red. A new tape stripe was included in the V-6 Sport Appearance group. Sixteen-inch wheels and tires were standard on base and deluxe V-6 coupes. A new speed-sensitive radio was now part of the Mach 1000 and Mach 460 audio systems. Also new was a four-piece two-tone leather steering wheel, a new storage net in coupes and optional Nudo leather-trimmed seats. Option program changes included a new MP3/CD radio for standard and deluxe configurations and a new Mach 1000 audio option for premium configurations.

BASE MUSTANG COUPE: Standard equipment included body color front and rear fascias with Mustang nomenclature, a composite hood with scoop, complex reflector halogen headlights with integral turn/park lamps, three-tiered taillights, dual electric remote-control outside rearview mirrors (right-hand with convex glass), clearcoat paint, color-keyed rocker panel moldings, 16 x 7-in five-spoke cast-aluminum wheels, a steel spare rim 15-in. mini spare tire, second generation driver and front passenger airbags, a three-point active restraint system, deluxe carpets, child seat tether anchor brackets on the package tray, a cigarette lighter port and auxiliary power point, a clock integrated with the radio, a console (with armrest, integral storage bin, tissue holder, dual cupholders and parking brake boot), a power-operated inside-the-trunk deck lid release with glow-in-the-dark handle, a driver's footrest, a locking glove box, an analog instrument cluster (including a tachometer, a trip odometer, a voltmeter, a temperature gauge, a fuel gauge, an oil pressure gauge and an "overdrive off" indicator with automatic transmission), a light group (with lamps in dome, front "door ajar" switches and a "headlamps on" chime), luggage compartment trim and carpeting, dual visor-vanity mirrors, reclining cloth bucket seats with cloth two-way head restraints, a split-folding rear seat, stalk-mounted controls (turn signals, wiper/washer, high-beam and flash-to-pass), a storage net between visors on the headliner, a tilt steering wheel with center horn, monochromatic full wrapover door trim, soft flow-through door trim panels with full-length armrests and vinyl inserts, color-keyed upper instrument panel finish, a color keyed headliner, color-keyed safety belts, a color-keyed shifter bezel, color-keyed A and C pillar appliqués, color-keyed instrument cluster finish, manual control air conditioning, a heavy-duty 130-amp alternator, a 58-amp/hr heavy-duty maintenance-free battery, four-wheel power disc brakes, side window demisters, power door locks, an electrodrive cooling fan, EEC-V electronic engine controls, a 3.8-liter SEFI V-6, a stainless steel exhaust system, a fuel pump inertia shutoff switch, a 15.5-gal. fuel tank with tethered cap, complete Solar-Tinted glass, power ventilation with four instrument panel registers and positive shutoff, a dual note horn, a tunnel mounted parking brake with integral boot, an electronic AM/FM stereo cassette tape player with single disc CD and premium speakers and 80-watt integrated amplifier, the SecuriLock™ passive anti-theft system, remote keyless entry, power rack-and-pinion steering, a modified MacPherson strut front suspension with front stabilizer bar, a rear coil spring four-bar-link suspension with increased travel for smoother ride, gas pressurized front struts and rear shock absorbers, P225/55R16 all-season black sidewall tires, a rear window defroster, a five-speed manual overdrive transmission, one touch power windows and interval windshield wipers.

BASE MUSTANG CONVERTIBLE: Standard equipment included body color front and rear fascias with Mustang nomenclature, a power retractable convertible top with semi-hard top boot, a composite hood with scoop, complex reflector halogen headlights with integral turn/park lamps, three-tiered taillights, dual electric remote-control outside rearview mirrors (right-hand with convex glass), clearcoat paint, color-keyed rocker panel moldings, 16 x 7-in five-spoke cast-aluminum wheels, a steel spare rim 15-in. mini spare tire, second generation driver and front passenger airbags, a three-point active restraint system, deluxe carpets, child seat tether anchor brackets on the seatback, a cigarette lighter port and auxiliary power point, a clock integrated with the radio, a console (with armrest, integral storage bin, tissue holder, dual cupholders and parking brake boot), a power-operated inside-the-trunk deck lid release with glow-in-the-dark handle, a driver's footrest, a locking glove box, an analog instrument cluster (including a tachometer, a trip odometer, a voltmeter, a temperature gauge, a fuel gauge, an oil pressure gauge and an "overdrive off" indicator with automatic transmission), a light group (with lamps in dome, front "door ajar" switches and a "headlamps on" chime), luggage compartment trim and carpeting, dual visor-vanity mirrors, reclining cloth bucket seats with cloth two-way head restraints, a bench rear seat, stalk-mounted controls (turn signals, wiper/washer, high-beam and flash-to-pass), a storage net between visors on the headliner, a tilt steering wheel with center horn, monochromatic full wrapover door trim, soft flow-through door trim panels with full-length armrests and vinyl inserts, color-keyed upper instrument panel finish, a color keyed headliner, color-keyed safety belts, a color-keyed shifter bezel, color-keyed A and C pillar appliqués, color-keyed instrument cluster finish, manual control air conditioning, a heavy-duty 130-amp alternator, a 58-amp/hr heavy-duty maintenance-free battery, four-wheel power disc brakes, side window demisters, power door locks, an electrodrive cooling fan, EEC-V electronic engine controls, a 3.8-liter SEFI V-6, a stainless steel exhaust system, a fuel pump inertia shutoff switch, a 15.5-gal. fuel tank with tethered cap, complete Solar-Tinted glass, power ventilation with four instrument panel registers and positive shutoff, a dual note horn, a tunnel mounted parking brake with integral boot, an electronic AM/FM stereo cassette tape player with single disc CD and premium speakers and 80-watt integrated amplifier, the SecuriLock™ passive anti-theft system, remote keyless entry, power rack-and-pinion steering, a modified MacPherson strut front suspension with front stabilizer bar, a rear coil spring four-bar-link suspension with increased travel for smoother ride, gas pressurized front struts and rear shock absorbers, P225/55R16 all-season black sidewall tires, a rear window defroster, a five-speed manual overdrive transmission, one touch power windows, power quarter windows and interval windshield wipers.

I.D. DATA: A 17-character Vehicle Identification Number is stamped on an aluminum tab on the instrument panel, viewable through the windshield. A vehicle certification label is found on the body side of where the driver's door closes. The first symbol indicates the nation of origin: 1=United States of America. The second symbol indicates the manufacturer: F=Ford Motor Co. The third symbol indicates vehicle type: A=passenger car. The fourth symbol indicates type of restraint system: L= driver and front passenger airbags with passive front belts and active rear belts. The fifth symbol is the designation number: P=passenger car. The sixth and seventh symbols indicate car line and body type: 40=two-door coupe; 42=two-door GT coupe; 44=two-door convertible; 45=two-door GT convertible; 46=two-door Cobra R convertible; 47=two-door Cobra/Cobra R coupe. The eighth symbol indicates engine type: 4=232 cid (3.8-liter) EFI V-6; X=281 cid (4.6-liter) EFI SOHC V-8; V=281 cid (4.6-liter) EFI DOHC V-8. The ninth symbol is a check digit. The 10th symbol indicates model year: 2=2002. The 11th symbol indicates assembly plant: F=Dearborn, Mich. The last six symbols are the consecutive unit production number staring at 100001 at each factory. Paint Codes: B7=Zinc Yellow; D3 Torch Red Clearcoat, E9=Laser Red, L2=True Blue, PY=Bullitt Green, SU=Amazon Green, SW=Electric Green, TK=Mineral Gray; TL=Satin Silver Clearcoat and Z1=Oxford White.

Model No.	Body/ Style No.	Body Type & Seating	Factory Price	Shipping Weight	Prod. Total
MUSTANG VALUE LEADER (V-6)					
P	40	2d Coupe-4P	17,820	3,069	Note 2
MUSTANG DELUXE (V-6)					
P	40	2d Coupe-4P	18,425	3,069	Note 2
P	44	2d Convertible-4P	23,140	3,111	Note 2
MUSTANG PREMIUM (V-6)					
P	40	2d Coupe-4P	19,540	3,069	Note 2
P	44	2d Convertible-4P	25,725	3,111	Note 2

Note 1: Prices include dealer destination charges.

Note 2: Production totals not available at publishing date.

MUSTANG GT - V-8 - SERIES P - The 2002 Mustang GT was a carryover of the 2001 model with the tall, non-functional hood scoop and side scoops that set it more apart from the V-6 models.

MUSTANG GT COUPE: Standard equipment included body color front and rear fascias with Mustang nomenclature and dual tailpipe outlets at rear, a GT hood and side scoop, complex reflector halogen headlights with integral turn/park lamps, front fog lamps, three-tiered taillights, dual electric remote-control outside rearview mirrors (right-hand with convex glass), a single-wing rear deck lid spoiler, clearcoat paint, color-keyed rocker panel moldings, 17 x 8-in five-spoke forged aluminum wheels with carryover ornaments, an aluminum spare wheel and 15-in. mini spare tire, second generation driver and front passenger airbags, a three-point

active restraint system, deluxe carpets, child seat tether anchor brackets on the package tray, a cigarette lighter port and auxiliary power point, a clock integrated with the radio, a console (with armrest, integral storage bin, tissue holder, dual cupholders and parking brake boot), a power-operated inside-the-trunk deck lid release with glow-in-the-dark handle, a driver's footrest, a locking glove box, an analog instrument cluster (including a tachometer, a trip odometer, a voltmeter, a temperature gauge, a fuel gauge, an oil pressure gauge and an "overdrive off" indicator with automatic transmission), a 150-mph speedometer, a light group (with lamps in dome, front "door ajar" switches and a "headlamps on" chime), luggage compartment trim and carpeting, dual visor-vanity mirrors, reclining two-tone cloth GT sport seats with two-way cloth head restraints, a split-folding rear seat, stalk-mounted controls, a leather-wrapped tilt steering wheel with center horn (two-tone in combination with Medium Graphite and Medium Parchment interior), a storage net between sun visors on headliner, monochromatic full wrapover door trim, soft flow-through door panels with full-length armrests and vinyl inserts, color-keyed upper instrument panel finish, a color keyed headliner, color-keyed safety belts, a color-keyed shifter bezel, color-keyed A and C pillar appliqués, color-keyed instrument cluster finish, manual control air conditioning, a heavy-duty 130-amp alternator, a Traction-Loc rear axle, a 58-amp/hr heavy-duty maintenance-free battery, four-wheel ABS disc brakes, side window demisters, power door locks, an electrodrive cooling fan, EEC-V electronic engine controls, a 4.6-liter SOHC two-valve V-8, a dual stainless steel exhaust system, a fuel pump inertia shutoff switch, a 15.5-gal. fuel tank with tethered cap, complete Solar-Tinted glass, power ventilation with four instrument panel registers and positive shutoff, a dual note horn, a tunnel mounted parking brake with integral boot, an electronic AM/FM stereo cassette tape player with single disc CD and premium speakers and 80-watt integrated amplifier, the SecuriLock™ passive anti-theft system, remote keyless entry, power rack-and-pinion steering, a modified MacPherson strut front suspension with front stabilizer bar, a rear coil spring four-bar-link suspension with increased travel for smoother ride, gas pressurized front struts and rear shock absorbers with unique GT calibrations, a GT suspension package with variable rate coil springs and a quadra-shock rear suspension, P245/45ZR17 sidewall performance tires, a rear window defroster, a five-speed manual overdrive transmission, interval windshield wipers and one touch power windows.

MUSTANG GT CONVERTIBLE: Standard equipment included body color front and rear fascias with Mustang nomenclature and dual tailpipe outlets at rear, a power retractable convertible top with semi-hard boot, a GT hood and side scoop, complex reflector halogen headlights with integral turn/park lamps, front fog lamps, three-tiered taillights, dual electric remote-control outside rearview mirrors (right-hand with convex glass), a single-wing rear deck lid spoiler, clearcoat paint, color-keyed rocker panel moldings, 16 x 7-in cast-aluminum wheels, a steel mini spare and 15-in. temporary tire, 17 x 8-in five-spoke forged aluminum wheels with carryover ornaments, an aluminum spare wheel and 15-in. mini spare tire, second generation driver and front passenger airbags, a three-point active restraint system, deluxe carpets, child seat tether anchor brackets on the seatbacks, a cigarette lighter port and auxiliary power point, a clock integrated with the radio, a console (with armrest, integral storage bin, tissue holder, dual cupholders and parking brake boot), a power-operated inside-the-trunk deck lid release with glow-in-the-dark handle, a driver's footrest, a locking glove box, an analog instrument cluster (including a tachometer, a trip odometer, a voltmeter, a temperature gauge, a fuel gauge, an oil pressure gauge and an "overdrive off" indicator with automatic transmission), a 150-mph speedometer, a light group (with dome lamps integrated in mirror, front "door ajar" switches and a "headlamps on" chime), luggage compartment trim and carpeting, dual illuminated visor-vanity mirrors, reclining two-tone cloth GT sport seats with cloth two-way head restraints, a bench rear seat, stalk-mounted controls, a leather-wrapped tilt steering wheel (two-tone in combination with Medium Graphite and Medium Parchment interior), a storage net between sun visors on headliner, monochromatic full wrapover door trim, soft flow-through door panels with full-length armrests and vinyl inserts, color-keyed upper instrument panel finish, a color keyed headliner, color-keyed safety belts, a color-keyed shifter bezel, color-keyed A and C pillar appliqués, color-keyed instrument cluster finish, manual control air conditioning, a Traction-Loc rear axle, a heavy-duty 130-amp alternator, a 58-amp/hr heavy-duty maintenance-free battery, four-wheel ABS disc brakes, side window demisters, power door locks, an electrodrive cooling fan, EEC-V electronic engine controls, a 4.6-liter SOHC two-valve V-8, a dual stainless steel exhaust system, a fuel pump inertia shutoff switch, a 15.5-gal. fuel tank with tethered cap, complete Solar-Tinted glass, power ventilation with four instrument panel registers and positive shutoff, a dual note horn, a tunnel mounted parking brake with integral boot, an electronic AM/FM stereo cassette tape player with single disc CD and premium speakers and 80-watt integrated amplifier, the SecuriLock™ passive anti-theft system, remote keyless entry, power rack-and-pinion steering, a modified MacPherson strut front suspension with front stabilizer bar, a rear coil spring four-bar-link suspension with increased travel for smoother ride, gas pressurized front struts and rear shock absorbers with unique GT calibrations, a GT suspension package with variable rate coil springs and a quadra-shock rear suspension, P245/45ZR17 black sidewall performance tires, a five-speed manual overdrive transmission, a rear window defroster, interval windshield wipers, one touch power windows and power rear quarter windows.

MUSTANG GT DELUXE (V-8)

P	42	2d Coupe-4P	23,360	3,242	Note 4
P	45	2d Convertible-4P	27,615	3,386	Note 4

MUSTANG GT PREMIUM (V-8)

P	42	2d Coupe-4P	24,530	3,242	Note 4
P	45	2d Convertible-4P	28,785	3,386	Note 4

Note 3: Prices include dealer destination charges.

Note 4: Production totals not available at publishing date.

MUSTANG SVT COBRA COUPE – V-8 – SERIES P – The 2002 SVT Mustang Cobra had not made its debut at the time this catalog deadlined, but was expected to appear later in the spring.

MUSTANG SVT COBRA COUPE: Anticipated standard equipment features for the 2002 Mustang SVT Cobra coupe included the 4.6-liter DOHC V-8, a five-speed manual transmission, rear-wheel drive, a rear limited-slip differential, a modified MacPherson strut front suspension with stabilizer bar and 500 lb./in. coil springs, an independent rear suspension with steel upper and aluminum lower control arms and 470 lb./in. coil springs, front ABS brakes with 13-in. vented Brembo™ discs and PBR™ twin-piston caliper, rear ABS brakes with 11.65-in. vented discs and single-piston caliper, 17 x 8-in. five-spoke cast aluminum alloy wheel rims with painted surfaces, P245/45ZR17 black sidewall performance tires, an alloy spare wheel with mini spare tire, variable intermittent windshield wipers, all-speed traction control, a rear defogger, a tachometer, a clock, a rear deck lid spoiler, the SecuriLock™ anti-theft system with engine immobilizer, an inside-the-trunk emergency deck lid release, remote power door locks, one touch power windows, dual power outside rearview mirrors, cruise control, a leather-wrapped tilt-adjustable steering wheel, power steering, front door pockets, a front console with storage provisions, sport front bucket seats with six-way power driver's seat and front seat adjustable lumbar support, a remote trunk release, a rear split-folding bench seat, air conditioning, dual illuminated visor-vanity mirrors, a leather-trimmed gearshift knob, front and rear floor mats, an AM/FM stereo cassette with six-disc in-dash multi-CD player and 460-watt speakers.

MUSTANG SVT COBRA CONVERTIBLE: Anticipated standard equipment features for the 2002 Mustang SVT Cobra coupe included the 4.6-liter DOHC V-8, included a five-speed manual transmission, rear-wheel drive, a rear limited-slip differential, a modified MacPherson strut front suspension with stabilizer bar and 500 lb./in. coil springs, an independent rear suspension with steel upper and aluminum lower control arms and 470 lb./in. coil springs, front ABS brakes with 13-in. vented Brembo™ discs and PBR™ twin-piston caliper, rear ABS brakes with 11.65-in. vented discs and single-piston calipers, 17 x 8-in. five-spoke cast aluminum alloy wheel rims with painted surfaces, P245/45ZR17 black sidewall performance tires, an alloy spare wheel with mini spare tire, variable intermittent windshield wipers, a power convertible roof, a glass rear window, all-speed traction control, a rear defogger, a tachometer, a clock, a rear deck lid spoiler, the SecuriLock™ anti-theft system with engine immobilizer, an inside-the-trunk emergency deck lid release, remote power door locks, one touch power windows, dual power outside rearview mirrors, cruise control, a leather-wrapped tilt-adjustable steering wheel, power steering, front door pockets, a front console with storage provisions, sport front bucket seats with six-way power driver's seat and front seat adjustable lumbar support, a remote trunk release, a rear bench seat, air conditioning, dual illuminated visor-vanity mirrors, a leather-trimmed gearshift knob, front and rear floor mats, an AM/FM stereo cassette with six-disc in-dash multi-CD player and 460-watt speakers.

MUSTANG SVT COBRA (V-8)

P	47	2d Coupe-4P	TBA	3,242	Note 5
P	46	2d Convertible-4P	TBA	3,386	Note 5

Note 5: Production totals not available at publishing date.

Note 6: TBA means "to be announced."

MUSTANG ENGINES

ENGINE [BASE]: Overhead valve V-6. Cast-iron block. Hydraulic valve lifters. Four main bearings. Displacement: 232 cid (3.8 liters). Bore & stroke: 3.80 x 3.40 in. Compression ratio: 9.36:1. Brake horsepower: 190 at 5250 rpm. Torque: 220 lbs.-ft. at 2750 rpm. Sequential electronic fuel injection. VIN code 4.

ENGINE [GT]: Single overhead camshaft V-8. Cast-iron block. Hydraulic valve lifters. Displacement: 281 cid (4.6 liters). Bore & stroke: 3.60 x 3.60 in. Compression ratio: 9.0:1. Brake horsepower: 260 at 5250 rpm. Torque: 302 lbs.-ft. at 4000 rpm. Sequential electronic fuel injection. VIN code W.

ENGINE [SVT COBRA]: Double overhead camshaft V-8. Aluminum block. Aluminum heads. Hydraulic valve lifters. Displacement: 330 cid (5.4 liters). Bore & stroke: 3.55 x 4.15 in. Compression ratio: 9.85:1. Brake horsepower: 320 at 6000 rpm. Torque: 317 lbs.-ft. at 4750 rpm. Sequential electronic fuel injection. VIN code V.

CHASSIS: Wheelbase: 101.3 in. Overall length: 183.2 inches. Height: (coupe) 53.1 in.; (convertible) 53.2 in. Width 73.1 in. Front tread: 60.2 in. Rear tread: 60.6 inches

TECHNICAL: [BASE V-6] Standard transmission: five-speed manual overdrive. Drive axle: rear. Steering: Power assisted rack-and-pinion. Front suspension: modified MacPherson gas-pressurized shock struts with coil springs and stabilizer bar. Rear suspension: four-bar link and coil spring system, gas shocks. Front brakes: power assisted discs. Rear brakes: power assisted discs. Ignition: electronic. Body construction: unibody with front isolated mini-frame. Fuel tank: 15.7 gal.

TECHNICAL: [GT] Standard transmission: five-speed manual overdrive. Drive axle: rear. Steering: Power assisted rack-and-pinion. Front suspension: modified MacPherson gas-pressurized shock struts with unique GT calibrations and coil springs and stabilizer bar. Rear suspension: four-bar link and GT-specific variable-rate coil springs, and quadra shocks. Front brakes: power assisted discs. Rear brakes: power assisted discs. Ignition: electronic. Body construction: unibody with front isolated mini-frame. Fuel tank: 15.7 gal.

TECHNICAL: [COBRA SVT] Standard transmission: five-speed manual overdrive. Drive axle: rear. Steering: Power assisted rack-and-pinion. Front suspension: modified MacPherson gas-pressurized shock struts with coil springs and stabilizer bar; lowered for enhanced handling. Rear suspension: four-bar link and coil spring system, gas shocks; lowered for enhanced handling. Brakes: power assisted four-wheel disc brakes with Brembo™ rotors and calipers. Ignition: electronic. Body construction: unibody with front isolated mini-frame. Fuel tank: 15.7 gal.

OPTIONS: [V-6 VALUE LEADER COUPE] 58Z AM/FM stereo with MP3 CD player (no cost). 422 California emissions system (no cost). 423 California emissions system not required (no cost). 44U four-speed automatic overdrive transmission ($815). 93N non-California emissions (no cost).

OPTIONS: [V-6 DELUXE COUPE] 58Z AM/FM stereo with MP3 CD player (no cost). 552 antilock braking system with all-speed traction control ($730). 422 California emissions system (no cost). 423 California emissions system not required (no cost). 44U four-speed automatic overdrive transmission ($815). 589 Mach 460 stereo system ($550). 93N non-California emissions (no cost). 54V Sport Appearance package ($125).

OPTIONS: [V-6 DELUXE CONVERTIBLE] 58Z AM/FM stereo with MP3 CD player (no cost). 552 antilock braking system with all-speed traction control ($730). 422 California emissions system (no cost). 423 California emissions system not required (no cost). 44U four-speed automatic overdrive transmission ($815). 88T leather bucket seats ($525). 589 Mach 460 stereo system ($550). 93N non-California emissions (no cost).

OPTIONS: [V-6 PREMIUM COUPE] 422 California emissions system (no cost). 423 California emissions system not required (no cost). 44U four-speed automatic overdrive transmission ($815). 88T leather bucket seats ($525). 918 Mach 1000 stereo ($1,295). 93N non-California emissions (no cost).

OPTIONS: [V-6 PREMIUM CONVERTIBLE] 422 California emissions system (no cost). 423 California emissions system not required (no cost). 918 Mach 1000 stereo ($1,295). 93N non-California emissions (no cost). 54V Sport Appearance package ($125).

OPTIONS: [V-6 GT DELUXE COUPE] 58Z AM/FM stereo with MP3 CD player (no cost). 422 California emissions system (no cost). 423 California emissions system not required (no cost). 44U four-speed automatic overdrive transmission ($815). 88X leather sport bucket seats ($525). 589 Mach 460 stereo system ($550). 93N non-California emissions (no cost).

OPTIONS: [GT DELUXE CONVERTIBLE] 58Z AM/FM stereo with MP3 CD player (no cost). 422 California emissions system (no cost). 423 California emissions system not required (no cost). 44U four-speed automatic overdrive transmission ($815). 88X leather front sport bucket seats ($500). 58M Mach 460 stereo system ($550). 93N non-California emissions (no cost).

OPTIONS: [GT PREMIUM COUPE] 422 California emissions system (no cost). 423 California emissions system not required (no cost). 44U four-speed automatic overdrive transmission ($815). 918 Mach 1000 stereo ($1,295). 93N non-California emissions (no cost).

OPTIONS: [GT PREMIUM CONVERTIBLE] 422 California emissions system (no cost). 423 California emissions system not required (no cost). 44U four-speed automatic overdrive transmission ($815). 918 Mach 1000 stereo ($1,295). 93N non-California emissions (no cost).

OPTIONS: [SVT COBRA COUPE] Not available at time of publication.

OPTIONS: [SVT COBRA CONVERTIBLE] Not available at time of publication.

HISTORICAL FOOTNOTES: Robert "Bob" Penninger, a dedicated SVT Mustang Cobra enthusiast and secretary-treasurer of the SVT Owner's Association (www.svtoa.com) was a passenger on the American Airlines flight that terrorists flew into the Pentagon, in Washington, DC, on Sept. 11, 2001. The SVTOA noted his contributions to getting the San Diego Chapter started and mourned his passing.

A WORD ABOUT OLD FORDS...

The market for cars more than 20 years old is strong. Some buyers of pre-1980 cars are collectors who invest in vehicles likely to increase in value the older they get. Other buyers prefer the looks, size, performance and reliability of yesterday's better-built automobiles.

With a typical 1998 model selling for $20,000 or more, some Americans find themselves priced out of the new-car market. Late-model used cars are pricey, too, although short on distinctive looks and roominess. The old cars may use a little more gas, but they cost a lot less.

New cars and late-model used cars depreciate rapidly in value. They can't tow large trailers or mobile homes. Their high-tech engineering is expensive to maintain or repair. In contrast, well-kept old cars are mechanically simpler, but very powerful. They appreciate in value as they grow more scarce and collectible.

Selecting a car and paying the right price for it are two considerations old car buyers face. What models did Ford offer in 1958? Which 1963 Ford is worth the most today? What should one pay for a 1970 Torino GT convertible?

The *Standard Catalog of Ford 1903-1998* answers such questions. The following Price Guide section shows most models made between 1903 and 1991. It helps to gauge what they sell for in six different, graded conditions. Models built since 1991 are generally considered "used cars" of which few, as yet, have achieved collectible status.

The price estimates contained in this book are current as of the publishing date of late-1998. After that date, more current prices may be obtained by referring to *Old Cars Price Guide*, which is available from Krause Publications, 700 E. State St., Iola, WI 54990, telephone (715)445-2214.

HOW TO USE THE FORD PRICE GUIDE

On the following pages is a **COLLECTOR CAR VALUE GUIDE.** The value of an old car is a "ballpark" estimate at best. The estimates contained here are based upon national and regional data compiled by the editors of *Old Cars* and **Old Cars Price Guide.** These data include actual auction bids and prices at collector car auctions and sales, classified and display advertising of such vehicles, verified reports of private sales and input from experts.

Value estimates are listed for cars in six different states of condition. These conditions (1-6) are illustrated and explained in the **VEHICLE CONDITION SCALE** on the following page(s). Values are for complete vehicles, not parts cars, except as noted. Modified car values are not included, but can be estimated by figuring the cost of restoring to original condition and adjusting the figures shown here.

Appearing below is a sample price table listing that illustrates the following elements:

A. MAKE: The make (or marque) appears in large, bold-faced type at the beginning of each value section.

B. DESCRIPTION: The extreme left-hand column indicates vehicle year, model name, body type, engine configuration and, in some cases, wheelbase.

C. CONDITION CODE: The six columns to the right are headed by the numbers 1-to-6 which correspond to the conditions described in the **VEHICLE CONDITION SCALE** in this book.

D. VALUE: The value estimates, in dollars, appear below their respective condition codes and across from the vehicle descriptions.

A. MAKE ——— **FORD**

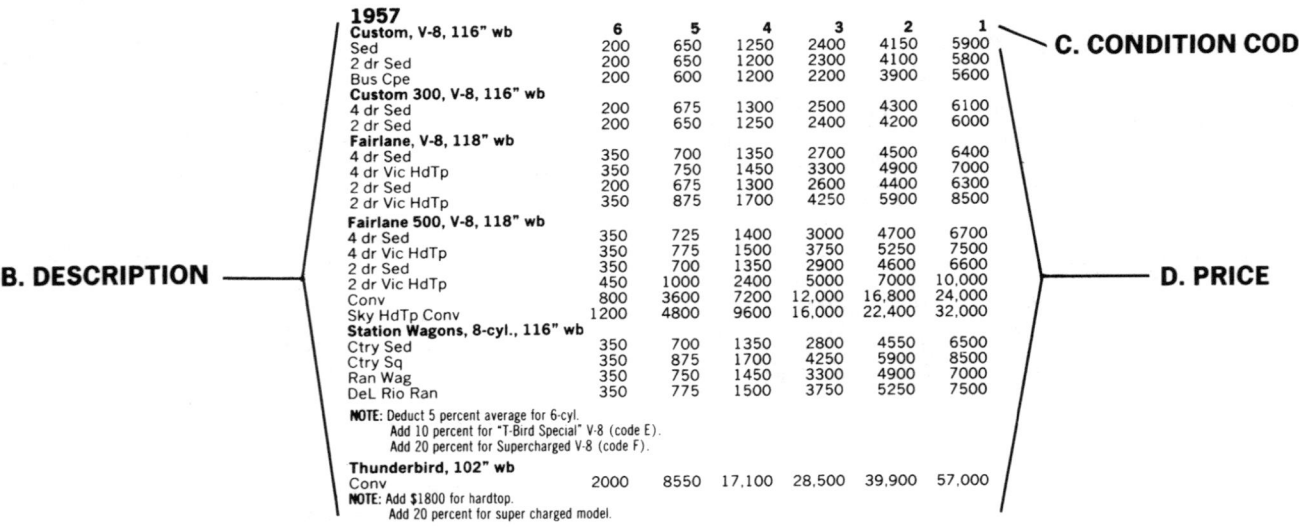

1957	6	5	4	3	2	1
Custom, V-8, 116" wb						
Sed	200	650	1250	2400	4150	5900
2 dr Sed	200	650	1200	2300	4100	5800
Bus Cpe	200	600	1200	2200	3900	5600
Custom 300, V-8, 116" wb						
4 dr Sed	200	675	1300	2500	4300	6100
2 dr Sed	200	650	1250	2400	4200	6000
Fairlane, V-8, 118" wb						
4 dr Sed	350	700	1350	2700	4500	6400
4 dr Vic HdTp	350	750	1450	3300	4900	7000
2 dr Sed	200	675	1300	2600	4400	6300
2 dr Vic HdTp	350	875	1700	4250	5900	8500
Fairlane 500, V-8, 118" wb						
4 dr Sed	350	725	1400	3000	4700	6700
4 dr Vic HdTp	350	775	1500	3750	5250	7500
2 dr Sed	350	700	1350	2900	4600	6600
2 dr Vic HdTp	450	1000	2400	5000	7000	10,000
Conv	800	3600	7200	12,000	16,800	24,000
Sky HdTp Conv	1200	4800	9600	16,000	22,400	32,000
Station Wagons, 8-cyl., 116" wb						
Ctry Sed	350	700	1350	2800	4550	6500
Ctry Sq	350	875	1700	4250	5900	8500
Ran Wag	350	750	1450	3300	4900	7000
DeL Rio Ran	350	775	1500	3750	5250	7500

NOTE: Deduct 5 percent average for 6-cyl.
Add 10 percent for "T-Bird Special" V-8 (code E).
Add 20 percent for Supercharged V-8 (code F).

Thunderbird, 102" wb						
Conv	2000	8550	17,100	28,500	39,900	57,000

NOTE: Add $1800 for hardtop.
Add 20 percent for super charged model.

B. DESCRIPTION

C. CONDITION CODE

D. PRICE

VEHICLE CONDITION SCALE

Excellent

1) EXCELLENT: Restored to current maxiumum professional standards of quality in every area, or perfect original with components operating and appearing as new. A 95-plus point show vehicle that is not driven.

Fine

2) FINE: Well-restored, or a combination of superior restoration and excellent original. Also, an *extremely* well-maintained original showing very minimal wear.

Very Good

3) VERY GOOD: Completely operable original or "older restoration" showing wear. Also, a good amateur restoration, all presentable and serviceable inside and out. Plus, combinations of well-done restoration and good operable components or a partially restored vehicle with all parts necessary to complete and/or valuable NOS parts.

Good

4) GOOD: A driveable vehicle needing no or only minor work to be functional. Also, a deteriorated restoration or a very poor amateur restoration. All components may need restoration to be "excellent," but the vehicle is mostly useable "as is."

Restorable

5) RESTORABLE: Needs *complete* restoration of body, chassis and interior. May or may not be running, but isn't weathered, wrecked or stripped to the point of being useful only for parts.

Parts Car

6) PARTS VEHICLE: May or may not be running, but is weathered, wrecked and/or stripped to the point of being useful primarily for parts.

FORD

	6	5	4	3	2	1

Model A 1903, 2-cyl., Ser. No. 1-670, 8 hp
1904, 2-cyl., Ser. No. 671-1708, 10 hp

	6	5	4	3	2	1
Rbt	1,920	5,760	9,600	19,200	33,600	48,000
Rbt W/ton	1,960	5,880	9,800	19,600	34,300	49,000

Model B 10 hp, 4-cyl.

Tr	value not estimable

Model C 10 hp, 2-cyl., Ser. No. 1709-2700

	6	5	4	3	2	1
Rbt	1,920	5,760	9,600	19,200	33,600	48,000
Rbt W/ton	1,960	5,880	9,800	19,600	34,300	49,000
Dr's Mdl	2,000	6,000	10,000	20,000	35,000	50,000

Model F 16 hp, 2-cyl., (Produced 1904-05-06)

	6	5	4	3	2	1
Tr	2,000	6,000	10,000	20,000	35,000	50,000

Model K 40 hp, 6-cyl., (Produced 1905-06-07-08)

	6	5	4	3	2	1
Tr	3,040	9,120	15,200	30,400	53,200	76,000
Rds	3,040	9,120	15,200	30,400	53,200	76,000

Model N 18 hp, 4-cyl., (Produced 1906-07-08)

	6	5	4	3	2	1
Rbt	1,840	5,520	9,200	18,400	32,200	46,000

Model R 4-cyl., (Produced 1907-08)

	6	5	4	3	2	1
Rbt	1,840	5,520	9,200	18,400	32,200	46,000

Model S 4-cyl.

	6	5	4	3	2	1
Rbt	1,840	5,520	9,200	18,400	32,200	46,000

1908 Model T, 4-cyl., 2 levers, 2 foot pedals (1,000 produced)

	6	5	4	3	2	1
Tr	1,960	5,880	9,800	19,600	34,300	49,000

1909 Model T, 4-cyl.

	6	5	4	3	2	1
Rbt	1,280	3,840	6,400	12,800	22,400	32,000
Tr	1,320	3,960	6,600	13,200	23,100	33,000
Trbt	1,240	3,720	6,200	12,400	21,700	31,000
Cpe	1,160	3,480	5,800	11,600	20,300	29,000
Twn Car	1,360	4,080	6,800	13,600	23,800	34,000
Lan'let	1,240	3,720	6,200	12,400	21,700	31,000

1910 Model T, 4-cyl.

	6	5	4	3	2	1
Rbt	1,240	3,720	6,200	12,400	21,700	31,000
Tr	1,280	3,840	6,400	12,800	22,400	32,000
Cpe	1,120	3,360	5,600	11,200	19,600	28,000
Twn Car	1,160	3,480	5,800	11,600	20,300	29,000
C'ml Rds	1,120	3,360	5,600	11,200	19,600	28,000

1911 Model T, 4-cyl.

	6	5	4	3	2	1
Rbt	1,200	3,600	6,000	12,000	21,000	30,000
Tor Rds	1,240	3,720	6,200	12,400	21,700	31,000
Tr	1,240	3,720	6,200	12,400	21,700	31,000
Trbt	1,200	3,600	6,000	12,000	21,000	30,000
Cpe	1,040	3,120	5,200	10,400	18,200	26,000
Twn Car	1,200	3,600	6,000	12,000	21,000	30,000
C'ml Rds	1,080	3,240	5,400	10,800	18,900	27,000
Dely Van	1,000	3,000	5,000	10,000	17,500	25,000

1912 Model T, 4-cyl.

	6	5	4	3	2	1
Rds	1,160	3,480	5,800	11,600	20,300	29,000
Tor Rds	1,200	3,600	6,000	12,000	21,000	30,000
Tr	1,240	3,720	6,200	12,400	21,700	31,000
Twn Car	1,200	3,600	6,000	12,000	21,000	30,000
Dely Van	1,040	3,120	5,200	10,400	18,200	26,000
C'ml Rds	1,120	3,360	5,600	11,200	19,600	28,000

1913 Model T, 4-cyl.

	6	5	4	3	2	1
Rds	1,160	3,480	5,800	11,600	20,300	29,000
Tr	1,240	3,720	6,200	12,400	21,700	31,000
Twn Car	1,120	3,360	5,600	11,200	19,600	28,000

1914 Model T, 4-cyl.

	6	5	4	3	2	1
Rds	1,160	3,480	5,800	11,600	20,300	29,000
Tr	1,240	3,720	6,200	12,400	21,700	31,000
Twn Car	1,160	3,480	5,800	11,600	20,300	29,000
Cpe	920	2,760	4,600	9,200	16,100	23,000

1915 & early 1916 Model T, 4-cyl., (brass rad.)

	6	5	4	3	2	1
Rds	1,160	3,480	5,800	11,600	20,300	29,000
Tr	1,200	3,600	6,000	12,000	21,000	30,000
Conv Cpe	1,240	3,720	6,200	12,400	21,700	31,000
Ctr dr Sed	960	2,880	4,800	9,600	16,800	24,000
Twn Car	1,120	3,360	5,600	11,200	19,600	28,000

1916 Model T, 4-cyl., (steel rad.)

	6	5	4	3	2	1
Rds	920	2,760	4,600	9,200	16,100	23,000
Tr	960	2,880	4,800	9,600	16,800	24,000
Conv Cpe	1,000	3,000	5,000	10,000	17,500	25,000
Ctr dr Sed	760	2,280	3,800	7,600	13,300	19,000
Twn Car	840	2,520	4,200	8,400	14,700	21,000

1917 Model T, 4-cyl.

	6	5	4	3	2	1
Rds	880	2,640	4,400	8,800	15,400	22,000
Tr	920	2,760	4,600	9,200	16,100	23,000
Conv Cpe	800	2,400	4,000	8,000	14,000	20,000
Twn Car	720	2,160	3,600	7,200	12,600	18,000
Ctr dr Sed	640	1,920	3,200	6,400	11,200	16,000
Cpe	680	2,040	3,400	6,800	11,900	17,000

1918 Model T, 4-cyl.

	6	5	4	3	2	1
Rds	880	2,640	4,400	8,800	15,400	22,000
Tr	920	2,760	4,600	9,200	16,100	23,000
Cpe	680	2,040	3,400	6,800	11,900	17,000
Ctr dr Sed	640	1,920	3,200	6,400	11,200	16,000

1919 Model T, 4-cyl.

	6	5	4	3	2	1
Rds	920	2,760	4,600	9,200	16,100	23,000
Tr	960	2,880	4,800	9,600	16,800	24,000
Cpe	680	2,040	3,400	6,800	11,900	17,000
Ctr dr Sed	680	2,040	3,400	6,800	11,900	17,000

1920-1921 Model T, 4-cyl.

	6	5	4	3	2	1
Rds	920	2,760	4,600	9,200	16,100	23,000
Tr	960	2,880	4,800	9,600	16,800	24,000
Cpe	640	1,920	3,200	6,400	11,200	16,000
Ctr dr Sed	640	1,920	3,200	6,400	11,200	16,000

1922-1923 Model T, 4-cyl.

	6	5	4	3	2	1
Rds	840	2,520	4,200	8,400	14,700	21,000
'22 Tr	880	2,640	4,400	8,800	15,400	22,000
'23 Tr	900	2,700	4,500	9,000	15,750	22,500
Cpe	640	1,920	3,200	6,400	11,200	16,000
4d Sed	540	1,620	2,700	5,400	9,450	13,500
2d Sed	532	1,596	2,660	5,320	9,310	13,300
Ctr dr Sed	650	1,900	3,200	6,400	11,200	16,000

1924 Model T, 4-cyl.

	6	5	4	3	2	1
Rds	840	2,520	4,200	8,400	14,700	21,000
Tr	900	2,700	4,500	9,000	15,750	22,500
Cpe	680	2,040	3,400	6,800	11,900	17,000
4d Sed	540	1,620	2,700	5,400	9,450	13,500
2d Sed	548	1,644	2,740	5,480	9,590	13,700
Rds PU	720	2,160	3,600	7,200	12,600	18,000

1925 Model T, 4-cyl.

	6	5	4	3	2	1
Rds	840	2,520	4,200	8,400	14,700	21,000
Tr	880	2,640	4,400	8,800	15,400	22,000
Cpe	680	2,040	3,400	6,800	11,900	17,000
2d	540	1,620	2,700	5,400	9,450	13,500
4d	560	1,680	2,800	5,600	9,800	14,000

1926 Model T, 4-cyl.

	6	5	4	3	2	1
Rds	880	2,640	4,400	8,800	15,400	22,000
Tr	920	2,760	4,600	9,200	16,100	23,000
Cpe	680	2,040	3,400	6,800	11,900	17,000
2d	560	1,680	2,800	5,600	9,800	14,000
4d	564	1,692	2,820	5,640	9,870	14,100

1927 Model T, 4-cyl.

	6	5	4	3	2	1
Rds	920	2,760	4,600	9,200	16,100	23,000
Tr	960	2,880	4,800	9,600	16,800	24,000
Cpe	700	2,100	3,500	7,000	12,250	17,500
2d	580	1,740	2,900	5,800	10,150	14,500
4d	572	1,716	2,860	5,720	10,010	14,300

1928 Model A, 4-cyl.

NOTE: Add 20 percent average for early 'AR' features.

	6	5	4	3	2	1
2d Rds	1,200	3,600	6,000	12,000	21,000	30,000
4d Phae	1,240	3,720	6,200	12,400	21,700	31,000
2d Cpe	680	2,040	3,400	6,800	11,900	17,000
2d Spl Cpe	700	2,100	3,500	7,000	12,250	17,500
2d Bus Cpe	680	2,040	3,400	6,800	11,900	17,000
2d Spt Cpe	720	2,160	3,600	7,200	12,600	18,000
2d Sed	620	1,860	3,100	6,200	10,850	15,500
4d Sed	624	1,872	3,120	6,240	10,920	15,600

1929 Model A, 4-cyl.

	6	5	4	3	2	1
2d Rds	1,200	3,600	6,000	12,000	21,000	30,000
4d Phae	1,240	3,720	6,200	12,400	21,700	31,000
2d Cabr	1,160	3,480	5,800	11,600	20,300	29,000
2d Cpe	660	1,980	3,300	6,600	11,550	16,500
2d Bus Cpe	640	1,920	3,200	6,400	11,200	16,000
2d Spl Cpe	660	1,980	3,300	6,600	11,550	16,500
2d Spt Cpe	700	2,100	3,500	7,000	12,250	17,500
2d Sed	620	1,860	3,100	6,200	10,850	15,500
4d 3W Sed	640	1,920	3,200	6,400	11,200	16,000
4d 5W Sed	620	1,860	3,100	6,200	10,850	15,500
4d DeL Sed	640	1,920	3,200	6,400	11,200	16,000
4d Twn Sed	660	1,980	3,300	6,600	11,550	16,500
4d Taxi	720	2,160	3,600	7,200	12,600	18,000
4d Twn Car	1,000	3,000	5,000	10,000	17,500	25,000
4d Sta Wag	880	2,640	4,400	8,800	15,400	22,000

1930 Model A, 4-cyl.

2d Rds	1,160	3,480	5,800	11,600	20,300	29,000
2d DeL Rds	1,200	3,600	6,000	12,000	21,000	30,000
4d Phae	1,240	3,720	6,200	12,400	21,700	31,000
2d DeL Phae	1,280	3,840	6,400	12,800	22,400	32,000
2d Cabr	1,120	3,360	5,600	11,200	19,600	28,000
2d Cpe	640	1,920	3,200	6,400	11,200	16,000
2d DeL Cpe	660	1,980	3,300	6,600	11,550	16,500
2d Spt Cpe	700	2,100	3,500	7,000	12,250	17,500
2d Std Sed	620	1,860	3,100	6,200	10,850	15,500
2d DeL Sed	640	1,920	3,200	6,400	11,200	16,000
2d 3W Cpe	640	1,920	3,200	6,400	11,200	16,000
2d 5W Cpe	620	1,860	3,100	6,200	10,850	15,500
4d DeL Sed	680	2,040	3,400	6,800	11,900	17,000
4d Twn Sed	640	1,920	3,200	6,400	11,200	16,000
2d Vic	800	2,400	4,000	8,000	14,000	20,000
4d Sta Wag	840	2,520	4,200	8,400	14,700	21,000

1931 Model A, 4-cyl.

2d Rds	1,160	3,480	5,800	11,600	20,300	29,000
2d DeL Rds	1,200	3,600	6,000	12,000	21,000	30,000
4d Phae	1,240	3,720	6,200	12,400	21,700	31,000
2d DeL Phae	1,280	3,840	6,400	12,800	22,400	32,000
2d Cabr	1,160	3,480	5,800	11,600	20,300	29,000
2d Conv Sed	1,240	3,720	6,200	12,400	21,700	31,000
2d Cpe	640	1,920	3,200	6,400	11,200	16,000
2d DeL Cpe	680	2,040	3,400	6,800	11,900	17,000
2d Spt Cpe	720	2,160	3,600	7,200	12,600	18,000
2d Sed	620	1,860	3,100	6,200	10,850	15,500
2d DeL Sed	640	1,920	3,200	6,400	11,200	16,000
4d Sed	640	1,920	3,200	6,400	11,200	16,000
4d DeL Sed	680	2,040	3,400	6,800	11,900	17,000
4d Twn Sed	700	2,100	3,500	7,000	12,250	17,500
2d Vic	800	2,400	4,000	8,000	14,000	20,000
4d Sta Wag	840	2,520	4,200	8,400	14,700	21,000

1932 Model B, 4-cyl.

2d Rds	1,400	4,200	7,000	14,000	24,500	35,000
4d Phae	1,440	4,320	7,200	14,400	25,200	36,000
2d Cabr	1,360	4,080	6,800	13,600	23,800	34,000
4d Conv Sed	1,400	4,200	7,000	14,000	24,500	35,000
2d Cpe	1,000	3,000	5,000	10,000	17,500	25,000
2d Spt Cpe	1,040	3,120	5,200	10,400	18,200	26,000
2d Sed	640	1,920	3,200	6,400	11,200	16,000
4d Sed	600	1,800	3,000	6,000	10,500	15,000
2d Vic	1,240	3,720	6,200	12,400	21,700	31,000
2d Sta Wag	1,120	3,360	5,600	11,200	19,600	28,000

1932 Model 18, V-8

2d Rds	1,560	4,680	7,800	15,600	27,300	39,000
2d DeL Rds	1,640	4,920	8,200	16,400	28,700	41,000
4d Phae	1,680	5,040	8,400	16,800	29,400	42,000
4d DeL Phae	1,720	5,160	8,600	17,200	30,100	43,000
2d Cabr	1,520	4,560	7,600	15,200	26,600	38,000
4d Conv Sed	1,560	4,680	7,800	15,600	27,300	39,000
2d Cpe	1,120	3,360	5,600	11,200	19,600	28,000
2d DeL Cpe	1,160	3,480	5,800	11,600	20,300	29,000
2d Spt Cpe	1,200	3,600	6,000	12,000	21,000	30,000
2d Sed	720	2,160	3,600	7,200	12,600	18,000
2d DeL Sed	760	2,280	3,800	7,600	13,300	19,000
4d Sed	680	2,040	3,400	6,800	11,900	17,000
4d DeL Sed	720	2,160	3,600	7,200	12,600	18,000
2d Vic	1,320	3,960	6,600	13,200	23,100	33,000
4d Sta Wag	1,360	4,080	6,800	13,600	23,800	34,000

1933 Model 40, V-8

4d Phae	1,440	4,320	7,200	14,400	25,200	36,000
4d DeL Phae	1,480	4,440	7,400	14,800	25,900	37,000
2d Rds	1,440	4,320	7,200	14,400	25,200	36,000
2d DeL Rds	1,480	4,440	7,400	14,800	25,900	37,000
2d 3W Cpe	880	2,640	4,400	8,800	15,400	22,000
2d 3W DeL Cpe	960	2,880	4,800	9,600	16,800	24,000
2d 5W Cpe	880	2,640	4,400	8,800	15,400	22,000
2d 5W DeL Cpe	1,000	3,000	5,000	10,000	17,500	25,000
2d Cabr	1,360	4,080	6,800	13,600	23,800	34,000
2d Sed	680	2,040	3,400	6,800	11,900	17,000
2d DeL Sed	720	2,160	3,600	7,200	12,600	18,000
4d Sed	600	1,800	3,000	6,000	10,500	15,000
4d DeL Sed	640	1,920	3,200	6,400	11,200	16,000
2d Vic	1,040	3,120	5,200	10,400	18,200	26,000
4d Sta Wag	1,240	3,720	6,200	12,400	21,700	31,000

1933 Model 40, 4-cyl.

NOTE: All models deduct 20 percent average from V-8 models.

1934 Model 40, V-8

2d Rds	1,560	4,680	7,800	15,600	27,300	39,000
4d Phae	1,600	4,800	8,000	16,000	28,000	40,000
2d Cabr	1,520	4,560	7,600	15,200	26,600	38,000
5W Cpe	880	2,640	4,400	8,800	15,400	22,000
2d 3W DeL Cpe	960	2,880	4,800	9,600	16,800	24,000
2d 5W DeL Cpe	920	2,760	4,600	9,200	16,100	23,000
2d Sed	600	1,800	3,000	6,000	10,500	15,000
2d DeL Sed	620	1,860	3,100	6,200	10,850	15,500
4d Sed	620	1,860	3,100	6,200	10,850	15,500
4d DeL Sed	628	1,884	3,140	6,280	10,990	15,700
2d Vic	1,040	3,120	5,200	10,400	18,200	26,000
4d Sta Wag	1,240	3,720	6,200	12,400	21,700	31,000

1935 Model 48, V-8

4d Phae	1,440	4,320	7,200	14,400	25,200	36,000
2d Rds	1,400	4,200	7,000	14,000	24,500	35,000
2d Cabr	1,400	4,200	7,000	14,000	24,500	35,000
4d Conv Sed	1,440	4,320	7,200	14,400	25,200	36,000
2d 3W DeL Cpe	1,040	3,120	5,200	10,400	18,200	26,000
2d 5W Cpe	960	2,880	4,800	9,600	16,800	24,000
2d 5W DeL Cpe	1,000	3,000	5,000	10,000	17,500	25,000
2d Sed	608	1,824	3,040	6,080	10,640	15,200
2d DeL Sed	628	1,884	3,140	6,280	10,990	15,700
4d Sed	604	1,812	3,020	6,040	10,570	15,100
4d DeL Sed	624	1,872	3,120	6,240	10,920	15,600
4d Sta Wag	1,240	3,720	6,200	12,400	21,700	31,000
4d C'ham Twn Car	1,240	3,720	6,200	12,400	21,700	31,000

1936 Model 68, V-8

2d Rds	1,440	4,320	7,200	14,400	25,200	36,000
4d Phae	1,480	4,440	7,400	14,800	25,900	37,000
2d Cabr	1,480	4,440	7,400	14,800	25,900	37,000
2d Clb Cabr	1,400	4,200	7,000	14,000	24,500	35,000
4d Conv Trk Sed	1,440	4,320	7,200	14,400	25,200	36,000
4d Conv Sed	1,400	4,200	7,000	14,000	24,500	35,000
2d 3W Cpe	1,080	3,240	5,400	10,800	18,900	27,000
2d 5W Cpe	1,000	3,000	5,000	10,000	17,500	25,000
2d 5W DeL Cpe	1,040	3,120	5,200	10,400	18,200	26,000
2d Sed	624	1,872	3,120	6,240	10,920	15,600
2d Tr Sed	644	1,932	3,220	6,440	11,270	16,100
2d DeL Sed	644	1,932	3,220	6,440	11,270	16,100
4d Sed	620	1,860	3,100	6,200	10,850	15,500
4d Tr Sed	640	1,920	3,200	6,400	11,200	16,000
4d DeL Sed	660	1,980	3,300	6,600	11,550	16,500
4d DeL Tr Sed	640	1,920	3,200	6,400	11,200	16,000
4d Sta Wag	1,280	3,840	6,400	12,800	22,400	32,000

1937 Model 74, V-8, 60 hp

2d Sed	564	1,692	2,820	5,640	9,870	14,100
2d Tr Sed	584	1,752	2,920	5,840	10,220	14,600
4d Sed	560	1,680	2,800	5,600	9,800	14,000
4d Tr Sed	580	1,740	2,900	5,800	10,150	14,500
2d Cpe	800	2,400	4,000	8,000	14,000	20,000
2d Cpe PU	840	2,520	4,200	8,400	14,700	21,000

1937 V-8 DeLuxe

4d Sta Wag	1,240	3,720	6,200	12,400	21,700	31,000

1937 Model 78, V-8, 85 hp

2d Rds	1,280	3,840	6,400	12,800	22,400	32,000
4d Phae	1,320	3,960	6,600	13,200	23,100	33,000
2d Cabr	1,320	3,960	6,600	13,200	23,100	33,000
2d Clb Cabr	1,360	4,080	6,800	13,600	23,800	34,000
4d Conv Sed	1,400	4,200	7,000	14,000	24,500	35,000
2d Cpe	760	2,280	3,800	7,600	13,300	19,000
2d Clb Cpe	800	2,400	4,000	8,000	14,000	20,000
2d Sed	584	1,752	2,920	5,840	10,220	14,600
2d Tr Sed	604	1,812	3,020	6,040	10,570	15,100
4d Sed	580	1,740	2,900	5,800	10,150	14,500
4d Tr Sed	600	1,800	3,000	6,000	10,500	15,000
4d Sta Wag	1,200	3,600	6,000	12,000	21,000	30,000

| | 6 | 5 | 4 | 3 | 2 | 1 |

1938 Model 81A Standard, V-8

	6	5	4	3	2	1
2d Cpe	740	2,220	3,700	7,400	12,950	18,500
2d Sed	564	1,692	2,820	5,640	9,870	14,100
4d Sed	560	1,680	2,800	5,600	9,800	14,000
4d Sta Wag	1,160	3,480	5,800	11,600	20,300	29,000

1938 Model 81A DeLuxe, V-8

	6	5	4	3	2	1
4d Phae	1,400	4,200	7,000	14,000	24,500	35,000
2d Conv	1,360	4,080	6,800	13,600	23,800	34,000
2d Clb Conv	1,400	4,200	7,000	14,000	24,500	35,000
4d Conv Sed	1,440	4,320	7,200	14,400	25,200	36,000
2d Cpe	720	2,160	3,600	7,200	12,600	18,000
2d Clb Cpe	800	2,400	4,000	8,000	14,000	20,000
2d Sed	604	1,812	3,020	6,040	10,570	15,100
4d Sed	600	1,800	3,000	6,000	10,500	15,000

NOTE: Deduct 10 percent average for 60 hp 82A Ford.

1939 Standard, V-8

	6	5	4	3	2	1
2d Cpe	840	2,520	4,200	8,400	14,700	21,000
2d Sed	584	1,752	2,920	5,840	10,220	14,600
4d Sed	580	1,740	2,900	5,800	10,150	14,500
4d Sta Wag	1,200	3,600	6,000	12,000	21,000	30,000

1939 DeLuxe, V-8

	6	5	4	3	2	1
2d Conv	1,560	4,680	7,800	15,600	27,300	39,000
4d Conv Sed	1,600	4,800	8,000	16,000	28,000	40,000
2d Cpe	880	2,640	4,400	8,800	15,400	22,000
2d Sed	604	1,812	3,020	6,040	10,570	15,100
4d Sed	600	1,800	3,000	6,000	10,500	15,000
4d Sta Wag	1,240	3,720	6,200	12,400	21,700	31,000

NOTE: Deduct 10 percent average for V-8, 60 hp models.

1940 Standard & DeLuxe, V-8

	6	5	4	3	2	1
2d Conv	1,680	5,040	8,400	16,800	29,400	42,000
2d Cpe	920	2,760	4,600	9,200	16,100	23,000
2d DeL Cpe	1,000	3,000	5,000	10,000	17,500	25,000
2d Sed	644	1,932	3,220	6,440	11,270	16,100
2d DeL Sed	664	1,992	3,320	6,640	11,620	16,600
4d Sed	640	1,920	3,200	6,400	11,200	16,000
4d DeL Sed	660	1,980	3,300	6,600	11,550	16,500
4d Sta Wag	1,280	3,840	6,400	12,800	22,400	32,000

NOTE: Deduct 10 percent average for V-8, 60 hp models.

1941 Model 11A Special, V-8

	6	5	4	3	2	1
2d Cpe	840	2,520	4,200	8,400	14,700	21,000
2d Sed	584	1,752	2,920	5,840	10,220	14,600
4d Sed	580	1,740	2,900	5,800	10,150	14,500

1941 DeLuxe

	6	5	4	3	2	1
3P Cpe	920	2,760	4,600	9,200	16,100	23,000
5P Cpe	920	2,760	4,600	9,200	16,100	23,000
2d Sed	644	1,932	3,220	6,440	11,270	16,100
4d Sed	640	1,920	3,200	6,400	11,200	16,000
4d Sta Wag	1,280	3,840	6,400	12,800	22,400	32,000

1941 Super DeLuxe

	6	5	4	3	2	1
2d Conv	1,520	4,560	7,600	15,200	26,600	38,000
3P Cpe	960	2,880	4,800	9,600	16,800	24,000
5P Cpe	960	2,880	4,800	9,600	16,800	24,000
2d Sed	664	1,992	3,320	6,640	11,620	16,600
4d Sed	660	1,980	3,300	6,600	11,550	16,500
4d Sta Wag	1,320	3,960	6,600	13,200	23,100	33,000

NOTE: Deduct 10 percent average for 6-cyl.

1942 Model 2GA Special, 6-cyl.

	6	5	4	3	2	1
3P Cpe	720	2,160	3,600	7,200	12,600	18,000
2d Sed	564	1,692	2,820	5,640	9,870	14,100
4d Sed	560	1,680	2,800	5,600	9,800	14,000

1942 Model 21A DeLuxe, V-8

	6	5	4	3	2	1
2d Cpe	760	2,280	3,800	7,600	13,300	19,000
5P Cpe	800	2,400	4,000	8,000	14,000	20,000
2d Sed	584	1,752	2,920	5,840	10,220	14,600
4d Sed	580	1,740	2,900	5,800	10,150	14,500

1942 Super DeLuxe

	6	5	4	3	2	1
2d Conv	1,240	3,720	6,200	12,400	21,700	31,000
3P Cpe	800	2,400	4,000	8,000	14,000	20,000
5P Cpe	840	2,520	4,200	8,400	14,700	21,000
2d Sed	580	1,740	2,900	5,800	10,150	14,500
4d Sed	568	1,704	2,840	5,680	9,940	14,200
4d Sta Wag	1,240	3,720	6,200	12,400	21,700	31,000

NOTE: Deduct 10 percent average for 6-cyl.

1946-1948 Model 89A DeLuxe, V-8

	6	5	4	3	2	1
3P Cpe	720	2,160	3,600	7,200	12,600	18,000
2d Sed	564	1,692	2,820	5,640	9,870	14,100
4d Sed	560	1,680	2,800	5,600	9,800	14,000

1946-1948 Model 89A Super DeLuxe, V-8

	6	5	4	3	2	1
2d Conv	1,280	3,840	6,400	12,800	22,400	32,000
2d Sptman Conv	2,800	8,400	14,000	28,000	49,000	70,000
2d 3P Cpe	760	2,280	3,800	7,600	13,300	19,000
2d 5P Cpe	800	2,400	4,000	8,000	14,000	20,000
2d Sed	584	1,752	2,920	5,840	10,220	14,600
4d Sed	580	1,740	2,900	5,800	10,150	14,500
4d Sta Wag	1,350	4,100	6,800	13,600	23,800	34,000

NOTE: Deduct 5 percent average for 6-cyl.

1949-1950 DeLuxe, V-8, 114" wb

	6	5	4	3	2	1
2d Bus Cpe	720	2,160	3,600	7,200	12,600	18,000
2d Sed	640	1,920	3,200	6,400	11,200	16,000
4d Sed	640	1,920	3,200	6,400	11,200	16,000

1949-1950 Custom DeLuxe, V-8, 114" wb

	6	5	4	3	2	1
2d Clb Cpe	760	2,280	3,800	7,600	13,300	19,000
2d Sed	700	2,100	3,500	7,000	12,250	17,500
4d Sed	700	2,100	3,500	7,000	12,250	17,500
2d Crest (1950 only)	800	2,400	4,000	8,000	14,000	20,000
2d Conv	1,200	3,600	6,000	12,000	21,000	30,000
2d Sta Wag	1,500	4,550	7,600	15,200	26,600	38,000

NOTE: Deduct 5 percent average for 6-cyl.

1951 DeLuxe, V-8, 114" wb

	6	5	4	3	2	1
2d Bus Cpe	720	2,160	3,600	7,200	12,600	18,000
2d Sed	680	2,040	3,400	6,800	11,900	17,000
4d Sed	680	2,040	3,400	6,800	11,900	17,000

1951 Custom DeLuxe, V-8, 114" wb

	6	5	4	3	2	1
2d Clb Cpe	800	2,400	4,000	8,000	14,000	20,000
2d Sed	760	2,280	3,800	7,600	13,300	19,000
4d Sed	760	2,280	3,800	7,600	13,300	19,000
2d Crest	840	2,520	4,200	8,400	14,700	21,000
2d HT	880	2,640	4,400	8,800	15,400	22,000
2d Conv	1,240	3,720	6,200	12,400	21,700	31,000
2d Sta Wag	1,550	4,600	7,700	15,400	27,000	38,500

NOTE: Deduct 5 percent average for 6-cyl.

1952-1953 Mainline, V-8, 115" wb

	6	5	4	3	2	1
2d Bus Cpe	640	1,920	3,200	6,400	11,200	16,000
2d Sed	564	1,692	2,820	5,640	9,870	14,100
4d Sed	560	1,680	2,800	5,600	9,800	14,000
2d Sta Wag	640	1,920	3,200	6,400	11,200	16,000

1952-1953 Customline, V-8, 115" wb

	6	5	4	3	2	1
2d Clb Cpe	720	2,160	3,600	7,200	12,600	18,000
2d Sed	660	1,980	3,300	6,600	11,550	16,500
4d Sed	656	1,968	3,280	6,560	11,480	16,400
4d Sta Wag	720	2,160	3,600	7,200	12,600	18,000

1952-1953 Crestline, 8-cyl., 115" wb

	6	5	4	3	2	1
2d HT	860	2,580	4,300	8,600	15,050	21,500
2d Conv	1,080	3,240	5,400	10,800	18,900	27,000
4d Sta Wag	740	2,220	3,700	7,400	12,950	18,500

NOTE: Deduct 5 percent average for 6-cyl. Add 50 percent for 1953 Indy Pace Car replica convertible.

1954 Mainline, 8-cyl., 115.5" wb

	6	5	4	3	2	1
2d Bus Cpe	600	1,800	3,000	6,000	10,500	15,000
2d Sed	564	1,692	2,820	5,640	9,870	14,100
4d Sed	560	1,680	2,800	5,600	9,800	14,000
2d Sta Wag	640	1,920	3,200	6,400	11,200	16,000

1954 Customline, V-8, 115.5" wb

	6	5	4	3	2	1
2d Clb Cpe	740	2,220	3,700	7,400	12,950	18,500
2d Sed	700	2,100	3,500	7,000	12,250	17,500
4d Sed	696	2,088	3,480	6,960	12,180	17,400
2/4d Sta Wag	760	2,280	3,800	7,600	13,300	19,000

1954 Crestline, V-8, 115.5" wb

	6	5	4	3	2	1
4d Sed	700	2,100	3,500	7,000	12,250	17,500
2d HT	920	2,760	4,600	9,200	16,100	23,000
2d Sky Cpe	1,160	3,480	5,800	11,600	20,300	29,000
2d Conv	1,240	3,720	6,200	12,400	21,700	31,000
4d Sta Wag	800	2,400	4,000	8,000	14,000	20,000

NOTE: Deduct 5 percent average for 6-cyl.

1955 Mainline, V-8, 115.5" wb

	6	5	4	3	2	1
2d Bus Sed	544	1,632	2,720	5,440	9,520	13,600
2d Sed	548	1,644	2,740	5,480	9,590	13,700
4d Sed	552	1,656	2,760	5,520	9,660	13,800

1955 Customline, V-8, 115.5" wb

	6	5	4	3	2	1
2d Sed	572	1,716	2,860	5,720	10,010	14,300
4d Sed	576	1,728	2,880	5,760	10,080	14,400

1955 Fairlane, V-8, 115.5" wb

	6	5	4	3	2	1
2d Sed	628	1,884	3,140	6,280	10,990	15,700
4d Sed	632	1,896	3,160	6,320	11,060	15,800
2d HT	880	2,640	4,400	8,800	15,400	22,000
2d Crn Vic	1,240	3,720	6,200	12,400	21,700	31,000
2d Crn Vic Plexi-top	1,360	4,080	6,800	13,600	23,800	34,000
2d Conv	1,560	4,680	7,800	15,600	27,300	39,000

1955 Station Wagon, V-8, 115.5" wb

	6	5	4	3	2	1
2d Custom Ran Wag	700	2,050	3,400	6,800	11,900	17,000
2d Ran Wag	660	1,980	3,300	6,600	11,550	16,500
4d Ctry Sed Customline	700	2,050	3,400	6,800	11,900	17,000
4d Ctry Sed Fairlane	700	2,150	3,600	7,200	12,600	18,000
4d Ctry Sq	760	2,280	3,800	7,600	13,300	19,000

NOTE: Deduct 5 percent average for 6-cyl.

1956 Mainline, V-8, 115.5" wb

	6	5	4	3	2	1
2d Bus Sed	548	1,644	2,740	5,480	9,590	13,700
2d Sed	556	1,668	2,780	5,560	9,730	13,900
4d Sed	552	1,656	2,760	5,520	9,660	13,800

1956 Customline, V-8, 115.5" wb

	6	5	4	3	2	1
2d Sed	580	1,740	2,900	5,800	10,150	14,500
4d Sed	576	1,728	2,880	5,760	10,080	14,400
2d HT Vic	800	2,400	4,000	8,000	14,000	20,000

1956 Fairlane, V-8, 115.5" wb

	6	5	4	3	2	1
2d Sed	632	1,896	3,160	6,320	11,060	15,800
4d Sed	628	1,884	3,140	6,280	10,990	15,700
4d HT Vic	880	2,640	4,400	8,800	15,400	22,000
2d HT Vic	1,080	3,240	5,400	10,800	18,900	27,000
2d Crn Vic	1,200	3,600	6,000	12,000	21,000	30,000
2d Crn Vic Plexi-top	1,360	4,080	6,800	13,600	23,800	34,000
2d Conv	1,680	5,040	8,400	16,800	29,400	42,000

1956 Station Wagons, V-8, 115.5" wb

	6	5	4	3	2	1
2d Ran Wag	640	1,920	3,200	6,400	11,200	16,000
2d Parklane	840	2,520	4,200	8,400	14,700	21,000
4d Ctry Sed Customline	700	2,050	3,400	6,800	11,900	17,000
4d Ctry Sed Fairlane	700	2,150	3,600	7,200	12,600	18,000
4d Ctry Sq	760	2,280	3,800	7,600	13,300	19,000

NOTE: Deduct 5 percent average for 6-cyl. Add 10 percent for "T-Bird Special" V-8.

1957 Custom, V-8, 116" wb

	6	5	4	3	2	1
2d Bus Cpe	404	1,212	2,020	4,040	7,070	10,100
2d Sed	416	1,248	2,080	4,160	7,280	10,400
4d Sed	412	1,236	2,060	4,120	7,210	10,300

1957 Custom 300, V-8, 116" wb

	6	5	4	3	2	1
2d Sed	520	1,560	2,600	5,200	9,100	13,000
4d Sed	424	1,272	2,120	4,240	7,420	10,600

1957 Fairlane, V-8, 118" wb

	6	5	4	3	2	1
2d Sed	524	1,572	2,620	5,240	9,170	13,100
4d Sed	520	1,560	2,600	5,200	9,100	13,000
4d HT Vic	760	2,280	3,800	7,600	13,300	19,000
2d Vic HT	840	2,520	4,200	8,400	14,700	21,000

1957 Fairlane 500, V-8, 118" wb

	6	5	4	3	2	1
2d Sed	532	1,596	2,660	5,320	9,310	13,300
4d Sed	528	1,584	2,640	5,280	9,240	13,200
4d HT Vic	760	2,280	3,800	7,600	13,300	19,000
2d HT Vic	920	2,760	4,600	9,200	16,100	23,000
2d Conv	1,400	4,200	7,000	14,000	24,500	35,000
2d Sky HT Conv	1,560	4,680	7,800	15,600	27,300	39,000

1957 Station Wagons, 8-cyl., 116" wb

	6	5	4	3	2	1
2d Ran Wag	560	1,680	2,800	5,600	9,800	14,000
2d DeL Rio Ran	580	1,740	2,900	5,800	10,150	14,500
4d Ctry Sed	680	2,040	3,400	6,800	11,900	17,000
4d Ctry Sq	640	1,920	3,200	6,400	11,200	16,000

NOTE: Deduct 5 percent average for 6-cyl. Add 20 percent for "T-Bird Special" V-8 (Code E). Add 30 percent for Supercharged V-8 (Code F).

1958 Custom 300, V-8, 116.03" wb

	6	5	4	3	2	1
2d Bus Cpe	268	804	1,340	2,680	4,690	6,700
2d Sed	400	1,200	2,000	4,000	7,000	10,000
4d Sed	372	1,116	1,860	3,720	6,510	9,300

1958 Fairlane, V-8, 116.03" wb

	6	5	4	3	2	1
2d Sed	380	1,140	1,900	3,800	6,650	9,500
4d Sed	376	1,128	1,880	3,760	6,580	9,400
4d HT	680	2,040	3,400	6,800	11,900	17,000
2d HT	720	2,160	3,600	7,200	12,600	18,000

1958 Fairlane 500, V-8, 118.04" wb

	6	5	4	3	2	1
2d Sed	412	1,236	2,060	4,120	7,210	10,300
4d Sed	396	1,188	1,980	3,960	6,930	9,900
4d HT	720	2,160	3,600	7,200	12,600	18,000
2d HT	800	2,400	4,000	8,000	14,000	20,000
2d Conv	1,080	3,240	5,400	10,800	18,900	27,000
2d Sky HT Conv	1,320	3,960	6,600	13,200	23,100	33,000

1958 Station Wagons, V-8, 116.03" wb

	6	5	4	3	2	1
2d Ran	548	1,644	2,740	5,480	9,590	13,700
4d Ran	540	1,620	2,700	5,400	9,450	13,500
4d Ctry Sed	580	1,740	2,900	5,800	10,150	14,500
2d DeL Rio Ran	600	1,800	3,000	6,000	10,500	15,000
4d Ctry Sq	620	1,860	3,100	6,200	10,850	15,500

NOTE: Deduct 5 percent average for 6-cyl.

1959 Custom 300, V-8, 118" wb

	6	5	4	3	2	1
2d Bus Cpe	380	1,140	1,900	3,800	6,650	9,500
2d Sed	384	1,152	1,920	3,840	6,720	9,600
4d Sed	380	1,140	1,900	3,800	6,650	9,500

1959 Fairlane, V-8, 118" wb

	6	5	4	3	2	1
2d Sed	276	828	1,380	2,760	4,830	6,900
4d Sed	272	816	1,360	2,720	4,760	6,800

1959 Fairlane 500, V-8, 118" wb

	6	5	4	3	2	1
2d Sed	364	1,092	1,820	3,640	6,370	9,100
4d Sed	360	1,080	1,800	3,600	6,300	9,000
4d HT	660	1,980	3,300	6,600	11,550	16,500
2d HT	780	2,340	3,900	7,800	13,650	19,500
2d Sun Conv	1,240	3,720	6,200	12,400	21,700	31,000
2d Sky HT Conv	1,640	4,920	8,200	16,400	28,700	41,000

1959 Galaxie, V-8, 118" wb

	6	5	4	3	2	1
2d Sed	372	1,116	1,860	3,720	6,510	9,300
4d Sed	368	1,104	1,840	3,680	6,440	9,200
4d HT	700	2,100	3,500	7,000	12,250	17,500
2d HT	820	2,460	4,100	8,200	14,350	20,500
2d Sun Conv	1,240	3,720	6,200	12,400	21,700	31,000
2d Sky HT Conv	1,560	4,680	7,800	15,600	27,300	39,000

1959 Station Wagons, V-8, 118" wb

	6	5	4	3	2	1
2d Ran	420	1,260	2,100	4,200	7,350	10,500
4d Ran	560	1,680	2,800	5,600	9,800	14,000
2d Ctry Sed	600	1,800	3,000	6,000	10,500	15,000
4d Ctry Sed	580	1,740	2,900	5,800	10,150	14,500
4d Ctry Sq	600	1,800	3,000	6,000	10,500	15,000

NOTE: Deduct 5 percent average for 6-cyl.

1960 Falcon, 6-cyl., 109.5" wb

	6	5	4	3	2	1
2d Sed	244	732	1,220	2,440	4,270	6,100
4d Sed	248	744	1,240	2,480	4,340	6,200
2d Sta Wag	248	744	1,240	2,480	4,340	6,200
4d Sta Wag	252	756	1,260	2,520	4,410	6,300

1960 Fairlane, V-8, 119" wb

	6	5	4	3	2	1
2d Bus Cpe	252	756	1,260	2,520	4,410	6,300
2d Sed	264	792	1,320	2,640	4,620	6,600
4d Sed	260	780	1,300	2,600	4,550	6,500

1960 Fairlane 500, V-8, 119" wb

	6	5	4	3	2	1
2d Sed	268	804	1,340	2,680	4,690	6,700
4d Sed	264	792	1,320	2,640	4,620	6,600

1960 Galaxie, V-8, 119" wb

	6	5	4	3	2	1
2d Sed	380	1,140	1,900	3,800	6,650	9,500
4d Sed	376	1,128	1,880	3,760	6,580	9,400
4d HT	600	1,800	3,000	6,000	10,500	15,000
2d HT	760	2,280	3,800	7,600	13,300	19,000

1960 Galaxie Special, V-8, 119" wb

	6	5	4	3	2	1
2d HT	840	2,520	4,200	8,400	14,700	21,000
2d Sun Conv	1,160	3,480	5,800	11,600	20,300	29,000

1960 Station Wagons, V-8, 119" wb

	6	5	4	3	2	1
2d Ran	532	1,596	2,660	5,320	9,310	13,300
4d Ran	520	1,560	2,600	5,200	9,100	13,000
4d Ctry Sed	540	1,620	2,700	5,400	9,450	13,500
4d Ctry Sq	560	1,680	2,800	5,600	9,800	14,000

NOTE: Deduct 5 percent average for 6-cyl.

1961 Falcon, 6-cyl., 109.5" wb

	6	5	4	3	2	1
2d Sed	268	804	1,340	2,680	4,690	6,700
4d Sed	272	816	1,360	2,720	4,760	6,800
2d Futura Sed	520	1,560	2,600	5,200	9,100	13,000
2d Sta Wag	276	828	1,380	2,760	4,830	6,900
4d Sta Wag	272	816	1,360	2,720	4,760	6,800

1961 Fairlane, V-8, 119" wb

	6	5	4	3	2	1
2d Sed	272	816	1,360	2,720	4,760	6,800
4d Sed	276	828	1,380	2,760	4,830	6,900

1961 Galaxie, V-8, 119" wb

	6	5	4	3	2	1
2d Sed	276	828	1,380	2,760	4,830	6,900
4d Sed	360	1,080	1,800	3,600	6,300	9,000
4d Vic HT	420	1,260	2,100	4,200	7,350	10,500
2d Vic HT	720	2,160	3,600	7,200	12,600	18,000
2d Star HT	760	2,280	3,800	7,600	13,300	19,000
2d Sun Conv	880	2,640	4,400	8,800	15,400	22,000

1961 Station Wagons, V-8, 119" wb

	6	5	4	3	2	1
4d Ran	500	1,500	2,500	5,000	8,750	12,500
2d Ran	500	1,500	2,550	5,100	8,900	12,700
4d 6P Ctry Sed	600	1,800	3,000	6,000	10,500	15,000
4d Ctry Sq	600	1,850	3,100	6,200	10,900	15,500

NOTE: Deduct 5 percent average for 6-cyl.

1962 Falcon, 6-cyl., 109.5" wb

	6	5	4	3	2	1
4d Sed	220	660	1,100	2,200	3,850	5,500
2d	216	648	1,080	2,160	3,780	5,400
2d Fut Spt Cpe	560	1,680	2,800	5,600	9,800	14,000
4d Sq Wag	250	800	1,350	2,700	4,750	6,800

1962 Falcon Station Bus, 6-cyl., 109.5" wb

	6	5	4	3	2	1
Sta Bus	212	636	1,060	2,120	3,710	5,300
Clb Wag	216	648	1,080	2,160	3,780	5,400
DeL Wag	220	660	1,100	2,200	3,850	5,500

1962 Fairlane, V-8, 115.5" wb

	6	5	4	3	2	1
4d Sed	216	648	1,080	2,160	3,780	5,400
2d Sed	212	636	1,060	2,120	3,710	5,300
4d Spt Sed	232	696	1,160	2,320	4,060	5,800

1962 Galaxie 500, V-8, 119" wb

	6	5	4	3	2	1
4d Sed	232	696	1,160	2,320	4,060	5,800
4d HT	380	1,140	1,900	3,800	6,650	9,500
2d Sed	228	684	1,140	2,280	3,990	5,700
2d HT	600	1,800	3,000	6,000	10,500	15,000
2d Conv	760	2,280	3,800	7,600	13,300	19,000

1962 Galaxie 500 XL, V-8, 119" wb

	6	5	4	3	2	1
2d HT	680	2,040	3,400	6,800	11,900	17,000
2d Conv	880	2,640	4,400	8,800	15,400	22,000

1962 Station Wagons, V-8, 119" wb

	6	5	4	3	2	1
4d Ranch	450	1,400	2,300	4,600	8,050	11,500
4d Ctry Sed	500	1,450	2,400	4,800	8,400	12,000
4d Ctry Sq	500	1,500	2,500	5,000	8,750	12,500

NOTE: Deduct 5 percent for 6-cyl. Add 30 percent for 406 V-8.

1963 Falcon, 6-cyl., 109.5" wb

	6	5	4	3	2	1
4d Sed	228	684	1,140	2,280	3,990	5,700
2d Sed	224	672	1,120	2,240	3,920	5,600
2d Spt Sed	240	720	1,200	2,400	4,200	6,000
2d HT	520	1,560	2,600	5,200	9,100	13,000
2d Spt HT	560	1,680	2,800	5,600	9,800	14,000
2d Conv	680	2,040	3,400	6,800	11,900	17,000
2d Spt Conv	720	2,160	3,600	7,200	12,600	18,000
4d Sq Wag	300	900	1,500	3,000	5,250	7,500
4d Sta Wag	300	850	1,400	2,800	4,900	7,000
2d Sta Wag	300	850	1,400	2,850	4,950	7,100

NOTE: Add 10 percent for V-8 models.

1963 Station Buses, 6-cyl., 90" wb

	6	5	4	3	2	1
Sta Bus	252	756	1,260	2,520	4,410	6,300
Clb Wag	256	768	1,280	2,560	4,480	6,400
DeL Clb Wag	240	720	1,200	2,400	4,200	6,000

1963 Sprint, V-8, 109.5" wb

	6	5	4	3	2	1
2d HT	640	1,920	3,200	6,400	11,200	16,000
2d Conv	760	2,280	3,800	7,600	13,300	19,000

1963 Fairlane, V-8, 115.5" wb

	6	5	4	3	2	1
4d Sed	216	648	1,080	2,160	3,780	5,400
2d Sed	212	636	1,060	2,120	3,710	5,300
2d HT	300	900	1,500	3,000	5,250	7,500
2d Spt Cpe	320	960	1,600	3,200	5,600	8,000
4d Sq Wag	450	1,400	2,300	4,600	8,050	11,500
4d Cus Ran	450	1,350	2,300	4,550	8,000	11,400

NOTE: Add 20 percent for 271 hp V-8.

1963 Ford 300, V-8, 119" wb

	6	5	4	3	2	1
4d Sed	220	660	1,100	2,200	3,850	5,500
2d Sed	216	648	1,080	2,160	3,780	5,400

1963 Galaxie 500, V-8, 119" wb

	6	5	4	3	2	1
4d Sed	224	672	1,120	2,240	3,920	5,600
4d HT	360	1,080	1,800	3,600	6,300	9,000
2d Sed	220	660	1,100	2,200	3,850	5,500
2d HT	680	2,040	3,400	6,800	11,900	17,000
2d FBk	760	2,280	3,800	7,600	13,300	19,000
2d Conv	840	2,520	4,200	8,400	14,700	21,000

1963 Galaxie 500 XL, V-8, 119" wb

	6	5	4	3	2	1
4d HT	420	1,260	2,100	4,200	7,350	10,500
2d HT	720	2,160	3,600	7,200	12,600	18,000
2d FBk	800	2,400	4,000	8,000	14,000	20,000
2d Conv	920	2,760	4,600	9,200	16,100	23,000

1963 Station Wagons, V-8, 119" wb

	6	5	4	3	2	1
4d Ctry Sed	500	1,450	2,400	4,800	8,400	12,000
4d Ctry Sq	500	1,500	2,500	5,000	8,750	12,500

NOTE: Deduct 5 percent average for 6-cyl. Add 30 percent for 406 & add 40 percent for 427. Add 5 percent for V-8 except Sprint.

1964 Falcon, 6-cyl., 109.5" wb

	6	5	4	3	2	1
4d Sed	224	672	1,120	2,240	3,920	5,600
2d Sed	220	660	1,100	2,200	3,850	5,500
2d HT	420	1,260	2,100	4,200	7,350	10,500
2d Spt HT	580	1,740	2,900	5,800	10,150	14,500
2d Conv	600	1,800	3,000	6,000	10,500	15,000
2d Spt Conv	640	1,920	3,200	6,400	11,200	16,000
4d Sq Wag	300	900	1,500	3,000	5,250	7,500
4d DeL Wag	300	850	1,400	2,800	4,900	7,000
4d Sta	300	850	1,400	2,800	4,900	7,000
2d Sta	300	850	1,400	2,850	4,950	7,100

NOTE: Add 10 percent for V-8 models.

1964 Station Bus, 6-cyl., 90" wb

	6	5	4	3	2	1
Sta Bus	240	720	1,200	2,400	4,200	6,000
Clb Wag	244	732	1,220	2,440	4,270	6,100
DeL Clb	252	756	1,260	2,520	4,410	6,300

1964 Sprint, V-8, 109.5" wb

	6	5	4	3	2	1
2d HT	620	1,860	3,100	6,200	10,850	15,500
2d Conv	680	2,040	3,400	6,800	11,900	17,000

1964 Fairlane, V-8, 115.5" wb

	6	5	4	3	2	1
4d Sed	208	624	1,040	2,080	3,640	5,200
2d Sed	204	612	1,020	2,040	3,570	5,100
2d HT	540	1,620	2,700	5,400	9,450	13,500
2d Spt HT	580	1,740	2,900	5,800	10,150	14,500
4d Sta Wag	400	1,200	2,000	4,050	7,050	10,100

NOTE: Add 20 percent for 271 hp V-8.

1964 Fairlane Thunderbolt

	6	5	4	3	2	1
2d Sed			value not estimable			

1964 Custom, V-8, 119" wb

	6	5	4	3	2	1
4d Sed	208	624	1,040	2,080	3,640	5,200
2d Sed	204	612	1,020	2,040	3,570	5,100

1964 Custom 500, V-8, 119" wb

	6	5	4	3	2	1
4d Sed	212	636	1,060	2,120	3,710	5,300
2d Sed	208	624	1,040	2,080	3,640	5,200

1964 Galaxie 500, V-8, 119" wb

	6	5	4	3	2	1
4d Sed	260	780	1,300	2,600	4,550	6,500
4d HT	400	1,200	2,000	4,000	7,000	10,000
2d Sed	256	768	1,280	2,560	4,480	6,400
2d HT	760	2,280	3,800	7,600	13,300	19,000
2d Conv	880	2,640	4,400	8,800	15,400	22,000

1964 Galaxie 500XL, V-8, 119" wb

	6	5	4	3	2	1
4d HT	560	1,680	2,800	5,600	9,800	14,000
2d HT	800	2,400	4,000	8,000	14,000	20,000
2d Conv	1,040	3,120	5,200	10,400	18,200	26,000

1964 Station Wagons, V-8, 119" wb

	6	5	4	3	2	1
4d Ctry Sed	600	1,800	3,000	6,000	10,500	15,000
4d Ctry Sq	600	1,850	3,100	6,200	10,900	15,500

NOTE: Add 40 percent for 427 V-8.

1965 Falcon, 6-cyl., 109.5" wb

	6	5	4	3	2	1
4d Sed	200	600	1,000	2,000	3,500	5,000
2d Sed	196	588	980	1,960	3,430	4,900
2d HT	360	1,080	1,800	3,600	6,300	9,000
2d Conv	640	1,920	3,200	6,400	11,200	16,000
4d Sq Wag	300	850	1,400	2,800	4,900	7,000
4d DeL Wag	250	800	1,300	2,600	4,550	6,500
4d Sta	250	700	1,200	2,400	4,200	6,000

	6	5	4	3	2	1
2d Sta	250	750	1,250	2,500	4,350	6,200

NOTE: Add 10 percent for V-8 models.

1965 Sprint, V-8, 109.5" wb

	6	5	4	3	2	1
2d HT	600	1,800	3,000	6,000	10,500	15,000
2d Conv	680	2,040	3,400	6,800	11,900	17,000

1965 Falcon Station Buses, 6-cyl., 90" wb

	6	5	4	3	2	1
Sta Bus	204	612	1,020	2,040	3,570	5,100
Clb Wag	212	636	1,060	2,120	3,710	5,300
DeL Wag	220	660	1,100	2,200	3,850	5,500

1965 Fairlane, V-8, 116" wb

	6	5	4	3	2	1
4d Sed	212	636	1,060	2,120	3,710	5,300
2d Sed	208	624	1,040	2,080	3,640	5,200
2d HT	360	1,080	1,800	3,600	6,300	9,000
2d Spt HT	540	1,620	2,700	5,400	9,450	13,500
4d Sta Wag	250	800	1,300	2,600	4,550	6,500

NOTE: Add 10 percent for 271 hp V-8.

1965 Custom, V-8, 119" wb

	6	5	4	3	2	1
4d Sed	200	600	1,000	2,000	3,500	5,000
2d Sed	196	588	980	1,960	3,430	4,900

1965 Custom 500, V-8, 119" wb

	6	5	4	3	2	1
4d Sed	204	612	1,020	2,040	3,570	5,100
2d Sed	200	600	1,000	2,000	3,500	5,000

1965 Galaxie 500, V-8, 119" wb

	6	5	4	3	2	1
4d Sed	240	720	1,200	2,400	4,200	6,000
4d HT	380	1,140	1,900	3,800	6,650	9,500
2d HT	560	1,680	2,800	5,600	9,800	14,000
2d Conv	640	1,920	3,200	6,400	11,200	16,000

1965 Galaxie 500 XL, V-8, 119" wb

	6	5	4	3	2	1
2d HT	600	1,800	3,000	6,000	10,500	15,000
2d Conv	680	2,040	3,400	6,800	11,900	17,000

1965 Galaxie 500 LTD, V-8, 119" wb

	6	5	4	3	2	1
4d HT	420	1,260	2,100	4,200	7,350	10,500
2d HT	660	1,980	3,300	6,600	11,550	16,500

1965 Station Wagons, V-8, 119" wb

	6	5	4	3	2	1
4d Ran	450	1,300	2,200	4,400	7,700	11,000
4d 9P Ctry Sed	450	1,400	2,300	4,600	8,050	11,500
4d 9P Ctry Sq	500	1,450	2,400	4,800	8,400	12,000

NOTE: Add 40 percent for 427 V-8.

1966 Falcon, 6-cyl., 110.9" wb

	6	5	4	3	2	1
4d Sed	200	600	1,000	2,000	3,500	5,000
2d Clb Cpe	196	588	980	1,960	3,430	4,900
2d Spt Cpe	212	636	1,060	2,120	3,710	5,300
4d 6P Wag	300	850	1,400	2,750	4,850	6,900
4d Sq Wag	300	850	1,400	2,800	4,900	7,000

1966 Falcon Station Bus, 6-cyl., 90" wb

	6	5	4	3	2	1
Clb Wag	192	576	960	1,920	3,360	4,800
Cus Clb Wag	196	588	980	1,960	3,430	4,900
DeL Clb Wag	200	600	1,000	2,000	3,500	5,000

1966 Fairlane, V-8, 116" wb

	6	5	4	3	2	1
4d Sed	204	612	1,020	2,040	3,570	5,100
2d Clb Cpe	200	600	1,000	2,000	3,500	5,000

1966 Fairlane 500, 6-cyl.

	6	5	4	3	2	1
4d Sed	250	700	1,150	2,300	4,050	5,800
2d Cpe	250	800	1,300	2,600	4,550	6,500
2d HT	450	1,400	2,300	4,600	8,050	11,500
2d Conv	750	2,300	3,800	7,600	13,300	19,000

1966 Fairlane 500 XL, V-8, 116" wb

	6	5	4	3	2	1
2d HT	540	1,620	2,700	5,400	9,450	13,500
2d Conv	840	2,520	4,200	8,400	14,700	21,000

1966 Fairlane 500 GT, V-8, 116" wb

	6	5	4	3	2	1
2d HT	600	1,800	3,000	6,000	10,500	15,000
2d Conv	880	2,640	4,400	8,800	15,400	22,000

1966 Station Wagons, V-8, 113" wb

	6	5	4	3	2	1
6P DeL	200	600	1,000	2,000	3,500	5,000
2d Sq Wag	250	750	1,250	2,500	4,350	6,200

1966 Custom, V-8, 119" wb

	6	5	4	3	2	1
4d Sed	208	624	1,040	2,080	3,640	5,200
2d Sed	204	612	1,020	2,040	3,570	5,100

1966 Galaxie 500, V-8, 119" wb

	6	5	4	3	2	1
4d Sed	240	720	1,200	2,400	4,200	6,000
4d HT	380	1,140	1,900	3,800	6,650	9,500
2d HT	420	1,260	2,100	4,200	7,350	10,500
2d Conv	640	1,920	3,200	6,400	11,200	16,000

1966 Galaxie 500, XL, V-8, 119" wb

	6	5	4	3	2	1
2d HT	540	1,620	2,700	5,400	9,450	13,500
2d Conv	680	2,040	3,400	6,800	11,900	17,000

1966 LTD, V-8, 119" wb

	6	5	4	3	2	1
4d HT	400	1,200	2,000	4,000	7,000	10,000
2d HT	520	1,560	2,600	5,200	9,100	13,000

1966 Galaxie 500, 7-litre V-8, 119" wb

	6	5	4	3	2	1
2d HT	640	1,920	3,200	6,400	11,200	16,000
2d Conv	760	2,280	3,800	7,600	13,300	19,000

NOTE: Add 50 percent for 427 engine option on 7-litre models.

1966 Station Wagons, V-8, 119" wb

	6	5	4	3	2	1
4d Ran Wag	450	1,400	2,300	4,600	8,050	11,500
4d Ctry Sed	500	1,450	2,400	4,800	8,400	12,000
4d Ctry Sq	500	1,500	2,500	5,000	8,750	12,500

NOTE: Add 40 percent for 427 or 30 percent for 428 engine option.

1967 Falcon, 6-cyl., 111" wb

	6	5	4	3	2	1
4d Sed	200	600	1,000	2,000	3,500	5,000
2d Sed	196	588	980	1,960	3,430	4,900
4d Sta Wag	250	700	1,200	2,400	4,200	6,000

1967 Futura

	6	5	4	3	2	1
4d Sed	204	612	1,020	2,040	3,570	5,100
2d Clb Cpe	200	600	1,000	2,000	3,500	5,000
2d HT	260	780	1,300	2,600	4,550	6,500

1967 Fairlane

	6	5	4	3	2	1
4d Sed	200	600	1,000	2,000	3,500	5,000
2d Cpe	196	588	980	1,960	3,430	4,900

1967 Fairlane 500, V-8, 116" wb

	6	5	4	3	2	1
4d Sed	204	612	1,020	2,040	3,570	5,100
2d Cpe	200	600	1,000	2,000	3,500	5,000
2d HT	380	1,140	1,900	3,800	6,650	9,500
2d Conv	580	1,740	2,900	5,800	10,150	14,500
4d Wag	250	800	1,300	2,600	4,550	6,500

1967 Fairlane 500 XL, V-8

	6	5	4	3	2	1
2d HT	400	1,200	2,000	4,000	7,000	10,000
2d Conv	680	2,040	3,400	6,800	11,900	17,000
2d HT GT	520	1,560	2,600	5,200	9,100	13,000
2d Conv GT	720	2,160	3,600	7,200	12,600	18,000

1967 Fairlane Wagons

	6	5	4	3	2	1
4d Sta Wag	250	700	1,200	2,400	4,200	6,000
4d 500 Wag	250	750	1,200	2,450	4,250	6,100
4d Sq Wag	250	750	1,250	2,500	4,400	6,300

1967 Ford Custom

	6	5	4	3	2	1
4d Sed	200	600	1,000	2,000	3,500	5,000
2d Sed	196	588	980	1,960	3,430	4,900

1967 Ford Custom 500

	6	5	4	3	2	1
4d Sed	204	612	1,020	2,040	3,570	5,100
2d Sed	200	600	1,000	2,000	3,500	5,000

1967 Galaxie 500, V-8, 119" wb

	6	5	4	3	2	1
4d Sed	212	636	1,060	2,120	3,710	5,300
4d HT	380	1,140	1,900	3,800	6,650	9,500
2d HT	540	1,620	2,700	5,400	9,450	13,500
2d Conv	680	2,040	3,400	6,800	11,900	17,000

1967 Galaxie 500 XL

	6	5	4	3	2	1
2d HT	580	1,740	2,900	5,800	10,150	14,500
2d Conv	720	2,160	3,600	7,200	12,600	18,000

1967 LTD, V-8, 119" wb

	6	5	4	3	2	1
4d HT	520	1,560	2,600	5,200	9,100	13,000
2d HT	600	1,800	3,000	6,000	10,500	15,000

1967 Station Wagons

	6	5	4	3	2	1
4d Ranch	450	1,300	2,200	4,400	7,700	11,000
4d Ctry Sed	450	1,400	2,300	4,600	8,050	11,500
4d Ctry Sq	500	1,450	2,400	4,800	8,400	12,000

NOTE: Add 5 percent for V-8. Add 40 percent for 427 or 428 engine option.

	6	5	4	3	2	1

1968 Standard Falcon

	6	5	4	3	2	1
4d Sed	180	540	900	1,800	3,150	4,500
2d Sed	176	528	880	1,760	3,080	4,400
4d Sta Wag	200	650	1,100	2,200	3,850	5,500

1968 Falcon Futura, 6-cyl., 110.0" wb

	6	5	4	3	2	1
4d Sed	184	552	920	1,840	3,220	4,600
2d Sed	180	540	900	1,800	3,150	4,800
2d Spt Cpe	192	576	960	1,920	3,360	4,800
4d Sta Wag	200	650	1,100	2,250	3,900	5,600

1968 Fairlane

	6	5	4	3	2	1
4d Sed	184	552	920	1,840	3,220	4,600
2d HT	260	780	1,300	2,600	4,550	6,500
4d Sta Wag	250	700	1,150	2,300	4,050	5,800

1968 Fairlane 500, V-8, 116" wb

	6	5	4	3	2	1
4d Sed	188	564	940	1,880	3,290	4,700
2d HT	360	1,080	1,800	3,600	6,300	9,000
2d FBk	320	960	1,600	3,200	5,600	8,000
2d Conv	600	1,800	3,000	6,000	10,500	15,000
4d Sta Wag	250	700	1,200	2,350	4,150	5,900

1968 Torino, V-8, 116" wb

	6	5	4	3	2	1
4d Sed	172	516	860	1,720	3,010	4,300
2d HT	380	1,140	1,900	3,800	6,650	9,500
4d Wag	250	700	1,200	2,400	4,200	6,000

1968 Torino GT, V-8

	6	5	4	3	2	1
2d HT	520	1,560	2,600	5,200	9,100	13,000
2d FBk	600	1,800	3,000	6,000	10,500	15,000
2d Conv	680	2,040	3,400	6,800	11,900	17,000

1968 Custom

	6	5	4	3	2	1
4d Sed	180	540	900	1,800	3,150	4,500
2d Sed	176	528	880	1,760	3,080	4,400

1968 Custom 500

	6	5	4	3	2	1
4d Sed	184	552	920	1,840	3,220	4,600
2d Sed	180	540	900	1,800	3,150	4,500

1968 Galaxie 500, V-8, 119" wb

	6	5	4	3	2	1
4d Sed	188	564	940	1,880	3,290	4,700
4d HT	192	576	960	1,920	3,360	4,800
2d HT	400	1,200	2,000	4,000	7,000	10,000
2d FBk	560	1,680	2,800	5,600	9,800	14,000
2d Conv	640	1,920	3,200	6,400	11,200	16,000

1968 XL

	6	5	4	3	2	1
2d FBk	600	1,800	3,000	6,000	10,500	15,000
2d Conv	680	2,040	3,400	6,800	11,900	17,000

1968 LTD

	6	5	4	3	2	1
4d Sed	200	600	1,000	2,000	3,500	5,000
4d HT	220	660	1,100	2,200	3,850	5,500
2d HT	420	1,260	2,100	4,200	7,350	10,500

1968 Ranch Wagon

	6	5	4	3	2	1
4d Std Wag	400	1,200	2,000	4,000	7,000	10,000
4d 500 Wag	400	1,200	2,050	4,100	7,150	10,200
4d DeL 500 Wag	400	1,250	2,050	4,100	7,200	10,300

1968 Country Sedan

	6	5	4	3	2	1
4d Std Wag	450	1,300	2,200	4,400	7,700	11,000
DeL Wag	450	1,350	2,250	4,500	7,850	11,200

1968 Country Squire

	6	5	4	3	2	1
4d Sta Wag	500	1,450	2,400	4,800	8,400	12,000
4d DeL Wag	500	1,500	2,500	4,950	8,700	12,400

NOTE: Add 50 percent for 429 engine option. Add 40 percent for 427 or 428 engine option.

1969 Falcon Futura, 6-cyl., 111" wb

	6	5	4	3	2	1
2d Spt Cpe	164	492	820	1,640	2,870	4,100
2d Sed	148	444	740	1,480	2,590	3,700

1969 Fairlane 500, V-8, 116" wb

	6	5	4	3	2	1
4d Sed	144	432	720	1,440	2,520	3,600
2d HT	260	780	1,300	2,600	4,550	6,500
2d FBk	240	720	1,200	2,400	4,200	6,000
2d Conv	520	1,560	2,600	5,200	9,100	13,000

1969 Torino, V-8, 116" wb

	6	5	4	3	2	1
4d Sed	160	480	800	1,600	2,800	4,000
2d HT	360	1,080	1,800	3,600	6,300	9,000

1969 Torino GT, V-8

	6	5	4	3	2	1
2d HT	520	1,560	2,600	5,200	9,100	13,000
2d FBk	600	1,800	3,000	6,000	10,500	15,000
2d Conv	720	2,160	3,600	7,200	12,600	18,000

1969 Cobra

	6	5	4	3	2	1
2d HT	760	2,280	3,800	7,600	13,300	19,000
2d FBk	800	2,400	4,000	8,000	14,000	20,000

1969 Galaxie 500, V-8, 121" wb

	6	5	4	3	2	1
4d HT	220	660	1,100	2,200	3,850	5,500
2d HT	260	780	1,300	2,600	4,550	6,500
2d FBk	400	1,200	2,000	4,000	7,000	10,000
2d Conv	600	1,800	3,000	6,000	10,500	15,000

1969 XL

	6	5	4	3	2	1
2d FBk	540	1,620	2,700	5,400	9,450	13,500
2d Conv	640	1,920	3,200	6,400	11,200	16,000

NOTE: Add 10 percent for GT option.

1969 LTD

	6	5	4	3	2	1
4d HT	240	720	1,200	2,400	4,200	6,000
2d HT	380	1,140	1,900	3,800	6,650	9,500

1969 Falcon Wagon, 6-cyl.

	6	5	4	3	2	1
4d Wag	160	480	800	1,600	2,800	4,000
4d Futura Sta Wag	200	600	1,000	2,050	3,550	5,100

1969 Fairlane, 6-cyl.

	6	5	4	3	2	1
4d Wag	250	750	1,200	2,450	4,250	6,100
4d 500 Sta Wag	250	800	1,350	2,700	4,700	6,700
4d Torino Sta Wag	250	750	1,250	2,500	4,400	6,300

NOTE: Add 30 percent for V-8 where available.

1969 Custom Ranch Wagon, V-8

	6	5	4	3	2	1
4d Wag	300	950	1,600	3,200	5,600	8,000
4d 500 Sta Wag 2S	300	950	1,600	3,250	5,650	8,100
4d 500 Sta Wag 4S	350	1,000	1,650	3,300	5,750	8,200

NOTE: Deduct 30 percent for 6-cyl.

1969 Galaxie 500 Country Sedan, V-8

	6	5	4	3	2	1
4d Wag 2S	350	1,000	1,650	3,300	5,750	8,200
4d Wag 4S	350	1,000	1,650	3,300	5,800	8,300

1969 LTD Country Squire, V-8

	6	5	4	3	2	1
4d Wag 2S	400	1,150	1,900	3,800	6,650	9,500
4d Wag 4S	400	1,150	1,900	3,850	6,700	9,600

NOTE: Add 40 percent for 428 engine option. Add 50 percent for 429 engine option.

1970 Falcon, 6-cyl., 110" wb

	6	5	4	3	2	1
4d Sed	176	528	880	1,760	3,080	4,400
2d Sed	172	516	860	1,720	3,010	4,300
4d Sta Wag	200	650	1,050	2,100	3,700	5,300

1970-1/2 Falcon, 6-cyl., 117" wb

	6	5	4	3	2	1
4d Sed	184	552	920	1,840	3,220	4,600
2d Sed	176	528	880	1,760	3,080	4,400
4d Sta Wag	200	650	1,100	2,200	3,850	5,500

1970 Futura, 6-cyl., 110" wb

	6	5	4	3	2	1
4d Sed	188	564	940	1,880	3,290	4,700
2d Sed	180	540	900	1,800	3,150	4,500
4d Sta Wag	200	650	1,100	2,200	3,850	5,500

NOTE: Add 10 percent for V-8.

1970 Maverick

	6	5	4	3	2	1
2d Sed	168	504	840	1,680	2,940	4,200

1970 Fairlane 500, V-8, 117" wb

	6	5	4	3	2	1
4d Sed	192	576	960	1,920	3,360	4,800
2d HT	240	720	1,200	2,400	4,200	6,000
4d Sta Wag	250	700	1,150	2,300	4,000	5,700

1970 Torino, V-8, 117" wb

	6	5	4	3	2	1
4d Sed	196	588	980	1,960	3,430	4,900
4d HT	240	720	1,200	2,400	4,200	6,000
2d HT	300	900	1,500	3,000	5,250	7,500
2d HT Sports Roof	420	1,260	2,100	4,200	7,350	10,500
4d Sta Wag	250	700	1,200	2,400	4,200	6,000

1970 Torino Brougham, V-8, 117" wb

	6	5	4	3	2	1
4d HT	260	780	1,300	2,600	4,550	6,500
2d HT	380	1,140	1,900	3,800	6,650	9,500
4d Sta Wag	250	700	1,150	2,300	4,050	5,800

1970 Torino GT, V-8, 117" wb

	6	5	4	3	2	1
2d HT	520	1,560	2,600	5,200	9,100	13,000
2d Conv	640	1,920	3,200	6,400	11,200	16,000

1970 Cobra, V-8, 117" wb

	6	5	4	3	2	1
2d HT	920	2,760	4,600	9,200	16,100	23,000

1970 Custom, V-8, 121" wb

	6	5	4	3	2	1
4d Sed	160	480	800	1,600	2,800	4,000
4d Sta Wag	250	700	1,150	2,300	4,000	5,700

1970 Custom 500, V-8, 121" wb

	6	5	4	3	2	1
4d Sed	164	492	820	1,640	2,870	4,100
4d Sta Wag	250	700	1,150	2,300	4,050	5,800

1970 Galaxie 500, V-8, 121" wb

	6	5	4	3	2	1
4d Sed	168	504	840	1,680	2,940	4,200
4d HT	220	660	1,100	2,200	3,850	5,500
2d HT	260	780	1,300	2,600	4,550	6,500
4d Sta Wag	250	700	1,200	2,350	4,150	5,900
2d FBk HT	400	1,200	2,000	4,000	7,000	10,000

1970 XL, V-8, 121" wb

	6	5	4	3	2	1
2d FBk HT	420	1,260	2,100	4,200	7,350	10,500
2d Conv	580	1,740	2,900	5,800	10,150	14,500

1970 LTD, V-8, 121" wb

	6	5	4	3	2	1
4d Sed	172	516	860	1,720	3,010	4,300
4d HT	188	564	940	1,880	3,290	4,700
2d HT	220	660	1,100	2,200	3,850	5,500
4d Sta Wag	250	700	1,200	2,400	4,200	6,000

1970 LTD Brougham, V-8, 121" wb

	6	5	4	3	2	1
4d Sed	176	528	880	1,760	3,080	4,400
4d HT	200	600	1,000	2,000	3,500	5,000
2d HT	240	720	1,200	2,400	4,200	6,000

NOTE: Add 40 percent for 428 engine option. Add 50 percent for 429 engine option.

1971 Pinto

	6	5	4	3	2	1
2d Rbt	168	504	840	1,680	2,940	4,200

1971 Maverick

	6	5	4	3	2	1
2d Sed	188	564	940	1,880	3,290	4,700
4d Sed	192	576	960	1,920	3,360	4,800
2d Grabber Sed	196	588	980	1,960	3,430	4,900

1971 Torino, V-8, 114" wb, Sta Wag 117" wb

	6	5	4	3	2	1
4d Sed	196	588	980	1,960	3,430	4,900
2d HT	260	780	1,300	2,600	4,550	6,500
4d Sta Wag	250	700	1,200	2,350	4,150	5,900

1971 Torino 500, V-8, 114" wb, Sta Wag 117" wb

	6	5	4	3	2	1
4d Sed	200	600	1,000	2,000	3,500	5,000
4d HT	244	732	1,220	2,440	4,270	6,100
2d HT Formal Roof	520	1,560	2,600	5,200	9,100	13,000
2d HT Spt Roof	540	1,620	2,700	5,400	9,450	13,500
4d Sta Wag	200	600	1,000	2,000	3,500	5,000
4d HT Brougham	244	732	1,220	2,440	4,270	6,100
2d HT Brougham	380	1,140	1,900	3,800	6,650	9,500
4d Sq Sta Wag	300	850	1,400	2,850	4,950	7,100
2d HT Cobra	920	2,760	4,600	9,200	16,100	23,000
2d HT GT	640	1,920	3,200	6,400	11,200	16,000
2d Conv	740	2,220	3,700	7,400	12,950	18,500

1971 Custom, V-8, 121" wb

	6	5	4	3	2	1
4d Sed	184	552	920	1,840	3,220	4,600
4d Sta Wag	300	850	1,400	2,800	4,900	7,000

1971 Custom 500, V-8, 121" wb

	6	5	4	3	2	1
4d Sed	188	564	940	1,880	3,290	4,700
4d Sta Wag	300	850	1,400	2,850	4,950	7,100

1971 Galaxie 500, V-8, 121" wb

	6	5	4	3	2	1
4d Sed	196	588	980	1,960	3,430	4,900
4d HT	200	600	1,000	2,000	3,500	5,000
2d HT	220	660	1,100	2,200	3,850	5,500
4d Sta Wag	300	900	1,500	2,950	5,200	7,400

1971 LTD

	6	5	4	3	2	1
4d Sed	200	600	1,000	2,000	3,500	5,000
4d HT	204	612	1,020	2,040	3,570	5,100
2d HT	220	660	1,100	2,200	3,850	5,500
2d Conv	540	1,620	2,700	5,400	9,450	13,500
Ctry Sq	450	1,300	2,200	4,400	7,700	11,000

1971 LTD Brougham, V-8, 121" wb

	6	5	4	3	2	1
4d Sed	204	612	1,020	2,040	3,570	5,100

	6	5	4	3	2	1
4d HT	220	660	1,100	2,200	3,850	5,500
2d HT	360	1,080	1,800	3,600	6,300	9,000

NOTE: Add 40 percent for 429 engine option.

1972 Pinto

	6	5	4	3	2	1
2d Sed	176	528	880	1,760	3,080	4,400
3d HBk	180	540	900	1,800	3,150	4,500
2d Wag	184	552	920	1,840	3,220	4,600

1972 Maverick

	6	5	4	3	2	1
4d Sed	176	528	880	1,760	3,080	4,400
2d Sed	180	540	900	1,800	3,150	4,500
2d Grabber Sed	196	588	980	1,960	3,430	4,900

NOTE: Deduct 20 percent for 6-cyl.

1972 Torino, V-8, 118" wb, 2d 114" wb

	6	5	4	3	2	1
4d Sed	176	528	880	1,760	3,080	4,400
2d HT	260	780	1,300	2,600	4,550	6,500
4d Sta Wag	250	700	1,150	2,300	4,000	5,700

1972 Gran Torino

	6	5	4	3	2	1
4d	180	540	900	1,800	3,150	4,500
2d HT	380	1,140	1,900	3,800	6,650	9,500

1972 Gran Torino Sport, V-8

	6	5	4	3	2	1
2d HT Formal	420	1,260	2,100	4,200	7,350	10,500
2d HT Sports	400	1,200	2,000	4,000	7,000	10,000
4d Sta Wag	250	800	1,300	2,600	4,550	6,500

1972 Custom, V-8, 121" wb

	6	5	4	3	2	1
4d Sed	184	552	920	1,840	3,220	4,600
4d Sta Wag	250	700	1,200	2,400	4,200	6,000

1972 Custom 500, V-8, 121" wb

	6	5	4	3	2	1
4d Sed	188	564	940	1,880	3,290	4,700
4d Sta Wag	250	800	1,300	2,600	4,550	6,500

1972 Galaxie 500, V-8, 121" wb

	6	5	4	3	2	1
4d Sed	192	576	960	1,920	3,360	4,800
4d HT	240	720	1,200	2,400	4,200	6,000
2d HT	360	1,080	1,800	3,600	6,300	9,000
4d Sta Wag	300	850	1,400	2,800	4,900	7,000

1972 LTD, V-8, 121" wb

	6	5	4	3	2	1
4d Sed	196	588	980	1,960	3,430	4,900
4d HT	208	624	1,040	2,080	3,640	5,200
2d HT	380	1,140	1,900	3,800	6,650	9,500
2d Conv	580	1,740	2,900	5,800	10,150	14,500
4d Sta Wag	300	850	1,450	2,900	5,050	7,200

1972 LTD Brougham, V-8, 121" wb

	6	5	4	3	2	1
4d Sed	200	600	1,000	2,000	3,500	5,000
4d HT	268	804	1,340	2,680	4,690	6,700
2d HT	400	1,200	2,000	4,000	7,000	10,000

NOTE: Add 40 percent for 429 engine option. Add 30 percent for 460 engine option.

1973 Pinto, 4-cyl.

	6	5	4	3	2	1
2d Sed	152	456	760	1,520	2,660	3,800
2d Rbt	156	468	780	1,560	2,730	3,900
2d Sta Wag	160	480	800	1,600	2,800	4,000

1973 Maverick, V-8

	6	5	4	3	2	1
2d Sed	150	500	800	1,650	2,850	4,100
4d Sed	168	504	840	1,680	2,940	4,200
2d Grabber Sed	188	564	940	1,880	3,290	4,700

1973 Torino, V-8

	6	5	4	3	2	1
4d Sed	156	468	780	1,560	2,730	3,900
2d HT	240	720	1,200	2,400	4,200	6,000
4d Sta Wag	164	492	820	1,640	2,870	4,100

1973 Gran Torino, V-8

	6	5	4	3	2	1
4d	160	480	800	1,600	2,800	4,000
2d HT	260	780	1,300	2,600	4,550	6,500
4d Sta Wag	200	600	1,050	2,100	3,650	5,200

1973 Gran Torino Sport, V-8

	6	5	4	3	2	1
2d SR HT	400	1,200	2,000	4,000	7,000	10,000
2d FR HT	420	1,260	2,100	4,200	7,350	10,500
4d Sq Wag	250	800	1,300	2,600	4,550	6,500

1973 Gran Torino Brgm, V-8

	6	5	4	3	2	1
4d	164	492	820	1,640	2,870	4,100
2d HT	400	1,200	2,000	4,000	7,000	10,000

1973 Custom 500, V-8

	6	5	4	3	2	1
4d	164	492	820	1,640	2,870	4,100

	6	5	4	3	2	1
4d Sta Wag	250	700	1,200	2,400	4,200	6,000

1973 Galaxie 500, V-8

	6	5	4	3	2	1
4d	168	504	840	1,680	2,940	4,200
2d HT	228	684	1,140	2,280	3,990	5,700
4d HT	172	516	860	1,720	3,010	4,300
4d Sta Wag	250	800	1,300	2,600	4,550	6,500

1973 LTD, V-8

	6	5	4	3	2	1
4d	172	516	860	1,720	3,010	4,300
2d HT	240	720	1,200	2,400	4,200	6,000
4d HT	180	540	900	1,800	3,150	4,500
4d Sta Wag	300	850	1,400	2,800	4,900	7,000

1973 LTD Brgm, V-8

	6	5	4	3	2	1
4d	176	528	880	1,760	3,080	4,400
2d HT	260	780	1,300	2,600	4,550	6,500
4d HT	220	660	1,100	2,200	3,850	5,500

NOTE: Add 30 percent for 429 engine option. Add 30 percent for 460 engine option.

1974 Pinto

	6	5	4	3	2	1
2d Sed	152	456	760	1,520	2,660	3,800
3d HBk	156	468	780	1,560	2,730	3,900
2d Sta Wag	150	500	800	1,600	2,800	4,000

1974 Maverick, V-8

	6	5	4	3	2	1
2d Sed	164	492	820	1,640	2,870	4,100
4d Sed	168	504	840	1,680	2,940	4,200
2d Grabber Sed	176	528	880	1,760	3,080	4,400

1974 Torino, V-8

	6	5	4	3	2	1
4d Sed	164	492	820	1,640	2,870	4,100
2d HT	228	684	1,140	2,280	3,990	5,700
4d Sta Wag	200	600	1,000	2,000	3,500	5,000

1974 Gran Torino, V-8

	6	5	4	3	2	1
4d Sed	168	504	840	1,680	2,940	4,200
2d HT	244	732	1,220	2,440	4,270	6,100
4d Sta Wag	200	600	1,000	2,050	3,550	5,100

1974 Gran Torino Sport, V-8

	6	5	4	3	2	1
2d HT	264	792	1,320	2,640	4,620	6,600

1974 Gran Torino Brgm, V-8

	6	5	4	3	2	1
4d Sed	172	516	860	1,720	3,010	4,300
2d HT	240	720	1,200	2,400	4,200	6,000

1974 Gran Torino Elite, V-8

	6	5	4	3	2	1
2d HT	260	780	1,300	2,600	4,550	6,500

1974 Gran Torino Squire, V-8

	6	5	4	3	2	1
4d Sta Wag	200	650	1,100	2,250	3,900	5,600

1974 Custom 500

	6	5	4	3	2	1
4d Sed	160	480	800	1,600	2,800	4,000
4d Sta Wag	200	650	1,100	2,200	3,850	5,500

1974 Galaxie 500, V-8

	6	5	4	3	2	1
4d Sed	164	492	820	1,640	2,870	4,100
2d HT	188	564	940	1,880	3,290	4,700
4d HT	176	528	880	1,760	3,080	4,400
4d Sta Wag	200	650	1,100	2,250	3,900	5,600

1974 LTD, V-8

	6	5	4	3	2	1
2d HT	200	600	1,000	2,000	3,500	5,000
4d Sed	168	504	840	1,680	2,940	4,200
4d HT	180	540	900	1,800	3,150	4,500
4d Sta Wag	250	800	1,300	2,600	4,550	6,500

1974 LTD Brgm, V-8

	6	5	4	3	2	1
4d Sed	168	504	840	1,680	2,940	4,200
2d HT	220	660	1,100	2,200	3,850	5,500
4d HT	200	600	1,000	2,000	3,500	5,000

NOTE: Add 30 percent for 460 engine option.

1975 Pinto

	6	5	4	3	2	1
2d Sed	160	480	800	1,600	2,800	4,000
3d HBk	164	492	820	1,640	2,870	4,100
2d Sta Wag	200	550	900	1,800	3,150	4,500

1975 Maverick

	6	5	4	3	2	1
2d Sed	176	528	880	1,760	3,080	4,400
4d Sed	180	540	900	1,800	3,150	4,500
2d Grabber Sed	184	552	920	1,840	3,220	4,600

1975 Torino

	6	5	4	3	2	1
2d Cpe	180	540	900	1,800	3,150	4,500
4d Sed	160	480	800	1,600	2,800	4,000
4d Sta Wag	164	492	820	1,640	2,870	4,100

1975 Gran Torino

	6	5	4	3	2	1
2d Cpe	184	552	920	1,840	3,220	4,600
4d Sed	168	504	840	1,680	2,940	4,200
4d Sta Wag	168	504	840	1,680	2,940	4,200

1975 Gran Torino Brougham

	6	5	4	3	2	1
2d Cpe	192	576	960	1,920	3,360	4,800
4d Sed	208	624	1,040	2,080	3,640	5,200

1975 Gran Torino Sport

	6	5	4	3	2	1
2d HT	200	600	1,000	2,000	3,500	5,000

1975 Torino Squire

	6	5	4	3	2	1
4d Sta Wag	200	650	1,100	2,200	3,850	5,500

1975 Elite

	6	5	4	3	2	1
2d HT	220	660	1,100	2,200	3,850	5,500

1975 Granada

	6	5	4	3	2	1
2d Cpe	172	516	860	1,720	3,010	4,300
4d Sed	148	444	740	1,480	2,590	3,700
2d Ghia Cpe	184	552	920	1,840	3,220	4,600
4d Ghia Sed	180	540	900	1,800	3,150	4,500

1975 Custom 500

	6	5	4	3	2	1
4d Sed	164	492	820	1,640	2,870	4,100
4d Sta Wag	164	492	820	1,640	2,870	4,100

1975 LTD

	6	5	4	3	2	1
2d Cpe	176	528	880	1,760	3,080	4,400
4d Sed	168	504	840	1,680	2,940	4,200

1975 LTD Brougham

	6	5	4	3	2	1
2d Cpe	180	540	900	1,800	3,150	4,500
4d Sed	172	516	860	1,720	3,010	4,300

1975 LTD Landau

	6	5	4	3	2	1
2d Cpe	188	564	940	1,880	3,290	4,700
4d Sed	176	528	880	1,760	3,080	4,400

1975 LTD Station Wagon

	6	5	4	3	2	1
4d Sta Wag	200	600	1,050	2,100	3,650	5,200
4d Ctry Sq	250	700	1,150	2,300	4,000	5,700

NOTE: Add 30 percent for 460 engine option.

1976 Pinto, 4-cyl.

	6	5	4	3	2	1
2d Sed	140	420	700	1,400	2,450	3,500
2d Rbt	144	432	720	1,440	2,520	3,600
2d Sta Wag	148	444	740	1,480	2,590	3,700
2d Sq Wag	152	456	760	1,520	2,660	3,800

NOTE: Add 10 percent for V-6.

1976 Maverick, V-8

	6	5	4	3	2	1
4d Sed	136	408	680	1,360	2,380	3,400
2d Sed	132	396	660	1,320	2,310	3,300

NOTE: Deduct 5 percent for 6-cyl.

1976 Torino, V-8

	6	5	4	3	2	1
4d Sed	140	420	700	1,400	2,450	3,500
2d HT	144	432	720	1,440	2,520	3,600

1976 Gran Torino, V-8

	6	5	4	3	2	1
4d Sed	144	432	720	1,440	2,520	3,600
2d HT	148	444	740	1,480	2,590	3,700

1976 Gran Torino Brougham, V-8

	6	5	4	3	2	1
4d Sed	148	444	740	1,480	2,590	3,700
2d HT	152	456	760	1,520	2,660	3,800

1976 Station Wagons, V-8

	6	5	4	3	2	1
4d 2S Torino	200	550	900	1,800	3,150	4,500
4d 2S Gran Torino	200	550	900	1,850	3,200	4,600
4d 2S Gran Torino Sq	200	550	950	1,900	3,300	4,700

1976 Granada, V-8

	6	5	4	3	2	1
4d Sed	128	384	640	1,280	2,240	3,200
2d Sed	132	396	660	1,320	2,310	3,300

1976 Granada Ghia, V-8

	6	5	4	3	2	1
4d Sed	132	396	660	1,320	2,310	3,300
2d Sed	136	408	680	1,360	2,380	3,400

Standard Catalog of® Ford

	6	5	4	3	2	1
1976 Elite, V-8						
2d HT	148	444	740	1,480	2,590	3,700
1976 Custom, V-8						
4d Sed	136	408	680	1,360	2,380	3,400
1976 LTD, V-8						
4d Sed	144	432	720	1,440	2,520	3,600
2d Sed	152	456	760	1,520	2,660	3,800
1976 LTD Brougham, V-8						
4d Sed	152	456	760	1,520	2,660	3,800
2d Sed	160	480	800	1,600	2,800	4,000
1976 LTD Landau, V-8						
4d Sed	160	480	800	1,600	2,800	4,000
2d Sed	168	504	840	1,680	2,940	4,200
1976 Station Wagons, V-8						
4d Ranch Wag	200	600	1,000	1,950	3,450	4,900
4d LTD Wag	200	600	1,050	2,100	3,650	5,200
4d Ctry Sq Wag	250	700	1,150	2,300	4,000	5,700
1977 Pinto, 4-cyl.						
2d Sed	144	432	720	1,440	2,520	3,600
2d Rbt	148	444	740	1,480	2,590	3,700
2d Sta Wag	150	500	850	1,700	2,950	4,200
2d Sq Wag	150	500	850	1,700	3,000	4,300
NOTE: Add 5 percent for V-6.						
1977 Maverick, V-8						
4d Sed	140	420	700	1,400	2,450	3,500
2d Sed	136	408	680	1,360	2,380	3,400
NOTE: Deduct 5 percent for 6-cyl.						
1977 Granada, V-8						
4d Sed	128	384	640	1,280	2,240	3,200
2d Sed	132	396	660	1,320	2,310	3,300
1977 Granada Ghia, V-8						
4d Sed	136	408	680	1,360	2,380	3,400
2d Sed	140	420	700	1,400	2,450	3,500
1977 LTD II "S", V-8						
4d Sed	132	396	660	1,320	2,310	3,300
2d Sed	136	408	680	1,360	2,380	3,400
1977 LTD II, V-8						
4d Sed	136	408	680	1,360	2,380	3,400
2d Sed	140	420	700	1,400	2,450	3,500
1977 LTD II Brougham, V-8						
4d Sed	144	432	720	1,440	2,520	3,600
2d Sed	148	444	740	1,480	2,590	3,700
1977 Station Wagons, V-8						
4d 2S LTD II	200	550	900	1,800	3,150	4,500
4d 3S LTD II	200	550	900	1,850	3,200	4,600
4d 3S LTD II Sq	200	600	950	1,900	3,350	4,800
1977 LTD, V-8						
4d Sed	148	444	740	1,480	2,590	3,700
2d Sed	152	456	760	1,520	2,660	3,800
1977 LTD Landau, V-8						
4d Sed	156	468	780	1,560	2,730	3,900
2d Sed	160	480	800	1,600	2,800	4,000
1977 Station Wagons, V-8						
4d 2S LTD	250	700	1,150	2,300	4,050	5,800
4d 3S LTD	250	700	1,200	2,350	4,150	5,900
4d 3S Ctry Sq	250	700	1,200	2,400	4,200	6,000
1978 Fiesta						
2d HBk	112	336	560	1,120	1,960	2,800
1978 Pinto						
2d	116	348	580	1,160	2,030	2,900
3d Rbt	144	432	720	1,440	2,520	3,600
2d Sta Wag	148	444	740	1,480	2,590	3,700
1978 Fairmont						
4d Sed	124	372	620	1,240	2,170	3,100
2d Sed	120	360	600	1,200	2,100	3,000
2d Cpe Futura	150	450	700	1,450	2,500	3,600
4d Sta Wag	150	400	700	1,400	2,450	3,500

	6	5	4	3	2	1
1978 Granada						
4d Sed	128	384	640	1,280	2,240	3,200
2d Sed	124	372	620	1,240	2,170	3,100
1978 LTD II "S"						
4d Sed	100	350	600	1,250	2,150	3,100
2d Cpe	100	350	600	1,200	2,100	3,000
1978 LTD II						
4d Sed	128	384	640	1,280	2,240	3,200
2d Cpe	124	372	620	1,240	2,170	3,100
1978 LTD II Brougham						
4d Sed	132	396	660	1,320	2,310	3,300
2d Cpe	128	384	640	1,280	2,240	3,200
1978 LTD						
4d	144	432	720	1,440	2,520	3,600
2d Cpe	148	444	740	1,480	2,590	3,700
4d 2S Sta Wag	250	700	1,200	2,400	4,200	6,000
1978 LTD Landau						
4d Sed	152	456	760	1,520	2,660	3,800
2d Cpe	156	468	780	1,560	2,730	3,900
1979 Fiesta, 4-cyl.						
3d HBk	116	348	580	1,160	2,030	2,900
1979 Pinto, V-6						
2d Sed	124	372	620	1,240	2,170	3,100
2d Rbt	144	432	720	1,440	2,520	3,600
2d Sta Wag	144	432	720	1,440	2,520	3,600
2d Sq Wag	148	444	740	1,480	2,590	3,700
NOTE: Deduct 5 percent for 4-cyl.						
1979 Fairmont, 6-cyl.						
4d Sed	128	384	640	1,280	2,240	3,200
2d Sed	124	372	620	1,240	2,170	3,100
2d Cpe	144	432	720	1,440	2,520	3,600
4d Sta Wag	132	396	660	1,320	2,310	3,300
4d Sq Wag	136	408	680	1,360	2,380	3,400
NOTE: Deduct 5 percent for 4-cyl. Add 5 percent for V-8.						
1979 Granada, V-8						
4d Sed	132	396	660	1,320	2,310	3,300
2d Sed	128	384	640	1,280	2,240	3,200
NOTE: Deduct 5 percent for 6-cyl.						
1979 LTD II, V-8						
4d Sed	128	384	640	1,280	2,240	3,200
2d Sed	124	372	620	1,240	2,170	3,100
1979 LTD II Brougham, V-8						
4d Sed	132	396	660	1,320	2,310	3,300
2d Sed	128	384	640	1,280	2,240	3,200
1979 LTD, V-8						
4d Sed	144	432	720	1,440	2,520	3,600
2d Sed	136	408	680	1,360	2,380	3,400
4d 2S Sta Wag	140	420	700	1,400	2,450	3,500
4d 3S Sta Wag	144	432	720	1,440	2,520	3,600
4d 2S Sq Wag	148	444	740	1,480	2,590	3,700
4d 3S Sq Wag	152	456	760	1,520	2,660	3,800
1979 LTD Landau						
4d Sed	152	456	760	1,520	2,660	3,800
2d Sed	144	432	720	1,440	2,520	3,600
1980 Fiesta, 4-cyl.						
2d HBk	124	372	620	1,240	2,170	3,100
1980 Pinto, 4-cyl.						
2d Cpe Pony	128	384	640	1,280	2,240	3,200
2d Sta Wag Pony	136	408	680	1,360	2,380	3,400
2d Cpe	132	396	660	1,320	2,310	3,300
2d HBk	136	408	680	1,360	2,380	3,400
2d Sta Wag	140	420	700	1,400	2,450	3,500
2d Sta Wag Sq	144	432	720	1,440	2,520	3,600
1980 Fairmont, 6-cyl.						
4d Sed	136	408	680	1,360	2,380	3,400
2d Sed	132	396	660	1,320	2,310	3,300
4d Sed Futura	144	432	720	1,440	2,520	3,600
2d Cpe Futura	164	492	820	1,640	2,870	4,100
4d Sta Wag	152	456	760	1,520	2,660	3,800
NOTE: Deduct 10 percent for 4-cyl. Add 12 percent for V-8.						

1980 Granada, V-8

	6	5	4	3	2	1
4d Sed	156	468	780	1,560	2,730	3,900
2d Sed	152	456	760	1,520	2,660	3,800
4d Sed Ghia	164	492	820	1,640	2,870	4,100
2d Sed Ghia	160	480	800	1,600	2,800	4,000
4d Sed ESS	168	504	840	1,680	2,940	4,200
2d Sed ESS	164	492	820	1,640	2,870	4,100

NOTE: Deduct 10 percent for 6-cyl.

1980 LTD, V-8

	6	5	4	3	2	1
4d Sed S	168	504	840	1,680	2,940	4,200
4d Sta Wag	176	528	880	1,760	3,080	4,400
4d Sed	172	516	860	1,720	3,010	4,300
2d Sed	168	504	840	1,680	2,940	4,200
4d Sta Wag	180	540	900	1,800	3,150	4,500
4d Sta Wag CS	188	564	940	1,880	3,290	4,700

1980 LTD Crown Victoria, V-8

	6	5	4	3	2	1
4d Sed	184	552	920	1,840	3,220	4,600
2d Sed	180	540	900	1,800	3,150	4,500

1981 Escort, 4-cyl.

	6	5	4	3	2	1
2d HBk SS	144	432	720	1,440	2,520	3,600
4d HBk SS	148	444	740	1,480	2,590	3,700

NOTE: Deduct 5 percent for lesser models.

1981 Fairmont, 6-cyl.

	6	5	4	3	2	1
2d Sed S	136	408	680	1,360	2,380	3,400
4d Sed	140	420	700	1,400	2,450	3,500
2d Sed	140	420	700	1,400	2,450	3,500
4d Futura	144	432	720	1,440	2,520	3,600
2d Cpe Futura	168	504	840	1,680	2,940	4,200
4d Sta Wag	156	468	780	1,560	2,730	3,900
4d Sta Wag Futura	160	480	800	1,600	2,800	4,000

NOTE: Deduct 10 percent for 4-cyl. Add 12 percent for V-8.

1981 Granada, 6-cyl.

	6	5	4	3	2	1
4d Sed GLX	160	480	800	1,600	2,800	4,000
2d Sed GLX	156	468	780	1,560	2,730	3,900

NOTE: Deduct 5 percent for lesser models. Deduct 10 percent for 4-cyl. Add 12 percent for V-8.

1981 LTD, V-8

	6	5	4	3	2	1
4d Sed S	172	516	860	1,720	3,010	4,300
4d Sta Wag S	180	540	900	1,800	3,150	4,500
4d Sed	176	528	880	1,760	3,080	4,400
2d Sed	172	516	860	1,720	3,010	4,300
4d Sta Wag	184	552	920	1,840	3,220	4,600
4d Sta Wag CS	192	576	960	1,920	3,360	4,800

1981 LTD Crown Victoria, V-8

	6	5	4	3	2	1
4d Sed	192	576	960	1,920	3,360	4,800
2d Sed	188	564	940	1,880	3,290	4,700

NOTE: Deduct 15 percent for 6-cyl.

1982 Escort, 4-cyl.

	6	5	4	3	2	1
2d HBk GLX	144	432	720	1,440	2,520	3,600
4d HBk GLX	148	444	740	1,480	2,590	3,700
4d Sta Wag GLX	152	456	760	1,520	2,660	3,800
2d HBk GT	156	468	780	1,560	2,730	3,900

NOTE: Deduct 5 percent for lesser models.

1982 EXP, 4-cyl.

	6	5	4	3	2	1
2d Cpe	180	540	900	1,800	3,150	4,500

1982 Fairmont Futura, 4-cyl.

	6	5	4	3	2	1
4d Sed	120	360	600	1,200	2,100	3,000
2d Sed	116	348	580	1,160	2,030	2,900
2d Cpe Futura	132	396	660	1,320	2,310	3,300

1982 Fairmont Futura, 6-cyl.

	6	5	4	3	2	1
4d Sed	148	444	740	1,480	2,590	3,700
2d Cpe Futura	172	516	860	1,720	3,010	4,300

1982 Granada, 6-cyl.

	6	5	4	3	2	1
4d Sed GLX	164	492	820	1,640	2,870	4,100
2d Sed GLX	160	480	800	1,600	2,800	4,000

NOTE: Deduct 10 percent for 4-cyl. Deduct 5 percent for lesser models.

1982 Granada Wagon, 6-cyl.

	6	5	4	3	2	1
4d Sta Wag GL	172	516	860	1,720	3,010	4,300

1982 LTD, V-8

	6	5	4	3	2	1
4d Sed S	176	528	880	1,760	3,080	4,400
4d Sed	180	540	900	1,800	3,150	4,500
2d Sed	176	528	880	1,760	3,080	4,400

1982 LTD Crown Victoria, V-8

	6	5	4	3	2	1
4d Sed	196	588	980	1,960	3,430	4,900
2d Sed	192	576	960	1,920	3,360	4,800

1982 LTD Station Wagon, V-8

	6	5	4	3	2	1
4d Sta Wag S	184	552	920	1,840	3,220	4,600
4d Sta Wag	188	564	940	1,880	3,290	4,700
4d Sta Wag CS	196	588	980	1,960	3,430	4,900

NOTE: Deduct 15 percent for V-6.

1983 Escort, 4-cyl.

	6	5	4	3	2	1
2d HBk GLX	144	432	720	1,440	2,520	3,600
4d HBk GLX	148	444	740	1,480	2,590	3,700
4d Sta Wag GLX	152	456	760	1,520	2,660	3,800
2d HBk GT	148	444	740	1,480	2,590	3,700

NOTE: Deduct 5 percent for lesser models.

1983 EXP, 4-cyl.

	6	5	4	3	2	1
2d Cpe	180	540	900	1,800	3,150	4,500

1983 Fairmont Futura, 6-cyl.

	6	5	4	3	2	1
4d Sed	148	444	740	1,480	2,590	3,700
2d Sed	144	432	720	1,440	2,520	3,600
2d Cpe	172	516	860	1,720	3,010	4,300

NOTE: Deduct 5 percent for 4-cyl.

1983 LTD, 6-cyl.

	6	5	4	3	2	1
4d Sed	168	504	840	1,680	2,940	4,200
4d Sed Brgm	176	528	880	1,760	3,080	4,400
4d Sta Wag	184	552	920	1,840	3,220	4,600

NOTE: Deduct 10 percent for 4-cyl.

1983 LTD Crown Victoria, V-8

	6	5	4	3	2	1
4d Sed	200	600	1,000	2,000	3,500	5,000
2d Sed	196	588	980	1,960	3,430	4,900
4d Sta Wag	204	612	1,020	2,040	3,570	5,100

1984 Escort, 4-cyl.

	6	5	4	3	2	1
4d HBk LX	140	420	700	1,400	2,450	3,500
2d HBk LX	140	420	700	1,400	2,450	3,500
4d Sta Wag LX	144	432	720	1,440	2,520	3,600
2d HBk GT	144	432	720	1,440	2,520	3,600
2d HBk Turbo GT	152	456	760	1,520	2,660	3,800

NOTE: Deduct 5 percent for lesser models.

1984 EXP, 4-cyl.

	6	5	4	3	2	1
2d Cpe	160	480	800	1,600	2,800	4,000
2d Cpe L	168	504	840	1,680	2,940	4,200
2d Cpe Turbo	184	552	920	1,840	3,220	4,600

1984 Tempo, 4-cyl.

	6	5	4	3	2	1
2d Sed GLX	140	420	700	1,400	2,450	3,500
4d Sed GLX	140	420	700	1,400	2,450	3,500

NOTE: Deduct 5 percent for lesser models.

1984 LTD, V-6

	6	5	4	3	2	1
4d Sed	168	504	840	1,680	2,940	4,200
4d Sed Brgm	172	516	860	1,720	3,010	4,300
4d Sta Wag	172	516	860	1,720	3,010	4,300
4d Sed LX, (V-8)	184	552	920	1,840	3,220	4,600

NOTE: Deduct 8 percent for 4-cyl.

1984 LTD Crown Victoria, V-8

	6	5	4	3	2	1
4d Sed S	188	564	940	1,880	3,290	4,700
4d Sed	196	588	980	1,960	3,430	4,900
2d Sed	196	588	980	1,960	3,430	4,900
4d Sta Wag S	200	600	1,000	2,000	3,500	5,000
4d Sta Wag	204	612	1,020	2,040	3,570	5,100
4d Sta Wag Sq	208	624	1,040	2,080	3,640	5,200

1985 Escort, 4-cyl.

	6	5	4	3	2	1
4d HBk LX	144	432	720	1,440	2,520	3,600
4d Sta Wag LX	144	432	720	1,440	2,520	3,600
2d HBk GT	148	444	740	1,480	2,590	3,700
2d HBk Turbo GT	156	468	780	1,560	2,730	3,900

NOTE: Deduct 5 percent for lesser models.

1985 EXP, 4-cyl.

	6	5	4	3	2	1
2d Cpe HBk	164	492	820	1,640	2,870	4,100
2d Cpe HBk Luxury	172	516	860	1,720	3,010	4,300
2d Cpe HBk Turbo	188	564	940	1,880	3,290	4,700

NOTE: Deduct 20 percent for diesel.

1985 Tempo, 4-cyl.

	6	5	4	3	2	1
2d Sed GLX	140	420	700	1,400	2,450	3,500

	6	5	4	3	2	1
4d Sed GLX	140	420	700	1,400	2,450	3,500

NOTE: Deduct 5 percent for lesser models. Deduct 20 percent for diesel.

1985 LTD

	6	5	4	3	2	1
4d V-6 Sed	172	516	860	1,720	3,010	4,300
4d V-6 Sed Brgm	176	528	880	1,760	3,080	4,400
4d V-6 Sta Wag	176	528	880	1,760	3,080	4,400
4d V-8 Sed LX	188	564	940	1,880	3,290	4,700

NOTE: Deduct 20 percent for 4-cyl. where available.

1985 LTD Crown Victoria, V-8

	6	5	4	3	2	1
4d Sed S	192	576	960	1,920	3,360	4,800
4d Sed	200	600	1,000	2,000	3,500	5,000
2d Sed	196	588	980	1,960	3,430	4,900
4d Sta Wag S	204	612	1,020	2,040	3,570	5,100
4d Sta Wag	208	624	1,040	2,080	3,640	5,200
4d Sta Wag Ctry Sq	216	648	1,080	2,160	3,780	5,400

1986 Escort

	6	5	4	3	2	1
2d HBk	144	432	720	1,440	2,520	3,600
4d HBk	140	420	700	1,400	2,450	3,500
4d Sta Wag	148	444	740	1,480	2,590	3,700
2d GT HBk	160	480	800	1,600	2,800	4,000

1986 EXP

	6	5	4	3	2	1
2d Cpe	184	552	920	1,840	3,220	4,600

1986 Tempo

	6	5	4	3	2	1
2d Sed	144	432	720	1,440	2,520	3,600
4d Sed	144	432	720	1,440	2,520	3,600

1986 Taurus

	6	5	4	3	2	1
4d Sed	188	564	940	1,880	3,290	4,700
4d Sta Wag	192	576	960	1,920	3,360	4,800

1986 LTD

	6	5	4	3	2	1
4d Sed	208	624	1,040	2,080	3,640	5,200
4d Brgm Sed	208	624	1,040	2,080	3,640	5,200
4d Sta Wag	216	648	1,080	2,160	3,780	5,400

1986 LTD Crown Victoria

	6	5	4	3	2	1
2d Sed	216	648	1,080	2,160	3,780	5,400
4d Sed	216	648	1,080	2,160	3,780	5,400
4d Sta Wag	220	660	1,100	2,200	3,850	5,500

NOTE: Add 10 percent for deluxe models. Deduct 5 percent for smaller engines.

1987 Escort, 4-cyl.

	6	5	4	3	2	1
2d HBk Pony	148	444	740	1,480	2,590	3,700
2d HBk GL	152	456	760	1,520	2,660	3,800
4d HBk GL	156	468	780	1,560	2,730	3,900
4d Sta Wag GL	156	468	780	1,560	2,730	3,900
2d HBk GT	160	480	800	1,600	2,800	4,000

1987 EXP, 4-cyl.

	6	5	4	3	2	1
2d HBk LX	188	564	940	1,880	3,290	4,700
2d HBk Spt	192	576	960	1,920	3,360	4,800

1987 Tempo

	6	5	4	3	2	1
2d Sed GL	148	444	740	1,480	2,590	3,700
4d Sed GL	152	456	760	1,520	2,660	3,800
2d Sed GL Spt	152	456	760	1,520	2,660	3,800
4d Sed GL Spt	156	468	780	1,560	2,730	3,900
2d Sed LX	156	468	780	1,560	2,730	3,900
4d Sed LX	160	480	800	1,600	2,800	4,000
2d Sed 4WD	180	540	900	1,800	3,150	4,500
4d Sed 4WD	184	552	920	1,840	3,220	4,600

1987 Taurus, 4-cyl.

	6	5	4	3	2	1
4d Sed	192	576	960	1,920	3,360	4,800
4d Sta Wag	196	588	980	1,960	3,430	4,900

1987 Taurus, V-6

	6	5	4	3	2	1
4d Sed L	196	588	980	1,960	3,430	4,900
4d Sta Wag L	200	600	1,000	2,000	3,500	5,000
4d Sed GL	200	600	1,000	2,000	3,500	5,000
4d Sta Wag GL	204	612	1,020	2,040	3,570	5,100
4d Sed LX	204	612	1,020	2,040	3,570	5,100
4d Sta Wag LX	208	624	1,040	2,080	3,640	5,200

1987 LTD Crown Victoria, V-8

	6	5	4	3	2	1
4d Sed S	220	660	1,100	2,200	3,850	5,500
4d Sta Wag S	224	672	1,120	2,240	3,920	5,600
4d Sed	224	672	1,120	2,240	3,920	5,600
2d Cpe	220	660	1,100	2,200	3,850	5,500
4d Sta Wag	224	672	1,120	2,240	3,920	5,600
4d Sta Wag Ctry Sq	232	696	1,160	2,320	4,060	5,800
4d Sed LX	228	684	1,140	2,280	3,990	5,700

	6	5	4	3	2	1
2d Cpe LX	224	672	1,120	2,240	3,920	5,600
4d Sta Wag LX	228	684	1,140	2,280	3,990	5,700
4d Sta Wag Ctry Sq LX	250	700	1,200	2,350	4,150	5,900

1988 Festiva, 4-cyl.

	6	5	4	3	2	1
2d HBk L	92	276	460	920	1,610	2,300
2d HBk L Plus	100	300	500	1,000	1,750	2,500
2d HBk LX	116	348	580	1,160	2,030	2,900

1988 Escort, 4-cyl.

	6	5	4	3	2	1
2d HBk Pony	88	264	440	880	1,540	2,200
2d HBk GL	100	300	500	1,000	1,750	2,500
4d HBk GL	104	312	520	1,040	1,820	2,600
4d Sta Wag GL	116	348	580	1,160	2,030	2,900
2d HBk GT	140	420	700	1,400	2,450	3,500
2d HBk LX	112	336	560	1,120	1,960	2,800
4d HBk LX	116	348	580	1,160	2,030	2,900
4d Sta Wag LX	124	372	620	1,240	2,170	3,100

1988 EXP, 4-cyl.

	6	5	4	3	2	1
2d HBk	120	360	600	1,200	2,100	3,000

1988 Tempo, 4-cyl.

	6	5	4	3	2	1
2d Sed GL	132	396	660	1,320	2,310	3,300
4d Sed GL	140	420	700	1,400	2,450	3,500
2d Sed GLS	140	420	700	1,400	2,450	3,500
4d Sed GLS	144	432	720	1,440	2,520	3,600
4d Sed LX	148	444	740	1,480	2,590	3,700
4d Sed 4x4	180	540	900	1,800	3,150	4,500

1988 Taurus, 4-cyl., V-6

	6	5	4	3	2	1
4d Sed	168	504	840	1,680	2,940	4,200
4d Sed L	176	528	880	1,760	3,080	4,400
4d Sta Wag L	184	552	920	1,840	3,220	4,600
4d Sed GL	180	540	900	1,800	3,150	4,500
4d Sta Wag GL	200	600	1,000	2,000	3,500	5,000
4d Sed LX	220	660	1,100	2,200	3,850	5,500
4d Sta Wag LX	228	684	1,140	2,280	3,990	5,700

1988 LTD Crown Victoria, V-8

	6	5	4	3	2	1
4d Sed	204	612	1,020	2,040	3,570	5,100
4d Sta Wag	212	636	1,060	2,120	3,710	5,300
4d Ctry Sq Sta Wag	232	696	1,160	2,320	4,060	5,800
4d Sed S	212	636	1,060	2,120	3,710	5,300
4d Sed LX	216	648	1,080	2,160	3,780	5,400
4d Sta Wag LX	220	660	1,100	2,200	3,850	5,500
4d Ctry Sq Sta Wag	240	720	1,200	2,400	4,200	6,000

1989 Festiva, 4-cyl.

	6	5	4	3	2	1
2d HBk L	128	384	640	1,280	2,240	3,200
2d HBk L Plus	132	396	660	1,320	2,310	3,300
2d HBk LX	136	408	680	1,360	2,380	3,400

1989 Escort, 4-cyl.

	6	5	4	3	2	1
2d HBk Pony	132	396	660	1,320	2,310	3,300
2d HBk LX	136	408	680	1,360	2,380	3,400
2d HBk GT	152	456	760	1,520	2,660	3,800
4d HBk LX	140	420	700	1,400	2,450	3,500
4d Sta Wag LX	144	432	720	1,440	2,520	3,600

1989 Tempo, 4-cyl.

	6	5	4	3	2	1
2d Sed GL	140	420	700	1,400	2,450	3,500
4d Sed GL	144	432	720	1,440	2,520	3,600
2d Sed GLS	152	456	760	1,520	2,660	3,800
4d Sed GLS	156	468	780	1,560	2,730	3,900
4d Sed LX	168	504	840	1,680	2,940	4,200
4d Sed 4x4	192	576	960	1,920	3,360	4,800

1989 Probe, 4-cyl.

	6	5	4	3	2	1
2d GL HBk	200	600	1,000	2,000	3,500	5,000
2d LX HBk	220	660	1,100	2,200	3,850	5,500
2d GT Turbo HBk	240	720	1,200	2,400	4,200	6,000

1989 Taurus, 4-cyl.

	6	5	4	3	2	1
4d Sed L	184	552	920	1,840	3,220	4,600
4d Sed GL	188	564	940	1,880	3,290	4,700

1989 V-6

	6	5	4	3	2	1
4d Sed L	192	576	960	1,920	3,360	4,800
4d Sta Wag L	200	600	1,000	2,000	3,500	5,000
4d Sed GL	204	612	1,020	2,040	3,570	5,100
4d Sta Wag GL	240	720	1,200	2,400	4,200	6,000
4d Sed LX	232	696	1,160	2,320	4,060	5,800
4d Sta Wag LX	360	1,080	1,800	3,600	6,300	9,000
4d Sed SHO	400	1,200	2,000	4,000	7,000	10,000

1989 LTD Crown Victoria, V-8

	6	5	4	3	2	1
4d Sed S	220	660	1,100	2,200	3,850	5,500

	6	5	4	3	2	1
4d Sed	228	684	1,140	2,280	3,990	5,700
4d Sed LX	252	756	1,260	2,520	4,410	6,300
4d Sta Wag	256	768	1,280	2,560	4,480	6,400
4d Sta Wag LX	260	780	1,300	2,600	4,550	6,500
4d Ctry Sq Sta Wag	264	792	1,320	2,640	4,620	6,600
4d Ctry Sq LX Sta Wag	250	800	1,350	2,700	4,700	6,700

1990 Festiva, 4-cyl.

	6	5	4	3	2	1
2d	112	336	560	1,120	1,960	2,800
2d L	120	360	600	1,200	2,100	3,000
2d LX	140	420	700	1,400	2,450	3,500

1990 Escort, 4-cyl.

	6	5	4	3	2	1
2d Pony HBk	120	360	600	1,200	2,100	3,000
2d LX HBk	140	420	700	1,400	2,450	3,500
4d LX HBk	144	432	720	1,440	2,520	3,600
4d LX Sta Wag	152	456	760	1,520	2,660	3,800
2d GT HBk	164	492	820	1,640	2,870	4,100

1990 Tempo, 4-cyl.

	6	5	4	3	2	1
2d GL Sed	144	432	720	1,440	2,520	3,600
4d GL Sed	148	444	740	1,480	2,590	3,700
2d GLS Sed	160	480	800	1,600	2,800	4,000
4d GLS Sed	164	492	820	1,640	2,870	4,100
4d LX Sed	168	504	840	1,680	2,940	4,200
4d Sed 4x4	220	660	1,100	2,200	3,850	5,500

1990 Probe

	6	5	4	3	2	1
2d GL HBk, 4-cyl.	220	660	1,100	2,200	3,850	5,500
2d LX HBk, V-6	260	780	1,300	2,600	4,550	6,500
2d GT HBk, Turbo	360	1,080	1,800	3,600	6,300	9,000

1990 Taurus, 4-cyl.

	6	5	4	3	2	1
4d L Sed	160	480	800	1,600	2,800	4,000
4d GL Sed	168	504	840	1,680	2,940	4,200

1990 V-6

	6	5	4	3	2	1
4d L Sed	188	564	940	1,880	3,290	4,700
4d L Sta Wag	200	600	1,000	2,000	3,500	5,000
4d GL Sed	196	588	980	1,960	3,430	4,900
4d GL Sta Wag	208	624	1,040	2,080	3,640	5,200
4d LX Sed	232	696	1,160	2,320	4,060	5,800
4d LX Sta Wag	256	768	1,280	2,560	4,480	6,400
4d SHO Sed	360	1,080	1,800	3,600	6,300	9,000

1990 LTD Crown Victoria, V-8

	6	5	4	3	2	1
4d S Sed	220	660	1,100	2,200	3,850	5,500
4d Sed	240	720	1,200	2,400	4,200	6,000
4d LX Sed	260	780	1,300	2,600	4,550	6,500
4d Sta Wag	232	696	1,160	2,320	4,060	5,800
4d LX Sta Wag	248	744	1,240	2,480	4,340	6,200
4d Ctry Sq Sta Wag	260	780	1,300	2,600	4,550	6,500
4d LX Ctry Sq Sta Wag	250	800	1,350	2,700	4,750	6,800

1991 Festiva, 4-cyl.

	6	5	4	3	2	1
2d HBk	124	372	620	1,240	2,170	3,100
2d GL HBk	132	396	660	1,320	2,310	3,300

1991 Escort, 4-cyl.

	6	5	4	3	2	1
2d Pony HBk	140	420	700	1,400	2,450	3,500
2d LX HBk	148	444	740	1,480	2,590	3,700
4d LX HBk	148	444	740	1,480	2,590	3,700
4d LX Sta Wag	156	468	780	1,560	2,730	3,900
2d GT HBk	164	492	820	1,640	2,870	4,100

1991 Tempo, 4-cyl.

	6	5	4	3	2	1
2d L Sed	144	432	720	1,440	2,520	3,600
4d L Sed	144	432	720	1,440	2,520	3,600
2d GL Sed	152	456	760	1,520	2,660	3,800
4d GL Sed	152	456	760	1,520	2,660	3,800
2d GLS Sed	160	480	800	1,600	2,800	4,000
4d GLS Sed	160	480	800	1,600	2,800	4,000
4d LX Sed	168	504	840	1,680	2,940	4,200
4d Sed 4x4	200	600	1,000	2,000	3,500	5,000

1991 Probe, 4-cyl.

	6	5	4	3	2	1
2d GL HBk	188	564	940	1,880	3,290	4,700
2d LX HBk	220	660	1,100	2,200	3,850	5,500
2d GT HBk Turbo	240	720	1,200	2,400	4,200	6,000

1991 Taurus, 4-cyl.

	6	5	4	3	2	1
4d L Sed	144	432	720	1,440	2,520	3,600
4d GL Sed	152	456	760	1,520	2,660	3,800

1991 Taurus, V-6

	6	5	4	3	2	1
4d L Sed	152	456	760	1,520	2,660	3,800
4d L Sta Wag	180	540	900	1,800	3,150	4,500
4d GL Sed	168	504	840	1,680	2,940	4,200
4d GL Sta Wag	220	660	1,100	2,200	3,850	5,500
4d LX Sed	208	624	1,040	2,080	3,640	5,200
4d LX Sta Wag	260	780	1,300	2,600	4,550	6,500
4d SHO Sed	380	1,140	1,900	3,800	6,650	9,500

1991 LTD Crown Victoria, V-8

	6	5	4	3	2	1
4d S Sed	180	540	900	1,800	3,150	4,500
4d Sed	220	660	1,100	2,200	3,850	5,500
4d LX Sed	240	720	1,200	2,400	4,200	6,000
4d 3S Sta Wag	196	588	980	1,960	3,430	4,900
4d 2S Sta Wag	236	708	1,180	2,360	4,130	5,900
4d LX 3S Sta Wag	256	768	1,280	2,560	4,480	6,400
4d Ctry Sq 3S Sta Wag	200	600	1,050	2,100	3,650	5,200
4d Ctry Sq 2S Sta Wag	250	750	1,250	2,500	4,350	6,200
4d Ctry Sq LX 3S Sta Wag	250	800	1,350	2,700	4,700	6,700

1992 Festiva, 4-cyl.

	6	5	4	3	2	1
2d L HBk	140	420	700	1,400	2,450	3,500
2d GL HBk	152	456	760	1,520	2,660	3,800

1992 Escort, 4-cyl.

	6	5	4	3	2	1
2d HBk	168	504	840	1,680	2,940	4,200
2d LX HBk	168	504	840	1,680	2,940	4,200
4d LX HBk	168	504	840	1,680	2,940	4,200
4d LX Sed	160	480	800	1,600	2,800	4,000
4d LX Sta Wag	176	528	880	1,760	3,080	4,400
4d LX-E Sta Wag	180	540	900	1,800	3,150	4,500
2d GT HBk	200	600	1,000	2,000	3,500	5,000

1992 Tempo, 4-cyl.

	6	5	4	3	2	1
2d GL Cpe	152	456	760	1,520	2,660	3,800
4d GL Sed	156	468	780	1,560	2,730	3,900
4d LX Sed	160	480	800	1,600	2,800	4,000
2d GLS Sed V-6	220	660	1,100	2,200	3,850	5,500
4d GLS Sed V-6	220	660	1,100	2,200	3,850	5,500

1992 Probe, 4-cyl.

	6	5	4	3	2	1
2d GL HBk	220	660	1,100	2,200	3,850	5,500
2d LX HBk V-6	256	768	1,280	2,560	4,480	6,400
2d GT HBk Turbo	260	780	1,300	2,600	4,550	6,500

1992 Taurus, V-6

	6	5	4	3	2	1
4d L Sed	200	600	1,000	2,000	3,500	5,000
4d L Sta Wag	200	600	1,000	2,000	3,500	5,000
4d GL Sed	220	660	1,100	2,200	3,850	5,500
4d GL Sta Wag	220	660	1,100	2,200	3,850	5,500
4d LX Sed	240	720	1,200	2,400	4,200	6,000
4d LX Sta Wag	240	720	1,200	2,400	4,200	6,000
4d SHO Sed	420	1,260	2,100	4,200	7,350	10,500

1992 Crown Victoria, V-8

	6	5	4	3	2	1
4d S Sed	240	720	1,200	2,400	4,200	6,000
4d Sed	260	780	1,300	2,600	4,550	6,500
4d LX Sed	380	1,140	1,900	3,800	6,650	9,500
4d Trg Sed	320	960	1,600	3,200	5,600	8,000

1993 Festiva, 4-cyl.

	6	5	4	3	2	1
2d Sed	144	432	720	1,440	2,520	3,600

1993 Escort, 4-cyl.

	6	5	4	3	2	1
2d HBk	172	516	860	1,720	3,010	4,300
2d LX HBk	176	528	880	1,760	3,080	4,400
2d GT HBk	180	540	900	1,800	3,150	4,500
4d HBk	176	528	880	1,760	3,080	4,400
4d LX Sed	180	540	900	1,800	3,150	4,500
4d LXE Sed	184	552	920	1,840	3,220	4,600
4d LX Sta Wag	188	564	940	1,880	3,290	4,700

1993 Tempo, 4-cyl.

	6	5	4	3	2	1
2d GL Sed	168	504	840	1,680	2,940	4,200
4d GL Sed	172	516	860	1,720	3,010	4,300
4d LX Sed	180	540	900	1,800	3,150	4,500

1993 Probe

	6	5	4	3	2	1
2d HBk, 4-cyl.	244	732	1,220	2,440	4,270	6,100
2d GT HBk, V-6	256	768	1,280	2,560	4,480	6,400

1993 Taurus, V-6

	6	5	4	3	2	1
4d GL Sed	248	744	1,240	2,480	4,340	6,200
4d LX Sed	252	756	1,260	2,520	4,410	6,300
4d GL Sta Wag	264	792	1,320	2,640	4,620	6,600
4d LX Sta Wag	268	804	1,340	2,680	4,690	6,700
4d SHO Sed	380	1,140	1,900	3,800	6,650	9,500

1993 Crown Victoria, V-8

	6	5	4	3	2	1
4d Sed S	284	852	1,420	2,840	4,970	7,100
4d Sed	292	876	1,460	2,920	5,110	7,300

	6	5	4	3	2	1
4d LX Sed	296	888	1,480	2,960	5,180	7,400

1994 Aspire, 4-cyl.

	6	5	4	3	2	1
2d HBk	128	384	640	1,280	2,240	3,200
2d SE HBk	140	420	700	1,400	2,450	3,500
4d HBk	136	408	680	1,360	2,380	3,400

1994 Escort, 4-cyl.

	6	5	4	3	2	1
2d HBk	156	468	780	1,560	2,730	3,900
2d LX HBk	180	540	900	1,800	3,150	4,500
4d LX HBk	180	540	900	1,800	3,150	4,500
2d GT HBk	200	600	1,000	2,000	3,500	5,000
4d LX Sed	188	564	940	1,880	3,290	4,700
4d LX Sta Wag	192	576	960	1,920	3,360	4,800

1994 Tempo, 4-cyl.

	6	5	4	3	2	1
2d GL Sed	168	504	840	1,680	2,940	4,200
4d GL Sed	172	516	860	1,720	3,010	4,300
4d LX Sed	180	540	900	1,800	3,150	4,500

1994 Probe

	6	5	4	3	2	1
2d HbK, 4-cyl.	250	750	1,200	2,450	4,250	6,100
2d GT HBk, V-6	250	750	1,300	2,550	4,500	6,400

1994 Taurus, V-6

	6	5	4	3	2	1
4d GL Sed	250	750	1,250	2,500	4,350	6,200
4d LX Sed	250	750	1,250	2,500	4,400	6,300
4d GL Sta Wag	250	800	1,300	2,650	4,600	6,600
4d LX Sta Wag	250	800	1,350	2,700	4,700	6,700
4d SHO Sed	400	1,150	1,900	3,800	6,650	9,500

1994 Crown Victoria, V-8

	6	5	4	3	2	1
4d Sed S	288	864	1,440	2,880	5,040	7,200
4d Sed	300	900	1,500	3,000	5,250	7,500
4d LX Sed	320	960	1,600	3,200	5,600	8,000

1995 Aspire, 4-cyl.

	6	5	4	3	2	1
2d HBk	150	400	650	1,300	2,250	3,200
2d SE HBk	150	400	700	1,400	2,450	3,500
4d HBk	150	400	700	1,350	2,400	3,400

1995 Escort, 4-cyl.

	6	5	4	3	2	1
2d HBk	150	450	800	1,550	2,750	3,900
2d LX HBk	200	550	900	1,800	3,150	4,500
4d LX HBk	200	550	900	1,800	3,150	4,500
4d LX Sed	200	550	950	1,900	3,300	4,700
4d LX Sta Wag	200	600	950	1,900	3,350	4,800
2d GT HBk	200	600	1,000	2,000	3,500	5,000

1995 Contour, 4-cyl. & V-6

	6	5	4	3	2	1
4d GL Sed	200	600	1,050	2,100	3,650	5,200
4d LX Sed	200	650	1,050	2,100	3,700	5,300
4d SE Sed (V-6 only)	200	650	1,100	2,250	3,900	5,600

1995 Probe, 4-cyl. & V-6

	6	5	4	3	2	1
2d HBk, 4-cyl.	250	750	1,200	2,450	4,250	6,100
2d GT HBk, V-6	250	750	1,300	2,550	4,500	6,400

1995 Taurus, V-6

	6	5	4	3	2	1
4d GL Sed	250	750	1,250	2,500	4,350	6,200
4d GL Sta Wag	250	800	1,300	2,650	4,600	6,600
4d LX Sed	250	750	1,250	2,500	4,400	6,300
4d LX Sta Wag	250	800	1,350	2,700	4,700	6,700
4d SE Sed	250	750	1,300	2,550	4,500	6,400
4d SHO Sed	400	1,150	1,900	3,800	6,650	9,500

1995 Crown Victoria, V-8

	6	5	4	3	2	1
4d S Sed	300	850	1,450	2,900	5,050	7,200
4d Sed	300	900	1,500	3,000	5,250	7,500
4d LX Sed	300	950	1,600	3,200	5,600	8,000

EDSEL

1958 Ranger Series, V-8, 118" wb

	6	5	4	3	2	1
2d Sed	540	1,620	2,700	5,400	9,450	13,500
4d Sed	540	1,620	2,700	5,400	9,450	13,500
4d HT	580	1,740	2,900	5,800	10,150	14,500
2d HT	680	2,040	3,400	6,800	11,900	17,000

1958 Pacer Series, V-8, 118" wb

	6	5	4	3	2	1
4d Sed	560	1,680	2,800	5,600	9,800	14,000
4d HT	600	1,800	3,000	6,000	10,500	15,000

	6	5	4	3	2	1
2d HT	720	2,160	3,600	7,200	12,600	18,000
2d Conv	1,200	3,600	6,000	12,000	21,000	30,000

1958 Corsair Series, V-8, 124" wb

	6	5	4	3	2	1
4d HT	640	1,920	3,200	6,400	11,200	16,000
2d HT	760	2,280	3,800	7,600	13,300	19,000

1958 Citation Series, V-8, 124" wb

	6	5	4	3	2	1
4d HT	720	2,160	3,600	7,200	12,600	18,000
2d HT	840	2,520	4,200	8,400	14,700	21,000
2d Conv	1,400	4,200	7,000	14,000	24,500	35,000

NOTE: Deduct 5 percent for 6-cyl.

1958 Station Wagons, V-8

	6	5	4	3	2	1
4d Vill	600	1,800	3,000	6,000	10,500	15,000
4d Ber	620	1,860	3,100	6,200	10,850	15,500
4d 9P Vill	608	1,824	3,040	6,080	10,640	15,200
4d 9P Ber	620	1,860	3,100	6,200	10,850	15,500
2d Rdup	560	1,680	2,800	5,600	9,800	14,000

1959 Ranger Series, V-8, 120" wb

	6	5	4	3	2	1
2d Sed	528	1,584	2,640	5,280	9,240	13,200
4d Sed	520	1,560	2,600	5,200	9,100	13,000
4d HT	580	1,740	2,900	5,800	10,150	14,500
2d HT	680	2,040	3,400	6,800	11,900	17,000

1959 Corsair Series, V-8, 120" wb

	6	5	4	3	2	1
4d Sed	540	1,620	2,700	5,400	9,450	13,500
4d HT	600	1,800	3,000	6,000	10,500	15,000
2d HT	720	2,160	3,600	7,200	12,600	18,000
2d Conv	1,160	3,480	5,800	11,600	20,300	29,000

1959 Station Wagons, V-8, 118" wb

	6	5	4	3	2	1
4d Vill	560	1,680	2,800	5,600	9,800	14,000
4d 9P Vill	580	1,740	2,900	5,800	10,150	14,500

NOTE: Deduct 5 percent for 6-cyl.

1960 Ranger Series, V-8, 120" wb

	6	5	4	3	2	1
2d Sed	528	1,584	2,640	5,280	9,240	13,200
4d Sed	524	1,572	2,620	5,240	9,170	13,100
4d HT	580	1,740	2,900	5,800	10,150	14,500
2d HT	920	2,760	4,600	9,200	16,100	23,000
2d Conv	1,320	3,960	6,600	13,200	23,100	33,000

1960 Station Wagons, V-8, 120" wb

	6	5	4	3	2	1
4d 9P Vill	600	1,800	3,000	6,000	10,500	15,000
4d 6P Vill	600	1,800	3,000	6,000	10,500	15,000

NOTE: Deduct 5 percent for 6-cyl.

LINCOLN

1920 V-8, 130" - 136" wb

	6	5	4	3	2	1
3P Rds	1,960	5,880	9,800	19,600	34,300	49,000
5P Phae	2,080	6,240	10,400	20,800	36,400	52,000
7P Tr	2,000	6,000	10,000	20,000	35,000	50,000
4P Cpe	1,500	4,500	7,500	15,000	26,250	37,500
5P Sed	1,460	4,380	7,300	14,600	25,550	36,500
Sub Sed	1,460	4,380	7,300	14,600	25,550	36,500
7P Town Car	1,540	4,620	7,700	15,400	26,950	38,500

1921 V-8, 130" - 136" wb

	6	5	4	3	2	1
3P Rds	1,920	5,760	9,600	19,200	33,600	48,000
5P Phae	2,000	6,000	10,000	20,000	35,000	50,000
7P Tr	1,960	5,880	9,800	19,600	34,300	49,000
4P Cpe	1,500	4,500	7,500	15,000	26,250	37,500
4P Sed	1,420	4,260	7,100	14,200	24,850	35,500
5P Sed	1,460	4,380	7,300	14,600	25,550	36,500
Sub Sed	1,460	4,380	7,300	14,600	25,550	36,500
Town Car	1,540	4,620	7,700	15,400	26,950	38,500

1922 V-8, 130" wb

	6	5	4	3	2	1
3P Rds	2,040	6,120	10,200	20,400	35,700	51,000
5P Phae	1,960	5,880	9,800	19,600	34,300	49,000
7P Tr	1,920	5,760	9,600	19,200	33,600	48,000
Conv Tr	1,960	5,880	9,800	19,600	34,300	49,000
4P Cpe	1,540	4,620	7,700	15,400	26,950	38,500
5P Sed	1,500	4,500	7,500	15,000	26,250	37,500

1922 V-8, 136" wb

	6	5	4	3	2	1
Spt Rds	2,000	6,000	10,000	20,000	35,000	50,000
DeL Phae	2,040	6,120	10,200	20,400	35,700	51,000
DeL Tr	1,960	5,880	9,800	19,600	34,300	49,000

	6	5	4	3	2	1
Std Sed	1,540	4,620	7,700	15,400	26,950	38,500
Jud Sed	1,580	4,740	7,900	15,800	27,650	39,500
FW Sed	1,580	4,740	7,900	15,800	27,650	39,500
York Sed	1,580	4,740	7,900	15,800	27,650	39,500
4P Jud Sed	1,620	4,860	8,100	16,200	28,350	40,500
7P Jud Limo	1,720	5,160	8,600	17,200	30,100	43,000
Sub Limo	1,800	5,400	9,000	18,000	31,500	45,000
Town Car	1,840	5,520	9,200	18,400	32,200	46,000
FW Limo	1,920	5,760	9,600	19,200	33,600	48,000
Std Limo	1,840	5,520	9,200	18,400	32,200	46,000
FW Cabr	2,120	6,360	10,600	21,200	37,100	53,000
FW Coll Cabr	2,320	6,960	11,600	23,200	40,600	58,000
FW Lan'let	1,920	5,760	9,600	19,200	33,600	48,000
FW Town Car	2,000	6,000	10,000	20,000	35,000	50,000
Holbrk Cabr	2,120	6,360	10,600	21,200	37,100	53,000
Brn Town Car	1,920	5,760	9,600	19,200	33,600	48,000
Brn OD Limo	2,000	6,000	10,000	20,000	35,000	50,000

1923 Model L, V-8

	6	5	4	3	2	1
Tr	1,920	5,760	9,600	19,200	33,600	48,000
Phae	1,960	5,880	9,800	19,600	34,300	49,000
Rds	1,920	5,760	9,600	19,200	33,600	48,000
Cpe	1,620	4,860	8,100	16,200	28,350	40,500
5P Sed	1,580	4,740	7,900	15,800	27,650	39,500
7P Sed	1,620	4,860	8,100	16,200	28,350	40,500
Limo	1,800	5,400	9,000	18,000	31,500	45,000
OD Limo	1,840	5,520	9,200	18,400	32,200	46,000
Town Car	1,880	5,640	9,400	18,800	32,900	47,000
4P Sed	1,540	4,620	7,700	15,400	26,950	38,500
Berl	1,580	4,740	7,900	15,800	27,650	39,500
FW Cabr	1,880	5,640	9,400	18,800	32,900	47,000
FW Limo	1,840	5,520	9,200	18,400	32,200	46,000
FW Town Car	1,880	5,640	9,400	18,800	32,900	47,000
Jud Cpe	1,620	4,860	8,100	16,200	28,350	40,500
Brn Town Car	1,880	5,640	9,400	18,800	32,900	47,000
Brn OD Limo	1,920	5,760	9,600	19,200	33,600	48,000
Jud 2W Berl	1,620	4,860	8,100	16,200	28,350	40,500
Jud 3W Berl	1,620	4,860	8,100	16,200	28,350	40,500
Holbrk Cabr	2,120	6,360	10,600	21,200	37,100	53,000

1924 V-8

	6	5	4	3	2	1
Tr	1,920	5,760	9,600	19,200	33,600	48,000
Phae	1,960	5,880	9,800	19,600	34,300	49,000
Rds	2,000	6,000	10,000	20,000	35,000	50,000
Cpe	1,660	4,980	8,300	16,600	29,050	41,500
5P Sed	1,580	4,740	7,900	15,800	27,650	39,500
7P Sed	1,540	4,620	7,700	15,400	26,950	38,500
Limo	1,620	4,860	8,100	16,200	28,350	40,500
4P Sed	1,540	4,620	7,700	15,400	26,950	38,500
Town Car	1,720	5,160	8,600	17,200	30,100	43,000
Twn Limo	1,760	5,280	8,800	17,600	30,800	44,000
FW Limo	1,800	5,400	9,000	18,000	31,500	45,000
Jud Cpe	1,580	4,740	7,900	15,800	27,650	39,500
Jud Berl	1,620	4,860	8,100	16,200	28,350	40,500
Brn Cabr	1,880	5,640	9,400	18,800	32,900	47,000
Brn Cpe	1,620	4,860	8,100	16,200	28,350	40,500
Brn OD Limo	1,800	5,400	9,000	18,000	31,500	45,000
Leb Sed	1,840	5,520	9,200	18,400	32,200	46,000

1925 Model L, V-8

	6	5	4	3	2	1
Tr	2,040	6,120	10,200	20,400	35,700	51,000
Spt Tr	2,200	6,600	11,000	22,000	38,500	55,000
Phae	2,080	6,240	10,400	20,800	36,400	52,000
Rds	2,040	6,120	10,200	20,400	35,700	51,000
Cpe	1,680	5,040	8,400	16,800	29,400	42,000
4P Sed	1,320	3,960	6,600	13,200	23,100	33,000
5P Sed	1,280	3,840	6,400	12,800	22,400	32,000
7P Sed	1,280	3,840	6,400	12,800	22,400	32,000
Limo	1,680	5,040	8,400	16,800	29,400	42,000
FW Limo	1,720	5,160	8,600	17,200	30,100	43,000
Jud Cpe	1,540	4,620	7,700	15,400	26,950	38,500
Jud Berl	1,580	4,740	7,900	15,800	27,650	39,500
Brn Cabr	2,080	6,240	10,400	20,800	36,400	52,000
FW Coll Clb Rds	2,040	6,120	10,200	20,400	35,700	51,000
FW Sed	1,840	5,520	9,200	18,400	32,200	46,000
FW Brgm	1,880	5,640	9,400	18,800	32,900	47,000
FW Cabr	2,000	6,000	10,000	20,000	35,000	50,000
3W Jud Berl	1,880	5,640	9,400	18,800	32,900	47,000
4P Jud Cpe	1,880	5,640	9,400	18,800	32,900	47,000
Jud Brgm	1,840	5,520	9,200	18,400	32,200	46,000
Mur OD Limo	2,000	6,000	10,000	20,000	35,000	50,000
Holbrk Brgm	1,920	5,760	9,600	19,200	33,600	48,000
Holbrk Coll	1,960	5,880	9,800	19,600	34,300	49,000
Brn OD Limo	1,960	5,880	9,800	19,600	34,300	49,000
Brn Spt Phae	2,200	6,600	11,000	22,000	38,500	55,000
Brn Lan Sed	1,960	5,880	9,800	19,600	34,300	49,000
Brn Town Car	2,000	6,000	10,000	20,000	35,000	50,000
Brn Pan Brgm	1,960	5,880	9,800	19,600	34,300	49,000
Hume Limo	2,040	6,120	10,200	20,400	35,700	51,000

	6	5	4	3	2	1
Hume Cpe	1,880	5,640	9,400	18,800	32,900	47,000
5P Leb Sed	2,000	6,000	10,000	20,000	35,000	50,000
4P Leb Sed	1,920	5,760	9,600	19,200	33,600	48,000
Leb DC Phae	2,640	7,920	13,200	26,400	46,200	66,000
Leb Clb Rds	2,320	6,960	11,600	23,200	40,600	58,000
Leb Limo	1,920	5,760	9,600	19,200	33,600	48,000
Leb Brgm	1,960	5,880	9,800	19,600	34,300	49,000
Leb Twn Brgm	2,000	6,000	10,000	20,000	35,000	50,000
Leb Cabr	2,120	6,360	10,600	21,200	37,100	53,000
Leb Coll Spt Cabr	2,320	6,960	11,600	23,200	40,600	58,000
Lke Cabr	2,240	6,720	11,200	22,400	39,200	56,000
Dtrch Coll Cabr	2,280	6,840	11,400	22,800	39,900	57,000

1926 Model L, V-8

	6	5	4	3	2	1
Tr	2,200	6,600	11,000	22,000	38,500	55,000
Spt Tr	2,400	7,200	12,000	24,000	42,000	60,000
Phae	2,320	6,960	11,600	23,200	40,600	58,000
Rds	2,240	6,720	11,200	22,400	39,200	56,000
Cpe	1,500	4,500	7,500	15,000	26,250	37,500
4P Sed	1,320	3,960	6,600	13,200	23,100	33,000
5P Sed	1,280	3,840	6,400	12,800	22,400	32,000
7P Sed	1,280	3,840	6,400	12,800	22,400	32,000
Limo	1,540	4,620	7,700	15,400	26,950	38,500
FW Limo	1,580	4,740	7,900	15,800	27,650	39,500
Jud Cpe	1,800	5,400	9,000	18,000	31,500	45,000
Jud Berl	1,760	5,280	8,800	17,600	30,800	44,000
Brn Cabr	2,160	6,480	10,800	21,600	37,800	54,000
Holbrk Coll Cabr	2,200	6,600	11,000	22,000	38,500	55,000
Hume Limo	1,760	5,280	8,800	17,600	30,800	44,000
W'by Limo	1,760	5,280	8,800	17,600	30,800	44,000
W'by Lan'let	1,800	5,400	9,000	18,000	31,500	45,000
Dtrch Sed	1,680	5,040	8,400	16,800	29,400	42,000
Dtrch Coll Cabr	2,240	6,720	11,200	22,400	39,200	56,000
Dtrch Brgm	1,840	5,520	9,200	18,400	32,200	46,000
Dtrch Cpe Rds	2,200	6,600	11,000	22,000	38,500	55,000
3W Jud Berl	1,720	5,160	8,600	17,200	30,100	43,000
Jud Brgm	1,680	5,040	8,400	16,800	29,400	42,000
Brn Phae	2,160	6,480	10,800	21,600	37,800	54,000
Brn Sed	1,660	4,980	8,300	16,600	29,050	41,500
Brn Brgm	1,680	5,040	8,400	16,800	29,400	42,000
Brn Semi-Coll Cabr	2,150	6,500	10,800	21,600	37,800	54,000
2W LeB Sed	1,660	4,980	8,300	16,600	29,050	41,500
3W LeB Sed	1,660	4,980	8,300	16,600	29,050	41,500
LeB Cpe	1,720	5,160	8,600	17,200	30,100	43,000
LeB Spt Cabr	2,200	6,600	11,000	22,000	38,500	55,000
LeB A-W Cabr	2,120	6,360	10,600	21,200	37,100	53,000
LeB Limo	1,800	5,400	9,000	18,000	31,500	45,000
LeB Clb Rds	2,240	6,720	11,200	22,400	39,200	56,000
Lke Rds	2,320	6,960	11,600	23,200	40,600	58,000
Lke Semi-Coll Cabr	2,100	6,350	10,600	21,200	37,100	53,000
Lke Cabr	2,240	6,720	11,200	22,400	39,200	56,000
LeB Conv Phae	2,320	6,960	11,600	23,200	40,600	58,000
LeB Conv	2,320	6,960	11,600	23,200	40,600	58,000

1927 Model L, V-8

	6	5	4	3	2	1
Spt Rds	2,880	8,640	14,400	28,800	50,400	72,000
Spt Tr	2,800	8,400	14,000	28,000	49,000	70,000
Phae	2,960	8,880	14,800	29,600	51,800	74,000
Cpe	1,720	5,160	8,600	17,200	30,100	43,000
2W Sed	1,360	4,080	6,800	13,600	23,800	34,000
3W Sed	1,320	3,960	6,600	13,200	23,100	33,000
Sed	1,280	3,840	6,400	12,800	22,400	32,000
FW Limo	1,840	5,520	9,200	18,400	32,200	46,000
Jud Cpe	1,800	5,400	9,000	18,000	31,500	45,000
Brn Cabr	2,800	8,400	14,000	28,000	49,000	70,000
Holbrk Cabr	2,960	8,880	14,800	29,600	51,800	74,000
Brn Brgm	2,160	6,480	10,800	21,600	37,800	54,000
Dtrch Conv Sed	3,040	9,120	15,200	30,400	53,200	76,000
Dtrch Conv Vic	3,040	9,120	15,200	30,400	53,200	76,000
Brn Conv	2,880	8,640	14,400	28,800	50,400	72,000
Brn Semi-Coll Cabr	2,950	8,900	14,800	29,600	51,800	74,000
Holbrk Coll Cabr	3,040	9,120	15,200	30,400	53,200	76,000
LeB A-W Cabr	3,040	9,120	15,200	30,400	53,200	76,000
LeB A-W Brgm	3,040	9,120	15,200	30,400	53,200	76,000
W'by Semi-Coll Cabr	2,950	8,900	14,800	29,600	51,800	74,000
Jud Brgm	2,160	6,480	10,800	21,600	37,800	54,000
Clb Rds	2,320	6,960	11,600	23,200	40,600	58,000
2W Jud Berl	1,720	5,160	8,600	17,200	30,100	43,000
3W Jud Berl	1,720	5,160	8,600	17,200	30,100	43,000
7P E d Limo	1,880	5,640	9,400	18,800	32,900	47,000
LeB Spt Cabr	3,040	9,120	15,200	30,400	53,200	76,000
W'by Lan'let	2,800	8,400	14,000	28,000	49,000	70,000
W'by Limo	1,920	5,760	9,600	19,200	33,600	48,000
LeB Cpe	1,840	5,520	9,200	18,400	32,200	46,000
Der Spt Sed	1,800	5,400	9,000	18,000	31,500	45,000
Lke Conv Sed	3,040	9,120	15,200	30,400	53,200	76,000
Dtrch Cpe Rds	2,960	8,880	14,800	29,600	51,800	74,000
Dtrch Spt Phae	3,040	9,120	15,200	30,400	53,200	76,000

1928 Model L, V-8

	6	5	4	3	2	1
164 Spt Tr	3,360	10,080	16,800	33,600	58,800	84,000
163 Lke Spt Phae	3,520	10,560	17,600	35,200	61,600	88,000
151 Lke Spt Rds	3,440	10,320	17,200	34,400	60,200	86,000
154 Clb Rds	3,280	9,840	16,400	32,800	57,400	82,000
156 Cpe	2,080	6,240	10,400	20,800	36,400	52,000
144W 2W Sed	1,360	4,080	6,800	13,600	23,800	34,000
144B Sed	1,360	4,080	6,800	13,600	23,800	34,000
152 Sed	1,320	3,960	6,600	13,200	23,100	33,000
147A Sed	1,320	3,960	6,600	13,200	23,100	33,000
147B Limo	2,080	6,240	10,400	20,800	36,400	52,000
161 Jud Berl	2,160	6,480	10,800	21,600	37,800	54,000
161C Jud Berl	2,160	6,480	10,800	21,600	37,800	54,000
Jud Cpe	2,320	6,960	11,600	23,200	40,600	58,000
159 Brn Cabr	3,360	10,080	16,800	33,600	58,800	84,000
145 Brn Brgm	2,800	8,400	14,000	28,000	49,000	70,000
155A Hlbrk Coll Cabr	3,500	10,600	17,600	35,200	61,500	88,000
155 LeB Spt Cabr	3,920	11,760	19,600	39,200	68,600	98,000
157 W'by Lan'let Berl	3,500	10,600	17,600	35,200	61,500	88,000
160 W'by Limo	3,760	11,280	18,800	37,600	65,800	94,000
162A LeB A-W Cabr	3,600	10,800	18,000	36,000	63,000	90,000
162 LeB A-W Lan'let	3,450	10,300	17,200	34,400	60,000	86,000
Jud Spt Cpe	3,200	9,600	16,000	32,000	56,000	80,000
LeB Cpe	3,360	10,080	16,800	33,600	58,800	84,000
Dtrch Conv Vic	3,760	11,280	18,800	37,600	65,800	94,000
Dtrch Cpe Rds	3,840	11,520	19,200	38,400	67,200	96,000
Dtrch Conv Sed	3,920	11,760	19,600	39,200	68,600	98,000
Holbrk Cabr	3,840	11,520	19,200	38,400	67,200	96,000
W'by Spt Sed	2,000	6,000	10,000	20,000	35,000	50,000
Der Spt Sed	2,000	6,000	10,000	20,000	35,000	50,000
Brn Spt Conv	3,440	10,320	17,200	34,400	60,200	86,000

1929 Model L, V-8 Standard Line

	6	5	4	3	2	1
Lke Spt Rds	3,760	11,280	18,800	37,600	65,800	94,000
Clb Rds	3,680	11,040	18,400	36,800	64,400	92,000
Lke Spt Phae	4,000	12,000	20,000	40,000	70,000	100,000
Lke TWS Spt Phae	4,400	13,200	22,000	44,000	77,000	110,000
Lke Spt Phae TC & WS	4,560	13,680	22,800	45,600	79,800	114,000
Lke Spt Tr	3,840	11,520	19,200	38,400	67,200	96,000
Lke Clb Rds	4,160	12,480	20,800	41,600	72,800	104,000
4P Cpe	2,120	6,360	10,600	21,200	37,100	53,000
Twn Sed	1,400	4,200	7,000	14,000	24,500	35,000
5P Sed	1,360	4,080	6,800	13,600	23,800	34,000
7P Sed	1,320	3,960	6,600	13,200	23,100	33,000
7P Limo	2,080	6,240	10,400	20,800	36,400	52,000
2W Jud Berl	2,240	6,720	11,200	22,400	39,200	56,000
3W Jud Berl	2,200	6,600	11,000	22,000	38,500	55,000
Brn A-W Brgm	3,520	10,560	17,600	35,200	61,600	88,000
Brn Cabr	3,680	11,040	18,400	36,800	64,400	92,000
Brn Non-Coll Cabr	3,520	10,560	17,600	35,200	61,600	88,000
Holbrk Coll Cabr	3,920	11,760	19,600	39,200	68,600	98,000
LeB A-W Cabr	4,000	12,000	20,000	40,000	70,000	100,000
LeB Semi-Coll Cabr	3,500	10,600	17,600	35,200	61,500	88,000
LeB Coll Cabr	3,920	11,760	19,600	39,200	68,600	98,000
W'by Lan'let	2,960	8,880	14,800	29,600	51,800	74,000
W'by Limo	2,800	8,400	14,000	28,000	49,000	70,000
Dtrch Cpe	2,560	7,680	12,800	25,600	44,800	64,000
Dtrch Sed	2,560	7,680	12,800	25,600	44,800	64,000
Dtrch Conv	3,760	11,280	18,800	37,600	65,800	94,000
LeB Spt Sed	2,640	7,920	13,200	26,400	46,200	66,000
LeB Aero Phae	3,760	11,280	18,800	37,600	65,800	94,000
LeB Sal Cabr	3,680	11,040	18,400	36,800	64,400	92,000
Brn Spt Conv	3,760	11,280	18,800	37,600	65,800	94,000
Dtrch Conv Sed	3,920	11,760	19,600	39,200	68,600	98,000
Dtrch Conv Vic	4,000	12,000	20,000	40,000	70,000	100,000

1930 Model L, V-8 Standard Line

	6	5	4	3	2	1
Conv Rds	3,760	11,280	18,800	37,600	65,800	94,000
5P Lke Spt Phae	4,160	12,480	20,800	41,600	72,800	104,000
5P Lke Spt Phae TC & WS	4,240	12,720	21,200	42,400	74,200	106,000
7P Lke Spt Phae	3,920	11,760	19,600	39,200	68,600	98,000
Lke Rds	4,160	12,480	20,800	41,600	72,800	104,000
4P Cpe	2,120	6,360	10,600	21,200	37,100	53,000
Twn Sed	1,400	4,200	7,000	14,000	24,500	35,000
5P Sed	1,360	4,080	6,800	13,600	23,800	34,000
7P Sed	1,320	3,960	6,600	13,200	23,100	33,000
7P Limo	2,080	6,240	10,400	20,800	36,400	52,000

1930 Custom Line

	6	5	4	3	2	1
Jud Cpe	2,480	7,440	12,400	24,800	43,400	62,000
2W Jud Berl	2,880	8,640	14,400	28,800	50,400	72,000
3W Jud Berl	2,880	8,640	14,400	28,800	50,400	72,000
Brn A-W Cabr	3,520	10,560	17,600	35,200	61,600	88,000
Brn Non-Coll Cabr	2,960	8,880	14,800	29,600	51,800	74,000
LeB A-W Cabr	4,400	13,200	22,000	44,000	77,000	110,000
LeB Semi-Coll Cabr	4,150	12,500	20,800	41,600	73,000	104,000
W'by Limo	2,880	8,640	14,400	28,800	50,400	72,000
Dtrch Cpe	2,640	7,920	13,200	26,400	46,200	66,000

	6	5	4	3	2	1
Dtrch Sed	2,640	7,920	13,200	26,400	46,200	66,000
2W W'by Twn Sed	2,640	7,920	13,200	26,400	46,200	66,000
3W W'by Twn Sed	2,800	8,400	14,000	28,000	49,000	70,000
W'by Pan Brgm	2,960	8,880	14,800	29,600	51,800	74,000
LeB Cpe	2,640	7,920	13,200	26,400	46,200	66,000
LeB Conv Rds	4,160	12,480	20,800	41,600	72,800	104,000
LeB Spt Sed	3,360	10,080	16,800	33,600	58,800	84,000
Der Spt Conv	4,240	12,720	21,200	42,400	74,200	106,000
Der Conv Phae	4,320	12,960	21,600	43,200	75,600	108,000
Brn Semi-Coll Cabr	4,150	12,500	20,800	41,600	73,000	104,000
Dtrch Conv Cpe	4,320	12,960	21,600	43,200	75,600	108,000
Dtrch Conv Sed	4,400	13,200	22,000	44,000	77,000	110,000
Wolf Conv Sed	4,400	13,200	22,000	44,000	77,000	110,000

1931 Model K, V-8 Type 201, V-8, 145" wb

	6	5	4	3	2	1
202B Spt Phae	4,960	14,880	24,800	49,600	86,800	124,000
202A Spt Phae	5,040	15,120	25,200	50,400	88,200	126,000
203 Spt Tr	4,560	13,680	22,800	45,600	79,800	114,000
214 Conv Rds	4,400	13,200	22,000	44,000	77,000	110,000
206 Cpe	2,560	7,680	12,800	25,600	44,800	64,000
204 Twn Sed	2,280	6,840	11,400	22,800	39,900	57,000
205 Sed	2,200	6,600	11,000	22,000	38,500	55,000
207A Sed	2,200	6,600	11,000	22,000	38,500	55,000
207B Limo	2,640	7,920	13,200	26,400	46,200	66,000
212 Conv Phae	4,560	13,680	22,800	45,600	79,800	114,000
210 Conv Cpe	4,400	13,200	22,000	44,000	77,000	110,000
211 Conv Sed	4,560	13,680	22,800	45,600	79,800	114,000
216 W'by Pan Brgm	2,900	8,650	14,400	28,800	50,400	72,000
213A Jud Berl	2,560	7,680	12,800	25,600	44,800	64,000
213B Jud Berl	2,560	7,680	12,800	25,600	44,800	64,000
Jud Cpe	2,560	7,680	12,800	25,600	44,800	64,000
Brn Cabr	4,400	13,200	22,000	44,000	77,000	110,000
LeB Cabr	4,400	13,200	22,000	44,000	77,000	110,000
W'by Limo	2,880	8,640	14,400	28,800	50,400	72,000
Lke Spt Rds	4,560	13,680	22,800	45,600	79,800	114,000
Der Conv Sed	4,880	14,640	24,400	48,800	85,400	122,000
LeB Conv Rds	4,640	13,920	23,200	46,400	81,200	116,000
Mur DC Phae	5,040	15,120	25,200	50,400	88,200	126,000
Dtrch Conv Sed	5,040	15,120	25,200	50,400	88,200	126,000
Dtrch Conv Cpe	4,960	14,880	24,800	49,600	86,800	124,000
Wtrhs Conv Vic	5,040	15,120	25,200	50,400	88,200	126,000

1932 Model KA, V-8, 8-cyl., 136" wb

	6	5	4	3	2	1
Rds	4,240	12,720	21,200	42,400	74,200	106,000
Phae	4,960	14,880	24,800	49,600	86,800	124,000
Twn Sed	2,400	7,200	12,000	24,000	42,000	60,000
Sed	2,320	6,960	11,600	23,200	40,600	58,000
Cpe	2,880	8,640	14,400	28,800	50,400	72,000
Vic	2,800	8,400	14,000	28,000	49,000	70,000
7P Sed	2,800	8,400	14,000	28,000	49,000	70,000
Limo	2,960	8,880	14,800	29,600	51,800	74,000

1932 Model KB, V-12 Standard, 12-cyl., 145" wb

	6	5	4	3	2	1
Phae	4,640	13,920	23,200	46,400	81,200	116,000
Spt Phae	4,800	14,400	24,000	48,000	84,000	120,000
Cpe	2,880	8,640	14,400	28,800	50,400	72,000
2W Tr Sed	2,560	7,680	12,800	25,600	44,800	64,000
3W Tr Sed	2,520	7,560	12,600	25,200	44,100	63,000
5P Sed	2,480	7,440	12,400	24,800	43,400	62,000
7P Sed	2,440	7,320	12,200	24,400	42,700	61,000
Limo	2,800	8,400	14,000	28,000	49,000	70,000

1932 Custom, 145" wb

	6	5	4	3	2	1
LeB Conv Cpe	5,200	15,600	26,000	52,000	91,000	130,000
2P Dtrch Cpe	3,600	10,800	18,000	36,000	63,000	90,000
4P Dtrch Cpe	3,440	10,320	17,200	34,400	60,200	86,000
Jud Cpe	3,680	11,040	18,400	36,800	64,400	92,000
Jud Berl	3,280	9,840	16,400	32,800	57,400	82,000
W'by Limo	3,360	10,080	16,800	33,600	58,800	84,000
Wtrhs Conv Vic	5,040	15,120	25,200	50,400	88,200	126,000
Dtrch Conv Sed	5,200	15,600	26,000	52,000	91,000	130,000
W'by Twn Brgm	3,920	11,760	19,600	39,200	68,600	98,000
Brn Brgm	3,840	11,520	19,200	38,400	67,200	96,000
Brn Non-Coll Cabr	4,300	13,000	21,600	43,200	75,500	108,000
Brn Semi-Coll Cabr	5,200	15,600	26,000	52,000	91,000	130,000
LeB Twn Cabr	5,600	16,800	28,000	56,000	98,000	140,000
Dtrch Spt Berl	4,400	13,200	22,000	44,000	77,000	110,000
5P Rlstn TwnC	5,040	15,120	25,200	50,400	88,200	126,000
7P Rlstn TwnC	5,040	15,120	25,200	50,400	88,200	126,000
Brn Phae	5,440	16,320	27,200	54,400	95,200	136,000
Brn dbl-entry Spt Sed	4,300	13,000	21,600	43,200	75,500	108,000
Brn A-W Brgm	5,440	16,320	27,200	54,400	95,200	136,000
Brn Clb Sed	4,320	12,960	21,600	43,200	75,600	108,000
Mur Conv Rds	7,400	22,200	37,000	74,000	129,500	185,000

1933 Model KA, V-12, 12-cyl., 136" wb

	6	5	4	3	2	1
512B Cpe	2,880	8,640	14,400	28,800	50,400	72,000
512A RS Cpe	2,960	8,880	14,800	29,600	51,800	74,000
513A Conv Rds	4,400	13,200	22,000	44,000	77,000	110,000

Model	6	5	4	3	2	1
514 Twn Sed	2,480	7,440	12,400	24,800	43,400	62,000
515 Sed	2,440	7,320	12,200	24,400	42,700	61,000
516 Cpe	2,880	8,640	14,400	28,800	50,400	72,000
517 Sed	2,440	7,320	12,200	24,400	42,700	61,000
517B Limo	2,800	8,400	14,000	28,000	49,000	70,000
518A DC Phae	5,200	15,600	26,000	52,000	91,000	130,000
518B Phae	5,040	15,120	25,200	50,400	88,200	126,000
519 7P Tr	4,880	14,640	24,400	48,800	85,400	122,000
520B RS Rds	4,480	13,440	22,400	44,800	78,400	112,000
520A Rds	4,400	13,200	22,000	44,000	77,000	110,000

1933 Model KB, V-8, 12-cyl., 145" wb

Model	6	5	4	3	2	1
252A DC Phae	5,440	16,320	27,200	54,400	95,200	136,000
252B Phae	5,200	15,600	26,000	52,000	91,000	130,000
253 7P Tr	5,200	15,600	26,000	52,000	91,000	130,000
Twn Sed	2,560	7,680	12,800	25,600	44,800	64,000
255 5P Sed	2,640	7,920	13,200	26,400	46,200	66,000
256 5P Cpe	2,960	8,880	14,800	29,600	51,800	74,000
257 7P Sed	2,560	7,680	12,800	25,600	44,800	64,000
257B Limo	3,040	9,120	15,200	30,400	53,200	76,000
258C Brn Semi-Coll Cabr	5,040	15,120	25,200	50,400	88,200	126,000
258D Brn Non-Coll Cabr	4,640	13,920	23,200	46,400	81,200	116,000
259 Brn Brgm	3,840	11,520	19,200	38,400	67,200	96,000
260 Brn Conv Cpe	7,400	22,200	37,000	74,000	129,500	185,000
Dtrch Conv Sed	7,600	22,800	38,000	76,000	133,000	190,000
2P Dtrch Cpe	3,760	11,280	18,800	37,600	65,800	94,000
4P Dtrch Cpe	3,760	11,280	18,800	37,600	65,800	94,000
Jud Berl	3,280	9,840	16,400	32,800	57,400	82,000
2P Jud Cpe	3,440	10,320	17,200	34,400	60,200	86,000
4P Jud Cpe	3,440	10,320	17,200	34,400	60,200	86,000
Jud Limo	3,600	10,800	18,000	36,000	63,000	90,000
LeB Conv Rds	6,000	18,000	30,000	60,000	105,000	150,000
W'by Limo	3,600	10,800	18,000	36,000	63,000	90,000
W'by Brgm	3,760	11,280	18,800	37,600	65,800	94,000

1934 Series K, V-12, 12-cyl., 136" wb

Model	6	5	4	3	2	1
4P Conv Rds	4,480	13,440	22,400	44,800	78,400	112,000
4P Twn Sed	2,200	6,600	11,000	22,000	38,500	55,000
5P Sed	2,560	7,680	12,800	25,600	44,800	64,000
5P Cpe	2,960	8,880	14,800	29,600	51,800	74,000
7P Sed	2,560	7,680	12,800	25,600	44,800	64,000
7P Limo	3,040	9,120	15,200	30,400	53,200	76,000
2P Cpe	3,040	9,120	15,200	30,400	53,200	76,000
5P Conv Phae	4,400	13,200	22,000	44,000	77,000	110,000
4P Cpe	2,800	8,400	14,000	28,000	49,000	70,000

1934 V-12, 145" wb

Model	6	5	4	3	2	1
Tr	4,320	12,960	21,600	43,200	75,600	108,000
Sed	2,640	7,920	13,200	26,400	46,200	66,000
Limo	2,960	8,880	14,800	29,600	51,800	74,000
2W Jud Berl	3,360	10,080	16,800	33,600	58,800	84,000
3W Jud Berl	3,280	9,840	16,400	32,800	57,400	82,000
Jud Sed Limo	3,040	9,120	15,200	30,400	53,200	76,000
Brn Brgm	3,280	9,840	16,400	32,800	57,400	82,000
Brn Semi-Coll Cabr	4,150	12,500	20,800	41,600	73,000	104,000
Brn Conv Cpe	5,040	15,120	25,200	50,400	88,200	126,000
W'by Limo	2,960	8,880	14,800	29,600	51,800	74,000
LeB Rds	5,040	15,120	25,200	50,400	88,200	126,000
Dtrch Conv Sed	5,440	16,320	27,200	54,400	95,200	136,000
Brn Conv Vic	5,440	16,320	27,200	54,400	95,200	136,000
LeB Cpe	3,280	9,840	16,400	32,800	57,400	82,000
Dtrch Conv Rds	5,040	15,120	25,200	50,400	88,200	126,000
W'by Spt Sed	2,960	8,880	14,800	29,600	51,800	74,000
LeB Conv Cpe	5,040	15,120	25,200	50,400	88,200	126,000
Brn Conv Sed	5,440	16,320	27,200	54,400	95,200	136,000
Brn Cus Phae	5,440	16,320	27,200	54,400	95,200	136,000
Brwstr Non-Coll Cabr	4,250	12,700	21,200	42,400	74,000	106,000

1935 Series K, V-12, 136" wb

Model	6	5	4	3	2	1
LeB Conv Rds	4,480	13,440	22,400	44,800	78,400	112,000
LeB Cpe	2,520	7,560	12,600	25,200	44,100	63,000
Cpe	2,440	7,320	12,200	24,400	42,700	61,000
Brn Conv Vic	4,560	13,680	22,800	45,600	79,800	114,000
2W Sed	2,080	6,240	10,400	20,800	36,400	52,000
3W Sed	2,040	6,120	10,200	20,400	35,700	51,000
LeB Conv Phae	4,640	13,920	23,200	46,400	81,200	116,000

1935 V-12, 145" wb

Model	6	5	4	3	2	1
7P Tr	4,400	13,200	22,000	44,000	77,000	110,000
7P Sed	2,120	6,360	10,600	21,200	37,100	53,000
7P Limo	2,520	7,560	12,600	25,200	44,100	63,000
LeB Conv Sed	5,040	15,120	25,200	50,400	88,200	126,000
Brn Semi-Coll Cabr	4,150	12,500	20,800	41,600	73,000	104,000
Brn Non-Coll Cabr	4,000	12,000	20,000	40,000	70,000	100,000
Brn Brgm	2,520	7,560	12,600	25,200	44,100	63,000
W'by Limo	2,480	7,440	12,400	24,800	43,400	62,000
W'by Spt Sed	2,520	7,560	12,600	25,200	44,100	63,000
2W Jud Berl	2,480	7,440	12,400	24,800	43,400	62,000

Model	6	5	4	3	2	1
3W Jud Berl	2,520	7,560	12,600	25,200	44,100	63,000
Jud Sed Limo	2,560	7,680	12,800	25,600	44,800	64,000

1936 Zephyr, V-12, 122" wb

Model	6	5	4	3	2	1
4d Sed	1,320	3,960	6,600	13,200	23,100	33,000
2d Sed	1,360	4,080	6,800	13,600	23,800	34,000

1936 12-cyl., 136" wb

Model	6	5	4	3	2	1
LeB Rds Cabr	3,600	10,800	18,000	36,000	63,000	90,000
2P LeB Cpe	1,960	5,880	9,800	19,600	34,300	49,000
5P Cpe	1,880	5,640	9,400	18,800	32,900	47,000
Brn Conv Vic	3,840	11,520	19,200	38,400	67,200	96,000
2W Sed	1,680	5,040	8,400	16,800	29,400	42,000
3W Sed	1,640	4,920	8,200	16,400	28,700	41,000
LeB Conv Sed	4,000	12,000	20,000	40,000	70,000	100,000

1936 V-12, 145" wb

Model	6	5	4	3	2	1
7P Tr	4,000	12,000	20,000	40,000	70,000	100,000
7P Sed	1,960	5,880	9,800	19,600	34,300	49,000
7P Limo	2,120	6,360	10,600	21,200	37,100	53,000
LeB Conv Sed w/part	4,250	12,700	21,200	42,400	74,000	106,000
Brn Semi-Coll Cabr	3,840	11,520	19,200	38,400	67,200	96,000
Brn Non-Coll Cabr	3,040	9,120	15,200	30,400	53,200	76,000
Brn Brgm	2,160	6,480	10,800	21,600	37,800	54,000
W'by Limo	2,240	6,720	11,200	22,400	39,200	56,000
W'by Spt Sed	2,080	6,240	10,400	20,800	36,400	52,000
2W Jud Berl	2,160	6,480	10,800	21,600	37,800	54,000
3W Jud Berl	2,200	6,600	11,000	22,000	38,500	55,000
Jud Limo	2,280	6,840	11,400	22,800	39,900	57,000

1937 Zephyr, V-12

Model	6	5	4	3	2	1
3P Cpe	1,240	3,720	6,200	12,400	21,700	31,000
2d Sed	1,120	3,360	5,600	11,200	19,600	28,000
4d Sed	1,080	3,240	5,400	10,800	18,900	27,000
Twn Sed	1,120	3,360	5,600	11,200	19,600	28,000

1937 Series K, V-12, 136" wb

Model	6	5	4	3	2	1
LeB Conv Rds	3,440	10,320	17,200	34,400	60,200	86,000
LeB Cpe	1,920	5,760	9,600	19,200	33,600	48,000
W'by Cpe	2,000	6,000	10,000	20,000	35,000	50,000
Brn Conv Vic	3,600	10,800	18,000	36,000	63,000	90,000
2W Sed	1,760	5,280	8,800	17,600	30,800	44,000
3W Sed	1,720	5,160	8,600	17,200	30,100	43,000

1937 V-12, 145" wb

Model	6	5	4	3	2	1
7P Sed	1,840	5,520	9,200	18,400	32,200	46,000
7P Limo	1,920	5,760	9,600	19,200	33,600	48,000
LeB Conv Sed	3,680	11,040	18,400	36,800	64,400	92,000
LeB Conv Sed w/part	3,850	11,500	19,200	38,400	67,000	96,000
Brn Semi-Coll Cabr	3,450	10,300	17,200	34,400	60,000	86,000
Brn Non-Coll Cabr	2,720	8,160	13,600	27,200	47,600	68,000
Brn Brgm	2,200	6,600	11,000	22,000	38,500	55,000
Brn Tr Cabr	3,600	10,800	18,000	36,000	63,000	90,000
2W Jud Berl	2,160	6,480	10,800	21,600	37,800	54,000
3W Jud Berl	2,120	6,360	10,600	21,200	37,100	53,000
Jud Limo	2,360	7,080	11,800	23,600	41,300	59,000
W'by Tr	2,480	7,440	12,400	24,800	43,400	62,000
W'by Limo	2,320	6,960	11,600	23,200	40,600	58,000
W'by Spt Sed	2,120	6,360	10,600	21,200	37,100	53,000
W'by Cpe	2,200	6,600	11,000	22,000	38,500	55,000
W'by Pan Brgm	2,240	6,720	11,200	22,400	39,200	56,000
Jud Cpe	2,200	6,600	11,000	22,000	38,500	55,000

1938 Zephyr, V-12

Model	6	5	4	3	2	1
3P Cpe	1,360	4,080	6,800	13,600	23,800	34,000
3P Conv Cpe	1,760	5,280	8,800	17,600	30,800	44,000
4d Sed	880	2,640	4,400	8,800	15,400	22,000
2d Sed	920	2,760	4,600	9,200	16,100	23,000
Conv Sed	2,400	7,200	12,000	24,000	42,000	60,000
Twn Sed	1,000	3,000	5,000	10,000	17,500	25,000

1938 Series K, V-12, 136" wb

Model	6	5	4	3	2	1
LeB Conv Rds	3,440	10,320	17,200	34,400	60,200	86,000
LeB Cpe	1,920	5,760	9,600	19,200	33,600	48,000
W'by Cpe	1,960	5,880	9,800	19,600	34,300	49,000
2W Sed	1,760	5,280	8,800	17,600	30,800	44,000
3W Sed	1,720	5,160	8,600	17,200	30,100	43,000
Brn Conv Vic	3,520	10,560	17,600	35,200	61,600	88,000

1938 V-12, 145" wb

Model	6	5	4	3	2	1
7P Sed	1,800	5,400	9,000	18,000	31,500	45,000
Sed Limo	1,840	5,520	9,200	18,400	32,200	46,000
LeB Conv Sed	3,840	11,520	19,200	38,400	67,200	96,000
LeB Conv Sed w/part	4,000	12,000	20,000	40,000	70,000	100,000
2W Jud Berl	1,840	5,520	9,200	18,400	32,200	46,000
3W Jud Berl	1,880	5,640	9,400	18,800	32,900	47,000
Jud Limo	1,960	5,880	9,800	19,600	34,300	49,000
Brn Tr Cabr	3,920	11,760	19,600	39,200	68,600	98,000

	6	5	4	3	2	1
W'by Tr	2,560	7,680	12,800	25,600	44,800	64,000
W'by Spt Sed	1,960	5,880	9,800	19,600	34,300	49,000
Brn Non-Coll Cabr	2,160	6,480	10,800	21,600	37,800	54,000
Brn Semi-Coll Cabr	3,450	10,300	17,200	34,400	60,000	86,000
Brn Brgm	1,960	5,880	9,800	19,600	34,300	49,000
W'by Pan Brgm	1,760	5,280	8,800	17,600	30,800	44,000
W'by Limo	2,160	6,480	10,800	21,600	37,800	54,000

1939 Zephyr, V-12

	6	5	4	3	2	1
3P Cpe	1,320	3,960	6,600	13,200	23,100	33,000
Conv Cpe	2,080	6,240	10,400	20,800	36,400	52,000
2d Sed	960	2,880	4,800	9,600	16,800	24,000
5P Sed	960	2,880	4,800	9,600	16,800	24,000
Conv Sed	2,360	7,080	11,800	23,600	41,300	59,000
Twn Sed	1,000	3,000	5,000	10,000	17,500	25,000

1939 Series K, V-12, 136" wb

	6	5	4	3	2	1
LeB Conv Rds	3,040	9,120	15,200	30,400	53,200	76,000
LeB Cpe	2,000	6,000	10,000	20,000	35,000	50,000
W'by Cpe	2,040	6,120	10,200	20,400	35,700	51,000
2W Sed	1,880	5,640	9,400	18,800	32,900	47,000
3W Sed	1,880	5,640	9,400	18,800	32,900	47,000
Brn Conv Vic	3,040	9,120	15,200	30,400	53,200	76,000

1939 V-12, 145" wb

	6	5	4	3	2	1
2W Jud Berl	1,920	5,760	9,600	19,200	33,600	48,000
3W Jud Berl	1,880	5,640	9,400	18,800	32,900	47,000
Jud Limo	2,000	6,000	10,000	20,000	35,000	50,000
Brn Tr Cabr	2,560	7,680	12,800	25,600	44,800	64,000
7P Sed	1,920	5,760	9,600	19,200	33,600	48,000
7P Limo	2,040	6,120	10,200	20,400	35,700	51,000
LeB Conv Sed	3,840	11,520	19,200	38,400	67,200	96,000
LeB Conv Sed w/part	4,000	12,000	20,000	40,000	70,000	100,000
W'by Spt Sed	2,160	6,480	10,800	21,600	37,800	54,000

1939 V-12, 145" wb, 6 wheels

	6	5	4	3	2	1
Brn Non-Coll Cabr	3,450	10,300	17,200	34,400	60,000	86,000
Brn Semi-Coll Cabr	3,850	11,500	19,200	38,400	67,000	96,000
Brn Brgm	2,280	6,840	11,400	22,800	39,900	57,000
W'by Limo	2,440	7,320	12,200	24,400	42,700	61,000

1940 Zephyr, V-12

	6	5	4	3	2	1
3P Cpe	1,240	3,720	6,200	12,400	21,700	31,000
OS Cpe	1,160	3,480	5,800	11,600	20,300	29,000
Clb Cpe	1,200	3,600	6,000	12,000	21,000	30,000
Conv Clb Cpe	1,800	5,400	9,000	18,000	31,500	45,000
6P Sed	960	2,880	4,800	9,600	16,800	24,000
Twn Limo	1,360	4,080	6,800	13,600	23,800	34,000
Cont Clb Cpe	2,120	6,360	10,600	21,200	37,100	53,000
Cont Conv Cabr	2,640	7,920	13,200	26,400	46,200	66,000

1940 Series K, V-12

NOTE: Available on special request, black emblems rather than blue.

1941 Zephyr, V-12

	6	5	4	3	2	1
3P Cpe	1,240	3,720	6,200	12,400	21,700	31,000
OS Cpe	1,160	3,480	5,800	11,600	20,300	29,000
Clb Cpe	1,200	3,600	6,000	12,000	21,000	30,000
Conv Cpe	1,760	5,280	8,800	17,600	30,800	44,000
Cont Cpe	2,080	6,240	10,400	20,800	36,400	52,000
Cont Conv Cabr	2,640	7,920	13,200	26,400	46,200	66,000
6P Sed	960	2,880	4,800	9,600	16,800	24,000
Cus Sed	1,000	3,000	5,000	10,000	17,500	25,000
8P Limo	1,200	3,600	6,000	12,000	21,000	30,000

1942 Zephyr, V-12

	6	5	4	3	2	1
3P Cpe	960	2,880	4,800	9,600	16,800	24,000
Clb Cpe	1,000	3,000	5,000	10,000	17,500	25,000
Conv Clb Cpe	1,720	5,160	8,600	17,200	30,100	43,000
Cont Cpe	2,080	6,240	10,400	20,800	36,400	52,000
Cont Conv Cabr	2,640	7,920	13,200	26,400	46,200	66,000
6P Sed	880	2,640	4,400	8,800	15,400	22,000
Cus Sed	920	2,760	4,600	9,200	16,100	23,000
8P Limo	1,240	3,720	6,200	12,400	21,700	31,000

1946-1948 8th Series, V-12, 125" wb

	6	5	4	3	2	1
2d Clb Cpe	960	2,880	4,800	9,600	16,800	24,000
2d Conv	1,640	4,920	8,200	16,400	28,700	41,000
4d Sed	880	2,640	4,400	8,800	15,400	22,000
2d Cont Cpe	2,120	6,360	10,600	21,200	37,100	53,000
2d Cont Conv	2,640	7,920	13,200	26,400	46,200	66,000

1949-1950 Model OEL, V-8, 121" wb

	6	5	4	3	2	1
4d Spt Sed	880	2,640	4,400	8,800	15,400	22,000
2d Cpe	1,040	3,120	5,200	10,400	18,200	26,000
2d Lido Cpe (1950 only)	1,240	3,720	6,200	12,400	21,700	31,000

1949-1950 Cosmopolitan, V-8, 125" wb

	6	5	4	3	2	1
4d Town Sed (1949 only)	920	2,760	4,600	9,200	16,100	23,000
4d Spt Sed	940	2,820	4,700	9,400	16,450	23,500

	6	5	4	3	2	1
2d Cpe	1,040	3,120	5,200	10,400	18,200	26,000
2d Capri (1950 only)	1,200	3,600	6,000	12,000	21,000	30,000
2d Conv	1,400	4,200	7,000	14,000	24,500	35,000

1951 Model Del, V-8, 121" wb

	6	5	4	3	2	1
4d Spt Sed	920	2,760	4,600	9,200	16,100	23,000
2d Cpe	1,000	3,000	5,000	10,000	17,500	25,000
2d Lido Cpe	1,300	3,900	6,500	13,000	22,750	32,500

1951 Cosmopolitan, V-8, 125" wb

	6	5	4	3	2	1
4d Spt Sed	960	2,880	4,800	9,600	16,800	24,000
2d Cpe	1,040	3,120	5,200	10,400	18,200	26,000
2d Capri	1,160	3,480	5,800	11,600	20,300	29,000
2d Conv	1,440	4,320	7,200	14,400	25,200	36,000

1952-1953 Cosmopolitan Model BH, V-8, 123" wb

	6	5	4	3	2	1
4d Sed	880	2,640	4,400	8,800	15,400	22,000
2d HT	1,080	3,240	5,400	10,800	18,900	27,000

1952-1953 Capri, V-8, 123" wb

	6	5	4	3	2	1
4d Sed	920	2,760	4,600	9,200	16,100	23,000
2d HT	1,120	3,360	5,600	11,200	19,600	28,000
2d Conv	1,440	4,320	7,200	14,400	25,200	36,000

1954 V-8, 123" wb

	6	5	4	3	2	1
4d Sed	880	2,640	4,400	8,800	15,400	22,000
2d HT	1,120	3,360	5,600	11,200	19,600	28,000

1954 Capri, V-8, 123" wb

	6	5	4	3	2	1
4d Sed	880	2,640	4,400	8,800	15,400	22,000
2d HT	1,200	3,600	6,000	12,000	21,000	30,000
2d Conv	1,480	4,440	7,400	14,800	25,900	37,000

1955 V-8, 123" wb

	6	5	4	3	2	1
4d Sed	880	2,640	4,400	8,800	15,400	22,000
2d HT	1,080	3,240	5,400	10,800	18,900	27,000

1955 Capri, V-8, 123" wb

	6	5	4	3	2	1
4d Sed	900	2,700	4,500	9,000	15,750	22,500
2d HT	1,160	3,480	5,800	11,600	20,300	29,000
2d Conv	1,600	4,800	8,000	16,000	28,000	40,000

1956 Capri, V-8, 126" wb

	6	5	4	3	2	1
4d Sed	900	2,700	4,500	9,000	15,750	22,500
2d HT	1,300	3,850	6,400	12,800	22,400	32,000

1956 Premiere, V-8, 126" wb

	6	5	4	3	2	1
4d Sed	920	2,760	4,600	9,200	16,100	23,000
2d HT	1,500	4,450	7,400	14,800	25,900	37,000
2d Conv	1,900	5,650	9,400	18,800	32,900	47,000

1956 Continental Mk II, V-8, 126" wb

	6	5	4	3	2	1
2d HT	1,900	5,750	9,600	19,200	33,600	48,000

1957 Capri, V-8, 126" wb

	6	5	4	3	2	1
4d Sed	760	2,280	3,800	7,600	13,300	19,000
4d HT	840	2,520	4,200	8,400	14,700	21,000
2d HT	1,150	3,500	5,800	11,600	20,300	29,000

1957 Premiere, V-8, 126" wb

	6	5	4	3	2	1
4d Sed	800	2,400	4,000	8,000	14,000	20,000
4d HT	880	2,640	4,400	8,800	15,400	22,000
2d HT	1,250	3,700	6,200	12,400	21,700	31,000
2d Conv	1,800	5,400	9,000	18,000	31,500	45,000

1957 Continental Mk II, V-8, 126" wb

	6	5	4	3	2	1
2d HT	1,900	5,750	9,600	19,200	33,600	48,000

1958-1959 Capri, V-8, 131" wb

	6	5	4	3	2	1
4d Sed	640	1,920	3,200	6,400	11,200	16,000
4d HT	720	2,160	3,600	7,200	12,600	18,000
2d HT	840	2,520	4,200	8,400	14,700	21,000

1958-1959 Premiere, V-8, 131" wb

	6	5	4	3	2	1
4d Sed	680	2,040	3,400	6,800	11,900	17,000
4d HT	760	2,280	3,800	7,600	13,300	19,000
2d HT	880	2,640	4,400	8,800	15,400	22,000

1958-1959 Continental Mk III and IV, V-8, 131" wb

	6	5	4	3	2	1
4d Sed	760	2,280	3,800	7,600	13,300	19,000
4d HT	840	2,520	4,200	8,400	14,700	21,000
2d HT	960	2,880	4,800	9,600	16,800	24,000
2d Conv	1,250	3,700	6,200	12,400	21,700	31,000
4d Town Car (1959 only)	960	2,880	4,800	9,600	16,800	24,000
4d Limo (1959 only)	1,000	3,000	5,000	10,000	17,500	25,000

1960 Lincoln, V-8, 131" wb

	6	5	4	3	2	1
4d Sed	680	2,040	3,400	6,800	11,900	17,000

	6	5	4	3	2	1
4d HT	760	2,280	3,800	7,600	13,300	19,000
2d HT	840	2,520	4,200	8,400	14,700	21,000

1960 Premiere, V-8, 131" wb

	6	5	4	3	2	1
4d Sed	720	2,160	3,600	7,200	12,600	18,000
4d HT	800	2,400	4,000	8,000	14,000	20,000
2d HT	880	2,640	4,400	8,800	15,400	22,000

1960 Continental Mk V, V-8, 131" wb

	6	5	4	3	2	1
4d Sed	800	2,400	4,000	8,000	14,000	20,000
4d HT	880	2,640	4,400	8,800	15,400	22,000
2d HT	1,040	3,120	5,200	10,400	18,200	26,000
2d Conv	1,350	4,100	6,800	13,600	23,800	34,000
4d Town Car	1,000	3,000	5,000	10,000	17,500	25,000
4d Limo	1,040	3,120	5,200	10,400	18,200	26,000

1961-1963 Continental, V-8, 123" wb

	6	5	4	3	2	1
4d Sed	640	1,920	3,200	6,400	11,200	16,000
4d Conv	1,080	3,240	5,400	10,800	18,900	27,000

1964-1965 Continental, V-8, 126" wb

	6	5	4	3	2	1
4d Sed	640	1,920	3,200	6,400	11,200	16,000
4d Conv	1,120	3,360	5,600	11,200	19,600	28,000
4d Exec Limo	720	2,160	3,600	7,200	12,600	18,000

1966 Continental, V-8, 126" wb

	6	5	4	3	2	1
4d Sed	640	1,920	3,200	6,400	11,200	16,000
2d HT	760	2,280	3,800	7,600	13,300	19,000
4d Conv	1,120	3,360	5,600	11,200	19,600	28,000

1967 Continental, V-8, 126" wb

	6	5	4	3	2	1
4d Sed	640	1,920	3,200	6,400	11,200	16,000
2d HT	760	2,280	3,800	7,600	13,300	19,000
4d Conv	1,120	3,360	5,600	11,200	19,600	28,000

1968 Continental, V-8, 126" wb

	6	5	4	3	2	1
4d Sed	600	1,800	3,000	6,000	10,500	15,000
2d HT	720	2,160	3,600	7,200	12,600	18,000

1968 Continental, V-8, 117" wb

	6	5	4	3	2	1
2d HT	760	2,280	3,800	7,600	13,300	19,000

1969 Continental, V-8, 126" wb

	6	5	4	3	2	1
4d Sed	560	1,680	2,800	5,600	9,800	14,000
2d HT	600	1,800	3,000	6,000	10,500	15,000

1969 Continental Mk III, V-8, 117" wb

	6	5	4	3	2	1
2d HT	920	2,760	4,600	9,200	16,100	23,000

1970 Continental

	6	5	4	3	2	1
4d Sed	560	1,680	2,800	5,600	9,800	14,000
2d HT	600	1,800	3,000	6,000	10,500	15,000

1970 Continental Mk III, V-8, 117" wb

	6	5	4	3	2	1
2d HT	940	2,820	4,700	9,400	16,450	23,500

1971 Continental

	6	5	4	3	2	1
4d Sed	560	1,680	2,800	5,600	9,800	14,000
2d	600	1,800	3,000	6,000	10,500	15,000

1971 Mk III

	6	5	4	3	2	1
2d	940	2,820	4,700	9,400	16,450	23,500

1972 Continental

	6	5	4	3	2	1
4d Sed	560	1,680	2,800	5,600	9,800	14,000
2d	600	1,800	3,000	6,000	10,500	15,000

1972 Mk IV

	6	5	4	3	2	1
2d	760	2,280	3,800	7,600	13,300	19,000

1973 Continental, V-8

	6	5	4	3	2	1
2d HT	580	1,740	2,900	5,800	10,150	14,500
4d HT	540	1,620	2,700	5,400	9,450	13,500

1973 Mk IV, V-8

	6	5	4	3	2	1
2d HT	760	2,280	3,800	7,600	13,300	19,000

1974 Continental, V-8

	6	5	4	3	2	1
4d Sed	520	1,560	2,600	5,200	9,100	13,000
2d Cpe	540	1,620	2,700	5,400	9,450	13,500

1974 Mk IV, V-8

	6	5	4	3	2	1
2d HT	720	2,160	3,600	7,200	12,600	18,000

1975 Continental, V-8

	6	5	4	3	2	1
4d Sed	532	1,596	2,660	5,320	9,310	13,300
2d Cpe	540	1,620	2,700	5,400	9,450	13,500

1975 Mk IV, V-8

	6	5	4	3	2	1
2d HT	720	2,160	3,600	7,200	12,600	18,000

1976 Continental, V-8

	6	5	4	3	2	1
4d Sed	520	1,560	2,600	5,200	9,100	13,000
2d Cpe	540	1,620	2,700	5,400	9,450	13,500

1976 Mk IV, V-8

	6	5	4	3	2	1
2d Cpe	720	2,160	3,600	7,200	12,600	18,000

NOTE: Add 10 percent for 460 cid engine.

1977 Versailles, V-8

	6	5	4	3	2	1
4d Sed	360	1,080	1,800	3,600	6,300	9,000

1977 Continental, V-8

	6	5	4	3	2	1
4d Sed	372	1,116	1,860	3,720	6,510	9,300
2d Cpe	380	1,140	1,900	3,800	6,650	9,500

1977 Mk V, V-8

	6	5	4	3	2	1
2d Cpe	680	2,040	3,400	6,800	11,900	17,000

NOTE: Add 10 percent for 460 cid engine.

1978 Versailles

	6	5	4	3	2	1
4d Sed	300	850	1,400	2,800	4,900	7,000

1978 Continental

	6	5	4	3	2	1
4d Sed	300	850	1,450	2,900	5,050	7,200
2d Cpe	300	900	1,500	3,050	5,300	7,600

1978 Mk V

	6	5	4	3	2	1
2d Cpe	720	2,160	3,600	7,200	12,600	18,000

NOTE: Add 10 percent for Diamond Jubilee. Add 5 percent for Collector Series. Add 5 percent for Designer Series. Add 10 percent for 460 cid engine.

1979 Versailles, V-8

	6	5	4	3	2	1
4d Sed	250	800	1,350	2,700	4,750	6,800

1979 Continental, V-8

	6	5	4	3	2	1
4d Sed	300	900	1,500	2,950	5,200	7,400
2d Cpe	300	950	1,600	3,150	5,550	7,900

1979 Mk V, V-8

	6	5	4	3	2	1
2d Cpe	680	2,040	3,400	6,800	11,900	17,000

NOTE: Add 5 percent for Collector Series. Add 5 percent for Designer Series.

1980 Versailles, V-8

	6	5	4	3	2	1
4d Sed	244	732	1,220	2,440	4,270	6,100

1980 Continental, V-8

	6	5	4	3	2	1
4d Sed	300	900	1,500	2,950	5,200	7,400
2d Cpe	300	950	1,600	3,150	5,550	7,900

1980 Mk VI, V-8

	6	5	4	3	2	1
4d Sed	360	1,080	1,800	3,600	6,300	9,000
2d Cpe	368	1,104	1,840	3,680	6,440	9,200

1981 Town Car, V-8

	6	5	4	3	2	1
4d Sed	300	900	1,450	2,900	5,100	7,300
2d Cpe	300	950	1,550	3,100	5,450	7,800

1981 Mk VI

	6	5	4	3	2	1
4d Sed	240	720	1,200	2,400	4,200	6,000
2d Cpe	248	744	1,240	2,480	4,340	6,200

1982 Town Car, V-8

	6	5	4	3	2	1
4d Sed	260	780	1,300	2,600	4,550	6,500

1982 Mk VI, V-8

	6	5	4	3	2	1
4d Sed	244	732	1,220	2,440	4,270	6,100
2d Cpe	248	744	1,240	2,480	4,340	6,200

1982 Continental, V-8

	6	5	4	3	2	1
4d Sed	520	1,560	2,600	5,200	9,100	13,000

1983 Town Car, V-8

	6	5	4	3	2	1
4d Sed	272	816	1,360	2,720	4,760	6,800

1983 Mk VI, V-8

	6	5	4	3	2	1
2d Cpe	248	744	1,240	2,480	4,340	6,200

1983 Continental, V-8

	6	5	4	3	2	1
4d Sed	520	1,560	2,600	5,200	9,100	13,000

1984 Town Car, V-8

	6	5	4	3	2	1
4d Sed	276	828	1,380	2,760	4,830	6,900

1984 Mk VII, V-8

	6	5	4	3	2	1
2d Cpe	360	1,080	1,800	3,600	6,300	9,000
2d LSC Cpe	540	1,620	2,700	5,400	9,450	13,500

1984 Continental, V-8

	6	5	4	3	2	1
4d Sed	520	1,560	2,600	5,200	9,100	13,000

1985 Town Car, V-8

	6	5	4	3	2	1
4d Sed	360	1,080	1,800	3,600	6,300	9,000

1985 Mk VII, V-8

	6	5	4	3	2	1
2d Cpe	368	1,104	1,840	3,680	6,440	9,200
2d LSC Cpe	540	1,620	2,700	5,400	9,450	13,500

1985 Continental, V-8

	6	5	4	3	2	1
4d Sed	536	1,608	2,680	5,360	9,380	13,400

1986 Town Car

	6	5	4	3	2	1
4d Sed	380	1,140	1,900	3,800	6,650	9,500

1986 Mk VII

	6	5	4	3	2	1
2d Cpe	520	1,560	2,600	5,200	9,100	13,000
2d LSC Cpe	540	1,620	2,700	5,400	9,450	13,500

1986 Continental

	6	5	4	3	2	1
4d Sed	552	1,656	2,760	5,520	9,660	13,800

NOTE: Add 20 percent for Designer Series.

1987 Town Car, V-8

	6	5	4	3	2	1
4d Sed	392	1,176	1,960	3,920	6,860	9,800
4d Sed Signature	420	1,260	2,100	4,200	7,350	10,500
4d Sed Cartier	540	1,620	2,700	5,400	9,450	13,500

1987 Mk VII, V-8

	6	5	4	3	2	1
2d Cpe	420	1,260	2,100	4,200	7,350	10,500
2d Cpe LSC	540	1,620	2,700	5,400	9,450	13,500
2d Cpe Bill Blass	560	1,680	2,800	5,600	9,800	14,000

1987 Continental, V-8

	6	5	4	3	2	1
4d Sed	380	1,140	1,900	3,800	6,650	9,500
4d Sed Givenchy	420	1,260	2,100	4,200	7,350	10,500

1988 Town Car, V-8

	6	5	4	3	2	1
4d Sed	400	1,200	2,000	4,000	7,000	10,000
4d Sed Signature	520	1,560	2,600	5,200	9,100	13,000
4d Sed Cartier	540	1,620	2,700	5,400	9,450	13,500

1988 Mk VII, V-8

	6	5	4	3	2	1
2d Cpe LSC	552	1,656	2,760	5,520	9,660	13,800
2d Cpe Bill Blass	556	1,668	2,780	5,560	9,730	13,900

1988 Continental, V-6

	6	5	4	3	2	1
4d Sed	412	1,236	2,060	4,120	7,210	10,300
4d Sed Signature	532	1,596	2,660	5,320	9,310	13,300

1989 Town Car, V-8

	6	5	4	3	2	1
4d Sed	540	1,620	2,700	5,400	9,450	13,500
4d Sed Signature	560	1,680	2,800	5,600	9,800	14,000
4d Sed Cartier	600	1,800	3,000	6,000	10,500	15,000

1989 Mk VII, V-8

	6	5	4	3	2	1
2d Cpe LSC	560	1,680	2,800	5,600	9,800	14,000
2d Cpe Bill Blass	560	1,680	2,800	5,600	9,800	14,000

1989 Continental, V-6

	6	5	4	3	2	1
4d Sed	420	1,260	2,100	4,200	7,350	10,500
4d Sed Signature	540	1,620	2,700	5,400	9,450	13,500

1990 Town Car, V-8

	6	5	4	3	2	1
4d Sed	600	1,800	3,000	6,000	10,500	15,000
4d Sed Signature	640	1,920	3,200	6,400	11,200	16,000
4d Sed Cartier	660	1,980	3,300	6,600	11,550	16,500

1990 Mk VII, V-8

	6	5	4	3	2	1
2d LSC Cpe	560	1,680	2,800	5,600	9,800	14,000
2d Cpe Bill Blass	580	1,740	2,900	5,800	10,150	14,500

1990 Continental, V-6

	6	5	4	3	2	1
4d Sed	520	1,560	2,600	5,200	9,100	13,000
4d Sed Signature	540	1,620	2,700	5,400	9,450	13,500

1991 Town Car, V-8

	6	5	4	3	2	1
4d Sed	520	1,560	2,600	5,200	9,100	13,000
4d Sed Signature	540	1,620	2,700	5,400	9,450	13,500
4d Sed Cartier	580	1,740	2,900	5,800	10,150	14,500

1991 Mk VII, V-8

	6	5	4	3	2	1
2d Cpe LSC	560	1,680	2,800	5,600	9,800	14,000
2d Cpe Bill Blass	580	1,740	2,900	5,800	10,150	14,500

1991 Continental, V-6

	6	5	4	3	2	1
4d Sed	420	1,260	2,100	4,200	7,350	10,500
4d Sed Signature	520	1,560	2,600	5,200	9,100	13,000

1992 Town Car, V-8

	6	5	4	3	2	1
4d Sed Executive	592	1,776	2,960	5,920	10,360	14,800
4d Sed Signature	600	1,800	3,000	6,000	10,500	15,000
4d Sed Cartier	620	1,860	3,100	6,200	10,850	15,500

1992 Mk VII, V-8

	6	5	4	3	2	1
2d Cpe LSC	640	1,920	3,200	6,400	11,200	16,000
2d Cpe Bill Blass	640	1,920	3,200	6,400	11,200	16,000

1992 Continental, V-6

	6	5	4	3	2	1
4d Executive	400	1,200	2,000	4,000	7,000	10,000
4d Signature	420	1,260	2,100	4,200	7,350	10,500

1993 Town Car, V-8

	6	5	4	3	2	1
4d Sed Executive	600	1,800	3,000	6,000	10,500	15,000
4d Sed Signature	640	1,920	3,200	6,400	11,200	16,000
4d Sed Cartier	660	1,980	3,300	6,600	11,550	16,500

1993 Mk VIII, V-8

	6	5	4	3	2	1
2d Sed Executive	648	1,944	3,240	6,480	11,340	16,200
2d Sed Signature	652	1,956	3,260	6,520	11,410	16,300

1993 Continental, V-6

	6	5	4	3	2	1
4d Sed Executive	600	1,800	3,000	6,000	10,500	15,000
4d Sed Signature	604	1,812	3,020	6,040	10,570	15,100

1994 Town Car, V-8

	6	5	4	3	2	1
4d Sed Executive	520	1,560	2,600	5,200	9,100	13,000
4d Sed Signature	540	1,620	2,700	5,400	9,450	13,500
4d Sed Cartier	580	1,740	2,900	5,800	10,150	14,500

1994 Mark VIII, V-8

	6	5	4	3	2	1
2d Cpe	520	1,560	2,600	5,200	9,100	13,000

1994 Continental, V-6

	6	5	4	3	2	1
4d Sed Executive	440	1,320	2,200	4,400	7,700	11,000
4d Sed Signature	480	1,440	2,400	4,800	8,400	12,000

1995 Town Car, V-8

	6	5	4	3	2	1
4d Executive Sed	500	1,550	2,600	5,200	9,100	13,000
4d Signature Sed	550	1,600	2,700	5,400	9,450	13,500
4d Cartier Sed	600	1,750	2,900	5,800	10,200	14,500

1995 Mark VIII, V-8

	6	5	4	3	2	1
2d Cpe	500	1,550	2,600	5,200	9,100	13,000

1995 Continental V-8

	6	5	4	3	2	1
4d Sed	500	1,500	2,500	5,000	8,750	12,500

MERCURY

1939 Series 99A, V-8, 116" wb

	6	5	4	3	2	1
2d Conv	1,450	4,300	7,200	14,400	25,200	36,000
2d Cpe	900	2,700	4,500	9,000	15,750	22,500
2d Sed	712	2,136	3,560	7,120	12,460	17,800
4d Sed	712	2,136	3,560	7,120	12,460	17,800

1940 Series O9A, V-8, 116" wb

	6	5	4	3	2	1
2d Conv	1,500	4,450	7,400	14,800	25,900	37,000
4d Conv Sed	1,120	3,360	5,600	11,200	19,600	28,000
2d Cpe	940	2,820	4,700	9,400	16,450	23,500
2d Sed	716	2,148	3,580	7,160	12,530	17,900
4d Sed	716	2,148	3,580	7,160	12,530	17,900

1941 Series 19A, V-8, 118" wb

	6	5	4	3	2	1
2d Conv	1,400	4,200	7,000	14,000	24,500	35,000
2d Bus Cpe	780	2,340	3,900	7,800	13,650	19,500
2d 5P Cpe	792	2,376	3,960	7,920	13,860	19,800
2d 6P Cpe	812	2,436	4,060	8,120	14,210	20,300
2d Sed	704	2,112	3,520	7,040	12,320	17,600
4d Sed	700	2,100	3,500	7,000	12,250	17,500
4d Sta Wag	1,320	3,960	6,600	13,200	23,100	33,000

1942 Series 29A, V-8, 118" wb

	6	5	4	3	2	1
2d Conv	1,200	3,600	6,000	12,000	21,000	30,000
2d Bus Cpe	728	2,184	3,640	7,280	12,740	18,200
2d 6P Cpe	740	2,220	3,700	7,400	12,950	18,500
2d Sed	680	2,040	3,400	6,800	11,900	17,000
4d Sed	676	2,028	3,380	6,760	11,830	16,900
4d Sta Wag	1,280	3,840	6,400	12,800	22,400	32,000

NOTE: Add 10 percent for liquamatic drive models.

1946-1948 Series 69M, V-8, 118" wb

	6	5	4	3	2	1
2d Conv	1,200	3,600	6,000	12,000	21,000	30,000
2d 6P Cpe	780	2,340	3,900	7,800	13,650	19,500
2d Sed	668	2,004	3,340	6,680	11,690	16,700
4d Sed	664	1,992	3,320	6,640	11,620	16,600
4d Sta Wag	1,280	3,840	6,400	12,800	22,400	32,000
2d Sptsman Conv (1946-47 only)	2,000	6,000	10,000	20,000	35,000	50,000

1949-1950 Series 0CM, V-8, 118" wb

	6	5	4	3	2	1
2d Conv	1,480	4,440	7,400	14,800	25,900	37,000
2d Cpe	1,120	3,360	5,600	11,200	19,600	28,000
2d Clb Cpe	1,160	3,480	5,800	11,600	20,300	29,000
2d Mon Cpe (1950 only)	1,200	3,600	6,000	12,000	21,000	30,000
4d Sed	760	2,280	3,800	7,600	13,300	19,000
2d Sta Wag	1,160	3,480	5,800	11,600	20,300	29,000

1951 Mercury, V-8, 118" wb

	6	5	4	3	2	1
4d Sed	780	2,340	3,900	7,800	13,650	19,500
2d Cpe	1,160	3,480	5,800	11,600	20,300	29,000
2d Conv	1,440	4,320	7,200	14,400	25,200	36,000
2d Sta Wag	1,100	3,350	5,600	11,200	19,600	28,000

1951 Monterey, V-8, 118" wb

	6	5	4	3	2	1
2d Clth Cpe	1,240	3,720	6,200	12,400	21,700	31,000
2d Lthr Cpe	1,280	3,840	6,400	12,800	22,400	32,000

1952-1953 Mercury Custom, V-8, 118" wb

	6	5	4	3	2	1
4d Sta Wag (1952 only)	700	2,150	3,600	7,200	12,600	18,000
4d Sed	644	1,932	3,220	6,440	11,270	16,100
2d Sed	680	2,040	3,400	6,800	11,900	17,000
2d HT	1,000	3,000	5,000	10,000	17,500	25,000

1952-1953 Monterey Special Custom, V-8, 118" wb

	6	5	4	3	2	1
4d Sed	652	1,956	3,260	6,520	11,410	16,300
2d HT	1,040	3,120	5,200	10,400	18,200	26,000
2d Conv	1,240	3,720	6,200	12,400	21,700	31,000
4d Sta Wag (1953 only)	800	2,400	4,000	8,000	14,000	20,000

1954 Mercury Custom, V-8, 118" wb

	6	5	4	3	2	1
4d Sed	704	2,112	3,520	7,040	12,320	17,600
2d Sed	700	2,100	3,500	7,000	12,250	17,500
2d HT	1,000	3,000	5,000	10,000	17,500	25,000

1954 Monterey Special Custom, V-8, 118" wb

	6	5	4	3	2	1
4d Sed	712	2,136	3,560	7,120	12,460	17,800
2d HT SV	1,320	3,960	6,600	13,200	23,100	33,000
2d HT	1,040	3,120	5,200	10,400	18,200	26,000
2d Conv	1,320	3,960	6,600	13,200	23,100	33,000
4d Sta Wag	840	2,520	4,200	8,400	14,700	21,000

1955 Custom Series, V-8, 119" wb

	6	5	4	3	2	1
4d Sed	660	1,980	3,300	6,600	11,550	16,500
2d Sed	656	1,968	3,280	6,560	11,480	16,400
2d HT	880	2,640	4,400	8,800	15,400	22,000
4d Sta Wag	680	2,040	3,400	6,800	11,900	17,000

1955 Monterey Series, V-8, 119" wb

	6	5	4	3	2	1
4d Sed	680	2,040	3,400	6,800	11,900	17,000
2d HT	920	2,760	4,600	9,200	16,100	23,000
4d Sta Wag	800	2,400	4,000	8,000	14,000	20,000

1955 Montclair Series, V-8, 119" wb

	6	5	4	3	2	1
4d Sed	700	2,100	3,500	7,000	12,250	17,500
2d HT	1,000	3,000	5,000	10,000	17,500	25,000
2d HT SV	1,320	3,960	6,600	13,200	23,100	33,000
2d Conv	1,360	4,080	6,800	13,600	23,800	34,000

1956 Medalist Series, V-8, 119" wb

	6	5	4	3	2	1
4d Sed	620	1,860	3,100	6,200	10,850	15,500
2d Sed	616	1,848	3,080	6,160	10,780	15,400
2d HT	800	2,400	4,000	8,000	14,000	20,000

1956 Custom Series, V-8, 119" wb

	6	5	4	3	2	1
4d Sed	640	1,920	3,200	6,400	11,200	16,000
2d Sed	648	1,944	3,240	6,480	11,340	16,200
2d HT	840	2,520	4,200	8,400	14,700	21,000
4d HT	720	2,160	3,600	7,200	12,600	18,000
2d Conv	1,280	3,840	6,400	12,800	22,400	32,000

(1956 Custom Series, continued)

	6	5	4	3	2	1
4d Sta Wag	740	2,220	3,700	7,400	12,950	18,500
2d Sta Wag	760	2,280	3,800	7,600	13,300	19,000

1956 Monterey Series, V-8, 119" wb

	6	5	4	3	2	1
4d Sed	660	1,980	3,300	6,600	11,550	16,500
4d Spt Sed	680	2,040	3,400	6,800	11,900	17,000
2d HT	920	2,760	4,600	9,200	16,100	23,000
4d HT	760	2,280	3,800	7,600	13,300	19,000
4d Sta Wag	780	2,340	3,900	7,800	13,650	19,500

1956 Montclair Series, V-8, 119" wb

	6	5	4	3	2	1
4d Spt Sed	700	2,100	3,500	7,000	12,250	17,500
2d HT	1,000	3,000	5,000	10,000	17,500	25,000
4d HT	800	2,400	4,000	8,000	14,000	20,000
2d Conv	1,400	4,200	7,000	14,000	24,500	35,000

1957 Monterey Series, V-8, 122" wb

	6	5	4	3	2	1
4d Sed	620	1,860	3,100	6,200	10,850	15,500
2d Sed	616	1,848	3,080	6,160	10,780	15,400
4d HT	760	2,280	3,800	7,600	13,300	19,000
2d HT	880	2,640	4,400	8,800	15,400	22,000
2d Conv	1,000	3,000	5,000	10,000	17,500	25,000

1957 Montclair Series, V-8, 122" wb

	6	5	4	3	2	1
4d Sed	640	1,920	3,200	6,400	11,200	16,000
4d HT	800	2,400	4,000	8,000	14,000	20,000
2d HT	920	2,760	4,600	9,200	16,100	23,000
2d Conv	1,160	3,480	5,800	11,600	20,300	29,000

1957 Turnpike Cruiser, V-8, 122" wb

	6	5	4	3	2	1
4d HT	960	2,880	4,800	9,600	16,800	24,000
2d HT	1,160	3,480	5,800	11,600	20,300	29,000
2d Conv	1,400	4,200	7,000	14,000	24,500	35,000

1957 Station Wagons, V-8, 122" wb

	6	5	4	3	2	1
2d Voy HT	960	2,880	4,800	9,600	16,800	24,000
4d Voy HT	940	2,820	4,700	9,400	16,450	23,500
2d Com HT	1,000	3,000	5,000	10,000	17,500	25,000
4d Com HT	980	2,940	4,900	9,800	17,150	24,500
4d Col Pk HT	1,080	3,240	5,400	10,800	18,900	27,000

1958 Mercury, V-8, 122" wb

	6	5	4	3	2	1
4d Sed	560	1,680	2,800	5,600	9,800	14,000
2d Sed	568	1,704	2,840	5,680	9,940	14,200

1958 Monterey, V-8, 122" wb

	6	5	4	3	2	1
4d Sed	568	1,704	2,840	5,680	9,940	14,200
2d Sed	572	1,716	2,860	5,720	10,010	14,300
4d HT	640	1,920	3,200	6,400	11,200	16,000
2d HT	720	2,160	3,600	7,200	12,600	18,000
2d Conv	1,000	3,000	5,000	10,000	17,500	25,000

1958 Montclair, V-8, 122" wb

	6	5	4	3	2	1
4d Sed	560	1,680	2,800	5,600	9,800	14,000
4d HT	760	2,280	3,800	7,600	13,300	19,000
2d HT	920	2,760	4,600	9,200	16,100	23,000
2d Conv	1,080	3,240	5,400	10,800	18,900	27,000

1958 Turnpike Cruiser, V-8, 122" wb

	6	5	4	3	2	1
4d HT	880	2,640	4,400	8,800	15,400	22,000
2d HT	1,040	3,120	5,200	10,400	18,200	26,000

1958 Station Wagons, V-8, 122" wb

	6	5	4	3	2	1
2d Voy HT	920	2,760	4,600	9,200	16,100	23,000
4d Voy HT	900	2,700	4,500	9,000	15,750	22,500
2d Com HT	980	2,940	4,900	9,800	17,150	24,500
4d Com HT	940	2,820	4,700	9,400	16,450	23,500
4d Col Pk HT	1,040	3,120	5,200	10,400	18,200	26,000

1958 Park Lane, V-8, 125" wb

	6	5	4	3	2	1
4d HT	800	2,400	4,000	8,000	14,000	20,000
2d HT	960	2,880	4,800	9,600	16,800	24,000
2d Conv	1,360	4,080	6,800	13,600	23,800	34,000

1959 Monterey, V-8, 126" wb

	6	5	4	3	2	1
4d Sed	540	1,620	2,700	5,400	9,450	13,500
2d Sed	544	1,632	2,720	5,440	9,520	13,600
4d HT	600	1,800	3,000	6,000	10,500	15,000
2d HT	720	2,160	3,600	7,200	12,600	18,000
2d Conv	1,040	3,120	5,200	10,400	18,200	26,000

1959 Montclair, V-8, 126" wb

	6	5	4	3	2	1
4d Sed	560	1,680	2,800	5,600	9,800	14,000
4d HT	640	1,920	3,200	6,400	11,200	16,000
2d HT	800	2,400	4,000	8,000	14,000	20,000

1959 Park Lane, V-8, 128" wb

	6	5	4	3	2	1
4d HT	680	2,040	3,400	6,800	11,900	17,000

	6	5	4	3	2	1
2d HT	840	2,520	4,200	8,400	14,700	21,000
2d Conv	1,080	3,240	5,400	10,800	18,900	27,000

1959 Country Cruiser Station Wagons, V-8, 126" wb

	6	5	4	3	2	1
2d Com HT	880	2,640	4,400	8,800	15,400	22,000
4d Com HT	860	2,580	4,300	8,600	15,050	21,500
4d Voy HT	920	2,760	4,600	9,200	16,100	23,000
4d Col Pk HT	940	2,820	4,700	9,400	16,450	23,500

1960 Comet, 6-cyl., 114" wb

	6	5	4	3	2	1
4d Sed	376	1,128	1,880	3,760	6,580	9,400
2d Sed	372	1,116	1,860	3,720	6,510	9,300
4d Sta Wag	380	1,140	1,900	3,800	6,650	9,500
2d Sta Wag	384	1,152	1,920	3,840	6,720	9,600

1960 Monterey, V-8, 126" wb

	6	5	4	3	2	1
4d Sed	380	1,140	1,900	3,800	6,650	9,500
2d Sed	376	1,128	1,880	3,760	6,580	9,400
4d HT	420	1,260	2,100	4,200	7,350	10,500
2d HT	640	1,920	3,200	6,400	11,200	16,000
2d Conv	920	2,760	4,600	9,200	16,100	23,000

1960 Country Cruiser Station Wagons, V-8, 126" wb

	6	5	4	3	2	1
4d Com HT	800	2,400	4,000	8,000	14,000	20,000
4d Col Pk HT	840	2,520	4,200	8,400	14,700	21,000

1960 Montclair, V-8, 126" wb

	6	5	4	3	2	1
4d Sed	392	1,176	1,960	3,920	6,860	9,800
4d HT	600	1,800	3,000	6,000	10,500	15,000
2d HT	680	2,040	3,400	6,800	11,900	17,000

1960 Park Lane, V-8, 126" wb

	6	5	4	3	2	1
4d HT	640	1,920	3,200	6,400	11,200	16,000
2d HT	760	2,280	3,800	7,600	13,300	19,000
2d Conv	1,120	3,360	5,600	11,200	19,600	28,000

1961 Comet, 6-cyl., 114" wb

	6	5	4	3	2	1
4d Sed	236	708	1,180	2,360	4,130	5,900
2d Sed	232	696	1,160	2,320	4,060	5,800
2d S-22 Cpe	520	1,560	2,600	5,200	9,100	13,000
4d Sta Wag	300	900	1,500	3,050	5,300	7,600
2d Sta Wag	300	900	1,550	3,100	5,400	7,700

1961 Meteor 600, V-8, 120" wb

	6	5	4	3	2	1
4d Sed	232	696	1,160	2,320	4,060	5,800
2d Sed	228	684	1,140	2,280	3,990	5,700

1961 Meteor 800, V-8, 120" wb

	6	5	4	3	2	1
4d Sed	240	720	1,200	2,400	4,200	6,000
4d HT	244	732	1,220	2,440	4,270	6,100
2d Sed	236	708	1,180	2,360	4,130	5,900
2d HT	260	780	1,300	2,600	4,550	6,500

1961 Monterey, V-8, 120" wb

	6	5	4	3	2	1
4d Sed	256	768	1,280	2,560	4,480	6,400
4d HT	260	780	1,300	2,600	4,550	6,500
2d HT	380	1,140	1,900	3,800	6,650	9,500
2d Conv	640	1,920	3,200	6,400	11,200	16,000

1961 Station Wagon, V-8, 120" wb

	6	5	4	3	2	1
4d Com	600	1,850	3,100	6,200	10,900	15,500
4d Col Pk	650	1,900	3,200	6,400	11,200	16,000

1962 Comet, 6-cyl.

	6	5	4	3	2	1
4d Sed	216	648	1,080	2,160	3,780	5,400
2d Sed	212	636	1,060	2,120	3,710	5,300
4d Sta Wag	212	636	1,060	2,120	3,710	5,300
2d Sta Wag	300	850	1,400	2,800	4,900	7,000
2d S-22 Cpe	520	1,560	2,600	5,200	9,100	13,000
4d Vill Sta Wag	300	850	1,450	2,900	5,050	7,200

NOTE: Add 10 percent for Custom line.

1962 Meteor, 8-cyl.

	6	5	4	3	2	1
4d Sed	220	660	1,100	2,200	3,850	5,500
2d Sed	216	648	1,080	2,160	3,780	5,400
2d S-33 Cpe	380	1,140	1,900	3,800	6,650	9,500

NOTE: Deduct 10 percent for 6-cyl. Add 10 percent for Custom line.

1962 Monterey, V-8

	6	5	4	3	2	1
4d Sed	224	672	1,120	2,240	3,920	5,600
4d HT Sed	228	684	1,140	2,280	3,990	5,700
2d Sed	216	648	1,080	2,160	3,780	5,400
2d HT	240	720	1,200	2,400	4,200	6,000
2d Conv	560	1,680	2,800	5,600	9,800	14,000
4d Sta Wag	500	1,450	2,400	4,800	8,400	12,000

NOTE: Add 10 percent for Custom line.

1962 Custom S-55 Sport Series, V-8

	6	5	4	3	2	1
2d HT	420	1,260	2,100	4,200	7,350	10,500
2d Conv	640	1,920	3,200	6,400	11,200	16,000

NOTE: Add 30 percent for 406 cid.

1963 Comet, 6-cyl.

	6	5	4	3	2	1
4d Sed	216	648	1,080	2,160	3,780	5,400
2d Sed	212	636	1,060	2,120	3,710	5,300
2d Cus HT	380	1,140	1,900	3,800	6,650	9,500
2d Cus Conv	560	1,680	2,800	5,600	9,800	14,000
2d S-22 Cpe	420	1,260	2,100	4,200	7,350	10,500
2d S-22 HT	540	1,620	2,700	5,400	9,450	13,500
2d S-22 Conv	640	1,920	3,200	6,400	11,200	16,000
4d Sta Wag	300	850	1,450	2,900	5,050	7,200
2d Sta Wag	300	900	1,450	2,900	5,100	7,300
4d Vill Sta Wag	300	950	1,550	3,100	5,450	7,800

NOTE: Add 10 percent for Custom line.

1963 Meteor, V-8

	6	5	4	3	2	1
4d Sed	220	660	1,100	2,200	3,850	5,500
2d Sed	216	648	1,080	2,160	3,780	5,400
4d Sta Wag	300	950	1,600	3,200	5,600	8,000
2d Cus HT	350	1,000	1,700	3,400	5,950	8,500
2d S-33 HT	400	1,200	2,000	4,000	7,000	10,000

NOTE: Deduct 10 percent for 6-cyl. Add 10 percent for Custom line.

1963 Monterey, V-8

	6	5	4	3	2	1
4d Sed	228	684	1,140	2,280	3,990	5,700
4d HT	240	720	1,200	2,400	4,200	6,000
2d Sed	224	672	1,120	2,240	3,920	5,600
2d HT	244	732	1,220	2,440	4,270	6,100
2d Cus Conv	368	1,104	1,840	3,680	6,440	9,200
2d S-55 HT	520	1,560	2,600	5,200	9,100	13,000
4d S-55 HT	436	1,308	2,180	4,360	7,630	10,900
2d S-55 Conv	680	2,040	3,400	6,800	11,900	17,000
2d Maraud FBk	420	1,260	2,100	4,200	7,350	10,500
2d Mar S-55 FBk	540	1,620	2,700	5,400	9,450	13,500
4d Col Pk	500	1,550	2,600	5,200	9,100	13,000

NOTE: Add 10 percent for Custom line. Add 30 percent for 406 cid. Add 60 percent for 427 cid.

1964 Comet, 6-cyl., 114" wb

	6	5	4	3	2	1
4d Sed	240	720	1,200	2,400	4,200	6,000
2d Sed	236	708	1,180	2,360	4,130	5,900
4d Sta Wag	300	850	1,450	2,900	5,050	7,200

1964 Comet 404, 6-cyl., 114" wb

	6	5	4	3	2	1
4d Sed	244	732	1,220	2,440	4,270	6,100
2d Sed	240	720	1,200	2,400	4,200	6,000
2d HT	380	1,140	1,900	3,800	6,650	9,500
2d Conv	560	1,680	2,800	5,600	9,800	14,000
4d DeL Wag	300	850	1,450	2,900	5,050	7,200
4d Sta Wag	300	850	1,400	2,850	4,950	7,100

1964 Comet Caliente, V-8 cyl., 114" wb

	6	5	4	3	2	1
4d Sed	248	744	1,240	2,480	4,340	6,200
2d HT	560	1,680	2,800	5,600	9,800	14,000
2d Conv	680	2,040	3,400	6,800	11,900	17,000

1964 Comet Cyclone, V-8 cyl., 114" wb

	6	5	4	3	2	1
2d HT	640	1,920	3,200	6,400	11,200	16,000

NOTE: Deduct 25 percent for 6-cyl. Caliente.

1964 Monterey, V-8

	6	5	4	3	2	1
4d Sed	236	708	1,180	2,360	4,130	5,900
4d HT	244	732	1,220	2,440	4,270	6,100
2d Sed	232	696	1,160	2,320	4,060	5,800
2d HT	252	756	1,260	2,520	4,410	6,300
2d HT FBk	380	1,140	1,900	3,800	6,650	9,500
2d Conv	580	1,740	2,900	5,800	10,150	14,500

1964 Montclair, V-8, 120" wb

	6	5	4	3	2	1
4d Sed	240	720	1,200	2,400	4,200	6,000
4d HT FBk	260	780	1,300	2,600	4,550	6,500
2d HT	400	1,200	2,000	4,000	7,000	10,000
2d HT FBk	420	1,260	2,100	4,200	7,350	10,500

1964 Park Lane, V-8, 120" wb

	6	5	4	3	2	1
4d Sed	248	744	1,240	2,480	4,340	6,200
4d HT	260	780	1,300	2,600	4,550	6,500
4d HT FBk	380	1,140	1,900	3,800	6,650	9,500
2d HT	520	1,560	2,600	5,200	9,100	13,000
2d HT FBk	560	1,680	2,800	5,600	9,800	14,000
2d Conv	680	2,040	3,400	6,800	11,900	17,000

1964 Station Wagon, V-8, 120" wb

	6	5	4	3	2	1
4d Col Pk	650	1,900	3,150	6,300	11,000	15,700

	6	5	4	3	2	1
4d Com	600	1,850	3,100	6,200	10,900	15,500

NOTE: Add 10 percent for Marauder. Add 5 percent for bucket seat option where available. Add 60 percent for 427 Super Marauder.

1965 Comet 202, V-8, 114" wb

	6	5	4	3	2	1
4d Sed	244	732	1,220	2,440	4,270	6,100
2d Sed	240	720	1,200	2,400	4,200	6,000
4d Sta Wag	300	900	1,450	2,900	5,100	7,300

NOTE: Deduct 20 percent for 6-cyl.

1965 Comet 404

	6	5	4	3	2	1
4d Sed	248	744	1,240	2,480	4,340	6,200
2d Sed	244	732	1,220	2,440	4,270	6,100
4d Vill Wag	300	900	1,500	2,950	5,200	7,400
4d Sta Wag	300	900	1,450	2,900	5,100	7,300

1965 Comet Caliente, V-8, 114" wb

	6	5	4	3	2	1
4d Sed	252	756	1,260	2,520	4,410	6,300
2d HT	400	1,200	2,000	4,000	7,000	10,000
2d Conv	680	2,040	3,400	6,800	11,900	17,000

1965 Comet Cyclone, V-8, 114" wb

	6	5	4	3	2	1
2d HT	640	1,920	3,200	6,400	11,200	16,000

1965 Monterey, V-8, 123" wb

	6	5	4	3	2	1
4d Sed	260	780	1,300	2,600	4,550	6,500
4d HT	360	1,080	1,800	3,600	6,300	9,000
4d Brzwy	380	1,140	1,900	3,800	6,650	9,500
2d Sed	256	768	1,280	2,560	4,480	6,400
2d HT	392	1,176	1,960	3,920	6,860	9,800
2d Conv	640	1,920	3,200	6,400	11,200	16,000

1965 Montclair, V-8, 123" wb

	6	5	4	3	2	1
4d Brzwy	400	1,200	2,000	4,000	7,000	10,000
4d HT	360	1,080	1,800	3,600	6,300	9,000
2d HT	400	1,200	2,000	4,000	7,000	10,000

1965 Park Lane, V-8, 123" wb

	6	5	4	3	2	1
4d Brzwy	420	1,260	2,100	4,200	7,350	10,500
4d HT	400	1,200	2,000	4,000	7,000	10,000
2d HT	420	1,260	2,100	4,200	7,350	10,500
2d Conv	680	2,040	3,400	6,800	11,900	17,000

1965 Station Wagon, V-8, 119" wb

	6	5	4	3	2	1
4d Col Pk	500	1,450	2,450	4,900	8,550	12,200
4d Com	450	1,400	2,350	4,700	8,200	11,700

NOTE: Add 60 percent for 427 cid engine.

1966 Comet Capri, V-8, 116" wb

	6	5	4	3	2	1
4d Sed	248	744	1,240	2,480	4,340	6,200
2d HT	360	1,080	1,800	3,600	6,300	9,000
4d Sta Wag	300	900	1,500	3,000	5,250	7,500

1966 Comet Caliente, V-8, 116" wb

	6	5	4	3	2	1
4d Sed	252	756	1,260	2,520	4,410	6,300
2d HT	520	1,560	2,600	5,200	9,100	13,000
2d Conv	680	2,040	3,400	6,800	11,900	17,000

1966 Comet Cyclone, V-8, 116" wb

	6	5	4	3	2	1
2d HT	560	1,680	2,800	5,600	9,800	14,000
2d Conv	800	2,400	4,000	8,000	14,000	20,000

1966 Comet Cyclone GT/GTA, V-8, 116" wb

	6	5	4	3	2	1
2d HT	640	1,920	3,200	6,400	11,200	16,000
2d Conv	920	2,760	4,600	9,200	16,100	23,000

1966 Comet 202, V-8, 116" wb

	6	5	4	3	2	1
4d Sed	240	720	1,200	2,400	4,200	6,000
2d Sed	248	744	1,240	2,480	4,340	6,200
4d Sta Wag	300	850	1,400	2,850	4,950	7,100

1966 Monterey, V-8, 123" wb

	6	5	4	3	2	1
4d Sed	252	756	1,260	2,520	4,410	6,300
4d Brzwy Sed	360	1,080	1,800	3,600	6,300	9,000
4d HT	380	1,140	1,900	3,800	6,650	9,500
2d Sed	256	768	1,280	2,560	4,480	6,400
2d HT FBk	400	1,200	2,000	4,000	7,000	10,000
2d Conv	580	1,740	2,900	5,800	10,150	14,500

1966 Montclair, V-8, 123" wb

	6	5	4	3	2	1
4d Sed	260	780	1,300	2,600	4,550	6,500
4d HT	388	1,164	1,940	3,880	6,790	9,700
2d HT	400	1,200	2,000	4,000	7,000	10,000

1966 Park Lane, V-8, 123" wb

	6	5	4	3	2	1
4d Brzwy Sed	400	1,200	2,000	4,000	7,000	10,000

	6	5	4	3	2	1
4d HT	400	1,200	2,000	4,000	7,000	10,000
2d HT	420	1,260	2,100	4,200	7,350	10,500
2d Conv	680	2,040	3,400	6,800	11,900	17,000

1966 S-55, V-8, 123" wb

	6	5	4	3	2	1
2d HT	560	1,680	2,800	5,600	9,800	14,000
2d Conv	640	1,920	3,200	6,400	11,200	16,000

1966 Station Wagons, V-8, 123" wb

	6	5	4	3	2	1
4d Comm	380	1,140	1,900	3,800	6,650	9,500
4d Col Pk	400	1,200	2,000	4,000	7,000	10,000

NOTE: Add 18 percent for 410 cid engine.

1967 Comet 202, V-8, 116" wb

	6	5	4	3	2	1
2d Sed	252	756	1,260	2,520	4,410	6,300
4d Sed	256	768	1,280	2,560	4,480	6,400

1967 Capri, V-8, 116" wb

	6	5	4	3	2	1
2d HT	268	804	1,340	2,680	4,690	6,700
4d Sed	252	756	1,260	2,520	4,410	6,300

1967 Caliante, V-8, 116" wb

	6	5	4	3	2	1
4d Sed	272	816	1,360	2,720	4,760	6,800
2d HT	420	1,260	2,100	4,200	7,350	10,500
2d Conv	620	1,860	3,100	6,200	10,850	15,500

1967 Cyclone, V-8, 116" wb

	6	5	4	3	2	1
2d HT	600	1,800	3,000	6,000	10,500	15,000
2d Conv	720	2,160	3,600	7,200	12,600	18,000

1967 Station Wagons, V-8, 113" wb

	6	5	4	3	2	1
4d Voyager	300	900	1,500	3,050	5,300	7,600
4d Villager	300	900	1,550	3,100	5,400	7,700

1967 Cougar, V-8, 111" wb

	6	5	4	3	2	1
2d HT	680	2,040	3,400	6,800	11,900	17,000
2d XR-7 HT	720	2,160	3,600	7,200	12,600	18,000

1967 Monterey, V-8, 123" wb

	6	5	4	3	2	1
4d Sed	252	756	1,260	2,520	4,410	6,300
4d Brzwy	360	1,080	1,800	3,600	6,300	9,000
2d Conv	600	1,800	3,000	6,000	10,500	15,000
2d HT	360	1,080	1,800	3,600	6,300	9,000
4d HT	260	780	1,300	2,600	4,550	6,500

1967 Montclair, V-8, 123" wb

	6	5	4	3	2	1
4d Sed	256	768	1,280	2,560	4,480	6,400
4d Brzwy	380	1,140	1,900	3,800	6,650	9,500
2d HT	400	1,200	2,000	4,000	7,000	10,000
4d HT	380	1,140	1,900	3,800	6,650	9,500

1967 Park Lane, V-8, 123" wb

	6	5	4	3	2	1
4d Brzwy	400	1,200	2,000	4,000	7,000	10,000
2d Conv	640	1,920	3,200	6,400	11,200	16,000
2d HT	420	1,260	2,100	4,200	7,350	10,500
4d HT	400	1,200	2,000	4,000	7,000	10,000

1967 Brougham, V-8, 123" wb

	6	5	4	3	2	1
4d Brzwy	428	1,284	2,140	4,280	7,490	10,700
4d HT	412	1,236	2,060	4,120	7,210	10,300

1967 Marquis, V-8, 123" wb

	6	5	4	3	2	1
2d HT	520	1,560	2,600	5,200	9,100	13,000

1967 Station Wagons, 119" wb

	6	5	4	3	2	1
4d Commuter	500	1,450	2,400	4,800	8,400	12,000
4d Col Park	500	1,500	2,500	5,000	8,750	12,500

NOTE: Add 10 percent for GT option. Add 15 percent for S-55 performance package. Add 60 percent for 427 cid engine.

1968 Comet, V-8

	6	5	4	3	2	1
2d HT	360	1,080	1,800	3,600	6,300	9,000

1968 Montego, V-8

	6	5	4	3	2	1
4d Sed	220	660	1,100	2,200	3,850	5,500
2d HT	240	720	1,200	2,400	4,200	6,000

1968 Montego MX

	6	5	4	3	2	1
4d Sta Wag	250	800	1,300	2,600	4,550	6,500
4d Sed	212	636	1,060	2,120	3,710	5,300
2d HT	360	1,080	1,800	3,600	6,300	9,000
2d Conv	580	1,740	2,900	5,800	10,150	14,500

1968 Cyclone, V-8

	6	5	4	3	2	1
2d FBk Cpe	600	1,800	3,000	6,000	10,500	15,000
2d HT	560	1,680	2,800	5,600	9,800	14,000

	6	5	4	3	2	1

1968 Cyclone GT 427, V-8

	6	5	4	3	2	1
2d FBk Cpe	920	2,760	4,600	9,200	16,100	23,000
2d HT	880	2,640	4,400	8,800	15,400	22,000

1968 Cyclone GT 428, V-8

	6	5	4	3	2	1
2d FBk Cpe	720	2,160	3,600	7,200	12,600	18,000

1968 Cougar, V-8

	6	5	4	3	2	1
2d HT Cpe	600	1,800	3,000	6,000	10,500	15,000
2d XR-7 Cpe	680	2,040	3,400	6,800	11,900	17,000

NOTE: Add 10 percent for GTE package. Add 5 percent for XR-7G.

1968 Monterey, V-8

	6	5	4	3	2	1
4d Sed	212	636	1,060	2,120	3,710	5,300
2d Conv	600	1,800	3,000	6,000	10,500	15,000
2d HT	260	780	1,300	2,600	4,550	6,500
4d HT	252	756	1,260	2,520	4,410	6,300

1968 Montclair, V-8

	6	5	4	3	2	1
4d Sed	216	648	1,080	2,160	3,780	5,400
2d HT	268	804	1,340	2,680	4,690	6,700
4d HT	260	780	1,300	2,600	4,550	6,500

1968 Park Lane, V-8

	6	5	4	3	2	1
4d Sed	232	696	1,160	2,320	4,060	5,800
2d Conv	620	1,860	3,100	6,200	10,850	15,500
2d HT	380	1,140	1,900	3,800	6,650	9,500
4d HT	276	828	1,380	2,760	4,830	6,900

1968 Marquis, V-8

	6	5	4	3	2	1
2d HT	400	1,200	2,000	4,000	7,000	10,000

1968 Station Wagons, V-8

	6	5	4	3	2	1
4d Commuter	500	1,500	2,500	5,000	8,750	12,500
4d Col Pk	500	1,550	2,600	5,200	9,100	13,000

NOTE: Deduct 5 percent for six-cylinder engine. Add 5 percent for Brougham package. Add 5 percent for "yacht paneling". Add 40 percent for 427 cid engine. Add 50 percent for 428 cid engine.

1969 Comet, 6-cyl.

	6	5	4	3	2	1
2d HT	240	720	1,200	2,400	4,200	6,000

1969 Montego, 6-cyl.

	6	5	4	3	2	1
4d Sed	192	576	960	1,920	3,360	4,800
2d HT	200	600	1,000	2,000	3,500	5,000

1969 Montego MX, V8

	6	5	4	3	2	1
4d Sed	196	588	980	1,960	3,430	4,900
2d HT	240	720	1,200	2,400	4,200	6,000
2d Conv	520	1,560	2,600	5,200	9,100	13,000
4d Sta Wag	300	900	1,500	3,000	5,250	7,500

1969 Cyclone, V-8

	6	5	4	3	2	1
2d HT	520	1,560	2,600	5,200	9,100	13,000

1969 Cyclone CJ, V-8

	6	5	4	3	2	1
2d HT	568	1,704	2,840	5,680	9,940	14,200

1969 Cougar, V-8

	6	5	4	3	2	1
2d HT	560	1,680	2,800	5,600	9,800	14,000
2d Conv	620	1,860	3,100	6,200	10,850	15,500
2d XR-7	600	1,800	3,000	6,000	10,500	15,000
2d XR-7 Conv	660	1,980	3,300	6,600	11,550	16,500
2d HT	720	2,160	3,600	7,200	12,600	18,000

NOTE: Add 30 percent for Boss 302. Add 50 percent for 428 CJ.

1969 Monterey, V-8

	6	5	4	3	2	1
4d Sed	232	696	1,160	2,320	4,060	5,800
4d HT	236	708	1,180	2,360	4,130	5,900
2d HT	248	744	1,240	2,480	4,340	6,200
2d Conv	500	1,450	2,400	4,800	8,400	12,000
4d Sta Wag	400	1,250	2,100	4,200	7,350	10,500

1969 Marauder, V-8

	6	5	4	3	2	1
2d HT	380	1,140	1,900	3,800	6,650	9,500
2d X-100 HT	560	1,680	2,800	5,600	9,800	14,000

1969 Marquis, V-8

	6	5	4	3	2	1
4d Sed	236	708	1,180	2,360	4,130	5,900
4d HT	240	720	1,200	2,400	4,200	6,000
2d HT	380	1,140	1,900	3,800	6,650	9,500
2d Conv	600	1,800	3,000	6,000	10,500	15,000
4d Sta Wag	450	1,300	2,200	4,400	7,700	11,000

1969 Marquis Brougham, V-8

	6	5	4	3	2	1
4d Sed	240	720	1,200	2,400	4,200	6,000

	6	5	4	3	2	1
4d HT	260	780	1,300	2,600	4,550	6,500
2d HT	450	1,400	2,300	4,600	8,050	11,500

NOTE: Add 10 percent for Montego/Comet V-8. Add 15 percent for GT option. Add 20 percent for GT Spoiler II. Add 10 percent for bucket seats (except Cougar). Add 10 percent for bench seats (Cougar only

1970 Montego

	6	5	4	3	2	1
4d Sed	236	708	1,180	2,360	4,130	5,900
2d HT	240	720	1,200	2,400	4,200	6,000

1970 Montego MX, V-8

	6	5	4	3	2	1
4d Sed	252	756	1,260	2,520	4,410	6,300
2d HT	360	1,080	1,800	3,600	6,300	9,000
4d Sta Wag	300	900	1,500	3,000	5,250	7,500

1970 Montego MX Brougham, V-8

	6	5	4	3	2	1
4d Sed	248	744	1,240	2,480	4,340	6,200
4d HT	260	780	1,300	2,600	4,550	6,500
2d HT	380	1,140	1,900	3,800	6,650	9,500
4d Vill Sta Wag	350	1,000	1,700	3,400	5,950	8,500

1970 Cyclone, V-8

	6	5	4	3	2	1
2d HT	580	1,740	2,900	5,800	10,150	14,500

1970 Cyclone GT, V-8

	6	5	4	3	2	1
2d HT	620	1,860	3,100	6,200	10,850	15,500

1970 Cyclone Spoiler, V-8

	6	5	4	3	2	1
2d HT	660	1,980	3,300	6,600	11,550	16,500

NOTE: Add 40 percent for 429 V-8 GT and Spoiler.

1970 Cougar, V-8

	6	5	4	3	2	1
2d HT	580	1,740	2,900	5,800	10,150	14,500
2d Conv	640	1,920	3,200	6,400	11,200	16,000

1970 Cougar XR-7, V-8

	6	5	4	3	2	1
2d HT	640	1,920	3,200	6,400	11,200	16,000
2d Conv	760	2,280	3,800	7,600	13,300	19,000
2d HT	720	2,160	3,600	7,200	12,600	18,000

NOTE: Add 30 percent for Boss 302. Add 50 percent for 428 CJ.

1970 Monterey, V-8

	6	5	4	3	2	1
4d Sed	240	720	1,200	2,400	4,200	6,000
4d HT	272	816	1,360	2,720	4,760	6,800
2d HT	372	1,116	1,860	3,720	6,510	9,300
2d Conv	540	1,620	2,700	5,400	9,450	13,500
4d Sta Wag	368	1,104	1,840	3,680	6,440	9,200

1970 Monterey Custom, V-8

	6	5	4	3	2	1
4d Sed	248	744	1,240	2,480	4,340	6,200
4d HT	360	1,080	1,800	3,600	6,300	9,000
2d HT	380	1,140	1,900	3,800	6,650	9,500

1970 Marauder, V-8

	6	5	4	3	2	1
2d HT	400	1,200	2,000	4,000	7,000	10,000
2d X-100 HT	560	1,680	2,800	5,600	9,800	14,000

1970 Marquis, V-8

	6	5	4	3	2	1
4d Sed	252	756	1,260	2,520	4,410	6,300
4d HT	368	1,104	1,840	3,680	6,440	9,200
2d HT	388	1,164	1,940	3,880	6,790	9,700
2d Conv	680	2,040	3,400	6,800	11,900	17,000
4d Sta Wag	400	1,150	1,900	3,800	6,650	9,500
4d Col Pk	400	1,200	1,950	3,900	6,850	9,800

1970 Marquis Brougham, V-8

	6	5	4	3	2	1
4d Sed	260	780	1,300	2,600	4,550	6,500
4d HT	360	1,080	1,800	3,600	6,300	9,000
2d HT	388	1,164	1,940	3,880	6,790	9,700

NOTE: Add 50 percent for any 429 engine option.

1971 Comet, V-8

	6	5	4	3	2	1
4d Sed	204	612	1,020	2,040	3,570	5,100
2d Sed	208	624	1,040	2,080	3,640	5,200
2d HT GT	360	1,080	1,800	3,600	6,300	9,000

1971 Montego, V-8

	6	5	4	3	2	1
4d Sed	200	600	1,000	2,000	3,500	5,000
2d HT	232	696	1,160	2,320	4,060	5,800

1971 Montego MX

	6	5	4	3	2	1
4 Sed	204	612	1,020	2,040	3,570	5,100
2d HT	228	684	1,140	2,280	3,990	5,700
4d Sta Wag	300	950	1,550	3,100	5,450	7,800

1971 Montego MX Brougham

	6	5	4	3	2	1
4d Sed	208	624	1,040	2,080	3,640	5,200

	6	5	4	3	2	1
4d HT	224	672	1,120	2,240	3,920	5,600
2d HT	240	720	1,200	2,400	4,200	6,000
4d Villager Sta Wag	300	950	1,600	3,150	5,550	7,900

1971 Cyclone, V-8

	6	5	4	3	2	1
2d HT	520	1,560	2,600	5,200	9,100	13,000

1971 Cyclone GT, V-8

	6	5	4	3	2	1
2d HT	560	1,680	2,800	5,600	9,800	14,000

1971 Cyclone Spoiler, V-8

	6	5	4	3	2	1
2d HT	580	1,740	2,900	5,800	10,150	14,500

NOTE: Add 40 percent for 429 V-8 GT and Spoiler.

1971 Cougar, V-8

	6	5	4	3	2	1
2d HT	520	1,560	2,600	5,200	9,100	13,000
2d Conv	560	1,680	2,800	5,600	9,800	14,000

1971 Cougar XR-7, V-8

	6	5	4	3	2	1
2d HT	580	1,740	2,900	5,800	10,150	14,500
2d Conv	620	1,860	3,100	6,200	10,850	15,500

1971 Monterey, V-8

	6	5	4	3	2	1
4d Sed	200	600	1,000	2,000	3,500	5,000
4d HT	216	648	1,080	2,160	3,780	5,400
2d HT	248	744	1,240	2,480	4,340	6,200
4d Sta Wag	350	1,100	1,800	3,650	6,350	9,100

1971 Monterey Custom, V-8

	6	5	4	3	2	1
4d Sed	204	612	1,020	2,040	3,570	5,100
4d HT	220	660	1,100	2,200	3,850	5,500
2d HT	260	780	1,300	2,600	4,550	6,500

1971 Marquis, V-8

	6	5	4	3	2	1
4d Sed	212	636	1,060	2,120	3,710	5,300
4d HT	228	684	1,140	2,280	3,990	5,700
2d HT	400	1,200	2,000	4,000	7,000	10,000
4d Sta Wag	350	1,100	1,850	3,700	6,450	9,200

1971 Marquis Brougham

	6	5	4	3	2	1
4d Sed	220	660	1,100	2,200	3,850	5,500
4d HT	240	720	1,200	2,400	4,200	6,000
2d HT	500	1,450	2,400	4,800	8,400	12,000
4d Col Pk	450	1,400	2,300	4,600	8,050	11,500

NOTE: Add 30 percent for 429.

1972 Comet, V-8

	6	5	4	3	2	1
4d Sed	204	612	1,020	2,040	3,570	5,100
2d Sed	220	660	1,100	2,200	3,850	5,500

1972 Montego, V-8

	6	5	4	3	2	1
4d Sed	200	600	1,000	2,000	3,500	5,000
2d HT	216	648	1,080	2,160	3,780	5,400

1972 Montego MX, V-8

	6	5	4	3	2	1
4d Sed	208	624	1,040	2,080	3,640	5,200
2d HT	300	950	1,600	3,200	5,600	8,000
4d Sta Wag	300	950	1,600	3,150	5,550	7,900

1972 Montego Brougham, V-8

	6	5	4	3	2	1
4d Sed	212	636	1,060	2,120	3,710	5,300
2d HT	260	780	1,300	2,600	4,550	6,500
4d Sta Wag	300	950	1,600	3,200	5,600	8,000

1972 Montego GT, V-8

	6	5	4	3	2	1
2d HT FBk	360	1,080	1,800	3,600	6,300	9,000

1972 Cougar, V-8

	6	5	4	3	2	1
2d HT	520	1,560	2,600	5,200	9,100	13,000
2d Conv	580	1,740	2,900	5,800	10,150	14,500

1972 Cougar XR-7, V-8

	6	5	4	3	2	1
2d HT	580	1,740	2,900	5,800	10,150	14,500
2d Conv	640	1,920	3,200	6,400	11,200	16,000

1972 Monterey, V-8

	6	5	4	3	2	1
4d Sed	300	950	1,600	3,200	5,600	8,000
4d HT	400	1,200	2,000	4,000	7,000	10,000
2d HT	500	1,500	2,500	5,000	8,750	12,500
4d Sta Wag	500	1,450	2,400	4,800	8,400	12,000

1972 Monterey Custom, V-8

	6	5	4	3	2	1
4d Sed	350	1,000	1,650	3,300	5,750	8,200
4d HT	400	1,200	2,050	4,100	7,150	10,200
2d HT	500	1,500	2,500	5,050	8,800	12,600

1972 Marquis, V-8

	6	5	4	3	2	1
4d Sed	300	900	1,500	3,000	5,250	7,500
4d HT	400	1,200	2,000	4,000	7,000	10,000
2d HT	500	1,450	2,400	4,800	8,400	12,000
4d Sta Wag	450	1,400	2,300	4,600	8,050	11,500

1972 Marquis Brougham, V-8

	6	5	4	3	2	1
4d Sed	350	1,050	1,700	3,450	6,000	8,600
4d HT	400	1,250	2,100	4,200	7,350	10,500
2d HT	500	1,500	2,500	5,000	8,750	12,500
4d Col Pk	500	1,450	2,400	4,800	8,400	12,000

1973 Comet, V-8

	6	5	4	3	2	1
4d Sed	204	612	1,020	2,040	3,570	5,100
2d Sed	220	660	1,100	2,200	3,850	5,500

1973 Montego, V-8

	6	5	4	3	2	1
4d Sed	200	600	1,000	2,000	3,500	5,000
2d HT	232	696	1,160	2,320	4,060	5,800

1973 Montego MX, V-8

	6	5	4	3	2	1
4d Sed	204	612	1,020	2,040	3,570	5,100
2d HT	240	720	1,200	2,400	4,200	6,000

1973 Montego MX Brougham, V-8

	6	5	4	3	2	1
4d Sed	208	624	1,040	2,080	3,640	5,200
2d HT	248	744	1,240	2,480	4,340	6,200

1973 Montego GT, V-8

	6	5	4	3	2	1
2d HT	360	1,080	1,800	3,600	6,300	9,000

1973 Montego MX

	6	5	4	3	2	1
4d Village Wag	300	950	1,550	3,100	5,450	7,800

1973 Cougar, V-8

	6	5	4	3	2	1
2d HT	420	1,260	2,100	4,200	7,350	10,500
2d Conv	540	1,620	2,700	5,400	9,450	13,500

1973 Cougar XR-7, V-8

	6	5	4	3	2	1
2d HT	540	1,620	2,700	5,400	9,450	13,500
2d Conv	580	1,740	2,900	5,800	10,150	14,500

1973 Monterey, V-8

	6	5	4	3	2	1
4d Sed	200	600	1,000	2,000	3,500	5,000
2d HT	204	612	1,020	2,040	3,570	5,100

1973 Monterey Custom, V-8

	6	5	4	3	2	1
4d Sed	204	612	1,020	2,040	3,570	5,100
2d HT	240	720	1,200	2,400	4,200	6,000

1973 Marquis, V-8

	6	5	4	3	2	1
4d Sed	350	1,000	1,700	3,400	5,950	8,500
4d HT	350	1,050	1,750	3,500	6,100	8,700
2d HT	400	1,150	1,900	3,800	6,650	9,500

1973 Marquis Brougham, V-8

	6	5	4	3	2	1
4d Sed	216	648	1,080	2,160	3,780	5,400
4d HT	240	720	1,200	2,400	4,200	6,000
2d HT	380	1,140	1,900	3,800	6,650	9,500

1973 Station Wagon, V-8

	6	5	4	3	2	1
4d Monterey	212	636	1,060	2,120	3,710	5,300
4d Marquis	216	648	1,080	2,160	3,780	5,400
4d Col Pk	372	1,116	1,860	3,720	6,510	9,300

1974 Comet, V-8

	6	5	4	3	2	1
4d Sed	204	612	1,020	2,040	3,570	5,100
2d Sed	220	660	1,100	2,200	3,850	5,500

1974 Montego, V-8

	6	5	4	3	2	1
4d Sed	208	624	1,040	2,080	3,640	5,200
2d HT	224	672	1,120	2,240	3,920	5,600

1974 Montego MX, V-8

	6	5	4	3	2	1
4d Sed	212	636	1,060	2,120	3,710	5,300
2d HT	228	684	1,140	2,280	3,990	5,700

1974 Montego MX Brougham, V-8

	6	5	4	3	2	1
4d Sed	216	648	1,080	2,160	3,780	5,400
2d HT	236	708	1,180	2,360	4,130	5,900
4d Villager	300	900	1,500	3,050	5,300	7,600

1974 Cougar, V-8

	6	5	4	3	2	1
2d HT	380	1,140	1,900	3,800	6,650	9,500

1974 Monterey, V-8

	6	5	4	3	2	1
4d Sed	204	612	1,020	2,040	3,570	5,100
2d HT	260	780	1,300	2,600	4,550	6,500

1974 Monterey Custom, V-8

	6	5	4	3	2	1
4d Sed	208	624	1,040	2,080	3,640	5,200
2d HT	260	780	1,300	2,600	4,550	6,500

1974 Marquis, V-8

	6	5	4	3	2	1
4d Sed	212	636	1,060	2,120	3,710	5,300
4d HT	220	660	1,100	2,200	3,850	5,500
2d HT	360	1,080	1,800	3,600	6,300	9,000

1974 Marquis Brougham, V-8

	6	5	4	3	2	1
4d Sed	216	648	1,080	2,160	3,780	5,400
4d HT	240	720	1,200	2,400	4,200	6,000
2d HT	360	1,080	1,800	3,600	6,300	9,000

1974 Station Wagons, V-8

	6	5	4	3	2	1
4d Monterey	360	1,080	1,800	3,600	6,300	9,000
4d Marquis	368	1,104	1,840	3,680	6,440	9,200
4d Col Pk	380	1,140	1,900	3,800	6,650	9,500

1975 Bobcat 4-cyl.

	6	5	4	3	2	1
2d HBk	204	612	1,020	2,040	3,570	5,100
4d Sta Wag	200	600	1,000	2,000	3,500	5,000

1975 Comet, V-8

	6	5	4	3	2	1
4d Sed	184	552	920	1,840	3,220	4,600
2d Sed	188	564	940	1,880	3,290	4,700

1975 Monarch, V-8

	6	5	4	3	2	1
4d Sed	196	588	980	1,960	3,430	4,900
2d Cpe	200	600	1,000	2,000	3,500	5,000

1975 Monarch Ghia, V-8

	6	5	4	3	2	1
4d Sed	200	600	1,000	2,000	3,500	5,000
2d Cpe	204	612	1,020	2,040	3,570	5,100

1975 Monarch Grand Ghia, V-8

	6	5	4	3	2	1
4d Sed	208	624	1,040	2,080	3,640	5,200

1975 Montego, V-8

	6	5	4	3	2	1
4d Sed	192	576	960	1,920	3,360	4,800
2d HT	196	588	980	1,960	3,430	4,900

1975 Montego MX, V-8

	6	5	4	3	2	1
4d Sed	196	588	980	1,960	3,430	4,900
2d HT	200	600	1,000	2,000	3,500	5,000

1975 Montego Brougham, V-8

	6	5	4	3	2	1
4d Sed	200	600	1,000	2,000	3,500	5,000
2d HT	204	612	1,020	2,040	3,570	5,100

1975 Station Wagons, V-8

	6	5	4	3	2	1
4d Villager	196	588	980	1,960	3,430	4,900

1975 Cougar, V-8

	6	5	4	3	2	1
2d HT	204	612	1,020	2,040	3,570	5,100

1975 Marquis, V-8

	6	5	4	3	2	1
4d Sed	196	588	980	1,960	3,430	4,900
2d HT	200	600	1,000	2,000	3,500	5,000

1975 Marquis Brougham, V-8

	6	5	4	3	2	1
4d Sed	200	600	1,000	2,000	3,500	5,000
2d HT	204	612	1,020	2,040	3,570	5,100

1975 Grand Marquis, V-8

	6	5	4	3	2	1
4d Sed	204	612	1,020	2,040	3,570	5,100
2d HT	208	624	1,040	2,080	3,640	5,200

1975 Station Wagons, V-8

	6	5	4	3	2	1
4d Marquis	300	850	1,400	2,800	4,900	7,000
4d Col Pk	350	1,000	1,700	3,400	5,950	8,500

1976 Bobcat, 4-cyl.

	6	5	4	3	2	1
3d HBk	184	552	920	1,840	3,220	4,600
4d Sta Wag	188	564	940	1,880	3,290	4,700

1976 Comet, V-8

	6	5	4	3	2	1
4d Sed	180	540	900	1,800	3,150	4,500
2d Sed	176	528	880	1,760	3,080	4,400

1976 Monarch, V-8

	6	5	4	3	2	1
4d Sed	172	516	860	1,720	3,010	4,300
2d Sed	196	588	980	1,960	3,430	4,900

1976 Monarch Ghia, V-8

	6	5	4	3	2	1
4d Sed	180	540	900	1,800	3,150	4,500
2d Sed	184	552	920	1,840	3,220	4,600

1976 Monarch Grand Ghia, V-8

	6	5	4	3	2	1
4d Sed	196	588	980	1,960	3,430	4,900

1976 Montego, V-8

	6	5	4	3	2	1
4d Sed	184	552	920	1,840	3,220	4,600
2d Cpe	188	564	940	1,880	3,290	4,700

1976 Montego MX, V-8

	6	5	4	3	2	1
4d Sed	192	576	960	1,920	3,360	4,800
2d Cpe	196	588	980	1,960	3,430	4,900

1976 Montego Brougham, V-8

	6	5	4	3	2	1
4d Sed	200	600	1,000	2,000	3,500	5,000
2d Cpe	204	612	1,020	2,040	3,570	5,100

1976 Station Wagons, V-8

	6	5	4	3	2	1
4d Montego MX	188	564	940	1,880	3,290	4,700
4d Montego Vill	192	576	960	1,920	3,360	4,800

1976 Cougar XR7, V-8

	6	5	4	3	2	1
2d HT	192	576	960	1,920	3,360	4,800

1976 Marquis, V-8

	6	5	4	3	2	1
4d Sed	184	552	920	1,840	3,220	4,600
2d Cpe	188	564	940	1,880	3,290	4,700

1976 Marquis Brougham, V-8

	6	5	4	3	2	1
4d Sed	192	576	960	1,920	3,360	4,800
2d Cpe	196	588	980	1,960	3,430	4,900

1976 Grand Marquis, V-8

	6	5	4	3	2	1
4d Sed	200	600	1,000	2,000	3,500	5,000
2d Cpe	204	612	1,020	2,040	3,570	5,100

1976 Station Wagons, V-8

	6	5	4	3	2	1
4d Marquis	220	660	1,100	2,200	3,850	5,500
4d Col Pk	240	720	1,200	2,400	4,200	6,000

1977 Bobcat, 4-cyl.

	6	5	4	3	2	1
3d HBk	200	550	900	1,800	3,150	4,500
4d Sta Wag	200	550	900	1,850	3,200	4,600
4d Vill Wag	200	550	950	1,900	3,300	4,700

NOTE: Add 5 percent for V-6.

1977 Comet, V-8

	6	5	4	3	2	1
4d Sed	144	432	720	1,440	2,520	3,600
2d Sed	148	444	740	1,480	2,590	3,700

1977 Monarch, V-8

	6	5	4	3	2	1
4d Sed	136	408	680	1,360	2,380	3,400
2d Sed	140	420	700	1,400	2,450	3,500

1977 Monarch Ghia, V-8

	6	5	4	3	2	1
4d Sed	144	432	720	1,440	2,520	3,600
2d Sed	148	444	740	1,480	2,590	3,700

1977 Cougar, V-8

	6	5	4	3	2	1
4d Sed	152	456	760	1,520	2,660	3,800
2d Sed	156	468	780	1,560	2,730	3,900

1977 Cougar Brougham, V-8

	6	5	4	3	2	1
4d Sed	156	468	780	1,560	2,730	3,900
2d Sed	160	480	800	1,600	2,800	4,000

1977 Cougar XR7, V-8

	6	5	4	3	2	1
2d HT	168	504	840	1,680	2,940	4,200

1977 Station Wagons, V-8

	6	5	4	3	2	1
4d Cougar	152	456	760	1,520	2,660	3,800
4d Vill	156	468	780	1,560	2,730	3,900

1977 Marquis, V-8

	6	5	4	3	2	1
4d Sed	156	468	780	1,560	2,730	3,900
2d Sed	160	480	800	1,600	2,800	4,000

1977 Marquis Brougham, V-8

	6	5	4	3	2	1
4d Sed	156	468	780	1,560	2,730	3,900
2d Sed	160	480	800	1,600	2,800	4,000

1977 Grand Marquis, V-8

	6	5	4	3	2	1
4d HT	164	492	820	1,640	2,870	4,100
2d HT	168	504	840	1,680	2,940	4,200

1977 Station Wagons, V-8

	6	5	4	3	2	1
4d 2S Marquis	250	700	1,200	2,400	4,200	6,000
4d 3S Marquis	250	750	1,200	2,450	4,250	6,100

1978 Bobcat

	6	5	4	3	2	1
3d Rbt	144	432	720	1,440	2,520	3,600
4d Sta Wag	200	550	900	1,800	3,150	4,500

1978 Zephyr

	6	5	4	3	2	1
4d Sed	132	396	660	1,320	2,310	3,300
2d Sed	128	384	640	1,280	2,240	3,200
2d Cpe	140	420	700	1,400	2,450	3,500
4d Sta Wag	150	450	750	1,500	2,600	3,700

1978 Monarch

	6	5	4	3	2	1
4d Sed	132	396	660	1,320	2,310	3,300
2d Sed	150	450	750	1,500	2,650	3,800

1978 Cougar

	6	5	4	3	2	1
4d Sed	140	420	700	1,400	2,450	3,500
2d HT	144	432	720	1,440	2,520	3,600

1978 Cougar XR7

	6	5	4	3	2	1
2d HT	164	492	820	1,640	2,870	4,100

1978 Marquis

	6	5	4	3	2	1
4d Sed	200	550	900	1,800	3,150	4,500
2d HT	250	800	1,350	2,700	4,750	6,800
4d Sta Wag	250	750	1,250	2,500	4,350	6,200

1978 Marquis Brougham

	6	5	4	3	2	1
4d Sed	156	468	780	1,560	2,730	3,900
2d HT	160	480	800	1,600	2,800	4,000

1978 Grand Marquis

	6	5	4	3	2	1
4d Sed	164	492	820	1,640	2,870	4,100
2d HT	168	504	840	1,680	2,940	4,200

1979 Bobcat, 4-cyl.

	6	5	4	3	2	1
3d Rbt	148	444	740	1,480	2,590	3,700
4d Wag	144	432	720	1,440	2,520	3,600
4d Villager Wag	148	444	740	1,480	2,590	3,700

1979 Capri, 4-cyl.

	6	5	4	3	2	1
2d Cpe	152	456	760	1,520	2,660	3,800
2d Ghia Cpe	160	480	800	1,600	2,800	4,000

NOTE: Add 5 percent for 6-cyl. Add 8 percent for V-8.

1979 Zephyr, 6-cyl.

	6	5	4	3	2	1
4d Sed	136	408	680	1,360	2,380	3,400
2d Cpe	144	432	720	1,440	2,520	3,600
2d Spt Cpe	152	456	760	1,520	2,660	3,800
4d Sta Wag	140	420	700	1,400	2,450	3,500

NOTE: Add 5 percent for V-8.

1979 Monarch, V-8

	6	5	4	3	2	1
4d Sed	136	408	680	1,360	2,380	3,400
2d Cpe	144	432	720	1,440	2,520	3,600

NOTE: Deduct 5 percent for 6-cyl.

1979 Cougar, V-8

	6	5	4	3	2	1
4d Sed	144	432	720	1,440	2,520	3,600
2d HT	148	444	740	1,480	2,590	3,700
2d HT XR7	164	492	820	1,640	2,870	4,100

1979 Marquis, V-8

	6	5	4	3	2	1
4d Sed	152	456	760	1,520	2,660	3,800
2d HT	156	468	780	1,560	2,730	3,900

1979 Marquis Brougham, V-8

	6	5	4	3	2	1
4d Sed	156	468	780	1,560	2,730	3,900
2d HT	160	480	800	1,600	2,800	4,000

1979 Grand Marquis, V-8

	6	5	4	3	2	1
4d Sed	160	480	800	1,600	2,800	4,000
2d HT	164	492	820	1,640	2,870	4,100

1979 Station Wagons, V-8

	6	5	4	3	2	1
4d 3S Marquis	152	456	760	1,520	2,660	3,800
4d 3S Colony Park	160	480	800	1,600	2,800	4,000

1980 Bobcat, 4-cyl.

	6	5	4	3	2	1
2d HBk	140	420	700	1,400	2,450	3,500
2d Sta Wag	144	432	720	1,440	2,520	3,600
2d Sta Wag Villager	152	456	760	1,520	2,660	3,800

1980 Capri, 6-cyl.

	6	5	4	3	2	1
2d HBk	188	564	940	1,880	3,290	4,700
2d HBk Ghia	200	600	1,000	2,000	3,500	5,000

NOTE: Deduct 10 percent for 4-cyl.

1980 Zephyr, 6-cyl.

	6	5	4	3	2	1
4d Sed	140	420	700	1,400	2,450	3,500
2d Sed	136	408	680	1,360	2,380	3,400
2d Cpe Z-7	168	504	840	1,680	2,940	4,200
4d Sta Wag	156	468	780	1,560	2,730	3,900

NOTE: Deduct 10 percent for 4-cyl.

1980 Monarch, V-8

	6	5	4	3	2	1
4d Sed	168	504	840	1,680	2,940	4,200
2d Cpe	164	492	820	1,640	2,870	4,100

NOTE: Deduct 10 percent for 4-cyl.

1980 Cougar XR7, V-8

	6	5	4	3	2	1
2d Cpe	232	696	1,160	2,320	4,060	5,800

1980 Marquis, V-8

	6	5	4	3	2	1
4d Sed	176	528	880	1,760	3,080	4,400
2d Sed	172	516	860	1,720	3,010	4,300

1980 Marquis Brougham, V-8

	6	5	4	3	2	1
4d Sed	184	552	920	1,840	3,220	4,600
2d Sed	180	540	900	1,800	3,150	4,500

1980 Grand Marquis, V-8

	6	5	4	3	2	1
4d Sed	188	564	940	1,880	3,290	4,700
2d Sed	184	552	920	1,840	3,220	4,600
4d Sta Wag	192	576	960	1,920	3,360	4,800
4d Sta Wag CP	200	600	1,000	2,000	3,500	5,000

1981 Lynx, 4-cyl.

	6	5	4	3	2	1
2d HBk RS	148	444	740	1,480	2,590	3,700
4d HBk RS	152	456	760	1,520	2,660	3,800
2d HBk LS	152	456	760	1,520	2,660	3,800

NOTE: Deduct 5 percent for lesser models.

1981 Zephyr, 6-cyl.

	6	5	4	3	2	1
4d Sed S	140	420	700	1,400	2,450	3,500
4d Sed	144	432	720	1,440	2,520	3,600
2d Sed	140	420	700	1,400	2,450	3,500
2d Cpe Z-7	172	516	860	1,720	3,010	4,300
4d Sta Wag	160	480	800	1,600	2,800	4,000

NOTE: Deduct 10 percent for 4-cyl.

1981 Capri, 6-cyl.

	6	5	4	3	2	1
2d HBk	180	540	900	1,800	3,150	4,500
2d HBk GS	188	564	940	1,880	3,290	4,700

NOTE: Deduct 10 percent for 4-cyl.

1981 Cougar, 6-cyl.

	6	5	4	3	2	1
4d Sed	168	504	840	1,680	2,940	4,200
2d Sed	164	492	820	1,640	2,870	4,100

NOTE: Deduct 10 percent for 4-cyl.

1981 Cougar XR7, V-8

	6	5	4	3	2	1
2d Cpe	236	708	1,180	2,360	4,130	5,900

NOTE: Deduct 12 percent for 6-cyl.

1981 Marquis, V-8

	6	5	4	3	2	1
4d Sed	176	528	880	1,760	3,080	4,400

1981 Marquis Brougham, V-8

	6	5	4	3	2	1
4d Sed	184	552	920	1,840	3,220	4,600
2d Sed	180	540	900	1,800	3,150	4,500

1981 Grand Marquis, V-8

	6	5	4	3	2	1
4d Sed	192	576	960	1,920	3,360	4,800
2d Sed	188	564	940	1,880	3,290	4,700
4d Sta Wag	196	588	980	1,960	3,430	4,900
4d Sta Wag CP	196	588	980	1,960	3,430	4,900

1982 Lynx, 4-cyl.

	6	5	4	3	2	1
2d HBk LS	152	456	760	1,520	2,660	3,800
4d HBk LS	156	468	780	1,560	2,730	3,900
4d Sta Wag LS	160	480	800	1,600	2,800	4,000
2d HBk RS	156	468	780	1,560	2,730	3,900

NOTE: Deduct 5 percent for lesser models.

1982 LN7, 4-cyl.

	6	5	4	3	2	1
2d HBk	184	552	920	1,840	3,220	4,600

1982 Zephyr, 6-cyl.

	6	5	4	3	2	1
4d Sed	148	444	740	1,480	2,590	3,700
2d Cpe Z-7	172	516	860	1,720	3,010	4,300
4d Sed GS	152	456	760	1,520	2,660	3,800
2d Cpe Z-7 GS	180	540	900	1,800	3,150	4,500

1982 Capri, 6-cyl.

	6	5	4	3	2	1
2d HBk L	212	636	1,060	2,120	3,710	5,300
2d HBk GS	220	660	1,100	2,200	3,850	5,500

1982 Capri, V-8

	6	5	4	3	2	1
2d HBk RS	224	672	1,120	2,240	3,920	5,600

NOTE: Deduct 10 percent for 4-cyl.

1982 Cougar, 6-cyl.

	6	5	4	3	2	1
4d Sed GS	160	480	800	1,600	2,800	4,000
2d Sed GS	156	468	780	1,560	2,730	3,900
4d Sta Wag GS	168	504	840	1,680	2,940	4,200
4d Sed LS	164	492	820	1,640	2,870	4,100
2d Sed LS	160	480	800	1,600	2,800	4,000

1982 Cougar XR7, V-8

	6	5	4	3	2	1
2d Cpe	240	720	1,200	2,400	4,200	6,000
2d Cpe LS	248	744	1,240	2,480	4,340	6,200

NOTE: Deduct 10 percent for 6-cyl.

1982 Marquis, V-8

	6	5	4	3	2	1
4d Sed	180	540	900	1,800	3,150	4,500

1982 Marquis Brougham, V-8

	6	5	4	3	2	1
4d Sed	188	564	940	1,880	3,290	4,700
2d Cpe	184	552	920	1,840	3,220	4,600

1982 Grand Marquis, V-8

	6	5	4	3	2	1
4d Sed	196	588	980	1,960	3,430	4,900
2d Cpe	192	576	960	1,920	3,360	4,800
4d Sta Wag	196	588	980	1,960	3,430	4,900
4d Sta Wag CP	200	600	1,000	2,000	3,500	5,000

1983 Lynx, 4-cyl.

	6	5	4	3	2	1
2d HBk LS	152	456	760	1,520	2,660	3,800
4d HBk LS	156	468	780	1,560	2,730	3,900
4d Sta Wag LS	160	480	800	1,600	2,800	4,000
2d HBk RS	156	468	780	1,560	2,730	3,900
4d HBk LTS	160	480	800	1,600	2,800	4,000

NOTE: Deduct 5 percent for lesser models.

1983 LN7, 4-cyl.

	6	5	4	3	2	1
2d HBk	188	564	940	1,880	3,290	4,700
2d HBk Spt	192	576	960	1,920	3,360	4,800
2d HBk GS	200	600	1,000	2,000	3,500	5,000
2d HBk RS	208	624	1,040	2,080	3,640	5,200

1983 Zephyr, V-6

	6	5	4	3	2	1
4d Sed	152	456	760	1,520	2,660	3,800
2d Cpe Z-7	176	528	880	1,760	3,080	4,400
4d Sed GS	156	468	780	1,560	2,730	3,900
2d Cpe Z-7 GS	184	552	920	1,840	3,220	4,600

NOTE: Deduct 10 percent for 4-cyl.

1983 Capri, 6-cyl.

	6	5	4	3	2	1
2d HBk L	216	648	1,080	2,160	3,780	5,400
2d HBk GS	224	672	1,120	2,240	3,920	5,600

1983 Capri, V-8

	6	5	4	3	2	1
2d HBk RS	228	684	1,140	2,280	3,990	5,700

NOTE: Deduct 10 percent for 4-cyl.

1983 Cougar, V-8

	6	5	4	3	2	1
2d Cpe	260	780	1,300	2,600	4,550	6,500
2d Cpe LS	268	804	1,340	2,680	4,690	6,700

NOTE: Deduct 15 percent for V-6.

1983 Marquis, 4-cyl.

	6	5	4	3	2	1
4d Sed	168	504	840	1,680	2,940	4,200
4d Brgm	176	528	880	1,760	3,080	4,400

1983 Marquis, 6-cyl.

	6	5	4	3	2	1
4d Sed	176	528	880	1,760	3,080	4,400
4d Sta Wag	188	564	940	1,880	3,290	4,700
4d Sed Brgm	192	576	960	1,920	3,360	4,800
4d Sta Wag Brgm	196	588	980	1,960	3,430	4,900

1983 Grand Marquis, V-8

	6	5	4	3	2	1
4d Sed	208	624	1,040	2,080	3,640	5,200
2d Cpe	204	612	1,020	2,040	3,570	5,100
4d Sed LS	216	648	1,080	2,160	3,780	5,400
2d Cpe LS	212	636	1,060	2,120	3,710	5,300
4d Sta Wag	220	660	1,100	2,200	3,850	5,500

1984 Lynx, 4-cyl.

	6	5	4	3	2	1
4d HBk LTS	140	420	700	1,400	2,450	3,500
2d HBk RS	144	432	720	1,440	2,520	3,600
2d HBk RS Turbo	152	456	760	1,520	2,660	3,800

NOTE: Deduct 5 percent for lesser models.

1984 Topaz, 4-cyl.

	6	5	4	3	2	1
2d Sed	132	396	660	1,320	2,310	3,300
4d Sed	132	396	660	1,320	2,310	3,300
2d Sed GS	136	408	680	1,360	2,380	3,400
4d Sed GS	136	408	680	1,360	2,380	3,400

1984 Capri, 4-cyl.

	6	5	4	3	2	1
2d HBk GS	176	528	880	1,760	3,080	4,400
2d HBk RS Turbo	192	576	960	1,920	3,360	4,800
2d HBk GS, V-6	184	552	920	1,840	3,220	4,600
2d HBk GS, V-8	192	576	960	1,920	3,360	4,800
2d HBk RS, V-8	200	600	1,000	2,000	3,500	5,000

1984 Cougar, V-6

	6	5	4	3	2	1
2d Cpe	168	504	840	1,680	2,940	4,200
2d Cpe LS	172	516	860	1,720	3,010	4,300

1984 Cougar, V-8

	6	5	4	3	2	1
2d Cpe	180	540	900	1,800	3,150	4,500
2d Cpe LS	192	576	960	1,920	3,360	4,800
2d Cpe XR7	220	660	1,100	2,200	3,850	5,500

1984 Marquis, 4-cyl.

	6	5	4	3	2	1
4d Sed	164	492	820	1,640	2,870	4,100
4d Sed Brgm	168	504	840	1,680	2,940	4,200

1984 Marquis, V-6

	6	5	4	3	2	1
4d Sed	168	504	840	1,680	2,940	4,200
4d Sed Brgm	172	516	860	1,720	3,010	4,300
4d Sta Wag	172	516	860	1,720	3,010	4,300
4d Sta Wag Brgm	176	528	880	1,760	3,080	4,400

1984 Grand Marquis, V-8

	6	5	4	3	2	1
4d Sed	196	588	980	1,960	3,430	4,900
2d Sed	196	588	980	1,960	3,430	4,900
4d Sed LS	200	600	1,000	2,000	3,500	5,000
2d Sed LS	200	600	1,000	2,000	3,500	5,000
4d Sta Wag Colony Park	200	600	1,000	2,000	3,500	5,000

1985 Lynx, 4-cyl.

	6	5	4	3	2	1
2d HBk GS	136	408	680	1,360	2,380	3,400
4d HBk GS	140	420	700	1,400	2,450	3,500
4d Sta Wag GS	140	420	700	1,400	2,450	3,500

NOTE: Deduct 20 percent for diesel. Deduct 5 percent for lesser models.

1985 Topaz, 4-cyl.

	6	5	4	3	2	1
2d Sed	136	408	680	1,360	2,380	3,400
4d Sed	136	408	680	1,360	2,380	3,400
2d Sed LS	136	408	680	1,360	2,380	3,400
4d Sed LS	140	420	700	1,400	2,450	3,500

NOTE: Deduct 20 percent for diesel.

1985 Capri, 4-cyl.

	6	5	4	3	2	1
2d HBk GS	180	540	900	1,800	3,150	4,500
2d HBk GS, V-6	184	552	920	1,840	3,220	4,600
2d HBk GS, V-8	196	588	980	1,960	3,430	4,900
2d HBk 5.0 liter, V-8	208	624	1,040	2,080	3,640	5,200

1985 Cougar, V-6

	6	5	4	3	2	1
2d Cpe	172	516	860	1,720	3,010	4,300
2d Cpe LS	176	528	880	1,760	3,080	4,400
2d Cpe, V-8	184	552	920	1,840	3,220	4,600
2d Cpe LS, V-8	196	588	980	1,960	3,430	4,900
2d Cpe XR7 Turbo, 4-cyl.	224	672	1,120	2,240	3,920	5,600

1985 Marquis, V-6

	6	5	4	3	2	1
4d Sed	172	516	860	1,720	3,010	4,300
4d Sed Brgm	176	528	880	1,760	3,080	4,400
4d Sta Wag	176	528	880	1,760	3,080	4,400
4d Sta Wag Brgm	180	540	900	1,800	3,150	4,500

NOTE: Deduct 20 percent for 4-cyl. where available.

	6	5	4	3	2	1

1985 Grand Marquis, V-8

	6	5	4	3	2	1
4d Sed	200	600	1,000	2,000	3,500	5,000
2d Sed	196	588	980	1,960	3,430	4,900
4d Sed LS	204	612	1,020	2,040	3,570	5,100
2d Sed LS	200	600	1,000	2,000	3,500	5,000
4d Sta Wag Colony Park	208	624	1,040	2,080	3,640	5,200

1986 Lynx

	6	5	4	3	2	1
2d HBk	140	420	700	1,400	2,450	3,500
4d HBk	148	444	740	1,480	2,590	3,700
4d Sta Wag	148	444	740	1,480	2,590	3,700

1986 Capri

	6	5	4	3	2	1
2d HBk	184	552	920	1,840	3,220	4,600

1986 Topaz

	6	5	4	3	2	1
2d Sed	144	432	720	1,440	2,520	3,600
4d Sed	144	432	720	1,440	2,520	3,600

1986 Marquis

	6	5	4	3	2	1
4d Sed	176	528	880	1,760	3,080	4,400
4d Sta Wag	180	540	900	1,800	3,150	4,500

1986 Marquis Brougham

	6	5	4	3	2	1
4d Sed	180	540	900	1,800	3,150	4,500
4d Sta Wag	184	552	920	1,840	3,220	4,600

1986 Cougar

	6	5	4	3	2	1
2d Cpe	192	576	960	1,920	3,360	4,800
2d LS Cpe	200	600	1,000	2,000	3,500	5,000
XR7 2d Cpe	228	684	1,140	2,280	3,990	5,700

1986 Grand Marquis

	6	5	4	3	2	1
2d Sed	204	612	1,020	2,040	3,570	5,100
4d Sed	208	624	1,040	2,080	3,640	5,200
4d Sta Wag	220	660	1,100	2,200	3,850	5,500

NOTE: Add 10 percent for deluxe models. Deduct 5 percent for smaller engines.

1987 Lynx, 4-cyl.

	6	5	4	3	2	1
2d HBk L	148	444	740	1,480	2,590	3,700
2d HBk GS	152	456	760	1,520	2,660	3,800
4d HBk GS	156	468	780	1,560	2,730	3,900
4d Sta Wag GS	156	468	780	1,560	2,730	3,900
2d HBk XR3	160	480	800	1,600	2,800	4,000

1987 Topaz, 4-cyl.

	6	5	4	3	2	1
2d Sed GS	152	456	760	1,520	2,660	3,800
4d Sed GS	156	468	780	1,560	2,730	3,900
2d Sed GS Spt	156	468	780	1,560	2,730	3,900
4d Sed GS Spt	160	480	800	1,600	2,800	4,000
4d Sed LS	164	492	820	1,640	2,870	4,100

1987 Cougar

	6	5	4	3	2	1
2d Cpe LS, V-6	256	768	1,280	2,560	4,480	6,400
2d Cpe LS, V-8	360	1,080	1,800	3,600	6,300	9,000
2d Cpe XR7, V-8	368	1,104	1,840	3,680	6,440	9,200

NOTE: Add 10 percent for Anniversary Model.

1987 Sable, V-6

	6	5	4	3	2	1
4d Sed GS	200	600	1,000	2,000	3,500	5,000
4d Sed LS	204	612	1,020	2,040	3,570	5,100
4d Sta Wag GS	204	612	1,020	2,040	3,570	5,100
4d Sta Wag LS	208	624	1,040	2,080	3,640	5,200

1987 Grand Marquis, V-8

	6	5	4	3	2	1
4d Sed GS	228	684	1,140	2,280	3,990	5,700
4d Sta Wag Col Park GS	236	708	1,180	2,360	4,130	5,900
2d Sed LS	228	684	1,140	2,280	3,990	5,700
4d Sed LS	232	696	1,160	2,320	4,060	5,800
4d Sta Wag Col Park LS	240	720	1,200	2,400	4,200	6,000

1988 Tracer, 4-cyl.

	6	5	4	3	2	1
2d HBk	120	360	600	1,200	2,100	3,000
4d HBk	124	372	620	1,240	2,170	3,100
4d Sta Wag	132	396	660	1,320	2,310	3,300

1988 Topaz, 4-cyl.

	6	5	4	3	2	1
2d Sed	128	384	640	1,280	2,240	3,200
4d Sed	132	396	660	1,320	2,310	3,300
4d Sed LS	144	432	720	1,440	2,520	3,600
4d Sed LTS	152	456	760	1,520	2,660	3,800
2d Sed XR5	160	480	800	1,600	2,800	4,000

1988 Cougar

	6	5	4	3	2	1
2d LS V-6	232	696	1,160	2,320	4,060	5,800
2d LS V-8	248	744	1,240	2,480	4,340	6,200
2d XR7 V-8	272	816	1,360	2,720	4,760	6,800

1988 Sable, V-6

	6	5	4	3	2	1
4d Sed GS	184	552	920	1,840	3,220	4,600
4d Sta Wag GS	208	624	1,040	2,080	3,640	5,200
4d Sed LS	192	576	960	1,920	3,360	4,800
4d Sta Wag LS	232	696	1,160	2,320	4,060	5,800

1988 Grand Marquis, V-8

	6	5	4	3	2	1
4d Sed GS	220	660	1,100	2,200	3,850	5,500
4d Sta Wag Col Park GS	232	696	1,160	2,320	4,060	5,800
4d Sed LS	224	672	1,120	2,240	3,920	5,600
4d Sta Wag Col Park LS	244	732	1,220	2,440	4,270	6,100

1989 Tracer, 4-cyl.

	6	5	4	3	2	1
4d HBk	156	468	780	1,560	2,730	3,900
2d HBk	152	456	760	1,520	2,660	3,800
4d Sta Wag	160	480	800	1,600	2,800	4,000

1989 Topaz, 4-cyl.

	6	5	4	3	2	1
2d Sed GS	144	432	720	1,440	2,520	3,600
4d Sed GS	148	444	740	1,480	2,590	3,700
4d Sed LS	156	468	780	1,560	2,730	3,900
4d Sed LTS	172	516	860	1,720	3,010	4,300
2d Sed XR5	196	588	980	1,960	3,430	4,900

1989 Cougar, V-6

	6	5	4	3	2	1
2d Cpe LS	360	1,080	1,800	3,600	6,300	9,000
2d Cpe XR7	400	1,200	2,000	4,000	7,000	10,000

1989 Sable, V-6

	6	5	4	3	2	1
4d Sed GS	212	636	1,060	2,120	3,710	5,300
4d Sta Wag GS	248	744	1,240	2,480	4,340	6,200
4d Sed LS	236	708	1,180	2,360	4,130	5,900
4d Sta Wag LS	368	1,104	1,840	3,680	6,440	9,200

1989 Grand Marquis, V-8

	6	5	4	3	2	1
4d Sed GS	252	756	1,260	2,520	4,410	6,300
4d Sed LS	256	768	1,280	2,560	4,480	6,400
4d Sta Wag Col Park GS	268	804	1,340	2,680	4,690	6,700
4d Sta Wag Col Park LS	276	828	1,380	2,760	4,830	6,900

1990 Topaz, 4-cyl.

	6	5	4	3	2	1
2d Sed GS	156	468	780	1,560	2,730	3,900
4d Sed GS	160	480	800	1,600	2,800	4,000
4d Sed LS	168	504	840	1,680	2,940	4,200
4d Sed LTS	184	552	920	1,840	3,220	4,600
2d Sed XR5	168	504	840	1,680	2,940	4,200

1990 Cougar, V-6

	6	5	4	3	2	1
2d Cpe LS	260	780	1,300	2,600	4,550	6,500
2d Cpe XR7	360	1,080	1,800	3,600	6,300	9,000

1990 Sable, V-6

	6	5	4	3	2	1
4d Sed GS	220	660	1,100	2,200	3,850	5,500
4d Sed LS	240	720	1,200	2,400	4,200	6,000
4d Sta Wag GS	240	720	1,200	2,400	4,200	6,000
4d Sta Wag LS	260	780	1,300	2,600	4,550	6,500

1990 Grand Marquis, V-8

	6	5	4	3	2	1
4d Sed GS	260	780	1,300	2,600	4,550	6,500
4d Sed LS	360	1,080	1,800	3,600	6,300	9,000
4d Sta Wag GS	360	1,080	1,800	3,600	6,300	9,000
4d Sta Wag LS	380	1,140	1,900	3,800	6,650	9,500

1991 Tracer, 4-cyl.

	6	5	4	3	2	1
4d NBk	140	420	700	1,400	2,450	3,500
4d NBk LTS	148	444	740	1,480	2,590	3,700
4d Sta Wag	156	468	780	1,560	2,730	3,900

1991 Topaz, 4-cyl.

	6	5	4	3	2	1
2d Sed GS	148	444	740	1,480	2,590	3,700
4d Sed GS	148	444	740	1,480	2,590	3,700
4d Sed LS	156	468	780	1,560	2,730	3,900
4d Sed LTS	160	480	800	1,600	2,800	4,000
2d Sed XR5	168	504	840	1,680	2,940	4,200

1991 Capri, 4-cyl.

	6	5	4	3	2	1
2d Conv	200	600	1,000	2,000	3,500	5,000
2d Conv XR2 Turbo	220	660	1,100	2,200	3,850	5,500

1991 Cougar

	6	5	4	3	2	1
2d Cpe LS, V-6	240	720	1,200	2,400	4,200	6,000
2d Cpe LS, V-8	360	1,080	1,800	3,600	6,300	9,000
2d Cpe XR7, V-8	380	1,140	1,900	3,800	6,650	9,500

1991 Sable, V-6

	6	5	4	3	2	1
4d Sed GS	148	444	740	1,480	2,590	3,700
4d Sta Wag GS	156	468	780	1,560	2,730	3,900

	6	5	4	3	2	1
4d Sed LS	152	456	760	1,520	2,660	3,800
4d Sta Wag LS	160	480	800	1,600	2,800	4,000

1991 Grand Marquis, V-8

	6	5	4	3	2	1
4d Sed GS	184	552	920	1,840	3,220	4,600
4d Sed LS	192	576	960	1,920	3,360	4,800

1991 Grand Marquis Colony Park, V-8

	6	5	4	3	2	1
4d Sta Wag GS35	220	660	1,100	2,200	3,850	5,500
4d Sta Wag GS25	216	648	1,080	2,160	3,780	5,400
4d Sta Wag LS35	224	672	1,120	2,240	3,920	5,600
4d Sta Wag LS25	220	660	1,100	2,200	3,850	5,500

1992 Tracer, 4-cyl.

	6	5	4	3	2	1
4d Sed	164	492	820	1,640	2,870	4,100
4d Sed LTS	168	504	840	1,680	2,940	4,200
4d Sta Wag	184	552	920	1,840	3,220	4,600

1992 Topaz, 4-cyl. & V-6

	6	5	4	3	2	1
2d Cpe GS	156	468	780	1,560	2,730	3,900
4d Sed GS	160	480	800	1,600	2,800	4,000
4d Sed LS	168	504	840	1,680	2,940	4,200
4d Sed LTS V-6	224	672	1,120	2,240	3,920	5,600
2d Cpe XR5 V-6	224	672	1,120	2,240	3,920	5,600

1992 Capri, 4-cyl.

	6	5	4	3	2	1
2d Conv	240	720	1,200	2,400	4,200	6,000
2d Conv XR2 Turbo	248	744	1,240	2,480	4,340	6,200

1992 Cougar

	6	5	4	3	2	1
2d Cpe LS, V-6	292	876	1,460	2,920	5,110	7,300
2d Cpe LS, V-8	308	924	1,540	3,080	5,390	7,700
2d Cpe XR7 V-8	316	948	1,580	3,160	5,530	7,900

1992 Sable, V-6

	6	5	4	3	2	1
4d Sed GS	240	720	1,200	2,400	4,200	6,000
4d Sta Wag GS	240	720	1,200	2,400	4,200	6,000
4d Sed LS	248	744	1,240	2,480	4,340	6,200
4d Sta Wag LS	248	744	1,240	2,480	4,340	6,200

1992 Grand Marquis, V-8

	6	5	4	3	2	1
4d Sed GS	280	840	1,400	2,800	4,900	7,000
4d Sed LS	288	864	1,440	2,880	5,040	7,200

1993 Tracer, 4-cyl.

	6	5	4	3	2	1
4d Sed	172	516	860	1,720	3,010	4,300
4d Sta Wag	184	552	920	1,840	3,220	4,600
4d Sed LTS	180	540	900	1,800	3,150	4,500

1993 Topaz, 4-cyl.

	6	5	4	3	2	1
2d Sed GS	168	504	840	1,680	2,940	4,200
4d Sed GS	176	528	880	1,760	3,080	4,400

1993 Capri, 4-cyl.

	6	5	4	3	2	1
2d Conv	280	840	1,400	2,800	4,900	7,000
2d Conv XR2 Turbo	288	864	1,440	2,880	5,040	7,200

1993 Cougar

	6	5	4	3	2	1
2d Cpe XR7, V-6	292	876	1,460	2,920	5,110	7,300
2d Cpe XR7, V-8	302	906	1,510	3,020	5,285	7,550

1993 Sable, V-6

	6	5	4	3	2	1
4d Sed GS	248	744	1,240	2,480	4,340	6,200
4d Sed LS	252	756	1,260	2,520	4,410	6,300
4d Sta Wag GS	260	780	1,300	2,600	4,550	6,500
4d Sta Wag LS	264	792	1,320	2,640	4,620	6,600

1993 Grand Marquis, V-8

	6	5	4	3	2	1
4d Sed GS	288	864	1,440	2,880	5,040	7,200
4d Sed LS	296	888	1,480	2,960	5,180	7,400

1994 Tracer, 4-cyl.

	6	5	4	3	2	1
4d Sed	200	600	1,000	2,000	3,500	5,000
4d Sed LTS	220	660	1,100	2,200	3,850	5,500
4d Sta Wag	240	720	1,200	2,400	4,200	6,000

1994 Topaz, 4-cyl.

	6	5	4	3	2	1
2d Sed GS	212	636	1,060	2,120	3,710	5,300
4d Sed GS	216	648	1,080	2,160	3,780	5,400

1994 Capri, 4-cyl.

	6	5	4	3	2	1
2d Conv	260	780	1,300	2,600	4,550	6,500
2d Conv XR2 Turbo	288	864	1,440	2,880	5,040	7,200

1994 Cougar

	6	5	4	3	2	1
2d Cpe XR7, V-6	260	780	1,300	2,600	4,550	6,500
2d Cpe XR7, V-8	280	840	1,400	2,800	4,900	7,000

1994 Sable, V-6

	6	5	4	3	2	1
4d Sed GS	220	660	1,100	2,200	3,850	5,500
4d Sed LS	240	720	1,200	2,400	4,200	6,000
4d Sta Wag GS	240	720	1,200	2,400	4,200	6,000
4d Sta Wag LS	260	780	1,300	2,600	4,550	6,500

1994 Grand Marquis, V-8

	6	5	4	3	2	1
4d Sed GS	300	900	1,500	3,000	5,250	7,500
4d Sed LS	320	960	1,600	3,200	5,600	8,000

1995 Tracer, 4-cyl.

	6	5	4	3	2	1
4d Sed	200	600	1,000	2,000	3,500	5,000
4d Sta Wag	250	700	1,200	2,400	4,200	6,000
4d LTS Sed	200	650	1,100	2,200	3,850	5,500

1995 Mystique, 4-cyl. & V-6

	6	5	4	3	2	1
4d GS Sed	200	650	1,050	2,100	3,700	5,300
4d LS Sed	200	650	1,100	2,200	3,850	5,500

1995 Cougar, V-6 & V-8

	6	5	4	3	2	1
2d XR7 Cpe, V-6	250	800	1,300	2,600	4,550	6,500
2d HR7 Cpe, V-8	300	850	1,400	2,800	4,900	7,000

1995 Sable, V-6

	6	5	4	3	2	1
4d GS Sed	200	650	1,100	2,200	3,850	5,500
4d GS Sta Wag	250	700	1,200	2,400	4,200	6,000
4d LS Sed	250	700	1,200	2,400	4,200	6,000
4d LS Sta Wag	250	800	1,300	2,600	4,550	6,500
4d LTS Sed	250	800	1,300	2,650	4,600	6,600

1995 Grand Marquis, V-8

	6	5	4	3	2	1
4d GS Sed	300	900	1,500	3,000	5,250	7,500
4d LS Sed	300	950	1,600	3,200	5,600	8,000

00

1993 Villager FWD, V-6

	6	5	4	3	2	1
Sta Wag GS	300	950	1,600	3,200	5,600	8,000
Sta Wag LS	350	1,100	1,800	3,600	6,300	9,000

1994 Villager, V-6

	6	5	4	3	2	1
Window Van GS	360	1,080	1,800	3,600	6,300	9,000
Window Van LS	432	1,296	2,160	4,320	7,560	10,800
Window Van Nautica	450	1,300	2,200	4,400	7,700	11,000

1995 Villager, V-6

	6	5	4	3	2	1
Window Van GS	350	1,100	1,800	3,600	6,300	9,000
Window Van LS	450	1,300	2,150	4,300	7,550	10,800
Window Van Nautica	450	1,300	2,200	4,400	7,700	11,000

MUSTANG

1964

	6	5	4	3	2	1
2d HT	940	2,820	4,700	9,400	16,450	23,500
Conv	1,320	3,960	6,600	13,200	23,100	33,000

NOTE: Deduct 20 percent for 6-cyl. Add 20 percent for Challenger Code "K" V-8. First Mustang introduced April 17, 1964 at N.Y. World's Fair.

1965

	6	5	4	3	2	1
2d HT	940	2,820	4,700	9,400	16,450	23,500
Conv	1,320	3,960	6,600	13,200	23,100	33,000
FBk	1,120	3,360	5,600	11,200	19,600	28,000

NOTE: Add 30 percent for 271 hp Hi-perf engine. Add 10 percent for "GT" Package. Add 10 percent for "original pony interior". Deduct 20 percent for 6-cyl.

1965 Shelby GT

	6	5	4	3	2	1
GT-350 FBk	2,320	6,960	11,600	23,200	40,600	58,000

1966

	6	5	4	3	2	1
2d HT	940	2,820	4,700	9,400	16,450	23,500
Conv	1,360	4,080	6,800	13,600	23,800	34,000
FBk	1,200	3,600	6,000	12,000	21,000	30,000

NOTE: Same as 1965.

1966 Shelby GT

	6	5	4	3	2	1
GT-350 FBk	2,120	6,360	10,600	21,200	37,100	53,000
GT-350H FBk	2,200	6,600	11,000	22,000	38,500	55,000
GT-350 Conv	3,040	9,120	15,200	30,400	53,200	76,000

1967

	6	5	4	3	2	1
2d HT	860	2,580	4,300	8,600	15,050	21,500

	6	5	4	3	2	1
Conv	1,200	3,600	6,000	12,000	21,000	30,000
FBk	980	2,940	4,900	9,800	17,150	24,500

NOTE: Same as 1964-65 plus. Add 10 percent for 390 cid V-8 (code "S"). Deduct 15 percent for 6-cyl.

1967 Shelby GT

	6	5	4	3	2	1
GT-350 FBk	1,840	5,520	9,200	18,400	32,200	46,000
GT-500 FBk	2,040	6,120	10,200	20,400	35,700	51,000

1968

	6	5	4	3	2	1
2d HT	860	2,580	4,300	8,600	15,050	21,500
Conv	1,200	3,600	6,000	12,000	21,000	30,000
FBk	980	2,940	4,900	9,800	17,150	24,500

NOTE: Same as 1964-67 plus. Add 10 percent for GT-390. Add 50 percent for 427 cid V-8 (code "W"). Add 30 percent for 428 cid V-8 (code "R"). Add 15 percent for "California Special" trim.

1968 Shelby GT

	6	5	4	3	2	1
350 Conv	2,360	7,080	11,800	23,600	41,300	59,000
350 FBk	1,440	4,320	7,200	14,400	25,200	36,000
500 Conv	2,880	8,640	14,400	28,800	50,400	72,000
500 FBk	1,960	5,880	9,800	19,600	34,300	49,000

NOTE: Add 30 percent for KR models.

1969

	6	5	4	3	2	1
2d HT	820	2,460	4,100	8,200	14,350	20,500
Conv	980	2,940	4,900	9,800	17,150	24,500
FBk	900	2,700	4,500	9,000	15,750	22,500
Mach 1	1,040	3,120	5,200	10,400	18,200	26,000
Boss 302	1,600	4,800	8,000	16,000	28,000	40,000
Boss 429	2,480	7,440	12,400	24,800	43,400	62,000
Grande	860	2,580	4,300	8,600	15,050	21,500

NOTE: Same as 1968; plus. Add 40 percent for "R" Code. Add 30 percent for Cobra Jet V-8. Add 40 percent for "Super Cobra Jet" engine.

1969 Shelby GT

	6	5	4	3	2	1
350 Conv	2,320	6,960	11,600	23,200	40,600	58,000
350 FBk	1,680	5,040	8,400	16,800	29,400	42,000
500 Conv	2,640	7,920	13,200	26,400	46,200	66,000
500 FBk	1,800	5,400	9,000	18,000	31,500	45,000

1970

	6	5	4	3	2	1
2d HT	820	2,460	4,100	8,200	14,350	20,500
Conv	960	2,880	4,800	9,600	16,800	24,000
FBk	880	2,640	4,400	8,800	15,400	22,000
Mach 1	960	2,880	4,800	9,600	16,800	24,000
Boss 302	1,520	4,560	7,600	15,200	26,600	38,000
Boss 429	2,400	7,200	12,000	24,000	42,000	60,000
Grande	860	2,580	4,300	8,600	15,050	21,500

NOTE: Add 30 percent for Cobra Jet V-8. Add 40 percent for "Super Cobra Jet". Deduct 20 percent for 6-cyl.

1970 Shelby GT

	6	5	4	3	2	1
350 Conv	2,240	6,720	11,200	22,400	39,200	56,000
350 FBk	1,680	5,040	8,400	16,800	29,400	42,000
500 Conv	2,640	7,920	13,200	26,400	46,200	66,000
500 FBk	1,800	5,400	9,000	18,000	31,500	45,000

1971

	6	5	4	3	2	1
2d HT	640	1,920	3,200	6,400	11,200	16,000
Grande	660	1,980	3,300	6,600	11,550	16,500
Conv	960	2,880	4,800	9,600	16,800	24,000
FBk	880	2,640	4,400	8,800	15,400	22,000
Mach 1	960	2,880	4,800	9,600	16,800	24,000
Boss 351	1,600	4,800	8,000	16,000	28,000	40,000

NOTE: Same as 1970. Deduct 20 percent for 6-cyl. Add 20 percent for HO option where available.

1972

	6	5	4	3	2	1
2d HT	640	1,920	3,200	6,400	11,200	16,000
Grande	660	1,980	3,300	6,600	11,550	16,500
FBk	800	2,400	4,000	8,000	14,000	20,000
Mach 1	880	2,640	4,400	8,800	15,400	22,000
Conv	920	2,760	4,600	9,200	16,100	23,000

NOTE: Deduct 20 percent for 6-cyl. Add 20 percent for HO option where available.

1973

	6	5	4	3	2	1
2d HT	620	1,860	3,100	6,200	10,850	15,500
Grande	660	1,980	3,300	6,600	11,550	16,500
FBk	760	2,280	3,800	7,600	13,300	19,000
Mach 1	880	2,640	4,400	8,800	15,400	22,000
Conv	960	2,880	4,800	9,600	16,800	24,000

1974 Mustang II, Mustang Four

	6	5	4	3	2	1
HT Cpe	240	720	1,200	2,400	4,200	6,000
FBk	252	756	1,260	2,520	4,410	6,300
Ghia	252	756	1,260	2,520	4,410	6,300

1974 Mustang Six

	6	5	4	3	2	1
HT Cpe	240	720	1,200	2,400	4,200	6,000
FBk	256	768	1,280	2,560	4,480	6,400
Ghia	256	768	1,280	2,560	4,480	6,400

1974 Mach 1 Six

	6	5	4	3	2	1
FBk	380	1,140	1,900	3,800	6,650	9,500

1975 Mustang

	6	5	4	3	2	1
HT Cpe	240	720	1,200	2,400	4,200	6,000
FBk	252	756	1,260	2,520	4,410	6,300
Ghia	252	756	1,260	2,520	4,410	6,300

1975 Mustang Six

	6	5	4	3	2	1
HT Cpe	244	732	1,220	2,440	4,270	6,100
FBk	256	768	1,280	2,560	4,480	6,400
Ghia	256	768	1,280	2,560	4,480	6,400
Mach 1	380	1,140	1,900	3,800	6,650	9,500

1975 Mustang, V-8

	6	5	4	3	2	1
HT Cpe	364	1,092	1,820	3,640	6,370	9,100
FBk Cpe	368	1,104	1,840	3,680	6,440	9,200
Ghia	380	1,140	1,900	3,800	6,650	9,500
Mach 1	420	1,260	2,100	4,200	7,350	10,500

1976 Mustang II, V-6

	6	5	4	3	2	1
2d	252	756	1,260	2,520	4,410	6,300
3d 2 plus 2	256	768	1,280	2,560	4,480	6,400
2d Ghia	268	804	1,340	2,680	4,690	6,700

NOTE: Deduct 20 percent for 4-cyl. Add 20 percent for V-8. Add 20 percent for Cobra II.

1976 Mach 1, V-6

	6	5	4	3	2	1
3d	360	1,080	1,800	3,600	6,300	9,000

1977 Mustang II, V-6

	6	5	4	3	2	1
2d	260	780	1,300	2,600	4,550	6,500
3d 2 plus 2	268	804	1,340	2,680	4,690	6,700
2d Ghia	276	828	1,380	2,760	4,830	6,900

NOTE: Deduct 20 percent for 4-cyl. Add 30 percent for Cobra II option. Add 20 percent for V-8.

1977 Mach 1, V-6

	6	5	4	3	2	1
2d	368	1,104	1,840	3,680	6,440	9,200

1978 Mustang II

	6	5	4	3	2	1
Cpe	244	732	1,220	2,440	4,270	6,100
3d 2 plus 2	252	756	1,260	2,520	4,410	6,300
Ghia Cpe	256	768	1,280	2,560	4,480	6,400

1978 Mach 1, V-6

	6	5	4	3	2	1
Cpe	360	1,080	1,800	3,600	6,300	9,000

NOTE: Add 20 percent for V-8. Add 30 percent for Cobra II option. Add 50 percent for King Cobra option. Deduct 20 percent for 4-cyl.

1979 V-6

	6	5	4	3	2	1
2d Cpe	248	744	1,240	2,480	4,340	6,200
3d Cpe	252	756	1,260	2,520	4,410	6,300
2d Ghia Cpe	260	780	1,300	2,600	4,550	6,500

1979 V-6

	6	5	4	3	2	1
3d Ghia Cpe	264	792	1,320	2,640	4,620	6,600

NOTE: Add 30 percent for Pace Car package. Add 30 percent for Cobra option.

1980 6-cyl.

	6	5	4	3	2	1
2d Cpe	212	636	1,060	2,120	3,710	5,300
2d HBk	216	648	1,080	2,160	3,780	5,400
2d Ghia Cpe	224	672	1,120	2,240	3,920	5,600
2d Ghia HBk	228	684	1,140	2,280	3,990	5,700

NOTE: Deduct 20 percent for 4-cyl. Add 30 percent for V-8.

1981 6-cyl.

	6	5	4	3	2	1
2d S Cpe	196	588	980	1,960	3,430	4,900
2d Cpe	204	612	1,020	2,040	3,570	5,100
2d HBk	208	624	1,040	2,080	3,640	5,200
2d Ghia Cpe	208	624	1,040	2,080	3,640	5,200
2d Ghia HBk	212	636	1,060	2,120	3,710	5,300

NOTE: Deduct 20 percent for 4-cyl. Add 35 percent for V-8.

1982 4-cyl.

	6	5	4	3	2	1
2d L Cpe	180	540	900	1,800	3,150	4,500
2d GL Cpe	184	552	920	1,840	3,220	4,600
2d GL HBk	188	564	940	1,880	3,290	4,700
2d GLX Cpe	196	588	980	1,960	3,430	4,900
2d GLX HBk	200	600	1,000	2,000	3,500	5,000

	6	5	4	3	2	1

1982 6-cyl.

	6	5	4	3	2	1
2d L Cpe	196	588	980	1,960	3,430	4,900
2d GL Cpe	200	600	1,000	2,000	3,500	5,000
2d GL HBk	204	612	1,020	2,040	3,570	5,100
2d GLX Cpe	212	636	1,060	2,120	3,710	5,300
2d GLX HBk	216	648	1,080	2,160	3,780	5,400

1982 V-8

	6	5	4	3	2	1
2d GT HBk	256	768	1,280	2,560	4,480	6,400

1983 4-cyl.

	6	5	4	3	2	1
2d L Cpe	184	552	920	1,840	3,220	4,600
2d GL Cpe	188	564	940	1,880	3,290	4,700
2d GL HBk	196	588	980	1,960	3,430	4,900
2d GLX Cpe	200	600	1,000	2,000	3,500	5,000
2d GLX HBk	204	612	1,020	2,040	3,570	5,100

1983 6-cyl.

	6	5	4	3	2	1
2d GL Cpe	204	612	1,020	2,040	3,570	5,100
2d GL HBk	208	624	1,040	2,080	3,640	5,200
2d GLX Cpe	216	648	1,080	2,160	3,780	5,400
2d GLX HBk	220	660	1,100	2,200	3,850	5,500
2d GLX Conv	240	720	1,200	2,400	4,200	6,000

1983 V-8

	6	5	4	3	2	1
2d GT HBk	360	1,080	1,800	3,600	6,300	9,000
2d GT Conv	400	1,200	2,000	4,000	7,000	10,000

1984 4-cyl.

	6	5	4	3	2	1
2d L Cpe	188	564	940	1,880	3,290	4,700
2d L HBk	192	576	960	1,920	3,360	4,800
2d LX Cpe	192	576	960	1,920	3,360	4,800
2d LX HBk	196	588	980	1,960	3,430	4,900
2d GT Turbo HBk	212	636	1,060	2,120	3,710	5,300
2d GT Turbo Conv	260	780	1,300	2,600	4,550	6,500

1984 V-6

	6	5	4	3	2	1
2d L Cpe	192	576	960	1,920	3,360	4,800
2d L HBk	196	588	980	1,960	3,430	4,900
2d LX Cpe	196	588	980	1,960	3,430	4,900
2d LX HBk	200	600	1,000	2,000	3,500	5,000
LX 2d Conv	280	840	1,400	2,800	4,900	7,000

1984 V-8

	6	5	4	3	2	1
2d L HBk	200	600	1,000	2,000	3,500	5,000
2d LX Cpe	204	612	1,020	2,040	3,570	5,100
2d LX HBk	204	612	1,020	2,040	3,570	5,100
2d LX Conv	320	960	1,600	3,200	5,600	8,000
2d GT HBk	212	636	1,060	2,120	3,710	5,300
2d GT Conv	340	1,020	1,700	3,400	5,950	8,500

NOTE: Add 20 percent for 20th Anniversary Edition. Add 40 percent for SVO Model.

1985 4-cyl.

	6	5	4	3	2	1
2d LX	196	588	980	1,960	3,430	4,900
2d LX HBk	200	600	1,000	2,000	3,500	5,000
2d SVO Turbo	240	720	1,200	2,400	4,200	6,000

1985 V-6

	6	5	4	3	2	1
2d LX	204	612	1,020	2,040	3,570	5,100
2d LX HBk	208	624	1,040	2,080	3,640	5,200
2d LX Conv	396	1,188	1,980	3,960	6,930	9,900

1985 V-8

	6	5	4	3	2	1
2d LX	220	660	1,100	2,200	3,850	5,500
2d LX HBk	224	672	1,120	2,240	3,920	5,600
2d LX Conv	420	1,260	2,100	4,200	7,350	10,500
2d GT HBk	400	1,200	2,000	4,000	7,000	10,000
2d GT Conv	560	1,680	2,800	5,600	9,800	14,000

NOTE: Add 40 percent for SVO Model.

1986 Mustang

	6	5	4	3	2	1
2d Cpe	200	600	1,000	2,000	3,500	5,000
2d HBk	200	600	1,000	2,000	3,500	5,000
2d Conv	380	1,140	1,900	3,800	6,650	9,500
2d Turbo HBk	240	720	1,200	2,400	4,200	6,000

1986 V-8

	6	5	4	3	2	1
2d HBk	240	720	1,200	2,400	4,200	6,000
2d Conv	420	1,260	2,100	4,200	7,350	10,500
2d GT HBk	400	1,200	2,000	4,000	7,000	10,000
2d GT Conv	560	1,680	2,800	5,600	9,800	14,000

NOTE: Add 40 percent for SVO Model.

1987 4-cyl.

	6	5	4	3	2	1
2d LX Sed	200	600	1,000	2,000	3,500	5,000
2d LX HBk	204	612	1,020	2,040	3,570	5,100
2d LX Conv	360	1,080	1,800	3,600	6,300	9,000

1987 V-8

	6	5	4	3	2	1
2d LX Sed	200	600	1,000	2,000	3,500	5,000
2d LX HBk	204	612	1,020	2,040	3,570	5,100
2d LX Conv	424	1,272	2,120	4,240	7,420	10,600
2d GT HBk	220	660	1,100	2,200	3,850	5,500
2d GT Conv	400	1,200	2,000	4,000	7,000	10,000

1988 V-6

	6	5	4	3	2	1
2d LX Sed	160	480	800	1,600	2,800	4,000
2d LX HBk	168	504	840	1,680	2,940	4,200
2d LX Conv	360	1,080	1,800	3,600	6,300	9,000

1988 V-8

	6	5	4	3	2	1
2d LX Sed	200	600	1,000	2,000	3,500	5,000
2d LX HBk	220	660	1,100	2,200	3,850	5,500
2d LX Conv	400	1,200	2,000	4,000	7,000	10,000
2d GT HBk	380	1,140	1,900	3,800	6,650	9,500
2d GT Conv	560	1,680	2,800	5,600	9,800	14,000

1989 4-cyl.

	6	5	4	3	2	1
2d LX Cpe	180	540	900	1,800	3,150	4,500
2d LX HBk	188	564	940	1,880	3,290	4,700
2d LX Conv	420	1,260	2,100	4,200	7,350	10,500

1989 V-8

	6	5	4	3	2	1
2d LX Spt Cpe	236	708	1,180	2,360	4,130	5,900
2d LX Spt HBk	240	720	1,200	2,400	4,200	6,000
2d LX Spt Conv	560	1,680	2,800	5,600	9,800	14,000
2d GT HBk	388	1,164	1,940	3,880	6,790	9,700
2d GT Conv	680	2,040	3,400	6,800	11,900	17,000

1990 4-cyl.

	6	5	4	3	2	1
2d LX	184	552	920	1,840	3,220	4,600
2d LX HBk	192	576	960	1,920	3,360	4,800
2d LX Conv	380	1,140	1,900	3,800	6,650	9,500

1990 V-8

	6	5	4	3	2	1
2d LX Spt	240	720	1,200	2,400	4,200	6,000
2d LX HBk Spt	248	744	1,240	2,480	4,340	6,200
2d LX Conv Spt	520	1,560	2,600	5,200	9,100	13,000
2d GT HBk	400	1,200	2,000	4,000	7,000	10,000
2d GT Conv	560	1,680	2,800	5,600	9,800	14,000

1991 4-cyl.

	6	5	4	3	2	1
2d LX Cpe	180	540	900	1,800	3,150	4,500
2d LX HBk	200	600	1,000	2,000	3,500	5,000
2d LX Conv	360	1,080	1,800	3,600	6,300	9,000

1991 V-8

	6	5	4	3	2	1
2d LX Cpe	220	660	1,100	2,200	3,850	5,500
2d LX HBk	240	720	1,200	2,400	4,200	6,000
2d LX Conv	400	1,200	2,000	4,000	7,000	10,000
2d GT HBk	380	1,140	1,900	3,800	6,650	9,500
2d GT Conv	540	1,620	2,700	5,400	9,450	13,500

1992 V-8, 4-cyl.

	6	5	4	3	2	1
2d LX Cpe	200	600	1,000	2,000	3,500	5,000
2d LX HBk	220	660	1,100	2,200	3,850	5,500
2d LX Conv	400	1,200	2,000	4,000	7,000	10,000

1992 V-8

	6	5	4	3	2	1
2d LX Sed	360	1,080	1,800	3,600	6,300	9,000
2d LX HBk	380	1,140	1,900	3,800	6,650	9,500
2d LX Conv	520	1,560	2,600	5,200	9,100	13,000
2d GT HBk	420	1,260	2,100	4,200	7,350	10,500
2d GT Conv	600	1,800	3,000	6,000	10,500	15,000

1993 4-cyl.

	6	5	4	3	2	1
2d LX Cpe	220	660	1,100	2,200	3,850	5,500
2d LX HBk	224	672	1,120	2,240	3,920	5,600
2d LX Conv	408	1,224	2,040	4,080	7,140	10,200

1993 V-8

	6	5	4	3	2	1
2d LX Cpe	360	1,080	1,800	3,600	6,300	9,000
2d LX HBk	368	1,104	1,840	3,680	6,440	9,200
2d LX Conv	552	1,656	2,760	5,520	9,660	13,800
2d GT HBk	400	1,200	2,000	4,000	7,000	10,000
2d GT Conv	620	1,860	3,100	6,200	10,850	15,500

1993 Cobra

	6	5	4	3	2	1
2d HBk	700	2,100	3,500	7,000	12,250	17,500

NOTE: Add 40 percent for Code R.

1994 V-6

	6	5	4	3	2	1
2d Cpe	320	960	1,600	3,200	5,600	8,000
2d Conv	440	1,320	2,200	4,400	7,700	11,000

1994 GT, V-8

	6	5	4	3	2	1
2d GT Cpe	420	1,260	2,100	4,200	7,350	10,500
2d GT Conv	480	1,440	2,400	4,800	8,400	12,000

1994 Cobra, V-8

	6	5	4	3	2	1
2d Cpe	560	1,680	2,800	5,600	9,800	14,000
2d Conv	640	1,920	3,200	6,400	11,200	16,000

1995 V-6

	6	5	4	3	2	1
2d Cpe	300	950	1,600	3,200	5,600	8,000
2d Conv	450	1,300	2,200	4,400	7,700	11,000

1995 V-8

	6	5	4	3	2	1
2d GTS Cpe	400	1,200	2,000	4,000	7,000	10,000
2d GT Cpe	400	1,250	2,100	4,200	7,350	10,500
2d GT Conv	500	1,450	2,400	4,800	8,400	12,000
2d Cobra Cpe	550	1,700	2,800	5,600	9,800	14,000
2d Cobra Conv	650	1,900	3,200	6,400	11,200	16,000

THUNDERBIRD

1955 102" wb

	6	5	4	3	2	1
Conv	2,560	7,680	12,800	25,600	44,800	64,000

NOTE: Add $1,800 for hardtop.

1956 102" wb

	6	5	4	3	2	1
Conv	2,480	7,440	12,400	24,800	43,400	62,000

NOTE: Add $1,800 for hardtop. Add 10 percent for 312 engine.

1957 102" wb

	6	5	4	3	2	1
Conv	2,520	7,560	12,600	25,200	44,100	63,000

NOTE: Add $1,800 for hardtop. Add 60 percent for supercharged V-8 (Code F). Add 20 percent for "T-Bird Special" V-8 (Code E).

1958 113" wb

	6	5	4	3	2	1
2d HT	1,200	3,600	6,000	12,000	21,000	30,000
Conv	1,600	4,800	8,000	16,000	28,000	40,000

1959 113" wb

	6	5	4	3	2	1
2d HT	1,160	3,480	5,800	11,600	20,300	29,000
Conv	1,560	4,680	7,800	15,600	27,300	39,000

NOTE: Add 30 percent for 430 engine option.

1960 113" wb

	6	5	4	3	2	1
SR HT	1,120	3,360	5,600	11,200	19,600	28,000
2d HT	1,080	3,240	5,400	10,800	18,900	27,000
Conv	1,560	4,680	7,800	15,600	27,300	39,000

NOTE: Add 30 percent for 430 engine option Code J.

1961 113" wb

	6	5	4	3	2	1
2d HT	960	2,880	4,800	9,600	16,800	24,000
Conv	1,400	4,200	7,000	14,000	24,500	35,000

NOTE: Add 20 percent for 390-375 hp engine. Add 25 percent for Indy Pace Car.

1962 113" wb

	6	5	4	3	2	1
2d HT	960	2,880	4,800	9,600	16,800	24,000
2d Lan HT	1,000	3,000	5,000	10,000	17,500	25,000
Conv	1,360	4,080	6,800	13,600	23,800	34,000
Spt Rds	1,520	4,560	7,600	15,200	26,600	38,000

NOTE: Add 20 percent for 390-340 hp engine. Add 40 percent for M Series option.

1963 113" wb

	6	5	4	3	2	1
2d HT	960	2,880	4,800	9,600	16,800	24,000
2d Lan HT	1,000	3,000	5,000	10,000	17,500	25,000
Conv	1,360	4,080	6,800	13,600	23,800	34,000
Spt Rds	1,520	4,560	7,600	15,200	26,600	38,000

NOTE: Add 12 percent for Monaco option. Add 20 percent for 390-340 hp engine. Add 40 percent for M Series option. Add 10 percent for 390-330 hp engine.

1964 113" wb

	6	5	4	3	2	1
2d HT	800	2,400	4,000	8,000	14,000	20,000
2d Lan HT	840	2,520	4,200	8,400	14,700	21,000
Conv	1,280	3,840	6,400	12,800	22,400	32,000

NOTE: Add 10 percent for Tonneau convertible option. Add 30 percent for tonneau option and wire wheels.

1965 113" wb

	6	5	4	3	2	1
2d HT	800	2,400	4,000	8,000	14,000	20,000
2d Lan HT	840	2,520	4,200	8,400	14,700	21,000

	6	5	4	3	2	1
Conv	1,300	3,950	6,600	13,200	23,100	33,000

NOTE: Add 5 percent for Special Landau option.

1966 113" wb

	6	5	4	3	2	1
2d HT Cpe	840	2,520	4,200	8,400	14,700	21,000
2d Twn Lan	920	2,760	4,600	9,200	16,100	23,000
2d HT Twn	880	2,640	4,400	8,800	15,400	22,000
Conv	1,350	4,100	6,800	13,600	23,800	34,000

NOTE: Add 20 percent for 428 engine.

1967 117" wb

	6	5	4	3	2	1
4d Lan	560	1,680	2,800	5,600	9,800	14,000

1967 115" wb

	6	5	4	3	2	1
2d Lan	600	1,800	3,000	6,000	10,500	15,000
2d HT	608	1,824	3,040	6,080	10,640	15,200

NOTE: Add 30 percent for 428 engine option.

1968 117" wb

	6	5	4	3	2	1
4d Lan Sed	560	1,680	2,800	5,600	9,800	14,000

1968 115" wb

	6	5	4	3	2	1
4d Lan Sed	580	1,740	2,900	5,800	10,150	14,500
2d Lan HT	588	1,764	2,940	5,880	10,290	14,700

NOTE: Add 30 percent for 429 engine option, Code K or 428 engine.

1969 117" wb

	6	5	4	3	2	1
4d Lan	560	1,680	2,800	5,600	9,800	14,000

1969 115" wb

	6	5	4	3	2	1
2d Lan HT	588	1,764	2,940	5,880	10,290	14,700
4d Lan	580	1,740	2,900	5,800	10,150	14,500

1970 117" wb

	6	5	4	3	2	1
4d Lan	560	1,680	2,800	5,600	9,800	14,000

1970 115" wb

	6	5	4	3	2	1
2d Lan HT	588	1,764	2,940	5,880	10,290	14,700
4d Lan	580	1,740	2,900	5,800	10,150	14,500

1971 117" wb

	6	5	4	3	2	1
4d HT	560	1,680	2,800	5,600	9,800	14,000

1971 115" wb

	6	5	4	3	2	1
2d HT	580	1,740	2,900	5,800	10,150	14,500
2d Lan HT	588	1,764	2,940	5,880	10,290	14,700

1972 120" wb

	6	5	4	3	2	1
2d HT	540	1,620	2,700	5,400	9,450	13,500

NOTE: Add 20 percent for 460 engine option.

1973 120" wb

	6	5	4	3	2	1
2d HT	520	1,560	2,600	5,200	9,100	13,000

1974 120" wb

	6	5	4	3	2	1
2d HT	520	1,560	2,600	5,200	9,100	13,000

1975 120" wb

	6	5	4	3	2	1
2d HT	432	1,296	2,160	4,320	7,560	10,800

1976 120" wb

	6	5	4	3	2	1
2d HT	412	1,236	2,060	4,120	7,210	10,300

1977 114" wb

	6	5	4	3	2	1
2d HT	364	1,092	1,820	3,640	6,370	9,100
2d Lan	368	1,104	1,840	3,680	6,440	9,200

1978 114" wb

	6	5	4	3	2	1
2d HT	380	1,140	1,900	3,800	6,650	9,500
2d Twn Lan	420	1,260	2,100	4,200	7,350	10,500
2d Diamond Jubilee	520	1,560	2,600	5,200	9,100	13,000

NOTE: Add 5 percent for T-tops.

1979 V-8, 114" wb

	6	5	4	3	2	1
2d HT	360	1,080	1,800	3,600	6,300	9,000
2d HT Lan	380	1,140	1,900	3,800	6,650	9,500
2d HT Heritage	400	1,200	2,000	4,000	7,000	10,000

NOTE: Add 5 percent for T-tops.

1980 V-8, 108" wb

	6	5	4	3	2	1
2d Cpe	240	720	1,200	2,400	4,200	6,000
2d Twn Lan Cpe	252	756	1,260	2,520	4,410	6,300
2d Silver Anniv. Cpe	260	780	1,300	2,600	4,550	6,500

1981 V-8, 108" wb

	6	5	4	3	2	1
2d Cpe	224	672	1,120	2,240	3,920	5,600

Standard Catalog of® Ford

	6	5	4	3	2	1
2d Twn Lan Cpe	232	696	1,160	2,320	4,060	5,800
2d Heritage Cpe	236	708	1,180	2,360	4,130	5,900

NOTE: Deduct 15 percent for 6-cyl.

1982 V-8, 108" wb

	6	5	4	3	2	1
2d Cpe	232	696	1,160	2,320	4,060	5,800
2d Twn Lan Cpe	240	720	1,200	2,400	4,200	6,000
2d Heritage Cpe	248	744	1,240	2,480	4,340	6,200

NOTE: Deduct 15 percent for V-6.

1983 V-6

	6	5	4	3	2	1
2d Cpe	364	1,092	1,820	3,640	6,370	9,100
2d Cpe Heritage	376	1,128	1,880	3,760	6,580	9,400

1983 V-8

	6	5	4	3	2	1
2d Cpe	376	1,128	1,880	3,760	6,580	9,400
2d Cpe Heritage	392	1,176	1,960	3,920	6,860	9,800

1983 4-cyl.

	6	5	4	3	2	1
2d Cpe Turbo	380	1,140	1,900	3,800	6,650	9,500

1984 V-6

	6	5	4	3	2	1
2d Cpe	276	828	1,380	2,760	4,830	6,900
2d Cpe Elan	368	1,104	1,840	3,680	6,440	9,200
2d Cpe Fila	372	1,116	1,860	3,720	6,510	9,300

1984 V-8

	6	5	4	3	2	1
2d Cpe	376	1,128	1,880	3,760	6,580	9,400
2d Cpe Elan	384	1,152	1,920	3,840	6,720	9,600
2d Cpe Fila	388	1,164	1,940	3,880	6,790	9,700

NOTE: Deduct 10 percent for V-6 non turbo.

1984 4-cyl.

	6	5	4	3	2	1
2d Cpe Turbo	376	1,128	1,880	3,760	6,580	9,400

1985 V-8, 104" wb

	6	5	4	3	2	1
2d Cpe	256	768	1,280	2,560	4,480	6,400
2d Elan Cpe	272	816	1,360	2,720	4,760	6,800
2d Fila Cpe	276	828	1,380	2,760	4,830	6,900

1985 4-cyl. Turbo

	6	5	4	3	2	1
2d Cpe	360	1,080	1,800	3,600	6,300	9,000

NOTE: Deduct 10 percent for V-6 non-turbo.

1986 104" wb

	6	5	4	3	2	1
2d Cpe	256	768	1,280	2,560	4,480	6,400
2d Elan Cpe	264	792	1,320	2,640	4,620	6,600
2d Turbo Cpe	368	1,104	1,840	3,680	6,440	9,200

1987 V-6, 104" wb

	6	5	4	3	2	1
2d Cpe	260	780	1,300	2,600	4,550	6,500
2d LX Cpe	264	792	1,320	2,640	4,620	6,600

1987 V-8, 104" wb

	6	5	4	3	2	1
2d Cpe	360	1,080	1,800	3,600	6,300	9,000
2d Spt Cpe	368	1,104	1,840	3,680	6,440	9,200
2d LX Cpe	372	1,116	1,860	3,720	6,510	9,300

1987 4-cyl. Turbo

	6	5	4	3	2	1
2d Cpe	368	1,104	1,840	3,680	6,440	9,200

1988 V-6

	6	5	4	3	2	1
2d Cpe	180	540	900	1,800	3,150	4,500
2d LX Cpe	200	600	1,000	2,000	3,500	5,000

1988 V-8

	6	5	4	3	2	1
2d Spt Cpe	220	660	1,100	2,200	3,850	5,500

1988 4-cyl. Turbo

	6	5	4	3	2	1
2d Cpe	188	564	940	1,880	3,290	4,700

NOTE: Add 20 percent for V-8 where available.

1989 V-6

	6	5	4	3	2	1
2d Cpe	272	816	1,360	2,720	4,760	6,800
2d LX Cpe	360	1,080	1,800	3,600	6,300	9,000
2d Sup Cpe	520	1,560	2,600	5,200	9,100	13,000

1990 V-6

	6	5	4	3	2	1
2d Cpe	260	780	1,300	2,600	4,550	6,500
2d LX Cpe	360	1,080	1,800	3,600	6,300	9,000
2d Sup Cpe	520	1,560	2,600	5,200	9,100	13,000

NOTE: Add 10 percent for Anniversary model.

1991 V-6

	6	5	4	3	2	1
2d Cpe	240	720	1,200	2,400	4,200	6,000
2d LX Cpe	260	780	1,300	2,600	4,550	6,500
2d Sup Cpe	340	1,020	1,700	3,400	5,950	8,500

1991 V-8

	6	5	4	3	2	1
2d Cpe	360	1,080	1,800	3,600	6,300	9,000
2d LX Cpe	380	1,140	1,900	3,800	6,650	9,500

1992 V-6

	6	5	4	3	2	1
2d Cpe	360	1,080	1,800	3,600	6,300	9,000
2d LX Cpe	368	1,104	1,840	3,680	6,440	9,200
2d Sup Cpe	380	1,140	1,900	3,800	6,650	9,500

1992 V-8

	6	5	4	3	2	1
2d Cpe	364	1,092	1,820	3,640	6,370	9,100
2d Spt Cpe	392	1,176	1,960	3,920	6,860	9,800
2d LX Cpe	380	1,140	1,900	3,800	6,650	9,500

1993 V-6

	6	5	4	3	2	1
2d LX Cpe	372	1,116	1,860	3,720	6,510	9,300
2d Sup Cpe	380	1,140	1,900	3,800	6,650	9,500

1993 V-8

	6	5	4	3	2	1
2d LX Cpe	404	1,212	2,020	4,040	7,070	10,100

1994 V-6

	6	5	4	3	2	1
2d LX Cpe	300	900	1,500	3,000	5,250	7,500
2d Sup Cpe	360	1,080	1,800	3,600	6,300	9,000

1994 V-8

	6	5	4	3	2	1
2d LX Cpe	320	960	1,600	3,200	5,600	8,000

1995 V-6

	6	5	4	3	2	1
2d LX Cpe	300	900	1,500	3,000	5,250	7,500
2d Sup Cpe	350	1,100	1,800	3,600	6,300	9,000

1995 V-8

	6	5	4	3	2	1
2d LX Cpe	300	950	1,600	3,200	5,600	8,000

The following press release excerpt is from the Ford Motor Company.

"We're committed to the number-one thing our customers want: enhanced performance."

— John Coletti, chief engineer for Ford SVT

Beginning with the original in 1993, every generation of the SVT Mustang Cobra has elevated its standard of performance. Now, the 2003 SVT Mustang Cobra raises the bar yet again, this time increasing power output to a level never before achieved in a production Mustang. The addition of a Roots-type supercharger and water-to-air intercooler to the Cobra's 4.6-liter, DOHC 4-valve V-8 engine bumps output to 390 horsepower and 390 foot-pounds of torque.

The new SVT Cobra also joins the 2002 SVT Focus in providing a six-speed gearbox as standard equipment. Additional enhancements for 2003 include exterior design alterations to the front and rear fascia, hood, rocker moldings and side scoops, as well as several changes to the interior appointments, including new multi-adjustable front seats trimmed in Nudo leather and Preferred suede.

"Every once in a while, a car comes along that really shakes up the status quo," said Tom Scarpello, marketing and sales manager for Ford's Special Vehicle Team. "Since the '64-1/2 Mustang was launched, there have been a number of Mustangs that set the standard for performance when they were introduced. The 2003 SVT Cobra is the new benchmark, and proudly carries on the tradition of Mustang performance leadership."

"We've had some pretty successful Mustangs, and specifically SVT Mustang Cobras," said John Coletti, chief engineer for Ford SVT, "but the whole idea is to improve. That's what we're committed to, and the number-one thing our customers want is enhanced performance. The supercharged engine allowed us to go where we needed to go — to give our customers a whole lot more car than ever before."

Powertrain

The 2003 SVT Mustang Cobra's 4.6-liter, DOHC V-8 is equipped with an Eaton™ supercharger and new aluminum alloy cylinder heads that provide increased flow capabilities. The engine produces 390 horsepower at 6,000 rpm and 390 foot-pounds of torque at 3,500 rpm, compared with the 2001 model's 320 hp at 6,000 rpm and 317 foot-pounds of torque at 4,750 rpm.

To provide strength necessary for the substantially increased torque output, the new Cobra engine is built on a cast-iron block.

The engine is mated to a TTC T-56 6-speed manual transmission.

Suspension and Brakes

The SVT Mustang Cobra's independent rear suspension system receives upgraded bushings and an additional tubular cross-brace for 2003, necessary for increased loading due to the higher power output and larger tires.

The 2003 SVT Cobra is equipped with gas-charged monotube Bilstein dampers at all four corners, and the pad material on the rear brakes has been upgraded for enhanced durability and brake performance.

Design and Equipment

Flow-through hood scoops help vent hot air from the engine compartment.

Exterior design changes distinguish the SVT Mustang Cobra from the regular production Mustang GT. While it retains the SVT-signature round fog lamps, the front fascia is more aggressive looking, and also helps to deliver more air to the engine compartment. The hood also has been redesigned, and now has flow-through scoops that help vent hot air from the engine compartment. Both the hood and rear deck are made of lightweight composite materials. Showing that SVT appreciates even the smallest details, the windshield wipers feature an aerodynamic "wing" to help keep the blades planted at speeds up to 130 mph.

New front face fascia helps deliver more air to the engine for intake and cooling systems. "Our customers want a more distinctive, recognizable Cobra," said Scarpello. "It's the top of the Mustang line, and also Ford's flagship performance car. So we put more emphasis on exterior differentiation and on interior touches that set it apart."

Inside, new front bucket seats are designed to provide enhanced support for both comfortable cruising and spirited driving. Seating surfaces have Nudo leather trim and Preferred suede inserts. The driver's seat has standard six-way power, plus new power-adjustable thigh and side bolsters, and power lumbar support. Switches for these new controls are in an easy-to-reach location on the right-front corner of the seat.

The gear shift knob is leather-wrapped, with a brushed-aluminum insert on the top, inscribed with the six-speed pattern. New metal-trimmed pedals and dead pedal complete the interior transformation. New front bucket seats provide enhanced support. Seating surfaces are Nudo leather with Preferred suede inserts.

Additional SVT Mustang Cobra standard features include a leather-wrapped steering wheel; leather boots for the shift and parking brake levers; tilt steering wheel; power windows, mirrors, door locks and trunk release; the SecuriLock™ passive anti-theft system; remote keyless entry; speed control; and a MACH 460 audio system with AM/FM stereo and an in-dash, six-disc CD player.

Exterior color choices for 2003 are Oxford White Clearcoat, Ebony Clearcoat, Torch Red Clearcoat, Sonic Blue Clearcoat, Satin Silver Clearcoat Metallic, Mineral Grey Clearcoat Metallic, and Zinc Yellow Clearcoat.

The interior is available in two color schemes; both feature a Dark Charcoal environment, with a choice of either Medium Parchment or Medium Graphite accents.

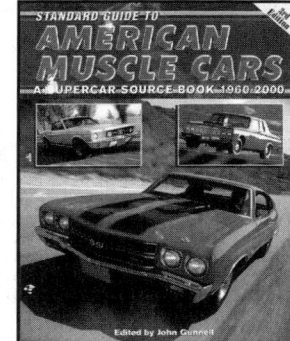
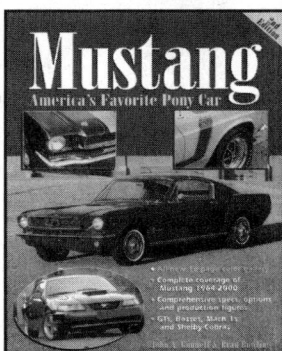

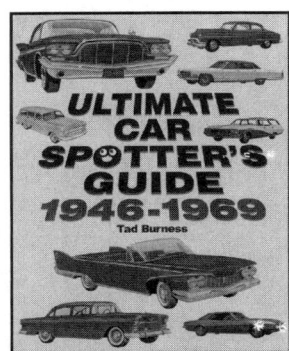